CONSTITUTIONAL LAW

ASPEN SELECT SERIES

CONSTITUTIONAL LAW
Cases and Materials
Third Edition

MARTIN L. LEVY
Professor of Law
Thurgood Marshall School of Law
Texas Southern University

CRAIG L. JACKSON
Professor of Law
Thurgood Marshall School of Law
Texas Southern University

To contact Customer Service, e-mail customer.service@aspenpublishing.com, call 1-800-950-5259, or mail correspondence to:

Aspen Publishing
Attn: Order Department
PO Box 990
Frederick, MD 21705

Printed in the United States of America.

1 2 3 4 5 6 7 8 9 0

ISBN 978-1-5438-5768-9

About Aspen Publishing

Aspen Publishing is a leading provider of educational content and digital learning solutions to law schools in the U.S. and around the world. Aspen provides best-in-class solutions for legal education through authoritative textbooks, written by renowned authors, and breakthrough products such as Connected eBooks, Connected Quizzing, and PracticePerfect.

The Aspen Casebook Series (famously known among law faculty and students as the "red and black" casebooks) encompasses hundreds of highly regarded textbooks in more than eighty disciplines, from large enrollment courses, such as Torts and Contracts to emerging electives such as Sustainability and the Law of Policing. Study aids such as the *Examples & Explanations* and the *Emanuel Law Outlines* series, both highly popular collections, help law students master complex subject matter.

Major products, programs, and initiatives include:

- **Connected eBooks** are enhanced digital textbooks and study aids that come with a suite of online content and learning tools designed to maximize student success. Designed in collaboration with hundreds of faculty and students, the Connected eBook is a significant leap forward in the legal education learning tools available to students.

- **Connected Quizzing** is an easy-to-use formative assessment tool that tests law students' understanding and provides timely feedback to improve learning outcomes. Delivered through CasebookConnect.com, the learning platform already used by students to access their Aspen casebooks, Connected Quizzing is simple to implement and integrates seamlessly with law school course curricula.

- **PracticePerfect** is a visually engaging, interactive study aid to explain commonly encountered legal doctrines through easy-to-understand animated videos, illustrative examples, and numerous practice questions. Developed by a team of experts, PracticePerfect is the ideal study companion for today's law students.

- The **Aspen Learning Library** enables law schools to provide their students with access to the most popular study aids on the market across all of their courses. Available through an annual subscription, the online library consists of study aids in e-book, audio, and video formats with full text search, note-taking, and highlighting capabilities.

- Aspen's **Digital Bookshelf** is an institutional-level online education bookshelf, consolidating everything students and professors need to ensure success. This program ensures that every student has access to affordable course materials from day one.

- **Leading Edge** is a community centered on thinking differently about legal education and putting those thoughts into actionable strategies. At the core of the program is the Leading Edge Conference, an annual gathering of legal education thought leaders looking to pool ideas and identify promising directions of exploration.

To the late Dean Otis H. King

"Otis without you not only would I not be at Thurgood Marshall, there would not be a Thurgood Marshall School of Law. This book's for you!!"

—Martin Levy

To my parents, James and Evelyn Jackson, who were teachers, for being wonderful parents and for instilling in me an appreciation for teaching and learning. Hopefully one day I will reach their level as a teacher.

—Craig Jackson

Table of Contents

Preface

I want to extend my thanks to my friend, colleague, and co-author, Craig Jackson, for his leadership in preparing the third edition of our casebook! So, thanks so much Craig, as well as to the editors at ASPEN!

Martin Levy
Houston
October 2022

This edition continues the inspired approach of the text's original author, Martin Levy, of presenting constitutional law within broader contexts than a simple progression of Supreme Court cases beginning with *Marbury v. Madison*. The text, now in its Third Edition as a collaborative work of the two of us, strives to demonstrate the role of social change and history in constitutional interpretation, as evident in the case selection and emphasis. For example, this book includes in certain core areas of the constitutional law canon cases that trace the nation's struggle with race — slavery is presented within the context of the drafting of the Constitution and in the Commerce Clause, as a reminder of the practice of human trafficking that influenced the writing of the Constitution and continues to influence social events today. Commercial regulation is presented as both a function of constitutional structure and international economics to demonstrate the kind of polity the Framers had in mind when drafting the Constitution. Procreative rights are the subject of several selected cases, including *Roe v. Wade,* and the case overturning *Roe, Dobbs v. Jackson Women's Health Organization*, to demonstrate judicial review and constitutional interpretation in addition to the jurisprudence of the Due Process Clause. The events leading up to and surrounding the nation's reaction to 9/11 are chronicled in cases addressing presidential power, separation of powers, the constitutional meaning of "war powers," and civil liberties. The economic history of the Great Depression serves as the backdrop to discussing the changes in the Court's interpretation of both the Commerce Clause and the Due Process Clause.

It has been an honor to work with Marty, my colleague of 32 years, on this latest edition of the textbook. Marty shares my view that constitutional law should be more than a collection of cases and descriptions of structures, fascinating perhaps to constitutional law scholars yet separated from the history and society that we all live in. Hopefully the use of historical and social contexts will be fascinating to students while demonstrating the real day-to-day impact of constitutional law on our lives.

Craig Jackson
Houston
October 2022

Acknowledgments

Michael J. Klarman, *Bush v. Gore* through the Lens of Constitutional History, 89 Cal. L. Rev. 1721 (2001). Available at: http://scholarship.law.berkeley.edu/californialawreview/vol89/iss6/2. Reprinted with permission from the author.

Mark Tushnet, Renormalizing *Bush v. Gore*: An Anticipatory Intellectual History, 90 Geo. L.J. 113 (2001). Reprinted with permission from the author.

PART I
GOVERNMENTAL POWERS

Chapter 1
The Supreme Court
and Judicial Review

The concept of "constitutional law" begs several questions as a means of introduction. What exactly is a Constitution? How does, or perhaps doesn't, it differ from any other concept of law as we know it? Or, for example, does it differ from statutory legislation? What is meant by "fundamental" law? Is, as is usually the scuttlebutt around the corridors of law schools, constitutional law different from other courses? These are questions relevant to the entire course, and beg your thoughts as we commence our study.

It is traditional for a course in constitutional law to begin with reading *Marbury v. Madison*. Why? What is judicial review? What does it have to do with constitutional law? Where does the Constitution allocate this power to the courts? Note that our study of governmental power focuses first on the judicial power, then on Congress (II) and the Executive Branch (III); yet each section commences with a judicial decision. What does this foretell about the Constitution and the Supreme Court?

As you read *Marbury*, keep in mind its contemporary relevance. Note that the next case included after *Marbury* is *Cooper v. Aaron*, where the principles inherent in *Marbury* are challenged in 1958, some 150 years after Justice Marshall's decision! You will soon see that the concept of judicial review in a democratic society will pose dilemmatic questions in regard to the American constitutional law that will be debated and analyzed as long as we maintain our present form of government.

As Alexander Bickel began his classic work, *The Least Dangerous Branch* (1962), so we begin our study:

> The least dangerous branch of the American government is the most extraordinarily powerful court of law the world has ever known. The power which distinguishes the Supreme Court of the United States is that of constitutional review of actions of the other branches of government, federal and state. Curiously enough, this power of judicial review, as it is called, does not derive from any explicit constitutional command. The authority to determine the meaning and application of a written constitution is nowhere defined or even mentioned in the document itself.[1]

Yet, Bickel foretells, "[i]f any social process can be said to have been 'done' at a given time and by a given act, it is Marshall's achievement. The time is 1803, the act was the decision in the case of *Marbury v. Madison*." An act that "plant[ed] the seed that would over time, grow into that many-rooted ever-proliferating banana tree which placed the Supreme Court . . . as the ultimate all-pervasive power in the republic." Gore Vidal, *Inventing a Nation* 144 (2003).

---

[1] Alexander Bickel, *The Least Dangerous Branch, 1* (Yale University Press (1962).

I. DEVELOPMENT OF JUDICIAL REVIEW

A. ORIGINS

Events Leading to *Marbury*. A central issue between the arising postrevolutionary American political factions was judicial review and the role of the Supreme Court in the country's "constitutional plan." The Federalists were advocates of judicial review. The classic defense of this "ultimate" judicial power was set forth in *The Federalist* No. 78, written by Alexander Hamilton and entitled "The judges as Guardians of the Constitution." The rival Anti-Federalists, or Democratic Republicans, led by Thomas Jefferson, vehemently opposed this role for the Court. The great democrats of their age perceived the Court, and therefore judicial review, as undemocratic. To Jefferson, the supremacy of the Constitution would be achieved by recourse to the people in their elective capacity: "The ultimate arbiter is the people of the Union." "But nothing in the Constitution has given them the right to decide for the Executive, more than the executive to decide for them." Thomas Jefferson, *Writings* 1426 (1984).

This issue so divided the Constitutional Convention that the lack of any mention of such a role for the Court, at least in explicit language, may have been a necessary compromise to achieve union. But if the issue was left to be resolved by the fledgling government, the ultimate energy of the debate would not disappoint. The election of 1800 became a center point for this controversy. Jefferson (Republican) referred to the election between Adams (Federalist) and himself as a "test of the ideals of the revolution," while assailing the monarchical tendencies of Adams himself. *Id.* at 669-73, 698-99.

The Jefferson victory left the Republicans in control of the "popularly elected" branches (executive and congressional), while the "life tenured" independence the Constitution afforded the judiciary remained the last bastion of Federalist power. Using legislation passed by the outgoing Federalist Congress, Adams, in an obvious attempt to extend Federalist control over the judiciary, nominated the now infamous "midnight judges" during the last two weeks of his term. Marbury and his co-petitioners were appointed on March 2, 1801, and confirmed on March 3, 1801, Adam's last day in office. These commissions were signed by Adams and sealed by the then Secretary of State, John Marshall himself, but Marbury's and some others' commissions were never delivered. Marshall's own brother, James, was to deliver the commissions but did not. When Jefferson assumed office he refused their delivery and considered them a "nullity." Thus the stage was set for Marbury to file suit to receive his commission against Jefferson's Secretary of State, James Madison. But in reality, this was a clash between two great Virginians, Jefferson and Marshall.

MARBURY v. MADISON
1 Cranch (5 U.S.) 137 (1803)

At the December term 1801, William Marbury, Dennis Ramsay, Robert Townsend Hooe, and William Harper, by their counsel severally moved the court for a rule to James Madison, secretary of state of the United States, to show cause why a mandamus should not issue commanding him to cause to be delivered to them respectively their several commissions as justices of the peace in the district of Columbia. This motion was supported by affidavits of the following facts: that notice of this motion had been given to Mr.

Madison; that Mr. Adams, the late president of the United States, nominated the applicants to the senate for their advice and consent to be appointed justices of the peace of the district of Columbia; that the senate advised and consented to the appointments; that commissions in due form were signed by the said president appointing them justices, &c. and that the seal of the United States was in due form affixed to the said commissions by the secretary of state; that the applicants have requested Mr. Madison to deliver them their said commissions, who has not complied with that request; and that their said commissions are withheld from them; that the applicants have made application to Mr. Madison as secretary of state of the United States at his office, for information whether the commissions were signed and sealed as aforesaid; that explicit and satisfactory information has not been given in answer to that inquiry, either by the secretary of state, or any officer in the department of state; that application has been made to the secretary of the senate for a certificate of the nomination of the applicants, and of the advice and consent of the senate, who has declined giving such a certificate; whereupon a rule was made to show cause on the fourth day of this term.

The questions argued by the counsel for the realtors were,

1. Whether the supreme court can award the writ of mandamus in any case.
2. Whether it will lie to a secretary of state, in any case whatever.
3. Whether in the present case the court may award a mandamus to James Madison, secretary of state.

Mr. Chief Justice MARSHALL delivered the opinion of the court.

At the last term, on the affidavits then read and filed with the clerk, a rule was granted in this case, requiring the secretary of state to show cause why a mandamus should not issue, directing him to deliver to William Marbury his commission as a justice of the peace for the county of Washington, in the district of Columbia.

No cause has been shown, and the present motion is for a mandamus. The peculiar delicacy of this case, the novelty of some of its circumstances, and the real difficulty attending the points which occur in it, require a complete exposition of the principles on which the opinion to be given by the court is founded.

These principles have been, on the side of the applicant, very ably argued at the bar. In rendering the opinion of the court, there will be some departure in form, though not in substance, from the points stated in that argument.

In the order in which the court has viewed this subject, the following questions have been considered and decided.

1. Has the applicant a right to the commission he demands?
2. If he has a right, and that right has been violated, do the laws of his country afford him a remedy?
3. If they do afford him a remedy, is it a mandamus issuing from this court?

The first object of inquiry is,

1. Has the applicant a right to the commission he demands?

[It] is therefore decidedly the opinion of the court, that when a commission has been signed by the president, the appointment is made; and that the commission is complete when the seal of the United States has been affixed to it by the secretary of state.

To withhold the commission, therefore, is an act deemed by the court not warranted by law, but violative of a vested legal right.

This brings us to the second inquiry; which is,

2. If he has a right, and that right has been violated, do the laws of his country afford him a remedy?

The very essence of civil liberty certainly consists in the right of every individual to claim the protection of the laws, whenever he receives an injury. One of the first duties of government is to afford that protection.

[T]he government of the United States has been emphatically termed a government of laws, and not of men. It will certainly cease to deserve this high appellation, if the laws furnish no remedy for the violation of a vested legal right.

If this obloquy is to be cast on the jurisprudence of our country, it must arise from the peculiar character of the case.

It behooves us then to inquire whether there be in its composition any ingredient which shall exempt from legal investigation, or exclude the injured party from legal redress.

[Is] it in the nature of the transaction? Is the act of delivering or withholding a commission to be considered as a mere political act belonging to the executive department alone, for the performance of which entire confidence is placed by our constitution in the supreme executive; and for any misconduct respecting which, the injured individual has no remedy.

That there may be such cases is not to be questioned; but that every act of duty to be performed in any of the great departments of government constitutes such a case, is not to be admitted.

It follows then that the question, whether the legality of an act of the head of a department be examinable in a court of justice or not, must always depend on the nature of that act.

[By] the constitution of the United States, the president is invested with certain important political powers, in the exercise of which he is to use his own discretion, and is accountable only to his country in his political character, and to his own conscience. To aid him in the performance of these duties, he is authorized to appoint certain officers, who act by his authority and in conformity with his orders.

In such cases, their acts are his acts; and whatever opinion may be entertained of the manner in which executive discretion may be used, still there exists, and can exist, no power to control that discretion. The subjects are political. They respect the nation, not individual rights, and being entrusted to the executive, the decision of the executive is conclusive. The application of this remark will be perceived by adverting to the act of congress for establishing the department of foreign affairs. This officer, as his duties were prescribed by that act, is to conform precisely to the will of the president. He is the mere organ by whom that will is communicated. The acts of such an officer, as an officer, can never be examinable by the courts.

But when the legislature proceeds to impose on that officer other duties; when he is directed peremptorily to perform certain acts; when the rights of individuals are dependent on the performance of those acts; he is so far the officer of the law; is amenable to the laws for his conduct; and cannot at his discretion sport away the vested rights of others.

The conclusion from this reasoning is, that where the heads of departments are the political or confidential agents of the executive, merely to execute the will of the president, or rather to act in cases in which the executive possesses a constitutional or legal discretion, nothing can be more perfectly clear than that their acts are only politically examinable. But where a specific duty is assigned by law, and individual rights depend upon the performance of that duty, it seems equally clear that the individual who considers himself injured has a right to resort to the laws of his country for a remedy.

It is then the opinion of the court, 1. That by signing the commission of Mr. Marbury, the president of the United States appointed him a justice of peace for the county of Washington in the district of Columbia; and that the seal of the United States, affixed thereto by the secretary of state, is conclusive testimony of the verity of the signature, and of the completion of the appointment; and that the appointment conferred on him a legal right to the office for the space of five years. 2. That, having this legal title to the office, he has a consequent right to the commission; a refusal to deliver which is a plain violation of that right, for which the laws of his country afford him a remedy.

It remains to be inquired whether, 3. He is entitled to the remedy for which he applies. This depends on, 1. The nature of the writ applied for. And, 2. The power of this court.

1. The nature of the writ.

[This] writ, if awarded, would be directed to an officer of government, and its mandate to him would be, to use the words of Blackstone, "to do a particular thing therein specified, which appertains to his office and duty, and which the court has previously determined or at least supposes to be consonant to right and justice." Or, in the words of Lord Mansfield, the applicant, in this case, has a right to execute an office of public concern, and is kept out of possession of that right.

These circumstances certainly concur in this case.

Still, to render the mandamus a proper remedy, the officer to whom it is to be directed, must be one to whom, on legal principles, such writ may be directed; and the person applying for it must be without any other specific and legal remedy.

1. With respect to the officer to whom it would be directed. The intimate political relation, subsisting between the president of the United States and the heads of departments, necessarily renders any legal investigation of the acts of one of those high officers peculiarly irksome, as well as delicate; and excites some hesitation with respect to the propriety of entering into such investigation. Impressions are often received without much reflection or examination; and it is not wonderful that in such a case as this, the assertion, by an individual, of his legal claims in a court of justice, to which claims it is the duty of that court to attend, should at first view be considered by some, as an attempt to intrude into the cabinet, and to intermeddle with the prerogatives of the executive.

It is scarcely necessary for the court to disclaim all pretensions to such a jurisdiction. An extravagance, so absurd and excessive, could not have been entertained for a moment. The province of the court is, solely, to decide on the rights of individuals, not to inquire how the executive, or executive officers, perform duties in which they have a discretion. Questions, in their nature political, or which are, by the constitution and laws, submitted to the executive, can never be made in this court.

But, if this be not such a question; if so far from being an intrusion into the secrets of the cabinet, it respects a paper, which, according to law, is upon record, and to a copy of which the law gives a right, on the payment of ten cents; if it be no intermeddling with a subject, over which the executive can be considered as having exercised any control; what is there in the exalted station of the officer, which shall bar a citizen from asserting, in a court of justice, his legal rights, or shall forbid a court to listen to the claim; or to issue a mandamus, directing the performance of a duty, not depending on executive discretion, but on particular acts of congress and the general principles of law?

[Where] the head of a department [is] directed by law to do a certain act affecting the absolute rights of individuals, [it] is not perceived on what ground the courts of the country are further excused from the duty of giving judgment, that right to be done to an injured [individual.]

This opinion seems not now for the first time to be taken up in this country.

This, then, is a plain case of a mandamus, either to deliver the commission, or a copy of it from the record; and it only remains to be inquired,

Whether it can issue from this court.

The act to establish the judicial courts of the United States authorizes the supreme court "to issue writs of mandamus, in cases warranted by the principles and usages of law, to any courts appointed, or persons holding office, under the authority of the United States."

The secretary of state, being a person, holding an office under the authority of the United States, is precisely within the letter of the description; and if this court is not authorized to issue a writ of mandamus to such an officer, it must be because the law is unconstitutional, and therefore absolutely incapable of conferring the authority, and assigning the duties which its words purport to confer and assign.

The constitution vests the whole judicial power of the United States in one supreme court, and such inferior courts as congress shall, from time to time, ordain and establish. This power is expressly extended to all cases arising under the laws of the United States; and consequently, in some form, may be exercised over the present case; because the right claimed is given by a law of the United States.

In the distribution of this power it is declared that "the supreme court shall have original jurisdiction in all cases affecting ambassadors, other public ministers and consuls, and those in which a state shall be a party. In all other cases, the supreme court shall have appellate jurisdiction."

It has been insisted at the bar, that as the original grant of jurisdiction to the supreme and inferior courts is general, and the clause, assigning original jurisdiction to the supreme court, contains no negative or restrictive words; the power remains to the legislature to assign original jurisdiction to that court in other cases than those specified in the article which has been recited; provided those cases belong to the judicial power of the United States.

If it had been intended to leave it in the discretion of the legislature to apportion the judicial power between the supreme and inferior courts according to the will of that body, it would certainly have been useless to have proceeded further than to have defined the judicial power, and the tribunals in which it should be vested. The subsequent part of the section is mere surplusage, is entirely without meaning, if such is to be the construction. If congress remains at liberty to give this court appellate jurisdiction, where the constitution has declared their jurisdiction shall be original; and original jurisdiction where the constitution has declared it shall be appellate; the distribution of jurisdiction made in the constitution, is form without substance.

Affirmative words are often, in their operation, negative of other objects than those affirmed; and in this case, a negative or exclusive sense must be given to them or they have no operation at all.

It cannot be presumed that any clause in the constitution is intended to be without effect; and therefore such construction is inadmissible, unless the words require it.

If the solicitude of the convention, respecting our peace with foreign powers, induced a provision that the supreme court should take original jurisdiction in cases which might be supposed to affect them; yet the clause would have proceeded no further than to provide for such cases, if no further restriction on the powers of congress had been intended. That they should have appellate jurisdiction in all other cases, with such exceptions as congress might make, is no restriction; unless the words be deemed exclusive of original jurisdiction.

When an instrument organizing fundamentally a judicial system, divides it into one supreme, and so many inferior courts as the legislature may ordain and establish; then enumerates its powers, and proceeds so far to distribute them, as to define the jurisdiction of the supreme court by declaring the cases in which it shall take original jurisdiction, and that in others it shall take appellate jurisdiction, the plain import of the words seems to be, that in one class of cases its jurisdiction is original, and not appellate; in the other it is appellate, and not original. If any other construction would render the clause inoperative, that is an additional reason for rejecting such other construction, and for adhering to the obvious meaning.

To enable this court then to issue a mandamus, it must be shown to be an exercise of appellate jurisdiction, or to be necessary to enable them to exercise appellate jurisdiction.

It has been stated at the bar that the appellate jurisdiction may be exercised in a variety of forms, and that if it be the will of the legislature that a mandamus should be used for that purpose, that will must be obeyed. This is true; yet the jurisdiction must be appellate, not original.

It is the essential criterion of appellate jurisdiction, that it revises and corrects the proceedings in a cause already instituted, and does not create that case. Although, therefore, a mandamus may be directed to courts, yet to issue such a writ to an officer for the delivery of a paper, is in effect the same as to sustain an original action for that paper, and therefore seems not to belong to appellate, but to original jurisdiction. Neither is it necessary in such a case as this, to enable the court to exercise its appellate jurisdiction.

The authority, therefore, given to the supreme court, by the act establishing the judicial courts of the United States, to issue writs of mandamus to public officers, appears not to be warranted by the constitution; and it becomes necessary to inquire whether a jurisdiction, so conferred, can be exercised.

The question, whether an act, repugnant to the constitution, can become the law of the land, is a question deeply interesting to the United States; but, happily, not of an intricacy proportioned to its interest. It seems only necessary to recognize certain principles, supposed to have been long and well established, to decide it.

That the people have an original right to establish, for their future government, such principles as, in their opinion, shall most conduce to their own happiness, is the basis on which the whole American fabric has been erected. The exercise of this original right is a very great exertion; nor can it nor ought it to be frequently repeated. The principles, therefore, so established are deemed fundamental. And as the authority, from which they proceed, is supreme, and can seldom act, they are designed to be permanent.

This original and supreme will organizes the government, and assigns to different departments their respective powers. It may either stop here; or establish certain limits not to be transcended by those departments.

The government of the United States is of the latter description. The powers of the legislature are defined and limited; and that those limits may not be mistaken or forgotten, the constitution is written. To what purpose are powers limited, and to what purpose is that limitation committed to writing; if these limits may, at any time, be passed by those intended to be restrained? The distinction between a government with limited and unlimited powers is abolished, if those limits do not confine the persons on whom they are imposed, and if acts prohibited and acts allowed are of equal obligation. It is a proposition too plain to be contested, that the constitution controls any legislative act repugnant to it; or, that the legislature may alter the constitution by an ordinary act.

Between these alternatives there is no middle ground. The constitution is either a superior, paramount law, unchangeable by ordinary means, or it is on a level with ordinary legislative acts, and like other acts, is alterable when the legislature shall please to alter it.

If the former part of the alternative be true, then a legislative act contrary to the constitution is not law: if the latter part be true, then written constitutions are absurd attempts, on the part of the people, to limit a power in its own nature illimitable.

Certainly all those who have framed written constitutions contemplate them as forming the fundamental and paramount law of the nation, and consequently the theory of every such government must be, that an act of the legislature repugnant to the constitution is void.

This theory is essentially attached to a written constitution, and is consequently to be considered by this court as one of the fundamental principles of our society. It is not therefore to be lost sight of in the further consideration of this subject.

If an act of the legislature, repugnant to the constitution, is void, does it, notwithstanding its invalidity, bind the courts and oblige them to give it effect? Or, in other words, though it be not law, does it constitute a rule as operative as if it was a law? This would be to overthrow in fact what was established in theory; and would seem, at first view, an absurdity too gross to be insisted on. It shall, however, receive a more attentive consideration.

It is emphatically the province and duty of the judicial department to say what the law is. Those who apply the rule to particular cases, must of necessity expound and interpret that rule. If two laws conflict with each other, the courts must decide on the operation of each.

So if a law be in opposition to the constitution: if both the law and the constitution apply to a particular case, so that the court must either decide that case conformably to the law, disregarding the constitution; or conformably to the constitution, disregarding the law: the court must determine which of these conflicting rules governs the case. This is of the very essence of judicial duty.

If then the courts are to regard the constitution; and the constitution is superior to any ordinary act of the legislature; the constitution, and not such ordinary act, must govern the case to which they both apply.

Those then who controvert the principle that the constitution is to be considered, in court, as a paramount law, are reduced to the necessity of maintaining that courts must close their eyes on the constitution, and see only the law.

This doctrine would subvert the very foundation of all written constitutions. It would declare that an act, which, according to the principles and theory of our government, is entirely void, is yet, in practice, completely obligatory. It would declare, that if the legislature shall do what is expressly forbidden, such act, notwithstanding the express prohibition, is in reality effectual. It would be giving to the legislature a practical and real omnipotence with the same breath which professes to restrict their powers within narrow limits. It is prescribing limits, and declaring that those limits may be passed at pleasure.

That it thus reduces to nothing what we have deemed the greatest improvement on political institutions — a written constitution, would of itself be sufficient, in America where written constitutions have been viewed with so much reverence, for rejecting the construction. But the peculiar expressions of the constitution of the United States furnish additional arguments in favor of its rejection.

The judicial power of the United States is extended to all cases arising under the constitution.

Could it be the intention of those who gave this power, to say that, in using it, the constitution should not be looked into? That a case arising under the constitution should be decided without examining the instrument under which it arises? This is too extravagant to be maintained.

In some cases then, the constitution must be looked into by the judges. And if they can open it at all, what part of it are they forbidden to read, or to obey?

There are many other parts of the constitution which serve to illustrate this subject.

It is declared that "no tax or duty shall be laid on articles exported from any state." Suppose a duty on the export of cotton, of tobacco, or of flour; and a suit instituted to recover it. Ought judgment to be rendered in such a case? ought the judges to close their eyes on the constitution, and only see the law.

The constitution declares that "no bill of attainder or ex post facto law shall be passed."

If, however, such a bill should be passed and a person should be prosecuted under it, must the court condemn to death those victims whom the constitution endeavors to preserve?

"No person," says the constitution, "shall be convicted of treason unless on the testimony of two witnesses to the same overt act, or on confession in open court."

Here the language of the constitution is addressed especially to the courts. It prescribes, directly for them, a rule of evidence not to be departed from. If the legislature should change that rule, and declare *one* witness, or a confession *out* of court, sufficient for conviction, must the constitutional principle yield to the legislative act?

From these and many other selections which might be made, it is apparent, that the framers of the constitution contemplated that instrument as a rule for the government of *courts*, as well as of the legislature.

Why otherwise does it direct the judges to take an oath to support it? This oath certainly applies, in an especial manner, to their conduct in their official character. How immoral to impose it on them, if they were to be used as the instruments, and the knowing instruments, for violating what they swear to support!

The oath of office, too, imposed by the legislature, is completely demonstrative of the legislative opinion on this subject. It is in these words: "I do solemnly swear that I will administer justice without respect to persons, and do equal right to the poor and to the rich; and that I will faithfully and impartially discharge all the duties incumbent on me as according to the best of my abilities and understanding, agreeably to the constitution and laws of the United States."

Why does a judge swear to discharge his duties agreeably to the constitution of the United States, if that constitution forms no rule for his government? if it is closed upon him and cannot be inspected by him.

If such be the real state of things, this is worse than solemn mockery. To prescribe, or to take this oath, becomes equally a crime.

It is also not entirely unworthy of observation, that in declaring what shall be the supreme law of the land, the constitution itself is first mentioned; and not the laws of the United States generally, but those only which shall be made in pursuance of the constitution, have that rank.

Thus, the particular phraseology of the constitution of the United States confirms and strengthens the principle, supposed to be essential to all written constitutions, that a law repugnant to the constitution is void, and that courts, as well as other departments, are bound by that instrument.

The rule must be discharged.

Comments on the Legitimacy of Review: The Weak Origins Argument. Do you agree with Marshall's conclusion in regard to judicial review in *Marbury*? If so, how can you explain, given the significance of the issue, the framers not granting such explicit authority to the Court? Yet, could the Constitution ever meet the mandates of the explicit language of the Supremacy Clause without judicial review? Whether one agrees with Marshall's delegation argument or not, the weak origins of the power is relevant to us *today* because of how it affects the manner in which the Court dispenses with judicial power. This is an important theme of this course offering.

Judicial Review in a Democratic Society. What is most significant to us is not whether the Court retains the power of judicial review today, for the process of history has entrenched the Court as the ultimate arbiter of the Constitution, but rather how the weak origins of the power affect how the Court exercises the power of judicial review in our contemporary democratic society. This is significant because a nonelected (undemocratic?) Court maintains the ultimate power of interpreting and enforcing the meaning of the Constitution as fundamental law by limiting the power of the "democratic branches" to its interpretations. These two themes, use of judicial review to limit the power of government to the Constitution as fundamental and supreme law, as set against the intent of the framers to establish a democratic form of government, will remain of great significance throughout our history and until the present day. The weak origins of judicial review and the nondemocratic makeup of the Supreme Court will thus assure the contemporary relevancy of these issues. Of importance to us will be their effect upon how the modern Court dispenses the judicial power. The cases that follow emphasize such via the real world of Supreme Court decisions: first is *Cooper v. Aaron*, a modern challenge to the power of judicial review in which southerners respond to the Supreme Court's decision in *Brown v. Board of Education* to desegregate the South, followed by the Court "selecting" the next president in *Bush v. Gore*. This case as well as the Brown case involves local actions. Just as in the case of Congressional legislation, judicial review is used to ensure that all levels of government, local as well as national government, operate according to the Court's interpretation of the Constitution.

COOPER v. AARON
358 U.S. 1 (1958)

Opinion of the Court by THE CHIEF JUSTICE, Mr. Justice BLACK, Mr. Justice FRANKFURTER, Mr. Justice DOUGLAS, Mr. Justice BURTON, Mr. Justice CLARK, Mr. Justice HARLAN, Mr. Justice BRENNAN, and Mr. Justice WHITTAKER.

As this case reaches us it raises questions of the highest importance to the maintenance of our federal system of government. It necessarily involves a claim by the Governor and Legislature of a State that there is no duty on state officials to obey federal court orders resting on this Court's considered interpretation of the United States Constitution. Specifically it involves actions by the Governor and Legislature of Arkansas upon the premise that they are not bound by our holding in Brown v. Board of Education, 347 U.S. 483, 74 S.Ct. 686, 98 L.Ed. 873. That holding was that the Fourteenth Amendment forbids States to use their governmental powers to bar children on racial grounds from attending schools where there is state participation through any arrangement, management, funds or property. We are urged to uphold a suspension of the Little Rock School Board's plan to do away with segregated public schools in Little Rock until state laws and efforts to upset and nullify our holding in Brown v. Board of Education have been further challenged and tested in the courts. We reject these contentions.

The constitutional rights of respondents are not to be sacrificed or yielded to the violence and disorder which have followed upon the actions of the Governor and Legislature. As this Court said some 41 years ago in a unanimous opinion in a case involving another aspect of racial segregation: "It is urged that this proposed segregation will promote the public peace by preventing race conflicts. Desirable as this is, and important as is the preservation of the public peace, this aim cannot be accomplished by laws or ordinances which deny rights created or protected by the federal Constitution." Buchanan v. Warley, 245 U.S. 60, 81, 38 S.Ct. 16, 20, 62 L.Ed. 149. Thus law and order are not here to be preserved by depriving the Negro children of their constitutional rights. The record before us clearly establishes that the growth of the Board's difficulties to a magnitude beyond its unaided power to control is the product of state action. Those difficulties, as counsel for the Board forthrightly conceded on the oral argument in this Court, can also be brought under control by state action.

What has been said, in the light of the facts developed, is enough to dispose of the case. However, we should answer the premise of the actions of the Governor and Legislature that they are not bound by our holding in the *Brown* case. It is necessary only to recall some basic constitutional propositions which are settled doctrine.

Article VI of the Constitution makes the Constitution the "supreme Law of the Land." In 1803, Chief Justice Marshall, speaking for a unanimous Court, referring to the Constitution as "the fundamental and paramount law of the nation," declared in the notable case of Marbury v. Madison, 1 Cranch 137, 177, 2 L.Ed. 60, that "It is emphatically the province and duty of the judicial department to say what the law is." This decision declared the basic principle that the federal judiciary is supreme in the exposition of the law of the Constitution, and that principle has ever since been respected by this Court and the Country as a permanent and indispensable feature of our constitutional system. It follows that the interpretation of the Fourteenth Amendment enunciated by this Court in the *Brown* case is the supreme law of the land, and Art. VI of the Constitution makes it of binding effect on the States "any Thing in the Constitution or Laws of any State to the Contrary notwithstanding." Every state legislator and executive and judicial officer is solemnly committed by oath taken pursuant to Art. VI, ¶ 3 "to support this Constitution." Chief Justice Taney, speaking for a unanimous Court in 1859, said that this requirement reflected the framers' "anxiety to preserve it [the Constitution] in full force, in all its powers, and to guard against resistance to or evasion of its authority, on the part of a State. . . ." Ableman v. Booth, 21 How. 506, 524, 16 L.Ed. 169.

No state legislator or executive or judicial officer can war against the Constitution without violating his undertaking to support it. Chief Justice Marshall spoke for a unanimous Court in saying that: "If the legislatures of the several states may, at will, annul the judgments of the courts of the United States, and destroy the rights acquired under those judgments, the constitution itself becomes a solemn mockery. . . ." United States v. Peters, 5 Cranch 115, 136, 3 L.Ed. 53. A Governor who asserts a power to nullify a federal court order is similarly restrained. If he had such power, said Chief Justice Hughes, in 1932, also for a unanimous Court, "it is manifest that the fiat of a state Governor, and not the Constitution of the United States, would be the supreme law of the land; that the restrictions of the Federal Constitution upon the exercise of state power would be but impotent phrases. . . ." Sterling v. Constantin, 287 U.S. 378, 397-398, 53 S.Ct. 190, 195, 77 L.Ed. 375.

[The] basic decision in *Brown* was unanimously reached by this Court only after the case had been briefed and twice argued and the issues had been given the most serious consideration. Since the first *Brown* opinion three new Justices have come to the Court. They are at one with the Justices still on the Court who participated in that basic decision as to its correctness, and that decision is now unanimously reaffirmed. The principles announced in that decision and the obedience of the States to them, according to the command of the Constitution, are indispensable for the protection of the freedoms guaranteed by our fundamental charter for all of us. Our constitutional ideal of equal justice under law is thus made a living truth.

BUSH v. GORE
531 U.S. 98 (2000)

PER CURIAM: . . .

[Following an agonizingly close presidential election in Florida, the Florida Supreme Court ordered a manual recount of undervotes, ballots on which no vote had been registered during the machine count, in all counties that had not yet completed a recount. In addition, it ordered that additional votes recovered during prior but untimely manual recounts in several other counties be included in the vote total.]

II

B

The individual citizen has no federal constitutional right to vote for electors for the President of the United States unless and until the state legislature chooses a statewide election as the means to implement its power to appoint members of the Electoral College. U.S. Const., Art. II, §1. This is the source for the statement in McPherson v. Blacker, 146 U.S. 1, 35 (1892), that the State legislature's power to select the manner for appointing electors is plenary; it may, if it so chooses, select the electors itself, which indeed was the manner used by State legislatures in several States for many years after the Framing of our Constitution. Id., at 28-33. History has now favored the voter, and in each of the several States the citizens themselves vote for Presidential electors. When the state legislature vests the right to vote for President in its people, the right to vote as the legislature has prescribed is fundamental; and one source of its fundamental nature lies in the equal weight accorded to each vote and the equal dignity owed to each voter. The State, of course, after granting the franchise in the special context of Article II, can take back the power to appoint electors. See id., at 35 ("[T]here is no doubt of the right of the legislature to resume the power at any time, for it can neither be taken away nor abdicated") (quoting S. Rep. No. 395, 43d Cong., 1st Sess.).

The right to vote is protected in more than the initial allocation of the franchise. Equal protection applies as well to the manner of its exercise. Having once granted the right to vote on equal terms, the State may not, by later arbitrary and disparate treatment, value one person's vote over that of another. See, e.g., Harper v. Virginia Bd. of Elections, 383 U.S. 663, 665 (1966) ("[O]nce the franchise is granted to the electorate, lines may not be drawn which are inconsistent with the Equal Protection Clause of the Fourteenth Amendment"). It must be remembered that "the right of suffrage can be denied by a debasement or dilution of the weight of a citizen's vote just as effectively as by wholly prohibiting the free exercise of the franchise." Reynolds v. Sims, 377 U.S. 533, 555 (1964). . . .

Much of the controversy seems to revolve around ballot cards designed to be perforated by a stylus but which, either through error or deliberate omission, have not been perforated with sufficient precision for a machine to count them. In some cases a piece of the card — a chad — is hanging, say by two corners. In other cases there is no separation at all, just an indentation.

The Florida Supreme Court has ordered that the intent of the voter be discerned from such ballots. For purposes of resolving the equal protection challenge, it is not necessary to decide whether the Florida Supreme Court had the authority under the legislative scheme for resolving election disputes to define what a legal vote is and to mandate a manual recount implementing that definition. The recount mechanisms implemented in response to the decisions of the Florida Supreme Court do not satisfy the minimum requirement for non-arbitrary treatment of voters necessary to secure the fundamental right. Florida's basic command for the count of legally cast votes is to consider the "intent of the voter." This is unobjectionable as an abstract proposition and a starting principle. The problem inheres in the absence of specific standards to ensure its equal application. The formulation of uniform rules to determine intent based on these recurring circumstances is practicable and, we conclude, necessary. . . .

An early case in our one person, one vote jurisprudence arose when a State accorded arbitrary and disparate treatment to voters in its different counties. Gray v. Sanders, 372 U.S. 368 (1963). The Court found a constitutional violation. We relied on these principles in the context of the Presidential selection process in Moore v. Ogilvie, 394 U.S. 814 (1969), where we invalidated a county-based procedure that diluted the influence of citizens in larger counties in the nominating process. There we observed that "[t]he idea that one group can be granted greater voting strength than another is hostile to the one man, one vote basis of our representative government." Id., at 819.

The State Supreme Court ratified this uneven treatment. It mandated that the recount totals from [several] counties [be] included in the certified total [even though] each of the counties used varying standards to determine what was a legal vote. Broward County used a more forgiving standard than Palm Beach County, and uncovered almost three times as many new votes, a result markedly disproportionate to the difference in population between the counties. . . .

In addition to these difficulties the actual process by which the votes were to be counted under the Florida Supreme Court's decision raises further concerns. That order did not specify who would recount the ballots. The county canvassing boards were forced to pull together ad hoc teams comprised of judges from various Circuits who had no previous training in handling and interpreting ballots. Furthermore, while others were permitted to observe, they were prohibited from objecting during the recount.

The recount process, in its features here described, is inconsistent with the minimum procedures necessary to protect the fundamental right of each voter in the special instance of a statewide recount under the authority of a single state judicial officer. Our consideration is limited to the present circumstances, for the problem of equal protection in election processes generally presents many complexities.

The question before the Court is not whether local entities, in the exercise of their expertise, may develop different systems for implementing elections. Instead, we are presented with a situation where a state court with the power to assure uniformity has ordered a statewide recount with minimal procedural safeguards. When a court orders a statewide remedy, there must be at least some assurance that the rudimentary requirements of equal treatment and fundamental fairness are satisfied. . . .

Upon due consideration of the difficulties identified to this point, it is obvious that the recount cannot be conducted in compliance with the requirements of equal protection and due process without substantial additional work. It would require not only the adoption (after opportunity for argument) of adequate statewide standards for determining what is a legal vote, and practicable procedures to implement them, but also orderly judicial review of any disputed matters that might arise. In addition, the Secretary of State has advised that the recount of only a portion of the ballots requires that the vote tabulation equipment be used to screen out undervotes, a function for which the machines were not designed. If a recount of overvotes were also required, perhaps even a second screening would be necessary. . . .

The Supreme Court of Florida has said that the legislature intended the State's electors to "participat[e] fully in the federal electoral process," as provided in 3 U.S.C. §5. [This provision is part of a complex scheme dealing with congressional procedures for the counting of electoral votes, enacted in the wake of the disputed presidential election of 1876. The statute provides that

> [if] any State shall have provided, by laws enacted prior to the day fixed for the appointment of the electors, for its final determination of any controversy or contest concerning the appointment of [electors] by judicial or other [methods], and such determination shall have been made at least six days before the time fixed for the meeting of the electors, such determination made pursuant to such law so existing on said day, and made at least six days prior to said time of meeting of the electors, shall be [conclusive].]

That statute, in turn, requires that any controversy or contest that is designed to lead to a conclusive selection of electors be completed by December 12. That date is upon us, and there is no recount procedure in place under the State Supreme Court's order that comports with minimal constitutional standards. Because it is evident that any recount seeking to meet the December 12 date will be unconstitutional for the reasons we have discussed, we reverse the judgment of the Supreme Court of Florida ordering a recount to proceed. . . .

None are more conscious of the vital limits on judicial authority than are the members of this Court, and none stand more in admiration of the Constitution's design to leave the selection of the President to the people, through their legislatures, and to the political sphere. When contending parties invoke the process of the courts, however, it becomes our unsought responsibility to resolve the federal and constitutional issues the judicial system has been forced to confront.

The judgment of the Supreme Court of Florida is reversed, and the case is remanded for further proceedings not inconsistent with this opinion.

Chief Justice REHNQUIST, with whom Justice SCALIA and Justice THOMAS join, concurring.

We join the per curiam opinion. We write separately because we believe there are additional grounds that require us to reverse the Florida Supreme Court's decision.

I

We deal here not with an ordinary election, but with an election for the President of the United States. . . .

[In] Anderson v. Celebrezze, 460 U.S. 780, 794-795 (1983), we said: "In the context of a Presidential election, state-imposed restrictions implicate a uniquely important national interest. For the President and the Vice President of the United States are the only elected officials who represent all the voters in the Nation."

In most cases, comity and respect for federalism compel us to defer to the decisions of state courts on issues of state law. That practice reflects our understanding that the decisions of state courts are definitive pronouncements of the will of the States as sovereigns. Cf. Erie R. Co. v. Tompkins, 304 U.S. 64 (1938). Of course, in ordinary cases, the distribution of powers among the branches of a State's government raises no questions of federal constitutional law, subject to the requirement that the government be republican in character. See U.S. Const., Art. IV, §4. But there are a few exceptional cases in which the Constitution imposes a duty or confers a power on a particular branch of a State's government. This is one of them. Article II, §1, cl. 2, provides that "each State shall appoint, in such Manner as the *Legislature* thereof may direct," electors for President and Vice President. (Emphasis added.) Thus, the text of the election law itself, and not just its interpretation by the courts of the States, takes on independent significance.

In McPherson v. Blacker, 146 U.S. 1 (1892), we explained that Art. II, §1, cl. 2, "conveys the broadest power of determination" and "leaves it to the legislature exclusively to define the method" of appointment. Id., at 27. A significant departure from the legislative scheme for appointing Presidential electors presents a federal constitutional question.

3 U.S.C. §5 informs our application of Art. II, §1, cl. 2, to the Florida statutory scheme, which, as the Florida Supreme Court acknowledged, took that statute into account. [If] we are to respect the legislature's Article II powers, therefore, we must ensure that post-election state court actions do not frustrate the legislative desire to attain the "safe harbor" provided by §5.

In Florida, the legislature has chosen to hold statewide elections to appoint the State's 25 electors. Importantly, the legislature has delegated the authority to run the elections and to oversee election disputes to the Secretary of State (Secretary), Fla. Stat. §97.012(1) (2000), and to state circuit courts, §§102.168(1), 102.168(8). Isolated sections of the code may well admit of more than one interpretation, but the general coherence of the legislative scheme may not be altered by judicial interpretation so as to wholly change the statutorily provided apportionment of responsibility among these various bodies. In any election but a Presidential election, the Florida Supreme Court can give as little or as much deference to Florida's executives as it chooses, so far as Article II is concerned, and this Court will have no cause to question the court's actions. But, with respect to a Presidential election, the court must be both mindful of the legislature's role under Article II in choosing the manner of appointing electors and deferential to those bodies expressly empowered by the legislature to carry out its constitutional mandate.

In order to determine whether a state court has infringed upon the legislature's authority, we necessarily must examine the law of the State as it existed prior to the action of the court. Though we generally defer to state courts on the interpretation of state law [there] are of course areas in which the Constitution requires this Court to undertake an independent, if still deferential, analysis of state law.

For example, in NAACP v. Alabama ex rel. Patterson, 357 U.S. 449 (1958), it was argued that we were without jurisdiction because the petitioner had not pursued the correct appellate remedy in Alabama's state courts. Petitioners had sought a state-law writ of certiorari in the Alabama Supreme Court when a writ of mandamus, according to that court, was proper. We found this state-law ground inadequate to defeat our jurisdiction because we were "unable to reconcile the procedural holding of the Alabama Supreme Court" with prior Alabama precedent. 357 U.S. at 456. The purported state-law ground was so novel, in our independent estimation, that "petitioner could not fairly be deemed to have been apprised of its existence." 357 U.S. at 457.

Six years later we decided Bouie v. City of Columbia, 378 U.S. 347 (1964), in which the state court had held, contrary to precedent, that the state trespass law applied to black sit-in demonstrators who had consent to enter private property but were then asked to leave. Relying upon *NAACP*, we concluded that the South Carolina Supreme Court's interpretation of a state penal statute had impermissibly broadened the scope of that statute beyond what a fair reading provided, in violation of due process. See 378 U.S. at 361-362. What we would do in the present case is precisely parallel: Hold that the Florida Supreme Court's interpretation of the Florida election laws impermissibly distorted them beyond what a fair reading required, in violation of Article II. . . .

II

Acting pursuant to its constitutional grant of authority, the Florida Legislature has created a detailed, if not perfectly crafted, statutory scheme that provides for appointment of Presidential electors by direct election. [The] legislature has designated the Secretary of State as the "chief election officer," with the responsibility to "obtain and maintain uniformity in the application, operation, and interpretation of the election laws." §97.012. The state legislature has delegated to county canvassing boards the duties of administering elections. §102.141. Those boards are responsible for providing results to the state Elections Canvassing [Commission]. Cf. Boardman v. Esteva, 323 So. 2d 259, 268, n. 5 (1975) ("The election process . . . is committed to the executive branch of government through duly designated officials all charged with specific duties. . . . [The] judgments [of these officials] are entitled to be regarded by the courts as presumptively correct. . . .").

After the election has taken place, [the] county canvassing boards must file certified election returns with the Department of State by 5 p.m. on the seventh day following the election. §102.112(1). . . .

The state legislature has also provided mechanisms both for protesting election returns and for contesting certified election results. Section 102.166 governs protests. Any protest must be filed prior to the certification of election results by the county canvassing board. §102.166(4)(b). Once a protest has been filed, "the county canvassing board may authorize a manual recount." §102.166(4)(c). If a sample recount conducted pursuant to §102.166(5) "indicates an error in the vote tabulation which could affect the outcome of the election," the county canvassing board is instructed to: "(a) Correct the error and recount the remaining precincts with the vote tabulation system; (b) Request the Department of State to verify the tabulation software; or (c) Manually recount all ballots," §102.166(5). In the event a canvassing board chooses to conduct a manual recount of all ballots, §102.166(7) prescribes procedures for such a recount.

Contests to the certification of an election, on the other hand, are controlled by §102.168. The grounds for contesting an election include "receipt of a number of illegal votes or rejection of a number of legal votes sufficient to change or place in doubt the result of the election." §102.168(3)(c). [Section] 102.168(8) provides that "the circuit judge to whom the contest is presented may fashion such orders as he or she deems necessary to ensure that each allegation in the complaint is investigated, examined, or checked, to prevent or correct any alleged wrong, and to provide any relief appropriate under such circumstances." In Presidential elections, the contest period necessarily terminates on the date set by 3 U.S.C. §5 for concluding the State's "final determination" of election controversies.

In its first decision, Palm Beach Canvassing Bd. v. Harris, 772 So. 2d 1220 (2000) (*Harris I*), the Florida Supreme Court extended the 7-day statutory certification deadline established by the legislature. This modification of the code, by lengthening the protest period, necessarily shortened the contest period for Presidential elections. Underlying the extension of the certification deadline and the shortchanging of the contest period was, presumably, the clear implication that certification was a matter of significance: The certified winner would enjoy presumptive validity, making a contest proceeding by the losing candidate an uphill battle. In its latest opinion, however, the court empties certification of virtually all legal consequence during the contest, and in doing so departs from the provisions enacted by the Florida Legislature.

The court determined that canvassing boards' decisions regarding whether to recount ballots past the certification deadline (even the certification deadline established by *Harris I*) are to be reviewed de novo, although the election code clearly vests discretion whether to recount in the boards, and sets strict deadlines subject to the Secretary's rejection of late tallies and monetary fines for tardiness. Moreover, the Florida court held that all late vote tallies arriving during the contest period should be automatically included in the certification regardless of the certification deadline (even the certification deadline established by *Harris I*), thus virtually eliminating both the deadline and the Secretary's discretion to disregard recounts that violate it.

Moreover, the court's interpretation of "legal vote," and hence its decision to order a contest-period recount, plainly departed from the legislative scheme. Florida statutory law cannot reasonably be thought to require the counting of improperly marked ballots. Each Florida precinct before election day provides instructions on how properly to cast a vote, §101.46; each polling place on election day contains a working model of the voting machine it uses, §101.5611; and each voting booth contains a sample ballot, §101.46. In precincts using punch-card ballots, voters are instructed to punch out the ballot cleanly:

AFTER VOTING, CHECK YOUR BALLOT CARD TO BE SURE YOUR VOTING SELECTIONS ARE CLEARLY AND CLEANLY PUNCHED AND THERE ARE NO CHIPS LEFT HANGING ON THE BACK OF THE CARD.

Instructions to Voters, quoted in Touchston v. McDermott, 2000 WL 1781942, *6 & n. 19 (CA11) (Tjoflat, J., dissenting). No reasonable person would call it "an error in the vote tabulation," Fla. Stat. §102.166(5), or a "rejection of legal votes," Fla. Stat. §102.168(3)(c), when electronic or electromechanical equipment performs precisely in the manner designed, and fails to count those ballots that are not marked in the manner that these voting instructions explicitly and prominently specify. The scheme that the Florida Supreme Court's opinion attributes to the legislature is one in which machines are required to be "capable of correctly counting votes," §101.5606(4), but which nonetheless regularly produces elections in which legal votes are predictably not tabulated, so that in close elections manual recounts are regularly required. This is of course absurd. The Secretary of State, who is authorized by law to issue binding interpretations of the election code, §§97.012, 106.23, rejected this peculiar reading of the statutes. See DE 00-13 (opinion of the Division of Elections). The Florida Supreme Court, although it must defer to the Secretary's interpretations, see Krivanek v. Take Back Tampa Political Committee, 625 So. 2d 840, 844 (Fla. 1993), rejected her reasonable interpretation and embraced the peculiar one. See Palm Beach County Canvassing Board v. Harris, No. SC00-2346 (Dec. 11, 2000) (*Harris III*).

But [in] a Presidential election the clearly expressed intent of the legislature must prevail. And there is no basis for reading the Florida statutes as requiring the counting of improperly marked ballots. . . .

III

The scope and nature of the remedy ordered by the Florida Supreme Court jeopardizes the "legislative wish" to take advantage of the safe harbor provided by 3 U.S.C. §5. December 12, 2000, is the last date for a final determination of the Florida electors that will satisfy §5. Yet in the late afternoon of December 8th — four days before this deadline — the Supreme Court of Florida ordered recounts of tens of thousands of so-called "undervotes" spread through 64 of the State's 67 counties. This was done in a search for elusive — perhaps delusive — certainty as to the exact count of 6 million votes. But no one claims that these ballots have not previously been tabulated; they were initially read by voting machines at the time of the election, and thereafter reread by virtue of Florida's automatic recount provision. No one claims there was any fraud in the election. The Supreme Court of Florida ordered this additional recount under the provision of the election code giving the circuit judge the authority to provide relief that is "appropriate under such circumstances." Fla. Stat. §102.168(8) (2000).

Surely when the Florida Legislature empowered the courts of the State to grant "appropriate" relief, it must have meant relief that would have become final by the cut-off date of 3 U.S.C. §5. In light of the inevitable legal challenges and ensuing appeals to the Supreme Court of Florida and petitions for certiorari to this Court, the entire recounting process could not possibly be completed by that date. . . .

Given all these factors, and in light of the legislative intent identified by the Florida Supreme Court to bring Florida within the "safe harbor" provision of 3 U.S.C. §5, the remedy prescribed by the Supreme Court of Florida cannot be deemed an "appropriate" one as of December 8. It significantly departed from the statutory framework in place on November 7, and authorized open-ended further proceedings which could not be completed by December 12, thereby preventing a final determination by that date.

For these reasons, in addition to those given in the per curiam, we would reverse.

Justice STEVENS, with whom Justice GINSBURG and Justice BREYER join, dissenting.

The Constitution assigns to the States the primary responsibility for determining the manner of selecting the Presidential electors. See Art. II, §1, cl. 2. When questions arise about the meaning of state laws, including election laws, it is our settled practice to accept the opinions of the highest courts of the States as providing the final answers. On rare occasions, however, either federal statutes or the Federal Constitution may require federal judicial intervention in state elections. This is not such an occasion.

The federal questions that ultimately emerged in this case are not substantial. Article II provides that "[e]ach State shall appoint, in such Manner as the Legislature thereof may direct, a Number of Electors." It does not create state legislatures out of whole cloth, but rather takes them as they come — as creatures born of, and constrained by, their state constitutions. [The] legislative power in Florida is subject to judicial review pursuant to Article V of the Florida Constitution, and nothing in Article II of the Federal Constitution frees the state legislature from the constraints in the state constitution that created it. [The] Florida Supreme Court's exercise of appellate jurisdiction therefore was wholly consistent with, and indeed contemplated by, the grant of authority in Article II. . . .

Nor are petitioners correct in asserting that the failure of the Florida Supreme Court to specify in detail the precise manner in which the "intent of the voter," Fla. Stat. §101.5614(5) (Supp. 2001), is to be determined rises to the level of a constitutional violation. We found such a violation when individual votes within the same State were weighted unequally, see, e.g., Reynolds v. Sims, but we have never before called into question the substantive standard by which a State determines that a vote has been legally cast. And there is no reason to think that the guidance provided to the factfinders, specifically the various canvassing boards, by the "intent of the voter" standard is any less sufficient — or will lead to results any less uniform than, for example, the "beyond a reasonable doubt" standard employed everyday by ordinary citizens in courtrooms across this country.

Admittedly, the use of differing substandards for determining voter intent in different counties employing similar voting systems may raise serious concerns. Those concerns are alleviated, if not eliminated, by the fact that a single impartial magistrate will ultimately adjudicate all objections arising from the recount process. . . .

What must underlie petitioners' entire federal assault on the Florida election procedures is an unstated lack of confidence in the impartiality and capacity of the state judges who would make the critical decisions if the vote count were to proceed. Otherwise, their position is wholly without merit. The endorsement of that position by the majority of this Court can only lend credence to the most cynical appraisal of the work of judges throughout the land. It is confidence in the men and women who administer the judicial system that is the true backbone of the rule of law. Time will one day heal the wound to that confidence that will be inflicted by today's decision. One thing, however, is certain. Although we may never know with complete certainty the identity of the winner of this year's Presidential election, the identity of the loser is perfectly clear. It is the Nation's confidence in the judge as an impartial guardian of the rule of law.

I respectfully dissent.

Justice SOUTER, with whom Justice BREYER joins, [dissenting]. . . .

Petitioners have raised an equal protection claim (or, alternatively, a due process claim), in the charge that unjustifiably disparate standards are applied in different electoral jurisdictions to otherwise identical facts. It is true that the Equal Protection Clause does not forbid the use of a variety of voting mechanisms within a jurisdiction, even though different mechanisms will have different levels of effectiveness in recording voters' intentions; local variety can be justified by concerns about cost, the potential value of innovation, and so on. But evidence in the record here suggests that a different order of disparity obtains under rules for determining a voter's intent that have been applied (and could continue to be applied) to identical types of ballots used in identical brands of machines and exhibiting identical physical characteristics (such as "hanging" or "dimpled" chads). I can conceive of no legitimate state interest served by these differing treatments of the expressions of voters' fundamental rights. The differences appear wholly arbitrary.

In deciding what to do about this, we should take account of the fact that electoral votes are due to be cast in six days. I would therefore remand the case to the courts of Florida with instructions to establish uniform standards for evaluating the several types of ballots that have prompted differing treatments, to be applied within and among counties when passing on such identical ballots in any further recounting (or successive recounting) that the courts might order.

Unlike the majority, I see no warrant for this Court to assume that Florida could not possibly comply with this requirement before the date set for the meeting of electors, December 18. . . .

I respectfully dissent.

Justice GINSBURG, with whom Justice STEVENS joins, and with whom Justice SOUTER and Justice BREYER join as to Part I, dissenting.

I . . .

Rarely has this Court rejected outright an interpretation of state law by a state high court. Fairfax's Devisee v. Hunter's Lessee, 7 Cranch 603 (1813), NAACP v. Alabama ex rel. Patterson, 357 U.S. 449 (1958), and Bouie v. City of Columbia, 378 U.S. 347 (1964), cited by The Chief Justice, are three such rare instances. But those cases are embedded in historical contexts hardly comparable to the situation here. *Fairfax's Devisee*, which held that the Virginia Court of Appeals had misconstrued its own forfeiture laws to deprive a British subject of lands secured to him by federal treaties, occurred amidst vociferous States' rights attacks on the Marshall Court. The Virginia court refused to obey this Court's *Fairfax's Devisee* mandate to enter judgment for the British subject's successor in interest. That refusal led to the Court's pathmarking decision in Martin v. Hunter's Lessee, 1 Wheat. 304 (1816). *Patterson*, a case decided three months after Cooper v. Aaron, 358 U.S. 1 (1958), in the face of Southern resistance to the civil rights movement, held that the Alabama Supreme Court had irregularly applied its own procedural rules to deny review of a contempt order against the NAACP arising from its refusal to disclose membership lists. [*Bouie*], stemming from a lunch counter "sit-in" at the height of the civil rights movement, held that the South Carolina Supreme Court's construction of its trespass laws — criminalizing conduct not covered by the text of an otherwise clear statute — was "unforeseeable" and thus violated due process when applied retroactively to the petitioners.

The Chief Justice's casual citation of these cases might lead one to believe they are part of a larger collection of cases in which we said that the Constitution impelled us to train a skeptical eye on a state court's portrayal of state law. But one would be hard pressed, I think, to find additional cases that fit the mold. As Justice Breyer convincingly explains, this case involves nothing close to the kind of recalcitrance by a state high court that warrants extraordinary action by this Court. The Florida Supreme Court concluded that counting every legal vote was the overriding concern of the Florida Legislature when it enacted the State's Election Code. The court surely should not be bracketed with state high courts of the Jim Crow South.

The Chief Justice says that Article II, by providing that state legislatures shall direct the manner of appointing electors, authorizes federal superintendence over the relationship between state courts and state legislatures, and licenses a departure from the usual deference we give to state court interpretations of state law. The Framers of our Constitution, however, understood that in a republican government, the judiciary would construe the legislature's enactments. See U.S. Const., Art. III; The Federalist No. 78 (A. Hamilton). In light of the constitutional guarantee to States of a "Republican Form of Government," U.S. Const., Art. IV, §4, Article II can hardly be read to invite this Court to disrupt a State's republican regime. Yet The Chief Justice today would reach out to do just that. By holding that Article II requires our revision of a state court's construction of state laws in order to protect one organ of the State from another, The Chief Justice contradicts the basic principle that a State may organize itself as it sees fit. See, e.g., Gregory v. Ashcroft, 501 U.S. 452, 460 (1991) ("Through the structure of its government, and the character of those who exercise government authority, a State defines itself as a sovereign."); Highland Farms Dairy v. Agnew, 300 U.S. 608, 612 (1937) ("How power shall be distributed by a state among its governmental organs is commonly, if not always, a question for the state itself."). Article II does not call for the scrutiny undertaken by this Court. . . .

II . . .

I cannot agree that the recount adopted by the Florida court, flawed as it may be, would yield a result any less fair or precise than the certification that preceded that recount. . . .

I dissent.

Justice BREYER . . . dissenting. . . .

II

[This portion of Justice Breyer's opinion was joined by Justices Stevens, Ginsburg, and Souter.]

Despite the reminder that this case involves "an election for the President of the United States," (Rehnquist, C.J., concurring), no preeminent legal concern, or practical concern related to legal questions, required this Court to hear this case, let alone to issue a stay that stopped Florida's recount process in its tracks. With one exception, petitioners' claims do not ask us to vindicate a constitutional provision designed to protect a basic human right. See, e.g., Brown v. Board of Education, 347 U.S. 483 (1954). Petitioners invoke fundamental fairness, namely, the need for procedural fairness, including finality. But with the one "equal protection" exception, they rely upon law that focuses, not upon that basic need, but upon the constitutional allocation of power. . . .

Of course, the selection of the President is of fundamental national importance. But that importance is political, not legal. And this Court should resist the temptation unnecessarily to resolve tangential legal disputes, where doing so threatens to determine the outcome of the election.

The Constitution and federal statutes themselves make clear that restraint is appropriate. They set forth a road map of how to resolve disputes about electors, even after an election as close as this one. That road map foresees resolution of electoral disputes by state courts. See 3 U.S.C. §5. [But] it nowhere provides for involvement by the United States Supreme Court.

To the contrary, the Twelfth Amendment commits to Congress the authority and responsibility to count electoral votes. A federal statute, the Electoral Count Act, enacted after the close 1876 Hayes-Tilden Presidential election, specifies that, after States have tried to resolve disputes (through "judicial" or other means), Congress is the body primarily authorized to resolve remaining disputes. See Electoral Count Act of 1887, 24 Stat. 373, 3 U.S.C. §§5, 6, and 15.

The legislative history of the Act makes clear its intent to commit the power to resolve such disputes to Congress, rather than the courts:

> "The two Houses are, by the Constitution, authorized to make the count of electoral votes. They can only count legal votes, and in doing so must determine, from the best evidence to be had, what are legal votes. . . . The power to determine rests with the two Houses, and there is no other constitutional tribunal." H. Rep. No. 1638, 49th Cong., 1st Sess., 2 (1886) (report submitted by Rep. Caldwell, Select Committee on the Election of President and Vice-President). . . .

Given this detailed, comprehensive scheme for counting electoral votes, there is no reason to believe that federal law either foresees or requires resolution of such a political issue by this Court. Nor, for that matter, is there any reason to think that the Constitution's Framers would have reached a different conclusion. Madison, at least, believed that allowing the judiciary to choose the presidential electors "was out of the question." Madison, July 25, 1787 (reprinted in 5 Elliot's Debates on the Federal Constitution 363 (2d ed. 1876)).

The decision by both the Constitution's Framers and the 1886 Congress to minimize this Court's role in resolving close federal presidential elections is as wise as it is clear. However awkward or difficult it may be for Congress to resolve difficult electoral disputes, Congress, being a political body, expresses the people's will far more accurately than does an unelected Court. And the people's will is what elections are about. . . .

[The history of the disputed election of 1876, including] the participation in the work of the electoral commission by five Justices, including Justice Bradley, did not lend that process legitimacy. Nor did it assure the public that the process had worked fairly, guided by the law. Rather, it simply embroiled Members of the Court in partisan conflict, thereby undermining respect for the judicial process. And the Congress that later enacted the Electoral Count Act knew it.

This history may help to explain why I think it not only legally wrong, but also most unfortunate, for the Court simply to have terminated the Florida recount. Those who caution judicial restraint in resolving political disputes have described the quintessential case for that restraint as a case marked, among other things, by the "strangeness of the issue," its "intractability to principled resolution," its "sheer momentousness, . . . which tends to unbalance judicial judgment," and "the inner vulnerability, the self-doubt of an institution which is electorally irresponsible and has no earth to draw strength from [citing A. Bickel, The Least Dangerous Branch 184 (1962)]." Those characteristics mark this case. . . .

I fear that in order to bring this agonizingly long election process to a definitive conclusion, we have not adequately attended to that necessary "check upon our own exercise of power," "our own sense of self-restraint." United States v. Butler, 297 U.S. 1, 79 (1936) (Stone, J., dissenting). Justice Brandeis once said of the Court, "The most important thing we do is not doing." Bickel, supra, at 71. What it does today, the Court should have left undone. I would repair the damage done as best we now can, by permitting the Florida recount to continue under uniform standards.

I respectfully dissent.

Comments on *Bush v. Gore.* Volumes have been written concerning this opinion "selecting a president." While the opinion underscores the modern significance of the power of judicial review and the Supreme Court in U.S. society, note the following commentators' views of the opinion.

CASS SUNSTEIN, ORDER WITHOUT LAW
68 U. Chi. L. Rev. 757, 758-59 (2001)

The Court's decision in Bush v. Gore did have two fundamental virtues. First, it produced a prompt and decisive conclusion to the chaotic post-election period of 2000. Indeed, it probably did so in a way that carried more simplicity and authority than anything that might have been expected from the United States Congress. The Court might even have avoided a genuine constitutional crisis. Second, the Court's equal protection holding carries considerable appeal. On its face, that holding has the potential to create the most expansive, and perhaps sensible, protection for voting rights since the Court's one-person, one-vote decisions of mid-century. . . .

The Court's decision also had two large vices. First, the Court effectively resolved the presidential election not unanimously, but by a 5-4 vote, with the majority consisting entirely of the Court's most conservative justices. Second, the Court's rationale was not only exceedingly ambitious but also embarrassingly weak. However appealing, its equal protection holding had no basis in precedent or in history. It also raises a host of puzzles for the future, which the Court appeared to try to resolve with its minimalist cry of "here, but nowhere else." . . .

From the standpoint of constitutional order, the Court might well have done the nation a service. From the standpoint of legal reasoning, the Court's decision was very bad. In short, the Court's decision produced order without law. . . .

PAMELA S. KARLAN, UNDULY PARTIAL: THE SUPREME COURT AND THE FOURTEENTH AMENDMENT IN *BUSH v. GORE*
29 Fla. St. U. L. Rev. 587, 600-01 (2001)

[Bush v. Gore] was political, in the broad sense of the word. The Court was trying to wrap its decision in the mantle of its most popularly and jurisprudentially successful intervention into the political process: the one-person, one-vote cases. This is a familiar strategy. Consider Planned Parenthood v. Casey, the case in which the Court reaffirmed the central right to reproductive autonomy recognized in Roe v. Wade. The joint opinion written by Justices O'Connor, Kennedy, and Souter invoked another iconic Equal Protection Clause case, Brown v. Board of Education. It too treated the responsibility of articulating binding principles of constitutional law as an unsought responsibility. And it saw a special dimension "present whenever the Court's interpretation of the Constitution calls the contending sides of a national controversy to end their national division by accepting a common mandate rooted in the Constitution." It identified only two such occasions "in our lifetime, . . . the decisions of *Brown* and *Roe*."

Perhaps the Supreme Court saw Bush v. Gore as a third such occasion. Once again, the Court was asking the nation to end its close division by accepting a common mandate rooted in the Constitution and accepting a judicial resolution. And as between the Equal Protection Clause — source of some of the Supreme Court's finest moments — and the other contenders, it was no contest. If the Supreme Court was going to stop the recount, it had to use a constitutional provision with a pedigree. The Equal Protection Clause provided exactly that. Moreover, it allowed the Court to invoke the specter of unfair treatment of voters, whereas the other available constitutional contenders protected either the prerogative of state legislatures (Article II, Section 1) or, even worse, the interests of candidate George W. Bush (the Due Process Clause . . .).

JOHN C. YOO, IN DEFENSE OF THE COURT'S LEGITIMACY
68 U. Chi. L. Rev. 775, 776, 779-81 (2001)

[C]oncerns about the Court's legitimacy are overblown. While it is certainly too early to be sure, the Court's actions, and their impact on the political system, come nowhere close to approaching the circumstances that surrounded earlier, real threats to the Court's standing. The Court did not decide any substantive issues — on a par with abortion or privacy rights, for example — that call upon the Court to remain continually at the center of political controversy for years. Instead, the Court issued a fairly narrow decision in a one-of-a-kind case — the procedures to govern presidential election counts — that is not likely to reappear in our lifetimes. Rather than acting hypocritically and lawlessly, the Court's decision to bring the Florida election dispute to a timely, and final, end not only restored stability to the political system but was also consistent with the institutional role the Court has shaped for itself over the last decade. . . .

The Court's authority has come under serious question four times in our history: the Marshall Court, the Taney Court's decision in *Dred Scott*, the Court's early resistance to the New Deal, and the Warren Court's fight against segregation and its expansion of individual liberties. Close inspection of these periods show that they bear little resemblance to Bush v. Gore. . . .

The defining characteristic of several of these periods was the persistent, central role of the Court in the political disputes of the day. Contrast these periods with Bush v. Gore. In Bush v. Gore, the Court sought to resolve a narrow legal issue involving the selection of presidential electors. The question bears no constitutional implications for the resolution of any significant and ongoing social issues of today — abortion, race relations, education, social security, defense. The decision poses no bar to a society that seeks to use the democratic process to resolve any pressing social problems. While the Democratic party has reason to be dissatisfied with the outcome of Bush v. Gore, it has no interest in challenging the legal reasoning of the decision in the future. It is highly unlikely that the Court will remain a central player in future presidential election contests. . . .

MICHAEL J. KLARMAN, *BUSH v. GORE* THROUGH THE LENS OF CONSTITUTIONAL HISTORY
89 Cal. L. Rev. 1721, 1722, 1747-48, 1761-64 (2001)

[H]istory's verdict on a Supreme Court ruling depends more on whether public opinion ultimately supports the outcome than on the quality of the legal reasoning or the craftsmanship of the Court's opinion. . . .

The principal variable influencing the Court's reputation is how popular or unpopular its decisions are. Second, . . . the intensity of that sentiment — how strongly supporters and opponents feel about the underlying issue — influences the Court's standing. Third, [is how convinced opponents are] . . . that the Court decision resolving that issue will be implemented, rather than evaded or even nullified. . . . Fourth, the relative power of the constituencies that support and oppose the Court's rulings may be relevant. . . . Fifth, some constitutional issues linger, while others fade away. Controversial decisions on topics that quickly become obsolete are unlikely to do the Court much long-term harm. Sixth, public opinion changes, often quite dramatically, on some constitutional issues but not others. . . . Seventh, Justices sometimes, but not always, enjoy subsequent opportunities to adjust their original decision, thus modulating results that initially proved controversial. Eighth, contentious constitutional decisions sometimes come in packages. A ruling that might not have significantly impaired the Court's standing had it been an isolated event, may weaken an institution already under siege because of contemporaneous decisions. . . .

Half the country, the half that voted for Al Gore, thinks the result in Bush v. Gore was wrong; many think it was egregiously so. . . . Yet, while nearly all Democrats criticize *Bush*, it is not clear how intense their opposition is. Surely most Americans are more energized by presidential elections than by flag burning. On the other hand, relatively few Gore supporters seem to have manifested an intensity of commitment for their candidate approaching that displayed by right-to-lifers in opposition to Roe v. Wade. Indeed, a principal reason that Gore found himself in the Florida predicament that he did (recall that all the political scientists' models predicted a relatively comfortable victory for him) was the relative lack of enthusiasm evinced by many Democrats for their party's candidate. Thus one might surmise that many Democrats' opposition to Bush v. Gore will be lukewarm at best. My hunch, however, is that this supposition is mistaken. . . . This efficacious a ruling, on this divisive an issue, is certain to generate tremendous resentment toward the Court.

As to the relative power of the constituencies impacted by the Court's decision, both Democrats and Republicans have plenty of political and economic clout in American society. Thus, Bush v. Gore is not a case where the Court's critics are relatively disadvantaged in the public relations battle that follows the ruling. On the other hand, it is hard to think of a constitutional issue that is more destined to become obsolete. George W. Bush will be president, possibly as a result of the Supreme Court's ruling, for four years. If he serves eight years, an intervening independent cause, a second electoral victory, will greatly reduce the Court's responsibility for the second term. . . . Moreover, the Supreme Court's ruling in *Bush*, by design, will have implications for no other constitutional issue. . . . Memories of what most Democrats will regard as the (at least attempted) judicial theft of a presidential election will survive, but they will be just that — memories. . . .

On the other hand, unlike with racial segregation, where public opinion transformed over time, popular attitudes toward Bush v. Gore probably never will change very much. Democrats are likely always to believe that the Supreme Court intervened in the 2000 presidential election because the conservative Justices preferred George W. Bush for president. Perhaps some attitudes will change if Bush proves to be a particularly good or bad President, but probably not too many. Moreover, unlike with the death penalty, the Supreme Court almost certainly will enjoy no future opportunities to revisit the issue in *Bush* . . . and thus to fix its "mistake." Once elected president, Bush cannot be "unelected."

Finally, from the "basket of issues" perspective, the Rehnquist Court might survive Bush v. Gore reasonably unscathed, because the remainder of the Court's constitutional jurisprudence has been such a political grab bag of results. . . . While the Rehnquist Court arguably has been the most activist in history, its activism does not manifest a consistent political valence. In recent years, liberals generally have won on issues involving abortion, school prayer, gender discrimination, and freedom of speech. Conservatives, on the other hand, have triumphed on issues such as affirmative action, minority voting districts, public aid to parochial schools, federalism, the death penalty, and (usually) criminal procedure. . . . Perhaps Democratic ire over Bush v. Gore is somewhat ameliorated by the Rehnquist Court's continuing propensity to distribute a substantial share of constitutional victories to liberals.

MARK TUSHNET, RENORMALIZING *BUSH v. GORE*: AN ANTICIPATORY INTELLECTUAL HISTORY
90 Geo. L.J. 113, 113-16, 124-25 (2001)

The critical legal studies claim that law, properly understood, was indistinguishable from politics, properly understood, was quite threatening to the self-understanding of legal elites. . . . Legal elites are heavily invested in insisting that there is a real difference between law and politics. They are also invested, though slightly less so, in insisting that judges typically do law rather than politics. These investments . . . meant that something had to be done to take the sting out of the criticisms that [Bush v. Gore] was infected by blatant partisanship . . . so that we can return to our belief that law is sensibly distinguishable from politics. . . .

I will identify several major techniques of renormalization. The first is simple enough: Ignore the case. Treat it as a unique event in the legal universe, unlikely ever to be repeated. . . . The difficulty that ignoring the case poses for legal elites is precisely that the decision presents itself as law, and for legal elites, judicial decisions are distinguished from executive ones, for example, precisely because executive decisions need have no implications for the future — can be sui generis — in ways that judicial decisions must.

The second renormalization technique . . . acknowledges that the decision in Bush v. Gore cannot really be regarded as an example of courts operating at anywhere near their best and may even be a (hopefully) isolated case in which law was in fact reduced to politics. . . . [T]he Court, and the nation, confronted a chaotic situation implicating both the selection of the nation's most important public official and an impending constitutional crisis. The Court, in this view, was in a position to resolve the crisis in a statesmanlike way. Perhaps the Court's legal theory was thin, but a barely adequate legal theory may be sufficient when invoked to avert a serious constitutional crisis. . . .

[A third] technique of renormalization . . . [tries] to work out the doctrinal implications of the Court's innovations. . . .

A final technique of renormalization is in some ways the most interesting. It involves the generalized invocation of rule-of-law norms, typically in the form of assertions that the

Supreme Court's decision, while perhaps incorrect, nonetheless deserves respect because the Court is our nation's voice of the law. . . . Not surprisingly, this creates something of a psychological difficulty, related to, but not quite the same as, the phenomenon of cognitive dissonance. People find it hard to think that decisions with which they disagree are nevertheless justified. People also find it hard to give up on the ideal of the rule of law. The outcome is predictable. As time passes, people come to think that the decisions with which they initially disagreed were actually not wrong. I think we can expect to see, and I think reasonably soon, progressives asserting that, as a matter of fact, Bush v. Gore was correctly decided.

As indeed it was. After all, the equal protection doctrine the case articulated can certainly be turned to progressive uses. . . . And that, to conclude, would be another vindication of a different critical legal studies claim, this one about the indeterminacy of legal doctrine.

B. CONTEMPORARY USE OF THE JUDICIAL POWER

Both the weak origins of judicial review and the ultimate power in a democratic society resting in a nonelected Court are meaningful today because of how they affect the Court's use of the judicial power. Justice Learned Hand, for example, supported his thesis that the Court should use the power of judicial review "sparingly" because he found the power only "implied" from the Constitution. To Hand, therefore, the power of judicial review was "not a logical deduction, but . . . a practical condition upon its [the Constitution's] successful operation, it need not be exercised whenever a Court sees an invasion of the Constitution." Learned Hand, *The Bill of Rights* (1958). Note how Hand uses the weak origins of judicial review to fashion a role of the Court where the use of the power is limited. When would Hand conclude that the Court should apply judicial review? What does he mean by "a practical condition upon its successful operation"? It is worthy of mention that implementation of Hand's approach requires that the Court maintain the discretion to decide whether or not it wants to hear a case. Thus, for example, to use the power sparingly the Court must have the ability to sidestep cases. Do democratic principles demand such?

To emphasize the interrelation of the "weak origins" thesis to the use of the judicial power, the views of another equally renowned constitutional scholar, Herbert Wechsler. Wechsler found that the power of judicial review was "anchored in the Constitution," much as Justice Marshall concluded in *Marbury*, and disagreed with Hand in asserting that because of such "there is no such escape from . . . judicial obligation; the duty cannot be attenuated in any way." Fearful of the discretion necessary for the Court to apply the power sparingly, Wechsler concluded that the Court must "decide the case and . . . decide it in accordance with the law." There should be no discretion to decline jurisdiction. See Herbert Wechsler, *Toward Neutral Principles of Constitutional Law*, 73 Harv. L. Rev. 1 (1959).

The conflicting themes of judicial review in a democratic society, as set against "weak origins," affects not only whether the Court might hear a case, but also how it should interpret the Constitution. Thus, because of weak origins of judicial review and democratic principles, can we argue that the Court should maintain a very limited, perhaps strictly construed, interpretation of the Constitution? Or, based upon the Supremacy Clause, should the concept of limiting the power of government to the document as fundamental law cause the Court to be more active and interpret the Constitution as a "living document"? These issues affect all of constitutional law and extend the vibrancy of *Marbury* to today: when the Court should hear cases and how it should go about interpreting the Constitution.

The articles that are assigned and available "on-line" provide a convenient basis for understanding judicial review and the operation of the Supreme Court. They address the classic themes concerning how the Court should apply judicial power. This is the case both in the sense of when the Court should hear cases and render the power and, once it has so decided, how it should interpret the Constitution. Each article is prefaced by a short description of the meaning and relevancy of the piece in relation to our purpose.

THE FEDERALIST NO. 78
(Alexander Hamilton)

[This is the classic defense for the ultimate power of constitutional interpretation resting in the "least dangerous branch."]

The Judiciary Department
Independent Journal
Saturday, June 14, 1788

To the People of the State of New York:

We proceed now to an examination of the judiciary department of the proposed government.

In unfolding the defects of the existing Confederation, the utility and necessity of a federal judicature have been clearly pointed out. It is the less necessary to recapitulate the considerations there urged, as the propriety of the institution in the abstract is not disputed; the only questions which have been raised being relative to the manner of constituting it, and to its extent. To these points, therefore, our observations shall be confined.

The manner of constituting it seems to embrace these several objects: 1st. The mode of appointing the judges. 2d. The tenure by which they are to hold their places. 3d. The partition of the judiciary authority between different courts, and their relations to each other.

First. As to the mode of appointing the judges; this is the same with that of appointing the officers of the Union in general, and has been so fully discussed in the two last numbers, that nothing can be said here which would not be useless repetition.

Second. As to the tenure by which the judges are to hold their places; this chiefly concerns their duration in office; the provisions for their support; the precautions for their responsibility.

According to the plan of the convention, all judges who may be appointed by the United States are to hold their offices *during good behavior*; which is conformable to the most approved of the State constitutions and among the rest, to that of this State. Its propriety having been drawn into question by the adversaries of that plan, is no light symptom of the rage for objection, which disorders their imaginations and judgments. The standard of good behavior for the continuance in office of the judicial magistracy, is certainly one of the most valuable of the modern improvements in the practice of government. In a monarchy it is an excellent barrier to the despotism of the prince; in a republic it is a no less excellent barrier to the encroachments and oppressions of the representative body. And it is the best expedient which can be devised in any government, to secure a steady, upright, and impartial administration of the laws.

Whoever attentively considers the different departments of power must perceive, that, in a government in which they are separated from each other, the judiciary, from the nature of its functions, will always be the least dangerous to the political rights of the Constitution; because it will be least in a capacity to annoy or injure them. The Executive not only dispenses the honors, but holds the sword of the community. The legislature not only commands the purse, but prescribes the rules by which the duties and rights of every citizen are to be regulated. The judiciary, on the contrary, has no influence over either the sword or the purse; no direction either of the strength or of the wealth of the society; and can take no active resolution whatever. It may truly be said to have neither *force* nor *will*, but merely judgment; and must ultimately depend upon the aid of the executive arm even for the efficacy of its judgments.

This simple view of the matter suggests several important consequences. It proves incontestably, that the judiciary is beyond comparison the weakest of the three departments of power; that it can never attack with success either of the other two; and that all possible care is requisite to enable it to defend itself against their attacks. It equally proves, that though individual oppression may now and then proceed from the courts of justice, the general liberty of the people can never be endangered from that quarter; I mean so long as the judiciary remains truly distinct from both the legislature and the Executive. For I agree, that "there is no liberty, if the power of judging be not separated from the legislative and executive powers." And it proves, in the last place, that as liberty can have nothing to fear from the judiciary alone, but would have every thing to fear from its union with either of the other departments; that as all the effects of such a union must ensue from a dependence of the former on the latter, notwithstanding a nominal and apparent separation; that as, from the natural feebleness of the judiciary, it is in continual jeopardy of being overpowered, awed, or influenced by its co-ordinate branches; and that as nothing can contribute so much to its firmness and independence as permanency in office, this quality may therefore be justly regarded as an indispensable ingredient in its constitution, and, in a great measure, as the citadel of the public justice and the public security.

The complete independence of the courts of justice is peculiarly essential in a limited Constitution. By a limited Constitution, I understand one which contains certain specified exceptions to the legislative authority; such, for instance, as that it shall pass no bills of attainder, no *ex post facto* laws, and the like. Limitations of this kind can be preserved in practice no other way than through the medium of courts of justice, whose duty it must be to declare all acts contrary to the manifest tenor of the Constitution void. Without this, all the reservations of particular rights or privileges would amount to nothing.

Some perplexity respecting the rights of the courts to pronounce legislative acts void, because contrary to the Constitution, has arisen from an imagination that the doctrine would imply a superiority of the judiciary to the legislative power. It is urged that the authority which can declare the acts of another void, must necessarily be superior to the one whose acts may be declared void. As this doctrine is of great importance in all the American constitutions, a brief discussion of the ground on which it rests cannot be unacceptable.

There is no position which depends on clearer principles, than that every act of a delegated authority, contrary to the tenor of the commission under which it is exercised, is void. No legislative act, therefore, contrary to the Constitution, can be valid. To deny this, would be to affirm, that the deputy is greater than his principal; that the servant is above his master; that the representatives of the people are superior to the people themselves; that men acting by virtue of powers, may do not only what their powers do not authorize, but what they forbid.

If it be said that the legislative body are themselves the constitutional judges of their own powers, and that the construction they put upon them is conclusive upon the other departments, it may be answered, that this cannot be the natural presumption, where it is not to be collected from any particular provisions in the Constitution. It is not otherwise to be supposed, that the Constitution could intend to enable the representatives of the people to substitute their *will* to that of their constituents. It is far more rational to suppose, that the courts were designed to be an intermediate body between the people and the legislature, in order, among other things, to keep the latter within the limits assigned to their authority. The interpretation of the laws is the proper and peculiar province of the courts. A constitution is, in fact, and must be regarded by the judges, as a fundamental law. It therefore belongs to them to ascertain its meaning, as well as the meaning of any particular act proceeding from the legislative body. If there should happen to be an irreconcilable variance between the two, that which has the superior obligation and validity ought, of course, to be preferred; or, in other words, the Constitution ought to be preferred to the statute, the intention of the people to the intention of their agents.

Nor does this conclusion by any means suppose a superiority of the judicial to the legislative power. It only supposes that the power of the people is superior to both; and that where the will of the legislature, declared in its statutes, stands in opposition to that of the people, declared in the Constitution, the judges ought to be governed by the latter rather than the former. They ought to regulate their decisions by the fundamental laws, rather than by those which are not fundamental.

This exercise of judicial discretion, in determining between two contradictory laws, is exemplified in a familiar instance. It not uncommonly happens, that there are two statutes existing at one time, clashing in whole or in part with each other, and neither of them containing any repealing clause or expression. In such a case, it is the province of the courts to liquidate and fix their meaning and operation. So far as they can, by any fair construction, be reconciled to each other, reason and law conspire to dictate that this should be done; where this is impracticable, it becomes a matter of necessity to give effect to one, in exclusion of the other. The rule which has obtained in the courts for determining their relative validity is, that the last in order of time shall be preferred to the first. But this is a mere rule of construction, not derived from any positive law, but from the nature and reason of the thing. It is a rule not enjoined upon the courts by legislative provision, but adopted by themselves, as consonant to truth and propriety, for the direction of their conduct as interpreters of the law. They thought it reasonable, that between the interfering acts of an *equal* authority, that which was the last indication of its will should have the preference.

But in regard to the interfering acts of a superior and subordinate authority, of an original and derivative power, the nature and reason of the thing indicate the converse of that rule as proper to be followed. They teach us that the prior act of a superior ought to be preferred to the subsequent act of an inferior and subordinate authority; and that accordingly, whenever a particular statute contravenes the Constitution, it will be the duty of the judicial tribunals to adhere to the latter and disregard the former.

It can be of no weight to say that the courts, on the pretense of a repugnancy, may substitute their own pleasure to the constitutional intentions of the legislature. This might as well happen in the case of two contradictory statutes; or it might as well happen in every adjudication upon any single statute. The courts must declare the sense of the law; and if they should be disposed to exercise *will* instead of *judgment*, the consequence would equally be the substitution of their pleasure to that of the legislative body. The observation, if it prove anything, would prove that there ought to be no judges distinct from that body.

If, then, the courts of justice are to be considered as the bulwarks of a limited Constitution against legislative encroachments, this consideration will afford a strong argument for the permanent tenure of judicial offices, since nothing will contribute so much as this to that independent spirit in the judges which must be essential to the faithful performance of so arduous a duty.

This independence of the judges is equally requisite to guard the Constitution and the rights of individuals from the effects of those ill humors, which the arts of designing men, or the influence of particular conjunctures, sometimes disseminate among the people themselves, and which, though they speedily give place to better information, and more deliberate reflection, have a tendency, in the meantime, to occasion dangerous innovations in the government, and serious oppressions of the minor party in the community. Though I trust the friends of the proposed Constitution will never concur with its enemies, in questioning that fundamental principle of republican government, which admits the right of the people to alter or abolish the established Constitution, whenever they find it inconsistent with their happiness, yet it is not to be inferred from this principle, that the representatives of the people, whenever a momentary inclination happens to lay hold of a majority of their constituents, incompatible with the provisions in the existing Constitution, would, on that account, be justifiable in a violation of those provisions; or that the courts would be under a greater obligation to connive at infractions in this shape, than when they had proceeded wholly from the cabals of the representative body. Until the people have, by some solemn and authoritative act, annulled or changed the established form, it is binding upon themselves collectively, as well as individually; and no presumption, or even knowledge, of their sentiments, can warrant their representatives in a departure from it, prior to such an act. But it is easy to see, that it would require an uncommon portion of fortitude in the judges to do their duty as faithful guardians of the Constitution, where legislative invasions of it had been instigated by the major voice of the community.

But it is not with a view to infractions of the Constitution only, that the independence of the judges may be an essential safeguard against the effects of occasional ill humors in the society. These sometimes extend no farther than to the injury of the private rights of particular classes of citizens, by unjust and partial laws. Here also the firmness of the judicial magistracy is of vast importance in mitigating the severity and confining the operation of such laws. It not only serves to moderate the immediate mischiefs of those which may have been passed, but it operates as a check upon the legislative body in passing them; who, perceiving that obstacles to the success of iniquitous intention are to be expected from the scruples of the courts, are in a manner compelled, by the very motives of the injustice they meditate, to qualify their attempts. This is a circumstance calculated to have more influence upon the character of our governments, than but few may be aware of. The benefits of the integrity and moderation of the judiciary have already been felt in more States than one; and though they may have displeased those whose sinister expectations they may have disappointed, they must have commanded the esteem and applause of all the virtuous and disinterested. Considerate men, of every description, ought to prize whatever will tend to beget or fortify that temper in the courts: as no man can be sure that he may not be to-morrow the victim of a spirit of injustice, by which he may be a gainer to-day. And every man must now feel, that the inevitable tendency of such a spirit is to sap the foundations of public and private confidence, and to introduce in its stead universal distrust and distress.

That inflexible and uniform adherence to the rights of the Constitution, and of individuals, which we perceive to be indispensable in the courts of justice, can certainly not be expected from judges who hold their offices by a temporary commission. Periodical appointments, however regulated, or by whomsoever made, would, in some way or other, be fatal to their necessary independence. If the power of making them was committed either to the Executive or legislature, there would be danger of an improper complaisance to the branch which possessed it; if to both, there would be an unwillingness to hazard the displeasure of either; if to the people, or to persons chosen by them for the special purpose, there would be too great a disposition to consult popularity, to justify a reliance that nothing would be consulted but the Constitution and the laws.

There is yet a further and a weightier reason for the permanency of the judicial offices, which is deducible from the nature of the qualifications they require. It has been frequently remarked, with great propriety, that a voluminous code of laws is one of the inconveniences necessarily connected with the advantages of a free government. To avoid an arbitrary discretion in the courts, it is indispensable that they should be bound down by strict rules and precedents, which serve to define and point out their duty in every particular case that comes before them; and it will readily be conceived from the variety of controversies which grow out of the folly and wickedness of mankind, that the records of those precedents must unavoidably swell to a very considerable bulk, and must demand long and laborious study to acquire a competent knowledge of them. Hence it is, that there can be but few men in the society who will have sufficient skill in the laws to qualify them for the stations of judges. And making the proper deductions for the ordinary depravity of human nature, the number must be still smaller of those who unite the requisite integrity with the requisite knowledge. These considerations apprise us, that the government can have no great option between fit character; and that a temporary duration in office, which would naturally discourage such characters from quitting a lucrative line of practice to accept a seat on the bench, would have a tendency to throw the administration of justice into hands less able, and less well qualified, to conduct it with utility and dignity. In the present circumstances of this country, and in those in which it is likely to be for a long time to come, the disadvantages on this score would be greater than they may at first sight appear; but it must be confessed, that they are far inferior to those which present themselves under the other aspects of the subject.

Upon the whole, there can be no room to doubt that the convention acted wisely in copying from the models of those constitutions which have established *good behavior* as the tenure of their judicial offices, in point of duration; and that so far from being blamable on this account, their plan would have been inexcusably defective, if it had wanted this important feature of good government. The experience of Great Britain affords an illustrious comment on the excellence of the institution.

PUBLIUS.

1. The celebrated Montesquieu, speaking of them, says: "Of the three powers above mentioned, the judiciary is next to nothing." — *Spirit of Laws*. Vol. I, page 186.

2. *Idem*, page 181.

3. Vide Protest of the Minority of the Convention of Pennsylvania, Martin's Speech, etc.

C. CONSTITUTIONAL INTERPRETATION: "WHEN AND HOW"

1. HEAD START — CONTRACEPTION/REPRODUCTION: A CASE STUDY

The ongoing debate in teaching constitutional law has always revolved around whether materials concerning Article III requirements for jurisdiction (case and controversy) should be covered prior to the "substance" of the Constitution (governmental powers, individual rights, and so on) or after. If, as has been the purpose of our inquiry thus far, the Court should maintain the discretion to decline jurisdiction when it feels the power of judicial review should be limited in a democratic society, the Court must have means of "opening or closing" the "judicial door" to accomplish such. After all, the Court, though it may maintain the "ultimate power" of constitutional interpretation, is still a court, and "abstention" still requires a legal basis upon which to so act. This necessitates law, if you will, that can be instrumental in allowing the Court to hear or not hear the issues presented in the case before it. Thus, for example and as discussed earlier, passive virtue to Bickel or use of the power sparingly to Hand requires a legal basis to avoid rendering the judicial power.

The Article III requirements of a "case and controversy" have served this end. The next section of the text will review these issues in detail. What makes organization of materials difficult is the fact that although the Court may decline jurisdiction citing to Article III requirements as not having been met, oftentimes it is the merits of the case (perhaps dealing with abortion or affirmative action) that are the actual bases for declining review. Consequently, it can be argued that the substantive constitutional issues should be covered before case and controversy, if denials of jurisdiction can be best explained by the merits of the case to be decided. Yet, one can also argue that such an approach takes the "horse before the cart," as it is illogical to review cases concerning jurisdiction, a ruling which must come before any consideration of the merits, after studying the merits.

The materials that follow — a mini-review of constitutional decision making — are structured to avoid these pitfalls and to allow you to see how the Constitution's jurisdiction requirements (Article III, case and controversy) are applied as a means of controlling the application of judicial power. This is, so to speak, a course within a course. We will use contraceptive/reproduction cases as means of exemplifying how the issues we have discussed up to this point affect the actual process of how the Supreme Court goes about deciding cases. The selection of these cases is no coincidence. The abortion cases have been quite controversial in the public eye, and the interest they generate becomes an attractive teaching tool and vehicle for our study. They are excellent examples of how the application of the power of judicial review is affected by the nature of the issues before the Court and the role of the Court in our democratic society.

We have asserted thus far, through cases, texts, and articles, that the dilemma of judicial review, given its weak origins and undemocratic character, affects not only *when* the Court should hear a case, but, and equally as important, *how* it should go about interpreting the Constitution. The controversy surrounding the abortion/reproductive decisions highlights all of the issues and, by means of example, illuminates how the nature of the issues before the Court affects both *when* and *how* the Court goes about deciding cases.

Tileston, *Poe*, and *Griswold* all deal with the same statute — the Connecticut ban on birth contraception. They are included as examples of how the controversy surrounding the statute affected not only *when* the Court would hear the case, but *how* the case and controversy requirement was applied as a determinative means. *Roe* and *Casey* (*Griswold* as well, once the Court decided to hear the case!) are included to underscore the fact that in constitutional decision making, how the Court goes about interpreting the Constitution is just as significant an issue as its decision to hear it. Thus, in the sense that we have studied interpretivism and noninterpretivism, the abortion decisions are a means of understanding that societal politics was not the only issue that generated controversy, but rather, for the "constitutionalist," the Court's decision that abortion was protected as a part of the right to privacy, when the Fourteenth Amendment does not mention either "abortion" or "privacy," stimulated just as much or more controversy.

TILESTON v. ULLMAN
318 U.S. 44 (1943)

PER CURIAM.

This case comes here on appeal to review a declaratory judgment of the Supreme Court of Errors of Connecticut that §§ 6246 and 6562 of the General Statutes of Connecticut of 1930 — prohibiting the use of drugs or instruments to prevent conception, and the giving of assistance or counsel in their use — are applicable to appellant, a registered physician, and as applied to him are constitutional. 129 Conn. 84, 26 A.2d 582, 588.

The suit was tried and judgment rendered on the allegations of the complaint which are stipulated to be true. Appellant alleged that the statute, if applicable to him, would prevent his giving professional advice concerning the use of contraceptives to three patients whose condition of health was such that their lives would be endangered by child-bearing, and that appellees, law enforcement officers of the state, intend to prosecute any offense against the statute and "claim or may claim" that the proposed professional advice would constitute such an offense. The complaint set out in detail the danger to the lives of appellant's patients in the event that they should bear children, but contained no allegations asserting any claim under the Fourteenth Amendment of infringement of appellant's liberty or his property rights. The relief prayed was a declaratory judgment as to whether the statutes are applicable to appellant and if so whether they constitute a valid exercise of constitutional power "within the meaning and intent of Amendment XIV of the Constitution of the United States prohibiting a state from depriving any person of life without due process of law." On stipulation of the parties the state superior court ordered these questions of law reserved for the consideration and advice of the Supreme Court of Errors. That court, which assumed without deciding that the case was an appropriate one for a declaratory judgment, ruled that the statutes "prohibit the action proposed to be done" by appellant and "are constitutional."

We are of the opinion that the proceedings in the state courts present no constitutional question which appellant has standing to assert. The sole constitutional attack upon the statutes under the Fourteenth Amendment is confined to their deprivation of life — obviously not appellant's but his patients'. There is no allegation or proof that appellant's life is in danger. His patients are not parties to this proceeding and there is no basis on which we can say that he has standing to secure an adjudication of his patients' constitutional right to life, which they do not assert in their own behalf. No question is raised in the record with respect to the deprivation of appellant's liberty or property in contravention of the Fourteenth Amendment, nor is there anything in the opinion or judgment of the Supreme Court of Errors which indicates or would support a decision of any question other than those raised in the superior court and reserved by it for decision of the Supreme Court of Errors. That court's practice is to decline to answer questions not reserved. General Statutes § 5652.

Since the appeal must be dismissed on the ground that appellant has no standing to litigate the constitutional question which the record presents, it is unnecessary to consider whether the record shows the existence of a genuine case or controversy essential to the exercise of the jurisdiction of this Court. Cf. Nashville, C. & St. L. Ry. v. Wallace, 288 U.S. 249, 259, 53 S.Ct. 345, 346, 77 L.Ed. 730, 87 A.L.R. 1191.

Dismissed.

POE v. ULLMAN
367 U.S. 497 (1961)

Mr. Justice FRANKFURTER announced the judgment of the Court and an opinion in which THE CHIEF JUSTICE, Mr. Justice CLARK and Mr. Justice WHITTAKER join.

These appeals challenge the constitutionality, under the Fourteenth Amendment, of Connecticut statutes which, as authoritatively construed by the Connecticut Supreme Court of Errors, prohibit the use of contraceptive devices and the giving of medical advice in the use of such devices. In proceedings seeking declarations of law, not on review of convictions for violation of the statutes, that court has ruled that these statutes would be applicable in the case of married couples and even under claim that conception would constitute a serious threat to the health or life of the female spouse.

No. 60 combines two actions brought in a Connecticut Superior Court for declaratory relief. The complaint in the first alleges that the plaintiffs, Paul and Pauline Poe, are a husband and wife, thirty and twenty-six years old respectively, who live together and have no children. Mrs. Poe has had three consecutive pregnancies terminating in infants with multiple congenital abnormalities from which each died shortly after birth. Plaintiffs have consulted Dr. Buxton, an obstetrician and gynecologist of eminence, and it is Dr. Buxton's opinion that the cause of the infants' abnormalities is genetic, although the underlying "mechanism" is unclear. In view of the great emotional stress already suffered by plaintiffs, the probable consequence of another pregnancy is psychological strain extremely disturbing to the physical and mental health of both husband and wife. Plaintiffs know that it is Dr. Buxton's opinion that the best and safest medical treatment which could be prescribed for their situation is advice in methods of preventing conception. Dr. Buxton knows of drugs, medicinal articles and instruments which can be safely used to effect contraception. Medically, the use of these devices is indicated as the best and safest preventive measure necessary for the protection of plaintiffs' health. Plaintiffs, however, have been unable to obtain this information for the sole reason that its delivery and use may or will be claimed by the defendant State's Attorney (appellee in this Court) to constitute offenses against Connecticut law. The State's Attorney intends to prosecute offenses against the State's laws, and claims that the giving of contraceptive advice and the use of contraceptive devices would be offenses forbidden by Conn. Gen. Stat. Rev.1958, §§ 53-32 and 54-196. Alleging irreparable injury and a substantial uncertainty of legal relations (a local procedural requisite for a declaration), plaintiffs ask a declaratory judgment that §§ 53-32 and 54-196 are unconstitutional, in that they deprive the plaintiffs of life and liberty without due process of law.

The second action in No. 60 is brought by Jane Doe, a twenty-five-year-old housewife. Mrs. Doe, it is alleged, lives with her husband, they have no children; Mrs. Doe recently underwent a pregnancy which induced in her a critical physical illness — two weeks' unconsciousness and a total of nine weeks' acute sickness which left her with partial paralysis, marked impairment of speech, and emotional instability. Another pregnancy would be exceedingly perilous to her life. She, too, has consulted Dr. Buxton, who believes that the best and safest treatment for her is contraceptive advice. The remaining allegations of Mrs. Doe's complaint, and the relief sought, are similar to those in the case of Mr. and Mrs. Poe.

In No. 61, also a declaratory judgment action, Dr. Buxton is the plaintiff. Setting forth facts identical to those alleged by Jane Doe, he asks that the Connecticut statutes prohibiting his giving of contraceptive advice to Mrs. Doe be adjudged unconstitutional, as depriving him of liberty and property without due process. . . .

The Connecticut law prohibiting the use of contraceptives has been on the State's books since 1879. Conn. Acts 1879, c. 78. During the more than three-quarters of a century since its enactment, a prosecution for its violation seems never to have been initiated, save in State v. Nelson, 126 Conn. 412, 11 A.2d 856. The circumstances of that case, decided in 1940, only prove the abstract character of what is before us. There, a test case was brought to determine the constitutionality of the Act as applied against two doctors and a nurse who had allegedly disseminated contraceptive information. After the Supreme Court of Errors sustained the legislation on appeal from a demurrer to the information, the State moved to dismiss the information. Neither counsel nor our own researches have discovered any other attempt to enforce the prohibition of distribution or use of contraceptive devices by criminal process. The unreality of these law suits is illumined by another circumstance. We were advised by counsel for appellants that contraceptives are commonly and notoriously sold in Connecticut drug stores. Yet no prosecutions are recorded; and certainly such ubiquitous, open, public sales would mere quickly invite the attention of enforcement officials than the conduct in which the present appellants wish to engage — the giving of private medical advice by a doctor to his individual patients, and their private use of the devices prescribed. The undeviating policy of nullification by Connecticut of its anti-contraceptive laws throughout all the long years that they have been on the statute books bespeaks more than prosecutorial paralysis. What was said in another context is relevant here. "Deeply embedded traditional ways of carrying out state policy . . ." — or not carrying it out — "are often tougher and truer law than the dead words of the written text." Nashville, C. & St. L.R. Co. v. Browning, 310 U.S. 362, 369, 60 S.Ct. 968, 972, 84 L.Ed. 1254.

The restriction of our jurisdiction to cases and controversies within the meaning of Article III of the Constitution, see Muskrat v. United States, 219 U.S. 346, 31 S.Ct. 250, 55 L.Ed. 246, is not the sole limitation on the exercise of our appellate powers, especially in cases raising constitutional questions. The policy reflected in numerous cases and over a long period was thus summarized in the oft-quoted statement of Mr. Justice Brandeis: "The Court (has) developed, for its own governance in the cases confessedly within its jurisdiction, a series of rules under which it has avoided passing upon a large part of all the constitutional questions pressed upon it for decision." Ashwander v. Tennessee Valley Authority, 297 U.S. 288, 341, 346, 56 S.Ct. 466, 482, 80 L.Ed. 688 (concurring opinion). In part the rules summarized in the *Ashwander* opinion have derived from the historically defined, limited nature and function of courts and from the recognition that, within the framework of our adversary system, the adjudicatory process is most securely founded when it is exercised under the impact of a lively conflict between antagonistic demands, actively pressed, which make resolution of the controverted issue a practical necessity. See Little v. Bowers, 134 U.S. 547, 558, 10 S.Ct. 620, 623, 33 L.Ed. 1016; People of State of California v. San Pablo & Tulare R. Co., 149 U.S. 308, 314, 13 S.Ct. 876, 878, 37 L.Ed. 747; United States v. Fruehauf, 365 U.S. 146, 157, 81 S.Ct. 547, 554, 5 L.Ed.2d 476. In part they derive from the fundamental federal and tripartite character of our National Government and from the role — restricted by its very responsibility — of the federal courts, and particularly this Court, within that structure. See the Note to Hayburn's Case, 2 Dall. 409, 1 L.Ed. 436; Commonwealth of Massachusetts v. Mellon, 262 U.S. 447, 488-489, 43 S.Ct. 597, 601, 67 L.Ed. 1078; Watson v. Buck, 313 U.S. 387, 400-403, 61 S.Ct. 962, 966-968, 85 L.Ed. 1416; Alabama State Federation of Labor, etc. v. McAdory, 325 U.S. 450, 471, 65 S.Ct. 1384, 1394, 89 L.Ed. 1725.

These considerations press with special urgency in cases challenging legislative action or state judicial action as repugnant to the Constitution. . . .

. . . [It] is clear that the mere existence of a state penal statute would constitute insufficient grounds to support a federal court's adjudication of its constitutionality in proceedings brought against the State's prosecuting officials if real threat of enforcement is wanting. See Ex parte La Prade, 289 U.S. 444, 458, 53 S.Ct. 682, 77 L.Ed. 1311. If the prosecutor expressly agrees not to prosecute, a suit against him for declaratory and injunctive relief is not such an adversary case as will be reviewed here. C.I.O. v. McAdory, 325 U.S. 472, 475, 65 S.Ct. 1395, 1397, 89 L.Ed. 1741. Eighty years of Connecticut history demonstrate a similar, albeit tacit agreement. The fact that Connecticut has not chosen to press the enforcement of this statute deprives these controversies of the immediacy which is an indispensable condition of constitutional adjudication. This Court cannot be umpire to debates concerning harmless, empty shadows. To find it necessary to pass on these statutes now, in order to protect appellants from the hazards of prosecution, would be to close our eyes to reality.

Nor does the allegation by the Poes and Doe that they are unable to obtain information concerning contraceptive devices from Dr. Buxton, "for the sole reason that the delivery and use of such information and advice may or will be claimed by the defendant State's Attorney to constitute offenses," disclose a necessity for present constitutional decision. It is true that this Court has several times passed upon criminal statutes challenged by persons who claimed that the effects of the statutes were to deter others from maintaining profitable or advantageous relations with the complainants. See, e.g., Truax v. Raich, 239 U.S. 33, 36 S.Ct. 7, 60 L.Ed. 131; Pierce v. Society of Sisters, 268 U.S. 510, 45 S.Ct. 571, 69 L.Ed. 1070. But in these cases the deterrent effect complained of was one which was grounded in a realistic fear of prosecution. We cannot agree that if Dr. Buxton's compliance with these statutes is uncoerced by the risk of their enforcement, his patients are entitled to a declaratory judgment concerning the statutes' validity. And, with due regard to Dr. Buxton's standing as a physician and to his personal sensitiveness, we cannot accept, as the basis of constitutional adjudication, other than as chimerical the fear of enforcement of provisions that have during so many years gone uniformly and without exception unenforced.

Justiciability is of course not a legal concept with a fixed content or susceptible of scientific verification. Its utilization is the resultant of many subtle pressures, including the appropriateness of the issues for decision by this Court and the actual hardship to the litigants of denying them the relief sought. Both these factors justify withholding adjudication of the constitutional issue raised under the circumstances and in the manner in which they are now before the Court. Dismissed.

Mr. Justice DOUGLAS, dissenting.

. . . [When] the Court goes outside the record to determine that Connecticut has adopted "The undeviating policy of nullification . . . of its anti-contraceptive laws," it selects a particularly poor case in which to exercise such a novel power. This is not a law which is a dead letter. Twice since 1940, Connecticut has reenacted these laws as part of general statutory revisions. Consistently, bills to remove the statutes from the books have been rejected by the legislature. In short, the statutes — far from being the accidental left-overs of another era — are the center of a continuing controversy in the State. See, e.g., The New Republic, May 19, 1947, p. 8.

Again, the Court relies on the inability of counsel to show any attempts, other than the Nelson case, "to enforce the prohibition of distribution or use of contraceptive devices by criminal process." Yet, on oral argument, counsel for the appellee stated on his own knowledge that several proprietors had been prosecuted in the "minor police courts of Connecticut" after they had been "picked up" for selling contraceptives. The enforcement of criminal laws in minor courts has just as much impact as in those cases where appellate courts are resorted to. The need of the protection of constitutional guarantees, and the right to them, are not less because the matter is small or the court lowly. See Thompson v. City of Louisville, 362 U.S. 199, 80 S.Ct. 624, 4 L.Ed.2d 654; Tumey v. State of Ohio, 273 U.S. 510, 47 S.Ct. 437, 71 L.Ed. 749. Nor is the need lacking because the dispensing of birth-control information is by a single doctor rather than by birth-control clinics. The nature of the controversy would not be changed one iota had a dozen doctors, representing a dozen birth-control clinics, sued for remedial relief.

What are these people — doctor and patients — to do? Flout the law and go to prison? Violate the law surreptitiously and hope they will not get caught? By today's decision we leave them no other alternatives. It is not the choice they need have under the regime of the declaratory judgment and our constitutional system. It is not the choice worthy of a civilized society. A sick wife, a concerned husband, a conscientious doctor seek a dignified, discrete, orderly answer to the critical problem confronting them. We should not turn them away and make them flout the law and get arrested to have their constitutional rights determined. See Railway Mail Ass'n v. Corsi, 326 U.S. 88, 65 S.Ct. 1483, 89 L.Ed. 2072. They are entitled to an answer to their predicament here and now.

Mr. Justice HARLAN, dissenting.

. . . [H]ere is the core of my disagreement with the present disposition. As I will develop later in this opinion, the most substantial claim which these married persons press is their right to enjoy the privacy of their marital relations free of the inquiry of the criminal law, whether it be in a prosecution of them or of a doctor whom they have consulted. And I cannot agreed that their enjoyment of this privacy is not substantially impinged upon, when they are told that if they use contraceptives, indeed whether they do so or not, the only thing which stands between them and being forced to render criminal account of their marital privacy is the whim of the prosecutor. Connecticut's highest court has told us in the clearest terms that, given proof, the prosecutor will succeed if he decides to bring a proceeding against one of the appellants for taking the precise actions appellants have announced they intend to take. The State Court does not agree that there has come into play a "tougher and truer law than the dead words of the written text," and in the light of twelve unsuccessful attempts since 1943 to change this legislation, Poe v. Ullman, 147 Conn. 48, 56, note 2, 156 A.2d 508, 513, this position is not difficult to understand. Prosecution and conviction for the clearly spelled-out actions the appellants wish to take is not made unlikely by any fortuitous factor outside the control of the parties, nor is it made uncertain by possible variations in the actions appellants actually take from those the state courts have already passed upon. All that stands between the appellants and jail is the legally unfettered whim of the prosecutor and the constitutional issue this Court today refuses to decide.

PART TWO. CONSTITUTIONALITY.

. . . [I] consider that this Connecticut legislation, as construed to apply to these appellants, violates the Fourteenth Amendment. I believe that a statute making it a criminal offense for married couples to use contraceptives is an intolerable and unjustifiable invasion of privacy in the conduct of the most intimate concerns of an individual's personal life. I reach this conclusion, even though I find it difficult and unnecessary at this juncture to accept appellants' other argument that the judgment of policy behind the statute, so applied, is so arbitrary and unreasonable as to render the enactment invalid for that reason alone. Since both the contentions draw their basis from no explicit language of the Constitution, and have yet to find expression in any decision of this Court, I feel it desirable at the outset to state the framework of constitutional principles in which I think the issue must be judged.

GRISWOLD v. CONNECTICUT
381 U.S. 479 (1965)

ROE v. WADE
410 U.S. 113 (1973)

PLANNED PARENTHOOD OF SOUTHEASTERN PENNSYLVANIA v. CASEY
505 U.S. 833 (1992)

THOMAS E. DOBBS, STATE HEALTH OFFICER OF THE MISSISSIPPI DEPARTMENT OF HEALTH, ET AL., PETITIONERS v. JACKSON WOMEN'S HEALTH ORGANIZATION
597 U.S. ___(2022)

The above decisions can be found in Chapter 5, Constitutionally Protected Rights—Due Process, sections I.C.1 and I.C.2.

D. SUPREMACY AND STATE COURTS

Despite *Marbury*, can the Constitution be the "supreme law of land" if the Court is not the ultimate arbiter of the meaning of the Constitution in regard to the states? This is the issue in controversy in *Martin v. Hunter's Lessee*. Note the Jeffersonian position advanced by Justice Roane of Virginia, as he challenges the Supreme Court and Justice Story. (Marshall recused himself because of his previous involvement with land in the Northern Neck.) Justice Holmes would state in regard to the significance of this issue, "I do not think the United States would come to an end if we lost our power to declare an Act of Congress void. I do think the Union would be imperiled if we could not make that declaration as to the laws of the several States." Oliver Wendell Holmes, *Collected Legal Papers* **295**, **296** (1990). Do you agree? Why would Holmes conclude that the "Union would be imperiled"?

MARTIN v. HUNTER'S LESSEE
14 U.S. (1 Wheat.) 304 (1816)

[This case arose out of a dispute over the ownership of land in the Northern Neck of Virginia in postrevolutionary America. In 1779 Virginia expropriated all property owned by British subjects. Hunter, an American citizen, claimed the land pursuant to a grant from the state of Virginia in 1789 based upon the 1779 confiscation of lands owned by British subjects. Martin, a British subject, claimed that the attempted confiscation was ineffective under anticonfiscation clauses of treaties between the United States and England. The Virginia trial court held in favor of Martin; the Virginia Court of Appeals reversed, concluding that the state's title to the land had vested before the relevant treaties via its Temporary Survey in 1782, and alternatively that Martin's claim was defeated by a 1796 Act of Compromise between the state and Martin's uncle, from whom Martin's claim derived. The U.S. Supreme Court reversed the Virginia Court of Appeals, neglecting to mention the Act of Compromise but claiming that Virginia had not perfected its title before the relevant treaties. Fairfax's Devisee v. Hunter's Lessee, 7 Cranch 603 (1813). The Supreme Court remanded the case to the Virginia Court of Appeals with instructions to enter judgment for the appellant. But on remand, the Virginia court declined. The court said that §25 of the Judiciary Act was unconstitutional insofar as it extended the appellate jurisdiction of the Supreme Court to the Virginia court.

Dates of Consequence in *Martin*:

1779: Virginia expropriates British property.
1781: Northern Neck — Fairfax dies — bequeath to Martin's Uncle — English resident.
1782: Temporary survey — alien enemies.
1783: Treaty with Britain — "no future confiscations."
1785: Virginia makes 1779 law applicable to Fairfax.
1789: Hunter receives some of the land.
1791: Hunter starts ejectment of Fairfax.
1794: "Jay Treaty" — British subjects who hold land continue to.
1796-1803: English Fairfax dies and leaves to land to Martin (Virginia citizen).
1809: Virginia Court holds Hunter takes land before Treaty of 1783.
1813: U.S. Supreme Court reverses, holds land taken after treaty, and to Martin.
1815: Justice Roane, Virginia court, holds not obligated to abide by Supreme Court decision.
1816: Present case.]

Mr. Justice STORY delivered the opinion of the Court. . . .
   [The] appellate power is not limited by the terms of the third article to any particular courts. The words are, "the judicial power (which includes appellate power) shall extend

to all cases," &c., and "in all other cases before mentioned the supreme court shall have appellate jurisdiction." It is the case, then, and not the court, that gives the jurisdiction. If the judicial power extends to the case, it will be in vain to search in the letter of the constitution for any qualification as to the tribunal where it depends. [If] the text be clear and distinct, no restriction upon its plain and obvious import ought to be admitted, unless the inference be irresistible.

If the constitution meant to limit the appellate jurisdiction to cases pending in the courts of the United States, it would necessarily follow that the jurisdiction of these courts would, in all the cases enumerated in the constitution, be exclusive of state tribunals. How otherwise could the jurisdiction extend to all cases arising under the constitution, laws, and treaties of the United States, or to all cases of admiralty and maritime jurisdiction? If some of these cases might be entertained by state tribunals, and no appellate jurisdiction as to them should exist, then the appellate power would not extend to all, but to some, cases. If state tribunals might exercise concurrent jurisdiction over all or some of the other classes of cases in the constitution without control, then the appellate jurisdiction of the United States might, as to such cases, have no real existence, contrary to the manifest intent of the constitution. [This] construction would abridge the jurisdiction of such court far more than has been ever contemplated in any act of congress. . . .

[It] is plain that the framers of the constitution did contemplate that cases within the judicial cognizance of the United States not only might but would arise in the state courts, in the exercise of their ordinary jurisdiction. With this view the sixth article declares, that "this constitution, and the laws of the United States, which shall be made in pursuance thereof, and all treaties made, or which shall be made, under the authority of the United States, shall be the supreme law of the land, and the judges in every state shall be bound thereby, any thing in the constitution or laws of any state to the contrary notwithstanding." It is obvious that this obligation is imperative upon the state judges in their official, and not merely in their private, capacities. From the very nature of their judicial duties they would be called upon to pronounce the law applicable to the case in judgment. They were not to decide merely according to the laws or constitution of the state, but according to the constitution, laws and treaties of the United States — "the supreme law of the land."

A moment's consideration will show us the necessity and propriety of this provision in cases where the jurisdiction of the state courts is unquestionable. Suppose a contract for the payment of money is made between citizens of the same state, and performance thereof is sought in the courts of that state; no person can doubt that the jurisdiction completely and exclusively attaches, in the first instance, to such courts. Suppose at the trial the defendant sets up in his defence a tender under a state law, making paper money a good tender, or a state law, impairing the obligation of such contract, which law, if binding, would defeat the suit. The constitution of the United States has declared that no state shall make any thing but gold or silver coin a tender in payment of debts, or pass a law impairing the obligation of contracts. If congress shall not have passed a law providing for the removal of such a suit to the courts of the United States, must not the state court proceed to hear and determine it? [Suppose] an indictment for a crime in a state court, and the defendant should allege in his defence that the crime was created by an ex post facto act of the state, must not the state court, in the exercise of a jurisdiction which has already rightfully attached, have a right to pronounce on the validity and sufficiency of the defence? It would be extremely difficult, upon any legal principles, to give a negative answer to these inquiries. Innumerable instances of the same sort might be stated, in illustration of the position; and unless the state courts could sustain jurisdiction in such cases, this clause of the sixth article would be without meaning or effect, and public mischiefs, of a most enormous magnitude, would inevitably ensue.

It must, therefore, be conceded that the constitution not only contemplated, but meant to provide for cases within the scope of the judicial power of the United States, which might yet depend before state tribunals. It was foreseen that in the exercise of their ordinary jurisdiction, state courts would incidentally take cognizance of cases arising under the constitution, the laws, and treaties of the United States. Yet to all these cases the judicial power, by the very terms of the constitution, is to extend. It cannot extend by original jurisdiction if that was already rightfully and exclusively attached in the state courts, which (as has been already shown) may occur; it must, therefore, extend by appellate jurisdiction, or not at all. It would seem to follow that the appellate power of the United States must, in such cases, extend to state tribunals; and if in such cases, there is no reason why it should not equally attach upon all others within the purview of the constitution.

It has been argued that such an appellate jurisdiction over state courts is inconsistent with the genius of our governments, and the spirit of the constitution. That the latter was never designed to act upon state sovereignties, but only upon the people, and that if the power exists, it will materially impair the sovereignty of the states, and the independence of their courts. . . .

It is a mistake that the constitution was not designed to operate upon states, in their corporate capacities. It is crowded with provisions which restrain or annul the sovereignty of the states in some of the highest branches of their prerogatives. The tenth section of the first article contains a long list of disabilities and prohibitions imposed upon the states. Surely, when such essential portions of state sovereignty are taken away, or prohibited to be exercised, it cannot be correctly asserted that the constitution does not act upon the states. The language of the constitution is also imperative upon the states as to the performance of many duties. It is imperative upon the state legislatures to make laws prescribing the time, places, and manner of holding elections for senators and representatives, and for electors of president and vice-president. And in these, as well as some other cases, congress have a right to revise, amend, or supercede the laws which may be passed by state legislatures. When, therefore, the states are stripped of some of the highest attributes of sovereignty, and the same are given to the United States; when the legislatures of the states are, in some respects, under the control of congress, and in every case are, under the constitution, bound by the paramount authority of the United States; it is certainly difficult to support the argument that the appellate power over the decisions of state courts is contrary to the genius of our institutions. The courts of the United States can, without question, revise the proceedings of the executive and legislative authorities of the states, and if they are found to be contrary to the constitution, may declare them to be of no legal validity. Surely the exercise of the same right over judicial tribunals is not a higher or more dangerous act of sovereign power.

Nor can such a right be deemed to impair the independence of state judges. It is assuming the very ground in controversy to assert that they possess an absolute independence of the United States. In respect to the powers granted to the United States, they are not independent; they are expressly bound to obedience by the letter of the constitution; and if they should unintentionally transcend their authority, or misconstrue the constitution, there is no more reason for giving their judgments an absolute and irresistible force, than for giving it to the acts of the other co-ordinate departments of state sovereignty.

The argument urged from the possibility of the abuse of the revising power, is equally unsatisfactory. It is always a doubtful course, to argue against the use or existence of a power, from the possibility of its abuse. It is still more difficult, by such an argument, to in graft upon a general power a restriction which is not to be found in the terms in which it is given. From the very nature of things, the absolute right of decision, in the last resort, must rest somewhere — wherever it may be vested it is susceptible of abuse. In all questions of jurisdiction the inferior, or appellate court, must pronounce the final judgment; and common sense, as well as legal reasoning, has conferred it upon the latter.

It is further argued, that no great public mischief can result from a construction which shall limit the appellate power of the United States to cases in their own courts: first, because state judges are bound by an oath to support the constitution of the United States, and must be presumed to be men of learning and integrity; and, secondly, because congress must have an unquestionable right to remove all cases within the scope of the judicial power from the state courts to the courts of the United States, at any time before final judgment, though not after final judgment. As to the first reason — admitting that the judges of the state courts are, and always will be, of as much learning, integrity, and wisdom, as those of the courts of the United States, (which we very cheerfully admit,) it does not aid the argument. It is manifest that the constitution has proceeded upon a theory of its own, and given or withheld powers according to the judgment of the American people, by whom it was adopted. [The] constitution has presumed (whether rightly or wrongly we do not inquire) that state attachments, state prejudices, state jealousies, and state interests, might sometimes obstruct, or control, or be supposed to obstruct or control, the regular administration of justice. Hence, in controversies between states; between citizens of different states; between citizens claiming grants under different states; between a state and its citizens, or foreigners, and between citizens and foreigners, it enables the parties, under the authority of congress, to have the controversies heard, tried, and determined before the national tribunals. No other reason than that which has been stated can be assigned, why some, at least, of those cases should not have been left to the cognizance of the state courts. In respect to the other enumerated cases — the cases arising under the constitution, laws, and treaties of the United States, cases affecting ambassadors and other public ministers, and cases of admiralty and maritime jurisdiction — reasons of a higher and more extensive nature, touching the safety, peace, and sovereignty of the nation, might well justify a grant of exclusive jurisdiction.

This is not all. A motive of another kind, perfectly compatible with the most sincere respect for state tribunals, might induce the grant of appellate power over their decisions. That motive is the importance, and even necessity of uniformity of decisions throughout the whole United States, upon all subjects within the purview of the constitution. Judges of equal learning and integrity, in different states, might differently interpret a statute, or a treaty of the United States, or even the constitution itself: If there were no revising authority to control these jarring and discordant judgments, and harmonize them into uniformity, the laws, the treaties, and the constitution of the United States would be different in different states, and might, perhaps, never have precisely the same construction, obligation, or efficacy, in any two states. The public mischiefs that would attend such a state of things would be truly deplorable; and it cannot be believed that they could have escaped the enlightened convention which formed the constitution. What, indeed, might then have been only prophecy, has now become fact; and the appellate jurisdiction must continue to be the only adequate remedy for such evils. There is an additional consideration, which is entitled to great weight. The constitution of the United States was designed for the common and equal benefit of all the people of the United States. The judicial power was granted for the same benign and salutary purposes. It was not to be exercised exclusively for the benefit of parties who might be plaintiffs, and would elect the national forum, but also for the protection of defendants who might be entitled to try their rights, or assert their privileges, before the same forum. Yet, if the construction contended for be correct, it will follow, that as the plaintiff may always elect the state court, the defendant may be deprived of all the security which the constitution intended in aid of his rights. Such a state of things can, in no respect, be considered as giving equal rights. . . .

On the whole, the court are of opinion, that the appellate power of the United States does extend to cases pending in the state courts; and that the 25th section of the judiciary act, which authorizes the exercise of this jurisdiction in the specified cases, by a writ of error, is supported by the letter and spirit of the constitution. We find no clause in that instrument which limits this power; and we dare not interpose a limitation where the people have not been disposed to create one. . . . [Reversed.]

1. REVIEW OF STATE COURTS "IN-ACTION": INDEPENDENT/ADEQUATE GROUNDS

The Court has long held that it lacks power to review state court decisions that rest on "adequate and independent state grounds." Efforts to obtain review of such decisions are dismissed for lack of jurisdiction. Thus, where a state court has addressed both state and federal questions in deciding a case, its decision is not reviewable if the state ground alone is sufficient to support its judgment. In such situations, an error in the state court's interpretation of federal law would not affect the result in the case. Determining whether a state court's reliance on a state law ground bars Supreme Court review is a frequently encountered and complex problem. State grounds of decision may be substantive or procedural: a state court ruling may rest on a mixture of state and federal substantive grounds; or a state court may fail to reach a federal issue because of an allegedly dispositive state procedural barrier. Justice Jackson, in *Herb v. Pitcairn*, 324 U.S. 117 (1945), summarized the theoretical bases of the doctrine as follows:

> This Court [has always] adhered to the principle that it will not review judgments of state courts that rest on adequate and independent state grounds. [The reason] is found in the partitioning of power between the state and federal judicial systems and in the limitations of our own jurisdiction. Our only power over state judgments is to correct them to the extent that they incorrectly adjudge federal rights. And our power is to correct wrong judgments, not to revise opinions. We are not permitted to render an advisory opinion, and if the same judgment would be rendered by the state court after we corrected its views of federal laws, our review could amount to nothing more than an advisory opinion.

Justice Jackson found the rule a constitutional mandate, in view of the Article III preclusion of advisory opinions by federal courts. Others have suggested that, whether or not the rule is constitutionally required, it is mandated by the jurisdictional statute.

In constitutional litigation, the most common example of an independent and adequate state substantive ground is a state court ruling that a state law violates both the federal constitution and an identical or similar provision in the state constitution. In principle, it is clear that even though the state court opinion may include an elaborate discussion of the meaning of the federal guarantee — an interpretation that may be wrong — the Supreme

Court will not review if the state judges rest their decision on their own constitutional provision as well. In such a situation, correction of the state court's interpretation would not change the outcome of the case; Court correction of the state court's error would accordingly be an unpermitted advisory opinion, even though the erroneous state court ruling would produce a nonuniform interpretation of federal law.

Prior to Story's finding in *Martin v. Hunter's Lessee*, Justice Roane asserted on behalf of the Virginia Court of Appeals that it was the province of the courts of Virginia to decide Virginia property law and that §25 of the Judiciary Act was unconstitutional insofar as it extended the appellate jurisdiction of the Supreme Court to the Virginia court. Was he correct? What result if the case was litigated today and subject to the "independent and adequate grounds" test? Do the facts and dates detailed prior to *Martin* support Roane's argument?

MICHIGAN v. LONG
463 U.S. 1032 (1983)

[Interrelated developments in recent years have made applications of the adequate state grounds principle controversial. These developments are products of the modern Court's occasional proclivity to cut back on federal constitutional guarantees announced by the Warren Court, especially in the area of criminal defendants' rights. One consequence was that a number of state courts began to invalidate state laws in opinions that, while primarily discussing the federal Constitution (although arguably out of line with narrower modern Court rulings), were nevertheless allegedly immune from Court review because of an additional, brief statement by the state court that a similar state constitutional provision had been violated as well. While that pattern was developing, some Justices of the Supreme Court were probably increasingly frustrated by the existence of such "erroneous" yet unreviewable federal constitutional rulings in the state court reports. The Court's response to this "problem" in *Long* provides its most recent statement in regard to the independent and adequate grounds test.]

Justice O'CONNOR delivered the opinion of the Court.
II
Before reaching the merits, we must consider Long's argument that we are without jurisdiction to decide this case because the decision below rests on an adequate and independent state ground. The court below referred twice to the state constitution in its opinion, but otherwise relied exclusively on federal law. Long argues that the Michigan courts have provided greater protection from searches and seizures under the state constitution than is afforded under the Fourth Amendment, and the references to the state constitution therefore establish an adequate and independent ground for the decision below.

It is, of course, "incumbent upon this Court . . . to ascertain for itself . . . whether the asserted non-federal ground independently and adequately supports the judgment." Abie State Bank v. Bryan, 282 U.S. 765, 773, 51 S.Ct. 252, 255, 75 L.Ed. 690 (1931). Although we have announced a number of principles in order to help us determine whether various forms of references to state law constitute adequate and independent state grounds,[2] we

---

[2] For example, we have long recognized that "where the judgment of a state court rests upon two grounds, one of which is federal and the other non-federal in character, our jurisdiction fails if the non-federal ground is independent of the federal ground and adequate to support the judgment." Fox Film Corp. v. Muller, 296 U.S.

openly admit that we have thus far not developed a satisfying and consistent approach for resolving this vexing issue. In some instances, we have taken the strict view that if the ground of decision was at all unclear, we would dismiss the case. See, e.g., Lynch v. New York, 293 U.S. 52, 55 S.Ct. 16, 79 L.Ed. 191 (1934). In other instances, we have vacated, see, e.g., Minnesota v. National Tea Co., 309 U.S. 551, 60 S.Ct. 676, 84 L.Ed. 20 (1940), or continued a case, see, e.g., Herb v. Pitcairn, 324 U.S. 117, 65 S.Ct. 459, 89 L.Ed. 789 (1945), in order to obtain clarification about the nature of a state court decision. See also California v. Krivda, 409 U.S. 33, 93 S.Ct. 32, 34 L.Ed.2d 45 (1972). In more recent cases, we have ourselves examined state law to determine whether state courts have used federal law to guide their application of state law or to provide the actual basis for the decision that was reached. See Texas v. Brown, 103 S.Ct. 1535, 1538, 75 L.Ed.2d 502 (1983) (plurality opinion). Cf. South Dakota v. Neville, 103 S.Ct. 916, 925, 74 L.Ed.2d 748 (1983) (Stevens, J., dissenting). In Oregon v. Kennedy, 456 U.S. 667, 670-671, 102 S.Ct. 2083, 2086-2087, 72 L.Ed.2d 416 (1982), we rejected an invitation to remand to the state court for clarification even when the decision rested in part on a case from the state court, because we determined that the state case itself rested upon federal grounds. We added that "[e]ven if the case admitted of more doubt as to whether federal and state grounds for decision were intermixed, the fact that the state court relied to the extent it did on federal grounds requires us to reach the merits." Id., at 671, 102 S.Ct., at 2087.

This *ad hoc* method of dealing with cases that involve possible adequate and independent state grounds is antithetical to the doctrinal consistency that is required when sensitive issues of federal-state relations are involved. Moreover, none of the various methods of disposition that we have employed thus far recommends itself as the preferred method that we should apply to the exclusion of others, and we therefore determine that it is appropriate to reexamine our treatment of this jurisdictional issue in order to achieve the consistency that is necessary.

The process of examining state law is unsatisfactory because it requires us to interpret state laws with which we are generally unfamiliar, and which often, as in this case, have not been discussed at length by the parties. Vacation and continuance for clarification have also been unsatisfactory both because of the delay and decrease in efficiency of judicial administration, see Dixon v. Duffy, 344 U.S. 143, 73 S.Ct. 193, 97 L.Ed. 153 (1952), and, more important, because these methods of disposition place significant burdens on state courts to demonstrate the presence or absence of our jurisdiction. See Philadelphia Newspapers, Inc. v. Jerome, 434 U.S. 241, 244, 98 S.Ct. 546, 548, 54 L.Ed.2d 506 (1978) (Rehnquist, J., dissenting); Department of Motor Vehicles v. Rios, 410 U.S. 425, 427, 93 S.Ct. 1019, 1021, 35 L.Ed.2d 398 (1973) (Douglas, J., dissenting). Finally, outright dismissal of cases is clearly not a panacea because it cannot be doubted that there is an

---

207, 210, 56 S.Ct. 183, 184, 80 L.Ed. 158 (1935). We may review a state case decided on a federal ground even if it is clear that there was an available state ground for decision on which the state court could properly have relied. Beecher v. Alabama, 389 U.S. 35, 37, n. 3, 88 S.Ct. 189, 190, 19 L.Ed.2d 35 (1967). Also, if, in our view, the state court "'felt compelled by what it understood to be federal constitutional considerations to construe . . . its own law in the manner that it did,'" then we will not treat a normally adequate state ground as independent, and there will be no question about our jurisdiction. Delaware v. Prouse, 440 U.S. 648, 653, 99 S.Ct. 1391, 1395, 59 L.Ed.2d 660 (1979) (quoting Zacchini v. Scripps-Howard Broadcasting Co., 433 U.S. 562, 568, 97 S.Ct. 2849, 2854, 53 L.Ed.2d 965 (1977)). See also South Dakota v. Neville, 103 S.Ct. 1535, 1540, n. 3, 75 L.Ed.2d 502 (1983). Finally, "where the non-federal ground is so interwoven with the [federal ground] as not to be an independent matter, or is not of sufficient breadth to sustain the judgment without any decision of the other, our jurisdiction is plain." Enterprise Irrigation District v. Farmers Mutual Canal Company, 243 U.S. 157, 164, 37 S.Ct. 318, 321, 61 L.Ed. 644 (1917).

important need for uniformity in federal law, and that this need goes unsatisfied when we fail to review an opinion that rests primarily upon federal grounds and where the *independence* of an alleged state ground is not apparent from the four corners of the opinion. We have long recognized that dismissal is inappropriate "where there is strong indication . . . that the federal constitution as judicially construed controlled the decision below." *National Tea Co., supra,* 309 U.S., at 556, 60 S.Ct., at 679 (1940).

Respect for the independence of state courts, as well as avoidance of rendering advisory opinions, have been the cornerstones of this Court's refusal to decide cases where there is an adequate and independent state ground. It is precisely because of this respect for state courts, and this desire to avoid advisory opinions, that we do not wish to continue to decide issues of state law that go beyond the opinion that we review, or to require state courts to reconsider cases to clarify the grounds of their decisions. Accordingly, when, as in this case, a state court decision fairly appears to rest primarily on federal law, or to be interwoven with the federal law, and when the adequacy and independence of any possible state law ground is not clear from the face of the opinion, we will accept as the most reasonable explanation that the state court decided the case the way it did because it believed that federal law required it to do so. If a state court chooses merely to rely on federal precedents as it would on the precedents of all other jurisdictions, then it need only make clear by a plain statement in its judgment or opinion that the federal cases are being used only for the purpose of guidance, and do not themselves compel the result that the court has reached. In this way, both justice and judicial administration will be greatly improved. If the state court decision indicates clearly and expressly that it is alternatively based on bona fide separate, adequate, and independent grounds, we, of course, will not undertake to review the decision.

This approach obviates in most instances the need to examine state law in order to decide the nature of the state court decision, and will at the same time avoid the danger of our rendering advisory opinions. It also avoids the unsatisfactory and intrusive practice of requiring state courts to clarify their decisions to the satisfaction of this Court. We believe that such an approach will provide state judges with a clearer opportunity to develop state jurisprudence unimpeded by federal interference, and yet will preserve the integrity of federal law. "It is fundamental that state courts be left free and unfettered by us in interpreting their state constitutions. But it is equally important that ambiguous or obscure adjudications by state courts do not stand as barriers to a determination by this Court of the validity under the federal constitution of state action." *National Tea Co., supra,* 309 U.S., at 557, 60 S.Ct., at 679.

The principle that we will not review judgments of state courts that rest on adequate and independent state grounds is based, in part, on "the limitations of our own jurisdiction." *Herb v. Pitcairn,* 324 U.S. 117, 125, 65 S.Ct. 459, 463, 89 L.Ed. 789 (1945). The jurisdictional concern is that we not "render an advisory opinion, and if the same judgment would be rendered by the state court after we corrected its views of federal laws, our review could amount to nothing more than an advisory opinion." Id., at 126, 65 S.Ct., at 463. Our requirement of a "plain statement" that a decision rests upon adequate and independent state grounds does not in any way authorize the rendering of advisory opinions. Rather, in determining, as we must, whether we have jurisdiction to review a case that is alleged to rest on adequate and independent state grounds, see *Abie State Bank v. Bryan, supra,* 282 U.S., at 773, 51 S.Ct., at 255, we merely assume that there are no such grounds when it is not clear from the opinion itself that the state court relied upon an adequate and independent state ground and when it fairly appears that the state court rested its decision primarily on federal law.

Our review of the decision below under this framework leaves us unconvinced that it rests upon an independent state ground. Apart from its two citations to the state constitution, the court below relied *exclusively* on its understanding of *Terry* and other federal cases. Not a single state case was cited to support the state court's holding that the search of the passenger compartment was unconstitutional. Indeed, the court declared that the search in this case was unconstitutional because "[t]he Court of Appeals erroneously applied the principles of *Terry v. Ohio* . . . to the search of the interior of the vehicle in this case." 413 Mich., at 471, 320 N.W.2d, at 869. The references to the state constitution in no way indicate that the decision below rested on grounds in any way *independent* from the state court's interpretation of federal law. Even if we accept that the Michigan constitution has been interpreted to provide independent protection for certain rights also secured under the Fourth Amendment, it fairly appears in this case that the Michigan Supreme Court rested its decision primarily on federal law.

Rather than dismissing the case, or requiring that the state court reconsider its decision on our behalf solely because of a mere possibility that an adequate and independent ground supports the judgment, we find that we have jurisdiction in the absence of a plain statement that the decision below rested on an adequate and independent state ground. It appears to us that the state court "felt compelled by what it understood to be federal constitutional considerations to construe . . . its own law in the manner it did." Zacchini v. Scripps-Howard Broadcasting Co., 433 U.S. 562, 568, 97 S.Ct. 2849, 2854, 53 L.Ed.2d 965 (1977).

The decision of the Michigan Supreme Court is reversed, and the case is remanded for further proceedings not inconsistent with this opinion.

II. JURISDICTIONAL LIMITATIONS ON THE SCOPE OF THE JUDICIAL POWER

A. CONGRESSIONAL/STATUTORY

The Constitution prescribes to Congress jurisdictional power over the judicial branch, which affords to Congress the ability to impose jurisdictional limitations on the scope of the judicial power. This congressional statutory authority speaks both to the appellate jurisdiction of the Supreme Court and to all lower federal courts:

> Article III. Section 2. (Exceptions Clause) In all other cases before mentioned, the Supreme Court shall have appellate Jurisdiction, both as to Law and Fact, with such Exceptions, and under such Regulations as the Congress shall make.
> Article III. Section 1. (Lower Courts) The judicial Power of the United States, shall be vested in one Supreme Court, and in such inferior Courts as the Congress may from time to time ordain and establish.

Is there a potential conflict between these jurisdictional powers allocated to Congress and the power of the federal courts, in particular the Supreme Court? Could judicial review be affected? Supremacy? Is this dilemmatic? Are these congressional powers simply a part of constitutional checks and balances, or do they threaten the separate power of the Court that we have detailed thus far, "the ultimate arbiter of the Constitution"? Keep these issues in mind as you read through the following sections.

At the conclusion of the materials below, evaluate the constitutionality of the following legislation introduced in Congress by Senator Jesse Helms in 1979:

> The Supreme Court shall not have jurisdiction to review, by appeal, writ of certiorari, or otherwise, any case arising out of any State statute, ordinance, rule, regulation, or any part thereof, or arising out of any act interpreting, applying, or enforcing a State statute, ordinance, rule, or regulation, which relates to voluntary prayers in public schools and public buildings.

On a similar basis, Senator Helms also introduced legislation withdrawing jurisdiction from the lower federal courts to hear any such cases. Do the materials that follow afford a constitutional support for this legislation? Once again, what of judicial review and supremacy? Are there arguments that can be made to the contrary, even given the explicit language of the Constitution?

1. SUPREME COURT/APPELLATE JURISDICTION

EX PARTE McCARDLE
74 U.S. (7 Wall.) 506 (1869)

[McCardle was arrested under charges of libel; disturbing the peace; inciting insurrection, disorder, and violence; and impeding reconstruction. McCardle sought habeas corpus from a federal court in Mississippi, claiming that Congress lacked constitutional authority to establish a system of military government in the states. The case was in this sense a fundamental challenge to Congress's reconstruction power. After losing in the trial court, McCardle appealed, invoking a habeas corpus act enacted in 1867. Congress feared that the case would be a vehicle for invalidating the reconstruction plan. Congress therefore enacted — while the case was pending and over presidential veto on constitutional grounds — a statute that repealed the provision of the 1867 habeas corpus act that McCardle had invoked.]

THE CHIEF JUSTICE [CHASE] delivered the opinion of the court.

The first question necessarily is that of jurisdiction; for, if the act of March, 1868, takes away the jurisdiction defined by the act of February, 1867, it is useless, if not improper, to enter into any discussion of other questions.

It is quite true, as was argued by the counsel for the petitioner, that the appellate jurisdiction of this court is not derived from acts of Congress. It is, strictly speaking, conferred by the Constitution. But it is conferred "with such exceptions and under such regulations as Congress shall make." It is unnecessary to consider whether, if Congress had made no exceptions and no regulations, this court might not have exercised general appellate jurisdiction under rules prescribed by itself. For among the earliest acts of the first Congress, at its first session, was the act of September 24th, 1789, to establish the judicial courts of the United States. That act provided for the organization of this court, and prescribed regulations for the exercise of its jurisdiction. . . .

The principle that the affirmation of appellate jurisdiction implies the negation of all such jurisdiction not affirmed having been thus established, it was an almost necessary consequence that acts of Congress, providing for the exercise of jurisdiction, should come to be spoken of as acts granting jurisdiction, and not as acts making exceptions to the constitutional grant of it.

The exception to appellate jurisdiction in the case before us, however, is not an inference from the affirmation of other appellate jurisdiction. It is made in terms. The provision of the act of 1867, affirming the appellate jurisdiction of this court in cases of habeas corpus is expressly repealed. It is hardly possible to imagine a plainer instance of positive exception.

We are not at liberty to inquire into the motives of the legislature. We can only examine into its power under the Constitution; and the power to make exceptions to the appellate jurisdiction of this court is given by express words. What, then, is the effect of the repealing act upon the case before us? We cannot doubt as to this. Without jurisdiction the court cannot proceed at all in any cause. Jurisdiction is power to declare the law, and when it ceases to exist, the only function remaining to the court is that of announcing the fact and dismissing the cause. And this is not less clear upon authority than upon principle.

Counsel seem to have supposed, if effect be given to the repealing act in question, that the whole appellate power of the court, in cases of habeas corpus, is denied. But this is an error. The act of 1868 does not except from that jurisdiction any cases but appeals from Circuit Courts under the act of 1867. It does not affect the jurisdiction which was previously exercised.

The appeal of the petitioner in this case must be dismissed for want of jurisdiction

---

The Scope of Congressional Power. How far-reaching is the congressional power sustained in *McCardle*? Can Congress legislatively void judicial review? Is this a clash of conflicting constitutional theses? Is congressional power under the Exceptions Clause more explicit that that of judicial review? Yet, what of supremacy?

The inherent danger to "our system of constitutional government" posed by these questions has mandated much attention by constitutional scholars. The struggle is, of course, to give meaning to the Exceptions Clause (the explicit language in Article III does make this unavoidable!), while salvaging judicial review and supremacy. What follows is a brief review of arguments that have been advanced to limit the jurisdiction-stripping power of Congress in light of judicial review. Is the Court vulnerable to political reprisals from Congress unless the reach of *McCardle* can be limited? Note how important it is to provide a constitutional effect to the explicit language of the Exceptions Clause, while at the same time limiting congressional exercise of this power to negate the Constitution as fundamental law via the Court's power of judicial review.

The Exigency of *McCardle*: Is *McCardle* "Good Law" Today? The *McCardle* case itself moved to a climax at the height of the tension generated between Congress and the president by the Civil War and reconstruction. Soon after the basic provisions of reconstruction legislation had been passed over the president's veto, challenges in the courts were launched. Prospects for success seemed good if the Court reached the merits: the military government features looked vulnerable in view of a case decided by the Supreme Court just before the reconstruction laws were passed. But then, while Congress was considering measures to avert the judicial threat to reconstruction, the Court took jurisdiction of McCardle's appeal. With that constitutional challenge formally before the Court and with argument on the merits already concluded (but, as the official report noted, "before conference in regard to the decision proper to be made"), Congress passed the 1868 law withdrawing appellate jurisdiction. By then, impeachment proceedings against President Johnson had begun. Nevertheless, he vetoed the law. With the Court standing by and withholding action on the case before it pending the outcome of the political battle, Congress overrode the veto. Argument on the jurisdiction-curtailing law was then sought in the Court. And, as one more manifestation of the political crisis hovering over the case, that argument was postponed because of "the Chief Justice being detained from his place here, by his duties in the Court of Impeachment." *Ex Parte McCardle* 74 U.S. 506, 509.

One post-*McCardle* effort to elicit a ruling on reconstruction seemed to limit the effect of the decision by ascribing it to exigencies of the Civil War and reconstruction. In *Ex parte Yerger*, 8 Wall. (75 U.S.) 85 (1869), the Court took jurisdiction of a proceeding by another petitioner in military detention in Mississippi, distinguished *McCardle* as opinion based upon "imperious public exigency," and found that "it was, doubtless, within the constitutional discretion of Congress to determine whether such an exigency existed; but it is not to be presumed that an act, passed under such circumstances, was intended to have any further effect than that plainly apparent from its terms." *Id.* at 104.

Justice Douglas, furthering this view of *McCardle*, in an oft-cited opinion, stated that "[t]here is a serious question whether the *McCardle* case could command a majority view today." *Glidden Co. v. Zdanok,* 370 U.S. 530, 605 (1962) (dissenting opinion).

Yet, even if *McCardle* would "not command a majority today," the Exceptions Clause remains. We turn next to scholarly responses to resolve this dilemmatic constitutional conflict.

The Essential Role for the Court in Our Constitutional Plan. Professor Henry Hart offers perhaps the most-cited resolution of this constitutional conflict. Hart offers a means of restraining the power of Congress by asserting that the Exception Clause could not be exercised in a way that would interfere with the "essential" or "core" functions of the Court. He argues that "the exceptions must not be such as will destroy the essential role of the *Supreme* Court in the constitutional plan." See Henry Hart, *The Power of Congress to Limit the Jurisdiction of Federal Courts: An Exercise in Dialectic*, 66 Harv. L. Rev. 1362, 1365 (1953). What is the "essential" or "core" role of the Court? Could this reading of the Exceptions Clause retain constitutional meaning in regard to congressional power over the Court's appellate jurisdiction, while limiting the negative effect of "jurisdiction stripping"?

Other scholars have amplified Hart's thesis. Leonard Ratner argues that the Exceptions Clause, "as it is sometimes claimed, is not consistent with the intended function of courts in the constitutional order." He defines "essential functions" as supremacy and the resolution of conflicting state interpretations of federal law. In particular, he argues that supremacy limits the exceptions power of Congress from barring or, in effect, deciding cases dealing with a "particular subject matter." See Leonard G. Ratner, *Congressional Power over the Appellate Jurisdiction of the Supreme Court*, 109 U. Pa. L. Rev. 157 (1960).

If one of the Court's essential functions is "resolution of conflicting state interpretations of federal law," is *Martin v. Hunter's Lessee* not worthy of mention? If access to the Supreme Court were barred, for example, decisions would be left to lower courts, with inconsistent results and a threat to the uniformity need articulated by Justice Story in *Martin*. Would this not eviscerate the constitutional mandate in *Martin*? Recall Justice Holmes comment in our discussion of *Martin*: "I do think the Union would be imperiled if we could not make that declaration as to the laws of the several States." Oliver Wendell Holmes, *Collected Legal Papers* 296 (1990). Should *Martin* serve as a limitation of the Exceptions Clause? Are there other constitutional mandates that should also so limit exceptions in order to effectuate their end?

Case Law. Perhaps influenced by scholarly response, the Court itself has laid forth a basis for limiting yet retaining congressional power under the Exceptions Clause, while minimizing constitutional conflict with the Court's "Separate Power."

Ex parte Yerger. *Yerger*, 8 Wall. (75 U.S.) 85 (1869), introduced above, like *McCardle*, unsuccessfully sought habeas in a lower federal court. But Yerger came to the Supreme Court by a route different from McCardle's: he did not invoke the appeal provision of the 1867 Act and instead sought relief under a preexisting law authorizing "original" jurisdiction in the Court for habeas petitions; accordingly, the Court found, the 1868 repeal did not apply. (Recall the final paragraph of *McCardle*.) Yet a decision on the constitutionality of the Reconstruction Acts was once again averted: before the Court could rule on the merits, Yerger was released from military custody. *Ex parte Yerger* played an important role 127 years later when the Court considered whether provisions of the 1996 Antiterrorism and Effective Death Penalty Act unconstitutionally curtailed the Supreme Court's appellate jurisdiction. ***Felker v. Turpin***, 518 U.S. 651 (1996). The Act included provisions curtailing state prisoners' *second or successive applications for federal habeas corpus relief. Among these was one* precluding Supreme Court review of any decision by a court of appeals granting or denying authorization for a state prisoner to file a second or successive application. (The courts of appeals were given a "gatekeeping" function requiring their permission for the consideration of prisoners' second or successive applications by the district courts.) Chief Justice Rehnquist's majority opinion in *Felker* concluded that the availability of relief in the Supreme Court by filing an "original" habeas petition "obviates any claim by petitioner under the Exceptions Clause of Article III, § 2." The Court had noted that route in the final paragraph of *Ex parte McCardle*, and, as noted, that route was utilized when Yerger filed a habeas petition soon after *McCardle*. The *Felker* opinion discussed *Yerger* at some length and found that, as in *Yerger*, there was no reason to find that the new 1996 law intended to repeal by implication the Court's habeas power in "original" jurisdiction cases. (Note that this jurisdiction is "original" only because it is filed in the first instance in the Supreme Court. For constitutional purposes, such an "original" petition is an exercise of the Court's appellate (rather than original) jurisdiction. See Dallin H. Oaks, *The "Original" Writ of Habeas Corpus in the Supreme Court*, 1962 Sup. Ct. Rev. 153.) The *Felker* Court noted that the 1996 law had "not repealed our authority to entertain original habeas petitions, for reasons similar to those stated in *Yerger*"; since the law did not "repeal our authority to entertain a petition for habeas corpus, there can be no plausible argument that the Act has deprived this Court of appellate jurisdiction in violation of Article III, § 2." A concurrence by Justice Souter, joined by Justices Stevens and Breyer, pointed out that "if it should later turn out that statutory avenues other than certiorari for reviewing a gatekeeping determination were closed, the question whether the statute exceeded Congress' Exceptions Clause power would be open. The question could arise if the Court of Appeals adopted divergent interpretations of the gatekeeper standard."

The *Klein* Case. Though Congress has not given the Court cause to reexamine *McCardle* directly, in *United States v. Klein*, 13 Wall. (80 U.S.) 128 (1872), the Court inferred a limitation on the reach of *McCardle*. In the *Klein* controversy, earlier rulings had held that a presidential pardon satisfied the statutory requirement that a property claimant was not a supporter of the "rebellion." The new statute enacted while Klein's appeal was pending provided that a pardon was to be taken as showing quite the opposite, that the claimant *had* aided the rebellion, and went on to provide that the courts were to dismiss such claims for want of jurisdiction. The opinion holding the law unconstitutional stated that the Court would have upheld it as an exercise of the "exceptions" power if "it simply denied the right of appeal in a particular class of cases." But here the jurisdictional language was only a means to an end: "to deny pardons granted by the President the effect which this court had adjudged them to have." The Court concluded that dismissing the appeal would allow Congress to "prescribe rules of decision to the Judicial Department of the government in cases pending before it," and this was a violation of separation of powers principles. In short, the Court found the statute unconstitutional on two separation of powers grounds: the law prescribed how a court should decide an issue and hence interfered with judicial autonomy; and it denied effect to a presidential pardon, thus interfering with executive autonomy.

It has been argued that the result in *Klein* rests on a principle of continuing utility as a limit on congressional power over jurisdiction. In this regard Justice Harlan made such a reference to *Klein* in the following passage in *Glidden*: "The authority [of Congress to curb the jurisdiction of Art. III courts] is not, of course, unlimited. In 1870, Congress purported to withdraw jurisdiction from the Court of Claims and from this Court on appeal over cases seeking indemnification for property captured during the Civil War, so far as eligibility therefore might be predicated upon an amnesty awarded by the President, as both courts had previously held that it might. Despite Ex parte McCardle, the Court refused to apply the statute to a case in which the claimant had already been adjudged entitled to recover by the Court of Claims, calling it an unconstitutional attempt to invade the judicial province by prescribing a rule of decision in a pending case. United States v. Klein."

Does this view of *Klein* resolve the conflict? Congress may make exceptions to the Court's appellate jurisdiction as long as the exceptions relate to "a class of cases," or are "jurisdictional" in nature, and do not have as their intent usurping the judicial power by deciding or having the effect of deciding a particular case or cases. Here the constitutional mandate of the Exceptions Clause is given substantive meaning while affording constitutional protection to the Court's ultimate power, judicial review, or the Court's "essential role in our constitutional plan." What of the Helms amendment discussed at the beginning of this section? What is the result if this reading of the Constitution is applied to it?

Practical Considerations. Assertions of broad congressional power to make exceptions to appellate jurisdiction, as in *McCardle*, understandably have proved tempting to some critics of modern Court decisions, prompting recurrent congressional efforts to curb the Court's jurisdiction. Indeed, it can be argued that the congressional power over appellate jurisdiction is ultimately a source of strength rather than weakness for the Court. Consider the suggestion in Henry Hart & Herbert Wechsler, *Federal Courts* 370 (4th ed. 1996), that it may be "politically healthy" that "the limits of congressional power have never been completely clarified": "In some circumstances, may not attempts to restrict jurisdiction be an appropriate and important way for the political branches to register disagreement with the Court? And is it not enormously significant that, ever since *McCardle*, such 'attempts' have, in the main, been just that — that Congress has not significantly cut back the Supreme Court's jurisdiction in a vindictive manner despite the great unpopularity of some of its rulings?" Note also Charles Black's argument that the existence of congressional power over federal court jurisdiction (and the traditional forbearance of Congress in using it) is "the rock on which rests the legitimacy of the judicial work in a democracy." Charles Black, *The Presidency and Congress*, 32 Wash. & Lee L. Rev. 841, 846 (1975).

In the last half century, Congress has recurrently threatened but rarely acted to curb the Supreme Court's appellate jurisdiction. A congressional attack on Court jurisdiction in the late 1950s, in hostile response to First Amendment decisions allegedly too soft on "subversiveness," was narrowly defeated. A 1968 crime control bill proposed, in hostile response to *Miranda v. Arizona*, 384 U.S. 436 (1966), stripping the Court of jurisdiction to reverse state decisions admitting confessions as voluntarily made, but these provisions were eliminated on the floor of the Senate. In the early 1980s, Senator Jesse Helms, as discussed above, led efforts to curb both Supreme Court and lower federal court jurisdiction in cases involving school prayer. Senator Edward Kennedy attacked that proposal on the Senate floor as an evisceration of the principle of *Martin v. Hunter's Lessee*. Senator Helms responded by referring to "the acknowledged power of Congress to make exceptions and prescribe regulations to the appellate power." During 1981 and 1982, some 30 other jurisdiction-stripping bills were introduced in Congress, with some eliciting extensive committee hearings. See Max Baucus & Kennerth Kay, *The Court Stripping Bills: Their Impact on the Constitution, the Courts, and Congress*, 27 Vill. L. Rev. 988 (1982). The proposals would have eliminated the Court's appellate jurisdiction in such controversial areas as busing and abortion as well as school prayer. All these proposals failed. By the mid-1980s, the momentum behind these efforts waned considerably, largely because many opponents of the challenged Court ruling shifted their energies to attempts to amend the Constitution and to influence the judicial nomination process.

2. LOWER FEDERAL COURTS

Congressional Control of Lower Federal Court Jurisdiction. Is the power to "create" the lower federal courts also the power to destroy? Once again, and much like *McCardle*, the Supreme Court in *Sheldon v. Sill*, 49 U.S. 441, 449 (1850), appeared to so find when it held, "Courts created by statute can have no jurisdiction but such as the statute confers," or, under constitution art. 3, vesting judicial power in supreme court and such inferior courts as Congress may from time to time ordain and establish, "Congress may withhold from any court of its creation jurisdiction of any of enumerated controversies."

Are the issues the same here as with the Exceptions Clause? Is the "essential role of the Court in our constitutional plan" affected by a ban on lower court jurisdiction if there is no "exception" to the Supreme Court's appellate jurisdiction? Is there potential for judicial review?

Does it take two to tango? In regard to the Helms amendment discussed above, can its constitutionality be reviewed by the Supreme Court even if there is a ban on lower federal court jurisdiction? What result in regard to the same inquiry if appellate review to the Supreme Court is denied? Is there a difference in impact between one and the other? What is the effect of the Helms amendment taken as a whole, that is, limitation both in regard to lower as well as appellate jurisdiction?

Yet, even if there is potential for judicial review despite congressional limitation on jurisdiction in the federal courts, other problems exist. Thus, for example, the ability of the Supreme Court to hear any cases would be limited to state appeals. This would present both substantive and administrative problems. Nonetheless, both the Constitution and recurrent statements by the Court itself suggest broad congressional authority over the jurisdiction of the lower federal courts. Because of these problems, scholars have argued that there are inherent Article III limitations on what Congress may do. Is there an "essential" role for lower federal courts analogous to that claimed regarding the Supreme Court's appellate jurisdiction? Here, for example, Justice Story has argued that the framers' constitutional language "Shall be vested" is mandatory in nature, so that in order to have an effective judiciary Congress must establish such courts. Theodore Eisenberg, in *Congressional Authority to Restrict Lower Federal Court Jurisdiction*, 83 Yale L.J. 498 (1974), argues in this regard that "[i]t can now be asserted that the [existence of lower federal courts] in some form is constitutionally required." Although Paul M. Bator, in *Congressional Power Over the Jurisdiction of the Federal Courts*, 27 Vill. L. Rev. 1030 (1982), points out that "[i]f the Congress decides that a certain category of case arising under a federal law should be litigated in a state court, subject to Supreme Court review, neither the letter nor the spirit of the Constitution has been violated. What has happened is that Congress has taken up one of the precise options which the constitutional Framers specifically envisioned." Yet, given the "essential role of the Court," can it at least be argued that Congress may not impose limits on lower federal courts when it is motivated by hostility to unpopular decisions?

Even if asserted constitutional restraints on congressional power are not persuasive with respect to curbs on Supreme Court or lower court jurisdiction, can a stronger case be made for restraints when Congress, as in the Helms prayer bill, seeks to strip jurisdiction from *all* federal courts — the Supreme Court as well as the lower courts — in a specified class of cases? Lawrence Sager has argued that Art. III requires that there must be *some* federal judicial forum for the enforcement of federal constitutional rights — either an "inferior" court or the Supreme Court. Lawrence Sager, *Foreword: Constitutional Limitations on Congress' Authority to Regulate the Jurisdiction of the Federal Courts*, 95 Harv. L. Rev. 17 (1981).

B. ARTICLE III "CASE AND CONTROVERSY"— CONSTITUTIONAL AND DISCRETIONARY ABSTENTION

1. THE CONSTITUTIONAL REQUIREMENTS

Article III, §2, of the Constitution limits the reach of the judicial power to "cases" and "controversies." Though we have already inferred that these requirements will be used by the Court as a means of limiting how the judicial power will be applied, we must first view them for what they are: constitutional limitations on the judicial power. Therefore the Constitution itself, at least at a minimum, is a significant limitation on the power of judicial review, for the Court can only be the "ultimate arbiter of the Constitution" when there is a case and controversy. A case has been defined as a "suit according to regular judicial process," and a controversy as the "existence of present or possible adverse parties whose contentions are submitted to adjudication." In short, the Constitution makes clear that the Court can only render judicial review while sitting as a court, not a super-legislature with a veto power over the other branches, limiting the exercise of their power to hearing cases *only* as a part of the "normal judicial process."

Are these unusual requirements for a court? Isn't the purpose of litigation to resolve controversies between parties via the judicial process? If you popped into any courtroom today, do you think you would find any litigation between parties not containing a case and controversy? Yet these requirements will be of significant import in constitutional adjudication. Why? If almost all lawsuits seem to be cases attempting to resolve controversies, if these appear to be rather normal requirements for any court, what's the big deal? Just the amount of material reviewing these issues in this work hints that there is more. What is it? What's judicial review got to do with it?

In the name of this Article III mandate, the Court will not render "advisory opinions" as well as "moot" or "collusive" lawsuits. As we shall see, the case and controversy requirement will not only limit review in regard to these unconstitutional no-no's, but the concept of "controversy" will also require affirmative proof of adversity before the constitutional mandate can be met.

2. ADVISORY OPINIONS: ADVERSITY, MOOTNESS, AND COLLUSION

Advisory Opinions. The case and controversy requirements, in their constitutional dimension, are threshold limitations on the scope of the judicial power. *Muskrat* emphasizes that it is unconstitutional for the Court to render review if there is not a case and controversy, holding that this would be an unconstitutional "advisory opinion." When there is no case or controversy, there is no jurisdiction and — of consequence — no judicial review. In this sense, these are constitutional no-nos.

MUSKRAT v. UNITED STATES
219 U.S. 346 (1911)

[In 1907 Congress, responding to previous legislation setting aside lands for the Cherokee Indians, passed legislation authorizing four individuals, including Muskrat, to file lawsuits challenging statutes promulgated in 1904 and 1906.]

Mr. Justice DAY delivered the opinion of the court:

The first question in these cases, as in others, involves the jurisdiction of the court to entertain the proceeding, and that depends upon whether the jurisdiction conferred is within the power of Congress, having in view the limitations of the judicial power, as established by the Constitution of the United States.

In 1793, by direction of the President, Secretary of State Jefferson addressed to the justices of the Supreme Court a communication soliciting their views upon the question whether their advice to the Executive would be available in the solution of important questions of the construction of treaties, laws of nations and laws of the land, which the Secretary said were often presented under circumstances which "*do not give a cognizance of them to the tribunals of the country.*" The answer to the question was postponed until the subsequent sitting of the Supreme Court, when Chief Justice Jay and his associates answered to President Washington that, in consideration of the lines of separation drawn by the Constitution between the three departments of government, and being judges of a court of last resort, afforded strong arguments against the propriety of extra-judicially deciding the questions alluded to, and expressing the view that the power given by the Constitution to the President, of calling on heads of departments for opinions, "seems to have been purposely, as well as expressly, united to the executive departments." Correspondence & Public Papers of John Jay, vol. 3, p. 486.

. . . [B]y the express terms of the Constitution, the exercise of the judicial power is limited to "cases" and "controversies." Beyond this it does not extend, and unless it is asserted in a case or controversy within the meaning of the Constitution, the power to exercise it is nowhere conferred.

What, then, does the Constitution mean in conferring this judicial power with the right to determine "cases" and "controversies." A "case" was defined by Mr. Chief Justice Marshall as early as the leading case of Marbury v. Madison, 1 Cranch, 137, 2 L. Ed. 60, to be a suit instituted according to the regular course of judicial procedure. And what more, if anything, is meant in the use of the term "controversy"?

Applying the principles thus long settled by the decisions of this court to the act of Congress undertaking to confer jurisdiction in this case, . . . the object and purpose of the suit is wholly comprised in the determination of the constitutional validity of certain acts of Congress; and furthermore, in the last paragraph of the section, should a judgment be rendered in the court of claims or this court, denying the constitutional validity of such acts, then the amount of compensation to be paid to attorneys employed for the purpose of testing the constitutionality of the law is to be paid out of funds in the Treasury of the United States belonging to the beneficiaries, the act having previously provided that the United States should be made a party, and the Attorney General be charged with the defense of the suits.

It is therefore evident that there is neither more nor less in this procedure than an attempt to provide for a judicial determination, final in this court, of the constitutional validity of an act of Congress. Is such a determination within the judicial power conferred by the Constitution, as the same has been interpreted and defined in the authoritative decisions to which we have referred? We think it is not. That judicial power, as we have seen, is the right to determine actual controversies arising between adverse litigants, duly instituted in courts of proper jurisdiction. The right to declare a law unconstitutional arises because an act of Congress relied upon by one or the other of such parties in determining their rights is in conflict with the fundamental law. The exercise of this, the most important and delicate duty of this court, is not given to it as a body with revisory power over the action of Congress, but because the rights of the litigants in justiciable controversies require the court to choose between the fundamental law and a law purporting to be enacted within constitutional authority, but in fact beyond the power delegated to the legislative branch of the government. This attempt to obtain a judicial declaration of the validity of the act of Congress is not presented in a "case" or "controversy," to which, under the Constitution of the United States, the judicial power alone extends. It is true the United States is made a defendant to this action, but it has no interest adverse to the claimants. The object is not to assert a property right as against the government, or to demand compensation for alleged wrongs because of action upon its part. The whole purpose of the law is to determine the constitutional validity of this class of legislation, in a suit not arising between parties concerning a property right necessarily involved in the decision in question, but in a proceeding against the government in its sovereign capacity, and concerning which the only judgment required is to settle the doubtful character of the legislation in question. Such judgment will not conclude private parties, when actual litigation brings to the court the question of the constitutionality of such legislation. In a legal sense the judgment could not be executed, and amounts in fact to no more than an expression of opinion upon the validity of the acts in question. Confining the jurisdiction of this court within the limitations conferred by the Constitution, which the court has hitherto been careful to observe, and whose boundaries it has refused to transcend, we think the Congress, in the act of March

1, 1907, exceeded the limitations of legislative authority, so far as it required of this court action not judicial in its nature within the meaning of the Constitution.

. . . [The] questions involved in this proceeding as to the validity of the legislation may arise in suits between individuals, and when they do and are properly brought before this court for consideration they, of course, must be determined in the exercise of its judicial functions. For the reasons we have stated, we are constrained to hold that these actions present no justiciable controversy within the authority of the court, acting within the limitations of the Constitution under which it was created. As Congress, in passing this act, as a part of the plan involved, evidently intended to provide a review of the judgment of the court of claims in this court, as the constitutionality of important legislation is concerned, we think the act cannot be held to intend to confer jurisdiction on that court separately considered.

The judgments will be reversed and the cases remanded to the Court of Claims, with directions to dismiss the petitions for want of jurisdiction.

———————

Note on Advisory Opinions. Under the first president, the Supreme Court said that it was constitutionally forbidden to issue "advisory opinions" — opinions on the constitutionality of legislative or executive actions that did not grow out of a case or controversy. President Washington, through Secretary of State Thomas Jefferson, asked the Justices whether he might request their views about legal questions growing out of a war, in which the United States was neutral, between England and France. The Justices responded: "The three departments of the government [being] in certain respects checks upon each other, and our being judges of a court in the last resort, are considerations which accord strong arguments against the propriety of our extra-judicially deciding the questions alluded to, especially as the power given by the Constitution to the President, of calling on the heads of departments for opinions, seems to have been purposely as well as expressly united to the executive departments. We exceedingly regret every event that may cause embarrassment to your administration, but we derive consolation from the reflection that your judgment will discern what is right." Quoted in P. Bator, P. Mishkin, D. Shapiro, & H. Wechsler, Hart & Wechsler's *The Federal Courts and the Federal System* 65-66 (2d ed. 1973).

What might be the advantages and disadvantages of permitting courts to issue advisory opinions? Is the Court's conclusion a natural or an inevitable interpretation of Article III? Would advisory opinions not be more efficient? Note that such a power would enable executive and legislative officials to obtain authoritative judgments on constitutional issues before relevant actions are taken, something that would have significant advantages. Some state supreme courts are authorized to issue advisory opinions. Note also that the Office of Legal Counsel of the Department of Justice has assumed an advice-giving role, at least for the executive branch, informing the president and other executive branch members of its views about the constitutionality of proposed courses of action. But perhaps advisory bodies of this kind end up having close collegial relations with those to whom they give advice; perhaps there is greater independence in an institution that decides only actual cases. Does the text of Article III support a judicial refusal to fulfill that role?

Mootness. What is a "moot" lawsuit? Was there ever a controversy in a suit determined to be moot? Why would one want to litigate a lawsuit that is moot? If the controversy is determined to be moot, are the parties asking for an "advisory opinion"?

DeFUNIS V. ODEGAARD
416 U.S. 312 (1974)

PER CURIAM.

In 1971 the petitioner Marco DeFunis, Jr., applied for admission as a first-year student at the University of Washington Law School, a state-operated institution. The size of the incoming first-year class was to be limited to 150 persons, and the Law School received some 1,600 applications for these 150 places. DeFunis was eventually notified that he had been denied admission. He thereupon commenced this suit in a Washington trial court, contending that the procedures and criteria employed by the Law School Admissions Committee invidiously discriminated against him on account of his race in violation of the Equal Protection Clause of the Fourteenth Amendment to the United States Constitution.

DeFunis brought the suit on behalf of himself alone, and not as the representative of any class, against the various respondents, who are officers, faculty members, and members of the Board of Regents of the University of Washington. He asked the trial court to issue a mandatory injunction commanding the respondents to admit him as a member of the first-year class entering in September 1971, on the ground that the Law School admissions policy had resulted in the unconstitutional denial of his application for admission. The trial court agreed with his claim and granted the requested relief. DeFunis was, accordingly, admitted to the Law School and began his legal studies there in the fall of 1971. On appeal, the Washington Supreme Court reversed the judgment of the trial court and held that the Law School admissions policy did not violate the Constitution. By this time DeFunis was in his second year at the Law School.

He then petitioned this Court for a writ of certiorari, and Mr. Justice Douglas, as Circuit Justice, stayed the judgment of the Washington Supreme Court pending the "final disposition of the case by this Court." By virtue of this stay, DeFunis has remained in law school, and was in the first term of his third and final year when this Court first considered his certiorari petition in the fall of 1973. Because of our concern that DeFunis' third-year standing in the Law School might have rendered this case moot, we requested the parties to brief the question of mootness before we acted on the petition. In response, both sides contended that the case was not moot. The respondents indicated that, if the decision of the Washington Supreme Court were permitted to stand, the petitioner could complete the term for which he was then enrolled but would have to apply to the faculty for permission to continue in the school before he could register for another term.[3]

In response to questions raised from the bench during the oral argument, counsel for the petitioner has informed the Court that DeFunis has now registered "for his final quarter in law school." Counsel for the respondents have made clear that the Law School will not in any way seek to abrogate this registration. In light of DeFunis' recent registration for the last quarter of his final law school year, and the Law School's assurance that his

---

[3] By contrast, in their response to the petition for certiorari, the respondents had stated that DeFunis "will complete his third year (of law school) and be awarded his J.D. degree at the end of the 1973-74 academic year regardless of the outcome of this appeal."

registration is fully effective, the insistent question again arises whether this case is not moot, and to that question we now turn.

The starting point for analysis is the familiar proposition that "federal courts are without power to decide questions that cannot affect the rights of litigants in the case before them." North Carolina v. Rice, 404 U.S. 244, 246, 92 S.Ct. 402, 404, 30 L.Ed.2d 413 (1971). The inability of the federal judiciary "to review moot cases derives from the requirement of Art. III of the Constitution under which the exercise of judicial power depends upon the existence of a case or controversy." Although as a matter of Washington state law it appears that this case would be saved from mootness by "the great public interest in the continuing issues raised by this appeal," 82 Wash.2d 11, 23 n. 6, 507 P.2d 1169, 1177 n. 6 (1973), the fact remains that under Art. III "[e]ven in cases arising in the state courts, the question of mootness is a federal one which a federal court must resolve before it assumes jurisdiction." North Carolina v. Rice, supra, 404 U.S., at 246, 92 S.Ct., at 404.

The respondents have represented that, without regard to the ultimate resolution of the issues in this case, DeFunis will remain a student in the Law School for the duration of any term in which he has already enrolled. Since he has now registered for his final term, it is evident that he will be given an opportunity to complete all academic and other requirements for graduation, and, if he does so, will receive his diploma regardless of any decision this Court might reach on the merits of this case. In short, all parties agree that DeFunis is now entitled to complete his legal studies at the University of Washington and to receive his degree from that institution. A determination by this Court of the legal issues tendered by the parties is no longer necessary to compel that result, and could not serve to prevent it. DeFunis did not cast his suit as a class action, and the only remedy he requested was an injunction commanding his admission to the Law School. He was not only accorded that remedy, but he now has also been irrevocably admitted to the final term of the final year of the Law School course. The controversy between the parties has thus clearly ceased to be "definite and concrete" and no longer "touch[es] the legal relations of parties having adverse legal interests." Aetna Life Ins. Co. v. Haworth, 300 U.S. 227, 240-241, 57 S.Ct. 461, 464, 81 L.Ed. 617 (1937).

It matters not that these circumstances partially stem from a policy decision on the part of the respondent Law School authorities. The respondents, through their counsel, the Attorney General of the State, have professionally represented that in no event will the status of DeFunis now be affected by any view this Court might express on the merits of this controversy. And it has been the settled practice of the Court, in contexts no less significant, fully to accept representations such as these as parameters for decision.

There is a line of decisions in this Court standing for the proposition that the "voluntary cessation of allegedly illegal conduct does not deprive the tribunal of power to hear and determine the case, i.e., does not make the case moot." These decisions and the doctrine they reflect would be quite relevant if the question of mootness here had arisen by reason of a unilateral change in the admissions procedures of the Law School. For it was the admissions procedures that were the target of this litigation, and a voluntary cessation of the admissions practices complained of could make this case moot only if it could be said with assurance "that 'there is no reasonable expectation that the wrong will be repeated.'" United States v. W. T. Grant Co., supra, 345 U.S., at 633, 73 S.Ct., at 897. Otherwise, "[t]he defendant is free to return to his old ways," id., at 632, 73 S.Ct., at 897, and this fact would be enough to prevent mootness because of the "public interest in having the legality of the practices settled." Ibid. But mootness in the present case depends not at all upon a "voluntary cessation" of the admissions practices that were the subject of this litigation. It depends, instead, upon the simple fact that DeFunis is now in the final quarter of the final year of his course of study, and the settled and unchallenged policy of the Law School to permit him to complete the term for which he is now enrolled.

It might also be suggested that this case presents a question that is "capable of repetition, yet evading review," Southern Pacific Terminal Co. v. ICC, 219 U.S. 498, 515, 31 S.Ct. 279, 283, 55 L.Ed. 310 (1911); Roe v. Wade, 410 U.S. 113, 125, 93 S.Ct. 705, 713, 35 L.Ed.2d 147 (1973), and is thus amenable to federal adjudication even though it might otherwise be considered moot. But DeFunis will never again be required to run the gantlet of the Law School's admission process, and so the question is certainly not "capable of repetition" so far as he is concerned. Moreover, just because this particular case did not reach the Court until the eve of the petitioner's graduation from Law School, it hardly follows that the issue he raises will in the future evade review. If the admissions procedures of the Law School remain unchanged, there is no reason to suppose that a subsequent case attacking those procedures will not come with relative speed to this Court, now that the Supreme Court of Washington has spoken. This case, therefore, in no way presents the exceptional situation in which the Southern Pacific Terminal doctrine might permit a departure from "[t]he usual rule in federal cases . . . that an actual controversy must exist at stages of appellate or certiorari review, and not simply at the date the action is initiated." Roe v. Wade, supra, at 125, 93 S.Ct., at 712; United States v. Munsingwear, Inc., 340 U.S. 36, 71 S.Ct. 104, 95 L.Ed. 36 (1950).

Because the petitioner will complete his law school studies at the end of the term for which he has now registered regardless of any decision this Court might reach on the merits of this litigation, we conclude that the Court cannot, consistently with the limitations of Art. III of the Constitution, consider the substantive constitutional issues tendered by the parties.[4] Accordingly, the judgment of the Supreme Court of Washington is vacated, and the cause is remanded for such proceedings as by that court may be deemed appropriate.

It is so ordered. Vacated and remanded.

Mr. Justice BRENNAN, with whom Mr. Justice DOUGLAS, Mr. Justice WHITE, and Mr. Justice MARSHALL concur, dissenting.

I respectfully dissent. Many weeks of the school term remain, and petitioner may not receive his degree despite respondents' assurances that petitioner will be allowed to complete this term's schooling regardless of our decision. Any number of unexpected events — illness, economic necessity, even academic failure — might prevent his graduation at the end of the term. Were that misfortune to befall, and were petitioner required to register for yet another term, the prospect that he would again face the hurdle of the admissions policy is real, not fanciful; for respondents warn that "Mr. DeFunis would have to take some appropriate action to request continued admission for the remainder of his law school education, and some discretionary action by the University on such request

---

[4] It is suggested in dissent that "[a]ny number of unexpected events — illness, economic necessity, even academic failure — might prevent his graduation at the end of the term." Post, at 1721. "But such speculative contingencies afford no basis for our passing on the substantive issues (the petitioner) would have us decide," Hall v. Beals, 396 U.S. 45, 49, 90 S.Ct. 200, 202, 24 L.Ed.2d 214 (1969), in the absence of "evidence that this is a prospect of 'immediacy and reality.'" Golden v. Zwickler, 394 U.S. 103, 109, 89 S.Ct. 956, 960, 22 L.Ed.2d 113 (1969); Maryland Casualty Co. v. Pacific Coal & Oil Co., 312 U.S. 270, 273, 61 S.Ct. 510, 512, 85 L.Ed. 826 (1941).

would have to be taken." Respondents' Memorandum on the Question of Mootness 3-4 (emphasis supplied). Thus, respondents' assurances have not dissipated the possibility that petitioner might once again have to run the gantlet of the University's allegedly unlawful admissions policy. The Court therefore proceeds on an erroneous premise in resting its mootness holding on a supposed inability to render any judgment that may affect one way or the other petitioner's completion of his law studies. For surely if we were to reverse the Washington Supreme Court, we could insure that, if for some reason petitioner did not graduate this spring, he would be entitled to re-enrollment at a later time on the same basis as others who have not faced the hurdle of the University's allegedly unlawful admissions policy.

In these circumstances, and because the University's position implies no concession that its admissions policy is unlawful, this controversy falls squarely within the Court's long line of decisions holding that the "[m]ere voluntary cessation of allegedly illegal conduct does not moot a case." Since respondents' voluntary representation to this Court is only that they will permit petitioner to complete this term's studies, respondents have not borne the "heavy burden," United States v. Concentrated Phosphate Export Assn., supra, 393 U.S., at 203, 89 S.Ct., at 364, of demonstrating that there was not even a "mere possibility" that petitioner would once again be subject to the challenged admissions policy. United States v. W. T. Grant Co., supra, 345 U.S., at 633, 73 S.Ct., at 898. On the contrary, respondents have positioned themselves so as to be "free to return to [their] old ways." Id., at 632, 73 S.Ct., at 897.

I can thus find no justification for the Court's straining to rid itself of this dispute. While we must be vigilant to require that litigants maintain a personal stake in the outcome of a controversy to assure that "the questions will be framed with the necessary specificity, that the issues will be contested with the necessity adverseness and that the litigation will be pursued with the necessary vigor to assure that the constitutional challenge will be made in a form traditionally thought to be capable of judicial resolution," Flast v. Cohen, 392 U.S. 83, 106, 88 S.Ct. 1942, 1955, 20 L.Ed.2d 947 (1968), there is no want of an adversary contest in this case. Indeed, the Court concedes that, if petitioner has lost his stake in this controversy, he did so only when he registered for the spring term. But appellant took that action only after the case had been fully litigated in the state courts, briefs had been filed in this Court, and oral argument had been heard. The case is thus ripe for decision on a fully developed factual record with sharply defined and fully canvassed legal issues. Cf. Sibron v. New York, 392 U.S. 40, 57, 88 S.Ct. 1889, 1899, 20 L.Ed.2d 917 (1968).

Moreover, in endeavoring to dispose of this case as moot, the Court clearly disserves the public interest. The constitutional issues which are avoided today concern vast numbers of people, organizations, and colleges and universities, as evidenced by the filing of twenty-six amicus curiae briefs. Few constitutional questions in recent history have stirred as much debate, and they will not disappear. They must inevitably return to the federal courts and ultimately again to this Court. Cf. Richardson v. Wright, 405 U.S. 208, 212, 92 S.Ct. 788, 791, 31 L.Ed.2d 151 (1972) (dissenting opinion). Because avoidance of repetitious litigation serves the public interest, that inevitability counsels against mootness determinations, as here, not compelled by the record. Cf. United States v. W. T. Grant Co., supra, 345 U.S., at 632, 73 S.Ct., at 897; Parker v. Ellis, 362 U.S. 574, 594, 80 S.Ct. 909, 920, 4 L.Ed.2d 963 (1960) (dissenting opinion). Although the Court should, of course, avoid unnecessary decisions of constitutional questions, we should not transform principles of avoidance of constitutional decisions into devices for sidestepping resolution of difficult cases. Cf. Cohens v. Virginia, 6 Wheat. 264, 404-405, 5 L.Ed. 257 (1821) (Marshall, C.J.).

On what appears in this case, I would find that there is an extant controversy and decide the merits of the very important constitutional questions presented.

———

Capable of Repetition yet Evading Review. Is there a loophole in *DeFunis* or perhaps in any lawsuit held to be moot? What would be the result if, upon filing the suit, the law school simply admits the student? Isn't the controversy that existed over, moot, and an advisory opinion?

The Supreme Court has held that jurisdiction can still be maintained in such a circumstance if the party can prove that the issue is "capable of repetition, yet evading review." Despite concrete arguments proving a moot controversy "capable of repetition, yet evading review," does this exception not hint that even given constitutional restraints the Court can maintain some discretion here? Was this the case in *DeFunis*? What of *Roe v. Wade*, below?

ROE v. WADE
410 U.S. 113 (1973)

[*Roe* is discussed supra; what follows is the Court's finding in regard to the mootness issue inherent in the subject matter.]

Mr. Justice BLACKMUN delivered the opinion of the Court.

The usual rule in federal cases is that an actual controversy must exist at stages of appellate or certiorari review, and not simply at the date the action is initiated. United States v. Munsingwear, Inc., 340 U.S. 36, 71 S.Ct. 104, 95 L.Ed. 36 (1950); Golden v. Zwickler, [394 U.S. 103 (1969)]; SEC v. Medical Committee for Human Rights, 404 U.S. 403, 92 S.Ct. 577, 30 L.Ed.2d 560 (1972).

But when, as here, pregnancy is a significant fact in the litigation, the normal 266-day human gestation period is so short that the pregnancy will come to term before the usual appellate process is complete. If that termination makes a case moot, pregnancy litigation seldom will survive much beyond the trial stage, and appellate review will be effectively denied. Our law should not be that rigid. Pregnancy often comes more than once to the same woman, and in the general population, if man is to survive, it will always be with us. Pregnancy provides a classic justification for a conclusion of nonmootness. It truly could be "capable of repetition, yet evading review." Southern Pacific Terminal Co. v. ICC, 219 U.S. 498, 515, 31 S.Ct. 279, 283, 55 L.Ed. 310 (1911). See Moore v. Ogilvie, 394 U.S. 814, 816, 89 S.Ct. 1493, 1494, 23 L.Ed.2d 1 (1969); Carroll v. President and Commissioners of Princess Anne, 393 U.S. 175, 178-179, 89 S.Ct. 347, 350, 351, 21 L.Ed.2d 325 (1968); United States v. W. T. Grant Co., 345 U.S. 629, 632-633, 73 S.Ct. 894, 897-898, 97 L.Ed. 1303 (1953).

We, therefore, agree with the District Court that Jane Roe had standing to undertake this litigation, that she presented a justiciable controversy, and that the termination of her 1970 pregnancy has not rendered her case moot.

———

Collusion. In a collusive lawsuit, the parties are feigning a controversy. Why would anyone want to fake a controversy? Lawsuits are not fun, are they? Once again, what's judicial review got to do with it? The Supreme Court has held that a collusive suit is an advisory opinion because there is not an "honest assertion of rights." United States v. Johnson, 319 U.S. 332 (1943). How does this differ from a moot lawsuit?

Assume that a son, a minority stockholder in his father's company, sues his father's company claiming that a piece of "new deal legislation" is unconstitutional as applied to the company. Is there a case and controversy? Why or why not? See Carter v. Carter Coal Co. 298 U.S. 238 (1936)

3. "MEASURING" CONTROVERSY/ADVERSITY

If it is unconstitutional for the Court to render advisory opinions, circumstances where there is not a case and controversy, then the converse is true as well: in order to attain jurisdiction, the parties must affirmatively prove that there is a case and controversy. If rendering advisory opinions is a constitutional no-no, then proving that there is a case and controversy is a constitutional yes-yes. Given the significance of these issues, the Court has developed a long train of decisional law setting forth the requisites for proving up a case and controversy. Since a case is simply "a suit according to the normal judicial process," most attention here centers on the word "controversy." A controversy is a "dispute between sides holding opposing views," and it is reasonable to assume that parties holding these opposing views are "adverse" to one another. Therefore, as noted earlier, the Court has required "an actual controversy between adverse litigants" to meet Article III requirements. So, out of the constitutional terminology, "controversy" becomes the defining requirement of "adversity." By proving adversity between the parties, a party can prove that there is a proper controversy.

The next question is, of course, how do you prove adversity? In the materials that follow, we will view the affirmative requirements (yes-yeses) that the Court has held as a measure of whether there is sufficient adversity to maintain a case and controversy. Here the Court will center on whether the prospective litigant has been harmed. The assumption is that if the plaintiffs in the lawsuit have been harmed by the defendants, the parties are adverse and there is a legitimate controversy.

4. STANDING/PERSONALIZED HARM

As set out below, the Court requires that there be an inquiry as to whether there is a sufficient harm in order for the litigants to have "standing." Litigants have standing if they can "personalize" the harm and prove that they are affected by it. Standing measures whether there has been a "personal harm" that has occurred to the claimant, so that the claimant has a sufficient "personal stake" in the outcome. (Controversy>Adversity>Standing/Personal Harm)

a. RIPENESS/CONCRETENESS

A second but related (to standing) measure of whether there is a sufficient harm deals with the timing of the harm — "ripeness." A harm may not be properly alleged if the harm has not occurred, is hypothetical, and has not sufficiently developed so that it is concrete and ready for judicial resolution. The doctrine of ripeness bars courts from deciding cases that are premature — too speculative or remote to warrant judicial intervention. Assume a challenge to a criminal statute before a prosecution is initiated. Is the circumstance "ripe"? Is there a sufficient harm when the mere existence of the statute has not produced an actual harm? It has been said in relation to proving up a harm that standing measures the "personal" nature of the harm while ripeness measures whether the "issues" have matured enough to substantiate the immediacy of the harm.

Declaratory Judgments and Ripeness. If the "harm" must have occurred in order for the circumstance to be "ripe," are declaratory judgments constitutional? Even given the importance in modern practice of declaratory relief (defining the rights of the parties and avoiding irreparable harms before they occur), this issue was unresolved before the Court sustained the Tennessee Declaratory Judgment Act in the case that follows. Note that a Federal Declaratory Judgment Act was soon to follow.

NASHVILLE, CINCINNATI & ST. LOUIS RAILWAY v. WALLACE
288 U.S. 249 (1933).

Mr. Justice STONE delivered the opinion of the Court.

. . . This preliminary question, which has been elaborately briefed and argued, must first be considered, for the judicial power with which this Court is invested by article 3, § 1, of the Constitution, extends by article 3, § 2, only to "cases" and "controversies"; if no "case" or "controversy" is presented for decision, we are without power to review the decree of the court below. Muskrat v. United States, 219 U.S. 346, 31 S.Ct. 250, 55 L.Ed. 246. . . .

Section 1 of the Tennessee Declaratory Judgments Act confers jurisdiction on courts of record "to declare rights . . . whether or not further relief is or could be claimed" and provides that "no action or proceeding shall be open to objection on the ground that a declaratory judgment or decree is prayed for. The declaration may be either affirmative or negative in form and effect; and such declaration shall have the force and effect of a final judgment or decree." By section 2 it is provided that "any person . . . whose rights, status or other legal relations are affected by a statute . . . may have determined any question of construction or validity arising under the . . . statute . . . and obtain a declaration of rights . . . thereunder."

This statute has often been considered by the highest court of Tennessee, which has consistently held that its provisions may only be invoked when the complainant asserts rights which are challenged by the defendant, and presents for decision an actual controversy to which he is a party, capable of final adjudication by the judgment or decree to be rendered. . . .

That the issues thus raised and judicially determined would constitute a case or controversy if raised and decided in a suit brought by the taxpayer to enjoin collection of the tax cannot be questioned. The proceeding terminating in the decree below . . . was between adverse parties, seeking a determination of their legal rights upon the facts alleged in the bill and admitted by the demurrer. [T]he question lends itself to judicial determination and is of the kind which this court traditionally decides. Thus the narrow question presented for determination is whether the controversy before us, which would be justiciable in this Court if presented in a suit for injunction, is any the less so because through a modified procedure appellant has been permitted to present it in the state courts, without praying for an injunction or alleging that irreparable injury will result from the collection of the tax.

The issues raised here are the same as those which under old forms of procedure could be raised only in a suit for an injunction or one to recover the tax after its payment. But the Constitution does not require that the case or controversy should be presented by traditional forms of procedure, invoking only traditional remedies. The judiciary clause of the Constitution defined and limited judicial power, not the particular method by which that power might be invoked. It did not crystallize into changeless form the procedure of 1789 as the only possible means for presenting a case or controversy otherwise cognizable by the federal courts. Whenever the judicial power is invoked to review a judgment of a state court, the ultimate constitutional purpose is the protection, by the exercise of the judicial function, of rights arising under the Constitution and laws of the United States. The states are left free to regulate their own judicial procedure. Hence changes merely in the form or method of procedure by which federal rights are brought to final adjudication in the state courts are not enough to preclude review of the adjudication by this Court, so long as the case retains the essentials of an adversary proceeding, involving a real, not a hypothetical, controversy, which is finally determined by the judgment below. As the prayer for relief by injunction is not a necessary prerequisite to the exercise of judicial power, allegations of threatened irreparable injury which are material only if an injunction is asked, may likewise be dispensed with if, in other respects, the controversy presented is, as in this case, real and substantial. Accordingly, we must consider the constitutional questions raised by the appeal.

Note on Declaratory Relief. Based upon the finding in *Nashville*, the Court has held that Article III requirements are met in a declaratory action if the requisites for declaratory relief are met. This normally means a declaratory action is deemed ripe and concrete if there is no adequate remedy at law and/or the harm itself is irreparable. Will ripeness nonetheless always be an issue in any federal declaratory action? Why?

5. MEASURING ADVERSITY: JUDICIAL RESTRAINT AND THE DISCRETIONARY USE OF THE JUDICIAL POWER— LIMITING JUDICIAL ACTIVISM

Despite the constitutional origin of the case and controversy requirements, the Court has nonetheless applied these requirements as a means of achieving judicial restraint — limiting the power of judicial review. To a degree, the materials in this work have had the intent of preparing you for this discretionary use of the judicial power. Thus, the theme of the weak origins of judicial review, particularly given the ultimate power in a democratic society resting in a nonelected Court, assumed some instrumental means of achieving judicial restraint. Recall our discussion of Judge Learned Hand's thesis that the Court should use the power of judicial review "sparingly" because he found the power only "implied" from the Constitution. Or Hand's view that in a democratic society the Court should not use the power of review to become "a third legislative chamber, . . . [f]or myself it would be most irksome to be ruled by a bevy of Platonic Guardians, even if I knew how to choose them, which . . . I do not." Learned Hand, *The Bill of Rights* (1958).

Though the judicial power is arguably secure today (see *Bush v. Gore,* supra, if there be any need to substantiate this thesis), it is nonetheless true that the Supreme Court throughout history, as well as in the modern era, has to one degree or another limited the power of judicial review because of the aforementioned rationale. If the Supreme Court has limited the judicial power, meaningful inquiry centers on the extent of such, for it is then a study of degree. This was true during the activist Warren era, as well as the more restraint-oriented Burger years. Yet, logic dictates that we should expect to see less discretionary avoidance in the Warren era as opposed to that in the Burger/Rehnquist years. What is most relevant, then, is that for any Court in any era there will be a need for a discretionary means to restrain judicial review. Yet, the Court must also serve as the ultimate arbiter of the Constitution in order to achieve the mandate of supremacy and maintain the Constitution as fundamental law. As one might assume, this is a tedious balance that will provide us a tedious study!

The desire to use discretion in restraining the judicial power, however, is one thing; finding a means to accomplish such is another. In this sense we can view law as having instrumental purpose or as using decisional law to achieve a desired ends. Here, and for the remainder of this section, we will see the case and controversy requirements applied as a means of achieving judicial restraint via a discretionary use of the judicial power.

The materials presented thus far have laid a foundation to understanding the reasons the Court exercises such discretion. This has been the method in the madness thus far. Discretion is never easy to contend with, particularly for a lawyer who wants to anticipate and predict results, but it is a reality in regard to the Supreme Court. In order to predict the outcome of an issue, one must understand and take discretion into account. This much we know: judicial restraint will be achieved by application of decisional law, namely by recourse to the language of case and controversy. So if you are ready, here we go!

6. STANDING: CITIZEN AND TAXPAYER SUITS

Citizen Standing. Is alleging a violation of the Constitution in and of itself a sufficient personal harm? To what extent should citizens be able to enforce the Constitution by recourse to the federal courts? Assume that you feel a statute promulgated by Congress violates freedom of speech as guaranteed by the First Amendment, even though you have not taken part in the proscribed activity. Should you be able to bring a cause of action to limit the power of Congress to the Constitution in this circumstance? Is this a sufficient personal harm? (You assert that the government has harmed you because you are a citizen protected by the Constitution and the First Amendment.) Would the denial of this personal right to others harm you?

In the context of a democratic society (recall the limitation on the Court's exercise of the power of judicial review "as a part of the normal judicial process"), what would be the result of finding such a harm sufficient to allow adjudication whenever a "citizen" filed a suit? Is it the constitutional responsibility of citizens to litigate such harms as a means of assuring that the Constitution is fundamental law? If any citizen could so easily assert such a harm, will this lead to government by Court rather than by democratic process?

These are significant questions that are not only byproducts of judicial review, but given the limitation against advisory opinions, are significant because a citizen can at least claim some quantum of personal harm by the adoption of an unconstitutional statute that denies personal rights. Yet, if the Court were to so hold, how would such affect our governing process?

What are the dangers of the Court finding that such a litigant has standing and therefore a constitutional controversy? Nonetheless, the Constitution does simply require a controversy and does not specify either the degree or nature of the controversy. But given the nature of the judicial power in a democratic society, how do you think the Court will respond? In *Schlesinger v. Reservists to Stop the War* 418 U.S. 208 (1974) the Court provides a contemporary response to the potential for citizen standing. Have you guessed the result?

In *Schlesinger* the Court rejected a claim of standing by plaintiffs who were past and present members of the Reserves and who sought to challenge the Reserve membership of certain members of Congress as being in violation of the Incompatibility Clause, the clause in Article I, § 6, cl. 2, stating that "no Person holding any Office under the United States shall be a Member of either House during his continuance in the Office.

Chief Justice Burger's majority opinion concluded that the plaintiffs lacked standing . . . as citizens. In the course of his opinion, he explained why a "generalized citizen interest" is not a sufficient basis for access to the federal courts. "The only interest [is one] shared by all citizens. [The] claimed nonobservance [of that Clause], standing alone, would adversely affect only the generalized interest of all citizens in constitutional governance, and that is an abstract injury. . . . To permit a complainant who has no concrete injury to require a court to rule on important constitutional issues in the abstract would create the potential for abuse of the judicial process, distort the role of the Judiciary in its relationship to the Executive and the Legislature and open the Judiciary to an arguable charge of government by injunction . . . The proposition that all constitutional provisions are enforceable by any citizen simply because citizens are the ultimate beneficiaries of those provisions has no boundaries . . . Our system of government leaves many crucial decisions to the political processes.

———

Taxpayer Standing. Can taxpayers make a better argument for a cognizable harm? If so, what would it be? One thing that should be obvious by now: the citizen and taxpayer standing cases bring into focus one of the central themes of constitutional law — if the Supreme Court in its exercise of the judicial power must "bow to the democratic process," how does it go about it? If the answer is by "manipulation" of the case and controversy requirements, then the taxpayer standing cases are not only an instructive means of teaching jurisdiction requirements, but are also an instrumental means of understanding how different Courts in different eras use these tools to effectuate their view of how the judicial power should be applied. Put simply, the more a majority on a Court desires to restrain the judicial power, the more stringent the standing barrier to review will be, or the converse, the more activist a given Court intends, the less restrictive the standing barrier will be.

The selection of the cases that follow was based upon an elucidation of this thesis. Thus, they should exemplify that the barrier to taxpayer standing depends upon a given Court's view of how the power of judicial review should be applied in a democratic society. See whether these cases live up to this billing.

MASSACHUSETTS v. MELLON [FROTHINGHAM V. MELLON]
262 U.S. 447 (1923)

Mr. Justice SUTHERLAND delivered the opinion of the Court.

These cases were argued and will be considered and disposed of together. [Both] cases challenge the constitutionality of the Act of November 23, 1921, 42 Stat. 224, c. 135, commonly called the Maternity Act. Briefly, it provides for an initial appropriation and thereafter annual appropriations for a period of five years, to be apportioned among such of the several states as shall accept and comply with its provisions, for the purpose of co-operating with them to reduce maternal and infant mortality and protect the health of mothers and infants. It creates a bureau to administer the act in co-operation with state agencies, which are required to make such reports concerning their operations and expenditures as may be prescribed by the federal bureau. Whenever that bureau shall determine that funds have not been properly expended in respect of any state, payments may be withheld.

[In] the Massachusetts Case it is alleged that the plaintiff's rights and powers as a sovereign state and the rights of its citizens have been invaded and usurped by these expenditures and acts, and that, although the state has not accepted the act, its constitutional rights are infringed by the passage thereof and the imposition upon the state of an illegal and unconstitutional option either to yield to the federal government a part of its reserved rights or lose the share which it would otherwise be entitled to receive of the moneys appropriated. In the Frothingham Case plaintiff alleges that the effect of the statute will be to take her property, under the guise of taxation, without due process of law.

We have reached the conclusion that the cases must be disposed of for want of jurisdiction, without considering the merits of the constitutional questions.

First. The state of Massachusetts in its own behalf, in effect, complains that the act in question invades the local concerns of the state, and is a usurpation of power, viz. the power of local self-government, reserved to the states.

Probably it would be sufficient to point out that the powers of the state are not invaded, since the statute imposes no obligation but simply extends an option which the state is free to accept or reject. [It] is plain that that question, as it is thus presented, is political, and not judicial in character, and therefore is not a matter which admits of the exercise of the judicial power.

[We] come next to consider whether the suit may be maintained by the state as the representative of its citizens. To this the answer is not doubtful. We need not go so far as to say that a state may never intervene by suit to protect its citizens against any form of enforcement of unconstitutional acts of Congress; but we are clear that the right to do so does not arise here. Ordinarily, at least, the only way in which a state may afford protection to its citizens in such cases is through the enforcement of its own criminal statutes, where that is appropriate, or by opening its courts to the injured persons for the maintenance of civil suits or actions. But the citizens of Massachusetts are also citizens of the United States. It cannot be conceded that a state, as parens patriae, may institute judicial proceedings to protect citizens of the United States from the operation of the statutes thereof. While the state, under some circumstances, may sue in that capacity for the protection of its citizens (Missouri v. Illinois and Chicago District, 180 U. S. 208, 241, 21 Sup. Ct. 331, 45 L. Ed. 497), it is no part of its duty or power to enforce their rights in respect of their relations with the federal government. In that field it is the United States, and not the state, which represents them as parens patriae, when such representation becomes appropriate; and to the former, and not to the latter, they must look for such protective measures as flow from that status.

Second. The attack upon the statute in the Frothingham Case is, generally, the same, but this plaintiff alleges, in addition that she is a taxpayer of the United States; and her contention, though not clear, seems to be that the effect of the appropriations complained of will be to increase the burden of future taxation and thereby take her property without due process of law. The right of a taxpayer to enjoin the execution of a federal appropriation act, on the ground that it is invalid and will result in taxation for illegal purposes, has never been passed upon by this court. In cases where it was presented, the question has either been allowed to pass sub silentio or the determination of it expressly withheld. Bradfield v. Roberts, 175 U. S. 291, 295, 20 Sup. Ct. 121, 44 L. Ed. 168. The case last cited came here from the Court of Appeals of the District of Columbia, and that court sustained the right of the plaintiff to sue by treating the case as one directed against the District of Columbia, and therefore subject to the rule, frequently stated by this court, that resident taxpayers may sue to enjoin an illegal use of the moneys of a municipal corporation. Roberts v. Bradfield, 12 App. D. C. 453, 459, 460. The interest of a taxpayer of a municipality in the application of its moneys is direct and immediate and the remedy by injunction to prevent their misuse is not inappropriate. It is upheld by a large number of state cases and is the rule of this court. Crampton v. Zabriskie, 101 U. S. 601, 609, 25 L. Ed. 1070. Nevertheless, there are decisions to the contrary. See, for example, Miller v. Grandy, 13 Mich. 540, 550. The reasons which support the extension of the equitable remedy to a single taxpayer in such cases are based upon the peculiar relation of the corporate taxpayer to the corporation, which is not without some resemblance to that subsisting between stockholder and private corporation. 4 Dillon, Municipal Corporations (5th Ed.) § 1580 et seq. But the relation of a taxpayer of the United States to the federal government is very different. His interest in the moneys of the treasury — partly realized from taxation and partly from other sources — is shared with millions of others, is comparatively minute and indeterminable, and the effect upon future taxation, of any payment out of the funds, so remote, fluctuating and uncertain, that no basis is afforded for an appeal to the preventive powers of a court of equity.

The administration of any statute, likely to produce additional taxation to be imposed upon a vast number of taxpayers, the extent of whose several liability is indefinite and constantly changing, is essentially a matter of public and not of individual concern. If one taxpayer may champion and litigate such a cause, then every other taxpayer may do the same, not only in respect of the statute here under review, but also in respect of every other appropriation act and statute whose administration requires the outlay of public money, and whose validity may be questioned. The bare suggestion of such a result, with its attendant inconveniences, goes far to sustain the conclusion which we have reached, that a suit of this character cannot be maintained. It is of much significance that no precedent sustaining the right to maintain suits like this has been called to our attention, although, since the formation of the government, as an examination of the acts of Congress will disclose, a large number of statutes appropriating or involving the expenditure of moneys for non-federal purposes have been enacted and carried into effect.

The functions of government under our system are apportioned. To the legislative department has been committed the duty of making laws, to the executive the duty of executing them, and to the judiciary the duty of interpreting and applying them in cases properly brought before the courts. The general rule is that neither department may invade the province of the other and neither may control, direct, or restrain the action of the other. We are not now speaking of the merely ministerial duties of officials. Gaines v. Thompson, 7 Wall. 347, 19 L. Ed. 62. We have no power per se to review and annul acts of Congress on the ground that they are unconstitutional. That question may be considered only when the justification for some direct injury suffered or threatened, presenting a justiciable issue, is made to rest upon such an act. Then the power exercised is that of ascertaining and declaring the law applicable to the controversy. It amounts to little more than the negative power to disregard an unconstitutional enactment, which otherwise would stand in the way of the enforcement of a legal right. The party who invokes the power must be able to show, not only that the statute is invalid, but that he has sustained or is immediately in danger of sustaining some direct injury as the result of its enforcement, and not merely that he suffers in some indefinite way in common with people generally. If a case for preventive relief be presented, the court enjoins, in effect, not the execution of the statute, but the acts of the official, the statute notwithstanding. Here the parties plaintiff have no such case. Looking through forms of words to the substance of their complaint, it is merely that officials of the executive department of the government are executing and will execute an act of Congress asserted to be unconstitutional; and this we are asked to prevent. To do so would be, not to decide a judicial controversy, but to assume a position of authority over the governmental acts of another and coequal department, an authority which plainly we do not possess.

———

Comment on *Mellon*. Does the Court deny there was a harm in *Mellon*, or was the nature of the harm the central issue? Was the *Mellon* decision based upon the constitutional requirement for a controversy or rather upon the Court's use of standing as a discretionary tool? Could a taxpayer achieve standing after *Mellon* based upon the harm he or she suffered as a taxpayer?

FLAST v. COHEN
392 U.S. 83 (1968)

Mr. Chief Justice WARREN delivered the opinion of the Court.
In Frothingham v. Mellon, 262 U.S. 447, 43 S.Ct. 597, 67 L.Ed. 1078 (1923), this Court ruled that a federal taxpayer is without standing to challenge the constitutionality of a federal statute. That ruling has stood for 45 years as an impenetrable barrier to suits against Acts of Congress brought by individuals who can assert only the interest of federal taxpayers. In this case, we must decide whether the *Frothingham* barrier should be lowered when a taxpayer attacks a federal statute on the ground that it violates the Establishment and Free Exercise Clauses of the First Amendment.
Appellants filed suit in the United States District Court for the Southern District of New York to enjoin the allegedly unconstitutional expenditure of federal funds under Titles I and II of the Elementary and Secondary Education Act of 1965, 79 Stat. 27, 20 U.S.C. §§ 241a et seq., 821 et seq. (1964 ed., Supp. II). The complaint alleged that the seven appellants had as a common attribute that "each pay(s) income taxes of the United States," and it is clear from the complaint that the appellants were resting their standing to maintain the action solely on their status as federal taxpayers. The appellees, who are charged by Congress with administering the Elementary and Secondary Education Act of 1965, were sued in their official capacities.
The gravamen of the appellants' complaint was that federal funds appropriated under the Act were being used to finance instruction in reading, arithmetic, and other subjects in religious schools, and to purchase textbooks and other instructional materials for use in such schools. Such expenditures were alleged to be in contravention of the Establishment and Free Exercise Clauses of the First Amendment. [The] complaint asked for a declaration that appellees' actions in approving the expenditure of federal funds for the alleged purposes were not authorized by the Act or, in the alternative, that if appellees' actions are deemed within the authority and intent of the Act, "the Act is to that extent

unconstitutional and void." The complaint also prayed for an injunction to enjoin appellees from approving any expenditure of federal funds for the allegedly unconstitutional purposes.

. . . [Although] the barrier *Frothingham* erected against federal taxpayer suits has never been breached, the decision has been the source of some confusion and the object of considerable criticism. The confusion has developed as commentators have tried to determine whether *Frothingham* establishes a constitutional bar to taxpayer suits or whether the Court was simply imposing a rule of self-restraint which was not constitutionally compelled. The conflicting viewpoints are reflected in the arguments made to this Court by the parties in this case. The Government has pressed upon us the view that *Frothingham* announced a constitutional rule, compelled by the Article III limitations on federal court jurisdiction and grounded in considerations of the doctrine of separation of powers. Appellants, however, insist that *Frothingham* expressed no more than a policy of judicial self-restraint which can be disregarded when compelling reasons for assuming jurisdiction over a taxpayer's suit exist. The opinion delivered in *Frothingham* can be read to support either position.

. . . [To] the extent that *Frothingham* has been viewed as resting on policy considerations, it has been criticized as depending on assumptions not consistent with modern conditions. For example, some commentators have pointed out that a number of corporate taxpayers today have a federal tax liability running into hundreds of millions of dollars, and such taxpayers have a far greater monetary stake in the Federal Treasury than they do in any municipal treasury. To some degree, the fear expressed in *Frothingham* that allowing one taxpayer to sue would inundate the federal courts with countless similar suits has been mitigated by the ready availability of the devices of class actions and joinder under the Federal Rules of Civil Procedure, adopted subsequent to the decision in *Frothingham*. Whatever the merits of the current debate over *Frothingham*, its very existence suggests that we should undertake a fresh examination of the limitations upon standing to sue in a federal court and the application of those limitations to taxpayer suits.

. . . [The] jurisdiction of federal courts is defined and limited by Article III of the Constitution. In terms relevant to the question for decision in this case, the judicial power of federal courts is constitutionally restricted to "cases" and "controversies." As is so often the situation in constitutional adjudication, those two words have an iceberg quality, containing beneath their surface simplicity submerged complexities which go to the very heart of our constitutional form of government. Embodied in the words "cases" and "controversies" are two complementary but somewhat different limitations. In part those words limit the business of federal courts to questions presented in an adversary context and in a form historically viewed as capable of resolution through the judicial process. And in part those words define the role assigned to the judiciary in a tripartite allocation of power to assure that the federal courts will not intrude into areas committed to the other branches of government. Justiciability is the term of art employed to give expression to this dual limitation placed upon federal courts by the case-and-controversy doctrine.

Additional uncertainty exists in the doctrine of justiciability because that doctrine has become a blend of constitutional requirements and policy considerations. And a policy limitation is "not always clearly distinguished from the constitutional limitation."

It is in this context that the standing question presented by this case must be viewed and that the Government's argument on that question must be evaluated. As we understand it, the Government's position is that the constitutional scheme of separation of powers, and the deference owed by the federal judiciary to the other two branches of government within that scheme, present an absolute bar to taxpayer suits challenging the validity of federal spending programs. The Government views such suits as involving no more than the mere disagreement by the taxpayer "with the uses to which tax money is put." According to the Government, the resolution of such disagreements is committed to other branches of the Federal Government and not to the judiciary. Consequently, the Government contends that, under no circumstances, should standing be conferred on federal taxpayers to challenge a federal taxing or spending program. An analysis of the function served by standing limitations compels a rejection of the Government's position.

Standing is an aspect of justiciability and, as such, the problem of standing is surrounded by the same complexities and vagaries that inhere in justiciability. Standing has been called one of "the must amorphous (concepts) in the entire domain of public law."

Despite the complexities and uncertainties, some meaningful form can be given to the jurisdictional limitations placed on federal court power by the concept of standing. The fundamental aspect of standing is that it focuses on the party seeking to get his complaint before a federal court and not on the issues he wishes to have adjudicated. The "gist of the question of standing" is whether the party seeking relief has "alleged such a personal stake in the outcome of the controversy as to assure that concrete adverseness which sharpens the presentation of issues upon which the court so largely depends for illumination of difficult constitutional questions." Baker v. Carr, 369 U.S. 186, 204, 82 S.Ct. 691, 703, 7 L.Ed.2d 663 (1962). In other words, when standing is placed in issue in a case, the question is whether the person whose standing is challenged is a proper party to request an adjudication of a particular issue and not whether the issue itself is justiciable. Thus, a party may have standing in a particular case, but the federal court may nevertheless decline to pass on the merits of the case because, for example, it presents a political question. A proper party is demanded so that federal courts will not be asked to decide "ill-defined controversies over constitutional issues," United Public Workers of America v. Mitchell, 330 U.S. 75, 90, 67 S.Ct. 556, 564, 91 L.Ed. 754 (1947), or a case which is of "a hypothetical or abstract character." Aetna Life Insurance Co. of Hartford, Conn. v. Haworth, 300 U.S. 27, 240, 57 S.Ct. 461, 463, 81 L.Ed. 617 (1937). So stated, the standing requirement is closely related to, although more general than, the rule that federal courts will not entertain friendly suits, Chicago & Grand Trunk R. Co. v. Wellman, supra, or those which are feigned or collusive in nature, United States v. Johnson, 319 U.S. 302, 63 S.Ct. 1075, 87 L.Ed. 1413 (1943); Lord v. Veazie, 8 How. 251, 12 L.Ed. 1067 (1850).

When the emphasis in the standing problem is placed on whether the person invoking a federal court's jurisdiction is a proper party to maintain the action, the weakness of the Government's argument in this case becomes apparent. The question whether a particular person is a proper party to maintain the action does not, by its own force, raise separation of powers problems related to improper judicial interference in areas committed to other branches of the Federal Government. Such problems arise, if at all, only from the substantive issues the individual seeks to have adjudicated. Thus, in terms of Article III limitations on federal court jurisdiction, the question of standing is related only to whether the dispute sought to be adjudicated will be presented in an adversary context and in a form historically viewed as capable of judicial resolution. It is for that reason that the emphasis in standing problems is on whether the party invoking federal court jurisdiction has "a personal stake in the outcome of the controversy," Baker v. Carr, supra, 369 U.S. at 204, 82 S.Ct. at 703, and whether the dispute touches upon "the legal relations of parties having adverse legal interests." Aetna Life Insurance Co. v. Haworth, supra, 300 U.S. at 240-241, 57 S.Ct. at 464. A taxpayer may or may not have the requisite personal stake in the outcome, depending upon the circumstances of the particular case. Therefore, we find no absolute bar in Article III to suits by federal taxpayers challenging allegedly unconstitutional federal taxing and spending programs. There remains, however, the problem of determining the circumstances under which a federal taxpayer will be deemed to have the personal stake and interest that impart the necessary concrete adverseness to such litigation so that standing can be conferred on the taxpayer qua taxpayer consistent with the constitutional limitations of Article III.

The various rules of standing applied by federal courts have not been developed in the abstract. Rather, they have been fashioned with specific reference to the status asserted by the party whose standing is challenged and to the type of question he wishes to have adjudicated. We have noted that, in deciding the question of standing, it is not relevant that the substantive issues in the litigation might be non-justiciable. However, our decisions establish that, in ruling on standing, it is both appropriate and necessary to look to the substantive issues for another purpose, namely, to determine whether there is a logical nexus between the status asserted and the claim sought to be adjudicated. For example, standing requirements will vary in First Amendment religion cases depending upon whether the party raises an Establishment Clause claim or a claim under the Free Exercise Clause. See McGowan v. State of Maryland, 366 U.S. 420, 429-430, 81 S.Ct. 1101, 1106-1107, 6 L.Ed.2d 393 (1961). Such inquiries into the nexus between the status asserted by the litigant and the claim he presents are essential to assure that he is a proper and appropriate party to invoke federal judicial power. Thus, our point of reference in this case is the standing of individuals who assert only the status of federal taxpayers and who challenge the constitutionality of a federal spending program. Whether such individuals have standing to maintain that form of action turns on whether they can demonstrate the necessary stake as taxpayers in the outcome of the litigation to satisfy Article III requirements.

The nexus demanded of federal taxpayers has two aspects to it. First, the taxpayer must establish a logical link between that status and the type of legislative enactment attacked. Thus, a taxpayer will be a proper party to allege the unconstitutionality only of exercises of congressional power under the taxing and spending clause of Art. I, § 8, of the Constitution. It will not be sufficient to allege an incidental expenditure of tax funds in the administration of an essentially regulatory statute. This requirement is consistent with the limitation imposed upon state-taxpayer standing in federal courts in Doremus v. Board of Education, 342 U.S. 429, 72 S.Ct. 394, 96 L.Ed. 475 (1952). Secondly, the taxpayer must establish a nexus between that status and the precise nature of the constitutional infringement alleged. Under this requirement, the taxpayer must show that the challenged enactment exceeds specific constitutional limitations imposed upon the exercise of the congressional taxing and spending power and not simply that the enactment is generally beyond the powers delegated to Congress by Art. I, § 8. When both nexuses are established, the litigant will have shown a taxpayer's stake in the outcome of the controversy and will be a proper and appropriate party to invoke a federal court's jurisdiction.

The taxpayer-appellants in this case have satisfied both nexuses to support their claim of standing under the test we announce today. Their constitutional challenge is made to an exercise by Congress of its power under Art. I, s 8, to spend for the general welfare, and the challenged program involves a substantial expenditure of federal tax funds. In addition, appellants have alleged that the challenged expenditures violate the Establishment and Free Exercise Clauses of the First Amendment. Our history vividly illustrates that one of the specific evils feared by those who drafted the Establishment Clause and fought for its adoption was that the taxing and spending power would be used to favor one religion over another or to support religion in general. James Madison, who is generally recognized as the leading architect of the religion clauses of the First Amendment, observed in his famous Memorial and Remonstrance Against Religious Assessments that "the same authority which can force a citizen to contribute three pence only of his property for the support of any one establishment, may force him to conform to any other establishment in all cases whatsoever." 2 Writings of James Madison 183, 186 (Hunt ed. 1901). The concern of Madison and his supporters was quite clearly that religious liberty ultimately would be the victim if government could employ its taxing and spending powers to aid one religion over another or to aid religion in general. The Establishment Clause was designed as a specific bulwark against such potential abuses of governmental power, and that clause of the First Amendment operates as a specific constitutional limitation upon the exercise by Congress of the taxing and spending power conferred by Art. I, § 8.

The allegations of the taxpayer in Frothingham v. Mellon, supra, were quite different from those made in this case, and the result in *Frothingham* is consistent with the test of taxpayer standing announced today. The taxpayer in *Frothingham* attacked a federal spending program and she, therefore, established the first nexus required. However, she lacked standing because her constitutional attack was not based on an allegation that Congress, in enacting the Maternity Act of 1921, had breached a specific limitation upon its taxing and spending power. The taxpayer in *Frothingham* alleged essentially that Congress, by enacting the challenged statute, had exceeded the general powers delegated to it by Art. I, § 8, and that Congress had thereby invaded the legislative province reserved to the States by the Tenth Amendment. To be sure, Mrs. Frothingham made the additional allegation that her tax liability would be increased as a result of the allegedly unconstitutional enactment, and she framed that allegation in terms of a deprivation of property without due process of law. However, the Due Process Clause of the Fifth Amendment does not protect taxpayers against increases in tax liability, and the taxpayer in *Frothingham* failed to make any additional claim that the harm she alleged resulted from a breach by Congress of the specific constitutional limitations imposed upon an exercise of the taxing and spending power. In essence, Mrs. Frothingham was attempting to assert the States' interest in their legislative prerogatives and not a federal taxpayer's interest in being free of taxing and spending in contravention of specific constitutional limitations imposed upon Congress' taxing and spending power.

We have noted that the Establishment Clause of the First Amendment does specifically limit the taxing and spending power conferred by Art. I, § 8. Whether the Constitution contains other specific limitations can be determined only in the context of future cases. However, whenever such specific limitations are found, we believe a taxpayer will have a clear stake as a taxpayer in assuring that they are not breached by Congress. Consequently, we hold that a taxpayer will have standing consistent with Article III to invoke federal judicial power when he alleges that congressional action under the taxing and spending clause is in derogation of those constitutional provisions which operate to restrict the exercise of the taxing and spending power. The taxpayer's allegation in such cases would be that his tax money is being extracted and spent in violation of specific constitutional protections against such abuses of legislative power. Such an injury is appropriate for judicial redress, and the taxpayer has established the necessary nexus between his status and the nature of the allegedly unconstitutional action to support his claim of standing to secure judicial review. Under such circumstances, we feel confident that the questions will be framed with the necessary specificity, that the issues will be contested with the necessary adverseness and that the litigation will be pursued with the necessary vigor to assure that the constitutional challenge will be made in a form traditionally thought to be capable of judicial resolution. We lack that confidence in cases such as *Frothingham* where a taxpayer seeks to employ a federal court as a forum in which to air his generalized grievances about the conduct of government or the allocation of power in the Federal System.

While we express no view at all on the merits of appellants' claims in this case, their complaint contains sufficient allegations under the criteria we have outlined to give them standing to invoke a federal court's jurisdiction for an adjudication on the merits.

Reversed.

———

Comment on *Flast*. Was it possible for a taxpayer to attain standing after *Flast*? How, and upon what basis? Did *Flast* overrule *Mellon*? If the door to taxpayer standing was opened after *Flast*, are you surprised that this would occur during what is viewed as the activism of the Warren Court? If it was opened, how far? How would you expect a more restraint-oriented Court in the Burger years to respond to these issues in the case that follows?

UNITED STATES v. RICHARDSON
418 U.S. 166 (1974)

Mr. Chief Justice BURGER delivered the opinion of the Court.

We granted certiorari in this case to determine whether the respondent has standing to bring an action as a federal taxpayer alleging that certain provisions concerning public reporting of expenditures under the Central Intelligence Agency Act of 1949, 63 Stat. 208, 50 U.S.C. § 403a et seq., violate Art. I, § 9, cl. 7, of the Constitution which provides:

> No Money shall be drawn from the Treasury, but in Consequence of Appropriations made by Law; and a regular Statement and Account of the Receipts and Expenditures of all public Money shall be published from time to time.

We conclude that respondent lacks standing to maintain a suit for the relief sought and we reverse. . . .

The Court [in *Flast*] then announced a two-pronged standing test which requires allegations: (a) challenging an enactment under the Taxing and Spending Clause of Art. I, § 8, of the Constitution; and (b) claiming that the challenged enactment exceeds specific constitutional limitations imposed on the taxing and spending power. While the "impenetrable barrier to suits against Acts of Congress brought by individuals who can assert only the interest of federal taxpayers," had been slightly lowered, the Court made clear it was reaffirming the principle of *Frothingham* precluding a taxpayer's use of "a federal court as a forum in which to air his generalized grievances about the conduct of government or the allocation of power in the Federal System."

. . . [Although] the Court made it very explicit in *Flast* that a "fundamental aspect of standing" is that it focuses primarily on the party seeking to get his complaint before the federal court rather than "on the issues he wishes to have adjudicated," id., at 99, 88 S.Ct., at 1952, it made equally clear that "in ruling on [taxpayer] standing, it is both appropriate and necessary to look to the substantive issues for another purpose, namely, to determine whether there is a logical nexus between the status asserted and the claim sought to be adjudicated," ibid., 88 S.Ct., at 1953.

We therefore turn to an examination of the issues sought to be raised by respondent's complaint to determine whether he is "a proper and appropriate party to invoke federal judicial power," id., at 102, 88 S.Ct., at 1953, with respect to those issues.

We need not and do not reach the merits of the constitutional attack on the statute; our inquiry into the "substantive issues" is for the limited purpose indicated above. The mere recital of the respondent's claims and an examination of the statute under attack demonstrate how far he falls short of the standing criteria of *Flast* and how neatly he falls within the *Frothingham* holding left undisturbed. Although the status he rests on is that he is a taxpayer, his challenge is not addressed to the taxing or spending power, but to the statutes regulating the CIA, specifically 50 U.S.C. § 403j(b). That section provides different accounting and reporting requirements and procedures for the CIA, as is also done with respect to other governmental agencies dealing in confidential areas.

Respondent makes no claim that appropriated funds are being spent in violation of a "specific constitutional limitation upon the . . . taxing and spending power . . ." 392 U.S., at 104, 88 S.Ct., at 1954. Rather, he asks the courts to compel the Government to give him information on precisely how the CIA spends its funds. Thus there is no "logical nexus" between the asserted status of taxpayer and the claimed failure of the Congress to require the Executive to supply a more detailed report of the expenditures of that agency.

The question presented thus is simply and narrowly whether these claims meet the standards for taxpayer standing set forth in *Flast*; we hold they do not. Respondent is seeking "to employ a federal court as a forum in which to air his generalized grievances about the conduct of government." 392 U.S., at 106, 88 S.Ct., at 1956. Both *Frothingham* and *Flast*, supra, reject that basis for standing.

The respondent's claim is that without detailed information on CIA expenditures — and hence its activities — he cannot intelligently follow the actions of Congress or the Executive, nor can he properly fulfill his obligations as a member of the electorate in voting for candidates seeking national office.

This is surely the kind of a generalized grievance described in both *Frothingham* and *Flast* since the impact on him is plainly undifferentiated and "common to all members of the public." Ex parte Le vitt, 302 U.S. 633, 634, 58 S.Ct. 1, 82 L.Ed. 493 (1937); Laird v. Tatum, 408 U.S. 1, 13, 92 S.Ct. 2318, 2325, 33 L.Ed.2d 154 (1972). While we can hardly dispute that this respondent has a genuine interest in the use of funds and that his interest may be prompted by his status as a taxpayer, he has not alleged that, as a taxpayer, he is in danger of suffering any particular concrete injury as a result of the operation of this statute. As the Court noted in Sierra Club v. Morton, 405 U.S. 727, 92 S.Ct. 1361, 31 L.Ed.2d 636 (1972):

> [A] mere "interest in a problem," no matter how long-standing the interest and no matter how qualified the organization is in evaluating the problem, is not sufficient by itself to render the organization "adversely affected" or "aggrieved" within the meaning of the APA.

Id., at 739, 92 S.Ct., at 1368.

Ex parte Levitt, supra, is especially instructive. There Levitt sought to challenge the validity of the commission of a Supreme Court Justice who had been nominated and confirmed as such while he was a member of the Senate. Levitt alleged that the appointee had voted for an increase in the emoluments provided by Congress for Justices of the Supreme Court during the term for which he was last elected to the United States Senate. The claim was that the appointment violated the explicit prohibition of Art. I, 6, cl. 2, of the Constitution. 10. The Court disposed of Levitt's claim, stating:

> It is an established principle that to entitle a private individual to invoke the judicial power to determine the validity of executive or legislative action he must show that he has sustained or is immediately in danger of sustaining a direct injury as the result of that action, and it is not sufficient that he has merely a general interest common to all members of the public.

Of course, if Levitt's allegations were true, they made out an arguable violation of an explicit prohibition of the Constitution. Yet even this was held insufficient to support standing because, whatever Levitt's injury, it was one he shared with "all members of the public." Respondent here, like the petitioner in Levitt, also fails to clear the threshold hurdle of Baker v. Carr, 369 U.S., at 204. See supra, at 171, and Flast, supra. 11.

It can be argued that if respondent is not permitted to litigate this issue, no one can do so. In a very real sense, the absence of any particular individual or class to litigate these claims gives support to the argument that the subject matter is committed to the surveillance of Congress, and ultimately to the political process. Any other conclusion would mean that the Founding Fathers intended to set up something in the nature of an Athenian democracy or a New England town meeting to oversee the conduct of the National Government by means of lawsuits in federal courts. The Constitution created a representative Government with the representatives directly responsible to their constituents at stated periods of two, four, and six years; that the Constitution does not afford a judicial remedy does not, of course, completely disable the citizen who is not satisfied with the "ground rules" established by the Congress for reporting expenditures of the Executive Branch. Lack of standing within the narrow confines of Art. III jurisdiction does not impair the right to assert his views in the political forum or at the polls. Slow, cumbersome, and unresponsive though the traditional electoral process may be thought at times, our system provides for changing members of the political branches when dissatisfied citizens convince a sufficient number of their fellow electors that elected representatives are delinquent in performing duties committed to them.

As our society has become more complex, our numbers more vast, our lives more varied, and our resources more strained, citizens increasingly request the intervention of the courts on a greater variety of issues than at any period of our national development. The acceptance of new categories of judicially cognizable injury has not eliminated the basic principle that to invoke judicial power the claimant must have a "personal stake in the outcome," Baker v. Carr, supra, at 204, 82 S.Ct., at 703, or a "particular, concrete injury," Sierra Club, supra, 405 U.S., at 740-741, n. 16, 92 S.Ct., at 1369, or "a direct injury," Ex parte Le vitt, supra, 302 U.S., at 634, 58 S.Ct., at 1; in short, something more than "generalized grievances," Flast, supra, 392 U.S., at 106, 88 S.Ct., at 1956. Respondent has failed to meet these fundamental tests; accordingly, the judgment of the Court of Appeals is reversed.

Mr. Justice POWELL, concurring.

[I] write solely to indicate that I would go further than the Court and would lay to rest the approach undertaken in *Flast*. I would not overrule *Flast* on its facts, because it is now settled that federal taxpayer standing exists in Establishment Clause cases. I would not, however, perpetuate the doctrinal confusion inherent in the *Flast* two-part "nexus" test. That test is not a reliable indicator of when a federal taxpayer has standing, and it has no sound relationship to the question whether such a plaintiff, with no other interest at stake, should be allowed to bring suit against one of the branches of the Federal Government. In my opinion, it should be abandoned.

I . . .

The ambiguities inherent in the *Flast* "nexus" limitations on federal taxpayer standing are illustrated by this case. There can be little doubt about respondent's fervor in pursuing his case, both within administrative channels and at every level of the federal courts. The intensity of his interest appears to bear no relationship to the fact that, literally speaking, he is not challenging directly a congressional exercise of the taxing and spending power. On the other hand, if the involvement of the taxing and spending power has some relevance, it requires no great leap in reasoning to conclude that the Statement and Account Clause, Art. I, § 9, cl. 7, on which respondent relies, is inextricably linked to that power. And that Clause might well be seen as a "specific" limitation on congressional spending. Indeed, it could be viewed as the most democratic of limitations. Thus, although the Court's application of *Flast* to the instant case is probably literally correct, adherence to the *Flast* test in this instance suggests, as does *Flast* itself, that the test is not a sound or logical limitation on standing.

The lack of real meaning and of principled content in the *Flast* "nexus" test renders it likely that it will in time collapse of its own weight. This will present several options for the Court. It may either reaffirm pre-*Flast* prudential limitations on federal and citizen taxpayer standing; attempt new doctrinal departures in this area, . . . or simply drop standing barriers altogether. I believe the first option to be the appropriate course, for reasons which may be emphasized by noting the difficulties I see with the other two. And, while I do not disagree at this late date with the Baker v. Carr statement of the constitutional indicia of standing, I further believe that constitutional limitations are not the only pertinent considerations.

III

Relaxation of standing requirements is directly related to the expansion of judicial power. It seems to me inescapable that allowing unrestricted taxpayer or citizen standing would significantly alter the allocation of power at the national level, with a shift away from a democratic form of government. I also believe that repeated and essentially head-on confrontations between the life tenured branch and the representative branches of government will not, in the long run, be beneficial to either. The public confidence essential to the former and the vitality critical to the latter may well erode if we do not exercise self-restraint in the utilization of our power to negative the actions of the other branches. We should be ever mindful of the contradictions that would arise if a democracy were to permit general oversight of the elected branches of government by a non-representative, and in large measure insulated, judicial branch. Moreover, the argument that the Court should allow unrestricted taxpayer or citizen standing underestimates the ability of the representative branches of the Federal Government to respond to the citizen pressure that has been responsible in large measure for the concurrent drift toward expanded standing. Indeed, taxpayer or citizen advocacy, given its potentially broad base, is precisely the type of leverage that in a democracy ought to be employed against the branches that were intended to be responsive to public attitudes about the appropriate operation of government. 'We must as judges recall that, as Mr. Justice Holmes wisely observed, the other branches of the Government "are ultimate guardians of the liberties and welfare of the people in quite as great a degree as the courts."

. . . The power recognized in Marbury v. Madison, 1 Cranch 137, 2 L.Ed. 60 (1803), is a potent one. Its prudent use seems to me incompatible with unlimited notions of taxpayer and citizen standing. Were we to utilize this power as indiscriminately as is now being urged, we may witness efforts by the representative branches drastically to curb its use. Due to what many have regarded as the unresponsiveness of the Federal Government to recognized needs or serious inequities in our society, recourse to the federal courts has attained an unprecedented popularity in recent decades. Those courts have often acted as a major instrument of social reform. But this has not always been the case, as experiences under the New Deal illustrate. The public reaction to the substantive due process holdings of the federal courts during that period requires no elaboration, and it is not unusual for history to repeat itself.

. . . The irreplaceable value of the power articulated by Mr. Chief Justice Marshall lies in the protection it has afforded the constitutional rights and liberties of individual citizens and minority groups against oppressive or discriminatory government action. It is this role, not some amorphous, general supervision of the operations of government, that has maintained public esteem for the federal courts and has permitted the peaceful coexistence of the counter-majoritarian implications of judicial review and the democratic principles upon which our Federal Government in the final analysis rests.

In sum, I believe we should limit the expansion of federal taxpayer and citizen standing in the absence of specific statutory authorization to an outer boundary drawn by the results in *Flast*. . . . I think we should face up to the fact that all such suits are an effort "to employ a federal court as a forum in which to air . . . generalized grievances about the conduct of government or the allocation of power in the Federal System." Flast v. Cohen, 392 U.S., at 106, 88 S.Ct., at 1956. The Court should explicitly reaffirm traditional prudential barriers against such public actions. My reasons for this view are rooted in respect for democratic processes and in the conviction that "[t]he powers of the federal judiciary will be adequate for the great burdens placed upon them only if they are employed prudently, with recognition of the strengths as well as the hazards that go with out kind of representative government."

The doctrine of standing has always reflected prudential as well as constitutional limitations. Indeed, it might be said that the correct reading of the *Flast* nexus test is as a prudential limit. . . . Whatever may have been the Court's initial perception of the intent of the Framers, it is now settled that such rules of self-restraint are not required by Art. III but are "judicially created overlays that Congress may strip away. . . ." But where Congress does so, my objections to public actions are ameliorated by the congressional mandate. Specific statutory grants of standing in such cases alleviate the conditions that make "judicial forbearance the part of wisdom."

———

Comment on *Richardson*. What exactly did the Court hold in *Richardson*? Was *Flast* overruled? Is *Mellon* now "good law"? Could a taxpayer maintain standing post-*Richardson*? How wide, or narrow, is the door now? Did the merits of *Richardson* affect the outcome? Is the Statement and Account Clause still a meaningful part of the

Constitution? This inquiry takes us back to our introductory comments on how an understanding of the merits at stake may be necessary to understand the application of jurisdictional restraints. The case that follows reviews the Court's present position in regard to taxpayer standing and the use of jurisdictional requirements as a means of enforcing a given Court's philosophy on how the judicial power should be applied.

VALLEY FORGE CHRISTIAN COLLEGE v. AMERICANS UNITED FOR SEPARATION OF CHURCH AND STATE
454 U.S. 464 (1982)

Justice REHNQUIST delivered the opinion of the Court.

The property which spawned this litigation was acquired by the Department of the Army in 1942, as part of a larger tract of approximately 181 acres of land northwest of Philadelphia. The Army built on that land the Valley Forge General Hospital, and for 30 years thereafter, that hospital provided medical care for members of the Armed Forces. In April 1973, as part of a plan to reduce the number of military installations in the United States, the Secretary of Defense proposed to close the hospital, and the General Services Administration declared it to be "surplus property."

The Department of Health, Education, and Welfare (HEW) eventually assumed responsibility for disposing of portions of the property, and in August 1976, it conveyed a 77-acre tract to petitioner, the Valley Forge Christian College. The appraised value of the property at the time of conveyance was $577,500. This appraised value was discounted, however, by the Secretary's computation of a 100% public benefit allowance, which permitted petitioner to acquire the property without making any financial payment for it. The deed from HEW conveyed the land in fee simple with certain conditions subsequent, which required petitioner to use the property for 30 years solely for the educational purposes described in petitioner's application.

Petitioner is a nonprofit educational institution operating under the supervision of a religious order known as the Assemblies of God. By its own description, petitioner's purpose is "to offer systematic training on the collegiate level to men and women for Christian service as either ministers or laymen." App. 34. Its degree programs reflect this orientation by providing courses of study "to train leaders for church related ministries." *Id.*, at 102. Faculty members must "have been baptized in the Holy Spirit and be living consistent Christian lives," *id.*, at 37, and all members of the college administration must be affiliated with the Assemblies of God, *id.*, at 36. In its application for the 77-acre tract, petitioner represented that, if it obtained the property, it would make "additions to its offerings in the arts and humanities," and would strengthen its "psychology" and "counseling" courses to provide services in inner-city areas.

[Respondents] Americans United for Separation of Church and State, Inc. (Americans United), and four of its employees, learned of the conveyance through a news release. Two months later, they brought suit in the United States District Court for the District of Columbia, later transferred to the Eastern District of Pennsylvania, to challenge the conveyance on the ground that it violated the Establishment Clause of the First Amendment. See *id.*, at 10. In its amended complaint, Americans United described itself as a nonprofit organization composed of 90,000 "taxpayer members." The complaint asserted that each member "would be deprived of the fair and constitutional use of his (her) tax dollar for constitutional purposes in violation of his (her) rights under the First

Amendment of the United States Constitution." *Ibid.* Respondents sought a declaration that the conveyance was null and void, and an order compelling petitioner to transfer the property back to the United States. *Id.*, at 12.

. . . [Unlike] the plaintiffs in *Flast*, respondents fail the first prong of the test for taxpayer standing. Their claim is deficient in two respects. First, the source of their complaint is not a congressional action, but a decision by HEW to transfer a parcel of federal property. *Flast* limited taxpayer standing to challenges directed "only [at] exercises of congressional power."

Second, and perhaps redundantly, the property transfer about which respondents complain was not an exercise of authority conferred by the Taxing and Spending Clause of Art. I, § 8. The authorizing legislation, the Federal Property and Administrative Services Act of 1949, was an evident exercise of Congress' power under the Property Clause, Art. IV, § 3, cl. 2. Respondents do not dispute this conclusion, see Brief for Respondents Americans United et al. 10, and it is decisive of any claim of taxpayer standing under the *Flast* precedent. [FN17]

> FN17. Although not necessary to our decision, we note that any connection between the challenged property transfer and respondents' tax burden is at best speculative and at worst nonexistent. Although public funds were expended to establish the Valley Forge General Hospital, the land was acquired and the facilities constructed 30 years prior to the challenged transfer. Respondents do not challenge this expenditure, and we do not immediately perceive how such a challenge might now be raised. Nor do respondents dispute the Government's conclusion that the property has become useless for federal purposes and ought to be disposed of in some productive manner. In fact, respondents' only objection is that the Government did not receive adequate consideration for the transfer, because petitioner's use of the property will not confer a public benefit. See Brief for Respondents Americans United et al. 13. Assuming, *arguendo*, that this proposition is true, an assumption by no means clear, there is no basis for believing that a transfer to a different purchaser would have added to Government receipts. As the Government argues, "the ultimate purchaser would, in all likelihood, have been another non-profit institution or local school district rather than a purchaser for cash." Brief for Federal Respondents 30. Moreover, each year of delay in disposing of the property *depleted* the Treasury by the amounts necessary to maintain a facility that had lost its value to the Government. Even if respondents had brought their claim within the outer limits of *Flast*, therefore, they still would have encountered serious difficulty in establishing that they "personally would benefit in a tangible way from the court's intervention." Warth v. Seldin, 422 U.S., at 508, 95 S.Ct., at 2210.

Any doubt that once might have existed concerning the rigor with which the *Flast* exception to the *Frothingham* principle ought to be applied should have been erased by this Court's recent decisions in United States v. Richardson, 418 U.S. 166, 94 S.Ct. 2940, 41 L.Ed.2d 678 (1974), and *Schlesinger v. Reservists Committee to Stop the War*, supra. In *Richardson*, the question was whether the plaintiff had standing as a federal taxpayer to argue that legislation which permitted the Central Intelligence Agency to withhold from the public detailed information about its expenditures violated the Accounts Clause of the Constitution. We rejected plaintiff's claim of standing because "his challenge [was] not addressed to the taxing or spending power, but to the statutes regulating the CIA." 418 U.S., at 175, 94 S.Ct., at 2945. The "mere recital" of those claims "demonstrate[d] how far he [fell] short of the standing criteria of *Flast* and how neatly he [fell] within the *Frothingham* holding left undisturbed." Id., at 174-175, 94 S.Ct., at 2945.

Although the Court of Appeals properly doubted respondents' ability to establish standing solely on the basis of their taxpayer status, it considered their allegations of taxpayer injury to be "essentially an assumed role." 619 F.2d, at 261. "Plaintiffs have no reason to expect, nor perhaps do they care about, any personal tax saving that might result should they prevail. The crux of the interest at stake, the plaintiffs argue, is found in the Establishment Clause, not in the supposed loss of money as such. As a matter of primary identity, therefore, the plaintiffs are not so much taxpayers as separationists. . . ." *Ibid.* In the court's view, respondents had established standing by virtue of an " 'injury in fact' to their shared individuated right to a government that 'shall make no law respecting the establishment of religion.'" *Ibid.* The court distinguished this "injury" from "the question of 'citizen standing' as such." Id., at 262. Although citizens generally could not establish standing simply by claiming an interest in governmental observance of the Constitution, respondents had "set forth instead a particular and concrete injury" to a "personal constitutional right." Id., at 265.

. . . [In] finding that respondents had alleged something more than "the generalized interest of all citizens in constitutional governance," Schlesinger, supra, 418 U.S., at 217, 94 S.Ct., at 2930, the Court of Appeals relied on factual differences which we do not think amount to legal distinctions. The court decided that respondents' claim differed from those in *Schlesinger* and *Richardson*, which were predicated, respectively, on the Incompatibility and Accounts Clauses, because "it is at the very least arguable that the Establishment Clause creates in each citizen a 'personal constitutional right' to a government that does not establish religion." 619 F.2d, at 265 (footnote omitted). The court found it unnecessary to determine whether this "arguable" proposition was correct, since it judged the mere allegation of a legal right sufficient to confer standing.

This reasoning process merely disguises, we think with a rather thin veil, the inconsistency of the court's results with our decisions in *Schlesinger* and *Richardson*. The plaintiffs in those cases plainly asserted a "personal right" to have the Government act in accordance with their views of the Constitution; indeed, we see no barrier to the *assertion* of such claims with respect to any constitutional provision. But assertion of a right to a particular kind of Government conduct, which the Government has violated by acting differently, cannot alone satisfy the requirements of Art. III without draining those requirements of meaning.

Nor can *Schlesinger* and *Richardson* be distinguished on the ground that the Incompatibility and Accounts Clauses are in some way less "fundamental" than the Establishment Clause. Each establishes a norm of conduct which the Federal Government is bound to honor — to no greater or lesser extent than any other inscribed in the Constitution. To the extent the Court of Appeals relied on a view of standing under which the Art. III burdens diminish as the "importance" of the claim on the merits increases, we reject that notion. The requirement of standing "focuses on the party seeking to get his complaint before a federal court and not on the issues he wishes to have adjudicated." Flast v. Cohen, supra, 392 U.S., at 99, 88 S.Ct., at 1952. Moreover, we know of no principled basis on which to create a hierarchy of constitutional values or a complementary "sliding scale" of standing which might permit respondents to invoke the judicial power of the United States. "The proposition that all constitutional provisions are enforceable by any citizen simply because citizens are the ultimate beneficiaries of those provisions has no boundaries." Schlesinger v. Reservists Committee to Stop the War, supra, 418 U.S., at 227, 94 S.Ct., at 2935.

The complaint in this case shares a common deficiency with those in *Schlesinger* and *Richardson*. Although respondents claim that the Constitution has been violated, they claim nothing else. They fail to identify any personal injury suffered by them *as a consequence* of the alleged constitutional error, other than the psychological consequence presumably produced by observation of conduct with which one disagrees. That is not an injury sufficient to confer standing under Art. III, even though the disagreement is phrased in constitutional terms. It is evident that respondents are firmly committed to the constitutional principle of separation of church and State, but standing is not measured by the intensity of the litigant's interest or the fervor of his advocacy. "[T]hat concrete adverseness which sharpens the presentation of issues," Baker v. Carr, 369 U.S., at 204, 82 S.Ct., at 703, is the anticipated consequence of proceedings commenced by one who has been injured in fact; it is not a permissible substitute for the showing of injury itself.

In reaching this conclusion, we do not retreat from our earlier holdings that standing may be predicated on noneconomic injury. See, e. g., United States v. SCRAP, 412 U.S., at 686-688, 93 S.Ct., at 2415-2416; Association of Data Processing Service Orgs. v. Camp, 397 U.S., at 153-154, 90 S.Ct., at 829-830. We simply cannot see that respondents have alleged an *injury* of *any* kind, economic or otherwise, sufficient to confer standing. Respondents complain of a transfer of property located in Chester County, Pa. The named plaintiffs reside in Maryland and Virginia; [FN23] their organizational headquarters are located in Washington, D.C. They learned of the transfer through a news release. Their claim that the Government has violated the Establishment Clause does not provide a special license to roam the country in search of governmental wrongdoing and to reveal their discoveries in federal court. [FN24] The federal courts were simply not constituted as ombudsmen of the general welfare.

FN23. Respondent Americans United claims that it has certain unidentified members who reside in Pennsylvania. It does not explain, however, how this fact establishes a cognizable injury where none existed before. Respondent is still obligated to allege facts sufficient to establish that one or more of its members has suffered, or is threatened with, an injury other than their belief that the transfer violated the Constitution.

FN24. Respondents also claim standing by reference to the Administrative Procedure Act, 5 U.S.C. § 702, which authorizes judicial review at the instance of any person who has been "adversely affected or aggrieved by agency action within the meaning of a relevant statute." Neither the Administrative Procedure Act, nor any other congressional enactment, can lower the threshold requirements of standing under Art. III. See, e. g., Gladstone, Realtors v. Village of Bellwood, 441 U.S., at 100, 99 S.Ct., at 1608; Warth v. Seldin, 422 U.S., at 501, 95 S.Ct., at 2206. Respondents do not allege that the Act creates a legal right, "the invasion of which creates standing," Linda R.S. v. Richard D., 410 U.S., at 617, n. 3, 93 S.Ct., at 1148, n. 3, and there is no other basis for arguing that its existence alters the rules of standing otherwise applicable to this case.

The Court of Appeals in this case ignored unambiguous limitations on taxpayer and citizen standing. It appears to have done so out of the conviction that enforcement of the Establishment Clause demands special exceptions from the requirement that a plaintiff allege "'distinct and palpable injury to himself,' . . . that is likely to be redressed if the requested relief is granted."

Implicit in the foregoing is the philosophy that the business of the federal courts is correcting constitutional errors, and that "cases and controversies" are at best merely convenient vehicles for doing so and at worst nuisances that may be dispensed with when they become obstacles to that transcendent endeavor. This philosophy has no place in our constitutional scheme. It does not become more palatable when the underlying merits concern the Establishment Clause. Respondents' claim of standing implicitly rests on the presumption that violations of the Establishment Clause typically will not cause injury sufficient to confer standing under the "traditional" view of Art. III. But "[t]he assumption that if respondents have no standing to sue, no one would have standing, is not a reason to find standing." Schlesinger v. Reservists Committee to Stop the War, 418 U.S., at 227, 94 S.Ct., at 2935. This view would convert standing into a requirement that must be observed only when satisfied. Moreover, we are unwilling to assume that injured parties are nonexistent simply because they have not joined respondents in their suit. The law of averages is not a substitute for standing.

Were we to accept respondents' claim of standing in this case, there would be no principled basis for confining our exception to litigants relying on the Establishment Clause. Ultimately, that exception derives from the idea that the judicial power requires nothing more for its invocation than important issues and able litigants. [FN26] The existence of injured parties who might not wish to bring suit becomes irrelevant. Because we are unwilling to countenance such a departure from the limits on judicial power contained in Art. III, the judgment of the Court of Appeals is reversed.

FN26. Were we to recognize standing premised on an "injury" consisting solely of an alleged violation of a " 'personal constitutional right' to a government that does not establish religion," *id.*, at 265, a principled consistency would dictate recognition of respondents' standing to challenge execution of every capital sentence on the basis of a personal right to a government that does not impose cruel and unusual punishment, or standing to challenge every affirmative-action program on the basis of a personal right to a government that does not deny equal protection of the laws, to choose but two among as many possible examples as there are commands in the Constitution.

It is so ordered.

7. "IN HOUSE RULES" AND CONTEMPORARY JUDICIAL SELF-GOVERNANCE

Were the results in the taxpayer standing cases based upon the constitutional requirements of case and controversy, or were they based upon the Court's own prerogative, a kind of Article III "plus"? If they are additional requirements based upon the Court applying its own discretion as to how it believes the judicial power should be applied, do they exemplify the impact of the weak origin of the power and its application by a nonelected body in a society supposedly governed by democratic process? If they are "Court created," may we describe them as "In-house of self governance" applied as "prudential barriers to review"? *Warth v. Seldin* is perhaps the most significant case presented in regard to these materials (Article III); this Burger Court "treatise" on the standing requirement is still the major source for the modern Court's view on the meaning of Article III in relation to application of the judicial power. Of even greater significance is that *Warth* provides direct and straightforward answers concerning the issue of constitutional versus discretionary requirements for judicial review.

WARTH v. SELDIN
422 U.S. 490 (1975)

Mr. Justice POWELL delivered the opinion of the Court.

Petitioners, various organizations and individuals resident in the Rochester, N.Y., metropolitan area, brought this action in the District Court for the Western District of New York against the town of Penfield, an incorporated municipality adjacent to Rochester, and against members of Penfield's Zoning, Planning and Town Boards. Petitioners claimed that the town's zoning ordinance, by its terms and as enforced by the defendant board members, respondents here, effectively excluded persons of low and moderate income from living in the town, in contravention of petitioners' First, Ninth, and Fourteenth Amendment rights and in violation of 42 U.S.C. §§ 1981, 1982, and 1983. The District Court dismissed the complaint and denied a motion to add petitioner Housing Council in the Monroe County Area, Inc., as party-plaintiff and also a motion by petitioner Rochester Home Builders Association, Inc., for leave to intervene as party-plaintiff. The Court of Appeals for the Second Circuit affirmed, holding that none of the plaintiffs, and neither Housing Council nor Home Builders Association, had standing to prosecute the action. 495 F.2d 1187 (1974). We granted the petition for certiorari. 419 U.S. 823, 95 S.Ct. 40, 42 L.Ed.2d 47 (1974). For reasons that differ in certain respects from those upon which the Court of Appeals relied, we affirm.

II

We address first the principles of standing relevant to the claims asserted by the several categories of petitioners in this case. In essence the question of standing is whether the litigant is entitled to have the court decide the merits of the dispute or of particular issues. This inquiry involves both constitutional limitations on federal-court jurisdiction and prudential limitations on its exercise. E.g., Barrows v. Jackson, 346 U.S. 249, 255-256, 73 S.Ct. 1031, 1034-1035, 97 L.Ed. 1586 (1953). In both dimensions it is founded in concern about the proper — and properly limited — role of the courts in a democratic society. See Schlesinger v. Reservists to Stop the War, 418 U.S. 208, 221-227, 94 S.Ct. 2925, 2932-2935, 41 L.Ed.2d 706 (1974); United States v. Richardson, 418 U.S. 166, 188-197, 94 S.Ct. 2940, 2952-2956, 41 L.Ed.2d 678 (1974) (Powell, J., concurring).

In its constitutional dimension, standing imports justiciability: whether the plaintiff has made out a "case or controversy" between himself and the defendant within the meaning of Art. III. This is the threshold question in every federal case, determining the power of the court to entertain the suit. As an aspect of justiciability, the standing question is whether the plaintiff has "alleged such a personal stake in the outcome of the controversy" as to warrant his invocation of federal-court jurisdiction and to justify exercise of the court's remedial powers on his behalf. Baker v. Carr, 369 U.S. 186, 204, 82 S.Ct. 691, 703, 7 L.Ed.2d 663 (1962). The Art. III judicial power exists only to redress or otherwise to protect against injury to the complaining party, even though the court's judgment may benefit others collaterally. A federal court's jurisdiction therefore can be invoked only when the plaintiff himself has suffered "some threatened or actual injury resulting from the putatively illegal action. . . ." Linda R.S. v. Richard D., 410 U.S. 614, 617, 93 S.Ct. 1146, 1148, 35 L.Ed.2d 536 (1973). See Data Processing Service v. Camp, 397 U.S. 150, 151-154, 90 S.Ct., 827, 829-830, 25 L.Ed.2d 184 (1970).

Apart from this minimum constitutional mandate, this Court has recognized other limits on the class of persons who may invoke the courts' decisional and remedial powers. First, the Court has held that when the asserted harm is a "generalized grievance" shared in substantially equal measure by all or a large class of citizens, that harm alone normally does not warrant exercise of jurisdiction. E.g., Schlesinger v. Reservists to Stop the War, supra; United States v. Richardson, supra; Ex parte Le vitt, 302 U.S. 633, 634, 58 S.Ct. 1, 82 L.Ed. 493 (1937), Second, even when the plaintiff has alleged injury sufficient to meet the "case or controversy" requirement, this Court has held that the plaintiff generally must assert his own legal rights and interests, and cannot rest his claim to relief on the legal rights or interests of third parties. E.g., Tileston v. Ullman, 318 U.S. 44, 63 S.Ct. 493, 87 L.Ed. 603 (1943). See United States v. Raines, 362 U.S. 17, 80 S.Ct. 519, 4 L.Ed.2d 524 (1960); Barrows v. Jackson, supra. Without such limitations — closely related to Art. III concerns but essentially matters of judicial self-governance — the courts would be called upon to decide abstract questions of wide public significance even though other governmental institutions may be more competent to address the questions and even though judicial intervention may be unnecessary to protect individual rights. See, e.g., Schlesinger v. Reservists to Stop the War, 418 U.S., at 222, 94 S.Ct., at 2932.

Although standing in no way depends on the merits of the plaintiff's contention that particular conduct is illegal, e.g., Flast v. Cohen, 392 U.S. 83, 99, 88 S.Ct. 1942, 1952, 20 L.Ed.2d 947 (1968), it often turns on the nature and source of the claim asserted. The actual or threatened injury required by Art. III may exist solely by virtue of "statutes creating legal rights, the invasion of which creates standing . . ." See Linda R.S. v. Richard D., supra, 410 U.S., at 617 n. 3, 93 S.Ct., at 1148; Sierra Club v. Morton, 405 U.S. 727, 732, 92 S.Ct. 1361, 1364, 31 L.Ed.2d 636 (1972). Moreover, the source of the plaintiff's claim to relief assumes critical importance with respect to the prudential rules of standing that, apart from Art. III's minimum requirements, serve to limit the role of the courts in resolving public disputes. Essentially, the standing question in such cases is whether the constitutional or statutory provision on which the claim rests properly can be understood as granting persons in the plaintiff's position a right to judicial relief. In some circumstances, countervailing considerations may outweigh the concerns underlying the usual reluctance to exert judicial power when the plaintiff's claim to relief rests on the legal rights of third parties. See United States v. Raines, 362 U.S., at 22-23, 80 S.Ct., at 523-524. In such instances, the Court has found, in effect, that the constitutional or statutory provision in question implies a right of action in the plaintiff. See Pierce v. Society of Sisters, 268 U.S. 510, 45 S.Ct. 571, 69 L.Ed. 1070 (1925); Sullivan v. Little Hunting Park, Inc., 396 U.S. 229, 237, 90 S.Ct. 400, 404, 24 L.Ed.2d 386 (1969). See generally Part IV, infra. Moreover, Congress may grant an express right of action to persons who otherwise would be barred by prudential standing rules. Of course, Art. III's requirement remains: the plaintiff still must allege a distinct and palpable injury to himself, even if it is an injury shared by a large class of other possible litigants. E.g., United States v. SCRAP, 412 U.S. 669, 93 S.Ct. 2405, 37 L.Ed.2d 254 (1973). But so long as this requirement is satisfied, persons to whom Congress has granted a right of action, either expressly or by clear implication, may have standing to seek relief on the basis of the legal rights and interests of others, and, indeed, may invoke the general public interest in support of their claim. E.g., Sierra Club v. Morton, supra, 405 U.S., at 737, 92 S.Ct., at 1367; FCC v. Sanders Radio Station, 309 U.S. 470, 477, 60 S.Ct. 693, 698, 84 L.Ed. 869 (1940).

III

With these general considerations in mind, we turn first to the claims of petitioners Ortiz, Reyes, Sinkler, and Broadnax, each of whom asserts standing as a person of low or moderate income and, coincidentally, as a member of a minority racial or ethnic group. We must assume, taking the allegations of the complaint as true, that Penfield's zoning ordinance and the pattern of enforcement by respondent officials have had the purpose and effect of excluding persons of low and moderate income, many of whom are members of racial or ethnic minority groups. We also assume, for purposes here, that such intentional exclusionary practices, if proved in a proper case, would be adjudged violative of the constitutional and statutory rights of the persons excluded.

But the fact that these petitioners share attributes common to persons who may have been excluded from residence in the town is an insufficient predicate for the conclusion that petitioners themselves have been excluded, or that the respondents' assertedly illegal actions have violated their rights. Petitioners must allege and show that they personally have been injured, not that injury has been suffered by other, unidentified members of the class to which they belong and which they purport to represent. Unless these petitioners can thus demonstrate the requisite case or controversy between themselves personally and respondents, "none may seek relief on behalf of himself or any other member of the class." O'Shea v. Littleton, 414 U.S. 488, 494, 94 S.Ct. 669, 675, 38 L.Ed.2d 674 (1974). See, e.g., Bailey v. Patterson, 369 U.S. 31, 32-33, 82 S.Ct. 549, 550-551, 7 L.Ed.2d 512 (1962).

In their complaint, petitioners Ortiz, Reyes, Sinkler, and Broadnax alleged in conclusory terms that they are among the persons excluded by respondents' actions. None of them has ever resided in Penfield; each claims at least implicitly that he desires, or has desired, to do so. Each asserts, moreover, that he made some effort, at some time, to locate housing in Penfield that was at once within his means and adequate for his family's needs. Each claims that his efforts proved fruitless. We may assume, as petitioners allege, that respondents' actions have contributed, perhaps substantially, to the cost of housing in Penfield. But there remains the question whether petitioners' inability to locate suitable housing in Penfield reasonably can be said to have resulted, in any concretely demonstrable way, from respondents' alleged constitutional and statutory infractions. Petitioners must allege facts from which it reasonably could be inferred that, absent the respondents' restrictive zoning practices, there is a substantial probability that they would have been able to purchase or lease in Penfield and that, if the court affords the relief requested, the asserted inability of petitioners will be removed. Linda R.S. v. Richard D., supra.

We find the record devoid of the necessary allegations. As the Court of Appeals noted, none of these petitioners has a present interest in any Penfield property; none is himself subject to the ordinance's strictures; and none has even been denied a variance or permit by respondent officials. 495 F.2d, at 1191. Instead, petitioners claim that respondents' enforcement of the ordinance against third parties — developers, builders, and the like — has had the consequence of precluding the construction of housing suitable to their needs at prices they might be able to afford. The fact that the harm to petitioners may have resulted indirectly does not in itself preclude standing. When a governmental prohibition or restriction imposed on one party causes specific harm to a third party, harm that a constitutional provision or statute was intended to prevent, the indirectness of the injury does not necessarily deprive the person harmed of standing to vindicate his rights. E.g., Roe v. Wade, 410 U.S. 113, 124, 93 S.Ct. 705, 712, 35 L.Ed.2d 147 (1973). But it may make it substantially more difficult to meet the minimum requirement of Art. III: to establish that, in fact, the asserted injury was the consequence of the defendants' actions, or that prospective relief will remove the harm.

Here, by their own admission, realization of petitioners' desire to live in Penfield always has depended on the efforts and willingness of third parties to build low- and moderate-cost housing. The record specifically refers to only two such efforts: that of Penfield Better Homes Corp., in late 1969, to obtain the rezoning of certain land in Penfield to allow the construction of subsidized cooperative townhouses that could be purchased by persons of moderate income; and a similar effort by O'Brien Homes, Inc., in late 1971. But the record is devoid of any indication that these projects, or other like projects, would have satisfied petitioners' needs at prices they could afford, or that, were the court to remove the obstructions attributable to respondents, such relief would benefit petitioners. Indeed, petitioners' descriptions of their individual financial situations and housing needs suggest precisely the contrary — that their inability to reside in Penfield is the consequence of the economics of the area housing market, rather than of respondents' assertedly illegal acts. In short, the facts alleged fail to support an actionable causal relationship between Penfield's zoning practices and petitioners' asserted injury.

We hold only that a plaintiff who seeks to challenge exclusionary zoning practices must allege specific, concrete facts demonstrating that the challenged practices harm him, and that he personally would benefit in a tangible way from the court's intervention. Absent the necessary allegations of demonstrable, particularized injury, there can be no confidence of "a real need to exercise the power of judicial review" or that relief can be framed "no (broader) than required by the precise facts to which the court's ruling would be applied." Schlesinger v. Reservists to Stop the War, 418 U.S., at 221-222, 94 S.Ct., at 2932.

IV

The petitioners who assert standing on the basis of their status as taxpayers of the city of Rochester present a different set of problems. These 'taxpayer-petitioners' claim that they are suffering economic injury consequent to Penfield's allegedly discriminatory and exclusionary zoning practices. Their argument, in brief, is that Penfield's persistent refusal to allow or to facilitate construction of low- and moderate-cost housing forces the city of Rochester to provide more such housing than it otherwise would do; that to provide such housing, Rochester must allow certain tax abatements; and that as the amount of tax-abated property increases, Rochester taxpayers are forced to assume an increased tax burden in order to finance essential public services.

. . . [Apart] from the conjectural nature of the asserted injury, the line of causation between Penfield's actions and such injury is not apparent from the complaint. Whatever may occur in Penfield, the injury complained of — increases in taxation — results only from decisions made by the appropriate Rochester authorities, who are not parties to this case.

But even if we assume that the taxpayer-petitioners could establish that Penfield's zoning practices harm them, their complaint nonetheless was properly dismissed. Petitioners do not, even if they could, assert any personal right under the Constitution or any statute to be free of action by a neighboring municipality that may have some incidental adverse effect on Rochester. On the contrary, the only basis of the taxpayer-petitioners' claim is that Penfield's zoning ordinance and practices violate the constitutional and statutory rights of third parties, namely, persons of low and moderate income who are said to be excluded from Penfield. In short the claim of these petitioners falls squarely within the prudential standing rule that normally bars litigants from asserting the rights or legal interests of others in order to obtain relief from injury to themselves. As we have observed above, this rule of judicial self-governance is subject to exceptions, the most prominent of which is that Congress may remove it by statute. Here, however, no statute expressly or by clear implication grants a right of action, and thus standing to seek relief, to persons in petitioners' position. In several cases, this Court has allowed standing to litigate the rights of third parties when enforcement of the challenged restriction against the litigant would result indirectly in the violation of third parties' rights. See, e.g., Doe v. Bolton, 410 U.S.

179, 188, 93 S.Ct. 739, 745, 35 L.Ed.2d 205 (1973); Griswold v. Connecticut, 381 U.S. 479, 481, 85 S.Ct. 1678, 1680, 14 L.Ed.2d 510 (1965); Barrows v. Jackson, 346 U.S. 249, 73 S.Ct. 1031, 97 L.Ed. 1586 (1953). But the taxpayer-petitioners are not themselves subject to Penfield's zoning practices. Nor do they allege that the challenged zoning ordinance and practices preclude or otherwise adversely affect a relationship existing between them and the persons whose rights assertedly are violated. E.g., Sullivan v. Little Hunting Park, Inc., 396 U.S., at 237, 90 S.Ct. 400, 404, 24 L.Ed.2d 386; NAACP v. Alabama, 357 U.S. 449, 458-460, 78 S.Ct. 1163, 1169-1171, 2 L.Ed.2d 1488 (1958); Pierce v. Society of Sisters, 368 U.S., at 534-536, 45 S.Ct. 571, 573-574, 69 L.Ed. 1070. No relationship, other than an incidental congruity of interest, is alleged to exist between the Rochester taxpayers and persons who have been precluded from living in Penfield. Nor do the taxpayer-petitioners show that their prosecution of the suit is necessary to insure protection of the rights asserted, as there is no indication that persons who in fact have been excluded from Penfield are disabled from asserting their own right in a proper case. In sum, we discern no justification for recognizing in the Rochester taxpayers a right of action on the asserted claim.

V

We turn next to the standing problems presented by the petitioner associations — Metro-Act of Rochester, Inc., one of the original plaintiffs; Housing Council in the Monroe County Area, Inc., which the original plaintiffs sought to join as a party-plaintiff; and Rochester Home Builders Association, Inc., which moved in the District Court for leave to intervene as plaintiff. There is no question that an association may have standing in its own right to seek judicial relief from injury to itself and to vindicate whatever rights and immunities the association itself may enjoy. Moreover, in attempting to secure relief from injury to itself the association may assert the rights of its members, at least so long as the challenged infractions adversely affect its members' associational ties. E.g., NAACP v. Alabama, supra, 357 U.S., at 458-460, 78 S.Ct. 1163, 1169-1171, 2 L.Ed.2d 1488; Anti-Fascist Committee v. McGrath, 341 U.S. 123, 183-187, 71 S.Ct. 624, 654-657, 95 L.Ed. 817 (1951) (Jackson J., concurring). With the limited exception of Metro-Act, however, none of the associational petitioners here has asserted injury to itself.

Even in the absence of injury to itself, an association may have standing solely as the representative of its members. E.g., National Motor Freight Assn. v. United States, 372 U.S. 246, 83 S.Ct. 688, 9 L.Ed.2d 709 (1963). The possibility of such representational standing, however, does not eliminate or attenuate the constitutional requirement of a case or controversy. See Sierra Club v. Morton, 405 U.S. 727, 92 S.Ct. 1361, 31 L.Ed.2d 636 (1972). The association must allege that its members, or any one of them, are suffering immediate or threatened injury as a result of the challenged action of the sort that would make out a justiciable case had the members themselves brought suit. Id., at 734-741, 92 S.Ct., at 1365-1369. So long as this can be established, and so long as the nature of the claim and of the relief sought does not make the individual participation of each injured party indispensable to proper resolution of the cause, the association may be an appropriate representative of its members, entitled to invoke the court's jurisdiction.

A

Petitioner Metro-Act's claims to standing on its own behalf as a Rochester taxpayer, and on behalf of its members who are Rochester taxpayers or persons of low or moderate income, are precluded by our holdings in Parts III and IV, supra, as to the individual petitioners, and require no further discussion. Metro-Act also alleges, however, that 9% of its membership is composed of present residents of Penfield. It claims that, as a result of the persistent pattern of exclusionary zoning practiced by respondents and the consequent exclusion of persons of low and moderate income, those of its members who are Penfield residents are deprived of the benefits of living in a racially and ethnically integrated community. Referring to our decision in Trafficante v. Metropolitan Life Ins. Co., 409 U.S. 205, 93 S.Ct. 364, 34 L.Ed.2d 415 (1972), Metro-Act argues that such deprivation is a sufficiently palpable injury to satisfy the Art. III case-or-controversy requirement, and that it has standing as the representative of its members to seek redress.

. . . [Metro-Act] does not assert on behalf of its members any right of action under the 1968 Civil Rights Act. [Even] if we assume, arguendo, that apart from any statutorily created right the asserted harm to Metro-Act's Penfield members is sufficiently direct and personal to satisfy the case-or-controversy requirement of Art. III, prudential considerations strongly counsel against according them or Metro-Act standing to prosecute this action. We do not understand Metro-Act to argue that Penfield residents themselves have been denied any constitutional rights, affording them a cause of action under 42 U.S.C. § 1983. Instead, their complaint is that they have been harmed indirectly by the exclusion of others. This is an attempt to raise putative rights of third parties, and none of the exceptions that allow such claims is present here. In these circumstances, we conclude that it is inappropriate to allow Metro-Act to invoke the judicial process.

B

Petitioner Home Builders, in its intervenor-complaint, asserted standing to represent its member firms engaged in the development and construction of residential housing in the Rochester area, including Penfield. Home Builders alleged that the Penfield zoning restrictions, together with refusals by the town officials to grant variances and permits for the construction of low- and moderate-cost housing, had deprived some of its members of "substantial business opportunities and profits." App. 156.

. . . [Home Builders'] prayer for prospective relief fails for a different reason. It can have standing as the representative of its members only if it has alleged facts sufficient to make out a case or controversy had the members themselves brought suit. No such allegations were made. The complaint refers to no specific project of any of its members that is currently precluded either by the ordinance or by respondents' action in enforcing it.

. . . [A] like problem is presented with respect to petitioner Housing Council. The affidavit accompanying the motion to join it as plaintiff states that the Council includes in its membership "at lease seventeen" groups that have been, are, or will be involved in the development of low- and moderate-cost housing. But with one exception, the complaint does not suggest that any of these groups has focused its efforts on Penfield or has any specific plan to do so. Again with the same exception, neither the complaint nor any materials of record indicate that any member of Housing Council has taken any step toward building housing in Penfield, or has had dealings of any nature with respondents. The exception is the Penfield Better Homes Corp. As we have observed above, it applied to respondents in late 1969 for a zoning variance to allow construction of a housing project designed for persons of moderate income. The affidavit in support of the motion to join Housing Council refers specifically to this effort, the supporting materials detail at some length the circumstances surrounding the rejection of Better Homes' application. It is therefore possible that in 1969, or within a reasonable time thereafter, Better Homes itself and possibly Housing Council as its representative would have had standing to seek review of respondents' action. The complaint, however, does not allege that the Penfield Better Homes project remained viable in 1972 when this complaint was filed, or that respondents' actions continued to block a then-current construction project. In short, neither the complaint nor the record supplies any basis from which to infer that the controversy between respondents and Better Homes, however vigorous it may once have been, remained a live, concrete dispute when this complaint was filed.

VI

The rules of standing, whether as aspects of the Art. III case-or-controversy requirement or as reflections of prudential considerations defining and limiting the role of the courts, are threshold determinants of the propriety of judicial intervention. It is the responsibility of the complainant clearly to allege facts demonstrating that he is a proper party to invoke judicial resolution of the dispute and the exercise of the court's remedial powers. We agree with the District Court and the Court of Appeals that none of the petitioners here has met this threshold requirement. Accordingly, the judgment of the Court of Appeals is

Affirmed.

Mr. Justice BRENNAN, with whom Mr. Justice WHITE and Mr. Justice MARSHALL join, dissenting.

In this case, a wide range of plaintiffs, alleging various kinds of injuries, claimed to have been affected by the Penfield zoning ordinance, on its face and as applied, and by other practices of the defendant officials of Penfield. Alleging that as a result of these laws and practices low- and moderate-income and minority people have been excluded from Penfield, and that this exclusion is unconstitutional, plaintiffs sought injunctive, declaratory, and monetary relief. The Court today, in an opinion that purports to be a "standing" opinion but that actually, I believe, has overtones of outmoded notions of pleading and of justiciability, refuses to find that any of the variously situated plaintiffs can clear numerous hurdles, some constructed here for the first time, necessary to establish "standing." While the Court gives lip service to the principle, oft repeated in recent years, that "standing in no way depends on the merits of the plaintiff's contention that particular conduct is illegal," ante, at 2206, in fact the opinion, which tosses out of court almost every conceivable kind of plaintiff who could be injured by the activity claimed to be unconstitutional, can be explained only by an indefensible hostility to the claim on the merits. I can appreciate the Court's reluctance to adjudicate the complex and difficult legal questions involved in determining the constitutionality of practices which assertedly limit residence in a particular municipality to those who are white and relatively well off, and I also understand that the merits of this case could involve grave sociological and political ramifications. But courts cannot refuse to hear a case on the merits merely because they would prefer not to, and it is quite clear, when the record is viewed with dispassion, that at least three of the groups of plaintiffs have made allegations, and supported them with affidavits and documentary evidence, sufficient to survive a motion to dismiss for lack of standing.

II. LOW-INCOME AND MINORITY PLAINTIFFS

. . . [Thus], the Court's real holding is not that these petitioners have not alleged an injury resulting from respondents' action, but that they are not to be allowed to prove one, because "realization of petitioners' desire to live in Penfield always has depended on the efforts and willingness of third parties to build low- and moderate-cost housing," ante, at 2208, and "the record is devoid of any indication that . . . (any) projects, would have satisfied petitioners' needs at prices they could afford." Ante, at 2208-2209.

Certainly, this is not the sort of demonstration that can or should be required of petitioners at this preliminary stage.

. . . [Here], the very fact that, as the Court stresses, these petitioner's claim rests in part upon proving the intentions and capabilities of third parties to build in Penfield suitable housing which they can afford, coupled with the exclusionary character of the claim on the merits, makes it particularly inappropriate to assume that these petitioners' lack of specificity reflects a fatal weakness in their theory of causation. Obviously they cannot be expected, prior to discover and trial, to know the future plans of building companies, the precise details of the housing market in Penfield, or everything which has transpired in 15 years of application of the Penfield zoning ordinance, including every housing plan suggested and refused. To require them to allege such facts is to require them to prove their case on paper in order to get into [court].

III. ASSOCIATIONS INCLUDING BUILDING CONCERNS

Again, the Court ignores the thrust of the complaints and asks petitioners to allege the impossible. According to the allegations, the building concerns' experience in the past with Penfield officials has shown any plans for low- and moderate-income housing to be futile for, again according to the allegations, the respondents are engaged in a purposeful, conscious scheme to exclude such housing. Particularly with regard to a low- or moderate-income project, the cost of litigating, with respect to any particular project, the legality of a refusal to approve it may well be prohibitive. And the merits of the exclusion of this or that project is not at the heart of the complaint; the claim is that respondents will not approve any project which will provide residences for low- and moderate-income people.

When this sort of pattern-and-practice claim is at the heart of the controversy, allegations of past injury, which members of both of these organizations have clearly made, and of a future intent, if the barriers are cleared, again to develop suitable housing for Penfield, should be more than sufficient. The past experiences, if proved at trial, will give credibility and substance to the claim of interest in future building activity in Penfield. These parties, if their allegations are proved, certainly have the requisite personal stake in the outcome of this controversy, and the Court's conclusion otherwise is only a conclusion that this controversy may not be litigated in a federal court.

I would reverse the judgment of the Court of Appeals.

***Warth* Comments.** Did the merits affect the outcome in *Warth*? Recall Justice Brennan's comment in this regard: "While the Court gives lip service to the principle, . . . that 'standing in no way depends on the merits of the plaintiff's contention that particular conduct is illegal,'. . . in fact the opinion, which tosses out of court almost every conceivable kind of plaintiff who could be injured by the activity claimed to be unconstitutional, can be explained only by an indefensible hostility to the claim on the merits." What issues in *Warth* do you think the Court might have wanted to avoid?

In-House Rules. Is there any doubt after *Warth* that the Court maintains its own in-house rules of self-governance that are additional barriers to review beyond what the Court describes as constitutional "Article III minimums"? Given the materials thus far, is this any surprise? What are the in-house rules? Which of the standing cases that we have studied thus far were denied review because of the "prudential" as opposed to constitutional rules?

Third-Party Standing: Exceptions. The Court has traditionally afforded exceptions to what can now be described as the "prudential" rule against third-party standing. A brief review of these exceptions is in order.

1. Associations/Class-Actions. The relationship between the third party and the claimant may serve as a predicate for such an exception. If an organization or "class" can maintain standing to represent its members, we arguably have an exception to the third-party barrier to review. In *Sierra Club v. Morton*, 405 U.S. 727 (1972), though the members seemed to have the required "nexus" to the purposes of the organization, standing was denied, and the case appeared to make "class action or associational standing" difficult to achieve. The case involved an effort by an organization with "a special interest in the conservation and sound maintenance of the national parks" to challenge construction of a recreation area in a national forest. In the plaintiffs' view, the construction would have violated federal law. The Court held that although the fact that an aesthetic, conservational, or recreational harm could be sufficient, the plaintiffs did not meet the "the requirement that the party seeking review must have himself suffered an injury." In this case, the "Sierra Club failed to allege that it or its members" used the site in question and suffered any personal harm.

The effect and meaning of *Sierra Club* was limited in United States v. SCRAP, 412 U.S. 669 (1973), in which the Court held that environmental groups could challenge the Interstate Commerce Commission's failure to suspend a surcharge on railroad freight rates as unlawful under the Interstate Commerce Commission Act. The plaintiffs claimed that their members "used the forests, streams, mountains, and other resources in the Washington metropolitan area for camping, hiking, fishing, and sightseeing," which because of the failure to suspend the surcharge "would cause increased use of nonrecyclable commodities as compared to recyclable goods," which would cause a littered and spoiled environment in these recreational areas. The Court's conclusions in *SCRAP* centered on the fact that the plaintiffs had shown how each individual member was personally harmed in relation to the purposes of the organization. *Sierra Club* was distinguished because "mere intellectual outrage" was insufficient to maintain standing. Therefore, class action and/or associational standing is permissible if a distinct and palpable injury that would affect each member is properly alleged.

2. The Litigants Cannot Protect Their Own Rights. The Court has held that where it is "impossible" for the actual parties to protect their own rights, it may be permissible to allow third parties to litigate on their behalf, as long as the third party can assert an injury in fact. See Gladstone, Realtors v. Village of Bellwood, 441 U.S. 91, 99 (1979) The Court in *Warth* seemed to validate this exception:

> Essentially, the standing question in such cases is whether the constitutional or statutory provision on which the claim rests properly can be understood as granting persons in the plaintiff's position a right to judicial relief. In some circumstances, countervailing considerations may outweigh the concerns underlying the usual reluctance to exert judicial power when the plaintiff's claim to relief rests on the legal rights of third parties. In such instances, the Court has found, in effect, that the constitutional or statutory provision in question implies a right of action in the plaintiff.

3. Lowering of the In-House Rules. The Court in *Warth* stipulated that standing may rest where a "constitutional or statutory provision in question implies a right of action in the plaintiff." In particular it held that

Congress may grant an express right of action to persons who otherwise would be barred by prudential standing rules. Of course, Art. III's requirement remains: the plaintiff still must allege a distinct and palpable injury to himself, even if it is an injury shared by a large class of other possible litigants. But so long as this requirement is satisfied, persons to whom Congress has granted a right of action, either expressly or by clear implication, may have standing to seek relief on the basis of the legal rights and interests of others, and, indeed, may invoke the general public interest in support of their claim.

When Congress so acts, is there a logical consistency in lowering the prudential rules? If the rules have been created by the Court as a means of invoking judicial restraint so as to "bow to the democratic process," is it not logical that they be lowered when the "democracy," speaking through Congress, creates "a cause in action" and asks that the Court hear the case? Must Article III constitutional minimums still be met? Do you think the Court will live up to this billing by doing away with "discretion" when the democratic branch wants the case heard? If Congress wants the case heard, though logic may dictate that the very purpose for prudential rules no longer exists, can we assume the case will be heard, whatever the merits? Some have questioned this likelihood, particularly given the history of the Court. Yet, with the in-house rules lowered, could the Court still maintain the discretion to decline? This, of course, takes us to the remaining requirements that are mandated by the Constitution, even if the in-house rules are lowered, Article III minimums! In *Valley Forge*, which follows and was reviewed earlier at the conclusion of taxpayer standing, the Court restated the *Warth* requirements, but in particular provided an extensive review of the meaning of Article III minimums, or constitutional requisites.

VALLEY FORGE CHRISTIAN COLLEGE v. AMERICANS UNITED FOR SEPARATION OF CHURCH AND STATE
454 U.S. 464 (1982)

[The facts for this case are set out at page 277, supra..]

Justice REHNQUIST delivered the opinion of the Court.
. . . [The] term "standing" subsumes a blend of constitutional requirements and prudential considerations, see Warth v. Seldin, 422 U.S. 490, 498, 95 S.Ct. 2197, 2204, 45 L.Ed.2d 343 (1975), and it has not always been clear in the opinions of this Court whether particular features of the "standing" requirement have been required by Art. III *ex proprio vigore*, or whether they are requirements that the Court itself has erected and which were not compelled by the language of the Constitution. See Flast v. Cohen, supra, at 97, 88 S.Ct., at 1951.
A recent line of decisions, however, has resolved that ambiguity, at least to the following extent: at an irreducible minimum, Art. III requires the party who invokes the court's authority to "show that he personally has suffered some actual or threatened injury as a result of the putatively illegal conduct of the defendant," Gladstone, Realtors v. Village of Bellwood, 441 U.S. 91, 99, 99 S.Ct. 1601, 1608, 60 L.Ed.2d 66 (1979), and that the injury "fairly can be traced to the challenged action" and "is likely to be redressed by a favorable decision," Simon v. Eastern Kentucky Welfare Rights Org., 426 U.S. 26, 38, 41, 96 S.Ct. 1917, 1924, 1925, 48 L.Ed.2d 450 (1976). In this manner does Art. III limit the

federal judicial power "to those disputes which confine federal courts to a role consistent with a system of separated powers and which are traditionally thought to be capable of resolution through the judicial process." Flast v. Cohen, 392 U.S., at 97, 88 S.Ct., at 1951.

The requirement of "actual injury redressable by the court," Simon, supra, 426 U.S., at 39, 96 S.Ct., at 1924, serves several of the "implicit policies embodied in Article III," *Flast*, supra, 392 U.S., at 96, 88 S.Ct., at 1950. It tends to assure that the legal questions presented to the court will be resolved, not in the rarified atmosphere of a debating society, but in a concrete factual context conducive to a realistic appreciation of the consequences of judicial action. The "standing" requirement serves other purposes. Because it assures an actual factual setting in which the litigant asserts a claim of injury in fact, a court may decide the case with some confidence that its decision will not pave the way for lawsuits which have some, but not all, of the facts of the case actually decided by the court.

The Art. III aspect of standing also reflects a due regard for the autonomy of those persons likely to be most directly affected by a judicial order. The federal courts have abjured appeals to their authority which would convert the judicial process into "no more than a vehicle for the vindication of the value interests of concerned bystanders." United States v. SCRAP, 412 U.S. 669, 687, 93 S.Ct. 2405, 2416, 37 L.Ed.2d 254 (1973). Were the federal courts merely publicly funded forums for the ventilation of public grievances or the refinement of jurisprudential understanding, the concept of "standing" would be quite unnecessary. But the "cases and controversies" language of Art. III forecloses the conversion of courts of the United States into judicial versions of college debating forums.

The exercise of judicial power, which can so profoundly affect the lives, liberty, and property of those to whom it extends, is therefore restricted to litigants who can show "injury in fact" resulting from the action which they seek to have the court adjudicate.

The exercise of the judicial power also affects relationships between the coequal arms of the National Government. The effect is, of course, most vivid when a federal court declares unconstitutional an act of the Legislative or Executive Branch. While the exercise of that "ultimate and supreme function," Chicago & Grand Trunk R. Co. v. Wellman, supra, at 345, 12 S.Ct., at 402, is a formidable means of vindicating individual rights, when employed unwisely or unnecessarily it is also the ultimate threat to the continued effectiveness of the federal courts in performing that role.

. . . [Proper] regard for the complex nature of our constitutional structure requires neither that the Judicial Branch shrink from a confrontation with the other two coequal branches of the Federal Government, nor that it hospitably accept for adjudication claims of constitutional violation by other branches of government where the claimant has not suffered cognizable injury.

. . . [Beyond] the constitutional requirements, the federal judiciary has also adhered to a set of prudential principles that bear on the question of standing. Thus, this Court has held that "the plaintiff generally must assert his own legal rights and interests, and cannot rest his claim to relief on the legal rights or interests of third parties." Warth v. Seldin, 422 U.S., at 499, 95 S.Ct., at 2205. [FN10] In addition, even when the plaintiff has alleged redressable injury sufficient to meet the requirements of Art. III, the Court has refrained from adjudicating "abstract questions of wide public significance" which amount to "generalized grievances," pervasively shared and most appropriately addressed in the representative branches. Id., at 499-500, 95 S.Ct., at 2205-2206. Finally, the Court has required that the plaintiff's complaint fall within "the zone of interests to be protected or regulated by the statute or constitutional guarantee in question." Association of Data

Processing Service Orgs. v. Camp, 397 U.S. 150, 153, 90 S.Ct. 827, 830, 25 L.Ed.2d 184 (1970).

Merely to articulate these principles is to demonstrate their close relationship to the policies reflected in the Art. III requirement of actual or threatened injury amenable to judicial remedy. But neither the counsels of prudence nor the policies implicit in the "case or controversy" requirement should be mistaken for the rigorous Art. III requirements themselves. Satisfaction of the former cannot substitute for a demonstration of "'distinct and palpable injury' . . . that is likely to be redressed if the requested relief is granted." Gladstone, Realtors v. Village of Bellwood, 441 U.S., at 100, 99 S.Ct., at 1608 (quoting Warth v. Seldin, supra, 422 U.S., at 501, 95 S.Ct., at 2206). That requirement states a limitation on judicial power, not merely a factor to be balanced in the weighing of so-called "prudential" considerations.

We need not mince words when we say that the concept of "Art. III standing" has not been defined with complete consistency in all of the various cases decided by this Court which have discussed it, nor when we say that this very fact is probably proof that the concept cannot be reduced to a one-sentence or one-paragraph definition. But of one thing we may be sure: Those who do not possess Art. III standing may not litigate as suitors in the courts of the United States. Article III, which is every bit as important in its circumscription of the judicial power of the United States as in its granting of that power, is not merely a troublesome hurdle to be overcome if possible so as to reach the "merits" of a lawsuit which a party desires to have adjudicated; it is a part of the basic charter promulgated by the Framers of the Constitution at Philadelphia in 1787, a charter which created a general government, provided for the interaction between that government and the governments of the several States, and was later amended so as to either enhance or limit its authority with respect to both States and individuals.

"Dear Prudence": *Elk Grove* **and the Establishment Clause — 2004 Term. ELK GROVE UNIFIED SCHOOL DISTRICT v. NEWDOW**, 542 U.S. 1 (2004). The Ninth Circuit had declared the phrase "under God" in the Pledge of Allegiance to be an unconstitutional establishment of religion in the context of daily recitation of the Pledge in public schools. The Supreme Court reversed, finding that the father, an atheist, who brought the action, lacked standing. The father and mother were engaged in a "protracted custody dispute," but the mother had legal custody and had intervened in the federal action to object to the father's representing their daughter's interests. Indeed, and of significance to the Court, she had obtained a state court order directing him not to undertake representation of the daughter or to bring suit as the daughter's "next friend." The federal district court nevertheless held that this did not deprive Newdow, "as a noncustodial parent, of Article III standing to object to unconstitutional government action affecting his child."

Justice Stevens, speaking for the majority, and quoting from *Allen v. Wright*, supra, found the circumstance governed by the "prudential limits to the powers of an unelected, unrepresentative judiciary in our kind of government."

The command to guard jealously and exercise rarely our power to make constitutional pronouncements requires strictest adherence when matters of great national significance are at stake. Even in cases concededly within our jurisdiction under Article III, we abide by "a series of rules under which [we have] avoided passing upon a large part of all the constitutional questions pressed upon [us] for decision. Always we must balance "the heavy obligation to exercise jurisdiction," against the "deeply rooted" commitment "not to pass on questions of constitutionality" unless adjudication of the constitutional issue is necessary. Without such limitations — closely related to Art. III concerns but essentially matters of judicial self-governance — the courts would be called upon to decide abstract questions of wide public significance even though other governmental institutions may be more competent to address the questions and even though judicial intervention may be unnecessary to protect individual rights.

Justice Stevens based this finding on "prudential standing, which embodies judicially self-imposed limits on the exercise of federal jurisdiction," particularly because the Court "has consistently declined to intervene is the realm of domestic relations. . . . [I]n general, it is appropriate for the federal courts to leave delicate issues of domestic relations to the state courts." Newdow had contended that despite the mother's final authority (the state courts had recognized that the mother had authority to make final decisions for the child if the two parents disagreed), he retained an "unrestricted right to inculcate in his daughter — free from governmental interference — in the atheistic beliefs he finds persuasive." To Justice Stevens, Newdow's rights had to be viewed against the rights of the child's mother as a parent and as legal custodian and, most important, the interests of the child. "What makes this case different is that Newdow's standing derives entirely from his relationship with his daughter, but he lacks the right to litigate as her next friend. In marked contrast to our case law on *jus tertii, see, e.g., Singleton v. Wulff,* the interests of this parent and this child are not parallel and, indeed, are potentially in conflict."

Though the court of appeals had determined that state law vested in Newdow "a cognizable right to influence his daughter's religious upbringing," Justice Stevens concluded that

> [n]othing that either Banning [the mother] or the School Board has done . . . impairs Newdow's right to instruct his daughter in his religious views. . . . He wishes to forestall his daughter's exposure to religious ideas that her mother, who wields a form of veto power, endorses, and to use his parental status to challenge the influences to which his daughter may be exposed in school when he and Banning disagree. The California cases simply do not stand for the proposition that Newdow has a right to dictate to others what they may and may not say to his child respecting religion. In our view, it is improper for the federal courts to entertain a claim by a plaintiff whose standing to sue is founded on family law rights that are in dispute when prosecution of the lawsuit may have an adverse effect on the person who is the source of the plaintiff's standing. When hard questions of domestic relations are sure to affect the outcome, the prudent course is for the federal court to stay its hand rather than reach out to resolve a weighty question of federal constitutional law. . . . There is a vast difference between Newdow's right to communicate with his child — which both California law and the First Amendment recognize — and his claimed right to shield his daughter from influences to which she is exposed in school despite the terms of the custody order. We conclude that, having been deprived under California law of the right to sue as next friend, Newdow lacks prudential standing to bring this suit in federal court.

Chief Justice Rehnquist, joined by Justices O'Connor and Thomas, dissented from the standing holding: The Court concludes that the California cases "do not stand for the proposition that Newdow has a right to dictate to others what they may or may not say to his child respecting religion." Surely, under California case law and the current custody order, respondent may not tell Banning what she may say to their child respecting religion, and respondent does not seek to. Just as surely, respondent cannot name his daughter as a party to a lawsuit against Banning's wishes. But his claim is different: Respondent does not seek to tell just anyone what he or she may say to his daughter, and he does not seek to vindicate solely her rights. "Respondent asserts that the School District's pledge ceremony infringes his right under California law to expose his daughter to his religious views. While she is intimately associated with the source of respondent's standing (the father-daughter relationship and respondent's rights thereunder), the daughter *is not the source* of respondent's standing; instead it is their relationship that provides respondent his standing, which is clear once respondent's interest is properly described."

Reaching the merits of the establishment claim, Chief Justice Rehnquist and Justice O'Connor both held that the phrase "under God" was neither an endorsement of religion nor itself a religious exercise so as to warrant condemnation as an establishment of religion. To the Chief Justice, the phrase is simply a recognition of the role of religion in the country's history: "Reciting the Pledge, or listening to others recite it, is a patriotic exercise, not a religious one; participants promise fidelity to our flag and our Nation, not to any particular God, faith, or church." To Justice O'Connor, the Establishment Clause allows a form of "ceremonial deism" that prefers no particular religion and endorses no particular religious belief.

Is the real reason for prudence in *Elk Grove* the majority's desire to side step the difficult Establishment Clause issue? Note, despite their usual call for restraint, no prudence from the dissenting justices!

Still Prudence "After All These Years." In *DaimlerChrysler,* in 2006, the Supreme Court reaffirmed *Flast* as a limited exception to the prohibition against taxpayer standing. Ohio plaintiffs alleged that they were harmed as state taxpayers because tax breaks offered by state and local government to attract companies to move into the area violated the Dormant Commerce Clause. (The Dormant Commerce Clause refers to the Court's "self-enforcement" of the principle that state and local governments act unconstitutionally if they place an undue burden on interstate commerce.) The U.S. Court of Appeals for the Sixth Circuit found the alleged harm sufficient to hear the case and concluded that there was a violation of the Dormant Commerce Clause. The Supreme Court dismissed the case for lack of standing. Reinforcing *Flast*, the Court held that standing based upon their asserted status as state taxpayers is not permitted.

DAIMLER CHRYSLER CORP. v. CUNO
547 U.S. 332 (2006)

Chief Justice ROBERTS delivered the opinion of the Court.
. . . [T]he city of Toledo and State of Ohio sought to encourage . . . DaimlerChrysler to expand its Jeep operation in Toledo, by offering local and state tax benefits for new investment. Taxpayers in Toledo sued, alleging that their local and state tax burdens were increased by the tax breaks for DaimlerChrysler, tax breaks that they asserted violated the Commerce Clause. The Court of Appeals agreed that a state tax credit offered under Ohio law violated the Commerce Clause, and state and local officials and DaimlerChrysler sought review in this Court. We are obligated before reaching this Commerce Clause question to determine whether the taxpayers who objected to the credit have standing to

press their complaint in federal court. We conclude that they do not, and we therefore can proceed no further.

Plaintiffs principally claim standing by virtue of their status as Ohio tax-payers, alleging that the franchise tax credit "depletes the funds of the State of Ohio to which the Plaintiffs contribute through their tax payments" and thus "diminish[es] the total funds available for lawful uses and impos[es] disproportionate burdens on" them. On several occasions, this Court has denied federal taxpayers standing under Article III to object to a particular expenditure of federal funds simply because they are taxpayers.

The animating principle behind these cases was announced in their progenitor, *Frothingham v. Mellon* (1923). In rejecting a claim that improper federal appropriations would "increase the burden of future taxation and thereby take [the plaintiffs'] property without due process of law," the Court observed that a federal taxpayer's "interest in the moneys of the Treasury is shared with millions of others; is comparatively minute and indeterminable; and the effect upon future taxation, of any payment out of the funds, so remote, fluctuating and uncertain, that no basis is afforded for an appeal to the preventive powers of a court of equity."

This logic is equally applicable to taxpayer challenges to expenditures that deplete the treasury, and to taxpayer challenges to so-called "tax expenditures," which reduce amounts available to the treasury by granting tax credits or exemptions. In either case, the alleged injury is based on the asserted effect of the allegedly illegal activity on public revenues, to which the taxpayer contributes. Standing has been rejected in such cases because the alleged injury is not "concrete and particularized," but instead a grievance the taxpayer suffers in some indefinite way in common with people generally." In addition, the injury is not "actual or imminent," but instead "conjectural or hypothetical." As an initial matter, it is unclear that tax breaks of the sort at issue here do in fact deplete the treasury: The very point of the tax benefits is to spur economic activity, which in turn increases government revenues. In this very action, the Michigan plaintiffs claimed that they were injured because they lost out on the added revenues that would have accompanied DaimlerChrysler's decision to expand facilities in Michigan.

Plaintiffs' alleged injury is also "conjectural or hypothetical" in that it depends on how legislators respond to a reduction in revenue, if that is the consequence of the credit. Establishing injury requires speculating that elected officials will increase a taxpayer-plaintiff's tax bill to make up a deficit; establishing redressability requires speculating that abolishing the challenged credit will redound to the benefit of the taxpayer because legislators will pass along the supposed increased revenue in the form of tax reductions. Neither sort of speculation suffices to support standing.

A taxpayer-plaintiff has no right to insist that the government dispose of any increased revenue it might experience as a result of his suit by decreasing his tax liability or bolstering programs that benefit him. To the contrary, the decision of how to allocate any such savings is the very epitome of a policy judgment committed to the "broad and legitimate discretion" of lawmakers, which "the courts cannot presume either to control or to predict." Under such circumstances, we have no assurance that the asserted injury is "imminent" — that it is "certainly impending."

The foregoing rationale for rejecting federal taxpayer standing applies with undiminished force to state taxpayers. We indicated as much in *Doremus v. Board of Ed. of Hawthorne* (1952). In that case, we noted our earlier holdings that "the interests of a taxpayer in the moneys of the federal treasury are too indeterminable, remote, uncertain and indirect" to support standing to challenge "their manner of expenditure." We then "reiterate[d]" what we had said in rejecting a federal taxpayer challenge to a federal statute "as equally true when a state Act is assailed: 'The [taxpayer] must be able to show . . . that he has sustained . . . some direct injury . . . and not merely that he suffers in some indefinite way in common with people generally.'" The allegations of injury that plaintiffs make in their complaint furnish no better basis for finding standing than those made in the cases where federal taxpayer standing was denied. Plaintiffs claim that DaimlerChrysler's tax credit depletes the Ohio fisc and "impos[es] disproportionate burdens on [them]." This is no different from similar claims by federal taxpayers we have already rejected under Article III as insufficient to establish standing. For the foregoing reasons, we hold that state taxpayers have no standing under Article III to challenge state tax or spending decisions simply by virtue of their status as taxpayers.

Plaintiffs argue that an exception to the general prohibition on taxpayer standing should exist for Commerce Clause challenges to state tax or spending decisions, analogizing their Commerce Clause claim to the Establishment Clause challenge we permitted in *Flast v. Cohen* (1968). *Flast* held that because "the Establishment Clause . . . specifically limit[s] the taxing and spending power conferred by Art. I, § 8, "a taxpayer will have standing consistent with Article III to invoke federal judicial power when he alleges that congressional action under the taxing and spending clause is in derogation of" the Establishment Clause. But as plaintiffs candidly concede, "only the Establishment Clause" has supported federal taxpayer suits since *Flast*. Quite apart from whether the franchise tax credit is analogous to an exercise of congressional power under Art. I, § 8, plaintiffs' reliance on *Flast* is misguided: Whatever rights plaintiffs have under the Commerce Clause, they are fundamentally unlike the right not to "contribute three pence . . . for the support of any one [religious] establishment." (2 Writings of James Madison 186 (G. Hunt ed. 1901)). Indeed, plaintiffs compare the Establishment Clause to the Commerce Clause at such a high level of generality that almost any constitutional constraint on government power would "specifically limit" a State's taxing and spending power for *Flast* purposes. [A] finding that the Commerce Clause satisfies the *Flast* test would leave no principled way of distinguishing those other constitutional provisions that we have recognized constrain governments' taxing and spending decisions. Yet such a broad application of *Flast*'s exception to the general prohibition on taxpayer standing would be quite at odds with its narrow application in our precedent and *Flast*'s own promise that it would not transform federal courts into forums for taxpayers' "generalized grievances." Plaintiffs thus do not have state taxpayer standing on the ground that their Commerce Clause challenge is just like the Establishment Clause challenge in *Flast*.

Plaintiffs also claim that their status as municipal taxpayers gives them standing to challenge the state franchise tax credit at issue here. The *Frothingham* Court noted with approval the standing of municipal residents to enjoin the "illegal use of the moneys of a municipal corporation," relying on "the peculiar relation of the corporate taxpayer to the corporation" to distinguish such a case from the general bar on taxpayer suits. Plaintiffs here challenged the municipal property tax exemption as municipal taxpayers. That challenge was rejected by the Court of Appeals on the merits, and no issue regarding plaintiffs' standing to bring it has been raised. In plaintiffs' challenge to the state franchise tax credit, however, they identify no municipal action contributing to any claimed injury.

. . . [P]laintiffs' challenge is still to the state law and state decision, not those of their municipality. We have already explained why a state taxpayer lacks standing to challenge a state fiscal decision on the grounds that it might affect his tax liability. All plaintiffs have done in recasting their claims as ones brought by municipal taxpayers whose municipalities receive funding from the State — the level of which might be affected by the same state fiscal decision — is introduce yet another level of conjecture to their already hypothetical claim of injury.

Because plaintiffs have no standing to challenge that credit, the lower courts erred by considering their claims against it on the merits.

————

Et Tu *Flast*? *Hein v. Freedom from Religion Foundation, Inc.* What is left of *Flast*? Is it even an exception? In *Hein*, an organization that was opposed to government endorsement of religion and three of its members brought an Establishment Clause challenge against a federal agency's use of federal money to fund conferences to promote the President George W. Bush's "faith-based initiatives."

HEIN v. FREEDOM FROM RELIGION FOUNDATION, INC.
551 U.S. 587 (2007)

Justice ALITO announced the judgment of the Court and delivered an opinion in which THE CHIEF JUSTICE and Justice KENNEDY join.

This is a lawsuit in which it was claimed that conferences held as part of the President's Faith-Based and Community Initiatives program violated the Establishment Clause of the First Amendment because, among other things, President Bush and former Secretary of Education Paige gave speeches that used "religious imagery" and praised the efficacy of faith-based programs in delivering social services. The plaintiffs contend that they meet the standing requirements of Article III of the Constitution because they pay federal taxes.

It has long been established, however, that the payment of taxes is generally not enough to establish standing to challenge an action taken by the Federal Government. [I]n *Flast v. Cohen* we recognized a narrow exception to the general rule against federal taxpayer standing. Under *Flast,* a plaintiff asserting an Establishment Clause claim has standing to challenge a law authorizing the use of federal funds in a way that allegedly violates the Establishment Clause. In the present case, Congress did not specifically authorize the use of federal funds to pay for the conferences or speeches that the plaintiffs challenged. Instead, the conferences and speeches were paid for out of general Executive Branch appropriations. The Court of Appeals, however, held that the plaintiffs have standing as taxpayers because the conferences were paid for with money appropriated by Congress.

The question that is presented here is whether this broad reading of *Flast* is correct. We hold that it is not. We therefore reverse the decision of the Court of Appeals.

I

A

In 2001, the President issued an executive order creating the White House Office of Faith-Based and Community Initiatives within the Executive Office of the President. Exec. Order No. 13199, Comp. The purpose of this new office was to ensure that "private and charitable community groups, including religious ones . . . have the fullest opportunity permitted by law to compete on a level playing field, so long as they achieve valid public purposes" and adhere to "the bedrock principles of pluralism, nondiscrimination, evenhandedness, and neutrality."

By separate executive orders, the President also created Executive Department Centers for Faith-Based and Community Initiatives within several federal agencies and departments. These centers were given the job of ensuring that faith-based community groups would be eligible to compete for federal financial support without impairing their independence or autonomy, as long as they did "not use direct Federal financial assistance to support any inherently religious activities, such as worship, religious instruction, or proselytization." To this end, the President directed that "[n]o organization should be discriminated against on the basis of religion or religious belief in the administration or distribution of Federal financial assistance under social service programs," and that "[a]ll organizations that receive Federal financial assistance under social services programs should be prohibited from discriminating against beneficiaries or potential beneficiaries of the social services programs on the basis of religion or religious belief." Petitioners, who have been sued in their official capacities, are the directors of the White House Office and various Executive Department Centers.

No congressional legislation specifically authorized the creation of the White House Office or the Executive Department Centers. Rather, they were "created entirely within the executive branch . . . by Presidential executive order." *Freedom From Religion Foundation, Inc. v. Chao,* 433 F.3d 989, 997 (C.A.7 2006). Nor has Congress enacted any law specifically appropriating money for these entities' activities. Instead, their activities are funded through general Executive Branch appropriations.

B

The respondents are Freedom From Religion Foundation, Inc., a nonstock corporation "opposed to government endorsement of religion." Respondents brought suit in the United States District Court for the Western District of Wisconsin, alleging that petitioners violated the Establishment Clause by organizing conferences at which faith-based organizations allegedly "are singled out as being particularly worthy of federal funding . . . , and the belief in God is extolled as distinguishing the claimed effectiveness of faith-based social services." [R]espondents alleged that the conferences were designed to promote, and had the effect of promoting, religious community groups over secular ones.

The only asserted basis for standing was that the individual respondents are federal taxpayers who are "opposed to the use of Congressional taxpayer appropriations to advance and promote religion." In their capacity as federal taxpayers, respondents sought to challenge Executive Branch expenditures for these conferences, which, they contended, violated the Establishment Clause.

C

The District Court dismissed the claims against petitioners for lack of standing. It concluded that under *Flast,* federal taxpayer standing is limited to Establishment Clause challenges to the constitutionality of "'exercises of congressional power under the taxing and spending clause of Art. I, § 8.'" Because petitioners in this case acted "at the President's request and on the President's behalf" and were not "charged with the administration of a congressional program," the District Court concluded that the challenged activities were "not 'exercises of congressional power'" sufficient to provide a basis for taxpayer standing under *Flast.*

A divided panel of the United States Court of Appeals for the Seventh Circuit reversed. The majority read *Flast* as granting federal taxpayers standing to challenge Executive Branch programs on Establishment Clause grounds so long as the activities are "financed by a congressional appropriation." This was the case, the majority concluded, even where "there is no statutory program" enacted by Congress and the funds are "from appropriations for the general administrative expenses, over which the President and other executive branch officials have a degree of discretionary power."

The Court of Appeals denied en banc review by a vote of seven to four. Concurring in the denial of rehearing, Chief Judge Flaum expressed doubt about the panel decision, but noted that "the obvious tension which has evolved in this area of jurisprudence . . . can only be resolved by the Supreme Court." We granted certiorari to resolve this question, 549 U.S. ____ (2006), and we now reverse.

II

A

Article III of the Constitution limits the judicial power of the United States to the resolution of "Cases" and "Controversies," and "'Article III standing . . . enforces the Constitution's case-or-controversy requirement.'" *DaimlerChrysler Corp. v. Cuno,* 547 U.S. ____, (2006) (quoting *Elk Grove Unified School Dist. v. Newdow,* "No principle is more fundamental to the judiciary's proper role in our system of government than the constitutional limitation of federal-court jurisdiction to actual cases or controversies.").

"[O]ne of the controlling elements in the definition of a case or controversy under Article III" is standing. The requisite elements of Article III standing are well established: "A plaintiff must allege personal injury fairly traceable to the defendant's allegedly unlawful conduct and likely to be redressed by the requested relief." *Allen v. Wright* (1984).

The constitutionally mandated standing inquiry is especially important in a case like this one, in which taxpayers seek "to challenge laws of general application where their own injury is not distinct from that suffered in general by other taxpayers or citizens." This is because "[t]he judicial power of the United States defined by Art. III is not an unconditioned authority to determine the constitutionality of legislative or executive acts." *Valley Forge Christian College v. Americans United for Separation of Church and State, Inc.,* 454 U.S. 464 (1982). The federal courts are not empowered to seek out and strike down any governmental act that they deem to be repugnant to the Constitution. Rather, federal courts sit "solely, to decide on the rights of individuals," *Marbury v. Madison,* 1 Cranch 137 (1803), and must " 'refrai[n] from passing upon the constitutionality of an act . . . unless obliged to do so in the proper performance of our judicial function, when the question is raised by a party whose interests entitle him to raise it.' As we held over 80 years ago, in another case involving the question of taxpayer standing: "We have no power *per se* to review and annul acts of Congress on the ground that they are unconstitutional. The question may be considered only when the justification for some direct injury suffered or threatened, presenting a justiciable issue, is made to rest upon such an act. . . . The party who invokes the power must be able to show not only that the statute is invalid but that he has sustained or is immediately in danger of sustaining some direct injury as the result of its enforcement, and not merely that he suffers in some indefinite way in common with people generally." " *Frothingham v. Mellon,* decided with *Massachusetts v. Mellon,* 262 U.S. 447, 488 (1923).

B

As a general matter, the interest of a federal taxpayer in seeing that Treasury funds are spent in accordance with the Constitution does not give rise to the kind of redressable "personal injury" required for Article III standing. [W]e have consistently held that this type of interest is too generalized and attenuated to support Article III standing. Because the interests of the taxpayer are, in essence, the interests of the public-at-large, deciding a constitutional claim based solely on taxpayer standing "would be[,] not to decide a judicial controversy, but to assume a position of authority over the governmental acts of another and co-equal department, an authority which plainly we do not possess."

C

In *Flast*, the Court carved out a narrow exception to the general constitutional prohibition against taxpayer standing. The Court set out a two-part test for determining whether a federal taxpayer has standing to challenge an allegedly unconstitutional expenditure: "First, the taxpayer must establish a logical link between that status and the type of legislative enactment attacked. Thus, a taxpayer will be a proper party to allege the unconstitutionality only of exercises of congressional power under the taxing and spending clause of Art. I, § 8, of the Constitution. It will not be sufficient to allege an incidental expenditure of tax funds in the administration of an essentially regulatory statute. . . . Secondly, the taxpayer must establish a nexus between that status and the precise nature of the constitutional infringement alleged. Under this requirement, the taxpayer must show that the challenged enactment exceeds specific constitutional limitations imposed upon the exercise of the congressional taxing and spending power and not simply that the enactment is generally beyond the powers delegated to Congress by Art. I, § 8." [T]he Court held that the taxpayer-plaintiff in *Flast* had satisfied both prongs of this test.

III

A

Respondents argue that this case falls within the *Flast* exception, which they read to cover any "expenditure of government funds in violation of the Establishment Clause." But this broad reading fails to observe "the rigor with which the *Flast* exception to the *Frothingham* principle ought to be applied."

The expenditures at issue in *Flast* were made pursuant to an express congressional mandate and a specific congressional appropriation. [The] expenditures challenged in *Flast*, then, were funded by a specific congressional appropriation and were disbursed to private schools (including religiously affiliated schools) pursuant to a direct and unambiguous congressional mandate. Indeed, the *Flast* taxpayer-plaintiff's constitutional claim was premised on the contention that if the Government's actions were "'within the authority and intent of the Act, the Act is to that extent unconstitutional and void.'" And the judgment reviewed by this Court in *Flast* solely concerned the question whether "if [the challenged] expenditures are authorized by the Act the statute constitutes a 'law respecting an establishment of religion' and law 'prohibiting the free exercise thereof'" under the First Amendment. [But] as this Court later noted, *Flast* "limited taxpayer standing to challenges directed 'only [at] exercises of congressional power'" under the Taxing and Spending Clause. *Valley Forge*, 454 U.S., at 479.

B

The link between congressional action and constitutional violation that supported taxpayer standing in *Flast* is missing here. Respondents do not challenge any specific congressional action or appropriation; nor do they ask the Court to invalidate any congressional enactment or legislatively created program as unconstitutional. That is because the expenditures at issue here were not made pursuant to any Act of Congress. Rather, Congress provided general appropriations to the Executive Branch to fund its day-to-day activities. These appropriations did not expressly authorize, direct, or even mention the expenditures of which respondents complain. Those expenditures resulted from executive discretion, not congressional action.

We have never found taxpayer standing under such circumstances. In *Valley Forge*, we held that a taxpayer lacked standing to challenge "a decision by [the federal Department of Health, Education and Welfare] to transfer a parcel of federal property" to a religious college because this transfer was "not a congressional action." [W]e found that the plaintiffs lacked standing because *Flast* "limited taxpayer standing to challenges directed 'only [at] exercises of congressional power'" under the Taxing and Spending Clause.

Bowen v. Kendrick, 487 U.S. 589, 108 S.Ct. 2562, 101 L.Ed.2d 520 (1988), on which respondents rely heavily, is not to the contrary. In that case, we held that the taxpayer-plaintiffs had standing to mount an as-applied challenge to the Adolescent Family Life Act (AFLA), which authorized federal grants to private community service groups including religious organizations. The Court found "a sufficient nexus between the taxpayer's standing as a taxpayer and the congressional exercise of taxing and spending power," notwithstanding the fact that the "the funding authorized by Congress ha[d] flowed through and been administered" by an Executive Branch official.

But the key to that conclusion was the Court's recognition that AFLA was "at heart a program of disbursement of funds pursuant to Congress' taxing and spending powers," and that the plaintiffs' claims "call[ed] into question how the funds authorized by Congress [were] being disbursed *pursuant to the AFLA's statutory mandate.*" AFLA not only expressly authorized and appropriated specific funds for grant-making, it also expressly contemplated that some of those moneys might go to projects involving religious groups.

Respondents attempt to paint their lawsuit as a *Kendrick*-style as-applied challenge, but this effort is unavailing for the simple reason that they can cite no statute whose application they challenge. The best they can do is to point to unspecified, lump-sum "Congressional budget appropriations" for the general use of the Executive Branch — the allocation of which "is a[n] administrative decision traditionally regarded as committed to agency discretion." Characterizing this case as an "as-applied challenge" to these general appropriations statutes would stretch the meaning of that term past its breaking point. It cannot be that every legal challenge to a discretionary Executive Branch action implicates the constitutionality of the underlying congressional appropriation.

In short, this case falls outside the "the narrow exception" that *Flast* "created to the general rule against taxpayer standing established in *Frothingham.*" Because the expenditures that respondents challenge were not expressly authorized or mandated by any specific congressional enactment, respondents' lawsuit is not directed at an exercise of congressional power, see *Valley Forge,* 454 U.S., at 479, and thus lacks the requisite "logical nexus" between taxpayer status "and the type of legislative enactment attacked."

IV

A

1

Respondents argue that it is "arbitrary" to distinguish between money spent pursuant to congressional mandate and expenditures made in the course of executive discretion, because "the injury to taxpayers in both situations is the very injury targeted by the Establishment Clause and *Flast* — the expenditure for the support of religion of funds exacted from taxpayers."

But *Flast* focused on congressional action, and we must decline this invitation to extend its holding to encompass discretionary Executive Branch expenditures. [W]e have repeatedly emphasized that the *Flast* exception has a "narrow application in our precedent," that only "slightly lowered" the bar on taxpayer standing, *Richardson,* 418 U.S., at 173, and that must be applied with "rigor," *Valley Forge.*

It is significant that, in the four decades since its creation, the *Flast* exception has largely been confined to its facts. We have declined to lower the taxpayer standing bar in suits alleging violations of any constitutional provision apart from the Establishment Clause. We have similarly refused to extend *Flast* to permit taxpayer standing for Establishment Clause challenges that do not implicate Congress' taxing and spending power. In effect, . . . we have adopted the position set forth by Justice Powell in his concurrence in *Richardson* and have "limit[ed] the expansion of federal taxpayer and citizen standing in the absence of specific statutory authorization to an outer boundary drawn by the *results* in *Flast*. . . ." 418 U.S., at 196.

2

While respondents argue that Executive Branch expenditures in support of religion are no different from legislative extractions, *Flast* itself rejected this equivalence: "It will not be sufficient to allege an incidental expenditure of tax funds in the administration of an essentially regulatory statute." Because almost all Executive Branch activity is ultimately funded by some congressional appropriation, extending the *Flast* exception to purely executive expenditures would effectively subject every federal action — be it a conference, proclamation or speech — to Establishment Clause challenge by any taxpayer in federal court.

It would also raise serious separation-of-powers concerns. As we have recognized, *Flast* itself gave too little weight to these concerns. By framing the standing question solely in terms of whether the dispute would be presented in an adversary context and in a form traditionally viewed as capable of judicial resolution, *Flast* "failed to recognize that this doctrine has a separation-of-powers component, which keeps courts within certain traditional bounds vis-a-vis the other branches, concrete adverseness or not."

The constitutional requirements for federal-court jurisdiction — including the standing requirements and Article III — "are an essential ingredient of separation and equilibration of powers." "Relaxation of standing requirements is directly related to the expansion of judicial power," and lowering the taxpayer standing bar to permit challenges of purely executive actions "would significantly alter the allocation of power at the national level, with a shift away from a democratic form of government." The rule respondents propose would enlist the federal courts to superintend, at the behest of any federal taxpayer, the speeches, statements, and myriad daily activities of the President, his staff, and other Executive Branch officials. This would "be quite at odds with . . . *Flast*'s own promise that it would not transform federal courts into forums for taxpayers' 'generalized grievances'" about the conduct of government, *Cuno,* and would "open the Judiciary to an arguable charge of providing 'government by injunction.'" It would deputize federal courts as "'virtually continuing monitors of the wisdom and soundness of Executive action,'" and that, most emphatically, "is not the role of the judiciary."

3

Respondents take a somewhat different approach, contending that their proposed expansion of *Flast* would be manageable because they would require that a challenged expenditure be "fairly traceable to the conduct alleged to violate the Establishment Clause." Applying this test, they argue, would "scree[n] out . . . challenge[s to] the content of one particular speech, for example the State of the Union address, as an Establishment Clause violation."

We find little comfort in this vague and ill-defined test. As an initial matter, respondents fail to explain why the (often substantial) costs that attend, for example, a Presidential address are any less "traceable" than the expenses related to the Executive Branch statements and conferences at issue here. [M]oreover, the "traceability" inquiry, depending on how it is framed, would appear to prove either too little or too much. If the question is whether an allegedly unconstitutional executive action can somehow be traced to taxpayer funds *in general,* the answer will always be yes: Almost all Executive Branch activities are ultimately funded by *some* congressional appropriation, whether general or specific, which is in turn financed by tax receipts. If, on the other hand, the question is whether the challenged action can be traced to the contributions of a *particular* taxpayer-plaintiff, the answer will almost always be no: As we recognized in *Frothingham,* the interest of any individual taxpayer in a particular federal expenditure "is comparatively minute and indeterminable . . . and constantly changing."

B

Respondents set out a parade of horribles that they claim could occur if *Flast* is not extended to discretionary Executive Branch expenditures. For example, they say, a federal agency could use its discretionary funds to build a house of worship or to hire clergy of one denomination and send them out to spread their faith. In the unlikely event that any of these executive actions did take place, Congress could quickly step in. And respondents make no effort to show that these improbable abuses could not be challenged in federal court by plaintiffs who would possess standing based on grounds other than taxpayer standing.

C

Over the years, *Flast* has been defended by some and criticized by others. But the present case does not require us to reconsider that precedent. The Court of Appeals did not apply *Flast*; it extended *Flast*. It is a necessary concomitant of the doctrine of *stare decisis* that a precedent is not always expanded to the limit of its logic. That was the approach that then-Justice Rehnquist took in his opinion for the Court in *Valley Forge,* and it is the approach we take here. We do not extend *Flast,* but we also do not overrule it. We leave *Flast* as we found it.

Justice Scalia says that we must either overrule *Flast* or extend it to the limits of its logic. His position is not "[in]sane," inconsistent with the "rule of law," or "utterly meaningless." But it is wrong. Justice Scalia does not seriously dispute either (1) that *Flast* itself spoke in terms of "legislative enactment[s]" and "exercises of congressional power," or (2) that in the four decades since *Flast* was decided, we have never extended its narrow exception to a purely discretionary Executive Branch expenditure. We need go no further to decide this case. Relying on the provision of the Constitution that limits our role to resolving the "Cases" and "Controversies" before us, we decide only the case at hand. For these reasons, the judgment of the Court of Appeals for the Seventh Circuit is reversed.

Justice KENNEDY, concurring.

The separation-of-powers design in the Constitution is implemented, among other means, by Article III's case-or-controversy limitation and the resulting requirement of standing. See, *e.g., Lujan v. Defenders of Wildlife,* 504 U.S. 555, 559-560, 112 S.Ct. 2130, 119 L.Ed.2d 351 (1992). The Court's decision in *Flast v. Cohen,* 392 U.S. 83, 88 S.Ct. 1942, 20 L.Ed.2d 947 (1968), and in later cases applying it, must be interpreted as respecting separation-of-powers principles but acknowledging as well that these principles, in some cases, must accommodate the First Amendment's Establishment Clause. The clause expresses the Constitution's special concern that freedom of conscience not be compromised by government taxing and spending in support of religion. In my view the result reached in *Flast* is correct and should not be called into question. For the reasons set forth by Justice Alito, however, *Flast* should not be extended to permit taxpayer standing in the instant matter. And I join his opinion in full.

It must be remembered that, even where parties have no standing to sue, members of the Legislative and Executive Branches are not excused from making constitutional determinations in the regular course of their duties. Government officials must make a conscious decision to obey the Constitution whether or not their acts can be challenged in a court of law and then must conform their actions to these principled determinations.

Justice SCALIA, with whom Justice THOMAS joins, concurring in the judgment.

Today's opinion is, in one significant respect, entirely consistent with our previous cases addressing taxpayer standing to raise Establishment Clause challenges to government expenditures. Unfortunately, the consistency lies in the creation of utterly meaningless distinctions which separate the case at hand from the precedents that have come out differently, but which cannot possibly be (in any sane world) the reason it comes out differently. If this Court is to decide cases by rule of law rather than show of hands, we must surrender to logic and choose sides: Either *Flast v. Cohen* should be applied to (at a minimum) *all* challenges to the governmental expenditure of general tax revenues in a manner alleged to violate a constitutional provision specifically limiting the taxing and spending power, or *Flast* should be repudiated. For me, the choice is easy. *Flast* is wholly irreconcilable with the Article III restrictions on federal-court jurisdiction that this Court has repeatedly confirmed are embodied in the doctrine of standing.

Overruling prior precedents, even precedents as disreputable as *Flast,* is nevertheless a serious undertaking, and I understand the impulse to take a minimalist approach. But laying just claim to be honoring *stare decisis* requires more than beating *Flast* to a pulp and then sending it out to the lower courts weakened, denigrated, more incomprehensible than ever, and yet somehow technically alive. Even before the addition of the new meaningless distinction devised by today's plurality, taxpayer standing in Establishment Clause cases has been a game of chance. We had an opportunity today to erase this blot on our jurisprudence, but instead have simply smudged it.

. . . [I] can think of few cases less warranting of *stare decisis* respect. It is time — it is past time — to call an end. *Flast* should be overruled.

Justice SOUTER, with whom Justice STEVENS, Justice GINSBURG, and Justice BREYER join, dissenting.

Flast v. Cohen, 392 U.S. 83, 102, 88 S.Ct. 1942, 20 L.Ed.2d 947 (1968), held that plaintiffs with an Establishment Clause claim could "demonstrate the necessary stake as taxpayers in the outcome of the litigation to satisfy Article III requirements." Here, the controlling, plurality opinion declares that *Flast* does not apply, but a search of that opinion for a suggestion that these taxpayers have any less stake in the outcome than the taxpayers in *Flast* will come up empty: the plurality makes no such finding, nor could it. Instead, the controlling opinion closes the door on these taxpayers because the Executive Branch, and not the Legislative Branch, caused their injury. I see no basis for this distinction in either logic or precedent, and respectfully dissent.

I

We held in *Flast,* and repeated just last Term, that the "'injury' alleged in Establishment Clause challenges to federal spending" is "the very 'extract[ion] and spen[ding]' of 'tax money' in aid of religion." *DaimlerChrysler Corp. v. Cuno,* 547 U.S. — , — (2006). As the Court said in *Flast,* the importance of that type of injury has deep historical roots going back to the ideal of religious liberty in James Madison's Memorial and Remonstrance Against Religious Assessments, that the government in a free society may not "force a citizen to contribute three pence only of his property for the support of any one establishment" of religion. Madison thus translated into practical terms the right of conscience described when he wrote that "[t]he Religion . . . of every man must be left to the conviction and conscience of every man; and it is the right of every man to exercise it as these may dictate."

Here, there is no dispute that taxpayer money in identifiable amounts is funding conferences, and these are alleged to have the purpose of promoting religion. Cf. *Doremus v. Board of Ed. of Hawthorne,* 342 U.S. 429 (1952). The taxpayers therefore seek not to "extend" *Flast,* but merely to apply it. When executive agencies spend identifiable sums of tax money for religious purposes, no less than when Congress authorizes the same thing, taxpayers suffer injury. And once we recognize the injury as sufficient for Article III, there can be no serious question about the other elements of the standing enquiry: the injury is indisputably "traceable" to the spending, and "likely to be redressed by" an injunction prohibiting it. *Allen v. Wright,* 468 U.S. 737 (1984); see also *Cuno* ("[A]n injunction against the spending would of course redress *that* injury").

The plurality points to the separation of powers to explain its distinction between legislative and executive spending decisions, but there is no difference on that point of view between a Judicial Branch review of an executive decision and a judicial evaluation of a congressional one. We owe respect to each of the other branches, no more to the former than to the latter, and no one has suggested that the Establishment Clause lacks applicability to executive uses of money. It would surely violate the Establishment Clause for the Department of Health and Human Services to draw on a general appropriation to build a chapel for weekly church services (no less than if a statute required it), and for good reason: if the Executive could accomplish through the exercise of discretion exactly what Congress cannot do through legislation, Establishment Clause protection would melt away.

So in *Bowen v. Kendrick,* 487 U.S. 589, 108 S.Ct. 2562, 101 L.Ed.2d 520 (1988), we recognized the equivalence between a challenge to a congressional spending bill and a claim that the Executive Branch was spending an appropriation, each in violation of the Establishment Clause. We held that the "claim that . . . funds [were] being used improperly by individual grantees [was no] less a challenge to congressional taxing and spending power simply because the funding authorized by Congress has flowed through and been administered by the Secretary," and we added that "we have not questioned the standing of taxpayer plaintiffs to raise Establishment Clause challenges, even when their claims raised questions about the administratively made grants."

The plurality points out that the statute in *Bowen* "expressly authorized and appropriated specific funds for grantmaking" and "expressly contemplated that some of those moneys might go to projects involving religious groups." That is all true, but there is no reason to think it should matter, and every indication in *Bowen* that it did not. Thus, after *Bowen,* the plurality's distinction between a "congressional mandate" on the one hand and "executive discretion" on the other, is at once arbitrary and hard to manage: if the statute itself is constitutional, all complaints must be about the exercise of "executive discretion," so there is no line to be drawn between *Bowen* and the case before us today.

II

While *Flast* standing to assert the right of conscience is in a class by itself, it would be a mistake to think that case is unique in recognizing standing in a plaintiff without injury to flesh or purse. Cognizable harm takes account of the nature of the interest protected, which is the reason that "the constitutional component of standing doctrine incorporates concepts concededly not susceptible of precise definition," leaving it impossible "to make application of the constitutional standing requirement a mechanical exercise." The question, ultimately, has to be whether the injury alleged is "too abstract, or otherwise not appropriate, to be considered judicially cognizable."

Thus, *Flast* speaks for this Court's recognition (shared by a majority of the Court today) that when the Government spends money for religious purposes a taxpayer's injury is serious and concrete enough to be "judicially cognizable." The judgment of sufficient injury takes account of the Madisonian relationship of tax money and conscience, but it equally reflects the Founders' pragmatic "conviction that individual religious liberty could be achieved best under a government which was stripped of all power to tax, to support, or otherwise to assist any or all religions," and the realization continuing to the modern day that favoritism for religion "'sends the . . . message to . . . nonadherents "that they are outsiders, not full members of the political community.""'"

Because the taxpayers in this case have alleged the type of injury this Court has seen as sufficient for standing, I would affirm.

ARIZONA CHRISTIAN SCHOOL TUITION ORGANIZATION v. WINN
563 U.S. 125 (2011)

Justice KENNEDY delivered the opinion of the Court.

Arizona provides tax credits for contributions to school tuition organizations, or STOs. STOs use these contributions to provide scholarships to students attending private schools, many of which are religious. Respondents are a group of Arizona taxpayers who challenge the STO tax credit as a violation of Establishment Clause principles under the First and Fourteenth Amendments. After the Arizona Supreme Court rejected a similar Establishment Clause claim on the merits, respondents sought intervention from the Federal Judiciary.

To obtain a determination on the merits in federal court, parties seeking relief must show that they have standing under Article III of the Constitution. Standing in Establishment Clause cases may be shown in various ways. Some plaintiffs may demonstrate standing based on the direct harm of what is claimed to be an establishment of religion, such as a mandatory prayer in a public school classroom. See *School Dist. Of Abington Township v. Schempp*, 374 U.S. 203, 224, n. 9, 83 S.Ct. 1560, 10 L.Ed.2d 844 (1963). Other plaintiffs may demonstrate standing on the ground that they have incurred a cost or been denied a benefit on account of their religion. Those costs and benefits can result from alleged discrimination in the tax code, such as when the availability of a tax exemption is conditioned on religious affiliation. See *Texas Monthly, Inc. v. Bullock*, 489 U.S. 1, 8, 109 S.Ct. 890, 103 L.Ed.2d 1 (1989) (plurality opinion).

For their part, respondents contend that they have standing to challenge Arizona's STO tax credit for one and only one reason: because they are Arizona taxpayers. But the mere fact that a plaintiff is a taxpayer is not generally deemed sufficient to establish standing in federal court. To overcome that rule, respondents must rely on an exception created in *Flast v. Cohen* (1968). For the reasons discussed below, respondents cannot take advantage of *Flast*'s narrow exception to the general rule against taxpayer standing. As a consequence, respondents lacked standing to commence this action, and their suit must be dismissed for want of jurisdiction.

Respondents challenged § 43-1089, a provision of the Arizona Tax Code [that] allows Arizona taxpayers to obtain dollar-for-dollar tax credits of up to $500 per person and $1,000 per married couple for contributions to STOs. [A] charitable organization could be deemed an STO only upon certain conditions. [It must] allocate "at least ninety per cent of its annual revenue for educational scholarships or tuition grants" to children attending qualified schools. A "qualified school," in turn, was defined in part as a private school in Arizona that did not discriminate on the basis of race, color, handicap, familial status, or national origin.

. . . Respondents alleged that § 43-1089 allows STOs "to use State income-tax revenues to pay tuition for students at religious schools," some of which "discriminate on the basis of religion in selecting students." Respondents requested, among other forms of relief, an injunction against the issuance of § 43-1089 tax credits for contributions to religious STOs. [T]he Arizona Christian School Tuition Organization and other interested parties intervened. [T]he Court of Appeals ruled that respondents had stated a claim that § 43-1089 violated the Establishment Clause of the First Amendment. . . .

Continued adherence to the case-or-controversy requirement of Article III maintains the public's confidence in an unelected but restrained Federal Judiciary. If the judicial power were "extended to every *question* under the constitution," Chief Justice Marshall once explained, federal courts might take possession of "almost every subject proper for legislative discussion and decision." 4 Papers of John Marshall 95 (C. Cullen ed.1984) (quoted in *DaimlerChrysler Corp. v. Cuno*, 547 U.S. 332, 341, 126 S.Ct. 1854, 164 L.Ed.2d 589 (2006)). . . .

Respondents suggest that their status as Arizona taxpayers provides them with standing to challenge the STO tax credit. Absent special circumstances, however, standing cannot be based on a plaintiff's mere status as a taxpayer. This Court has rejected the general proposition that an individual who has paid taxes has a "continuing, legally cognizable interest in ensuring that those funds are not *used* by the Government in a way that violates the Constitution." *Hein v. Freedom From Religion Foundation, Inc.*, 551 U.S. 587, 599, 127 S.Ct. 2553, 168 L.Ed.2d 424 (2007) (plurality opinion). This precept has been referred to as the rule against taxpayer standing.

The doctrinal basis for the rule was discussed in Frothingham v. Mellon (1923) (decided with *Massachusetts v. Mellon*). [Later, in] *Doremus v. Board of Ed. of Hawthorne*, 342 U.S. 429, 72 S.Ct. 394, 96 L.Ed. 475 (1952), the Court considered *Frothingham*'s prohibition on taxpayer standing in connection with an alleged Establishment Clause violation. A New Jersey statute had provided that public school teachers would read Bible verses to their students at the start of each school day. A plaintiff sought to have the law enjoined, asserting standing based on her status as a taxpayer. . . . The plaintiff in *Doremus* lacked any "direct and particular financial interest" in the suit, and, as a result, a decision on the merits would have been merely "advisory." It followed that the plaintiff's allegations did not give rise to a case or controversy subject to judicial resolution under Article III. Cf. *School Dist. of Abington Township v. Schempp*, 374 U.S., at 224, n. 9, 83 S.Ct. 1560 (finding standing where state laws required Bible readings or prayer in public schools, not because plaintiffs were state taxpayers but because their children were enrolled in public schools and so were "directly affected" by the challenged laws).

In holdings consistent with *Frothingham* and *Doremus*, more recent decisions have explained that claims of taxpayer standing rest on unjustifiable economic and political speculation. When a government expends resources or declines to impose a tax, its budget does not necessarily suffer. On the contrary, the purpose of many governmental expenditures and tax benefits is "to spur economic activity, which in turn *increases* government revenues."

Difficulties persist even if one assumes that an expenditure or tax benefit depletes the government's coffers. To find injury, a court must speculate "that elected officials will increase a taxpayer-plaintiff's tax bill to make up a deficit." And to find redressability, a court must assume that, were the remedy the taxpayers seek to be allowed, "legislators will pass along the supposed increased revenue in the form of tax reductions." It would be "pure speculation" to conclude that an injunction against a government expenditure or tax benefit "would result in any actual tax relief" for a taxpayer-plaintiff.

These well-established principles apply to the present cases. Respondents may be right that Arizona's STO tax credits have an estimated annual value of over $50 million. . . . By helping students obtain scholarships to private schools, both religious and secular, the STO program might relieve the burden placed on Arizona's public schools. The result could be an immediate and permanent cost savings for the State. . . .

Even assuming the STO tax credit has an adverse effect on Arizona's annual budget, problems would remain. To conclude there is a particular injury in fact would require speculation that Arizona lawmakers react to revenue shortfalls by increasing respondents' tax liability. . . . Respondents have not established that an injunction against application of the STO tax credit would prompt Arizona legislators to "pass along the supposed increased revenue in the form of tax reductions." Those matters, too, are conjectural. . . .

The primary contention of respondents, of course, is that, despite the general rule that taxpayers lack standing to object to expenditures alleged to be unconstitutional, their suit falls within the exception established by *Flast v. Cohen* [which] found support for its finding of personal injury in "the history of the Establishment Clause," particularly James Madison's Memorial and Remonstrance Against Religious Assessments. . . . Respondents contend that these principles demonstrate their standing to challenge the STO tax credit. In their view the tax credit is, for *Flast* purposes, best understood as a governmental expenditure. That is incorrect.

It is easy to see that tax credits and governmental expenditures can have similar economic consequences, at least for beneficiaries whose tax liability is sufficiently large to take full advantage of the credit. Yet tax credits and governmental expenditures do not both implicate individual taxpayers in sectarian activities. A dissenter whose tax dollars are "extracted and spent" knows that he has in some small measure been made to contribute to an establishment in violation of conscience. *Flast.* In that instance the taxpayer's direct and particular connection with the establishment does not depend on economic speculation or political conjecture. The connection would exist even if the conscientious dissenter's tax liability were unaffected or reduced. When the government declines to impose a tax, by contrast, there is no such connection between dissenting taxpayer and alleged establishment. Any financial injury remains speculative. And awarding some citizens a tax credit allows other citizens to retain control over their own funds in accordance with their own consciences.

The distinction between governmental expenditures and tax credits refutes respondents' assertion of standing. When Arizona taxpayers choose to contribute to STOs, they spend their own money, not money the State has collected from respondents or from other taxpayers. Arizona's § 43-1089 does not "extract[t] and spent[d]" a conscientious dissenter's funds in service of an establishment, *Flast,* or "'force a citizen to contribute three pence only of his property'" to a sectarian organization. On the contrary, respondents and other Arizona taxpayers remain free to pay their own tax bills, without contributing to an STO. Respondents are likewise able to contribute to an STO of their choice, either religious or secular. And respondents also have the option of contributing to other charitable organizations, in which case respondents may become eligible for a tax deduction or a different tax credit. . . .

Furthermore, respondents cannot satisfy the requirements of causation and redressability. When the government collects and spends taxpayer money, governmental choices are responsible for the transfer of wealth. In that case a resulting subsidy of religious activity is, for purposes of *Flast,* traceable to the government's expenditures. And an injunction against those expenditures would address the objections of conscience raised by taxpayer-plaintiffs. Here, by contrast, contributions result from the decisions of private taxpayers regarding their own funds. Private citizens create private STOs; STOs choose beneficiary schools; and taxpayers then contribute to STOs. While the State, at the outset, affords the opportunity to create and contribute to an STO, the tax credit system is implemented by private action and with no state intervention. Objecting taxpayers know that their fellow citizens, not the State, decide to contribute and in fact make the contribution. These considerations prevent any injury the objectors may suffer from being fairly traceable to the government. And while an injunction against application of the tax credit most likely would reduce contributions to STOs, that remedy would not affect noncontributing taxpayers or their tax payments. As a result, any injury suffered by respondents would not be remedied by an injunction limiting the tax credit's operation.

. . . Like contributions that lead to charitable tax deductions, contributions yielding STO tax credits are not owed to the State and, in fact, pass directly from taxpayers to private organizations. Respondents' contrary position assumes that income should be treated as if it were government property even if it has not come into the tax collector's hands. That premise finds no basis in standing jurisprudence. Private bank accounts cannot be equated with the Arizona State Treasury.

The conclusion that the *Flast* exception is inapplicable at first may seem in tension with several earlier cases, all addressing Establishment Clause issues and all decided after *Flast.* See *Mueller,* 463 U.S. 388, 103 S.Ct. 3062, 77 L.Ed.2d 721; *Committee for Public Ed. & Religious Liberty. Nyquist,* 413 U.S. 756, 93 S.Ct. 2955, 37 L.Ed.2d 948 (1973); *Hunt v. McNair,* 413 U.S. 734, 93 S.Ct. 2868, 37 L.Ed.2d 923 (1973); *Walz v. Tax Comm'n of City of New York,* 397 U.S. 664, 90 S.Ct. 1409, 25 L.Ed.2d 697 (1970); cf. *Hibbs v. Winn,* 542 U.S. 88, 124 S.Ct. 2276, 159 L.Ed.2d 172 (reaching only threshold jurisdictional issues). But those cases do not mention standing and so are not contrary to the conclusion reached here. When a potential jurisdictional defect is neither noted nor discussed in a federal decision, the decision does not stand for the proposition that no defect existed. See, *e.g., Hagans v. Lavine,* 415 U.S. 528, 535, n. 5, 94 S.Ct. 1372, 39 L.Ed.2d 577 (1974) ("[W]hen questions of jurisdiction have been passed on in prior decisions *sub silentio,* this Court has never considered itself bound when a subsequent case finally brings the jurisdictional issue before us"). . . .

Furthermore, if a law or practice, including a tax credit, disadvantages a particular religious group or a particular nonreligious group, the disadvantaged party would not have to rely on *Flast* to obtain redress for a resulting injury. See *Texas Monthly, Inc. v. Bullock* (plurality opinion) (finding standing where a general interest magazine sought to recover tax payments on the ground that religious periodicals were exempt from the tax). Because standing in Establishment Clause cases can be shown in various ways, it is far from clear that any nonbinding *sub silentio* holdings in the cases respondents cite would have depended on *Flast.* See, *e.g., Walz,* supra (explaining that the plaintiff was an "owner of real estate" in New York City who objected to the city's issuance of "property tax exemptions to religious organizations"). That the plaintiffs in those cases could have advanced arguments for jurisdiction independent of *Flast* makes it particularly inappropriate to determine whether or why standing should have been found where the issue was left unexplored. . . .

The present suit serves as an illustration of these principles. The fact that respondents are state taxpayers does not give them standing to challenge the subsidies that § 43-1089 allegedly provides to religious STOs. To alter the rules of standing or weaken their requisite elements would be inconsistent with the case-or-controversy limitation on federal jurisdiction imposed by Article III.

The judgment of the Court of Appeals is reversed.

It is so ordered.

Justice SCALIA, with whom Justice THOMAS joins, concurring.

. . . *Flast* is an anomaly in our jurisprudence, irreconcilable with the Article III restrictions on federal judicial power that our opinions have established. I would repudiate that misguided decision and enforce the Constitution. I nevertheless join the Court's opinion because it finds respondents lack standing by applying *Flast* rather than distinguishing it away on unprincipled grounds.

Justice KAGAN, with whom Justice GINSBURG, Justice BREYER, and Justice SOTOMAYOR join, dissenting.

. . . [The Court's] novel distinction in standing law between appropriations and tax expenditures has as little basis in principle as it has in our precedent. Cash grants and targeted tax breaks are means of accomplishing the same government objective — to provide financial support to select individuals or organizations. Taxpayers who oppose state aid of religion have equal reason to protest whether that aid flows from the one form of subsidy or the other. Either way, the government has financed the religious activity. And so either way, taxpayers should be able to challenge the subsidy.

Still worse, the Court's arbitrary distinction threatens to eliminate *all* occasions for a taxpayer to contest the government's monetary support of religion. Precisely because appropriations and tax breaks can achieve identical objectives, the government can easily substitute one for the other. Today's opinion thus enables the government to end-run *Flast*'s guarantee of access to the Judiciary. From now on, the government need follow just one simple rule — subsidize through the tax system — to preclude taxpayer challenges to state funding of religion.

. . . [Plaintiffs] attack a provision of the Arizona tax code that the legislature enacted pursuant to the State Constitution's taxing and spending clause (*Flast* nexus, part 1). And they allege that this provision violates the Establishment Clause (*Flast* nexus, part 2). . . .

. . . A taxpayer has standing to challenge state subsidies to religion, the Court announces, when the mechanism used is an appropriation, but not when the mechanism is a targeted tax break, otherwise called a "tax expenditure." In the former case, but not in the latter, the Court declares, the taxpayer suffers cognizable injury. But this distinction finds no support in case law, and just as little in reason. In the decades since *Flast,* no court — not one — has differentiated between appropriations and tax expenditures in deciding whether litigants have standing.

. . . The Court's ruling today will not shield all state subsidies for religion from review; as the Court notes, some persons alleging Establishment Clause violations have suffered individualized injuries, and therefore have standing, independent of their taxpayer status. But *Flast* arose because "the taxing and spending power [may] be used to favor one religion over another or to support religion in general," without causing particularized harm to discrete persons. It arose because state sponsorship of religion sometimes harms individuals only (but this "only" is no small matter) in their capacity as contributing members of our national community. In those cases, the *Flast* Court thought, our Constitution's guarantee of religious neutrality still should be enforced.

Because that judgment was right then, and remains right today, I respectfully dissent.

CLAPPER v. AMNESTY INTERNATIONAL ET AL
568 U.S. ___ (2013)

JUSTICE ALITO delivered the opinion of the Court.

Section 702 of the Foreign Intelligence Surveillance Act of 1978, 50 U. S. C. §1881a (2006 ed., Supp. V), allows the Attorney General and the Director of National Intelligence to acquire foreign intelligence information by jointly authorizing the surveillance of individuals who are not "United States persons"[5] and are reasonably believed to be located outside the United States. Before doing so, the Attorney General and the Director of National Intelligence normally must obtain the Foreign Intelligence Surveillance Court's approval. Respondents are United Statespersons whose work, they allege, requires them to engage in sensitive international communications with individuals who they believe are likely targets of surveillance under §1881a. Respondents seek a declaration that §1881a is unconstitutional, as well as an injunction against §1881a-authorized surveillance. The question before us is whether respondents have Article III standing to seek this prospective relief.

Respondents assert that they can establish injury in fact because there is an objectively reasonable likelihood that their communications will be acquired under §1881a at some point in the future. But respondents' theory of *future* injury is too speculative to satisfy the well-established requirement that threatened injury must be "certainly impending." *E.g.*, *Whitmore* v. *Arkansas*, 495 U. S. 149, 158 (1990). And even if respondents could demonstrate that the threatened injury is certainly impending, they still would not be able to establish that this injury is fairly traceable to §1881a. As an alternative argument, respondents contend that they are suffering *present* injury because the risk of §1881a-authorized surveillance already has forced them to take costly and burdensome measures to protect the confidentiality of their international communications. But respondents cannot manufacture standing by choosing to make expenditures based on hypothetical future harm that is not certainly impending. We therefore hold that respondents lack Article III standing.

I
A

In 1978, after years of debate, Congress enacted the Foreign Intelligence Surveillance Act (FISA) to authorize and regulate certain governmental electronic surveillance of communications for foreign intelligence purposes. See 92 Stat. 1783, 50 U. S. C. §1801 *et seq.*; 1 D. Kris & J. Wilson, National Security Investigations & Prosecutions §§3.1, 3.7 (2d ed. 2012) (hereinafter Kris & Wilson). In enacting FISA, Congress legislated against the backdrop of our decision in *United States* v. *United States Dist. Court for Eastern Dist. of Mich.*, 407 U. S. 297 (1972) (*Keith*), in which we explained that the standards and procedures that law enforcement officials must follow when conducting "surveillance of

---

[5] The term "United States person" includes citizens of the United States, aliens admitted for permanent residence, and certain associations and corporations. 50 U. S. C. §1801(i); see §1881(a).

'ordinary crime'" might not be required in the context of surveillance conducted for domestic national-security purposes. *Id.*, at 322–323. Although the *Keith* opinion expressly disclaimed any ruling "on the scope of the President's surveillance power with respect to the activities of foreign powers," *id.*, at 308, it implicitly suggested that a special framework for foreign intelligence surveillance might be constitutionally permissible, see *id.*, at 322–323.

In constructing such a framework for foreign intelligence surveillance, Congress created two specialized courts. In FISA, Congress authorized judges of the Foreign Intelligence Surveillance Court (FISC) to approve electronic surveillance for foreign intelligence purposes if there is probable cause to believe that "the target of the electronic surveillance is a foreign power or an agent of a foreign power," and that each of the specific "facilities or places at which the electronic surveillance is directed is being used, or is about to be used, by a foreign power or an agent of a foreign power." §105(a)(3), 92 Stat. 1790; see §§105(b)(1)(A), (b)(1)(B), *ibid.*; 1 Kris & Wilson §7:2, at 194–195; *id.*, §16:2, at 528–529. Additionally, Congress vested the Foreign Intelligence Surveillance Court of Review with jurisdiction to review any denials by the FISC of applications for electronic surveillance. §103(b),92 Stat. 1788; 1 Kris & Wilson §5:7, at 151–153.

In the wake of the September 11th attacks, President George W. Bush authorized the National Security Agency (NSA) to conduct warrantless wiretapping of telephone and e-mail communications where one party to the communication was located outside the United States and a participant in "the call was reasonably believed to be a member or agent of al Qaeda or an affiliated terrorist organization," [In] January 2007, the FISC issued orders authorizing the Government to target international communications into or out of the United States where there was probable cause to believe that one participant to the communication was a member or agent of al Qaeda or an associated terrorist organization. [After] a FISC Judge subsequently narrowed the FISC's authorization of such surveillance, however, the Executive asked Congress to amend FISA so that it would provide the intelligence community with additional authority to meet the challenges of modern technology and international terrorism. *Id.*, at 315a–318a, 331a–333a, 398a; see *id.*, at 262a, 277a–279a, 287a.

When Congress enacted the FISA Amendments Act of 2008 (FISA Amendments Act), 122 Stat. 2436, it left much of FISA intact, but it "established a new and independent source of intelligence collection authority, beyond that granted in traditional FISA." 1 Kris & Wilson §9:11, at 349–350. As relevant here, §702 of FISA, 50 U. S. C. §1881a (2006 ed., Supp. V), which was enacted as part of the FISA Amendments Act, supplements pre-existing FISA authority by creating a new framework under which the Government may seek the FISC's authorization of certain foreign intelligence surveillance targeting the communications of non-U. S. persons located abroad. Unlike traditional FISA surveillance, §1881a does not require the Government to demonstrate probable cause that the target of the electronic surveillance is a foreign power or agent of a foreign power. [And], unlike traditional FISA, §1881a does not require the Government to specify the nature and location of each of the particular facilities or places at which the electronic surveillance will occur. Compare §§1805(a)(2)(B), (c)(1) (2006 ed. and Supp. V), with §§1881a(d)(1), (g)(4), (i)(3)(A);638 F. 3d, at 125–126; 1 Kris & Wilson §16:16, at 585.[6]

The present case involves a constitutional challenge to §1881a. Surveillance under §1881a is subject to statutory conditions, judicial authorization, congressional supervision, and compliance with the Fourth Amendment. Section 1881a provides that, upon the issuance of an order from the Foreign Intelligence Surveillance Court, "the Attorney General and the Director of National Intelligence may authorize jointly, for a period of up

---

[6] Congress recently reauthorized the FISA Amendments Act for another five years. See 126 Stat. 1631.

to 1 year . . . , the targeting of persons reasonably believed to be located outside the United States to acquire foreign intelligence information." §1881a(a). Surveillance under §1881a may not be intentionally targeted at any person known to be in the United States or any U.S. person reasonably believed to be located abroad. §§1881a(b)(1)–(3); see also §1801(i). Additionally, acquisitions under §1881a must comport with the Fourth Amendment. §1881a(b)(5). Moreover, surveillance under §1881a is subject to congressional oversight and several types of Executive Branch review. See §§1881a(f)(2), (*l*); *Amnesty Int'l USA* v. *McConnell*, 646 F. Supp. 2d 633, 640–641 (SDNY 2009).

[B]

Respondents are attorneys and human rights, labor, legal, and media organizations whose work allegedly requires them to engage in sensitive and sometimes privileged telephone and e-mail communications with colleagues, clients, sources, and other individuals located abroad. Respondents believe that some of the people with whom they exchange foreign intelligence information are likely targets of surveillance under §1881a. Specifically, respondents claim that they communicate by telephone and e-mail with people the Government "believes or believed to be associated with terrorist organizations," "people located in geographic areas that are a special focus" of the Government's counterterrorism or diplomatic efforts, and activists who oppose governments that are supported by the United States Government. App. to Pet. for Cert. 399a.

Respondents claim that §1881a compromises their ability to locate witnesses, cultivate sources, obtain information, and communicate confidential information to their clients. Respondents also assert that they "have ceased engaging" in certain telephone and e-mail conversations. *Id.,* at 400a. According to respondents, the threat of surveillance will compel them to travel abroad in order to have in-person conversations. In addition, respondents declare that they have undertaken "costly and burdensome measures" to protect the confidentiality of sensitive communications. *Ibid.*

C

[Respondents] assert what they characterize as two separate theories of Article III standing. First, they claim that there is an objectively reasonable likelihood that their communications will be acquired under §1881a at some point in the future, thus causing them injury. Second, respondents maintain that the risk of surveillance under §1881a is so substantial that they have been forced to take costly and burdensome measures to protect the confidentiality of their international communications; in their view, the costs they have incurred constitute present injury that is fairly traceable to §1881a.

After both parties moved for summary judgment, the District Court held that respondents do not have standing. *McConnell*, 646 F. Supp. 2d, at 635. On appeal, however, a panel of the Second Circuit reversed. The panel agreed with respondents' argument that they have standing due to the objectively reasonable likelihood that their communications will be intercepted at some time in the future. 638 F. 3d, at 133, 134, 139. In addition, the panel held that respondents have established that they are suffering "*present injuries in fact*—economic and professional harms—stemming from a reasonable fear of *future* harmful government conduct." *Id.*, at 138. The Second Circuit denied rehearing en banc by an equally divided vote. 667 F. 3d 163 (2011).

Because of the importance of the issue and the novel view of standing adopted by the Court of Appeals, we granted certiorari, 566 U. S. __ (2012), and we now reverse.

II

Article III of the Constitution limits federal courts' jurisdiction to certain "Cases" and "Controversies." As we have explained, "[n]o principle is more fundamental to the judiciary's proper role in our system of government than the constitutional limitation of federal-court jurisdiction to actual cases or controversies." *DaimlerChrysler Corp.* v.

Cuno, 547 U. S. 332, 341 (2006) (internal quotation marks omitted); *Raines* v. *Byrd*, 521 U. S. 811, 818 (1997) (internal quotation marks omitted); see, *e.g.*, *Summers* v. *Earth Island Institute*, 555 U. S. 488, 492–493 (2009). "One element of the case-or-controversy requirement" is that plaintiffs "must establish that they have standing to sue." *Raines*, *supra,* at 818; see also *Summers*, *supra*, at 492– 493; *DaimlerChrysler Corp.*, *supra*, at 342; *Lujan* v. *Defenders of Wildlife*, 504 U. S. 555, 560 (1992).

The law of Article III standing, which is built on separation-of-powers principles, serves to prevent the judicial process from being used to usurp the powers of the political branches. [In] keeping with the purpose of this doctrine, "[o]ur standing inquiry has been especially rigorous when reaching the merits of the dispute would force us to decide whether an action taken by one of the other two branches of the Federal Government was unconstitutional." *Raines*, *supra*, at 819–820; see *Valley Forge Christian College*, *supra*, at 473–474; *Schlesinger*, *supra*, at 221–222. "Relaxation of standing requirements is directly related to the expansion of judicial power," *United States* v. *Richardson*, 418 U. S. 166, 188 (1974) (Powell, J., concurring); see also *Summers*, *supra*, at 492–493; *Schlesinger*, *supra*, at 222, and we have often found a lack of standing in cases in which the Judiciary has been requested to review actions of the political branches in the fields of intelligence gathering and foreign affairs, see, *e.g.*, *Richardson*, *supra*, at 167–170 (plaintiff lacked standing to challenge the constitutionality of a statute permitting the Central Intelligence Agency to account for its expenditures solely on the certificate of the CIA Director).

To establish Article III standing, an injury must be "concrete, particularized, and actual or imminent; fairly traceable to the challenged action; and redressable by a favorable ruling." *Monsanto Co.* v. *Geertson Seed Farms*, 561 U. S.___, ___ (2010) (slip op., at 7); see also *Summers*, *supra*, at 493; *Defenders of Wildlife*, 504 U. S., at 560–561. "Although imminence is concededly a somewhat elastic concept, it cannot be stretched beyond its purpose, which is to ensure that the alleged injury is not too speculative for Article III purposes—that the injury is *certainly* impending." *Id.*, at 565, n. 2 (internal quotation marks omitted). Thus, we have repeatedly reiterated that "threatened injury must be *certainly impending* to constitute injury in fact," and that "[a]llegations of *possible* future injury" are not sufficient. *Whitmore*, 495 U. S., at 158 (emphasis added; internal quotation marks omitted); see also *Defenders of Wildlife*, *supra*, at 565, n. 2, 567, n. 3; see *DaimlerChrysler Corp.*, *supra*, at 345; *Friends of the Earth, Inc.* v. *Laidlaw Environmental Services (TOC), Inc.*, 528 U. S. 167, 190 (2000); *Babbitt* v. *Farm Workers*, 442 U. S. 289, 298 (1979).

III

A

Respondents assert that they can establish injury in fact that is fairly traceable to §1881a because there is an objectively reasonable likelihood that their communications with their foreign contacts will be intercepted under §1881a at some point in the future. This argument fails. As an initial matter, the Second Circuit's "objectively reasonable likelihood" standard is inconsistent with our requirement that "threatened injury must be certainly impending to constitute injury in fact."

Furthermore, respondents' argument rests on their highly speculative fear that: (1) the Government will decide to target the communications of non-U. S. persons with whom they communicate; (2) in doing so, the Government will choose to invoke its authority under §1881a rather than utilizing another method of surveillance; (3) the Article III judges who serve on the Foreign Intelligence Surveillance Court will conclude that the Government's proposed surveillance procedures satisfy §1881a's many safeguards and are consistent with the Fourth Amendment; (4) the Government will succeed in intercepting the communications of respondents' contacts; and (5) respondents will be parties to the particular communications that the Government intercepts. As discussed below, respondents' theory of standing, which relies on a highly attenuated chain of possibilities, does not satisfy the requirement that threatened injury must be certainly impending. See *Summers, supra*, at 496 (rejecting a standing theory premised on a speculative chain of possibilities); *Whitmore, supra*, at 157–160 (same). Moreover, even if respondents could demonstrate injury in fact, the second link in the above-described chain of contingencies—which amounts to mere speculation about whether surveillance would be under §1881a or some other authority—shows that respondents cannot satisfy the requirement that any injury in fact must be fairly traceable to §1881a.

First, it is speculative whether the Government will imminently target communications to which respondents are parties. Section 1881a expressly provides that respondents, who are U. S. persons, cannot be targeted for surveillance under §1881a. See §§1881a(b)(1)–(3); 667 F. 3d, at 173 (Raggi, J., dissenting from denial of rehearing en banc). Accordingly, it is no surprise that respondents fail to offer any evidence that their communications have been monitored under §1881a, a failure that substantially undermines their standing theory. See *ACLU*, 493 F. 3d, at 655–656, 673–674 (opinion of Batchelder, J.) (concluding that plaintiffs who lacked evidence that their communications had been intercepted did not have standing to challenge alleged NSA surveillance). Indeed, respondents do not even allege that the Government has sought the FISC's approval for surveillance of their communications. Accordingly, respondents' theory necessarily rests on their assertion that the Government will target *other individuals*—namely, their foreign contacts.

Yet respondents have no actual knowledge of the Government's §1881a targeting practices. Instead, respondents merely speculate and make assumptions about whether their communications with their foreign contacts will be acquired under §1881a. See 667 F. 3d, at 185–187 (opinion of Raggi, J.). For example, journalist Christopher Hedges states: "I have no choice but to *assume* that any of my international communications *may* be subject to government surveillance, and I have to make decisions . . . in light of that *assumption*." App. to Pet. for Cert. 366a (emphasis added and deleted). Similarly, attorney Scott McKay asserts that, "[b]ecause of the [FISA Amendments Act], we now have to *assume* that every one of our international communications *may* be monitored by the government." *Id.*, at 375a (emphasis added); see also *id.*, at 337a, 343a–344a, 350a, 356a. "The party invoking federal jurisdiction bears the burden of establishing" standing—and, at the summary judgment stage, such a party "can no longer rest on . . . 'mere allegations,' but must 'set forth' by affidavit or other evidence 'specific facts.'" *Defenders of Wildlife*, 504 U. S., at 561. Respondents, however, have set forth no specific facts demonstrating that the communications of their foreign contacts will be targeted. Moreover, because §1881a at most *authorizes*—but does not *mandate* or *direct*—the surveillance that respondents fear, respondents' allegations are necessarily conjectural. See *United Presbyterian Church in U. S. A. v. Reagan*, 738 F. 2d 1375, 1380 (CADC 1984) (Scalia, J.); 667 F. 3d, at 187 (opinion of Raggi, J.). Simply put, respondents can only speculate as to how the Attorney General and the Director of National Intelligence will exercise their discretion in determining which communications to target.[7]

---

[7] It was suggested at oral argument that the Government could help resolve the standing inquiry by disclosing to a court, perhaps through an *in camera* proceeding, (1) whether it is intercepting respondents' communications and (2) what targeting or minimization procedures it is using. See Tr. of Oral Arg. 13–14, 44, 56. This suggestion is puzzling. As an initial matter, it is *respondents'* burden to prove their standing by pointing to specific facts, *Lujan* v. *Defenders of Wildlife*, 504 U. S. 555, 561 (1992), not the Government's burden to disprove standing by revealing details of its surveillance priorities. Moreover, this type of hypothetical disclosure proceeding would allow a terrorist(or his attorney) to determine whether he is currently under U. S. surveillance simply by filing a lawsuit challenging the Government's surveillance program. Even if the terrorist's attorney were to comply with a protective order prohibiting him from sharing the Government's disclosures with his client, the court's post disclosure decision about whether to dismiss the suit for lack of

Second, even if respondents could demonstrate that the targeting of their foreign contacts is imminent, respondents can only speculate as to whether the Government will seek to use §1881a-authorized surveillance (rather than other methods) to do so. The Government has numerous other methods of conducting surveillance, none of which is challenged here. Even after the enactment of the FISA Amendments Act, for example, the Government may still conduct electronic surveillance of persons abroad under the older provisions of FISA so long as it satisfies the applicable requirements, including a demonstration of probable cause to believe that the person is a foreign power or agent of a foreign power. See §1805. The Government may also obtain information from the intelligence services of foreign nations. Brief for Petitioners 33. And, although we do not reach the question, the Government contends that it can conduct FISA-exempt human and technical surveillance programs that are governed by Executive Order 12333. See Exec. Order No. 12333, §§1.4,2.1–2.5, 3 CFR 202, 210–212 (1981), reprinted as amended, note following 50 U. S. C. §401, pp. 543, 547–548. Even if respondents could demonstrate that their foreign contacts will imminently be targeted—indeed, even if they could show that interception of their own communications will imminently occur—they would still need to show that their injury is fairly traceable to §1881a. But, because respondents can only speculate as to whether any (asserted) interception would be under §1881a or some other authority, they cannot satisfy the "fairly traceable" requirement.

Third, even if respondents could show that the Government will seek the Foreign Intelligence Surveillance Court's authorization to acquire the communications of respondents' foreign contacts under §1881a, respondents can only speculate as to whether that court will authorize such surveillance. In the past, we have been reluctant to endorse standing theories that require guesswork as to how independent decision makers will exercise their judgment. In *Whitmore*, for example, the plaintiff 's theory of standing hinged largely on the probability that he would obtain federal habeas relief and be convicted upon retrial. In holding that the plaintiff lacked standing, we explained that "[i]t is just not possible for a litigant to prove in advance that the judicial system will lead to any particular result in his case." 495 U. S., at 159–160; see *Defenders of Wildlife*, 504 U. S., at 562.

We decline to abandon our usual reluctance to endorse standing theories that rest on speculation about the decisions of independent actors. Section 1881a mandates that the Government must obtain the Foreign Intelligence Surveillance Court's approval of targeting procedures, minimization procedures, and a governmental certification regarding proposed surveillance. §§1881a(a), (c)(1), (i)(2), (i)(3). The Court must, for example, determine whether the Government's procedures are "reasonably designed . . .to minimize the acquisition and retention, and prohibit the dissemination, of non publicly available information concerning unconsenting United States persons." §1801(h); see §§1881a(i)(2), (i)(3)(A). And, critically, the Court must also assess whether the Government's targeting and minimization procedures comport with the Fourth Amendment. §1881a(i)(3)(A).

Fourth, even if the Government were to obtain the Foreign Intelligence Surveillance Court's approval to target respondents' foreign contacts under §1881a, it is unclear whether the Government would succeed in acquiring the communications of respondents' foreign contacts. And fifth, even if the Government were to conduct surveillance of respondents' foreign contacts, respondents can only speculate as to whether *their own communications* with their foreign contacts would be incidentally acquired.

---

standing would surely signal to the terrorist whether his name was on the list of surveillance targets.

In sum, respondents' speculative chain of possibilities does not establish that injury based on potential future surveillance is certainly impending or is fairly traceable to se. 1881a.[8]

B

Respondents' alternative argument—namely, that they can establish standing based on the measures that they have undertaken to avoid §1881a-authorized surveillance—fares no better. Respondents assert that they are suffering ongoing injuries that are fairly traceable to §1881a because the risk of surveillance under §1881a requires them to take costly and burdensome measures to protect the confidentiality of their communications. Respondents claim, for instance, that the threat of surveillance sometimes compels them to avoid certain e-mail and phone conversations, to "tal[k] in generalities rather than specifics," or to travel so that they can have in-person conversations. The Second Circuit panel concluded that, because respondents are already suffering such ongoing injuries, the likelihood of interception under §1881a is relevant only to the question whether respondents' ongoing injuries are "fairly traceable" to §1881a. See 638 F. 3d, at 133–134; 667 F. 3d, at 180 (opinion of Raggi,J.). Analyzing the "fairly traceable" element of standing under a relaxed reasonableness standard, see 638 F. 3d, at 133–134, the Second Circuit then held that "plaintiffs have established that they suffered *present* injuries in fact—economic and professional harms—stemming from a reasonable fear of *future* harmful government conduct," *id.*, at 138.

The Second Circuit's analysis improperly allowed respondents to establish standing by asserting that they suffer present costs and burdens that are based on a fear of surveillance, so long as that fear is not "fanciful, paranoid, or otherwise unreasonable." See *id.*, at 134. This improperly waters down the fundamental requirements of Article III. Respondents' contention that they have standing because they incurred certain costs as a reasonable reaction to a risk of harm is unavailing—because the harm respondents seek to avoid is not certainly impending. In other words, respondents cannot manufacture standing merely by inflicting harm on themselves based on their fears of hypothetical future harm that is not certainly impending. See *Pennsylvania* v. *New Jersey*, 426 U. S. 660, 664 (1976) (*per curium*); *National Family Planning & Reproductive Health Assn., Inc.*, 468 F. 3d 826, 831 (CADC 2006). Any ongoing injuries that respondents are suffering are not fairly traceable to §1881a. [Because] respondents do not face a threat of certainly impending interception under §1881a, the costs that they have incurred to avoid surveillance are simply the product of their fear of surveillance,[9] and our decision in *Laird* makes it clear that such a fear is insufficient to create standing. See 408 U. S., at 10–15.

---

[8] Our cases do not uniformly require plaintiffs to demonstrate that it is literally certain that the harms they identify will come about. In some instances, we have found standing based on a "substantial risk" that the harm will occur, which may prompt plaintiffs to reasonably incur costs to mitigate or avoid that harm. *Monsanto Co.* v. *Geertson Seed Farms*, 561 U. S. ___, ___ (2010) (slip op., at 11–12). See also *Pennell* v. *City of San Jose*, 485 U. S. 1, 8 (1988); *Blum* v. *Yaretsky*, 457 U. S. 991, 1000–1001 (1982); *Babbitt* v. *Farm Workers*, 442 U. S. 289, 298 (1979). But to the extent that the "substantial risk" standard is relevant and is distinct from the "clearly impending" requirement, respondents fall short of even that standard, in light of the attenuated chain of inferences necessary to find harm here. See *supra*, at 11–15. In addition, plaintiffs bear the burden of pleading and proving concrete facts showing that the defendant's actual action has caused the substantial risk of harm. Plaintiffs cannot rely on speculation about "'the unfettered choices made by independent actors not before the court.'" *Defenders of Wildlife*, 504 U. S., at 562.

[9] Although respondents' alternative theory of standing rests primarily on choices that *they* have made based on their subjective fear of surveillance, respondents also assert that third parties might be disinclined to speak with them due to a fear of surveillance. See App. to Pet. for Cert. 372a–373a, 352a–353a. To the extent that such assertions are based on anything other than conjecture, see *Defenders of Wildlife*, 504 U. S., at 560, they do not establish injury that is fairly traceable to §1881a, because they are based on third parties' subjective fear of surveillance, see *Laird*, 408 U. S., at 10–14.

For the reasons discussed above, respondents' self inflicted injuries are not fairly traceable to the Government's purported activities under §1881a, and their subjective fear of surveillance does not give rise to standing.

[B]

Respondents also suggest that they should be held to have standing because otherwise the constitutionality of §1881a could not be challenged. It would be wrong, they maintain, to "insulate the government's surveillance activities from meaningful judicial review." Brief for Respondents 60. Respondents' suggestion is both legally and factually incorrect. First, "'[t]he assumption that if respondents have no standing to sue, no one would have standing, is not a reason to find standing.'" *Valley Forge Christian College*, 454 U. S., at 489; *Schlesinger*, 418 U. S., at 227; see also *Richardson*, 418 U. S., at 179; *Raines*, 521U. S., at 835 (Souter, J., joined by GINSBURG, J., concurring in judgment).

Second, our holding today by no means insulates §1881a from judicial review. As described above, Congress created a comprehensive scheme in which the Foreign Intelligence Surveillance Court evaluates the Government's certifications, targeting procedures, and minimization procedures—including assessing whether the targeting and minimization procedures comport with the Fourth Amendment. §§1881a(a), (c)(1), (i)(2), (i)(3). Any dissatisfaction that respondents may have about the Foreign intelligence Surveillance Court's rulings—or the congressional delineation of that court's role—is irrelevant to our standing analysis.

Additionally, if the Government intends to use or disclose information obtained or derived from a §1881a acquisition in judicial or administrative proceedings, it must provide advance notice of its intent, and the affected person may challenge the lawfulness of the acquisition. §§1806(c), 1806(e), 1881e(a) (2006 ed. and Supp. V).[10]

Thus, if the Government were to prosecute one of respondent-attorney's foreign clients using §1881a-authorized surveillance, the Government would be required to make a disclosure. Although the foreign client might not have a viable Fourth Amendment claim, see, *e.g., United States* v. *Verdugo-Urquidez*, 494 U. S. 259, 261 (1990), it is possible that the monitoring of the target's conversations with his or her attorney would provide grounds for a claim of standing on the part of the attorney. Such an attorney would certainly have a stronger evidentiary basis for establishing standing than do respondents in the present case. In such a situation, unlike in the present case, it would at least be clear that the Government had acquired the foreign client's communications using §1881a authorized surveillance.

Finally, any electronic communications service provider that the Government directs to assist in §1881a surveillance may challenge the lawfulness of that directive before the FISC. §§1881a(h)(4), (6). Indeed, at the behest of a service provider, the Foreign Intelligence Surveillance Court of Review previously analyzed the constitutionality of electronic surveillance directives issued pursuant to a now-expired set of FISA amendments. See *In re Directives Pursuant to Section 105B of Foreign Intelligence Surveillance Act*, 551 F. 3d 1004, 1006–1016 (2008) (holding that the provider had standing and that the directives were constitutional).

* * *

We hold that respondents lack Article III standing because they cannot demonstrate that the future injury they purportedly fear is certainly impending and because they cannot

---

[10] The possibility of judicial review in this context is not farfetched. In *United States v. Damrah*, 412 F. 3d 618 (CA6 2005), for example, the Government made a pretrial disclosure that it intended to use FISA evidence in a prosecution; the defendant (unsuccessfully) moved to suppress the FISA evidence, even though he had not been the *target* of the surveillance; and the Sixth Circuit ultimately held that FISA's procedures are consistent with the Fourth Amendment. See *id.*, at 622, 623, 625.

manufacture standing by incurring costs in anticipation of non-imminent harm. We therefore reverse the judgment of the Second Circuit and remand the case for further proceedings consistent with this opinion.

It is so ordered.

[The dissenting opinions of Justice Breyer, joined by Justices Ginsburg, Sotomayor and Kagan is omitted].

ARIZONA STATE LEGISLATURE
v. ARIZONA INDEPENDENT REDISTRICTING COMMISSION ET AL.
576 U.S. 787 (2015)

JUSTICE GINSBURG delivered the opinion of the Court. [See pages _____ for the Court's opinion regarding the merits of the case].

II

We turn first to the threshold question: Does the Arizona Legislature have standing to bring this suit? Trained on "whether the plaintiff is [a] proper party to bring [a particular lawsuit,]" standing is "[o]ne element" of the Constitution's case-or-controversy limitation on federal judicial authority, expressed in Article III of the Constitution. *Raines* v. *Byrd*, 521 U. S. 811, 818 (1997). "To qualify as a party with standing to litigate," the Arizona Legislature "must show, first and foremost," injury in the form of "'invasion of a legally protected interest' that is 'concrete and particularized' and 'actual or imminent.'" *Arizonans for Official English* v. *Arizona*, 520 U. S. 43, 64 (1997) (quoting *Lujan* v. *Defenders of Wildlife*, 504 U. S. 555, 560 (1992)). The Legislature's injury also must be" fairly traceable to the challenged action" and "redressableby a favorable ruling." *Clapper* v. *Amnesty Int'l USA*, 568 U. S. 398 (2013) (slip op., at 10) (internal quotation marks omitted).

The Arizona Legislature maintains that the Elections Clause vests in it "primary responsibility" for redistricting. Brief for Appellant 51, 53. To exercise that responsibility, the Legislature urges, it must have at least the opportunity to engage (or decline to engage) in redistricting before the State may involve other actors in the redistricting process. See *id.*, at 51–53. Proposition 106, which gives the AIRC binding authority over redistricting, regardless of the Legislature's action or inaction, strips the Legislature of its alleged prerogative to initiate redistricting. That asserted deprivation would be remedied by a court order enjoining the enforcement of Proposition 106. Although we conclude that the Arizona Legislature does not have the exclusive, constitutionally guarded role it asserts, see *infra*, at 24–35, one must not "confus[e] weakness on the merits with absence of Article III standing." *Davis* v. *United States*, 564 U. S. ___, ___, n. 10 (2011) (slip op., at 19, n. 10); see *Warth* v. *Seldin*, 422 U. S. 490, 500 (1975) (standing "often turns on the nature and source of the claim asserted," but it "in no way depends on the merits" of the claim).

The AIRC argues that the Legislature's alleged injury is insufficiently concrete to meet the standing requirement absent some "specific legislative act that would have taken effect but for Proposition 106." Brief for Apelles 20. The United States, as *amicus curiae*, urges that even more is needed: the Legislature's injury will remain speculative, the United States contends, unless and until the Arizona Secretary of State refuses to implement a competing redistricting plan passed by the Legislature. Brief for United States 14–17. In our view, the Arizona Legislature's suit is not premature, nor is its alleged injury too "conjectural" or "hypothetical" to establish standing. *Defenders of Wildlife*, 504 U. S., at 560 (internal quotation marks omitted).

Two prescriptions of Arizona's Constitution would render the Legislature's passage of a competing plan and submission of that plan to the Secretary of State unavailing. Indeed, those actions would directly and immediately conflict with the regime Arizona's Constitution establishes. Cf. *Sporhase v. Nebraska ex rel. Douglas*, 458 U. S. 941, 944, n. 2 (1982) (failure to apply for permit which" would not have been granted" under existing law did not deprive plaintiffs of standing to challenge permitting regime). First, the Arizona Constitution instructs that the Legislature "shall not have the power to adopt any measure that supersedes [an initiative], in whole or in part, . . . unless the superseding measure furthers the purposes" of the initiative. Art. IV, pt. 1, §1(14). Any redistricting map passed by the Legislature in an effort to supersede the AIRC's map surely would not "furthe[r] the purposes" of Proposition 106. Second, once the AIRC certifies its redistricting plan to the Secretary of State, Arizona's Constitution requires the Secretary to implement that plan and no other. [To] establish standing, the Legislature need not violate the Arizona Constitution and show that the Secretary of State would similarly disregard the State's fundamental instrument of government.

Raines v. *Byrd*, 521 U. S. 811 (1997), does not aid AIRC's argument that there is no standing here. In *Raines*, this Court held that six *individual Members* of Congress lacked standing to challenge the Line Item Veto Act. *Id.*, at 813–814, 829–830 (holding specifically and only that "individual members of Congress [lack] Article III standing"). The Act, which gave the President authority to cancel certain spending and tax benefit measures after signing them into law, allegedly diluted the efficacy of the Congress members' votes. *Id.*, at 815–817. The "institutional injury" at issue, we reasoned, scarcely zeroed in on any individual Member. *Id.*, at 821. "[W]idely dispersed," the alleged injury "necessarily [impacted] all Members of Congress and both Houses . . . equally." *Id.*, at 829, 821. None of the plaintiffs, therefore, could tenably claim a "personal stake" in the suit. *Id.*, at 830.

In concluding that the individual Members lacked standing, the Court "attach[ed] some importance to the fact that [the *Raines* plaintiffs had] not been authorized to represent their respective Houses of Congress." *Id.*, at 829. "[I]ndeed," the Court observed, "both houses actively oppose[d] their suit." *Ibid.* Having failed to prevail in their own Houses, the suitors could not repair to the Judiciary to complain. The Arizona Legislature, in contrast, is an institutional plaintiff asserting an institutional injury, and it commenced this action after authorizing votes in both of its chambers, App. 26–27, 46. That "different . . . circumstanc[e]," 521 U. S., at 830, was not *sub judice* in *Raines*.

Closer to the mark is this Court's decision in *Coleman* v. *Miller*, 307 U. S. 433 (1939). There, plaintiffs were 20 (of 40) Kansas State Senators, whose votes "would have been sufficient to defeat [a] resolution ratifying [a] proposed [federal] constitutional amendment." *Id.*, at 446.[11] We held they had standing to challenge, as impermissible under Article V of the Federal Constitution, the State Lieutenant Governor's tie-breaking vote for the amendment. *Ibid. Coleman*, as we later explained in *Raines*, stood "for the proposition that legislators whose votes would have been sufficient to defeat (or enact) a specific legislative Act have standing to sue if that legislative action goes into effect (or does not go into effect), on the ground that their votes have been completely nullified." 521 U. S., at 823.[12] Our conclusion that the Arizona Legislature has standing fits that bill. Proposition 106, together with the Arizona Constitution's ban on efforts to undermine the purposes of an initiative, see *supra*, at 11, would "completely nullif[y]" any vote by the Legislature, now or "in the future," purporting to adopt a redistricting plan. *Raines*, 521 U. S., at 823–824.[13]

This dispute, in short, "will be resolved . . . in a concrete factual context conducive to a realistic appreciation of the consequences of judicial action." *Valley Forge Christian*

College v. *Americans United for Separation of Church and State, Inc.*, 454 U. S. 464, 472 (1982).

ALABAMA LEGISLATIVE BLACK CAUCUS ET AL.
v. ALABAMA ET AL.
575 U.S. 254 (2015)

JUSTICE BREYER delivered the opinion of the Court.

[The discussion of the redistricting issue, raised by the Alabama Democratic Conference, is discussed at pages_____. This excerpt is the Court's opinion on the lower federal court's determination that the Conference lacked standing to bring its complaint on redistricting.]

III

We next consider the District Court's holding with respect to standing. The District Court, *sua sponte*, held that the Conference lacked standing—either to bring racial gerrymandering claims with respect to the four individual districts that the court specifically considered (*i.e.*, Senate Districts 7, 11, 22, and 26) or to bring a racial gerrymandering claim with respect to the "State as a whole." 989 F. Supp. 2d, at 1292. The District Court recognized that ordinarily "[a]n association has standing to bring suit on behalf of its members *when its members would have standing to sue in their own right*, the interests at stake are germane to the organization's purpose, and neither the claim asserted nor the relief requested requires individuals members' participation in the lawsuit." *Id.*, at 1291 (quoting *Friends of the Earth, Inc.* v. *Laidlaw Environmental Services (TOC), Inc.*, 528 U. S. 167, 181 (2000); emphasis added).

It also recognized that a "member" of an association "would have standing to sue" in his or her "own right" when that member "resides in the district that he alleges was the product of a racial gerrymander." 989 F. Supp. 2d, at 1291 (citing *Hays*, 515 U. S., at 744–745). But, the District Court nonetheless denied standing because it believed that the "record" did "not clearly identify the districts in which the individual members of the [Conference] reside," and the Conference had "not proved that it has members who have standing to pursue any district-specific claims of racial gerrymandering." 989 F. Supp. 2d, at 1292.

The District Court conceded that Dr. Joe Reed, a representative of the Conference, testified that the Conference "has members in almost every county in Alabama." *Ibid.* But, the District Court went on to say that "the counties in Alabama are split into many districts." *Ibid.* And the "Conference offered no testimony or evidence that it has members in all of the districts in Alabama or in any of the [four] specific districts that it challenged." *Ibid.*

The record, however, lacks adequate support for the District Court's conclusion. Dr. Reed's testimony supports, and nothing in that record undermines, the Conference's own statement, in its post-trial brief, that it is a "statewide political caucus founded in 1960." Conference Post-Trial Brief 3. It has the "purpose" of "endors[ing]candidates for political office who will be responsible to the needs of the blacks and other minorities and poor people." *Id.*, at 3–4. These two statements (the second of which the principal dissent ignores), taken together with Dr. Reed's testimony, support an inference that the organization has members in all of the State's majority-minority districts, other things being equal, which is sufficient to meet the Conference's burden of establishing standing. That is to say, it seems highly likely that a "statewide" organization with members in "almost every county," the purpose of which is to help "blacks and other minorities and poor people," will have members in each majority-minority district. But cf. *post,* at 3–5 (SCALIA, J., dissenting).

At the very least, the common sense inference is strong enough to lead the Conference reasonably to believe that, in the absence of a state challenge or a court request for more detailed information, it need not provide additional information such as a specific membership list. We have found nothing in the record, nor has the State referred us to anything in the record, that suggests the contrary. Cf. App. 204–205, 208 (State arguing lack of standing, not because of inadequate member residency but because an association "lives" nowhere and that the Conference should join individual members). The most the State argued was that "[n]one of the *individual* [p]laintiffs [who brought the case with the Conference] claims to live in" Senate District 11, *id.*, at 205 (emphasis added), but the Conference would likely not have understood that argument as a request that *it* provide a membership list. In fact, the Conference might have understood the argument as an indication that the State did *not* contest its membership in every district.

To be sure, the District Court had an independent obligation to confirm its jurisdiction, even in the absence of a state challenge. See *post,* at 4–5 (SCALIA, J., dissenting). But, in these circumstances, elementary principles of procedural fairness required that the District Court, rather than acting *sua sponte*, give the Conference an opportunity to provide evidence of member residence. Cf. *Warth* v. *Seldin*, 422 U. S. 490, 501–502 (1975) (explaining that a court may "allow or [r]equire" a plaintiff to supplement the record to show standing and that "[i]f, *after this opportunity*, the plaintiff 's standing does not adequately appear from all materials of record, the complaint must be dismissed" (emphasis added)). Moreover, we have no reason to believe that the Conference would have been unable to provide a list of members, at least with respect to the majority-minority districts, had it been asked. It has filed just such a list in this Court. See Affidavit of Joe L. Reed. Pursuant to this Court's Rule 32.3 (Lodging of Conference affidavit listing members residing in each majority-minority district in the State); see also *Parents Involved in Community Schools* v. *Seattle School Dist. No. 1*, 551 U. S. 701, 718 (2007) (accepting a lodged affidavit in similar circumstances). Thus, the District Court on remand should reconsider the Conference's standing by permitting the Conference to file its list of members and permitting the State to respond, as appropriate.

The Alabama Legislative Black Caucus and the Alabama Democratic Conference appeal a three-judge Federal District Court decision rejecting their challenges to the lawfulness of Alabama's 2012 redistricting of its State House of Representatives and State Senate. The appeals focus upon the appellants' claims that new district boundaries create "racial gerrymanders" in violation of the Fourteenth Amendment's Equal Protection Clause. See, *e.g., Shaw* v. *Hunt*, 517 U. S. 899, 907–908 (1996) (*Shaw II*) (Fourteenth Amendment forbids use of race as "'predominant'" district boundary-drawing "'factor'" unless boundaries are "narrowly tailored" to achieve a "'compelling state interest'" (citations omitted)). We find that the District Court applied incorrect legal standards in evaluating the claims. We consequently vacate its decision and remand the cases for further proceedings.

UNITED STATES v. WINDSOR
570 U. S. 744 (2013)

JUSTICE KENNEDY delivered the opinion of the Court.

Two women then resident in New York were married in a lawful ceremony in Ontario, Canada, in 2007. Edith Windsor and Thea Spyer returned to their home in New York City.

When Spyer died in 2009, she left her entire state to Windsor. Windsor sought to claim the estate tax exemption for surviving spouses. She was barred from doing so, however, by a federal law, the Defense of Marriage Act, which excludes a same-sex partner from the definition of "spouse" as that term is used in federal statutes. Windsor paid the taxes but filed suit to challenge the constitutionality of this provision. The United States District Court and the Court of Appeals ruled that this portion of the statute is unconstitutional and ordered the United States to pay Windsor a refund. This Court granted certiorari and now affirms the judgment in Windsor's favor.

[II]

It is appropriate to begin by addressing whether either the Government or BLAG, or both of them, were entitled to appeal to the Court of Appeals and later to seek certiorari and appear as parties here. There is no dispute that when this case was in the District Court it presented a concrete disagreement between opposing parties, a dispute suitable for judicial resolution. "[A] taxpayer has standing to challenge the collection of a specific tax assessment as unconstitutional; being forced to pay such a tax causes a real and immediate economic injury to the individual taxpayer." *Hein* v. *Freedom From Religion Foundation, Inc.*, 551 U. S. 587, 599 (2007) (plurality opinion) (emphasis deleted). Windsor suffered a redressable injury when she was required today estate taxes from which, in her view, she was exempt but for the alleged invalidity of §3 of DOMA.

The decision of the Executive not to defend the constitutionality of §3 in court while continuing to deny refunds and to assess deficiencies does introduce a complication. Even though the Executive's current position was announced before the District Court entered its judgment, the Government's agreement with Windsor's position would not have deprived the District Court of jurisdiction to entertain and resolve the refund suit; for her injury (failure to obtain a refund allegedly required by law) was concrete, persisting, and un-redressed. The Government's position—agreeing with Windsor's legal contention but refusing to give it effect—meant that there was a justiciable controversy between the parties, despite what the claimant would find to be an inconsistency in that stance. Windsor, the Government, BLAG, and the *amicus* appear to agree upon that point. The disagreement is over the standing of the parties, or aspiring parties, to take an appeal in the Court of Appeals and to appear as parties in further proceedings in this Court.

The *amicus'* position is that, given the Government's concession that §3 is unconstitutional, once the District Court ordered the refund the case should have ended; and the *amicus* argues the Court of Appeals should have dismissed the appeal. The *amicus* submits that once the President agreed with Windsor's legal position and the District Court issued its judgment, the parties were no longer adverse. From this standpoint the United States was a prevailing party below, just as Windsor was. Accordingly, the *amicus* reasons, it is inappropriate for this Court to grant certiorari and proceed to rule on the merits; for the United States seeks no redress from the judgment entered against it.

This position, however, elides the distinction between two principles: the jurisdictional requirements of Article III and the prudential limits on its exercise. See *Warth* v. *Seldin*, 422 U. S. 490, 498 (1975). The latter are "essentially matters of judicial self-governance." *Id.*, at 500. The Court has kept these two strands separate: "Article III standing, which enforces the Constitution's case-or controversy requirement, see *Lujan* v. *Defenders of Wildlife*, 504 U. S. 555, 559–562 (1992); and prudential standing, which embodies 'judicially self-imposed limits on the exercise of federal jurisdiction,' *Allen* [v. *Wright*,] 468 U. S. [737,] 751 [(1984)]." *Elk Grove Unified School Dist.* v. *Newdow*, 542 U. S. 1, 11–12 (2004).

The requirements of Article III standing are familiar:

> "First, the plaintiff must have suffered an 'injury in fact'—an invasion of a legally protected interest which is (a) concrete and particularized, and (b) 'actual or imminent, not "conjectural or hypothetical."' Second, there must be a causal connection between the injury and the conduct complained of—the injury has to be 'fairly . . . trace[able] to the challenged action of the defendant, and not . . . th[e] result [of] the independent action of some third party not before the court.' Third, it must be 'likely,' as opposed to merely 'speculative,' that the injury will be 'redressed by a favorable decision.'" *Lujan, supra,* at 560–561 (footnote and citations omitted).

Rules of prudential standing, by contrast, are more flexible "rule[s] . . . of federal appellate practice," *Deposit Guaranty Nat. Bank* v. *Roper,* 445 U. S. 326, 333 (1980), designed to protect the courts from "decid[ing] abstract questions of wide public significance even [when] other governmental institutions may be more competent to address the questions and even though judicial intervention may be unnecessary to protect individual rights." *Warth, supra,* at 500.

In this case the United States retains a stake sufficient to support Article III jurisdiction on appeal and in proceedings before this Court. The judgment in question orders the United States to pay Windsor the refund she seeks. An order directing the Treasury to pay money is "a real and immediate economic injury," *Hein,* 551 U. S., at 599, indeed as real and immediate as an order directing an individual to pay a tax. That the Executive may welcome this order to pay the refund if it is accompanied byte constitutional ruling it wants does not eliminate the injury to the national Treasury if payment is made, or to the taxpayer if it is not. The judgment orders the United States to pay money that it would not disburse but for the court's order. The Government of the United States has a valid legal argument that it is injured even if the Executive disagrees with §3 of DOMA, which results in Windsor's liability for the tax. Windsor's ongoing claim for funds that the United States refuses to pay thus establishes a controversy sufficient for Article III jurisdiction. It would be a different case if the Executive had taken the further step of paying Windsor the refund to which she was entitled under the District Court's ruling.

This Court confronted a comparable case in *INS* v. *Chadha,* 462 U. S. 919 (1983). A statute by its terms allowed one House of Congress to order the Immigration and Naturalization Service (INS) to deport the respondent Chadha. There, as here, the Executive determined that the statute was unconstitutional, and "the INS presented the Executive's views on the constitutionality of the House action to the Court of Appeals." *Id.,* at 930. The INS, however, continued to abide by the statute, and "the INS brief to the Court of Appeals did not alter the agency's decision to comply with the House action ordering deportation of Chadha." *Ibid.* This Court held "that the INS was sufficiently aggrieved by the Court of Appeals decision prohibiting it from taking action it would otherwise take," *ibid.,* regardless of whether the agency welcomed the judgment. The necessity of a "case or controversy" to satisfy Article III was defined as a requirement that the Court's "'decision will have real meaning: if we rule for Chadha, he will not be deported; if we uphold [the statute], the INS will execute its order and deport him.'" *Id.,* at 939–940 (quoting *Chadha* v. *INS,* 634 F. 2d 408, 419 (CA9 1980)). This conclusion was not dictum. It was a necessary predicate to the Court's holding that "prior to Congress' intervention, there was adequate Art. III adverseness." 462 U. S., at 939. The holdings of cases are instructive, and the words of *Chadha* make clear its holding that the refusal of the Executive to provide the relief sought suffices to preserve a justiciable dispute as required by Article III. In short, even where "the Government largely agree[s] with the opposing party on the merits of the controversy," there is sufficient adverseness and an "adequate basis for jurisdiction in the fact that the Government intended to enforce the challenged law against that party." *Id.*, at 940, n. 12.

It is true that "[a] party who receives all that he has sought generally is not aggrieved by the judgment affording the relief and cannot appeal from it." *Roper, supra,* at 333, see also *Camreta v. Greene,* 563 U. S. ___, ___ (2011) (slip op., at 8) ("As a matter of practice and prudence, we have generally declined to consider cases at the request of a prevailing party, even when the Constitution allowed us to do so"). But this rule "does not have its source in the jurisdictional limitations of Art. III. In an appropriate case, appeal may be permitted . . . at the behest of the party who has prevailed on the merits, so long as that party retains a stake in the appeal satisfying the requirements of Art. III." *Roper, supra,* at 333–334.

While these principles suffice to show that this case presents a justiciable controversy under Article III, the prudential problems inherent in the Executive's unusual position require some further discussion. The Executive's agreement with Windsor's legal argument raises the risk that instead of a "'real, earnest and vital controversy,'" the Court faces a "friendly, non-adversary, proceeding . . . [in which] 'a party beaten in the legislature [seeks to]transfer to the courts an inquiry as to the constitutionality of the legislative act.'" *Ashwander v. TVA,* 297 U. S. 288, 346 (1936) (Brandeis, J., concurring) (quoting *Chicago & Grand Trunk R. Co.* v. *Wellman,* 143 U. S. 339, 345 (1892)). Even when Article III permits the exercise of federal jurisdiction, prudential considerations demand that the Court insist upon "that concrete adverseness which sharpens the presentation of issues upon which the court so largely depends for illumination of difficult constitutional questions." *Baker* v. *Carr,* 369 U. S. 186, 204 (1962).

There are, of course, reasons to hear a case and issue a ruling even when one party is reluctant to prevail in its position. Unlike Article III requirements—which must be satisfied by the parties before judicial consideration is appropriate—the relevant prudential factors that counsel against hearing this case are subject to "countervailing considerations [that] may outweigh the concerns underlying the usual reluctance to exert judicial power." *Warth,* 422 U. S., at 500–501. One consideration is the extent to which adversarial presentation of the issues is assured by the participation of *amici curiae* prepared to defend with vigor the constitutionality of the legislative act. With respect to this prudential aspect of standing as well, the *Chadha* Court encountered a similar situation. It noted that "there may be prudential, as opposed to Art. III, concerns about sanctioning the adjudication of [this case]in the absence of any participant supporting the validity of [the statute]. The Court of Appeals properly dispelled any such concerns by inviting and accepting briefs from both Houses of Congress." 462 U. S., at 940. *Chadha* was not an anomaly in this respect. The Court adopts the practice of entertaining arguments made by an *amicus* when the Solicitor General confesses error with respect to a judgment below, even if the confession is in effect an admission that an Act of Congress is unconstitutional. See, *e.g., Dickerson* v. *United States,* 530 U. S. 428 (2000).

In the case now before the Court the attorneys for BLAG present a substantial argument for the constitutionality of §3 of DOMA. BLAG's sharp adversarial presentation of the issues satisfies the prudential concerns that otherwise might counsel against hearing an appeal from a decision with which the principal parties agree. Were this Court to hold that prudential rules require it to dismiss the case, and, in consequence, that the Court of Appeals erred in failing to dismiss it as well, extensive litigation would ensue. The district courts in 94 districts throughout the Nation would be without precedential guidance not only in tax refund suits but also in cases involving the whole of DOMA's sweep involving over 1,000 federal statutes and myriad of federal regulations. For instance, the opinion of the Court of Appeals for the First Circuit, addressing the validity of DOMA in a case involving regulations of the Department of Health and Human Services, likely would be vacated with instructions to dismiss, its ruling and guidance also then erased. See *Massachusetts* v. *United States Dept. of Health and Human Servs.*, 682 F. 3d 1 (CA1 2012). Rights and privileges of hundreds of thousands of persons would be adversely affected, pending a case in which all prudential concerns about justiciability are absent. That numerical prediction may not be certain, but it is certain that the cost in judicial resources and expense of litigation for all persons adversely affected would be immense. True, the very extent of DOMA's mandate means that at some point a case likely would arise without the prudential concerns raised here; but the costs, uncertainties, and alleged harm and injuries likely would continue for a time measured in years before the issue is resolved. In these unusual and urgent circumstances, the very term "prudential" counsels that it is a proper exercise of the Court's responsibility to take jurisdiction. For these reasons, the prudential and Article III requirements are met here; and, as a consequence, the Court need not decide whether BLAG would have standing to challenge the District Court's ruling and its affirmance in the Court of Appeals on BLAG's own authority.

The Court's conclusion that this petition may be heard on the merits does not imply that no difficulties would ensue if this were a common practice in ordinary cases. The Executive's failure to defend the constitutionality of an Act of Congress based on a constitutional theory not yet established in judicial decisions has created a procedural dilemma. On the one hand, as noted, the Government's agreement with Windsor raises questions about the propriety of entertaining a suit in which it seeks affirmance of an order invalidating a federal law and ordering the United States to pay money. On the other hand, if the Executive's agreement with a plaintiff that a law is unconstitutional is enough to preclude judicial review, then the Supreme Court's primary role in determining the constitutionality of a law that has inflicted real injury on a plaintiff who has brought a justiciable legal claim would become only secondary to the President's. This would undermine the clear dictate of the separation-of-powers principle that "when an Act of Congress is alleged to conflict with the Constitution, '[i]t is emphatically the province and duty of the judicial department to say what the law is.'" *Zivotofsky* v. *Clinton*, 566 U. S. ___, ___ (2012) (slip op., at 7) (quoting *Marbury* v. *Madison*, 1 Cranch 137, 177 (1803)). Similarly, with respect to the legislative power, when Congress has passed a statute and a President has signed it, it poses grave challenges to the separation of powers for the Executive at a particular moment to be able to nullify Congress' enactment solely on its own initiative and without any determination from the Court. The Court's jurisdictional holding, it must be underscored, does not mean the arguments for dismissing this dispute on prudential grounds lack substance. Yet the difficulty the Executive faces should be acknowledged. When the Executive makes a principled determination that a statute is unconstitutional, it faces a difficult choice. Still, there is no suggestion here that it is appro-priate for the Executive as a matter of course to challenge statutes in the judicial forum rather than making the case to Congress for their amendment or repeal. The integrity of the political process would be at risk if difficult constitutional issues were simply referred to the Court as a routine exercise. But this case is not routine. And the capable defense of the law by BLAG ensures that these prudential issues do not cloud the merits question, which is one of immediate importance to the Federal Government and to hundreds of thousands of persons. These circumstances support the Court's decision to proceed to the merits.

JUSTICE SCALIA, with whom JUSTICE THOMAS joins, and with whom THE CHIEF JUSTICE joins as to Part I, dissenting.

I

A

The Court is eager—*hungry*—to tell everyone its view of the legal question at the heart of this case. Standing in the way is an obstacle, a technicality of little interest to anyone but the people of We the People, who created it as a barrier against judges' intrusion into their lives. They gave judges, in Article III, only the "judicial Power," a power to decide not abstract questions but real, concrete "Cases" and "Controversies." Yet the plaintiff and the Government agree entirely on what should happen in this lawsuit. They agree that the court below got it right; and they agreed in the court below that the court below that one got it right as well. What, then, are we *doing* here?

The answer lies at the heart of the jurisdictional portion of today's opinion, where a single sentence lays bare the majority's vision of our role. The Court says that we have the power to decide this case because if we did not, then our "primary role in determining the constitutionality of a law" (at least one that "has inflicted real injury on a plaintiff") would "become only secondary to the President's." *Ante,* at 12. But wait, the reader wonders—Windsor won below, and so *cured* her injury, and the President was glad to see it. True, says the majority, but judicial review must march on regardless, lest we "undermine the clear dictate of the separation-of-powers principle that when an Act of Congress is alleged to conflict with the Constitution, it is emphatically the province and duty of the judicial department to say what the law is." *Ibid.* (internal quotation marks and brackets omitted).

That is jaw-dropping. It is an assertion of judicial supremacy over the people's Representatives in Congress and the Executive. It envisions a Supreme Court standing (or rather enthroned) at the apex of government, empowered to decide all constitutional questions, always and everywhere "primary" in its role.

This image of the Court would have been unrecognizable to those who wrote and ratified our national charter. They knew well the dangers of "primary" power, and so created branches of government that would be "perfectly coordinate by the terms of their common commission," none of which branches could "pretend to an exclusive or superior right of settling the boundaries between their respective powers." The Federalist, No. 49, p. 314 (C. Rossiter ed. 1961) (J. Madison). The people did this to protect themselves. They did it to guard their right to self-rule against the black-robed supremacy that today's majority finds so attractive. So it was that Madison could confidently state, with no fear of contradiction, that there was nothing of "greater intrinsic value" or "stamped with the authority of more enlightened patrons of liberty" than a government of separate and coordinate powers. *Id.,* No. 47, at 301.

For this reason we are quite forbidden to say what the law is whenever (as today's opinion asserts) "'an Act of Congress is alleged to conflict with the Constitution.'" *Ante,* at 12. We can do so only when that allegation will determine the outcome of a lawsuit, and is contradicted byte other party. The "judicial Power" is not, as the majority believes, the power "'to say what the law is,'" *ibid.,* giving the Supreme Court the "primary role in determining the constitutionality of laws." The majority must have in mind one of the foreign constitutions that pronounces such primacy for its constitutional court and allows that primacy to be exercised in contexts other than a law suit. See, *e.g.,* Basic Law for the Federal Republic of Germany, Art. 93. The judicial power as Americans have understood it (and their English ancestors before them) is the power to adjudicate, with conclusive effect, disputed government claims (civil or criminal) against private persons, and disputed claims by private persons against the government or other private persons. Sometimes (though not always) the parties before the court disagree not with regard to the facts of their case (or not *only* with regard to the facts) but with regard to the applicable law—in which event (and *only* in which event) it becomes the "'province and duty of the judicial department to say what the law is.'" *Ante,* at 12.

In other words, declaring the compatibility of state or federal laws with the Constitution is not only not the "primary role" of this Court, it is not a separate, free standing role *at all.* We perform that role incidentally—by accident, as it were—when that is necessary to resolve the dispute before us. Then, and only then, does it become "'the province and duty of the judicial department to say what the law is.'" That is why, in 1793, we politely declined the Washington Administration's request to "say what the law is" on a particular treaty matter that was not the subject of a concrete legal controversy. 3 Correspondence and Public Papers of John Jay 486–489 (H.Johnston ed. 1893). And that is why, as our opinions have said, some questions of law will *never* be presented to this Court, because there will never be anyone with standing to bring a lawsuit. See *Schlesinger* v. *Reservists Comm. to Stop the War*, 418 U. S. 208, 227 (1974); *United States* v. *Richardson*, 418 U. S. 166, 179 (1974). As Justice Brandeis put it, we cannot "pass upon the constitutionality of legislation in a friendly, non-adversary, proceeding"; absent a "'real, earnest and vital controversy between individuals,'" we have neither any work to do nor any power to do it. *Ashwander* v. *TVA*, 297 U. S. 288, 346 (1936) (concurring opinion) (quoting *Chicago & Grand Trunk R. Co.*v. *Wellman*, 143 U. S. 339, 345 (1892)). Our authority begins and ends with the need to adjudge the rights of an injured party who stands before us seeking redress. *Lujan* v. *Defenders of Wildlife*, 504 U. S. 555, 560 (1992).

That is completely absent here. Windsor's injury was cured by the judgment in her favor. And while, in ordinary circumstances, the United States is injured by a directive to pay a tax refund, this suit is far from ordinary. Whatever injury the United States has suffered will surely not be redressed by the action that it, as a litigant, asks us to take. The final sentence of the Solicitor General's brief on the merits reads: "For the foregoing reasons, the judgment of the court of appeals *should be affirmed.*" Brief for United States (merits) 54 (emphasis added). That will not cure the Government's injury, but carve it into stone. One could spend many fruitless afternoons ransacking our library for any other petitioner's brief seeking an affirmance of the judgment against it. What the petitioner United States asks us to do in the case before us is exactly what the respondent Windsor asks us to do: not to provide relief from the judgment below but to say that that judgment was correct. And the same was true in the Court of Appeals: Neither party sought to undo the judgment for Windsor, and so that court should have dismissed the appeal (just as we should dismiss) for lack of jurisdiction. Since both parties agreed with the judgment of the District Court for the Southern District of New York, the suit should have ended there. The further proceedings have been a contrivance, having no object in mind except to elevate a District Court judgment that has no precedential effect in other courts, to one that has precedential effect throughout the Second Circuit, and then (in this Court) precedential effect throughout the United States.

We have never before agreed to speak—to "say what the law is"—where there is no controversy before us. In the more than two centuries that this Court has existed as an institution, we have never suggested that we have the power to decide a question when every party agrees with both its nominal opponent *and the court below* on that question's answer. The United States reluctantly conceded that at oral argument. See Tr. of Oral Arg. 19–20.

The closest we have ever come to what the Court blesses today was our opinion in *INS* v. *Chadha*, 462 U. S. 919 (1983). But in that case, two parties to the litigation disagreed with the position of the United States and with the court below: the House and Senate, which had intervened in the case. Because *Chadha* concerned the validity of a mode of congressional action—the one-house legislative veto—the House and Senate were threatened with destruction of what they claimed to be one of their institutional powers.

The Executive choosing not to defend that power,[11] we permitted the House and Senate to intervene. Nothing like that is present here.

To be sure, the Court in *Chadha* said that statutory aggrieved-party status was "not altered by the fact that the Executive may agree with the holding that the statute in question is unconstitutional." *Id.,* at 930–931. But in a footnote to that statement, the Court acknowledged Article III's separate requirement of a "justiciable case or controversy," and stated that *this* requirement was satisfied "because of the presence of the two Houses of Congress as adverse parties." *Id.,* at 931, n. 6. Later in its opinion, the *Chadha* Court remarked that the United States' announced intention to enforce the statute also sufficed to permit judicial review, even absent congressional participation. *Id.,* at 939. That remark is true, as a description of the judicial review conducted in the Court of Appeals, where the Houses of Congress had not intervened. (The case originated in the Court of Appeals, since it sought review of agency action under 8 U. S. C. §1105a(a) (1976 ed.).) There, absent a judgment setting aside the INS order, Chadha faced deportation. This passage of our opinion seems to be addressing that initial standing in the Court of Appeals, as indicated by its quotation from the lower court's opinion, 462 U. S., at 939–940. But if it was addressing standing to pursue the appeal, the remark was both the purest dictum (as congressional intervention at that point made the required adverseness "beyond doubt," *id.,* at 939), and quite incorrect. When a private party has a judicial decree safely in hand to prevent his injury, additional judicial action requires that a party injured by the decree *seek to undo it.* In *Chadha,* the intervening House and Senate fulfilled that requirement. Here no one does.

The majority's discussion of the requirements of Article III bears no resemblance to our jurisprudence. It accuses the *amicus* (appointed to argue against our jurisdiction) of "elid[ing] the distinction between . . . the jurisdictional requirements of Article III and the prudential limits on its exercise." *Ante,* at 6. It then proceeds to call the requirement of adverseness a "prudential" aspect of standing. *Of standing.* That is incomprehensible. A plaintiff (or appellant) can have all the standing in the world—satisfying all three standing requirements of *Lujan* that the majority so carefully quotes, *ante,* at 7—and yet no Article III controversy may be before the court. Article III requires not just a plaintiff (or appellant) who has standing to complain but *an opposing party* who denies the validity of the complaint. It is not the *amicus* that has done the eliding of distinctions, but the majority, calling the quite separate Article III requirement of adverseness between the parties an element (which it then pronounces a "prudential" element) of standing. The question here is not whether, as the majority puts it, "the United States retains a stake sufficient to support Article III jurisdiction," *ibid.* the question is whether there is any controversy (which requires *contradiction*) between the United States and Ms. Windsor. There is not.

I find it wryly amusing that the majority seeks to dismiss the requirement of party-adverseness as nothing more than a "prudential" aspect of the sole Article III requirement of standing. (Relegating a jurisdictional requirement to "prudential" status is a wondrous device, enabling courts to ignore the requirement whenever they believe it "prudent"—which is to say, a good idea.) Half a century ago, a Court similarly bent upon announcing its view regarding the constitutionality of a federal statute achieved that goal by effecting

---

[11] There the Justice Department's refusal to defend the legislation was in accord with its longstanding (and entirely reasonable) practice of declining to defend legislation that in its view infringes upon Presidential powers. There is no justification for the Justice Department's abandoning the law in the present case. The majority opinion makes a point of scolding the President for his "failure to defend the constitutionality of an Act of Congress based on a constitutional theory not yet established in judicial decisions," *ante,* at 12. But the rebuke is tongue in-cheek, for the majority gladly gives the President what he wants. Contrary to all precedent, it decides this case (and even decides it the way the President wishes) *despite* his abandonment of the defense and the consequent absence of a case or controversy.

a remarkably similar *but completely opposite* distortion of the principles limiting our jurisdiction. The Court's notorious opinion in *Flast* v. *Cohen*, 392 U. S. 83, 98–101 (1968), held that *standing* was merely an element (which it pronounced to be a "prudential" element) of the sole Article III requirement of *adverseness*. We have been living with the chaos created by that power-grabbing decision ever since, see *Hein* v. *Freedom From Religion Foundation, Inc.*, 551 U. S. 587 (2007), as we will have to live with the chaos created by this one.

[It] may be argued that if what we say is true some Presidential determinations that statutes are unconstitutional will not be subject to our review. That is as it should be, when both the President and the plaintiff agree that the statute is unconstitutional. Where the Executive is enforcing an unconstitutional law, suit will of course lie; but if, in that suit, the Executive admits the unconstitutionality of the law, the litigation should end in an order or a consent decree enjoining enforcement. This suit saw the light of day only because the President enforced the Act (and thus gave Windsor standing to sue) even though he believed it unconstitutional. He could have equally chosen (more appropriately, some would say) neither to enforce nor to defend the statute he believed to be unconstitutional, see Presidential Authority to Decline to Execute Unconstitutional Statutes, 18 Op. Off. Legal Counsel 199(Nov. 2, 1994)—in which event Windsor would not have been injured, the District Court could not have refereed this friendly scrimmage, and the Executive's determination of unconstitutionality would have escaped this Court's desire to blurt out its view of the law. The matter would have been left, as so many matters ought to be left, to a tug of war between the President and the Congress, which has innumerable means (up to and including impeachment) of compelling the President to enforce the laws it has written. Or the President could have evaded presentation of the constitutional issue to this Court simply by declining to appeal the District Court and Court of Appeals dispositions he agreed with. Be sure of this much: If a President wants to insulate his judgment of unconstitutionality from our review, he can. What the views urged in this dissent produce is not insulation from judicial review but insulation from Executive contrivance.

The majority brandishes the famous sentence from *Marbury* v. *Madison*, 1 Cranch 137, 177 (1803) that "[i]t is emphatically the province and duty of the judicial department to say what the law is." *Ante*, at 12 (internal quotation marks omitted). But that sentence neither says nor implies that it is *always* the province and duty of the Court to say what the law is—much less that its responsibility in that regard is a "primary" one. The very next sentence of Chief Justice Marshall's opinion makes the crucial qualification that today's majority ignores: "*Those who apply the rule to particular cases*, must of necessity expound and interpret that rule." 1 Cranch, at 177 (emphasis added). Only when a "particular case" is before us—that is, a controversy that it is our business to resolve under Article III—do we have the province and duty to pronounce the law. For the views of our early Court more precisely addressing the question before us here, the majority ought instead to have consulted the opinion of Chief Justice Taney in *Lord* v. *Veazie*, 8 How. 251 (1850):

> "The objection in the case before us is . . . that the plaintiff and defendant have the same interest, and that interest adverse and in conflict with the interest of third persons, whose rights would be seriously affected if the question of law was decided in the manner that both of the parties to this suit desire it to be.

> "A judgment entered under such circumstances, and for such purposes, is a mere form. The whole proceeding was in contempt of the court, and highly reprehensible . . . . A judgment in form, thus procured, in the eye of the law is no judgment of the court. It is a nullity, and no writ of error will lie upon it. This writ is, therefore, dismissed." *Id.*, at 255–256.

There is, in the words of *Marbury,* no "necessity [to] expound and interpret" the law in this case; just a desire to place this Court at the center of the Nation's life. 1 Cranch, at 177.

[JUSTICE] ALITO, with whom JUSTICE THOMAS joins as to Parts II and III, dissenting.

I

I turn first to the question of standing. In my view, the United States clearly is not a proper petitioner in this case. The United States does not ask us to overturn the judgment of the court below or to alter that judgment in any way. Quite to the contrary, the United States argues emphatically in favor of the correctness of that judgment. We have never before reviewed a decision at the sole behest of a party that took such a position, and to do so would be to render an advisory opinion, in violation of Article III's dictates. For the reasons given in JUSTICE SCALIA's dissent, I do not find the Court's arguments to the contrary to be persuasive.

Whether the Bipartisan Legal Advisory Group of the House of Representatives (BLAG) has standing to petition is a much more difficult question. It is also a significantly closer question than whether the intervenors in *Hollingsworth* v. *Perry, ante,* p.___—which the Court also decides today—have standing to appeal. It is remarkable that the Court has simultaneously decided that the United States, which "receive[d] all that [it] ha[d] sought" below, *Deposit Guaranty Nat. Bank* v. *Roper,* 445 U. S. 326, 333 (1980), is a proper petitioner in this case but that the intervenors in *Hollingsworth,* who represent the party that lost in the lower court, are not. In my view, both the *Hollingsworth* intervenors and BLAG have standing.[12] A party invoking the Court's authority has a sufficient stake to permit it to appeal when it has "'suffered an injury in fact' that is caused by 'the conduct complained of' and that 'will be redressed by a favorable decision.'" *Camreta* v. *Greene,* 563 U. S. ___, ___ (2011) (slip op., at 5) (quoting *Lujan* v. *Defenders of Wildlife,* 504 U. S. 555, 560–561 (1992)). In the present case, the House of Representatives, which has authorized BLAG to represent its interests in this matter, suffered just such an injury.

In *INS* v. *Chadha,* 462 U. S. 919 (1983), the Court held that the two Houses of Congress were "proper parties" to file a petition in defense of the constitutionality of the one-house veto statute, *id.,* at 930, n. 5 (internal quotation marks omitted). Accordingly, the Court granted and decided petitions by both the Senate and the House, in addition to the Executive's petition. *Id.,* at 919, n.*. That the two Houses had standing to petition is not surprising: The Court of Appeals' decision in *Chadha,* by holding the one-house veto to be unconstitutional, had limited Congress' power to legislate. In discussing Article III standing, the Court suggested that Congress suffered a similar injury whenever federal legislation it had passed was struck down, noting that it had "long held that Congress is the proper party to defend the validity of a statute when an agency of government, as a defendant charged with enforcing the statute, agrees with plaintiffs that the statute is inapplicable or unconstitutional." *Id.,* at 940.

---

12 Our precedents make clear that, in order to support our jurisdiction, BLAG must demonstrate that it had Article III standing in its own right, quite apart from its status as an intervenor. See *Diamond* v. *Charles,* 476 U. S. 54, 68 (1986) ("Although intervenors are considered parties entitled, among other things, to seek review by this Court, an intervenor's right to continue a suit in the absence of the party on whose side intervention was permitted is contingent upon a showing by the intervenor that he fulfills the requirements of Art. III" (citation omitted)); *Arizonans for Official English* v. *Arizona,* 520 U. S. 43, 64 (1997) ("Standing to defend on appeal in the place of an original defendant, no less than standing to sue, demands that the litigant possess a direct stake in the outcome" (internal quotation marks omitted)); *id.,* at 65 ("An intervenor cannot step into the shoes of the original party unless the intervenor independently fulfills the requirements of Article III" (internal quotation marks omitted)).

The United States attempts to distinguish *Chadha* on the ground that it "involved an unusual statute that vested the House and the Senate themselves each with special procedural rights—namely, the right effectively to veto Executive action." Brief for United States (jurisdiction) 36. But that is a distinction without a difference: just as the Court of Appeals decision that the *Chadha* Court affirmed impaired Congress' power by striking down throne-house veto, so the Second Circuit's decision here impairs Congress' legislative power by striking down an Act of Congress. The United States has not explained why the fact that the impairment at issue in *Chadha* was "special" or "procedural" has any relevance to whether Congress suffered an injury. Indeed, because legislating is Congress' central function, any impairment of that function is a more grievous injury than the impairment of a procedural add-on.

The Court's decision in *Coleman* v. *Miller*, 307 U. S. 433 (1939), bolsters this conclusion. In *Coleman*, we held that a group of state senators had standing to challenge a lower court decision approving the procedures used to ratify an amendment to the Federal Constitution. We reasoned that the senators' votes—which would otherwise have carried the day—were nullified by that action. See *id.,* at 438 ("Here, the plaintiffs include twenty senators, whose votes against ratification have been overridden and virtually held for naught although if they are right in their contentions their votes would have been sufficient to defeat ratification. We think that these senators have a plain, direct and adequate interest in maintaining the effectiveness of their votes"); *id.*, at 446 ("[W]e find no departure from principle in recognizing in the instant case that at least the twenty senators whose votes, if their contention were sustained, would have been sufficient to defeat the resolution ratifying the proposed constitutional amendment, have an interest in the controversy which, treated by the state court as a basis for entertaining and deciding the federal questions, is sufficient to give the Court jurisdiction to review that decision"). By striking down §3 of DOMA as unconstitutional, the Second Circuit effectively "held for naught" an Act of Congress. Just as the state-senator-petitioners in *Coleman* were necessary parties to the amendment's ratification, the House of Representatives was a necessary party to DOMA's passage; indeed, the House's vote would have been sufficient to prevent DOMA's repeal if the Court had not chosen to execute that repeal judicially.

Both the United States and the Court-appointed *amicus* err in arguing that *Raines* v. *Byrd*, 521 U. S. 811 (1997), is to the contrary. In that case, the Court held that Members of Congress who had voted "nay" to the Line Item Veto Act did not have standing to challenge that statute in federal court. *Raines* is inapposite for two reasons. First, *Raines* dealt with individual Members of Congress and specifically pointed to the individual Members' lack of institutional endorsement as a sign of their standing problem: "We attach some importance to the fact that appellees have not been authorized to represent their respective Houses of Congress in this action, and indeed both Houses actively oppose their suit." *Id.*, at 829; see also *ibid.*, n.10 (citing cases to the effect that "members of collegial bodies do not have standing to perfect an appeal the body itself has declined to take" (internal quotation marks omitted)).

Second, the Members in *Raines*—unlike the state senators in *Coleman*—were not the pivotal figures whose votes would have caused the Act to fail absent some challenged action. Indeed, it is telling that *Raines* characterized *Coleman* as standing "for the proposition that legislators whose votes would have been sufficient to defeat (or enact) a specific legislative Act have standing to sue if that legislative action goes into effect (or does not go into effect), on the ground that their votes have been completely nullified." 521 U. S., at 823. Here, by contrast, passage by the House was needed for DOMA to become law. U. S. Const., Art. I, §7 (bicameralism and presentment requirements for legislation).

I appreciate the argument that the Constitution confers on the President alone the authority to defend federal law in litigation, but in my view, as I have explained, that argument is contrary to the Court's holding in *Chadha*, and it is certainly contrary to the *Chadha* Court's endorsement of the principle that "Congress is the proper party to defend the validity of a statute" when the Executive refuses to do so on constitutional grounds. 462 U. S., at 940. See also 2 U. S. C. §288h(7) (Senate Legal Counsel shall defend the constitutionality of Acts of Congress when placed in issue). Accordingly, in the narrow category of cases in which a court strikes down an Act of Congress and the Executive declines to defend the Act, Congress both has standing to defend the undefended statute and is a proper party to do so.

HOLLINGSWORTH v. PERRY
570 U. S. 693 (2013)

CHIEF JUSTICE ROBERTS delivered the opinion of the Court.

The public is currently engaged in an active political debate over whether same-sex couples should be allowed to marry. That question has also given rise to litigation. In this case, petitioners, who oppose same-sex marriage, ask us to decide whether the Equal Protection Clause "prohibits the State of California from defining marriages the union of a man and a woman." Pet. for Cert. i. Respondents, same-sex couples who wish to marry, view the issue in somewhat different terms: For them, it is whether California—having previously recognized the right of same-sex couples to marry—may reverse that decision through a referendum.

Federal courts have authority under the Constitution to answer such questions only if necessary to do so in the course of deciding an actual "case" or "controversy." As used in the Constitution, those words do not include every sort of dispute, but only those "historically viewed as capable of resolution through the judicial process." *Flast* v. *Cohen*, 392 U. S. 83, 95 (1968). This is an essential limit on our power: It ensures that we act *as judges*, and do not engage in policymaking properly left to elected representatives.

For there to be such a case or controversy, it is not enough that the party invoking the power of the court have a keen interest in the issue. That party must also have "standing," which requires, among other things, that it have suffered a concrete and particularized injury. Because we find that petitioners do not have standing, we have no authority to decide this case on the merits, and neither did the Ninth Circuit.

I

In 2008, the California Supreme Court held that limiting the official designation of marriage to opposite-sex couples violated the equal protection clause of the California Constitution. *In re Marriage Cases*, 43 Cal. 4th 757, 183 P. 3d 384. Later that year, California voters passed the ballot initiative at the center of this dispute, known as Proposition 8. That proposition amended the California Constitution to provide that "[o]nly marriage between a man and a woman is valid or recognized in California." Cal. Const., Art. I, §7.5. Shortly thereafter, the California Supreme Court rejected a procedural challenge to the amendment, and held that the Proposition was properly enacted under California law. *Strauss* v. *Horton*, 46 Cal. 4th 364, 474–475, 207 P. 3d 48, 122 (2009). According to the California Supreme Court, Proposition 8 created a "narrow and limited exception" to the state constitutional rights otherwise guaranteed to same-sex couples. *Id.,* at 388, 207 P. 3d, at 61. Under California law, same-sex couples have a right to enter into relationships recognized by the State as "domestic partnerships," which carry "the same rights, protections, and benefits, and shall be subject to the same responsibilities, obligations, and duties under law . . . as are granted to and imposed upon spouses." Cal. Fam. Code Ann. §297.5(a) (West 2004). In *In re Marriage Cases*, the

California Supreme Court concluded that the California Constitution further guarantees same-sex couples "all of the constitutionally based incidents of marriage," including the right to have that marriage "officially recognized" as such by the State. 43 Cal. 4th, at 829, 183 P. 3d, at 433–434. Proposition 8, the court explained in *Strauss*, left those rights largely undisturbed, reserving only "the official *designation* of the term 'marriage' for the union of opposite-sex couples as a matter of state constitutional law." 46 Cal. 4th, at 388, 207 P. 3d, at 61.

Respondents, two same-sex couples who wish to marry, filed suit in federal court, challenging Proposition 8 under the Due Process and Equal Protection Clauses of the Fourteenth Amendment to the Federal Constitution. The complaint named as defendants California's Governor, attorney general, and various other state and local officials responsible for enforcing California's marriage laws. Those officials refused to defend the law, although they have continued to enforce it throughout this litigation. The District Court allowed petitioners—the official proponents of the initiative, see Cal. Elec. Code Ann. §342 (West 2003)—to intervene to defend it. After a 12-day bench trial, the District Court declared Proposition 8 unconstitutional, permanently enjoining the California officials named as defendants from enforcing the law, and "directing the official defendants that all persons under their control or supervision" shall not enforce it. *Perry* v. *Schwarzenegger*, 704 F. Supp. 2d 921, 1004 (ND Cal. 2010).

Those officials elected not to appeal the District Court order. When petitioners did, the Ninth Circuit asked them to address "why this appeal should not be dismissed for lack of Article III standing." *Perry* v. *Schwarzenegger*, Civ. No. 10–16696 (CA9, Aug. 16, 2010), p. 2. After briefing and argument, the Ninth Circuit certified a question to the California Supreme Court:

> "Whether under Article II, Section 8 of the California Constitution, or otherwise under California law, the official proponents of an initiative measure possess either a particularized interest in the initiative's validity or the authority to assert the State's interest in the initiative's validity, which would enable them to defend the constitutionality of the initiative upon its adoption or appeal a judgment invalidating the initiative, when the public officials charged with that duty refuse to do so." *Perry* v. *Schwarzenegger*, 628 F. 3d 1191, 1193 (2011).

The California Supreme Court agreed to decide the certified question, and answered in the affirmative. Without addressing whether the proponents have a particularized interest of their own in an initiative's validity, the court concluded that "[i]n a postelection challenge to a voter-approved initiative measure, the official proponents of the initiative are authorized under California law to appear and assert the state's interest in the initiative's validity and to appeal a judgment invalidating the measure when the public officials who ordinarily defend the measure or appeal such a judgment decline to do so." *Perry* v. *Brown*, 52 Cal. 4th 1116, 1127, 265 P. 3d 1002, 1007 (2011).

Relying on that answer, the Ninth Circuit concluded that petitioners had standing under federal law to defend the constitutionality of Proposition 8. California, it reasoned, "'has standing to defend the constitutionality of its [laws],'" and States have the "prerogative, as independent sovereigns, to decide for themselves who may assert their interests." *Perry* v. *Brown*, 671 F. 3d 1052, 1070, 1071 (2012) (quoting *Diamond* v. *Charles*, 476 U. S. 54, 62 (1986)). "All a federal court need determine is that the state has suffered a harm sufficient to confer standing and that the party seeking to invoke the jurisdiction of the court is authorized by the state to represent its interest in remedying that harm." 671 F. 3d, at 1072.

On the merits, the Ninth Circuit affirmed the District Court. The court held the Proposition unconstitutional under the rationale of our decision in *Romer* v. *Evans*, 517 U.

S. 620 (1996). 671 F. 3d, at 1076, 1095. In the Ninth Circuit's view, *Romer* stands for the proposition that "the Equal Protection Clause requires the state to have a legitimate reason for withdrawing a right or benefit *from one group but not others*, whether or not it was required to confer that right or benefit in the first place." 671 F. 3d, at 1083–1084. The Ninth Circuit concluded that "taking away the official designation" of "marriage" from same-sex couples, while continuing to afford those couples all the rights and obligations of marriage, did not further any legitimate interest of the State. *Id.,* at 1095. Proposition 8, in the court's view, violated the Equal Protection Clause because it served no purpose "but to impose on gays and lesbians, through the public law, a majority's private disapproval of them and their relationships." *Ibid.*

We granted certiorari to review that determination, and directed that the parties also brief and argue "Whether petitioners have standing under Article III, §2, of the Constitution in this case." 568 U. S. ___ (2012).

II

Article III of the Constitution confines the judicial power of federal courts to deciding actual "Cases" or "Controversies." §2. One essential aspect of this requirement is that any person invoking the power of a federal court must demonstrate standing to do so. This requires the litigant to prove that he has suffered a concrete and particularized injury that is fairly traceable to the challenged conduct, and is likely to be redressed by a favorable judicial decision. *Lujan* v. *Defenders of Wildlife*, 504 U. S. 555, 560– 561 (1992). In other words, for a federal court to have authority under the Constitution to settle a dispute, the party before it must seek a remedy for a personal and tangible harm. "The presence of a disagreement, however sharp and acrimonious it may be, is insufficient by itself to meet Art. III's requirements." *Diamond, supra,* at 62.

The doctrine of standing, we recently explained, "serves to prevent the judicial process from being used to usurp the powers of the political branches." *Clapper* v. *Amnesty Int'l USA*, 568 U. S. ___, ___ (2013) (slip op., at 9). In light of this "overriding and time-honored concern about keeping the Judiciary's power within its proper constitutional sphere, we must put aside the natural urge to proceed directly to the merits of [an] important dispute and to 'settle' it for the sake of convenience and efficiency." *Raines* v. *Byrd*, 521 U. S. 811, 820 (1997) (footnote omitted).

Most standing cases consider whether a plaintiff has satisfied the requirement when filing suit, but Article III demands that an "actual controversy" persist throughout all stages of litigation. *Already, LLC* v. *Nike, Inc.*, 568 U. S. ___, ___ (2013) (slip op., at 4) (internal quotation marks omitted). That means that standing "must be met by persons seeking appellate review, just as it must be met by persons appearing in courts of first instance." *Arizonans for Official English* v. *Arizona*, 520 U. S. 43, 64 (1997). We therefore must decide whether petitioners had standing to appeal the District Court's order.

Respondents initiated this case in the District Court against the California officials responsible for enforcing Proposition 8. The parties do not contest that respondents had Article III standing to do so. Each couple expressed a desire to marry and obtain "official sanction" from the State, which was unavailable to them given the declaration in Proposition 8 that "marriage" in California is solely between a man and a woman. App. 59.

After the District Court declared Proposition 8 unconstitutional and enjoined the state officials named as defendants from enforcing it, however, the inquiry under Article III changed. Respondents no longer had any injury to redress—they had won—and the state officials chose not to appeal.

The only individuals who sought to appeal that order were petitioners, who had intervened in the District Court. But the District Court had not ordered them to do or refrain from doing anything. To have standing, a litigant must seek relief for an injury that affects him in a "personal and individual way." *Defenders of Wildlife, supra,* at 560, n. 1. He must possess a "direct stake in the outcome" of the case. *Arizonans for Official English, supra,* at 64 (internal quotation marks omitted). Here, however, petitioners had no "direct stake" in the outcome of their appeal. Their only interest in having the District Court order reversed was to vindicate the constitutional validity of a generally applicable California law.

We have repeatedly held at such a "generalized grievance," no matter how sincere, is insufficient to confer standing. A litigant "raising only a generally available grievance about government—claiming only harm to his and every citizen's interest in proper application of the Constitution and laws, and seeking relief that no more directly and tangibly benefits him than it does the public at large—does not state an Article III case or controversy." *Defenders of Wildlife, supra,* at 573–574; see *Lance* v. *Coffman,* 549 U. S. 437, 439 (2007) (*per curiam*) ("Our refusal to serve as a forum for generalized grievances has a lengthy pedigree."); *Allen* v. *Wright,* 468 U. S. 737, 754 (1984) ("an asserted right to have the Government act in accordance with law is not sufficient, standing alone, to confer jurisdiction on a federal court"); *Massachusetts* v. *Mellon,* 262 U. S. 447, 488 (1923) ("The party who invokes the [judicial] power must be able to show . . . that he has sustained or is immediately in danger of sustaining some direct injury . . . and not merely that he suffers in some indefinite way in common with people generally.").

Petitioners argue that the California Constitution and its election laws give them a "'unique,' 'special,' and 'distinct' role in the initiative process—one 'involving both authority and responsibilities that differ from other supporters of the measure.'" Reply Brief 5 (quoting 52 Cal. 4th, at 1126, 1142, 1160, 265 P. 3d, at 1006, 1017–1018, 1030). True enough—but only when it comes to the process of enacting the law. Upon submitting the proposed initiative to the attorney general, petitioners became the official "proponents" of Proposition 8. Cal. Elec. Code Ann. §342 (West 2003). As such, they were responsible for collecting the signatures required to qualify the measure for the ballot. §§9607–9609. After those signatures were collected, the proponents alone had the right to file the measure with election officials to put it on the ballot. §9032. Petitioners also possessed control over the arguments in favor of the initiative that would appear in California's ballot pamphlets. §§9064, 9065, 9067, 9069.

But once Proposition 8 was approved by the voters, the measure became "a duly enacted constitutional amendment or statute." 52 Cal. 4th, at 1147, 265 P. 3d, at 1021. Petitioners have no role—special or otherwise—in the enforcement of Proposition 8. See *id.,* at 1159, 265 P. 3d, at 1029 (petitioners do not "possess any official authority . . . to directly enforce the initiative measure in question"). They therefore have no "personal stake" in defending its enforcement that is distinguishable from the general interest of every citizen of California. *Defenders of Wildlife, supra,* at 560–561.

Article III standing "is not to be placed in the hands of 'concerned bystanders,' who will use it simply as a 'vehicle for the vindication of value interests.'" *Diamond,* 476 U. S., at 62. No matter how deeply committed petitioners may be to upholding Proposition 8 or how "zealous [their]advocacy," *post,* at 4 (KENNEDY, J., dissenting), that is not a "particularized" interest sufficient to create a case or controversy under Article III. *Defenders of Wildlife,* 504 U. S., at 560, and n. 1; see *Arizonans for Official English,* 520 U. S., at 65 ("Nor has this Court ever identified initiative proponents as Article-III-qualified defenders of the measures they advocated."); *Don't Bankrupt Washington Committee* v. *Continental Ill. Nat. Bank & Trust Co. of Chicago,* 460 U. S. 1077 (1983) (summarily dismissing, for lack of standing, appeal by an initiative proponent from a decision holding the initiative unconstitutional).

III

A

Without a judicially cognizable interest of their own, petitioners attempt to invoke that of someone else. They assert that even if *they* have no cognizable interest in appealing the District Court's judgment, the State of California does, and they may assert that interest on the State's behalf. It is, however, a "fundamental restriction on our authority" that "[i]n the ordinary course, a litigant must assert his or her own legal rights and interests, and cannot rest a claim to relief on the legal rights or interests of third parties." *Powers* v. *Ohio*, 499 U. S. 400, 410 (1991). There are "certain, limited exceptions" to that rule. *Ibid.* But even when we have allowed litigants to assert the interests of others, the litigants themselves still "must have suffered an injury in fact, thus giving [them] a sufficiently concrete interest in the outcome of the issue in dispute." *Id.,* at 411 (internal quotation marks omitted).

For the reasons we have explained, petitioners have likewise not suffered an injury in fact, and therefore would ordinarily have no standing to assert the State's interests.

B

Petitioners contend that this case is different, because the California Supreme Court has determined that they are "authorized under California law to appear and assert the state's interest" in the validity of Proposition 8. 52 Cal. 4th, at 1127, 265 P. 3d, at 1007. The court below agreed: "All a federal court need determine is that the state has suffered a harm sufficient to confer standing and that the party seeking to invoke the jurisdiction of the court is authorized by the state to represent its interest in remedying that harm." 671 F. 3d, at 1072. As petitioners put it, they "need no more show a personal injury, separate from the State's indisputable interest in the validity of its law, than would California's Attorney General or did the legislative leaders held to have standing in *Karcher v. May,* 484 U. S. 72 (1987)." Reply Brief 6.

In *Karcher,* we held that two New Jersey state legislators—Speaker of the General Assembly Alan Karcher and President of the Senate Carmen Orechio—could intervene in a suit against the State to defend the constitutionality of a New Jersey law, after the New Jersey attorney general had declined to do so. 484 U. S., at 75, 81–82. "Since the New Jersey Legislature had authority under state law to represent the State's interests in both the District Courtland the Court of Appeals," we held that the Speaker and the President, in their official capacities, could vindicate that interest in federal court on the legislature's behalf. *Id.,* at 82.

Far from supporting petitioners' standing, however, *Karcher* is compelling precedent against it. The legislators in that case intervened in their official capacities as Speaker and President of the legislature. No one doubts that a State has a cognizable interest "in the continued enforceability" of its laws that is harmed by a judicial decision declaring a state law unconstitutional. *Maine* v. *Taylor,* 477 U. S. 131, 137 (1986). To vindicate that interest or any other, a State must be able to designate agents to represent it in federal court. See *Poindexter* v. *Greenhow,* 114 U. S. 270, 288 (1885) ("The State is a political corporate body [that] can act only through agents"). That agent is typically the State's attorney general. But state law may provide for other officials to speak for the State in federal court, as New Jersey law did for the State's presiding legislative officers in *Karcher.* See 484 U. S., at 81–82.

What is significant about *Karcher* is what happened after the Court of Appeals decision in that case. Karcher and Orechio lost their positions as Speaker and President, but nevertheless sought to appeal to this Court. We held that they could not do so. We explained that while they were able to participate in the lawsuit in their official capacities as presiding officers of the incumbent legislature, "since they no longer hold those offices, they lack authority to pursue this appeal." *Id.,* at 81.

The point of *Karcher* is not that a State could authorize *private parties* to represent its interests; Karcher and Orechio were permitted to proceed only because they were state officers, acting in an official capacity. As soon as they lost that capacity, they lost standing. Petitioners here hold no office and have always participated in this litigation solely as private parties.

The cases relied upon by the dissent, see *post,* at 11–12, provide petitioners no more support. The dissent's primary authorities, in fact, do not discuss standing at all. See *Young* v. *United States ex rel. Vuitton et Fils S. A.,* 481 U. S. 787 (1987); *United States* v. *Providence Journal Co.,* 485 U. S. 693 (1988). And none comes close to establishing that mere authorization to represent a third party's interests is sufficient to confer Article III standing on private parties with no injury of their own.

The dissent highlights the discretion exercised by special prosecutors appointed by federal courts to pursue contempt charges. See *post,* at 11 (citing *Young, supra,* at 807). Such prosecutors do enjoy a degree of independence in carrying out their appointed role, but no one would suppose that they are not subject to the ultimate authority of the court that appointed them. See also *Providence Journal, supra,* at 698–707 (recognizing further control exercised by the Solicitor General over special prosecutors).

The dissent's remaining cases, which at least consider standing, are readily distinguishable. See *Vermont Agency of Natural Resources* v. *United States ex rel. Stevens,* 529 U. S. 765, 771–778 (2000) (justifying *qui tam* actions based on a partial assignment of the Government's damages claim and a "well nigh conclusive" tradition of such actions in English and American courts dating back to the 13th century); *Whitmore* v. *Arkansas,* 495 U. S. 149, 162–164 (1989) (justifying "next friend" standing based on a similar history dating back to the 17th century, requiring the next friend to prove a disability of the real party in interest and a "significant relationship" with that party); *Gollust* v. *Mendell,* 501 U. S. 115, 124–125 (1990) (requiring plaintiff in shareholder-derivative suit to maintain a financial stake in the outcome of the litigation, to avoid "serious constitutional doubt whether that plaintiff could demonstrate the standing required by Article III's case-or controversy limitation").

[IV]

The dissent eloquently recounts the California Supreme Court's reasons for deciding that state law authorizes petitioners to defend Proposition 8. See *post,* at 3–5. We do not "disrespect[ ]" or "disparage[ ]" those reasons. *Post,* at 12. Nor do we question California's sovereign right to maintain an initiative process, or the right of initiative proponents to defend their initiatives in California courts, where Article III does not apply. But as the dissent acknowledges, see *post,* at 1, standing in federal court is a question of federal law, not state law. And no matter its reasons, the fact that a State thinks a private party should have standing to seek relief for a generalized grievance cannot override our settled law to the contrary. The Article III requirement that a party invoking the jurisdiction of a federal court seek relief for a personal, particularized injury serves vital interests going to the role of the Judiciary in our system of separated powers. "Refusing to entertain generalized grievances ensures that . . . courts exercise power that is judicial in nature," *Lance,* 549 U. S., at 441, and ensures that the Federal Judiciary respects "the proper—and properly limited—role of the courts in a democratic society," *DaimlerChrysler Corp.* v. *Cuno,* 547 U. S. 332, 341 (2006) (internal quotation marks omitted). States cannot alter that role simply by issuing to private parties who otherwise lack standing a ticket to the federal courthouse.

* * *

We have never before upheld the standing of a private party to defend the constitutionality of a state statute when state officials have chosen not to. We decline to do so for the first time here.

Because petitioners have not satisfied their burden to demonstrate standing to appeal the judgment of the District Court, the Ninth Circuit was without jurisdiction to consider the appeal. The judgment of the Ninth Circuit is vacated, and the case is remanded with instructions to dismiss the appeal for lack of jurisdiction.

It is so ordered.
[The dissent of Justice Kennedy is omitted. Eds.]

Note

After *Hollingsworth v. Perry* and *Arizona Legislature v. Arizona Independent Redistricting Commission*, the Court revisited the issues in those cases in Virginia House of Delegates v. Bethune-Hill, 587 U.S. ___ (2019). The Court was asked to rule on whether the Virginia House of Delegates, one chamber of the two-chamber Virginia General Assembly, had standing to appeal a lower federal court decision invalidating a redistricting plan held to be a racial gerrymander enacted by the entire Assembly. The Court found that House lacked standing.

The majority, in an opinion written by Justice Ginsburg, noted that a party must demonstrate the standing criteria at every stage of litigation. This requirement was drawn into question after the state attorney general, statutorily empowered to represent state interests in litigation, declined to appeal the lower court's decision. The House of Delegates, interveners at the earlier stage, sought to appeal the decision of the lower court.

The majority noted that Virginia, unlike some other states, authorizes the state Attorney General only to represent its interest in litigation. Hence, according to that reasoning, the standing the state has to defend its legislation would not transfer to the House of Delegate, an intervener, after the "state" chooses to accept a negative court ruling. The House of Delegates was found to lack standing to appeal the decision in this case.

Also, like in *Hollingsworth* where private citizens were found without standing to defend on appeal (following the state's withdrawal), a ruling nullifying a state constitutional amendment banning same-sex marriage as unconstitutional due to any cognizable interests in the matter, the Court rejected the House's claim that it suffered its own injury from the lower court ruling. The majority found that position unpersuasive as well. The Court reasoned that the House of Delegates, being only one of two chambers in the General Assembly which passed the redistricting plan in both houses, could not claim injury separate from the entire assembly. Nor could the House of Delegates claim injury in the fact that the lower court decision would alter the composition of the chamber. The majority noted that the chamber's standing position was different from that in *Arizona State Legislature v. Arizona Independent Redistricting Commission* in that in the Arizona case the entire legislature was challenging the loss of its entire authority to engage in redistricting where that authority had been transferred to a non-partisan commission by virtue of a state-wide referendum. In the present case, Virginia lawmakers had not been relieved of redistricting authority. The Assembly, working as a bicameral unit, could pass redistricting plans subject to judicial review of the constitutionality of its actions, which is what happened here.

To the House's argument that the ruling would alter district boundaries, hence affecting the composition of the House of Delegates, the majority opinion noted that any change in the composition of that body is a matter of voter discretion and does not create cognizable injury on the House.

SUSAN B. ANTHONY LIST v. DRIEHAUS
573 U. S. 149 (2014)

JUSTICE THOMAS delivered the opinion of the Court.

Petitioners in this case seek to challenge an Ohio statute that prohibits certain "false statements" during the course of a political campaign. The question in this case is whether their pre enforcement challenge to that law is justiciable — and in particular, whether they have alleged a sufficiently imminent injury for the purposes of Article III. We conclude that they have.

I

The Ohio statute at issue prohibits certain "false statement[s]" "during the course of any campaign for nomination or election to public office or office of a political party." As relevant here, the statute makes it a crime for any person to "[m]ake a false statement concerning the voting record of a candidate or public official," or to "[p]ost, publish, circulate, distribute, or otherwise disseminate a false statement concerning a candidate, either knowing the same to be false or with reckless disregard of whether it was false or not." "[A]ny person" acting on personal knowledge may file a complaint with the Ohio Elections Commission (or Commission) alleging a violation of the false statement statute. If filed within 60 days of a primary election or 90 days of a general election, the complaint is referred to a panel of at least three Commission members. The panel must then hold an expedited hearing, generally within two business days, to determine whether there is probable cause to believe the alleged violation occurred. Upon a finding of probable cause, the full Commission must, within 10 days, hold a hearing on the complaint. . . .

II

Petitioner Susan B. Anthony List (SBA) is a "pro-life advocacy organization." During the 2010 election cycle, SBA publicly criticized various Members of Congress who voted for the Patient Protection and Affordable Care Act (ACA). In particular, it issued a press release announcing its plan to "educat[e] voters that their representative voted for a health care bill that includes taxpayer-funded abortion." The press release listed then-Congressman Steve Driehaus, a respondent here, who voted for the ACA. SBA also sought to display a billboard in Driehaus' district condemning that vote. The planned billboard would have read:

"Shame on Steve Driehaus! Driehaus voted FOR taxpayer-funded abortion."

The advertising company that owned the billboard space refused to display that message, however, after Driehaus' counsel threatened legal action.

On October 4, 2010, Driehaus filed a complaint with the Ohio Elections Commission alleging, as relevant here, that SBA had violated [the statute] by falsely stating that he had voted for "taxpayer-funded abortion." Because Driehaus filed his complaint 29 days before the general election, a Commission panel held an expedited hearing. On October 14, 2010, the panel voted 2 to 1 to find probable cause that a violation had been committed. The full Commission set a hearing date for 10 business days later, and the parties commenced discovery. Driehaus noticed depositions of three SBA employees as well as individuals affiliated with similar advocacy groups. He also issued discovery requests for all evidence that SBA would rely on at the Commission hearing, as well as SBA's communications with allied organizations, political party committees, and Members of Congress and their staffs.

On October 18, 2010 — after the panel's probable-cause determination, but before the scheduled Commission hearing — SBA filed suit in Federal District Court, seeking declaratory and injunctive relief on the ground that [the statute] violate[s] the First and

Fourteenth Amendments of the United States Constitution. The District Court stayed the action under Younger v. Harris, 401 U.S. 37 (1971), pending completion of the Commission proceedings. The Sixth Circuit denied SBA's motion for an injunction pending appeal. Driehaus and SBA eventually agreed to postpone the full Commission hearing until after the election. When Driehaus lost the election in November 2010, he moved to withdraw his complaint against SBA. The Commission granted the motion with SBA's consent. Once the Commission proceedings were terminated, the District Court lifted the stay and SBA amended its complaint. As relevant here, the amended complaint alleged that [the statute is] unconstitutional both facially and as applied. Specifically, the complaint alleged that SBA's speech about Driehaus had been chilled; that SBA "intends to engage in substantially similar activity in the future"; and that it "face[d] the prospect of its speech and associational rights again being chilled and burdened," because "[a]ny complainant can hale [it] before the [Commission], forcing it to expend time and resources defending itself." The District Court consolidated SBA's suit with a separate suit brought by petitioner Coalition Opposed to Additional Spending and Taxes (COAST), an advocacy organization that also alleged that the same Ohio false statement provisions are unconstitutional both facially and as applied. According to its amended complaint, COAST intended to disseminate a mass e-mail and other materials criticizing Driehaus' vote for the ACA as a vote "to fund abortions with tax dollars," but refrained from doing so because of the Commission proceedings against SBA. COAST further alleged that it "desires to make the same or similar statements about other federal candidates who voted for" the ACA, but that fear "of finding itself subject to the same fate" as SBA has deterred it from doing so. . . .

III

A

[This] case concerns the injury-in-fact requirement, which helps to ensure that the plaintiff has a "personal stake in the outcome of the controversy." Warth v. Seldin, 422 U.S. 490, 498 (1975) (internal quotation marks omitted). An injury sufficient to satisfy Article III must be "concrete and particularized" and "actual or imminent, not 'conjectural' or 'hypothetical.' " [Lujan.] An allegation of future injury may suffice if the threatened injury is "certainly impending," or there is a " 'substantial risk' that the harm will occur." [Clapper.]

B

One recurring issue in our cases is determining when the threatened enforcement of a law creates an Article III injury. When an individual is subject to such a threat, an actual arrest, prosecution, or other enforcement action is not a prerequisite to challenging the law. . . .

IV

Here, SBA and COAST contend that the threat of enforcement of the false statement statute amounts to an Article III injury in fact. We agree: Petitioners have alleged a credible threat of enforcement.

A

First, petitioners have alleged "an intention to engage in a course of conduct arguably affected with a constitutional interest." Both petitioners have pleaded specific statements they intend to make in future election cycles. SBA has already stated that representatives who voted for the ACA supported "taxpayer-funded abortion," and it has alleged an "inten[t] to engage in substantially similar activity in the future." COAST has alleged that it previously intended to disseminate materials criticizing a vote for the ACA as a vote "to fund abortions with tax dollars," and that it "desires to make the same or similar statements about other federal candidates who voted for [the ACA]." Because petitioners' intended future conduct concerns political speech, it is certainly "affected with a constitutional interest."

B

Next, petitioners' intended future conduct is "arguably . . . proscribed by [the] statute" they wish to challenge. The Ohio false statement law sweeps broadly, and covers the subject matter of petitioners' intended speech. Both SBA and COAST have alleged an intent to "[m]ake" statements "concerning the voting record of a candidate or public official," and to "disseminate" statements "concerning a candidate . . . to promote the election, nomination, or defeat of the candidate[.]" And, a Commission panel here already found probable cause to believe that SBA violated the statute when it stated that Driehaus had supported "taxpayer-funded abortion" — the same sort of statement petitioners plan to disseminate in the future. Under these circumstances, we have no difficulty concluding that petitioners' intended speech is "arguably proscribed" by the law. Respondents incorrectly rely on Golden v. Zwickler, 394 U.S. 103 (1969). In that case, the plaintiff had previously distributed anonymous leaflets criticizing a particular Congressman who had since left office. The Court dismissed the plaintiff's challenge to the electoral leafleting ban as nonjusticiable because his "*sole concern* was literature relating to the Congressman and his record," and "it was most unlikely that the Congressman would again be a candidate." (emphasis added). Under those circumstances, any threat of future prosecution was "wholly conjectural."

Here, by contrast, petitioners' speech focuses on the broader issue of support for the ACA, not on the voting record of a single candidate. Because petitioners' alleged future speech is not directed exclusively at Driehaus, it does not matter whether he "may run for office again." As long as petitioners continue to engage in comparable electoral speech regarding support for the ACA, that speech will remain arguably proscribed by Ohio's false statement statute. Respondents, echoing the Sixth Circuit, contend that SBA's fears of enforcement are misplaced because SBA has not said it " 'plans to lie or recklessly disregard the veracity of its speech.' " The Sixth Circuit reasoned that because SBA "can only be liable for making a statement 'knowing' it is false," SBA's insistence that its speech is factually true "makes the possibility of prosecution for uttering such statements exceedingly slim."

The Sixth Circuit misses the point. SBA's insistence that the allegations in its press release were true did not prevent the Commission panel from finding probable cause to believe that SBA had violated the law the first time around. And, there is every reason to think that similar speech in the future will result in similar proceedings, notwithstanding SBA's belief in the truth of its allegations. Nothing in this Court's decisions requires a plaintiff who wishes to challenge the constitutionality of a law to confess that he will in fact violate that law.

C

Finally, the threat of future enforcement of the false statement statute is substantial. Most obviously, there is a history of past enforcement here . . . . [Commission] proceedings are not a rare occurrence. Petitioners inform us that the Commission " 'handles about 20 to 80 false statement complaints per year,' " and respondents do not deny that the Commission frequently fields complaints alleging violations of the false statement statute. Moreover, respondents have not disavowed enforcement if petitioners make similar statements in the future. In fact, the specter of enforcement is so substantial that the owner of the billboard refused to display SBA's message after receiving a letter threatening Commission proceedings. On these facts, the prospect of future enforcement is far from "imaginary or speculative."

We take the threatened Commission proceedings into account because administrative action, like arrest or prosecution, may give rise to harm sufficient to justify pre-enforcement review. The burdens that Commission proceedings can impose on electoral speech are of particular concern here. As the Ohio Attorney General himself notes, the "practical effect" of the Ohio false statement scheme is "to permit a private complainant . . . to gain a campaign advantage without ever having to prove the falsity of a statement." [Moreover], the target of a false statement complaint may be forced to divert significant time and resources to hire legal counsel and respond to discovery requests in the crucial days leading up to an election. And where, as here, a Commission panel issues a preelection probable-cause finding, "such a determination itself may be viewed [by the electorate] as a sanction by the State.

Although the threat of Commission proceedings is a substantial one, we need not decide whether that threat standing alone gives rise to an Article III injury. The burdensome Commission proceedings here are backed by the additional threat of criminal prosecution. We conclude that the combination of those two threats suffices to create an Article III injury under the circumstances of this case That conclusion holds true as to both SBA and COAST. Respondents, relying on Younger v. Harris, 401 U.S. 37 (1971), appear to suggest that COAST lacks standing because it refrained from actually disseminating its planned speech in order to avoid Commission proceedings of its own. In *Younger,* the plaintiff had been indicted for distributing leaflets in violation of the California Criminal Syndicalism Act. When he challenged the constitutionality of the law in federal court, several other plaintiffs intervened, arguing that their own speech was inhibited by Harris' prosecution. The Court concluded that only the plaintiff had standing because the intervenors "d[id] not claim that they ha[d] ever been threatened with prosecution, that a prosecution [wa]s likely, or even that a prosecution [wa]s remotely possible."

That is not this case. Unlike the intervenors in *Younger,* COAST has alleged an intent to engage in the same speech that was the subject of a prior enforcement proceeding. Also unlike the intervenors in *Younger,* who had never been threatened with prosecution, COAST has been the subject of Commission proceedings in the past. . . .

In sum, we find that both SBA and COAST have alleged a credible threat of enforcement. . . .

Petitioners in this case have demonstrated an injury in fact sufficient for Article III standing. We accordingly reverse the judgment of the United States Court of Appeals for the Sixth Circuit and remand the case for further proceedings consistent with this opinion, including a determination whether the remaining Article III standing requirements are met.

It is so ordered.

———

How much redressability is required for a party to have standing? In Uzuegbunam v. Preczewski, 592 US___(2021), the Supreme Court answered that question by allowing that a nominal damages award for a completed injury is enough to satisfy the redressability requirement for constitutional standing. The case involved a claim by a college student that his First Amendment rights were violated when the university invoked a campus policy which prevented him from speaking of his religion and distributing related literature on campus. After the plaintiff and another student filed for injunctive relief and nominal damages against university officials, the University abandoned the policy and argued that the change rendered the lawsuit moot, claiming that the plaintiffs could not receive any further relief and moved for dismissal on the grounds that the action lacked redressability, rendering the plaintiff without standing to sue. The Court issued a judgment on behalf of the plaintiff on the basis that the request for nominal damages was sufficient to maintain standing as the damages requested met the redressability requirement.

Justice Thomas, writing for the majority, applied English and American common law rulings for the Court's conclusion that nominal damages "affect the behavior of the defendant towards the plaintiff," Hewitt v. Helms, 482 U.S. 755 (1992). However, though several of the English and American cases broadly supported the narrow issue of the value of nominal damages as settling a case, others appear to have been taken out of context and not clearly in support of the proposition that nominal damages can redress a claim raised by a plaintiff in the most literal sense for purposes of maintaining standing. See Church of Scientology of Cal. v. United States, 506 U.S. 9, 13 (describing the return or destruction of records improperly confiscated by the IRS as a "partial remedy" though not nominal damages). At best the decision appears to be a widening of the meaning of redressability for standing purposes to include nominal damages and other measures that may not have a direct positive effect on redressing a plaintiff's injury.

Perhaps a bit less theoretical and more coherent resolution to the standing issue is in the third major challenge to the Patient Protection and Affordable Care Act (ACA), Texas v. California, 592 U.S. ____ (2021). Texas and other states as well as individuals sued the United States over the constitutionality of the act after the tax provision enforcement of the personal mandate, the basis for the Court finding the law constitutional in the first challenge in 2012, was removed from the law as part of the tax changes enacted in 2017 by Congress. Justice Breyer, writing for the Court in a 8-1 decision, held that the lack of an enforcement mechanism undermined both the causation and redressability of the claims by both the individual and state plaintiffs for purposes of standing.

With regard to the claim by the individual plaintiffs that they were injured by out-of-pocket payments for required health insurance coverage, the Court rhetorically posed the question of "why were the payments made in the first place" with no enforcement provision on the books after the repeal of the tax provision for uninsured persons. No satisfactory answer was provided, destroying the causation prong of constitutional standing since nothing on the part of the federal government was responsible for the out-of-pocket insurance expenditures. Furthermore, absent causation from a federally enforced tax measure, the Court reasoned that there was nothing to redress and hence the individuals had not met the standing requirement.

A similar path of reasoning animated the Court's opinion with regard to the challenging states that referred to additional expenses incurred to state-run health insurance programs as a result persons signing up for that health insurance because of the ACA. Again the Court raised the rhetorical question of why were individuals taking out state health insurance coverage in the absence of a federal enforcement mechanism of a tax. No satisfactory answer as to causation other than the implied encouragement by the ACA for persons to take out discounted coverage came from the states. Absent causation from a federal action or threatened action, and no redressability that the Court could provide under these facts, the Court found that the states too had failed the standing requirement. As Justice Thomas noted in his concurrence, the parties "have not identified any unlawful action that has injured them."

Of course, the repeal of the tax enforcement provision (which was ruled not a penalty for persons not obtaining insurance in *NFIB v. Sibelius*, 567 U.S. 519, a ruling which saved the constitutionality of the ACA, see page 373 infra) made it impossible for the plaintiffs to claim standing under the Court's reasoning. And, on the other hand, had the tax not been repealed, the ruling in NFIB v. Sibelius would have had stare decisis effect, making it unlikely that the Court would overrule itself just nine years after rendering the decision. Is this the last challenge to the Affordable Care Act?

In Trump v. New York, 592 U.S. ___(2020), the Court, in a per curiam opinion, addressed a challenge to President Trump's direction to the Department of Commerce to conduct the decennial census count in 2020 "to provide information permitting the President, to the extent practicable, to exercise the President's discretion to carry out the policy" of excluding persons not in the country legally from the census count. The census data is used by the federal government to apportion Congressional representation, by state governments for intrastate redistricting and by Congress for legislating funding for federal government services and programs. Several states, local governments, organizations, and individuals challenged the President's direction that the Commerce Department develop the information to carry out the President's policy.

Inasmuch as the President's policy had not been carried out as of the date of the suit and subsequent submission to the Supreme Court, the Court ruled that the suit was premature, hence not ripe for litigation. Also, the Court ruled that the plaintiffs did not have standing to challenge on the basis of claims that the President's direction to Commerce would result in an unconstitutional undercount, due to the speculative nature of the claims. The Court, relying on the substantial risk of harm standard in Clapper v. Amnesty Int'l USA, 568 U. S. 398, 414, n. 5 (2013), expressed doubt of the degree of certainty that the data on the population of persons not in the country legally would not be reported in final census calculations, or to what extent. With regard to funding, the per curiam opinion relied on the Federal Government's representation to the Court that funding decisions are not necessarily based on apportionment formulas submitted to Congress in making its lack of standing decision.

Justice Breyer, writing for fellow dissenters Justices Sotomayor and Kagan, found less uncertainty in the future use of the data ordered by the President, or in its effects on funding and Congressional apportionment, a conclusion based primarily on the clarity of the President's direction and the fact that the Federal Government already has substantial data, unrelated to the census count, of individuals in the country without legal documentation; data that Justice Breyer reasons is not speculative, but certain. Based on this, the dissenters argued that the case is ripe for litigation and that the plaintiffs have standing.

8. STANDING AND FEDERALISM: PRUDENCE AND ENFORCING THE TENTH AMENDMENT

Do prudential limits on Article III standing preclude standing for an individual indicted under a federal statute to challenge the indictment as exceeding Congress's powers by intruding upon the reserved autonomy of the states? In *Bond v. United States*, 564 U.S. 211 (2011), Justice Kennedy wrote for a unanimous Court that a woman indicted under the Chemical Weapons Convention Implementation Act of 1998 for placing chemicals on the mailbox of her husband's pregnant lover had standing to challenge the indictment on federalism grounds, even though no state was a party to the federal proceedings. Ruling that she clearly had Article III standing, Justice Kennedy stated that her challenge was not precluded as an attempt to assert third-party standing: "An individual has a direct interest in objecting to laws that upset the constitutional balance between the National Government and the States when the enforcement of those laws causes injury that is concrete, particular, and redressable. Fidelity to principles of federalism is not for the States alone to vindicate." Justices Ginsburg, joined by Justice Breyer, filed a concurrence specifying that "Bond, like any other defendant, has a personal right not to be convicted under a constitutionally invalid law," and thus was asserting first-party, not third-party rights.

9. Article III Minimums:
HOW MINIMUM IS MINIMUM? OR "HOW LOW CAN YOU GO"?

What are the Article III minimum requirements as opposed to the prudential rules? Does the fact that they extend from a constitutional source make them significant? Could Congress lower them? How straightforward will their application be? Will the nature of the case affect their application? Will they inevitably be applied in a discretionary fashion? If Congress has created a cause in action that lowers the in-house rules, is there any principled or doctrinal basis for the Court to abstain? The case that follows serves as our basis for studying these questions.

ALLEN v. WRIGHT
468 U.S. 737 (1984)

[This nationwide class action suit was brought by parents of black schoolchildren against the Internal Revenue Service (IRS), contending that the IRS had not carried out its obligation to deny tax-exempt status to private schools that discriminated on the basis of race. The IRS generally does require, as a condition for tax-exempt status (and eligibility to receive deductible charitable contributions), that schools not discriminate on that basis. In *Bob Jones University v. United States*, 461 U.S. 574 (1983), the Court held that the governing statute disqualified such schools from receiving tax-exempt status as "charities."

According to the parents — respondents in this case representing several million people — the IRS's regulations, procedures, and policies resulted in a failure to enforce the statutory mandate: the IRS had not denied tax-exempt status to many schools that in fact discriminated on the basis of race. Some schools, for example, received the exemption as a result of the tax-exempt status of "umbrella" organizations that support or operate such schools. According to the parents, the failure to carry out the statutory mandate (1) amounted to federal support for segregated schools and (2) fostered the organization and expansion of such schools, thus interfering with the efforts of federal agencies and courts to bring about desegregation in public school districts that had been segregated in the past. Respondents did not allege that they had applied to the private schools in question, but claimed instead that the IRS's unlawful activities had harmed their children attending schools that were undergoing or might undergo desegregation. They claimed that by failing to deny the exemption, the IRS subsidized discriminatory private schools and thus decreased the likelihood that desegregation plans would be effective. Respondents sought declaratory and injunctive relief requiring the IRS to issue guidelines so as to deny tax exemptions to all private schools that discriminated on the basis of race. The court of appeals held in their favor.]

Justice O'CONNOR delivered the opinion of the Court.

Article III of the Constitution confines the federal courts to adjudicating actual "cases" and "controversies." As the Court explained in Valley Forge Christian College v. Americans United for Separation of Church and State, Inc., 454 U.S. 464, 471-476 (1982), the "case or controversy" requirement defines with respect to the Judicial Branch the idea of separation of powers on which the Federal Government is founded. The several doctrines that have grown up to elaborate that requirement are "founded in concern about the proper — and properly limited — role of the courts in a democratic society."

All of the doctrines that cluster about Article III — not only standing but mootness, ripeness, political question, and the like — relate in part, and in different though overlapping ways, to an idea, which is more than an intuition but less than a rigorous and explicit theory, about the constitutional and prudential limits to the powers of an unelected, unrepresentative judiciary in our kind of government. Vander Jagt v. O'Neill, 699 F.2d 1166, 1178-1179 (1983) (Bork, J., concurring). The case-or-controversy doctrines state fundamental limits on federal judicial power in our system of government.

The Art. III doctrine that requires a litigant to have "standing" to invoke the power of a federal court is perhaps the most important of these doctrines. "In essence the question of standing is whether the litigant is entitled to have the court decide the merits of the dispute or of particular issues." Standing doctrine embraces several judicially self-imposed limits on the exercise of federal jurisdiction, such as the general prohibition on a litigant's raising another person's legal rights, the rule barring adjudication of generalized grievances more appropriately addressed in the representative branches, and the requirement that a plaintiff's complaint fall within the zone of interests protected by the law invoked. [The] requirement of standing, however, has a core component derived directly from the Constitution. A plaintiff must allege personal injury fairly traceable to the defendant's allegedly unlawful conduct and likely to be redressed by the requested relief.

Like the prudential component, the constitutional component of standing doctrine incorporates concepts concededly not susceptible of precise definition. The injury alleged must be, for example, "'distinct and palpable,'" [and] not "abstract" or "conjectural" or "hypothetical." [The] injury must be "fairly" traceable to the challenged action, and relief from the injury must be "likely" to follow from a favorable decision. [These] terms cannot be defined so as to make application of the constitutional standing requirement a mechanical exercise.

In many cases the standing question can be answered chiefly by comparing the allegations of the particular complaint to those made in prior standing cases. [More] important, the law of Art. III standing is built on a single basic idea — the idea of separation of powers. Determining standing in a particular case may be facilitated by clarifying principles or even clean rules developed in prior cases. Typically, however, the standing inquiry requires careful judicial examination of a complaint's allegations to ascertain whether the particular plaintiff is entitled to an adjudication of the particular claims asserted. Is the injury too abstract, or otherwise not appropriate, to be considered judicially cognizable? Is the line of causation between the illegal conduct and injury too attenuated? Is the prospect of obtaining relief from the injury as a result of a favorable ruling too speculative? These questions and any others relevant to the standing inquiry must be answered by reference to the Art. III notion that federal courts may exercise power only "in the last resort, and as a necessity," and only when adjudication is "consistent with a system of separated powers and [the dispute is one] traditionally thought to be capable of resolution through the judicial process."

Respondents allege two injuries in their complaint to support their standing to bring this lawsuit. First, they say that they are harmed directly by the mere fact of Government financial aid to discriminatory private schools. Second, they say that the federal tax exemptions to racially discriminatory private schools in their communities impair their ability to have their public schools desegregated. [Respondents'] first claim of injury [might] be a claim simply to have the Government avoid the violation of law alleged in respondents' complaint. Alternatively, it might be a claim of stigmatic injury, or denigration, suffered by all members of a racial group when the Government discriminates on the basis of race. Under neither interpretation is this claim of injury judicially cognizable.

This Court has repeatedly held that an asserted right to have the Government act in accordance with law is not sufficient, standing alone, to confer jurisdiction on a federal court. [Recently,] in [*Valley Forge, infra*] we rejected a claim of standing to challenge a Government conveyance of property to a religious institution. Insofar as the plaintiffs relied simply on "'their shared individuated right'" to a Government that made no law respecting an establishment of religion [we] held that plaintiffs had not alleged a judicially cognizable injury. . . .

Neither do they have standing to litigate their claims based on the stigmatizing injury often caused by racial discrimination. There can be no doubt that this sort of noneconomic injury is one of the most serious consequences of discriminatory government action and is sufficient in some circumstances to support standing.

. . . [Our] cases make clear, however, that such injury accords a basis for standing only to "those persons who are personally denied equal treatment" by the challenged discriminatory conduct. . . . [If] the abstract stigmatic injury were cognizable, standing would extend nationwide to all members of the particular racial groups against which the Government was alleged to be discriminating by its grant of a tax exemption to a racially discriminatory school, regardless of the location of that school. All such persons could claim the same sort of abstract stigmatic injury respondents assert in their first claim of injury. A black person in Hawaii could challenge the grant of a tax exemption to a racially discriminatory school in Maine. Recognition of standing in such circumstances would transform the federal courts into "no more than a vehicle for the vindication of the value interests of concerned bystanders." It is in their complaint's second claim of injury that respondents allege harm to a concrete, personal interest that can support standing in some circumstances. The injury they identify — their children's diminished ability to receive an education in a racially integrated school — is, beyond any doubt, not only judicially cognizable but, as shown by cases from Brown v. Board of Education, 347 U.S. 483 (1954), to Bob Jones University v. United States, 461 U.S. — (1983), one of the most serious injuries recognized in our legal system. Despite the constitutional importance of curing the injury alleged by respondents, however, the federal judiciary may not redress it unless standing requirements are met. In this case, respondents' second claim of injury cannot support standing because the injury alleged is not fairly traceable to the Government conduct respondents challenge as unlawful.

The illegal conduct challenged by respondents is the IRS's grant of tax exemptions to some racially discriminatory schools. The line of causation between that conduct and desegregation of respondents' schools is attenuated at best. From the perspective of the IRS, the injury to respondents is highly indirect and "results from the independent action of some third party not before the court."

The diminished ability of respondents' children to receive a desegregated education would be fairly traceable to unlawful IRS grants of tax exemptions only if there were enough racially discriminatory private schools receiving tax exemptions in respondents' communities for withdrawal of those exemptions to make an appreciable difference in public-school integration. Respondents have made no such allegation. It is, first, uncertain how many racially discriminatory private schools are in fact receiving tax exemptions. Moreover, it is entirely speculative [whether] withdrawal of a tax exemption from any particular school would lead the school to change its policies. [It] is just as speculative whether any given parent of a child attending such a private school would decide to transfer the child to public school as a result of any changes in educational or financial policy made by the private school once it was threatened with loss of tax-exempt status. It is also pure speculation whether, in a particular community, a large enough number of the numerous relevant school officials and parents would reach decisions that collectively would have a significant impact on the racial composition of the public schools.

The links in the chain of causation between the challenged Government conduct and the asserted injury are far too weak for the chain as a whole to sustain respondents' standing. In [*Eastern Kentucky Welfare Rights Organization*, infra], the Court held that standing to challenge a Government grant of a tax exemption to hospitals could not be founded on the asserted connection between the grant of tax-exempt status and the hospitals' policy concerning the provision of medical services to indigents. The causal connection depended on the decisions hospitals would make in response to withdrawal of tax-exempt status, and those decisions were sufficiently uncertain to break the chain of causation between the plaintiff's injury and the challenged Government action. [The] chain of causation is even weaker in this case. It involves numerous third parties (officials of racially discriminatory schools receiving tax exemptions and the parents of children attending such schools) who may not even exist in respondents' communities and whose independent decisions may not collectively have a significant effect on the ability of public-school students to receive a desegregated education.

The idea of separation of powers that underlies standing doctrine explains why our cases preclude the conclusion that respondents' alleged injury "fairly can be traced to the challenged action" of the IRS. That conclusion would pave the way generally for suits challenging, not specifically identifiable Government violations of law, but the particular programs agencies establish to carry out their legal obligations. Such suits, even when premised on allegations of several instances of violations of law, are rarely if ever appropriate for federal-court adjudication.

Carried to its logical end, [respondents'] approach would have the federal courts as virtually continuing monitors of the wisdom and soundness of Executive action; such a role is appropriate for the Congress acting through its committees and the "power of the purse"; it is not the role of the judiciary, absent actual present or immediately threatened injury resulting from unlawful governmental action.

The same concern for the proper role of the federal courts is reflected in cases like O'Shea v. Littleton, 414 U.S. 488 (1974), Rizzo v. Goode, 423 U.S. 362 (1976), and City of Los Angeles v. Lyons, 461 U.S. 95 (1983). In all three cases plaintiffs sought injunctive relief directed at certain system-wide law enforcement practices. The Court held in each case that, absent an allegation of a specific threat of being subject to the challenged practices, plaintiffs had no standing to ask for an injunction. Animating this Court's holdings was the principle that "[a] federal court . . . is not the proper forum to press" general complaints about the way in which government goes about its business. . . .

Case-or-controversy considerations, the Court observed in O'Shea v. Littleton, supra, 414 U.S., at 499, "obviously shade into those determining whether the complaint states a sound basis for equitable relief." The latter set of considerations should therefore inform our judgment about whether respondents have standing. Most relevant to this case is the principle articulated in [*Rizzo v. Goode* 423 U.S. 362, 378, 379 (1976)]: "When a plaintiff seeks to enjoin the activity of a government agency, ...even within a unitary court system, his case must contend with 'the well-established rule that the Government has traditionally been granted the widest latitude in the "dispatch of its own internal affairs." When transported into the Art. III context, that principle, grounded as it is in the idea of separation of powers, counsels against recognizing standing in a case brought, not to enforce specific legal obligations whose violation works a direct harm, but to seek a restructuring of the apparatus established by the Executive Branch to fulfill its legal duties. The Constitution, after all, assigns to the Executive Branch, and not to the Judicial Branch, the duty to "take Care that the Laws be faithfully executed." U.S. Const., Art. II, §3. We could not recognize respondents' standing in this case without running afoul of that structural principle. . . .

"The necessity that the plaintiff who seeks to invoke judicial power stand to profit in some personal interest remains an Art. III requirement." Respondents have not met this fundamental requirement. The judgment of the Court of Appeals is accordingly reversed, and the injunction issued by that court is vacated.

It is so ordered.

Justice BRENNAN, dissenting.

[By] relying on generalities concerning our tripartite system of government, the Court is able to conclude that the respondents lack standing to maintain this action without acknowledging the precise nature of the injuries they have alleged. In so doing, the Court displays a startling insensitivity to the historical role played by the federal courts in eradicating race discrimination from our nation's schools — a role that has played a prominent part in this Court's decisions from [*Brown*]. . . .

In these cases, the respondents have alleged at least one type of injury that satisfies the constitutional requirement of "distinct and palpable injury." In particular, they claim that the IRS' grant of tax-exempt status to racially discriminatory private schools directly injures their children's opportunity and ability to receive a desegregated education. . . .

Viewed in light of the injuries they claim, the respondents have alleged a direct causal relationship between the government action they challenge and the injury they suffer: their inability to receive an education in a racially integrated school is directly and adversely affected by the tax-exempt status granted by the IRS to racially discriminatory schools in their respective school districts. [The] elimination of tax-exempt status for racially discriminatory private schools would serve to lessen the impact that those institutions have in defeating efforts to desegregate the public schools.

More than one commentator has noted that the causation component of the Court's standing inquiry is no more than a poor disguise for the Court's view of the merits of the underlying claims. The Court today does nothing to avoid that criticism.

————

The Causation Requirement. Is *Allen v. Wright* a straightforward application of constitutional standards, or does it create a prudential basis for declining jurisdiction in the name of the Constitution? Is this inherent in any requirement that is based upon the concept of "causation"? Is causation always a speculative inquiry? If it is, and if it is an Article III minimum requirement, might minimum not necessarily be so minimum? Was it in *Allen*? Did the merits affect the outcome in *Allen*? Isn't it quite possible that what is speculative and lacking causation to you might not be so to me? Is this Brennan's point?

Assume that the IRS is challenged under § 10 of the APA, which gives a right to judicial review to any person "adversely affected or aggrieved by agency action," because it has not enforced a congressionally mandated requirement to withdraw "charitable" tax status to nonprofit hospitals that do not meet federal requirements to offer indigent/emergency services. Plaintiffs seek enforcement of this requirement (withdrawal of nonprofit and nontaxable status) against hospitals that have not met the requirement to offer indigent services. Do they have standing? What result?

TRUMP v. HAWAII 585 U. S. ____ (2018)

[In December 2015, a candidate for the Republican nomination for president, Donald Trump, issued the following press release, which was followed by a public announcement: "Donald J. Trump is calling for a total and complete shutdown of Muslims entering the United States until our country's representatives can figure out what is going on." Shortly after winning the presidential election in 2016 and taking office in 2017, the Trump Administration issued executive orders to implement restrictions on travel to the United States of persons from certain Muslim majority states. The first two were stayed by federal courts. The third executive order, designed to address deficiencies related to religious discrimination identified by the lower federal courts staying those earlier orders, reached the Supreme Court in 2017, and in 2018, the Court, by a 5-4 margin, held that executive order to be constitutional.]

Chief Justice Roberts delivered the opinion of the Court

[I]

[B]

Plaintiffs in this case are the State of Hawaii, three individuals (Dr. Ismail Elshikh, John Doe #1, and John Doe #2), and the Muslim Association of Hawaii. The State operates the University of Hawaii system, which recruits students and faculty from the designated countries. The three individual plaintiffs are U.S. citizens or lawful permanent residents who have relatives from Iran, Syria, and Yemen applying for immigrant or nonimmigrant visas. The Association is a nonprofit organization that operates a mosque in Hawaii.

[IV.]

[A.]

Because we have an obligation to assure ourselves of jurisdiction under Article III, we begin by addressing the question whether plaintiffs have standing to bring their constitutional challenge.

Federal courts have authority under the Constitution to decide legal questions only in the course of resolving "Cases" or "Controversies." Art. III, §2. One of the essential elements of a legal case or controversy is that the plaintiff have standing to sue. Standing requires more than just a "keen interest in the issue." *Hollingsworth v. Perry*, 570 U. S. 693, 700 (2013). It requires allegations—and, eventually, proof—that the plaintiff "personal[ly]" suffered a concrete and particularized injury in connection with the conduct about which he complains. Spokeo, Inc. v. Robins, 578 U. S. ___, ___ (2016) (slip op., at 7). In a case arising from an alleged violation of the Establishment Clause, a plaintiff must show, as in other cases, that he is "directly affected by the laws and practices against which [his] complaints are directed." *School Dist. of Abington Township v. Schempp*, 374 U. S. 203, 224, n. 9 (1963). That is an issue here because the entry restrictions apply not to plaintiffs themselves but to others seeking to enter the United States.

Plaintiffs first argue that they have standing on the ground that the Proclamation "establishes a disfavored faith" and violates "their own right to be free from federal [religious] establishments." Brief for Respondents 27–28 (emphasis deleted). They describe such injury as "spiritual and dignitary." Id., at 29.

We need not decide whether the claimed dignitary interest establishes an adequate ground for standing. The three individual plaintiffs assert another, more concrete injury: the alleged real-world effect that the Proclamation has had in keeping them separated from certain relatives who seek to enter the country. See ibid.; *Town of Chester v. Laroe Estates, Inc.,* 581 U. S. ___, _137 S.Ct. 1645 (2017) (slip op., at 5–6) ("At least one plaintiff must have standing to seek each form of relief requested in the complaint."). We agree that a person's interest in being united with his relatives is sufficiently concrete and particularized to form the basis of an Article III injury in fact. This Court has previously considered the merits of claims asserted by United States citizens regarding violations of their personal rights allegedly caused by the Government's exclusion of particular foreign nationals. Likewise, one of our prior stay orders in this litigation recognized that an American individual who has "a bona fide relationship with a particular person seeking to enter the country . . . can legitimately claim concrete hardship if that person is excluded." *Trump v. IRAP*, 582 U. S., at ___ (slip op., at 13).

The Government responds that plaintiffs' Establishment Clause claims are not justiciable because the Clause does not give them a legally protected interest in the admission of particular foreign nationals. But that argument—which depends upon the scope of plaintiffs' Establishment Clause rights—concerns the merits rather than the justiciability of plaintiffs' claims. We therefore conclude that the individual plaintiffs have Article III standing to challenge the exclusion of their relatives under the Establishment Clause.

10. ARTICLE III MINIMUMS: CAN CONGRESS "CREATE" STANDING?

Lujan is a most appropriate summation of the materials we have reviewed thus far. It is the most recent "treatise" on modern standing from Article III minimums to "in-house rules." Yet, it also explores a significant issue that we have yet to detail, namely, if Congress can lower the in-house rules by creating a cause in action, can it in effect "create" standing? Can you make an argument that advances this thesis? What of Article III minimums?

If one concludes that Congress can create standing, then must one assert that Congress can meet Article III requirements? Why, or why not? Is this problematic? Can you make such an argument? Isn't it true that if the only reason to exercise judicial restraint is to bow to the democratic process, that this is not a concern when Congress so acts? How does the Court in *Lujan* respond to these issues? Can Congress create standing?

LUJAN v. DEFENDERS OF WILDLIFE
504 U.S. 555 (1992)

Justice SCALIA delivered the opinion of the Court with respect to Parts I, II, III-A, and IV, and an opinion with respect to Part III-B, in which THE CHIEF JUSTICE, Justice WHITE, and Justice THOMAS join.

This case involves a challenge to a rule promulgated by the Secretary of the Interior interpreting § 7 of the Endangered Species Act of 1973 (ESA), 87 Stat. 884, 892, as amended, 16 U.S.C. § 1536, in such fashion as to render it applicable only to actions within the United States or on the high seas. The preliminary issue, and the only one we reach, is whether respondents here, plaintiffs below, have standing to seek judicial review of the rule.

I

The ESA, 87 Stat. 884, as amended, 16 U.S.C. § 1531 *et seq.*, seeks to protect species of animals against threats to their continuing existence caused by man. See generally TVA v. Hill, 437 U.S. 153, 98 S.Ct. 2279, 57 L.Ed.2d 117 (1978). The ESA instructs the Secretary of the Interior to promulgate by regulation a list of those species which are either endangered or threatened under enumerated criteria, and to define the critical habitat of these species. 16 U.S.C. §§ 1533, 1536. Section 7(a)(2) of the Act then provides, in pertinent part:

> Each Federal agency shall, in consultation with and with the assistance of the Secretary [of the Interior], insure that any action authorized, funded, or carried out by such agency . . . is not likely to jeopardize the continued existence of any endangered species or threatened species or result in the destruction or adverse modification of habitat of such species which is determined by the Secretary, after consultation as appropriate with affected States, to be critical.

16 U.S.C. § 1536(a)(2).

In 1978, the Fish and Wildlife Service (FWS) and the National Marine Fisheries Service (NMFS), on behalf of the Secretary of the Interior and the Secretary of Commerce respectively, promulgated a joint regulation stating that the obligations imposed by § 7(a)(2) extend to actions taken in foreign nations. 43 Fed.Reg. 874 (1978). The next year, however, the Interior Department began to reexamine its position. Letter from Leo Kuliz, Solicitor, Department of the Interior, to Assistant Secretary, Fish and Wildlife and Parks, Aug. 8, 1979. A revised joint regulation, reinterpreting § 7(a)(2) to require consultation only for actions taken in the United States or on the high seas, was proposed in 1983, 48 Fed.Reg. 29990, and promulgated in 1986, 51 Fed.Reg. 19926; 50 CFR 402.01 (1991).

Shortly thereafter, respondents, organizations dedicated to wildlife conservation and other environmental causes, filed this action against the Secretary of the Interior, seeking a declaratory judgment that the new regulation is in error as to the geographic scope of § 7(a)(2) and an injunction requiring the Secretary to promulgate a new regulation restoring the initial interpretation. The District Court granted the Secretary's motion to dismiss for lack of standing. Defenders of Wildlife v. Hodel, 658 F.Supp. 43, 47-48 (Minn.1987). The Court of Appeals for the Eighth Circuit reversed by a divided vote. Defenders of Wildlife v. Hodel, 851 F.2d 1035 (1988). On remand, the Secretary moved for summary judgment on the standing issue, and respondents moved for summary judgment on the merits. The District Court denied the Secretary's motion, on the ground that the Eighth Circuit had already determined the standing question in this case; it granted respondents' merits motion, and ordered the Secretary to publish a revised regulation. Defenders of Wildlife v. Hodel, 707 F.Supp. 1082 (Minn.1989). The Eighth Circuit affirmed. 911 F.2d 117 (1990). We granted certiorari, 500 U.S. 915, 111 S.Ct. 2008, 114 L.Ed.2d 97 (1991).

II

One of those landmarks, setting apart the "Cases" and "Controversies" that are of the justiciable sort referred to in Article III — "serv[ing] to identify those disputes which are appropriately resolved through the judicial process," Whitmore v. Arkansas, 495 U.S. 149, 155, 110 S.Ct. 1717, 1722, 109 L.Ed.2d 135 (1990) — is the doctrine of standing. Though some of its elements express merely prudential considerations that are part of judicial self-government, the core component of standing is an essential and unchanging part of the case-or-controversy requirement of Article III. See, *e.g.,* Allen v. Wright, 468 U.S. 737, 751, 104 S.Ct. 3315, 3324, 82 L.Ed.2d 556 (1984).

Over the years, our cases have established that the irreducible constitutional minimum of standing contains three elements. First, the plaintiff must have suffered an "injury in fact" — an invasion of a legally protected interest which is (a) concrete and particularized, see id., at 756, 104 S.Ct., at 3327; Warth v. Seldin, 422 U.S. 490, 508, 95 S.Ct. 2197, 2210, 45 L.Ed.2d 343 (1975); Sierra Club v. Morton, 405 U.S. 727, 740-741, n. 16, 92 S.Ct. 1361, 1368-1369, n. 16, 31 L.Ed.2d 636 (1972); and (b) "actual or imminent, not 'conjectural' or 'hypothetical,'" Whitmore, supra, 495 U.S., at 155, 110 S.Ct., at 1723 (quoting Los Angeles v. Lyons, 461 U.S. 95, 102, 103 S.Ct. 1660, 1665, 75 L.Ed.2d 675 (1983)). Second, there must be a causal connection between the injury and the conduct complained of — the injury has to be "fairly . . . trace[able] to the challenged action of the defendant, and not . . . th[e] result [of] the independent action of some third party not before the court." Simon v. Eastern Ky. Welfare Rights Organization, 426 U.S. 26, 41-42, 96 S.Ct. 1917, 1926, 48 L.Ed.2d 450 (1976). Third, it must be "likely," as opposed to merely "speculative," that the injury will be "redressed by a favorable decision." Id., at 38, 43, 96 S.Ct., at 1924, 1926.

III

Respondents had not made the requisite demonstration of (at least) injury and redressability.

A

Respondents' claim to injury is that the lack of consultation with respect to certain funded activities abroad "increas[es] the rate of extinction of endangered and threatened species." Complaint ¶ 5, App. 13. Of course, the desire to use or observe an animal species, even for purely esthetic purposes, is undeniably a cognizable interest for purpose of standing. See, *e.g.,* Sierra Club v. Morton, 405 U.S., at 734, 92 S.Ct., at 1366. "But the 'injury in fact' test requires more than an injury to a cognizable interest. It requires that the party seeking review be himself among the injured." Id., at 734-735, 92 S.Ct., at 1366.

[With] respect to this aspect of the case, the Court of Appeals focused on the affidavits of two Defenders' members — Joyce Kelly and Amy Skilbred. Ms. Kelly stated that she traveled to Egypt in 1986 and "observed the traditional habitat of the endangered nile crocodile there and intend[s] to do so again, and hope[s] to observe the crocodile directly," and that she "will suffer harm in fact as the result of [the] American . . . role . . . in overseeing the rehabilitation of the Aswan High Dam on the Nile . . . and [in] develop[ing] . . . Egypt's . . . Master Water Plan." App. 101. Ms. Skilbred averred that she traveled to Sri Lanka in 1981 and "observed th[e] habitat" of "endangered species such as the Asian elephant and the leopard" at what is now the site of the Mahaweli project funded by the Agency for International Development (AID), although she "was unable to see any of the endangered species"; "this development project," she continued, "will seriously reduce endangered, threatened, and endemic species habitat including areas that I visited . . . [, which] may severely shorten the future of these species"; that threat, she concluded, harmed her because she "intend[s] to return to Sri Lanka in the future and hope[s] to be more fortunate in spotting at least the endangered elephant and leopard." Id., at 145-146. When Ms. Skilbred was asked at a subsequent deposition if and when she had any plans to return to Sri Lanka, she reiterated that "I intend to go back to Sri Lanka," but confessed that she had no current plans: "I don't know [when]. There is a civil war going on right now. I don't know. Not next year, I will say. In the future." Id., at 318.

We shall assume for the sake of argument that these affidavits contain facts showing that certain agency-funded projects threaten listed species — though that is questionable. They plainly contain no facts, however, showing how damage to the species will produce "imminent" injury to Mses. Kelly and Skilbred. That the women "had visited" the areas of the projects before the projects commenced proves nothing. As we have said in a related context, "'Past exposure to illegal conduct does not in itself show a present case or controversy regarding injunctive relief . . . if unaccompanied by any continuing, present adverse effects.'" *Lyons*, 461 U.S., at 102, 103 S.Ct., at 1665 (quoting O'Shea v. Littleton, 414 U.S. 488, 495-496, 94 S.Ct. 669, 676, 38 L.Ed.2d 674 (1974)). And the affiants' profession of an "inten[t]" to return to the places they had visited before — where they will presumably, this time, be deprived of the opportunity to observe animals of the endangered species — is simply not enough. Such "some day" intentions — without any description of concrete plans, or indeed even any specification of *when* the some day will be — do not support a finding of the "actual or imminent" injury that our cases require. See supra, at 2136.

Besides relying upon the Kelly and Skilbred affidavits, respondents propose a series of novel standing theories.

. . . [Other] theories are called, alas, the "animal nexus" approach, whereby anyone who has an interest in studying or seeing the endangered animals anywhere on the globe has standing; and the "vocational nexus" approach, under which anyone with a professional interest in such animals can sue. Under these theories, anyone who goes to see Asian elephants in the Bronx Zoo, and anyone who is a keeper of Asian elephants in the Bronx Zoo, has standing to sue because the Director of the Agency for International Development (AID) did not consult with the Secretary regarding the AID-funded project in Sri Lanka. This is beyond all reason. Standing is not "an ingenious academic exercise in the conceivable," United States v. Students Challenging Regulatory Agency Procedures (SCRAP), 412 U.S. 669, 688, 93 S.Ct. 2405, 2416, 37 L.Ed.2d 254 (1973), but as we have said requires, at the summary judgment stage, a factual showing of perceptible harm. It is clear that the person who observes or works with a particular animal threatened by a federal decision is facing perceptible harm, since the very subject of his interest will no longer exist. It is even plausible — though it goes to the outermost limit of plausibility — to think that a person who observes or works with animals of a particular species in the very area of the world where that species is threatened by a federal decision is facing such harm, since some animals that might have been the subject of his interest will no longer exist, see Japan Whaling Assn. v. American Cetacean Society, 478 U.S. 221, 231, n. 4, 106 S.Ct. 2860, 2866, n. 4, 92 L.Ed.2d 166 (1986). It goes beyond the limit, however, and into pure speculation and fantasy, to say that anyone who observes or works with an endangered species, anywhere in the world, is appreciably harmed by a single project affecting some portion of that species with which he has no more specific connection.

B

Besides failing to show injury, respondents failed to demonstrate redressability. [Since] the agencies funding the projects were not parties to the case, the District Court could accord relief only against the Secretary: He could be ordered to revise his regulation to require consultation for foreign projects. But this would not remedy respondents' alleged injury unless the funding agencies were bound by the Secretary's regulation, which is very much an open question.

IV

The Court of Appeals found that respondents had standing for an additional reason: because they had suffered a "procedural injury." The so-called "citizen-suit" provision of the ESA provides, in pertinent part, that "any person may commence a civil suit on his own behalf (A) to enjoin any person, including the United States and any other governmental instrumentality or agency . . . who is alleged to be in violation of any provision of this chapter." 16 U.S.C. § 1540(g). The court held that, because § 7(a)(2) requires interagency consultation, the citizen-suit provision creates a "procedural righ[t]" to consultation in all "persons" — so that *anyone* can file suit in federal court to challenge the Secretary's (or presumably any other official's) failure to follow the assertedly correct consultative procedure, notwithstanding his or her inability to allege any discrete injury flowing from that failure. 911 F.2d, at 121-122. To understand the remarkable nature of this holding one must be clear about what it does *not* rest upon: This is not a case where plaintiffs are seeking to enforce a procedural requirement the disregard of which could impair a separate concrete interest of theirs (*e.g.,* the procedural requirement for a hearing prior to denial of their license application, or the procedural requirement for an environmental impact statement before a federal facility is constructed next door to them). Nor is it simply a case where concrete injury has been suffered by many persons, as in mass fraud or mass tort situations. Nor, finally, is it the unusual case in which Congress has created a concrete private interest in the outcome of a suit against a private party for the government's benefit, by providing a cash bounty for the victorious plaintiff. Rather, the court held that the injury-in-fact requirement had been satisfied by congressional conferral upon *all* persons of an abstract, self-contained, non-instrumental "right" to have the Executive observe the procedures required by law. We reject this view.

We have consistently held that a plaintiff raising only a generally available grievance about government — claiming only harm to his and every citizen's interest in proper application of the Constitution and laws, and seeking relief that no more directly and tangibly benefits him than it does the public at large — does not state an Article III case or controversy. [In] Massachusetts v. Mellon, 262 U.S. 447, 43 S.Ct. 597, 67 L.Ed. 1078 (1923), we dismissed for lack of Article III standing a taxpayer suit challenging the propriety of certain federal expenditures. We said:

> The party who invokes the power [of judicial review] must be able to show not only that the statute is invalid but that he has sustained or is immediately in danger of sustaining some direct injury as the result of its enforcement, and not merely that he suffers in some indefinite way in common with people generally. . . . Here the parties plaintiff have no such case. . . . [T]heir complaint . . . is merely that officials of the executive department of the government are executing and will execute an act of Congress asserted to be unconstitutional; and this we are asked to prevent. To do so would be not to decide a judicial controversy, but to assume a position of authority over the governmental acts of another and co-equal department, an authority which plainly we do not possess.

Id., at 488-489, 43 S.Ct., at 601.

[In] United States v. Richardson, 418 U.S. 166, 94 S.Ct. 2940, 41 L.Ed.2d 678 (1974), we dismissed for lack of standing a taxpayer suit challenging the Government's failure to disclose the expenditures of the Central Intelligence Agency, in alleged violation of the constitutional requirement, Art. I, § 9, cl. 7, that "a regular Statement and Account of the Receipts and Expenditures of all public Money shall be published from time to time."

We held that such a suit rested upon an impermissible "generalized grievance," and was inconsistent with "the framework of Article III" because "the impact on [plaintiff] is plainly undifferentiated and 'common to all members of the public.'" *Richardson*, supra, at 171, 176-177, 94 S.Ct., at 2944, 2946. And in Schlesinger v. Reservists Comm. to Stop the War, 418 U.S. 208, 94 S.Ct. 2925, 41 L.Ed.2d 706 (1974), we dismissed for the same reasons a citizen-taxpayer suit contending that it was a violation of the Incompatibility Clause, Art. I, § 6, cl. 2, for Members of Congress to hold commissions in the military Reserves. We said that the challenged action, "standing alone, would adversely affect only the generalized interest of all citizens in constitutional governance." . . . [S]ince *Schlesinger* we have on two occasions held that an injury amounting only to the alleged violation of a right to have the Government act in accordance with law was not judicially cognizable because "'assertion of a right to a particular kind of Government conduct, which the Government has violated by acting differently, cannot alone satisfy the requirements of Art. III without draining those requirements of meaning.'" *Allen*, 468 U.S., at 754, 104 S.Ct., at 3326; Valley Forge Christian College v. Americans United for Separation of Church and State, Inc., 454 U.S. 464, 483, 102 S.Ct. 752, 764, 70 L.Ed.2d 700 (1982). And only two Terms ago, we rejected the notion that Article III permits a citizen suit to prevent a condemned criminal's execution on the basis of "'the public interest protections of the Eighth Amendment'"; once again, "[t]his allegation raise[d] only the 'generalized interest of all citizens in constitutional governance' . . . and [was] an inadequate basis on which to grant . . . standing." *Whitmore*, 495 U.S., at 160, 110 S.Ct., at 1725.

To be sure, our generalized-grievance cases have typically involved Government violation of procedures assertedly ordained by the Constitution rather than the Congress. But there is absolutely no basis for making the Article III inquiry turn on the source of the asserted right. Whether the courts were to act on their own, or at the invitation of Congress, in ignoring the concrete injury requirement described in our cases, they would be discarding a principle fundamental to the separate and distinct constitutional role of the Third Branch — one of the essential elements that identifies those "Cases" and "Controversies" that are the business of the courts rather than of the political branches. "The province of the court," as Chief Justice Marshall said in Marbury v. Madison, 5 U.S. (1 Cranch) 137, 170, 2 L.Ed. 60 (1803), "is, solely, to decide on the rights of individuals." Vindicating the *public* interest (including the public interest in Government observance of the Constitution and laws) is the function of Congress and the Chief Executive. The question presented here is whether the public interest in proper administration of the laws (specifically, in agencies' observance of a particular, statutorily prescribed procedure) can be converted into an individual right by a statute that denominates it as such, and that permits all citizens (or, for that matter, a subclass of citizens who suffer no distinctive concrete harm) to sue. If the concrete injury requirement has the separation-of-powers significance we have always said, the answer must be obvious: To permit Congress to convert the undifferentiated public interest in executive officers' compliance with the law into an "individual right" vindicable in the courts is to permit Congress to transfer from the President to the courts the Chief Executive's most important constitutional duty, to "take Care that the Laws be faithfully executed," Art. II, § 3. It would enable the courts, with the permission of Congress, "to assume a position of authority over the governmental acts of another and co-equal department," Massachusetts v. Mellon, 262 U.S., at 489, 43 S.Ct., at 601, and to become "'virtually continuing monitors of the wisdom and soundness of Executive action.'" *Allen*, supra, 468 U.S., at 760, 104 S.Ct., at 3329 (quoting Laird v.

Tatum, 408 U.S. 1, 15, 92 S.Ct. 2318, 2326, 33 L.Ed.2d 154 (1972)). We have always rejected that vision of our role:

> [But] under Article III, Congress established courts to adjudicate cases and controversies as to claims of infringement of individual rights whether by unlawful action of private persons or by the exertion of unauthorized administrative power.

Stark v. Wickard, 321 U.S. 288, 309-310, 64 S.Ct. 559, 571, 88 L.Ed. 733 (1944) (footnote omitted).

"Individual rights," within the meaning of this passage, do not mean public rights that have been legislatively pronounced to belong to each individual who forms part of the public. See also *Sierra Club,* 405 U.S., at 740-741, n. 16, 92 S.Ct., at 1369, n. 16.

Nothing in this contradicts the principle that "[t]he . . . injury required by Art. III may exist solely by virtue of 'statutes creating legal rights, the invasion of which creates standing.'" *Warth,* 422 U.S., at 500, 95 S.Ct., at 2206 (quoting Linda R. S. v. Richard D., 410 U.S. 614, 617, n. 3, 93 S.Ct. 1146, 1148, n. 3, 35 L.Ed.2d 536 (1973)). [Whether] or not the principle set forth in *Warth* can be extended beyond that distinction, it is clear that in suits against the Government, at least, the concrete injury requirement must remain.

[We] hold that respondents lack standing to bring this action.

Justice KENNEDY, with whom Justice SOUTER joins, concurring in part and concurring in the judgment.

Although I agree with the essential parts of the Court's analysis, I write separately to make several observations.

[I] join Part IV of the Court's opinion with the following observations. As Government programs and policies become more complex and far reaching, we must be sensitive to the articulation of new rights of action that do not have clear analogs in our common-law tradition. Modern litigation has progressed far from the paradigm of Marbury suing Madison to get his commission, Marbury v. Madison, 5 U.S. (1 Cranch) 137, 2 L.Ed. 60 (1803), or Ogden seeking an injunction to halt Gibbons' steamboat operations, Gibbons v. Ogden, 22 U.S. (9 Wheat.) 1, 6 L.Ed. 23 (1824). In my view, Congress has the power to define injuries and articulate chains of causation that will give rise to a case or controversy where none existed before, and I do not read the Court's opinion to suggest a contrary view. See Warth v. Seldin, 422 U.S. 490, 500, 95 S.Ct. 2197, 2205, 45 L.Ed.2d 343 (1975); *ante,* at 2145-2146. In exercising this power, however, Congress must at the very least identify the injury it seeks to vindicate and relate the injury to the class of persons entitled to bring suit. The citizen-suit provision of the Endangered Species Act does not meet these minimal requirements, because while the statute purports to confer a right on "any person . . . to enjoin . . . the United States and any other governmental instrumentality or agency . . . who is alleged to be in violation of any provision of this chapter," it does not of its own force establish that there is an injury in "any person" by virtue of any "violation." 16 U.S.C. § 1540(g)(1)(A).

The Court's holding that there is an outer limit to the power of Congress to confer rights of action is a direct and necessary consequence of the case and controversy limitations found in Article III. I agree that it would exceed those limitations if, at the behest of Congress and in the absence of any showing of concrete injury, we were to entertain citizen suits to vindicate the public's non-concrete interest in the proper administration of the laws. While it does not matter how many persons have been injured by the challenged action, the party bringing suit must show that the action injures him in a concrete and personal way. This requirement is not just an empty formality. It preserves the vitality of the adversarial process by assuring both that the parties before the court have an actual, as opposed to professed, stake in the outcome, and that "the legal questions presented . . . will be resolved, not in the rarified atmosphere of a debating society, but in a concrete factual context conducive to a realistic appreciation of the consequences of judicial action." Valley Forge Christian College v. Americans United for Separation of Church and State, Inc., 454 U.S. 464, 472, 102 S.Ct. 752, 758, 70 L.Ed.2d 700 (1982). In addition, the requirement of concrete injury confines the Judicial Branch to its proper, limited role in the constitutional framework of Government.

Justice STEVENS, concurring in the judgment.

Because I am not persuaded that Congress intended the consultation requirement in § 7(a)(2) of the Endangered Species Act of 1973 (ESA), 16 U.S.C. § 1536(a)(2), to apply to activities in foreign countries, I concur in the judgment of reversal. I do not, however, agree with the Court's conclusion that respondents lack standing because the threatened injury to their interest in protecting the environment and studying endangered species is not "imminent." Nor do I agree with the plurality's additional conclusion that respondents' injury is not "redressable" in this litigation.

Justice BLACKMAN, with whom Justice O'CONNOR joins, dissenting.

I part company with the Court in this case in two respects. First, I believe that respondents have raised genuine issues of fact — sufficient to survive summary judgment — both as to injury and as to redressability. Second, I question the Court's breadth of language in rejecting standing for "procedural" injuries. I fear the Court seeks to impose fresh limitations on the constitutional authority of Congress to allow citizen suits in the federal courts for injuries deemed "procedural" in nature. I dissent.

II

The Court concludes that any "procedural injury" suffered by respondents is insufficient to confer standing. It rejects the view that the "injury-in-fact requirement [is] satisfied by congressional conferral upon *all* persons of an abstract, self-contained, non-instrumental 'right' to have the Executive observe the procedures required by law." *Ante,* at 2143. Whatever the Court might mean with that very broad language, it cannot be saying that "procedural injuries" *as a class* are necessarily insufficient for purposes of Article III standing.

Congress legislates in procedural shades of gray not to aggrandize its own power but to allow maximum Executive discretion in the attainment of Congress' legislative goals. Congress could simply impose a substantive prohibition on Executive conduct; it could say that no agency action shall result in the loss of more than 5% of any listed species. Instead, Congress sets forth substantive guidelines and allows the Executive, within certain procedural constraints, to decide how best to effectuate the ultimate goal. See American Power & Light Co. v. SEC, 329 U.S. 90, 105, 67 S.Ct. 133, 142, 91 L.Ed. 103 (1946). The Court never has questioned Congress' authority to impose such procedural constraints on Executive power. Just as Congress does not violate separation of powers by structuring the procedural manner in which the Executive shall carry out the laws, surely the federal courts do not violate separation of powers when, at the very instruction and command of Congress, they enforce these procedures.

To prevent Congress from conferring standing for "procedural injuries" is another way of saying that Congress may not delegate to the courts authority deemed "executive" in nature. [Here] Congress seeks not to delegate "executive" power but only to strengthen the procedures it has legislatively mandated.

[Ironically], this Court has previously justified a relaxed review of congressional delegation to the Executive on grounds that Congress, in turn, has subjected the exercise of that power to judicial review. INS v. Chadha, 462 U.S. 919, 953-954, n. 16, 103 S.Ct. 2764, 2785-2786, n. 16, 77 L.Ed.2d 317 (1983); American Power & Light Co. v. SEC, 329 U.S., at 105-106, 67 S.Ct. at 142-143. The Court's intimation today that procedural injuries are not constitutionally cognizable threatens this understanding upon which Congress has undoubtedly relied. In no sense is the Court's suggestion compelled by our "common understanding of what activities are appropriate to legislatures, to executives, and to courts." *Ante,* at 2136. In my view, it reflects an unseemly solicitude for an expansion of power of the Executive Branch. [There] is no room for a *per se* rule or presumption excluding injuries labeled "procedural" in nature.

III

In conclusion, I cannot join the Court on what amounts to a slash-and-burn expedition through the law of environmental standing. In my view, "[t]he very essence of civil liberty certainly consists in the right of every individual to claim the protection of the laws, whenever he receives an injury." Marbury v. Madison, 1 Cranch 137, 163, 2 L.Ed. 60 (1803).

I dissent.

MASSACHUSETTS v. ENVIRONMENTAL PROTECTION AGENCY
549 U.S. 497 (2007)

Justice STEVENS delivered the opinion of the Court, in which Justices KENNEDY, SOUTER, GINSBURG, and BREYER joined.

A well-documented rise in global temperatures has coincided with a significant increase in the concentration of carbon dioxide in the atmosphere. Respected scientists believe the two trends are related. For when carbon dioxide is released into the atmosphere, it acts like the ceiling of a greenhouse, trapping solar energy and retarding the escape of reflected heat. It is therefore a species — the most important species — of a "greenhouse gas." Calling global warming "the most pressing environmental challenge of our time," a group of States, local governments, and private organizations, alleged [that] the Environmental Protection Agency (EPA) has abdicated its responsibility under the Clean Air Act to regulate the emissions of four greenhouse gases, including carbon dioxide.

[Article III] of the Constitution limits federal-court jurisdiction to "Cases" and "Controversies." [No] justiciable "controversy" exists when parties seek adjudication of a political question, when they ask for an advisory opinion, or when the question sought to be adjudicated has been mooted by subsequent developments. This case suffers from none of these defects. The parties' dispute turns on the proper construction of a congressional statute, a question eminently suitable to resolution in federal court. Congress has moreover authorized this type of challenge to EPA action. [EPA] maintains that because greenhouse gas emissions inflict widespread harm, the doctrine of standing presents an insuperable jurisdictional obstacle. We do not agree. [Lujan] holds that a litigant must demonstrate that it has suffered a concrete and particularized injury that is either actual or imminent, that the injury is fairly traceable to the defendant, and that it is likely that a favorable decision will redress that injury. However, a litigant to whom Congress has "accorded a procedural right to protect his concrete interests" — here, the right to challenge agency action unlawfully withheld — "can assert that right without meeting all the normal standards for redressability and immediacy." When a litigant is vested with a procedural right, that litigant has standing if there is some possibility that the requested relief will prompt the injury-causing party to reconsider the decision that allegedly harmed the litigant.

Only one of the petitioners needs to have standing to permit us to consider the petition for review. We stress here [the] special position and interest of Massachusetts. It is of considerable relevance that the party seeking review here is a sovereign State and not, as it was in *Lujan*, a private individual. Well before the creation of the modern administrative state, we recognized that States are not normal litigants for the purposes of invoking federal jurisdiction. As Justice Holmes explained in Georgia v. Tennessee Copper Co., 206 U.S. 230 (1907), a case in which Georgia sought to protect its citizens from air pollution originating outside its borders; "This is a suit by a State for an injury to it in its capacity of quasi-sovereign. In that capacity the State has an interest independent of and behind the titles of its citizens, in all the earth and air within its domain." [Just] as Georgia's "independent interest in all the earth and air within its domain" supported federal jurisdiction a century ago, so too does Massachusetts' well-founded desire to preserve its sovereign territory today.

[The Injury.] The harms associated with climate change are serious and well recognized. [That] these climate-change risks are "widely shared" does not minimize Massachusetts' interest in the outcome of this litigation. According to petitioners' unchallenged affidavits, global sea levels rose somewhere between 10 and 20 centimeters over the 20th century as a result of global warming. These rising seas have already begun to swallow Massachusetts' coastal land. Because the Commonwealth "owns a substantial portion of the state's coastal property," it has alleged a particularized injury in its capacity as a landowner.

[Causation.] EPA does not dispute the existence of a causal connection between man-made greenhouse gas emissions and global warming. At a minimum, therefore, EPA's refusal to regulate such emissions "contributes" to Massachusetts' injuries. EPA nevertheless maintains that its decision not to regulate greenhouse gas emissions from new motor vehicles contributes so insignificantly to petitioners' injuries that the agency cannot be hauled into federal court to answer for them. For the same reason, EPA does not believe that any realistic possibility exists that the relief petitioners seek would mitigate global climate change and remedy their injuries. That is especially so because predicted increases in greenhouse gas emissions from developing nations, particularly China and India, are likely to offset any marginal domestic decrease.

But EPA overstates its case. Its argument rests on the erroneous assumption that a small incremental step, because it is incremental, can never be attacked in a federal judicial forum. Yet accepting that premise would doom most challenges to regulatory action. Agencies, like legislatures, do not generally resolve massive problems in one fell regulatory swoop. [That] a first step might be tentative does not by itself support the notion that federal courts lack jurisdiction to determine whether that step conforms to law. And reducing domestic automobile emissions is hardly a tentative step. [Considering] just emissions from the transportation sector, which represent less than one-third of this country's total carbon dioxide emissions, the United States would still rank as the third-largest emitter of carbon dioxide in the world, outpaced only by the European Union and China. Judged by any standard, U.S. motor-vehicle emissions make a meaningful contribution to greenhouse gas concentrations and hence, according to petitioners, to global warming.

[The Remedy.] While it may be true that regulating motor-vehicle emissions will not by itself reverse global warming, it by no means follows that we lack jurisdiction to decide whether EPA has a duty to take steps to slow or reduce it. Because of the enormity of the potential consequences associated with manmade climate change, the fact that the effectiveness of a remedy might be delayed during the (relatively short) time it takes for a new motor-vehicle fleet to replace an older one is essentially irrelevant. Nor is it dispositive that developing countries such as China and India are poised to increase greenhouse gas emissions substantially over the next century: A reduction in domestic emissions would slow the pace of global emissions increases, no matter what happens elsewhere.

In sum [the] rise in sea levels associated with global warming has already harmed and will continue to harm Massachusetts. The risk of catastrophic harm, though remote, is nevertheless real. That risk would be reduced to some extent if petitioners received the relief they seek. We therefore hold that petitioners have standing to challenge the EPA's denial of their rulemaking petition.

Chief Justice ROBERTS, with whom Justices SCALIA, THOMAS, and ALITO join, dissenting.

[This] Court's standing jurisprudence [recognizes] that redress of grievances of the sort at issue here "is the function of Congress and the Chief Executive," not the federal courts. *Lujan.* [Petitioners] bear the burden of alleging an injury that is fairly traceable to the Environmental Protection Agency's failure to promulgate new motor vehicle greenhouse gas emission standards, and that is likely to be redressed by the prospective issuance of such standards. [Relaxing] Article III standing requirements because asserted injuries are pressed by a State [has] no basis in our jurisprudence. [Far] from being a substitute for Article III injury, parens patriae actions raise an additional hurdle for a state litigant: the articulation of a "quasi-sovereign interest" "apart from the interests of particular private parties." [In] the context of parens patriae standing, however, we have characterized state ownership of land as a "nonsovereign interes[t]" because a State "is likely to have the same interests as other similarly situated proprietors."

[The] status of Massachusetts as a State cannot compensate for petitioners' failure to demonstrate injury in fact, causation, and redressability. [If] petitioners rely on loss of land, [that] alleged injury must be "concrete and particularized." [The] very concept of global warming seems inconsistent with this particularization requirement. Global warming is a phenomenon "harmful to humanity at large," and the redress petitioners seek is focused no more on them than on the public generally — it is literally to change the atmosphere around the world. If petitioners' particularized injury is loss of coastal land, it is also that injury that must be "actual or imminent, not conjectural or hypothetical," "real and immediate," and "certainly impending." [But] aside from a single conclusory statement, there is nothing in petitioners' 43 standing declarations and accompanying exhibits to support an inference of actual loss of Massachusetts coastal land from 20th century global sea level increases. It is pure conjecture. [One] of petitioners' declarants predicts global warming will cause sea level to rise by 20 to 70 centimeters by the year 2100. [But] accepting a century-long time [renders] requirements of imminence and immediacy utterly toothless.

Petitioners' reliance on Massachusetts's loss of coastal land as their injury in fact for standing purposes creates insurmountable problems for them with respect to causation and redressability. [As] EPA explained in its denial of petitioners' request for rulemaking, "predicting future climate change necessarily involves a complex web of economic and physical factors." [Petitioners] are never able to trace their alleged injuries back through this complex web to the fractional amount of global emissions that might have been limited with EPA standards. In light of the bit-part domestic new motor vehicle greenhouse gas emissions have played in what petitioners describe as a 150-year global phenomenon, and the myriad additional factors bearing on petitioners' alleged injury — the loss of Massachusetts coastal land — the connection is far too speculative to establish causation.

Redressability is even more problematic. [Petitioners] cannot meaningfully predict what will come of the 80 percent of global greenhouse gas emissions that originate outside the United States. As the Court acknowledges, "developing countries such as China and India are poised to increase greenhouse gas emissions substantially over the next century," so the domestic emissions at issue here may become an increasingly marginal portion of global emissions, and any decreases produced by petitioners' desired standards are likely to be overwhelmed many times over by emissions increases elsewhere in the world.

Petitioners offer declarations attempting to address this uncertainty, contending that "[i]f the U.S. takes steps to reduce motor vehicle emissions, other countries are very likely to take similar actions regarding their own motor vehicles using technology developed in response to the U.S. program." [But] when the existence of an element of standing "depends on the unfettered choices made by independent actors not before the courts and whose exercise of broad and legitimate discretion the courts cannot presume either to control or to predict," a party must present facts supporting an assertion that the actor will proceed in such a manner. The declarations' conclusory (not to say fanciful) statements do not even come close. No matter, the Court reasons, because any decrease in domestic emissions will "slow the pace of global emissions increases, no matter what happens elsewhere." Every little bit helps, so Massachusetts can sue over any little bit.

[Today's] decision recalls the previous high-water mark of diluted standing requirements, United States v. Students Challenging Regulatory Agency Procedures (SCRAP), 412 U.S. 669 (1973). *SCRAP* involved "[p]robably the most attenuated injury conferring Art. III standing" and "surely went to the very outer limit of the law" — until today. In *SCRAP*, the Court based an environmental group's standing to challenge a railroad freight rate surcharge on the group's allegation that increases in railroad rates would cause an increase in the use of nonrecyclable goods, resulting in the increased need for natural resources to produce such goods. According to the group, some of these resources might be taken from the Washington area, resulting in increased refuse that might find its way into area parks, harming the group's members.

Over time, *SCRAP* became emblematic not of the looseness of Article III standing requirements, but of how utterly manipulable they are if not taken seriously as a matter of judicial self-restraint. *SCRAP* made standing seem a lawyer's game, rather than a fundamental limitation ensuring that courts function as courts and not intrude on the politically accountable branches. Today's decision is *SCRAP* for a new generation.

[The portions of the opinion of the Court going to the merits of the claim are omitted.]

11. ARTICLE III MINIMUMS: "INJURY IN FACT" AND "CAUSAL CONNECTION"

SUMMERS v. EARTH ISLAND INSTITUTE, 555 U.S. 488 (2009). In *Summers* the Court once again emphasized that even under "minimum" standards it might scrutinize the "concreteness" of the cited harm in regard to the injury-in-fact requirement. Environmental organizations sued to enjoin the U.S. Forest Service from applying its regulations to exempt the sale of certain timber on 238 acres of fire-damaged federal land from the notice, comment, and appeal process set forth in the Forest Service Decisionmaking and Appeals Reform Act. Justice Scalia, speaking for the Court (5 to 4), held that plaintiffs did not have standing to challenge regulations when there was no concrete dispute over application of those regulations. The plaintiffs claimed that they had suffered procedural injury, the ability to file comments on some of the Forest Service actions. "But deprivation of a procedural right without some concrete interest that is affected by the deprivation — a procedural right *in* vacuo — is insufficient to create Article III standing."

The Court acknowledged that Congress can loosen the requirements of the redressability prong of standing so that standing exists despite the possibility that plaintiffs' alleged right to comment would not be successful in persuading the Forest Service to avoid impairment of plaintiffs' concrete interests. "Unlike redressability, however, the requirement of injury in fact is a hard floor of Article III jurisdiction that cannot be removed by statute." The Court also rejected additional affidavits because plaintiffs had filed them *after* the trial was over, judgment was entered, and notice of appeal filed. The affidavits the Court did consider failed to establish that any member had any concrete plans to visit a site where the challenged regulations were being applied in a manner that would harm that member's concrete interests.

C. DISCRETIONARY ABSTENTION/THE POWER TO DECLINE JURISDICTION

1. AVOIDING CONSTITUTIONAL QUESTIONS

Given our review of constitutional decision making and the conclusion of the Court in *Warth*, it seems somewhat anticlimatic to introduce the thesis that the Court will apply discretionary abstention and decline jurisdiction to avoid constitutional questions. This concept did not commence with *Warth v. Seldin*, though the Court in *Warth* did make prudence a part of legal doctrine in constitutional law. Such abstention had a history before *Warth*, although prior to its holding, one had to make "analytical" arguments in support of such rather than the straightforward "law" articulated in the opinion. In cases such as *Rescue Army v. Municipal Court of Los Angeles*, 331 U.S. 549 (1947), where Justice Rutledge argued "that the Court will not adjudicate constitutional issues unless such rulings are unavoidable;" to the Connecticut anticontraceptive cases reviewed earlier (*Tileston* and *Poe*); or to the famous summary dismissals in the *Naim v. Naim* litigation (350 U.S. 891 (1955) and 350 U.S. 985 (1956)), there has been a history of such judicial restraint in constitutional matters. As we have asserted, the legacy of judicial review and the democratic nature of the U.S. system of government make these dilemmatic issues unavoidable. So it should certainly not be news that the Court so acts.

The question that remains was well put by Gerard Gunther when he responded to the virtues of Alexander Bickel's judicial "passivity": "we have never confronted one issue of great significance[:] is avoidance of the judicial power, where constitutional requirements are satisfied, in and of itself constitutional?" Gerard Gunther, *The Subtle Vices of the Passive Virtues*, 64 Colum. L. Rev. 1 (1964). Note Chief Justice Marshall's views on this issue in the next case, a restatement of the principal holding of *Martin v. Hunter's Lessee*, but in regard to state criminal rather than civil proceedings.

COHENS v. VIRGINIA
6 Wheat. (19 U.S.) 264 (1821)

Mr. Chief Justice MARSHALL delivered the opinion of the Court. . . .

It is most true that this Court will not take jurisdiction if it should not: but it is equally true, that it must take jurisdiction if it should. The judiciary cannot, as the legislature may, avoid a measure because it approaches the confines of the constitution. We cannot pass it by because it is doubtful. With whatever doubts, with whatever difficulties, a case may be attended, we must decide it, if it be brought before us. We have no more right to decline the exercise of jurisdiction which is given, than to usurp that which is not given. The one or the other would be treason to the constitution. Questions may occur which we would gladly avoid; but we cannot avoid them. All we can do is, to exercise our best judgment, and conscientiously to perform our duty. In doing this, on the present occasion, we find this tribunal invested with appellate jurisdiction in *all* cases arising under the constitution and laws of the United States. We find no exception to this grant, and we cannot insert one.

Comments on *Cohens*. This statement has become known as Marshall's "dicta" in *Cohens*. Are you surprised that it has been so distinguished? Marshall certainly raised interesting issues, particularly, "We have no more right to decline the exercise of jurisdiction which is given, than to usurp that which is not given. The one or the other would be *treason* to the constitution." (emphasis added). For our purposes perhaps being a "realist" is the best posture: as the materials in this text emphasize, and as has been made clear in the modern era by the Court itself, the Supreme Court and the federal courts *will* exercise discretionary abstention even when the Constitution's jurisdictional requirements are met, and we had best be prepared to deal with it.

Would it surprise you to find out that political liberals argued for restraint by the Court when political conservatives dominated the Court and pursued judicial activism, and that political conservatives argued for restraint by the Court when political liberals dominated the Court and pursued judicial activism? Is this "human nature," or if life is "bull*hit", why would you assume the Supreme Court and its judges would be any different. (Ah, but there we are playing "realist" once again.) Consequently, the classic statement summarizing Supreme Court discretionary abstention came from perhaps the most liberal Justice of his age, Louis Brandeis, in his concurring opinion in *Ashwander,* responding to the judicial activism of a politically conservative Court.

ASHWANDER v. TENNESSEE VALLEY AUTHORITY
297 U.S. 288 (1936)

Mr. Chief Justice HUGHES delivered the opinion of the Court.

On January 4, 1934, the Tennessee Valley Authority, an agency of the federal government, entered into a contract with the Alabama Power Company, providing (1) for the purchase by the Authority from the Power Company of certain transmission lines, substations, and auxiliary properties for $1,000,000; (2) for the purchase by the Authority from the Power Company of certain real property for $150,000; (3) for an interchange of hydroelectric energy, and, in addition, for the sale by the Authority to the Power Company of its 'surplus power,' on stated terms; and (4) for mutual restrictions as to the areas to be served in the sale of power. The contract was amended and supplemented in minor particulars on February 13 and May 24, 1934.

. . . [P]laintiffs are holders of preferred stock of the Alabama Power Company. Conceiving the contract with the Tennessee Valley Authority to be injurious to the corporate interests and also invalid, because beyond the constitutional power of the federal government, they submitted their protest to the board of directors of the Power Company and demanded that steps should be taken to have the contract annulled. The board refused, and the Commonwealth & Southern Corporation, the holder of all the common stock of the Power Company, declined to call a meeting of the stockholders to take action. [A]s the protest was unavailing, plaintiffs brought this suit to have the invalidity of the contract determined and its performance enjoined. Going beyond that particular challenge, and setting forth the pronouncements, policies, and programs of the Authority, plaintiffs sought a decree restraining these activities as repugnant to the Constitution, and also asked a general declaratory decree with respect to the rights of the Authority in various relations.

Mr. Justice BRANDEIS (concurring).

"Considerations of propriety, as well as long-established practice, demand that we refrain from passing upon the constitutionality of an act of Congress unless obliged to do so in the proper performance of our judicial function, when the question is raised by a party whose interests entitle him to raise it." Blair v. United States, 250 U.S. 273, 279, 39 S.Ct. 468, 470, 63 L.Ed. 979.

. . . [T]he Court developed, for its own governance in the cases confessedly within its jurisdiction, a series of rules under which it has avoided passing upon a large part of all the constitutional questions pressed upon it for decision. They are:

1.   The Court will not pass upon the constitutionality of legislation in a friendly, non-adversary, proceeding, declining because to decide such questions "is legitimate only in the last resort, and as a necessity in the determination of real, earnest, and vital controversy between individuals. It never was the thought that, by means of a friendly suit, a party beaten in the legislature could transfer to the courts an inquiry as to the constitutionality of the legislative act." Chicago & Grand Trunk Ry. Co. v. Wellman, 143 U.S. 339, 345, 12 S.Ct. 400, 402, 36 L.Ed. 176. Compare Lord v. Veazie, 8 How. 251, 12 L.Ed. 1067; Atherton Mills v. Johnston, 259 U.S. 13, 15, 42 S.Ct. 422, 66 L.Ed. 814.

2. The Court will not "anticipate a question of constitutional law in advance of the necessity of deciding it." Liverpool, N.Y. & Phila. Steamship Co. v. Emigration Commissioners, 113 U.S. 33, 39, 5 S.Ct. 352, 355, 28 L.Ed. 899; Abrams v. Van Schaick, 293 U.S. 188, 55 S.Ct. 135, 79 L.Ed. 278; Wilshire Oil Co. v. United States, 295 U.S. 100, 55 S.Ct. 673, 79 L.Ed. 1329. "It is not the habit of the court to decide questions of a constitutional nature unless absolutely necessary to a decision of the case." Burton v. United States, 196 U.S. 283, 295, 25 S.Ct. 243, 245, 49 L.Ed. 482.

3. The Court will not "formulate a rule of constitutional law broader than is required by the precise facts to which it is to be applied." Liverpool, N.Y. & Phila. Steamship Co. v. Emigration Commissioners, supra. Compare Hammond v. Schappi Bus Line, Inc., 275 U.S. 164, 169-172, 48 S.Ct. 66, 72 L.Ed. 218.

4. The Court will not pass upon a constitutional question although properly presented by the record, if there is also present some other ground upon which the case may be disposed of. This rule has found most varied application. Thus, if a case can be decided on either of two grounds, one involving a constitutional question, the other a question of statutory construction or general law, the Court will decide only the latter. Siler v. Louisville & Nashville R. Co., 213 U.S. 175, 191, 29 S.Ct. 451, 53 L.Ed. 753; Light v. United States, 220 U.S. 523, 538, 31 S.Ct. 485, 55 L.Ed. 570. Appeals from the highest court of a state challenging its decision of a question under the Federal Constitution are frequently dismissed because the judgment can be sustained on an independent state ground. Berea College v. Kentucky, 211 U.S. 45, 53, 29 S.Ct. 33, 53 L.Ed. 81.

5. The Court will not pass upon the validity of a statute upon complaint of one who fails to show that he is injured by its operation. Tyler v. Judges, etc., 179 U.S. 405, 21 S.Ct. 206, 45 L.Ed. 252; Hendrick v. Maryland, 235 U.S. 610, 621, 35 S.Ct. 140, 59 L.Ed. 385. Among the many applications of this rule, none is more striking than the denial of the right of challenge to one who lacks a personal or property right. Thus, the challenge by a public official interested only in the performance of his official duty will not be entertained. Columbus & Greenville Ry. Co. v. Miller, 283 U.S. 96, 99, 100, 51 S.Ct. 392, 75 L.Ed. 861. In Fairchild v. Hughes, 258 U.S. 126, 42 S.Ct. 274, 66 L.Ed. 499, the Court affirmed the dismissal of a suit brought by a citizen who sought to have the Nineteenth Amendment declared unconstitutional. In Massachusetts v. Mellon, 262 U.S. 447, 43 S.Ct. 597, 67 L.Ed. 1078, the challenge of the federal Maternity Act was not entertained although made by the commonwealth on behalf of all its citizens.

6. The Court will not pass upon the constitutionality of a statute at the instance of one who has availed himself of its benefits. Great Falls Mfg. Co. v. Attorney General, 124 U.S. 581, 8 S.Ct. 631, 31 L.Ed. 527; Wall v. Parrot Silver & Copper Co., 244 U.S. 407, 411, 412, 37 S.Ct. 609, 61 L.Ed. 1229; St. Louis Malleable Casting Co. v. Prendergast Construction Co., 260 U.S. 469, 43 S.Ct. 178, 67 L.Ed. 351.

7. "When the validity of an act of the Congress is drawn in question, and even if a serious doubt of constitutionality is raised, it is a cardinal principle that this Court will first ascertain whether a construction of the statute is fairly possible by which the question may be avoided." Crowell v. Benson, 285 U.S. 22, 62, 52 S.Ct. 285, 296, 76 L.Ed. 598.

[Mr]. Justice Iredell said, as early as 1798, in Calder v. Bull, 3 Dall. 386, 399, 1 L.Ed. 648: "If any act of congress, or of the legislature of a state, violates those constitutional provisions, it is unquestionably void; though, I admit, that as the authority to declare it void is of a delicate and awful nature, the court will never resort to that authority, but in a clear and urgent case.'"

Mr. Chief Justice Marshall said, in Dartmouth College v. Woodward, 4 Wheat. 518, 625, 4 L.Ed. 629: "On more than one occasion, this court has expressed the cautious circumspection with which it approaches the consideration of such questions; and has declared, that in no doubtful case, would it pronounce a legislative act to be contrary to the constitution."

———————

Comments on the "Neo-Brandeisian" Rules. To what extent are these rules created by the Court or extracted from the Constitution? Does this make a difference? With whom do you agree, Marshall or Brandeis? If Marshall's views in *Cohens* are dicta, note that the "neo-Brandeisian" rules extend from a concurring opinion! Does all of this become mere conjecture when the Court, in the section that follows, stipulates that it will abstain from cases that are political questions?

2. POLITICAL QUESTIONS

The Court, in *Baker v. Carr*, below, summarized the two bases upon which it will abstain from hearing a case because it is a political question: 1. "a textually demonstrable constitutional commitment of the issue to a coordinate political department"; or 2. "a lack of judicially discoverable and manageable standards for resolving it." Are both of these discretionary? A textually committed power to a coordinate branch is arguably constitutionally based, but what of judicially unmanageable standards? How do you think Herbert Wechsler and Alexander Bicker, discussed earlier, would have viewed the above cited bases for political questions? Recall that they differed in regard to discretion in application of the judicial power.

The most significant debate over the political question doctrine in the modern era concerned the "mal-apportionment" of both state and federal legislatures. Justice Frankfurter's views in *Colegrove*, following, in the neo-Brandeisian spirit, draw upon both of the above-cited bases for political question abstention.

Baker is the Warren era response to *Colegrove* and set the stage for reapportionment (ordered in *Reynolds v. Sims*, supra) and revitalization of democracy in America. Earl Warren, in his biography, would conclude that *Baker* was the most significant decision during his tenure as Chief Justice. See Earl Warren, *The Memoirs of Earl Warren* 306-310 (1977). Why do you think he would so conclude, particularly given the numerous decisions of great impact decided while he served as Chief Justice?

COLEGROVE v. GREEN
328 U.S. 549 (1946)

Mr. Justice FRANKFURTER announced the judgment of the Court and an opinion in which Mr. Justice REED and Mr. Justice BURTON concur.

. . . [Petitioners] are three qualified voters in Illinois districts which have much larger populations than other Illinois congressional districts. They brought this suit against the Governor, the Secretary of State, and the Auditor of the State of Illinois, as members ex officio of the Illinois Primary Certifying Board, to restrain them, in effect, from taking proceedings for an election in November 1946, under the provisions of Illinois law governing congressional districts. Illinois Laws of 1901, p. 3. Formally, the appellees asked for a decree, with its incidental relief, § 274d Judicial Code, 28 U.S.C. § 400, 28 U.S.C.A. § 400, declaring these provisions to be invalid because they violated various provisions of the United States Constitution and § 3 of the Reapportionment Act of August 8, 1911, 37 Stat. 13, 2 U.S.C.A. § 3, as amended, 2 U.S.C. § 2a, 2 U.S.C.A. § 2a, in that by reason of subsequent changes in population the congressional districts for the election of Representatives in the Congress created by the Illinois Laws of 1901, Ill.Rev.Stat.Ch. 46, 1945, §§ 154-156, lacked compactness of territory and approximate equality of population. The District Court, feeling bound by this Court's opinion in Wood v. Broom, 287 U.S. 1, 53 S.Ct. 1, 77 L.Ed. 131, dismissed the bill. 64 F.Supp. 632.

. . . [W]e are of opinion that the petitioners ask of this Court what is beyond its competence to grant. This is one of those demands on judicial power which cannot be met by verbal fencing about "jurisdiction." It must be resolved by considerations on the basis of which this Court, from time to time, has refused to intervene in controversies. It has refused to do so because due regard for the effective working of our Government revealed this issue to be of a peculiarly political nature and therefore not meet for judicial determination.

. . . [The] basis for the suit is not a private wrong, but a wrong suffered by Illinois as a polity. Compare Nixon v. Herndon, 273 U.S. 536, 47 S.Ct. 446, 71 L.Ed. 759 and Lane v. Wilson, 307 U.S. 268, 59 S.Ct. 872, 83 L.Ed. 1281, with Giles v. Harris, 189 U.S. 475, 23 S.Ct. 639, 47 L.Ed. 909. In effect this is an appeal to the federal courts to reconstruct the electoral process of Illinois in order that it may be adequately represented in the councils of the Nation. Because the Illinois legislature has failed to revise its congressional Representative districts in order to reflect great changes, during more than a generation, in the distribution of its population, we are asked to do this, as it were, for Illinois.

Of course no court can affirmatively remap the Illinois districts so as to bring them more in conformity with the standards of fairness for a representative system. At best we could only declare the existing electoral system invalid. The result would be to leave Illinois undistricted and to bring into operation, if the Illinois legislature chose not to act, the choice of members for the House of Representatives on a state-wide ticket. The last stage may be worse than the first. The upshot of judicial action may defeat the vital political principle which led Congress, more than a hundred years ago, to require districting.

The petitioners urge with great zeal that the conditions of which they complain are grave evils and offend public morality. The Constitution of the United States gives ample power to provide against these evils. But due regard for the Constitution as a viable system precludes judicial correction. Authority for dealing with such problems resides elsewhere. Article I, section 4 of the Constitution provides that "The Times, Places and Manner of holding Elections for . . . Representative, shall be prescribed in each State by the Legislature thereof; but the Congress may at any time by Law make or alter such Regulations. . . ." The short of it is that the Constitution has conferred upon Congress exclusive authority to secure fair representation by the States in the popular House and left to that House determination whether States have fulfilled their responsibility. If Congress failed in exercising its powers, whereby standards of fairness are offended, the remedy ultimately lies with the people. Whether Congress faithfully discharges its duty or not, the subject has been committed to the exclusive control of Congress. An aspect of government from which the judiciary, in view of what is involved, has been excluded by the clear intention of the Constitution cannot be entered by the federal courts because Congress may have been in default in exacting from States obedience to its mandate.

The one stark fact that emerges from a study of the history of congressional apportionment is its embroilment in politics, in the sense of party contests and party interests. The Constitution enjoins upon Congress the duty of apportioning Representatives "among the several States . . . according to their respective Numbers. . . ." Article I, § 2.

. . . [To] sustain this action would cut very deep into the very being of Congress. Courts ought not to enter this political thicket. The remedy for unfairness in districting is to secure State legislatures that will apportion properly, or to invoke the ample powers of Congress. The Constitution has many commands that are not enforceable by courts because they clearly fall outside the conditions and purposes that circumscribe judicial action. [Violation] of the great guaranty of a republican form of government in States cannot be challenged in the courts. Pacific States Telephone & Telegraph Co. v. Oregon, 223 U.S. 118, 32 S.Ct. 224, 56 L.Ed. 377. The Constitution has left the performance of many duties in our governmental scheme to depend on the fidelity of the executive and legislative action and, ultimately, on the vigilance of the people in exercising their political rights.

Dismissal of the complaint is affirmed.

BAKER v. CARR
369 U.S. 186 (1962)

Action under the civil rights statute, by qualified voters of certain counties of Tennessee for a declaration that a state apportionment statute was an unconstitutional deprivation of equal protection of the laws. [A] three-judge District Court, for the Middle District of Tennessee, 179 F.Supp. 824, entered an order dismissing the complaint, and plaintiffs appealed.

Mr. Justice BRENNAN delivered the opinion of the Court.

[We] hold that this challenge to an apportionment presents no non-justiciable "political question." . . .

Of course the mere fact that the suit seeks protection of a political right does not mean it presents a political question. Such an objection "is little more than a play upon words." Rather, it is argued that apportionment cases, whatever the actual wording of the complaint, can involve no federal constitutional right except one resting on the guaranty of a republican form of government, and that complaints based on that clause have been held to present political questions which are non-justiciable.

We hold that the claim pleaded here neither rests upon nor implicates the Guaranty Clause. [To] show why we reject the argument based on the Guaranty Clause, we must examine the authorities under it. But because there appears to be some uncertainty as to why those cases did present political questions, and specifically as to whether this apportionment case is like those cases, we deem it necessary first to consider the contours of the "political question" doctrine.

Our discussion [requires] review of a number of political question cases, in order to expose the attributes of the doctrine — attributes which, in various settings, diverge, combine, appear, and disappear in seeming disorderliness.

We have said that "In determining whether a question falls within [the political question] category, the appropriateness under our system of government of attributing finality to the action of the political departments and also the lack of satisfactory criteria for a judicial determination are dominant considerations." The non-justiciability of a political question is primarily a function of the separation of powers. Much confusion results from the capacity of the "political question" label to obscure the need for case-by-case inquiry. Deciding whether a matter has in any measure been committed by the Constitution to another branch of government, or whether the action of that branch exceeds whatever authority has been committed, is itself a delicate exercise in constitutional interpretation, and is a responsibility of this Court as ultimate interpreter of the Constitution.

Foreign relations: There are sweeping statements to the effect that all questions touching foreign relations are political questions. Not only does resolution of such issues frequently turn on standards that defy judicial application, or involve the exercise of a discretion demonstrably committed to the executive or legislature; but many such questions uniquely demand single-voiced statement of the Government's views. Yet it is error to suppose that every case or controversy which touches foreign relations lies beyond judicial cognizance. Our cases in this field seem invariably to show a discriminating analysis of the particular question posed, in terms of the history of its management by the political branches, of its susceptibility to judicial handling in the light of its nature and posture in the specific case, and of the possible consequences of judicial action. Dates of duration of hostilities: Though it has been stated broadly that "the power which declared the necessity is the power to declare its cessation, and what the cessation requires," here too analysis reveals isolable reasons for the presence of political questions, underlying this Court's refusal to review the political departments' determination of when or whether a war has ended. Dominant is the need for finality in the political determination, for emergency's nature demands "A prompt and unhesitating obedience." . . . Further, clearly definable criteria for decision may be available. In such cases the political question barrier falls away. . . . Validity of enactments: In Coleman v. Miller, [307 U.S. 433 (1939)], this Court held that the questions of how long a proposed amendment to the Federal Constitution remained open to ratification, and what effect a prior rejection had on a subsequent ratification, were committed to congressional resolution and involved criteria of decision that necessarily escaped the judicial grasp. Similar considerations apply to the enacting process: "The respect due to coequal and independent departments," and the need for finality and certainty about the status of a statute contribute to judicial reluctance to inquire whether, as passed, it complied with all requisite formalities. . . .

[It] is apparent that several formulations which vary slightly according to the settings in which the questions arise may describe a political question, although each has one or more elements which identify it as essentially a function of the separation of powers. Prominent on the surface of any case held to involve a political question is found a textually demonstrable constitutional commitment of the issue to a coordinate political department; or a lack of judicially discoverable and manageable standards for resolving it; or the impossibility of deciding without an initial policy determination of a kind clearly for nonjudicial discretion; or the impossibility of a court's undertaking independent resolution without expressing lack of the respect due coordinate branches of government; or an unusual need for unquestioning adherence to a political decision already made; or the potentiality of embarrassment from multifarious pronouncements by various departments on one question.

Unless one of these formulations is inextricable from the case at bar, there should be no dismissal for non-justiciability on the ground of a political question's presence. The doctrine of which we treat is one of "political questions," not one of "political cases." . . .

But it is argued that this case shares the characteristics of decisions that constitute a category not yet considered, cases concerning the Constitution's guaranty [of] a republican form of government. [Guaranty] Clause claims involve those elements which define a "political question," and for that reason and no other, they are non-justiciable. In particular, [the] non-justiciability of such claims has nothing to do with their touching upon matters of state governmental organization. Luther v. Borden, [7 How. 1 (1849)], though in form simply an action for damages for trespass was, as Daniel Webster said in opening the argument for the defense, "an unusual case." The defendants, admitting an otherwise tortious breaking and entering, sought to justify their action on the ground that they were agents of the established lawful government of Rhode Island, which State was then under martial law to defend itself from active insurrection; that the plaintiff was engaged in that insurrection; and that they entered under orders to arrest the plaintiff. The case arose "out of the unfortunate political differences which agitated the people of Rhode Island in 1841 and 1842," [and] which had resulted in a situation wherein two groups laid competing claims to recognition as the lawful government. The plaintiff's right to recover depended upon which of the two groups was entitled to such recognition; but the lower court's refusal to receive evidence or hear argument on that issue, its charge to the jury that the earlier established or "charter" government was lawful, and the verdict for the defendants, were affirmed upon appeal to this Court.

Chief Justice Taney's opinion for the Court reasoned as follows: (1) If a court were to hold the defendants' acts unjustified because the charter government had no legal existence during the period in question, it would follow that all of that government's actions — laws enacted, taxes collected, salaries paid, accounts settled, sentences passed — were of no effect; and that "the officers who carried their decisions into operation [were] answerable as trespassers, if not in some cases as criminals." [A] decision for the plaintiff would inevitably have produced some significant measure of chaos. . . . (2) No state court had recognized as a judicial responsibility settlement of the issue of the locus of state governmental authority. Indeed, the courts of Rhode Island had in several cases held that "it rested with the political power to decide whether the charter government had been displaced or not," and that that department had acknowledged no change. (3) Since "[t]he question relates, altogether, to the constitution and laws of [the] . . . State," the courts of the United States had to follow the state courts' decisions unless there was a federal constitutional ground for overturning them. (4) No provision of the Constitution could be or had been invoked for this purpose except Art. IV, §4, the Guaranty Clause. Having already noted the absence of standards whereby the choice between governments could be made by a court acting independently, Chief Justice Taney now found further textual and practical reasons for concluding that, if any department of the United States was empowered by the Guaranty Clause to resolve the issue, it was not the judiciary: Under this article of the Constitution it rests with Congress to decide what government is the established one in a State. . . . [After] the President has acted and called out the militia, is a Circuit Court of the United States authorized to inquire whether his decision was right? . . .

If the judicial power extends so far, the guarantee contained in the Constitution of the United States is a guarantee of anarchy, and not of order. . . . Clearly, several factors were thought by the Court in Luther to make the question there "political": the commitment to the other branches of the decision as to which is the lawful state government; the unambiguous action by the President, in recognizing the charter government as the lawful authority; the need for finality in the executive's decision; and the lack of criteria by which a court could determine which form of government was republican.

But the only significance that Luther could have for our immediate purposes is in its holding that the Guaranty Clause is not a repository of judicially manageable standards which a court could utilize independently in order to identify a State's lawful government.

. . .

We come, finally, to the ultimate inquiry whether our precedents as to what constitutes a non-justiciable "political question" bring the case before us under the umbrella of that doctrine. A natural beginning is to note whether any of the common characteristics which we have been able to identify and label descriptively are present. We find none: The question here is the consistency of state action with the Federal Constitution. We have no question decided, or to be decided, by a political branch of government coequal with this Court. Nor do we risk embarrassment of our government abroad, or grave disturbance at home if we take issue with Tennessee as to the constitutionality of her action here challenged. Nor need the appellants, in order to succeed in this action, ask the Court to enter upon policy determinations for which judicially manageable standards are lacking. Judicial standards under the Equal Protection Clause are well developed and familiar, and it has been open to courts since the enactment of the Fourteenth Amendment to determine, if on the particular facts they must, that a discrimination reflects no policy, but simply arbitrary and capricious action.

This case does, in one sense, involve the allocation of political power within a State, and the appellants might conceivably have added a claim under the Guaranty Clause. Of course, as we have seen, any reliance on that clause would be futile. But because any reliance on the Guaranty Clause could not have succeeded it does not follow that appellants may not be heard on the equal protection claim which in fact they tender. True, it must be clear that the Fourteenth Amendment claim is not so enmeshed with those political question elements which render Guaranty Clause claims non-justiciable as actually to present a political question itself. But we have found that not to be the case here.

Reversed and remanded.

Mr. Justice FRANKFURTER, whom Mr. Justice HARLAN joins, dissenting.

[A] hypothetical claim resting on abstract assumptions is now for the first time made the basis for affording illusory relief for a particular evil even though it foreshadows deeper and more pervasive difficulties in consequence. The claim is hypothetical and the assumptions are abstract because the Court does not vouchsafe the lower courts — state and federal — guidelines for formulating specific, definite, wholly unprecedented remedies for the inevitable litigations that today's umbrageous disposition is bound to stimulate in connection with politically motivated reapportionments in so many States. In such a setting, to promulgate jurisdiction in the abstract is meaningless. It is as devoid of reality as "a brooding omnipresence in the sky," for it conveys no intimation what relief, if any, a District Court is capable of affording that would not invite legislatures to play ducks and drakes with the judiciary. [To] charge courts with the task of accommodating the incommensurable factors of policy that underlie these mathematical puzzles is to attribute, however flatteringly, omnicompetence to judges. . . .

[In] a democratic society like ours, relief must come through an aroused popular conscience that sears the conscience of the people's representatives. In any event there is nothing judicially more unseemly nor more self-defeating than for this Court to make in terrorem pronouncements, to indulge in merely empty rhetoric, sounding a word of promise to the ear, sure to be disappointing to the hope.

[From] its earliest opinions this Court has consistently recognized a class of controversies which do not lend themselves to judicial standards and judicial remedies. . .
.

The present case involves all of the elements that have made the Guarantee Clause cases non-justiciable. It is, in effect, a Guarantee Clause claim masquerading under a different label. But it cannot make the case more fit for judicial action that appellants invoke the Fourteenth Amendment rather than Art. IV, §4, where, in fact, the gist of their complaint is the same — unless it can be found that the Fourteenth Amendment speaks with greater particularity to their situation. We have been admonished to avoid "the tyranny of labels." Art. IV, §4, is not committed by express constitutional terms to Congress. It is the nature of the controversies arising under it, nothing else, which has made it judicially unenforceable. But where judicial competence is wanting, it cannot be created by invoking one clause of the Constitution rather than another.

––––––––

Comment on *Baker* and Reapportionment. Was *Baker* an activist case? How did the majority in *Baker* circumvent the issues raised by Frankfurter in *Colegrove*? Was *Baker* an "end-around" *Colegrove*? If so, how might it affect political question doctrine?

Did the Court in *Baker* conclude that reapportionment was not "textually committed"? Upon what rationale did the Court base its decision? Did *Baker* make the decision in *Powell,* which follows, possible? Does the Court's decision in *Powell* answer the first question asked: "Was *Baker* an activist case?" Why or why not?

POWELL v. McCORMACK
395 U.S. 486 (1969)

Mr. Chief Justice WARREN delivered the opinion of the Court.

In November 1966, petitioner Adam Clayton Powell, Jr., was duly elected from the 18th congressional District of New York to serve in the United States House of Representatives for the 90th Congress. However, pursuant to a House resolution, he was not permitted to take his seat. Powell (and some of the voters of his district) then filed suit in Federal District Court, claiming that the House could exclude him only if it found he failed to meet the standing requirements of age, citizenship, and residence contained in Art. I, § 2, of the Constitution — requirements the House specifically found Powell met — and thus had excluded him unconstitutionally. The District Court dismissed petitioners' complaint "for want of jurisdiction of the subject matter." A panel of the Court of Appeals affirmed the dismissal, although on somewhat different grounds, each judge filing a separate opinion. We have determined that it was error to dismiss the complaint and that petitioner Powell is entitled to a declaratory judgment that he was unlawfully excluded from the 90th Congress.

[B. POLITICAL QUESTION DOCTRINE]
1. Textually Demonstrable Constitutional Commitment

Respondents maintain that even if this case is otherwise justiciable, it presents only a political question. It is well established that the federal courts will not adjudicate political questions. See, e.g., Coleman v. Miller, 307 U.S. 433, 59 S.Ct. 972, 83 L.Ed. 1385 (1939); Oetjen v. Central Leather Co., 246 U.S. 297, 38 S.Ct. 309, 62 L.Ed. 726 (1918). In Baker v. Carr, supra, we noted that political questions are not justiciable primarily because of the separation of powers within the Federal Government. After reviewing our decisions in this area, we concluded that on the surface of any case held to involve a political question was at least one of the following formulations:

> a textually demonstrable constitutional commitment of the issue to a co-ordinate political department; or a lack of judicially discoverable and manageable standards for resolving it; or the impossibility of deciding without an initial policy determination of a kind clearly for nonjudicial discretion; or the impossibility of a court's undertaking independent resolution without expressing lack of the respect due co-ordinate branches of government; or an unusual need for unquestioning adherence to a political decision already made; or the potentiality of embarrassment from multifarious pronouncements by various departments on one question.

369 U.S., at 217, 82 S.Ct., at 710.

Respondents' first contention is that this case presents a political question because under Art. I, § 5, there has been a "textually demonstrable constitutional commitment" to the House of the "adjudicatory power" to determine Powell's qualifications. Thus it is argued that the House, and the House alone, has power to determine who is qualified to be a member.

In order to determine whether there has been a textual commitment to a coordinate department of the Government, we must interpret the Constitution. In other words, we must first determine what power the Constitution confers upon the House through Art. I, § 5, before we can determine to what extent, if any, the exercise of that power is subject to judicial review. Respondents maintain that the House has broad power under § 5, and, they argue, the House may determine which are the qualifications necessary for membership. On the other hand, petitioners allege that the Constitution provides that an elected representative may be denied his seat only if the House finds he does not meet one of the standing qualifications expressly prescribed by the Constitution.

If examination of § 5 disclosed that the Constitution gives the House judicially unreviewable power to set qualifications for membership and to judge whether prospective members meet those qualifications, further review of the House determination might well be barred by the political question doctrine. On the other hand, if the Constitution gives the House power to judge only whether elected members possess the three standing qualifications set forth in the Constitution, further consideration would be necessary to determine whether any of the other formulations of the political question doctrine are "inextricable from the case at bar."[13] Baker v. Carr, supra, at 217, 82 S.Ct. at 710.

In other words, whether there is a "textually demonstrable constitutional commitment of the issue to a coordinate political department" of government and what is the scope of such commitment are questions we must resolve for the first time in this case. For, as we pointed out in Baker v. Carr, supra, "[d]eciding whether a matter has in any measure been committed by the Constitution to another branch of government, or whether the action of that branch exceeds whatever authority has been committed, is itself a delicate exercise in

---

[13] Consistent with this interpretation, federal courts might still be barred by the political question doctrine from reviewing the House's factual determination that a member did not meet one of the standing qualifications. This is an issue not presented in this case and we express no view as to its resolution.

constitutional interpretation, and is a responsibility of this Court as ultimate interpreter of the Constitution." Id., at 211, 82 S.Ct. at 706.

In order to determine the scope of any "textual commitment" under Art. I, § 5, we necessarily must determine the meaning of the phrase to "be the Judge of the Qualifications of its own Members." Petitioners argue that the records of the debates during the constitutional Convention; available commentary from the post-Convention, pre-ratification period; and early congressional applications of Art. I, § 5, support their construction of the section. Respondents insist, however, that a careful examination of the pre-Convention practices of the English Parliament and American colonial assemblies demonstrates that by 1787, a legislature's power to judge the qualifications of its members was generally understood to encompass exclusion or expulsion on the ground that an individual's character or past conduct rendered him unfit to serve. When the Constitution and the debates over its adoption are thus viewed in historical perspective, argue respondents, it becomes clear that the "qualifications" expressly set forth in the Constitution were not meant to limit the long-recognized legislative power to exclude or expel at will, but merely to establish "standing incapacities," which could be altered only by a constitutional amendment. Our examination of the relevant historical materials leads us to the conclusion that petitioners are correct and that the Constitution leaves the House without authority to exclude any person, duly elected by his constituents, who meets all the requirements for membership expressly prescribed in the Constitution.

d. Conclusion

Had the intent of the Framers emerged from these materials with less clarity, we would nevertheless have been compelled to resolve any ambiguity in favor of a narrow construction of the scope of Congress' power to exclude members-elect. A fundamental principle of our representative democracy is, in Hamilton's words, "that the people should choose whom they please to govern them." 2 Elliot's Debates 257. As Madison pointed out at the Convention, this principle is undermined as much by limiting whom the people can select as by limiting the franchise itself. In apparent agreement with this basic philosophy, the Convention adopted his suggestion limiting the power to expel. To allow essentially that same power to be exercised under the guise of judging qualifications, would be to ignore Madison's warning, borne out in the Wilkes case and some of Congress' own post–Civil War exclusion cases, against "vesting an improper & dangerous power in the Legislature." 2 Farrand 249. Moreover, it would effectively nullify the Convention's decision to require a two-thirds vote for expulsion. Unquestionably, Congress has an interest in preserving its institutional integrity, but in most cases that interest can be sufficiently safeguarded by the exercise of its power to punish its members for disorderly behavior and, in extreme cases, to expel a member with the concurrence of two-thirds. In short, both the intention of the Framers, to the extent it can be determined, and an examination of the basic principles of our democratic system persuade us that the Constitution does not vest in the Congress a discretionary power to deny membership by a majority vote.

For these reasons, we have concluded that Art. I, § 5, is at most a 'textually demonstrable commitment' to Congress to judge only the qualifications expressly set forth in the Constitution. Therefore, the 'textual commitment' formulation of the political question doctrine does not bar federal courts from adjudicating petitioners' claims.

2. Other Considerations

Respondents' alternate contention is that the case presents a political question because judicial resolution of petitioners' claim would produce a "potentially embarrassing confrontation between coordinate branches" of the Federal Government. But, as our interpretation of Art. I, § 5, discloses, a determination of petitioner Powell's right to sit would require no more than an interpretation of the Constitution. Such a determination falls within the traditional role accorded courts to interpret the law, and does not involve a "lack of the respect due (a) coordinate (branch) of government," nor does it involve an "initial policy determination of a kind clearly for nonjudicial discretion." Baker v. Carr, 369 U.S. 186, at 217, 82 S.Ct. 691, at 710. Our system of government requires that federal courts on occasion interpret the Constitution in a manner at variance with the construction given the document by another branch. The alleged conflict that such an adjudication may cause cannot justify the courts' avoiding their constitutional responsibility.[14] See United States v. Brown, 381 U.S. 437, 462, 85 S.Ct. 1707, 1722, 14 L.Ed.2d 484 (1965); Youngstown Sheet & Tube Co. v. Sawyer, 343 U.S. 579, 613-614, 72 S.Ct. 863, 898, 96 L.Ed. 1153 (1952) (Frankfurter, J., concurring); Myers v. United States, 272 U.S. 52, 293, 47 S.Ct. 21, 84 (1926) (Brandeis, J., dissenting).

Nor are any of the other formulations of a political question "inextricable from the case at bar." Baker v. Carr, supra, at 217, 82 S.Ct. at 710. Petitioners seek a determination that the House was without power to exclude Powell from the 90th Congress, which, we have seen, requires an interpretation of the Constitution — a determination for which clearly there are "judicially . . . manageable standards." Finally, a judicial resolution of petitioners' claim will not result in "multifarious pronouncements by various departments on one question." For, as we noted in Baker v. Carr, supra, at 211, 82 S.Ct., at 706 it is the responsibility of this Court to act as the ultimate interpreter of the Constitution. Marbury v. Madison, 1 Cranch (5 U.S.) 137, 2 L.Ed. 60 (1803). Thus, we conclude that petitioners' claim is not barred by the political question doctrine, and, having determined that the claim is otherwise generally justiciable, we hold that the case is justiciable.

VII. CONCLUSION

[Therefore], we hold that, since Adam Clayton Powell, Jr., was duly elected by the voters of the 18th congressional District of New York and was not ineligible to serve under any provision of the Constitution, the House was without power to exclude him from its membership.

Petitioners seek additional forms of equitable relief, including mandamus for the release of petitioner Powell's back pay. The propriety of such remedies, however, is more appropriately considered in the first instance by the courts below. Therefore, as to respondents McCormack, Albert, Ford, Celler, and Moore, the judgment of the Court of Appeals for the District of Columbia Circuit is affirmed. As to respondents Jennings, Johnson, and Miller, the judgment of the Court of Appeals for the District of Columbia Circuit is reversed and the case is remanded to the United States District Court for the District of Columbia with instructions to enter a declaratory judgment and for further proceedings consistent with this opinion.

It is so ordered.

———————

Comment on *Powell*. Is *Powell* simply an application of the *Baker* rationale, or does it expand it? Is the "qualification" clause still a "textual commitment" to Congress

———————

[14] In fact, the Court has noted that it is an "inadmissible suggestion" that action might be taken in disregard of a judicial determination. McPherson v. Blacker, 146 U.S. 1, 24, 13 S.Ct. 3, 6, 36 L.Ed.2d 869 (1892).

after *Powell*? If so, on what basis does the Court reach the merits? The case that follows is the most recent statement on "textual commitments" and political questions.

NIXON v. UNITED STATES
506 U.S. 224 (1993)

Nixon, a former district court judge who was convicted of making false statements before a federal grand jury, sought judicial review of his subsequent removal from office by impeachment. He claimed that the Senate had failed to "try" him within the meaning of the impeachment clause of article I. Upon receiving articles of impeachment from the House, the Senate referred the matter to a committee, which reported to the full body. Although the committee presented the Senate with a transcript of the proceedings and Nixon was permitted to make a personal appeal to the Senate, the full body did not receive any of the evidence.

Chief Justice REHNQUIST delivered the opinion of the Court:
[Before] we reach the merits of such a claim, we must decide whether it is "justiciable," that is, whether it is a claim that may be resolved by the courts. We conclude that it is not. . . .
A controversy is non-justiciable — i.e., involves a political question — where there is "a textually demonstrable constitutional commitment of the issue to a coordinate political department; or a lack of judicially discoverable and manageable standards for resolving it" [*Baker*]. But the courts must, in the first instance, interpret the text in question and determine whether and to what extent the issue is textually committed. [The] concept of a textual commitment to a coordinate political department is not completely separate from the concept of a lack of judicially discoverable and manageable standards for resolving it; the lack of judicially manageable standards may strengthen the conclusion that there is a textually demonstrable commitment to a coordinate branch. . . .
In this case, we must examine Art. I, §3, cl. 6 [which provides that "[t]he Senate shall have the sole Power to try all Impeachments." This provision] is a grant of authority to the Senate, and the word "sole" indicates that this authority is reposed in the Senate, and nowhere else. . . .
Petitioner argues that the word "try" [requires that] the proceedings must be in the nature of a judicial trial. . . .
The word "try," both in 1787 and later, has considerably broader meanings than those to which petitioner would limit it. [Based] on the variety of definitions, [we] cannot say that the Framers used the word [as] an implied limitation on the method by which the Senate might proceed in trying impeachments. . . .
The conclusion that the use of the word "try" [lacks] sufficient precision to afford any judicially manageable standard of review of the Senate's actions is fortified by the existence of the three very specific requirements that the Constitution does impose on the Senate when trying impeachments: the members must be under oath, a two-thirds vote is required to convict, and the Chief Justice presides when the President is tried. These limitations are quite precise, and their nature suggests that the Framers did not intend to impose additional limitations on the form of the Senate proceedings by the use of the word ["try"].

[The] common sense meaning of the word "sole" is that the Senate alone shall have authority to determine whether an individual should be acquitted or convicted. . . .

[Judicial] review would be inconsistent with the Framers' insistence that our system be one of checks and balances. In our constitutional system, impeachment was designed to be the only check on the Judicial Branch by the Legislature. [Judicial] involvement in impeachment proceedings, even if only for purposes of judicial review, is counterintuitive because it would eviscerate the "important constitutional check" placed on the Judiciary by the Framers. Nixon's argument would place final reviewing authority with respect to impeachments in the hands of the same body that the impeachment process is meant to regulate. . . .

In addition to the textual commitment argument, we are persuaded that the lack of finality and the difficulty of fashioning relief counsel against justiciability. [Opening] the door of judicial review to the procedures used by the Senate in trying impeachments would "expose the political life of the country to months, or perhaps years, of chaos." This lack of finality would manifest itself most dramatically if the President were impeached. The legitimacy of any successor, and hence his effectiveness, would be impaired severely, not merely while the judicial process was running its course, but during any retrial that a differently constituted Senate might conduct if its first judgment of conviction were invalidated. Equally uncertain is the question of what relief a court may give other than simply setting aside the judgment of conviction. Could it order the reinstatement of a convicted federal judge, or order Congress to create an additional judgeship if the seat had been filled in the interim? . . .

We agree with Nixon that courts possess power to review either legislative or executive action that transgresses identifiable textual limits. As we have made clear, "whether the action of [either the Legislative or the Executive Branch] exceeds whatever authority has been committed, is itself a delicate exercise in constitutional interpretation, and is a responsibility of this Court as ultimate interpreter of the Constitution." [*Baker*]. But we conclude, after exercising that delicate responsibility, that the word "try" in the Impeachment Clause does not provide an identifiable textual limit on the authority which is committed to the Senate.

Note on Foreign Affairs. Is the president, given the executive branch's broad power in foreign affairs (see the next section), protected from judicial intrusion by political question abstention? Which basis of political question doctrine would be most applicable here? Textual commitment? Judicially unmanageable standards? Goldwater, which follows and reviews presidential authority and the treaty power, is a contemporary view of these issues, with Justice Rehnquist providing his opinion in regard to the questions just raised. On what basis does Justice Powell reach a decision?

GOLDWATER v. CARTER
444 U.S. 996 (1979)

[The Court, without hearing oral argument, in setting aside the lower court's decisions, did not resolve whether the president could terminate a treaty without participation of the Senate. While holding the case nonjusticiable, the Court could not agree on a rationale.]

Mr. Justice POWELL, concurring.

Although I agree with the result reached by the Court, I would dismiss the complaint as not ripe for judicial review.

I

This Court has recognized that an issue should not be decided if it is not ripe for judicial review. Buckley v. Valeo, 424 U.S. 1, 113-114, 96 S.Ct. 612, 46 L.Ed.2d 659 (1976) (per curiam). Prudential considerations persuade me that a dispute between Congress and the President is not ready for judicial review unless and until each branch has taken action asserting its constitutional authority. Differences between the President and the Congress are commonplace under our system. The differences should, and almost invariably do, turn on political rather than legal considerations. The Judicial Branch should not decide issues affecting the allocation of power between the President and Congress until the political branches reach a constitutional impasse. Otherwise, we would encourage small groups or even individual Members of Congress to seek judicial resolution of issues before the normal political process has the opportunity to resolve the conflict.

[In] this case, a few Members of Congress claim that the President's action in terminating the treaty with Taiwan has deprived them of their constitutional role with respect to a change in the supreme law of the land. Congress has taken no official action. In the present posture of this case, we do not know whether there ever will be an actual confrontation between the Legislative and Executive Branches. Although the Senate has considered a resolution declaring that Senate approval is necessary for the termination of any mutual defense treaty, see 125 Cong.Rec. S7015, S7038-S7039 (June 6, 1979), no final vote has been taken on the resolution. See id., at S16683-S16692 (Nov. 15, 1979). Moreover, it is unclear whether the resolution would have retroactive effect. See id., at S7054-S7064 (June 6, 1979); id., at S7862 (June 18, 1979). It cannot be said that either the Senate or the House has rejected the President's claim. If the Congress chooses not to confront the President, it is not our task to do so. I therefore concur in the dismissal of this case.

II

Mr. Justice Rehnquist suggests, however, that the issue presented by this case is a nonjusticiable political question which can never be considered by this Court. I cannot agree. In my view, reliance upon the political-question doctrine is inconsistent with our precedents. As set forth in the seminal case of Baker v. Carr, 369 U.S. 186, 217, 82 S.Ct. 691, 7 L.Ed.2d 663 (1962), the doctrine incorporates three inquiries: (i) Does the issue involve resolution of questions committed by the text of the Constitution to a coordinate branch of Government? (ii) Would resolution of the question demand that a court move beyond areas of judicial expertise? (iii) Do prudential considerations counsel against judicial intervention? In my opinion the answer to each of these inquiries would require us to decide this case if it were ready for review.

First, the existence of "a textually demonstrable constitutional commitment of the issue to a coordinate political department," ibid., turns on an examination of the constitutional provisions governing the exercise of the power in question. Powell v. McCormack, 395 U.S. 486, 519, 89 S.Ct. 1944, 23 L.Ed.2d 491 (1969). No constitutional provision explicitly confers upon the President the power to terminate treaties. Further, Art. II, § 2, of the Constitution authorizes the President to make treaties with the advice and consent of the Senate. Article VI provides that treaties shall be a part of the supreme law of the land. These provisions add support to the view that the text of the Constitution does not unquestionably commit the power to terminate treaties to the President alone. Cf.

Gilligan v. Morgan, 413 U.S. 1, 6, 93 S.Ct. 2440, 37 L.Ed.2d 407 (1973); Luther v. Borden, 7 How. 1, 42, 12 L.Ed. 581 (1849).

Second, there is no "lack of judicially discoverable and manageable standards for resolving" this case; nor is a decision impossible "without an initial policy determination of a kind clearly for nonjudicial discretion." Baker v. Carr, supra, 369 U.S., at 217, 82 S.Ct. 691. We are asked to decide whether the President may terminate a treaty under the Constitution without congressional approval. Resolution of the question may not be easy, but it only requires us to apply normal principles of interpretation to the constitutional provisions at issue. See Powell v. McCormack, supra, 395 U.S., at 548-549, 89 S.Ct. 1944. The present case involves neither review of the President's activities as Commander in Chief nor impermissible interference in the field of foreign affairs. Such a case would arise if we were asked to decide, for example, whether a treaty required the President to order troops into a foreign country. But "it is error to suppose that every case or controversy which touches foreign relations lies beyond judicial cognizance." Baker v. Carr, supra, 369 U.S., at 211, 82 S.Ct. 691. This case "touches" foreign relations, but the question presented to us concerns only the constitutional division of power between Congress and the President.

If this case were ripe for judicial review, see Part I supra, none of these prudential considerations would be present. Interpretation of the Constitution does not imply lack of respect for a coordinate branch. Powell v. McCormack, supra, 395 U.S., at 548, 89 S.Ct. 1944. If the President and the Congress had reached irreconcilable positions, final disposition of the question presented by this case would eliminate, rather than create, multiple constitutional interpretations. The specter of the Federal Government brought to a halt because of the mutual intransigence of the President and the Congress would require this Court to provide a resolution pursuant to our duty "'to say what the law is.'" United States v. Nixon, 418 U.S. 683, 703, 94 S.Ct. 3090, 41 L.Ed.2d 1039 (1974), quoting Marbury v. Madison, 1 Cranch 137, 177, 2 L.Ed. 60 (1803).

Mr. Justice REHNQUIST, with whom THE CHIEF JUSTICE, Mr. Justice STEWART, and Mr. Justice STEVENS join, concurring in the judgment.

[In addition to the statements below, Justice Rehnquist pointedly cited Chief Justice Hughes' opinion in *Coleman v. Miller*, 307 U.S. 433 (1939), where Chief Justice Hughes spoke of "relevant conditions, political, social and economic" as an apparently broad discretionary bases for a determination of non-justiciability based on a lack of judicially manageable standards.]

I am of the view that the basic question presented by the petitioners in this case is "political" and therefore non-justiciable because it involves the authority of the President in the conduct of our country's foreign relations and the extent to which the Senate or the Congress is authorized to negate the action of the President.

. . . [I] believe . . . that the controversy in the instant case is a non-justiciable political dispute that should be left for resolution by the Executive and Legislative Branches of the Government. Here, while the Constitution is express as to the manner in which the Senate shall participate in the ratification of a treaty, it is silent as to that body's participation in the abrogation of a treaty.

. . . [I]n light of the absence of any constitutional provision governing the termination of a treaty, and the fact that different termination procedures may be appropriate for different treaties, the instant case in my view also "must surely be controlled by political standards."

Mr. Justice BRENNAN, dissenting.

I respectfully dissent from the order directing the District Court to dismiss this case, and would affirm the judgment of the Court of Appeals insofar as it rests upon the President's well-established authority to recognize, and withdraw recognition from, foreign governments. App. to Pet. for Cert. 27A-29A.

In stating that this case presents a non-justiciable "political question," Mr. Justice Rehnquist, in my view, profoundly misapprehends the political-question principle as it applies to matters of foreign relations. Properly understood, the political-question doctrine restrains courts from reviewing an exercise of foreign policy judgment by the coordinate political branch to which authority to make that judgment has been "constitutional[ly] commit[ted]." Baker v. Carr, 369 U.S. 186, 211-213, 217, 82 S.Ct. 691, 7 L.Ed.2d 663 (1962). But the doctrine does not pertain when a court is faced with the *antecedent* question whether a particular branch has been constitutionally designated as the repository of political decision-making power. Cf. Powell v. McCormack, 395 U.S. 486, 519-521, 89 S.Ct. 1944, 23 L.Ed.2d 491 (1969). The issue of decision-making authority must be resolved as a matter of constitutional law, not political discretion; accordingly, it falls within the competence of the courts.

. . . [Our] cases firmly establish that the Constitution commits to the President alone the power to recognize, and withdraw recognition from, foreign regimes. See Banco Nacional de Cuba v. Sabbatino, 376 U.S. 398, 410, 84 S.Ct. 923, 11 L.Ed.2d 804 (1964); Baker v. Carr, supra, 369 U.S., at 212, 82 S.Ct. 691; United States v. Pink, 315 U.S. 203, 228-230, 62 S.Ct. 552, 86 L.Ed. 796 (1942). That mandate being clear, our judicial inquiry into the treaty rupture can go no further. See Baker v. Carr, supra, 369 U.S., at 212, 82 S.Ct. 691; United States v. Pink, supra, 315 U.S., at 229, 62 S.Ct. 552.

Recognition of Foreign Sovereigns. Where Congress enacts a statute providing that Americans born in Jerusalem may elect to have Israel listed as the place of birth on their passports, but the State Department disagrees based on a policy not to take a position on the political status of Jerusalem, does a U.S. citizen's lawsuit seeking to vindicate his statutory right present a nonjusticiable political question? In *Zivotofsky v. Clinton*, 566 U.S. 189 (2012), the Court decided that it does not, holding the case justiciable but declining to opine upon its merits. Section 214(d) of the 2002 Foreign Relations Authorization Act provides that "[f]or purposes of the United States citizen born in the city of Jerusalem, the Secretary [of State] shall, upon the request of the citizen or the citizen's legal guardian, record the place of birth as Israel." Petitioner Menachem Binyamin Zivotofsky, a U.S. citizen because both his parents were U.S. citizens, was born in Jerusalem in 2002, shortly after § 214(d) was enacted. His parents requested that his consular report of birth and U.S. passport list his place of birth as "Jerusalem, Israel," but U.S. officials declined, citing long-standing State Department policy. Zivotofsky's parents filed a complaint on his behalf against the Secretary of State. The district court found that the case presented a nonjusticiable political question and the D.C. Circuit affirmed, reasoning that the Constitution gives the executive the exclusive power to recognize foreign sovereigns, and that the exercise of this power cannot be reviewed by the courts.

In an 8 to 1 decision, the Supreme Court vacated and remanded, holding that the courts "are fully capable of determining whether this statute may be given effect, or instead must be struck down in light of authority conferred on the Executive by the Constitution." Chief Justice Roberts wrote for the Court: "Zivotofsky does not ask the courts to determine whether Jerusalem is the capital of Israel. He instead seeks to determine whether he may vindicate his statutory right, under § 214(d), to choose to have Israel recorded on his passport as his place of birth. [The] federal courts are not being asked to supplant a foreign policy decision of the political branches with the courts' own unmoored determination of what United States policy toward Jerusalem should be. [To] resolve [Zivotovsky's] claim, the Judiciary must decide if Zivotofsky's interpretation of the statute is correct, and whether the statute is constitutional. This is a familiar judicial exercise. Moreover, because the parties do not dispute the interpretation of § 214(d), the only real question for the courts is whether the statute is constitutional. At least since Marbury v. Madison, we have recognized that when an Act of Congress is alleged to conflict with the Constitution, '[i]t is emphatically the province and duty of the judicial department to say what the law is.'" Because the Court found the sole issue to be the constitutionality of § 214(d), it found no textually demonstrable commitment of the issue exclusively to the executive branch and no lack of judicially administrable standards. While acknowledging the clash on the merits between Secretary Clinton's position that "the Constitution gives the Executive the exclusive power to formulate recognition policy" based on the president's power to "receive Ambassadors and other public Ministers," Art. II, § 3, and Zivotofsky's position that § 214(d) is instead a permissible exercise of Congress's "authority to legislate on the form and content of a passport" based on its powers over naturalization, Art. I, § 8, cl. 4, and foreign commerce, Art. I § 8, cl. 3, the Chief Justice left the resolution of the merits questions in the first instance for the lower courts to decide.

Justice Sotomayor, joined in relevant part by Justice Breyer, concurred in part and in the judgment, writing separately to clarify her view that she understood "the inquiry required by the political question doctrine to be more demanding than that suggested by the Court." Justice Alito concurred in the judgment. Justice Breyer filed the lone dissent, arguing that the prudential considerations set forth in the *Baker v. Carr* factors should have led the Court "not to decide a case otherwise properly before it": "First, the issue before us arises in the field of foreign affairs. [The] Constitution primarily delegates the foreign affairs powers 'to the political departments of the government, Executive and Legislative,' not to the Judiciary. [Second,] if the courts must answer the constitutional question before us, they may well have to evaluate the foreign policy implications of foreign policy decisions. [In] the Middle East, administrative matters can have implications that extend far beyond the purely administrative. Political reactions in that region can prove uncertain. [Third,] the countervailing interests in obtaining judicial resolution of the constitutional determination are not particularly strong ones. Zivotofsky does not assert the kind of interest, *e.g.*, an interest in property or bodily integrity, which courts have traditionally sought to protect. [The] interest that Zivotofsky asserts [is] akin to an ideological interest. [Fourth,] insofar as the controversy reflects different foreign policy views among the political branches of Government, those branches have nonjudicial methods of working out their differences [, which] minimizes the need for judicial intervention here."

D. SUPREME COURT PRACTICE

The Federal Judicial System. Though the Supreme Court is the only Court created and mandated by the Constitution, given the statutorily based lower federal court system, it sits "on top" of the federal and state (where appropriate independent and adequate grounds exist) judicial hierarchy. The nation is divided geographically into 11 judicial circuits, with each circuit headed by a circuit court of appeal. Each circuit is subdivided into geographical districts containing several district courts (trial courts). The circuit courts of appeal, absent Supreme Court decision, maintain precedential value for all of the district courts within their circuit. It is important to remember that all of the material we have reviewed in this section applies to all federal courts as well as the Supreme Court.

The two major functions of the Supreme Court in the modern era have been to decide and articulate significant principles of constitutional law, as well as to resolve conflicting decisions between the circuits.

Supreme Court Jurisdiction. Though the constitutional basis for the jurisdiction of the Supreme Court is set out in Article III, Congress has never granted litigants access to the Court in all cases for which Article III provides authorization. The governing provisions are set out in 28 U.S.C. §§1251-1257. These provisions furnished two principal routes to the Supreme Court. The first is through "appeal" where jurisdiction is mandatory, meaning that the Court must hear an appeal from the losing party below. Although the Court traditionally provided "brief" memorandum decisions if it desired to avoid the "mandatory" nature of an appeal, the significance of this issue was mooted in 1988 when Congress limited jurisdiction by "appeal" to only the rarest of cases.

The second, and now major basis for the Court's appellate jurisdiction, is via "certiorari." Certiorari jurisdiction is discretionary. The Court can deny certiorari for any reason, and in fact does not have to articulate any reason. The Court, for example, may deny certiorari for reasons other than its agreement with the decision below: the unimportance of the issue, the unusual character of the particular facts, the desire to see the issue "percolate" in the lower courts, the controversial character of the problem, or the wish to allow the political process time to consider the problem before an authoritative resolution is obtained. Certiorari is so discretionary that it is an extension of the judicial discretion previously reviewed. Recall the views of Alexander Bickel in regard to "passive virtues." The precedential value of a denial of "cert.," is quite simply that, "a denial of cert.," nothing more and nothing less. It is important to note, though, that the decision below still stands.

Parties seeking certiorari must file a petition for certiorari, articulating the rationale for why the case deserves review. Rule 17 of the Supreme Court rules states:

> The following, while neither controlling nor fully measuring the Court's discretion, indicate the character of the reasons that will be considered:
>
> (a) When a federal court of appeals has rendered a decision in conflict with the decision of another federal court of appeals on the same matter; or has decided a federal question in a way in conflict with a state court of last resort; or has so far departed from the accepted and usual course of judicial proceedings [as] to call for an exercise of this Court's power of supervision.
>
> (b) When a state court of last resort has decided a federal question in a way in conflict with the decision of another state court of last resort or of a federal court of appeals.
>
> (c) When a state court or a federal court of appeals has decided an important question of federal law which has not been, but should be, settled by this Court, or has decided a federal question in way in conflict with applicable decisions of this Court.

Rules of the Supreme Court, 445 U.S. 983, 1003 (1980).

Screening certiorari cases has varied with different Courts and Chief Justices. Even the Justices themselves differ. Some rely on law clerks to write brief memoranda about cases presented for certiorari; others read all or some of the petitions themselves; and many participate in a "cert pool" in which one law clerk is assigned responsibility for writing a memorandum circulated to many of the chambers. Cases perceived to be of importance are placed on the "Discuss List" — the list of cases to be discussed by the Justices in conference. From that list, the Court decides which cases to hear by application of the "Rule of Four." Certiorari is granted when four of the Justices so concur. The requirement of four Justices, who for whatever individual reason desire to grant certiorari, is not a coincidence — four is of course one short of a majority. This process has had political overtones. Frankfurter once referred to the "Rule of Four" as the "Rule of Three" because once three Justices wanted to hear a case it wasn't much trouble to get another to agree. He accused Justice Black of having three other Justices in his "back pocket" so that he could have a case granted certiorari whenever he so chose. See Joseph Lash, *From the Diaries of Felix Frankfurter* 331-333 (1975). There was much controversy, for example, when Chief Justice Burger created the "collective cert pool," so, in the eyes of Burger's critics, he could centralize control over the process. See Bob Woodward & Scott Armstrong, *The Brethren* 272-273 (1979).

Chapter 2
Congress and Federal Authority

I. AUTHORITY TO LEGISLATE: NATIONAL POWERS IN FEDERAL UNION

Federalism brought the colonies together in union as the several states of the United States of America. The division of power and authority between the states and federal government has remained a significant issue throughout the nation's history. In the last decade a narrow majority of the Supreme Court has once again placed this issue at the forefront in what has been described as an "anti-federalist" revival. Whatever the merits of this "revival," it has certainly made the study of federal power and federalism a most spirited and contemporary issue.

The first attempt at union, the Articles of Confederation, succeeded only in bringing the former colonies together as one nation. Under the Articles the states ceded so little authority to the national government that this attempt at a loose confederation of states failed. In particular, the Articles' denial of a centralized or national power over commerce and "economic union" was unsatisfactory. Thus, the lack of a central authority that could raise tax revenues to both provide for the national security and stimulate economic growth was so debilitating that the states themselves realized that increased federal authority was necessary. This led to a convention, nominally gathered to amend the Articles, but with most political leaders (still the "founding fathers") realizing that a new Constitution to replace the Articles was needed.

As it has every other aspect of the American experience, slavery proved to be a driving issue in regard to state prerogative. The initial de-centralization of power under the Articles may well have been driven by attempting to avoid the divergent views, essentially between the north and south, over the maintenance of slavery. Adopting a new Constitution would prove to be no different in regard to these differences, and most historians would concur that a compromise over the Constitutional reference supporting the maintenance of slavery was necessary before the southern states would cede necessary authority to the new central government.

Those attending what became our "constitutional convention" were in general agreement that the new national government needed broader power, the only debate was over "how much." Here, much the same as our discussion concerning the power and authority of the Supreme Court, most of the framers joined together to achieve a more functional national authority, setting aside their differences to a future date. Much as they did in The Federalist No. 78, Madison and Hamilton joined together to provide extensive thoughts of the framers in regard to state and federal authority under the new Constitution in several chapters of the Federalist Papers.

The most significant issue to arise concerning federalism and the debates concerning the adoption of the Constitution was the fact that the document did not detail what powers would be retained or remain with the states. Hamilton, in The Federalist No. 84, defended the omission as inconsequential because the federal government had only those powers enumerated to it. Broad displeasure with this response, as well as a lack of any "bill of rights" to limit further reaches of federal authority, produced a compromise which promised both a bill of rights and an amendment securing state powers upon the meeting of the first Congress after the successful adoption of the new Constitution.

After adoption and while the meaning of the Constitution was a work in progress, political factions were soon to form. Once again, the Federalists, the conservatives of their age, sought expansive federal authority, with the Anti-Federalist, or Democratic Republicans, fearing central authority and defending the "sovereign" rights of the several states. Nowhere are these differences better seen than in the counter play between the "necessary and proper clause" and the 10th Amendment.

A major failure of the "Articles" was its lack of granting any "implied" power to the central government. The lack of any reference to any implied power necessary to effectuate those powers granted to the central government was particularly debilitating. The framers, both Federalist and Republican, sought to remedy this by inclusion of a grant of implied power in the new document. This was accomplished by the "necessary and proper clause."

> Article I. Section 8. The Congress shall have the power . . . To make all law which shall be necessary and proper for carrying into Execution the foregoing Powers, and all other Powers vested by this Constitution in the Government of the United States, or in any Department or Officer thereof.

Though there was consensus on the new federal government having implied power, the question of "how much" once again divided the factions that formed. The Republicans, led by Jefferson, sought to limit the clause by allowing Congress only those implied powers that were "absolutely necessary." The Federalists, pursued the Hamiltonian position which afforded a broad and flexible bases for implied authority. In fact, the Hamiltonian position might well have allowed Congress to achieve via the necessary and proper clause a power which the framers had denied to so enumerate. Hamilton argued that it was the "intent of the Convention [to] give a liberal latitude" in allowing for implied powers. Note how different the operation of each government would be depending upon the position adopted. The nature of implied power was a major issue in the decennial case of *McCulloch v. Maryland*, which follows.

The 10th Amendment seems clear, at least in its language:

> The powers not delegated to the United States by the Constitution, nor prohibited by it to the States, are reserved to the States respectively, or to the people.

Yet, it is evident that there is an inherent ambiguity between the concept of implied power resting in the federal government via the necessary and proper clause and the reservation of non-enumerated powers to the states. Can one assume, for example, that a power that is not delegated to the United States by the Constitution will be reserved to the States? This seems to be the intent of the language of the 10th Amendment. But what if a power supposedly reserved to the states "is necessary and proper" for the federal government to carry out an enumerated power? Is not the power we thought reserved to the states now an implied power of the federal government? Not so simple! Should both governments be able to maintain the power? Both do have a Constitutional basis to so assert. The "grayness" here is significant and not easily resolved. This is even more significant given the fact that the framers themselves had such divergent views on the meaning of the necessary and proper clause. It is certainly another reason why Marshall's threshold definitions in *McCulloch* are so important.

That the framers meant "what they said" in regard to this "counter play" between implied power and the Tenth Amendment is made even more apparent when one views the Articles of Confederation equivalent to the Constitution's reservation of state power. Art. II of the Articles stated that each state retained, "every Power, Jurisdiction and rights, which is not by this confederation *expressly* delegated to the United States." (emphasis added) This reservation was unclouded, if the power was not "expressly" granted to the federal government under the Articles it was retained by the States. Thus, not only was "implied" authority not an issue, but the Articles provided a very limited basis for national power. The Tenth Amendment to the Constitution's deletion of the adverb "expressly," while reserving to the States powers not delegated to the United States, expressed the framers intent to allow for implied power extending from the necessary and proper clause. This deletion indicates that the federal government might still retain a power not expressly granted to it, via the necessary and proper clause. This substantiates the inherent ambiguity discussed above — a power not delegated to the national government may still be retained by it if "necessary and proper" to carry out a enumerated power, even though it might also be reserved to the states.

Though, in the words of Jefferson at his inaugural, "We are all Federalists, we are all Republicans," might well have described the framers at the adoption of the Constitution, such was not the case as issues of state versus federal power developed and political "factions" formed in the fledgling regime. As discussed above, divergent views on the meaning of the necessary and proper clause and the 10th amendment, and the nature of sovereignty that remained with the states, found finite and profound differences abounding in the political atmosphere of the new republic.

As this drama was to play itself out, the Federalist retained control over the federal judiciary and in particular the Supreme Court through the dominance of its Chief Justice John Marshall. The significance of his opinion in Marbury v. Madison, reserving for the Court the ultimate power as final arbiter of the meaning of the new Constitution, reached epic proportions as in exercising the Court's power Marshall provided threshold decisions that would shape and institutionalize the nature of the new Constitution and the nation. None of these is more significant, particularly given the modern "anti-federalist" revival, then the delineation of federal authority to legislate in *McCullough v. Maryland*, which follows.

In relation to the issues posed, do you think Marshall will advance national or state authority? Marshall's opinion in *McCullough* has been called "a lesson in nation building," see if you can determine why. Finally, Marshall states in *McCulloch*, "We must never forget it is a constitution we expounding." What does Marshall mean by this statement, and how does it illuminate his or anyone's view of the how the Court should go about rendering the power of judicial review and interpreting the Constitution?

A. A LESSON IN NATION BUILDING

McCULLOCH v. MARYLAND
17 U.S. 316 (1819)

MARSHALL, Ch. J., delivered the opinion of the court.

In the case now to be determined, the defendant, a sovereign state, denies the obligation of a law enacted by the legislature of the Union, and the plaintiff, on his part, contests the validity of an act which has been passed by the legislature of that state. The constitution of our country, in its most interesting and vital parts, is to be considered; the conflicting powers of the government of the Union and of its members, as marked in that constitution, are to be discussed; and an opinion given, which may essentially influence the great operations of the government. No tribunal can approach such a question without a deep sense of its importance, and of the awful responsibility involved in its decision. But it must be decided peacefully, or remain a source of hostile legislation, perhaps, of hostility of a still more serious nature; and if it is to be so decided, by this tribunal alone can the decision be made. On the supreme court of the United States has the constitution of our country devolved this important duty.

The first question made in the cause is — has congress power to incorporate a bank?

. . .

[In] discussing this question, the counsel for the state of Maryland have deemed it of some importance, in the construction of the constitution, to consider that instrument, not as emanating from the people, but as the act of sovereign and independent states. The powers of the general government, it has been said, are delegated by the states, who alone are truly sovereign; and must be exercised in subordination to the states, who alone possess supreme dominion. It would be difficult to sustain this proposition. The convention which framed the constitution was indeed elected by the state legislatures. But the instrument, when it came from their hands, was a mere proposal, without obligation, or pretensions to it. It was reported to the then existing congress of the United States, with a request that it might "be submitted to a convention of delegates, chosen in each state by the people thereof, under the recommendation of its legislature, for their assent and ratification." This mode of proceeding was adopted; and by the convention, by congress, and by the state legislatures, the instrument was submitted to the *people*. They acted upon it in the only manner in which they can act safely, effectively and wisely, on such a subject, by assembling in convention. It is true, they assembled in their several states — and where else should they have assembled? No political dreamer was ever wild enough to think of breaking down the lines which separate the states, and of compounding the American people into one common mass. Of consequence, when they act, they act in their states. But the measures they adopt do not, on that account, cease to be the measures of the people themselves, or become the measures of the state governments.

From these conventions, the constitution derives its whole authority. The government proceeds directly from the people; is "ordained and established," in the name of the people; and is declared to be ordained, "in order to form a more perfect union, establish justice, insure domestic tranquility, and secure the blessings of liberty to themselves and to their posterity." The assent of the states, in their sovereign capacity, is implied, in calling a convention, and thus submitting that instrument to the people. But the people were at perfect liberty to accept or reject it; and their act was final. It required not the affirmance, and could not be negatived, by the state governments. The constitution, when thus adopted, was of complete obligation, and bound the state sovereignties. . . .

This government is acknowledged by all, to be one of enumerated powers. The principle, that it can exercise only the powers granted to it, would seem too apparent, to have required to be enforced by all those arguments, which its enlightened friends, while it was depending before the people, found it necessary to urge; that principle is now universally admitted. But the question respecting the extent of the powers actually granted, is perpetually arising, and will probably continue to arise, so long as our system shall exist. In discussing these questions, the conflicting powers of the general and state governments must be brought into view, and the supremacy of their respective laws, when they are in opposition, must be settled.

If any one proposition could command the universal assent of mankind, we might expect it would be this — that the government of the Union, though limited in its powers, is supreme within its sphere of action. This would seem to result, necessarily, from its nature. It is the government of all; its powers are delegated by all; it represents all, and acts for all. Though any one state may be willing to control its operations, no state is willing to allow others to control them. The nation, on those subjects on which it can act, must necessarily bind its component parts. But this question is not left to mere reason: the people have, in express terms, decided it, by saying, "this constitution, and the laws of the United States, which shall be made in pursuance thereof," "shall be the supreme law of the land," and by requiring that the members of the state legislatures, and the officers of the executive and judicial departments of the states, shall take the oath of fidelity to it. The government of the United States, then, though limited in its powers, is supreme; and its laws, when made in pursuance of the constitution, form the supreme law of the land, "anything in the constitution or laws of any state to the contrary notwithstanding."

Among the enumerated powers, we do not find that of establishing a bank or creating a corporation. But there is no phrase in the instrument which, like the articles of confederation, excludes incidental or implied powers; and which requires that everything granted shall be expressly and minutely described. Even the 10th amendment, which was framed for the purpose of quieting the excessive jealousies which had been excited, omits the word "expressly," and declares only, that the powers "not delegated to the United States, nor prohibited to the states, are reserved to the states or to the people;" thus leaving the question, whether the particular power which may become the subject of contest, has been delegated to the one government, or prohibited to the other, to depend on a fair construction of the whole instrument. The men who drew and adopted this amendment had experienced the embarrassments resulting from the insertion of this word in the articles of confederation, and probably omitted it, to avoid those embarrassments. A constitution, to contain an accurate detail of all the subdivisions of which its great powers will admit, and of all the means by which they may be carried into execution, would partake of the prolixity of a legal code, and could scarcely be embraced by the human mind. It would, probably, never be understood by the public. Its nature, therefore, requires, that only its great outlines should be marked, its important objects designated, and the minor ingredients which compose those objects, be deduced from the nature of the objects themselves. That this idea was entertained by the framers of the American constitution, is not only to be inferred from the nature of the instrument, but from the language. Why else were some of the limitations, found in the 9th section of the 1st article, introduced? It is also, in some degree, warranted, by their having omitted to use any restrictive term which might prevent its receiving a fair and just interpretation. In considering this question, then, we must never forget that it is a *constitution* we are expounding.

Although, among the enumerated powers of government, we do not find the word "bank" or "incorporation," we find the great powers, to lay and collect taxes; to borrow money; to regulate commerce; to declare and conduct a war; and to raise and support armies and navies. The sword and the purse, all the external relations, and no inconsiderable portion of the industry of the nation, are entrusted to its government. It can never be pretended, that these vast powers draw after them others of inferior importance, merely because they are inferior. Such an idea can never be advanced. But it may with great reason be contended, that a government, entrusted with such ample powers, on the due execution of which the happiness and prosperity of the nation so vitally depends, must also be entrusted with ample means for their execution. The power being given, it is the interest of the nation to facilitate its execution. It can never be their interest, and cannot be presumed to have been their intention, to clog and embarrass its execution, by withholding the most appropriate means. Throughout this vast republic, from the St. Croix to the Gulf of Mexico, from the Atlantic to the Pacific, revenue is to be collected and expended, armies are to be marched and supported. The exigencies of the nation may require, that the treasure raised in the north should be transported to the south, that raised in the east, conveyed to the west, or that this order should be reversed. Is that construction of the constitution to be preferred, which would render these operations difficult, hazardous and expensive? Can we adopt that construction (unless the words imperiously require it), which would impute to the framers of that instrument, when granting these powers for the public good, the intention of impeding their exercise, by withholding a choice of means? If, indeed, such be the mandate of the constitution, we have only to obey; but that instrument does not profess to enumerate the means by which the powers it confers may be executed; nor does it prohibit the creation of a corporation, if the existence of such a being be essential, to the beneficial exercise of those powers. It is, then, the subject of fair inquiry, how far such means may be employed.

It is not denied, that the powers given to the government imply the ordinary means of execution. That, for example, of raising revenue, and applying it to national purposes, is admitted to imply the power of conveying money from place to place, as the exigencies of the nation may require, and of employing the usual means of conveyance. But it is denied, that the government has its choice of means; or, that it may employ the most convenient means, if, to employ them, it be necessary to erect a corporation. On what foundation does this argument rest? On this alone: the power of creating a corporation, is one appertaining to sovereignty, and is not expressly conferred on congress. This is true. But all legislative powers appertain to sovereignty. The original power of giving the law on any subject whatever, is a sovereign power; and if the government of the Union is restrained from creating a corporation, as a means for performing its functions, on the single reason that the creation of a corporation is an act of sovereignty; if the sufficiency of this reason be acknowledged, there would be some difficulty in sustaining the authority of congress to pass other laws for the accomplishment of the same objects. The government which has a right to do an act, and has imposed on it, the duty of performing that act, must, according to the dictates of reason, be allowed to select the means; and those who contend that it may not select any appropriate means, that one particular mode of effecting the object is excepted, take upon themselves the burden of establishing that exception. . . .

[T]he constitution of the United States has not left the right of congress to employ the necessary means, for the execution of the powers conferred on the government, to general reasoning. To its enumeration of powers is added, that of making "all laws which shall be necessary and proper, for carrying into execution the foregoing powers, and all other powers vested by this constitution, in the government of the United States, or in any department thereof."

[T]he argument on which most reliance is placed, is drawn from that peculiar language of this clause. Congress is not empowered by it to make all laws, which may have relation to the powers conferred on the government, but such only as may be *"necessary and proper"* for carrying them into execution. The word *"necessary"* is considered as controlling the whole sentence, and as limiting the right to pass laws for the execution of the granted powers, to such as are indispensable, and without which the power would be nugatory. That it excludes the choice of means, and leaves to congress, in each case, that only which is most direct and simple. . . .

The subject is the execution of those great powers on which the welfare of a nation essentially depends. It must have been the intention of those who gave these powers, to insure, so far as human prudence could insure, their beneficial execution. This could not be done, by confiding the choice of means to such narrow limits as not to leave it in the power of congress to adopt any which might be appropriate, and which were conducive to the end. This provision is made in a constitution, intended to endure for ages to come, and consequently, to be adapted to the various *crises* of human affairs. To have prescribed the means by which government should, in all future time, execute its powers, would have been to change, entirely, the character of the instrument, and give it the properties of a legal code. It would have been an unwise attempt to provide, by immutable rules, for exigencies which, if foreseen at all, must have been seen dimly, and which can be best provided for as they occur. To have declared, that the best means shall not be used, but those alone, without which the power given would be nugatory, would have been to deprive the legislature of the capacity to avail itself of experience, to exercise its reason, and to accommodate its legislation to circumstances.

If we apply this principle of construction to any of the powers of the government, we shall find it so pernicious in its operation that we shall be compelled to discard it. The powers vested in congress may certainly be carried into execution, without prescribing an oath of office. The power to exact this security for the faithful performance of duty, is not given, nor is it indispensably necessary. The different departments may be established; taxes may be imposed and collected; armies and navies may be raised and maintained; and money may be borrowed, without requiring an oath of office. It might be argued, with as much plausibility as other incidental powers have been assailed, that the convention was not unmindful of this subject. The oath which might be exacted — that of fidelity to the constitution — is prescribed, and no other can be required. Yet, he would be charged with insanity, who should contend, that the legislature might not superadd, to the oath directed by the constitution, such other oath of office as its wisdom might suggest.

So, with respect to the whole penal code of the United States: whence arises the power to punish, in cases not prescribed by the constitution? All admit, that the government may, legitimately, punish any violation of its laws; and yet, this is not among the enumerated powers of congress. The right to enforce the observance of law, by punishing its infraction, might be denied, with the more plausibility, because it is expressly given in some cases.

Congress is empowered "to provide for the punishment of counterfeiting the securities and current coin of the United States," and "to define and punish piracies and felonies committed on the high seas, and offences against the law of nations." The several powers of congress may exist, in a very imperfect state, to be sure, but they may exist and be carried into execution, although no punishment should be inflicted, in cases where the right to punish is not expressly given.

Take, for example, the power "to establish post-offices and post-roads." This power is executed, by the single act of making the establishment. But, from this has been inferred the power and duty of carrying the mail along the post-road, from one post-office to another. And from this implied power, has again been inferred the right to punish those who steal letters from the post-office, or rob the mail. It may be said, with some plausibility, that the right to carry the mail, and to punish those who rob it, is not indispensably necessary to the establishment of a post-office and post-road. This right is indeed essential to the beneficial exercise of the power, but not indispensably necessary to its existence. So, of the punishment of the crimes of stealing or falsifying a record or process of a court of the United States, or of perjury in such court. To punish these offences, is certainly conducive to the due administration of justice. But courts may exist, and may decide the causes brought before them, though such crimes escape punishment.

The baneful influence of this narrow construction on all the operations of the government, and the absolute impracticability of maintaining it, without rendering the government incompetent to its great objects, might be illustrated by numerous examples drawn from the constitution, and from our laws. The good sense of the public has pronounced, without hesitation, that the power of punishment appertains to sovereignty, and may be exercised, whenever the sovereign has a right to act, as incidental to his constitutional powers. It is a means for carrying into execution all sovereign powers, and may be used, although not indispensably necessary. It is a right incidental to the power, and conducive to its beneficial exercise.

If this limited construction of the word "necessary" must be abandoned, in order to punish, whence is derived the rule which would reinstate it, when the government would carry its powers into execution, by means not vindictive in their nature? If the word "necessary" means "needful," "requisite," "essential," "conducive to," in order to let in the power of punishment for the infraction of law; why is it not equally comprehensive, when required to authorize the use of means which facilitate the execution of the powers of government, without the infliction of punishment?

In ascertaining the sense in which the word "necessary" is used in this clause of the constitution, we may derive some aid from that with which it is associated. Congress shall have power "to make all laws which shall be necessary and proper to carry into execution" the powers of the government. If the word "necessary" was used in that strict and rigorous sense for which the counsel for the state of Maryland contend, it would be an extraordinary departure from the usual course of the human mind, as exhibited in composition, to add a word, the only possible effect of which is, to qualify that strict and rigorous meaning; to present to the mind the idea of some choice of means of legislation, not strained and compressed within the narrow limits for which gentlemen contend.

But the argument which most conclusively demonstrates the error of the construction contended for by the counsel for the state of Maryland, is founded on the intention of the convention, as manifested in the whole clause. To waste time and argument in proving that, without it, congress might carry its powers into execution, would be not much less idle, than to hold a lighted taper to the sun. As little can it be required to prove, that in the absence of this clause, congress would have some choice of means. That it might employ those which, in its judgment, would most advantageously effect the object to be accomplished. That any means adapted to the end, any means which tended directly to the execution of the constitutional powers of the government, were in themselves constitutional. This clause, as construed by the state of Maryland, would abridge, and almost annihilate, this useful and necessary right of the legislature to select its means. That this could not be intended, is, we should think, had it not been already controverted, too apparent for controversy.

We think so for the following reasons: 1st. The clause is placed among the powers of congress, not among the limitations on those powers. 2d. Its terms purport to enlarge, not to diminish the powers vested in the government. It purports to be an additional power, not a restriction on those already granted. No reason has been, or can be assigned, for thus concealing an intention to narrow the discretion of the national legislature, under words which purport to enlarge it. The framers of the constitution wished its adoption, and well knew that it would be endangered by its strength, not by its weakness. Had they been capable of using language which would convey to the eye one idea, and, after deep reflection, impress on the mind, another, they would rather have disguised the grant of power, than its limitation. If, then, their intention had been, by this clause, to restrain the free use of means which might otherwise have been implied, that intention would have been inserted in another place, and would have been expressed in terms resembling these. "In carrying into execution the foregoing powers, and all others," &c., "no laws shall be passed but such as are necessary and proper." Had the intention been to make this clause restrictive, it would unquestionably have been so in form as well as in effect.

The result of the most careful and attentive consideration bestowed upon this clause is, that if it does not enlarge, it cannot be construed to restrain the powers of congress, or to impair the right of the legislature to exercise its best judgment in the selection of measures to carry into execution the constitutional powers of the government. If no other motive for its insertion can be suggested, a sufficient one is found in the desire to remove all doubts respecting the right to legislate on that vast mass of incidental powers which must be involved in the constitution, if that instrument be not a splendid bauble.

We admit, as all must admit, that the powers of the government are limited, and that its limits are not to be transcended. But we think the sound construction of the constitution must allow to the national legislature that discretion, with respect to the means by which the powers it confers are to be carried into execution, which will enable that body to perform the high duties assigned to it, in the manner most beneficial to the people. Let the end be legitimate, let it be within the scope of the constitution, and all means which are appropriate, which are plainly adapted to that end, which are not prohibited, but consist with the letter and spirit of the constitution, are constitutional. . . .

After this declaration, it can scarcely be necessary to say, that the existence of state banks can have no possible influence on the question. No trace is to be found in the constitution, of an intention to create a dependence of the government of the Union on those of the states, for the execution of the great powers assigned to it. Its means are adequate to its ends; and on those means alone was it expected to rely for the accomplishment of its ends. To impose on it the necessity of resorting to means which it cannot control, which another government may furnish or withhold, would render its course precarious, the result of its measures uncertain, and create a dependence on other governments, which might disappoint its most important designs, and is incompatible with the language of the constitution. But were it otherwise, the choice of means implies a right to choose a national bank in preference to state banks, and congress alone can make the election.

After the most deliberate consideration, it is the unanimous and decided opinion of this court, that the act to incorporate the Bank of the United States is a law made in pursuance of the constitution, and is a part of the supreme law of the land.

The branches, proceeding from the same stock, and being conducive to the complete accomplishment of the object, are equally constitutional. It would have been unwise, to locate them in the charter, and it would be unnecessarily inconvenient, to employ the legislative power in making those subordinate arrangements. The great duties of the bank are prescribed; those duties require branches; and the bank itself may, we think, be safely trusted with the selection of places where those branches shall be fixed; reserving always to the government the right to require that a branch shall be located where it may be deemed necessary.

It being the opinion of the court, that the act incorporating the bank is constitutional; and that the power of establishing a branch in the state of Maryland might be properly exercised by the bank itself, we proceed to inquire. . . . .

2. Whether the state of Maryland may, without violating the constitution, tax that branch? That the power of taxation is one of vital importance; that it is retained by the states; that it is not abridged by the grant of a similar power to the government of the Union; that it is to be concurrently exercised by the two governments — are truths which have never been denied. But such is the paramount character of the constitution, that its capacity to withdraw any subject from the action of even this power, is admitted. The states are expressly forbidden to lay any duties on imports or exports, except what may be absolutely necessary for executing their inspection laws. If the obligation of this prohibition must be conceded — if it may restrain a state from the exercise of its taxing power on imports and exports — the same paramount character would seem to restrain, as it certainly may restrain, a state from such other exercise of this power, as is in its nature incompatible with, and repugnant to, the constitutional laws of the Union. A law, absolutely repugnant to another, as entirely repeals that other as if express terms of repeal were used.

On this ground, the counsel for the bank place its claim to be exempted from the power of a state to tax its operations. There is no express provision for the case, but the claim has been sustained on a principle which so entirely pervades the constitution, is so intermixed with the materials which compose it, so interwoven with its web, so blended with its texture, as to be incapable of being separated from it, without rending it into shreds. This great principle is, that the constitution and the laws made in pursuance thereof are supreme; that they control the constitution and laws of the respective states, and cannot be controlled by them. From this, which may be almost termed an axiom, other propositions are deduced as corollaries, on the truth or error of which, and on their application to this case, the cause has been supposed to depend. These are, 1st. That a power to create implies a power to preserve: 2d. That a power to destroy, if wielded by a different hand, is hostile to, and incompatible with these powers to create and to preserve: 3d. That where this repugnancy exists, that authority which is supreme must control, not yield to that over which it is supreme. . . .

The power of congress to create, and of course, to continue, the bank, was the subject of the preceding part of this opinion; and is no longer to be considered as questionable. That the power of taxing it by the states may be exercised so as to destroy it, is too obvious to be denied. But taxation is said to be an absolute power, which acknowledges no other limits than those expressly prescribed in the constitution, and like sovereign power of every other description, is entrusted to the discretion of those who use it. But the very terms of this argument admit, that the sovereignty of the state, in the article of taxation itself, is subordinate to, and may be controlled by the constitution of the United States. How far it has been controlled by that instrument, must be a question of construction. In making this construction, no principle, not declared, can be admissible, which would defeat the legitimate operations of a supreme government. It is of the very essence of supremacy, to remove all obstacles to its action within its own sphere, and so to modify every power vested in subordinate governments, as to exempt its own operations from their own influence. This effect need not be stated in terms. It is so involved in the declaration of supremacy, so necessarily implied in it, that the expression of it could not make it more certain. We must, therefore, keep it in view, while construing the constitution.

The argument on the part of the state of Maryland, is, not that the states may directly resist a law of congress, but that they may exercise their acknowledged powers upon it, and that the constitution leaves them this right, in the confidence that they will not abuse it. Before we proceed to examine this argument, and to subject it to test of the constitution, we must be permitted to bestow a few considerations on the nature and extent of this original right of taxation, which is acknowledged to remain with the states. It is admitted, that the power of taxing the people and their property, is essential to the very existence of government, and may be legitimately exercised on the objects to which it is applicable, to the utmost extent to which the government may choose to carry it. The only security against the abuse of this power, is found in the structure of the government itself. In imposing a tax, the legislature acts upon its constituents. This is, in general, a sufficient security against erroneous and oppressive taxation.

The people of a state, therefore, give to their government a right of taxing themselves and their property, and as the exigencies of government cannot be limited, they prescribe no limits to the exercise of this right, resting confidently on the interest of the legislator, and on the influence of the constituent over their representative, to guard them against its abuse. But the means employed by the government of the Union have no such security, nor is the right of a state to tax them sustained by the same theory. Those means are not given by the people of a particular state, not given by the constituents of the legislature, which claim the right to tax them, but by the people of all the states. They are given by all, for the benefit of all — and upon theory, should be subjected to that government only which belongs to all.

It may be objected to this definition, that the power of taxation is not confined to the people and property of a state. It may be exercised upon every object brought within its jurisdiction. This is true. But to what source do we trace this right? It is obvious, that it is an incident of sovereignty, and is co-extensive with that to which it is an incident. All subjects over which the sovereign power of a state extends, are objects of taxation; but those over which it does not extend, are, upon the soundest principles, exempt from taxation. This proposition may almost be pronounced self-evident.

The sovereignty of a state extends to everything which exists by its own authority, or is introduced by its permission; but does it extend to those means which are employed by congress to carry into execution powers conferred on that body by the people of the United States? We think it demonstrable, that it does not. Those powers are not given by the people of a single state. They are given by the people of the United States, to a government whose laws, made in pursuance of the constitution, are declared to be supreme. Consequently, the people of a single state cannot confer a sovereignty which will extend over them.

If we measure the power of taxation residing in a state, by the extent of sovereignty which the people of a single state possess, and can confer on its government, we have an intelligible standard, applicable to every case to which the power may be applied. We have a principle which leaves the power of taxing the people and property of a state unimpaired; which leaves to a state the command of all its resources, and which places beyond its reach, all those powers which are conferred by the people of the United States on the government of the Union, and all those means which are given for the purpose of carrying those powers into execution. We have a principle which is safe for the states, and safe for the Union. We are relieved, as we ought to be, from clashing sovereignty; from interfering powers; from a repugnancy between a right in one government to pull down, what there is an acknowledged right in another to build up; from the incompatibility of a right in one government to destroy, what there is a right in another to preserve. We are not driven to the perplexing inquiry, so unfit for the judicial department, what degree of taxation is the legitimate use, and what degree may amount to the abuse of the power. The attempt to use it on the means employed by the government of the Union, in pursuance of the constitution, is itself an abuse, because it is the usurpation of a power which the people of a single state cannot give. We find, then, on just theory, a total failure of this original right to tax the means employed by the government of the Union, for the execution of its powers. The right never existed, and the question whether it has been surrendered, cannot arise. . . .

If we apply the principle for which the state of Maryland contends, to the constitution, generally, we shall find it capable of changing totally the character of that instrument. We shall find it capable of arresting all the measures of the government, and of prostrating it at the foot of the states. The American people have declared their constitution and the laws made in pursuance thereof, to be supreme; but this principle would transfer the supremacy, in fact, to the states. If the states may tax one instrument, employed by the government in the execution of its powers, they may tax any and every other instrument. They may tax the mail; they may tax the mint; they may tax patent-rights; they may tax the papers of the custom-house; they may tax judicial process; they may tax all the means employed by the government, to an excess which would defeat all the ends of government. This was not intended by the American people. They did not design to make their government dependent on the states. . . .

It has also been insisted, that, as the power of taxation in the general and state governments is acknowledged to be concurrent, every argument which would sustain the right of the general government to tax banks chartered by the states, will equally sustain the right of the states to tax banks chartered by the general government. But the two cases are not on the same reason. The people of all the states have created the general government, and have conferred upon it the general power of taxation. The people of all the states, and the states themselves, are represented in congress, and, by their representatives, exercise this power. When they tax the chartered institutions of the states, they tax their constituents; and these taxes must be uniform. But when a state taxes the operations of the government of the United States, it acts upon institutions created, not by their own constituents, but by people over whom they claim no control. It acts upon the measures of a government created by others as well as themselves, for the benefit of others in common with themselves. The difference is that which always exists, and always must exist, between the action of the whole on a part, and the action of a part on the whole — between the laws of a government declared to be supreme, and those of a government which, when in opposition to those laws, is not supreme.

But if the full application of this argument could be admitted, it might bring into question the right of congress to tax the state banks, and could not prove the rights of the states to tax the Bank of the United States.

The court has bestowed on this subject its most deliberate consideration. The result is a conviction that the states have no power, by taxation or otherwise, to retard, impede, burden, or in any manner control, the operations of the constitutional laws enacted by congress to carry into execution the powers vested in the general government. This is, we think, the unavoidable consequence of that supremacy which the constitution has declared. We are unanimously of opinion, that the law passed by the legislature of Maryland, imposing a tax on the Bank of the United States, is unconstitutional and void.

This opinion does not deprive the states of any resources which they originally possessed. It does not extend to a tax paid by the real property of the bank, in common with the other real property within the state, nor to a tax imposed on the interest which the citizens of Maryland may hold in this institution, in common with other property of the same description throughout the state. But this is a tax on the operations of the bank, and is, consequently, a tax on the operation of an instrument employed by the government of the Union to carry its powers into execution. Such a tax must be unconstitutional.

———

Comments on *McCulloch*: Constitutional Interpretation and *McCulloch*. Does Justice Marshall set forth a credo for positional interpretation in *McCulloch*? What is it? Justice Frankfurter called Marshall's statement that, "We must never forget it is a constitutional we expounding," ". . . the single most important utterance in the literature of constitutional law." See, Frankfurter, "John Marshall and the Judicial Function," 69 Harv. L. Rev. 217, 219 (1955). Why would Frankfurter so assert? Is this a preference for a "clause bound" or "living Constitution"? Note that Frankfurter advocated judicial restraint throughout his tenure on the Court and once commented, "precisely because 'it is a constitution we are expounding,' we ought not to take liberties with it." *National Mutual Insurance Co. v. Tidewater Transfer Co.*, 337 U.S. 581, 647 (1949) (Frankfurter, J., dissenting).

"Consider the following possible interpretations of Chief Justice Marshall's position. (a) The power-granting provisions of the Constitution should be broadly construed. Those provisions are meant to endure over time. They should be interpreted flexibly as new and unforeseen problems arise. But to say this is emphatically not to say that courts ought to have a license, often or ever, to strike down legislative action on grounds of changed circumstances. (b) All provisions of the Constitution, including those granting powers and those creating rights, should be broadly construed. Constitutions simply do not contain specific answers to all questions for all times. (c) The meaning of the Constitution changes with changing circumstances, in accordance with changing social norms and needs. Judges need not adhere to the specific "intent" of the framers or the original meaning of the text, but must interpret the document flexibly in light of contemporary necessities." (Stone, Seidman, Sustein, Tushnet, *Constitutional Law* 68 (1996).)

Necessary and Proper Clause — Implied Power. Marshall adopts Hamilton's view allowing a broad "latitude" implied power extending from the necessary and proper clause. Were you surprised? What are the long term effects of this aspect of the decision? Are there any limits on what powers may be implied from the exercise of an enumerated power? Marshall states in *McCulloch*, "[W]e think the sound construction of the constitution must allow to the national legislature that discretion to the means by which the powers it confers are to be carried into execution. . . . Let the end be legitimate, let it be within the scope of the Constitution, and all means which are appropriate, which are plainly adapted to that end, which are not prohibited, but consist with the letter and spirit of the Constitution, are constitutional." Is this an appropriate limit? As we move through the materials you will find that whenever the Court exercises judicial review and defers to Congress or "bows to the democratic process," it will apply a "rational purpose" review. Is *McCulloch* the origin of this minimum level of scrutiny?

Federalism-based Limits on the Necessary and Proper Clause? In *McCulloch,* the Supreme Court read the Necessary and Proper Clause of Article I, § 8, cl. 18, broadly in support of Congress's power to charter a national bank. Does the current Court's federalism-based limits on the commerce power developed in the line of cases from *Lopez* to *Raich* (Chapter 2), have any application to the Necessary and Proper Clause?

In *United States v. Comstock*, 560 U.S. 126 (2010), the Court considered the question whether the Necessary and Proper Clause grants authority to Congress to enact a statute, 18 U.S.C. § 4248, allowing federal district courts to order the civil commitment of mentally ill, sexually dangerous federal prisoners beyond the dates they would otherwise be released. The Court found, by a vote of 7–2, that the Clause does grant such authority. Justice Breyer wrote for the Court, joined significantly by Chief Justice Roberts as well as Justices Stevens, Ginsburg, and Sotomayor:

> Here we ask whether the Federal Government has the authority under Article I of the Constitution to enact this federal civil-commitment program or whether its doing so falls beyond the reach of a government "of enumerated powers." McCulloch v. Maryland. [We] conclude that the Constitution grants Congress legislative power sufficient to enact § 4248. We base this conclusion on five considerations, taken together.
>
> First, the Necessary and Proper Clause grants Congress broad authority to enact federal legislation [that is] "convenient, or useful" or "conducive" to the authority's "beneficial exercise." [McCulloch.] Neither Congress' power to criminalize conduct, nor its power to imprison individuals who engage in that conduct, nor its power to enact laws governing prisons and prisoners, is explicitly mentioned in the Constitution. But Congress nonetheless possesses broad authority to do each of those things in the course of "carrying into Execution" [its] enumerated powers. Second, the civil-commitment statute before us constitutes a modest addition to a set of federal prison-related mental-health statutes that have existed [since] 1855. Third, Congress reasonably extended its longstanding civil-commitment system to cover mentally ill and sexually dangerous persons who are already in federal custody, even if doing so detains them beyond the termination of their criminal sentence. [The] Federal Government is the custodian of its prisoners [and] has the constitutional power to act in order to protect nearby (and other) communities from the danger federal prisoners may pose. [Moreover,] § 4248 is "reasonably adapted" to Congress' power to act as a responsible federal custodian. Congress could have reasonably concluded that federal inmates who suffer from a mental illness that causes them to "have serious difficulty in refraining from sexually violent conduct" would pose an especially high danger to the public if released. And Congress could also have reasonably concluded [that] a reasonable number of such individuals would likely not be detained by the States if released from federal custody. Fourth, the statute properly accounts for state interests. [Section 4248 does not] invade state sovereignty [but rather] requires accommodation of state interests: [it] requires the Attorney General to encourage the relevant States to take custody of the individual without inquiring into the "suitability" of their intended care or treatment, and to relinquish federal authority whenever a State asserts its own. Fifth, the links between § 4248 and an enumerated Article I power are not too attenuated. [We need not] fear that our holding today confers on Congress a general "police power" [for] § 4248 is narrow in scope. It has been applied to only a small fraction of federal prisoners. And its reach is limited to individuals already "in the custody of the" Federal Government. [Taken] together, these considerations lead us to conclude that the statute is a "necessary and

proper" means of exercising the federal authority that permits Congress to create federal criminal laws, to punish their violation, to imprison violators, to provide appropriately for those imprisoned, and to maintain the security of those who are not imprisoned but who may be affected by the federal imprisonment of others.

Justice Kennedy, joined by Justice Alito, filed a concurrence in the judgment, agreeing that § 4248 was a necessary and proper exercise of congressional authority, but emphasizing that the rationality review applicable to a Necessary and Proper Clause inquiry should not be as deferential as the minimal rationality test employed in due process inquiries: "[U]nder the Necessary and Proper Clause, application of a 'rational basis' test should be at least as exacting as it has been in the Commerce Clause cases, if not more so. [Those] precedents require a tangible link to commerce, not a mere conceivable rational relation, as in [the due process cases]. The rational basis referred to in the Commerce Clause context is a demonstrated link in fact, based on empirical demonstration."

Justice Alito filed a separate concurrence in the judgment, opining that it is "necessary and proper for Congress to protect the public from dangers created by the federal criminal justice and prison systems. [Just] as it is necessary and proper for Congress to provide for the apprehension of escaped federal prisoners, it is necessary and proper for Congress to provide for the civil commitment of dangerous federal prisoners who would otherwise escape civil commitment as a result of federal imprisonment."

Justice Thomas, joined for the most part by Justice Scalia, filed a dissent objecting that the statute intrudes too far upon the authority of the States: "§ 4248 can be a valid exercise of congressional authority only if it is 'necessary and proper for carrying into Execution' one or more of those federal powers actually enumerated in the Constitution. [The] Government identifies no specific enumerated power or powers as a constitutional predicate for § 4248, and none are readily discernable. Indeed, not even the Commerce Clause [can] justify federal civil detention of sex offenders [as sexual violence is a noneconomic activity]. [The] power to care for the mentally ill and, where necessary, the power 'to protect the community from the dangerous tendencies of some' mentally ill persons, are among the numerous powers that remain with the States. [True,] 29 States appear as amici and argue that § 4248 is constitutional. They tell us that they do not object to Congress retaining custody of 'sexually dangerous persons' after their criminal sentences expire because the cost of detaining such persons is 'expensive' [and] these States would rather the Federal Government bear this expense. Congress' power, however, is fixed by the Constitution; it does not expand merely to suit the States' policy preferences, or to allow State officials to avoid difficult choices regarding the allocation of state funds. [Today's] opinion [comes] perilously close to transforming the Necessary and Proper Clause into a basis for [a] federal police power."

A Lesson in Nation Building? Why such a grandiose description of a judicial decision? The significance of the "ultimate power" of judicial review resting in a Court is apparent when the judiciary makes a threshold decision delineating the balance of power under the new Constitution in the fledgling republic. Though Marshall applied a rather deferential review, he was quick to point out in response to critics of the decision (Justice Roan, for example) that it was review nonetheless and that the Court would "invalidate laws for the accomplishment of objects not entrusted to the national government."

Does Marshall rely on "political safeguards" as the major means of resolving conflicts over "federalism" in *McCulloch*? (See Wechsler, "The Political Safeguards of Federalism," 54 Colum.L.Rev. 543 (1954), or Choper, Judicial Review and the National

Political Process (1980).) Here, the deference of allowing Congress to "choose the means" reinforces a broad basis for federal power under the necessary and proper clause and portends that the balance of power between state and federal government should be decided via the political process as opposed to the Court applying the Constitution as fundamental law. What are the advantages or disadvantages of each approach?

Is the inherent flexibility of the "political process" a better alternative for successful government — by not "fixing" and "limiting" the question of power between state and federal governments to the inflexible mandates of the Constitution as fundamental law. If such is the case the people through their elected officials in Congress can adjust state versus federal power to the needs of the times. This would allow for greater federal authority when necessary (the Great Depression for example), yet the ability to cede more authority to the states when that alternative might be necessary (the Reagan revolution?). Is the flexibility afforded by the balance of power between state and federal government being left to the political process, with minimum judicial oversight, a "lesson in nation building" or birth of "big brother"? These are more than academic questions given the current Court's "anti-federalist" revival challenging the views of Marshall in *McCulloch.*

Representation (Without Taxation) — State v. Federal Power. Marshall is troubled by the fact that when a state taxes a national entity we have "taxation without representation" because the state is in effect taxing citizens who are not represented in the state legislature imposing the tax. Yet, when the federal government taxes a state, "In imposing a tax the legislature acts upon its constituents." This, he argues, "is in general a sufficient security against erroneous and oppressive taxation," and in "the legislature of the Union alone, all are represented." (See the discussion of intergovernmental immunity, below) Does this rationale also support the deference in bowing to the national political process to resolve this issue? The claim here is that the power to elect representatives will act as a safeguard against the abuse of political power by elected officials. Does Marshall's view on the "representative" nature of power support the inherent flexibility afforded by deferring to the political process? The judicial role is then limited to an "oversight" that will ensure that the political process itself will ensure against improper conduct.

Note, by contrast, Chief Justice Marshall's suggestion that while the federal government has an (implicit) immunity from state taxation, states may not be immune from federal taxation. How does Chief Justice Marshall's theory of representation operate differently here? The central idea is that the judicial role is to make up for defects in the ordinary operation of representative government; the source of judicial decision is a breakdown in political processes. Is this not similar to the theory advanced by John Ely in *Democracy and Distrust* (1980).

B. OTHER ASPECTS OF FEDERAL POWER

Preemption. What is given may not be reserved. If the Constitution enumerates a power to Congress and Congress so chooses to exercise it, may it "preempt the states" from acting in the field? The argument is yes because if the power is enumerated, and Congress in exercise of the power displaces or preempts the states, then there is nothing left to be reserved. The Court has held that whether or not there is preemption is a matter of congressional intent. Where the intent to preempt is clear and express, this is not problematic. Such, however, may not always be the case, and in limited circumstances preemption may be implied. Mere silence on behalf of Congress is presumed, nonetheless, to intend that state regulation in the field is permissible. (But see the discussion of the "dormant" or self-enforcing commerce power, infra)

The Court has held that there are three ways in which Congress may preempt state regulation: by expressly stating the preemption, or by enacting a regulation with which the state regulation in fact conflicts, or by enacting a system of regulations so comprehensive as to displace all state regulations even if they do not conflict with any specific federal one ("occupying the field").

1. Express preemption. A federal statute may state that it preempts state law, but a question as to the "extent" of the "express" preemption may still be exist. Does, for example, the state law at issue fall within the category of laws that are preempted?

2. Conflicting regulations. Conflicts may occur when it is impossible to comply with both state and federal laws or when the state law "stands as an obstacle to the accomplishment of the full purposes and objectives of Congress." (See *Hines v. Davidowitz*, 312 U.S. 52 (1941).)

3. Occupying the field. Given the state "displacement" resulting from preemption, the Court is reticent against finding that Congress intended to preempt by occupying the field. Yet, with strong support and proof that Congress' occupation of the field shows their intent to preemption the Court has so concluded. (See *Rice v. Santa Fe Elevator Co*, 331 U.S. 218 (1947).)

Preemption is not the norm, in fact where Congress is silent and none of the above cited circumstances are present the presumption is that Congress intended that the states may also occupy the field. Often times, Congress may preempt in part but save to suitors other state or common law remedies. The issues raised therein are often quite complex, and are best reviewed in a course offering specialized coverage in this area.

Recent Preemption Decisions. Of interest given the views of several of the current Justices in regard to protecting the power of the States as against the Federal Government, are several recent decisions finding that federal law preempts state common law in regard to civil (tort) damage liability. In *Riegel v. Medtronic, Inc.*, 552 U.S. 312 (2008), for example, the Court examined whether the Medical Device Amendments of 1976 (MDA) bar a state court action challenging the allegedly tortious design and manufacture of a defective medical device. The MDA charges the Food and Drug Administration (FDA) with conducting premarket review of certain medical devices to determine if there is reasonable assurance of "safety and effectiveness" in general and for the particular uses indicated in the labeling. If the FDA gives premarket approval, the manufacturer cannot make changes in a device's design, manufacture, or labeling without further FDA approval. The MDA also contains a preemption provision providing that no state may adopt a "requirement" that is "different from, or in addition to, any requirement applicable under this chapter to the device" and that "relates to the safety or effectiveness of the device or to any other matter included in a requirement applicable to the device." 21 U.S.C. § 360k(a). At issue was a state common law claim brought by petitioner alleging that a heart catheter used on her husband had been designed, labeled, and manufactured defectively, in violation of New York common law. The Court held that common law duties imposed on device manufacturers fit within the "normal meaning" of "requirement[s]" for purposes of the MDA. This reading of "the broad language chosen by Congress," moreover, made sense because "[s]tate tort law that requires a manufacturer's catheters to be safer, but hence less effective, than the model the FDA has approved disrupts the federal scheme no less than state regulatory law to the same effect." Although the dissent found it difficult to believe that Congress would deny consumers all forms of judicial recourse for alleged product defects in such devices, the Court replied that "this is exactly what a pre-emption clause for medical devices does by its terms." See also *Rowe v. New Hampshire Motor Transport Ass'n,* 552 U.S. 364 (2008), for a similar result concerning the Motor Carrier Act of 1980 and a state regulation which limited shipment of tobacco products to minors. Do these cases portend a "showdown" between this majority's protection of business interests as against its protection of state versus federal power, perhaps detailing a new approach in these circumstances, or are they simply "express statutory preemption" cases? With litigation in the Federal Courts concerning issues similar to those in *Riegel,* but dealing with FDA approved drugs, an answer came in the Court's 2008-09 term. In *Wyeth v. Levine,* 129 S.Ct. 1187 (2009), plaintiff sued a drug manufacturer claiming negligence because the warning label for the drug did not provide a warning concerning the danger of administering a nausea medication directly into the patient's vein. The doctor failed to use this technique, which ultimately led to gangrene and amputation of plaintiff's arm. The jury concluded that had the doctor administered the drug by an intravenous drip into her vein, her injury would not have occurred. Wyeth (the drug company), citing the "preemption argument" of *Riegel,* defended the doctor's action by arguing that the FDA had approved the warning label thus preempting state law. A divided Court (6 to 3) held that the federal law did not preempt state tort liability because Wyeth should have added a stronger warning label, which would not have made the drug "misbranded," rejecting the extensive ramification of extending *Riegel* to the FDA's general "drug approval."

Justice Alito, joined by Justices Robert and Scalia, dissented and argued that this case "cannot be reconciled with *Geier v. American Honda Motor Co.,* 529 U.S. 861, 120 S.Ct. 1913, 146 L.Ed.2d 914 (2000), or general principles of conflict pre-emption."

The Court recently suggested that the trigger for preemption is lighter in the immigration context than in the usual case. In *Arizona v. United States,* 567 U.S. 387 (2012), a divided Court held that federal immigration law occupies the field such that Arizona could not (a) make it a crime for an alien to fail to comply with federal registration requirements; (b) make it a crime for an unauthorized alien to work or apply for employment in the state; and (c) authorize state law enforcement to arrest a person on probable cause that he or she has committed an offense that makes that individual removable. At the outset of its analysis, the Court emphasized the federal government's "broad, undoubted power" over immigration and the potential foreign relations implications of the treatment of foreign nationals within U.S. borders. The Court also noted the pervasiveness of federal regulation of immigration. From that starting point, the Court found it relatively straightforward to conclude that the three provisions of state law mentioned above either entered a field that federal law had fully occupied or stood as an obstacle to the purposes of federal law. Citing Hines v. Davidovitz, 312 U.S. 52 (1941), the Court reasoned that Congress had "struck a careful balance" about the appropriate requirements for the registration of aliens and about the sanctions for nonregistration, and that this "comprehensive" federal scheme precludes state regulation of the same field. Similarly, the Court found that because federal law imposed "comprehensive" sanctions on employers who hired unauthorized aliens — but deliberately omitted criminal sanctions on the employees themselves — states could not impose such sanctions on employees without interposing an obstacle to federal purposes. Finally, the Court found that the state's authorization to arrest persons based on probable cause of removability interfered with the purposes of federal law by intruding on the enforcement discretion of federal immigration officers. The Court upheld only one provision of the Arizona law, which provides that an officer who makes a lawful stop or arrest must take steps to ascertain immigration status if he or she has reasonable suspicion that the subject is an unauthorized alien.

Justices Scalia, Thomas, and Alito filed separate partial dissents. Justice Scalia argued that states have a traditional sovereign interest in the preservation of the integrity of their borders, and that courts should insist on a clear statement of legislative intent before reading a statute to abrogate that sovereign authority. Because none of the Arizona provisions squarely conflicts with federal law, Justice Scalia would have upheld them all. The fact that state laws strike a different balance from the federal laws on some issues, he argued, should not alone provide a ground for preemption. For example, he added, "[t]he sale of illegal drugs TTT violates state law as well as federal law, and no one thinks that the state penalties cannot exceed the federal." With respect to the employment provision in particular, Justice Scalia emphasized that Congress adopted an *express* preemption provision displacing "any state or local law imposing civil or criminal sanctions TTT upon those who employ, or recruit or refer for a fee for employment, unauthorized aliens." 8 U.S.C. § 1324a(h)(2). For him, Congress's adoption of an express preemption provision precluded the Court's finding implied preemption of laws that did not fall within scope of the express provision.

Justice Alito agreed with the Court that under *Hines v. Davidovitz*, Arizona's registration provision was preempted. Relying on both the presumption against preemption and the limited scope of the express preemption provision cited above, he argued, however, that there was insufficient evidence that Congress wished to preempt the state's prescription of sanctions for unauthorized aliens seeking employment. Finally, he argued that the arrest authority conferred by the Arizona statute added little to state enforcement officers' background authority to arrest aliens for removable offenses, and that there is nothing in the state law that necessarily places its enforcement in conflict with the discretion of federal officials. Justice Thomas wrote a brief dissent reiterating his previously stated concerns about doctrines of implied preemption.

One interesting aspect of the case is that both the majority and Justice Scalia's dissent framed their respective analyses against the backdrop of broad structural presumptions — in the former case, a presumption of overriding federal interest and, in the latter, a presumption that a state possesses sovereign authority to exclude persons from its borders. Where do these presumptions come from and how far do they go? Do they help or confuse judicial analysis? More generally, in other opinions, Justice Thomas has stated his reluctance to find implied preemption at all, reasoning that the analysis is too malleable and requires judges to delve into the unknowable realm of unstated congressional purpose. Does the complexity of the competing arguments in this case lend any support to this position? Or is it standard judicial practice to determine when Congress has struck an intricate federal balance that deliberately goes so far and no farther? Compare *Buckman Co. v. Plaintiffs' Legal Comm.*, 531 U.S. 341, 347-348 (2001); *Wisconsin Dept. of Industry, Labor & Human Relations v. Gould Inc.*, 475 U.S. 282, 288-289 (1986); *Silkwood v. Kerr-McGee Corp.*, 464 U.S. 238, 249 (1984).

Sports Betting and Preemption

MURPHY v. NATIONAL COLLEGIATE ATHLETIC ASSOCIATION
584 U. S. _____ (2018)

[In addressing whether or not a federal law prohibiting states from authorizing sports betting constituted a case of federal overreach into state power (the Anti-commandeering Doctrine, at 2.II.G.2), the court also addressed the claim that the federal statute preempted any state actions on the betting issue in this excerpt.

The portion of the Court's opinion specifically addressing the Anti-commandeering doctrine is included at page 326.]

[V]

Respondents and the United States defend the antiauthorization prohibition on the ground that it constitutes a valid preemption provision, but it is no such thing. Preemption is based on the Supremacy Clause, and that Clause is not an independent grant of legislative power to Congress. Instead, it simply provides "a rule of decision." Armstrong v. Exceptional Child Center, Inc., 575 U. S. ___, ___ (2015) (slip op., at 3). It specifies that federal law is supreme in case of a conflict with state law. Therefore, in order for the PASPA provision to preempt state law, it must satisfy two requirements. First, it must represent the exercise of a power conferred on Congress by the Constitution; pointing to the Supremacy Clause will not do. Second, since the Constitution "confers upon Congress the power to regulate individuals, not States," New York, 505 U. S., at 166, the PASPA provision at issue must be best read as one that regulates private actors. Our cases have identified three different types of preemption—"conflict," "express," and "field," see English v. General Elec. Co., 496 U. S. 72, 78–79 (1990)—but all of them work in the same way: Congress enacts a law that imposes restrictions or confers rights on private actors; a state law confers rights or imposes restrictions that conflict with the federal law; and therefore the federal law takes precedence and the state law is preempted.

This mechanism is shown most clearly in cases involving "conflict preemption." A recent example is Mutual Pharmaceutical Co. v. Bartlett, 570 U. S. 472 (2013). In that case, a federal law enacted under the Commerce Clause regulated manufacturers of generic drugs, prohibiting them from altering either the composition or labeling approved by the Food and Drug Administration. A State's tort law, however, effectively required a manufacturer to supplement the warnings included in the FDA-approved label. Id., at 480–486. We held that the state law was preempted because it imposed a duty that was inconsistent—i.e., in conflict—with federal law. Id., at 493.

"Express preemption" operates in essentially the same way, but this is often obscured by the language used by Congress in framing preemption provisions. The provision at issue in Morales v. Trans World Airlines, Inc., 504 U. S. 374 (1992), is illustrative. The Airline Deregulation Act of 1978 lifted prior federal regulations of airlines, and "[t]o ensure that the States would not undo federal deregulation with regulation of their own," id., at 378, the Act provided that "no State or political subdivision thereof . . . shall enact or enforce any law, rule, regulation, standard, or other provision having the force and effect of law relating to rates, routes, or services of any [covered] air carrier." 49 U. S. C. App. §1305(a)(1) (1988 ed.).

This language might appear to operate directly on the States, but it is a mistake to be confused by the way in which a preemption provision is phrased. As we recently explained, "we do not require Congress to employ a particular linguistic formulation when preempting state law." Coventry Health Care of Mo., Inc. v. Nevils, 581 U. S. ___, ___–___ (2017) (slip op., at 10–11). And if we look beyond the phrasing employed in the Airline Deregulation Act's preemption provision, it is clear that this provision operates just like any other federal law with preemptive effect. It confers on private entities (i.e., covered carriers) a federal right to engage in certain conduct subject only to certain (federal) constraints. "Field preemption" operates in the same way.

Field preemption occurs when federal law occupies a "field" of regulation "so comprehensively that it has left no room for supplementary state legislation." R. J. Reynolds Tobacco Co. v. Durham County, 479 U. S. 130, 140 (1986). In describing field preemption, we have sometimes used the same sort of shorthand employed by Congress in express preemption provisions. See, e.g., Oneok, Inc. v. Learjet, Inc., 575 U. S. ___, ___ (2015) (slip op., at 2) ("Congress has forbidden the State to take action in the field that the federal statute pre-empts"). But in substance, field preemption does not involve congressional commands to the States. Instead, like all other forms of preemption, it concerns a clash between a constitutional exercise of Congress's legislative power and conflicting state law. See Crosby v. National Foreign Trade Council, 530 U. S. 363, 372, n. 6 (2000).

The Court's decision in Arizona v. United States, 567 U. S. 387 (2012), shows how this works. Noting that federal statutes "provide a full set of standards governing alien registration," we concluded that these laws "reflect[] a congressional decision to foreclose any state regulation in the area, even if it is parallel to federal standards." Id., at 401. What this means is that the federal registration provisions not only impose federal registration obligations on aliens but also confer a federal right to be free from any other registration requirements.

In sum, regardless of the language sometimes used by Congress and this Court, every form of preemption is based on a federal law that regulates the conduct of private actors, not the States.

Once this is understood, it is clear that the PASPA provision prohibiting state authorization of sports gambling is not a preemption provision because there is no way in which this provision can be understood as a regulation of private actors. It certainly does not confer any federal rights on private actors interested in conducting sports gambling operations. (It does not give them a federal right to engage in sports gambling.) Nor does it impose any federal restrictions on private actors. If a private citizen or company started a sports gambling operation, either with or without state authorization, §3702(1) would not be violated and would not provide any ground for a civil action by the Attorney General or any other party. Thus, there is simply no way to understand the provision prohibiting state authorization as anything other than a direct command to the States. And that is exactly what the anti-commandeering rule does not allow.

———

Intergovernmental Tax Immunity. As McCulloch v. Maryland has illustrated one of the constitutional principles that governs relations between state and nation is that neither may destroy the autonomy of the other. In McCulloch itself, John Marshall struck down Maryland's tax on the operations of a federal instrumentality, the Bank of the United States. For over a century after McCulloch, constitutional tax immunities expanded in a number of directions. Marshall in McCulloch had indicated that his views of federal immunity from state taxation did not imply a reciprocal immunity of state operations from federal taxes. Nevertheless, the post–Civil War Court held that state activities did enjoy a reciprocal immunity from federal taxation. Collector v. Day, 11 Wall. (78 U.S.) 113 (1871). Moreover, the Court steadily expanded the circle of immunities, from the primary immunity of the government itself to the derivative immunity of third persons — employees, lessees, patentees — in some ways related to governmental activities. In the late 1930s, that circle began to contract. For example, Helvering v. Gerhardt, 304 U.S. 405 (1938), and Graves v. New York ex rel. O'Keefe, 306 U.S. 466 (1939), held that the salaries of the employees of one government are not immune from income taxes imposed by the other. In recent years, intergovernmental tax immunities have continued to wane, although the Court continues to enforce a few constitutional tax immunities, as when states impose property taxes directly on federal property. See Rohr Aircraft Corp. v. San Diego County, 362 U.S. 628 (1960); see generally Massachusetts v. United States, 435 U.S. 444 (1978).

Increasingly, however, the modern scope of federal immunities turns on congressional statements recognizing or waiving immunities. Thus, when the specific *McCulloch* issue resurfaced in the Court a century and a half later, in *First Agric. Nat. Bank v. State Tax Comm'n*, 392 U.S. 339 (1968), the Court emphasized the dimensions of the *statutory* grant of immunity. Justice Marshall's dissent, joined by Justices Harlan and Stewart, argued that, in light of the "present functions and role of national banks," they should not be considered "constitutionally immune from nondiscriminatory state taxation." He suggested that *McCulloch* and other "hoary cases" could "and perhaps should" be read as banning only discriminatory taxes. That would "require a re-evaluation of the validity of the doctrine of intergovernmental tax immunities — a doctrine which does not rest upon any specific provisions of the Constitution, but rather upon this Court's concepts of federalism." Since Congress is able to provide statutory immunities, "there is little reason for this Court to cling to the view that the Constitution itself makes federal instrumentalities immune from state taxation in the absence of authorizing legislation."

For an effort to articulate "a narrow approach to governmental tax immunity," see *United States v. New Mexico*, 455 U.S. 720 (1982). There Justice Blackmun stated the basic principles as follows: "The one constant [is] simple enough to express: a State may not, consistent with the Supremacy Clause, lay a tax 'directly upon the United States.' [But] the limits on the immunity doctrine are [as] significant as the rule itself. [What] the Court's cases leave room for, then, is the conclusion that tax immunity is appropriate in only one circumstance: when the levy falls on the United States itself, or on an agency or instrumentality so closely connected to the Government, that the two cannot realistically be viewed as separate entities. [This] view, we believe, comports with the principal purpose of the immunity doctrine, that of forestalling 'clashing sovereignty' [McCulloch], by preventing the States from laying demands directly on the Federal Government." But even under this "narrow approach," the Court continues to scrutinize closely those taxes alleged to discriminate against the federal government. See, e.g., *Davis v. Michigan Dept. of Treasury*, 489 U.S. 803 (1989).

The issues that demand further study in a course specializing in the same is the degree to which federal immunities may extend to "private" companies that contract with the Federal government, and the limitation of the reciprocal nature of the immunity to state entities that are not related to "sovereignty" and particularly those that are proprietary.

C. THE MODERN ANTI-FEDERALIST REVIVAL

As we commence our study of congressional power and federalism, it is worth noting the impact of the current Court on these issues. *U.S. Term Limits* has been selected to articulate not only the nature of the present views, but also the divisions between the present Justices in this regard. This review is not just for "background"; the *Term Limits* dissenters have helped form majorities to spearhead the "anti-federalist" revival.

The origins of the disagreements between the Justices in *Term Limits* dates to positions advanced by the Federalists and Republicans after adoption of the Constitution. The essential question was whether the national government was an independent entity created by the people, or whether the national government was formed by and extended from the several states. The preamble to the Constitution seems to speak to this question:

We the People of the United States, in Order to form a more perfect Union, establish Justice, insure domestic Tranquility, provide for the common defense, promote the general Welfare, and secure the Blessings of Liberty to ourselves and our Posterity, *do ordain and establish this Constitution for the United States of America.* (Emphasis added)

Though one might think "We the people" would lay this issue to rest, it did not. The Republicans would assert that the states retained the power of "nullification" over what they considered to be unconstitutional federal laws. The Kentucky and Virginia resolution, authored by Jefferson and Madison, and adopted by two state legislatures in 1798, protested the adoption of the Federal Alien and Sedition Acts. The resolutions asserted that the federal government was a compact among the states, its power being limited to those delegated to it, and that the states were not obligated to abide by an unconstitutional exercise of federal power — nullification. The civil war and the constitutional amendments that followed would seem to negate this contention (and *Cooper v. Aaron*, infra, as well). Note, nonetheless, how the majority and dissenting opinions in *Term Limits* are a modern "rehashing" of the views as to whether the people or the states created the national government.

To the majority in *Term Limits*, the nation was commenced by "We the people," and therefore the states cannot maintain any reserved power over the federal government or over what did not exist. The states could enjoy only those powers that were delegated to them by the Constriction itself. To the dissenters, asserting that the pre-existing states formed the federation under the Constitution, the states retained all power they held prior to union, including over the federal government itself, except only those taken away by the new Constitution. Given the result in *Term Limits*, all of this might not seem so significant, yet the remainder of this section makes this revival of these pre–Civil War issues relevant and controversial. Kathleen Sullivan even suggests that the "dissenters may have lost the battle but won the war," given the Court's recent decisions limiting the federal commerce power and federal power over the states themselves via the 11th Amendment, both of which rest ahead.

U.S. TERM LIMITS, INC. v. THORNTON
514 U.S. 779 (1995)

Justice STEVENS delivered the opinion of the Court.

The Constitution sets forth qualifications for membership in the Congress of the United States. [The age, citizenship, and residence requirements of Art. I, §2, cl. 2, and Art I, § 3, cl. 3.]

[Today's] cases present a challenge to an amendment to the Arkansas State Constitution that prohibits the name of an otherwise-eligible candidate for Congress from appearing on the general election ballot if that candidate has already served three terms in the House of Representatives or two terms in the Senate. The Arkansas Supreme Court held that the amendment violates the Federal Constitution. We agree with that holding. Such a state-imposed restriction is contrary to the "fundamental principle of our representative democracy," embodied in the Constitution, that "the people should choose whom they please to govern them." Powell v. McCormack, 395 U.S. 486, 547, 89 S.Ct. 1944, 1977, 23 L.Ed.2d 491 (1969) (internal quotation marks omitted). Allowing individual States to adopt their own qualifications for congressional service would be inconsistent with the Framers' vision of a uniform National Legislature representing the people of the United States. If the qualifications set forth in the text of the Constitution are to be changed, that text must be amended.

Petitioners argue somewhat half-heartedly that the narrow holding in Powell, which involved the power of the House to exclude a Member pursuant to Art. I, § 5, does not control the more general question whether Congress has the power to add qualifications. Powell, however, is not susceptible to such a narrow reading. Our conclusion that Congress may not alter or add to the qualifications in the Constitution was integral to our analysis and outcome.

Our reaffirmation of Powell does not necessarily resolve the specific questions presented in these cases. For petitioners argue that whatever the constitutionality of additional qualifications for membership imposed by Congress, the historical and textual materials discussed in Powell do not support the conclusion that the Constitution prohibits additional qualifications imposed by States. In the absence of such a constitutional prohibition, petitioners argue, the Tenth Amendment and the principle of reserved powers require that States be allowed to add such qualifications.

[We] disagree for two independent reasons. First, we conclude that the power to add qualifications is not within the "original powers" of the States, and thus is not reserved to the States by the Tenth Amendment. Second, even if States possessed some original power in this area, we conclude that the Framers intended the Constitution to be the exclusive source of qualifications for Members of Congress, and that the Framers thereby "divested" States of any power to add qualifications.

The "plan of the convention" as illuminated by the historical materials, our opinions, and the text of the Tenth Amendment draws a basic distinction between the powers of the newly created Federal Government and the powers retained by the pre-existing sovereign States. As Chief Justice Marshall explained, "it was neither necessary nor proper to define the powers retained by the States. These powers proceed, not from the people of America, but from the people of the several States; and remain, after the adoption of the constitution, what they were before, except so far as they may be abridged by that instrument." Sturges v. Crowninshield, 4 Wheat. 122, 193, 4 L.Ed. 529 (1819).

This classic statement by the Chief Justice endorsed Hamilton's reasoning in The Federalist No. 32 that the plan of the Constitutional Convention did not contemplate "[a]n entire consolidation of the States into one complete national sovereignty," but only a partial consolidation in which "the State governments would clearly retain all the rights of sovereignty which they before had, and which were not, by that act, *exclusively* delegated to the United States." The Federalist No. 32, at 198. The text of the Tenth Amendment unambiguously confirms this principle.

SOURCE OF THE POWER

Contrary to petitioners' assertions, the power to add qualifications is not part of the original powers of sovereignty that the Tenth Amendment reserved to the States. Petitioners' Tenth Amendment argument misconceives the nature of the right at issue because that Amendment could only "reserve" that which existed before. As Justice Story recognized, "the states can exercise no powers whatsoever, which exclusively spring out of the existence of the national government, which the constitution does not delegate to them. . . . No state can say, that it has reserved, what it never possessed." 1 Story § 627.

Justice Story's position thus echoes that of Chief Justice Marshall in McCulloch v. Maryland, 4 Wheat. 316, 4 L.Ed. 579 (1819). In McCulloch, the Court rejected the argument that the Constitution's silence on the subject of state power to tax corporations chartered by Congress implies that the States have "reserved" power to tax such federal instrumentalities. As Chief Justice Marshall pointed out, an "original right to tax" such federal entities "never existed, and the question whether it has been surrendered, cannot arise."

[With] respect to setting qualifications for service in Congress, no such right existed before the Constitution was ratified. [The] Framers envisioned a uniform national system, rejecting the notion that the Nation was a collection of States, and instead creating a direct link between the National Government and the people of the United States. In that National Government, representatives owe primary allegiance not to the people of a State, but to the people of the Nation.

[In] short, as the Framers recognized, electing representatives to the National Legislature was a new right, arising from the Constitution itself. The Tenth Amendment thus provides no basis for concluding that the States possess reserved power to add qualifications to those that are fixed in the Constitution. Instead, any state power to set the qualifications for membership in Congress must derive not from the reserved powers of state sovereignty, but rather from the delegated powers of national sovereignty. In the absence of any constitutional delegation to the States of power to add qualifications to those enumerated in the Constitution, such a power does not exist.

[Our] conclusion that States lack the power to impose qualifications vindicates the same "fundamental principle of our representative democracy" that we recognized in *Powell*, namely, that "the people should choose whom they please to govern them."

[An] aspect of sovereignty is the right of the people to vote for whom they wish. Finally, state-imposed restrictions, unlike the congressionally imposed restrictions at issue in Powell, violate a third idea central to this basic principle: that the right to choose representatives belongs not to the States, but to the people. From the start, the Framers recognized that the "great and radical vice" of the Articles of Confederation was "the principle of LEGISLATION for STATES or GOVERNMENTS, in their CORPORATE or COLLECTIVE CAPACITIES, and as contradistinguished from the INDIVIDUALS of whom they consist." The Federalist No. 15, at 108 (Hamilton). Thus the Framers, in perhaps their most important contribution, conceived of a Federal Government directly responsible to the people, possessed of direct power over the people, and chosen directly, not by States, but by the people. The Framers implemented this ideal most clearly in the provision, extant from the beginning of the Republic, that calls for the Members of the House of Representatives to be "chosen every second Year by the People of the several States." Art. I, § 2, cl. 1. Following the adoption of the Seventeenth Amendment in 1913, this ideal was extended to elections for the Senate. The Congress of the United States, therefore, is not a confederation of nations in which separate sovereigns are represented by appointed delegates, but is instead a body composed of representatives of the people. As Chief Justice John Marshall observed: "The government of the Union, then, . . . is, emphatically, and truly, a government of the people. In form and in substance it emanates from them. Its powers are granted by them, and are to be exercised directly on them, and for their benefit." McCulloch v. Maryland, 4 Wheat., at 404-405. Ours is a "government of the people, by the people, for the people." A. Lincoln, Gettysburg Address (1863).

Petitioners argue that, even if States may not add qualifications, Amendment 73 is constitutional because it is not such a qualification, and because Amendment 73 is a permissible exercise of state power to regulate the "Times, Places and Manner of holding Elections." We reject these contentions.

Unlike § 1 and 2 of Amendment 73, which create absolute bars to service for long-term incumbents running for state office, § 3 merely provides that certain Senators and Representatives shall not be certified as candidates and shall not have their names appear on the ballot. They may run as write-in candidates and, if elected, they may serve. Petitioners contend that only a legal bar to service creates an impermissible qualification, and that Amendment 73 is therefore consistent with the Constitution.

[We] need not decide whether petitioners' narrow understanding of qualifications is correct because, even if it is, Amendment 73 may not stand.

[In] our view, Amendment 73 is an indirect attempt to accomplish what the Constitution prohibits Arkansas from accomplishing directly. As the plurality opinion of the Arkansas Supreme Court recognized, Amendment 73 is an "effort to dress eligibility to stand for Congress in ballot access clothing," because the "intent and the effect of Amendment 73 are to disqualify congressional incumbents from further service."

[A] necessary consequence of petitioners' argument is that Congress itself would have the power to "make or alter" a measure such as Amendment 73. Art. I, § 4, cl. 1. That the Framers would have approved of such a result is unfathomable.

[Moreover], petitioners' broad construction of the Elections Clause is fundamentally inconsistent with the Framers' view of that Clause. The Framers intended the Elections Clause to grant States authority to create procedural regulations, not to provide States with license to exclude classes of candidates from federal office.

[Members] of Congress are chosen by separate constituencies, but that they become, when elected, servants of the people of the United States. They are not merely delegates appointed by separate, sovereign States; they occupy offices that are integral and essential components of a single National Government. In the absence of a properly passed constitutional amendment, allowing individual States to craft their own qualifications for Congress would thus erode the structure envisioned by the Framers, a structure that was designed, in the words of the Preamble to our Constitution, to form a "more perfect Union." The judgment is affirmed.

Justice KENNEDY, concurring.
I join the opinion of the Court.

Federalism was our Nation's own discovery. The Framers split the atom of sovereignty. It was the genius of their idea that our citizens would have two political capacities, one state and one federal, each protected from incursion by the other. The resulting Constitution created a legal system unprecedented in form and design, establishing two orders of government, each with its own direct relationship, its own privity, its own set of mutual rights and obligations to the people who sustain it and are governed by it.

A distinctive character of the National Government, the mark of its legitimacy, is that it owes its existence to the act of the whole people who created it. It must be remembered that the National Government, too, is republican in essence and in theory.

[Once] the National Government was formed under our Constitution, the same republican principles continued to guide its operation and practice. As James Madison explained, the House of Representatives "derive[s] its powers from the people of America," and "the operation of the government on the people in their individual capacities" makes it "a national government," not merely a federal one. *Id.,* No. 39, at 244, 245 (emphasis deleted). The Court confirmed this principle in McCulloch v. Maryland, 4 Wheat. 316, 404-405, 4 L.Ed. 579 (1819), when it said: "The government of the Union, then, . . . is, emphatically, and truly, a government of the people.

[In] one sense it is true that "the people of each State retained their separate political identities," *post,* at 1877, for the Constitution takes care both to preserve the States and to make use of their identities and structures at various points in organizing the federal union. It does not at all follow from this that the sole political identity of an American is with the State of his or her residence. It denies the dual character of the Federal Government which is its very foundation to assert that the people of the United States do not have a political identity as well, one independent of, though consistent with, their identity as citizens of the State of their residence.

[It] might be objected that because the States ratified the Constitution, the people can delegate power only through the States or by acting in their capacities as citizens of particular States. But in McCulloch v. Maryland, the Court set forth its authoritative rejection of this idea:

[The] political identity of the entire people of the Union is reinforced by the proposition, which I take to be beyond dispute, that, though limited as to its objects, the National Government is, and must be, controlled by the people without collateral interference by the States. McCulloch affirmed this proposition as well, when the Court rejected the suggestion that States could interfere with federal powers. "This was not intended by the American people. They did not design to make their government dependent on the States." Id., at 432. The States have no power, reserved or otherwise, over the exercise of federal authority within its proper sphere. That the States may not invade the sphere of federal sovereignty is as incontestable, in my view, as the corollary proposition that the Federal Government must be held within the boundaries of its own power when it intrudes upon matters reserved to the States. See United States v. Lopez.

It is maintained by our dissenting colleagues that the State of Arkansas seeks nothing more than to grant its people surer control over the National Government, a control, it is said, that will be enhanced by the law at issue here. The arguments for term limitations (or ballot restrictions having the same effect) are not lacking in force; but the issue, as all of us must acknowledge, is not the efficacy of those measures but whether they have a legitimate source, given their origin in the enactments of a single State. There can be no doubt, if we are to respect the republican origins of the Nation and preserve its federal character, that there exists a federal right of citizenship, a relationship between the people of the Nation and their National Government, with which the States may not interfere. Because the Arkansas enactment intrudes upon this federal domain, it exceeds the boundaries of the Constitution.

Justice THOMAS, with whom THE CHIEF JUSTICE, Justice O'CONNOR, and Justice SCALIA join, dissenting.

I dissent. Nothing in the Constitution deprives the people of each State of the power to prescribe eligibility requirements for the candidates who seek to represent them in Congress. The Constitution is simply silent on this question. And where the Constitution is silent, it raises no bar to action by the States or the people.

Because the majority fundamentally misunderstands the notion of "reserved" powers, I start with some first principles. Contrary to the majority's suggestion, the people of the States need not point to any affirmative grant of power in the Constitution in order to prescribe qualifications for their representatives in Congress, or to authorize their elected state legislators to do so.

Our system of government rests on one overriding principle: All power stems from the consent of the people. To phrase the principle in this way, however, is to be imprecise about something important to the notion of "reserved" powers. The ultimate source of the Constitution's authority is the consent of the people of each individual State, not the consent of the undifferentiated people of the Nation as a whole.

The ratification procedure erected by Article VII makes this point clear. The Constitution took effect once it had been ratified by the people gathered in convention in nine different States. But the Constitution went into effect only "between the States so ratifying the same," Art. VII; it did not bind the people of North Carolina until they had accepted it. In Madison's words, the popular consent upon which the Constitution's authority rests was "given by the people, not as individuals composing one entire nation, but as composing the distinct and independent States to which they respectively belong." The Federalist No. 39

[When] they adopted the Federal Constitution, of course, the people of each State surrendered some of their authority to the United States (and hence to entities accountable to the people of other States as well as to themselves). They affirmatively deprived their States of certain powers, see, *e.g.,* Art. I, § 10, and they affirmatively conferred certain powers upon the Federal Government, see, *e.g.,* Art. I, § 8. Because the people of the several States are the only true source of power, however, the Federal Government enjoys no authority beyond what the Constitution confers: The Federal Government's powers are limited and enumerated.

[In] each State, the remainder of the people's powers — "[t]he powers not delegated to the United States by the Constitution, nor prohibited by it to the States," Amdt. 10 — are either delegated to the state government or retained by the people. The Federal Constitution does not specify which of these two possibilities obtains; it is up to the various state constitutions to declare which powers the people of each State have delegated to their state government. As far as the Federal Constitution is concerned, then, the States can exercise all powers that the Constitution does not withhold from them. The Federal Government and the States thus face different default rules: Where the Constitution is silent about the exercise of a particular power — that is, where the Constitution does not speak either expressly or by necessary implication — the Federal Government lacks that power and the States enjoy it. These basic principles are enshrined in the Tenth Amendment.

[To] be sure, when the Tenth Amendment uses the phrase "the people," it does not specify whether it is referring to the people of each State or the people of the Nation as a whole. But the latter interpretation would make the Amendment pointless: There would have been no reason to provide that where the Constitution is silent about whether a particular power resides at the state level, it might or might not do so. In addition, it would make no sense to speak of powers as being reserved to the undifferentiated people of the Nation as a whole, because the Constitution does not contemplate that those people will either exercise power or delegate it. The Constitution simply does not recognize any mechanism for action by the undifferentiated people of the Nation.

[In] short, the notion of popular sovereignty that undergirds the Constitution does not erase state boundaries, but rather tracks them. The people of each State obviously did trust their fate to the people of the several States when they consented to the Constitution; not only did they empower the governmental institutions of the United States, but they also agreed to be bound by constitutional amendments that they themselves refused to ratify. At the same time, however, the people of each State retained their separate political identities. As Chief Justice Marshall put it, "[n]o political dreamer was ever wild enough to think of breaking down the lines which separate the States, and of compounding the American people into one common mass." McCulloch v. Maryland.

[If] we are to invalidate Arkansas' Amendment 73, we must point to something in the Federal Constitution that deprives the people of Arkansas of the power to enact such measures.

[According] to the majority, the States possess only those powers that the Constitution affirmatively grants to them or that they enjoyed before the Constitution was adopted; the Tenth Amendment "could only 'reserve' that which existed before."

[The] majority also seeks support for its view of the Tenth Amendment in *McCulloch*. But this effort is misplaced. McCulloch did make clear that a power need not be "expressly" delegated to the United States or prohibited to the States in order to fall outside the Tenth Amendment's reservation; delegations and prohibitions can also arise by necessary implication. True to the text of the Tenth Amendment, however, McCulloch indicated that all powers as to which the Constitution does not speak (whether expressly or by necessary implication) are "reserved" to the state level.

[For] the past 175 years, McCulloch has been understood to rest on the proposition that the Constitution affirmatively barred Maryland from imposing its tax on the bank's operations. For the majority, however, McCulloch apparently turned on the fact that before the Constitution was adopted, the States had possessed no power to tax the instrumentalities of the governmental institutions that the Constitution created. This understanding of McCulloch makes most of Chief Justice Marshall's opinion irrelevant; according to the majority, there was no need to inquire into whether federal law deprived Maryland of the power in question, because the power could not fall into the category of "reserved" powers anyway.

[Despite] the majority's citation of Garcia and McCulloch, the only true support for its view of the Tenth Amendment comes from Joseph Story's 1833 treatise on constitutional law. See 2 J. Story, Commentaries on the Constitution of the United States §§ 623-628. Justice Story was a brilliant and accomplished man, and one cannot casually dismiss his views. On the other hand, he was not a member of the Founding generation, and his Commentaries on the Constitution were written a half century after the framing. Rather than representing the original understanding of the Constitution, they represent only his own understanding. In a range of cases concerning the federal/state relation, moreover, this Court has deemed positions taken in Story's commentaries to be more nationalist than the Constitution warrants. In this case too, Story's position that the only powers reserved to the States are those that the States enjoyed before the framing conflicts with both the plain language of the Tenth Amendment and the underlying theory of the Constitution.

The majority . . . asserts that because Congress as a whole is an institution of the National Government, the individual Members of Congress "owe primary allegiance not to the people of a State, but to the people of the Nation."

Political scientists can debate about who commands the "primary allegiance" of Members of Congress once they reach Washington. From the framing to the present, however, the *selection* of the Representatives and Senators from each State has been left entirely to the people of that State or to their state legislature. The very name "congress" suggests a coming together of representatives from distinct entities. But the selection of representatives in Congress is indisputably an act of the people of each State, not some abstract people of the Nation as a whole.

[Although] the United States obviously is a Nation, and although it obviously has citizens, the Constitution does not call for Members of Congress to be elected by the undifferentiated national citizenry; indeed, it does not recognize any mechanism at all (such as a national referendum) for action by the undifferentiated people of the Nation as a whole. [When] it comes to the selection of Members of Congress, the people of each State have retained their independent political identity. As a result, there is absolutely nothing strange about the notion that the people of the States or their state legislatures possess "reserved" powers in this area.

[I] take it to be established, then, that the people of Arkansas do enjoy "reserved" powers over the selection of their representatives in Congress. Purporting to exercise those reserved powers, they have agreed among themselves that the candidates covered by § 3 of Amendment 73 — those whom they have already elected to three or more terms in the House of Representatives or to two or more terms in the Senate — should not be eligible to appear on the ballot for reelection, but should nonetheless be returned to Congress if enough voters are sufficiently enthusiastic about their candidacy to write in their names. Whatever one might think of the wisdom of this arrangement, we may not override the decision of the people of Arkansas unless something in the Federal Constitution deprives them of the power to enact such measures.

The majority settles on "the Qualifications Clauses" as the constitutional provisions that Amendment 73 violates. [The] Qualifications Clauses are merely straightforward recitations of the minimum eligibility requirements that the Framers thought it essential for every Member of Congress to meet. They restrict state power only in that they prevent the States from *abolishing* all eligibility requirements for membership in Congress.

Because the text of the Qualifications Clauses does not support its position, the majority turns instead to its vision of the democratic principles that animated the Framers. But the majority's analysis goes to a question that is not before us: whether Congress has the power to prescribe qualifications for its own members. As I discuss in Part B, the democratic principles that contributed to the Framers' decision to withhold this power from Congress do not prove that the Framers also deprived the people of the States of their reserved authority to set eligibility requirements for their own representatives.

[The] reason for Congress' incapacity is not that the Qualifications Clauses deprive Congress of the authority to set qualifications, but rather that nothing in the Constitution grants Congress this power. In the absence of such a grant, Congress may not act. But deciding whether the Constitution denies the qualification-setting power to the States and the people of the States requires a fundamentally different legal analysis.

[When] the people of a State themselves decide to restrict the field of candidates whom they are willing to send to Washington as their representatives, they simply have not violated the principle that "the people should choose whom they please to govern them." See 2 Elliot 257 (remarks of Alexander Hamilton at the New York Convention).

It is radical enough for the majority to hold that the Constitution implicitly precludes the people of the States from prescribing any eligibility requirements for the congressional candidates who seek their votes. This holding, after all, does not stop with negating the term limits that many States have seen fit to impose on their Senators and Representatives. Today's decision also means that no State may disqualify congressional candidates whom a court has found to be mentally incompetent, who are currently in prison,), or who have past vote-fraud convictions.

The majority's opinion may not go so far, although it does not itself suggest any principled stopping point. No matter how narrowly construed, however, today's decision reads the Qualifications Clauses to impose substantial implicit prohibitions on the States and the people of the States. I would not draw such an expansive negative inference from the fact that the Constitution requires Members of Congress to be a certain age, to be inhabitants of the States that they represent, and to have been United States citizens for a specified period. Rather, I would read the Qualifications Clauses to do no more than what they say. I respectfully dissent.

———————

Comments on *Term-Limits*. What do you think of all of this? Is this a nation created by the people, or a national entity created by the states, and thus "Dual Sovereigns?" Did the preamble and post–Civil War amendments settle these issues? Do the dissenters recall the "Lessons of *McCulloch*"? Would they fix state and federal power denying the flexibility inherent in *McCulloch*? Should the power balance between state and federal governments be established by the activism of the Supreme Court and fixed as a matter of fundamental law, or should the Court defer to the political process? These are question of consequence, and the controversy over this Court's "fetish with federalism" will play itself out through the remainder of this Chapter.

II. COMMERCE POWER

If the major weakness in the Articles of Confederation was a lack of national control over economic activity, the most significant power enumerated to Congress in the new Constitution spoke to that deficiency, "To Regulate Commerce with Foreign Nations, and among the Several States, and with Indian Tribes." (Art. I, § 8, cl. 3) There is no doubt (See Hamilton's *Federalist* No. 22) that the framers intended broad congressional power over national commerce not only to limit "interfering and unneighborly regulations by some states," but also to create a national market as a predicate to expand the nation's economy.

The modern American economic monolith is no doubt a byproduct of our success in creating a national market as per the intent of the framers. As the framers may have anticipated, this new power to "regulate commerce among the several states" has not only become the most significant basis for federal authority, but has, from its inception, been the center of controversy and debate over the balance of power between state and federal governments.

For the student of constitutional law, however, a study of the commerce power is most instructive in bringing into "life" the issues discussed earlier concerning the role of the Supreme Court in our system of government. A study of the commerce power is a study of the socio-economic development of this nation, as set against the power balance between federal government and the states. The Supreme Court will be no idle spectator.

The potential for bias and rule by "platonic" guardians that we studied in the first section will become more than theory as we study the Court and the commerce power. We will see the Court accused of bias toward industrialism by reading capitalism and their own economic views into the Constitution, as well as the post "Court packing" Court accused of bias toward federal authority in the creation of "big brother." This pattern will continue as the modern Court sets about limiting the commerce for the first time in forty years. It has become almost axiomatic in the study of Constitutional law to follow the study of the judicial power with a study of the Commerce Clause, as the latter is the perfect vehicle for translating "theory" into "practice."

The sections that follow are divided by eras to elucidate this history. So here we go, as we review the socioeconomic history of the Court and the Commerce power from *Gibbons* to *Lopez*. First, one more "threshold" decision by Chief Justice Marshall, as he defines the extent of federal authority under the new commerce power in *Gibbons v. Ogden*.

A. THE COURT AT THE THRESHOLD: "FULTON'S FOLLY"

GIBBONS v. OGDEN
22 U.S. 1 (1824)

[The New York legislature enacted a statute granting Robert Fulton and Robert Livingston the exclusive right to operate steamboats in New York waters. The statute was designed to encourage investment in the development of the then-novel technology of steamboats. Fulton and Livingston licensed Ogden to operate a ferry between New York City and Elizabethtown Point in New Jersey. Gibbons began operating a competing ferry service that, because it necessarily entered New York waters, violated the grant to Fulton and Livingston and the license to Ogden. Gibbons's ferries were, however, licensed as "vessels [in] the coasting trade" under a statute enacted by Congress in 1793. Ogden obtained an injunction against Gibbons from the New York courts.]

Chief Justice MARSHALL delivered the opinion for the Court.

[The] subject to be regulated is commerce; and our constitution being, as was aptly said at the bar, one of enumeration, and not of definition, to ascertain the extent of the power, it becomes necessary to settle the meaning of the word. The counsel for the appellee would limit it to traffic, to buying and selling, or the interchange of commodities, and do not admit that it comprehends navigation. This would restrict a general term, applicable to many objects, to one of its significations. Commerce, undoubtedly, is traffic, but it is something more: it is intercourse. It describes the commercial intercourse between nations, and parts of nations, in all its branches, and is regulated by prescribing rules for carrying on that intercourse.

[The] subject to which the power is next applied, is to commerce "among the several States." The word "among" means intermingled with. A thing which is among others, is intermingled with them. Commerce among the States, cannot stop at the external boundary line of each State, but may be introduced into the interior. It is not intended to say that these words comprehend that commerce, which is completely internal, which is carried on between man and man in a State, or between different parts of the same State, and which does not extend to or affect other States. Such a power would be inconvenient, and is certainly unnecessary.

[Comprehensive] as the word "among" is, it may very properly be restricted to that commerce which concerns more States than one. The phrase is not one which would probably have been selected to indicate the completely interior traffic of a State. [The] enumeration presupposes something not enumerated; and that something, if we regard the language or the subject of the sentence, must be the exclusively internal commerce of a State. The genius and character of the whole government seem to be, that its action is to be applied to all the external concerns of the nation, and to those internal concerns which affect the States generally; but not to those which are completely within a particular State, which do not affect other States, and with which it is not necessary to interfere, for the purpose of executing some of the general powers of the government. The completely internal commerce of a State, then, may be considered as reserved for the State itself.

[It] is the power to regulate; that is, to prescribe the rule by which commerce is to be governed. This power, like all others vested in Congress, is complete in itself, may be exercised to its utmost extent, and acknowledges no limitations, other than are prescribed in the constitution. These are expressed in plain terms, and do not affect the questions which arise in this case, or which have been discussed at the bar. If, as has always been understood, the sovereignty of Congress, though limited to specified objects, is plenary as to those objects, the power over commerce with foreign nations, and among the several States, is vested in Congress as absolutely as it would be in a single government, having in its constitution the same restrictions on the exercise of the power as are found in the constitution of the United States. The wisdom and the discretion of Congress, their identity with the people, and the influence which their constituents possess at elections, are, in this, as in many other instances, as that, for example, of declaring war, the sole restraints on which they have relied, to secure them from its abuse. They are the restraints on which the people must often they solely, in all representative governments.

[That] inspection laws may have a remote and considerable influence on commerce, will not be denied; but that a power to regulate commerce is the source from which the right to pass them is derived, cannot be admitted. The object of inspection laws, is to improve the quality of articles produced by the labour of a country; to fit them for exportation; or, it may be, for domestic use. They act upon the subject before it becomes an article of foreign commerce, or of commerce among the States, and prepare it for that purpose. They form a portion of that immense mass of legislation, which embraces everything within the territory of a State, not surrendered to the general government: all which can be most advantageously exercised by the States themselves. Inspection laws, quarantine laws, health laws of every description, as well as laws for regulating the internal commerce of a State, and those which respect turnpike roads, ferries, &c., are component parts of this mass.

[No] direct general power over these objects is granted to Congress; and, consequently, they remain subject to State legislation. If the legislative power of the Union can reach them, it must be for national purposes; it must be where the power is expressly given for a special purpose, or is clearly incidental to some power which is expressly given."

[Powerful] and ingenious minds, taking, as postulates, that the powers expressly granted to the government of the Union, are to be contracted by construction, into the narrowest possible compass, and that the original powers of the States are retained, if any possible construction will retain them, may, by a course of well digested, but refined and metaphysical reasoning, founded on these premises, explain away the constitution of our country, and leave it, a magnificent structure, indeed, to look at, but totally unfit for use. They may so entangle and perplex the understanding, as to obscure principles, which were before thought quite plain, and induce doubts where, if the mind were to pursue its own course, none would be perceived. In such a case, it is peculiarly necessary to recur to safe and fundamental principles to sustain those principles, and when sustained, to make them the tests of the arguments to be examined.

Comments on *Gibbons*. Does Justice Marshall provide for an expansive commerce power in *Gibbons*? Once again, are you surprised? How important is the constitutional term "among" to the opinion? Would there have been a different outcome if the framers had chosen the word "between" instead of "among"? What is the difference between these words, and how would this affect both the framers' intent and the reach of federal authority? Despite the framers' choice of "among," see whether the Court actually reads the clause as if it reads "between."

Immediately following the decision in *Gibbons*, interstate commerce in the Union increased. Warren, in his *The Supreme Court in United States History,* commented that the opening of the navigational waters by allowing free passage to all steamboats was, "the emancipation proclamation of American commerce." After *Gibbons,* Congress made little use of the power to regulate commerce until the late nineteenth century.

B. THE INDIRECT-DIRECT TEST: LAISSEZ-FAIRE AND LIMITATION OF NATIONAL POWER

By the turn of the century, American industrial development was in full swing. While industrial capitalism would help develop American resources, national market, and economic power, it would not do such without cost. A new immigrant impoverished working class would develop in that nation's cities. Despite the great wealth generated by the economic monopolies of the capitalist "Robber Barons," the working class suffered such horrors as poor working conditions, long hours, and child labor. The Congress, led by the Sherman Antitrust Act's response to the monopolies (see *Knight,* below), attempted to provide a federal regulatory response to control these social horrors. As the cases that follow illustrate, between the industrial capitalist and the Congress stood the Supreme Court. Are the cases that follow explainable in light of *Gibbons*? What of the lessons of *McCulloch*?

UNITED STATES v. KNIGHT
156 U.S. 1 (1895)

Mr. Chief Justice FULLER, delivered the opinion of the court.

[By] the purchase of the stock of the four Philadelphia refineries with shares of its own stock the American Sugar Refining Company acquired nearly complete control of the manufacture of refined sugar within the United States. The bill charged that the contracts under which these purchases were made constituted combinations in restraint of trade, and that in entering into them the defendants combined and conspired to restrain the trade and commerce in refined sugar among the several states and with foreign nations, contrary to the act of congress of July 2, 1890.

The fundamental question is whether, conceding that the existence of a monopoly in manufacture is established by the evidence, that monopoly can be directly suppressed under the act of congress in the mode attempted by this bill.

That which belongs to commerce is within the jurisdiction of the United States, but that which does not belong to commerce is within the jurisdiction of the police power of the state. Gibbons v. Ogden, 9 Wheat. 1, 210; Brown v. Maryland, 12 Wheat. 419, 448; The License Cases, 5 How. 599; Mobile Co. v. Kimball, 102 U. S. 691; Bowman v. Railway Co., 125 U. S. 465, 8 Sup. Ct. 689, 1062; Leisy v. Hardin, 135 U. S. 100, 10 Sup. Ct. 681; In re Rahrer, 140 U. S. 545, 555, 11 Sup. Ct. 865.

[Doubtless] the power to control the manufacture of a given thing involves, in a certain sense, the control of its disposition, but this is a secondary, and not the primary, sense; and, although the exercise of that power may result in bringing the operation of commerce into play, it does not control it, and affects it only incidentally and indirectly. Commerce succeeds to manufacture, and is not a part of it. The power to regulate commerce is the power to prescribe the rule by which commerce shall be governed, and is a power independent of the power to suppress monopoly. But it may operate in repression of monopoly whenever that comes within the rules by which commerce is governed, or whenever the transaction is itself a monopoly of commerce.

[It] will be perceived how far-reaching the proposition is that the power of dealing with a monopoly directly may be exercised by the general government whenever interstate or international commerce may be ultimately affected. The regulation of commerce applies to the subjects of commerce, and not to matters of internal police. Contracts to buy, sell, or exchange goods to be transported among the several states, the transportation and its instrumentalities, and articles bought, sold, or exchanged for the purposes of such transit among the states, or put in the way of transit, may be regulated; but this is because they form part of interstate trade or commerce. The fact that an article is manufactured for export to another state does not of itself make it an article of interstate commerce, and the intent of the manufacturer does not determine the time when the article or product passes from the control of the state and belongs to commerce. This was so ruled in Coe v. Errol, 116 U. S. 517, 6 Sup. Ct. 475, in which the question before the court was whether certain logs cut at a place in New Hampshire, and hauled to a river town for the purpose of transportation to the state of Maine, were liable to be taxed like other property in the state of New Hampshire. Mr. Justice Bradley, delivering the opinion of the court, said: "Does the owner's state of mind in relation to the goods — that is, his intent to export them, and his partial preparation to do so — exempt them from taxation? This is the precise question for solution. . . . There must be a point of time when they cease to be governed exclusively by the domestic law, and begin to be governed and protected by the national law of commercial regulation; and that moment seems to us to be a legitimate one for this purpose in which they commence their final movement from the state of their origin to that of their destination."

And again, in Kidd v. Pearson, 128 U. S. 1, 20, 24, 9 Sup. Ct. 6, where the question was discussed whether the right of a state to enact a statute prohibiting within its limits the manufacture of intoxicating liquors, except for certain purposes, could be overthrown by the fact that the manufacturer intended to export the liquors when made, it was held that the intent of the manufacturer did not determine the time when the article or product passed from the control of the state and belonged to commerce, and that, therefore, the statute, in omitting to except from its operation the manufacture of intoxicating liquors within the limits of the state for export, did not constitute an unauthorized interference with the right of congress to regulate commerce. And Mr. Justice Lamar remarked: No distinction is more popular to the common mind, or more clearly expressed in economic and political literature, than that between manufacture and commerce. Manufacture is transformation, — the fashioning of raw materials into a change of form for use. The functions of commerce are different. The buying and selling, and the transportation incidental thereto, constitute commerce; and the regulation of commerce in the constitutional sense embraces the regulation at least of such transportation. . . . If it be held that the term includes the regulation of all such manufactures as are intended to be the subject of commercial transactions in the future, it is impossible to deny that it would also include all productive industries that contemplate the same thing. The result would be that congress would be invested, to the exclusion of the states, with the power to regulate, not only manufactures, but also agriculture, horticulture, stock-raising, domestic fisheries, mining; in short, every branch of human industry. For is there one of them that does not contemplate, more or less clearly, an interstate or foreign market? Does not the wheat grower of the Northwest, and the cotton planter of the South, plant, cultivate, and harvest his crop with an eye on the prices at Liverpool, New York, and Chicago? The power being vested in congress and denied to the states, it would follow as an inevitable result that the duty would devolve on congress to regulate all of these delicate, multiform, and vital interests, — interests which in their nature are, and must be, local. . . ."

[I]n Gibbons v. Ogden, Brown v. Maryland, and other cases often cited, the state laws, which were held inoperative, were instances of direct interference with, or regulations of, interstate or international commerce; yet in Kidd v. Pearson the refusal of a state to allow articles to be manufactured within her borders, even for export, was held not to directly affect external commerce; and state legislation which, in a great variety of ways, affected interstate commerce and persons engaged in it, has been frequently sustained because the interference was not direct.

Contracts, combinations, or conspiracies to control domestic enterprise in manufacture, agriculture, mining, production in all its forms, or to raise or lower prices or wages, might unquestionably tend to restrain external as well as domestic trade, but the restraint would be an indirect result, however inevitable, and whatever its extent, and such result would not necessarily determine the object of the contract, combination, or conspiracy.

Again, all the authorities agree that, in order to vitiate a contract or combination, it is not essential that its result should be a complete monopoly; it is sufficient if it really tends to that end, and to deprive the public of the advantages which flow from free competition. Slight reflection will show that, if the national power extends to all contracts and combinations in manufacture, agriculture, mining, and other productive industries, whose ultimate result may affect external commerce, comparatively little of business operations and affairs would be left for state control.

[B]ut the contracts and acts of the defendants related exclusively to the acquisition of the Philadelphia refineries and the business of sugar refining in Pennsylvania, and bore no direct relation to commerce between the states. [There] was nothing in the proofs to indicate any intention to put a restraint upon trade or commerce, and the fact, as we have seen, that trade or commerce might be indirectly affected, was not enough to entitle complainants to a decree.

Decree affirmed.

HOUSTON, E. & W. RY. CO. v. UNITED STATES
(The Shreveport Rate Case)
234 U.S. 342 (1914)

Mr. Justice HUGHES delivered the opinion of the court:

These suits were brought in the commerce court by the Houston, East & West Texas Railway Company and the Houston & Shreveport Railroad Company, and by the Texas & Pacific Railway Company, respectively, to set aside an order of the Interstate Commerce Commission, dated March 11, 1912, upon the ground that it exceeded the Commission's authority.

[Congress] is empowered to regulate, — that is, to provide the law for the government of interstate commerce; to enact "all appropriate legislation" for its "protection and advancement" (The Daniel Ball, 10 Wall. 557, 564, 19 L. Ed. 999, 1001); to adopt measures "to promote its growth and insure its safety" (Mobile County v. Kimball, 102 U. S. 691, 696, 697, 29 L. Ed. 238-240); "to foster, protect, control, and restrain" (Second Employers' Liability Cases [Mondou v. New York, N. H. & H. R. Co.] 223 U. S. 1, 47, 53, 54, 56 L. ed. 327, 345, 347, 348, 38 L.R.A.(N.S.) 44, 32 Sup. Ct. Rep. 169, 1 N. C. C. A. 875). Its authority, extending to these interstate carriers as instruments of interstate commerce, necessarily embraces the right to control their operations in all matters having such a close and substantial relation to interstate traffic that the control is essential or appropriate to the security of that traffic, to the efficiency of the interstate service, and to the maintenance of conditions under which interstate commerce may be conducted upon fair terms and without molestation or hindrance. As it is competent for Congress to legislate to these ends, unquestionably it may seek their attainment by requiring that the agencies of interstate commerce shall not be used in such manner as to cripple, retard, or destroy it. The fact that carriers are instruments of intrastate commerce, as well as of interstate commerce, does not derogate from the complete and paramount authority of Congress over the latter, or preclude the Federal power from being exerted to prevent the intrastate operations of such carriers from being made a means of injury to that which has been confided to Federal care. Wherever the interstate and intrastate transactions of carriers are so related that the government of the one involves the control of the other, it is Congress, and not the state, that is entitled to prescribe the final and dominant rule, for otherwise Congress would be denied the exercise of its constitutional authority, and the state, and not the nation, would be supreme within the national field.

[This] is not to say that Congress possesses the authority to regulate the internal commerce of a state, as such, but that it does possess the power to foster and protect interstate commerce, and to take all measures necessary or appropriate to that end, although intrastate transactions of interstate carriers may thereby be controlled.

SWIFT & CO. v. UNITED STATES
196 U.S. 375 (1905)

[The Court sustaining a Sherman Act injunction for price fixing.]

Mr. Justice HOLMES delivered the opinion of the court:

[It] is said that this charge is too vague and that it does not set forth a case of commerce among the states. Taking up the latter objection first, commerce among the states is not a technical legal conception, but a practical one, drawn from the course of business. When cattle are sent for sale from a place in one state, with the expectation that they will end their transit, after purchase, in another, and when in effect they do so, with only the interruption necessary to find a purchaser at the stock yards, and when this is a typical, constantly recurring course, the current thus existing is a current of commerce among the states, and the purchase of the cattle is a part and incident of such commerce.

[But] it may be that the question of taxation does not depend upon whether the article taxed may or may not be said to be in the course of commerce between the states . . .

HAMMER v. DAGENHART
247 U.S. 251 (1918)

Mr. Justice DAY delivered the opinion of the Court.

[Bill was filed by a father in his own behalf and as next friend of his two minor sons, employees in a cotton mill, to enjoin the enforcement of the act of Congress intended to prevent interstate commerce in the products of child labor. The District Court held the act unconstitutional and entered a decree enjoining its enforcement. This appeal brings the case here.]

The controlling question for decision is: Is it within the authority of Congress in regulating commerce among the states to prohibit the transportation in interstate commerce of manufactured goods, the product of a factory in which, within thirty days prior to their removal there from, children under the age of fourteen have been employed or permitted to work, or children between the ages of fourteen and sixteen years have been employed or permitted to work more than eight hours in any day, or more than six days in any week, or after the hour of 7 o'clock p. m., or before the hour of 6 o'clock a. m.?

In Gibbons v. Ogdon, 9 Wheat. 1, 6 L. Ed. 23, Chief Justice Marshall, speaking for this court, and defining the extent and nature of the commerce power, said, "It is the power to regulate; that is, to prescribe the rule by which commerce is to be governed." In other words, the power is one to control the means by which commerce is carried on, which is directly the contrary of the assumed right to forbid commerce from moving and thus destroying it as to particular commodities. But it is insisted that adjudged cases in this court establish the doctrine that the power to regulate given to Congress incidentally includes the authority to prohibit the movement of ordinary commodities and therefore that the subject is not open for discussion. The cases demonstrate the contrary. They rest upon the character of the particular subjects dealt with and the fact that the scope of governmental authority, state or national, possessed over them is such that the authority to prohibit is as to them but the exertion of the power to regulate.

In each of these instances [Lottery Case, Hipolite and Hoke] the use of interstate transportation was necessary to the accomplishment of harmful results. In other words, although the power over interstate transportation was to regulate, that could only be accomplished by prohibiting the use of the facilities of interstate commerce to effect the evil intended. This element is wanting in the present case. The thing intended to be accomplished by this statute is the denial of the facilities of interstate commerce to those manufacturers in the states who employ children within the prohibited ages. The act in its effect does not regulate transportation among the states, but aims to standardize the ages at which children may be employed in mining and manufacturing within the states. The goods shipped are of themselves harmless. The act permits them to be freely shipped after thirty days from the time of their removal from the factory. When offered for shipment, and before transportation begins, the labor of their production is over, and the mere fact that they were intended for interstate commerce transportation does not make their production subject to federal control under the commerce power.

Over interstate transportation, or its incidents, the regulatory power of Congress is ample, but the production of articles, intended for interstate commerce, is a matter of local regulation. "When the commerce begins is determined, not by the character of the commodity, nor by the intention of the owner to transfer it to another state for sale, nor by his preparation of it for transportation, but by its actual delivery to a common carrier for transportation, or the actual commencement of its transfer to another state." Mr. Justice Jackson in Re Greene (C. C.) 52 Fed. 113. This principle has been recognized often in this court. Coe v. Errol, 116 U. S. 517, 6 Sup. Ct. 475, 29 L. Ed. 715; Bacon v. Illinois, 227 U. S. 504, 33 Sup. Ct. 299, 57 L. Ed. 615, and cases cited. If it were otherwise, all manufacture intended for interstate shipment would be brought under federal control to the practical exclusion of the authority of the states, a result certainly not contemplated by the framers of the Constitution when they vested in Congress the authority to regulate commerce among the States. Kidd v. Pearson, 128 U. S. 1, 21, 9 Sup. Ct. 6, 32 L. Ed. 346.

It is further contended that the authority of Congress may be exerted to control interstate commerce in the shipment of child made goods because of the effect of the circulation of such goods in other states where the evil of this class of labor has been recognized by local legislation, and the right to thus employ child labor has been more rigorously restrained than in the state of production. In other words, that the unfair competition, thus engendered, may be controlled by closing the channels of interstate commerce to manufacturers in those states where the local laws do not meet what Congress deems to be the more just standard of other states.

There is no power vested in Congress to require the states to exercise their police power so as to prevent possible unfair competition. Many causes may co-operate to give one state, by reason of local laws or conditions, an economic advantage over others. The commerce clause was not intended to give to Congress a general authority to equalize such conditions. In some of the states laws have been passed fixing minimum wages for women, in others the local law regulates the hours of labor of women in various employments. Business done in such states may be at an economic disadvantage when compared with states which have no such regulations; surely, this fact does not give Congress the power to deny transportation in interstate commerce to those who carry on business where the hours of labor and the rate of compensation for women have not been fixed by a standard in use in other states and approved by Congress.

The grant of power of Congress over the subject of interstate commerce was to enable it to regulate such commerce, and not to give it authority to control the states in their exercise of the police power over local trade and manufacture.

The grant of authority over a purely federal matter was not intended to destroy the local power always existing and carefully reserved to the states in the Tenth Amendment to the Constitution.

In interpreting the Constitution it must never be forgotten that the nation is made up of states to which are entrusted the powers of local government. And to them and to the people the powers not expressly delegated to the national government are reserved.

[We] have neither authority nor disposition to question the motives of Congress in enacting this legislation. The purposes intended must be attained consistently with constitutional limitations and not by an invasion of the powers of the states. This court has no more important function than that which devolves upon it the obligation to preserve inviolate the constitutional limitations upon the exercise of authority federal and state to the end that each may continue to discharge, harmoniously with the other, the duties entrusted to it by the Constitution.

In our view the necessary effect of this act is, by means of a prohibition against the movement in interstate commerce of ordinary commercial commodities to regulate the hours of labor of children in factories and mines within the states, a purely state authority. Thus the act in a two-fold sense is repugnant to the Constitution. It not only transcends the authority delegated to Congress over commerce but also exerts a power as to a purely local matter to which the federal authority does not extend. The far reaching result of upholding the act cannot be more plainly indicated than by pointing out that if Congress can thus regulate matters entrusted to local authority by prohibition of the movement of commodities in interstate commerce, all freedom of commerce will be at an end, and the power of the states over local matters may be eliminated, and thus our system of government be practically destroyed.

Affirmed.

Mr. Justice HOLMES, dissenting.

The single question in this case is whether Congress has power to prohibit the shipment in interstate or foreign commerce of any product of a cotton mill situated in the United States, in which within thirty days before the removal of the product children under fourteen have been employed, or children between fourteen and sixteen have been employed more than eight hours in a day, or more than six days in any week, or between seven in the evening and six in the morning. The objection urged against the power is that the States have exclusive control over their methods of production and that Congress cannot meddle with them, and taking the proposition in the sense of direct intermeddling I agree to it and suppose that no one denies it. But if an act is within the powers specifically conferred upon Congress, it seems to me that it is not made any less constitutional because of the indirect effects that it may have, however obvious it may be that it will have those effects, and that we are not at liberty upon such grounds to hold it void.

The first step in my argument is to make plain what no one is likely to dispute — that the statute in question is within the power expressly given to Congress if considered only as to its immediate effects and that if invalid it is so only upon some collateral ground. The statute confines itself to prohibiting the carriage of certain goods in interstate or foreign commerce. Congress is given power to regulate such commerce in unqualified terms. It would not be argued today that the power to regulate does not include the power to prohibit. Regulation means the prohibition of something, and when interstate commerce is the matter to be regulated I cannot doubt that the regulation may prohibit any part of such commerce that Congress sees fit to forbid. At all events it is established by the Lottery Case and others that have followed it that a law is not beyond the regulative power of Congress merely because it prohibits certain transportation out and out. Champion v. Ames, 188 U. S. 321, 355, 359, 23 Sup. Ct. 321, 47 L. Ed. 492, et seq. So I repeat that this statute in its immediate operation is clearly within the Congress's constitutional power.

The question then is narrowed to whether the exercise of its otherwise constitutional power by Congress can be pronounced unconstitutional because of its possible reaction upon the conduct of the States in a matter upon which I have admitted that they are free from direct control. I should have thought that that matter had been disposed of so fully as to leave no room for doubt. I should have thought that the most conspicuous decisions of this Court had made it clear that the power to regulate commerce and other constitutional powers could not be cut down or qualified by the fact that it might interfere with the carrying out of the domestic policy of any State.

The manufacture of oleomargarine is as much a matter of State regulation as the manufacture of cotton cloth. Congress levied a tax upon the compound when colored so as to resemble butter that was so great as obviously to prohibit the manufacture and sale. In a very elaborate discussion the present Chief Justice excluded any inquiry into the purpose of an act which apart from that purpose was within the power of Congress.

[The] notion that prohibition is any less prohibition when applied to things now thought evil I do not understand. But if there is any matter upon which civilized countries have agreed — far more unanimously than they have with regard to intoxicants and some other matters over which this country is now emotionally aroused — it is the evil of premature and excessive child labor. I should have thought that if we were to introduce our own moral conceptions where is my opinion they do not belong, this was preeminently a case for upholding the exercise of all its powers by the United States.

But I had thought that the propriety of the exercise of a power admitted to exist in some cases was for the consideration of Congress alone and that this Court always had disavowed the right to intrude its judgment upon questions of policy or morals. It is not for this Court to pronounce when prohibition is necessary to regulation if it ever may be necessary — to say that it is permissible as against strong drink but not as against the product of ruined lives.

The Act does not meddle with anything belonging to the States. They may regulate their internal affairs and their domestic commerce as they like. But when they seek to send their products across the State line they are no longer within their rights. If there were no Constitution and no Congress their power to cross the line would depend upon their neighbors. Under the Constitution such commerce belongs not to the States but to Congress to regulate. It may carry out its views of public policy whatever indirect effect they may have upon the activities of the States. Instead of being encountered by a prohibitive tariff at her boundaries the State encounters the public policy of the United States which it is for Congress to express. The public policy of the United States is shaped with a view to the benefit of the nation as a whole. If, as has been the case within the memory of men still living, a State should take a different view of the propriety of sustaining a lottery from that which generally prevails, I cannot believe that the fact would require a different decision from that reached in Champion v. Ames. Yet in that case it would be said with quite as much force as in this that Congress was attempting to intermeddle with the State's domestic affairs. The national welfare as understood by Congress may require a different attitude within its sphere from that of some self-seeking State. It seems to me entirely constitutional for Congress to enforce its understanding by all the means at its command.

Mr. Justice McKenna, Mr. Justice Brandeis, and Mr. Justice Clarke concur in this opinion.

———

Bias, the Commerce Clause, and the Court. The allegation of a Supreme Court bias toward "big business" and "laissez-faire" capitalism has been leveled at the judicial approach represented by the above cited cases. A close look at the opinions seems to substantiate these allegations.

Note, for example, Justice Day's citation to the Commerce Clause in *Hammer* as if the Constitution reserved to the states powers not "expressly" delegated to the federal government, despite the significant deletion of this adverb from the Articles in the new Constitution (see our discussion of such and the Necessary and Proper Clause, above).

> In interpreting the Constitution it must never be forgotten that the nation is made up of states to which are entrusted the powers of local government. And to them and to the people the *powers not expressly delegated to the national government are reserved.* (Emphasis added)

While Day and the activist five to four majority in *Hammer* may have limited application of the Commerce Clause as if the document so read, the fact that it did not, and the history surrounding such, raises questions as to the Court's intent and its veracity.

If the reach of the clause was only to commerce in "traffic," the Court's interpretation seems to avoid the meaning of the framers' choice of "among." For, to regulate only traffic, and not manufacture, seems to read the clause as if Congress had the power to regulate commerce "between" the several states rather than among them. Given Day's use of "expressly," it is not surprising to see the Court also refer to the commerce as if it did read "between":

> [But] it may be that the question of taxation does not depend upon whether the article taxed may or may not be said to be in the course of commerce between the states. . . . (See *Swift & Co. v. United States*, above.)

In *The Daniel Ball*, 77 U.S. (10 Wall.) 557 (1871), the Court further evidenced the use of "between" as opposed to "among," while sustaining a federal safety regulation applied to small ship navigation, "whenever a commodity has begun to move as an article of trade from one State to another, commerce in that commodity *between* the States has commenced" (emphasis added).

Viewed today, one is struck by the boldness of the Justices in supplanting the actual text of the Constitution. Herbert Wechsler underscored this bias of the Court by pointing out that despite their limiting the reach of the Sherman Antitrust Act to businesses, they nonetheless applied the Act to labor unions. (See *Lowe v. Lawlor* 208 U.S. 274 (1908).) Wechsler would call this disparity on behalf of the Court, "Strangely deficient in principal." See Wechsler, "The Political Safeguards Federalism," 54 Colum.L.Rev. 543 (1954).

It is, of course, at least possible to ascribe these decisions to the Court's principled view of the 10th Amendment as opposed to advancing the cause of big business, but as you will see, the Court would also limit state attempts to regulate these activities as well. (See *Lochner v. New York*, 198 U.S. 45 (1905).) In the end, and in response to this conservative judicial activism, the political liberals would become the major advocates of judicial restraint — recall the "neo-Brandeisian" rules of restraint and the position advanced by Justice Frankfurter against the Court's conclusions in *Baker v. Carr*.

The Great Depression and Limited Federal Power. The limits on national power by the Court's Commerce Clause dogma: "direct-indirect," "commerce is traffic," reached dramatic proportion at the onset of the Great Depression. Notably, the Court, as represented by the majority opinion in *Hammer*, decided Commerce Clause cases based upon the "manner" of the activity, as opposed to the "magnitude" of its impact upon commerce and the nation as a whole. The crisis generated by the depression left Holmes's plea in his *Hammer* dissent unattended, "The national welfare as understood by Congress may require a different attitude within its sphere from that of some self-seeking State."

The economic emergency generated by the depression seemed to call for a dramatic federal response. The election of Franklin D. Roosevelt in 1932, with his call for a "new deal," and the economic action invoked in his famous first "100 days" in office, certainly exemplified such. The stage was set as the Supreme Court faced this new deal legislation which was a profound national response to the economic chaos of the depression, with Commerce Clause decisional law that "fixed" and limited federal power. Here the Court faced a conflict with the expressed desires of the people through their elected representative in Congress as well as the President. A backdrop to all of this remained Marshall's plea in *McCulloch* that "it is a Constitution" we are expounding. Recall that Marshall called for a Constitution that could meet the test of time, and emergencies like the economic crises the nation faced, with the "flexibility" inherent in resolution via the political process. This test of *McCulloch* came before a Court much accused of bias in limiting federal power. The stage was set for this dramatic test of constitutional process, as the "least dangerous branch" faced Roosevelt's new deal. The resulting confrontation would not disappoint.

1. No "NEW DEAL"

A.L.A. SCHECHTER POULTRY CORP. v. UNITED STATES
295 U.S. 495 (1935)

Mr. Chief Justice HUGHES delivered the opinion of the Court.

Petitioners in No. 854 were convicted in the District Court of the United States for the Eastern District of New York on eighteen counts of an indictment charging violations of what is known as the "Live Poultry Code," and on an additional count for conspiracy to commit such violations. By demurrer to the indictment and appropriate motions on the trial, the defendants contended (1) that the code had been adopted pursuant to an unconstitutional delegation by Congress of legislative power; (2) that it attempted to regulate intrastate transactions which lay outside the authority of Congress; and (3) that in certain provisions it was repugnant to the due process clause of the Fifth Amendment.

New York City is the largest live poultry market in the United States. Ninety-six percent of the live poultry there marketed comes from other states. Three-fourths of this amount arrives by rail and is consigned to commission men or receivers. Most of these freight shipments (about 75 per cent.) come in at the Manhattan Terminal of the New York Central Railroad, and the remainder at one of the four terminals in New Jersey serving New York City. The commission men transact by far the greater part of the business on a commission basis, representing the shippers as agents, and remitting to them the proceeds of sale, less commissions, freight, and handling charges. Otherwise, they buy for their own account. They sell to slaughterhouse operators who are also called marketmen.

The defendants are slaughterhouse operators of the latter class. A.L.A. Schechter Poultry Corporation and Schechter Live Poultry Market are corporations conducting wholesale poultry slaughterhouse markets in Brooklyn, New York City. Joseph Schechter operated the latter corporation and also guaranteed the credits of the former corporation, which was operated by Martin, Alex, and Aaron Schechter. Defendants ordinarily purchase their live poultry from commission men at the West Washington Market in New York City or at the railroad terminals serving the city, but occasionally they purchase from commission men in Philadelphia. They buy the poultry for slaughter and resale. After the poultry is trucked to their slaughterhouse markets in Brooklyn, it is there sold, usually within twenty-four hours, to retail poultry dealers and butchers who sell directly to consumers. Defendants do not sell poultry in interstate commerce.

The "Live Poultry Code" was promulgated under section 3 of the National Industrial Recovery Act. That section, the pertinent provisions of which are set forth in the margin, authorizes the President to approve "codes of fair competition." [. . .] Violation of any provision of a code (so approved or prescribed) 'in any transaction in or affecting interstate or foreign commerce' is made a misdemeanor punishable by a fine of not more than $500 for each offense, and each day the violation continues is to be deemed a separate offense. . . .

The code fixes the number of hours for workdays. It provides that no employee, with certain exceptions, shall be permitted to work in excess of forty hours in any one week, and that no employees, save as stated, "shall be paid in any pay period less than at the rate of fifty (50) cents per hour." The article containing "general labor provisions" prohibits the employment of any person under 16 years of age, and declares that employees shall have the right of "collective bargaining" and freedom of choice with respect to labor organizations, in the terms of section 7(a) of the act (15 USCA § 707(a). The minimum number of employees, who shall be employed by slaughterhouse operators, is fixed; the number being graduated according to the average volume of weekly sales. . . .

We are told that the provision of the statute authorizing the adoption of codes must be viewed in the light of the grave national crisis with which Congress was confronted. Undoubtedly, the conditions to which power is addressed are always to be considered when the exercise of power is challenged. Extraordinary conditions may call for extraordinary remedies. But the argument necessarily stops short of an attempt to justify action which lies outside the sphere of constitutional authority. Extraordinary conditions do not create or enlarge constitutional power. The Constitution established a national government with powers deemed to be adequate, as they have proved to be both in war and peace, but these powers of the national government are limited by the constitutional grants. Those who act under these grants are not at liberty to transcend the imposed limits because they believe that more or different power is necessary. Such assertions of extra constitutional authority were anticipated and precluded by the explicit terms of the Tenth Amendment — "The powers not delegated to the United States by the Constitution, nor prohibited by it to the States, are reserved to the States respectively, or to the people."

The Question of the Application of the Provisions of the Live Poultry Code to Intrastate Transactions. — Although the validity of the codes (apart from the question of delegation) rests upon the commerce clause of the Constitution, section 3(a) of the act (15 USCA § 703(a) is not in terms limited to interstate and foreign commerce. From the generality of its terms, and from the argument of the government at the bar, it would appear that section 3(a) was designed to authorize codes without that limitation. But under section 3(f) of the act (15 USCA § 73(f) penalties are confined to violations of a code provision "in any transaction in or affecting interstate or foreign commerce." This aspect of the case presents the question whether the particular provisions of the Live Poultry Code, which the defendants were convicted for violating and for having conspired to violate, were within the regulating power of Congress.

These provisions relate to the hours and wages of those employed by defendants in their slaughterhouses in Brooklyn and to the sales there made to retail dealers and butchers. [Were] these transactions "in" interstate commerce? Much is made of the fact that almost all the poultry coming to New York is sent there from other states. But the code provisions, as here applied, do not concern the transportation of the poultry from other states to New York, or the transactions of the commission men or others to whom it is consigned, or the sales made by such consignees to defendants. When defendants had made their purchases, whether at the West Washington Market in New York City or at the railroad terminals serving the city, or elsewhere, the poultry was trucked to their slaughterhouses in Brooklyn for local disposition. The interstate transactions in relation to that poultry then ended. Defendants held the poultry at their slaughterhouse markets for slaughter and local sale to retail dealers and butchers who in turn sold directly to consumers. Neither the slaughtering nor the sales by defendants were transactions in interstate commerce.

The undisputed facts thus afford no warrant for the argument that the poultry handled by defendants at their slaughterhouse markets was in a "current" or "flow" of interstate commerce, and was thus subject to congressional regulation. The mere fact that there may be a constant flow of commodities into a state does not mean that the flow continues after the property has arrived and has become commingled with the mass of property within the state and is there held solely for local disposition and use. So far as the poultry here in question is concerned, the flow in interstate commerce had ceased. The poultry had come to a permanent rest within the state. It was not held, used, or sold by defendants in relation to any further transactions in interstate commerce and was not destined for transportation to other states. Hence decisions which deal with a stream of interstate commerce — where goods come to rest within a state temporarily and are later to go forward in interstate commerce — and with the regulations of transactions involved in that practical continuity of movement, are not applicable here.

Did the defendants' transactions directly "affect" interstate commerce so as to be subject to federal regulation? [In] determining how far the federal government may go in controlling intrastate transactions upon the ground that they 'affect' interstate commerce, there is a necessary and well-established distinction between direct and indirect effects. The precise line can be drawn only as individual cases arise, but the distinction is clear in principle. Direct effects are illustrated by the railroad cases we have cited, as, e.g., the effect of failure to use prescribed safety appliances on railroads which are the highways of both interstate and intrastate commerce, injury to an employee engaged in interstate transportation by the negligence of an employee engaged in an intrastate movement, the fixing of rates for intrastate transportation which unjustly discriminate against interstate commerce. But where the effect of intrastate transactions upon interstate commerce is merely indirect, such transactions remain within the domain of state power. If the commerce clause were construed to reach all enterprises and transactions which could be said to have an indirect effect upon interstate commerce, the federal authority would embrace practically all the activities of the people, and the authority of the state over its domestic concerns would exist only by sufferance of the federal government. Indeed, on such a theory, even the development of the state's commercial facilities would be subject to federal control. As we said in Simpson v. Shepard (Minnesota Rate Case), 230 U.S. 352, 410, 33 S.Ct. 729, 745, 57 L.Ed. 1511, 48 L.R.A. (N.S.) 1151, Ann. Cas. 1916A, 18: "In the intimacy of commercial relations, much that is done in the superintendence of local matters may have an indirect bearing upon interstate commerce. The development of local resources and the extension of local facilities may have a very important effect upon communities less favored, and to an appreciable degree alter the course of trade. The freedom of local trade may stimulate interstate commerce, while restrictive measures within the police power of the state, enacted exclusively with respect to internal business, as distinguished from interstate traffic, may in their reflex or indirect influence diminish the latter and reduce the volume of articles transported into or out of the state." See, also, Kidd v. Pearson, 128 U.S. 1, 21, 9 S.Ct. 6, 32 L.Ed. 346; Heisler v. Thomas Colliery Co., 260 U.S. 245, 259, 260, 43 S.Ct. 83, 67 L.Ed. 237.

[The] distinction between direct and indirect effects of intrastate transactions upon interstate commerce must be recognized as a fundamental one, essential to the maintenance of our constitutional system. Otherwise, as we have said, there would be virtually no limit to the federal power, and for all practical purposes we should have a completely centralized government. We must consider the provisions here in question in the light of this distinction.

The question of chief importance relates to the provisions of the code as to the hours and wages of those employed in defendants' slaughterhouse markets. It is plain that these requirements are imposed in order to govern the details of defendants' management of their local business. The persons employed in slaughtering and selling in local trade are not employed in interstate commerce. Their hours and wages have no direct relation to interstate commerce. The question of how many hours these employees should work and what they should be paid differs in no essential respect from similar questions in other local businesses which handle commodities brought into a state and there dealt in as a part of its internal commerce. This appears from an examination of the considerations urged by the government with respect to conditions in the poultry trade. Thus, the government argues that hours and wages affect prices; that slaughterhouse men sell at a small margin above operating costs; that labor represents 50 to 60 per cent. of these costs; that a slaughterhouse operator paying lower wages or reducing his cost by exacting long hours of work translates his saving into lower prices; that this results in demands for a cheaper grade of goods: and that the cutting of prices brings about a demoralization of the price structure. Similar conditions may be adduced in relation to other businesses. The argument of the government proves too much. If the federal government may determine the wages and hours of employees in the internal commerce of a state, because of their relation to cost and prices and their indirect effect upon interstate commerce, it would seem that a similar control might be exerted over other elements of cost, also affecting prices, such as the number of employees, rents, advertising, methods of doing business, etc. All the processes of production and distribution that enter into cost could likewise be controlled. If the cost of doing an intrastate business is in itself the permitted object of federal control, the extent of the regulation of cost would be a question of discretion and not of power.

The government also makes the point that efforts to enact state legislation establishing high labor standards have been impeded by the belief that, unless similar action is taken generally, commerce will be diverted from the states adopting such standards, and that this fear of diversion has led to demands for federal legislation on the subject of wages and hours. The apparent implication is that the federal authority under the commerce clause should be deemed to extend to the establishment of rules to govern wages and hours in intrastate trade and industry generally throughout the country, thus overriding the authority of the states to deal with domestic problems arising from labor conditions in their internal commerce.

It is not the province of the Court to consider the economic advantages or disadvantages of such a centralized system. It is sufficient to say that the Federal Constitution does not provide for it. Our growth and development have called for wide use of the commerce power of the federal government in its control over the expanded activities of interstate commerce and in protecting that commerce from burdens, interferences, and conspiracies to restrain and monopolize it. But the authority of the federal government may not be pushed to such an extreme as to destroy the distinction, which the commerce clause itself establishes, between commerce "among the several States" and the internal concerns of a state. The same answer must be made to the contention that is based upon the serious economic situation which led to the passage of the Recovery Act — the fall in prices, the decline in wages and employment, and the curtailment of the market for commodities. Stress is laid upon the great importance of maintaining wage distributions which would provide the necessary stimulus in starting 'the cumulative forces making for expanding commercial activity.' Without in any way disparaging this motive, it is enough to say that the recuperative efforts of the federal government must be made in a manner consistent with the authority granted by the Constitution.

We are of the opinion that the attempt through the provisions of the code to fix the hours and wages of employees of defendants in their intrastate business was not a valid exercise of federal power. . . .

[W]e hold the code provisions here in question to be invalid and that the judgment of conviction must be reversed.

Comments on *Schechter*. The National Industrial Recovery Act of 1933 was the "heart" of the New Deal, Roosevelt's first response to the depression. Though it had been in effect for two years before the Court's finding it unconstitutional in *Schechter*, F.D.R., as you can imagine, was not pleased at the result. In effect, battle lines between the administration and the Court were drawn, and Roosevelt commented after the decision that "it [*Schechter*] clarifies the issue," as he referred to the Supreme Court as a "horse and buggy Court," out of touch with contemporary needs. A most activist Court would face a most activist President in the midst of the nation's greatest economic crisis.

The opinion in *Schechter* can certainly be contrasted with the "flexibility" of resolving these issues via the political process advanced by Marshall in *McCulloch*. If there had ever been a need for "national" action, the economic collapse of the Great Depression appeared to be such a time. Though the Congress cited the N.I.R.A. as an "emergency economic regulation," the Court, in response to these needs, and contrary to Marshall's lesson in nation building, nonetheless struck down the "New Deal" as unconstitutional as beyond the reach of national power. The Court continued to limit federal authority under the Commerce Clause to the "manner" of the activity (Local v. National), making the magnitude of the national economic crisis irrelevant to its decision. In response to the pleas for national action to face the emergency, the Court appeared unfazed, as is evidenced by Chief Justice Hughes's comments on behalf of the majority:

Extraordinary conditions may call for extraordinary remedies. But the argument necessarily stops short of an attempt to justify action which lies outside the sphere of constitutional authority. Extraordinary conditions do not create or enlarge constitutional power.

It is not the province of the Court to consider the economic advantages or disadvantages of such a centralized system. It is sufficient to say that the Federal Constitution does not provide for it.

Could the individual states provide any meaningful response to the national problem? Under the *Schechter* Court's reading this appeared to be irrelevant, or, let the nation be doomed in the name of the Supreme Court's reading of the Constitution. Did Learned Hand forewarn of this type of activism and government by Court if judicial review was not restrained? Here, it was the judicial conservatives actively pursuing a liberal use of the judicial power, arguable to further their political ends, and, au contraire, the political liberals (Brandeis, Frankfurter) argued in response for a restrained and conservative application of the judicial power. Where is Wechsler's "neutral principal"? What was worse, of course, was that this reading of the Constitution itself may not have been tenable. Most arguably not to Marshall either in *McCulloch* or *Gibbons*.

Whether or not the Court was imposing its own economic views on the nation, the lack of federal authority to respond to the depression placed the nation not only in the utmost exigency, but in a potential conflict between the political branches and the Court. As the 1936 presidential election loomed, the impending nature of the conflict was heightened by the opinion in *Carter Coal*, which follows.

CARTER v. CARTER COAL CO.
298 U.S. 238 (1936)

Mr. Justice SUTHERLAND delivered the opinion of the Court.

[Without] repeating the long and involved provisions with regard to the fixing of minimum prices, it is enough to say that the act confers the power to fix the minimum price of coal at each and every coal mine in the United States, with such price variations as the board may deem necessary and proper. There is also a provision authorizing the commission, when deemed necessary in the public interest, to establish maximum prices in order to protect the consumer against unreasonably high prices.

[The] labor provisions of the code, found in part 3 of the same section (15 U.S.C.A. § 808), require that in order to effectuate the purposes of the act the district boards and code members shall accept specified conditions contained in the code, [hours and wage rates].

[It] is no longer open to question that the general government, unlike the states, Hammer v. Dagenhart, 247 U.S. 251, 275, 38 S.Ct. 529, 62 L.Ed. 1101, 3 A.L.R. 649, Ann.Cas.1918E 724, possesses no inherent power in respect of the internal affairs of the states; and emphatically not with regard to legislation.

[Since] the validity of the act depends upon whether it is a regulation of interstate commerce, the nature and extent of the power conferred upon Congress by the commerce clause becomes the determinative question in this branch of the case. The commerce clause (art. 1, § 8, cl. 3) vests in Congress the power "To regulate Commerce with foreign Nations, and among the several States, and with the Indian Tribes." The function to be exercised is that of regulation. The distinction between manufacture and commerce was discussed in Kidd v. Pearson, 128 U.S. 1, 20, 21, 22, 9 S.Ct. 6, 10, 32 L.Ed. 346, and it was said:

No distinction is more popular to the common mind, or more clearly expressed in economic and political literature, than that between manufactures and commerce. Manufacture is transformation — the fashioning of raw materials into a change of form for use. The functions of commerce are different. . . . If it be held that the term includes the regulation of all such manufactures as are intended to be the subject of commercial transactions in the future, it is impossible to deny that it would also include all productive industries that contemplate the same thing. The result would be that congress would be invested, to the exclusion of the states, with the power to regulate, not only manufacture, but also agriculture, horticulture, stock-raising, domestic fisheries, mining, — in short, every branch of human industry. For is there one of them that does not contemplate, more or less clearly, an interstate or foreign market? Does not the wheat-grower of the northwest, and the cotton-planter of the south, plant, cultivate, and harvest his crop with an eye on the prices at Liverpool, New York, and Chicago? The power being vested in congress and denied to the states, it would follow as an inevitable result that the duty would devolve on congress to regulate all of these delicate, multiform, and vital interests, — interests which in their nature are, and must be, local in all the details of their successful management.

[We] have seen that the word "commerce" is the equivalent of the phrase "intercourse for the purposes of trade." Plainly, the incidents leading up to and culminating in the mining of coal do not constitute such intercourse. The employment of men, the fixing of their wages, hours of labor, and working conditions, the bargaining in respect of these things — whether carried on separately or collectively — each and all constitute intercourse for the purposes of production, not of trade. The latter is a thing apart from the relation of employer and employee, which in all producing occupations is purely local in character. Extraction of coal from the mine is the aim and the completed result of local activities. Commerce in the coal mined is not brought into being by force of these activities, but by negotiations, agreements and circumstances entirely apart from production. Mining brings the subject-matter of commerce into existence. Commerce disposes of it.

Whether the effect of a given activity or condition is direct or indirect is not always easy to determine. The word "direct" implies that the activity or condition invoked or blamed shall operate proximately — not immediately, remotely, or collaterally — to produce the effect. It connotes the absence of an efficient intervening agency or condition. And the extent of the effect bears no logical relation to its character. The distinction between a direct and an indirect effect turns, not upon the magnitude of either the cause or the effect, but entirely upon the manner in which the effect has been brought about. If the production by one man of a single ton of coal intended for interstate sale and shipment, and actually so sold and shipped, affects interstate commerce indirectly, the effect does not become direct by multiplying the tonnage, or increasing the number of men employed, or adding to the expense or complexities of the business, or by all combined. It is quite true that rules of law are sometimes qualified by considerations of degree, as the government argues. But the matter of degree has no bearing upon the question here, since that question is not — What is the extent of the local activity or condition, or the extent of the effect produced upon interstate commerce? but — What is the relation between the activity or condition and the effect?

Much stress is put upon the evils which come from the struggle between employers and employees over the matter of wages, working conditions, the right of collective bargaining, etc., and the resulting strikes, curtailment, and irregularity of production and effect on prices; and it is insisted that interstate commerce is greatly affected thereby. But, in addition to what has just been said, the conclusive answer is that the evils are all local evils over which the federal government has no legislative control. The relation of employer and employee is a local relation.

———————

Comments on *Carter*. Could the Court have refused to reach the merits because the suit was "collusive," i.e., father v. son? Did the government's entrance as a party provide the necessary adverse litigants, or does this opportunity to sidestep the controversy not underscore the majority's desire exercise its activism? Does the fact that the Court refused to find the price control section of the statute separable, and thus salvageable, despite the fact that Congress expressed such intent, further support the Court's bias and activism?

2. "COURT PACKING"

Roosevelt's Response and the Election of 1936. After *Carter*, and particularly *U.S. v. Butler*, where the Court invalidated the Agricultural Adjustment Act (supra), a vital component of the New Deal, Roosevelt felt that, "strong measures were needed to save the New Deal" from the Court "and the Court from itself." A total of seven pieces of New Deal legislation had been held unconstitutional by the Court. With the election of 1936 approaching, Roosevelt decided to wait for a sweeping victory to serve as support for executive action against the Court.

In the campaign, F.D.R. did not specifically make the Court an issue. Yet, the national economic crisis, and the government's ability to deal with such problems, were the focal points of his attack. For example, in his acceptance speech at the Democratic Convention in Philadelphia, Roosevelt launched into one of the most blatant attacks on big business and the industrial capitalists ever attempted by a President. Roosevelt saw economic tyranny threatening Americans, and he warned:

> It was natural and perhaps human that the privileged princes of these new economic dynasties, thirsting for power, reached out for control over Government itself. They created a new despotism and wrapped it in the robes of legal sanction. . . .
>
> The Royalists, of the economic order, have conceded that political freedom was the business of the Government, but they have maintained that economic slavery was nobody's business. . . . [T]hey deny that the Government could do anything to protect the citizen in his, right to work and his right to live. . . .
>
> These economic royalists complain that we seek to overthrow the institutions of America. What they really complain of, is that we seek to take away their power.

Those "economic royalists" attacked by Roosevelt were quick to respond, asserting that as an individual born into the "aristocracy" of American society, he had "deserted his class."

Roosevelt assumed office with an overwhelming victory (523 of 531 electoral votes), and took his oath from Chief Justice Hughes. He was to comment concerning this occasion that after swearing to uphold the Constitution, he wanted to tell Hughes that it was to "the Constitution as I understand it." F.D.R.'s last indication of future action took place in his 1937 inaugural address when he asserted, "we must find practical control over blind economic forces and blindly selfish men."

The Plan. In February of 1937, Roosevelt acted. Rejecting a constitutional amendment, he proposed legislation that encompassed an ingenious plan that would have as its covert purpose, yet, as its obvious intent, the "packing" of the Supreme Court to favor his "New Deal." Roosevelt adopted this approach from previous debate concerning congressional reform of the lower federal courts, which had been discussed from 1913 to 1916. That this plan was purposely selected to legitimize his action can be seen from the fact that the then Supreme Court Justice McReynolds, before his appointment to the Court, had previously been associated with this reform package when it was originally discussed.

The plan quite simply allowed the President to appoint one Justice to the bench for every sitting Justice who had reached the retirement age of 70. The only limitation allowed a maximum total of 15 sitting Justices. Consequently, with six Justices over the retirement age of 70 at that time, Roosevelt proposed that he be allowed to add 6 justices, and thus reach the ceiling of 15. It was all too obvious that the final result of this plan would be to "stack" the Court in favor of Roosevelt.

On March 9, 1937, in one of his famous "fireside chats," the President told the American people, "We have . . . reached the point . . . where we must take action to save the Constitution from the Court and the Court from itself. We must take an appeal from the Court to the Constitution itself."

The Response. Roosevelt's dramatic move quickly backfired. To many, his attempted court packing was in disregard of the Constitution, and some argued he was assuming dictatorial powers. This attack on the Constitution even split New Dealers. Hatton Sumners, chairman of the House Judiciary Committee, was to comment, after hearing the proposed plan outlined, "Boys, here's where I cash in."

Roosevelt's attack spurred responses from the Justices themselves, even though they normally attempted to remain above "political squabbles." Chief Justice Hughes, in a letter to Senator Wheeler, co-signed by Justices Brandeis and Van Devanter, stated that the Court was "fully abreast of its work" and that, "apart from any question of policy, which I do not discuss, [an increase] would not promote the efficiency of the Court."

In July of 1937, after the Senate Judiciary Committee had rejected the proposal in June, the plan was defeated. Yet, the story does not end here, for the Senate defeat was anticlimactic. Dramatically, before the plan officially failed, and while the turmoil concerning it raged, the Supreme Court reversed itself, and sustained New Deal legislation. In *N.L.R.B. v. Jones & Laughlin Steel*, the Court sustained the Wagner Act, reversing its previous views, and Roosevelt was to claim that though he "lost the battle [the court packing plan], he had won the war."

Though it is certainly reasonable to assume that the pressure exerted by Roosevelt may have affected the Court, recent evidence seems to indicate that the change in the Court's view occurred before introduction of the plan and the pressure that followed. A Supreme Court memo, taken from a discussion of *West Coast Hotel v. Parish* (see Chapter 1), seems to indicate that Justice Roberts, a Roosevelt opponent, had been persuaded to shift his opinion before the reorganization was instituted. Thus, the issue may well have been settled before Roosevelt's action.

Is "court packing" proof that the Court truly is "the least powerful" branch, and, in a constitutional conflict with the executive branch (Congress as well?) concerning their exercise of judicial review in regard to the meaning of the Constitution, the political power of the President can "bring them in line"? The resignation of Richard Nixon (*Nixon v. United States*, Chapter 3) and the "selection" of George Bush (*Bush v. Gore*, Chapter 1) might well attest to the institutionalization the Court's power in the modern era; yet, for whatever the rationale, is such political influence a sufficient check on the Court itself?

When Justice Van Devanter resigned in 1937, the swing vote for Roosevelt was available, and the makeup of the Court and its views on the constitutional balance of power between the state and federal governments changed accordingly. Between 1937 and 1941, Roosevelt was to make seven more appointments to the Court due to retirement, and thus provide a new Court, and as we shall see, to a great extent a new Commerce Clause. The cases that follow in the next section serve as a basis for defining the dimensions of the expanded commerce authority that was to occur either because of, or despite, Roosevelt's court packing. The question remains as to whether Justice Roberts's switch was "a switch in time to save the nine." (Sources for the material discussed herein were drawn from Burns, "Roosevelt: The Lion And The Fox" (1956), 291-315; Jackson, "The Struggle For Judicial Supremacy" (1941), 176-196; Leuchtenburg, "Franklin D. Roosevelt and The New Deal" (1963), 231-251.)

C. SUBSTANTIAL EFFECT: EXPANSION OF FEDERAL AUTHORITY, 1937-1995—"A SWITCH IN TIME TO SAVE THE NINE"

On April 12, 1937, with the nation and Roosevelt looking on, the Court reviewed the constitutionality of the National Labor Relations Act of 1935. In dramatic fashion, the Court sustained the legislation and applied an expanded commerce power, with the previous dissenters now joined by Hughes and Roberts.

NLRB v. JONES & LAUGHLIN STEEL CORP.
301 U.S. 1 (1937)

Mr. Chief Justice HUGHES delivered the opinion of the Court.

In a proceeding under the National Labor Relations Act of 1935 the National Labor Relations Board found that the respondent, Jones & Laughlin Steel Corporation, had violated the act by engaging in unfair labor practices affecting commerce. The proceeding was instituted by the Beaver Valley Lodge No. 200, affiliated with the Amalgamated Association of Iron, Steel and Tin Workers of America, a labor organization. The unfair labor practices charged were that the corporation was discriminating against members of the union with regard to hire and tenure of employment, and was coercing and intimidating its employees in order to interfere with their self-organization. The discriminatory and coercive action alleged was the discharge of certain employees.

The [NLRB] has found: The corporation is organized under the laws of Pennsylvania and has its principal office at Pittsburgh. It is engaged in the business of manufacturing iron and steel in plants situated in Pittsburgh and nearby Aliquippa, Pa. It manufactures and distributes a widely diversified line of steel and pig iron, being the fourth largest producer of steel in the United States. With its subsidiaries — nineteen in number — it is a completely integrated enterprise, owning and operating ore, coal and limestone properties, lake and river transportation facilities and terminal railroads located at its manufacturing plants. It owns or controls mines in Michigan and Minnesota. It operates four ore steamships on the Great Lakes, used in the transportation of ore to its factories. It owns coal mines in Pennsylvania. It operates towboats and steam barges used in carrying coal to its factories. It owns limestone properties in various places in Pennsylvania and West Virginia. It owns the Monongahela connecting railroad which connects the plants of the Pittsburgh works and forms an interconnection with the Pennsylvania, New York

Central and Baltimore & Ohio Railroad systems. It owns the Aliquippa & Southern Railroad Company, which connects the Aliquippa works with the Pittsburgh & Lake Erie, part of the New York Central system. Much of its product is shipped to its warehouses in Chicago, Detroit, Cincinnati and Memphis, — to the last two places by means of its own barges and transportation equipment. In Long Island City, New York, and in New Orleans it operates structural steel fabricating shops in connection with the warehousing of semifinished materials sent from its works. Through one of its wholly-owned subsidiaries it owns, leases, and operates stores, warehouses, and yards for the distribution of equipment and supplies for drilling and operating oil and gas wells and for pipe lines, refineries and pumping stations. It has sales offices in twenty cities in the United States and a wholly-owned subsidiary which is devoted exclusively to distributing its product in Canada. Approximately 75 per cent. of its product is shipped out of Pennsylvania.

Summarizing these operations, the Labor Board concluded that the works in Pittsburgh and Aliquippa "might be likened to the heart of a self-contained, highly integrated body. They draw in the raw materials from Michigan, Minnesota, West Virginia, Pennsylvania in part through arteries and by means controlled by the respondent; they transform the materials and then pump them out to all parts of the nation through the vast mechanism which the respondent has elaborated."

[The] act is challenged in its entirety as an attempt to regulate all industry, thus invading the reserved powers of the States over their local concerns. It is asserted that the references in the act to interstate and foreign commerce are colorable at best; that the act is not a true regulation of such commerce or of matters which directly affect it, but on the contrary has the fundamental object of placing under the compulsory supervision of the federal government all industrial labor relations within the nation. The argument seeks support in the broad words of the preamble (section 1) and in the sweep of the provisions of the act, and it is further insisted that its legislative history shows an essential universal purpose in the light of which its scope cannot be limited by either construction or by the application of the severability clause.

If this conception of terms, intent and consequent inseparability were sound, the act would necessarily fall by reason of the limitation upon the federal power which inheres in the constitutional grant, as well as because of the explicit reservation of the Tenth Amendment. Schechter Corporation v. United States, 295 U.S. 495, 549, 550, 554, 55 S.Ct. 837, 851, 853, 79 L.Ed. 1570, 97 A.L.R. 947. The authority of the federal government may not be pushed to such an extreme as to destroy the distinction, which the commerce clause itself establishes, between commerce 'among the several States' and the internal concerns of a state. That distinction between what is national and what is local in the activities of commerce is vital to the maintenance of our federal system. Id.

But we are not at liberty to deny effect to specific provisions, which Congress has constitutional power to enact, by superimposing upon them inferences from general legislative declarations of an ambiguous character, even if found in the same statute. The cardinal principle of statutory construction is to save and not to destroy. We have repeatedly held that as between two possible interpretations of a statute, by one of which it would be unconstitutional and by the other valid, our plain duty is to adopt that which will save the act. Even to avoid a serious doubt the rule is the same. Federal Trade Commission v. American Tobacco Co., 264 U.S. 298, 307, 44 S.Ct. 336, 337, 68 L.Ed. 696, 32 A.L.R. 786; Panama R.R. Co. v. Johnson, 264 U.S. 375, 390, 44 S.Ct. 391, 395, 68 L.Ed. 748; Missouri Pacific R.R. Co., v. Boone, 270 U.S. 466, 472, 46 S.Ct. 341, 343, 70 L.Ed. 688; Blodgett v. Holden, 275 U.S. 142, 148, 276 U.S. 594, 48 S.Ct. 105, 107, 72 L.Ed. 206;

Richmond Screw Anchor Co. v. United States, 275 U.S. 331, 346, 48 S.Ct. 194, 198, 72 L.Ed. 303.

We think it clear that the National Labor Relations Act may be construed so as to operate within the sphere of constitutional authority. The jurisdiction conferred upon the Board, and invoked in this instance, is found in section 10(a), 29 U.S.C.A. § 160(a), which provides:

> "Sec. 10(a). The Board is empowered, as hereinafter provided, to prevent any person from engaging in any unfair labor practice (listed in section 8 (section 158)) affecting commerce."

The critical words of this provision, prescribing the limits of the Board's authority in dealing with the labor practices, are "affecting commerce." The act specifically defines the "commerce" to which it refers (section 2(6), 29 U.S.C.A. § 152(6):

> "The term 'commerce' means trade, traffic, commerce, transportation, or communication among the several States, or between the District of Columbia or any Territory of the United States and any State or other Territory, or between any foreign country and any State, Territory, or the District of Columbia, or within the District of Columbia or any Territory, or between points in the same State but through any other State or any Territory or the District of Columbia or any foreign country."

There can be no question that the commerce thus contemplated by the act (aside from that within a Territory or the District of Columbia) is interstate and foreign commerce in the constitutional sense. The act also defines the term "affecting commerce" section 2(7), 29 U.S.C.A. § 152(7):

> "The term 'affecting commerce' means in commerce, or burdening or obstructing commerce or the free flow of commerce, or having led or tending to lead to a labor dispute burdening or obstructing commerce or the free flow of commerce."

This definition is one of exclusion as well as inclusion. The grant of authority to the Board does not purport to extend to the relationship between all industrial employees and employers. Its terms do not impose collective bargaining upon all industry regardless of effects upon interstate or foreign commerce. It purports to reach only what may be deemed to burden or obstruct that commerce and, thus qualified, it must be construed as contemplating the exercise of control within constitutional bounds. It is a familiar principle that acts which directly burden or obstruct interstate or foreign commerce, or its free flow, are within the reach of the congressional power. Acts having that effect are not rendered immune because they grow out of labor disputes. See Texas & N.O.R. Co. v. Railway & S.S. Clerks, 281 U.S. 548, 570, 50 S.Ct. 427, 433, 434, 74 L.Ed. 1034; Schechter Corporation v. United States, supra, 295 U.S. 495, at pages 544, 545, 55 S.Ct. 837, 849, 79 L.Ed. 1570, 97 A.L.R. 947; Virginian Railway Co. v. System Federation No. 40, 300 U.S. 515, 57 S.Ct. 592, 81 L.Ed. 789, decided March 29, 1937. It is the effect upon commerce, not the source of the injury, which is the criterion. Second Employers' Liability Cases (Mondou v. New York, N.H. & H.R. Co.), 223 U.S. 1, 51, 32 S.Ct. 169, 56 L.Ed. 327, 38 L.R.A.(N.S.) 44. Whether or not particular action does affect commerce in such a close and intimate fashion as to be subject to federal control, and hence to lie within the authority conferred upon the Board, is left by the statute to be determined as individual cases arise.

We are thus to inquire whether in the instant case the constitutional boundary has been passed.

The congressional authority to protect interstate commerce from burdens and obstructions is not limited to transactions which can be deemed to be an essential part of a "flow" of interstate or foreign commerce. Burdens and obstructions may be due to injurious action springing from other sources. [Although] activities may be intrastate in character when separately considered, if they have such a close and substantial relation to interstate commerce that their control is essential or appropriate to protect that commerce from burdens and obstructions, Congress cannot be denied the power to exercise that control. Schechter Corporation v. United States, supra. Undoubtedly the scope of this power must be considered in the light of our dual system of government and may not be extended so as to embrace effects upon interstate commerce so indirect and remote that to embrace them, in view of our complex society, would effectually obliterate the distinction between what is national and what is local and create a completely centralized government. Id. The question is necessarily one of degree.

[The] close and intimate effect which brings the subject within the reach of federal power may be due to activities in relation to productive industry although the industry when separately viewed is local. It is thus apparent that the fact that the employees here concerned were engaged in production is not determinative. The question remains as to the effect upon interstate commerce of the labor practice involved. In the Schechter Case, supra, we found that the effect there was so remote as to be beyond the federal power. [In] the Carter Case, supra, the Court was of the opinion that the provisions of the statute relating to production were invalid upon several grounds, — that there was improper delegation of legislative power, and that the requirements not only went beyond any sustainable measure of protection of interstate commerce but were also inconsistent with due process. These cases are not controlling here.

[I]t is idle to say that the effect would be indirect or remote. It is obvious that it would be immediate and might be catastrophic. We are asked to shut our eyes to the plainest facts of our national life and to deal with the question of direct and indirect effects in an intellectual vacuum. Because there may be but indirect and remote effects upon interstate commerce in connection with a host of local enterprises throughout the country, it does not follow that other industrial activities do not have such a close and intimate relation to interstate commerce as to make the presence of industrial strife a matter of the most urgent national concern. When industries organize themselves on a national scale, making their relation to interstate commerce the dominant factor in their activities, how can it be maintained that their industrial labor relations constitute a forbidden field into which Congress may not enter when it is necessary to protect interstate commerce from the paralyzing consequences of industrial war? We have often said that interstate commerce itself is a practical conception. It is equally true that interferences with that commerce must be appraised by a judgment that does not ignore actual experience.

Experience has abundantly demonstrated that the recognition of the right of employees to self-organization and to have representatives of their own choosing for the purpose of collective bargaining is often an essential condition of industrial peace.

Reversed and remanded.

Mr. Justice MCREYNOLDS delivered the following dissenting opinion. [Joined by Justices VAN DEVANTER, SUTHERLAND, and BUTLER]

Any effect on interstate commerce by the discharge of employees shown here would be indirect and remote in the highest degree, as consideration of the facts will show. In No. 419 ten men out of ten thousand were discharged; in the other cases only a few. The immediate effect in the factor may be to create discontent among all those employed and a strike may follow, which, in turn, may result in reducing production, which ultimately may reduce the volume of goods moving in interstate commerce. By this chain of indirect and progressively remote events we finally reach the evil with which it is said the legislation under consideration undertakes to deal. A more remote and indirect interference with interstate commerce or a more definite invasion of the powers reserved to the states is difficult, if not impossible, to imagine. [Whatever] effect any cause of discontent may ultimately have upon commerce is far too indirect to justify congressional regulation. Almost anything — marriage, birth, death — may in some fashion affect commerce.

Comments on *Jones & Laughlin*. The Court offered a new basis for evaluating federal authority under the Commerce Clause in *Jones & Laughlin*. What was it? What did it have to do with "magnitude" and "manner"? How do you think the new test will expand congressional power?

UNITED STATES v. DARBY
312 U.S. 100 (1941)

[Darby challenged a charge of violating the Fair Labor Standards Act of 1938. The act provided for a minimum wage and hours for workers engaged in the production of goods manufactured for interstate commerce. The district court sustained Darby's objections to the constitutionality of the act.]

Mr. Justice STONE delivered the opinion of the Court. . . .

[The purpose of the act] is to exclude from interstate commerce goods produced for the commerce and to prevent their production for interstate commerce, under conditions detrimental to the maintenance of the minimum standards of living necessary for health and general well-being; and to prevent the use of interstate commerce as the means of competition in the distribution of goods so produced, and as the means of spreading and perpetuating such substandard labor conditions among the workers of the several states. . .

THE PROHIBITION OF SHIPMENT OF THE PROSCRIBED GOODS IN INTERSTATE COMMERCE . . .

While manufacture is not of itself interstate commerce, the shipment of manufactured goods interstate is such commerce and the prohibition of such shipment by Congress is indubitably a regulation of the commerce. The power to regulate commerce is the power "to prescribe the rule by which commerce is governed." Gibbons v. Ogden. It extends not only to those regulations which aid, foster and protect the commerce, but embraces those which prohibit it. [Lottery Case.] It is conceded that the power of Congress to prohibit transportation in interstate commerce includes noxious articles, [Lottery Case; Hipolite Egg Co.], stolen articles, kidnapped persons, and articles such as intoxicating liquor or convict made goods, traffic in which is forbidden or restricted by the laws of the state of destination. Kentucky Whip & Collar Co. v. Illinois Central R. Co., 299 U.S. 334.

But it is said that the present prohibition falls within the scope of none of these categories; that while the prohibition is nominally a regulation of the commerce its motive or purpose is regulation of wages and hours of persons engaged in manufacture, the control of which has been reserved to the states and upon which Georgia and some of the states of destination have placed no restriction.

The power of Congress over interstate commerce "is complete in itself, may be exercised to its utmost extent, and acknowledges no limitations other than are prescribed in the Constitution." Gibbons v. Ogden. [Congress,] following its own conception of public policy concerning the restrictions which may appropriately be imposed on interstate commerce, is free to exclude from the commerce articles whose use in the states for which they are destined it may conceive to be injurious to the public health, morals, or welfare, even though the state has not sought to regulate their use. [Lottery Case.]

Such regulation is not a forbidden invasion of state power merely because either its motive or its consequence is to restrict the use of articles of commerce within the states of destination; and is not prohibited unless by other Constitutional provisions. It is no objection to the assertion of the power to regulate interstate commerce that its exercise is attended by the same incidents which attend the exercise of the police power of the states.

The motive and purpose of the present regulation are plainly to make effective the Congressional conception of public policy that interstate commerce should not be made the instrument of competition in the distribution of goods produced under substandard labor conditions, which competition is injurious to the commerce and to the states from and to which the commerce flows. The motive and purpose of a regulation of interstate commerce are matters for the legislative judgment upon the exercise of which the Constitution places no restriction and over which the courts are given no control. "The judicial cannot prescribe to the legislative department of the government limitations upon the exercise of its acknowledged power." Veazie Bank v. Fenno, 8 Wall. 533. Whatever their motive and purpose, regulations of commerce which do not infringe some constitutional prohibition are within the plenary power conferred on Congress by the Commerce Clause. Subject only to that limitation, [we] conclude that the prohibition of the shipment interstate of goods produced under the forbidden substandard labor conditions is within the constitutional authority of Congress.

In the more than a century which has elapsed since the decision of Gibbons v. Ogden, these principles of constitutional interpretation have been so long and repeatedly recognized by this Court as applicable to the Commerce Clause, that there would be little occasion for repeating them now were it not for the decision of this Court twenty-two years ago in Hammer v. Dagenhart, 247 U.S. 251. . . .

Hammer v. Dagenhart has not been followed. The distinction on which the decision was rested that Congressional power to prohibit interstate commerce is limited to articles which in themselves have some harmful or deleterious property — a distinction which was novel when made and unsupported by any provision of the Constitution — has long since been abandoned. The thesis of the opinion that the motive of the prohibition or its effect to control in some measure the use or production within the states of the article thus excluded from the commerce can operate to deprive the regulation of its constitutional authority has long since ceased to have force. . . .

The conclusion is inescapable that Hammer v. Dagenhart was a departure from the principles which have prevailed in the interpretation of the Commerce Clause both before and since the decision and that such vitality, as a precedent, as it then had has long since been exhausted. It should be and now is overruled.

Validity of the Wage and Hour Requirements. Section 15(a)(2) and 6 and 7 require employers to conform to the wage and hour provisions with respect to all employees engaged in the production of goods for interstate commerce. As appellee's employees are not alleged to be "engaged in interstate commerce" the validity of the prohibition turns on the question whether the employment, under other than the prescribed labor standards, of employees engaged in the production of goods for interstate commerce is so related to the commerce and so affects it as to be within the reach of the power of Congress to regulate it. . . .

[The] phrase "produced for interstate commerce" [embraces] at least the case where an employer [manufactures] his product with the intent or expectation that according to the normal course of his business all or some part of it will be selected for shipment to those customers.

[The] obvious purpose of the Act was not only to prevent the interstate transportation of the proscribed product, but to stop the initial step toward transportation, production with the purpose of so transporting it. . . .

There remains the question whether such restriction on the production of goods for commerce is a permissible exercise of the commerce power. The power of Congress over interstate commerce is not confined to the regulation of commerce among the states. It extends to those activities intrastate which so affect interstate commerce or the exercise of the power of Congress over it as to make regulation of them appropriate means to the attainment of a legitimate end, the exercise of the granted power of Congress to regulate interstate commerce.

[Congress], having by the present Act adopted the policy of excluding from interstate commerce all goods produced for the commerce which do not conform to the specified labor standards, it may choose the means reasonably adapted to the attainment of the permitted end, even though they involve control of intrastate activities. Such legislation has often been sustained with respect to powers, other than the commerce power granted to the national government, when the means chosen, although not themselves within the granted power, were nevertheless deemed appropriate aids to the accomplishment of some purpose within an admitted power of the national government. A familiar like exercise of power is the regulation of intrastate transactions which are so commingled with or related to interstate commerce that all must be regulated if the interstate commerce is to be effectively controlled. [Shreveport Rate Case.] . . .

We think also that §15(a)(2), now under consideration, is sustainable independently of §15(a)(1), which prohibits shipment or transportation of the proscribed goods. As we have said the evils aimed at by the Act are the spread of substandard labor conditions through the use of the facilities of interstate commerce for competition by the goods so produced with those produced under the prescribed or better labor conditions; and the consequent dislocation of the commerce itself caused by the impairment or destruction of local businesses by competition made effective through interstate commerce. The Act is thus directed at the suppression of a method or kind of competition in interstate commerce which it has in effect condemned as "unfair," as the Clayton Act has condemned other "unfair methods of competition" made effective through interstate commerce. . . .

The means adopted by §15(a)(2) for the protection of interstate commerce by the suppression of the production of the condemned goods for interstate commerce is so related to the commerce and so affects it as to be within the reach of the commerce power. Congress, to attain its objective in the suppression of nationwide competition in interstate commerce by goods produced under substandard labor conditions, has made no distinction as to the volume or amount of shipments in the commerce or of production for commerce by any particular shipper or producer. It recognized that in present day industry, competition by a small part may affect the whole and that the total effect of the competition of many small producers may be great. The legislation aimed at a whole embraces all its parts. . . .

Our conclusion is unaffected by the Tenth Amendment. [The] amendment states but a truism that all is retained which has not been surrendered. There is nothing in the history of its adoption to suggest that it was more than declaratory of the relationship between the national and state governments as it had been established by the Constitution before the amendment or that its purpose was other than to allay fears that the new national government might seek to exercise powers not granted, and that the states might not be able to exercise fully their reserved powers. [Reversed.]

Comments on *Darby*. Scholars have argued that *Jones & Laughlin* may have provided the drama, but the birth of the new commerce power took place in *Darby*. Why? Does *Darby* do away with all of the previous limitations on the commerce power? Is the Court's finding that "[t]he commerce power extends to those intrastate activities which so affect interstate commerce . . . ," a basis for unlimited federal power?

Once an activity is "within" the reach of the commerce power, can Congress do what it will, because the power is "complete in itself, [and] may be exercised to its utmost extent"? The Court in *Darby* justified the regulation as a "necessary and proper" means of enforcing the ban on interstate shipment. Are there any limitations to the use of this technique? Is the power now so broad and plenary that Congress may regulate any activity that substantially affects commerce, even if the goal is to effectuate "social policy"?

Another interesting aspect of *Darby* is that despite all of the court-packing hoopla, Roosevelt named seven (still out of nine) new Justices to the Court between 1937 and 1941. Does this explain the significance of *Darby*?

If the Commerce Clause became the broadest basis for federal authority, the "centerpiece" case that afforded such, at least in regard to the leaders of the modern "anti-federalist revival," was *Wickard v. Filburn*, which follows. See if you can determine why.

WICKARD v. FILBURN
317 U.S. 111 (1942)

Mr. Justice JACKSON delivered the opinion of the Court. . . .

The appellee filed his complaint against the Secretary of Agriculture of the United States. [He] sought to enjoin enforcement against himself of the marketing penalty imposed by . . . the Agricultural Adjustment Act of 1938 upon that part of his 1941 wheat crop which was available for marketing in excess of the marketing quota established for his farm. He also sought a declaratory judgment that the wheat marketing quota provisions of the Act as amended and applicable to him were unconstitutional because not sustainable under the Commerce Clause or consistent with the Due Process Clause of the Fifth Amendment.

In July of 1940, pursuant to the Agricultural Adjustment Act of 1938, there were established for the appellee's 1941 crop a wheat acreage allotment of 11.1 acres and a normal yield of 20.1 bushels of wheat an acre. He was given notice of such allotment in

July of 1940 before the Fall planting of his 1941 crop of wheat, and again in July of 1941, before it was harvested. He sowed, however, 23 acres, and harvested from his 11.9 acres of excess acreage 239 bushels, which under the terms of the Act, . . . constituted farm marketing excess, subject to a penalty of 49 cents a bushel, or $117.11 in all. The appellee has not paid the penalty and he has not postponed or avoided it by storing the excess under regulations of the Secretary of Agriculture, or by delivering it up to the Secretary. The Committee, therefore, refused him a marketing card, which was, under the terms of Regulations promulgated by the Secretary, necessary to protect a buyer from liability to the penalty and upon its protecting lien.

The general scheme of the Agricultural Adjustment Act of 1938 as related to wheat is to control the volume moving in interstate and foreign commerce in order to avoid surpluses and shortages and the consequent abnormally low or high wheat prices and obstructions to commerce. Within prescribed limits and by prescribed standards the Secretary of Agriculture is directed to ascertain and proclaim each year a national acreage allotment for the next crop of wheat, which is then apportioned to the states and their counties, and is eventually broken up into allotments for individual farms. Loans and payments to wheat farmers are authorized in stated circumstances.

The Act provides further that whenever it appears that the total supply of wheat as of the beginning of any marketing year, beginning July 1, will exceed a normal year's domestic consumption and export by more than 35 per cent, the Secretary shall so proclaim not later than May 15 prior to the beginning of such marketing year; and that during the marketing year a compulsory national marketing quota shall be in effect with respect to the marketing of wheat. Between the issuance of the proclamation and June 10, the Secretary must, however, conduct a referendum of farmers who will be subject to the quota to determine whether they favor or oppose it; and if more than one-third of the farmers voting in the referendum do oppose, the Secretary must prior to the effective date of the quota by proclamation suspend its operation.

It is urged that under the Commerce Clause, [Congress] does not possess the power it has in this instance sought to exercise. The question would merit little consideration [except] for that fact that this Act extends federal regulation to production not intended in any part for commerce but wholly for consumption on the farm. [Marketing] quotas not only embrace all that may be sold without penalty but also what may be consumed on the premises. . . .

Appellee says that this is a regulation of production and consumption of wheat. Such activities are, he urges, [local] in character, and their effects upon interstate commerce are at most "indirect." . . . [Questions] of the power of Congress are not to be decided by reference to any formula which would give controlling force to nomenclature such as "production" and "indirect" and foreclose consideration of the actual effects of the activity in question upon interstate commerce.

At the beginning Chief Justice Marshall described the federal commerce power with a breadth never yet exceeded. [Gibbons v. Ogden.] He made emphatic the embracing and penetrating nature of this power by warning that effective restraints on its exercise must proceed from political rather than from judicial processes. . . .

The Court's recognition of the relevance of the economic effects in the application of the Commerce Clause [has] made the mechanical application of legal formulas no longer feasible. Once an economic measure of the reach of the power granted to Congress in the Commerce Clause is accepted, questions of federal power cannot be decided simply by finding the activity in question to be "production," nor can consideration of its economic effects be foreclosed by calling them "indirect." . . .

Whether the subject of the regulation in question was "production," "consumption," or "marketing" is, therefore, not material for purposes of deciding the question of federal power before us. That an activity is of local character may help in a doubtful case to determine whether Congress intended to reach it. [But] even if appellee's activity be local and though it may not be regarded as commerce, it may still, whatever its nature, be reached by Congress if it exerts a substantial economic effect on interstate commerce, and this irrespective of whether such effect is what might at some earlier time have been defined as "direct" or "indirect."

The parties have stipulated a summary of the economics of the wheat industry. Commerce among the states in wheat is large and important. Although wheat is raised in every state but one, production in most states is not equal to consumption. Sixteen states on average have had a surplus of wheat above their own requirements for feed, seed, and food. Thirty-two states and the District of Columbia, where production has been below consumption, have looked to these surplus-producing states for their supply as well as for wheat for export and carry-over.

The wheat industry has been a problem industry for some years. Largely as a result of increased foreign production and import restrictions, annual exports of wheat and flour from the United States during the ten-year period ending in 1940 averaged less than 10 per cent of total production, while during the 1920's they averaged more than 25 per cent. The decline in the export trade has left a large surplus in production which, in connection with an abnormally large supply of wheat and other grains in recent years, caused congestion in a number of markets; tied up railroad cars; and caused elevators in some instances to turn away grains, and railroads to institute embargoes to prevent further congestion. . . .

In the absence of regulation, the price of wheat in the United States would be much affected by world conditions. During 1941, producers who cooperated with the Agricultural Adjustment program received an average price on the farm of about $1.16 a bushel, as compared with the world market price of 40 cents a bushel. . . .

The effect of consumption of home-grown wheat on interstate commerce is due to the fact that it constitutes the most variable factor in the disappearance of the wheat crop. Consumption on the farm where grown appears to vary in an amount greater than 20 per cent of average production. The total amount of wheat consumed as food varies but relatively little, and use as seed is relatively constant.

The maintenance by government regulation of a price for wheat undoubtedly can be accomplished as effectively by sustaining or increasing the demand as by limiting the supply. The effect of the statute before us is to restrict the amount which may be produced for market and the extent as well to which one may forestall resort to the market by producing to meet his own needs. That appellee's own contribution to the demand for wheat may be trivial by itself is not enough to remove him from the scope of federal regulation where, as here, his contribution, taken together with that of many others similarly situated, is far from trivial.

[A] factor of such volume and variability as home-consumed wheat would have a substantial influence on price and market conditions. This may arise because being in marketable condition such wheat overhangs the market and, if induced by rising prices, tends to flow into the market and check price increases. But if we assume that it is never marketed, it supplies a need of the man who grew it which would otherwise be reflected by purchases in the open market. Home-grown wheat in this sense competes with wheat in commerce. The stimulation of commerce is a use of the regulatory function quite as definitely as prohibitions or restrictions thereon. This record leaves us in no doubt that Congress may properly have considered that wheat consumed on the farm where grown, if wholly outside the scheme of regulation, would have a substantial effect in defeating and obstructing its purpose to stimulate trade therein at increased prices.

It is said, however, that this Act, forcing some farmers into the market to buy what they could provide for themselves, is an unfair promotion of the markets and prices of specializing wheat growers. It is of the essence of regulation that it lays a restraining hand on the self-interest of the regulated and that advantages from the regulation commonly fall to others. The conflicts of economic interest between the regulated and those who advantage by it are wisely left under our system to resolution by the Congress under its more flexible and responsible legislative process. Such conflicts rarely lend themselves to judicial determination. And with the wisdom, workability, or fairness, of the plan of regulation we have nothing to do. [Reversed.]

Comments on *Wickard*. Is there any activity that does not have a "substantial economic effect on interstate commerce," after *Wickard*? Isn't the effect of one farmer trivial? How does the Court conclude that the activity substantially affects commerce? Is this a circumstance where big brother is telling a farmer how much home feed he can grow, or is the government correct in asserting that all farmers taken as whole could subvert the purpose of the AAA and its quotas?

Wickard turns on the "aggregate affect" of the regulated activity: "taken together with that of many others similarly situated." Given this rationale, can't we make the effect of any activity substantial? Does the term "substantial" serve as an effective limitation on the reach of the commerce power? Or, is the breadth of the power due to the fact that we have succeeded beyond the framers' wildest intent in establishing a national market? A national market so extensive, intertwined, and inter-state dependent in character that there is no longer any activity that is truly "local" or purely inter-state. We will reconsider the concerns about the aggregation approach when we review *United States v. Lopez*, supra, decided in 1995 and the first significant limitation on commerce power in the modern era.

D. THE USE OF THE EXPANDED COMMERCE POWER AS A REGULATORY TOOL FOR FEDERAL AUTHORITY—EARLY PRECEDENTS

Although the Court limited the reach of the commerce clause in this era, they did such by limiting what was considered commerce, or what was "within commerce." Note, however, that once an activity was "within commerce" the Court allowed a very broad basis for federal authority. *Champion v. Ames* serves as an example of the breadth of the historic "scope" of the commerce power once an activity was reachable.

CHAMPION v. AMES
(The Lottery Case)
188 U.S. 321 (1903)

[The Federal Lottery Act of 1895 prohibited the interstate transportation of foreign lottery tickets. Champion was indicted for shipping a box of Paraguayan lottery tickets from Texas to California.]

Mr. Justice HARLAN delivered the opinion of the court:

[Undoubtedly,] the carrying from one State to another by independent carriers of things or commodities that are ordinary subjects of traffic, and which have in themselves a recognized value in money, constitutes interstate commerce.

[It] is said that the statute in question does not regulate the carrying of lottery tickets from State to State, but by punishing those who cause them to be so carried Congress in effect prohibits such carrying. [Are] we prepared to say that a provision which is, in effect, a prohibition of the carriage of such articles from State to State is not a fit or appropriate mode for the regulation of that particular kind of commerce? If lottery traffic, carried on through interstate commerce, is a matter of which Congress may take cognizance and over which its power may be exerted, can it be possible that it must tolerate the traffic, and simply regulate the manner in which it may be carried on? Or may not Congress, for the protection of the people of all the States, and under the power to regulate interstate commerce, devise such means, within the scope of the Constitution, and not prohibited by it, as will drive that traffic out of commerce among the States? . . .

[It] must not be forgotten that the power of Congress to regulate commerce among the States is plenary, is complete in itself, and is subject to no limitations except such as may be found in the Constitution. What provision in that instrument can be regarded as limiting the exercise of the power granted? What clause can be cited which, in any degree, countenances the suggestion that one may, of right, carry or cause to be carried from one State to another that which will harm the public morals? [We] have said that the liberty protected by the Constitution embraces the right to be free in the enjoyment of one's faculties; "to be free to use them in all lawful ways; to live and work where he will; to earn his livelihood by any lawful calling; to pursue any livelihood or avocation, and for that purpose to enter into all contracts that may be proper." Allgeyer v. Louisiana, 165 U.S. 578, 589. But surely it will not be said to be a part of any one's liberty, as recognized by the supreme law of the land, that he shall be allowed to introduce into commerce among the States an element that will be confessedly injurious to the public morals.

Congress [does] not assume to interfere with traffic or commerce in lottery tickets carried on exclusively within the limits of any State, but has in view only commerce of that kind among the several States. It has not assumed to interfere with the completely internal affairs of any State, and has only legislated in respect of a matter which concerns the people of the United States. As a State may, for the purpose of guarding the morals of its own people, forbid all sales of lottery tickets within its limits, so Congress, for the purpose of guarding the people of the United States against the 'widespread pestilence of lotteries' and to protect the commerce which concerns all the States, may prohibit the carrying of lottery tickets from one State to another. In legislating upon the subject of the traffic in lottery tickets, as carried on through interstate commerce, Congress only supplemented the action of those States — perhaps all of them — which, for the protection of the public morals, prohibit the drawing of lotteries, as well as the sale or circulation of lottery tickets, within their respective limits. It said, in effect, that it would not permit the declared policy of the States, which sought to protect their people against the mischief's of the lottery business, to be overthrown or disregarded by the agency of interstate commerce.

It is said, however, that if, in order to suppress lotteries carried on through interstate commerce, Congress may exclude lottery tickets from such commerce, that principle leads necessarily to the conclusion that Congress may arbitrarily exclude from commerce among the States any article, commodity or thing, of whatever kind or nature, or however useful or valuable, which it may choose, no matter with what motive, to declare shall not be carried from one State to another. It will be time enough to consider the constitutionality of such legislation when we must do so. The present case does not require the court to declare the full extent of the power that Congress may exercise in the regulation of commerce among the States. We may, however, repeat, in this connection, what the court has heretofore said, that the power of Congress to regulate commerce among the States, although plenary, cannot be deemed arbitrary, since it is subject to such limitations or restrictions as are prescribed by the Constitution. This power, therefore, may not be exercised so as to infringe rights secured or protected by that instrument. It would not be difficult to imagine legislation that would be justly liable to such an objection as that stated, and be hostile to the objects for the accomplishment of which Congress was invested with the general power to regulate commerce among the several States. But, as often said, the possible abuse of a power is not an argument against its existence. There is probably no governmental power that may not be exerted to the injury of the public. If what is done by Congress is manifestly in excess of the powers granted to it, then upon the courts will rest the duty of adjudging that its action is neither legal nor binding upon the people. But if what Congress does is within the limits of its power, and is simply unwise or injurious, the remedy is that suggested by Chief Justice Marshall in Gibbons v. Ogden, when he said: The wisdom and the discretion of Congress, their identity with the people, and the influence which their constituents possess at elections, are, in this, as in many other instances, as that, for example, of declaring war, the sole restraints on which they have relied, to secure them from its abuse. They are the restraints on which the people must often rely solely, in all representative governments.

Mr. Chief Justice FULLER, with whom concur Mr. Justice BREWER, Mr. Justice SHIRAS, and Mr. Justice PECKHAM, dissenting.

[Everything] is an article of commerce the moment it is taken to be transported from place to place, and of interstate commerce if from State to State. . . .

An invitation to dine, or to take a drive, or a note of introduction, all become articles of commerce under the ruling in this case, by being deposited with an express company for transportation. This in effect breaks down all the differences between that which is, and that which is not, an article of commerce, and the necessary consequence is to take from the States all jurisdiction over the subject so far as interstate communication is concerned. It is a long step in the direction of wiping out all traces of state lines, and the creation of a centralized Government.

———

Implications of *Darby*. The broad scope and plenary nature of the commerce power set out in the *Lottery Case* — "[It] must not be forgotten that the power of Congress to regulate commerce among the States is plenary, is complete in itself, and is subject to no limitations except such as may be found in the Constitution" — was ready and waiting for "substantial effect" and the expanded basis of activity reachable under the clause. The combination of the broad "scope" of the power, with the expanded basis for what was "within" commerce, provided a powerful one-two "punch" for federal regulation. *Perez* exemplifies such.

PEREZ v. UNITED STATES
402 U.S. 146 (1971)

Mr. Justice DOUGLAS delivered the opinion of the Court.

The question in this case is whether Title II of the Consumer Credit Protection Act, 82 Stat. 159, 18 U.S.C. § 891 et seq. (1964 ed., Supp. V), as construed and applied to petitioner, is a permissible exercise by Congress of its powers under the Commerce Clause of the Constitution. . . .

Petitioner is one of the species commonly known as "loan sharks" which Congress found are in large part under the control of "organized crime." "Extortionate credit transactions" are defined as those characterized by the use or threat of the use of "violence or other criminal means" in enforcement. There was ample evidence showing petitioner was a "loan shark" who used the threat of violence as a method of collection. He loaned money to one Miranda, owner of a new butcher shop, making a $1,000 advance to be repaid in installments of $105 per week for 14 weeks. After paying at this rate for six or eight weeks, petitioner increased the weekly payment to $130. In two months Miranda asked for an additional loan of $2,000 which was made, the agreement being that Miranda was to pay $205 a week. In a few weeks petitioner increased the weekly payment to $330. When Miranda objected, petitioner told him about a customer who refused to pay and ended up in a hospital. So Miranda paid. In a few months petitioner increased his demands to $500 weekly which Miranda paid, only to be advised that at the end of the week petitioner would need $1,000. Miranda made that payment by not paying his suppliers; but, faced with a $1,000 payment the next week, he sold his butcher shop. Petitioner pursued Miranda, first making threats to Miranda's wife and then telling Miranda he could have him castrated. When Miranda did not make more payments, petitioner said he was turning over his collections to people who would not be nice but who would put him in the hospital if he did not pay. Negotiations went on, Miranda finally saying he could only pay $25 a week. Petitioner said that was not enough, that Miranda should steal or sell drugs if necessary to get the money to pay the loan, and that if he went to jail it would be better than going to a hospital with a broken back or legs. He added, "I could have sent you to the hospital, you and your family, any moment I want with my people."

Petitioner's arrest followed. Miranda, his wife, and an employee gave the evidence against petitioner who did not testify or call any witnesses. Petitioner's attack was on the constitutionality of the Act, starting with a motion to dismiss the indictment.

The constitutional question is a substantial one. . . .

The House debates include a long article from the New York Times Magazine for January 28, 1968, on the connection between the "loan shark" and organized crime. Id., at 1428-1431. The gruesome and stirring episodes related have the following as a prelude: "The loan shark, then, is the indispensable 'moneymover' of the underworld. He takes 'black' money tainted by its derivation from the gambling or narcotics rackets and turns it 'white' by funneling it into channels of legitimate trade. In so doing, he exacts usurious interest that doubles the black-white money in no time; and, by his special decrees, by his imposition of impossible penalties, he greases the way for the underworld takeover of entire businesses." Id., at 1429. . . .

The Commerce Clause reaches, in the main, three categories of problems. First, the use of channels of interstate or foreign commerce which Congress deems are being misused, as, for example, the shipment of stolen goods (18 U.S.C. §§ 2312-2315) or of persons who have been kidnapped (18 U.S.C. § 1201). Second, protection of the instrumentalities of interstate commerce, as for example, the destruction of an aircraft (18 U.S.C. § 32), or persons or things in commerce, as, for example, thefts from interstate shipments (18 U.S.C. § 659). Third, those activities affecting commerce. It is with this last category that we are here concerned. . . .

[E]ven if appellee's activity be local and though it may not be regarded as commerce, it may still, whatever its nature, be reached by Congress if it exerts a substantial economic effect on interstate commerce, and this irrespective of whether such effect is what might at some earlier time have been defined as "direct" or "indirect." . . . .

Where the class of activities is regulated and that class is within the reach of federal power, the courts have no power "to excise, as trivial, individual instances" of the class. Maryland v. Wirtz, 392 U.S. 183, 193, 88 S.Ct. 2017, 2022, 20 L.Ed.2d 1020, 1029.

[Justice Douglas reviewed the congressional support for the conclusion that these transactions affected interstate commerce.] The essence of all these reports and hearings was summarized and embodied in formal congressional findings. They supplied Congress with the knowledge that the loan shark racket provides organized crime with its second most lucrative source of revenue, exacts millions from the pockets of people, coerces its victims into the commission of crimes against property, and causes the takeover by racketeers of legitimate businesses. See generally 114 Cong.Rec. 14391, 14392, 14395, 14396.

We have mentioned in detail the economic, financial, and social setting of the problem as revealed to Congress. We do so not to infer that Congress need make particularized findings in order to legislate. We relate the history of the Act in detail to answer the impassioned plea of petitioner that all that is involved in loan sharking is a traditionally local activity. It appears, instead, that loan sharking in its national setting is one way organized interstate crime holds its guns to the heads of the poor and the rich alike and syphons funds from numerous localities to finance its national operations.

Affirmed.

Mr. Justice STEWART, dissenting.

Congress surely has power under the Commerce Clause to enact criminal laws to protect the instrumentalities of interstate commerce, to prohibit the misuse of the channels or facilities of interstate commerce, and to prohibit or regulate those intrastate activities that have a demonstrably substantial effect on interstate commerce. But under the statute before us a man can be convicted without any proof of interstate movement, of the use of the facilities of interstate commerce, or of facts showing that his conduct affected interstate commerce. I think the Framers of the Constitution never intended that the National Government might define as a crime and prosecute such wholly local activity through the enactment of federal criminal laws.

In order to sustain this law we would, in my view, have to be able at the least to say that Congress could rationally have concluded that loan sharking is an activity with interstate attributes that distinguish it in some substantial respect from other local crime. But it is not enough to say that loan sharking is a national problem, for all crime is a national problem. It is not enough to say that some loan sharking has interstate characteristics, for any crime may have an interstate setting. And the circumstance that loan sharking has an adverse impact on interstate business is not a distinguishing attribute, for interstate business suffers from almost all criminal activity, be it shoplifting or violence in the streets.

Because I am unable to discern any rational distinction between loan sharking and other local crime, I cannot escape the conclusion that this statute was beyond the power of Congress to enact. The definition and prosecution of local, intrastate crime are reserved to the States under the Ninth and Tenth Amendments.

Comments on *Perez*. Does loan sharking have a substantial effect on commerce? Are there elements of both *Darby* and *Wickard* necessary to reach the result? What are they? Is Congress regulating commerce or social policy in *Perez*? Does or should such make a difference?

The reach of the commerce power as a tool for regulating "social evils" (we've come a long way from *Hammer*) is nowhere more evidenced than in the Civil Rights Act of 1964 — an attempt to prohibit private parties from discrimination on the basis of race in denial of public facilities and accommodations. The Supreme Court's review of the constitutionality of this legislation follows. Does *Perez* set forth a precedent in support of this legislation?

E. DRAWING ON THE EXPANSIVE COMMERCE POWER TO PROTECT CIVIL RIGHTS

In 1964 the ever-expanding use of the commerce power received further amplification when the clause was used as a means of protecting civil rights. With much social pressure (from the civil rights movement as well as a byproduct of the assassination of President John Kennedy, who first proposed the legislation) on the federal government to provide civil rights protection against denial of access to public accommodation, Congress responded with passage of the Civil Right Act of 1964, based upon both the Commerce Clause and the 14th amendment.

The use of the commerce power to support the legislation caused much debate concerning the passage of the bill. Some Senators argued that this was an extension of the commerce power beyond its original intent. They argued that the administration offered it as a basis for the statute simply because the commerce power was the most expansive source of federal authority. They argued that this legislation should more properly be based on the 14th amendment and its guarantee of "equal protection of the law." (Most federal laws, including the Civil Rights Act of 1883, which is much the same as the 1964 act, protected civil rights via the post–Civil War amendments.) In committee hearings, Senator Thurmond (Rep., S.C.) stated, "isn't it true that all of the acts of Congress based on the Commerce Clause . . . were primarily designed to regulate economic affairs of life and that the basic purpose of this bill is to regulate moral and social affairs." Senator Cooper (Rep., Ky.) bluntly concluded, "If there is a right to the equal use of accommodations held out to the public, it is a right of citizenship and a constitutional right under the 14th amendment. It has nothing to do with whether a business is in interstate commerce. . . ."

The rationale for these arguments, however, extended from previous Supreme Court rulings in relation to the 14th amendment, with the southern Senators assuming that the bill, if so based, would be held unconstitutional. Thus, their noble support of "constitutional principle" masked their racist purpose of continuing "Jim Crow" and segregation. In the *Slaughter House Cases*, 10 Wall. 36 (1873), discussed infra, the Court had limited application of the equal protection clause to only those circumstances where there had been "state action." The 1883 Act, for example, had been held unconstitutional because the attempt to reach "public accommodations" that were in private hands lacked "state action." Though the state action limitation had been somewhat broadened by 1964, it had none the less remained as a prerequisite for application of the equal protection clause. Viewed in this light, the 1964 Act attempted to reach "private" discrimination, and there was fear amongst supporters of the bill that basing it upon the 14th amendment might lead to the Court declaring the legislation unconstitutional. Given the broad reach of Commerce Clause jurisprudence, the Act's supporters embraced the commerce power to support the enactment. The ignoble opponents of the bill argued for the 14th amendment, in hope that it would be declared unconstitutional.

Mr. Burke Marshall (Assistant Attorney General, Civil Rights Division) seemed to admit such in the hearing when he concluded, "Senator, I think it would be a mistake to rely solely on the 14th amendment. This bill . . . relies on the 14th amendment, and also relies on the Commerce Clause. I think if it relied solely on the 14th amendment, it might not be held constitutional." Attorney General Robert Kennedy, in supporting the bill before the Committee, and after admitting possible problems with the 14th amendment approach, argued for the Commerce Clause and stated, "Senator, I think that there is an injustice that needs to be remedied. We have to find the tools with which to remedy that injustice. . . . We need to obtain a remedy. The commerce clause will obtain a remedy and there won't be a problem about the constitutionality. . . ." Kennedy also argued, in support of the statute and the Court's commerce clause decisional law, that "I think that the discrimination that is taking place at the present time is having a very adverse effect on our economy."

The bill, when adopted, laid a clear predicate for application of the commerce clause, though it was based upon both constitutional provisions. Should Congress frame legislation based upon the Supreme Court's interpretation of the Constitution, or their own? In the sense of "separation of powers" and "advisory opinions," what are the ramifications of each approach, or is the matter likely to be resolved, as Attorney General Kennedy suggests, by "practical realities."

Levy, in "The Supreme Court — Minority Rights and Principled Adjudication," 2 Tex.So.L.Rev. 208 (1972), forewarned of the possibility that since the principled basis for the statute, the 14th amendment, had been bypassed for the "convenience of the Commerce power," that a Court at any given time could assert that "civil rights" were not "commerce" and void the legislation as *beyond* the reach of the Commerce Clause. Is this exactly what occurred in *United States v. Lopez,* 514 U.S. 549 (1995), supra, or can the cases below be distinguished from *Lopez*?

In the cases that follow, the Court reviewed the constitutionality of the Act as based upon the Commerce Clause. In *Heart of Atlanta* the Court responded to the debates in Congress, specifically in relation to Title II, Sec. 201(b)1, making discrimination in the denial of facilities in inns, hotels, and motels, on the grounds of race, unconstitutional. In the companion case, *Katzenbach v. McClung*, the Court reviewed Section 201(b)2, which guaranteed the same as above in relation to establishments such as restaurants and lunchrooms.

HEART OF ATLANTA MOTEL v. UNITED STATES
379 U.S. 241 (1964)

Mr. Justice CLARK delivered the opinion of the Court

The case comes here on admissions and stipulated facts. Appellant owns and operates the Heart of Atlanta Motel which has 216 rooms available to transient guests. The motel is located on Courtland Street, two blocks from downtown Peachtree Street. It is readily accessible to interstate highways 75 and 85 and state highways 23 and 41. Appellant solicits patronage from outside the State of Georgia through various national advertising media, including magazines of national circulation; it maintains over 50 billboards and highway signs within the State, soliciting patronage for the motel; it accepts convention trade from outside Georgia and approximately 75% of its registered guests are from out of State. Prior to passage of the Act the motel had followed a practice of refusing to rent rooms to Negroes, and it alleged that it intended to continue to do so. In an effort to perpetuate that policy this suit was filed.

The appellant contends that Congress in passing this Act exceeded its power to regulate commerce under Art. I, § 8, cl. 3, of the Constitution of the United States; that the Act violates the Fifth Amendment because appellant is deprived of the right to choose its customers and operate its business as it wishes, resulting in a taking of its liberty and property without due process of law and a taking of its property without just compensation; and, finally, that by requiring appellant to rent available rooms to Negroes against its will, Congress is subjecting it to involuntary servitude in contravention of the Thirteenth Amendment.

The appellees counter that the unavailability to Negroes of adequate accommodations interferes significantly with interstate travel, and that Congress, under the Commerce Clause, has power to remove such obstructions and restraints; that the Fifth Amendment does not forbid reasonable regulation and that consequential damage does not constitute a "taking" within the meaning of that amendment; that the Thirteenth Amendment claim fails because it is entirely frivolous to say that an amendment directed to the abolition of human bondage and the removal of widespread disabilities associated with slavery places discrimination in public accommodations, beyond the reach of both federal and state law.

At the trial the appellant offered no evidence, submitting the case on the pleadings, admissions and stipulation of facts; however, appellees proved the refusal of the motel to accept Negro transients after the passage of the Act. The District Court sustained the constitutionality of the sections of the Act under attack (§§ 201(a), (b)(1) and (c)(1)) and issued a permanent injunction on the counterclaim of the appellees. It restrained the appellant from "[r]efusing to accept Negroes as guests in the motel by reason of their race or color" and from "[m]aking any distinction whatever upon the basis of race or color in the availability of the goods, services, facilities privileges, advantages or accommodations offered or made available to the guests of the motel, or to the general public, within or upon any of the premises of the Heart of Atlanta Motel, Inc."

It is admitted that the operation of the motel brings it within the provisions of § 201(a) of the Act and that appellant refused to provide lodging for transient Negroes because of their race or color and that it intends to continue that policy unless restrained.

The sole question posed is, therefore, the constitutionality of the Civil Rights Act of 1964 as applied to these facts. The legislative history of the Act indicates that Congress based the Act on § 5 and the Equal Protection Clause of the Fourteenth Amendment as well as its power to regulate interstate commerce under Art. I, § 8, cl. 3, of the Constitution.

The Senate Commerce Committee made it quite clear that the fundamental object of Title II was to vindicate "the deprivation of personal dignity that surely accompanies denials of equal access to public establishments." At the same time, however, it noted that such an objective has been and could be readily achieved "by congressional action based on the commerce power of the Constitution." S.Rep. No. 872, supra, at 16-17. Our study of the legislative record, made in the light of prior cases, has brought us to the conclusion that Congress possessed ample power in this regard, and we have therefore not considered the other grounds relied upon. This is not to say that the remaining authority upon which it acted was not adequate, a question upon which we do not pass, but merely that since the commerce power is sufficient for our decision here we have considered it alone. Nor is § 201(d) or § 202, having to do with state action, involved here and we do not pass upon either of those sections. 5. The Civil Rights Cases, 109 U.S. 3, 3 S.Ct. 18 (1883), and their Application.

While the Act as adopted carried no congressional findings the record of its passage through each house is replete with evidence of the burdens that discrimination by race or color places upon interstate commerce. See Hearings before Senate Committee on Commerce on S. 1732, 88th Cong., 1st Sess.; S.Rep. No. 872, supra; Hearings before Senate Committee on the Judiciary on S. 1731, 88th Cong., 1st Sess.; Hearings before House Subcommittee No. 5 of the Committee on the Judiciary on miscellaneous proposals regarding Civil Rights, 88th Cong., 1st Sess., ser. 4; H.R.Rep. No. 914, supra. This testimony included the fact that our people have become increasingly mobile with millions of people of all races traveling from State to State; that Negroes in particular have been the subject of discrimination in transient accommodations, having to travel great distances to secure the same; that often they have been unable to obtain accommodations and have had to call upon friends to put them up overnight, S.Rep. No. 872, supra, at 14-22; and that these conditions had become so acute as to require the listing of available lodging for Negroes in a special guidebook which was itself 'dramatic testimony to the difficulties' Negroes encounter in travel. Senate Commerce Committee Hearings, supra, at 692-694. These exclusionary practices were found to be nationwide, the Under Secretary of Commerce testifying that there is "no question that this discrimination in the North still exists to a large degree" and in the West and Midwest as well. Id., at 735, 744. This testimony indicated a qualitative as well as quantitative effect on interstate travel by Negroes. The former was the obvious impairment of the Negro traveler's pleasure and convenience that resulted when he continually was uncertain of finding lodging. As for the latter, there was evidence that this uncertainty stemming from racial discrimination had the effect of discouraging travel on the part of a substantial portion of the Negro community.

[T]he determinative test of the exercise of power by the Congress under the Commerce Clause is simply whether the activity sought to be regulated is "commerce which concerns more States than one" and has a real and substantial relation to the national interest.

The same interest in protecting interstate commerce which led Congress to deal with segregation in interstate carriers and the white-slave traffic has prompted it to extend the exercise of its power to gambling, Lottery Case (Champion v Ames), 188 U.S. 321, 23 S.Ct. 321, 47 L.Ed. 492 (1903); to criminal enterprises, Brooks v. United States, 267 U.S. 432, 45 S.Ct. 345, 69 L.Ed. 699 (1925); to deceptive practices in the sale of products, Federal Trade Comm. v. Mandel Bros., Inc., 359 U.S. 385, 79 S.Ct. 818, 3 L.Ed.2d 893 (1959); to fraudulent security transactions, Securities & Exchange Comm. v. Ralston Purina Co., 346 U.S. 119, 73 S.Ct. 981, 97 L.Ed. 1494 (1953); to misbranding of drugs,

Weeks v. United States, 245 U.S. 618, 38 S.Ct. 219, 62 L.Ed. 513 (1918); to wages and hours, United States v. Darby, 312 U.S. 100, 657, 61 S.Ct. 451, 85 L.Ed. 609 (1941); to members of labor unions, National Labor Relations Board v. Jones & Laughlin Steel Corp., 301 U.S. 1, 57 S.Ct. 615, 81 L.Ed. 893 (1937); to crop control, Wickard v. Filburn, 317 U.S. 111, 63 S.Ct. 82, 87 L.Ed. 122 (1942); to discrimination against shippers, United States v. Baltimore & Ohio R. Co., 333 U.S. 169, 68 S.Ct. 494, 92 L.Ed. 618 (1948); to the protection of small business from injurious price cutting, Moore v. Mead's Fine Bread Co., 348 U.S. 115, 75 S.Ct. 148, 99 L.Ed. 145 (1954); to resale price maintenance, Hudson Distributors, Inc. v. Eli Lilly & Co., 377 U.S. 386, 84 S.Ct. 1273, 12 L.Ed.2d 394 (1964), Schwegmann Bros. v. Calvert Distillers Corp., 341 U.S. 384, 71 S.Ct. 745, 95 L.Ed. 1035 (1951); to professional football, Radovich v. National Football League, 352 U.S. 445, 77 S.Ct. 390, 1 L.Ed.2d 456 (1957); and to racial discrimination by owners and managers of terminal restaurants, Boynton v. Com. of Virginia, 364 U.S. 454, 81 S.Ct. 182, 5 L.Ed.2d 206 (1960).

That Congress was legislating against moral wrongs in many of these areas rendered its enactments no less valid. In framing Title II of this Act Congress was also dealing with what it considered a moral problem. But that fact does not detract from the overwhelming evidence of the disruptive effect that racial discrimination has had on commercial intercourse. It was this burden which empowered Congress to enact appropriate legislation, and, given this basis for the exercise of its power, Congress was not restricted by the fact that the particular obstruction to interstate commerce with which it was dealing was also deemed a moral and social wrong.

It is said that the operation of the motel here is of a purely local character. But, assuming this to be true, "[i]f it is interstate commerce that feels the pinch, it does not matter how local the operation which applies the squeeze." United States v. Women's Sportswear Mfg. Ass'n, 336 U.S. 460, 464, 69 S.Ct. 714, 716, 93 L.Ed. 805 (1949). See National Labor Relations Board v. Jones & Laughlin Steel Corp., supra. As Chief Justice Stone put it in United States v. Darby, supra: "The power of Congress over interstate commerce is not confined to the regulation of commerce among the states. It extends to those activities intrastate which so affect interstate commerce or the exercise of the power of Congress over it as to make regulation of them appropriate means to the attainment of a legitimate end, the exercise of the granted power of Congress to regulate interstate commerce. See McCulloch v. Maryland, 4 Wheat. 316, 421, 4 L.Ed. 579." 312 U.S. at 118, 61 S.Ct. at 459.

Thus the power of Congress to promote interstate commerce also includes the power to regulate the local incidents thereof, including local activities in both the States of origin and destination, which might have a substantial and harmful effect upon that commerce. One need only examine the evidence which we have discussed above to see that Congress may — as it has — prohibit racial discrimination by motels serving travelers, however "local" their operations may appear.

KATZENBACH v. McCLUNG
379 U.S. 294 (1964)

Mr. Justice CLARK delivered the opinion of the Court.

This case was argued with No. 515, Heart of Atlanta Motel v. United States, decided this date, 379 U.S. 241, 85 S.Ct. 348, in which we upheld the constitutional validity of Title

II of the Civil Rights Act of 1964 against an attack no hotels, motels, and like establishments. This complaint for injunctive relief against appellants attacks the constitutionality of the Act as applied to a restaurant. [An] injunction was issued restraining appellants from enforcing the Act against the restaurant. 233 F.Supp. 815. We now reverse the judgment.

Ollie's Barbecue is a family-owned restaurant in Birmingham, Alabama, specializing in barbecued meats and homemade pies, with a seating capacity of 220 customers. It is located on a state highway 11 blocks from an interstate one and a somewhat greater distance from railroad and bus stations. The restaurant caters to a family and white-collar trade with a take-out service for Negroes. It employs 36 persons, two-thirds of whom are Negroes.

In the 12 months preceding the passage of the Act, the restaurant purchased locally approximately $150,000 worth of food, $69,683 or 46% of which was meat that it bought from a local supplier who had procured it from outside the State. The District Court expressly found that a substantial portion of the food served in the restaurant had moved in interstate commerce. The restaurant has refused to serve Negroes in its dining accommodations since its original opening in 1927, and since July 2, 1964, it has been operating in violation of the Act. The court below concluded that if it were required to serve Negroes it would lose a substantial amount of business.

[Sections] 201(b)(2) and (c) place any "restaurant . . . principally engaged in selling food for consumption on the premises' under the Act 'if . . . it serves or offers to serve interstate travelers or a substantial portion of the food which it serves . . . has moved in commerce."

Ollie's Barbecue admits that it is covered by these provisions of the Act. The Government makes no contention that the discrimination at the restaurant was supported by the State of Alabama. There is no claim that interstate travelers frequented the restaurant. The sole question, therefore, narrows down to whether Title II, as applied to a restaurant annually receiving about $70,000 worth of food which has moved in commerce, is a valid exercise of the power of Congress. The Government has contended that Congress had ample basis upon which to find that racial discrimination at restaurants which receive from out of state a substantial portion of the food served does, in fact, impose commercial burdens of national magnitude upon interstate commerce. The appellees' major argument is directed to this premise. They urge that no such basis existed.

4. THE CONGRESSIONAL HEARINGS

As we noted in Heart of Atlanta Motel both Houses of Congress conducted prolonged hearings on the Act. And, as we said there, while no formal findings were made, which of course are not necessary, it is well that we make mention of the testimony at these hearings the better to understand the problem before Congress and determine whether the Act is a reasonable and appropriate means toward its solution. The record is replete with testimony of the burdens placed on interstate commerce by racial discrimination in restaurants. A comparison of per capita spending by Negroes in restaurants, theaters, and like establishments indicated less spending, after discounting income differences, in areas where discrimination is widely practiced. This condition, which was especially aggravated in the South, was attributed in the testimony of the Under Secretary of Commerce to racial segregation. See Hearings before the Senate Committee on Commerce on S. 1732, 88th Cong., 1st Sess., 695. This diminutive spending springing from a refusal to serve Negroes and their total loss as customers has, regardless of the absence of direct evidence, a close connection to interstate commerce. The fewer customers a restaurant enjoys the less food it sells and consequently the less it buys. S.Rep. No. 872, 88th Cong., 2d Sess., at 19; Senate Commerce Committee Hearings, at 207. In addition, the Attorney General testified that this type of discrimination imposed "an artificial restriction on the market" and interfered with the flow of merchandise. Id., at 18-19; also, on this point, see testimony of Senator Magnuson, 110 Cong.Rec. 7402-7403. In addition, there were many references to discriminatory situations causing wide unrest and having a depressant effect on general business conditions in the respective communities. See, e.g., Senate Commerce Committee Hearings, at 623-630, 695-700, 1384-1385.

Moreover there was an impressive array of testimony that discrimination in restaurants had a direct and highly restrictive effect upon interstate travel by Negroes. This resulted, it was said, because discriminatory practices prevent Negroes from buying prepared food served on the premises while on a trip, except in isolated and unkempt restaurants and under most unsatisfactory and often unpleasant conditions. This obviously discourages travel and obstructs interstate commerce for one can hardly travel without eating. Likewise, it was said, that discrimination deterred professional, as well as skilled, people from moving into areas where such practices occurred and thereby caused industry to be reluctant to establish there. S.Rep. No. 872, supra, at 18-19.

We believe that this testimony afforded ample basis for the conclusion that established restaurants in such areas sold less interstate goods because of the discrimination, that interstate travel was obstructed directly by it, that business in general suffered and that many new businesses refrained from establishing there as a result of it. Hence the District Court was in error in concluding that there was no connection between discrimination and the movement of interstate commerce. The court's conclusion that such a connection is outside "common experience" flies in the face of stubborn fact.

It goes without saying that, viewed in isolation, the volume of food purchased by Ollie's Barbecue from sources supplied from out of state was insignificant when compared with the total foodstuffs moving in commerce. But, as our late Brother Jackson said for the Court in Wickard v. Filburn, 317 U.S. 111, 63 S.Ct. 82, 87 L.Ed. 122 (1942): "That appellee's own contribution to the demand for wheat may be trivial by itself is not enough to remove him from the scope of federal regulation where, as here, his contribution, taken together with that of many others similarly situated, is far from trivial." At 127-128, 63 S.Ct. at 90. We noted in Heart of Atlanta Motel that a number of witnesses attested to the fact that racial discrimination was not merely a state or regional problem but was one of nationwide scope. Against this background, we must conclude that while the focus of the legislation was on the individual restaurant's relation to interstate commerce, Congress appropriately considered the importance of that connection with the knowledge that the discrimination was but "representative of many others throughout the country, the total incidence of which if left unchecked may well become far-reaching in its harm to commerce." Polish National Alliance of U.S. v. National Labor Relations Board, 322 U.S. 643, 648, 64 S.Ct. 1196, 1199, 88 L.Ed. 1509 (1944).

With this situation spreading as the record shows, Congress was not required to await the total dislocation of commerce. [Much] is said about a restaurant business being local but "even if appellee's activity be local and though it may not be regarded as commerce, it may still, whatever its nature, be reached by Congress if it exerts a substantial economic effect on interstate commerce. . . ."

The appellees contend that Congress has arbitrarily created a conclusive presumption that all restaurants meeting the criteria set out in the Act "affect commerce." Stated another way, they object to the omission of a provision for a case-by-case determination — judicial or administrative — that racial discrimination in a particular restaurant affects commerce.

But Congress' action in framing this Act was not unprecedented. In United States v. Darby, 312 U.S. 100, 657, 61 S.Ct. 451, 85 L.Ed. 609 (1941), this Court held constitutional the Fair Labor Standards Act of 1938. There Congress determined that the payment of substandard wages to employees engaged in the production of goods for commerce, while not itself commerce, so inhibited it as to be subject to federal regulation. The appellees in that case argued, as do the appellees here, that the Act was invalid because it included no provision for an independent inquiry regarding the effect on commerce of substandard wages in a particular business. (Brief for appellees, pp. 76-77, United States v. Darby, 312 U.S. 100, 657, 61 S.Ct. 451, 85 L.Ed. 609.) But the Court rejected the argument, observing that:

> "[S]ometimes Congress itself has said that a particular activity affects the commerce, as it did in the present Act, the Safety Appliance Act . . . and the Railway Labor Act . . . .. In passing on the validity of legislation of the class last mentioned the only function of courts is to determine whether the particular activity regulated or prohibited is within the reach of the federal power." At 120-121, 61 S.Ct. at 460.

Here, as there, Congress has determined for itself that refusals of service to Negroes have imposed burdens both upon the interstate flow of food and upon the movement of products generally. Of course, the mere fact that Congress has said when particular activity shall be deemed to affect commerce does not preclude further examination by this Court. But where we find that the legislators, in light of the facts and testimony before them, have a rational basis for finding a chosen regulatory scheme necessary to the protection of commerce, our investigation is at an end. The only remaining question — one answered in the affirmative by the court below — is whether the particular restaurant either serves or offers to serve interstate travelers or serves food a substantial portion of which has moved in interstate commerce.

The appellees urge that Congress, in passing the Fair Labor Standards Act and the National Labor Relations Act, made specific findings which were embodied in those statutes. Here, of course, Congress had included no formal findings. But their absence is not fatal to the validity of the statute, see United States v. Carolene Products Co., 304 U.S. 144, 152, 58 S.Ct. 778, 783, 82 L.Ed. 1234 (1938), for the evidence presented at the hearings fully indicated the nature and effect of the burdens on commerce which Congress meant to alleviate.

Confronted as we are with the facts laid before Congress, we must conclude that it had a rational basis for finding that racial discrimination in restaurants had a direct and adverse effect on the free flow of interstate commerce. [We] think in so doing that Congress acted well within its power to protect and foster commerce in extending the coverage of Title II only to those restaurants offering to serve interstate travelers or serving food, a substantial portion of which has moved in interstate commerce.

The absence of direct evidence connecting discriminatory restaurant service with the flow of interstate food, a factor on which the appellees place much reliance, is not, given the evidence as to the effect of such practices on other aspects of commerce, a crucial matter.

The power of Congress in this field is broad and sweeping; where it keeps within its sphere and violates no express constitutional limitation it has been the rule of this Court, going back almost to the founding days of the Republic, not to interfere. The Civil Rights Act of 1964, as here applied, we find to be plainly appropriate in the resolution of what the Congress found to be a national commercial problem of the first magnitude. Reversed.

———

Comments on *Heart of Atlanta* and *Katzenbach*. Why the companion case? What is the purpose in reviewing the statute in both cases? Would the Court have reached the same result in *Katzenbach* if all the "meat" was "intrastate"?

A new day and a new look at the Civil Rights Act of 1964. The October 2019 term saw a long awaited interpretation of the Civil Rights Act of 1964's prohibition of discrimination on the basis of sex and its applicability to discrimination in both public (based on the Equal Protection Clause) and private sectors (based on the Commerce Clause). Justice Gorsuch writing for the Court in *Bostock v. Clayton County Georgia*, 590 U.S.___(2020) reasoned that despite the fact that LGBT rights were likely not within the contemplation of the Congress which passed the law, the language dictates that discriminatory hiring and work condition decisions based on the sex of an individual for a sexual orientation or gender identity that would be acceptable for a person of the opposite sex is sex discrimination prohibited by the act. Perhaps put more simply, to refuse to hire or retain a man whose orientation is to have intimate romantic or sexual relations with other men but not treat a woman with the same orientation toward men is discrimination on the basis of sex. Or to put it in "Court-speak":

> "From the ordinary public meaning of the statute's language at the time of the law's adoption, a straightforward rule emerges: An employer violates Title VII when it intentionally fires an individual employee based in part on sex. It doesn't matter if other factors besides the plaintiff's sex contributed to the decision. And it doesn't matter if the employer treated women as a group the same when compared to men as a group. If the employer intentionally relies in part on an individual employee's sex when deciding to discharge the employee—put differently, if changing the employee's sex would have yielded a different choice by the employer—a statutory violation has occurred. Title VII's message is 'simple but momentous': An individual employee's sex is 'not relevant to the selection, evaluation, or compensation of employees.'"

F. LIMITS ON THE COMMERCE POWER IN THE MODERN ERA

United States v. Lopez may have been the first significant denial of federal power under the Commerce Clause in more than forty years, but it was not the Rehnquist Court's first attempt in advancing "state sovereignty" against federal authority. This story is told in section G below, which discusses the Court's attempt to limit the reach of the commerce power against the states in *National League of Cities v. Usery* (Chapter 2, infra) and was eventually overruled in *Garcia v. San Antonio Metropolotian Transit Authority* (Chapter 2, infra). Chief Justice Rehnquist, who wrote the opinion for the 5-4 majority in *National League*, commented in his *Garcia* dissent, while asserting his displeasure with the overrule, "I do not think it incumbent on those of us in dissent to spell out further the fine points of a principle that will, I am confident, in time again command the support of a majority of this Court." Is *Lopez* such a case?

UNITED STATES v. LOPEZ
514 U.S. 549 (1995)

Chief Justice REHNQUIST delivered the opinion of the Court.

In the Gun-Free School Zones Act of 1990, Congress made it a federal offense "for any individual knowingly to possess a firearm at a place that the individual knows, or has reasonable cause to believe, is a school zone." 18 U.S.C. § 922(q)(1)(A) (1988 ed., Supp. V). The Act neither regulates a commercial activity nor contains a requirement that the possession be connected in any way to interstate commerce. We hold that the Act exceeds the authority of Congress "[t]o regulate Commerce . . . among the several States. . . ." U.S. Const., Art. I, § 8, cl. 3.

On March 10, 1992, respondent, who was then a 12th-grade student, arrived at Edison High School in San Antonio, Texas, carrying a concealed .38-caliber handgun and five bullets. The Court of Appeals reversed, ruling that the law was beyond the reach of the commerce power. We now affirm.

[We] start with first principles. The Constitution creates a Federal Government of enumerated powers. See Art. I, § 8. As James Madison wrote: "The powers delegated by the proposed Constitution to the federal government are few and defined. Those which are to remain in the State governments are numerous and indefinite." The Federalist No. 45, pp. 292-293 (C. Rossiter ed. 1961). This constitutionally mandated division of authority "was adopted by the Framers to ensure protection of our fundamental liberties.

[The] Constitution delegates to Congress the power "[t]o regulate Commerce with foreign Nations, and among the several States, and with the Indian Tribes." Art. I, § 8, cl. 3. The Court, through Chief Justice Marshall, first defined the nature of Congress' commerce power in Gibbons v. Ogden, 9 Wheat. 1, 189-190, 6 L.Ed. 23 (1824):

> "Commerce, undoubtedly, is traffic, but it is something more: it is intercourse. It describes the commercial intercourse between nations, and parts of nations, in all its branches, and is regulated by prescribing rules for carrying on that intercourse."

The commerce power "is the power to regulate; that is, to prescribe the rule by which commerce is to be governed. This power, like all others vested in congress, is complete in itself, may be exercised to its utmost extent, and acknowledges no limitations, other than are prescribed in the constitution." Id., at 196. The Gibbons Court, however, acknowledged that limitations on the commerce power are inherent in the very language of the Commerce Clause:

> "It is not intended to say that these words comprehend that commerce, which is completely internal, which is carried on between man and man in a State, or between different parts of the same State, and which does not extend to or affect other States. Such a power would be inconvenient, and is certainly unnecessary."

> "Comprehensive as the word 'among' is, it may very properly be restricted to that commerce which concerns more States than one. . . . The enumeration presupposes something not enumerated; and that something, if we regard the language, or the subject of the sentence, must be the exclusively internal commerce of a State." Id., at 194-195.

For nearly a century thereafter, the Court's Commerce Clause decisions dealt but rarely with the extent of Congress' power, and almost entirely with the Commerce Clause as a limit on state legislation that discriminated against interstate commerce. Under this line of precedent, the Court held that certain categories of activity such as "production," "manufacturing," and "mining" were within the province of state governments, and thus were beyond the power of Congress under the Commerce Clause. See Wickard v. Filburn, 317 U.S. 111, 121, 63 S.Ct. 82, 87, 87 L.Ed. 122 (1942) (describing development of Commerce Clause jurisprudence).

In 1887, Congress enacted the Interstate Commerce Act, 24 Stat. 379, and in 1890, Congress enacted the Sherman Antitrust Act, 26 Stat. 209, as amended, 15 U.S.C. § 1 *et seq.* These laws ushered in a new era of federal regulation under the commerce power. When cases involving these laws first reached this Court, we imported from our negative Commerce Clause cases the approach that Congress could not regulate activities such as "production," "manufacturing," and "mining." See, *e.g.,* United States v. E.C. Knight Co., 156 U.S. 1, 12, 15 S.Ct. 249, 253-254, 39 L.Ed. 325 (1895) ("Commerce succeeds to manufacture, and is not part of it"); Carter v. Carter Coal Co., 298 U.S. 238, 304, 56 S.Ct. 855, 869, 80 L.Ed. 1160 (1936) ("Mining brings the subject matter of commerce into existence. Commerce disposes of it"). Simultaneously, however, the Court held that, where the interstate and intrastate aspects of commerce were so mingled together that full regulation of interstate commerce required incidental regulation of intrastate commerce, the Commerce Clause authorized such regulation. See, *e.g.,* Shreveport Rate Cases, 234 U.S. 342, 34 S.Ct. 833, 58 L.Ed. 1341 (1914).

In A.L.A. Schechter Poultry Corp. v. United States, 295 U.S. 495, 550, 55 S.Ct. 837, 851-52, 79 L.Ed. 1570 (1935), the Court struck down regulations that fixed the hours and wages of individuals employed by an intrastate business because the activity being regulated related to interstate commerce only indirectly. In doing so, the Court characterized the distinction between direct and indirect effects of intrastate transactions upon interstate commerce as "a fundamental one, essential to the maintenance of our constitutional system." Id., at 548, 55 S.Ct., at 851. Activities that affected interstate commerce directly were within Congress' power; activities that affected interstate commerce indirectly were beyond Congress' reach. Id., at 546, 55 S.Ct., at 850. The justification for this formal distinction was rooted in the fear that otherwise "there would be virtually no limit to the federal power and for all practical purposes we should have a completely centralized government." Id., at 548, 55 S.Ct., at 851.

Two years later, in the watershed case of NLRB v. Jones & Laughlin Steel Corp., 301 U.S. 1, 57 S.Ct. 615, 81 L.Ed. 893 (1937), the Court upheld the National Labor Relations Act against a Commerce Clause challenge, and in the process, departed from the distinction between "direct" and "indirect" effects on interstate commerce. Id., at 36-38, 57 S.Ct., at 623-624 ("The question [of the scope of Congress' power] is necessarily one of degree"). The Court held that intrastate activities that "have such a close and substantial relation to interstate commerce that their control is essential or appropriate to protect that commerce from burdens and obstructions" are within Congress' power to regulate. Id., at 37, 57 S.Ct., at 624.

In United States v. Darby, 312 U.S. 100, 61 S.Ct. 451, 85 L.Ed. 609 (1941), the Court upheld the Fair Labor Standards Act, stating:

> "The power of Congress over interstate commerce is not confined to the regulation of commerce among the states. It extends to those activities intrastate which so affect interstate commerce or the exercise of the power of Congress over it as to make regulation

of them appropriate means to the attainment of a legitimate end, the exercise of the granted power of Congress to regulate interstate commerce." Id., at 118, 61 S.Ct., at 459.

[In] Wickard v. Filburn, the Court upheld the application of amendments to the Agricultural Adjustment Act of 1938 to the production and consumption of homegrown wheat. 317 U.S., at 128-129, 63 S.Ct., at 90-91. The Wickard Court explicitly rejected earlier distinctions between direct and indirect effects on interstate commerce, stating:

> "[E]ven if appellee's activity be local and though it may not be regarded as commerce, it may still, whatever its nature, be reached by Congress if it exerts a substantial economic effect on interstate commerce, and this irrespective of whether such effect is what might at some earlier time have been defined as 'direct' or 'indirect.'" Id., at 125, 63 S.Ct., at 89.

The Wickard Court emphasized that although Filburn's own contribution to the demand for wheat may have been trivial by itself, that was not "enough to remove him from the scope of federal regulation where, as here, his contribution, taken together with that of many others similarly situated, is far from trivial." Id., at 127-128, 63 S.Ct., at 90-91.

Jones & Laughlin Steel, Darby, and Wickard ushered in an era of Commerce Clause jurisprudence that greatly expanded the previously defined authority of Congress under that Clause. In part, this was a recognition of the great changes that had occurred in the way business was carried on in this country. Enterprises that had once been local or at most regional in nature had become national in scope. But the doctrinal change also reflected a view that earlier Commerce Clause cases artificially had constrained the authority of Congress to regulate interstate commerce.

But even these modern-era precedents which have expanded congressional power under the Commerce Clause confirm that this power is subject to outer limits. In Jones & Laughlin Steel, the Court warned that the scope of the interstate commerce power "must be considered in the light of our dual system of government and may not be extended so as to embrace effects upon interstate commerce so indirect and remote that to embrace them, in view of our complex society, would effectually obliterate the distinction between what is national and what is local and create a completely centralized government." 301 U.S., at 37, 57 S.Ct., at 624; see also Darby, supra, 312 U.S., at 119-120, 61 S.Ct., at 459-460 (Congress may regulate intrastate activity that has a "substantial effect" on interstate commerce); Wickard, supra, at 125, 63 S.Ct., at 89 (Congress may regulate activity that "exerts a substantial economic effect on interstate commerce"). Since that time, the Court has heeded that warning and undertaken to decide whether a rational basis existed for concluding that a regulated activity sufficiently affected interstate commerce.

[Similarly], in Maryland v. Wirtz, 392 U.S. 183, 88 S.Ct. 2017, 20 L.Ed.2d 1020 (1968), the Court reaffirmed that "the power to regulate commerce, though broad indeed, has limits" that "[t]he Court has ample power" to enforce. In response to the dissent's warnings that the Court was powerless to enforce the limitations on Congress' commerce powers because "[a]ll activities affecting commerce, even in the minutest degree, [Wickard], may be regulated and controlled by Congress," (Douglas, J., dissenting), the Wirtz Court replied that the dissent had misread precedent as "[n]either here nor in Wickard has the Court declared that Congress may use a relatively trivial impact on commerce as an excuse for broad general regulation of state or private activities," Rather, "[t]he Court has said only that where *a general regulatory statute bears a substantial relation to commerce,* the *de minimis* character of individual instances arising under that statute is of no consequence."

Consistent with this structure, we have identified three broad categories of activity that Congress may regulate under its commerce power. First, Congress may regulate the use of the channels of interstate commerce. See, *e.g.,* Darby, 312 U.S., at 114, 61 S.Ct., at 457; Heart of Atlanta Motel, supra, at 256, 85 S.Ct., at 357 Second, Congress is empowered to regulate and protect the instrumentalities of interstate commerce, or persons or things in interstate commerce, even though the threat may come only from intrastate activities. Finally, Congress' commerce authority includes the power to regulate those activities having a substantial relation to interstate commerce, Jones & Laughlin Steel, 301 U.S., at 37, 57 S.Ct., at 624, *i.e.,* those activities that substantially affect interstate commerce, Wirtz, supra, at 196, n. 27, 88 S.Ct., at 2024, n. 27.

Within this final category, admittedly, our case law has not been clear whether an activity must "affect" or "substantially affect" interstate commerce in order to be within Congress' power to regulate it under the Commerce Clause. We conclude, consistent with the great weight of our case law, that the proper test requires an analysis of whether the regulated activity "substantially affects" interstate commerce.

We now turn to consider the power of Congress, in the light of this framework, to enact § 922(q). The first two categories of authority may be quickly disposed of: § 922(q) is not a regulation of the use of the channels of interstate commerce, nor is it an attempt to prohibit the interstate transportation of a commodity through the channels of commerce; nor can § 922(q) be justified as a regulation by which Congress has sought to protect an instrumentality of interstate commerce or a thing in interstate commerce. Thus, if § 922(q) is to be sustained, it must be under the third category as a regulation of an activity that substantially affects interstate commerce.

First, we have upheld a wide variety of congressional Acts regulating intrastate economic activity where we have concluded that the activity substantially affected interstate commerce. Examples include the regulation of intrastate coal mining; intrastate extortionate credit transactions, restaurants utilizing substantial interstate supplies, inns and hotels catering to interstate guests, and production and consumption of homegrown wheat. These examples are by no means exhaustive, but the pattern is clear. Where economic activity substantially affects interstate commerce, legislation regulating that activity will be sustained.

Even Wickard, which is perhaps the most far reaching example of Commerce Clause authority over intrastate activity, involved economic activity in a way that the possession of a gun in a school zone does not.

Section 922(q) is a criminal statute that by its terms has nothing to do with "commerce" or any sort of economic enterprise, however broadly one might define those terms. Section 922(q) is not an essential part of a larger regulation of economic activity, in which the regulatory scheme could be undercut unless the intrastate activity were regulated. It cannot, therefore, be sustained under our cases upholding regulations of activities that arise out of or are connected with a commercial transaction, which viewed in the aggregate, substantially affects interstate commerce.

Second, § 922(q) contains no jurisdictional element which would ensure, through case-by-case inquiry, that the firearm possession in question affects interstate commerce. For example, in United States v. Bass, 404 U.S. 336, 92 S.Ct. 515, 30 L.Ed.2d 488 (1971), the Court interpreted former 18 U.S.C. § 1202(a), which made it a crime for a felon to "receiv[e], posses[s], or transpor[t] in commerce or affecting commerce . . . any firearm."

The Court interpreted the possession component of § 1202(a) to require an additional nexus to interstate commerce both because the statute was ambiguous and because "unless Congress conveys its purpose clearly, it will not be deemed to have significantly changed the federal-state balance." Id., at 349, 92 S.Ct., at 523. The Bass Court set aside the conviction because, although the Government had demonstrated that Bass had possessed a firearm, it had failed "to show the requisite nexus with interstate commerce." Id., at 347, 92 S.Ct., at 522. The Court thus interpreted the statute to reserve the constitutional question whether Congress could regulate, without more, the "mere possession" of firearms. See id., at 339, n. 4, 92 S.Ct., at 518, n. 4; see also United States v. Five Gambling Devices, 346 U.S. 441, 448, 74 S.Ct. 190, 194, 98 L.Ed. 179 (1953) (plurality opinion) ("The principle is old and deeply imbedded in our jurisprudence that this Court will construe a statute in a manner that requires decision of serious constitutional questions only if the statutory language leaves no reasonable alternative"). Unlike the statute in Bass, § 922(q) has no express jurisdictional element which might limit its reach to a discrete set of firearm possessions that additionally have an explicit connection with or effect on interstate commerce.

Although as part of our independent evaluation of constitutionality under the Commerce Clause we of course consider legislative findings, and indeed even congressional committee findings, regarding effect on interstate commerce, see, e.g., Preseault v. ICC, 494 U.S., at 17, 110 S.Ct., at 924-925, (1990), the Government concedes that "[n]either the statute nor its legislative history contain[s] express congressional findings regarding the effects upon interstate commerce of gun possession in a school zone." We agree with the Government that Congress normally is not required to make formal findings as to the substantial burdens that an activity has on interstate commerce. But to the extent that congressional findings would enable us to evaluate the legislative judgment that the activity in question substantially affected interstate commerce, even though no such substantial effect was visible to the naked eye, they are lacking here.

[The] Government's essential contention, in fine, is that we may determine here that § 922(q) is valid because possession of a firearm in a local school zone does indeed substantially affect interstate commerce. Brief for United States 17. The Government argues that possession of a firearm in a school zone may result in violent crime and that violent crime can be expected to affect the functioning of the national economy in two ways. First, the costs of violent crime are substantial, and, through the mechanism of insurance, those costs are spread throughout the population. Second, violent crime reduces the willingness of individuals to travel to areas within the country that are perceived to be unsafe. The Government also argues that the presence of guns in schools poses a substantial threat to the educational process by threatening the learning environment. A handicapped educational process, in turn, will result in a less productive citizenry. That, in turn, would have an adverse effect on the Nation's economic well-being. As a result, the Government argues that Congress could rationally have concluded that § 922(q) substantially affects interstate commerce.

We pause to consider the implications of the Government's arguments. The Government admits, under its "costs of crime" reasoning, that Congress could regulate not only all violent crime, but all activities that might lead to violent crime, regardless of how tenuously they relate to interstate commerce. Similarly, under the Government's "national productivity" reasoning, Congress could regulate any activity that it found was related to the economic productivity of individual citizens: family law (including marriage, divorce, and child custody), for example. Under the theories that the Government presents in support of § 922(q), it is difficult to perceive any limitation on federal power, even in areas such as criminal law enforcement or education where States historically have been sovereign. Thus, if we were to accept the Government's arguments, we are hard pressed to posit any activity by an individual that Congress is without power to regulate.

Although Justice Breyer argues that acceptance of the Government's rationales would not authorize a general federal police power, he is unable to identify any activity that the States may regulate but Congress may not. Justice Breyer posits that there might be some limitations on Congress' commerce power, such as family law or certain aspects of education. These suggested limitations, when viewed in light of the dissent's expansive analysis, are devoid of substance.

Justice Breyer focuses, for the most part, on the threat that firearm possession in and near schools poses to the educational process and the potential economic consequences flowing from that threat. Specifically, the dissent reasons that (1) gun-related violence is a serious problem; (2) that problem, in turn, has an adverse effect on classroom learning; and (3) that adverse effect on classroom learning, in turn, represents a substantial threat to trade and commerce. This analysis would be equally applicable, if not more so, to subjects such as family law and direct regulation of education.

For instance, if Congress can, pursuant to its Commerce Clause power, regulate activities that adversely affect the learning environment, then, *a fortiori,* it also can regulate the educational process directly. Congress could determine that a school's curriculum has a "significant" effect on the extent of classroom learning. As a result, Congress could mandate a federal curriculum for local elementary and secondary schools because what is taught in local schools has a significant "effect on classroom learning," and that, in turn, has a substantial effect on interstate commerce.

Justice Breyer rejects our reading of precedent and argues that "Congress . . . could rationally conclude that schools fall on the commercial side of the line." Again, Justice Breyer's rationale lacks any real limits because, depending on the level of generality, any activity can be looked upon as commercial. Under the dissent's rationale, Congress could just as easily look at child rearing as "fall[ing] on the commercial side of the line" because it provides a "valuable service — namely, to equip [children] with the skills they need to survive in life and, more specifically, in the workplace." *Ibid.* We do not doubt that Congress has authority under the Commerce Clause to regulate numerous commercial activities that substantially affect interstate commerce and also affect the educational process. That authority, though broad, does not include the authority to regulate each and every aspect of local schools.

Admittedly, a determination whether an intrastate activity is commercial or noncommercial may in some cases result in legal uncertainty. But, so long as Congress' authority is limited to those powers enumerated in the Constitution, and so long as those enumerated powers are interpreted as having judicially enforceable outer limits, congressional legislation under the Commerce Clause always will engender "legal uncertainty."

[The] Constitution mandates this uncertainty by withholding from Congress a plenary police power that would authorize enactment of every type of legislation. See Art. I, § 8. Congress has operated within this framework of legal uncertainty ever since this Court determined that it was the Judiciary's duty "to say what the law is." Any possible benefit from eliminating this "legal uncertainty" would be at the expense of the Constitution's system of enumerated powers.

In Jones & Laughlin Steel, 301 U.S., at 37, 57 S.Ct., at 624, we held that the question of congressional power under the Commerce Clause "is necessarily one of degree." To the same effect is the concurring opinion of Justice Cardozo in Schechter Poultry:

> "There is a view of causation that would obliterate the distinction between what is national and what is local in the activities of commerce. Motion at the outer rim is communicated perceptibly, though minutely, to recording instruments at the center. A society such as ours 'is an elastic medium which transmits all tremors throughout its territory; the only question is of their size.'" 295 U.S., at 554, 55 S.Ct., at 853 (quoting United States v. A.L.A. Schechter Poultry Corp., 76 F.2d 617, 624 (CA2 1935) (L. Hand, J., concurring)).

These are not precise formulations, and in the nature of things they cannot be. But we think they point the way to a correct decision of this case. The possession of a gun in a local school zone is in no sense an economic activity that might, through repetition elsewhere, substantially affect any sort of interstate commerce. Respondent was a local student at a local school; there is no indication that he had recently moved in interstate commerce, and there is no requirement that his possession of the firearm have any concrete tie to interstate commerce.

To uphold the Government's contentions here, we would have to pile inference upon inference in a manner that would bid fair to convert congressional authority under the Commerce Clause to a general police power of the sort retained by the States. Admittedly, some of our prior cases have taken long steps down that road, giving great deference to congressional action. The broad language in these opinions has suggested the possibility of additional expansion, but we decline here to proceed any further. To do so would require us to conclude that the Constitution's enumeration of powers does not presuppose something not enumerated, cf. Gibbons v. Ogden, supra, at 195, and that there never will be a distinction between what is truly national and what is truly local, cf. Jones & Laughlin Steel, supra, at 30, 57 S.Ct., at 621. This we are unwilling to do.

Affirmed.

Justice KENNEDY, with whom Justice O'CONNOR joins, concurring.

The history of the judicial struggle to interpret the Commerce Clause during the transition from the economic system the Founders knew to the single, national market still emergent in our own era counsels great restraint before the Court determines that the Clause is insufficient to support an exercise of the national power. That history gives me some pause about today's decision, but I join the Court's opinion with these observations on what I conceive to be its necessary though limited holding.

[The] progression of our Commerce Clause cases from Gibbons to the present was not marked, however, by a coherent or consistent course of interpretation; for neither the course of technological advance nor the foundational principles for the jurisprudence itself were self-evident to the courts that sought to resolve contemporary disputes by enduring principles.

Furthermore, for almost a century after the adoption of the Constitution, the Court's Commerce Clause decisions did not concern the authority of Congress to legislate. Rather, the Court faced the related but quite distinct question of the authority of the States to regulate matters that would be within the commerce power had Congress chosen to act. The simple fact was that in the early years of the Republic, Congress seldom perceived the necessity to exercise its power.

[The] history of our Commerce Clause decisions contains at least two lessons of relevance to this case. The first, as stated at the outset, is the imprecision of content-based boundaries used without more to define the limits of the Commerce Clause. The second, related to the first but of even greater consequence, is that the Court as an institution and the legal system as a whole have an immense stake in the stability of our Commerce Clause jurisprudence as it has evolved to this point. *Stare decisis* operates with great force in counseling us not to call in question the essential principles now in place respecting the congressional power to regulate transactions of a commercial nature. That fundamental restraint on our power forecloses us from reverting to an understanding of commerce that would serve only an 18th-century economy, dependent then upon production and trading practices that had changed but little over the preceding centuries; it also mandates against returning to the time when congressional authority to regulate undoubted commercial activities was limited by a judicial determination that those matters had an insufficient connection to an interstate system. Congress can regulate in the commercial sphere on the assumption that we have a single market and a unified purpose to build a stable national economy.

[It] does not follow, however, that in every instance the Court lacks the authority and responsibility to review congressional attempts to alter the federal balance. This case requires us to consider our place in the design of the Government and to appreciate the significance of federalism in the whole structure of the Constitution.

Of the various structural elements in the Constitution, separation of powers, checks and balances, judicial review, and federalism, only concerning the last does there seem to be much uncertainty respecting the existence, and the content, of standards that allow the Judiciary to play a significant role in maintaining the design contemplated by the Framers.

[There] is irony in this, because of the four structural elements in the Constitution just mentioned, federalism was the unique contribution of the Framers to political science and political theory. Though on the surface the idea may seem counterintuitive, it was the insight of the Framers that freedom was enhanced by the creation of two governments, not one.

[The] theory that two governments accord more liberty than one requires for its realization two distinct and discernable lines of political accountability: one between the citizens and the Federal Government; the second between the citizens and the States. If, as Madison expected, the Federal and State Governments are to control each other, see The Federalist No. 51, and hold each other in check by competing for the affections of the people, see The Federalist No. 46, those citizens must have some means of knowing which of the two governments to hold accountable for the failure to perform a given function. "Federalism serves to assign political responsibility, not to obscure it." Were the Federal Government to take over the regulation of entire areas of traditional state concern, areas having nothing to do with the regulation of commercial activities, the boundaries between the spheres of federal and state authority would blur and political responsibility would become illusory. The resultant inability to hold either branch of the government answerable to the citizens is more dangerous even than devolving too much authority to the remote central power.

To be sure, one conclusion that could be drawn from The Federalist Papers is that the balance between national and state power is entrusted in its entirety to the political process. Madison's observation that "the people ought not surely to be precluded from giving most of their confidence where they may discover it to be most due," The Federalist No. 46, p. 295 (C. Rossiter ed. 1961), can be interpreted to say that the essence of responsibility for a shift in power from the State to the Federal Government rests upon a political judgment, though he added assurance that "the State governments could have little to apprehend, because it is only within a certain sphere that the federal power can, in the nature of things, be advantageously administered," *ibid*. Whatever the judicial role, it is axiomatic that Congress does have substantial discretion and control over the federal balance.

[Some] Congresses have accepted responsibility to confront the great questions of the proper federal balance in terms of lasting consequences for the constitutional design. The political branches of the Government must fulfill this grave constitutional obligation if democratic liberty and the federalism that secures it are to endure.

At the same time, the absence of structural mechanisms to require those officials to undertake this principled task, and the momentary political convenience often attendant upon their failure to do so, argue against a complete renunciation of the judicial role. Although it is the obligation of all officers of the Government to respect the constitutional design, the federal balance is too essential a part of our constitutional structure and plays too vital a role in securing freedom for us to admit inability to intervene when one or the other level of Government has tipped the scales too far.

[The] substantial element of political judgment in Commerce Clause matters leaves our institutional capacity to intervene more in doubt than when we decide cases, for instance, under the Bill of Rights even though clear and bright lines are often absent in the latter class of disputes. But our cases do not teach that we have no role at all in determining the meaning of the Commerce Clause.

Our position in enforcing the dormant Commerce Clause is instructive. The Court's doctrinal approach in that area has likewise "taken some turns." Yet in contrast to the prevailing skepticism that surrounds our ability to give meaning to the explicit text of the Commerce Clause, there is widespread acceptance of our authority to enforce the dormant Commerce Clause, which we have but inferred from the constitutional structure as a limitation on the power of the States. True, if we invalidate a state law, Congress can in effect overturn our judgment, whereas in a case announcing that Congress has transgressed its authority, the decision is more consequential, for it stands unless Congress can revise its law to demonstrate its commercial character. This difference no doubt informs the circumspection with which we invalidate an Act of Congress, but it does not mitigate our duty to recognize meaningful limits on the commerce power of Congress.

The statute before us upsets the federal balance to a degree that renders it an unconstitutional assertion of the commerce power, and our intervention is required. As The Chief Justice explains, unlike the earlier cases to come before the Court here neither the actors nor their conduct has a commercial character, and neither the purposes nor the design of the statute has an evident commercial nexus. The statute makes the simple possession of a gun within 1,000 feet of the grounds of the school a criminal offense. In a sense any conduct in this interdependent world of ours has an ultimate commercial origin or consequence, but we have not yet said the commerce power may reach so far. If Congress attempts that extension, then at the least we must inquire whether the exercise of national power seeks to intrude upon an area of traditional state concern.

An interference of these dimensions occurs here, for it is well established that education is a traditional concern of the States. The proximity to schools, including of course schools owned and operated by the States or their subdivisions, is the very premise for making the conduct criminal. In these circumstances, we have a particular duty to ensure that the federal-state balance is not destroyed.

[The] statute now before us forecloses the States from experimenting and exercising their own judgment in an area to which States lay claim by right of history and expertise, and it does so by regulating an activity beyond the realm of commerce in the ordinary and usual sense of that term. The tendency of this statute to displace state regulation in areas of traditional state concern is evident from its territorial operation. There are over 100,000 elementary and secondary schools in the United States. Each of these now has an invisible federal zone extending 1,000 feet beyond the (often irregular) boundaries of the school property. In some communities no doubt it would be difficult to navigate without infringing on those zones. Yet throughout these areas, school officials would find their own programs for the prohibition of guns in danger of displacement by the federal authority unless the State chooses to enact a parallel rule.

This is not a case where the etiquette of federalism has been violated by a formal command from the National Government directing the State to enact a certain policy, cf. New York v. United States, 505 U.S. 144, 112 S.Ct. 2408, 120 L.Ed.2d 120 (1992), or to organize its governmental functions in a certain way, cf. FERC v. Mississippi, 456 U.S., at 781, 102 S.Ct., at 2149 (O'Connor, J., concurring in judgment in part and dissenting in part). While the intrusion on state sovereignty may not be as severe in this instance as in some of our recent Tenth Amendment cases, the intrusion is nonetheless significant. Absent a stronger connection or identification with commercial concerns that are central to the Commerce Clause, that interference contradicts the federal balance the Framers designed and that this Court is obliged to enforce.

For these reasons, I join in the opinion and judgment of the Court.

Justice THOMAS, concurring.

[Although] I join the majority, I write separately to observe that our case law has drifted far from the original understanding of the Commerce Clause. In a future case, we ought to temper our Commerce Clause jurisprudence in a manner that both makes sense of our more recent case law and is more faithful to the original understanding of that Clause.

We have said that Congress may regulate not only "Commerce . . . among the several States," U.S. Const., Art. I, § 8, cl. 3, but also anything that has a "substantial effect" on such commerce. This test, if taken to its logical extreme, would give Congress a "police power" over all aspects of American life. Unfortunately, we have never come to grips with this implication of our substantial effects formula.

[In] an appropriate case, I believe that we must further reconsider our "substantial effects" test with an eye toward constructing a standard that reflects the text and history of the Commerce Clause without totally rejecting our more recent Commerce Clause jurisprudence.

Today, however, I merely support the Court's conclusion with a discussion of the text, structure, and history of the Commerce Clause and an analysis of our early case law. My goal is simply to show how far we have departed from the original understanding and to demonstrate that the result we reach today is by no means "radical," see *post,* at 1651 (Stevens, J., dissenting). I also want to point out the necessity of refashioning a coherent test that does not tend to "obliterate the distinction between what is national and what is local and create a completely centralized government."

At the time the original Constitution was ratified, "commerce" consisted of selling, buying, and bartering, as well as transporting for these purposes.

[As] one would expect, the term "commerce" was used in contradistinction to productive activities such as manufacturing and agriculture.

[The] Constitution not only uses the word "commerce" in a narrower sense than our case law might suggest, it also does not support the proposition that Congress has authority over all activities that "substantially affect" interstate commerce. The Commerce Clause does not state Congress may regulate all matters that substantially affect commerce, there is no need for the Constitution to specify that Congress may enact bankruptcy laws, cl. 4, or coin money and fix the standard of weights and measures, cl. 5, or punish counterfeiters of United States coin and securities, cl. 6. Likewise, Congress would not need the separate authority to establish post offices and post roads, cl. 7, or to grant patents and copyrights, cl. 8, or to "punish Piracies and Felonies committed on the high Seas," cl. 10. It might not even need the power to raise and support an Army and Navy, cls. 12 and 13, for fewer people would engage in commercial shipping if they thought that a foreign power could expropriate their property with ease. Indeed, if Congress could regulate matters that substantially affect interstate commerce, there would have been no need to specify that Congress can regulate international trade and commerce with the Indians. As the Framers surely understood, these other branches of trade substantially affect interstate commerce.

Put simply, much if not all of Art. I, § 8 (including portions of the Commerce Clause itself), would be surplusage if Congress had been given authority over matters that substantially affect interstate commerce. An interpretation of cl. 3 that makes the rest of § 8 superfluous simply cannot be correct. Yet this Court's Commerce Clause jurisprudence has endorsed just such an interpretation: The power we have accorded Congress has swallowed Art. I, § 8.

[Indeed], if a "substantial effects" test can be appended to the Commerce Clause, why not to every other power of the Federal Government? There is no reason for singling out the Commerce Clause for special treatment. Accordingly, Congress could regulate all matters that "substantially affect" the Army and Navy, bankruptcies, tax collection, expenditures, and so on. In that case, the Clauses of § 8 all mutually overlap, something we can assume the Founding Fathers never intended.

Our construction of the scope of congressional authority has the additional problem of coming close to turning the Tenth Amendment on its head. Our case law could be read to reserve to the United States all powers not expressly *prohibited* by the Constitution. Taken together, these fundamental textual problems should, at the very least, convince us that the "substantial effects" test should be reexamined.

The exchanges during the ratification campaign reveal the relatively limited reach of the Commerce Clause and of federal power generally. The Founding Fathers confirmed that most areas of life (even many matters that would have substantial effects on commerce) would remain outside the reach of the Federal Government. Such affairs would continue to be under the exclusive control of the States.

[In] short, the Founding Fathers were well aware of what the principal dissent calls "'economic . . . realities.'" See *post,* at 1662 (Breyer, J.) (quoting North American Co. v. SEC, 327 U.S. 686, 705, 66 S.Ct. 785, 796, 90 L.Ed. 945 (1946)). Even though the boundary between commerce and other matters may ignore "economic reality" and thus seem arbitrary or artificial to some, we must nevertheless respect a constitutional line that does not grant Congress power over all that substantially affects interstate commerce.

If the principal dissent's understanding of our early case law were correct, there might be some reason to doubt this view of the original understanding of the Constitution. According to that dissent, Chief Justice Marshall's opinion in Gibbons v. Ogden, 9 Wheat. 1, 6 L.Ed. 23 (1824), established that Congress may control all local activities that "significantly affect interstate commerce."

[In] my view, the dissent is wrong about the holding and reasoning of Gibbons. Because this error leads the dissent to characterize the first 150 years of this Court's case law as a "wrong turn," I feel compelled to put the last 50 years in proper perspective.

[First], the Court made the uncontroversial claim that federal power does not encompass "*commerce*" that "does not extend to or affect other States." 9 Wheat., at 194 (emphasis added). From this statement, the principal dissent infers that whenever an activity affects interstate commerce, it necessarily follows that Congress can regulate such activities. Of course, Chief Justice Marshall said no such thing and the inference the dissent makes cannot be drawn.

There is a much better interpretation of the "affect[s]" language: Because the Court had earlier noted that the commerce power did not extend to wholly intrastate commerce, the Court was acknowledging that although the line between intrastate and interstate/foreign commerce would be difficult to draw, federal authority could not be construed to cover purely intrastate commerce. Commerce that did not affect another State could *never* be said to be commerce "among the several States."

But even if one were to adopt the dissent's reading, the "affect[s]" language, at most, permits Congress to regulate only intrastate *commerce* that substantially affects interstate and foreign commerce. There is no reason to believe that Chief Justice Marshall was asserting that Congress could regulate *all* activities that affect interstate commerce.

[I] am aware of no cases prior to the New Deal that characterized the power flowing from the Commerce Clause as sweepingly as does our substantial effects test. My review of the case law indicates that the substantial effects test is but an innovation of the 20th century.

[These] cases all establish a simple point: From the time of the ratification of the Constitution to the mid-1930's, it was widely understood that the Constitution granted Congress only limited powers, notwithstanding the Commerce Clause. Moreover, there was no question that activities wholly separated from business, such as gun possession, were beyond the reach of the commerce power. If anything, the "wrong turn" was the Court's dramatic departure in the 1930's from a century and a half of precedent.

Apart from its recent vintage and its corresponding lack of any grounding in the original understanding of the Constitution, the substantial effects test suffers from the further flaw that it appears to grant Congress a police power over the Nation. When asked at oral argument if there were *any* limits to the Commerce Clause, the Government was at a loss for words. Likewise, the principal dissent insists that there are limits, but it cannot muster even one example. Indeed, the dissent implicitly concedes that its reading has no limits when it criticizes the Court for "threaten[ing] legal uncertainty in an area of law that . . . seemed reasonably well settled." The one advantage of the dissent's standard is certainty: It is certain that under its analysis everything may be regulated under the guise of the Commerce Clause.

The substantial effects test suffers from this flaw, in part, because of its "aggregation principle." Under so-called "class of activities" statutes, Congress can regulate whole categories of activities that are not themselves either "interstate" or "commerce." In applying the effects test, we ask whether the class of activities *as a whole* substantially affects interstate commerce, not whether any specific activity within the class has such effects when considered in isolation. See Maryland v. Wirtz, 392 U.S., at 192-193, 88 S.Ct., at 2021-2022 (if class of activities is "'within the reach of federal power,'" courts may not excise individual applications as trivial) (quoting Darby, 312 U.S., at 120-121, 61 S.Ct., at 460-461).

The aggregation principle is clever, but has no stopping point. Suppose all would agree that gun possession within 1,000 feet of a school does not substantially affect commerce, but that possession of weapons generally (knives, brass knuckles, nunchakus, etc.) does. Under our substantial effects doctrine, even though Congress cannot single out gun possession, it can prohibit weapon possession generally. But one *always* can draw the circle broadly enough to cover an activity that, when taken in isolation, would not have substantial effects on commerce. Under our jurisprudence, if Congress passed an omnibus "substantially affects interstate commerce" statute, purporting to regulate every aspect of human existence, the Act apparently would be constitutional. Even though particular sections may govern only trivial activities, the statute in the aggregate regulates matters that substantially affect commerce.

This extended discussion of the original understanding and our first century and a half of case law does not necessarily require a wholesale abandonment of our more recent opinions. It simply reveals that our substantial effects test is far removed from both the Constitution and from our early case law and that the Court's opinion should not be viewed as "radical" or another "wrong turn" that must be corrected in the future. The analysis also suggests that we ought to temper our Commerce Clause jurisprudence.

[Unless] the dissenting Justices are willing to repudiate our long-held understanding of the limited nature of federal power, I would think that they, too, must be willing to reconsider the substantial effects test in a future case. If we wish to be true to a Constitution that does not cede a police power to the Federal Government, our Commerce Clause's boundaries simply cannot be "defined" as being "'commensurate with the national needs'" or self-consciously intended to let the Federal Government "'defend itself against economic forces that Congress decrees inimical or destructive of the national economy.'" Such a formulation of federal power is no test at all: It is a blank check.

At an appropriate juncture, I think we must modify our Commerce Clause jurisprudence. Today, it is easy enough to say that the Clause certainly does not empower Congress to ban gun possession within 1,000 feet of a school.

Justice BREYER, with whom Justice STEVENS, Justice SOUTER, and Justice GINSBURG join, dissenting.

[First], the power to "regulate Commerce . . . among the several States," U.S. Const., Art. I, § 8, cl. 3, encompasses the power to regulate local activities insofar as they significantly affect interstate commerce.

[Second], in determining whether a local activity will likely have a significant effect upon interstate commerce, a court must consider, not the effect of an individual act (a single instance of gun possession), but rather the cumulative effect of all similar instances (*i.e.,* the effect of all guns possessed in or near schools).

[Third], the Constitution requires us to judge the connection between a regulated activity and interstate commerce, not directly, but at one remove. Courts must give Congress a degree of leeway in determining the existence of a significant factual connection between the regulated activity and interstate commerce — both because the Constitution delegates the commerce power directly to Congress and because the determination requires an empirical judgment of a kind that a legislature is more likely than a court to make with accuracy. The traditional words "rational basis" capture this leeway. Thus, the specific question before us, as the Court recognizes, is not whether the "regulated activity sufficiently affected interstate commerce," but, rather, whether Congress could have had "*a rational basis*" for so concluding.

I recognize that we must judge this matter independently. "[S]imply because Congress may conclude that a particular activity substantially affects interstate commerce does not necessarily make it so."

Applying these principles to the case at hand, we must ask whether Congress could have had a *rational basis* for finding a significant (or substantial) connection between gun-related school violence and interstate commerce. Or, to put the question in the language of the *explicit* finding that Congress made when it amended this law in 1994: Could Congress rationally have found that "violent crime in school zones," through its effect on the "quality of education," significantly (or substantially) affects "interstate" or "foreign commerce"? 18 U.S.C. §§ 922(q)(1)(F), (G). As long as one views the commerce connection, not as a "technical legal conception," but as "a practical one," Swift & Co. v. United States, 196 U.S. 375, 398, 25 S.Ct. 276, 280, 49 L.Ed. 518 (1905) (Holmes, J.), the answer to this question must be yes. Numerous reports and studies — generated both inside and outside government — make clear that Congress could reasonably have found the empirical connection that its law, implicitly or explicitly, asserts. (See Appendix, *infra*, at 1665, for a sample of the documentation, as well as for complete citations to the sources referenced below.)

For one thing, reports, hearings, and other readily available literature make clear that the problem of guns in and around schools is widespread and extremely serious.

[To] hold this statute constitutional is not to "obliterate" the "distinction between what is national and what is local," nor is it to hold that the Commerce Clause permits the Federal Government to "regulate any activity that it found was related to the economic productivity of individual citizens," to regulate "marriage, divorce, and child custody," or to regulate any and all aspects of education. First, this statute is aimed at curbing a particularly acute threat to the educational process — the possession (and use) of life-threatening firearms in, or near, the classroom. The empirical evidence that I have discussed above unmistakably documents the special way in which guns and education are incompatible. See *supra*, at 1659. This Court has previously recognized the singularly disruptive potential on interstate commerce that acts of violence may have. See Perez, supra, 402 U.S., at 156-157, 91 S.Ct., at 1362-1363. Second, the immediacy of the connection between education and the national economic well-being is documented by scholars and accepted by society at large in a way and to a degree that may not hold true for other social institutions. It must surely be the rare case, then, that a statute strikes at conduct that (when considered in the abstract) seems so removed from commerce, but which (practically speaking) has so significant an impact upon commerce.

In sum, a holding that the particular statute before us falls within the commerce power would not expand the scope of that Clause. Rather, it simply would apply preexisting law to changing economic circumstances. It would recognize that, in today's economic world, gun-related violence near the classroom makes a significant difference to our economic, as well as our social, well-being. In accordance with well-accepted precedent, such a holding would permit Congress "to act in terms of economic . . . realities," would interpret the commerce power as "an affirmative power commensurate with the national needs," and would acknowledge that the "commerce clause does not operate so as to render the nation powerless to defend itself against economic forces that Congress decrees inimical or destructive of the national economy."

The majority's holding — that § 922 falls outside the scope of the Commerce Clause — creates three serious legal problems. First, the majority's holding runs contrary to modern Supreme Court cases that have upheld congressional actions despite connections to interstate or foreign commerce that are less significant than the effect of school violence.

[The] second legal problem the Court creates comes from its apparent belief that it can reconcile its holding with earlier cases by making a critical distinction between "commercial" and noncommercial "transaction[s]." That is to say, the Court believes the Constitution would distinguish between two local activities, each of which has an identical effect upon interstate commerce, if one, but not the other, is "commercial" in nature. As a general matter, this approach fails to heed this Court's earlier warning not to turn "questions of the power of Congress" upon "formula[s]" that would give "controlling force to nomenclature such as 'production' and 'indirect' and foreclose consideration of the actual effects of the activity in question upon interstate commerce." Wickard, supra, 317 U.S., at 120, 63 S.Ct., at 87.

[Moreover], the majority's test is not consistent with what the Court saw as the point of the cases that the majority now characterizes. Although the majority today attempts to categorize Perez, McClung, and Wickard as involving intrastate "economic activity," the Courts that decided each of those cases did *not* focus upon the economic nature of the activity regulated. Rather, they focused upon whether that activity *affected* interstate or foreign commerce. In fact, the Wickard Court expressly held that Filburn's consumption of home-grown wheat, "*though it may not be regarded as commerce,*" could nevertheless be regulated — "*whatever its nature*" — so long as "it exerts a substantial economic effect on interstate commerce."

More importantly, if a distinction between commercial and noncommercial activities is to be made, this is not the case in which to make it. The majority clearly cannot intend such a distinction to focus narrowly on an act of gun possession standing by itself, for such a reading could not be reconciled with either the civil rights cases (McClung and Daniel) or Perez — in each of those cases the specific transaction (the race-based exclusion, the use of force) was not itself "commercial." And, if the majority instead means to distinguish generally among broad categories of activities, differentiating what is educational from what is commercial, then, as a practical matter, the line becomes almost impossible to draw. Schools that teach reading, writing, mathematics, and related basic skills serve *both* social and commercial purposes, and one cannot easily separate the one from the other. American industry itself has been, and is again, involved in teaching. When, and to what extent, does its involvement make education commercial? Does the number of vocational classes that train students directly for jobs make a difference? Does it matter if the school is public or private, nonprofit or profit seeking? Does it matter if a city or State adopts a voucher plan that pays private firms to run a school? Even if one were to ignore these practical questions, why should there be a theoretical distinction between education, when it significantly benefits commerce, and environmental pollution, when it causes economic harm?

Regardless, if there is a principled distinction that could work both here and in future cases, Congress (even in the absence of vocational classes, industry involvement, and private management) could rationally conclude that schools fall on the commercial side of the line. In 1990, the year Congress enacted the statute before us, primary and secondary schools spent $230 billion — that is, nearly a quarter of a trillion dollars — which accounts for a significant portion of our $5.5 trillion gross domestic product for that year. The business of schooling requires expenditure of these funds on student transportation, food and custodial services, books, and teachers' salaries. These expenditures enable schools to provide a valuable service — namely, to equip students with the skills they need to survive in life and, more specifically, in the workplace. Certainly, Congress has often analyzed school expenditure as if it were a commercial investment, closely analyzing whether schools are efficient, whether they justify the significant resources they spend, and whether they can be restructured to achieve greater returns. Why could Congress, for Commerce Clause purposes, not consider schools as roughly analogous to commercial investments from which the Nation derives the benefit of an educated work force?

The third legal problem created by the Court's holding is that it threatens legal uncertainty in an area of law that, until this case, seemed reasonably well settled. Congress has enacted many statutes (more than 100 sections of the United States Code), including criminal statutes (at least 25 sections), that use the words "affecting commerce" to define their scope, see, *e.g.,* 18 U.S.C. § 844(i) (destruction of buildings used in activity affecting interstate commerce), and other statutes that contain no jurisdictional language at all, see, *e.g.,* 18 U.S.C. § 922(o)(1) (possession of machineguns). Do these, or similar, statutes regulate noncommercial activities? If so, would that alter the meaning of "affecting commerce" in a jurisdictional element? More importantly, in the absence of a jurisdictional element, are the courts nevertheless to take Wickard, (and later similar cases) as inapplicable, and to judge the effect of a single noncommercial activity on interstate commerce without considering similar instances of the forbidden conduct? However these questions are eventually resolved, the legal uncertainty now created will restrict Congress' ability to enact criminal laws aimed at criminal behavior that, considered problem by problem rather than instance by instance, seriously threatens the economic, as well as social, well-being of Americans.

In sum, to find this legislation within the scope of the Commerce Clause would permit "Congress . . . to act in terms of economic . . . realities." North American Co. v. SEC, 327 U.S., at 705, 66 S.Ct., at 796 (citing Swift & Co. v. United States, 196 U.S., at 398, 25 S.Ct., at 280 (Holmes, J.)). It would interpret the Clause as this Court has traditionally interpreted it, with the exception of one wrong turn subsequently corrected. See Gibbons v. Ogden, 9 Wheat., at 195 (holding that the commerce power extends "to all the external concerns of the nation, and to those internal concerns which affect the States generally"); United States v. Darby, 312 U.S., at 116-117, 61 S.Ct., at 458 ("The conclusion is inescapable that Hammer v. Dagenhart [the child labor case] was a departure from the principles which have prevailed in the interpretation of the Commerce Clause both before and since the decision. . . . It should be and now is overruled"). Upholding this legislation would do no more than simply recognize that Congress had a "rational basis" for finding a significant connection between guns in or near schools and (through their effect on education) the interstate and foreign commerce they threaten. For these reasons, I would reverse the judgment of the Court of Appeals. Respectfully, I dissent.

Comments on *Lopez*. Is *Lopez* a "magnitude" or "manner" case? Does the "substantial effect" test survive? If so, where and when? What of "aggregation" — is it still with us? Where exactly does *Lopez* stand in relation to the pre- and post-court-packing Commerce Clause standards?

We have located the *Lopez* decision immediately after *Heart of Atlanta* and *Katzenbach*, the cases reviewing the Civil Rights Act of 1964. Why? How would those cases be decided post-*Lopez*?

Does the Court in *Lopez* apply the "traditional deferential rational purpose test" in reviewing congressional support for finding that the activity substantially affects interstate commerce? The Court in *Lopez* concluded that Congress had made no findings with respect to the impact of the regulated activity on interstate commerce. How would you advise a Congressperson to overcome the *Lopez* result in regard to prospective legislation? Would a more comprehensive set of congressional findings change the result? Would any findings be sufficient to satisfy the Court? The case that follows, with the same 5-4 majority as *Lopez*, offers insight into these questions.

UNITED STATES v. MORRISON
529 U.S. 598 (2000)

[Christy Brzonkala, a former university student, brought claims under Violence Against Women Act (VAWA) against two football players who allegedly raped her at Virginia Polytechnic Institute, a state-operated school. When, under the University disciplinary system, one of the accused students was not punished and the other had his punishment suspended, she dropped out of school and sued both the men and Virginia Tech in the United States District Court for the Western District of Virginia.]

Chief Justice REHNQUIST delivered the opinion of the Court.

In these cases we consider the constitutionality of 42 U.S.C. § 13981, which provides a federal civil remedy for the victims of gender-motivated violence. . . .

Section 13981 was part of the Violence Against Women Act of 1994, § 40302, 108 Stat. 1941-1942. It states that "[a]ll persons within the United States shall have the right to be free from crimes of violence motivated by gender." 42 U.S.C. § 13981(b). To enforce that right, subsection (c) declares:

"A person (including a person who acts under color of any statute, ordinance, regulation, custom, or usage of any State) who commits a crime of violence motivated by gender and thus deprives another of the right declared in subsection (b) of this section shall be liable to the party injured, in an action for the recovery of compensatory and punitive damages, injunctive and declaratory relief, and such other relief as a court may deem appropriate."

[We] turn to the question whether § 13981 falls within Congress' power under Article I, § 8, of the Constitution. Brzonkala and the United States rely upon the third clause of the section, which gives Congress power "[t]o regulate Commerce with foreign Nations, and among the several States, and with the Indian Tribes."

Lopez emphasized [that] even under our modern, expansive interpretation of the Commerce Clause, Congress' regulatory authority is not without effective bounds. Id., at 557, 115 S.Ct. 1624.

[Petitioners] seek to sustain § 13981 as a regulation of activity that substantially affects interstate commerce. Given § 13981's focus on gender-motivated violence wherever it occurs (rather than violence directed at the instrumentalities of interstate commerce, interstate markets, or things or persons in interstate commerce), we agree that this is the proper inquiry.

Since Lopez most recently canvassed and clarified our case law governing this third category of Commerce Clause regulation, it provides the proper framework for conducting the required analysis of § 13981. In Lopez, we held that the Gun-Free School Zones Act of 1990, 18 U.S.C. § 922(q)(1)(A), which made it a federal crime to knowingly possess a firearm in a school zone, exceeded Congress' authority under the Commerce Clause. See 514 U.S., at 551, 115 S.Ct. 1624. Several significant considerations contributed to our decision.

First, we observed that § 922(q) was "a criminal statute that by its terms has nothing to do with 'commerce' or any sort of economic enterprise, however broadly one might define those terms." Id., at 561, 115 S.Ct. 1624. [Both] petitioners and Justice Souter's dissent downplay the role that the economic nature of the regulated activity plays in our Commerce Clause analysis. But a fair reading of Lopez shows that the noneconomic, criminal nature of the conduct at issue was central to our decision in that case. See, *e.g.,* id., at 551, 115 S.Ct. 1624 ("The Act [does not] regulat[e] a commercial activity"), 560 ("Even which is perhaps the most far reaching example of Commerce Clause authority over intrastate activity, involved economic activity in a way that the possession of a gun in a school zone does not"), 561 ("Section 922(q) is not an essential part of a larger regulation of economic activity"); [see] also id., at 573-574, 115 S.Ct. 1624 (Kennedy, J., concurring) (stating that Lopez did not alter our "practical conception of commercial regulation" and that Congress may "regulate in the commercial sphere on the assumption that we have a single market and a unified purpose to build a stable national economy"), 577 ("Were the Federal Government to take over the regulation of entire areas of traditional state concern, areas having nothing to do with the regulation of commercial activities, the boundaries between the spheres of federal and state authority would blur"), 580 ("[U]nlike the earlier cases to come before the Court here neither the actors nor their conduct has a commercial character, and neither the purposes nor the design of the statute has an evident commercial nexus. The statute makes the simple possession of a gun within 1,000 feet of the grounds of the school a criminal offense. In a sense any conduct in this interdependent world of ours has an ultimate commercial origin or consequence, but we have not yet said the commerce power may reach so far" (citation omitted)). Lopez's review of Commerce Clause case law demonstrates that in those cases where we have sustained federal regulation of intrastate activity based upon the activity's substantial effects on interstate commerce, the activity in question has been some sort of economic endeavor. See id., at 559-560, 115 S.Ct. 1624.

The second consideration that we found important in analyzing § 922(q) was that the statute contained "no express jurisdictional element which might limit its reach to a discrete set of firearm possessions that additionally have an explicit connection with or effect on interstate commerce." Id., at 562, 115 S.Ct. 1624. Such a jurisdictional element may establish that the enactment is in pursuance of Congress' regulation of interstate commerce.

Third, we noted that neither § 922(q) "'nor its legislative history contain[s] express congressional findings regarding the effects upon interstate commerce of gun possession in a school zone.'" Ibid. (quoting Brief for United States, O.T.1994, No. 93-1260, pp. 5-6). While "Congress normally is not required to make formal findings as to the substantial burdens that an activity has on interstate commerce," 514 U.S., at 562, 115 S.Ct. 1624 (citing McClung, supra, at 304, 85 S.Ct. 377; Perez, 402 U.S., at 156, 91 S.Ct. 1357), the existence of such findings may "enable us to evaluate the legislative judgment that the activity in question substantially affect[s] interstate commerce, even though no such substantial effect [is] visible to the naked eye." 514 U.S., at 563, 115 S.Ct. 1624.

Finally, our decision in Lopez rested in part on the fact that the link between gun possession and a substantial effect on interstate commerce was attenuated. Id., at 563-567, 115 S.Ct. 1624.

With these principles underlying our Commerce Clause jurisprudence as reference points, the proper resolution of the present cases is clear. Gender-motivated crimes of violence are not, in any sense of the phrase, economic activity. While we need not adopt a categorical rule against aggregating the effects of any noneconomic activity in order to decide these cases, thus far in our Nation's history our cases have upheld Commerce Clause regulation of intrastate activity only where that activity is economic in nature. See, *e.g.,* id., at 559-560, 115 S.Ct. 1624, and the cases cited therein.

Like the Gun-Free School Zones Act at issue in Lopez, § 13981 contains no jurisdictional element establishing that the federal cause of action is in pursuance of Congress' power to regulate interstate commerce. Although Lopez makes clear that such a jurisdictional element would lend support to the argument that § 13981 is sufficiently tied to interstate commerce, Congress elected to cast § 13981's remedy over a wider, and more purely intrastate, body of violent crime.

In contrast with the lack of congressional findings that we faced in Lopez, § 13981 *is* supported by numerous findings regarding the serious impact that gender-motivated violence has on victims and their families. See, *e.g.,* H.R. Conf. Rep. No. 103-711, p. 385 (1994), U.S.Code Cong. & Admin.News 1994, pp. 1803, 1853; S.Rep. No. 103-138, p. 40 (1993); S.Rep. No. 101-545, p. 33 (1990). But the existence of congressional findings is not sufficient, by itself, to sustain the constitutionality of Commerce Clause legislation. As we stated in Lopez, "'[S]imply because Congress may conclude that a particular activity substantially affects interstate commerce does not necessarily make it so.'" 514 U.S., at 557, n. 2, 115 S.Ct. 1624 (quoting Hodel, 452U.S., at 311, 101 S.Ct. 2389 (Rehnquist, J., concurring in judgment)). Rather, "'[w]hether particular operations affect interstate commerce sufficiently to come under the constitutional power of Congress to regulate them is ultimately a judicial rather than a legislative question, and can be settled finally only by this Court.'" 514 U.S., at 557, n. 2, 115 S.Ct. 1624 (quoting Heart of Atlanta Motel, 379 U.S., at 273, 85 S.Ct. 348 (Black, J., concurring)).

In these cases, Congress' findings are substantially weakened by the fact that they rely so heavily on a method of reasoning that we have already rejected as unworkable if we are to maintain the Constitution's enumeration of powers. Congress found that gender-motivated violence affects interstate commerce "by deterring potential victims from traveling interstate, from engaging in employment in interstate business, and from transacting with business, and in places involved in interstate commerce; . . . by diminishing national productivity, increasing medical and other costs, and decreasing the supply of and the demand for interstate products." H.R. Conf. Rep. No. 103-711, at 385, U.S.Code Cong. & Admin.News 1994, pp. 1803, 1853.

[The] reasoning that petitioners advance seeks to follow the but-for causal chain from the initial occurrence of violent crime (the suppression of which has always been the prime object of the States' police power) to every attenuated effect upon interstate commerce. If accepted, petitioners' reasoning would allow Congress to regulate any crime as long as the nationwide, aggregated impact of that crime has substantial effects on employment, production, transit, or consumption. Indeed, if Congress may regulate gender-motivated violence, it would be able to regulate murder or any other type of violence since gender-motivated violence, as a subset of all violent crime, is certain to have lesser economic impacts than the larger class of which it is a part.

Petitioners' reasoning, moreover, will not limit Congress to regulating violence but may, as we suggested in Lopez, be applied equally as well to family law and other areas of traditional state regulation since the aggregate effect of marriage, divorce, and childrearing on the national economy is undoubtedly significant. . . .

We accordingly reject the argument that Congress may regulate noneconomic, violent criminal conduct based solely on that conduct's aggregate effect on interstate commerce. The Constitution requires a distinction between what is truly national and what is truly local. Lopez, 514 U.S., at 568, 115 S.Ct. 1624 (citing Jones & Laughlin Steel, 301 U.S., at 30, 57 S.Ct. 615). In recognizing this fact we preserve one of the few principles that has been consistent since the Clause was adopted. The regulation and punishment of intrastate violence that is not directed at the instrumentalities, channels, or goods involved in interstate commerce has always been the province of the States. Indeed, we can think of no better example of the police power, which the Founders denied the National Government and reposed in the States, than the suppression of violent crime and vindication of its victims.

[In part III of the opinion, the Chief Justice also denied the reach of federal power as based upon the Equal Protection Clause of the 14th Amendment.]

Affirmed.

Justice THOMAS, concurring.

The majority opinion correctly applies our decision in United States v. Lopez, 514 U.S. 549, 115 S.Ct. 1624, 131 L.Ed.2d 626 (1995), and I join it in full. I write separately only to express my view that the very notion of a "substantial effects" test under the Commerce Clause is inconsistent with the original understanding of Congress' powers and with this Court's early Commerce Clause cases. By continuing to apply this rootless and malleable standard, however circumscribed, the Court has encouraged the Federal Government to persist in its view that the Commerce Clause has virtually no limits. Until this Court replaces its existing Commerce Clause jurisprudence with a standard more consistent with the original understanding, we will continue to see Congress appropriating state police powers under the guise of regulating commerce.

Justice SOUTER, with whom Justice STEVENS, Justice GINSBURG, and Justice BREYER join, dissenting.

Our cases, which remain at least nominally undisturbed, stand for the following propositions. Congress has the power to legislate with regard to activity that, in the aggregate, has a substantial effect on interstate commerce. See Wickard v. Filburn, 317 U.S. 111, 124-128, 63 S.Ct. 82, 87 L.Ed. 122 (1942); Hodel v. Virginia Surface Mining & Reclamation Assn., Inc., 452 U.S. 264, 277, 101 S.Ct. 2352, 69 L.Ed.2d 1 (1981). The fact of such a substantial effect is not an issue for the courts in the first instance, ibid., but for the Congress, whose institutional capacity for gathering evidence and taking testimony far exceeds ours. By passing legislation, Congress indicates its conclusion, whether explicitly or not, that facts support its exercise of the commerce power. The business of the courts is to review the congressional assessment, not for soundness but simply for the rationality of concluding that a jurisdictional basis exists in fact. See ibid. Any explicit findings that Congress chooses to make, though not dispositive of the question of rationality, may advance judicial review by identifying factual authority on which Congress relied. Applying those propositions in these cases can lead to only one conclusion.

One obvious difference from United States v. Lopez, 514 U.S. 549, 115 S.Ct. 1624, 131 L.Ed.2d 626 (1995), is the mountain of data assembled by Congress, here showing the effects of violence against women on interstate commerce. Passage of the Act in 1994 was preceded by four years of hearings held which included testimony from physicians and law professors; from survivors of rape and domestic violence; and from representatives of state law enforcement and private business. The record includes reports on gender bias from task forces in 21 States, and we have the benefit of specific factual findings in the eight separate Reports issued by Congress and its committees over the long course leading to enactment.

Congress thereby explicitly stated the predicate for the exercise of its Commerce Clause power. Is its conclusion irrational in view of the data amassed? True, the methodology of particular studies may be challenged, and some of the figures arrived at may be disputed. But the sufficiency of the evidence before Congress to provide a rational basis for the finding cannot seriously be questioned.

If the analogy to the Civil Rights Act of 1964 is not plain enough, one can always look back a bit further. In Wickard, we upheld the application of the Agricultural Adjustment Act to the planting and consumption of homegrown wheat. The effect on interstate commerce in that case followed from the possibility that wheat grown at home for personal consumption could either be drawn into the market by rising prices, or relieve its grower of any need to purchase wheat in the market. See 317 U.S., at 127-129, 63 S.Ct. 82. The Commerce Clause predicate was simply the effect of the production of wheat for home consumption on supply and demand in interstate commerce. Supply and demand for goods in interstate commerce will also be affected by the deaths of 2,000 to 4,000 women annually at the hands of domestic abusers, see S.Rep. No. 101-545, at 36, and by the reduction in the work force by the 100,000 or more rape victims who lose their jobs each year or are forced to quit, see *id.*, at 56; H.R.Rep. No. 103-395, at 25-26. Violence against women may be found to affect interstate commerce and affect it substantially.

The Act would have passed muster at any time between Wickard in 1942 and Lopez in 1995, a period in which the law enjoyed a stable understanding that congressional power under the Commerce Clause, complemented by the authority of the Necessary and Proper Clause, Art. I, § 8, cl. 18, extended to all activity that, when aggregated, has a substantial effect on interstate commerce.

[History] has shown that categorical exclusions have proven as unworkable in practice as they are unsupportable in theory. [For] significant periods of our history, the Court has defined the commerce power as plenary, unsusceptible to categorical exclusions, and this was the view expressed throughout the latter part of the 20th century in the substantial effects test. These two conceptions of the commerce power, plenary and categorically limited, are in fact old rivals, and today's revival of their competition summons up familiar history, a brief reprise of which may be helpful in posing what I take to be the key question going to the legitimacy of the majority's decision to breathe new life into the approach of categorical limitation.

In the half century following the modern activation of the commerce power with passage of the Interstate Commerce Act in 1887, this Court from time to time created categorical enclaves beyond congressional reach by declaring such activities as "mining," "production," "manufacturing," and union membership to be outside the definition of "commerce" and by limiting application of the effects test to "direct" rather than "indirect" commercial consequences.

Since adherence to these formalistically contrived confines of commerce power in large measure provoked the judicial crisis of 1937, one might reasonably have doubted that Members of this Court would ever again toy with a return to the days before NLRB v. Jones & Laughlin Steel Corp., 301 U.S. 1, 57 S.Ct. 615, 81 L.Ed. 893 (1937), which brought the earlier and nearly disastrous experiment to an end. And yet today's decision can only be seen as a step toward recapturing the prior mistakes.

Just as the old formalism had value in the service of an economic conception [laissez-faire], the new one is useful in serving a conception of federalism. It is the instrument by which assertions of national power are to be limited in favor of preserving a supposedly discernible, proper sphere of state autonomy to legislate or refrain from legislating as the individual States see fit.

The Court finds it relevant that the statute addresses conduct traditionally subject to state prohibition under domestic criminal law. [Again] history seems to be recycling, for the theory of traditional state concern as grounding a limiting principle has been rejected previously. [See] Garcia v. San Antonio Metropolitan Transit Authority, 469 U.S. 528, 105 S.Ct. 1005, 83 L.Ed.2d 1016 (1985), which held that the concept of "traditional governmental function" (as an element of the immunity doctrine under Hodel) was incoherent.

[The] objection to reviving traditional state spheres of action as a consideration in commerce analysis, however, not only rests on the portent of incoherence, but is compounded by a further defect just as fundamental. The defect, in essence, is the majority's rejection of the Founders' considered judgment that politics, not judicial review, should mediate between state and national interests as the strength and legislative jurisdiction of the National Government inevitably increased through the expected growth of the national economy. . . .

Today's majority, however, finds no significance whatever in the state support for the Act based upon the States' acknowledged failure to deal adequately with gender-based violence in state courts, and the belief of their own law enforcement agencies that national action is essential.

The National Association of Attorneys General supported the Act unanimously, see Violence Against Women: Victims of the System, Hearing on S. 15 before the Senate Committee on the Judiciary, 102d Cong., 1st Sess., 37-38 (1991), and Attorneys General from 38 States urged Congress to enact the Civil Rights Remedy, representing that "the current system for dealing with violence against women is inadequate," see Crimes of Violence Motivated by Gender, Hearing before the Subcommittee on Civil and Constitutional Rights of the House Committee on the Judiciary, 103d Cong., 1st Sess., 34-36 (1993). It was against this record of failure at the state level that the Act was passed to provide the choice of a federal forum in place of the state-court systems found inadequate to stop gender-biased violence. See Women and Violence, Hearing before the Senate Committee on the Judiciary, 101st Cong., 2d Sess., 2 (1990) (statement of Sen. Biden) (noting importance of federal forum). The Act accordingly offers a federal civil rights remedy aimed exactly at violence against women, as an alternative to the generic state tort causes of action found to be poor tools of action by the state task forces. See S.Rep. No. 101-545, at 45 (noting difficulty of fitting gender-motivated crimes into common-law categories). As the 1993 Senate Report put it, "The Violence Against Women Act is intended to respond both to the underlying attitude that this violence is somehow less serious than other crime and to the resulting failure of our criminal justice system to address such violence. Its goals are both symbolic and practical. . . ." S.Rep. No. 103-138, at 38.

The collective opinion of state officials that the Act was needed continues virtually unchanged, and when the Civil Rights Remedy was challenged in court, the States came to its defense. Thirty-six of them and the Commonwealth of Puerto Rico have filed an *amicus* brief in support of petitioners in these cases, and only one State has taken respondents' side. It is, then, not the least irony of these cases that the States will be forced to enjoy the new federalism whether they want it or not. For with the Court's decision today, Antonio Morrison, like Carter Coal's James Carter before him, has "won the states' rights plea against the states themselves." R. Jackson, The Struggle for Judicial Supremacy 160 (1941).

All of this convinces me that today's ebb of the commerce power rests on error, and at the same time leads me to doubt that the majority's view will prove to be enduring law. There is yet one more reason for doubt. Although we sense the presence of Carter Coal, Schechter, and Usery once again, the majority embraces them only at arm's-length. [As] our predecessors learned then, the practice of such ad hoc review cannot preserve the distinction between the judicial and the legislative, and this Court, in any event, lacks the institutional capacity to maintain such a regime for very long. This one will end when the majority realizes that the conception of the commerce power for which it entertains hopes would inevitably fail the test expressed in Justice Holmes's statement that "[t]he first call of a theory of law is that it should fit the facts." O. Holmes, The Common Law 167 (Howe ed.1963). The facts that cannot be ignored today are the facts of integrated national commerce and a political relationship between States and Nation much affected by their respective treasuries and constitutional modifications adopted by the people. The federalism of some earlier time is no more adequate to account for those facts today than the theory of laissez-faire was able to govern the national economy 70 years ago.

Justice BREYER, with whom Justice STEVENS joins, and with whom Justice SOUTER and Justice GINSBURG join as to Part I-A, dissenting.

Consider the problems. The "economic/noneconomic" distinction is not easy to apply. Does the local street corner mugger engage in "economic" activity or "noneconomic" activity when he mugs for money? Would evidence that desire for economic domination underlies many brutal crimes against women save the present statute?

[More] important, why should we give critical constitutional importance to the economic, or noneconomic, nature of an interstate-commerce-affecting *cause?* If chemical emanations through indirect environmental change cause identical, severe commercial harm outside a State, why should it matter whether local factories or home fireplaces release them?

[Most] importantly, the Court's complex rules seem unlikely to help secure the very object that they seek, namely, the protection of "areas of traditional state regulation" from federal intrusion. . . .

How much would be gained, for example, were Congress to reenact the present law in the form of "An Act Forbidding Violence Against Women Perpetrated at Public Accommodations or by Those Who Have Moved in, or through the Use of Items that Have Moved in, Interstate Commerce"?

[We] live in a Nation knit together by two centuries of scientific, technological, commercial, and environmental change. Those changes, taken together, mean that virtually every kind of activity, no matter how local, genuinely can affect commerce, or its conditions, outside the State — at least when considered in the aggregate. Heart of Atlanta Motel, 379 U.S., at 251, 85 S.Ct. 348. And that fact makes it close to impossible for courts to develop meaningful subject-matter categories that would exclude some kinds of local activities from ordinary Commerce Clause "aggregation" rules without, at the same time, depriving Congress of the power to regulate activities that have a genuine and important effect upon interstate commerce.

Since judges cannot change the world, the "defect" means that, within the bounds of the rational, Congress, not the courts, must remain primarily responsible for striking the appropriate state/federal balance.

Comments on *Morrison*. What does *Morrison* add to *Lopez*? Is *Morrison* more "activist" then *Lopez*? Would the outcome in *Morrison* change any of your answers to the following questions posed after the *Lopez* decision: "How would you advise a Congressperson to overcome the *Lopez* (*Morrison* as well) result in regard to prospective legislation? Would a more comprehensive set of congressional findings change the result? Would any findings be sufficient to satisfy the Court?"

Justice Souter, in his opinion joined by the dissenters, comments:

> Since adherence to these formalistically contrived confines of commerce power in large measure provoked the judicial crisis of 1937, one might reasonably have doubted that Members of this Court would ever again toy with a return to the days before NLRB v. Jones & Laughlin Steel Corp., 301 U.S. 1, 57 S.Ct. 615, 81 L.Ed. 893 (1937), which brought the earlier and nearly disastrous experiment to an end. And yet today's decision can only be seen as a step toward recapturing the prior mistakes. Just as the old formalism had value in the service of an economic conception [laissez-faire], the new one is useful in serving a conception of federalism.

What do you think?

1. "IS HOME WEED HOME FEED?"

GONZALES v. RAICH
545 U.S. 1 (2005)

Justice STEVENS delivered the opinion of the Court.

California is one of at least nine States that authorize the use of marijuana for medicinal purposes. The question presented in this case is whether the power vested in Congress by Article I, §8, of the Constitution "[t]o make all Laws which shall be necessary and proper for carrying into Execution" its authority to "regulate Commerce with foreign Nations, and among the several States" includes the power to prohibit the local cultivation and use of marijuana in compliance with California law.

I

California has been a pioneer in the regulation of marijuana. In 1913, California was one of the first States to prohibit the sale and possession of marijuana, and at the end of the century, California became the first State to authorize limited use of the drug for medicinal purposes. In 1996, California voters passed Proposition 215, now codified as the Compassionate Use Act of 1996. The proposition was designed to ensure that "seriously ill" residents of the State have access to marijuana for medical purposes, and to encourage Federal and State Governments to take steps towards ensuring the safe and affordable distribution of the drug to patients in need. The Act creates an exemption from criminal prosecution for physicians, as well as for patients and primary caregivers who possess or cultivate marijuana for medicinal purposes with the recommendation or approval of a physician. A "primary caregiver" is a person who has consistently assumed responsibility for the housing, health, or safety of the patient.

Respondents Angel Raich and Diane Monson are California residents who suffer from a variety of serious medical conditions and have sought to avail themselves of medical marijuana pursuant to the terms of the Compassionate Use Act. They are being treated by licensed, board-certified family practitioners, who have concluded, after prescribing a host of conventional medicines to treat respondents' conditions and to alleviate their associated symptoms, that marijuana is the only drug available that provides effective treatment. Both women have been using marijuana as a medication for several years pursuant to their doctors' recommendation, and both rely heavily on cannabis to function on a daily basis. Indeed, Raich's physician believes that forgoing cannabis treatments would certainly cause Raich excruciating pain and could very well prove fatal.

Respondent Monson cultivates her own marijuana, and ingests the drug in a variety of ways including smoking and using a vaporizer. Respondent Raich, by contrast, is unable to cultivate her own, and thus relies on two caregivers, litigating as "John Does," to provide her with locally grown marijuana at no charge. These caregivers also process the cannabis into hashish or keif, and Raich herself processes some of the marijuana into oils, balms, and foods for consumption.

On August 15, 2002, county deputy sheriffs and agents from the federal Drug Enforcement Administration (DEA) came to Monson's home. After a thorough investigation, the county officials concluded that her use of marijuana was entirely lawful as a matter of California law. Nevertheless, after a 3-hour standoff, the federal agents seized and destroyed all six of her cannabis plants.

Respondents thereafter brought this action against the Attorney General of the United States and the head of the DEA seeking injunctive and declaratory relief prohibiting the enforcement of the federal Controlled Substances Act (CSA), 84 Stat. 1242, 21 U.S.C. § 801 *et seq.*, to the extent it prevents them from possessing, obtaining, or manufacturing cannabis for their personal medical use. In their complaint and supporting affidavits, Raich and Monson described the severity of their afflictions, their repeatedly futile attempts to obtain relief with conventional medications, and the opinions of their doctors concerning their need to use marijuana. Respondents claimed that enforcing the CSA against them would violate the Commerce Clause, the Due Process Clause of the Fifth Amendment, the Ninth and Tenth Amendments of the Constitution, and the doctrine of medical necessity.

The District Court denied respondents' motion for a preliminary injunction. [A] divided panel of the Court of Appeals for the Ninth Circuit reversed and ordered the District Court to enter a preliminary injunction. *Raich* v. *Ashcroft*, 352 F.3d 1222 (2003). The court found that respondents had "demonstrated a strong likelihood of success on their claim that, as applied to them, the CSA is an unconstitutional exercise of Congress' Commerce Clause authority." *Id.,* at 1227. The Court of Appeals distinguished prior Circuit cases upholding the CSA in the face of Commerce Clause challenges by focusing on what it deemed to be the "*separate and distinct class of activities*" at issue in this case: "the intrastate, noncommercial cultivation and possession of cannabis for personal medical purposes as recommended by a patient's physician pursuant to valid California state law." *Id.,* at 1228. The court found the latter class of activities "different in kind from drug trafficking" because interposing a physician's recommendation raises different health and safety concerns, and because "this limited use is clearly distinct from the broader illicit drug market — as well as any broader commercial market for medicinal marijuana —

insofar as the medicinal marijuana at issue in this case is not intended for, nor does it enter, the stream of commerce." *Ibid.*

The majority placed heavy reliance on our decisions in *United States* v. *Lopez,* 514 U.S. 549 (1995), and *United States* v. *Morrison,* 529 U.S. 598 (2000), as interpreted by recent Circuit precedent, to hold that this separate class of purely local activities was beyond the reach of federal power. In contrast, the dissenting judge concluded that the CSA, as applied to respondents, was clearly valid under *Lopez* and *Morrison;* moreover, he thought it "simply impossible to distinguish the relevant conduct surrounding the cultivation and use of the marijuana crop at issue in this case from the cultivation and use of the wheat crop that affected interstate commerce in *Wickard* v. *Filburn.*" 352 F.3d, at 1235 (Beam, J., dissenting) (citation omitted).

The obvious importance of the case prompted our grant of certiorari. 542 U.S. 936 (2004). The case is made difficult by respondents' strong arguments that they will suffer irreparable harm because, despite a congressional finding to the contrary, marijuana does have valid therapeutic purposes. The question before us, however, is not whether it is wise to enforce the statute in these circumstances; rather, it is whether Congress' power to regulate interstate markets for medicinal substances encompasses the portions of those markets that are supplied with drugs produced and consumed locally. Well-settled law controls our answer. The CSA is a valid exercise of federal power, even as applied to the troubling facts of this case. We accordingly vacate the judgment of the Court of Appeals.

II

Shortly after taking office in 1969, President Nixon declared a national "war on drugs." As the first campaign of that war, Congress set out to enact legislation that would consolidate various drug laws on the books into a comprehensive statute, provide meaningful regulation over legitimate sources of drugs to prevent diversion into illegal channels, and strengthen law enforcement tools against the traffic in illicit drugs. That effort culminated in the passage of the Comprehensive Drug Abuse Prevention and Control Act of 1970, 84 Stat. 1236.

This was not, however, Congress' first attempt to regulate the national market in drugs. Rather, as early as 1906 Congress enacted federal legislation imposing labeling regulations on medications and prohibiting the manufacture or shipment of any adulterated or misbranded drug traveling in interstate commerce.

[In] 1970, after declaration of the national "war on drugs," federal drug policy underwent a significant transformation. A number of noteworthy events precipitated this policy shift. First, in *Leary* v. *United States,* 395 U.S. 6 (1969), this Court held certain provisions of the Marihuana Tax Act and other narcotics legislation unconstitutional. Second, at the end of his term, President Johnson fundamentally reorganized the federal drug control agencies. The Bureau of Narcotics, then housed in the Department of Treasury, merged with the Bureau of Drug Abuse Control, then housed in the Department of Health, Education, and Welfare (HEW), to create the Bureau of Narcotics and Dangerous Drugs, currently housed in the Department of Justice. Finally, prompted by a perceived need to consolidate the growing number of piecemeal drug laws and to enhance federal drug enforcement powers, Congress enacted the Comprehensive Drug Abuse Prevention and Control Act.

Title II of that Act, the CSA, repealed most of the earlier anti-drug laws in favor of a comprehensive regime to combat the international and interstate traffic in illicit drugs. The main objectives of the CSA were to conquer drug abuse and to control the legitimate and illegitimate traffic in controlled substances. Congress was particularly concerned with the need to prevent the diversion of drugs from legitimate to illicit channels.

To effectuate these goals, Congress devised a closed regulatory system making it unlawful to manufacture, distribute, dispense, or possess any controlled substance except in a manner authorized by the CSA. 21 U.S.C. § 841(a)(1), 844(a). The CSA categorizes all controlled substances into five schedules. §812. The drugs are grouped together based on their accepted medical uses, the potential for abuse, and their psychological and physical effects on the body. §§811, 812. Each schedule is associated with a distinct set of controls regarding the manufacture, distribution, and use of the substances listed therein. §§821-830.

In enacting the CSA, Congress classified marijuana as a Schedule I drug. U.S.C. § 812(c). This preliminary classification was based, in part, on the recommendation of the Assistant Secretary of HEW "that marihuana be retained within schedule I at least until the completion of certain studies now underway." Schedule I drugs are categorized as such because of their high potential for abuse, lack of any accepted medical use, and absence of any accepted safety for use in medically supervised treatment. §812(b)(1). These three factors, in varying gradations, are also used to categorize drugs in the other four schedules. For example, Schedule II substances also have a high potential for abuse which may lead to severe psychological or physical dependence, but unlike Schedule I drugs, they have a currently accepted medical use. §812(b)(2). By classifying marijuana as a Schedule I drug, as opposed to listing it on a lesser schedule, the manufacture, distribution, or possession of marijuana became a criminal offense, with the sole exception being use of the drug as part of a Food and Drug Administration pre-approved research study. §§823(f), 841(a)(1), 844(a); see also *United States* v. *Oakland Cannabis Buyers' Cooperative,* 532 U.S. 483, 490 (2001).

The CSA provides for the periodic updating of schedules and delegates authority to the Attorney General, after consultation with the Secretary of Health and Human Services, to add, remove, or transfer substances to, from, or between schedules. §811. Despite considerable efforts to reschedule marijuana, it remains a Schedule I drug.

III

Respondents in this case do not dispute that passage of the CSA, as part of the Comprehensive Drug Abuse Prevention and Control Act, was well within Congress' commerce power. Brief for Respondents 22, 38. Nor do they contend that any provision or section of the CSA amounts to an unconstitutional exercise of congressional authority. Rather, respondents' challenge is actually quite limited; they argue that the CSA's categorical prohibition of the manufacture and possession of marijuana as applied to the intrastate manufacture and possession of marijuana for medical purposes pursuant to California law exceeds Congress' authority under the Commerce Clause.

In assessing the validity of congressional regulation, none of our Commerce Clause cases can be viewed in isolation. As charted in considerable detail in *United States* v. *Lopez*, our understanding of the reach of the Commerce Clause, as well as Congress' assertion of authority thereunder, has evolved over time. The Commerce Clause emerged as the Framers' response to the central problem giving rise to the Constitution itself: the absence of any federal commerce power under the Articles of Confederation. For the first century of our history, the primary use of the Clause was to preclude the kind of discriminatory state legislation that had once been permissible. Then, in response to rapid industrial development and an increasingly interdependent national economy, Congress "ushered in a new era of federal regulation under the commerce power," beginning with the enactment of the Interstate Commerce Act in 1887, 24 Stat. 379, and the Sherman Antitrust Act in 1890, 26 Stat. 209, as amended, 15 U.S.C. § 2 et seq.

Cases decided during that "new era," which now spans more than a century, have identified three general categories of regulation in which Congress is authorized to engage under its commerce power. First, Congress can regulate the channels of interstate commerce. *Perez* v. *United States,* 402 U.S. 146, 150 (1971). Second, Congress has authority to regulate and protect the instrumentalities of interstate commerce, and persons or things in interstate commerce. *Ibid.* Third, Congress has the power to regulate activities that substantially affect interstate commerce. *Ibid.; NLRB* v. *Jones & Laughlin Steel Corp.,* 301 U.S. 1, 37 (1937). Only the third category is implicated in the case at hand.

Our case law firmly establishes Congress' power to regulate purely local activities that are part of an economic "class of activities" that have a substantial effect on interstate commerce. See, *e.g., Perez,* 402 U.S., at 151; *Wickard* v. *Filburn,* 317 U.S. 111, 128-129 (1942). As we stated in *Wickard,* "even if appellee's activity be local and though it may not be regarded as commerce, it may still, whatever its nature, be reached by Congress if it exerts a substantial economic effect on interstate commerce." *Id.,* at 125. We have never required Congress to legislate with scientific exactitude. When Congress decides that the "'total incidence'" of a practice poses a threat to a national market, it may regulate the entire class. See *Perez,* 402 U.S., at 154-155 (quoting *Westfall* v. *United States,* 274 U.S. 256, 259 (1927) ("[W]hen it is necessary in order to prevent an evil to make the law embrace more than the precise thing to be prevented it may do so")). In this vein, we have reiterated that when "'a general regulatory statute bears a substantial relation to commerce, the *de minimis* character of individual instances arising under that statute is of no consequence.'" *E.g., Lopez,* 514 U.S., at 558 (emphasis deleted) (quoting *Maryland* v. *Wirtz,* 392 U.S. 183, 196, n. 27 (1968)).

Our decision in *Wickard,* 317 U.S. 111, is of particular relevance. In *Wickard,* we upheld the application of regulations promulgated under the Agricultural Adjustment Act of 1938, 52 Stat. 31, which were designed to control the volume of wheat moving in interstate and foreign commerce in order to avoid surpluses and consequent abnormally low prices. The regulations established an allotment of 11.1 acres for Filburn's 1941 wheat crop, but he sowed 23 acres, intending to use the excess by consuming it on his own farm. Filburn argued that even though we had sustained Congress' power to regulate the production of goods for commerce, that power did not authorize "federal regulation [of] production not intended in any part for commerce but wholly for consumption on the farm." *Wickard,* 317 U.S., at 118. Justice Jackson's opinion for a unanimous Court rejected this submission. He wrote:

> "The effect of the statute before us is to restrict the amount which may be produced for market and the extent as well to which one may forestall resort to the market by producing to meet his own needs. That appellee's own contribution to the demand for wheat may be trivial by itself is not enough to remove him from the scope of federal regulation where, as here, his contribution, taken together with that of many others similarly situated, is far from trivial." *Id.,* at 127-128.

Wickard thus establishes that Congress can regulate purely intrastate activity that is not itself "commercial," in that it is not produced for sale, if it concludes that failure to regulate that class of activity would undercut the regulation of the interstate market in that commodity.

The similarities between this case and *Wickard* are striking. Like the farmer in *Wickard*, respondents are cultivating, for home consumption, a fungible commodity for which there is an established, albeit illegal, interstate market. Just as the Agricultural Adjustment Act was designed "to control the volume [of wheat] moving in interstate and foreign commerce in order to avoid surpluses . . ." and consequently control the market price, *id.*, at 115, a primary purpose of the CSA is to control the supply and demand of controlled substances in both lawful and unlawful drug markets. See nn. 20-21, *supra*. In *Wickard*, we had no difficulty concluding that Congress had a rational basis for believing that, when viewed in the aggregate, leaving home-consumed wheat outside the regulatory scheme would have a substantial influence on price and market conditions. Here too, Congress had a rational basis for concluding that leaving home-consumed marijuana outside federal control would similarly affect price and market conditions.

More concretely, one concern prompting inclusion of wheat grown for home consumption in the 1938 Act was that rising market prices could draw such wheat into the interstate market, resulting in lower market prices. *Wickard*, 317 U.S., at 128. The parallel concern making it appropriate to include marijuana grown for home consumption in the CSA is the likelihood that the high demand in the interstate market will draw such marijuana into that market. While the diversion of homegrown wheat tended to frustrate the federal interest in stabilizing prices by regulating the volume of commercial transactions in the interstate market, the diversion of homegrown marijuana tends to frustrate the federal interest in eliminating commercial transactions in the interstate market in their entirety. In both cases, the regulation is squarely within Congress' commerce power because production of the commodity meant for home consumption, be it wheat or marijuana, has a substantial effect on supply and demand in the national market for that commodity.

Nonetheless, respondents suggest that *Wickard* differs from this case in three respects: (1) the Agricultural Adjustment Act, unlike the CSA, exempted small farming operations; (2) *Wickard* involved a "quintessential economic activity" — a commercial farm — whereas respondents do not sell marijuana; and (3) the *Wickard* record made it clear that the aggregate production of wheat for use on farms had a significant impact on market prices. Those differences, though factually accurate, do not diminish the precedential force of this Court's reasoning.

The fact that Wickard's own impact on the market was "trivial by itself" was not a sufficient reason for removing him from the scope of federal regulation. 317 U.S., at 127. That the Secretary of Agriculture elected to exempt even smaller farms from regulation does not speak to his power to regulate all those whose aggregated production was significant, nor did that fact play any role in the Court's analysis. Moreover, even though Wickard was indeed a commercial farmer, the activity he was engaged in — the cultivation of wheat for home consumption — was not treated by the Court as part of his commercial farming operation. And while it is true that the record in the *Wickard* case itself established the causal connection between the production for local use and the national market, we have before us findings by Congress to the same effect.

Findings in the introductory sections of the CSA explain why Congress deemed it appropriate to encompass local activities within the scope of the CSA. See n. 20, *supra*. The submissions of the parties and the numerous *amici* all seem to agree that the national, and international, market for marijuana has dimensions that are fully comparable to those defining the class of activities regulated by the Secretary pursuant to the 1938 statute. Respondents nonetheless insist that the CSA cannot be constitutionally applied to their activities because Congress did not make a specific finding that the intrastate cultivation and possession of marijuana for medical purposes based on the recommendation of a physician would substantially affect the larger interstate marijuana market. Be that as it may, we have never required Congress to make particularized findings in order to legislate, see *Lopez*, 514 U.S., at 562; *Perez*, 402 U.S., at 156, absent a special concern such as the protection of free speech, see, *e.g., Turner Broadcasting System, Inc.* v. *FCC*, 512 U.S. 622, 664-668 (1994) (plurality opinion). While congressional findings are certainly helpful in reviewing the substance of a congressional statutory scheme, particularly when the connection to commerce is not self-evident, and while we will consider congressional findings in our analysis when they are available, the absence of particularized findings does not call into question Congress' authority to legislate.

In assessing the scope of Congress' authority under the Commerce Clause, we stress that the task before us is a modest one. We need not determine whether respondents' activities, taken in the aggregate, substantially affect interstate commerce in fact, but only whether a "rational basis" exists for so concluding. *Lopez*, 514 U.S., at 557; see also *Hodel* v. *Virginia Surface Mining & Reclamation Assn., Inc.*, 452 U.S. 264, 276-280 (1981); *Perez*, 402 U.S., at 155-156; *Katzenbach* v. *McClung*, 379 U.S. 294, 299-301 (1964); *Heart of Atlanta Motel, Inc.* v. *United States*, 379 U.S. 241, 252-253 (1964). Given the enforcement difficulties that attend distinguishing between marijuana cultivated locally and marijuana grown elsewhere, 21 U.S.C. § 801(5), and concerns about diversion into illicit channels, we have no difficulty concluding that Congress had a rational basis for believing that failure to regulate the intrastate manufacture and possession of marijuana would leave a gaping hole in the CSA. Thus, as in *Wickard*, when it enacted comprehensive legislation to regulate the interstate market in a fungible commodity, Congress was acting well within its authority to "make all Laws which shall be necessary and proper" to "regulate Commerce . . . among the several States." U.S. Const., Art. I, §8. That the regulation ensnares some purely intrastate activity is of no moment. As we have done many times before, we refuse to excise individual components of that larger scheme.

IV

To support their contrary submission, respondents rely heavily on two of our more recent Commerce Clause cases. In their myopic focus, they overlook the larger context of modern-era Commerce Clause jurisprudence preserved by those cases. Moreover, even in the narrow prism of respondents' creation, they read those cases far too broadly. Those two cases, of course, are *Lopez*, 514 U.S. 549, and *Morrison*, 529 U.S. 598. As an initial matter, the statutory challenges at issue in those cases were markedly different from the challenge respondents pursue in the case at hand. Here, respondents ask us to excise individual applications of a concededly valid statutory scheme. In contrast, in both *Lopez* and *Morrison*, the parties asserted that a particular statute or provision fell outside Congress' commerce power in its entirety. This distinction is pivotal for we have often reiterated that "[w]here the class of activities is regulated and that class is within the reach of federal power, the courts have no power 'to excise, as trivial, individual instances' of the class." *Perez*, 402 U.S., at 154 (emphasis deleted) (quoting *Wirtz*, 392 U.S., at 193); see also *Hodel*, 452 U.S., at 308.

At issue in *Lopez*, 514 U.S. 549, was the validity of the Gun-Free School Zones Act of 1990, which was a brief, single-subject statute making it a crime for an individual to possess a gun in a school zone. 104 Stat. 4844-4845, 18 U.S.C. § 922(q)(1)(A). The Act did not regulate any economic activity and did not contain any requirement that the possession of a gun have any connection to past interstate activity or a predictable impact on future commercial activity. Distinguishing our earlier cases holding that comprehensive regulatory statutes may be validly applied to local conduct that does not, when viewed in isolation, have a significant impact on interstate commerce, we held the statute invalid. We explained:

> "Section 922(q) is a criminal statute that by its terms has nothing to do with 'commerce' or any sort of economic enterprise, however broadly one might define those terms. Section 922(q) is not an essential part of a larger regulation of economic activity, in which the regulatory scheme could be undercut unless the intrastate activity were regulated. It cannot, therefore, be sustained under our cases upholding regulations of activities that arise out of or are connected with a commercial transaction, which viewed in the aggregate, substantially affects interstate commerce." 514 U.S., at 561.

The statutory scheme that the Government is defending in this litigation is at the opposite end of the regulatory spectrum. As explained above, the CSA, enacted in 1970 as part of the Comprehensive Drug Abuse Prevention and Control Act, 84 Stat. 1242-1284, was a lengthy and detailed statute creating a comprehensive framework for regulating the production, distribution, and possession of five classes of "controlled substances." Most of those substances — those listed in Schedules II through V — have a useful and legitimate medical purpose and are necessary to maintain the health and general welfare of the American people." 21 U.S.C. § 801(1). The regulatory scheme is designed to foster the beneficial use of those medications, to prevent their misuse, and to prohibit entirely the possession or use of substances listed in Schedule I, except as a part of a strictly controlled research project.

While the statute provided for the periodic updating of the five schedules, Congress itself made the initial classifications. It identified 42 opiates, 22 opium derivatives, and 17 hallucinogenic substances as Schedule I drugs. 84 Stat. 1248. Marijuana was listed as the 10th item in the third subcategory. That classification, unlike the discrete prohibition established by the Gun-Free School Zones Act of 1990, was merely one of many "essential part[s] of a larger regulation of economic activity, in which the regulatory scheme could be undercut unless the intrastate activity were regulated." *Lopez*, 514 U.S., at 561. Our opinion in *Lopez* casts no doubt on the validity of such a program.

Nor does this Court's holding in *Morrison*, 529 U.S. 598. The Violence Against Women Act of 1994, 108 Stat. 1902, created a federal civil remedy for the victims of gender-motivated crimes of violence. 42 U.S.C. § 13981. The remedy was enforceable in both state and federal courts, and generally depended on proof of the violation of a state law. Despite congressional findings that such crimes had an adverse impact on interstate commerce, we held the statute unconstitutional because, like the statute in *Lopez*, it did not regulate economic activity. We concluded that "the noneconomic, criminal nature of the conduct at issue was central to our decision" in *Lopez*, and that our prior cases had identified a clear pattern of analysis: "'Where economic activity substantially affects interstate commerce, legislation regulating that activity will be sustained.'" *Morrison*, 529 U.S., at 610.

Unlike those at issue in *Lopez* and *Morrison*, the activities regulated by the CSA are quintessentially economic. "Economics" refers to "the production, distribution, and consumption of commodities." Webster's Third New International Dictionary 720 (1966). The CSA is a statute that regulates the production, distribution, and consumption of commodities for which there is an established, and lucrative, interstate market. Prohibiting the intrastate possession or manufacture of an article of commerce is a rational (and commonly utilized) means of regulating commerce in that product. Such prohibitions include specific decisions requiring that a drug be withdrawn from the market as a result of the failure to comply with regulatory requirements as well as decisions excluding Schedule I drugs entirely from the market. Because the CSA is a statute that directly regulates economic, commercial activity, our opinion in *Morrison* casts no doubt on its constitutionality.

The Court of Appeals was able to conclude otherwise only by isolating a "separate and distinct" class of activities that it held to be beyond the reach of federal power, defined as "the intrastate, noncommercial cultivation, possession and use of marijuana for personal medical purposes on the advice of a physician and in accordance with state law." 352 F.3d, at 1229. The court characterized this class as "different in kind from drug trafficking." *Id.,* at 1228. The differences between the members of a class so defined and the principal traffickers in Schedule I substances might be sufficient to justify a policy decision exempting the narrower class from the coverage of the CSA. The question, however, is whether Congress' contrary policy judgment, *i.e.*, its decision to include this narrower "class of activities" within the larger regulatory scheme, was constitutionally deficient. We have no difficulty concluding that Congress acted rationally in determining that none of the characteristics making up the purported class, whether viewed individually or in the aggregate, compelled an exemption from the CSA; rather, the subdivided class of activities defined by the Court of Appeals was an essential part of the larger regulatory scheme.

First, the fact that marijuana is used "for personal medical purposes on the advice of a physician" cannot itself serve as a distinguishing factor. 352 F.3d, at 1229. The CSA designates marijuana as contraband for *any* purpose; in fact, by characterizing marijuana as a Schedule I drug, Congress expressly found that the drug has no acceptable medical uses. Moreover, the CSA is a comprehensive regulatory regime specifically designed to regulate which controlled substances can be utilized for medicinal purposes, and in what manner. Indeed, most of the substances classified in the CSA "have a useful and legitimate medical purpose." 21 U.S.C. § 801(1). Thus, even if respondents are correct that marijuana does have accepted medical uses and thus should be re-designated as a lesser schedule drug, the CSA would still impose controls beyond what is required by California law. The CSA requires manufacturers, physicians, pharmacies, and other handlers of controlled substances to comply with statutory and regulatory provisions mandating registration with the DEA, compliance with specific production quotas, security controls to guard against diversion, recordkeeping and reporting obligations, and prescription requirements. See 21 U.S.C. § 821-830; 21 CFR §1301 *et seq.* (2004). Furthermore, the dispensing of new drugs, even when doctors approve their use, must await federal approval. *United States* v. *Rutherford*, 442 U.S. 544 (1979). Accordingly, the mere fact that marijuana — like virtually every other controlled substance regulated by the CSA — is used for medicinal purposes cannot possibly serve to distinguish it from the core activities regulated by the CSA.

Nor can it serve as an "objective marke[r]" or "objective facto[r]" to arbitrarily narrow the relevant class as the dissenters suggest, *post*, at 6 (O'Connor, J., dissenting); *post*, at 12 (Thomas, J., dissenting). More fundamentally, if, as the principal dissent contends, the personal cultivation, possession, and use of marijuana for medicinal purposes is beyond the "'outer limits' of Congress' Commerce Clause authority," *post*, at 1 (O'Connor, J., dissenting), it must also be true that such personal use of marijuana (or any other homegrown drug) for recreational purposes is also beyond those "'outer limits,'" whether or not a State elects to authorize or even regulate such use. Justice Thomas' separate dissent suffers from the same sweeping implications. That is, the dissenters' rationale logically extends to place *any* federal regulation (including quality, prescription, or quantity controls) of *any* locally cultivated and possessed controlled substance for *any* purpose beyond the "'outer limits'" of Congress' Commerce Clause authority. One need not have a degree in economics to understand why a nationwide exemption for the vast quantity of marijuana (or other drugs) locally cultivated for personal use (which presumably would include use by friends, neighbors, and family members) may have a substantial impact on the interstate market for this extraordinarily popular substance. The congressional judgment that an exemption for such a significant segment of the total market would undermine the orderly enforcement of the entire regulatory scheme is entitled to a strong presumption of validity. Indeed, that judgment is not only rational, but "visible to the naked eye," *Lopez*, 514 U.S., at 563, under any commonsense appraisal of the probable consequences of such an open-ended exemption.

Second, limiting the activity to marijuana possession and cultivation "in accordance with state law" cannot serve to place respondents' activities beyond congressional reach. The Supremacy Clause unambiguously provides that if there is any conflict between federal and state law, federal law shall prevail. It is beyond peradventure that federal power over commerce is "'superior to that of the States to provide for the welfare or necessities of their inhabitants,'" however legitimate or dire those necessities may be. *Wirtz*, 392 U.S., at 196 (quoting *Sanitary Dist. of Chicago* v. *United States*, 266 U.S. 405, 426 (1925)). See also 392 U.S., at 195-196; *Wickard*, 317 U.S., at 124 ("'[N]o form of state activity can constitutionally thwart the regulatory power granted by the commerce clause to Congress'"). Just as state acquiescence to federal regulation cannot expand the bounds of the Commerce Clause, see, *e.g.*, *Morrison*, 529 U.S., at 661-662 (Breyer, J., dissenting) (noting that 38 States requested federal intervention), so too state action cannot circumscribe Congress' plenary commerce power. See *United States* v. *Darby*, 312 U.S. 100, 114 (1941) ("That power can neither be enlarged nor diminished by the exercise or non-exercise of state power").

Respondents acknowledge this proposition, but nonetheless contend that their activities were not "an essential part of a larger regulatory scheme" because they had been "isolated by the State of California, and [are] policed by the State of California," and thus remain "entirely separated from the market." Tr. of Oral Arg. 27. The dissenters fall prey to similar reasoning. See n. 38, *supra* this page. The notion that California law has surgically excised a discrete activity that is hermetically sealed off from the larger interstate marijuana market is a dubious proposition, and, more importantly, one that Congress could have rationally rejected.

Indeed, that the California exemptions will have a significant impact on both the supply and demand sides of the market for marijuana is not just "plausible" as the principal dissent concedes, *post*, at 16 (O'Connor, J., dissenting), it is readily apparent. The exemption for physicians provides them with an economic incentive to grant their patients permission to use the drug. In contrast to most prescriptions for legal drugs, which limit the dosage and duration of the usage, under California law the doctor's permission to recommend marijuana use is open-ended. The authority to grant permission whenever the doctor determines that a patient is afflicted with "any other illness for which marijuana provides relief," Cal. Health & Safety Code Ann. §11362.5(b)(1)(A) (West Supp. 2005), is broad enough to allow even the most scrupulous doctor to conclude that some recreational uses would be therapeutic. And our cases have taught us that there are some unscrupulous physicians who over prescribe when it is sufficiently profitable to do so.

The exemption for cultivation by patients and caregivers can only increase the supply of marijuana in the California market. The likelihood that all such production will promptly terminate when patients recover or will precisely match the patients' medical needs during their convalescence seems remote; whereas the danger that excesses will satisfy some of the admittedly enormous demand for recreational use seems obvious. Moreover, that the national and international narcotics trade has thrived in the face of vigorous criminal enforcement efforts suggests that no small number of unscrupulous people will make use of the California exemptions to serve their commercial ends whenever it is feasible to do so. Taking into account the fact that California is only one of at least nine States to have authorized the medical use of marijuana, a fact Justice O'Connor's dissent conveniently disregards in arguing that the demonstrated effect on commerce while admittedly "plausible" is ultimately "unsubstantiated," *post*, at 14, 16, Congress could have rationally concluded that the aggregate impact on the national market of all the transactions exempted from federal supervision is unquestionably substantial.

So, from the "separate and distinct" class of activities identified by the Court of Appeals (and adopted by the dissenters), we are left with "the intrastate, noncommercial cultivation, possession and use of marijuana." 352 F.3d, at 1229. Thus the case for the exemption comes down to the claim that a locally cultivated product that is used domestically rather than sold on the open market is not subject to federal regulation. Given the findings in the CSA and the undisputed magnitude of the commercial market for marijuana, our decisions in *Wickard* v. *Filburn* and the later cases endorsing its reasoning foreclose that claim.

V

Respondents also raise a substantive due process claim and seek to avail themselves of the medical necessity defense. These theories of relief were set forth in their complaint but were not reached by the Court of Appeals. We therefore do not address the question whether judicial relief is available to respondents on these alternative bases. We do note, however, the presence of another avenue of relief. As the Solicitor General confirmed during oral argument, the statute authorizes procedures for the reclassification of Schedule I drugs. But perhaps even more important than these legal avenues is the democratic process, in which the voices of voters allied with these respondents may one day be heard in the halls of Congress. Under the present state of the law, however, the judgment of the Court of Appeals must be vacated. The case is remanded for further proceedings consistent with this opinion.

It is so ordered.

Justice SCALIA, concurring in the judgment.

I agree with the Court's holding that the Controlled Substances Act (CSA) may validly be applied to respondents' cultivation, distribution, and possession of marijuana for personal, medicinal use. I write separately because my understanding of the doctrinal foundation on which that holding rests is, if not inconsistent with that of the Court, at least more nuanced.

Since *Perez* v. *United States,* 402 U.S. 146 (1971), our cases have mechanically recited that the Commerce Clause permits congressional regulation of three categories: (1) the channels of interstate commerce; (2) the instrumentalities of interstate commerce, and persons or things in interstate commerce; and (3) activities that "substantially affect" interstate commerce. *Id.*, at 150; see *United States* v. *Morrison,* 529 U.S. 598, 608-609 (2000); *United States* v. *Lopez,* 514 U.S. 549, 558-559 (1995); *Hodel* v. *Virginia Surface*

Mining & Reclamation Assn., Inc., 452 U.S. 264, 276-277 (1981). The first two categories are self-evident, since they are the ingredients of interstate commerce itself. See *Gibbons* v. *Ogden,* 9 Wheat. 1, 189-190 (1824). The third category, however, is different in kind, and its recitation without explanation is misleading and incomplete.

It is *misleading* because, unlike the channels, instrumentalities, and agents of interstate commerce, activities that substantially affect interstate commerce are not themselves part of interstate commerce, and thus the power to regulate them cannot come from the Commerce Clause alone. Rather, as this Court has acknowledged since at least *United States* v. *Coombs,* 12 Pet. 72 (1838), Congress's regulatory authority over intrastate activities that are not themselves part of interstate commerce (including activities that have a substantial effect on interstate commerce) derives from the Necessary and Proper Clause. *Id.,* at 78; *Katzenbach* v. *McClung,* 379 U.S. 294, 301-302 (1964); *United States* v. *Wrightwood Dairy Co.,* 315 U.S. 110, 119 (1942); *Shreveport Rate Cases,* 234 U.S. 342, 353 (1914); *United States* v. *E. C. Knight Co.,* 156 U.S. 1, 39-40 (1895) (Harlan, J., dissenting). And the category of "activities that substantially affect interstate commerce," *Lopez, supra,* at 559, is *incomplete* because the authority to enact laws necessary and proper for the regulation of interstate commerce is not limited to laws governing intrastate activities that substantially affect interstate commerce. Where necessary to make a regulation of interstate commerce effective, Congress may regulate even those intrastate activities that do not themselves substantially affect interstate commerce.

I

Our cases show that the regulation of intrastate activities may be necessary to and proper for the regulation of interstate commerce in two general circumstances. Most directly, the commerce power permits Congress not only to devise rules for the governance of commerce between States but also to facilitate interstate commerce by eliminating potential obstructions, and to restrict it by eliminating potential stimulants. See *NLRB* v. *Jones & Laughlin Steel Corp.,* 301 U.S. 1, 36-37 (1937). That is why the Court has repeatedly sustained congressional legislation on the ground that the regulated activities had a substantial effect on interstate commerce. See, *e.g., Hodel, supra,* at 281 (surface coal mining); *Katzenbach, supra,* at 300 (discrimination by restaurants); *Heart of Atlanta Motel, Inc.* v. *United States,* 379 U.S. 241, 258 (1964) (discrimination by hotels); *Mandeville Island Farms* v. *American Crystal Sugar Co.,* 334 U.S. 219, 237 (1948) (intrastate price-fixing); *Board of Trade of Chicago* v. *Olsen,* 262 U.S. 1, 40 (1923) (activities of a local grain exchange); *Stafford* v. *Wallace,* 258 U.S. 495, 517, 524-525 (1922) (intrastate transactions at stockyard). *Lopez* and *Morrison* recognized the expansive scope of Congress's authority in this regard: "[T]he pattern is clear. Where economic activity substantially affects interstate commerce, legislation regulating that activity will be sustained." *Lopez, supra,* at 560; *Morrison, supra,* at 610 (same).

This principle is not without limitation. In *Lopez* and *Morrison,* the Court — conscious of the potential of the "substantially affects" test to "'obliterate the distinction between what is national and what is local,'" *Lopez, supra,* at 566-567 (quoting *A. L. A. Schechter Poultry Corp.* v. *United States,* 295 U.S. 495, 554 (1935)); see also *Morrison, supra,* at 615-616 — rejected the argument that Congress may regulate *noneconomic* activity based solely on the effect that it may have on interstate commerce through a remote chain of inferences. *Lopez, supra,* at 564-566; *Morrison, supra,* at 617-618. "[I]f we were to accept [such] arguments," the Court reasoned in *Lopez,* "we are hard pressed to posit any activity by an individual that Congress is without power to regulate." *Lopez, supra,* at 564; see also *Morrison, supra,* at 615-616. Thus, although Congress's authority to regulate intrastate activity that substantially affects interstate commerce is broad, it does not permit the Court to "pile inference upon inference," *Lopez, supra,* at 567, in order to establish that noneconomic activity has a substantial effect on interstate commerce.

As we implicitly acknowledged in *Lopez,* however, Congress's authority to enact laws necessary and proper for the regulation of interstate commerce is not limited to laws directed against economic activities that have a substantial effect on interstate commerce. Though the conduct in *Lopez* was not economic, the Court nevertheless recognized that it could be regulated as "an essential part of a larger regulation of economic activity, in which the regulatory scheme could be undercut unless the intrastate activity were regulated." 514 U.S., at 561. This statement referred to those cases permitting the regulation of intrastate activities "which in a substantial way interfere with or obstruct the exercise of the granted power." *Wrightwood Dairy Co.,* 315 U.S., at 119; see also *United States* v. *Darby,* 312 U.S. 100, 118-119 (1941); *Shreveport Rate Cases,* 234 U.S., at 353. As the Court put it in *Wrightwood Dairy,* where Congress has the authority to enact a regulation of interstate commerce, "it possesses every power needed to make that regulation effective." 315 U.S., at 118-119.

Although this power "to make . . . regulation effective" commonly overlaps with the authority to regulate economic activities that substantially affect interstate commerce, and may in some cases have been confused with that authority, the two are distinct. The regulation of an intrastate activity may be essential to a comprehensive regulation of interstate commerce even though the intrastate activity does not itself "substantially affect" interstate commerce. Moreover, as the passage from *Lopez* quoted above suggests, Congress may regulate even noneconomic local activity if that regulation is a necessary part of a more general regulation of interstate commerce. See *Lopez, supra,* at 561. The relevant question is simply whether the means chosen are "reasonably adapted" to the attainment of a legitimate end under the commerce power. See *Darby, supra,* at 121.

In *Darby,* for instance, the Court explained that "Congress, having . . . adopted the policy of excluding from interstate commerce all goods produced for the commerce which do not conform to the specified labor standards," 312 U.S., at 121, could not only require employers engaged in the production of goods for interstate commerce to conform to wage and hour standards, *id.,* at 119-121, but could also require those employers to keep employment records in order to demonstrate compliance with the regulatory scheme, *id.,* at 125. While the Court sustained the former regulation on the alternative ground that the activity it regulated could have a "great effect" on interstate commerce, *id.,* at 122-123, it affirmed the latter on the sole ground that "[t]he requirement for records even of the intrastate transaction is an appropriate means to a legitimate end," *id.,* at 125.

As the Court said in the *Shreveport Rate Cases,* the Necessary and Proper Clause does not give "Congress . . . the authority to regulate the internal commerce of a State, as such," but it does allow Congress "to take all measures necessary or appropriate to" the effective regulation of the interstate market, "although intrastate transactions . . . may thereby be controlled." 234 U.S., at 353; see also *Jones & Laughlin Steel Corp.,* 301 U.S., at 38 (the logic of the *Shreveport Rate Cases* is not limited to instrumentalities of commerce).

II

Today's principal dissent objects that, by permitting Congress to regulate activities necessary to effective interstate regulation, the Court reduces *Lopez* and *Morrison* to "little more than a drafting guide." *Post,* at 5 (opinion of O'Connor, J.). I think that criticism unjustified. Unlike the power to regulate activities that have a substantial effect on interstate commerce, the power to enact laws enabling effective regulation of interstate commerce can only be exercised in conjunction with congressional regulation of an interstate market, and it extends only to those measures necessary to make the interstate regulation effective. As *Lopez* itself states, and the Court affirms today, Congress may regulate noneconomic intrastate activities only where the failure to do so "could . . . undercut" its regulation of interstate commerce. See *Lopez, supra,* at 561; *ante,* at 15, 21, 22. This is not a power that threatens to obliterate the line between "what is truly national and what is truly local." *Lopez, supra,* at 567-568.

Lopez and *Morrison* affirm that Congress may not regulate certain "purely local" activity within the States based solely on the attenuated effect that such activity may have in the interstate market. But those decisions do not declare noneconomic intrastate activities to be categorically beyond the reach of the Federal Government. Neither case involved the power of Congress to exert control over intrastate activities in connection with a more comprehensive scheme of regulation; *Lopez* expressly disclaimed that it was such a case, 514 U.S., at 561, and *Morrison* did not even discuss the possibility that it was. (The Court of Appeals in *Morrison* made clear that it was not. See *Brzonkala* v. *Virginia Polytechnic Inst.,* 169 F.3d 820, 834-835 (CA4 1999) (en banc).) To dismiss this distinction as "superficial and formalistic," see *post,* at 6 (O'Connor, J., dissenting), is to misunderstand the nature of the Necessary and Proper Clause, which empowers Congress to enact laws in effectuation of its enumerated powers that are not within its authority to enact in isolation. See *McCulloch* v. *Maryland,* 4 Wheat. 316, 421-422 (1819).

And there are other restraints upon the Necessary and Proper Clause authority. As Chief Justice Marshall wrote in *McCulloch* v. *Maryland,* even when the end is constitutional and legitimate, the means must be "appropriate" and "plainly adapted" to that end. *Id.,* at 421. Moreover, they may not be otherwise "prohibited" and must be "consistent with the letter and spirit of the constitution." *Ibid.* These phrases are not merely hortatory. For example, cases such as *Printz* v. *United States,* 521 U.S. 898 (1997), and *New York* v. *United States,* 505 U.S. 144 (1992), affirm that a law is not "'*proper* for carrying into Execution the Commerce Clause'" "[w]hen [it] violates [a constitutional] principle of state sovereignty." *Printz, supra,* at 923-924; see also *New York, supra,* at 166.

III

The application of these principles to the case before us is straightforward. In the CSA, Congress has undertaken to extinguish the interstate market in Schedule I controlled substances, including marijuana. The Commerce Clause unquestionably permits this. The power to regulate interstate commerce "extends not only to those regulations which aid, foster and protect the commerce, but embraces those which prohibit it." *Darby,* 312 U.S., at 113. See also *Hipolite Egg Co.* v. *United States,* 220 U.S. 45, 58 (1911); *Lottery Case,* 188 U.S. 321, 354 (1903). To effectuate its objective, Congress has prohibited almost all intrastate activities related to Schedule I substances — both economic activities (manufacture, distribution, possession with the intent to distribute) and noneconomic activities (simple possession). See 21 U.S.C. § 841(a), 844(a). That simple possession is a noneconomic activity is immaterial to whether it can be prohibited as a necessary part of a larger regulation. Rather, Congress's authority to enact all of these prohibitions of intrastate controlled-substance activities depends only upon whether they are appropriate means of achieving the legitimate end of eradicating Schedule I substances from interstate commerce.

By this measure, I think the regulation must be sustained. Not only is it impossible to distinguish "controlled substances manufactured and distributed intrastate" from "controlled substances manufactured and distributed interstate," but it hardly makes sense to speak in such terms. Drugs like marijuana are fungible commodities. As the Court explains, marijuana that is grown at home and possessed for personal use is never more than an instant from the interstate market — and this is so whether or not the possession is for medicinal use or lawful use under the laws of a particular State. See *ante*, at 23-30. Congress need not accept on faith that state law will be effective in maintaining a strict division between a lawful market for "medical" marijuana and the more general marijuana market. See *id.*, at 26-27, and n. 38. "To impose on [Congress] the necessity of resorting to means which it cannot control, which another government may furnish or withhold, would render its course precarious, the result of its measures uncertain, and create a dependence on other governments, which might disappoint its most important designs, and is incompatible with the language of the constitution." *McCulloch, supra*, at 424.

Finally, neither respondents nor the dissenters suggest any violation of state sovereignty of the sort that would render this regulation "inappropriate," *id.*, at 421 — except to argue that the CSA regulates an area typically left to state regulation. See *post*, at 6-7, 11 (opinion of O'Connor, J.); *post*, at 8-9 (opinion of Thomas, J.); Brief for Respondents 39-42. That is not enough to render federal regulation an inappropriate means. The Court has repeatedly recognized that, if authorized by the commerce power, Congress may regulate private endeavors "even when [that regulation] may pre-empt express state-law determinations contrary to the result which has commended itself to the collective wisdom of Congress." *National League of Cities* v. *Usery*, 426 U.S. 833, 840 (1976); see *Cleveland* v. *United States*, 329 U.S. 14, 19 (1946); *McCulloch, supra*, at 424. At bottom, respondents' state-sovereignty argument reduces to the contention that federal regulation of the activities permitted by California's Compassionate Use Act is not sufficiently necessary to be "necessary and proper" to Congress's regulation of the interstate market. For the reasons given above and in the Court's opinion, I cannot agree.

I thus agree with the Court that, however the class of regulated activities is subdivided, Congress could reasonably conclude that its objective of prohibiting marijuana from the interstate market "could be undercut" if those activities were excepted from its general scheme of regulation. See *Lopez*, 514 U.S., at 561. That is sufficient to authorize the application of the CSA to respondents.

Justice O'CONNOR, with whom THE CHIEF JUSTICE and Justice THOMAS join as to all but Part III, dissenting.

We enforce the "outer limits" of Congress' Commerce Clause authority not for their own sake, but to protect historic spheres of state sovereignty from excessive federal encroachment and thereby to maintain the distribution of power fundamental to our federalist system of government. *United States* v. *Lopez*, 514 U.S. 549, 557 (1995); *NLRB* v. *Jones & Laughlin Steel Corp.*, 301 U.S. 1, 37 (1937). One of federalism's chief virtues, of course, is that it promotes innovation by allowing for the possibility that "a single courageous State may, if its citizens choose, serve as a laboratory; and try novel social and economic experiments without risk to the rest of the country." *New State Ice Co.* v. *Liebmann*, 285 U.S. 262, 311 (1932) (Brandeis, J., dissenting).

This case exemplifies the role of States as laboratories. The States' core police powers have always included authority to define criminal law and to protect the health, safety, and welfare of their citizens. *Brecht* v. *Abrahamson*, 507 U.S. 619, 635 (1993); *Whalen* v. *Roe*, 429 U.S. 589, 603, n. 30 (1977). Exercising those powers, California (by ballot initiative and then by legislative codification) has come to its own conclusion about the difficult and sensitive question of whether marijuana should be available to relieve severe pain and suffering. Today the Court sanctions an application of the federal Controlled Substances

Act that extinguishes that experiment, without any proof that the personal cultivation, possession, and use of marijuana for medicinal purposes, if economic activity in the first place, has a substantial effect on interstate commerce and is therefore an appropriate subject of federal regulation. In so doing, the Court announces a rule that gives Congress a perverse incentive to legislate broadly pursuant to the Commerce Clause — nestling questionable assertions of its authority into comprehensive regulatory schemes — rather than with precision. That rule and the result it produces in this case are irreconcilable with our decisions in *Lopez, supra,* and *United States* v. *Morrison,* 529 U.S. 598 (2000). Accordingly I dissent.

I

In *Lopez,* we considered the constitutionality of the Gun-Free School Zones Act of 1990, which made it a federal offense "for any individual knowingly to possess a firearm . . . at a place the individual knows, or has reasonable cause to believe, is a school zone," 18 U.S.C. § 922(q)(2)(A). We explained that "Congress' commerce authority includes the power to regulate those activities having a substantial relation to interstate commerce . . . , *i.e.,* those activities that substantially affect interstate commerce." 514 U.S., at 558-559 (citation omitted). This power derives from the conjunction of the Commerce Clause and the Necessary and Proper Clause. *Garcia* v. *San Antonio Metropolitan Transit Authority,* 469 U.S. 528, 585-586 (1985) (O'Connor, J., dissenting) (explaining that *United States* v. *Darby,* 312 U.S. 100 (1941), *United States* v. *Wrightwood Dairy Co.,* 315 U.S. 110 (1942), and *Wickard* v. *Filburn,* 317 U.S. 111 (1942), based their expansion of the commerce power on the Necessary and Proper Clause, and that "the reasoning of these cases underlies every recent decision concerning the reach of Congress to activities affecting interstate commerce"); *ante,* at 2 (Scalia, J., concurring in judgment). We held in *Lopez* that the Gun-Free School Zones Act could not be sustained as an exercise of that power.

Our decision about whether gun possession in school zones substantially affected interstate commerce turned on four considerations. *Lopez, supra,* at 559-567; see also *Morrison, supra,* at 609-613. First, we observed that our "substantial effects" cases generally have upheld federal regulation of economic activity that affected interstate commerce, but that §922(q) was a criminal statute having "nothing to do with 'commerce' or any sort of economic enterprise." *Lopez,* 514 U.S., at 561. In this regard, we also noted that "[s]ection 922(q) is not an essential part of a larger regulation of economic activity, in which the regulatory scheme could be undercut unless the intrastate activity were regulated. It cannot, therefore, be sustained under our cases upholding regulations of activities that arise out of or are connected with a commercial transaction, which viewed in the aggregate, substantially affects interstate commerce." *Ibid.* Second, we noted that the statute contained no express jurisdictional requirement establishing its connection to interstate commerce. *Ibid.*

Third, we found telling the absence of legislative findings about the regulated conduct's impact on interstate commerce. We explained that while express legislative findings are neither required nor, when provided, dispositive, findings "enable us to evaluate the legislative judgment that the activity in question substantially affect[s] interstate commerce, even though no such substantial effect [is] visible to the naked eye." *Id.,* at 563. Finally, we rejected as too attenuated the Government's argument that firearm possession in school zones could result in violent crime which in turn could adversely affect the national economy. *Id.,* at 563-567. The Constitution, we said, does not tolerate reasoning that would "convert congressional authority under the Commerce Clause to a general police power of the sort retained by the States." *Id.,* at 567. Later in *Morrison, supra*, we relied on the same four considerations to hold that §40302 of the Violence Against Women Act of 1994, 42 U.S.C. § 13981 exceeded Congress' authority under the Commerce Clause.

In my view, the case before us is materially indistinguishable from *Lopez* and *Morrison* when the same considerations are taken into account.

II

A

What is the relevant conduct subject to Commerce Clause analysis in this case? The Court takes its cues from Congress, applying the above considerations to the activity regulated by the Controlled Substances Act (CSA) in general. The Court's decision rests on two facts about the CSA: (1) Congress chose to enact a single statute providing a comprehensive prohibition on the production, distribution, and possession of all controlled substances, and (2) Congress did not distinguish between various forms of intrastate noncommercial cultivation, possession, and use of marijuana. See 21 U.S.C. § 841(a)(1), 844(a). Today's decision suggests that the federal regulation of local activity is immune to Commerce Clause challenge because Congress chose to act with an ambitious, all-encompassing statute, rather than piecemeal. In my view, allowing Congress to set the terms of the constitutional debate in this way, *i.e.*, by packaging regulation of local activity in broader schemes, is tantamount to removing meaningful limits on the Commerce Clause.

The Court's principal means of distinguishing *Lopez* from this case is to observe that the Gun-Free School Zones Act of 1990 was a "brief, single-subject statute," *ante*, at 20, see also *ante,* at 19, whereas the CSA is "a lengthy and detailed statute creating a comprehensive framework for regulating the production, distribution, and possession of five classes of 'controlled substances,'" *ibid*. Thus, according to the Court, it was possible in *Lopez* to evaluate in isolation the constitutionality of criminalizing local activity (there gun possession in school zones), whereas the local activity that the CSA targets (in this case cultivation and possession of marijuana for personal medicinal use) cannot be separated from the general drug control scheme of which it is a part.

Today's decision allows Congress to regulate intrastate activity without check, so long as there is some implication by legislative design that regulating intrastate activity is essential (and the Court appears to equate "essential" with "necessary") to the interstate regulatory scheme. Seizing upon our language in *Lopez* that the statute prohibiting gun possession in school zones was "not an essential part of a larger regulation of economic activity, in which the regulatory scheme could be undercut unless the intrastate activity were regulated," 514 U.S., at 561, the Court appears to reason that the placement of local activity in a comprehensive scheme confirms that it is essential to that scheme. *Ante*, at 21-22. If the Court is right, then *Lopez* stands for nothing more than a drafting guide: Congress should have described the relevant crime as "transfer or possession of a firearm anywhere in the nation" — thus including commercial and noncommercial activity, and clearly encompassing some activity with assuredly substantial effect on interstate commerce. Had it done so, the majority hints, we would have sustained its authority to regulate possession of firearms in school zones. Furthermore, today's decision suggests we would readily sustain a congressional decision to attach the regulation of intrastate activity to a pre-existing comprehensive (or even not-so-comprehensive) scheme. If so, the Court invites increased federal regulation of local activity even if, as it suggests, Congress would not enact a *new* interstate scheme exclusively for the sake of reaching intrastate activity, see *ante*, at 22, n. 33; *ante*, at 6 (Scalia, J., concurring in judgment).

I cannot agree that our decision in *Lopez* contemplated such evasive or overbroad legislative strategies with approval. Until today, such arguments have been made only in dissent. See *Morrison*, 529 U.S., at 657 (Breyer, J., dissenting) (given that Congress can regulate "'an essential part of a larger regulation of economic activity,'" "can Congress save the present law by including it, or much of it, in a broader 'Safe Transport' or 'Worker Safety' act?"). *Lopez* and *Morrison* did not indicate that the constitutionality of federal regulation depends on superficial and formalistic distinctions. Likewise I did not understand our discussion of the role of courts in enforcing outer limits of the Commerce Clause for the sake of maintaining the federalist balance our Constitution requires, see *Lopez*, 514 U.S., at 557; *id.*, at 578 (Kennedy, J., concurring), as a signal to Congress to enact legislation that is more extensive and more intrusive into the domain of state power. If the Court always defers to Congress as it does today, little may be left to the notion of enumerated powers.

The hard work for courts, then, is to identify objective markers for confining the analysis in Commerce Clause cases. Here, respondents challenge the constitutionality of the CSA as applied to them and those similarly situated. I agree with the Court that we must look beyond respondents' own activities. Otherwise, individual litigants could always exempt themselves from Commerce Clause regulation merely by pointing to the obvious — that their personal activities do not have a substantial effect on interstate commerce. See *Maryland* v. *Wirtz*, 392 U.S. 183, 193 (1968); *Wickard*, 317 U.S., at 127-128. The task is to identify a mode of analysis that allows Congress to regulate more than nothing (by declining to reduce each case to its litigants) and less than everything (by declining to let Congress set the terms of analysis). The analysis may not be the same in every case, for it depends on the regulatory scheme at issue and the federalism concerns implicated. See generally *Lopez*, 514 U.S., at 567; *id.*, at 579 (Kennedy, J., concurring).

A number of objective markers are available to confine the scope of constitutional review here. Both federal and state legislation — including the CSA itself, the California Compassionate Use Act, and other state medical marijuana legislation — recognize that medical and nonmedical (*i.e.*, recreational) uses of drugs are realistically distinct and can be segregated, and regulate them differently. See 21 U.S.C. § 812; Cal. Health & Safety Code Ann. §11362.5 (West Supp. 2005); *ante*, at 1 (opinion of the Court). Respondents challenge only the application of the CSA to medicinal use of marijuana. Cf. *United States* v. *Raines*, 362 U.S. 17, 20-22 (1960) (describing our preference for as-applied rather than facial challenges). Moreover, because fundamental structural concerns about dual sovereignty animate our Commerce Clause cases, it is relevant that this case involves the interplay of federal and state regulation in areas of criminal law and social policy, where "States lay claim by right of history and expertise." *Lopez*, *supra*, at 583 (Kennedy, J., concurring); see also *Morrison*, *supra*, at 617-619; *Lopez*, *supra*, at 580 (Kennedy, J., concurring) ("The statute before us upsets the federal balance to a degree that renders it an unconstitutional assertion of the commerce power, and our intervention is required"); cf. *Garcia*, 469 U.S., at 586 (O'Connor, J., dissenting) ("[S]tate autonomy is a relevant factor in assessing the means by which Congress exercises its powers" under the Commerce Clause). California, like other States, has drawn on its reserved powers to distinguish the regulation of medicinal marijuana. To ascertain whether Congress' encroachment is constitutionally justified in this case, then, I would focus here on the personal cultivation, possession, and use of marijuana for medicinal purposes.

B

Having thus defined the relevant conduct, we must determine whether, under our precedents, the conduct is economic and, in the aggregate, substantially affects interstate commerce. Even if intrastate cultivation and possession of marijuana for one's own medicinal use can properly be characterized as economic, and I question whether it can, it has not been shown that such activity substantially affects interstate commerce. Similarly, it is neither self-evident nor demonstrated that regulating such activity is necessary to the interstate drug control scheme.

The Court's definition of economic activity is breathtaking. It defines as economic any activity involving the production, distribution, and consumption of commodities. And it appears to reason that when an interstate market for a commodity exists, regulating the intrastate manufacture or possession of that commodity is constitutional either because that intrastate activity is itself economic, or because regulating it is a rational part of regulating its market. Putting to one side the problem endemic to the Court's opinion — the shift in focus from the activity at issue in this case to the entirety of what the CSA regulates, see *Lopez, supra*, at 565 ("depending on the level of generality, any activity can be looked upon as commercial") — the Court's definition of economic activity for purposes of Commerce Clause jurisprudence threatens to sweep all of productive human activity into federal regulatory reach.

The Court uses a dictionary definition of economics to skirt the real problem of drawing a meaningful line between "what is national and what is local," *Jones & Laughlin Steel*, 301 U.S., at 37. It will not do to say that Congress may regulate noncommercial activity simply because it may have an effect on the demand for commercial goods, or because the noncommercial endeavor can, in some sense, substitute for commercial activity. Most commercial goods or services have some sort of privately producible analogue. Home care substitutes for daycare. Charades games substitute for movie tickets. Backyard or windowsill gardening substitutes for going to the supermarket. To draw the line wherever private activity affects the demand for market goods is to draw no line at all, and to declare everything economic. We have already rejected the result that would follow — a federal police power. *Lopez, supra*, at 564.

In *Lopez* and *Morrison*, we suggested that economic activity usually relates directly to commercial activity. See *Morrison*, 529 U.S., at 611, n. 4 (intrastate activities that have been within Congress' power to regulate have been "of an apparent commercial character"); *Lopez*, 514 U.S., at 561 (distinguishing the Gun-Free School Zones Act of 1990 from "activities that arise out of or are connected with a commercial transaction"). The homegrown cultivation and personal possession and use of marijuana for medicinal purposes has no apparent commercial character. Everyone agrees that the marijuana at issue in this case was never in the stream of commerce, and neither were the supplies for growing it. (Marijuana is highly unusual among the substances subject to the CSA in that it can be cultivated without any materials that have traveled in interstate commerce.) *Lopez* makes clear that possession is not itself commercial activity. *Ibid*. And respondents have not come into possession by means of any commercial transaction; they have simply grown, in their own homes, marijuana for their own use, without acquiring, buying, selling, or bartering a thing of value. Cf. *id.*, at 583 (Kennedy, J., concurring) ("The statute now before us forecloses the States from experimenting . . . and it does so by regulating an activity beyond the realm of commerce in the ordinary and usual sense of that term").

The Court suggests that *Wickard*, which we have identified as "perhaps the most far reaching example of Commerce Clause authority over intrastate activity," *Lopez, supra*, at

560, established federal regulatory power over any home consumption of a commodity for which a national market exists. I disagree. *Wickard* involved a challenge to the Agricultural Adjustment Act of 1938 (AAA), which directed the Secretary of Agriculture to set national quotas on wheat production, and penalties for excess production. 317 U.S., at 115-116. The AAA itself confirmed that Congress made an explicit choice not to reach — and thus the Court could not possibly have approved of federal control over — small-scale, noncommercial wheat farming. In contrast to the CSA's limitless assertion of power, Congress provided an exemption within the AAA for small producers. When Filburn planted the wheat at issue in *Wickard*, the statute exempted plantings less than 200 bushels (about six tons), and when he harvested his wheat it exempted plantings less than six acres. *Id.*, at 130, n. 30. *Wickard,* then, did not extend Commerce Clause authority to something as modest as the home cook's herb garden. This is not to say that Congress may never regulate small quantities of commodities possessed or produced for personal use, or to deny that it sometimes needs to enact a zero tolerance regime for such commodities. It is merely to say that *Wickard* did not hold or imply that small-scale production of commodities is always economic, and automatically within Congress' reach.

Even assuming that economic activity is at issue in this case, the Government has made no showing in fact that the possession and use of homegrown marijuana for medical purposes, in California or elsewhere, has a substantial effect on interstate commerce. Similarly, the Government has not shown that regulating such activity is necessary to an interstate regulatory scheme. Whatever the specific theory of "substantial effects" at issue (*i.e.*, whether the activity substantially affects interstate commerce, whether its regulation is necessary to an interstate regulatory scheme, or both), a concern for dual sovereignty requires that Congress' excursion into the traditional domain of States be justified.

That is why characterizing this as a case about the Necessary and Proper Clause does not change the analysis significantly. Congress must exercise its authority under the Necessary and Proper Clause in a manner consistent with basic constitutional principles. *Garcia*, 469 U.S., at 585 (O'Connor, J., dissenting) ("It is not enough that the 'end be legitimate'; the means to that end chosen by Congress must not contravene the spirit of the Constitution"). As Justice Scalia recognizes, see *ante*, at 7 (opinion concurring in judgment), Congress cannot use its authority under the Clause to contravene the principle of state sovereignty embodied in the Tenth Amendment. *Ibid.* Likewise, that authority must be used in a manner consistent with the notion of enumerated powers — a structural principle that is as much part of the Constitution as the Tenth Amendment's explicit textual command. Accordingly, something more than mere assertion is required when Congress purports to have power over local activity whose connection to an intrastate market is not self-evident. Otherwise, the Necessary and Proper Clause will always be a back door for unconstitutional federal regulation. Cf. *Printz* v. *United States*, 521 U.S. 898, 923 (1997) (the Necessary and Proper Clause is "the last, best hope of those who defend ultra vires congressional action"). Indeed, if it were enough in "substantial effects" cases for the Court to supply conceivable justifications for intrastate regulation related to an interstate market, then we could have surmised in *Lopez* that guns in school zones are "never more than an instant from the interstate market" in guns already subject to extensive federal regulation, *ante*, at 8 (Scalia, J., concurring in judgment), recast *Lopez* as a Necessary and Proper Clause case, and thereby upheld the Gun-Free School Zones Act of 1990. (According to the Court's and the concurrence's logic, for example, the *Lopez* court should have reasoned that the prohibition on gun possession in school zones could be an appropriate means of effectuating a related prohibition on "sell[ing]" or "deliver[ing]" firearms or ammunition to "any individual who the licensee knows or has reasonable cause to believe is less than eighteen years of age." 18 U.S.C. § 922(b)(1) (1988 ed., Supp. II).)

There is simply no evidence that homegrown medicinal marijuana users constitute, in the aggregate, a sizable enough class to have a discernable, let alone substantial, impact on the national illicit drug market — or otherwise to threaten the CSA regime. Explicit evidence is helpful when substantial effect is not "visible to the naked eye." See *Lopez*, 514 U.S., at 563. And here, in part because common sense suggests that medical marijuana users may be limited in number and that California's Compassionate Use Act and similar state legislation may well isolate activities relating to medicinal marijuana from the illicit market, the effect of those activities on interstate drug traffic is not self-evidently substantial.

In this regard, again, this case is readily distinguishable from *Wickard*. To decide whether the Secretary could regulate local wheat farming, the Court looked to "the actual effects of the activity in question upon interstate commerce." 317 U.S., at 120. Critically, the Court was able to consider "actual effects" because the parties had "stipulated a summary of the economics of the wheat industry." *Id.*, at 125. After reviewing in detail the picture of the industry provided in that summary, the Court explained that consumption of homegrown wheat was the most variable factor in the size of the national wheat crop, and that on-site consumption could have the effect of varying the amount of wheat sent to market by as much as 20 percent. *Id.*, at 127. With real numbers at hand, the *Wickard* Court could easily conclude that "a factor of such volume and variability as home-consumed wheat would have a substantial influence on price and market conditions" nationwide. *Id.*, at 128; see also *id.*, at 128-129 ("This record leaves us in no doubt" about substantial effects).

The Court recognizes that "the record in the *Wickard* case itself established the causal connection between the production for local use and the national market" and argues that "we have before us findings by Congress *to the same effect*." *Ante*, at 17 (emphasis added). The Court refers to a series of declarations in the introduction to the CSA saying that (1) local distribution and possession of controlled substances causes "swelling" in interstate traffic; (2) local production and distribution cannot be distinguished from interstate production and distribution; (3) federal control over intrastate incidents "is essential to effective control" over interstate drug trafficking. 21 U.S.C. § 801(1)-(6). These bare declarations cannot be compared to the record before the Court in *Wickard*.

They amount to nothing more than a legislative insistence that the regulation of controlled substances must be absolute. They are asserted without any supporting evidence — descriptive, statistical, or otherwise. "[S]imply because Congress may conclude a particular activity substantially affects interstate commerce does not necessarily make it so." *Hodel* v. *Virginia Surface Mining & Reclamation Assn., Inc.*, 452 U.S. 264, 311 (1981) (Rehnquist, J., concurring in judgment). Indeed, if declarations like these suffice to justify federal regulation, and if the Court today is right about what passes rationality review before us, then our decision in *Morrison* should have come out the other way. In that case, Congress had supplied numerous findings regarding the impact gender-motivated violence had on the national economy. 529 U.S., at 614; *id.*, at 628-636 (Souter, J., dissenting) (chronicling findings). But, recognizing that ""'[w]hether particular operations affect interstate commerce sufficiently to come under the constitutional power of Congress to regulate them is ultimately a judicial rather than a legislative question,'"" we found Congress' detailed findings inadequate. *Id.*, at 614 (quoting *Lopez, supra*, at 557, n. 2, in turn quoting *Heart of Atlanta Motel, Inc.* v. *United States*, 379 U.S. 241, 273 (1964) (Black,

J., concurring)). If, as the Court claims, today's decision does not break with precedent, how can it be that voluminous findings, documenting extensive hearings about the specific topic of violence against women, did not pass constitutional muster in *Morrison*, while the CSA's abstract, unsubstantiated, generalized findings about controlled substances do?

[The] Government has not overcome empirical doubt that the number of Californians engaged in personal cultivation, possession, and use of medical marijuana, or the amount of marijuana they produce, is enough to threaten the federal regime. Nor has it shown that Compassionate Use Act marijuana users have been or are realistically likely to be responsible for the drug's seeping into the market in a significant way. The Government does cite one estimate that there were over 100,000 Compassionate Use Act users in California in 2004, but does not explain, in terms of proportions, what their presence means for the national illicit drug market. [It] also provides anecdotal evidence about the CSA's enforcement. See Reply Brief for Petitioners 17-18. The Court also offers some arguments about the effect of the Compassionate Use Act on the national market. It says that the California statute might be vulnerable to exploitation by unscrupulous physicians, that Compassionate Use Act patients may overproduce, and that the history of the narcotics trade shows the difficulty of cordoning off any drug use from the rest of the market. These arguments are plausible; if borne out in fact they could justify prosecuting Compassionate Use Act patients under the federal CSA. But, without substantiation, they add little to the CSA's conclusory statements about diversion, essentiality, and market effect. Piling assertion upon assertion does not, in my view, satisfy the substantiality test of *Lopez* and *Morrison*.

III

We would do well to recall how James Madison, the father of the Constitution, described our system of joint sovereignty to the people of New York: "The powers delegated by the proposed constitution to the federal government are few and defined. Those which are to remain in the State governments are numerous and indefinite. . . . The powers reserved to the several States will extend to all the objects which, in the ordinary course of affairs, concern the lives, liberties, and properties of the people, and the internal order, improvement, and prosperity of the State." The Federalist No. 45, pp. 292-293 (C. Rossiter ed. 1961).

Relying on Congress' abstract assertions, the Court has endorsed making it a federal crime to grow small amounts of marijuana in one's own home for one's own medicinal use. This overreaching stifles an express choice by some States, concerned for the lives and liberties of their people, to regulate medical marijuana differently. If I were a California citizen, I would not have voted for the medical marijuana ballot initiative; if I were a California legislator I would not have supported the Compassionate Use Act. But whatever the wisdom of California's experiment with medical marijuana, the federalism principles that have driven our Commerce Clause cases require that room for experiment be protected in this case. For these reasons I dissent.

Justice Thomas filed a separate dissenting opinion.

Comments on *Gonzales* — Where Are We at Now? Is *Gonzales* consistent with the holdings in *Lopez* and *Morrison*? On what basis are these cases distinguishable? Is this simply a matter of economic versus non-economic activity? Is *Wickard* revived? When is it applicable and when is it not? Note the alignment of Justices in *Gonzales*: the dissenting Justices in *Lopez* and *Morrison* become the "majority" in *Gonzales* with the addition of

Justice Kennedy's vote, and a concurring opinion of Justice Scalia "tagging along." What meaning here? To what degree did the nature of the issue, federal drug control, affect the outcome? Does this underscore Justice Scalia's opinion, or was it his view of the reach of federal regulatory power? Given the nature of the issues, the realignment of Justices, and the replacement of the Chief Justice and Justice O'Connor (both in the dissent here), what next?

Environmental Protection and the Commerce Clause. If gun possession and domestic violence are subject matters too far removed from the national commerce power to permit congressional regulation, then what of environmental protection laws? May Congress, within the meaning of the commerce power, regulate seasonal streams and intermittent wetlands that are not themselves part of the nation's navigable waterways? In *Rapanos v. United States*, 547 U.S. 715 (2006), the Court did not reach the constitutional question of the breadth of Congress's power to protect the environment, but offered a narrowing construction of the term "waters" in the Clean Water Act that some Justices suggested was necessary to avoid that constitutional question. The Act prohibits certain discharges into "navigable waters," defined as "the waters of the United States." Army Corps of Engineer regulations interpreted such waters to include "wetlands adjacent to" such waters even if only intermittently wet. In *Solid Waste Agency of Northern Cook Co. v. Army Corps of Engineers*, 531 U.S. 159 (2001), the Court had previously rejected the Corps' assertion of jurisdiction over an abandoned sand and gravel pit that provided a habitat for migratory birds, reasoning that such an isolated intrastate location had no "significant nexus" to traditionally navigable waters.

Writing for a plurality of the Court in Rapanos and consolidated cases, Justice Scalia, joined by Chief Justice Roberts and Justices Thomas and Alito, opined that the Corps' interpretation exceeded its authority under the Act: "[W]e consider whether four Michigan wetlands, which lie near ditches or man-made drains that eventually empty into traditional navigable waters, constitute 'waters of the United States' within the meaning of the Act. [The term] 'the waters' refers [to] water 'as found in streams and bodies forming geographical features such as oceans, rivers, [and] lakes,' or 'the flowing or moving masses, as of waves or floods, making up such streams or bodies.' Webster's New International Dictionary 2882 (2d ed. 1954). On this definition, 'the waters of the United States' include only relatively permanent, standing or flowing bodies of water [as] opposed to ordinarily dry channels through which water occasionally or intermittently flows."

The plurality suggested that the Corps' more expansive definition "presses the envelope of constitutional validity" and thus requires a plainer statement of authority from Congress: "Regulation of land use, as through the issuance of the development permits sought by petitioners in [these] cases, is a quintessential state and local power. The extensive federal jurisdiction urged by the Government would authorize the Corps to function as a de facto regulator of immense stretches of intrastate land. [We] ordinarily expect a 'clear and manifest' statement from Congress to authorize an unprecedented intrusion into traditional state authority. Likewise, [the] Corps' interpretation stretches the outer limits of Congress's commerce power and raises difficult questions about the ultimate scope of that power. [W]e would expect a clearer statement from Congress to authorize [such] an agency theory of jurisdiction."

Justice Kennedy provided the fifth vote for remanding the case for further proceedings, but concurred only in the judgment. In his reading of the relevant provision of the Clean Water Act, a wetland need only "possess a 'significant nexus' to waters that are or were navigable in fact or that could reasonably be so made" — a test that Justice Scalia's plurality opinion dismissed as "perfectly opaque." Justice Kennedy insisted that his "interpretation of the Act does not raise federalism or Commerce Clause concerns sufficient to support a presumption against its adoption. ['The] exercise of the granted power of Congress to regulate interstate commerce may be aided by appropriate and needful control of activities and agencies which, though intrastate, affect that commerce.'"

Justice Stevens filed a dissent joined by Justices Souter, Ginsburg, and Breyer. The dissenters found reasonable the Army Corps' determination "that wetlands adjacent to tributaries of traditionally navigable waters preserve the quality of our Nation's waters by, among other things, providing habitat for aquatic animals, keeping excessive sediment and toxic pollutants out of adjacent waters, and reducing downstream flooding by absorbing water at times of high flow." The dissent rejected as unwarranted the plurality's concern that "the Corps' approach might exceed the limits of our Commerce Clause authority," reasoning that "[t]he wetlands in these cases are not 'isolated' but instead are adjacent to tributaries of traditionally navigable waters and play important roles in the watershed, such as keeping water out of the tributaries or absorbing water from the tributaries. 'There is no constitutional reason why Congress cannot, under the commerce power, treat the watersheds as a key to flood control on navigable streams and their tributaries.'" Justice Breyer filed a brief separate dissent emphasizing the breadth of Congress' power under the Commerce Clause over the nation's "intricately interconnected" waters.

2. THE AFFORDABLE HEALTH CARE ACT AND THE COMMERCE CLAUSE

NATIONAL FEDERATION OF INDEPENDENT BUSINESS v. SEBELIUS
132 S. Ct. 2566 (2012)

Chief Justice ROBERTS announced the judgment of the Court and delivered an opinion with respect to Part III-A.

[In 2010, Congress enacted the Patient Protection and Affordable Care Act. The Act aims to increase the number of Americans covered by health insurance and decrease the cost of health care. The individual mandate requires most Americans to maintain "minimum essential" health insurance coverage. The mandate does not apply to some individuals, such as prisoners and undocumented aliens. Many individuals will receive the required coverage through their employer or from a government program such as Medicaid or Medicare. But for individuals who are not exempt and do not receive health insurance through a third party, the means of satisfying the requirement is to purchase insurance from a private company. Beginning in 2014, those who do not comply with the mandate must make a "[s]hared responsibility payment" to the federal government. That payment, which the Act describes as a "penalty," is calculated as a percentage of household income, subject to a floor based on a specified dollar amount and a ceiling based on the average annual premium the individual would have to pay for qualifying private health insurance. The Act provides that the penalty will be paid to the Internal Revenue Service with an individual's taxes, and "shall be assessed and collected in the same manner" as tax penalties, such as the penalty for claiming too large an income tax refund.]

III.A.[The] Government's first argument is that the individual mandate is a valid exercise of Congress's power under the Commerce Clause and the Necessary and Proper Clause. According to the Government, the health care market is characterized by a significant cost-shifting problem. Everyone will eventually need health care at a time and to an extent they cannot predict, but if they do not have insurance, they often will not be able to pay for it. Because state and federal laws nonetheless require hospitals to provide a certain degree of care to individuals without regard to their ability to pay, hospitals end up receiving compensation for only a portion of the services they provide. To recoup the losses, hospitals pass on the cost to insurers through higher rates, and insurers, in turn, pass on the cost to policy holders in the form of higher premiums. Congress estimated that the cost of uncompensated care raises family health insurance premiums, on average, by over $1,000 per year.

In the Affordable Care Act, Congress addressed the problem of those who cannot obtain insurance coverage because of preexisting conditions or other health issues. It did so through the Act's "guaranteed-issue" and "community-rating" provisions. These provisions together prohibit insurance companies from denying coverage to those with such conditions or charging unhealthy individuals higher premiums than healthy individuals. The guaranteed-issue and community-rating reforms do not, however, address the issue of healthy individuals who choose not to purchase insurance to cover potential health care needs. In fact, the reforms sharply exacerbate that problem, by providing an incentive for individuals to delay purchasing health insurance until they become sick, relying on the promise of guaranteed and affordable coverage. The reforms also threaten to impose massive new costs on insurers, who are required to accept unhealthy individuals but prohibited from charging them rates necessary to pay for their coverage. This will lead insurers to significantly increase premiums on everyone. The individual mandate was Congress's solution to these problems. By requiring that individuals purchase health insurance, the mandate prevents cost-shifting by those who would otherwise go without it. In addition, the mandate forces into the insurance risk pool more healthy individuals, whose premiums on average will be higher than their health care expenses. This allows insurers to subsidize the costs of covering the unhealthy individuals the reforms require them to accept.

1. [The] Government contends that the individual mandate is within Congress's power because the failure to purchase insurance "has a substantial and deleterious effect on interstate commerce" by creating the cost-shifting problem. [Given] its expansive scope, it is no surprise that Congress has employed the commerce power in a wide variety of ways to address the pressing needs of the time. But Congress has never attempted to rely on that power to compel individuals not engaged in commerce to purchase an unwanted product.

[The] power to regulate commerce presupposes the existence of commercial activity to be regulated. If the power to "regulate" something included the power to create it, many of the provisions in the Constitution would be superfluous. [Our] precedent also reflects this understanding. As expansive as our cases construing the scope of the commerce power have been, they all have one thing in common: They uniformly describe the power as reaching "activity." [The] individual mandate, however, does not regulate existing commercial activity. It instead compels individuals to become active in commerce by purchasing a product, on the ground that their failure to do so affects interstate commerce. Construing the Commerce Clause to permit Congress to regulate individuals precisely because they are doing nothing would open a new and potentially vast domain to congressional authority.

[Applying] the Government's logic to the familiar case of Wickard v. Filburn [17th ed., p. 102] shows how far that logic would carry us from the notion of a government of limited powers. [Wickard] has long been regarded as "perhaps the most far reaching example of Commerce Clause authority over intrastate activity," but the Government's theory in this case would go much further. [The] farmer in Wickard was at least actively engaged in the production of wheat, and the Government could regulate that activity because of its effect on commerce. The Government's theory here would effectively override that limitation, by establishing that individuals may be regulated under the Commerce Clause whenever enough of them are not doing something the Government would have them do.

Indeed, the Government's logic would justify a mandatory purchase to solve almost any problem. To consider a different example in the health care market, many Americans do not eat a balanced diet. That group makes up a larger percentage of the total population than those without health insurance. The failure of that group to have a healthy diet increases health care costs, to a greater extent than the failure of the uninsured to purchase insurance. Those increased costs are borne in part by other Americans who must pay more, just as the uninsured shift costs to the insured. Congress addressed the insurance problem by ordering everyone to buy insurance. Under the Government's theory, Congress could address the diet problem by ordering everyone to buy vegetables. People, for reasons of their own, often fail to do things that would be good for them or good for society. Those failures — joined with the similar failures of others — can readily have a substantial effect on interstate commerce. Under the Government's logic, that authorizes Congress to use its commerce power to compel citizens to act as the Government would have them act. That is not the country the Framers of our Constitution envisioned.

[The] Government [argues] that because sickness and injury are unpredictable but unavoidable, "the uninsured as a class are active in the market for health care, which they regularly seek and obtain." [But] we have never permitted Congress to anticipate that activity itself in order to regulate individuals not currently engaged in commerce. [Everyone] will likely participate in the markets for food, clothing, transportation, shelter, or energy; that does not authorize Congress to direct them to purchase particular products in those or other markets today. The Commerce Clause is not a general license to regulate an individual from cradle to grave, simply because he will predictably engage in particular transactions. Any police power to regulate individuals as such, as opposed to their activities, remains vested in the States. [The] individual mandate forces individuals into commerce precisely because they elected to refrain from commercial activity. Such a law cannot be sustained under a clause authorizing Congress to "regulate Commerce."

2.The Government next contends that Congress has the power under the Necessary and Proper Clause to enact the individual mandate because the mandate is an "integral part of a comprehensive scheme of economic regulation" — the guaranteed-issue and community-rating insurance reforms. Under this argument, it is not necessary to consider the effect that an individual's inactivity may have on interstate commerce; it is enough that Congress regulate commercial activity in a way that requires regulation of inactivity to be effective. [The] individual mandate cannot be sustained under the Necessary and Proper Clause as an essential component of the insurance reforms. Each of our prior cases upholding laws under that Clause involved exercises of authority derivative of, and in service to, a granted power. [The] individual mandate, by contrast, vests Congress with the extraordinary ability to create the necessary predicate to the exercise of an enumerated power. [The] Government relies primarily on our decision in Gonzales v. Raich, [but] Raich did not involve the exercise of any "great substantive and independent power," McCulloch, of the sort at issue here. Instead, it concerned only the constitutionality of "individual applications of a concededly valid statutory scheme." Just as the individual mandate cannot be sustained as a law regulating the substantial effects of the failure to purchase health insurance, neither can it be upheld as a "necessary and proper" component of the insurance reforms.

Justices SCALIA, KENNEDY, THOMAS, and ALITO, dissenting.

[Whatever] may be the conceptual limits upon the Commerce Clause, [they] cannot be such as will enable the Federal Government to regulate all private conduct and to compel the States to function as administrators of federal programs. [The] striking case of Wickard v. Filburn, which held that the economic activity of growing wheat, even for one's own consumption, affected commerce sufficiently that it could be regulated, always has been regarded as the *ne plus ultra* of expansive Commerce Clause jurisprudence. To go beyond that, and to say the failure to grow wheat (which is not an economic activity, or any activity at all) nonetheless affects commerce and therefore can be federally regulated, is to make mere breathing in and out the basis for federal prescription and to extend federal power to virtually all human activity.

I.[The] Government offers two theories as to why the Individual Mandate is [constitutional.] Neither theory suffices to sustain its validity. A.[The] Government presents the Individual Mandate as a unique feature of a complicated regulatory scheme governing many parties with countervailing incentives that must be carefully balanced. Congress has imposed an extensive set of regulations on the health insurance industry, and compliance with those regulations will likely cost the industry a great deal. If the industry does not respond by increasing premiums, it is not likely to survive. And if the industry does increase premiums, then there is a serious risk that its products-insurance plans will become economically undesirable for many and prohibitively expensive for the rest. This is not a dilemma unique to regulation of the health insurance industry. Government regulation typically imposes costs on the regulated industry — especially regulation that prohibits economic behavior in which most market participants are already engaging. [Here,] however, Congress has impressed into service third parties, healthy individuals who could be but are not customers of the relevant industry, to offset the undesirable consequences of the regulation. Congress' desire to force these individuals to purchase insurance is motivated by the fact that they are further removed from the market than unhealthy individuals with pre-existing conditions, because they are less likely to need extensive care in the near future. If Congress can reach out and command even those furthest removed from an interstate market to participate in the market, then the Commerce Clause becomes a font of unlimited power.

[Gonzales v. Raich] is no precedent for what Congress has done here. That case's prohibition of growing and of possession [did] not represent the expansion of the federal power to direct into a broad new field. [Moreover, the] Court's opinion in Raich pointed out that the growing and possession prohibitions were the only practicable way of enabling the prohibition of interstate traffic in marijuana to be effectively enforced. [With] the present statute, by contrast, there are many ways other than this unprecedented Individual Mandate by which the regulatory scheme's goals of reducing insurance premiums and ensuring the profitability of insurers could be achieved. For instance, those who did not purchase insurance could be subjected to a surcharge when they do enter the health insurance system. Or they could be denied a full income tax credit given to those who do purchase the insurance.

B. The Government's second theory in support of the Individual Mandate is that [it] directs the manner in which individuals purchase health care services and related goods (directing that they be purchased through insurance) and is therefore a straightforward exercise of the commerce power. The primary problem with this argument is that [the Mandate] does not apply only to persons who purchase all, or most, or even any, of the health care services or goods that the mandated insurance covers. [The] decision to forgo participation in an interstate market is not itself commercial activity (or indeed any activity at all) within Congress' power to regulate. It is true that, at the end of the day, it is inevitable that each American will affect commerce and become a part of it, even if not by choice. But if every person comes within the Commerce Clause power of Congress to regulate by the simple reason that he will one day engage in commerce, the idea of a limited Government power is at an end.

C.[The] dissent dismisses the conclusion that the power to compel entry into the health-insurance market would include the power to compel entry into the new-car or broccoli markets. The latter purchasers, it says, "will be obliged to pay at the counter before receiving the vehicle or nourishment," whereas those refusing to purchase health-insurance will ultimately get treated anyway, at others' expense. But those differences do not show that the failure to enter the health-insurance market, unlike the failure to buy cars and broccoli, is an activity that Congress can "regulate."

Justice GINSBURG, with whom Justices BREYER, SOTOMAYOR and KAGAN join, dissenting in part.

Unlike the Chief Justice, [I would hold] that the Commerce Clause authorizes Congress to enact the minimum coverage provision. In enacting the [ACA,] Congress comprehensively reformed the national market for healthcare products and services. By any measure, that market is immense. Collectively, Americans spent $2.5 trillion on health care in 2009, accounting for 17.6% of our Nation's economy. Within the next decade, it is anticipated, spending on health care will nearly double. [Unlike] the market for almost any other product or service, the market for medical care is one in which all individuals inevitably participate. Virtually every person residing in the United States, sooner or later, will visit a doctor or other health-care professional. When individuals make those visits, they face another reality of the current market for medical care: its high cost. In 2010, on average, an individual in the United States incurred over $7,000 in health-care expenses. Over a lifetime, costs mount to hundreds of thousands of dollars. When a person requires nonroutine care, the cost will generally exceed what he or she can afford to pay. [Although] every U.S. domiciliary will incur significant medical expenses during his or her lifetime, the time when care will be needed is often unpredictable. An accident, a heart attack, or a cancer diagnosis commonly occurs without warning. Inescapably, we are all at peril of needing medical care without a moment's notice.

To manage the risks associated with medical care — its high cost, its unpredictability, and its inevitability — most people in the United States obtain health insurance. [Not] all U.S. residents, however, have health insurance. In 2009, approximately 50 million people were uninsured, either by choice or, more likely, because they could not afford private insurance and did not qualify for government aid. [Unlike] markets for most products, however, the inability to pay for care does not mean that an uninsured individual will receive no care. Federal and state law, as well as professional obligations and embedded social norms, require hospitals and physicians to provide care when it is most needed, regardless of the patient's ability to pay. [As] a consequence, medical-care providers deliver significant amounts of care to the uninsured for which the providers receive no payment. Health-care providers do not absorb these bad debts. Instead, they raise their prices, passing along the cost of uncompensated care to those who do pay reliably: the government and private insurance companies. In response, private insurers increase their premiums, shifting the cost of the elevated bills from providers onto those who carry insurance. The net result: Those with health insurance subsidize the medical care of those without it. As economists would describe what happens, the uninsured "free ride" on those who pay for health insurance. The size of this subsidy is considerable. Congress found that the cost-shifting just described "increases family [insurance] premiums by on average over $1,000 a year."

States cannot resolve the problem of the uninsured on their own. [An] influx of unhealthy individuals into a State with universal health care would result in increased spending on medical services. To cover the increased costs, a State would have to raise taxes, and private health-insurance companies would have to increase premiums. Higher taxes and increased insurance costs would, in turn, encourage businesses and healthy individuals to leave the State. [Facing] that risk, individual States are unlikely to take the initiative in addressing the problem of the uninsured, even though solving that problem is in all States' best interests. Congress' intervention was needed to overcome this collective-action impasse.

Aware that a national solution was required, Congress could have taken over the health-insurance market by establishing a tax-and-spend federal program like Social Security. Such a program, commonly referred to as a singlepayer system (where the sole payer is the Federal Government), would have left little, if any, room for private enterprise or the States. Instead of going this route, Congress enacted the ACA, a solution that retains a robust role for private insurers and state governments. [To] ensure that individuals with medical histories have access to affordable insurance, Congress [imposed] a "guaranteed issue" requirement, which bars insurers from denying coverage to any person on account of that person's medical condition or history [and required] insurers to use "community rating" to price their insurance policies, [barring] insurance companies from charging higher premiums to those with preexisting conditions. But these two provisions, Congress comprehended, could not work effectively unless individuals were given a powerful incentive to obtain insurance. [When] insurance companies are required to insure the sick at affordable prices, individuals can wait until they become ill to buy insurance. Pretty soon, those in need of immediate medical care [become] the insurance companies' main customers. This "adverse selection" problem leaves insurers with two choices: They can either raise premiums dramatically to cover their ever-increasing costs or they can exit the market. [Massachusetts,] Congress was told, cracked the adverse selection problem. By requiring most residents to obtain insurance, the Commonwealth ensured that insurers would not be left with only the sick as customers. In coupling the minimum coverage provision with guaranteed-issue and community-rating prescriptions, Congress followed Massachusetts' lead.

[Consistent] with the Framers' intent, we have repeatedly emphasized that Congress' authority under the Commerce Clause is dependent upon "practical" considerations, including "actual experience." We afford Congress the leeway "to undertake to solve national problems directly and realistically." [Congress] had a rational basis for concluding that the uninsured, as a class, substantially affect interstate commerce [and that] their inability to pay for a significant portion of [their health care] consumption drives up market prices, foists costs on other consumers, and reduces market efficiency and stability. [The] minimum coverage provision, furthermore, bears a "reasonable connection" to Congress' goal of protecting the health-care market from the disruption caused by individuals who fail to obtain insurance. By requiring those who do not carry insurance to pay a toll, the minimum coverage provision gives individuals a strong incentive to insure. This incentive, Congress had good reason to believe, would reduce the number of uninsured and, correspondingly, mitigate the adverse impact the uninsured have on the national health-care market.

[The] inevitable yet unpredictable need for medical care and the guarantee that emergency care will be provided when required are conditions nonexistent in other markets. That is so of the market for cars, and of the market for broccoli as well. Although an individual might buy a car or a crown of broccoli one day, there is no certainty she will ever do so. And if she eventually wants a car or has a craving for broccoli, she will be obliged to pay at the counter before receiving the vehicle or nourishment. She will get no free ride or food, at the expense of another consumer forced to pay an inflated price. Upholding the minimum coverage provision on the ground that all are participants or will be participants in the health-care market would therefore carry no implication that Congress may justify under the Commerce Clause a mandate to buy other products and services.

[For] the reasons explained above, the minimum coverage provision is valid Commerce Clause legislation. When viewed as a component of the entire ACA, the provision's constitutionality becomes even plainer. The Necessary and Proper Clause "empowers Congress to enact laws in effectuation of its [commerce] powe[r] that are not within its authority to enact in isolation." Raich. [One] of Congress' goals in enacting the Affordable Care Act was to eliminate the insurance industry's practice of charging higher prices or denying coverage to individuals with preexisting medical conditions. The commerce power allows Congress to ban this practice, a point no one disputes. Congress knew, however, that simply barring insurance companies from relying on an applicant's medical history would not work in practice. Without the individual mandate, Congress learned, guaranteed-issue and community-rating requirements would trigger an adverse-selection death-spiral in the health-insurance market: Insurance premiums would skyrocket, the number of uninsured would increase, and insurance companies would exit the market. When complemented by an insurance mandate, on the other hand, guaranteed issue and community rating would work as intended, increasing access to insurance and reducing uncompensated care. [The] minimum coverage provision is thus an "essential par[t] of a larger regulation of economic activity"; without the provision, "the regulatory scheme [w]ould be undercut." Raich.

———————

How much damage did Chief Justice Roberts' opinion do to the previous understanding of the Congressional power under the Commerce Clause? For an overview of this case and its relationship to previous Commerce Clause cases from the New Deal decisions discussed earlier and a critique of Justice Roberts decision, see Jackson, *The Limiting Principle Strategy and the New Deal Commerce Clause*, 15 U. Pa. J. Const. L. 11 (2014).

One Last Try: King v. Burwell, 576 U.S. 473 (2015). [Though it found that the Commerce Clause would not support the individual mandate, the Court upheld it as a tax measure. See later Section III.A.1 of this chapter] In King v. Burwell, the Supreme Court, in an opinion written by Chief Justice Roberts, dealt with a statutory challenge to the Affordable Care Act. The act itself was designed to make insurance available to most Americans by guaranteeing health insurance coverage regardless of prior health condition.

To do that, the Act provided for the formation of market exchanges from which insurance consumers could select coverage. The act anticipated that either states or the federal government would set up the insurance exchanges and negotiate the terms as consistent with the act. The act also provided for three coverage formulas: Iit made insurance coverage mandatory for all Americans that could afford to pay for coverage (subject to a tax penalty for non-compliance), provided for tax credits for those within a defined range of the poverty line to assist in acquiring coverage as a condition to the mandate, and provided for the continuation of traditional state-funded coverage for those at or below the poverty line. The purpose for the mandate was to ensure a premium pool to incentivize insurance companies to provide guaranteed coverage.

Plaintiffs in the case were from Virginia, a state which declined to provide a state organized exchange, leaving Virginia residents to pick insurance carriers from a federally organized exchange. Based on language in the legislation that appeared to limit tax credits to persons acquiring insurance on exchange markets set up by states ("an Exchange established by the State under [42 U. S. C. §18031],") the plaintiffs claimed that they were exempt from the insurance mandate because Virginia did not have a state exchange. They argued that without tax credits, which they claimed were only available for participants in state exchanges, the Act exempted them from the insurance coverage mandate. As it turned out, a significant number of states declined to set up state exchanges, leaving those residents dependent upon federal insurance exchanges. The net result of the plaintiff's argument would be to undermine the viability of the act by reducing the size of the premium pool needed to make guaranteed coverage a reality, if tax credits were not available to a substantial number of Americans within the plaintiff's economic demographic.

The Court initially declined to apply the rule in *Chevron USA v. National Resources Defense Council* 467 U. S. 837 (1984), which requires federal courts to defer to the interpretation of the federal agency to whom interpretive authority in administering laws is delegated. The Court held that the tax credit issue was an economic policy issue that would not have been delegated to the IRS, a tax collection agency without expertise in such matters. As a result, the Court declined to follow the interpretation of the Internal Revenue Service, which equated the "established by a State" language to more general language covering both state and federal exchanges.

However, noting that the act contained several examples of inartful drafting, the Court declined the plaintiffs' plain meaning arguments. Instead, in light of the fact that a plain reading of the statute would significantly undermine the viability of the legislative scheme, the Court found the language vague and held that Congress did not intend to undermine the very legislation that it passed by limiting tax credits to state exchanges alone.

G. STATE AUTONOMY, FEDERALISM, AND THE 10TH AND 11TH AMENDMENTS: MODERN LIMITS ON THE COMMERCE POWER

1. PRE-*GARCIA* "STATE SOVEREIGNTY AND THE 10TH AMENDMENT"

As stated in Section F, above, in regard to *United States v. Lopez*, "[it] may have been the first significant denial of Congress power under the Commerce Clause in over forty years, but it was not the "Rehnquist" Court's first attempt in advancing "state sovereignty" against federal authority. This story is told in the next Section, "State Autonomy, Federalism," where the Court's attempt to limit the reach of the commerce power against the states in National League of Cities v. Usery, was eventually overruled in Garcia v. San

Antonio Metropolitan Transit Authority." These cases are significant for both institutional and substantive reasons.

First, as Justice Blackmun points out in *Garcia*, overturning significant and historic principles of constitutional law by a narrow 5–4 majority has institutional pitfalls. The judicial activism represented by overturning congressional statutes with such a narrow majority questions the value of stare decisis and the meaning of precedent in Supreme Court decision making. Note how much discussion as to the meaning of stare decisis is offered by Justice Blackmun in *Garcia*. This is not just conjecture, when new dogma, arguably overruling past precedent, is promulgated on a 5–4 basis in *National League*, the future value of the decision and the meaning of stare decisis hinges on "just one vote (Blackmun's)." Should institutional concern for the respect afforded the Supreme Court in this 5–4 back and forth of significant constitutional values affect how Justices reach decisions in cases such as these?

Chief Justice Rehnquist appeared unconcerned about these values in his *Garcia* dissent: "I do not think it incumbent on those of us in dissent to spell out further the fine points of a principle that will, I am confident, in time again command the support of a majority of this Court." Justice Stewart is said to have refused to provide the fifth vote to overrule the controversial *Miranda* decision, even though he dissented in *Miranda* itself, and commented that he would provide a sixth vote to overrule, but not a fifth. Why would Stewart so state? Whose view do you prefer, Rehnquist's or Stewart's?

Second, and in relation to the "issues," even more important, Rehnquist would prove partially correct is his dissenting prediction in *Garcia*. The Court, despite the ruling in *Garcia*, will resurrect a similar "sovereignty" protection for state governments in the cases reviewed at the close of this section, "Other Ways to Skin a Cat," and in section H below.

The following summaries describe the path the Court took leading to Garcia, the decision which reinstated certain congressional authority, via the Commerce Clause, over state activities.

NATIONAL LEAGUE OF CITIES v. USERY, 426 U.S. 833 (1976). In a "threshold" opinion by the Chief Justice (Rehnquist), which overruled the reach of the commerce power for the first time in some forty years, the Court in a narrow 5-4 decision held that the commerce clause did not empower Congress to enforce the minimum-wage and overtime provisions of the Fair Labor Standards Act (FLSA) against the states "in areas of traditional governmental functions" protected by the 10th Amendment. Though the Court concluded that the wages and hours of state employees affected interstate commerce, it nonetheless determined that the statute was unconstitutional and beyond the scope of Federal authority.

Based upon a fragile five-person majority, contingent on Justice Blackmun's concurrence, the Court "battled" over the implications of *National League* prior to the *Garcia* decision. A brief review of several of these decisions follows.

HODEL v. VIRGINIA SURFACE MINING ASSOCIATION, 452 U.S. 264 (1981). The Court upheld the constitutionality of a federal statute governing state regulatory authority over the operation of strip mines, raising the issue of what amounted to a traditional government function. Mr. Justice Marshall found "four conditions [that] must be satisfied before a state activity may be deemed immune from a particular federal regulation under the Commerce Clause. First, [the] federal statute at issue must regulate 'the "States as States."' Second, the statute must 'address matters that are indisputably "attribute[s] of state sovereignty."' Third, state compliance with the federal obligation must 'directly impair [the States'] ability "to structure integral operations in areas of traditional governmental functions."' Finally, the relation of state and federal interests must not be such that 'the nature of the federal interest . . . justifies state submission.'"

In rejecting the argument that based upon National League the State's inherent control of its "property law" was an aspect of "state sovereignty protected by the 10th amendment," the Court held that the "strip-mining" legislation did not regulate the "State as States," and was a permissible exercise of the commerce power.

UNITED TRANSPORTATION UNION v. LONG ISLAND RAILROAD, 455 U.S. 678 (1982). The Court unanimously rejected another National League challenge to the constitutionality of applying the Railway Labor Act's collective bargaining provisions to the state-owned Long Island Railroad. The Court held that the third part of the Hodel test was not meet, because the operation of a railroad was not a "traditional state function," and that the National League of Cities test "was not meant to impose a static historical view of state functions."

FEDERAL ENERGY REGULATORY COMMISSION v. MISSISSIPPI, 456 U.S. 742 (1982). During a national "energy crisis," the Court rejected a *National League* challenge to a congressional response to the "emergency," the Public Utilities Regulatory Policies Act (PURPA) of 1978. Justice Blackman, speaking for the majority upheld congressional policy finding that Congress, "Could have pre-empted the field and that PURPA should not be invalid simply because out of deference to state authority, Congress adopted a less intrusive scheme."

EEOC v. WYOMING, 460 U.S. 226 (1983). Justice Blackmun, now joined by the four "dissenters" in National League, formed a majority to reject a challenge to the application of the Age Discrimination in Employment Act of 1974 to state employees. The opinion by Justice Brennan found that the act did not impair states' abilities to structure their integral operations to a degree making the act unconstitutional. (Note the present Court's view of this statute as applied to state governments in *Kimel v. Florida Bd. of Regents*, supra, a different way to skin the same cat.)

GARCIA v. SAN ANTONIO METROPOLITAN TRANSIT AUTHORITY
469 U.S. 528 (1985)

Justice Blackmun delivered the opinion of the Court.

We revisit in these cases an issue raised in National League of Cities v. Usery, 426 U.S. 833, 96 S.Ct. 2465, 49 L.Ed.2d 245 (1976). In that litigation, this Court, by a sharply divided vote, ruled that the Commerce Clause does not empower Congress to enforce the minimum-wage and overtime provisions of the Fair Labor Standards Act (FLSA) against the States "in areas of traditional governmental functions." Id., at 852, 96 S.Ct., at 2474. Although *National League of Cities* supplied some examples of "traditional governmental functions," it did not offer a general explanation of how a "traditional" function is to be distinguished from a "nontraditional" one. Since then, federal and state courts have struggled with the task, thus imposed, of identifying a traditional function for purposes of state immunity under the Commerce Clause.

In the present cases, a Federal District Court concluded that municipal ownership and operation of a mass transit system is a traditional governmental function and thus, under *National League of Cities,* is exempt from the obligations imposed by the FLSA. Faced with the identical question, three Federal Courts of Appeals and one state appellate court have reached the opposite conclusion.

Our examination of this "function" standard applied in these and other cases over the last eight years now persuades us that the attempt to draw the boundaries of state regulatory immunity in terms of "traditional governmental function" is not only unworkable but is also inconsistent with established principles of federalism and, indeed, with those very federalism principles on which *National League of Cities* purported to rest. That case, accordingly, is overruled.

We therefore now reject, as unsound in principle and unworkable in practice, a rule of state immunity from federal regulation that turns on a judicial appraisal of whether a particular governmental function is "integral" or "traditional." Any such rule leads to inconsistent results at the same time that it disserves principles of democratic self-governance, and it breeds inconsistency precisely because it is divorced from those principles. If there are to be limits on the Federal Government's power to interfere with state functions — as undoubtedly there are — we must look elsewhere to find them.

[T]he principal means chosen by the Framers to ensure the role of the States in the federal system lies in the structure of the Federal Government itself. [T]he Framers chose to rely on a federal system in which special restraints on federal power over the States inhered principally in the workings of the National Government itself, rather than in discrete limitations on the objects of federal authority. State sovereign interests, then, are more properly protected by procedural safeguards inherent in the structure of the federal system than by judicially created limitations on federal power.

[The] effectiveness of the federal political process in preserving the States' interests is apparent even today in the course of federal legislation. [Nonetheless], against this background, we are convinced that the fundamental limitation that the constitutional scheme imposes on the Commerce Clause to protect the "States as States" is one of process rather than one of result. Any substantive restraint on the exercise of Commerce Clause powers must find its justification in the procedural nature of this basic limitation, and it must be tailored to compensate for possible failings in the national political process rather than to dictate a "sacred province of state autonomy

Of course, we continue to recognize that the States occupy a special and specific position in our constitutional system and that the scope of Congress' authority under the Commerce Clause must reflect that position. But the principal and basic limit on the federal commerce power is that inherent in all congressional action — the built-in restraints that our system provides through state participation in federal governmental action. The political process ensures that laws that unduly burden the States will not be promulgated. In the factual setting of these cases the internal safeguards of the political process have performed as intended.

These cases do not require us to identify or define what affirmative limits the constitutional structure might impose on federal action affecting the States under the Commerce Clause. See *Coyle v. Oklahoma*, 221 U.S. 559, 31 S.Ct. 688, 55 L.Ed. 853 (1911). We note and accept Justice Frankfurter's observation in *New York v. United States*, 326 U.S. 572, 583, 66 S.Ct. 310, 314, 90 L.Ed. 326 (1946): "The process of Constitutional adjudication does not thrive on conjuring up horrible possibilities that never happen in the real world and devising doctrines sufficiently comprehensive in detail to cover the remotest contingency. Nor need we go beyond what is required for a reasoned disposition of the kind of controversy now before the Court."

Though the separate concurrence providing the fifth vote in *National League of Cities* was "not untroubled by certain possible implications" of the decision, 426 U.S., at 856, 96 S.Ct., at 2476, the Court in that case attempted to articulate affirmative limits on the Commerce Clause power in terms of core governmental functions and fundamental attributes of state sovereignty. But the model of democratic decision making the Court there identified underestimated, in our view, the solicitude of the national political process for the continued vitality of the States. Attempts by other courts since then to draw guidance from this model have proved it both impracticable and doctrinally barren. In sum, in *National League of Cities* the Court tried to repair what did not need repair.

We do not lightly overrule recent precedent. We have not hesitated, however, when it has become apparent that a prior decision has departed from a proper understanding of congressional power under the Commerce Clause. See *United States v. Darby*, 312 U.S. 100, 116-117, 61 S.Ct. 451, 458-459, 85 L.Ed. 609 (1941). Due respect for the reach of congressional power within the federal system mandates that we do so now.

SOUTH CAROLINA v. BAKER, 485 U.S. 505 (1988). *Baker* represents the Court's only review of the *Garcia* exception for judicial intervention, "to compensate for possible failings in the national political process."

A 1982 tax reform statute removed the exemption from federal taxes of income from certain state bonds. The Supreme Court, with only Justice O'Connor dissenting, held that the statute was not unconstitutional. "Garcia holds that the limits [on Congress's power] are structural, not substantive — i.e., that States must find their protection from congressional regulation through the national political process, not through judicially defined spheres of unregulable state activity. South Carolina contends that the political process failed here because Congress had no concrete evidence quantifying the tax evasion attributable [to the affected bonds] and relied instead on anecdotal evidence. [It] also argues that Congress chose an ineffective remedy. [Although] Garcia left open the possibility that some extraordinary defects in the national political process might render congressional regulation of state activities invalid, [South] Carolina has not even alleged that it was deprived of any right to participate in the national political process or that it was singled out in a way that left it politically isolated and powerless." The Court also rejected the argument that the statute "commandeered" states by "coercing [them] into enacting legislation" that would allow them to issue bonds that would continue to receive federal tax-exempt status. The Court said that the federal statute simply regulated state activity, and that any "commandeering" that occurred was "an inevitable consequence of regulating a state activity."

Justice O'Connor dissented, arguing that the statute was unconstitutional because the Court failed "to inquire into the substantial adverse effects on state and local governments

326 PART I. GOVERNMENTAL POWERS

that would follow from state taxation of the interest on state and local bonds." Chief Justice Rehnquist, in contrast, concurred in the result, relying on the Special Master's finding that depriving the particular bonds in question of tax exempt status would have "no substantial effect on the abilities of States to raise debt capital."

———

Comment on *Garcia*. Blackmun portends in *Garcia* a return to the "national political process," as opposed to the Court, to supervise federalism: "State sovereign interests, then, are more properly protected by procedural safeguards inherent in the structure of the federal system than by judicially created limitations on federal power. Any substantive restraint on the exercise of Commerce Clause powers must find its justification in the procedural nature of this basic limitation, and it must be tailored to compensate for possible failings in the national political process rather than to dictate a 'sacred province of state autonomy.'" Is this a return to "the lessons" of *McCulloch*?

But recalling Rehnquist's "words for the wise," that his views would once again "command the support of a majority of this Court," are the cases below, *New York v. United States* and *Printz v. United States*, another "Way to Skin a Cat"? Did Powell win the battle but lose the war?

2. THE ANTI-COMMANDEERING DOCTRINE, OR "OTHER WAYS TO SKIN A CAT"

NEW YORK v. UNITED STATES
505 U.S. 144 (1992)

Justice O'CONNOR delivered the opinion of the Court.

The constitutional question is as old as the Constitution: It consists of discerning the proper division of authority between the Federal Government and the States. We conclude that while Congress has substantial power under the Constitution to encourage the States to provide for the disposal of the radioactive waste generated within their borders, the Constitution does not confer upon Congress the ability simply to compel the States to do so. We therefore find that only two of the Act's three provisions at issue are consistent with the Constitution's allocation of power to the Federal Government.

In some cases the Court has inquired whether an Act of Congress is authorized by one of the powers delegated to Congress in Article I of the Constitution. See, *e.g., Perez v. United States*, 402 U.S. 146, 91 S.Ct. 1357, 28 L.Ed.2d 686 (1971); *McCulloch v. Maryland*, 4 Wheat. 316, 4 L.Ed. 579 (1819). In other cases the Court has sought to determine whether an Act of Congress invades the province of state sovereignty reserved by the Tenth Amendment. See, *e.g., Garcia v. San Antonio Metropolitan Transit Authority*, 469 U.S. 528, 105 S.Ct. 1005, 83 L.Ed.2d 1016 (1985); *Lane County v. Oregon*, 7 Wall. 71, 19 L.Ed. 101 (1869). In a case like these, involving the division of authority between federal and state governments, the two inquiries are mirror images of each other. If a power is delegated to Congress in the Constitution, the Tenth Amendment expressly disclaims any reservation of that power to the States; if a power is an attribute of state sovereignty reserved by the Tenth Amendment, it is necessarily a power the Constitution has not conferred on Congress.

It is in this sense that the Tenth Amendment "states but a truism that all is retained which has not been surrendered."

[Congress] exercises its conferred powers subject to the limitations contained in the Constitution. Thus, for example, under the Commerce Clause Congress may regulate publishers engaged in interstate commerce, but Congress is constrained in the exercise of that power by the First Amendment. The Tenth Amendment likewise restrains the power of Congress, but this limit is not derived from the text of the Tenth Amendment itself, which, as we have discussed, is essentially a tautology. Instead, the Tenth Amendment confirms that the power of the Federal Government is subject to limits that may, in a given instance, reserve power to the States. The Tenth Amendment thus directs us to determine, as in this case, whether an incident of state sovereignty is protected by a limitation on an Article I power.

Petitioners do not contend that Congress lacks the power to regulate the disposal of low level radioactive waste. Space in radioactive waste disposal sites is frequently sold by residents of one State to residents of another. Regulation of the resulting interstate market in waste disposal is therefore well within Congress' authority under the Commerce Clause. Petitioners contend only that the Tenth Amendment limits the power of Congress to regulate in the way it has chosen. Rather than addressing the problem of waste disposal by directly regulating the generators and disposers of waste, petitioners argue, Congress has impermissibly directed the States to regulate in this field.

Most of our recent cases interpreting the Tenth Amendment have concerned the authority of Congress to subject state governments to generally applicable laws. This litigation presents no occasion to apply or revisit the holdings of any of these cases, as this is not a case in which Congress has subjected a State to the same legislation applicable to private parties. Cf. *FERC v. Mississippi,* 456 U.S. 742, 758-759, 102 S.Ct. 2126, 2137, 72 L.Ed.2d 532 (1982).

This litigation instead concerns the circumstances under which Congress may use the States as implements of regulation; that is, whether Congress may direct or otherwise motivate the States to regulate in a particular field or a particular way. Our cases have established a few principles that guide our resolution of the issue.

As an initial matter, Congress may not simply "commandee[r] the legislative processes of the States by directly compelling them to enact and enforce a federal regulatory program." *Hodel v. Virginia Surface Mining & Reclamation Assn., Inc.,* 452 U.S. 264, 288, 101 S.Ct. 2352, 2366, 69 L.Ed.2d 1 (1981).

While Congress has substantial powers to govern the Nation directly, including in areas of intimate concern to the States, the Constitution has never been understood to confer upon Congress the ability to require the States to govern according to Congress' instructions. See *Coyle v. Smith,* 221 U.S. 559, 565, 31 S.Ct. 688, 689, 55 L.Ed. 853 (1911).

Indeed, the question whether the Constitution should permit Congress to employ state governments as regulatory agencies was a topic of lively debate among the Framers. Under the Articles of Confederation, Congress lacked the authority in most respects to govern the people directly. In practice, Congress "could not directly tax or legislate upon individuals; it had no explicit 'legislative' or 'governmental' power to make binding 'law' enforceable as such." Amar, Of Sovereignty and Federalism, 96 Yale L.J. 1425, 1447 (1987).

The inadequacy of this governmental structure was responsible in part for the Constitutional Convention. Alexander Hamilton observed: "The great and radical vice in the construction of the existing Confederation is in the principle of LEGISLATION for STATES or GOVERNMENTS, in their CORPORATE or COLLECTIVE CAPACITIES, and as contra-distinguished from the INDIVIDUALS of whom they consist." The Federalist No. 15, p. 108 (C. Rossiter ed. 1961). As Hamilton saw it, "we must resolve to incorporate into our plan those ingredients which may be considered as forming the characteristic difference between a league and a government; we must extend the authority of the Union to the persons of the citizens — the only proper objects of government." *Id.,* at 109.

The Convention generated a great number of proposals for the structure of the new Government, but two quickly took center stage. Under the Virginia Plan, as first introduced by Edmund Randolph, Congress would exercise legislative authority directly upon individuals, without employing the States as intermediaries. 1 Records of the Federal Convention of 1787, p. 21 (M. Farrand ed. 1911). Under the New Jersey Plan, as first introduced by William Paterson, Congress would continue to require the approval of the States before legislating, as it had under the Articles of Confederation.

In the end, the Convention opted for a Constitution in which Congress would exercise its legislative authority directly over individuals rather than over States; for a variety of reasons, it rejected the New Jersey Plan in favor of the Virginia Plan. 1 *id.,* at 313. This choice was made clear to the subsequent state ratifying conventions.

[We] have always understood that even where Congress has the authority under the Constitution to pass laws requiring or prohibiting certain acts, it lacks the power directly to compel the States to require or prohibit those acts. *E.g., FERC v. Mississippi,* 456 U.S., at 762-766, 102 S.Ct., at 2138-2141; *Hodel v. Virginia Surface Mining & Reclamation Assn., Inc.,* 452 U.S., at 288-289, 101 S.Ct., at 2366; *Lane County v. Oregon,* 7 Wall., at 76. The allocation of power contained in the Commerce Clause, for example, authorizes Congress to regulate interstate commerce directly; it does not authorize Congress to regulate state governments' regulation of interstate commerce.

This is not to say that Congress lacks the ability to encourage a State to regulate in a particular way, or that Congress may not hold out incentives to the States as a method of influencing a State's policy choices.

[First], under Congress' spending power, "Congress may attach conditions on the receipt of federal funds." *South Dakota v. Dole,* 483 U.S., at 206, 107 S.Ct., at 2795. [Second], where Congress has the authority to regulate private activity under the Commerce Clause, we have recognized Congress' power to offer States the choice of regulating that activity according to federal standards or having state law pre-empted by federal regulation. *Hodel v. Virginia Surface Mining & Reclamation Assn., Inc., supra,* 452 U.S., at 288, 101 S.Ct., at 2366. See also *FERC v. Mississippi, supra,* 456 U.S., at 764-765, 102 S.Ct., at 2140.

[By] either of these methods, as by any other permissible method of encouraging a State to conform to federal policy choices, the residents of the State retain the ultimate decision as to whether or not the State will comply. If a State's citizens view federal policy as sufficiently contrary to local interests, they may elect to decline a federal grant. If state residents would prefer their government to devote its attention and resources to problems other than those deemed important by Congress, they may choose to have the Federal Government rather than the State bear the expense of a federally mandated regulatory program, and they may continue to supplement that program to the extent state law is not pre-empted. Where Congress encourages state regulation rather than compelling it, state governments remain responsive to the local electorate's preferences; state officials remain accountable to the people.

By contrast, where the Federal Government compels States to regulate, the accountability of both state and federal officials is diminished. If the citizens of New York, for example, do not consider that making provision for the disposal of radioactive waste is in their best interest, they may elect state officials who share their view. That view can always be pre-empted under the Supremacy Clause if it is contrary to the national view, but in such a case it is the Federal Government that makes the decision in full view of the public, and it will be federal officials that suffer the consequences if the decision turns out to be detrimental or unpopular. But where the Federal Government directs the States to regulate, it may be state officials who will bear the brunt of public disapproval, while the federal officials who devised the regulatory program may remain insulated from the electoral ramifications of their decision. Accountability is thus diminished when, due to federal coercion, elected state officials cannot regulate in accordance with the views of the local electorate in matters not pre-empted by federal regulation.

The first of these steps is an unexceptionable exercise of Congress' power to authorize the States to burden interstate commerce. While the Commerce Clause has long been understood to limit the States' ability to discriminate against interstate commerce, see, *e.g.*, *Wyoming v. Oklahoma*, 502 U.S. 437, 454-455, 112 S.Ct. 789, 800, 117 L.Ed.2d 1 (1992); *Cooley v. Board of Wardens of Port of Philadelphia ex rel. Society for Relief of Distressed Pilots*, 12 How. 299, 13 L.Ed. 996 (1852), that limit may be lifted, as it has been here, by an expression of the "unambiguous intent" of Congress. *Wyoming, supra*, 502 U.S., at 458, 112 S.Ct., at 802; *Prudential Ins. Co. v. Benjamin*, 328 U.S. 408, 427-431, 66 S.Ct. 1142, 1153-1156, 90 L.Ed. 1342 (1946). Whether or not the States would be permitted to burden the interstate transport of low level radioactive waste in the absence of Congress' approval, the States can clearly do so *with* Congress' approval, which is what the Act gives them.

The second step, the Secretary's collection of a percentage of the surcharge, is no more than a federal tax on interstate commerce, which petitioners do not claim to be an invalid exercise of either Congress' commerce or taxing power. Cf. *United States v. Sanchez*, 340 U.S. 42, 44-45, 71 S.Ct. 108, 110, 95 L.Ed. 47 (1950); *Steward Machine Co. v. Davis*, 301 U.S. 548, 581-583, 57 S.Ct. 883, 888-889, 81 L.Ed. 1279 (1937).

[12] The third step is a conditional exercise of Congress' authority under the Spending Clause: Congress has placed conditions — the achievement of the milestones — on the receipt of federal funds. Petitioners do not contend that Congress has exceeded its authority in any of the four respects our cases have identified. See generally *South Dakota v. Dole*, 483 U.S., at 207-208, 107 S.Ct., at 2796. The expenditure is for the general welfare, *Helvering v. Davis*, 301 U.S. 619, 640-641, 57 S.Ct. 904, 908, 81 L.Ed. 1307 (1937); the States are required to use the money they receive for the purpose of assuring the safe disposal of radioactive waste. 42 U.S.C. § 2021e(d)(2)(E). The conditions imposed are unambiguous, *Pennhurst State School and Hospital v. Halderman*, 451 U.S., at 17, 101 S.Ct., at 1540; the Act informs the States exactly what they must do and by when they must do it in order to obtain a share of the escrow account. The conditions imposed are reasonably related to the purpose of the expenditure, *Massachusetts v. United States*, 435 U.S., at 461, 98 S.Ct., at 1164; both the conditions and the payments embody Congress' efforts to address the pressing problem of radioactive waste disposal. Finally, petitioners do not claim that the conditions imposed by the Act violate any independent constitutional prohibition. *Lawrence County v. Lead-Deadwood School Dist. No. 40-1*, 469 U.S. 256, 269-270, 105 S.Ct. 695, 702-703, 83 L.Ed.2d 635 (1985).

Petitioners contend nevertheless that the *form* of these expenditures removes them from the scope of Congress' spending power. Petitioners emphasize the Act's instruction to the Secretary of Energy to "deposit all funds received in a special escrow account. The funds so deposited shall not be the property of the United States." 42 U.S.C. § 2021e(d)(2)(A). Petitioners argue that because the money collected and redisbursed to the

States is kept in an account separate from the general treasury, because the Secretary holds the funds only as a trustee, and because the States themselves are largely able to control whether they will pay into the escrow account or receive a share, the Act "in no manner calls for the spending of federal funds." Reply Brief for Petitioner State of New York 6.

The Constitution's grant to Congress of the authority to "pay the Debts and provide for the . . . general Welfare" has never, however, been thought to mandate a particular form of accounting. A great deal of federal spending comes from segregated trust funds collected and spent for a particular purpose. See, *e.g.,* 23 U.S.C. § 118 (Highway Trust Fund); 42 U.S.C. § 401(a) (Federal Old-Age and Survivors Insurance Trust Fund); 42 U.S.C. § 401(b) (Federal Disability Insurance Trust Fund); 42 U.S.C. § 1395t (Federal Supplementary Medical Insurance Trust Fund). The Spending Clause has never been construed to deprive Congress of the power to structure federal spending in this manner. Petitioners' argument regarding the States' ability to determine the escrow account's income and disbursements ignores the fact that Congress specifically provided the States with this ability as a method of encouraging the States to regulate according to the federal plan. That the States are able to choose whether they will receive federal funds does not make the resulting expenditures any less federal; indeed, the location of such choice in the States is an inherent element in any conditional exercise of Congress' spending power.

The Act's first set of incentives, in which Congress has conditioned grants to the States upon the States' attainment of a series of milestones, is thus well within the authority of Congress under the Commerce and Spending Clauses. Because the first set of incentives is supported by affirmative constitutional grants of power to Congress, it is not inconsistent with the Tenth Amendment.

In the second set of incentives, Congress has authorized States and regional compacts with disposal sites gradually to increase the cost of access to the sites, and then to deny access altogether, to radioactive waste generated in States that do not meet federal deadlines. As a simple regulation, this provision would be within the power of Congress to authorize the States to discriminate against interstate commerce. See *Northeast Bancorp, Inc. v. Board of Governors, FRS,* 472 U.S. 159, 174-175, 105 S.Ct. 2545, 2554, 86 L.Ed.2d 112 (1985). Where federal regulation of private activity is within the scope of the Commerce Clause, we have recognized the ability of Congress to offer States the choice of regulating that activity according to federal standards or having state law pre-empted by federal regulation. See *Hodel v. Virginia Surface Mining & Reclamation Assn., Inc.,* 452 U.S., at 288, 101 S.Ct., at 2366; *FERC v. Mississippi,* 456 U.S., at 764-765, 102 S.Ct., at 2140.

The affected States are not compelled by Congress to regulate, because any burden caused by a State's refusal to regulate will fall on those who generate waste and find no outlet for its disposal, rather than on the State as a sovereign. A State whose citizens do not wish it to attain the Act's milestones may devote its attention and its resources to issues its citizens deem more worthy; the choice remains at all times with the residents of the State, not with Congress.

The take title provision is of a different character. This third so-called "incentive" offers States, as an alternative to regulating pursuant to Congress' direction, the option of taking title to and possession of the low level radioactive waste generated within their borders and becoming liable for all damages waste generators suffer as a result of the States' failure to do so promptly. In this provision, Congress has crossed the line distinguishing encouragement from coercion.

The take title provision offers state governments a "choice" of either accepting ownership of waste or regulating according to the instructions of Congress. Respondents do not claim that the Constitution would authorize Congress to impose either option as a freestanding requirement. On one hand, the Constitution would not permit Congress simply to transfer radioactive waste from generators to state governments. Such a forced transfer, standing alone, would in principle be no different than a congressionally compelled subsidy from state governments to radioactive waste producers. The same is true of the provision requiring the States to become liable for the generators' damages. Standing alone, this provision would be indistinguishable from an Act of Congress directing the States to assume the liabilities of certain state residents. Either type of federal action would "commandeer" state governments into the service of federal regulatory purposes, and would for this reason be inconsistent with the Constitution's division of authority between federal and state governments. On the other hand, the second alternative held out to state governments — regulating pursuant to Congress' direction — would, standing alone, present a simple command to state governments to implement legislation enacted by Congress. As we have seen, the Constitution does not empower Congress to subject state governments to this type of instruction.

[T]he United States argues that the Constitution's prohibition of congressional directives to state governments can be overcome where the federal interest is sufficiently important to justify state submission. This argument contains a kernel of truth: In determining whether the Tenth Amendment limits the ability of Congress to subject state governments to generally applicable laws, the Court *has* in some cases stated that it will evaluate the strength of federal interests in light of the degree to which such laws would prevent the State from functioning as a sovereign; that is, the extent to which such generally applicable laws would impede a state government's responsibility to represent and be accountable to the citizens of the State. But whether or not a particularly strong federal interest enables Congress to bring state governments within the orbit of generally applicable *federal* regulation, no Member of the Court has ever suggested that such a federal interest would enable Congress to command a state government to enact *state* regulation. No matter how powerful the federal interest involved, the Constitution simply does not give Congress the authority to require the States to regulate. The Constitution instead gives Congress the authority to regulate matters directly and to pre-empt contrary state regulation. Where a federal interest is sufficiently strong to cause Congress to legislate, it must do so directly; it may not conscript state governments as its agents.

Because an instruction to state governments to take title to waste, standing alone, would be beyond the authority of Congress, and because a direct order to regulate, standing alone, would also be beyond the authority of Congress, it follows that Congress lacks the power to offer the States a choice between the two. A choice between two unconstitutionally coercive regulatory techniques is no choice at all.

Whether one views the take title provision as lying outside Congress' enumerated powers, or as infringing upon the core of state sovereignty reserved by the Tenth Amendment, the provision is inconsistent with the federal structure of our Government established by the Constitution.

Respondents note that the Act embodies a bargain among the sited and United States, a compromise to which New York was a willing participant and from which New York has reaped much benefit. Respondents then pose what appears at first to be a troubling question: How can a federal statute be found an unconstitutional infringement of state sovereignty when state officials consented to the statute's enactment?

The answer follows from an understanding of the fundamental purpose served by our Government's federal structure. The Constitution does not protect the sovereignty of States for the benefit of the States or state governments as abstract political entities, or even for the benefit of the public officials governing the States. To the contrary, the Constitution divides authority between federal and state governments for the protection of individuals. State sovereignty is not just an end in itself: "Rather, federalism secures to citizens the liberties that derive from the diffusion of sovereign power." *Coleman v. Thompson*, 501 U.S. 722, 759, 111 S.Ct. 2546, 2570, 115 L.Ed.2d 640 (1991) (BLACKMUN, J., dissenting). "Just as the separation and independence of the coordinate branches of the Federal Government serves to prevent the accumulation of excessive power in any one branch, a healthy balance of power between the States and the Federal Government will reduce the risk of tyranny and abuse from either front." Gregory v. Ashcroft, 501 U.S., at 458, 111 S.Ct., at 2400 (1991). See The Federalist No. 51, p. 323 (C. Rossiter ed. 1961).

Where Congress exceeds its authority relative to the States, therefore, the departure from the constitutional plan cannot be ratified by the "consent" of state officials.

State officials thus cannot consent to the enlargement of the powers of Congress beyond those enumerated in the Constitution. Indeed, the facts of these cases raise the possibility that powerful incentives might lead both federal and state officials to view departures from the federal structure to be in their personal interests. Most citizens recognize the need for radioactive waste disposal sites, but few want sites near their homes. As a result, while it would be well within the authority of either federal or state officials to choose where the disposal sites will be, it is likely to be in the political interest of each individual official to avoid being held accountable to the voters for the choice of location. If a federal official is faced with the alternatives of choosing a location or directing the States to do it, the official may well prefer the latter, as a means of shifting responsibility for the eventual decision. If a state official is faced with the same set of alternatives — choosing a location or having Congress direct the choice of a location — the state official may also prefer the latter, as it may permit the avoidance of personal responsibility. The interests of public officials thus may not coincide with the Constitution's intergovernmental allocation of authority. Where state officials purport to submit to the direction of Congress in this manner, federalism is hardly being advanced.

The shortage of disposal sites for radioactive waste is a pressing national problem, but a judiciary that licensed extra-constitutional government with each issue of comparable gravity would, in the long run, be far worse.

States are not mere political subdivisions of the United States. State governments are neither regional offices nor administrative agencies of the Federal Government. The positions occupied by state officials appear nowhere on the Federal Government's most detailed organizational chart. The Constitution instead "leaves to the several States a residuary and inviolable sovereignty," The Federalist No. 39, p. 245 (C. Rossiter ed. 1961), reserved explicitly to the States by the Tenth Amendment.

Whatever the outer limits of that sovereignty may be, one thing is clear: The Federal Government may not compel the States to enact or administer a federal regulatory program. The Constitution permits both the Federal Government and the States to enact legislation regarding the disposal of low level radioactive waste. The Constitution enables the Federal Government to pre-empt state regulation contrary to federal interests, and it permits the Federal Government to hold out incentives to the States as a means of encouraging them to adopt suggested regulatory schemes. It does not, however, authorize Congress simply to direct the States to provide for the disposal of the radioactive waste generated within their borders. While there may be many constitutional methods of achieving regional self-sufficiency in radioactive waste disposal, the method Congress has chosen is not one of them. The judgment of the Court of Appeals is accordingly

Affirmed in part and reversed in part.

Justice WHITE, with whom Justice BLACKMUN and Justice STEVENS join, concurring in part and dissenting in part.

My disagreement with the Court's analysis begins at the basic descriptive level of how the legislation at issue in this case came to be enacted. [The] Low-Level Radioactive Waste Policy Act [resulted] from the efforts of state leaders to achieve a state-based set of remedies to the waste problem. They sought not federal pre-emption or intervention, but rather congressional sanction of interstate compromises they had reached. . . .

[The] attempts by States to enter into compacts and to gain congressional approval sparked a new round of political squabbling between elected officials from unsited States, who generally opposed ratification of the compacts that were being formed, and their counterparts from the sited States, who insisted that the promises made [be] honored. In its effort to keep the States at the forefront of the policy amendment process, the National Governors' Association organized more than a dozen meetings to achieve a state consensus.

These discussions were not merely academic. The sited States grew increasingly and justifiably frustrated by the seeming inaction of unsited States in meeting the projected actions called for in the 1980 Act. Thus, as the end of 1985 approached, the sited States viewed the January 1, 1986 deadline established in the 1980 Act as a "drop-dead" date, on which the regional compacts could begin excluding the entry of out-of-region waste. Since by this time the three disposal facilities operating in 1980 were still the only such plants accepting low-level radioactive waste, the unsited States perceived a very serious danger if the three existing facilities actually carried out their threat to restrict access to the waste generated solely within their respective compact regions.

A movement thus arose to achieve a compromise [in] which the sited States agreed to continue accepting waste in exchange for the imposition of stronger measures to guarantee compliance with the unsited States' assurances that they would develop alternate disposal facilities. As Representative Derrick explained, the compromise 1985 legislation "gives non sited States more time to develop disposal sites, but also establishes a very firm timetable and sanctions for failure to live up [to] the agreement." Representative Markey added that "this compromise became the basis for our amendments to the Low-Level Radioactive Waste Policy Act of 1980. In the process of drafting such amendments, various concessions have been made by all sides in an effort to arrive at a bill which all parties could accept." The bill that in large measure became the 1985 Act "represented the diligent negotiating undertaken by" the National Governors' Association and "embodied" the "fundamentals of their settlement." In sum, the 1985 Act was very much the product of cooperative federalism, in which the States bargained among themselves to achieve compromises for Congress to sanction. . . .

In my view, New York's actions subsequent to enactment of the 1980 and 1985 Acts fairly indicate its approval of the interstate agreement process embodied in those laws. [The] States — including New York — worked through their Governors to petition Congress for the 1980 and 1985 Acts. [These] statutes are best understood as the products of collective state action, rather than as impositions placed on States by the Federal Government. . . .

[Seen] as a term of an agreement entered into between the several States, this measure proves to be less constitutionally odious than the Court opines. First, the practical effect of New York's position is that because it is unwilling to honor its obligations to provide in-state storage facilities for its low-level radioactive waste, other States with such plants must accept New York's waste, whether they wish to or not. Otherwise, the many economically and socially-beneficial producers of such waste in the State would have to cease their operations. The Court's refusal to force New York to accept responsibility for its own problem inevitably means that some other State's sovereignty will be impinged by it being forced, for public health reasons, to accept New York's low-level radioactive waste. I do not understand the principle of federalism to impede the National Government from acting as referee among the States to prohibit one from bullying another.

Moreover, it is utterly reasonable that, in crafting a delicate compromise between the three overburdened States that provided low-level radioactive waste disposal facilities and the rest of the States, Congress would have to ratify some punitive measure as the ultimate sanction for noncompliance. The take title provision, though surely onerous, does not take effect if the generator of the waste does not request such action, or if the State lives up to its bargain of providing a waste disposal facility either within the State or in another State pursuant to a regional compact arrangement or a separate contract. . . .

The Court announces that it has no occasion to revisit such decisions as [Gregory v. Ashcroft, Garcia], and [National League of Cities], because "this is not a case in which Congress has subjected a State to the same legislation applicable to private parties." Although this statement sends the welcome signal that the Court does not intend to cut a wide swath through our recent Tenth Amendment precedents, it nevertheless is unpersuasive. . . .

The Court's distinction between a federal statute's regulation of States and private parties for general purposes, as opposed to a regulation solely on the activities of States, is unsupported by our recent Tenth Amendment cases. [The] Court makes no effort to explain why this purported distinction should affect the analysis of Congress' power under general principles of federalism and the Tenth Amendment. [An] incursion on state sovereignty hardly seems more constitutionally acceptable if the federal statute that "commands" specific action also applies to private parties. The alleged diminution in state authority over its own affairs is not any less because the federal mandate restricts the activities of private parties. . . .

[The] more appropriate analysis should flow from Garcia. . . .

[Where] it addresses this aspect of respondents' argument, the Court tacitly concedes that a failing of the political process cannot be shown in this case because it refuses to rebut the unassailable arguments that the States were well able to look after themselves in the legislative process that culminated in the 1985 Act's passage. [The] Court rejects this process-based argument by resorting to generalities and platitudes about the purpose of federalism being to protect individual rights.

Ultimately, I suppose, the entire structure of our federal constitutional government can be traced to an interest in establishing checks and balances to prevent the exercise of tyranny against individuals. But these fears seem extremely far distant to me in a situation such as this. We face a crisis of national proportions in the disposal of low-level radioactive waste, and Congress has acceded to the wishes of the States by permitting local decisionmaking rather than imposing a solution from Washington. New York itself participated and supported passage of this legislation at both the gubernatorial and federal representative levels, and then enacted state laws specifically to comply with the deadlines and timetables agreed upon by the States in the 1985 Act. For me, the Court's civics lecture has a decidedly hollow ring at a time when action, rather than rhetoric, is needed to solve a national problem.

The ultimate irony of the decision today is that in its formalistically rigid obeisance to "federalism," the Court gives Congress fewer incentives to defer to the wishes of state officials in achieving local solutions to local problems. This legislation was a classic example of Congress acting as arbiter among the States in their attempts to accept responsibility for managing a problem of grave import. The States urged the National Legislature not to impose from Washington a solution to the country's low-level radioactive waste management problems. Instead, they sought a reasonable level of local and regional autonomy consistent with Art. I, §10, cl. 3, of the Constitution. By invalidating the measure designed to ensure compliance for recalcitrant States, such as New York, the Court upsets the delicate compromise achieved among the States and forces Congress to erect several additional formalistic hurdles to clear before achieving exactly the same objective. Because the Court's justifications for undertaking this step are unpersuasive to me, I respectfully dissent.

Justice STEVENS, concurring in part and dissenting in part.

Under the Articles of Confederation, the Federal Government had the power to issue commands to the States. Because that indirect exercise of federal power proved ineffective, the Framers of the Constitution empowered the Federal Government to exercise legislative authority directly over individuals within the States, even though that direct authority constituted a greater intrusion on State sovereignty. Nothing in that history suggests that the Federal Government may not also impose its will upon the several States as it did under the Articles. The Constitution enhanced, rather than diminished, the power of the Federal Government.

The notion that Congress does not have the power to issue "a simple command to state governments to implement legislation enacted by Congress," is incorrect and unsound. [To] the contrary, the Federal Government directs state governments in many realms. The Government regulates state-operated railroads, state school systems, state prisons, state elections, and a host of other state functions. Similarly, there can be no doubt that, in time of war, Congress could either draft soldiers itself or command the States to supply their quotas of troops. I see no reason why Congress may not also command the States to enforce federal water and air quality standards or federal standards for the disposition of low-level radioactive wastes.

The Constitution gives this Court the power to resolve controversies between the States. Long before Congress enacted pollution-control legislation, this Court crafted a body of "interstate common law," Illinois v. City of Milwaukee, 406 U.S. 91, 106 (1972), to govern disputes between States involving interstate waters. In such contexts, we have not hesitated to direct States to undertake specific actions. For example, we have "imposed on States an affirmative duty to take reasonable steps to conserve and augment the water supply of an interstate stream." Thus, we unquestionably have the power to command an upstream State that is polluting the waters of a downstream State to adopt appropriate regulations to implement a federal statutory command.

With respect to the problem presented by the case at hand, if litigation should develop between States that have joined a compact, we would surely have the power to grant relief in the form of specific enforcement of the take title provision. Indeed, even if the statute had never been passed, if one State's radioactive waste created a nuisance that harmed its neighbors, it seems clear that we would have had the power to command the offending State to take remedial action. If this Court has such authority, surely Congress has similar authority.

PRINTZ v. UNITED STATES
521 U.S. 898 (1997)

Justice SCALIA delivered the opinion of the Court.

The question presented in these cases is whether certain interim provisions of the Brady Handgun Violence Prevention Act, Pub.L. 103-159, 107 Stat. 1536, commanding state and local law enforcement officers to conduct background checks on prospective handgun purchasers and to perform certain related tasks, violate the Constitution.

The Gun Control Act of 1968 (GCA), 18 U.S.C. § 921 *et seq.*, establishes a detailed federal scheme governing the distribution of firearms. It prohibits firearms dealers from transferring handguns to any person under 21, not resident in the dealer's State, or prohibited by state or local law from purchasing or possessing firearms, § 922(b). It also forbids possession of a firearm by, and transfer of a firearm to, convicted felons, fugitives from justice, unlawful users of controlled substances, persons adjudicated as mentally defective or committed to mental institutions, aliens unlawfully present in the United States, persons dishonorably discharged from the Armed Forces, persons who have renounced their citizenship, and persons who have been subjected to certain restraining orders or been convicted of a misdemeanor offense involving domestic violence. §§ 922(d) and (g).

In 1993, Congress amended the GCA by enacting the Brady Act. The Act requires the Attorney General to establish a national instant background-check system by November 30, 1998, Pub.L. 103-159, as amended, Pub.L. 103-322, 103 Stat. 2074, note following 18 U.S.C. § 922, and immediately puts in place certain interim provisions until that system becomes operative. Under the interim provisions, a firearms dealer who proposes to transfer a handgun must first: (1) receive from the transferee a statement (the Brady Form), § 922(s)(1)(A)(i)(I), containing the name, address, and date of birth of the proposed transferee along with a sworn statement that the transferee is not among any of the classes of prohibited purchasers, § 922(s)(3); (2) verify the identity of the transferee by examining an identification document, § 922(s)(1)(A)(i)(II); and (3) provide the "chief law enforcement officer" (CLEO) of the transferee's residence with notice of the contents (and a copy) of the Brady Form, §§ 922(s)(1)(A)(i)(III) and (IV). [The] CLEO must "make a reasonable effort to ascertain within 5 business days whether receipt or possession would be in violation of the law, including research in whatever State and local recordkeeping systems are available and in a national system designated by the Attorney General." § 922(s)(2). The Act does not require the CLEO to take any particular action if he determines that a pending transaction would be unlawful; he may notify the firearms dealer to that effect, but is not required to do so. If, however, the CLEO notifies a gun dealer that a prospective purchaser is ineligible to receive a handgun, he must, upon request, provide the would-be purchaser with a written statement of the reasons for that determination. § 922(s)(6)(C). Moreover, if the CLEO does not discover any basis for objecting to the sale, he must destroy any records in his possession relating to the transfer, including his copy of the Brady Form. § 922(s)(6)(B)(i). Under a separate provision of the GCA, any person who "knowingly violates [the section of the GCA amended by the Brady Act] shall be fined under this title, imprisoned for not more than 1 year, or both." § 924(a)(5).

Petitioners Jay Printz and Richard Mack, the CLEOs for Ravalli County, Montana, and Graham County, Arizona, respectively, filed separate actions challenging the constitutionality of the Brady Act's interim provisions. In each case, the District Court held that the provision requiring CLEOs to perform background checks was unconstitutional, but concluded that that provision was severable from the remainder of the Act, effectively leaving a voluntary background-check system in place. 856 F.Supp. 1372 (D.Ariz.1994); 854 F.Supp. 1503 (D.Mont.1994). A divided panel of the Court of Appeals for the Ninth Circuit reversed, finding none of the Brady Act's interim provisions to be unconstitutional.

[T]he Brady Act purports to direct state law enforcement officers to participate, albeit only temporarily, in the administration of a federally enacted regulatory scheme.

Petitioners here object to being pressed into federal service, and contend that congressional action compelling state officers to execute federal laws is unconstitutional. Because there is no constitutional text speaking to this precise question, the answer to the CLEOs' challenge must be sought in historical understanding and practice, in the structure of the Constitution, and in the jurisprudence of this Court.

The Government contends, to the contrary, that "the earliest Congresses enacted statutes that required the participation of state officials in the implementation of federal laws," Brief for United States 28. The Government's contention demands our careful consideration, since early congressional enactments "provid[e] 'contemporaneous and weighty evidence' of the Constitution's meaning."

The Government observes that statutes enacted by the first Congresses required state courts to record applications for citizenship, Act of Mar. 26, 1790, ch. 3, § 1, 1 Stat. 103, to transmit abstracts of citizenship applications and other naturalization records to the Secretary of State, Act of June 18, 1798, ch. 54, § 2, 1 Stat. 567, and to register aliens seeking naturalization and issue certificates of registry, Act of Apr. 14, 1802, ch. 28, § 2, 2 Stat. 154-155. It may well be, however, that these requirements applied only in States that authorized their courts to conduct naturalization proceedings. See Act of Mar. 26, 1790, ch. 3, § 1, 1 Stat. 103; Holmgren v. United States, 217 U.S. 509, 516-517, 30 S.Ct. 588, 589, 54 L.Ed. 861 (1910) (explaining that the Act of March 26, 1790, "conferred authority upon state courts to admit aliens to citizenship" and refraining from addressing the question "whether the States can be required to enforce such naturalization laws against their consent"); United States v. Jones, 109 U.S. 513, 519-520, 3 S.Ct. 346, 351, 27 L.Ed. 1015 (1883) (stating that these obligations were imposed "with the consent of the States" and "could not be enforced against the consent of the States"). Other statutes of that era apparently or at least arguably required state courts to perform functions unrelated to naturalization, such as resolving controversies between a captain and the crew of his ship concerning the seaworthiness of the vessel, Act of July 20, 1790, ch. 29, § 3, 1 Stat. 132, hearing the claims of slave owners who had apprehended fugitive slaves and issuing certificates authorizing the slave's forced removal to the State from which he had fled, Act of Feb. 12, 1793, ch. 7, § 3, 1 Stat. 302-305, taking proof of the claims of Canadian refugees who had assisted the United States during the Revolutionary War, Act of Apr. 7, 1798, ch. 26, § 3, 1 Stat. 548, and ordering the deportation of alien enemies in times of war, Act of July 6, 1798, ch. 66, § 2, 1 Stat. 577-578.

These early laws establish, at most, that the Constitution was originally understood to permit imposition of an obligation on state *judges* to enforce federal prescriptions, insofar as those prescriptions related to matters appropriate for the judicial power. [We] do not think the early statutes imposing obligations on state courts imply a power of Congress to impress the state executive into its service. Indeed, it can be argued that the numerousness of these statutes, contrasted with the utter lack of statutes imposing obligations on the States' executive (notwithstanding the attractiveness of that course to Congress), suggests an assumed *absence* of such power. The only early federal law the Government has brought to our attention that imposed duties on state executive officers is the Extradition Act of 1793, which required the "executive authority" of a State to cause the arrest and delivery of a fugitive from justice upon the request of the executive authority of the State from which the fugitive had fled. See Act of Feb. 12, 1793, ch. 7, § 1, 1 Stat. 302. That was in direct implementation, however, of the Extradition Clause of the Constitution itself, see Art. IV, § 2.

Not only do the enactments of the early Congresses, as far as we are aware, contain no evidence of an assumption that the Federal Government may command the States' executive power in the absence of a particularized constitutional authorization, they contain some indication of precisely the opposite assumption. On September 23, 1789 — the day before its proposal of the Bill of Rights, see 1 Annals of Congress 912-913 — the First Congress enacted a law aimed at obtaining state assistance of the most rudimentary and necessary sort for the enforcement of the new Government's laws: the holding of federal prisoners in state jails at federal expense. Significantly, the law issued not a command to the States' executive, but a recommendation to their legislatures.

[T]he Government also appeals to other sources we have usually regarded as indicative of the original understanding of the Constitution. It points to portions of The Federalist which reply to criticisms that Congress's power to tax will produce two sets of revenue officers — for example, "Brutus's" assertion in his letter to the New York Journal of December 13, 1787, that the Constitution "opens a door to the appointment of a swarm of revenue and excise officers to prey upon the honest and industrious part of the community, eat up their substance, and riot on the spoils of the country," reprinted in 1 Debate on the Constitution 502 (B. Bailyn ed.1993). "Publius" responded that Congress will probably "make use of the State officers and State regulations, for collecting" federal taxes, The Federalist No. 36, p. 221 (C. Rossiter ed. 1961) (A. Hamilton) (hereinafter The Federalist), and predicted that "the eventual collection [of internal revenue] under the immediate authority of the Union, will generally be made by the officers, and according to the rules, appointed by the several States," *id.,* No. 45, at 292 (J. Madison). The Government also invokes The Federalist's more general observations that the Constitution would "enable the [national] government to employ the ordinary magistracy of each [State] in the execution of its laws," *id.,* No. 27, at 176 (A. Hamilton), and that it was "extremely probable that in other instances, particularly in the organization of the judicial power, the officers of the States will be clothed with the correspondent authority of the Union," *id.,* No. 45, at 292 (J. Madison). But none of these statements necessarily implies — what is the critical point here — that Congress could impose these responsibilities *without the consent of the States.* They appear to rest on the natural assumption that the States would consent to allowing their officials to assist the Federal Government, see *FERC v. Mississippi,* 456 U.S. 742, 796, n. 35, 102 S.Ct. 2126, 2157, n. 35, 72 L.Ed.2d 532 (1982) (O'Connor, J., concurring in judgment in part and dissenting in part), an assumption proved correct by the extensive mutual assistance the States and Federal Government voluntarily provided one another in the early days of the Republic.

Another passage of The Federalist reads as follows:

> "It merits particular attention . . . that the laws of the Confederacy as to the *enumerated* and *legitimate* objects of its jurisdiction will become the SUPREME LAW of the land; to the observance of which all officers, legislative, executive, and judicial in each State will be bound by the sanctity of an oath. Thus, the legislatures, courts, and magistrates, of the respective members will be incorporated into the operations of the national government *as far as its just and constitutional authority extends;* and will be rendered auxiliary to the enforcement of its laws." The Federalist No. 27, at 177 (A. Hamilton) (emphasis in original).

The Government does not rely upon this passage, but Justice Souter (with whose conclusions on this point the dissent is in agreement, see *post,* at 2390 makes it the very foundation of his position; so we pause to examine it in some detail. Justice Souter finds "[t]he natural reading" of the phrases "'will be incorporated into the operations of the national government'" and "'will be rendered auxiliary to the enforcement of its laws'" to be that the National Government will have "authority . . . , when exercising an otherwise legitimate power (the commerce power, say), to require state 'auxiliaries' to take appropriate action." *Post,* at 2402. There are several obstacles to such an interpretation. First, the consequences in question ("incorporated into the operations of the national government" and "rendered auxiliary to the enforcement of its laws") are said in the quoted passage to flow *automatically* from the officers' oath to observe "the laws of the Confederacy as to the *enumerated* and *legitimate* objects of its jurisdiction." Thus, if the passage means that state officers must take an active role in the implementation of federal law, it means that they must do so without the necessity for a congressional directive that they implement it. But no one has ever thought, and no one asserts in the present litigation, that that is the law. The second problem with Justice Souter's reading is that it makes state *legislatures* subject to federal direction. (The passage in question, after all, does not include legislatures merely incidentally, as by referring to "all state officers"; it refers to legislatures *specifically* and *first of all.*) We have held, however, that state legislatures are *not* subject to federal direction. *New York v. United States,* 505 U.S. 144, 112 S.Ct. 2408, 120 L.Ed.2d 120 (1992).

Justice Souter contends that his interpretation of The Federalist No. 27 is "supported by No. 44," written by Madison, wherefore he claims that "Madison and Hamilton" together stand opposed to our view. *Post,* at 2402, 2404. In fact, The Federalist No. 44 quite clearly contradicts Justice Souter's reading. In that Number, Madison justifies the requirement that state officials take an oath to support the Federal Constitution on the ground that they "will have an essential agency in giving effect to the federal Constitution." If the dissent's reading of The Federalist No. 27 were correct (and if Madison agreed with it), one would surely have expected that "essential agency" of state executive officers (if described further) to be described as their responsibility to execute the laws enacted under the Constitution. Instead, however, The Federalist No. 44 continues with the following description:

> "The election of the President and Senate will depend, in all cases, on the legislatures of the several States. And the election of the House of Representatives will equally depend on the same authority in the first instance; and will, probably, forever *be conducted by the officers* and according to the laws *of the States.*" *Id.,* at 287 (emphasis added).

It is most implausible that the person who labored for that example of state executive officers' assisting the Federal Government believed, but neglected to mention, that they had a responsibility to execute federal laws.

To complete the historical record, we must note that there is not only an absence of executive-commandeering statutes in the early Congresses, but there is an absence of them in our later history as well, at least until very recent years. The Government points to the Act of August 3, 1882, ch. 376, § § 2, 4, 22 Stat. 214, which enlisted state officials "to take charge of the local affairs of immigration in the ports within such State, and to provide for the support and relief of such immigrants therein landing as may fall into distress or need of public aid"; to inspect arriving immigrants and exclude any person found to be a "convict, lunatic, idiot," or indigent; and to send convicts back to their country of origin "without compensation." The statute did not, however, *mandate* those duties, but merely empowered the Secretary of the Treasury "to *enter into contracts* with such State . . . officers as *may be designated* for that purpose *by the governor* of any State." (Emphasis added.)

The Government cites the World War I selective draft law that authorized the President "to utilize the service of any or all departments and any or all officers or agents of the United States *and of the several States,* Territories, and the District of Columbia, and subdivisions thereof, in the execution of this Act," and made any person who refused to comply with the President's directions guilty of a misdemeanor. Act of May 18, 1917, ch. 15, § 6, 40 Stat. 80-81 (emphasis added). However, it is far from clear that the authorization "to utilize the service" of state officers was an authorization to *compel* the service of state officers; and the misdemeanor provision surely applied only to refusal to comply with the President's *authorized* directions, which might not have included directions to officers of States whose Governors had not volunteered their services. It is interesting that in implementing the Act President Wilson did not commandeer the services of state officers, but instead requested the assistance of the States' Governors, see Proclamation of May 18, 1917, 40 Stat. 1665 ("call[ing] upon the Governor of each of the several States . . . and all officers and agents of the several States . . . to perform certain duties"); Registration Regulations Prescribed by the President Under the Act of Congress Approved May 18, 1917, pt. 1, § 7 ("[T]he governor [of each State] is *requested* to act under the regulations and rules prescribed by the President or under his direction" (emphasis added)), obtained the consent of each of the Governors, see Note, The President, the Senate, the Constitution, and the Executive Order of May 8, 1926, 21 Ill. L.Rev. 142, 144 (1926), and left it to the Governors to issue orders to their subordinate state officers, see Selective Service Regulations Prescribed by the President Under the Act of May 18, 1917, § 27 (1918); J. Clark, The Rise of a New Federalism 91 (1965). See generally Note, 21 Ill. L.Rev., at 144. It is impressive that even with respect to a wartime measure the President should have been so solicitous of state independence.

The Government points to a number of federal statutes enacted within the past few decades that require the participation of state or local officials in implementing federal regulatory schemes. Some of these are connected to federal funding measures, and can perhaps be more accurately described as conditions upon the grant of federal funding than as mandates to the States; others, which require only the provision of information to the Federal Government, do not involve the precise issue before us here, which is the forced participation of the States' executive in the actual administration of a federal program. We of course do not address these or other currently operative enactments that are not before us; it will be time enough to do so if and when their validity is challenged in a proper case.

For deciding the issue before us here, they are of little relevance. Even assuming they represent assertion of the very same congressional power challenged here, they are of such recent vintage that they are no more probative than the statute before us of a constitutional tradition that lends meaning to the text. Their persuasive force is far outweighed by almost two centuries of apparent congressional avoidance of the practice.

We turn next to consideration of the structure of the Constitution, to see if we can discern among its "essential postulate[s]," *Principality of Monaco v. Mississippi,* 292 U.S. 313, 322, 54 S.Ct. 745, 748, 78 L.Ed. 1282 (1934), a principle that controls the present cases.

A

It is incontestable that the Constitution established a system of "dual sovereignty." *Gregory v. Ashcroft,* 501 U.S. 452, 457, 111 S.Ct. 2395, 2399, 115 L.Ed.2d 410 (1991); *Tafflin v. Levitt,* 493 U.S. 455, 458, 110 S.Ct. 792, 795, 107 L.Ed.2d 887 (1990). Although the States surrendered many of their powers to the new Federal Government, they retained "a residuary and inviolable sovereignty," The Federalist No. 39, at 245 (J. Madison). This is reflected throughout the Constitution's text, *Lane County v. Oregon,* 7 Wall. 71, 76, 19 L.Ed. 101 (1869); *Texas v. White,* 7 Wall. 700, 725, 19 L.Ed. 227 (1869), including (to mention only a few examples) the prohibition on any involuntary reduction or combination of a State's territory, Art. IV, § 3; the Judicial Power Clause, Art. III, § 2, and the Privileges and Immunities Clause, Art. IV, § 2, which speak of the "Citizens" of the States; the amendment provision, Article V, which requires the votes of three-fourths of the States to amend the Constitution; and the Guarantee Clause, Art. IV, § 4, which "presupposes the continued existence of the states and . . . those means and instrumentalities which are the creation of their sovereign and reserved rights," *Helvering v. Gerhardt,* 304 U.S. 405, 414-415, 58 S.Ct. 969, 973, 82 L.Ed. 1427 (1938). Residual state sovereignty was also implicit, of course, in the Constitution's conferral upon Congress of not all governmental powers, but only discrete, enumerated ones, Art. I, § 8, which implication was rendered express by the Tenth Amendment's assertion that "[t]he powers not delegated to the United States by the Constitution, nor prohibited by it to the States, are reserved to the States respectively, or to the people."

[T]he Framers rejected the concept of a central government that would act upon and through the States, and instead designed a system in which the State and Federal Governments would exercise concurrent authority over the people — who were, in Hamilton's words, "the only proper objects of government," The Federalist No. 15, at 109. We have set forth the historical record in more detail elsewhere, see *New York v. United States,* 505 U.S., at 161-166, 112 S.Ct., at 2420-2423, and need not repeat it here. It suffices to repeat the conclusion: "the Framers explicitly chose a Constitution that confers upon Congress the power to regulate individuals, not States." *Id.,* at 166, 112 S.Ct., at 2423. The great innovation of this design was that "our citizens would have two political capacities, one state and one federal, each protected from incursion by the other" — "a legal system unprecedented in form and design, establishing two orders of government, each with its own direct relationship, its own privity, its own set of mutual rights and obligations to the people who sustain it and are governed by it." *U.S. Term Limits, Inc. v. Thornton,* 514 U.S. 779, 838, 115 S.Ct. 1842, 1872, 131 L.Ed.2d 881 (1995) (Kennedy, J., concurring). The Constitution thus contemplates that a State's government will represent and remain accountable to its own citizens. *See New York, supra,* at 168-169, 112 S.Ct., at 2424; *United States v. Lopez,* 514 U.S. 549, 576-577, 115 S.Ct. 1624, 1638-1639, 131 L.Ed.2d 626 (1995) (Kennedy, J., concurring). Cf. *Edgar v. MITE Corp.,* 457 U.S. 624, 644, 102

S.Ct. 2629, 2641, 73 L.Ed.2d 269 (1982) ("the State has no legitimate interest in protecting nonresident [s]"). As Madison expressed it: "[T]he local or municipal authorities form distinct and independent portions of the supremacy, no more subject, within their respective spheres, to the general authority than the general authority is subject to them, within its own sphere." The Federalist No. 39, at 245.

This separation of the two spheres is one of the Constitution's structural protections of liberty. "Just as the separation and independence of the coordinate branches of the Federal Government serve to prevent the accumulation of excessive power in any one branch, a healthy balance of power between the States and the Federal Government will reduce the risk of tyranny and abuse from either front." 501 U.S., *supra,* at 458, 111 S.Ct., at 2400. To quote Madison once again:

> "In the compound republic of America, the power surrendered by the people is first divided between two distinct governments, and then the portion allotted to each subdivided among distinct and separate departments. Hence a double security arises to the rights of the people. The different governments will control each other, at the same time that each will be controlled by itself." The Federalist No. 51, at 323.

See also The Federalist No. 28, at 180-181 (A. Hamilton). The power of the Federal Government would be augmented immeasurably if it were able to impress into its service — and at no cost to itself — the police officers of the 50 States.

[F]ederal control of state officers would have upon the first element of the "double security" alluded to by Madison: the division of power between State and Federal Governments. It would also have an effect upon the second element: the separation and equilibration of powers between the three branches of the Federal Government itself. The Constitution does not leave to speculation who is to administer the laws enacted by Congress; the President, it says, "shall take Care that the Laws be faithfully executed," Art. II, § 3, personally and through officers whom he appoints (save for such inferior officers as Congress may authorize to be appointed by the "Courts of Law" or by "the Heads of Departments" who are themselves Presidential appointees), Art. II, § 2. The Brady Act effectively transfers this responsibility to thousands of CLEOs in the 50 States, who are left to implement the program without meaningful Presidential control (if indeed meaningful Presidential control is possible without the power to appoint and remove). The insistence of the Framers upon unity in the Federal Executive — to ensure both vigor and accountability — is well known. See The Federalist No. 70 (A.Hamilton); 2 Documentary History of the Ratification of the Constitution 495 (M. Jensen ed.1976) (statement of James Wilson); see also Calabresi & Prakash, The President's Power to Execute the Laws, 104 Yale L.J. 541 (1994). That unity would be shattered, and the power of the President would be subject to reduction, if Congress could act as effectively without the President as with him, by simply requiring state officers to execute its laws.

The Brady Act effectively transfers the President's responsibility to administer the laws enacted by Congress, Art. II, § § 2 and 3, to thousands of CLEOs in the 50 States, who are left to implement the program without meaningful Presidential control. The Federal Executive's unity would be shattered, and the power of the President would be subject to reduction, if Congress could simply require state officers to execute its laws.

The dissent of course resorts to the last, best hope of those who defend ultra vires congressional action, the Necessary and Proper Clause. It reasons, *post,* at 2387, that the power to regulate the sale of handguns under the Commerce Clause, coupled with the power to "make all Laws which shall be necessary and proper for carrying into Execution the foregoing Powers," Art. I, § 8, conclusively establishes the Brady Act's constitutional validity, because the Tenth Amendment imposes no limitations on the exercise of *delegated* powers but merely prohibits the exercise of powers "*not* delegated to the United States." What destroys the dissent's Necessary and Proper Clause argument, however, is not the Tenth Amendment but the Necessary and Proper Clause itself. When a "La [w] . . . for carrying into Execution" the Commerce Clause violates the principle of state sovereignty reflected in the various constitutional provisions we mentioned earlier, *supra,* at 2376-2377, it is not a "La[w] . . . *proper* for carrying into Execution the Commerce Clause," and is thus, in the words of The Federalist, "merely [an] ac[t] of usurpation" which "deserve[s] to be treated as such." The Federalist No. 33, at 204 (A. Hamilton).

Finally, and most conclusively in the present litigation, we turn to the prior jurisprudence of this Court. Federal commandeering of state governments is such a novel phenomenon that this Court's first experience with it did not occur until the 1970's, when the Environmental Protection Agency promulgated regulations requiring States to prescribe auto emissions testing, monitoring and retrofit programs, and to designate preferential bus and carpool lanes. The Courts of Appeals for the Fourth and Ninth Circuits invalidated the regulations on statutory grounds in order to avoid what they perceived to be grave constitutional issues, see *Maryland v. EPA,* 530 F.2d 215, 226 (C.A.4 1975); *Brown v. EPA,* 521 F.2d 827, 838-842 (C.A.9 1975); and the District of Columbia Circuit invalidated the regulations on both constitutional and statutory grounds, see *District of Columbia v. Train,* 521 F.2d 971, 994 (1975). After we granted certiorari to review the statutory and constitutional validity of the regulations, the Government declined even to defend them, and instead rescinded some and conceded the invalidity of those that remained, leading us to vacate the opinions below and remand for consideration of mootness. *EPA v. Brown,* 431 U.S. 99, 97 S.Ct. 1635, 52 L.Ed.2d 166 (1977) (*per curiam*).

Although we had no occasion to pass upon the subject in *Brown,* later opinions of ours have made clear that the Federal Government may not compel the States to implement, by legislation or executive action, federal regulatory programs.

When we were at last confronted squarely with a federal statute that unambiguously required the States to enact or administer a federal regulatory program, our decision should have come as no surprise. We concluded that Congress could constitutionally require the States to do neither. *Id.,* at 176, 112 S.Ct., at 2428. "The Federal Government," we held, "may not compel the States to enact or administer a federal regulatory program." *Id.,* at 188, 112 S.Ct., at 2435.

The Government contends that *New York* is distinguishable on the following ground: Unlike the "take title" provisions invalidated there, the background-check provision of the Brady Act does not require state legislative or executive officials to make policy, but instead issues a final directive to state CLEOs.

The Government's distinction between "making" law and merely "enforcing" it, between "policymaking" and mere "implementation," is an interesting one. Executive action that has utterly no policymaking component is rare, particularly at an executive level as high as a jurisdiction's chief law enforcement officer. [Is] this decision whether to devote maximum "reasonable efforts" or minimum "reasonable efforts" not preeminently a matter of policy? It is quite impossible, in short, to draw the Government's proposed line at "no policymaking," and we would have to fall back upon a line of "not too much policymaking." How much is too much is not likely to be answered precisely; and an imprecise barrier against federal intrusion upon state authority is not likely to be an effective one.

Even assuming, moreover, that the Brady Act leaves no "policymaking" discretion with the States, we fail to see how that improves rather than worsens the intrusion upon state sovereignty. Preservation of the States as independent and autonomous political entities is arguably less undermined by requiring them to make policy in certain fields than (as Judge Sneed aptly described it over two decades ago) by "reduc[ing] [them] to puppets of a ventriloquist Congress," *Brown v. EPA*, 521 F.2d, at 839. It is an essential attribute of the States' retained sovereignty that they remain independent and autonomous within their proper sphere of authority. See *Texas v. White*, 7 Wall., at 725. It is no more compatible with this independence and autonomy that their officers be "dragooned" (as Judge Fernandez put it in his dissent below, 66 F.3d, at 1035) into administering federal law, than it would be compatible with the independence and autonomy of the United States that its officers be impressed into service for the execution of state laws.

The Government purports to find support for its proffered distinction of *New York* in our decisions in *Testa v. Katt*, 330 U.S. 386, 67 S.Ct. 810, 91 L.Ed. 967 (1947), and *FERC v. Mississippi*, 456 U.S. 742, 102 S.Ct. 2126, 72 L.Ed.2d 532 (1982). We find neither case relevant. *Testa* stands for the proposition that state courts cannot refuse to apply federal law — a conclusion mandated by the terms of the Supremacy Clause ("the Judges in every State shall be bound [by federal law]"). As we have suggested earlier, *supra*, at 2370, that says nothing about whether state executive officers must administer federal law.

The Government also maintains that requiring state officers to perform discrete, ministerial tasks specified by Congress does not violate the principle of *New York* because it does not diminish the accountability of state or federal officials. This argument fails even on its own terms. By forcing state governments to absorb the financial burden of implementing a federal regulatory program, Members of Congress can take credit for "solving" problems without having to ask their constituents to pay for the solutions with higher federal taxes. And even when the States are not forced to absorb the costs of implementing a federal program, they are still put in the position of taking the blame for its burdensomeness and for its defects. See Merritt, Three Faces of Federalism: Finding a Formula for the Future, 47 Vand. L.Rev. 1563, 1580, n. 65 (1994). Under the present law, for example, it will be the CLEO and not some federal official who stands between the gun purchaser and immediate possession of his gun.

Finally, the Government puts forward a cluster of arguments that can be grouped under the heading: "The Brady Act serves very important purposes, is most efficiently administered by CLEOs during the interim period, and places a minimal and only temporary burden upon state officers." There is considerable disagreement over the extent of the burden, but we need not pause over that detail. Assuming *all* the mentioned factors were true, they might be relevant if we were evaluating whether the incidental application to the States of a federal law of general applicability excessively interfered with the functioning of state governments. See, *e.g., Fry v. United States*, 421 U.S. 542, 548, 95 S.Ct. 1792, 1796, 44 L.Ed.2d 363 (1975); *National League of Cities v. Usery*, 426 U.S. 833, 853, 96 S.Ct. 2465, 2475, 49 L.Ed.2d 245 (1976) (overruled by *Garcia v. San Antonio Metropolitan Transit Authority*, 469 U.S. 528, 105 S.Ct. 1005, 83 L.Ed.2d 1016 (1985)); *South Carolina v. Baker*, 485 U.S. 505, 529, 108 S.Ct. 1355, 1370, 99 L.Ed.2d 592 (1988) (Rehnquist, C.J., concurring in judgment). But where, as here, it is the whole *object* of the law to direct the functioning of the state executive, and hence to compromise the structural framework of dual sovereignty, such a "balancing" analysis is inappropriate. It is the very *principle* of separate state sovereignty that such a law offends, and no comparative assessment of the various interests can overcome that fundamental defect.

We held in *New York* that Congress cannot compel the States to enact or enforce a federal regulatory program. Today we hold that Congress cannot circumvent that prohibition by conscripting the State's officers directly. The Federal Government may neither issue directives requiring the States to address particular problems, nor command the States' officers, or those of their political subdivisions, to administer or enforce a federal regulatory program. It matters not whether policymaking is involved, and no case-by-case weighing of the burdens or benefits is necessary; such commands are fundamentally incompatible with our constitutional system of dual sovereignty. Accordingly, the judgment of the Court of Appeals for the Ninth Circuit is reversed.

It is so ordered.

Justice O'CONNOR, concurring.

Our precedent and our Nation's historical practices support the Court's holding today. [T]he Court appropriately refrains from deciding whether other purely ministerial reporting requirements imposed by Congress on state and local authorities pursuant to its Commerce Clause powers are similarly invalid. See, *e.g.,* 42 U.S.C. § 5779(a) (requiring state and local law enforcement agencies to report cases of missing children to the Department of Justice). The provisions invalidated here, however, which directly compel state officials to administer a federal regulatory program, utterly fail to adhere to the design and structure of our constitutional scheme.

Justice THOMAS, concurring.

In my "revisionist" view, see *post,* at 2387, (Stevens, J., dissenting), the Federal Government's authority under the Commerce Clause, which merely allocates to Congress the power "to regulate Commerce . . . among the several States," does not extend to the regulation of wholly *intra*state, point-of-sale transactions. See *United States v. Lopez,* 514 U.S. 549, 584, 115 S.Ct. 1624, 1642, 131 L.Ed.2d 626 (1995) (concurring opinion). Absent the underlying authority to regulate the intrastate transfer of firearms, Congress surely lacks the corollary power to impress state law enforcement officers into administering and enforcing such regulations.

[If], however, the Second Amendment is read to confer a *personal* right to "keep and bear arms," a colorable argument exists that the Federal Government's regulatory scheme, at least as it pertains to the purely intrastate sale or possession of firearms, runs afoul of that Amendment's protections. As the parties did not raise this argument, however, we need not consider it here.

Justice STEVENS, with whom Justice SOUTER, Justice GINSBURG, and Justice BREYER join, dissenting.

When Congress exercises the powers delegated to it by the Constitution, it may impose affirmative obligations on executive and judicial officers of state and local governments as well as ordinary citizens. [Article] I, § 8, grants Congress the power to regulate commerce among the States. Putting to one side the revisionist views expressed by Justice Thomas in his concurring opinion in *United States v. Lopez,* 514 U.S. 549, 584, 115 S.Ct. 1624, 1642, 131 L.Ed.2d 626 (1995), there can be no question that that provision adequately supports the regulation of commerce in handguns effected by the Brady Act. Moreover, the additional grant of authority in that section of the Constitution "[t]o make all Laws which shall be necessary and proper for carrying into Execution the foregoing Powers" is surely adequate to support the temporary enlistment of local police officers in the process of identifying persons who should not be entrusted with the possession of handguns. [The] Amendment confirms the principle that the powers of the Federal Government are limited to those affirmatively granted by the Constitution, but it does not purport to limit the scope or the effectiveness of the exercise of powers that are delegated to Congress Thus, the Amendment provides no support for a rule that immunizes local officials from obligations that might be imposed on ordinary citizens. Indeed, it would be more reasonable to infer that federal law may impose greater duties on state officials than on private citizens because another provision of the Constitution requires that "all executive and judicial Officers, both of the United States and of the several States, shall be bound by Oath or Affirmation, to support this Constitution." Art. VI, cl. 3.

[T]he historical materials strongly suggest that the founders intended to enhance the capacity of the Federal Government by empowering it — as a part of the new authority to make demands directly on individual citizens — to act through local officials. Hamilton made clear that the new Constitution, "by extending the authority of the federal head to the individual citizens of the several States, will enable the government to employ the ordinary magistracy of each in the execution of its laws." The Federalist No. 27, at 180. Hamilton's meaning was unambiguous; the Federal Government was to have the power to demand that local officials implement national policy programs.

More specifically, during the debates concerning the ratification of the Constitution, it was assumed that state agents would act as tax collectors for the Federal Government. Opponents of the Constitution had repeatedly expressed fears that the new Federal Government's ability to impose taxes directly on the citizenry would result in an overbearing presence of federal tax collectors in the States. Federalists rejoined that this problem would not arise because, as Hamilton explained, "the United States . . . will make use of the State officers and State regulations for collecting" certain taxes. *Id.*, No. 36, at 235. Similarly, Madison made clear that the new central Government's power to raise taxes directly from the citizenry would "not be resorted to, except for supplemental purposes of revenue . . . and that the eventual collection, under the immediate authority of the Union, will generally be made by the officers . . . appointed by the several States." *Id.*, No. 45, at 318.

The Court's response to this powerful historical evidence is weak. The majority suggests that "none of these statements necessarily implies . . . Congress could impose these responsibilities without the consent of the States." *Ante,* at 2372 (emphasis deleted). No fair reading of these materials can justify such an interpretation.

Bereft of support in the history of the founding, the Court rests its conclusion on the claim that there is little evidence the National Government actually exercised such a power in the early years of the Republic. [We] have never suggested that the failure of the early Congresses to address the scope of federal power in a particular area or to exercise a particular authority was an argument against its existence. That position, if correct, would undermine most of our post-New Deal Commerce Clause jurisprudence. [More] importantly, the fact that Congress did elect to rely on state judges and the clerks of state courts to perform a variety of executive functions, see *ante,* at 2369-2372, is surely evidence of a contemporary understanding that their status as state officials did not immunize them from federal service.

For example, statutes of the early Congresses required in mandatory terms that state judges and their clerks perform various executive duties with respect to applications for citizenship. [Similarly], the First Congress enacted legislation requiring state courts to serve, functionally, like contemporary regulatory agencies in certifying the seaworthiness of vessels.

[The] use of state judges and their clerks to perform executive functions was, in historical context, hardly unusual. [The] majority's insistence that this evidence of federal enlistment of state officials to serve executive functions is irrelevant simply because the assistance of "judges" was at issue rests on empty formalistic reasoning of the highest order.

The Court's "structural" arguments are not sufficient to rebut that presumption. [As] we explained in *Garcia v. San Antonio Metropolitan Transit Authority,* 469 U.S. 528, 105 S.Ct. 1005, 83 L.Ed.2d 1016 (1985): "[T]he principal means chosen by the Framers to ensure the role of the States in the federal system lies in the structure of the Federal Government itself. [Given] the fact that the Members of Congress are elected by the people of the several States, with each State receiving an equivalent number of Senators in order to ensure that even the smallest States have a powerful voice in the Legislature, it is quite unrealistic to assume that they will ignore the sovereignty concerns of their constituents. It is far more reasonable to presume that their decisions to impose modest burdens on state officials from time to time reflect a considered judgment that the people in each of the States will benefit there from.

Recent developments demonstrate that the political safeguards protecting Our Federalism are effective. The majority expresses special concern that were its rule not adopted the Federal Government would be able to avail itself of the services of state government officials "at no cost to itself." *Ante,* at 2378; see also *ante,* at 2382 (arguing that "Members of Congress can take credit for 'solving' problems without having to ask their constituents to pay for the solutions with higher federal taxes"). But this specific problem of federal actions that have the effect of imposing so-called "unfunded mandates" on the States has been identified and meaningfully addressed by Congress in recent legislation. See Unfunded Mandates Reform Act of 1995, Pub.L. 104-4, 109 Stat. 48.

The statute was designed "to end the imposition, in the absence of full consideration by Congress, of Federal mandates on State . . . governments without adequate Federal funding, in a manner that may displace other essential State . . . governmental priorities." 2 U.S.C. § 1501(2) (1994 ed., Supp. II). It functions, *inter alia,* by permitting Members of Congress to raise an objection by point of order to a pending bill that contains an "unfunded mandate," as defined by the statute, of over $50 million. The mandate may not then be enacted unless the Members make an explicit decision to proceed anyway. See Recent Legislation, Unfunded Mandates Reform Act of 1995, 109 Harv. L.Rev. 1469 (1996) (describing functioning of statute). Whatever the ultimate impact of the new legislation, its passage demonstrates that unelected judges are better off leaving the protection of federalism to the political process in all but the most extraordinary circumstances.

Perversely, the majority's rule seems more likely to damage than to preserve the safeguards against tyranny provided by the existence of vital state governments. By limiting the ability of the Federal Government to enlist state officials in the implementation of its programs, the Court creates incentives for the National Government to aggrandize itself. In the name of State's rights, the majority would have the Federal Government create vast national bureaucracies to implement its policies. This is exactly the sort of thing that the early Federalists promised would not occur, in part as a result of the National Government's ability to rely on the magistracy of the States.

Finally, the majority provides an incomplete explanation of our decision in *Testa v. Katt*, 330 U.S. 386, 67 S.Ct. 810, 91 L.Ed. 967 (1947), and demeans its importance. In that case the Court unanimously held that state courts of appropriate jurisdiction must occupy themselves adjudicating claims brought by private litigants under the federal Emergency Price Control Act of 1942, regardless of how otherwise crowded their dockets might be with state-law matters. [It] is impossible to reconcile the Court's present view that *Testa* rested entirely on the specific reference to state judges in the Supremacy Clause with our extension of that early case in *FERC*.

Even if the Court were correct in its suggestion that it was the reference to judges in the Supremacy Clause, rather than the central message of the entire Clause, that dictated the result in *Testa*, the Court's implied *expressio unius* argument that the Framers therefore did *not* intend to permit the enlistment of other state officials is implausible. Throughout our history judges, state as well as federal, have merited as much respect as executive agents. The notion that the Framers would have had no reluctance to "press state judges into federal service" against their will but would have regarded the imposition of a similar — indeed, far lesser — burden on town constables as an intolerable affront to principles of state sovereignty can only be considered perverse.

The provision of the Brady Act that crosses the Court's newly defined constitutional threshold is more comparable to a statute requiring local police officers to report the identity of missing children to the Crime Control Center of the Department of Justice than to an offensive federal command to a sovereign State. If Congress believes that such a statute will benefit the people of the Nation, and serve the interests of cooperative federalism better than an enlarged federal bureaucracy, we should respect both its policy judgment and its appraisal of its constitutional power.

Accordingly, I respectfully dissent.

Justice SOUTER, dissenting.

In deciding these cases, which I have found closer than I had anticipated, it is The Federalist that finally determines my position. I believe that the most straightforward reading of No. 27 is authority for the Government's position here, and that this reading is both supported by No. 44 and consistent with Nos. 36 and 45.

Two such examples of anticipated state collection of federal revenue are instructive, each of which is put forward to counter fears of a proliferation of tax collectors. In No. 45, Hamilton says that if a State is not given (or declines to exercise) an option to supply its citizens' share of a federal tax, the "eventual collection [of the federal tax] under the immediate authority of the Union, will generally be made by the officers, and according to the rules, appointed by the several States." *Id.*, No. 45, at 313. And in No. 36, he explains that the National Government would more readily "employ the State officers as much as possible, and to attach them to the Union by an accumulation of their emoluments," *id.*, No. 36, at 228, than by appointing separate federal revenue collectors.

In the light of all these passages, I cannot persuade myself that the statements from No. 27 speak of anything less than the authority of the National Government, when exercising an otherwise legitimate power (the commerce power, say), to require state "auxiliaries" to take appropriate action. To be sure, it does not follow that any conceivable requirement may be imposed on any state official. I continue to agree, for example, that Congress may not require a state legislature to enact a regulatory scheme and that *New York v. United States*, 505 U.S. 144, 112 S.Ct. 2408, 120 L.Ed.2d 120 (1992), was rightly decided[.]

Justice BREYER, with whom Justice STEVENS joins, dissenting.

I would add to the reasons Justice Stevens sets forth the fact that the United States is not the only nation that seeks to reconcile the practical need for a central authority with the democratic virtues of more local control. At least some other countries, facing the same basic problem, have found that local control is better maintained through application of a principle that is the direct opposite of the principle the majority derives from the silence of our Constitution. The federal systems of Switzerland, Germany, and the European Union, for example, all provide that constituent states, not federal bureaucracies, will themselves implement many of the laws, rules, regulations, or decrees enacted by the central "federal" body. Lenaerts, Constitutionalism and the Many Faces of Federalism, 38 Am. J. Comp. L. 205, 237 (1990); D. Currie, The Constitution of the Federal Republic of Germany 66, 84 (1994); Mackenzie-Stuart, Foreword, Comparative Constitutional Federalism: Europe and America ix (M. Tushnet ed.1990); Kimber, A Comparison of Environmental Federalism in the United States and the European Union, 54 Md. L.Rev. 1658, 1675-1677 (1995). They do so in part because they believe that such a system interferes less, not more, with the independent authority of the "state," member nation, or other subsidiary government, and helps to safeguard individual liberty as well. See Council of European Communities, European Council in Edinburgh, 11-12 Dec. 1992, Conclusions of the Presidency 20-21 (1993); D. Lasok & K. Bridge, Law and Institutions of the European Union 114 (1994); Currie, *supra,* at 68, 81-84, 100-101; Frowein, Integration and the Federal Experience in Germany and Switzerland, in 1 Integration Through Law 573, 586-587 (M. Cappelletti, M. Seccombe, & J. Weiler eds.1986); Lenaerts, *supra,* at 232, 263.

Of course, we are interpreting our own Constitution, not those of other nations, and there may be relevant political and structural differences between their systems and our own. Cf. The Federalist No. 20, pp. 134-138 (C. Rossiter ed. 1961) (J. Madison and A. Hamilton) (rejecting certain aspects of European federalism). But their experience may nonetheless cast an empirical light on the consequences of different solutions to a common legal problem — in this case the problem of reconciling central authority with the need to preserve the liberty-enhancing autonomy of a smaller constituent governmental entity. Cf. *id.,* No. 42, at 268 (J. Madison) (looking to experiences of European countries); *id.,* No. 43, at 275, 276 (J. Madison) (same). And that experience here offers empirical confirmation of the implied answer to a question Justice Stevens asks: Why, or how, would what the majority sees as a constitutional alternative — the creation of a new federal gun-law bureaucracy, or the expansion of an existing federal bureaucracy — better promote either state sovereignty or individual liberty? See *ante,* at 2389, 2396 (Stevens, J., dissenting).

As comparative experience suggests, there is no need to interpret the Constitution as containing an absolute principle — forbidding the assignment of virtually any federal duty to any state official.

Comments on *New York* and *Printz*. Was Rehnquist right, do the *Garcia* dissenters now "command the support of a majority"? Was *Garcia* overruled? Sidestepped? Is the Court in *New York* and *Printz* using procedural or substantive safeguards to protect state power?

Has the *National League* 10th Amendment–based protection of state sovereignty been resurrected? Note, Justice O'Connor in *New York*, "[if] a power is an attribute of state sovereignty reserved by the Tenth Amendment, it is necessarily a power the Constitution has not conferred on Congress. . . .The Tenth Amendment likewise restrains the power of Congress, but this limit is not derived from the text of the Tenth Amendment itself, which, as we have discussed, is essentially a tautology. Instead, the Tenth Amendment confirms that the power of the Federal Government is subject to limits that may, in a given instance, reserve power to the States. *The Tenth Amendment thus directs us to determine, as in this case, whether an incident of state sovereignty is protected by a limitation on an Article I power.*" (emphasis added). Just a sheep of a different color, i.e., once again the Court reads the 10th Amendment as an "unarticulated" limitation on Article I powers.

As the dissenters point out, where is the necessary and proper clause? Does the Court just avoid it? No necessary and proper clause makes it easier for the majority to reach their ends — no ambiguity between reserved powers and implied powers. The Court applies the 10th Amendment, where by their own admission their finding is "not derived from the text," and then pays no attention to the text of the Constitution, the necessary and proper clause. Can they be accused of a biased activism in support of their own views as to federalism, strangely absent, if you recall, in the *Bush v. Gore* opinion.

Is there a difference in application between the findings in *National League* and *New York/Printz*? What does "compel" got to do with this? Is that the primary distinction? If so, how significant is the difference? Would subsidies "compel"? What of conditional spending? What of O'Connor's "voluntary"?

What does *Printz* add to *New York*? Is it the application of "anticommandeering" to state executive officials or the Brady Act's enforcement through state officers? Both the majorities in *New York* and *Printz* continue to support requiring state courts to enforce national laws (*Testa v. Katt*). Why should "commandeering" of state judges be allowed but not state executive officials? Prakash, in "Field Office Federalism," 79 Va. L. Rev 1957 (1993), argues that both state executives and judges must administer the laws of the land, so why the difference?

The majority in *Printz* (5–4 again) holds that "[t]he federal government may not compel the States to enact or administer a federal regulatory program," declaring "our constitutional system [a] dual sovereignty." Are we back to who created the nation, "We the People," or "the States"? If there is any doubt as to a new "dual sovereignty," supported by a majority of five, our review of the 11th Amendment, which follows, puts any doubt to rest.

The Anti Commandeering Doctrine and State Authorized Sports Betting

MURPHY v. NATIONAL COLLEGIATE ATHLETIC ASSOCIATION
584 U. S. ____ (2018)

Justice ALITO delivered the opinion of the Court.

The State of New Jersey wants to legalize sports gambling at casinos and horseracing tracks, but a federal law, the Professional and Amateur Sports Protection Act, generally makes it unlawful for a State to "authorize" sports gambling schemes. 28 U. S. C. §3702(1). We must decide whether this provision is compatible with the system of "dual sovereignty" embodied in the Constitution.

I

A

Americans have never been of one mind about gambling, and attitudes have swung back and forth. By the end of the 19th century, gambling was largely banned throughout the country, but beginning in the 1920s and 1930s, laws prohibiting gambling were gradually loosened.

New Jersey's experience is illustrative. In 1897, New Jersey adopted a constitutional amendment that barred all gambling in the State. But during the Depression, the State permitted pari-mutuel betting on horse races as a way of increasing state revenue, and in 1953, churches and other nonprofit organizations were allowed to host bingo games. In 1970, New Jersey became the third State to run a state lottery, and within five years, 10 other States followed suit.

By the 1960s, Atlantic City, "once the most fashionable resort of the Atlantic Coast," had fallen on hard times, and casino gambling came to be seen as a way to revitalize the city. In 1974, a referendum on statewide legalization failed, but two years later, voters approved a narrower measure allowing casino gambling in Atlantic City alone. At that time, Nevada was the only other State with legal casinos, and thus for a while the Atlantic City casinos had an east coast monopoly. "With 60 million people living within a one-tank car trip away," Atlantic City became "the most popular tourist destination in the United States." But that favorable situation eventually came to an end.

With the enactment of the Indian Gaming Regulatory Act in 1988, 25 U. S. C. §2701 et seq., casinos opened on Indian land throughout the country. Some were located within driving distance of Atlantic City, and nearby States (and many others) legalized casino gambling. But Nevada remained the only state venue for legal sports gambling in casinos, and sports gambling is immensely popular.

Sports gambling, however, has long had strong opposition. Opponents argue that it is particularly addictive and especially attractive to young people with a strong interest in sports, and in the past gamblers corrupted and seriously damaged the reputation of professional and amateur sports. Apprehensive about the potential effects of sports gambling, professional sports leagues and the National Collegiate Athletic Association (NCAA) long opposed legalization.

B

By the 1990s, there were signs that the trend that had brought about the legalization of many other forms of gambling might extend to sports gambling, and this sparked federal efforts to stem the tide. Opponents of sports gambling turned to the legislation now before us, the Professional and Amateur Sports Protection Act (PASPA). 28 U. S. C. §3701 et seq. PASPA's proponents argued that it would protect young people, and one of the bill's sponsors, Senator Bill Bradley of New Jersey, a former college and professional basketball star, stressed that the law was needed to safeguard the integrity of sports. The Department of Justice opposed the bill, but it was passed and signed into law. PASPA's most important provision, part of which is directly at issue in these cases, makes it "unlawful" for a State or any of its subdivisions "to sponsor, operate, advertise, promote, license, or authorize by law or compact . . . a lottery, sweepstakes, or other betting, gambling, or wagering scheme based . . . on" competitive sporting events. §3702(1). In parallel, §3702(2) makes it "unlawful" for "a person to sponsor, operate, advertise, or promote" those same gambling schemes23—but only if this is done "pursuant to the law or compact of a governmental entity." PASPA does not make sports gambling a federal crime (and thus was not anticipated to impose a significant law enforcement burden on the Federal Government).24

Instead, PASPA allows the Attorney General, as well as professional and amateur sports organizations, to bring civil actions to enjoin violations. §3703.

[B]y 2011, with Atlantic City facing stiff competition . . . [New Jersey] voters approved an amendment to the State Constitution making it lawful for the legislature to authorize sports gambling . . . . and in 2012 the legislature enacted a law doing just that.

The 2012 Act quickly came under attack. The major professional sports leagues and the NCAA brought an action in federal court against the New Jersey Governor and other state officials (hereinafter New Jersey), seeking to enjoin the new law on the ground that it violated PASPA. In response, the State argued, among other things, that PASPA unconstitutionally infringed the State's sovereign authority to end its sports gambling ban. See National Collegiate Athletic Assn. v. Christie, 926 F. Supp. 2d 551, 561 (NJ 2013).

In making this argument, the State relied primarily on two cases, New York v. United States, 505 U. S. 144 (1992), and Printz v. United States, 521 U. S. 898 (1997), in which we struck down federal laws based on what has been dubbed the "anti-commandeering" principle. In New York, we held that a federal law unconstitutionally ordered the State to regulate in accordance with federal standards, and in Printz, we found that another federal statute unconstitutionally compelled state officers to enforce federal law.

Relying on these cases, New Jersey argued that PASPA is similarly flawed because it regulates a State's exercise of its lawmaking power by prohibiting it from modifying or repealing its laws prohibiting sports gambling. See National Collegiate Athletic Assn. v. Christie, 926 F. Supp. 2d, at 561–562. The plaintiffs countered that PASPA is critically different from the commandeering cases because it does not command the States to take any affirmative act. Id., at 562. Without an affirmative federal command to do something, the plaintiffs insisted, there can be no claim of commandeering. Ibid.

The District Court found no anti-commandeering violation, id., at 569–573, and a divided panel of the Third Circuit affirmed, National Collegiate Athletic Assn. v. Christie, 730 F. 3d 208 (2013) (Christie I). The panel thought it significant that PASPA does not impose any affirmative command. Id., at 231. In the words of the panel, "PASPA does not require or coerce the states to lift a finger." Ibid. (emphasis deleted). The panel recognized that an affirmative command (for example, "Do not repeal") can often be phrased as a prohibition ("Repeal is prohibited"), but the panel did not interpret PASPA as prohibiting the repeal of laws outlawing sports gambling. Id., at 232. A repeal, it thought, would not amount to "authoriz[ation]" and thus would fall outside the scope of §3702(1). "[T]he lack of an affirmative prohibition of an activity," the panel wrote, "does not mean it is affirmatively authorized by law. The right to do that which is not prohibited derives not from the authority of the state but from the inherent rights of the people." Id., at 232 (emphasis deleted).

New Jersey filed a petition for a writ of certiorari, raising the anti-commandeering issue. Opposing certiorari, the United States told this Court that PASPA does not require New Jersey "to leave in place the state-law prohibitions against sports gambling that it had chosen to adopt prior to PASPA's enactment. To the contrary, New Jersey is free to repeal those prohibitions in whole or in part." Brief for United States in Opposition in Christie v. National Collegiate Athletic Assn., O. T. 2013, No. 13–967 etc., p. 11. See also Brief for Respondents in Opposition in No. 13–967 etc., p. 23 ("Nothing in that unambiguous language compels states to prohibit or maintain any existing prohibition on sports gambling"). We denied review.

Picking up on the suggestion that a partial repeal would be allowed, the New Jersey Legislature enacted the law now before us. 2014 N. J. Laws p. 602 (2014 Act). The 2014

Act declares that it is not to be interpreted as causing the State to authorize, license, sponsor, operate, advertise, or promote sports gambling. Ibid. Instead, it is framed as a repealer. Specifically, it repeals the provisions of state law prohibiting sports gambling insofar as they concerned the "placement and acceptance of wagers" on sporting events by persons 21 years of age or older at a horseracing track or a casino or gambling house in Atlantic City. Ibid. The new law also specified that the repeal was effective only as to wagers on sporting events not involving a New Jersey college team or a collegiate event taking place in the State. Ibid.

Predictably, the same plaintiffs promptly commenced a new action in federal court. They won in the District Court, National Collegiate Athletic Assn. v. Christie, 61 F. Supp. 3d 488 (NJ 2014), and the case was eventually heard by the Third Circuit sitting en banc. The en banc court affirmed, finding that the new law, no less than the old one, violated PASPA by "author[izing]" sports gambling. National Collegiate Athletic Assn. v. Governor of N. J., 832 F. 3d 389 (2016) (case below). The court was unmoved by the New Jersey Legislature's "artful[]" attempt to frame the 2014 Act as a repealer. Id., at 397. Looking at what the law "actually does," the court concluded that it constitutes an authorization because it "selectively remove[s] a prohibition on sports wagering in a manner that permissively channels wagering activity to particular locations or operators." Id., at 397, 401. The court disavowed some of the reasoning in the Christie I opinion, finding its discussion of "the relationship between a 'repeal' and an 'authorization' to have been too facile." 832 F. 3d, at 401. But the court declined to say whether a repeal that was more complete than the 2014 Act would still amount to an authorization. The court observed that a partial repeal that allowed only "de minimis wagers between friends and family would not have nearly the type of authorizing effect" that it found in the 2014 Act, and it added: "We need not . . . articulate a line whereby a partial repeal of a sports wagering ban amounts to an authorization under PASPA, if indeed such a line could be drawn." Id., at 402 (emphasis added).

Having found that the 2014 Act violates PASPA's prohibition of state authorization of sports gambling schemes, the court went on to hold that this prohibition does not contravene the anti-commandeering principle because it "does not command states to take affirmative actions." Id., at 401.

We granted review to decide the important constitutional question presented by these cases, sub nom. Christie v. National Collegiate Athletic Assn., 582 U. S. ___ (2017).

II

Before considering the constitutionality of the PASPA provision prohibiting States from "author[izing]" sports gambling, we first examine its meaning. The parties advance dueling interpretations, and this dispute has an important bearing on the constitutional issue that we must decide. Neither respondents nor the United States, appearing as an amicus in support of respondents, contends that the provision at issue would be constitutional if petitioners' interpretation is correct.

[Petitioners] argue that the anti-authorization provision requires States to maintain their existing laws against sports gambling without alteration. One of the accepted meanings of the term "authorize," they point out, is "permit." Brief for Petitioners in No. 16–476, p. 42 (citing Black's Law Dictionary 133 (6th ed. 1990); Webster's Third New International Dictionary 146 (1992)). They therefore contend that any state law that has the effect of permitting sports gambling, including a law totally or partially repealing a prior prohibition, amounts to an authorization.

Respondents interpret the provision more narrowly. They claim that the primary definition of "authorize" requires affirmative action. Brief for Respondents 39. To authorize, they maintain, means "'[t]o empower; to give a right or authority to act; to endow with authority.'" Ibid. (quoting Black's Law Dictionary, at 133). And this, they say, is precisely what the 2014 Act does: It empowers a defined group of entities, and it endows them with the authority to conduct sports gambling operations.

[The United States as amicus in support of Respondents argued that] PASPA...does not prohibit a State from enacting a complete repeal because "one would not ordinarily say that private conduct is 'authorized by law' simply because the government has not prohibited it." Brief for United States 17. But the United States claims that "[t]he 2014 Act's selective and conditional permission to engage in conduct that is generally prohibited certainly qualifies" as an authorization. Ibid. The United States does not argue that PASPA outlaws all partial repeals, but it does not set out any clear rule for distinguishing between partial repeals that constitute the "authorization" of sports gambling and those that are permissible. The most that it is willing to say is that a State could "eliminat[e] prohibitions on sports gambling involving wagers by adults or wagers below a certain dollar threshold."

B

In our view, petitioners' interpretation is correct: When a State completely or partially repeals old laws banning sports gambling, it "authorize[s]" that activity. This is clear when the state-law landscape at the time of PASPA's enactment is taken into account. At that time, all forms of sports gambling were illegal in the great majority of States, and in that context, the competing definitions offered by the parties lead to the same conclusion. The repeal of a state law banning sports gambling not only "permits" sports gambling (petitioners' favored definition); it also gives those now free to conduct a sports betting operation the "right or authority to act"; it "empowers" them (respondents' and the United Status's definition).

The concept of state "authorization" makes sense only against a backdrop of prohibition or regulation. A State is not regarded as authorizing everything that it does not prohibit or regulate. No one would use the term in that way. For example, no one would say that a State "authorizes" its residents to brush their teeth or eat apples or sing in the shower. We commonly speak of state authorization only if the activity in question would otherwise be restricted.

[The] interpretation adopted by the Third Circuit and advocated by respondents and the United States not only ignores the situation that Congress faced when it enacted PASPA but also leads to results that Congress is most unlikely to have wanted. This is illustrated by the implausible conclusions that all of those favoring alternative interpretations have been forced to reach about the extent to which the provision permits the repeal of laws banning sports gambling. The Third Circuit could not say which, if any, partial repeals are allowed. 832 F. 3d, at 402. Respondents and the United States tell us that the PASPA ban on state authorization allows complete repeals, but beyond that they identify no clear line. It is improbable that Congress meant to enact such a nebulous regime.

[III]

A

The anti-commandeering doctrine may sound arcane, but it is simply the expression of a fundamental structural decision incorporated into the Constitution, i.e., the decision to withhold from Congress the power to issue orders directly to the States. When the original States declared their independence, they claimed the powers inherent in sovereignty—in the words of the Declaration of Independence, the authority "to do all . . . Acts and Things which Independent States may of right do." ¶32. The Constitution limited but did not abolish the sovereign powers of the States, which retained "a residuary and inviolable sovereignty." The Federalist No. 39, p. 245 (C. Rossiter ed. 1961). Thus, both the Federal Government and the States wield sovereign powers, and that is why our system of government is said to be one of "dual sovereignty." Gregory v. Ashcroft, 501 U. S. 452, 457 (1991). The Constitution limits state sovereignty in several ways. It directly prohibits the States from exercising some attributes of sovereignty. See, e.g., Art. I, §10. Some grants of power to the Federal Government have been held to impose implicit restrictions on the States. See, e.g., Department of Revenue of Ky. v. Davis, 553 U. S. 328. [And] the Constitution indirectly restricts the States by granting certain legislative powers to Congress, see Art. I, §8, while providing in the Supremacy Clause that federal law is the "supreme Law of the Land . . . any Thing in the Constitution or Laws of any State to the Contrary notwithstanding," Art. VI, cl. 2. This means that when federal and state law conflict, federal law prevails and state law is preempted.

The legislative powers granted to Congress are sizable, but they are not unlimited. The Constitution confers on Congress not plenary legislative power but only certain enumerated powers. Therefore, all other legislative power is reserved for the States, as the Tenth Amendment confirms. And conspicuously absent from the list of powers given to Congress is the power to issue direct orders to the governments of the States. The anti-commandeering doctrine simply represents the recognition of this limit on congressional authority.

Although the anti-commandeering principle is simple and basic, it did not emerge in our cases until relatively recently, when Congress attempted in a few isolated instances to extend its authority in unprecedented ways. The pioneering case was New York v. United States, 505 U. S. 144 (1992), which concerned a federal law that required a State, under certain circumstances, either to "take title" to low-level radioactive waste or to "regulat[e] according to the instructions of Congress." Id., at 175. In enacting this provision, Congress issued orders to either the legislative or executive branch of state government (depending on the branch authorized by state law to take the actions demanded). Either way, the Court held, the provision was unconstitutional because "the Constitution does not empower Congress to subject state governments to this type of instruction." Id., at 176. Justice O'Connor's opinion for the Court traced this rule to the basic structure of government established under the Constitution. The Constitution, she noted, "confers upon Congress the power to regulate individuals, not States." Id., at 166. In this respect, the Constitution represented a sharp break from the Articles of Confederation. "Under the Articles of Confederation, Congress lacked the authority in most respects to govern the people directly." Id., at 163. Instead, Congress was limited to acting "'only upon the States.'" Id., at 162 (quoting Lane County v. Oregon, 7 Wall. 71, 76 (1869)). Alexander Hamilton, among others, saw this as "'[t]he great and radical vice in . . . the existing Confederation.'" 505 U. S., at 163 (quoting The Federalist No. 15, at 108). The Constitutional Convention considered plans that would have preserved this basic structure, but it rejected them in favor of a plan under which "Congress would exercise its legislative authority directly over individuals rather than over States." 505 U. S., at 165.

As to what this structure means with regard to Congress's authority to control state legislatures, New York was clear and emphatic. The opinion recalled that "no Member of the Court ha[d] ever suggested" that even "a particularly strong federal interest" "would enable Congress to command a state government to enact state regulation." Id., at 178 (emphasis in original). "We have always understood that even where Congress has the authority under the Constitution to pass laws requiring or prohibiting certain acts, it lacks the power directly to compel the States to require or prohibit those acts." Id., at 166. "Congress may not simply 'commandee[r] the legislative processes of the States by directly compelling them to enact and enforce a federal regulatory program.'" Id., at 161 (quoting Hodel v. Virginia Surface Mining & Reclamation Assn., Inc., 452 U. S. 264, 288 (1981)). "Where a federal interest is sufficiently strong to cause Congress to legislate, it must do so directly; it may not conscript state governments as its agents." 505 U. S., at 178.

Five years after New York, the Court applied the same principles to a federal statute requiring state and local law enforcement officers to perform background checks and related tasks in connection with applications for handgun licenses. Printz, 521 U. S. 898. Holding this provision unconstitutional, the Court put the point succinctly: "The Federal Government" may not "command the States' officers, or those of their political subdivisions, to administer or enforce a federal regulatory program." Id., at 935. This rule applies, Printz held, not only to state officers with policymaking responsibility but also to those assigned more mundane tasks. Id., at 929–930.

[IV]

A

The PASPA provision at issue here—prohibiting state authorization of sports gambling—violates the anti-commandeering rule. That provision unequivocally dictates what a state legislature may and may not do. And this is true under either our interpretation or that advocated by respondents and the United States. In either event, state legislatures are put under the direct control of Congress. It is as if federal officers were installed in state legislative chambers and were armed with the authority to stop legislators from voting on any offending proposals. A more direct affront to state sovereignty is not easy to imagine. Neither respondents nor the United States contends that Congress can compel a State to enact legislation, but they say that prohibiting a State from enacting new laws is another matter. Noting that the laws challenged in New York and Printz "told states what they must do instead of what they must not do," respondents contend that commandeering occurs "only when Congress goes beyond precluding state action and affirmatively commands it."

This distinction is empty. It was a matter of happenstance that the laws challenged in New York and Printz commanded "affirmative" action as opposed to imposing a prohibition. The basic principle—that Congress cannot issue direct orders to state legislatures—applies in either event. Here is an illustration. PASPA includes an exemption for States that permitted sports betting at the time of enactment, §3704, but suppose Congress did not adopt such an exemption. Suppose Congress ordered States with legalized sports betting to take the affirmative step of criminalizing that activity and ordered the remaining States to retain their laws prohibiting sports betting. There is no good reason why the former would intrude more deeply on state sovereignty than the latter.

[The] legalization of sports gambling is a controversial subject. Supporters argue that legalization will produce revenue for the States and critically weaken illegal sports betting operations, which are often run by organized crime. Opponents contend that legalizing sports gambling will hook the young on gambling, encourage people of modest means to squander their savings and earnings, and corrupt professional and college sports. The legalization of sports gambling requires an important policy choice, but the choice is not ours to make.

Congress can regulate sports gambling directly, but if it elects not to do so, each State is free to act on its own. Our job is to interpret the law Congress has enacted and decide whether it is consistent with the Constitution. PASPA is not. PASPA "regulate[s] state governments' regulation" of their citizens, New York, 505 U. S., at 166. The Constitution gives Congress no such power. The judgment of the Third Circuit is reversed.

It is so ordered.

[Section V addressing the issue of the federal preemption doctrine is excerpted in the Preemption section. Section VI addressing severability is not included in this excerpt. A concurrence by Justice Thomas, an opinion concurring in part and dissenting in part by Justice Breyer and an opinion dissenting by Justice Sotomayor are not included.]

H. THE REHNQUIST COURT FETISH—"DUAL SOVEREIGNTY," THE 11TH AMENDMENT: LIMITATION OF CONGRESSIONAL POWER

The 11th Amendment and Sovereign Immunity. The 11th Amendment has traditionally been reserved for course offerings in federal jurisdiction. The Amendment states: "The judicial power of the United States shall not be construed to extend to any [suit] commenced or prosecuted against one of the United States by Citizens of another State, or by Citizens or Subjects of any Foreign States." Since the Amendment limits and speaks only to the jurisdiction of the federal courts, a reasonable question might be: "What's it doing here?" Well, the answer relates to the "fetish" of the Rehnquist Court, which we have just reviewed in relation to the Commerce Clause and the 10th Amendment — the anti-federalist revival and the modern reincarnate of the notion of dual sovereignty.

Having failed in the *National League* concept of a 10th Amendment sovereign immunity limiting federal power, the Court has not only revived this theme in the above cited *New York* and *Printz*, but has also elucidated a new approach to protect state sovereignty by substituting the 11th Amendment for such protection rather than the 10th. This significant decisional law applies the jurisdiction barrier of the 11th Amendment to achieve substantive effect. In the lead case, *Seminole Tribe of Florida v. Florida*, 517 U.S. 44 (1996), the Court held that the 11th Amendment embodies "a principle of [state] sovereign immunity" that limits federal court jurisdiction of state governments in Congress's exercise of its Article I powers. Though the intricacies of the 11th Amendment are best left to federal jurisdiction, the substantive effect of this line of cases on the power of Congress as against the states is so significant that we cannot conclude our study of the commerce power without a brief review of this decisional law, if only to remind us that when "procedure" denies jurisdiction, it most certainly has a "substantive" effect.

The 11th Amendment was adopted because the Court in *Chisholm v. Georgia*, 2 U.S. (2 Dall.) 419 (1793), took original jurisdiction of a suit against Georgia by a South Carolina creditor seeking payment for goods purchased by Georgia during the Revolution. The response to the Court taking jurisdiction of an out-of-state litigant suing another state government was so dramatic that the adoption of the 11th Amendment soon followed.

The Supreme Court, in *Hans v. Louisiana*, 134 U.S. 1 (1890), an oft-criticized ruling, extended the 11th Amendment beyond its text and held that its jurisdictional limitation applied to in-state citizens as well. Thus the dubious history of the amendment so commences. *Hans* put in question the ability to enforce any of the post–Civil War amendments and civil rights legislation in federal court when a state citizen claimed such a right based depravation against his or her state government. The Court responded to this problem in *Ex parte Young*, 209 U.S. 123 (1908), allowing jurisdiction for such depravations by holding that a federal court could issue an injunction against state officials who sought to enforce an unconstitutional state law by applying the judicial fiction that the defendant was not really the state but rather the official, acting beyond his constitutional authority.

More was in store in the early "Burger Court" years when the Court, in *Edelman v. Jordan*, 415 U.S. 651 (1974), limited *Ex parte Young* and found that the 11th Amendment only permitted lawsuits for prospective injunctive relief against state officers, denying lawsuits for retrospective relief via a judgment for damages. The plot thickened in *Fitzpatrick v. Bitzer*, 427 U.S. 445 (1976), when the Court held that Congress could abrogate the state's 11th Amendment immunity and allow states to be sued directly (for retrospective damages as well), pursuant to its enforcement power under the 14th Amendment. The Court's rationale was the fact that the 14th Amendment was adopted during the Reconstruction era partially based upon the framers suspectness as to whether the southern state governments would adequately protect the new federal rights, and that it was adopted well after the 11th. The Court also imposed a clear statement rule on the applicability of *Fitzpatrick*, stipulating that "Congress may abrogate the States' constitutionally secured immunity from suit in federal court only by making its intention unmistakably clear in the language of the statute." *Atascadero State Hospital v. Scanlon*, 473 U.S. 234, 242 (1985).

Post-*Fitzpatrick* the question remained as to whether Congress could also abrogate state sovereign immunity when it exercised its Art. I, § 8, powers, such as the commerce power, as opposed to its civil rights enforcement powers. In *Pennsylvania v. Union Gas Co.*, 491 U.S. 1 (1989), a divided Court held that "Congress has the authority to create such a course of action when legislating pursuant to the Commerce Clause." Then, "along came Jones."

Still Skinning the Cat, *Seminole Tribe*. In *Seminole Tribe of Florida v. Florida*, 517 U.S. 44 (1996), the majority overruled *Union Gas* and rejected the claim that Congress, acting under its commerce power, could abrogate a state's 11th Amendment immunity. Chief Justice Rehnquist's majority opinion held that "notwithstanding Congress' clear attempt to abrogate the States' sovereign immunity, the Indian Commerce Clause does not grant Congress that power, and therefore [the law] cannot grant jurisdiction over a state that does not consent to be sued." Though the Court reaffirmed *Fitzpatrick v. Bitzer*, it explicitly held that *Pennsylvania v. Union Gas Co.*, the only other case sustaining congressional abrogation of the states' immunity, was overruled. Rehnquist claimed that *Union Gas* had "deviated sharply from our established federalism jurisprudence and essentially eviscerated our decision in *Hans*." The Court supported its conclusion in regard to the inapplicability of the Commerce Clause, because "the Fourteenth Amendment, adopted well after the adoption of the Eleventh Amendment and the ratification of the Constitution, operated to alter the preexisting balance between state and federal power achieved by Article III and the Eleventh Amendment. [In] overruling *Union Gas* today, we can reconfirm that . . . the Eleventh Amendment restricts the judicial power under Article III, and Article I cannot be used to circumvent the constitutional limitations placed upon federal jurisdiction."

The Court has continued to apply and expand the doctrine announced in *Seminole Tribe*. What about federal law suits brought in state court? In *Alden v. Maine*, 527 U.S. 706 (1999), the Court extended the state sovereign immunity bar to lawsuits against states in state court. In another 5–4 decision, the Court held that Congress, in exercising its Article I powers, may not abrogate state sovereign immunity by authorizing private actions for money damages against nonconsenting states in their own courts. Justice Kennedy acknowledged that this limitation on congressional power could not be derived from the text of the 11th Amendment, which merely limits the exercise of federal judicial power. He rooted it instead in "the Constitution's structure, and its history, [which] make clear [that] the States' immunity from suit is a fundamental aspect of the sovereignty which the

States enjoyed before the ratification of the Constitution, and which they retain today." To Kennedy, "sovereign immunity derives not from the Eleventh Amendment but from the structure of the original Constitution itself."

More recently, the Court continued its more than two-hundred-year-old attempt to provide a coherent explanation of the state sovereignty issue in the 2018 term. It is not clear that the effort was successful. In *Franchise Tax Board of California v. Hyatt*, 587 U.S. ___(2019), Justice Thomas, writing for a Court split 5-4, decided that a private suit by an individual against a state in the court of another state violated the principle of state sovereign immunity (in this case a common lawsuit brought in Nevada against the state of California involving torts and not based on federal statutory law). Like *Alden v. Maine*, the decision was not based on the specific language of the Eleventh Amendment, but on the structural considerations of the federal system and Justice Thomas's view of the historical record of the intentions of the framers. Thomas reasoned that the understanding at the time of the original Constitution was that states were equal sovereigns and not subject to the authority of sister states. Though this reasoning formed, somewhat, the basis for the *Alden v. Maine* decision, the key difference is that *Hyatt* did not involve a federal law and Congressional abrogation of state sovereignty. In essence where *Alden* established limits on Congressional authority to abrogate state sovereign immunity in a matter involving a federal question, *Hyatt* addressed the more general matter of state sovereign immunity outside of Congressional abrogation authority. The Court reasoned that nothing in the Constitution, the Eleventh Amendment notwithstanding, undermined the basic principle and understanding of the framers at the beginning of the constitutional era that the states had an independent sovereignty, and hence sovereign immunity, limited only by clear constitutional design. Absent such a design in the Constitution, the Court reasoned, the original understanding of the states as sovereign entities precluded being subjected to the judicial authority of another state.

Congress, Abrogation, and the 14th Amendment. With the Court continuing to emphasize and reaffirm viability of *Fitzpatrick* — "sovereign immunity does not bar suits brought under federal statutes authorized by § 5 of the Fourteenth Amendment" — attention turned to how the Court would scrutinize such congressional legislation. Do you think the Court would apply a deferential rational purpose review here? In *Florida Prepaid Postsecondary Education Expense Board v. College Savings Bank*, 527 U.S. 627 (1999), and *College Savings Bank v. Florida Prepaid Postsecondary Education Expense Board*, 527 U.S. 666 (1999), the Court invalidated two federal statutes that expressly abrogated states' sovereign immunity with respect to patent and trademark infringement actions brought against state entities (such as public universities) in federal court. The Court's activism seemed to continue as it once again imposed its judgment as opposed to that of Congress's in finding that Congress had not adequately justified the exercise of its powers under § 5 of the 14th Amendment.

This pattern continued in *Kimel v. Florida Board of Regents*, 528 U.S. 62 (2000), where the Court again invalidated a congressional attempt to abrogate state sovereign immunity — this time under the Age Discrimination in Employment Act of 1967 (ADEA). Of note, the Court so concluded despite a congressional attempt to provide thorough support for the legislation under its § 5 power. The 5–4 majority (Rehnquist, Scalia, Kennedy, Thomas, and O'Connor) reiterated that Congress lacked power under Article I to subject state employers to suit at the hands of private individuals, and went on to find such suits against the states unauthorized under Congress's civil rights enforcement powers under § 5 of the 14th Amendment. The dissenters (Stevens, Souter, Ginsburg, and Breyer) reiterated their objection that the 11th Amendment "only places a textual limitation on [diversity suits in] federal courts," not a limitation on federal courts' power to entertain suits against a state by that state's own citizens, and argued that *Seminole Tribe's* understanding of sovereign immunity "is so profoundly mistaken and so fundamentally inconsistent with the Framers' conception of the constitutional order that it has forsaken any claim to the usual deference or respect owed to decisions of this Court."

In 2001 in *Alabama v. Garrett,* 531 U.S. 356, with the same 5–4 "line-up," the majority found Congress's support for its conclusion that the states had discriminated against disabled citizens inadequate and held that the Americans with Disabilities Act unconstitutionally abrogated the states' immunity from suit. By now, it became clear that the 14th Amendment would "not be a road" so easily traveled.

In the 2002 term the Court extended this 11th Amendment sovereign immunity doctrine to adjudicative proceedings by federal administrative agencies (*Federal Maritime Commission*). This doctrine had now "covered it all" — federal courts, state courts, and federal administrative agencies.

Comment on *Seminole*. These cases are certainly "billboard" opinions for this Court and its anti-federalist revival. But how significant are they in practice? *Garcia,* for example, has not been overruled, and these statutes are still applicable to state governments; only their remedial enforcement has been affected. Alternative avenues of enforcement are also available: *Ex parte Young* is still in force and can be used against the states through private injunctions against state officials; and the application of federal conditional spending and conditions that require the states to waive their 11th Amendment immunity remain viable. Yet, Meltzer argues in "Overcoming Immunity: The Case of Federal Regulations of Intellectual Property," 53 Stan. L. Rev. 1331 (2001), "[t]aking a significant bite out of the enforcement apparatus for a vast range of federal statutes is every bit as significant as holding that one or two particular schemes may not be imposed against the states at all."

Changes Afoot? Of interest, the Court, in the 2003 term, found congressional findings adequate to support abrogation of the states' 11th Amendment immunity in the furtherance of its § 5 power to enforce the 14th Amendment. In *Nevada Department of Human Resources v. Hibbs,* 538 U.S. 721 (2003), the Court found the Family and Medical Leave Act of 1993 (FMLA) within the scope of Congress's civil rights enforcement powers. Chief Justice Rehnquist, writing for the majority, stated, "[The] Constitution does not provide for federal jurisdiction over suits against nonconsenting States. Congress may, however, abrogate such immunity in federal court if it makes its intention to abrogate unmistakably clear in the language of the statute and acts pursuant to a valid exercise of its power under § 5 of the Fourteenth Amendment." The Court, viewing the congressional findings in support of the legislation, concluded that, "the States' record of unconstitutional participation in, and fostering of, gender-based discrimination in the administration of leave benefits is weighty enough to justify the enactment of prophylactic § 5 legislation." The Court relied heavily on the increased scrutiny the Court itself applied in areas concerning gender-based discrimination, in support of congressional findings. Thus, a somewhat "we're ok, then you're ok" analysis.

Why this result? Was the Court "backing off," or was the record that Congress had made on a past history of state discrimination enough to muster the result? Or, was it the judicial lineup? Interestingly enough the majority opinion, written by Chief Justice Rehnquist and joined by Justice O'Connor, also included three of the *Seminole* cases dissenters, Justices Souter, Ginsburg, and Breyer. With Justice Stevens concurring, we actually had a 6–3 opinion. Congressional findings may have been enough to convince these Justices, but it was still not enough to gain the support of the remaining "three" of the *Seminole* 5-4 majority, for Justices Scalia, Kennedy, and Thomas dissented. As is often the case in regard to disputes of this nature, a new majority may be forming around § 5 as another means of avoiding the *Seminole* result.

The "*Hibbs*" reading of the Court's own interpretation of the Equal Protection clause "enhancing" the ability of Congress to abrogate the 11th Amendment immunity seemed to be set a bit more in "cement" during the 2004 term in *Tennessee v. Lane*, 124 S. Ct. 1978. The Court, despite the conclusion in *Garrett* and much like *Hibbs*, held that a paraplegic who had to crawl up two flights of stairs to appear in criminal court could maintain a cause in action against the state under the ADA, once again applying a different analysis where fundamental federal rights were at stake, such as due process and access to courts, because of the strict scrutiny applied by the Court itself in these circumstances.

All Article I Powers? In *Central Virginia Community College v. Katz*, 546 U.S. 356 (2006), the Court held, by a 5–4 vote, that Congress could abrogate state sovereign immunity under the Bankruptcy Clause, Article I, § 8, cl. 4, which provides that Congress shall have the power to establish "uniform Laws on the subject of Bankruptcies throughout the United States." Justice Stevens, writing for the majority, concluded that despite the assumption in *Seminole* that the "case would apply to the Bankruptcy Clause," the framers intended the clause "as a grant of legislative authority to Congress . . . to authorize limited subordination of state sovereign immunity in the bankruptcy arena." The necessary fifth vote was provided by Justice O'Connor, in her last term on the Court, joining the *Seminole, Alden, Kimel, Garrett,* and *FMC* dissenters. Justice Thomas dissented, joined by the newly appointed Chief Justice Roberts and Justices Scalia and Kennedy. Asserting that it was "settled doctrine," he found it, "[difficult] to discern an intention to abrogate state sovereign immunity through [the] Bankruptcy Clause when no such intention has been found in any of the other clauses in Article I." Given the adamancy of the dissenters, the views of Justice Alito, Justice O'Connor's successor, might prove pivotal in relation to a final resolution of this issue.

III. OTHER NATIONAL POWERS

A. THE TAXING AND SPENDING POWERS

Though most would agree that the primary bases for assertion of congressional authority in the modern era has been the commerce power, among other Article I powers, the taxing and spending powers also stand as paramount with a broad basis for federal prerogative. The ability of the federal government to tax has not only been a source of revenue for spending purposes, but has also provided the government with the power to use a tax for regulatory purposes.

The Constitution, in Article 9, § 9(4), originally stipulated that "No Capitation, or other direct tax shall be laid, unless in Proportion to the Census or Enumeration here-in before directed to be taken," thus denying the federal government the authority to institute an income tax. In 1913, through the XVI Amendment to the Constitution, the power, "to lay and collect taxes on incomes" was granted to the Congress. It is certainly not a coincidence that this additional power closely parallels expanded federal power by providing the means of raising revenues for both spending and regulatory purpose.

Of interest is the fact that the "pre-court-packing Court," contrary to its limited definitions of commerce, provided a broad basis for both the federal taxing and spending powers, although it struck down legislation based upon those powers being limited by the Tenth Amendment.

Nonetheless, in the modern era, both powers have been elements of evolving federal power, and in regard to the most recent limitations on the commerce power (see *Lopez* and *Morrison*, supra) have become viable alternatives for federal authority.

1. THE TAXING POWER

After the failure to curb child labor in *Hammer*, Congress promulgated the Child Labor Tax Law, entitled an act "to Provide Revenue and for other Purposes," as a means of accomplishing the same. Congress intended to use its power to tax for regulatory purpose and circumvent the Court's invalidation of the Commerce Clause as a means for limiting child labor. The statute required that anyone who employed child labor, defined as it had been in the statute invalidated in *Hammer*, pay an excise tax equivalent to 10 percent of the entire net profits of the mine or factory. The opinion that follows in the Child Labor Tax Case is significant not only in the Court's continued denial of federal authority, but also in the fact that it still provided a broad predicate for federal regulatory power under the taxing power.

BAILEY v. DREXEL FURNITURE CO.
(Child Labor Tax Case)
259 U.S. 20 (1922)

Mr. Chief Justice TAFT delivered the opinion of the Court.

This case presents the question of the constitutional validity of the Child Labor Tax Law. The plaintiff below, the Drexel Furniture Company, is engaged in the manufacture of furniture in the Western district of North Carolina. On September 20, 1921, it received a notice from Bailey, United States collector of internal revenue for the district, that it had been assessed $6,312.79 for having during the taxable year 1919 employed and permitted to work in its factory a boy under 14 years of age, thus incurring the tax of 10 percent on its net profits for that year. The company paid the tax under protest, and, after rejection of its claim for a refund, brought this suit. On demurrer to an amended complaint, judgment was entered for the company against the collector for the full amount, with interest. The writ of error is prosecuted by the collector direct from the District Court under section 238 of the Judicial Code (Comp. St. § 1215).

[The] law is attacked on the ground that it is a regulation of the employment of child labor in the states — an exclusively state function under the federal Constitution and within the reservations of the Tenth Amendment. It is defended on the ground that it is a mere excise tax levied by the Congress of the United States under its broad power of taxation conferred by section 8, article 1, of the federal Constitution. We must construe the law and interpret the intent and meaning of Congress from the language of the act. The words are to be given their ordinary meaning unless the context shows that they are differently used. Does this law impose a tax with only that incidental restraint and regulation which a tax must inevitably involve? Or does it regulate by the use of the so-called tax as a penalty? If a tax, it is clearly an excise. If it were an excise on a commodity or other thing of value, we might not be permitted under previous decisions of this court to infer solely from its heavy burden that the act intends a prohibition instead of a tax. But this act is more. It provides a heavy exaction for a departure from a detailed and specified course of conduct in business. That course of business is that employers shall employ in mines and quarries, children of an age greater than 16 years; in mills and factories, children of an age greater than 14 years, and shall prevent children of less than 16 years in mills and factories from working more than 8 hours a day or 6 days in the week. If an employer departs from this prescribed course of business, he is to pay to the government one-tenth of his entire net income in the business for a full year. The amount is not to be proportioned in any degree to the extent or frequency of the departures, but is to be paid by the employer in full measure whether he employs 500 children for a year, or employs only one for a day. Moreover, if he does not know the child is within the named age limit, he is not to pay; that is to say, it is only where he knowingly departs from the prescribed course that payment is to be exacted. Scienters are associated with penalties, not with taxes. The employer's factory is to be subject to inspection at any time not only by the taxing officers of the Treasury, the Department normally charged with the collection of taxes, but also by the Secretary of Labor and his subordinates, whose normal function is the advancement and protection of the welfare of the workers. In the light of these features of the act, a court must be blind not to see that the so-called tax is imposed to stop the employment of children within the age limits prescribed. Its prohibitory and regulatory effect and purpose are palpable. All others can see and understand this. How can we properly shut our minds to it?

[Out] of a proper respect for the acts of a co-ordinate branch of the government, this court has gone far to sustain taxing acts as such, even though there has been ground for suspecting, from the weight of the tax, it was intended to destroy its subject. But in the act before us the presumption of validity cannot prevail, because the proof of the contrary is found on the very face of its provisions. Grant the validity of this law, and all that Congress would need to do, hereafter, in seeking to take over to its control any one of the great number of subjects of public interest, jurisdiction of which the states have never parted with, and which are reserved to them by the Tenth Amendment, would be to enact a detailed measure of complete regulation of the subject and enforce it by a so called tax upon departures from it. To give such magic to the word "tax" would be to break down all constitutional limitation of the powers of Congress and completely wipe out the sovereignty of the states.

The difference between a tax and a penalty is sometimes difficult to define, and yet the consequences of the distinction in the required method of their collection often are important. Where the sovereign enacting the law has power to impose both tax and penalty, the difference between revenue production and mere regulation may be immaterial, but not so when one sovereign can impose a tax only, and the power of regulation rests in another. Taxes are occasionally imposed in the discretion of the Legislature on proper subjects with the primary motive of obtaining revenue from them and with the incidental motive of discouraging them by making their continuance onerous. They do not lose their character as taxes because of the incidental motive. But there comes a time in the extension of the penalizing features of the so-called tax when it loses its character as such and becomes a mere penalty, with the characteristics of regulation and punishment. Such is the case in the law before us. [The] case before us cannot be distinguished from that of Hammer v. Dagenhart. This case requires as did the Dagenhart Case the application of the principle announced by Chief Justice Marshall in McCulloch v. Maryland, 4 Wheat. 316, 423 (4 L. Ed. 579), in a much-quoted passage: "Should Congress, in the execution of its powers, adopt measures which are prohibited by the Constitution; or should Congress, under the pretext of executing its powers, pass laws for the accomplishment of objects not intrusted to the government; it would become the painful duty of this tribunal, should a case requiring such a decision come before it, to say that such an act was not the law of the land."

But it is pressed upon us that this court has gone so far in sustaining taxing measures the effect and tendency of which was to accomplish purposes not directly within congressional power that we are bound by authority to maintain this law.

[The] first of these is Veazie Bank v. Fenno, 8 Wall. 533, 19 L. Ed. 482. In that case, the validity of a law which increased a tax on the circulating notes of persons and state banks from one per centum to 10 per centum was in question. The main question was whether this was a direct tax to be apportioned among the several states 'according to their respective numbers.' This was answered in the negative. The second objection was stated by the court:

[It] will be observed that the sole objection to the tax here was its excessive character. Nothing else appeared on the face of the act. It was an increase of a tax admittedly legal to a higher rate and that was all. There were no elaborate specifications on the face of the act, as here, indicating the purpose to regulate matters of state concern and jurisdiction through an exaction so applied as to give it the qualities of a penalty for violation of law rather than a tax.

[But] more than this, what was charged to be the object of the excessive tax was within the congressional authority, as appears from the second answer which the court gave to the objection. After having pointed out the legitimate means taken by Congress to secure a national medium or currency, the court said (8 Wall. 549, 19 L. Ed. 482): "Having thus, in the exercise of undisputed constitutional powers, undertaken to provide a currency for the whole country, it cannot be questioned that Congress may, constitutionally, secure the benefit of it to the people by appropriate legislation. To this end, Congress has denied the quality of legal tender to foreign coins, and has provided by law against the imposition of counterfeit and base coin on the community. To the same end, Congress may restrain, by suitable enactments, the circulation as money of any notes not issued under its own authority. Without this power, indeed, its attempts to secure a sound and uniform currency for the country must be futile."

The next case is that of McCray v. United States, 195 U. S. 27, 24 Sup. Ct. 769, 49 L. Ed. 78, 1 Ann. Cas. 561. That, like the Veazie Bank Case, was the increase of an excise tax upon a subject properly taxable in which the taxpayers claimed that the tax had become invalid because the increase was excessive. It was a tax on oleomargarine, a substitute for butter. The tax on the white oleomargarine was one-quarter of a cent a pound, and on the yellow oleomargarine was first 2 cents and was then by the act in question increased to 10 cents per pound. This court held that the discretion of Congress in the exercise of its constitutional powers to levy excise taxes could not be controlled or limited by the courts because the latter might deem the incidence of the tax oppressive or even destructive. It was the same principle as that applied in the Veazie Bank Case. This was that Congress, in selecting its subjects for taxation, might impose the burden where and as it would, and that a motive disclosed in its selection to discourage sale or manufacture of an article by a higher tax than on some other did not invalidate the tax. In neither of these cases did the law objected to show on its face as does the law before us the detailed specifications of a regulation of a state concern and business with a heavy exaction to promote the effecicacy of such regulation.

[The] fourth case is United States v. Doremus, 249 U. S. 86, 39 Sup. Ct. 214, 63 L. Ed. 493. That involved the validity of the Narcotic Drug Act (38 Stat. 785 [Comp. St. § 6287g et seq.]), which imposed a special tax on the manufacture, importation and sale or gift of opium or cocoa leaves or their compounds or derivatives. It required every person subject to the special tax, to register with the collector of internal revenue his name and place of business and forbade him to sell except upon the written order of the person to whom the sale was made on a form prescribed by the Commissioner of Internal Revenue. The vendor was required to keep the order for two years, and the purchaser to keep a duplicate for the same time and all were to be subject to official inspection. Similar requirements were made as to sales upon prescriptions of a physician and as to the dispensing of such drugs directly to a patient by a physician. The validity of a special tax in the nature of an excise tax on the manufacture, importation, and sale of such drugs was, of course, unquestioned. The provisions for subjecting the sale and distribution of the drugs to official supervision and inspection were held to have a reasonable relation to the enforcement of the tax and were therefore held valid.

The court said that the act could not be declared invalid just because another motive than taxation, not shown on the face of the act, might have contributed to its passage. This case does not militate against the conclusion we have reached in respect to the law now before us. The court, there, made manifest its view that the provisions of the so-called taxing act must be naturally and reasonably adapted to the collection of the tax and not solely to the achievement of some other purpose plainly within state power. Affirmed.

Comment on the Child Labor Tax Case. What limitation does the Court place on the taxing power? How significant is the limitation? How would you advise Congress on how to enact legislation under the taxing power post-*Bailey*? Which is more significant in support of the Court's decision: its definition of the federal taxing power or its view of the Tenth Amendment?

The opinion that follows reflects a "modern" view of the taxing power. Has *Bailey* been overruled? What's changed, the Court's view of the taxing power or the Tenth Amendment?

UNITED STATES v. KAHRIGER
345 U.S. 22 (1953)

Defendant was indicted for failure to register in accordance with provisions of the Gamblers' Occupational Tax Act and for failure to pay the tax. The United States District

Court for the Eastern District of Pennsylvania, 105 F.Supp. 322, granted defendant's motion to dismiss the information on the ground of unconstitutionality of the Act, and the United States appealed. The Supreme Court, Mr. Justice Reed, held, inter alia, that the Act was not unconstitutional as a usurpation of the police powers of the states under the guise of a taxing Act.

Mr. Justice REED delivered the opinion of the Court.

The issue raised by this appeal is the constitutionality of the occupational tax provisions of the Revenue Act of 1951, which levy a tax on persons engaged in the business of accepting wagers, and require such persons to register with the Collector of Internal Revenue. The unconstitutionality of the tax is asserted on two grounds. First, it is said that Congress, under the pretense of exercising its power to tax has attempted to penalize illegal intrastate gambling through the regulatory features of the Act, 26 U.S.C. (Supp. V) § 3291, 26 U.S.C.A. § 3291, and has thus infringed the police power which is reserved to the states. Secondly, it is urged that the registration provisions of the tax violate the privilege against self-incrimination and are arbitrary and vague, contrary to the guarantees of the Fifth Amendment.

Appellee would have us say that because there is legislative history indicating a congressional motive to suppress wagering, this tax is not a proper exercise of such taxing power. In the License Cases, supra, it was admitted that the federal license "discouraged" the activities. The intent to curtail and hinder, as well as tax, was also manifest in the following cases, and in each of them the tax was upheld: Veazie Bank v. Fenno, 8 Wall. 533, 19 L.Ed. 482 (tax on paper money issued by state banks); McCray v. United States, 195 U.S. 27, 59, 24 S.Ct. 769, 777, 49 L.Ed. 78 (tax on colored oleomargarine; United States v. Doremus, 249 U.S. 86, 39 S.Ct. 214, 63 L.Ed. 493 and Nigro v. United States, 276 U.S. 332, 48 S.Ct. 388, 72 L.Ed. 600 (tax on narcotics); Sonzinsky v. United States, 300 U.S. 506, 57 S.Ct. 554, 81 L.Ed. 772 (tax on firearms); United States v. Sanchez, 340 U.S. 42, 71 S.Ct. 108, 95 L.Ed. 47 (tax on marihuana).

It is conceded that a federal excise tax does not cease to be valid merely because it discourages or deters the activities taxed. Nor is the tax invalid because the revenue obtained its negligible. Appellee, however, argues that the sole purpose of the statute is to penalize only illegal gambling in the states through the guise of a tax measure. As with the above excise taxes which we have held to be valid, the instant tax has a regulatory effect. But regardless of its regulatory effect, the wagering tax produces revenue. As such it surpasses both the narcotics and firearms taxes which we have found valid.

While the Court has never questioned the above-quoted statement of Mr. Chief Justice Marshall in the McCulloch case, the application of the rule has brought varying holdings on constitutionality. Where federal legislation has rested on other congressional powers, such as the Necessary and Proper Clause or the Commerce Clause, this Court has generally sustained the statutes, despite their effect on matters ordinarily considered state concern. When federal power to regulate is found, its exercise is a matter for Congress. Where Congress has employed the taxing clause a greater variation in the decisions has resulted. The division in this Court has been more acute. Without any specific differentiation between the power to tax and other federal powers, the indirect results from the exercise of the power to tax have raised more doubts. This is strikingly illustrated by the shifting course of adjudication in taxation of the handling of narcotics. The tax ground in the Veazie Bank case, supra, recognized that strictly state governmental activities such as the right to pass laws were beyond the federal taxing power. That case allowed a tax, however, that obliterated from circulation all state bank notes. A reason was that "the judicial cannot prescribe to the legislative departments of the government limitations upon the exercise of its acknowledged powers." 8 Wall. at page 548. The tax cases cited above in the third preceding paragraph followed that theory. It is hard to understand why the power to tax should raise more doubts because of indirect effects than other federal powers.

Penalty provisions in tax statutes added for breach of a regulation concerning activities in themselves subject only to state regulation have caused this Court to declare the enactments invalid. Unless there are provisions, extraneous to any tax need, courts are without authority to limit the exercise of the taxing power. All the provisions of this excise are adapted to the collection of a valid tax.

Mr. Justice JACKSON, concurring.

I concur in the judgment and opinion of the Court, but with such doubt that if the minority agreed upon an opinion which did not impair legitimate use of the taxing power I probably would join it. But we deal here with important and contrasting values in our scheme of government, and it is important that neither be allowed to destroy the other.

Of course, all taxation has a tendency proportioned to its burdensomeness to discourage the activity taxed. One cannot formulate a revenue-raising plan that would not have economic and social consequences. Congress may and should place the burden of taxes where it will least handicap desirable activities and bear most heavily on useless or harmful ones. If Congress may tax one citizen to the point of discouragement for making an honest living, it is hard to say that it may not do the same to another just because he makes a sinister living. If the law-abiding must tell all to the tax collector, it is difficult to excuse one because his business is law-breaking. Strangely enough, Fifth Amendment protection against self-incrimination has been refused to business as against inquisition by the regulatory power, Shapiro v. United States, 335 U.S. 1, 68 S.Ct. 1375, 92 L.Ed. 1787, in what seemed to me a flagrant violation of it. See dissenting opinion, 335 U.S. at page 70, 68 S.Ct. 1410.

But here is a purported tax law which requires no reports and lays no tax except on specified gamblers whose calling in most states is illegal. It requires this group to step forward and identify themselves, not because they like others have income, but because of its source. This is difficult to regard as a rational or good-faith revenue measure, despite the deference that is due Congress. On the contrary, it seems to be a plan to tax out of existence the professional gambler whom it has been found impossible to prosecute out of existence. Few pursuits are entitled to less consideration at our hands than professional gambling, but the plain unwelcome fact is that it continues to survive because a large and influential part of our population patronizes and protects it.

The United States has a system of taxation by confession. That a people so numerous, scattered and individualistic annually assesses itself with a tax liability, often in highly burdensome amounts, is a reassuring sign of the stability and vitality of our system of self-government. What surprised me in once trying to help administer these laws was not to discover examples of recalcitrance, fraud or self-serving mistakes in reporting, but to discover that such derelictions were so few. It will be a sad day for the revenues if the good will of the people toward their taxing system is frittered away in efforts to accomplish by taxation moral reforms that cannot be accomplished by direct legislation. But the evil that can come from this statute will probably soon make itself manifest to Congress. The evil of a judicial decision impairing the legitimate taxing power by extreme constitutional interpretations might not be transient. Even though this statute approaches the fair limits of constitutionality, I join the decision of the Court.

Mr. Justice FRANKFURTER, dissenting.

The Court's opinion manifests a natural difficulty in reaching its conclusion. Constitutional issues are likely to arise whenever Congress draws on the taxing power not to raise revenue but to regulate conduct. This is so, of course, because of the distribution of legislative power as between the Congress and the State Legislatures in the regulation of conduct.

When oblique use is made of the taxing power as to matters which substantively are not within the powers delegated to Congress, the Court cannot shut its eyes to what is obviously, because designedly, an attempt to control conduct which the Constitution left to the responsibility of the States, merely because Congress wrapped the legislation in the verbal cellophane of a revenue measure.

What is relevant to judgment here is that, even if the history of this legislation as it went through Congress did not give one the libretto to the song, the context of the circumstances which brought forth this enactment — sensationally exploited disclosures regarding gambling in big cities and small, the relation of this gambling to corrupt politics, the impatient public response to these disclosures, the feeling of ineptitude or paralysis on the part of local law-enforcing agencies — emphatically supports what was revealed on the floor of Congress, namely, that what was formally a means of raising revenue for the Federal Government was essentially an effort to check if not to stamp out professional gambling.

A nominal taxing measure must be found an inadmissible intrusion into a domain of legislation reserved for the States not merely when Congress requires that such a measure is to be enforced through a detailed scheme of administration beyond the obvious fiscal needs, as in the Child Labor Tax Case, supra. That is one ground for holding that Congress was constitutionally disrespectful of what is reserved to the States. Another basis for deeming such a formal revenue measure inadmissible is presented by this case. In addition to the fact that Congress was concerned with activity beyond the authority of the Federal Government, the enforcing provision of this enactment is designed for the systematic confession of crimes with a view to prosecution for such crimes under State law.

The motive of congressional legislation is not for our scrutiny, provided only that the ulterior purpose is not expressed in ways which negative what the revenue words on their face express and, which do not seek enforcement of the formal revenue purpose through means that offend those standards of decency in our civilization against which due process.

I would affirm this judgment.

Comment on the Taxing Power. How significant was the fact that if the parties complied in *Bailey* no revenue would be raised, while such was not the case in *Kahriger*? When can Congress *not* tax for regulatory purposes? Is the present limitation on the taxing power meaningful? How easy is it for Congress to overcome it? Is the real change the Court's view of the Tenth Amendment as opposed to limits on the taxing power? Could the current Court's views on the nature of the Tenth Amendment affect prospective limits on the taxing power?

Postscript: The Court later held that the occupational tax violated the self-incrimination clause of the Fifth Amendment. Marchetti v. United States, 390 U.S. 39 (1968).

Mandatory Health Insurance Purchase as a Tax. In upholding the "individual mandate" provision of the Patient Protection and Affordable Care Act of 2010 (ACA), a 5–4 majority of the Court relied upon the taxing power rather than the Commerce Clause as the proper source of Congress's authority to require individuals to maintain "minimum essential" health insurance coverage or pay a "penalty" to the Internal Revenue Service for failing to do so. Chief Justice Roberts wrote for the Court on the taxing power; for the opinions on the commerce power holding, in which he spoke for a different 5–4 lineup. In reaching the conclusion that the taxing power authorized Congress to impose the mandate, the Chief Justice also, elsewhere in the opinion, rejected the argument that the mandate was a tax for purposes of the Anti-Injunction Act, which bars certain suits for injunctive relief against Congress's imposition of a tax.

NATIONAL FEDERATION OF INDEPENDENT BUSINESS v. SEBELIUS
132 S. Ct. 2566 (2012)

Chief Justice ROBERTS announced the judgment of the Court and delivered the opinion of the Court with respect to Part III-C, in which Justices GINSBURG, BREYER, SOTOMAYOR, and KAGAN joined; and an opinion with respect to Parts III-B, and III-D.

III. B. Because the Commerce Clause does not support the individual mandate, it is necessary to turn to the Government's second argument: that the mandate may be upheld as within Congress's enumerated power to "lay and collect Taxes." Art. I, § 8, cl. 1. The Government's tax power argument asks us to view the statute differently than we did in considering its commerce power theory. In making its Commerce Clause argument, the Government defended the mandate as a regulation requiring individuals to purchase health insurance. The Government does not claim that the taxing power allows Congress to issue such a command. Instead, the Government asks us to read the mandate not as ordering individuals to buy insurance, but rather as imposing a tax on those who do not buy that product.

[Under] the mandate, if an individual does not maintain health insurance, the only consequence is that he must make an additional payment to the IRS when he pays his taxes. That, according to the Government, means the mandate can be regarded as establishing a condition — not owning health insurance — that triggers a tax — the required payment to the IRS. Under that theory, the mandate is not a legal command to buy insurance. Rather, it makes going without insurance just another thing the Government taxes, like buying gasoline or earning income. And if the mandate is in effect just a tax hike on certain taxpayers who do not have health insurance, it may be within Congress's constitutional power to tax.

C. [The] exaction the Affordable Care Act imposes on those without health insurance looks like a tax in many respects. The "[s]hared responsibility payment," as the statute entitles it, is paid into the Treasury by "taxpayer[s]" when they file their tax returns. [The] requirement to pay is found in the Internal Revenue Code and enforced by the IRS, which [must] assess and collect it "in the same manner as taxes." This process yields the essential feature of any tax: it produces at least some revenue for the Government. [It] is of course true that the Act describes the payment as a "penalty," not a "tax." [But] that label [does] not determine whether the payment may be viewed as an exercise of Congress's taxing power. It is up to Congress whether to apply the Anti-Injunction Act to any particular statute, so it makes sense to be guided by Congress's choice of label on that question. That choice does not, however, control whether an exaction is within Congress's constitutional power to tax.

[In] Drexel Furniture [17th ed., p. 152], we focused on three practical characteristics of the so-called tax on employing child laborers that convinced us the "tax" was actually a penalty. First, the tax imposed an exceedingly heavy burden — 10 percent of a company's net income — on those who employed children, no matter how small their infraction. Second, it imposed that exaction only on those who knowingly employed underage laborers. Such scienter requirements are typical of punitive statutes, because Congress often wishes to punish only those who intentionally break the law. Third, this "tax" was enforced in part by the Department of Labor, an agency responsible for punishing violations of labor laws, not collecting revenue. The same analysis here suggests that the shared responsibility payment may for constitutional purposes be considered a tax, not a penalty: First, for most Americans the amount due will be far less than the price of insurance, and, by statute, it can never be more. It may often be a reasonable financial decision to make the payment rather than purchase insurance, unlike the "prohibitory" financial punishment in Drexel Furniture. Second, the individual mandate contains no scienter requirement. Third, the payment is collected solely by the IRS through the normal means of taxation.

None of this is to say that the payment is not intended to affect individual conduct. Although the payment will raise considerable revenue, it is plainly designed to expand health insurance coverage. But taxes that seek to influence conduct are nothing new. [Today,] federal and state taxes can compose more than half the retail price of cigarettes, not just to raise more money, but to encourage people to quit smoking. [Indeed,] "[e]very tax is in some measure regulatory." That [the mandate] seeks to shape decisions about whether to buy health insurance does not mean that it cannot be a valid exercise of the taxing power. In distinguishing penalties from taxes, this Court has explained that "if the concept of penalty means anything, it means punishment for an unlawful act or omission." While the individual mandate clearly aims to induce the purchase of health insurance, it need not be read to declare that failing to do so is unlawful. Neither the Act nor any other law attaches negative legal consequences to not buying health insurance, beyond requiring a payment to the IRS.

[Congress's] ability to use its taxing power to influence conduct is not without limits. A few of our cases policed these limits aggressively, invalidating punitive exactions obviously designed to regulate behavior otherwise regarded at the time as beyond federal authority. See, e.g., United States v. Butler [Levy, 4th ed., p. 438]; Drexel Furniture. [We] have already explained that the shared responsibility payment's practical characteristics pass muster as a tax under our narrowest interpretations of the taxing power. Because the tax at hand is within even those strict limits, we need not here decide the precise point at which an exaction becomes so punitive that the taxing power does not authorize it. [Although] the breadth of Congress's power to tax is greater than its power to regulate commerce, the taxing power does not give Congress the same degree of control over individual behavior. Once we recognize that Congress may regulate a particular decision under the Commerce Clause, the Federal Government can bring its full weight to bear. Congress may simply command individuals to do as it directs. [By] contrast, Congress's authority under the taxing power is limited to requiring an individual to pay money into the Federal Treasury, no more. [The] Affordable Care Act's requirement that certain individuals pay a financial penalty for not obtaining health insurance may reasonably be characterized as a tax. Because the Constitution permits such a tax, it is not our role to forbid it, or to pass upon its wisdom or fairness.

Justices SCALIA, KENNEDY, THOMAS, and ALITO, dissenting.

[Our] cases establish a clear line between a tax and a penalty: "'[A] tax is an enforced contribution to provide for the support of government; a penalty . . . is an exaction imposed by statute as punishment for an unlawful act.'" [We] have never held [that] a penalty imposed for violation of the law was so trivial as to be in effect a tax. We have never held that *any* exaction imposed for violation of the law is an exercise of Congress' taxing power — even when the statute calls it a tax, much less when (as here) the statute repeatedly calls it a penalty. When an act "adopt[s] the criteria of wrongdoing" and then imposes a monetary penalty as the "principal consequence on those who transgress its standard," it creates a regulatory penalty, not a tax. Child Labor Tax Case [Levy 4th ed., p. 432].

[To] say that the Individual Mandate merely imposes a tax is not to interpret the statute but to rewrite it. Judicial tax-writing is particularly troubling. Taxes have never been popular, see, *e.g.,* Stamp Act of 1765, and in part for that reason, the Constitution requires tax increases to originate in the House of Representatives. See Art. I, § 7, cl. 1. That is to say, they must originate in the legislative body most accountable to the people, where legislators must weigh the need for the tax against the terrible price they might pay at their next election, which is never more than two years off. The Federalist No. 58 "defend[ed] the decision to give the origination power to the House on the ground that the Chamber that is more accountable to the people should have the primary role in raising revenue." [Imposing] a tax through judicial legislation inverts the constitutional scheme, and places the power to tax in the branch of government least accountable to the citizenry.

2. THE SPENDING POWER

The Constitution provides at the commencement of Art.1, § 8, that "[t]he Congress shall have the power to . . . provide for the common Defense and general Welfare of the United States." As noted above, "the "pre-Court-packing Court," contrary to its limited definition of commerce, provided a broad basis for both the federal taxing and spending powers, although it nonetheless struck down legislation based upon its view that the exercise of those powers were limited by the Tenth Amendment." Even given such in regard to the spending power, this is one of the least litigated areas of constitutional law. The first significant definition of the power to spend for the general welfare did not take place until 1927, in *U.S. v. Butler*, cited below. Why do you think a threshold decision in regard to the spending power did not take place until 1927? What's Article III and the Court's in-house rules got to do with it?

Once again, albeit in 1927, we are back to the differing views on federal power, here the "general welfare clause," between Hamilton (Federalists) and Madison (Republicans). The essential controversy was the meaning of Congress's power to spend for the general welfare. Madison, espousing a more limited view of this power, argued that spending for the "general welfare" was limited to expenditures directly related to the "enumerated" fields of legislative power. Hamilton, on the other hand, asserted a broader view and argued that "general welfare" was a separate and distinct enumeration of power to the Congress, not confined or limited to other enumerated powers. Thus, for example, to Hamilton, Congress's substantive power to spend was limited only by the requirement that it be spent for the *general* welfare. Knowing that the pre-court-packing Court would most likely strike down another piece of new deal legislation, which view do you think the Court in *Butler* adopts. Might you be surprised?

Roosevelt's Agricultural Adjustment Act of 1933 was a system of farm subsidies from taxable revenue. It was a cornerstone of the new deal. In the opinion that follows, the last before a reversal in Supreme Court views, the Court considers the constitutionality of the AAA and makes threshold decisions in relation to the extent of the federal spending power.

UNITED STATES v. BUTLER
297 U.S. 1 (1936)

Receivership suit by the Franklin Process Company against the Hoosac Mills Corporation, in which William M. Butler and another were appointed as receivers for defendant. A decree allowing a claim of the United States for a balance due on processing and floor stock taxes assessed against defendant (8 F.Supp. 552) was reversed, and the cause remanded by the Circuit Court of Appeals (78 F.(2d) 1), and the United States brings certiorari. Judgment of the Circuit Court of Appeals affirmed.

Mr. Justice ROBERTS delivered the opinion of the Court.

In this case we must determine whether certain provisions of the Agricultural Adjustment Act, 1933, conflict with the Federal Constitution.

The United States presented a claim to the respondents as receivers of the Hoosac Mills Corporation for processing and floor taxes on cotton levied under sections 9 and 16 of the act. The receivers recommended that the claim be disallowed. The District Court found the taxes valid and ordered them paid. Upon appeal the Circuit Court of Appeals reversed the order. The judgment under review was entered prior to the adoption of the amending act of August 24, 1935, and we are therefore concerned only with the original act.

[The] government asserts that even if the respondents may question the propriety of the appropriation embodied in the statute, their attack must fail because article 1, § 8 of the Constitution, authorizes the contemplated expenditure of the funds raised by the tax. This contention presents the great and the controlling question in the case.

[There] should be no misunderstanding as to the function of this court in such a case. It is sometimes said that the court assumes a power to overrule or control the action of the people's representatives. This is a misconception. The Constitution is the supreme law of the land ordained and established by the people. All legislation must conform to the principles it lays down. When an act of Congress is appropriately challenged in the courts as not conforming to the constitutional mandate, the judicial branch of the government has only one duty; to lay the article of the Constitution which is invoked beside the statute which is challenged and to decide whether the latter squares with the former. All the court does, or can do, is to announce its considered judgment upon the question. The only power it has, if such it may be called, is the power of judgment. This court neither approves nor condemns any legislative policy. Its delicate and difficult office is to ascertain and declare whether the legislation is in accordance with, or in contravention of, the provisions of the Constitution; and, having done that, its duty ends.

[The] clause thought to authorize the legislation, the first, confers upon the Congress power "to lay and collect Taxes, Duties, Imposts and Excises, to pay the Debts and provide for the common Defense and general Welfare of the United States. . . ." It is not contended that this provision grants power to regulate agricultural production upon the theory that such legislation would promote the general welfare. The government concedes that the phrase "to provide for the general welfare" qualifies the power "to lay and collect taxes." The view that the clause grants power to provide for the general welfare, independently of the taxing power, has never been authoritatively accepted. Mr. Justice Story points out that, if it were adopted, "it is obvious that under color of the generality of the words, to 'provide for the common defense and general welfare,' the government of the United States is, in reality, a government of general and unlimited powers, notwithstanding the subsequent enumeration of specific powers." The true construction undoubtedly is that the only thing granted is the power to tax for the purpose of providing funds for payment of the nation's debts and making provision for the general welfare.

[Nevertheless], the government asserts that warrant is found in this clause for the adoption of the Agricultural Adjustment Act. The argument is that Congress may appropriate and authorize the spending of moneys for the "general welfare"; that the phrase should be liberally construed to cover anything conducive to national welfare; that decision as to what will promote such welfare rests with Congress alone, and the courts may not review its determination; and, finally, that the appropriation under attack was in fact for the general welfare of the United States.

[Since] the foundation of the nation, sharp differences of opinion have persisted as to the true interpretation of the phrase. Madison asserted it amounted to no more than a reference to the other powers enumerated in the subsequent clauses of the same section; that, as the United States is a government of limited and enumerated powers, the grant of power to tax and spend for the general national welfare must be confined to the enumerated legislative fields committed to the Congress. In this view the phrase is mere tautology, for taxation and appropriation are or may be necessary incidents of the exercise of any of the enumerated legislative powers. Hamilton, on the other hand, maintained the clause confers a power separate and distinct from those later enumerated is not restricted in meaning by the grant of them, and Congress consequently has a substantive power to tax and to appropriate, limited only by the requirement that it shall be exercised to provide for the general welfare of the United States. Each contention has had the support of those whose views are entitled to weight. This court has noticed the question, but has never found it necessary to decide which is the true construction. Mr. Justice Story, in his Commentaries, espouses the Hamiltonian position. We shall not review the writings of public men and commentators or discuss the legislative practice. Study of all these leads us to conclude that the reading advocated by Mr. Justice Story is the correct one. While, therefore, the power to tax is not unlimited, its confines are set in the clause which confers it, and not in those of section 8 which bestow and define the legislative powers of the Congress. It results that the power of Congress to authorize expenditure of public moneys for public purposes is not limited by the direct grants of legislative power found in the Constitution.

[We] are not now required to ascertain the scope of the phrase "general welfare of the United States" or to determine whether an appropriation in aid of agriculture falls within it. Wholly apart from that question, another principle embedded in our Constitution prohibits the enforcement of the Agricultural adjustment Act. The act invades the reserved rights of the states. It is a statutory plan to regulate and control agricultural production, a matter beyond the powers delegated to the federal government. The tax, the appropriation of the funds raised, and the direction for their disbursement, are but parts of the plan. They are but means to an unconstitutional end.

[It] is an established principle that the attainment of a prohibited end may not be accomplished under the pretext of the exertion of powers which are granted.

[If] the taxing power may not be used as the instrument to enforce a regulation of matters of state concern with respect to which the Congress has no authority to interfere, may it, as in the present case, be employed to raise the money necessary to purchase a compliance which the Congress is powerless to command? The government asserts that whatever might be said against the validity of the plan, if compulsory, it is constitutionally sound because the end is accomplished by voluntary co-operation. There are two sufficient answers to the contention. The regulation is not in fact voluntary. The farmer, of course, may refuse to comply, but the price of such refusal is the loss of benefits. The amount offered is intended to be sufficient to exert pressure on him to agree to the proposed regulation. The power to confer or withhold unlimited benefits is the power to coerce or destroy. If the cotton grower elects not to accept the benefits, he will receive less for his crops; those who receive payments will be able to undersell him. The result may well to financial ruin. The coercive purpose and intent of the statute is not obscured by the fact that it has not been perfectly successful. [The] asserted power of choice is illusory. [But] if the plan were one for purely voluntary co-operation it would stand no better so far as federal power is concerned. At best, it is a scheme for purchasing with federal funds submission to federal regulation of a subject reserved to the states.

It is said that Congress has the undoubted right to appropriate money to executive officers for expenditure under contracts between the government and individuals; that much of the total expenditures is so made. But appropriations and expenditures under contracts for proper governmental purposes cannot justify contracts which are not within federal power. And contracts for the reduction of acreage and the control of production are outside the range of that power. An appropriation to be expended by the United States under contracts calling for violation of a state law clearly would offend the Constitution. Is a statute less objectionable which authorizes expenditure of federal moneys to induce action in a field in which the United States has no power to intermeddle? The Congress cannot invade state jurisdiction to compel individual action; no more can it purchase such action.

[We] are not here concerned with a conditional appropriation of money, nor with a provision that if certain conditions are not complied with the appropriation shall no longer be available. By the Agricultural Adjustment Act the amount of the tax is appropriated to be expended only in payment under contracts whereby the parties bind themselves to regulation by the federal government. There is an obvious difference between a statute stating the conditions upon which moneys shall be expended and one effective only upon assumption of a contractual obligation to submit to a regulation which otherwise could not be enforced. Many examples pointing the distinction might be cited. We are referred to appropriations in aid of education, and it is said that no one has doubted the power of Congress to stipulate the sort of education for which money shall be expended. But an appropriation to an educational institution which by its terms is to become available only if the beneficiary enters into a contract to teach doctrines subversive of the Constitution is clearly bad. An affirmance of the authority of Congress so to condition the expenditure of an appropriation would tend to nullify all constitutional limitations upon legislative power.

Congress has no power to enforce its commands on the farmer to the ends sought by the Agricultural Adjustment Act. It must follow that it may not indirectly accomplish those ends by taxing and spending to purchase compliance. The Constitution and the entire plan of our government negative any such use of the power to tax and to spend as the act undertakes to authorize. It does not help to declare that local conditions throughout the nation have created a situation of national concern; for this is but to say that whenever there is a widespread similarity of local conditions, Congress may ignore constitutional limitations upon its own powers and usurp those reserved to the states.

[If] the act before us is a proper exercise of the federal taxing power, evidently the regulation of all industry throughout the United States may be accomplished by similar exercises of the same power.

[The] sole premise is that, though the makers of the Constitution, in erecting the federal government, intended sedulously to limit and define its powers, so as to reserve to the states and the people sovereign power, to be wielded by the states and their citizens and not to be invaded by the United States, they nevertheless by a single clause gave power to the Congress to tear down the barriers, to invade the states' jurisdiction, and to become a parliament of the whole people, subject to no restrictions save such as are self-imposed. The argument, when seen in its true character and in the light of its inevitable results, must be rejected.

The judgment is affirmed.

Mr. Justice STONE (dissenting).

The power of courts to declare a statute unconstitutional is subject to two guiding principles of decision which ought never to be absent from judicial consciousness. One is that courts are concerned only with the power to enact statutes, not with their wisdom. The other is that while unconstitutional exercise of power by the executive and legislative branches of the government is subject to judicial restraint, the only check upon our own exercise of power is our own sense of self-restraint. For the removal of unwise laws from the statute books appeal lies, not to the courts, but to the ballot and to the processes of democratic government.

[As] the present depressed state of agriculture is nation wide in its extent and effects, there is no basis for saying that the expenditure of public money in aid of farmers is not within the specifically granted power of Congress to levy taxes to "provide for the . . . general welfare." The opinion of the Court does not declare otherwise.

[Of] the assertion that the payments to farmers are coercive, it is enough to say that no such contention is pressed by the taxpayer, and no such consequences were to be anticipated or appear to have resulted from the administration of the act. The suggestion of coercion finds no support in the record or in any data showing the actual operation of the act. Threat of loss, not hope of gain, is the essence of economic coercion.

[It] is upon the contention that state power is infringed by purchased regulation of agricultural production that chief reliance is placed. It is insisted that, while the Constitution gives to Congress, in specific and unambiguous terms, the power to tax and spend, the power is subject to limitations which do not find their origin in any express provision of the Constitution and to which other expressly delegated powers are not subject.

The Constitution requires that public funds shall be spent for a defined purpose, the promotion of the general welfare. Their expenditure usually involves payment on terms which will insure use by the selected recipients within the limits of the constitutional purpose. Expenditures would fail of their purpose and thus lose their constitutional sanction if the terms of payment were not such that by their influence on the action of the recipients the permitted end would be attained. The power of Congress to spend is inseparable from persuasion to action over which Congress has no legislative control. Congress may not command that the science of agriculture be taught in state universities. But if it would aid the teaching of that science by grants to state institutions, it is appropriate, if not necessary, that the grant be on the condition, incorporated in the Morrill Act, 12 Stat. 503, 7 U.S.C.A. § 301 et seq., 26 Stat. 417, 7 U.S.C.A. § 321 et seq., that it be used for the intended purpose. Similarly it would seem to be compliance with the Constitution, not violation of it, for the government to take and the university to give a contract that the grant would be so used. It makes no difference that there is a promise to do an act which the condition is calculated to induce. Condition and promise are alike valid since both are in furtherance of the national purpose for which the money is appropriated.

[It] is a contradiction in terms to say that there is power to spend for the national welfare, while rejecting any power to impose conditions reasonably adapted to the attainment of the end which alone would justify the expenditure.

The limitation now sanctioned must lead to absurd consequences. The government may give seeds to farmers, but may not condition the gift upon their being planted in places where they are most needed or even planted at all. The government may give money to the unemployed, but may not ask that those who get it shall give labor in return, or even use it to support their families. [It] may support rural schools, 39 Stat. 929 (20 U.S.C.A. § 11 et seq.), 45 Stat. 1151 (20 U.S.C.A. §§ 15a to 15c), 48 Stat. 792 (20 U.S.C.A. §§ 15d to 15g), but may not condition its grant by the requirement that certain standards be maintained. It may appropriate moneys to be expended by the Reconstruction Finance Corporation "to aid in financing agriculture, commerce and industry," and to facilitate "the exportation of agricultural and other products." Do all its activities collapse because, in order to effect the permissible purpose in myriad ways the money is paid out upon terms and conditions which influence action of the recipients within the states, which Congress cannot command? The answer would seem plain. If the expenditure is for a national public purpose, that purpose will not be thwarted because payment is on condition which will advance that purpose. The action which Congress induces by payments of money to promote the general welfare, but which it does not command or coerce, is but an incident to a specifically granted power, but a permissible means to a legitimate end. If appropriation in aid of a program of curtailment of agricultural production is constitutional, and it is not denied that it is, payment to farmers on condition that they reduce their crop acreage is constitutional. It is not any the less so because the farmer at his own option promises to fulfill the condition.

That the governmental power of the purse is a great one is not now for the first time announced.

[The] suggestion that it must now be curtailed by judicial fiat because it may be abused by unwise use hardly rises to the dignity of argument. So may judicial power be abused. "The power to tax is the power to destroy," but we do not, for that reason, doubt its existence, or hold that its efficacy is to be restricted by its incidental or collateral effects upon the states. See Veazie Bank v. Fenno, 8 Wall. 533, 19 L.Ed. 482; McCray v. United States, 195 U.S. 27, 24 S.Ct. 769, 49 L.Ed. 78, 1 Ann.Cas. 561; compare Magnano Co. v. Hamilton, 292 U.S. 40, 54 S.Ct. 599, 78 L.Ed. 1109. The power to tax and spend is not without constitutional restraints. One restriction is that the purpose must be truly national. Another is that it may not be used to coerce action left to state control. Another is the conscience and patriotism of Congress and the Executive. "It must be remembered that legislatures are ultimate guardians of the liberties and welfare of the people in quite as great a degree as the courts." Justice Holmes, in Missouri, Kansas & Texas R. Co. v. May, 194 U.S. 267, 270, 24 S.Ct. 638, 639, 48 L.Ed. 971.

A tortured construction of the Constitution is not to be justified by recourse to extreme examples of reckless congressional spending which might occur if courts could not prevent — expenditures which, even if they could be thought to effect any national purpose, would be possible only by action of a legislature lost to all sense of public responsibility. Such suppositions are addressed to the mind accustomed to believe that it is the business of courts to sit in judgment on the wisdom of legislative action. Courts are not the only agency of government that must be assumed to have capacity to govern. Congress and the courts both unhappily may falter or be mistaken in the performance of their constitutional duty. But interpretation of our great charter of government which proceeds on any assumption that the responsibility for the preservation of our institutions is the exclusive concern of any one of the three branches of government, or that it alone can save them from destruction is far more likely, in the long run, "to obliterate the constituent members" of "an indestructible union of indestructible states" than the frank recognition that language, even of a constitution, may mean what it says: that the power to tax and spend includes the power to relieve a nationwide economic maladjustment by conditional gifts of money.

Mr. Justice STONE, Mr. Justice BRANDEIS, and Mr. Justice CARDOZO, dissenting.

Comments on *Butler*. Given that the Court adopts the Hamiltonian position on the scope of the spending power, is the Court consistent in finding the act unconstitutional? If the spending power is an "enumerated" power, limited by its application to the *general* welfare, on what basis does the Court deny federal authority? It is the Tenth Amendment, or is it "coercion?" Does Justice Roberts take the position that although there are no judicially enforceable internal limitations on the spending power (i.e., Congress, not the Court, should determine whether an expenditure promotes the "general welfare"), there are judicially enforceable "federalism-based" external limitations on that power?

In *Steward Machine Co.*, the Court will find that the Social Security Act is a valid exercise of the spending power. The case represents not only the post-court-packing view of the federal spending power, but will also set forth a predicate for "conditional spending" that is with us until today. Other than the outcome, how does *Steward Machine Co.* differ from *Butler*?

STEWARD MACHINE CO. v. DAVIS
301 U.S. 548 (1937)

Mr. Justice CARDOZO delivered the opinion of the Court.

The validity of the tax imposed by the Social Security Act (42 U.S.C.A. §§ 301 — 1305) on employers of eight or more is here to be determined.

Petitioner, an Alabama corporation, paid a tax in accordance with the statute, filed a claim for refund with the Commissioner of Internal Revenue, and sued to recover the payment ($46.14), asserting a conflict between the statute and the Constitution of the United States.

[The] caption of title IX is "Tax on Employers of Eight or More." Every employer (with stated exceptions) is to pay for each calendar year "an excise tax, with respect to having individuals in his employ," the tax to be measured by prescribed percentages of the total wages payable by the employer during the calendar year with respect to such employment. §901. One is not, however, an "employer" within the meaning of the act unless he employs eight persons or more.

[For] the moment, it is enough to say that the Fund is to be held by the Secretary of the Treasury, who is to invest in government securities any portion not required in his judgment to meet current withdrawals. He is authorized and directed to pay out of the fund to any competent state agency such sums as it may duly requisition from the amount standing to its credit. Section 904(f).

[The] excise is not void as involving the coercion of the states in contravention of the Tenth Amendment or of restrictions implicit in our federal form of government.

[There] must be a showing in the second place that the tax and the credit in combination are weapons of coercion, destroying or impairing the autonomy of the states. The truth of each proposition being essential to the success of the assault, we pass for convenience to a consideration of the second, without pausing to inquire whether there has been a demonstration of the first.

[To] draw the line intelligently between duress and inducement, there is need to remind ourselves of facts as to the problem of unemployment that are now matters of common knowledge.

[The] relevant statistics are gathered in the brief of counsel for the government. Of the many available figures a few only will be mentioned. During the years 1929 to 1936, when the country was passing through a cyclical depression, the number of the unemployed mounted to unprecedented heights. Often the average was more than 10 million; at times a peak was attained of 16 million or more. Disaster to the breadwinner meant disaster to dependents. Accordingly the roll of the unemployed, itself formidable enough, was only a partial roll of the destitute or needy. The fact developed quickly that the states were unable to give the requisite relief. The problem had become national in area and dimensions. There was need of help from the nation if the people were not to starve.

[In] the presence of this urgent need for some remedial expedient, the question is to be answered whether the expedient adopted has overlept the bounds of power. The assailants of the statute say that its dominant end and aim is to drive the state Legislatures under the whip of economic pressure into the enactment of unemployment compensation laws at the bidding of the central government. Supporters of the statute say that its operation is not constraint, but the creation of a larger freedom, the states and the nation joining in a co-operative endeavor to avert a common evil. Before Congress acted, unemployment compensation insurance was still, for the most part, a project and no more.

[Many] held back through alarm lest in laying such a toll upon their industries, they would place themselves in a position of economic disadvantage as compared with neighbors or competitors. Two consequences ensued. One was that the freedom of a state to contribute its fair share to the solution of a national problem was paralyzed by fear. The other was that in so far as there was failure by the states to contribute relief according to the measure of their capacity, a disproportionate burden, and a mountainous one, was laid upon the resources of the government of the nation.

[The] Social Security Act is an attempt to find a method by which all these public agencies may work together to a common end. Every dollar of the new taxes will continue in all likelihood to be used and needed by the nation as long as states are unwilling, whether through timidity or for other motives, to do what can be done at home. At least the inference is permissible that Congress so believed, though retaining undiminished freedom to spend the money as it pleased. On the other hand, fulfillment of the home duty will be lightened and encouraged by crediting the taxpayer upon his account with the Treasury of the nation to the extent that his contributions under the laws of the locality have simplified or diminished the problem of relief and the probable demand upon the resources of the fisc.

[Who] then is coerced through the operation of this statute? Not the taxpayer. He pays in fulfillment of the mandate of the local legislature. Not the state. Even now she does not offer a suggestion that in passing the unemployment law she was affected by duress. See Carmichael v. Southern Coal & Coke Co. (Carmichael v. Gulf States Paper Corporation), supra. For all that appears, she is satisfied with her choice, and would be sorely disappointed if it were now to be annulled. The difficulty with the petitioner's contention is that it confuses motive with coercion.

[Every] rebate from a tax when conditioned upon conduct is in some measure a temptation. But to hold that motive or temptation is equivalent to coercion is to plunge the law in endless difficulties. The outcome of such a doctrine is the acceptance of a philosophical determinism by which choice becomes impossible. Till now the law has been guided by a robust common sense which assumes the freedom of the will as a working hypothesis in the solution of its problems. The wisdom of the hypothesis has illustration in this case. There would be a strange irony, indeed, if her choice were now to be annulled on the basis of an assumed duress in the enactment of a statute which her courts have accepted as a true expression of her will.

In ruling as we do, we leave many questions open. We do not say that a tax is valid, when imposed by act of Congress, if it is laid upon the condition that a state may escape its operation through the adoption of a statute unrelated in subject-matter to activities fairly within the scope of national policy and power. No such question is before us. In the tender of this credit Congress does not intrude upon fields foreign to its function. The purpose of its intervention, as we have shown, is to safeguard its own treasury and as an incident to that protection to place the states upon a footing of equal opportunity. Drains upon its own resources are to be checked; obstructions to the freedom of the states are to be leveled. It is one thing to impose a tax dependent upon the conduct of the taxpayers, or of the state in which they live, where the conduct to be stimulated or discouraged is unrelated to the fiscal need subserved by the tax in its normal operation, or to any other end legitimately national. The Child Labor Tax Case, 259 U.S. 20, 42 S.Ct. 449, 66 L.Ed. 817, 21 A.L.R. 1432, and Hill v. Wallace, 259 U.S. 44, 42 S.Ct. 453, 66 L.Ed. 822, were decided in the belief that the statutes there condemned were exposed to that reproach. Cf. United States v. Constantine, 296 U.S. 287, 56 S.Ct. 223, 80 L.Ed. 233. It is quite another thing to say that a tax will be abated upon the doing of an act that will satisfy the fiscal need, the tax and the alternative being approximate equivalents. In such circumstances, if in no others, inducement or persuasion does not go beyond the bounds of power. We do not fix the outermost line. Enough for present purposes that wherever the line may be, this statute is within it. Definition more precise must abide the wisdom of the future.

[The] statute does not call for a surrender by the states of powers essential to their quasi sovereign existence. [A] credit to taxpayers for payments made to a state under a state unemployment law will be manifestly futile in the absence of some assurance that the law leading to the credit is in truth what it professes to be. An unemployment law framed in such a way that the unemployed who look to it will be deprived of reasonable protection is one in name and nothing more. What is basic and essential may be assured by suitable conditions. The terms embodied in these sections are directed to that end. A wide range of judgment is given to the several states as to the particular type of statute to be spread upon their books.

[What] they may not do, if they would earn the credit, is to depart from those standards which in the judgment of Congress are to be ranked as fundamental. Even if opinion may differ as to the fundamental quality of one or more of the conditions, the difference will not avail to vitiate the statute. In determining essentials, Congress must have the benefit of a fair margin of discretion.

Comments on *Butler* and *Steward Machine*. Is *Steward Machine Co.* consistent with *Butler*? What are the differences? Is it the Tenth Amendment, or is it "coercion?" Does the Court's view of the Tenth Amendment in *Butler* make the Act "coercive," and its view of the Tenth Amendment in *Steward* make it "voluntary"?

3. CONDITIONAL SPENDING

Steward Machine's resolution of the conflict between powers reserved to the states in the Tenth Amendment, as against the broad enumerated power of Congress to spend for the general welfare, has made cooperation between the states and federal government via "conditional spending" a most popular legislative alternative.

Does the concept of conditional spending, which now serves as the basis for many federal grants-in-aid programs to the states, affect the power balance between state and federal governments? Was Justice McReynolds correct when he forewarned that *Steward Machine* was the "beginning of the end" of federal union, that conditional spending inherently meant that the "States become humble suppliants of the Federal government," thus "reversing their true relations to this Union"? Or, is the logic of Justice Cardozo, that these cases simply recognize that "only a power that is national can serve the interests of all," more persuasive? Are these cases simply dissertations on the best way to run a nation, with the Constitution broad enough to support both views?

SOUTH DAKOTA v. DOLE
483 U.S. 203 (1978)

State of South Dakota brought action challenging constitutionality of federal statute conditioning states' receipt of portion of federal highway funds on adoption of minimum drinking age of 21. The United States District Court for the District of South Dakota, Andrew W. Bogue, J., dismissed complaint, and state appealed. The Court of Appeals for the Eighth Circuit, 791 F.2d 628, affirmed, and state petitioned for writ of certiorari. The Supreme Court, Chief Justice Rehnquist, held that statute conditioning receipt of highway funds on adoption of minimum drinking age is valid use of Congress' spending power.

Chief Justice REHNQUIST delivered the opinion of the Court.

[W]e need not decide in this case whether [the Twenty-first] Amendment would prohibit an attempt by Congress to legislate directly a national minimum drinking age. Here, Congress has acted indirectly under its spending power to encourage uniformity in the States' drinking ages. As we explain below, we find this legislative effort within constitutional bounds even if Congress may not regulate drinking ages directly.

The Constitution empowers Congress to "lay and collect Taxes, Duties, Imposts, and Excises, to pay the Debts and provide for the common Defense and general Welfare of the United States." Art. I, § 8, cl. 1. Incident to this power, Congress may attach conditions on the receipt of federal funds, and has repeatedly employed the power "to further broad policy objectives by conditioning receipt of federal moneys upon compliance by the recipient with federal statutory and administrative directives." *Fullilove v. Klutznick,* 448 U.S. 448, 474, 100 S.Ct. 2758, 2772, 65 L.Ed.2d 902 (1980) (opinion of Burger, C.J.). *Steward Machine Co. v. Davis,* 301 U.S. 548, 57 S.Ct. 883, 81 L.Ed. 1279 (1937). The breadth of this power was made clear in *United States v. Butler,* 297 U.S. 1, 66, 56 S.Ct. 312, 319, 80 L.Ed. 477 (1936), where the Court, resolving a longstanding debate over the scope of the Spending Clause, determined that "the power of Congress to authorize expenditure of public moneys for public purposes is not limited by the direct grants of legislative power found in the Constitution." Thus, objectives not thought to be within Article I's "enumerated legislative fields," *id.,* at 65, 56 S.Ct., at 319, may nevertheless be attained through the use of the spending power and the conditional grant of federal funds.

The remaining question about the validity of § 158 — and the basic point of disagreement between the parties — is whether the Twenty-first Amendment constitutes an "independent constitutional bar" to the conditional grant of federal funds. *Lawrence County v. Lead-Deadwood School Dist., supra,* at 269-270, 105 S.Ct., at 702-703. Petitioner, relying on its view that the Twenty-first Amendment prohibits *direct* regulation of drinking ages by Congress, asserts that "Congress may not use the spending power to regulate that which it is prohibited from regulating directly under the Twenty-first Amendment." Brief for Petitioner 52-53. But our cases show that this "independent constitutional bar" limitation on the spending power is not of the kind petitioner suggests. *United States v. Butler, supra,* 297 U.S., at 66, 56 S.Ct., at 319, for example, established that the constitutional limitations on Congress when exercising its spending power are less exacting than those on its authority to regulate directly.

We have also held that a perceived Tenth Amendment limitation on congressional regulation of state affairs did not concomitantly limit the range of conditions legitimately placed on federal grants. In *Oklahoma v. Civil Service Comm'n,* 330 U.S. 127, 67 S.Ct. 544, 91 L.Ed. 794 (1947), the Court considered the validity of the Hatch Act insofar as it was applied to political activities of state officials whose employment was financed in whole or in part with federal funds. The State contended that an order under this provision to withhold certain federal funds unless a state official was removed invaded its sovereignty in violation of the Tenth Amendment. Though finding that "the United States is not concerned with, and has no power to regulate, local political activities as such of state officials," the Court nevertheless held that the Federal Government "does have power to fix the terms upon which its money allotments to states shall be disbursed." *Id.,* at 143, 67 S.Ct., at 553. The Court found no violation of the State's sovereignty because the State could, and did, adopt "the 'simple expedient' of not yielding to what she urges is federal coercion. The offer of benefits to a state by the United States dependent upon cooperation by the state with federal plans, assumedly for the general welfare, is not unusual."

These cases establish that the "independent constitutional bar" limitation on the spending power is not, as petitioner suggests, a prohibition on the indirect achievement of objectives which Congress is not empowered to achieve directly. Instead, we think that the language in our earlier opinions stands for the unexceptionable proposition that the power may not be used to induce the States to engage in activities that would themselves be unconstitutional. Thus, for example, a grant of federal funds conditioned on invidiously discriminatory state action or the infliction of cruel and unusual punishment would be an illegitimate exercise of the Congress' broad spending power. But no such claim can be or is made here. Were South Dakota to succumb to the blandishments offered by Congress and raise its drinking age to 21, the State's action in so doing would not violate the constitutional rights of anyone.

Our decisions have recognized that in some circumstances the financial inducement offered by Congress might be so coercive as to pass the point at which "pressure turns into compulsion." *Steward Machine Co. v. Davis, supra,* 301 U.S., at 590, 57 S.Ct., at 892. Here, however, Congress has directed only that a State desiring to establish a minimum drinking age lower than 21 lose a relatively small percentage of certain federal highway funds. Petitioner contends that the coercive nature of this program is evident from the degree of success it has achieved. We cannot conclude, however, that a conditional grant of federal money of this sort is unconstitutional simply by reason of its success in achieving the congressional objective.

When we consider, for a moment, that all South Dakota would lose if she adheres to her chosen course as to a suitable minimum drinking age is 5% of the funds otherwise obtainable under specified highway grant programs, the argument as to coercion is shown to be more rhetoric than fact. As we said a half century ago in *Steward Machine Co. v. Davis:* "[E]very rebate from a tax when conditioned upon conduct is in some measure a temptation. But to hold that motive or temptation is equivalent to coercion is to plunge the law in endless difficulties. The outcome of such a doctrine is the acceptance of a philosophical determinism by which choice becomes impossible. Till now the law has been guided by a robust common sense which assumes the freedom of the will as a working hypothesis in the solution of its problems." 301 U.S., at 589-590, 57 S.Ct., at 891-892.

Here Congress has offered relatively mild encouragement to the States to enact higher minimum drinking ages than they would otherwise choose. But the enactment of such laws remains the prerogative of the States not merely in theory but in fact. Even if Congress might lack the power to impose a national minimum drinking age directly, we conclude that encouragement to state action found in § 158 is a valid use of the spending power. Accordingly, the judgment of the Court of Appeals is affirmed.

Justice O'CONNOR, dissenting.

§ 158 is not a condition on spending reasonably related to the expenditure of federal funds and cannot be justified on that ground. Rather, it is an attempt to regulate the sale of liquor, an attempt that lies outside Congress' power to regulate commerce because it falls within the ambit of § 2 of the Twenty-first Amendment.

My disagreement with the Court is relatively narrow on the spending power issue: it is a disagreement about the application of a principle rather than a disagreement on the principle itself. I agree with the Court that Congress may attach conditions on the receipt of federal funds to further "the federal interest in particular national projects or programs." *Massachusetts v. United States,* 435 U.S. 444, 461, 98 S.Ct. 1153, 1164, 55 L.Ed.2d 403 (1978); see *Oklahoma v. Civil Service Comm'n,* 330 U.S. 127, 143-144, 67 S.Ct. 544, 553-554, 91 L.Ed. 794 (1947); *Steward Machine Co. v. Davis,* 301 U.S. 548, 57 S.Ct. 883, 81 L.Ed. 1279 (1937). I also subscribe to the established proposition that the reach of the spending power "is not limited by the direct grants of legislative power found in the Constitution." *United States v. Butler,* 297 U.S. 1, 66, 56 S.Ct. 312, 319, 80 L.Ed. 477

(1936). Finally, I agree that there are four separate types of limitations on the spending power: the expenditure must be for the general welfare, *Helvering v. Davis,* 301 U.S. 619, 640-641, 57 S.Ct. 904, 908-909, 81 L.Ed. 1307 (1937), the conditions imposed must be unambiguous, *Pennhurst State School and Hospital v. Halderman,* 451 U.S. 1, 17, 101 S.Ct. 1531 (1981), they must be reasonably related to the purpose of the expenditure, *Massachusetts v. United States, supra,* 435 U.S., at 461, 98 S.Ct., at 1164, and the legislation may not violate any independent constitutional prohibition, *Lawrence County v. Lead-Deadwood School Dist.,* 469 U.S. 256, 269-270, 105 S.Ct. 695, 703-704, 83 L.Ed.2d 635 (1985). *Ante,* at 2796-2797. Insofar as two of those limitations are concerned, the Court is clearly correct that § 158 is wholly unobjectionable. Establishment of a national minimum drinking age certainly fits within the broad concept of the general welfare and the statute is entirely unambiguous. I am also willing to assume, *arguendo,* that the Twenty-first Amendment does not constitute an "independent constitutional bar" to a spending condition. See *ante,* at 2797-2798.

But the Court's application of the requirement that the condition imposed be reasonably related to the purpose for which the funds are expended is cursory and unconvincing. We have repeatedly said that Congress may condition grants under the spending power only in ways reasonably related to the purpose of the federal program. *Massachusetts v. United States, supra,* 435 U.S., at 461, 98 S.Ct., at 1164; *Ivanhoe Irrigation Dist. v. McCracken,* 357 U.S. 275, 295, 78 S.Ct. 1174, 1185, 2 L.Ed.2d 313 (1958) (the United States may impose "reasonable conditions relevant to federal interest in the project and to the over-all objectives thereof"); *Steward Machine Co. v. Davis, supra,* 301 U.S. at 590, 57 S.Ct., at 892 ("We do not say that a tax is valid, when imposed by act of Congress, if it is laid upon the condition that a state may escape its operation through the adoption of a statute unrelated in subject matter to activities fairly within the scope of national policy and power"). In my view, establishment of a minimum drinking age of 21 is not sufficiently related to interstate highway construction to justify so conditioning funds appropriated for that purpose.

In support of its contrary conclusion, the Court relies on a supposed concession by counsel for South Dakota that the State "has never contended that the congressional action was . . . unrelated to a national concern in the absence of the Twenty-first Amendment." Brief for Petitioner 52. In the absence of the Twenty-first Amendment, however, there is a strong argument that the Congress might regulate the conditions under which liquor is sold under the commerce power, just as it regulates the sale of many other commodities that are in or affect interstate commerce. The fact that the Twenty-first Amendment is crucial to the State's argument does not, therefore, amount to a concession that the condition imposed by § 158 is reasonably related to highway construction. The Court also relies on a portion of the argument transcript in support of its claim that South Dakota conceded the reasonable relationship point. *Ante,* at 2797, n. 3, citing Tr. of Oral Arg. 19-21. But counsel's statements there are at best ambiguous. Counsel essentially said no more than that he was not prepared to argue the reasonable relationship question discussed at length in the Brief for the National Conference of State Legislatures et al. as *Amicus Curiae.*

Aside from these "concessions" by counsel, the Court asserts the reasonableness of the relationship between the supposed purpose of the expenditure — "safe interstate travel" — and the drinking age condition. *Ante,* at 2797. The Court reasons that Congress wishes that the roads it builds may be used safely, that drunken drivers threaten highway safety, and that young people are more likely to drive while under the influence of alcohol under existing law than would be the case if there were a uniform national drinking age of 21. It hardly needs saying, however, that if the purpose of § 158 is to deter drunken driving, it is far too over and under-inclusive. It is over-inclusive because it stops teenagers from drinking even when they are not about to drive on interstate highways. It is under-inclusive because teenagers pose only a small part of the drunken driving problem in this Nation.

When Congress appropriates money to build a highway, it is entitled to insist that the highway be a safe one. But it is not entitled to insist as a condition of the use of highway funds that the State impose or change regulations in other areas of the State's social and economic life because of an attenuated or tangential relationship to highway use or safety. Indeed, if the rule were otherwise, the Congress could effectively regulate almost any area of a State's social, political, or economic life on the theory that use of the interstate transportation system is somehow enhanced. If, for example, the United States were to condition highway moneys upon moving the state capital, I suppose it might argue that interstate transportation is facilitated by locating local governments in places easily accessible to interstate highways — or, conversely, that highways might become overburdened if they had to carry traffic to and from the state capital. In my mind, such a relationship is hardly more attenuated than the one which the Court finds supports § 158.

There is a clear place at which the Court can draw the line between permissible and impermissible conditions on federal grants. It is the line identified in the Brief for the National Conference of State Legislatures et al. as *Amicus Curiae:* "Congress has the power to *spend* for the general welfare, it has the power to *legislate* only for delegated purposes. . . . "The appropriate inquiry, then, is whether the spending requirement or prohibition is a condition on a grant or whether it is regulation. The difference turns on whether the requirement specifies in some way how the money should be spent, so that Congress' intent in making the grant will be effectuated. Congress has no power under the Spending Clause to impose requirements on a grant that go beyond specifying how the money should be spent. A requirement that is not such a specification is not a condition, but a regulation, which is valid only if it falls within one of Congress' delegated regulatory powers." *Id.,* at 19-20.

This approach harks back to *United States v. Butler,* 297 U.S. 1, 56 S.Ct. 312, 80 L.Ed. 477 (1936), the last case in which this Court struck down an Act of Congress as beyond the authority granted by the Spending Clause. There the Court wrote that "[t]here is an obvious difference between a statute stating the conditions upon which moneys shall be expended and one effective only upon assumption of a contractual obligation to submit to a regulation which otherwise could not be enforced." *Id.,* at 73, 56 S.Ct., at 322. The *Butler* Court saw the Agricultural Adjustment Act for what it was — an exercise of regulatory, not spending, power. The error in *Butler* was not the Court's conclusion that the Act was essentially regulatory, but rather its crabbed view of the extent of Congress' regulatory power under the Commerce Clause. The Agricultural Adjustment Act was regulatory but it was regulation that today would likely be considered within Congress' commerce power. See, *e.g., Katzenbach v. McClung,* 379 U.S. 294, 85 S.Ct. 377, 13 L.Ed.2d 290 (1964); *Wickard v. Filburn,* 317 U.S. 111, 63 S.Ct. 82, 87 L.Ed. 122 (1942).

While *Butler's* authority is questionable insofar as it assumes that Congress has no regulatory power over farm production, its discussion of the spending power and its description of both the power's breadth and its limitations remain sound. The Court's decision in *Butler* also properly recognizes the gravity of the task of appropriately limiting the spending power. If the spending power is to be limited only by Congress' notion of the general welfare, the reality, given the vast financial resources of the Federal Government, is that the Spending Clause gives "power to the Congress to tear down the barriers, to invade the states' jurisdiction, and to become a parliament of the whole people, subject to no restrictions save such as are self-imposed." *United States v. Butler, supra,* 297 U.S., at 78, 56 S.Ct., at 324. This, of course, as *Butler* held, was not the Framers' plan and it is not the meaning of the Spending Clause.

Our later cases are consistent with the notion that, under the spending power, the Congress may only condition grants in ways that can fairly be said to be related to the expenditure of federal funds. [Other] conditions that have been upheld by the Court may be viewed as independently justified under some regulatory power of the Congress. This case, however, falls into neither class. As discussed above, a condition that a State will raise its drinking age to 21 cannot fairly be said to be reasonably related to the expenditure of funds for highway construction. The only possible connection, highway safety, has nothing to do with how the funds Congress has appropriated are expended. Rather than a condition determining how federal highway money shall be expended, it is a regulation determining who shall be able to drink liquor. As such it is not justified by the spending power.

Of the other possible sources of congressional authority for regulating the sale of liquor only the commerce power comes to mind. But in my view, the regulation of the age of the purchasers of liquor, just as the regulation of the price at which liquor may be sold, falls squarely within the scope of those powers reserved to the States by the Twenty-first Amendment. Accordingly, Congress simply lacks power under the Commerce Clause to displace state regulation of this kind. *Ibid.*

The immense size and power of the Government of the United States ought not obscure its fundamental character. It remains a Government of enumerated powers. *McCulloch v. Maryland,* 4 Wheat. 316, 405, 4 L.Ed. 579 (1819). Because 23 U.S.C. § 158 (1982 ed., Supp. III) cannot be justified as an exercise of any power delegated to the Congress, it is not authorized by the Constitution.

———

Comments on *Dole*. If Congress can regulate directly under the Commerce Clause, can it regulate indirectly, by granting tax exemptions or subsidies to people who meet specified conditions, under the taxing and spending clauses? Does the Court so hold in *Dole*? Note Chief Justice Rehnquist's observations about the scope of the conditional spending power: "The spending power is of course not unlimited, but is instead subject to several general restrictions. [First,] the exercise of the spending power must be in pursuit of 'the general welfare.' [Butler.] In considering whether a particular expenditure is intended to serve general public purposes, courts should defer substantially to the judgment of Congress. Second, [if] Congress desires to condition the States' receipt of federal funds, it 'must do so [unambiguously.'] Third, our cases have suggested (without significant elaboration) that conditions on federal grants might be illegitimate if they are unrelated 'to the federal interest in particular national projects or programs.' Finally, [other] constitutional provisions may provide an independent bar to the conditional grant of federal funds."

Yet, in the end, is this all about what is and what is not coercion? The Court in *Dole* finds, supported by *Steward Machine,* that at some point, "pressure turns into coercion." "[A]ll South Dakota would lose if she adheres to her chosen course as to a suitable minimum drinking age is 5% of the funds otherwise obtainable under specified highway grant programs, the argument as to coercion is shown to be more rhetoric than fact. [Here]

Congress has offered relatively mild encouragement to the States to enact higher minimum drinking ages than they would otherwise choose. [But] the enactment of such laws remains the prerogative of the States not merely in theory but in fact."

Given the broad reading of the spending power in *Dole*, is it an alternative power for Congress because of the modern limits placed on direct regulation in *Lopez* and *Morrison*? Are *New York v. United States* and *Prinz v. United States* limitations on *Dole,* or, when is coercion, coercion?

NATIONAL FEDERATION OF INDEPENDENT BUSINESS v. SEBELIUS
132 S. Ct. 2566 (2012)

Chief Justice ROBERTS announced the judgment of the Court and delivered an opinion with respect to Part IV, in which Justices BREYER and KAGAN join.

[In this excerpt from the landmark case, the Court grappled with the issue of the Medicaid Expansion provisions of the Affordable Care Act, which would have required states to increase the eligibility for the low-income medical care program to accommodate the goals of the Act in order to receive federal funding for the program under the Spending Clause.]

IV.

A.

The States [contend] that the Medicaid expansion exceeds Congress's authority under the Spending Clause. They claim that Congress is coercing the States to adopt the changes it wants by threatening to withhold all of a State's Medicaid grants, unless the State accepts the new expanded funding and complies with the conditions that come with it. This, they argue, violates the basic principle that the "Federal Government may not compel the States to enact or administer a federal regulatory program." New York v. United States [Levy, 4th ed., p. 403].

[The] Spending Clause grants Congress the power "to pay the Debts and provide for the . . . general Welfare of the United States." U.S. Const., Art. I, § 8, cl. 1. We have long recognized that Congress may use this power to grant federal funds to the States, and may condition such a grant upon the States' "taking certain actions that Congress could not require them to take." [The] conditions imposed by Congress ensure that the funds are used by the States to "provide for the . . . general Welfare" in the manner Congress intended. At the same time, our cases have recognized limits on Congress's power under the Spending Clause to secure state compliance with federal objectives. "We have repeatedly characterized . . . Spending Clause legislation as 'much in the nature of a contract.'" The legitimacy of Congress's exercise of the spending power "thus rests on whether the State voluntarily and knowingly accepts the terms of the 'contract.'" This limitation is critical to ensuring that Spending Clause legislation does not undermine the status of the States as independent sovereigns in our federal system.

That insight has led this Court [to] scrutinize Spending Clause legislation to ensure that Congress is not using financial inducements to exert a "power akin to undue influence." Steward Machine Co. v. Davis, [17th ed., p. 160]. Congress may use its spending power to create incentives for States to act in accordance with federal policies. But when "pressure turns into compulsion," the legislation runs contrary to our system of federalism. [We] addressed such concerns in Steward Machine. That case involved a federal tax on employers that was abated if the businesses paid into a state unemployment plan that met certain federally specified conditions. An employer sued, alleging that the tax was impermissibly "driv[ing] the state legislatures under the whip of economic pressure into the enactment of unemployment compensation laws at the bidding of the central government." [We] observed that Congress adopted the challenged tax and abatement program to channel money to the States that would otherwise have gone into the Federal Treasury for use in providing national unemployment services. Congress was willing to direct businesses to instead pay the money into state programs only on the condition that the money be used for the same purposes. Predicating tax abatement on a State's adoption of a particular type of unemployment legislation was therefore a means to "safeguard [the Federal Government's] own treasury." We held that "[i]n such circumstances, if in no others, inducement or persuasion does not go beyond the bounds of power." In rejecting the argument that the federal law was a "weapon[] of coercion, destroying or impairing the autonomy of the states," the Court noted that there was no reason to suppose that the State in that case acted other than through "her unfettered will."

[The States here] object that Congress has "crossed the line distinguishing encouragement from coercion" in the way it has structured the funding: Instead of simply refusing to grant the new funds to States that will not accept the new conditions, Congress has also threatened to withhold those States' existing Medicaid funds. The States claim that this threat serves no purpose other than to force unwilling States to sign up for the dramatic expansion in health care coverage effected by the Act. Given the nature of the threat and the programs at issue here, we must agree. We have upheld Congress's authority to condition the receipt of funds on the States' complying with restrictions on the use of those funds, because that is the means by which Congress ensures that the funds are spent according to its view of the "general Welfare." Conditions that do not here govern the use of the funds, however, cannot be justified on that basis. When, for example, such conditions take the form of threats to terminate other significant independent grants, the conditions are properly viewed as a means of pressuring the States to accept policy changes.

In South Dakota v. Dole [Levy 4th ed., p. 447], we considered a challenge to a federal law that threatened to withhold five percent of a State's federal highway funds if the State did not raise its drinking age to 21. The Court found that the condition was "directly related to one of the main purposes for which highway funds are expended-safe interstate travel." At the same time, the condition was not a restriction on how the highway funds — set aside for specific highway improvement and maintenance efforts — were to be used. [We] found that the inducement was not impermissibly coercive, because Congress was offering only "relatively mild encouragement to the States." We observed that "all South Dakota would lose if she adheres to her chosen course as to a suitable minimum drinking age is 5%" of her highway funds.

[In] this case, the financial "inducement" Congress has chosen is much more than "relatively mild encouragement" — it is a gun to the head. Section 1396c of the Medicaid Act provides that if a State's Medicaid plan does not comply with the Act's requirements, the Secretary of Health and Human Services may declare that "further payments will not be made to the State." A State that opts out of the [ACA's] expansion in health care coverage thus stands to lose not merely "a relatively small percentage" of its existing Medicaid funding, but all of it. Medicaid spending accounts for over 20 percent of the average State's total budget, with federal funds covering 50 to 83 percent of those costs. [It] is easy to see how the Dole Court could conclude that the threatened loss of less than half of one percent of South Dakota's budget left that State with a "prerogative" to reject

Congress's desired policy, "not merely in theory but in fact." The threatened loss of over 10 percent of a State's overall budget, in contrast, is economic dragooning that leaves the States with no real option but to acquiesce in the Medicaid expansion.

Here, the Government claims that the Medicaid expansion is properly viewed merely as a modification of the existing program because the States agreed that Congress could change the terms of Medicaid when they signed on in the first place. [The] Medicaid expansion, however, accomplishes a shift in kind, not merely degree. [It] is no longer a program to care for the neediest among us, but rather an element of a comprehensive national plan to provide universal health insurance coverage. [While] Congress may have styled the expansion a mere alteration of existing Medicaid, it recognized it was enlisting the States in a new health care program. "[Though] Congress' power to legislate under the spending power is broad, it does not include surprising participating States with post acceptance or 'retroactive' conditions." A State could hardly anticipate that Congress's reservation of the right to "alter" or "amend" the Medicaid program included the power to transform it so dramatically.

The Court in Steward Machine did not attempt to "fix the outermost line" where persuasion gives way to coercion. The Court found it "[e]nough for present purposes that wherever the line may be, this statute is within it." We have no need to fix a line either. It is enough for today that wherever that line may be, this statute is surely beyond it.

B. Nothing in our opinion precludes Congress from offering funds under the Affordable Care Act to expand the availability of health care, and requiring that States accepting such funds comply with the conditions on their use. What Congress is not free to do is to penalize States that choose not to participate in that new program by taking away their existing Medicaid funding. [In] light of the Court's holding, the Secretary cannot apply § 1396c to withdraw existing Medicaid funds for failure to comply with the requirements set out in the expansion. That fully remedies the constitutional violation we have identified. The chapter of the United States Code that contains § 1396c includes a severability clause confirming that we need go no further.

[The] question remains whether Congress would have wanted the rest of the Act to stand, had it known that States would have a genuine choice whether to participate in the new Medicaid expansion. Unless it is "evident" that the answer is no, we must leave the rest of the Act intact. We are confident that Congress would have wanted to preserve the rest of the Act. [The] Court today limits the financial pressure the Secretary may apply to induce States to accept the terms of the Medicaid expansion. [We] have no way of knowing how many States will accept the terms of the expansion, but we do not believe Congress would have wanted the whole Act to fall, simply because some may choose not to participate.

Justice GINSBURG, joined by Justice SOTOMAYOR, concurring in part, concurring in the judgment in part, and dissenting in part.

[The] Chief Justice [concludes] that the 2010 expansion is unduly coercive [because] the Medicaid expansion is [a] new grant program, not an addition to the Medicaid program existing before the ACA's enactment, [the] expansion was unforeseeable by the States when they first signed on to Medicaid, [and] the threatened loss of funding is so large that the States have no real choice but to participate in the Medicaid expansion. The Chief Justice therefore — for the first time ever — finds an exercise of Congress' spending power unconstitutionally coercive. Medicaid, as amended by the ACA, however, is not two spending programs; it is a single program with a constant aim — to enable poor persons to receive basic health care when they need it. Given past expansions, plus express statutory warning that Congress may change the requirements participating States must meet, there can be no tenable claim that the ACA fails for lack of notice. Moreover, States have no entitlement to receive any Medicaid funds; they enjoy only the opportunity to accept funds on Congress' terms. [Congress] is simply requiring States to do what States have long been required to do to receive Medicaid funding: comply with the conditions Congress prescribes for participation.

A. Expansion has been characteristic of the Medicaid program. Akin to the ACA in 2010, the Medicaid Act as passed in 1965 augmented existing federal grant programs jointly administered with the States. States were not required to participate in Medicaid. But if they did, the Federal Government paid at least half the costs. [Since] 1965, Congress has amended the Medicaid program on more than 50 occasions, sometimes quite sizably, [adding] millions to the Medicaid-eligible population. [Nor] will the expansion exorbitantly increase state Medicaid spending. The Congressional Budget Office (CBO) projects that States will spend 0.8% more than they would have, absent the ACA. Whatever the increase in state obligations after the ACA, it will pale in comparison to the increase in federal funding.

[Any] fair appraisal of Medicaid would require acknowledgment of the considerable autonomy States enjoy under the Act. Far from "conscript[ing] state agencies into the national bureaucratic army," Medicaid "is designed to advance cooperative federalism." Subject to its basic requirements, the Medicaid Act empowers States to "select dramatically different levels of funding and coverage, alter and experiment with different financing and delivery modes, and opt to cover (or not to cover) a range of particular procedures and therapies." [The] ACA does not jettison this approach. States, as first-line administrators, will continue to guide the distribution of substantial resources among their needy populations.

The alternative to conditional federal spending, it bears emphasis, is not state autonomy but state marginalization. In 1965, Congress elected to nationalize health coverage for seniors through Medicare. It could similarly have established Medicaid as an exclusively federal program. Instead, Congress gave the States the opportunity to partner in the program's administration and development. Absent from the nationalized model, of course, is the state-level policy discretion and experimentation that is Medicaid's hallmark; undoubtedly the interests of federalism are better served when States retain a meaningful role in the implementation of a program of such importance.

B. [Prior] to today's decision, [the] Court has never ruled that the terms of any grant crossed the indistinct line between temptation and coercion. [This] case does not present the concerns that led the Court in Dole even to consider the prospect of coercion. In Dole, the condition — set 21 as the minimum drinking age — did not tell the States how to use funds Congress provided for highway construction. Further, in view of the Twenty-First Amendment, it was an open question whether Congress could directly impose a national minimum drinking age. The ACA, in contrast, relates solely to the federally funded Medicaid program; if States choose not to comply, Congress has not threatened to withhold funds earmarked for any other program. Nor does the ACA use Medicaid funding to induce States to take action Congress itself could not undertake. The Federal Government undoubtedly could operate its own healthcare program for poor persons, just as it operates Medicare for seniors' health care.

C. [The] Chief Justice calls the ACA new, but in truth, it simply reaches more of America's poor than Congress originally covered. Medicaid was created to enable States to provide medical assistance to "needy persons." By bringing health care within the reach of a larger population of Americans unable to afford it, the Medicaid expansion is an extension of that basic aim. [Congress] has broad authority to construct or adjust spending programs to meet its contemporary understanding of "the general Welfare." [Consider] also that Congress could have repealed Medicaid. Thereafter, Congress could have enacted Medicaid II, a new program combining the pre–2010 coverage with the expanded coverage required by the ACA.

[The] Chief Justice finds the Medicaid expansion vulnerable because it took participating States by surprise. ["If] Congress intends to impose a condition on the grant of federal moneys, it must do so unambiguously." That requirement is met in this case. Section 2001 does not take effect until 2014. The ACA makes perfectly clear what will be required of States that accept Medicaid funding after that date: They must extend eligibility to adults with incomes no more than 133% of the federal poverty line. [Conditions] on federal funds [must] be unambiguously clear at the time a State receives and uses the money — not at the time, perhaps years earlier, when Congress passed the law establishing the program. In any event, from the start, the Medicaid Act put States on notice that the program could be changed: "The right to alter, amend, or repeal any provision of [Medicaid]," the statute has read since 1965, "is hereby reserved to the Congress." [Given] the enlargement of Medicaid in the years since 1965, a State would be hard put to complain that it lacked fair notice when, in 2010, Congress altered Medicaid to embrace a larger portion of the Nation's poor.

The Chief Justice sees no need to "fix the outermost line where persuasion gives way to coercion." Neither do the joint dissenters. [When] future Spending Clause challenges arrive, as they likely will in the wake of today's decision, how will litigants and judges assess whether "a State has a legitimate choice whether to accept the federal conditions in exchange for federal funds"? Are courts to measure the number of dollars the Federal Government might withhold for noncompliance? The portion of the State's budget at stake? And which State's — or States' — budget is determinative: the lead plaintiff, all challenging States (26 in this case, many with quite different fiscal situations), or some national median? Does it matter that Florida, unlike most States, imposes no state income tax, and therefore might be able to replace foregone federal funds with new state revenue? Or that the coercion state officials in fact fear is punishment at the ballot box for turning down a politically popular federal grant? [The] coercion inquiry, therefore, appears to involve political judgments that defy judicial calculation.

D. [The Chief Justice] holds that the Constitution precludes the Secretary from withholding "existing" Medicaid funds based on States' refusal to comply with the expanded Medicaid program. For the foregoing reasons, I disagree that any such withholding would violate the Spending Clause. But in view of The Chief Justice's disposition, I agree with him that the Medicaid Act's severability clause determines the appropriate remedy. [I] therefore concur in the judgment with respect to Part IV-B of The Chief Justice's opinion.

Justices SCALIA, KENNEDY, THOMAS, and ALITO, dissenting.

IV. [The] ACA does not legally compel the States to participate in the expanded Medicaid program, but the Act authorizes a severe sanction for any State that refuses to go along: termination of all the State's Medicaid funding. For the average State, the annual federal Medicaid subsidy is equal to more than one-fifth of the State's expenditures. A State forced out of the program would not only lose this huge sum but would almost certainly find it necessary to increase its own health-care expenditures substantially, requiring either a drastic reduction in funding for other programs or a large increase in state taxes. And these new taxes would come on top of the federal taxes already paid by the State's citizens to fund the Medicaid program in other States.

[When] Congress makes grants to the States, it customarily attaches conditions. [This] practice of attaching conditions to federal funds greatly increases federal power. "[O]bjectives not thought to be within Article I's enumerated legislative fields, may nevertheless be attained through the use of the spending power and the conditional grant of federal funds." Dole. This formidable power, if not checked in any way, would present a grave threat to the system of federalism created by our Constitution. If Congress' "Spending Clause power to pursue objectives outside of Article I's enumerated legislative fields," is "limited only by Congress' notion of the general welfare, the reality, given the vast financial resources of the Federal Government, is that the Spending Clause gives 'power to the Congress to tear down the barriers, to invade the states' jurisdiction, and to become a parliament of the whole people, subject to no restrictions save such as are self-imposed,'" Dole (O'Connor, J., dissenting) (quoting Butler).

[The] legitimacy of attaching conditions to federal grants to the States depends on the voluntariness of the States' choice to accept or decline the offered package. Therefore, if States really have no choice other than to accept the package, the offer is coercive, and the conditions cannot be sustained under the spending power. And as our decision in South Dakota v. Dole makes clear, theoretical voluntariness is not enough. [The] Federal Government's argument in this case at best pays lip service to the anticoercion principle. The Federal Government suggests that it is sufficient if States are "free, as a matter of law, to turn down" federal funds. [This] argument ignores reality. When a heavy federal tax is levied to support a federal program that offers large grants to the States, States may, as a practical matter, be unable to refuse to participate in the federal program and to substitute a state alternative. Even if a State believes that the federal program is ineffective and inefficient, withdrawal would likely force the State to impose a huge tax increase on its residents, and this new state tax would come on top of the federal taxes already paid by residents to support subsidies to participating States.

[The] dimensions of the Medicaid program lend strong support to the petitioner States' argument that refusing to accede to the conditions set out in the ACA is not a realistic option. [Medicaid] has long been the largest federal program of grants to the States. In 2010, the Federal Government directed more than $552 billion in federal funds to the States. Of this, more than $233 billion went to pre-expansion Medicaid. This amount equals nearly 22% of all state expenditures combined. [The] States devote a larger percentage of their budgets to Medicaid than to any other item. Federal funds account for anywhere from 50% to 83% of each State's total Medicaid expenditures; most States receive more than $1 billion in federal Medicaid funding; and a quarter receive more than $5 billion. These federal dollars total nearly two thirds [of] all Medicaid expenditures nationwide. [The] sheer size of this federal spending program in relation to state expenditures means that a State would be very hard pressed to compensate for the loss of federal funds by cutting other spending or raising additional revenue. [The] States are far less reliant on federal funding for any other program.

For these reasons, the offer that the ACA makes to the States — go along with a dramatic expansion of Medicaid or potentially lose all federal Medicaid funding — is quite unlike anything that we have seen in a prior spending-power case. In South Dakota v. Dole, the total amount that the States would have lost if every single State had refused to comply with the 21-year-old drinking age was approximately $614 million — or about 0.19% of all state expenditures combined. South Dakota stood to lose, at most, funding that amounted to less than 1% of its annual state expenditures. Under the ACA, by contrast, the Federal Government has threatened to withhold 42.3% of all federal outlays to the states, or approximately $233 billion. South Dakota stands to lose federal funding equaling 28.9% of its annual state expenditures. Withholding $614.7 million, equaling only 0.19% of all state expenditures combined, is aptly characterized as "relatively mild encouragement," but threatening to withhold $233 billion, equaling 21.86% of all state expenditures combined, is a different matter.

What the statistics suggest is confirmed by the goal and structure of the ACA. In crafting the ACA, Congress clearly expressed its informed view that no State could possibly refuse the offer that the ACA extends. The stated goal of the ACA is near-universal health care coverage. [If] Congress had thought that States might actually refuse to go along with the expansion of Medicaid, Congress would surely have devised a backup scheme so that the most vulnerable groups in our society, those previously eligible for Medicaid, would not be left out in the cold. But nowhere in the over 900-page Act is such a scheme to be found. [In sum,] it is perfectly clear from the goal and structure of the ACA that the offer of the Medicaid Expansion was one that Congress understood no State could refuse. The Medicaid Expansion therefore exceeds Congress' spending power and cannot be implemented.

Seven Members of the Court agree that the Medicaid Expansion, as enacted by Congress, is unconstitutional. Because the Medicaid Expansion is unconstitutional, the question of remedy arises. The most natural remedy would be to invalidate the Medicaid Expansion. [We] should not accept the Government's invitation to attempt to solve a constitutional problem by rewriting the Medicaid Expansion so as to allow States that reject it to retain their pre-existing Medicaid funds.

The Affordable Care Act and the Revival of Limits on the Spending Power. In the twenty-five years following *Dole*, the Court never found that a condition on the expenditure of federal funds exceeded Congress's spending power by being impermissibly coercive or otherwise intruding upon the role of the states in the federalist system. That changed in the challenge to the Medicaid expansion provision of the Patient Protection and Affordable Care Act of 2010 (ACA) in the excerpt from *N.F.I.B v. Sebelius* above. By now you have noticed that the dissenters, Scalia, Thomas, Alito, and Kennedy, dissented with regard to this and the Commerce Clause portions of the opinion with reasoning not terribly different from Chief Justice Roberts's opinion. The only difference here has to do with the remedy—the conservative dissenters would have denied the Government's request to sever the offending coercive characteristics of the expansion provision of the bill whereas the Chief Justice allowed that portion to be severed from the bill, allowing the Medicaid expansion to proceed but without the mandatory acceptance by the states. Only in their Tax Clause dissent did the dissenters actually depart from the core reasoning in the Chief Justice's holding.

B. THE WAR AND TREATY POWERS

1. THE WAR POWER

"The war power to wage . . . is a power to wage war successfully." *Home Building & Loan Ass'n v. Blaisdell*, 290 U.S. 398, 426, (1934). Is this a pseudonym for the case that follows?

WOODS v. MILLER CO.
333 U.S. 138 (1948)

[The Supreme Court upheld the constitutionality of the Housing and Rent Act of 1947, which froze rents at their wartime levels. It concluded that "the war power sustains this legislation." Even though the President had declared hostilities terminated on December 31, 1946, before the statute was enacted, "the war power does not necessarily end with the cessation of hostilities." When Congress acted, there was a deficit in housing that, in considerable measure, was caused by the heavy demobilization of veterans and by the cessation or reduction in residential construction during the period of hostilities due to the allocation of building materials to military projects. Since the war effort contributed heavily to that deficit, Congress had the power even after the cessation of hostilities to act to control the forces that a short supply of the needed article created.]

Mr. Justice DOUGLAS delivered the opinion of the Court.

We recognize the force of the argument that the effects of war under modern conditions may be felt in the economy for years and years, and that if the war power can be used in days of peace to treat all the wounds which war inflicts on our society, it may not only swallow up all other powers of Congress but largely obliterate the Ninth and Tenth Amendments as well. There are no such implications in today's decision. We deal here with the consequences of a housing deficit greatly intensified during the period of hostilities by the war effort. Any power, of course, can be abused. But we cannot assume that Congress is not alert to its constitutional responsibilities. And the question whether the war power has been properly employed in cases such as this is open to judicial inquiry.

The question of the constitutionality of action taken by Congress does not depend on recitals of the power which it undertakes to exercise. Here it is plain from the legislative history that Congress was invoking its war power to cope with a current condition of which the war was a direct and immediate cause.

Justice JACKSON, concurring.

[He expressed "misgivings" about "this vague, undefined and indefinable 'war power.'"]

No one will question that this power is the most dangerous one to free government in the whole catalogue of powers. It is usually invoked in haste and excitement when calm legislative consideration of constitutional limitation is difficult. It is executed in a time of patriotic fervor that makes moderation unpopular. And, worst of all, it is interpreted by judges under the influence of the same passions and pressures. Always, [the] Government urges hasty decision to forestall some emergency or serve some purposes and pleads that paralysis will result if its claims to power are denied or their confirmation delayed.

Particularly when the war power is invoked to do things to the liberties of people, or to their property or economy that only indirectly affect conduct of the war and do not relate to the management of the war itself, the constitutional basis should be scrutinized with care. [The] present state of war [was not] merely technical, and the statute [is] constitutional.

---

2. THE TREATY POWER

Article II, § 2, of the Constitution allocates to the President the power to negotiate treaties, subject to the "Advice and Consent" of the Senate by a two-thirds vote. Once the Senate has concurred with a treaty negotiated by the Executive, the Supreme Court has held that it takes its place as "Supreme Law of the Land" with the same effect as the Constitution and laws of the United States.

In the case that follows, the Supreme Court faced the question as to whether or not it was possible for the government to proceed with, and bind the states to, a treaty whose subject matter had previously been held beyond the law-making powers granted to Congress.

MISSOURI v. HOLLAND
252 U.S. 416 (1920)

Mr. Justice HOLMES delivered the opinion of the court.

This is a bill in equity brought by the State of Missouri to prevent a game warden of the United States from attempting to enforce the Migratory Bird Treaty Act of 1918 and the regulations made by the Secretary of Agriculture in pursuance of the same. The ground of the bill is that the statute is an unconstitutional interference with the rights reserved to the States by the Tenth Amendment, and that the acts of the defendant done and threatened under that authority invade the sovereign right of the State and contravene its will manifested in statutes. . . .

On December 8, 1916, a treaty between the United States and Great Britain was proclaimed by the President. It recited that many species of birds in their annual migrations traversed certain parts of the United States and of Canada, that they were of great value as a source of food and in destroying insects injurious to vegetation, but were in danger of extermination through lack of adequate protection. It therefore provided for specified close seasons [and] agreed that the two powers would take or propose to their law-making bodies the necessary measures for carrying the treaty out. [The act] prohibited the killing, capturing or selling any of the migratory birds included in the terms of the treaty except as permitted by regulations [to] be made by the Secretary of Agriculture. . .

[It] is not enough to refer to the Tenth Amendment, reserving the powers not delegated to the United States, because by Article II, §2, the power to make treaties is delegated expressly, and by Article VI treaties made under the authority of the United States [are] declared the supreme law of the land. If the treaty is valid there can be no dispute about the validity of the statute under Article I, §8, as a necessary and proper means to execute the powers of the Government. . . .

It is said that a treaty cannot be valid if it infringes the Constitution, that there are limits, therefore, to the treaty-making power, and that one such limit is that what an act of

Congress could not do unaided, in derogation of the powers reserved to the States, a treaty cannot do. An earlier act of Congress that attempted by itself and not in pursuance of a treaty to regulate the killing of migratory birds within the States had been held bad in the District Court. . . .

Whether the [cases] were decided rightly or not they cannot be accepted as a test of the treaty power. Acts of Congress are the supreme law of the land only when made in pursuance of the Constitution, while treaties are declared to be so when made under the authority of the United States. It is open to question whether the authority of the United States means more than the formal acts prescribed to make the convention. We do not mean to imply that there are no qualifications to the treaty-making power; but they must be ascertained in a different way. It is obvious that there may be matters of the sharpest exigency for the national well being that an act of Congress could not deal with but that a treaty followed by such an act could, and it is not lightly to be assumed that, in matters requiring national action, "a power which must belong to and somewhere reside in every civilized government" is not to be found. [When] we are dealing with words that also are a constituent act, like the Constitution of the United States, we must realize that they have called into life a being the development of which could not have been foreseen completely by the most gifted of its begetters. It was enough for them to realize or to hope that they had created an organism; it has taken a century and has cost their successors much sweat and blood to prove that they created a nation. The case before us must be considered in the light of our whole experience and not merely in that of what was said a hundred years ago. The treaty in question does not contravene any prohibitory words to be found in the Constitution. The only question is whether it is forbidden by some invisible radiation from the general terms of the Tenth Amendment. We must consider what this country has become in deciding what that Amendment has reserved. . . .

Here a national interest of very nearly the first magnitude is involved. It can be protected only by national action in concert with that of another power. The subject matter is only transitorily within the State and has no permanent habitat therein. But for the treaty and the statute there soon might be no birds for any powers to deal with. We see nothing in the Constitution that compels the Government to sit by while a food supply is cut off and the protectors of our forests and our crops are destroyed. It is not sufficient to rely upon the States. The reliance is vain, and were it otherwise, the question is whether the United States is forbidden to act. We are of opinion that the treaty and statute must be upheld.

Affirmed.

Mr. Justice Van Devanter and Mr. Justice Pitney dissent.

Comments on *Holland*. Though the Court held that the treaty in question did "not contravene any prohibitory words . . . in the Constitution," they did state that "[i]t is obvious that there may be matters of the sharpest exigency for the national well-being that an act of Congress could not deal with but that a treaty followed by such an act could, and it is not lightly to be assumed that, in matters requiring national action, 'a power which must belong to and somewhere reside in every civilized government'" is not to be found." Consequently, under the urgency of foreign affairs, the government may well act through a treaty where a statute would not suffice.

What is the "different way" that federalism-based limits on the treaty power are to be ascertained? Is it "different" in light of the commerce clause doctrine in 1920? "Different" in light of today's Commerce Clause doctrine? Can courts determine what are "matters requiring national action" by treaty followed by legislation, rather than by legislation alone? How likely is the President to negotiate and the Senate to ratify a treaty on a matter not requiring national action in Holmes's sense? What different issues would arise had the treaty been "self-executing," that is, had the treaty, as a matter of U.S. law, not required implementing legislation in order to impose legally enforceable obligations on Americans? How would the political process differ?

MEDELLÍN v. TEXAS, 552 U.S. 491 (2008). In 2004, the International Court of Justice (ICJ) ruled that the United States violated the Vienna Convention when state authorities did not give Medellín (and 50 other Mexican nationals) information about their Vienna Convention rights to have their consulates notified of their arrest. This violation, the ICJ said, entitled the detainees to have their convictions and sentences reviewed, notwithstanding any other state or federal law that might normally bar review. *Sanchez-Llamas v. Oregon*, 548 U.S. 331 (2006), issued after the ICI ruling (but involving individuals who were not named in the ICI judgment), held that, contrary to the ICJ's determination, the Convention did not preclude the application of state procedural default rules. President Bush then issued a Presidential Memorandum stating that the United States would "discharge its international obligations" under the ICI ruling "by having State courts give effect to the decision" in "cases filed by the 51 Mexican nationals addressed in that decision." Relying on the ICI ruling and the President's Memorandum, Medellín filed a second state habeas corpus application, which the state courts dismissed, concluding that neither the ICI judgment nor the President's Memorandum was binding federal law that could displace the state's limitations on filing successive habeas corpus applications. The Court (7 to 2) agreed. Relying on *Foster v. Neilson*, the Court concluded that the treaty and ICI judgment are not self-executing. Chief Justice Roberts, for the Court, agreed that the ICJ decision creates an "international law obligation," but an ICJ decision under the Vienna Convention on Consular Relations does not automatically become binding federal law that is judicially enforceable in any U.S. court. Indeed, Roberts pointed out, 171 nations are parties to the Vienna Convention, and none of them treat ICI judgments as binding in their domestic courts. The President's Memorandum does not change that. "The responsibility for transforming an international obligation arising from a non-self-executing treaty into domestic law falls to Congress." Justice Stevens concurred in the judgment. Justice Breyer, joined by Justices Souter and Ginsburg, dissented.

IV. STATE REGULATION AND THE NATIONAL ECONOMY: THE DORMANT COMMERCE CLAUSE

United States Constitution, Article I Section 8: "To regulate Commerce with foreign Nations, and among the several States, and with the Indian Tribes."

A. INTRODUCTION

You will recall from the previous materials the discussion on the use of the federal legislative power pursuant to the Commerce Clause. There, you learned that the authority to regulate commerce enumerated in the Constitution touched on a variety of issues having to do specifically with the role of the Congress in regulating commercial activity. The central issue in those cases had to do with whether congressional exercise of the commerce power interfered with state authority within state borders.

Implicit in that discussion is the question of whether the alternative to congressional regulation would be state regulation. In other words, if Congress is prevented from regulating certain commercial activity that occurs within the borders of the states, is this because of a verbatim reading of the Commerce Clause, stressing the language "among the several states" as a limiting term, or because the scheme of our government relies on a division of responsibility between the states and the federal government? Consider the language of the Supreme Court in *Schecter Poultry Corp. v. United States:* "But the authority of the federal government may not be pushed to such an extreme as to destroy the distinction, which the commerce clause itself establishes, between commerce 'among the several States' and the internal concerns of a State." 295 U.S. 495 at 550.

What are the internal concerns of a state that Chief Justice Hughes spoke of in *Schecter*? What is the constitutional basis for the above statement? The Chief Justice stated at an earlier point in the opinion, referring to the federal government's argument that the federal assertion of power was needed due to the economic crisis of the times, that "[s]uch assertions of extra-constitutional authority were anticipated and precluded by the explicit terms of the Tenth Amendment. The powers not delegated to the United States by the Constitution, nor prohibited by it to the States, are reserved to the States respectively, or to the people." *Id.* at 529.

These powers reserved for the states are frequently called police powers, which is another way of describing that body of state laws that regulate matters within its concern, both geographically and jurisdictionally. The only reference to so-called police powers is in this quoted language from the Tenth Amendment. Yet the language conceptualizes the nature of our federal system — a division of authority between the federal government and the states.

To some, at best the Tenth Amendment merely refers to a limitation on the federal government. It has been argued that if there is to be a limitation on the states that limitation would have to be inferred from other parts of the Constitution, or from conclusions based on various interpretations of the Constitution. Certainly there is nothing specific in the Commerce Clause that suggests a limitation on the state regulation of interstate commerce. Nonetheless, a limitation on state power over commerce has been read into the clause. This limitation has been given a name, as if to describe actual language in the document. The Dormant Commerce Clause, or as some refer to it, the Negative Commerce Clause, is not a clause at all. It is the conclusion drawn by Supreme Court Justices as far back as the 19th century that states are limited in their dealings with internal commercial matters only to the extent that those dealings do not interfere with interstate commerce.

So, what is the Dormant Commerce Clause? Under the clause, the court invalidates some protectionist or burdensome state legislation even in areas where Congress is silent. Where Congress passes legislation regulating an activity, whether or not commercial, the doctrine of pre-emption prohibits state activity that conflicts with the legislation, or interferes with the field in which Congress has legislated on the theory that Congress by its action has staked out its ground. The Dormant Commerce Clause takes this notion of congressional prerogative a step further. Even where Congress has been silent with regard to an area of interstate commercial activity, authority over that area is limited to Congress, and states may not regulate to the extent that such regulation interferes with interstate commerce.

The reason for this remarkable limitation has been explained as a means to prevent states from engaging in destructive trade wars in areas that would affect the national commerce. [See Comment, "The American Common Market," below.] So the solution arrived at over time is that certain areas, because of the nature of their effect on interstate commerce, should, if regulated at all, be regulated solely by the Congress. As such, this is the converse of the controversy outlined in the 10th Amendment debate earlier, where the question was how far can the federal government dip into the state area. The rhetorical answer was, as far as the implied powers allow. But in the ambit of the Dormant Commerce Clause, the states do not have anything analogous to the implied powers, or powers necessary and proper for implementing its authorized powers. At one time, it was believed by some members of the Supreme Court that it was possible to interpret the Commerce Clause as to carving out an area of concurrent power to regulate the flow of commerce. Yet, that view has been discarded to allow a limited role for the states, allowing them to engage in matters of state preeminence, such as health or safety regulation, even over subjects of interstate commerce. But the states do not have a constitutional, philosophical, or political science rationale for dipping into the area of federal pre-eminence — the actual regulation of commercial activity among the several states.

But the key question in the cases is how is this area of state prohibition covered by the Dormant Commerce Clause properly articulated.

1. COMMENT: THE AMERICAN COMMON MARKET

In *Hughes v. Alexandria Scrap Corp.*, 426 U.S. 794 (1976), the Supreme Court offered an economic description of the national economy within the federal system: "[t]he argument starts from the premise, well established by the history of the Commerce Clause, that this Nation is a common market in which state lines cannot be made barriers to the free flow of both raw materials and finished goods in response to the economic laws of supply and demand."

By attaching the Commerce Clause in both its overt and dormant aspects to the economic concept of common market, the Court opened a wide theoretical basis for understanding the reasons a Dormant Commerce Clause is needed. However, economic theory alone does not justify the invocation of legal doctrine. Justices Scalia and Thomas do not accept the notion of a Dormant Commerce Clause, and no doubt would not be persuaded by the economic theory of common market, preferring to rely on textual sources for their understanding of the Commerce Clause. On the other hand, the history of trade wars between the several states during the period of the Articles of Confederation do suggest that the constitutional framers had in mind a halt to state economic self-interest in contravention of national economic goals when they were drafting the new Constitution.

Whatever the history or proper interpretation of the Commerce Clause, the economic theory behind common markets may be helpful in understanding and critiquing the approaches taken by the Supreme Court in Dormant Commerce Clause cases.

Economics and History of Common Markets. In addition to being the first republic to experiment with a written constitution and a federal system of sovereign states, the United States was also among the first grouping of states to engage in what is known as economic integration. Economic integration is the larger term to describe a variety of economic schemes where the economies of various states are interwoven at different levels depending upon the type of economic goals desired by the parties. A common market is a kind of economic integration arrangement. When a common market is formed, members agree not to engage in discrimination of any kind against the products, services, and economic activity of another member state. A central goal of a common market is free flow of goods, labor, and capital across state borders.[1] The principal anticipated result from the formation of a common market is to enlarge access to productive capacities and opportunities. Another kind of economic arrangement is the customs union, where each member nation has the same tariff policies affecting goods from non-member states.[2] A common market is distinguished from a customs union in this respect: where a customs union allows free trade in goods among state units who share the same trade policies towards the goods of non-member states, a common market has the same attributes of a customs union, but also allows labor services, and other economic factors including capital originating in one member state to do cross the border of a fellow common market member. An economic union has the same characteristics as a common market, but also requires harmonization of national economic and social (labor laws for example) policies so that each member nation is not at a disadvantage because of macroeconomic policy differences affecting traded goods and services.[3] Finally total economic integration is an economic union that also *unifies* monetary policy, fiscal policy, and social economic policy.[4] Where an economic union requires that national policies are harmonized so that however a nation chooses to accomplish a goal, each nation must reach the same result, a unification of policies results in economic policy decisions being made from a central authority.

The purpose of all of this is so that firms can have larger markets to take advantage of and can utilize the natural resources and labor pools of any state in the economic integration to enlarge its business activity, individuals can have access to available employment wherever it can be found, while at the same time being able to rely on common economic policies so that each firm and each individual stands on equal footing economically regardless of where business is conducted or employment is sought within the integration setting. Such economic freedom is believed to create opportunities for economies of scale enhancing the international competitiveness of the market's industrial, manufacturing, agriculture, and services sectors.[5]

Consider the United States and the labor pool, for example. If past trends hold, most students reading this will take the bar and practice in the state of their legal education. But because there are no impediments to considering jobs in other states, many students will accept positions away from their state of legal education and take the bar there. On the other hand, a decision to take the bar and practice in say, Canada or Mexico will be fraught with significant barriers. Because the United States is essentially an advanced form of economic integration, the legal labor pool is said to be mobile.

---

[1] BELA BELASSA, THE THEORY OF ECONOMIC INTEGRATION 2 (1961).

[2] *Id.*

[3] *Id.*

[4] *Id.*

[5] In his classic work on customs unions, economist Jacob Viner suggests that the idea that customs unions would produce economies of scale is oversold. This orthodox economic theory consists of comparing trade creation and trade diverting effects of a regional integration scheme. Under orthodox analysis, the regional integration is a valid strategy only if the economic effect would be to create trade where none existed before. Viner offers the rationale that customs unions may cause the diversion of trade in less expensive goods in favor of more expensive goods produced within a customs union. JACOB VINER, THE CUSTOMS UNION ISSUE, Chapter IV, *The Economics of Customs Unions* (1950) in Miraslav Jovanovic, INTERNATIONAL ECONOMIC INTEGRATION: THEORY AND MEASUREMENT 169 (1998).

Since the end of the Second World War, economic integration has been the foreign policy of preference and choice among nation-states from Europe, to Africa, Latin America, and Asia.[6] The European Union is an economic union comprised of 27 nation states that have a harmonized market policy in commerce in goods, services, monetary affairs, social, and a single currency. In Africa, the African Union is at the beginning stages of forming what leaders there anticipate will become as cohesive a single market as the European effort has become. In North America, the United States, Mexico, and Canada have formed an elementary example of economic integration. Originally known as the North American Free Trade Agreement, it was renegotiated and went into effect as the United States Mexico Canada Agreement (USMCA). Under the USMCA, goods and some services are allowed to flow freely through the national borders of the three countries. However, the USMCA is not nearly the massive and comprehensive economic integration seen in Europe. Falling short of the requisites of a customs union, each of the three USMCA states have their own tariff and trade policies regarding non-USMCA nations.[7]

Because judges and constitutional and historical commentators have termed the American economic experience as a common market, the term will continue to be used here. However, the American version of economic integration is really a hybrid somewhere between an economic union and total integration. The U.S. states have, for example, a common monetary policy — none, as the Constitution denies the states the authority to mint or coin money, and implicitly to have any control over the money supply. The Constitution opts instead to delegate this power to the central government. The Constitution also denies states the authority to engage in separate trade policies with other nations.

On the other hand, due to our nation's concept of federalism, not all economic policy authority is removed from state hands. States may continue to regulate corporations, have state tax policies, regulate industry and banking, all within constitutional limits that will be studied in this chapter. The result, because of our notions of federalism, is a partial, not total economic integration with key economic regulatory authority remaining with the states.

This kind of federal nation requires extraordinary measures to keep the federal units, the states, from engaging in economic warfare against each other, as was the case during the period governed by the Articles of Confederation.[8] Indeed, the principal purpose for establishing the Constitution was to "form a more perfect union," and among the imperfections of the Union under the Articles of Confederation, if not the primary imperfection, was the multitude of ruinous economic policies setting states against each other.[9] The economic chaos resulted from the failure of the drafters of the Articles to include a central authority over national commerce. The new Constitution of 1789 was designed in large part to solve this problem. Given that the competition among states for economic advantage was the principal reason the Constitutional Convention of 1787 was called in the first place, it should be obvious that some sort of limitation on the ability of

---

[6] BELASSA, supra note 1, at 3-4.

[7] Jackson, *Social Policy Harmonization and Worker Rights in the European Union: A Model for North America?* 21 N.C. J. Int'l L. & Comm. Reg. 3 n.4 (1995).

[8] Indeed, Belassa describes similar economic dislocation within Europe during the interwar years between World Wars I and II. The sort of economic competition among states created the impetus for economic integration with in Europe following World War II. BELASSA, supra note 1, at 5.

[9] Nowak Sixth Ed. 4.3.

states to compete against other states was intended to be part of the Constitution by the framers.

B. THE AMERICAN COMMON MARKET AS SEEN IN THE CONSTITUTION AND SUPREME COURT DECISIONS

1. CONSTITUTIONAL PROVISIONS

The Commerce Clause may be the primary example of the intent of the framers to create a conflict-free common market among the states, but other provisions in the Constitution exemplify this goal as well. While giving Congress the power to lay "[D]uties and [E]xcises" that are "uniform throughout the United States,"[10] the Constitution also disempowers the states from exercising similar authority with regard to internal and international commerce, except as necessary, with regard to the latter, to fund inspection obligations for incoming products.[11] Other commercial and economic policies made exclusive to the federal government include a uniform bankruptcy law[12] and monetary policy.[13]

The Commerce Clause covers a wide variety of economic activity, the breadth of which, as was demonstrated in the previous section, depends upon what the Supreme Court is calling commerce at any given moment in history. While the Constitution does express limitations on the regulatory authority of states in the areas mentioned above, it does not express similar limitations with regard to general commercial activity. This has led dissenters from the concept of a Dormant Commerce Clause to conclude that such limitation was not intended by the framers. In other words, according to the dissent, where the framers wanted to limit the states' authority in economic matters, they said so in express provisions of the Constitution. The dormancy of the negative Commerce Clause suggests that the framers never intended to restrict state authority over commercial regulation, at least not through the Commerce Clause.[14]

Nonetheless, the prevalent view is that the Commerce Clause does in fact include a negative component. Lest states be allowed to restrict, or even embargo goods or other economic activity from other regions of the country, an interpretation that prevents such discrimination is clearly in keeping with the needs of a common market.

Most of the substance of the Commerce Clause, in either its positive or dormant states, has been developed through case law, as the clause is a scant seventeen words. Other economic integration settings have settled once and for all the kind of internal economic intercourse that will be allowed by detailed provisions in their governing documents. For

---

[10] Art. I, § 8, cl. 1.

[11] At Art. I, § 9, cl. 5, the Constitution prohibits states from taxing or applying a duty on exports. Artcle I, § 10, prohibits states from laying "any [i]mpost or [d]uties on [i]mports or [e]xports, except what may be absolutely necessary for executing its inspection laws, without Congressional consent.

[12] Art. I, § 8, cl. 4.

[13] Art. I, § 8, cl. 5, empowers the Congress in this area. Art. I, § 10, cl. 1, prohibits the states from coining money or providing bills of credit, or otherwise altering the nature of legal tender for paying debts.

[14] In Camps Newfound/Owatonna Inc v. Town of Harrison Maine, 520 U.S. 564 (1997), Justice Thomas, in dissent, argued that the Import Export clause is the appropriate place to limit state imposition of duties on articles from other states. His basis was that the terms "imports" and "exports" as understood in the eighteenth century and in the several states referred to trade between the states as well as other nations. Justice Thomas's position would limit the prohibition to the actual imposition of duties. Other forms of commercial regulation, even to the extent such regulation would discriminate, would be allowed.

example, the European Union has over nearly 80 articles devoted directly to economic management and guidelines for member state economic harmonization.[15] Among those rules are provisions prohibiting restrictions entry of member state goods, capital, services and labor.[16] In other words, under the rules of the European Union, states may not impede economic trade and intercourse within the union either by discriminatory or burdensome measures.

2. SUPREME COURT DECISIONS

As will be demonstrated in more detail in part D the court opinions based on the Dormant Commerce Clause have fairly consistently issued rulings facilitating the creation and maintenance of an economic integration scheme. For example, the Court has frequently found that any type of discrimination violates the Dormant Commerce Clause unless a legitimate state purpose cannot be achieved any other way. Similar to the specific provisions of the treaty governing the European Union, these cases assure that economic activity of one state can flow unimpeded to another state by duties or taxes imposed by the receiving state, whether discriminatorily applied, or simply burdensome on the free flow. In the case of discriminatory state policies designed to benefit in state economic activity, the Court has also found that services, such as landfill services, should remain available to any generator of waste regardless of state of origin.[17] Again, as a single economic unit, these decisions ensure that one state is not more burdened by the lack of access to landfill services than a state with adequate landfill capacity.

Discrimination can also take the form of measures designed to make it more difficult for out-of-state goods and services to sell or do business in the receiving state. A minimum price for a product set by a receiving state that is above the wholesale price for that same product from a neighboring state undercuts the benefit in the form of lower prices for the receiving state consumer market that the out-of-state producer is entitled to receive because he or she was able to achieve certain levels of efficiency in production processes. Such programs violate the Dormant Commerce Clause. This is true even though it is also possible that out-of-state products might be priced lower because of subsidization from the home state, allowing the exportation to the receiving state at lower cost (and hence lower prices in the latter market). In addition, producers in the producing state could engage in anti-competitive activity designed to artificially and temporarily lower prices to undercut prices in the receiving state. Though the latter practice may be actionable in anti-trust law, and both practices would, under international trade law, invite legal retaliation on the part of the receiving state in the form of anti-dumping and countervailing duties, the Dormant Commerce Clause forbids states from any retaliatory action, such as placing either a pricing restriction or a tax on those out-of-state products. Such a policy is inconsistent with the competitive goals of economic integration and is routinely prohibited in other economic integration schemes worldwide.[18]

---

[15] Treaty Establishing the European Economic Community Articles 30-109.

[16] *Id.* at pts. 2.1 and 2.3.

[17] *City of Philadelphia v. New Jersey*, 437 U.S. 617 (1978), (Chapter 2).

[18] A state's subsidization policy that encourages the importation to other states of lower priced goods and services are generally prohibited or subject to tight controls in other unions and common markets. Outside of economic integration agreements, national subsidization policies can subject local goods to countervailing duties in international markets. In the United States, however, a state's subsidization policy is considered an appropriate prerogative of state lawmakers. Concerns emanating from the Tenth Amendment are, under the Constitution, more protective of state sovereignty in this area than general principles of national sovereignty

In addition to invalidating state laws that discriminate against the economic interests of other states, the Supreme Court has also ruled that even absent discrimination, state measures that burden the free flow of economic activity violates the clause if that burden is not offset by superior benefits to the state resulting from the measure.[19] Hence, even if the economic activity of the legislating state are treated in the same manner as out-of-state activity, that measure may still have to pass constitutional muster. Hence, traffic safety regulations affecting commercial drivers from other states were found to be invalid despite the universality of coverage because of limited to non-existent safety benefits, and that investment restrictions that affect in-state and out-of-state takeover efforts was burdensome on interstate commerce.[20] The cases of this sort demonstrate that, at least in the Supreme Court's view, non-discriminatory yet burdensome regulation interferes with the common market as is the case with outright discrimination.

C. DEVELOPMENT OF THE DORMANT COMMERCE CLAUSE

1. EARLY CASES

The idea that the Commerce Clause has a dormant aspect was not one that was immediately understood. The concept of dormancy — that Congress's pre-eminence in the area of the actual regulation of commerce was protected even in Congress's silence — was developed in the nineteenth century by the Court. As the first case below indicates, questions about the exclusivity of the congressional power, what exclusivity meant, the relation between that power and the reservation of authority still held by the states, and whether the states may exercise their own legitimate power even where the Congress's authority over commerce might be impacted were addressed, though not always clearly and absolutely.

The next case, *Gibbons v. Ogden*, was presented in the previous section on the Commerce Clause for the purpose of demonstrating the early Court's approach to the meaning of interstate commerce. This excerpt demonstrates how Chief Justice Marshall addressed the power of states vis-à-vis the power of the federal government to regulate commerce.

GIBBONS v. OGDEN
22 U.S. 1 (1824)

[See section II.A for background.]

Mr. Chief Justice MARSHALL delivered the opinion of the Court, and, after stating the case, proceeded as follows:

. . . The words are, "Congress shall have power to regulate commerce with foreign nations, and among the several States, and with the Indian tribes." . . .

The subject to which the power is next applied is to commerce "among the several States." The word "among" means intermingled with. A thing which is among others is

---

under international law.
[19] See Chapter 2, infra.
[20] *Edgar v. Mite Corp.*, 457 U.S. 624 (1982).

intermingled with them. Commerce among the States cannot stop at the external boundary line of each State, but may be introduced into the interior. . . .

The power of Congress, then, comprehends navigation, within the limits of every State in the Union, so far as that navigation may be in any manner connected with "commerce with foreign nations, or among the several States, or with the Indian tribes." It may, of consequence, pass the jurisdictional line of New York and act upon the very waters to which the prohibition now under consideration applies.

But it has been urged with great earnestness that, although the power of Congress to regulate commerce with foreign nations and among the several States be coextensive with the subject itself, and have no other limits than are prescribed in the Constitution, yet the States may severally exercise the same power, within their respective jurisdictions. In support of this argument, it is said that they possessed it as an inseparable attribute of sovereignty, before the formation of the Constitution, and still retain it except so far as they have surrendered it by that instrument; that this principle results from the nature of the government, and is secured by the tenth amendment; that an affirmative grant of power is not exclusive unless in its own nature it be such that the continued exercise of it by the former possessor is inconsistent with the grant, and that this is not of that description.

The appellant, conceding these postulates except the last, contends that full power to regulate a particular subject implies the whole power, and leaves no residuum; that a grant of the whole is incompatible with the existence of a right in another to any part of it. . . .

In discussing the question whether this power is still in the States, in the case under consideration, we may dismiss from it the inquiry whether it is surrendered by the mere grant to Congress, or is retained until Congress shall exercise the power. We may dismiss that inquiry because it has been exercised, and the regulations which Congress deemed it proper to make are now in full operation. The sole question is can a State regulate commerce with foreign nations and among the States while Congress is regulating it?

. . . [T]he inspection laws are said to be regulations of commerce, and are certainly recognised in the Constitution as being passed in the exercise of a power remaining with the States.

That inspection laws may have a remote and considerable influence on commerce will not be denied, but that a power to regulate commerce is the source from which the right to pass them is derived cannot be admitted. The object of inspection laws is to improve the quality of articles produced by the labour of a country, to fit them for exportation, or, it may be, for domestic use. They act upon the subject before it becomes an article of foreign commerce or of commerce among the States, and prepare it for that purpose. They form a portion of that immense mass of legislation which embraces everything within the territory of a State not surrendered to the General Government; all which can be most advantageously exercised by the States themselves. Inspection laws, quarantine laws, health laws of every description, as well as laws for regulating the internal commerce of a State, and those which respect turnpike roads, ferries, &c., are component parts of this mass.

No direct general power over these objects is granted to Congress, and, consequently, they remain subject to State legislation. If the legislative power of the Union can reach them, it must be for national purposes, it must be where the power is expressly given for a special purpose or is clearly incidental to some power which is expressly given. It is obvious that the government of the Union, in the exercise of its express powers — that, for example, of regulating commerce with foreign nations and among the States — may use means that may also be employed by a State in the exercise of its acknowledged powers —

that, for example, of regulating commerce within the State. If Congress license vessels to sail from one port to another in the same State, the act is supposed to be necessarily incidental to the power expressly granted to Congress, and implies no claim of a direct power to regulate the purely internal commerce of a State or to act directly on its system of police. So, if a State, in passing laws on subjects acknowledged to be within its control, and with a view to those subjects, shall adopt a measure of the same character with one which Congress may adopt, it does not derive its authority from the particular power which has been granted, but from some other, which remains with the State and may be executed by the same means. All experience shows that the same measures, or measures scarcely distinguishable from each other, may flow from distinct powers, but this does not prove that the powers themselves are identical.

. . . In our complex system, presenting the rare and difficult scheme of one General Government whose action extends over the whole but which possesses only certain enumerated powers, and of numerous State governments which retain and exercise all powers not delegated to the Union, contests respecting power must arise. Were it even otherwise, the measures taken by the respective governments to execute their acknowledged powers would often be of the same description, and might sometimes interfere. This, however, does not prove that the one is exercising, or has a right to exercise, the powers of the other. . . .

Since, however, in exercising the power of regulating their own purely internal affairs, whether of trading or police, the States may sometimes enact laws the validity of which depends on their interfering with, and being contrary to, an act of Congress passed in pursuance of the Constitution, the Court will enter upon the inquiry whether the laws of New York, as expounded by the highest tribunal of that State, have, in their application to this case, come into collision with an act of Congress and deprived a citizen of a right to which that act entitles him. Should this collision exist, it will be immaterial whether those laws were passed in virtue of a concurrent power "to regulate commerce with foreign nations and among the several States" or in virtue of a power to regulate their domestic trade and police. In one case and the other, the acts of New York must yield to the law of Congress, and the decision sustaining the privilege they confer against a right given by a law of the Union must be erroneous.

Comments on *Gibbons*. This is an additional excerpt from the opinion that we studied earlier. The earlier portion deals with the propriety of federal regulation in the area of ferries between states. As such, it defined the use of the Commerce Clause. This portion deals with the question of whether the states should have been regulating the ferries between New York and New Jersey in the first place. In other words, does the Dormant Commerce Clause preclude state regulation whether or not there is federal regulation?

Marshall's approach is not as complex as it seems. He just writes that way. First, he acknowledges that the states and the federal government may sometimes do the same thing on the same object of regulation, but for different purposes: Congress in pursuit of its enumerated powers and states in pursuit of their police powers, such as in the areas of taxation or health and safety. This contrasts with the position argued by one of the parties that the federal power is plenary not only in purpose, but in object and method as well. Marshall counters with the inspection laws, which at times might look like regulations of commerce because the same items subject to the Interstate Commerce Clause could be regulated by the state under the police power to inspect goods entering state jurisdiction.

The appellant argues a bit more broadly, that the power to do a thing, in pursuance of the commerce power and the responsibility over that thing, when granted to the federal government, means full power over that thing, and such an architecture cannot contemplate activity outside of the federal government even if Congress has not acted. This seems to be a special case of the Commerce Clause, which, the argument goes, cannot tolerate concurrent activity, while many of the other enumerated powers might. By concurrent activity this criticism seems to imply that any state regulation over a thing within interstate commerce interferes with congressional authority, even when silent. But Marshall avoids a direct answer and sticks to his guns, so to speak, acknowledging that when the states and the national government pursue their own powers, conflicts are bound to arise, but "[t]his, however, does not prove that the one is exercising, or has a right to exercise, the powers of the other." Missing in Marshall's commentary is the answer to the question of whether the states may regulate without state police power motives, which would be the ultimate notion of concurrent authority.

In the end, Marshall rules, based on the Supremacy Clause, that where Congress has spoken, that's it; the acts of Congress are the supreme law of the land. Here, Congress had spoken: it had set up a licensing system for navigating the Hudson River, and New York's licensing system was preempted. Even state law that does not offend the Dormant Commerce Clause can be struck down under the pre-emption doctrine where Congress has acted on a particular subject matter.

Is the Commerce Clause discussion in this case merely dictum?

COOLEY v. BOARD OF WARDENS
53 U.S. 299 (1852)

[The Court was asked to consider Pennsylvania state legislation requiring ships entering the ports of that state to hire pilots to navigate ships into port. This requirement cost shipowners the pilotage fee and carried with it fines for non-compliance. Because the regulation covered ships arriving from out-of-state destinations, the Court was asked to consider whether it interfered with the power of Congress to regulate commerce.]

Mr. Justice CURTIS delivered the opinion of the court.

. . . It remains to consider the objection that it is repugnant to the third clause of the eighth section of the first article: "The Congress shall have power to regulate commerce with foreign nations and among the several states, and with the Indian tribes."

That the power to regulate commerce includes the regulation of navigation we consider settled. And when we look to the nature of the service performed by pilots, to the relations which that service and its compensations bear to navigation between the several states and between the ports of the United States and foreign countries, we are brought to the conclusion that the regulation of the qualifications of pilots, of the modes and times of offering and rendering their services, of the responsibilities which shall rest upon them, of the powers they shall possess, of the compensation they may demand, and of the penalties by which their rights and duties may be enforced, do constitute regulations of navigation, and consequently of commerce, within the just meaning of this clause of the Constitution.
. . .

The act of Congress of the 7th of August, 1789, sect. 4, is as follows:

That all pilots in the bays, inlets, rivers, harbors, and ports of the United States shall continue to be regulated in conformity with the existing laws of the states, respectively, wherein such pilots may be, or with such laws as the states may respectively hereafter enact for the purpose, until further legislative provision shall be made by Congress.

. . . If the states were divested of the power to legislate on this subject by the grant of the commercial power to Congress, it is plain this act could not confer upon them power thus to legislate. If the Constitution excluded the states from making any law regulating commerce, certainly Congress cannot re-grant, or in any manner re-convey to the states that power. And yet this act of 1789 gives its sanction only to laws enacted by the states. This necessarily implies a constitutional power to legislate. . . . Entertaining these views, we are brought directly and unavoidably to the consideration of the question whether the grant of the commercial power to Congress did *per se* deprive the states of all power to regulate pilots. This question has never been decided by this court, nor, in our judgment, has any case depending upon all the considerations which must govern this one come before this court. The grant of commercial power to Congress does not contain any terms which expressly exclude the states from exercising an authority over its subject matter. If they are excluded, it must be because the nature of the power thus granted to Congress requires that a similar authority should not exist in the states. . . . And, on the other hand, if it were admitted that the existence of this power in Congress, like the power of taxation, is compatible with the existence of a similar power in the states, then it would be in conformity with the contemporary exposition of the Constitution (Federalist, No. 32), and with the judicial construction given from time to time by this court, after the most deliberate consideration, to hold that the mere grant of such a power to Congress did not imply a prohibition on the states to exercise the same power, that it is not the mere existence of such a power, but its exercise by Congress, which may be incompatible with the exercise of the same power by the states, and that the states may legislate in the absence of congressional regulations. *Sturges v. Crowninshield,* 4 Wheat. 193; *Moore v. Houston,* 5 *id.* 1; *Wilson v. Blackbird Creek Co.,* 2 Pet. 251.

The diversities of opinion, therefore, which have existed on this subject have arisen from the different views taken of the nature of this power. But when the nature of a power like this is spoken of, when it is said that the nature of the power requires that it should be exercised exclusively by Congress, it must be intended to refer to the subjects of that power, and to say they are of such a nature as to require exclusive legislation by Congress. Now the power to regulate commerce embraces a vast field containing not only many but exceedingly various subjects quite unlike in their nature, some imperatively demanding a single uniform rule operating equally on the commerce of the United States in every port and some, like the subject now in question, as imperatively demanding that diversity which alone can meet the local necessities of navigation.

Either absolutely to affirm or deny that the nature of this power requires exclusive legislation by Congress is to lose sight of the nature of the subjects of this power and to assert concerning all of them what is really applicable but to a part. Whatever subjects of this power are in their nature national, or admit only of one uniform system or plan of regulation, may justly be said to be of such a nature as to require exclusive legislation by Congress. That this cannot be affirmed of laws for the regulation of pilots and pilotage is plain. The act of 1789 contains a clear and authoritative declaration by the first Congress that the nature of this subject is such that, until Congress should find it necessary to exert its power, it should be left to the legislation of the states, that it is local and not national, that it is likely to be the best provided for not by one system or plan of regulations, but by as many as the legislative discretion of the several states should deem applicable to the local peculiarities of the ports within their limits. . . .

It is the opinion of a majority of the court that the mere grant to Congress of the power to regulate commerce did not deprive the states of power to regulate pilots, and that, although Congress has legislated on this subject, its legislation manifests an intention, with a single exception, not to regulate this subject, but to leave its regulation to the several states. To these precise questions, which are all we are called on to decide, this opinion must be understood to be confined. It does not extend to the question what other subjects, under the commercial power are within the exclusive control of Congress, or may be regulated by the states in the absence of all congressional legislation, nor to the general question how far any regulation of a subject by Congress may be deemed to operate as an exclusion of all legislation by the states upon the same subject. We decide the precise questions before us, upon what we deem sound principles, applicable to this particular subject in the state in which the legislation of Congress has left it. We go no further. . . .

If the grant of commercial power in the Constitution has deprived the states of all power to legislate for the regulation of pilots, if their laws on this subject are mere usurpations upon the exclusive power of the general government, and utterly void, it may be doubted whether Congress could, with propriety, recognize them as laws and adopt them as its own acts; and how are the legislatures of the states to proceed in future, to watch over and amend these laws, as the progressive wants of a growing commerce will require, when the members of those legislatures are made aware that they cannot legislate on this subject without violating the oaths they have taken to support the Constitution of the United States?

We are of opinion that this state law was enacted by virtue of a power residing in the state to legislate; that it is not in conflict with any law of Congress; that it does not interfere with any system which Congress has established by making regulations, or by intentionally leaving individuals to their own unrestricted action; that this law is therefore valid, and the judgment of the Supreme Court of Pennsylvania in each case must be affirmed.

Mr. Justice McLean and Mr. Justice Wayne dissented, and Mr. Justice Daniel, although he concurred in the judgment of the court, yet dissented from its reasoning.

Notes and Questions

1. This case is similar to *Gibbons v. Ogden* in that both involved potential conflicts between state laws and federal law. Take this opportunity to synthesize the two decisions, comparing and contrasting the facts, law involved, reasoning, and holdings. Are the two cases consistent? Are they different in ways that suggest different approaches to the law? The remaining comments may help.

2. Chief Justice Marshall, in *Gibbons*, distinguished state laws that purport to regulate interstate commerce and other kinds of state legislation. Describe the distinctions made by the Chief Justice.

3. Does the *Gibbons* opinion decide that the commerce power may be exercised exclusively by Congress, or does it suggest that the power is concurrent and may also be exercised by the states? Consider the following language from the case:

That inspection laws may have a remote and considerable influence on commerce will not be denied, but that a power to regulate commerce is the source from which the right to pass them is derived cannot be admitted. The object of inspection laws is to improve the quality of articles produced by the labour of a country, to fit them for exportation, or, it may be, for domestic use. They act upon the subject before it becomes an article of foreign commerce or of commerce among the States, and prepare it for that purpose. They form a portion of that immense mass of legislation which embraces everything within the territory of a State not surrendered to the General Government; all which can be most advantageously exercised by the States themselves. Inspection laws, quarantine laws, health laws of every description, as well as laws for regulating the internal commerce of a State, and those which respect turnpike roads, ferries, &c., are component parts of this mass.

4. On the other hand, does the Court in *Cooley* suggest exclusivity or concurrence between the states and the federal government in its discussion of the commerce power? Consider this portion of the opinion:

[S]o much of this act of 1789 as declares that pilots shall continue to be regulated "by such laws as the states may respectively hereafter enact for that purpose," instead of being held to be inoperative as an attempt to confer on the states a power to legislate of which the Constitution had deprived them, is allowed an appropriate and important signification It manifests the understanding of Congress, at the outset of the government, that the nature of this subject is not such as to require its exclusive legislation.

5. In the opinion, Justice Curtis said:

If the grant of commercial power in the Constitution has deprived the states of all power to legislate for the regulation of pilots, if their laws on this subject are mere usurpations upon the exclusive power of the general government, and utterly void, it may be doubted whether Congress could, with propriety, recognize them as laws and adopt them as its own acts.

What does this mean, and is it still law today? In the case of *Prudential Insurance v. Benjamin*, 328 U.S. 408 (1946) the Supreme Court upheld legislation by Congress allowing state taxes that, through preferences for local commerce, regulated interstate commerce. Consider the following language:

It has never been the law that what the states may do in the regulation of commerce, Congress being silent, is the full measure of its power. Much less has this boundary been thought to confine what Congress and the states, acting together, may accomplish. So to regard the matter would invert the constitutional grant into a limitation upon the very power it confers.

The commerce clause is in no sense a limitation upon the power of Congress over interstate and foreign commerce. On the contrary, it is, as Marshall declared in *Gibbons v. Ogden,* a grant to Congress of plenary and supreme authority over those subjects. The only limitation it places upon Congress's power is in respect to what constitutes commerce, including whatever rightly may be found to affect it sufficiently to make Congressional regulation necessary or appropriate. This limitation, of course, is entirely distinct from the implied prohibition of the commerce clause

. . . The power of Congress over commerce, exercised entirely without reference to coordinated action of the states, is not restricted, except as the Constitution expressly provides, by any limitation which forbids it to discriminate against interstate commerce and in favor of local trade. Its plenary scope enables Congress not only to promote, but also to prohibit, interstate commerce, as it has done frequently and for a great variety of reasons. That power does not run down a one-way street, or one of narrowly fixed dimensions. Congress may keep the way open, confine it broadly or closely, or close it entirely, subject only to the restrictions placed upon its authority by other constitutional provisions and the requirement that it shall not invade the domains of action reserved exclusively for the states.

This broad authority Congress may exercise alone, subject to those limitations, or in conjunction with coordinated action by the states in which case limitations imposed for the preservation of their powers become inoperative, and only those designed to forbid action altogether by any power or combination of powers in our governmental system remain effective. Here, both Congress and South Carolina have acted, and in complete coordination, to sustain the tax. It is therefore reinforced by the exercise of all the power of government residing in our scheme. Clear and gross must be the evil which would nullify such an exertion, one which could arise only by exceeding beyond cavil some explicit and compelling limitation imposed by a constitutional provision or provisions designed and intended to outlaw the action taken entirely from our constitutional framework.

Gibbons and *Cooley* left us with two approaches to the commerce power and the states. Chief Justice Marshall focused on what the state was doing in addressing, mostly in dicta, the kind of state legislation involved. If the legislation touched upon things in interstate commerce, the *Gibbons* opinion would require invalidation on constitutional grounds unless the state regulation was a matter of the state police power. *Cooley*, on the other hand, focused instead on the nature of the commercial activity involved. This could have a narrowing effect on state authority since a state would have to establish that a thing is local in character.

Though *Cooley* was the later word on the subject, *Gibbons* did make an invaluable contribution to the discussion. *Cooley* established the authority of states to regulate in pursuit of matters of local concern. Gibbons suggested that police regulation would be permissible. Together a rule can be articulated that allows for police-type regulation on matters of local concern. To the extent that something is in interstate commerce, if it is a matter of local concern, regulations in pursuit of a state's police powers would be constitutional.

2. RACE, SLAVERY, AND THE DORMANT COMMERCE CLAUSE

The beginning of the development of both versions of the Commerce Clause came at a time when the ownership of human beings was legal in this country. Because of slavery, it seems natural to ponder whether any cases exist that treated African Americans as merchandise subject to state regulation only if, as a matter of local concern, the regulations dealt with traditional state police powers. While none of the majority opinions discussed below took such an odious leap in characterization, we can note that in a few of the cases the Commerce Clause was a matter of consideration.

At the time *Elkison v. Delieseline*, 8 Fed. Cas. 493, NO. 4366 (C.C.D.S.C. 1823), was decided, Supreme Court Justices routinely sat as circuit court judges in circuits assigned to them. This practice still exists today, though fewer opportunities are taken to sit on lower courts by the nine. This case is an appellate case heard by Supreme Court Justice William Johnson. The court essentially rules that the state interest is not sufficient. Concurrent authority is not paramount authority, and whatever the reason of the regulation, it amounts to a regulation of commerce, even if Congress has not acted.

The case dealt with the question of whether or not a South Carolina law called the Negro Seaman's Act that requires the imprisonment of free Negro sailors and others when docked in the ports of that state at a time when African slavery was legal. Under that law, free Negro sailors could be sold out of imprisonment if the ship captain did not pay for the imprisonment during the period of the ship's dockage. South Carolina and its council claimed a sovereign right to such legislation, founded in notions of federalism in existence at that time, even a willingness to dissolve the Union if they did not get their way here. This case, an appellate case, was heard by Supreme Court Justice Johnson on circuit.

Implicit in South Carolina's position is the need to protect itself from free Negroes lest they encourage insurrection of the enslaved Negroes. Yet Johnson did not treat blacks as commerce. But he did indicate that such a regulation would affect all persons of color on board ships, and hence those ships, and hence the commerce on those ships inhibiting their entry into South Carolinian ports, and this would be a regulation of interstate commerce of a national character, which is the business of Congress, not the states. In response to the argument that the law was passed in exercise of a state's concurrent right, Johnson states: "'Concurrent' does not mean paramount and yet in order to divest a right conferred by the general government, it is very clear that the state right must be more than concurrent. But the right of the general government to regulate commerce with the sister states and foreign nations is a paramount and exclusive right; and this conclusion we arrive at wither we examine it with reference to the words of the constitution, or the nature of the grant." Johnson goes on further to say: "It is true that it contains no prohibition on the states to regulate foreign commerce. Nor was such a prohibition necessary, for the words of the grant sweep away the whole subject and leave nothing for the states to act upon."

In *Mayor of New York v. Miln*, 36 U.S. 102 (1837), the Supreme Court was called upon to rule on a law that requires ship captains to provide the city of New York with a list of passengers, failure of which will result in fine. Though not a slavery case, *Miln* has implications for *Elkisseliene* and *Groves v. Slaughter* (below). The Court found the interest of the state to be important and that the list requirement was not a regulation of commerce. The Court acknowledges that the power to regulate interstate commerce is not extended to states, and cites *Gibbons v. Ogden* for the proposition. However, the Court notes that persons are not commerce. "[W]hilst a state is acting within the scope of its legitimate power as to the end to be attained, it may use whatever means, being appropriate to the end, it may think fit; although they may be the same or so nearly the same, as scarcely to be distinguished from those adopted by the Congress acting under a different power (Commerce): subject only . . . to this limitation, that in the event of collision, the law of the state must yield to the law of Congress." The Court went on to say that "[a]ll those powers which relate to merely municipal legislation, or which may more properly be called internal police, are not surrendered or restrained. . . ."

Is this an implicit reversal of *Elkison*? What about the other commercial effects of the "free Negro law" in *Elkison*? Is that a legitimate distinction?

GROVES v. SLAUGHTER
40 U.S. 449 (1841)

[In 1832, the Mississippi Constitution prohibited the introduction of slaves from out of state for sale. Under the Mississippi law, blacks could be purchased outside of the state and brought to the state for personal use. In 1836 the parties entered into a business agreement that resulted in the sale of imported slaves. The buyer subsequently declined payment of a promissory note tendered for the blacks, resulting in litigation. The buyer claimed that the sale was void due to the Mississippi Constitution, which outlawed such importation for commercial reasons. The question before the Supreme Court of the United States was whether the sale was void under the Mississippi Constitution and whether the provision in the state's constitution was constitutional under the Commerce Clause of the United States Constitution. If the constitutional provision was found to be in violation of the as of yet unnamed Dormant Commerce Clause, the transaction would have been considered valid and enforceable.

The majority held that the failure of the legislature to pass implementing legislation meant that the constitutional provision was not in effect. Because the note was hence enforceable, the majority declined to rule on the Commerce Clause issue. However, three members of the court issued separate opinions. These separate opinions are important for what they say about the mores of the time, and the development of the Dormant Commerce Clause. Notice that this case preceded *Cooley*.]

McLEAN, Justice.

As one view of this case involves the construction of the constitution of the United States in a most important part, and in regard to its bearing upon a momentous and most delicate subject, I will state in a few words my own views on that branch [40 U.S. 449, 504] of the case. The case has been argued with surpassing ability on both sides. And although the question I am to consider, is not necessary to a decision of the case; yet, it is so intimately connected with it, and has been so elaborately argued, that under existing circumstances, I deem it fit and proper to express my opinion upon it. . . .

In the case of Gibbons v. Ogden, 9 Wheat. 186, this court decided, that the power to regulate commerce is exclusively vested in congress, and that no part of it can be exercised by a state. The necessity of a uniform commercial regulation, more than any other consideration, led to the adoption of the federal constitution. And unless the power be not only paramount, but exclusive, the constitution must fail to attain one of the principal objects of its formation. It has been contended, that a state may exercise a commercial power, if the same has not been exercised by congress. And that this power of the state ceased, when the federal authority was exerted over the same subject-matter. This argument is founded upon the supposition, that a state may exercise a power which is expressly given to the federal government, if it shall not exert the power, in all the modes, and over all the subjects to which it can be applied. If this rule of construction were generally adopted and practically enforced, it would be as fatal to the spirit of the constitution, as it is opposed to its letter. If a commercial power may be exercised by a state, because it has not been exercised by congress, the same rule must apply to other powers expressly delegated to the federal government.

It is admitted, that the power of taxation is common to the state and federal governments; but this is not, in its nature or effect, a repugnant power; and its exercise is vital to both governments. A power may remain dormant, though the expediency of its exercise has been fully considered. It is often wiser and more politic, to forbear, than to exercise a power. A state regulates its own internal commerce, may pass inspection and police laws, designed to guard the health aud protect the rights of its citizens. But these laws must not be extended so as to come in conflict with a power expressly given to the federal government. It is enough to say, that the commercial power, as it regards foreign commerce, and commerce among the several states, has been decided by this court to be exclusively vested in congress. . . .

The transportation of slaves from a foreign country, before the abolition of that traffic, was subject to this commercial power. This would seem to be admitted in the constitution, as it provides 'the importation of such persons as any of the states, now existing, shall think proper to admit, shall not be prohibited by congress, prior to the year 1808: but a tax or duty, may be imposed on such importation, not exceeding ten dollars for each person.' An exception to a rule is said to prove the existence of the rule; and this exception to the exercise of the commercial power, may well be considered as a clear recognition of the power in the case stated. The United States are considered as a unit, in all regulations of foreign commerce. But this cannot be the case, where the regulations are to operate among the several states. The law must be equal and general in its provisions. Congress cannot pass a non-intercourse law, as among the several states; nor impose an embargo that shall affect only a part of them. Navigation, whether on the high seas, or in the coasting trade, is a part of our commerce; and when extended beyond the limits of any state, is subject to the power of congress. And as regards this intercourse, internal or foreign, it is immaterial, whether the cargo of the vessel consists of passengers, or articles of commerce.

Can the transfer and sale of slaves from one state to another, be regulated by congress, under the commercial power? If a state may admit or prohibit slaves at its discretion, this power must be in the state, and not in congress. The constitution seems to recognise the power to be in the states. The importation of certain persons, meaning slaves, which was not to be prohibited before 1808, was limited to such states, then existing, as shall think proper to admit them. Some of the states, at that time, prohibited the admission of slaves, and their right to do so was as strongly implied by this provision, as the right of other stares that admitted them.

The constitution treats slaves as persons. In the second section of the first article, which apportions representatives and directs taxes among the states, it provides, "the numbers shall be determined, by adding to the whole number of free persons, including those bound to service for a term of years, and excluding Indians not taxed, three-fifths of all other persons." And again, in the third section of the fourth article, it is declared, that "no person, held to service or labor in one state, under the laws thereof, escaping into another, shall, in consequence of any law or regulation therein, be discharged from such service or labor, but shall be delivered up on claim of the party to whom such service or labor may be due." By the laws of certain states, slaves are treated as property; and the constitution of Mississippi prohibits their being brought into that state, by citizens of other states, for sale, or as merchandize. Merchandize is a comprehensive term, and may include every article of traffic, whether foreign or domestic, which is properly embraced by a commercial regulation. But if slaves are considered in some of the states, as merchandize, that cannot divest them of the leading and controlling quality of persons, by which they are designated in the constitution. The character of property is given them by the local law. This law is respected, and all rights under it are protected by the federal anthorities; but the constitution acts upon slaves as persons, and not as property.

In all the old states, at the time of the revolution, slavery existed in a greater or less degree. By more than one-half of them, including those that have been since admitted into the Union, it has been abolished or prohibited. And in these states, a slave cannot be brought as merchandize, or held to labor. in any of them, except as a transient person. The constitution of Ohio declares, that there shall be neither slavery nor involuntary servitude in the state, except for the punishment of crimes. Is this provision in conflict with the power in congress to regulate commerce? . . . If Ohio may prohibit the introduction of slaves into it altogether, may not the state of Mississippi regulate their admission? The constitution of the United States operates alike on all the states; and one state has the same power over the subject of slavery as every other state. If it be constitutional in one state, to abolish or prohibit slavery, it cannot be unconstitutional in another, within its discretion, to regulate it. Could Ohio, in her constitution, have prohibited the introduction into the state, of the cotton of the south, or the manufactured articles of the north? If a state may exercise this power, it may establish a non-intercourse with the other states. This, no one will pretend, is within the power of a state. Such a measure would be repugnant to the constitution, and it would strike at the foundation of the Union. The power vested in congress to regulate commerce among the several states, was designed to prevent commercial conflicts among them. But whilst Ohio [40 U.S. 449, 508] could not proscribe the productions of the south, nor the fabrics of the north, no one doubts its power to prohibit slavery. And what can more unanswerably establish the doctrine, that a state may prohibit slavery, or, in its discretion, regulate it, without trenching upon the commercial power of congress? The power over slavery belongs to the states respectively. It is local in its character, and in its effects; and the transfer or sale of slaves cannot be separated from this power. It is, indeed, an essential part of it. Each state has a right to protect itself against the avarice and intrusion of the slave-dealer; to guard its citizens against the inconveniences and dangers of a slave population. The right to exercise this power, by a state, is higher and deeper than the constitution. The evil involves the prosperity, and may endanger the existence of a state. Its power to guard against, or to remedy the evil, rests upon the law of self-preservation; a law vital to every community, and especially to a sovereign state.

TANEY, Ch. J.

I had not intended to express an opinion upon the question raised in the argument, in relation to the power of congress to regulate the traffic in slaves between the different states, because the court have come to the conclusion, in which I concur, that the point is not involved in the case before us. But as my brother McLean has stated his opinion upon it, I am not willing, by remaining silent, to leave any doubt as to mine.

In my judgment, the power over this subject is exclusively with the several states; and each of them has a right to decide for itself, whether it will, or will not, allow persons of this description to be brought within its limits, from another state, either for sale, or for any other purpose; and also to prescribe the manner and mode in which they may be introduced, and to determine their condition and treatment within their respective territories: and the action of the several states upon this subject cannot be controlled by congress, either by virtue of its power to regulate commerce, or by virtue of any power conferred by the constitution of the United States. I do not, however, mean to argue this question; and I state my opinion upon it, on account of the interest which a large portion of the Union naturally feel in this matter, and from an apprehension that may silence, when another member of the court has delivered his opinion, might be misconstrued.

Another question of constitutional law has also been brought into discussion, that is to say: whether the grant of power to the general government, to regulate commerce, does not carry with it an implied prohibition to the states to make any regulations upon the subject, even although they should be altogether consistent with those made by congress. I decline expressing any opinion upon this question, because it is one step further out of the case really before us; and there is nothing in the character of the point that seems to require a voluntary declaration of opinion by the members of the court. . . . But the question upon which different opinions have been entertained, is this: would a regulation of commerce, by a state, be valid, until congress should otherwise direct; provided such regulation was consistent with the regulations of congress, and did not, in any manner, conflict with them? No case has yet arisen, which made it necessary, in the judgment of the court, to decide this question. . . .

BALDWIN, Justice.

As this case has been decided on its merits, and the opinion of the court covers every point directly involved, I had not thought that any merely collateral question would have been noticed; for I cannot believe, that in the opinion of any of the judges, it is at all necessary to inquire, what would have been the result, if the court had held that the contract on which this suit was brought, was void by the laws or constitution of Mississippi. The questions which would have arisen, in such an event, are of the highest importance to the country; and in my opinion, ought not to be considered by us, unless a case arise in which their decision becomes indispensable, when too much deliberation cannot be had, before a judgment is pronounced upon them. But since a different course has been taken by the judges who have preceded me, I am not willing to remain silent; lest it may be inferred, that my opinion coincides with that of the judges who have now expressed theirs.

That the power of congress "to regulate commerce among [40 U.S. 449, 511] the several states," is exclusive of any interference by the states, has been in my opinion, conclusively settled by the solemn opinions of this court, in *Gibbons v. Ogden*, 9 Wheat. 186-222, and in *Brown v. Maryland*, 12 Wheat. 438-46. If these decisions are not to be taken as the established construction of this clause of the constitution, I know of none which are not yet open to doubt; nor can there be any adjudications of this court, which must be considered as authoritative upon any question, if these are not to be so on this. . . .

Other judges consider the constitution as referring to slaves only as persons, and as property, in no other sense than as persons escaping from service; they do not consider them to be recognised as subjects of commerce, either "with foreign nations," or "among the several states"; but I cannot acquiesce in this position. In other times, and in another department of this government, I have expressed my opinion on this subject. . . . That I may stand alone among the members of this court, does not deter me from declaring that I feel bound to consider slaves as property, by the law of the states, before the adoption of the constitution, and from the first settlement of the colonies; that this right of property exists independently of the constitution, which does not create, but recognises and protects it from violation, by any law or regulation of any state, in the cases to which the constitution applies.

It was a principle of the revolution, and the practical construction of the Declaration of Independence, that "necessity or expediency" justified "the refusal of liberty, in certain circumstances, to persons of a particular color"; and that "those to whom their services and labor were due, were their owners." (1 Laws U. S. 24-5.) In the 7th article of the preliminary treaty of peace with Great Britain, there is this expression, "negroes, or other property"

(Ibid. 198); also, in the 7th article of the definitive treaty (Ibid. 204); which conclusively shows the then accepted understanding of the country. . . .

Slaves, then, being articles of commerce with foreign nations, up to 1808, and until their importation was prohibited by congress, they were also articles of commerce among the several states, which recognised them as property capable of being transferred from hand to hand as chattels. Whether they should be so held or not, or what should be the extent of the right of property in the owner of a slave, depended on the law of each state; that was and is a subject on which no power is granted by the constitution to congress; consequently, none can be exercised, directly or indirectly. It is a matter of internal police, over which the states have reserved the entire control; they, and they alone, can declare what is property capable of ownership, absolute or qualified; they may continue or abolish slavery at their pleasure, as was done before, and has been done since the constitution; which leaves this subject untouched and intangible, except by the states.

As each state has plenary power to legislate on this subject, its laws are the test of what is property; if they recognise slaves as the property of those who hold them, they become the subjects of commerce between the states which so recognise them, and the traffic in them may be regulated by congress, as the traffic in other articles; but no further. . . .

. . . It is fully within the power of any state to entirely prohibit the importation of slaves, of all descriptions, or of those who are diseased, convicts, or of dangerous or immoral habits or conduct; this is a regulation of police, for purposes of internal safety to the state, or the health and morals of its citizens, or to effectuate its system of policy in the abolition of slavery. But where no object of police is discernible in a state law of constitution, nor any rule of policy, other than that which gives to its own citizens a "privilege," which is denied to citizens of other states, it is wholly different. . . . To consider them as persons merely, and not property, is, in my settled opinion, the first step towards state of things to be avoided only by a firm adherence to the fundamental principles of the state and federal governments, in relation to this species of property. If the first step taken be a mistaken one, the successive ones will be fatal to the whole system. I have taken my stand on the only position which, in my judgment, is impregnable; and feel confident in its strength, however it may be assailed in public opinion, here or elsewhere.

Notes and Questions

1. McLean and Taney both agreed that the sale of African Americans did not fall under the Commerce Clause. Is their reasoning the same? If it is, why did Taney feel obliged to write separately? Recall that Taney, as Chief Justice, wrote the opinion in the *Dred Scott* case.

2. Baldwin found that African American slaves were property and subject to the Commerce Clause. Is Baldwin pro-slavery? If so, what is the risk of his argument?

3. McLean's opinion suggests that a state may have a legitimate reason for resisting the institution of slavery. McLean would affirm the legitimacy of such a legislative choice by a state. Later you will learn that the modern approach to the Dormant Commerce Clause recognizes as an exception a state's legitimate purpose in discriminating against out-of-state commerce.

D. THE MODERN DORMANT COMMERCE CLAUSE

Cooley's prescription for deciding Dormant Commerce Clause cases was whether or not the subject matter was national or local in character. This turned out to be harder to implement in practice than anticipated. Over the years the Court experimented with various approaches to implement this standard. At one time the Court veered into an approach designed to assist in determining whether an activity imposed a direct or indirect burden on interstate commerce as a surrogate for the national/local distinction. Ultimately this approach was discarded because the task of determining whether a state law had a direct or indirect burden on commerce or whether an activity was national or local in character was deemed too unwieldy. The dissents in the following case, perhaps, pointed a new way.

DI SANTO v. PENNSYLVANIA
273 U.S. 34 (1927)

[A Pennsylvania statute required licenses of persons engaged in the selling of tickets for international travel on ships from Pennsylvania ports. DiSanto was convicted of failing to acquire a license, though he conducted a travel business which focused on international travel by ship. He appealed his conviction by challenging the validity of the statute under the foreign commerce clause. The principles of direct/indirect burden applied to the interstate commerce clause also applied to the foreign commerce clause.]

Justice BUTLER delivered the opinion of the Court:
. . . The soliciting of passengers and the sale of steamship tickets and orders for passage between the United States [273 U.S. 34, 37] and Europe constitute a well-recognized part of foreign commerce. See Davis v. Farmers' Co-operative Co., 262 U.S. 312, 315, 43 S. Ct. 556. A state statute which by its necessary operation directly interferes with or burdens foreign commerce is a prohibited regulation and invalid, regardless of the purpose with which it was passed. Shafer v. Farmers' Grain Co., 268 U.S. 189, 199 , 45 S. Ct. 481, and cases cited. Such legislation cannot be sustained as an exertion of the police power of the state to prevent possible fraud. Real Silk Mills v. Portland, 268 U.S. 325, 336, 45 S. Ct. 525. The Congress has complete and paramount authority to regulate foreign commerce and, by appropriate measures, to protect the public against the frauds of those who sell these tickets and orders. The sales here in question are related to foreign commerce as directly as are sales made in ticket offices maintained by the carriers and operated by their servants and employees. The license fee and other things imposed by the act on plaintiff in error, who initiates for his principals a transaction in foreign commerce, constitute a direct burden on that commerce.
Judgment reversed.

Mr. Justice BRANDEIS, with whom Mr. Justice HOLMES concurs, dissenting.
The statute is an exertion of the police power of the state. It's evident purpose is to prevent a particular species of fraud and imposition found to have been practiced in Pennsylvania upon persons of small means, unfamiliar with our language and institutions. Much of the immigration into the United States is effected by arrangements made here for remittance of the means of travel. The individual immigrant is often an advance. After

gaining a foothold here, he has his wife and children, aged parents, brothers, sisters or other relatives follow. To this end he remits steamship tickets or orders for transportation. The purchase of the tickets involves trust in the dealer. This is so not only because of the nature of the transaction, but also because a purchaser when unable to pay the whole price at one time makes successive deposits on account, the ticket or order not being delivered until full payment is made. The facilities for remitting both cash and steamship tickets are commonly furnished by private bankers of the same nationality as the immigrant. It was natural that the supervision of persons engaged in the business of supplying steamship tickets should be committed by the statute to the commissioner of banking.

Although the purchase made is of an ocean steamship ticket, the transaction regulated is wholly intrasate-as much so as if the purchase were of local real estate or of local theater tickets. There is no purpose on the part of the state to regulate foreign commerce. The statute is not an obstruction to foreign commerce. It does not discriminate against foreign commerce. It places no direct burden upon such commerce. It does not affect the commerce except indirectly. Congress could, of course, deal with the subject, because it is connected with foreign commrce. But it has not done so. Nor has it legislated on any allied subject. Thus, there can be no contention that Congress has occupied the field. And obviously, also, this is not a case in which the silence of Congress can be interpreted as a prohibition of state action-as a declaration that in the sale of ocean steamship tickets fraud may be practiced without let or hindrance. If Pennsylvania must submit to seeing its citizens defrauded, it is not because Congress has so willed, but because the Constitution so commands. I cannot believe that it does.

Mr. Justice STONE, dissenting. . . .

As this court has many times decided, the purpose of the commerce clause was not to preclude all state regulation of commerce crossing state lines but to prevent discrimination and the erection of barriers or obstacles to the free flow of commerce, interstate or foreign.

The recognition of the power of the states to regulate commerce within certain limits is a recognition that there are matters of local concern which may properly be subject to state regulation and which, because of their local character, as well as their number and diversity, can never be adequately dealt with by Congress. Such regulation, so long as it does not impede the free flow of commerce, may properly be and for the most part has been left to the state by the decisions of this court.

In this case the traditional test of the limit of state action by inquiring whether the interference with commerce is direct or indirect seems to me too mechanical, too uncertain in its application, and too remote from actualities, to be of value. . . .

But it seems clear that those interferences not deemed forbidden are to be sustained, not because the effect on commerce is nominally indirect, but because a consideration of all the facts and circumstances, such as the nature of the regulation, its function, the character of the business involved and the actual effect on the flow of commerce, lead to the conclusion that the regulation concerns interests peculiarly local and does not infringe the national interest in maintaining the freedom of commerce across state lines.

Mr. Justice Holmes and Mr. Justice Brandeis concur in this opinion.

Notes

The more holistic approach suggested by Justice Stone became the basis of the modern approach to the Commerce Clause. What eventually came out of several decisions and became the modern approach is summarized below:

1. State and federal governments may sometimes do the same thing on the same object of regulation, but for different purposes (state police power to regulate disease or other evils and feds to regulate commerce).

2. Such actions by states may amount to regulation of interstate commerce, but as long as they are not protectionist or burdensome without appreciable local benefits, the acts are constitutional.

3. However, the power to regulate commerce is plenary to the federal government. This is true whether or not the federal government has acted on the thing.

4. Where federal government has acted in the area by passing legislation, there can be no conflict with that legislation, even if the state is not trying to emulate Congress's authority. Commerce cannot tolerate concurrent activity; neither may bankruptcy power, copyright power, patent power, and so on. Other enumerated powers may tolerate concurrent activity. (This represents the preemption doctrine, which is addressed at ___supra.)

The following section will explore the means by which the Court has addressed the Dormant Commerce Clause through most of the twentieth century and in the present. Two categories of cases emerge from the Court's decisions. Category one involves protectionism — cases where state legislation prefers in-state economic interests to out-of-state competition.

Category two involves state practices that do not discriminate, but do burden all commerce, local and out-of-state alike. In this case, the Court will weigh the burdens against the benefits to the state to determine whether the latter outweigh the burdens. If they do, the Court will find the measure constitutional. The analytical method under this category is known as the Pike Balancing test from *Pike v. Bruce Church, Inc.*, 397 U.S. 137 (1970), a case that is covered in section IV. D. 2.

1. CATEGORY ONE: DISCRIMINATION

Consider the description in *Brown-Forman Distillers v. New York State Liquor Authority*, 476 U.S. 573 (1986), of the approach to Dormant Commerce Clause litigation:

> When a state statute directly regulates or discriminates against interstate commerce, or when its effect is to favor in-state economic interests over out-of-state interests, it is generally struck down without further inquiry, but when a statute has only indirect effects on interstate commerce and regulates evenhandedly, the courts examine whether the state's interest is legitimate and whether the burden on interstate commerce clearly exceeds the local benefits; there is no clear line separating these categories of state regulation, and in either situation the critical consideration is the overall effect of the statute on both local and interstate activities.

Hence in the modern era of Dormant Commerce Clause litigation the Court will look to whether the state is acting on something that would be covered by the Commerce Clause. In some cases the state action may be functionally identical to a federal action (collecting a tax on the part of the state, collecting a duty or fine on the part of the federal government). The purpose of the federal measure would be to regulate commerce. The state measure should be in pursuit of legitimate purpose under state police powers or simply a regulation of commerce as a local matter without burden or discrimination.

However, the trap for states is when they attempt to legislate, presumably in pursuit of legitimate state police purposes, but wind up favoring in state economic reasons for no good reasons other than the fact that they can. These kinds of legislation are routinely invalidated by the Court in the modern Dormant Commerce Clause jurisprudence, as protectionist.

However, if it is determined that the purpose of the state legislation is indeed legitimate, the state may be able to avoid invalidation. To do so, the state must demonstrate that there is no other less discriminatory means of achieving the legislative goals. This judicial review of state legislation is often called strict scrutiny.[21] When the Court decides in this manner, the measure is considered protectionist.

Opinions from the Court that address discriminatory state legislation can be divided into two analytical groups: one where the statute is discriminatory on its face, and the second where the statute may appear neutral, but represents an underlying motive or effect that results in discrimination.

a. CATEGORY ONE (A) — FACIAL DISCRIMINATION

Though it is rare that a state will express discriminatory motives in the body or face of legislation, such legislation does exist. By restricting or making the commercial conditions for sale less favorable for the out-of-state products, the state is effectively regulating commerce and is virtually per se invalid. However, the Supreme Court has recognized, in limited instances, that a legitimate state purpose may reside in such a discriminatory measure. The result is that such discriminatory measures are *virtually* per se invalid, pending the state proving that the purpose for the discrimination was legitimate (i.e., not to favor the competitive position of local business), and that the method chosen to effect the legitimate purpose was the only reasonable option.

Putting these principles to use as we study facial discrimination against out-of-state commerce by the states, it is important to be aware of the process the Court uses in its analysis. First, discriminatory purpose is determined (which in a case of facial discrimination would be apparent on the face of the legislation). Then protectionism is determined. A state statute is protectionist (and thus prohibited) when the purpose of the regulation is not legitimate, or if legitimate, there is a less protectionist means of accomplishing that purpose.

The cases discussed below address state laws or regulations that were found to be protectionist or those that were found to be discriminatory, though not protectionist (that is, laws that were passed to pursue legitimate purposes in the least discriminatory manner). Cases that were found not to be either protectionist or simply discriminatory are discussed under Category Two—laws that burden interstate commerce.

The following case addresses the protectionism issue from an unusual place — garbage. While one might think of protectionism as a means of protecting local industries'

---

[21] The term "strict scrutiny" is used later in this book when the Due Process and Equal Protection Clauses are studied. Here, as in due process and equal protection, the term denotes an exacting scrutiny to determine whether a government policy will be excepted from the constitutional rule. However, in equal protection and due process cases, the process of strict scrutiny is different. See Chapter V. infra.

market positions for the purpose of selling products, these garbage cases expand the notion of what kinds of commercial advantages a state may seek to protect. Consider how the Court applies the analysis to the case below.

CITY OF PHILADELPHIA v. NEW JERSEY
437 U.S. 617 (1978)

Mr. Justice STEWART delivered the opinion of the Court.

A New Jersey law prohibits the importation of most "solid or liquid waste which originated or was collected outside the territorial limits of the State. . . ." In this case, we are required to decide whether this statutory prohibition violates the Commerce Clause of the United States Constitution.

I

The statutory provision in question is ch. 363 of 1973 N.J. Laws, which took effect in early 1974. In pertinent part it provides:

> No person shall bring into this State any solid or liquid waste which originated or was collected outside the territorial limits of the State, except garbage to be fed to swine in the State of New Jersey, until the commissioner [of the State Department of Environmental Protection] shall determine that such action can be permitted without endangering the public health, safety and welfare and has promulgated regulations permitting and regulating the treatment and disposal of such waste in this State.

N.J.Stat.Ann. § 13*I*-10 (West Supp. 1978). As authorized by ch. 363, the Commissioner promulgated regulations permitting four categories of waste to enter the State. Apart from these narrow exceptions, however, New Jersey closed its borders to all waste from other States.

Immediately affected by these developments were the operators of private landfills in New Jersey and several cities in other States that had agreements with these operators for waste disposal. They brought suit against New Jersey and its Department of Environmental Protection in state court, attacking the statute and regulations on a number of state and federal grounds. In an oral opinion granting the plaintiffs' motion for summary judgment, the trial court declared the law unconstitutional because it discriminated against interstate commerce. The New Jersey Supreme Court consolidated this case with another reaching the same conclusion, *Hackensack Meadowlands Development Comm'n v. Municipal Sanitary Landfill Auth.*, 127 N.J.Super. 160, 316 A.2d 711, *and reversed,* 68 N.J. 451, 348 A.2d 505. It found that ch. 363 advanced vital health and environmental objectives with no economic discrimination against, and with little burden upon, interstate commerce, and that the law was therefore permissible under the Commerce Clause of the Constitution. The court also found no congressional intent to preempt ch. 363 by enacting in 1965 the Solid Waste Disposal Act, 79 Stat. 997, 42 U.S.C. § 3251 *et seq.,* as amended by the Resource Recovery Act of 1970, 84 Stat. 1227. . . .

II

Before it addressed the merits of the appellants' claim, the New Jersey Supreme Court questioned whether the interstate movement of those wastes banned by ch. 363 is "commerce" at all within the meaning of the Commerce Clause. Any doubts on that score should be laid to rest at the outset.

The state court expressed the view that there may be two definitions of "commerce" for constitutional purposes. When relied on "to support some exertion of federal control or regulation," the Commerce Clause permits "a very sweeping concept" of commerce. 68 N.J. at 469, 348 A.2d at 514. But when relied on "to strike down or restrict state legislation," that Clause and the term "commerce" have a "much more confined . . . reach." *Ibid.*

The state court reached this conclusion in an attempt to reconcile modern Commerce Clause concepts with several old cases of this Court holding that States can prohibit the importation of some objects because they "are not legitimate subjects of trade and commerce." . . .

We think the state court misread our cases, and thus erred in assuming that they require a two-tiered definition of commerce. . . .

III
A

Although the Constitution gives Congress the power to regulate commerce among the States, many subjects of potential federal regulation under that power inevitably escape congressional attention "because of their local character and their number and diversity." *South Carolina State Highway Dept. v. Barnwell Bros., Inc.,* 303 U.S. 177, 185. In the absence of federal legislation, these subjects are open to control by the States so long as they act within the restraints imposed by the Commerce Clause itself. *See Raymond Motor Transportation, Inc. v. Rice,* 434 U.S. 429, 440. The bounds of these restraints appear nowhere in the words of the Commerce Clause, but have emerged gradually in the decisions of this Court giving effect to its basic purpose. That broad purpose was well expressed by Mr. Justice Jackson in his opinion for the Court in *H. P. Hood & Sons, Inc. v. Du Mond,* 336 U.S. 525, 537-538:

> This principle that our economic unit is the Nation, which alone has the gamut of powers necessary to control of the economy, including the vital power of erecting customs barriers against foreign competition, has as its corollary that the states are not separable economic units. As the Court said in *Baldwin v. Seelig,* 294 U.S. [511], 527, "what is ultimate is the principle that one state, in its dealings with another, may not place itself in a position of economic isolation."

The opinions of the Court through the years have reflected an alertness to the evils of "economic isolation" and protectionism, while at the same time recognizing that incidental burdens on interstate commerce may be unavoidable when a State legislates to safeguard the health and safety of its people. Thus, where simple economic protectionism is effected by state legislation, a virtually *per se* rule of invalidity has been erected. *See, e.g., H. P. Hood & Sons, Inc., v. DuMond, supra; Toomer v. Witsell,* 334 U.S. 385, 403-406; *Baldwin v. G.A.F. Seelig, Inc., supra; Buck v. Kuykendall,* 267 U.S. 307, 315-316. The clearest example of such legislation is a law that overtly blocks the flow of interstate commerce at a State's borders. *Cf. Welton v. Missouri,* 91 U.S. 275. . . .

The crucial inquiry, therefore, must be directed to determining whether ch. 363 is basically a protectionist measure, or whether it can fairly be viewed as a law directed to legitimate local concerns, with effects upon interstate commerce that are only incidental.

B

The purpose of ch. 363 is set out in the statute itself as follows:

> The Legislature finds and determines that . . . the volume of solid and liquid waste continues to rapidly increase, that the treatment and disposal of these wastes continues to pose an even greater threat to the quality of the environment of New Jersey, that the available and appropriate land fill sites within the State are being diminished, that the environment continues to be threatened by the treatment and disposal of waste which originated or was collected outside the State, and that the public health, safety and welfare require that the treatment and disposal within this State of all wastes generated outside of the State be prohibited.

[New Jersey] has every right to protect its residents' pocketbooks, as well as their environment. And it may be assumed as well that New Jersey may pursue those ends by slowing the flow of all waste into the State's remaining landfills, even though interstate commerce may incidentally be affected. But whatever New Jersey's ultimate purpose, it may not be accomplished by discriminating against articles of commerce coming from outside the State unless there is some reason, apart from their origin, to treat them differently. Both on its face and in its plain effect, ch. 363 violates this principle of nondiscrimination.

The New Jersey law at issue in this case falls squarely within the area that the Commerce Clause puts off limits to state regulation. On its face, it imposes on out-of-state commercial interests the full burden of conserving the State's remaining landfill space. It is true that, in our previous cases, the scarce natural resource was itself the article of commerce, whereas here the scarce resource and the article of commerce are distinct. But that difference is without consequence. In both instances, the State has overtly moved to slow or freeze the flow of commerce for protectionist reasons. It does not matter that the State has shut the article of commerce inside the State in one case, and outside the State in the other. What is crucial is the attempt by one State to isolate itself from a problem common to many by erecting a barrier against the movement of interstate trade.

The appellees argue that not all laws which facially discriminate against out-of-state commerce are forbidden protectionist regulations. In particular, they point to quarantine laws, which this Court has repeatedly upheld even though they appear to single out interstate commerce for special treatment. *See Baldwin v. G.A.F. Seelig, Inc., supra* at 525; *Bowman v. Chicago & Northwestern R. Co.,* 125 U.S. at 489. In the appellees' view, ch. 363 is analogous to such health-protective measures, since it reduces the exposure of New Jersey residents to the allegedly harmful effects of landfill sites.

It is true that certain quarantine laws have not been considered forbidden protectionist measures, even though they were directed against out-of-state commerce. *See Asbell v. Kansas,* 209 U.S. 251; *Reid v. Colorado,* 187 U.S. 137; *Bowman v. Chicago & Northwestern R. Co., supra* at 489. But those quarantine laws banned the importation of articles such as diseased livestock that required destruction as soon as possible because their very movement risked contagion and other evils. Those laws thus did not discriminate against interstate commerce as such, but simply prevented traffic in noxious articles, whatever their origin.

The New Jersey statute is not such a quarantine law. There has been no claim here that the very movement of waste into or through New Jersey endangers health, or that waste must be disposed of as soon and as close to its point of generation as possible. The harms caused by waste are said to arise after its disposal in landfill sites, and, at that point, as New Jersey concedes, there is no basis to distinguish out-of-state waste from domestic waste. If one is inherently harmful, so is the other. Yet New Jersey has banned the former, while leaving its landfill sites open to the latter. The New Jersey law blocks the importation of waste in an obvious effort to saddle those outside the State with the entire burden of slowing the flow of refuse into New Jersey's remaining landfill sites. That legislative effort is clearly impermissible under the Commerce Clause of the Constitution.

Today, cities in Pennsylvania and New York find it expedient or necessary to send their waste into New Jersey for disposal, and New Jersey claims the right to close its borders to such traffic. Tomorrow, cities in New Jersey may find it expedient or necessary to send their waste into Pennsylvania or New York for disposal, and those States might then claim the right to close their borders. The Commerce Clause will protect New Jersey in the future, just as it protects her neighbors now, from efforts by one State to isolate itself in the stream of interstate commerce from a problem shared by all. The judgment is

Reversed.

Notes and Questions

1. In your study of this case, take note of how the Court applied the analytical technique described earlier. How did the Court characterize the protectionism, considering that the commerce banned by New Jersey was garbage? Is that a commodity worth protecting against? In other words, is New Jersey protecting in-state producers of garbage? Is the ban protectionist? Why? Then Justice Rehnquist, in dissent, complained that the majority was denying New Jersey the right to protect itself from hazardous waste:

> Under them, New Jersey may require germ-infected rags or diseased meat to be disposed of as best as possible within the State, but at the same time prohibit the importation of such items for disposal at the facilities that are set up within New Jersey for disposal of such material generated within the State. The physical fact of life that New Jersey must somehow dispose of its own noxious items does not mean that it must serve as a depository for those of every other State. Similarly, New Jersey should be free under our past precedents to prohibit the importation of solid waste because of the health and safety problems that such waste poses to its citizens. The fact that New Jersey continues to, and indeed must continue to, dispose of its own solid waste does not mean that New Jersey may not prohibit the importation of even more solid waste into the State. I simply see no way to distinguish solid waste, on the record of this case, from germ-infected rags, diseased meat, and other noxious items.

Does the majority have an answer to Rehnquist's criticism? Do you agree with it?

Philadelphia v. New Jersey is about a basic unadulterated restriction, discriminatory in the sense that New Jersey sought to solve a real problem on the backs of out-of-state economic interests, so that in-state economic interests will benefit from landfill room. There are many reasons why states seek to discriminate in favor of local in-state interests. Seldom will a state be quite as bold as New Jersey in legislating an outright prohibition. Other methods are typically used to restrain competition to the benefit of in-state interests. The next several cases highlight taxation policy as a means of limiting the impact that out-of-state business trade can have on in-state business. The legislation in these cases, because the pertinent distinction between in-state and out-of-state products, goods, and services are drawn in the legislation, are considered examples of facial discrimination.

The Court found that an exemption for locally produced alcoholic beverages from a general liquor tax in Hawaii violated the Dormant Commerce Clause. In *Bacchus Imports v. Dias*, 468 U.S. 263 (1984), beverages produced from locally grown fruits and manufactured in Hawaii would not be liable for a general liquor tax. The Court found this tax program unconstitutionally assisted locally produced and locally grown liquors and fruits in competition with out-of-state liquor products.

In *West Lynn Creamery v. Healy,* 512 U.S. 186 (1994), Massachusetts devised a scheme to tax milk dealers with proceeds to go to a fund to subsidize Massachusetts dairy farmers suffering from depressed milk prices. On its face, the scheme taxed all milk dealers the same, whether in or out of state. Yet, also on its face, a subsidy from that fund went to Massachusetts dairy farmers. The effect of such taxes was that retail milk prices rose to accommodate the additional costs. On the other hand, the rebate/subsidy from the fund created by the tax to Massachusetts farmers allowed that the farmers could lower their prices to dealers accordingly to adjust to the new pricing structure caused by the tax. Out-of-state farmers, because they were not privy to the subsidy, could not make the same adjustment. In defense of the scheme, Massachusetts argued that the tax in the case was non-discriminatory, and hence constitutional, and that state subsidies have long been considered to be acceptable devices for implementing state business policy. The fact that both legal devices were administered together should not work to the prejudice of the scheme.

The Court, in an opinion written by Justice Stevens, responded by examining its jurisprudence in non-discriminatory taxation cases. The opinion allowed that such taxes are generally upheld apparently despite the burden on interstate commerce, because of the "'existence of major in state interests adversely affected . . .'" (quoting from *Minnesota v. Clover Leaf Creamery*, 449 U.S. 456, 473, n. 17). The quoted language describes one of the values in Dormant Commerce Clause jurisprudence, that of protecting out of state interests from excesses of in state political processes. This is because out of state interests have little or no influence over those in state processes. However, where in state interests, which presumably have a check on in state political processes, are adversely affected by those processes in the same way as out of state interests, there is no need for the Court to intervene to curtail legislative abuse. However, in this case, whatever internal political opposition that might have arisen over the tax would in effect be placated by the subsidy to Massachusetts farmers, whose subsidized prices are passed on downstream to the dealers paying the tax. Hence, even though state tax and subsidization policies are not offensive to the Constitution separately, together in the same scheme, they create a perfect storm of discriminatory economic policy. And by discriminatory policy, the Court explained that the purpose of the scheme was "to enable higher cost Massachusetts dairy farmers to compete with lower cost dairy farmers in other States." The majority went on to state that the policy "violates the cardinal principle that a State may not 'benefit in state economic interest by burdening out of state competitors'" (quoting *New Energy Co. of Indiana v. Limbach*, 486 U.S. 269 at 273-274). By this language, while ruling that the scheme was a violation of the Dormant Commerce Clause because of the un-rebated tax on out of state milk dealers, the Court distinguished state assistance programs like subsidies from measures that burden out of state business. In other words, subsidies alone are not problematic even though they could have the same effect of lowering consumer prices of subsidized producers to the harm of out of state competitors.

In a concurrence joined by Justice Thomas, Justice Scalia points to this distinction and questions the logic. "And even where the funding does not come in any part from taxes on out-of-state goods, 'merely assist[ing]' in-state businesses . . . unquestionably neutralizes advantages possessed by out-of-state enterprises. Such subsidies, particularly where they are in the form of cash or (what turns out to be the same thing) tax forgiveness, are often admitted to have as their purpose — indeed, are nationally advertised as having as their purpose — making it more profitable to conduct business in-state than elsewhere, i.e., distorting normal market incentives." Instead of relying upon unsustainable justifications of subsidization policies, Scalia would have focused on the scheme as a tax scheme in which a tax is levied, and then returned to local farmers. In this light, under Scalia's characterization, the scheme is nothing more than a discriminatory tax.

Chief Justice Rehnquist's dissenting opinion found exception to the majority's position on federalism grounds as well as doubts about the laissez-faire economic policy he suggested animated the majority opinion. To Rehnquist, the fact that Massachusetts taxed one set of players in the milk distribution industry (dealers) and subsidized another set of players (farmers/producers) was significant because "[n]o decided case supports the Court's conclusion that the negative Commerce Clause prohibits the State from using money that it has lawfully obtained through a neutral tax on milk dealers and distributing it as a subsidy to dairy farmers."

Notes and Questions

1. The majority argued in *West Lynn* that a non-discriminatory tax alone would not be offensive to the Constitution since a state's taxpayers are just as negatively affected by the tax as out-of-state taxpayers. Because one of the values of the Dormant Commerce Clause is to prevent legislative abuse against out-of-state interests, a non-discriminatory tax alone (without the subsidy) does not indicate such legislative abuse.

Is this political process rationale convincing? Do the economic reasons discussed in the comment on the American Common Market provide a weaker or stronger justification for the court's policy?

2. Can Chief Justice Rehnquist's position be justified from an economic standpoint?

Compensatory Tax Schemes. In *Chemical Waste Management, Inc v. Hunt*, 504 U.S. 334 (1992), Justice White, writing for the majority, reiterated the Court's position in *City of Philadelphia*, when addressing whether a differential tax on out-of-state waste was constitutional. Justice White, writing for the majority, recalled the analytical standard discussed above when stating that a less discriminatory means of reducing waste volume should have been considered by the state of Alabama when it charged a differential fee on out-of-state waste. The opinion re-established the market principle for waste disposal that the Court held in *City of Philadelphia* and went on to explain:

> The Act's additional fee facially discriminates against hazardous waste generated in States other than Alabama, and the Act overall has plainly discouraged the full operation of petitioner's facility. Such burdensome taxes imposed on interstate commerce alone are generally forbidden. . . .
>
> [Protection of health and the environment, collecting compensation for out of state waste, and the reduction of waste transportation on Alabama highways] may all be legitimate local interests, and petitioner has not attacked them. But only rhetoric, and not explanation, emerges as to why Alabama targets *only* interstate hazardous waste to meet these goals. . . . In the face of such findings, invalidity under the Commerce Clause necessarily follows, for "whatever [Alabama's] ultimate purpose, it may not be accomplished by discriminating against articles of commerce coming from outside the State unless there is some reason, apart from their origin, to treat them differently."

Philadelphia v. *New Jersey*, 437 U. S., at 626-627; see *New Energy Co., supra*, at 279-280. The burden is on the State to show that "the *discrimination* is demonstrably justified by a valid factor unrelated to economic protectionism," . . . and it has not carried this burden.

The Court reached a similar result in *Oregon Waste Systems, Inc. v. Department of Environmental Quality of Oregon*, 511 U.S. 93 (1994). Justice Thomas, normally an opponent of the Dormant Commerce Clause concept, wrote that the basic principles applied in *Chemical Waste Management* and *City of Philadelphia* would apply in the present case. Oregon charged waste from out of state a fee of $2.25 per ton for disposal at Oregon landfill sites. The fee was borne by landfill site owners. In-state waste was charged $0.85 per ton for disposal. Finding this arrangement discriminatory, Justice Thomas's opinion found the tax discriminatory and rejected Oregon's claim that the fee was a compensatory tax based on the cost to Oregon to receive imported waste because it was not "the rough equivalent of an identifiable and 'substantially similar' tax on intrastate commerce." Thomas explained that substantially similar taxes on intrastate and out-of-state items are those assessments based on a substantially equivalent taxing event. Oregon did not establish either that the fees were the rough equivalent of each other or that the differential fees were based upon the same taxing event. The fee on out-of-state waste was based upon, according to Oregon, the cost of storage, yet the claim that the difference between the two fees was made up by other taxable assessments on businesses that produced waste was not found by the Court to be substantially equivalent taxing events.

Justice Thomas called the sale and use of goods as the prototypical example of equivalent taxing events. To demonstrate an example of a compensatory tax scheme that was not offensive to the Dormant Commerce Clause, he referenced *Henneford v. Silas Mason Co.,* 300 U.S. 577 (1937), which dealt with compensatory taxes on the use of both intrastate and imported out-of-state property. In that case, Washington State collected a use tax on all tangible personal property purchased at retail, excepting from tax those items for which had already been subjected to a tax equal to or greater than the tax at the rate imposed in Washington. The exception applied to property acquired both in state and out of state. Justice Cardozo wrote that the tax did not violate the Constitution because the taxes on the two categories of property were equivalent and not discriminatory.

Notes

1. In *Comptroller of the Treasury of Md v. Wynne* **575 U.S. 542 (2015),** Justice Alito, writing for the Court, either announced a new rule applying the double taxation prohibition under the Dormant Commerce Clause's jurisprudence to individual income, or reiterated that the prohibition is not limited to the corporate income which was the subject of the previous double taxation decisions. To the majority, the decision simply reiterated a principle which it believed was implied in previous decisions. The opinion laid out the logic of the case law, focusing on internal and external inconsistencies. In the case, individuals with investment income coming from out of state were subject to county income taxation, though state income taxation was waived or allowed a credit for out of state income. Non-residents not subject to the county tax were subject to a special non-resident tax on out of state income. Despite attempts by the dissent of Justice Ginsburg (joined by Justices Kagan and Scalia) in the case to make the argument that income taxation in the present case, and the excise taxes in the main corporate taxation cases (where double taxation was found where out of state goods were subject to excise taxes from both origin

and destination states), were not the same and hence not properly analyzed as either internally or externally inconsistent, the majority treated the two types of taxation as the same and relied significantly on the double corporate excise tax cases discussed in this chapter. The reason offered by the dissenters was that under the Due Process clause states have the jurisdiction to tax all income earned by residents, regardless of where it is earned, eliminating any unfairness that such a scheme might represent.

Justice Alito and the majority maintained that authority of a taxing jurisdiction to tax all income under the Due Process Clause does not, in and of itself, answer the dormant commerce clause question. Justice Alito noted, mathematically in the opinion, that income that is taxed both in state and out of state is subject to double taxation. Such a tax scheme subjects interstate commerce to discriminatory impediments and hence violated the Dormant Commerce Clause even if the Due Process Clause would otherwise authorize the assertion of governmental power to so tax.

It should be noted that Justice Scalia and Thomas stood by their oft stated position that the Dormant Commerce Clause is the result of incorrect interpretations of the Commerce Clause by past Court panels over the years. Justice Thomas noted that lack of a historical record indicating that the Framers intended such an interpretation of the Commerce Clause, which resulted in the following response by Justice Alito, alluding to the fact that double taxation of income has a particularly pernicious effect on cross state commuters:

> We are unaware of records showing, for example, that it was common in 1787 for workers to commute to Manhattan from New Jersey by rowboat or from Connecticut by stagecoach.

Justice Scalia, using his preferred phrase "Negative Commerce Clause," termed the whole Dormant Commerce Clause exercise a "judicial fraud," which elicited a sharp response from the majority opinion author, Justice Alito, who noted that such "was not the view of the Court in *Gibbons* v. *Ogden*, 9 Wheat, at 209, where Chief Justice Marshall wrote that there was "great force" in the argument that the Commerce Clause by itself limits the power of the States to enact laws regulating interstate commerce. Since that time, this supposedly fraudulent doctrine has been applied in dozens of our opinions, joined by dozens of Justices."

2. In the 2018 term the Court addressed the nexus between the Dormant Commerce Clause, liquor sales, and the history of the interpretation of the prohibition against state discriminatory and protectionist legislation.

At issue in *Tennessee Wine and Spirits Retailers Ass'n v. Thomas,* 587 U.S. ___(2019), were state residency requirements for licenses to operate liquor stores in Tennessee. The requirements were that in order "[t]o obtain an initial retail license, an individual must demonstrate that he or she has "been a bona fide resident" of the State for the previous two years. And to renew such a license—which Tennessee law requires after only one year of operation—an individual must show continuous residency in the State for a period of 10 consecutive years." These same requirements applied to directors and officers of any corporation seeking to operate such establishments within the state, a requirement that effectively precluded publicly traded corporations from the business.

In addressing the constitutionality of the Tennessee law, Justice Alito explained the history and purpose of the Dormant Commerce Clause:

We have long held that this Clause also prohibits state laws that unduly restrict interstate commerce. See, *e.g.*, *ibid.*; *Philadelphia v. New Jersey*, 437 U. S. 617, 623– 624 (1978); *Cooley v. Board of Wardens of Port of Philadelphia ex rel. Soc. for Relief of Distressed Pilots*, 12 How. 299, 318–319 (1852); *Willson v. Black Bird Creek Marsh Co.*, 2 Pet. 245, 252 (1829). "This 'negative' aspect of the Commerce Clause" prevents the States from adopting protectionist measures and thus preserves a national market for goods and services. *New Energy Co. of Ind. v. Limbach*, 486 U. S. 269, 273 (1988).

[That] is so because removing state trade barriers was a principal reason for the adoption of the Constitution. Under the Articles of Confederation, States notoriously obstructed the interstate shipment of goods. "Interference with the arteries of commerce was cutting off the very life-blood of the nation." M. Farrand, The Framing of the Constitution of the United States 7 (1913). The Annapolis Convention of 1786 was convened to address this critical problem, and it culminated in a call for the Philadelphia Convention that framed the Constitution in the summer of 1787. At that Convention, discussion of the power to regulate interstate commerce was almost uniformly linked to the removal of state trade barriers, see Abel, *The Commerce Clause in the Constitutional Convention and in Contemporary Comment*, 25 Minn. L. Rev. 432, 470–471 (1941), and when the Constitution was sent to the state conventions, fostering free trade among the States was prominently cited as a reason for ratification. In The Federalist No. 7, Hamilton argued that state protectionism could lead to conflict among the States, see The Federalist No. 7, pp. 62– 63 (C. Rossiter ed. 1961), and in No. 11, he touted the benefits of a free national market, *id.*, at 88–89. In The Federalist No. 42, Madison sounded a similar theme. *Id.*, at 267–268.

In light of this background, it would be strange if the Constitution contained no provision curbing state protectionism, and at this point in the Court's history, no provision other than the Commerce Clause could easily do the job. The only other provisions that the Framers might have thought would fill that role, at least in part, are the Import-Export Clause, Art. I, §10, cl. 2, which generally prohibits a State from "lay[ing] any Imposts or Duties on Imports or Exports," and the Privileges and Immunities Clause, Art. IV, §2, which provides that "[t]he Citizens of each State shall be entitled to all Privileges and Immunities of Citizens in the several States." But the Import-Export Clause was long ago held to refer only to international trade. See *Woodruff v. Parham*, 8 Wall. 123, 136–137 (1869). And the Privileges and Immunities Clause has been interpreted not to protect corporations, *Western & Southern Life Ins. Co.* v. *State Bd. of Equalization of Cal.*, 451 U. S. 648, 656 (1981) (citing *Hemphill* v. *Orloff*, 277 U. S. 537, 548–550 (1928)), and may not guard against certain discrimination scrutinized under the dormant Commerce Clause, see Denning, Why the Privileges and Immunities Clause of Article IV Cannot Replace the Dormant Commerce Clause Doctrine, 88 Minn. L. Rev. 384, 393–397 (2003). So if we accept the Court's established interpretation of those provisions, that leaves the Commerce Clause as the primary safeguard against state protectionism.

It is not surprising, then, that our cases have long emphasized the connection between the trade barriers that prompted the call for a new Constitution and our dormant Commerce Clause jurisprudence. In *Guy* v. *Baltimore*, 100 U. S. 434, 440 (1880), for example, the Court wrote that state protectionist measures, "if maintained by this court, would ultimately bring our commerce to that 'oppressed and degraded state,' existing at the adoption of the present Constitution, when the helpless, inadequate Confederation was abandoned and the national government instituted." More recently, we observed that our dormant Commerce Clause cases reflect a "'central concern of the Framers that was an immediate reason for calling the Constitutional Convention: the conviction that in order to succeed, the new Union would have to avoid the tendencies toward economic Balkanization that had plagued relations among the Colonies and later among the States under the Articles of Confederation.' " *Granholm*, 544 U.S., at 472 (quoting *Hughes* v. *Oklahoma*, 441 U. S. 322, 325–326 (1979)).

In light of this history and our established case law, we reiterate that the Commerce Clause by its own force restricts state protectionism.

The Court found that the requirements did in fact violate the Constitution's Commerce Clause in that the residency requirements discriminated facially against interstate commerce. But because liquor was involved, the Court had to deal with the complicating factor of the Twenty-first Amendment, which repealed Prohibition. Section 2 of the Amendment states: "transportation or importation into any State, Territory, or possession of the United States for delivery or use therein of intoxicating liquors, in violation of the laws thereof, is hereby prohibited". Does this language mean that even discriminatory laws are protected by the Twenty-first? The Court said no, and discussed the state of the law and Court decisions before Prohibition. The repealing amendment, according to Justice Alito's opinion, simply returns the state of affairs with regard to liquor regulation to the state of affairs prior to Prohibition, which included the Dormant Commerce Clause's prohibition of discriminatory legislation. Given that Tennessee's law was clearly discriminatory, the Court ruled it unconstitutional, the Twenty-first Amendment notwithstanding.

Question

Is Justice Thomas's distinction between the facts in *Oregon Waste Systems* and *Henneford* persuasive?

Restrictions on Both Out-of-State and Intrastate Activity. On the same day it decided *Chemical Waste Management*, the Court decided *Fort Gratiot Sanitary Landfill, Inc. v. Michigan Department of Natural Resources*, 504 U.S. 353 (1992). Michigan law gave counties the option of restricting use of landfill resources to garbage collected in the county's jurisdiction. A local landfill operator filed for and was rejected in an attempt to receive out-of-state waste. Petitioner sued, claiming that the restrictions were unconstitutional under the Commerce Clause. Michigan argued, among other things, that the option giving counties the choice to restrict landfill usage to in-county waste was not discriminatory against out-of-state imports, but that it treated intrastate and interstate waste identically. The Court, in an opinion written by Justice Stevens, disagreed and cited to previous cases in which discrimination by political subdivisions were no more tolerable under the Dormant Commerce Clause than statewide discrimination against out-of-state parties, even though the former entailed some discrimination against in-state commercial interests.

For this proposition, Justice Stevens referenced *Dean Milk v. Madison*, 340 U.S. 349 (1951). In that case, a city law barring the sale of milk in Madison, Wisconsin, that had been processed and bottled outside of a 5 mile radius, was found to be discriminatory even though the discrimination applied to some Wisconsin processors as well as out-of-state processors. The Court noted that the fact that Wisconsin milk producers are discriminated against as well is immaterial. The fact remained that the regulation discriminated against out-of-state milk, and did so even though there were reasonable alternatives to discrimination to achieve the goal of milk safety. Among those reasonable alternatives would be to rely upon federal standards and inspections to ensure the safety of out-of-state milk, standards which, it was acknowledged by both parties, would reach the same safety goals as Madison's plan.

Discrimination That Does Not Offend the Dormant Commerce Clause. *Dean Milk* and other discrimination/protectionism cases leave some leeway for governments at the state and political subdivision level to actually discriminate "if reasonable nondiscriminatory alternatives, adequate to conserve legitimate local interests, are available," 340 U.S. at 354. For an example of a law that allowed discrimination under this standard, consider *Maine v. Taylor*, 477 U.S. 131 (1986). In that case, the Court gave deference to a finding that there existed legitimate uncertainty about possible ecological effects on the presence of parasites in baitfish from out of state and that these concerns could not be adequately served in nondiscriminatory ways. Writing for the majority, Justice Blackmun reiterated the special scrutiny the Court devotes to protectionist legislation. In upholding Maine's law, the Court held that discriminatory laws may be upheld only if they serve "a legitimate local purpose that could not be served as well by available nondiscriminatory means."

As for the first prong, the facts of the case indicate that it was quite likely that parasites would have a significantly damaging effect on Maine's baitfish population. The Court acknowledged the legitimacy of Maine's efforts to protect its local fish population from the damage, even though local fish could be exposed to parasites through continuous river flows from other jurisdictions. The possibility that these efforts might prove to be negligible did not sway the Court. The opinion argued that the Commerce Clause did not require Maine to do nothing in the face of a real problem. As for the second prong of the test, the Court accepted evidence that testing procedures for determining the existence of parasites in imported baitfish had not been developed. Hence, a crucial nondiscriminatory alternative to a total quarantine, testing supplies of baitfish as they enter Maine, was held not to be a reasonable alternative to an outright prohibition.

The Market Participant Exception. The cases in this section can be discussed in either facial or non-facial categories. Here the state acts as a consumer for services or goods, or as a vender of services or goods. The choices made by the state, to engage in transactions with the freedom of a market participant—to make market decisions that are deemed non-regulatory—can be compared to the choices made by an individual or firm who would not be limited to transactions involving parties of the same state. The exception applies, however, as long as the state does not use its regulatory power to dictate downstream transactions of the party with whom the state is doing business.

SOUTH-CENTRAL TIMBER DEVELOPMENT, INC. v. WUNNICKE
467 U.S. 82 (1984)

Justice WHITE announced the judgment of the Court and delivered the opinion of the Court with respect to Parts I and II, and an opinion with respect to Parts III and IV, in which Justice BRENNAN, Justice BLACKMUN, and Justice STEVENS joined.

I

In September 1980, the Alaska Department of Natural Resources published a notice that it would sell approximately 49 million board-feet of timber in the area of Icy Cape, Alaska, on October 23, 1980. The notice of sale, the prospectus, and the proposed contract for the sale all provided, pursuant to 11 Alaska Admin. Code 76.130 (1974), that "[p]rimary manufacture within the State of Alaska will be required as a special provision of the contract." App. 35a. Under the primary-manufacture requirement, the successful bidder must partially process the timber prior to shipping it outside of the State. The requirement is imposed by contract and does not limit the export of unprocessed timber not owned by the State. The stated purpose of the requirement is to "protect existing industries, provide for the establishment of new industries, derive revenue from all timber resources, and manage the State's forests on a sustained yield basis." Governor's Policy Statement, App. 28a. When it imposes the requirement, the State charges a significantly lower price for the timber than it otherwise would. . . .

Petitioner, South-Central Timber Development, Inc., is an Alaska corporation engaged in the business of purchasing standing timber, logging the timber, and shipping the logs into foreign commerce, almost exclusively to Japan. 4 It does not operate a mill in Alaska and customarily sells unprocessed logs. When it learned that the primary-manufacture requirement was to be imposed on the Icy Cape sale, it brought an action in Federal District Court seeking an injunction, arguing that the requirement violated the negative implications of the Commerce Clause. . . .

III

[Are] Alaska's restrictions on export of unprocessed timber from state-owned lands are exempt from Commerce Clause scrutiny under the "market-participant doctrine."

Our cases make clear that if a State is acting as a market participant, rather than as a market regulator, the Dormant Commerce Clause places no limitation on its activities. See *White v. Massachusetts Council of Construction Employers, Inc.*, 460 U.S., at 206 -208; *Reeves, Inc. v. Stake*, 447 U.S. 429, 436 -437 (1980); *Hughes v. Alexandria Scrap Corp.*, 426 U.S. 794, 810 (1976). The precise contours of the market-participant doctrine have yet to be established, however, the doctrine having been applied in only three cases of this Court to date.

The first of the cases, *Hughes v. Alexandria Scrap Corp.*, supra, involved a Maryland program designed to reduce the number of junked automobiles in the State. A "bounty" was established on Maryland-licensed junk cars, and the State imposed more stringent documentation requirements on out-of-state scrap processors than on in-state ones. The Court rejected a Commerce Clause attack on the program, although it noted that under traditional Commerce Clause analysis the program might well be invalid because it had the effect of reducing the flow of goods in interstate commerce. Id., at 805. The Court concluded that Maryland's action was not "the kind of action with which the Commerce Clause is concerned," ibid., because "[n]othing in the purposes animating the Commerce Clause prohibits a State, in the absence of congressional action, from participating in the market and exercising the right to favor its own citizens over others." Id., at 810 (footnote omitted).

In *Reeves, Inc. v. Stake*, supra, the Court upheld a South Dakota policy of restricting the sale of cement from a state-owned plant to state residents, declaring that "[t]he basic distinction drawn in Alexandria Scrap between States as market participants and States as market regulators makes good sense and sound law." Id., at 436. The Court relied upon "'the long recognized right of trader or manufacturer, engaged in an entirely private business, freely to exercise his own independent discretion as to parties with whom he will deal.'" Id., at 438-439 (quoting United States v. Colgate & Co., 250 U.S. 300, 307 (1919)). In essence, the Court recognized the principle that the Commerce Clause places no limitations on a State's refusal to deal with particular parties when it is participating in the interstate market in goods.

The most recent of this Court's cases developing the market-participant doctrine is *White v. Massachusetts Council of Construction Employers, Inc.*, supra, in which the Court sustained against a Commerce Clause challenge an executive order of the Mayor of Boston that required all construction projects funded in whole or in part by city funds or city-administered funds to be performed by a work force of at least 50% city residents. The Court rejected the argument that the city was not entitled to the protection of the doctrine because the order had the effect of regulating employment contracts between public contractors and their employees. Id., [467 U.S. 82, 95] at 211, n. 7. Recognizing that "there are some limits on a state or local government's ability to impose restrictions that reach beyond the immediate parties with which the government transacts business," the Court found it unnecessary to define those limits because "[e]veryone affected by the order [was], in a substantial if informal sense, 'working for the city.'" Ibid. The fact that the employees were "working for the city" was "crucial" to the market-participant analysis in White. *United Building and Construction Trades Council v. Mayor of Camden*, 465 U.S. 208, 219 (1984).

The State of Alaska contends that its primary-manufacture requirement fits squarely within the market-participant doctrine, arguing that "Alaska's entry into the market may be viewed as precisely the same type of subsidy to local interests that the Court found unobjectionable in Alexandria Scrap." . . . However, when Maryland became involved in the scrap market it was as a purchaser of scrap; Alaska, on the other hand, participates in the timber market, but imposes conditions downstream in the timber-processing market. Alaska is not merely subsidizing local timber processing in an amount "roughly equal to the difference between the price the timber would fetch in the absence of such a requirement and the amount the state actually receives." If the State directly subsidized the timber-processing industry by such an amount, the purchaser would retain the option of taking advantage of the subsidy by processing timber in the State or forgoing the benefits of the subsidy and exporting unprocessed timber. Under the Alaska requirement, however, the choice is made for him: if he buys timber from the State he is not free to take the timber out of state prior to processing.

The State also would have us find Reeves controlling. It states that "Reeves made it clear that the Commerce Clause imposes no limitation on Alaska's power to choose the terms on which it will sell its timber." . . . Such an unrestrained reading of Reeves is unwarranted. Although the Court in Reeves did strongly endorse the right of a State to deal with whomever it chooses when it participates in the market, it did not — and did not purport to — sanction the imposition of any terms that the State might desire. For example, the Court expressly noted in Reeves that "Commerce Clause scrutiny may well be more rigorous when a restraint on foreign commerce is alleged," 447 U.S., at 438, n. 9; that a natural resource "like coal, timber, wild game, or minerals," was not involved, but instead the cement was "the end product of a complex process whereby a costly physical plant and human labor act on raw materials," id., at 443-444; and that South Dakota did not bar resale of South Dakota cement to out-of-state purchasers, id., at 444, n. 17. In this case, all three of the elements that were not present in Reeves — foreign commerce, a natural resource, and restrictions on resale — are present.

Finally, Alaska argues that since the Court in White upheld a requirement that reached beyond "the boundary of formal privity of contract," 460 U.S., at 211, n. 7, then, a fortiori, the primary-manufacture requirement is permissible, because the State is not regulating contracts for resale of timber or regulating the buying and selling of timber, but is instead "a seller of timber, pure and simple." Brief for Respondents 28. Yet it is clear that the State is more than merely a seller of timber. In the commercial context, the seller usually has no say over, and no interest in, how the product is to be used after sale; in this case, however, payment for the timber does not end the obligations of the purchaser, for, despite the fact that the purchaser has taken delivery of the timber and has paid for it, he cannot do with it as he pleases. Instead, he is obligated to deal with a stranger to the contract after completion of the sale. That privity of contract is not always the outer boundary of permissible state activity does not necessarily mean that the Commerce Clause has no application within the boundary of formal privity. The market-participant doctrine permits a State to influence "a discrete, identifiable class of economic activity in which [it] is a major participant." *White v. Massachusetts Council of Construction Workers, Inc.*, 460 U.S., at 211, n. 7. Contrary to the State's contention, the doctrine is not carte blanche to impose any conditions that the State has the economic power to dictate, and does not validate any requirement merely because the State imposes it upon someone with whom it is in contractual privity.

The limit of the market-participant doctrine must be that it allows a State to impose burdens on commerce within the market in which it is a participant, but allows it to go no further. The State may not impose conditions, whether by statute, regulation, or contract, that have a substantial regulatory effect outside of that particular market. 10 Unless the "market" is relatively narrowly defined, the doctrine has the potential of swallowing up the rule that States may not impose substantial burdens on interstate commerce even if they act with the permissible state purpose of fostering local industry. . . .

[D]ownstream restrictions have a greater regulatory effect than do limitations on the immediate transaction. Instead of merely choosing its own trading partners, the State is attempting to govern the private, separate economic relationships of its trading partners; that is, it restricts the post-purchase activity of the purchaser, rather than merely the purchasing activity. In contrast to the situation in White, this restriction on private economic activity takes place after the completion of the parties' direct commercial obligations, rather than during the course of an ongoing commercial relationship in which the city retained a continuing proprietary interest in the subject of the contract. 11 In sum, the State may not avail itself of the market-participant doctrine to immunize its downstream regulation of the timber-processing market in which it is not a participant.

IV

Viewed as a naked restraint on export of unprocessed logs, there is little question that the processing requirement cannot survive scrutiny under the precedents of the Court. For example, in Pike v. Bruce Church, Inc., 397 U.S. 137 (1970), we . . . held that if the Commerce Clause forbids a State to require work to be done within the State for the purpose of promoting employment, then, a fortiori, it forbids a State to impose such a requirement to enhance the reputation of its producers. Because of the protectionist nature of Alaska's local-processing requirement and the burden on commerce resulting therefrom, we conclude that it falls within the rule of virtual per se invalidity of laws that "bloc[k] the flow of interstate commerce at a State's borders." City of Philadelphia v. New Jersey, 437 U.S. 617, 624 (1978).

We are buttressed in our conclusion that the restriction is invalid by the fact that foreign commerce is burdened by the restriction. It is a well-accepted rule that state restrictions burdening foreign commerce are subjected to a more rigorous and searching scrutiny. It is crucial to the efficient execution of the Nation's foreign policy that "the Federal Government . . . speak with one voice when regulating commercial relations with foreign governments." Michelin Tire Corp. v. Wages, 423 U.S. 276, 285 (1976); see also Japan Line, Ltd. v. County of Los Angeles, 441 U.S. 434 (1979). In light of the substantial attention given by Congress to the subject of export restrictions on unprocessed timber, it would be peculiarly inappropriate to permit state regulation of the subject. See Prohibit Export of Unprocessed Timber: Hearing on H. R. 639 before the Subcommittee on Forests, Family Farms, and Energy of the House Committee on Agriculture, 97th Cong., 1st Sess. (1981).

. . . It is so ordered. Justice Marshall took no part in the decision of this case.

Justice REHNQUIST, with whom Justice O'CONNOR joins, dissenting. . . .

The contractual term at issue here no more transforms Alaska's sale of timber into "regulation" of the processing industry than the resident-hiring preference imposed by the city of Boston in White v. Massachusetts Council of Construction Employers, Inc., 460 U.S. 204 (1983), constituted regulation of the construction industry. Alaska is merely paying the buyer of the timber indirectly, by means of a reduced price, to hire Alaska residents to process the timber. Under existing precedent, the State could accomplish that same result in any number of ways. For example, the State could choose to sell its timber only to those companies that maintain active primary-processing plants in Alaska. Reeves, Inc. v. Stake, 447 U.S. 429 (1980). Or the State could directly subsidize the primary-processing industry within the State. Hughes v. Alexandria Scrap Corp., 426 U.S. 794 (1976). The State could even pay to have the logs processed and then enter the market only to sell processed logs. See ante, at 99. It seems to me unduly formalistic to conclude that the one path chosen by the State as best suited to promote its concerns is the path forbidden it by the Commerce Clause. For these reasons, I would affirm the judgment of the Court of Appeals.

Notes and Questions

1. The key part of the case was decided by a plurality of the Court. Eight Justices took part in the deliberations as Justice Marshall was not involved. Justice Rehnquist and Justice O'Connor dissented. Justice Powell wrote separately, concurring in part and in the judgment and was joined by Chief Justice Burger.

2. Is the plurality argument (parts III and IV) that downstream requirements have to be within the same market in which it is a participant persuasive? Critique the argument.

3. Justice Rehnquist (soon to be Chief Justice Rehnquist) argues that the requirement of local processing is really a term of the contract with the timber buyers. In other words, it is consideration given by the timber buyers in exchange for the concessionary price for the timber. Is Rehnquist correct?

DEPARTMENT OF REVENUE OF KENTUCKY v. DAVIS
553 U.S. 328 (2008)

[Earlier, this case was used to discuss the emerging public function doctrine. This excerpt of the opinion addresses a rather curious argument by Justice Souter that Kentucky's bonds and tax programs qualified them for the market participant exception because of Kentucky's involvement in the private bond market.]

This case, like *United Haulers,* may also be seen under the broader rubric of the market participation doctrine, although the Davises say that market participant cases are inapposite here. In their view, we may not characterize state action under the Kentucky statutes as market activity for public purposes, because this would ignore a fact absent in *United Haulers* but central here: this is a case about differential taxation, and a difference that amounts to a heavier tax burden on interstate activity is forbidden, see, *e.g., Camps Newfound/Owatonna, Inc.* v. *Town of Harrison,* 520 U. S. 564 (1997) (invalidating statute exempting charities from real estate and personal property taxes unless conducted or operated principally for the benefit of out-of-state residents); *Fulton Corp.,* 516 U. S. 325 (striking down tax on corporate stock held by state residents, where rate of tax was inversely proportional to the corporation's exposure to the State's income tax); *Bacchus Imports, Ltd.* v. *Dias,* 468 U. S. 263 (1984) (holding excise tax on sale of liquor at wholesale unconstitutional because it exempted some locally produced alcoholic beverages).

The Davises make a fair point to the extent that they argue that Kentucky acts in two roles at once, issuing bonds and setting taxes, and if looked at as a taxing authority it seems to invite dormant Commerce Clause scrutiny of its regulatory activity, see *Walling* v. *Michigan,* 116 U. S. 446, 455 (1886) ("A discriminating tax imposed by a State operating to the disadvantage of the products of other States when introduced into the first mentioned State, is, in effect, a regulation in restraint of commerce among the States, and as such is a usurpation of the power conferred by the Constitution upon the Congress"); see also *Camps Newfound, supra,* at 578 ("[I]t is clear that discriminatory burdens on interstate commerce imposed by regulation or taxation may . . . violate the Commerce Clause"); *Tracy, supra,* at 287 ("The negative or dormant implication of the Commerce Clause prohibits state taxation . . . that discriminates against or unduly burdens interstate commerce").

But there is no ignoring the fact that imposing the differential tax scheme makes sense only because Kentucky is also a bond issuer. The Commonwealth has entered the market for debt securities, just as Maryland entered the market for automobile hulks, see *Alexandria Scrap,* 426 U. S., at 806, and South Dakota entered the cement market, see *Reeves,* 447 U. S., at 440. It simply blinks this reality to disaggregate the Commonwealth's two roles and pretend that in exempting the income from its securities, Kentucky is independently regulating or regulating in the garden variety way that has made a State vulnerable to the dormant Commerce Clause. States that regulated the price of milk, see, *e.g., West Lynn Creamery, Inc.* v. *Healy,* 512 U. S. 186 (1994) ; *Baldwin* v. *G. A. F. Seelig, Inc.,* 294 U. S. 511 (1935), did not keep herds of cows or compete against dairy producers for the dollars of milk drinkers. But when Kentucky exempts its bond interest, it is competing in the market for limited investment dollars, alongside private bond issuers and its sister States, and its tax structure is one of the tools of competition.

The failure to appreciate that regulation by taxation here goes hand in hand with market participation by selling bonds allows the Davises to advocate the error of focusing exclusively on the Commonwealth as regulator and ignoring the Commonwealth as bond seller, see Brief for Respondents 36-39, just as the state court did in saying that "'when a state chooses to tax its citizens, it is acting as a market regulator[,]' not as a market participant." 197 S. W. 3d, at 564 (quoting *Shaper,* 97 Ohio App. 3d, at 764, 647 N. E. 2d, at 552). To indulge in this single vision, however, would require overruling most, if not all, of the cases on point decided since *Alexandria Scrap. White,* for example, also scrutinized a government acting in dual roles. The mayor of Boston promulgated an executive order that bore the hallmarks of regulation: it applied to every construction project funded wholly or partially by city funds (or funds administered by the city), and it imposed general restrictions on the hiring practices of private contractors, mandating that 50% of their work forces be bona fide Boston residents and setting thresholds for minorities (25%) and women (10%) as well. See 460 U. S., at 205, n. 1; see also *id.,* at 218–219 (Blackmun, J., concurring in part and dissenting in part) ("The executive order in this case . . . is a direct attempt to govern private economic relationships. . . . [It] is the essence of regulation"). At the same time, the city took part in the market by "expend[ing] its own funds in entering into construction contracts for public projects." *Id.,* at 214–215 (opinion of the Court). After speaking of "'[t]he basic distinction . . . between States as market participants and States as market regulators,'" *id.,* at 207 (quoting *Reeves, supra,* at 436-437), *White* did not dissect Boston's conduct and ignore the former. Instead, the Court treated the regulatory activity in favor of local and minority labor as terms or conditions of the government's efforts in its market role, which was treated as dispositive. Similarly, in *Alexandria Scrap,* Maryland employed the tools of regulation to invigorate its participation in the market for automobile hulks. The specific controversy there was over documentation requirements included in a "comprehensive statute designed to speed up the scrap cycle." 426 U. S., at 796. Superficially, the scheme was regulatory in nature; but the Court's decision was premised on its view that, in practical terms, Maryland had not only regulated but had also "entered into the market itself to bid up [the] price" of automobile hulks. See *id.,* at 806In each of these cases the commercial activities by the governments and their regulatory efforts complemented each other in some way, and in each of them the fact of tying the regulation to the public object of the foray into the market was understood to give the regulation a civic objective different from the discrimination traditionally held to be unlawful: in the paradigm of unconstitutional discrimination the law chills interstate activity by creating a commercial advantage for goods or services marketed by local private actors, not by governments and those they employ to fulfill their civic objectives, see, . . . In sum, our cases on market regulation without market participation prescribe standard dormant Commerce Clause analysis; our cases on market participation joined with regulation (the usual situation) prescribe exceptional treatment for this direct governmental activity in commercial markets for the public's benefit. The Kentucky tax scheme falls outside the forbidden paradigm because the Commonwealth's direct participation favors, not local private entrepreneurs, but the Commonwealth and local governments. The Commonwealth enacted its tax code with an eye toward making some or all of its bonds more marketable. When it issues them for sale in the bond market, it relies on that tax code, and seller and purchaser treat the bonds and the tax rate as joined just as intimately, say, as the work force requirements and city construction contracts were in Boston. Issuing bonds must therefore have the same significance under the dormant Commerce Clause as government trash processing, junk car disposal, or construction; and *United Haulers, Alexandria Scrap,* and *White* can be followed only by rejecting the Davises' argument that Kentucky's regulatory activity should be viewed in isolation as Commerce Clause discrimination.

Notes and Questions

This portion, III-B, was joined only by Justices Stevens and Breyer, a total of three out of nine Justices. Is it valid as precedent? Does this portion of the opinion expand the market participant doctrine?

The New Public Function Exception. The following decision, *Carbone v. Clarkstown*, could easily have been presented under the earlier heading "Restrictions on Both Out-of-State and Intrastate Activity." However, we are presenting it here because the decision was crucial in the formulation of a new doctrine in the Dormant Commerce Clause jurisprudence, the public function exception. Though the *Carbone* decision does not address the exception, the decision following it, *United Haulers v. Oneida-Herkimer*, articulates and develops the exception in large part based on distinctions between it and *Carbone*.

C & A CARBONE, INC. v. TOWN OF CLARKSTOWN
511 U.S. 383 (1993)

Justice KENNEDY delivered the opinion of the Court.

As solid waste output continues apace and landfill capacity becomes more costly and scarce, state and local governments are expending significant resources to develop trash control systems that are efficient, lawful, and protective of the environment. The difficulty of their task is evident from the number of recent cases that we have heard involving waste transfer and treatment. The case decided today, while perhaps a small new chapter in that course of decisions, rests nevertheless upon well-settled principles of our Commerce Clause jurisprudence.

We consider a so-called flow control ordinance, which requires all solid waste to be processed at a designated transfer station before leaving the municipality. The avowed purpose of the ordinance is to retain the processing fees charged at the transfer station to amortize the cost of the facility. Because it attains this goal by depriving competitors, including out-of-state firms, of access to a local market, we hold that the flow control ordinance violates the Commerce Clause. . . .

In August, 1989, Clarkstown entered into a consent decree with the New York State Department of Environmental Conservation. The town agreed to close its landfill located on Route 303 in West Nyack and build a new solid waste transfer station on the same site. The station would receive bulk solid waste and separate recyclable from nonrecyclable items. Recyclable waste would be baled for shipment to a recycling facility; nonrecyclable waste, to a suitable landfill or incinerator.

The cost of building the transfer station was estimated at $1.4 million. A local private contractor agreed to construct the facility and operate it for five years, after which the town would buy it for one dollar. During those five years, the town guaranteed a minimum waste flow of 120,000 tons per year, for which the contractor could charge the hauler a so-called tipping fee of $81 per ton. If the station received less than 120,000 tons in a year, the town promised to make up the tipping fee deficit. The object of this arrangement was to amortize the cost of the transfer station: the town would finance its new facility with the income generated by the tipping fees.

The problem, of course, was how to meet the yearly guarantee. This difficulty was compounded by the fact that the tipping fee of $81 per ton exceeded the disposal cost of unsorted solid waste on the private market. The solution the town adopted was the flow control ordinance here in question. The ordinance requires all nonhazardous solid waste within the town to be deposited at the Route 303 transfer station. Noncompliance is punishable by as much as a $1,000 fine and up to 15 days in jail.

The petitioners in this case are C & A Carbone, Inc., a company engaged in the processing of solid waste, and various related companies or persons, all of whom we designate Carbone. Carbone operates a recycling center in Clarkstown, where it receives bulk solid waste, sorts and bales it, and then ships it to other processing facilities — much as occurs at the town's new transfer station. While the flow control ordinance permits recyclers like Carbone to continue receiving solid waste, 3.C, it requires them to bring the nonrecyclable residue from that waste to the Route 303 station. It thus forbids Carbone to ship the nonrecyclable waste itself, and it requires Carbone to pay a tipping fee on trash that Carbone has already sorted.

[State officials discovered that Carbone had been sending collected waste out of state in violation of the local ordinance. The city of Clarkstown eventually sued Carbone to enjoin it from sending waste to any other collection point other than the one designated by the ordinance. The litigation reached the Supreme Court.]

At the outset, we confirm that the flow control ordinance does regulate interstate commerce, despite the town's position to the contrary. The town says that its ordinance reaches only waste within its jurisdiction, and is, in practical effect, a quarantine: it prevents garbage from entering the stream of interstate commerce until it is made safe. This reasoning is premised, however, on an outdated and mistaken concept of what constitutes interstate commerce.

While the immediate effect of the ordinance is to direct local transport of solid waste to a designated site within the local jurisdiction, its economic effects are interstate in reach. The Carbone facility in Clarkstown receives and processes waste from places other than Clarkstown, including from out of State. By requiring Carbone to send the non-recyclable portion of this waste to the Route 303 transfer station at an additional cost, the flow control ordinance drives up the cost for out-of-state interests to dispose of their solid waste. [The] ordinance prevents everyone except the favored local operator from performing the initial processing step. The ordinance thus deprives out-of-state businesses of access to a local market. These economic effects are more than enough to bring the Clarkstown ordinance within the purview of the Commerce Clause. It is well settled that actions are within the domain of the Commerce Clause if they burden interstate commerce or impede its free flow. NLRB v. Jones & Laughlin Steel Corp., 301 U.S. 1, 31 (1937). . . .

Our initial discussion of the effects of the ordinance on interstate commerce goes far toward refuting the town's contention that there is no discrimination in its regulatory scheme. The town's own arguments go the rest of the way. As the town itself points out, what makes garbage a profitable business is not its own worth but the fact that its possessor must pay to get rid of it. In other words, the article of commerce is not so much the solid waste itself, but rather the service of processing and disposing of it.

The ordinance is no less discriminatory because in-state or in-town processors are also covered by the prohibition. In Dean Milk Co. v. Madison, 340 U.S. 349 (1951), we struck down a city ordinance that required all milk sold in the city to be pasteurized within five miles of the city lines. We found it "immaterial that Wisconsin milk from outside the Madison area is subjected to the same proscription as that moving in interstate commerce." Id., at 354, n. 4.

. . . In this light, the flow control ordinance is just one more instance of local processing requirements that we long have held invalid. . . . The essential vice in laws of this sort is that they bar the import of the processing service. . . . Put another way, the offending local laws hoard a local resource . . . for the benefit of local businesses that treat it.

The flow control ordinance has the same design and effect. It hoards solid waste, and the demand to get rid of it, for the benefit of the preferred processing facility. . . .

Discrimination against interstate commerce in favor of local business or investment is per se invalid, save in a narrow class of cases in which the municipality can demonstrate, under rigorous scrutiny, that it has no other means to advance a legitimate local interest. Maine v. Taylor, 477 U.S. 131 (1986). . . .

The flow control ordinance does serve a central purpose that a non-protectionist regulation would not: it ensures that the town-sponsored facility will be profitable, so that the local contractor can build it and Clarkstown can buy it back at nominal cost in five years. In other words, as the most candid of amici and even Clarkstown admit, the flow control ordinance is a financing measure. By itself, of course, revenue generation is not a local interest that can justify discrimination against interstate commerce. Otherwise, States could impose discriminatory taxes against solid waste originating outside the State.

Clarkstown maintains that special financing is necessary to ensure the long-term survival of the designated facility. If so, the town may subsidize the facility through general taxes or municipal bonds. New Energy Co. of Indiana v. Limbach, 486 U.S. 269, 278 (1988). But having elected to use the open market to earn revenues for its project, the town may not employ discriminatory regulation to give that project an advantage over rival businesses from out of State.

Though the Clarkstown ordinance may not in explicit terms seek to regulate interstate commerce, it does so nonetheless by its practical effect and design. In this respect the ordinance is not far different from the state law this Court found invalid in Buck v. Kuykendall, 267 U.S. 307 (1925). That statute prohibited common carriers from using state highways over certain routes without a certificate of public convenience. Writing for the Court, Justice Brandeis said of the law: "Its primary purpose is not regulation with a view to safety or to conservation of the highways, but the prohibition of competition. It determines not the manner of use, but the persons by whom the highways may be used. It prohibits such use to some persons while permitting it to others for the same purpose and in the same manner." Id., at 315-316.

State and local governments may not use their regulatory power to favor local enterprise by prohibiting patronage of out-of-state competitors or their facilities. We reverse the judgment and remand the case for proceedings not inconsistent with this decision.

It is so ordered

———————

In the next decision, *United Haulers v. Oneida-Herkimer,* Chief Justice John Roberts establishes for the first time an exception from the anti-discrimination rule for state-run operations. Examine Chief Justice Roberts's reasoning in the decision. Does he base his analysis on previous cases, constitutional interpretation independent of previous cases, or judicial policy? Is the distinction made by the Chief Justice between *Carbone* and *United Haulers* convincing? You may wish to synthesize the two cases to help in answering these questions. Consider when reading the excerpt of Justice Thomas's dissent whether his critique of the majority's approach is warranted.

UNITED HAULERS ASSOCIATION v. ONEIDA-HERKIMER SOLID WASTE MANAGEMENT AUTHORITY
550 U.S. 330 (2007)

Chief Justice ROBERTS delivered the opinion of the Court, except as to Part II-D.

"Flow control" ordinances require trash haulers to deliver solid waste to a particular waste processing facility. In *C & A Carbone, Inc.* v. *Clarkstown*, 511 U. S. 383 (1994), this Court struck down under the Commerce Clause a flow control ordinance that forced haulers to deliver waste to a particular *private* processing facility. In this case, we face flow control ordinances quite similar to the one invalidated in *Carbone*. The only salient difference is that the laws at issue here require haulers to bring waste to facilities owned and operated by a state-created public benefit corporation. We find this difference constitutionally significant. Disposing of trash has been a traditional government activity for years, and laws that favor the government in such areas — but treat every private business, whether in-state or out-of-state, exactly the same — do not discriminate against interstate commerce for purposes of the Commerce Clause. . . .

I

. . . In 1989, the [Oneida-Herkimer Solid Waste Management Authority, a government agency] and the Counties entered into a Solid Waste Management Agreement, under which the Authority agreed to manage all solid waste within the Counties. Private haulers would remain free to pick up citizens' trash from the curb, but the Authority would take over the job of processing the trash, sorting it, and sending it off for disposal. To fulfill its part of the bargain, the Authority agreed to purchase and develop facilities for the processing and disposal of solid waste and recyclables generated in the Counties.

The Authority collected "tipping fees" to cover its operating and maintenance costs for these facilities. The tipping fees significantly exceeded those charged for waste removal on the open market, but they allowed the Authority to do more than the average private waste disposer. . . .

. . . Counties enacted "flow control" ordinances requiring that all solid waste generated within the Counties be delivered to the Authority's processing sites. Private haulers must obtain a permit from the Authority to collect waste in the Counties. Penalties for noncompliance with the ordinances include permit revocation, fines, and imprisonment.

Petitioners are United Haulers Association, Inc., a trade association made up of solid waste management companies, and six haulers that operated in Oneida and Herkimer Counties when this action was filed. . . .

II

A

To determine whether a law violates this so-called "dormant" aspect of the Commerce Clause, we first ask whether it discriminates on its face against interstate commerce. . . .

B

. . . In *Carbone*, the town of Clarkstown, New York, hired a private contractor to build a waste transfer station. According to the terms of the deal, the contractor would operate the facility for five years, charging an above-market tipping fee of $81 per ton; after five years, the town would buy the facility for one dollar. The town guaranteed that the facility would receive a certain volume of trash per year. To make good on its promise, Clarkstown passed a flow control ordinance requiring that all nonhazardous solid waste within the town be deposited at the transfer facility. See 511 U. S., at 387.

This Court struck down the ordinance, holding that it discriminated against interstate commerce by "hoard[ing] solid waste, and the demand to get rid of it, for the benefit of the preferred processing facility." *Id.,* at 392. The dissent pointed out that all of this Court's local processing cases involved laws that discriminated in favor of *private* entities, not public ones. *Id.,* at 411 (opinion of Souter, J.). According to the dissent, Clarkstown's ostensibly private transfer station was "essentially a municipal facility," *id.,* at 419, and this distinction should have saved Clarkstown's ordinance because favoring local government is by its nature different from favoring a particular private company. The majority did not comment on the dissent's public-private distinction.

The parties in this case draw opposite inferences from the majority's silence. The haulers say it proves that the majority agreed with the dissent's characterization of the facility, but thought there was no difference under the dormant Commerce Clause between laws favoring private entities and those favoring public ones. The Counties disagree, arguing that the majority studiously avoided the issue because the facility in *Carbone* was private, and therefore the question whether *public* facilities may be favored was not properly before the Court.

We believe the latter interpretation of *Carbone* is correct. . . . "[I]n *Carbone* the Justices were divided over the *fact of whether* the favored facility was public or private, rather than on the import of that distinction." The *Carbone* dissent offered a number of reasons why public entities should be treated differently from private ones under the dormant Commerce Clause. It is hard to suppose that the *Carbone* majority definitively rejected these arguments without explaining why.

The *Carbone* majority viewed Clarkstown's flow control ordinance as "just one more instance of local processing requirements that we long have held invalid." *Id.,* at 391. It then cited six local processing cases, every one of which involved discrimination in favor of *private* enterprise. The Court's own description of the cases acknowledges that the "offending local laws hoard a local resource — be it meat, shrimp, or milk — for the benefit of *local businesses* that treat it." *Id.,* at 392 (emphasis added). If the Court were extending this line of local processing cases to cover discrimination in favor of local government, one would expect it to have said so. . . .

C

The flow control ordinances in this case benefit a clearly public facility, while treating all private companies exactly the same. Because the question is now squarely presented on the facts of the case before us, we decide that such flow control ordinances do not discriminate against interstate commerce for purposes of the dormant Commerce Clause.

Given these differences, it does not make sense to regard laws favoring local government and laws favoring private industry with equal skepticism. As our local processing cases demonstrate, when a law favors in-state business over out-of-state competition, rigorous scrutiny is appropriate because the law is often the product of "simple economic protectionism." *Wyoming* v. *Oklahoma*, 502 U. S. 437, 454 (1992); *Philadelphia* v. *New Jersey*, 437 U. S., at 626-627. Laws favoring local government, by contrast, may be directed toward any number of legitimate goals unrelated to protectionism. Here the flow control ordinances enable the Counties to pursue particular policies with respect to the handling and treatment of waste generated in the Counties, while allocating the costs of those policies on citizens and businesses according to the volume of waste they generate.

The contrary approach of treating public and private entities the same under the dormant Commerce Clause would lead to unprecedented and unbounded interference by the courts with state and local government. The dormant Commerce Clause is not a roving license for federal courts to decide what activities are appropriate for state and local government to undertake, and what activities must be the province of private market competition. In this case, the citizens of Oneida and Herkimer Counties have chosen the government to provide waste management services, with a limited role for the private sector in arranging for transport of waste from the curb to the public facilities. The citizens could have left the entire matter for the private sector, in which case any regulation they undertook could not discriminate against interstate commerce. But it was also open to them to vest responsibility for the matter with their government, and to adopt flow control ordinances to support the government effort. It is not the office of the Commerce Clause to control the decision of the voters on whether government or the private sector should provide waste management services. "The Commerce Clause significantly limits the ability of States and localities to regulate or otherwise burden the flow of interstate commerce, but it does not elevate free trade above all other values." *Maine* v. *Taylor*, 477 U. S., at 151. See *Exxon Corp.* v. *Governor of Maryland*, 437 U. S. 117, 127 (1978) (Commerce Clause does not protect "the particular structure or method of operation" of a market). . . .

We hold that the Counties' flow control ordinances, which treat in-state private business interests exactly the same as out-of-state ones, do not "discriminate against interstate commerce" for purposes of the dormant Commerce Clause. . . .

The judgments of the United States Court of Appeals for the Second Circuit are affirmed.

It is so ordered.

Justice THOMAS, concurring in the judgment.

I concur in the judgment. Although I joined *C & A Carbone, Inc.* v. *Clarkstown*, 511 U. S. 383 (1994), I no longer believe it was correctly decided. The negative Commerce Clause has no basis in the Constitution and has proved unworkable in practice. . . .

Under the Commerce Clause, "Congress shall have Power . . . [t]o regulate Commerce with foreign Nations, and among the several States, and with the Indian Tribes." U. S. Const., Art. I, §8, cl. 3. The language of the Clause allows Congress not only to regulate interstate commerce but also to prevent state regulation of interstate commerce. *State Bd. of Ins.* v. *Todd Shipyards Corp.*, 370 U. S. 451, 456 (1962); *Gibbons* v. *Ogden*, 9 Wheat. 1, 210 (1824). Expanding on the interstate-commerce powers explicitly conferred on Congress, this Court has interpreted the Commerce Clause as a tool for courts to strike down state laws that it believes inhibit interstate commerce. But there is no basis in the Constitution for that interpretation.

. . . Court proceeds to analyze whether the ordinances "discriminat[e] on [their] face against interstate commerce." *Ante*, at 6. Again, none of the cases the Court cites explains how the absence or presence of discrimination is relevant to deciding whether the ordinances are constitutionally permissible, and at least one case affirmatively admits that the nondiscrimination rule has no basis in the Constitution. *Philadelphia* v. *New Jersey*, 437 U. S. 617, 623 (1978) ("The bounds of these restraints appear nowhere in the words of the Commerce Clause, but have emerged gradually in the decisions of this Court giving effect to its basic purpose"). Thus cloaked in the "purpose" of the Commerce Clause, the rule against discrimination that the Court applies to decide this case exists untethered from the written Constitution. The rule instead depends upon the policy preferences of a majority of this Court.

. . . [Today's majority and dissent] rest on the erroneous assumption that the Court must choose between economic protectionism and the free market. But the Constitution vests that fundamentally legislative choice in Congress. To the extent that Congress does not exercise its authority to make that choice, the Constitution does not limit the States' power to regulate commerce. In the face of congressional silence, the States are free to set the balance between protectionism and the free market. Instead of accepting this constitutional reality, the Court's negative Commerce Clause jurisprudence gives nine Justices of this Court the power to decide the appropriate balance.

II . . .

Explaining why the ordinances do not discriminate against interstate commerce, the Court states that "government is vested with the responsibility of protecting the health, safety, and welfare of its citizens." *Ante,* at 10. According to the Court, a law favoring in-state business requires rigorous scrutiny because the law "is often the product of 'simple economic protectionism.'" *Ante,* at 11. A law favoring local government, however, "may be directed toward any number of legitimate goals unrelated to protectionism." *Ibid.* This distinction is razor thin: In contrast to today's deferential approach (apparently based on the Court's trust of local government), the Court has applied the equivalent of strict scrutiny in other cases even where it is unchallenged that the state law discriminated in favor of in-state private entities for a legitimate, nonprotectionist reason. See *Barber, supra,* at 319 (striking down the State's inspection law for livestock even though it did not challenge "[t]he presumption that this statute was enacted, in good faith, . . . to protect the health of the people of Minnesota").

In *Carbone,* which involved discrimination in favor of private entities, we did not doubt the good faith of the municipality in attempting to deal with waste through a flow-control ordinance. 511 U. S., at 386-389. But we struck down the ordinance because it did not allow interstate entities to participate in waste disposal. *Id.,* at 390-395. The majority distinguishes *Carbone* by deciding that favoritism of a government monopoly is less suspect than government regulation of private entities. I see no basis for drawing such a conclusion, which, if anything, suggests a policy-driven preference for government monopoly over privatization. *Ante,* at 12 (stating that "waste disposal is both typically and traditionally a local government function" (alteration and internal quotation marks omitted)). Whatever the reason, the choice is not the Court's to make. Like all of the Court's previous negative Commerce Clause cases, today's decision leaves the future of state and local regulation of commerce to the whim of the Federal Judiciary.

III

Despite its acceptance of negative Commerce Clause jurisprudence, the Court expresses concern about "unprecedented and unbounded interference by the courts with state and local government." It explains:

> The dormant Commerce Clause is not a roving license for federal courts to decide what activities are appropriate for state and local government to undertake, and what activities must be the province of private market competition. . . .
> There is no reason to step in and hand local businesses a victory they could not obtain through the political process.

I agree that the Commerce Clause is not a "roving license" and that the Court should not deliver to businesses victories that they failed to obtain through the political process. I differ with the Court because I believe its powerful rhetoric is completely undermined by the doctrine it applies. . . .

Because I believe that the power to regulate interstate commerce is a power given to Congress and not the Court, I concur in the judgment of the Court.

Notes and Questions

1.   Justice Thomas, along with Justice Scalia, has frequently repeated his opposition to the Dormant Commerce Clause as a concept.   Inasmuch as the Constitution does not expressly place limits on state regulatory activities, does Justice Thomas have a point? If, however, the Constitution was authored because of divisions between the states, frequently for economic reasons, does allowing state discrimination against the economic interests of other states make sense?   For a critique of the economic rationale behind the Dormant Commerce Clause, see McGreal, *The Flawed Economics of the Dormant Commerce Clause,* 39 Wm. & Mary L. Rev. 1206 (1997-1998)

2.   Does Justice Thomas accurately portray the argument of the majority on the discrimination point? He equates the majority's holding in favor of state-run operations with prior decisions finding discrimination in legislation favoring local business where the purposes were legitimate. Is this a valid comparison?

3.   Does the majority base its public function doctrine on case law or constitutional text, or does the opinion represent a policy preference on the part of the majority?

4.   In ruling in favor of the waste authority, does the majority claim that New York discriminates for a legitimate purpose and that there is no less discriminatory means of achieving that purpose, or does the majority hold that there is no discrimination?

In the following term, in 2008, the Court picked up the public function test where it left off in *Department of Revenue of Kentucky v. Davis,* 553 U.S. __328_ (2008). The case involved a Kentucky state tax policy that exempted Kentucky government bonds from state taxes while taxing all other bonds, both public and private, at the normal rate. A result of the policy was an increase in demand for local government bonds over bonds from other jurisdictions and private bonds. Justice Souter, writing for a plurality, applied the public function test in declining to find discrimination in the policy, stating that the policy was not subject to standard Commerce Clause scrutiny "owing to its likely motivation by legitimate objectives distinct from the simple economic protectionism the Clause abhors." Noting that private bond issuers in Kentucky were not favored under the policy, the opinion underscored that traditional notions of protectionism did not apply to the facts. Justice Stevens concurred by explaining his dissent in *United Haulers.* "A State's reliance on 'general taxes or municipal bonds' to finance public projects does not merit the same Commerce Clause scrutiny as operating a fee-for-service business enterprise in an area in which there is an established interstate market."

b. CATEGORY ONE (B) — DISCRIMINATORY PURPOSE OR EFFECT (NON-FACIAL DISCRIMINATION)

In this category of cases, the law does not state a discriminatory purpose on the face by stating a treatment of economic interest differently by locale.   In other words, legislatures can word statutes artfully to not betray a discriminatory purpose. At other times, a discriminatory effect may not even have been anticipated by the lawmakers. However, the same virtual per se invalidity of protectionism applies here where the Court can establish a protectionist purpose or a protectionist effect. First, discriminatory purpose or effect is determined. Then the protectionism is determined. A state statute is protectionist and thus prohibited when the purpose of the regulation is not legitimate, or if legitimate, there is a less protectionist means of accomplishing that purpose.

BALDWIN v. G.A.F. SEELIG, INC.
294 U.S. 511 (1935)

Mr. Justice CARDOZO delivered the opinion of the Court.

Whether and to what extent the New York Milk Control Act (N.Y. Laws of 1933, c. 158; Laws of 1934, c. 126) may be applied against a dealer who has acquired title to the milk as the result of a transaction in interstate commerce is the question here to be determined.

G.A.F. Seelig, Inc. is engaged in business as a milk dealer in the city of New York. It buys its milk, including cream, in Fair Haven, Vermont, from the Seelig Creamery Corporation, which, in turn, buys from the producers on the neighboring farms. . . .

The New York Milk Control Act, with the aid of regulations made thereunder, has set up a system of minimum prices to be paid by dealers to producers. The validity of that system in its application to producers doing business in New York State has support in our decisions. *Nebbia v. New York*, 291 U.S. 502; *Hegeman Farms Corp. v. Baldwin*, 293 U.S. 163. *Cf. Borden's Farm Products Co. v. Baldwin*, 293 U.S. 194. . . . To keep the system unimpaired by competition from afar, the Act has a provision whereby the protective prices are extended to that part of the supply (about 30%) which comes from other states. The substance of the provision is that, so far as such a prohibition is permitted by the Constitution, there shall be no sale within the state of milk bought outside unless the price paid to the producers was one that would be lawful upon a like transaction within the state.

. . . Seelig buys its milk from the Creamery in Vermont at prices lower than the minimum payable to producers in New York. The Commissioner of Farms and Markets refuses to license the transaction of its business unless it signs an agreement to conform to the New York statute and regulations in the sale of the imported product. . . . This suit has been brought to restrain the enforcement of the Act in its application to the complainant, repugnancy being charged between its provisions, when so applied, and limitations imposed by the Constitution of the United States. United States Constitution, Art. I, § 8, clause 3. . . .

First. An injunction was properly granted restraining the enforcement of the Act in its application to sales in the original packages.

New York has no power to project its legislation into Vermont by regulating the price to be paid in that state for milk acquired there. So much is not disputed. New York is equally without power to prohibit the introduction within her territory of milk of wholesome quality acquired in Vermont, whether at high prices or at low ones. This again is not disputed. Accepting those postulates, New York asserts her power to outlaw milk so introduced by prohibiting its sale thereafter if the price that has been paid for it to the farmers of Vermont is less than would be owing in like circumstances to farmers in New York. The importer, in that view, may keep his milk or drink it, but sell it, he may not.

Such a power, if exerted, will set a barrier to traffic between one state and another as effective as if customs duties equal to the price differential had been laid upon the thing transported. . . .

It is the established doctrine of this court that a state may not, in any form or under any guise, directly burden the prosecution of interstate business. . . . We are reminded in the opinion below that a chief occasion of the commerce clauses was "the mutual jealousies and aggressions of the States, taking form in customs barriers and other economic retaliation." . . . If New York, in order to promote the economic welfare of her farmers, may guard them against competition with the cheaper prices of Vermont, the door has been opened to rivalries and reprisals that were meant to be averted by subjecting commerce between the states to the power of the nation.

The argument is pressed upon us, however, that the end to be served by the Milk Control Act is something more than the economic welfare of the farmers or of any other class or classes. The end to be served is the maintenance of a regular and adequate supply of pure and wholesome milk, the supply being put in jeopardy when the farmers of the state are unable to earn a living income. *Nebbia v. New York, supra.* Price security, we are told, is only a special form of sanitary security; the economic motive is secondary and subordinate; the state intervenes to make its inhabitants healthy, and not to make them rich. On that assumption we are asked to say that intervention will be upheld as a valid exercise by the state of its internal police power, though there is an incidental obstruction to commerce between one state and another. This would be to eat up the rule under the guise of an exception. Economic welfare is always related to health, for there can be no health if men are starving. Let such an exception be admitted, and all that a state will have to do in times of stress and strain is to say that its farmers and merchants and workmen must be protected against competition from without, lest they go upon the poor relief lists, or perish altogether. To give entrance to that excuse would be to invite a speedy end of our national solidarity. The Constitution was framed under the dominion of a political philosophy less parochial in range. It was framed upon the theory that the peoples of the several states must sink or swim together, and that, in the long run, prosperity and salvation are in union, and not division. . . .

Affirmed.

Notes and Questions

1. Does the Court rule that a state may not set prices for goods produced and/or sold in the state? If so, is the Court suggesting that states must adhere strictly to laissez-faire capitalist policies or unregulated markets for the sale of goods and services? See *Lochner v. New York*, 198 U.S. 45 (1905), and the materials following the case, section V infra.

2. Is the statute in *Baldwin* discriminatory in purpose? In effect? Both? While reading the note cases below, ask yourself whether the statutes are invalidated because they were discriminatory in purpose or effect.

H.P. Hood & Sons v. Du Mond, 336 U.S. 525 (1949), is another case involving that highly regulated and perishable commodity — milk. In the industry, milk dealers rely on local milk depots where area farmers deposit their milk for transport and sale. Milk collected at the depots are sold by dealers, sometimes in different locations. Dealers will seek access to local production by owning facilities for the collection of milk. H.P. Hood and Sons, which sells milk in the Boston, Massachusetts, area, decided to add to its battery of dealer-owned receiving depots in New York State and sought a license from the state.

The license was denied by the state agriculture commissioner to set up such a fourth station. Under the statute the commissioner had to be satisfied that a license to set up a station would not have a negative effect on competition in a market already adequately served. Hood's plan failed that test. The commissioner's conclusion was that a new depot would divert farmers from other local depots serving other areas, milk supply would be threatened in those areas, and cost of handling milk in the underperforming depots would increase.

The Court invalidated the law. Justice Jackson writing for the Court made it clear that the state's action in denying Hood the license was really about hoarding for economic advantage just as *Baldwin* was about economic advantage — protectionism. The purpose behind the statute as applied, as described in the opinion, to assure local supply within regions of the state, was not a legitimate one. Justice Jackson described the economic policy policed by the Dormant Commerce Clause as a "federal free trade unit." "Our system, fostered by the Commerce Clause, is that every farmer and every craftsman shall be encouraged to produce by the certainty that he will have free access to every market in the Nation, that no home embargoes will withhold his export, and no foreign state will by customs duties or regulations exclude them." The discrimination in this case is undoubtedly against exports, and those engaged in exporting to other states — in particular H.P. Hood and Sons. The need to assure supply, according to Justice Jackson, is one that requires interstate commercial regulation, a federal role.

The question raised by the dissent by Justice Black was straight to the question about the legitimacy of the policy. Because the license requirements apply to local dealers as well, where is the protectionism? Black suggested that it certainly is not in the policy which, in addition to being evenly applied, legitimately gives the state the tools to guard against a kind of competition among milk dealers that would undermine the safety and quantity of the milk supply for the region in question. To Black, the standard suggested by Justice Stone in his dissent in *DiSanto v. Commonwealth of Pennsylvania*, to engage in "a consideration of all the facts and circumstances, such as the nature of the regulation, its function, the character of the business involved and the actual effect on the flow of commerce," should have been used to determine the legitimacy of the purpose behind this statute. To Justice Black, the purpose was absolutely legitimate and the statute should not have been invalidated by the Court.

But consider Justice Clark's rationalization in *Cities Service Gas v. Peerless Oil & Gas,* 340 U.S. 179 (1950), dealing with regulation of natural gas prices designed to conserve gas. Pipeline companies, which sold mostly out of state, had to pay the state price rather than the world market price, which was cheaper. This was allowed, and the distinction between this case and *Hood* was supposedly that the law in *Hood* solely denied facilities to foreign distributors to protect local consumers. In *Cities Service* the state price applied to all gas coming out of that source (of which 90% was sold out of state). Justice Clark also held "that a legitimate local interest is at stake in this case. . . . A state is justifiably concerned with preventing rapid and uneconomic dissipation of one of its chief natural resources. The basis of the law was to conserve the state's gas resources." *Hood* is distinguished as being a total denial of facilities for the collection of milk for out-of-state consumption. The Court might have also added that milk supplies, while shortages were reported, are not in danger of dissipation as is the case with petroleum products.

Is destination discrimination really discrimination of the kind the Dormant Commerce Clause was designed to root out? Most cases that we have looked at dealt with supply-side discrimination, that is, discrimination against the entry of supply. *Hood* and *Cities Service* (and *Philadelphia v. New York, Chemical Waste Management, Inc v. Hunt, Oregon Waste*

Systems, Inc. v. Department of Environmental Quality of Oregon, and *Fort Gratiot Sanitary Landfill, Inc. v. Michigan Department of Natural Resources* cases discussed earlier) dealt with demand-side discrimination — cutting off out-of-state customers from local supply (in the case of the garbage cases, the supply was in-state landfill access). Who benefits from these policies?

As far as effects cases, consider *Hunt v. Washington State Apple Advertising Comm'n,* 432 U.S. 333 (1977). In invalidating the statute at issue, the Court did not ascribe a protectionist motive to a North Carolina law prohibiting labeling advertising apples as grade other than USDA. The labeling law had the effect of discriminating against Washington apples, which are usually superior to USDA grade. Washington apples are labeled under that state's system. Because of the unusually high quality of Washington apples, labeling that reflects that state's agricultural standards benefits the sale of the state's apples. To remove labeling for sale in a small part of the Washington apples' national market would be expensive and burdensome, resulting in additional cost in order to compete in North Carolina, which had its own apple industry. The law also had the effect of eliminating the competitive advantage built in the Washington apple industry that state labeling would allow, equating Washington apples with all other apples sold in North Carolina.

The law was found to be discriminatory and protectionist in effect. North Carolina's offered reason for the law was to rectify the confusion caused by the sale of the apple production from 13 different states, 7 of which had their own labeling systems. North Carolina's solution was a uniform labeling law applied to all apples, regardless of origin.

The Court found North Carolina's labeling law to be ineffective and inefficient in pursuit in an otherwise legitimate purpose. State and USDA labeling could have been used allowing Washington apples to retain their competitive advantage brand identification. The law was also found not to be effective as a consumer protection measure since the effect of the uniform labeling is only noticed by wholesalers and brokers, and not average consumers.

2. CATEGORY TWO: NONDISCRIMINATORY, YET BURDENSOME, STATE LEGISLATION (PIKE BALANCING)

This category deals with a different kind of problem than protectionism. Some state legislation objectionable to the Dormant Commerce Clause does not discriminate in favor of local products and economic interest, but, in the name of safety or some other interest, places requirements on all commerce resulting in a burden on interstate commerce. When the Court meets this kind of legislation, it applies what is called the Pike balancing test from the case *Pike v. Bruce Church Inc.,* 397 U.S. 137 (1970). What is important about that case is the test. "Where the statute regulates even-handedly to effectuate a legitimate local public interest, and its effects on interstate commerce are only incidental, it will be upheld unless the burden imposed on such commerce is clearly excessive in relation to the putative local benefits. . . . [T]he extent of the burden that will be tolerated will . . . depend on the nature of the local interest involved, and on whether it could be promoted as well with a lesser impact on interstate activities."

At this point it might be helpful to visualize the landscape of the Dormant Commerce Clause in the following way:

- Certain acts of the state are so local that they have virtually no relation to interstate commerce.

- Even regulation of interstate commerce is permissible if it is not substantial.
- Some acts on the part of the state amount to an actual regulation of commerce which is so far beyond appropriate state authority as to be virtually per se illegal.
- Discrimination is such a state action. Yet, even discrimination can be justified for legitimate reasons where there are no more benign ways of achieving the legitimate goals.
- In between the two extremes above are those actions on the part of the state that to some degree affect interstate commerce, even to the point of regulation, but do not discriminate in favor of local economic activity. Sometimes these state laws are constitutional, and sometimes they are not, depending upon whether the legislation is in pursuit of a legitimate purpose that outweighs the burden, and inconvenience placed on the free flow of trade in the American "common market" (Pike balancing).

Focus on the balancing standard. It brings to mind a major critique of Pike balancing, frequently offered by Justice Scalia. Scalia has stated that using Pike balancing in a dispute between parties is problematic because, in his view, the balancing "scale analogy is not really appropriate, since the interests on both sides are incommensurate. It is more like judging whether a particular line is longer than a particular rock is heavy." *Bendix Autolite v. Midwesco Enterprises*, 486 U.S. 888, 897 (1988).

Consider Justice Scalia's position within the context of the following case. *Southern Pacific Co. v. Arizona* is one of the key decisions recognizing even non-discriminatory legislation has the potential to be offensive to the Constitution. While reading the case, consider whether the Supreme Court runs the risk of second-guessing elected legislatures. How is this concern different, if at all, from the discrimination cases? How does Justice Scalia's critique of Pike balancing affect this issue?

SOUTHERN PACIFIC CO. v. ARIZONA ex rel. SULLIVAN
325 U.S. 761 (1945)

Mr. Chief Justice STONE delivered the opinion of the Court.

The Arizona Train Limit Law of May 16, 1912, Arizona Code Ann., 1039, § 69-119, makes it unlawful for any person or corporation to operate within the state a railroad train of more than fourteen passenger or seventy freight cars, and authorizes the state to recover a money penalty for each violation of the Act. . . .

Although the commerce clause conferred on the national government power to regulate commerce, its possession of the power does not exclude all state power of regulation. Ever since *Willson v. Black-Bird Creek Marsh Co.*, 2 Pet. 245, and *Cooley v. Board of Wardens*, 12 How. 299, it has been recognized that, in the absence of conflicting legislation by Congress, there is a residuum of power in the state to make laws governing matters of local concern which nevertheless in some measure affect interstate commerce or even, to some extent, regulate it. *Minnesota Rate Cases*, 230 U.S. 352, 399-400; *South Carolina Highway Dept. v. Barnwell Bros.*, 303 U.S. 177, 187, *et seq.; California v. Thompson*, 313 U.S. 109, 113-114, and cases cited; *Parker v. Brown*, 317 U.S. 341, 359-360. Thus, the states may regulate matters which, because of their number and diversity, may never be adequately dealt with by Congress. *Cooley v. Board of Wardens, supra*, 319; *South Carolina Highway Dept. v. Barnwell Bros., supra*, 185; *California v. Thompson, supra*, 113; *Duckworth v. Arkansas*, 314 U.S. 390, 394; *Parker v. Brown, supra*, 362, 363.

When the regulation of matters of local concern is local in character and effect, and its impact on the national commerce does not seriously interfere with its operation, and the consequent incentive to deal with them nationally is slight, such regulation has been generally held to be within state authority. *South Carolina Highway Dept. v. Barnwell Bros., supra,* 188 and cases cited; *Lone Star Gas Co. v. Texas,* 304 U.S. 224, 238; *Milk Board v. Eisenberg Co.,* 306 U.S. 346, 351; *Maurer v. Hamilton,* 309 U.S. 598, 603; *California v. Thompson, supra,* 113-114, and cases cited.

But ever since *Gibbons v. Ogden.* 9 Wheat. 1, the states have not been deemed to have authority to impede substantially the free flow of commerce from state to state, or to regulate those phases of the national commerce which, because of the need of national uniformity, demand that their regulation, if any, be prescribed by a single authority. . . .

For a hundred years, it has been accepted constitutional doctrine that the commerce clause, without the aid of Congressional legislation, thus affords some protection from state legislation inimical to the national commerce, and that, in such cases, where Congress has not acted, this Court, and not the state legislature, is, under the commerce clause, the final arbiter of the competing demands of state and national interests. . . .

Congress has undoubted power to redefine the distribution of power over interstate commerce. It may either permit the states to regulate the commerce in a manner which would otherwise not be permissible, . . . or exclude state regulation even of matters of peculiarly local concern which nevertheless affect interstate commerce. . . .

But, in general, Congress has left it to the courts to formulate the rules thus interpreting the commerce clause in its application, doubtless because it has appreciated the destructive consequences to the commerce of the nation if their protection were withdrawn, *Gwin, White & Prince v. Henneford, supra,* 441, and has been aware that, in their application, state laws will not be invalidated without the support of relevant factual material which will "afford a sure basis" for an informed judgment. *Terminal Railroad Assn. v. Brotherhood, supra,* 8; *Southern R. Co. v. King,* 217 U.S. 524. Meanwhile, Congress has accommodated its legislation, as have the states, to these rules as an established feature of our constitutional system. There has thus been left to the states wide scope for the regulation of matters of local state concern, even though it in some measure affects the commerce, provided it does not materially restrict the free flow of commerce across state lines, or interfere with it in matters with respect to which uniformity of regulation is of predominant national concern.

Hence, the matters for ultimate determination here are the nature and extent of the burden which the state regulation of interstate trains, adopted as a safety measure, imposes on interstate commerce, and whether the relative weights of the state and national interests involved are such as to make inapplicable the rule, generally observed, that the free flow of interstate commerce and its freedom from local restraints in matters requiring uniformity of regulation are interests safeguarded by the commerce clause from state interference. . .

.

The findings [of the state trial court, ed.] show that the operation of long trains, that is, trains of more than fourteen passenger and more than seventy freight cars, is standard practice over the main lines of the railroads of the United States, and that, if the length of trains is to be regulated at all, national uniformity in the regulation adopted, such as only Congress can prescribe, is practically indispensable to the operation of an efficient and economical national railway system. On many railroads, passenger trains of more than fourteen cars and freight trains of more than seventy cars are operated, and, on some systems, freight trains are run ranging from one hundred and twenty-five to one hundred and sixty cars in length. Outside of Arizona, where the length of trains is not restricted, appellant runs a substantial proportion of long trains. In 1939, on its comparable route for through traffic through Utah and Nevada, from 66 to 85% of its freight trains were over seventy cars in length, and over 43% of its passenger trains included more than fourteen passenger cars.

In Arizona, approximately 93% of the freight traffic and 95% of the passenger traffic is interstate. Because of the Train Limit Law appellant is required to haul over 300 more trains in Arizona than would otherwise have been necessary. . . . The additional cost of operation of trains complying with the Train Limit Law in Arizona amounts, for the two railroads traversing that state, to about $1,000,000 a year. The reduction in train lengths also impedes efficient operation. More locomotives and more manpower are required; the necessary conversion and reconversion of train lengths at terminals, and the delay caused by breaking up and remaking long trains upon entering and leaving the state in order to comply with the law, delay the traffic and diminishes its volume moved in a given time, especially when traffic is heavy. . . .

The unchallenged findings leave no doubt that the Arizona Train Limit Law imposes a serious burden on the interstate commerce conducted by appellant. It materially impedes the movement of appellant's interstate trains through that state, and interposes a substantial obstruction to the national policy proclaimed by Congress, to promote adequate, economical and efficient railway transportation service. Interstate Commerce Act, preceding § 1, 54 Stat. 899. . . . Compliance with a state statute limiting train lengths requires interstate trains of a length lawful in other states to be broken up and reconstituted as they enter each state according as it may impose varying limitations upon train lengths. The alternative is for the carrier to conform to the lowest train limit restriction of any of the states through which its trains pass, whose laws thus control the carriers' operations both within and without the regulating state.

. . . With such laws in force in states which are interspersed with those having no limit on train lengths, the confusion and difficulty with which interstate operations would be burdened under the varied system of state regulation and the unsatisfied need for uniformity in such regulation, if any, are evident.

At present, the seventy freight car laws are enforced only in Arizona and Oklahoma, with a fourteen car passenger car limit in Arizona. The record here shows that the enforcement of the Arizona statute results in freight trains' being broken up and reformed at the California border and in New Mexico, some distance from the Arizona line. Frequently, it is not feasible to operate a newly assembled train from the New Mexico yard nearest to Arizona, with the result that the Arizona limitation governs the flow of traffic as far east as El Paso, Texas. For similar reasons, the Arizona law often controls the length of passenger trains all the way from Los Angeles to El Paso.

If one state may regulate train lengths, so may all the others, and they need not prescribe the same maximum limitation. The practical effect of such regulation is to control train operations beyond the boundaries of the state exacting it because of the necessity of breaking up and reassembling long trains at the nearest terminal points before entering and after leaving the regulating state. The serious impediment to the free flow of commerce by the local regulation of train lengths, and the practical necessity that such regulation, if any, must be prescribed by a single body having a nationwide authority are apparent.

The trial court found that the Arizona law had no reasonable relation to safety, and made train operation more dangerous. Examination of the evidence and the detailed findings makes it clear that this conclusion was rested on facts found which indicate that such increased danger of accident and personal injury as may result from the greater length of trains is more than offset by the increase in the number of accidents resulting from the larger number of trains when train lengths are reduced. In considering the effect of the statute as a safety measure, therefore, the factor of controlling significance for present purposes is not whether there is basis for the conclusion of the Arizona Supreme Court that the increase in length of trains beyond the statutory maximum has an adverse effect upon safety of operation. The decisive question is whether, in the circumstances, the total effect of the law as a safety measure in reducing accidents and casualties is so slight or problematical as not to outweigh the national interest in keeping interstate commerce free from interferences which seriously impede it and subject it to local regulation which does not have a uniform effect on the interstate train journey which it interrupts. . . .

Upon an examination of the whole case, the trial court found that, "if short-train operation may or should result in any decrease in the number or severity of the 'slack' or 'slack-surge' type of accidents or casualties, such decrease is substantially more than offset by the increased number of accidents and casualties from other causes that follow the arbitrary limitation of freight trains to 70 cars . . . and passenger trains to 14 cars."

We think, as the trial court found, that the Arizona Train Limit Law, viewed as a safety measure, affords, at most, slight and dubious advantage, if any, over unregulated train lengths, because it results in an increase in the number of trains and train operations and the consequent increase in train accidents of a character generally more severe than those due to slack action. . . .

Appellees especially rely . . . on *South Carolina Highway Dept. v. Barnwell Bros., supra.* . . . *South Carolina Highway Dept. v. Barnwell Bros., supra,* was concerned with the power of the state to regulate the weight and width of motor cars passing interstate over its highways, a legislative field over which the state has a far more extensive control than over interstate railroads. In that case, and in *Maurer v. Hamilton, supra,* we were at pains to point out that there are few subjects of state regulation affecting interstate commerce which are so peculiarly of local concern as is the use of the state's highways. Unlike the railroads, local highways are built, owned and maintained by the state or its municipal subdivisions. The state is responsible for their safe and economical administration. Regulations affecting the safety of their use must be applied alike to intrastate and interstate traffic. The fact that they affect alike shippers in interstate and intrastate commerce in great numbers, within as well as without the state, is a safeguard against regulatory abuses. Their regulation is akin to quarantine measures, game laws, and like local regulations of rivers, harbors, piers, and docks, with respect to which the state has exceptional scope for the exercise of its regulatory power, and which, Congress not acting, have been sustained even though they materially interfere with interstate commerce (303 U.S. at 187-188, and cases cited).

Reversed.

Mr. Justice Rutledge concurs in the result.

Mr. Justice BLACK, dissenting.

In *Hennington v. Georgia,* 163 U.S. 299, 304, a case which involved the power of a state to regulate interstate traffic, this Court said, "The whole theory of our government, federal and state, is hostile to the idea that questions of legislative authority may depend . . . upon opinions of judges as to the wisdom or want of wisdom in the enactment of laws under powers clearly conferred upon the legislature."

What the Court decides today is that it is unwise governmental policy to regulate the length of trains. I am therefore constrained to note my dissent. . . .

In 1912, the year Arizona became a state, its legislature adopted and referred to the people several safety measures concerning the operation of railroads. . . . The third safety statute which the Arizona legislature submitted to the electorate, and which was adopted by it, is the train limitation statute now under consideration. By its enactment, the legislature and the people adopted the viewpoint that long trains were more dangerous than short trains, and limited the operation of train units to 14 cars for passenger and 70 cars for freight. This same question was considered in other states, and some of them, over the vigorous protests of railroads, adopted laws similar to the Arizona statute.

This controversy between the railroads and their employees, which was nationwide, was carried to Congress. Extensive hearings took place. The employees' position was urged by members of the various Brotherhoods. The railroads' viewpoint was presented through representatives of their National Association. In 1937, the Senate Interstate Commerce Committee, after its own exhaustive hearings, unanimously recommended that trains be limited to 70 cars as a safety measure. The Committee, in its Report, reviewed the evidence and specifically referred to the large and increasing number of injuries and deaths suffered by railroad employees; it concluded that the admitted danger from slack movement was greatly intensified by the operation of long trains; that short trains reduce this danger; that the added cost of short trains to the railroad was no justification for jeopardizing the safety of railroad employees, and that the legislation would provide a greater degree of safety for persons and property, increase protection for railway employees and the public, and improve transportation services for shippers and consumers. The Senate passed the bill, but the House Committee failed to report it out. . . .

In the state court, a rather extraordinary "trial" took place. Charged with violating the law, the railroad admitted the charge. It alleged that the law was unconstitutional, however, and sought a trial of facts on that issue. The essence of its charge of unconstitutionality rested on one of these two grounds: (1) the legislature and people of Arizona erred in 1912 in determining that the running of long trains was dangerous; or (2) railroad conditions had so improved since 1912 that previous dangers did not exist to the same extent, and that the statute should be stricken down either because it cast an undue burden on interstate commerce by reason of the added cost or because the changed conditions had rendered the Act "arbitrary and unreasonable." Thus, the issue which the court "tried" was not whether the railroad was guilty of violating the law, but whether the law was unconstitutional, either because the legislature had been guilty of misjudging the facts concerning the degree of the danger of long trains or because the 1912 conditions of danger no longer existed.

. . . We can best understand the nature of this "trial" by analogizing the same procedure to a defendant charged with violating a state or national safety appliance act, where the defendant comes into court and admits violation of the act. In such cases, the ordinary procedure would be for the court to pass upon the constitutionality of the act, and either discharge or convict the defendants. The procedure here, however, would justify quite a different trial method. Under it, a defendant is permitted to offer voluminous evidence to show that a legislative body has erroneously resolved disputed facts in finding a danger great enough to justify the passage of the law. This new pattern of trial procedure makes it necessary for a judge to hear all the evidence offered as to why a legislature passed a law, and to make findings of fact as to the validity of those reasons. If, under today's ruling, a court does make findings as to a danger contrary to the findings of the legislature, and the evidence heard "lends support" to those findings, a court can then invalidate the law. In this respect, the Arizona County Court acted, and this Court today is acting, as a "super legislature."

Even if this method of invalidating legislative acts is a correct one, I still think that the "findings" of the state court do not authorize today's decision. That court did not find that there is no unusual danger from slack movements in long trains. It did decide on disputed evidence that the long train "slack movement" dangers were more than offset by prospective dangers as a result of running a larger number of short trains, since many people might be hurt at grade crossings. There was undoubtedly some evidence before the state court from which it could have reached such a conclusion. There was undoubtedly as much evidence before it which would have justified a different conclusion.

Under those circumstances, the determination of whether it is in the interest of society for the length of trains to be governmentally regulated is a matter of public policy. Someone must fix that policy — either the Congress, or the state, or the courts. A century and a half of constitutional history and government admonishes this Court to leave that choice to the elected legislative representatives of the people themselves, where it properly belongs both on democratic principles and the requirements of efficient government.

I think that legislatures, to the exclusion of courts, have the constitutional power to enact laws limiting train lengths, for the purpose of reducing injuries brought about by "slack movements." Their power is not less because a requirement of short trains might increase grade crossing accidents. This latter fact raises an entirely different element of danger which is itself subject to legislative regulation. For legislatures may, if necessary, require railroads to take appropriate steps to reduce the likelihood of injuries at grade crossings. *Denver & R.G. R. Co. v. Denver,* 250 U.S. 241. And the fact that grade crossing improvements may be expensive is no sufficient reason to say that an unconstitutional "burden" is put upon a railroad, even though it be an interstate road. *Erie R. Co. v. Public Utility Commissioners,* 254 U.S. 394, 408-411. . . .

. . . It may be that offsetting dangers are possible in the operation of short trains. The balancing of these probabilities, however, is not, in my judgment, a matter for judicial determination, but one which calls for legislative consideration. Representatives elected by the people to make their laws, rather than judges appointed to interpret those laws, can best determine the policies which govern the people. That, at least, is the basic principle on which our democratic society rests. I would affirm the judgment of the Supreme Court of Arizona.

Notes

1. Justice William O. Douglas issued a brief dissent in this case which foreshadowed part of Justice Scalia's position regarding balancing:

> I have expressed my doubts whether the courts should intervene in situations like the present and strike down state legislation on the grounds that it burdens interstate commerce. My view has been that the courts should intervene only where the state legislation discriminated against interstate commerce or was out of harmony with laws which Congress had enacted.
>
> . . . I think the legislation is entitled to a presumption of validity. If a State passed a law prohibiting the hauling of more than one freight car at a time, we would have a situation comparable in effect to a state law requiring all railroads within its borders to operate on narrow gauge tracks. The question is one of degree, and calls for a close appraisal of the facts. I am not persuaded that the evidence adduced by the railroads overcomes the

presumption of validity to which this train limit law is entitled. For the reasons stated by Mr. Justice Black, Arizona's train limit law should stand as an allowable regulation enacted to protect the lives and limbs of the men who operate the trains.

Does the balancing formula used to determine the constitutionality of non-discriminatory state legislation invite the kind of process criticized in both dissents? Recall Justice Scalia's critique. To place matters into perspective, consider the process in *Southern Pacific*. The Court had to decide not only whether the state legislation burdened commerce, but it had to decide whether that burden was outweighed by the benefits. This involved a case-by-case and fact-intensive analysis. Many constitutional decisions require this kind of analysis, however; balancing under the dormant commerce clause also requires value judgments deduced from this fact finding.

Is this process different from the process in the discrimination cases? Are courts, especially appellate courts which do not conduct fact finding, well suited for balancing? Is this a proper role for any court? Recall the considerations raised in our discussion of judicial review, and review the arguments raised in the article by Professor Thayer, *The Origin and Scope of the American Doctrine of Constitutional Law* discussed at the beginning of the course. Does *Southern Pacific* raise alarm bells?

2. Arizona argued that the holding in *South Carolina Highway Department v. Barnwell Brothers*, 303 U.S. 177 (1938), required a holding in the present case in its favor. In *Barnwell Brothers*, the Court upheld a state law regulating the weight and length of vehicles on state maintained highways. The Court stated:

> Few subjects of state regulation are so peculiarly of local concern as is the use of state highways. There are few, local regulation of which is so inseparable from a substantial effect on interstate commerce. Unlike the railroads, local highways are built, owned and maintained by the state or its municipal subdivisions. The state has a primary and immediate concern in their safe and economical administration. The present regulations, or any others of like purpose, if they are to accomplish their end, must be applied alike to interstate and intrastate traffic both moving in large volume over the highways. The fact that they affect alike shippers in interstate and intrastate commerce in large number within as well as without the state is a safeguard against their abuse.

Id. at 187. Is the Court's distinction between highways and railroads convincing?

The *Barnwell Brothers* rationale is really a remnant of the old local/national distinction and used in that case to justify the outcome. However, subsequent cases make clear that even if non-discriminatory, state laws affecting commerce will not get an automatic pass without passing the balancing test. Such an example is *Bibb v. Navajo Freight Lines, Inc.*, 359 U.S. 520 (1959). The case dealt with, believe it or not, mudguards and an Illinois law requiring contour mudguards on trucks, apparently for safety reasons. The Court started off, in this Douglas opinion, acknowledging the *Barnwell* decision. "The power of the state to regulate the use of its highways is broad and pervasive." The opinion then noted that safety "measures carry a strong presumption of validity. If there are alternative ways of solving a problem, we do not sit to determine which of them is best suited to achieve a valid state objective." In *Bibb* the Court decided to allow discretion for the states in these category two cases. However, in a slight change of heart from *Barnwell*, Douglas stated that *Barnwell* did not wholly reflect the proper commerce clause standard for highway safety. He goes on to find that the law did in fact burden interstate commerce because when a truck entered Illinois, it had to shift its cargo to a differently designed vehicle (presumably with contour mudguards), and this was a burden on interstate commerce. But that is not enough. Does this burden outweigh the safety benefits? The Court said yes.

A more recent decision is the decision in *Kassel v. Consolidated Freightways Corp.*, 450 U.S. 662 (1981). The Court held that safety benefits of a ban on double-rigged trucks were too slight to outweigh the significant costs to interstate commerce (higher fuel and operating costs of diverting trucks around the state (Iowa) on cross-country trips). In addition to the category two problem, there was a category one problem. Exemptions in favor of local trucks were uncovered as well as discriminatory statements on the part of the Governor of Iowa. This indicated that there was discrimination that would subject the ban to the virtually per se invalidity standard.

Other cases covered focused on state burdens on trade, as opposed to simply transportation. In *Exxon Corp v. Governor of Maryland,* 437 U.S. 117 (1978), the Court dealt with a ban on oil company–owned gasoline retail outlets. These oil companies could still sell their petroleum products to independent retailers. The Court found no undue burden on interstate commerce, certainly no discrimination as there were no oil companies in Maryland, and hence, no competitive advantage. As far as burden, petroleum still could come into Maryland. Noting that the out-of-state oil firms themselves were burdened by the Maryland law, the Court held that the "Clause protects the interstate market, not particular interstate firms, from prohibitive or burdensome regulations."

Ponder whether that last statement seems consistent with the following cases.

The Court found in *Edgar v. Mite Corp.*, 457 U.S. 624 (1982), that state regulations on takeover offers requiring registration with the state of Illinois prior to the offer, during which time the offeror could not communicate with shareholders but the target company could, were invalid as a burden on interstate commerce that outweighed local benefits. [Note, this law applied to out-of-state corporations as well as in-state corporations.]

In *CTS Corp. v. Dynamics Corp*, 481 U.S. 69 (1987), an Indiana law required that a purchaser acquiring control shares in a corporation had to seek shareholder approval to acquire voting rights. Because the law applied to offerors who were Indiana residents or out of state, there was no discrimination. But on the issue of whether there was a burden, the Court found that the local benefits of state regulation of corporate law outweighed the burden on interstate commerce. States incorporate corporations. That carries with it a power to regulate. The benefits of such a system are established. Now this case was distinguished fron *Mite* because the law in Illinois applied to out-of-state corporations as well as in-state corporations. The burden there was apparently because of the burden on out-of-state corporations. There was apparently no benefit to the state of such a burden. Here, as the object of the measure was Indiana incorporated companies, there is a putative local benefit. Justice Scalia in concurrence would have found the law valid simply because there was no discrimination (categories one and two) — he does not like the Pike balancing test. Justice White in his dissent believed that the law inhibited interstate commerce, in that it is regulating the purchase of stock, even if it is the stock of Indiana corporations, because the buyers, at least some of them, were from out of state.

In *McBurney v. Young,* **569** U.S. 221 (2013), the Court declined to extend the definition of commerce to public records, the result being that discrimination under

Freedom of Information Act against out of state applicants was found not violative of the Constitution. Justice Alito, writing for a unanimous Court stated:

> Virginia's FOIA law neither "regulates" nor "burdens" interstate commerce; rather, it merely provides a service to local citizens that would not otherwise be available at all. The "common thread" among those cases in which the Court has found a dormant Commerce Clause violation is that "the State interfered with the natural functioning of the interstate market either through prohibition or through burdensome regulation." *Hughes* v. *Alexandria Scrap Corp.*, 426 U. S. 794, 806 (1976). Here, by contrast, Virginia neither prohibits access to an interstate market nor imposes burdensome regulation on that market. Rather, it merely creates and provides to its own citizens copies—which would not otherwise exist—of state records. As discussed above, the express purpose of Virginia's FOIA law is to "ensur[e] the people of the Commonwealth ready access to public records in the custody of a public body or its officers and employees, and free entry to meetings of public bodies wherein the business of the people is being conducted." Va. Code Ann. §2.2–3700(B). This case is thus most properly brought under the Privileges and Immunities Clause: It quite literally poses the question whether Virginia can deny out-of-state citizens a benefit that it has conferred on its own citizens. Cf. *Missouri Pacific R. Co.*, 257 U. S., at 535 (analyzing whether the privilege of access to a State's courts must be made available to out-of-state citizens equally with the citizens of the relevant State). Because it does not pose the question of the constitutionality of a state law that interferes with an interstate market through prohibition or burdensome regulations, this case is not governed by the dormant Commerce Clause.
>
> Even shoehorned into our dormant Commerce Clause framework, however, Hurlbert's claim would fail. Insofar as there is a "market" for public documents in Virginia, it is a market for a product that the Commonwealth has created and of which the Commonwealth is the sole manufacturer. We have held that a State does not violate the dormant Commerce Clause when, having created a market through a state program, it "limits benefits generated by [that] state program to those who fund the state treasury and whom the State was created to serve." *Reeves, Inc.* v. *Stake*, 447 U. S. 429, 442 (1980). "Such policies, while perhaps 'protectionist' in a loose sense, reflect the essential and patently unobjectionable purpose of state government—to serve the citizens of the State." *Ibid.*; cf. *Department of Revenue of Ky.* v. *Davis*, 553 U. S. 328, 341 (2008) ("[A] government function is not susceptible to standard dormant Commerce Clause scrutiny owing to its likely motivation by legitimate objectives distinct from the simple economic protectionism the Clause abhors"). For these reasons, Virginia's citizens-only FOIA provision does not violate the dormant Commerce Clause.

Is Justice Alito's reasoning persuasive? Is he using the Market Participant exception, discussed in the next section, without saying so? After reading the cases under that exception, return to this excerpt and evaluate the Court's position.

Chapter 3
The President, Executive Authority, and Separation of Power

The modern American presidency has ascended in both the authority and power to rival the emperors who ruled over the Republic of Rome. Much debate has existed in the nation in relation to the extent of authority that should rest in the nation's chief executive. Despite being a "minority (non-majoritarian) President," anointed by the Supreme Court in Bush v. Gore (Chapter 1), the catastrophic events of 9/11 and the ensuing American response made George W. Bush a center of controversy concerning presidential power. The Bush administration asserted unprecedented executive authority and power to combat the war on terrorism. All of the materials in this chapter, in regard to the President's power in both foreign and domestic affairs, must be viewed against this background.

Though the founding fathers recognized a need for a unified head of state and government in creation of the office, they nonetheless limited allocation of power to the Executive and provided numerous checks on that power by the Congress. They steadfastly attempted to withhold from the office the prerogatives of monarchs, both in relation to "kingly regalia" and autocratic authority. Examples of this can be seen in the fact that although the framers titled the President "Commander-in-Chief," they nonetheless left the power to "declare war" to Congress. Though they allowed him to negotiate treaties and appoint Supreme Court justices, they also required the advice and consent of the Senate. Most specifically, they charged him with faithfully executing the laws of the nation, or the laws promulgated by the Congress. Though the framers feared "executive majesty," they also feared unchecked "democratic rule" by Congress, and they consequently allotted to the President the authority to veto acts of Congress, with the veto subject to being overridden by a two-thirds vote of the bodies.

Arthur M. Schlesinger, Jr., in his *The Imperial Presidency* (1973), asserted that "[b]y the early 1970's the American President had become on issues of war and peace the most absolute monarch among the great powers of the world." As Commander-in-Chief, providing the nation with a singular voice abroad, the President ultimately retained sweeping power in regard to foreign relations. Notably in this regard, James Madison wrote to Tomas Jefferson, "Perhaps it is a universal truth that the loss of liberty at home is to be charged to provisions against danger, real or apprehended, from abroad." From the nation's inception to the war on terrorism, the extent of power resting in the President in domestic affairs has been ascribed to the threat to "national security" from abroad. This expansive presidential power, even in a post-Watergate world, calls into question whether a significant change in the constitutional balance of power in the federal government has replaced that originally articulated in the Constitution by its framers.

The most difficult question concerning presidential power is the level of authority which may accrue to the President as Commander-in-Chief in instances of national emergency, where the constitutional balance of power may not provide for prompt or adequate response — situations that are so grave that "necessity may know no law." Does the Constitution, as a "living" document, allow the President unilateral authority to meet situations such as these through his "inherent" power to protect the national security? Is it worth, for example, limiting presidential power, and preserving constitutional values and liberties, if the end result is the loss of the Constitution itself? Yet, if we allow the Constitution to "bend" in these situations, how will we know when presidential actions are justified, and might we not also see the liberties the document guarantees lost to the ambition of tyrannical rulers? The present war on terrorism and the adoption of the "PATRIOT Act" makes this a question of a most consequential value.

In this section, we will confront these issues and the sources of presidential power in domestic and then foreign affairs. In this context, we will also view the clashes of such authority against the other branches of government (separation of powers).

I. PRESIDENTIAL POWER: DOMESTIC AFFAIRS

The Imperial Presidency was essentially the creation of foreign policy. A combination of doctrines and emotions — belief in permanent and universal crisis fear of communism, faith in the duty and the right of the United States to intervene swiftly in every part of the world — had brought about the unprecedented centralization of decisions over war and peace in the Presidency. [Schlesinger, *The Imperial Presidency* (1973).]

The argument for presidential power in domestic affairs, based upon inherent constitutional power over foreign affairs, raises most difficult questions. Recent events have focused on the level of "inherent emergency power" granted to the executive to protect national security from threats that are external. The degree unto which a President can assert "inherent" power over internal affairs, as based upon national security and threats from abroad, will be our focus. Asserting broad-based presidential prerogative in this circumstance may well contradict the balance of power intended by the Constitution, specifically in relation to the law making powers of Congress. Once again the perplexing issue of what type of authority rests in the Executive to protect the national security, set against the limits on such in the Constitution's balance of power and liberties, is before us. The issue in relation to domestic affairs is of great magnitude, for allowing the Executive "emergency" powers in domestic affairs similar to those granted in foreign affairs could complete a full circle of dictatorial authority to a President. Does "necessity know no law"? Can we be assured that in granting the President these inherent emergency powers that they will not be abused — keeping in mind the particularly devastating effects of such abuse in relation to domestic affairs? Is it even possible for the Court to allow for such presidential prerogative when necessary, yet limit such when not? Or, so to speak, is the "cat already out of the bag"?

In the opinion that follows, the Supreme Court confronted just these issues. With President Truman fighting an undeclared war, a "police action" in Korea, a labor dispute led to a strike called by the United Steel Workers against the steel companies in 1952. In a controversial action, President Truman "nationalized" the steel companies until the strike was settled, citing the need for steel production to provide armaments for the undeclared Korean War as a necessity to protect the national security. Though the steel companies argued that the seizure was unconstitutional, Truman asserted his inherent emergency powers as Commander-in-Chief in defense of his action. In his memoirs, *Year of Trial and*

Hope (1956), he stated that "Russia would believe us so weakened by an extended strike as to invite further aggression, and there might be other Koreas."

Thus, the issue of how far-reaching the President's emergency powers were was placed squarely before the Court. Some individuals felt that the Court would not reach the merits by classifying the issue as a political question, controlled by the President's knowledge and prerogatives in foreign affairs, and consequently lacking "judicially manageable standards." But, as if to underscore the importance of the issues, the Court did not hesitate to render jurisdiction over the subject matter and reach the merits of the case.

The opinions that follow have provided a "rule of thumb" for judicial evaluation of presidential power in domestic affairs until the present day. Pay particular attention to Justice Jackson's concurring opinion, as it is now viewed as the most significant in terms of future guidance. It is worth noting that the Chief Justice (Rehnquist) served as Justice Jackson's law clerk.

YOUNGSTOWN SHEET & TUBE CO. v. SAWYER
(The Steel Seizure Case)
343 U.S. 579 (1952)

Mr. Justice BLACK delivered the opinion of the Court.

We are asked to decide whether President Truman was acting within his constitutional power when he issued an order directing the Secretary of Commerce to take possession of and operate most of the Nation's steel mills. The mill owners argue that the President's order amounts to lawmaking, a legislative function which the Constitution has expressly confided to the Congress and not to the President. The Government's position is that the order was made on findings of the President that his action was necessary to avert a national catastrophe which would inevitably result from a stoppage of steel production, and that in meeting this grave emergency the President was acting within the aggregate of his constitutional powers as the Nation's Chief Executive and the Commander in Chief of the Armed Forces of the United States. The issue emerges here from the following series of events:

In the latter part of 1951, a dispute arose between the steel companies and their employees over terms and conditions that should be included in new collective bargaining agreements. Long-continued conferences failed to resolve the dispute. On December 18, 1951, the employees' representative, United Steelworkers of America, C.I.O., gave notice of an intention to strike when the existing bargaining agreements expired on December 31. The Federal Mediation and Conciliation Service then intervened in an effort to get labor and management to agree. This failing, the President on December 22, 1951, referred the dispute to the Federal Wage Stabilization Board to investigate and make recommendations for fair and equitable terms of settlement. This Board's report resulted in no settlement. On April 4, 1952, the Union gave notice of a nation-wide strike called to begin at 12:01 A.M. April 9. The indispensability of steel as a component of substantially all weapons and other war materials led the President to believe that the proposed work stoppage would immediately jeopardize our national defense and that governmental seizure of the steel mills was necessary in order to assure the continued availability of steel. Reciting these considerations for his action, the President, a few hours before the strike was to begin, issued Executive Order 10340. [The] order directed the Secretary of Commerce to take possession of most of the steel mills and keep them running. The Secretary immediately issued his own possessory orders, calling upon the presidents of the various seized companies to serve as operating managers for the United States. They were directed to carry on their activities in accordance with regulations and directions of the Secretary. The next morning the President sent a message to Congress reporting his action.

[Twelve] days later he sent a second message. [Congress] has taken no action. . . .

[The Court noted that the companies had obeyed the Secretary's order under protest and brought suit against him in district court. On April 30, that court issued a temporary restraining order prohibiting the Secretary from continuing the seizure and possession of the plants. On the same day, the district court's order was stayed by the court of appeals. The Supreme Court granted certiorari on May 3 and heard argument on May 12; the decision was announced on June 2.]

The President's power, if any, to issue the order must stem either from an act of Congress or from the Constitution itself. There is no statute that expressly authorizes the President to take possession of property as he did here. Nor is there any act of Congress to which our attention has been directed from which such a power can fairly be implied. [There] are two statutes which do authorize the President to take both personal and real property under certain conditions. However, the Government admits that these conditions were not met and that the President's order was not rooted in either of the statutes. The Government refers to the seizure provisions of one of these statutes as "much too cumbersome, involved, and time-consuming for the crisis which was at hand."

Moreover, the use of the seizure technique to solve labor disputes in order to prevent work stoppages was not only unauthorized by any congressional enactment; prior to this controversy, Congress had refused to adopt that method of settling labor disputes. When the Taft-Hartley Act was under consideration in 1947, Congress rejected an amendment which would have authorized such governmental seizures in cases of emergency. . . .

It is clear that if the President had authority to issue the order he did, it must be found in some provision of the Constitution. And it is not claimed that express constitutional language grants this power to the President. The contention is that presidential power should be implied from the aggregate of his powers under the Constitution. Particular reliance is placed on provisions in Article II which say that "The executive Power shall be vested in a President . . ."; that "he shall take Care that the Laws be faithfully executed"; and that he "shall be Commander in Chief of the Army and Navy of the United States."

The order cannot properly be sustained as an exercise of the President's military power as Commander in Chief of the Armed Forces. The Government attempts to do so by citing a number of cases upholding broad powers in military commanders engaged in day-to-day fighting in a theater of war. Such cases need not concern us here. Even though "theater of war" be an expanding concept, we cannot with faithfulness to our constitutional system hold that the Commander in Chief of the Armed Forces has the ultimate power as such to take possession of private property in order to keep labor disputes from stopping production. This is a job for the Nation's lawmakers, not for its military authorities.

Nor can the seizure order be sustained because of the several constitutional provisions that grant executive power to the President. In the framework of our Constitution, the President's power to see that the laws are faithfully executed refutes the idea that he is to be a lawmaker. The Constitution limits his functions in the lawmaking process to the recommending of laws he thinks wise and the vetoing of laws he thinks bad. And the Constitution is neither silent nor equivocal about who shall make laws which the President is to execute. The first section of the first article says that "All legislative Powers herein granted shall be vested in a Congress of the United States. . . ." After granting many powers to the Congress, Article I goes on to provide that Congress may "make all Laws which shall be necessary and proper for carrying into Execution the foregoing Powers, and all other Powers vested by this Constitution in the Government of the United States, or in any Department or Officer thereof."

The President's order does not direct that a congressional policy be executed in a manner prescribed by Congress — it directs that a presidential policy be executed in a manner prescribed by the President. The preamble of the order itself, like that of many statutes, sets out reasons why the President believes certain policies should be adopted, proclaims these policies as rules of conduct to be followed, and again, like a statute, authorizes a government official to promulgate additional rules and regulations consistent with the policy proclaimed and needed to carry that policy into execution. The power of Congress to adopt such public policies as those proclaimed by the order is beyond question. It can authorize the taking of private property for public use. It can make laws regulating the relationships between employers and employees, prescribing rules designed to settle labor disputes, and fixing wages and working conditions in certain fields of our economy. The Constitution does not subject this lawmaking power of Congress to presidential or military supervision or control.

It is said that other Presidents without congressional authority have taken possession of private business enterprises in order to settle labor disputes. But even if this be true, Congress has not thereby lost its exclusive constitutional authority to make laws necessary and proper to carry out the powers vested by the Constitution "in the Government of the United States, or any Department or Officer thereof."

The Founders of this Nation entrusted the lawmaking power to the Congress alone in both good and bad times. It would do no good to recall the historical events, the fears of power and the hopes for freedom that lay behind their choice. Such a review would but confirm our holding that this seizure order cannot stand.

The judgment of the District Court is affirmed.

Mr. Justice FRANKFURTER, concurring.

[Not] so long ago it was fashionable to find our system of checks and balances obstructive to effective government. It was easy to ridicule that system as outmoded — too easy. The experience through which the world has passed in our own day has made vivid the realization that the Framers of our Constitution were not inexperienced doctrinaires. These long-headed statesmen had no illusion that our people enjoyed biological or psychological or sociological immunities from the hazards of concentrated power. It is absurd to see a dictator in a representative product of the sturdy democratic traditions of the Mississippi Valley. The accretion of dangerous power does not come in a day. It does come, however slowly, from the generative force of unchecked disregard of the restrictions that fence in even the most disinterested assertion of authority. . . .

Marshall's admonition [in McCulloch] that "it is a constitution we are expounding" is especially relevant when the Court is required to give legal sanctions to an underlying principle of the Constitution — that of separation of powers. "The great ordinances of the Constitution do not establish and divide fields of black and white." . . .

[We] must therefore put to one side consideration of what powers the President would have had if there had been no legislation whatever bearing on the authority asserted by the seizure, or if the seizure had been only for a short, explicitly temporary period, to be terminated automatically unless Congressional approval were given. . . .

The question before the Court comes in this setting. Congress has frequently — at least 16 times since 1916 — specifically provided for executive seizure of production, transportation, communications, or storage facilities. In every case it has qualified this grant of power with limitations and safeguards. This body of enactments demonstrates that Congress deemed seizure so drastic a power as to require that it be carefully circumscribed whenever the President was vested with this extraordinary authority. . . .

In any event, nothing can be plainer than that Congress made a conscious choice of policy in a field full of perplexity and peculiarly within legislative responsibility for choice. In formulating legislation for dealing with industrial conflicts, Congress could not more clearly and emphatically have withheld authority than it did in [the Taft-Hartley Act of] 1947. . . .

It cannot be contended that the President would have had power to issue this order had Congress explicitly negated such authority in formal legislation. Congress has expressed its will to withhold this power from the President as though it had said so in so many words. . . .

Apart from his vast share of responsibility for the conduct of our foreign relations, the embracing function of the President is that "he shall take Care that the Laws be faithfully executed. . . ." Art. II, §3. The nature of that authority has for me been comprehensively indicated by Mr. Justice Holmes. "The duty of the President to see that the laws be executed is a duty that does not go beyond the laws or require him to achieve more than Congress sees fit to leave within his power." Myers v. United States, 272 U.S. 52, 177. The powers of the President are not as particularized as are those of Congress. But unenumerated powers do not mean undefined powers. . . .

To be sure, the content of the three authorities of government is not to be derived from an abstract analysis. The areas are partly interacting, not wholly disjointed. The Constitution is a framework for government. Therefore the way the framework has consistently operated fairly establishes that it has operated according to its true nature. Deeply embedded traditional ways of conducting government cannot supplant the Constitution or legislation, but they give meaning to the words of a text or supply them. It is an inadmissibly narrow conception of American constitutional law to confine it to the words of the Constitution and to disregard the gloss which life has written upon them. In short, a systematic, unbroken, executive practice, long pursued to the knowledge of the Congress and never before questioned, engaged in by Presidents who have also sworn to uphold the Constitution, making as it were such exercise of power part of the structure of our government, may be treated as a gloss on "executive Power" vested in the President by § 1 of Art. II.

Down to the World War II period, [the] record is barren of instances comparable to the one before us. [In] this case, reliance on the powers that flow from declared war has been commendably disclaimed by the Solicitor General. Thus the list of executive assertions of the power of seizure in circumstances comparable to the present reduces to three in the six-month period from June to December of 1941. [Without] passing on their validity, as we are not called upon to do, it suffices to say that these three isolated instances do not add up, either in number, scope, duration or contemporaneous legal justification, to the necessary kind of executive construction of the Constitution. [Nor] do they come to us sanctioned by long-continued acquiescence of Congress giving decisive weight to a construction by the Executive of its powers. [No] doubt a government with distributed authority, subject to be challenged in the courts of law, at least long enough to consider and adjudicate the challenge, labors under restrictions from which other governments are free. It has not been our tradition to envy such governments. In any event our government was designed to have such restrictions. The price was deemed not too high in view of the safeguards which these restrictions afford. . . .

Mr. Justice JACKSON, concurring in the judgment and opinion of the Court.

[A] judge, like an executive adviser, may be surprised at the poverty of really useful and unambiguous authority applicable to concrete problems of executive power as they actually present themselves. Just what our forefathers did envision, or would have envisioned had they foreseen modern conditions, must be divined from materials almost as enigmatic as the dreams Joseph was called upon to interpret for Pharaoh. A century and a half of partisan debate and scholarly speculation yields no net result but only supplies more or less apt quotations from respected sources on each side of any question. They largely cancel each other. And court decisions are indecisive because of the judicial practice of dealing with the largest questions in the most narrow way.

The actual art of governing under our Constitution does not and cannot conform to judicial definitions of the power of any of its branches based on isolated clauses or even single Articles torn from context. While the Constitution diffuses power the better to secure liberty, it also contemplates that practice will integrate the dispersed powers into a workable government. It enjoins upon its branches separateness but interdependence, autonomy but reciprocity. Presidential powers are not fixed but fluctuate, depending upon their disjunction or conjunction with those of Congress. We may well begin by a somewhat over-simplified grouping of practical situations in which a President may doubt, or others may challenge, his powers, and by distinguishing roughly the legal consequences of this factor of relativity.

1. When the President acts pursuant to an express or implied authorization of Congress, his authority is at its maximum, for it includes all that he possesses in his own right plus all that Congress can delegate. In these circumstances, and in these only, may he be said (for what it may be worth) to personify the federal sovereignty. If his act is held unconstitutional under these circumstances, it usually means that the Federal Government as an undivided whole lacks power. A seizure executed by the President pursuant to an Act of Congress would be supported by the strongest of presumptions and the widest latitude of judicial interpretation, and the burden of persuasion would rest heavily upon any who might attack it.

2. When the President acts in absence of either a congressional grant or denial of authority, he can only rely upon his own independent powers, but there is a zone of twilight in which he and Congress may have concurrent authority, or in which its distribution is uncertain. Therefore, congressional inertia, indifference or quiescence may sometimes, at least as a practical matter, enable, if not invite, measures on independent presidential responsibility. In this area, any actual test of power is likely to depend on the imperatives of events and contemporary imponderables rather than on abstract theories of law.

3. When the President takes measures incompatible with the expressed or implied will of Congress, his power is at its lowest ebb, for then he can rely only upon his own constitutional powers minus any constitutional powers of Congress over the matter. Courts can sustain exclusive presidential control in such a case only by disabling the Congress from acting upon the subject. Presidential claim to a power at once so conclusive and preclusive must be scrutinized with caution, for what is at stake is the equilibrium established by our constitutional system.

Into which of these classifications does this executive seizure of the steel industry fit? It is eliminated from the first by admission, for it is conceded that no congressional authorization exists for this seizure. . . .

Can it then be defended under flexible tests available to the second category? It seems clearly eliminated from that class because Congress has not left seizure of private property an open field but has covered it by three statutory policies inconsistent with this seizure. . . .

This leaves the current seizure to be justified only by the severe tests under the third grouping, where it can be supported only by any remainder of executive power after subtraction of such powers as Congress may have over the subject. In short, we can sustain the President only by holding that seizure of such strike-bound industries is within his domain and beyond control by Congress. . . .

The Solicitor General seeks the power of seizure in three clauses of the Executive Article, the first reading, "The executive Power shall be vested in a President of the United States of America." [I] quote the interpretation which his brief puts upon it: "In our view, this clause constitutes a grant of all the executive powers of which the Government is capable." If that be true, it is difficult to see why the forefathers bothered to add several specific items, including some trifling ones.

The example of such unlimited executive power that must have most impressed the forefathers was the prerogative exercised by George III, and the description of its evils in the Declaration of Independence leads me to doubt that they were creating their new Executive in his image. [And] if we seek instruction from our own times, we can match it only from the executive powers in those governments we disparagingly describe as totalitarian. I cannot accept the view that this clause is a grant in bulk of all conceivable executive power but regard it as an allocation to the presidential office of the generic powers thereafter stated.

The clause on which the Government next relies is that "The President shall be Commander in Chief of the Army and Navy of the United States. . . ." These cryptic words [imply] something more than an empty title. But just what authority goes with the name has plagued presidential advisers who would not waive or narrow it by nonassertion yet cannot say where it begins or ends. It undoubtedly puts the Nation's armed forces under presidential command. Hence, this loose appellation is sometimes advanced as support for any presidential action, internal or external, involving use of force, the idea being that it vests power to do anything, anywhere, that can be done with an army or navy.

That seems to be the logic of an argument tendered at our bar — that the President having, on his own responsibility, sent American troops abroad derives from that act "affirmative power" to seize the means of producing a supply of steel for them. . . .

I cannot foresee all that it might entail if the Court should indorse this argument. Nothing in our Constitution is plainer than that declaration of a war is entrusted only to Congress. Of course, a state of war may in fact exist without a formal declaration. But no doctrine that the Court could promulgate would seem to me more sinister and alarming than that a President whose conduct of foreign affairs is so largely uncontrolled, and often even is unknown, can vastly enlarge his mastery over the internal affairs of the country by his own commitment of the Nation's armed forces to some foreign venture. I do not, however, find it necessary or appropriate to consider the legal status of the Korean enterprise to discountenance argument based on it.

Assuming that we are in a war de facto, whether it is or is not a war de jure, does that empower the Commander in Chief to seize industries he thinks necessary to supply our army? The Constitution expressly places in Congress power "to raise and support Armies" and "to provide and maintain a Navy." (Emphasis supplied.) This certainly lays upon Congress primary responsibility for supplying the armed forces. Congress alone controls the raising of revenues and their appropriation and may determine in what manner and by what means they shall be spent for military and naval procurement. . . .

There are indications that the Constitution did not contemplate that the title Commander in Chief of the Army and Navy will constitute him also Commander in Chief of the country, its industries and its inhabitants. He has no monopoly of "war powers," whatever they are. . . .

The third clause in which the Solicitor General finds seizure powers is that "he shall take Care that the Laws be faithfully executed. . . ." That authority must be matched against words of the Fifth Amendment that "No person shall be . . . deprived of life, liberty or property, without due process of law. . . ." One gives a governmental authority that reaches so far as there is law, the other gives a private right that authority shall go no farther. These signify about all there is of the principle that ours is a government of laws, not of men, and that we submit ourselves to rulers only if under rules.

The Solicitor General lastly grounds support of the seizure upon nebulous, inherent powers never expressly granted but said to have accrued to the office from the customs and claims of preceding administrations. The plea is for a resulting power to deal with a crisis or an emergency according to the necessities of the case, the unarticulated assumption being that necessity knows no law.

Loose and irresponsible use of adjectives colors all nonlegal and much legal discussion of presidential powers. "Inherent" powers, "implied" powers, "incidental" powers, "plenary" powers, "war" powers and "emergency" powers are used, often interchangeably and without fixed or ascertainable meanings.

The vagueness and generality of the clauses that set forth presidential powers afford a plausible basis for pressures within and without an administration for presidential action beyond that supported by those whose responsibility it is to defend his actions in court. The claim of inherent and unrestricted presidential powers has long been a persuasive dialectical weapon in political controversy. While it is not surprising that counsel should grasp support from such unadjudicated claims of power, a judge cannot accept self-serving press statements of the attorney for one of the interested parties as authority in answering a constitutional question, even if the advocate was himself. But prudence has counseled that actual reliance on such nebulous claims stop short of provoking a judicial test. . . .

The appeal, however, that we declare the existence of inherent powers ex necessitate to meet an emergency asks us to do what many think would be wise, although it is something the forefathers omitted. They knew what emergencies were, knew the pressures they engender for authoritative action, knew, too, how they afford a ready pretext for usurpation. We may also suspect that they suspected that emergency powers would tend to kindle emergencies. Aside from suspension of the privilege of the writ of habeas corpus in time of rebellion or invasion, when the public safety may require it, they made no express provision for exercise of extraordinary authority because of a crisis. I do not think we rightfully may so amend their work. . . .

In view of the ease, expedition and safety with which Congress can grant and has granted large emergency powers, certainly ample to embrace this crisis, I am quite unimpressed with the argument that we should affirm possession of them without statute. Such power either has no beginning or it has no end. If it exists, it need submit to no legal restraint. I am not alarmed that it would plunge us straightway into dictatorship, but it is at least a step in that wrong direction.

As to whether there is imperative necessity for such powers, it is relevant to note the gap that exists between the President's paper powers and his real powers. The Constitution does not disclose the measure of the actual controls wielded by the modern presidential office. That instrument must be understood as an Eighteenth-Century sketch of a government hoped for, not as a blueprint of the Government that is. Vast accretions of federal power, eroded from that reserved by the States, have magnified the scope of presidential activity. Subtle shifts take place in the centers of real power that do not show in the face of the Constitution.

Executive power has the advantage of concentration in a single head in whose choice the whole Nation has a part, making him the focus of public hopes and expectations. In drama, magnitude and finality his decisions so far overshadow any others that almost alone he fills the public eye and ear. No other personality in public life can begin to compete with him in access to the public mind through modern methods of communications. By his prestige as head of state and his influence upon public opinion he exerts a leverage upon those who are supposed to check and balance his power which often cancels their effectiveness.

Moreover, rise of the party system has made a significant extraconstitutional supplement to real executive power. No appraisal of his necessities is realistic which overlooks that he heads a political system as well as a legal system. Party loyalties and interests, sometimes more binding than law, extend his effective control into branches of government other than his own and he often may win, as a political leader, what he cannot command under the Constitution. . . .

But I have no illusion that any decision by this Court can keep power in the hands of Congress if it is not wise and timely in meeting its problems. A crisis that challenges the President equally, or perhaps primarily, challenges Congress. If not good law, there was worldly wisdom in the maxim attributed to Napoleon that "The tools belong to the man who can use them." We may say that power to legislate for emergencies belongs in the hands of Congress, but only Congress itself can prevent power from slipping through its fingers.

The essence of our free Government is "leave to live by no man's leave, underneath the law" — to be governed by those impersonal forces which we call law. Our Government is fashioned to fulfill this concept so far as humanly possible. [The] executive action we have here originates in the individual will of the President and represents an exercise of authority without law. No one, perhaps not even the President, knows the limits of the power he may seek to exert in this instance and the parties affected cannot learn the limit of their rights. We do not know today what powers over labor or property would be claimed to flow from Government possession if we should legalize it, what rights to compensation would be claimed or recognized, or on what contingency it would end. With all its defects, delays and inconveniences, men have discovered no technique for long preserving free government except that the Executive be under the law, and that the law be made by parliamentary deliberations.

Such institutions may be destined to pass away. But it is the duty of the Court to be last, not first, to give them up.

[The concurring opinions of Justices Burton, Clark and Douglas are omitted.]

Mr. Chief Justice VINSON, with whom Mr. Justice REED and Mr. Justice MINTON join, dissenting.

The President of the United States directed the Secretary of Commerce to take temporary possession of the Nation's steel mills during the existing emergency because "a work stoppage would immediately jeopardize and imperil our national defense and the defense of those joined with us in resisting aggression, and would add to the continuing danger of our soldiers, sailors, and airmen engaged in combat in the field." . . .

In passing upon the question of Presidential powers in this case, we must first consider the context in which those powers were exercised. . . .

The President has the duty to execute [legislative programs.] Their successful execution depends upon continued production of steel and stabilized prices for steel. Accordingly, when the collective bargaining agreements between the Nation's steel producers and their employees, represented by the United Steel Workers, were due to expire on December 31, 1951, and a strike shutting down the entire basic steel industry was threatened, the President acted to avert a complete shutdown of steel production. . . .

One is not here called upon even to consider the possibility of executive seizure of a farm, a corner grocery store or even a single industrial plant. Such considerations arise only when one ignores the central fact of this case — that the Nation's entire basic steel production would have shut down completely if there had been no Government seizure. Even ignoring for the moment whatever confidential information the President may possess as "the Nation's organ for foreign affairs," the uncontroverted affidavits in this record amply support the finding that "a work stoppage would immediately jeopardize and imperil our national defense."

Plaintiffs do not remotely suggest any basis for rejecting the President's finding that any stoppage of steel production would immediately place the Nation in peril. [Under the plaintiffs'] view, the President is left powerless at the very moment when the need for action may be most pressing and when no one, other than he, is immediately capable of action. Under this view, he is left powerless because a power not expressly given to Congress is nevertheless found to rest exclusively with Congress. [But the] whole of the "executive Power" is vested in the President. . . .

This comprehensive grant of the executive power to a single person was bestowed soon after the country had thrown the yoke of monarchy. Only by instilling initiative and vigor in all of the three departments of Government, declared Madison, could tyranny in any form be avoided. [It] is thus apparent that the Presidency was deliberately fashioned as an office of power and independence. Of course, the Framers created no autocrat capable of arrogating any power unto himself at any time. But neither did they create an automaton impotent to exercise the powers of Government at a time when the survival of the Republic itself may be at stake.

In passing upon the grave constitutional question presented in this case, we must never forget, as Chief Justice Marshall admonished, that the Constitution is "intended to endure for ages to come, and, consequently, to be adapted to the various crises of human affairs," and that "[i]ts means are adequate to its ends." Cases do arise presenting questions which could not have been foreseen by the Framers. In such cases, the Constitution has been treated as a living document adaptable to new situations. But we are not called upon today to expand the Constitution to meet a new situation. For, in this case, we need only look to history and time-honored principles of constitutional law. . . .

A review of executive action demonstrates that our Presidents have on many occasions exhibited the leadership contemplated by the Framers when they made the President

Commander in Chief, and imposed upon him the trust to "take Care that the Laws be faithfully executed." With or without explicit statutory authorization, Presidents have at such times dealt with national emergencies by acting promptly and resolutely to enforce legislative programs, at least to save those programs until Congress could act. Congress and the courts have responded to such executive initiative with consistent approval. . . .

[Chief Justice Vinson discussed historical practices.]

Much of the argument in this case has been directed at straw men. We do not now have before us the case of a President acting solely on the basis of his own notions of the public welfare. Nor is there any question of unlimited executive power in this case. The President himself closed the door to any such claim when he sent his Message to Congress stating his purpose to abide by any action of Congress, whether approving or disapproving his seizure action. Here, the President immediately made sure that Congress was fully informed of the temporary action he had taken only to preserve the legislative programs from destruction until Congress could act.

The absence of a specific statute authorizing seizure of the steel mills as a mode of executing the laws — both the military procurement program and the anti-inflation program — has not until today been thought to prevent the President from executing the laws. Unlike an administrative commission confined to the enforcement of the statute under which it was created, or the head of a department when administering a particular statute, the President is a constitutional officer charged with taking care that a "mass of legislation" be executed. Flexibility as to mode of execution to meet critical situations is a matter of practical necessity. . . .

The broad executive power granted by Article II to an officer on duty 365 days a year cannot, it is said, be invoked to avert disaster. Instead, the President must confine himself to sending a message to Congress recommending action. Under this messenger-boy concept of the Office, the President cannot even act to preserve legislative programs from destruction so that Congress will have something left to act upon. There is no judicial finding that the executive action was unwarranted because there was in fact no basis for the President's finding of the existence of an emergency for, under this view, the gravity of the emergency and the immediacy of the threatened disaster are considered irrelevant as a matter of law. . . .

[There] is no question that the possession was other than temporary in character and subject to congressional direction — either approving, disapproving or regulating the manner in which the mills were to be administered and returned to the owners. The President immediately informed Congress of his action and clearly stated his intention to abide by the legislative will. No basis for claims of arbitrary action, unlimited powers or dictatorial usurpation of congressional power appears from the facts of this case. On the contrary, judicial, legislative and executive precedents throughout our history demonstrate that in this case the President acted in full conformity with his duties under the Constitution. . . .

————————

Comments on the Steel Seizure Case. The *Youngstown* decision was reached *only* two months after Truman seized the industries. Should the Court have waited three weeks before hearing the case? Were the issues "ripe" before the actual takeover? The Court has been criticized for this rapid movement, especially in light of the importance of the issues. Is this an indication of the Court's desire to reach the merits? If it had waited until the actual takeover, the strike may have been settled, perhaps based on Truman's "threat" alone.

Does the Court recognize any presidential emergency power? Did Justice Black? Justice Jackson? Why has Jackson's opinion become the "lead" opinion in the case? Why not Black's? Is Black's opinion so "textual" that it denies necessary flexibility? Is Black's opinion too confining in relation to the possible need for emergency presidential action? Does Jackson's opinion allow for a "living document," based upon the facts and "realities of a given circumstance"? Are the issues here more important than the constitutional text? Justice Jackson allowed for presidential authority when an absolute "necessity," yet limited arbitrary prerogatives. Do you agree? Is it the best-reasoned opinion in the case? Yet, because Jackson's rationale does allow for inherent emergency power, does it allow for abuse of such power? Is the ultimate test of his standards the gravity of the danger? Can the Court adequately police under such a criteria? How does he limit abuse of presidential authority? What has "democracy got to do with it"? How does Jackson use the "will of the majority" and the democratic process as a means of resolving these issues? Does the "will of Congress" replace constitutional limits? Is Jackson's guiding principle that the President cannot interfere in domestic affairs through a policy contra to congressional stipulations? If one accepts the need for presidential emergency action, is the "public will" as expressed by elected representatives an adequate control? How important is "openness" in government if such is to be the case?

What does Jackson mean by a "zone of twilight," and how should these circumstances be resolved? Does "history" provide a "gloss" on the text? Can the Court provide effective control here?

Does the President have any implied or emergency powers after *Youngstown*? Is this also a matter of circumstance? Note that Art. I refers to "legislative powers herein granted," while Art. II refers to "executive power" without a "herein granted" qualification. In Alexander Hamilton's view, the "different modes of expression in regard to the two powers confirm the inference that the authority vested in the President is not limited to the specific cases of executive power delineated in Article II." 7 *Works of Alexander Hamilton* 80 (1851). This line of reasoning led to the conclusion, reached by Theodore Roosevelt and adhered to by many subsequent Presidents, that the President "was a steward of the people bound actively and affirmatively to do all he could for the people [unless] such action was forbidden by the Constitution or by the law." T. Roosevelt, *Autobiography* 372 (1914). Contrast with this the view of President Taft and others, that the President may exercise only those powers traceable to a constitutional grant of authority. Does *Youngstown* resolve this dispute? (Stone, et al., *Constitutional Law* (1996).)

Truman asserted in his memoirs that

> [w]hatever the six justices of the Supreme Court meant by their differing opinions about the constitutional powers of the President, he must always act in a national emergency. We live in an age when hostilities begin without polite exchanges of diplomatic notes. There are no longer sharp distinctions between combatants and noncombatants, between military targets and the sanctuary of civilian areas. Nor can we separate the economic facts from the problems of defense and security. [The] President, who is Commander in Chief and who represents the interests of all the people, must be able to act at all times to meet any sudden threat to the national security." [Truman, *Memoirs: Years of Trial and Hope* 478, 541 (1956).]

Does the Court reject this view in *Youngstown*? Is Truman right? In a post–9/11 world, does "necessity know no law"?

DAMES & MOORE v. REGAN
453 U.S. 654 (1981)

Justice REHNQUIST delivered the opinion of the Court.

[This] dispute involves various Executive Orders and regulations by which the President nullified attachments and liens on Iranian assets in the United States, directed that these assets be transferred to Iran, and suspended claims against Iran that may be presented to an International Claims Tribunal. This action was taken in an effort to comply with an Executive Agreement between the United States and Iran. We granted certiorari before judgment in this case, and set an expedited briefing and argument schedule, because lower courts had reached conflicting conclusions on the validity of the President's actions and, as the Solicitor General informed us, unless the Government acted by July 19, 1981, Iran could consider the United States to be in breach of the Executive Agreement.

[On] November 4, 1979, the American Embassy in Tehran was seized and our diplomatic personnel were captured and held hostage. In response to that crisis, President Carter, acting pursuant to the International Emergency Economic Powers Act, 91 Stat. 1626, (hereinafter IEEPA), declared a national emergency on November 14, 1979, and blocked the removal or transfer of "all property and interests in property of the Government of Iran, its instrumentalities and controlled entities and the Central Bank of Iran which are or become subject to the jurisdiction of the United States. . . ." Exec. Order No. 12170, 3 CFR 457 (1980), note following President Carter authorized the Secretary of the Treasury to promulgate regulations carrying out the blocking order. On November 15, 1979, the Treasury Department's Office of Foreign Assets Control issued a regulation providing that "[u]nless licensed or authorized . . . any attachment, judgment, decree, lien, execution, garnishment, or other judicial process is null and void with respect to any property in which on or since [November 14, 1979,] there existed an interest of Iran." 31 CFR § 535.203(e) (1980). The regulations also made clear that any licenses or authorizations granted could be "amended, modified, or revoked at any time." § 535.805.

[On] November 26, 1979, the President granted a general license authorizing certain judicial proceedings against Iran but which did not allow the "entry of any judgment or of any decree or order of similar or analogous effect. . . ." § 535.504(a). On December 19, 1979, a clarifying regulation was issued stating that "the general authorization for judicial proceedings contained in § 535.504(a) includes pre-judgment attachment." § 535.418.

On December 19, 1979, petitioner Dames & Moore filed suit in the United States District Court for the Central District of California against the Government of Iran, the Atomic Energy Organization of Iran, and a number of Iranian banks. In its complaint, petitioner alleged that its wholly owned subsidiary, Dames & Moore International, S. R. L., was a party to a written contract with the Atomic Energy Organization, and that the subsidiary's entire interest in the contract had been assigned to petitioner. Under the contract, the subsidiary was to conduct site studies for a proposed nuclear power plant in Iran. As provided in the terms of the contract, the Atomic Energy Organization terminated the agreement for its own convenience on June 30, 1979. Petitioner contended, however, that it was owed $3,436,694.30 plus interest for services performed under the contract prior to the date of termination. The District Court issued orders of attachment directed against property of the defendants, and the property of certain Iranian banks was then attached to secure any judgment that might be entered against them.

[On] January 20, 1981, the Americans held hostage were released by Iran pursuant to an Agreement entered into the day before and embodied in two Declarations of the Democratic and Popular Republic of Algeria. Declaration of the Government of the Democratic and Popular Republic of Algeria (App. to Pet. for Cert. 21-29), and Declaration of the Government of the Democratic and Popular Republic of Algeria Concerning the Settlement of Claims by the Government of the United States of America and the Government of the Islamic Republic of Iran (*id.*, at 30-35). The Agreement stated that "[i]t is the purpose of [the United States and Iran] . . . to terminate all litigation as between the Government of each party and the nationals of the other, and to bring about the settlement and termination of all such claims through binding arbitration." In furtherance of this goal, the Agreement called for the establishment of an Iran-United States Claims Tribunal which would arbitrate any claims not settled within six months. Awards of the Claims Tribunal are to be "final and binding" and "enforceable . . . in the courts of any nation in accordance with its laws." *Id.*, at 32. Under the Agreement, the United States is obligated "to terminate all legal proceedings in United States courts involving claims of United States persons and institutions against Iran and its state enterprises, to nullify all attachments and judgments obtained therein, to prohibit all further litigation based on such claims, and to bring about the termination of such claims through binding arbitration." *Id.*, at 22.

In addition, the United States must "act to bring about the transfer" by July 19, 1981, of all Iranian assets held in this country by American banks. *Id.*, at 24-25. One billion dollars of these assets will be deposited in a security account in the Bank of England, to the account of the Algerian Central Bank, and used to satisfy awards rendered against Iran by the Claims Tribunal. *Ibid.*

On January 19, 1981, President Carter issued a series of Executive Orders implementing the terms of the agreement. These Orders revoked all licenses permitting the exercise of "any right, power, or privilege" with regard to Iranian funds, securities, or deposits; "nullified" all non-Iranian interests in such assets acquired subsequent to the blocking order of November 14, 1979; and required those banks holding Iranian assets to transfer them "to the Federal Reserve Bank of New York, to be held or transferred as directed by the Secretary of the Treasury."

On February 24, 1981, President Reagan issued an Executive Order in which he "ratified" the January 19th Moreover, he "suspended" all "claims which may be presented to the . . . Tribunal" and provided that such claims "shall have no legal effect in any action now pending in any court of the United States." *Ibid.* The suspension of any particular claim terminates if the Claims Tribunal determines that it has no jurisdiction over that claim; claims are discharged for all purposes when the Claims Tribunal either awards some recovery and that amount is paid, or determines that no recovery is due. *Ibid.*

[The] parties and the lower courts, confronted with the instant questions, have all agreed that much relevant analysis is contained in *Youngstown Sheet & Tube Co. v. Sawyer*, 343 U.S. 579, 72 S.Ct. 863, 96 L.Ed. 1153 (1952). Justice Black's opinion for the Court in that case, involving the validity of President Truman's effort to seize the country's steel mills in the wake of a nationwide strike, recognized that "[t]he President's power, if any, to issue the order must stem either from an act of Congress or from the Constitution itself." *Id.*, at 585, 72 S.Ct. at 864. Justice Jackson's concurring opinion elaborated in a general way the consequences of different types of interaction between the two democratic branches in assessing Presidential authority to act in any given case. When the President acts pursuant to an express or implied authorization from Congress, he exercises not only his powers but also those delegated by Congress. In such a case the executive action "would be supported by the strongest of presumptions and the widest latitude of judicial interpretation, and the burden of persuasion would rest heavily upon any who might attack it." When the President acts in the absence of congressional authorization he may enter "a zone of twilight in which he and Congress may have concurrent authority, or in which its distribution is uncertain." *Ibid.* In such a case the analysis becomes more complicated, and the validity of the President's action, at least so far as separation-of-powers principles are concerned, hinges on a consideration of all the circumstances which might shed light on the views of the Legislative Branch toward such action, including "congressional inertia, indifference or quiescence." *Ibid.* Finally, when the President acts in contravention of the will of Congress, "his power is at its lowest ebb," and the Court can sustain his actions "only by disabling the Congress from acting upon the subject.".

Although we have in the past found and do today find Justice Jackson's classification of executive actions into three general categories analytically useful, we should be mindful of Justice Holmes' admonition, quoted by Justice Frankfurter in *Youngstown, supra,* at 597, 72 S.Ct., at 890 (concurring opinion), that "[t]he great ordinances of the Constitution do not establish and divide fields of black and white." Justice Jackson himself recognized that his three categories represented "a somewhat over-simplified grouping," and it is doubtless the case that executive action in any particular instance falls, not neatly in one of three pigeonholes, but rather at some point along a spectrum running from explicit congressional authorization to explicit congressional prohibition. This is particularly true as respects cases such as the one before us, involving responses to international crises the nature of which Congress can hardly have been expected to anticipate in any detail.

[The] Government, however, has principally relied on § 203 of the IEEPA, 91 Stat. 1626, 50 U.S.C. § 1702(a)(1) (1976 ed., Supp. III), as authorization for these actions. Section 1702(a)(1) provides in part:

> At the times and to the extent specified in section 1701 of this title, the President may, under such regulations as he may prescribe, by means of instructions, licenses, or otherwise —
>> (A) investigate, regulate, or prohibit —
>>> (i) any transactions in foreign exchange,
>>> (ii) transfers of credit or payments between, by, through, or to any banking institution, to the extent that such transfers or payments involve any interest of any foreign country or a national thereof,
>>> (iii) the importing or exporting of currency or securities, and
>>> (B) investigate, regulate, direct and compel, nullify, void, prevent or prohibit, any acquisition, holding, withholding, use, transfer, withdrawal, transportation, importation or exportation of, or dealing in, or exercising any right, power, or privilege with respect to, or transactions involving, any property in which any foreign country or a national thereof has any interest;
>> by any person, or with respect to any property, subject to the jurisdiction of the United States."

The Government contends that the acts of "nullifying" the attachments and ordering the "transfer" of the frozen assets are specifically authorized by the plain language of the above statute.

[Because] the President's action in nullifying the attachments and ordering the transfer of the assets was taken pursuant to specific congressional authorization, it is "supported by the strongest of presumptions and the widest latitude of judicial interpretation, and the burden of persuasion would rest heavily upon any who might attack it." *Youngstown* (Jackson, J., concurring). Under the circumstances of this case, we cannot say that petitioner has sustained that heavy burden. A contrary ruling would mean that the Federal Government as a whole lacked the power exercised by the President, and that we are not prepared to say.

Although we have concluded that the IEEPA constitutes specific congressional authorization to the President to nullify the attachments and order the transfer of Iranian assets, there remains the question of the President's authority to suspend claims pending in American courts. Such claims have, of course, an existence apart from the attachments which accompanied them. In terminating these claims through Executive Order No. 12294 the President purported to act under authority of both the IEEPA and, the so-called "Hostage Act."

[We] conclude that although the IEEPA authorized the nullification of the attachments, it cannot be read to authorize the suspension of the claims. The claims of American citizens against Iran are not in themselves transactions involving Iranian property or efforts to exercise any rights with respect to such property. An *in personam* lawsuit, although it might eventually be reduced to judgment and that judgment might be executed upon, is an effort to establish liability and fix damages and does not focus on any particular property within the jurisdiction. The terms of the IEEPA therefore do not authorize the President to suspend claims in American courts. This is the view of all the courts which have considered the question.

[Concluding] that neither the IEEPA nor the Hostage Act constitutes specific authorization of the President's action suspending claims, however, is not to say that these statutory provisions are entirely irrelevant to the question of the validity of the President's action. We think both statutes highly relevant in the looser sense of indicating congressional acceptance of a broad scope for executive action in circumstances such as those presented in this case. As noted in Part III, *supra*, at 2982-2983, the IEEPA delegates broad authority to the President to act in times of national emergency with respect to property of a foreign country. The Hostage Act similarly indicates congressional willingness that the President have broad discretion when responding to the hostile acts of foreign sovereigns.

[Although] we have declined to conclude that the IEEPA or the Hostage Act directly authorizes the President's suspension of claims for the reasons noted, we cannot ignore the general tenor of Congress' legislation in this area in trying to determine whether the President is acting alone or at least with the acceptance of Congress. As we have noted, Congress cannot anticipate and legislate with regard to every possible action the President may find it necessary to take or every possible situation in which he might act. Such failure of Congress specifically to delegate authority does not, "especially . . . in the areas of foreign policy and national security," imply "congressional disapproval" of action taken by the Executive. On the contrary, the enactment of legislation closely related to the question of the President's authority in a particular case which evinces legislative intent to accord the President broad discretion may be considered to "invite" "measures on independent presidential responsibility," *Youngstown* (Jackson, J., concurring). At least this is so where there is no contrary indication of legislative intent and when, as here, there is a history of congressional acquiescence in conduct of the sort engaged in by the President. It is to that history which we now turn.

Not infrequently in affairs between nations, outstanding claims by nationals of one country against the government of another country are "sources of friction" between the two sovereigns. *United States v. Pink* To resolve these difficulties, nations have often entered into agreements settling the claims of their respective nationals. As one treatise writer puts it, international agreements settling claims by nationals of one state against the government of another "are established international practice reflecting traditional international theory." L. Henkin, Foreign Affairs and the Constitution 262 (1972). Consistent with that principle, the United States has repeatedly exercised its sovereign authority to settle the claims of its nationals against foreign countries. Though those settlements have sometimes been made by treaty, there has also been a longstanding practice of settling such claims by executive agreement without the advice and consent of the Senate. Under such agreements, the President has agreed to renounce or extinguish claims of United States nationals against foreign governments in return for lump-sum payments or the establishment of arbitration procedures. To be sure, many of these settlements were encouraged by the United States claimants themselves, since a claimant's only hope of obtaining any payment at all might lie in having his Government negotiate a diplomatic settlement on his behalf. But it is also undisputed that the "United States has sometimes disposed of the claims of its citizens without their consent, or even without consultation with them, usually without exclusive regard for their interests, as distinguished from those of the nation as a whole." President "may waive or settle a claim against a foreign state . . . [even] without the consent of the [injured] national"). It is clear that the practice of settling claims continues today. Since 1952, the President has entered into at least 10 binding settlements with foreign nations, including an $80 million settlement with the People's Republic of China.

[Crucial] to our decision today is the conclusion that Congress has implicitly approved the practice of claim settlement by executive agreement. This is best demonstrated by Congress' enactment of the International Claims Settlement Act of 1949.

[Over] the years Congress has frequently amended the International Claims Settlement Act to provide for particular problems arising out of settlement agreements, thus demonstrating Congress' continuing acceptance of the President's claim settlement authority. Finally, the legislative history of the IEEPA further reveals that Congress has accepted the authority of the Executive to enter into settlement agreements. Though the IEEPA was enacted to provide for some limitation on the President's emergency powers, Congress stressed that "[n]othing in this act is intended . . . to interfere with the authority of the President to [block assets], or to impede the settlement of claims of U. S. citizens against foreign countries."

[In] addition to congressional acquiescence in the President's power to settle claims, prior cases of this Court have also recognized that the President does have some measure of power to enter into executive agreements without obtaining the advice and consent of the Senate. *United States v. Pink*.

[In] light of all of the foregoing — the inferences to be drawn from the character of the legislation Congress has enacted in the area, such as the IEEPA and the Hostage Act, and from the history of acquiescence in executive claims settlement — we conclude that the President was authorized to suspend pending claims pursuant to Executive Order No. 12294. As Justice Frankfurter pointed out in *Youngstown* "a systematic, unbroken, executive practice, long pursued to the knowledge of the Congress and never before questioned . . . may be treated as a gloss on 'Executive Power' vested in the President by § 1 of Art. II." Past practice does not, by itself, create power, but "long-continued practice, known to and acquiesced in by Congress, would raise a presumption that the [action] had been [taken] in pursuance of its consent. . . . In light of the fact that Congress may be considered to have consented to the President's action in suspending claims, we cannot say that action exceeded the President's powers.

Our conclusion is buttressed by the fact that the means chosen by the President to settle the claims of American nationals provided an alternative forum, the Claims Tribunal, which is capable of providing meaningful relief.

[Just] as importantly, Congress has not disapproved of the action taken here. Though Congress has held hearings on the Iranian Agreement itself, Congress has not enacted legislation, or even passed a resolution, indicating its displeasure with the Agreement. Quite the contrary, the relevant Senate Committee has stated that the establishment of the Tribunal is "of vital importance to the United States." We are thus clearly not confronted with a situation in which Congress has in some way resisted the exercise of Presidential authority.

[Finally], we re-emphasize the narrowness of our decision. We do not decide that the President possesses plenary power to settle claims, even as against foreign governmental entities. As the Court of Appeals for the First Circuit stressed, "[t]he sheer magnitude of such a power, considered against the background of the diversity and complexity of modern international trade, cautions against any broader construction of authority than is necessary." But where, as here, the settlement of claims has been determined to be a necessary incident to the resolution of a major foreign policy dispute between our country and another, and where, as here, we can conclude that Congress acquiesced in the President's action, we are not prepared to say that the President lacks the power to settle such claims.

The judgment of the District Court is accordingly affirmed, and the mandate shall issue forthwith.

———

Comments on *Dames & Moore*. *Dames & Moore* must be understood in the context of the Iranian hostage crisis. President Carter was able to secure the release of the hostages in return for the various agreements at issue in the Court's opinion. As you can imagine, there was considerable pressure for the Court to affirm the basis for their release. Miller, in "Dames & Moore v. Regan: A Political Decision by a Political Court," 29 UCLA L. Rev. 1104, 1105, 1127 (1982), comments in this regard: "Although crafted in familiar lawyers' language, Justice Rehnquist's opinion for the Court reeks with the odor of compromise forced by necessity. Principle, as usual, gave way to realpolitik. The Justices had, in the last analysis, no choice save to sustain the validity of President Carter's hurried deal for the release of the hostages. Invalidation of the executive agreement would have placed the prospective conduct of American policy in an intolerable position. [I] do not suggest that the Constitution, as written, is irrelevant in such cases as Dames & Moore. Of course it has pertinence, but only as a point of departure for political decisions politically made." Or, see H. Koh, *The National Security Constitution: Sharing Power after the Iran-Contra Affair* 139-140 (1990): "It is hard to fault the result in Dames & Moore, given the crisis atmosphere that surrounded its decision and the national mood of support for the hostage accord. Yet [the] Court should have demanded more specific legislative approval for the president's far-reaching measures. The hostages had returned home months earlier and the hostage accord had given the United States government six months before the frozen Iranian assets were to be transferred — plenty of time for the president to ask a supportive Congress for a swift joint resolution of approval."

Does this exigency explain the result in the case? Does it defend the result, or do you agree with Koh? The events did produce a need for a decision that required flexibility that Black's opinion in *Youngstown* could not offer. In fact, Justice Rehnquist, Jackson's former law clerk, while applying Jackson's *Youngstown* "three-part formula," mixes in a little of Frankfurter's *Youngstown* concurrence, " 'As Justice Frankfurter pointed out in *Youngstown*, 343 U.S., at 610-611, 72 S.Ct., at 897-898, "a systematic, unbroken, executive practice, long pursued to the knowledge of the Congress and never before questioned . . . may be treated as a gloss on 'Executive Power' vested in the President by § 1 of Art. II." Past practice does not, by itself, create power, but "long-continued practice, known to and acquiesced in by Congress, would raise a presumption that the [action] had been [taken] in pursuance of its consent. . . ." ' " Should this be the guiding light when we are in Justice Jackson's "zone of twilight"?

Because there was no record of specific congressional action, does the majority need even more flexibility than Jackson offered? Thus, Frankfurter's concurrence? Koh argues in his above cited article, "[By] finding legislative 'approval' when Congress had given none, [the Dames & Moore Court] not only inverted the Steel Seizure holding — which construed statutory nonapproval of the president's act to mean legislative disapproval — but also condoned legislative inactivity at a time that demanded interbranch dialogue and bipartisan consensus."

Dames & Moore and Youngstown. Did *Dames & Moore* affect the present meaning of *Youngstown* as precedent? Did the *Dames & Moore* Court search for congressional approval (silence can mean approval) in order to avoid Jackson's "zone of twilight" and the pressure it places on the Court? Is the Court's approach a rejection of Justice Black's opinion, in favor of an approach that borrows from both Justices Frankfurter and Jackson?

Steel Seizure, 9/11, and the War on Terrorism. The executive responses to the terrorism represented by 9/11 have raised serious questions concerning the issues in *Youngstown*. President Bush has cited the war on terror as a basis for his authority to defend the national security. Based upon such, he has asserted executive authority to unilaterally define any American citizen as an "enemy combatant" and, without any due process, place the individual in military custody, imprisoned indefinitely and incommunicado. Given these tactics, what result in relation to *Youngstown*? Is this a *Youngstown* case, presidential power in domestic affairs to protect the national security, or a *Korematsu* case? In *Korematsu* (Chapter 6), the Supreme Court held that the relocation of Japanese Americans to concentration camps without any process was constitutional, based upon emergency needs during the Second World War. Korematsu v. United States, 323 U.S. 214 (1944). Does it make any difference that the Second World War was "declared," but the war on terrorism was not? Should it? Does it make any difference that the war on terrorism may continue beyond our lifetimes and not have a definitive end, as was the case in previous wars?

The NSA Wiretaps and Youngstown. In December 2005, the New York Times reported that shortly after September 11, 2001, President Bush authorized the National Security Agency (NSA) to secretly, and without warrants, tap the phones of American citizens the agency suspected of having ties to foreign terrorists. This of course raised serious questions in regard to the power of the President in domestic affairs as based upon national security concerns.

The Bush administration supported this action based upon the "inherent" power of the President, arguing that Article II of the Constitution gives the President the inherent authority to authorize such warrantless wiretapping to protect national security, and/or that Congress gave the President such authority when it adopted the "Authorization for Use of Military Force Act" to use "all necessary and appropriate force" to catch those responsible for the September 11, 2001, attacks. The administration argued that warrantless wiretapping should be "included in any natural reading" of Congress's Authorization for Use of Military Force.

Critics have responded that this warrantless wiretapping violates the Fourth Amendment's guarantee against unreasonable search and seizure. Specifically they argue that it is illegal because the President is circumventing the court established by the Foreign Intelligence Surveillance Act of 1978, 50 U.S.C. § 1801, to review and expedite warrant applications from the federal government for this exact purpose. The Act, as amended, also allows warrantless surveillance if approved by the United States Foreign Intelligence Court within 72 hours. In adopting this legislation, Congress specifically denied the government and the President the authority to conduct warrantless wiretapping.

What is the likely outcome if the issue of presidential power is litigated? How applicable would Justice Jackson's three-part analysis in *Youngstown* be in reaching a resolution? Is the *Dames & Moore* analysis necessary or not? Are these facts distinguishable from *Youngstown*? If so, or if not, upon what basis?

A. THE "WAR ON TERRORISM"

The Court, in its 2004 Term, faced these issues in regard to the unilateral authority cited by the Executive Branch, in three cases. The significance of the decisions cannot be overstated given the nature of the "unbridled power," perhaps unique in our history, asserted by President Bush. Given that the same Court that selected Mr. Bush as President reviewed these broad-based assertions of presidential power, the Court's reluctance to allow such unilateral presidential prerogative to combat terrorism is quite significant.

Of the three cases in which opinions were rendered, Hamdi v. Rumsfeld, 542 U.S. 507 (2004), Rumsfeld v. Padilla, 542 U.S. 426 (2004), and Rasul v. Bush, 542 U.S. 466 (2004), *Hamdi* proved to be most significant. Hamdi, an American citizen, was arrested in Afghanistan. The government asserted the authority to hold him indefinitely, denying him the right to a hearing or, for that matter, any due process, by defining him an "enemy combatant," based upon his capture in a "combat zone." The extent of the power over American citizens sought by Bush was reviewed by the Court in the context of a writ of habeas corpus filed by Hamdi's father.

In *Padilla*, the government arrested an American citizen, Jose Padilla, in the United States for preparing a "dirty bomb" for explosion. At first, the government held Padilla as a material witness, but shortly before a hearing at which it would have been required to present evidence against him, the government placed him in military custody and asserted the authority to hold him indefinitely, incommunicado, and "without any available process," as an "enemy combatant." Many thought the *Padilla* case would be most significant because he was an American citizen arrested in America, thus raising the issue as to whether "any" American might be arrested and so held if the President so desired. Yet the Court limited its decision to *Padilla*'s "improper filing" of his habeas petition.

In the third decision, *Rasul v. Bush*, the Court reviewed the legality of the detention of foreign nationals captured abroad in connection with hostilities and incarcerated at the Guantanamo Bay Naval Base, Cuba, as against the government's claim that the Court lacked jurisdiction to consider these challenges. Given the government's claim (arguably that Guantanamo Bay was the only "lawless" place in the world), the Court's decision extending its jurisdiction was most meaningful.

HAMDI v. RUMSFELD
542 U.S. 507 (2004)

O'CONNOR, J., announced the judgment of the Court and delivered an opinion, in which REHNQUIST, C.J., and KENNEDY and BREYER, JJ., joined. SOUTER, J., filed an opinion concurring in part, dissenting in part, and concurring in the judgment, in which GINSBURG, J., joined. SCALIA, J., filed a dissenting opinion, in which STEVENS, J., joined. THOMAS, J., filed a dissenting opinion.

Justice O'CONNOR announced the judgment of the Court and delivered an opinion, in which THE CHIEF JUSTICE, Justice KENNEDY, and Justice BREYER join.

At this difficult time in our Nation's history, we are called upon to consider the legality of the Government's detention of a United States citizen on United States soil as an "enemy combatant" and to address the process that is constitutionally owed to one who seeks to challenge his classification as such. The United States Court of Appeals for the Fourth Circuit held that petitioner's detention was legally authorized and that he was entitled to no further opportunity to challenge his enemy-combatant label. We now vacate and remand. We hold that although Congress authorized the detention of combatants in the narrow circumstances alleged here, due process demands that a citizen held in the United States as an enemy combatant be given a meaningful opportunity to contest the factual basis for that detention before a neutral decisionmaker.

II. The threshold question before us is whether the Executive has the authority to detain citizens who qualify as "enemy combatants." There is some debate as to the proper scope of this term, and the Government has never provided any court with the full criteria that it uses in classifying individuals as such. It has made clear, however, that, for purposes of this case, the "enemy combatant" that it is seeking to detain is an individual who, it alleges, was "'part of or supporting forces hostile to the United States or coalition partners'" in Afghanistan and who "'engaged in an armed conflict against the United States'" there. We therefore answer only the narrow question before us: whether the detention of citizens falling within that definition is authorized.

The Government maintains that no explicit congressional authorization is required, because the Executive possesses plenary authority to detain pursuant to Article II of the Constitution. We do not reach the question whether Article II provides such authority, however, because we agree with the Government's alternative position, that Congress has in fact authorized Hamdi's detention, through the AUMF.

Our analysis on that point, set forth below, substantially overlaps with our analysis of Hamdi's principal argument for the illegality of his detention. He posits that his detention is forbidden by 18 U.S.C. § 4001(a). Section 4001(a) states that "no citizen shall be imprisoned or otherwise detained by the United States except pursuant to an Act of Congress." Congress passed § 4001(a) in 1971 as part of a bill to repeal the Emergency

Detention Act of 1950, which provided procedures for executive detention, during times of emergency, of individuals deemed likely to engage in espionage or sabotage. Congress was particularly concerned about the possibility that the Act could be used to reprise the Japanese internment camps of World War II. The Government again presses two alternative positions. First, it argues that § 4001(a), in light of its legislative history and its location in Title 18, applies only to "the control of civilian prisons and related detentions," not to military detentions. Second, it maintains that § 4001(a) is satisfied, because Hamdi is being detained "pursuant to an Act of Congress" — the AUMF. Again, because we conclude that the Government's second assertion is correct, we do not address the first. In other words, for the reasons that follow, we conclude that the AUMF is explicit congressional authorization for the detention of individuals in the narrow category we describe (assuming, without deciding, that such authorization is required), and that the AUMF satisfied § 4001(a)'s requirement that a detention be "pursuant to an Act of Congress" (assuming, without deciding, that § 4001(a) applies to military detentions).

The AUMF authorizes the President to use "all necessary and appropriate force" against "nations, organizations, or persons" associated with the September 11, 2001, terrorist attacks. There can be no doubt that individuals who fought against the United States in Afghanistan as part of the Taliban, an organization known to have supported the al Qaeda terrorist network responsible for those attacks, are individuals Congress sought to target in passing the AUMF. We conclude that detention of individuals falling into the limited category we are considering, for the duration of the particular conflict in which they were captured, is so fundamental and accepted an incident to war as to be an exercise of the "necessary and appropriate force" Congress has authorized the President to use.

The capture and detention of lawful combatants and the capture, detention, and trial of unlawful combatants, by "universal agreement and practice," are "important incidents of war." The purpose of detention is to prevent captured individuals from returning to the field of battle and taking up arms once again.

There is no bar to this Nation's holding one of its own citizens as an enemy combatant. In *Quirin*, one of the detainees, Haupt, alleged that he was a naturalized United States citizen. We held that "citizens who associate themselves with the military arm of the enemy government, and with its aid, guidance and direction enter this country bent on hostile acts, are enemy belligerents within the meaning of . . . the law of war." While Haupt was tried for violations of the law of war, nothing in *Quirin* suggests that his citizenship would have precluded his mere detention for the duration of the relevant hostilities. Nor can we see any reason for drawing such a line here. A citizen, no less than an alien, can be "part of or supporting forces hostile to the United States or coalition partners" and "engaged in an armed conflict against the United States;" such a citizen, if released, would pose the same threat of returning to the front during the ongoing conflict.

In light of these principles, it is of no moment that the AUMF does not use specific language of detention. Because detention to prevent a combatant's return to the battlefield is a fundamental incident of waging war, in permitting the use of "necessary and appropriate force," Congress has clearly and unmistakably authorized detention in the narrow circumstances considered here.

Hamdi objects, nevertheless, that Congress has not authorized the *indefinite* detention to which he is now subject. The Government responds that "the detention of enemy combatants during World War II was just as 'indefinite' while that war was being fought." We take Hamdi's objection to be not to the lack of certainty regarding the date on which the conflict will end, but to the substantial prospect of perpetual detention. We recognize that the national security underpinnings of the "war on terror," although crucially important, are broad and malleable. As the Government concedes, "given its unconventional nature, the current conflict is unlikely to end with a formal cease-fire agreement." The prospect Hamdi raises is therefore not far-fetched. If the Government does not consider this unconventional war won for two generations, and if it maintains during that time that Hamdi might, if released, rejoin forces fighting against the United States, then the position it has taken throughout the litigation of this case suggests that Hamdi's detention could last for the rest of his life.

It is a clearly established principle of the law of war that detention may last no longer than active hostilities. *See* Article 118 of the Geneva Convention (III) Relative to the Treatment of Prisoners of War ("Prisoners of war shall be released and repatriated without delay after the cessation of active hostilities").

Hamdi contends that the AUMF does not authorize indefinite or perpetual detention. Certainly, we agree that indefinite detention for the purpose of interrogation is not authorized. Further, we understand Congress' grant of authority for the use of "necessary and appropriate force" to include the authority to detain for the duration of the relevant conflict, and our understanding is based on longstanding law-of-war principles. If the practical circumstances of a given conflict are entirely unlike those of the conflicts that informed the development of the law of war, that understanding may unravel. But that is not the situation we face as of this date. Active combat operations against Taliban fighters apparently are ongoing in Afghanistan. The United States may detain, for the duration of these hostilities, individuals legitimately determined to be Taliban combatants who "engaged in an armed conflict against the United States." If the record establishes that United States troops are still involved in active combat in Afghanistan, those detentions are part of the exercise of "necessary and appropriate force," and therefore are authorized by the AUMF.

Ex parte Milligan, 4 Wall. 2, 125 (1866), does not undermine our holding about the Government's authority to seize enemy combatants, as we define that term today. In that case, the Court made repeated reference to the fact that its inquiry into whether the military tribunal had jurisdiction to try and punish Milligan turned in large part on the fact that Milligan was not a prisoner of war, but a resident of Indiana arrested while at home there. That fact was central to its conclusion. Had Milligan been captured while he was assisting Confederate soldiers by carrying a rifle against Union troops on a Confederate battlefield, the holding of the Court might well have been different.

Quirin was a unanimous opinion. It both postdates and clarifies *Milligan,* providing us with the most apposite precedent that we have on the question of whether citizens may be detained in such circumstances. Brushing aside such precedent — particularly when doing so gives rise to a host of new questions never dealt with by this Court — is unjustified and unwise.

III. Even in cases in which the detention of enemy combatants is legally authorized, there remains the question of what process is constitutionally due to a citizen who disputes his enemy-combatant status. Hamdi argues that he is owed a meaningful and timely hearing and that "extra-judicial detention [that] begins and ends with the submission of an affidavit based on third-hand hearsay" does not comport with the Fifth and Fourteenth Amendments. The Government counters that any more process than was provided below would be both unworkable and "constitutionally intolerable." Our resolution of this dispute requires a careful examination both of the writ of habeas corpus, which Hamdi now seeks to employ as a mechanism of judicial review, and of the Due Process Clause, which informs the procedural contours of that mechanism in this instance.

Though they reach radically different conclusions on the process that ought to attend the present proceeding, the parties begin on common ground. All agree that, absent suspension, the writ of habeas corpus remains available to every individual detained within the United States. All agree suspension of the writ has not occurred here. Thus, it is undisputed that Hamdi was properly before an Article III court to challenge his detention under 28 U.S.C. § 2241.

B. [T]he Government urges the adoption of the Fourth Circuit's holding below — that because it is "undisputed" that Hamdi's seizure took place in a combat zone, the habeas determination can be made purely as a matter of law, with no further hearing or factfinding necessary. This argument is easily rejected. [T]he circumstances surrounding Hamdi's seizure cannot in any way be characterized as "undisputed," as "those circumstances are neither conceded in fact, nor susceptible to concession in law, because Hamdi has not been permitted to speak for himself or even through counsel as to those circumstances." Further, the "facts" that constitute the alleged concession are insufficient to support Hamdi's detention. Under the definition of enemy combatant that we accept today as falling within the scope of Congress' authorization, Hamdi would need to be "part of or supporting forces hostile to the United States or coalition partners" and "engaged in an armed conflict against the United States" to justify his detention in the United States for the duration of the relevant conflict. The habeas petition states only that "when seized by the United States Government, Mr. Hamdi resided in Afghanistan." An assertion that one *resided* in a country in which combat operations are taking place is not a concession that one was "*captured* in a zone of active combat operations in a foreign theater of war," and certainly is not a concession that one was "part of or supporting forces hostile to the United States or coalition partners" and "engaged in an armed conflict against the United States." Accordingly, we reject any argument that Hamdi has made concessions that eliminate any right to further process.

C. The Government's second argument requires closer consideration. This is the argument that further factual exploration is unwarranted and inappropriate in light of the extraordinary constitutional interests at stake. Under the Government's most extreme rendition of this argument, "respect for separation of powers and the limited institutional capabilities of courts in matters of military decision-making in connection with an ongoing conflict" ought to eliminate entirely any individual process, restricting the courts to investigating only whether legal authorization exists for the broader detention scheme. At most, the Government argues, courts should review its determination that a citizen is an enemy combatant under a very deferential "some evidence" standard. Under this review, a court would assume the accuracy of the Government's articulated basis for Hamdi's detention, as set forth in the Mobbs Declaration, and assess only whether that articulated basis was a legitimate one.

In response, Hamdi emphasizes that this Court consistently has recognized that an individual challenging his detention may not be held at the will of the Executive without recourse to some proceeding before a neutral tribunal to determine whether the Executive's asserted justifications for that detention have basis in fact and warrant in law.

Both of these positions highlight legitimate concerns. And both emphasize the tension that often exists between the autonomy that the Government asserts is necessary in order to pursue effectively a particular goal and the process that a citizen contends he is due before he is deprived of a constitutional right. The ordinary mechanism that we use for balancing such serious competing interests, and for determining the procedures that are necessary to ensure that a citizen is not "deprived of life, liberty, or property, without due process of law," is the test that we articulated in *Mathews v. Eldridge,* 424 U.S. 319 (1976). *Mathews* dictates that the process due in any given instance is determined by weighing "the private interest that will be affected by the official action" against the Government's asserted interest, "including the function involved" and the burdens the Government would face in providing greater process.

1. It is beyond question that substantial interests lie on both sides of the scale in this case. Hamdi's "private interest . . . affected by the official action," is the most elemental of liberty interests — the interest in being free from physical detention by one's own government. We have always been careful not to 'minimize the importance and fundamental nature' of the individual's right to liberty, and we will not do so today.

Nor is the weight on this side of the *Mathews* scale offset by the circumstances of war or the accusation of treasonous behavior, for "it is clear that commitment for *any* purpose constitutes a significant deprivation of liberty that requires due process protection," and at this stage in the *Mathews* calculus, we consider the interest of the *erroneously* detained individual.

2. On the other side of the scale are the weighty and sensitive governmental interests in ensuring that those who have in fact fought with the enemy during a war do not return to battle against the United States. As discussed above, the law of war and the realities of combat may render such detentions both necessary and appropriate, and our due process analysis need not blink at those realities. Without doubt, our Constitution recognizes that core strategic matters of warmaking belong in the hands of those who are best positioned and most politically accountable for making them. *Youngstown Sheet & Tube Co. v. Sawyer* (acknowledging "broad powers in military commanders engaged in day-to-day fighting in a theater of war").

The Government also argues at some length that its interests in reducing the process available to alleged enemy combatants are heightened by the practical difficulties that would accompany a system of trial-like process. In its view, military officers who are engaged in the serious work of waging battle would be unnecessarily and dangerously distracted by litigation half a world away, and discovery into military operations would both intrude on the sensitive secrets of national defense and result in a futile search for evidence buried under the rubble of war. To the extent that these burdens are triggered by heightened procedures, they are properly taken into account in our due process analysis.

3. Striking the proper constitutional balance here is of great importance to the Nation during this period of ongoing combat. But it is equally vital that our calculus not give short shrift to the values that this country holds dear or to the privilege that is American citizenship. It is during our most challenging and uncertain moments that our Nation's commitment to due process is most severely tested; and it is in those times that we must preserve our commitment at home to the principles for which we fight abroad.

With due recognition of these competing concerns, we believe that neither the process proposed by the Government nor the process apparently envisioned by the District Court below strikes the proper constitutional balance when a United States citizen is detained in the United States as an enemy combatant. That is, "the risk of erroneous deprivation" of a detainee's liberty interest is unacceptably high under the Government's proposed rule, while some of the "additional or substitute procedural safeguards" suggested by the District Court are unwarranted in light of their limited "probable value" and the burdens they may impose on the military in such cases.

We therefore hold that a citizen-detainee seeking to challenge his classification as an enemy combatant must receive notice of the factual basis for his classification, and a fair opportunity to rebut the Government's factual assertions before a neutral decisionmaker.

At the same time, the exigencies of the circumstances may demand that, aside from these core elements, enemy combatant proceedings may be tailored to alleviate their uncommon potential to burden the Executive at a time of ongoing military conflict. Hearsay, for example, may need to be accepted as the most reliable available evidence from the Government in such a proceeding. Likewise, the Constitution would not be offended by a presumption in favor of the Government's evidence, so long as that presumption remained a rebuttable one and fair opportunity for rebuttal were provided. Thus, once the Government puts forth credible evidence that the habeas petitioner meets the enemy-combatant criteria, the onus could shift to the petitioner to rebut that evidence with more persuasive evidence that he falls outside the criteria. A burden-shifting scheme of this sort would meet the goal of ensuring that the errant tourist, embedded journalist, or local aid worker has a chance to prove military error while giving due regard to the Executive once it has put forth meaningful support for its conclusion that the detainee is in fact an enemy combatant. In the words of *Mathews*, process of this sort would sufficiently address the "risk of erroneous deprivation" of a detainee's liberty interest while eliminating certain procedures that have questionable additional value in light of the burden on the *Government*.

We think it unlikely that this basic process will have the dire impact on the central functions of warmaking that the Government forecasts. The parties agree that initial captures on the battlefield need not receive the process we have discussed here; that process is due only when the determination is made to *continue* to hold those who have been seized. The Government has made clear in its briefing that documentation regarding battlefield detainees already is kept in the ordinary course of military affairs. Any factfinding imposition created by requiring a knowledgeable affiant to summarize these records to an independent tribunal is a minimal one. Likewise, arguments that military officers ought not have to wage war under the threat of litigation lose much of their steam when factual disputes at enemy-combatant hearings are limited to the alleged combatant's acts. This focus meddles little, if at all, in the strategy or conduct of war, inquiring only into the appropriateness of continuing to detain an individual claimed to have taken up arms against the United States. While we accord the greatest respect and consideration to the judgments of military authorities in matters relating to the actual prosecution of a war, and recognize that the scope of that discretion necessarily is wide, it does not infringe on the core role of the military for the courts to exercise their own time-honored and constitutionally mandated roles of reviewing and resolving claims like those presented here.

D. In so holding, we necessarily reject the Government's assertion that separation of powers principles mandate a heavily circumscribed role for the courts in such circumstances. Indeed, the position that the courts must forgo any examination of the individual case and focus exclusively on the legality of the broader detention scheme cannot be mandated by any reasonable view of separation of powers, as this approach serves only to *condense* power into a single branch of government. We have long since made clear that a state of war is not a blank check for the President when it comes to the rights of the Nation's citizens. *Youngstown Sheet & Tube.* Whatever power the United States Constitution envisions for the Executive in its exchanges with other nations or with enemy organizations in times of conflict, it most assuredly envisions a role for all three branches when individual liberties are at stake. Likewise, we have made clear that, unless Congress acts to suspend it, the Great Writ of habeas corpus allows the Judicial Branch to play a necessary role in maintaining this delicate balance of governance, serving as an important judicial check on the Executive's discretion in the realm of detentions. Thus, while we do not question that our due process assessment must pay keen attention to the particular burdens faced by the Executive in the context of military action, it would turn our system of checks and balances on its head to suggest that a citizen could not make his way to court with a challenge to the factual basis for his detention by his government, simply because the Executive opposes making available such a challenge. Absent suspension of the writ by Congress, a citizen detained as an enemy combatant is entitled to this process.

Because we conclude that due process demands some system for a citizen detainee to refute his classification, the proposed "some evidence" standard is inadequate. Any process in which the Executive's factual assertions go wholly unchallenged or are simply presumed correct without any opportunity for the alleged combatant to demonstrate otherwise falls constitutionally short. Aside from unspecified "screening" processes, and military interrogations in which the Government suggests Hamdi could have contested his classification, Hamdi has received no process. An interrogation by one's captor, however effective an intelligence-gathering tool, hardly constitutes a constitutionally adequate factfinding before a neutral decisionmaker. Plainly, the "process" Hamdi has received is not that to which he is entitled under the Due Process Clause.

There remains the possibility that the standards we have articulated could be met by an appropriately authorized and properly constituted military tribunal. Indeed, it is notable that military regulations already provide for such process in related instances, dictating that tribunals be made available to determine the status of enemy detainees who assert prisoner-of-war status under the Geneva Convention. In the absence of such process, however, a court that receives a petition for a writ of habeas corpus from an alleged enemy combatant must itself ensure that the minimum requirements of due process are achieved. Both courts below recognized as much, focusing their energies on the question of whether Hamdi was due an opportunity to rebut the Government's case against him. The Government, too, proceeded on this assumption, presenting its affidavit and then seeking that it be evaluated under a deferential standard of review based on burdens that it alleged would accompany any greater process.

IV. Hamdi asks us to hold that the Fourth Circuit also erred by denying him immediate access to counsel upon his detention and by disposing of the case without permitting him to meet with an attorney. Since our grant of certiorari in this case, Hamdi has been appointed counsel, with whom he has met for consultation purposes on several occasions, and with whom he is now being granted unmonitored meetings. He unquestionably has the right to access to counsel in connection with the proceedings on remand. No further consideration of this issue is necessary at this stage of the case.

Justice SOUTER, with whom Justice GINSBURG joins, concurring in part, dissenting in part, and concurring in the judgment.

The plurality rejects any such limit on the exercise of habeas jurisdiction and so far I agree with its opinion. The plurality does, however, accept the Government's position that if Hamdi's designation as an enemy combatant is correct, his detention (at least as to some period) is authorized by an Act of Congress as required by § 4001(a), that is, by the Authorization for Use of Military Force. Here, I disagree and respectfully dissent. The Government has failed to demonstrate that the Force Resolution authorizes the detention complained of here even on the facts the Government claims. If the Government raises nothing further than the record now shows, the Non-Detention Act entitles Hamdi to be released.

[I]n requiring that any Executive detention be "pursuant to an Act of Congress," then, Congress necessarily meant to require a congressional enactment that clearly authorized detention or imprisonment.

[T]he defining character of American constitutional government is its constant tension between security and liberty, serving both by partial helpings of each. In a government of separated powers, deciding finally on what is a reasonable degree of guaranteed liberty whether in peace or war (or some condition in between) is not well entrusted to the Executive Branch of Government, whose particular responsibility is to maintain security. For reasons of inescapable human nature, the branch of the Government asked to counter a serious threat is not the branch on which to rest the Nation's entire reliance in striking the balance between the will to win and the cost in liberty on the way to victory; the responsibility for security will naturally amplify the claim that security legitimately raises. A reasonable balance is more likely to be reached on the judgment of a different branch, just as Madison said in remarking that "the constant aim is to divide and arrange the several offices in such a manner as that each may be a check on the other — that the private interest of every individual may be a sentinel over the public rights." The Federalist No. 51. Hence the need for an assessment by Congress before citizens are subject to lockup, and likewise the need for a clearly expressed congressional resolution of the competing claims.

Next, there is the Government's claim, accepted by the Court, that the terms of the Force Resolution are adequate to authorize detention of an enemy combatant under the circumstances described, a claim the Government fails to support sufficiently to satisfy § 4001(a) as read to require a clear statement of authority to detain. Since the Force Resolution was adopted one week after the attacks of September 11, 2001, it naturally speaks with some generality, but its focus is clear, and that is on the use of military power. It is fairly read to authorize the use of armies and weapons, whether against other armies or individual terrorists. But it never so much as uses the word detention, and there is no reason to think Congress might have perceived any need to augment Executive power to deal with dangerous citizens within the United States, given the well-stocked statutory arsenal of defined criminal offenses covering the gamut of actions that a citizen sympathetic to terrorists might commit.

Because I find Hamdi's detention forbidden by § 4001(a) and unauthorized by the Force Resolution, I would not reach any questions of what process he may be due in litigating disputed issues in a proceeding under the habeas statute or prior to the habeas enquiry itself. For me, it suffices that the Government has failed to justify holding him in the absence of a further Act of Congress, criminal charges, a showing that the detention conforms to the laws of war, or a demonstration that § 4001(a) is unconstitutional. I would therefore vacate the judgment of the Court of Appeals and remand for proceedings consistent with this view.

Since this disposition does not command a majority of the Court, however, the need to give practical effect to the conclusions of eight members of the Court rejecting the Government's position calls for me to join with the plurality in ordering remand on terms closest to those I would impose. Although I think litigation of Hamdi's status as an enemy combatant is unnecessary, the terms of the plurality's remand will allow Hamdi to offer evidence that he is not an enemy combatant, and he should at the least have the benefit of that opportunity.

It should go without saying that in joining with the plurality to produce a judgment, I do not adopt the plurality's resolution of constitutional issues that I would not reach. It is not that I could disagree with the plurality's determinations (given the plurality's view of the Force Resolution) that someone in Hamdi's position is entitled at a minimum to notice of the Government's claimed factual basis for holding him, and to a fair chance to rebut it before a neutral decision maker; nor, of course, could I disagree with the plurality's affirmation of Hamdi's right to counsel. On the other hand, I do not mean to imply agreement that the Government could claim an evidentiary presumption casting the burden of rebuttal on Hamdi, or that an opportunity to litigate before a military tribunal might obviate or truncate enquiry by a court on habeas.

Subject to these qualifications, I join with the plurality in a judgment of the Court vacating the Fourth Circuit's judgment and remanding the case.

Justice SCALIA, with whom Justice STEVENS joins, dissenting.

Where the Government accuses a citizen of waging war against it, our constitutional tradition has been to prosecute him in federal court for treason or some other crime. Where the exigencies of war prevent that, the Constitution's Suspension Clause, allows Congress to relax the usual protections temporarily. Absent suspension, however, the Executive's assertion of military exigency has not been thought sufficient to permit detention without charge. No one contends that the congressional Authorization for Use of Military Force, on which the Government relies to justify its actions here, is an implementation of the Suspension Clause. Accordingly, I would reverse the decision below.

I. The very core of liberty secured by our Anglo-Saxon system of separated powers has been freedom from indefinite imprisonment at the will of the Executive.

The gist of the Due Process Clause, as understood at the founding and since, was to force the Government to follow those common-law procedures traditionally deemed necessary before depriving a person of life, liberty, or property. When a citizen was deprived of liberty because of alleged criminal conduct, those procedures typically required committal by a magistrate followed by indictment and trial. The Due Process Clause "in effect affirms the right of trial according to the process and proceedings of the common law."

These due process rights have historically been vindicated by the writ of habeas corpus. In England before the founding, the writ developed into a tool for challenging executive confinement. It was not always effective. [As a result, the Habeas Corpus Act of 1679 added additional protections.]

The writ of habeas corpus was preserved in the Constitution — the only common-law writ to be explicitly mentioned. Hamilton lauded "the establishment of the writ of *habeas corpus*" in his Federalist defense as a means to protect against "the practice of arbitrary imprisonments . . . in all ages, [one of] the favourite and most formidable instruments of tyranny." The Federalist No. 84.

II. The allegations here, of course, are no ordinary accusations of criminal activity. Yaser Esam Hamdi has been imprisoned because the Government believes he participated in the waging of war against the United States. The relevant question, then, is whether there is a different, special procedure for imprisonment of a citizen accused of wrongdoing *by aiding the enemy in wartime*.

A. Justice O'Connor, writing for a plurality of this Court, asserts that captured enemy combatants (other than those suspected of war crimes) have traditionally been detained until the cessation of hostilities and then released. That is probably an accurate description of wartime practice with respect to enemy *aliens*. The tradition with respect to American citizens, however, has been quite different. Citizens aiding the enemy have been treated as traitors subject to the criminal process.

The only citizen other than Hamdi known to be imprisoned in connection with military hostilities in Afghanistan against the United States *was* subjected to criminal process and convicted upon a guilty plea. See *United States v. Lindh*, 212 F. Supp. 2d 541 (ED Va. 2002).

III. *Milligan* is not exactly this case, of course, since the petitioner was threatened with death, not merely imprisonment. But the reasoning and conclusion of *Milligan* logically cover the present case. The Government justifies imprisonment of Hamdi on principles of the law of war and admits that, absent the war, it would have no such authority. But if the law of war cannot be applied to citizens where courts are open, then Hamdi's imprisonment without criminal trial is no less unlawful than Milligan's trial by military tribunal.

IV. The Government argues that our more recent jurisprudence ratifies its indefinite imprisonment of a citizen within the territorial jurisdiction of federal courts. It places primary reliance upon *Ex parte Quirin* [*Q*]*uirin* would still not justify denial of the writ here. In *Quirin* it was uncontested that the petitioners were members of enemy forces. They were "*admitted* enemy invaders," and it was "undisputed" that they had landed in the United States in service of German forces. The specific holding of the Court was only that, "upon the *conceded* facts," the petitioners were "plainly within [the] boundaries" of military jurisdiction. But where those jurisdictional facts are *not* conceded — where the petitioner insists that he is *not* a belligerent — *Quirin* left the pre-existing law in place: Absent suspension of the writ, a citizen held where the courts are open is entitled either to criminal trial or to a judicial decree requiring his release.

V. It follows from what I have said that Hamdi is entitled to a habeas decree requiring his release unless (1) criminal proceedings are promptly brought, or (2) Congress has suspended the writ of habeas corpus. A suspension of the writ could, of course, lay down conditions for continued detention, similar to those that today's opinion prescribes under the Due Process Clause. But there is a world of difference between the people's representatives' determining the need for that suspension (and prescribing the conditions for it), and this Court's doing so.

The plurality finds justification for Hamdi's imprisonment in the Authorization for Use of Military Force. [The AUMF] is not remotely a congressional suspension of the writ, and no one claims that it is. Contrary to the plurality's view, I do not think this statute even authorizes detention of a citizen with the clarity necessary to satisfy the interpretive canon that statutes should be construed so as to avoid grave constitutional concerns; with the clarity necessary to comport with cases such as *Ex parte Endo* and *Duncan v. Kahanamoku* or with the clarity necessary to overcome the statutory prescription that "no citizen shall be imprisoned or otherwise detained by the United States except pursuant to an Act of Congress." 18 U.S.C. § 4001(a). But even if it did, I would not permit it to overcome Hamdi's entitlement to habeas corpus relief. The Suspension Clause of the Constitution, which carefully circumscribes the conditions under which the writ can be withheld, would be a sham if it could be evaded by congressional prescription of requirements *other than the common-law requirement of committal for criminal prosecution* that render the writ, though available, unavailing. If the Suspension Clause does not guarantee the citizen that he will either be tried or released, unless the conditions for suspending the writ exist and the grave action of suspending the writ has been taken; if it merely guarantees the citizen that he will not be detained unless Congress by ordinary legislation says he can be detained; it guarantees him very little indeed.

It should not be thought, however, that the plurality's evisceration of the Suspension Clause augments, principally, the power of Congress. As usual, the major effect of its constitutional improvisation is to increase the power of the Court. Having found a congressional authorization for detention of citizens where none clearly exists; and having discarded the categorical procedural protection of the Suspension Clause; the plurality then proceeds, under the guise of the Due Process Clause, to prescribe what procedural protections *it* thinks appropriate.

Having distorted the Suspension Clause, the plurality finishes up by transmogrifying the Great Writ — disposing of the present habeas petition by remanding for the District Court to "engage in a factfinding process that is both prudent and incremental." "In the absence of [the Executive's prior provision of procedures that satisfy due process], . . . a court that receives a petition for a writ of habeas corpus from an alleged enemy combatant must itself ensure that the minimum requirements of due process are achieved." This judicial remediation of executive default is unheard of. The role of habeas corpus is to determine the legality of executive detention, not to supply the omitted process necessary to make it legal. It is not the habeas court's function to make illegal detention legal by supplying a process that the Government could have provided, but chose not to. If Hamdi is being imprisoned in violation of the Constitution (because without due process of law), then his habeas petition should be granted; the Executive may then hand him over to the criminal authorities, whose detention for the purpose of prosecution will be lawful, or else must release him.

VI. Several limitations give my views in this matter a relatively narrow compass. They apply only to citizens, accused of being enemy combatants, who are detained within the territorial jurisdiction of a federal court. This is not likely to be a numerous group; currently we know of only two, Hamdi and Jose Padilla. Where the citizen is captured outside and held outside the United States, the constitutional requirements may be different. Moreover, even within the United States, the accused citizen-enemy combatant may lawfully be detained once prosecution is in progress or in contemplation. The Government has been notably successful in securing conviction, and hence long-term custody or execution, of those who have waged war against the state.

I frankly do not know whether these tools are sufficient to meet the Government's security needs, including the need to obtain intelligence through interrogation. It is far beyond my competence, or the Court's competence, to determine that. But it is not beyond Congress's. If the situation demands it, the Executive can ask Congress to authorize suspension of the writ — which can be made subject to whatever conditions Congress deems appropriate, including even the procedural novelties invented by the plurality today. To be sure, suspension is limited by the Constitution to cases of rebellion or invasion. But whether the attacks of September 11, 2001, constitute an "invasion," and whether those attacks still justify suspension several years later, are questions for Congress rather than this Court. If civil rights are to be curtailed during wartime, it must be done openly and democratically, as the Constitution requires, rather than by silent erosion through an opinion of this Court

Many think it not only inevitable but entirely proper that liberty give way to security in times of national crisis — that, at the extremes of military exigency, *inter arma silent leges*. Whatever the general merits of the view that war silences law or modulates its voice, that view has no place in the interpretation and application of a Constitution designed precisely to confront war and, in a manner that accords with democratic principles, to accommodate it. Because the Court has proceeded to meet the current emergency in a manner the Constitution does not envision. I respectfully dissent.

Justice THOMAS, dissenting.

The Executive Branch, acting pursuant to the powers vested in the President by the Constitution and with explicit congressional approval, has determined that Yaser Hamdi is an enemy combatant and should be detained. This detention falls squarely within the Federal Government's war powers, and we lack the expertise and capacity to second-guess that decision. As such, petitioners' habeas challenge should fail, and there is no reason to remand the case. The plurality reaches a contrary conclusion by failing adequately to consider basic principles of the constitutional structure as it relates to national security and foreign affairs and by using the balancing scheme of *Mathews v. Eldridge*. I do not think that the Federal Government's war powers can be balanced away by this Court. Arguably, Congress could provide for additional procedural protections, but until it does, we have no right to insist upon them. But even if I were to agree with the general approach the plurality takes, I could not accept the particulars. The plurality utterly fails to account for the Government's compelling interests and for our own institutional inability to weigh competing concerns correctly. I respectfully dissent.

I. "It is 'obvious and unarguable' that no governmental interest is more compelling than the security of the Nation." The national security, after all, is the primary responsibility and purpose of the Federal Government. But because the Founders understood that they could not foresee the myriad potential threats to national security that might later arise, they chose to create a Federal Government that necessarily possesses sufficient power to handle any threat to the security of the Nation.

The Founders intended that the President have primary responsibility -along with the necessary power — to protect the national security and to conduct the Nation's foreign relations. They did so principally because the structural advantages of a unitary Executive are essential in these domains. This is because "decision, activity, secrecy, and dispatch will generally characterise the proceedings of one man, in a much more eminent degree, than the proceedings of any greater number."

These structural advantages are most important in the national-security and foreign-affairs contexts. "Of all the cares or concerns of government, the direction of war most peculiarly demands those qualities which distinguish the exercise of power by a single hand." The Federalist No. 74 (A. Hamilton). Also for these reasons, John Marshall explained that "the President is the sole organ of the nation in its external relations, and its sole representative with foreign nations." To this end, the Constitution vests in the President "the executive Power," provides that he "shall be Commander in Chief of the" armed forces, and places in him the power to recognize foreign governments.

This Court has long recognized these features and has accordingly held that the President has *constitutional* authority to protect the national security and that this authority carries with it broad discretion.

Congress, to be sure, has a substantial and essential role in both foreign affairs and national security. But it is crucial to recognize that *judicial* interference in these domains destroys the purpose of vesting primary responsibility in a unitary Executive. Several points, made forcefully by Justice Jackson, are worth emphasizing. First, with respect to certain decisions relating to national security and foreign affairs, the courts simply lack the relevant information and expertise to second-guess determinations made by the President based on information properly withheld. Second, even if the courts could compel the Executive to produce the necessary information, such decisions are simply not amenable to judicial determination because "they are delicate, complex, and involve large elements of prophecy." Third, the Court has correctly recognized the primacy of the political branches in the foreign-affairs and national-security contexts.

For these institutional reasons and because "Congress cannot anticipate and legislate with regard to every possible action the President may find it necessary to take or every possible situation in which he might act," it should come as no surprise that "such failure of Congress . . . does not, 'especially . . . in the areas of foreign policy and national security,' imply 'congressional disapproval' of action taken by the Executive." *Dames & Moore v. Regan.* Rather, in these domains, the fact that Congress has provided the President with broad authorities does not imply — and the Judicial Branch should not infer — that Congress intended to deprive him of particular powers not specifically enumerated.

To be sure, the Court has at times held, in specific circumstances, that the military acted beyond its warmaking authority. But these cases are distinguishable in important ways. In *Ex parte Endo,* the Court held unlawful the detention of an admittedly law-abiding and loyal American of Japanese ancestry. It did so because the Government's asserted reason for the detention had nothing to do with the congressional and executive authorities upon which the Government relied. Those authorities permitted detention for the purpose of preventing espionage and sabotage and thus could not be pressed into service for detaining a loyal citizen. And in *Youngstown,* Justice Jackson emphasized that "Congress had not left seizure of private property an open field but had covered it by three statutory policies inconsistent with the seizure."

I acknowledge that the question whether Hamdi's executive detention is lawful is a question properly resolved by the Judicial Branch, though the question comes to the Court with the strongest presumptions in favor of the Government. The plurality agrees that Hamdi's detention is lawful if he is an enemy combatant. But the question whether Hamdi is actually an enemy combatant is "of a kind for which the Judiciary has neither aptitude, facilities nor responsibility and which has long been held to belong in the domain of political power not subject to judicial intrusion or inquiry." That is, although it is appropriate for the Court to determine the judicial question whether the President has the asserted authority, we lack the information and expertise to question whether Hamdi is actually an enemy combatant, a question the resolution of which is committed to other branches.

II. Although the President very well may have inherent authority to detain those arrayed against our troops, I agree with the plurality that we need not decide that question because Congress has authorized the President to do so. The Authorization for Use of Military Force (AUMF), authorizes the President to "use all necessary and appropriate force against those nations, organizations, or persons he determines planned, authorized, committed, or aided the terrorist attacks" of September 11, 2001.

The plurality, however, qualifies its recognition of the President's authority to detain enemy combatants in the war on terrorism in ways that are at odds with our precedent. Thus, the plurality relies primarily on Article 118 of the Geneva Convention (III) Relative to the Treatment of Prisoners of War, for the proposition that "it is a clearly established principle of the law of war that detention may last no longer than active hostilities." It then appears to limit the President's authority to detain by requiring that the record establish that United States troops are still involved in active combat in Afghanistan because, in that case, detention would be "part of the exercise of 'necessary and appropriate force.'" But I do not believe that we may diminish the Federal Government's war powers by reference to a treaty and certainly not to a treaty that does not apply. Further, we are bound by the political branches' determination that the United States is at war. And, in any case, the power to detain does not end with the cessation of formal hostilities.

Accordingly, the President's action here is "supported by the strongest of presumptions and the widest latitude of judicial interpretation." The question becomes whether the Federal Government (rather than the President acting alone) has power to detain Hamdi as an enemy combatant. More precisely, we must determine whether the Government may detain Hamdi given the procedures that were used.

III. I agree with the plurality that the Federal Government has power to detain those that the Executive Branch determines to be enemy combatants. But I do not think that the plurality has adequately explained the breadth of the President's authority to detain enemy combatants, an authority that includes making virtually conclusive factual findings. In my view, the structural considerations discussed above, as recognized in our precedent, demonstrate that we lack the capacity and responsibility to second-guess this determination.

In this context, due process requires nothing more than a good-faith executive determination. To be clear: The Court has held that an executive, acting pursuant to statutory and constitutional authority may, consistent with the Due Process Clause, unilaterally decide to detain an individual if the executive deems this necessary for the public safety *even if he is mistaken*. The Government's asserted authority to detain an individual that the President has determined to be an enemy combatant, at least while hostilities continue, comports with the Due Process Clause. As these cases also show, the Executive's decision that a detention is necessary to protect the public need not and should not be subjected to judicial second-guessing. Indeed, at least in the context of enemy-combatant determinations, this would defeat the unity, secrecy, and dispatch that the Founders believed to be so important to the warmaking function.

Justice Scalia relies heavily upon *Ex parte Milligan*. I admit that *Milligan* supports his position. But because the Executive Branch there, unlike here, did not follow a specific statutory mechanism provided by Congress, the Court did not need to reach the broader question of Congress' power, and its discussion on this point was arguably dicta. More importantly, the Court referred frequently and pervasively to the criminal nature of the proceedings instituted against Milligan. In fact, this feature serves to distinguish the state cases as well.

Although I do acknowledge that the reasoning of these cases might apply beyond criminal punishment, the punishment-nonpunishment distinction harmonizes all of the precedent. And, subsequent cases have at least implicitly distinguished *Milligan* in just this way. Because the Government does not detain Hamdi in order to punish him, as the plurality acknowledges, *Milligan* and the New York cases do not control.

Accordingly, I conclude that the Government's detention of Hamdi as an enemy combatant does not violate the Constitution.

RUMSFELD v. PADILLA
542 U.S. 426 (2004)

Chief Justice REHNQUIST delivered the opinion of the Court.

Respondent Jose Padilla is a United States citizen detained by the Department of Defense pursuant to the President's determination that he is an "enemy combatant" who conspired with al Qaeda to carry out terrorist attacks in the United States. We confront two questions: First, did Padilla properly file his habeas petition in the Southern District of New York; and second, did the President possess authority to detain Padilla militarily. We answer the threshold question in the negative and thus do not reach the second question presented.

Because we do not decide the merits, we only briefly recount the relevant facts. On May 8, 2002, Padilla flew from Pakistan to Chicago's O'Hare International Airport. As he stepped off the plane, Padilla was apprehended by federal agents executing a material witness warrant issued by the United States District Court for the Southern District of New York (Southern District) in connection with its grand jury investigation into the September 11th terrorist attacks. Padilla was then transported to New York, where he was held in federal criminal custody. On May 22, acting through appointed counsel, Padilla moved to vacate the material witness warrant.

Padilla's motion was still pending when, on June 9, the President issued an order to Secretary of Defense Donald H. Rumsfeld designating Padilla an "enemy combatant" and directing the Secretary to detain him in military custody. In support of this action, the President invoked his authority as "Commander in Chief of the U.S. armed forces" and the Authorization for Use of Military Force Joint Resolution, enacted by Congress on September 18, 2001.

That same day, Padilla was taken into custody by Department of Defense officials and transported to the Consolidated Naval Brig in Charleston, South Carolina. He has been held there ever since.

On June 11, Padilla's counsel, claiming to act as his next friend, filed in the Southern District a habeas corpus petition under 28 U.S.C. § 2241. The amended petition named as respondents President Bush, Secretary Rumsfeld, and Melanie A. Marr, Commander of the Consolidated Naval Brig.

The Government moved to dismiss, arguing that Commander Marr, as Padilla's immediate custodian, is the only proper respondent to his habeas petition, and that the

District Court lacks jurisdiction over Commander Marr because she is located outside the Southern District.

The District Court issued its decision in December 2002. The court held that the Secretary's "personal involvement" in Padilla's military custody renders him a proper respondent to Padilla's habeas petition, and that it can assert jurisdiction over the Secretary under New York's long-arm statute, notwithstanding his absence from the Southern District. On the merits, however, the court accepted the Government's contention that the President has authority to detain as enemy combatants citizens captured on American soil during a time of war.

The Court of Appeals for the Second Circuit reversed. The court agreed with the District Court that Secretary Rumsfeld is a proper respondent, reasoning that in cases where the habeas petitioner is detained for "other than federal criminal violations, the Supreme Court has recognized exceptions to the general practice of naming the immediate physical custodian as respondent." Reaching the merits, the Court of Appeals held that the President lacks authority to detain Padilla militarily. The court concluded that neither the President's Commander-in-Chief power nor the AUMF authorizes military detentions of American citizens captured on American soil.

We granted the Government's petition for certiorari to review the Court of Appeals' rulings with respect to the jurisdictional and the merits issues, both of which raise important questions of federal law. The question whether the Southern District has jurisdiction over Padilla's habeas petition breaks down into two related subquestions. First, who is the proper respondent to that petition? And second, does the Southern District have jurisdiction over him or her? We address these questions in turn.

The federal habeas statute straightforwardly provides that the proper respondent to a habeas petition is "the person who has custody over [the petitioner]." The consistent use of the definite article in reference to the custodian indicates that there is generally only one proper respondent to a given prisoner's habeas petition. This custodian, moreover, is "the person" with the ability to produce the prisoner's body before the habeas court. We summed up the plain language of the habeas statute over 100 years ago in this way: "These provisions contemplate a proceeding against some person who has the *immediate custody* of the party detained, with the power to produce the body of such party before the court or judge, that he may be liberated if no sufficient reason is shown to the contrary."

In accord with the statutory language, longstanding practice confirms that in habeas challenges to present physical confinement — "core challenges" — the default rule is that the proper respondent is the warden of the facility where the prisoner is being held, not the Attorney General or some other remote supervisory official. No exceptions to this rule, either recognized or proposed, apply here. [An exception for citizens held overseas does not apply.]

We turn now to the second subquestion. District courts are limited to granting habeas relief "within their respective jurisdictions." 28 U.S.C. § 2241(a). We have interpreted this language to require "nothing more than that the court issuing the writ have jurisdiction over the custodian." Thus, jurisdiction over Padilla's habeas petition lies in the Southern District only if it has jurisdiction over Commander Marr. We conclude it does not.

The proviso that district courts may issue the writ only "within their respective jurisdictions" forms an important corollary to the immediate custodian rule in challenges to present physical custody under § 2241. Together they compose a simple rule that has been consistently applied in the lower courts, including in the context of military detentions: Whenever a § 2241 habeas petitioner seeks to challenge his present physical custody within the United States, he should name his warden as respondent and file the petition in the district of confinement. [The exception to the "immediate custodian" rule for citizens held overseas also carries and exception for place of filing.]

The District of South Carolina, not the Southern District of New York, was the district court in which Padilla should have brought his habeas petition. We therefore reverse the judgment of the Court of Appeals and remand the case for entry of an order of dismissal without prejudice.

Justice KENNEDY, with whom Justice O'CONNOR joins, concurring.

Both Padilla's change in location and his change of custodian reflected a change in the Government's rationale for detaining him. He ceased to be held under the authority of the criminal justice system, and began to be held under that of the military detention system. Rather than being designed to play games with forums, the Government's removal of Padilla reflected the change in the theory on which it was holding him. Whether that theory is a permissible one, of course, is a question the Court does not reach today.

Justice STEVENS, with whom Justice SOUTER, Justice GINSBURG, and Justice BREYER join, dissenting.

The petition for a writ of habeas corpus filed in this case raises questions of profound importance to the Nation. The arguments set forth by the Court do not justify avoidance of our duty to answer those questions. It is quite wrong to characterize the proceeding as a "simple challenge to physical custody," that should be resolved by slavish application of a "bright-line rule" designed to prevent "rampant forum shopping" by litigious prison inmates. As the Court's opinion itself demonstrates, that rule is riddled with exceptions fashioned to protect the high office of the Great Writ. This is an exceptional case that we clearly have jurisdiction to decide.

All Members of this Court agree that the immediate custodian rule should control in the ordinary case and that habeas petitioners should not be permitted to engage in forum shopping. More narrowly, we agree that if jurisdiction was proper when the petition was filed, it cannot be defeated by a later transfer of the prisoner to another district.

It is reasonable to assume that if the Government had given Newman, who was then representing respondent in an adversary proceeding, notice of its intent to ask the District Court to vacate the outstanding material witness warrant and transfer custody to the Department of Defense, Newman would have filed the habeas petition then and there, rather than waiting two days. Under that scenario, respondent's immediate custodian would then have been physically present in the Southern District of New York carrying out orders of the Secretary of Defense. Surely at that time Secretary Rumsfeld, rather than the lesser official who placed the handcuffs on petitioner, would have been the proper person to name as a respondent to that petition.

The difference between that scenario and the secret transfer that actually occurred should not affect our decision, for we should not permit the Government to obtain a tactical advantage as a consequence of an *ex parte* proceeding. The departure from the time-honored practice of giving one's adversary fair notice of an intent to present an important motion to the court justifies treating the habeas application as the functional equivalent of one filed two days earlier.

At stake in this case is nothing less than the essence of a free society. Even more important than the method of selecting the people's rulers and their successors is the character of the constraints imposed on the Executive by the rule of law. Unconstrained

Executive detention for the purpose of investigating and preventing subversive activity is the hallmark of the Star Chamber. Access to counsel for the purpose of protecting the citizen from official mistakes and mistreatment is the hallmark of due process.

Executive detention of subversive citizens, like detention of enemy soldiers to keep them off the battlefield, may sometimes be justified to prevent persons from launching or becoming missiles of destruction. It may not, however, be justified by the naked interest in using unlawful procedures to extract information. Incommunicado detention for months on end is such a procedure. Whether the information so procured is more or less reliable than that acquired by more extreme forms of torture is of no consequence. For if this Nation is to remain true to the ideals symbolized by its flag, it must not wield the tools of tyrants even to resist an assault by the forces of tyranny.

I respectfully dissent.

RASUL v. BUSH
542 U.S. 466 (2004)

Justice STEVENS delivered the opinion of the Court.

These two cases present the narrow but important question whether United States courts lack jurisdiction to consider challenges to the legality of the detention of foreign nationals captured abroad in connection with hostilities and incarcerated at the Guantanamo Bay Naval Base, Cuba.

Since early 2002, the U.S. military has held [petitioners' relatives, Kuwaitis and Australians] — along with, according to the Government's estimate, approximately 640 other non-Americans captured abroad — at the Naval Base at Guantanamo Bay. The United States occupies the Base, which comprises 45 square miles of land and water along the southeast coast of Cuba, pursuant to a 1903 Lease Agreement executed with the newly independent Republic of Cuba in the aftermath of the Spanish-American War. Under the Agreement, "the United States recognizes the continuance of the ultimate sovereignty of the Republic of Cuba over the [leased areas]," while "the Republic of Cuba consents that during the period of the occupation by the United States . . . the United States shall exercise complete jurisdiction and control over and within said areas." In 1934, the parties entered into a treaty providing that, absent an agreement to modify or abrogate the lease, the lease would remain in effect "so long as the United States of America shall not abandon the . . . naval station of Guantanamo."

In 2002, petitioners, through relatives acting as their next friends, filed various actions in the U.S. District Court for the District of Columbia challenging the legality of their detention at the Base. All alleged that none of the petitioners has ever been a combatant against the United States or has ever engaged in any terrorist acts. They also alleged that none has been charged with any wrongdoing, permitted to consult with counsel, or provided access to the courts or any other tribunal.

[T]he District Court dismissed for want of jurisdiction. The court held, in reliance on our opinion in *Johnson v. Eisentrager,* 339 U.S. 763 (1950), that "aliens detained outside the sovereign territory of the United States [may not] invoke a petition for a writ of habeas corpus." The Court of Appeals affirmed. We granted certiorari and now reverse.

Congress has granted federal district courts, "within their respective jurisdictions," the authority to hear applications for habeas corpus by any person who claims to be held "in custody in violation of the Constitution or laws or treaties of the United States." 28 U.S.C.

§ § 2241(a), (c)(3). Habeas corpus is, however, "a writ antecedent to statute, . . . throwing its root deep into the genius of our common law." The writ appeared in English law several centuries ago, became "an integral part of our common-law heritage" by the time the Colonies achieved independence, and received explicit recognition in the Constitution, which forbids suspension of "the Privilege of the Writ of Habeas Corpus . . . unless when in Cases of Rebellion or Invasion the public Safety may require it."

As it has evolved over the past two centuries, the habeas statute clearly has expanded habeas corpus "beyond the limits that obtained during the 17th and 18th centuries." *Swain v. Pressley, 430 U.S. 372, 380, n. 13 (1977).* But "at its historical core, the writ of habeas corpus has served as a means of reviewing the legality of Executive detention, and it is in that context that its protections have been strongest." As Justice Jackson wrote in an opinion respecting the availability of habeas corpus to aliens held in U.S. custody: "Executive imprisonment has been considered oppressive and lawless since John, at Runnymede, pledged that no free man should be imprisoned, dispossessed, outlawed, or exiled save by the judgment of his peers or by the law of the land. The judges of England developed the writ of habeas corpus largely to preserve these immunities from executive restraint." *Shaughnessy v. United States ex rel. Mezei* (dissenting opinion).

Consistent with the historic purpose of the writ, this Court has recognized the federal courts' power to review applications for habeas relief in a wide variety of cases involving Executive detention, in wartime as well as in times of peace. The Court has, for example, entertained the habeas petitions of an American citizen who plotted an attack on military installations during the Civil War, *Ex parte Milligan,* and of admitted enemy aliens convicted of war crimes during a declared war and held in the United States, *Ex parte Quirin,* and its insular possessions, *In re Yamashita.*

The question now before us is whether the habeas statute confers a right to judicial review of the legality of Executive detention of aliens in a territory over which the United States exercises plenary and exclusive jurisdiction, but not "ultimate sovereignty."

Respondents' primary submission is that the answer to the jurisdictional question is controlled by our decision in *Eisentrager.* In that case, we held that a Federal District Court lacked authority to issue a writ of habeas corpus to 21 German citizens who had been captured by U.S. forces in China, tried and convicted of war crimes by an American military commission headquartered in Nanking, and incarcerated in the Landsberg Prison in occupied Germany. The Court of Appeals in *Eisentrager* had found jurisdiction, reasoning that "any person who is deprived of his liberty by officials of the United States, acting under purported authority of that Government, and who can show that his confinement is in violation of a prohibition of the Constitution, has a right to the writ." In reversing that determination, this Court summarized the six critical facts in the case:

> We are here confronted with a decision whose basic premise is that these prisoners are entitled, as a constitutional right, to sue in some court of the United States for a writ of *habeas corpus.* To support that assumption we must hold that a prisoner of our military authorities is constitutionally entitled to the writ, even though he (a) is an enemy alien; (b) has never been or resided in the United States; (c) was captured outside of our territory and there held in military custody as a prisoner of war; (d) was tried and convicted by a Military Commission sitting outside the United States; (e) for offenses against laws of war committed outside the United States; (f) and is at all times imprisoned outside the United States.

On this set of facts, the Court concluded, "no right to the writ of *habeas corpus* appears."

Petitioners in these cases differ from the *Eisentrager* detainees in important respects: They are not nationals of countries at war with the United States, and they deny that they have engaged in or plotted acts of aggression against the United States; they have never been afforded access to any tribunal, much less charged with and convicted of wrongdoing; and for more than two years they have been imprisoned in territory over which the United States exercises exclusive jurisdiction and control.

Application of the habeas statute to persons detained at the base is consistent with the historical reach of the writ of habeas corpus. At common law, courts exercised habeas jurisdiction over the claims of aliens detained within sovereign territory of the realm, as well as the claims of persons detained in the so-called "exempt jurisdictions," where ordinary writs did not run, and all other dominions under the sovereign's control. As Lord Mansfield wrote in 1759, even if a territory was "no part of the realm," there was "no doubt" as to the court's power to issue writs of habeas corpus if the territory was "under the subjection of the Crown."

In the end, the answer to the question presented is clear. Petitioners contend that they are being held in federal custody in violation of the laws of the United States. No party questions the District Court's jurisdiction over petitioners' custodians. Section 2241, by its terms, requires nothing more. We therefore hold that § 2241 confers on the District Court jurisdiction to hear petitioners' habeas corpus challenges to the legality of their detention at the Guantanamo Bay Naval Base.

In addition to invoking the District Court's jurisdiction under § 2241, the *Al Odah* petitioners' complaint invoked the court's jurisdiction under 28 U.S.C. § 1331, the federal question statute, as well as § 1350, the Alien Tort Statute. The Court of Appeals, again relying on *Eisentrager*, held that the District Court correctly dismissed the claims founded on § 1331 and § 1350 for lack of jurisdiction, even to the extent that these claims "deal only with conditions of confinement and do not sound in habeas," because petitioners lack the "privilege of litigation" in U.S. courts.

As explained above, *Eisentrager* itself erects no bar to the exercise of federal court jurisdiction over the petitioners' habeas corpus claims. The courts of the United States have traditionally been open to nonresident aliens. And indeed, 28 U.S.C. § 1350 explicitly confers the privilege of suing for an actionable "tort . . . committed in violation of the law of nations or a treaty of the United States" on aliens alone. The fact that petitioners in these cases are being held in military custody is immaterial to the question of the District Court's jurisdiction over their nonhabeas statutory claims.

VI

Whether and what further proceedings may become necessary after respondents make their response to the merits of petitioners' claims are matters that we need not address now. What is presently at stake is only whether the federal courts have jurisdiction to determine the legality of the Executive's potentially indefinite detention of individuals who claim to be wholly innocent of wrongdoing. Answering that question in the affirmative, we reverse the judgment of the Court of Appeals and remand for the District Court to consider in the first instance the merits of petitioners' claims.

It is so ordered.

Justice KENNEDY, concurring in the judgment.

The Court is correct, in my view, to conclude that federal courts have jurisdiction to consider challenges to the legality of the detention of foreign nationals held at the Guantanamo Bay Naval Base in Cuba. While I reach the same conclusion, my analysis follows a different course. In my view, the correct course is to follow the framework of *Eisentrager*.

Eisentrager considered the scope of the right to petition for a writ of habeas corpus against the backdrop of the constitutional command of the separation of powers. The issue before the Court was whether the Judiciary could exercise jurisdiction over the claims of German prisoners held in the Landsberg prison in Germany following the cessation of hostilities in Europe. The Court concluded the petition could not be entertained. The petition was not within the proper realm of the judicial power. It concerned matters within the exclusive province of the Executive, or the Executive and Congress, to determine.

The decision in *Eisentrager* indicates that there is a realm of political authority over military affairs where the judicial power may not enter. The existence of this realm acknowledges the power of the President as Commander in Chief, and the joint role of the President and the Congress, in the conduct of military affairs. A faithful application of *Eisentrager*, then, requires an initial inquiry into the general circumstances of the detention to determine whether the Court has the authority to entertain the petition and to grant relief after considering all of the facts presented. A necessary corollary of *Eisentrager* is that there are circumstances in which the courts maintain the power and the responsibility to protect persons from unlawful detention even where military affairs are implicated.

The facts here are distinguishable from those in *Eisentrager* in two critical ways, leading to the conclusion that a federal court may entertain the petitions. First, Guantanamo Bay is in every practical respect a United States territory, and it is one far removed from any hostilities. What matters is the unchallenged and indefinite control that the United States has long exercised over Guantanamo Bay. From a practical perspective, the indefinite lease of Guantanamo Bay has produced a place that belongs to the United States, extending the "implied protection" of the United States to it.

The second critical set of facts is that the detainees at Guantanamo Bay are being held indefinitely, and without benefit of any legal proceeding to determine their status. In *Eisentrager*, the prisoners were tried and convicted by a military commission of violating the laws of war and were sentenced to prison terms. Having already been subject to procedures establishing their status, they could not justify "a limited opening of our courts" to show that they were "of friendly personal disposition" and not enemy aliens. Indefinite detention without trial or other proceeding presents altogether different considerations. It allows friends and foes alike to remain in detention. It suggests a weaker case of military necessity and much greater alignment with the traditional function of habeas corpus. Perhaps, where detainees are taken from a zone of hostilities, detention without proceedings or trial would be justified by military necessity for a matter of weeks; but as the period of detention stretches from months to years, the case for continued detention to meet military exigencies becomes weaker.

In light of the status of Guantanamo Bay and the indefinite pretrial detention of the detainees, I would hold that federal-court jurisdiction is permitted in these cases. This approach would avoid creating automatic statutory authority to adjudicate the claims of persons located outside the United States, and remains true to the reasoning of *Eisentrager*. For these reasons, I concur in the judgment of the Court.

Justice SCALIA, with whom THE CHIEF JUSTICE and Justice THOMAS join, dissenting.

The Court today holds that the habeas statute, 28 U.S.C. § 2241, extends to aliens detained by the United States military overseas, outside the sovereign borders of the United States and beyond the territorial jurisdictions of all its courts. This is not only a novel holding; it contradicts a half-century-old precedent on which the military undoubtedly relied, *Johnson v. Eisentrager.* This is an irresponsible overturning of settled law in a matter of extreme importance to our forces currently in the field. I would leave it to Congress to change § 2241, and dissent from the Court's unprecedented holding.

In abandoning the venerable statutory line drawn in *Eisentrager*, the Court boldly extends the scope of the habeas statute to the four corners of the earth. Part III of its opinion asserts that "a district court acts 'within [its] respective jurisdiction' within the meaning of § 2241 as long as 'the custodian can be reached by service of process.'"

The consequence of this holding, as applied to aliens outside the country, is breathtaking. It permits an alien captured in a foreign theater of active combat to bring a § 2241 petition against the Secretary of Defense. Over the course of the last century, the United States has held millions of alien prisoners abroad. A great many of these prisoners would no doubt have complained about the circumstances of their capture and the terms of their confinement. The military is currently detaining over 600 prisoners at Guantanamo Bay alone; each detainee undoubtedly has complaints — real or contrived — about those terms and circumstances. The Court's unheralded expansion of federal-court jurisdiction is not even mitigated by a comforting assurance that the legion of ensuing claims will be easily resolved on the merits. To the contrary, the Court says that the "petitioners' allegations . . . unquestionably describe 'custody in violation of the Constitution or laws or treaties of the United States.'" From this point forward, federal courts will entertain petitions from these prisoners, and others like them around the world, challenging actions and events far away, and forcing the courts to oversee one aspect of the Executive's conduct of a foreign war.

Today's carefree Court disregards, without a word of acknowledgment, the dire warning of a more circumspect Court in *Eisentrager*:

> To grant the writ to these prisoners might mean that our army must transport them across the seas for hearing. This would require allocation for shipping space, guarding personnel, billeting and rations. It might also require transportation for whatever witnesses the prisoners desired to call as well as transportation for those necessary to defend legality of the sentence. The writ, since it is held to be a matter of right, would be equally available to enemies during active hostilities as in the present twilight between war and peace. Such trials would hamper the war effort and bring aid and comfort to the enemy. They would diminish the prestige of our commanders, not only with enemies but with wavering neutrals. It would be difficult to devise more effective fettering of a field commander than to allow the very enemies he is ordered to reduce to submission to call him to account in his own civil courts and divert his efforts and attention from the military offensive abroad to the legal defensive at home. Nor is it unlikely that the result of such enemy litigiousness would be conflict between judicial and military opinion highly comforting to enemies of the United States.

The Court gives only two reasons why the presumption against extraterritorial effect does not apply to Guantanamo Bay. First, the Court says (without any further elaboration) that "the United States exercises 'complete jurisdiction and control' over the Guantanamo Bay Naval Base [under the terms of a 1903 lease agreement], and may continue to exercise such control permanently if it so chooses [under the terms of a 1934 Treaty]." The Court does not explain how "complete jurisdiction and control" without sovereignty causes an enclave to be part of the United States for purposes of its domestic laws. Since "jurisdiction and control" obtained through a lease is no different in effect from "jurisdiction and control" acquired by lawful force of arms, parts of Afghanistan and Iraq should logically be regarded as subject to our domestic laws. Indeed, if "jurisdiction and control" rather than sovereignty were the test, so should the Landsberg Prison in Germany, where the United States held the *Eisentrager* detainees.

The second and last reason the Court gives for the proposition that domestic law applies to Guantanamo Bay is the Solicitor General's concession that there would be habeas jurisdiction over a United States citizen in Guantanamo Bay. "Considering that the statute draws no distinction between Americans and aliens held in federal custody, there is little reason to think that Congress intended the geographical coverage of the statute to vary depending on the detainee's citizenship." But the reason the Solicitor General conceded there would be jurisdiction over a detainee who was a United States citizen had *nothing to do* with the special status of Guantanamo Bay: "Our answer to that question, Justice Souter, is that citizens of the United States, because of their constitutional circumstances, may have greater rights with respect to the scope and reach of the Habeas Statute as the Court has or would interpret it." And *that* position — the position that United States citizens throughout the world may be entitled to habeas corpus rights — is precisely the position that this Court adopted in *Eisentrager,* even while holding that aliens abroad *did not have* habeas corpus rights.

To the extent the writ's "extraordinary territorial ambit" did extend to exempt jurisdictions, outlying dominions, and the like, that extension applied only to British *subjects*. Blackstone explained that the writ "runs into all parts of the king's dominions" because "the king is at all times entitled to have an account why the liberty of any of his *subjects* is restrained."

Departure from our rule of *stare decisis* in statutory cases is always extraordinary; it ought to be unthinkable when the departure has a potentially harmful effect upon the Nation's conduct of a war. The Commander in Chief and his subordinates had every reason to expect that the internment of combatants at Guantanamo Bay would not have the consequence of bringing the cumbersome machinery of our domestic courts into military affairs. Congress is in session. If it wished to change federal judges' habeas jurisdiction from what this Court had previously held that to be, it could have done so. And it could have done so by intelligent revision of the statute, instead of by today's clumsy, countertextual reinterpretation that confers upon wartime prisoners greater habeas rights than domestic detainees. The latter must challenge their present physical confinement in the district of their confinement, see *Rumsfeld* v. *Padilla*, whereas under today's strange holding Guantanamo Bay detainees can petition in any of the 94 federal judicial districts. The fact that extraterritorially located detainees lack the district of detention that the statute requires has been converted from a factor that precludes their ability to bring a petition at all into a factor that frees them to petition wherever they wish — and, as a result, to forum shop. For this Court to create such a monstrous scheme in time of war, and in frustration of our military commanders' reliance upon clearly stated prior law, is judicial adventurism of the worst sort.

———————

Comments on *Hamdi*, *Padilla*, and *Rasul*. How significant is *Hamdi*? How protective will "the minimum requirements of due process," let alone the "possibility" that a "military tribunal" may meet these requisites, be? Can we assume that the Court's rejection of the government's arguments by requiring judicial review in the *Hamdi* circumstance will be applied to "Americans arrested on American soil (*Padilla*)"? Any basis for a contrary result? Then why the remand?

Is *Rasul* the real surprise? We may have expected the *Hamdi* result, particularly in regard to the *Padilla* facts, but the reach of federal jurisdiction and habeas corpus outside U.S. territory appears to "make the point." Yet, a denial of jurisdiction to the federal courts is a challenge to them by a coordinate branch, though one that, in the end, the Court itself will decide. Is this the real issue in *Rasul*? Can we expect the due process requirements that might be made applicable to American citizens to be more extensive than those required in the *Rasul* circumstance? Should we?

Though all of these cases rest their import on the availability of federal court review, the issue on the merits —what process requirements are due — is significant as well. This begs observation as these cases move through the federal courts. Is it meaningful in the twenty-first century that application of the basic magna carta right to habeas corpus has been challenged by the President and the Executive Branch, terror or not?

Hamdan. On the final day of the October 2005 Term, the Court, in the opinion below, reviewed military tribunals and, although finding them unauthorized by statute and contrary to international law, laid a predicate for their future application. Drama pervaded as both the majority and dissenting opinions were read aloud from the bench.

HAMDAN v. RUMSFELD
548 U.S. 557 (2006)

Justice STEVENS announced the judgment of the Court and delivered the opinion of the Court [and an opinion with respect to Parts V and VI-D-iv, in which Justices SOUTER, GINSBURG, and BREYER joined].

Petitioner Salim Ahmed Hamdan, a Yemeni national, is in custody at an American prison in Guantanamo Bay, Cuba. In November 2001, during hostilities between the United States and the Taliban (which then governed Afghanistan), Hamdan was captured by militia forces and turned over to the U.S. military. In June 2002, he was transported to Guantanamo Bay. Over a year later, the President deemed him eligible for trial by military commission for then-unspecified crimes. After another year had passed, Hamdan was charged with one count of conspiracy "to commit . . . offenses triable by military commission." Hamdan [petitioned] for [a] writ of habeas corpus.

[We] conclude that the military commission convened to try Hamdan lacks power to proceed because its structure and procedures violate both the Uniform Code of Military Justice (UCMJ) and the Geneva Conventions.

I. [On] September 11, 2001, agents of the al Qaeda terrorist organization hijacked commercial airplanes and attacked the World Trade Center in New York City and the national headquarters of the Department of Defense in Arlington, Virginia. Americans will never forget the devastation wrought by these acts. Nearly 3,000 civilians were killed. Congress responded by adopting [the AUMF, see 4th ed., p.555], pursuant to [which] the President ordered the Armed Forces of the United States to invade Afghanistan. In the ensuing hostilities, hundreds of individuals, Hamdan among them, were captured and eventually detained at Guantanamo Bay. On November 13, 2001, while the United States was still engaged in active combat with the Taliban, the President issued a comprehensive military order intended to govern the "Detention, Treatment, and Trial of Certain Non-Citizens in the War Against Terrorism," [providing that] any noncitizen for whom the President determines "there is reason to believe" that he or she (1) "is or was" a member of al Qaeda or (2) has engaged or participated in terrorist activities aimed at or harmful to the United States ["shall,] when tried, be tried by military commission for any and all offenses triable by military commission that such individual is alleged to have committed, and may be punished in accordance with the penalties provided under applicable law, including imprisonment or death." The November 13 Order vested in the Secretary of Defense the power to appoint military commissions [but] that power has since been delegated to [a] retired Army major general.

II. [The majority rejected the Government's motion to dismiss for lack of jurisdiction under the Detainee Treatment Act of 2005 (DTA), reading the jurisdiction-stripping provisions of that Act not to apply to cases such as Hamdan's that were pending at the time of enactment.]

III. [The majority likewise rejected the Government's argument that the Court should abstain out of comity from interrupting nonfinal military proceedings, concluding:] Hamdan and the Government both have a compelling interest in knowing in advance whether Hamdan may be tried by a military commission that arguably is without any basis in law and operates free from many of the procedural rules prescribed by Congress for courts-martial — rules intended to safeguard the accused and ensure the reliability of any conviction.

IV. [The] military commission, a tribunal neither mentioned in the Constitution nor created by statute, was born of military necessity, [foreshadowed] by earlier tribunals like the Board of General Officers that General Washington convened to try British Major John Andre for spying during the Revolutionary War. [Exigency] alone, of course, will not justify the establishment and use of penal tribunals not contemplated by Article I, § 8 and Article III, § 1 of the Constitution unless some other part of that document authorizes a response to the felt need. And that authority, if it exists, can derive only from the powers granted jointly to the President and Congress in time of war. The Constitution makes the President the "Commander in Chief" of the Armed Forces, Art. II, § 2, cl. 1, but vests in Congress the powers to "declare War . . . and make Rules concerning Captures on Land and Water," Art. I, § 8, cl. 11, to "raise and support Armies," cl. 12, to "define and punish . . . Offences against the Law of Nations," cl. 10, and "To make Rules for the Government and Regulation of the land and naval Forces," cl. 14.

[Whether] the President may constitutionally convene military commissions "without the sanction of Congress" in cases of "controlling necessity" is a question this Court has not answered definitively, and need not answer today. For we held in Quirin that Congress had, through Article of War 15 [adopted in 1916], sanctioned the use of military commissions in such circumstances. Article 21 of the UCMJ, the language of which is substantially identical to the old Article 15, [was] preserved by Congress after World War II. [But] even Quirin did not view the authorization as a sweeping mandate for the President to "invoke military commissions when he deems them necessary." Rather, [Quirin] recognized that Congress had simply preserved what power, under the Constitution and the common law of war, the President had had before 1916 to convene military commissions

— with the express condition that the President and those under his command comply with the law of war.

The Government would have us [find] in either the AUMF or the DTA specific, overriding authorization for the very commission that has been convened to try Hamdan. Neither of these congressional Acts, however, expands the President's authority to convene military commissions. First, while we assume that the AUMF activated the President's war powers, see Hamdi v. Rumsfeld, and that those powers include the authority to convene military commissions in appropriate circumstances, there is nothing in the text or legislative history of the AUMF even hinting that Congress intended to expand or alter the authorization set forth in Article 21 of the UCMJ.

[Although] the DTA, unlike either Article 21 or the AUMF, was enacted after the President had convened Hamdan's commission, it contains no language authorizing that tribunal or any other at Guantanamo Bay. [Together,] the UCMJ, the AUMF, and the DTA at most acknowledge a general Presidential authority to convene military commissions in circumstances where justified under the "Constitution and laws," including the law of war.

V. The common law governing military commissions may be gleaned from past practice and what sparse legal precedent exists. Commissions historically have been used in three situations. First, they have substituted for civilian courts at times and in places where martial law has been declared. [Second,] commissions have been established, to try civilians "as part of a temporary military government over occupied enemy territory or territory regained from an enemy where civilian government cannot and does not function." The third type of commission, convened as an "incident to the conduct of war" when there is a need "to seize and subject to disciplinary measures those enemies who in their attempt to thwart or impede our military effort have violated the law of war," [serves to] determine, typically on the battlefield itself, whether the defendant has violated the law of war. The last time the U.S. Armed Forces used the law-of-war military commission was during World War II. In Quirin, this Court sanctioned President Roosevelt's use of such a tribunal to try Nazi saboteurs captured on American soil during the War. [Since] Guantanamo Bay is neither enemy-occupied territory nor under martial law, the law-of-war commission is the only model available.

[The] charge against Hamdan [alleges] a conspiracy extending over a number of years, from 1996 to November 2001. All but two months of that more than 5-year-long period preceded the attacks of September 11, 2001, and the enactment of the AUMF. [Neither] the purported agreement with Osama bin Laden and others to commit war crimes, nor a single overt act, is alleged to have occurred in a theater of war or on any specified date after September 11, 2001. None of the overt acts that Hamdan is alleged to have committed violates the law of war. [These] facts alone cast doubt on the legality of the charge and, hence, the commission; [the] offense alleged must have been committed both in a theater of war and *during,* not before, the relevant conflict.

But the deficiencies in the time and place allegations also underscore — indeed are symptomatic of — the most serious defect of this charge: The offense it alleges is not triable by law-of-war military commission. There is no suggestion that Congress has, in exercise of its constitutional authority to "define and punish . . . Offences against the Law of Nations," U.S. Const., Art. I, § 8, cl. 10, positively identified "conspiracy" as a war crime. [While] Congress, through Article 21 of the UCMJ, has "incorporated by reference" the common law of war, which may render triable by military commission certain offenses not defined by statute, [the] precedent must be plain and unambiguous, [and that] burden is far from satisfied here. The crime of "conspiracy" has rarely if ever been tried as such in this country by any law-of-war military commission not exercising some other form of jurisdiction, and does not appear in either the Geneva Conventions or the Hague Conventions — the major treaties on the law of war. [Finally,] international sources confirm that the crime charged here is not a recognized violation of the law of war. [None] of the major treaties governing the law of war identifies conspiracy as a violation thereof. And the only "conspiracy" crimes that have been recognized by international war crimes tribunals (whose jurisdiction often extends beyond war crimes proper to crimes against humanity and crimes against the peace) are conspiracy to commit genocide and common plan to wage aggressive war. [The] International Military Tribunal at Nuremberg, over the prosecution's objections, pointedly refused to recognize as a violation of the law of war conspiracy to commit war crimes.

[Because] the charge does not support the commission's jurisdiction, the commission lacks authority to try Hamdan. [Hamdan] is charged not with an overt act for which he was caught red-handed in a theater of war and which military efficiency demands be tried expeditiously, but with an *agreement* the inception of which long predated the attacks of September 11, 2001 and the AUMF. That may well be a crime [prosecutable by court-martial or in federal court] but it is not an offense that "by the law of war may be tried by military commission."

VI. Whether or not the Government has charged Hamdan with an offense against the law of war cognizable by military commission, the commission lacks power to proceed. The UCMJ conditions the President's use of military commissions on compliance not only with the American common law of war, but also with the rest of the UCMJ itself [and] with the "rules and precepts of the law of nations," including, *inter alia,* the four Geneva Conventions signed in 1949. The procedures that the Government has decreed will govern Hamdan's trial by commission violate these laws.

A. [Every commission] must have a presiding officer and at least three other members, all of whom must be commissioned officers. [The] accused is entitled to appointed military counsel and may hire civilian counsel at his own expense. [The] accused also is entitled to a copy of the charge(s) against him, both in English and his own language (if different), to a presumption of innocence, and to certain other rights typically afforded criminal defendants in civilian courts and courts-martial. These rights are subject, however, to one glaring condition: The accused and his civilian counsel may be excluded from, and precluded from ever learning what evidence was presented during, any part of the proceeding that either the Appointing Authority or the presiding officer decides to "close." [Appointed] military defense counsel must be privy to these closed sessions, but may, at the presiding officer's discretion, be forbidden to reveal to his or her client what took place therein. Another striking feature of the rules [is] that they permit the admission of *any* evidence that, in the opinion of the presiding officer, "would have probative value to a reasonable person." Under this test, not only is testimonial hearsay and evidence obtained through coercion fully admissible, but neither live testimony nor witnesses' written statements need be sworn.

B. [Hamdan objects] that the procedures' admitted deviation from those governing courts-martial itself renders the commission illegal, [that] he may [be] convicted based on evidence he has not seen or heard, and that any evidence admitted against him need not comply with the admissibility or relevance rules typically applicable in criminal trials and court-martial proceedings.

C. [Article 36] of the UCMJ [provides that] the rules applied to military commissions must be the same as those applied to courts-martial unless such uniformity proves impracticable. [Nothing] in the record before us demonstrates that it would be impracticable to apply court-martial rules in this case. There is no suggestion, for example, of any logistical difficulty in securing properly sworn and authenticated evidence or in applying the usual principles of relevance and admissibility. [The] only reason offered [is] the danger posed by international terrorism. Without for one moment underestimating that danger, it is not evident to us why it should require, in the case of Hamdan's trial, any variance from the rules that govern courts-martial. The absence of any showing of impracticability is particularly disturbing when considered in light of the clear and admitted failure to apply one of the most fundamental protections afforded not just by the Manual for Courts — Martial but also by the UCMJ itself: the right to be present. [Under] the circumstances, then, the rules applicable in courts-martial must apply.

D. [The] procedures adopted to try Hamdan also violate the Geneva Conventions.

i. [The] Court of Appeals [held] that "the 1949 Geneva Convention does not confer upon Hamdan a right to enforce its provisions in court." [But] regardless of the nature of the rights conferred on Hamdan, they are [part] of the law of war. And compliance with the law of war is the condition upon which the authority set forth in Article 21 is granted.

ii. [The] Court of Appeals [also] reasoned that the war with al Qaeda evades the reach of the Geneva Conventions. We [disagree.] [Although] al Qaeda, unlike Afghanistan, is not [a] signatory of the Conventions, there is at least one provision of the Geneva Conventions that applies here even if the relevant conflict is not one between signatories. Article 3 [provides] that in a "conflict not of an international character occurring in the territory of one of the [signatories], each Party to the conflict shall be bound to apply, as a minimum," certain provisions [including one that] prohibits "the passing of sentences and the carrying out of executions [upon detainees] without previous judgment pronounced by a regularly constituted court affording all the judicial guarantees which are recognized as indispensable by civilized peoples."

iii. Common Article 3, then, is applicable here and [requires] that Hamdan be tried by a "regularly constituted court." ["The] regular military courts in our system are the courts-martial established by congressional statutes." At a minimum, a military commission "can be 'regularly constituted' by the standards of our military justice system only if some practical need explains deviations from court-martial practice." [No] such need has been demonstrated here.

iv. ["The] judicial guarantees which are recognized as indispensable by civilized peoples" [must] be understood to incorporate at least the barest of those trial protections that have been recognized by customary international law. Many of these are described in Article 75 of Protocol I to the Geneva Conventions of 1949, adopted in 1977. [Among] the rights set forth in Article 75 is the "right to be tried in [one's] presence." [The military commission procedures] dispense with the principles, articulated in Article 75 and indisputably part of the customary international law, that an accused must, absent disruptive conduct or consent, be present for his trial and must be privy to the evidence against him. That the Government has a compelling interest in denying Hamdan access to certain sensitive information is not doubted. But, at least absent express statutory provision to the contrary, information used to convict a person of a crime must be disclosed to him.

v. Common Article 3 obviously tolerates a great degree of flexibility in trying individuals captured during armed conflict; its requirements are general ones, crafted to accommodate a wide variety of legal systems. But *requirements* they are nonetheless. The commission that the President has convened to try Hamdan does not meet those requirements.

vi. [It] bears emphasizing that Hamdan does not challenge, and we do not today address, the Government's power to detain him for the duration of active hostilities in order to prevent such harm. But in undertaking to try Hamdan and subject him to criminal punishment, the Executive is bound to comply with the Rule of Law that prevails in this jurisdiction.
[Reversed.]

Justice BREYER, with whom Justices KENNEDY, SOUTER, and GINSBURG join, concurring.
[The] Court's conclusion ultimately rests upon a single ground: Congress has not issued the Executive a "blank check." [Nothing] prevents the President from returning to Congress to seek the authority he believes necessary. Where, as here, no emergency prevents consultation with Congress, judicial insistence upon that consultation does not weaken our Nation's ability to deal with danger.

Justice KENNEDY, with whom Justices SOUTER, GINSBURG, and BREYER join as to Parts I and II, concurring in part.
Military Commission Order No. 1, which governs the military commission established to try petitioner Salim Hamdan for war crimes, exceeds limits that certain statutes, duly enacted by Congress, have placed on the President's authority to convene military courts. This is not a case, then, where the Executive can assert some unilateral authority to fill a void left by congressional inaction. It is a case where Congress, in the proper exercise of its powers as an independent branch of government, and as part of a long tradition of legislative involvement in matters of military justice, has considered the subject of military tribunals and set limits on the President's authority. [If] Congress, after due consideration, deems it appropriate to change the controlling statutes [it] has the power and prerogative to do so. I join the Court's opinion, save Parts V and VI-D-iv.

I. Trial by military commission raises separation-of-powers concerns of the highest order. Located within a single branch, these courts carry the risk that offenses will be defined, prosecuted, and adjudicated by executive officials without independent review. Concentration of power puts personal liberty in peril of arbitrary action by officials, an incursion the Constitution's three-part system is designed to avoid. It is imperative, then, that when military tribunals are established, full and proper authority exists for the Presidential directive.
The proper framework for assessing whether Executive actions are authorized is the three-part scheme used by Justice Jackson in his opinion in Youngstown Sheet & Tube

Co. v. Sawyer [15th ed., p. 344]. In this case, [the] President has acted in a field with a history of congressional participation and regulation. In the [UCMJ], Congress has set forth governing principles for military courts. The UCMJ as a whole establishes an intricate system of military justice. It authorizes courts-martial in various forms; it regulates the organization and procedure of those courts; it defines offenses and rights for the accused; and it provides mechanisms for appellate review. [It] further recognizes that special military commissions may be convened to try war crimes. While these laws provide authority for certain forms of military courts, they also impose limitations. If the President has exceeded these limits, this becomes a case of conflict between Presidential and congressional action — a case within Justice Jackson's third category, not the second or first.

II. [The] circumstances of Hamdan's trial present no exigency requiring special speed or precluding careful consideration of evidence. For roughly four years, Hamdan has been detained at a permanent United States military base in Guantanamo Bay, Cuba. And regardless of the outcome of the criminal proceedings at issue, the Government claims authority to continue to detain him based on his status as an enemy combatant.

[The] Court is correct to conclude that the military commission the President has convened to try Hamdan is unauthorized. [Structural] differences between the military commissions and courts-martial — the concentration of functions, including legal decisionmaking, in a single executive official; the less rigorous standards for composition of the tribunal; and the creation of special review procedures in place of institutions created and regulated by Congress — remove safeguards that are important to the fairness of the proceedings and the independence of the court. Congress has prescribed these guarantees for courts-martial; and no evident practical need explains the departures here. For these reasons the commission cannot be considered regularly constituted under United States law and thus does not satisfy Congress' requirement that military commissions conform to the law of war. [Moreover,] the basic procedures for the commissions deviate from procedures for courts-martial, in violation of [UCMJ Article 36]. [The] Military Commission Order abandons the detailed Military Rules of Evidence [and] could permit admission of multiple hearsay and other forms of evidence generally prohibited on grounds of unreliability. [The] Government has made no demonstration of practical need for these special rules and procedures.

III. In light of the conclusion that the military commission here is unauthorized under the UCMJ, I see no need to consider several further issues addressed in the plurality opinion [and] dissent. [First,] I would not decide whether [Geneva Convention] Article 3's standard [necessarily] requires that the accused have the right to be present at all stages of a criminal trial. [I] likewise see no need to address the validity of the conspiracy charge against Hamdan. [Congress,] not the Court, is the branch in the better position to undertake the "sensitive task of establishing a principle not inconsistent with the national interest or international justice."

Justice THOMAS, with whom Justice SCALIA joins, and with whom Justice ALITO joins in all but Parts I, II-C-1, and III-B-2, dissenting.[1]

[The] Court's evident belief that *it* is qualified to pass on the "military necessity" of the Commander in Chief's decision to employ a particular form of force against our enemies [is] antithetical to our constitutional structure.

I. [When] "the President acts pursuant to an express or implied authorization from Congress," his actions are "'supported by the strongest of presumptions,'" Youngstown (Jackson, J., concurring). [Under] this framework, the President's decision to try Hamdan before a military commission for his involvement with al Qaeda is entitled to a heavy measure of deference. In the present conflict, Congress has authorized the President "to use all necessary and appropriate force against those nations, organizations, or persons *he determines* planned, authorized, committed, or aided the terrorist attacks that occurred on September 11, 2001 . . . in order to prevent any future acts of international terrorism against the United States by such nations, organizations or persons." [AUMF (emphasis added)]. As a plurality of the Court observed in Hamdi, the "capture, detention, and *trial* of unlawful combatants, by 'universal agreement and practice,' are 'important incidents of war.'" [Accordingly,] congressional authorization for military commissions pertaining to the instant conflict derives not only from Article 21 of the UCMJ, but also from the more recent, and broader, authorization contained in the AUMF. [In] such circumstances, [our] duty to defer to the Executive's military and foreign policy judgment is at its zenith; it does not countenance the kind of second-guessing the Court repeatedly engages in today.

II. A. [The Executive has easily satisfied the considerations] that a law-of-war military commission may only assume jurisdiction of "offences committed within the field of the command of the convening commander," and that such offenses "must have been committed within the period of the war." [Even] before September 11, 2001, al Qaeda was involved in the bombing of the World Trade Center in New York City in 1993, the bombing of the Khobar Towers in Saudi Arabia in 1996, the bombing of the U.S. Embassies in Kenya and Tanzania in 1998, and the attack on the U.S. *S. Cole* in Yemen in 2000. [Based] on the foregoing, the President's judgment — that the present conflict substantially predates the AUMF, extending at least as far back as al Qaeda's 1996 declaration of war on our Nation, and that the theater of war extends at least as far as the localities of al Qaeda's principal bases of operations — is beyond judicial reproach.

B. [Law-of-war] military commissions have jurisdiction over "'individuals of the enemy's army who have been guilty of illegitimate warfare or other offences in violation of the laws of war.'" [This] consideration is easily satisfied here, as Hamdan is an unlawful combatant charged with joining and conspiring with a terrorist network dedicated to flouting the laws of war.

C. [The] common law of war is [flexible] and evolutionary in nature, building upon the experience of the past and taking account of the exigencies of the present [and] affords a measure of respect for the judgment of military commanders. [The] plurality's newly

---

[1] Justice Scalia also filed a dissent objecting that the Court lacked jurisdiction under the Detainee Treatment Act of 2005 or should have abstained on comity grounds. Chief Justice Roberts, having sat on the D.C. Circuit panel below, took no part in the decision.

minted clear-statement rule is [fundamentally] inconsistent with the nature of the common law [and] with the nature of warfare, which also evolves and changes over time.

1. Under either the correct, flexible approach to evaluating the adequacy of Hamdan's charge, or under the plurality's new, clear-statement approach, Hamdan has been charged with conduct constituting two distinct violations of the law of war cognizable before a military commission: membership in a war-criminal enterprise and conspiracy to commit war crimes. [Unlawful] combat-ants, such as Hamdan, violate the law of war merely by joining an organization, such as al Qaeda, whose principal purpose is the "killing [and] disabling . . . of peaceable citizens or soldiers."

2. ["The] experience of our wars" is rife with evidence that establishes beyond any doubt that conspiracy to violate the laws of war is [also] itself an offense cognizable before a law-of-war military commission. 3. Ultimately, the plurality's determination that Hamdan has not been charged with an offense triable before a military commission rests not upon any historical example or authority, but upon the plurality's raw judgment [of] "military necessity." This judgment starkly confirms that the plurality has appointed itself the ultimate arbiter of what is quintessentially a policy and military judgment. The judgment of the political branches that Hamdan, and others like him, must be held accountable before military commissions for their involvement with and membership in an unlawful organization dedicated to inflicting massive civilian casualties is supported by virtually every relevant authority. [It] is also supported by the nature of the present conflict. We are not engaged in a traditional battle with a nation-state, but with a worldwide, hydra-headed enemy, who lurks in the shadows conspiring to reproduce the atrocities of September 11, 2001, and who has boasted of sending suicide bombers into civilian gatherings, has proudly distributed videotapes of beheadings of civilian workers, and has tortured and dismembered captured American soldiers. But according to the plurality, [our] troops must catch the terrorists "redhanded," in the midst of *the attack itself,* in order to bring them to justice. Not only is this conclusion fundamentally inconsistent with the cardinal principal of the law of war, namely protecting non-combatants, but it would sorely hamper the President's ability to confront and defeat a new and deadly enemy.

III. A. [Far] from constraining the President's authority, Article 36 recognizes the President's prerogative to depart from the procedures applicable in criminal cases whenever *he alone* does not deem such procedures "practicable." [Nothing] in the text of Article 36 supports the Court's sweeping conclusion that it represents an unprecedented congressional effort to change the nature of military commissions from common-law war courts to tribunals that must presumptively function like courts-martial. [The] Court provides no explanation why the President's determination that employing court-martial procedures in the military commissions [would] hamper our war effort is in any way inadequate to satisfy its newly minted "practicability" requirement.

B. [Parts 1 and 2 of this section of the dissent argue that the Geneva Conventions are not judicially enforceable and do not apply to war with al Qaeda.] 3. [Even if] Article 3 were judicially enforceable and applicable to the present conflict, petitioner would not be entitled to relief. [Hamdan's] military commission [is] plainly "regularly constituted" because such commissions have been employed throughout our history to try unlawful combatants for crimes against the law of war. [Similarly,] the procedures to be employed by Hamdan's commission afford "all the judicial guarantees which are recognized as indispensable by civilized peoples." [The] plurality concludes that Hamdan's commission is unlawful because of the possibility that Hamdan will be barred from proceedings and denied access to evidence that may be used to convict him. But, under the commissions' rules, the Government may not impose such bar or denial on Hamdan if it would render his trial unfair. ["Civilized peoples"] would take into account the context of military commission trials against unlawful combatants in the war on terrorism, including the need to keep certain information secret in the interest of preventing future attacks on our Nation and its foreign installations so long as it did not deprive the accused of a fair trial.

Justice ALITO, with whom Justices SCALIA and THOMAS join, dissenting.

[The] holding of the Court, as I understand it, rests on the following reasoning. A military commission is lawful only if it is authorized by [UCMJ Article 21]; this provision permits the use of a commission to try "offenders or offenses" that "by statute or by the law of war may be tried by" such a commission; because no statute provides that an offender such as petitioner or an offense such as the one with which he is charged may be tried by a military commission, he may be tried by military commission only if the trial is authorized by "the law of war"; the Geneva Conventions are part of the law of war; and Common Article 3 of the Conventions prohibits petitioner's trial because the commission before which he would be tried is not "a regularly constituted court," I disagree with this holding because petitioner's commission is "a regularly constituted court."

[I] interpret this element to require that the court be appointed or established in accordance with the appointing country's domestic law. [I] see no basis for the Court's holding that a military commission cannot be regarded as "a regularly constituted court" unless it is similar in structure and composition to a regular military court or unless there is an "evident practical need" for the divergence. [Tribunals] that vary significantly in structure, composition, and procedures may all be "regularly" or "properly" constituted. [I] cannot agree with the Court's conclusion that the military commission at issue here is not a "regularly constituted court" because its structure and composition differ from those of a court-martial. [Whatever] else may be said about the system that was created by Military Commission Order No. 1 and augmented by the Detainee Treatment Act, this system — which features formal trial procedures, multiple levels of administrative review, and the opportunity for review by a United States Court of Appeals and by this Court — does not dispense "summary justice."

———

Events After *Hamdan*: Congressional Response. After the decision in *Hamdan*, Congress enacted the Military Commissions Act of 2006 (MCA), Pub. L. No. 109-366, 120 Stat. 2600. The MCA states that it "shall apply to all cases, without exception, pending on or after the date of the enactment of this Act which relate to any aspect of the detention, transfer, treatment, trial, or conditions of detention of an alien detained by the United States since Sept. 11, 2001." The Act defines "unlawful combatant" as "a person who has engaged in hostilities or who has purposefully and materially supported hostilities against the United States or its co-belligerents who is not a lawful enemy combatant (including a person who is part of the Taliban, al Qaeda, or associated forces); or [] a person who, before, on, or after the date of the enactment of the [MCA], has been determined to be an unlawful enemy combatant by a [CSRT] or another competent tribunal established under the authority of the President or the Secretary of Defense."

The MCA provides the President with authority to try such alien unlawful enemy combatants by military commissions, for any offense made punishable by the law of war. The MCA also expanded the DTA's removal of habeas jurisdiction to all overseas enemy combatant detainees, regardless of where they were being held: "No court, justice, or judge shall have jurisdiction to hear or consider an application for a writ of habeas corpus filed by or on behalf of an alien detained by the United States who has been determined by the United States to have been properly detained as an enemy combatant or is awaiting such determination. Except as provided in [the DTA,] no court, justice, or judge shall have jurisdiction to hear or consider any other action against the United States or its agents relating to any aspect of the detention, transfer, treatment, trial, or conditions of confinement of an alien who is or was detained by the United States and has been determined by the United States to have been properly detained as an enemy combatant or is awaiting such determination."

Was Congress's enactment of the MCA sufficient to cure the lack of executive authority found by the *Hamdan* Court? Note that Justice Breyer concurred separately, in an opinion joined by Justices Kennedy, Souter, and Ginsburg, to emphasize that "[n]othing prevents the President from returning to Congress to seek the authority he believes necessary." Did the MCA provide that authority? Consider the view that "Hamdan is not a constitutional ruling, but rather a decision about the presence vel non of congressional authorization and the content of any congressional limits on the President's use of military commissions." Estreicher & O'Scannlain, "The Limits of Hamdan v. Rumsfeld," 9 Green Bag 353 (2006).

Hamdi and Hamdan. Does the Court's holding in *Hamdi* suggest that congressional action may be insufficient to remedy potential constitutional flaws in executive detention and trial? May a noncitizen detainee argue that habeas relief is still constitutionally required, despite the elimination of statutory habeas in the MCA? Is the MCA's attempt to strip federal courts of habeas jurisdiction for detainees constitutional in light of separation of powers, the Suspension Clause, and Equal Protection guarantees? Even if habeas relief may be negated generally, may alien unlawful enemy combatants object to their selective excision from the right to habeas corpus? Does a detainee retain the ability to use habeas to challenge the *jurisdiction* of the court before which he or she is tried?

Habeas Corpus Rights After *Hamdan*. On remand, the district court in Hamdan's case found that the MCA had deprived it of statutory jurisdiction over Hamdan's habeas claims, and that, like the enemy combatants in Johnson v. Eisentrager, he lacked "the geographical and volitional predicates necessary to claim a constitutional entitlement to habeas corpus." In February 2007, a divided panel of the Court of Appeals for the D.C. Circuit upheld the habeas-stripping provisions of the Military Commissions Act, finding that "the Constitution does not confer rights on aliens without property or presence within the United States." Boumediene v. Bush, 476 F.3d 981 (D.C. Cir. 2007).

The Supreme Court denied immediate certiorari review of the D.C. Circuit's opinion in April 2007 (Boumediene v. Bush, 549 U.S. 1328), with Justices Kennedy and Stevens including a statement defending the denial and explaining that "[d]espite the obvious importance of the issues raised in these cases, we are persuaded that traditional rules governing our decision of constitutional questions, and our practice of requiring the exhaustion of available remedies as a precondition to accepting jurisdiction over applications for the writ of habeas corpus, make it appropriate to deny these petitions at this time." Of even greater interest, Justice Breyer, joined by Justices Souter and Ginsburg, dissented from the denial, asserting that they would "grant the petitions for certiorari and the motions to expedite the cases." Given Justice Stevens's opinion in *Hamdan*, the lack of his providing the necessary fourth vote to allow certiorari review "tickled Court watchers' fantasy." This was particularly the case because Justice Stevens joined Justice Kennedy, forewarned in their joint statement that if necessary the Court "should act promptly to ensure that the office and purposes of the writ of habeas corpus are not compromised."

All of this seemed to make sense when the Court reversed itself in late June 2007 (Boumediene v. Bush, 549 U.S. 1328) and indicated that it would nonetheless grant certiorari and render a decision in the matter. This rarely granted motion for reconsideration required five as opposed to the four votes necessary for certiorari. Was there an agreement between Kennedy and Stevens to so act if necessary? This would have supplied the necessary five votes. What might have occurred to cause them to so act? Though the Court offered no explanation, the answer became apparent in a dramatic decision announced at the close of the Court's 2008 term in Boumediene v. Bush.

BOUMEDIENE v. BUSH
553 U.S. 723 (2008)

[The Court reached the question as to whether the MCA, as modified by the DTA, unconstitutionally suspended the writ of habeas corpus. Section 7 of the MCA provides: "No court, justice, or judge shall have jurisdiction to hear or consider an application for a writ of habeas corpus filed by or on behalf of an alien detained by the United States who has been determined by the United States to have been properly detained as an enemy combatant or is awaiting such determination." The DTA provides for the exclusive jurisdiction of the Court of Appeals for the District of Columbia Circuit to review decisions by CSRTs concerning alien enemy combatants.]

Justice KENNEDY delivered the opinion of the Court, in which Justices STEVENS, SOUTER, GINSBURG, and BREYER joined.

Petitioners are aliens designated as enemy combatants and detained at the United States Naval Station at Guantanamo Bay, Cuba. [Petitioners] present a question not resolved by our earlier cases relating to the detention of aliens at Guantanamo: whether they have the constitutional privilege of habeas corpus, a privilege not to be withdrawn except in conformance with the Suspension Clause, Art. I, § 9, cl. 2. We hold these petitioners do have the habeas corpus privilege. Congress has enacted a statute, the Detainee Treatment Act of 2005 (DTA), that provides certain procedures for review of the detainees' status. We hold that those procedures are not an adequate and effective substitute for habeas corpus. Therefore § 7 of the Military Commissions Act of 2006 (MCA) operates as an unconstitutional suspension of the writ.

II. [As] a threshold matter, we must decide whether MCA § 7 denies the federal courts jurisdiction to hear habeas corpus actions pending at the time of its enactment. We hold the statute does deny that jurisdiction, so that, if the statute is valid, petitioners' cases must be dismissed.

III. [In] deciding the constitutional questions now presented we must determine whether petitioners are barred from seeking the writ or invoking the protections of the Suspension Clause either because of their status, *i.e.*, petitioners' designation by the Executive Branch as enemy combatants, or their physical location, *i.e.*, their presence at Guantanamo Bay.

A. [The] Framers viewed freedom from unlawful restraint as a fundamental precept of liberty, and they understood the writ of habeas corpus as a vital instrument to secure that freedom. Experience taught, however, that the common-law writ all too often had been insufficient to guard against the abuse of monarchial power. That history counseled the necessity for specific language in the Constitution to secure the writ and ensure its place in our legal system. [That] the Framers considered the writ a vital instrument for the protection of individual liberty is evident from the care taken to specify the limited grounds for its suspension: "The Privilege of the Writ of Habeas Corpus shall not be suspended, unless when in Cases of Rebellion or Invasion the public Safety may require it." Art. I, § 9, cl. 2.

[The] Clause protects the rights of the detained by a means consistent with the essential design of the Constitution. It ensures that, except during periods of formal suspension, the Judiciary will have a time-tested device, the writ, to maintain the "delicate balance of governance" that is itself the surest safeguard of liberty. The Clause protects the rights of the detained by affirming the duty and authority of the Judiciary to call the jailer to account. The separation-of-powers doctrine, and the history that influenced its design, therefore must inform the reach and purpose of the Suspension Clause.

B. ["At] the absolute minimum" the Clause protects the writ as it existed when the Constitution was drafted and ratified. [The] Government argues the common-law writ ran only to those territories over which the Crown was sovereign. Petitioners argue that jurisdiction followed the King's officers. Diligent search by all parties reveals no certain conclusions. In none of the cases cited do we find that a common-law court would or would not have granted, or refused to hear for lack of jurisdiction, a petition for a writ of habeas corpus brought by a prisoner deemed an enemy combatant, under a standard like the one the Department of Defense has used in these cases, and when held in a territory, like Guantanamo, over which the Government has total military and civil control. [Each] side in the present matter argues that the very lack of a precedent on point supports its position. The Government points out there is no evidence that a court sitting in England granted habeas relief to an enemy alien detained abroad; petitioners respond there is no evidence that a court refused to do so for lack of jurisdiction. [We decline] to infer too much, one way or the other, from the lack of historical evidence on point.

IV. [Drawing] from its position that at common law the writ ran only to territories over which the Crown was sovereign, the Government says the Suspension Clause affords petitioners no rights because the United States does not claim sovereignty over the place of detention. Guantanamo Bay is not formally part of the United States. [We] accept the Government's position that Cuba, and not the United States, retains de jure sovereignty over Guantanamo Bay. As we did in Rasul, however, we take notice of the obvious and uncontested fact that the United States, by virtue of its complete jurisdiction and control over the base, maintains de facto sovereignty over this territory.

A. [The] Court has discussed the issue of the Constitution's extraterritorial application on many occasions. These decisions undermine the Government's argument that, at least as applied to noncitizens, the Constitution necessarily stops where de jure sovereignty ends. [Nothing] in Eisentrager says that de jure sovereignty is or has ever been the only relevant consideration in determining the geographic reach of the Constitution or of habeas corpus. [Questions] of extraterritoriality turn on objective factors and practical concerns, not formalism.

B. The Government's formal sovereignty-based test raises troubling separation-of-powers concerns as well. The political history of Guantanamo illustrates the deficiencies of this approach. The United States has maintained complete and uninterrupted control of the bay for over 100 years. At the close of the Spanish-American War, Spain ceded control over the entire island of Cuba to the United States and specifically "relinquishe[d] all claim[s] of sovereignty . . . and title." [Although] it recognized, by entering into the 1903 Lease Agreement, that Cuba retained "ultimate sovereignty" over Guantanamo, the United States continued to maintain the same plenary control it had enjoyed since 1898. [The] Constitution grants Congress and the President the power to acquire, dispose of, and govern territory, not the power to decide when and where its terms apply. Even when the United States acts outside its borders, its powers are not "absolute and unlimited" but are subject "to such restrictions as are expressed in the Constitution."

C. [At] least three factors are relevant in determining the reach of the Suspension Clause: (1) the citizenship and status of the detainee and the adequacy of the process through which that status determination was made; (2) the nature of the sites where apprehension and then detention took place; and (3) the practical obstacles inherent in resolving the prisoner's entitlement to the writ.

Applying this framework, we note at the onset that the status of these detainees is a matter of dispute. The petitioners, like those in Eisentrager, are not American citizens. But the petitioners in Eisentrager did not contest, it seems, the Court's assertion that they were "enemy alien[s]." In the instant cases, by contrast, the detainees deny they are enemy combatants. [As] to the second factor relevant to this analysis, the detainees here are similarly situated to the Eisentrager petitioners in that the sites of their apprehension and detention are technically outside the sovereign territory of the United States, [a] factor that weighs against finding they have rights under the Suspension Clause. But there are critical differences between Landsberg Prison, circa 1950, and the United States Naval Station at Guantanamo Bay in 2008. Unlike its present control over the naval station, the United States' control over the prison in Germany was neither absolute nor indefinite. [In] every practical sense Guantanamo is not abroad; it is within the constant jurisdiction of the United States. [As] to the third factor, we recognize, as the Court did in Eisentrager, that there are costs to holding the Suspension Clause applicable in a case of military detention abroad. Habeas corpus proceedings may require expenditure of funds by the Government and may divert the attention of military personnel from other pressing tasks. While we are sensitive to these concerns, we do not find them dispositive. Compliance with any judicial process requires some incremental expenditure of resources.

[We] hold that Art. I, § 9, cl. 2, of the Constitution has full effect at Guantanamo Bay. If the privilege of habeas corpus is to be denied to the detainees now before us, Congress must act in accordance with the requirements of the Suspension Clause. [The] MCA does not purport to be a formal suspension of the writ; and the Government, in its submissions to us, has not argued that it is. Petitioners, therefore, are entitled to the privilege of habeas corpus to challenge the legality of their detention.

V. In light of this holding the question becomes whether the statute stripping jurisdiction to issue the writ avoids the Suspension Clause mandate because Congress has provided adequate substitute procedures for habeas corpus. [When] Congress has intended to replace traditional habeas corpus with habeas-like substitutes, [it] has granted to the courts broad remedial powers to secure the historic office of the writ. [In] contrast the DTA's jurisdictional grant is quite limited. The Court of Appeals has jurisdiction not to inquire into the legality of the detention generally but only to assess whether the CSRT complied with the "standards and procedures specified by the Secretary of Defense" and whether those standards and procedures are lawful. If Congress had envisioned DTA review as coextensive with traditional habeas corpus, it would not have drafted the statute in this manner.

B. We do not endeavor to offer a comprehensive summary of the requisites for an adequate substitute for habeas corpus. We do consider it uncontroversial, however, that the privilege of habeas corpus entitles the prisoner to a meaningful opportunity to demonstrate that he is being held pursuant to "the erroneous application or interpretation" of relevant law. [We hold] that when the judicial power to issue habeas corpus properly is invoked the judicial officer must have adequate authority to make a determination in light of the relevant law and facts and to formulate and issue appropriate orders for relief, including, if necessary, an order directing the prisoner's release.

C. [Even assuming] the DTA can be construed to allow the Court of Appeals to review or correct the CSRT's factual determinations, as opposed to merely certifying that the tribunal applied the correct standard of proof, we see no way to construe the statute to allow what is also constitutionally required in this context: an opportunity for the detainee to present relevant exculpatory evidence that was not made part of the record in the earlier proceedings. [This] evidence, however, may be critical to the detainee's argument that he is not an enemy combatant and there is no cause to detain him. [Petitioners] have met their burden of establishing that the DTA review process is, on its face, an inadequate substitute for habeas corpus.

IV. A. [The] question remains whether there are prudential barriers to habeas corpus review under these circumstances. [In] some of these cases six years have elapsed without the judicial oversight that habeas corpus or an adequate substitute demands. And there has been no showing that the Executive faces such onerous burdens that it cannot respond to habeas corpus actions. [While] some delay in fashioning new procedures is unavoidable, the costs of delay can no longer be borne by those who are held in custody. The detainees in these cases are entitled to a prompt habeas corpus hearing.

[Our] opinion does not undermine the Executive's powers as Commander in Chief. On the contrary, the exercise of those powers is vindicated, not eroded, when confirmed by the Judicial Branch. Within the Constitution's separation-of-powers structure, few exercises of judicial power are as legitimate or as necessary as the responsibility to hear challenges to the authority of the Executive to imprison a person.

Justice SOUTER, with whom Justices GINSBURG and BREYER join, concurring.

[A fact] insufficiently appreciated by the dissents is the length of the disputed imprisonments, some of the prisoners represented here today having been locked up for six years. Hence the hollow ring when the dissenters suggest that the Court is somehow precipitating the judiciary into reviewing claims that the military (subject to appeal to the Court of Appeals for the District of Columbia Circuit) could handle within some reasonable period of time. [After] six years of sustained executive detentions in Guantanamo, subject to habeas jurisdiction but without any actual habeas scrutiny, today's decision is no judicial victory, but an act of perseverance in trying to make habeas review, and the obligation of the courts to provide it, mean something of value both to prisoners and to the Nation.

Chief Justice ROBERTS, with whom Justices SCALIA, THOMAS, and ALITO join, dissenting.

Today the Court strikes down as inadequate the most generous set of procedural protections ever afforded aliens detained by this country as enemy combatants. The political branches crafted these procedures amidst an ongoing military conflict, after much careful investigation and thorough debate. [I] believe the system the political branches constructed adequately protects any constitutional rights aliens captured abroad and detained as enemy combatants may enjoy. I therefore would dismiss these cases on that ground.

[CSRT] review is just the first tier of collateral review in the DTA system. The statute provides additional review in an Article III court. [A] *court* determines whether the CSRT procedures are constitutional, and a *court* determines whether those procedures were followed in a particular case. [The] Hamdi plurality concluded that this type of review would be enough to satisfy due process, even for citizens. Congress followed the Court's lead, only to find itself the victim of a constitutional bait and switch. [Hamdi] said the Constitution guarantees citizen detainees only "basic" procedural rights, and that the process for securing those rights can "be tailored to alleviate [the] uncommon potential to burden the Executive at a time of ongoing military conflict." [All told,] the DTA provides the prisoners held at Guantanamo Bay adequate opportunity to contest the bases of their detentions, which is all habeas corpus need allow.

[The] Court finds the DTA system an inadequate habeas substitute, for one central reason: Detainees are unable to introduce at the appeal stage exculpatory evidence discovered after the conclusion of their CSRT proceedings. [If] this is the most the Court can muster, the ice beneath its feet is thin indeed. [The] CSRT procedures provide ample opportunity for detainees to introduce exculpatory evidence — whether documentary in nature or from live witnesses — before the military tribunals. [The] Court's hand wringing over the DTA's treatment of later-discovered exculpatory evidence is the most it has to show after a roving search for constitutionally problematic scenarios. But "[t]he delicate power of pronouncing an Act of Congress unconstitutional," we have said, "is not to be exercised with reference to hypothetical cases thus imagined." The Court today invents a sort of reverse facial challenge and applies it with gusto: If there is *any* scenario in which the statute *might* be constitutionally infirm, the law must be struck down.

[The] majority rests its decision on abstract and hypothetical concerns. Step back and consider what, in the real world, Congress and the Executive have actually granted aliens captured by our Armed Forces overseas and found to be enemy combatants:

The right to hear the bases of the charges against them, including a summary of any classified evidence.

The ability to challenge the bases of their detention before military tribunals modeled after Geneva Convention procedures

[The] right, before the CSRT, to testify, introduce evidence, call witnesses, question those the Government calls, and secure release, if and when appropriate.

The right to the aid of a personal representative in arranging and presenting their cases before a CSRT.

Before the D.C. Circuit, the right to employ counsel, challenge the factual record, contest the lower tribunal's legal determinations, ensure compliance with the Constitution and laws, and secure release, if any errors below establish their entitlement to such relief.

In sum, the DTA satisfies the majority's own criteria for assessing adequacy. This statutory scheme provides the combatants held at Guantanamo greater procedural protections than have ever been afforded alleged enemy detainees — whether citizens or aliens — in our national history.

Justice SCALIA, with whom THE CHIEF JUSTICE and Justices THOMAS and ALITO join, dissenting.

Today, for the first time in our Nation's history, the Court confers a constitutional right to habeas corpus on alien enemies detained abroad by our military forces in the course of an ongoing war. The Chief Justice's dissent, which I join, shows that the procedures prescribed by Congress in the Detainee Treatment Act provide the essential protections that habeas corpus guarantees; there has thus been no suspension of the writ, and no basis exists for judicial intervention beyond what the Act allows. My problem with today's opinion is more fundamental still: The writ of habeas corpus does not, and never has, run in favor of aliens abroad; the Suspension Clause thus has no application, and the Court's intervention in this military matter is entirely ultra vires.

[The] Suspension Clause of the Constitution provides: "The Privilege of the Writ of Habeas Corpus shall not be suspended, unless when in Cases of Rebellion or Invasion the public Safety may require it." Art. I, § 9, cl. 2. As a court of law operating under a written Constitution, our role is to determine whether there is a conflict between that Clause and the Military Commissions Act. A conflict arises only if the Suspension Clause preserves the privilege of the writ for aliens held by the United States military as enemy combatants at the base in Guantanamo Bay, located within the sovereign territory of Cuba.

[The] Court purports to derive from our precedents a "functional" test for the extraterritorial reach of the writ, which shows that the Military Commissions Act unconstitutionally restricts the scope of habeas. That is remarkable because the most pertinent of those precedents, Johnson v. Eisentrager, conclusively establishes the opposite. There we were confronted with the claims of 21 Germans held at Landsberg Prison, an American military facility located in the American Zone of occupation in postwar Germany. They had been captured in China, and an American military commission sitting there had convicted them of war crimes — collaborating with the Japanese after Germany's surrender. Like the petitioners here, the Germans claimed that their detentions violated the Constitution and international law, and sought a writ of habeas corpus. Writing for the Court, Justice Jackson held that American courts lacked habeas jurisdiction. Eisentrager thus held — held beyond any doubt — that the Constitution does not ensure habeas for aliens held by the United States in areas over which our Government is not sovereign. [Eisentrager] nowhere mentions a "functional" test, and the notion that it is based upon such a principle is patently false. [There] is simply no support for the Court's assertion that constitutional rights extend to aliens held outside U.S. sovereign territory, and Eisentrager could not be clearer that the privilege of habeas corpus does not extend to aliens abroad. By blatantly distorting Eisentrager, the Court avoids the difficulty of explaining why it should be overruled.

[Putting] aside the conclusive precedent of Eisentrager, it is clear that the original understanding of the Suspension Clause was that habeas corpus was not available to aliens abroad. It is entirely clear that, at English common law, the writ of habeas corpus did not extend beyond the sovereign territory of the Crown. To be sure, the writ had an "extraordinary territorial ambit," because it was a so-called "prerogative writ," which, unlike other writs, could extend beyond the realm of England to other places where the Crown was sovereign. But prerogative writs could not issue to foreign countries, even for British subjects; they were confined to the King's dominions — those areas over which the Crown was sovereign. [In sum,] *all* available historical evidence points to the conclusion that the writ would not have been available at common law for aliens captured and held outside the sovereign territory of the Crown.

[What] history teaches is confirmed by the nature of the limitations that the Constitution places upon suspension of the common-law writ. It can be suspended only "in Cases of Rebellion or Invasion." Art. I, § 9, cl. 2. The latter case (invasion) is plainly limited to the territory of the United States; and while it is conceivable that a rebellion could be mounted by American citizens abroad, surely the overwhelming majority of its occurrences would be domestic. [Because] I conclude that the text and history of the Suspension Clause provide no basis for our jurisdiction, I would affirm the Court of Appeals even if Eisentrager did not govern these cases.

Boudmediene: What's Next? How is *Boudmediene* going to be enforced? Can the military trials continue? Could they meet habeas requirements? What other constitutional rights might the detainees retain? Of interest in regard to these questions as well as the remedial enforcement of the *Boudmediene* decision is the Court's finding in Parhat v. Gates, 532 F.3d 834 (D.C. Cir. 2008), decided the same term. There, the D.C. Circuit overturned the Department of Defense's classification of Huzaifa Parhat as an enemy combatant. Parhat is a Chinese Muslin known as a Uighur. He has said that he went to Afghanistan (where he was captured during the war) for military training so that he could return to fight Chinese oppression of ethnic Uighurs. The Uighurs are a Chinese separatist group that the U.S. government has designated as a terrorist organization, though it is not in a conflict with the United States. The military says that this group has ties to al Qaeda. A U.S. military official said that the military has cleared these Uighurs for release, but it has been unable to find a country willing to accept them. (The government persuaded Albania to accept five Uighurs in 2006.) It could return them to China but refuses to do so because of fear that the Chinese government will torture them. The D.C. Circuit said that the government must release or transfer Parhat or hold a new hearing consistent with the D.C. Circuit's classified opinion. Or, the court said, Parhat may seek release immediately by filing a writ of habeas corpus pursuant to *Boumediene*.

Note also, Munaf v. Geren, 553 U.S. 674 (2008), was decided the same term. Two American citizens voluntarily traveled to Iraq and allegedly committed crimes there. Munaf is a dual American Iraqi citizen, and Omar is a dual American Jordanian citizen. Multinational forces in Iraq (MNF-I) captured them, American military officers conducted

MNF-I hearings, and they concluded that Munaf and Omar posed threats to Iraq's security and detained them. MNF-I said Munaf was involved with a kidnapping-for-profit scheme of journalists and Omar was harboring an Iraqi terrorist and four Jordanian terrorists. It also found several weapons and explosive-making materials in Omar's home. One of Omar's wives and a son filed a habeas petition. Munaf's sister filed for him. They were held in a detainee camp operated by the MNF-I, and sought to enjoin transfer to the custody of the Central Criminal Court of Iraq (CCCI). Chief Justice Roberts, for a unanimous Court ruled, first, that the federal habeas statute does extend to American citizens held overseas by American forces operating subject to an American chain of command. However, courts may not use habeas to enjoin the United States from transferring alleged criminals to a foreign sovereign where the crimes were allegedly committed. Quoting Wilson v. Girard, the Court said that enjoining the transfers "would interfere with Iraq's sovereign right to 'punish offenses against its laws committed within its borders.'" The Court noted that it has long held that courts may not use habeas corpus to defeat the extradition of an American citizen accused of violating the laws of a foreign sovereign, "even when application of that sovereign's law would allegedly violate the Constitution." The detainees claim that they "would be denied constitutional rights if transferred" to Iraq, but "we have recognized that it is for the political branches, not the judiciary, to assess practices in foreign countries and to determine national policy in light of those assessments." It is up to the Executive Branch, not the courts, to "decline to surrender a detainee for many reasons, including humanitarian ones." Justice Souter, joined by Justices Ginsburg and Breyer, also filed a concurrence that said that habeas relief might exist if there was evidence that torture or other inhuman conditions would result from a transfer.

The *Padilla* "Wars." After the decision in Rumsfeld v. Padilla, Jose Padilla filed his cause in the proper court naming the proper respondent. In its February 28, 2005 decision, the U.S. District Court in South Carolina found in Padilla v. Hafnt, 389 F. Supp. 2d 678 (D.S.C. 2005), that Congress did not authorize the prisoner's indefinite detention without trial and that the President's inherent constitutional power did not allow him to subject a prisoner to indefinite military detention. The Fourth Circuit Court of Appeals reversed the district court's decision in Padilla v. Hafnt, 423 F.3d 386 (4th Cir. 2005). The unanimous three-judge panel held that the President possessed the authority under the Authorization for Use of Military Force Act to detain an enemy combatant.

While Padilla was appealing his case to the Supreme Court, the Justice Department indicted him in Florida for various federal crimes. President Bush then ordered that Padilla be transferred from military custody as an "enemy combatant" to the custody of the Attorney General of the United States so that Padilla could be tried in federal court subject to all constitutional rights. Pursuant to Supreme Court Rule 36, which requires that in a habeas corpus proceedings the person who has custody of the individual cannot transfer him without authorization from the court, the government filed such a request to the Fourth Circuit. In a somewhat surprising but noteworthy finding, the Fourth Circuit Court of Appeals denied the government's request for emergency authorization to transfer Padilla to a federal facility because the government was "trying to avoid the Supreme Court's review." Further indicating its displeasure, the Fourth Circuit also denied the government's request that it vacate its September 9 decision that found in its favor. The Fourth Circuit decisions were appealed to the Supreme Court, and on January 4, 2006, without comment, the Supreme Court allowed Padilla to be transferred.

On April 3, 2006, the Supreme Court denied certiorari in the matter based upon "strong prudential considerations," because Padilla was no longer in military custody and had been indicted and was awaiting trial in the federal district court in Florida (Padilla v. Hanft, 547 U.S. 1062 (2006)). Responding to the argument that at any time before or after the trial Padilla could be placed back into military custody, and certainly a message from the Court that they would closely follow future proceedings regarding Padilla, Justice Kennedy forewarned that "[i]n the course of its supervision over Padilla's custody and trial the District Court will be obliged to afford him the protection, including the right to a speedy trial, guaranteed to all federal criminal defendants. See, *e.g.,* U.S. Const., Amdt. 6; 18 U.S.C. § 3161. Were the Government to seek to change the status or conditions of Padilla's custody, that court would be in a position to rule quickly on any responsive filings submitted by Padilla. In such an event, the District Court, as well as other courts of competent jurisdiction, should act promptly to ensure that the office and purposes of the writ of habeas corpus are not compromised. Padilla, moreover, retains the option of seeking a writ of habeas corpus in this Court."

With three Justices dissenting, just one short of the necessary four required for certiorari (Souter, Breyer, and Ginsburg — where-oh-where was Justice Stevens?), Justice Ginsburg provided a written dissent and would have granted certiorari citing exceptions to the mootness requirement in finding that just because the government had voluntarily ceased detaining Padilla "does not make the case less capable for repetition or less evasive for review."

II. Presidential Power: Foreign Affairs

The Constitutional declaration that the President would be Commander-in-Chief has provided a basis for expansive presidential authority in conducting the foreign affairs of the nation. In the modern era this role has been expanded by those who have argued that the necessities of the "nuclear age" demand a great amount of freedom for the Chief Executive in conducting foreign policy so as to assure that the nation can adequately respond to any emergency. In fact, the Constitution's stipulation that only Congress can "declare war" has all but lost its meaning.

It is important to recall the issues discussed in regard to presidential power in domestic affairs because the question that must be posed is whether the necessities of the day require that the President's role in conducting foreign affairs be dramatically broadened, perhaps beyond that envisioned by the framers. The question is whether this would destroy the delicate balancing of powers articulated by the framers, and perhaps the very meaning of our constitutional government.

Though the Court has been rather particular about citing to the Constitution's textual allocation of separate power between the President, Congress, and the Court in domestic affairs (see *Youngstown* above), such has not been the case concerning foreign affairs. In foreign affairs, the Court has based its decisions more on what it sees are the practical realties of the circumstance, as opposed to constitutional sources of authority. Thus, executive prerogative in foreign affairs,

is not determined by any "natural" division. As they have evolved, the foreign relations powers appear [fissured]: [some] powers and functions belong to the President, some to Congress, some to the President-and-Senate; some can be exercised by either the President or the Congress, some require the joint authority of both. Irregular, uncertain division renders claims of usurpation more difficult to establish and the courts have not been available to adjudicate them. [L. Henkin, *Foreign Affairs and the Constitution* 32 (1972).]

Though, as noted by Henkin, the Constitution itself provides a distributive allocation of power in foreign affairs to both the President and Congress, historical practice and practical accommodations, formal and informal, have become the governing agenda.

The opinion that follows has been cited as setting the seeds of the "Imperial Presidency" in the conduct of the nation's foreign affairs. *Curtiss-Wright* concerned the American sale of arms (lend-lease) to our future allies before our entry into the Second World War. Those who argue that the President has too broad of latitude in the conduct of foreign affairs often cite to the *Curtiss-Wright* opinion as significant sources of such. See if you can determine why this view of *Curtiss-Wright* is meaningful in analyzing the power of the President in foreign affairs.

UNITED STATES v. CURTISS-WRIGHT CORP.
299 U.S. 304 (1936)

Mr. Justice SUTHERLAND delivered the opinion of the Court.

[An] indictment was returned in the court below, the first count of which charges that appellees [conspired] to sell in the United States certain arms of war, namely fifteen machine guns, to Bolivia, a country then engaged in armed conflict in the Chaco, in violation of the Joint Resolution of Congress approved May 28, 1934, and the provisions of a proclamation issued on the same day by the President [pursuant] to authority conferred by §1 of the resolution. [The joint resolution authorized the President to prohibit the sale of arms if he found that such a prohibition would contribute to establishment of peace in the region. The lower court held that the joint resolution was an unconstitutional delegation of legislative power to the President.]

Whether, if the Joint Resolution had related solely to internal affairs it would be open to the challenge that it constituted an unlawful delegation of legislative power to the Executive, we find it unnecessary to determine. [Curtiss-Wright was decided one year after the Court invalidated the National Industrial Recovery Act on the ground that it impermissibly delegated a legislative function to the President. See Schecter Poultry Corp. v. United States, (Chapter 2).] The whole aim of the resolution is to affect a situation entirely external to the United States, and falling within the category of foreign affairs. [Assuming] (but not deciding) that the challenged delegation, if it were confined to internal affairs, would be invalid, may it nevertheless be sustained on the ground that its exclusive aim is to afford a remedy for a hurtful condition within foreign territory?

It will contribute to the elucidation of the question if we first consider the differences between the powers of the federal government in respect of foreign or external affairs and those in respect of domestic or internal affairs. . . .

The two classes of powers are different, both in respect of their origin and their nature. The broad statement that the federal government can exercise no powers except those specifically enumerated in the Constitution, and such implied powers as are necessary and proper to carry into effect the enumerated powers, is categorically true only in respect of our internal affairs. In that field, the primary purpose of the Constitution was to carve from the general mass of legislative powers then possessed by the states such portions as it was thought desirable to vest in the federal government, leaving those not included in the enumeration still in the states. [That] this doctrine applies only to powers which the states had, is self evident. And since the states severally never possessed international powers, such powers could not have been carved from the mass of state powers but obviously were transmitted to the United States from some other source. . . .

As a result of the separation from Great Britain by the colonies acting as a unit, the powers of external sovereignty passed from the Crown not to the colonies severally, but to the colonies in their collective and corporate capacity as the United States of America. [Rulers] come and go; governments end and forms of government change; but sovereignty survives. A political society cannot endure without a supreme will somewhere. Sovereignty is never held in suspense. When, therefore, the external sovereignty of Great Britain in respect of the colonies ceased, it immediately passed to the Union. . . .

It results that the investment of the federal government with the powers of external sovereignty did not depend upon the affirmative grants of the Constitution. The powers to declare and wage war, to conclude peace, to make treaties, to maintain diplomatic relations with other sovereignties, if they had never been mentioned in the Constitution, would have vested in the federal government as necessary concomitants of nationality. . . . Not only, as we have shown, is the federal power over external affairs in origin and essential character different from that over internal affairs, but participation in the exercise of the power is significantly limited. In this vast external realm, with its important, complicated, delicate and manifold problems, the President alone has the power to speak or listen as a representative of the nation. He makes treaties with the advice and consent of the Senate; but he alone negotiates. Into the field of negotiation the Senate cannot intrude; and Congress itself is powerless to invade it. As Marshall said [in] the House of Representatives, "The President is the sole organ of the nation in its external relations, and its sole representative with foreign nations." . . .

It is important to bear in mind that we are here dealing not alone with an authority vested in the President by an exertion of legislative power, but with such an authority plus the very delicate, plenary and exclusive power of the President as the sole organ of the federal government in the field of international relations — a power which does not require as a basis for its exercise an act of Congress. [It] is quite apparent that if, in the maintenance of our international relations, embarrassment — perhaps serious embarrassment — is to be avoided and success for our aims achieved, congressional legislation [must] often accord to the President a degree of discretion and freedom from statutory restriction which would not be admissible were domestic affairs alone involved. Moreover, he, not Congress, has the better opportunity of knowing the conditions which prevail in foreign countries, and especially is this true in time of war. He has his confidential sources of information. He has his agents in the form of diplomatic, consular and other officials. Secrecy in respect of information gathered by them may be highly necessary, and the premature disclosure of it productive of harmful results. . . .

In the light of the foregoing observations, it is evident that this court should not be in haste to apply a general rule which will have the effect of condemning legislation like that under review as constituting an unlawful delegation of legislative power. The principles which justify such legislation find overwhelming support in the unbroken legislative practice which has prevailed almost from the inception of the national government to the present day. . .

[Reversed.]

Mr. Justice McReynolds dissented without opinion

Comments on *Curtiss-Wright*. Should the rationale that the necessities of government in the realm of foreign affairs do not require affirmative grants of constitutional power to the President, because he "knows best," be the business of the Court? Why not Congress? Is the Court interpreting the Constitution or acting the role of a political scientist? Did Vietnam prove that the President "might not know best"?

How viable is the Court's thesis that in order to compete with other nations we must allocate similar authority to the President? Or, to confront a "ruthless Hitler," we must be ruthless; to confront Russian secret police and intelligence actions, we must create agencies to do the same; and to confront and deal with dictators and terrorists, we must allow similar amounts of dictatorial power to the President. If this be our guiding principle, do we not become like the authoritarian regimes we oppose? President Richard Nixon, for example, asked Congress to grant him absolute authority to establish trade agreements and tariffs in a meeting with the Russians. He asserted that the Russian leaders would already maintain such authority, and that he required the same in order to bargain with them as an equal. Yet, the Russian leaders had such power as an extension of their authoritarian rule, while our Constitution required that the President act only with the advice and consent of the Senate. Is this an example of our democratic rule as opposed to that of the Russians? If we abide by the Court's and Nixon's logic, will we not be sacrificing what we presumably stand for? If the President has to act like a dictator to combat dictators, then how different are we from them? Are these questions for a court or political scientists? Can we say that the Constitution's distribution of power between Congress and the President may provide some weakness in the short run, but that in the end it is our greatest strength? By limiting authoritarian rule in this country, will we not assure ourselves that our freedom will not be swept away, and we will then be able to espouse the most attractive of all foreign policies — the fact that we are a free people?

A. EXECUTIVE AGREEMENTS

In Art. II, Section 2, the Constitution allocates to the President the power to negotiate treaties, subject to the "advice and consent" of the Senate via a two-thirds vote. Once the Senate has concurred with a treaty negotiated by the Executive, the Supreme Court has held it takes its place as "Supreme Law of the Land," with the same effect as the Constitution and laws of the United States. The executive branch has frequently resorted in foreign relations to unilateral executive agreements rather than treaties confirmed by the Senate according to the procedures set forth in Art. II. Concerns have recurrently been voiced that the executive agreements route may unduly intrude upon the Senate's role by bypassing treaty making. Fears have also been voiced that executive agreements may be on a par with treaties and may thus be able to supersede state legislation under the Supremacy Clause. Recall Missouri v. Holland (Chapter 2). Are such agreements supportable on the basis of inherent presidential authority? To what extent can executive agreements be justified as incidental to specified Art. II powers? Must all executive agreements be made in pursuance of a statute?

In an important consideration of executive agreements, United States v. Belmont, 301 U.S. 324 (1937), the Court sustained the validity of an executive agreement and held that it took precedence over conflicting state policy. Justice Sutherland, who had written *Curtiss-Wright* a year earlier, wrote for the majority. The agreement arose out of the

American diplomatic recognition of the Soviet Union in 1933. At the same time as President Roosevelt recognized the U.S.S.R., an exchange of diplomatic correspondence between the President and Maxim Litvinov effected an assignment to the United States of all Soviet claims against Americans who held funds of Russian companies seized after the Revolution. The *Belmont* suit was brought by the United States in reliance upon that assignment, in order to recover funds deposited by a Russian corporation with a private New York banker. The lower courts dismissed the action on the ground that implementing the U.S.S.R.'s confiscation would violate the public policy of New York. Justice Sutherland's majority opinion emphasized that recognition, the establishment of diplomatic relations, assignment "were all parts of one transaction, resulting in an international compact between the two governments." He had no doubt that the negotiations and the agreements "were within the competence of the President": "in respect of what was done here, the Executive had authority to speak as the sole organ." And the assignment and agreement, unlike treaties, did not require the Senate's participation. He stated that "an international compact, as this was, is not always a treaty which requires the participation of the Senate. There are many such compacts, of which a protocol, a modus vivendi, a postal convention, and agreements like that now under consideration are illustrations." And the supremacy clause required that contrary state policies must give way. The Litvinov Assignment resurfaced in the Court in United States v. Pink, 315 U.S. 203 (1942). Justice Douglas's opinion for the Court stated that the President "has the power to determine the policy [to] govern the question of recognition" and that, under the supremacy clause, such "international compacts and agreements as the Litvinov Assignment have a similar dignity" as treaties.

Does *Belmont*, against the background of *Curtiss-Wright*, support a broad autonomous presidential authority to enter into executive agreements? Or is it important to distinguish among constitutional sources for particular agreements? Is it useful to invoke the three-pronged analysis of Justice Jackson in the Steel Seizure Case? Many executive agreements fall within his category: they are adopted pursuant to statutory authority, as in trade agreements legislation, authorizing modification of tariffs through presidential agreements. The Litvinov Agreement involved in *Belmont*, by contrast, rested on the specifically delegated presidential authority regarding diplomatic recognition, in Art. II, § 3 (stating that the President "shall receive ambassadors and other public Ministers"). As to such agreements, it is arguable that Congress possesses no authority to interfere with executive power. Could Congress, under the necessary and proper clause, enact guidelines for the negotiation of executive agreements? Is there a broader inherent executive power such as that suggested in *Curtiss-Wright* that may justify executive agreements? Consider the permissible scope of executive agreements outlined in *Dames & Moore*, above.

MENACHEM BINYAMIN ZIVOTOFSKY v. JOHN KERRY
576 U.S. 1 (2015)

Justice KENNEDY delivered the opinion of the Court.

A delicate subject lies in the background of this case. That subject is Jerusalem. Questions touching upon the history of the ancient city and its present legal and international status are among the most difficult and complex in international affairs. In our constitutional system these matters are committed to the Legislature and the Executive, not the Judiciary.

As a result, in this opinion the Court does no more, and must do no more, than note the existence of international debate and tensions respecting Jerusalem. Those matters are for Congress and the President to discuss and consider as they seek to shape the Nation's foreign policies.

The Court addresses two questions to resolve the inter-branch dispute now before it. First, it must determine whether the President has the exclusive power to grant formal recognition to a foreign sovereign. Second, if he has that power, the Court must determine whether Congress can command the President and his Secretary of State to issue a formal statement that contradicts the earlier recognition. The statement in question here is a congressional mandate that allows a United States citizen born in Jerusalem to direct the President and Secretary of State, when issuing his passport, to state that his place of birth is "Israel."

I

A

Jerusalem's political standing has long been, and remains, one of the most sensitive issues in American foreign policy, and indeed it is one of the most delicate issues in current international affairs. In 1948, President Truman formally recognized Israel in a signed statement of "recognition." See Statement by the President Announcing Recognition of the State of Israel, Public Papers of the Presidents, May 14, 1948, p. 258 (1964). That statement did not recognize Israeli sovereignty over Jerusalem. Over the last 60 years, various actors have sought to assert full or partial sovereignty over the city, including Israel, Jordan, and the Palestinians. Yet, in contrast to a consistent policy of formal recognition of Israel, neither President Truman nor any later United States President has issued an official statement or declaration acknowledging any country's sovereignty over Jerusalem. Instead, the Executive Branch has maintained that "'the status of Jerusalem . . . should be decided not unilaterally but in consultation with all concerned.'" United Nations Gen. Assembly Official Records, 5th Emergency Sess., 1554th Plenary Meetings, United Nations Doc. No. 1 A/PV.1554, p. 10 (July 14, 1967); see, e.g., Remarks by President Obama in Address to the United Nations Gen. Assembly (Sept. 21, 2011), 2011 Daily Comp. of Pres. Doc. No. 00661, p. 4 ("Ultimately, it is the Israelis and the Palestinians, not us, who must reach agreement on the issues that divide them," including "Jerusalem"). In a letter to Congress then-Secretary of State Warren Christopher expressed the Executive's concern that "[t]here is no issue related to the Arab-Israeli negotiations that is more sensitive than Jerusalem." See 141 Cong. Rec. 28967 (1995) (letter to Robert Dole, Majority Leader, (June 20, 1995)). He further noted the Executive's opinion that "any effort . . . to bring it to the forefront" could be "very damaging to the success of the peace process." *Ibid.*

The President's position on Jerusalem is reflected in State Department policy regarding passports and consular reports of birth abroad. Understanding that passports will be construed as reflections of American policy, the State Department's Foreign Affairs Manual instructs its employees, in general, to record the place of birth on a passport as the "country [having] present sovereignty over the actual area of birth." Dept. of State, 7 Foreign Affairs Manual (FAM) §1383.4 (1987). If a citizen objects to the country listed as sovereign by the State Department, he or she may list the city or town of birth rather than the country. See *id.*, §1383.6. The FAM, however, does not allow citizens to list a sovereign that conflicts with Executive Branch policy. See generally *id.*, §1383. Because the United States does not recognize any country as having sovereignty over Jerusalem, the FAM instructs employees to record the place of birth for citizens born there as "Jerusalem." *Id.*, §1383.5–6 (emphasis deleted).

In 2002, Congress passed the Act at issue here, the Foreign Relations Authorization Act, Fiscal Year 2003,116 Stat. 1350. Section 214 of the Act is titled "United States Policy with Respect to Jerusalem as the Capital of Israel." *Id.*, at 1365. The subsection that lies at the heart of this case, §214(d), addresses passports. That subsection seeks to override the FAM by allowing citizens born in Jerusalem to list their place of birth as "Israel." Titled "Record of Place of Birth as Israel for Passport Purposes," §214(d) states "[f]or purposes of the registration of birth, certification of nationality, or issuance of a passport of a United States citizen born in the city of Jerusalem, the Secretary shall, upon the request of the citizen or the citizen's legal guardian, record the place of birth as Israel." *Id.*, at 1366.

When he signed the Act into law, President George W. Bush issued a statement declaring his position that §214 would, "if construed as mandatory rather than advisory, impermissibly interfere with the President's constitutional authority to formulate the position of the United States, speak for the Nation in international affairs, and determine the terms on which recognition is given to foreign states." Statement on Signing the Foreign Relations Authorization Act, Fiscal Year 2003, Public Papers of the Presidents, George W. Bush, Vol. 2, Sept. 30, 2002, p. 1698(2005). The President concluded, "U. S. policy regarding Jerusalem has not changed." *Ibid.*

[In] response [to protests from the Palestine Liberation Organization and others interested in the role of Palestinians in the peace process, eds.] the Secretary of State advised diplomats to express their understanding of "Jerusalem's importance to both sides and to many others around the world." App. 228. He noted his belief that America's "policy towards Jerusalem" had not changed. *Ibid.*

B

In 2002, petitioner Menachem Binyamin Zivotofsky was born to United States citizens living in Jerusalem. App.24–25. In December 2002, Zivotofsky's mother visited the American Embassy in Tel Aviv to request both a passport and a consular report of birth abroad for her son. *Id.*, at 25. She asked that his place of birth be listed as "'Jerusalem, Israel.'" *Ibid.* The Embassy clerks explained that, pursuant to State Department policy, the passport would list only "Jerusalem." *Ibid.* Zivotofsky's parents objected and, as his guardians, brought suit on his behalf in the United States District Court for the District of Columbia, seeking to enforce §214(d).

Pursuant to §214(d), Zivotofsky claims the right to have "Israel" recorded as his place of birth in his passport. See *Zivotofsky* v. *Clinton*, 566 U. S. ___, ___ (2012) (slip op., at 4) ("[W]hile Zivotofsky had originally asked that 'Jerusalem, Israel' be recorded on his passport, '[b]oth sides agree that the question now is whether §214(d) entitles [him] to have just 'Israel' listed' ").

[After] Zivotofsky brought suit, the District Court dismissed his case, reasoning that it presented a nonjusticiable political question and that Zivotofsky lacked standing. App. 28–39. The Court of Appeals for the District of Columbia Circuit reversed on the standing issue, *Zivotofsky* v. *Secretary of State*, 444 F. 3d 614, 617–619 (2006), but later affirmed the District Court's political question determination. See *Zivotofsky* v. *Secretary of State*, 571 F. 3d 1227, 1228 (2009).

This Court granted certiorari, vacated the judgment, and remanded the case. Whether §214(d) is constitutional, the Court held, is not a question reserved for the political branches. In reference to Zivotofsky's claim the Court observed "the Judiciary must decide if Zivotofsky's interpretation of the statute is correct, and whether the statute is constitutional"—not whether Jerusalem is, in fact, part of Israel. *Zivotofsky* v. *Clinton*, *supra*, at___ (slip op., at 7).

On remand the Court of Appeals held the statute unconstitutional. It determined that "the President exclusively holds the power to determine whether to recognize a foreign sovereign," 725 F. 3d, at 214, and that "section 214(d) directly contradicts a carefully considered exercise of the Executive branch's recognition power." *Id.*, at 217.

This Court again granted certiorari. 572 U. S. ___ (2014).

II

In considering claims of Presidential power this Court refers to Justice Jackson's familiar tripartite framework from *Youngstown Sheet & Tube Co.* v. *Sawyer*, 343 U. S. 579, 635–638 (1952) (concurring opinion). The framework divides exercises of Presidential power into three categories: First, when "the President acts pursuant to an express or implied authorization of Congress, his authority is at its maximum, for it includes all that he possesses in his own right plus all that Congress can delegate." *Id.*, at 635. Second, "in absence of either a congressional grant or denial of authority" there is a "zone of twilight in which he and Congress may have concurrent authority," and where "congressional inertia, indifference or quiescence may" invite the exercise of executive power. *Id.*, at 637. Finally, when "the President takes measures incompatible with the expressed or implied will of Congress . . . he can rely only upon his own constitutional powers minus any constitutional powers of Congress over the matter." *Ibid.* To succeed in this third category, the President's asserted power must be both "exclusive" and "conclusive" on the issue. *Id.*, at 637–638.

In this case the Secretary contends that §214(d) infringes on the President's exclusive recognition power by "requiring the President to contradict his recognition position regarding Jerusalem in official communications with foreign sovereigns."

[To] determine whether the President possesses the exclusive power of recognition the Court examines the Constitution's text and structure, as well as precedent and history bearing on the question.

A

Recognition is a "formal acknowledgement" that a particular "entity possesses the qualifications for statehood" or "that a particular regime is the effective government of a state." Restatement (Third) of Foreign Relations Law of the United States §203, Comment *a*, p. 84 (1986). It may also involve the determination of a state's territorial bounds. See 2 M. Whiteman, Digest of International Law §1, p. 1 (1963) (Whiteman) ("[S]tates may recognize or decline to recognize territory as belonging to, or under the sovereignty of, or having been acquired or lost by, other states"). Recognition is often effected by an express "written or oral declaration." 1 J. Moore, Digest of International Law §27, p. 73 (1906) (Moore). It may also be implied— for example, by concluding a bilateral treaty or by sending or receiving diplomatic agents. *Ibid.*; I. Brownlie, Principles of Public International Law 93 (7th ed. 2008)(Brownlie).

Legal consequences follow formal recognition. Recognized sovereigns may sue in United States courts, see *Guaranty Trust Co.* v. *United States*, 304 U. S. 126, 137 (1938), and may benefit from sovereign immunity when they are sued, see *National City Bank of N. Y.* v. *Republic of China*, 348 U. S. 356, 358–359 (1955). The actions of a recognized sovereign committed within its own territory also receive deference in domestic courts under the act of state doctrine. See *Oetjen* v. *Central Leather Co.*, 246 U. S. 297, 302–303 (1918). Recognition at international law, furthermore, is a precondition of regular diplomatic relations. 1 Moore §27, at 72. Recognition is thus "useful, even necessary," to the existence of a state. *Ibid.*

Despite the importance of the recognition power in foreign relations, the Constitution does not use the term "recognition," either in Article II or elsewhere. The Secretary asserts that the President exercises the recognition power based on the Reception Clause, which directs that the President "shall receive Ambassadors and other public Ministers." Art. II, §3. As Zivotofsky notes, the Reception Clause received little attention at the Constitutional Convention. See Reinstein, Recognition: A Case Study on the Original Understanding of Executive Power, 45 U.Rich. L. Rev. 801, 860–862 (2011). In fact, during the ratification debates, Alexander Hamilton claimed that the power to receive ambassadors was "more a matter of dignity than of authority," a ministerial duty largely "without consequence." The Federalist No. 69, p. 420 (C. Rossiter ed. 1961).

At the time of the founding, however, prominent international scholars suggested that receiving an ambassador was tantamount to recognizing the sovereignty of the sending state. [It] is a logical and proper inference, then, that a Clause directing the President alone to receive ambassadors would be understood to acknowledge his power to recognize other nations.

[The] inference that the President exercises the recognition power is further supported by his additional Article II powers. It is for the President, "by and with the Advice and Consent of the Senate," to "make Treaties, provided two thirds of the Senators present concur." Art. II, §2, cl. 2. In addition, "he shall nominate, and by and with the Advice and Consent of the Senate, shall appoint Ambassadors" as well as "other public Ministers and Consuls." *Ibid.*

[At] international law, recognition may be effected by different means, but each means is dependent upon Presidential power. In addition to receiving an ambassador, recognition may occur on "the conclusion of a bilateral treaty," or the "formal initiation of diplomatic relations, "including the dispatch of an ambassador. Brownlie 93; see also 1 Moore §27, at 73. The President has the sole power to negotiate treaties, see *United States v. Curtiss-Wright Export Corp.*, 299 U. S. 304, 319 (1936), and the Senate may not conclude or ratify a treaty without Presidential action. The President, too, nominates the Nation's ambassadors and dispatches other diplomatic agents. Congress may not send an ambassador without his involvement. Beyond that, the President himself has the power to open diplomatic channels simply by engaging in direct diplomacy with foreign heads of state and their ministers. The Constitution thus assigns the President means to effect recognition on his own initiative. Congress, by contrast, has no constitutional power that would enable it to initiate diplomatic relations with a foreign nation.

[The] text and structure of the Constitution grant the President the power to recognize foreign nations and governments. The question then becomes whether that power is exclusive. The various ways in which the President may unilaterally effect recognition— and the lack of any similar power vested in Congress—suggest that it is. So, too, do functional considerations. Put simply, the Nation must have a single policy regarding which governments are legitimate in the eyes of the United States and which are not. Foreign countries need to know, before entering into diplomatic relations or commerce with the United States, whether their ambassadors will be received; whether their officials will be immune from suit in federal court; and whether they may initiate lawsuits hereto vindicate their rights. These assurances cannot be equivocal.

[It] remains true, of course, that many decisions affecting foreign relations—including decisions that may determine the course of our relations with recognized countries— require congressional action. Congress may "regulate Commerce with foreign Nations," "establish an uniform Rule of Naturalization," "define and punish Piracies and Felonies committed on the high Seas, and Offences against the Law of Nations," "declare War," "grant Letters of Marque and Reprisal," and "make Rules for the Government and Regulation of the land and naval Forces." U. S. Const., Art. I, §8. In addition, the President cannot make a treaty or appoint an ambassador without the approval of the Senate. Art. II, §2, cl. 2. The President, furthermore, could not build an American Embassy abroad without congressional appropriation of the necessary funds. Art. I, §8, cl. 1. Under basic separation-of-powers principles, it is for the Congress to enact the laws, including "all Laws which shall be necessary and proper for carrying into Execution" the powers of the Federal Government. §8, cl. 18.

In foreign affairs, as in the domestic realm, the Constitution "enjoins upon its branches separateness but interdependence, autonomy but reciprocity." *Youngstown*, 343 U. S., at 635 (Jackson, J., concurring). Although the President alone effects the formal act of recognition, Congress' powers, and its central role in making laws, give it substantial authority regarding many of the policy determinations that precede and follow the act of recognition itself. If Congress disagrees with the President's recognition policy, there may be consequences. Formal recognition may seem a hollow act if it is not accompanied by the dispatch of an ambassador, the easing of trade restrictions, and the conclusion of treaties. And those decisions require action by the Senate or the whole Congress.

In practice, then, the President's recognition determination is just one part of a political process that may require Congress to make laws. The President's exclusive recognition power encompasses the authority to acknowledge, in a formal sense, the legitimacy of other states and governments, including their territorial bounds. Albeit limited, the exclusive recognition power is essential to the conduct of Presidential duties. The formal act of recognition is an executive power that Congress may not qualify. If the President is to be effective in negotiations over a formal recognition determination, it must be evident to his counterparts abroad that he speaks for the Nation on that precise question.

A clear rule that the formal power to recognize a foreign government subsists in the President therefore serves a necessary purpose in diplomatic relations. All this, of course, underscores that Congress has an important role in other aspects of foreign policy, and the President may be bound by any number of laws Congress enacts. In this way ambition counters ambition, ensuring that the democratic will of the people is observed and respected in foreign affairs as in the domestic realm. See The Federalist No. 51, p. 322 (J. Madison).

B

No single precedent resolves the question whether the President has exclusive recognition authority and, if so, how far that power extends. In part that is because, until today, the political branches have resolved their disputes over questions of recognition. The relevant cases, though providing important instruction, address the division of recognition power between the Federal Government and the States, see, *e.g., Pink*, 315 U. S. 203, or between the courts and the political branches, see, *e.g., Banco Nacional de Cuba*, 376 U. S., at 410—not between the President and Congress. As the parties acknowledge, some isolated statements in those cases lend support to the position that Congress has a role in the recognition process. In the end, however, a fair reading of the cases shows that the President's role in the recognition process is both central and exclusive.

[The Court discusses the issue of exclusivity over recognition of foreign governments by citing to *United States* v. *Belmont*, 301 U. S. 324 (1937), and *Pink*, 315 U. S. 203, two cases from the 1930s that pit New York state laws denying access to nationalized funds in New York banks to the Soviet Union, against the Presidential recognition of the Soviet

Union. The Court argues that the language in the decisions point to presidential exclusivity, even though the cases addresses state laws and not Congressional enactments.]

[The] Secretary [c]ontends that under the Court's precedent the President has "exclusive authority to conduct diplomatic relations," along with "the bulk of foreign-affairs powers." Brief for Respondent 18, 16. In support of his submission that the President has broad, undefined powers over foreign affairs, the Secretary quotes *United States* v. *Curtiss-Wright Export Corp.*, which described the President as "the sole organ of the federal government in the field of international relations." 299 U. S., at 320. This Court declines to acknowledge that unbounded power. A formulation broader than the rule that the President alone determines what nations to formally recognize as legitimate—and that he consequently controls his statements on matters of recognition—presents different issues and is unnecessary to the resolution of this case.

The *Curtiss-Wright* case does not extend so far as the Secretary suggests. In *Curtiss-Wright*, the Court considered whether a congressional delegation of power to the President was constitutional. Congress had passed a joint resolution giving the President the discretion to prohibit arms sales to certain militant powers in South America. The resolution provided criminal penalties for violation of those orders. *Id.,* at 311–312. The Court held that the delegation was constitutional, reasoning that Congress may grant the President substantial authority and discretion in the field of foreign affairs. *Id.,* at 315–329. Describing why such broad delegation may be appropriate, the opinion stated:

> "In this vast external realm, with its important, complicated, delicate and manifold problems, the President alone has the power to speak or listen as a representative of the nation. He *makes* treaties with the advice and consent of the Senate; but he alone negotiates. Into the field of negotiation the Senate cannot intrude; and Congress itself is powerless to invade it. As Marshall said in his great argument of March 7,1800, in the House of Representatives, 'The President is the sole organ of the nation in its external relations, and its sole representative with foreign nations.' [10Annals of Cong.] 613." *Id.,* at 319.

This description of the President's exclusive power was not necessary to the holding of *Curtiss-Wright*—which, after all, dealt with congressionally authorized action, not a unilateral Presidential determination. Indeed, *Curtiss-Wright* did not hold that the President is free from Congress' lawmaking power in the field of international relations. The President does have a unique role in communicating with foreign governments, as then Congressman John Marshall acknowledged. See 10 Annals of Cong. 613 (1800) (cited in *Curtiss-Wright, supra,* at 319). But whether the realm is foreign or domestic, it is still the Legislative Branch, not the Executive Branch, that makes the law.

[That] said, judicial precedent and historical practice teach that it is for the President alone to make the specific decision of what foreign power he will recognize as legitimate, both for the Nation as a whole and for the purpose of making his own position clear within the context of recognition in discussions and negotiations with foreign nations. Recognition is an act with immediate and powerful significance for international relations, so the President's position must be clear. Congress cannot require him to contradict his own statement regarding a determination of formal recognition.

[III]

As the power to recognize foreign states resides in the President alone, the question becomes whether §214(d) infringes on the Executive's consistent decision to withhold recognition with respect to Jerusalem. See *Nixon* v. *Administrator of General Services*, 433

U. S. 425, 443 (1977) (action unlawful when it "prevents the Executive Branch from accomplishing its constitutionally assigned functions").

Section 214(d) requires that, in a passport or consular report of birth abroad, "the Secretary shall, upon the request of the citizen or the citizen's legal guardian, record the place of birth as Israel" for a "United States citizen born in the city of Jerusalem." 116 Stat. 1366. That is, §214(d) requires the President, through the Secretary, to identify citizens born in Jerusalem who so request as being born in Israel. But according to the President, those citizens were not born in Israel.

[If] the power over recognition is to mean anything, it must mean that the President not only makes the initial, formal recognition determination but also that he may maintain that determination in his and his agent's statements.

[As] Justice Jackson wrote in *Youngstown*, when a Presidential power is "exclusive," it "disabl[es] the Congress from acting upon the subject." 343 U. S., at 637–638 (concurring opinion). Here, the subject is quite narrow: The Executive's exclusive power extends no further than his formal recognition determination. But as to that determination, Congress may not enact a law that directly contradicts it. This is not to say Congress may not express its disagreement with the President in myriad ways. For example, it may enact an embargo, decline to confirm an ambassador, or even declare war. But none of these acts would alter the President's recognition decision.

[Although] the statement required by §214(d) would not itself constitute a formal act of recognition, it is a mandate that the Executive contradict his prior recognition determination in an official document issued by the Secretary of State. See *Urtetiqui* v. *D'Arcy*, 9 Pet. 692, 699 (1835) (a passport "from its nature and object, is addressed to foreign powers" and "is to be considered . . . in the character of a political document"). As a result, it is unconstitutional. This is all the more clear in light of the longstanding treatment of a passport's place-of-birth section as an official executive statement implicating recognition.

* * *

In holding §214(d) invalid the Court does not question the substantial powers of Congress over foreign affairs in general or passports in particular. This case is confined solely to the exclusive power of the President to control recognition determinations, including formal statements by the Executive Branch acknowledging the legitimacy of a state or government and its territorial bounds. Congress cannot command the President to contradict an earlier recognition determination in the issuance of passports.

The judgment of the Court of Appeals for the District of Columbia Circuit is *Affirmed.*

JUSTICE BREYER, concurring.

I continue to believe that this case presents a political question inappropriate for judicial resolution. See *Zivotofsky* v. *Clinton*, 566 U. S. ___, ___ (2012) (BREYER, J., dissenting). But because precedent precludes resolving this case on political question grounds, see *id.*, at ___ (majority opinion) (slip op., at 1), I join the Court's opinion.

[An opinion by Justice Thomas, concurring in part and dissenting in part, along with dissents by Chief Justice Roberts and Justice Scalia have been omitted. Eds]

B. MILITARY AFFAIRS: THE PRESIDENT AND USE OF ARMED FORCE

The issue of the President and the use of armed force has been debated throughout our history. Though the framers well understood the need for bold and unified action during time of war, they also recognized the threat to our system of government and its guaranteed liberties by withholding from the Commander-in-Chief the power to declare war, and granting such to the Congress. The President was to be the leader in waging war, but not without an open commitment by the people as expressed through their representatives in Congress. The framers were well aware of the dangers and disaster that war reaps, and reserved this commitment to the democratic process.

The framers themselves thought the issue resolved. They felt that even with the division of the "war-making" and "war-declaring" powers, the Constitution could still meet the needs of any emergency. Madison, in Federalist No. 44, stated in relation to this question, "It is vain to oppose constitutional barriers to the impulse of self preservation . . . . this . . . plants in the Constitution itself the necessary usurpation of power . . . which is a germ." Hamilton, even though he proposed that the Senate have the sole power to declare war, later argued in Federalist No. 25, "A nation incapacitated by its Constitution to prepare for defense, before it was actually invaded," was in deep danger.

The final resolution of these issues is evident from Madison's notes taken at the Constitutional Convention:

"To make war."

Mr. Pinkney opposed the vesting this power in the Legislature. Its proceedings were too slow. It wd. meet but once a year. The Hs. of Reps. would be too numerous for such deliberations. The Senate would be the best depositary, being more acquainted with foreign affairs, and most capable of proper resolutions. If the States are equally represented in Senate, so as to give no advantage to large States, the power will notwithstanding be safe, as the small have their all at stake in such cases as well as the large States. It would be singular for one authority to make war, and another peace.

Mr. Butler. The Objections agst the Legislature lie in a great degree agst the Senate. He was for vesting the power in the President, who will have all the requisite qualities, and will not make war but when the Nation will support it.

Mr. M[adison] and Mr. Gerry moved to insert "declare," striking out "make" war; leaving to the Executive the power to repel sudden attacks.

Mr. Sharman thought it stood very well. The Executive shd. be able to repel and not to commence war. "Make" better than "declare" the latter narrowing the power too much.

Mr. Gerry never expected to hear in a republic a motion to empower the Executive alone to declare war.

Mr. Elseworth. There is a material difference between the cases of making war, and making peace. It shd. be more easy to get out of war, than into it. War also is a simple and overt declaration, peace attended with intricate & secret negotiations.

Mr. Mason was agst giving the power of war to the Executive, because not [safely] to be trusted with it; or to the Senate, because not so constructed as to be entitled to it. He was for clogging rather than facilitating war; but for facilitating peace. He preferred "declare" to "make."

On the Motion to insert declare — in place of Make, [it was agreed to.]

When Madison and Gerry interjected and moved to insert "declare," striking out "make" war, in order to allow the President to repel sudden attacks, the framers' mindset seemed clear. They sought to limit arbitrary Executive wars, but to allow the President to respond to emergency threats by repelling sudden attacks if there was not time for a congressional declaration: in other words, to allow the nation to protect itself if the need for a declaration endangered the republic.

The question advanced today is whether, with limited second chances in the nuclear age, presidential use of armed force need be expanded beyond its original intent, based upon the inherent power of the President as Commander-in-Chief? Simply put, the question is whether the President can affirmatively commit troops to battle in order to protect the national security without a congressional declaration of war. Even if such defensive power exists, is there an inherent power in the presidency to wage offensive strikes?

Dean John Hart Ely has argued that the constitutional assignment of the war declaration power to Congress was specifically designed to ensure that the decision to go to war would not be made lightly or quickly, or without public support adequate to sustain a full prosecution of the war. "What is at stake [is] the judgment that no single individual should be able to take the nation into war and thereby risk the lives of all of us, especially our young people." And, Ely argues, this constitutional requirement serves to increase the effectiveness of the nation's military commitments: "Unless Congress has unequivocally authorized a war at the outset, it is a good deal more likely later to undercut the effort." Ely advocates a strong judicial role to "induce" Congress "to discharge its constitutional responsibilities." Ely, *War and Responsibility: Constitutional Lessons of Vietnam and Its Aftermath* 4 (1993). Consider the countervailing view that efforts to have courts "pass on the legality of executive decisions to involve the nation in hostilities" would generally be "not only futile, but harmful to our national interests" because they tend "to create hard-and-fast rules in areas of overlapping authority [that] are intensely political and often require subtle handling." Or, that the "President does not act irresponsibly merely because Congress has not specifically authorized the action taken" so long as he acts "in the absence of legislative direction to the contrary," see Sofaer, "The Power over War," 50 U. Miami L. Rev. 33 (1995). Should courts resolve questions as to whether there has been adequate congressional authorization for war? Should courts view such questions as justiciable? For the view that separation of powers issues, including war powers disputes, should be nonjusticiable, see Choper, *Judicial Review and the National Political Process* (1980). For one judicial assessment, see, e.g., Dellums v. Bush, 752 F. Supp. 1141 (D.D.C. 1990).

If presidential war powers are to be restrained, is a greater assertion of congressional authority preferable to judicial intervention? In the wake of the Vietnam War (and the Watergate controversy), Congress sought to provide guidelines for the future use of armed forces. It adopted (overriding President Nixon's veto) a joint resolution, the War Powers Resolution of 1973, an unusual, structural, quasi-constitutional variety of congressional action, focusing not on substantive policy but on processes and relationships. The War Powers Resolution provides: "It is the purpose of this joint resolution to fulfill the intent of the framers of the Constitution of the United States and insure that the collective judgment of both the Congress and the President will apply to the introduction of United States Armed Forces into hostilities, or into situations where imminent involvement in hostilities is clearly indicated by the circumstances, and to the continued use of such forces in hostilities or in such situations." Its procedures specify that the President may introduce troops into hostilities pursuant only to "(1) a declaration of war, (2) specific statutory authorization, or (3) a national emergency created by attack *upon* the United States, its territories or possessions, or its armed forces;" that "[t]he President in every possible instance shall consult with Congress before introducing United States Armed Forces into hostilities" and during those hostilities; that when troops are introduced into or readied for hostilities abroad, "the President shall submit within 48 hours to the Speaker of the House of Representatives and to the President pro tempore of the Senate a report, in writing," setting forth the circumstances necessitating the introduction of armed forces, the constitutional and legislative authority therefore, and such other information as the Congress may request; and that "[w]ithin sixty calendar days after a report is submitted or is required to be submitted, [the] President shall terminate any use of United States Armed Forces with respect to which such report was submitted (or required to be submitted), unless the Congress (1) has declared war or has enacted a specific authorization for such use of United States Armed Forces, (2) has extended by law such sixty-day period, or (3) is physically unable to meet as a result of an armed attack upon the United States," a period extendable for an additional thirty days in cases of "unavoidable military necessity"; and finally, providing that at any time, forces abroad "shall be removed by President if the Congress so directs by concurrent [resolution]."

In vetoing the War Powers Resolution, President Nixon rested heavily on alleged constitutional defects, arguing that the resolution "would attempt to take away, by a mere legislative act, authorities which the President has properly exercised under the constitution for almost 200 years." He was "particularly disturbed by the fact that certain of the President's constitutional powers as Commander in Chief of the Armed Forces would terminate automatically" without congressional action. Note too that the resolution does not limit the use of armed forces to formal declarations of war but also mentions "specific statutory authorization," although it excludes mere congressional appropriations. Are the congressional "authorization[s]" recognized by the resolution constitutionally adequate alternatives for formal declarations of war? For a defense of the resolution arguing that it "is nothing more or less than a congressional definition of the word 'war' in article [that] does not intrude on any presidential prerogative," see Carter, "The Constitutionality of the War Powers Resolution," 70 Va. L. Rev. 101 (1984). For the view that the War Powers Resolution should have been even more forceful, see Ely, *War and Responsibility: Constitutional Lessons of Vietnam and Its Aftermath* (1993), elaborating the argument in Ely, "Suppose Congress Wanted a War Powers Act That Worked," 88 Colum. L. Rev. 1379 (1988), that "[in] large measure the tale of the [resolution] has been a tale of congressional spinelessness" in the face of unanticipated presidential defiance, but that this "defect can be repaired, if Congress still has the will to be held accountable."

Is the statute constitutional? Does it amend the Constitution by legislative act? Despite Nixon's assertion that it curtails the Commander-in-Chief's constitutional obligations, does it not pose an even greater conflict with the Constitution by allowing the President to commit troops to action at his will for 60 days, without a declaration of war? Some have argued that despite its intent, the Act encourages presidential war by allowing war for at least 60 to 90 days without a declaration. Further, is Congress likely to cut off funds after troops are in battle for 90 days?

Prize Cases and Judicial Review. Although the existence and scope of the President's power to use the armed forces have been controversial throughout U.S. history, the courts have rarely addressed the issue. The Supreme Court's most extensive discussion appears in The Prize Cases, 67 U.S. (2 Black) 635 (1863). At issue was the lawfulness of President Lincoln's proclamation establishing a blockade of southern ports after the secession of the southern states. The Court, in an opinion by Justice Grier, upheld the blockade. Justice Grier began his analysis by arguing that a state of war existed between the northern and southern states. "As a civil war is never publicly proclaimed, [its] actual existence is a fact in our domestic history which the Court is bound to notice and to know." Although Congress had the exclusive power to declare a national or foreign war, it could not

> declare war against a State, or any number of States, by virtue of any clause in the Constitution. The Constitution confers on the President the whole Executive power. [He] has no power to initiate or declare a war either against a foreign nation or a domestic State. But by [Acts] of Congress, [he] is authorized to [call] out the militia and use the military and naval forces of the United States in case of invasion by foreign nations, and to suppress insurrection against the government of a State or of the United States.
>
> If a war be made by invasion of a foreign nation, the President is not only authorized but bound to resist force by force. He does not initiate the war, but is bound to accept the challenge without waiting for any special legislative authority. And whether the hostile party be a foreign invader, or States organized in rebellion, it is none the less a war, although the declaration of it be "unilateral."
>
> Justice Nelson, joined by Chief Justice Taney and Justices Castrom and Clifford, dissented:
>
> By our Constitution [the] war power is lodged in Congress. . . .
>
> [It] has [been] argued that [the President's commander-in-chief power] from necessity should be construed as vesting him with the war power, or the Republic might greatly suffer or be in danger from the attacks of the hostile party before the assembling of Congress. But we have seen that the whole military and naval force are in his hands under the municipal laws of the country. He can meet the adversary upon land and water with all the forces of the Government. The truth is, this idea of the existence of any necessity for clothing the President with the war power [is] simply a monstrous exaggeration; for besides having the command of the whole of the army and navy, Congress can be assembled within thirty days, if the safety of the country requires that the war power shall be brought into operation.

The Precedent of "Presidential Wars." In the absence of authoritative judicial pronouncements, most of the "law" of war-making power has been made by the actual practice of Congress and the President. The case studies that follow illustrate this interaction in four contemporary contexts (least we also not recall the Vietnam War). With respect to each of them, consider whether the results would have been any different if the courts had played a larger role.

a. The First Persian Gulf War. On August 8, 1990, six days after Iraq invaded Kuwait, President George H.W. Bush deployed the largest American combat force since the Vietnam War to protect Saudi Arabia from an Iraqi attack. Throughout the fall, soldiers and reservists from around the nation were sent to the Persian Gulf region. In October, both the House and the Senate passed resolutions that supported the defensive operations but stopped short of declaring war. On November 8, notwithstanding the limited congressional authorization, President Bush doubled the existing 230,000 American troops in the Gulf in order to provide the United States with "an adequate offensive military operation." On November 29, at the behest of the Bush administration, the United Nations Security Council passed a resolution demanding that Iraq unconditionally withdraw from Kuwait by January 15, 1991, and authorizing member nations to "use necessary means" to free Kuwait and force Iraqi compliance.

Tensions escalated throughout the next month, and on January 8 the President formally requested Congress to pass a joint resolution supporting "the use of all necessary means" to achieve the goals of the United Nations resolution. Four days later, Congress complied. House Joint Resolution 77, 105 Stat. 3 (1991), approved the use of American military force against Iraq after January 15, provided that the President determined and reported to Congress that all diplomatic efforts had been exhausted. Five days later, on January 17, the United States and its allies unleashed Operation Desert Storm, flying over 1,400 air sorties against Iraqi targets. On February 24, the allies launched a land invasion of Kuwait. Three days later, President Bush asserted that Kuwait had been liberated and ordered a cease-fire. Iraq immediately announced that it would comply with all United Nations Security Council resolutions passed during the crisis.

Did the President have the constitutional authority to approve the buildup in Saudi Arabia without congressional approval? Would it have been constitutional for him to have launched Operation Desert Storm in the absence of House Joint Resolution 77? After President Bush's November 8 announcement of an intent to gain an offensive capability, fifty-four members of Congress filed suit to enjoin the President from ordering American forces into war "absent meaningful consultation with and genuine approval by Congress." In Dellums v. Bush, 752 F. Supp. 1141 (D.D.C. 1990), the district court rejected the plaintiffs' motion for a preliminary injunction for lack of ripeness. In the course of so holding, however, the court said that it had "no hesitation in concluding that an offensive entry into Iraq by several hundred thousand United States servicemen [could] be described as a 'war' within the meaning of [the Constitution]," and that, "in principle, an injunction may issue at the request of members of Congress to prevent the conduct of war which is about to be carried on without congressional authorization."

Was House Joint Resolution 77 constitutionally adequate to authorize Operation Desert Storm? During debate on the floor, both sponsors and opponents of the resolution spoke of it as equivalent to a declaration of war. But consider Sidak, "To Declare War," 41 Duke L.J. 29, 33, 68 (1991):

> To commence warfare on the scale witnessed against Iraq, the President needed to receive a formal declaration of war. He did not. [Although] politically significant, [the joint resolution] was a legal nullity, a merely prefatory or hortatory gesture.

For an opposing point of view, see Koh, "The Coase Theorem and the War Power: A Response," 41 Duke L.J. 122, 127 (1991):

> [Members] of Congress were painfully aware not only that they were voting on the functional equivalent of a declaration of war, but also that their votes would be intensely scrutinized. Pre-vote speeches were nationally televised, and the roll-call votes were published in every newspaper. [Given] these indicia of public accountability, it is difficult to see what additional accountability would have been gained had the resolution been styled as a declaration of war.

b. The War in Kosovo. On March 24, 1999, the United States commenced its largest military operation since the Gulf War. Americans joined a NATO air operation designed to deter and, subsequently, to reverse the "ethnic cleansing" of Kosovo, a province of Yugoslavia. Once again, the operation was undertaken without benefit of a formal congressional declaration of war.

The air strikes began after Yugoslavia's rejection of NATO demands designed to ensure Kosovo's autonomy. On March 26, 1999, President Bill Clinton submitted a formal report to Congress that, he said, was "part of my efforts to keep Congress fully informed consistent with the War Powers Resolution." In the report, he asserted that he was undertaking the action "pursuant to my constitutional authority to conduct U.S. foreign relations and as Commander-in-Chief and Chief Executive."

Congress took a number of seemingly inconsistent actions with regard to the war. On March 23, 1999, the Senate passed a resolution authorizing the President to conduct military air operations in Yugoslavia, but the House rejected a similar measure in a tie vote on April 28, 1999. On the same day, the House defeated a measure declaring a state of war between the United States and Yugoslavia and a measure directing the President to remove all U.S. armed forces from the operations against Yugoslavia, but adopted a measure prohibiting the use of funds for the deployment of ground troops. On May 6, 1999, the House passed a measure providing emergency funding for the war.

On April 30, 1999, several members of Congress filed suit in U.S. district court seeking a declaratory judgment that the Kosovo action was unconstitutional without a congressional declaration of war and that under § 1544(b) of the War Powers Resolution, the President was obligated to terminate hostilities within sixty calendar days of his report to Congress. In Campbell v. Clinton, 203 F.3d 19 (D.C. Cir. 2000), decided after hostilities had ended, the court held that the plaintiffs lacked standing to maintain the action. Should the court have considered the claim? If so, how should it have ruled on the merits?

c. The War on Terrorism. On September 18, 2001, Congress enacted a joint resolution, granting President George W. Bush authority to

> use all necessary and appropriate force against those nations, organizations, or persons he determines planned, authorized, committed, or aided the terrorist attacks that occurred on September 11, 2001, or harbored such organizations or persons, in order to prevent any future acts of international terrorism against the United States by such nations, organizations or persons. [Joint Resolution of Congress Authorizing the Use of Force, Pub. L. No. 107-40, 115 Stat. 224 (2001).]

Is the joint resolution the equivalent of a declaration of war? If not, why did Congress avoid an official declaration of war? Senate Foreign Relations Committee Chairman Joseph Biden stated that the resolution was "the constitutional equivalent of a declaration of war." Turner, "The War on Terrorism and the Modern Relevance of the Congressional Power to Declare War," 25 Harv. J. of Law & Pol. 519, 521 (2002).) Representative Conyers stated that "[by] not declaring war the resolution preserves our precious civil liberties" and that "[this] is important because declarations of war trigger broad statutes that not only criminalize interference with troops and recruitment but also authorize the President to apprehend 'alien enemies.'" Katyal & Tribe, "Waging War, Deciding Guilt: Trying the Military Tribunals," 111 Yale L.J. 1259, 1285 (2002).

Whom is the war being waged against? Does a declared war require an end by treaty, subject to ratification by the Senate? Is there some comparable event that will demarcate the end of the war against terrorism? How will we know when the war is over? Paulsen, in "Youngstown Goes to War," 19 Const. Com. 215 (2002), acknowledges that the Joint Resolution constitutes "a truly extraordinary congressional grant to the President of extraordinary discretion in the use of military power for an indefinite period of time." Yet he concludes that Congress's position articulated in the resolution is within the "twilight zone" described in Justice Jackson's *Youngstown* concurrence. Congress's September 18, 2001, resolution stipulates that "the President has authority under the Constitution to take action to deter and prevent acts of international terrorism against the United States — is a legitimate and constitutionally proper one."

Notice that the Resolution authorizes military action only with respect to those involved in the destruction of the World Trade Center. Does the President have constitutional authority to conduct a broader "war" against alleged terrorists not associated with that attack?

d. The War in Iraq. On October 16, 2002, Congress enacted the following resolution:

(a) Authorization. The President is authorized to use the Armed Forces of the United States as he determines to be necessary and appropriate in order to (1) defend the national security of the United States against the continuing threat posed by Iraq; and (2) enforce all relevant United Nations Security Council resolutions regarding Iraq.

(b) Presidential Determination. In connection with the exercise of the authority granted in subsection (a) to use force the President shall, prior to such exercise or as soon thereafter as may be feasible, but no later than 48 hours after exercising such authority, make available to the Speaker of the House of Representatives and the President pro tempore of the Senate his determination that (1) reliance by the United States on further diplomatic or other peaceful means alone either (A) will not adequately protect the national security of the United States against the continuing threat posed by Iraq or (B) is not likely to lead to enforcement of all relevant United Nations Security Council resolutions regarding Iraq; and (2) acting pursuant to this joint resolution is consistent with the United States and other countries continuing to take the necessary actions against international terrorist and terrorist organizations, including those nations, organizations, or persons who planned, authorized, committed or aided the terrorist attacks that occurred on September 11, 2001.

(c) War Powers Resolution Requirements.

(1) Specific Statutory Authorization. Consistent with section [1547(A)(1)] of the War Powers Resolution, the Congress declares that this section is intended to constitute specific statutory authorization within the meaning of section [1544(B)] of the War Powers Resolution.

(2) Applicability of Other Requirements. Nothing in this joint resolution supersedes any requirement of the War Powers Resolution. Authorization for Use of Military Force against Iraq Resolution of 2002, PL 107-243, 116 Stat. 1498 (2002).

Months later, acting pursuant to this authority, the President committed American military forces to Iraq. Does a congressional authorization for military action at some point in the indefinite future constitute a declaration of war within the meaning of Article I, §8? Consider in this regard the implications of United States v. Curtiss-Wright Corp., above. If the Use of Military Force Resolution is not a declaration of war, does the War Powers Resolution make the President's actions legal?

Final Comment on Presidential Use of Armed Force. The question posed after the Vietnam debacle was how can we avoid "one-person presidential wars"? Is a compromise that allows such wars to start, either tenable or constitutional? Can we rely on the courts or Congress to curtail such actions? Is the problem, as Madison forewarned, not letting presidential wars even start, so the "germ will not spread"? Should a congressional declaration be required for all such actions as the Constitution and the framers appear to stipulate? Yet, does this allow for adequate defense in the nuclear age? Are things so different from the time of the founding of the country? After all, the framers realized that action might be necessary for self-defense ("to repel sudden attack"), but stipulated that in order to preserve our freedoms that the Congress must declare war. Can we conclude that the issue was resolved by the Constitution, and should we not live up to its principle? Is this entire problem simply another outgrowth of the "Imperial Presidency" and the disregard of the balance of powers retained in the Constitution? If the Constitution is antedated in regard to these issues, are we not better off amending it rather than getting around its text and intent for contemporary convenience? If we do not, where does this type of "convenient" constitutional interpretation stop once started? Many Justices who labor to discover "original intent" change "their shoes" on this issue.

Was Lincoln correct when he forewarned in response to the Mexican war, "Allow the President to invade a neighboring nation, whenever he shall deem it necessary to repel an invasion and you allow him to make war at pleasure. Study to see if you can fix any limit to his power in this respect." How could you stop him? Lincoln hypothesized, "You may say to him, 'I see no probability of the British invading us' but he will say to you be silent; I see it, if you don't." To Lincoln, the Constitution resolved that "no one man should hold the power of bringing this oppression upon us." Are contemporary needs so different from the age of Lincoln? Does he not speak to the same issues that are pressed upon us today as new demands, beyond the anticipation of the framers, that call for reallocation of power?

III. SEPARATION OF POWERS

In designing the structure of our Government and dividing and allocating the sovereign power among three co-equal branches, the Framers of the Constitution sought to provide a comprehensive system, but the separate powers were not intended to operate with absolute independence. [United States v. Nixon, 418 U.S. 683, 708 (1974).]

The constitutional "balance of power" is an outgrowth of our system of separation of powers. The framers sought this separation between three co-equal branches to limit "autocratic" centralization of power in one branch. Madison, in Federalist Nos. 47 and 48, articulated the framers' purpose in such a system. In advancing the concept of "separate powers," Madison drew upon the philosophy of Montesquieu, and in Federalist No. 47 he made citation to Montesquieu's famous statement, "There can be no liberty where the legislative and executive powers are united in the same person, or body of magistrates" or "if the power of judging be not separated from the legislative and executive powers. . . ."

Nonetheless, the framers were also well aware of the need for the three branches to coordinate and work together to achieve efficient government. They recognized that "separate power" could lead to one of the branches attempting to centralize its authority at the sake of the others. Control of these separate powers was to be preserved and maintained by a system of "checks and balances" between the branches. In Madison's own words, "The several departments of power are distributed and blended in such a manner as at once to destroy all symmetry and beauty of form, and to expose some of the essential parts of the edifice to the danger of being crushed by the disproportionate weight of other parts." Federalist No. 47, 336. Consequently, the separate powers allocated to each branch were made dependent, for operative effect, on powers resting in another branch. This was to ensure that the units would have to work and function together in order to govern, as well as to ensure that no one branch would attempt to assert control over the others. The framers hoped that a grasp for power by one branch against another would be limited by these checks and balances.

The importance of "blended, separate powers" to the operation of government is evident by Madison forewarning in Federalist No. 48 that "unless these departments be so far connected and blended as to give each a constitutional control over the others, the degree of separation which the maxim requires, as essential to free government, can never in practice be duly maintained."

The materials in this section will highlight several of the most significant power-based "clashes" between the coordinate branches: legislative veto, impoundment, control of executive personnel, and executive privilege. (Note that our previous discussion of the "war power," as between Congress and the President, could be included within these materials as well, with particular reference to the War Powers Act.) It is also worth mentioning that these "clashes" are often the result of Congress and the President trying to achieve "workable government" when they feel that the Constitution is antiquated in terms of contemporary needs. The Supreme Court has been active in policing the needs of workable government, particularly when they confront what the Court views as constitutional mandates to the contrary.

A. LEGISLATIVE VETO

INS v. CHADHA
462 U.S. 919 (1983)

Chief Justice BURGER delivered the opinion of the Court.

Chadha is an East Indian who was born in Kenya and holds a British passport. He was lawfully admitted to the United States in 1966 on a nonimmigrant student visa. His visa expired on June 30, 1972. On October 11, 1973, the District Director of the Immigration and Naturalization Service ordered Chadha to show cause why he should not be deported for having "remained in the United States for a longer time than permitted." [After a hearing, an immigration judge ordered] that Chadha's deportation be suspended. The immigration judge found that Chadha met the requirements of [the statute]: he had resided continuously in the United States for over seven years, was of good moral character, and would suffer "extreme hardship" if deported. Pursuant to [the statute the] immigration judge suspended Chadha's deportation and a report of the suspension was transmitted to Congress.

Once the Attorney General's recommendation for suspension of Chadha's deportation was conveyed to Congress, Congress had the power under [the statute to] veto the Attorney General's determination that Chadha should not be deported. . . .

On December 12, 1975, Representative Eilberg, Chairman of the Judiciary Subcommittee on Immigration, Citizenship, and International Law, introduced a resolution opposing "the granting of permanent residence in the United States to [six] aliens," including Chadha. [The] resolution was passed without debate or recorded vote. Since the House action was pursuant to [the statute] the resolution was not treated as an Article I legislative act; it was not submitted to the Senate or presented to the President for his action.

After the House veto of the Attorney General's decision to allow Chadha to remain in the United States, the immigration judge reopened the deportation proceedings and [Chadha] was ordered deported pursuant to the House action. . .

We turn now to the question whether action of one House of Congress under [the statute] violates strictures of the Constitution. [The] fact that a given law or procedure is efficient, convenient, and useful in facilitating functions of the government, standing alone, will not save it if it is contrary to the Constitution. Convenience and efficiency are not the primary objectives — or the hallmarks — of democratic government and our inquiry is sharpened rather than blunted by the fact that Congressional veto provisions are appearing with increasing frequency in statutes which delegate authority to executive and independent agencies: Since 1932, when the first veto provision was enacted into law, 295 congressional veto-type procedures have been inserted in 196 different statutes as follows: from 1932 to 1939, five statutes were affected; from 1940-49, nineteen statutes; between 1950-59, thirty-four statutes; and from 1960-69, forty-nine. From the year 1970 through 1975, at least one hundred sixty-three such provisions were included in eighty-nine laws.

Justice White undertakes to make a case for the proposition that the one-House veto is a useful "political invention." [But] policy arguments supporting even useful "political inventions" are subject to the demands of the Constitution which defines powers and, with respect to this subject, sets out just how those powers are to be exercised.

Explicit and unambiguous provisions of the Constitution prescribe and define the respective functions of the Congress and of the Executive in the legislative process. [Article] I provides: All legislative Powers herein granted shall be vested in a Congress of the United States, which shall consist of a Senate and a House of Representatives. Art. I, §1. Every Bill which shall have passed the House of Representatives and the Senate, shall, before it becomes a Law, be presented to the President of the United States; . . . Art. I, §7, cl. 2. Every Order, Resolution, or Vote to which the Concurrence of the Senate and House of Representatives may be necessary (except on a question of Adjournment) shall be presented to the President of the United States; and before the Same shall take Effect, shall be approved by him, or being disapproved by him, shall be repassed by two thirds of the Senate and House of Representatives, according to the Rules and Limitations prescribed in the Case of a Bill. Art. I, §7, cl. 3.

These provisions of Art. I are integral parts of the constitutional design for the separation of powers. . . . The records of the Constitutional Convention reveal that the requirement that all legislation be presented to the President before becoming law was uniformly accepted by the Framers. . . . The decision to provide the President with a limited and qualified power to nullify proposed legislation by veto was based on the profound conviction of the Framers that the powers conferred on Congress were the powers to be most carefully circumscribed. . . .

The bicameral requirement of Art. I, §§1, 7 was of scarcely less concern to the Framers than was the Presidential veto and indeed the two concepts are interdependent. By providing that no law could take effect without the concurrence of the prescribed majority of the Members of both Houses, the Framers reemphasized their belief [that] legislation should not be enacted unless it has been carefully and fully considered by the Nation's elected officials. . . .

We see therefore that the Framers were acutely conscious that the bicameral requirement and the Presentment Clauses would serve essential constitutional functions. [It] emerges clearly that the prescription for legislative action in Art. I, §§1, 7 represents the Framers' decision that the legislative power of the Federal government be exercised in accord with a single, finely wrought and exhaustively considered, procedure.

[When] the Executive acts, it presumptively acts in an executive or administrative capacity as defined in Art. II. And when, as here, one House of Congress purports to act, it is presumptively acting within its assigned sphere. Beginning with this presumption, we must nevertheless establish that the challenged action under [the statute] is of the kind to which the procedural requirements of Art. I, §7 apply. Not every action taken by either House is subject to the bicameralism and presentment requirements of Art. I. [Whether] actions taken by either House are, in law and fact, an exercise of legislative power depends not on their form but upon "whether they contain matter which is properly to be regarded as legislative in its character and effect." . . .

Examination of the action taken here by one House [reveals] that it was essentially legislative in purpose and effect. In purporting to exercise power defined in Art. I, §8, cl. 4 to "establish an uniform Rule of Naturalization," the House took action that had the purpose and effect of altering the legal rights, duties and relations of persons, including the Attorney General, Executive Branch officials and Chadha, all outside the legislative branch. [The] one-House veto operated in this case to overrule the Attorney General and mandate Chadha's deportation; absent the House action, Chadha would remain in the United States. Congress has acted and its action has altered Chadha's status.

The legislative character of the one-House veto in this case is confirmed by the character of the Congressional action it supplants. Neither the House of Representatives nor the Senate contends that, absent the veto provision, [either] of them, or both of them acting together, could effectively require the Attorney General to deport an alien once the Attorney General, in the exercise of legislatively delegated authority, 16 had determined the alien should remain in the United States. Without the challenged provision, [this] could have been achieved, if at all, only by legislation requiring deportation. . . .

The nature of the decision implemented by the one-House veto in this case further manifests its legislative character. After long experience with the clumsy, time consuming private bill procedure, Congress made a deliberate choice to delegate to the Executive Branch, [the] authority to allow deportable aliens to remain in this country in certain specified circumstances. It is not disputed that this choice to delegate authority is precisely the kind of decision that can be implemented only in accordance with the procedures set out in Art. I. Disagreement with the Attorney General's decision on Chadha's deportation — that is, Congress' decision to deport Chadha — no less than Congress' original choice to delegate to the Attorney General the authority to make that decision, involves determinations of policy that Congress can implement in only one way, bicameral passage followed by presentment to the President. Congress must abide by its delegation of authority until that delegation is legislatively altered or revoked.

Finally, we see that when the Framers intended to authorize either House of Congress to act alone and outside of its prescribed bicameral legislative role, they narrowly and precisely defined the procedure for such action. There are but four provisions in the Constitution, explicit and unambiguous, by which one House may act alone with the unreviewable force of law, not subject to the President's veto.

[The House's power to initiate impeachments, the Senate's power to conduct trials following impeachment, the Senate's power over presidential appointments, and the Senate's power to ratify treaties.]

[These provisions give] further support for the conclusion that Congressional authority is not to be implied. . . . The choices we discern as having been made in the Constitutional Convention impose burdens on governmental processes that often seem clumsy, inefficient, even unworkable, but those hard choices were consciously made by men who had lived under a form of government that permitted arbitrary governmental acts to go unchecked. There is no support in the Constitution or decisions of this Court for the proposition that the cumbersomeness and delays often encountered in complying with explicit Constitutional standards may be avoided, either by the Congress or by the President. See [Youngstown]. With all the obvious flaws of delay, untidiness, and potential for abuse, we have not yet found a better way to preserve freedom than by making the exercise of power subject to the carefully crafted restraints spelled out in the Constitution.

We hold that the Congressional veto provision [is unconstitutional]. Accordingly, the judgment of the Court of Appeals is affirmed.

Justice POWELL, concurring in the judgment.

On its face, the House's action appears clearly adjudicatory. The House did not enact a general rule; rather it made its own determination that six specific persons did not comply with certain statutory criteria. It thus undertook the type of decision that traditionally has been left to other branches.

The impropriety of the House's assumption of this function is confirmed by the fact that its action raises the very danger the Framers sought to avoid — the exercise of unchecked power. In deciding whether Chadha deserves to be deported, Congress is not subject to any internal constraints that prevent it from arbitrarily depriving him of the right to remain in this country. Unlike the judiciary or an administrative agency, Congress is not bound by established substantive rules. Nor is it subject to the procedural safeguards, such as the right to counsel and a hearing before an impartial tribunal, that are present when a court or an agency adjudicates individual rights. The only effective constraint on Congress' power is political, but Congress is most accountable politically when it prescribes rules of general applicability. When it decides rights of specific persons, those rights are subject to "the tyranny of a shifting majority."

[In] my view, when Congress undertook to apply its rules to Chadha, it exceeded the scope of its constitutionally prescribed authority. I would not reach the broader question whether legislative vetoes are invalid under the Presentment Clauses.

Justice WHITE, dissenting.

Today the Court not only invalidates §244(c)(2) of the Immigration and Nationality Act, but also sounds the death knell for nearly 200 other statutory provisions in which Congress has reserved a "legislative veto." For this reason, the Court's decision is of surpassing importance. And it is for this reason that the Court would have been well-advised to decide the case, if possible, on the narrower grounds of separation of powers, leaving for full consideration the constitutionality of other congressional review statutes operating on such varied matters as war powers and agency rulemaking, some of which concern the independent regulatory agencies.

The prominence of the legislative veto mechanism in our contemporary political system and its importance to Congress can hardly be overstated. It has become a central means by which Congress secures the accountability of executive and independent agencies. Without the legislative veto, Congress is faced with a Hobson's choice: either to refrain from delegating the necessary authority, leaving itself with a hopeless task of writing laws with the requisite specificity to cover endless special circumstances across the entire policy landscape, or in the alternative, to abdicate its lawmaking function to the executive branch and independent agencies. To choose the former leaves major national problems unresolved; to opt for the latter risks unaccountable policymaking by those not elected to fill that role. Accordingly, over the past five decades, the legislative veto has been placed in nearly 200 statutes. The device is known in every field of governmental concern: reorganization, budgets, foreign affairs, war powers, and regulation of trade, safety, energy, the environment and the economy.

[Justice White summarized the history of the legislative veto, noting that it was a response to "the sprawling government structure" created after the Depression; that it "balanced delegations of statutory authority in new areas"; and that it played an important role in disputes in the 1970s over impoundment, war, and national emergency powers.]

Even this brief review suffices to demonstrate that the legislative veto [is an] important if not indispensable political invention that allows the President and Congress to resolve major constitutional and policy differences, assures the accountability of independent regulatory agencies, and preserves Congress' control over lawmaking. . . .

The history of the legislative veto also makes clear that it has not been a sword with which Congress has struck out to aggrandize itself at the expense of the other branches — the concerns of Madison and Hamilton. Rather, the veto has been a means of defense, a reservation of ultimate authority necessary if Congress is to fulfill its designated role under Article I as the nation's lawmaker. While the President has often objected to particular legislative vetoes, generally those left in the hands of congressional committees, the Executive has more often agreed to legislative review as the price for a broad delegation of authority. To be sure, the President may have preferred unrestricted power, but that could be precisely why Congress thought it essential to retain a check on the exercise of delegated authority. . . .

[The] Constitution does not directly authorize or prohibit the legislative veto. Thus, our task should be to determine whether the legislative veto is consistent with the purposes of Art. I and the principles of Separation of Powers. [We] should not find the lack of a specific constitutional authorization for the legislative veto surprising, and I would not infer disapproval of the mechanism from its absence. From the summer of 1787 to the present the government of the United States has become an endeavor far beyond the contemplation of the Framers. Only within the last half century has the complexity and size of the Federal Government's responsibilities grown so greatly that the Congress must rely on the legislative veto as the most effective if not the only means to insure their role as the nation's lawmakers. But the wisdom of the Framers was to anticipate that the nation would grow and new problems of governance would require different solutions. Accordingly, our Federal Government was intentionally chartered with the flexibility to respond to contemporary needs without losing sight of fundamental democratic principles. . . .

[The presentment and bicameralism requirements do] not [answer] the constitutional question before us. The power to exercise a legislative veto is not the power to write new law without bicameral approval or presidential consideration. The veto must be authorized by statute and may only negative what an Executive department or independent agency has proposed. On its face, the legislative veto no more allows one House of Congress to make law than does the presidential veto confer such power upon the President. Accordingly, the Court properly recognizes that it "must establish that the challenged action [is] of the kind to which the procedural requirements of Art. I, §7 apply." . . .

The terms of the Presentment Clauses suggest only that bills and their equivalent are subject to the requirements of bicameral passage and presentment to the President.

Although the Clause does not specify the actions for which the concurrence of both Houses is "necessary," the proceedings at the Philadelphia Convention suggest its purpose was to prevent Congress from circumventing the presentation requirement in the making of new legislation. . . .

When the Convention did turn its attention to the scope of Congress' lawmaking power, the Framers were expansive. The Necessary and Proper Clause, Art. I, §8, cl. 18, vests Congress with the power "to make all laws which shall be necessary and proper for carrying into Execution the foregoing Powers [the enumerated powers of §8], and all other Powers vested by this Constitution in the government of the United States, or in any Department or Officer thereof." It is long-settled that Congress may "exercise its best judgment in the selection of measures, to carry into execution the constitutional powers of the government," and "avail itself of experience, to exercise its reason, and to accommodate its legislation to circumstances." [McCulloch.]

The Court heeded this counsel in approving the modern administrative state. The Court's holding today that all legislative type action must be enacted through the lawmaking process ignores that legislative authority is routinely delegated to the Executive Branch, to the independent regulatory agencies, and to private individuals and groups. "The rise of administrative bodies probably has been the most significant legal trend of the last century. . . . They have become a veritable fourth branch of the Government, which has deranged our three-branch legal theories. . . ."

This Court's decisions sanctioning such delegations make clear that Article I does not require all action with the effect of legislation to be passed as a law.

Theoretically, agencies and officials were asked only to "fill up the details," and the rule was that "Congress cannot delegate any part of its legislative power except under a limitation of a prescribed standard." In practice, however, restrictions on the scope of the power that could be delegated diminished and all but disappeared. . . .

The wisdom and the constitutionality of these broad delegations are matters that still have not been put to rest. But for present purposes, these cases establish that by virtue of congressional delegation, legislative power can be exercised by independent agencies and Executive departments without the passage of new legislation. For some time, the sheer amount of law — the substantive rules that regulate private conduct and direct the operation of government — made by the agencies has far outnumbered the lawmaking engaged in by Congress through the traditional process. There is no question but that agency rulemaking is lawmaking in any functional or realistic sense of the term.

If Congress may delegate lawmaking power to independent and executive agencies, it is most difficult to understand Article I as forbidding Congress from also reserving a check on Legislative power for itself. Absent the veto, the agencies receiving delegations of legislative or quasi-legislative power may issue regulations having the force of law without bicameral approval and without the President's signature. It is thus not apparent why the reservation of a veto over the exercise of that legislative power must be subject to a more exacting test. In both cases, it is enough that the initial statutory authorizations comply with the Article I requirements. . . .

Nor are there strict limits on the agents that may receive such delegations of legislative authority so that it might be said that the legislature can delegate authority to others but not to itself. While most authority to issue rules and regulations is given to the executive branch and the independent regulatory agencies, statutory delegations to private persons have also passed this Court's scrutiny. [More] fundamentally, even if the Court correctly characterizes the Attorney General's authority under [the statute] as an Article II Executive power, the Court concedes that certain administrative agency action, such as rulemaking, "may resemble lawmaking" and recognizes that "[t]his Court has referred to agency activity as being 'quasi-legislative' in character." [Such] rules and adjudications by the agencies meet the Court's own definition of legislative action for they "alter[ ] the legal rights, duties, and relations of persons . . . outside the legislative branch," and involve "determinations of policy." Under the Court's analysis, the Executive Branch and the independent agencies may make rules with the effect of law while Congress, in whom the Framers confided the legislative power, Art. I, §1, may not exercise a veto which precludes such rules from having operative force. If the effective functioning of a complex modern government requires the delegation of vast authority which, by virtue of its breadth, is legislative or "quasi-legislative" in character, I cannot accept that Article I — which is, after all, the source of the non-delegation doctrine — should forbid Congress from qualifying that grant with a legislative veto.

The Court also takes no account of perhaps the most relevant consideration: However resolutions of disapproval under [the statute] are formally characterized, in reality, a departure from the status quo occurs only upon the concurrence of opinion among the House, Senate, and President. Reservations of legislative authority to be exercised by Congress should be upheld if the exercise of such reserved authority is consistent with the distribution of and limits upon legislative power that Article I provides. . . .

[Justice White argued that the veto "did not alter the division of actual authority between Congress and the executive," since a change in the alien's legal status could occur only with the concurrence of the President and both Houses. Thus, the purposes of the presentment and bicameralism requirements were satisfied.]

[The] history of the separation of powers doctrine is also a history of accommodation and practicality. Apprehensions of an overly powerful branch have not led to undue prophylactic measures that handicap the effective working of the national government as a whole. The Constitution does not contemplate total separation of the three branches of Government.

[The] legislative veto provision does not "prevent the Executive Branch from accomplishing its constitutionally assigned functions." First, it is clear that the Executive Branch has no "constitutionally assigned" function of suspending the deportation of aliens. " 'Over no conceivable subject is the legislative power of Congress more complete than it is over' the admission of aliens."

Moreover, the Court believes that the legislative veto [is] best characterized as an exercise of legislative or quasi-legislative authority. Under this characterization, the practice does not, even on the surface, constitute an infringement of executive or judicial prerogative. The Attorney General's suspension of deportation is equivalent to a proposal for legislation. . . .

Nor does [the statute] infringe on the judicial power, as Justice Powell would hold. [The statute] makes clear that Congress has reserved its own judgment as part of the statutory process. Congressional action does not substitute for judicial review of the Attorney General's decisions. . . . I do not suggest that all legislative vetoes are necessarily consistent with separation of powers principles. A legislative check on an inherently executive function, for example that of initiating prosecutions, poses an entirely different question. But the legislative veto device here — and in many other settings — is far from an instance of legislative tyranny over the Executive. It is a necessary check on the unavoidably expanding power of the agencies, both executive and independent, as they engage in exercising authority delegated by Congress.

[The court's decision] reflects a profoundly different conception of the Constitution than that held by the Courts which sanctioned the modern administrative state. Today's decision strikes down in one fell swoop provisions in more laws enacted by Congress than the Court has cumulatively invalidated in its history. I fear it will now be more difficult "to insure that the fundamental policy decisions in our society will be made not by an appointed official but by the body immediately responsible to the people," Arizona v. California, 373 U.S. 546, 625 (1963) (Harlan, J., dissenting). I must dissent.

[Justice Rehnquist dissented on the ground that the legislative veto provision was not severable.]

B. IMPOUNDMENT

CLINTON v. CITY OF NEW YORK
524 U.S. 417 (1998)

[City, health-care providers, unions, and farmers' cooperatives, and individual members commenced separate actions challenging the constitutionality of the Line Item Veto Act after President Clinton exercised his authority under the Act to cancel provisions of the Balanced Budget Act and Taxpayer Relief Act. The United States District Court for the District of Columbia, 985 F. Supp. 168, entered an order holding that the Line Item Veto Act was unconstitutional. On expedited appeal, the Supreme Court held that the Line Item Veto Act violated the Presentment Clause by departing from "finely wrought" constitutional procedure for enactment of law.]

Justice STEVENS delivered the opinion of the Court.

The Line Item Veto Act (Act), 110 Stat. 1200, 2 U.S.C. § 691 *et seq.* (1994 ed., Supp. II), was enacted in April 1996 and became effective on January 1, 1997. The following day, six Members of Congress who had voted against the Act brought suit in the District Court for the District of Columbia challenging its constitutionality. On April 10, 1997, the District Court entered an order holding that the Act is unconstitutional. *Byrd v. Raines,* 956 F.Supp. 25 (D.D.C.1997). In obedience to the statutory direction to allow a direct, expedited appeal to this Court, see §§ 692(b)-(c), we promptly noted probable jurisdiction and expedited review, 520 U.S. 1194, 117 S.Ct. 1489, 137 L.Ed.2d 699 (1997). We determined, however, that the Members of Congress did not have standing to sue because they had not "alleged a sufficiently concrete injury to have established Article III standing," *Raines v. Byrd,* 521 U.S. 811, 830, 117 S.Ct. 2312, 2322, 138 L.Ed.2d 849 (1997); thus, "[i]n . . . light of [the] overriding and time-honored concern about keeping the Judiciary's power within its proper constitutional sphere," *id.,* at 820, 117 S.Ct., at 2318, we remanded the case to the District Court with instructions to dismiss the complaint for lack of jurisdiction.

Less than two months after our decision in that case, the President exercised his authority to cancel one provision in the Balanced Budget Act of 1997, Pub.L. 105-33, 111 Stat. 251, 515, and two provisions in the Taxpayer Relief Act of 1997, Pub.L. 105-34, 111 Stat. 788, 895-896, 990-993. Appellees, claiming that they had been injured by two of those cancellations, filed these cases in the District Court. That Court again held the statute invalid, 985 F.Supp. 168, 177-182 (1998), and we again expedited our review, 522 U.S. 1144, 118 S.Ct. 1123, 140 L.Ed.2d 172 (1998). We now hold that these appellees have standing to challenge the constitutionality of the Act and, reaching the merits, we agree that the cancellation procedures set forth in the Act violate the Presentment Clause, Art. I, § 7, cl. 2, of the Constitution.

The Line Item Veto Act gives the President the power to "cancel in whole" three types of provisions that have been signed into law: "(1) any dollar amount of discretionary budget authority; (2) any item of new direct spending; or (3) any limited tax benefit." In identifying items for cancellation he must consider the legislative history, the purposes, and other relevant information about the items. He must determine, with respect to each cancellation, that it will "(i) reduce the Federal budget deficit; (ii) not impair any essential Government functions; and (iii) not harm the national interest." Moreover, he must transmit a special message to Congress notifying it of each cancellation within five calendar days (excluding Sundays) after the enactment of the canceled provision. It is undisputed that the President meticulously followed these procedures in these cases.

A cancellation takes effect upon receipt by Congress of the special message from the President. See § 691b(a). If, however, a "disapproval bill" pertaining to a special message is enacted into law, the cancellations set forth in that message become "null and void." *Ibid.* The Act sets forth a detailed expedited procedure for the consideration of a "disapproval bill," see § 691d, but no such bill was passed for either of the cancellations involved in these cases. A majority vote of both Houses is sufficient to enact a disapproval bill. The Act does not grant the President the authority to cancel a disapproval bill, see § 691(c), but he does, of course, retain his constitutional authority to veto such a bill.

In both legal and practical effect, the President has amended two Acts of Congress by repealing a portion of each. "[R]epeal of statutes, no less than enactment, must conform with Art. I." *INS v. Chadha*, 462 U.S. 919, 954, 103 S.Ct. 2764, 2785-2786, 77 L.Ed.2d 317 (1983). There is no provision in the Constitution that authorizes the President to enact, to amend, or to repeal statutes. Both Article I and Article II assign responsibilities to the President that directly relate to the lawmaking process, but neither addresses the issue presented by these cases. The President "shall from time to time give to the Congress Information on the State of the Union, and recommend to their Consideration such Measures as he shall judge necessary and expedient. . . ." Art. II, § 3. Thus, he may initiate and influence legislative proposals. Moreover, after a bill has passed both Houses of Congress, but "before it become[s] a Law," it must be presented to the President. If he approves it, "he shall sign it, but if not he shall return it, with his Objections to that House in which it shall have originated, who shall enter the Objections at large on their Journal, and proceed to reconsider it." Art. I, § 7, cl. 2. His "return" of a bill, which is usually described as a "veto," is subject to being overridden by a two-thirds vote in each House.

There are important differences between the President's "return" of a bill pursuant to Article I, § 7, and the exercise of the President's cancellation authority pursuant to the Line Item Veto Act. The constitutional return takes place *before* the bill becomes law; the statutory cancellation occurs *after* the bill becomes law. The constitutional return is of the entire bill; the statutory cancellation is of only a part. Although the Constitution expressly authorizes the President to play a role in the process of enacting statutes, it is silent on the subject of unilateral Presidential action that either repeals or amends parts of duly enacted statutes.

There are powerful reasons for construing constitutional silence on this profoundly important issue as equivalent to an express prohibition. The procedures governing the enactment of statutes set forth in the text of Article I were the product of the great debates and compromises that produced the Constitution itself. Familiar historical materials provide abundant support for the conclusion that the power to enact statutes may only "be exercised in accord with a single, finely wrought and exhaustively considered, procedure." *Chadha*, 462 U.S., at 951, 103 S.Ct., at 2784. Our first President understood the text of the

Presentment Clause as requiring that he either "approve all the parts of a Bill, or reject it in toto." What has emerged in these cases from the President's exercise of his statutory cancellation powers, however, are truncated versions of two bills that passed both Houses of Congress. They are not the product of the "finely wrought" procedure that the Framers designed.

The Government advances two related arguments to support its position that despite the unambiguous provisions of the Act, cancellations do not amend or repeal properly enacted statutes in violation of the Presentment Clause. First, relying primarily on *Field v. Clark*, 143 U.S. 649, 12 S.Ct. 495, 36 L.Ed. 294 (1892), the Government contends that the cancellations were merely exercises of discretionary authority granted to the President by the Balanced Budget Act and the Taxpayer Relief Act read in light of the previously enacted Line Item Veto Act. Second, the Government submits that the substance of the authority to cancel tax and spending items "is, in practical effect, no more and no less than the power to 'decline to spend' specified sums of money, or to 'decline to implement' specified tax measures."

In *Field v. Clark*, the Court upheld the constitutionality of the Tariff Act of 1890. Act of Oct. 1, 1890, 26 Stat. 567. That statute contained a "free list" of almost 300 specific articles that were exempted from import duties "unless otherwise specially provided for in this act." *Id.*, at 602. Section 3 was a special provision that directed the President to suspend that exemption for sugar, molasses, coffee, tea, and hides "whenever, and so often" as he should be satisfied that any country producing and exporting those products imposed duties on the agricultural products of the United States that he deemed to be "reciprocally unequal and unreasonable. . . ." *Id.*, at 612, quoted in *Field*, 143 U.S., at 680, 12 S.Ct., at 500. The section then specified the duties to be imposed on those products during any such suspension. The Court provided this explanation for its conclusion that § 3 had not delegated legislative power to the President: "Nothing involving the expediency or the just operation of such legislation was left to the determination of the President. . . . [W]hen he ascertained the fact that duties and exactions, reciprocally unequal and unreasonable, were imposed upon the agricultural or other products of the United States by a country producing and exporting sugar, molasses, coffee, tea or hides, it became his duty to issue a proclamation declaring the suspension, as to that country, which Congress had determined should occur. He had no discretion in the premises except in respect to the duration of the suspension so ordered. But that related only to the enforcement of the policy established by Congress. As the suspension was absolutely required when the President ascertained the existence of a particular fact, it cannot be said that in ascertaining that fact and in issuing his proclamation, in obedience to the legislative will, he exercised the function of making laws. . . . It was a part of the law itself as it left the hands of Congress that the provisions, full and complete in themselves, permitting the free introduction of sugars, molasses, coffee, tea and hides, from particular countries, should be suspended, in a given contingency, and that in case of such suspensions certain duties should be imposed." *Id.*, at 693, 12 S.Ct., at 504-505.

This passage identifies three critical differences between the power to suspend the exemption from import duties and the power to cancel portions of a duly enacted statute. First, the exercise of the suspension power was contingent upon a condition that did not exist when the Tariff Act was passed: the imposition of "reciprocally unequal and unreasonable" import duties by other countries. In contrast, the exercise of the cancellation power within five days after the enactment of the Balanced Budget and Tax Reform Acts necessarily was based on the same conditions that Congress evaluated when it passed those statutes. Second, under the Tariff Act, when the President determined that the contingency had arisen, he had a duty to suspend; in contrast, while it is true that the President was required by the Act to make three determinations before he canceled a provision, see 2 U.S.C. § 691(a)(A) (1994 ed., Supp. II), those determinations did not qualify his discretion to cancel or not to cancel. Finally, whenever the President suspended an exemption under the Tariff Act, he was executing the policy that Congress had embodied in the statute. In contrast, whenever the President cancels an item of new direct spending or a limited tax benefit he is rejecting the policy judgment made by Congress and relying on his own policy judgment. Thus, the conclusion in *Field v. Clark* that the suspensions mandated by the Tariff Act were not exercises of legislative power does not undermine our opinion that cancellations pursuant to the Line Item Veto Act are the functional equivalent of partial repeals of Acts of Congress that fail to satisfy Article I, § 7.

Neither are we persuaded by the Government's contention that the President's authority to cancel new direct spending and tax benefit items is no greater than his traditional authority to decline to spend appropriated funds. The Government has reviewed in some detail the series of statutes in which Congress has given the Executive broad discretion over the expenditure of appropriated funds. For example, the First Congress appropriated "sum[s] not exceeding" specified amounts to be spent on various Government operations. See, *e.g.,* Act of Sept. 29, 1789, ch. 23, § 1, 1 Stat. 95; Act of Mar. 26, 1790, ch. 4, 1 Stat. 104; Act of Feb. 11, 1791, ch. 6, 1 Stat. 190. In those statutes, as in later years, the President was given wide discretion with respect to both the amounts to be spent and how the money would be allocated among different functions. It is argued that the Line Item Veto Act merely confers comparable discretionary authority over the expenditure of appropriated funds. The critical difference between this statute and all of its predecessors, however, is that unlike any of them, this Act gives the President the unilateral power to change the text of duly enacted statutes. None of the Act's predecessors could even arguably have been construed to authorize such a change.

[We] express no opinion about the wisdom of the procedures authorized by the Line Item Veto Act. Thus, because we conclude that the Act's cancellation provisions violate Article I, § 7, of the Constitution, we find it unnecessary to consider the District Court's alternative holding that the Act "impermissibly disrupts the balance of powers among the three branches of government." [Our] decision rests on the narrow ground that the procedures authorized by the Line Item Veto Act are not authorized by the Constitution. [If] the Line Item Veto Act were valid, it would authorize the President to create a different law — one whose text was not voted on by either House of Congress or presented to the President for signature. Something that might be known as "Public Law 105-33 as modified by the President" may or may not be desirable, but it is surely not a document that may "become a law" pursuant to the procedures designed by the Framers of Article I, § 7, of the Constitution. If there is to be a new procedure in which the President will play a different role in determining the final text of what may "become a law," such change must come not by legislation but through the amendment procedures set forth in Article V of the Constitution.

The judgment of the District Court is affirmed.

Justice KENNEDY, concurring.

A Nation cannot plunder its own treasury without putting its Constitution and its survival in peril. The statute before us, then, is of first importance, for it seems undeniable the Act will tend to restrain persistent excessive spending. Nevertheless, for the reasons given by Justice Stevens in the opinion for the Court, the statute must be found invalid. Failure of political will does not justify unconstitutional remedies. [Liberty] is always at stake when one or more of the branches seek to transgress the separation of powers. Separation of powers was designed to implement a fundamental insight: Concentration of power in the hands of a single branch is a threat to liberty. [It] follows that if a citizen who is taxed has the measure of the tax or the decision to spend determined by the Executive alone, without adequate control by the citizen's Representatives in Congress, liberty is threatened.

Justice SCALIA, with whom Justice O'CONNOR joins, and with whom Justice BREYER joins as to Part III, concurring in part and dissenting in part.

The Presentment Clause requires, in relevant part, that "[e]very Bill which shall have passed the House of Representatives and the Senate, shall, before it become a Law, be presented to the President of the United States; If he approve he shall sign it, but if not he shall return it." U.S. Const., Art. I, § 7, cl. 2. There is no question that enactment of the Balanced Budget Act complied with these requirements: the House and Senate passed the bill, and the President signed it into law. It was only *after* the requirements of the Presentment Clause had been satisfied that the President exercised his authority under the Line Item Veto Act to cancel the spending item. Thus, the Court's problem with the Act is not that it authorizes the President to veto parts of a bill and sign others into law, but rather that it authorizes him to "cancel" — prevent from "having legal force or effect" — certain parts of duly enacted statutes.

Article I, § 7, of the Constitution obviously prevents the President from canceling a law that Congress has not authorized him to cancel. [But] that is not this case. It was certainly arguable, as an original matter, that Art. I, § 7, also prevents the President from canceling a law which itself *authorizes* the President to cancel it. But as the Court acknowledges, that argument has long since been made and rejected. In 1809, Congress passed a law authorizing the President to cancel trade restrictions against Great Britain and France if either revoked edicts directed at the United States. Act of Mar. 1, 1809, § 11, 2 Stat. 528. Joseph Story regarded the conferral of that authority as entirely unremarkable in *The Orono,* 18 F. Cas. 830, No. 10,585 (CCD Mass. 1812). The Tariff Act of 1890 authorized the President to "suspend, by proclamation to that effect" certain of its provisions if he determined that other countries were imposing "reciprocally unequal and unreasonable" duties. Act of Oct. 1, 1890, § 3, 26 Stat. 612. This Court upheld the constitutionality of that Act in *Field v. Clark,* 143 U.S. 649, 12 S.Ct. 495, 36 L.Ed. 294 (1892).

As much as the Court goes on about Art. I, § 7, therefore, that provision does not demand the result the Court reaches. It no more categorically prohibits the Executive *reduction* of congressional dispositions in the course of implementing statutes that authorize such reduction, than it categorically prohibits the Executive *augmentation* of congressional dispositions in the course of implementing statutes that authorize such augmentation — generally known as substantive rulemaking. There are, to be sure, limits upon the former just as there are limits upon the latter — and I am prepared to acknowledge that the limits upon the former may be much more severe. Those limits are established, however, not by some categorical prohibition of Art. I, § 7, which our cases conclusively disprove, but by what has come to be known as the doctrine of unconstitutional delegation of legislative authority: When authorized Executive reduction or augmentation is allowed to go too far, it usurps the nondelegable function of Congress and violates the separation of powers.

I turn, then, to the crux of the matter: whether Congress's authorizing the President to cancel an item of spending gives him a power that our history and traditions show must reside exclusively in the Legislative Branch. [The] President's discretion under the Line Item Veto Act is certainly broader than the Comptroller General's discretion was under the 1985 Act, but it is no broader than the discretion traditionally granted the President in his execution of spending laws.

Insofar as the degree of political, "lawmaking" power conferred upon the Executive is concerned, there is not a dime's worth of difference between Congress's authorizing the President to *cancel* a spending item, and Congress's authorizing money to be spent on a particular item at the President's discretion. [Examples] of appropriations committed to the discretion of the President abound in our history. The constitutionality of such appropriations has never seriously been questioned.

Certain Presidents have claimed Executive authority to withhold appropriated funds even *absent* an express conferral of discretion to do so. [President] Nixon, the Mahatma Gandhi of all impounders, asserted at a press conference in 1973 that his "constitutional right" to impound appropriated funds was "absolutely clear." The President's News Conference of Jan. 31, 1973, 9 Weekly Comp. of Pres. Doc. 109-110 (1973). Our decision two years later in *Train v. City of New York,* 420 U.S. 35, 95 S.Ct. 839, 43 L.Ed.2d 1 (1975), proved him wrong, but it implicitly confirmed that Congress may confer discretion upon the Executive to withhold appropriated funds, even funds appropriated for a specific purpose.

The short of the matter is this: Had the Line Item Veto Act authorized the President to "decline to spend" any item of spending contained in the Balanced Budget Act of 1997, there is not the slightest doubt that authorization would have been constitutional. What the Line Item Veto Act does instead — authorizing the President to "cancel" an item of spending — is technically different. But the technical difference does *not* relate to the technicalities of the Presentment Clause, which have been fully complied with; and the doctrine of unconstitutional delegation, which *is* at issue here, is preeminently *not* a doctrine of technicalities. The title of the Line Item Veto Act, which was perhaps designed to simplify for public comprehension, or perhaps merely to comply with the terms of a campaign pledge, has succeeded in faking out the Supreme Court. The President's action it authorizes in fact is not a line-item veto and thus does not offend Art. I, § 7; and insofar as the substance of that action is concerned, it is no different from what Congress has permitted the President to do since the formation of the Union.

For the foregoing reasons, I respectfully dissent.

Justice BREYER, with whom Justice O'CONNOR and Justice SCALIA join as to Part III, dissenting.

I. I agree with the Court that the parties have standing, but I do not agree with its ultimate conclusion. In my view the Line Item Veto Act (Act) does not violate any specific textual constitutional command, nor does it violate any implicit separation-of-powers principle. Consequently, I believe that the Act is constitutional.

II. I approach the constitutional question before us with three general considerations in mind. *First,* the Act represents a legislative effort to provide the President with the power to give effect to some, but not to all, of the expenditure and revenue-diminishing provisions contained in a single massive appropriations bill. And this objective is constitutionally proper. When our Nation was founded, Congress could easily have provided the President with this kind of power. In that time period, our population was less than 4 million, federal employees numbered fewer than 5,000, annual federal budget outlays totaled approximately $4 million. At that time, a Congress, wishing to give a President the power to select among appropriations, could simply have embodied each appropriation in a separate bill, each bill subject to a separate Presidential veto.

Today, however, our population is about 250 million, see U.S. Dept. of Commerce, Census Bureau, 1990 Census, the Federal Government employs more than 4 million people, see Office of Management and Budget, Budget of the United States Government, Fiscal Year 1998: Analytical Perspectives 207 (1997) (hereinafter Analytical Perspectives), the annual federal budget is $1.5 trillion, see Office of Management and Budget, Budget of the United States Government, Fiscal Year 1998: Budget 303 (1997) (hereinafter Budget), and a typical budget appropriations bill may have a dozen titles, hundreds of sections, and spread across more than 500 pages of the Statutes at Large. See, *e.g.,* Balanced Budget Act of 1997, Pub.L. 105-33, 111 Stat. 251. Congress cannot divide such a bill into thousands, or tens of thousands, of separate appropriations bills, each one of which the President would have to sign, or to veto, separately. Thus, the question is whether the Constitution permits Congress to choose a particular novel *means* to achieve this same, constitutionally legitimate, *end.*

Second, the case in part requires us to focus upon the Constitution's generally phrased structural provisions, provisions that delegate all "legislative" power to Congress and vest all "executive" power in the President. See Part IV, *infra.* The Court, when applying these provisions, has interpreted them generously in terms of the institutional arrangements that they permit. [Indeed], Chief Justice Marshall, in a well-known passage, explained, "To have prescribed the means by which government should, in all future time, execute its powers, would have been to change, entirely, the character of the instrument, and give it the properties of a legal code. It would have been an unwise attempt to provide, by immutable rules, for exigencies which, if foreseen at all, must have been seen dimly, and which can be best provided for as they occur." *McCulloch v. Maryland,* 4 Wheat. 316, 415, 4 L.Ed. 579 (1819). This passage, like the cases I have just mentioned, calls attention to the genius of the Framers' pragmatic vision, which this Court has long recognized in cases that find constitutional room for necessary institutional innovation. *Third,* we need not here referee a dispute among the other two branches. And, as the majority points out: 'When this Court is asked to invalidate a statutory provision that has been approved by both Houses of the Congress and signed by the President, particularly an Act of Congress that confronts a deeply vexing national problem, it should only do so for the most compelling constitutional reasons.'" *Ante,* at 2107, n. 42 (quoting *Bowsher v. Synar,* 478 U.S. 714, 736, 106 S.Ct. 3181, 3192-3193, 92 L.Ed.2d 583 (1986) (Stevens, J., concurring in judgment)). Cf. *Youngstown Sheet and Tube Co., supra,* at 635, 72 S.Ct., at 870 (Jackson, J., concurring) ("Presidential powers are not fixed but fluctuate, depending on their disjunction or conjunction with those of Congress . . . [and when] the President acts pursuant to an express or implied authorization of Congress, his authority is at its maximum").

The background circumstances also mean that we are to interpret nonliteral separation-of-powers principles in light of the need for "workable government." *Youngstown Sheet and Tube Co., supra,* at 635, 72 S.Ct., at 870 (Jackson, J., concurring).

If we apply those principles in light of that objective, as this Court has applied them in the past, the Act is constitutional.

III. The Court believes that the Act violates the literal text of the Constitution. A simple syllogism captures its basic reasoning: Major Premise: The Constitution sets forth an exclusive method for enacting, repealing, or amending laws. See *ante,* at 2103-2104. Minor Premise: The Act authorizes the President to "repea[l] or amen[d]" laws in a different way, namely by announcing a cancellation of a portion of a previously enacted law. See *ante,* at 2102-2103. Conclusion: The Act is inconsistent with the Constitution. I find this syllogism unconvincing, however, because its Minor Premise is faulty. When the President "canceled" the two appropriation measures now before us, he did not *repeal* any law nor did he *amend* any law. He simply *followed* the law, leaving the statutes, as they are literally written, intact.

[Imagine] that the canceled New York health care tax provision at issue here, Pub.L. 105-33, § 4722(c), 111 Stat. 515 (quoted in full *ante,* at 2095, n. 2), had instead said the following: "Section One. Taxes . . . that were collected by the State of New York from a health care provider before June 1, 1997, and for which a waiver of the provisions [requiring payment] have been sought . . . are deemed to be permissible health care related taxes . . . *provided however that the President may prevent the just-mentioned provision from having legal force or effect if he determines x, y, and z.* (Assume x, y and z to be the same determinations required by the Line Item Veto Act). [One] could not say that a President who "prevent[s]" the deeming language from "having legal force or effect," see 2 U.S.C. § 691e(4)(B) (1994 ed., Supp. II), has either *repealed* or *amended* this particular hypothetical statute. Rather, the President has *followed* that law to the letter. He has exercised the power it explicitly delegates to him. He has executed the law, not repealed it.

It could make no significant difference to this linguistic point were the italicized proviso to appear, not as part of what I have called Section One, but, instead, at the bottom of the statute page, say, referenced by an asterisk, with a statement that it applies to every spending provision in the Act next to which a similar asterisk appears. And that being so, it could make no difference if that proviso appeared, instead, in a different, earlier enacted law, along with legal language that makes it applicable to every future spending provision picked out according to a specified formula. But, of course, this last mentioned possibility is this very case.

[For] that reason, one cannot dispose of this case through a purely literal analysis as the majority does. Literally speaking, the President has not "repealed" or "amended" anything. He has simply *executed* a power conferred upon him by Congress, which power is contained in laws that were enacted in compliance with the exclusive method set forth in the Constitution.

Because one cannot say that the President's exercise of the power the Act grants is, literally speaking, a "repeal" or "amendment," the fact that the Act's procedures differ from the Constitution's exclusive procedures for enacting (or repealing) legislation is beside the point. The Act *itself* was enacted in accordance with these procedures, and its failure to require the President to satisfy those procedures does not make the Act unconstitutional.

IV. Because I disagree with the Court's holding of literal violation, I must consider whether the Act nonetheless violates separation-of-powers principles — principles that arise out of the Constitution's vesting of the "executive Power" in "a President," U.S. Const., Art. II, § 1, and "[a]ll legislative Powers" in "a Congress," Art. I, § 1. There are three relevant separation-of-powers questions here: (1) Has Congress given the President the wrong kind of power, *i.e.,* "non-Executive" power? (2) Has Congress given the President the power to "encroach" upon Congress' own constitutionally reserved territory? (3) Has Congress given the President too much power, violating the doctrine of "nondelegation"? These three limitations help assure "adequate control by the citizen's Representatives in Congress," upon which Justice Kennedy properly insists. See *ante,* at 2109 (concurring opinion). And with respect to *this* Act, the answer to all these questions is "no."

Viewed conceptually, the power the Act conveys is the right kind of power. It is "executive."   As explained above, an exercise of that power "executes" the Act. Conceptually speaking, it closely resembles the kind of delegated authority — to spend or not to spend appropriations, to change or not to change tariff rates — that Congress has frequently granted the President, any differences being differences in degree, not kind. See Part IV-C, *infra.*

The fact that one could also characterize this kind of power as "legislative," say, if Congress itself (by amending the appropriations bill) prevented a provision from taking effect, is beside the point. This Court has frequently found that the exercise of a particular power, such as the power to make rules of broad applicability, *American Trucking Assns., Inc. v. United States,* 344 U.S. 298, 310-313, 73 S.Ct. 307, 314-316, 97 L.Ed. 337 (1953), or to adjudicate claims, *Crowell v. Benson,* 285 U.S., at 50-51, 54, 52 S.Ct., at 292-293; *Wiener v. United States,* 357 U.S. 349, 354-356, 78 S.Ct. 1275, 1278-1279, 2 L.Ed.2d 1377 (1958), can fall within the constitutional purview of more than one branch of Government. See *Wayman v. Southard,* 10 Wheat. 1, 43, 6 L.Ed. 253 (1825) (Marshall, C.J.) ("Congress may certainly delegate to others, powers which the legislature may rightfully exercise itself"). The Court does not "carry out the distinction between legislative and executive action with mathematical precision" or "divide the branches into watertight compartments," *Springer v. Philippine Islands,* 277 U.S. 189, 211, 48 S.Ct. 480, 485-486, 72 L.Ed. 845 (1928) (Holmes, J., dissenting), for, as others have said, the Constitution "blend[s]" as well as "separat[es]" powers in order to create a workable government. 1 K. Davis, Administrative Law § 1.09, p. 68 (1958).

In contrast to these cases, one cannot say that the Act "encroaches" upon Congress' power, when Congress retained the power to insert, by simple majority, into any future appropriations bill, into any section of any such bill, or into any phrase of any section, a provision that says the Act will not apply.   Congress also retained the power to "disapprov[e]," and thereby reinstate, any of the President's cancellations. See 2 U.S.C. § 691b(a). And it is Congress that drafts and enacts the appropriations statutes that are subject to the Act in the first place — and thereby defines the outer limits of the President's cancellation authority.

Nor can one say the Act's grant of power "aggrandizes" the Presidential office. The grant is limited to the context of the budget. It is limited to the power to spend, or not to spend, particular appropriated items, and the power to permit, or not to permit, specific limited exemptions from generally applicable tax law from taking effect. These powers, as I will explain in detail, resemble those the President has exercised in the past on other occasions. See Part IV-C, *infra.* The delegation of those powers to the President may strengthen the Presidency, but any such change in Executive Branch authority seems minute when compared with the changes worked by delegations of other kinds of authority that the Court in the past has upheld.

[T]he Constitution permits only those delegations where Congress "shall lay down by legislative act an *intelligible principle* to which the person or body authorized to [act] is directed to conform." Indeed, the Court has only twice in its history found that a congressional delegation of power violated the "nondelegation" doctrine. One such case, *Panama Refining Co. v. Ryan,* 293 U.S. 388, 55 S.Ct. 241, 79 L.Ed. 446 (1935), was in a sense a special case, for it was discovered in the midst of the case that the particular exercise of the power at issue, the promulgation of a Petroleum Code under the National Industrial Recovery Act, did not contain any legally operative sentence. *Id.,* at 412-413, 55 S.Ct., at 244-245. The other case, *A.L.A. Schechter Poultry Corp. v. United States,* 295 U.S. 495, 55 S.Ct. 837, 79 L.Ed. 1570 (1935), involved a delegation through the National Industrial Recovery Act, 48 Stat. 195, that contained not simply a broad standard ("fair competition"), but also the conferral of power on private parties to promulgate rules applying that standard to virtually all of American industry, *id.,* at 521-525, 55 S.Ct., at 839-841. As Justice Cardozo put it, the legislation exemplified "delegation running riot," which created a "roving commission to inquire into evils and upon discovery correct them." *Id.,* at 553, 551, 55 S.Ct., at 853, 852 (concurring opinion).

The case before us does not involve any such "roving commission," nor does it involve delegation to private parties, nor does it bring all of American industry within its scope. It is limited to one area of Government, the budget, and it seeks to give the President the power, in one portion of that budget, to tailor spending and special tax relief to what he concludes are the demands of fiscal responsibility. Nor is the standard that governs his judgment, though broad, any broader than the standard that currently governs the award of television licenses, namely, "public convenience, interest, *or* necessity." 47 U.S.C. § 303 (emphasis added). To the contrary, (a) the broadly phrased limitations in the Act, together with (b) its evident deficit reduction purpose, and (c) a procedure that guarantees Presidential awareness of the reasons for including a particular provision in a budget bill, taken together, guide the President's exercise of his discretionary powers.

On the other hand, I must recognize that there are important differences between the delegation before us and other broad, constitutionally acceptable delegations to Executive Branch agencies — differences that argue against my conclusion. In particular, a broad delegation of authority to an administrative agency differs from the delegation at issue here in that agencies often develop subsidiary rules under the statute, rules that explain the general "public interest" language. Doing so diminishes the risk that the agency will use the breadth of a grant of authority as a cloak for unreasonable or unfair implementation. See 1 K. Davis, Administrative Law § 3:15, pp. 207-208 (2d ed.1978). Moreover, agencies are typically subject to judicial review, which review provides an additional check against arbitrary implementation. See, *e.g., Motor Vehicle Mfrs. Assn. of United States, Inc. v. State Farm Mut. Automobile Ins. Co.,* 463 U.S. 29, 40-42, 103 S.Ct. 2856, 2865-2866, 77 L.Ed.2d 443 (1983). The President has not so narrowed his discretionary power through rule, nor is his implementation subject to judicial review under the terms of the Administrative Procedure Act. See, *e.g., Franklin v. Massachusetts,* 505 U.S. 788, 801, 112 S.Ct. 2767, 2775-2776, 120 L.Ed.2d 636 (1992) (APA does not apply to President absent express statement by Congress).

While I believe that these last mentioned considerations are important, they are not determinative. The President, unlike most agency decision makers, is an elected official. He is responsible to the voters, who, in principle, will judge the manner in which he exercises his delegated authority.

Consequently I believe that the power the Act grants the President to prevent spending items from taking effect does not violate the "nondelegation" doctrine.

In sum, I recognize that the Act before us is novel. In a sense, it skirts a constitutional edge. But that edge has to do with means, not ends. The means chosen do not amount literally to the enactment, repeal, or amendment of a law. Nor, for that matter, do they amount literally to the "line item veto" that the Act's title announces. Those means do not violate any basic separation-of-powers principle. They do not improperly shift the constitutionally foreseen balance of power from Congress to the President. Nor, since they comply with separation-of-powers principles, do they threaten the liberties of individual citizens. They represent an experiment that may, or may not, help representative government work better. The Constitution, in my view, authorizes Congress and the President to try novel methods in this way. Consequently, with respect, I dissent.

C. EXECUTIVE OFFICERS

BOWSHER v. SYNAR
478 U.S. 714 (1986)

Chief Justice BURGER delivered the opinion of the Court.

The question presented by these appeals is whether the assignment by Congress to the Comptroller General of the United States of certain functions under the Balanced Budget and Emergency Deficit Control Act of 1985 violates the doctrine of separation of powers.

On December 12, 1985, the President signed into law the Balanced Budget and Emergency Deficit Control Act of 1985, Pub.L. 99-177, 99 Stat. 1038, 2 U.S.C. § 901 *et seq.* (1982 ed., Supp. III), popularly known as the "Gramm-Rudman-Hollings Act." The purpose of the Act is to eliminate the federal budget deficit. To that end, the Act sets a "maximum deficit amount" for federal spending for each of fiscal years 1986 through 1991. The size of that maximum deficit amount progressively reduces to zero in fiscal year 1991. If in any fiscal year the federal budget deficit exceeds the maximum deficit amount by more than a specified sum, the Act requires across-the-board cuts in federal spending to reach the targeted deficit level, with half of the cuts made to defense programs and the other half made to nondefense programs. The Act exempts certain priority programs from these cuts. § 255.

These "automatic" reductions are accomplished through a rather complicated procedure, spelled out in § 251, the so-called "reporting provisions" of the Act. Each year, the Directors of the Office of Management and Budget (OMB) and the Congressional Budget Office (CBO) independently estimate the amount of the federal budget deficit for the upcoming fiscal year. If that deficit exceeds the maximum targeted deficit amount for that fiscal year by more than a specified amount, the Directors of OMB and CBO independently calculate, on a program-by-program basis, the budget reductions necessary to ensure that the deficit does not exceed the maximum deficit amount. The Act then requires the Directors to report jointly their deficit estimates and budget reduction calculations to the Comptroller General.

The Comptroller General, after reviewing the Directors' reports, then reports his conclusions to the President. § 251(b). The President in turn must issue a "sequestration" order mandating the spending reductions specified by the Comptroller General. § 252.

There follows a period during which Congress may by legislation reduce spending to obviate, in whole or in part, the need for the sequestration order. If such reductions are not enacted, the sequestration order becomes effective and the spending reductions included in that order are made.

Anticipating constitutional challenge to these procedures, the Act also contains a "fallback" deficit reduction process to take effect "[i]n the event that any of the reporting procedures described in section 251 are invalidated." § 274(f). Under these provisions, the report prepared by the Directors of OMB and the CBO is submitted directly to a specially created Temporary Joint Committee on Deficit Reduction, which must report in five days to both Houses a joint resolution setting forth the content of the Directors' report. Congress then must vote on the resolution under special rules, which render amendments out of order. If the resolution is passed and signed by the President, it then serves as the basis for a Presidential sequestration order.

[The] Constitution does not contemplate an active role for Congress in the supervision of officers charged with the execution of the laws it enacts. The President appoints "Officers of the United States" with the "Advice and Consent of the Senate. . . ." Art. II, § 2. Once the appointment has been made and confirmed, however, the Constitution explicitly provides for removal of Officers of the United States by Congress only upon impeachment by the House of Representatives and conviction by the Senate. An impeachment by the House and trial by the Senate can rest only on "Treason, Bribery or other high Crimes and Misdemeanors." Article II, § 4. A direct congressional role in the removal of officers charged with the execution of the laws beyond this limited one is inconsistent with separation of powers.

[In] light of these precedents, we conclude that Congress cannot reserve for itself the power of removal of an officer charged with the execution of the laws except by impeachment. To permit the execution of the laws to be vested in an officer answerable only to Congress would, in practical terms, reserve in Congress control over the execution of the laws. As the District Court observed: "Once an officer is appointed, it is only the authority that can remove him, and not the authority that appointed him, that he must fear and, in the performance of his functions, obey." 626 F.Supp., at 1401. The structure of the Constitution does not permit Congress to execute the laws; it follows that Congress cannot grant to an officer under its control what it does not possess. Our decision in *INS v. Chadha*, 462 U.S. 919, 103 S.Ct. 2764, 77 L.Ed.2d 317 (1983), supports this conclusion. [To] permit an officer controlled by Congress to execute the laws would be, in essence, to permit a congressional veto. Congress could simply remove, or threaten to remove, an officer for executing the laws in any fashion found to be unsatisfactory to Congress. This kind of congressional control over the execution of the laws, *Chadha* makes clear, is constitutionally impermissible.

[Appellants] urge that the Comptroller General performs his duties independently and is not subservient to Congress. We agree with the District Court that this contention does not bear close scrutiny.

The critical factor lies in the provisions of the statute defining the Comptroller General's office relating to removability. Although the Comptroller General is nominated by the President from a list of three individuals recommended by the Speaker of the House of Representatives and the President *pro tempore* of the Senate, see 31 U.S.C. § 703(a)(2), and confirmed by the Senate, he is removable only at the initiative of Congress. He may be removed not only by impeachment but also by joint resolution of Congress "at any time" resting on any one of the following bases:

(i) permanent disability;
(ii) inefficiency;
(iii) neglect of duty;
(iv) malfeasance; or
(v) a felony or conduct involving moral turpitude.

[These] terms are very broad and, as interpreted by Congress, could sustain removal of a Comptroller General for any number of actual or perceived transgressions of the legislative will. The Constitutional Convention chose to permit impeachment of executive officers only for "Treason, Bribery, or other high Crimes and Misdemeanors." It rejected language that would have permitted impeachment for "maladministration," with Madison arguing that "[s]o vague a term will be equivalent to a tenure during pleasure of the Senate." 2 M. Farrand, Records of the Federal Convention of 1787, p. 550 (1911).

We need not decide whether "inefficiency" or "malfeasance" are terms as broad as "maladministration" in order to reject the dissent's position that removing the Comptroller General requires "a feat of bipartisanship more difficult than that required to impeach and convict."

[Justice] White, however, assures us that "[r]ealistic consideration" of the "practical result of the removal provision," reveals that the Comptroller General is unlikely to be removed by Congress. The separated powers of our Government cannot be permitted to turn on judicial assessment of whether an officer exercising executive power is on good terms with Congress. The Framers recognized that, in the long term, structural protections against abuse of power were critical to preserving liberty. In constitutional terms, the removal powers over the Comptroller General's office dictate that he will be subservient to Congress.

[It] is clear that Congress has consistently viewed the Comptroller General as an officer of the Legislative Branch. The Reorganization Acts of 1945 and 1949, for example, both stated that the Comptroller General and the GAO are "a part of the legislative branch of the Government." 59 Stat. 616; 63 Stat. 205. Similarly, in the Accounting and Auditing Act of 1950, Congress required the Comptroller General to conduct audits "as an agent of the Congress." 64 Stat. 835.

Over the years, the Comptrollers General have also viewed themselves as part of the Legislative Branch. [Against] this background, we see no escape from the conclusion that, because Congress has retained removal authority over the Comptroller General, he may not be entrusted with executive powers. The remaining question is whether the Comptroller General has been assigned such powers in the Balanced Budget and Emergency Deficit Control Act of 1985.

[Appellants] suggest that the duties assigned to the Comptroller General in the Act are essentially ministerial and mechanical so that their performance does not constitute "execution of the law" in a meaningful sense. On the contrary, we view these functions as plainly entailing execution of the law in constitutional terms. Interpreting a law enacted by Congress to implement the legislative mandate is the very essence of "execution" of the law. Under § 251, the Comptroller General must exercise judgment concerning facts that affect the application of the Act. He must also interpret the provisions of the Act to determine precisely what budgetary calculations are required. Decisions of that kind are typically made by officers charged with executing a statute.

The executive nature of the Comptroller General's functions under the Act is revealed in § 252(a)(3) which gives the Comptroller General the ultimate authority to determine the budget cuts to be made. Indeed, the Comptroller General commands the President himself to carry out, without the slightest variation (with exceptions not relevant to the constitutional issues presented), the directive of the Comptroller General as to the budget reductions:

[Congress] of course initially determined the content of the Balanced Budget and Emergency Deficit Control Act; and undoubtedly the content of the Act determines the nature of the executive duty. However, as *Chadha* makes clear, once Congress makes its choice in enacting legislation, its participation ends. Congress can thereafter control the execution of its enactment only indirectly — by passing new legislation. *Chadha*, 462 U.S., at 958, 103 S.Ct., at 2787-2789. By placing the responsibility for execution of the Balanced Budget and Emergency Deficit Control Act in the hands of an officer who is subject to removal only by itself, Congress in effect has retained control over the execution of the Act and has intruded into the executive function. The Constitution does not permit such intrusion.

[No] one can doubt that Congress and the President are confronted with fiscal and economic problems of unprecedented magnitude, but "the fact that a given law or procedure is efficient, convenient, and useful in facilitating functions of government, standing alone, will not save it if it is contrary to the Constitution. Convenience and efficiency are not the primary objectives — or the hallmarks — of democratic government. . . ." *Chadha, supra,* 462 U.S., at 944, 103 S.Ct., at 2781.

It is so ordered.

Justice WHITE, dissenting.

The Court, acting in the name of separation of powers, takes upon itself to strike down the Gramm-Rudman-Hollings Act, one of the most novel and far-reaching legislative responses to a national crisis since the New Deal. The basis of the Court's action is a solitary provision of another statute that was passed over 60 years ago and has lain dormant since that time. I cannot concur in the Court's action. Like the Court, I will not purport to speak to the wisdom of the policies incorporated in the legislation the Court invalidates; that is a matter for the Congress and the Executive, *both* of which expressed their assent to the statute barely half a year ago. I will, however, address the wisdom of the Court's willingness to interpose its distressingly formalistic view of separation of powers as a bar to the attainment of governmental objectives through the means chosen by the Congress and the President in the legislative process established by the Constitution. Twice in the past four years I have expressed my view that the Court's recent efforts to police the separation of powers have rested on untenable constitutional propositions leading to regrettable results. Today's result is even more misguided. As I will explain, the Court's decision rests on a feature of the legislative scheme that is of minimal practical significance and that presents no substantial threat to the basic scheme of separation of powers. In attaching dispositive significance to what should be regarded as a triviality, the Court neglects what has in the past been recognized as a fundamental principle governing consideration of disputes over separation of powers: "The actual art of governing under our Constitution does not and cannot conform to judicial definitions of the power of any of its branches based on isolated clauses or even single Articles torn from context. While the Constitution diffuses power the better to secure liberty, it also contemplates that practice will integrate the dispersed powers into a workable government." *Youngstown Sheet & Tube Co. v. Sawyer,* 343 U.S. 579, 635, 72 S.Ct. 863, 870, 96 L.Ed. 1153 (1952) (Jackson, J., concurring).

[Before] examining the merits of the Court's argument, I wish to emphasize what it is that the Court quite pointedly and correctly does *not* hold: namely, that "executive" powers of the sort granted the Comptroller by the Act may only be exercised by officers removable at will by the President.

[The] Court's recognition of the legitimacy of legislation vesting "executive" authority in officers independent of the President does not imply derogation of the President's own constitutional authority — indeed, duty — to "take Care that the Laws be faithfully executed," Art. II, § 3, for any such duty is necessarily limited to a great extent by the content of the laws enacted by the Congress. As Justice Holmes put it: "The duty of the President to see that the laws be executed is a duty that does not go beyond the laws or require him to achieve more than Congress sees fit to leave within his power." *Myers v. United States, supra,* at 177, 47 S.Ct., at 85 (dissenting). Justice Holmes perhaps overstated his case, for there are undoubtedly executive functions that, regardless of the enactments of Congress, must be performed by officers subject to removal at will by the President. Whether a particular function falls within this class or within the far larger class that may be relegated to independent officers "will depend upon the character of the office." *Humphrey's Executor, supra,* 295 U.S., at 631, 55 S.Ct., at 875.

[It] is evident (and nothing in the Court's opinion is to the contrary) that the powers exercised by the Comptroller General under the Gramm-Rudman-Hollings Act are not such that vesting them in an officer not subject to removal at will by the President would in itself improperly interfere with Presidential powers. Determining the level of spending by the Federal Government is not by nature a function central either to the exercise of the President's enumerated powers or to his general duty to ensure execution of the laws; rather, appropriating funds is a peculiarly legislative function.

[The] question remains whether, as the Court concludes, the fact that the officer to whom Congress has delegated the authority to implement the Act is removable by a joint resolution of Congress should require invalidation of the Act. The Court's decision, as I have stated above, is based on a syllogism: the Act vests the Comptroller with "executive power"; such power may not be exercised by Congress or its agents; the Comptroller is an agent of Congress because he is removable by Congress; therefore the Act is invalid. I have no quarrel with the proposition that the powers exercised by the Comptroller under the Act may be characterized as "executive" in that they involve the interpretation and carrying out of the Act's mandate. I can also accept the general proposition that although Congress has considerable authority in designating the officers who are to execute legislation, the constitutional scheme of separated powers does prevent Congress from reserving an executive role for itself or for its "agents." *Buckley v. Valeo,* 424 U.S., at 120-141, 96 S.Ct., at 682-692, *id.,* at 267-282, 96 S.Ct., at 749-756 (White, J., concurring in part and dissenting in part). I cannot accept, however, that the exercise of authority by an officer removable for cause by a joint resolution of Congress is analogous to the impermissible execution of the law by Congress itself, nor would I hold that the congressional role in the removal process renders the Comptroller an "agent" of the Congress, incapable of receiving "executive" power.

[As] the majority points out, however, the Court's decision in *INS v. Chadha,* 462 U.S. 919, 103 S.Ct. 2764, 77 L.Ed.2d 317 (1983), recognizes additional limits on the ability of Congress to participate in or influence the execution of the laws. As interpreted in *Chadha,* the Constitution prevents Congress from interfering with the actions of officers of the United States through means short of legislation satisfying the demands of bicameral passage and presentment to the President for approval or disapproval. *Id.,* at 954-955, 103

S.Ct., at 2785-2786. Today's majority concludes that the same concerns that underlay *Chadha* indicate the invalidity of a statutory provision allowing the removal by joint resolution for specified cause of any officer performing executive functions. Such removal power, the Court contends, constitutes a "congressional veto" analogous to that struck down in *Chadha,* for it permits Congress to "remove, or threaten to remove, an officer for executing the laws in any fashion found to be unsatisfactory." *Ante,* at 3189. The Court concludes that it is "[t]his kind of congressional control over the execution of the laws" that *Chadha* condemns. *Ibid.*

The deficiencies in the Court's reasoning are apparent. First, the Court baldly mischaracterizes the removal provision when it suggests that it allows Congress to remove the Comptroller for "executing the laws in any fashion found to be unsatisfactory"; in fact, Congress may remove the Comptroller only for one or more of five specified reasons, which "although not so narrow as to deny Congress any leeway, circumscribe Congress' power to some extent by providing a basis for judicial review of congressional removal." *Ameron, Inc. v. United States Army Corps of Engineers,* 787 F.2d 875, 895 (CA3 1986) (Becker, J., concurring in part). Second, and more to the point, the Court overlooks or deliberately ignores the decisive difference between the congressional removal provision and the legislative veto struck down in *Chadha:* under the Budget and Accounting Act, Congress may remove the Comptroller only through a joint resolution, which by definition must be passed by both Houses and signed by the President. See *United States v. California,* 332 U.S. 19, 28, 67 S.Ct. 1658, 1663, 91 L.Ed. 1889 (1947). In other words, a removal of the Comptroller under the statute *satisfies the requirements of bicameralism and presentment laid down in* Chadha. The majority's citation of *Chadha* for the proposition that Congress may only control the acts of officers of the United States "by passing new legislation," *ante,* at 3192, in no sense casts doubt on the legitimacy of the removal provision, for that provision allows Congress to effect removal only through action that constitutes legislation as defined in *Chadha.*

To the extent that it has any bearing on the problem now before us, *Chadha* would seem to suggest the legitimacy of the statutory provision making the Comptroller removable through joint resolution, for the Court's opinion in *Chadha* reflects the view that the bicameralism and presentment requirements of Art. I represent the principal assurances that Congress will remain within its legislative role in the constitutionally prescribed scheme of separated powers. Action taken in accordance with the "single, finely wrought, and exhaustively considered, procedure" established by Art. I, *Chadha, supra,* at 951, 103 S.Ct., at 2784, should be presumptively viewed as a legitimate exercise of legislative power. That such action may represent a more or less successful attempt by Congress to "control" the actions of an officer of the United States surely does not in itself indicate that it is unconstitutional, for no one would dispute that Congress has the power to "control" administration through legislation imposing duties or substantive restraints on executive officers, through legislation increasing or decreasing the funds made available to such officers, or through legislation actually abolishing a particular office. Indeed, *Chadha* expressly recognizes that while congressional meddling with administration of the laws outside of the legislative process is impermissible, congressional control over executive officers exercised through the legislative process is valid. 462 U.S., at 955, n. 19, 103 S.Ct., at 2786, n. 19. Thus, if the existence of a statute permitting removal of the Comptroller through joint resolution (that is, through the legislative process) renders his exercise of executive powers unconstitutional, it is for reasons having virtually nothing to do with *Chadha.*

[That] a joint resolution removing the Comptroller General would satisfy the requirements for legitimate legislative action laid down in *Chadha* does not fully answer the separation of powers argument, for it is apparent that even the results of the constitutional legislative process may be unconstitutional if those results are in fact destructive of the scheme of separation-of-powers. *Nixon v. Administrator of General Services,* 433 U.S. 425, 97 S.Ct. 2777, 53 L.Ed.2d 867 (1977). The question to be answered is whether the threat of removal of the Comptroller General for cause through joint resolution as authorized by the Budget and Accounting Act renders the Comptroller sufficiently subservient to Congress that investing him with "executive" power can be realistically equated with the unlawful retention of such power by Congress itself; more generally, the question is whether there is a genuine threat of "encroachment or aggrandizement of one branch at the expense of the other," *Buckley v. Valeo,* 424 U.S., at 122, 96 S.Ct., at 684. Common sense indicates that the existence of the removal provision poses no such threat to the principle of separation of powers.

The statute does not permit anyone to remove the Comptroller at will; removal is permitted only for specified cause, with the existence of cause to be determined by Congress following a hearing. Any removal under the statute would presumably be subject to post-termination judicial review to ensure that a hearing had in fact been held and that the finding of cause for removal was not arbitrary. See *Ameron, Inc. v. United States Army Corps of Engineers,* 787 F.2d, at 895 (Becker, J., concurring in part). These procedural and substantive limitations on the removal power militate strongly against the characterization of the Comptroller as a mere agent of Congress by virtue of the removal authority. Indeed, similarly qualified grants of removal power are generally deemed to protect the officers to whom they apply and to establish their independence from the domination of the possessor of the removal power. See *Humphrey's Executor v. United States,* 295 U.S., at 625-626, 629-630, 55 S.Ct., at 874-875. Removal authority limited in such a manner is more properly viewed as motivating adherence to a substantive standard established by law than as inducing subservience to the particular institution that enforces that standard. That the agent enforcing the standard is Congress may be of some significance to the Comptroller, but Congress' substantively limited removal power will undoubtedly be less of a spur to subservience than Congress' unquestionable and unqualified power to enact legislation reducing the Comptroller's salary, cutting the funds available to his department, reducing his personnel, limiting or expanding his duties, or even abolishing his position altogether.

More importantly, the substantial role played by the President in the process of removal through joint resolution reduces to utter insignificance the possibility that the threat of removal will induce subservience to the Congress. As I have pointed out above, a joint resolution must be presented to the President and is ineffective if it is vetoed by him, unless the veto is overridden by the constitutionally prescribed two-thirds majority of both Houses of Congress. The requirement of Presidential approval obviates the possibility that the Comptroller will perceive himself as so completely at the mercy of Congress that he will function as its tool. If the Comptroller's conduct in office is not so unsatisfactory to the President as to convince the latter that removal is required under the statutory standard, Congress will have no independent power to coerce the Comptroller unless it can muster a two-thirds majority in both Houses — a feat of bipartisanship more difficult than that required to impeach and convict. The incremental *in terrorem* effect of the possibility of congressional removal in the face of a Presidential veto is therefore exceedingly unlikely to have any discernible impact on the extent of congressional influence over the Comptroller.

The practical result of the removal provision is not to render the Comptroller unduly dependent upon or subservient to Congress, but to render him one of the most independent officers in the entire federal establishment. Those who have studied the office agree that the procedural and substantive limits on the power of Congress and the President to remove the Comptroller make dislodging him against his will practically impossible.

[Realistic] consideration of the nature of the Comptroller General's relation to Congress thus reveals that the threat to separation of powers conjured up by the majority is wholly chimerical.

[The] majority's contrary conclusion rests on the rigid dogma that, outside of the impeachment process, any "direct congressional role in the removal of officers charged with the execution of the laws . . . is inconsistent with separation of powers." *Ante,* at 3187. Reliance on such an unyielding principle to strike down a statute posing no real danger of aggrandizement of congressional power is extremely misguided and insensitive to our constitutional role. I dissent.

MORRISON v. OLSON
487 U.S. 654 (1988)

Chief Justice REHNQUIST delivered the opinion of the Court.

This case presents us with a challenge to the independent counsel provisions of the Ethics in Government Act of 1978. We hold today that these provisions of the Act do not violate the Appointments Clause of the Constitution, Art. II, §2, cl. 2, or the limitations of Article III, nor do they impermissibly interfere with the President's authority under Article II in violation of the constitutional principle of separation of powers.

Briefly stated, Title VI of the Ethics of Government Act allows for the appointment of an "independent counsel" to investigate and, if appropriate, prosecute certain high ranking government officials for violations of federal criminal laws. The Act requires the Attorney General, upon receipt of information that he determines is "sufficient to constitute grounds to investigate whether any person [covered by the Act] may have violated any Federal criminal law," to conduct a preliminary investigation of the matter. When the Attorney General has completed this investigation, or 90 days has elapsed, he is required to report to a special court (the Special Division) created by the Act "for the purpose of appointing independent counsels." If the Attorney General determines that "there are no reasonable grounds to believe that further investigation is warranted," then he must notify the Special Division of this result. In such a case, "the division of the court shall have no power to appoint an independent counsel." If, however, the Attorney General has determined that there are "reasonable grounds to believe that further investigation or prosecution is warranted," then he "shall apply to the division of the court for the appointment of an independent counsel." The Attorney General's application to the court "shall contain sufficient information to assist the [court] in selecting an independent counsel and in defining that independent counsel's prosecutorial jurisdiction." Upon receiving this application, the Special Division "shall appoint an appropriate independent counsel and shall define that independent counsel's prosecutorial jurisdiction." . . .

[The act provides that the independent counsel can be removed from office only by impeachment or by personal action of the Attorney General for good cause, physical disability, mental incapacity, "or any other condition that substantially impairs the performance of such independent counsel's duties." It also provides that the counsel can be "terminated" if the Special Division finds that "the investigation of all matters within the prosecutorial jurisdiction of such independent counsel . . . have been completed or so substantially completed that it would be appropriate for the Department of Justice to complete such investigations and prosecutions."]

A divided Court of Appeals [invalidated the act]. We now reverse. . . .

III. The line between "inferior" and "principal" officers is one that is far from clear, and the Framers provided little guidance into where it should be drawn. . . . We need not attempt here to decide exactly where the line falls between the two types of officers, because in our view appellant clearly falls on the "inferior officer" side of that line. Several factors lead to this conclusion. [The Court relies on the fact that the special prosecutor could be removed by the Attorney General, that she was authorized to perform only certain limited duties, and that her office was limited in jurisdiction and tenure.]

This does not, however, end our inquiry under the Appointments Clause. Appellees argue that even if appellant is an "inferior" officer, the Clause does not empower Congress to place the power to appoint such an officer outside the Executive Branch. They contend that the Clause does not contemplate congressional authorization of "interbranch appointments," in which an officer of one branch is appointed by officers of another branch. The relevant language of the Appointments Clause is worth repeating. It reads: ". . . but the Congress may by Law vest the Appointment of such inferior Officers, as they think proper, in the President alone, in the courts of Law, or in the Heads of Departments." On its face, the language of this "excepting clause" admits of no limitation on interbranch appointments. Indeed, the inclusion of "as they think proper" seems clearly to give Congress significant discretion to determine whether it is "proper" to vest the appointment of, for example, executive officials in the "courts of Law." . . .

We do not mean to say that Congress' power to provide for interbranch appointments of "inferior officers" is unlimited. In addition to separation of powers concerns, which would arise if such provisions for appointment had the potential to impair the constitutional functions assigned to one of the branches, [Congress'] decision to vest the appointment power in the courts would be improper if there was some "incongruity" between the functions normally performed by the courts and the performance of their duty to appoint. [In] this case, however, we do not think it impermissible for Congress to vest the power to appoint independent counsels in a specially created federal court. We thus disagree with the Court of Appeals' conclusion that there is an inherent incongruity about a court having the power to appoint prosecutorial officers.12 We have recognized that courts may appoint private attorneys to act as prosecutor for judicial contempt judgments. . . .

Congress of course was concerned when it created the office of independent counsel with the conflicts of interest that could arise in situations when the Executive Branch is called upon to investigate its own high-ranking officers. If it were to remove the appointing authority from the Executive Branch, the most logical place to put it was in the Judicial Branch. In the light of the Act's provision making the judges of the Special Division ineligible to participate in any matters relating to an independent counsel they have appointed, we do not think that appointment of the independent counsels by the court runs afoul of the constitutional limitation on "incongruous" interbranch appointments.

IV. Appellees next contend that the powers vested in the Special Division by the Act conflict with Article III of the Constitution. . . .

[The Court concludes that miscellaneous powers granted to the Special Division are mostly either "passive" or "ministerial" in nature and therefore pose no serious Article III difficulty. Although the provision authorizing the Special Division to terminate the office of independent counsel was more troubling, the Court interprets the provision as no more than "a device for removing from the public payroll an independent counsel who has served her purpose, but is unwilling to acknowledge the fact." As so construed, the termination power did not "pose a sufficient threat of judicial intrusion into matters that are more properly within the Executive's authority to require that the Act be invalidated as inconsistent with Article III."]

V. Two related issues must be addressed: The first is whether the provision of the Act restricting the Attorney General's power to remove the independent counsel to only those instances in which he can show "good cause," taken by itself, impermissibly interferes with the President's exercise of his constitutionally appointed functions. The second is whether, taken as a whole, the Act violates the separation of powers by reducing the President's ability to control the prosecutorial powers wielded by the independent counsel.

a. We held in Bowsher that "Congress cannot reserve for itself the power of removal of an officer charged with the execution of the laws except by impeachment." A primary antecedent for this ruling was our 1925 decision in [Myers]. . . .

Unlike both Bowsher and Myers, this case does not involve an attempt by Congress itself to gain a role in the removal of executive officials other than its established powers of impeachment and conviction. The Act instead puts the removal power squarely in the hands of the Executive Branch; an independent counsel may be removed from office, "only by the personal action of the Attorney General, and only for good cause." There is no requirement of congressional approval of the Attorney General's removal decision, though the decision is subject to judicial review. In our view, the removal provisions of the Act make this case more analogous to Humphrey's Executor v. United States, and Weiner v. United States, than to Myers or Bowsher. . . .

Appellees contend that Humphrey's Executor and Wiener are distinguishable from this case because they did not involve officials who performed a "core executive function." They argue that our decision in Humphrey's Executor rests on a distinction between "purely executive" officials and officials who exercise "quasi-legislative" and "quasi-judicial" powers. . . .

We undoubtedly did rely on the terms "quasi-legislative" and "quasi-judicial" to distinguish the officials involved in Humphrey's Executor and Wiener from those in Myers, but our present considered view is that the determination of whether the Constitution allows Congress to impose a "good cause"-type restriction on the President's power to remove an official cannot be made to turn on whether or not that official is classified as "purely executive." The analysis contained in our removal cases is designed not to define rigid categories of those officials who may or may not be removed at will by the President, but to ensure that Congress does not interfere with the President's exercise of the "executive power" and his constitutionally appointed duty to "take care that the laws be faithfully executed" under Article II. . . .

We do not mean to suggest that an analysis of the functions served by the officials at issue is irrelevant. But the real question is whether the removal restrictions are of such a nature that they impede the President's ability to perform his constitutional duty, and the functions of the officials in question must be analyzed in that light. Considering for the moment the "good cause" removal provision in isolation from the other parts of the Act at issue in this case, we cannot say that the imposition of a "good cause" standard for removal by itself unduly trammels on executive authority. . . .

Although the counsel exercises no small amount of discretion and judgment in deciding how to carry out her duties under the Act, we simply do not see how the President's need to control the exercise of that discretion is so central to the functioning of the Executive Branch as to require as a matter of constitutional law that the counsel be terminable at will by the President.

Nor do we think that the "good cause" removal provision at issue here impermissibly burdens the President's power to control or supervise the independent counsel, as an executive official, in the execution of her duties under the Act. This is not a case in which the power to remove an executive official has been completely stripped from the President, thus providing no means for the President to ensure the "faithful execution" of the laws. Rather, because the independent counsel may be terminated for "good cause," the Executive, through the Attorney General, retains ample authority to assure that the counsel is competently performing her statutory responsibilities in a manner that comports with the provisions of the Act. Although we need not decide in this case exactly what is encompassed with the term "good cause" under the Act, the legislative history of the removal provision also makes clear that the Attorney General may remove an independent counsel for "misconduct." . . .

We do not think that this limitation as it presently stands sufficiently deprives the President of control over the independent counsel to interfere impermissibly with his constitutional obligation to ensure the faithful execution of the laws.

b. The final question to be addressed is whether the Act, taken as a whole, violates the principle of separation of powers by unduly interfering with the role of the Executive Branch. . . .

[We] have never held that the Constitution requires that the three Branches of Government "operate with absolute independence." . . .

We observe first that this case does not involve an attempt by Congress to increase its own powers at the expense of the Executive Branch. Unlike some of our previous cases, most recently Bowsher v. Synar, this case simply does not pose a "dange[r] of congressional usurpation of Executive Branch functions," [See] also [Chadha]. . . .

Similarly, we do not think that the Act works any judicial usurpation of properly executive functions. . . .

Finally, we do not think that the Act "impermissibly undermine[s]" the powers of the Executive Branch, or "disrupts the proper balance between the coordinate branches [by] prevent[ing] the Executive Branch from accomplishing its constitutionally assigned functions." It is undeniable that the Act reduces the amount of control or supervision that the Attorney General and, through him, the President exercises over the investigation and prosecution of a certain class of alleged criminal activity. . . .

Nonetheless, the Act does give the Attorney General several means of supervising or controlling the prosecutorial powers that may be wielded by an independent counsel. . . .

The decision of the Court of Appeals is therefore reversed.

Justice Kennedy took no part in the consideration or decision of this case.

Justice SCALIA, dissenting. . . .

II. If to describe this case is not to decide it, the concept of a government of separate and coordinate powers no longer has meaning. The Court devotes most of its attention to such relatively technical details as the Appointments Clause and the removal power, addressing briefly and only at the end of its opinion the separation of powers. [I] think that has it backwards. Our opinions are full of the recognition that it is the principle of separation of powers, and the inseparable corollary that each department's "defense must . . . be made commensurate to the danger of attack," Federalist No. 51, p. 322 (J. Madison), which gives comprehensible content to the appointments clause, and determines the appropriate scope of the removal power. . . .

Art. II, §1, cl. 1 of the Constitution provides: "The executive Power shall be vested in a President of the United States." [T]his does not mean some of the executive power, but all of the executive power. It seems to me, therefore, that the decision of the Court of Appeals invalidating the present statute must be upheld on fundamental separation-of-powers principles if the following two questions are answered affirmatively: (1) Is the conduct of a criminal prosecution (and of an investigation to decide whether to prosecute) the exercise of purely executive power? (2) Does the statute deprive the President of the United States of exclusive control over the exercise of that power? Surprising to say, the Court appears to concede an affirmative answer to both questions, but seeks to avoid the inevitable conclusion that since the statute vests some purely executive power in a person who is not the President of the United States it is void.

The Court concedes that "[t]here is no real dispute that the functions performed by the independent counsel are 'executive'," though it qualifies that concession by adding "in the sense that they are 'law enforcement' functions that typically have been undertaken by officials within the Executive Branch." The qualifier adds nothing but atmosphere. In what other sense can one identify "the executive Power" that is supposed to be vested in the President (unless it includes everything the Executive Branch is given to do) except by reference to what has always and everywhere — if conducted by Government at all — been conducted never by the legislature, never by the courts, and always by the executive. There is no possible doubt that the independent counsel's functions fit this description. . . .

As for the second question, whether the statute before us deprives the President of exclusive control over that quintessentially executive activity, the Court does not, and could not possibly, assert that it does not. That is indeed the whole object of the statute. Instead, the Court points out that the President, through his Attorney General, has at least some control. That concession is alone enough to invalidate the statute, but I cannot refrain from pointing out that the Court greatly exaggerates the extent of that "some" presidential control. . . .

The utter incompatibility of the Court's approach with our constitutional traditions can be made more clear, perhaps, by applying it to the powers of the other two Branches. Is it conceivable that if Congress passed a statute depriving itself of less than full and entire control over some insignificant area of legislation, we would inquire whether the matter was "so central to the functioning of the Legislative Branch" as really to require complete control, or whether the statute gives Congress "sufficient control over the surrogate legislator to ensure that Congress is able to perform its constitutionally assigned duties"? Of course we would have none of that. Once we determined that a purely legislative power was at issue we would require it to be exercised, wholly and entirely, by Congress. Or to bring the point closer to home, consider a statute giving to non-Article III judges just a tiny bit of purely judicial power in a relatively insignificant field, with substantial control, though not total control, in the courts — perhaps "clear error" review, which would be a fair judicial equivalent of the Attorney General's "for cause" removal power here. Is there any doubt that we would not pause to inquire whether the matter was "so central to the functioning of the Judicial Branch" as really to require complete control, or whether we retained "sufficient control over the matters to be decided that we are able to perform our constitutionally assigned duties"? We would say that our "constitutionally assigned duties" include complete control over all exercises of the judicial power — or, as the plurality opinion said in Northern Pipeline Construction Co. v. Marathon Pipe Line Co., that "[t]he inexorable command of [article III] is clear and definite: The judicial power of the United States must be exercised by courts having the attributes prescribed in Art. III." We should say here that the President's constitutionally assigned duties include complete control over investigation and prosecution of violations of the law, and that the inexorable command of Article II is clear and definite: the executive power must be vested in the President of the United States.

Is it unthinkable that the President should have such exclusive power, even when alleged crimes by him or his close associates are at issue? No more so than that Congress should have the exclusive power of legislation, even when what is at issue is its own exemption from the burdens of certain laws. No more so than that this Court should have the exclusive power to pronounce the final decision on justiciable cases and controversies, even those pertaining to the constitutionality of a statute reducing the salaries of the Justices. A system of separate and coordinate powers necessarily involves an acceptance of exclusive power that can theoretically be abused. . . .

The Court has, nonetheless, replaced the clear constitutional prescription that the executive power belongs to the President with a "balancing test." What are the standards to determine how the balance is to be struck, that is, how much removal of presidential power is too much? Many countries of the world get along with an Executive that is much weaker than ours — in fact, entirely dependent upon the continued support of the legislature. Once we depart from the text of the Constitution, just where short of that do we stop? The most amazing feature of the Court's opinion is that it does not even purport to give an answer. It simply announces, with no analysis, that the ability to control the decision whether to investigate and prosecute the President's closest advisors, and indeed the President himself, is not "so central to the functioning of the Executive Branch" as to be constitutionally required to be within the President's control. . . .

Besides weakening the Presidency by reducing the zeal of his staff, it must also be obvious that the institution of the independent counsel enfeebles him more directly in his constant confrontations with Congress, by eroding his public support. Nothing is so politically effective as the ability to charge that one's opponent and his associates are not merely wrong-headed, naive, ineffective, but, in all probability, "crooks." And nothing so effectively gives an appearance of validity to such charges as a Justice Department investigation and, even better, prosecution. The present statute provides ample means for that sort of attack, assuring that massive and lengthy investigations will occur, not merely when the Justice Department in the application of its usual standards believes they are called for, but whenever it cannot be said that there are "no reasonable grounds to believe" they are called for. . . .

[The] Court does not attempt to "decide exactly" what establishes the line between principal and "inferior" officers, but is confident that, whatever the line may be, appellant "clearly falls on the 'inferior officer' side" of it. . . .

[Justice Scalia points out that most principal officers are removable at will and not simply for cause and argues that the majority understates the scope of the independent counsel's powers.] I think it preferable to look to the text of the Constitution and the division of power that it establishes. These demonstrate, I think, that the independent counsel is not an inferior officer because she is not subordinate to any officer in the Executive Branch (indeed, not even to the President). Dictionaries in use at the time of the Constitutional Convention gave the word "inferiour" two meanings which it still bears today: (1) "[l]ower in place, . . . station, . . . rank of life, . . . value or excellency," and (2) "[s]ubordinate." S. Johnson, Dictionary of the English Language (6th ed. 1785). In a document dealing with the structure (the constitution) of a government, one would naturally expect the word to bear the latter meaning — indeed, in such a context it would be unpardonably careless to use the word unless a relationship of subordination was intended. . . .

IV . . . There is of course no provision in the Constitution stating who may remove executive officers, except the provisions for removal by impeachment. Before the present decision it was established, however, (1) that the President's power to remove principal officers who exercise purely executive powers could not be restricted, see [Myers], and (2) that his power to remove inferior officers who exercise purely executive powers, and whose appointment Congress had removed from the usual procedure of presidential appointment with Senate consent, could be restricted, at least where the appointment had been made by an officer of the Executive Branch. . . .

Since our 1935 decision in [Humphrey's Executor] — which was considered by many at the time the product of an activist, anti-New Deal court bent on reducing the power of President Franklin Roosevelt — it has been established that the line of permissible restriction upon removal of principal officers lies at the point at which the powers exercised by those officers are no longer purely executive. . . .

What Humphrey's Executor (and presumably Myers) really means, we are now told, is not that there are any "rigid categories of those officials who may or may not be removed at will by the President," but simply that Congress cannot "interfere with the President's exercise of the 'executive power' and his constitutionally appointed duty to 'take care that the laws be faithfully executed.'" . . . Humphrey's Executor at least had the decency formally to observe the constitutional principle that the President had to be the repository of all executive power, which, as Myers carefully explained, necessarily means that he must be able to discharge those who do not perform executive functions according to his liking. . . .

By contrast, "our present considered view" is simply that any Executive officer's removal can be restricted, so long as the President remains "able to accomplish his constitutional role." There are now no lines. If the removal of a prosecutor, the virtual embodiment of the power to "take care that the laws be faithfully executed," can be restricted, what officer's removal cannot? This is an open invitation for Congress to experiment. What about a special Assistant Secretary of State, with responsibility for one very narrow area of foreign policy, who would not only have to be confirmed by the Senate but could also be removed only pursuant to certain carefully designed restrictions? Could this possibly render the President "[un]able to accomplish his constitutional role"? Or a special Assistant Secretary of Defense for Procurement? The possibilities are endless, and the Court does not understand what the separation of powers, what "[a]mbition . . . counteract[ing] ambition," Federalist No. 51, p. 322 (Madison), is all about, if it does not expect Congress to try them. As far as I can discern from the Court's opinion, it is now open season upon the President's removal power for all executive officers, with not even the superficially principled restriction of Humphrey's Executor as cover. The Court essentially says to the President "Trust us. We will make sure that you are able to accomplish your constitutional role." I think the Constitution gives the President — and the people — more protection than that.

V. The purpose of the separation and equilibration of powers in general, and of the unitary Executive in particular, was not merely to assure effective government but to preserve individual freedom. Those who hold or have held offices covered by the Ethics in Government Act are entitled to that protection as much as the rest of us, and I conclude my discussion by considering the effect of the Act upon the fairness of the process they receive.

Only someone who has worked in the field of law enforcement can fully appreciate the vast power and the immense discretion that are placed in the hands of a prosecutor with respect to the objects of his investigation. . . .

Under our system of government, the primary check against prosecutorial abuse is a political one. The prosecutors who exercise this awesome discretion are selected and can be removed by a President, whom the people have trusted enough to elect. Moreover, when crimes are not investigated and prosecuted fairly, nonselectively, with a reasonable sense of proportion, the President pays the cost in political damage to his administration. . . .

That is the system of justice the rest of us are entitled to, but what of that select class consisting of present or former high-level executive-branch officials? If an allegation is made against them of any violation of any federal criminal law (except Class B or C misdemeanors or infractions) the Attorney General must give it his attention. That in itself is not objectionable. But if, after a 90-day investigation without the benefit of normal investigatory tools, the Attorney General is unable to say that there are "no reasonable grounds to believe" that further investigation is warranted, a process is set in motion that is not in the full control of persons "dependent on the people," and whose flaws cannot be blamed on the President. An independent counsel is selected, and the scope of her authority prescribed, by a panel of judges. What if they are politically partisan, as judges have been known to be, and select a prosecutor antagonistic to the administration, or even to the particular individual who has been selected for this special treatment? There is no remedy for that, not even a political one. . . .

It is, in other words, an additional advantage of the unitary Executive that it can achieve a more uniform application of the law. Perhaps that is not always achieved, but the mechanism to achieve it is there. The mini-Executive that is the independent counsel, however, operating in an area where so little is law and so much is discretion, is intentionally cut off from the unifying influence of the Justice Department, and from the perspective that multiple responsibilities provide. What would normally be regarded as a technical violation (there are no rules defining such things), may in her small world assume the proportions of an indictable offense. . . .

The ad hoc approach to constitutional adjudication has real attraction, even apart from its work-saving potential. It is guaranteed to produce a result, in every case, that will make a majority of the Court happy with the law. The law is, by definition, precisely what the majority thinks, taking all things into account, it ought to be. I prefer to rely upon the judgment of the wise men who constructed our system, and of the people who approved it, and of two centuries of history that have shown it to be sound. Like it or not, that judgment says, quite plainly, that "[t]he executive Power shall be vested in a President of the United States."

———————

FREE ENTERPRISE FUND v. PUBLIC COMPANY ACCOUNTING OVERSIGHT BOARD, 561 U.S. 477 (2010). Established as part of a series of accounting reforms in the Sarbanes-Oxley Act of 2002, the Public Company Accounting Oversight Board is composed of five members appointed by the Securities and Exchange Commission (SEC), which is required by statute to be bipartisan. The Board has broad authority to inspect and investigate private accounting firms and impose sanctions against them. The SEC may remove Board members only for "good cause," and the President may remove SEC Commissioners only for "inefficiency, neglect of duty, or malfeasance in office."

In a 5–4 decision invalidating the removal provision as violating the separation of powers, Chief Justice Roberts wrote for the Court, joined by Justices Scalia, Kennedy, Thomas, and Alito:

We have previously [e.g., in Humphrey's Executor and Morrison v. Olson (1988); upheld limited restrictions on the President's removal power. In those cases, however, only one level of protected tenure separated the President from an officer exercising executive power. It was the President — or a subordinate he could remove at will — who decided whether the officer's conduct merited removal under the good-cause standard. The Act before us does something quite different. It not only protects Board members from removal except for good cause, but withdraws from the President any decision on whether that good cause exists. That decision is vested instead in other tenured officers — the Commissioners — none of whom is subject to the President's direct control. The result is a Board that is not accountable to the President, and a President who is not responsible for the Board.

The added layer of tenure protection makes a difference. Without a layer of insulation between the Commission and the Board, the Commission could remove a Board member at any time, and therefore would be fully responsible for what the Board does. The President could then hold the Commission to account for its supervision of the Board, to the same extent that he may hold the Commission to account for everything else it does. A second level of tenure protection changes the nature of the President's review. Now the Commission cannot remove a Board member at will. The President therefore cannot hold the Commission fully accountable for the Board's conduct, to the same extent that he may hold the Commission accountable for everything else that it does. The Commissioners are not responsible for the Board's actions. They are only responsible for their own determination of whether the Act's rigorous good cause standard is met. And even if the President disagrees with their determination, he is powerless to intervene — unless that determination is so unreasonable as to constitute "inefficiency, neglect of duty, or malfeasance in office." This novel structure does not merely add to the Board's independence, but transforms it. Neither the President, nor anyone directly responsible to him, nor even an officer whose conduct he may review only for good cause, has full control over the Board. The President is stripped of the power our precedents have preserved, and his ability to execute the laws — by holding his subordinates accountable for their conduct — is impaired. That arrangement is contrary to Article II's vesting of the executive power in the President." The majority found the invalid removal provisions severable, excising them and leaving Board members removable by the SEC at will while leaving the rest of Sarbanes-Oxley intact.

Justice Breyer filed a dissent joined by Justices Stevens, Ginsburg and Sotomayor:

In Myers, the Court invalidated — for the first and only time — a congressional statute on the ground that it unduly limited the President's authority to remove an Executive Branch official. But soon thereafter the Court expressly disapproved most of Myers' broad reasoning. See Humphrey's Executor. [The] Court has since said that "the essence of the decision in Myers" [was] the judgment that the Constitution prevents Congress from "draw[ing] to itself . . . the power to remove or the right to participate in the exercise of that power." Morrison. [Congress] has not granted itself any role in removing the members of the Accounting Board. [When] previously deciding this kind of nontextual question, the Court has emphasized the importance of examining how a particular provision, taken in context, is likely to function. [E.g., Steel Seizure.] It is not surprising that the Court in these circumstances has looked to function and context, and not to bright-line rules. For one thing, that approach embodies the intent of the Framers. As Chief Justice Marshall long ago observed, our Constitution is fashioned so as to allow the three coordinate branches, including this Court, to exercise practical judgment in response to changing conditions and "exigencies." McCulloch. For another, a functional approach permits Congress and the President the flexibility needed to adapt statutory law to changing circumstances.

[The] "for cause" restriction before us will not restrict presidential power significantly. For one thing, the restriction directly limits, not the President's power, but the power of an already independent agency. [The] statute provides the Commission with full authority and virtually comprehensive control over all of the Board's functions. [The] Commission's control over the Board's investigatory and legal functions is virtually absolute. Moreover, the Commission [controls] the Board's budget, [can] assign to the Board any "duties or functions" that it "determines are necessary or appropriate," [and] has full "oversight and enforcement authority over the Board," including the authority to inspect the Board's activities whenever it believes it "appropriate" to do so. [Everyone] concedes that the President's control over the Commission is constitutionally sufficient. See Humphrey's Executor. And if the President's control over the Commission is sufficient, and the Commission's control over the Board is virtually absolute, then, as a practical matter, the President's control over the Board should prove sufficient as well. [This] Court has long recognized the appropriateness of using "for cause" provisions to protect the personal independence of those who [engage] in adjudicatory functions. Humphrey's Executor. Moreover, in addition to their adjudicative functions, the Accounting Board members supervise, and are themselves, technical professional experts. This Court has recognized [the] constitutional legitimacy of a justification that rests agency independence upon the need for technical expertise. Humphrey's Executor. [Congress] and the President could reasonably have thought it prudent to insulate the adjudicative Board members from fear of purely politically based removal.

Notes

Following up on the structural approach laid out in *Free Enterprise Fund* Chief Justice Roberts, writing for the majority in Seila Law v. Consumer Financial Protection Bureau 590 U.S.___(2020), decided that an agency such as the CFPB exercised sufficient executive functions including enforcement of financial statutes, assessing administrative penalties, and policy-making, to be an executive agency that should be subject to the President's direct control, and that would include removal at will. Like in *Free Enterprise*, Roberts found the provision that limited the President's removal discretion of the lone officer of the CFPB (the Director) insufficient under the Congressional legislation creating the agency and hence a violation of the principle of separation of powers. Under the law, the President's removal discretion over the Director, who is appointed for a five-year term, is limited to removal for "inefficiency, neglect of duty, or malfeasance in office"—but not at will as would be the case of any other executive officer such as a Cabinet secretary, making the Director, under Robert's reasoning, not subject to the kind of Presidential oversight over policy and enforcement that, according to Roberts, is required within the

Executive Branch. Important also to Roberts's view that the legislation did not allow direct presidential control over the agency is the fact that "[t]he CFPB receives its funding outside the annual appropriations process from the Federal Reserve, which is itself funded outside the appropriations process through bank assessments."

Justice Kagan, in a dissent joined by Justices Sotomayor, Ginsburg, and Breyer, took issue with the Chief Justice's model of executive power. Kagan's argument begins with the position that, traditionally, Congress and the executive branch have worked out the structure and power distribution over regulatory agencies among themselves, implying that such questions are political in the sense that they are beyond the competency of the courts. Furthermore, regarding Roberts's association of at-will removal power as a feature of constitutional executive power, Justice Kagan argued that "[t]he majority relies for its contrary vision on Article II's Vesting Clause [defining the powers of the three branches, eds] but the provision can't carry all that weight. Or as Chief Justice Rehnquist wrote of a similar claim in Morrison v. Olson, 487 U. S. 654 (1988), "extrapolat[ing]" an unrestricted removal power from such "general constitutional language"—which says only that "[t]he executive Power shall be vested in a President"—is 'more than the text will bear.'" Instead, Kagan argued, the Court precedent has recognized that "Congress could protect from at-will removal the officials it deemed to need some independence from political pressures. Nowhere do those precedents suggest what the majority announces today: that the President has an 'unrestricted removal power' subject to two bounded exceptions."

The debate over executive power, or the "Unitary Executive Theory" continues.

NLRB v. NOEL CANNING
573 U.S. 513 (2014)

Justice BREYER delivered the opinion of the Court.

Ordinarily the President must obtain "the Advice and Consent of the Senate" before appointing an "Office[r] of the United States." But the Recess Appointments Clause creates an exception. It gives the President alone the power "to fill up all Vacancies that may happen during the Recess of the Senate, by granting Commissions which shall expire at the End of their next Session." Art. II, §2, cl. 3. We here consider three questions about the application of this Clause.

The first concerns the scope of the words "recess of the Senate." Does that phrase refer only to an inter-session recess (*i.e.*, a break between formal sessions of Congress), or does it also include an intra-session recess, such as a summer recess in the midst of a session? We conclude that the Clause applies to both kinds of recess.

The second question concerns the scope of the words "vacancies that may happen." Does that phrase refer only to vacancies that first come into existence during a recess, or does it also include vacancies that arise prior to a recess but continue to exist during the recess? We conclude that the Clause applies to both kinds of vacancy.

The third question concerns calculation of the length of a "recess." The President made the appointments here at issue on January 4, 2012. At that time the Senate was in recess pursuant to a December 17, 2011, resolution providing for a series of brief recesses punctuated by "*pro forma* session[s]," with "no business . . . transacted," every Tuesday and Friday through January 20, 2012. In calculating the length of a recess are we to ignore the *pro forma* sessions, thereby treating the series of brief recesses as a single, month-long recess? We conclude that we cannot ignore these *pro forma* sessions.

Our answer to the third question means that, when the appointments before us took place, the Senate was in the midst of a 3-day recess. Three days is too short a time to bring a recess within the scope of the Clause. Thus we conclude that the President lacked the power to make the recess appointments here at issue.

I

The case before us arises out of a labor dispute. The National Labor Relations Board (NLRB) found that a Pepsi-Cola distributor, Noel Canning, had unlawfully refused to reduce to writing and execute a collective-bargaining agreement with a labor union. The Board ordered the distributor to execute the agreement and to make employees whole for any losses. The Pepsi-Cola distributor subsequently asked the Court of Appeals for the District of Columbia Circuit to set the Board's order aside. It claimed that three of the five Board members had been invalidly appointed, leaving the Board without the three lawfully appointed members necessary for it to act.

The three members in question were Sharon Block, Richard Griffin, and Terence Flynn. In 2011 the President had nominated each of them to the Board. As of January 2012, Flynn's nomination had been pending in the Senate awaiting confirmation for approximately a year. The nominations of each of the other two had been pending for a few weeks. On January 4, 2012, the President, invoking the Recess Appointments Clause, appointed all three to the Board.

II

Before turning to the specific questions presented, we shall mention two background considerations that we find relevant to all three. First, *the Recess Appointments Clause sets forth a subsidiary, not a primary, method for appointing officers of the United States.* The immediately preceding Clause — Article II, Section 2, Clause 2 — provides the primary method of appointment. It says that the President "shall nominate, *and by and with the Advice and Consent of the Senate,* shall appoint Ambassadors, other public Ministers and Consuls, Judges of the supreme Court, and all other Officers of the United States." The Federalist Papers make clear that the Founders intended this method of appointment, requiring Senate approval, to be the norm (at least for principal officers). Thus the Recess Appointments Clause reflects the tension between, on the one hand, the President's continuous need for "the assistance of subordinates," and, on the other, the Senate's practice, particularly during the Republic's early years, of meeting for a single brief session each year.

Second, in interpreting the Clause, we put significant weight upon historical practice. For one thing, the interpretive questions before us concern the allocation of power between two elected branches of Government. We recognize, of course, that the separation of powers can serve to safeguard individual liberty, and that it is the "duty of the judicial department" — in a separation-of-powers case as in any other — "to say what the law is." But it is equally true that the longstanding "practice of the government," can inform our determination of "what the law is." That principle is neither new nor controversial.

There is a great deal of history to consider here. Presidents have made recess appointments since the beginning of the Republic. Their frequency suggests that the Senate and President have recognized that recess appointments can be both necessary and appropriate in certain circumstances. We have not previously interpreted the Clause, and, when doing so for the first time in more than 200 years, we must hesitate to upset the compromises and working arrangements that the elected branches of Government themselves have reached.

III

The first question concerns the scope of the phrase "*the recess* of the Senate." The Constitution provides for congressional elections every two years. And the 2-year life of each elected Congress typically consists of two formal 1-year sessions, each separated from the next by an "intersession recess." The Senate or the House of Representatives announces an inter-session recess by approving a resolution stating that it will "adjourn *sine die*," i.e., without specifying a date to return (in which case Congress will reconvene when the next formal session is scheduled to begin).

The Senate and the House also take breaks in the midst of a session. The Senate or the House announces any such "intra-session recess" by adopting a resolution stating that it will "adjourn" to a fixed date, a few days or weeks or even months later. All agree that the phrase "the recess of the Senate" covers inter-session recesses. The question is whether it includes intra-session recesses as well.

In our view, the phrase "the recess" includes an intra-session recess of substantial length. Its words taken literally can refer to both types of recess. Founding-era dictionaries define the word "recess," much as we do today, simply as "a period of cessation from usual work." We recognize that the word "the" in "*the* recess" might suggest that the phrase refers to the single break separating formal sessions of Congress. That is because the word "the" frequently (but not always) indicates "a particular thing." But the word can also refer "to a term used generically or universally." Reading "the" generically in this way, there is no linguistic problem applying the Clause's phrase to both kinds of recess. And, in fact, the phrase "the recess" was used to refer to intra-session recesses at the time of the founding.

The constitutional text is thus ambiguous. And we believe the Clause's purpose demands the broader interpretation. The Clause gives the President authority to make appointments during "the recess of the Senate" so that the President can ensure the continued functioning of the Federal Government when the Senate is away. The Senate is equally away during both an inter-session and an intra-session recess, and its capacity to participate in the appointments process has nothing to do with the words it uses to signal its departure.

History also offers strong support for the broad interpretation. We concede that pre-Civil War history is not helpful. But it shows only that Congress generally took long breaks between sessions, while taking no significant intra-session breaks at all (five times it took a break of a week or so at Christmas). Obviously, if there are no significant intra-session recesses, there will be no intra-session recess appointments. In 1867 and 1868, Congress for the first time took substantial, nonholiday intrasession breaks, and President Andrew Johnson made dozens of recess appointments.

In all, between the founding and the Great Depression, Congress took substantial intra-session breaks (other than holiday breaks) in four years: 1867, 1868, 1921, and 1929. And in each of those years the President made intra-session recess appointments.

Since 1929, and particularly since the end of World War II, Congress has shortened its inter-session breaks as it has taken longer and more frequent intra-session breaks; Presidents have correspondingly made more intra-session recess appointments. Indeed, if we include military appointments, Presidents have made thousands of intra-session recess appointments.

The upshot is that restricting the Clause to inter-session recesses would frustrate its purpose. It would make the President's recess-appointment power dependent on a formalistic distinction of Senate procedure. Moreover, the President has consistently and frequently interpreted the word "recess" to apply to intra-session recesses, and has acted on that interpretation. The Senate as a body has done nothing to deny the validity of this practice for at least three-quarters of a century. And three-quarters of a century of settled practice is long enough to entitle a practice to "great weight in a proper interpretation" of the constitutional provision. The greater interpretive problem is determining how long a recess must be in order to fall within the Clause. Is a break of a week, or a day, or an hour too short to count as a "recess"? The Clause itself does not say. And Justice Scalia claims that this silence itself shows that the Framers intended the Clause to apply only to an inter-session recess. We disagree. For one thing, the most likely reason the Framers did not place a textual floor underneath the word "recess" is that they did not foresee the *need* for one. They might have expected that the Senate would meet for a single session lasting at most half a year. Moreover, the lack of a textual floor raises a problem that plagues *both* interpretations — Justice Scalia's and ours. Today a brief inter-session recess is just as possible as a brief intra-session recess.

Even the Solicitor General, arguing for a broader interpretation, acknowledges that there is a lower limit applicable to both kinds of recess. He argues that the lower limit should be three days by analogy to the Adjournments Clause of the Constitution.

We agree with the Solicitor General that a 3-day recess would be too short. A Senate recess that is so short that it does not require the consent of the House is not long enough to trigger the President's recess-appointment power.

That is not to say that the President may make recess appointments during any recess that is "more than three days." The Recess Appointments Clause seeks to permit the Executive Branch to function smoothly when Congress is unavailable. And though Congress has taken short breaks for almost 200 years, and there have been many thousands of recess appointments in that time, we have not found a single example of a recess appointment made during an intra-session recess that was shorter than 10 days.

In sum, we conclude that the phrase "the recess" applies to both intrasession and inter-session recesses. If a Senate recess is so short that it does not require the consent of the House, it is too short to trigger the Recess Appointments Clause. And a recess lasting less than 10 days is presumptively too short as well.

IV

The second question concerns the scope of the phrase "vacancies *that may happen* during the recess of the Senate." All agree that the phrase applies to vacancies that initially occur during a recess. But does it also apply to vacancies that initially occur before a recess and continue to exist during the recess? In our view the phrase applies to both kinds of vacancy.

We believe that the Clause's language, read literally, permits, though it does not naturally favor, our broader interpretation. We concede that the most natural meaning of "happens" as applied to a "vacancy" (at least to a modern ear) is that the vacancy "happens" when it initially occurs. But that is not the only possible way to use the word. In any event, the linguistic question here is not whether the phrase can be, but whether it must be, read more narrowly. The question is whether the Clause is ambiguous. And the broader reading, we believe, is at least a permissible reading of a " 'doubtful' " phrase. We consequently go on to consider the Clause's purpose and historical practice. The Clause's purpose strongly supports the broader interpretation. That purpose is to permit the President to obtain the assistance of subordinate officers when the Senate, due to its recess, cannot confirm them. At the same time, we recognize one important purpose-related consideration that argues in the opposite direction. A broad interpretation might permit a President to avoid Senate confirmations as a matter of course. If the Clause gives the President the power to "fill up all vacancies" that occur before, and continue to exist during, the Senate's recess, a President might not submit any nominations to the Senate. He might simply wait for a recess and then provide all potential nominees with recess appointments. He might thereby routinely avoid the constitutional need to obtain the Senate's "advice and consent." A recess appointee only serves a limited term. That, combined with the lack of Senate approval, may diminish the recess appointee's ability, as a practical matter, to get a controversial job done. And even where the President and Senate are at odds over politically sensitive appointments, compromise is normally possible. In an unusual instance, where a matter is important enough to the Senate, that body can remain in session, preventing recess appointments by refusing to take a recess. In any event, the Executive Branch has adhered to the broader interpretation for two centuries, and Senate confirmation has always remained the norm for officers that require it.

While we concede that both interpretations carry with them some risk of undesirable consequences, we believe the narrower interpretation risks undermining constitutionally conferred powers more seriously and more often. It would prevent the President from making any recess appointment that arose before a recess, no matter who the official, no matter how dire the need, no matter how uncontroversial the appointment, and no matter how late in the session the office fell vacant. Historical practice over the past 200 years strongly favors the broader interpretation. The tradition of applying the Clause to pre-recess vacancies dates at least to President James Madison.

The upshot is that the President has consistently and frequently interpreted the Recess Appointments Clause to apply to vacancies that initially occur before, but continue to exist during, a recess of the Senate. The Senate as a body has not countered this practice for nearly three-quarters of a century, perhaps longer. The tradition is long enough to entitle the practice "to great regard in determining the true construction" of the constitutional provision. And we are reluctant to upset this traditional practice where doing so would seriously shrink the authority that Presidents have believed existed and have exercised for so long. In light of some linguistic ambiguity, the basic purpose of the Clause, and the historical practice we have described, we conclude that the phrase "all vacancies" includes vacancies that come into existence while the Senate is in session.

V

The third question concerns the calculation of the length of the Senate's "recess." On December 17, 2011, the Senate by unanimous consent adopted a resolution to convene "*pro forma* session[s]" only, with "no business . . . transacted," on every Tuesday and Friday from December 20, 2011, through January 20, 2012. At the end of each *pro forma* session, the Senate would "adjourn until" the following *pro forma* session. During that period, the Senate convened and adjourned as agreed. It held *pro forma* sessions on December 20, 23, 27, and 30, and on January 3, 6, 10, 13, 17, and 20; and at the end of each *pro forma* session, it adjourned until the time and date of the next.

The President made the recess appointments before us on January 4, 2012, in between the January 3 and the January 6 *pro forma* sessions. We must determine the significance of these sessions — that is, whether, for purposes of the Clause, we should treat them as periods when the Senate was in session or as periods when it was in recess. If the former, the period between January 3 and January 6 was a 3-day recess, which is too short to trigger the President's recess-appointment power. If the latter, however, then the 3-day period was part of a much longer recess during which the President did have the power to make recess appointments. The Solicitor General argues that we must treat the *pro forma* sessions as periods of recess. He says that these "sessions" were sessions in name only because the Senate was in recess as a *functional* matter. The Senate, he contends, remained in a single, unbroken recess from January 3, when the second session of the 112th Congress began by operation of the Twentieth Amendment, until January 23, when the Senate reconvened to do regular business.

In our view, however, the *pro forma* sessions count as sessions, not as periods of recess. We hold that, for purposes of the Recess Appointments Clause, the Senate is in session when it says it is, provided that, under its own rules, it retains the capacity to transact Senate business. The Senate met that standard here.

The standard we apply is consistent with the Constitution's broad delegation of authority to the Senate to determine how and when to conduct its business. The Constitution explicitly empowers the Senate to "determine the Rules of its Proceedings." Art. I, §5, cl. 2 .

For these reasons, we conclude that we must give great weight to the Senate's own determination of when it is and when it is not in session. But our deference to the Senate cannot be absolute. When the Senate is without the *capacity* to act, under its own rules, it is not in session even if it so declares. In that circumstance, the Senate is not simply unlikely or unwilling to act upon nominations of the President. It is *unable* to do so. The purpose of the Clause is to ensure the continued functioning of the Federal Government while the Senate is unavailable. This purpose would count for little were we to treat the Senate as though it were in session even when it lacks the ability to provide its "advice and consent." Accordingly, we conclude that when the Senate declares that it is in session and possesses the capacity, under its own rules, to conduct business, it is in session for purposes of the Clause.

Applying this standard, we find that the *pro forma* sessions were sessions for purposes of the Clause. First, the Senate said it was in session. The Journal of the Senate and the Congressional Record indicate that the Senate convened for a series of twice-weekly "sessions" from December 20 through January 20. And these reports of the Senate "must be assumed to speak the truth."

Second, the Senate's rules make clear that during its *pro forma* sessions, despite its resolution that it would conduct no business, the Senate retained the power to conduct business. During any *pro forma* session, the Senate could have conducted business simply by passing a unanimous consent agreement. The Senate in fact conducts much of its business through unanimous consent. Senate rules presume that a quorum is present unless a present Senator questions it. And when the Senate has a quorum, an agreement is unanimously passed if, upon its proposal, no present Senator objects. It is consequently unsurprising that the Senate *has* enacted legislation during *pro forma* sessions even when it has said that no business will be transacted.

By way of contrast, we do not see how the Senate could conduct business during a recess. It could terminate the recess and then, when in session, pass a bill. But in that case, of course, the Senate would no longer be in recess. It would be in session. And that is the crucial point. Senate rules make clear that, once in session, the Senate can act even if it has earlier said that it would not.

VI

The Recess Appointments Clause responds to a structural difference between the Executive and Legislative Branches: The Executive Branch is perpetually in operation, while the Legislature only acts in intervals separated by recesses. The purpose of the Clause is to allow the Executive to continue operating while the Senate is unavailable. We believe that the Clause's text, standing alone, is ambiguous. It does not resolve whether the President may make appointments during intra-session recesses, or whether he may fill pre-recess vacancies. But the broader reading better serves the Clause's structural function. Moreover, that broader reading is reinforced by centuries of history, which we are hesitant to disturb. We thus hold that the Constitution empowers the President to fill any existing vacancy during any recess — intra-session or inter-session — of sufficient length. Justice Scalia would render illegitimate thousands of recess appointments reaching all the way back to the founding era. More than that:

Calling the Clause an "anachronism," he would basically read it out of the Constitution. He performs this act of judicial excision in the name of liberty. We fail to see how excising the Recess Appointments Clause preserves freedom.

Given our answer to the last question before us, we conclude that the Recess Appointments Clause does not give the President the constitutional authority to make the appointments here at issue. Because the Court of Appeals reached the same ultimate conclusion (though for reasons we reject), its judgment is affirmed.

Justice SCALIA, with whom THE CHIEF JUSTICE, Justice THOMAS, and Justice ALITO join, concurring in the judgment. To prevent the President's recess-appointment power from nullifying the Senate's role in the appointment process, the Constitution cabins that power in two significant ways. First, it may be exercised only in "the Recess of the Senate," that is, the intermission between two formal legislative sessions. Second, it may be used to fill only those vacancies that "happen during the Recess," that is, offices that become vacant during that intermission. Both conditions are clear from the Constitution's text and structure, and both were well understood at the founding. The Court of Appeals correctly held that the appointments here at issue are invalid because they did not meet either condition.

Today's Court agrees that the appointments were in-valid, but for the far narrower reason that they were made during a 3-day break in the Senate's session. On its way to that result, the majority sweeps away the key textual limitations on the recess-appointment power. It holds, first, that the President can make appointments without the Senate's participation even during short breaks in the middle of the Senate's session, and second, that those appointments can fill offices that became vacant long before the break in which they were filled. The majority justifies those textual results on an adverse-possession theory of executive authority: Presidents have long claimed the powers in question, and the Senate has not disputed those claims with sufficient vigor, so the Court should not "upset the compromises and working arrangements that the elected branches of Government themselves have reached."

The Court's decision transforms the recess-appointment power from a tool carefully designed to fill a narrow and specific need into a weapon to be wielded by future Presidents against future Senates. To reach that result, the majority casts aside the plain, original meaning of the constitutional text in deference to late-arising historical practices that are ambiguous at best. The majority's insistence on deferring to the Executive's untenably broad interpretation of the power is in clear conflict with our precedent and forebodes a diminution of this Court's role in controversies involving the separation of powers and the structure of government. I concur in the judgment only.

I. OUR RESPONSIBILITY

Today's majority disregards two overarching principles that ought to guide our consideration of the questions presented here. First, the Constitution's core, government-structuring provisions are no less critical to preserving liberty than are the later adopted provisions of the Bill of Rights. Indeed, "[s]o convinced were the Framers that liberty of the person inheres in structure that at first they did not consider a Bill of Rights necessary."

Second and relatedly, when questions involving the Constitution's government-structuring provisions are presented in a justiciable case, it is the solemn responsibility of the Judicial Branch "to say what the law is." This Court does not defer to the other branches' resolution of such controversies; our role is in no way "lessened" because it might be said that "the two political branches are adjusting their own powers between themselves." Since the separation of powers exists for the protection of individual liberty, its vitality "does not depend" on "whether 'the encroached-upon branch approves the encroachment.' " Rather, policing the "enduring structure" of constitutional government when the political branches fail to do so is "one of the most vital functions of this Court."

II. INTRA-SESSION BREAKS

The first question presented is whether "the Recess of the Senate," during which the President's recess-appointment power is active, is (a) the period between two of the Senate's formal sessions, or (b) any break in the Senate's proceedings. I would hold that "the Recess" is the gap between sessions and that the appointments at issue here are invalid because they undisputedly were made *during* the Senate's session. The Court's contrary conclusion — that "the Recess" includes "breaks in the midst of a session," — is inconsistent with the Constitution's text and structure, and it requires judicial fabrication of vague, unadministrable limits on the recess-appointment power (thus defined) that overstep the judicial role. And although the majority relies heavily on "historical practice," no practice worthy of our deference supports the majority's conclusion on this issue.

A. PLAIN MEANING

A sensible interpretation of the Recess Appointments Clause should start by recognizing that the Clause uses the term "Recess" in contradistinction to the term "Session." In the founding era, the terms "recess" and "session" had well-understood meanings in the marking-out of legislative time. The life of each elected Congress typically consisted (as it still does) of two or more formal sessions separated by adjournments "*sine die*," that is, without a specified return date.

To be sure, in colloquial usage both words, "recess" and "session," could take on alternative, less precise meanings. A session could include any short period when a legislature's members were "assembled for business," and a recess could refer to any brief "suspension" of legislative "business." But as even the majority acknowledges, the Constitution's use of "the word 'the' in '*the* [R]ecess' " tends to suggest "that the phrase refers to the single break separating formal sessions." Besides being linguistically unsound, the majority's reading yields the strange result that an appointment made during a short break near the beginning of one official session will not terminate until the end of the *following* official session, enabling the appointment to last for up to two years.

To avoid the absurd results that follow from its colloquial reading of "the Recess," the majority is forced to declare that some intra-session breaks-though undisputedly within the phrase's colloquial meaning are simply "too short to trigger the Recess Appointments Clause." But it identifies no textual basis whatsoever for limiting the length of "the

Recess," nor does it point to any clear standard for determining how short is too short. It is inconceivable that the Framers would have left the circumstances in which the President could exercise such a significant and potentially dangerous power so utterly indeterminate. And what about breaks longer than three days? The majority says that a break of four to nine days is "presumptively too short" but that the presumption may be rebutted in an "unusual circumstance," such as a "national catastrophe . . . that renders the Senate unavailable but calls for an urgent response." The majority must hope that the *in terrorem* effect of its "presumptively too short" pronouncement will deter future Presidents from making any recess appointments during 4-to-9-day breaks and thus save us from the absurd spectacle of unelected judges evaluating (after an evidentiary hearing?) whether an alleged "catastrophe" was sufficiently "urgent" to trigger the recess-appointment power. As for breaks of 10 or more days: We are presumably to infer that such breaks do not trigger any "presumpt[ion]" against recess appointments, but does that mean the President has an utterly free hand? Or can litigants seek invalidation of an appointment made during a 10-day break by pointing to an absence of "unusual" or "urgent" circumstances necessitating an immediate appointment, albeit without the aid of a "presumpt[ion]" in their favor? Or, to put the question as it will present itself to lawyers in the Executive Branch: Can the President make an appointment during a 10-day break simply to overcome "political opposition in the Senate" despite the absence of any "national catastrophe," even though it "go[es] without saying" that he cannot do so during a 9-day break? Who knows? The majority does not say, and neither does the Constitution. Even if the many questions raised by the majority's failure to articulate a standard could be answered, a larger question would remain: If the Constitution's text empowers the President to make appointments during any break in the Senate's proceedings, by what right does the majority subject the President's exercise of that power to vague, court-crafted limitations with no textual basis? The majority claims its temporal guideposts are informed by executive practice, but a President's self-restraint cannot "bind his successors by diminishing their powers."

B. HISTORICAL PRACTICE

For the foregoing reasons, the Constitution's text and structure unambiguously refute the majority's freewheeling interpretation of "the Recess." It is not plausible that the Constitution uses that term in a sense that authorizes the President to make unilateral appointments during *any* break in Senate proceedings, subject only to hazy, a textual limits crafted by this Court centuries after ratification. The majority, however, insists that history "offers strong support" for its interpretation. The historical practice of the political branches is, of course, irrelevant when the Constitution is clear. But even if the Constitution were thought ambiguous on this point, history does not support the majority's interpretation. What does all this amount to? In short: Intra-session recess appointments were virtually unheard of for the first 130 years of the Republic, were deemed unconstitutional by the first Attorney General to address them, were not openly defended by the Executive until 1921, were not made in significant numbers until after World War II, and have been repeatedly criticized as unconstitutional by Senators of both parties. It is astonishing for the majority to assert that this history lends "strong support," to its interpretation of the Recess Appointments Clause. And the majority's contention that recent executive practice in this area merits deference because the Senate has not done more to oppose it is utterly divorced from our precedent. "The structural interests protected by the Appointments Clause are not those of any one branch of Government but of the entire Republic," and the Senate could not give away those protections even if it wanted to.

III. PRE-RECESS VACANCIES

The second question presented is whether vacancies that "happen during the Recess of the Senate," which the President is empowered to fill with recess appointments, are (a) vacancies that *arise* during the recess, or (b) all vacancies that *exist* during the recess, regardless of when they arose. I would hold that the recess-appointment power is limited to vacancies that arise during the recess in which they are filled, and I would hold that the appointments at issue here-which undisputedly filled pre-recess vacancies-are invalid for that reason as well as for the reason that they were made during the session. The Court's contrary conclusion is inconsistent with the Constitution's text and structure, and it further undermines the balance the Framers struck between Presidential and Senatorial power. Historical practice also fails to support the majority's conclusion on this issue.

A. PLAIN MEANING

As the majority concedes, "the most natural meaning of 'happens' as applied to a 'vacancy' . . . is that the vacancy 'happens' when it initially occurs." The majority adds that this meaning is most natural "to a modern ear," but it fails to show that founding-era ears heard it differently. "Happen" meant then, as it does now, "[t]o fall out; to chance; to come to pass." Thus, a vacancy that *happened* during the Recess was most reasonably understood as one that *arose* during the recess. It was, of course, possible in certain contexts for the word "happen" to mean "happen to be" rather than "happen to occur," as in the idiom "it so happens." But that meaning is not at all natural when the subject is a vacancy, a state of affairs that comes into existence at a particular moment in time. In any event, no reasonable reader would have understood the Recess Appointments Clause to use the word "happen" in the majority's "happen to be" sense, and thus to empower the President to fill all vacancies that might *exist* during a recess, regardless of when they arose. For one thing, the Clause's language would have been a surpassingly odd way of giving the President that power. The Clause easily could have been written to convey that meaning clearly: It could have referred to "all Vacancies that may exist during the Recess," or it could have omitted the qualifying phrase entirely and simply authorized the President to "fill up all Vacancies during the Recess." Given those readily available alternative phrasings, the reasonable reader might have wondered, why would any intelligent drafter intending the majority's reading have inserted the words "that may happen" — words that, as the majority admits, make the majority's desired reading awkward and unnatural, and that must be effectively read out of the Clause to achieve that reading?

For another thing, the majority's reading not only strains the Clause's language but distorts its constitutional role, which was meant to be subordinate. As Hamilton explained, appointment with the advice and consent of the Senate was to be "the general mode of appointing officers of the United States."

If, however, the Clause had allowed the President to fill *all* pre-existing vacancies during the recess by granting commissions that would last throughout the following session, it would have been impossible to regard it — as the Framers plainly did — as a mere codicil to the Constitution's principal, power-sharing scheme for filling federal offices. On the majority's reading, the President would have had no need *ever* to seek the Senate's advice and consent for his appointments: Whenever there was a fair prospect of the Senate's rejecting his preferred nominee, the President could have appointed that individual unilaterally during the recess, allowed the appointment to expire at the end of the next session, renewed the appointment the following day, and so on *ad infinitum*. (Circumvention would have been especially easy if, as the majority also concludes, the President was authorized to make such appointments during any intra-session break of more than a few days.) It is unthinkable that such an obvious means for the Executive to expand its power would have been overlooked during the ratification debates.

B. HISTORICAL PRACTICE

For the reasons just given, it is clear that the Constitution authorizes the President to fill unilaterally only those vacancies that arise during a recess, not every vacancy that happens to exist during a recess. Again, however, the majority says "[h]istorical practice" requires the broader interpretation. And again the majority is mistaken. Even if the Constitution were wrongly thought to be ambiguous on this point, a fair recounting of the relevant history does not support the majority's interpretation. In sum: Washington's and Adams' Attorneys General read the Constitution to restrict recess appointments to vacancies arising during the recess, and there is no evidence that any of the first four Presidents consciously departed from that reading. The contrary reading was first defended by an executive official in 1823, was vehemently rejected by the Senate in 1863, was vigorously resisted by legislation in place from 1863 until 1940, and is arguably inconsistent with legislation in place from 1940 to the present. The Solicitor General has identified only about 100 appointments that have ever been made under the broader reading, and while it seems likely that a good deal more have been made in the last few decades, there is good reason to doubt that many were made before 1940 (since the appointees could not have been compensated). I can conceive of no sane constitutional theory under which this evidence of "historical practice"—which is actually evidence of a long-simmering inter-branch conflict-would require us to defer to the views of the Executive Branch.

IV. CONCLUSION

What the majority needs to sustain its judgment is an ambiguous text and a clear historical practice. What it has is a clear text and an at-best ambiguous historical practice. Even if the Executive could accumulate power through adverse possession by engaging in a *consistent* and *unchallenged* practice over a long period of time, the oft-disputed practices at issue here would not meet that standard. Nor have those practices created any justifiable expectations that could be disappointed by enforcing the Constitution's original meaning. There is thus no ground for the majority's deference to the unconstitutional recess-appointment practices of the Executive Branch.

The majority replaces the Constitution's text with a new set of judge made rules to govern recess appointments. Henceforth, the Senate can avoid triggering the President's now-vast recess-appointment power by the odd contrivance of never adjourning for more than three days without holding a *pro forma* session at which it is understood that no business will be conducted. How this new regime will work in practice remains to be seen. Perhaps it will reduce the prevalence of recess appointments. But perhaps not: Members of the President's party in Congress may be able to prevent the Senate from holding *pro forma* sessions with the necessary frequency, and if the House and Senate disagree, the President may be able to adjourn both "to such Time as he shall think proper." U.S. Const., Art. II, §3. In any event, the limitation upon the President's appointment power is there not for the benefit of the Senate, but for the protection of the people; it should not be dependent on Senate action for its existence. The real tragedy of today's decision is not simply the abolition of the Constitution's limits on the recess-appointment power and the substitution of a novel framework invented by this Court. It is the damage done to our separation-of-powers jurisprudence more generally. It is not every day that we encounter a proper case or controversy requiring interpretation of the Constitution's structural provisions. Most of the time, the interpretation of those provisions is left to the political branches—which, in deciding how much respect to afford the constitutional text, often take their cues from this Court. We should therefore take every opportunity to affirm the primacy of the Constitution's enduring principles over the politics of the moment. Our failure to do so today will resonate well beyond the particular dispute at hand. Sad, but true: The Court's embrace of the adverse-possession theory of executive power (a characterization the majority resists but does not refute) will be cited in diverse contexts, including those presently unimagined, and will have the effect of aggrandizing the Presidency beyond its constitutional bounds and undermining respect for the separation of powers.

D. WATERGATE AND EXECUTIVE PRIVILEGE

Watergate and the Nixon resignation are constitutional footnotes to the fears of the framers that one branch would assert unilateral authority by expanding its separate powers. The ensuing check provided by Congress and the Supreme Court exemplified how the framers envisioned such a grasp for separate power would be curtailed. These events depict the meaning and operation of checks and balances within a system of separate powers. Note that in regard to the Court's opinion in United States v. Nixon, scholars have argued that although Nixon may have "lost the battle," the presidency may have "won the war." See whether you agree.

UNITED STATES v. NIXON
418 U.S. 683 (1974)

Chief Justice BURGER delivered the opinion of the Court.

This litigation presents for review the denial of a motion, filed in the District Court on behalf of the President of the United States, in the case of United States v. Mitchell et al. (D.C.Crim. No. 74-110), to quash a third-party subpoena duces tecum issued by the United States District Court for the District of Columbia, pursuant to Fed.Rule Crim.Proc. 17(c). The subpoena directed the President to produce certain tape recordings and documents relating to his conversations with aides and advisers. The court rejected the President's claims of absolute executive privilege, of lack of jurisdiction, and of failure to satisfy the requirements of Rule 17(c).

On March 1, 1974, a grand jury of the United States District Court for the District of Columbia returned an indictment charging seven named individuals with various offenses, including conspiracy to defraud the United States and to obstruct justice. Although he was not designated as such in the indictment, the grand jury named the President, among others, as an unindicted coconspirator. On April 18, 1974, upon motion of the Special Prosecutor, see n. 8, infra, a subpoena duces tecum was issued pursuant to Rule 17(c) to the President by the United States District Court and made returnable on May 2, 1974. This subpoena required the production, in advance of the September 9 trial date, of certain tapes, memoranda, papers, transcripts or other writings relating to certain precisely identified meetings between the President and others. The Special Prosecutor was able to fix the time, place, and persons present at these discussions because the White House daily logs and appointment records had been delivered to him. On April 30, the President publicly released edited transcripts of 43 conversations; portions of 20 conversations subject to subpoena in the present case were included. On May 1, 1974, the President's counsel, filed a "special appearance" and a motion to quash the subpoena under Rule 17(c). This motion was accompanied by a formal claim of privilege.

[On] May 20, 1974, the District Court denied the motion to quash and the motions to expunge and for protective orders. 377 F.Supp. 1326. It further ordered "the President or any subordinate officer, official, or employee with custody or control of the documents or objects subpoenaed," id., at 1331 to deliver to the District Court, on or before May 31, 1974, the originals of all subpoenaed items, as well as an index and analysis of those items, together with tape copies of those portions of the subpoenaed recordings for which transcripts had been released to the public by the President on April 30.

[On] May 24, 1974, the President filed a timely notice of appeal from the District Court order, and the certified record from the District Court was docketed in the United States Court of Appeals for the District of Columbia Circuit. On the same day, the President also filed a petition for writ of mandamus in the Court of Appeals seeking review of the District Court order.

Later on May 24, the Special Prosecutor also filed, in this Court, a petition for a writ of certiorari before judgment. On May 31, the petition was granted with an expedited briefing schedule.

A. [Having] determined that the requirements of Rule 17(c) were satisfied, we turn to the claim that the subpoena should be quashed because it demands "confidential conversations between a President and his close advisors that it would be inconsistent with the public interest to produce." The first contention is a broad claim that the separation of powers doctrine precludes judicial review of a President's claim of privilege. The second contention is that if he does not prevail on the claim of absolute privilege, the court should hold as a matter of constitutional law that the privilege prevails over the subpoena duces tecum.

In the performance of assigned constitutional duties each branch of the Government must initially interpret the Constitution, and the interpretation of its powers by any branch is due great respect from the others. The President's counsel, as we have noted, reads the Constitution as providing an absolute privilege of confidentiality for all Presidential communications. Many decisions of this Court, however, have unequivocally reaffirmed the holding of Marbury v. Madison, 1 Cranch, 137, 2 L.Ed. 60 (1803), that "[i]t is emphatically the province and duty of the judicial department to say what the law is."

No holding of the Court has defined the scope of judicial power specifically relating to the enforcement of a subpoena for confidential Presidential communications for use in a criminal prosecution, but other exercises of power by the Executive Branch and the Legislative Branch have been found invalid as in conflict with the Constitution. Powell v. McCormack, 395 U.S. 486, 89 S.Ct. 1944, 23 L.Ed.2d 491 (1969); Youngstown, Sheet & Tube Co. v. Sawyer, 343 U.S. 579, 72 S.Ct. 863, 96 L.Ed. 1153 (1952). In a series of cases, the Court interpreted the explicit immunity conferred by express provisions of the Constitution on Members of the House and Senate by the Speech or Debate Clause, U.S.Const. Art. I, § 6. Since this Court has consistently exercised the power to construe and delineate claims arising under express powers, it must follow that the Court has authority to interpret claims with respect to powers alleged to derive from enumerated powers.

[Notwithstanding] the deference each branch must accord the others, the "judicial Power of the United States" vested in the federal courts by Art. III, § 1, of the Constitution can no more be shared with the Executive Branch than the Chief Executive, for example, can share with the Judiciary the veto power, or the Congress share with the Judiciary the power to override a Presidential veto. Any other conclusion would be contrary to the basic concept of separation of powers and the checks and balances that flow from the scheme of a tripartite government. We therefore reaffirm that it is the province and duty of this Court 'to say what the law is' with respect to the claim of privilege presented in this case. Marbury v. Madison, supra, 1 Cranch. at 177, 2 L.Ed. 60.

B. In support of his claim of absolute privilege, the President's counsel urges two grounds, one of which is common to all governments and one of which is peculiar to our system of separation of powers. The first ground is the valid need for protection of communications between high Government officials and those who advise and assist them in the performance of their manifold duties; the importance of this confidentiality is too plain to require further discussion. Human experience teaches that those who expect public dissemination of their remarks may well temper candor with a concern for appearances and for their own interests to the detriment of the decisionmaking process. Whatever the nature of the privilege of confidentiality of Presidential communications in the exercise of Art. II powers, the privilege can be said to derive from the supremacy of each branch within its own assigned area of constitutional duties. Certain powers and privileges flow from the nature of enumerated powers; the protection of the confidentiality of Presidential communications has similar constitutional underpinnings.

The second ground asserted by the President's counsel in support of the claim of absolute privilege rests on the doctrine of separation of powers. Here it is argued that the independence of the Executive Branch within its own sphere, Humphrey's Executor v. United States, 295 U.S. 602, 629-630, 55 S.Ct. 869, 874-875, 79 L.Ed. 1611 (1935); Kilbourn v. Thompson, 103 U.S. 168, 190-191, 26 L.Ed. 377 (1881), insulates a President from a judicial subpoena in an ongoing criminal prosecution, and thereby protects confidential Presidential communications.

However, neither the doctrine of separation of powers, nor the need for confidentiality of high-level communications, without more, can sustain an absolute, unqualified Presidential privilege of immunity from judicial process under all circumstances. The President's need for complete candor and objectivity from advisers calls for great deference from the courts. However, when the privilege depends solely on the broad, undifferentiated claim of public interest in the confidentiality of such conversations, a confrontation with other values arises. Absent a claim of need to protect military, diplomatic, or sensitive national security secrets, we find it difficult to accept the argument that even the very important interest in confidentiality of Presidential communications is significantly diminished by production of such material for in camera inspection with all the protection that a district court will be obliged to provide.

The impediment that an absolute, unqualified privilege would place in the way of the primary constitutional duty of the Judicial Branch to do justice in criminal prosecutions would plainly conflict with the function of the courts under Art. III. In designing the structure of our Government and dividing and allocating the sovereign power among three co-equal branches, the Framers of the Constitution sought to provide a comprehensive system, but the separate powers were not intended to operate with absolute independence.

[To] read the Art. II powers of the President as providing an absolute privilege as against a subpoena essential to enforcement of criminal statutes on no more than a generalized claim of the public interest in confidentiality of nonmilitary and nondiplomatic discussions would upset the constitutional balance of "a workable government" and gravely impair the role of the courts under Art. III.

C. Since we conclude that the legitimate needs of the judicial process may outweigh Presidential privilege, it is necessary to resolve those competing interests in a manner that preserves the essential functions of each branch. The right and indeed the duty to resolve that question does not free the Judiciary from according high respect to the representations made on behalf of the President.

[But] this presumptive privilege must be considered in light of our historic commitment to the rule of law. This is nowhere more profoundly manifest than in our view that the 'twofold aim (of criminal justice) is that guilt shall not escape or innocence suffer.' We have elected to employ an adversary system of criminal justice in which the parties contest all issues before a court of law. The need to develop all relevant facts in the adversary system is both fundamental and comprehensive. To ensure that justice is done, it is imperative to the function of courts that compulsory process be available for the production of evidence needed either by the prosecution or by the defense.

[In] this case the President challenges a subpoena served on him as a third party requiring the production of materials for use in a criminal prosecution; he does so on the claim that he has a privilege against disclosure of confidential communications. He does not place his claim of privilege on the ground they are military or diplomatic secrets. As to these areas of Art. II duties the courts have traditionally shown the utmost deference to Presidential responsibilities.

[No] case of the Court, however, has extended this high degree of deference to a President's generalized interest in confidentiality. Nowhere in the Constitution, as we have noted earlier, is there any explicit reference to a privilege of confidentiality, yet to the extent this interest relates to the effective discharge of a President's powers, it is constitutionally based.

[In] this case we must weigh the importance of the general privilege of confidentiality of Presidential communications in performance of the President's responsibilities against the inroads of such a privilege on the fair administration of criminal justice. The interest in preserving confidentiality is weighty indeed and entitled to great respect. However, we cannot conclude that advisers will be moved to temper the candor of their remarks by the infrequent occasions of disclosure because of the possibility that such conversations will be called for in the context of a criminal prosecution.

On the other hand, the allowance of the privilege to withhold evidence that is demonstrably relevant in a criminal trial would cut deeply into the guarantee of due process of law and gravely impair the basic function of the courts. A President's acknowledged need for confidentiality in the communications of his office is general in nature, whereas the constitutional need for production of relevant evidence in a criminal proceeding is specific and central to the fair adjudication of a particular criminal case in the administration of justice. Without access to specific facts a criminal prosecution may be totally frustrated. The President's broad interest in confidentiality of communications will not be vitiated by disclosure of a limited number of conversations preliminarily shown to have some bearing on the pending criminal cases.

D. [If] a President concludes that compliance with a subpoena would be injurious to the public interest he may properly, as was done here, invoke a claim of privilege on the return of the subpoena. Upon receiving a claim of privilege from the Chief Executive, it became the further duty of the District Court to treat the subpoenaed material as presumptively privileged and to require the Special Prosecutor to demonstrate that the Presidential material was "essential to the justice of the (pending criminal) case." Accordingly we affirm the order of the District Court that subpoenaed materials be transmitted to that court. We now turn to the important question of the District Court's responsibilities in conducting the in camera examination of Presidential materials or communications delivered under the compulsion of the subpoena duces tecum.

E. [Statements] that meet the test of admissibility and relevance must be isolated; all other material must be excised. At this stage the District Court is not limited to representations of the Special Prosecutor as to the evidence sought by the subpoena; the material will be available to the District Court. It is elementary that in camera inspection of evidence is always a procedure calling for scrupulous protection against any release or publication of material not found by the court, at that stage, probably admissible in evidence and relevant to the issues of the trial for which it is sought. That being true of an ordinary situation, it is obvious that the District Court has a very heavy responsibility to see to it that Presidential conversations, which are either not relevant or not admissible, are accorded that high degree of respect due the President of the United States. Mr. Chief Justice Marshall, sitting as a trial judge in the Burr case, supra, was extraordinarily careful to point out that "[i]n no case of this kind would a court be required to proceed against the president as against an ordinary individual."

Marshall's statement cannot be read to mean in any sense that a President is above the law, but relates to the singularly unique role under Art. II of a President's communications and activities, related to the performance of duties under that Article. Moreover, a President's communications and activities encompass a vastly wider range of sensitive material than would be true of any "ordinary individual." It is therefore necessary in the public interest to afford Presidential confidentiality the greatest protection consistent with the fair administration of justice. The need for confidentiality even as to idle conversations with associates in which casual reference might be made concerning political leaders within the country or foreign statesmen is too obvious to call for further treatment. We have no doubt that the District Judge will at all times accord to Presidential records that high degree of deference suggested in United States v. Burr, supra and will discharge his responsibility to see to it that until released to the Special Prosecutor no in camera material is revealed to anyone. This burden applies with even greater force to excised material; once the decision is made to excise, the material is restored to its privileged status and should be returned under seal to its lawful custodian.

Since this matter came before the Court during the pendency of a criminal prosecution, and on representations that time is of the essence, the mandate shall issue forthwith.

Affirmed.

[Justice Rehnquist did not participate.]

CLINTON v. JONES
520 U.S. 681 (1997)

Justice STEVENS delivered the opinion of the Court.

This case raises a constitutional and a prudential question concerning the Office of the President of the United States. Respondent, a private citizen, seeks to recover damages from the current occupant of that office based on actions allegedly taken before his term began. The President submits that in all but the most exceptional cases the Constitution requires federal courts to defer such litigation until his term ends and that, in any event, respect for the office warrants such a stay. Despite the force of the arguments supporting the President's submissions, we conclude that they must be rejected.

I. Petitioner, William Jefferson Clinton, was elected to the Presidency in 1992, and re-elected in 1996. His term of office expires on January 20, 2001. In 1991 he was the Governor of the State of Arkansas. Respondent, Paula Corbin Jones, is a resident of California. In 1991 she lived in Arkansas, and was an employee of the Arkansas Industrial Development Commission.

On May 6, 1994, she commenced this action in the United States District Court for the Eastern District of Arkansas by filing a complaint naming petitioner and Danny Ferguson, a former Arkansas State Police officer, as defendants. The complaint alleges two federal claims, and two state-law claims over which the federal court has jurisdiction because of the diverse citizenship of the parties. As the case comes to us, we are required to assume the truth of the detailed — but as yet untested — factual allegations in the complaint.

Those allegations principally describe events that are said to have occurred on the afternoon of May 8, 1991, during an official conference held at the Excelsior Hotel in Little Rock, Arkansas. The Governor delivered a speech at the conference; respondent — working as a state employee — staffed the registration desk. She alleges that Ferguson persuaded her to leave her desk and to visit the Governor in a business suite at the hotel, where he made "abhorrent" sexual advances that she vehemently rejected. She further claims that her superiors at work subsequently dealt with her in a hostile and rude manner, and changed her duties to punish her for rejecting those advances. Finally, she alleges that after petitioner was elected President, Ferguson defamed her by making a statement to a reporter that implied she had accepted petitioner's alleged overtures, and that various persons authorized to speak for the President publicly branded her a liar by denying that the incident had occurred.

Respondent seeks actual damages of $75,000 and punitive damages of $100,000. Her complaint contains four counts. The first charges that petitioner, acting under color of state law, deprived her of rights protected by the Constitution, in violation of Rev. Stat. § 1979, 42 U.S.C. § 1983. The second charges that petitioner and Ferguson engaged in a conspiracy to violate her federal rights, also actionable under federal law. See Rev. Stat. § 1980, 42 U.S.C. § 198520. The third is a state common law claim for intentional infliction of emotional distress, grounded primarily on the incident at the hotel. The fourth count, also based on state law, is for defamation, embracing both the comments allegedly made to the press by Ferguson and the statements of petitioner's agents. Inasmuch as the legal sufficiency of the claims has not yet been challenged, we assume, without deciding, that each of the four counts states a cause of action as a matter of law. With the exception of the last charge, which arguably may involve conduct within the outer perimeter of the President's official responsibilities, it is perfectly clear that the alleged misconduct of petitioner was unrelated to any of his official duties as President of the United States and, indeed, occurred before he was elected to that office.

II. In response to the complaint, petitioner promptly advised the District Court that he intended to file a motion to dismiss on grounds of Presidential immunity, and requested the court to defer all other pleadings and motions until after the immunity issue was resolved. The District Judge denied the motion to dismiss on immunity grounds and ruled that discovery in the case could go forward, but ordered any trial stayed until the end of petitioner's Presidency. Both parties appealed. A divided panel of the Court of Appeals affirmed the denial of the motion to dismiss, but because it regarded the order postponing the trial until the President leaves office as the "functional equivalent" of a grant of temporary immunity, it reversed that order.

IV. Petitioner's [The President] principal submission — that "in all but the most exceptional cases," Brief for Petitioner i, the Constitution affords the President temporary immunity from civil damages litigation arising out of events that occurred before he took office — cannot be sustained on the basis of precedent.

The principal rationale for affording certain public servants immunity from suits for money damages arising out of their official acts is inapplicable to unofficial conduct. In cases involving prosecutors, legislators, and judges we have repeatedly explained that the immunity serves the public interest in enabling such officials to perform their designated functions effectively without fear that a particular decision may give rise to personal liability

That rationale provided the principal basis for our holding that a former President of the United States was "entitled to absolute immunity from damages liability predicated on his official acts," *Fitzgerald,* 457 U.S., at 749, 102 S.Ct., at 2701. See *id.,* at 752, 102 S.Ct., at 2702 (citing *Ferri v. Ackerman*). Our central concern was to avoid rendering the President "unduly cautious in the discharge of his official duties." 457 U.S., at 752, n. 32, 102 S.Ct., at 2702, n. 32.

This reasoning provides no support for an immunity for *unofficial* conduct. As we explained in *Fitzgerald,* "the sphere of protected action must be related closely to the immunity's justifying purposes." *Id.,* at 755, 102 S.Ct., at 2704. Because of the President's broad responsibilities, "we recognized in that case an immunity from damages claims arising out of official acts extending to the "outer perimeter of his authority." *Id.,* at 757, 102 S.Ct., at 2705. But we have never suggested that the President, or any other official, has an immunity that extends beyond the scope of any action taken in an official capacity. As our opinions have made clear, immunities are grounded in "the nature of the function performed, not the identity of the actor who performed it." *Id.,* at 229, 108 S.Ct., at 545.

V. We are also unpersuaded by the evidence from the historical record to which petitioner has called our attention. He points to a comment by Thomas Jefferson protesting the subpoena *duces tecum* Chief Justice Marshall directed to him in the Burr trial, a statement in the diaries kept by Senator William Maclay of the first Senate debates, in which then-Vice President John Adams and Senator Oliver Ellsworth are recorded as having said that "the President personally [is] not . . . subject to any process whatever," lest it be "put . . . in the power of a common Justice to exercise any Authority over him and Stop the Whole Machine of Government," and to a quotation from Justice Story's Commentaries on the Constitution. None of these sources sheds much light on the question at hand. Finally, Justice Story's comments in his constitutional law treatise provide no substantial support for petitioner's position. Story wrote that because the President's "incidental powers" must include "the power to perform [his duties], without any obstruction," he "cannot, therefore, be liable to arrest, imprisonment, or detention, while he is in the discharge of the duties of his office; and *for this purpose* his person must be deemed, in civil cases at least, to possess an official inviolability." 3 Story § 1563, at 418-419 (emphasis added). Story said only that "*an* official inviolability," *ibid.* (emphasis added), was necessary to preserve the President's ability to perform the functions of the office; he did not specify the dimensions of the necessary immunity. While we have held that an immunity from suits grounded on official acts is necessary to serve this purpose, see *Fitzgerald,* 457 U.S., at 749, 102 S.Ct., at 2701, it does not follow that the broad immunity from *all* civil damages suits that petitioner seeks is also necessary.

Respondent, in turn, has called our attention to conflicting historical evidence. Speaking in favor of the Constitution's adoption at the Pennsylvania Convention, James Wilson — who had participated in the Philadelphia Convention at which the document was drafted — explained that, although the President "is placed [on] high," "not a single privilege is annexed to his character; far from being above the laws, he is amenable to them in his private character as a citizen, and in his public character by impeachment." 2 J. Elliot, Debates on the Federal Constitution 480 (2d ed. 1863) (emphasis deleted). This description is consistent with both the doctrine of Presidential immunity as set forth in *Fitzgerald* and rejection of the immunity claim in this case.

In the end, as applied to the particular question before us, we reach the same conclusion about these historical materials that Justice Jackson described when confronted with an issue concerning the dimensions of the President's power. "Just what our forefathers did envision, or would have envisioned had they foreseen modern conditions, must be divined from materials almost as enigmatic as the dreams Joseph was called upon to interpret for Pharoah. A century and a half of partisan debate and scholarly speculation yields no net result but only supplies more or less apt quotations from respected sources on each side. . . . They largely cancel each other." *Youngstown Sheet & Tube Co. v. Sawyer,* 343 U.S. 579, 634-635, 72 S.Ct. 863, 869-870, 96 L.Ed. 1153 (1952) (concurring opinion).

VI. Petitioner's [The President] strongest argument supporting his immunity claim is based on the text and structure of the Constitution. He does not contend that the occupant of the Office of the President is "above the law," in the sense that his conduct is entirely immune from judicial scrutiny. The President argues merely for a postponement of the judicial proceedings that will determine whether he violated any law. His argument is grounded in the character of the office that was created by Article II of the Constitution, and relies on separation-of-powers principles that have structured our constitutional arrangement since the founding.

As a starting premise, petitioner contends that he occupies a unique office with powers and responsibilities so vast and important that the public interest demands that he devote his undivided time and attention to his public duties. He submits that — given the nature of the office — the doctrine of separation of powers places limits on the authority of the Federal Judiciary to interfere with the Executive Branch that would be transgressed by allowing this action to proceed.

We have no dispute with the initial premise of the argument. Former Presidents, from George Washington to George Bush, have consistently endorsed petitioner's characterization of the office. After serving his term, Lyndon Johnson observed: "Of all the 1,886 nights I was President, there were not many when I got to sleep before 1 or 2 a.m., and there were few mornings when I didn't wake up by 6 or 6:30." In 1967, the Twenty-fifth Amendment to the Constitution was adopted to ensure continuity in the performance of the powers and duties of the office; one of the sponsors of that Amendment stressed the importance of providing that "at all times" there be a President "who has complete control and will be able to perform" those duties. As Justice Jackson has pointed out, the Presidency concentrates executive authority "in a single head in whose choice the whole Nation has a part, making him the focus of public hopes and expectations. In drama, magnitude and finality his decisions so far overshadow any others that almost alone he fills the public eye and ear." *Youngstown Sheet & Tube Co. v. Sawyer*, 343 U.S., at 653, 72 S.Ct., at 879 (concurring opinion). We have, in short, long recognized the "unique position in the constitutional scheme" that this office occupies. *Fitzgerald*, 457 U.S., at 749, 102 S.Ct., at 2701.

It does not follow, however, that separation-of-powers principles would be violated by allowing this action to proceed. Of course the lines between the powers of the three branches are not always neatly defined. See *Mistretta v. United States*, 488 U.S. 361, 380-381, 109 S.Ct. 647, 659-660, 102 L.Ed.2d 714 (1989). But in this case there is no suggestion that the Federal Judiciary is being asked to perform any function that might in some way be described as "executive." Whatever the outcome of this case, there is no possibility that the decision will curtail the scope of the official powers of the Executive Branch.

Rather than arguing that the decision of the case will produce either an aggrandizement of judicial power or a narrowing of executive power, petitioner contends that — as a byproduct of an otherwise traditional exercise of judicial power — burdens will be placed on the President that will hamper the performance of his official duties. We have recognized that "[e]ven when a branch does not arrogate power to itself . . . the separation-of-powers doctrine requires that a branch not impair another in the performance of its constitutional duties." *Loving v. United States*, 517 U.S. 748, 757, 116 S.Ct. 1737, 1743, 135 L.Ed.2d 36 (1996); see also *Nixon v. Administrator of General Services*, 433 U.S. 425, 443, 97 S.Ct. 2777, 2790, 53 L.Ed.2d 867 (1977). As a factual matter, petitioner contends that this particular case — as well as the potential additional litigation that an affirmance of the Court of Appeals judgment might spawn — may impose an unacceptable burden on the President's time and energy, and thereby impair the effective performance of his office.

Petitioner's predictive judgment finds little support in either history or the relatively narrow compass of the issues raised in this particular case. As we have already noted, in the more than 200-year history of the Republic, only three sitting Presidents have been subjected to suits for their private actions. See *supra*, at 1643. If the past is any indicator, it seems unlikely that a deluge of such litigation will ever engulf the Presidency. As for the case at hand, if properly managed by the District Court, it appears to us highly unlikely to occupy any substantial amount of petitioner's time.

The fact that a federal court's exercise of its traditional Article III jurisdiction may significantly burden the time and attention of the Chief Executive is not sufficient to establish a violation of the Constitution. [We] have long held that when the President takes official action, the Court has the authority to determine whether he has acted within the law. Perhaps the most dramatic example of such a case is our holding that President Truman exceeded his constitutional authority when he issued an order directing the Secretary of Commerce to take possession of and operate most of the Nation's steel mills in order to avert a national catastrophe. *Youngstown Sheet & Tube Co. v. Sawyer*, 343 U.S. 579, 72 S.Ct. 863, 96 L.Ed. 1153 (1952). Despite the serious impact of that decision on the ability of the Executive Branch to accomplish its assigned mission, and the substantial time that the President must necessarily have devoted to the matter as a result of judicial involvement, we exercised our Article III jurisdiction to decide whether his official conduct conformed to the law. Our holding was an application of the principle established in *Marbury v. Madison,* 1 Cranch 137, 2 L.Ed. 60 (1803), that "[i]t is emphatically the province and duty of the judicial department to say what the law is." *Id* at 177.

[It] is also settled that the President is subject to judicial process in appropriate circumstances. Although Thomas Jefferson apparently thought otherwise, Chief Justice Marshall, when presiding in the treason trial of Aaron Burr, ruled that a subpoena *duces tecum* could be directed to the President. *United States v. Burr,* 25 F. Cas. 30 (No. 14,692d) (C.C.Va. 1807). We unequivocally and emphatically endorsed Marshall's position when we held that President Nixon was obligated to comply with a subpoena commanding him to produce certain tape recordings of his conversations with his aides. *United States v. Nixon,* 418 U.S. 683, 94 S.Ct. 3090, 41 L.Ed.2d 1039 (1974). As we explained, "neither the doctrine of separation of powers, nor the need for confidentiality of high-level communications, without more, can sustain an absolute, unqualified Presidential privilege of immunity from judicial process under all circumstances." *Id.,* at 706, 94 S.Ct., at 3106.

In sum, "[i]t is settled law that the separation-of-powers doctrine does not bar every exercise of jurisdiction over the President of the United States." *Fitzgerald,* 457 U.S., at 753-754, 102 S.Ct., at 2703. If the Judiciary may severely burden the Executive Branch by reviewing the legality of the President's official conduct, and if it may direct appropriate process to the President himself, it must follow that the federal courts have power to determine the legality of his unofficial conduct. The burden on the President's time and energy that is a mere byproduct of such review surely cannot be considered as onerous as the direct burden imposed by judicial review and the occasional invalidation of his official actions. We therefore hold that the doctrine of separation of powers does not require federal courts to stay all private actions against the President until he leaves office.

The reasons for rejecting such a categorical rule apply as well to a rule that would require a stay "in all but the most exceptional cases." Brief for Petitioner i. Indeed, if the Framers of the Constitution had thought it necessary to protect the President from the burdens of private litigation, we think it far more likely that they would have adopted a categorical rule than a rule that required the President to litigate the question whether a specific case belonged in the "exceptional case" subcategory. In all events, the question whether a specific case should receive exceptional treatment is more appropriately the subject of the exercise of judicial discretion than an interpretation of the Constitution. Accordingly, we turn to the question whether the District Court's decision to stay the trial until after petitioner leaves office was an abuse of discretion.

VII. The Court of Appeals described the District Court's discretionary decision to stay the trial as the "functional equivalent" of a grant of temporary immunity. 72 F.3d, at 1361, n. 9. Concluding that petitioner was not constitutionally entitled to such an immunity, the court held that it was error to grant the stay. *Ibid.* Although we ultimately conclude that the stay should not have been granted, we think the issue is more difficult than the opinion of the Court of Appeals suggests.

The District Court has broad discretion to stay proceedings as an incident to its power to control its own docket. See, *e.g., Landis v. North American Co.,* 299 U.S. 248, 254, 57 S.Ct. 163, 165-166, 81 L.Ed. 153 (1936). As we have explained, "[e]specially in cases of extraordinary public moment, [a plaintiff] may be required to submit to delay not immoderate in extent and not oppressive in its consequences if the public welfare or convenience will thereby be promoted." *Id.,* at 256, 57 S.Ct., at 166. Although we have rejected the argument that the potential burdens on the President violate separation-of-powers principles, those burdens are appropriate matters for the District Court to evaluate in its management of the case. The high respect that is owed to the office of the Chief Executive, though not justifying a rule of categorical immunity, is a matter that should inform the conduct of the entire proceeding, including the timing and scope of discovery.

Nevertheless, we are persuaded that it was an abuse of discretion for the District Court to defer the trial until after the President leaves office. Such a lengthy and categorical stay takes no account whatever of the respondent's interest in bringing the case to trial. The complaint was filed within the statutory limitations period — albeit near the end of that period — and delaying trial would increase the danger of prejudice resulting from the loss of evidence, including the inability of witnesses to recall specific facts, or the possible death of a party.

The decision to postpone the trial was, furthermore, premature. The proponent of a stay bears the burden of establishing its need. *Id.,* at 255, 57 S.Ct., at 166. In this case, at the stage at which the District Court made its ruling, there was no way to assess whether a stay of trial after the completion of discovery would be warranted. Other than the fact that a trial may consume some of the President's time and attention, there is nothing in the record to enable a judge to assess the potential harm that may ensue from scheduling the trial promptly after discovery is concluded. We think the District Court may have given undue weight to the concern that a trial might generate unrelated civil actions that could conceivably hamper the President in conducting the duties of his office. If and when that should occur, the court's discretion would permit it to manage those actions in such fashion (including deferral of trial) that interference with the President's duties would not occur. But no such impingement upon the President's conduct of his office was shown here.

VIII. We add a final comment on two matters that are discussed at length in the briefs: the risk that our decision will generate a large volume of politically motivated harassing and frivolous litigation, and the danger that national security concerns might prevent the President from explaining a legitimate need for a continuance.

We are not persuaded that either of these risks is serious. Most frivolous and vexatious litigation is terminated at the pleading stage or on summary judgment, with little if any personal involvement by the defendant. See Fed. Rules Civ. Proc. 12, 56. Moreover, the availability of sanctions provides a significant deterrent to litigation directed at the President in his unofficial capacity for purposes of political gain or harassment. History indicates that the likelihood that a significant number of such cases will be filed is remote. Although scheduling problems may arise, there is no reason to assume that the district courts will be either unable to accommodate the President's needs or unfaithful to the tradition — especially in matters involving national security — of giving "the utmost deference to Presidential responsibilities." Several Presidents, including petitioner, have given testimony without jeopardizing the Nation's security. See *supra,* at 1649. In short, we have confidence in the ability of our federal judges to deal with both of these concerns. If Congress deems it appropriate to afford the President stronger protection, it may respond with appropriate legislation. [Affirmed.]

Justice BREYER, concurring in the judgment.

I agree with the majority that the Constitution does not automatically grant the President an immunity from civil lawsuits based upon his private conduct. Nor does the "doctrine of separation of powers . . . require federal courts to stay" virtually "all private actions against the President until he leaves office." To obtain a postponement the President must "bea[r] the burden of establishing its need." *Ante,* at 1651.

In my view, however, once the President sets forth and explains a conflict between judicial proceeding and public duties, the matter changes. At that point, the Constitution permits a judge to schedule a trial in an ordinary civil damages action (where postponement normally is possible without overwhelming damage to a plaintiff only within the constraints of a constitutional principle — a principle that forbids a federal judge in such a case to interfere with the President's discharge of his public duties. I have no doubt that the Constitution contains such a principle applicable to civil suits, based upon Article II's vesting of the entire "executive Power" in a single individual, implemented through the Constitution's structural separation of powers, and revealed both by history and case precedent.

The Constitution states that the "executive Power shall be vested in a President." Art. II, § 1. This constitutional delegation means that a sitting President is unusually busy, that his activities have an unusually important impact upon the lives of others, and that his conduct embodies an authority bestowed by the entire American electorate. He (along with his constitutionally subordinate Vice President) is the only official for whom the entire Nation votes, and is the only elected officer to represent the entire Nation both domestically and abroad.

This constitutional delegation means still more. Article II makes a single President responsible for the actions of the Executive Branch in much the same way that the entire Congress is responsible for the actions of the Legislative Branch, or the entire Judiciary for those of the Judicial Branch. It thereby creates a constitutional equivalence between a single President, on the one hand, and many legislators, or judges, on the other.

The Founders created this equivalence by consciously deciding to vest Executive authority in one person rather than several. They did so in order to focus, rather than to spread, Executive responsibility thereby facilitating accountability. They also sought to encourage energetic, vigorous, decisive, and speedy execution of the laws by placing in the hands of a single, constitutionally indispensable, individual the ultimate authority that, in respect to the other branches, the Constitution divides among many.

For present purposes, this constitutional structure means that the President is not like Congress, for Congress can function as if it were whole, even when up to half of its members are absent, see U.S. Const., Art. I, § 5, cl. 1. It means that the President is not like the Judiciary, for judges often can designate other judges, *e.g.,* from other judicial circuits, to sit even should an entire court be detained by personal litigation. It means that, unlike Congress, which is regularly out of session, U.S. Const., Art. I, § § 4, 5, 7, the President never adjourns.

More importantly, these constitutional objectives explain why a President, though able to delegate duties to others, cannot delegate ultimate responsibility or the active obligation to supervise that goes with it. And the related constitutional equivalence between President, Congress, and the Judiciary means that judicial scheduling orders in a private civil case must not only take reasonable account of, say, a particularly busy schedule, or a job on which others critically depend, or an underlying electoral mandate. They must also reflect the fact that interference with a President's ability to carry out his public responsibilities is constitutionally equivalent to interference with the ability of the entirety of Congress, or the Judicial Branch, to carry out its public obligations.

Precedent that suggests . . .that the Constitution does *not* offer a sitting President significant protections from potentially distracting civil litigation — consists of the following: (1) In several instances sitting Presidents have given depositions or testified at criminal trials, and (2) this Court has twice authorized the enforcement of subpoenas seeking documents from a sitting President for use in a criminal case. I agree with the majority that these precedents reject any absolute Presidential immunity from all court process. But they do not cast doubt upon Justice Story's basic conclusion that "in civil cases," a sitting President "possess[es] an official inviolability" as necessary to permit him to "perform" the duties of his office without "obstruction or impediment."

The first set of precedents tells us little about what the Constitution commands, for they amount to voluntary actions on the part of a sitting President. The second set of precedents amounts to a search for documents, rather than a direct call upon Presidential time. More important, both sets of precedents involve *criminal* proceedings in which the President participated as a witness. Criminal proceedings, unlike private civil proceedings, are public acts initiated and controlled by the Executive Branch; see *United States v. Nixon,* 418 U.S., at 693-696, 94 S.Ct., at 3100-3102; they are not normally subject to postponement, see U.S. Const., Amdt. 6; and ordinarily they put at risk, not a private citizen's hope for monetary compensation, but a private citizen's freedom from enforced confinement, 418 U.S., at 711-712, and n. 19, 94 S.Ct., at 3109-3110, and n. 19; *Fitzgerald,* 457 U.S., at 754, n. 37, 102 S.Ct., at 2703, n. 37. See also *id.,* at 758, n. 41, 102 S.Ct., at 2705, n. 41. Nor is it normally possible in a criminal case, unlike many civil cases, to provide the plaintiff with interest to compensate for scheduling delay. See, *e.g., Winter v. Cerro Gordo County Conservation Bd.,* 925 F.2d 1069, 1073 (C.A.8 1991); *Foley v. Lowell,* 948 F.2d 10, 17-18 (C.A.1 1991); *Wooten v. McClendon,* 272 Ark. 61, 62-63, 612 S.W.2d 105, 106 (1981).

The remaining precedent to which the majority refers does not seem relevant in this case. That precedent, *Youngstown Sheet & Tube Co. v. Sawyer,* 343 U.S. 579, 585, 72 S.Ct. 863, 865-866, 96 L.Ed. 1153 (1952), concerns *official* action. And any Presidential time spent dealing with, or action taken in response to, that kind of case *is* part of a President's official duties. Hence court review in such circumstances could not interfere with, or distract from, official duties. Insofar as a court orders a President, in any such a proceeding, to act or to refrain from action, it defines, or determines, or clarifies the legal scope of an official duty. By definition (if the order itself is lawful), it cannot impede, or obstruct, or interfere with the President's basic task — the lawful exercise of his Executive authority.

Case law, particularly, *Nixon v. Fitzgerald,* strongly supports the principle that judges hearing a private civil damages action against a sitting President may not issue orders that could significantly distract a President from his official duties. [The] Court rested its conclusion in important part upon the fact that civil lawsuits "could distract a President from his public duties, to the detriment of not only the President and his office but also the Nation that the Presidency was designed to serve."

[Fitzgerald's] key paragraph, explaining why the President enjoys an absolute immunity rather than a qualified immunity, contains seven sentences, four of which focus primarily upon time and energy *distraction* and three of which focus primarily upon official decision *distortion.* Indeed, that key paragraph begins by stating: "Because of the singular importance of the President's duties, diversion of his energies by concern with private lawsuits would raise unique risks to the effective functioning of government." 457 U.S., at 751, 102 S.Ct., at 2702.

Moreover, the Court, in numerous other cases, has found the problem of time and energy distraction a critically important consideration militating in favor of a grant of immunity.

The majority points to the fact that private plaintiffs have brought civil damages lawsuits against a sitting President only three times in our Nation's history; and it relies upon the threat of sanctions to discourage, and "the court's discretion" to manage, such actions so that "interference with the President's duties would not occur." *Ante,* at 1651. I am less sanguine. Since 1960, when the last such suit was filed, the number of civil lawsuits filed annually in Federal District Courts has increased from under 60,000 to about 240,000, see Administrative Office of the United States Courts, Statistical Tables for the Federal Judiciary 27 (1995); Annual Report of the Director of the Administrative Office of the United States Courts — 1960, p. 224 (1961); the number of federal district judges has increased from 233 to about 650, see Administrative Office of United States Courts, Judicial Business of United States Courts 7 (1994); Annual Report of the Director of the Administrative Office of the United States Courts — 1960, *supra,* at 205; the time and expense associated with both discovery and trial have increased, see, *e.g.,* Bell, Varner, & Gottschalk, Automatic Disclosure in Discovery — The Rush To Reform, 27 Ga. L.Rev. 1, 9-11 (1992); see also S.Rep. No. 101-416, p. 1 (1990); Judicial Improvements Act of 1990, Pub.L. 101-650, 104 Stat. 5089; an increasingly complex economy has led to increasingly complex sets of statutes, rules, and regulations that often create potential liability, with, or without fault. And this Court has now made clear that such lawsuits may proceed against a sitting President. The consequence, as the Court warned in *Fitzgerald,* is that a sitting President, given "the visibility of his office," could well become "an easily identifiable target for suits for civil damages," 457 U.S., at 753, 102 S.Ct., at 2703.

I concede the possibility that district courts, supervised by the Courts of Appeals and perhaps this Court, might prove able to manage private civil damages actions against sitting Presidents without significantly interfering with the discharge of Presidential duties. [I] agree with the majority's determination that a constitutional defense must await a more specific showing of need; I do not agree with what I believe to be an understatement of the "danger." And I believe that ordinary case-management principles are unlikely to prove sufficient to deal with private civil lawsuits for damages unless supplemented with a constitutionally based requirement that district courts schedule proceedings so as to avoid significant interference with the President's ongoing discharge of his official responsibilities. [The] District Court in this case determined that the Constitution required the postponement of trial during the sitting President's term. It may well be that the trial of this case cannot take place without significantly interfering with the President's ability to carry out his official duties. Yet, I agree with the majority that there is no automatic temporary immunity and that the President should have to provide the District Court with a reasoned explanation of why the immunity is needed; and I also agree that, in the absence of that explanation, the court's postponement of the trial date was premature. For those reasons, I concur in the result.

Comments on *Clinton v. Jones.* Just as the *Nixon* opinion may have precipitated his impeachment, did the opinion in *Jones* have the same effect in regard to President Clinton? Would President Clinton's impeachment have occurred if the Court in *Jones* had not concluded that in regard to "the risk that our decision will generate a large volume of politically motivated harassing and frivolous litigation, and the danger that national security concerns might prevent the President from explaining a legitimate need for a continuance[,] *[w]e are not persuaded that either of these risks is serious*" (emphasis added)?

The *Cheney* opinion, which follows, is the most contemporary statement concerning executive privilege.

CHENEY v. U.S. DISTRICT COURT
542 U.S. 367 (2004)

[Public interest groups filed suit under the Federal Advisory Committee Act (FACA) seeking information from the Vice President and other senior Executive Branch officials about the members and activities of a task force (NEPDG) established to develop a national energy policy for the President. To show FACA's applicability, plaintiffs obtained an extensive discovery order regarding NEPDG's activities that requested even more information than they would be entitled to if they succeeded in proving that FACA applied. The D.C. Circuit, relying on *Nixon,* denied the government's petition for mandamus to vacate the district court's discovery order and to dismiss the Vice President as a defendant because of principles of separation of powers. The Court, per Justice Kennedy, remanded to the D.C. Circuit to reconsider:]

Accepted mandamus standards are broad enough to allow a court to prevent a lower court from interfering with a coequal branch's ability to discharge its constitutional responsibilities. [The] need for information for use in civil cases, while far from negligible, does not share the urgency or significance of the criminal subpoena requests in *Nixon*. . . . Withholding materials from a tribunal in an ongoing criminal case. when the information is necessary to the court in carrying out its tasks "conflict[s] with the function of the courts under Art. III." [Withholding] the information in this case, however, does not hamper another branch's ability to perform its "essential functions" in quite the same way. [Even if] FACA's statutory objectives would be to some extent frustrated, [it] cannot, in fairness, be compared to *Nixon,* where a court's ability to fulfill its constitutional responsibility to resolve cases and controversies within its jurisdiction hinges on the availability of certain indispensable information.

[This] Court has held, on more than one occasion, that "[t]he high respect that is owed to the office of the Chief Executive . . . is a matter that should inform the conduct of the entire proceeding, including the timing and scope of discovery," *Clinton,* and that the Executive's "constitutional responsibilities and status [are] factors counseling judicial deference and restraint" in the conduct of litigation against it, *Nixon v. Fitzgerald.* [Given] the breadth of the discovery requests in this case compared to the narrow subpoena orders in *Nixon,* our precedent provides no support for the proposition [adopted by the district court] that the Executive Branch "shall bear the burden" of invoking executive privilege with sufficient specificity and of making particularized objections. [Our] precedents suggest just the opposite. See, *e.g., Clinton v. Jones,* 520 U.S. 681, 117 S.Ct. 1636, 137 L.Ed.2d 945 (1997); *id.,* at 705, 117 S.Ct. 1636 (holding that the Judiciary may direct "appropriate process" to the Executive); *Nixon v. Fitzgerald,* 457 U.S., at 753, 102 S.Ct. 2690.

[In] recognition of these concerns, there is sound precedent in the District of Columbia itself for district courts to explore other avenues, short of forcing the Executive to invoke privilege, when they are asked to enforce against the Executive Branch unnecessarily broad subpoenas. [But the D.C. Circuit] labored under the mistaken assumption that the assertion of executive privilege is a necessary precondition to the Government's separation-of-powers objections.

E. THE TRUMP PROCEEDINGS

Perhaps not since Watergate has the issue of presidential power and, in particular, presidential privilege and immunity been so vigorously considered by the three branches of government. Of course the prelude to this period of litigation are the cases we just covered.

United States v. Nixon and *Clinton v. Jones* had one key point in common: both had to do with judicial proceedings. *Nixon's* judicial proceeding was criminal in nature and the Jones suit was of course civil. Nixon also dealt with a claim of executive privilege involving official documents while President Clinton claimed absolute immunity from suit. Both were rejected by the Court; in the Nixon case the Court saying that accommodations could be made to protect sensitive information but making clear that there was no absolute immunity from responding to a court subpoena in a criminal proceeding. In *Clinton* the Court rejected any notion of executive immunity from suit having to do with activities before Clinton was President, and any immunity due to the taxing nature of defending a civil suit was rejected outright by the Court.

During the prelude to the first impeachment of President Donald Trump, several House committees issued subpoenas for what has been characterized as personal tax and business information of the President regarding activities before the Trump presidency. At about the same period of time, the district attorney for New York County (Manhattan) subpoenaed tax and business records of the President's businesses and those of associates and relatives as part of an undisclosed grand jury investigation. The latter case is summarized below, and the excerpted opinion in the former decision is included afterward. Both are from the 2019 October Term.

Crucial to the understanding of *Trump v. Vance*, 590 U.S. ___ (2020), is the history of similar subpoena controversies involving court proceedings dating back to the treason trial of Aaron Burr in 1807. The Court in *Vance* was unanimous in concluding that the President did not have absolute immunity, dismissing claims that state court subpoenas could create a diversion of the President from his duties, that there would be a stigma on the President to comply with a subpoena, or that such actions could be a tool of harassment by state prosecutors. As for the latter, legal prohibitions against grand jury fishing expeditions should protect the President and the Supremacy Clause provided a particularly strong layer of protection against state interference with federal matters. The majority also believed that subpoenas need not be subjected to a scrutiny any higher than a showing by the DA that the information was needed, citing to *United States v. Aaron Burr*, 25 F Cas 55 (1807) (the Burr treason trial) for the proposition that a president stands in "*nearly* the same situation with any other individual" when it comes to judicial process. The majority interpreted the term "nearly" as allowing a president to present evidence of interference with his duties to a judge who may exercise her judicial prerogative of modifying or quashing such a subpoena.

However, two dissents by Justices Thomas and Alito, while agreeing that there is no absolute immunity, would seemingly grant greater deference to the President's representation that the subpoena interfered with executive duties.

Chief Justice Roberts's recounting of the history of Presidential subpoenas, beginning with the Burr treason trial, is quite illuminating as well as interesting:

> In the summer of 1807, all eyes were on Richmond, Virginia. Aaron Burr, the former Vice President, was on trial for treason. Fallen from political grace after his fatal

duel with Alexander Hamilton, and with a murder charge pending in New Jersey, Burr followed the path of many down-and-out Americans of his day—he headed West in search of new opportunity. But Burr was a man with outsized ambitions. Together with General James Wilkinson, the Governor of the Louisiana Territory, he hatched a plan to establish a new territory in Mexico, then controlled by Spain. Both men anticipated that war between the United States and Spain was imminent, and when it broke out they intended to invade Spanish territory at the head of a private army.

But while Burr was rallying allies to his cause, tensions with Spain eased and rumors began to swirl that Burr was conspiring to detach States by the Allegheny Mountains from the Union. Wary of being exposed as the principal co-conspirator, Wilkinson took steps to ensure that any blame would fall on Burr. He sent a series of letters to President Jefferson accusing Burr of plotting to attack New Orleans and revolutionize the Louisiana Territory.

Jefferson, who despised his former running mate Burr for trying to steal the 1800 presidential election from him, was predisposed to credit Wilkinson's version of events. The President sent a special message to Congress identifying Burr as the "prime mover" in a plot "against the peace and safety of the Union." 16 Annals of Cong. 39–40 (1807). Ac- cording to Jefferson, Burr contemplated either the "severance of the Union" or an attack on Spanish territory. Id., at 41. Jefferson acknowledged that his sources contained a "mixture of rumors, conjectures, and suspicions" but, citing Wilkinson's letters, he assured Congress that Burr's guilt was "beyond question."

The trial that followed was "the greatest spectacle in the short history of the republic," complete with a Founder-studded cast. N. Isenberg, Fallen Founder: The Life of Aaron Burr 351 (2007). People flocked to Richmond to watch, massing in tents and covered wagons along the banks of the James River, nearly doubling the town's population of 5,000. Burr's defense team included Edmund Randolph and Luther Martin, both former delegates at the Constitutional Convention and renowned advocates. Chief Justice John Marshall, who had recently squared off with the Jefferson administration in Marbury v. Madison, 1 Cranch 137 (1803), presided as Circuit Justice for Virginia. Meanwhile Jefferson, intent on conviction, orchestrated the prosecution from afar, dedicating Cabinet meetings to the case, peppering the prosecutors with directions, and spending nearly $100,000 from the Treasury on the five-month proceedings.

In the lead-up to trial, Burr, taking aim at his accusers, moved for a subpoena duces tecum directed at Jefferson. The draft subpoena required the President to produce an October 21, 1806 letter from Wilkinson and accompanying documents, which Jefferson had referenced in his message to Congress. The prosecution opposed the request, arguing that a President could not be subjected to such a subpoena and that the letter might contain state secrets. Following four days of argument, Marshall announced his ruling to a packed chamber.

The President, Marshall declared, does not "stand exempt from the general provisions of the constitution" or, in particular, the Sixth Amendment's guarantee that those accused have compulsory process for obtaining witnesses for their defense. United States v. Burr, 25 F. Cas. 30, 33–34 (No. 14,692d) (CC Va. 1807). At common law the "single reservation" to the duty to testify in response to a subpoena was "the case of the king," whose "dignity" was seen as "incompatible" with appearing "under the process of the court." Id., at 34. But, as Marshall explained, a king is born to power and can "do no wrong." Ibid. The President, by contrast, is "of the people" and subject to the law. Ibid. According to Marshall, the sole argument for exempting the President from testimonial obligations was that his "duties as chief magistrate demand his whole time for national objects." Ibid. But, in Marshall's assessment, those demands were "not unremitting." Ibid. And should the President's duties preclude his attendance at a particular time and place, a court could work that out upon return of the subpoena.

Marshall also rejected the prosecution's argument that the President was immune from a subpoena duces tecum because executive papers might contain state secrets. "A subpoena duces tecum," he said, "may issue to any person to whom an ordinary subpoena may issue." Ibid. As he explained, no "fair construction" of the Constitution supported the conclusion that the right "to compel the attendance of witnesses[ ] does not extend" to requiring those witnesses to "bring[] with them such papers as may be material in the defense." Id., at 35. And, as a matter of basic fairness, permitting such information to be withheld would "tarnish the reputation of the court." Id., at 37. As for "the propriety of introducing any papers," that would "depend on the character of the paper, not on the character of the person who holds it." Id., at 34. Marshall acknowledged that the papers sought by Burr could contain information "the disclosure of which would endanger the public safety," but stated that, again, such concerns would have "due consideration" upon the return of the subpoena.

While the arguments unfolded, Jefferson, who had received word of the motion, wrote to the prosecutor indicating that he would—subject to the prerogative to decide which executive communications should be withheld—"furnish on all occasions, whatever the purposes of justice may require." Letter from T. Jefferson to G. Hay (June 12,1807), in 10 Works of Thomas Jefferson 398, n. (P. Ford ed. 1905). His "personal attendance," however, was out of the question, for it "would leave the nation without" the "sole branch which the constitution requires to be always in function." Letter from T. Jefferson to G. Hay (June 17, 1807), in id., at 400–401, n.

Before Burr received the subpoenaed documents, Marshall rejected the prosecution's core legal theory for treason and Burr was accordingly acquitted. Jefferson, however, was not done. Committed to salvaging a conviction, he directed the prosecutors to proceed with a misdemeanor (yes, misdemeanor) charge for inciting war against Spain. Burr then renewed his request for Wilkinson's October 21 letter, which he later received a copy of, and subpoenaed a second letter, dated November 12, 1806, which the prosecutor claimed was privileged. Acknowledging that the President may withhold information to protect public safety, Marshall instructed that Jefferson should "state the particular reasons" for withholding the letter. United States v. Burr, 25 F. Cas. 187, 192 (No. 14,694) (CC Va. 1807). The court, paying "all proper respect" to those reasons, would then decide whether to compel disclosure. Ibid. But that decision was averted when the misdemeanor trial was cut short after it became clear that the prosecution lacked the evidence to convict.

In the two centuries since the Burr trial, successive Presidents have accepted Marshall's ruling that the Chief Executive is subject to subpoena. In 1818, President Monroe received a subpoena to testify in a court-martial against one of his appointees. See Rotunda, Presidents and Ex-Presidents as Witnesses: A Brief Historical Footnote, 1975 U. Ill. L. Forum 1, 5. His Attorney General, William Wirt—who had served as a prosecutor during Burr's trial—advised Monroe that, per Marshall's ruling, a subpoena to testify may "be properly awarded to the President." Id., at 5–6. Monroe offered to sit for a deposition and ultimately submitted answers to written interrogatories.

Following Monroe's lead, his successors have uniformly agreed to testify when called in criminal proceedings, provided they could do so at a time and place of their choosing. In 1875, President Grant submitted to a three-hour deposition in the criminal prosecution of a political appointee embroiled in a network of tax-evading whiskey distillers. See 1 R. Rotunda & J. Nowak, Constitutional Law §7.1(b)(ii), p. 996 (5th ed. 2012) (Rotunda & Nowak). A century later, President Ford's attempted assassin subpoenaed him to testify in her defense. See United States v. Fromme, 405 F. Supp. 578 (ED Cal. 1975). Ford obliged—from a safe distance—in the first videotaped deposition of a President. President Carter testified via the same means in the trial of two local officials who, while Carter was Governor of Georgia, had offered to contribute to his campaign in exchange for advance warning of any state gambling raids. See Carter's

Testimony, on Videotape, Is Given to Georgia Gambling Trial, N. Y. Times, Apr. 20, 1978, p. A20 (Carter recounted that he "rejected the proposition instantly."). Two years later, Carter gave videotaped testimony to a federal grand jury investigating whether a fugitive financier had entreated the White House to quash his extradition proceedings. See Rotunda & Nowak §7.1(b)(vi), at 997. President Clinton testified three times, twice via deposition pursuant to subpoenas in federal criminal trials of associates implicated during the Whitewater investigation, and once by video for a grand jury investigating possible perjury. See id., §7.1(c)(viii), at 1007–1008.

The bookend to Marshall's ruling came in 1974 when the question he never had to decide—whether to compel the disclosure of official communications over the objection of the President—came to a head. That spring, the Special Prosecutor appointed to investigate the break-in of the Democratic National Committee Headquarters at the Watergate complex filed an indictment charging seven defendants associated with President Nixon and naming Nixon as an unindicted co-conspirator. As the case moved toward trial, the Special Prosecutor secured a subpoena duces tecum directing Nixon to produce, among other things, tape recordings of Oval Office meetings. Nixon moved to quash the subpoena, claiming that the Constitution provides an absolute privilege of confidentiality to all presidential communications. This Court rejected that argument in United States v. Nixon, 418 U. S. 683 (1974), a decision we later described as "unequivocally and emphatically endorsing Marshall's" holding that Presidents are subject to subpoena. Clinton v. Jones, 520 U. S. 681, 704 (1997).

The Nixon Court readily acknowledged the importance of preserving the confidentiality of communications "between high Government officials and those who advise and assist them." 418 U. S., at 705. "Human experience," the Court explained, "teaches that those who expect public dissemination of their remarks may well temper candor with a concern for appearances and for their own interests to the detriment of the decision-making process." Ibid. Confidentiality thus promoted the "public interest in can- did, objective, and even blunt or harsh opinions in Presidential decision-making." Id., at 708.

But, like Marshall two centuries prior, the Court recognized the countervailing interests at stake. Invoking the common law maxim that "the public has a right to every man's evidence," the Court observed that the public interest in fair and accurate judicial proceedings is at its height in the criminal setting, where our common commitment to justice demands that "guilt shall not escape" nor "innocence suffer." Id., at 709 (internal quotation marks and alteration omitted). Because these dual aims would be "defeated if judgments" were "founded on a partial or speculative presentation of the facts," the Nixon Court recognized that it was "imperative" that "compulsory process be available for the production of evidence needed either by the prosecution or the defense." Ibid.

The Court thus concluded that the President's "generalized assertion of privilege must yield to the demonstrated, specific need for evidence in a pending criminal trial." Id., at 713. Two weeks later, President Nixon dutifully released the tapes.

TRUMP v. MAZARS, LLP
590 U.S.___(2020)

Chief Justice ROBERTS delivered the opinion of the Court.

Over the course of five days in April 2019, three committees of the U. S. House of Representatives issued four subpoenas seeking information about the finances of President Donald J. Trump, his children, and affiliated businesses. We have held that the House has authority under the Constitution to issue subpoenas to assist it in carrying out its legislative responsibilities. The House asserts that the financial information sought here—

encompassing a decade's worth of transactions by the President and his family—will help guide legislative reform in areas ranging from money laundering and terrorism to foreign involvement in U. S. elections. The President contends that the House lacked a valid legislative aim and instead sought these records to harass him, expose personal matters, and conduct law enforcement activities beyond its authority. The question presented is whether the subpoenas exceed the authority of the House under the Constitution.

We have never addressed a congressional subpoena for the President's information. Two hundred years ago, it was established that Presidents may be subpoenaed during a federal criminal proceeding, United States v. Burr, 25 F. Cas. 30 (No. 14,692d) (CC Va. 1807) (Marshall, Cir. J.), and earlier today we extended that ruling to state criminal proceedings, Trump v. Vance, ante, p. ___. Nearly fifty years ago, we held that a federal prosecutor could obtain information from a President despite assertions of executive privilege, United States v. Nixon, 418 U. S. 683 (1974), and more recently we ruled that a private litigant could subject a President to a damages suit and appropriate discovery obligations in federal court, Clinton v. Jones, 520 U. S. 681 (1997).

This case is different. Here the President's information is sought not by prosecutors or private parties in connection with a particular judicial proceeding, but by committees of Congress that have set forth broad legislative objectives. Congress and the President—the two political branches established by the Constitution—have an ongoing relation- ship that the Framers intended to feature both rivalry and reciprocity. See The Federalist No. 51, p. 349 (J. Cooke ed. 1961) (J. Madison); Youngstown Sheet & Tube Co. v. Sawyer, 343 U. S. 579, 635 (1952) (Jackson, J., concurring). That distinctive aspect necessarily informs our analysis of the question before us.

[I]
[A]

[According] to the House, the Financial Services Committee issued these subpoenas pursuant to House Resolution 206, which called for "efforts to close loopholes that allow corruption, terrorism, and money laundering to infiltrate our country's financial system." H. Res. 206, 116th Cong., 1st Sess., 5 (Mar. 13, 2019). Such loopholes, the resolution explained, had allowed "illicit money, including from Russian oligarchs," to flow into the United States through "anonymous shell companies" using investments such as "luxury high-end real estate." Id., at 3. The House also invokes the oversight plan of the Financial Services Committee, which stated that the Committee intends to review banking regulation and "examine the implementation, effectiveness, and enforcement" of laws designed to prevent money laundering and the financing of terrorism. H. R. Rep. No. 116–40, p. 84 (2019). The plan further provided that the Committee would "consider proposals to pre- vent the abuse of the financial system" and "address any vulnerabilities identified" in the real estate market. Id., at 85.

On the same day as the Financial Services Committee, the Permanent Select Committee on Intelligence issued an identical subpoena to Deutsche Bank—albeit for different reasons. According to the House, the Intelligence Committee subpoenaed Deutsche Bank as part of an investigation into foreign efforts to undermine the U. S. political process. Committee Chairman Adam Schiff had described that investigation in a previous statement, explaining that the Committee was examining alleged attempts by Russia to influence the 2016 election; potential links between Russia and the President's campaign; and whether the President and his associates had been compromised by foreign actors or interests. Press Release, House Permanent Select Committee on Intelligence, Chairman Schiff Statement on House Intelligence Committee Investigation (Feb. 6, 2019).

Chairman Schiff added that the Committee planned "to develop legislation and policy reforms to ensure the U. S. government is better positioned to counter future efforts to undermine our political process and national security." Ibid.

Four days after the Financial Services and Intelligence Committees, the House Committee on Oversight and Reform issued another subpoena, this time to the President's personal accounting firm, Mazars USA, LLP. The subpoena demanded information related to the President and several affiliated business entities from 2011 through 2018, including statements of financial condition, independent auditors' reports, financial reports, underlying source documents, and communications between Mazars and the President or his businesses. The subpoena also requested all engagement agreements and contracts "[w]ithout regard to time." App. to Pet. for Cert. in 19–715, p. 230.

Chairman Elijah Cummings explained the basis for the subpoena in a memorandum to the Oversight Committee. According to the chairman, recent testimony by the President's former personal attorney Michael Cohen, along with several documents prepared by Mazars and supplied by Cohen, raised questions about whether the President had accurately represented his financial affairs. Chairman Cummings asserted that the Committee had "full authority to investigate" whether the President: (1) "may have engaged in illegal conduct before and during his tenure in office," (2) "has undisclosed conflicts of interest that may impair his ability to make impartial policy decisions," (3) "is complying with the Emoluments Clauses of the Constitution," and (4) "has accurately reported his finances to the Office of Government Ethics and other federal entities." App. in No. 19–5142 (CADC), p. 107. "The Committee's interest in these matters," Chairman Cummings concluded, "informs its review of multiple laws and legislative proposals under our jurisdiction." Ibid.

[II

A]

The question presented is whether the subpoenas exceed the authority of the House under the Constitution. Historically, disputes over congressional demands for presidential documents have not ended up in court. Instead, they have been hashed out in the "hurly-burly, the give-and-take of the political process between the legislative and the executive." Hearings on S. 2170 et al. before the Subcommittee on Intergovernmental Relations of the Senate Committee on Government Operations, 94th Cong., 1st Sess., 87 (1975) (A. Scalia, Assistant Attorney General, Office of Legal Counsel).

[The opinion then went through an historical survey of congressional requests for information from the President beginning with President George Washington through the Clinton administration. The opinion noted that each request had been resolve through Executive and Legislative branches negotiations.]

[This] dispute therefore represents a significant departure from historical practice. Although the parties agree that this particular controversy is justiciable, we recognize that it is the first of its kind to reach this Court; that disputes of this sort can raise important issues concerning relations between the branches; that related disputes involving congressional efforts to seek official Executive Branch information recur on a regular basis, including in the context of deeply partisan controversy; and that Congress and the Executive have nonetheless managed for over two centuries to resolve such disputes among themselves without the benefit of guidance from us. Such longstanding practice " 'is a consideration of great weight' " in cases concerning "the allocation of power between [the] two elected branches of Government," and it imposes on us a duty of care to ensure that we not needlessly disturb "the compromises and working arrangements that [those] branches . . . themselves have reached." NLRB v. Noel Canning, 573 U. S. 513, 524–526 (2014) (quoting The Pocket Veto Case, 279 U. S. 655, 689 (1929)). With that in mind, we turn to the question presented.

B

[Because] [Congress's power to subpoena]is "justified solely as an adjunct to the legislative process," it is subject to several limitations. Id., at 197. Most importantly, a congressional subpoena is valid only if it is "related to, and in furtherance of, a legitimate task of the Congress." Id., at 187. The subpoena must serve a "valid legislative purpose," Quinn v. United States, 349 U. S. 155, 161 (1955); it must "concern[] a subject on which legislation 'could be had,' " Eastland v. United States Servicemen's Fund, 421 U.S. 491, 506 (1975) (quoting McGrain, 273 U. S., at 177).

Furthermore, Congress may not issue a subpoena for the purpose of "law enforcement," because "those powers are assigned under our Constitution to the Executive and the Judiciary." Quinn, 349 U. S., at 161. Thus Congress may not use subpoenas to "try" someone "before [a] committee for any crime or wrongdoing." McGrain, 273 U. S., at 179. Congress has no " 'general' power to inquire into private affairs and compel disclosures," id., at 173–174, and "there is no congressional power to expose for the sake of exposure," Watkins, 354 U. S., at 200. "Investigations conducted solely for the personal aggrandizement of the investigators or to 'punish' those investigated are indefensible." Id., at 187.

Finally, recipients of legislative subpoenas retain their constitutional rights throughout the course of an investigation. See id., at 188, 198. And recipients have long been understood to retain common law and constitutional privileges with respect to certain materials, such as attorney-client communications and governmental communications protected by executive privilege.

C

The President contends, as does the Solicitor General appearing on behalf of the United States, that the usual rules for congressional subpoenas do not govern here because the President's papers are at issue. They argue for a more demanding standard based in large part on cases involving the Nixon tapes—recordings of conversations between President Nixon and close advisers discussing the break-in at the Democratic National Committee's headquarters at the Watergate complex. The tapes were subpoenaed by a Senate committee and the Special Prosecutor investigating the break-in, prompting President Nixon to invoke executive privilege and leading to two cases addressing the showing necessary to require the President to comply with the subpoenas. See Nixon, 418 U. S. 683; Senate Select Committee, 498 F. 2d 725.

Those cases, the President and the Solicitor General now contend, establish the standard that should govern the House subpoenas here. Quoting Nixon, the President asserts that the House must establish a "demonstrated, specific need" for the financial information, just as the Watergate special prosecutor was required to do in order to obtain the tapes. 418 U. S., at 713. And drawing on Senate Select Committee—the D. C. Circuit case refusing to enforce the Senate subpoena for the tapes—the President and the Solicitor General argue that the House must show that the financial information is "demonstrably critical" to its legislative purpose. 498 F. 2d, at 731.

We disagree that these demanding standards apply here. Unlike the cases before us, Nixon and Senate Select Committee involved Oval Office communications over which the President asserted executive privilege. That privilege safeguards the public interest in candid, confidential deliberations within the Executive Branch; it is "fundamental to the operation of Government." Nixon, 418 U. S., at 708. As a result, information subject to executive privilege deserves "the greatest protection consistent with the fair administration of justice." Id., at 715. We decline to transplant that protection root and branch to cases involving non-privileged, private information, which by definition does not implicate sensitive Executive Branch deliberations.

The standards proposed by the President and the Solicitor General—if applied outside the context of privileged information—would risk seriously impeding Congress in carrying out its responsibilities. The President and the Solicitor General would apply the same exacting standards to all subpoenas for the President's information, without recognizing distinctions between privileged and non-privileged information, between official and personal information, or between various legislative objectives. Such a categorical approach would represent a significant departure from the longstanding way of doing business between the branches, giving short shrift to Congress's important interests in conducting inquiries to obtain the information it needs to legislate effectively.

[Legislative] inquiries might involve the President in appropriate cases; as noted, Congress's responsibilities extend to "every affair of government." Ibid. (internal quotation marks omitted). Because the President's approach does not take adequate account of these significant congressional interests, we do not adopt it.

D

The House meanwhile would have us ignore that these suits involve the President. Invoking our precedents concerning investigations that did not target the President's papers, the House urges us to uphold its subpoenas because they "relate[] to a valid legislative purpose" or "concern[] a subject on which legislation could be had." That approach is appropriate, the House argues, because the cases before us are not "momentous separation-of-powers disputes."

[The Court at this point of the opinion discusses what it considers significant separation of powers concerns. The Chief Justice appears to be using the concept of the "President's papers" and "President's personal papers" interchangeably, though that is not really clear from the discussion in this portion. Assuming the latter, the Court's assertion that this case is different from cases going back to George Washington (having to do with official papers and materials), or necessary for a judicial proceeding (United States v. Nixon) has merit. With regard to separation of powers concerns, the opinion expresses concern with the political use to which such a subpoena power could be put, allowing Congress to aggrandize its power through the use of the subpoena that could at some level of analysis be deemed "demonstrably critical" to a "valid legislative purpose."]

E

Congressional subpoenas for the President's personal information implicate weighty concerns regarding the separation of powers. Neither side, however, identifies an approach that accounts for these concerns. For more than two centuries, the political branches have resolved information disputes using the wide variety of means that the Constitution puts at their disposal. The nature of such interactions would be transformed by judicial enforcement of either of the approaches suggested by the parties, eroding a "[d]eeply embedded traditional way[] of conducting government." Youngstown Sheet & Tube Co., 343 U. S., at 610 (Frankfurter, J., concurring).

A balanced approach is necessary, one that takes a "considerable impression" from "the practice of the government," McCulloch v. Maryland, 4 Wheat. 316, 401 (1819); see Noel Canning, 573 U. S., at 524–526, and "resist[s]" the "pressure inherent within each of the separate Branches to exceed the outer limits of its power," INS v. Chadha, 462 U. S. 919, 951 (1983). We therefore conclude that, in assessing whether a subpoena directed at the President's personal information is "related to, and in furtherance of, a legitimate task of the Congress," Watkins, 354 U. S., at 187, courts must perform a careful analysis that takes adequate account of the separation of powers principles at stake, including both the significant legislative interests of Congress and the "unique position" of the President, Clinton, 520 U. S., at 698 (internal quotation marks omitted). Several special considerations inform this analysis.

First, courts should carefully assess whether the asserted legislative purpose warrants the significant step of involving the President and his papers. "'[O]ccasion[s] for constitutional confrontation between the two branches' should be avoided whenever possible." Cheney v. United States Dist. Court for D. C., 542 U. S. 367, 389–390 (2004) (quoting Nixon, 418 U. S., at 692). Congress may not rely on the President's information if other sources could reasonably provide Congress the information it needs in light of its particular legislative objective. The President's unique constitutional position means that Congress may not look to him as a "case study" for general legislation. Cf. 943 F. 3d, at 662–663, n. 67.

Unlike in criminal proceedings, where "[t]he very integrity of the judicial system" would be undermined without "full disclosure of all the facts," Nixon, 418 U. S., at 709, efforts to craft legislation involve predictive policy judgments that are "not hamper[ed] . . . in quite the same way" when every scrap of potentially relevant evidence is not available, Cheney, 542 U. S., at 384; see Senate Select Committee, 498 F. 2d, at 732. While we certainly recognize Congress's important interests in obtaining information through appropriate inquiries, those interests are not sufficiently powerful to justify access to the President's personal papers when other sources could provide Congress the information it needs.

Second, to narrow the scope of possible conflict between the branches, courts should insist on a subpoena no broader than reasonably necessary to support Congress's legislative objective. The specificity of the subpoena's request "serves as an important safeguard against unnecessary intrusion into the operation of the Office of the President." Cheney, 542 U. S., at 387.

Third, courts should be attentive to the nature of the evidence offered by Congress to establish that a subpoena advances a valid legislative purpose. The more detailed and substantial the evidence of Congress's legislative purpose, the better. See Watkins, 354 U. S., at 201, 205 (preferring such evidence over "vague" and "loosely worded" evidence of Congress's purpose). That is particularly true when Congress contemplates legislation that raises sensitive constitutional issues, such as legislation concerning the Presidency. In such cases, it is "impossible" to conclude that a subpoena is designed to advance a valid legislative purpose unless Congress adequately identifies its aims and explains why the President's information will advance its consideration of the possible legislation. Id., at 205–206, 214–215.

Fourth, courts should be careful to assess the burdens imposed on the President by a subpoena. We have held that burdens on the President's time and attention stemming from judicial process and litigation, without more, generally do not cross constitutional lines. See Vance, ante, at 12–14; Clinton, 520 U. S., at 704–705. But burdens imposed by a congressional subpoena should be carefully scrutinized, for they stem from a rival political branch that has an ongoing relationship with the President and incentives to use subpoenas for institutional advantage.

Other considerations may be pertinent as well; one case every two centuries does not afford enough experience for an exhaustive list.

When Congress seeks information "needed for intelligent legislative action," it "unquestionably" remains "the duty of all citizens to cooperate." Watkins, 354 U. S., at 187 (emphasis added). Congressional subpoenas for information from the President, however, implicate special concerns regarding the separation of powers. The courts below did not take adequate account of those concerns. The judgments of the Courts of Appeals for the D. C. Circuit and the Second Circuit are vacated, and the cases are remanded for further proceedings consistent with this opinion.

It is so ordered.

Justice THOMAS, dissenting.

Three Committees of the U. S. House of Representatives issued subpoenas to several accounting and financial firms to obtain the personal financial records of the President, his family, and several of his business entities. The Committees do not argue that these subpoenas were issued pursuant to the House's impeachment power. Instead, they argue that the subpoenas are a valid exercise of their legislative powers.

Petitioners challenge the validity of these subpoenas. In doing so, they call into question our precedents to the extent that they allow Congress to issue legislative subpoenas for the President's private, nonofficial documents. I would hold that Congress has no power to issue a legislative subpoena for private, nonofficial documents—whether they belong to the President or not. Congress may be able to obtain these documents as part of an investigation of the President, but to do so, it must proceed under the impeachment power. Accordingly, I would reverse the judgments of the Courts of Appeals.

[The remainder of Justice Thomas's dissent is omitted. Justice Alito also filed a dissent objecting to the lack of specificity of the majority's remand. Alito would require a more exacting description from Congress of the purpose of the subpoenas, a specific description of Congressional authority, and why other sources would be inadequate for Congress's legislative business or otherwise unavailable.]

PART II
INDIVIDUAL RIGHTS AND LIBERTIES

Chapter 4
Application of the Bill of Rights

I. ADOPTION OF THE BILL OF RIGHTS

Liberty lies in the hearts of men and women, when it dies there, no constitution, no law, no court can save it; no constitution, no law, no court can even do much to help it. While it lies there it needs no constitution, no law, no court to save it. [Judge Learned Hand, *The Spirit of Liberty* 190 (1944).]

Though the Constitution itself was to assure liberty through a government of limited powers, powers that were to be separated and allocated to three distinct branches that could "check and balance" each other, the inclusion of a bill of rights via the amendment process was to become the nation's most important source of liberty. The concept of judicial review placed the United States Supreme Court in the primary role as protector of these rights for all citizens. This was particularly true for the nation's minorities, for the bill of rights, as fundamental law, could protect the rights declared within against majority intrusion. The Supreme Court's life tenure and non-elected status placed it in a most appropriate role to enforce and protect these rights since the Court was not responsible to any majority. Though we are not guaranteed that a given Supreme Court will serve this function, this status, particularly as against the "majoritarian" nature of the other branches of the central government, makes the Court an important and integral part of our study of individual rights and liberties.

Though the framers chose not to include an enumerated list of rights in the original document, Article I nonetheless provided immunity in congressional debates; freedom of movement through the commerce clause; prohibitions against bills of attainder and ex post facto laws; and the privilege of habeas corpus. Article III guaranteed the right of a jury trial and specifically defined the meaning of treasonable acts. Article IV entitled citizens of each state "to all Privileges and Immunities of Citizens of the several states" and guaranteed that each state would maintain "a Republican form of government." Yet, the inclusion of these guarantees in the body of the document fell short of enumerating other vital and important rights. We will first turn to the failure of the framers to include a "bill of rights" in the Constitution itself, and the eventual corrective measure of adopting a list of such rights as the first Ten Amendments to the document.

A. THE FAILURE TO INCLUDE A WRITTEN BILL OF RIGHTS

Though English precedent had provided the framers with a basis for enumerating the rights of the people in the Constitution itself (the famous English grants in Magna Carta (1215); Petition of Right (1628); and Bill of Rights (1689)), the framers chose not to include such at the Constitutional Convention. Their rationale for such, and its effect upon the eventual inclusion of a bill of rights, is our first inquiry.

It would seem that "non-inclusion" was "rights negative," or that the framers believed that the federal government should not afford such protection. Appearances here, however, may have been deceiving, for upon close observation this may not have been the case. The debates at the Constitutional Convention (here, Madison's notes) are a meaningful point of reference.

The concept of including a bill of rights surfaced several times at the Convention, and the failure of these efforts can serve as a means of understanding the rationale for non-enumeration in the document. Col. Mason first proposed such in the following discussion:

Col. Mason: . . . He wishes the plan had been prefaced with a bill of rights, and would second a motion, if made for the purpose. It would give great quiet to the people, and, with the aid of the state declarations, a bill might be prepared in a few hours.

Mr. Gerry concurred in the idea, and moved for a committee to prepare a bill of rights.

Col. Mason seconded the motion.

Mr. Sherman was for securing the rights of the people, where requisite. The state declarations of rights are not repealed by this Constitution, and being in force are sufficient. . . . The legislature may be safely trusted.

Col. Mason. The laws of the United States are to be paramount to state bill of rights.

On the question for a committee to prepare a bill of rights — New Hampshire, Connecticut, New Jersey, Pennsylvania, Delaware, ay; Maryland, Virginia, North Carolina, South Carolina, Georgia, no; Massachusetts, absent.

It appears that the failure of Mason's motion to carry was based on Sherman's response that the states maintained such enumerated rights. Though Mason raised the issue of federal supremacy in relation to such, it is nonetheless true that the states themselves had secured enumerated rights to their citizens, most famous of which was Virginia's Bill of Rights, structured in part by Thomas Jefferson, and closely paralleling the first Ten Amendments that were later adopted by the central government at Jefferson's urging.

The problem here is the nature of our "federalism," the two hats worn by all citizens, federal and state citizenship. Here a state's protection of rights, given federal supremacy, would not affect federal citizenship, and thus could not afford any such protection.

A second rational for non-inclusion surfaces in the following interchange between Pinckney, Gerry and Sherman:

Mr. Pinckney & Gerry, moved to insert a declaration "that the liberty of the press should be inviolably observed."

Mr. Sherman: It is unnecessary — The power of Congress does not extend to the Press. . . . On the question, (it passed in the negative).

The defeat of this motion seems to indicate that the framers believed that the rights of the people could not be limited by the federal government since it maintained only those powers enumerated to it by the Constitution. As a government limited to enumerated powers, if a power was not allocated to the government it would have no basis upon which to act. How, so to speak, could the government act in disregard of a right when it was not granted such power. Hamilton supported this view and argued in the Federalist No. 8 "[t]hat the provision against restraining the liberty of the press afforded a clear implication that a power to prescribe proper regulations concerning [the press] was intended to be vested in the national government."

This view does not seem to take into account the Constitution's grant of "implied" power to the federal Congress via the necessary and proper clause. In this sense the limitation of the Congress to exercise only enumerated powers was nominal, because it was conceivable that the government could infringe on liberties by exercising implied authority that was necessary and proper to carrying out an enumerated power. Thus, for example, might the government, despite no affirmative grant of power, limit speech during a war because it was necessary and proper to execute the war power?

The greatest libertarian of the age and author of the Declaration of Independence, Thomas Jefferson, had been absent from the Constitutional Convention while serving as the American Minister to France in Paris. Some have argued that his absence alone precipitated the failure of the framers to enumerate rights. From Paris, Jefferson had vehemently protested the framers' decision, via correspondence with them and especially his compatriot James Madison. On October 17, 1788, Madison wrote to Jefferson of the problems concerning a bill of rights, reviewing the rationales for non-inclusion:

> My own opinion has always been in favor of a bill of rights; provided it be so framed as not to imply powers not meant to be included in the enumeration. At the same time I have never thought the omission a material defect, . . . I have not viewed it in an important light 1. because I conceive that in a certain degree, . . . the rights in question are reserved by the manner in which the federal powers are granted. 2. because there is great reason to fear that a positive declaration of some of the most essential rights could not be obtained in the requisite latitude. 3. because the limited powers of the federal government and the jealousy of the subordinate Governments, afford a security which has not existed in the case of State Governments, and exists in no other. 4. because experience proves the inefficacy of a bill of rights on those occasions when its control is most needed. Repeated violations of these parchment barriers have been committed by overbearing majorities in every State. In Virginia I have seen the bill of rights violated in every instance where it has been opposed to a popular current. In our government the real power lies in the majority of the Community, and the invasion of private rights is chiefly to be apprehended, not from acts of Government contrary to the sense of its constituents, but from acts in which the Government is the mere instrument of the major number of the Constituents. (i.e. "Tyranny of the majority")

Here Madison raised a meaningful rationale for not including a written bill — the fear that enumeration of certain rights would *limit* those not enumerated. Hamilton also argued in Federalist No. 8 that the enumeration of specific liberties "would disparage those rights which were not placed in that enumeration." The answer to this question has plagued "constitutionalists" throughout history. Is it possible to detail a list of rights which includes all rights that are necessary forevermore? Would any such enumeration not inevitably be limiting in character because one could assume that any right not enumerated was *not* intended. This argument against enumeration is consequential because "more" (a written bill) might protect less. Was the Ninth Amendment ("The enumeration in the Constitution, of certain rights, shall not be construed to deny or disparage others retained by the people") the framers' response to this problem? Though the Ninth Amendment appears to indicate that the bill of rights would not be exhaustive, the Court has never adopted this position. Despite the apparent specificity of the language in the Ninth Amendment, is does not articulate who is to construe any "unarticulated" rights. Though judicial review lingers, the framers do not so specify either in the Amendment or, as we have seen, in the Constitution itself. Furthermore, and as we have also seen in our study of the judicial power, the Court's ability to declare unarticulated rights, whether it be based upon the Ninth Amendment or substantive due process, is in itself most controversial.

Jefferson provided Madison with a response to this and other issues raised in Madison's letter of October 17, 1788. From Paris, on March 15, 1789, Jefferson forwarded an articulate defense of a written bill of rights, thus becoming the major proponent for such among the founding fathers. Interestingly, given his position on judicial review, he also provided a specific role for the Supreme Court in relation to application of a bill of rights:

> Your thoughts on the subject of the Declaration of rights in the letter of Oct. 17. I have weighed with great satisfaction. In the arguments in favor of a declaration of rights, you omit one which has great weight with me, the legal check which it puts into the hands of the judiciary. This is a body, which if rendered independent and kept strictly to their own department merits great confidence for their learning and integrity. The Declaration of rights is like all other human blessings alloyed with some inconveniences, . . . But the good in the instance vastly overweighs the evil. I cannot refrain from making short answers to the objection which your letter states to have been ignored. 1. That the rights in question are reserved by the manner in which the federal powers are granted. Answer . . . in a constitutive act which leaves some precious articles unnoticed, and raise implication against their (Executive and Legislative branches) abuses of power within the field submitted to them. 2. A positive declaration of some essential rights could not be obtained in the requisite latitude. Answer. Half a loaf is better than no bread. If we cannot secure all our rights, let us secure what we can. 3. The limited powers of the federal government and jealousy of the subordinate governments afford a security which exists in no other instance. Answer. The first member of this seems resolvably into the first objection before stated. 4. Expedience proves the inefficacy of a bill of rights. Answer. There is a remarkable difference between the characters of the Inconveniences which attend a Declaration of Rights, and those which attend the want of it. The inconveniences of the Declaration are that it may cramp government in it's useful exertions. But the evil of this is short-lived, trivial and reparable. The inconveniences of the want of a Declaration are permanent, afflicting and irreparable. The tyranny of the legislature is the most formable dread at present, . . . That of the executive will come its turn. . . .

Several State Conventions that considered ratification of the new Constitution expressed dismay as to the lack of an enumerated bill of rights. The seeds for its eventual inclusion via the amendment process were sown in these debates. Massachusetts, for example, so strongly protested the failure of the framers to include such that a quasi-compromise was reached wherein Massachusetts agreed to ratify the document, subject to the promise that efforts would be made to attach a bill of rights to the Constitution.

With the urging of Jefferson and a mandate from the State ratifications, on June 8, 1789, Madison rose in the House of Representatives and proposed a Bill of Rights as the first amendments to the Constitution. In doing such he, as had Jefferson, also articulated a specific role for the judiciary in relation to the declarations of rights:

> If they are incorporated into the Constitution, independent tribunals of justice will consider themselves in a peculiar manner the guardians of those rights; they will be an impenetrable bulwark against every assumption of power in the legislative or executive; they will be naturally led to resist every encroachment upon rights stipulated for in the Constitution by the declaration of rights.

Madison's purpose was not only reinforced by Jefferson's arguments, but also by the demands for such from the states, particularly in relation to North Carolina and Rhode Island, two states which had not joined the union as of that date.   Several of the proposed amendments were not adopted. Congress itself did not adopt a provision that would have made several of the rights binding upon the states.   In support of such, Madison had articulated the need for binding the states: "[I]t must be admitted, on all hands, that the state governments are as liable to attach these invaluable privileges as the general government is, and therefore ought to be as cautiously guarded against."   The states themselves failed to ratify provisions adopted by Congress that called for changing the size of the House of Representatives and changing the compensation for congressmen and senators.

Thus, for all practical purposes the Bill of Rights was part and parcel of the Constitution, for the ratification of the document itself was contingent on an inclusion of a declaration of rights. When that commitment was fulfilled by Madison proposing the aforesaid amendments, by 1791 the states themselves ratified the amendments.

Were the arguments against a written bill of rights persuasive?   What light has our history shed on this debate?   How meaningful was the criticism that a written bill of rights would limit liberties by not encompassing all that might be necessary?   Is the Ninth Amendment a sufficient answer?   Who will define these "reserved" rights which are not articulated?   Can the Supreme Court serve such a purpose through judicial review?   Yet, if the Court so functions, will it not be "writing a Constitution" rather than interpreting it? Is the Ninth Amendment a defense for such?   What of the "broad" constitutional clauses? One of the means the framers used to avoid the limitation of being too specific in defining rights was the use of broad language, such as "due process of law."   How important is all of this to Marshall's concept that it is "a Constitution we are expounding"?

Does the fact that the Congress rejected a provision making some rights applicable to the states become a persuasive reason for so concluding?   How significant is this issue? In relation to State power, especially during the 19th century, what problems do you anticipate might evolve in protecting rights if they were not made applicable to the states?

What can a bill of rights offer us if, as Hand asserted, liberty ultimately must rest "in the hearts of men and women"?   Does the fact that we have had a bill of rights for more than two hundred years contribute to liberty resting in our hearts today?   If it has, the problem of whether protected rights should be limited only to those specified in the Amendments still remains.   Can we overcome this problem?   Is it a problem?   How important are the broad phrases such as "due process"; "privileges and immunities"; "life, liberty and the pursuit of happiness"; and "equal protection of the Law" in keeping our liberties in touch with the times?   What should be the role of the Court in this regard? What do you think Jefferson meant when he spoke of "a legal check" in the hands of the judiciary?   What role might he have foreseen for the Court in relation to the questions we have posed?

II. THE BILL OF RIGHTS AND THE STATES

The struggle to adopt a bill of rights as the first ten amendments to the Constitution was only the first battle fought for civil liberties.   The second battle was to be fought over the framework and meaning of these rights, and the protection they offered to all citizens. Americans were to wear two citizenship "hats," one as national citizens in their relation to the federal government, and the other as state citizens in their relation to their state governments.   In the opinion that follows, the Supreme Court faced the question as to whether the bill of rights was applicable to the states or whether state citizens could claim the protection of these federal rights as against their state governments.   This was a question of consequence not only in regard to the civil liberties retained by state citizens, but also in regard to the continued maintenance of slavery and the balance of power between the federal and state governments.   Once again, in another threshold decision, Chief Justice Marshall delivered the opinion of the Court.

BARRON v. BALTIMORE
32 U.S. (7 Pet.) 243 (1833)

Barron sued the City for ruining his wharf in Baltimore harbor. Barron claimed that municipal street construction had diverted the flow of streams so that they deposited silt in front of his wharf, and that this made the water too shallow for most vessels. Barron maintained that this action violated the fifth amendment, which provides that private property shall not be "taken for public use, without just compensation." The Court rejected Barron's contention that the fifth amendment, "being in favor of the liberty of the citizens, ought to be so construed as to restrain the legislative power of a state, as well as that of the United States."

Chief Justice MARSHALL delivered the opinion:
    The question [is] of great importance, but not of much difficulty. The constitution was ordained and established by the people of the United States for themselves, for their own government, and not for the government of the individual states. Each state established a constitution for itself, and in that constitution, provided such limitations and restrictions on the powers of its particular government, as its judgment dictated. The people of the United States framed such a government for the United States as they supposed best adapted to their situation and best calculated to promote their interests. The powers they conferred on this government were to be exercised by itself; and the limitations on power, if expressed in general terms, are naturally, and, we think, necessarily, applicable to the government created by the instrument. . . .
    [Article I, section 10, of the original constitution expressly enumerates those limitations] which were to operate on the state legislatures. [Had] the framers of [the] amendments intended them to be limitations on the powers of the state governments, they

would have imitated the framers of the original constitution, and have expressed that intention. Had congress engaged in the extraordinary occupation of improving the constitutions of the several states, by affording the people additional protection from the exercise of power by their own governments, in matters which concerned themselves alone, they would have declared this purpose in plain and intelligible language. But it is universally understood, it is a part of the history of the day, that the great revolution which established the constitution of the United States, was not affected without immense opposition. Serious fears were extensively entertained, that those powers which the patriot statesmen, who then watched over the interests of our country, deemed essential to union, and to the attainment of those invaluable objects for which union was sought, might be exercised in a manner dangerous to liberty. In almost every convention by which the constitution was adopted, amendments to guard against the abuse of power were recommended. These amendments demanded security against the apprehended encroachments of the general government — not against those of the local governments. In compliance with a sentiment thus generally expressed, to quiet fears thus extensively entertained, amendments were proposed by the required majority in congress, and adopted by the states. These amendments contain no expression indicating an intention to apply them to the state governments. This court cannot so apply them.

We are of opinion, that the [just compensation] provision in the fifth amendment [is] intended solely as a limitation on the exercise of power by the government of the United States, and is not applicable to legislation of the states.

———

Comments on *Barron*.   Was Marshall correct in his conclusion that the bill of rights was not intended to apply to the states?   Was the defeat of Madison's proposal to make the bill of rights effective against the states conclusive proof in support of Marshall?   Is it possible to make an argument that "some" of the rights declared in the first ten amendments were applicable to the states? Could such a division be drawn along the lines of those that "prohibit" activity from the central government, as against those that speak to protecting "persons" from having their rights violated?   Did Marshall avoid such an interpretation? Are you surprised that Marshall, the federalist, sides with the states in *Barron*?

Though most historians concur with Marshall's analysis, the decision nonetheless had significant effect on the evolvement of civil rights and liberties in the nation's development. The states themselves maintained much autonomy at the time of the adoption of the Constitution, and the 10th amendment was to reserve local "police powers" to them as well. Of consequence, the most serious problems relating to liberty concerned state citizens and their state governments.   If the bill of rights was held applicable to the states, state citizens would have had recourse to them in protection of their liberties.   When these federally protected rights were held as inapplicable to the states, the liberties retained by citizens of each state would be entirely dependent on those protected by their state governments. Though most states maintained some form of right-based protection in their own constitutions, the rights and liberties of Americans were not "nationalized" and were thus dependent on the states in which they resided.   The inherent danger of this dependence is evidenced by the fact that many of these states maintained slavery at the same time they maintained rights!   Given the result in *Barron*, the issue of national protection of rights and liberties would not be resolved until well into the twentieth century.

Nonetheless, the holding in *Barron* had pronounced effects on civil liberties in the early years of the nation. First, by holding that the bill of rights affected only the federal government, all citizens held two types of distinct and meaningful citizenship — state and national. In their role as national citizens, they would receive protection from the federal bill of rights, yet in their role as state citizens they would not. Second, since most criminal sanctions remained with the states (the Supreme Court did not maintain jurisdiction in the appeal of criminal cases during most of the era), enforcement and application of the bill of rights by the Supreme Court was almost nonexistent for three-quarters of a century, and only became an issue with the adoption of the post–Civil War amendments.

The result in *Barron* may have been predetermined by the framers' desire to allow slavery to be maintained in the South. It is impossible to tell the story of individual rights and liberties in America without reviewing the hypocrisy of adopting a bill of rights while the Constitution and the nation allowed the maintenance of the most ignoble of human practice, slavery, to be maintained in the South. It is to this issue and its hypocrisy that we turn next.

III. SLAVERY AND THE CONSTITUTION: THE IGNOBLE COMPROMISE

American history has been dominated by slavery and racism. Any study of civil rights must focus on racism. Southern economies depended on slavery before the adoption of the Constitution, and the document itself, even accompanied by a bill of rights, recognized and thus condoned this most abhorrent of evil. The Constitution spoke to slavery at three essential clauses:

Art. IV., Sec. 2. "The Return Clause." No Person held to Service or Labour in one State, under the Laws thereof, escaping into another, shall, in Consequence of any Law or Regulation therein, be discharged from such Service or Labour, but shall be delivered up on Claim of the Party to whom such Service or Labour may be due.

Art. I., Sec. 9. "The Importation Clause." The Migration or Importation of such Persons as any of the States now existing shall think proper to admit, shall not be prohibited by the Congress prior to the Year one thousand eight hundred and eight, but a Tax or duty may be imposed on such Importation, not exceeding ten dollars for each Person.

Art. I. Sec. 2. "The Three-Fifths Clause." Representatives and direct Taxes shall be apportioned among the several States which may be included within this Union, according to their respective Numbers, which shall be determined by adding to the whole Number of free Persons, including those bound to Service for a Term of Years, and excluding Indians not taxed, three fifths of all other Persons.

These references to slavery promoted its existence (at least until 1808) and unaugustly intertwined crimes against humanity into the idealism of the Constitution and the American experience. As if this was not enough, the framers engaged in "sleight of hand" in their terminology: The importation clause speaks to "such Person"; the return clause to "Person held to Service or Labour"; the three-fifths clause limits apportionment to a "whole Number for free Persons" and "three fifths of all other Persons." To the heritage of "We the People" the framers not only "constitutionalized" slavery, but used language as if to hide their ignoble deed from posterity.

The purpose of the three-fifths clause was to ensure political dominance of the South. When the House was apportioned, and electors for the President selected, the South was to get an additional three-fifths vote/apportion for the "other Persons," their slaves. Gary Wills, in his *"Negro President," Jefferson and the Slave Power* (2003), argues that Jefferson's election as President in 1800 was not due to a populist "Second Revolution," as billed by Jefferson, but rather to the South's additional apportionment in the electoral college because of the three-fifths clause.

> If real votes alone had been counted, Adams would have been returned to office. But, of course, the "vote" did not depend solely on voters. Though Jefferson, admittedly, received eight more votes than Adams in the Electoral College, at least twelve of his votes were not based on the citizenry that could express its will but on the blacks owned by southern masters. It galled the Federalists that Jefferson hailed his 1800 victory as a triumph of democracy and majority rule when, as the *Mercury and New-England Palladium* of Boston said (January 20, 1801), he had made his "ride into the temple of Liberty on the shoulders of slaves." [*Id.* at 2.]

The return clause is the most chilling of the three. Hope may spring eternal, but as the essence of the human spirit it must be broken to maintain slavery. The framers sought to chill hope by making escape to freedom in the North "unconstitutional," and requiring that any escaped slave "shall be delivered up on Claim of the Party to whom such Service or Labour may be due." The history of our Constitution has been a history of limiting the power of the state to reach private conduct. Even today the Supreme Court has condoned racism and segregation if purely "private" in its form. (See *Moose Lodge*, infra.) Note here, however, that the framers had little trouble making the private conduct of freeing a slave unconstitutional. For a fortunate few, the "underground railroad" to Canada became the only "safe" means to avoid the Constitution itself.

The most interesting of the clauses is the importation clause. On one hand, it condoned slavery by making importation of slaves constitutionally permissible, even denying an exorbitant "excise tax" to curb the practice. Yet on the other hand, it prohibited importation "to the Year one thousand eight hundred and eight." Beneath this apparent inconsistency lurks "the ignoble compromise."

By 1776 there were one-half million slaves in America, about one-sixth of the population. This was not an insignificant number, and the struggle for union and the adoption of a new Constitution made the status of these individuals a central issue. Why a compromise? In order to form a union with the slave-holding South, the North agreed to allow the slave system to continue in the South until the "prohibition" on importation of slaves in 1808 (the Importation Clause). Was this a compromise, at least until 1808, in order to form a nation and adopt a new Constitution?

Some have argued such. Certainly there were abolitionist sentiments in the North, and the Virginia contingent, Washington, Madison, and Jefferson, though slave holders, had openly expressed hostility to slavery. It is true that this clause was added to the Constitution as a "compromise" to ensure that several southern states would join the Union. In the words of Governor Morris, "this part of the Constitution was a compliance with [the] states of North Carolina, South Carolina, and Georgia," and there was some hope that banning importation after 1808 would curtail the system. But in reality the compromise was "ignoble." The framers knew, or should have known, that such a prohibition on importation would not be successful and would not curtail slavery. James Madison commented in this regard, "Twenty years will produce all the mischief that can be apprehended from a liberty to import slaves."

Madison proved to be correct.   Whether the supposed comprise was ignoble by intent or effect, slavery did not cease in the South after the 1808 prohibition.   In fact, the invention of the cotton gin reinvigorated the oppressive use of slave labor in the cotton fields and provided significant economic gain for the southern economy.   The Louisiana Purchase further strengthened the South's political influence, already significant because of geographic representation in the Senate and the three-fifths clause in apportioning the House.   As Wills comments,

> A bargain had been struck at the Constitutional Convention — one of the famous compromises on which the document was formed, this one intended to secure ratification in the South. The negotiated agreement decreed that each slave held in the United States would count as three-fifths of a person — the so-called federal ratio — for establishing the representation of a state in the House of Representatives (and consequently in the Electoral College, which was based on the House and Senate numbers for each state in Congress). [Wills, *supra*, at 2.]

Just as all rights of African Americans were sacrificed to achieve union, so they also became, under the bondage of slavery, the sacrificial lamb for the economic development of the southern economy. Rather than seeing slavery abolished after 1808, the South was to respond with its own system of "regenerating" the slave race, and in doing such found a new business — raising slaves for market in the South and Southwest.   This was a most ignoble compromise and a blight on the history of our nation.

The Supreme Court was no idle spectator to the Constitution's condoning slavery.   It "sealed" the deal.   The two cases that follow are exemplary of such.

PRIGG v. PENNSYLVANIA
41 U.S. 539 (1842)

Story, Justice, delivered the opinion of the court.

The facts are briefly these:

The plaintiff in error was indicted in the court of over and terminer for York county, for having, with force and violence, taken and carried away from that county, to the state of Maryland, a certain negro woman, named Margaret Morgan, with a design and intention of selling and disposing of, and keeping her, as a slave or servant for life, contrary to a statute of Pennsylvania, passed on the 26th of March 1826. That statute, in the first section, in substance, provides, that if any person or persons shall, from and after the passing of the act, by force and violence, take and carry away, or cause to be taken and carried away, and shall, by fraud or false pretense, seduce, or cause to be seduced, or shall attempt to take, carry away or seduce, any negro or mulatto, from any part of that commonwealth, with a design and intention of selling and disposing of, or causing to be sold, or of keeping and detaining, or of causing to be kept and detained, such negro or mulatto, as a slave or servant for life, or for any term whatsoever; every such person or persons, his or their aiders or abettors, shall, on conviction thereof, be deemed guilty of felony, and shall forfeit and pay a sum not less than five hundred, nor more than one thousand dollars; and moreover, shall be sentenced to undergo servitude for any term or terms of years, not less than seven years nor exceeding twenty-one years; and shall be confined and kept to hard labor, &c. There are many other provisions in the statute, which is recited at large in the record, but to which it is in our view unnecessary to advert upon the present occasion.

The plaintiff in error pleaded not guilty to the indictment; and at the trial, the jury found a special verdict, which, in substance, states, that the negro woman, Margaret Morgan, was a slave for life, and held to labor and service under and according to the laws of Maryland, to a certain Margaret Ashmore, a citizen of Maryland; that the slave escaped and fled from Maryland, into Pennsylvania, in 1832; that the plaintiff in error, being legally constituted the agent and attorney of the said Margaret Ashmore, in 1837, caused the said negro woman to be taken and apprehended as a fugitive from labor, by a state constable, under a warrant from a Pennsylvania magistrate; that the said negro woman was thereupon brought before the said magistrate, who refused to take further cognisance of the case; and thereupon, the plaintiff in error did remove, take and carry away the said negro woman and her children, out of Pennsylvania, into Maryland, and did deliver the said negro woman and her children into the custody and possession of the said Margaret Ashmore. The special verdict further finds, that one of the children was born in Pennsylvania, more than a year after the said negro woman had fled and escaped from Maryland. Upon this special verdict, the court of oyer and terminer of York county adjudged that the plaintiff in error was guilty of the offence charged in the indictment. A writ of error was brought from that judgment to the supreme court of Pennsylvania, where the judgment was, *pro forma*, affirmed. From this latter judgment, the present writ of error has been brought to this court.

Before proceeding to discuss the very important and interesting questions involved in this record, it is fit to say, that the cause has been conduced in the court below, and has been brought here by the co-operation and sanction, both of the state of Maryland, and the state of Pennsylvania, in the most friendly and courteous spirit, with a view to have those questions finally disposed of by the adjudication of this court; so that the agitations on this subject, in both states, which have had a tendency to interrupt the harmony between them, may subside, and the conflict of opinion be put at rest. It should also be added, that the statute of Pennsylvania of 1826, was (as has been suggested at the bar) passed with a view of meeting the supposed wishes of Maryland on the subject of fugitive slaves; and that, although it has failed to produce the good effects intended in its practical construction, the result was unforeseen and undesigned.

The question arising in the case, as to the constitutionality of the statute of Pennsylvania, has been most elaborately argued at the bar. The counsel for the plaintiff in error have contended, that the statute of Pennsylvania is unconstitutional; first, because congress has the exclusive power of legislation upon the subject-matter, under the constitution of the United States, and under the act of the 12th of February 1793, ch. 51, which was passed in pursuance thereof; secondly, that if this power is not exclusive in congress, still the concurrent power of the state legislatures is suspended by the actual exercise of the power of congress; and thirdly, that if not suspended, still the statute of Pennsylvania, in all its provisions applicable to this case, is in direct collision with the act of congress, and therefore, is unconstitutional and void. The counsel for Pennsylvania maintain the negative of all those points.

There are two clauses in the constitution upon the subject of fugitives, which stands in juxtaposition with each other, and have been thought mutually to illustrate each other. They are both contained in the second section of the fourth article, and are in the following words: "A person charged in any state with treason, felony or other crime, who shall flee from justice, and be found in another state, shall, on demand of the executive authority of the state from which he fled, be delivered up, to be removed to the state having jurisdiction of the crime." "No person held to service or labor in one state, under the laws thereof, escaping into another, shall, in consequence of any law or regulation therein, be discharged from such service or labor; but shall be delivered up, on claim of the party to whom such service or labor may be due."

The last clause is that, the true interpretation whereof is directly in judgment before us. Historically, it is well known, that the object of this clause was to secure to the citizens of the slave-holding states the complete right and title of ownership in their slaves, as property, in every state in the Union into which they might escape from the state where they were held in servitude. The full recognition of this right and title was indispensable to the security of this species of property in all the slave-holding states; and, indeed, was so vital to the preservation of their domestic interests and institutions, that it cannot be doubted, that it constituted a fundamental article, without the adoption of which the Union could not have been formed. Its true design was, to guard against the doctrines and principles prevalent in the non-slave-holding states, by preventing them from intermeddling with, or obstructing, or abolishing the rights of the owners of slaves.

By the general law of nations, no nation is bound to recognise the state of slavery, as to foreign slaves found within its territorial dominions, when it is in opposition to its own policy and institutions, in favor of the subjects of other nations where slavery is recognised. If it does it, it is as a matter of comity, and not as a matter of international right. The state of slavery is deemed to be a mere municipal regulation, founded upon and limited to the range of the territorial laws. This was fully recognised in *Somerset's Case*, Lofft 1; s. c. 11 State Trials, by Harg. 340; s. c. 20 How. State Trial 79; which decided before the American revolution. It is manifest, from this consideration, that if the constitution had not contained this clause, every non-slave-holding state in the Union would have been at liberty to have been at liberty to have declared free all runaway slaves coming within its limits, and to have given them entire immunity and protection against the claims of their masters; a course which would have created the most bitter animosities, and engendered perpetual strife between the different states. The clause was, therefore, of the last importance to the safety and security of the southern states, and could not have been surrendered by them, without endangering their whole property in slaves. The clause was accordingly adopted into the constitution, by the unanimous consent of the framers of it; a proof at once of its intrinsic and practical necessity.

How, then, are we to interpret the language of the clause? The true answer is, in such a manner as, consistently with the words, shall fully and completely effectuate the whole objects of it. If, by one mode of interpretation, the right must become shadowy and unsubstantial, and without any remedial power adequate to the end, and by another mode, it will attain its just end and secure its manifest purpose, it would seem, upon principles of reasoning, absolutely irresistible, that the latter ought to prevail. No court of justice can be authorized so to construe any clause of the constitution as to defeat its obvious ends, when another construction, equally accordant with the words and sense thereof, will enforce and protect them.

The clause manifestly contemplates the existence of a positive, unqualified right on the part of the owner of the slave, which no state law or regulation can in any way qualify, regulate, control or restrain. The slave is not to be discharged from service or labor, in consequence of any state law or regulation. Now, certainly, without indulging in any nicety of criticism upon words, it may fairly and reasonably be said, that any state law or state regulation, which interrupts, limits, delays or postpones the right of the owner to the immediate possession of the slave, and the immediate command of his service and labor, operates, *pro tanto*, a discharge of the slave therefrom. The question can never be, how much the slave is discharged from; but whether he is discharged from any, by the natural or necessary operation of state laws or state regulations. The question is not one of quantity or degree, but of withholding or controlling the incidents of a positive and absolute right.

We have said, that the clause contains a positive and unqualified recognition of the right of the owner in the slave, unaffected by any state law or legislation whatsoever, because there is no qualification or restriction of it to be found therein; and we have no right to insert any, which is not expressed, and cannot be fairly implied. Especially, are we estopped from so doing, when the clause puts the right to the service or labor upon the same ground, and to the same extent, in every other state as in the state from which the slave escaped, and in which he was held to the service or labor. If this be so, then all the incidents to that right attach also. The owner must, therefore, have the right to seize and repossess the slave, which the local laws of his own state confer upon him, as property; and we all know that this right of seizure and recaption is universally acknowledged in all the slave-holding states. Indeed, this is no more than a mere affirmance of the principles of the common law applicable to this very subject. Mr. Justice Blackstone (3 Bl. Com. 4) lays it down as unquestionable doctrine. "Recaption or reprisal (says he) is another species of remedy by the mere act of the party injured. This happens, when any one hath deprived another of his property in goods or chattels personal, or wrongfully detains one's wife, child or servant; in which case, the owner of the goods, and the husband, parent or master, may lawfully claim and retake them, wherever he happens to find them, so it be not in a riotous manner, or attended with a breach of the peace." Upon this ground, we have not the slightest hesitation in holding, that under and in virtue of the constitution, the owner of a slave is clothed with entire authority, in every state in the Union, to seize and recapture his slave, whenever he can do it, without any breach of the peace or any illegal violence. In this sense, and to this extent, this clause of the constitution may properly be said to execute itself, and to require no aid from legislation, state or national.

But the clause of the constitution does not stop here; nor, indeed, consistently with its professed objects, could it do so. Many cases must arise, in which, if the remedy of the owner were confined to the mere right of seizure and recaption, he would be utterly without any adequate redress. He may not be able to lay his hands upon the slave. He may not be able to enforce his rights against persons, who either secrete or conceal, or withhold the slave. He may be restricted by local legislation, as to the mode of proofs of his ownership; as to the courts in which he shall sue, and as to the actions which he may bring; or the process be may use to compel the delivery of the slave. Nay! the local legislation may be utterly inadequate to furnish the appropriate redress, by authorizing no process *in rem*, or no specific mode of repossessing the slave, leaving the owner, at best, not that right which the constitution designed to secure, a specific delivery and repossession of the slave, but a mere remedy in damages; and that, perhaps, against persons utterly insolvent or worthless. The state legislation may be entirely silent on the whole subject, and its ordinary remedial process framed with different views and objects; and this may be innocently as well as designedly done, since every state is perfectly competent, and has the exclusive right, to prescribe the remedies in its own judicial tribunals, to limit the time as well as the mode of redress, and to deny jurisdiction over cases, which its own policy and its own institutions either prohibit or discountenance. If, therefore, the clause of the constitution had stopped at the mere recognition of the right, without providing or contemplating any means by which it might be established and enforced, in cases where it did not execute itself, it is plain, that it would have been, in a great variety of cases, a delusive and empty annunciation. If it did not contemplate any action, either through state or national legislation, as auxiliaries to its more perfect enforcement in the form of remedy, or of protection, then, as there would be no duty on either to aid the right, it would be left to the mere comity of the states, to act as they should please, and would depend for its security upon the changing course of public opinion, the mutations of public policy, and the general adaptations of remedies for purposes strictly according to the *lex fori*.

And this leads us to the consideration of the other part of the clause, which implies at once a guarantee and duty. It says, 'but he (the slave) shall be delivered up, on claim of the party to whom such service or labor may be due.' Now, we think it exceedingly difficult, if not impracticable, to read this language, and not to feel, that it contemplated some further remedial redress than that which might be administered at the hands of the owner himself. A claim is to be made! What is a claim? It is, in a just jurisdical sense, a demand of some matter, as of right, made by one person upon another, to do or to forbear to do some act or thing as a matter of duty. A more limited, but at the same time, an equally expressive, definition was given by Lord DYER, as cited in *Stowel* v. *Zouch*, 1 Plowd. 359; and it is equally applicable to the present case: that "a claim is a challenge by a man of the propriety or ownership of a thing, which he has not in possession, but which is wrongfully detained from him." The slave is to be delivered up on the claim. By whom to be delivered up? In what mode to be delivered up? How, if a refusal takes place, is the right of delivery to be enforced? Upon what proofs? What shall be the evidence of a rightful recaption or delivery? When and under what circumstances shall the possession of the owner, after it is obtained, be conclusive of his right, so as to preclude any further inquiry or examination into it by local tribunals or otherwise, while the slave, in possession of the owner, is *in transitu* to the state from which he fled? These and many other questions will readily occur upon the slightest attention to the clause; and it is obvious, that they can receive but one satisfactory answer. They require the aid of legislation, to protect the right, to enforce the delivery, and to secure the subsequent possession of the slave. If, indeed, the constitution guaranties the right, and if it requires the delivery upon the claim of the owner (as cannot well be doubted), the natural inference certainly is, that the national government is clothed with the appropriate authority and functions to enforce it. The fundamental principle, applicable to all cases of this sort, would seem to be, that where the end is required, the means are given; and where the duty is enjoined, the ability to perform it is contemplated to exist, on the part of the functionaries to whom it is intrusted. The clause is found in the national constitution, and not in that of any state. It does not point out any state functionaries, or any state action, to carry its provisions into effect. The states cannot, therefore, be compelled to enforce them; and it might well be deemed an unconstitutional exercise of the power of interpretation, to insist, that the states are bound to provide means to carry into effect the duties of the national government, nowhere delegated or intrusted to them by the constitution. On the contrary, the natural, if not the necessary, conclusion is, that the national government, in the absence of all positive provisions to the contrary, is bound, through its own proper departments, legislative, judicial or executive, as the case may require, to carry into effect all the rights and duties imposed upon it by the constitution. The remark of Mr. Madison, in the Federalist (No. 43), would seem in such cases to apply with peculiar force. "A right (says he) implies a remedy; and where else would the remedy be deposited, than where it is deposited by the constitution?" meaning, as the context shows, in the government of the United States.

It is plain, then, that where a claim is made by the owner, out of possession, for the delivery of a slave, it must be made, if at all, against some other person; and inasmuch as the right is a right of property, capable of being recognised and asserted by proceedings before a court of justice, between parties adverse to each other, it constitutes, in the strictest sense, a controversy between the parties, and a case "arising under the constitution" of the United States, within the express delegation of judicial power given by that instrument. Congress, then, may call that power into activity, for the very purpose of giving effect to that right; and if so, then it may prescribe the mode and extent in which it shall be applied, and how, and under what circumstances, the proceedings shall afford a complete protection and guarantee to the right.

Congress has taken this very view of the power and duty of the national government. As early as the year 1791, the attention of congress was drawn to it (as we shall hereafter more fully see), in consequence of some practical difficulties arising under the other clause, respecting fugitives from justice escaping into other states. The result of their deliberations was the passage of the act of the 12th of February 1793, ch. 51, which, after having, in the first and second sections, provided by the case of fugitives from justice, by a demand to be made of the delivery, through the executive authority of the state where they are found, proceeds, in the third section, to provide, that when a person held to labor or service in any of the United States, shall escape into any other of the states or territories, the person to whom such labor or service may be due, his agent or attorney, is hereby empowered to seize or arrest such fugitive from labor, and take him or her before any judge of the circuit or district courts of the United States, residing or being within the state, or before any magistrate of a county, city or town corporate, wherein such seizure or arrest shall be made; and upon proof, to the satisfaction of such judge or magistrate, either by oral evidence or affidavit, &c., that the person so seized or arrested, does, under the laws of the state or territory from which he or she fled, owe service or labor to the person claiming him or her, it shall be the duty of such judge or magistrate, to give a certificate thereof to such claimant, his agent or attorney, which shall be sufficient warrant for removing the said fugitive from labor, to the state or territory from which he or she fled. The fourth section provides a penalty against any person, who shall knowingly and willingly obstruct or hinder such claimant, his agent or attorney, in so seizing or arresting such fugitive from labor, or rescue such fugitive from the claimant, or his agent or attorney, when so arrested, or who shall harbor or conceal such fugitive, after notice that he is such; and it also saves to the person claiming such labor or service, his right of action for or on account of such injuries.

In a general sense, this act may be truly said to cover the whole ground of the constitution, both as to fugitives from justice, and fugitive slaves; that is, it covers both the subjects, in its enactments; not because it exhausts the remedies which may be applied by congress to enforce the rights, if the provisions of the act shall in practice be found not to attain the object of the constitution; but because it points out fully all the modes of attaining those objects, which congress, in their discretion, have as yet deemed expedient or proper to meet the exigencies of the constitution. If this be so, then it would seem, upon just principles of construction, that the legislation of congress, if constitutional, must supersede all state legislation upon the same subject; and by necessary implication prohibit it. For, if congress have a constitutional power to regulate a particular subject, and they do actually regulate it in a given manner, and in a certain form, it cannot be, that the state legislatures have a right to interfere, and as it were, by way of compliment to the legislation of congress, to prescribe additional regulations, and what they may deem auxiliary provisions for the same purpose. In such a case, the legislation of congress, in what it does prescribe, manifestly indicates, that it does not intend that there shall be any further legislation to act upon the subject-matter. Its silence as to what it does not do, is as expressive of what its intention is, as the direct provisions made by it. This doctrine was fully recognised by this court, in the case of Houston v. Moore, 5 Wheat. 1, 21-2; where it was expressly held, that where congress have exercised a power over a particular subject given them by the constitution, it is not competent for state legislation to add to the provisions of congress upon that subject; for that the will of congress upon the whole subject is as clearly established by what it has not declared, as by what it has expressed.

But it has been argued, that the act of congress is unconstitutional, because it does not fall within the scope of any of the enumerated powers of legislation confided to that body; and therefore, it is void. Stripped of its artificial and technical structure, the argument comes to this, that although rights are exclusively secured by, or duties are exclusively imposed upon, the national government, yet, unless the power to enforce these rights or to execute these duties, can be found among the express powers of legislation enumerated in the constitution, they remain without any means of giving them effect by any act of congress; and they must operate solely *proprio vigore*, however defective may be their operation; nay! even although, in a practical sense, they may become a nullity, from the want of a proper remedy to enforce them, or to provide against their violation. If this be the true interpretation of the constitution, it must, in a great measure, fail to attain many of its avowed and positive objects, as a security of rights, and a recognition of duties. Such a limited construction of the constitution has never yet been adopted as correct, either in theory or practice. No one has ever supposed, that congress could, constitutionally, by its legislation, exercise powers, or enact laws, beyond the powers delegated to it by the constitution. But it has, on various occasions, exercised powers which were necessary and proper as means to carry into effect rights expressly given, and duties expressly enjoined thereby. The end being required, it has been deemed a just and necessary implication, that the means to accomplish it are given also; or, in other words, that the power flows as a necessary means to accomplish the end.

Thus, for example, although the constitution has declared, that representatives shall be apportioned among the states according to their respective federal numbers; and for this purpose, it has expressly authorized congress, by law, to provide for an enumeration of the population every ten years; yet the power to apportion representatives, after this enumeration is made, is nowhere found among the express powers given to congress, but it has always been acted upon, as irresistibly flowing from the duty positively enjoined by the constitution. Treaties made between the United States and foreign powers, often contain special provisions, which do not execute themselves, but require the interposition of congress to carry them into effect, and congress has constantly, in such cases, legislated on the subject; yet, although the power is given to the executive, with the consent of the senate, to make treaties, the power is nowhere in positive terms conferred upon congress to make laws to carry the stipulations of treaties into effect; it has been supposed to result from the duty of the national government to fulfill all the obligations of treaties. The senators and representatives in congress are, in all cases, except treason, felony and breach of the peace, exempted from arrest, during their attendance at the sessions thereof, and in going to and returning from the same. May not congress enforce this right, by authorizing a writ of *habeas corpus*, to free them from an illegal arrest, in violation of this clause of the constitution? If it may not, then the specific remedy to enforce it must exclusively depend upon the local legislation of the states; and may be granted or refused, according to their own varying policy or pleasure. The constitution also declares, that the privilege of the writ of *habeas corpus* shall not be suspended, unless, when in cases of rebellion or invasion, the public safety may require it. No express power is given to congress to secure this invaluable right in the non-enumerated cases, or to suspend the writ in cases of rebellion or invasion. And yet it would be difficult to say, since this great writ of liberty is usually provided for by the ordinary functions of legislation, and can be effectually provided for only in this way, that it ought not to be deemed, by necessary implication, within the scope of the legislative power of congress. These cases are put merely by way of illustration, to show, that the rule of interpretation, insisted upon at the argument, is quite too narrow to provide for the ordinary exigencies of the national government, in cases where rights are intended to be absolutely secured, and duties are positively enjoined by the constitution.

The very act of 1793, now under consideration, affords the most conclusive proof, that congress has acted upon a very different rule of interpretation, and has supposed, that the right as well as the duty of legislation on the subject of fugitives from justice, and fugitive slaves, was within the scope of the constitutional authority conferred on the national legislature. In respect to fugitives from justice, the constitution, although it expressly provides, that the demand shall be made by the executive authority of the state from which the fugitive has fled, is silent as to the party upon whom the demand is to be made, and as to the mode in which it shall be made. This very silence occasioned embarrassments in enforcing the right and duty, at an early period after the adoption of the constitution; and produced a hesitation on the part of the executive authority of Virginia to deliver up a fugitive from justice, upon the demand of the executive of Pennsylvania, in the year 1791; and as we historically know from the message of President Washington, and the public documents of that period, it was the immediate cause of the passing of the act of 1793, which designated the person (the state executive) upon whom the demand should be made, and the mode and proofs upon and in which it should be made. From that time down to the present hour, not a doubt has been breathed upon the constitutionality of this part of the act; and every executive in the Union has constantly acted upon and admitted its validity. Yet the right and the duty are dependent, as to their mode of execution, solely on the act of congress; and but for that, they would remain a nominal right and passive duty, the execution of which being intrusted to and required of no one in particular, all persons might be at liberty to disregard it. This very acquiescence, under such circumstances, of the highest state functionaries, is a most decisive proof of the universality of the opinion, that the act is founded in a just construction of the constitution, independent of the vast influence, which it ought to have as a contemporaneous exposition of the provisions, by those who were its immediate framers, or intimately connected with its adoption.

The same uniformity of acquiescence in the validity of the act of 1793, upon the other part of the subject-matter, that of fugitive slaves, has prevailed throughout the whole Union, until a comparatively recent period. Nay! being from its nature and character more readily susceptible of being brought into controversy in courts of justice, than the former, and of enlisting in opposition to it, the feelings, and it may be, the prejudices, of some portions of the non-slaveholding states, it has naturally been brought under adjudication in several states in the Union, and particularly in Massachusetts, New York and Pennsylvania; and on all these occasions its validity has been affirmed. The cases cited at the bar, of Wright v. Deacon, 5 Serg. & Rawle 62; Glen v. Hodges, 9 Johns. 67; Jack v. Martin, 12 Wend. 311; s. c. 12 Ibid. 507; and Commonwealth v. Griffin, 2 Pick. 11, are directly in point. So far as the judges of the courts of the United States have been called upon to enforce it, and to grant the certificate required by it, it is believed, that it has been uniformly recognised as a binding and valid law, and as imposing a constitutional duty. Under such circumstances, if the question were one of doubtful construction, such long acquiescence in it, such contemporaneous expositions of it, and such extensive and uniform recognition of its validity, would, in our judgment, entitle the question to be considered at rest; unless, indeed, the interpretation of the constitution is to be delivered over to interminable doubt throughout the whole progress of legislation and of national operations. Congress, the executive, and the judiciary, have, upon various occasions, acted upon this as a sound and reasonable doctrine. Especially did this court, in the cases of Stuart v. Laird, 1 Cranch 299, and Martin v. Hunter, 1 Wheat. 304, and in *Cohens* v. *Commonwealth of Virginia*, 6 Ibid. 264, rely upon contemporaneous expositions of the constitution, and long acquiescence in it, with great confidence, in the discussion of questions of a highly interesting and important nature.

But we do not wish to rest our present opinion upon the ground either of contemporaneous exposition, or long acquiescence, or even practical action; neither do we mean to admit the question to be of a doubtful nature, and therefore, as properly calling for the aid of such considerations. On the contrary, our judgment would be the same, if the question were entirely new, and the act of congress were of recent enactment. We hold the act to be clearly constitutional, in all its leading provisions, and, indeed, with the exception of that part which confers authority upon state magistrates, to be free from reasonable doubt and difficulty, upon the grounds already stated. As to the authority so conferred upon state magistrates, while a difference of opinion has existed, and may exist still, on the point, in different states, whether state magistrates are bound to act under it, none is entertained by this court, that state magistrates may, if they choose, exercise that authority, unless prohibited by state legislation.

The remaining question is, whether the power of legislation upon this subject is exclusive in the national government, or concurrent in the states, until it is exercised by congress. In our opinion, it is exclusive; and we shall now proceed briefly to state our reasons for that opinion. The doctrine stated by this court, in Sturges v. Crowninshield, 4 Wheat. 122, 193, contains the true, although not the sole, rule or consideration, which is applicable to this particular subject. "Wherever," said Mr. Chief Justice Marshall, in delivering the opinion of the court, "the terms in which a power is granted to congress, or the nature of the power, require, that it should be exercised exclusively by congress, the subject is as completely taken from the state legislatures, as if they had been forbidden to act." The nature of the power, and the true objects to be attained by it, are then as important to be weighed, in considering the question of its exclusiveness, as the words in which it is granted.

In the first place, it is material to state (what has been already incidentally hinted at), that the right to seize and retake fugitive slaves and the duty to deliver them up, in whatever state of the Union they may be found, and, of course, the corresponding power in congress to use the appropriate means to enforce the right and duty, derive their whole validity and obligation exclusively from the constitution of the United States, and are there, for the first time, recognised and established in that peculiar character. Before the adoption of the constitution, no state had any power whatsoever over the subject, except within its own territorial limits, and could not bind the sovereignty or the legislation of other states. Whenever the right was acknowledged, or the duty enforced, in any state, it was as a matter of comity, and not as a matter of strict moral, political or international obligation or duty. Under the constitution, it is recognised as an absolute, positive right and duty, pervading the whole Union with an equal and supreme force, uncontrolled and uncontrollable by state sovereignty or state legislation. It, therefore, in a just sense, a new and positive right, independent of comity, confined to no territorial limits, and bounded by no state institutions or policy. The natural inference deductible from this consideration certainly is, in the absence of any positive delegation of power to the state legislatures, that it belongs to the legislative department of the national government, to which it owes its origin and establishment. It would be a strange anomaly, and forced construction, to suppose, that the national government meant to rely for the due fulfillment of its own proper duties, and the rights it intended to secure, upon state legislation, and not upon that of the Union. *A fortiori*, it would be more objectionable, to suppose, that a power, which was to be the same throughout the Union, should be confided to state sovereignty, which could not rightfully act beyond its own territorial limits.

In the next place, the nature of the provision and the objects to be attained by it, require that it should be controlled by one and the same will, and act uniformly by the same system of regulations throughout the Union. If, then, the states have a right, in the absence of legislation by congress, to act upon the subject, each state is at liberty to prescribe just such regulations as suit its own policy, local convenience and local feelings. The legislation of one state may not only be different from, but utterly repugnant to and incompatible with, that of another. The time and mode, and limitation of the remedy, the proofs of the title, and all other incidents applicable thereto, may be prescribed in one state, which are rejected or disclaimed in another. One state may require the owner to sue in one mode, another, in a different mode. One state may make a statute of limitations as to the remedy, in its own tribunals, short and summary; another may prolong the period, and yet restrict the proofs. Nay, some states may utterly refuse to act upon the subject of all; and others may refuse to open its courts to any remedies *in rem*, because they would interfere with their own domestic policy, institutions or habits. The right, therefore, would never, in a practical sense, be the same in all the states. It would have no unity of purpose, or uniformity of operation. The duty might be enforced in some states; retarded or limited in others; and denied, as compulsory, in many, if not in all. Consequences like these must have been foreseen as very likely to occur in the non-slave-holding states, where legislation, if not silent on the subject, and purely voluntary, could scarcely be presumed to be favorable to the exercise of the rights of the owner.

It is scarcely conceivable, that the slave-holding states would have been satisfied with leaving to the legislation of the non-slave-holding states, a power of regulation, in the absence of that of congress, which would or might practically amount to a power to destroy the rights of the owner. If the argument, therefore, of a concurrent power in the states to act upon the subject-matter, in the absence of legislation by congress, be well founded; then, if congress had never acted at all, or if the act of congress should be repealed, without providing a substitute, there would be a resulting authority in each of the states to regulate the whole subject, at its pleasure, and to dole out its own remedial justice, or withhold it, at its pleasure, and according to its own views of policy and expediency. Surely, such a state of things never could have been intended, under such a solemn guarantee of right and duty. On the other hand, construe the right of legislation as exclusive in congress, and every evil and every danger vanishes. The right and the duty are then co-extensive and uniform in remedy and operation throughout the whole Union. The owner has the same security, and the same remedial justice, and the same exemption from state regulation and control, through however many states he may pass with his fugitive slave in his possession, *in transitu* to his own domicile. But upon the other supposition, the moment he passes the state line, he becomes amenable to the laws of another sovereignty, whose regulations may greatly embarrass or delay the exercise of his rights, and even be repugnant to those of the state where he first arrested the fugitive. Consequences like these show, that the nature and objects of the provisions imperiously require, that to make it effectual, it should be construed to be exclusive of state authority. We adopt the language of this court in Sturges v. Crowninshield, 4 Wheat. 193, and say, that 'it has never been supposed, that the concurrent power of legislation extended to every possible case in which its exercise by the states has not been expressly prohibited; the confusion of such a practice would be endless.' And we know no case in which the confusion and public inconvenience and mischiefs thereof could be more completely exemplified than the present.

These are some of the reasons, but by no means all, upon which we hold the power of legislation on this subject to be exclusive in congress. To guard, however, against any possible misconstruction of our views, it is proper to state, that we are by no means to be understood, in any manner whatsoever, to doubt or to interfere with the police power belonging to the states, in virtue of their general sovereignty. That police power extends over all subjects within territorial limits of the states, and has never been conceded to the United States. It is wholly distinguishable from the right and duty secured by the provision now under consideration; which is exclusively derived from and secured by the constitution of the United States, and owes its whole efficacy thereto. We entertain no doubt whatsoever, that the states, in virtue of their general police power, possesses full jurisdiction to arrest and restrain runaway slaves, and remove them from their borders, and otherwise to secure themselves against their depredations and evil example, as they certainly may do in cases of idlers, vagabonds and paupers. The rights of the owners of fugitive slaves are in no just sense interfered with, or regulated, by such a course; and in many cases, the operations of this police power, although designed generally for other purposes, for protection, safety and peace of the state, may essentially promote and aid the interests of the owners. But such regulations can never be permitted to interfere with, or to obstruct, the just rights of the owner to reclaim his slave, derived from the constitution of the United States, or with the remedies prescribed by congress to aid and enforce the same.

Upon these grounds, we are of opinion, that the act of Pennsylvania upon which this indictment is founded, is unconstitutional and void. It purports to punish as a public offence against that state, the very act of seizing and removing a slave, by his master, which the constitution of the United States was designed to justify and uphold. The special verdict finds this fact, and the state courts have rendered judgment against the plaintiff in error upon that verdict. That judgment must, therefore, be reversed, and the cause remanded to the supreme court of Pennsylvania, with directions to carry into effect the judgment of this court rendered upon the special verdict, in favor of the plaintiff in error.

————

Comment on *Prigg*.   Was Justice Story's opinion an accurate interpretation of the framers' intent?   He certainly substantiates the tenant of the ignoble compromise,

Historically, it is well known, that the object of this clause was to secure to the citizens of the slave-holding states the complete right and title of ownership in their slaves, as property, in every state in the Union into which they might escape from the state where they were held in servitude. The full recognition of this right and title was indispensable to the security of this species of property in all the slave-holding states; and, indeed, was so vital to the preservation of their domestic interests and institutions, that it cannot be doubted, that it constituted a fundamental article, without the adoption of which the Union could not have been formed. Its true design was, to guard against the doctrines and principles prevalent in the non-slave-holding states, by preventing them from intermeddling with, or obstructing, or abolishing the rights of the owners of slaves.

Even if Story accurately interpreted the intent of the Constitution, should his opinion securing "title of ownership of . . . slaves" and the "indispensable . . . security of this species of property" be viewed as a "crime against humanity"? Would it be so viewed against the present-day landscape in international law? Should it have been so viewed at the time of the decision?

As alluded to earlier, note that the Court does not hesitate to enforce the private action of slave-owners in forcefully returning their slaves. As we shall soon see, the Supreme Court has held that both the 14th Amendment and congressional enforcement of the rights guaranteed therein are quite limited in their ability to reach private conduct that racially discriminates, even against these very slaves as well as their heirs.

The opinion that follows has been cited as one of the most heinous decisions ever reached by any adjudicative body. It has played a central role in American history, from the civil war and postwar amendments to the present day. Given our study of judicial review and the power of the Supreme Court, it is worth remembering that the same Court that gave us *Brown v. Board of Education* also gave us *Dred Scott*.

DRED SCOTT v. SANDFORD
60 U.S. (19 How.) 393 (1857)

[With the nation on the brink of Civil War over the issue of abolition, the Supreme Court faced slavery, and the status of those individuals so encumbered, in one of the most infamous decisions ever reached by a judicial body. The suit was commenced in 1853 in the Federal Circuit Court of Missouri by an American black, Dred Scott, against a New Yorker, John Sandford, to whom Scott had been sold in Missouri in 1838. Federal jurisdiction was premised on diversity of citizenship. Scott instituted an action in trespass against Sandford claiming he could not be sold because he was no longer a slave but a free man. Scott rested this claim on the fact that in 1834 he had been transported by a former master into the free state of Illinois ("'Free' by state statute") where he resided for two years, and then into the northern reaches of the Louisiana territory (Minnesota), which was governed by the Missouri Compromise of 1820, 3 Stat. 545, that stipulated, as a means of postponing conflict over abolition, that territories north of 36° 30′ longitude would remain "free" (Minnesota) and those below would remain "slave" (Missouri). Scott argued that these provisions made him a free man. In response, Sandford contended that, even if Scott were free, he was not a citizen of Missouri, and that the court therefore lacked jurisdiction under the diversity of citizenship provisions of Article III. Moreover, Sanford asserted that Scott was not free, since his presence in Illinois and the Louisiana Territory could not deprive his former owner of his property interest in Scott when he returned to Missouri. Having lost in trial court, Scott petitioned the United States Supreme Court on writ of error.]

Mr. Chief Justice TANEY delivered the opinion of the Court. . . .

[The Court first addressed the question whether Scott was a citizen of Missouri for diversity purposes.]

The words "people of the United States" and "citizens" are synonymous terms, and mean the same thing. They both describe the political body who, according to our republican institutions, form the sovereignty, and who hold the power and conduct the Government through their representatives. They are what we familiarly call the "sovereign people," and every citizen is one of this people, and a constituent member of this sovereignty. The question before us is, whether the class of persons described in the plea in abatement compose a portion of this people, and are constituent members of this sovereignty? We think they are not, and that they are not included, and were not intended to be included, under the word "citizens" in the Constitution, and can therefore claim none of the rights and privileges which that instrument provides for and secures to citizens of the United States. On the contrary, they were at that time considered as a subordinate and inferior class of beings, who had been subjugated by the dominant race, and, whether emancipated or not, yet remained subject to their authority, and had no rights or privileges but such as those who held the power and the Government might choose to grant them.

It is not the province of the court to decide upon the justice or injustice, the policy or impolicy, of these laws. The decision of that question belonged to the political or law-making power; to those who formed the sovereignty and framed the Constitution. The duty of the court is, to interpret the instrument they have framed, with the best lights we can obtain on the subject, and to administer it as we find it, according to its true intent and meaning when it was adopted.

In discussing this question, we must not confound the rights of citizenship which a State may confer within its own limits, and the rights of citizenship as a member of the Union. [The] Constitution has conferred on Congress the right to establish an uniform rule of naturalization, and this right is evidently exclusive, and has always been held by this court to be so. Consequently, no State, since the adoption of the Constitution, can by naturalizing an alien invest him with the rights and privileges secured to a citizen of a State under the Federal Government, although, so far as the State alone was concerned, he would undoubtedly be entitled to the rights of a citizen, and clothed with all the rights and immunities which the Constitution and laws of the State attached to that character. . . .

In the opinion of the court, the legislation and histories of the times, and the language used in the Declaration of Independence, show, that neither the class of persons who had been imported as slaves, nor their descendants, whether they had become free or not, were then acknowledged as a part of the people, nor intended to be included in the general words used in that memorable instrument.

It is difficult at this day to realize the state of public opinion in relation to that unfortunate race, which prevailed in the civilized and enlightened portions of the world at the time of the Declaration of Independence, and when the Constitution of the United States was framed and adopted. But the public history of every European nation displays it in a manner too plain to be mistaken.

They had for more than a century before been regarded as beings of an inferior order, and altogether unfit to associate with the white race, either in social or political relations; and so far inferior, that they had no rights which the white man was bound to respect; and that the negro might justly and lawfully be reduced to slavery for his benefit. He was bought and sold, and treated as an ordinary article of merchandise and traffic, whenever a profit could be made by it. This opinion was at that time fixed and universal in the civilized portion of the white race. It was regarded as an axiom in morals as well as in politics, which no one thought of disputing, or supposed to be open to dispute; and men in every grade and position in society daily and habitually acted upon it in their private pursuits, as well as in

matters of public concern, without doubting for a moment the correctness of this opinion.
. . .

[Upon] a full and careful consideration of the subject, the court is of opinion, that, upon the facts stated in the plea in abatement, Dred Scott was not a citizen of Missouri within the meaning of the Constitution of the United States, and not entitled as such to sue in its courts; and, consequently, that the Circuit Court had no jurisdiction of the case, and that the judgment on the plea in abatement is erroneous. . . .

II

[The Court then discussed whether Scott remained a slave after his sojourn in the Louisiana Territory and Illinois.]

The act of Congress, upon which the plaintiff relies, declares that slavery and involuntary servitude, except as a punishment for crime, shall be forever prohibited in all that part of the territory ceded by France, under the name of Louisiana, which lies north of thirty-six degrees thirty minutes north latitude, and not included within the limits of Missouri. And the difficulty which meets us at the threshold of this part of the inquiry is, whether Congress was authorized to pass this law under any of the powers granted to it by the Constitution; for if the authority is not given by that instrument, it is the duty of this court to declare it void and inoperative, and incapable of conferring freedom upon any one who is held as a slave under the laws of any one of the States. . . .

[The] power of Congress over the person or property of a citizen can never be a mere discretionary power under our Constitution and form of Government. The powers of the Government and the rights and privileges of the citizen are regulated and plainly defined by the Constitution itself. [An] act of Congress which deprives a citizen of the United States of his liberty or property, merely because he came himself or brought his property into a particular Territory of the United States, and who had committed no offence against the laws, could hardly be dignified with the name of due process of law. . . .

[The] right of property in a slave is distinctly and expressly affirmed in the Constitution. The right to traffic in it, like an ordinary article of merchandise and property, was guaranteed to the citizens of the United States, in every State that might desire it, for twenty years. And the Government in express terms is pledged to protect it in all future time, if the slave escapes from his owner. This is done in plain words — too plain to be misunderstood. And no word can be found in the Constitution which gives Congress a greater power over slave property, or which entitles property of that kind to less protection than property of any other description. The only power conferred is the power coupled with the duty of guarding and protecting the owner in his rights.

Upon these considerations, it is the opinion of the court that the act of Congress which prohibited a citizen from holding and owning property of this kind in the territory of the United States north of the line therein mentioned, is not warranted by the Constitution, and is therefore void; and that neither Dred Scott himself, nor any of his family, were made free by being carried into this territory; even if they had been carried there by the owner, with the intention of becoming a permanent resident.

[Finally the Court addressed Scott's contention that he had been made free by his visit to Illinois, a free state. The Court held that his status on his return to Missouri was to be determined by Missouri law, rather than Illinois law, and that under that law, he remained a slave.

Justices Wayne, Daniel, Campbell, Grier, Nelson, and Catron each wrote separate concurring opinions. Justices McLean and Curtis dissented.]

Comments on _Dred Scott._ Should the Court have reached the merits on all three issues, given the lack of jurisdiction based upon citizenship? Why did they so proceed? Did the majority want to find the Missouri Compromise unconstitutional for political purpose? Some say this aspect of the decision led to civil war. Did "dicta" cause a civil war?

Was this a biased decision? History has provided support for this thesis. The Justices, it seems, were directly involved in the political struggle against abolition. Charles Warren, in his definitive work, _The Supreme Court in United States History_ (1922), pointed out that remarkably, Justice James Wayne wrote to President-elect Buchanan and urged him to write a letter to Justice Grier to bring him in line with the majority that planned on using the case as a vehicle for declaring the Missouri Compromise unconstitutional. That Buchanan did such is evidenced by a letter sent back to him by Grier, thanking him for his views, and then outlining the exact decision the Court was to reach in the case before the opinion itself was rendered:

> But the opinion will not be delivered before Friday the 6th of March. We will not let any others of our brethren know anything about the cause of our anxiety to produce this result, and though contrary to our usual practice, we have thought it due to you to state to you in candor confidence the real state of the matter.

What institutional danger rests within this type of conduct by Justices of the Supreme Court? Has the role of the Court as protector of the slave system advanced in _Prigg_ and _Dred Scott_ changed your view in regard to the nature and application of judicial review? Should it? What recourse is there to this type of judicial conduct? Is the Court best suited to protect minority rights? Have your views changed?

The Court supported its finding that the Missouri Compromise was unconstitutional by application of what has been termed Fifth Amendment "substantive" due process. Though this substantive application of due process was novel then, it will be applied in a latter era (see the "_Lochner_ era," Chapter 5) when the Court is once again accused of "bias" by protecting the interests of "big business" and laissez-faire capitalism. One result of the _Dred Scott_ decision was to deny Congress the ability to protect African Americans because the Court would view any such action as an unconstitutional denial of "property" rights. The Court, raising racism to constitutional law, supported this finding by holding that the Constitution itself recognized slaves not as persons but as property, "Now . . . the right of property in a slave is distinctly and expressly affirmed in the Constitution. The right to traffic in it, like an ordinary article of merchandise and property." Where does the Constitution so state? Does this "substantive" use of due process pose potential dangers to constitutional interpretation? Recall our discussion of substantive due process (there the Fourteenth Amendment) and the right of privacy in our study of the judicial power and constitutional decision-making (Chapter 1).

A civil war followed the Court's decision in _Dred Scott_ — and no wonder! Given the lack of any "national" protection of rights and liberties, the post–Civil War amendments would serve as a means of changing the constitutional framework of the bill of rights.

IV. THE CIVIL WAR AND THE POST–CIVIL WAR AMENDMENTS

If the operations by which the middle classes of England broke the paver of the king and aristocracy are to be known collectively as the Puritan Revolution, if the series of acts by which the bourgeois and peasants of France overthrew the king, nobility and clergy is to be called the French Revolution, then accuracy compels us to characterize by the same farm the social cataclysm in which the capitalists,' laborers, and farmers of the North and West drove from power in the national government the planting aristocracy of' the South. Viewed under the fight of universal history, the fighting was a fleeting incident; the social revolution was the essential, portentous outcome. . . . The so-called civil war was in reality a Second American Revolution and in a strict sense, the First.   I Charles & Mary Beard, *The Rise of American Civilization* 53 (1909).]

To Charles and Mary Beard, the famed American historians, the "civil war was in reality a Second American Revolution": a revolution, if you will, in its "revolutionary" effects on every aspect of American society.   These effects were most notable in three areas.   First, the socio-economic character of postwar America found the northern industrial capitalist triumphant in his vision of an industrially based economy creating a national market to sell and disseminate manufactured goods.   Second, and though its ultimate effect would take more than one hundred years, protection of rights and liberties would be nationalized and rest with the federal as opposed to state governments.   Finally, the war, its amendments and legislation, would in effect commence a transfer of political power from a governing order dominated by the states to domination by the national government.

This effect was dynamic in changing the nature of America as prophesized by the Beards.   Much has been written of the "economic" causes of the war.   Yet, the truth of this thesis need not minimize the significance of "abolition" at the center of the controversy. This is the case if only because it is difficult to lead men to fight and risk death in order to create a "national market."   History has proven that men will risk their lives for "freedom," and as the Civil War's central theme, abolition provided the necessary "rallying cry."   Nowhere is this more evident than Abraham Lincoln's emancipation proclamation, which while absent of legal effect, nonetheless served as the ethical motivation for the northern cause.

The politics of this era were much the same as politics of any American era.   The Republican party ascended to power to fight the war and reconstruct the nation supported by a political coalition that provided both the economic and political support necessary to pursue its cause: northern industrial capitalists, midwestern farmers, and, of course, abolitionists.   As alluded to above, though these three groups joined together in pursuit of the benefits they shared from fighting a successful war, the rationale for their support differed.   While the abolitionists sought emancipation and freedom for the enslaved African Americans in the South, the northern industrial capitalists and midwestern farmers sought national markets, particularly in the South, to sell their goods and commodities. Much of this was based upon the politics of "self-interest," as opposed to any unifying ideology other than winning the war.   H. J. Graham, in his article "Conspiracy Theory of the Fourteenth Amendment," 47 Yale L.J. 37 (1938), brought much attention to this hypothesis.   Graham asserted, for example, that the industrial capitalists agreed to support the adoption of the Fourteenth Amendment if the "abolitionists" would provide a record in committee to support the inclusion of corporations as "persons" entitled to the protection secured by the Amendment's "equal protection clause." Politics in this sense makes strange "bed fellows." What is significant here is the fact that although these groups joined together in support of the northern cause, they did such for diverse reasons and potentially conflicting interests. They may have joined together for the mutual benefits gained by the war's success, but in regard to reconstruction their mutuality would dissipate as their interests diverged. This is politics now, and it was politics then — it would shape reconstruction.

A.   THE AMENDMENTS "ANNOTATED"

1. Amendment XIII [1865]

Section 1. Neither slavery nor involuntary servitude, except as a punishment for crime whereof the party shall have been duly convicted, shall exist within the United States, or any place subject to their jurisdiction.
Section 2. Congress shall have power to enforce this article by appropriate legislation.

With the emancipation proclamation of questionable legal merit, the first order of postwar business was amending the Constitution and abolishing slavery. Note that the Amendment's abolishment of slavery and involuntary servitude reaches private as well as governmental conduct. This is significant because the language of the Fourteenth Amendment's guarantees addresses "State[s]." The major issue concerning the meaning and intent of the Thirteenth Amendment, particularly because it embraces private action, is whether the Amendment could reach "the badges" of slavery — the conditions that the former slaves faced as a   result of the bondage and oppression that they had suffered.

The reach of the Amendment was of particular significance because Section 2 stipulates that "Congress shall have power to enforce this article by appropriate legislation." The fact that the framers of the Amendments intended broad-based congressional support of the postwar Amendments is evidenced by the fact that all three Amendments conclude with a grant of such enforcement power to Congress. Though it is clear that the framers intended that Congress could reach private activity in enforcing the Thirteenth Amendment, the question that remained was whether they could reach the "badges of slavery" as well as enforce abolition.

Though it appears that the framers themselves intended that Congress could reach the badges of slavery under its enforcement power, the framers feared that a still conservative Supreme Court might limit the Amendments and Congress's enforcement power might reach to abolition alone. This concern served as the predicate for the adoption of the most far-reaching constitutional protection of civil rights and liberties, the adoption of the Fourteenth Amendment in 1868.

2. Amendment XIV [1868]

Section 1. All persons born or naturalized in the United States, and subject to the jurisdiction thereof, are citizens of the United States and of the State wherein they reside. No State shall make or enforce any law which shall abridge the privileges or immunities of citizens of the United States; nor shall any State deprive any person of life, liberty, or property, without due process of law; nor deny to any person within its jurisdiction the equal protection of the laws.

Section 2. Representatives shall be apportioned among the several States according to their respective numbers, counting the whole number of persons in each State, excluding Indians not taxed. But when the right to vote at any election for the choice of electors for President and Vice President of the United States, Representatives in Congress, the Executive and Judicial officers of a State, or the members of the Legislature thereof, is denied to any of the male inhabitants of such State, being twenty-one years of age, and citizens of the United States, or in any way abridged, except for participation in rebellion, or other crime, the basis of representation therein shall be reduced in the proportion which the number of such male citizens shall bear to the whole number of male citizens twenty-one years of age in such State.

Section 3. No person shall be a Senator or Representative in Congress, or elector of President and Vice President, or hold any office, civil or military, under the United States, or under any State, who, having previously taken an oath, as a member of Congress, or as an officer of the United States, or as a member of any State legislature, or as an executive or judicial officer of any State, to support the Constitution of the United States, shall have engaged in insurrection or rebellion against the same, or given aid or comfort to the enemies thereof. But Congress may by a vote of two-thirds of each House, remove such disability.

Section 4. The validity of the public debt of the United States, authorized by law, including debts incurred for payment of pensions and bounties for services in suppressing insurrection or rebellion, shall not be questioned. But neither the United States nor any State shall assume or pay any debt or obligation incurred in aid of insurrection or rebellion against the United States, or any claim for the loss of emancipation of any slave; but all such debts, obligations and claims shall be held illegal and void.

Section 5. The Congress shall have power to enforce, by appropriate legislation, the provisions of this article.

There is no doubt the first sentence of the Fourteenth Amendment (Section 1) had as its intent overruling the heinous *Dred Scott* decision.   For despite the Court's conclusion that slaves were not "citizens" of the national government because there were mere chattels, now, "All persons born or naturalized in the United States, and subject to the jurisdiction thereof, are citizens of the United States and of the State wherein they reside." The meaning of the second sentence, however, has produced as much debate concerning its intent than perhaps any other verbiage in the Constitution: "No State shall make or enforce any law which shall abridge the privileges or immunities of citizens of the United States."   What are the "privileges or immunities" of federal citizenship?   If the first sentence overruled *Dred Scott*, did the second sentence overrule *Barron v. Baltimore*? Was this "shorthand" language for the "Bill of Rights"?   If it was, *Barron* would be overruled, the Bill of Rights would be applicable to the states, and the nation would have national protection of civil rights and liberties for the first time in its history.   It would seem logical to so conclude based upon the language of these two sentences, particularly because the now abolished slavery has been a major reason for limiting the applicability of the Bill of Rights to the states.   Yet, as the Beards forewarned, to so conclude would provide a profound change in the power balance between state and federal government, most particularly in the "new" postwar South.   This was a question of great meaning, and it awaited application of judicial review by the Supreme Court.

Next the framers dictated that "nor shall any State deprive any person of life, liberty, or property, without due process of law; nor deny to any person within its jurisdiction the equal protection of the laws."   The meaning and application (when or how can a state "deprive" and "deny?") of these great "personal" guarantees of "due process" and "equal protection" also awaited threshold interpretation by the postwar Supreme Court. Certainly the framers' resort to "broad" language in these clauses left unmistakable latitude in judicial application.   How would the Court respond?

Finally, and of particular significance given the framers' intent of adopting the Fourteenth Amendment to support the constitutionality of postwar civil rights legislation, the framers granted to Congress the power to enforce these "broad clauses" by appropriate legislation.

3. Amendment XV [1870]

Section 1. The right of citizens of the United States to vote shall not be denied or abridged by the United States or by any State on account of race, color, or previous condition of servitude.

Section 2. The Congress shall have power to enforce this article by appropriate legislation.

The Fifteenth Amendment, with a most pointed specificity, guaranteed that the voting rights of both the national and state governments "shall not be denied or abridged" on account of race.   The narrowness of the reach of this Amendment has found it perhaps the least "controversial" and "reviewed" of the three.   Yet, its inclusion when such discrimination might have been actionable under the equal protection clause of the Fourteenth Amendment underscores the importance of these voting rights to the framers. How African Americans would nonetheless be denied the right to vote despite the Fifteenth Amendment is an American tale that will be told by the Supreme Court.

B. RECONSTRUCTION AND A RETURN TO NORMALCY

1. "Radical" Reconstruction

The pseudonym for reconstruction in the South after the Civil War was "radical." Why "radical reconstruction"?   At least one reason was that from the southern perspective, it was radical to force the civil rights of the former slaves "down the throats" of southerners.   The South's resistance to the rights of the freed persons was evident from the onset of the postwar era. (See John Hope Franklin, *Reconstruction After the Civil War* (1961).)   With the assassination of Lincoln, Vice President Andrew Johnson, who had been a slave owner, assumed the presidency.   Johnson, a "southern sympathizer," adopted a position in regard to the South and reconstruction that confronted congressional postwar policy.   This created a clash in regard to reconstruction policies between Congress and the President that led to the impeachment of Johnson.

Certainly the views expressed by Johnson did not seem consistent with a civil war fought over "abolition" and followed by the adoption of the postwar Amendments. Johnson was to veto numerous civil rights bills promulgated by Congress.   John Hope Franklin, quoting Johnson, highlights his racism:

The blacks of the South, [Johnson] said, not only had no regard for the rights of property, but were "utterly so ignorant of public affairs that their voting can consist in nothing more than carrying a ballot to the place where they are directed to deposit it. . . . *Of all the dangers which our nation has yet encountered, none are equal to those which must result from the success of the effort now making to Africanize the half of our country."* [*Id.* at 74) (emphasis added).]

Given the overt racism of Johnson, one might have wondered "who won the war."

Southern resistance to the newly established rights of the freed slaves stepped in tow with Johnson's urging and views.   The southern slave system was ultimately replaced by the infamous "black codes."   A Mississippi statute provided, for example, "Every civil officer shall, and every person, may, arrest, and carry back to his or her legal employer any freedman, free negro, or mulatto who shall have quit the service of his or her employer before the expiration of his or her term of service without good cause."   Other "codes" forbid African Americans from a variety of activities, even renting or leasing certain lands. To many, these codes where simply another form of slavery.   (*Id.* at 48-52.)

Ultimately, the Southern response had significant political consequences.   Without the cooperation of southern whites, how could a national market be created?   The clash over the freedom and rights of the former slaves broke the northern coalition that had formed to support the war.   The northern industrial capitalists and midwestern farmers' ultimate goal was creation of a national market, and to them this could be accomplished only with the cooperation of the South and its former leaders.   If they had to choose between "black rights" and their economic goals, they would choose the latter rather than the former.   Thus, despite the drive for civil rights on behalf of northern abolitionists, the capitalists and farmers' dominant elements of their civil war coalition sought a "return to normalcy" and therefore cooperation with southern whites, at the cost of the new found freedoms of the former slaves.   Once again, African American rights, despite the Civil War, abolition, and adoption of the great postwar amendments, would become sacrificial lambs to the development of the southern economy and creation of a national market.

2. "A Return to Normalcy"

The breakdown of this coalition and the changing goals of the post–Civil War era found the nation's rallying cry "A Return to Normalcy" — shorthand language for economic reunion at the sacrifice of "black" rights.   Consequently, a death penalty was served upon the only legal means the nation had for protecting blacks. The editors of Scribner's Monthly, a popular northern journal, best expressed this attitude:

Men of the South, We want you . . . Men of the South, We Long for resonation of your peace and your prosperity. We should see your cities thriving, your homes happy, your plantations *teeming* with plenteous harvests, your schools overflowing, your *wisest statesmen leading you,* and all causes and all memories of discord *wiped out forever.* [Coulter, *The South During Reconstruction 1865-1877*, at 166 (1947) (emphasis added).]

The prevailing attitude became reunion with the South.   To many this furthered what they considered to be the major purpose of the Civil War itself, the advancement of industrial capitalism.   The longing for a "return to normalcy" made this possible. Miller, in *The Supreme Court and the Uses of History* 115 (1969), makes this state of affairs quite clear:

With the energies of the country directed elsewhere, the political and social gap dividing the radical Republican spirit of the postwar decade from the late nineteenth century

America grew wider. In the South where any change would be most evident, the tentatively planted practices of Jim Crow developed a tenacious root-system to which few whites objected.

The postwar radicals were gone, and

the new radicals wanted peace. As representatives of industrial capitalism, they saw that the South was an important element in establishment of a vast domestic market. [See Hatcher, *The Shaping of American Tradition* 593 (1947).]

The ultimate "codification" of this "return" occurred amidst the confusion created by the lack of a victorious candidate in the presidential election of 1876. Though the democrat Tilden had won the popular vote in the contest against the republican Hays, Tilden was "one" vote short of the necessary votes to elect a President in the electoral college. A special electoral commission was formed made up of 8 Republicans and 7 Democrats (5 Senators, 5 Congressmen, 5 Supreme Court Justices) to resolve the conflict and elect a President. In order to certify Republican electors and install Hayes as President, a compromise was struck with southern Democrats:

[I]n return for their co-operation in seating Hayes and their promise not to mistreat the Negro, Southerners were to be rewarded with withdrawal of federal troops and recognition of democratic governments in South Carolina, and Louisiana. [Magrath, *Waite-Triumph of Character* 136-149 (1963); see also Reunion and Reaction (1956).]

In fact the "Hayes-Tilden compromise" stood for the recognition and acceptance of Jim Crow, the desire for a "return to normalcy," and the transformation of the Republican party along national lines. All of this served the economic benefit of the northern industrialists.

The Supreme Court became the "guardian of the compromise of 1876." As the desire for normalcy expressed itself politically, "the Supreme Court was no idle spectator"; its decisions showed, in fact, "that the Court in facing the Southern question marched in step with the national mood." Radical reconstruction had ended, "the Hayes-Tilden election crisis provided the excuse for the desired accommodation — an accommodation which had as one of its essential elements the remission of the Negroes destiny to the states. The Supreme Court saw to it that this bargain was *not violated.*" M. Levy, "The Supreme Court Minority Rights and Principled Adjudication," 2 Tex. So. L. Rev. 208, 217-220 (1973) (emphasis added).

C. A SUPREME COURT TRILOGY

Given the adoption of the Amendments and supporting civil rights legislation, one might reasonably question why more than one hundred years of "Jim Crow" and apartheid would follow. If this was a sacrifice of "black" rights for economic gain and a national market, the "culprit" was none other than the Supreme Court.

In a trilogy of cases the Court provided threshold interpretations of the postwar Amendments and civil rights legislation adopted under Congress's enforcement power. These three cases, *Slaughter-House, Civil Rights, and Plessy v. Ferguson,* are presented as a "trilogy" because taken together these decisions so "watered down" the effect of the Amendments so as to deny their intended benefit not only to the freed persons in the South but to the nation as a whole.   The impact of these decisions set back individual rights and liberties until the present day, both doctrinally and substantively.   It would be more than one hundred years before the noble goals of the postwar era would meet fruition — though, as we shall see in the following sections, that day would come.

In the *Slaughter-House Cases,* and most assuredly by the *Civil Rights Cases,* the Court faced a national mood dedicated to "reunion." Placed in proper perspective, the Court faced public pressure for reconciliation, and for the normalcy of a return to the previous "federal equilibrium" that the new amendments challenged. The reconciliation that the Court provided allowed the Union to reunite and continue the process of industrial development.   This was done at the expense of rights of African Americans by diluting the meaning and effect of the Amendments and their accompanying legislation.

SLAUGHTER-HOUSE CASES
83 U.S. 36 (1872)

[In the context of "slaughter-houses" claiming the protection of the postwar Amendments against local economic regulation (recall Graham's "Conspiracy Theory of the Fourteenth Amendment"), the Court faced perhaps the most central question in regard to interpreting the Fourteenth Amendment: Did the "privileges and immunities clause" incorporate the bill of rights and make it applicable to the states?   The nature of the protection of rights and liberties nationwide, as well as the status of the freed slaves, hung in the balance.]

Error to the Supreme Court of Louisiana.

The three cases — the parties to which as plaintiffs and defendants in error, are given specifically as a sub-title, at the head of this report, but which are reported together also under the general name which, in common parlance, they had acquired — grew out of an act of the legislature of the State of Louisiana, entitled: "*An act to protect the health of the City of New Orleans, to locate the stock landings and slaughter-houses, and to incorporate 'The Crescent City Live-Stock Landing and Slaughter-House Company,'*" which was approved on the 8th of March, 1869, and went into operation on the 1st of June following; and the three cases were argued together.

Mr. Justice MILLER, now, April 14th, 1873, delivered the opinion of the court.

[The] regulation of the place and manner of conducting the slaughtering of animals, and the business of butchering within a city, and the inspection of the animals to be killed for meat, and of the meat afterwards, are among the most necessary and frequent exercises of this power. It is not, therefore, needed that we should seek for a comprehensive definition, but rather look for the proper source of its exercise.

[It] cannot be denied that the statute under consideration is aptly framed to remove from the more densely populated part of the city, the noxious slaughter-houses, and large and offensive collections of animals necessarily incident to the slaughtering business of a large city, and to locate them where the convenience, health, and comfort of the people require they shall be located. And it must be conceded that the means adopted by the act for this purpose are appropriate, are stringent, and effectual. But it is said that in creating a corporation for this purpose, and conferring upon it exclusive privileges — privileges which it is said constitute a monopoly — the legislature has exceeded its power. If this statute had imposed on the city of New Orleans precisely the same duties, accompanied by the same privileges. [The] plaintiffs in error accepting this issue, allege that the statute is a violation of the Constitution of the United States in these several particulars:

That it creates an involuntary servitude forbidden by the thirteenth article of amendment;

That it abridges the privileges and immunities of citizens of the United States;

That it denies to the plaintiffs the equal protection of the laws; and

[This] court is thus called upon for the first time to give construction to these articles.

[The] most cursory glance at these articles discloses a unity of purpose, when taken in connection with the history of the times, which cannot fail to have an important bearing on any question of doubt concerning their true meaning. Nor can such doubts, when any reasonably exist, be safely and rationally solved without a reference to that history; for in it is found the occasion and the necessity for recurring again to the great source of power in this country, the people of the States, for additional guarantees of human rights; additional powers to the Federal government; additional restraints upon those of the States. Fortunately that history is fresh within the memory of us all, and its leading features, as they bear upon the matter before us, free from doubt.

[Undoubtedly] the overshadowing and efficient cause was African slavery.

In that struggle slavery, as a legalized social relation, perished. It perished as a necessity of the bitterness and force of the conflict. When the armies of freedom found themselves upon the soil of slavery they could do nothing less than free the poor victims whose enforced servitude was the foundation of the quarrel. And when hard pressed in the contest these men (for they proved themselves men in that terrible crisis) offered their services and were accepted by thousands to aid in suppressing the unlawful rebellion, slavery was at an end wherever the Federal government succeeded in that purpose. The proclamation of President Lincoln expressed an accomplished fact as to a large portion of the insurrectionary districts, when he declared slavery abolished in them all. But the war being over, those who had succeeded in re-establishing the authority of the Federal government were not content to permit this great act of emancipation to rest on the actual results of the contest or the proclamation of the Executive, both of which might have been questioned in after times, and they determined to place this main and most valuable result in the Constitution of the restored Union as one of its fundamental articles. Hence the thirteenth article of amendment of that instrument. Its two short sections seem hardly to admit of construction, so vigorous is their expression and so appropriate to the purpose we have indicated.

[To] withdraw the mind from the contemplation of this grand yet simple declaration of the personal freedom of all the human race within the jurisdiction of this government — a declaration designed to establish the freedom of four millions of slaves — and with a microscopic search endeavor to find in it a reference to servitudes, which may have been attached to property in certain localities, requires an effort, to say the least of it.

That a personal servitude was meant is proved by the use of the word "involuntary," which can only apply to human beings. The exception of servitude as a punishment for crime gives an idea of the class of servitude that is meant. The word servitude is of larger meaning than slavery, as the latter is popularly understood in this country, and the obvious purpose was to forbid all shades and conditions of African slavery. It was very well understood that in the form of apprenticeship for long terms, as it had been practiced in the West India Islands, on the abolition of slavery by the English government, or by reducing the slaves to the condition of serfs attached to the plantation, the purpose of the article might have been evaded, if only the word slavery had been used. The case of the apprentice slave, held under a law of Maryland, liberated by Chief Justice Chase, on a writ of habeas corpus under this article, illustrates this course of observation. And it is all that we deem necessary to say on the application of that article to the statute of Louisiana, now under consideration.

The process of restoring to their proper relations with the Federal government and with the other States those which had sided with the rebellion, undertaken under the proclamation of President Johnson in 1865, and before the assembling of Congress, developed the fact that, notwithstanding the formal recognition by those States of the abolition of slavery, the condition of the slave race would, without further protection of the Federal government, be almost as bad as it was before. Among the first acts of legislation adopted by several of the States in the legislative bodies which claimed to be in their normal relations with the Federal government, were laws which imposed upon the colored race onerous disabilities and burdens, and curtailed their rights in the pursuit of life, liberty, and property to such an extent that their freedom was of little value, while they had lost the protection which they had received from their former owners from motives both of interest and humanity.

They were in some States forbidden to appear in the towns in any other character than menial servants. They were required to reside on and cultivate the soil without the right to purchase or own it. They were excluded from many occupations of gain, and were not permitted to give testimony in the courts in any case where a white man was a party. It was said that their lives were at the mercy of bad men, either because the laws for their protection were insufficient or were not enforced.

These circumstances, whatever of falsehood or misconception may have been mingled with their presentation, forced upon the statesmen who had conducted the Federal government in safety through the crisis of the rebellion, and who supposed that by the thirteenth article of amendment they had secured the result of their labors, the conviction that something more was necessary in the way of constitutional protection to the unfortunate race who had suffered so much. They accordingly passed through Congress the proposition for the fourteenth amendment.

[A] few years' experience satisfied the thoughtful men who had been the authors of the other two amendments that, notwithstanding the restraints of those articles on the States, and the laws passed under the additional powers granted to Congress, these were inadequate for the protection of life, liberty, and property, without which freedom to the slave was no boon. They were in all those States denied the right of suffrage. The laws were administered by the white man alone. It was urged that a race of men distinctively marked as was the negro, living in the midst of another and dominant race, could never be fully secured in their person and their property without the right of suffrage. Hence [the 15th Amendment].

[We] repeat, then, in the light of this recapitulation of events, almost too recent to be called history, but which are familiar to us all; and on the most casual examination of the language of these amendments, no one can fail to be impressed with the one pervading purpose found in them all, lying at the foundation of each, and without which none of them would have been even suggested; we mean the freedom of the slave race, the security and firm establishment of that freedom, and the protection of the newly-made freeman and citizen from the oppressions of those who had formerly exercised unlimited dominion over him. It is true that only the fifteenth amendment, in terms, mentions the negro by speaking of his color and his slavery. But it is just as true that each of the other articles was addressed to the grievances of that race, and designed to remedy them as the fifteenth.

We do not say that no one else but the negro can share in this protection. Both the language and spirit of these articles are to have their fair and just weight in any question of construction. Undoubtedly while negro slavery alone was in the mind of the Congress which proposed the thirteenth article, it forbids any other kind of slavery, now or hereafter. If Mexican peonage or the Chinese coolie labor system shall develop slavery of the Mexican or Chinese race within our territory, this amendment may safely be trusted to make it void. And so if other rights are assailed by the States which properly and necessarily fall within the protection of these articles, that protection will apply, though the party interested may not be of African descent. But what we do say, and what we wish to be understood is, that in any fair and just construction of any section or phrase of these amendments, it is necessary to look to the purpose which we have said was the pervading spirit of them all, the evil which they were designed to remedy, and the process of continued addition to the Constitution, until that purpose was supposed to be accomplished, as far as constitutional law can accomplish it.

The first section of the fourteenth article, to which our attention is more specially invited, opens with a definition of citizenship. It overturns the Dred Scott decision by making *all persons* born within the United States and subject to its jurisdiction citizens of the United States. That its main purpose was to establish the citizenship of the negro can admit of no doubt.

[The] next observation is more important in view of the arguments of counsel in the present case. It is, that the distinction between citizenship of the United States and citizenship of a State is clearly recognized and established. Not only may a man be a citizen of the United States without being a citizen of a State, but an important element is necessary to convert the former into the latter. He must reside within the State to make him a citizen of it, but it is only necessary that he should be born or naturalized in the United States to be a citizen of the Union.

It is quite clear, then, that there is a citizenship of the United States, and a citizenship of a State, which are distinct from each other, and which depend upon different characteristics or circumstances in the individual.

We think this distinction and its explicit recognition in this amendment of great weight in this argument, because the next paragraph of this same section, which is the one mainly relied on by the plaintiffs in error, speaks only of privileges and immunities of citizens of the United States, and does not speak of those of citizens of the several States. The argument, however, in favor of the plaintiffs rests wholly on the assumption that the citizenship is the same, and the privileges and immunities guaranteed by the clause are the same.

The language is, "No State shall make or enforce any law which shall abridge the privileges or immunities of citizens of *the United States*." It is a little remarkable, if this clause was intended as a protection to the citizen of a State against the legislative power of his own State, that the word citizen of the State should be left out when it is so carefully used, and used in contradistinction to citizens of the United States, in the very sentence which precedes it. It is too clear for argument that the change in phraseology was adopted understandingly and with a purpose.

Of the privileges and immunities of the citizen of the United States, and of the privileges and immunities of the citizen of the State, and what they respectively are, we will presently consider; but we wish to state here that it is only the former which are placed by this clause under the protection of the Federal Constitution, and that the latter, whatever they may be, are not intended to have any additional protection by this paragraph of the amendment.

If, then, there is a difference between the privileges and immunities belonging to a citizen of the United States as such, and those belonging to the citizen of the State as such the latter must rest for their security and protection where they have heretofore rested; for they are not embraced by this paragraph of the amendment.

[In] the Constitution of the United States, which superseded the Articles of Confederation, the corresponding provision is found in section two of the fourth article, in the following words: "The citizens of each State shall be entitled to all the privileges and immunities of citizens of the several States."

[Fortunately] we are not without judicial construction of this clause of the Constitution. The first and the leading case on the subject is that of *Corfield* v. *Coryell*, decided by Mr. Justice Washington in the Circuit Court for the District of Pennsylvania in 1823.

"The inquiry," he says, "is, what are the privileges and immunities of citizens of the several States? We feel no hesitation in confining these expressions to those privileges and immunities which are *fundamental;* which belong of right to the citizens of all free governments, and which have at all times been enjoyed by citizens of the several States which compose this Union, from the time of their becoming free, independent, and sovereign. What these fundamental principles are, it would be more tedious than difficult to enumerate. They may all, however, be comprehended under the following general heads: protection by the government, with the right to acquire and possess property of every kind, and to pursue and obtain happiness and safety, subject, nevertheless, to such restraints as the government may prescribe for the general good of the whole."

[The] description, when taken to include others not named, but which are of the same general character, embraces nearly every civil right for the establishment and protection of which organized government is instituted. They are, in the language of Judge Washington, those rights which are fundamental. Throughout his opinion, they are spoken of as rights belonging to the individual as a citizen of a State. They are so spoken of in the constitutional provision which he was construing. And they have always been held to be the class of rights which the State governments were created to establish and secure.

[The] constitutional provision there alluded to did not create those rights, which it called privileges and immunities of citizens of the States. It threw around them in that clause no security for the citizen of the State in which they were claimed or exercised. Nor did it profess to control the power of the State governments over the rights of its own citizens.

Its sole purpose was to declare to the several States, that whatever those rights, as you grant or establish them to your own citizens, or as you limit or qualify, or impose restrictions on their exercise, the same, neither more nor less, shall be the measure of the rights of citizens of other States within your jurisdiction.

It would be the vainest show of learning to attempt to prove by citations of authority, that up to the adoption of the recent amendments, no claim or pretence was set up that those rights depended on the Federal government for their existence or protection, beyond the very few express limitations which the Federal Constitution imposed upon the States —

such, for instance, as the prohibition against ex post facto laws, bills of attainder, and laws impairing the obligation of contracts. But with the exception of these and a few other restrictions, the entire domain of the privileges and immunities of citizens of the States, as above defined, lay within the constitutional and legislative power of the States, and without that of the Federal government. Was it the purpose of the fourteenth amendment, by the simple declaration that no State should make or enforce any law which shall abridge the privileges and immunities of *citizens of the United States*, to transfer the security and protection of all the civil rights which we have mentioned, from the States to the Federal government? And where it is declared that Congress shall have the power to enforce that article, was it intended to bring within the power of Congress the entire domain of civil rights heretofore belonging exclusively to the States?

All this and more must follow, if the proposition of the plaintiffs in error be sound. For not only are these rights subject to the control of Congress whenever in its discretion any of them are supposed to be abridged by State legislation, but that body may also pass laws in advance, limiting and restricting the exercise of legislative power by the States, in their most ordinary and usual functions, as in its judgment it may think proper on all such subjects. And still further, such a construction followed by the reversal of the judgments of the Supreme Court of Louisiana in these cases, would constitute this court a perpetual censor upon all legislation of the States, on the civil rights of their own citizens, with authority to nullify such as it did not approve as consistent with those rights, as they existed at the time of the adoption of this amendment. The argument we admit is not always the most conclusive which is drawn from the consequences urged against the adoption of a particular construction of an instrument. But when, as in the case before us, these consequences are so serious, so far-reaching and pervading, so great a departure from the structure and spirit of our institutions; when the effect is to fetter and degrade the State governments by subjecting them to the control of Congress, in the exercise of powers heretofore universally conceded to them of the most ordinary and fundamental character; when in fact it radically changes the whole theory of the relations of the State and Federal governments to each other and of both these governments to the people; the argument has a force that is irresistible, in the absence of language which expresses such a purpose too clearly to admit of doubt.

We are convinced that no such results were intended by the Congress which proposed these amendments, nor by the legislatures of the States which ratified them.

Having shown that the privileges and immunities relied on in the argument are those which belong to citizens of the States as such, and that they are left to the State governments for security and protection, and not by this article placed under the special care of the Federal government, we may hold ourselves excused from defining the privileges and immunities of citizens of the United States which no State can abridge, until some case involving those privileges may make it necessary to do so.

But lest it should be said that no such privileges and immunities are to be found if those we have been considering are excluded, we venture to suggest some which own their existence to the Federal government, its National character, its Constitution, or its laws.

One of these is well described in the case of *Crandall* v. *Nevada*. It is said to be the right of the citizen of this great country, protected by implied guarantees of its Constitution, "to come to the seat of government to assert any claim he may have upon that government, to transact any business he may have with it, to seek its protection, to share its offices, to engage in administering its functions. He has the right of free access to its seaports, through which all operations of foreign commerce are conducted, to the subtreasuries, land offices, and courts of justice in the several States."

[Another] privilege of a citizen of the United States is to demand the care and protection of the Federal government over his life, liberty, and property when on the high seas or within the jurisdiction of a foreign government. Of this there can be no doubt, nor that the right depends upon his character as a citizen of the United States. The right to peaceably assemble and petition for redress of grievances, the privilege of the writ of *habeas corpus*, are rights of the citizen guaranteed by the Federal Constitution. The right to use the navigable waters of the United States, however they may penetrate the territory of the several States, all rights secured to our citizens by treaties with foreign nations, are dependent upon citizenship of the United States, and not citizenship of a State. One of these privileges is conferred by the very article under consideration. It is that a citizen of the United States can, of his own volition, become a citizen of any State of the Union by a *bona fide* residence therein, with the same rights as other citizens of that State. To these may be added the rights secured by the thirteenth and fifteenth articles of amendment, and by the other clause of the fourteenth, next to be considered.

But it is useless to pursue this branch of the inquiry, since we are of opinion that the rights claimed by these plaintiffs in error, if they have any existence, are not privileges and immunities of citizens of the United States within the meaning of the clause of the fourteenth amendment under consideration.

[The] argument has not been much pressed in these cases that the defendant's charter deprives the plaintiffs of their property without due process of law, or that it denies to them the equal protection of the law. The first of these paragraphs has been in the Constitution since the adoption of the fifth amendment, as a restraint upon the Federal power. It is also to be found in some form of expression in the constitutions of nearly all the States, as a restraint upon the power of the States.

[We] are not without judicial interpretation, therefore, both State and National, of the meaning of this clause. And it is sufficient to say that under no construction of that provision that we have ever seen, or any that we deem admissible, can the restraint imposed by the State of Louisiana upon the exercise of their trade by the butchers of New Orleans be held to be a deprivation of property within the meaning of that provision.

"Nor shall any State deny to any person within its jurisdiction the equal protection of the laws."

In the light of the history of these amendments, and the pervading purpose of them, which we have already discussed, it is not difficult to give a meaning to this clause. The existence of laws in the States where the newly emancipated negroes resided, which discriminated with gross injustice and hardship against them as a class, was the evil to be remedied by this clause, and by it such laws are forbidden.

If, however, the States did not conform their laws to its requirements, then by the fifth section of the article of amendment Congress was authorized to enforce it by suitable legislation. We doubt very much whether any action of a State not directed by way of discrimination against the negroes as a class, or on account of their race, will ever be held to come within the purview of this provision. It is so clearly a provision for that race and that emergency, that a strong case would be necessary for its application to any other. But as it is a State that is to be dealt with, and not alone the validity of its laws, we may safely leave that matter until Congress shall have exercised its power, or some case of State oppression, by denial of equal justice in its courts, shall have claimed a decision at our hands. We find no such case in the one before us, and do not deem it necessary to go over the argument again, as it may have relation to this particular clause of the amendment.

[Unquestionably] this has given great force to the argument, and added largely to the number of those who believe in the necessity of a strong National government.

But, however pervading this sentiment, and however it may have contributed to the adoption of the amendments we have been considering, we do not see in those amendments any purpose to destroy the main features of the general system. Under the pressure of all the excited feeling growing out of the war, our statemen have still believed that the existence of the State with powers for domestic and local government, including the regulation of civil rights — the rights of person and of property — was essential to the perfect working of our complex form of government, though they have thought proper to impose additional limitations on the States, and to confer additional power on that of the Nation.

[The] judgments of the Supreme Court of Louisiana in these cases are affirmed.

Mr. Justice FIELD, dissenting:

[The] question presented is, therefore, one of the gravest importance, not merely to the parties here, but to the whole country. It is nothing less than the question whether the recent amendments to the Federal Constitution protect the citizens of the United States against the deprivation of their common rights by State legislation. In my judgment the fourteenth amendment does afford such protection, and was so intended by the Congress which framed and the States which adopted it.

That amendment prohibits slavery and involuntary servitude, except as a punishment for crime, but I have not supposed it was susceptible of a construction which would cover the enactment in question. I have been so accustomed to regard it as intended to meet that form of slavery which had previously prevailed in this country, and to which the recent civil war owed its existence, that I was not prepared, nor am I yet, to give to it the extent and force ascribed by counsel. Still it is evidence that the language of the amendment is not used in a restrictive sense. It is not confined to African slavery alone. It is general and universal in its application. Slavery of white men as well as of black men is prohibited, and not merely slavery in the strict sense of the term, but involuntary servitude in every form.

The words "involuntary servitude" have not been the subject of any judicial or legislative exposition, that I am aware of, in this country, except that which is found in the Civil Rights Act, which will be hereafter noticed. It is, however, plaintiffs in error therefore contend that "wherever a law of a State, or a law of the United States, makes a discrimination between classes of persons, which deprives the one class of their freedom or their property, or which makes a caste of them to subserve the power, pride, avarice, vanity, or vengeance of others," there involuntary servitude exists within the meaning of the thirteenth amendment.

[The] amendment does not attempt to confer any new privileges or immunities upon citizens, or to enumerate or define those already existing. It assumes that there are such privileges and immunities which belong of right to citizens as such, and ordains that they shall not be abridged by State legislation. If this inhibition has no reference to privileges and immunities of this character, but only refers, as held by the majority of the court in their opinion, to such privileges and immunities as were before its adoption specially designated in the Constitution or necessarily implied as belonging to citizens of the United States, it was a vain and idle enactment, which accomplished nothing, and most unnecessarily excited Congress and the people on its passage. With privileges and immunities thus designated or implied no State could ever have interfered by its laws, and no new constitutional provision was required to inhibit such interference. The supremacy of the Constitution and the laws of the United States always controlled any State legislation of that character. But if the amendment refers to the natural and inalienable rights which belong to all citizens, the inhibition has a profound significance and consequence.

[The] terms, privileges and immunities, are not new in the amendment; they were in the Constitution before the amendment was adopted. They are found in the second section of the fourth article, which declares that "the citizens of each State shall be entitled to all privileges and immunities of citizens in the several States," and they have been the subject of frequent consideration in judicial decisions. In *Corfield* v. *Coryell*, [the] privileges and immunities designated in the second section of the fourth article of the Constitution are, then, according to the decision cited, those which of right belong to the citizens of all free governments, and they can be enjoyed under that clause by the citizens of each State in the several States upon the same terms and conditions as they are enjoyed by the citizens of the latter States. No discrimination can be made by one State against the citizens of other States in their enjoyment, nor can any greater imposition be levied than such as is laid upon its own citizens. It is a clause which insures equality in the enjoyment of these rights between citizens of the several States whilst in the same State.

[If] under the fourth article of the Constitution equality of privileges and immunities is secured between citizens of different States, under the fourteenth amendment the same equality is secured between citizens of the United States.

[This] equality of right, with exemption from all disparaging and partial enactments, in the lawful pursuits of life, throughout the whole country, is the distinguishing privilege of citizens of the United States. To them, everywhere, all pursuits, all professions, all avocations are open without other restrictions than such as are imposed equally upon all others of the same age, sex, and condition. The State may prescribe such regulations for every pursuit and calling of life as will promote the public health, secure the good order and advance the general prosperity of society, but when once prescribed, the pursuit or calling must be free to be followed by every citizen who is within the conditions designated, and will conform to the regulations. This is the fundamental idea upon which our institutions rest, and unless adhered to in the legislation of the country our government will be a republic only in name. The fourteenth amendment, in my judgment, makes it essential to the validity of the legislation of every State that this equality of right should be respected. How widely this equality has been departed from, how entirely rejected and trampled upon by the act of Louisiana, I have already shown. And it is to me a matter of profound regret that its validity is recognized by a majority of this court, for by it the right of free labor, one of the most sacred and imprescriptible rights of man, is violated. As stated by the Supreme Court of Connecticut, in the case cited, grants of exclusive privileges, such as is made by the act in question, are opposed to the whole theory of free government, and it requires no aid from any bill of rights to render them void. That only is a free government, in the American sense of the term, under which the inalienable right of every citizen to pursue his happiness is unrestrained, except by just, equal, and impartial laws.

I am authorized by The Chief Justice, Mr. Justice Swayne, and Mr. Justice Bradley, to state that they concur with me in this dissenting opinion.

Mr. Justice BRADLEY, also dissenting:

[In] my judgment, it was the intention of the people of this country in adopting that amendment to provide National security against violation by the States of the fundamental rights of the citizen.

[If] my views are correct with regard to what are the privileges and immunities of citizens, it follows conclusively that any law which establishes a sheer monopoly, depriving a large class of citizens of the privilege of pursuing a lawful employment, does abridge the privileges of those citizens.

The amendment also prohibits any State from depriving any person (citizen or otherwise) of life, liberty, or property, without due process of law.

In my view, a law which prohibits a large class of citizens from adopting a lawful employment, or from following a lawful employment previously adopted, does deprive them of liberty as well as property, without due process of law. Their right of choice is a portion of their liberty; their occupation is their property. Such a law also deprives those citizens of the equal protection of the laws, contrary to the last clause of the section.

[It] is futile to argue that none but persons of the African race are intended to be benefited by this amendment. They may have been the primary cause of the amendment, but its language is general, embracing all citizens, and I think it was purposely so expressed.

[But] great fears are expressed that this construction of the amendment will lead to enactments by Congress interfering with the internal affairs of the States, and establishing therein civil and criminal codes of law for the government of the citizens, and thus abolishing the State governments in everything but name; or else, that it will lead the Federal courts to draw to their cognizance the supervision of State tribunals on every subject of judicial inquiry, on the plea of ascertaining whether the privileges and immunities of citizens have not been abridged.

In my judgment no such practical inconveniences would arise. Very little, if any, legislation on the part of Congress would be required to carry the amendment into effect. Like the prohibition against passing a law impairing the obligation of a contract, it would execute itself. The point would   be regularly raised, in a suit at law, and settled by final reference to the Federal court. As the privileges and immunities protected are only those fundamental ones which belong to every citizen, they would soon become so far defined as to cause but a slight accumulation of business in the Federal courts. Besides, the recognized existence of the law would prevent its frequent violation. But even if the business of the National courts should be increased, Congress could easily supply the remedy by increasing their number and efficiency. The great question is, What is the true construction of the amendment? When once we find that, we shall find the means of giving it effect. The argument from inconvenience ought not to have a very controlling influence in questions of this sort. The National will and National interest are of far greater importance.

[A dissenting opinion by Justice Swayne is omitted.]

Comments on *Slaughter-House* and the Privileges and Immunities Clause. Justice Miller's opinion in *Slaughter-House* placed the privileges and immunities clause in the constitutional "waste paper basket," where it still rests. As Corwin commented in relation to the decision, "Unique among constitutional provisions, the privileges and immunities clause of the Fourteenth Amendment enjoys the distinction of having been rendered a 'practical nullity' by a single decision of the Supreme Court within five years after its ratification." E. Corwin, *The Constitution of the United States of America* 965

(1953).   This was so because the Court not only rejected "incorporation," but also provided a limited nature of rights that Miller concluded would be protected.   As David Currie commented, the problem was

> Miller's . . . conclusion that the sole office of the clause was to protect rights already given by some other federal law. Apart from the amendment's less than conclusive reference to dual citizenship, his sole justification was that a broader holding would "radically [change] the whole theory of the relations of the State and Federal governments to each other and of both these governments to the people" — which quite arguably was precisely what the authors of the amendment had in mind.   [David Currie, "The Constitution in the Supreme Court: Limitations on State Power," 1865-1873, 51 U. Chi. L. Rev. 329, 348 (1983).]

Offhand it does not appear likely that the Civil War was fought, and the Fourteenth Amendment adopted, for access to navigable water, seaports, parks, and to redress only the national government.   Much has been made of the "bias" of the Court's decision in relation to the intent of those who framed the clause.   A typical criticism follows:

> A single change was made in Section One after it had been reported by the Joint Committee. This was the addition of the first sentence defining citizenship. [Significantly,] no one observed that while citizenship was made dual in this first sentence, only the privileges or immunities of "citizens of the United States" were specifically protected in the second sentence against abridgment by the states. The reason for this apparent oversight is that [opponents] of slavery had regarded all the important "natural" and constitutional rights as being privileges or immunities of citizens of the United States. This had been the cardinal premise of antislavery theory. [The] real purpose of adding this citizenship definition was to [overrule Dred Scott]. [To] reach the conclusion of Justice Miller and the majority, one must disregard not only all antislavery from 1834 on, but one must ignore virtually every word said in the debates of 1865-66.   [Graham, *Our "Declaratory" Fourteenth Amendment*, 7 Stan. L. Rev. 3, 23, 25 (1954); see also Fairman, *Does the Fourteenth Amendment Incorporate the Bill of Rights? The Original Understanding*, 2 Stan. L. Rev. 5, 132, 137-139 (1949); and a more recent criticism, Amar, *The Bill of Rights and the Fourteenth Amendment*, 101 Yale L.J. 1193 (1992).]

Almost one hundred years later the dissents of Field and Bradley would reach fruition in regard to "fundamental rights" incorporation, but by application of the due process clause of the Fourteenth Amendment as opposed to the privileges and immunities clause. (Incorporation is discussed later in this chapter.)   For all practical purposes *Slaughter-House* remains "good law" today and "[t]he Court has generally adhered to the *Slaughter-House* interpretation of the privileges or immunities clause, thus rendering the clause essentially superfluous." Laurence Tribe, *American Constitutional Law* 423 (1978).

In regard to our present inquiry, the first in our trilogy of cases limiting the meaning and effect of the postwar Amendments is in.   The Court arguably placed a "return to normalcy" and its own view of federalism as more significant than the words and intent of the Amendments.   In a most ignoble first step, the Court rejected incorporation and the "nationalization" of civil rights and liberties.   This not only limited right-based protection across the land, but had the most incongruous effect of returning freed slaves to their former masters in order to secure such protection.

THE CIVIL RIGHTS CASES
109 U.S. 3 (1883)

[The next case helped the Court "seal the deal." If the freed slaves could not rely on incorporated federal rights to protect them from their state governments, they still maintained those substantive rights secured by the Fourteenth Amendment: Due Process and Equal Protection. Justice Bradley turned to the meaning of the Amendment's terminology that "No state shall" deprive or deny, as the Court continued its emasculation of African American rights.]

Mr. Justice BRADLEY delivered the opinion of the Court.

Has congress constitutional power to make such a law? Of course, no one will contend that the power to pass it was contained in the constitution before the adoption of the last three amendments. The power is sought, first, in the fourteenth amendment, and the views and arguments of distinguished senators, advanced while the law was under consideration, claiming authority to pass it by virtue of that amendment, are the principal arguments adduced in favor of the power. We have carefully considered those arguments, as was due to the eminent ability of those who put them forward, and have felt, in all its force, the weight of authority which always invests a law that congress deems itself competent to pass. But the responsibility of an independent judgment is now thrown upon this court; and we are bound to exercise it according to the best lights we have.

The first section of the fourteenth amendment, — which is the one relied on, — after declaring who shall be citizens of the United States, and of the several states, is prohibitory in its character, and prohibitory upon the states. It declares that "no state shall make or enforce any law which shall abridge the privileges or immunities of citizens of the United States; nor shall any state deprive any person of life, liberty, or property without due process of law; nor deny to any person within its jurisdiction the equal protection of the laws." It is state action of a particular character that is prohibited. Individual invasion of individual rights is not the subject-matter of the amendment. It has a deeper and broader scope. It nullifies and makes void all state legislation, and state action of every kind, which impairs the privileges and immunities of citizens of the United States, or which injures them in life, liberty, or property without due process of law, or which denies to any of them the equal protection of the laws. It not only does this, but, in order that the national will, thus declared, may not be a mere *brutum fulmen*, the last section of the amendment invests congress with power to enforce it by appropriate legislation. To enforce what? To enforce the prohibition. To adopt appropriate legislation for correcting the effects of such prohibited state law and state acts, and thus to render them effectually null, void, and innocuous. This is the legislative power conferred upon congress, and this is the whole of it. It does not invest congress with power to legislate upon subjects which are within the domain of state legislation; but to provide modes of relief against state legislation, or state action, of the kind referred to. It does not authorize congress to create a code of municipal law for the regulation of private rights; but to provide modes of redress against the operation of state laws, and the action of state officers, executive or judicial, when these are subversive of the fundamental rights specified in the amendment. Positive rights and privileges are undoubtedly secured by the fourteenth amendment; but they are secured by way of prohibition against state laws and state proceedings affecting those rights and privileges, and by power given to congress to legislate for the purpose of carrying such prohibition into effect; and such legislation must necessarily be predicated upon such supposed state laws or state proceedings, and be directed to the correction of their operation and effect.   A quite full discussion of this aspect of the amendment may be found in U. S. v. *Cruikshank*, 92 U. S. 542; *Virginia* v. *Rives*, 100 U. S. 313, and *Ex parte Virginia*, Id. 339.

An apt illustration of this distinction may be found in some of the provisions of the original constitution.   Take the subject of contracts, for example.   The constitution prohibited the states from passing any law impairing the obligation of contracts.   This did not give to congress power to provide laws for the general enforcement of contracts; nor power to invest the courts of the United States with jurisdiction over contracts, so as to enable parties to sue upon them in those courts.   It did, however, give the power to provide remedies by which the impairment of contracts by state legislation might be counteracted and corrected; and this power was exercised.   The remedy which congress actually provided was that contained in the twenty-fifth section of the judiciary act of 1789, giving to the supreme court of the United States jurisdiction by writ of error to review the final decisions of state courts whenever they should sustain the validity of a state statute or authority, alleged to be repugnant to the constitution or laws of the United States.   By this means, if a state law was passed impairing the obligation of a contract, and the state tribunals sustained the validity of the law, the mischief could be corrected in this court. The legislation of congress, and the proceedings provided for under it, were corrective in their character.   No attempt was made to draw into the United States courts the litigation of contracts generally, and no such attempt would have been sustained.   We do not say that the remedy provided was the only one that might have been provided in that case. Probably congress had power to pass a law giving to the courts of the United States direct jurisdiction over contracts alleged to be impaired by a state law; and, under the broad provisions of the act of March 3, 1875, giving to the circuit courts jurisdiction of all cases arising under the constitution and laws of the United States, it is possible that such jurisdiction now exists.   But under that or any other law, it must appear, as well by allegation as proof at the trial, that the constitution had been violated by the action of the state legislature.   Some obnoxious state law passed, or that might be passed, is necessary to be assumed in order to lay the foundation of any federal remedy in the case, and for the very sufficient reason that the constitutional prohibition is against *state laws* impairing the obligation of contracts.

And so in the present case, until some state law has been passed, or some state action through its officers or agents has been taken, adverse to the rights of citizens sought to be protected by the fourteenth amendment, no legislation of the United States under said amendment, nor any proceeding under such legislation, can be called into activity, for the prohibitions of the amendment are against state laws and acts done under state authority. Of course, legislation may and should be provided in advance to meet the exigency when it arises, but it should be adapted to the mischief and wrong which the amendment was intended to provide against; and that is, state laws or state action of some kind adverse to the rights of the citizen secured by the amendment.   Such legislation cannot properly cover the whole domain of rights appertaining to life, liberty, and property, defining them and providing for their vindication.   That would be to establish a code of municipal law regulative of all private rights between man and man in society.   It would be to make congress take the place of the state legislatures and to supersede them.   It is absurd to affirm that, because the rights of life, liberty, and property (which include all civil rights that men have) are by the amendment sought to be protected against invasion on the part of the state without due process of law, congress may, therefore, provide due process of law for their vindication in every case; and that, because the denial by a state to any persons of the equal protection of the laws is prohibited by the amendment, therefore congress may establish laws for their equal protection. In fine, the legislation which congress is authorized to adopt in this behalf is not general legislation upon the rights of the citizen, but corrective legislation; that is, such as may be necessary and proper for counteracting such laws as the states may adopt or enforce, and which by the amendment they are prohibited from making or enforcing, or such acts and proceedings as the states may commit or take, and which by the amendment they are prohibited from committing or taking. It is not necessary for us to state, if we could, what legislation would be proper for congress to adopt. It is sufficient for us to examine whether the law in question is of that character.

An inspection of the law shows that it makes no reference whatever to any supposed or apprehended violation of the fourteenth amendment on the part of the states. It is not predicated on any such view. It proceeds *ex directo* to declare that certain acts committed by individuals shall be deemed offenses, and shall be prosecuted and punished by proceedings in the courts of the United States. It does not profess to be corrective of any constitutional wrong committed by the states; it does not make its operation to depend upon any such wrong committed. It applies equally to cases arising in states which have the justest laws respecting the personal rights of citizens, and whose authorities are ever ready to enforce such laws as to those which arise in states that may have violated the prohibition of the amendment. In other words, it steps into the domain of local jurisprudence, and lays down rules for the conduct of individuals is society towards each other, and imposes sanctions for the enforcement of those rules, without referring in any manner to any supposed action of the state or its authorities.

[I]t is proper to state that civil rights, such as are guarantied by the constitution against state aggression, cannot be impaired by the wrongful acts of individuals, unsupported by state authority in the shape of laws, customs, or judicial or executive proceedings. The wrongful act of an individual, unsupported by any such authority, is simply a private wrong, or a crime of that individual; an invasion of the rights of the injured party, it is true, whether they affect his person, his property, or his reputation; but if not sanctioned in some way by the state, or not done under state authority, his rights remain in full force, and may presumably be vindicated by resort to the laws of the state for redress. An individual cannot deprive a man of his right to vote, to hold property, to buy and to sell, to sue in the courts, or to be a witness or a juror; he may, by force or fraud, interfere with the enjoyment of the right in a particular case; he may commit an assault against the person, or commit murder, or use ruffian violence at the polls, or slander the good name of a fellow-citizen; but unless protected in these wrongful acts by some shield of state law or state authority, he cannot destroy or injure the right; he will only render himself amenable to satisfaction or punishment; and amenable therefor to the laws of the state where the wrongful acts are committed. Hence, in all those cases where the constitution seeks to protect the rights of the citizen against discriminative and unjust laws of the state by prohibiting such laws, it is not individual offenses, but abrogation and denial of rights, which it denounces, and for which it clothes the congress with power to provide a remedy. This abrogation and denial of rights, for which the states alone were or could be responsible, was the great seminal and fundamental wrong which was intended to be remedied. And the remedy to be provided must necessarily be predicated upon that wrong. It must assume that in the cases provided for, the evil or wrong actually committed rests upon some state law or state authority for its excuse and perpetration.

Of course, these remarks do not apply to those cases in which congress is clothed with direct and plenary powers of legislation over the whole subject, accompanied with an express or implied denial of such power to the states, as in the regulation of commerce with foreign nations, among the several states, and with the Indian tribes, the coining of money, the establishment of post-offices and post-roads, the declaring of war, etc. In these cases congress has power to pass laws for regulating the subjects specified, in every detail, and the conduct and transactions of individuals respect thereof. But where a subject is not submitted to the general legislative power of congress, but is only submitted thereto for the purpose of rendering effective some prohibition against particular state legislation or state action in reference to that subject, the power given is limited by its object, and any legislation by congress in the matter must necessarily be corrective in its character, adapted to counteract and redress the operation of such prohibited state laws or proceedings of state officers.

If the principles of interpretation which we have laid down are correct, as we deem them to be, — and they are in accord with the principles laid down in the cases before referred to, as well as in the recent case of U. S. v. *Harris*, decided at the last term of this court, [1 Sup. Ct. Rep. 601,] — it is clear that the law in question cannot be sustained by any grant of legislative power made to congress by the fourteenth amendment. That amendment prohibits the states from denying to any person the equal protection of the laws, and declares that congress shall have power to enforce, by appropriate legislation, the provisions of the amendment. The law in question, without any reference to adverse state legislation on the subject, declares that all persons shall be entitled to equal accommodation and privileges of inns, public conveyances, and places of public amusement, and imposes a penalty upon any individual who shall deny to any citizen such equal accommodations and privileges. This is not corrective legislation; it is primary and direct; it takes immediate and absolute possession of the subject of the right of admission to inns, public conveyances, and places of amusement. It supersedes and displaces state legislation on the same subject, or only allows it permissive force. It ignores such legislation, and assumes that the matter is one that belongs to the domain of national regulation. Whether it would not have been a more effective protection of the rights of citizens to have clothed congress with plenary power over the whole subject, is not now the question. What we have to decide is, whether such plenary power has been conferred upon congress by the fourteenth amendment, and, in our judgment, it has not.

We have discussed the question presented by the law on the assumption that a right to enjoy equal accommodations and privileges in all inns, public conveyances, and places of public amusement, is one of the essential rights of the citizen which no state can abridge or interfere with. Whether it is such a right or not is a different question, which, in the view we have taken of the validity of the law on the ground already stated, it is not necessary to examine.

We have also discussed the validity of the law in reference to cases arising in the states only; and not in reference to cases arising in the territories or the District of Columbia, which are subject to the plenary legislation of congress in every branch of municipal regulation. Whether the law would be a valid one as applied to the territories and the district is not a question for consideration in the cases before us; they all being cases arising within the limits of states. And whether congress, in the exercise of its power to regulate commerce among the several states, might or might not pass a law regulating rights in public conveyances passing from one state to another, is also a question which is not now before us, as the sections in question are not conceived in any such view.

[L]egislation may be necessary and proper to meet all the various cases and circumstances to be affected by it, and to prescribe proper modes of redress for its violation in letter or spirit.   And such legislation may be primary and direct in its character; for the amendment is not a mere prohibition of state laws establishing or upholding slavery, but an absolute declaration that slavery or involuntary servitude shall not exist in any part of the United States.

It is true that slavery cannot exist without law any more than property in lands and goods can exist without law, and therefore the thirteenth amendment may be regarded as nullifying all state laws which establish or uphold slavery.   But it has a reflex character also, establishing and decreeing universal civil and political freedom throughout the United States; and it is assumed that the power vested in congress to enforce the article by appropriate legislation, clothes congress with power to pass all laws necessary and proper for abolishing all badges and incidents of slavery in the United Stated; and upon this assumption it is claimed that this is sufficient authority for declaring by law that all persons shall have equal accommodations and privileges in all inns, public conveyances, and places of public amusement; the argument being that the denial of such equal accommodations and privileges is in itself a subjection to a species of servitude within the meaning of the amendment.   Conceding the major proposition to be true, that that congress has a right to enact all necessary and proper laws for the obliteration and prevention of slavery, with all its badges and incidents, is the minor proposition also true, that the denial to any person of admission to the accommodations and privileges of an inn, a public conveyance, or a theater, does subject that person to any form of servitude, or tend to fasten upon him any badge of slavery?   If it does not, then power to pass the law is not found in the thirteenth amendment.

In a very able and learned presentation of the cognate question as to the extent of the rights, privileges, and immunities of citizens which cannot rightfully be abridged by state laws under the fourteenth amendment, made in a former case, a long list of burdens and disabilities of a servile character, incident to feudal vasslage in France, and which were abolished by the decrees of the national assembly, was presented for the purpose of showing that all inequalities and observances exacted by one man from another, were servitudes or badges of slavery, which a great nation, in its effort to establish universal liberty, made haste to wipe out and destroy.   But these were servitudes imposed by the old law, or by long custom which had the force of law, and exacted by one man from another without the latter's consent. Should any such servitudes be imposed by a state law, there can be no doubt that the law would be repugnant to the fourteenth, no less than to the thirteenth, amendment; nor any greater doubt that congress has adequate power to forbid any such servitude from being exacted.

But is there any similarity between such servitudes and a denial by the owner of an inn, a public conveyance, or a theater, of its accommodations and privileges to an individual, even through the denial be founded on the race or color of that individual? Where does any slavery or servitude, or badge of either, arise from such an act of denial? Whether it might not be a denial of a right which, if sanctioned by the state law, would be obnoxious to the prohibitions of the fourteenth amendment, is another question.   But what has it to do with the question of slavery?   It may be that by the black code, (as it was called,) in the times when slavery prevailed, the proprietors of inns and public conveyances were forbidden to receive persons of the African race, because it might assist slaves to escape from the control of their masters.   This was merely a means of preventing such escapes, and was no part of the servitude itself.   A law of that kind could not have any such object now, however justly it might be deemed an invasion of the party's legal right as a citizen, and amenable to the prohibitions of the fourteenth amendment.

The long existence of African slavery in this country gave us very distinct notions of what it was, and what were its necessary incidents. Compulsory service of the slave for the benefit of the master, restraint of his movements except by the master's will, disability to hold property, to make contracts, to have a standing in court, to be a witness against a white person, and such like burdens and incapacities were the inseparable incidents of the institution. Severer punishments for crimes were imposed on the slave than on free persons guilty of the same offenses. Congress, as we have seen, by the civil rights bill of 1866, passed in view of the thirteenth amendment, before the fourteenth was adopted, undertook to wipe out these burdens and disabilities, the necessary incidents of slavery, constituting its substance and visible from; and to secure to all citizens of every race and color, and without regard to previous servitude, those fundamental rights which are the essence of civil freedom, namely, the same right to make and enforce contracts, to sue, be parties, give evidence, and to inherit, purchase, lease, sell, and convey property, as is enjoyed by white citizens. Whether this legislation was fully authorized by the thirteenth amendment alone, without the support which it afterwards received from the fourteenth amendment, after the adoption of which it was re-enacted with some additions, it is not necessary to inquire. It is referred to for the purpose of showing that at that time (in 1866) congress did not assume, under the authority given by the thirteenth amendment, to adjust what may be called the social rights of men and races in the community; but only to declare and vindicate those fundamental rights which appertain to the essence of citizenship, and the enjoyment or deprivation of which constitutes the essential distinction between freedom and slavery.

We must not forget that the province and scope of the thirteenth and fourteenth amendments are different: the former simply abolished slavery, the latter prohibited the states from abridging the privileges or immunities of citizens of the United States, from depriving them of life, liberty, or property without due process of law, and from denying to any the equal protection of the laws. The amendments are different, and the powers of congress under them are different. What congress has power to do under one, it may not have power to do under the other. Under the thirteenth amendment, it has only to do with slavery and its incidents. Under the fourteenth amendment, it has power to counteract and render nugatory all state laws and proceedings which have the effect to abridge any of the privileges or immunities which have the effect to abridge any deprive them of life, liberty, or property without due process of law, or to deny to any of them the equal protection of the laws. Under the thirteenth amendment the legislation, so far as necessary or proper to eradicate all forms and incidents of slavery and involuntary servitude, may be direct and primary, operating upon the acts of individuals, whether sanctioned by state legislation or not; under the fourteenth, as we have already shown, it must necessarily be, and can only be, corrective in its character, addressed to counteract and afford relief against state regulations or proceedings.

The only question under the present head, therefore, is, whether the refusal to any persons of the accommodations of an inn, or a public conveyance, or a place of public amusement, by an individual, and without any sanction or support from any state law or regulation, does inflict upon such persons any manner of servitude, or form of slavery, as those terms are understood in this country? Many wrongs may be obnoxious to the prohibitions of the fourteenth amendment which are not, in any just sense, incidents or elements of slavery. Such, for example, would be the taking of private property without due process of law; or allowing persons who have committed certain crimes (horse-stealing, for example) to be seized and hung by the *posse comitatus* without regular trial; or denying to any person, or class of persons, the right to pursue any peaceful avocations allowed to others. What is called class legislation would belong to this category, and would be obnoxious to the prohibitions of the fourteenth amendment, but would not to the prohibitions of the fourteenth when not involving the idea of any subjection of one man to another. The thirteenth amendment has respect, not to distinctions of race, or class, or color, but to slavery. The fourteenth amendment extends its protection to races and classes, and prohibits any state legislation which has the effect of denying to any race or class, or to any individual, the equal protection of the laws.

Now, conceding, for the sake of the argument, that the admission to an inn, a public conveyance, or a place of public amusement, on equal terms with all other citizens, is the right of every man and all classes of men, is it any more than one of those rights which the states by the fourteenth amendment are forbidden to deny to any person? and is the constitution violated until the denial of the right has some state sanction or authority? Can the act of a mere individual, the owner of the inn, the public conveyance, or place of amusement, refusing the accommodation, be justly regarded as imposing any badge of slavery or servitude upon the applicant, or only as inflicting an ordinary civil injury, properly cognizable by the laws of the state, and presumably subject to redress by those laws until the contrary appears?

After giving to these questions all the consideration which their importance demands, we are forced to the conclusion that such an act of refusal has nothing to do with slavery or involuntary servitude, and that if it is volatile of any right of the party, his redress is to be sought under the laws of the state; or, if those laws are adverse to his rights and do not protect him, his remedy will be found in the corrective legislation which congress has adopted, or may adopt, for counteracting the effect of state laws, or state action, prohibited by the fourteenth amendment. It would be running the slavery argument into the ground to make it apply to every act of discrimination which a person may see fit to make as to the guests he will entertain, or as to the people he will take into his coach or cab or car, or admit to his concert or theater, or deal with in other matters of intercourse or business. Innkeepers and public carriers, by the laws of all the states, so far as we are aware, are bound, to the extent of their facilities, to furnish proper accommodation to all unobjectionable persons who in good faith apply for them. If the laws themselves make any unjust discrimination, amenable to the prohibitions of the fourteenth amendment, congress has full power to afford a remedy under that amendment and in accordance with it.

When a man has emerged from slavery, and by the aid of beneficent legislation has shaken off the inseparable concomitants of that state, there must be some stage in the progress of his elevation when he takes the rank of a mere citizen, and ceases to be the special favorite of the laws, and when his rights as a citizen, or a man, are to be protected in the ordinary modes by which other men's rights are protected.

This conclusion disposes of the cases now under consideration. In the cases of *U. S.* v. *Ryan*, and of *Robinson* v. *Memphis & C. R. Co.*, the judgments must be affirmed. In the other cases, the answer to be given will be, that the first and second sections of the act of congress of March 1, 1875, entitled "An act to protect all citizens in their civil and legal rights," are unconstitutional and void, and that judgment should be rendered upon the several indictments in those cases accordingly. And it is so ordered.

Justice HARLAN, dissenting.

The opinion in these cases proceeds, as it seems to me, upon grounds entirely too narrow and artificial.   The substance and spirit of the recent amendments of the constitution have been sacrificed by a subtle and ingenious verbal criticism.   The thirteenth amendment, my brethren concede, did something more than to prohibit slavery as an *institution*, resting upon distinctions of race, and upheld by positive law.   They admit that it established and decreed universal *civil freedom* throughout the United States.   But did the freedom thus established involve nothing more than exemption from actual slavery? Was nothing more intended than to forbid one man from owning another as property? Was it the purpose of the nation simply to destroy the institution, and then remit the race, theretofore held in bondage, to the several states for such protection, in their civil rights, necessarily growing out of freedom, as those states, in their discretion, choose to provide? Were the states, against whose solemn protest the institution was destroyed, to be left perfectly free, so far as national interference was concerned, to make or allow discriminations against that race, as such, in the enjoyment of those fundamental rights that inhere in a state of freedom?   Had the thirteenth amendment stopped with the sweeping declaration, in its first section, against the existence of slavery and involuntary servitude, except for crime, congress would have had the power, by implication, according to the doctrines of *Prigg* v. *Com.*, repeated in *Strauder* v. *West Virginia*, to protect the freedom thus established, and consequently to secure the enjoyment of such civil rights as were fundamental in freedom.   But that it can exert its authority to that extent is now made clear, and was intended to be made clear, by the express grant of power contained in the second section of that amendment.

That there are burdens and disabilities which constitute badges of slavery and servitude, and that the express power delegated to congress to enforce, by appropriate legislation, the thirteenth amendment, may be exerted by legislation of a direct and primary character, for the eradication, not simply of the institution, but of its badges and incidents, are propositions which ought to be deemed indisputable. [I] do not contend that the thirteenth amendment invests congress with authority, by legislation, to regulate the entire body of the civil rights which citizens enjoy, or may enjoy, in the several states.   But I do hold that since slavery, as the court has repeatedly declared, was the moving or principal cause of the adoption of that amendment, and since that institution rested wholly upon the inferiority, as a race, of those held in bondage, their freedom necessarily involved immunity from, and protection against, all discrimination against them, because of their race, in respect of such civil rights as belong to freemen of other races.   Congress, therefore, under its express power to enforce that amendment, by appropriate legislation, may enact laws to protect that people against the deprivation, *on account of their race*, of any civil rights enjoyed by other freemen in the same state; and such legislation may be of a direct and primary character, operating upon states, their officers and agents, and also upon, at least, such individuals and corporations as exercise public functions and wield power and authority under the state.

It remains now to inquire what are the legal rights of colored persons in respect of the accommodations, privileges, and facilities of public conveyances, inns, and places of public amusement.

1.   As to public conveyances on land and water.   The sum of the adjudged cases is that a railroad corporation is a governmental agency, created primarily for public purposes, and subject to be controlled for the public benefit.   Such being the relations these corporations hold to the public, it would seem that the right of a colored person to use an

improved public highway, upon the terms accorded to freemen of other races, is as fundamental in the state of freedom, established in this country, as are any of the rights which my brethren concede to be so far fundamental as to be deemed the essence of civil freedom. "Personal liberty consists," says Blackstone, "in the power of locomotion, of changing situation, or removing one's person to whatever place one's own inclination may direct, without restraint, unless by due course of law." But of what value is this right of locomotion, if it may be clogged by such burdens as congress intended by the act of 1875 to remove? They are burdens which lay at the very foundation of the institution of slavery as it once existed. They are not to be sustained, except upon the assumption that there is still, in this land of universal liberty, a class which may yet be discriminated against, even in respect of rights of a character so essential and so supreme, that, deprived of their enjoyment, in common with others, a freeman is not only branded as one inferior and infected, but, in the competitions of life, is robbed of some of the most necessary means of existence; and all this solely because they belong to a particular race which the nation has liberated. The thirteenth amendment alone obliterated the race line, so far as all rights fundamental in a state of freedom are concerned.

2. As to inns. [A] keeper of an inn is in the exercise of a *quasi* public employment. The law gives him special privileges, and he is charged with certain duties and responsibilities to the public. The public nature of his employment forbids him from discriminating against any person asking admission as a guest on account of the race or color of that person.

3. As to places of public amusement. [Within] the meaning of the act of 1875, they are such as are established and maintained under direct license of the law. The authority to establish and maintain them comes from the public. The colored race is a part of that public. The local government granting the license represents them as well as all other races within its jurisdiction. A license from the public to establish a place of public amusement, imports, in law, equality of right, at such places, among all the members of that public. I am of the, opinion that such [racial] discrimination practiced [sic] by corporations and individuals in the exercise of their public or quasi-public functions is a badge of servitude, the imposition of which congress may prevent under its power. By appropriate legislation, to enforce the thirteenth amendment; and consequently, without reference to its enlarged power under the fourteenth amendment, the act of March 1, 1875, is not, in my judgment, repugnant to the constitution.

[Much] that has been said as to the power of Congress under the 13th Amendment is applicable [to the 14th]. The assumption that this amendment consists wholly of prohibitions upon state laws and state proceedings in hostility to its provisions, is unauthorized by its language. The first clause of the first section — "all persons born or naturalized in the United States, and subject to the jurisdiction thereof, are citizens of the United States, and of the state wherein they reside" — is of a distinctly affirmative character. In its application to the colored race, previously liberated, it created and granted, as well citizenship of the United States, as citizenship of the state in which they respectively resided. It introduced all of that race, whose ancestors had been imported and sold as slaves, at once, into the political community known as the "People of the United States." They became, instantly, citizens of the United States, and of their respective states. Further, they were brought, by this supreme act of the nation, within the direct operation of that provision of the constitution which declares that "the citizens of each state shall be entitled to all privileges and immunities of citizens in the several states." Article 4, § 2.

The citizenship thus acquired by that race, in virtue of an affirmative grant by the nation, may be protected, not alone by the judicial branch of the government, but by congressional legislation of a primary direct character; this, because the power of congress is not restricted to the enforcement of prohibitions upon state laws or state action. It is, in terms distinct and positive, to enforce "the *provisions* of *this article*" of amendment; not simply those of a prohibitive character, but the provisions, — *all* of the provisions, — affirmative and prohibitive, of the amendment. It is, therefore, a grave misconception to suppose that the fifth section of the amendment has reference exclusively to express prohibitions upon state laws or state action. But what was secured to colored citizens of the United States — as between them and their respective states — by the grant to them of state citizenship? With what rights, privileges, or immunities did this grant from the nation invest them? There is one, if there be no others — exemption from race discrimination in respect of any civil right belonging to citizens of the white race in the same state. If any right was created by that amendment, the grant of power, through appropriate legislation, to enforce its provisions authorizes congress, by means of legislation operating throughout the entire Union, to guard, secure, and protect that right. It is fundamental in American citizenship that, in respect of such rights, there shall be no discrimination by the state, or its officers, or by individuals, or corporations exercising public functions or authority, against any citizen because of his race or previous condition of servitude.

[But] if it were conceded that the power of congress could not be brought into activity until the rights specified in the act of 1875 had been abridged or denied by some state law or state action, I maintain that the decision of the court is erroneous. [In] every material sense applicable to the practical enforcement of the fourteenth amendment, railroad corporations, keepers of inns, and managers of places of public amusement are agents of the state, because amenable, in respect of their public duties and functions, to public regulation.

[I] agree that if one citizen chooses not to hold social intercourse with another, he is not and cannot be made amenable to the law for his conduct in that regard; for no legal right of a citizen is violated by the refusal of others to maintain merely social relations with him, even upon grounds of race. What I affirm is that no state, nor the officers of any state, nor any corporation or individual wielding power under state authority for the public benefit or the public convenience, can, consistently either with the freedom established by the fundamental law, or with that equality of civil rights which now belongs to every citizen, discriminate against freemen or citizens, in their civil rights, because of their race, or because they once labored under disabilities imposed upon them as a race. The rights which congress, by the act of 1875, endeavored to secure and protect are legal, not social, rights. The right, for instance, of a colored citizen to use the accommodations of a public highway upon the same terms as are permitted to white citizens is no more a social right than his right, under the law, to use the public streets of a city, or a town, or a turnpike road, or a public market, or a post-office, or his right to sit in a public building with others, of whatever race, for the purpose of hearing the political questions of the day discussed.

[Today] it is the colored race which is denied, by corporations and individuals wielding public authority, rights fundamental in their freedom and citizenship. At some future time it may be some other race that will fall under the ban. If the constitutional amendments be enforced, according to the intent with which, as I conceive, they were adopted, there cannot be, in this republic, any class of human beings in practical subjection to another [class.] The supreme law of the land has decreed that no authority shall be exercised in this country upon the basis of discrimination, in respect of civil rights, against freemen and citizens because of their race, color, or previous condition of servitude. To that decree — for the due enforcement of which, by appropriate legislation, congress has been invested with express power — every one must bow, whatever may have been, or whatever now are, his individual views as to the wisdom or policy, either of the recent changes in the fundamental law, or of the legislation which has been enacted to give them effect.

Comments on the *Civil Rights Cases*. As Albert Blaustein asserted in *Civil Rights and the American Negro* 241 (1968), "The Civil Rights Cases of 1883 confirmed the fact that the national government was officially abandoning the Negro to the caprice of state control. The next thirty years indicated the extent to which the Negro, . . . could be repressed and reduced to the status of second class citizenship by the force of law and the force of custom sustained by that state control." He concluded, "This was the era of Jim Crow. . . ."

The *Civil Rights Cases* also exemplified the Court's bias in voiding the 1875 act. For, while voiding the Civil Rights Act of 1875, the Court upheld the Removal Act of 1875 — when both were enacted in the closing days of the forty-third Congress, and "both were an ultimate expression of Republican reconstruction politics." The Court voided the Act advancing civil rights, yet upheld the Removal Act because it enhanced a "national market." This inconsistency is explained by the fact that the Removal Act advanced the Court's bias toward economic development, while the Civil Rights Act inhibited such. *Id.*

The effect of the case upon the enforcement clause was so great that "the very idea of civil rights legislation lapsed into a Constitutional limbo for three quarters of a Century." The Supreme Court not only allowed discrimination to flourish, but allowed such under the infamous Jim Crow state legislation. *Id.*

In a nation where activities that society's very existence depends on — travel, communication, medical care, energy, etc. — are in "private hands," the impact of the Court's decision was broad and, in the South, oppressive. In effect, the Court allowed the South to "drape the robes of their discrimination in private sanction." In this sense the "white robes" worn by Klan members had practical intent; they were worn to hide the fact that many members were local and state officials who, if discovered, may well have provided the necessary state action to make the activity reachable by federal authorities. The fact that Congress itself was aware of this tactic and intended this type of private activity to be reached via its Fourteenth Amendment enforcement power is evidenced by the language of the Civil Rights Acts of 1870 and 1871 reaching "private" deprivations of federal rights, "If two or more persons *go in disguise* on the highway, or the premises of another, with intent to prevent or hinder his free exercise of enjoyment of any right or privilege so secured." (Language is from the 1870 statute, now 18 U.S.C. § 241; similar language in the 1871 statute is now 42 U.S.C. § 1985(3) (emphasis added).) Since roughly the same Congress framed both the Fourteenth Amendment (1868) and this civil rights legislation (1870, 1871), the Court's finding that the legislation was unconstitutional because Congress could not reach private conduct seemed to be contrary to the expressed intent of the framers themselves.

The "State Action" limitation imposed by the Court is still with us today. Recall our discussion of the Civil Rights Act of 1964, with almost the exact same "Public Accommodation Language" as the 1875 statute. There, and in order to avoid the problem posed by the state action limitation, the Court found the 1964 Act constitutional based upon the ability of Congress to reach private activity under the commerce power. Yet, Congress's intent in regard to both the Fourteenth Amendment and the 1875 Act did not reach fruition for almost one-hundred years.

Much the same as Justice Bradley's dissent in *Slaughter-House* would set forth the predicate for a "fundamental rights" approach to due process incorporation in the modern era, so too would Justice Harlan's dissent in the *Civil Rights Cases*. The "public function" rationale that Justice Harlan asserted as a basis for allowing Congress to reach these activities via its enforcement power will serve as the basis for a retrenching by the Supreme Court in regard to these issues at the onset of the civil rights movement in the mid-twentieth century.

The final of our trilogy of cases, *Plessy v. Ferguson*, followed the *Civil Rights Cases* by thirteen years. Though the impact of the *Slaughter-House* and *Civil Rights Cases* dramatically affected and endangered the circumstances that African Americans faced in the South, the guarantee that no state could "deny to any person within its jurisdiction the equal protection of the laws" nonetheless remained. Given the fact that by this time both "Jim Crow" and apartheid were already entrenched in the South, the guarantee that a state could not deprive its citizens of equal protection was unaffected by these decisions. The application of the equal protection clause to state governments could still have provided significant protection — that is, until the decision in *Plessy*.

PLESSY v. FERGUSON
163 U.S. 537 (1896)

That petitioner was a citizen of the United States and a resident of the state of Louisiana, of mixed descent, in the proportion of seven-eighths Caucasian and one-eighth African blood; that the mixture of colored blood was not discernible in him, and that he was entitled to every recognition, right, privilege, and immunity secured to the citizens of the United States of the white race by its constitution and laws; that on June 7, 1892, he engaged and paid for a first-class passage on the East Louisiana Railway, from New Orleans to Covington, in the same state, and thereupon entered a passenger train, and took possession of a vacant seat in a coach where passengers of the white race were accommodated; that such railroad company was incorporated by the laws of Louisiana as a common carrier, and was not authorized to distinguish between citizens according to their race, but, notwithstanding this, petitioner was required by the conductor, under penalty of ejection from said train and imprisonment, to vacate said coach, and occupy another seat, in a coach assigned by said company for persons not of the white race, and for no other reason than that petitioner was of the colored race; that, upon petitioner's refusal to comply with such order, he was, with the aid of a police officer, forcibly ejected from said coach, and hurried off to, and imprisoned in, the parish jail of New Orleans, and there held to answer a charge made by such officer to the effect that he was guilty of having criminally violated an act of the general assembly of the state, approved July 10, 1890, in such case made and provided.

[Mr.] Justice BROWN, after stating the facts in the foregoing language, delivered the opinion of the court.

[The] object of the amendment was undoubtedly to enforce the absolute equality of the two races before the law, but, in the nature of things, it could not have been intended to abolish distinctions based upon color, or to enforce social, as distinguished from political, equality, or a commingling of the two races upon terms unsatisfactory to either. Laws permitting, and even requiring, their separation, in places where they are liable to be brought into contact, do not necessarily imply the inferiority of either race to the other, and have been generally, if not universally, recognized as within the competency of the state legislatures in the exercise of their police power. The most common instance of this is connected with the establishment of separate schools for white and colored children, which have been held to be a valid exercise of the legislative power even by courts of states where the political rights of the colored race have been longest and most earnestly enforced.

[Laws] forbidding the intermarriage of the two races may be said in a technical sense to interfere with the freedom of contract, and yet have been universally recognized as within the police power of the state.

The distinction between laws interfering with the political equality of the negro and those requiring the separation of the two races in schools, theaters, and railway carriages has been frequently drawn by this court. [Strauder].

[In] this connection, it is also suggested by the learned counsel for the plaintiff in error that the same argument that will justify the state legislature in requiring railways to provide separate accommodations for the two races will also authorize them to require separate cars to be provided for people whose hair is of a certain color, or who are aliens, or who belong to certain nationalities, or to enact laws requiring colored people to walk upon one side of the street, and white people upon the other, or requiring white men's houses to be painted white, and colored men's black, or their vehicles or business signs to be of different colors, upon the theory that one side of the street is as good as the other, or that a house or vehicle of one color is as good as one of another color. The reply to all this is that every exercise of the police power must be reasonable, and extend only to such laws as are enacted in good faith for the promotion of the public good, and not for the annoyance or oppression of a particular class.

[In] determining the question of reasonableness, it is at liberty to act with reference to the established usages, customs, and traditions of the people, and with a view to the promotion of their comfort, and the preservation of the public peace and good order. gauged by this standard, we cannot say that a law which authorizes or even requires the separation of the two races in public conveyances is unreasonable, or more obnoxious to the fourteenth amendment than the acts of congress requiring separate schools for colored children in the District of Columbia, the constitutionality of which does not seem to have been questioned, or the corresponding acts of state legislatures.

We consider the underlying fallacy of the plaintiff's argument to consist in the assumption that the enforced separation of the two races stamps the colored race with a badge of inferiority. If this be so, it is not by reason of anything found in the act, but solely because the colored race chooses to put that construction upon it. The argument necessarily assumes that if, as has been more than once the case, and is not unlikely to be so again, the colored race should become the dominant power in the state legislature, and should enact a law in precisely similar terms, it would thereby relegate the white race to an inferior position. We imagine that the white race, at least, would not acquiesce in this assumption. The argument also assumes that social prejudices may be overcome by legislation, and that equal rights cannot be secured to the negro except by an enforced commingling of the two races. We cannot accept this proposition. If the two races are to meet upon terms of social equality, it must be the result of natural affinities, a mutual appreciation of each other's merits, and a voluntary consent of individuals. Legislation is powerless to eradicate racial instincts, or to abolish distinctions based upon physical differences, and the attempt to do so can only result in accentuating the difficulties of the present situation.   If the civil and political rights of both races be equal, one cannot be inferior to the other civilly or politically.   If one race be inferior to the other socially, the constitution of the United States cannot put them upon the same plane.

Mr. Justice HARLAN, dissenting.

[I] deny that any legislative body or judicial tribunal may have regard to the   race of citizens when the civil rights of those citizens are involved.   Indeed, such legislation as that here in question is inconsistent not only with that equality of rights which pertains to citizenship, national and state, but with the personal liberty enjoyed by every one within the United States.

[It] was said in argument that the statute of Louisiana does not discriminate against either race, but prescribes a rule applicable alike to white and colored citizens.   But this argument does not meet the difficulty. Every one knows that the statute in question had its origin in the purpose, not so much to exclude white persons from railroad cars occupied by blacks, as to exclude colored people from coaches occupied by or assigned to white persons. Railroad corporations of Louisiana did not make discrimination among whites in the matter of commodation for travelers.   The thing to accomplish was, under the guise of giving equal accommodation for whites and blacks, to compel the latter to keep to themselves while traveling in railroad passenger coaches.   No one would be so wanting in candor as to assert the contrary.   The fundamental objection, therefore, to the statute, is that it interferes with the personal freedom of citizens.   "Personal liberty," it has been well said, "consists in the power of locomotion, of changing situation, or removing one's person to whatsoever places one's own inclination may direct, without imprisonment or restraint, unless by due course of law."   1 Bl. Comm. *134.   If a white man and a black man choose to occupy the same public conveyance on a public highway, it is their right to do so; and no government, proceeding alone on grounds of race, can prevent it without infringing the personal liberty of each.

[The] white race deems itself to be the dominant race in this country.   And so it is, in prestige, in achievements, in education, in wealth, and in power. So, I doubt not, it will continue to be for all time, if it remains true to its great heritage, and holds fast to the principles of constitutional liberty. But in view of the constitution, in the eye of the law, there is in this country no superior, dominant, ruling class of citizens.   There is no caste here.   Our constitution is color-blind, and neither knows nor tolerates classes among citizens.   In respect of civil rights, all citizens are equal before the law.   The humblest is the peer of the most powerful.   The law regards man as man, and takes no account of his surroundings or of his color when his civil rights as guaranteed by the supreme law of the land are involved.   It is therefore to be regretted that this high tribunal, the final expositor of the fundamental law of the land, has reached the conclusion that it is competent for a state to regulate the enjoyment by citizens of their civil rights solely upon the basis of race.

In my opinion, the judgment this day rendered will, in time, prove to be quite as pernicious as the decision made by this tribunal in the Dred Scott Case.

[The] present decision, it may well be apprehended, will not only stimulate aggressions, more or less brutal and irritating, upon the admitted rights of colored citizens, but will encourage the belief that it is possible, by means of state enactments, to defeat the beneficent purposes which the people of the United States had in view when they adopted the recent amendments of the constitution, by one of which the blacks of this country were made citizens of the United States and of the states in which they respectively reside, and whose privileges and immunities, as citizens, the states are forbidden to abridge. Sixty millions of whites are in no danger from the presence here of eight millions of blacks. The destinies of the two races, in this country, are indissolubly linked together, and the interests of both require that the common government of all shall not permit the seeds of race hate to be planted under the sanction of law.   What can more certainly arouse race hate, what more certainly create and perpetuate a feeling of distrust between these races, than state enactments which, in fact, proceed on the ground that colored citizens are so inferior and degraded that they cannot be allowed to sit in public coaches occupied by white citizens?   That, as all will admit, is the real meaning of such legislation as was enacted in Louisiana.

[If] evils will result from the commingling of the two races upon public highways established for the benefit of all, they will be infinitely less than those that will surely come from state legislation regulating the enjoyment of civil rights upon the basis of race.   We boast of the freedom enjoyed by our people above all other peoples.   But it is difficult to reconcile that boast with a state of the law which, practically, puts the brand of servitude and degradation upon a large class of our fellow citizens, — our equals before the law. The thin disguise of 'equal' accommodations for passengers in railroad coaches will not mislead any one, nor atone for the wrong this day done.

Comments on *Plessy* and "Separate but Equal."   If the question is how could African Americans suffer the oppression and discrimination they faced for some one hundred years despite the adoption of the great   postwar amendments and civil rights legislation, the answer, at least as far as the Supreme Court is concerned, is in: Despite the privileges and immunities clause, the freed persons were placed at the mercy of their former masters, with no federal right-based protection; the 14th Amendment itself could not reach any form of "private" racism and discrimination generated in the South, inclusive of "public accommodations"; and finally, separation of the races by force of law did not violate equal protection — separate but equal was equal.

It is worth reminding ourselves, once again, that, "[a]s the desire for normalcy expressed itself politically, the Supreme Court was no idle spectator"; its decisions showed, in fact, "that the Court in facing the Southern question marched in step with the national mood."   Radical reconstruction had ended, "the Hayes-Tilden election crisis provided the excuse for the desired accommodation — an accommodation which had as one of its essential elements the remission of the Negroes' destiny to the states.   The Supreme Court saw to it that this bargain was *not violated*." (Levy, 2 Tex. So. L. Rev. at 217-220.)

V. THE STRUGGLE FOR INCORPORATION

A. "NOR SHALL ANY STATE DEPRIVE ANY PERSON OF LIFE, LIBERTY, OR PROPERTY, WITHOUT DUE PROCESS OF LAW"

Though *Slaughter-House* may be "good law" when it comes to privileges and immunities incorporation, it was not the end of the road when it came to the issue of incorporation and national protection of civil rights and liberties.   As inferred by Justice Bradley's dissenting opinion, the "struggle for incorporation," because of the *Slaughter-*

House decision, would turn to the due process clause and the Fourteenth Amendment's guarantee that "nor shall any State deprive any person of life, liberty, or property, without due process of law."

Though due process seems to conjure "procedural" as opposed to "substantive" rights, the use of the term "liberty" in the clause, and the plain and simple "need" for at least some national protection of civil rights and liberties, found it the most likely alternative for incorporating rights. By the *Palko* decision in 1937, there was no longer any doubt that "due process" could embrace not only procedural rights but substantive rights as well. Paramount in this move to "due process" incorporation was the Court, in 1925, applying the free speech protection of the First Amendment to the states based upon the due process clause of the Fourteenth Amendment by finding that freedom of speech was "among the fundamental personal rights and liberties." Gitlow v. New York, 268 U.S. 652 (1925).

If the due process clause was to serve as the basis for incorporation, particularly given the procedural nature of the "right," the most significant question was how one would decide which rights were protected. This might have been a less difficult inquiry under the privileges and immunities clause. Recall the argument that the privileges and immunities of national citizenship must have been the bill of rights, and that this terminology was shorthand language for such. Yet, the "textual" problem of incorporating via due process made this question quite difficult. The *Palko* and *Adamson* opinions, which followed the debate among Justices Black, Cardozo, and Frankfurter over this very issue, reached historic proportion as the Justices debated how this process should be invoked.

See whether you can stake out the positions of each of the Justices in the opinions that follow. How does each Justice go about determining how rights should be incorporated and made applicable to the states?

PALKO v. CONNECTICUT
302 U.S. 319 (1937)

[A Connecticut statute permitted the state to appeal in criminal cases. Although the Court "assumed for the purpose of the case" that such a statute, if enacted by the United States, would violate the double jeopardy clause of the Fifth Amendment, it rejected appellant's contention that the same standard applied, via the due process clause of the Fourteenth Amendment, to the states. In so deciding, Justice Cardozo articulated his "selective" approach to incorporation.]

Justice CARDOZO delivered the opinion of the Court:

[T]he due process clause of the Fourteenth Amendment may make it unlawful for a state to abridge by its statutes the freedom of speech which the First Amendment safeguards against encroachment by the Congress, *De Jonge v. Oregon,* 299 U. S. 353, 299 U. S. 364; *Herndon v. Lowry,* 301 U. S. 242, 301 U. S. 259; or the like freedom of the press, *Grosjean v. American Press Co.,*297 U. S. 233; *Near v. Minnesota ex rel. Olson,* 283 U. S. 697, 283 U. S. 707; or the free exercise of religion, *Hamilton v. Regents,*293 U. S. 245, 293 U. S. 262; *cf. Grosjean v. American Press Co., supra; Pierce v. Society of Sisters,* 268 U. S. 510; or the right of peaceable assembly, without which speech would be unduly trammeled, *De Jonge v. Oregon, supra; Herndon v. Lowry, supra;* or the right of one accused of crime to the benefit of counsel, *Powell v. Alabama,* 287 U. S. 45. In these and other situations, immunities that are valid as against the federal government by force of the specific pledges of particular amendments have been found to be implicit in the concept of ordered liberty, and thus, through the Fourteenth Amendment, become valid as against the states.

The line of division may seem to be wavering and broken if there is a hasty catalogue of the cases on the one side and the other. [But] there emerges the perception of a rationalizing principle which gives to discrete instances a proper order and coherence. The right to trial by jury and the immunity from prosecution except as the result of an indictment may have value and importance. Even so, they are not of the very essence of a scheme of ordered liberty. To abolish them is not to violate a "principle of justice so rooted in the tradition and conscience of our people as to be ranked as fundamental." [Few] would be so narrow or provincial as to maintain that a fair and enlightened system of justice would be impossible without them. What is true of jury trials and indictments is true also [of] the immunity from compulsory self-incrimination. This too might be lost, and justice still be done.

We reach a different plane of social and moral values when we pass to the privileges and immunities that have been taken over from the earlier articles of the federal bill of rights and brought within the Fourteenth Amendment by a process of absorption. [The] process of absorption has had its source in the belief that neither liberty nor justice would exist if they were sacrificed. [This] is true, for illustration, of freedom of thought and speech. Of that freedom one may say that it is the matrix, and indispensable condition, of nearly every other form of freedom. [Fundamental] too in the concept of due process, and so in that of liberty, is the thought that condemnation shall be rendered only after trial.

Is that kind of double jeopardy to which the statute has subjected him a hardship so acute and shocking that our polity will not endure it? Does it violate those "fundamental principles of liberty and justice which lie at the base of all our civil and political institutions"? [The] answer must surely be "no."

Justice Butler dissented.

ADAMSON v. CALIFORNIA
332 U.S. 46 (1947)

[In a state court prosecution, the prosecution was permitted to comment on the defendant's failure to take the witness stand. The Court assumed that such comment "would infringe defendant's privilege against self-incrimination [if] this were a trial in a court of the United States." In Justice Reed's 5–4 majority opinion, the Court held that the 14th Amendment did not incorporate the privilege, based upon Court's finding in *Palko* that not all guarantees of the Bill of Rights were protected by the 14th Amendment. Given such, he concluded that the self-incrimination privilege was not "fundamental to ordered liberty" and therefore not applicable to the states. In a lengthy dissenting opinion, Justice Black, joined by Justice Douglas, set forth his theory of "total" incorporation.]

Mr. Justice BLACK, dissenting.

This decision reasserts a constitutional theory spelled out in [Twining], that this Court is endowed by the Constitution with boundless power under "natural law" periodically to expand and contract constitutional standards to conform to the Court's conception of what at a particular time constitutes "civilized decency" and "fundamental liberty and justice."

[I] would not reaffirm the Twining decision. I think that decision and the "natural law" theory of the Constitution upon which it relies degrade the constitutional safeguards of the Bill of Rights and simultaneously appropriate for this Court a broad power which we are not authorized by the Constitution to exercise. . . .

My study of the historical events that culminated in the Fourteenth Amendment, and the expressions of those who sponsored and favored, as well as those who opposed its submission and passage, persuades me that one of the chief objects that the provisions of the Amendment's first section, separately, and as a whole, were intended to accomplish was to make the Bill of Rights applicable to the states. With full knowledge of the import of the Barron decision, the framers and backers of the Fourteenth Amendment proclaimed its purpose to be to overturn the constitutional rule that case had announced. . . .

[I] fear to see the consequences of the Court's practice of substituting its own concepts of decency and fundamental justice for the language of the Bill of Rights as its point of departure in interpreting and enforcing that Bill of Rights. [I] would follow what I believe was the original purpose of the Fourteenth Amendment — to extend to all the people of the nation the complete protection of the Bill of Rights. . . ."

Mr. Justice FRANKFURTER (concurring).

Less than 10 years ago, Mr. Justice Cardozo announced as settled constitutional law that while the Fifth Amendment, "which is not directed to the States, but solely to the federal government," provides that no person shall be compelled in any criminal case to be a witness against himself, the process of law assured by the Fourteenth Amendment does not require such immunity from self-crimination: "in prosecutions by a state, the exemption will fail if the state elects to end it." Palko v. Connecticut, 302 U.S. 319, 322, 324, 58 S.Ct. 149, 150, 151, 82 L.Ed. 288. Mr. Justice Cardozo spoke for the Court, consisting of Mr. Chief Justice Hughes, and McReynolds, Brandeis, Sutherland, Stone, Roberts, Black, JJ. (Mr. Justice Butler dissented.) The matter no longer called for discussion; a reference to Twining v. New Jersey, 211 U.S. 78, 29 S.Ct. 14, 53 L.Ed. 97, decided 30 years before the Palko case, sufficed.

Decisions of this Court do not have equal intrinsic authority. The Twining case shows the judicial process at its best — comprehensive briefs and powerful arguments on both sides, followed by long deliberation, resulting in an opinion by Mr. Justice Moody which at once gained and has ever since retained recognition as one of the outstanding opinions in the history of the Court. After enjoying unquestioned prestige for 40 years, the Twining case should not now be diluted, even unwittingly, either in its judicial philosophy or in its particulars. As the surest way of keeping the Twining case intact, I would affirm this case on its authority.

[Between] the incorporation of the Fourteenth Amendment into the Constitution and the beginning of the present membership of the Court — a period of 70 years — the scope of that Amendment was passed upon by 43 judges. Of all these judges, only one, who may respectfully be called an eccentric exception, ever indicated the belief that the Fourteenth Amendment was a shorthand summary of the first eight Amendments theretofore limiting only the Federal Government, and that due process incorporated those eight Amendments as restrictions upon the powers of the States. Among these judges were not only those who would have to be included among the greatest in the history of the Court, but — it is especially relevant to note — they included those whose services in the cause of human rights and the spirit of freedom are the most conspicuous in our history. It is not invidious to single out Miller, Davis, Bradley, Waite, Matthews, Gray,

Fuller, Holmes, Brandeis, Stone and Cardozo (to speak only of the dead) as judges who were alert in safeguarding and promoting the interests of liberty and human dignity through law. But they were also judges mindful of the relation of our federal system to a progressively democratic society and therefore duly regardful of the scope of authority that was left to the States even after the Civil War. And so they did not find that the Fourteenth Amendment, concerned as it was with matters fundamental to the pursuit of justice, fastened upon the States procedural arrangements which, in the language of Mr. Justice Cardozo, only those who are 'narrow or provincial' would deem essential to 'a fair and enlightened system of justice.' Palko v. Connecticut, 302 U.S. 319, 325, 58 S.Ct. 149, 151, 152, 82 L.Ed. 288. To suggest that it is inconsistent with a truly free society to begin prosecutions without an indictment, to try petty civil cases without the paraphernalia of a common law jury, to take into consideration that one who has full opportunity to make a defense remains silent is, in de Tocqueville's phrase, to confound the familiar with the necessary.

The short answer to the suggestion that the provision of the Fourteenth Amendment, which ordains 'nor shall any State deprive any person of life, liberty, or property, without due process of law,' was a way of saying that every State must thereafter initiate prosecutions through indictment by a grand jury, must have a trial by a jury of 12 in criminal cases, and must have trial by such a jury in common law suits where the amount in controversy exceeds $20, is that it is a strange way of saying it. It would be extraordinarily strange for a Constitution to convey such specific commands in such a roundabout and inexplicit way. After all, an amendment to the Constitution should be read in a "sense most obvious to the common understanding at the time of its adoption.' . . . For it was for public adoption that it was proposed.' Those reading the English language with the meaning which it ordinarily conveys, those conversant with the political and legal history of the concept of due process, those sensitive to the relations of the States to the central government as well as the relation of some of the provisions of the Bill of Rights to the process of justice, would hardly recognize the Fourteenth Amendment as a cover for the various explicit provisions of the first eight Amendments. Some of these are enduring reflections of experience with human nature, while some express the restricted views of Eighteenth-Century England regarding the best methods for the ascertainment of facts. The notion that the Fourteenth Amendment was a covert way of imposing upon the States all the rules which it seemed important to Eighteenth Century statesmen to write into the Federal Amendments, was rejected by judges who were themselves witnesses of the process by which the Fourteenth Amendment became part of the Constitution. Arguments that may now be adduced to prove that the first eight Amendments were concealed within the historic phrasing of the Fourteenth Amendment were not unknown at the time of its adoption. A surer estimate of their bearing was possible for judges at the time than distorting distance is likely to vouchsafe. Any evidence of design or purpose not contemporaneously known could hardly have influenced those who ratified the Amendment. Remarks of a particular proponent of the Amendment, no matter how influential, are not to be deemed part of the Amendment. What was submitted for ratification was his proposal, not his speech. Thus, at the time of the ratification of the Fourteenth Amendment the constitutions of nearly half of the ratifying States did not have the rigorous requirements of the Fifth Amendment for instituting criminal proceedings through a grand jury. It could hardly have occurred to these States that by ratifying the Amendment they uprooted their established methods for prosecuting crime and fastened upon themselves a new prosecutorial system.

Indeed, the suggestion that the Fourteenth Amendment incorporates the first eight Amendments as such is not unambiguously urged.   Even the boldest innovator would shrink from suggesting to more than half the States that they may no longer initiate prosecutions without indictment by grand jury, or that thereafter all the States of the Union must furnish a jury of 12 for every case involving a claim above $20.   There is suggested merely a selective incorporation of the first eight Amendments into the Fourteenth Amendment.   Some are in and some are out, but we are left in the dark as to which are in and which are out.   Nor are we given the calculus for determining which go in and which stay out.   If the basis of selection is merely that those provisions of the first eight Amendments are incorporated which commend themselves to individual justices as indispensable to the dignity and happiness of a free man, we are thrown back to a merely subjective test.   The protection against unreasonable search and seizure might have primacy for one judge, while trial by a jury of 12 for every claim above $20 might appear to another as an ultimate need in a free society.   In the history of thought 'natural law' has a much longer and much better founded meaning and justification than such subjective selection of the first eight Amendments for incorporation into the Fourteenth.   If all that is meant is that due process contains within itself certain minimal standards which are "of the very essence of a scheme of ordered liberty," Palko v. Connecticut, 302 U.S. 319, 325, 58 S.Ct. 149, 151, 152, 82 L.Ed. 288, putting upon this Court the duty of applying these standards from time to time, then we have merely arrived at the insight which our predecessors long ago expressed.   [As] judges charged with the delicate task of subjecting the government of a continent to the Rule of Law we must be particularly mindful that it is "a constitution we are expounding," so that it should not be imprisoned in what are merely legal forms even though they have the sanction of the Eighteenth Century.

[The] Amendment neither comprehends the specific provisions by which the founders deemed it appropriate to restrict the federal government nor is it confined to them.   The Due Process Clause of the Fourteenth Amendment has an independent potency, precisely as does the Due Process Clause of the Fifth Amendment in relation to the Federal Government.   It ought not to require argument to reject the notion that due process of law meant one thing in the Fifth Amendment and another in the Fourteenth.   The Fifth Amendment specifically prohibits prosecution of an "infamous crime" except upon indictment; it forbids double jeopardy; it bars compelling a person to be a witness against himself in any criminal case; it precludes deprivation of "life, liberty, or property, without due process of law."   Are Madison and his contemporaries in the framing of the Bill of Rights to be charged with writing into it a meaningless clause?   To consider "due process of law" as merely a shorthand statement of other specific clauses in the same amendment is to attribute to the authors and proponents of this Amendment ignorance of, or indifference to, a historic conception which was one of the great instruments in the arsenal of constitutional freedom which the Bill of Rights was to protect and strengthen.

A construction which gives to due process no independent function but turns it into a summary of the specific provisions of the Bill of Rights would, as has been noted, tear up by the roots much of the fabric of law in the several States, and would deprive the States of opportunity for reforms in legal process designed for extending the area of freedom.   It would assume that no other abuses would reveal themselves in the course of time than those which had become manifest in 1791.   Such a view not only disregards the historic meaning of "due process."   It leads inevitably to a warped construction of specific provisions of the Bill of Rights to bring within their scope conduct clearly condemned by due process but not easily fitting into the pigeon-holes of the specific provisions.   It seems pretty late in the day to suggest that a phrase so laden with historic meaning should be given an improvised content consisting of some but not all of the provisions of the first eight Amendments, selected on an undefined basis, with improvisation of content for the provisions so selected.

And so, when, as in a case like the present, a conviction in a State court is here for review under a claim that a right protected by the Due Process Clause of the Fourteenth Amendment has been denied, the issue is not whether an infraction of one of the specific provisions of the first eight Amendments is disclosed by the record.   The relevant question is whether the criminal proceedings which resulted in conviction deprived the accused of the due process of law to which the United States Constitution entitled him.   Judicial review of that guaranty of the Fourteenth Amendment inescapably imposes upon this Court an exercise of judgment upon the whole course of the proceedings in order to ascertain whether they offend those canons of decency and fairness which express the notions of justice of English-speaking peoples even toward those charged with the most heinous offenses.   These standards of justice are not authoritatively formulated anywhere as though they were prescriptions in a pharmacopoeia.   But neither does the application of the Due Process Clause imply that judges are wholly at large.   The judicial judgment in applying the Due Process Clause must move within the limits of accepted notions of justice and is not to be based upon the idiosyncrasies of a merely personal judgment.   The fact that judges among themselves may differ whether in a particular case a trial offends accepted notions of justice is not disproof that general rather than idiosyncratic standards are applied.   An important safeguard against such merely individual judgment is an alert deference to the judgment of the State court under review.

————

"Complete" Incorporation.   The "complete" incorporation argument advanced by Justice Black has never commanded a majority of the Court.   Black's position is, as he argues, better advanced by the privileges and immunities clause, though he is well prepared to make the same total incorporation argument based upon due process.   Making the bill of rights, "part and parcel," applicable to the states not only better suited Justice Black's renowned strict constructionist position, but was further advanced by his view that the history of the Fourteenth Amendment supported the framers' intent for complete incorporation.   Black's history was soon challenged by Professor Charles Fairmen's:

> Apart from a few isolated references, the theory that [the] privileges and immunities clause incorporated Amendments I to VIII found no recognition in the practice of Congress, or the action of state legislatures, constitutional conventions, or courts. [The] freedom that the states traditionally [had] exercised to develop their own systems for administering justice repels any thought that the [Bill of Rights] provisions on grand jury, criminal jury, and civil jury were fastened upon them in 1868. Congress would not have attempted such a thing, the country would not have stood for it, the legislatures would not have ratified. . .
>
> .
>
> If the founders of the Fourteenth Amendment did not intend the privileges and immunities clause to impose Amendments I to VIII, then what, it may be asked, did they mean? [If] one seeks some inclusive and exclusive definition, such that one could say, this is precisely what they had in mind — pretty clearly there never was any such clear conception. [The opponents of the measure magnified] the proposal to render it odious. [The advocates] offered illustrations of particular evils that would be repressed; [but] stayed away from any explanation of a fundamental principle. [Brooding] over the matter

[has] slowly brought [me to] the conclusion that [the protection of those rights that are] "implicit in the concept of ordered liberty" [comes] as close as one can to catching the vague aspirations that were hung upon the privileges and immunities clause. [Charles Fairmen, "Does the Fourteenth Amendment Incorporate the Bill of Rights? The Original Understanding," 2 Stan. L. Rev. 5, 132, 137-139 (1949).]

Black, however, was somewhat triumphant when he smugly concurred in *Duncan v. Louisiana* (cited below) in 1968, "I am very happy to support this selective process through which our Court has since the Adamson test held most of the specific Bill of Right's protections applicable to the states."

Fundamental Fairness/Natural Law Incorporation. The opinions of Justices Cordozo and Frankfurter have been described as natural law/fundamental fairness incorporation because they call for an independent Fourteenth Amendment inquiry in regard to the significance and meaning of any particular right. The "trademark" language in both *Palko* (double jeopardy) and *Adamson* (self-incrimination) is whether the right is "implicit in our concept of ordered liberty," a "principle of justice so rooted in the conscience of our people as to be ranked as fundamental," or "deeply rooted in our civil and political institutions." Though Justice Frankfurter desired to avoid "the idiosyncrasies of a merely personal judgment," this approach was criticized by Justice Black precisely because it was "entirely too speculative."

"Select" Incorporation. What are the rights most likely to be deemed "fundamental" via the above detailed nomenclature? The rights detailed in the first nine amendments would no doubt come to mind. The Warren Court looked increasingly to the bill of rights to "selectively" incorporate the specific guarantees of the bill of rights into the due process clause of the Fourteenth Amendment. This might be described as fundamental fairness/natural law select incorporation. The concept being that the "fundamental fairness" inquiry would be used to decide which of the protections in the bill of rights should be selectively incorporated. To be sure, though this form of selective incorporation centered on the first nine amendments, only those protections of the bill of rights deemed fundamental would be included, though it was also possible that an unarticulated right not so specified could be deemed "fundamental" and held applicable to the states as well.

In this sense, recall the discussion of the issues extending from the right of privacy (*Roe v. Wade*) in our study of the judicial power (Chapter 1). It is worth noting that the same "fundamental fairness" inquiry used by the court to selectively incorporate fundamental rights is also applied by the Court to create unarticulated rights by a substantive application of the due process clause of the Fourteenth Amendment. Thus, we might say that substantive due process is substantive due process, is substantive due process. The intent being that the inquiry as to which rights are incorporated and made applicable to the states is the approximate inquiry the Court uses to create fundamental rights that are not delineated in the Constitution — and that the due process clause of the Fourteenth Amendment is the source for both.

Duncan articulates the present position of the Court in regard to fundamental fairness selective incorporation, as the Court reviews whether the Sixth Amendment right to a jury trial is fundamental and applicable to the states.

DUNCAN v. LOUISIANA
391 U.S. 145 (1968)

Mr. Justice WHITE delivered the opinion of the Court.

Appellant, Gary Duncan, was convicted of simple battery in the Twenty-fifth Judicial District Court of Louisiana. Under Louisiana law simple battery is a misdemeanor, punishable by a maximum of two years' imprisonment and a $300 fine. Appellant sought trial by jury, but because the Louisiana Constitution grants jury trials only in cases in which capital punishment or imprisonment at hard labor may be imposed, the trial judge denied the request. Appellant was convicted and sentenced to serve 60 days in the parish prison and pay a fine of $150. Appellant sought review in the Supreme Court of Louisiana, asserting that the denial of jury trial violated rights guaranteed to him by the United States Constitution. The Supreme Court, finding "[n]o error of law in the ruling complained of," denied appellant a writ of certiorari. Pursuant to 28 U.S.C. § 1257(2) appellant sought review in this Court, alleging that the Sixth and Fourteenth Amendments to the United States Constitution secure the right to jury trial in state criminal prosecutions where a sentence as long as two years may be imposed.

In resolving conflicting claims concerning the meaning of this spacious language, the Court has looked increasingly to the Bill of Rights for guidance; many of the rights guaranteed by the first eight Amendments to the Constitution have been held to be protected against state action by the Due Process Clause of the Fourteenth Amendment. That clause now protects the right to compensation for property taken by the State; the rights of speech, press, and religion covered by the First Amendment; the Fourth Amendment rights to be free from unreasonable searches and seizures and to have excluded from criminal trials any evidence illegally seized; the right guaranteed by the Fifth Amendment to be free of compelled self-incrimination; and the Sixth Amendment rights to counsel, to a speedy and public trial, to confrontation of opposing witnesses, and to compulsory process for obtaining witnesses.

The test for determining whether a right extended by the Fifth and Sixth Amendments with respect to federal criminal proceedings is also protected against state action by the Fourteenth Amendment has been phrased in a variety of ways in the opinions of this Court. The question has been asked whether a right is among those "fundamental principles of liberty and justice which lie at the base of all our civil and political institutions," Powell v. State of Alabama, 287 U.S. 45, 67, 53 S.Ct. 55, 63, 77 L.Ed. 158 (1932); whether it is "basic in our system of jurisprudence," In re Oliver, 333 U.S. 257, 273, 68 S.Ct. 499, 507, 92 L.Ed. 682 (1948); and whether it is "a fundamental right, essential to a fair trial," Gideon v. Wainwright, 372 U.S. 335, 343-344, 83 S.Ct. 792, 796, 9 L.Ed.2d 799 (1963); Malloy v. Hogan, 378 U.S. 1, 6, 84 S.Ct. 1489, 1492, 12 L.Ed.2d 653 (1964); Pointer v. State of Texas, 380 U.S. 400, 403, 85 S.Ct. 1065, 1067, 13 L.Ed.2d 923 (1965). The claim before us is that the right to trial by jury guaranteed by the Sixth Amendment meets these tests. The position of Louisiana, on the other hand, is that the Constitution imposes upon the States no duty to give a jury trial in any criminal case, regardless of the seriousness of the crime or the size of the punishment which may be imposed. Because we believe that trial by jury in criminal cases is fundamental to the American scheme of justice, we hold that the Fourteenth Amendment guarantees a right of jury trial in all criminal cases which — were they to be tried in a federal court — would come within the Sixth Amendment's guarantee. Since we consider the appeal before us to be such a case, we hold that the Constitution was violated when appellant's demand for jury trial was refused.

The history of trial by jury in criminal cases has been frequently told.   It is sufficient for present purposes to say that by the time our Constitution was written, jury trial in criminal cases had been in existence in England for several centuries and carried impressive credentials traced by many to Magna Carta.   Its preservation and proper operation as a protection against arbitrary rule were among the major objectives of the revolutionary settlement which was expressed in the Declaration and Bill of Rights of 1689.   In the 18th century Blackstone could write: "Our law has therefore wisely placed this strong and two-fold barrier, of a presentment and a trial by jury, between the liberties of the people and the prerogative of the crown.   It was necessary, for preserving the admirable balance of our constitution, to vest the executive power of the laws in the prince: and yet this power might be dangerous and destructive to that very constitution, if exerted without check or control, by justices of oyer and terminer occasionally named by the crown; who might then, as in France or Turkey, imprison, dispatch, or exile any man that was obnoxious to the government, by an instant declaration that such is their will and pleasure. But the founders of the English law have, with excellent forecast, contrived that . . . the truth of every accusation, whether preferred in the shape of indictment, information, or appeal, should afterwards be confirmed by the unanimous suffrage of twelve of his equals and neighbours, indifferently chosen and superior to all suspicion."

Jury trial came to America with English colonists, and received strong support from them.   Royal interference with the jury trial was deeply resented.   Among the resolutions adopted by the First Congress of the American Colonies (the Stamp Act Congress) on October 19, 1765 — resolutions deemed by their authors to state "the most essential rights and liberties of the colonists"   — was the declaration: "That trial by jury is the inherent and invaluable right of every British subject in these colonies."

The First Continental Congress, in the resolve of October 14, 1774, objected to trials before judges dependent upon the Crown alone for their salaries and to trials in England for alleged crimes committed in the colonies; the Congress therefore declared: "That the respective colonies are entitled to the common law of England, and more especially to the great and inestimable privilege of being tried by their peers of the vicinage, according to the course of that law."

The Declaration of Independence stated solemn objections to the King's making "judges dependent on his will alone, for the tenure of their offices, and the amount and payment of their salaries," to his "depriving us in many cases, of the benefits of Trial by Jury," and to his "transporting us beyond Seas to be tried for pretended offenses."   The Constitution itself, in Art. III, § 2, commanded: "The Trial of all Crimes, except in Cases of Impeachment, shall be by Jury; and such Trial shall be held in the State where the said Crimes shall have been committed."

Objections to the Constitution because of the absence of a bill of rights were met by the immediate submission and adoption of the Bill of Rights.   Included was the Sixth Amendment which, among other things, provided: "In all criminal prosecutions, the accused shall enjoy the right to a speedy and public trial, by an impartial jury of the State and district wherein the crime shall have been committed."

The constitutions adopted by the original States guaranteed jury trial.   Also, the constitution of every State entering the Union thereafter in one form or another protected the right to jury trial in criminal cases.

Even such skeletal history is impressive support for considering the right to jury trial in criminal cases to be fundamental to our system of justice, an importance frequently recognized in the opinions of this Court.   For example, the Court has said: "Those who emigrated to this country from England brought with them this great privilege 'as their birthright and inheritance, as a part of that admirable common law which had fenced around and interposed barriers on every side against the approaches of arbitrary power."

Jury trial continues to receive strong support. The laws of every State guarantee a right to jury trial in serious criminal cases; no State has dispensed with it; nor are there significant movements underway to do so. Indeed, the three most recent state constitutional revisions, in Maryland, Michigan, and New York, carefully preserved the right of the accused to have the judgment of a jury when tried for a serious crime.

We are aware of prior cases in this Court in which the prevailing opinion contains statements contrary to our holding today that the right to jury trial in serious criminal cases is a fundamental right and hence must be recognized by the States as part of their obligation to extend due process of law to all persons within their jurisdiction. Louisiana relies especially on Maxwell v. Dow, 176 U.S. 581, 20 S.Ct. 448, 44 L.Ed. 597 (1900); Palko v. State of Connecticut, 302 U.S. 319, 58 S.Ct. 149, 82 L.Ed. 288 (1937); and Snyder v. Commonwealth of Massachusetts, 291 U.S. 97, 54 S.Ct. 330, 78 L.Ed. 674 (1934). None of these cases, however, dealt with a State which had purported to dispense entirely with a jury trial in serious criminal cases. Maxwell held that no provision of the Bill of Rights applied to the States — a position long since repudiated — and that the Due Process Clause of the Fourteenth Amendment did not prevent a State from trying a defendant for a non-capital offense with fewer than 12 men on the jury. It did not deal with a case in which no jury at all had been provided. In neither Palko nor Snyder was jury trial actually at issue, although both cases contain important dicta asserting that the right to jury trial is not essential to ordered liberty and may be dispensed with by the States regardless of the Sixth and Fourteenth Amendments. These observations, though weighty and respectable, are nevertheless dicta, unsupported by holdings in this Court that a State may refuse a defendant's demand for a jury trial when he is charged with a serious crime. Perhaps because the right to jury trial was not directly at stake, the Court's remarks about the jury in Palko and Snyder took no note of past or current developments regarding jury trials, did not consider its purposes and functions, attempted no inquiry into how well it was performing its job, and did not discuss possible distinctions between civil and criminal cases. In Malloy v. Hogan, supra, the Court rejected Palko's discussion of the self-incrimination clause. Respectfully, we reject the prior dicta regarding jury trial in criminal cases.

The guarantees of jury trial in the Federal and State Constitutions reflect a profound judgment about the way in which law should be enforced and justice administered. A right to jury trial is granted to criminal defendants in order to prevent oppression by the Government. Those who wrote our constitutions knew from history and experience that it was necessary to protect against unfounded criminal charges brought to eliminate enemies and against judges too responsive to the voice of higher authority. The framers of the constitutions strove to create an independent judiciary but insisted upon further protection against arbitrary action. Providing an accused with the right to be tried by a jury of his peers gave him an inestimable safeguard against the corrupt or overzealous prosecutor and against the compliant, biased, or eccentric judge. If the defendant preferred the common-sense judgment of a jury to the more tutored but perhaps less sympathetic reaction of the single judge, he was to have it. Beyond this, the jury trial provisions in the Federal and State Constitutions reflect a fundamental decision about the exercise of official power — a reluctance to entrust plenary powers over the life and liberty of the citizen to one judge or to a group of judges. Fear of unchecked power, so typical of our State and Federal Governments in other respects, found expression in the criminal law in this insistence upon community participation in the determination of guilt or innocence. The deep commitment of the Nation to the right of jury trial in serious criminal cases as a defense against arbitrary law enforcement qualifies for protection under the Due Process Clause of the Fourteenth Amendment, and must therefore be respected by the States.

Of course jury trial has "its weaknesses and the potential for misuse," Singer v. United States, 380 U.S. 24, 35, 85 S.Ct. 783, 790, 13 L.Ed.2d 630 (1965). We are aware of the long debate, especially in this century, among those who write about the administration of justice, as to the wisdom of permitting untrained laymen to determine the facts in civil and criminal proceedings. Although the debate has been intense, with powerful voices on either side, most of the controversy has centered on the jury in civil cases. Indeed, some of the severest critics of civil juries acknowledge that the arguments for criminal juries are much stronger. In addition, at the heart of the dispute have been express or implicit assertions that juries are incapable of adequately understanding evidence or determining issues of fact, and that they are unpredictable, quixotic, and little better than a roll of dice. Yet, the most recent and exhaustive study of the jury in criminal cases concluded that juries do understand the evidence and come to sound conclusions in most of the cases presented to them and that when juries differ with the result at which the judge would have arrived, it is usually because they are serving some of the very purposes for which they were created and for which they are now employed.

The State of Louisiana urges that holding that the Fourteenth Amendment assures a right to jury trial will cast doubt on the integrity of every trial conducted without a jury. Plainly, this is not the import of our holding. Our conclusion is that in the American States, as in the federal judicial system, a general grant of jury trial for serious offenses is a fundamental right, essential for preventing miscarriages of justice and for assuring that fair trials are provided for all defendants. We would not assert, however, that every criminal trial — or any particular trial — held before a judge alone is unfair or that a defendant may never be as fairly treated by a judge as he would be by a jury. Thus we hold no constitutional doubts about the practices, common in both federal and state courts, of accepting waivers of jury trial and prosecuting petty crimes without extending a right to jury trial.

II. Louisiana's final contention is that even if it must grant jury trials in serious criminal cases, the conviction before us is valid and constitutional because here the petitioner was tried for simple battery and was sentenced to only 60 days in the parish prison. We are not persuaded. It is doubtless true that there is a category of petty crimes or offenses which is not subject to the Sixth Amendment jury trial provision and should not be subject to the Fourteenth Amendment jury trial requirement here applied to the States. Crimes carrying possible penalties up to six months do not require a jury trial if they otherwise qualify as petty offenses, Cheff v. Schnackenberg, 384 U.S. 373, 86 S.Ct. 1523, 16 L.Ed.2d 629 (1966). But the penalty authorized for a particular crime is of major relevance in determining whether it is serious or not and may in itself, if severe enough, subject the trial to the mandates of the Sixth Amendment. District of Columbia v. Clawans, 300 U.S. 617, 57 S.Ct. 660, 81 L.Ed. 843 (1937). The penalty authorized by the law of the locality may be taken "as a gauge of its social and ethical judgments." 300 U.S., at 628, 57 S.Ct., at 663, of the crime in question. In Clawans the defendant was jailed for 60 days, but it was the 90-day authorized punishment on which the Court focused in determining that the offense was not one for which the Constitution assured trial by jury.   In the case before us the Legislature of Louisiana has made simple battery a criminal offense punishable by imprisonment for up to two years and a fine. The question, then, is whether a crime carrying such a penalty is an offense which Louisiana may insist on trying without a jury.

We think not. Reversed and remanded.

Mr. Justice BLACK, with whom Mr. Justice DOUGLAS joins, concurring.

With this holding I agree for reasons given by the Court.   I also agree because of reasons given in my dissent in Adamson v. People of State of California, 332 U.S. 47, 68, 67 S.Ct. 1672, 1683, 91 L.Ed. 1903.   In that dissent, at 90, 67 S.Ct., at 1695, I took the position, contrary to the holding in Twining v. State of New Jersey, 211 U.S. 78, 29 S.Ct. 14, 53 L.Ed. 97, that the Fourteenth Amendment made all of the provisions of the Bill of Rights applicable to the States. This Court in Palko v. State of Connecticut, 302 U.S. 319, 323, 58 S.Ct. 149, 151, 82 L.Ed. 288, decided in 1937, although saying "[t]here is no such general rule," went on to add that the Fourteenth Amendment may make it unlawful for a State to abridge by its statutes the "freedom of speech which the First Amendment safeguards against encroachment by the Congress . . . or the like freedom of the press . . . or the free exercise of religion . . . or the right of peaceable assembly . . . or the right of one accused of crime to the benefit of counsel. . . .   In these and other situations immunities that are valid as against the federal government by force of the specific pledges of particular amendments have been found to be implicit in the concept of ordered liberty, and thus, through the Fourteenth Amendment, become valid as against the states."   Id., at 324-325, 58 S.Ct., at 151-152.

And the Palko opinion went on to explain, 302 U.S., at 326, 58 S.Ct., at 152, that certain Bill of Rights' provisions were made applicable to the States by bringing them "within the Fourteenth Amendment by a process of absorption." Thus Twining v. State of New Jersey, supra, refused to hold that any one of the Bill of Rights' provisions was made applicable to the States by the Fourteenth Amendment, but Palko, which must be read as overruling Twining on this point, concluded that the Bill of Rights Amendments that are "implicit in the concept of ordered liberty" are "absorbed" by the Fourteenth as protections against state invasion.   In this situation I said in Adamson v. People of State of California, 332 U.S., at 89, 67 S.Ct., at 1695 that, while "I would . . . extend to all the people of the nation the complete protection of the Bill of Rights," that "[i]f the choice must be between the selective process of the Palko decision applying some of the Bill of Rights to the States, or the Twining rule applying none of them, I would choose the Palko selective process." See Gideon v. Wainwright, 372 U.S. 335, 83 S.Ct. 792, 9 L.Ed.2d 799.   And I am very happy to support this selective process through which our Court has since the Adamson case held most of the specific Bill of Rights' protections applicable to the States to the same extent they are applicable to the Federal Government.   Among these are the right to trial by jury decided today, the right against compelled self-incrimination, the right to counsel, the right to compulsory process for witnesses, the right to confront witnesses, the right to a speedy and public trial, and the right to be free from unreasonable searches and seizures.

All of these holdings making Bill of Rights' provisions applicable as such to the States mark, of course, a departure from the Twining doctrine holding that none of those provisions were enforceable as such against the States.   The dissent in this case, however, makes a spirited and forceful defense of that now discredited doctrine.   I do not believe that it is necessary for me to repeat the historical and logical reasons for my challenge to the Twining holding contained in my Adamson dissent and Appendix to it.   What I wrote there in 1947 was the product of years of study and research. My appraisal of the legislative history followed 10 years of legislative experience as a Senator of the United States, not a bad way, I suspect, to learn the value of what is said in legislative debates, committee discussions, committee reports, and various other steps taken in the course of passage of bills, resolutions, and proposed constitutional amendments. My Brother Harlan's objections to my Adamson dissent history, like that of most of the objectors, relies most heavily on a criticism written by Professor Charles Fairman and published in the Stanford Law Review. 2 Stan.L.Rev. 5 (1949). I have read and studied this article extensively, including the historical references, but am compelled to add that in my view it has completely failed to refute the inferences and arguments that I suggested in my Adamson dissent. Professor Fairman's "history" relies very heavily on what was not said in the state legislatures that passed on the Fourteenth Amendment. Instead of relying on this kind of negative pregnant, my legislative experience has convinced me that it is far wiser to rely on what was said, and most importantly, said by the men who actually sponsored the Amendment in the Congress. I know from my years in the United States Senate that it is to men like Congressman Bingham, who steered the Amendment through the House, and Senator Howard, who introduced it in the Senate, that members of Congress look when they seek the real meaning of what is being offered. And they vote for or against a bill based on what the sponsors of that bill and those who oppose it tell them it means. The historical appendix to my Adamson dissent leaves no doubt in my mind that both its sponsors and those who opposed it believed the Fourteenth Amendment made the first eight Amendments of the Constitution (the Bill of Rights) applicable to the States.

In addition to the adoption of Professor Fairman's "history," American citizenship could there be than that privilege to claim the protections of our great Bill of Rights? I suggest that any reading of "privileges or immunities of citizens of the United States" which excludes the Bill of Rights' safeguards renders the words of this section of the Fourteenth Amendment meaningless. Senator Howard, who introduced the Fourteenth Amendment for passage in the Senate, certainly read the words this way. Although I have cited his speech at length in my Adamson dissent appendix, I believe it would be worthwhile to reproduce a part of it here.

While I do not wish at this time to discuss at length my disagreement with Brother Harlan's forthright and frank restatement of the now discredited Twining doctrine, I do want to point out what appears to me to be the basic difference between us. His view, as was indeed the view of Twining, is that "due process is an evolving concept" and therefore that it entails a "gradual process of judicial inclusion and exclusion" to ascertain those "immutable principles . . . of free government which no member of the Union may disregard." Thus the Due Process Clause is treated as prescribing no specific and clearly ascertainable constitutional command that judges must obey in interpreting the Constitution, but rather as leaving judges free to decide at any particular time whether a particular rule or judicial formulation embodies an "immutable principl[e] of free government" or is "implicit in the concept of ordered liberty," or whether certain conduct "shocks the judge's conscience" or runs counter to some other similar, undefined and undefinable standard. Thus due process, according to my Brother Harlan, is to be a phrase with no permanent meaning, but one which is found to shift from time to time in accordance with judges' predilections and understandings of what is best for the country. If due process means this, the Fourteenth Amendment, in my opinion, might as well have been written that "no person shall be deprived of life, liberty or property except by laws that the judges of the United States Supreme Court shall find to be consistent with the immutable principles of free government." It is impossible for me to believe that such unconfined power is given to judges in our Constitution that is a written one in order to limit governmental power.

Another tenet of the Twining doctrine as restated by my Brother Harlan is that "due process of law requires only fundamental fairness." But the "fundamental fairness" test is one on a par with that of shocking the conscience of the Court. Each of such tests depends entirely on the particular judge's idea of ethics and morals instead of requiring him to depend on the boundaries fixed by the written words of the Constitution. Nothing in the history of the phrase "due process of law" suggests that constitutional controls are to depend on any particular judge's sense of values. The origin of the Due Process Clause is Chapter 39 of Magna Carta which declares that "No free man shall be taken, outlawed, banished, or in any way destroyed, nor will We proceed against or prosecute him, except by the lawful judgment of his peers and by the law of the land." As early as 1354 the words "due process of law" were used in an English statute interpreting Magna Carta, and by the end of the 14th century "due process of law" and "law of the land" were interchangeable. Thus the origin of this clause was an attempt by those who wrote Magna Carta to do away with the so-called trials of that period where people were liable to sudden arrest and summary conviction in courts and by judicial commissions with no sure and definite procedural protections and under laws that might have been improvised to try their particular cases. Chapter 39 of Magna Carta was a guarantee that the government would take neither life, liberty, nor property without a trial in accord with the law of the land that already existed at the time the alleged offense was committed. This means that the Due Process Clause gives all Americans, whoever they are and wherever they happen to be, the right to be tried by independent and unprejudiced courts using established procedures and applying valid pre-existing laws. There is not one word of legal history that justifies making the term "due process of law" mean a guarantee of a trial free from laws and conduct which the courts deem at the time to be "arbitrary," "unreasonable," "unfair," or "contrary to civilized standards." The due process of law standard for a trial is one in accordance with the Bill of Rights and laws passed pursuant to constitutional power, guaranteeing to all alike a trial under the general law of the land.

Finally I want to add that I am not bothered by the argument that applying the Bill of Rights to the States "according to the same standards that protect those personal rights against federal encroachment," interferes with our concept of federalism in that it may prevent States from trying novel social and economic experiments. I have never believed that under the guise of federalism the States should be able to experiment with the protections afforded our citizens through the Bill of Rights. As Justice Goldberg said so wisely in his concurring opinion in Pointer v. State of Texas, 380 U.S. 400, 85 S.Ct. 1065, 13 L.Ed.2d 923:

> To deny to the States the power to impair a fundamental constitutional right is not to increase federal power, but, rather, to limit the power of both federal and state governments in favor of safeguarding the fundamental rights and liberties of the individual. In my view this promotes rather than undermines the basic policy of avoiding excess concentration of power in government, federal or state, which underlies our concepts of federalism. 380 U.S., at 414, 85 S.Ct., at 1073.

It seems to me totally inconsistent to advocates on the one hand, the power of this Court to strike down any state law or practice which it finds "unreasonable" or "unfair" and, on the other hand, urge that the States be given maximum power to develop their own laws and procedures. Yet the due process approach of my Brothers Harlan and Fortas (see other concurring opinion, post, p. 1459) does just that since in effect it restricts the States to practices which a majority of this Court is willing to approve on a case-by-case basis. No one is more concerned than I that the States be allowed to use the full scope of their powers as their citizens sees fit. And that is why I have continually fought against the expansion of this Court's authority over the States through the use of a broad, general interpretation of due process that permits judges to strike down state laws they do not like.

In closing I want to emphasize that I believe as strongly as ever that the Fourteenth Amendment was intended to make the Bill of Rights applicable to the States.

Mr. Justice HARLAN, whom Mr. Justice STEWART joins, dissenting.

The States have always borne primary responsibility for operating the machinery of criminal justice within their borders, and adapting it to their particular circumstances. In exercising this responsibility, each State is compelled to conform its procedures to the requirements of the Federal Constitution. The Due Process Clause of the Fourteenth Amendment requires that those procedures be fundamentally fair in all respects. It does not, in my view, impose or encourage nationwide uniformity for its own sake; it does not command adherence to forms that happen to be old; and it does not impose on the States the rules that may be in force in the federal courts except where such rules are also found to be essential to basic fairness.

The Court's approach to this case is an uneasy and illogical compromise among the views of various Justices on how the Due Process Clause should be interpreted. The Court does not say that those who framed the Fourteenth Amendment intended to make the Sixth Amendment applicable to the States. And the Court concedes that it finds nothing unfair about the procedure by which the present appellant was tried. Nevertheless, the Court reverses his conviction: it holds, for some reason not apparent to me, that the Due Process Clause incorporates the particular clause of the Sixth Amendment that requires trial by jury in federal criminal cases — including, as I read its opinion, the sometimes trivial accompanying baggage of judicial interpretation in federal contexts. I have raised my voice many times before against the Court's continuing undiscriminating insistence upon fastening on the States federal notions of criminal justice, and I must do so again in this instance. With all respect, the Court's approach and its reading of history are altogether topsy-turvy.

I. In my view, often expressed elsewhere, the first section of the Fourteenth Amendment was meant neither to incorporate, nor to be limited to, the specific guarantees of the first eight Amendments. The overwhelming historical evidence marshalled by Professor Fairman demonstrates, to me conclusively, that the Congressmen and state legislators who wrote, debated, and ratified the Fourteenth Amendment did not think they were "incorporating" the Bill of Rights and the very breadth and generality of the Amendment's provisions suggest that its authors did not suppose that the Nation would always be limited to mid-19th century conceptions of "liberty" and "due process of law" but that the increasing experience and evolving conscience of the American people would add new "intermediate premises." In short, neither history, nor sense, supports using the Fourteenth Amendment to put the States in a constitutional straitjacket with respect to their own development in the administration of criminal or civil law.

Although I therefore fundamentally disagree with the total incorporation view of the Fourteenth Amendment, it seems to me that such a position does at least have the virtue, lacking in the Court's selective incorporation approach, of internal consistency: we look to the Bill of Rights, word for word, clause for clause, precedent for precedent because, it is said, the men who wrote the Amendment wanted it that way.   For those who do not accept this "history," a different source of "intermediate premises" must be found.   The Bill of Rights is not necessarily irrelevant to the search for guidance in interpreting the Fourteenth Amendment, but the reason for and the nature of its relevance must be articulated.

Apart from the approach taken by the absolute incorporationists, I can see only one method of analysis that has any internal logic. That is to start with the words "liberty" and "due process of law" and attempt to define them in a way that accords with American traditions and our system of government.   This approach, involving a much more discriminating process of adjudication than does "incorporation," is, albeit difficult, the one that was followed throughout the 19th and most of the present century.   It entails a "gradual process of judicial inclusion and exclusion," seeking, with due recognition of constitutional tolerance for state experimentation and disparity, to ascertain those "immutable principles . . . of justice which inhere in the very idea of free government which no member of the Union may disregard."   Due process was not restricted to rules fixed in the past, for that "would be to deny every quality of the law but its age, and to render it incapable of progress or improvement."   Nor did it impose nationwide uniformity in details, for "[t]he Fourteenth Amendment does not profess to secure to all persons in the United States the benefit of the same laws and the same remedies.   Great diversities in these respects may exist in two States separated only by an imaginary line.   On one side of this line there may be a right of trial by jury, and on the other side no such right.   Each State prescribes its own modes of judicial proceeding."

Through this gradual process, this Court sought to define "liberty" by isolating freedoms that Americans of the past and of the present considered more important than any suggested countervailing public objective.   The Court also, by interpretation of the phrase "due process of law," enforced the Constitution's guarantee that no State may imprison an individual except by fair and impartial procedures.

The relationship of the Bill of Rights to this "gradual process" seems to me to be twofold.   In the first place it has long been clear that the Due Process Clause imposes some restrictions on state action that parallel Bill of Rights restrictions on federal action. Second, and more important than this accidental overlap, is the fact that the Bill of Rights is evidence, at various points, of the content Americans find in the term 'liberty' and of American standards of fundamental fairness.

Today's Court still remains unwilling to accept the total incorporationists' view of the history of the Fourteenth Amendment. This, if accepted, would afford a cogent reason for applying the Sixth Amendment to the States.   The Court is also, apparently, unwilling to face the task of determining whether denial of trial by jury in the situation before us, or in other situations, is fundamentally unfair.   Consequently, the Court has compromised on the ease of the incorporationist position, without its internal logic.   It has simply assumed that the question before us is whether the Jury Trial Clause of the Sixth Amendment should be incorporated into the Fourteenth, jot-for-jot and case-for-case, or ignored. Then the Court merely declares that the clause in question is "in" rather than "out."

The Court has justified neither its starting place nor its conclusion.   If the problem is to discover and articulate the rules of fundamental fairness in criminal proceedings, there is no reason to assume that the whole body of rules developed in this Court constituting

Sixth Amendment jury trial must be regarded as a unit. The requirement of trial by jury in federal criminal cases has given rise to numerous subsidiary questions respecting the exact scope and content of the right. It surely cannot be that every answer the Court has given, or will give, to such a question is attributable to the Founders; or even that every rule announced carries equal conviction of this Court; still less can it be that every such subprinciple is equally fundamental to ordered liberty.

Examples abound. I should suppose it obviously fundamental to fairness that a "jury" means an "impartial jury." I should think it equally obvious that the rule, imposed long ago in the federal courts, that "jury" means "jury of exactly twelve," is not fundamental to anything: there is no significance except to mystics in the number 12. Again, trial by jury has been held to require a unanimous verdict of jurors in the federal courts, although unanimity has not been found essential to liberty in Britain, where the requirement has been abandoned.

Even if I could agree that the question before us is whether Sixth Amendment jury trial is totally "in" or totally "out," I can find in the Court's opinion no real reasons for concluding that it should be "in." The basis for differentiating among clauses in the Bill of Rights cannot be that only some clauses are in the Bill of Rights, or that only some are old and much praised, or that only some have played an important role in the development of federal law. These things are true of all. The Court says that some clauses are more "fundamental" than others, but it turns out to be using this word in a sense that would have astonished Mr. Justice Cardozo and which, in addition, is of no help. The word does not mean "analytically critical to procedural fairness" for no real analysis of the role of the jury in making procedures fair is even attempted. Instead, the word turns out to mean "old," "much praised," and "found in the Bill of Rights." The definition of "fundamental" thus turns out to be circular.

II. Since, as I see it, the Court has not even come to grips with the issues in this case, it is necessary to start from the beginning. When a criminal defendant contends that his state conviction lacked "due process of law," the question before this Court, in my view, is whether he was denied any element of fundamental procedural fairness. Believing, as I do, that due process is an evolving concept and that old principles are subject to re-evaluation in light of later experience, I think it appropriate to deal on its merits with the question whether Louisiana denied appellant due process of law when it tried him for simple assault without a jury.

The obvious starting place is the fact that this Court has, in the past, held that trial by jury is not a requisite of criminal due process. Numerous [cases] in this Court have assumed that jury trial is not fundamental to ordered liberty.

Although it is of course open to this Court to re-examine these decisions, I can see no reason why they should now be overturned. It can hardly be said that time has altered the question, or brought significant new evidence to bear upon it. The virtues and defects of the jury system have been hotly debated for a long time, and are hotly debated today, without significant change in the lines of argument.

The argument that jury trial is not a requisite of due process is quite simple. The central proposition of Palko, supra, a proposition to which I would adhere, is that "due process of law" requires only that criminal trials be fundamentally fair. As stated above, apart from the theory that it was historically intended as a mere shorthand for the Bill of Rights, I do not see what else "due process of law" can intelligibly be thought to mean. If due process of law requires only fundamental fairness, then the inquiry in each case must be whether a state trial process was a fair one. The Court has held, properly I think, that in an adversary process it is a requisite of fairness, for which there is no adequate substitute, that a criminal defendant be afforded a right to counsel and to cross-examine opposing witnesses. But it simply has not been demonstrated, nor, I think, can it be demonstrated, that trial by jury is the only fair means of resolving issues of fact.

Indeed, even if I were persuaded that trial by jury is a fundamental right in some criminal cases, I could see nothing fundamental in the rule, not yet formulated by the Court, that places the prosecution of appellant for simple battery within the category of "jury crimes" rather than "petty crimes." Trial by jury is ancient, it is true. Almost equally ancient, however, is the discovery that, because of it, "the King's most loving Subjects are much travailed and otherwise encumbered in coming and keeping of the said six Weeks Sessions, to their Costs, Charges, Unquietness."

As a result, through the long course of British and American history, summary procedures have been used in a varying category of lesser crimes as a flexible response to the burden jury trial would otherwise impose.

The point is not that many offenses that English-speaking communities have, at one time or another, regarded as triable without a jury are more serious, and carry more serious penalties, than the one involved here. The point is rather that until today few people would have thought the exact location of the line mattered very much. There is no obvious reason why a jury trial is a requisite of fundamental fairness when the charge is robbery, and not a requisite of fairness when the same defendant, for the same actions, is charged with assault and petty theft. The reason for the historic exception for relatively minor crimes is the obvious one: the burden of jury trial was thought to outweigh its marginal advantages. Exactly why the States should not be allowed to make continuing adjustments, based on the state of their criminal dockets and the difficulty of summoning jurors, simply escapes me.

In sum, there is a wide range of views on the desirability of trial by jury, and on the ways to make it most effective when it is used; there is also considerable variation from State to State in local conditions such as the size of the criminal caseload, the ease or difficulty of summoning jurors, and other trial conditions bearing on fairness. We have before us, therefore, an almost perfect example of a situation in which the celebrated dictum of Mr. Justice Brandeis should be invoked. It is, he said, "one of the happy incidents of the federal system that a single courageous state may, if its citizens choose, serve as a laboratory. . . ." New State Ice Co. v. Liebmann, 285 U.S. 262, 280, 311, 52 S.Ct. 371, 386, 76 L.Ed. 747 (dissenting opinion).

This Court, other courts, and the political process are available to correct any experiments in criminal procedure that prove fundamentally unfair to defendants. That is not what is being done today: instead, and quite without reason, the Court has chosen to impose upon every State one means of trying criminal cases; it is a good means, but it is not the only fair means, and it is not demonstrably better than the alternatives States might devise.

I would affirm the judgment of the Supreme Court of Louisiana.

———

Comments on *Duncan*. Justice Black's boast, cited earlier and taken from his *Duncan* concurrence, "I am very happy to support this selective process through which our Court has since the Adamson test held most of the specific Bill of Right's protections applicable to the states," is fairly accurate. To those rights enumerated in *Duncan*, we can add the fifth amendment prohibition on "double jeopardy," Benton v. Maryland, 395 U.S. 784 (1969), overruling *Palko*; the eighth amendment prohibition on "cruel and unusual punishment," Robinson v. California, 370 U.S. 660 (1962); and the eighth amendment prohibition on "excessive" bail, Schilb v. Kuebel, 404 U.S. 357 (1971). The only provisions of the first eight amendments that have not been incorporated are the second and third amendments, the fifth amendment requirement of grand jury indictment, and the seventh amendment right to a jury trial in civil cases.

The Court in *Duncan* concludes, "[We] hold that the Fourteenth Amendment guarantees a right of jury trial in all criminal cases which — were they to be tried in a federal court — would come within the Sixth Amendment's guarantee."   Is this statement still viable after the findings in the cases that follow: *Williams*, *Apodaca*, and *Burch*?   Or was *Duncan* overruled?

WILLIAMS v. FLORIDA
399 U.S. 78 (1970)

Mr. Justice WHITE delivered the opinion of the Court.

Petitioner [f]iled a pretrial motion to impanel a 12-man jury instead of the six-man jury provided by Florida law in all but capital cases. That motion too was denied. Petitioner was convicted as charged and was sentenced to life imprisonment.   The District Court of Appeal affirmed, rejecting petitioner's claims that his Fifth and Sixth Amendment rights had been violated.   We granted certiorari. 396 U.S. 955, 90 S.Ct. 439, 24 L.Ed.2d 420 (1969).

II. In Duncan v. Louisiana, 391 U.S. 145, 88 S.Ct. 1444, 20 L.Ed.2d 491 (1968), we held that the Fourteenth Amendment guarantees a right to trial by jury in all criminal cases that — were they to be tried in a federal court — would come within the Sixth Amendment's guarantee. Petitioner's trial for robbery on July 3, 1968, clearly falls within the scope of that holding. See Baldwin v. New York, 399 U.S. 66, 90 S.Ct. 1886, 26 N.E.2d 437; DeStefano v. Woods, 392 U.S. 631, 88 S.Ct. 2093, 20 L.Ed.2d 1308 (1968). The question in this case then is whether the constitutional guarantee of a trial by "jury" necessarily requires trial by exactly 12 persons, rather than some lesser number — in this case six.   We hold that the 12-man panel is not a necessary ingredient of 'trial by jury,' and that respondent's refusal to impanel more than the six members provided for by Florida law did not violate petitioner's Sixth Amendment rights as applied to the States through the Fourteenth.

We had occasion in Duncan v. Louisiana, supra, to review briefly the oft-told history of the development of trial by jury in criminal cases. That history revealed a long tradition attaching great importance to the concept of relying on a body of one's peers to determine guilt or innocence as a safeguard against arbitrary law enforcement.   That same history, however, affords little insight into the considerations that gradually led the size of that body to be generally fixed at 12.   Some have suggested that the number 12 was fixed upon simply because that was the number of the presentment jury from the hundred, from which the petit jury developed. Other, less circular but more fanciful reasons for the number 12 have been given, "but they were all brought forward after the number was fixed," and rest on little more than mystical or superstitious insights into the significance of "12." Lord Coke's explanation that the "number of twelve is much respected in holy writ, as 12 apostles, 12 stones, 12 tribes, etc.," is typical. In short, while sometime in the 14th century the size of the jury at common law came to be fixed generally at 12, that particular feature of the jury system appears to have been a historical accident, unrelated to the great purposes which gave rise to the jury in the first place. The question before us is whether this accidental feature of the jury has been immutably codified into our Constitution.

This Court's earlier decisions have assumed an affirmative answer to this question. The leading case so construing the Sixth Amendment is Thompson v. Utah, 170 U.S. 343, 18 S.Ct. 620, 42 L.Ed. 1061 (1898). There the defendant had been tried and convicted by a 12-man jury for a crime committed in the Territory of Utah. A new trial was granted, but by that time Utah had been admitted as a State. The defendant's new trial proceeded under Utah's Constitution, providing for a jury of only eight members. This Court reversed the resulting conviction, holding that Utah's constitutional provision was an ex post facto law as applied to the defendant. In reaching its conclusion, the Court announced that the Sixth Amendment was applicable to the defendant's trial when Utah was a Territory, and that the jury referred to in the Amendment was a jury "constituted, as it was at common law, of twelve persons, neither more nor less." 170 U.S., at 349, 18 S.Ct., at 622. Arguably unnecessary for the result, this announcement was supported simply by referring to the Magna Carta, and by quoting passages from treatises which noted — what has already been seen — that at common law the jury did indeed consist of 12. Noticeably absent was any discussion of the essential step in the argument: namely, that every feature of the jury as it existed at common law — whether incidental or essential to that institution — was necessarily included in the Constitution wherever that document referred to a "jury." Subsequent decisions have reaffirmed the announcement in Thompson often in dictum and usually by relying — where there was any discussion of the issue at all — solely on the fact that the common-law jury consisted of 12. See Patton v. United States, 281 U.S. 276, 288, 50 S.Ct. 253, 254, 74 L.Ed. 854 (1930); Rassmussen v. United States, 197 U.S. 516, 519, 25 S.Ct. 514, 515, 49 L.Ed. 862 (1905); Maxwell v. Dow, 176 U.S. 581, 586, 20 S.Ct. 448, 450, 451, 44 L.Ed. 597 (1900).

While "the intent of the Framers" is often an elusive quarry, the relevant constitutional history casts considerable doubt on the easy assumption in our past decisions that if a given feature existed in a jury at common law in 1789, then it was necessarily preserved in the Constitution. Provisions for jury trial were first placed in the Constitution in Article III's provision that "[t]he Trial of all Crimes . . . shall be by Jury; and such Trial shall be held in the State where the said Crimes shall have been committed." The "very scanty history (of this provision) in the records of the Constitutional Convention" sheds little light either way on the intended correlation between Article III's "jury" and the features of the jury at common law. Indeed, pending and after the adoption of the Constitution, fears were expressed that Article III's provision failed to preserve the common-law right to be tried by a "jury of the vicinage." That concern, as well as the concern to preserve the right to jury in civil as well as criminal cases, furnished part of the impetus for introducing amendments to the Constitution that ultimately resulted in the jury trial provisions of the Sixth and Seventh Amendments. As introduced by James Madison in the House, the Amendment relating to jury trial in criminal cases would have provided that:

> The trial of all crimes . . . shall be by an impartial jury of freeholders of the vicinage, with the requisite of unanimity for conviction, of the right of challenge, and other accustomed requisites. . . .

The Amendment passed the House in substantially this form, but after more than a week of debate in the Senate it returned to the House considerably altered. While records of the actual debates that occurred in the Senate are not available, a letter from Madison to Edmund Pendleton on September 14, 1789, indicates that one of the Senate's major objections was to the "vicinage" requirement in the House version. A conference committee was appointed. As reported in a second letter by Madison on September 23, 1789, the Senate remained opposed to the vicinage requirement, partly because in its view the then pending judiciary bill — which was debated at the same time as the Amendments — adequately preserved the common-law vicinage feature, making it unnecessary to freeze that requirement into the Constitution. "The Senate," wrote Madison: "are . . . inflexible in opposing a definition of the locality of Juries. The vicinage they contend is either too vague or too strict a term; too vague if depending on limits to be fixed by the pleasure of the law, too strict if limited to the county. It was proposed to insert after the word Juries, "with the accustomed requisites," leaving the definition to be construed according to the judgment of professional men. Even this could not be obtained. . . . The Senate suppose, also, that the provision for vicinage in the Judiciary bill will sufficiently quiet the fears which called for an amendment on this point."

The version that finally emerged from the Committee was the version that ultimately became the Sixth Amendment, ensuring an accused: "the right to a speedy and public trial, by an impartial jury of the State and district wherein the crime shall have been committed, which district shall have been previously ascertained by law. . . ."

Gone were the provisions spelling out such common-law features of the jury as "unanimity," or "the accustomed requisites." And the "vicinage" requirement itself had been replaced by wording that reflected a compromise between broad and narrow definitions of that term, and that left Congress the power to determine the actual size of the "vicinage" by its creation of judicial districts.

Three significant features may be observed in this sketch of the background of the Constitution's jury trial provisions. First, even though the vicinage requirement was as much a feature of the common-law jury as was the 12-man requirement, the mere reference to "trial by jury" in Article III was not interpreted to include that feature. Indeed, as the subsequent debates over the Amendments indicate, disagreement arose over whether the feature should be included at all in its common-law sense, resulting in the compromise described above. Second, provisions that would have explicitly tied the "jury" concept to the "accustomed requisites" of the time were eliminated. Such action is concededly open to the explanation that the "accustomed requisites" were thought to be already included in the concept of a "jury." But that explanation is no more plausible than the contrary one: that the deletion had some substantive effect. Indeed, given the clear expectation that a substantive change would be effected by the inclusion or deletion of an explicit "vicinage" requirement, the latter explanation is, if anything, the more plausible. Finally, contemporary legislative and constitutional provisions indicate that where Congress wanted to leave no doubt that it was incorporating existing common-law features of the jury system, it knew how to use express language to that effect. Thus, the Judiciary bill, signed by the President on the same day that the House and Senate finally agreed on the form of the Amendments to be submitted to the States, provided in certain cases for the narrower "vicinage" requirements that the House had wanted to include in the Amendments. And the Seventh Amendment, providing for jury trial in civil cases, explicitly added that "no fact tried by a jury, shall be otherwise re-examined in any Court of the United States, than according to the rules of the common law."

We do not pretend to be able to divine precisely what the word "jury" imported to the Framers, the First Congress, or the States in 1789. It may well be that the usual expectation was that the jury would consist of 12, and that hence, the most likely conclusion to be drawn is simply that little thought was actually given to the specific question we face today. But there is absolutely no indication in "the intent of the Framers" of an explicit decision to equate the constitutional and common-law characteristics of the jury. Nothing in this history suggests, then, that we do violence to the letter of the Constitution by turning to other than purely historical considerations to determine which features of the jury system, as it existed at common law, were preserved in the Constitution. The relevant inquiry, as we see it, must be the function that the particular feature performs and its relation to the purposes of the jury trial. Measured by this standard, the 12-man requirement cannot be regarded as an indispensable component of the Sixth Amendment.

The purpose of the jury trial, as we noted in Duncan, is to prevent oppression by the Government. "Providing an accused with the right to be tried by a jury of his peers gave him an inestimable safeguard against the corrupt or overzealous prosecutor and against the compliant, biased, or eccentric judge." Duncan v. Louisiana, supra, 391 U.S., at 156, 88 S.Ct., at 1451. Given this purpose, the essential feature of a jury obviously lies in the interposition between the accused and his accuser of the commonsense judgment of a group of laymen, and in the community participation and shared responsibility that results from that group's determination of guilt or innocence. The performance of this role is not a function of the particular number of the body that makes up the jury. To be sure, the number should probably be large enough to promote group deliberation, free from outside attempts at intimidation, and to provide a fair possibility for obtaining a representatives cross-section of the community. But we find little reason to think that these goals are in any meaningful sense less likely to be achieved when the jury numbers six, than when it numbers 12 — particularly if the requirement of unanimity is retained. And, certainly the reliability of the jury as a factfinder hardly seems likely to be a function of its size.

It might be suggested that the 12-man jury gives a defendant a greater advantage since he has more "chances" of finding a juror who will insist on acquittal and thus prevent conviction. But the advantage might just as easily belong to the State, which also needs only one juror out of twelve insisting on guilt to prevent acquittal. What few experiments have occurred — usually in the civil area — indicate that there is no discernible difference between the results reached by the two different-sized juries. In short, neither currently available evidence nor theory suggests that the 12-man jury is necessarily more advantageous to the defendant than a jury composed of fewer members.

Similarly, while in theory the number of viewpoints represented on a randomly selected jury ought to increase as the size of the jury increases, in practice the difference between the 12-man and the six-man jury in terms of the cross-section of the community represented seems likely to be negligible. Even the 12-man jury cannot insure representation of every distinct voice in the community, particularly given the use of the peremptory challenge. As long as arbitrary exclusions of a particular class from the jury rolls are forbidden, see, e.g., Carter v. Jury Commission, 396 U.S. 320, 329-330, 90 S.Ct. 518, 523, 24 L.Ed.2d 549 (1970), the concern that the cross-section will be significantly diminished if the jury is decreased in size from 12 to six seems an unrealistic one.

We conclude, in short, as we began: the fact that the jury at common law was composed of precisely 12 is a historical accident, unnecessary to effect the purposes of the jury system and wholly without significance "except to mystics." Duncan v. Louisiana, supra, 391 U.S., at 182, 88 S.Ct. at 1466 (Harlan, J., dissenting). To read the Sixth

Amendment as forever codifying a feature so incidental to the real purpose of the Amendment is to ascribe a blind formalism to the Framers which would require considerably more evidence than we have been able to discover in the history and language of the Constitution or in the reasoning of our past decisions. We do not mean to intimate that legislatures can never have good reasons for concluding that the 12-man jury is preferable to the smaller jury, or that such conclusions — reflected in the provisions of most States and in our federal system — are in any sense unwise. Legislatures may well have their own views about the relative value of the larger and smaller juries, and may conclude that, wholly apart from the jury's primary function, it is desirable to spread the collective responsibility for the determination of guilt among the larger group. In capital cases, for example, it appears that no State provides for less than 12 jurors — a fact that suggests implicit recognition of the value of the larger body as a means of legitimating society's decision to impose the death penalty. Our holding does no more than leave these considerations to Congress and the States, unrestrained by an interpretation of the Sixth Amendment that would forever dictate the precise number that can constitute a jury. Consistent with this holding, we conclude that petitioner's Sixth Amendment rights, as applied to the States through the Fourteenth Amendment, were not violated by Florida's decision to provide a six-man rather than a 12-man jury. The judgment of the Florida District Court of Appeal is affirmed.

BURCH v. LOUISIANA
441 U.S. 130 (1979)

Mr. Justice REHNQUIST delivered the opinion of the Court.

The Louisiana Constitution and Code of Criminal Procedure provide that criminal cases in which the punishment imposed may be confinement for a period in excess of six months "shall be tried before a jury of six persons, five of whom must concur to render a verdict." We granted certiorari to decide whether conviction by a nonunanimous six-person jury in a state criminal trial for a nonpetty offense as contemplated by these provisions of Louisiana law violates the rights of an accused to trial by jury guaranteed by the Sixth and Fourteenth Amendments. 439 U.S. 925, 99 S.Ct. 307, 58 L.Ed.2d 317 (1978).

Petitioners, an individual and a Louisiana corporation, were jointly charged in two counts with the exhibition of two obscene motion pictures. Pursuant to Louisiana law, they were tried before a six-person jury, which found both petitioners guilty as charged. A poll of the jury after verdict indicated that the jury had voted unanimously to convict petitioner Wrestle, Inc., and had voted 5-1 to convict petitioner Burch. Burch was sentenced to two consecutive 7-month prison terms, which were suspended, and fined $1,000; Wrestle, Inc., was fined $600 on each count.

[T]he court (Louisiana) concluded that none of this Court's decisions precluded use of a nonunanimous six-person jury. "'If 75 percent concurrence (9/12) was enough for a verdict as determined in Johnson v. Louisiana, 406 U.S. 356, 92 S.Ct. 1620, 32 L.Ed.2d 152 (1972), then requiring 83 percent concurrence (5/6) ought to be within the permissible limits of *Johnson*.'" *Ibid.*, quoting Hargrave, The Declaration of Rights of the Louisiana Constitution of 1974, 35 La.L.Rev. 1, 56 n. 300 (1974). And our recent decision in Ballew v. Georgia, 435 U.S. 223, 98 S.Ct. 1029, 55 L.Ed.2d 234 (1978), striking down a Georgia law allowing conviction by a unanimous five-person jury in nonpetty criminal cases, was distinguishable in the Louisiana Supreme Court's view: "[I]n Williams [v. Florida, 399 U.S.

78, 90 S.Ct. 1893, 26 L.Ed.2d 446 (1970)] the court held that a six-person jury was of sufficient size to promote adequate group deliberation, to insulate members from outside intimidation, and to provide a representative cross-section of the community. These values, which *Ballew* held a five-person jury is inadequate to serve, are not necessarily defeated because the six-person jury's verdict may be rendered by five instead of by six persons." 360 So.2d, at 838.

[We] agree with the Louisiana Supreme Court that the question presented is a "close" one. Nonetheless, we believe that conviction by a nonunanimous six-member jury in a state criminal trial for a nonpetty offense deprives an accused of his constitutional right to trial by jury.

Only in relatively recent years has this Court had to consider the practices of the several States relating to jury size and unanimity. Duncan v. Louisiana, 391 U.S. 145, 88 S.Ct. 1444, 20 L.Ed.2d 491 (1968), marked the beginning of our involvement with such questions. The Court in *Duncan* held that because trial by jury in "serious" criminal cases is "fundamental to the American scheme of justice" and essential to due process of law, the Fourteenth Amendment guarantees a state criminal defendant the right to a jury trial in any case which, if tried in a federal court, would require a jury under the Sixth Amendment. Id., at 149, 158-159, 88 S.Ct., at 1447, 1452-1453.

Two Terms later in Williams v. Florida, 399 U.S. 78, 86, 90 S.Ct. 1893, 1898, 26 L.Ed.2d 446 (1970), the Court held that this constitutional guarantee of trial by jury did not require a State to provide an accused with a jury of 12 members and that Florida did not violate the jury trial rights of criminal defendants charged with nonpetty offenses by affording them jury panels comprised of only 6 persons.

A similar analysis led us to conclude in 1972 that a jury's verdict need not be unanimous to satisfy constitutional requirements, even though unanimity had been the rule at common law. Thus, in Apodaca v. Oregon, 406 U.S. 404, 92 S.Ct. 1628, 32 L.Ed.2d 184 (1972), we upheld a state statute providing that only 10 members of a 12-person jury need concur to render a verdict in certain noncapital cases. In terms of the role of the jury as a safeguard against oppression, the plurality opinion perceived no difference between those juries required to act unanimously and those permitted to act by votes of 10 to 2. Nor was unanimity viewed by the plurality as contributing materially to the exercise of the jury's common-sense judgment or as a necessary precondition to effective application of the requirement that jury panels represent a fair cross section of the community.[9]

Last Term, in Ballew v. Georgia, 435 U.S. 223, 98 S.Ct. 1029, 55 L.Ed.2d 234 (1978), we considered whether a jury of less than six members passes constitutional scrutiny, a question that was explicitly reserved in Williams v. Florida. See 399 U.S., at 91 n. 28, 90 S.Ct., at 1901 n. 28. The Court, in separate opinions, held that conviction by a unanimous five-person jury in a trial for a nonpetty offense deprives an accused of his right to trial by jury. While readily admitting that the line between six members and five was not altogether easy to justify, at least five Members of the Court believed that reducing a jury to five persons in nonpetty cases raised sufficiently substantial doubts as to the fairness of the proceeding and proper functioning of the jury to warrant drawing the line at six. See

---

[9] Mr. Justice Powell concurred in the judgment in Apodaca v. Oregon, 406 U.S., at 366, 92 S.Ct., at 1635. He concluded that although Sixth Amendment history and precedent required jury unanimity in federal trials, the Due Process Clause of the Fourteenth Amendment does not incorporate all the elements of a jury trial required by the Sixth Amendment and does not prevent Oregon from permitting conviction by a verdict of 10-2. Id., at 369-380, 92 S.Ct., at 1637-1642.

435 U.S., at 239, 98 S.Ct., at 1038 (opinion of Blackmun, J.); id., at 245-246, 98 S.Ct., at 1042 (opinion of Powell, J.).[10]

We thus have held that the Constitution permits juries of less than 12 members, but that it requires at least 6.   Ballew v. Georgia, supra; *Williams v. Florida, supra*.   And we have approved the use of certain nonunanimous verdicts in cases involving 12-person juries.   *Apodaca v. Oregon, supra* (10-2); Johnson v. Louisiana, 406 U.S. 356, 92 S.Ct. 1620, 32 L.Ed.2d 152 (1972) (9-3).   These principles are not questioned here.   Rather, this case lies at the intersection of our decisions concerning jury size and unanimity.   As in *Ballew*, we do not pretend the ability to discern *a priori* a bright line below which the number of jurors participating in the trial or in the verdict would not permit the jury to function in the manner required by our prior cases.

[T]his line-drawing process, "although essential, cannot be wholly satisfactory, for it requires attaching different consequences to events which, when they lie near the line, actually differ very little."   Duncan v. Louisiana, supra, at 161, 88 S.Ct., at 1453; see Baldwin v. New York, supra, 399 U.S. at 72-73, 90 S.Ct. at 1890-1891 (plurality opinion). However, much the same reasons that led us in *Ballew* to decide that use of a five-member jury threatened the fairness of the proceeding and the proper role of the jury, lead us to conclude now that conviction for a nonpetty offense by only five members of a six-person jury presents a similar threat to preservation of the substance of the jury trial guarantee and justifies our requiring verdicts rendered by six-person juries to be unanimous.[11]   We are buttressed in this view by the current jury practices of the several States.   It appears that of those States that utilize six-member juries in trials of nonpetty offenses, only two, including Louisiana, also allow nonunanimous verdicts. We think that this near-uniform judgment of the Nation provides a useful guide in delimiting the line between those jury practices that are constitutionally permissible and those that are not.

[W]e think that when a State has reduced the size of its juries to the minimum number of jurors permitted by the Constitution, the additional authorization of nonunanimous verdicts by such juries sufficiently threatens the constitutional principles that led to the establishment of the size threshold that any countervailing interest of the State should yield.

The judgment of the Louisiana Supreme Court affirming the conviction of petitioner Burch is, therefore, reversed, and its judgment affirming the conviction of petitioner Wrestle, Inc., is affirmed.   The case is remanded to the Louisiana Supreme Court for proceedings not inconsistent with this opinion.

II

Our inquiry must focus upon the function served by the jury in contemporary society. Cf. Williams v. Florida, supra, at 99-100, 90 S.Ct., at 1905.   As we said in Duncan, the purpose of trial by jury is to prevent oppression by the Government by providing a "safeguard against the corrupt or overzealous prosecutor and against the complaint, biased, or eccentric judge."   Duncan v. Louisiana, 391 U.S., at 156, 88 S.Ct., at 1451.   "Given this purpose, the essential feature of a jury obviously lies in the interposition between the accused and his accuser of the commonsense judgment of a group of laymen . . ." Williams

---

[10] Mr. Justice White concurred in the judgment on the ground that a jury of fewer than six persons would not satisfy the fair-cross-section requirement of the Sixth and Fourteenth Amendments.   435 U.S., at 245, 98 S.Ct., at 1042.   See also id., at 246, 98 S.Ct., at 1042 (opinion of Brennan, J., joining opinion of Blackmun, J., insofar as it holds that the Sixth and Fourteenth Amendments require juries in criminal trials to contain more than five persons).

[11] We, of course, intimate no view as to the constitutionality of nonunanimous verdicts rendered by juries comprised of more than six members.

v. Florida, supra, 399 U.S., at 100, 90 S.Ct., at 1906.   A requirement of unanimity, however, does not materially contribute to the exercise of this commonsense judgment. As we said in Williams, a jury will come to such a judgment as long as it consists of a group of laymen representative of a cross section of the community who have the duty and the opportunity to deliberate, free from outside attempts at intimidation, on the question of a defendant's guilt.   In terms of this function we perceive no difference between juries required to act unanimously and those permitted to convict or acquit by votes of 10 to two or 11 to one. Requiring unanimity would obviously produce hung juries in some situations where nonunanimous juries will convict or acquit.   But in either case, the interest of the defendant in having the judgment of his peers interposed between himself and the officers of the State who prosecute and judge him is equally well served.

III

Petitioners nevertheless argue that unanimity serves other purposes constitutionally essential to the continued operation of the jury system. Their principal contention is that a Sixth Amendment "jury trial" made mandatory on the States by virtue of the Due Process Clause of the Fourteenth Amendment, Duncan v. Louisiana, supra, should be held to require a unanimous jury verdict in order to give substance to the reasonable-doubt standard otherwise mandated by the Due Process Clause.   See In re Winship, 397 U.S. 358, 363-364, 90 S.Ct. 1068, 1072, 25 L.Ed.2d 368 (1970).

We are quite sure, however, that the Sixth Amendment itself has never been held to require proof beyond a reasonable doubt in criminal cases.   The reasonable-doubt standard developed separately from both the jury trial and the unanimous verdict.   As the Court noted in the Winship case, the rule requiring proof of crime beyond a reasonable doubt did not crystallize in this country until after the Constitution was adopted.   See id., at 361, 90 S.Ct., at 1070.   And in that case, which held such a burden of proof to be constitutionally required, the Court purported to draw no support from the Sixth Amendment.

Petitioners' argument that the Sixth Amendment requires jury unanimity in order to give effect to the reasonable-doubt standard thus founders on the fact that the Sixth Amendment does not require proof beyond a reasonable doubt at all.   The reasonable-doubt argument is rooted, in effect, in due process and has been rejected in Johnson v. Louisiana, 406 U.S. 356, 92 S.Ct. 1620, 32 L.Ed.2d 152.

IV

Petitioners also cite quite accurately a long line of decisions of this Court upholding the principle that the Fourteenth Amendment requires jury panels to reflect a cross section of the community.   They then contend that unanimity is a necessary precondition for effective application of the cross-section requirement, because a rule permitting less than unanimous verdicts will make it possible for convictions to occur without the acquiescence of minority elements within the community.

There are two flaws in this argument. One is petitioners' assumption that every distinct voice in the community has a right to be represented on every jury and a right to prevent conviction of a defendant in any case. All that the Constitution forbids, however, is systematic exclusion of identifiable segments of the community from jury panels and from the juries ultimately drawn from those panels; a defendant may not, for example, challenge the makeup of a jury merely because no members of his race are on the jury, but must prove that his race has been systematically excluded.   No group, in short, has the right to block convictions; it has only the right to participate in the overall legal processes by which criminal guilt and innocence are determined.

We also cannot accept petitioners' second assumption — that minority groups, even when they are represented on a jury, will not adequately represent the viewpoint of those groups simply because they may be outvoted in the final result. They will be present during all deliberations, and their views will be heard. We cannot assume that the majority of the jury will refuse to weigh the evidence and reach a decision upon rational grounds, just as it must now do in order to obtain unanimous verdicts, or that a majority will deprive a man of his liberty on the basis of prejudice when a minority is presenting a reasonable argument in favor of acquittal. We simply find no proof for the notion that a majority will disregard its instructions and cast its votes for guilt or innocence based on prejudice rather than the evidence. Judgment affirmed.

Mr. Justice Powell concluded that:

1. Although on the basis of history and precedent the Sixth Amendment mandates unanimity in a federal jury trial, the Due Process Clause of the Fourteenth Amendment, while requiring States to provide jury trials for serious crimes, does not incorporate all the elements of a jury trial within the meaning of the Sixth Amendment and does not require jury unanimity. Oregon's "ten of twelve" rule is not violative of due process.

2. Nor is the Oregon provision inconsistent with the due process requirement that a jury be drawn from a representative cross section of the community as the jury majority remains under the duty to consider the minority viewpoint in the course of deliberation, and the usual safeguards exist to minimize the possibility of jury irresponsibility.

———————

Comments on Contemporary Incorporation. Was *Duncan* overruled? If a right is deemed a "fundamental principle of liberty and justice which lie at the base of all our civil and political institutions," will it be held applicable to the states? If so, how do you explain the results in the above cited cases in regard to "number of jurors" (*Williams*) and "unanimity" (*Apodaca*, finding unanimity not constitutionally mandated—but see *Ramos* below)? Is the issue in *Burch* "how low you can go"? If *Duncan* has not been overruled, do the decisions in *Williams* and *Apodaca* force the result in *Burch*? What is the difference between a process being "a part of the right itself" as against a conclusion that it is not? How does this question affect contemporary incorporation law?

How would you describe the present standards for incorporating rights and making them applicable to the states?

1. THE SECOND AMENDMENT, AND INCORPORATION PART I

a. "THE RIGHT OF THE PEOPLE TO KEEP . . . ARMS, SHALL NOT BE INFRINGED"

Though this section addresses enumerated rights made incumbent upon the states to enforce through incorporation, the Second Amendment was not a part of this incorporation debate originally—that is until the Supreme Court for the first time in our constitutional history enforced the Second Amendment as a matter of individual right to keep arms unconnected with service in a militia by a 5–4 majority (and, as we shall see below, the right to bear arms, as in carry arms, was found to be just as protected as the right to keep arms during the Court's 2021 term). In *District of Columbia v. Heller, 554 U.S. 570 (2008)* the Court invalidated a D.C. law that effectively banned the possession of handguns. It was later found to be a fundamental right, and a candidate for incorporation to the states in the case following this note, *McDonald v. City of Chicago, 561 U.S. 742 (2010).*

In *Heller*, Justice Scalia, joined by Chief Justice Roberts and Justices Kennedy, Thomas, and Alito, explained the late-breaking nature of the decision: "It should be unsurprising that such a significant matter has been for so long judicially unresolved. For most of our history, the Bill of Rights was not thought applicable to the States, and the Federal Government did not significantly regulate the possession of firearms by law-abiding citizens. Other provisions of the Bill of Rights have similarly remained unilluminated for lengthy periods."

Justice Scalia's majority opinion began by reviewing the linguistic and historical meaning of the right to keep and bear arms, concluding that it confers individual rather than collective rights and is unconnected to militia service: "The first salient feature of the operative clause is that it codifies a 'right of the people.' The unamended Constitution and the Bill of Rights use the phrase 'right of the people' two other times, in the First Amendment's Assembly-and-Petition Clause and in the Fourth Amendment's Search-and-Seizure Clause. The Ninth Amendment uses very similar terminology ('The enumeration in the Constitution, of certain rights, shall not be construed to deny or disparage others retained by the people'). All three of these instances unambiguously refer to individual rights, not 'collective' rights, or rights that may be exercised only through participation in some corporate body. [Reading] the Second Amendment as protecting only the right to 'keep and bear Arms' in an organized militia therefore fits poorly with the operative clause's description of the holder of that right as 'the people.' We start therefore with a strong presumption that the Second Amendment right is exercised individually and belongs to all Americans."

Turning to the meaning of the phrase "to keep and bear Arms," Justice Scalia concluded that "Arms" means the same now as in the 18th century: "The 1773 edition of Samuel Johnson's dictionary defined 'arms' as 'weapons of offence, or armour of defence.' [The] term was applied, then as now, to weapons that were not specifically designed for military use and were not employed in a military capacity." Again, looking to Johnson's dictionary, he concluded further that "the most natural reading of 'keep Arms' in the Second Amendment is to 'have weapons,'" again with no necessary connection to a militia. And while he read the phrase "bear Arms" to imply the carrying of a weapon for the purpose of offensive or defensive confrontation, he suggested that this "in no way connotes participation in a structured military organization." Justice Scalia concluded: "Putting all of these textual elements together, we find that they guarantee the individual right to possess and carry weapons in case of confrontation. This meaning is strongly confirmed by the historical background of the Second Amendment. We look to this because it has always been widely understood that the Second Amendment, like the First and Fourth Amendments, codified a *pre-existing* right. The very text of the Second Amendment implicitly recognizes the pre-existence of the right and declares only that it 'shall not be infringed.'"

Turning to the prefatory clause, "A well regulated Militia, being necessary to the security of a free State," Justice Scalia asked, "Does the preface fit with an operative clause that creates an individual right to keep and bear arms? It fits perfectly, once one knows the history that the founding generation knew. [That] history showed that the way tyrants had eliminated a militia consisting of all the able-bodied men was not by banning the militia but simply by taking away the people's arms, enabling a select militia or standing army to suppress political opponents. This is what had occurred in England that prompted codification of the right to have arms in the English Bill of Rights. [It] is therefore entirely sensible that the Second Amendment's prefatory clause announces the purpose for which the right was codified: to prevent elimination of the militia. The prefatory clause does not suggest that preserving the militia was the only reason Americans valued the ancient right; most undoubtedly thought it even more important for self-defense and hunting. But the threat that the new Federal Government would destroy the citizens' militia by taking away their arms was the reason that right — unlike some other English rights — was codified in a written Constitution."

Finding that post-Ratification history supported this historical account, Justice Scalia then turned to the aftermath of the Civil War, when "there was an outpouring of discussion of the Second Amendment in Congress and in public discourse, as people debated whether and how to secure constitutional rights for newly free slaves. [Blacks] were routinely disarmed by Southern States after the Civil War. Those who opposed these injustices frequently stated that they infringed blacks' constitutional right to keep and bear arms. Needless to say, the claim was not that blacks were being prohibited from carrying arms in an organized state militia. [It] was plainly the understanding in the post-Civil War Congress that the Second Amendment protected an individual right to use arms for self-defense."

Justice Scalia's majority opinion cautioned that, "[l]ike most rights, the right secured by the Second Amendment is not unlimited. From Blackstone through the 19th-century cases, commentators and courts routinely explained that the right was not a right to keep and carry any weapon whatsoever in any manner whatsoever and for whatever purpose." He noted the "historical tradition of prohibiting the carrying of 'dangerous and unusual weapons.'" But, turning to the D.C. law at issue, he found it incapable of constitutional defense: "[T]he law totally bans handgun possession in the home. It also requires that any lawful firearm in the home be disassembled or bound by a trigger lock at all times, rendering it inoperable. [The] inherent right of self-defense has been central to the Second Amendment right. The handgun ban amounts to a prohibition of an entire class of 'arms' that is overwhelmingly chosen by American society for that lawful purpose. The prohibition extends, moreover, to the home, where the need for defense of self, family, and property is most acute. Under any of the standards of scrutiny that we have applied to enumerated constitutional rights, banning from the home 'the most preferred firearm in the nation to "keep" and use for protection of one's home and family,' would fail constitutional muster." He concluded: "We are aware of the problem of handgun violence in this country. [The] Constitution leaves the District of Columbia a variety of tools for combating that problem, including some measures regulating handguns. But the enshrinement of constitutional rights necessarily takes certain policy choices off the table. These include the absolute prohibition of handguns held and used for self-defense in the home."

Justice Stevens wrote a dissent, joined by Justices Souter, Ginsburg, and Breyer, taking a very different view of the founding text and history: "The question presented by this case is not whether the Second Amendment protects a 'collective right' or an 'individual right.' Surely it protects a right that can be enforced by individuals. But a conclusion that the Second Amendment protects an individual right does not tell us anything about the scope of that right. Guns are used to hunt, for self-defense, to commit crimes, for sporting activities, and to perform military duties. The Second Amendment plainly does not protect the right to use a gun to rob a bank; it is equally clear that it *does* encompass the right to use weapons for certain military purposes. Whether it also protects the right to possess and use guns for nonmilitary purposes like hunting and personal self-defense is the question presented by this case. The text of the Amendment, its history, and our decision in United States v. Miller, 307 U.S. 174 (1939), provide a clear answer to that question.

"The Second Amendment was adopted to protect the right of the people of each of the several States to maintain a well-regulated militia. It was a response to concerns raised during the ratification of the Constitution that the power of Congress to disarm the state militias and create a national standing army posed an intolerable threat to the sovereignty of the several States. Neither the text of the Amendment nor the arguments advanced by its proponents evidenced the slightest interest in limiting any legislature's authority to regulate private civilian uses of firearms. Specifically, there is no indication that the Framers of the Amendment intended to enshrine the common-law right of self-defense in the Constitution. [The] view of the Amendment we took in Miller — that it protects the right to keep and bear arms for certain military purposes, but that it does not curtail the Legislature's power to regulate the nonmilitary use and ownership of weapons — is both the most natural reading of the Amendment's text and the interpretation most faithful to the history of its adoption."

Justice Breyer's separate dissent, joined by Justices Stevens, Souter, and Ginsburg, agreed with Justice Stevens that the Amendment does not protect an interest in individual self-defense, but argued that, even assuming arguendo that it did, under an appropriate balancing of interests, D.C.'s regulation, "which focuses upon the presence of handguns in high-crime urban areas, represents a permissible legislative response to a serious, indeed life-threatening, problem."

Heller — What's Next? Even given the Court's revolutionary and threshold conclusion that the Second Amendment is in fact a "personal constitutional right," one question, most significant in regard to the meaning and effect of the *Heller* decision, was left unresolved.

Although the majority concluded that a state still maintains an interest in protecting "health and safety" sufficient to regulate gun use, they did not specifically identify the standard of review to be applied. Given that the Court has traditionally applied a strict scrutiny standard requiring proof of a narrowly tailored compelling interest to regulate a fundamental right, this is now a central issue yet to be decided. Can we assume that a state or local government must meet the stringent compelling purpose standard before it can so regulate? Justice Breyer assumes such in his dissent and comments:

> What kind of constitutional standard should the court use? How high a protective hurdle does the Amendment erect? [T]he question matters. The majority is wrong when it says that the District's law is unconstitutional "[u]nder any of the standards of scrutiny that we have applied to enumerated constitutional rights." How could that be? It certainly would not be unconstitutional under, for example, a "rational basis" standard, which requires a court to uphold regulation so long as it bears a "rational relationship" to a "legitimate governmental purpose." The law at issue here, which in part seeks to prevent gun-related accidents, at least bears a "rational relationship" to that "legitimate" life-saving objective. And nothing in the three 19th-century state cases to which the majority turns for support mandates the conclusion that the present District law must fall. These cases were decided well (80, 55, and 49 years, respectively) after the framing; they neither claim nor provide any special insight into the intent of the Framers; they involve laws much less narrowly tailored that the one before us; and state cases in any event are not determinative of federal constitutional questions.

Respondent proposes that the Court adopt a "strict scrutiny" test, which would require reviewing with care each gun law to determine whether it is "narrowly tailored to achieve a compelling governmental interest." But the majority implicitly, and appropriately, rejects that suggestion by broadly approving a set of laws-prohibitions on concealed weapons, forfeiture by criminals of the Second Amendment right, prohibitions on firearms in certain locales, and governmental regulation of commercial firearm sales whose constitutionality under a strict scrutiny standard would be far from clear.

Indeed, adoption of a true strict-scrutiny standard for evaluating gun regulations would be impossible. That is because almost every gun-control regulation will seek to advance (as the one here does) a "primary concern of every government—a concern for the safety and indeed the lives of its citizens." The Court has deemed that interest, as well as "the Government's general interest in preventing crime," to be "compelling," and the Court has in a wide variety of constitutional contexts found such public-safety concerns sufficiently forceful to justify restrictions on individual liberties. Thus, any attempt *in theory* to apply strict scrutiny to gun regulations will *in practice* turn into an interest-balancing inquiry, with the interests protected by the Second Amendment on one side and the governmental public-safety concerns on the other, the only question being whether the regulation at issue impermissibly burdens the former in the course of advancing the latter.

b. "AND BEAR ARMS"—

Heller dealt with the core right to keep arms. The Second Amendment also includes the term "bear" as in "bear arms." The "bear arms" part of the Amendment was addressed in the 2021 term with regard to the kinds of restrictions, if any, that can be imposed by government on weapons being carried or possessed outside of the home. This issue was explored in *New York State Rifle and Pistol Association v. Bruen*, 597 U.S. ____(2022). *Bruen* also addressed the issue "left hanging" in *Heller*—the standard of scrutiny to be employed in cases involving the rights to keep and bear arms.

As Justice Thomas pointed out in *Bruen,* federal Courts of Appeal have (out of necessity since the Supreme Court had not addressed the issue in any meaningful way since *McDonald,* below) developed a standard of scrutiny that combine the historic focus of Justice Scalia's opinion in *Heller* and a traditional standard for evaluating fundamental rights (determined to be so in *McDonald,* below, when the right was incorporated to the states two years later), the means-end a heightened scrutiny in determining whether government regulation of Second Amendment Rights was constitutional. Justice Thomas, writing for the 6-3 majority, announced that that process included one too many standards. Noting that the *Heller* opinion only relied on historical evidence to support the right, and to invalidate the local law at issue abridging that right, Justice Thomas established that the only scrutiny applicable to Second Amendment rights regulations would be their consistency with regulatory standards in place when the Second Amendment became part of the Constitution, essentially an originalist approach.

The opinion attempted to explain the historical approach, embracing contemporaneous understandings of the right to bear arms, the issue in this case, modified only for the identity of the arms, but not for the reasons for the right, personal protection. Acknowledging that originalist historical analysis is nuanced, if not downright difficult,

Justice Thomas, like Justice Scalia in *Heller*, explained that such an approach was more consistent with the proper role of the judiciary.

New York state required a government-issued license before individuals could carry handguns. In order to receive such a license, an individual had to satisfy the licensing agency that "proper cause" existed for issuing the license, essentially a subjective determination by the agency, though not necessarily arbitrary. To Thomas, this procedure did not conform to historical regulatory standards at the time of the Second Amendment's inclusion in the Constitution. Evidence submitted by New York that the ability to carry a weapon was heavily regulated under the common law and statute in England, dating back centuries before the Founding as well as during the colonial period, was countered in the opinion clarifying the laws at issue in some cases, or dismissing others as outlier rules. Laws during the early U.S. Constitutional period were evaluated by the majority opinion in much the same way, leading to a general discounting of legal history counter to the majority's theory of the case. At the end of the day, the historical regulatory guidance that government could rely on for constitutional regulation of the right to bear arms was described as follows:

> Those restrictions, for example, limited the intent for which one could carry arms, the manner by which one carried arms, or the exceptional circumstances under which one could not carry arms, such as before justices of the peace and other government officials. Apart from a few late-19th- century outlier jurisdictions, American governments simply have not broadly prohibited the public carry of commonly used firearms for personal defense. Nor, subject to a few late-in-time outliers, have American governments required law-abiding, responsible citizens to "demonstrate a special need for self-protection distinguishable from that of the general community" in order to carry arms in public.

2. THE SECOND AMENDMENT, AND INCORPORATION PART II

McDONALD v. CITY OF CHICAGO
561 U.S. 742 (2010)

Justice ALITO announced the judgment of the Court and delivered the opinion of the Court with respect to Parts I, II–A, II–B, II–D, III–A, and III–B, in which ROBERTS, C. J., and SCALIA, KENNEDY, and THOMAS, JJ., joined, and an opinion with respect to Parts II–C, IV, and V, in which ROBERTS, C. J., and SCALIA and KENNEDY, JJ., join. SCALIA, J., filed a concurring opinion. THOMAS, J., filed an opinion concurring in part and concurring in the judgment. STEVENS, J., filed a dissenting opinion. BREYER, J., filed a dissenting opinion, in which GINSBURG and SOTOMAYOR, JJ., joined.

Two years ago, in *District of Columbia v. Heller*, 554 U.S. 570, 128 S.Ct. 2783, 171 L.Ed.2d 637 (2008), we held that the Second Amendment protects the right to keep and bear arms for the purpose of self-defense, and we struck down a District of Columbia law that banned the possession of handguns in the home. The city of Chicago (City) and the village of Oak Park, a Chicago suburb, have laws that are similar to the District of Columbia's, but Chicago and Oak Park argue that their laws are constitutional because the Second Amendment has no application to the States. We have previously held that most of the provisions of the Bill of Rights apply with full force to both the Federal Government and the States. Applying the standard that is well established in our case law, we hold that the Second Amendment right is fully applicable to the States.

[II]

[A]

Petitioners argue that the Chicago and Oak Park laws violate the right to keep and bear arms for two reasons. Petitioners' primary submission is that this right is among the "privileges or immunities of citizens of the United States" and that the narrow interpretation of the Privileges or Immunities Clause adopted in the *Slaughter-House Cases, supra,* should now be rejected. As a secondary argument, petitioners contend that the Fourteenth Amendment's Due Process Clause "incorporates" the Second Amendment right.

Chicago and Oak Park (municipal respondents) maintain that a right set out in the Bill of Rights applies to the States only if that right is an indispensable attribute of *any* "'civilized'" legal system. Brief for Municipal Respondents 9. If it is possible to imagine a civilized country that does not recognize the right, the municipal respondents tell us, then that right is not protected by due process. *Ibid.* And since there are civilized countries that ban or strictly regulate the private possession of handguns, the municipal respondents maintain that due process does not preclude such measures. *Id.,* at 21-23. In light of the parties' far-reaching arguments, we begin by recounting this Court's analysis over the years of the relationship between the provisions of the Bill of Rights and the States.

B

The Bill of Rights, including the Second Amendment, originally applied only to the Federal Government. In *Barron ex rel. Tiernan v. Mayor of Baltimore,* 7 Pet. 243, 8 L.Ed. 672 (1833), the Court, in an opinion by Chief Justice Marshall, explained that this question was "of great importance" but "not of much difficulty." *Id.,* at 247. In less than four pages, the Court firmly rejected the proposition that the first eight Amendments operate as limitations on the States, holding that they apply only to the Federal Government. See also *Lessee of Livingston v. Moore,* 7 Pet. 469, 551-552, 8 L.Ed. 751 (1833) ("[I]t is now settled that those amendments [in the Bill of Rights] do not extend to the states").

The constitutional Amendments adopted in the aftermath of the Civil War fundamentally altered our country's federal system. The provision at issue in this case, § 1 of the Fourteenth Amendment, provides, among other things, that a State may not abridge "the privileges or immunities of citizens of the United States" or deprive "any person of life, liberty, or property, without due process of law."

Four years after the adoption of the Fourteenth Amendment, this Court was asked to interpret the Amendment's reference to "the privileges or immunities of citizens of the United States." The *Slaughter-House Cases, supra,* involved challenges to a Louisiana law permitting the creation of a state-sanctioned monopoly on the butchering of animals within the city of New Orleans. Justice Samuel Miller's opinion for the Court concluded that the Privileges or Immunities Clause protects only those rights "which owe their existence to the Federal government, its National character, its Constitution, or its laws." *Id.,* at 79. The Court held that other fundamental rights—rights that predated the creation of the Federal Government and that "the State governments were created to establish and secure"— were not protected by the Clause. *Id.,* at 76.

In drawing a sharp distinction between the rights of federal and state citizenship, the Court relied on two principal arguments. First, the Court emphasized that the Fourteenth Amendment's Privileges or Immunities Clause spoke of "the privileges or immunities of *citizens of the United States,*" and the Court contrasted this phrasing with the wording in the first sentence of the Fourteenth Amendment and in the Privileges and Immunities Clause of Article IV, both of which refer to *state* citizenship. (Emphasis added.) Second, the Court stated that a contrary reading would "radically chang[e] the whole theory of the relations of the State and Federal governments to each other and of both these governments to the people," and the Court refused to conclude that such a change had been made "in the absence of language which expresses such a purpose too clearly to admit of doubt." *Id.,* at 78. Finding the phrase "privileges or immunities of citizens of the United States" lacking by this high standard, the Court reasoned that the phrase must mean something more limited.

Under the Court's narrow reading, the Privileges or Immunities Clause protects such things as the right "to come to the seat of government to assert any claim [a citizen] may have upon that government, to transact any business he may have with it, to seek its protection, to share its offices, to engage in administering its functions . . . [and to] become a citizen of any State of the Union by a *bonafide* residence therein, with the same rights as other citizens of that State." *Id.,* at 79-80 (internal quotation marks omitted).

Finding no constitutional protection against state intrusion of the kind envisioned by the Louisiana statute, the Court upheld the statute. Four Justices dissented. Justice Field, joined by Chief Justice Chase and Justices Swayne and Bradley, criticized the majority for reducing the Fourteenth Amendment's Privileges or Immunities Clause to "a vain and idle enactment, which accomplished nothing, and most unnecessarily excited Congress and the people on its passage." *Id.,* at 96; see also *id.,* at 104. Justice Field opined that the Privileges or Immunities Clause protects rights that are "in their nature . . . fundamental," including the right of every man to pursue his profession without the imposition of unequal or discriminatory restrictions. *Id.,* at 96-97 (internal quotation marks omitted). Justice Bradley's dissent observed that "we are not bound to resort to implication . . . to find an authoritative declaration of some of the most important privileges and immunities of citizens of the United States. It is in the Constitution itself." *Id.,* at 118. Justice Bradley would have construed the Privileges or Immunities Clause to include those rights enumerated in the Constitution as well as some unenumerated rights. *Id.,* at 119. Justice Swayne described the majority's narrow reading of the Privileges or Immunities Clause as "turn[ing] . . . what was meant for bread into a stone." *Id.,* at 129 (dissenting opinion).

Today, many legal scholars dispute the correctness of the narrow *Slaughter-House* interpretation. See, *e.g., Saenz v. Roe,* 526 U.S. 489, 522, n. 1, 527, 119 S.Ct. 1518, 143 L.Ed.2d 689 (1999) (Thomas, J., dissenting) (scholars of the Fourteenth Amendment agree "that the Clause does not mean what the Court said it meant in 1873"); Amar, Substance and Method in the Year 2000, 28 Pepperdine L.Rev. 601, 631, n. 178 (2001) ("Virtually no serious modern scholar—left, right, and center—thinks that this [interpretation] is a plausible reading of the Amendment"); Brief for Constitutional Law Professors as *Amici Curiae* 33 (claiming an "overwhelming consensus among leading constitutional scholars" that the opinion is "egregiously wrong"); C. Black, A New Birth of Freedom 74-75 (1997).

Three years after the decision in the *Slaughter-House Cases,* the Court decided *Cruikshank,* the first of the three 19th-century cases on which the Seventh Circuit relied. 92 U.S. 542, 23 L.Ed. 588. In that case, the Court reviewed convictions stemming from the infamous Colfax Massacre in Louisiana on Easter Sunday 1873. Dozens of blacks, many unarmed, were slaughtered by a rival band of armed white men. Cruikshank himself allegedly marched unarmed African-American prisoners through the streets and then had them summarily executed. Ninety-seven men were indicted for participating in the massacre, but only nine went to trial. Six of the nine were acquitted of all charges; the remaining three were acquitted of murder but convicted under the Enforcement Act of 1870, 16 Stat. 140, for banding and conspiring together to deprive their victims of various constitutional rights, including the right to bear arms.

The Court reversed all of the convictions, including those relating to the deprivation of the victims' right to bear arms. *Cruikshank,* 92 U.S., at 553, 559. The Court wrote that the right of bearing arms for a lawful purpose "is not a right granted by the Constitution" and is not "in any manner dependent upon that instrument for its existence." *Id.,* at 553. "The second amendment," the Court continued, "declares that it shall not be infringed; but this . . . means no more than that it shall not be infringed by Congress." *Ibid.* "Our later decisions in *Presser v. Illinois,* 116 U.S. 252, 265[, 6 S.Ct. 580, 29 L.Ed. 615] (1886), and *Miller v. Texas,* 153 U.S. 535, 538[, 14 S.Ct. 874, 38 L.Ed. 812] (1894), reaffirmed that the Second Amendment applies only to the Federal Government." *Heller,* 554 U.S., at 620, n. 23, 128 S.Ct., at 2813 n. 23.

C

[We] see no need to reconsider that interpretation here. For many decades, the question of the rights protected by the Fourteenth Amendment against state infringement has been analyzed under the Due Process Clause of that Amendment and not under the Privileges or Immunities Clause. We therefore decline to disturb the Slaughter-House holding.

[D]
[3]

[After describing previous Court definitions of substantive due process, Justice Alito turned to the standard he describes as controlling. Eds.]

The Court made it clear that the governing standard is not whether any "civilized system [can] be imagined that would not accord the particular protection." Instead, the Court inquired whether a particular Bill of Rights guarantee is fundamental to our scheme of ordered liberty and system of justice. Id., at 149, and n. 14; see also id., at 148 (referring to those "fundamental principles of liberty and justice which lie at the base of all our civil and political institutions".

[III]

With this framework in mind, we now turn directly to the question whether the Second Amendment right to keep and bear arms is incorporated in the concept of due process. In answering that question, as just explained, we must decide whether the right to keep and bear arms is fundamental to our scheme of ordered liberty, Duncan, 391 U. S., at 149, or as we have said in a related context, whether this right is "deeply rooted in this Nation's history and tradition," Washington v. Glucksberg, 521 U. S. 702, 721 (1997) (internal quotation marks omitted).

A

Our decision in Heller points unmistakably to the answer. Self-defense is a basic right, recognized by many legal systems from ancient times to the present day, and in Heller, we held that individual self-defense is "the central component" of the Second Amendment right. 554 U. S., at ____ (slip op., at 26); see also id., at ____ (slip op., at 56) (stating that the "inherent right of self-defense has been central to the Second Amendment right"). Explaining that "the need for defense of self, family, and property is most acute" in the home, ibid., we found that this right applies to handguns because they are "the most preferred firearm in the nation to 'keep' and use for protection of one's home and family," id., at ____ (slip op., at 57) (some internal quotation marks omitted); see also id., at ____ (slip op., at 56) (noting that handguns are "overwhelmingly chosen by American society for [the] lawful purpose" of self-defense); id., at ___ (slip op., at 57) ("[T]he American people have considered the handgun to be the quintessential self-defense weapon"). Thus, we concluded, citizens must be permitted "to use [handguns] for the core lawful purpose of self-defense." Id., at ___ (slip op., at 58).

Heller makes it clear that this right is "deeply rooted in this Nation's history and tradition." Glucksberg, supra, at 721 (internal quotation marks omitted). Heller explored the right's origins, noting that the 1689 English Bill of Rights explicitly protected a right to keep arms for self-defense, 554 U. S., at ___–___ (slip op., at 19–20), and that by 1765, Blackstone was able to assert that the right to keep and bear arms was "one of the fundamental rights of Englishmen," id., at ___ (slip op., at 20).

Blackstone's assessment was shared by the American colonists. As we noted in Heller, King George III's attempt to disarm the colonists in the 1760's and 1770's "provoked polemical reactions by Americans invoking their rights as Englishmen to keep arms." Id., at ___ (slip op., at 21); see also L. Levy, Origins of the Bill of Rights 137–143 (1999) (hereinafter Levy).

The right to keep and bear arms was considered no less fundamental by those who drafted and ratified the Bill of Rights. "During the 1788 ratification debates, the fear that the federal government would disarm the people in order to impose rule through a standing army or select militia was pervasive in Antifederalist rhetoric." Heller, supra, at ___ (slip op., at 25) (citing Letters from the Federal Farmer III (Oct. 10, 1787), in 2 The Complete Anti-Federalist 234, 242 (H. Storing ed. 1981)); see also Federal Farmer: An Additional Number of Letters to the Republican, Letter XVIII (Jan. 25, 1788), in 17 Documentary History of the Ratification of the Constitution 360, 362–363 (J. Kaminski & G. Saladino eds. 1995); S. Halbrook, The Founders' Second Amendment 171–278 (2008). Federalists responded, not by arguing that the right was insufficiently important to warrant protection but by contending that the right was adequately protected by the Constitution's assignment of only limited powers to the Federal Government.

[This] understanding persisted in the years immediately following the ratification of the Bill of Rights. In addition to the four States that had adopted Second Amendment analogues before ratification, nine more States adopted state constitutional provisions protecting an individual right to keep and bear arms between 1789 and 1820. Heller, supra, at ___ (slip op., at 27–30). Founding-era legal commentators confirmed the importance of the right to early Americans.

[B]

1

By the 1850's, the perceived threat that had prompted the inclusion of the Second Amendment in the Bill of Rights—the fear that the National Government would disarm the universal militia—had largely faded as a popular concern, but the right to keep and bear arms was highly valued for purposes of self-defense. See M. Doubler, Civilian in Peace, Soldier in War 87–90 (2003); Amar, Bill of Rights 258–259. Abolitionist authors wrote in support of the right.

[After] the Civil War, many of the over 180,000 African Americans who served in the Union Army returned to the States of the old Confederacy, where systematic efforts were made to disarm them and other blacks. See Heller, 554 U. S., at ___ (slip op., at 42); E. Foner, Reconstruction: America's Unfinished Revolution 1863–1877, p. 8 (1988) (hereinafter Foner). The laws of some States formally prohibited African Americans from possessing firearms. For example, a Mississippi law provided that "no freedman, free negro or mulatto, not in the military service of the United States government, and not licensed so to do by the board of police of his or her county, shall keep or carry firearms of any kind, or any ammunition, dirk or bowie knife." Certain Offenses of Freedmen, 1865 Miss. Laws p. 165, §1, in 1 Documentary History of Reconstruction 289 (W. Fleming ed. 1950).

[Throughout] the South, armed parties, often consisting of ex-Confederate soldiers serving in the state militias, forcibly took firearms from newly freed slaves. In the first session of the 39th Congress, Senator Wilson told his colleagues: "In Mississippi rebel State forces, men who were in the rebel armies, are traversing the State, visiting the freedmen, disarming them, perpetrating murders and outrages upon them; and the same things are done in other sections of the country." 39th Cong. Globe 40 (1865).

Union Army commanders took steps to secure the right of all citizens to keep and bear arms, but the 39th Congress concluded that legislative action was necessary. Its efforts to safeguard the right to keep and bear arms demonstrate that the right was still recognized to be fundamental.

The most explicit evidence of Congress' aim appears in §14 of the Freedmen's Bureau Act of 1866, which provided that "the right . . . to have full and equal benefit of all laws and proceedings concerning personal liberty, personal security, and the acquisition, enjoyment, and disposition of estate, real and personal, including the constitutional right to bear arms, shall be secured to and enjoyed by all the citizens . . . without respect to race or color, or previous condition of slavery." 14 Stat. 176–177 (emphasis added). Section 14 thus explicitly guaranteed that "all the citizens," black and white, would have "the constitutional right to bear arms."

The Civil Rights Act of 1866, 14 Stat. 27, which was considered at the same time as the Freedmen's Bureau Act, similarly sought to protect the right of all citizens to keep and bear arms. Section 1 of the Civil Rights Act guaranteed the "full and equal benefit of all laws and proceedings for the security of person and property, as is enjoyed by white citizens."

Congress, however, ultimately deemed these legislative remedies insufficient. Southern resistance, Presidential vetoes, and this Court's pre-Civil-War precedent persuaded Congress that a constitutional amendment was necessary to provide full protection for the rights of blacks. Today, it is generally accepted that the Fourteenth Amendment was understood to provide a constitutional basis for protecting the rights set out in the Civil Rights Act of 1866. See General Building Contractors Assn., Inc. v. Pennsylvania, 458 U. S. 375, 389 (1982); see also Amar, Bill of Rights 187; Calabresi, Two Cheers for Professor Balkin's Originalism, 103 Nw. U. L. Rev. 663, 669–670 (2009).

In debating the Fourteenth Amendment, the 39th Congress referred to the right to keep and bear arms as a fundamental right deserving of protection. Senator Samuel Pomeroy described three "indispensable" "safeguards of liberty under our form of Government." 39th Cong. Globe 1182. One of these, he said, was the right to keep and bear arms: "Every man . . . should have the right to bear arms for the defense of himself and family and his homestead. And if the cabin door of the freedman is broken open and the intruder enters for purposes as vile as were known to slavery, then should a well-loaded musket be in the hand of the occupant to send the polluted wretch to another world, where his wretchedness will forever remain complete." Ibid.

[In] sum, it is clear that the Framers and ratifiers of the Fourteenth Amendment counted the right to keep and bear arms among those fundamental rights necessary to our system of ordered liberty.

* * *

[In] Heller, we held that the Second Amendment protects the right to possess a handgun in the home for the purpose of self-defense. Unless considerations of stare decisis counsel otherwise, a provision of the Bill of Rights that protects a right that is fundamental from an American perspective applies equally to the Federal Government and the States. See Duncan, 391 U. S., at 149, and n. 14. We therefore hold that the Due Process Clause of the Fourteenth Amendment incorporates the Second Amendment right recognized in Heller. The judgment of the Court of Appeals is reversed, and the case is remanded for further proceedings.

It is so ordered.

Comment on *McDonald*. Justice Scalia, while part of the majority for the core holding that the Second Amendment described a fundamental right to bear arms incorporated to the states, did not join the majority opinion's discussion of the privileges and immunities clause, the City's position on the meaning of fundamental rights, and the opinion's critiques of the dissents.

Justice Scalia concurred, in his words, "[d]espite my misgivings about Substantive Due Process as an original matter": "I have acquiesced in the Court's incorporation of certain guarantees in the Bill of Rights 'because it is both long established and narrowly limited.' This case does not require me to reconsider that view, since straightforward application of settled doctrine suffices to decide it."

Justice Thomas filed a partial concurrence and concurrence in the judgment, arguing that the Privileges or Immunities rather than the Due Process Clause is the appropriate vehicle for incorporating the Second Amendment right against the States: "Applying what is now a well-settled test, the plurality opinion concludes that the right to keep and bear arms applies to the States through the Fourteenth Amendment's Due Process Clause because it is 'fundamental' to the American 'scheme of ordered liberty,' and 'deeply rooted in this Nation's history and tradition.' I agree with that description of the right. But I cannot agree that it is enforceable against the States through a clause that speaks only to 'process.' Instead, the right to keep and bear arms is a privilege of American citizenship that applies to the States through the Fourteenth Amendment's Privileges or Immunities Clause."

Justice Thomas acknowledged that the Court's precedents had defined the privileges or immunities of national citizenship "narrowly," noting that the *Slaughter-House Cases* had "defined that category to include only those rights 'which owe their existence to the Federal government, its National character, its Constitution, or its laws,'" and that later cases had "interpret[ed] the Privileges or Immunities Clause even more narrowly": "Chief among those cases is United States v. Cruikshank, 92 U.S. 542 (1876). There, the Court held that members of a white militia who had brutally murdered as many as 165 black Louisianans congregating outside a courthouse had not deprived the victims of their privileges as American citizens to peaceably assemble or to keep and bear arms. According to the Court, the right to peaceably assemble codified in the First Amendment was not a privilege of United States citizenship because '[t]he right . . . existed long before the adoption of the Constitution.' Similarly, the Court held that the right to keep and bear arms was not a privilege of United States citizenship because it was not 'in any manner dependent upon that instrument for its existence.'" After an exhaustive review of the contemporaneous history and legislative history surrounding enactment of the Fourteenth Amendment, he concluded: "This history confirms what the text of the Privileges or Immunities Clause most naturally suggests: Consistent with its command that '[n]o State shall . . . abridge' the rights of United States citizens, the Clause establishes a minimum baseline of federal rights, and the constitutional right to keep and bear arms plainly was among them."

Justice Thomas rejected the view that stare decisis compels deference to the *Slaughter-House Cases'* interpretation of "the rights of state and federal citizenship as mutually exclusive": "The better view, in light of the States and Federal Government's shared history of recognizing certain inalienable rights in their citizens, is that the privileges and immunities of state and federal citizenship overlap. [A] separate question is whether the privileges and immunities of American citizenship include any rights besides those enumerated in the Constitution. [Because] this case does not involve an unremunerated right, it is not necessary to resolve the question whether the Clause protects such rights."

Finally, Justice Thomas argued, *Cruikshank*, which "squarely held that the right to keep and bear arms was not a privilege of American citizenship, thereby overturning the convictions of militia members responsible for the brutal Colfax Massacre, [is] not a precedent entitled to any respect": "Cruikshank's holding that blacks could look only to state governments for protection of their right to keep and bear arms enabled private forces, often with the assistance of local governments, to subjugate the newly freed slaves and their descendants through a wave of private violence designed to drive blacks from the voting booth and force them into peonage, an effective return to slavery. Without federal enforcement of the inalienable right to keep and bear arms, these militias and mobs were tragically successful in waging a campaign of terror against the very people the Fourteenth Amendment had just made citizens." Justice Thomas concluded: "I agree with the Court that the Second Amendment is fully applicable to the States. I do so because the right to keep and bear arms is guaranteed by the Fourteenth Amendment as a privilege of American citizenship."

Justice Stevens filed an exhaustive solo dissent, stating "[t]his is a substantive due process case." In an extended discussion of substantive due process methodology, he stressed that interpretation of the Due Process Clause should not be too rigidly historical: "The Court hinges its entire decision on one mode of intellectual history, culling selected pronouncements and enactments from the 18th and 19th centuries to ascertain what Americans thought about firearms. [The] plurality suggests that only interests that have proved 'fundamental from an American perspective,' or 'deeply rooted in this Nation's history and tradition,' to the Court's satisfaction, may qualify for incorporation into the Fourteenth Amendment. To the extent the Court's opinion could be read to imply that the historical pedigree of a right is the exclusive or dispositive determinant of its status under the Due Process Clause, the opinion is seriously mistaken." At the same time, he emphasized the need for judicial modesty and self-restraint in substantive due process interpretation, stating that "it is incumbent upon us, as federal judges contemplating a novel rule that would bind all 50 States, to proceed cautiously and to decide only what must be decided."

Having laid out general interpretive principles, Justice Stevens continued: "Understood as a plea to keep their preferred type of firearm in the home, petitioners' argument has real force. The decision to keep a loaded handgun in the house is often motivated by the desire to protect life, liberty, and property. It is comparable, in some ways, to decisions about the education and upbringing of one's children. For it is the kind of decision that may have profound consequences for every member of the family, and for the world beyond. [Bolstering] petitioners' claim, our law has long recognized that the home provides a kind of special sanctuary in modern life. [The] State generally has a lesser basis for regulating private as compared to public acts, and firearms kept inside the home generally pose a lesser threat to public welfare as compared to firearms taken outside."

He concluded, however, that, "[w]hile I agree with the Court that our substantive due process cases offer a principled basis for holding that petitioners have a constitutional right to possess a usable firearm in the home, I am ultimately persuaded that a better reading of our case law supports the city of Chicago. I would not foreclose the possibility that a particular plaintiff — say, an elderly widow who lives in a dangerous neighborhood and does not have the strength to operate a long gun — may have a cognizable liberty interest in possessing a handgun. But I cannot accept petitioners' broader submission. A number of factors, taken together, lead me to this conclusion.

"First, firearms have a fundamentally ambivalent relationship to liberty. Just as they can help homeowners defend their families and property from intruders, they can help thugs and insurrectionists murder innocent victims. The threat that firearms will be misused is far from hypothetical, for gun crime has devastated many of our communities. [Second,] the right to possess a firearm of one's choosing is different in kind from the liberty interests we have recognized under the Due Process Clause. [It] does not appear to be the case that the ability to own a handgun, or any particular type of firearm, is critical to leading a life of autonomy, dignity, or political equality. [Third,] the experience of other advanced democracies, including those that share our British heritage, undercuts the notion that an expansive right to keep and bear arms is intrinsic to ordered liberty. Many of these countries place restrictions on the possession, use, and carriage of firearms far more onerous than the restrictions found in this Nation. [Fourth,] the Second Amendment differs in kind from the Amendments that surround it, [in that it] was the States, not private persons, on whose immediate behalf the Second Amendment was adopted. Notwithstanding [Heller's] efforts to write the Second Amendment's preamble out of the Constitution, the Amendment still serves the structural function of protecting the States from encroachment by an overreaching Federal Government. [Fifth,] although it may be true that Americans' interest in firearm possession and state-law recognition of that interest are 'deeply rooted' in some important senses, it is equally true that the States have a long and unbroken history of regulating firearms. [Finally, this] is a quintessential area in which federalism ought to be allowed to flourish without this Court's meddling.

[States] and localities vary significantly in the patterns and problems of gun violence they face, as well as in the traditions and cultures of lawful gun use they claim. The city of Chicago, for example, faces a pressing challenge in combating criminal street gangs. Most rural areas do not."

Justice Breyer, joined by Justices Ginsburg and Sotomayor, filed a separate dissent. Noting that Justice Stevens's dissent focused on substantive due process concerns, Justice Breyer wrote to "separately consider the question of 'incorporation,'" stating that "I can find nothing in the Second Amendment's text, history, or underlying rationale that could warrant characterizing it as 'fundamental' insofar as it seeks to protect the keeping and bearing of arms for private self-defense purposes. [The] majority here [relies] almost exclusively upon history to make the necessary showing. But to do so for incorporation purposes is both wrong and dangerous. [Where] history provides no clear answer, [it is proper] to look to other factors in considering whether a right is sufficiently 'fundamental' to remove it from the political process in every State. I would include among those factors the nature of the right; any contemporary disagreement about whether the right is fundamental; the extent to which incorporation will further other, perhaps more basic, constitutional aims; and the extent to which incorporation will advance or hinder the Constitution's structural aims, including its division of powers among different governmental institutions (and the people as well). Is incorporation needed, for example, to further the Constitution's effort to ensure that the government treats each individual with equal respect? Will it help maintain the democratic form of government that the Constitution foresees?

"[How] do these considerations apply here? [There] is no popular consensus that the private self-defense right described in Heller is fundamental. [One] side believes the right essential to protect the lives of those attacked in the home; the other side believes it essential to regulate the right in order to protect the lives of others attacked with guns. It seems unlikely that definitive evidence will develop one way or the other. [Moreover,] there is no reason here to believe that incorporation of the private self-defense right will further any other or broader constitutional objective. We are aware of no argument that gun-control regulations target or are passed with the purpose of targeting 'discrete and insular minorities.' Carolene Products. Nor will incorporation help to assure equal respect for individuals. Unlike the First Amendment's rights of free speech, free press, assembly, and petition, the private self-defense right does not comprise a necessary part of the democratic process that the Constitution seeks to establish. Unlike the First Amendment's religious protections, the Fourth Amendment's protection against unreasonable searches and seizures, the Fifth and Sixth Amendments' insistence upon fair criminal procedure, and the Eighth Amendment's protection against cruel and unusual punishments, the private self-defense right does not significantly seek to protect individuals who might otherwise suffer unfair or inhumane treatment at the hands of a majority. Unlike the protections offered by many of these same Amendments, it does not involve matters as to which judges possess a comparative expertise, by virtue of their close familiarity with the justice system and its operation.

"[Finally,] incorporation of the right will work a significant disruption in the constitutional allocation of decision-making authority. [First, the] incorporation of the right recognized in Heller would amount to a significant incursion on a traditional and important area of state concern, altering the constitutional relationship between the States and the Federal Government. [Second, determining] the constitutionality of a particular state gun law requires finding answers to complex empirically based questions of a kind that legislatures are better able than courts to make. [Third, the] ability of States to reflect local preferences and conditions — both key virtues of federalism — here has particular importance. The incidence of gun ownership varies substantially as between crowded cities and uncongested rural communities, as well as among the different geographic regions of the country. [The] nature of gun violence also varies as between rural communities and cities. [Fourth,] incorporation of any right removes decisions from the democratic process."

After concluding that all of these factors militated against incorporation, Justice Breyer ended by emphasizing that history too was an equivocal source of support for incorporation: "Although the majority does not discuss 20th- or 21st-century evidence concerning the Second Amendment at any length, I think that it is essential to consider the recent history of the right to bear arms for private self-defense when considering whether the right is 'fundamental.' [By] the end of the 20th century, in every State and many local communities, highly detailed and complicated regulatory schemes governed (and continue to govern) nearly every aspect of firearm ownership. [And] state courts in States with constitutions that provide gun rights have almost uniformly interpreted those rights as providing protection only against unreasonable regulation of guns. [Ambiguous] history cannot show that the Fourteenth Amendment incorporates a private right of self-defense against the States."

EVANGELISTO RAMOS, PETITIONER v. LOUISIANA
590 U.S.__(2020)

Justice GORSUCH announced the judgment of the Court and delivered the opinion of the Court with respect to Parts I, II–A, III, and IV–B–1, an opinion with respect to Parts II–B, IV–B–2, and V, in which Justice GINSBURG, Justice BREYER, and Justice SOTOMAYOR join, and an opinion with respect to Part IV–A, in which Justice GINSBURG and Justice BREYER join.

Accused of a serious crime, Evangelisto Ramos insisted on his innocence and invoked his right to a jury trial. Eventually, 10 jurors found the evidence against him persuasive. But a pair of jurors believed that the State of Louisiana had failed to prove Mr. Ramos's guilt beyond reasonable doubt; they voted to acquit.

In 48 States and federal court, a single juror's vote to ac- quit is enough to prevent a conviction. But not in Louisiana. Along with Oregon, Louisiana has long punished people based on 10-to-2 verdicts like the one here. So instead of the mistrial he would have received almost anywhere else, Mr. Ramos was sentenced to life in prison without the possibility of parole.

Why do Louisiana and Oregon allow non-unanimous convictions? Though it's hard to say why these laws persist, their origins are clear. Louisiana first endorsed non-unanimous verdicts for serious crimes at a constitutional convention in 1898. According to one committee chairman, the avowed purpose of that convention was to "establish the supremacy of the white race," and the resulting document included many of the trappings of the Jim Crow era: a poll tax, a combined literacy and property ownership test, and a grandfather clause that in practice exempted white residents from the most onerous of these requirements.

[We] took this case to decide whether the Sixth Amendment right to a jury trial—as incorporated against the States by way of the Fourteenth Amendment—requires a unanimous verdict to convict a defendant of a serious offense. Louisiana insists that this Court has never definitively passed on the question and urges us to find its practice consistent with the Sixth Amendment. By contrast, the dissent doesn't try to defend Louisiana's law on Sixth or Fourteenth Amendment grounds; tacitly, it seems to admit that the Constitution forbids States from using non-unanimous juries. Yet, unprompted by Louisiana, the dissent suggests our precedent requires us to rule for the State any- way. What explains all this? To answer the puzzle, it's necessary to say a bit more about the merits of the question presented, the relevant precedent, and, at last, the consequences that follow from saying what we know to be true.

I

The Sixth Amendment promises that "[i]n all criminal prosecutions, the accused shall enjoy the right to a speedy and public trial, by an impartial jury of the State and district wherein the crime shall have been committed, which district shall have been previously ascertained by law." The Amendment goes on to preserve other rights for criminal defendants but says nothing else about what a "trial by an impartial jury" entails.

Still, the promise of a jury trial surely meant *something*—otherwise, there would have been no reason to write it down. Nor would it have made any sense to spell out the places from which jurors should be drawn if their powers as jurors could be freely abridged by statute. Imagine a constitution that allowed a "jury trial" to mean nothing but a single person rubber-stamping convictions without hearing any evidence—but simultaneously insisting that the lone juror come from a specific judicial district "previously ascertained by law." And if that's not enough, imagine a constitution that included the same hollow guarantee twice—not only in the Sixth Amendment, but also in Article III.8 No: The text and structure of the Constitution clearly suggest that the term "trial by an impartial jury" carried with it some meaning about the content and requirements of a jury trial.

One of these requirements was unanimity. Wherever we might look to determine what the term "trial by an impartial jury trial" meant at the time of the Sixth Amendment's adoption—whether it's the common law, state practices in the founding era, or opinions and treatises written soon afterward—the answer is unmistakable. A jury must reach a unanimous verdict in order to convict.

The requirement of juror unanimity emerged in 14th-century England and was soon accepted as a vital right protected by the common law. As Blackstone explained, no person could be found guilty of a serious crime unless "the truth of every accusation . . . should . . . be confirmed by the unanimous suffrage of twelve of his equals and neighbors, indifferently chosen, and superior to all suspicion."

It was against this backdrop that James Madison drafted and the States ratified the Sixth Amendment in 1791. By that time, unanimous verdicts had been required for about 400 years. If the term "trial by an impartial jury" carried any meaning at all, it surely included a requirement as long and widely accepted as unanimity.

II

A

How, despite these seemingly straightforward principles, have Louisiana's and Oregon's laws managed to hang on for so long? It turns out that the Sixth Amendment's otherwise simple story took a strange turn in 1972. That year, the Court confronted these States' unconventional schemes for the first time—in Apodaca v. Oregon and a companion case, Johnson v. Louisiana. Ultimately, the Court could do no more than issue a badly fractured set of opinions. Four dissenting Justices would not have hesitated to strike down the States' laws, recognizing that the Sixth Amendment requires unanimity and that this guarantee is fully applicable against the States under the Fourteenth Amendment. But a four-Justice plurality took a very different view of the Sixth Amendment. These Justices declared that the real question before them was whether unanimity serves an important "function" in "contemporary society." Then, having reframed the question, the plurality wasted few words before concluding that unanimity's costs out- weigh its benefits in the modern era, so the Sixth Amendment should not stand in the way of Louisiana or Oregon.

The ninth Member of the Court adopted a position that was neither here nor there. On the one hand, Justice Powell agreed that, as a matter of "history and precedent, . . . the Sixth Amendment requires a unanimous jury verdict to convict." But, on the other hand, he argued that the Fourteenth Amendment does not render this guarantee against the federal government fully applicable against the States. In this way, Justice Powell doubled down on his belief in "dual-track" incorporation—the idea that a single right can mean two different things depending on whether it is being invoked against the federal or a state government.

Justice Powell acknowledged that his argument for dual-track incorporation came "late in the day." Late it was. The Court had already, nearly a decade earlier, "rejected the notion that the Fourteenth Amendment applies to the States only a 'watered-down, subjective version of the individual guarantees of the Bill of Rights.' "It's a point we've restated many times since, too, including as recently as last year. Still, Justice Powell frankly explained, he was "unwillin[g]" to follow the Court's precedents. So he offered up the essential fifth vote to uphold Mr. Apodaca's conviction—if based only on a view of the Fourteenth Amendment that he knew was (and remains) foreclosed by precedent.

III

Louisiana's approach may not be quite as tough as trying to defend Justice Powell's dual-track theory of incorporation, but it's pretty close. How does the State deal with the fact this Court has said 13 times over 120 years that the Sixth Amendment does require unanimity? Or the fact that five Justices in Apodaca said the same? The best the State can offer is to suggest that all these statements came in dicta. But even supposing (without granting) that Louisiana is right and it's dicta all the way down, why would the Court now walk away from many of its own statements about the Constitution's meaning? And what about the prior 400 years of English and American cases requiring unanimity—should we dismiss all those as dicta too?

Sensibly, Louisiana doesn't dispute that the common law required unanimity. Instead, it argues that the drafting history of the Sixth Amendment reveals an intent by the framers to leave this particular feature behind. The State points to the fact that Madison's proposal for the Sixth Amendment originally read: "The trial of all crimes . . . shall be by an impartial jury of freeholders of the vicinage, with the requisite of unanimity for conviction, of the right of challenge, and other accustomed requisites. . . ." Louisiana notes that the House of Representatives approved this text with minor modifications. Yet, the State stresses, the Senate replaced "impartial jury of freeholders of the vicinage" with "impartial jury of the State and district wherein the crime shall have been committed" and also removed the explicit references to unanimity, the right of challenge, and "other accustomed requisites." In light of these revisions, Louisiana would have us infer an intent to abandon the common law's traditional unanimity requirement.

But this snippet of drafting history could just as easily support the opposite inference. Maybe the Senate deleted the language about unanimity, the right of challenge, and "other accustomed prerequisites" because all this was so plainly included in the promise of a "trial by an impartial jury" that Senators considered the language surplusage. The truth is that we have little contemporaneous evidence shedding light on why the Senate acted as it did. So rather than dwelling on text left on the cutting room floor, we are much better served by interpreting the language Congress retained and the States ratified. And, as we've seen, at the time of the Amendment's adoption, the right to a jury trial meant a trial in which the jury renders a unanimous verdict.

Further undermining Louisiana's inference about the drafting history is the fact it proves too much. If the Senate's deletion of the word "unanimity" changed the meaning of the text that remains, then the same would seemingly have to follow for the other deleted words as well. So it's not just unanimity that died in the Senate, but all the "other accustomed requisites" associated with the common law jury trial right—i.e., everything history might have taught us about what it means to have a jury trial. Taking the State's argument from drafting history to its logical conclusion would thus leave the right to a "trial by jury" devoid of meaning. A right mentioned twice in the Constitution would be reduced to an empty promise. That can't be right.

[V]

On what ground would anyone have us leave Mr. Ramos in prison for the rest of his life? Not a single Member of this Court is prepared to say Louisiana secured his conviction constitutionally under the Sixth Amendment. No one be- fore us suggests that the error was harmless. Louisiana does not claim precedent commands an affirmance. In the end, the best anyone can seem to muster against Mr. Ramos is that, if we dared to admit in his case what we all know to be true about the Sixth Amendment, we might have to say the same in some others. But where is the justice in that? Every judge must learn to live with the fact he or she will make some mistakes; it comes with the territory. But it is something else entirely to perpetuate something we all know to be wrong only because we fear the consequences of being right. The judgment of the Court of Appeals is Reversed.

Comment. In 2020-2021 term the Court revisited its 2019-2020 term decision in *Ramos v. Louisiana*, 590 U. S. ___ (2020) which held that the fundamental right to a jury trial for serious offenses, applied to the states via the Incorporation Doctrine of the Due Process Clause of the Fourteenth Amendment, included the right to be convicted on the basis of a unanimous jury verdict. Though the basic right was not altered, the Court ruled in *Edwards v. Vannoy*, 593 U.S. ___(2021) that the right could not be applied retroactively in federal collateral proceedings.   A bit of explaining may be in order.

The *Ramos* decision reached the Supreme Court on appeal from the Louisiana Supreme Court by way of the defendant Ramos' habeas corpus appeal of his conviction for murder by a 10-2 verdict, legal in Louisiana at the time (see summary this section). Procedurally, this was a direct appeal to the U.S. Supreme Court on the constitutional issue of non-unanimous jury verdict in serious crime cases. There the Court issued the ruling that the Louisiana law was unconstitutional. In the *Edwards* case, after appeals of the conviction before the state criminal courts, the case became final. Edwards then filed a petition for a federal writ of habeas corpus in the U. S. District Court for the Middle District of Louisiana. Before the habeas action reached the U.S. Supreme Court, *Ramos* was decided.

The habeas action is considered a separate case from the original criminal trial and appeals, and because it was filed with the federal courts, it is considered a federal collateral action. The issue before the Supreme Court was whether new criminal procedure rules have retroactive effect in federal collateral actions. The majority decided that such rules (which would include the unanimous rule newly announced in *Ramos*) were not retroactive.

VI. THE STATE ACTION LIMITATION

The state action limitation had its source in the Court's post–Civil War decision in the *Civil Rights Cases*, discussed earlier.   Though our discussion therein dramatized the broad-based nature of the limitation the Court imposed, even alleging the Court's bias toward forsaking the rights of African Americans in the postwar South, this was not to say that the language of the Fourteenth Amendment was not directed at state governments ("No state shall make or enforce, . . . nor shall any state deprive, . . . nor deny."), for it was.   The modern "story" of state action emphasizes the ability to reach some forms of what had previously been considered private and unreachable conduct, and was closely associated with the rise of the civil rights movement in America in the mid-twentieth century, reaching its "zenith" in the 1960s and the Warren Court.

These decisions changed the landscape of the state action doctrine, perhaps bringing it more in touch with the framers' intent — Harlan's dissenting opinion in the *Civil Rights Cases*, for example, would be drawn upon in this regard.   Yet, as the nation turned away from the civil rights era, the more conservative and privacy-oriented Burger and Rehnquist

Courts would limit and retreat from the Warren Court's doctrine liberalizing the ability to reach private activity.

Though we will study this history in the context of decisional law, it is worth spending some time discussing the significance of private as opposed to governmental conduct, given the nature of our society and the framers' choice of language in structuring the Fourteenth Amendment.

While we are certainly not the only capitalist country in the world, we arguably maintain more activity as private than any other society in the world. In the United States, activity that society's very existence is dependent on remains in private hands. These activities are maintained by governments themselves in most other nations in order to ensure the public good. Thus, for example, almost all modes of transportation (Amtrak being the exception) and all forms of communications, production of energy, and health care are in "private hands." Most of these services are so "public dependent" (quasi-public) that our civilization could not function without them. In the United States when private conduct cannot be reached by the Fourteenth Amendment the results are serious. In fact, the extent of the often complained of bureaucratic regulation that has existed in the United States is not, as is often misunderstood, a by-product of a powerful government interfering in private affairs, but is necessary because without such regulation the nation could be put at the mercy of private entrepreneurs. Most reports now cite the energy shortage in the State of California as a by-product of profiteers benefiting from a lack of regulation. The issues in the United States of private versus public (government) are most consequential.

Given this circumstance, two doctrines have emerged unto which the Court will treat private activity as state action. First, capsulizing the discussion above, certain private activities are so public in character that they satisfy state action because they serve a "public function." Note the potential breadth here since many activities that are in private hands arguably serve a "public function." Next, the government may be so involved in regulating private activities that the Court may find state action because of "significant state involvement." Thus, as a by-product of state regulation to ensure the public good when "quasi-public" activity is in private hands, this very regulation can provide enough state involvement to convert private activity into state action. Because the private market mandates regulation, this approach has even greater potential to find state action.

Finally, it is worthy to note that even given the difficult issues that these quasi-public activities pose, there is "some" point where human activity is so private that personal freedom mandates that we do not want any involvement of the government or the Fourteenth Amendment. Though there may be such a point, there is much debate about when we have reached it. Thus, for example, should a private club have the "freedom" to advocate racial exclusion? (See *Moose Lodge,* infra.) Do we want the government to make our private thoughts actionable, even they are racist? At some point, private activity is so "public" in its significance that we may want to invoke the Fourteenth Amendment, yet at some point we may well want to protect our privacy from government intrusion. At what point does individual autonomy end and the Fourteenth Amendment begin? In the materials that follow, different Courts in different eras will provide varying responses to these questions of great social import.

A. PUBLIC FUNCTION

MARSH v. ALABAMA
326 U.S. 501 (1946)

Mr. Justice BLACK delivered the opinion of the Court.

In this case we are asked to decide whether a State, consistently with the First and Fourteenth Amendments, can impose criminal punishment on a person who undertakes to distribute religious literature on the premises of a company-owned town contrary to the wishes of the town's management. The town, a suburb of Mobile, Alabama, known as Chickasaw, is owned by the Gulf Shipbuilding Corporation. Except for that it has all the characteristics of any other American town. The property consists of residential buildings, streets, a system of sewers, a sewage disposal plant and a "business block" on which business places are situated. A deputy of the Mobile County Sheriff, paid by the company, serves as the town's policeman. Merchants and service establishments have rented the stores and business places on the business block and the United States uses one of the places as a post office from which six carriers deliver mail to the people of Chickasaw and the adjacent area. The town and the surrounding neighborhood, which can not be distinguished from the Gulf property by anyone not familiar with the property lines, are thickly settled, and according to all indications the residents use the business block as their regular shopping center. To do so, they now, as they have for many years, make use of a company-owned paved street and sidewalk located alongside the store fronts in order to enter and leave the stores and the post office. Intersecting company-owned roads at each end of the business block lead into a four-lane public highway which runs parallel to the business block at a distance of thirty feet. There is nothing to stop highway traffic from coming onto the business block and upon arrival a traveler may make free use of the facilities available there. In short the town and its shopping district are accessible to and freely used by the public in general and there is nothing to distinguish them from any other town and shopping center except the fact that the title to the property belongs to a private corporation.

Appellant, a Jehovah's Witness, came onto the sidewalk we have just described, stood near the post-office and undertook to distribute religious literature. In the stores the corporation had posted a notice which read as follows: "This Is Private Property, and Without Written Permission, No Street, or House Vendor, Agent or Solicitation of Any Kind Will Be Permitted." Appellant was warned that she could not distribute the literature without a permit and told that no permit would be issued to her. She protested that the company rule could not be constitutionally applied so as to prohibit her from distributing religious writings. When she was asked to leave the sidewalk and Chickasaw she declined. The deputy sheriff arrested her and she was charged in the state court with violating Title 14, Section 426 of the 1940 Alabama Code which makes it a crime to enter or remain on the premises of another after having been warned not to do so. Appellant contended that to construe the state statute as applicable to her activities would abridge her right to freedom of press and religion contrary to the First and Fourteenth Amendments to the Constitution. This contention was rejected and she was convicted. The Alabama Court of Appeals affirmed the conviction, holding that the statute as applied was constitutional because the title to the sidewalk was in the corporation and because the public use of the sidewalk had not been such as to give rise to a presumption under Alabama law of its irrevocable dedication to the public.   The case is here on Appeal.

Had the title to Chickasaw belonged not to a private but to a municipal corporation and had appellant been arrested for violating a municipal ordinance rather than a ruling by those appointed by the corporation to manage a company-town it would have been clear that appellant's conviction must be reversed. [Neither] a state nor a municipality can completely bar the distribution of literature containing religious or political ideas on its streets, sidewalks and public places or make the right to distribute dependent on a flat license tax or permit to be issued by an official who could deny it at will.   We have also held that an ordinance completely prohibiting the dissemination of ideas on the city streets can not be justified on the ground that the municipality holds legal title to them. And we have recognized that the preservation of a free society is so far dependent upon the right of each individual citizen to receive such literature as he himself might desire that a municipality could not without jeopardizing that vital individual freedom, prohibit door to door distribution of literature.   From these decisions it is clear that had the people of Chickasaw owned all the homes, and all the stores, and all the streets, and all the sidewalks, all those owners together could not have set up a municipal government with sufficient power to pass an ordinance completely barring the distribution of religious literature.   Our question then narrows down to this: Can those people who live in or come to Chickasaw be denied freedom of press and religion simply because a single company has legal title to all the town? For it is the state's contention that the mere fact that all the property interests in the town are held by a single company is enough to give that company power, enforceable by a state statute, to abridge these freedoms.

We do not agree that the corporation's property interests settle the question.   The State urges in effect that the corporation's right to control the inhabitants of Chickasaw is coextensive with the right of a homeowner to regulate the conduct of his guests.   We can not accept that contention.   Ownership does not always mean absolute dominion.   The more an owner, for his advantage, opens up his property for use by the public in general, the more do his rights become circumscribed by the statutory and constitutional rights of those who use it.   Thus, the owners of privately held bridges, ferries, turnpikes and railroads may not operate them as freely as a farmer does his farm.   Since these facilities are built and operated primarily to benefit the public and since their operation is essentially a public function, it is subject to state regulation.   And, though the issue is not directly analogous to the one before us we do want to point out by way of illustration that such regulation may not result in an operation of these facilities, even by privately owned companies, which unconstitutionally interferes with and discriminates against interstate commerce.   Had the corporation here owned the segment of the four-lane highway which runs parallel to the "business block" and operated the same under a State franchise, doubtless no one would have seriously contended that the corporation's property interest in the highway gave it power to obstruct through traffic or to discriminate against interstate commerce.   And even had there been no express franchise but mere acquiescence by the State in the corporation's use of its property as a segment of the four-lane highway, operation of all the highway, including the segment owned by the corporation, would still have been performance of a public function and discrimination would certainly have been illegal.

We do not think it makes any significant constitutional difference as to the relationship between the rights of the owner and those of the public that here the State, instead of permitting the corporation to operate a highway, permitted it to use its property as a town, operate a "business block" in the town and a street and sidewalk on that business block. Whether a corporation or a municipality owns or possesses the town the public in either case has an identical interest in the functioning of the community in such manner that the channels of communication remain free.   As we have heretofore stated, the town of Chickasaw does not function differently from any other town.   The "business block" serves as the community shopping center and is freely accessible and open to the people in the area and those passing through.   The managers appointed by the corporation cannot curtail the liberty of press and religion of these people consistently with the purposes of the Constitutional guarantees, and a state statute, as the one here involved, which enforces such action by criminally punishing those who attempt to distribute religious literature clearly violates the First and Fourteenth Amendments to the Constitution.

Many people in the United States live in company-owned towns.   These people, just as residents of municipalities, are free citizens of their State and country.   Just as all other citizens they must make decisions which affect the welfare of community and nation.   To act as good citizens they must be informed.   In order to enable them to be properly informed their information must be uncensored.   There is no more reason for depriving these people of the liberties guaranteed by the First and Fourteenth Amendments than there is for curtailing these freedoms with respect to any other citizen.

When we balance the Constitutional rights of owners of property against those of the people to enjoy freedom of press and religion, as we must here, we remain mindful of the fact that the latter occupy a preferred position.   As we have stated before, the right to exercise the liberties safeguarded by the First Amendment "lies at the foundation of free government by free men" and we must in all cases "weigh the circumstances and appraise . . . the reasons . . . in support of the regulation of [those] rights." In our view the circumstance that the property rights to the premises where the deprivation of liberty, here involved, took place, were held by others than the public, is not sufficient to justify the State's permitting a corporation to govern a community of citizens so as to restrict their fundamental liberties and the enforcement of such restraint by the application of a State statute.   Insofar as the State has attempted to impose criminal punishment on appellant for undertaking to distribute religious literature in a company town, its action cannot stand. The case is reversed and the cause remanded for further proceedings not inconsistent with this opinion.   Reversed and remanded.

EVANS v. NEWTON
382 U.S. 296 (1966)

Mr. Justice DOUGLAS delivered the opinion of the Court.

In 1911 United States Senator Augustus O. Bacon executed a will that devised to the Mayor and Council of the City of Macon, Georgia, a tract of land which, after the death of the Senator's wife and daughters, was to be used as 'a park and pleasure ground' for white people only, the Senator stating in the will that while he had only the kindest feeling for the Negroes he was of the opinion that "in their social relations the two races (white and negro) should be forever separate."   The will provided that the park should be under the control of a Board of Managers of seven persons, all of whom were to be white. The city kept the park segregated for some years but in time let Negroes use it, taking the position that the park was a public facility which it could not constitutionally manage and maintain on a segregated basis.

Thereupon, individual members of the Board of Managers of the park brought this suit in a state court against the City of Macon and the trustees of certain residuary beneficiaries of Senator Bacon's estate, asking that the city be removed as trustee and that the court appoint new trustees, to whom title to the park would be transferred. The city answered, alleging it could not legally enforce racial segregation in the park. The other defendants admitted the allegation and requested that the city be removed as trustee.

Several Negro citizens of Macon intervened, alleging that the racial limitation was contrary to the laws and public policy of the United States, and asking that the court refuse to appoint private trustees. Thereafter the city resigned as trustee and amended its answer accordingly. Moreover, other heirs of Senator Bacon intervened and they and the defendants other than the city asked for reversion of the trust property to the Bacon estate in the event that the prayer of the petition were denied.

The Georgia court accepted the resignation of the city as trustee and appointed three individuals as new trustees, finding it unnecessary to pass on the other claims of the heirs. On appeal by the Negro intervenors, the Supreme Court of Georgia affirmed, holding that Senator Bacon had the right to give and bequeath his property to a limited class, that charitable trusts are subject to supervision of a court of equity, and that the power to appoint new trustees so that the purpose of the trust would not fail was clear. 220 Ga. 280, 138 S.E.2d 573. The case is here on a writ of certiorari. 380 U.S. 971, 85 S.Ct. 1338, 14 L.Ed.2d 267.

There are two complementary principles to be reconciled in this case. One is the right of the individual to pick his own associates so as to express his preferences and dislikes, and to fashion his private life by joining such clubs and groups as he chooses. The other is the constitutional ban in the Equal Protection Clause of the Fourteenth Amendment against state-sponsored racial inequality, which of course bars a city from acting as trustee under a private will that serves the racial segregation cause. Com. of Pennsylvania v. Board of Directors of City Trusts, 353 U.S. 230, 77 S.Ct. 806, 1 L.Ed.2d 792. A private golf club, however, restricted to either Negro or white membership is one expression of freedom of association. But a municipal golf course that serves only one race is state activity indicating a preference on a matter as to which the State must be neutral. What is "private" action and what is "state" action is not always easy to determine. See Burton v. Wilmington Parking Authority, 365 U.S. 715, 81 S.Ct. 856, 6 L.Ed.2d 45. Conduct that is formally "private" may become so entwined with governmental policies or so impregnated with a governmental character as to become subject to the constitutional limitations placed upon state action. The action of a city in serving as trustee of property under a private will serving the segregated cause is an obvious example.

The range of government activities is broad and varied, and the fact that government has engaged in a particular activity does not necessarily mean that an individual entrepreneur or manager of the same kind of undertaking suffers the same constitutional inhibitions. [This] park, however, is in a different posture. For years it was an integral part of the City of Macon's activities. From the pleadings we assume it was swept, manicured, watered, patrolled, and maintained by the city as a public facility for whites only, as well as granted tax exemption under Ga.Code Ann. § 92-201. The momentum it acquired as a public facility is certainly not dissipated ipso facto by the appointment of "private" trustees. So far as this record shows, there has been no change in municipal maintenance and concern over this facility. Whether these public characteristics will in time be dissipated is wholly conjectural. If the municipality remains entwined in the management or control of the park, it remains subject to the restraints of the Fourteenth Amendment. [We] only hold that where the tradition of municipal control had become firmly established, we cannot take judicial notice that the mere substitution of trustees instantly transferred this park from the public to the private sector.

This conclusion is buttressed by the nature of the service rendered the community by a park. The service rendered even by a private park of this character is municipal in nature. It is open to every white person, there being no selective element other than race. Golf clubs, social centers, luncheon clubs, schools such as Tuskegee was at least in origin, and other like organizations in the private sector are often racially oriented. A park, on the other hand, is more like a fire department or police department that traditionally serves the community. Mass recreation through the use of parks is plainly in the public domain, and state courts that aid private parties to perform that public function on a segregated basis implicate the State in conduct proscribed by the Fourteenth Amendment. Like the streets of the company town in Marsh v. State of Alabama, supra, the elective process of Terry v. Adams, supra, and the transit system of Public Utilities Commission of District of Columbia v. Pollak, supra, the predominant character and purpose of this park are municipal.

Under the circumstances of this case, we cannot but conclude that the public character of this park requires that it be treated as a public institution subject to the command of the Fourteenth Amendment, regardless of who now has title under state law. We may fairly assume that had the Georgia courts been of the view that even in private hands the park may not be operated for the public on a segregated basis, the resignation would not have been approved and private trustees appointed. We put the matter that way because on this record we cannot say that the transfer of title per se disentangled the park from segregation under the municipal regime that long controlled it. Since the judgment below gives effect to that purpose, it must be and is. Reversed.

AMALGAMATED FOOD EMPLOYEES UNION LOCAL 590
v. LOGAN VALLEY PLAZA
391 U.S. 308 (1968)

Mr. Justice MARSHALL delivered the opinion of the Court.

This case presents the question whether peaceful picketing of a business enterprise located within a shopping center can be enjoined on the ground that it constitutes an unconsented invasion of the property rights of the owners of the land on which the center is situated. We granted certiorari to consider petitioners' contentions that the decisions of the state courts enjoining their picketing as a trespass are violative of their rights under the First and Fourteenth Amendments of the United States Constitution.

Logan Valley Plaza, Inc. (Logan), one of the two respondents herein, owns a large, newly developed shopping center complex, known as the Logan Valley Mall, located near the City of Altoona, Pennsylvania. The shopping center is situated at the intersection of Plank Road, which is to the east of the center, and Good's Lane, which is to the south. Plank Road, also known as U.S. Route 220, is a heavily traveled highway along which traffic moves at a fairly high rate of speed. There are five entrance roads into the center, three from Plank Road and two from Good's Lane. Aside from these five entrances, the shopping center is totally separated from the adjoining roads by earthen berms. The berms are 15 feet wide along Good's Lane and 12 feet wide along Plank Road.

At the time of the events in this case, Logan Valley Mall was occupied by two businesses, Weis Markets, Inc. (Weis), the other respondent herein, and Sears, Roebuck and Co. (Sears)[.]

[On] December 8, 1965, Weis opened for business, employing a wholly nonunion staff of employees. A few days after it opened for business, Weis posted a sign on the exterior of its building prohibiting trespassing or soliciting by anyone other than its employees on its porch or parking lot. On December 17, 1965, members of Amalgamated Food Employees Union, Local 590, began picketing Weis. They carried signs stating that the Weis market was nonunion and that its employees were not "receiving union wages or other union benefits." The pickets did not include any employees of Weis, but rather were all employees of competitors of Weis. The picketing continued until December 27, during which time the number of pickets varied between four and 13 and averaged around six. The picketing was carried out almost entirely in the parcel pickup area and that portion of the parking lot immediately adjacent thereto. Although some congestion of the parcel pickup area occurred, such congestion was sporadic and infrequent. The picketing was peaceful at all times and unaccompanied by either threats or violence.

On December 27, Weis and Logan instituted an action in equity in the Court of Common Pleas of Blair County, and that court immediately issued an ex parte order enjoining petitioners from, inter alia, "[p]icketing and trespassing upon . . . the [Weis] storeroom, porch and parcel pick-up area . . . [and] the [Logan] parking area and all entrances and exits leading to said parking area." The effect of this order was to require that all picketing be carried on along the berms beside the public roads outside the shopping center. Picketing continued along the berms and, in addition, handbills asking the public not to patronize Weis because it was nonunion were distributed, while petitioners contested the validity of the ex parte injunction. After an evidentiary hearing, which resulted in the establishment of the facts set forth above, the Court of Common Pleas continued indefinitely its original ex parte injunction without modification.

That court explicitly rejected petitioners' claim under the First Amendment that they were entitled to picket within the confines of the shopping center, and their contention that the suit was within the primary jurisdiction of the NLRB. The trial judge held that the injunction was justified both in order to protect respondents' property rights and because the picketing was unlawfully aimed at coercing Weis to compel its employees to join a union. On appeal the Pennsylvania Supreme Court, with three Justices dissenting, affirmed the issuance of the injunction on the sole ground that petitioners' conduct constituted a trespass on respondents' property.

We start from the premise that peaceful picketing carried on in a location open generally to the public is, absent other factors involving the purpose or manner of the picketing, protected by the First Amendment.

[The] case squarely presents, therefore, the question whether Pennsylvania's generally valid rules against trespass to private property can be applied in these circumstances to bar petitioners from the Weis and Logan premises. It is clear that if the shopping center premises were not privately owned but instead constituted the business area of a municipality, which they to a large extent resemble, petitioners could not be barred from exercising their First Amendment rights there on the sole ground that title to the property was in the municipality. [The] streets, sidewalks, parks, and other similar public places are so historically associated with the exercise of First Amendment rights that access to them for the purpose of exercising such rights cannot constitutionally be denied broadly and absolutely. [That] the manner in which handbilling, or picketing, is carried out may be regulated does not mean that either can be barred under all circumstances on publicly owned property simply by recourse to traditional concepts of property law concerning the incidents of ownership of real property.

This Court has also held, in Marsh v. State of Alabama, 326 U.S. 501, 66 S.Ct. 276, 90 L.Ed. 265 (1946), that under some circumstances property that is privately owned may, at least for First Amendment purposes, be treated as though it were publicly held.   In Marsh, the appellant, a Jehovah's Witness, had undertaken to distribute religious literature on a sidewalk in the business district of Chickasaw, Alabama.   Chickasaw, a so-called company town, was wholly owned by the Gulf Shipbuilding Corporation.   "The property consists of residential buildings, streets, a system of sewers, a sewage disposal plant and a 'business block' on which business places are situated. . . . [T]he residents use the business block as their regular shopping center.   To do so, they now, as they have for many years, make use of a company-owned paved street and sidewalk located alongside the store fronts in order to enter and leave the stores and the post office.   Intersecting company-owned roads at each end of the business block lead into a four-lane public highway which runs parallel to the business block at a distance of thirty feet.   There is nothing to stop highway traffic from coming onto the business block and upon arrival a traveler may make free use of the facilities available there.   In short, the town and its shopping district are accessible to and freely used by the public in general and there is nothing to distinguish them from any other town and shopping center except the fact that the title to the property belongs to a private corporation."

The corporation had posted notices in the stores stating that the premises were private property and that no solicitation of any kind without written permission would be permitted.   Appellant Marsh was told that she must have a permit to distribute her literature and that a permit would not be granted to her.   When she declared that the company rule could not be utilized to prevent her from exercising her constitutional rights under the First Amendment, she was ordered to leave Chickasaw.   She refused to do so and was arrested for violating Alabama's criminal trespass statute.   In reversing her conviction under the statute, this Court held that the fact that the property from which appellant was sought to be ejected for exercising her First Amendment rights was owned by a private corporation rather than the State was an insufficient basis to justify the infringement on appellant's right to free expression occasioned thereby.   Likewise the fact that appellant Marsh was herself not a resident of the town was not considered material.

The similarities between the business block in Marsh and the shopping center in the present case are striking.   The perimeter of Logan Valley Mall is a little less than 1.1 miles. Inside the mall were situated, at the time of trial, two substantial commercial enterprises with numerous others soon to follow.   Immediately adjacent to the mall are two roads, one of which is a heavily traveled state highway and from both of which lead entrances directly into the mall.   Adjoining the buildings in the middle of the mall are sidewalks for the use of pedestrians going to and from their cars and from building to building.   In the parking areas, roadways for the use of vehicular traffic entering and leaving the mall are clearly marked out.   The general public has unrestricted access to the mall property.   The shopping center here is clearly the functional equivalent of the business district of Chickasaw involved in Marsh.

We see no reason why access to a business district in a company town for the purpose of exercising First Amendment rights should be constitutionally required, while access for the same purpose to property functioning as a business district should be limited simply because the property surrounding the "business district" is not under the same ownership.

Here the roadways provided for vehicular movement within the mall and the sidewalks leading from building to building are the functional equivalents of the streets and sidewalks of a normal municipal business district. The shopping center premises are open to the public to the same extent as the commercial center of a normal town. So far as can be determined, the main distinction in practice between use by the public of the Logan Valley Mall and of any other business district, were the decisions of the state courts to stand, would be that those members of the general public who sought to use the mall premises in a manner contrary to the wishes of the respondents could be prevented from so doing.

All we decide here is that because the shopping center serves as the community business block "and is freely accessible and open to the people in the area and those passing through," Marsh v. State of Alabama, 326 U.S., at 508, 66 S.Ct. at 279, the State may not delegate the power, through the use of its trespass laws, wholly to exclude those members of the public wishing to exercise their First Amendment rights on the premises in a manner and for a purpose generally consonant with the use to which the property is actually put.

[A]s to the sufficiency of respondents' ownership of the Logan Valley Mall premises as the sole support of the injunction issued against petitioners, we simply repeat what was said in Marsh v. State of Alabama, 326 U.S. at 506, 66 S.Ct. at 278, "Ownership does not always mean absolute dominion. The more an owner, for his advantage, opens up his property for use by the public in general, the more do his rights become circumscribed by the statutory and constitutional rights of those who use it." Logan Valley Mall is the functional equivalent of a "business block" and for First Amendment purposes must be treated in substantially the same manner.

The judgment of the Supreme Court of Pennsylvania is reversed and the case is remanded for further proceedings not inconsistent with this opinion. It is so ordered.

———

Comments on *Logan Valley Plaza*. *Logan Valley Plaza* marks the end of the Warren Court's expansion in regard to the public function doctrine. In the cases that follow, the Burger Court, with the civil rights era waning and privacy and free enterprise values increasing, will place significant limitations on public functions.

HUDGENS v. NATIONAL LABOR RELATIONS BOARD
424 U.S. 507 (1976)

Mr. Justice STEWART delivered the opinion of the Court.

A group of labor union members who engaged in peaceful primary picketing within the confines of a privately owned shopping center were threatened by an agent of the owner with arrest for criminal trespass if they did not depart. The question presented is whether this threat violated the National Labor Relations Act, 49 Stat. 449, as amended, 61 Stat. 136, 29 U.S.C. § 151 et seq. The National Labor Relations Board concluded that it did, and the Court of Appeals for the Fifth Circuit agreed. We granted certiorari because of the seemingly important questions of federal law presented.

The petitioner, Scott Hudgens, is the owner of the North DeKalb Shopping Center, located in suburban Atlanta, Ga. The center consists of a single large building with an enclosed mall. Surrounding the building is a parking area which can accommodate 2,640 automobiles. The shopping center houses 60 retail stores leased to various businesses. One of the lessees is the Butler Shoe Co. Most of the stores, including Butler's, can be entered only from the interior mall.

In January 1971, warehouse employees of the Butler Shoe Co. went on strike to protest the company's failure to agree to demands made by their union in contract negotiations. The strikers decided to picket not only Butler's warehouse but its nine retail stores in the Atlanta area as well, including the store in the North DeKalb Shopping Center. On January 22, 1971, four of the striking warehouse employees entered the center's enclosed mall carrying placards which read: "Butler Shoe Warehouse on Strike, AFL-CIO, Local 315." The general manager of the shopping center informed the employees that they could not picket within the mall or on the parking lot and threatened them with arrest if they did not leave. The employees departed but returned a short time later and began picketing in an area of the mall immediately adjacent to the entrances of the Butler store. After the picketing had continued for approximately 30 minutes, the shopping center manager again informed the pickets that if they did not leave they would be arrested for trespassing. The pickets departed.

The union subsequently filed with the Board an unfair labor practice charge against Hudgens, alleging interference with rights protected by § 7 of the Act. Relying on this Court's decision in *Food Employees v. Logan Valley Plaza*, 391 U.S. 308, 88 S.Ct. 1601, 20 L.Ed.2d 603, the Board entered a cease-and-desist order against Hudgens. Hudgens filed a petition for review in the Court of Appeals for the Fifth Circuit. Soon thereafter this Court decided Lloyd Corp. v. Tanner, 407 U.S. 551, 92 S.Ct. 2219, 33 L.Ed.2d 131, and Central Hardware Co. v. NLRB, 407 U.S. 539, 92 S.Ct. 2238, 33 L.Ed.2d 122, and the Court of Appeals remanded the case to the Board for reconsideration in light of those two decisions.

[It] is, of course, a commonplace that the constitutional guarantee of free speech is a guarantee only against abridgment by government, federal or state. Thus, while statutory or common law may in some situations extend protection or provide redress against a private corporation or person who seeks to abridge the free expression of others, no such protection or redress is provided by the Constitution itself.

This elementary proposition is little more than a truism. But even truisms are not always unexceptionably true, and an exception to this one was recognized almost 30 years ago in Marsh v. Alabama, 326 U.S. 501, 66 S.Ct. 276, 90 L.Ed. 265. In Marsh, a Jehovah's Witness who had distributed literature without a license on a sidewalk in Chickasaw, Ala., was convicted of criminal trespass.

The Court pointed out that if the "title" to Chickasaw had "belonged not to a private but to a municipal corporation and had appellant been arrested for violating a municipal ordinance rather than a ruling by those appointed by the corporation to manage a company town it would have been clear that appellant's conviction must be reversed." Concluding that Gulf's "property interests" should not be allowed to lead to a different result in Chickasaw, which did "not function differently from any other town," the Court invoked the First and Fourteenth Amendments to reverse the appellant's conviction.

It was the Marsh case that in 1968 provided the foundation for the Court's decision in Amalgamated Food Employees Union v. Logan Valley Plaza, 391 U.S. 308, 88 S.Ct. 1601, 20 L.Ed.2d 603. [The] Court's opinion . . . reviewed the Marsh case in detail, emphasized the similarities between the business block in Chickasaw, Ala., and the Logan Valley shopping center and unambiguously concluded: "The shopping center here is clearly the functional equivalent of the business district of Chickasaw involved in Marsh." 391 U.S., at 318, 88 S.Ct., at 1608. Upon the basis of that conclusion, the Court held that the First and Fourteenth Amendments required reversal of the judgment of the Pennsylvania Supreme Court.

Four years later the Court had occasion to reconsider the Logan Valley doctrine in Lloyd Corp. v. Tanner, 407 U.S. 551, 92 S.Ct. 2219, 33 L.Ed.2d 131. That case involved a shopping center covering some 50 acres in downtown Portland, Ore. On a November day in 1968 five young people entered the mall of the shopping center and distributed handbills protesting the then ongoing American military operations in Vietnam. Security guards told them to leave, and they did so, "to avoid arrest." Id., at 556, 92 S.Ct., at 2223. They subsequently brought suit in a Federal District Court, seeking declaratory and injunctive relief. The trial court ruled in their favor, holding that the distribution of handbills on the shopping center's property was protected by the First and Fourteenth Amendments. The Court of Appeals for the Ninth Circuit affirmed the judgment, 446 F.2d 545, expressly relying on this Court's Marsh and Logan Valley decisions. This Court reversed the judgment of the Court of Appeals.

The Court in its Lloyd opinion did not say that it was overruling the Logan Valley decision. Indeed a substantial portion of the Court's opinion in Lloyd was devoted to pointing out the differences between the two cases, noting particularly that, in contrast to the hand-billing in Lloyd, the picketing in Logan Valley had been specifically directed to a store in the shopping center and the pickets had had no other reasonable opportunity to reach their intended audience. But the fact is that the reasoning of the Court's opinion in Lloyd cannot be squared with the reasoning of the Court's opinion in Logan Valley.

It matters not that some Members of the Court may continue to believe that the Logan Valley case was rightly decided.   Our institutional duty is to follow until changed the law as it now is, not as some Members of the Court might wish it to be. And in the performance of that duty we make clear now, if it was not clear before, that the rationale of Logan Valley did not survive the Court's decision in the Lloyd case.   Not only did the Lloyd opinion incorporate lengthy excerpts from two of the dissenting opinions in Logan Valley, the ultimate holding in Lloyd amounted to a total rejection of the holding in Logan Valley : "The basic issue in this case is whether respondents, in the exercise of asserted First Amendment rights, may distribute handbills on Lloyd's private property contrary to its wishes and contrary to policy enforced against all handbilling. In addressing this issue, it must be remembered that the First and Fourteenth Amendments safeguard the rights of free speech and assembly by limitations on State action, not on action by the owner of private property used nondiscriminatorily for private purposes only. . . ."

> Respondents contend . . . that the property of a large shopping center is "open to the public," serves the same purposes as a "business district" of a municipality, and therefore has been dedicated to certain types of public use. The argument is that such a center has sidewalks, streets, and parking areas which are functionally similar to facilities customarily provided by municipalities. It is then asserted that all members of the public, whether invited as customers or not, have the same right of free speech as they would have on the similar public facilities in the streets of a city or town.
>
> The argument reaches too far. The Constitution by no means requires such an attenuated doctrine of dedication of private property to public use. The closest decision in theory, Marsh v. Alabama, supra, involved the assumption by a private enterprise of all of the attributes of a state-created municipality and the exercise by that enterprise of semi-official municipal functions as a delegate of the State. In effect, the owner of the company town was performing the full spectrum of municipal powers and stood in the shoes of the

State. In the instant case there is no comparable assumption or exercise of municipal functions or power.

We hold that there has been no such dedication of Lloyd's privately owned and operated shopping center to public use as to entitle respondents to exercise therein the asserted First Amendment rights. . . .

It conversely follows, therefore, that if the respondents in the Lloyd case did not have a First Amendment right to enter that shopping center distribute handbills concerning Vietnam, then the pickets in the present case did not have a First Amendment right to enter this shopping center for the purpose of advertising their strike against the Butler Shoe Co.

We conclude, in short, that under the present state of the law the constitutional guarantee of free expression has no part to play in a case such as this.

For the reasons stated in this opinion, the judgment is vacated and the case is remanded to the Court of Appeals with directions to remand to the National Labor Relations Board, so that the case may be there considered under the statutory criteria of the National Labor Relations Act alone.   It is so ordered.   Vacated and remanded.

JACKSON v. METROPOLITAN EDISON CO.
419 U.S. 345 (1974)

Mr. Justice REHNQUIST delivered the opinion of the Court.

Respondent Metropolitan Edison Co. is a privately owned and operated Pennsylvania corporation which holds a certificate of public convenience issued by the Pennsylvania Public Utility Commission empowering it to deliver electricity to a service area which includes the city of York, Pa.

Petitioner Catherine Jackson is a resident of York, who has received electricity in the past from respondent. Until September 1970, petitioner received electric service to her home in York under an account with respondent in her own name. When her account was terminated because of asserted delinquency in payments due for service, a new account with respondent was opened in the name of one James Dodson, another occupant of the residence, and service to the residence was resumed. There is a dispute as to whether payments due under the Dodson account for services provided during this period were ever made. In August 1971, Dodson left the residence. Service continued thereafter but concededly no payments were made. Petitioner states that no bills were received during this period.

On October 6, 1971, employees of Metropolitan came to the residence and inquired as to Dodson's present address. Petitioner stated that it was unknown to her. On the following day, another employee visited the residence and informed petitioner that the meter had been tampered with so as not to register amounts used. She disclaimed knowledge of this and requested that the service account for her home be shifted from Dodson's name to that of the Robert Jackson, later identified as her 12-year-old son. Four days later on October 11, 1971, without further notice to petitioner, Metropolitan employees disconnected her service.

Petitioner then filed suit against Metropolitan in the United States District Court. [She] urged that . . . Metropolitan's termination of her service for alleged nonpayment constituted "state action" depriving her of property in violation of the Fourteenth Amendment's guarantee of due process of law.

Petitioner next urges that state action is present because respondent provides an essential public service required to be supplied on a reasonably continuous basis by Pa.Stat.Ann., Tit. 66, § 1171 (1959), and hence performs a "public function." We have, of course, found state action present in the exercise by a private entity of powers traditionally exclusively reserved to the State. If we were dealing with the exercise by Metropolitan of some power delegated to it by the State which is traditionally associated with sovereignty, such as eminent domain, our case would be quite a different one. But while the Pennsylvania statute imposes an obligation to furnish service on regulated utilities, it imposes no such obligation on the State. The Pennsylvania courts have rejected the contention that the furnishing of utility services is either a state function or a municipal duty.

Perhaps in recognition of the fact that the supplying of utility service is not traditionally the exclusive prerogative of the State, petitioner invites the expansion of the doctrine of this limited line of cases into a broad principle that all businesses "affected with the public interest" are state actors in all their actions. We decline the invitation for reasons stated long ago in Nebbia v. New York, 291 U.S. 502, 54 S.Ct. 505, 78 L.Ed. 940 (1934), in the course of rejecting a substantive due process attack on state legislation: "It is clear that there is no closed class or category of businesses affected with a public interest. . . . The phrase 'affected with a public interest' can, in the nature of things, mean no more than that an industry, for adequate reason, is subject to control for the public good. In several of the decisions of this court wherein the expressions 'affected with a public interest,' and 'clothed with a public use,' have been brought forward as the criteria . . . it has been admitted that they are not susceptible of definition and form an unsatisfactory test. . . ." Id., at 536, 54 S.Ct. at 515.

Doctors, optometrists, lawyers, Metropolitan, and Nebbia's upstate New York grocery selling a quart of milk are all in regulated businesses, providing arguably essential goods and services, "affected with a public interest." We do not believe that such a status converts their every action, absent more, into that of the State. Affirmed.

Mr. Justice MARSHALL, dissenting.

The Metropolitan Edison Co. provides an essential public service to the people of York, Pa. It is the only entity public or private, that is authorized to supply electric service to most of the community.

The fact that the Metropolitan Edison Co. supplies an essential public service that is in many communities supplied by the government weighs more heavily for me than for the majority. The Court concedes that state action might be present if the activity in question were "traditionally associated with sovereignty," but it then undercuts that point by suggesting that a particular service is not a public function if the State in question has not required that it be governmentally operated. This reads the "public function" argument too narrowly. The whole point of the "public function" cases is to look behind the State's decision to provide public services through private parties. See Evans v. Newton, 382 U.S. 296, 86 S.Ct. 486, 15 L.Ed.2d 373 (1966); Terry v. Adams, 345 U.S. 461, 73 S.Ct. 809, 97 L.Ed. 1152 (1953); Marsh v. Alabama, 326 U.S. 501, 66 S.Ct. 276, 90 L.Ed. 265 (1946). In my view, utility service is traditionally identified with the State through universal public regulation or ownership to a degree sufficient to render it a "public function."

I agree with the majority that it requires more than a finding that a particular business is "affected with the public interest" before constitutional burdens can be imposed on that business. But when the activity in question is of such public importance that the State invariably either provides the service itself or permits private companies to act as state surrogates in providing it, much more is involved than just a matter of public interest. In those cases, the State has determined that if private companies wish to enter the field, they will have to surrender many of the prerogatives normally associated with private enterprise and behave in many ways like a governmental body. And when the State's regulatory scheme has gone that far, it seems entirely consistent to impose on the public utility the constitutional burdens normally reserved for the State.   I dissent.

FLAGG BROTHERS v. BROOKS
436 U.S. 149 (1978)

Mr. Justice REHNQUIST delivered the opinion of the Court.

[The question presented by this litigation is whether a warehouseman's proposed sale of goods entrusted to him for storage, as permitted by New York Uniform Commercial Code §7-210, is an action properly attributable to the State of New York. Section 7-210 provides that after proper notification, a warehouseman may satisfy a lien on goods in his possession by selling the goods.]

I. [When respondent Brooks was evicted from her apartment, the city marshal arranged for storage of her possessions in petitioner's warehouse. After a series of disputes over the validity of petitioner's charges for moving and storage, petitioner sent Brooks a letter threatening sale of the possessions. Brooks thereupon initiated this action, claiming, inter alia, that the sale pursuant to section 7-210 without a prior judicial hearing would violate the due process clause. She relied on a series of decisions in which the Court had held that due process requires that debtors be afforded a hearing before a creditor can utilize remedies involving the deprivation of property. See North Georgia Finishing, Inc. v. Di-Chem, Inc., 419 U.S. 601 (1975); Fuentes v. Shevin, 407 U.S. 67 (1972); Sniadach v. Family Finance Corp., 395 U.S. 337 (1969). Brooks was later joined in her action by respondent Jones, whose goods had also been stored by petitioner following her eviction.]

II. [The] only issue presented by this case is whether Flagg Brothers' action may fairly be attributed to the State of New York. We conclude that it may not.

III. Respondents' primary contention is that New York has delegated to Flagg Brothers a power "traditionally exclusively reserved to the State." [Jackson.] They argue that the resolution of private disputes is a traditional function of civil government, and that the State in §7-210 has delegated this function to Flagg Brothers. Respondents, however, have read too much into the language of our previous cases. While many functions have been traditionally performed by governments, very few have been "exclusively reserved to the State."

These two branches of the public-function doctrine have in common the feature of exclusivity.   Although the elections held by the Democratic Party and its affiliates were the only meaningful elections in Texas, and the streets owned by the Gulf Shipbuilding Corp. were the only streets in Chickasaw, the proposed sale by Flagg Brothers under § 7-210 is not the only means of resolving this purely private dispute.   Respondent Brooks has never alleged that state law barred her from seeking a waiver of Flagg Brothers' right to sell her goods at the time she authorized their storage.   Presumably, respondent Jones, who alleges that she never authorized the storage of her goods, could have sought to replevy her goods at any time under state law. The challenged statute itself provides a damages remedy against the warehouseman for violations of its provisions. This system of rights and remedies, recognizing the traditional place of private arrangements in ordering relationships in the commercial world, can hardly be said to have delegated to Flagg Brothers an exclusive prerogative of the sovereign. [Whatever] the particular remedies available under New York law, we do not consider a more detailed description of them necessary to our conclusion that the settlement of disputes between debtors and creditors is not traditionally an exclusive public function. Creditors and debtors have had available to them historically a far wider number of choices than has one who would be an elected public official, or a member of Jehovah's Witnesses who wished to distribute literature in Chickasaw, Ala., at the time *Marsh* was decided.

Thus, even if we were inclined to extend the sovereign-function doctrine outside of its present carefully confined bounds, the field of private commercial transactions would be a particularly inappropriate area into which to expand it. We conclude that our sovereign-function cases do not support a finding of state action here.

[We] would be remiss if we did not note that there are a number of state and municipal functions not covered by our election cases or governed by the reasoning of *Marsh* which have been administered with a greater degree of exclusivity by States and municipalities than has the function of so-called "dispute resolution." Among these are such functions as education, fire and police protection, and tax collection. We express no view as to the extent, if any, to which a city or State might be free to delegate to private parties the performance of such functions and thereby avoid the strictures of the Fourteenth Amendment.

Mr. Justice STEVENS, with whom Mr. Justice WHITE and Mr. Justice MARSHALL join, dissenting. . . .

New York has authorized the warehouseman to perform what is clearly a state function. The test of what is a state function for purposes of the Due Process Clause has been variously phrased. Most frequently the issue is presented in terms of whether the State has delegated a function traditionally and historically associated with sovereignty.

In this Court, petitioners have attempted to argue that the nonconsensual transfer of property rights is not a traditional function of the sovereign. The overwhelming historical evidence is to the contrary, however, and the Court wisely does not adopt this position. Instead, the Court reasons that state action cannot be found because the State has not delegated to the warehouseman an *exclusive* sovereign function.[8] This distinction, however, is not consistent with our prior decisions on state action; is not even adhered to by the Court in this case; and, most importantly, is inconsistent with the line of cases beginning with Sniadach v. Family Finance Corp., 395 U.S. 337, 89 S.Ct. 1820, 23 L.Ed.2d 349.

If it is unconstitutional for a State to allow a private party to exercise a traditional state power because the state supervision of that power is purely mechanical, the State surely

---

[8] See *ante*, at 1734. As I understand the Court's notion of "exclusivity," the sovereign function here is not exclusive because there may be other state remedies, under different statutes or common-law theories, available to respondents. *Ante*, at 1735. Even if I were to accept the notion that sovereign functions must be "exclusive," the Court's description of exclusivity is incomprehensible. The question is whether a particular action is a uniquely sovereign function, not whether state law forecloses any possibility of recovering for damages for such activity.

cannot immunize its actions from constitutional *scrutiny* by removing even the mechanical supervision.

Whether termed "traditional," "exclusive," or "significant," the state power to order binding, nonconsensual resolution of a conflict between debtor and creditor is exactly the sort of power with which the Due Process Clause is concerned. And the State's delegation of that power to a private party is, accordingly, subject to due process scrutiny. . . .

MANHATTAN COMMUNITY ACCESS CORPORATION, ET AL., PETITIONERS v. DEEDEE HALLECK, ET AL.
587 U.S. ___ (2019)

Justice KAVANAUGH delivered the opinion of the Court.

The Free Speech Clause of the First Amendment constrains governmental actors and protects private actors. To draw the line between governmental and private, this Court applies what is known as the state-action doctrine. Under that doctrine, as relevant here, a private entity may be considered a state actor when it exercises a function "traditionally exclusively reserved to the State." *Jackson* v. *Metropolitan Edison Co.*, 419 U. S. 345, 352 (1974).

This state-action case concerns the public access channels on Time Warner's cable system in Manhattan. Public access channels are available for private citizens to use. The public access channels on Time Warner's cable system in Manhattan are operated by a private nonprofit corporation known as MNN. The question here is whether MNN—even though it is a private entity—nonetheless is a state actor when it operates the public access channels. In other words, is operation of public access channels on a cable system a traditional, exclusive public function? If so, then the First Amendment would restrict Minnesota's exercise under the state-action doctrine as it has been articulated and applied by our precedents, we conclude that operation of public access channels on a cable system is not a traditional, exclusive public function. Moreover, a private entity such as MNN who opens its property for speech by others is not transformed by that fact alone into a state actor. In operating the public access channels, MNN is a private actor, not a state actor, and MNN therefore is not subject to First Amendment constraints on its editorial discretion. We reverse in relevant part the judgment of the Second Circuit, and we remand the case for further proceedings consistent with this opinion.

[Time] Warner operates a cable system in Manhattan. Under state law, Time Warner must set aside some channels on its cable system for public access. New York City (the City) has designated a private nonprofit corporation named Manhattan Neighborhood Network, commonly referred to as MNN, to operate Time Warner's public access channels in Manhattan. This case involves a complaint against MNN regarding its management of the public access channels.

B

DeeDee Halleck and Jesus Papoleto Melendez produced public access programming in Manhattan. They made a film about MNN's alleged neglect of the East Harlem community. Halleck submitted the film to MNN for airing on MNN's public access channels, and MNN later televised the film. Afterwards, MNN fielded multiple complaints about the film's content. In response, MNN temporarily suspended Halleck from using the public access channels.

Halleck and Melendez soon became embroiled in another dispute with MNN staff. In the wake of that dispute, MNN ultimately suspended Halleck and Melendez from all MNN services and facilities. Halleck and Melendez then sued MNN, among other parties, in Federal District Court. The two producers claimed that MNN violated their First Amendment free-speech rights when MNN restricted their access to the public access channels because of the content of their film. MNN moved to dismiss the producers' First Amendment claim on the ground that MNN is not a state actor and therefore is not subject to First Amendment restrictions on its editorial discretion. The District Court agreed with MNN and dismissed the producers' First Amendment claim.

The Second Circuit reversed in relevant part. 882 F. 3d 300, 308 (2018). In the majority opinion authored by Judge Newman and joined by Judge Lohier, the court stated that the public access channels in Manhattan are a public forum for purposes of the First Amendment. Reasoning that "public forums are usually operated by governments," the court concluded that MNN is a state actor subject to First Amendment constraints. *Id.*, at 306–307. Judge Lohier added a concurring opinion, explaining that MNN also qualifies as a state actor for the independent reason that "New York City delegated to MNN the traditionally public function of administering and regulating speech in the public forum of Manhattan's public access channels." *Id.*, at 309.

[We] granted certiorari to resolve disagreement among the Courts of Appeals on the question whether private operators of public access cable channels are state actors subject to the First Amendment.

II

[Here], the producers claim that MNN, a private entity, restricted their access to MNN's public access channels because of the content of the producers' film. The producers have advanced a First Amendment claim against MNN. The threshold problem with that First Amendment claim is a fundamental one: MNN is a private entity.

Relying on this Court's state-action precedents, the producers assert that MNN is nonetheless a state actor subject to First Amendment constraints on its editorial discretion. Under this Court's cases, a private entity can qualify as a state actor in a few limited circumstances—including, for example, (i) when the private entity performs a traditional, exclusive public function, see, *e.g., Jackson*, 419 U. S., at 352–354; (ii) when the government compels the private entity to take a particular action, see, *e.g., Blum* v. *Yaretsky*, 457 U. S. 991, 1004–1005 (1982); or (iii) when the government acts jointly with the private entity, see, *e.g., Lugar* v. *Edmondson Oil Co.*, 457 U. S. 922, 941–942 (1982).

The producers' primary argument here falls into the first category: The producers contend that MNN exercises a traditional, exclusive public function when it operates the public access channels on Time Warner's cable system in Manhattan. We disagree.

A

[Under] the Court's cases, a private entity may qualify as a state actor when it exercises "powers traditionally exclusively reserved to the State." *Jackson*, 419 U. S., at 352. It is not enough that the federal, state, or local government exercised the function in the past, or still does. And it is not enough that the function serves the public good or the public interest in some way. Rather, to qualify as a traditional, exclusive public function within the meaning of our state-action precedents, the government must have traditionally *and* exclusively performed the function. See *Rendell-Baker* v. *Kohn*, 457 U. S. 830, 842 (1982); *Jackson*, 419 U. S., at 352–353; *Evans* v. *Newton*, 382 U. S. 296, 300 (1966).

The Court has stressed that "very few" functions fall into that category. *Flagg Bros., Inc.* v. *Brooks*, 436 U. S. 149, 158 (1978). Under the Court's cases, those functions include, for example, running elections and operating a company town. See *Terry* v. *Adams*, 345 U. S. 461, 468– 470 (1953) (elections); *Marsh* v. *Alabama*, 326 U. S. 501, 505–509 (1946) (company town); *Smith* v. *Allwright*, 321 U. S. 649, 662–666 (1944) (elections); *Nixon* v. *Condon*, 286 U. S. 73, 84–89 (1932) (elections).

Relatedly, this Court has recognized that a private entity may, under certain circumstances, be deemed a state actor when the government has outsourced one of its constitutional obligations to a private entity. In *West* v. *Atkins*, for example, the State was constitutionally obligated to provide medical care to prison inmates. 487 U. S. 42, 56 (1988). That scenario is not present here because the government has no such obligation to operate public access channels.

The Court has ruled that a variety of functions do not fall into that category, including, for example: running sports associations and leagues, administering insurance payments, operating nursing homes, providing special education, representing indigent criminal defendants, resolving private disputes, and supplying electricity.

The relevant function in this case is operation of public access channels on a cable system. That function has not traditionally and exclusively been performed by government. [In] short, operating public access channels on a cable system is not a traditional, exclusive public function within the meaning of this Court's cases.

B

To avoid that conclusion, the producers widen the lens and contend that the relevant function here is not simply the operation of public access channels on a cable system, but rather is more generally the operation of a public forum for speech. And according to the producers, operation of a public forum for speech is a traditional, exclusive public function.

That analysis mistakenly ignores the threshold state- action question. When the government provides a forum for speech (known as a public forum), the government may be constrained by the First Amendment, meaning that the government ordinarily may not exclude speech or speakers from the forum on the basis of viewpoint, or sometimes even on the basis of content.

By contrast, when a private entity provides a forum for speech, the private entity is not ordinarily constrained by the First Amendment because the private entity is not a state actor. The private entity may thus exercise editorial discretion over the speech and speakers in the forum. This Court so ruled in its 1976 decision in *Hudgens v. NLRB*. There, the Court held that a shopping center owner is not a state actor subject to First Amendment requirements such as the public forum doctrine.

The *Hudgens* decision reflects a commonsense principle: Providing some kind of forum for speech is not an activity that only governmental entities have traditionally performed. Therefore, a private entity who provides a forum for speech is not transformed by that fact alone into a state actor. [In] short, merely hosting speech by others is not a traditional, exclusive public function and does not alone transform private entities into state actors subject to First Amendment constraints.

[C]

Next, the producers retort that this case differs from *Hudgens* because New York City has designated MNN to operate the public access channels on Time Warner's cable system, and because New York State heavily regulates MNN with respect to the public access channels. Under this Court's cases, however, those facts do not establish that MNN is a state actor.

New York City's designation of MNN to operate the public access channels is analogous to a government license, a government contract, or a government-granted monopoly. But as the Court has long held, the fact that the government licenses, contracts with, or grants a monopoly to a private entity does not convert the private entity into a state actor—unless the private entity is performing a traditional, exclusive public function. [The] same principle applies if the government funds or subsidizes a private entity. See *Blum*, 457 U. S., at 1011; *Rendell-Baker*, 457 U. S., at 840.

[Here], therefore, the City's designation of MNN to operate the public access channels on Time Warner's cable system does not make MNN a state actor.

So, too, New York State's extensive regulation of MNN's operation of the public access channels does not make MNN a state actor. Under the State's regulations, air time on the public access channels must be free, and programming must be aired on a first-come, first-served basis. Those regulations restrict MNN's editorial discretion and in effect require MNN to operate almost like a common carrier. But under this Court's cases, those restrictions do not render MNN a state actor.

In *Jackson* v. *Metropolitan Edison Co.*, the leading case on point, the Court stated that the "fact that a business is subject to state regulation does not by itself convert its action into that of the State." 419 U. S., at 350. In that case, the Court held that "a heavily regulated, privately owned utility, enjoying at least a partial monopoly in the providing of electrical service within its territory," was not a state actor. *Id.*, at 358. The Court explained that the "mere existence" of a "regulatory scheme"—even if "extensive and detailed"—did not render the utility a state actor. *Id.,* at 350, and n. 7. Nor did it matter whether the State had authorized the utility to provide electric service to the community, or whether the utility was the only entity providing electric service to much of that community.

This case closely parallels *Jackson*. Like the electric utility in *Jackson*, MNN is "a heavily regulated, privately owned" entity. *Id.*, at 358. As in *Jackson*, the regulations do not transform the regulated private entity into a state actor.

[In] sum, we conclude that MNN is not subject to First Amendment constraints on how it exercises its editorial discretion with respect to the public access channels. To be sure, MNN is subject to state-law constraints on its editorial discretion (assuming those state laws do not violate a federal statute or the Constitution). If MNN violates those state laws, or violates any applicable con- tracts, MNN could perhaps face state-law sanctions or liability of some kind. We of course take no position on any potential state-law questions. We simply conclude that MNN, as a private actor, is not subject to First Amendment constraints on how it exercises editorial discretion over the speech and speakers on its public access channels.

III

Perhaps recognizing the problem with their argument that MNN is a state actor under ordinary state-action principles applicable to private entities and private property, the producers alternatively contend that the public access channels are actually the property of New York City, not the property of Time Warner or MNN. On this theory, the producers say (and the dissent agrees) that MNN is in essence simply managing government property on behalf of New York City.

The short answer to that argument is that the public access channels are not the property of New York City. Nothing in the record here suggests that a government (federal, state, or city) owns or leases either the cable system or the public access channels at issue here. Both Time Warner and MNN are private entities. Time Warner is the cable operator, and it owns its cable network, which contains the public access channels. MNN operates those public access channels with its own facilities and equipment. The City does not own or lease the public access channels, and the City does not possess a formal easement or other property interest in those channels. The franchise agreements between the City and Time Warner do not say that the City has any property interest in the public access channels. On the contrary, the franchise agreements expressly place the public access channels "under the jurisdiction" of MNN. App. 22. Moreover, the producers did not allege in their complaint that the City has a property interest in the channels. And the producers have not cited any basis in state law for such a conclusion. Put simply, the City does not have "any formal easement or other property interest in those channels." *Denver Area*, 518 U. S., at 828 (opinion of THOMAS, J.).

It does not matter that a provision in the franchise agreements between the City and Time Warner allowed the City to designate a private entity to operate the public access channels on Time Warner's cable system. Time Warner still owns the cable system. And MNN still operates the public access channels. To reiterate, nothing in the franchise agreements suggests that the City possesses any property interest in Time Warner's cable system, or in the public access channels on that system.

[Having] said all that, our point here should not be read too broadly. Under the laws in certain States, including New York, a local government may decide to itself operate the public access channels on a local cable system (as many local governments in New York State and around the country already do), or could take appropriate steps to obtain a property interest in the public access channels. Depending on the circumstances, the First Amendment might then constrain the local government's operation of the public access channels. We decide only the case before us in light of the record before us.

[MNN] is a private entity that operates public access channels on a cable system. Operating public access channels on a cable system is not a traditional, exclusive public function. A private entity such as MNN who opens its property for speech by others is not transformed by that fact alone into a state actor. Under the text of the Constitution and our precedents, MNN is not a state actor subject to the First Amendment. We reverse in relevant part the judgment of the Second Circuit, and we remand the case for further proceedings consistent with this opinion.

It is so ordered.

Justice SOTOMAYOR, with whom Justice GINSBURG, Justice BREYER, and Justice KAGAN join, dissenting.

II
[A]
[2]

[I]t should become clear that the public-access channels are a public forum. Outside of classic examples like sidewalks and parks, a public forum exists only where the government has deliberately opened up the setting for speech by at least a subset of the public. *Cornelius*, 473 U. S., at 802. "Accordingly, the Court has looked to the policy and practice of the government," as well as the nature of the property itself, "to ascertain whether it intended to designate a place not traditionally open to assembly and debate as a public forum." See *ibid.* For example, a state college might make its facilities open to student groups, or a municipality might open up an auditorium for certain public meetings. See *id.*, at 802–803.

The requisite governmental intent is manifest here. As noted above, New York State regulations require that the channels be made available to the public "on a first-come, first-served, nondiscriminatory basis." 16 N. Y. Codes, Rules & Regs. §895.4(c)(4); see also §§895.4(c)(8)–(9). The State, in other words, mandates that the doors be wide open for public expression. MNN's contract with Time Warner follows suit. App. 23. And that is essentially how MNN itself describes things. See Tr. of Oral Arg. 9 ("We do not prescreen videos. We—they come into the door. We put them on the air"). These regulations "evidenc[e] a clear intent to create a public forum." *Cornelius*, 473 U. S., at 802.

[III]

[B]

To see more clearly the difference between the cases on which the majority fixates and the present case, leave aside the majority's private comedy club. Imagine instead that a state college runs a comedy showcase each year, renting out a local theater and, pursuant to state regulations mandating open access to certain kinds of student activities, allowing students to sign up to perform on a first-come, first-served basis. Cf. *Rosenberger* v. *Rector and Visitors of Univ. of Va.*, 515 U. S. 819 (1995). After a few years, the college decides that it is tired of running the show, so it hires a performing-arts nonprofit to do the job. The nonprofit prefers humor that makes fun of a certain political party, so it allows only student acts that share its views to participate. Does the majority believe that the nonprofit is indistinguishable, for purposes of state action, from a private comedy club opened by local entrepreneurs?

I hope not. But two dangers lurk here regardless. On the one hand, if the City's decision to outsource the channels to a private entity did render the First Amendment irrelevant, there would be substantial cause to worry about the potential abuses that could follow. Can a state university evade the First Amendment by hiring a non- profit to apportion funding to student groups? Can a city do the same by appointing a corporation to run a municipal theater? What about its parks?

On the other hand, the majority hastens to qualify its decision, see *ante*, at 7, n. 1, 15, and to cabin it to the specific facts of this case, *ante*, at 15. Those are prudent limitations. Even so, the majority's focus on *Jackson* still risks sowing confusion among the lower courts about how and when government outsourcing will render any abuses that follow beyond the reach of the Constitution.

[IV]

This is not a case about bigger governments and smaller individuals, *ante*, at 16; it is a case about principals and agents. New York City opened up a public forum on public-access channels in which it has a property interest. It asked MNN to run that public forum, and MNN accepted the job. That makes MNN subject to the First Amendment, just as if the City had decided to run the public forum itself.

While the majority emphasizes that its decision is narrow and fact bound, *ante*, at 15, that does not make it any less misguided. It is crucial that the Court does not continue to ignore the reality, fully recognized by our precedents, that private actors who have been delegated constitutional responsibilities like this one should be accountable to the Constitution's demands. I respectfully

———

Comment on Public Function. Is there anything left of public function doctrine? Is *Marsh* still good law? Why or why not? In a society that in some sense is run as much by private as government hands, given the Court's views at present, how many functions can be public? What would you have to prove? Given the roots of modern state action law being seeded by almost the same civil rights issues that spawned the Fourteenth Amendment itself, one particular line of cases has yet to be challenged, "The White Primary Cases," and given such they mandate particular attention.

1. "THE WHITE PRIMARY CASES"

This series of cases involved the effective exclusion of blacks from Texas elections, with the "primary election" being used to "privatize" the discrimination. The Court held that the discriminatory policies of private political organizations could be attributed to the state. These cases stand out today as perhaps the "last bastion" of public function doctrine.

NIXON v. HERNDON, 273 U.S. 536 (1927). The Court held that the Fourteenth Amendment had been violated when blacks were denied ballots in the State Democratic Party primary pursuant to a Texas statute that stated, "[I]n no event shall a Negro be eligible to participate in a Democratic Party primary election held in the State of Texas."

NIXON v. CONDON, 286 U.S. 73 (1932). Texas, unfettered by the decision in *Herndon*, rewrote the statute to provide that the State Executive Committee of the party in power could prescribe the qualifications of its members for voting. The Court once again found that the denial of the franchise to blacks was unconstitutional. Since the Committee was acting under authority expressly delegated by the state, the Court reasoned that its decisions could be attributed to the state.

GROVEY v. TOWNSEND, 295 U.S. 45 (1935). Texas, still flaunting its goal of racial exclusion, next allowed this policy to be applied by the state party convention without specific statutory authorization. The Court, now complicit in the effort, held that there was no state action and therefore no constitutional violation. In the Court's view, the exclusionary policy was voluntarily adopted by the Democratic Party, which was not an organ of the state. The policy was no more than a refusal of party membership with which "the State need have no concern."

SMITH v. ALLWRIGHT, 321 U.S. 649 (1944). *Grovey* was nonetheless overruled in *Allwright*. The Court held that "[t]he privilege of membership in a party may be, as this Court said in [*Grovey*,] no concern of a State. But when, as here, that privilege is also the essential qualification for voting in a primary to select nominees for a general election, the State makes the action of the party the action of the State." Of interest, the Court based its conclusion on the 15th Amendment, rather than the 14th, and cited to an intervening decision, *U.S. v. Classic*, 313 U.S. 299 (1941), as a basis for the decision.

The Court based its finding on the fact that the Democratic Party's exclusionary policy could be attributed to the state, and seemed to rest this analysis on the "public function" performed by party officials. Thus, the Court stated that "the place of the primary in the electoral scheme makes clear that state delegation to a party of the power to fix the qualifications of primary elections is delegation of a state function that may make the party's action the action of the State."

To the Court, "when primaries become a part of the machinery for choosing officials, state and national, as they have here, the same tests to determine the character of discrimination or abridgement should be applied to the primary as are applied to the general election. If the State requires a certain electoral procedure, prescribes a general election ballot made up of party nominees so chosen and limits the choice of the electorate in general elections for state offices, practically speaking, to those whose names appear on such a ballot, it endorses, adopts and enforces the discrimination against Negroes, practiced by a party entrusted by Texas law with the determination of the qualifications of participants in the primary."

The opinion also suggested that the state had an affirmative constitutional obligation to prevent private organizations from abridging electoral rights: "The United States is a constitutional democracy. Its organic law grants to all citizens a right to participate in the choice of elected officials without restriction by any State because of race. This grant to the people of the opportunity for choice is not to be nullified by a State through casting its electoral process in a form which permits a private organization to practice racial discrimination in the election. Constitutional rights would be of little value if they could be thus indirectly denied."

TERRY v. ADAMS, 345 U.S. 461 (1953). Texas was still undeterred. In a final effort to exclude its African American citizens from voting, "pre-primary, primaries" were held by the Jaybird Democratic Association, a Texas political organization. The Jaybirds maintained that they were not a political party at all, but rather a self-governing voluntary club. Their election was not regulated by the state, and there was no legal connection between victory in that election and nomination by the Democratic Party to run in the subsequent general election. As a practical matter, however, white voters generally abided by the "recommendations" of the Jaybirds, and the Jaybird president testified that a purpose of his organization was to exclude blacks from the voting process. The Jaybirds were so successful in this endeavor that victors in the Jaybird primary had almost without exception run and won without opposition in the Democratic primaries and the general election that followed.

Although eight Justices agreed that exclusion of blacks from the Jaybird primary violated the Fifteenth Amendment, no opinion attracted a majority. Writing for three justices, Justice Black focused on the state's failure to control private conduct that effectively deprived blacks of political power: "The only election that has counted in this Texas county for more than fifty years has been that held by the Jaybirds from which Negroes were excluded. The Democratic primary and the general election have become no more than the perfunctory ratifiers of the choice that has already been made in Jaybird elections from which Negroes have been excluded. It is immaterial that the state does not control that part of this elective process which it leaves for the Jaybirds to manage. [The] effect of the whole procedure, Jaybird primary plus Democratic primary plus general election, is to do precisely that which the Fifteenth Amendment forbids — strip Negroes of every vestige of influence in selecting the officials who control the local county matters that intimately touch the daily lives of citizens."

Writing only for himself, Justice Frankfurter found state involvement because state election officials had participated as voters in the Jaybird primary. The four other Justices who found the requisite state action joined an opinion by Justice Clark. In his view, the record established that the Jaybirds operated "as part and parcel of the Democratic Party, an organization existing under the auspices of Texas law." It followed that the result was dictated by Smith v. Allwright. "[When] a state structures its electoral apparatus in a form which devolves upon a political organization the uncontested choice of public officials, that organization itself, in whatever disguise, takes on those attributes of government which draw the Constitution's safeguards into play."

Justice Minton cast the sole dissenting vote.

B. STATE INVOLVEMENT

SHELLEY v. KRAEMER
334 U.S. 1 (1948)

Mr. Chief Justice VINSON delivered the opinion of the Court.

These cases present for our consideration questions relating to the validity of court enforcement of private agreements, generally described as restrictive covenants, which have as their purpose the exclusion of persons of designated race or color from the Basic constitutional issues of obvious importance have been raised.

The first of these cases comes to this Court on certiorari to the Supreme Court of Missouri. On February 16, 1911, thirty out of a total of thirty-nine owners of property fronting both sides of Labadie Avenue between Taylor Avenue and Cora Avenue in the city of St. Louis, signed an agreement, which was subsequently recorded, providing in part:

> The said property is hereby restricted to the use and occupancy for the term of Fifty (50) years from this date, so that it shall be a condition all the time and whether recited and referred to as [sic] not in subsequent conveyances and shall attach to the land, as a condition precedent to the sale of the same, that hereafter no part of said property or any portion thereof shall be, for said term of Fifty-years, occupied by any person not of the Caucasian race, it being intended hereby to restrict the use of said property for said period of time against the occupancy as owners or tenants of any portion of said property for resident or other purpose by people of the Negro or Mongolian Race.

On August 11, 1945, pursuant to a contract of sale, petitioners Shelley, who are Negroes, for valuable consideration received from one Fitzgerald a warranty deed to the parcel in question. The trial court found that petitioners had no actual knowledge of the restrictive agreement at the time of the purchase.

On October 9, 1945, respondents, as owners of other property subject to the terms of the restrictive covenant, brought suit in Circuit Court of the city of St. Louis praying that petitioners Shelley be restrained from taking possession of the property and that judgment be entered divesting title out of petitioners Shelley and revesting title in the immediate grantor or in such other person as the court should direct. The trial court denied the requested relief on the ground that the restrictive agreement, upon which respondents based their action, had never become final and complete because it was the intention of the parties to that agreement that it was not to become effective until signed by all property owners in the district, and signatures of all the owners had never been obtained.

The agreement provided that the restrictions were to remain in effect until January 1, 1960. The contract was subsequently recorded; and similar agreements were executed with respect to eighty percent of the lots in the block in which the property in question is situated.

Whether the equal protection clause of the Fourteenth Amendment inhibits judicial enforcement by state courts of restrictive covenants based on race or color is a question which this Court has not heretofore been called upon to consider. It cannot be doubted that among the civil rights intended to be protected from discriminatory state action by the

Fourteenth Amendment are the rights to acquire, enjoy, own and dispose of property. Equality in the enjoyment of property rights was regarded by the framers of that Amendment as an essential pre-condition to the realization of other basic civil rights and liberties which the Amendment was intended to guarantee. Thus, 1978 of the Revised Statutes, derived from § 1 of the Civil Rights Act of 1866 which was enacted by Congress while the Fourteenth Amendment was also under consideration, provides: "All citizens of the United States shall have the same right, in every State and Territory, as is enjoyed by white citizens thereof to inherit, purchase, lease, sell, hold, and convey real and personal property." This Court has given specific recognition to the same principle.

It is likewise clear that restrictions on the right of occupancy of the sort sought to be created by the private agreements in these cases could not be squared with the requirements of the Fourteenth Amendment if imposed by state statute or local ordinance. We do not understand respondents to urge the contrary.

But the present cases, unlike those just discussed, do not involve action by state legislatures or city councils. Here the particular patterns of discrimination and the areas in which the restrictions are to operate, are determined, in the first instance, by the terms of agreements among private individuals. Participation of the State consists in the enforcement of the restrictions so defined. The crucial issue with which we are here confronted is whether this distinction removes these cases from the operation of the prohibitory provisions of the Fourteenth Amendment.

Since the decision of this Court in the Civil Rights Cases, 1883, 109 U.S. 3, 3 S.Ct. 18, 27 L.Ed. 835, the principle has become firmly embedded in our constitutional law that the action inhibited by the first section of the Fourteenth Amendment is only such action as may fairly be said to be that of the States. That Amendment erects no shield against merely private conduct, however discriminatory or wrongful.

We conclude, therefore, that the restrictive agreements standing alone cannot be regarded as a violation of any rights guaranteed to petitioners by the Fourteenth Amendment. So long as the purposes of those agreements are effectuated by voluntary adherence to their terms, it would appear clear that there has been no action by the State and the provisions of the Amendment have not been violated.

But here there was more. These are cases in which the purposes of the agreements were secured only by judicial enforcement by state courts of the restrictive terms of the agreements. The respondents urge that judicial enforcement of private agreements does not amount to state action; or, in any event, the participation of the State is so attenuated in character as not to amount to state action within the meaning of the Fourteenth Amendment. Finally, it is suggested, even if the States in these cases may be deemed to have acted in the constitutional sense, their action did not deprive petitioners of rights guaranteed by the Fourteenth Amendment. We move to a consideration of these matters.

That the action of state courts and of judicial officers in their official capacities is to be regarded as action of the State within the meaning of the Fourteenth Amendment, is a proposition which has long been established by decisions of this Court.

We have no doubt that there has been state action in these cases in the full and complete sense of the phrase. The undisputed facts disclose that petitioners were willing purchasers of properties upon which they desired to establish homes. The owners of the properties were willing sellers; and contracts of sale were accordingly consummated. It is clear that but for the active intervention of the state courts, supported by the full panoply of state power, petitioners would have been free to occupy the properties in question without restraint.

These are not cases, as has been suggested, in which the States have merely abstained from action, leaving private individuals free to impose such discriminations as they see fit. Rather, these are cases in which the States have made available to such individuals the full coercive power of government to deny to petitioners, on the grounds of race or color, the enjoyment of property rights in premises which petitioners are willing and financially able to acquire and which the grantors are willing to sell. The difference between judicial enforcement and nonenforcement of the restrictive covenants is the difference to petitioners between being denied rights of property available to other members of the community and being accorded full enjoyment of those rights on an equal footing.

The enforcement of the restrictive agreements by the state courts in these cases was directed pursuant to the common-law policy of the States as formulated by those courts in earlier decisions. The judicial action in each case bears the clear and unmistakable imprimatur of the State. We have noted that previous decisions of this Court have established the proposition that judicial action is not immunized from the operation of the Fourteenth Amendment simply because it is taken pursuant to the state's common-law policy. Nor is the Amendment ineffective simply because the particular pattern of discrimination, which the State has enforced, was defined initially by the terms of a private agreement. State action, as that phrase is understood for the purposes of the Fourteenth Amendment, refers to exertions of state power in all forms. And when the effect of that action is to deny rights subject to the protection of the Fourteenth Amendment, it is the obligation of this Court to enforce the constitutional commands.

We hold that in granting judicial enforcement of the restrictive agreements in these cases, the States have denied petitioners the equal protection of the laws and that, therefore, the action of the state courts cannot stand. We have noted that freedom from discrimination by the States in the enjoyment of property rights was among the basic objectives sought to be effectuated by the framers of the Fourteenth Amendment. That such discrimination has occurred in these cases is clear.

Respondents urge, however, that since the state courts stand ready to enforce restrictive covenants excluding white persons from the ownership or occupancy of property covered by such agreements, enforcement of covenants excluding colored persons may not be deemed a denial of equal protection of the laws to the colored persons who are thereby affected. This contention does not bear scrutiny. The parties have directed our attention to no case in which a court, state or federal, has been called upon to enforce a covenant excluding members of the white majority from ownership or occupancy of real property on grounds of race or color. But there are more fundamental considerations. The rights created by the first section of the Fourteenth Amendment are, by its terms, guaranteed to the individual. The rights established are personal rights. It is, therefore, no answer to these petitioners to say that the courts may also be induced to deny white persons rights of ownership and occupancy on grounds of race or color. Equal protection of the laws is not achieved through indiscriminate imposition of inequalities.

For the reasons stated, the judgment of the Supreme Court of Missouri and the judgment of the Supreme Court of Michigan must be reversed. Reversed.

Comments on *Shelley*. Did the Court in *Shelley* hold private restrictive covenants illegal or unenforceable? What would be the difference? What is the "equal protection" issue in *Shelley*? Did the Court resolve it? Was the Fair Housing Act of 1964, which outlawed racial discrimination in covenants of this nature, necessary after *Shelley*? Could the FHA be supported by the Fourteenth Amendment?   What constitutional basis do you think Congress used to support the statute?

How broad is *Shelley*?   Vinson states, "State action, as that phrase is understood for the purposes of the Fourteenth Amendment, refers to exertions of state power in all forms." Is this far-reaching, particularly given the amount of state regulation of activities that are "quasi-public" but in private hands?   How would you expect the "modern court" to view the potential breadth of *Shelley*?

The cases that follow, *Pennsylvania v. Board* and *Evans*, apply *Shelley* to other "property" circumstances.

PENNSYLVANIA v. BOARD OF DIRECTORS OF CITY TRUSTS OF CITY OF PHILADELPHIA
353 U.S. 230 (1957)

The motion to dismiss the appeal for want of jurisdiction is granted.   28 U.S.C. § 1257(2), 28 U.S.C.A. § 1257(2).   Treating the papers whereon the appeal was taken as a petition for writ of certiorari, 28 U.S.C. § 2103, 28 U.S.C.A. § 2103, the petition is granted. 28 U.S.C. § 1257(3), 28 U.S.C.A. § 1257(3).   Stephen Girard, by a will probated in 1831, left a fund in trust for the erection, maintenance, and operation of a "college."   The will provided that the college was to admit "as many poor white male orphans, between the ages of six and ten years, as the said income shall be adequate to maintain."   The will named as trustee the City of Philadelphia.   The provisions of the will were carried out by the State and City and the college was opened in 1848.   Since 1869, by virtue of an act of the Pennsylvania Legislature, the trust has been administered and the college operated by the "Board of Directors of City Trusts of the City of Philadelphia."   Pa.Laws 1869, No. 1258, p. 1276; Purdon's Pa.Stat.Ann., 1957, Tit. 53, § 16365.

In February 1954, the petitioners Foust and Felder applied for admission to the college.   They met all qualifications except that they were Negroes.   For this reason the Board refused to admit them.   They petitioned the Orphans' Court of Philadelphia County for an order directing the Board to admit them, alleging that their exclusion because of race violated the Fourteenth Amendment to the Constitution.   The State of Pennsylvania and the City of Philadelphia joined in the suit also contending the Board's action violated the Fourteenth Amendment.   The Orphans' Court rejected the constitutional contention and refused to order the applicant's admission.   In re Girard's Estate, 4 Pa.Dist. & Co.R.2d 671 (Orph.Ct.Philadelphia).   This was affirmed by the Pennsylvania Supreme Court. 386 Pa. 548, 127 A.2d 287.

The Board which operates Girard College is an agency of the State of Pennsylvania. Therefore, even though the Board was acting as a trustee, its refusal to admit Foust and Felder to the college because they were Negroes was discrimination by the State. Such discrimination is forbidden by the Fourteenth Amendment.   Brown v. Board of Education, 347 U.S. 483, 74 S.Ct. 686, 98 L.Ed. 873.   Accordingly, the judgment of the Supreme Court of Pennsylvania is reversed and the cause is remanded for further proceedings not inconsistent with this opinion.

Reversed and remanded with directions.

EVANS v. ABNEY
396 U.S. 435 (1970)

Mr. Justice BLACK delivered the opinion of the Court.

Once again this Court must consider the constitutional implications of the 1911 will of United States Senator A. O. Bacon of Georgia which conveyed property in trust to Senator Bacon's home city of Macon for the creation of a public park for the exclusive use of the white people of that city. As a result of our earlier decision in this case which held that the park, Baconsfield, could not continue to be operated on a racially discriminatory basis, Evans v. Newton, 382 U.S. 296, 86 S.Ct. 486, 15 L.Ed.2d 373 (1966), the Supreme Court of Georgia ruled that Senator Bacon's intention to provide a park for whites only had become impossible to fulfill and that accordingly the trust had failed and the parkland and other trust property had reverted by operation of Georgia law to the heirs of the Senator. 224 Ga. 826, 165 S.E.2d 160 (1968). Petitioners, the same Negro citizens of Macon who have sought in the courts to integrate the park, contend that this termination of the trust violates their rights to equal protection and due process under the Fourteenth Amendment. We granted certiorari because of the importance of the questions involved. 394 U.S. 1012, 89 S.Ct. 1628, 23 L.Ed.2d 38 (1969). For the reasons to be stated, we are of the opinion that the judgment of the Supreme Court of Georgia should be, and it is, affirmed.

Any harshness that may have resulted from the state court's decision can be attributed solely to its intention to effectuate as nearly as possible the explicit terms of Senator Bacon's will.

Similarly, the situation presented in this case is also easily distinguishable from that presented in Shelley v. Kraemer, 334 U.S. 1, 68 S.Ct. 836, 92 L.Ed. 1161 (1948), where we held unconstitutional state judicial action which had affirmatively enforced a private scheme of discrimination against Negroes. Here the effect of the Georgia decision eliminated all discrimination against Negroes in the park by eliminating the park itself, and the termination of the park was a loss shared equally by the white and Negro citizens of Macon since both races would have enjoyed a constitutional right of equal access to the park's facilities had it continued. The judgment is affirmed.

Mr. Justice BRENNAN, dissenting.

Shelley v. Kraemer, 334 U.S. 1, 68 S.Ct. 836, 92 L.Ed. 1161 (1948), stands at least for the proposition that where parties of different races are willing to deal with one another a state court cannot keep them from doing so by enforcing a privately devised racial restriction.

This, then, is not a case of private discrimination. It is rather discrimination in which the State of Georgia is "significantly involved," and enforcement of the reverter is therefore unconstitutional. Cf. Burton v. Wilmington Parking Authority, 365 U.S. 715, 81 S.Ct. 856, 6 L.Ed.2d 45 (1961); Robinson v. Florida, 378 U.S. 153, 84 S.Ct. 1693, 12 L.Ed.2d 771 (1964). I would reverse the judgment of the Supreme Court of Georgia.

BURTON v. WILMINGTON PARKING AUTHORITY
365 U.S. 715 (1961)

Mr. Justice CLARK delivered the opinion of the Court.

In this action for declaratory and injunctive relief it is admitted that the Eagle Coffee Shoppe, Inc., a restaurant located within an off-street automobile parking building in Wilmington, Delaware, has refused to serve appellant food or drink solely because he is a Negro.   The parking building is owned and operated by the Wilmington Parking Authority, an agency of the State of Delaware, and the restaurant is the Authority's lessee. Appellant claims that such refusal abridges his rights under the Equal Protection Clause of the Fourteenth Amendment to the United States Constitution.   The Supreme Court of Delaware has held that Eagle was acting in "a purely private capacity" (157 A.2d 902) under its lease; that its action was not that of the Authority and was not, therefore, state action within the contemplation of the prohibitions contained in that Amendment.   It also held that under 24 Del.Code § 1501, Eagle was a restaurant, not an inn, and that as such it "is not required (under Delaware law) to serve any and all persons entering its place of business."   Del.1960, 157 A.2d 894, 902.   On appeal here from the judgment as having been based upon a statute construed unconstitutionally, we postponed consideration of the question of jurisdiction under 28 U.S.C. § 1257(2), 28 U.S.C.A. § 1257(2), to the hearing on the merits. 364 U.S. 810, 81 S.Ct. 52, 5 L.Ed.2d 40.   We agree with the respondents that the appeal should be dismissed and accordingly the motion to dismiss is granted. However, since the action of Eagle in excluding appellant raises an important constitutional question, the papers whereon the appeal was taken are treated as a petition for a writ of certiorari, 28 U.S.C. § 2103, 28 U.S.C.A. § 2103, and the writ is granted. 28 U.S.C. § 1257(3), 28 U.S.C.A. § 1257(3).   On the merits we have concluded that the exclusion of appellant under the circumstances shown to be present here was discriminatory state action in violation of the Equal Protection Clause of the Fourteenth Amendment.

The Authority was created by the City of Wilmington pursuant to 22 Del.Code, §§ 501-515.   It is "a public body corporate and politic, exercising public powers of the State as an agency thereof." § 504.   Its statutory purpose is to provide adequate parking facilities for the convenience of the public and thereby relieve the 'parking crisis, which threatens the welfare of the community. . .'

The first project undertaken by the Authority was the erection of a parking facility on Ninth Street in downtown Wilmington.

Before it began actual construction of the facility, the Authority was advised by its retained experts that the anticipated revenue from the parking of cars and proceeds from sale of its bonds would not be sufficient to finance the construction costs of the facility. Moreover, the bonds were not expected to be marketable if payable solely out of parking revenues.   To secure additional capital needed for its "debt-service" requirements, and thereby to make bond financing practicable, the Authority decided it was necessary to enter long-term leases with responsible tenants for commercial use of some of the space available in the projected "garage building."   The public was invited to bid for these leases.

In April 1957 such a private lease, for 20 years and renewable for another 10 years, was made with Eagle Coffee Shoppe, Inc., for use as a "restaurant, dining room, banquet hall, cocktail lounge and bar and for no other use and purpose."

Its lease, however, contains no requirement that its restaurant services be made available to the general public on a nondiscriminatory basis, in spite of the fact that the Authority has power to adopt rules and regulations respecting the use of its facilities except any as would impair the security of its bondholders. § 511.

Other portions of the structure were leased to other tenants, including a bookstore, a retail jeweler, and a food store.   Upon completion of the building, the Authority located at appropriate places thereon official signs indicating the public character of the building, the flew from mastheads on the roof both the state and national flags.

It is clear, as it always has been since the Civil Rights Cases, supra, that "Individual invasion of individual rights is not the subject-matter of the amendment," 109 U.S. at page 11, 3 S.Ct. at page 21, and that private conduct abridging individual rights does no violence to the Equal Protection Clause unless to some significant extent the State in any of its manifestations has been found to have become involved in it. Because the virtue of the right to equal protection of the laws could lie only in the breadth of its application, its constitutional assurance was reserved in terms whose imprecision was necessary if the right were to be enjoyed in the variety of individual-state relationships which the Amendment was designed to embrace. For the same reason, to fashion and apply a precise formula for recognition of state responsibility under the Equal Protection Clause is an "impossible task" which "This Court has never attempted." Kotch v. Board of River Port Pilot Com'rs, 330 U.S. 552, 556, 67 S.Ct. 910, 912, 91 L.Ed. 1093. Only by sifting facts and weighing circumstances can the nonobvious involvement of the State in private conduct be attributed its true significance.

The Delaware Supreme Court seems to have placed controlling emphasis on its conclusion, as to the accuracy of which there is doubt, that only some 15% of the total cost of the facility was "advanced" from public funds; that the cost of the entire facility was allocated three-fifths to the space for commercial leasing and two-fifths to parking space; that anticipated revenue from parking was only some 30.5% of the total income, the balance of which was expected to be earned by the leasing; that the Authority had no original intent to place a restaurant in the building, it being only a happenstance resulting from the bidding; that Eagle expended considerable moneys on furnishings; that the restaurant's main and marked public entrance is on Ninth Street without any public entrance direct from the parking area; and that "the only connection Eagle has with the public facility . . . is the furnishing of the sum of $28,700 annually in the form of rent which is used by the Authority to defray a portion of the operating expense of an otherwise unprofitable enterprise." 157 A.2d 894, 901. While these factual considerations are indeed validly accountable aspects of the enterprise upon which the State has embarked, we cannot say that they lead inescapably to the conclusion that state action is not present. Their persuasiveness is diminished when evaluated in the context of other factors which must be acknowledged.

The land and building were publicly owned. As an entity, the building was dedicated to "public uses" in performance of the Authority's "essential governmental functions." 22 Del.Code, §§ 501, 514. The costs of land acquisition, construction, and maintenance are defrayed entirely from donations by the City of Wilmington, from loans and revenue bonds and from the proceeds of rentals and parking services out of which the loans and bonds were payable. Assuming that the distinction would be significant, cf. Derrington v. Plummer, 5 Cir., 240 F.2d 922, 925, the commercially leased areas were not surplus state property, but constituted a physically and financially integral and, indeed, indispensable part of the State's plan to operate its project as a self-sustaining unit. It cannot be doubted that the peculiar relationship of the restaurant to the parking facility in which it is located confers on each an incidental variety of mutual benefits. Neither can it be ignored, especially in view of Eagle's affirmative allegation that for it to serve Negroes would injure its business, that profits earned by discrimination not only contribute to, but also are indispensable elements in, the financial success of a governmental agency.

Addition of all these activities, obligations and responsibilities of the Authority, the benefits mutually conferred, together with the obvious fact that the restaurant is operated as an integral part of a public building devoted to a public parking service, indicates that degree of state participation and involvement in discriminatory action which it was the design of the Fourteenth Amendment to condemn.   It is irony amounting to grave injustice that in one part of a single building, erected and maintained with public funds by an agency of the State to serve a public purpose, all persons have equal rights, while in another portion, also serving the public, a Negro is a second-class citizen, offensive because of his race, without rights and unentitled to service, but at the same time fully enjoys equal access to nearby restaurants in wholly privately owned buildings.   As the Chancellor pointed out, in its lease with Eagle the Authority could have affirmatively required Eagle to discharge the responsibilities under the Fourteenth Amendment imposed upon the private enterprise as a consequence of state participation.   But no State may effectively abdicate its responsibilities by either ignoring them or by merely failing to discharge them whatever the motive may be.   It is of no consolation to an individual denied the equal protection of the laws that it was done in good faith.   Certainly the conclusions drawn in similar cases by the various Courts of Appeals do not depend upon such a distinction. By its inaction, the Authority, and through it the State, has not only made itself a party to the refusal of service, but has elected to place its power, property and prestige behind the admitted discrimination.   The State has so far insinuated itself into a position of interdependence with Eagle that it must be recognized as a joint participant in the challenged activity, which, on that account, cannot be considered to have been so "purely private" as to fall without the scope of the Fourteenth Amendment.

Because readily applicable formulae may not be fashioned, the conclusions drawn from the facts and circumstances of this record are by no means declared as universal truths on the basis of which every state leasing agreement is to be tested.   Owing to the very "largeness" of government, a multitude of relationships might appear to some to fall within the Amendment's embrace, but that, it must be remembered, can be determined only in the framework of the peculiar facts or circumstances present.   Therefore respondents' prophecy of nigh universal application of a constitutional precept so peculiarly dependent for its invocation upon appropriate facts fails to take into account "Differences in circumstances [which] beget appropriate differences in law," Whitney v. State Tax Comm., 309 U.S. 530, 542, 60 S.Ct. 635, 640, 84 L.Ed. 909.   Specifically defining the limits of our inquiry, what we hold today is that when a State leases public property in the manner and for the purpose shown to have been the case here, the proscriptions of the Fourteenth Amendment must be complied with by the lessee as certainly as though they were binding covenants written into the agreement itself.   Reversed and remanded.

Mr. Justice STEWART, concurring.

I agree that the judgment must be reversed, but I reach that conclusion by a route much more direct than the one traveled by the Court.   In upholding Eagle's right to deny service to the appellant solely because of his race, the Supreme Court of Delaware relied upon a statute of that State which permits the proprietor of a restaurant to refuse to serve "persons whose reception or entertainment by him would be offensive to the major part of his customers." . . . There is no suggestion in the record that the appellant as an individual was such a person.   The highest court of Delaware has thus construed this legislative enactment as authorizing discriminatory classification based exclusively on color.   Such a law seems to me clearly violative of the Fourteenth Amendment.

Mr. Justice HARLAN, whom Mr. Justice WHITTAKER joins, dissenting.

The Court's opinion, by a process of first undiscriminatingly throwing together various factual bits and pieces and then undermining the resulting structure by an equally vague disclaimer, seems to me to leave completely at sea just what it is in this record that satisfies the requirement of "state action."

If in the context of this record this means, as my Brother Stewart suggests, that the Delaware court construed this state statute "as authorizing discriminatory classification based exclusively on color," I would certainly agree, without more, that the enactment is offensive to the Fourteenth Amendment. It would then be quite unnecessary to reach the much broader questions dealt with in the Court's opinion. If, on the other hand, the state court meant no more than that under the statute, as at common law, Eagle was free to serve only those whom it pleased, then, and only then, would the question of "state action" be presented in full-blown form.

―――――

Comments on *Burton*. The policy of the Wilmington Parking Authority was arguably "neutral" in regard to racial discrimination by its tenants. On what basis did the Court find state action? Was it the state's "inaction"? Can the state involve itself through its "inaction" as well as "action"? Or was the symbiotic relationship between the parties more significant? Some have cited *Burton* as the source for contemporary state involvement doctrine. Which of the above cited bases would be the most likely candidate for such?

Did the state in *Burton* "encourage" the illegal activity? What would be the result if there was such a finding (encouragement) in regard to determining state involvement? The Court deals with such a circumstance in *Reitman*.

1. "STATE ENCOURAGEMENT"

REITMAN v. MULKEY
387 U.S. 369 (1967)

[Between 1959 and 1963, California enacted various fair housing acts that prohibited racial discrimination in the sale or rental of private dwellings. In 1964, through the initiative process, California voters enacted Proposition 14, which amended the state's constitution to prohibit the state from denying the "right of any person [to] decline to sell, lease or rent [property] to such person or persons as he, in his absolute discretion, chooses." Respondents, alleging that petitioners had refused to rent them an apartment because of their race, brought an action in state court based on the fair housing acts. They contended that Proposition 14, which had the effect of repealing the acts, violated the equal protection clause. The California Supreme Court ruled in their favor, and in a five-to-four decision, the U.S. Supreme Court affirmed.]

Mr. Justice WHITE delivered the opinion of the Court.

The question here is whether Art. I, § 26, of the California Constitution denies "to any person . . . the equal protection of the laws" within the meaning of the Fourteenth Amendment of the Constitution of the United States. Section 26 of Art. I, an initiated measure submitted to the people as Proposition 14 in a statewide ballot in 1964, provides in part as follows:

[Proposition 14's] immediate design and intent, the California court said, were "to overturn state laws that bore on the right of private sellers and lessors to discriminate," the Unruh and Rumford Acts, and "to forestall future state action that might circumscribe this right." This aim was successfully achieved: the adoption of Proposition 14 "generally nullifies both the Rumford and Unruh Acts as they apply to the housing market," and establishes "a purported constitutional right to privately discriminate on grounds which admittedly would be unavailable under the Fourteenth Amendment should state action be involved."

[The] court conceded that the State was permitted a neutral position with respect to private racial discriminations and that the State was not bound by the Federal Constitution to forbid them. But, because a significant state involvement in private discriminations could amount to unconstitutional state action, Burton v. Wilmington Parking Authority, 365 U.S. 715, 81 S.Ct. 856, 6 L.Ed.2d 45, the court deemed it necessary to determine whether Proposition 14 invalidly involved the State in racial discriminations in the housing market. Its conclusion was that it did.

The state court concluded that a prohibited state involvement could be found "even where the state can be charged with only encouraging," rather than commanding discrimination. Also of particular interest to the court was Mr. Justice Stewart's concurrence in Burton v. Wilmington Parking Authority, 365 U.S. 715, 726, 81 S.Ct. 856, 862, 6 L.Ed.2d 45, where it was said that the Delaware courts had construed an existing Delaware statute as "authorizing" racial discrimination in restaurants and that the statute was therefore invalid. To the California court "[t]he instant case presents an undeniably analogous situation" wherein the State had taken affirmative action designed to make private discriminations legally possible. Section 26 was said to have changed the situation from one in which discrimination was restricted "to one wherein it is encouraged, within the meaning of the cited decisions"; § 26 was legislative action "which authorized private discrimination" and made the State "at least a partner in the instant act of discrimination. . . ." The court could "conceive of no other purpose for an application of section 26 aside from authorizing the perpetration of a purported private discrimination. . . ." The judgment of the California court was that § 26 unconstitutionally involves the State in racial discriminations and is therefore invalid under the Fourteenth Amendment.

There is so sound reason for rejecting this judgment. Petitioners contend that the California court has misconstrued the Fourteenth Amendment since the repeal of any statute prohibiting racial discrimination, which is constitutionally permissible, may be said to "authorize" and "encourage" discrimination because it makes legally permissible that which was formerly proscribed. But, as we understand the California court, it did not posit a constitutional violation on the mere repeal of the Unruh and Rumford Acts. It did not read either our cases or the Fourteenth Amendment as establishing an automatic constitutional barrier to the repeal of an existing law prohibiting racial discriminations in housing; nor did the court rule that a State may never put in statutory form an existing policy of neutrality with respect to private discriminations. What the court below did was first to reject the notion that the State was required to have a statute prohibiting racial discriminations in housing. Second, it held the intent of § 26 was to authorize private racial discriminations in the housing market, to repeal the Unruh and Rumford Acts and to create a constitutional right to discriminate on racial grounds in the sale and leasing of real property. Hence, the court dealt with § 26 as though it expressly authorized and constitutionalized the private right to discriminate.   Third, the court assessed the ultimate impact of § 26 in the California environment and concluded that the section would encourage and significantly involve the State in private racial discrimination contrary to the Fourteenth Amendment.

The California court could very reasonably conclude that § 26 would and did have wider impact than a mere repeal of existing statutes.   Section 26 mentioned neither the Unruh nor Rumford Act in so many words.   Instead, it announced the constitutional right of any person to decline to sell or lease his real property to anyone to whom he did not desire to sell or lease. Unruh and Rumford were thereby pro tanto repealed.   But the section struck more deeply and more widely.   Private discriminations in housing were now not only free from Rumford and Unruh but they also enjoyed a far different status than was true before the passage of those statutes.   The right to discriminate, including the right to discriminate on racial grounds, was now embodied in the State's basic charter, immune from legislative, executive, or judicial regulation at any level of the state government. Those practicing racial discriminations need no longer rely solely on their personal choice. They could now invoke express constitutional authority, free from censure or interference of any kind from official sources.   All individuals, partnerships, corporations and other legal entities, as well as their agents and representatives, could now discriminate with respect to their residential real property, which is defined as any interest in real property of any kind or quality, "irrespective of how obtained or financed," and seemingly irrespective of the relationship of the State to such interests in real property.   Only the State is excluded with respect to property owned by it.

This Court has never attempted the "impossible task" of formulating an infallible test for determining whether the State 'in any of its manifestations' has become significantly involved in private discriminations. "Only by sifting facts and weighing circumstances" on a case-by-case basis can a "nonobvious involvement of the State in private conduct be attributed its true significance."   Burton v. Wilmington Parking Authority, 365 U.S. 715, 722, 81 S.Ct. 856, 860. Here the California court, armed as it was with the knowledge of the facts and circumstances concerning the passage and potential impact of § 26, and familiar with the milieu in which that provision would operate, has determined that the provision would involve the State in private racial discriminations to an unconstitutional degree. We accept this holding of the California court.

In Burton v. Wilmington Parking Authority, 365 U.S. 715, 81 S.Ct. 856, the operator-lessee of a restaurant located in a building owned by the State and otherwise operated for public purposes, refused service to Negroes. Although the State neither commanded nor expressly authorized or encouraged the discriminations, the State had "elected to place its power, property and prestige behind the admitted discrimination" and by "its inaction . . . has . . . made itself a party to the refusal of service . . ." which therefore could not be considered the purely private choice of the restaurant operator.

None of these cases squarely controls the case we now have before us.   But they do illustrate the range of situations in which discriminatory state action has been identified. They do exemplify the necessity for a court to assess the potential impact of official action in determining whether the State has significantly involved itself with invidious discriminations.   Here we are dealing with a provision which does not just repeal an existing law forbidding private racial discriminations.   Section 26 was intended to authorize, and does authorize, racial discrimination in the housing market. The right to discriminate is now one of the basic policies of the State.   The California Supreme Court believes that the section will significantly encourage and involve the State in private discriminations. We have been presented with no persuasive considerations indicating that these judgments should be overturned.

Affirmed.

Mr. Justice HARLAN, whom Mr. Justice BLACK, Mr. Justice CLARK, and Mr. Justice STEWART join, dissenting.

In short, all that has happened is that California has effected a pro tanto repeal of its prior statutes forbidding private discrimination. This runs no more afoul of the Fourteenth Amendment than would have California's failure to pass any such anti-discrimination statutes in the first instance. The fact that such repeal was also accompanied by a constitutional prohibition against future enactment of such laws by the California Legislature cannot well be thought to affect, from a federal constitutional standpoint, the validity of what California has done.

[There] were no disputed issues of fact at all. The only "factual" matter relied on by the majority of the California Supreme Court was the context in which Proposition 14 was adopted. This, of course, is nothing but a legal conclusion as to federal constitutional law.

There is no question that the adoption of § 26, repealing the former state anti-discrimination laws and prohibiting the enactment of such state laws in the future, constituted "state action" within the meaning of the Fourteenth Amendment. The only issue is whether this provision impermissibly deprives any person of equal protection of the laws. As a starting point, it is clear that any statute requiring unjustified discriminatory treatment is unconstitutional. E.g., Nixon v. Herndon, 273 U.S. 536, 47 S.Ct. 446; Brown v. Board of Education, supra; Peterson v. City of Greenville, 373 U.S. 244, 83 S.Ct. 1119, 10 L.Ed.2d 323. And it is no less clear that the Equal Protection Clause bars as well discriminatory governmental administration of a statute fair on its face. E.g., Yick Wo v. Hopkins, 118 U.S. 356, 6 S.Ct. 1064, 30 L.Ed. 220. This case fits within neither of these two categories: Section 26 is by its terms inoffensive, and its provisions require no affirmative governmental enforcement of any sort. A third category of equal-protection cases, concededly more difficult to characterize, stands for the proposition that when governmental involvement in private discrimination reaches a level at which the State can be held responsible for the specific act of private discrimination, the strictures of the Fourteenth Amendment come into play. In dealing with this class of cases, the inquiry has been framed as whether the State has become "a joint participant in the challenged activity, which, on that account, cannot be considered to have been so 'purely private' as to fall without the scope of the Fourteenth Amendment."

By focusing on "encouragement" the Court, I fear, is forging a slippery and unfortunate criterion by which to measure the constitutionality of a statute simply permissive in purpose and effect, and inoffensive on its face. This conclusion appears to me to state only a truism.

A moment of thought will reveal the far-reaching possibilities of the Court's new doctrine, which I am sure the Court does not intend. Every act of private discrimination is either forbidden by state law or permitted by it. There can be little doubt that such permissiveness — whether by express constitutional or statutory provision, or implicit in the common law — to some extent "encourages" those who wish to discriminate to do so. Under this theory "state action" in the form of laws that do nothing more than passively permit private discrimination could be said to tinge all private discrimination with the taint of unconstitutional state encouragement.

I believe the state action required to bring the Fourteenth Amendment into operation must be affirmative and purposeful, actively fostering discrimination.

I think that this decision is not only constitutionally unsound, but in its practical potentialities short-sighted. Opponents of state anti-discrimination statutes are now in a position to argue that such legislation should be defeated because, if enacted, it may be unrepealable.

Comments on *Reitman*. Did the Court in *Burton* find that the state "facilitated" the discrimination as opposed to a finding in *Reitman* that the state "encouraged" the discrimination? If so, what would be the difference?

MOOSE LODGE NO. 107 v. IRVIS
407 U.S. 163 (1972)

[*Moose Lodge*, perhaps more than any other contemporary state action case, captures the most provocative public/private distinction in America — private versus state racism. As we have emphasized in this work, the issue of "racism" has dominated American life from the inception of the Constitution until today. This was the case both in regard to the Constitution's explicit condemnation of slavery and the Court's limitations on the reach of the post–Civil War Amendments that spurned the racism of "Jim Crow." Because of such, when there is a finding of state action, race-based discrimination has been singled out for the most arduous of legal protection. But what of "private racism"? Are thoughts actionable? Should they be? What is the state's role in this regard? When is racism private, and when does it contain the necessary state action? How did *Burton* resolve this issue?

What of a racist private club? Is the state involved with such a club? Could such a club exist without water, electricity, safety, or liquor codes? Could we make a "but not for" argument here? Is the social value of privacy more important than these indirect means of the government condoning, or at least allowing, private racism? These are not only significant constitutional questions, but are meaningful moral questions, most particularly in regard to our nation, what it is about, and what its most cherished values are. Here the value of privacy and racism potentially clash — forcing a choice between the two. The Burger Court faced these issues in *Moose Lodge* and provided its answer.]

Appellee Irvis, a Negro guest of a member of appellant, a private club, was refused service at the club's dining room and bar solely because of his race. In suing for injunctive relief, appellee contended that the discrimination was state action, and thus a violation of the Equal Protection Clause of the Fourteenth Amendment, because the Pennsylvania liquor board had issued appellant a private club liquor license. The District Court found appellant's membership and guest practices discriminatory, agreed with appellee's view that state action was present, and declared the liquor license invalid as long as appellant continued its discriminatory practices. Appellant's motion to have the final decree limited to its guest policy was opposed by appellee, and the court denied the motion. Following the District Court's decision, the applicable bylaws were amended to exclude as guests those who would be excluded as members.

Mr. Justice REHNQUIST delivered the opinion of the Court.

Our cases make clear that the impetus for the forbidden discrimination need not originate with the State if it is state action that enforces privately originated discrimination. Shelley v. Kraemer, supra.

The Court has never held, of course, that discrimination by an otherwise private entity would be violative of the Equal Protection Clause if the private entity receives any sort of benefit or service at all from the State, or if it is subject to state regulation in any degree whatever. Since state-furnished services include such necessities of life as electricity, water, and police and fire protection, such a holding would utterly emasculate the distinction between private as distinguished from state conduct set forth in The Civil Rights Cases, supra, and adhered to in subsequent decisions. Our holdings indicate that where the impetus for the discrimination is private, the State must have "significantly involved itself with invidious discriminations," in order for the discriminatory action to fall within the ambit of the constitutional prohibition.

Here there is nothing approaching the symbiotic relationship between lessor and lessee that was present in Burton, where the private lessee obtained the benefit of locating in a building owned by the state-created parking authority, and the parking authority was enabled to carry out its primary public purpose of furnishing parking space by advantageously leasing portions of the building constructed for that purpose to commercial lessees such as the owner of the Eagle Restaurant. Unlike Burton, the Moose Lodge building is located on land owned by it, not by any public authority. Far from apparently holding itself out as a place of public accommodation, Moose Lodge quite ostentatiously proclaims the fact that it is not open to the public at large. Nor is it located and operated in such surroundings that although private in name, it discharges a function or performs a service that would otherwise in all likelihood be performed by the State. In short, while Eagle was a public restaurant in a public building, Moose Lodge is a private social club in a private building.

With the exception hereafter noted, the Pennsylvania Liquor Control Board plays absolutely no part in establishing or enforcing the membership or guest policies of the club that it licenses to serve liquor. There is no suggestion in this record that Pennsylvania law, either as written or as applied, discriminates against minority groups either in their right to apply for club licenses themselves or in their right to purchase and be served liquor in places of public accommodation. The only effect that the state licensing of Moose Lodge to serve liquor can be said to have on the right of any other Pennsylvanian to buy or be served liquor on premises other than those of Moose Lodge is that for some purposes club licenses are counted in the maximum number of licenses that may be issued in a given municipality. . . .

The District Court was at pains to point out in its opinion what it considered to be the "pervasive" nature of the regulation of private clubs by the Pennsylvania Liquor Control Board. . . .

However detailed this type of regulation may be in some particulars, it cannot be said to in any way foster or encourage racial discrimination. Nor can it be said to make the State in any realistic sense a partner or even a joint venturer in the club's enterprise. The limited effect of the prohibition against obtaining additional club licenses when the maximum number of retail licenses allotted to a municipality has been issued, when considered together with the availability of liquor from hotel, restaurant, and retail licensees, falls far short of conferring upon club licensees a monopoly in the dispensing of liquor in any given municipality or in the State as a whole. We therefore hold that, with the exception hereafter noted, the operation of the regulatory scheme enforced by the

Pennsylvania Liquor Control Board does not sufficiently implicate the State in the discriminatory guest policies of Moose Lodge to make the latter "state action" within the ambit of the Equal Protection Clause of the Fourteenth Amendment.

Reversed and remanded.

Mr. Justice DOUGLAS, with whom Mr. Justice MARSHALL joins, dissenting.

My view of the First Amendment and the related guarantees of the Bill of Rights is that they create a zone of privacy which precludes government from interfering with private clubs or groups. The associational rights which our system honors permit all white, all black, all brown, and all yellow cubs to be formed. They also permit all Catholic, all Jewish, or all agnostic clubs to be established. Government may not tell a man or woman who his or her associates must be. The individual can be as selective as he desires. So the fact that the Moose Lodge allows only Caucasians to join or come as guests is constitutionally irrelevant, as is the decision of the Black Muslims to admit to their services only members of their race.

The problem is different, however, where the public domain is concerned. I have indicated in Garner v. Louisiana, 368 U.S. 157, 82 S.Ct. 248, 7 L.Ed.2d 207, and Lombard v. Louisiana, 373 U.S. 267, 83 S.Ct. 1122, 10 L.Ed.2d 338, that where restaurants or other facilities serving the public are concerned and licenses are obtained from the State for operating the business, the "public" may not be defined by the proprietor to include only people of his choice; nor may a state or municipal service be granted only to some. Evans v. Newton, 382 U.S. 296, 298-299, 86 S.Ct. 486, 487-488, 15 L.Ed.2d 373.

Those cases are not precisely apposite, however, for a private club, by definition, is not in the public domain. And the fact that a private club gets some kind of permit from the State or municipality does not make it ipso facto a public enterprise or undertaking, any more than the grant to a householder of a permit to operate an incinerator puts the householder in the public domain. We must, therefore, examine whether there are special circumstances involved in the Pennsylvania scheme which differentiate the liquor license possessed by Moose Lodge from the incinerator permit.

It is argued that this regulation only aims at the prevention of subterfuge and at enforcing Pennsylvania's differentiation between places of public accommodation and bona fide private clubs. It is also argued that the regulation only gives effect to the constitutionally protected rights of privacy and of association. But I cannot so read the regulation. While those other purposes are embraced in it, so is the restrictive membership clause. And we have held that "a State is responsible for the discriminatory act of a private party when the State, by its law, has compelled the act." Adickes v. S.H. Kress & Co., 398 U.S. 144, 170, 90 S.Ct. 1598, 1615, 26 L.Ed.2d 142. See Peterson v. City of Greenville, 373 U.S. 244, 248, 83 S.Ct. 1119, 1121, 10 L.Ed.2d 323. It is irrelevant whether the law is statutory, or an administrative regulation. Robinson v. Florida, 378 U.S. 153, 84 S.Ct. 1693, 1695, 12 L.Ed.2d 771. And it is irrelevant whether the discriminatory act was instigated by the regulation, or was independent of it. Peterson v. City of Greenville, supra. The result, as I see it, is the same as though Pennsylvania had put into its liquor licenses a provision that the license may not be used to dispense liquor to blacks, browns, yellows — or atheists or agnostics. Regulation § 113.09 is thus an invidious form of state action.

Were this regulation the only infirmity in Pennsylvania's licensing scheme, I would perhaps agree with the majority that the appropriate relief would be a decree enjoining its enforcement. But there is another flaw in the scheme not so easily cured. Liquor licenses in Pennsylvania, unlike driver's licenses, or marriage licenses, are not freely available to those who meet racially neutral qualifications. There is a complex quota system, which the majority accurately describes. Ante, at 1973. What the majority neglects to say is that the quota for Harrisburg, where Moose Lodge No. 107 is located, has been full for many years. No more club licenses may be issued in that city.

This state-enforced scarcity of licenses restricts the ability of blacks to obtain liquor, for liquor is commercially available only at private clubs for a significant portion of each week. Access by blacks to places that serve liquor is further limited by the fact that the state quota is filled. A group desiring to form a nondiscriminatory club which would serve blacks must purchase a license held by an existing club, which can exact a monopoly price for the transfer. The availability of such a license is speculative at best, however, for, as Moose Lodge itself concedes, without a liquor license a fraternal organization would be hard pressed to survive.

Comments on *Moose Lodge*. Do you agree with the Court's finding in *Moose Lodge*? Does this mean that African Americans can "ban" whites from their private clubs? Mexicans, Chicanos, Jews, Asians, and other groups as well? Could a racially restrictive private club exist without any state involvement? If not, on what basis does the Court conclude that there is not state action? Would the *Shelly* opinion support a conclusion that there was state action? Has the reach of *Shelly* been limited? Is the Court applying the *Burton* analysis here, or is it different?

What is the message here? Is the Court condoning private racism? Is "moral" leadership something the Court should pay attention to, particularly when it uses natural law inquires to establish fundamental rights? Or have we reached a level of privacy where we do not want governmental intrusion?

What is the state of "state involvement" law post–*Moose Lodge*? When can state involvement produce a finding of state action? What has "nexus" got to do with it? See whether *Moose Lodge*, and *Burton* provide the theoretical basis for modern state action doctrine in the cases that follow.

2. "CONTEMPORARY STANDARDS"

JACKSON v. METROPOLITAN EDISON CO.
419 U.S. 345 (1974)

Petitioner brought suit against respondent, a privately owned and operated utility corporation which holds a certificate of public convenience issued by the Pennsylvania Utility Commission, seeking damages and injunctive relief under 42 U.S.C. § 1983 for termination of her electric service allegedly before she had been afforded notice, a hearing, and an opportunity to pay any amounts found due. Petitioner claimed that under state law she was entitled to reasonably continuous electric service and that respondent's termination for alleged nonpayment, permitted by a provision of its general tariff filed with the Commission, was state action depriving petitioner of her property without due process of law and giving rise to a cause of action under § 1983. The Court of Appeals affirmed the District Court's dismissal of petitioner's complaint.

483 F.2d 754, affirmed.

Mr. Justice REHNQUIST delivered the opinion of the Court.

[The] mere fact that a business is subject to state regulation does not by itself convert its action into that of the State for purposes of the Fourteenth Amendment. 407 U.S., at 176-177, 92 S.Ct., at 1973. Nor does the fact that the regulation is extensive and detailed, as in the case of most public utilities, do so. Public Utilities Comm'n v. Pollak, 343 U.S. 451, 462, 72 S.Ct. 813, 820, 96 L.Ed. 1068 (1952). It may well be that acts of a heavily regulated utility with at least something of a governmentally protected monopoly will more readily be found to be "state" acts than will the acts of an entity lacking these characteristics. But the inquiry must be whether there is a sufficiently close nexus between the State and the challenged action of the regulated entity so that the action of the latter may be fairly treated as that of the State itself. Moose Lodge No. 107, supra, 407 U.S. at 176, 92 S.Ct. at 1973. The true nature of the State's involvement may not be immediately obvious, and detailed inquiry may be required in order to determine whether the test is met. Burton v. Wilmington Parking Authority, supra. Petitioner advances a series of contentions which, in her view, lead to the conclusion that this case should fall on the Burton side of the line drawn in the Civil Rights Cases, supra, rather than on the Moose Lodge side of that line. We find none of them persuasive. Petitioner first argues that "state action" is present because of the monopoly status allegedly conferred upon Metropolitan by the State of Pennsylvania. As a factual matter, it may well be doubted that the State ever granted or guaranteed Metropolitan a monopoly.[8] But assuming that it had, this fact is not determinative in considering whether Metropolitan's termination of service to petitioner was 'state action' for purposes of the Fourteenth Amendment. In Pollak, supra, where the Court dealt with the activities of the District of Columbia Transit Co., a congressionally established monopoly, we expressly disclaimed reliance on the monopoly status of the transit authority. Similarly, although certain monopoly aspects were presented in Moose Lodge No. 107, supra, we found that the Lodge's action was not subject to the provisions of the Fourteenth Amendment. In each of those cases, there was insufficient relationship between the challenged actions of the entities involved and their monopoly status. There is no indication of any greater connection here. Petitioner next urges that state action is present because respondent provides an essential public service required to be supplied on a reasonably continuous basis by Pa.Stat.Ann., Tit. 66, § 1171 (1959), and hence performs a "public function."

We also reject the notion that Metropolitan's termination is state action because the State "has specifically authorized and approved" the termination practice. In the instant case, Metropolitan filed with the Public Utility Commission a general tariff — a provision of which states Metropolitan's right to terminate service for nonpayment. This provision has appeared in Metropolitan's previously filed tariffs for many years and has never been the subject of a hearing or other scrutiny by the Commission. Although the Commission did hold hearings on portions of Metropolitan's general tariff relating to a general rate increase, it never even considered the reinsertion of this provision in the newly filed general tariff. The provision became effective 60 days after filing when not disapproved by the Commission. As a threshold matter, it is less than clear under state law that Metropolitan was even required to file this provision as part of its tariff or that the Commission would have had the power to disapprove it. The District Court observed that the sole connection

---

[8] As petitioner admits, such public utility companies are natural monopolies created by the economic forces of high threshold capital requirements and virtually unlimited economy of scale. Regulation was superimposed on such natural monopolies as a substitute for competition and not to eliminate it.

of the Commission with this regulation was Metropolitan's simple notice filing with the Commission and the lack of any Commission action to prohibit it.

The case most heavily relied on by petitioner is Public Utilities Comm'n v. Pollak, supra. There the Court dealt with the contention that Capital Transit's installation of a piped music system on its buses violated the First Amendment rights of the bus riders. It is not entirely clear whether the Court alternatively held that Capital Transit's action was action of the "State" for First Amendment purposes, or whether it merely assumed, arguendo, that it was and went on to resolve the First Amendment question adversely to the bus riders. In either event, the nature of the state involvement there was quite different than it is here. The District of Columbia Public Utilities Commission, on its own motion, commenced an investigation of the effects of the piped music, and after a full hearing concluded not only that Capital Transit's practices were "not inconsistent with public convenience, comfort, and safety," 81 P.U.R. (N.S.) 122, 126 (1950), but also that the practice "in fact, through the creation of better will among passengers, . . . tends to improve the conditions under which the public ride." Ibid. Here, on the other hand, there was no such imprimatur placed on the practice of Metropolitan about which petitioner complains. The nature of governmental regulation of private utilities is such that a utility may frequently be required by the state regulatory scheme to obtain approval for practices a business regulated in less detail would be free to institute without any approval from a regulatory body. Approval by a state utility commission of such a request from a regulated utility, where the commission has not put its own weight on the side of the proposed practice by ordering it, does not transmute a practice initiated by the utility and approved by the commission into "state action."   At most, the Commission's failure to overturn this practice amounted to no more than a determination that a Pennsylvania utility was authorized to employ such a practice if it so desired. Respondent's exercise of the choice allowed by state law where the initiative comes from it and not from the State, does not make its action in doing so 'state action' for purposes of the Fourteenth Amendment.

We also find absent in the instant case the symbiotic relationship presented in Burton v. Wilmington Parking Authority, 365 U.S. 715, 81 S.Ct. 856, 6 L.Ed.2d 45 (1961). There where a private lessee, who practiced racial discrimination, leased space for a restaurant from a state parking authority in a publicly owned building, the Court held that the State had so far insinuated itself into a position of interdependence with the restaurant that it was a joint participant in the enterprise. We cautioned, however, that while 'a multitude of relationships might appear to some to fall within the Amendment's embrace,' differences in circumstances beget differences in law, limiting the actual holding to lessees of public property.   Metropolitan is a privately owned corporation, and it does not lease its facilities from the State of Pennsylvania. It alone is responsible for the provision of power to its customers. In common with all corporations of the State it pays taxes to the State, and it is subject to a form of extensive regulation by the State in a way that most other business enterprises are not. But this was likewise true of the appellant club in Moose Lodge No. 107 v. Irvis, supra, where we said: "However detailed this type of regulation may be in some particulars, it cannot be said to in any way foster or encourage racial discrimination. Nor can it be said to make the State in any realistic sense a partner or even a joint venturer in the club's enterprise."

All of petitioner's arguments taken together show no more than that Metropolitan was a heavily regulated, privately owned utility, enjoying at least a partial monopoly in the providing of electrical service within its territory, and that it elected to terminate service to petitioner in a manner which the Pennsylvania Public Utility Commission found permissible under state law. Under our decision this is not sufficient to connect the State of Pennsylvania with respondent's action so as to make the latter's conduct attributable to the State for purposes of the Fourteenth Amendment.

We conclude that the State of Pennsylvania is not sufficiently connected with respondent's action in terminating petitioner's service so as to make respondent's conduct in so doing attributable to the State for purposes of the Fourteenth Amendment. We therefore have no occasion to decide whether petitioner's claim to continued service was "property" for purposes of that Amendment, or whether "due process of law" would require a State taking similar action to accord petitioner the procedural rights for which she contends. The judgment of the Court of Appeals for the Third Circuit is therefore affirmed.

Mr. Justice MARSHALL, dissenting.

Our state-action cases have repeatedly relied on several factors clearly presented by this case: a state-sanctioned monopoly; an extensive pattern of cooperation between the "private" entity and the State; and a service uniquely public in nature. Today the Court takes a major step in repudiating this line of authority and adopts a stance that is bound to lead to mischief when applied to problems beyond the narrow sphere of due process objections to utility terminations.   When the State confers a monopoly on a group or organization, this Court has held that the organization assumes many of the obligations of the State. Even when the Court has not found state action based solely on the State's conferral of a monopoly, it has suggested that the monopoly factor weighs heavily in determining whether constitutional obligations can be imposed on formally private entities.

[The] majority distinguishes this line of cases with a cryptic assertion that public utility companies are "natural monopolies."   The theory behind the distinction appears to be that since the State's purpose in regulating a natural monopoly is not to aid the company but to prevent its charging monopoly prices, the State's involvement is somehow less significant for state-action purposes. I cannot agree that so much should turn on so narrow a distinction.   [The] difficulty inherent in this kind of economic analysis counsels against excusing natural monopolies from the reach of state-action principles. [The] suggestion that the State would have to "put its own weight on the side of the proposed practice by ordering it" seems to me to mark a sharp departure from our previous state-action cases. From The Civil Rights Cases, 109 U.S. 3, 3 S.Ct. 18, 27 L.Ed. 835 (1883), to Moose Lodge, supra, we have consistently indicated that state authorization and approval of "private" conduct would support a finding of state action.

[I] question the wisdom of giving such short shrift to the extensive interaction between the company and the State, and focusing solely on the extent of state support for the particular activity under challenge. In cases where the State's only significant involvement is through financial support or limited regulation of the private entity, it may be well to inquire whether the State's involvement suggests state approval of the objectionable conduct. But where the State has so thoroughly insinuated itself into the operations of the enterprise, it should not be fatal if the State has not affirmatively sanctioned the particular practice in question.

Finally, it seems to me in any event that the State has given its approval to Metropolitan Edison's termination procedures.   What is perhaps most troubling about the Court's opinion is that it would appear to apply to a broad range of claimed constitutional violations by the company. The Court has not adopted the notion, accepted elsewhere, that different standards should apply to state action analysis when different constitutional claims are presented. Thus, the majority's analysis would seemingly apply as well to a company that refused to extend service to Negroes, welfare recipients, or any other group that the company preferred, for its own reasons, not to serve. I cannot believe that this Court would hold that the State's involvement with the utility company was not sufficient to impose upon the company an obligation to meet the constitutional mandate of nondiscrimination. Yet nothing in the analysis of the majority opinion suggests otherwise. I dissent.

FLAGG BROTHERS v. BROOKS
436 U.S. 149 (1978)

Mr. Justice REHNQUIST delivered the opinion of the Court.

[For the facts and review of the Court's decision concerning the "public function" doctrine, see supra (public function cases). The discussion that follows deals with the claim of state involvement.]

IV. Respondents further urge that Flagg Brothers' proposed action is properly attributable to the State because the State has authorized and encouraged it in enacting §7-210. [This] Court, however, has never held that a State's mere acquiescence in a private action converts that action into that of the State. The Court rejected a similar argument in Jackson. The clearest demonstration of this distinction appears in Moose Lodge No. 107 v. Irvis. These cases clearly rejected the notion that our prior cases permitted the imposition of Fourteenth Amendment restraints on private action by the simple device of characterizing the State's inaction as "authorization" or "encouragement."

It is quite immaterial that the State has embodied its decision not to act in statutory form. If New York had no commercial statutes at all, its courts would still be faced with the decision whether to prohibit or to permit the sort of sale threatened here the first time an aggrieved bailor came before them for relief. [It] is quite immaterial that the State has embodied its decision not to act in statutory form. If New York had no commercial statutes at all, its courts would still be faced with the decision whether to prohibit or to permit the sort of sale threatened here the first time an aggrieved bailor came before them for relief. A judicial decision to deny relief would be no less an "authorization" or "encouragement" of that sale than the legislature's decision embodied in this statute. [If] the mere denial of judicial relief is considered sufficient encouragement to make the State responsible for those private acts, all private deprivations of property would be converted into public acts whenever the State, for whatever reason, denies relief sought by the putative property owner.

[Here,] the State of New York has not compelled the sale of a bailor's goods, but has merely announced the circumstances under which its courts will not interfere with a private sale. Indeed, the crux of respondents' complaint is not that the State has acted, but that it has refused to act. This statutory refusal to act is no different in principle from an ordinary statute of limitations whereby the State declines to provide a remedy for private deprivations of property after the passage of a given period of time. [Reversed.]

Mr. Justice STEVENS, with whom Mr. Justice WHITE and Mr. Justice MARSHALL join, dissenting.

The claimed power derives solely from the State, and specifically from §7-210 of the New York Uniform Commercial Code. The question is whether a state statute which authorizes a private party to deprive a person of his property without his consent must meet the requirements of the Due Process Clause of the Fourteenth Amendment. This question must be answered in the affirmative unless the State has virtually unlimited power to transfer interests in private property without any procedural protections. . . .

In determining that New York's statute cannot be scrutinized under the Due Process Clause, the Court reasons that the warehouseman's proposed sale is solely private action because the state statute "permits but does not compel" the sale, and because the warehouseman has not been delegated a power "exclusively reserved to the State." Under this approach a State could enact laws authorizing private citizens to use self-help in countless situations without any possibility of federal challenge. A state statute could authorize the warehouseman to retain all proceeds of the lien sale, even if they far exceeded the amount of the alleged debt; it could authorize finance companies to enter private homes to repossess merchandise; or indeed, it could authorize "any person with sufficient physical power," to acquire and sell the property of his weaker neighbor. An attempt to challenge the validity of any such outrageous statute would be defeated by the reasoning the Court uses today: The Court's rationale would characterize action pursuant to such a statute as purely private action, which the State permits but does not compel, in an area not exclusively reserved to the State. As these examples suggest, the distinctions between "permission" and "compulsion" on the one hand, and "exclusive" and "nonexclusive," on the other, cannot be determinative factors in state-action analysis. There is no great chasm between "permission" and "compulsion" requiring particular state action to fall within one or the other definitional camp. [In] this case, the State of New York, by enacting §7-210 of the Uniform Commercial Code, has acted in the most effective and unambiguous way a State can act. This section specifically authorizes petitioner Flagg Brothers to sell respondents' possessions; it details the procedures that petitioner must follow; and it grants petitioner the power to convey good title to goods that are now owned by respondents to a third party.

[Cases] such as North Georgia Finishing must be viewed as reflecting this Court's recognition of the significance of the State's role in defining and controlling the debtor-creditor relationship. The Court's language to this effect in the various debtor-creditor cases has been unequivocal. In Fuentes v. Shevin the Court stressed that the statutes in question "abdicate[d] effective state control over state power." And it is clear that what was of concern in Shevin was the private use of state power to achieve a nonconsensual resolution of a commercial dispute. The state statutes placed the state power to repossess property in the hands of an interested private party, just as the state statute in this case places the state power to conduct judicially binding sales in satisfaction of a lien in the hands of the warehouseman. Private parties, serving their own private advantage, may unilaterally invoke state power to replevy goods from another. No state official participates in the decision to seek a writ; no state official reviews the basis for the claim to repossession; and no state official evaluates the need for immediate seizure. There is not even a requirement that the plaintiff provide any information to the court on these matters.

[Yet] the very defect that made the statutes in Shevin and North Georgia Finishing unconstitutional — lack of state control — is, under today's decision, the factor that precludes constitutional review of the state statute. The Due Process Clause cannot command such incongruous results. If it is unconstitutional for a State to allow a private party to exercise a traditional state power because the state supervision of that power is purely mechanical, the State surely cannot immunize its actions from constitutional scrutiny by removing even the mechanical supervision.

It is important to emphasize that, contrary to the Court's apparent fears, this conclusion does not even remotely suggest that "all private deprivations of property [will] be converted into public acts whenever the State, for whatever reason, denies relief sought by the putative property owner." The focus is not on the private deprivation but on the state authorization. "[W]hat is always vital to remember is that it is the state's conduct, whether action or inaction, not the private conduct, that gives rise to constitutional attack." Friendly, The Dartmouth College Case and The Public-Private Penumbra, 12 Texas Quarterly, No. 2, p. 17 (1969) (Supp.). The State's conduct in this case takes the concrete form of a statutory enactment, and it is that statute that may be challenged. . . .

Finally, it is obviously true that the overwhelming majority of disputes in our society are resolved in the private sphere. But it is no longer possible, if it ever was, to believe that a sharp line can be drawn between private and public actions. The Court today holds that our examination of state delegations of power should be limited to those rare instances where the State has ceded one of its "exclusive" powers. As indicated, I believe that this limitation is neither logical nor practical. More troubling, this description of what is state action does not even attempt to reflect the concerns of the Due Process Clause, for the state-action doctrine is, after all, merely one aspect of this broad constitutional protection. In the broadest sense, we expect government "to provide a reasonable and fair framework of rules which facilitate commercial transactions. . . ." This "framework of rules" is premised on the assumption that the State will control nonconsensual deprivations of property and that the State's control will, in turn, be subject to the restrictions of the Due Process Clause. The power to order legally binding surrenders of property and the constitutional restrictions on that power are necessary correlatives in our system. In effect, today's decision allows the State to divorce these two elements by the simple expedient of transferring the implementation of its policy to private parties. Because the Fourteenth Amendment does not countenance such a division of power and responsibility, I respectfully dissent.

Comments on *Jackson* and *Flagg Bros.* Were you surprised at the result in *Jackson*? How limited is the present view of state action? In both cases the Court describes the involvement of the state as "mere acquiescence." Do you agree? Do these findings mean that whenever a private utility is challenged, state action could not be proven? What would one have to allege in order to convert both of the cases to a circumstance where the Court would make a finding that there was state action? Once again, what's nexus got to do with it? What might *Lugar*, which follows, have to do with it?

LUGAR v. EDMONDSON OIL CO.
457 U.S. 922 (1982)

This case concerns the relationship between the requirement of "state action" to establish a violation of the Fourteenth Amendment, and the requirement of action "under color of state law" to establish a right to recover under 42 U.S.C. § 1983, which provides a remedy for deprivation of constitutional rights when that deprivation takes place "under color of any statute, ordinance, regulation, custom, or usage" of a State. Respondents filed suit in Virginia state court on a debt owed by petitioner, and sought prejudgment attachment of certain of petitioner's property. Pursuant to Virginia law, respondents alleged, in an *ex parte* petition, a belief that petitioner was disposing of or might dispose of his property in order to defeat his creditors; acting upon that petition, a Clerk of the state court issued a writ of attachment, which was executed by the County Sheriff; a hearing on the propriety of the attachment was later conducted; and 34 days after the levy the trial judge dismissed the attachment for respondents' failure to establish the alleged statutory grounds for attachment. Petitioner then brought this action in Federal District Court under § 1983, alleging that in attaching his property respondents had acted jointly with the State to deprive him of his property without due process of law. The District Court held that the alleged actions of the respondents did not constitute state action as required by the Fourteenth Amendment, and that the complaint therefore did not state a valid claim under § 1983. The Court of Appeals affirmed, but on the basis that the complaint failed to allege conduct under color of state law for purposes of § 1983 because there was neither usurpation or corruption of official power by a private litigant nor a surrender of judicial power to the private litigant in such a way that the independence of the enforcing officer was compromised to a significant degree.

Justice WHITE delivered the opinion of the Court.

Turning to this case, the first question is whether the claimed deprivation has resulted from the exercise of a right or privilege having its source in state authority. The second question is whether, under the facts of this case, respondents, who are private parties, may be appropriately characterized as "state actors."

[We] have consistently held that a private party's joint participation with state officials in the seizure of disputed property is sufficient to characterize that party as a "state actor" for purposes of the Fourteenth Amendment. [The] Court of Appeals erred in holding that in this context "joint participation" required something more than invoking the aid of state officials to take advantage of state-created attachment procedures. That holding is contrary to the conclusions we have reached as to the applicability of due process standards to such procedures. Whatever may be true in other contexts, this is sufficient when the State has created a system whereby state officials will attach property on the *ex parte* application of one party to a private dispute.[21]

In summary, petitioner was deprived of his property through state action; respondents were, therefore, acting under color of state law in participating in that deprivation. Petitioner did present a valid cause of action under § 1983 insofar as he challenged the constitutionality of the Virginia statute; he did not insofar as he alleged only misuse or abuse of the statute.

The judgment is reversed in part and affirmed in part, and the case is remanded for further proceedings consistent with this opinion. So ordered.

Chief Justice BURGER, dissenting.

Respondents did no more than invoke a presumptively valid state prejudgment attachment procedure available to all. Relying on a dubious "but for" analysis, the Court erroneously concludes that the subsequent procedural steps taken by the State in attaching a putative debtor's property in some way transforms respondents' acts into actions of the

---

[21] Contrary to the suggestion of Justice Powell's dissent, we do not hold today that "a private party's mere invocation of state legal procedures constitutes 'joint participation' or 'conspiracy' with state officials satisfying the § 1983 requirement of action under color of law." *Post*, at 2761. The holding today, as the above analysis makes clear, is limited to the particular context of prejudgment attachment.

State. This case is no different from the situation in which a private party commences a lawsuit and secures injunctive relief which, even if temporary, may cause significant injury to the defendant. Invoking a judicial process, of course, implicates the State and its officers but does not transform essentially private conduct into actions of the State. Dennis v. Sparks, 449 U.S. 24, 101 S.Ct. 183, 66 L.Ed.2d 185 (1980).

Justice POWELL, with whom Justice REHNQUIST and Justice O'CONNOR join, dissenting.

This Court today reverses the judgment of those lower courts. It holds that respondent, a private citizen who did no more than commence a legal action of a kind traditionally initiated by private parties, thereby engaged in "state action." This decision is as unprecedented as it is implausible. It is plainly unjust to the respondent, and the Court makes no argument to the contrary. Today's decision therefore is as unprecedented as it is unjust.

Comments on *Lugar*. Is *Lugar* distinguishable from *Jackson* and *Flagg Bros.* on the facts or the "law" applied? Does *Lugar* indicate the limits of the earlier decisions? If so, what are they?

EDMONSON v. LEESVILLE CONCRETE CO.
500 U.S. 614 (1991)

Petitioner Edmonson sued respondent Leesville Concrete Co. in the District Court, alleging that Leesville's negligence had caused him personal injury. During *voir dire*, Leesville used two of its three peremptory challenges authorized by statute to remove black persons from the prospective jury. Citing Batson v. Kentucky, 476 U.S. 79, 106 S.Ct. 1712, 90 L.Ed.2d 69, Edmonson, who is black, requested that the court require Leesville to articulate a race-neutral explanation for the peremptory strikes. The court refused on the ground that Batson does not apply in civil proceedings, and the empaneled jury, which consisted of 11 white persons and 1 black, rendered a verdict unfavorable to Edmonson. The Court of Appeals affirmed, holding that a private litigant in a civil case can exercise peremptory challenges without accountability for alleged racial classifications.

Justice KENNEDY delivered the opinion of the Court.

We must decide in the case before us whether a private litigant in a civil case may use peremptory challenges to exclude jurors on account of their race. Recognizing the impropriety of racial bias in the courtroom, we hold the race-based exclusion violates the equal protection rights of the challenged jurors.

We begin our discussion within the framework for state-action analysis set forth in Lugar, supra, 457 U.S., at 937, 102 S.Ct., at 2753-54. There we considered the state-action question in the context of a due process challenge to a State's procedure allowing private parties to obtain prejudgment attachments. We asked first whether the claimed constitutional deprivation resulted from the exercise of a right or privilege having its source in state authority, 457 U.S., at 939-941, 102 S.Ct., at 2754-2756; and second, whether the private party charged with the deprivation could be described in all fairness as a state actor, id., at 941-942, 102 S.Ct., at 2755-2756.

There can be no question that the first part of the Lugar inquiry is satisfied here. By their very nature, peremptory challenges have no significance outside a court of law. Their sole purpose is to permit litigants to assist the government in the selection of an impartial trier of fact.

Given that the statutory authorization for the challenges exercised in this case is clear, the remainder of our state-action analysis centers around the second part of the Lugar test, whether a private litigant in all fairness must be deemed a government actor in the use of peremptory challenges. Although we have recognized that this aspect of the analysis is often a factbound inquiry, see Lugar, supra, 457 U.S., at 939, 102 S.Ct., at 2754-55, our cases disclose certain principles of general application. Our precedents establish that, in determining whether a particular action or course of conduct is governmental in character, it is relevant to examine the following: the extent to which the actor relies on governmental assistance and benefits, see Burton v. Wilmington Parking Authority, 365 U.S. 715, 81 S.Ct. 856, 6 L.Ed.2d 45 (1961); whether the actor is performing a traditional governmental function, see Terry v. Adams, 345 U.S. 461, 73 S.Ct. 809, 97 L.Ed. 1152 (1953); Marsh v. Alabama, 326 U.S. 501, 66 S.Ct. 276, 90 L.Ed. 265 (1946); cf. San Francisco Arts & Athletics, Inc. v. United States Olympic Comm., 483 U.S. 522, 544-545, 107 S.Ct. 2971, 2985-2986, 97 L.Ed.2d 427 (1987); and whether the injury caused is aggravated in a unique way by the incidents of governmental authority, see Shelley v. Kraemer, 334 U.S. 1, 68 S.Ct. 836, 92 L.Ed. 1161 (1948). Based on our application of these three principles to the circumstances here, we hold that the exercise of peremptory challenges by the defendant in the District Court was pursuant to a course of state action.

Our cases have found state action when private parties make extensive use of state procedures with "the overt, significant assistance of state officials." Id., at 486, 108 S.Ct., at 1345; see Lugar v. Edmondson Oil Co., 457 U.S. 922, 102 S.Ct. 2744, 73 L.Ed.2d 482 (1982); Sniadach v. Family Finance Corp. of Bay View, 395 U.S. 337, 89 S.Ct. 1820, 23 L.Ed.2d 349 (1969). It cannot be disputed that, without the overt, significant participation of the government, the peremptory challenge system, as well as the jury trial system of which it is a part, simply could not exist.

As we have outlined here, a private party could not exercise its peremptory challenges absent the overt, significant assistance of the court. The government summons jurors, constrains their freedom of movement, and subjects them to public scrutiny and examination. The party who exercises a challenge invokes the formal authority of the court, which must discharge the prospective juror, thus effecting the "final and practical denial" of the excluded individual's opportunity to serve on the petit jury. Virginia v. Rives, 100 U.S. 313, 322, 25 L.Ed. 667 (1880). Without the direct and indispensable participation of the judge, who beyond all question is a state actor, the peremptory challenge system would serve no purpose. By enforcing a discriminatory peremptory challenge, the court "has not only made itself a party to the [biased act], but has elected to place its power, property and prestige behind the [alleged] discrimination." Burton v. Wilmington Parking Authority, 365 U.S., at 725, 81 S.Ct., at 862. In so doing, the government has "create[d] the legal framework governing the [challenged] conduct," National Collegiate Athletic Assn., 488 U.S., at 192, 109 S.Ct., at 462, and in a significant way has involved itself with invidious discrimination.

If a government confers on a private body the power to choose the government's employees or officials, the private body will be bound by the constitutional mandate of race neutrality. Cf. Tarkanian, 488 U.S., at 192-193, 109 S.Ct., at 462-463; Rendell-Baker v. Kohn, 457 U.S. 830, 102 S.Ct. 2764, 73 L.Ed.2d 418 (1982). At least a plurality of the

Court recognized this principle in Terry v. Adams, 345 U.S. 461, 73 S.Ct. 809, 97 L.Ed. 1152 (1953). There we found from Smith v. Allwright, 321 U.S. 649, 664, 64 S.Ct. 757, 765, 88 L.Ed. 987 (1944), the principle that "any 'part of the machinery for choosing officials' becomes subject to the Constitution's constraints."

Finally, we note that the injury caused by the discrimination is made more severe because the government permits it to occur within the courthouse itself.

Race discrimination within the courtroom raises serious questions as to the fairness of the proceedings conducted there. Racial bias mars the integrity of the judicial system and prevents the idea of democratic government from becoming a reality. Rose v. Mitchell, 443 U.S. 545, 556, 99 S.Ct. 2993, 3000, 61 L.Ed.2d 739 (1979); Smith v. Texas, 311 U.S. 128, 130, 61 S.Ct. 164, 165, 85 L.Ed. 84 (1940). In the many times we have addressed the problem of racial bias in our system of justice, we have not "questioned the premise that racial discrimination in the qualification or selection of jurors offends the dignity of persons and the integrity of the courts." Powers, 499 U.S., at 402, 111 S.Ct., at 1366. To permit racial exclusion in this official forum compounds the racial insult inherent in judging a citizen by the color of his or her skin.

The judgment is reversed, and the case is remanded for further proceedings consistent with our opinion.

Justice O'CONNOR, with whom THE CHIEF JUSTICE and Justice SCALIA join, dissenting.

The peremptory challenge "allow[s] parties," in this case *private* parties, to exclude potential jurors. It is the nature of a peremptory that its exercise is left wholly within the discretion of the litigant. In both criminal and civil trials, the peremptory challenge is a mechanism for the exercise of *private* choice in the pursuit of fairness. The peremptory is, by design, an enclave of private action in a government-managed proceeding.

[That these] actions may be necessary to a peremptory challenge — in the sense that there could be no such challenge without a venire from which to select — no more makes the challenge state action than the building of roads and provision of public transportation makes state action of riding on a bus.

[Trials] in this country are adversarial proceedings. Attorneys for private litigants do not act on behalf of the government, or even the public as a whole; attorneys represent their clients. An attorney's job is to "advanc[e] the 'undivided interests of his client.' This is essentially a private function . . . for which state office and authority are not needed."

The Court is plainly wrong when it asserts that "[i]n the jury selection process, the government and private litigants work for the same end." See *ante,* at 2086. In a civil trial, the attorneys for each side are in "an adversarial relation," *ibid.;* they use their peremptory strikes in direct opposition to one another, and for precisely contrary ends. The government cannot "work for the same end" as both parties. In fact, the government is neutral as to private litigants' use of peremptory strikes. That's the point. The government does not encourage or approve these strikes, or direct that they be used in any particular way, or even that they be used at all. The government is simply not "responsible" for the use of peremptory strikes by private litigants.

Constitutional "liability attaches only to those wrongdoers 'who carry a badge of authority of [the government] and represent it in some capacity.'" Tarkanian, 488 U.S., at 191, 109 S.Ct., at 461. A government attorney who uses a peremptory challenge on behalf of the client is, by definition, representing the government. The challenge thereby becomes state action. It is antithetical to the nature of our adversarial process, however, to say that a private attorney acting on behalf of a private client represents the government for constitutional purposes.

Beyond "significant participation" and "traditional function," the Court's final argument is that the exercise of a peremptory challenge by a private litigant is state action because it takes place in a courtroom. *Ante,* at 2087. In the end, this is all the Court is left with; peremptories do not involve the "overt, significant participation of the government," nor do they constitute a "traditional function of the government." The Court is also wrong in its ultimate claim. If Dodson stands for anything, it is that the actions of a lawyer in a courtroom do not become those of the government by virtue of their location. This is true even if those actions are based on race.

Racism is a terrible thing. It is irrational, destructive, and mean. Arbitrary discrimination based on race is particularly abhorrent when manifest in a courtroom, a forum established by the government for the resolution of disputes through "quiet rationality." See *ante,* at 2088. But not every opprobrious and inequitable act is a constitutional violation. The Fifth Amendment's Due Process Clause prohibits only actions for which the Government can be held responsible. The Government is not responsible for everything that occurs in a courtroom. The Government is not responsible for a peremptory challenge by a private litigant. I respectfully dissent.

Justice SCALIA, dissenting.

I join Justice O'Connor's dissent, which demonstrates that today's opinion is wrong in principle. I write to observe that it is also unfortunate in its consequences.

Although today's decision neither follows the law nor produces desirable concrete results, it certainly has great symbolic value. To overhaul the doctrine of state action in this fashion — what a magnificent demonstration of this institution's uncompromising hostility to race-based judgments, even by private actors! The price of the demonstration is, alas, high, and much of it will be paid by the minority litigants who use our courts. I dissent.

———

Comments on *Edmonson*. Does *Edmonson* underscore the significance of the *Lugar* analysis? Justice Kennedy applies the *Lugar* analysis (test). What is it? Justice Kennedy also speaks of "certain general principles" that "our cases disclose." What are they?

BRENTWOOD ACADEMY v. TENNESSEE SECONDARY SCHOOL ATHLETIC ASSOCIATION
531 U.S. 288 (2001)

[Respondent not-for-profit athletic association (Association) regulates interscholastic sport among Tennessee public and private high schools. Most of the State's public high schools are members, representing 84% of the Association's membership. School officials make up the voting membership of the Association's governing council and control board, which typically hold meetings during regular school hours. The Association is largely funded by gate receipts. Association staff, although not state employees, may join the state retirement system. The Association sets membership standards and student eligibility rules and has the power to penalize any member school that violates those rules. The

State Board of Education (State Board) has long acknowledged the Association's role in regulating interscholastic competition in public schools, and its members sit as nonvoting members of the Association's governing bodies. When the Association penalized petitioner Brentwood Academy for violating a recruiting rule, Brentwood sued the Association and its executive director under 42 U.S.C. § 1983, claiming that the rule's enforcement was state action that violated the First and Fourteenth Amendments. The District Court granted Brentwood summary judgment, enjoining the rule's enforcement, but the Sixth Circuit found no state action and reversed.]

Justice SOUTER delivered the opinion of the Court.

The issue is whether a statewide association incorporated to regulate interscholastic athletic competition among public and private secondary schools may be regarded as engaging in state action when it enforces a rule against a member school. The association in question here includes most public schools located within the State, acts through their representatives, draws its officers from them, is largely funded by their dues and income received in their stead, and has historically been seen to regulate in lieu of the State Board of Education's exercise of its own authority. We hold that the association's regulatory activity may and should be treated as state action owing to the pervasive entwinement of state school officials in the structure of the association, there being no offsetting reason to see the association's acts in any other way.

[Examples] of public entwinement in the management and control of ostensibly separate trusts or corporations foreshadow this case, as this Court itself anticipated in Tarkanian. Tarkanian arose when an undoubtedly state actor, the University of Nevada, suspended its basketball coach, Tarkanian, in order to comply with rules and recommendations of the National Collegiate Athletic Association (NCAA). The coach charged the NCAA with state action, arguing that the state university had delegated its own functions to the NCAA, clothing the latter with authority to make and apply the university's rules, the result being joint action making the NCAA a state actor.

To be sure, it is not the strict holding in Tarkanian that points to our view of this case, for we found no state action on the part of the NCAA. We could see, on the one hand, that the university had some part in setting the NCAA's rules, and the Supreme Court of Nevada had gone so far as to hold that the NCAA had been delegated the university's traditionally exclusive public authority over personnel. 488 U.S., at 190, 109 S.Ct. 454. But on the other side, the NCAA's policies were shaped not by the University of Nevada alone, but by several hundred member institutions, most of them having no connection with Nevada, and exhibiting no color of Nevada law. Id., at 193, 109 S.Ct. 454. Since it was difficult to see the NCAA, not as a collective membership, but as surrogate for the one State, we held the organization's connection with Nevada too insubstantial to ground a state-action claim. Id., at 193, 196, 109 S.Ct. 454.

But dictum in Tarkanian pointed to a contrary result on facts like ours, with an organization whose member public schools are all within a single State. "The situation would, of course, be different if the [Association's] membership consisted entirely of institutions located within the same State, many of them public institutions created by the same sovereign." Id., at 193, n. 13, 109 S.Ct. 454. To support our surmise, we approvingly cited two cases: Clark v. Arizona Interscholastic Assn., 695 F.2d 1126 (C.A.9 1982), cert. denied, 464 U.S. 818, 104 S.Ct. 79, 78 L.Ed.2d 90 (1983), a challenge to a state high school athletic association that kept boys from playing on girls' interscholastic volleyball teams in Arizona; and Louisiana High School Athletic Assn. v. St. Augustine

High School, 396 F.2d 224 (C.A.5 1968), a parochial school's attack on the racially segregated system of interscholastic high school athletics maintained by the athletic association. In each instance, the Court of Appeals treated the athletic association as a state actor.

Just as we foresaw in Tarkanian, the "necessarily fact-bound inquiry," Lugar, 457 U.S., at 939, 102 S.Ct. 2744, leads to the conclusion of state action here. The nominally private character of the Association is overborne by the pervasive entwinement of public institutions and public officials in its composition and workings, and there is no substantial reason to claim unfairness in applying constitutional standards to it.

The Association is not an organization of natural persons acting on their own, but of schools, and of public schools to the extent of 84% of the total. Under the Association's bylaws, each member school is represented by its principal or a faculty member, who has a vote in selecting members of the governing legislative council and board of control from eligible principals, assistant principals, and superintendents.

[By] giving these jobs to the Association, the 290 public schools of Tennessee belonging to it can sensibly be seen as exercising their own authority to meet their own responsibilities.

[In] sum, to the extent of 84% of its membership, the Association is an organization of public schools represented by their officials acting in their official capacity to provide an integral element of secondary public schooling. There would be no recognizable Association, legal or tangible, without the public school officials, who do not merely control but overwhelmingly perform all but the purely ministerial acts by which the Association exists and functions in practical terms.

To complement the entwinement of public school officials with the Association from the bottom up, the State of Tennessee has provided for entwinement from top down. State Board members are assigned ex officio to serve as members of the board of control and legislative council, and the Association's ministerial employees are treated as state employees to the extent of being eligible for membership in the state retirement system.

The judgment of the Court of Appeals for the Sixth Circuit is reversed, and the case is remanded for further proceedings consistent with this opinion.

It is so ordered.

Justice THOMAS, with whom THE CHIEF JUSTICE, Justice SCALIA, and Justice KENNEDY join, dissenting.

We have never found state action based upon mere "entwinement." Until today, we have found a private organization's acts to constitute state action only when the organization performed a public function; was created, coerced, or encouraged by the government; or acted in a symbiotic relationship with the government. The majority's holding — that the Tennessee Secondary School Athletic Association's (TSSAA) enforcement of its recruiting rule is state action — not only extends state-action doctrine beyond its permissible limits but also encroaches upon the realm of individual freedom that the doctrine was meant to protect. I respectfully dissent. . .

I am not prepared to say that any private organization that permits public entities and public officials to participate acts as the State in anything or everything it does, and our state-action jurisprudence has never reached that far. The state-action doctrine was developed to reach only those actions that are truly attributable to the State, not to subject private citizens to the control of federal courts hearing § 1983 actions.

Comment on *Brentwood Academy*. Is the "public entanglement" rationale in *Brentwood* enough to distinguish *NCAA v. Tarkanian*, 488 U.S. 179 (1988)? Could NCAA activities ever be held as state action?

Chapter 5
Constitutionally Protected Rights
— Due Process

Having reviewed issues relating to the general application of constitutional rights — incorporation and state action — we now turn to the Constitution's protection of specific substantive rights. In this section we will review those rights protected by the due process clause and equal protection clause of the Fourteenth Amendment. While it is evident that the rights to due process and equal protection are protected, recall from our study of constitutional decision making at the commencement of this work, and our study of incorporation, that the due process clause has also been used to both incorporate most of the bill of rights to the states and to create additional non-articulated constitutional rights. This we call "substantive due process," and we will commence our inquiry with a study of the due process clause, first in its controversial "substantive" application, and then in its more normative "procedural" application.

I. SUBSTANTIVE DUE PROCESS

A. INTRODUCTION

"Substantive due process," John Ely asserted, "sounds like a contradiction in terms — sort of like 'green pastel redness.'" Ely, *Democracy and Distrust* 18 (1980). A contradiction in terms because the concept of due process normally conjures procedural rights. When the framers adopted the Fifth Amendment right to due process, their intent that it be procedural was evidenced by their delineation of a variety of specific procedural rights as well: indictment, double jeopardy, self-incrimination, speedy and public trial, jury trial, information, confrontation, compulsory process, and assistance of counsel. The term "due process" itself is defined as "[a]n established course for judicial proceedings or other governmental activities designed to safeguard the legal rights of the individual." *American Heritage Dictionary of the English Language* (4th ed. 2003).

When we speak of a substantive application of the due process clause we do not speak of the right as procedural, we speak of the verbiage that "[n]o state may deprive any citizen of life, liberty or property without due process of law," as a source for creating additional "substantive rights." Consequently, we use the term in a substantive as opposed to a procedural sense. Therein lies the confusion of "green pastel redness"! This substantive application of a procedural right may make more sense when we recall that the opinion in *Slaughter-House*, in closing the door to privileges and immunities incorporation, left the door ajar for incorporation via the due process clause. Remember, if you will, that substantive due process is substantive due process, is substantive due process, or that fundamental fairness select incorporation is no different than our present inquiry, except that we are using the due process clause's "fundamental fairness" litany to create additional unarticulated fundamental rights.

Our study of substantive due process differs only in its concentration on applying the fundamental fairness dogma to create rights that are not articulated in the Constitution. As we noted at the onset of our study, though creation of unarticulated rights may help provide a "living constitution," it is a most controversial and oft debated role for the Court. Offhand it might seem that allowing the Court to create additional unarticulated rights could only benefit our society by affording greater protection against government intrusion. But before we are so sure of such we must learn the "Lessons of *Lochner*."

LOCHNER v. NEW YORK
198 U.S. 45 (1905)

Mr. Justice PECKHAM delivered the opinion of the Court.

[The Court held a New York statute that attempted to regulate minimum hours by "providing that no employee shall . . . work in a biscuit, bread or cake bakery or confectionary establishment more than sixty hours in any one week, or more than ten hours in any one day," unconstitutional.]

The statute necessarily interferes with the right of contract between the employer and employees, concerning the number of hours in which the latter may labor in the bakery of the employer. The general right to make a contract in relation to his business is part of the liberty of the individual protected by the Fourteenth Amendment of the Federal Constitution. Under that provision no State can deprive any person of life, liberty or property without due process of law. The right to purchase or to sell labor is part of the liberty protected by this amendment, unless there are circumstances which exclude the right. There are, however, certain powers, existing in the sovereignty of each State in the Union, somewhat vaguely termed police powers, the exact description and limitation of which have not been attempted by the courts. Those powers [relate] to the safety, health, morals and general welfare of the public. Both property and liberty are held on such reasonable conditions as may be imposed by the governing power of the State in the exercise of those powers, and with such conditions the Fourteenth Amendment was not designed to interfere.

This court has recognized the existence and upheld the exercise of the police powers of the States in many cases. [Among] the [cases] where the state law has been upheld by this court is that of Holden v. Hardy, 169 U.S. 366 [1898]. A provision in the act of the legislature of Utah was there under consideration, the act limiting the employment of workmen in all underground mines or workings, to eight hours per day, "except in cases of emergency, where life or property is in imminent danger." [The] act was held to be a valid exercise of the police powers of the State. [It] was held that the kind of employment [and] the character of the employees [were] such as to make it reasonable and proper for the State to interfere to prevent the employees from being constrained by the rules laid down by the proprietors in regard to labor. [There] is nothing in Holden v. Hardy which covers the case now before us. . . .

It must, of course, be conceded that there is a limit to the valid exercise of the police power by the State. There is no dispute concerning this general proposition. Otherwise the Fourteenth Amendment would have no efficacy and the legislatures of the States would have unbounded power. [In] every case that comes before this court, therefore, where legislation of this character is concerned and where the protection of the Federal Constitution is sought, the question necessarily arises: Is this a fair, reasonable and appropriate exercise of the police power of the State, or is it an unreasonable, unnecessary and arbitrary interference with the right of the individual to his personal liberty or to enter into those contracts in relation to labor which may seem to him appropriate or necessary for the support of himself and his family? Of course the liberty of contract relating to labor includes both parties to it. The one has as much right to purchase as the other to sell labor.

This is not a question of substituting the judgment of the court for that of the legislature. If the act be within the power of the State it is valid, although the judgment of the court might be totally opposed to the enactment of such a law. But the question would still remain: Is it within the police power of the State? and that question must be answered by the court.

The question whether this act is valid as a labor law, pure and simple, may be dismissed in a few words. There is no reasonable ground for interfering with the liberty of person or the right of free contract, by determining the hours of labor, in the occupation of a baker. There is no contention that bakers as a class are not equal in intelligence and capacity to men in other trades or manual occupations, or that they are not able to assert their rights and care for themselves without the protecting arm of the State, interfering with their independence of judgment and of action. They are in no sense wards of the State. Viewed in the light of a purely labor law, with no reference whatever to the question of health, we think that a law like the one before us involves neither the safety, the morals nor the welfare of the public, and that the interest of the public is not in the slightest degree affected by such an act. The law must be upheld, if at all, as a law pertaining to the health of the individual engaged in the occupation of a baker. It does not affect any other portion of the public than those who are engaged in that occupation. Clean and wholesome bread does not depend upon whether the baker works but ten hours per day or only sixty hours a week. . . .

It is a question of which of two powers or rights shall prevail — the power of the State to legislate or the right of the individual to liberty of person and freedom of contract. The mere assertion that the subject relates though but in a remote degree to the public health does not necessarily render the enactment valid. The act must have a more direct relation, as a means to an end, and the end itself must be appropriate and legitimate, before an act can be held to be valid which interferes with the general right of an individual to be free in his person and in his power to contract in relation to his own labor. . . .

We think the limit of the police power has been reached and passed in this case. There is, in our judgment, no reasonable foundation for holding this to be necessary or appropriate as a health law to safeguard the public health or the health of the individuals who are following the trade of a baker. If this statute be valid, [there] would seem to be no length to which legislation of this nature might not go. . . .

We think that there can be no fair doubt that the trade of a baker, in and of itself, is not an unhealthy one to that degree which would authorize the legislature to interfere with the right to labor, and with the right of free contract on the part of the individual, either as employer or employee. In looking through statistics regarding all trades and occupations, it may be true that the trade of a baker does not appear to be as healthy as some other trades, and is also vastly more healthy than still others. To the common understanding the trade of a baker has never been regarded as an unhealthy one. [It] might be safely affirmed that almost all occupations more or less affect the health. There must be more than the mere fact of the possible existence of some small amount of unhealthiness to warrant legislative interference with liberty. It is unfortunately true that labor, even in any department, may possibly carry with it the seeds of unhealthiness. But are we all, on that account, at the mercy of legislative majorities? . . .

It is also urged, pursuing the same line of argument, that it is to the interest of the State that its population should be strong and robust, and therefore any legislation which may be said to tend to make people healthy must be valid as health laws, enacted under the police power. If this be a valid argument and a justification for this kind of legislation, it follows that the protection of the Federal Constitution from undue interference with liberty of person and freedom of contract is visionary, wherever the law is sought to be justified as a valid exercise of the police power. Scarcely any law but might find shelter under such assumptions. . . . Not only the hours of employees, but the hours of employers, could be regulated, and doctors, lawyers, scientists, all professional men, as well as athletes and artisans, could be forbidden to fatigue their brains and bodies by prolonged hours of exercise, lest the fighting strength of the State be impaired. We mention these extreme cases because the contention is extreme. We do not believe in the soundness of the views which uphold this law. [The] act is not, within any fair meaning of the term, a health law, but is an illegal interference with the rights of individuals, both employers and employees, to make contracts regarding labor upon such terms as they may think best, or which they may agree upon with the other parties to such contracts. Statutes of the nature of that under review, limiting the hours in which grown and intelligent men may labor to earn their living, are mere meddlesome interferences with the rights of the individual, and they are not saved from condemnation by the claim that they are passed in the exercise of the police power and upon the subject of the health of the individual whose rights are interfered with, unless there be some fair ground, reasonable in and of itself, to say that there is material danger to the public health or to the health of the employees, if the hours of labor are not curtailed. [All that the State] could properly do has been done by it with regard to the conduct of bakeries, as provided for in the other sections of the act, [which] provide for the inspection of the premises where the bakery is carried on, with regard to furnishing proper wash-rooms and water-closets, [with] regard to providing proper drainage, plumbing and painting [and] for other things of that nature. . . .

It was further urged [that] restricting the hours of labor in the case of bakers was valid because it tended to cleanliness on the part of the workers, as a man was more apt to be cleanly when not overworked, and if cleanly then his "output" was also more likely to be so. [In] our judgment it is not possible in fact to discover the connection between the number of hours a baker may work in the bakery and the healthful quality of the bread made by the workman. The connection, if any exists, is too shadowy and thin to build any argument for the interference of the legislature. [When] assertions such as we have adverted to become necessary in order to give, if possible, a plausible foundation for the contention that the law is a "health law," it gives rise to at least a suspicion that there was some other motive dominating the legislature than the purpose to subserve the public health or welfare.

This interference on the part of the legislatures of the several States with the ordinary trades and occupations of the people seems to be on the increase. . . .

It is impossible for us to shut our eyes to the fact that many of the laws of this character, while passed under what is claimed to be the police power for the purpose of protecting the public health or welfare, are, in reality, passed from other motives. We are justified in saying so when, from the character of the law and the subject upon which it legislates, it is apparent that the public health or welfare bears but the most remote relation to the law. The purpose of a statute must be determined from the natural and legal effect of the language employed; and whether it is or is not repugnant to the Constitution of the United States must be determined from the natural effect of such statutes when put into operation, and not from their proclaimed purpose. [The] court looks beyond the mere letter of the law in such cases. Yick Wo v. Hopkins, 118 U.S. 356.

It is manifest to us that the [law here] has no such direct relation to and no such substantial effect upon the health of the employee, as to justify us in regarding the section as really a health law. It seems to us that the real object and purpose were simply to regulate the hours of labor between the master and his employees (all being men, sui juris), in a private business, not dangerous in any degree to morals or in any real and substantial degree, to the health of the employees. Under such circumstances the freedom of master and employee to contract with each other in relation to their employment [cannot] be prohibited or interfered with, without violating the Federal Constitution. . . . Reversed.

Mr. Justice HARLAN, with whom Mr. Justice WHITE and Mr. Justice DAY concurred, dissenting. . . .

[The] statute must be taken as expressing the belief of the people of New York that, as a general rule, and in the case of the average man, labor in excess of sixty hours during a week in such establishments may endanger the health of those who thus labor. Whether or not this be wise legislation it is not the province of the court to inquire. Under our systems of government the courts are not concerned with the wisdom or policy of legislation. So that in determining the question of power to interfere with liberty of contract, the court may inquire whether the means devised by the State are germane to an end which may be lawfully accomplished and have a real or substantial relation to the protection of health, as involved in the daily work of the persons, male and female, engaged in bakery and confectionery establishments. But when this inquiry is entered upon I find it impossible, in view of common experience, to say that there is here no real or substantial relation between the means employed by the State and the end sought to be accomplished by its legislation. . . .

Professor Hirt in his treatise on the "Diseases of the Workers" has said: The labor of the bakers is among the hardest and most laborious imaginable, because it has to be performed under conditions injurious to the health of those engaged in it. It is hard, very hard work, not only because it requires a great deal of physical exertion in an overheated workshop and during unreasonably long hours, but more so because of the erratic demands of the public, compelling the baker to perform the greater part of his work at night, thus depriving him of an opportunity to enjoy the necessary rest and sleep, a fact which is highly injurious to his health.

Another writer says: The constant inhaling of flour dust causes inflammation of the lungs and of the bronchial tubes. The eyes also suffer through this dust. . . . The long hours of toil to which all bakers are subjected produce rheumatism, cramps and swollen legs. The intense heat in the workshops [is] another source of a number of diseases of various organs. [The] average age of a baker is below that of other workmen; they seldom live over their fiftieth year, most of them dying between the ages of forty and fifty. . . .

We judicially know that the question of the number of hours during which a workman should continuously labor has been, for a long period, and is yet, a subject of serious consideration among civilized peoples, and by those having special knowledge of the laws of health. . . .

We also judicially know that the number of hours that should constitute a day's labor in particular occupations involving the physical strength and safety of workmen has been the subject of enactments by Congress and by nearly all of the States. Many, if not most, of those enactments fix eight hours as the proper basis of a day's labor.

I do not stop to consider whether any particular view of this economic question presents the sounder theory. What the precise facts are it may be difficult to say. It is enough for the determination of this case, and it is enough for this court to know, that the question is one about which there is room for debate and for an honest difference of opinion. There are many reasons of a weighty, substantial character, based upon the experience of mankind, in support of the theory that, all things considered, more than ten hours' steady work each day, from week to week, in a bakery or confectionery establishment, may endanger the health, and shorten the lives of the workmen, thereby diminishing their physical and mental capacity to serve the State, and to provide for those dependent upon them.

If such reasons exist that ought to be the end of this case, for the State is not amenable to the judiciary, in respect of its legislative enactments, unless such enactments are plainly, palpably, beyond all question inconsistent with the Constitution of the United States. . . .

Mr. Justice HOLMES dissenting. . . .

This case is decided upon an economic theory which a large part of the country does not entertain. If it were a question whether I agreed with that theory, I should desire to study it further and long before making up my mind. But I do not conceive that to be my duty, because I strongly believe that my agreement or disagreement has nothing to do with the right of a majority to embody their opinions in law. It is settled by various decisions of this court that state constitutions and state laws may regulate life in many ways which we as legislators might think as injudicious or if you like as tyrannical as this, and which equally with this interfere with the liberty to contract. Sunday laws and usury laws are ancient examples. A more modern one is the prohibition of lotteries. The liberty of the citizen to do as he likes so long as he does not interfere with the liberty of others to do the same, which has been a shibboleth for some well-known writers, is interfered with by school laws, by the Post Office, by every state or municipal institution which takes his money for purposes thought desirable, whether he likes it or not. The Fourteenth Amendment does not enact Mr. Herbert Spencer's Social Statics. The other day we sustained the Massachusetts vaccination law. Jacobson v. Massachusetts, 197 U.S. 11. United States and state statutes and decisions cutting down the liberty to contract by way of combination are familiar to this court. [The] decision sustaining an eight hour law for miners is still recent. [Holden v. Hardy.] Some of these laws embody convictions or prejudices which judges are likely to share. Some may not. But a constitution is not intended to embody a particular economic theory, whether of paternalism and the organic relation of the citizen to the State or of laissez faire. It is made for people of fundamentally differing views, and the accident of our finding certain opinions natural and familiar or novel and even shocking ought not to conclude our judgment upon the question whether statutes embodying them conflict with the Constitution of the United States.

General propositions do not decide concrete cases. The decision will depend on a judgment or intuition more subtle than any articulate major premise. But I think that the proposition just stated, if it is accepted, will carry us far toward the end. Every opinion tends to become a law. I think that the word liberty in the Fourteenth Amendment is perverted when it is held to prevent the natural outcome of a dominant opinion, unless it can be said that a rational and fair man necessarily would admit that the statute proposed would infringe fundamental principles as they have been understood by the traditions of our people and our law. It does not need research to show that no such sweeping condemnation can be passed upon the statute before us. A reasonable man might think it a proper measure on the score of health. Men whom I certainly could not pronounce unreasonable would uphold it as a first installment of a general regulation of the hours of work. . . .

––––––––

The *Lochner* Era. Does *Lochner* convince you that allowing the Court to create unarticulated fundamental rights may not always be positive? Is *Lochner*'s "liberty of contract" really a fundamental right to be poor? Is this a "catch-22" of a "living constitution" — allowing the Court to create contemporary rights via a substantive due process application might allow it to create rights that we might not view as positive? Even potentially biased, given the discretion afforded? Is there a means of controlling the Court in this regard? Can you articulate such a means?

The accusation of bias against the Court centers not only on the denial of state regulation, but the concurrent denial of federal regulation as well. Thus, the net effect of these decisions was "no regulation," raising "laissez-fare" economics to constitutional status. As Justice Holmes asserted in his *Lochner* dissent, "But a constitution is not intended to embody a particular economic theory, whether of paternalism and the organic relation of the citizen to the State or of laissez faire."

The Court's bias toward reading laissez-faire capitalism as constitutionally mandated is substantiated by that fact that from the decision in *Lochner* in 1905 to the mid-1930s, the Court invalidated approximately 200 economic regulations, usually under the due process clause of the Fourteenth Amendment. As we noted at the outset of the materials, in this era the judicial "liberals," responding to *Lochner*, argued for a "conservative" application of the judicial power, while the judicial "conservatives" defended their activist and liberal use of the judicial power. Does the absence of principle here, as well as the shift in these views in the Warren era, indicate the Court is subject to the "constraints" of human nature, and that any neutrality we can expect from the Court is misplaced?

The retreat from the *Lochner* era commenced shortly before "Court packing" — recall Justice Roberts's "switch in time to save the nine"[1] — and continued beyond the New Deal given Roosevelt's impact on the makeup of the Supreme Court. This retreat, spurned by increasing judicial and academic criticism, and, perhaps most importantly, the economic realities of the Great Depression, seemed to undermine *Lochner*'s central premises, and is evidenced in the opinion that follows.

––––––––

[1] See West Coast Hotel Co. v. Parrish, 300 U.S. 379 (1937). Justice Roberts's "switch" provided a five-to-four decision where the Court upheld a state law establishing a minimum wage for women. Chief Justice Hughes delivered the opinion of the Court: "[The] violation alleged by those attacking minimum wage regulation for women is deprivation of freedom of contract. What is this freedom of contract? The Constitution does not speak of freedom of contract. It speaks of liberty and prohibits the deprivation of liberty without due process of law. [Regulation] which is reasonable in relation to its subject and is adopted in the interests of the community is due process. . . ."

1. DECLINE OF JUDICIAL INTERVENTION

NEBBIA v. NEW YORK
291 U.S. 502 (1934)

[During 1932, the prices received by farmers for milk fell much below the cost of production, and the situation of the families of dairy producers in New York grew "desperate." A legislative committee, established to investigate the matter, concluded that milk "is an essential item of diet," and that the failure "of producers to receive a reasonable return for their labor and investment over an extended period threatens a relaxation of vigilance against contamination." The committee further found that the "production and distribution of milk is a paramount industry of the state" and that the "milk industry is affected by factors of [price] instability [which] call for special methods of control." The legislature thus established the Milk Control Board, which was authorized to fix minimum and maximum retail prices for milk. Nebbia, the owner of a grocery store in Rochester, was convicted of selling milk below the minimum price fixed by the board. The Court, in a five-to-four decision, upheld the law.]

Justice ROBERTS delivered the opinion of the Court:
The legislature adopted [the law] as a method of correcting the evils, which the report of the committee showed could not be expected to right themselves through the ordinary play of the forces of supply and demand, owing to the peculiar and uncontrollable factors affecting the industry. [Under] our form of government the use of property and the making of contracts are normally matters of private and not of public concern. The general rule is that both shall be free of governmental interference. But neither property rights nor contract rights are absolute; for government cannot exist if the citizen may at will use his property to the detriment of his fellows, or exercise his freedom of contract to work them harm. [Thus] has this court from the early days affirmed that the power to promote the general welfare is inherent in government. [These] correlative rights, that of the citizen to exercise exclusive dominion over property and freely to contract about his affairs, and that of the state to regulate the use of property and the conduct of business, are always in collision. [But] subject only to constitutional restraint the private right must yield to the public need.

The Fifth Amendment, in the field of federal activity, and the Fourteenth, as respects state action, do not prohibit governmental regulation for the public welfare. They merely condition the exertion of the admitted power, by securing that the end shall be accomplished by methods consistent with due process. And the guaranty of due process, as has often been held, demands only that the law shall not be unreasonable, arbitrary or capricious, and that the means selected shall have a real and substantial relation to the object sought to be attained. [The] Constitution does not guarantee the unrestricted privilege to engage in a business or to conduct it as one pleases. . . .

But we are told that because the law essays to control prices it denies due process. Notwithstanding the admitted power to correct existing economic ills by appropriate regulation of business, [the] appellant urges that direct fixation of prices [is] per se unreasonable and unconstitutional, save as applied to businesses affected with a public interest; [and that no] business is so affected [unless it is in the nature of a public utility or a monopoly]. But this is a misconception. [There] is no closed class or category of businesses affected with a public interest, and the function of courts in the application of the Fifth and Fourteenth Amendments is to determine in each case whether circumstances vindicate the challenged regulation as a reasonable exertion of governmental authority or condemn it as arbitrary or discriminatory. [The] phrase "affected with a public interest" can, in the nature of things, mean no more than that an industry, for adequate reason, is subject to control for the public good. . . .

So far as the requirement of due process is concerned, [a] state is free to adopt whatever economic policy may reasonably be deemed to promote public welfare, and to enforce that policy by legislation adapted to its purpose. The courts are without authority either to declare such policy, or, when it is declared by the legislature, to override it. [If] the legislative policy be to curb unrestrained and harmful competition [it] does not lie with the courts to determine that the rule is unwise. [Times] without number we have said that the legislature is primarily the judge of the necessity of such an enactment, that every possible presumption is in favor of its validity, and that though the court may hold views inconsistent with the wisdom of the law, it may not be annulled unless palpably in excess of legislative power. [Price] control, like any other form of regulation, is unconstitutional only if arbitrary, discriminatory, or demonstrably irrelevant to the policy the legislature is free to adopt, and hence an unnecessary and unwarranted interference with individual liberty.

Justice MCREYNOLDS, joined by Justices VAN DEVANTER, SUTHERLAND, and BUTLER, dissented.

This is not regulation, but management, control, dictation — it amounts to the deprivation of the fundamental right which one has to conduct his own affairs honestly and along customary lines. [It is the duty of this Court to inquire] whether the means proposed have reasonable relation to something within legislative power. [Here,] we find direct interference with guaranteed rights defended upon the ground that the purpose was to promote the public welfare by increasing milk prices at the farm. [But it is unclear] how higher charges at stores to impoverished customers when the output is excessive [can] possibly increase receipts at the farm. [I]t appears to me wholly unreasonable to expect this legislation to accomplish the proposed end.

———

The "Lessons of *Lochner*." What are the lessons of *Lochner*? Should the Court avoid creating unarticulated fundamental rights? Should the Court defer to the democratic branches in regard to issues that are socio-economic in character? Much as Holmes's dissent, *Lochner* has laid a predicate for the Court retreating from scrutiny, let alone activism, in matters concerning socio-economics. The *Nebbia* opinion represents this "change" in direction:

> So far as the requirement of due process is concerned, [a] state is free to adopt whatever economic policy may reasonably be deemed to promote public welfare, and to enforce that policy by legislation adapted to its purpose. The courts are without authority either to declare such policy, or, when it is declared by the legislature, to override it. [If] the legislative policy be to curb unrestrained and harmful competition [it] does not lie with the courts to determine that the rule is unwise. [Times] without number we have said that the legislature is primarily the judge of the necessity of such an enactment, that every possible presumption is in favor of its validity, and that though the court may hold views inconsistent

with the wisdom of the law, it may not be annulled unless palpably in excess of legislative power.

Should this retreat from socio-economics mean that the Court should defer to the legislature in all instances? This issue will be of particular significance in the modern era. Are there any areas where the Court should provide a greater degree of scrutiny than dictated by the "lessons of *Lochner*"? What of state regulations that affect other fundamental rights or racial minorities? Despite decisions like *Nebbia*, should the Court maintain a more active presence in these areas? Should there be a "double standard"? If these are the present views of the Court in such matters, many trace the origin of this approach to Justice Stone's footnote 4 in *Carolene Products*.

UNITED STATES v. CAROLENE PRODUCTS CO.
304 U.S. 144 (1938)

[After extensive hearings, two congressional committees made the following findings: "There is an extensive commerce in milk compounds made of condensed milk from which the butter fat has been extracted and an equivalent amount of vegetable oil [has been] substituted. [By] reason of the extraction of the natural milk fat the compounded product [known as 'filled milk'] can be manufactured and sold at a lower cost than pure milk. Butter fat [is] rich in vitamins [that] are wanting in vegetable oils. The use of filled milk as a dietary substitute for pure milk results [in] undernourishment. [Despite] compliance with the branding and labeling requirements of the Pure Food and Drugs Act, there is widespread use of filled milk as a substitute for pure milk. This is aided by their identical taste and appearance, by the similarity of the containers in which they are sold, by the practice of dealers in offering the inferior product to customers as being as good as or better than pure condensed milk sold at a higher price, by customers' ignorance of the respective food values of the two products, and in many sections of the country by their inability to read the labels."

Based on these findings, Congress enacted the Filled Milk Act of 1923, which declared that "filled milk" is an "adulterated article of food, injurious to the public health," and that "its sale constitutes a fraud upon the public." The act therefore prohibited any person to ship filled milk in interstate commerce. In *Carolene Products*, the Court upheld the act.]

Justice STONE delivered the opinion of the Court:

We may assume for present purposes that no pronouncement of a legislature can forestall attack upon the constitutionality of [a prohibition] by applying opprobrious epithets to the prohibited act, and that a statute would deny due process which precluded the disproof in judicial proceedings of all facts which would show or tend to show that a statute depriving the suitor of life, liberty or property had a rational basis.

But such we think is not the purpose [of] the statutory characterization of filled milk as injurious to health and as a fraud upon the public. There is no need to consider it here as more than a declaration of the legislative findings deemed to support and justify the action taken, [aiding] informed judicial review, as do the reports of legislative committees, by revealing the rationale of the legislation. Even in the absence of such aids the existence of facts supporting the legislative judgment is to be presumed, for regulatory legislation affecting ordinary commercial transactions is not to be pronounced unconstitutional unless in the light of the facts made known or generally assumed it is of such a character as to preclude the assumption that it rests upon some rational basis. . . .[4]

Where the existence of a rational basis for legislation [depends] upon facts beyond the sphere of judicial notice, such facts may properly be made the subject of judicial inquiry, [and] the constitutionality of a statute predicated upon the existence of a particular state of facts may be challenged by showing to the court that those facts have ceased to exist. [Similarly] we recognize that the constitutionality of a statute, valid on its face, may be assailed by proof of facts tending to show that the statute as applied to a particular article is without support in reason because the article, although within the prohibited class, is so different from others of the class as to be without the reason for the prohibition, [though] the effect of such proof depends on the relevant circumstances of each case, as for example the administrative difficulty of excluding the article from the regulated class. [But] by their very nature such inquiries, where the legislative judgment is drawn in question, must be restricted to the issue whether any state of facts either known or which could reasonably be assumed affords support for it. Here the [appellee] challenges the validity of the statute on its face and it is evident from all the considerations presented to Congress, and those of which we may take judicial notice, that the question is at least debatable whether commerce in filled milk should be left unregulated, or in some measure restricted, or wholly prohibited. As that decision was for Congress, neither the finding of a court arrived at by weighing the evidence, nor the verdict of a jury can be substituted for it. [The Act is] constitutional.

---

[4] There may be narrower scope for operation of the presumption of constitutionality when legislation appears on its face to be within a specific prohibition of the Constitution, such as those of the first ten Amendments, which are deemed equally specific when held to be embraced within the Fourteenth. See Stromberg v. California, 283 U.S. 359, 369, 370, 51 S.Ct. 532, 535, 536, 75 L.Ed. 1117, 73 A.L.R. 1484; Lovell v. Griffin, 303 U.S. 444, 58 S.Ct. 666, 82 L.Ed. 949, decided March 28, 1938.

It is unnecessary to consider now whether legislation which restricts those political processes which can ordinarily be expected to bring about repeal of undesirable legislation, is to be subjected to more exacting judicial scrutiny under the general prohibitions of the Fourteenth Amendment than are most other types of legislation. On restrictions upon the right to vote, see Nixon v. Herndon, 273 U.S. 536, 47 S.Ct. 446, 71 L.Ed. 759; Nixon v. Condon, 286 U.S. 73, 52 S.Ct. 484, 76 L.Ed. 984, 88 A.L.R. 458; on restraints upon the dissemination of information, see Near v. Minnesota, 283 U.S. 697, 713-714, 718-720, 722, 51 S.Ct. 625, 630, 632, 633, 75 L.Ed. 1357; Grosjean v. American Press Co., 297 U.S. 233, 56 S.Ct. 444, 80 L.Ed. 660; Lovell v. Griffin, supra; on interferences with political organizations, see Stromberg v. California, supra, 283 U.S. 359, 369, 51 S.Ct. 532, 535, 75 L.Ed. 1117, 73 A.L.R. 1484; Fiske v. Kansas, 274 U.S. 380, 47 S.Ct. 655, 71 L.Ed. 1108; Whitney v. California, 274 U.S. 357, 373-378, 47 S.Ct. 641, 647, 649, 71 L.Ed. 1095; Herndon v. Lowry, 301 U.S. 242, 57 S.Ct. 732, 81 L.Ed. 1066; and see Holmes, J., in Gitlow v. New York, 268 U.S. 652, 673, 45 S.Ct. 625, 69 L.Ed. 1138; as to prohibition of peaceable assembly, see De Jonge v. Oregon, 299 U.S. 353, 365, 57 S.Ct. 255, 260, 81 L.Ed. 278.

Nor need we enquire whether similar considerations enter into the review of statutes directed at particular religious, Pierce v. Society of Sisters, 268 U.S. 510, 45 S.Ct. 571, 69 L.Ed. 1070, 39 A.L.R. 468, or national, Meyer v. Nebraska, 262 U.S. 390, 43 S.Ct. 625, 67 L.Ed. 1042, 29 A.L.R. 1446; Bartels v. Iowa, 262 U.S. 404, 43 S.Ct. 628, 67 L.Ed. 1047; Farrington v. Tokushige, 273 U.S. 284, 47 S.Ct. 406, 71 L.Ed. 646, or racial minorities. Nixon v. Herndon, supra; Nixon v. Condon, supra; whether prejudice against discrete and insular minorities may be a special condition, which tends seriously to curtail the operation of those political processes ordinarily to be relied upon to protect minorities, and which may call for a correspondingly more searching judicial inquiry. Compare McCulloch v. Maryland, 4 Wheat. 316, 428, 4 L.Ed. 579; South Carolina State Highway Department v. Barnwell Bros., 303 U.S. 177, 58 S.Ct. 510, 82 L.Ed. 734, decided February 14, 1938, note 2, and cases cited.

Comments on Stone's Footnote in *Carolene*.   Can cases dealing with fundamental rights and racial minorities be distinguished from *Lochner*?   If so, on what basis?   What if they also deal with socio-economic policy? Should the "lessons of *Lochner*" limit judicial scrutiny?   Having reviewed these issues in the context of the *Roe* (abortion) decision (Chapter 1), can *Roe* be distinguished from *Lochner*?   Though we will discuss these issues when we review the right of privacy/substantive due process and race-based discrimination/equal protection, the seeds of this double standard were arguably set in Stone's footnote.

Socio-economics and Deference: The Instrumental Nature of Law.   It is one thing for the Court to reject *Lochner* and another thing for the Court to provide decisional law that produces the intended result — deference to the legislature.   It is in this sense that law is instrumental — the Court must create and evolve legal principles that achieve their desired end.   The test applied in *Williams v. Lee Optical* is intended to reach this result. See whether you can define the test applied and whether you have seen the Court apply it thus far in our study.

WILLIAMSON v.   LEE OPTICAL
348 U.S. 483 (1955)

Justice DOUGLAS delivered the opinion of the Court:
The District Court held unconstitutional portions of three sections of the Act. First, it held invalid under the Due Process Clause of the Fourteenth Amendment the portions of § 2 which make it unlawful for any person not a licensed optometrist or ophthalmologist to fit lenses to a face or to duplicate or replace into frames lenses or other optical appliances, except upon written prescriptive authority of an Oklahoma licensed ophthalmologist or optometrist   The court held that "Although on this precise issue of duplication, the legislature in the instant regulation was dealing with a matter of public interest, the particular means chosen are neither reasonably necessary nor reasonably related to the end sought to be achieved."   An ophthalmologist is a duly licensed physician who specializes in the care of the eyes.   An optometrist examines eyes for refractive error, recognizes (but does not treat) diseases of the eye, and fills prescriptions for eyeglasses.   The optician is an artisan qualified to grind lenses, fill prescriptions, and fit frames.

The effect of § 2 is to forbid the optician from fitting or duplicating lenses without a prescription from an ophthalmologist or optometrist.   In practical effect, it means that no optician can fit old glasses into new frames or supply a lens, whether it be a new lens or one to duplicate a lost or broken lens, without a prescription.   The District Court conceded that it was in the competence of the police power of a State to regulate the examination of the eyes.   But it rebelled at the notion that a State could require a prescription from an optometrist or ophthalmologist 'to take old lenses and place them in new frames and then fit the completed spectacles to the face of the eyeglass wearer.'   It held that such a requirement was not 'reasonably and rationally related to the health and welfare of the people.'   The court found that through mechanical devices and ordinary skills the optician could take a broken lens or a fragment thereof, measure its power, and reduce it to prescriptive terms.   The court held that "Although on this precise issue of duplication, the legislature in the instant regulation was dealing with a matter of public interest, the particular means chosen are neither reasonably necessary nor reasonably related to the end sought to be achieved."

The Oklahoma law may exact a needless, wasteful requirement in many cases. But it is for the legislature, not the courts, to balance the advantages and disadvantages of the new requirement. It appears that in many cases the optician can easily supply the new frames or new lenses without reference to the old written prescription. [But] in some cases the directions contained in the prescription are essential. [The] legislature might have concluded that the frequency of occasions when a prescription is necessary was sufficient to justify this regulation of the fitting of eyeglasses. [Or] the legislature may have concluded that eye examinations were so critical, not only for correction of vision but also for detection of latent ailments or diseases, that every change in frames and every duplication of a lens should be accompanied by a prescription from a medical expert. To be sure, the present law does not require a new examination of the eyes every time the frames are changed or the lenses duplicated. [But] the law need not be in every respect logically consistent with its aims to be constitutional. It is enough that there is an evil at hand for correction, and that it might be thought that the particular legislative measure was a rational way to correct it. [The] day is gone when this Court uses the Due Process Clause [to] strike down state laws, regulatory of business and industrial conditions, because they may be unwise, improvident, or out of harmony with a particular school of thought.

Comment on the Rational Purpose Test.   The test applied in *Williams* has been described as the "rational purpose test."   The "purpose" being to defer to the legislative process and provide minimal judicial scrutiny by requiring proof only that "the particular means chosen are *reasonably* related to the end sought to be achieved" (emphasis added). It is worthy of mention that the rational purpose test is the rational purpose test, is the rational purpose test!   The point being that this same test may be applied to varying subject matters.   This "deferential" inquiry, for example, was arguably the same test applied by Marshall in *McCullough v Maryland*: "[W]e think the sound construction of the constitution must allow to the national legislature that discretion to the means by which the powers it confers are to be carried into execution. . . . Let the end be legitimate, let it be within the scope of the Constitution, and all means which are appropriate, which are plainly adapted to that end, which are not prohibited, but consist with the letter and spirit of the Constitution, are constitutional."   As we stated at that time, "As we move through the materials you will find that whenever the Court exercises judicial review and defers to Congress or 'bows to the democratic process,' it will apply a 'rational purpose' review." Well, we are there!   The final lesson of the *Lochner* era is that when socioeconomic policy is at issue, the deference of "rational purpose" review is the test.   Furthermore, the rational purpose review applied here will also be applied in regard to the equal protection clause, or anytime the Court wants to defer to the legislative process.

Punitive Damages and the Return to Substantive Due Process.   The most recent revival of substantive due process to protect economic liberty has involved limitations on punitive damage awards in civil cases. Such awards are often grossly disproportionate to actual damages. Yet no independent textual provision in the Constitution limits such civil awards.   The substantive due process issue in such cases is whether a punitive damages verdict rendered by a jury without sufficiently clear and objective criteria amounts to a naked wealth transfer or is even properly described as "law." After a series of decisions upholding challenged awards but intimating that some limits might apply (see, e.g., Pacific Mutual Life Insurance Co. v. Haslip, 499 U.S. 1 (1991); TXO Production Corp. v. Alliance Resources Corp., 509 U.S. 443 (1993); Honda Motor Co., Ltd. v. Oberg, 512 U.S. 415 (1994)), the Court finally did invalidate an award as excessive in *BMW of North American, Inc. v. Gore*, 517 U.S. 559 (1996), which involved a $2 million punitive damages award for the concealed paint touch-up of a new car, compensatory damages for which were assessed at only $4000. The opinion of the Court, written by Justice Stevens and joined by Justices O'Connor, Kennedy, Souter, and Breyer, reiterated that this limit is partly a matter of procedural due process — i.e., fair notice to the defendant of potential legal liability. But as Justice Breyer clarified in his concurrence, joined by Justices O'Connor and Souter, such limits might also be seen as a matter of substantive due process: "This constitutional concern, itself harkening back to the Magna Carta, arises out of the basic unfairness of depriving citizens of life, liberty, or property, through the application, not of law and legal processes, but of arbitrary coercion. Requiring the application of law, rather than a decisionmaker's caprice, does more than simply provide citizens notice of what actions may subject them to punishment; it also helps to assure the uniform general treatment of similarly situated persons that is the essence of law itself." Justice Scalia, joined by Justice Thomas, dissented: "I do not regard the Fourteenth Amendment's Due Process Clause as a secret repository of substantive guarantees against 'unfairness' — neither the unfairness of an excessive civil compensatory award, nor the unfairness of an 'unreasonable' punitive award." Justice Ginsburg also dissented, joined by Chief Justice Rehnquist.

In *State Farm Mutual Automobile Insurance Company v. Campbell*, 538 U.S. 408 (2003), the Court again returned to the constitutionality of punitive damage awards, holding 6–3 that a punitive damage award of $145 million, where compensatory damages are $1 million, is excessive and violates the Due Process Clause.

In the next case involving a challenge to a punitive damages award after *State Farm*, the first to be considered by the new Roberts Court, the Court relied on the procedural aspects of due process without reaching the substantive aspects. In *Philip Morris USA v. Williams*, 549 U.S. 346   (2007), the Court split 5–4 in vacating an award to the estate of a deceased smoker of $821,000 in compensatory damages and $79.5 million in punitive damages against a tobacco manufacturer on a claim for fraud for having knowingly and falsely led him to believe that smoking was safe. The tobacco company argued that the roughly 100-to-1 ratio of the $79.5 million punitive damages to the compensatory damages was "grossly excessive" under *State Farm*. Justice Breyer wrote the opinion of the Court, joined by Chief Justice Roberts and Justices Kennedy, Souter, and Alito, vacating the award and remanding without reaching the question whether the award was in fact "grossly excessive." He focused on the trial court's failure to instruct the jury clearly not to punish Philip Morris for possible harm to persons other than Williams. The plaintiff's attorney had told the jury to "think about how many other Jesse Williams in the last 40 years in the State of Oregon there have been. [Cigarettes] are going to kill ten [of every hundred]." Philip Morris asked the trial court to tell the jury that "you may consider the extent of harm suffered by others in determining what [the] reasonable relationship is" between any punitive award and "the harm caused to Jesse Williams" by Philip Morris's misconduct, "[but] you are not to punish the defendant for the impact of its alleged misconduct on other persons, who may bring lawsuits of their own in which other juries can resolve their claims." The judge rejected this proposal and instead told the jury that "[p]unitive damages are awarded against a defendant to punish misconduct and to deter misconduct" and "are not intended to compensate the plaintiff or anyone else for damages caused by the defendant's conduct."

Justice Breyer held the trial court's instruction insufficient: "In our view, the Constitution's Due Process Clause forbids a State to use a punitive damages award to punish a defendant for injury that it inflicts upon nonparties [who are] strangers to the litigation. [A] defendant threatened with punishment for injuring a nonparty victim has no opportunity to defend against the charge, by showing, for example in a case such as this, that the other victim was not entitled to damages because he or she knew that smoking was dangerous or did not rely upon the defendant's statements to the contrary. [And] to permit punishment for injuring a nonparty victim would add a near standardless dimension to the punitive damages equation. How many such victims are there? How seriously were they injured? Under what circumstances did injury occur? The trial will not likely answer such questions as to nonparty victims. The jury will be left to speculate.

"[Evidence] of actual harm to nonparties can help to show that the conduct that harmed the plaintiff also posed a substantial risk of harm to the general public, and so was particularly reprehensible. [But] a jury may not go further than this and use a punitive damages verdict to punish a defendant directly on account of harms it is alleged to have visited on nonparties. [We] therefore conclude that the Due Process Clause requires States to provide assurance that juries are not asking the wrong question, i.e., seeking, not simply to determine reprehensibility, but also to punish for harm caused strangers. [State] courts cannot authorize procedures that create an unreasonable and unnecessary risk of any such confusion occurring." The Court remanded to the Oregon courts to fashion such safeguards in any new trial.

Justice Stevens dissented, reiterating his commitment to the limits imposed in *Gore* and *State Farm* but objecting to "the Court's imposition of a novel limit on the State's power to impose punishment in civil litigation. Unlike the Court, I see no reason why an interest in punishing a wrongdoer 'for harming persons who are not before the court,' should not be taken into consideration when assessing the appropriate sanction for reprehensible conduct." He charged the majority with drawing an unworkable distinction: "[The] majority relies on a distinction between taking third-party harm into account in order to assess the reprehensibility of the defendant's conduct — which is permitted — from doing so in order to punish the defendant 'directly' — which is forbidden. This nuance eludes me." Justices Scalia, Thomas, and Ginsburg also dissented.

The Court returned to the issue of excessive punitive damages once again during the 2008 term in *Exxon Shipping Co. v. Baker*, 554 U.S. 471. This litigation extended from the infamous "Exxon Valdez" accident, when an Exxon tanker was grounded on a reef along the Alaska coast and spilled millions of gallons of crude oil into Prince William Sound. Though Exxon had pled guilty to criminal violations, paid fines, settled with state and federal governments as well as some private parties, the plaintiffs in this cause had sued for economic damages. A jury awarded $287 million in compensatory damages, along with $5 billion in punitive damages. Though the Court avoided the constitutional due process issues as framed by their *BMW* and *Philip Morris* decisions, they nonetheless continued the practice of limiting business exposure to punitive damages, holding that the judgment was excessive as based upon maritime common law. Justice Souter, speaking for a divided Court, held that the punitive award should be limited to an amount equal to compensatory damages. To Souter a punitive-to-compensatory ratio of 1:1 was the maximum allowable punitive damages in cases like this one "where the tortious action was worse than negligent but less than malicious," a "case of reckless action, profitless to the tortfeasor." Of interest, he added in a footnote, "In this case, then, the constitutional outer limit may well be 1:1." Thus, this Court's sympathy for "big business" exposure to the jury sanction of punitive damages marches on.

B. THE CONTRACT AND TAKINGS CLAUSES

Though the contract and takings clauses have not been applied to create unarticulated fundamental rights in the sense of our substantive due process discussion, their close association with the Court's decision making in the *Lochner* era mandates treatment. The clauses are united both conceptually and by judicial application. The clauses are underscored by the concept of non-interference by the government to the detriment of the individual. But the individual may also be a business entity, and therein lies the rub. Much as the Court was accused of bias during the *Lochner* era toward laissez-faire capitalism, the same accusations of bias were made when the Court employed both the takings and contract clauses to limit similar government regulations. Though this history alone is enough to interrupt our discussion of substantive due process to cover these materials, a revival in the modern era by a Court that may share a similar conceptual framework mandates such attention.

Both clauses also affect the concept of redistribution of wealth that has become an important socio-economic issue from the New Deal hence. Though there has been considerable pressure to limit the force of the contract and the takings clauses in the face of the "public interest," redistribution, particularly to the disadvantaged, "raised the eyes" of the Burger and Rehnquist Courts and has produced the attempts to reinvigorate both clauses.

1. THE CONTRACT CLAUSE

No State shall [pass] any [Law] impairing the Obligation of Contracts. [U.S. Const. art. I, §10, cl.]

The "Pragmatization" of the Contract Clause: From Absolute Limiter of State Government Action to Subordinate to State Police Power.

"[L]iteralism in the construction of the Contract Clause would make it destructive of the public interest by depriving the State of its prerogative of self-protection." W.B. Worthen v. Thomas, 292 U.S. 426 (1934).

a. NINETEENTH-CENTURY DEVELOPMENTS

FLETCHER v. PECK
6 Cranch (10 U.S.) 87 (1810)

[A year after the grant of land claimed by Native Americans known as Yazoo by the Georgia Legislature to white Georgia residents, that same body, reconstituted, passed legislation rescinding that grant in large part because of the fraud and corruption that accompanied the previous legislature's action. Claiming that he held the property without knowledge of the corruption accompanying the original conveyance to his seller, Peck sued to have the new law nullified.]

Chief Justice MARSHALL gave the opinion of the Court: . . .

The validity of this rescinding act, then, might well be doubted, were Georgia a single sovereign power. But Georgia cannot be viewed as a single, unconnected, sovereign power, on whose legislature no other restrictions are imposed than may be found in its own Constitution. She is a part of a large empire; she is a member of the American Union; and that Union has a Constitution the supremacy of which all acknowledge, and which imposes limits to the legislatures of the several States which none claim a right to pass. The Constitution of the United States declares that no State shall pass . . . law impairing the obligation of contracts. . . .

A contract is a compact between two or more parties, and is either executory or executed. An executory contract is one in which a party binds himself to do, or not to do, a particular thing; such was the law under which the conveyance was made by the Governor. A contract executed is one in which the object of contract is performed, and this, says Blackstone, differs in nothing from a grant. The contract between Georgia and the purchasers was executed by the grant. A contract executed, as well as one which is executory, contains obligations binding on the parties. A grant, in its own nature, amounts to an extinguishment of the right of the grantor, and implies a contract not to reassert that right. A party is therefore always estopped by his own grant.

Since, then, in fact, a grant is a contract executed, the obligation of which still continues, and since the Constitution uses the general term "contract" without distinguishing between those which are executory and those which are executed, it must be construed to comprehend the latter as well as the former. A law annulling conveyances between individuals, and declaring that the grantors should stand seised of their former estates, notwithstanding those grants, would be as repugnant to the Constitution as a law discharging the vendors of property from the obligation of executing their contracts by conveyances. It would be strange if a contract to convey was secured by the Constitution, while an absolute conveyance remained unprotected.

If, under a fair construction the Constitution, grants are comprehended under the term "contracts," is a grant from the State excluded from the operation of the provision? Is the clause to be considered as inhibiting the State from impairing the obligation of contracts between two individuals, but as excluding from that inhibition contracts made with itself?

The words themselves contain no such distinction. They are general, and are applicable to contracts of every description. If contracts made with the State are to be exempted from their operation, the exception must arise from the character of the contracting party, not from the words which are employed. . . .

It is, then, the unanimous opinion of the Court that, in this case, the estate having passed into the hands of a purchaser for a valuable consideration, without notice, the State of Georgia was restrained, either by general principles which are common to our free institutions or by the particular provisions of the Constitution of the United States, from passing a law whereby the estate of the plaintiff in the premises so purchased could be constitutionally and legally impaired and rendered null and void. . . .

Judgment affirmed with costs.

_____

Comments on *Fletcher*. Much in the same way Chief Justice Marshall felt the need to characterize the legislative grant to apply the Contract Clause, he also made the effort in *Trustees of Dartmouth College v. Woodward*, 4 Wheat (17 U.S.) 518 (1819), to characterize the charter from the British Monarchy that created Dartmouth College. By 1816 the legislature of New Hampshire, which succeeded into the role of Great Britain in this charter after the Revolution, decided that it wanted more control over the workings of the college and passed legislation significantly altering the terms of the Charter and reconfiguring the structure of the Board of Trustees. Certainly if the Charter is a contract, a valid legal argument can be made that the Contract Clause applies and that the actions of the New Hampshire legislature "[impairs] the obligation of contracts." However, considering the original purpose of the clause, to maintain private obligations that were entered into during the Revolution and beyond and to prohibit states from passing legislation forgiving such obligations, is the case of what was to become an Ivy League university, as compelling as maintaining debt obligations in a new economy? Here is how Chief Justice Marshall explained the characterization:

> It can require no argument to prove that the circumstances of this case constitute a contract. An application is made to the Crown for a charter to incorporate a religious and literary institution. In the application, it is stated that large contributions have been made for the object, which will be conferred on the corporation as soon as it shall be created. The charter is granted, and on its faith the property is conveyed. Surely, in this transaction, every ingredient of a complete and legitimate contract is to be found. The points for consideration are, 1. Is this contract protected by the Constitution of the United States? 2. Is it impaired by the acts under which the defendant holds?

Though the concept of reliance was not a solid one in the law at the time of this opinion, Chief Justice Marshall essentially is describing an enforceable promise made so by reliance. As contracts were understood at the time of *Dartmouth*, a promise producing reliance was considered a true exchange of consideration as one party suffered a detriment (Dartmouth College for arranging to take in and hold the contributions from third parties that were provided on the faith of the royal charter). But as Professor Jackson notes, such arrangements are best described as benefit-free reliance in that one of the parties, in this case Dartmouth College, is not receiving any benefit even if viewed subjectively. See Jackson, *Traditional Contract Law: Old and New Doctrine and Old and New Excuses,* _33_New Eng. L. Rev._365_(1999). If the principle of the Contract Clause was to prevent debtors from being relieved of their financial obligations, the Clause is inappropriate to *Dartmouth*. However, if the clause was designed to protect legitimate expectations whether based upon the exchange of consideration or the inducement to substantial detrimental reliance, a circumstance that might describe the contributors to Dartmouth, and Dartmouth itself in its efforts to handle and manage funds and property contributed, the Clause may achieve its purpose of protecting expectations, even if those expectations might not be quite as economic or dire as in the debtor circumstance. On the other hand, because third party gifts, like those the Chief Justice refers to, are just that, gifts, and managing gifts can hardly be seen as a substantial detriment, what exigency does applying the clause serve in this instance? Or does the clause represent not merely a response to or strategy against economic crisis, but a principle woven into our notions of ownership and property rights? Whatever the reason, the Supreme Court determined that the New Hampshire law was unconstitutional under the Contract Clause. Is this a case of judicial overreaching? The Chief Justice continued:

It is more than possible, that the preservation of rights of this description was not particularly in the view of the framers of the constitution, when the clause under consideration was introduced into that instrument. It is probable, that interferences of more frequent recurrence, to which the temptation was stronger, and of which the mischief was more extensive, constituted the great motive for imposing this restriction on the State legislatures. But although a particular and a rare case may not, in itself, be of sufficient magnitude to induce a rule, yet it must be governed by the rule, when established, unless some plain and strong reason for excluding it can be given. It is not enough to say, that this particular case was not in the mind of the Convention, when the article was framed, nor of the American people, when it was adopted. It is necessary to go farther, and to say that, had this particular case been suggested, the language would have been so varied, as to exclude it, or it would have been made a special exception.

Because economic arrangements invariably involve contracts, has the Supreme Court as early as these previous two cases effectively limited if not eliminated state economic regulation by such a wide description of contract?

Perhaps not. The Court allowed state regulation of contracts entered into after the challenged legislation in Ogden v. Saunders, 12 Wheat. (25 U.S.) 213 (1827), distinguishing between legislation impairing contracts in existence (unconstitutional — Sturges v. Crowninshield, 4 Wheat. (17 U.S.) 122 (1819) and legislation regulating contracts that might later come into existence, the situation in Ogden. The message of the Court at this point in its Contract Clause jurisprudence is that impairment means interfering with contractual expectations. If a law has been passed and parties voluntarily enter into a contract contrary to a provision of previous legislation, it cannot be supposed that the parties had expectations since their contract, in so many words, flouted existing law. Hence, the power of the government to engage in economic regulation was not dead.

Even legislation affecting the remedy of earlier contracts was not automatically subject to the clause's prohibition according to the Court in Bronson v. Kinzie, 1 How. (42 U.S.) 311 (1843). The case involved legislative changes in the means of executing on land and personal property by a court of law or equity. While acknowledging that legislation that affected the manner in which a party can be "made whole" after a breach by a buyer to purchase property was not an impairment of rights because of the distinction between rights and remedies, a law that legislated upon a remedy in such a way as to impair rights under contract would be prohibited under the clause. In this case the legislation included requirements that made it more difficult for a mortgagor to actually foreclose and sell mortgaged property upon default. This, the Court reasoned, went to the rights under the contract and could not stand.

Though it could have been read to keep states out of private economic transactions, this interpretation eventually gave way to either principled or practical interpretations to prevent the "hamstringing" of government in its regulatory capacity. By the time of the previous cases, the Court had gone only so far as to limit the clause's effects to prior contracts and remedial measures not affecting rights. Much of this jurisprudence certainly was cognizant of the proposition that state government needed economic regulatory capacity in order to function, and in ruling as it did, the Court perhaps saved the clause from obsolescence.

However, these decisions did not address the principle that in our Republic government has certain responsibilities that require regulation. The decisions manipulated the clause in pragmatic ways, but a head to head confrontation with the police power of the state started slowly with cases involving charters (again) between the state and private entities.   The Court decided *Charles River Bridge v. Warren Bridge*, 11 Pet. (29 U.S.) 514 (1830), essentially on contract principles, reasoning that there was no obligation that could be impaired when the State of Massachusetts chartered a competing bridge, the Warren, to provide traffic access over the Charles River with an earlier chartered bridge, the Charles River Bridge.   Massachusetts had not obligated itself in the earlier charter not to charter competing businesses, and "any ambiguity in the terms of the contract must operate against the adventurers and in favor of the public, and the plaintiffs can claim nothing that is not clearly given them by the act."   A more definitive (or perhaps defiant) statement by the Court came in *West River Bridge v. Dix*, 6 How. (47 U.S.) 507 (1848), where the proprietors of West River claimed that its charter with the state immunized it from eminent domain actions.   The Court addressed that argument, noting that all private rights are held subject to the right of eminent domain:

> The Constitution of the United States, although adopted by the sovereign states of this Union, and proclaimed in its own language to be the supreme law for their government, can by no rational interpretation be brought to conflict with this attribute in the states

By definition of the term "eminent domain," it remained fundamental to state police power rights, and hence the Constitution is understood within the context of this state right.

The direction of these two cases, by putting the public and state's interest ahead of the private rights under contracts signaled another "pragmatization" of the Contracts Clause, a theme that would be carried through to the twentieth century, a point that will be apparent in the next section.

b.   TWENTIETH-CENTURY DEVELOPMENTS

The context of the developments in Contracts Clause jurisprudence in the twentieth century included a conservative court philosophically oriented toward laissez-faire policies of state and federal government, an economic depression, and a belief among many in government that regulation of economic matters was a necessary antidote to the troubles in the economy.   As already discussed, the jurisprudence of the Court in the Due Process and Commerce Clause areas went through a   period from the beginning of the century to the mid-1930s where it repeatedly turned back efforts by state and local governments to regulate economic matters.   In matters regarding the states' police powers, the language of the Contracts Clause itself could not have stated more clearly the limits of state government, though the groundwork for a pragmatic approach to the clause's seeming absolutism had long since been developed.   Whether the Court's economic conservatism marked a return to the clause's absolutist roots or whether the Court would continue to regard the clause as subordinate to state police power, as it had in the nineteenth century charter cases, was the question on the minds of the litigants in the decisions below.   This question would be answered most definitively in the 1934 case excerpted below.   Though it came at a time when the Court did not mince words or decisions critical of government economic activism as abhorrent to the Constitution, the Court did continue its jurisprudence of allowing state governments room to maneuver in the management of local economic matters.

HOME BUILDING & LOAN ASS'N v. BLAISDELL
290 U.S. 398 (1934)

Chief Justice HUGHES delivered the opinion of the Court.

Appellant contests the validity of Chapter 339 of the Laws of Minnesota of 1933, p. 514, approved April 18, 1933, called the Minnesota Mortgage Moratorium Law, as being repugnant to the contract clause (Art. I, § 10) and the due process and equal protection clauses of the Fourteenth Amendment, of the Federal Constitution. The statute was sustained by the Supreme Court of Minnesota, 189 Minn. 422, 448, 249 N.W. 334, 893, and the case comes here on appeal.

The Act provides that, during the emergency declared to exist, relief may be had through authorized judicial proceedings with respect to foreclosures of mortgages, and execution sales, of real estate; that sales may be postponed and periods of redemption may be extended. The Act does not apply to mortgages subsequently made, nor to those made previously which shall be extended for a period ending more than a year after the passage of the Act (Part One, § 8). There are separate provisions in Part Two relating to homesteads, but these are to apply "only to cases not entitled to relief under some valid provision of Part One." The Act is to remain in effect "only during the continuance of the emergency and in no event beyond May 1, 1935." No extension of the period for redemption and no postponement of sale is to be allowed which would have the effect of extending the period of redemption beyond that date. Part Two, § 8.

The Act declares that the various provisions for relief are severable; that each is to stand on its own footing with respect to validity. Part One, § 9. We are here concerned with the provisions of Part One, § 4, authorizing the District Court of the county to extend the period of redemption from foreclosure sales "for such additional time as the court may deem just and equitable," subject to the above described limitation. The extension is to be made upon application to the court, on notice, for an order determining the reasonable value of the income on the property involved in the sale, or, if it has no income, then the reasonable rental value of the property, and directing the mortgagor to pay all or a reasonable part of such income or rental value, in or toward the payment of taxes, insurance, interest, mortgage . . . indebtedness at such times and in such manner as shall be determined by the court. The section also provides that the time for redemption from foreclosure sales theretofore made, which otherwise would expire less than thirty days after the approval of the Act shall be extended to a date thirty days after its approval, and application may be made to the court within that time for a further extension as provided in the section. By another provision of the Act, no action, prior to May 1, 1935, may be maintained for a deficiency judgment until the period of redemption as allowed by existing law or as extended under the provisions of the Act has expired. Prior to the expiration of the extended period of redemption, the court may revise or alter the terms of the extension as changed circumstances may require. Part One, § 5. . . .

In determining whether the provision for this temporary and conditional relief exceeds the power of the State by reason of the clause in the Federal Constitution prohibiting impairment of the obligations of contracts, we must consider the relation of emergency to constitutional power, the historical setting of the contract clause, the development of the jurisprudence of this Court in the construction of that clause, and the principles of construction which we may consider to be established.

Emergency does not create power. Emergency does not increase granted power or remove or diminish the restrictions imposed upon power granted or reserved. The

Constitution was adopted in a period of grave emergency. Its grants of power to the Federal Government and its limitations of the power of the States were determined in the light of emergency, and they are not altered by emergency. What power was thus granted and what limitations were thus imposed are questions which have always been, and always will be, the subject of close examination under our constitutional system.

While emergency does not create power, emergency may furnish the occasion for the exercise of power.

Although an emergency may not call into life a power which has never lived, nevertheless emergency may afford a reason for the exertion of a living power already enjoyed. . . .

In the construction of the contract clause, the debates in the Constitutional Convention are of little aid. But the reasons which led to the adoption of that clause, and of the other prohibitions of Section 10 of Article I, are not left in doubt, and have frequently been described with eloquent emphasis. The widespread distress following the revolutionary period, and the plight of debtors, had called forth in the States an ignoble array of legislative schemes for the defeat of creditors and the invasion of contractual obligations. Legislative interferences had been so numerous and extreme that the confidence essential to prosperous trade had been undermined and the utter destruction of credit was threatened. "The sober people of America" were convinced that some "thorough reform" was needed which would "inspire a general prudence and industry, and give a regular course to the business of society." The Federalist, No. 44. It was necessary to interpose the restraining power of a central authority in order to secure the foundations even of "private faith." . . .

But full recognition of the occasion and general purpose of the clause does not suffice to fix its precise scope. Nor does an examination of the details of prior legislation in the States yield criteria which can be considered controlling. To ascertain the scope of the constitutional prohibition, we examine the course of judicial decisions in its application. These put it beyond question that the prohibition is not an absolute one, and is not to be read with literal exactness, like a mathematical formula. Justice Johnson, in *Ogden v. Saunders, supra,* p. 286, adverted to such a misdirected effort in these words:

> It appears to me that a great part of the difficulties of the cause arise from not giving sufficient weight to the general intent of this clause in the constitution and subjecting it to a severe literal construction which would be better adapted to special pleadings.

And after giving his view as to the purport of the clause —

> that the States shall pass no law attaching to the acts of individuals other effects or consequences than those attached to them by the laws existing at their date, and all contracts thus construed shall be enforced according to their just and reasonable purport

— Justice Johnson added:

> But to assign to contracts, universally, a literal purport, and to exact for them a rigid literal fulfillment could not have been the intent of the constitution. It is repelled by a hundred examples. Societies exercise a positive control as well over the inception, construction and fulfillment of contracts as over the form and measure of the remedy to enforce them.

The inescapable problems of construction have been: what is a contract? What are the obligations of contracts? What constitutes impairment of these obligations? What residuum of power is there still in the States in relation to the operation of contracts, to protect the vital interests of the community? Questions of this character,

> of no small nicety and intricacy, have vexed the legislative halls, as well as the judicial tribunals, with an uncounted variety and frequency of litigation and speculation. Story on the Constitution, § 1375. . . .

It is competent for the States to change the form of the remedy, or to modify it otherwise, as they may see fit, provided no substantial right secured by the contract is thereby impaired. No attempt has been made to fix definitely the line between alterations of the remedy, which are to be deemed legitimate, and those which, under the form of modifying the remedy, impair substantial rights. Every case must be determined upon its own circumstances.

And Chief Justice Waite, quoting this language in *Antoni v. Greenhow*, 107 U.S. 769, 775, added: "In all such cases, the question becomes, therefore, one of reasonableness, and of that the legislature is primarily the judge."

The obligations of a contract are impaired by a law which renders them invalid, or releases or extinguishes them (*Sturges v. Crowninshield, supra,* pp. 197, 198) and impairment, as above noted, has been predicated of laws which, without destroying contracts, derogate from substantial contractual rights. In *Sturges v. Crowninshield, supra,* a state insolvent law which discharged the debtor from liability was held to be invalid as applied to contracts in existence when the law was passed. *See Ogden v. Saunders, supra.* In *Green v. Biddle,* 8 Wheat. 1, the legislative acts, which were successfully assailed, exempted the occupant of land from the payment of rents and profits to the rightful owner and were parts of a system the object of which was to compel the rightful owner to relinquish his lands or pay for all lasting improvements made upon them, without his consent or default. . . .

Not only is the constitutional provision qualified by the measure of control which the State retains over remedial processes, but the State also continues to possess authority to safeguard the vital interests of its people. It does not matter that legislation appropriate to that end "has the result of modifying or abrogating contracts already in effect." *Stephenson v. Binford,* 287 U.S. 251, 276. Not only are existing laws read into contracts in order to fix obligations as between the parties, but the reservation of essential attributes of sovereign power is also read into contracts as a postulate of the legal order. The policy of protecting contracts against impairment presupposes the maintenance of a government by virtue of which contractual relations are worthwhile — a government which retains adequate authority to secure the peace and good order of society. This principle of harmonizing the constitutional prohibition with the necessary residuum of state power has had progressive recognition in the decisions of this Court. . . .

The argument is pressed that, in the cases we have cited, the obligation of contracts was affected only incidentally. This argument proceeds upon a misconception. The question is not whether the legislative action affects contracts incidentally, or directly, or indirectly, but whether the legislation is addressed to a legitimate end and the measures taken are reasonable and appropriate to that end. Another argument, which comes more closely to the point, is that the state power may be addressed directly to the prevention of the enforcement of contracts only when these are of a sort which the legislature in its discretion may denounce as being in themselves hostile to public morals, or public health, safety or welfare, or where the prohibition is merely of injurious practices; that interference with the enforcement of other and valid contracts according to appropriate legal procedure, although the interference is temporary and for a public purpose, is not permissible. This is but to contend that, in the latter case, the end is not legitimate in the view that it cannot be reconciled with a fair interpretation of the constitutional provision.

Undoubtedly, whatever is reserved of state power must be consistent with the fair intent of the constitutional limitation of that power. The reserved power cannot be construed so as to destroy the limitation, nor is the limitation to be construed to destroy the reserved power in its essential aspects. They must be construed in harmony with each other. This principle precludes a construction which would permit the State to adopt as its policy the repudiation of debts or the destruction of contracts or the denial of means to enforce them. But it does not follow that conditions may not arise in which a temporary restraint of enforcement may be consistent with the spirit and purpose of the constitutional provision, and thus be found to be within the range of the reserved power of the State to protect the vital interests of the community. It cannot be maintained that the constitutional prohibition should be so construed as to prevent limited and temporary interpositions with respect to the enforcement of contracts if made necessary by a great public calamity such as fire, flood, or earthquake. *See American Land Co. v. Zeiss*, 219 U.S. 47. The reservation of state power appropriate to such extraordinary conditions may be deemed to be as much a part of all contracts as is the reservation of state power to protect the public interest in the other situations to which we have referred. And if state power exists to give temporary relief from the enforcement of contracts in the presence of disasters due to physical causes such as fire, flood or earthquake, that power cannot be said to be nonexistent when the urgent public need demanding such relief is produced by other and economic causes.

Whatever doubt there may have been that the protective power of the State, its police power, may be exercised — without violating the true intent of the provision of the Federal Constitution — in directly preventing the immediate and literal enforcement of contractual obligations, by a temporary and conditional restraint, where vital public interests would otherwise suffer, was removed by our decisions relating to the enforcement of provisions of leases during a period of scarcity of housing. . . .

In these cases of leases, it will be observed that the relief afforded was temporary and conditional, that it was sustained because of the emergency due to scarcity of housing, and that provision was made for reasonable compensation to the landlord during the period he was prevented from regaining possession. . . .

It is manifest from this review of our decisions that there has been a growing appreciation of public needs and of the necessity of finding ground for a rational compromise between individual rights and public welfare. The settlement and consequent contraction of the public domain, the pressure of a constantly increasing density of population, the interrelation of the activities of our people and the complexity of our economic interests, have inevitably led to an increased use of the organization of society in order to protect the very bases of individual opportunity. Where, in earlier days, it was thought that only the concerns of individuals or of classes were involved, and that those of the State itself were touched only remotely, it has later been found that the fundamental interests of the State are directly affected, and that the question is no longer merely that of one party to a contract as against another, but of the use of reasonable means to safeguard the economic structure upon which the good of all depends.

It is no answer to say that this public need was not apprehended a century ago, or to insist that what the provision of the Constitution meant to the vision of that day it must mean to the vision of our time. If, by the statement that what the Constitution meant at the time of its adoption it means today, it is intended to say that the great clauses of the Constitution must be confined to the interpretation which the framers, with the conditions and outlook of their time, would have placed upon them, the statement carries its own refutation. It was to guard against such a narrow conception that Chief Justice Marshall uttered the memorable warning — "We must never forget that it is a *constitution* we are expounding" (*McCulloch v. Maryland,* 4 Wheat. 316, 407) — "a constitution intended to endure for ages to come, and, consequently, to be adapted to the various crises of human affairs." *Id.,* p. 415. When we are dealing with the words of the Constitution, said this Court in *Missouri v. Holland,* 252 U.S. 416, 433, we must realize that they have called into life a being the development of which could not have been foreseen completely by the most gifted of its begetters. . . . The case before us must be considered in the light of our whole experience, and not merely in that of what was said a hundred years ago.

Nor is it helpful to attempt to draw a fine distinction between the intended meaning of the words of the Constitution and their intended application. When we consider the contract clause and the decisions which have expounded it in harmony with the essential reserved power of the States to protect the security of their peoples, we find no warrant for the conclusion that the clause has been warped by these decisions from its proper significance, or that the founders of our Government would have interpreted the clause differently had they had occasion to assume that responsibility in the conditions of the later day. The vast body of law which has been developed was unknown to the fathers, but it is believed to have preserved the essential content and the spirit of the Constitution. With a growing recognition of public needs and the relation of individual right to public security, the court has sought to prevent the perversion of the clause through its use as an instrument to throttle the capacity of the States to protect their fundamental interests. This development is a growth from the seeds which the fathers planted. It is a development forecast by the prophetic words of Justice Johnson in *Ogden v. Saunders,* already quoted. And the germs of the later decisions are found in the early cases of the *Charles River Bridge* and the *West River Bridge, supra,* which upheld the public right against strong insistence upon the contract clause. The principle of this development is, as we have seen, that the reservation of the reasonable exercise of the protective power of the State is read into all contracts, and there is no greater reason for refusing to apply this principle to Minnesota mortgages than to New York leases.

Applying the criteria established by our decisions we conclude:

1. An emergency existed in Minnesota which furnished a proper occasion for the exercise of the reserved power of the State to protect the vital interests of the community. The declarations of the existence of this emergency by the legislature and by the Supreme Court of Minnesota cannot be regarded as a subterfuge, or as lacking in adequate basis. *Block v. Hirsh, supra.* The finding of the legislature and state court has support in the facts of which we take judicial notice. *Atchison, T. & S.F. Ry. Co. v. United States,* 284 U.S. 248, 260. It is futile to attempt to make a comparative estimate of the seriousness of the emergency shown in the leasing cases from New York and of the emergency disclosed here. The particular facts differ, but that there were in Minnesota conditions urgently demanding relief, if power existed to give it, is beyond cavil. As the Supreme Court of Minnesota said, the economic emergency which threatened "the loss of homes and lands which furnish those in possession the necessary shelter and means of subsistence" was a "potent cause" for the enactment of the statute.

2. The legislation was addressed to a legitimate end, that is, the legislation was not for the mere advantage of particular individuals, but for the protection of a basic interest of society.

3. In view of the nature of the contracts in question — mortgages of unquestionable validity — the relief afforded and justified by the emergency, in order not to contravene the constitutional provision, could only be of a character appropriate to that emergency, and could be granted only upon reasonable conditions.

4. The conditions upon which the period of redemption is extended do not appear to be unreasonable. The initial extension of the time of redemption for thirty days from the approval of the Act was obviously to give a reasonable opportunity for the authorized application to the court. As already noted, the integrity of the mortgage indebtedness is not impaired; interest continues to run; the validity of the sale and the right of a mortgagee-purchaser to title or to obtain a deficiency judgment if the mortgagor fails to redeem within the extended period are maintained, and the conditions of redemption, if redemption there be, stand as they were under the prior law. The mortgagor, during the extended period, is not ousted from possession, but he must pay the rental value of the premises as ascertained in judicial proceedings, and this amount is applied to the carrying of the property and to interest upon the indebtedness. The mortgagee-purchaser, during the time that he cannot obtain possession, thus is not left without compensation for the withholding of possession. Also important is the fact that mortgagees, as is shown by official reports of which we may take notice, are predominantly corporations, such as insurance companies, banks, and investment and mortgage companies. These, and such individual mortgagees as are small investors, are not seeking homes or the opportunity to engage in farming. Their chief concern is the reasonable protection of their investment security. It does not matter that there are, or may be, individual cases of another aspect. The legislature was entitled to deal with the general or typical situation. The relief afforded by the statute has regard to the interest of mortgagees as well as to the interest of mortgagors. The legislation seeks to prevent the impending ruin of both by a considerate measure of relief.

In the absence of legislation, courts of equity have exercised jurisdiction in suits for the foreclosure of mortgages to fix the time and terms of sale and to refuse to confirm sales upon equitable grounds where they were found to be unfair or inadequacy of price was so gross as to shock the conscience. The "equity of redemption" is the creature of equity. While courts of equity could not alter the legal effect of the forfeiture of the estate at common law on breach of condition, they succeeded, operating on the conscience of the mortgagee, in maintaining that it was unreasonable that he should retain for his own benefit what was intended as a mere security; that the breach of condition was in the nature of a penalty, which ought to be relieved against, and that the mortgagor had an equity to redeem on payment of principal, interest and costs,   notwithstanding the forfeiture at law. This principle of equity was victorious against the strong opposition of the common law judges, who thought that, by "the Growth of Equity on Equity, the Heart of the Common Law is eaten out." The equitable principle became firmly established, and its application could not be frustrated even by the engagement of the debtor entered into at the time of the mortgage, the courts applying the equitable maxim "once a mortgage, always a mortgage, and nothing but a mortgage." Although the courts would have no authority to alter a statutory period of redemption, the legislation in question permits the courts to extend that period, within limits and upon equitable terms, thus providing a procedure and relief which are cognate to the historic exercise of the equitable jurisdiction. If it be determined, as it must be, that the contract clause is not an absolute and utterly unqualified restriction of the State's protective power, this legislation is clearly so reasonable as to be within the legislative competency.

5. The legislation is temporary in operation. It is limited to the exigency which called it forth. While the postponement of the period of redemption from the foreclosure sale is to May 1, 1935, that period may be reduced by the order of the court under the statute, in case of a change in circumstances, and the operation of the statute itself could not validly outlast the emergency or be so extended as virtually to destroy the contracts.

We are of the opinion that the Minnesota statute, as here applied, does not violate the contract clause of the Federal Constitution. Whether the legislation is wise or unwise as a matter of policy is a question with which we are not concerned. . . .

The judgment of the Supreme Court of Minnesota is affirmed.

Mr. Justice SUTHERLAND, dissenting. . . .

If the contract impairment clause, when framed and adopted, meant that the terms of a contract for the payment of money could not be altered *in invitum* by a state statute enacted for the relief of hardly pressed debtors to the end and with the effect of postponing payment or enforcement during and because of an economic or financial emergency, it is but to state the obvious to say that it means the same now. . . .

Chief Justice Taney, in *Dred Scott v. Sandford,* 19 How. 393, 426, said that, while the Constitution remains unaltered, it must be construed now as it was understood at the time of its adoption; that it is not only the same in words, but the same in meaning, and as long as it continues to exist in its present form, it speaks not only in the same words, but with the same meaning and intent with which it spoke when it came from the hands of its framers, and was voted on and adopted by the people of the United States. Any other rule of construction would abrogate the judicial character of this court, and make it the mere reflex of the popular opinion or passion of the day. . . .

The words of Judge Campbell, speaking for the Supreme Court of Michigan in *Twitchell v. Blodgett,* 13 Mich. 127, 139-140, are peculiarly apposite. "But it may easily happen," he said, "that specific provisions may, in unforeseen emergencies, turn out to have been inexpedient. This does not make these provisions any less binding. Constitutions cannot be changed by events alone. They remain binding as the acts of the people in their sovereign capacity, as the framers of Government, until they are amended or abrogated by the action prescribed by the authority which created them. It is not competent for any department of the Government to change a constitution, or declare it changed, simply because it appears ill-adapted to a new state of things." . . .

The provisions of the Federal Constitution, undoubtedly, are pliable in the sense that, in appropriate cases, they have the capacity of bringing within their grasp every new condition which falls within their meaning. But their *meaning* is changeless; it is only their *application* which is extensible. . . . Constitutional grants of power and restrictions upon the exercise of power are not flexible as the doctrines of the common law are flexible. These doctrines, upon the principles of the common law itself, modify or abrogate themselves whenever they are or whenever they become plainly unsuited to different or changed conditions.

An application of these principles to the question under review removes any doubt, if otherwise there would be any, that the contract impairment clause denies to the several states the power to mitigate hard consequences resulting to debtors from financial or economic exigencies by an impairment of the obligation of contracts of indebtedness. A candid consideration of the history and circumstances which led up to and accompanied the framing and adoption of this clause will demonstrate conclusively that it was framed and adopted with the specific and studied purpose of preventing legislation designed to relieve debtors especially in time of financial distress. . . .

If it be possible by resort to the testimony of history to put any question of constitutional intent beyond the domain of uncertainty, the foregoing leaves no reasonable ground upon which to base a denial that the clause of the Constitution now under consideration was meant to foreclose state action impairing the obligation of contracts *primarily and especially* in respect of such action aimed at giving relief to debtors *in time of emergency*. . . .

As this court has well said, whatever tends to postpone or retard the enforcement of a contract, to that extent weakens the obligation. According to one Latin proverb, "He who gives quickly gives twice," and, according to another, "He who pays too late pays less."

> Any authorization of the postponement of payment, or of means by which such postponement may be effected, is in conflict with the constitutional inhibition.

Louisiana v. New Orleans, 102 U.S. 203, 207. I am not able to see any real distinction between a statute which in substantive terms alters the obligation of a debtor-creditor contract so as to extend the time of its performance for a period of two years, and a statute which, though in terms acting upon the remedy, is aimed at the obligation (as distinguished, for example, from the judicial procedure incident to the enforcement thereof), and which does, in fact, withhold from the creditor, for the same period of time, the stipulated fruits of his contract. . . .

Being unable to reach any other conclusion than that the Minnesota statute infringes the constitutional restriction under review, I have no choice but to say so.

I am authorized to say that MR. JUSTICE VAN DEVANTER, MR. JUSTICE McREYNOLDS, and MR. JUSTICE BUTLER concur in this opinion.

Notes and Questions

Justice Sutherland makes an impassioned plea against the interpretation of the Contracts Clause in the dissent above. In his view, the jurisprudence of the Clause militates against the majority opinion which found state legislation requiring the temporary cessation of mortgage foreclosures to be permissible under the Constitution to address an economic emergency. According to Sutherland, any delay in foreclosure amounts to a different obligation and a different contract — one that the government has written for the contract partners. To Sutherland, past cases do not support this view of either the Clause itself, or the theory of interpretation employed by Chief Justice Hughes. Sutherland's reasoning is curious — in one of the rare citations to the infamous Dred Scott decision, he paraphrases Chief Justice Taney when he says:

> while the Constitution remains unaltered, it must be construed now as it was understood at the time of its adoption; that it is not only the same in words, but the same in meaning.

Sutherland might be correct in describing Taney's view regarding the status of Blacks in the US, or for that matter, with regard to the circumstances and original meaning surrounding the Contracts Clause. But he does not cite either *Charles River Bridge* or

West Bridge in making his argument. The Court in both cases showed a preference for public interests, with West Bridge imposing the ultimate impairment that the state can impose on any obligation — the power of eminent domain. To be sure, both cases involved the state as a contract party and the interests of the public might refer simply to contract interests. And the power of eminent domain is a state police power explicitly mentioned in the Constitution, and a comparison between that power and a legislative policy preference as in the present case, might not be justified.

With this in mind, which opinion stays more closely to the Constitution? Which is preferable from a policy standpoint? Should constitutional interpretation ever be based upon what is the best policy? Re-examine Chief Justice Hughes' five point check list of qualifications needed to approve of state legislation affecting a contract. Are the reasons substantially different from the nineteenth-century approach?

To Professor Richard Epstein, a literal reading of the Contracts Clause with exceptions (which means literal to a point) is the proper policy in order to keep government from interfering in private economic liberty. In his article *Toward a Revitalization of the Contracts Clause,* 51 University of Chicago Law Review. 703 (1984), Professor Epstein argues that an underlying purpose of the clause was to keep a lid on the attendant corruption possible when political pressure can be used to foster legislation that impairs obligations to the advantage of one political pressure group or another. To deter such corruption, the clause must be interpreted as applying prospectively to contracts not yet in existence as well as antecedent in effect — the effect of this interpretation would be that even future obligations would be beyond legislative control, an obvious rejection of Ogden. That along with, in his view, the overall policy of the Constitution being to limit government means that the only appropriate interpretation of the clause is to use it to limit state intervention. In a critique of Blaisdell, Epstein suggests that an appropriate exception to the austere language of the clause (which by his admission would prevent legislation such as the Uniform Commercial Code due to its affect prospectively on future obligations) would be to use state police power to protect third parties — and little else. Chief Justice Hughes' interpreted the clause to mean that an emergency gives the Congress the authority to authorize debt relief — the very thing the prevention of which, history suggests, was the motivation for the clause in the first place. Hughes reasoning strikes Epstein as "some of the most misguided thinking on constitutional interpretation imaginable."

————

Comments on *Blaisdell*. Since *Blaisdell*, the Court has continued the tradition of allowing state regulation with contract impairment under circumstances of either emergency or, as will be seen, important and legitimate public purpose. However, the Court did appear to reintroduce a more stringent standard when contracts involved the state as parties.

United States Trust Co. v. New Jersey was a case in which the legislature of New Jersey pledged in 1962 to protect New York/New Jersey bondholders from additional risks on their bonds by legislating a prohibition of additional encumbrances for mass transit projects between the two states. In the early 70s, in large part because of the energy crisis of the time, the two states sought to repeal their bond protections (New York had passed similar legislation) so that new mass transit projects could be financed, a financing that would have an effect on the security and value of the bonds purchased under the 1962 legislative assurances. Noting that the 1962 legislation was in effect contractual, Justice Blackmun writing for the Court noted that state sovereign police powers said to be reserved powers of states cannot be bargained away, the Contract Clause notwithstanding. In cases not involving reserved powers, such as financial obligations, states may still be allowed to exercise their authority, though they should be allowed less discretion to the state to determine necessity, importance, and reasonableness under the *Blaisdell* standard because it is a party to the contract.

This limited discretion led the Court to evaluate the necessity, importance, and reasonableness of the impairment closely. It ruled that the plan to encumber the Port Authority with additional mass transit projects for the purpose of encouraging less automobile use was not a new development, and hence not reasonable, since the need certainly existed at the time the covenant was entered into in 1962. Furthermore, a total repeal of the 1962 law was not necessary for the purpose because less financially risky measures were available to the Port Authority than repealing the moratorium on mass transit projects.

United States Trust notwithstanding, Epstein's position is for tighter application of the clause to contracts involving purely private interests, a position that would applaud the *United States Trust* decision. But Professor Epstein's position is for more of the same in cases where the state is not a party, a position that puts him to the right of Contracts Clause jurisprudence to date. On the other side of this jurisprudence is the position that the Court has, according to Justice Brennan in a dissent, joined by Justices Marshall and White, "construed the Contract Clause largely to be powerless in binding a State to contracts limiting the authority of successor legislatures to enact laws in furtherance of the health safety and similar collective interests." Brennan did not believe that states needed to identify special reserved powers in order to be accorded discretion in making policy decisions for the general welfare of the state.

Similarly misguided, according to Epstein, are more recent Contract Clause cases. When reviewing the summaries below, consider whether Epstein's narrow sense of exception — the protection of third parties — and his willingness to expand the clause's prohibition to cover not only impairment of existing obligations, but future contracts and the expansion of rights under contract as an anti-corruption interpretation, would be preferable to the holdings offered by the Court in these decisions.

ALLIED STRUCTURAL STEEL v. SPANNAUS
438 U.S. 234 (1978)

Justice STEWART delivered the opinion of the Court:

Although it was perhaps the strongest single constitutional check on state legislation during our early years as a Nation, the Contract Clause receded into comparative desuetude with the adoption of the Fourteenth Amendment, and particularly with the development of the large body of jurisprudence under the Due Process Clause of that Amendment in modern constitutional history. Nonetheless, the Contract Clause remains part of the Constitution. It is not a dead letter. And its basic contours are brought into focus by several of this Court's 20th-century decisions.

First of all, it is to be accepted as a commonplace that the Contract Clause does not operate to obliterate the police power of the States.

"It is the settled law of this court that the interdiction of statutes impairing the obligation of contracts does not prevent the State from exercising such powers as are vested in it for the promotion of the common weal, or are necessary for the general good of the public, though contracts previously entered into between individuals may thereby be affected. This power, which in its various ramifications is known as the police power, is an exercise of the sovereign right of the Government to protect the lives, health, morals, comfort and general welfare of the people, and is paramount to any rights under contracts between individuals." *Manigault v. Springs,* 199 U. S. 473, 199 U. S. 480.

[II]

[B]

If the Contract Clause is to retain any meaning at all, however, it must be understood to impose some limits upon the power of a State to abridge existing contractual relationships, even in the exercise of its otherwise legitimate police power. The existence and nature of those limits were clearly indicated in a series of cases in this Court arising from the efforts of the States to deal with the unprecedented emergencies brought on by the severe economic depression of the early 1930's.

In *Home Building & Loan Assn. v. Blaisdell,* 290 U.S. 398, the Court upheld against a Contract Clause attack a mortgage moratorium law that Minnesota had enacted to provide relief for homeowners threatened with foreclosure. Although the legislation conflicted directly with lenders' contractual foreclosure rights, the Court there acknowledged that, despite the Contract Clause, the States retain residual authority to enact laws "to safeguard the vital interests of [their] people." *Id.* at 434. In upholding the state mortgage moratorium law, the Court found five factors significant. First, the state legislature had declared in the Act itself that an emergency need for the protection of homeowners existed. *Id.* at 444. Second, the state law was enacted to protect a basic societal interest, not a favored group. *Id.* at 445. Third, the relief was appropriately tailored to the emergency that it was designed to meet. *Ibid.* Fourth, the imposed conditions were reasonable. *Id.* at 445-447. And, finally, the legislation was limited to the duration of the emergency. *Id.* at 447.

The *Blaisdell* opinion thus clearly implied that, if the Minnesota moratorium legislation had not possessed the characteristics attributed to it by the Court, it would have been invalid under the Contract Clause of the Constitution.

[III]

In applying these principles to the present case, the first inquiry must be whether the state law has, in fact, operated as a substantial impairment of a contractual relationship. The severity of the impairment measures the height of the hurdle the state legislation must clear. Minimal alteration of contractual obligations may end the inquiry at its first stage. Severe impairment, on the other hand, will push the inquiry to a careful examination of the nature and purpose of the state legislation.

Here, the company's contracts of employment with its employees included as a fringe benefit or additional form of compensation, the pension plan. The company's maximum obligation was to set aside each year an amount based on the plan's requirements for vesting. The plan satisfied the current federal income tax code and was subject to no other legislative requirements. And, of course, the company was free to amend or terminate the pension plan at any time. The company thus had no reason to anticipate that its employees' pension rights could become vested except in accordance with the terms of the plan. It relied heavily, and reasonably, on this legitimate contractual expectation in calculating its annual contributions to the pension fund.

The effect of Minnesota's Private Pension Benefits Protection Act on this contractual obligation was severe. The company was required in 1974 to have made its contributions throughout the pre-1974 life of its plan as if employees' pension rights had vested after 10 years, instead of vesting in accord with the terms of the plan. Thus, a basic term of the pension contract — one on which the company had relied for 10 years — was substantially modified. The result was that, although the company's past contributions were adequate when made, they were not adequate when computed under the 10-year statutory vesting requirement. The Act thus forced a current recalculation of the past 10 years' contributions based on the new, unanticipated 10-year vesting requirement.

Not only did the state law thus retroactively modify the compensation that the company had agreed to pay its employees from 1963 to 1974, but also it did so by changing the company's obligations in an area where the element of reliance was vital — the funding of a pension plan.

[Moreover], the retroactive state-imposed vesting requirement was applied only to those employers who terminated their pension plans or who, like the company, closed their Minnesota offices. The company was thus forced to make all the retroactive changes in its contractual obligations at one time. By simply proceeding to close its office in Minnesota, a move that had been planned before the passage of the Act, the company was assessed an immediate pension funding charge of approximately $185,000.

Thus, the statute in question here nullifies express terms of the company's contractual obligations and imposes a completely unexpected liability in potentially disabling amounts. There is not even any provision for gradual applicability or grace periods. *Cf.* the Employee Retirement Income Security Act of 1974 (ERISA), 29 U.S.C. §§ 1061(b)(2), 1086(b), and 1144 (1976 ed.). Yet there is no showing in the record before us that this severe disruption of contractual expectations was necessary to meet an important general social problem.

[But] whether or not the legislation was aimed largely at a single employer, it clearly has an extremely narrow focus. It applies only to private employers who have at least 100 employees, at least one of whom works in Minnesota, and who have established voluntary private pension plans, qualified under 401 of the Internal Revenue Code. And it applies only when such an employer closes his Minnesota office or terminates his pension plan. Thus, this law can hardly be characterized, like the law at issue in the *Blaisdell* case, as one enacted to protect a broad societal interest, rather than a narrow class.

Moreover, in at least one other important respect, the Act does not resemble the mortgage moratorium legislation whose constitutionality was upheld in the *Blaisdell* case. This legislation, imposing a sudden, totally unanticipated, and substantial retroactive obligation upon the company to its employees, was not enacted to deal with a situation remotely approaching the broad and desperate emergency economic conditions of the early 1930's — conditions of which the Court in *Blaisdell* took judicial notice.

Entering a field it had never before sought to regulate, the Minnesota Legislature grossly distorted the company's existing contractual relationships with its employees by superimposing retroactive obligations upon the company substantially beyond the terms of its employment contracts. And that burden was imposed upon the company only because it closed its office in the State.

This Minnesota law simply does not possess the attributes of those state laws that, in the past, have survived challenge under the Contract Clause of the Constitution. The law was not even purportedly enacted to deal with a broad, generalized economic or social problem. *Cf. Home Building & Loan Assn. v. Blaisdell,* 290 U.S. at 445. It did not operate in an area already subject to state regulation at the time the company's contractual obligations were originally undertaken, but invaded an area never before subject to regulation by the State. *Cf. Veix v. Sixth Ward Building & Loan Assn.,* 310 U.S. 32, 38. It did not effect simply a temporary alteration of the contractual relationships of those within its coverage, but worked a severe, permanent, and immediate change in those relationships

— irrevocably and retroactively. *Cf. United States Trust Co. v. New Jersey,* 431 U.S. at 22. And its narrow aim was leveled not at every Minnesota employer, not even at every Minnesota employer who left the State, but only at those who had, in the past, been sufficiently enlightened as voluntarily to agree to establish pension plans for their employees.

[The] judgment of the District Court is reversed.

Notes and Questions

Spannaus applies part of the Blaisdell test and finds the new Minnesota law lacking (as both Blaisdell and Spannaus are Minnesota cases). In addition to the distinction between the two cases, notice how the Court addressed the addition of rights as the same thing as the impairment of obligations. As discussed earlier, the concern of the drafters was the trend among post-Revolution state legislatures to pass laws forgiving debt taken on during the war. It can be said that such forgiveness amounted to an impairment of the obligation — harming the obligation to the detriment of the recipient of the performance — the debt holder will not get paid. Expanding the same concept to other kinds of performance, the Court declined to allow New Hampshire to get out of its obligation to Dartmouth College in that case. Similar focus on obligation can be seen in the other cases reviewed in this chapter. Though not the first, Spannaus is a case that addresses the adding on of rights, and not the impairment of obligation. Professor Epstein justifies this interpretation by arguing for a "functional interpretation of the clause." If the clause was to prevent contract legislation from favoring promisors over promisees, a circumstance that could be rife with corruption, would not it be reasonable to follow up on the other side and prevent well placed promisee interests from seeking the passage of legislation increasing the obligations of promisors?

Again we see an expansion beyond the words of the text of the Constitution in the interpretation of constitutional language — and in this case supported by Professor Epstein, whom you might well have realized by now is a conservative constitutional law theorist. Continue to consider the questions surrounding literalism that have been raised in this chapter and consider how you feel about conservative claims of judicial legislating from the bench — a charge often lodged against liberal judges in light of this process.

So far we can articulate the conservative view of the Contracts Clause as being one in favor of strict enforcement of the literal terms as well as the addition of legislated contract rights to the definition of impairment. Finally, in a nod to the practical needs of government, contracts that impair third party rights need not be as protected under the clause. With this blueprint, do the following cases that are described below mark a departure from the format developed in Blaisdell, and applied in Spannaus (albeit to different effect)?

In *Energy Reserves Group, Inc. v. Kansas Power and Light Co.,* Kansas passed legislation prohibiting price escalation of natural gas that would otherwise be in line with federal law. The federal law allowed states to stop price escalation and the plaintiff claimed that notwithstanding the federal permission, the Kansas law nullified provisions in contracts with parties it was supplying giving it the right to raise rates in accordance with federal law. Echoing previous cases, Justice Blackmun articulated a kind of "strict scrutiny" analysis for deciding when state regulatory legislation did not run afoul of the Contracts Clause. According to Justice Blackmun, the threshold inquiry would be whether the state has impaired substantially a contractual relationship. The severity of the impairment would determine the degree of scrutiny applied. If a substantial impairment is found, the Court will look to whether there is a significant and legitimate public purpose behind the regulation. Finally, legislation meeting these qualifications will be upheld only if the adjustment (impairment) of rights is based on reasonable conditions and is appropriate to the public purpose justifying the legislation. This latter requirement is similar to the narrow tailoring requirement in due process, equal protection, and First Amendment cases. Justice Blackmun argued that the parties, operating in a heavy regulated industry, did not suffer a substantial impairment of their expectations especially since the federal deregulation was not a sure thing when the parties contracted. Nonetheless, even if the impairment were substantial, it was in pursuit of a legitimate state interest, that of protecting consumers from excessive price escalation during deregulation. The law was determined to meet the narrow tailoring requirement because it was found to be neither underinclusive or overinclusive. Only the gas contracts susceptible to escalator price increases were affected and were the only contracts that were capable of causing the mischief sought to be regulated.

In *Exxon Corp. v. Eagerton*, Justice Marshall declined to find any impairment in an Alabama law that exempted royalty holders from a tax on oil and gas, and that part of the law that prohibited passing that tax on down the production line was found not to be violative of the Contracts Clause. For the latter portion of the law, Justice Marshall did not use Justice Blackmun's strict scrutiny approach, focusing on a looser standard that stressed a state's police power and whether the law addressed a "generally applicable rule of conduct" that advanced wide societal interest.

2. THE TAKINGS CLAUSE

[N]or shall private property be taken for public use, without just compensation. [U.S. Const. amend V.]

The Takings Clause addresses an authority of governments that is both basic and ancient — the ability of government to confiscate private property. The twist on this authority within liberal democracies is the obligation of governments to meet two requirements: that all such takings be for public uses and that just compensation be provided in such a case. Governments take property for a variety of public purposes, under the law of eminent domain or condemnation, to build freeways, schools, universities, right of ways for transportation projects such as light rail and subways. And not only is the issue of government takings important within the constitutional scheme of the United States, it is also a matter of international law, with implications of the ability of states to nationalize industries or expropriate private property in the national interest. International law, like U.S. constitutional law, generally requires that the reason for taking be for the public, with the definition of that concept ranging from strictly public use to the national interest a broader concept that gives government more room to expropriate than the more narrow public use.

Similarly in the United States we have seen a broadening of the core concept in eminent domain law. The constitutional term, *public use* has implications to some commentators including members of the Court, that the use be open to members of the public. However more recently, the term has come to refer to a broader concept of use. Public purpose, perhaps a derivative of the meaning Public Use, has been used to describe government takings that were characterized as benefiting the public, even though physical public access were not contemplated or possible.

Another controversy that has produced constitutional litigation in the takings field has been where government regulations on property so encumbered the "investment backed expectations" or the owner's anticipated   use of property by regulation that it amounts to a taking.   Such regulatory encumbrance can be temporary or partial, or both.   The Court has had to address that phenomenon to determine if such regulations can even be termed a taking before the standards for takings discussed above would even apply.

A third and perhaps less contentious topic has been the definition of just compensation.   In determining what constitutes "just compensation," the government does not need to take into account any speculative schemes that the owner claims the property was intended for use in. (See *Olson v. United States*, 292 U.S. 246 (1934).) Normally, the fair market value of the property determines just compensation. If the property is taken before the payment is made, interest may also accrue.   *Id.*   Deviation from this measure of just compensation has been required only "when market value has been too difficult to find, or when its application would result in manifest injustice to owner or public." (See United States v. Commodities Trading Corp., 339 U.S. 121, 123 (1950).)

The discussion of the Takings Clause in this chapter will focus on the first two questions, whether the government's plans for private property after condemnation meet the public use requirement, and what government regulations so encumber the private owner's use of property that it amounts to a taking.

a. PUBLIC USE

Exhibiting the same spirit of deference demonstrated in his opinion in Williamson v. Lee Optical, Justice Douglas's opinion in the case below defers to the legislative department, in this case Congress, in a case involving its police powers to govern the District of Columbia.

BERMAN v. PARKER
348 U.S. 26 (1954)

Mr. Justice DOUGLAS delivered the opinion of the Court.

The power of Congress over the District of Columbia includes all the legislative powers which a state may exercise over its affairs. *See District of Columbia v. Thompson Co.,* 346 U.S. 100, 108. We deal, in other words, with what traditionally has been known as the police power. An attempt to define its reach or trace its outer limits is fruitless, for each case must turn on its own facts. The definition is essentially the product of legislative determinations addressed to the purposes of government, purposes neither abstractly nor historically capable of complete definition. Subject to specific constitutional limitations, when the legislature has spoken, the public interest has been declared in terms well nigh conclusive. In such cases, the legislature, not the judiciary, is the main guardian of the public needs to be served by social legislation, whether it be Congress legislating concerning the District of Columbia [o]r the States legislating concerning local affairs. [T]his principle admits of no exception merely because the power of eminent domain is involved. The role of the judiciary in determining whether that power is being exercised for a public purpose is an extremely narrow one.

Public safety, public health, morality, peace and quiet, law and order — these are some of the more conspicuous examples of the traditional application of the police power to municipal affairs. [Once] the object is within the authority of Congress, the right to realize it through the exercise of eminent domain is clear. For the power of eminent domain is merely the means to the end. Once the object is within the authority of Congress, the means by which it will be attained is also for Congress to determine. Here, one of the means chosen is the use of private enterprise for redevelopment of the area. Appellants argue that this makes the project a taking from one businessman for the benefit of another businessman. But the means of executing the project are for Congress, and Congress alone, to determine once the public purpose has been established. The public end may be as well or better served through an agency of private enterprise than through a department of government — or so the Congress might conclude. We cannot say that public ownership is the sole method of promoting the public purposes of community redevelopment projects. What we have said also disposes of any contention concerning the fact that certain property owners in the area may be permitted to repurchase their properties for redevelopment in harmony with the over-all plan. That, too, is a legitimate means which Congress and its agencies may adopt, if they choose.

In the present case, Congress and its authorized agencies attack the problem of the blighted parts of the community on an area, rather than on a structure-by-structure, basis. That, too, is opposed by appellants. They maintain that, since their building does not imperil health or safety nor contribute to the making of a slum or a blighted area, it cannot be swept into a redevelopment plan by the mere dictum of the Planning Commission or the Commissioners. The particular uses to be made of the land in the project were determined with regard to the needs of the particular community. The experts concluded that, if the community were to be healthy, if it were not to revert again to a blighted or slum area, as though possessed of a congenital disease, the area must be planned as a whole. It was not enough, they believed, to remove existing buildings that were insanitary or unsightly. It was important to redesign the whole area so as to eliminate the conditions that cause slums — the overcrowding of dwellings, the lack of parks, the lack of adequate streets and alleys, the absence of recreational areas, the lack of light and air, the presence of outmoded street patterns. It was believed that the piecemeal approach, the removal of individual structures that were offensive, would be only a palliative. The entire area needed redesigning so that a balanced, integrated plan could be developed for the region, including not only new homes, but also schools, churches, parks, streets, and shopping centers. In this way, it was hoped that the cycle of decay of the area could be controlled, and the birth of future slums prevented. [S]uch diversification in future use is plainly relevant to the maintenance of the desired housing standards, and therefore within congressional power.

[Property] may, of course, be taken for this redevelopment which, standing by itself, is innocuous and unoffending. But we have said enough to indicate that it is the need of the area as a whole which Congress and its agencies are evaluating. If owner after owner were permitted to resist these redevelopment programs on the ground that his particular property was not being used against the public interest, integrated plans for redevelopment would suffer greatly. The argument pressed on us is, indeed, a plea to substitute the landowner's standard of the public need for the standard prescribed by Congress. But as we have already stated, community redevelopment programs need not, by force of the Constitution, be on a piecemeal basis — lot by lot, building by building.

It is not for the courts to oversee the choice of the boundary line, nor to sit in review on the size of a particular project area. Once the question of the public purpose has been decided, the amount and character of land to be taken for the project and the need for a particular tract to complete the integrated plan rests in the discretion of the legislative branch.

[T]he District Court indicated grave doubts concerning the Agency's right to take full title to the land as distinguished from the objectionable buildings located on it. 117 F.Supp. 705, 715-719. We do not share those doubts. If the Agency considers it necessary in carrying out the redevelopment project to take full title to the real property involved, it may do so. It is not for the courts to determine whether it is necessary for successful consummation of the project that unsafe, unsightly, or insanitary buildings alone be taken or whether title to the land be included, any more than it is the function of the courts to sort and choose among the various parcels selected for condemnation.

The rights of these property owners are satisfied when they receive that just compensation which the Fifth Amendment exacts as the price of the taking.

The judgment of the District Court, as modified by this opinion, is affirmed.

———————

Comments on *Berman*. The unanimous Court deferred to Congress on two crucial determinations regarding public use: Is slum removal public use, and can a public use be effectuated by passing title to private parties? Part of the land taken would be sold or leased for redevelopment purposes to private interests who agree to make certain land use provisions in their redevelopment plans. Is this a public use? Is slum removal a public use? Does the language used in the opinion, "public purpose," a more accurate term? How does the Court use the new term and get around the fact that that language is not used in the Constitution?

Most cases addressing the Takings Clause of the Fifth Amendment involve states and municipalities and state subdivisions. Of course the Fifth Amendment is made incumbent upon the states through the Fourteenth Amendment's due process clause, which is said to incorporate certain rights "implicit in the concept of ordered liberty" (Palko v. Connecticut) or "fundamental to the American scheme of justice." One of these cases is *Hawaii Housing Authority v. Midkiff*, 467 U.S. 229 (1984). In order to address a problem involving extreme concentrations of land ownership in a small percentage of private landowners in the state, the Hawaii legislature came up with a plan to redistribute land through the process of eminent domain. At the request of renters on the property at issue, property could be condemned and that property subdivided for sale to the former lessees. Private landowners among the small minority of large landowners protested the condemnation as a taking from one private party for the benefit of another and that such a taking could never be for public use. Responding to that argument, the unanimous court, in an opinion written by Justice O'Connor, relied upon the police power of the states and the traditional deference accorded that power as justification for its ruling. After quoting important passages from *Berman v. Parker*, the Court stated:

> The "public use" requirement is thus coterminous with the scope of a sovereign's police powers.
>
> There is, of course, a role for courts to play in reviewing a legislature's judgment of what constitutes a public use, even when the eminent domain power is equated with the police power. But the Court in *Berman* made clear that it is "an extremely narrow" one. *Id.*, at 32. The Court in *Berman* cited with approval the Court's decision in Old Dominion Co. v. United States, 269 U. S. 55, 66 (1925), which held that deference to the legislature's

"public use" determination is required "until it is shown to involve an impossibility." [To] be sure, the Court's cases have repeatedly stated that "one person's property may not be taken for the benefit of another private person without a justifying public purpose, even though compensation be paid." where the "order in question was not, *and was not claimed to be, . . .* a taking of private property for a public use under the right of eminent domain," *id.,* at 416 (emphasis added), the Court invalidated a compensated taking of property for lack of a justifying public purpose. But where the exercise of the eminent domain power is rationally related to a conceivable public purpose, the Court has never held a compensated taking to be proscribed by the Public Use Clause. [The] mere fact that property taken outright by eminent domain is transferred in the first instance to private beneficiaries does not condemn that taking as having only a private purpose. The Court long ago rejected any literal requirement that condemned property be put into use for the general public. "It is not essential that the entire community, nor even any considerable portion, . . . directly enjoy or participate in any improvement in order [for it] to constitute a public use." Rindge Co. v. Los Angeles, 262 U. S., at 707. "[W]hat in its immediate aspect [is] only a private transaction may . . . be raised by its class or character to a public affair." Block v. Hirsh, 256 U. S., at 155.

What kinds of checks can be placed on this police power? Is there a real possibility of governmental abuse of the power of eminent domain to benefit favored parties, interest groups, minorities, or members of majority communities? Does the court in *Midkiff* and *Berman* adequately take these dangers into account? Does the following case go beyond the holdings in *Berman* and *Midkiff?*

KELO v. NEW LONDON
545 U.S. 469 (2005)

Justice STEVENS delivered the opinion of the Court.

In 2000, the city of New London approved a development plan that, in the words of the Supreme Court of Connecticut, was "projected to create in excess of 1,000 jobs, to increase tax and other revenues, and to revitalize an economically distressed city, including its downtown and waterfront areas." 268 Conn. 1, 5, 843 A. 2d 500, 507 (2004). In assembling the land needed for this project, the city's development agent has purchased property from willing sellers and proposes to use the power of eminent domain to acquire the remainder of the property from unwilling owners in exchange for just compensation. The question presented is whether the city's proposed disposition of this property qualifies as a "public use" within the meaning of the Takings Clause of the Fifth Amendment to the Constitution.

I

The city of New London (hereinafter City) sits at the junction of the Thames River and the Long Island Sound in southeastern Connecticut. Decades of economic decline led a state agency in 1990 to designate the City a "distressed municipality." In 1996, the Federal Government closed the Naval Undersea Warfare Center, which had been located in the Fort Trumbull area of the City and had employed over 1,500 people. In 1998, the City's unemployment rate was nearly double that of the State, and its population of just under 24,000 residents was at its lowest since 1920.

These conditions prompted state and local officials to target New London, and particularly its Fort Trumbull area, for economic revitalization. To this end, respondent New London Development Corporation (NLDC), a private nonprofit entity established some years earlier to assist the City in planning economic development, was reactivated. In January 1998, the State authorized a $5.35 million bond issue to support the NLDC's planning activities and a $10 million bond issue toward the creation of a Fort Trumbull State Park. In February, the pharmaceutical company Pfizer Inc. announced that it would build a $300 million research facility on a site immediately adjacent to Fort Trumbull; local planners hoped that Pfizer would draw new business to the area, thereby serving as a catalyst to the area's rejuvenation. After receiving initial approval from the city council, the NLDC continued its planning activities and held a series of neighborhood meetings to educate the public about the process. In May, the city council authorized the NLDC to formally submit its plans to the relevant state agencies for review. Upon obtaining state-level approval, the NLDC finalized an integrated development plan focused on 90 acres of the Fort Trumbull area.

[II]

Petitioner Susette Kelo has lived in the Fort Trumbull area since 1997. She has made extensive improvements to her house, which she prizes for its water view. Petitioner Wilhelmina Dery was born in her Fort Trumbull house in 1918 and has lived there her entire life. Her husband Charles (also a petitioner) has lived in the house since they married some 60 years ago. In all, the nine petitioners own 15 properties in Fort Trumbull—4 in parcel 3 of the development plan and 11 in parcel 4A. Ten of the parcels are occupied by the owner or a family member; the other five are held as investment properties. There is no allegation that any of these properties is blighted or otherwise in poor condition; rather, they were condemned only because they happen to be located in the development area.

In December 2000, petitioners brought this action in the New London Superior Court. They claimed, among other things, that the taking of their properties would violate the "public use" restriction in the Fifth Amendment. After a 7-day bench trial, the Superior Court granted a permanent restraining order prohibiting the taking of the properties located in parcel 4A (park or marina support). It, however, denied petitioners relief as to the properties located in parcel 3 (office space).

After the Superior Court ruled, both sides took appeals to the Supreme Court of Connecticut. That court held, over a dissent, that all of the City's proposed takings were valid. It began by upholding the lower court's determination that the takings were authorized by chapter 132, the State's municipal development statute. That statute expresses a legislative determination that the taking of land, even developed land, as part of an economic development project is a "public use" and in the "public interest." Next, relying on cases such as *Hawaii Housing Authority* v. *Midkiff*, 467 U.S. 229 (1984), and *Berman* v. *Parker*, 348 U.S. 26 (1954), the court held that such economic development qualified as a valid public use under both the Federal and State Constitutions. 268 Conn., at 40, 843 A. 2d, at 527.

[III]

Two polar propositions are perfectly clear. On the one hand, it has long been accepted that the sovereign may not take the property of *A* for the sole purpose of transferring it to another private party *B*, even though *A* is paid just compensation. On the other hand, it is equally clear that a State may transfer property from one private party to another if future "use by the public" is the purpose of the taking; the condemnation of land for a railroad with common-carrier duties is a familiar example. Neither of these propositions, however, determines the disposition of this case.

As for the first proposition, the City would no doubt be forbidden from taking petitioners' land for the purpose of conferring a private benefit on a particular private party.

See *Midkiff,* 467 U.S., at 245 ("A purely private taking could not withstand the scrutiny of the public use requirement; it would serve no legitimate purpose of government and would thus be void"); *Missouri Pacific R. Co.* v. *Nebraska,* 164 U.S. 403 (1896).5 Nor would the City be allowed to take property under the mere pretext of a public purpose, when its actual purpose was to bestow a private benefit. The takings before us, however, would be executed pursuant to a "carefully considered" development plan. 268 Conn., at 54, 843 A. 2d, at 536. The trial judge and all the members of the Supreme Court of Connecticut agreed that there was no evidence of an illegitimate purpose in this case. Therefore, as was true of the statute challenged in *Midkiff,* 467 U.S., at 245, the City's development plan was not adopted "to benefit a particular class of identifiable individuals."

On the other hand, this is not a case in which the City is planning to open the condemned land — at least not in its entirety — to use by the general public. Nor will the private lessees of the land in any sense be required to operate like common carriers, making their services available to all comers. But although such a projected use would be sufficient to satisfy the public use requirement, this "Court long ago rejected any literal requirement that condemned property be put into use for the general public." *Id.,* at 244. Indeed, while many state courts in the mid-19th century endorsed "use by the public" as the proper definition of public use, that narrow view steadily eroded over time. Not only was the "use by the public" test difficult to administer (*e.g.,* what proportion of the public need have access to the property? at what price?), but it proved to be impractical given the diverse and always evolving needs of society. Accordingly, when this Court began applying the Fifth Amendment to the States at the close of the 19th century, it embraced the broader and more natural interpretation of public use as "public purpose." Thus, in a case upholding a mining company's use of an aerial bucket line to transport ore over property it did not own, Justice Holmes' opinion for the Court stressed "the inadequacy of use by the general public as a universal test." *Strickley* v. *Highland Boy Gold Mining Co.,* 200 U.S. 527, 531 (1906). We have repeatedly and consistently rejected that narrow test ever since.

The disposition of this case therefore turns on the question whether the City's development plan serves a "public purpose." Without exception, our cases have defined that concept broadly, reflecting our longstanding policy of deference to legislative judgments in this field.

In *Berman* v. *Parker,* 348 U.S. 26 (1954), this Court upheld a redevelopment plan targeting a blighted area of Washington, D. C., in which most of the housing for the area's 5,000 inhabitants was beyond repair. Under the plan, the area would be condemned and part of it utilized for the construction of streets, schools, and other public facilities. The remainder of the land would be leased or sold to private parties for the purpose of redevelopment, including the construction of low-cost housing.

The owner of a department store located in the area challenged the condemnation, pointing out that his store was not itself blighted and arguing that the creation of a "better balanced, more attractive community" was not a valid public use. *Id.,* at 31. Writing for a unanimous Court, Justice Douglas refused to evaluate this claim in isolation, deferring instead to the legislative and agency judgment that the area "must be planned as a whole" for the plan to be successful. *Id.,* at 34. The Court explained that "community redevelopment programs need not, by force of the Constitution, be on a piecemeal basis — lot by lot, building by building." *Id.,* at 35. The public use underlying the taking was unequivocally affirmed.

[In] *Hawaii Housing Authority* v. *Midkiff,* 467 U.S. 229 (1984), the Court considered a Hawaii statute whereby fee title was taken from lessors and transferred to lessees (for just compensation) in order to reduce the concentration of land ownership. We unanimously upheld the statute and rejected the Ninth Circuit's view that it was "a naked attempt on the part of the state of Hawaii to take the property of A and transfer it to B solely for B's private use and benefit." *Id.*, at 235 (internal quotation marks omitted). Reaffirming *Berman*'s deferential approach to legislative judgments in this field, we concluded that the State's purpose of eliminating the "social and economic evils of a land oligopoly" qualified as a valid public use. 467 U.S., at 241-242. Our opinion also rejected the contention that the mere fact that the State immediately transferred the properties to private individuals upon condemnation somehow diminished the public character of the taking. "[I]t is only the taking's purpose, and not its mechanics," we explained, that matters in determining public use. *Id.*, at 244.

[IV]

Those who govern the City were not confronted with the need to remove blight in the Fort Trumbull area, but their determination that the area was sufficiently distressed to justify a program of economic rejuvenation is entitled to our deference. The City has carefully formulated an economic development plan that it believes will provide appreciable benefits to the community, including — but by no means limited to — new jobs and increased tax revenue. As with other exercises in urban planning and development, the City is endeavoring to coordinate a variety of commercial, residential, and recreational uses of land, with the hope that they will form a whole greater than the sum of its parts. To effectuate this plan, the City has invoked a state statute that specifically authorizes the use of eminent domain to promote economic development. Given the comprehensive character of the plan, the thorough deliberation that preceded its adoption, and the limited scope of our review, it is appropriate for us, as it was in *Berman*, to resolve the challenges of the individual owners, not on a piecemeal basis, but rather in light of the entire plan. Because that plan unquestionably serves a public purpose, the takings challenged here satisfy the public use requirement of the Fifth Amendment.

To avoid this result, petitioners urge us to adopt a new bright-line rule that economic development does not qualify as a public use. Putting aside the unpersuasive suggestion that the City's plan will provide only purely economic benefits, neither precedent nor logic supports petitioners' proposal. Promoting economic development is a traditional and long accepted function of government. There is, moreover, no principled way of distinguishing economic development from the other public purposes that we have recognized. In our cases upholding takings that facilitated agriculture and mining, for example, we emphasized the importance of those industries to the welfare of the States in question, see, *e.g., Strickley*, 200 U.S. 527; in *Berman,* we endorsed the purpose of transforming a blighted area into a "well-balanced" community through redevelopment, 348 U.S., at 33; in *Midkiff*, we upheld the interest in breaking up a land oligopoly that "created artificial deterrents to the normal functioning of the State's residential land market," 467 U.S., at 242; and in *Monsanto*, we accepted Congress' purpose of eliminating a "significant barrier to entry in the pesticide market," 467 U.S., at 1014-1015. It would be incongruous to hold that the City's interest in the economic benefits to be derived from the development of the Fort Trumbull area has less of a public character than any of those other interests. Clearly, there is no basis for exempting economic development from our traditionally broad understanding of public purpose.

Petitioners contend that using eminent domain for economic development impermissibly blurs the boundary between public and private takings. Again, our cases foreclose this objection. Quite simply, the government's pursuit of a public purpose will often benefit individual private parties. For example, in *Midkiff*, the forced transfer of property conferred a direct and significant benefit on those lessees who were previously unable to purchase their homes. In *Monsanto*, we recognized that the "most direct beneficiaries" of the data-sharing provisions were the subsequent pesticide applicants, but benefiting them in this way was necessary to promoting competition in the pesticide market. 467 U.S., at 1014. The owner of the department store in *Berman* objected to "taking from one businessman for the benefit of another businessman," 348 U.S., at 33, referring to the fact that under the redevelopment plan land would be leased or sold to private developers for redevelopment. Our rejection of that contention has particular relevance to the instant case: "The public end may be as well or better served through an agency of private enterprise than through a department of government — or so the Congress might conclude. We cannot say that public ownership is the sole method of promoting the public purposes of community redevelopment projects." *Id.*, at 34.

It is further argued that without a bright-line rule nothing would stop a city from transferring citizen *A*'s property to citizen *B* for the sole reason that citizen *B* will put the property to a more productive use and thus pay more taxes. Such a one-to-one transfer of property, executed outside the confines of an integrated development plan, is not presented in this case. While such an unusual exercise of government power would certainly raise a suspicion that a private purpose was afoot, the hypothetical cases posited by petitioners can be confronted if and when they arise. They do not warrant the crafting of an artificial restriction on the concept of public use.

Alternatively, petitioners maintain that for takings of this kind we should require a "reasonable certainty" that the expected public benefits will actually accrue. Such a rule, however, would represent an even greater departure from our precedent. "When the legislature's purpose is legitimate and its means are not irrational, our cases make clear that empirical debates over the wisdom of takings — no less than debates over the wisdom of other kinds of socioeconomic legislation — are not to be carried out in the federal courts." *Midkiff*, 467 U.S., at 242. Indeed, earlier this Term we explained why similar practical concerns (among others) undermined the use of the "substantially advances" formula in our regulatory takings doctrine. See *Lingle* v. *Chevron U. S. A. Inc.*, 544 U.S. ___, ___ (2005) (slip op., at 14-15) (noting that this formula "would empower — and might often require — courts to substitute their predictive judgments for those of elected legislatures and expert agencies"). The disadvantages of a heightened form of review are especially pronounced in this type of case. Orderly implementation of a comprehensive redevelopment plan obviously requires that the legal rights of all interested parties be established before new construction can be commenced. A constitutional rule that required postponement of the judicial approval of every condemnation until the likelihood of success of the plan had been assured would unquestionably impose a significant impediment to the successful consummation of many such plans.

Just as we decline to second-guess the City's considered judgments about the efficacy of its development plan, we also decline to second-guess the City's determinations as to what lands it needs to acquire in order to effectuate the project. "It is not for the courts to oversee the choice of the boundary line nor to sit in review on the size of a particular project area. Once the question of the public purpose has been decided, the amount and character of land to be taken for the project and the need for a particular tract to complete the integrated plan rests in the discretion of the legislative branch." *Berman*, 348 U.S., at 35-36.

In affirming the City's authority to take petitioners' properties, we do not minimize the hardship that condemnations may entail, notwithstanding the payment of just compensation. We emphasize that nothing in our opinion precludes any State from placing further restrictions on its exercise of the takings power. Indeed, many States already impose "public use" requirements that are stricter than the federal baseline. Some of these requirements have been established as a matter of state constitutional law, while others are expressed in state eminent domain statutes that carefully limit the grounds upon which takings may be exercised. As the submissions of the parties and their *amici* make clear, the necessity and wisdom of using eminent domain to promote economic development are certainly matters of legitimate public debate. This Court's authority, however, extends only to determining whether the City's proposed condemnations are for a "public use" within the meaning of the Fifth Amendment to the Federal Constitution. Because over a century of our case law interpreting that provision dictates an affirmative answer to that question, we may not grant petitioners the relief that they seek.

The judgment of the Supreme Court of Connecticut is affirmed.

It is so ordered.

Justice KENNEDY, concurring.

I join the opinion for the Court and add these further observations.

This Court has declared that a taking should be upheld as consistent with the Public Use Clause, U.S. Const., Amdt. 5., as long as it is "rationally related to a conceivable public purpose." *Hawaii Housing Authority* v. *Midkiff,* 467 U.S. 229, 241 (1984); see also *Berman* v. *Parker,* 348 U.S. 26 (1954). This deferential standard of review echoes the rational-basis test used to review economic regulation under the Due Process and Equal Protection Clauses, see, *e.g., FCC* v. *Beach Communications, Inc.,* 508 U.S. 307, 313-314 (1993); *Williamson* v. *Lee Optical of Okla., Inc.,* 348 U.S. 483 (1955). The determination that a rational-basis standard of review is appropriate does not, however, alter the fact that transfers intended to confer benefits on particular, favored private entities, and with only incidental or pretextual public benefits, are forbidden by the Public Use Clause.

A court applying rational-basis review under the Public Use Clause should strike down a taking that, by a clear showing, is intended to favor a particular private party, with only incidental or pretextual public benefits, just as a court applying rational-basis review under the Equal Protection Clause must strike down a government classification that is clearly intended to injure a particular class of private parties, with only incidental or pretextual public justifications. As the trial court in this case was correct to observe, "Where the purpose [of a taking] is economic development and that development is to be carried out by private parties or private parties will be benefited, the court must decide if the stated public purpose–economic advantage to a city sorely in need of it — is only incidental to the benefits that will be confined on private parties of a development plan."

A court confronted with a plausible accusation of impermissible favoritism to private parties should treat the objection as a serious one and review the record to see if it has merit, though with the presumption that the government's actions were reasonable and intended to serve a public purpose. Here, the trial court conducted a careful and extensive inquiry into "whether, in fact, the development plan is of primary benefit to . . . the developer [*i.e.,* Corcoran Jennison], and private businesses which may eventually locate in the plan area [*e.g.,* Pfizer], and in that regard, only of incidental benefit to the city." The trial court considered testimony from government officials and corporate officers; *id.,* at 266-271; documentary evidence of communications between these parties, *ibid.*;

respondents' awareness of New London's depressed economic condition and evidence corroborating the validity of this concern, *id.,* at 272-273, 278-279; the substantial commitment of public funds by the State to the development project before most of the private beneficiaries were known, *id.,* at 276; evidence that respondents reviewed a variety of development plans and chose a private developer from a group of applicants rather than picking out a particular transferee beforehand, *id.,* at 273, 278; and the fact that the other private beneficiaries of the project are still unknown because the office space proposed to be built has not yet been rented, *id.,* at 278.

The trial court concluded, based on these findings, that benefiting Pfizer was not "the primary motivation or effect of this development plan"; instead, "the primary motivation for [respondents] was to take advantage of Pfizer's presence." *Id.,* at 276. Likewise, the trial court concluded that "[t]here is nothing in the record to indicate that . . . [respondents] were motivated by a desire to aid [other] particular private entities." *Id.,* at 278. Even the dissenting justices on the Connecticut Supreme Court agreed that respondents' development plan was intended to revitalize the local economy, not to serve the interests of Pfizer, Corcoran Jennison, or any other private party. 268 Conn. 1, 159, 843 A. 2d 500, 595 (2004) (Zarella, J., concurring in part and dissenting in part). This case, then, survives the meaningful rational basis review that in my view is required under the Public Use Clause.

Petitioners and their *amici* argue that any taking justified by the promotion of economic development must be treated by the courts as *per se* invalid, or at least presumptively invalid. Petitioners overstate the need for such a rule, however, by making the incorrect assumption that review under *Berman* and *Midkiff* imposes no meaningful judicial limits on the government's power to condemn any property it likes. A broad *per se* rule or a strong presumption of invalidity, furthermore, would prohibit a large number of government takings that have the purpose and expected effect of conferring substantial benefits on the public at large and so do not offend the Public Use Clause. . . .

For the foregoing reasons, I join in the Court's opinion.

Justice O'CONNOR, with whom THE CHIEF JUSTICE, Justice SCALIA, and Justice THOMAS join, dissenting.

[U]nder the banner of economic development, all private property is now vulnerable to being taken and transferred to another private owner, so long as it might be upgraded — *i.e.,* given to an owner who will use it in a way that the legislature deems more beneficial to the public — in the process. To reason, as the Court does, that the incidental public benefits resulting from the subsequent ordinary use of private property render economic development takings "for public use" is to wash out any distinction between private and public use of property — and thereby effectively to delete the words "for public use" from the Takings Clause of the Fifth Amendment. Accordingly I respectfully dissent.

Petitioners are nine resident or investment owners of 15 homes in the Fort Trumbull neighborhood of New London, Connecticut. Petitioner Wilhelmina Dery, for example, lives in a house on Walbach Street that has been in her family for over 100 years. She was born in the house in 1918; her husband, petitioner Charles Dery, moved into the house when they married in 1946. Their son lives next door with his family in the house he received as a wedding gift, and joins his parents in this suit. Two petitioners keep rental properties in the neighborhood.

[P]etitioners own properties in two of the plan's seven parcels — Parcel 3 and Parcel 4A. Under the plan, Parcel 3 is slated for the construction of research and office space as a market develops for such space. It will also retain the existing Italian Dramatic Club (a private cultural organization) though the homes of three plaintiffs in that parcel are to be demolished. Parcel 4A is slated, mysteriously, for "'park support.'" *Id.*, at 345-346. At oral argument, counsel for respondents conceded the vagueness of this proposed use, and offered that the parcel might eventually be used for parking. Tr. of Oral Arg. 36.

To save their homes, petitioners sued New London and the NLDC, to whom New London has delegated eminent domain power. Petitioners maintain that the Fifth Amendment prohibits the NLDC from condemning their properties for the sake of an economic development plan. Petitioners are not hold-outs; they do not seek increased compensation, and none is opposed to new development in the area. Theirs is an objection in principle: They claim that the NLDC's proposed use for their confiscated property is not a "public" one for purposes of the Fifth Amendment. While the government may take their homes to build a road or a railroad or to eliminate a property use that harms the public, say petitioners, it cannot take their property for the private use of other owners simply because the new owners may make more productive use of the property.

[W]hile the Takings Clause presupposes that government can take private property without the owner's consent, the just compensation requirement spreads the cost of condemnations and thus "prevents the public from loading upon one individual more than his just share of the burdens of government." [T]he public use requirement, in turn, imposes a more basic limitation, circumscribing the very scope of the eminent domain power: Government may compel an individual to forfeit her property for the *public's* use, but not for the benefit of another private person. This requirement promotes fairness as well as security.

[T]his case returns us for the first time in over 20 years to the hard question of when a purportedly "public purpose" taking meets the public use requirement. It presents an issue of first impression: Are economic development takings constitutional? I would hold that they are not. We are guided by two precedents about the taking of real property by eminent domain. In *Berman*, we upheld takings within a blighted neighborhood of Washington, D. C. The neighborhood had so deteriorated that, for example, 64.3% of its dwellings were beyond repair. 348 U.S., at 30. It had become burdened with "overcrowding of dwellings," "lack of adequate streets and alleys," and "lack of light and air." *Id.,* at 34. Congress had determined that the neighborhood had become "injurious to the public health, safety, morals, and welfare" and that it was necessary to "eliminat[e] all such injurious conditions by employing all means necessary and appropriate for the purpose," including eminent domain. *Id.*, at 28. Mr. Berman's department store was not itself blighted. Having approved of Congress' decision to eliminate the harm to the public emanating from the blighted neighborhood, however, we did not second-guess its decision to treat the neighborhood as a whole rather than lot-by-lot. *Id.*, at 34-35; see also *Midkiff*, 467 U.S., at 244 ("it is only the taking's purpose, and not its mechanics, that must pass scrutiny").

In *Midkiff*, we upheld a land condemnation scheme in Hawaii whereby title in real property was taken from lessors and transferred to lessees. [T]he Hawaii Legislature had concluded that the oligopoly in land ownership was "skewing the State's residential fee simple market, inflating land prices, and injuring the public tranquility and welfare," and therefore enacted a condemnation scheme for redistributing title. *Ibid.*

In those decisions, we emphasized the importance of deferring to legislative judgments about public purpose. Because courts are ill-equipped to evaluate the efficacy of proposed legislative initiatives, we rejected as unworkable the idea of courts' "'deciding on what is and is not a governmental function and . . . invalidating legislation on the basis of their view on that question at the moment of decision, a practice which has proved impracticable in other fields.'" *Id.*, at 240-241 (quoting *United States ex rel. TVA* v. *Welch*, 327 U.S. 546, 552 (1946)); see *Berman*, *supra*, at 32 ("[T]he legislature, not the judiciary, is the main guardian of the public needs to be served by social legislation"); Likewise, we recognized our inability to evaluate whether, in a given case, eminent domain is a necessary means by which to pursue the legislature's ends. *Midkiff*, *supra*, at 242; *Berman*, *supra*, at 103.

Yet for all the emphasis on deference, *Berman* and *Midkiff* hewed to a bedrock principle without which our public use jurisprudence would collapse: "A purely private taking could not withstand the scrutiny of the public use requirement; it would serve no legitimate purpose of government and would thus be void." *Midkiff*, 467 U.S., at 245; *id.*, at 241.

[The] Court's holdings in *Berman* and *Midkiff* were true to the principle underlying the Public Use Clause. In both those cases, the extraordinary, precondemnation use of the targeted property inflicted affirmative harm on society — in *Berman* through blight resulting from extreme poverty and in *Midkiff* through oligopoly resulting from extreme wealth. And in both cases, the relevant legislative body had found that eliminating the existing property use was necessary to remedy the harm. *Berman*, *supra*, at 28-29; *Midkiff*, *supra*, at 232. Thus a public purpose was realized when the harmful use was eliminated. Because each taking *directly* achieved a public benefit, it did not matter that the property was turned over to private use. Here, in contrast, New London does not claim that Susette Kelo's and Wilhelmina Dery's well-maintained homes are the source of any social harm. Indeed, it could not so claim without adopting the absurd argument that any single-family home that might be razed to make way for an apartment building, or any church that might be replaced with a retail store, or any small business that might be more lucrative if it were instead part of a national franchise, is inherently harmful to society and thus within the government's power to condemn.

In moving away from our decisions sanctioning the condemnation of harmful property use, the Court today significantly expands the meaning of public use. It holds that the sovereign may take private property currently put to ordinary private use, and give it over for new, ordinary private use, so long as the new use is predicted to generate some secondary benefit for the public — such as increased tax revenue, more jobs, maybe even aesthetic pleasure. But nearly any lawful use of real private property can be said to generate some incidental benefit to the public. Thus, if predicted (or even guaranteed) positive side-effects are enough to render transfer from one private party to another constitutional, then the words "for public use" do not realistically exclude *any* takings, and thus do not exert any constraint on the eminent domain power.

There is a sense in which this troubling result follows from errant language in *Berman* and *Midkiff*. In discussing whether takings within a blighted neighborhood were for a public use, *Berman* began by observing: "We deal, in other words, with what traditionally has been known as the police power." 348 U.S., at 32. From there it declared that "[o]nce the object is within the authority of Congress, the right to realize it through the exercise of eminent domain is clear." *Id.*, at 33. Following up, we said in *Midkiff* that "[t]he 'public use' requirement is coterminous with the scope of a sovereign's police powers." 467 U.S., at 240. This language was unnecessary to the specific holdings of those decisions. *Berman* and *Midkiff* simply did not put such language to the constitutional test, because the takings in those cases were within the police power but also for "public use" for the reasons I have described. The case before us now demonstrates why, when deciding if a taking's purpose is constitutional, the police power and "public use" cannot always be equated. The Court protests that it does not sanction the bare transfer from A to B for B's benefit. It suggests two limitations on what can be taken after today's decision. First, it maintains a role for courts in ferreting out takings whose sole purpose is to bestow a benefit on the private transferee — without detailing how courts are to conduct that complicated inquiry. *Ante*, at 7.

[After discussing means for isolating private benefit motives that might discredit an eminent domain proceeding making it unconstitutional under the Public Use Clause, the dissent continued:]

Even if there were a practical way to isolate the motives behind a given taking, the gesture toward a purpose test is theoretically flawed. [T]he logic of today's decision is that eminent domain may only be used to upgrade — not downgrade — property. At best this makes the Public Use Clause redundant with the Due Process Clause, which already prohibits irrational government action. See *Lingle*, 544 U.S. __. The Court rightfully admits, however, that the judiciary cannot get bogged down in predictive judgments about whether the public will actually be better off after a property transfer. In any event, this constraint has no realistic import. For who among us can say she already makes the most productive or attractive possible use of her property? The specter of condemnation hangs over all property. Nothing is to prevent the State from replacing any Motel 6 with a Ritz-Carlton, any home with a shopping mall, or any farm with a factory.

[It] was possible after *Berman* and *Midkiff* to imagine unconstitutional transfers from A to B. Those decisions endorsed government intervention when private property use had veered to such an extreme that the public was suffering as a consequence. Today nearly all real property is susceptible to condemnation on the Court's theory. In the prescient words of a dissenter from the infamous decision in *Poletown*, "[n]ow that we have authorized local legislative bodies to decide that a different commercial or industrial use of property will produce greater public benefits than its present use, no homeowner's, merchant's or manufacturer's property, however productive or valuable to its owner, is immune from condemnation for the benefit of other private interests that will put it to a 'higher' use." 410 Mich., at 644-645, 304 N. W. 2d, at 464 (opinion of Fitzgerald, J.). This is why economic development takings "seriously jeopardiz[e] the security of all private property ownership." *Id.*, at 645, 304 N. W. 2d, at 465 (Ryan, J., dissenting).

Any property may now be taken for the benefit of another private party, but the fallout from this decision will not be random. The beneficiaries are likely to be those citizens with disproportionate influence and power in the political process, including large corporations and development firms. As for the victims, the government now has license to transfer property from those with fewer resources to those with more. The Founders cannot have intended this perverse result. "[T]hat alone is a *just* government," wrote James Madison, "which *impartially* secures to every man, whatever is his *own*." For the National Gazette, Property, (Mar. 29, 1792), reprinted in 14 Papers of James Madison 266 (R. Rutland et al. eds. 1983).

I would hold that the takings in both Parcel 3 and Parcel 4A are unconstitutional, reverse the judgment of the Supreme Court of Connecticut, and remand for further proceedings.

[Justice Thomas also wrote a dissent in this case.]

Comments on *Kelo*. Justice O'Connor wrote the Court's opinion in the *Midkiff* decision, which she describes above as having errant language. What is the effect of that errant language? Is Justice O'Connor trying to retract her opinion from 22 years earlier? If not, what is the difference between the situations in *Berman* and *Midkiff*, and the one in *Kelo* that she does not like?

Justice O'Connor suggests a difference between the earlier cases, in particular the *Berman* case, and *Kelo* as being a matter of degree — circumstances of extreme poverty in *Berman* and extreme wealth in *Midkiff*, both determined to be serious problems by the legislature. However, whereas the majority would defer to the legislative actions in all three cases, Justice O'Connor would pull back on deference — some would say substitute judicial judgment — in cases where the problems are not as extreme, as the dissent suggests is the case in *Kelo*.

Justice O'Connor's dissent, if followed, would put the Court in a position of substituting judicial judgment for that of politically elected legislatures, in interpreting the public use clause and the public purpose concept that has emanated from the clause by virtue of cases like *Berman* and *Midkiff*, and now *Kelo*. Professor Asmara Tekle's critique of the majority's opinion perhaps offers an alternative, and perhaps more objective reason for courts to intervene, and explains a bit of the difference between *Berman* and *Kelo*, which are similar in that they share the economic development motive:

> [A]lthough in *Berman* the Court attempted to outline the contours of a "balanced, integrated plan" by noting that it would have to include "new homes, schools, churches, parks, streets, and shopping centers," in the hope that the plan would halt the "cycle of decay" of slum-ridden neighborhoods, the *Kelo* Court failed to allude to or to require such specific qualifications. Indeed, without defining any terms, the most specific delineation of an integrated or comprehensive development plan that *Kelo* gives is one that will "provide appreciable benefits to the community," such as additional jobs and tax revenue, as well as the hope that a city's plan will "coordinate a variety of commercial, residential, and recreational uses of land," such that the plan "will form a whole greater than the sum of its parts." In addition, the Court specifically declined to review the effectiveness of the economic development plan put forward by the city of New London.
>
> Outside of suggesting an almost exact replica of the economic plan for the Fort Trumbull neighborhood, *Kelo* provides little guidance as to how a constitutional economic development plan would amount to an unconstitutional taking. Not only does this lack of clarity provide little comfort to ordinary citizens whose property may be subject to takings, however amorphous or ineffective the plan may be, but the opaqueness of *Kelo*, with respect to constitutional criteria for an economic development plan, also opens the door wide to potential abuse of citizens by powerful institutional forces.

Tekle-Johnson, *Correcting for* Kelo: *Social Impact Assessments and the Re-Balancing of Power between "Desperate Cities," Corporate Interests, and the Average Joe*, 16 Cornell J. L. & Pub. Pol'y 187 (2006-2007).

b. REGULATORY TAKINGS

A governmental regulation by nature limits personal, social, and business choices of those regulated. To what extent does a regulation deprive persons of property, not in the sense of actual taking, but in the sense that the regulation removes all value from the property that is severely limited by the government regulation? As a start on this way of looking at the Takings Clause, the following early case lays out some of the ground rules.

PENNSYLVANIA COAL CO. v. MAHON
260 U.S. 393 (1922)

Mr. Justice HOLMES delivered the opinion of the Court.

This is a bill in equity brought by the defendants in error to prevent the Pennsylvania Coal Company from mining under their property in such way as to remove the supports and cause a subsidence of the surface and of their house. The bill sets out a deed executed by the Coal Company in 1878, under which the plaintiffs claim. The deed conveys the surface, but in express terms reserves the right to remove all the coal under the same, and the grantee takes the premises with the risk, and waives all claim for damages that may arise from mining out the coal. But the plaintiffs say that whatever may have been the Coal Company's rights, they were taken away by an Act of Pennsylvania, approved May 27, 1921, P.L. 1198, commonly known there as the Kohler Act. The Court of Common Pleas found that if not restrained the defendant would cause the damage to prevent which the bill was brought, but denied an injunction, holding that the statute if applied to this case would be unconstitutional. On appeal the Supreme Court of the State agreed that the defendant had contract and property rights protected by the Constitution of the United States, but held that the statute was a legitimate exercise of the police power and directed a decree for the plaintiffs. A writ of error was granted bringing the case to this Court.

The statute forbids the mining of anthracite coal in such way as to cause the subsidence of, among other things, any structure used as a human habitation, with certain exceptions, including among them land where the surface is owned by the owner of the underlying coal and is distant more than one hundred and fifty feet from any improved property belonging to any other person. As applied to this case the statute is admitted to destroy previously existing rights of property and contract. The question is whether the police power can be stretched so far.

Government hardly could go on if to some extent values incident to property could not be diminished without paying for every such change in the general law. As long recognized, some values are enjoyed under an implied limitation and must yield to the police power. But obviously the implied limitation must have its limits, or the contract and due process clauses are gone. One fact for consideration in determining such limits is the extent of the diminution. When it reaches a certain magnitude, in most if not in all cases there must be an exercise of eminent domain and compensation to sustain the act. So the question depends upon the particular facts. The greatest weight is given to the judgment of the legislature, but it always is open to interested parties to contend that the legislature has gone beyond its constitutional power.

This is the case of a single private house. No doubt there is a public interest even in this, as there is in every purchase and sale and in all that happens within the commonwealth. Some existing rights may be modified even in such a case. Rideout v. Knox, 148 Mass. 368. But usually in ordinary private affairs the public interest does not warrant much of this kind of interference. A source of damage to such a house is not a public nuisance even if similar damage is inflicted on others in different places. The damage is not common or public. Wesson v. Washburn Iron Co., 13 Allen, 95, 103. The extent of the public interest is shown by the statute to be limited, since the statute ordinarily does not apply to land when the surface is owned by the owner of the coal. Furthermore, it is not justified as a protection of personal safety. That could be provided for by notice. Indeed the very foundation of this bill is that the defendant gave timely notice of its intent to mine under the house. On the other hand the extent of the taking is great. It purports to abolish what is recognized in Pennsylvania as an estate in land — a very valuable estate — and what is declared by the Court below to be a contract hitherto binding the plaintiffs. If we were called upon to deal with the plaintiffs' position alone, we should think it clear that the statute does not disclose a public interest sufficient to warrant so extensive a destruction of the defendant's constitutionally protected rights.

But the case has been treated as one in which the general validity of the act should be discussed. The Attorney General of the State, the City of Scranton, and the representatives of other extensive interests were allowed to take part in the argument below and have submitted their contentions here. It seems, therefore, to be our duty to go farther in the statement of our opinion, in order that it may be known at once, and that further suits should not be brought in vain.

It is our opinion that the act cannot be sustained as an exercise of the police power, so far as it affects the mining of coal under streets or cities in places where the right to mine such coal has been reserved. As said in a Pennsylvania case, "For practical purposes, the right to coal consists in the right to mine it." Commonwealth v. Clearview Coal Co., 256 Pa. St. 328, 331. What makes the right to mine coal valuable is that it can be exercised with profit. To make it commercially impracticable to mine certain coal has very nearly the same effect for constitutional purposes as appropriating or destroying it. This we think that we are warranted in assuming that the statute does.

It is true that in Plymouth Coal Co. v. Pennsylvania, 232 U.S. 531, it was held competent for the legislature to require a pillar of coal to be left along the line of adjoining property, that, with the pillar on the other side of the line, would be a barrier sufficient for the safety of the employees of either mine in case the other should be abandoned and allowed to fill with water. But that was a requirement for the safety of employees invited into the mine, and secured an average reciprocity of advantage that has been recognized as a justification of various laws.

The rights of the public in a street purchased or laid out by eminent domain are those that it has paid for. If in any case its representatives have been so short sighted as to acquire only surface rights without the right of support, we see no more authority for supplying the latter without compensation than there was for taking the right of way in the first place and refusing to pay for it because the public wanted it very much. The protection of private property in the Fifth Amendment presupposes that it is wanted for public use, but provides that it shall not be taken for such use without compensation. A similar assumption is made in the decisions upon the Fourteenth Amendment. Hairston v. Danville & Western Ry. Co., 208 U.S. 598, 605. When this seemingly absolute protection is found to be qualified by the police power, the natural tendency of human nature is to extend the qualification more and more until at last private property disappears. But that cannot be accomplished in this way under the Constitution of the United States.

The general rule at least is, that while property may be regulated to a certain extent, if regulation goes too far it will be recognized as a taking. It may be doubted how far exceptional cases, like the blowing up of a house to stop a conflagration, go — and if they go beyond the general rule, whether they do not stand as much upon tradition as upon principle. Bowditch v. Boston, 101 U.S. 16. In general it is not plain that a man's misfortunes or necessities will justify his shifting the damages to his neighbor's shoulders.

Spade v. Lynn & Boston R.R. Co., 172 Mass. 488, 489. We are in danger of forgetting that a strong public desire to improve the public condition is not enough to warrant achieving the desire by a shorter cut than the constitutional way of paying for the change. As we already have said, this is a question of degree — and therefore cannot be disposed of by general propositions. But we regard this as going beyond any of the cases decided by this Court. The late decisions upon laws dealing with the congestion of Washington and New York, caused by the war, dealt with laws intended to meet a temporary emergency and providing for compensation determined to be reasonable by an impartial board. They went to the verge of the law but fell far short of the present act. Block v. Hirsh, 256 U.S. 135. Marcus Brown Holding Co. v. Feldman, 256 U.S. 170. Levy Leasing Co. v. Siegel, 258 U.S. 242.

We assume, of course, that the statute was passed upon the conviction that an exigency existed that would warrant it, and we assume that an exigency exists that would warrant the exercise of eminent domain. But the question at bottom is upon whom the loss of the changes desired should fall. So far as private persons or communities have seen fit to take the risk of acquiring only surface rights, we cannot see that the fact that their risk has become a danger warrants the giving to them greater rights than they bought.

Decree reversed.

Mr. Justice BRANDEIS, dissenting.

The Kohler Act prohibits, under certain conditions, the mining of anthracite coal within the limits of a city in such a manner or to such an extent "as to cause the . . . subsidence of any dwelling or other structure used as a human habitation, or any factory, store, or other industrial or mercantile establishment in which human labor is employed." Coal in place is land; and the right of the owner to use his land is not absolute. He may not so use it as to create a public nuisance; and uses, once harmless, may, owing to changed conditions, seriously threaten the public welfare. Whenever they do, the legislature has power to prohibit such uses without paying compensation; and the power to prohibit extends alike to the manner, the character and the purpose of the use. Are we justified in declaring that the Legislature of Pennsylvania has, in restricting the right to mine anthracite, exercised this power so arbitrarily as to violate the Fourteenth Amendment?

Every restriction upon the use of property imposed in the exercise of the police power deprives the owner of some right theretofore enjoyed, and is, in that sense, an abridgment by the State of rights in property without making compensation. But restriction imposed to protect the public health, safety or morals from dangers threatened is not a taking. The restriction here in question is merely the prohibition of a noxious use. The property so restricted remains in the possession of its owner. The State does not appropriate it or make any use of it. The State merely prevents the owner from making a use which interferes with paramount rights of the public. Whenever the use prohibited ceases to be noxious — as it may because of further change in local or social conditions, — the restriction will have to be removed and the owner will again be free to enjoy his property as heretofore.

The restriction upon the use of this property can not, of course, be lawfully imposed, unless its purpose is to protect the public. But the purpose of a restriction does not cease to be public, because incidentally some private persons may thereby receive gratuitously valuable special benefits. Thus, owners of low buildings may obtain, through statutory restrictions upon the height of neighboring structures, benefits equivalent to an easement of light and air. Welch v. Swasey, 214 U.S. 91. Compare Lindsley v. Natural Carbonic Gas Co., 220 U.S. 61; Walls v. Midland Carbon Co., 254 U.S. 300. Furthermore, a restriction, though imposed for a public purpose, will not be lawful, unless the restriction is an appropriate means to the public end. But to keep coal in place is surely an appropriate means of preventing subsidence of the surface; and ordinarily it is the only available means. Restriction upon use does not become inappropriate as a means, merely because it deprives the owner of the only use to which the property can then be profitably put. The liquor and the oleomargarine cases settled that. Mugler v. Kansas, 123 U.S. 623, 668, 669; Powell v. Pennsylvania, 127 U.S. 678, 682. See also Hadacheck v. Los Angeles, 239 U.S. 394; Pierce Oil Corporation v. City of Hope, 248 U.S. 498. Nor is a restriction imposed through exercise of the police power inappropriate as a means, merely because the same end might be affected through exercise of the power of eminent domain, or otherwise at public expense. Every restriction upon the height of buildings might be secured through acquiring by eminent domain the right of each owner to build above the limiting height; but it is settled that the State need not resort to that power. Compare Laurel Hill Cemetery v. San Francisco, 216 U.S. 358; Missouri Pacific Ry. Co. v. Omaha, 235 U.S. 121. If by mining anthracite coal the owner would necessarily unloose poisonous gasses, I suppose no one would doubt the power of the State to prevent the mining, without buying his coal fields. And why may not the State, likewise, without paying compensation, prohibit one from digging so deep or excavating so near the surface, as to expose the community to like dangers? In the latter case, as in the former, carrying on the business would be a public nuisance.

It is said that one fact for consideration in determining whether the limits of the police power have been exceeded is the extent of the resulting diminution in value; and that here the restriction destroys existing rights of property and contract. But values are relative. If we are to consider the value of the coal kept in place by the restriction, we should compare it with the value of all other parts of the land. That is, with the value not of the coal alone, but with the value of the whole property. The rights of an owner as against the public are not increased by dividing the interests in his property into surface and subsoil. The sum of the rights in the parts can not be greater than the rights in the whole. The estate of an owner in land is grandiloquently described as extending *ab orco usque ad coelum*. But I suppose no one would contend that by selling his interest above one hundred feet from the surface he could prevent the State from limiting, by the police power, the height of structures in a city. And why should a sale of underground rights bar the State's power? For aught that appears the value of the coal kept in place by the restriction may be negligible as compared with the value of the whole property, or even as compared with that part of it which is represented by the coal remaining in place and which may be extracted despite the statute. Ordinarily a police regulation, general in operation, will not be held void as to a particular property, although proof is offered that owing to conditions peculiar to it the restriction could not reasonably be applied. See Powell v. Pennsylvania, 127 U.S. 678, 681, 684; Murphy v. California, 225 U.S. 623, 629. But even if the particular facts are to govern, the statute should, in my opinion, be upheld in this case. For the defendant has failed to adduce any evidence from which it appears that to restrict its mining operations was an unreasonable exercise of the police power. Compare Reinman v. Little Rock, 237 U.S. 171, 177, 180; Pierce Oil Corporation v. City of Hope, 248 U.S. 498, 500. Where the surface and the coal belong to the same person, self-interest would ordinarily prevent mining to such an extent as to cause a subsidence. It was, doubtless, for this reason that the legislature, estimating the degrees of danger, deemed statutory restriction unnecessary for the public safety under such conditions.

[This] case involves only mining which causes subsidence of a dwelling house. But the Kohler Act contains provisions in addition to that quoted above; and as to these, also, an opinion is expressed. These provisions deal with mining under cities to such an extent as to cause subsidence of —

> (a) Any public building or any structure customarily used by the public as a place of resort, assemblage, or amusement, including, but not being limited to, churches, schools, hospitals, theatres, hotels, and railroad stations.
> (b) Any street, road, bridge, or other public passageway, dedicated to public use or habitually used by the public.
> (c) Any track, roadbed, right of way, pipe, conduct, wire, or other facility, used in the service of the public by any municipal corporation or public service company as defined by the Public Service Company Law.

A prohibition of mining which causes subsidence of such structures and facilities is obviously enacted for a public purpose; and it seems, likewise, clear that mere notice of intention to mine would not in this connection secure the public safety. Yet it is said that these provisions of the act cannot be sustained as an exercise of the police power where the right to mine such coal has been reserved. The conclusion seems to rest upon the assumption that in order to justify such exercise of the police power there must be "an average reciprocity of advantage" as between the owner of the property restricted and the rest of the community; and that here such reciprocity is absent. Reciprocity of advantage is an important consideration, and may even be an essential, where the State's power is exercised for the purpose of conferring benefits upon the property of a neighborhood, as in drainage projects, or upon adjoining owners, as by party wall provisions. But where the police power is exercised, not to confer benefits upon property owners, but to protect the public from detriment and danger, there is, in my opinion, no room for considering reciprocity of advantage. There was no reciprocal advantage to the owner prohibited from using his oil tanks in 248 U.S. 498; his brickyard, in 239 U.S. 394; his livery stable, in 237 U.S. 171; his billiard hall, in 225 U.S. 623; his oleomargarine factory, in 127 U.S. 678; his brewery, in 123 U.S. 623; unless it be the advantage of living and doing business in a civilized community. That reciprocal advantage is given by the act to the coal operators.

———

Comments on *Pennsylvania Coal*. The concept of reciprocity of advantage addresses the basis for regulatory takings, which, according to Justice Holmes, are constitutional where both the public and the party being regulated can point to some advantage to each by virtue of the regulation. Absent that, it is a taking, and compensation would be required. Mere impairment, inconvenience, or interference alone would not amount to a taking because the value of the property has not been diminished totally. But in *Pennsylvania Coal*, a right to mine, purchased by contract, was regulated away, destroying the total value to the owners of that contract right. Regulation in such a way must evidence some sort of reciprocal advantage or benefit from the regulation, as Holmes would explain, lest the government be required to provide some compensation. Brandeis, on the other hand, sees no purpose in mandating reciprocity of advantage where a proper use of the police power is in question: "But where the police power is exercised, not to confer benefits upon property owners, but to protect the public from detriment and danger, there is, in my opinion, no room for considering reciprocity of advantage."

Six years later, in *Miller v. Schoene*, 276 U.S. 272 (1928), a regulation requiring the destruction of red cedar, found to carry an infestation dangerous to apple orchards, was found not to be a taking and not covered by the Takings Clause. In finding the statute constitutional in a unanimous decision, the opinion written by Justice Stone made no mention of *Pennsylvania Coal*. It did contain the following language:

> On the evidence we may accept the conclusion of the Supreme Court of Appeals that the state was under the necessity of making a choice between the preservation of one class of property and that of the other wherever both existed in dangerous proximity. It would have been none the less a choice if, instead of enacting the present statute, the state, by doing nothing, had permitted serious injury to the apple orchards within its borders to go on unchecked. When forced to such a choice the state does not exceed its constitutional powers by deciding upon the destruction of one class of property in order to save another which, in the judgment of the legislature, is of greater value to the public. It will not do to say that the case is merely one of a conflict of two private interests and that the misfortune of apple growers may not be shifted to cedar owners by ordering the destruction of their property; for it is obvious that there may be, and that here there is, a preponderant public concern in the preservation of the one interest over the other. [And] where the public interest is involved preferment of that interest over the property interest of the individual, to the extent even of its destruction, is one of the distinguishing characteristics of every exercise of the police power which affects property.

Could the difference be explained by Holmes's concern in *Pennsylvania Coal* that in that case, owners of surface rights passed on the chance to purchase the very property right the regulation was essentially destroying — mining rights? Is the fact that no similar opportunity was at issue in *Miller* — there was no continuous opportunity to protect the investment of apple orchard owners by purchasing all red cedar trees in existence — determinative of the holding? Was the Court concerned in *Pennsylvania Coal* about the state using its police power to recover a lost investment opportunity (admittedly for the benefit of surface landowners) and that no such lost opportunity existed in *Miller*? Is this explainable by the need to balance private interests? Was the public interest so much weaker in Pennsylvania Coal, especially where surface rights owners could have protected themselves better by purchasing mining rights? Are the public interests in the apple orchards in Miller a matter of a popularity poll?

———

At this point in the narrative of regulatory takings, one could be forgiven for concluding that there are no coherent and principled means of deciding a case. Though we focused on only two decisions, *Miller* did not even try to make sense of the doctrinal problem apparent between it and *Pennsylvania Coal*. Though incoherence in Supreme Court jurisprudence is certainly not a new or rare matter, it is unusual for a decision to be as dismissive of a prior decision with similar facts as *Miller* was of *Pennsylvania Coal*. Perhaps the next decision will clarify the rule (or rules) regarding regulatory takings.

When a case has facts that are extremely close to previous cases on a question that has not been resolved or is captured in a morass of incoherency, Court watchers usually get excited at the prospect of the Court addressing a problem directly and finally clearing up the matter. *Keystone Bituminous Coal Ass'n v. Debenedictis,* 480 U.S. 470 (1987), is such a case. But did it provide a clear standard for determining when a regulatory action was in fact a compensable taking?

KEYSTONE BITUMINOUS COAL ASS'N v. DeBENEDICTIS
480 U.S. 470 (1987)

Justice STEVENS delivered the opinion of the Court:

In *Pennsylvania Coal Co. v. Mahon,* 260 U.S. 393 (1922), the Court reviewed the constitutionality of a Pennsylvania statute that admittedly destroyed "previously existing rights of property and contract.". . . In that case the "particular facts" led the Court to hold that the Pennsylvania Legislature had gone beyond its constitutional powers when it enacted a statute prohibiting the mining of anthracite coal in a manner that would cause the subsidence of land on which certain structures were located.

Now, 65 years later, we address a different set of "particular facts," involving the Pennsylvania Legislature's 1966 conclusion that the Commonwealth's existing mine subsidence legislation had failed to protect the public interest in safety, land conservation, preservation of affected municipalities' tax bases, and land development in the Commonwealth. Based on detailed findings, the legislature enacted the Bituminous Mine Subsidence and Land Conservation Act (the "Subsidence Act" or the "Act"), Pa. Stat. Ann., Tit. 52, § 1406.1 et seq. (Purdon Supp. 1986). Petitioners contend, relying heavily on our decision in *Pennsylvania Coal,* that § 4 and § 6 of the Subsidence Act and certain implementing regulations violate the Takings Clause, and that § 6 of the Act violates the Contracts Clause of the Federal Constitution. The District Court and the Court of Appeals concluded that *Pennsylvania Coal* does not control for several reasons and that our subsequent cases make it clear that neither § 4 nor § 6 is unconstitutional on its face. We agree.

I

Coal mine subsidence is the lowering of strata overlying a coal mine, including the land surface, caused by the extraction of underground coal. This lowering of the strata can have devastating effects. It often causes substantial damage to foundations, walls, other structural members, and the integrity of houses and buildings. Subsidence frequently causes sinkholes or troughs in land which make the land difficult or impossible to develop. Its effect on farming has been well documented — many subsided areas cannot be plowed or properly prepared. Subsidence can also cause the loss of groundwater and surface ponds. In short, it presents the type of environmental concern that has been the focus of so much federal, state, and local regulation in recent decades.

[II]

In 1982, petitioners filed a civil rights action in the United States District Court for the Western District of Pennsylvania seeking to enjoin officials of the DER from enforcing the Subsidence Act and its implementing regulations. The petitioners are an association of coal mine operators, and four corporations that are engaged, either directly or through affiliates, in underground mining of bituminous coal in western Pennsylvania.

[In] the portions of the complaint that are relevant to us, petitioners alleged that both [§ 4 of the Subsidence Act, as implemented by the and § 6 of the Subsidence Act] constitute a taking of their private property without compensation in violation of the Fifth and Fourteenth Amendments. They also alleged that § 6 impairs their contractual agreements in violation of Article I, § 10 of the Constitution. The parties entered into a stipulation of facts pertaining to petitioners' facial challenge, and filed cross motions for summary judgment on the facial challenge. The District Court granted respondent's motion. [We] granted certiorari, and now affirm.

III

Petitioners assert that disposition of their takings claim calls for no more than a straightforward application of the Court's decision in *Pennsylvania Coal Co. v. Mahon*. Although there are some obvious similarities between the cases, we agree with the Court of Appeals and the District Court that the similarities are far less significant than the differences, and that *Pennsylvania Coal* does not control this case.

[The Court reviewed the basic facts of *Pennsylvania Coal Co. v. Mahon*:] [After the mining company suffered a defeat at the state supreme court level] [t]he company promptly appealed to this Court, asserting that the impact of the statute was so severe that "a serious shortage of domestic fuel is threatened." Motion to Advance for Argument in *Pennsylvania Coal* v. *Mahon*, O. T. 1922, No. 549, p. 3. The company explained that until the Court ruled, "no anthracite coal which is likely to cause surface subsidence can be mined," and that strikes were threatened throughout the anthracite coal fields. In its argument in this Court, the company contended that the Kohler Act was not a bona fide exercise of the police power, but in reality was nothing more than "'robbery under the forms of law'" because its purpose was "not to protect the lives or safety of the public generally but merely to augment the property rights of a favored few." Over Justice Brandeis' dissent, this Court accepted the company's argument. In his opinion for the Court, Justice Holmes first characteristically decided the specific case at hand in a single, terse paragraph:

> This is the case of a single private house. No doubt there is a public interest even in this, as there is in every purchase and sale and in all that happens within the commonwealth. Some existing rights may be modified even in such a case. Rideout v. Knox, 148 Mass. 368. But usually in ordinary private affairs the public interest does not warrant much of this kind of interference. A source of damage to such a house is not a public nuisance even if similar damage is inflicted on others in different places. The damage is not common or public. *Wesson* v. *Washburn Iron Co.*, 13 Allen, 95, 103. The extent of the public interest is shown by the statute to be limited, since the statute ordinarily does not apply to land when the surface is owned by the owner of the coal. Furthermore, it is not justified as a protection of personal safety. That could be provided for by notice. Indeed the very foundation of this bill is that the defendant gave timely notice of its intent to mine under the house. On the other hand the extent of the taking is great. It purports to abolish what is recognized in Pennsylvania as an estate in land — a very valuable estate — and what is declared by the Court below to be a contract hitherto binding the plaintiffs. If we were called upon to deal with the plaintiffs' position alone, we should think it clear that the statute does not disclose a public interest sufficient to warrant so extensive a destruction of the defendant's constitutionally protected rights."

260 U.S., at 413-414. Then — uncharacteristically — Justice Holmes provided the parties with an advisory opinion discussing "the general validity of the Act." In the advisory portion of the Court's opinion, Justice Holmes rested on two propositions, both critical to the Court's decision. First, because it served only private interests, not health or safety, the Kohler Act could not be "sustained as an exercise of the police power." Id., at 414. Second, the statute made it "commercially impracticable" to mine "certain coal" in the areas affected by the Kohler Act.

The holdings and assumptions of the Court in *Pennsylvania Coal* provide obvious and necessary reasons for distinguishing *Pennsylvania Coal* from the case before us today. The two factors that the Court considered relevant, have become integral parts of our takings analysis. We have held that land use regulation can effect a taking if it "does not substantially advance legitimate state interests, . . . or denies an owner economically viable use of his land." (citations omitted); see also *Penn Central Transportation Co.* v. New York City, 438 U.S. 104, 124 (1978).Application of these tests to petitioners' challenge demonstrates that they have not satisfied their burden of showing that the Subsidence Act constitutes a taking. First, unlike the Kohler Act, the character of the governmental action involved here leans heavily against finding a taking; the Commonwealth of Pennsylvania has acted to arrest what it perceives to be a significant threat to the common welfare. Second, there is no record in this case to support a finding, similar to the one the Court made in *Pennsylvania Coal*, that the Subsidence Act makes it impossible for petitioners to profitably engage in their business, or that there has been undue interference with their investment-backed expectations.

The Public Purpose

Unlike the Kohler Act, which was passed upon in *Pennsylvania Coal*, the Subsidence Act does not merely involve a balancing of the private economic interests of coal companies against the private interests of the surface owners. The Pennsylvania Legislature specifically found that important public interests are served by enforcing a policy that is designed to minimize subsidence in certain areas.

[The] District Court and the Court of Appeals were both convinced that the legislative purposes set forth in the statute were genuine, substantial, and legitimate, and we have no reason to conclude otherwise.

None of the indicia of a statute enacted solely for the benefit of private parties identified in Justice Holmes' opinion are present here. First, Justice Holmes explained that the Kohler Act was a "private benefit" statute since it "ordinarily does not apply to land when the surface is owned by the owner of the coal." 260 U.S., at 414. The Subsidence Act, by contrast, has no such exception. The current surface owner may only waive the protection of the Act if the DER consents. See 25 Pa. Code § 89.145(b) (1983). Moreover, the Court was forced to reject the Commonwealth's safety justification for the Kohler Act because it found that the Commonwealth's interest in safety could as easily have been accomplished through a notice requirement to landowners. The Subsidence Act, by contrast, is designed to accomplish a number of widely varying interests, with reference to which petitioners have not suggested alternative methods through which the Commonwealth could proceed.

[Thus], the Subsidence Act differs from the Kohler Act in critical and dispositive respects. With regard to the Kohler Act, the Court believed that the Commonwealth had acted only to ensure against damage to some private landowners' homes. Justice Holmes stated that if the private individuals needed support for their structures, they should not have "[taken] the risk of acquiring only surface rights." 260 U.S., at 416. Here, by contrast, the Commonwealth is acting to protect the public interest in health, the environment, and the fiscal integrity of the area. That private individuals erred in taking a risk cannot estop the Commonwealth from exercising its police power to abate activity akin to a public nuisance. The Subsidence Act is a prime example that "circumstances may so change in time . . . as to clothe with such a [public] interest what at other times . . . would be a matter of purely private concern." Block v. Hirsh, 256 U.S. 135, 155 (1921).

[The] Court's hesitance to find a taking when the State merely restrains uses of property that are tantamount to public nuisances is consistent with the notion of "reciprocity of advantage" that Justice Holmes referred to in *Pennsylvania Coal*. Under our system of government, one of the State's primary ways of preserving the public weal is restricting the uses individuals can make of their property. While each of us is burdened somewhat by such restrictions, we, in turn, benefit greatly from the restrictions that are placed on others.

[Diminution] of Value and Investment-Backed Expectations

The second factor that distinguishes this case from *Pennsylvania Coal* is the finding in that case that the Kohler Act made mining of "certain coal" commercially impracticable. In this case, by contrast, petitioners have not shown any deprivation significant enough to satisfy the heavy burden placed upon one alleging a regulatory taking. For this reason, their takings claim must fail.

In addressing petitioners' claim we must not disregard the posture in which this case comes before us. The District Court granted summary judgment to respondents only on the facial challenge to the Subsidence Act. The court explained that "[because] plaintiffs have not alleged any injury due to the enforcement of the statute, there is as yet no concrete controversy regarding the application of the specific provisions and regulations. Thus, *the only question before this court is whether the mere enactment of the statutes and regulations constitutes a taking.*" 581 F.Supp., at 513 (emphasis added). The next phase of the case was to be petitioners' presentation of evidence about the actual effects the Subsidence Act had and would have on them. Instead of proceeding in this manner, however, the parties filed a joint motion asking the court to certify the facial challenge for appeal. The parties explained that an assessment of the actual impact that the Act has on petitioners' operations "will involve complex and voluminous proofs," which neither party was currently in a position to present, App. 15-17, and stressed that if an appellate court were to reverse the District Court on the facial challenge, then all of their expenditures in adjudicating the as-applied challenge would be wasted. Based on these considerations, the District Court certified three questions relating to the facial challenge.

[Petitioners] thus face an uphill battle in making a facial attack on the Act as a taking.

The hill is made especially steep because petitioners have not claimed, at this stage, that the Act makes it commercially impracticable for them to continue mining their bituminous coal interests in western Pennsylvania. Indeed, petitioners have not even pointed to a single mine that can no longer be mined for profit.

[The] judgment of the Court of Appeals is affirmed.

Any Clearer Now? Consider the following excerpts from Chief Justice Rehnquist's dissent, first addressing Justice Stevens's suggestion that the *Pennsylvania Coal* case as originally heard was about a single house and hence in the interest of private parties, and not a matter of public purpose, the opposite of the current case:

> In apparent recognition of the obstacles presented by *Pennsylvania Coal* to the decision it reaches, the Court attempts to undermine the authority of Justice Holmes' opinion as to the validity of the Kohler Act, labeling it "uncharacteristically . . . advisory." *Ante*, at 484. I would not so readily dismiss the precedential value of this opinion. There is, to be sure, some language in the case suggesting that it could have been decided simply by addressing the particular application of the Kohler Act at issue in the case. See, *e. g.*, Pennsylvania Coal, supra, at 414 ("If we were called upon to deal with the plaintiffs' position alone, we should think it clear that the statute does not disclose a public interest sufficient to warrant so extensive a destruction of the defendant's constitutionally protected rights"). The Court, however, found that the validity of the Act itself was properly drawn into question: "[The] case has been treated as one in which the general validity of the

[Kohler] act should be discussed." *Ibid*. The coal company clearly had an interest in obtaining a determination that the Kohler Act was unenforceable if it worked a taking without providing for compensation. For these reasons, I would not find the opinion of the Court in *Pennsylvania Coal* advisory in any respect.

Having argued that the Kohler Act in *Pennsylvania Coal* was not limited to a single house, but had broader impact, the Chief Justice went on to demonstrate how in both *Pennsylvania Coal* and *Keystone* that broader impact implicated the same public interest:

> Though several aspects of the Kohler Act limited its protection of these interests [t]his Court did not ignore the public interests served by the Act. [It] recognized that the Act "affects the mining of coal under streets or cities in places where the right to mine such coal has been reserved." Id., at 414. [T]he strong public interest in the stability of streets and cities, however, was insufficient "to warrant achieving the desire by a shorter cut than the constitutional way of paying for the change." *Ibid*. Thus, the Court made clear that the mere existence of a public purpose was insufficient to release the government from the compensation requirement: "The protection of private property in the Fifth Amendment presupposes that it is wanted for public use, but provides that it shall not be taken for such use without compensation." Id., at 415.
>
> The Subsidence Act rests on similar public purposes. These purposes were clearly stated by the legislature: "[To] aid in the protection of the safety of the public, to enhance the value of [surface area] lands for taxation, to aid in the preservation of surface water drainage and public water supplies and generally to improve the use and enjoyment of such lands. . . ." The Act's declaration of policy states that mine subsidence "has seriously impeded land development . . . has caused a very clear and present danger to the health, safety and welfare of the people of Pennsylvania [and] erodes the tax base of the affected municipalities." §§ 1406.3(2), (3), (4). The legislature determined that the prevention of subsidence would protect surface structures, advance the economic future and well-being of Pennsylvania, and ensure the safety and welfare of the Commonwealth's residents. *Ibid*. Thus, it is clear that the Court has severely understated the similarity of purpose between the Subsidence Act and the Kohler Act. The public purposes in this case are not sufficient to distinguish it from *Pennsylvania Coal*.

Is Chief Justice Rehnquist's dissent persuasive in its depiction of the majority opinion as not dealing fairly with the issues and mischaracterizing the present case as presenting a stronger case for public purpose?

Is the public purpose at issue in this case the same public purpose that must be satisfied when an actual taking is attempted by government? Later in his dissent, the Chief Justice addresses this issue by stating that the existence of matter of public concern over subsidence in either case

> does not resolve the question whether a taking has occurred; the existence of such a public purpose is merely a necessary prerequisite to the government's exercise of its taking power. See Hawaii Housing Authority v. Midkiff, 467 U.S. 229, 239-243, 245 (1984); Berman v. Parker, 348 U.S. 26, 32-33 (1954). The *nature* of these purposes may be relevant, for we have recognized that a taking does not occur where the government exercises its unquestioned authority to prevent a property owner from using his property to injure others without having to compensate the value of the forbidden use.

Chief Justice Rehnquist's opinion does appear to clear up some issues. First of all, the depiction of *Pennsylvania Coal* as being a single-issue case involving a single private interest may be a bit far-fetched on Justice Stevens's part. The dissent also points out that we really are talking about two different public interests in the takings cases.   There is the public interest that must exist before a taking can occur, along with compensation; and then there is the kind of public interest that determines whether a governmental action is in fact a taking — not as a legal condition for a taking, but as part of the definition of the act of taking.   As Rehnquist says in the excerpt above, "a taking does not occur where the government exercises its unquestioned authority to prevent a property owner from using his property to injure others without having to compensate the value of the forbidden use." This kind of public interest does not, according to Chief Justice Rehnquist, alone mean that a taking has not occurred.   The Court must still look to the degree the regulation interferes with the economic use of the property.   The majority did not find any significant diminution of property, finding the loss of the right to exploit that part of its property that could cause subsidence is but one part of the petitioner's property.   On the other hand, the dissent found that the property interests of the petitioners were separate and that the support interest had been completely destroyed, even if other interests had survived the regulation. This amounted to a taking requiring compensation.

This relative value of the diminution of property usage as a determinant of whether a regulation amounted to a taking is evident in several other cases before the Court.   The standard for evaluating regulations couples an important public interest (which could include ridding the community of noxious uses, nuisances, or injurious uses, or more broadly, to require a use beneficial to the public), with an evaluation of the economic interference with the owner's property.   Applying this to historic preservation in *Penn Central Transportation Co. v. New York City*, 438 U.S. 104 (1978), the Court approved of an historic landmark ordinance requiring the owners of Grand Central Station to refrain from building atop the historic train station in midtown Manhattan, referencing the value of historic preservation and the fact that the owner could transfer development rights forbidden to the station, to other properties aligning the property — minimizing the loss of economic value to the owner.   Crucial to that decision, in an opinion written by Justice Brennan, is the recognition that   "a 'taking' may more readily be found when the interference with property can be characterized as a physical invasion by government, than when interference arises from some public program adjusting the benefits and burdens of economic life to promote the common good."

But the Court did not reach the same conclusion in *Loretto v. Teleprompter Manhattan CATV*, 458 U.S. 19 (1982), where a permanent physical occupation of owner's property was sanctioned by the government as part of New York City's cable television startup; the installation of cable wire on private property amounted to a complete occupation, taking, however minor.   Even though the law passed the legitimate public purpose (injurious-to-beneficial to society/police power) part of the test, the law did not pass the interference with owner's property portion of the test.

Another permanent restriction on property use was struck down in *Lucas v. South Carolina Coastal Council*, 505 U.S. 1003 (1992).   Moving from an actual occupation in *Loretto* to a regulation so constricting in terms of actual use of property, the Court, in an opinion by Justice Scalia, held that a beachfront regulation prohibiting development of certain beachfront property was a taking.   Declining to expand the per se physical occupation rule from *Loretto* to the case, Justice Scalia instead addressed the nature of the property right that was constrained to determine whether the property interests were "part of the title to begin with."   As an alternative to the legitimate public purpose standard, or an elaboration on that standard, Justice Scalia argued that government restrictions on land use that would interfere with a government-held easement, as in government interests in navigation on its waters, would be an example of an interest that was not contained in the private landowner's title. Accordingly in such a case compensation under the Fifth and/or Fourteenth Amendments would not be necessary. In remanding the case back to the state court, the decision called for a determination as to whether under state law there was a common law prohibition on the kind of use (development) in light of the environmental interests of the state at issue. If so, the landowner would not have been entitled to the kind of use prohibited and, hence, would not be entitled to compensation.

Penn Central stands for the case by case evaluation of the circumstances involved, such as looking to the degree of deprivation of economic use by the governmental regulation and whether other economic uses are available to the landowner as well as the public purpose and the benefits to the public. *Pennsylvania Coal* and *Keystone* would be examples of such a case by case approach, with the economic prong of the test being the determining factor in each: a deprivation of economic use of property *in Pennsylvania Coal* not at all the case in *Keystone*. Whether one agrees with these conclusions, did the Justices in both cases consistently apply the standard as they articulated it?

Loretto, on the other hand, approved a per se rule in favor of finding a compensable taking where a permanent occupation is authorized by government. Perhaps similarly, in *Lucas*, a deprivation of all economic use of land was found to be a taking where the economic use was a property right that was part of the title itself, and not subject to common law government restrictions or easements. And since all such common law restrictions or easements would have existed prior to the acquisition of the property, a property owner cannot be said to have been deprived of any use that he or she was entitled to.

Instead of outright land use commands that may or may not pursue legitimate state interests or public purposes, or that may or may not amount to an outright occupation or deprivation of economic use of property, would a condition to a linked to a government permit resulting in the same end as a command be constitutional? Justice Scalia believed so in *Nollan v. California Coastal Commission*, 483 U.S. 825 (1987), but only where the condition was related to the legitimate government purpose. Concerned that private building on a stretch of private beach between public beaches would interfere with sight lines and general public enjoyment of the beach, the California Coastal Commission conditioned homeowners' permit to build a home on the privately owned property on their agreeing to provide access between the two beaches. Justice Scalia found the condition to be a taking. Like the physical occupation in *Loretto*, a per se rule would apply but for the fact that the case involved a condition. Furthermore, Justice Scalia acknowledged that the state could use its police powers to prohibit the building of the home — a more direct way of preserving sight lines according to the Court — than requiring the access easement. But inasmuch as the easement did not further public viewing of the ocean and simply provided access, the condition, according to the Court, was a taking not supported by countervailing public interests furthered by the occupation.

KOONTZ v. ST. JOHNS RIVER WATER MANAGEMENT DISTRICT
570 U. S. ____ (2013)

JUSTICE ALITO delivered the opinion of the Court.

Our decisions in *Nollan* v. *California Coastal Comm'n*, 483 U. S. 825 (1987), and *Dolan* v. *City of Tigard*, 512 U. S. 374 (1994), provide important protection against the misuse of the power of land-use regulation. In those cases, we held that a unit of government may not condition the approval of a land-use permit on the owner's relinquishment of a portion of his property unless there is a "nexus" and "rough proportionality" between the government's demand and the effects of the proposed land use. In this case, the St. Johns River Water Management District (District) believes that it circumvented *Nollan* and *Dolan* because of the way in which it structured its handling of a permit application submitted by Coy Koontz, Sr., whose estate is represented in this Court by Coy Koontz, Jr. The District did not approve his application on the condition that he surrender an interest in his land. Instead, the District, after suggesting that he could obtain approval by signing over such an interest, denied his application because he refused to yield. The Florida Supreme Court blessed this maneuver and thus effectively interred those important decisions. Because we conclude that *Nollan* and *Dolan* cannot be evaded in this way, the Florida Supreme Court's decision must be reversed.

I

A

[Petitioner] decided to develop the 3.7-acre northern section of his property, and in 1994 he applied to the District for MSSW and WRM permits. Under his proposal, petitioner would have raised the elevation of the northernmost section of his land to make it suitable for a building, graded the land from the southern edge of the building site down to the elevation of the high-voltage electrical lines, and installed a dry-bed pond for retaining and gradually releasing storm water runoff from the building and its parking lot. To mitigate the environmental effects of his proposal, petitioner offered to foreclose any possible future development of the approximately 11-acre southern section of his land by deeding to the District a conservation easement on that portion of his property.

The District considered the 11-acre conservation easement to be inadequate, and it informed petitioner that it would approve construction only if he agreed to one of two concessions. First, the District proposed that petitioner reduce the size of his development to 1 acre and deed to the District a conservation easement on the remaining 13.9 acres. To reduce the development area, the District suggested that petitioner could eliminate the dry-bed pond from his proposal and instead install a more costly subsurface storm water management system beneath the building site. The District also suggested that petitioner install retaining walls rather than gradually sloping the land from the building site down to the elevation of the rest of his property to the south.

In the alternative, the District told petitioner that he could proceed with the development as proposed, building on 3.7 acres and deeding a conservation easement to the government on the remainder of the property, if heal so agreed to hire contractors to make improvements to District-owned land several miles away. Specifically, petitioner could pay to replace culverts on one parcel or fill in ditches on another. Either of those projects would have enhanced approximately 50 acres of District-owned wetlands. When the District asks permit applicants to fund offsite mitigation work, its policy is never to require any particular offsite project, and it did not do so here. Instead, the District said that it "would also favorably consider" alternatives to its suggested offsite mitigation projects if petitioner proposed something "equivalent." App. 75.

Believing the District's demands for mitigation to be excessive in light of the environmental effects that
building proposal would have caused, petitioner filed suit in state court. Among other claims, he argued that he was entitled to relief under Fla. Stat. §373.617(2), which allows

owners to recover "monetary damages" if a state agency's action is "an unreasonable exercise of the state's police power constituting a taking without just compensation."

B

[A] majority of [the Florida Supreme Court] distinguished *Nollan* and *Dolan* on two grounds. First, the majority thought it significant that in this case, unlike *Nollan* or *Dolan*, the District did not approve petitioner's application on the condition that he accede to the District's demands; instead, the District denied his application because he refused to make concessions. 77 So. 3d, at 1230. Second, the majority drew a distinction between a demand for an interest in real property (what happened in *Nollan* and *Dolan*) and a demand for money. 77 So. 3d, at 1229–1230. The majority acknowledged a division of authority over whether a demand for money can give rise to a claim under *Nollan* and *Dolan*, and sided with those courts that have said it cannot.

[II]

A

[Our]decisions in [Nollan and Dolan] reflect two realities of the permitting process. The first is that land-use permit applicants are especially vulnerable to the type of coercion that the unconstitutional conditions doctrine prohibits because the government often has broad discretion to deny a permit that is worth far more than property it would like to take. By conditioning a building permit on the owner's deeding over a public right-of-way, for example, the government can pressure an owner into voluntarily giving up property for which the Fifth Amendment would otherwise require just compensation. See *id.*, at 384; *Nollan*, 483 U. S., at 831. So long as the building permit is more valuable than any just compensation the owner could hope to receive for the right-of-way, the owner is likely to accede to the government's demand, no matter how unreasonable. Extortionate demands of this sort frustrate the Fifth Amendment right to just compensation, and the unconstitutional conditions doctrine prohibits them.

A second reality of the permitting process is that many proposed land uses threaten to impose costs on the public that dedications of property can offset. Where a building proposal would substantially increase traffic congestion, for example, officials might condition permit approval on the owner's agreement to deed over the land needed to widen a public road. Respondent argues that a similar rationale justifies the exaction at issue here: petitioner's proposed construction project, it submits, would destroy wetlands on his property, and in order to compensate for this loss, respondent demands that he enhance wetlands elsewhere. Insisting that landowners internalize the negative externalities of their conduct is a hallmark of responsible land-use policy, and we have long sustained such regulations against constitutional attack. See *Village of Euclid* v. *Ambler Realty Co.*, 272 U. S. 365 (1926).

Nollan and *Dolan* accommodate both realities by allowing the government to condition approval of a permit on the dedication of property to the public so long as there is a "nexus" and "rough proportionality" between the property that the government demands and the social costs of the applicant's proposal. *Dolan, supra*, at 391; *Nollan*, 483 U. S., at 837. Our precedents thus enable permitting authorities to insist that applicants bear the full costs of their proposals while still forbidding the government from engaging in "out-and-out . . . extortion" that would thwart the Fifth Amendment right to just compensation. *Ibid.* (internal quotation marks omitted). Under *Nollan* and *Dolan* the government may choose whether and how a permit applicant is required to mitigate the impacts of a proposed development, but it may not leverage its legitimate interest in mitigation to pursue governmental ends that lack an essential nexus and rough proportionality to those impacts.

B

The principles that undergird our decisions in *Nollan* and *Dolan* do not change depending on whether the government *approves* a permit on the condition that the applicant turn over property or *denies* a permit because the applicant refuses to do so. We have often concluded that denials of governmental benefits were impermissible under the unconstitutional conditions doctrine. See, *e.g., Perry*, 408 U. S., at 597 (explaining that the government "*may not deny* a benefit to a person on a basis that infringes his constitutionally protected interests" (emphasis added)); *Memorial Hospital*, 415 U. S. 250 (finding unconstitutional condition where government denied health care benefits). In so holding, we have recognized that regardless of whether the government ultimately succeeds in pressuring someone into forfeiting a constitutional right, the unconstitutional conditions doctrine forbids burdening the Constitution's enumerated rights by coercively withholding benefits from those who exercise them.

A contrary rule would be especially untenable in this case because it would enable the government to evade the limitations of *Nollan* and *Dolan* simply by phrasing its demands for property as conditions precedent to permit approval. Under the Florida Supreme Court's approach, a government order stating that a permit is "approved if "the owner turns over property would be subject to *Nollan* and *Dolan*, but an identical order that uses the words "denied until" would not. Our unconstitutional conditions cases have long refused to attach significance to the distinction between conditions precedent and conditions subsequent.

[Nor] does it make a difference, as respondent suggests, that the government might have been able to deny petitioner's application outright without giving him the option of securing a permit by agreeing to spend money to improve public lands. [Yet] we have repeatedly rejected the argument that if the government need not confer a benefit at all, it can withhold the benefit because someone refuses to give up constitutional rights. *E.g., United States* v. *American Library Assn., Inc.*, 539 U. S. 194, 210 (2003) ("[T]he government may not deny a benefit to a person on a basis that infringes his constitutionally protected . . . freedom of speech *even if he has no entitlement to that benefit*".

[That] is not to say, however, that there is *no* relevant difference between a consummated taking and the denial of a permit based on an unconstitutionally extortionate demand. Where the permit is denied and the condition is never imposed, nothing has been taken. While the unconstitutional conditions doctrine recognizes that this *burdens* a constitutional right, the Fifth Amendment mandates a particular *remedy*—just compensation—only for takings. In cases where there is an excessive demand but no taking, whether money damages are available is not a question of federal constitutional law but of the cause of action—whether state or federal—on which the landowner relies. Because petitioner brought his claim pursuant to a state law cause of action, the Court has no occasion to discuss what remedies might be available for a *Nollan/Dolan* unconstitutional conditions violation either here or in other cases.

[III]

We turn to the Florida Supreme Court's alternative holding that petitioner's claim fails because respondent asked him to spend money rather than give up an easement on his land. A predicate for any unconstitutional conditions claim is that the government could not have constitutionally ordered the person asserting the claim to do what it attempted to pressure that person into doing. See *Rumsfeld*, 547 U. S., at 59–60. For that reason, we began our analysis in both *Nollan* and *Dolan* by observing that if the government had directly seized the easements it sought to obtain through the permitting process, it would have committed a *per se* taking. See *Dolan*, 512 U. S., at 384; *Nollan*, 483 U. S., at 831. The Florida Supreme Court held that petitioner's claim fails at this first step because the subject of the exaction at issue here was money rather than a more tangible interest in real property. 77 So. 3d, at 1230. Respondent and the dissent take the same position, citing the concurring and dissenting opinions in *Eastern Enterprises* v. *Apfel*, 524 U. S. 498 (1998), for the proposition that an obligation to spend money can never provide the basis for a takings claim. See *post,* at 5–8 (opinion of KAGAN, J.).

We note as an initial matter that if we accepted this argument it would be very easy for land-use permitting officials to evade the limitations of *Nollan* and *Dolan*. Because the government need only provide a permit applicant with one alternative that satisfies the nexus and rough proportionality standards, a permitting authority wishing to exact an easement could simply give the owner a choice of either surrendering an easement or making a payment equal to the easement's value. Such so-called "in lieu of" fees are utterly commonplace, Rosenberg, The Changing Culture of American Land Use Regulation: Paying for Growth with Impact Fees, 59 S. M. U. L. Rev. 177, 202–203 (2006), and they are functionally equivalent to other types of land use exactions. For that reason and those that follow, we reject respondent's argument and hold that so-called "monetary exactions" must satisfy the nexus and rough proportionality requirements of *Nollan* and *Dolan*.

[We] hold that the government's demand for property from a land-use permit applicant must satisfy the requirements of *Nollan* and *Dolan* even when the government denies the permit and even when its demand is for money. The Court expresses no view on the merits of petitioner's claim that respondent's actions here failed to comply with the principles set forth in this opinion and those two cases. The Florida Supreme Court's judgment is reversed, and this case is remanded for further proceedings not inconsistent with this opinion.

It is so ordered.

[A dissent by Justice Kagan, joined by Justices Ginsburg, Breyer, and Sotomayor is omitted].

Note on *Koontz*. A majority of the Court found that the case law applicable to physical takings of land applied as well to physical property in *Horne v. Department of Agriculture* 576 U. S. 350 (2015). The issue there was whether a government law, still in force though passed during the New Deal, which mandated certain percentages of a farmer's raisin crop to be reserved for possession by the Department of Agriculture as part of the Department's efforts to stabilize markets for raisin sales, was a physical taking. The United States relied on language from the regulatory takings case of *Lucas* v. *South Carolina Coastal Council*, 505 U. S. 1003 (1992) that owners of personal property "ought to be aware of the possibility that new regulation might even render his property economically worthless," such an "implied limitation" was not reasonable in the case of land. 505 U. S., at 1027–1028. This language keyed in on the theory behind the difference between regulatory takings as those takings that go too far, as measured by the degree of the government's interference with reasonable investment backed expectations. This standard heretofore had been applied to land holdings, though the language in Lucas implied that there are no reasonable expectations in personal property ownership because such owners "ought to be aware" that regulations could render their property useless. However, the majority noted that the taking in the present case involved a physical appropriation of the raisin farmers' property, and not a mere regulatory taking, and that the reasonable expectation formula is not applicable to actual physical takings.   Because the Department of Agriculture, through the Raisin Committee, actually took title in the raisins under the law,   whether the raisins were physically spirited away, or kept on farmer's premises, the Department has sole control on the disposal and use of the raisins, and not the growers.   The majority equated that to a physical taking, even though a regulatory restriction on farmers' use of raisin production would have the same economic effect on the growers.

The government further argued that because the growers could get something from   any proceeds received from government sales of the raisins, the action on the part of the Department did not amount to a taking since growers could get some monetary value. The government considered this to be the most important interest in the raisin crop, the monetary value, though possessory interest, and the right to do as pleases the growers is relinquished under the law.   The majority dismisses this argument as another mistaken use of regulatory taking jurisprudence in a case involving physical taking.   As a physical appropriation, the question of whether there is a constitutional taking does not rely on whether the owners are deprived of only a part of their interest in property, but on whether owners are deprived of property possession.   Any proceeds received in a physical possession case do not represent a remaining interest in property, but can only be considered part of compensation for the physical taking by the government.

Another argument offered by the government and dissent had to do with Congress' power to regulate interstate commerce.   The government suggested that the raisin reserve was a mere condition to the benefit of doing business in the raisin industry.   The Court noted that where it had previously recognized the authority of the government via Congressional legislation to apply certain conditions to the sale of hazardous materials under its regulatory authority, it had never extended that principle to more traditional non-hazardous uses of property.

C. REVIVAL OF SUBSTANTIVE DUE PROCESS

As underscored by our study of constitutional decision making at the commencement of this work, the significance of the "lessons of the *Lochner*" is not just a matter of history, for application of substantive due process has been revived in the modern era.   Though this evolution may have had its seeds set in Griswold v. Connecticut, decided at the height of the Warren Court, the ultimate resurrection of using the due process clause of the Fourteenth Amendment to create unarticulated fundamental rights occurred at the onset of the conservative Burger Court in Roe v. Wade.   To this controversial revival we now turn.

1. "FUNDAMENTAL" RIGHT TO PRIVACY

GRISWOLD v. CONNECTICUT
381 U.S. 479 (1965)

Mr. Justice DOUGLAS delivered the opinion of the Court.

Appellant Griswold is Executive Director of the Planned Parenthood League of Connecticut. Appellant Buxton is a licensed physician and a professor at the Yale Medical School who served as Medical Director for the League. . . .

They gave information, instruction, and medical advice to married persons as to the means of preventing conception. [Fees] were usually charged, although some couples were serviced free.

[The relevant Connecticut statute prohibits use of "any drug, medicinal article or instrument for the purpose of preventing conception."]

The appellants were found guilty as accessories and fined $100 each, against the claim that the accessory statute as so applied violated the Fourteenth Amendment. . . .

We think that appellants have standing to raise the constitutional rights of the married people with whom they had a professional relationship. [Certainly] the accessory should have standing to assert that the offense which he is charged with assisting is not, or cannot constitutionally be, a crime. . . .

Coming to the merits, we are met with a wide range of questions that implicate the Due Process Clause of the Fourteenth Amendment. Overtones of some arguments suggest that [Lochner] should be our guide. But we decline that invitation as we did in [West Coast Hotel Co. v. Parrish and Williamson v. Lee Optical, section D supra]. We do not sit as a super-legislature to determine the wisdom, need, and propriety of laws that touch economic problems, business affairs, or social conditions. This law, however, operates directly on an intimate relation of husband and wife and their physician's role in one aspect of that relation.

The association of people is not mentioned in the Constitution nor in the Bill of Rights. The right to educate a child in a school of the parents' choice — whether public or private or parochial — is also not mentioned. Nor is the right to study any particular subject or any foreign language. Yet the First Amendment has been construed to include certain of those rights. [As Pierce v. Society of Sisters, Meyer v. Nebraska, and other decisions suggest, the] right of freedom of speech and press includes not only the right to utter or to print, but the right to distribute, the right to receive, the right to read and freedom of inquiry, freedom of thought, and freedom to teach — indeed the freedom of the entire university community. Without those peripheral rights the specific rights would be less secure. And so we reaffirm the principle of the Pierce and the Meyer cases.   In NAACP v. Alabama, we protected the "freedom to associate and privacy in one's associations," noting that freedom of association was a peripheral First Amendment right. Disclosure of membership lists of a constitutionally valid association, we held, was invalid. [In] other words, the First Amendment has a penumbra where privacy is protected from governmental intrusion. In like context, we have protected forms of "association" that are not political in the customary sense but pertain to the social, legal, and economic benefit of the members. NAACP v. Button. [While association] is not expressly included in the First Amendment its existence is necessary in making the express guarantees fully meaningful.

The foregoing cases suggest that specific guarantees in the Bill of Rights have penumbras, formed by emanations from those guarantees that help give them life and substance. See Poe v. Ullman, 367 U.S. 497, 516-522 [Douglas, J., dissenting]. Various guarantees create zones of privacy. The right of association contained in the penumbra of the First Amendment is one, as we have seen. The Third Amendment in its prohibition against the quartering of soldiers "in any house" in time of peace without the consent of the owner is another facet of that privacy. The Fourth Amendment explicitly affirms the "right of the people to be secure in their persons, houses, papers, and effects, against unreasonable searches and seizures." The Fifth Amendment in its Self-Incrimination Clause enables the citizen to create a zone of privacy which government may not force him to surrender to his detriment. The Ninth Amendment provides: "The enumeration in the

Constitution, of certain rights, shall not be construed to deny or disparage others retained by the people."

The Fourth and Fifth Amendments were described in Boyd v. United States, 116 U.S. 616, 630, as protection against all governmental invasions "of the sanctity of a man's home and the privacies of life." We recently referred in Mapp v. Ohio, 367 U.S. 643, 656, to the Fourth Amendment as creating a "right to privacy, no less important than any other right carefully and particularly reserved to the people."

We have had many controversies over these penumbral rights of "privacy and repose." [Skinner v. Oklahoma and other] cases bear witness that the right of privacy which presses for recognition here is a legitimate one.

The present case, then, concerns a relationship lying within the zone of privacy created by several fundamental constitutional guarantees. And it concerns a law which, in forbidding the use of contraceptives rather than regulating their manufacture or sale, seeks to achieve its goals by means having a maximum destructive impact upon that relationship. Such a law cannot stand in light of the familiar principle, so often applied by this Court, that a "governmental purpose to control or prevent activities constitutionally subject to state regulation may not be achieved by means which sweep unnecessarily broadly and thereby invade the area of protected freedoms." [NAACP v. Alabama.] Would we allow the police to search the sacred precincts of marital bedrooms for telltale signs of the use of contraceptives? The very idea is repulsive to the notions of privacy surrounding the marriage relationship.

We deal with a right of privacy older than the Bill of Rights. [Marriage] is a coming together for better or for worse, hopefully enduring, and intimate to the degree of being sacred. It is an association that promotes a way of life, not causes; a harmony in living, not political faiths; a bilateral loyalty, not commercial or social projects. Yet it is an association for as noble a purpose as any involved in our prior decisions.

Reversed.

Mr. Justice GOLDBERG, whom THE CHIEF JUSTICE [WARREN] and Mr. Justice BRENNAN join, concurring.

I [join the Court's opinion]. Although I have not accepted the view that "due process" as used in the Fourteenth Amendment incorporates all of the first eight Amendments, [I] do agree that the concept of liberty protects those personal rights that are fundamental, and is not confined to the specific terms of the Bill of Rights. My conclusion that the concept of liberty [embraces] the right of marital privacy though that right is not mentioned explicitly in the Constitution is supported both by numerous decisions of this Court, referred to in the Court's opinion, and by the language and history of the Ninth Amendment [which] reveal that the Framers of the Constitution believed that there are additional fundamental rights, protected from governmental infringement. . . .

The Ninth Amendment [was] proffered to quiet expressed fears that a bill of specifically enumerated rights could not be sufficiently broad to cover all essential rights and that the specific mention of certain rights would be interpreted as a denial that others were protected. . . .

While this Court has had little occasion to interpret the Ninth Amendment, "[i]t cannot be presumed that any clause in the constitution is intended to be without effect." [To] hold that a right so basic and fundamental and so deep-rooted in our society as the right of privacy in marriage may be infringed because that right is not guaranteed in so many words by the first eight amendments to the Constitution is to ignore the Ninth Amendment and to give it no effect whatsoever. . . .

I do not mean to imply that the Ninth Amendment is applied against the States by the Fourteenth. [Rather,] the Ninth Amendment [simply] lends strong support to the view that the "liberty" protected by the Fifth and Fourteenth Amendments from infringement by the Federal Government or the States is not restricted to rights specifically mentioned in the first eight amendments. . . .

In determining which rights are fundamental, judges are not left at large to decide cases in light of their personal and private notions. Rather, they must look to the "traditions and [collective] conscience of our people" to determine whether a principle is "so rooted [there] . . . as to be ranked as fundamental." The inquiry is whether a right involved "is of such a character that it cannot be denied without violating those 'fundamental principles of liberty and justice which lie at the base of all our civil and political institutions.' . . .'"

The entire fabric of the Constitution and the purposes that clearly underlie its specific guarantees demonstrate that the rights to marital privacy and to marry and raise a family are of similar order and magnitude as the fundamental rights specifically protected.

Although the Constitution does not speak in so many words of the right of privacy in marriage, I cannot believe that it offers these fundamental rights no protection. The fact that no particular provision of the Constitution explicitly forbids the State from disrupting the traditional relation of the family — a relation as old and as fundamental as our entire civilization — surely does not show that the Government was meant to have the power to do so. . . .

The logic of the dissents would sanction federal or state legislation that seems to me even more plainly unconstitutional than the statute before us. Surely the Government, absent a showing of a compelling subordinating state interest, could not decree that all husbands and wives must be sterilized after two children have been born to them. Yet by their reasoning such an invasion of marital privacy would not be subject to constitutional challenge because, while it might be "silly," no provision of the Constitution specifically prevents the Government from curtailing the marital right to bear children and raise a family. . . .

In a long series of cases this Court has held that where fundamental personal liberties are involved, they may not be abridged by the States simply on a showing that a regulatory statute has some rational relationship to the effectuation of a proper state purpose. "Where there is a significant encroachment upon personal liberty, the State may prevail only upon showing a subordinating interest which is compelling." The law must be shown "necessary, and not merely rationally related, to the accomplishment of a permissible state policy."

[The] State, at most, argues that there is some rational relation between this statute and what is admittedly a legitimate subject of state concern — the discouraging of extra-marital relations. It says that preventing the use of birth-control devices by married persons helps prevent the indulgence by some in such extra-marital relations. The rationality of this justification is dubious, particularly in light of the admitted widespread availability to all persons [in] Connecticut, unmarried as well as married, of birth-control devices for the prevention of disease, as distinguished from the prevention of conception. But, in any event, it is clear that the state interest in safeguarding marital fidelity can be served by a more discriminately tailored statute, which does not, like the present one, sweep unnecessarily broadly, reaching far beyond the evil sought to be dealt with and intruding upon the privacy of all married couples. [Connecticut] does have statutes, the constitutionality of which is beyond doubt, which prohibit adultery and fornication. These statutes demonstrate that means for achieving the same basic purpose of protecting marital fidelity are available to Connecticut without the need to "invade the area of protected freedoms." . . .

In sum, I believe that the right of privacy in the marital relation is fundamental and basic — a personal right "retained by the people" within the meaning of the Ninth Amendment. Connecticut cannot constitutionally abridge this fundamental right, which is protected by the Fourteenth Amendment from infringement by the States. . . .

Mr. Justice HARLAN, concurring in the judgment.

[I] fully agree with the judgment of reversal, but [cannot] join the Court's opinion [because it evinces the view that] the Due Process Clause of the Fourteenth Amendment does not touch this Connecticut statute unless the enactment is found to violate some right assured by the letter or penumbra of the Bill of Rights. . . .

In my view, the proper constitutional inquiry in this case is whether this Connecticut statute infringes the Due Process Clause of the Fourteenth Amendment because the enactment violates basic values "implicit in the concept of ordered liberty," [Palko v. Connecticut]. For reasons stated at length in my dissenting opinion in Poe v. Ullman, [367 U. S. 497 (1961)], I believe that it does. While the relevant inquiry may be aided by resort to one or more of the provisions of the Bill of Rights, it is not dependent on them or any of their radiations. The Due Process Clause of the Fourteenth Amendment stands, in my opinion, on its own bottom. . . .

While I could not more heartily agree that judicial "self restraint" is an indispensable ingredient of sound constitutional adjudication, I do submit that the formula suggested [by the dissenters] for achieving it is more hollow than real. "Specific" provisions of the Constitution, no less than "due process," lend themselves as readily to "personal" interpretations by judges whose constitutional outlook is simply to keep the Constitution in supposed "tune with the times.". . .

Judicial self-restraint will not, I suggest, be brought about in the "due process" area by the historically unfounded incorporation formula long advanced by my Brother Black. It will be achieved in this area, as in other constitutional areas, only by continual insistence upon respect for the teachings of history, solid recognition of the basic values that underlie our society, and wise appreciation of the great roles that the doctrines of federalism and separation of powers have played in establishing and preserving American freedoms. *See Adamson v. California*, 332 U. S. 46,   332 U. S. 59 (Mr. Justice Frankfurter, concurring). Adherence to these principles will not, of course, obviate all constitutional differences of opinion among judges, nor should it. Their continued recognition will, however, go farther toward keeping most judges from roaming at large in the constitutional field than will the interpolation into the Constitution of an artificial and largely illusory restriction on the content of the Due Process Clause.

Mr. Justice WHITE, concurring in the judgment.

[This] is not the first time this Court has had occasion to articulate that the liberty entitled to protection under the Fourteenth Amendment includes the right "to marry, establish a home and bring up children," [Meyer v. Nebraska], and "the liberty . . . to direct the upbringing and education of children," [Pierce v. Society of Sisters], and that these are among "the basic civil rights of man." [Skinner.] These decisions affirm that there is a "realm of family life which the state cannot enter" without substantial justification. Surely the right invoked in this case, to be free of regulation of the intimacies of the marriage relationship, "come[s] to this Court with a momentum for respect lacking when appeal is made to liberties which derive merely from shifting economic arrangements." . . .

[The] State claims [that] its anti-use statute [serves its] policy against all forms of promiscuous or illicit sexual relationships, be they premarital or extramarital, concededly a permissible and legitimate legislative goal. [But I] fail to see how the ban on the use of contraceptives by married couples in any way reinforces the State's ban on illicit sexual relationships. [Perhaps] the theory is that the flat ban on use prevents married people from possessing contraceptives and without the ready availability of such devices for use in the marital relationship, there will be no or less temptation to use them in extramarital ones. This reasoning rests on the premise that married people will comply with the ban in regard to their marital relationship, notwithstanding total nonenforcement in this context and apparent nonenforcibility, but will not comply with criminal statutes prohibiting extramarital affairs and the anti-use statute in respect to illicit sexual relationships, a premise whose validity has not been demonstrated and whose intrinsic validity is not very evident. [I] find nothing in this record justifying the sweeping scope of this statute. . . .

Mr. Justice BLACK, with whom Mr. Justice STEWART joins, dissenting. . . .

The Court talks about a constitutional "right of privacy" as though there is some constitutional [provision] forbidding any law ever to be passed which might abridge the "privacy" of individuals. But there is not. There are, of course, guarantees in certain specific constitutional provisions which are designed in part to protect privacy at certain times and places with respect to certain activities. Such, for example, is the Fourth Amendment's guarantee against "unreasonable searches and seizures." But I think it belittles that Amendment to talk about it as though it protects nothing but "privacy." [The] average man would very likely not have his feelings soothed any more by having his property seized openly than by having it seized privately and by stealth. [I] get nowhere in this case by talk about a constitutional "right of privacy" as an emanation from one or more constitutional provisions. I like my privacy as well as the next one, but I am nevertheless compelled to admit that government has a right to invade it unless prohibited by some specific constitutional provision. . . .

I discuss the due process and Ninth Amendment arguments together because on analysis they turn out to be the same thing — merely using different words to claim for this Court and the federal judiciary power to invalidate any legislative act which the judges find irrational, unreasonable or offensive. [If] these formulas based on "natural justice" [are] to prevail, they require judges to determine what is or is not constitutional on the basis of their own appraisal of what laws are unwise or unnecessary. The power to make such decisions is [that] of a legislative body. [No] provision of the Constitution specifically gives such blanket power to courts. . . .

Of the cases on which my Brothers White and Goldberg rely so heavily, undoubtedly the reasoning of two of them supports their result here — as would that of a number of others which they do not bother to name, e.g., [Lochner]. The two they do cite and quote from, [Meyer and Pierce], elaborated the same natural law due process philosophy found in [Lochner]. [That was a] philosophy which many later opinions repudiated, and which I cannot accept. . . .

My Brother Goldberg has adopted the recent discovery that the Ninth Amendment as well as the Due Process Clause can be used by this Court as authority to strike down all state legislation which this Court thinks violates "fundamental principles of liberty and justice," or is contrary to the "traditions and [collective] conscience of our people." He also states [that] in making decisions on this basis judges will not consider "their personal and private notions." One may ask how they can avoid considering them. Our Court certainly has no machinery with which to take a Gallup Poll. And the scientific miracles of this age have not yet produced a gadget which the Court can use to determine what traditions are rooted in the "[collective] conscience of our people." Moreover, one would certainly have to look far beyond the language of the Ninth Amendment to find that the Framers vested in this Court any such awesome veto powers over lawmaking, either by the States or by the Congress. [That] Amendment was passed [to] assure the people that the Constitution in all its provisions was intended to limit the Federal Government to the powers granted expressly or by necessary implication. [This] fact is perhaps responsible for the peculiar phenomenon that for a period of a century and a half no serious suggestion was ever made that the Ninth Amendment [could] be used as a weapon of federal power to prevent state legislatures from passing laws they consider appropriate to govern local affairs. . . .

I realize that many good and able men have eloquently spoken and written [about] the duty of this Court to keep the Constitution in tune with the times. [For] myself, I must with all deference reject that philosophy. The Constitution makers knew the need for change and provided for it. [The] Due Process Clause with an "arbitrary and capricious" or "shocking to the conscience" formula was liberally used by this Court to strike down economic legislation in the early decades of this century, threatening, many people thought, the tranquility and stability of the Nation. That formula, based on subjective considerations of "natural justice," is no less dangerous when used to enforce this Court's views about personal rights than those about economic rights. . .

Mr. Justice STEWART, whom Mr. Justice BLACK joins, dissenting. . . .

I think this is an uncommonly silly law. [But] we are not asked in this case to say whether we think this law is unwise, or even asinine. We are asked to hold that it violates the United States Constitution. And that I cannot do.

In the course of its opinion the Court refers to no less than six Amendments to the Constitution: the First, the Third, the Fourth, the Fifth, the Ninth, and the Fourteenth. But the Court does not say which of these Amendments, if any, it thinks is infringed by this Connecticut law.

We are told that the Due Process Clause of the Fourteenth Amendment is not, as such, the "guide" in this case. With that much I agree.

As to the First, Third, Fourth, and Fifth Amendments, I can find nothing in any of them to invalidate this Connecticut law. [And to] say that the Ninth Amendment has anything to do with this case is to turn somersaults with history. The Ninth Amendment, like its companion the Tenth, [was adopted] to make clear that the adoption of the Bill of Rights did not alter the plan that the Federal Government was to be a government of express and limited powers. . . .

What provision of the Constitution, then, does make this state law invalid? The Court says it is the right of privacy "created by several fundamental constitutional guarantees." With all deference, I can find no such general right of privacy in the Bill of Rights, in any other part of the Constitution, or in any case ever before decided by this Court.

Comments on *Griswold*. True or false: The Court in *Griswold* agreed that the Constitution guarantees a fundamental right of privacy, but could not agree on exactly where the Constitution did so guarantee. Does this in itself describe the dilemma of Court-created rights? What was the source of the right to the *Griswold* majority?

Penumbras? Ninth Amendment? Fourteenth Amendment? Does this make a difference? Was the *Griswold* Court attempting to distinguish the decision from *Lochner*? Can *Griswold* be distinguished from *Lochner*?

What of the Ninth Amendment argument? Is it a "clause-bound" argument for a "living" non-interpretivist Constitution? How does Justice Black, the strict constructionist, counter this argument? Is he successful? Note the comments of John Ely, cited earlier:

> The received account of the Ninth Amendment, [offered by Justice Black in Griswold, goes] like this. There was fear that the inclusion of a bill of rights [would] be taken to imply that federal power was [not] limited to the authorities enumerated in Article I, Section 8, [but] extended all the way up to the edge of the rights stated in the first eight amendments. [The] Ninth Amendment, the received version goes, was attached to the Bill of Rights [to] negate that inference. [But the] Tenth Amendment, submitted and ratified at the same time, completely fulfills [that] function. [Moreover, the legislative history of the Ninth Amendment is consistent with Justice Goldberg's view, and] the conclusion that the Ninth Amendment was intended to signal the existence of federal constitutional rights beyond those specifically enumerated in the Constitution is the only conclusion its language seems comfortably able to support. [J. Ely, *Democracy and Distrust* 34-38 (1980).]

Even if the framers intended the Court to be the "actor" to create rights, do you think we will ever see the Court apply the view expressed by Justice Goldberg?   Why or why not?

Harlan's dissent in *Poe v. Ullman*. This Justice Harlan was the grandson of the Justice Harlan whose dissent in *Plessy v. Ferguson* [Chapter 4 section IV.C] was noteworthy for its depiction of racial mores of his time and the changes that were to come. Consider whether the grandson's (Justice Harlan II) dissent in *Poe v. Ullman* [Chapter 1 section I.C] is as prophetic as the grandfather's on the doctrine of substantive Due Process:

> [I] believe that a statute making it a criminal offense for married couples to use contraceptives is an intolerable and unjustifiable invasion of privacy in the conduct of the most intimate concerns of an individual's personal life. [Since this contention draws its] basis from no explicit language of the Constitution, [I] feel it desirable [to] state the framework of Constitutional principles in which I think the issue must be judged. [Because] it is the Constitution alone which warrants judicial interference in sovereign operations of the State, the basis of judgment as to the Constitutionality of state action must be a rational one, approaching the text [not] in a literalistic way, as if we had a tax statute before us, but as the basic charter of our society, setting out in spare but meaningful terms the principles of government. . . .
>
> It is but a truism to say that [the Due Process Clause] is not self-explanatory. [It] is important to note, however, that two views of the [Fourteenth] Amendment have not been accepted. . . . One view [sought] to limit the provision to a guarantee of procedural fairness. [The] other [would] have it that the Fourteenth Amendment, whether by way of the Privileges and Immunities Clause or the Due Process Clause, applied against the States only and precisely those restraints which [are embodied in the Bill of Rights]. However, "due process" in the consistent view of this Court has ever been a broader concept than the first view and more flexible than the second. . . .
>
> [It] is not the particular enumeration of rights in the first eight Amendments which spells out the reach of Fourteenth Amendment due process, but rather, as was suggested in another context long before the adoption of that Amendment, those concepts which

are considered to embrace those rights "which are . . . fundamental; which belong . . . to the citizens of all free governments," [Corfield v. Coryell], for "the purposes [of securing] which men enter into society," [Calder v. Bull]. . . .

Due process has not been reduced to any formula; its content cannot be determined by reference to any code. The best that can be said is that through the course of this Court's decisions it has represented the balance which our Nation, built upon postulates of respect for the liberty of the individual, has struck between that liberty and the demands of organized society. If the supplying of content to this Constitutional concept has of necessity been a rational process, it certainly has not been one where judges have felt free to roam where unguided speculation might take them. The balance of which I speak is the balance struck by this country, having regard to what history teaches are the traditions from which it developed as well as the traditions from which it broke. That tradition is a living thing. . . .

[The] liberty guaranteed by the Due Process Clause [is] not a series of isolated points [represented by the Bill of Rights]. It is a rational continuum which, broadly speaking, includes a freedom from all substantial arbitrary impositions and purposeless restraints, [citing, e.g., Allgeyer v. Louisiana, Skinner v. Oklahoma], and which also recognizes, what a reasonable and sensitive judgment must, that certain interests require particularly careful scrutiny of the state needs asserted to justify their abridgment. . . .

The State [asserts] that it is acting to protect the moral welfare of its citizenry. [Society] has traditionally concerned itself with the moral soundness of its people. [Certainly,] Connecticut's judgment [here] is no more demonstrably correct or incorrect than are the varieties of judgment, expressed in law, on marriage and divorce, on adult consensual homosexuality, abortion, and sterilization, or euthanasia and suicide. If we had a case before us which required us to decide simply, and in abstraction, whether the moral judgment implicit in the [present statute] was a sound one, the very controversial nature of these questions would, I think, require us to hesitate long before concluding that the Constitution precluded Connecticut from choosing as it has. . . .

But, as might be expected, we are not presented simply with this moral judgment to be passed on as an abstract proposition. The secular state [must] operate in the realm of behavior, [and] where it does so operate, not only the underlying, moral purpose of its operations, but also the choice of means becomes relevant to any Constitutional judgment on what is done. . . .

Precisely what is involved here is this: the State is asserting the right to enforce its moral judgment by intruding upon the most intimate details of the marital relation with the full power of the criminal law. Potentially, this could allow the deployment of all the incidental machinery of the criminal law, arrests, searches and seizures; inevitably, it must mean at the very least the lodging of criminal charges, a public trial, and testimony as the corpus delicti. [The] statute allows the State to enquire into, prove and punish married people for the private use of their marital intimacy.

[This] enactment involves what, by common understanding throughout the English-speaking world, must be granted to be a most fundamental aspect of "liberty," the privacy of the home in its most basic sense, and it is this which requires that the statute be subjected to "strict scrutiny." [Skinner v. Oklahoma.]

That aspect of liberty which embraces the concept of the privacy of the home receives explicit Constitutional protection at two places only. These are the Third [and Fourth Amendments]. . . .

It is clear, of course, that this Connecticut statute does not invade the privacy of the home in the usual sense, since the invasion involved here may [be] accomplished without any physical intrusion [into] the home. [But it] would surely be an extreme instance of sacrificing substance to form were it to be held that the Constitutional principle of privacy against arbitrary official intrusion comprehends only physical invasions by the police. [If] the physical curtilage of the home is protected, it is surely as a result of solicitude to protect the privacies of the life within. Certainly the safeguarding of the home does not follow merely from the sanctity of property rights. The home derives its pre-eminence as the seat of family life. [Of the] whole "private realm of family life" it is difficult to imagine what is more private or more intimate than a husband and wife's marital relations. . . .

Of course, [there] are countervailing considerations. "[T]he family . . . is not beyond regulation," and it would be an absurdity to suggest either that offenses may not be committed in the bosom of the family or that the home can be made a sanctuary for crime. The right of privacy [is] not an absolute. Thus, I would not suggest that adultery, homosexuality, fornication and incest are immune from criminal enquiry, however privately practiced. [But] not to discriminate between what is involved in this case and either the traditional offenses against good morals or crimes which, though they may be committed anywhere, happen to have been committed or concealed in the home, would entirely misconceive the argument that is being made.

[The] intimacy of husband and wife is necessarily an essential and accepted feature of the institution of marriage, an institution which the State not only must allow, but which always and in every age it has fostered and protected. It is one thing when the State exerts its power either to forbid extra-marital sexuality altogether, or to say who may marry, but it is quite another when, having acknowledged a marriage and the intimacies inherent in it, it undertakes to regulate by means of the criminal law the details of that intimacy. . . .

[Since,] as it appears to me, the statute marks an abridgment of important fundamental liberties protected by the Fourteenth Amendment, it will not do to urge [that it] is rationally related to the effectuation of a proper state purpose. A closer scrutiny and stronger justification than that are required.

[Though] the State has argued the Constitutional permissibility of the moral judgment underlying this statute, [it does not] even remotely [suggest] a justification for the obnoxiously intrusive means it has chosen to effectuate that policy. To me the very circumstance that Connecticut has not chosen to press the enforcement of this statute against individual users [conduces] to the inference either that it does not consider the policy of the statute a very important one, or that it does not regard the means it has chosen for its effectuation as appropriate or necessary. But conclusive, in my view, is the utter novelty of this enactment. Although the Federal Government and many States have at one time or other had on their books statutes forbidding or regulating the distribution of contraceptives, none, so far as I can find, has made the use of contraceptives a crime. . . .

2. ABORTION

ROE v. WADE
410 U.S. 113 (1973)

Mr. Justice BLACKMUN delivered the opinion of the Court.

This [appeal presents] constitutional challenges to state criminal abortion legislation. The Texas statutes under attack here [make procuring an abortion a crime except "by medical advice for the purpose of saving the life of the mother." These statutes] are typical of those that have been in effect in many States for approximately a century. . . .

We forthwith acknowledge our awareness of the sensitive and emotional nature of the abortion controversy, of the vigorous opposing views, even among physicians, and of the deep and seemingly absolute convictions that the subject inspires. . . .

Our task, of course, is to resolve the issue by constitutional measurement, free of emotion and of predilection. We seek earnestly to do this, and, because we do, we have inquired into, and in this opinion place some emphasis upon, medical and medical-legal history and what that history reveals about man's attitudes toward the abortion procedure over the centuries. . . .

[The] restrictive criminal abortion laws in effect in a majority of States today are of relatively recent vintage.

[They] derive from statutory changes effected, for the most part, in the latter half of the 19th century.

[Abortion] was practiced in Greek times as well as in the Roman Era. [Most] Greek thinkers [commended] abortion, at least prior to viability. [At] common law, abortion performed before "quickening" — the first recognizable movement of the fetus in utero, appearing usually from the 16th to the 18th week of pregnancy — was not an indictable offense. [It] was not until [the] middle and late 19th century [that] the quickening distinction [was abandoned] and the degree of the offense [increased]. [Thus,] at common law, at the time of the adoption of our Constitution, and throughout the major portion of the 19th century, [a] woman enjoyed a substantially broader right to terminate a pregnancy than she does in most States today. . . .

Three reasons have been advanced to explain historically the enactment of criminal abortion laws in the 19th century and to justify their continued existence. It has been argued occasionally that these laws were [designed] to discourage illicit sexual conduct. Texas, however, does not advance this justification in the present case. . . .

A second reason is concerned with abortion as a medical procedure. When most criminal abortion laws were first enacted, the procedure was [hazardous]. [Thus,] it has been argued that a State's real concern in enacting a criminal abortion law was to protect the pregnant woman. [Modern] medical techniques have altered this situation. [Mortality] rates for women undergoing early abortions [appear] to be as low as or lower than the rates for normal childbirth. [Of] course, important state interests in the areas of health and medical standards do remain. The State has a legitimate interest in seeing to it that abortion, like any other medical procedure, is performed under circumstances that insure maximum safety for the patient [and] the State retains a definite interest in protecting the woman's own health and safety when an abortion is proposed at a late stage of pregnancy.

The third reason is the State's interest [in] protecting prenatal life. Some of the argument for this justification rests on the theory that a new human life is present from the moment of conception. [But in] assessing the State's interest, recognition may [also] be given to the less rigid claim that [at] least potential life is involved. . . .

The Constitution does not explicitly mention any right of privacy. [But] the Court has recognized that a right of personal privacy, or a guarantee of certain areas or zones of privacy, does exist under the Constitution. In varying contexts, the Court or individual Justices have, indeed, found at least the roots of that right in the First Amendment, Stanley v. Georgia; in the Fourth and Fifth Amendments; in the penumbras of the Bill of Rights, [Griswold]; in the Ninth Amendment, id., (Goldberg, J., concurring); or in the concept of liberty guaranteed by the first section of the Fourteenth Amendment, see Meyer v. Nebraska. These decisions make it clear that only personal rights that can be deemed "fundamental" or "implicit in the concept of ordered liberty," are included in this guarantee of personal privacy. They also make it clear that the right has some extension to activities relating to marriage, Loving v. Virginia; procreation, [Skinner]; contraception, [Eisenstadt]; family relationships, Prince v. Massachusetts, 321 U.S. 158 (1944); and child rearing and education, [Pierce; Meyer].

This right of privacy, whether it be founded in the Fourteenth Amendment's concept of personal liberty [as] we feel it is, or [in] the Ninth [Amendment], is broad enough to encompass a woman's decision whether or not to terminate her pregnancy. The detriment that the State would impose upon the pregnant woman by denying this choice altogether is apparent. Specific and direct harm medically diagnosable even in early pregnancy may be involved. Maternity, or additional offspring, may force upon the woman a distressful life and future. Psychological harm may be imminent. Mental and physical health may be taxed by child care. There is also the distress, for all concerned, associated with the unwanted child, and there is the problem of bringing a child into a family already unable, psychologically and otherwise, to care for it. In other cases, [the] additional difficulties and continuing stigma of unwed motherhood may be involved. All these are factors the woman and her responsible physician necessarily will consider in consultation. On the basis of elements such as these, appellant [argues] that the woman's right is absolute and that she is entitled to terminate her pregnancy at whatever time, in whatever way, and for whatever reason she alone chooses. With this we do not agree. [The] Court's decisions recognizing a right of privacy also acknowledge that some state regulation in areas protected by that right is appropriate. . . .

Where certain "fundamental rights" are involved, the Court has held that regulation limiting these rights may be justified only by a "compelling state interest," and that legislative enactments must be narrowly drawn to express only the legitimate state interests at stake. . . .

The appellee [argues] that the fetus is a "person" within the language and meaning of the Fourteenth Amendment. [If] this suggestion of personhood is established, the appellant's case, of course, collapses, for the fetus' right to life would then be guaranteed specifically by the Amendment. . . .

The Constitution does not define "person" in so many words. Section 1 of the Fourteenth Amendment contains three references to "person." ["Person"] is used in other places in the Constitution: in the listing of qualifications for Representatives and Senators, Art. I, §2, cl. 2, and §3, cl. 3; in the Apportionment Clause, Art. I, §2, cl. 3; 53 in the Migration and Importation provision, Art. I, §9, cl. 1; in the Emolument Clause, Art. I, §9, cl. 8; in the Electors provisions, Art. II, §1, cl. 2, and the superseded cl. 3; in the provision outlining qualifications for the office of President, Art. II, §1, cl. 5; in the Extradition provisions, Art. IV, §2, cl. 2, and the superseded Fugitive Slave Clause 3; and in the Fifth, Twelfth, and Twenty-second Amendments, as well as in §§2 and 3 of the Fourteenth Amendment. But in nearly all these instances, the use of the word is such that it has application only post-natally. None indicates, with any assurance, that it has any possible pre-natal application.

All this, together with our observation that throughout the major portion of the 19th century prevailing legal abortion practices were far freer than they are today, persuades us that the word "person," as used in the Fourteenth Amendment, does not include the unborn. [Thus,] we pass on to other considerations.

The pregnant woman cannot be isolated in her privacy. She carries an embryo and, later, a fetus. [The] situation therefore is inherently different from marital intimacy, or bedroom possession of obscene material, or marriage, or procreation, or education, with which Eisenstadt and Griswold, Stanley, Loving, Skinner, and Pierce and Meyer were respectively concerned. [It] is reasonable and appropriate for a State to decide that at some point in time another interest, that of health of the mother or that of potential human life, becomes significantly involved.

Texas urges that, apart from the Fourteenth Amendment, life begins at conception and is present throughout pregnancy, and that, therefore, the State has a compelling interest in protecting that life from and after conception. We need not resolve the difficult question of when life begins. When those trained [in] medicine, philosophy, and theology are unable to arrive at any consensus, the judiciary, at this point in the development of man's knowledge, is not in a position to speculate as to the answer.

It should be sufficient to note briefly the wide divergence of thinking on [this] question. There has always been strong support for the view that life does not begin until live birth.   This was the belief of the Stoics. It appears to be the predominant, though not the unanimous, attitude of the Jewish faith. It may be taken to represent also the position of a large segment of the Protestant community. [The] common law found greater significance in quickening. Physicians and their scientific colleagues have [tended] to focus either upon conception, upon live birth, or upon the interim point at which the fetus becomes "viable," that is, potentially able to live outside the mother's womb, albeit with artificial aid. Viability is usually placed at about seven months (28 weeks) but may occur earlier, even at 24 weeks. [The Catholic church recognizes] the existence of life from the moment of conception. . . .

In areas other than criminal abortion [such as torts and inheritance], the law has been reluctant to endorse any theory that life, as we recognize it, begins before live birth or to accord legal rights to the unborn except in narrowly defined situations and except when the rights are contingent upon live birth. . . .

In view of all this, we do not agree that, by adopting one theory of life, Texas may override the rights of the pregnant woman that are at stake. We repeat, however, that the State does have an important and legitimate interest in preserving and protecting the health of the pregnant woman [and] that it has still another important and legitimate interest in protecting the potentiality of Human life. These interests are separate and distinct. Each grows in substantiality as the woman approaches term and, at a point during pregnancy, each becomes "compelling."

With respect to [the] interest in the health of the mother, the "compelling" point, in the light of present medical knowledge, is at approximately the end of the first trimester. This is so because of the now-established medical fact [that] until the end of the first trimester mortality in abortion may be less than mortality in normal childbirth. It follows that, from and after this point, a State may regulate the abortion procedure to the extent that the regulation reasonably relates to the preservation and protection of maternal health. Examples of permissible state regulation in this area are requirements as to the qualifications of the person who is to perform the abortion; [as] to the facility in which the procedure is to be performed; [and] the like.

This means, on the other hand, that, for the period of pregnancy prior to this "compelling" point, the attending physician, in consultation with his patient, is free to determine, without regulation by the State, that, in his medical judgment, the patient's pregnancy should be terminated. If that decision is reached, the judgment may be effectuated by an abortion free of interference by the State.

With respect to [the] interest in potential life, the "compelling" point is at viability. This is so because the fetus then presumably has the capability of meaningful life outside the mother's womb. State regulation protective of fetal life after viability thus has both logical and biological justifications. If the State is interested in protecting fetal life during that period, it may go so far as to proscribe abortion during that period, except when it is necessary to preserve the life or health of the mother.

Measured against these standards, [the Texas statute] sweeps too broadly [and] therefore, cannot survive the constitutional attack made upon it here. . . .

To summarize and to repeat: . . .

(a) For the stage prior to approximately the end of the first trimester, the abortion decision and its effectuation must be left to the medical judgment of the pregnant woman's attending physician.

(b) For the stage subsequent to approximately the end of the first trimester, the State, in promoting its interest in the health of the mother, may, if it chooses, regulate the abortion procedure in ways that are reasonably related to maternal health.

(c) For the stage subsequent to viability, the State in promoting its interest in the potentiality of human life may, if it chooses, regulate, and even proscribe, abortion except where it is necessary, in appropriate medical judgment, for the preservation of the life or health of the mother. . . .

This holding, we feel, is consistent with the relative weights of the respective interests involved, with the lessons and examples of medical and legal history, with the lenity of the common law, and with the demands of the profound problems of the present day. . . .

Mr. Justice STEWART, concurring.

In 1963, this Court, in Ferguson v. Skrupa, purported to sound the death knell for the doctrine of substantive due process. [Barely] two years later, in [Griswold], the Court held a Connecticut birth control law unconstitutional. In view of what had been so recently said in Skrupa, the Court's opinion in Griswold understandably did its best to avoid reliance on the Due Process Clause of the Fourteenth Amendment as the ground for decision. [But] it was clear to me then, and it is equally clear to me now, that the Griswold decision can be rationally understood only as a holding that the Connecticut statute substantively invaded the "liberty" that is protected by the Due Process Clause of the Fourteenth Amendment. As so understood, Griswold stands as one in a long line of pre-Skrupa cases decided under the doctrine of substantive due process, and I now accept it as such.

[The] Constitution nowhere mentions a specific right of personal choice in matters of marriage and family life, but the "liberty" protected by the Due Process Clause of the Fourteenth Amendment covers more than those freedoms explicitly named in the Bill of Rights. [In Eisenstadt], we recognized "the right of the individual, married or single, to be free from unwarranted governmental intrusion into matters so fundamentally affecting a person as the decision whether to bear or beget a child." That right necessarily includes the right of a woman to decide whether or not to terminate her pregnancy. . . .

It is evident that the Texas abortion statute infringes that right directly. [The] question then becomes whether the state interests advanced to justify this abridgment can survive the "particularly careful scrutiny" that the Fourteenth Amendment here requires.

The asserted state interests are protection of the health and safety of the pregnant woman, and protection of the potential future human life within her. These are legitimate objectives, [but as] the Court today has thoroughly demonstrated, [these] state interests cannot constitutionally support the broad abridgment of personal liberty worked by the existing Texas law. . . .

Mr. Justice DOUGLAS, concurring.

[The] Ninth Amendment [does] not create federally enforceable rights. [But] a catalogue of [the rights "retained by the people"] includes customary, traditional, and time-honored rights, amenities, privileges, and immunities that come within the sweep of "the Blessings of Liberty" mentioned in the preamble to the Constitution. Many of them, in my view, come within the meaning of the term "liberty" as used in the Fourteenth Amendment. First is the autonomous control over the development and expression of one's intellect, interests, tastes, and personality.   Second is freedom of choice in the basic decisions of one's life respecting marriage, divorce, procreation, contraception, and the education and upbringing of children.   Third is the freedom to care for one's health and person, freedom from bodily restraint or compulsion, freedom to walk, stroll, or loaf.

These rights, though fundamental, are likewise subject to regulation on a showing of "compelling state interest." . . .

[While] childbirth endangers the lives of some women, voluntary abortion at any time and place regardless of medical standards would impinge on a rightful concern of society. The woman's health is part of that concern; as is the life of the fetus after quickening. These concerns justify the State in treating the procedure as a medical one. . . .

Mr. Justice WHITE, with whom Mr. Justice REHNQUIST joins, dissenting.

[I] find nothing in the language or history of the Constitution to support the Court's judgment. The Court simply fashions and announces a new constitutional right for pregnant mothers and, with scarcely any reason or authority for its action, invests that right with sufficient substance to override most existing state abortion statutes. The upshot is that the people and the legislatures of the 50 States are constitutionally disentitled to weigh the relative importance of the continued existence and development of the fetus, on the one hand, against a spectrum of possible impacts on the mother, on the other hand. As an exercise of raw judicial power, the Court perhaps has authority to do what it does today; but in my view its judgment is an improvident and extravagant exercise of the power of judicial review that the Constitution extends to this Court. . . .

Mr. Justice REHNQUIST, dissenting. . . .

I have difficulty in concluding [that] the right of "privacy" is involved in this case. Texas [bars] the performance of a medical abortion by a licensed physician on a plaintiff such as Roe. A transaction resulting in an operation such as this is not "private" in the ordinary usage of that word. Nor is the "privacy" that the Court finds here even a distant relative of the freedom from searches and seizures protected by the Fourth Amendment. . .
.

If the Court means by the term "privacy" no more than that the claim of a person to be free from unwanted state regulation of consensual transactions may be a form of "liberty" protected by the Fourteenth Amendment, there is no doubt that similar claims have been upheld in our earlier decisions on the basis of that liberty. [The] test traditionally applied in the area of social and economic legislation is whether or not a law such as that challenged has a rational relation to a valid state objective. The Due Process Clause of the Fourteenth Amendment undoubtedly does place a limit, albeit a broad one, on legislative power to enact laws such as this. If the Texas statute were to prohibit an abortion even where the mother's life is in jeopardy, I have little doubt that such a statute would lack a rational relation to a valid state objective. But the Court's sweeping invalidation of any restrictions on abortion during the first trimester is impossible to justify under that standard, and the conscious weighing of competing factors that the Court's opinion apparently substitutes for the established test is far more appropriate to a legislative judgment than to a judicial one. While the Court's opinion quotes from the dissent of Mr. Justice Holmes in [Lochner], the result it reaches is more closely attuned to the majority opinion of Mr. Justice Peckham in that case.

The fact that a majority of the States reflecting, after all, the majority sentiment in those States, have had restrictions on abortions for at least a century is a strong indication, it seems to me, that the asserted right to an abortion is not "so rooted in the traditions and conscience of our people as to be ranked as fundamental." Even today, when society's views on abortion are changing, the very existence of the debate is evidence that the "right" to an abortion is not so universally accepted as the appellant would have us believe.

To reach its result, the Court necessarily has had to find within the scope of the Fourteenth Amendment a right that was apparently completely unknown to the drafters of the Amendment. [By] the time of the adoption of the Fourteenth Amendment in 1868, there were at least 36 laws enacted by state or territorial legislatures limiting abortion. [The] only conclusion possible from this history is that the drafters did not intend to have the Fourteenth Amendment withdraw from the States the power to legislate with respect to this matter. . . .

––––––––––

Comments on *Roe*. As we will learn below, *Roe v. Wade* was overruled in 2022 by the Court in *Dobbs v. Jackson Women's Health Organization* 597 U.S. ____(2022). However, understanding *Roe* is still crucial to understanding the reasoning in *Dobbs,* and the rationale behind other associated rights falling under substantive due process. What is the constitutional source of the right of privacy in *Roe*? Is the source of the right finally resolved? Is this for better or for worse? Have we returned to the *Lochner* era, or is *Roe* distinguishable from *Lochner*? Can privacy rights be distinguished from economic rights? Recall our discussion concerning *Griswold* and "socio-economics."

Jon Ely, a constitutional law scholar cited by the majority opinion in *Dobbs*, argued in "The Wages of Crying Wolf: A Comment on *Roe v. Wade*," 82 Yale L.J. 920 (1973), that *Griswold* was distinguishable from *Lochner* and defensible because "government snooping in our bedrooms" related to and was inferred from definable constitutional norms. Yet he asserted that *Roe* was not distinguishable because "abortion [was] not an inferable constitutional norm." To him, though *Roe* could not be distinguished from *Lochner* like judicial abuse, *Griswold* could be, thus, room for a right of privacy but not abortion. Thomas Grey argued to the contrary, using the "four corners" of a "living" Constitution to protect such private choices and limit the government from interfering with our lives in this regard. What do you think?

Trimesters and Compelling Purpose. Justice Blackman based much of his majority opinion in *Roe* on the inherent privacy of the doctor-patient relationship. Though he shunned "viability" as decisional, he could not avoid the trimesters of pregnancy as they related to the state's purpose in regulation. Thus, the later the term of the pregnancy the greater the state's interest in regulation.

This aspect of *Roe* is particularly relevant to the Court's current application of the "compelling purpose" test. Recall Justice Stone's footnote in *Carolene Products*, where he asserted a need for stricter judicial scrutiny in areas concerning race and fundamental rights than afforded by the post-*Lochner* "rational purpose test." Under strict scrutiny as applied in *Roe,* the Court will apply strict scrutiny and require the state to prove a compelling purpose when a fundamental right is involved. This has proven to be a very difficult, often impossible, burden of proof for a state to sustain.

Yet, *Roe* also stood for the premise that even where there is a fundamental right (privacy), states may still regulate if they can prove a compelling purpose. So, for example, even early "in term," health concerns advanced by the state could be held compelling. The Court's current application of the compelling purpose test, much of which rests ahead in our study of equal protection, is similar to the analysis applied by the Court in *Roe.*

3. THE NATURE OF THE RIGHT

Was there a difference between a fundamental right to have an abortion and a fundamental right to make a "personal choice" to have an abortion? This became an issue of significance in shaping the nature of the right articulated in *Roe*, particularly in regard to governmental funding. Framed another way, does it make a difference whether an indigent woman has a right to an abortion if she cannot afford to have one? And to add to that consideration is the question of whether the state or federal governments can deny the right if neither will fund the right through health care programs. *Maher v. Roe*, 432 U.S. 464 (1977), and *Harris v. McRae*, 448 U.S. 297 (1980), addressed this issue with regard to state and federal healthcare funding for the procedure.

In both cases state and federal funding was legislatively withheld from the abortion procedure under programs designed to assist the needy. *Maher* involved a prohibition of state administered Medicaid funding for nontherapeutic (not medically necessary) abortions, and *Harris* involved legislation known as the Hyde Amendment, which was a Congressional prohibition of federal Medicaid funding for abortions, whether or not medically necessary (though funding would be allowed where necessary to save the life of the mother or in cases of rape or incest). The majority in both opinions found government withholding of funding for the abortion procedure to be constitutional and the reasoning in both cases are largely similar. Both cases addressed a distinction between a right to choose to have an abortion and a right to have the government to fund that choice. Both decisions said no to the latter, while acknowledging that for women unable to pay for an abortion would normally mean that they would not be able to exercise that right. Justice Stewart put it this way:

> Although the liberty protected by the Due Process Clause affords protection against unwarranted government interference with freedom of choice in the context of certain personal decisions, it does not confer an entitlement to such funds as may be necessary to realize all the advantages of that freedom. To hold otherwise would mark a drastic change in our understanding of the Constitution. It cannot be that, because government may not prohibit the use of contraceptives, Griswold v. Connecticut, 381 U. S. 479, or prevent parents from sending their child to a private school, Pierce v. Society of Sisters, 268 U. S. 510, government therefore has an affirmative constitutional obligation to ensure that all persons have the financial resources to obtain contraceptives or send their children to private schools. [Nothing] in the Due Process Clause supports such an extraordinary result. Whether freedom of choice that is constitutionally protected warrants federal subsidization is a question for Congress to answer, not a matter of constitutional entitlement.

The beginning of the end. The path to overruling *Roe v. Wade* had its beginning during the interim period between the decision and the decision that follows next. Beginning with the funding cases just discussed, and continuing with decisions such as *Webster v. Reproductive Health Services*, 492 U.S. 490 (1989), it became apparent that the core holding in regarding a woman's right to choose was not infallible as long as the Court sanctioned small practical encroachments on that right, not to mention a close call in the *Webster* case where a plurality of the Court even called for an overrule of *Roe*. Only Justice O'Conner's vote (a concurrence finding, "the plurality has proceeded in a manner unnecessary to deciding the question at hand [an overrule])" saved an overrule. It seemed that only one additional vote would bring such to fruition.

Beyond these doctrinal debates, the politics of abortion also festered throughout our society. Most significant have been the attempts by state legislatures to use their power to regulate health and safety to "so burden" the right as to in effect deny it. This has led to a clash between state legislatures and the rights guaranteed by *Roe*. State attempts to require consent of husbands and parents of minor children; to limit the right as against viability; and to counsel against abortion have required the Court to determine whether these regulations so burdened the right as to be unconstitutional. Confirmations of Justices by the Senate seemed to become a pro-choice or anti-abortion "litmus test." The politics of *Roe* also took to the streets in the form of protects by both sides. All of these issues seemed to surface in what has become the seminal case dealing with abortion in the modern era, *Planned Parenthood v. Casey*.

PLANNED PARENTHOOD OF SOUTHEASTERN PENNSYLVANIA v. CASEY
505 U.S. 833 (1992)

Justice O'CONNOR, Justice KENNEDY, and Justice SOUTER announced the judgment of the Court and delivered the opinion of the Court with respect to Parts I, II, III, V-A, V-C, and VI, an opinion with respect to Part V-E, in which Justice STEVENS joins, and an opinion with respect to Parts IV, V-B, and V-D.

I

Liberty finds no refuge in a jurisprudence of doubt. Yet 19 years after our holding that the Constitution protects a woman's right to terminate her pregnancy in its early stages, that definition of liberty is still questioned. Joining the respondents as amicus curiae, the United States, as it has done in five other cases in the last decade, again asks us to overrule Roe.

At issue in these cases are five provisions of the Pennsylvania Abortion Control Act of 1982 as amended in 1988 and 1989. [The] Act requires that a woman seeking an abortion give her informed consent prior to the abortion procedure, and specifies that she be provided with certain information at least 24 hours before the abortion is performed. For a minor to obtain an abortion, the Act requires the informed consent of one of her parents, but provides for a judicial bypass option if the minor does not wish to or cannot obtain a parent's consent. Another provision of the Act requires that, unless certain exceptions apply, a married woman seeking an abortion must sign a statement indicating that she has notified her husband of her intended abortion. The Act exempts compliance with these three requirements in the event of a "medical emergency." [In] addition to the above provisions regulating the performance of abortions, the Act imposes certain reporting requirements on facilities that provide abortion services.

[After] considering the fundamental constitutional questions resolved by Roe, principles of institutional integrity, and the rule of stare decisis, we are led to conclude this: the essential holding of Roe v. Wade should be retained and once again reaffirmed.

It must be stated at the outset and with clarity that Roe's essential holding, the holding we reaffirm, has three parts. First is a recognition of the right of the woman to choose to have an abortion before viability and to obtain it without undue interference from the State. Before viability, the State's interests are not strong enough to support a prohibition of abortion or the imposition of a substantial obstacle to the woman's effective right to elect the procedure. Second is a confirmation of the State's power to restrict abortions after fetal viability, if the law contains exceptions for pregnancies which endanger a woman's life or health. And third is the principle that the State has legitimate interests from the outset of the pregnancy in protecting the health of the woman and the life of the fetus that may become a child.

II

Constitutional protection of the woman's decision to terminate her pregnancy derives from the Due Process Clause of the Fourteenth Amendment. [A]lthough a literal reading of the Clause might suggest that it governs only the procedures by which a State may deprive persons of liberty, for at least 105 years, [t]he Clause has been understood to contain a substantive component as well.

[I]t is also tempting [t]o suppose that the Due Process Clause protects only those practices, defined at the most specific level, that were protected against government interference by other rules of law when the Fourteenth Amendment was ratified. See Michael H. v. Gerald D., 491 U.S. 110, 127-128, n.6 (1989) (opinion of Scalia, J.). But such a view would be inconsistent with our law. It is a promise of the Constitution that there is a realm of personal liberty which the government may not enter. We have vindicated this principle before. Marriage is mentioned nowhere in the Bill of Rights and interracial marriage was illegal in most States in the 19th century, but the Court was no doubt correct in finding it to be an aspect of liberty protected against state interference by the substantive component of the Due Process Clause in Loving v. Virginia. [N]either the Bill of Rights nor the specific practices of States at the time of the adoption of the Fourteenth Amendment marks the outer limits of the substantive sphere of liberty which the Fourteenth Amendment protects. See U.S. Const., Amend. 9.

[Abortion] is a unique act. It is an act fraught with consequences for others: for the woman who must live with the implications of her decision; for the persons who perform and assist in the procedure; for the spouse, family, and society which must confront the knowledge that these procedures exist, procedures some deem nothing short of an act of violence against innocent human life; and, depending on one's beliefs, for the life or potential life that is aborted. [The] mother who carries a child to full term is subject to anxieties, to physical constraints, to pain that only she must bear. That these sacrifices have from the beginning of the human race been endured by woman with a pride that ennobles her in the eyes of others and gives to the infant a bond of love cannot alone be grounds for the State to insist she make the sacrifice. Her suffering is too intimate and personal for the State to insist, without more, upon its own vision of the woman's role, however dominant that vision has been in the course of our history and our culture. The destiny of the woman must be shaped to a large extent on her own conception of her spiritual imperatives and her place in society. It should be recognized, moreover, that in some critical respects the abortion decision is of the same character as the decision to use contraception, to which Griswold v. Connecticut, Eisenstadt v. Baird, and Carey v. Population Services International, afford constitutional protection. We have no doubt as to the correctness of those decisions. They support the reasoning in Roe relating to the woman's liberty because they involve personal decisions concerning not only the meaning of procreation but also human responsibility and respect for it.

[W]hile we appreciate the weight of the arguments made on behalf of the State in the case before us, arguments which in their ultimate formulation conclude that Roe should be overruled, the reservations any of us may have in reaffirming the central holding of Roe are outweighed by the explication of individual liberty we have given combined with the force of stare decisis. We turn now to that doctrine.

III

A

[In] this case we may inquire whether Roe's central rule has been found unworkable; whether the rule's limitation on state power could be removed without serious inequity to those who have relied upon it or significant damage to the stability of the society governed by the rule in question; whether the law's growth in the intervening years has left Roe's central rule a doctrinal anachronism discounted by society; and whether Roe's premises of fact have so far changed in the ensuing two decades as to render its central holding somehow irrelevant or unjustifiable in dealing with the issue it addressed.

1

Although Roe has engendered opposition, it has in no sense proven "unworkable," see Garcia v. San Antonio Metropolitan Transit Authority, 469 U.S. 528, 546 (1985), representing as it does a simple limitation beyond which a state law is unenforceable. While Roe has, of course, required judicial assessment of state laws affecting the exercise of the choice guaranteed against government infringement, and although the need for such review will remain as a consequence of today's decision, the required determinations fall within judicial competence.

2

The inquiry into reliance counts the cost of a rule's repudiation as it would fall on those who have relied reasonably on the rule's continued application. . . .

While neither respondents nor their amici in so many words deny that the abortion right invites some reliance prior to its actual exercise, one can readily imagine an argument stressing the dissimilarity of this case to one involving property or contract. Abortion is customarily chosen as an unplanned response to the consequence of unplanned activity or to the failure of conventional birth control, and except on the assumption that no intercourse would have occurred but for Roe's holding, such behavior may appear to justify no reliance claim.

[To] eliminate the issue of reliance that easily, however, one would need to limit cognizable reliance to specific instances of sexual activity. But to do this would be simply to refuse to face the fact that for two decades of economic and social developments, people have organized intimate relationships and made choices that define their views of themselves and their places in society, in reliance on the availability of abortion in the event that contraception should fail. The ability of women to participate equally in the economic and social life of the Nation has been facilitated by their ability to control their reproductive lives. See, e.g., R. Petchesky, Abortion and Woman's Choice 109, 133, n.7 (rev. ed. 1990). The Constitution serves human values, and while the effect of reliance on Roe cannot be exactly measured, neither can the certain cost of overruling Roe for people who have ordered their thinking and living around that case being dismissed.

3

No evolution of legal principle has left Roe's doctrinal footings weaker than they were in 1973. No development of constitutional law since the case was decided has implicitly or explicitly left Roe behind as a mere survivor of obsolete constitutional thinking.

It will be recognized, of course, that Roe stands at an intersection of two lines of decisions, but in whichever doctrinal category one reads the case, the result for present purposes will be the same. The Roe Court itself placed its holding in the succession of cases most prominently exemplified by Griswold v. Connecticut, 381 U.S. 479 (1965), see Roe, 410 U.S., at 152-153. [Roe,] however, may be seen not only as an exemplar of Griswold liberty but as a rule (whether or not mistaken) of personal autonomy and bodily integrity, with doctrinal affinity to cases recognizing limits on governmental power to mandate medical treatment or to bar its rejection. If so, our cases since Roe accord with Roe's view that a State's interest in the protection of life falls short of justifying any plenary override of individual liberty claims. Cruzan v. Director, Missouri Dept. of Health. Finally, one could classify Roe as sui generis. If the case is so viewed, then there clearly has been no erosion of its central determination.

[The] soundness of this prong of the Roe analysis is apparent from a consideration of the alternative. If indeed the woman's interest in deciding whether to bear and beget a child had not been recognized as in Roe, the State might as readily restrict a woman's right to choose to carry a pregnancy to term as to terminate it, to further asserted state interests in population control, or eugenics, for example. Yet Roe has been sensibly relied upon to counter any such suggestions. E.g., Arnold v. Board of Education of Escambia County, Ala., 880 F.2d 305, 311 (CA11 1989) (relying upon Roe and concluding that government officials violate the Constitution by coercing a minor to have an abortion); Avery v. County of Burke, 660 F.2d 111, 115 (CA4 1981) (county agency inducing teenage girl to undergo unwanted sterilization on the basis of misrepresentation that she had sickle cell trait); see also In re Quinlan, 70 N.J. 10, 355 A.2d 647, cert. denied sub nom. Garger v. New Jersey, 429 U.S. 922 (1976) (relying on Roe in finding a right to terminate medical treatment).

4

[Time] has overtaken some of Roe's factual assumptions: advances in maternal health care allow for abortions safe to the mother later in pregnancy than was true in 1973. But these facts go only to the scheme of time limits on the realization of competing interests, and the divergences from the factual premises of 1973 have no bearing on the validity of Roe's central holding, that viability marks the earliest point at which the State's interest in fetal life is constitutionally adequate to justify a legislative ban on nontherapeutic abortions.

5

The sum of the precedential inquiry to this point shows Roe's underpinnings unweakened in any way affecting its central holding. [Within] the bounds of normal stare decisis analysis, then, and subject to the considerations on which it customarily turns, the stronger argument is for affirming Roe's central holding, with whatever degree of personal reluctance any of us may have, not for overruling it.

B

In a less significant case, stare decisis analysis could, and would, stop at the point we have reached. But the sustained and widespread debate Roe has provoked calls for some comparison between that case and others of comparable dimension that have responded to national controversies and taken on the impress of the controversies addressed. Only two such decisional lines from the past century present themselves for examination, and in each instance the result reached by the Court accorded with the principles we apply today.

The first example is that line of cases identified with Lochner v. New York. [West] Coast Hotel Co. v. Parrish signaled the demise of Lochner by overruling Adkins. In the meantime, the Depression had come and, with it, the lesson that seemed unmistakable to most people by 1937, that the interpretation of contractual freedom protected in Adkins rested on fundamentally false factual assumptions about the capacity of a relatively unregulated market to satisfy minimal levels of human welfare. As Justice Jackson wrote of the constitutional crisis of 1937 shortly before he came on the bench, "The older world of laissez faire was recognized everywhere outside the Court to be dead." R. Jackson, The Struggle for Judicial Supremacy 85 (1941). The facts upon which the earlier case had premised a constitutional resolution of social controversy had proved to be untrue, and history's demonstration of their untruth not only justified but required the new choice of constitutional principle that West Coast Hotel announced. Of course, it was true that the Court lost something by its misperception, or its lack of prescience, and the Court-packing crisis only magnified the loss; but the clear demonstration that the facts of economic life were different from those previously assumed warranted the repudiation of the old law.

The second comparison that 20th century history invites is with the cases employing the separate-but-equal rule for applying the Fourteenth Amendment's equal protection guarantee. They began with Plessy v. Ferguson. [The] Plessy Court considered "the underlying fallacy of the plaintiff's argument to consist in the assumption that the enforced separation of the two races stamps the colored race with a badge of inferiority. If this be so, it is not by reason of anything found in the act, but solely because the colored race chooses to put that construction upon it." [But] this understanding of the facts and the rule it was stated to justify were repudiated in Brown. As one commentator observed, the question before the Court in Brown was "whether discrimination inheres in that segregation which is imposed by law in the twentieth century in certain specific states in the American Union. And that question has meaning and can find an answer only on the ground of history and of common knowledge about the facts of life in the times and places aforesaid." Black, The Lawfulness of the Segregation Decisions, 69 Yale L.J. 421, 427 (1960).

The Court in Brown addressed these facts of life by observing that whatever may have been the understanding in Plessy's time of the power of segregation to stigmatize those who were segregated with a "badge of inferiority," it was clear by 1954 that legally sanctioned segregation had just such an effect, to the point that racially separate public educational facilities were deemed inherently unequal. Society's understanding of the facts upon which a constitutional ruling was sought in 1954 was thus fundamentally different from the basis claimed for the decision in 1896. While we think Plessy was wrong the day it was decided, see Plessy (Harlan, J., dissenting), we must also recognize that the Plessy Court's explanation for its decision was so clearly at odds with the facts apparent to the Court in 1954 that the decision to reexamine Plessy was on this ground alone not only justified but required. West Coast Hotel and Brown each rested on facts, or an understanding of facts, changed from those which furnished the claimed justifications for the earlier constitutional resolutions. Each case was comprehensible as the Court's response to facts that the country could understand, or had come to understand already, but which the Court of an earlier day, as its own declarations disclosed, had not been able to perceive. As the decisions were thus comprehensible they were also defensible, not merely as the victories of one doctrinal school over another by dint of numbers (victories though they were), but as applications of constitutional principle to facts as they had not been seen by the Court before. In constitutional adjudication as elsewhere in life, changed circumstances may impose new obligations, and the thoughtful part of the Nation could accept each decision to overrule a prior case as a response to the Court's constitutional duty.

Because the case before us presents no such occasion it could be seen as no such response. Because neither the factual underpinnings of Roe's central holding nor our understanding of it has changed (and because no other indication of weakened precedent has been shown) the Court could not pretend to be reexamining the prior law with any justification beyond a present doctrinal disposition to come out differently from the Court of 1973. To overrule prior law for no other reason than that would run counter to the view repeated in our cases, that a decision to overrule should rest on some special reason over and above the belief that a prior case was wrongly decided.

C

The examination of the conditions justifying the repudiation of Adkins by West Coast Hotel and Plessy by Brown is enough to suggest the terrible price that would have been paid if the Court had not overruled as it did. In the present case, however, as our analysis to this point makes clear, the terrible price would be paid for overruling. Our analysis would not be complete, however, without explaining why overruling Roe's central holding would not only reach an unjustifiable result under principles of stare decisis, but would seriously weaken the Court's capacity to exercise the judicial power and to function as the Supreme Court of a Nation dedicated to the rule of law.

[The] underlying substance of [the Court's] legitimacy is of course the warrant for the Court's decisions in the Constitution and the lesser sources of legal principle on which the Court draws. That substance is expressed in the Court's opinions, and our contemporary understanding is such that a decision without principled justification would be no judicial act at all. But even when justification is furnished by apposite legal principle, something more is required. Because not every conscientious claim of principled justification will be accepted as such, the justification claimed must be beyond dispute. The Court must take care to speak and act in ways that allow people to accept its decisions on the terms the Court claims for them, as grounded truly in principle, not as compromises with social and political pressures having, as such, no bearing on the principled choices that the Court is obliged to make.

[The] need for principled action to be perceived as such is implicated to some degree whenever this, or any other appellate court, overrules a prior case. [In] two circumstances, however, the Court would almost certainly fail to receive the benefit of the doubt in overruling prior cases. There is, first, a point beyond which frequent overruling would overtax the country's belief in the Court's good faith. [That] first circumstance can be described as hypothetical; the second is to the point here and now. Where, in the performance of its judicial duties, the Court decides a case in such a way as to resolve the sort of intensely divisive controversy reflected in Roe and those rare, comparable cases, its decision has a dimension that the resolution of the normal case does not carry. It is the dimension present whenever the Court's interpretation of the Constitution calls the contending sides of a national controversy to end their national division by accepting a common mandate rooted in the Constitution.

The Court is not asked to do this very often, having thus addressed the Nation only twice in our lifetime, in the decisions of Brown and Roe. But when the Court does act in this way, its decision requires an equally rare precedential force to counter the inevitable efforts to overturn it and to thwart its implementation. [To] overrule under fire in the absence of the most compelling reason to reexamine a watershed decision would subvert the Court's legitimacy beyond any serious question.

[The] Court's duty in the present case is clear. In 1973, it confronted the already-divisive issue of governmental power to limit personal choice to undergo abortion, for which it provided a new resolution based on the due process guaranteed by the Fourteenth Amendment. Whether or not a new social consensus is developing on that issue, its divisiveness is no less today than in 1973, and pressure to overrule the decision, like pressure to retain it, has grown only more intense. A decision to overrule Roe's essential holding under the existing circumstances would address error, if error there was, at the cost of both profound and unnecessary damage to the Court's legitimacy, and to the Nation's commitment to the rule of law. It is therefore imperative to adhere to the essence of Roe's original decision, and we do so today.

IV

[We] conclude that the basic decision in Roe was based on a constitutional analysis which we cannot now repudiate. The woman's liberty is not so unlimited, however, that from the outset the State cannot show its concern for the life of the unborn, and at a later point in fetal development the State's interest in life has sufficient force so that the right of the woman to terminate the pregnancy can be restricted.

[We] conclude the line should be drawn at viability, so that before that time the woman has a right to choose to terminate her pregnancy. We adhere to this principle for two reasons. First, as we have said, is the doctrine of stare decisis. [The] second reason is that the concept of viability, as we noted in Roe, is the time at which there is a realistic possibility of maintaining and nourishing a life outside the womb, so that the independent existence of the second life can in reason and all fairness be the object of state protection that now overrides the rights of the woman. . . .

On the other side of the equation is the interest of the State in the protection of potential life. [The] weight to be given this state interest, not the strength of the woman's interest, was the difficult question faced in Roe. We do not need to say whether each of us, had we been Members of the Court when the valuation of the State interest came before it as an original matter, would have concluded, as the Roe Court did, that its weight is insufficient to justify a ban on abortions prior to viability even when it is subject to certain exceptions. [Yet] it must be remembered that Roe v. Wade speaks with clarity in establishing not only the woman's liberty but also the State's "important and legitimate interest in potential life." That portion of the decision in Roe has been given too little acknowledgment and implementation by the Court in its subsequent cases. Those cases decided that any regulation touching upon the abortion decision must survive strict scrutiny, to be sustained only if drawn in narrow terms to further a compelling state interest. Not all of the cases decided under that formulation can be reconciled with the holding in Roe itself that the State has legitimate interests in the health of the woman and in protecting the potential life within her. In resolving this tension, we choose to rely upon Roe, as against the later cases.

[We] reject the trimester framework, which we do not consider to be part of the essential holding of Roe.

[The] trimester framework suffers from these basic flaws: in its formulation it misconceives the nature of the pregnant woman's interest; and in practice it undervalues the State's interest in potential life, as recognized in Roe. . . .

[Numerous] forms of state regulation might have the incidental effect of increasing the cost or decreasing the availability of medical care, whether for abortion or any other medical procedure. The fact that a law which serves a valid purpose, one not designed to strike at the right itself, has the incidental effect of making it more difficult or more expensive to procure an abortion cannot be enough to invalidate it. Only where state regulation imposes an undue burden on a woman's ability to make this decision does the power of the State reach into the heart of the liberty protected by the Due Process Clause.
. . .

These considerations of the nature of the abortion right illustrate that it is an overstatement to describe it as a right to decide whether to have an abortion "without interference from the State." [Not] all governmental intrusion is of necessity unwarranted; and that brings us to the other basic flaw in the trimester framework: even in Roe's terms, in practice it undervalues the State's interest in the potential life within the woman. . . .

[Not] all burdens on the right to decide whether to terminate a pregnancy will be undue. In our view, the undue burden standard is the appropriate means of reconciling the State's interest with the woman's constitutionally protected liberty. . . .

A finding of an undue burden is a shorthand for the conclusion that a state regulation has the purpose or effect of placing a substantial obstacle in the path of a woman seeking an abortion of a nonviable fetus. A statute with this purpose is invalid because the means chosen by the State to further the interest in potential life must be calculated to inform the woman's free choice, not hinder it. And a statute which, while furthering the interest in potential life or some other valid state interest, has the effect of placing a substantial obstacle in the path of a woman's choice cannot be considered a permissible means of serving its legitimate ends. [Understood] another way, we answer the question, left open in previous opinions discussing the undue burden formulation, whether a law designed to further the State's interest in fetal life which imposes an undue burden on the woman's decision before fetal viability could be constitutional. The answer is no.

Some guiding principles should emerge. What is at stake is the woman's right to make the ultimate decision, not a right to be insulated from all others in doing so. Regulations which do no more than create a structural mechanism by which the State, or the parent or guardian of a minor, may express profound respect for the life of the unborn are permitted, if they are not a substantial obstacle to the woman's exercise of the right to choose. Unless it has that effect on her right of choice, a state measure designed to persuade her to choose childbirth over abortion will be upheld if reasonably related to that goal. Regulations designed to foster the health of a woman seeking an abortion are valid if they do not constitute an undue burden.

[We] give this summary:

(a) To protect the central right recognized by Roe v. Wade while at the same time accommodating the State's profound interest in potential life, we will employ the undue burden analysis as explained in this opinion. An undue burden exists, and therefore a provision of law is invalid, if its purpose or effect is to place a substantial obstacle in the path of a woman seeking an abortion before the fetus attains viability.

(b) We reject the rigid trimester framework of Roe v. Wade. To promote the State's profound interest in potential life, throughout pregnancy the State may take measures to ensure that the woman's choice is informed, and measures designed to advance this interest will not be invalidated as long as their purpose is to persuade the woman to choose childbirth over abortion. These measures must not be an undue burden on the right.

(c) As with any medical procedure, the State may enact regulations to further the health or safety of a woman seeking an abortion. Unnecessary health regulations that have the purpose or effect of presenting a substantial obstacle to a woman seeking an abortion impose an undue burden on the right.

(d) Our adoption of the undue burden analysis does not disturb the central holding of Roe v. Wade, and we reaffirm that holding. Regardless of whether exceptions are made for particular circumstances, a State may not prohibit any woman from making the ultimate decision to terminate her pregnancy before viability.

(e) We also reaffirm Roe's holding that "subsequent to viability, the State in promoting its interest in the potentiality of human life may, if it chooses, regulate, and even proscribe, abortion except where it is necessary, in appropriate medical judgment, for the preservation of the life or health of the mother."

V

A

Because it is central to the operation of various other requirements, we begin with the statute's definition of medical emergency. Under the statute, a medical emergency is that condition which, on the basis of the physician's good faith clinical judgment, so complicates the medical condition of a pregnant woman as to necessitate the immediate abortion of her pregnancy to avert her death or for which a delay will create serious risk of substantial and irreversible impairment of a major bodily function.

[The] District Court found that there were three serious conditions which would not be covered by the statute: preeclampsia, inevitable abortion, and premature ruptured membrane. Yet, as the Court of Appeals observed, it is undisputed that under some circumstances each of these conditions could lead to an illness with substantial and irreversible consequences. While the definition could be interpreted in an unconstitutional manner, the Court of Appeals construed the phrase "serious risk" to include those circumstances. [We] conclude that, as construed by the Court of Appeals, the medical emergency definition imposes no undue burden on a woman's abortion right.

B

[Except] in a medical emergency, the statute requires that at least 24 hours before performing an abortion a physician inform the woman of the nature of the procedure, the health risks of the abortion and of childbirth, and the "probable gestational age of the unborn child." The physician or a qualified nonphysician must inform the woman of the availability of printed materials published by the State describing the fetus and providing information about medical assistance for childbirth, information about child support from the father, and a list of agencies which provide adoption and other services as alternatives to abortion. An abortion may not be performed unless the woman certifies in writing that she has been informed of the availability of these printed materials and has been provided them if she chooses to view them. . . .

To the extent Akron I and Thornburgh find a constitutional violation when the government requires, as it does here, the giving of truthful, nonmisleading information about the nature of the procedure, the attendant health risks and those of childbirth, and the "probable gestational age" of the fetus, those cases go too far, are inconsistent with Roe's acknowledgment of an important interest in potential life, and are overruled. [In] attempting to ensure that a woman apprehend the full consequences of her decision, the State furthers the legitimate purpose of reducing the risk that a woman may elect an abortion, only to discover later, with devastating psychological consequences, that her decision was not fully informed. If the information the State requires to be made available to the woman is truthful and not misleading, the requirement may be permissible.

We also see no reason why the State may not require doctors to inform a woman seeking an abortion of the availability of materials relating to the consequences to the fetus, even when those consequences have no direct relation to her health. . . .

All that is left of petitioners' argument is an asserted First Amendment right of a physician not to provide information about the risks of abortion, and childbirth, in a manner mandated by the State. To be sure, the physician's First Amendment rights not to speak are implicated, but only as part of the practice of medicine, subject to reasonable licensing and regulation by the State. We see no constitutional infirmity in the requirement that the physician provide the information mandated by the State here.

The Pennsylvania statute also requires us to reconsider the holding in Akron I that the State may not require that a physician, as opposed to a qualified assistant, provide information relevant to a woman's informed consent. Since there is no evidence on this record that requiring a doctor to give the information as provided by the statute would amount in practical terms to a substantial obstacle to a woman seeking an abortion, we conclude that it is not an undue burden. . . .

Our analysis of Pennsylvania's 24-hour waiting period between the provision of the information deemed necessary to informed consent and the performance of an abortion under the undue burden standard requires us to reconsider the premise behind the decision in Akron I invalidating a parallel requirement. In Akron I we said: "Nor are we convinced that the State's legitimate concern that the woman's decision be informed is reasonably served by requiring a 24-hour delay as a matter of course." We consider that conclusion to be wrong. The idea that important decisions will be more informed and deliberate if they follow some period of reflection does not strike us as unreasonable, particularly where the statute directs that important information become part of the background of the decision. . . .

Whether the mandatory 24-hour waiting period is nonetheless invalid because in practice it is a substantial obstacle to a woman's choice to terminate her pregnancy is a closer question. The findings of fact by the District Court indicate that because of the distances many women must travel to reach an abortion provider, the practical effect will often be a delay of much more than a day because the waiting period requires that a woman seeking an abortion make at least two visits to the doctor. The District Court also found that in many instances this will increase the exposure of women seeking abortions to "the harassment and hostility of anti-abortion protestors demonstrating outside a clinic." As a result, the District Court found that for those women who have the fewest financial resources, those who must travel long distances, and those who have difficulty explaining their whereabouts to husbands, employers, or others, the 24-hour waiting period will be "particularly burdensome."

These findings are troubling in some respects, but they do not demonstrate that the waiting period constitutes an undue burden. [As] we have stated, under the undue burden standard a State is permitted to enact persuasive measures which favor childbirth over abortion, even if those measures do not further a health interest. And while the waiting period does limit a physician's discretion, that is not, standing alone, a reason to invalidate it.

We also disagree with the District Court's conclusion that the "particularly burdensome" effects of the waiting period on some women require its invalidation. . . .

We are left with the argument that the various aspects of the informed consent requirement are unconstitutional because they place barriers in the way of abortion on demand. Even the broadest reading of Roe, however, has not suggested that there is a constitutional right to abortion on demand. Rather, the right protected by Roe is a right to decide to terminate a pregnancy free of undue interference by the State. Because the informed consent requirement facilitates the wise exercise of that right it cannot be classified as an interference with the right Roe protects. The informed consent requirement is not an undue burden on that right.

C

Section 3209 of Pennsylvania's abortion law provides, except in cases of medical emergency, that no physician shall perform an abortion on a married woman without receiving a signed statement from the woman that she has notified her spouse that she is about to undergo an abortion. The woman has the option of providing an alternative signed statement certifying that her husband is not the man who impregnated her; that her husband could not be located; that the pregnancy is the result of spousal sexual assault which she has reported; or that the woman believes that notifying her husband will cause him or someone else to inflict bodily injury upon her. A physician who performs an abortion on a married woman without receiving the appropriate signed statement will have his or her license revoked, and is liable to the husband for damages.

The District Court heard the testimony of numerous expert witnesses, and made detailed findings of fact regarding the effect of this statute. These included:

273. The vast majority of women consult their husbands prior to deciding to terminate their pregnancy. . . .

279. The "bodily injury" exception could not be invoked by a married woman whose husband, if notified, would, in her reasonable belief, threaten to (a) publicize her intent to have an abortion to family, friends or acquaintances; (b) retaliate against her in future child custody or divorce proceedings; (c) inflict psychological intimidation or emotional harm upon her, her children or other persons; (d) inflict bodily harm on other persons such as children, family members or other loved ones; or (e) use his control over finances to deprive of necessary monies for herself or her children. . . .

281. Studies reveal that family violence occurs in two million families in the United States. This figure, however, is a conservative one that substantially understates (because battering is usually not reported until it reaches life-threatening proportions) the actual number of families affected by domestic violence. In fact, researchers estimate that one of every two women will be battered at some time in their life. . . .

282. A wife may not elect to notify her husband of her intention to have an abortion for a variety of reasons, including the husband's illness, concern about her own health, the imminent failure of the marriage, or the husband's absolute opposition to the abortion. . . .

284. Women of all class levels, educational backgrounds, and racial, ethnic and religious groups are battered. . . .

285. Wife-battering or abuse can take on many physical and psychological forms. The nature and scope of the battering can cover a broad range of actions and be gruesome and torturous. . . .

286. Married women, victims of battering, have been killed in Pennsylvania and throughout the United States. . . .

288. In a domestic abuse situation, it is common for the battering husband to also abuse the children in an attempt to coerce the wife. . . .

289. Mere notification of pregnancy is frequently a flashpoint for battering and violence within the family. The number of battering incidents is high during the pregnancy and often the worst abuse can be associated with pregnancy. . . . The battering husband may deny parentage and use the pregnancy as an excuse for abuse. . . .

290. Secrecy typically shrouds abusive families. Family members are instructed not to tell anyone, especially police or doctors, about the abuse and violence. Battering husbands often threaten their wives or her children with further abuse if she tells an outsider of the violence and tells her that nobody will believe her. A battered woman, therefore, is highly unlikely to disclose the violence against her for fear of retaliation by the abuser. . . .

294. A woman in a shelter or a safe house unknown to her husband is not reasonably likely to have bodily harm inflicted upon her by her batterer, however her attempt to notify her husband pursuant to section 3209 could accidentally disclose her whereabouts to her husband. Her fear of future ramifications would be realistic under the circumstances.

298. Because of the nature of the battering relationship, battered women are unlikely to avail themselves of the exceptions to section 3209 of the Act, regardless of whether the section applies to them.

These findings are supported by studies of domestic violence. [Thus] on an average day in the United States, nearly 11,000 women are severely assaulted by their male partners. Many of these incidents involve sexual assault. [Physical] violence is only the most visible form of abuse. Psychological abuse, particularly forced social and economic isolation of women, is also common. L. Walker, The Battered Woman Syndrome 27-28 (1984). Many victims of domestic violence remain with their abusers, perhaps because they perceive no superior alternative. Returning to one's abuser can be dangerous. Recent Federal Bureau of Investigation statistics disclose that 8.8% of all homicide victims in the United States are killed by their spouse. Thirty percent of female homicide victims are killed by their male partners.   The limited research that has been conducted with respect to notifying one's husband about an abortion, although involving samples too small to be representative, also supports the District Court's findings of fact. [There] are millions of women in this country who are the victims of regular physical and psychological abuse at the hands of their husbands. Should these women become pregnant, they may have very good reasons for not wishing to inform their husbands of their decision to obtain an abortion. Many may have justifiable fears of physical abuse, but may be no less fearful of the consequences of reporting prior abuse to the Commonwealth of Pennsylvania. If anything in this field is certain, it is that victims of spousal sexual assault are extremely reluctant to report the abuse to the government; hence, a great many spousal rape victims will not be exempt from the notification requirement imposed by §3209.

[Respondents] attempt to avoid the conclusion that §3209 is invalid by pointing out that [the] effects of §3209 are felt by only one percent of the women who obtain abortions. [We] disagree with respondents' basic method of analysis.

The analysis does not end with one percent of women upon whom the statute operates; it begins there. Legislation is measured for consistency with the Constitution by its impact on those whose conduct it affects. [The] unfortunate yet persisting conditions we document above will mean that in a large fraction of the cases in which §3209 is relevant, it will operate as a substantial obstacle to a woman's choice to undergo an abortion. It is an undue burden, and therefore invalid.

This conclusion is in no way inconsistent with our decisions upholding parental notification or consent requirements. Those enactments, and our judgment that they are constitutional, are based on the quite reasonable assumption that minors will benefit from consultation with their parents and that children will often not realize that their parents have their best interests at heart. We cannot adopt a parallel assumption about adult women.

. . .

Before birth, however, the issue takes on a very different cast. It is an inescapable biological fact that state regulation with respect to the child a woman is carrying will have a far greater impact on the mother's liberty than on the father's. The effect of state regulation on a woman's protected liberty is doubly deserving of scrutiny in such a case, as the State has touched not only upon the private sphere of the family but upon the very bodily integrity of the pregnant woman. The Court has held that "when the wife and the husband disagree on this decision, the view of only one of the two marriage partners can prevail. Inasmuch as it is the woman who physically bears the child and who is the more directly and immediately affected by the pregnancy, as between the two, the balance weighs in her favor." Danforth. This conclusion rests upon the basic nature of marriage and the nature of our Constitution: "The marital couple is not an independent entity with a mind and heart of its own, but an association of two individuals each with a separate intellectual and emotional makeup. If the right of privacy means anything, it is the right of the individual, married or single, to be free from unwarranted governmental intrusion into matters so fundamentally affecting a person as the decision whether to bear or beget a child." Eisenstadt v. Baird[, 405 U.S. 438 (1972)]. The Constitution protects individuals, men and women alike, from unjustified state interference, even when that interference is enacted into law for the benefit of their spouses.   There was a time, not so long ago, when a different understanding of the family and of the Constitution prevailed. In Bradwell v. Illinois, 16 Wall. 130 (1873), three Members of this Court reaffirmed the common-law principle that "a woman had no legal existence separate from her husband, who was regarded as her head and representative in the social state; and, notwithstanding some recent modifications of this civil status, many of the special rules of law flowing from and dependent upon this cardinal principle still exist in full force in most States." Id., at 141 (Bradley, J., joined by Swayne and Field, JJ., concurring in judgment). Only one generation has passed since this Court observed that "woman is still regarded as the center of home and family life," with attendant "special responsibilities" that precluded full and independent legal status under the Constitution. Hoyt v. Florida, 368 U.S. 57, 62 (1961). These views, of course, are no longer consistent with our understanding of the family, the individual, or the Constitution.

[The] husband's interest in the life of the child his wife is carrying does not permit the State to empower him with this troubling degree of authority over his wife. The contrary view leads to consequences reminiscent of the common law. A husband has no enforceable right to require a wife to advise him before she exercises her personal choices. If a husband's interest in the potential life of the child outweighs a wife's liberty, the State could require a married woman to notify her husband before she uses a postfertilization contraceptive. Perhaps next in line would be a statute requiring pregnant married women to notify their husbands before engaging in conduct causing risks to the fetus. After all, if the husband's interest in the fetus' safety is a sufficient predicate for state regulation, the State could reasonably conclude that pregnant wives should notify their husbands before drinking alcohol or smoking. Perhaps married women should notify their husbands before using contraceptives or before undergoing any type of surgery that may have complications affecting the husband's interest in his wife's reproductive organs. And if a husband's interest justifies notice in any of these cases, one might reasonably argue that it justifies exactly what the Danforth Court held it did not justify — a requirement of the husband's consent as well. A State may not give to a man the kind of dominion over his wife that parents exercise over their children.

Section 3209 embodies a view of marriage consonant with the common-law status of married women but repugnant to our present understanding of marriage and of the nature of the rights secured by the Constitution. Women do not lose their constitutionally protected liberty when they marry. The Constitution protects all individuals, male or female, married or unmarried, from the abuse of governmental power, even where that power is employed for the supposed benefit of a member of the individual's family.

D

We next consider the parental consent provision. Except in a medical emergency, an unemancipated young woman under 18 may not obtain an abortion unless she and one of her parents (or guardian) provides informed consent as defined above. If neither a parent nor a guardian provides consent, a court may authorize the performance of an abortion upon a determination that the young woman is mature and capable of giving informed consent and has in fact given her informed consent, or that an abortion would be in her best interests. . . .

The only argument made by petitioners respecting this provision and to which our prior decisions do not speak is the contention that the parental consent requirement is invalid because it requires informed parental consent. For the most part, petitioners' argument is a reprise of their argument with respect to the informed consent requirement in general, and we reject it for the reasons given above. . . .

E

Under the recordkeeping and reporting requirements of the statute, every facility which performs abortions is required to file a report stating its name and address as well as the name and address of any related entity, such as a controlling or subsidiary organization. In the case of state-funded institutions, the information becomes public. . . .

In Danforth, we held that recordkeeping and reporting provisions "that are reasonably directed to the preservation of maternal health and that properly respect a patient's confidentiality and privacy are permissible." We think that under this standard, all the provisions at issue here except that relating to spousal notice are constitutional. Although they do not relate to the State's interest in informing the woman's choice, they do relate to health. The collection of information with respect to actual patients is a vital element of medical research, and so it cannot be said that the requirements serve no purpose other than to make abortions more difficult. Nor do we find that the requirements impose a substantial obstacle to a woman's choice. At most they might increase the cost of some abortions by a slight amount. While at some point increased cost could become a substantial obstacle, there is no such showing on the record before us. . . .

VI

Our Constitution is a covenant running from the first generation of Americans to us and then to future generations. It is a coherent succession. Each generation must learn anew that the Constitution's written terms embody ideas and aspirations that must survive more ages than one. We accept our responsibility not to retreat from interpreting the full meaning of the covenant in light of all of our precedents. We invoke it once again to define the freedom guaranteed by the Constitution's own promise, the promise of liberty.

Justice BLACKMUN, concurring in part, concurring in the judgment in part, and dissenting in part. . . .

[Today,] no less than yesterday, the Constitution and decisions of this Court require that a State's abortion restrictions be subjected to the strictest of judicial scrutiny. Our precedents and the joint opinion's principles require us to subject all non-de minimis abortion regulations to strict scrutiny. Under this standard, the Pennsylvania statute's provisions requiring content-based counseling, a 24-hour delay, informed parental consent, and reporting of abortion-related information must be invalidated. . . .

State restrictions on abortion violate a woman's right of privacy in two ways. First, compelled continuation of a pregnancy infringes upon a woman's right to bodily integrity by imposing substantial physical intrusions and significant risks of physical harm. During pregnancy, women experience dramatic physical changes and a wide range of health consequences. Labor and delivery pose additional health risks and physical demands. In short, restrictive abortion laws force women to endure physical invasions far more substantial than those this Court has held to violate the constitutional principle of bodily integrity in other contexts. See, e.g., Winston v. Lee, 470 U.S. 753 (1985) (invalidating surgical removal of bullet from murder suspect); Rochin v. California, 342 U.S. 165 (1952) (invalidating stomach-pumping).

Further, when the State restricts a woman's right to terminate her pregnancy, it deprives a woman of the right to make her own decision about reproduction and family planning — critical life choices that this Court long has deemed central to the right to privacy. The decision to terminate or continue a pregnancy has no less an impact on a woman's life than decisions about contraception or marriage. Because motherhood has a dramatic impact on a woman's educational prospects, employment opportunities, and self-determination, restrictive abortion laws deprive her of basic control over her life. For these reasons, "the decision whether or not to beget or bear a child" lies at "the very heart of this cluster of constitutionally protected choices."

A State's restrictions on a woman's right to terminate her pregnancy also implicate constitutional guarantees of gender equality. State restrictions on abortion compel women to continue pregnancies they otherwise might terminate. By restricting the right to terminate pregnancies, the State conscripts women's bodies into its service, forcing women to continue their pregnancies, suffer the pains of childbirth, and in most instances, provide years of maternal care. The State does not compensate women for their services; instead, it assumes that they owe this duty as a matter of course. This assumption — that women can simply be forced to accept the "natural" status and incidents of motherhood — appears to rest upon a conception of women's role that has triggered the protection of the Equal Protection Clause. The joint opinion recognizes that these assumptions about women's place in society "are no longer consistent with our understanding of the family, the individual, or the Constitution." . . .

The 24-hour waiting period following the provision of the foregoing information is [clearly] unconstitutional. The District Court found that the mandatory 24-hour delay could lead to delays in excess of 24 hours, thus increasing health risks, and that it would require two visits to the abortion provider, thereby increasing travel time, exposure to further harassment, and financial cost. Finally, the District Court found that the requirement would pose especially significant burdens on women living in rural areas and those women that have difficulty explaining their whereabouts.

[The] Pennsylvania statute requires every facility performing abortions to report its activities to the Commonwealth. [The] Commonwealth attempts to justify its required reports on the ground that the public has a right to know how its tax dollars are spent. A regulation designed to inform the public about public expenditures does not further the Commonwealth's interest in protecting maternal health. Accordingly, such a regulation cannot justify a legally significant burden on a woman's right to obtain an abortion.

[Even] more shocking than The Chief Justice's cramped notion of individual liberty is his complete omission of any discussion of the effects that compelled childbirth and motherhood have on women's lives. The only expression of concern with women's health is purely instrumental — for The Chief Justice, only women's psychological health is a concern, and only to the extent that he assumes that every woman who decides to have an abortion does so without serious consideration of the moral implications of their decision. In short, The Chief Justice's view of the State's compelling interest in maternal health has less to do with health than it does with compelling women to be maternal.

Nor does The Chief Justice give any serious consideration to the doctrine of stare decisis. . . .

But, we are reassured, there is always the protection of the democratic process. While there is much to be praised about our democracy, our country since its founding has recognized that there are certain fundamental liberties that are not to be left to the whims of an election. A woman's right to reproductive choice is one of those fundamental liberties. Accordingly, that liberty need not seek refuge at the ballot box.

In one sense, the Court's approach is worlds apart from that of The Chief Justice and Justice Scalia. And yet, in another sense, the distance between the two approaches is short — the distance is but a single vote.

I am 83 years old. I cannot remain on this Court forever, and when I do step down, the confirmation process for my successor well may focus on the issue before us today. That, I regret, may be exactly where the choice between the two worlds will be made.

Justice STEVENS, concurring in part and dissenting in part. . . .

[The] societal costs of overruling Roe at this late date would be enormous. Roe is an integral part of a correct understanding of both the concept of liberty and the basic equality of men and women. . . .

My disagreement with the joint opinion begins with its understanding of the trimester framework established in Roe. [It] is not a "contradiction" to recognize that the State may have a legitimate interest in potential human life and, at the same time, to conclude that that interest does not justify the regulation of abortion before viability (although other interests, such as maternal health, may). The fact that the State's interest is legitimate does not tell us when, if ever, that interest outweighs the pregnant woman's interest in personal liberty. It is appropriate, therefore, to consider more carefully the nature of the interests at stake.

First, it is clear that, in order to be legitimate, the State's interest must be secular; consistent with the First Amendment the State may not promote a theological or sectarian interest. . . .

Identifying the State's interests — which the States rarely articulate with any precision — makes clear that the interest in protecting potential life is not grounded in the Constitution. It is, instead, an indirect interest supported by both humanitarian and pragmatic concerns. Many of our citizens believe that any abortion reflects an unacceptable disrespect for potential human life and that the performance of more than a million abortions each year is intolerable; many find third-trimester abortions performed when the fetus is approaching personhood particularly offensive. The State has a legitimate interest in minimizing such offense. The State may also have a broader interest in expanding the population, believing society would benefit from the services of additional productive citizens — or that the potential human lives might include the occasional Mozart or Curie.

[Under] these principles, §§3205(a)(2)(i)-(iii) of the Pennsylvania statute are unconstitutional. Those sections require a physician or counselor to provide the woman with a range of materials clearly designed to persuade her to choose not to undergo the abortion. While the State is free, pursuant to §3208 of the Pennsylvania law, to produce and disseminate such material, the State may not inject such information into the woman's deliberations just as she is weighing such an important choice.   Under this same analysis, §§3205(a)(1)(i) and (iii) of the Pennsylvania statute are constitutional. Those sections, which require the physician to inform a woman of the nature and risks of the abortion procedure and the medical risks of carrying to term, are neutral requirements comparable to those imposed in other medical procedures. Those sections indicate no effort by the State to influence the woman's choice in any way. If anything, such requirements enhance, rather than skew, the woman's decisionmaking.

The 24-hour waiting period required by §§3205(a)(1)-(2) of the Pennsylvania statute raises even more serious concerns. Such a requirement arguably furthers the State's interests in two ways, neither of which is constitutionally permissible.

In my opinion, a correct application of the "undue burden" standard leads to the same conclusion concerning the constitutionality of these requirements. A state-imposed burden on the exercise of a constitutional right is measured both by its effects and by its character: A burden may be "undue" either because the burden is too severe or because it lacks a legitimate, rational justification.

The 24-hour delay requirement fails both parts of this test. . . .

The counseling provisions are similarly infirm. Whenever government commands private citizens to speak or to listen, careful review of the justification for that command is particularly appropriate. In this case, the Pennsylvania statute directs that counselors provide women seeking abortions with information concerning alternatives to abortion, the availability of medical assistance benefits, and the possibility of child-support payments. The statute requires that this information be given to all women seeking abortions, including those for whom such information is clearly useless, such as those who are married, those who have undergone the procedure in the past and are fully aware of the options, and those who are fully convinced that abortion is their only reasonable option. Moreover, the statute requires physicians to inform all of their patients of "the probable gestational age of the unborn child." This information is of little decisional value in most cases, because 90% of all abortions are performed during the first trimester when fetal age has less relevance than when the fetus nears viability. . . .

Chief Justice REHNQUIST, with whom Justice WHITE, Justice SCALIA, and Justice THOMAS join, concurring in the judgment in part and dissenting in part.

The joint opinion, following its newly-minted variation on stare decisis, retains the outer shell of Roe v. Wade, but beats a wholesale retreat from the substance of that case. We believe that Roe was wrongly decided, and that it can and should be overruled consistently with our traditional approach to stare decisis in constitutional cases. We would adopt the approach of the plurality in Webster v. Reproductive Health Services, and uphold the challenged provisions of the Pennsylvania statute in their entirety.

I

[In] Roe v. Wade, the Court recognized a "guarantee of personal privacy" which "is broad enough to encompass a woman's decision whether or not to terminate her pregnancy." We are now of the view that, in terming this right fundamental, the Court in Roe read the earlier opinions upon which it based its decision much too broadly. Unlike marriage, procreation and contraception, abortion "involves the purposeful termination of potential life." Harris v. McRae, 448 U.S. 297, 325 (1980). [One] cannot ignore the fact that a woman is not isolated in her pregnancy, and that the decision to abort necessarily involves the destruction of a fetus.

Nor do the historical traditions of the American people support the view that the right to terminate one's pregnancy is "fundamental." The common law which we inherited from England made abortion after "quickening" an offense. At the time of the adoption of the Fourteenth Amendment, statutory prohibitions or restrictions on abortion were commonplace; in 1868, at least 28 of the then-37 States and 8 Territories had statutes banning or limiting abortion. By the turn of the century virtually every State had a law prohibiting or restricting abortion on its books. By the middle of the present century, a liberalization trend had set in. But 21 of the restrictive abortion laws in effect in 1868 were still in effect in 1973 when Roe was decided, and an overwhelming majority of the States prohibited abortion unless necessary to preserve the life or health of the mother.

[We] think, therefore, both in view of this history and of our decided cases dealing with substantive liberty under the Due Process Clause, that the Court was mistaken in Roe when it classified a woman's decision to terminate her pregnancy as a "fundamental right" that could be abridged only in a manner which withstood "strict scrutiny."

II

[The] joint opinion [cannot] bring itself to say that Roe was correct as an original matter, but the authors are of the view that "the immediate question is not the soundness of Roe's resolution of the issue, but the precedential force that must be accorded to its holding." Instead of claiming that Roe was correct as a matter of original constitutional interpretation, the opinion therefore contains an elaborate discussion of stare decisis. This discussion of the principle of stare decisis appears to be almost entirely dicta, because the joint opinion does not apply that principle in dealing with Roe. Roe decided that a woman had a fundamental right to an abortion. The joint opinion rejects that view. Roe decided that abortion regulations were to be subjected to "strict scrutiny" and could be justified only in the light of "compelling state interests." The joint opinion rejects that view. Roe analyzed abortion regulation under a rigid trimester framework, a framework which has guided this Court's decisionmaking for 19 years. The joint opinion rejects that framework.

[In] our view, authentic principles of stare decisis do not require that any portion of the reasoning in Roe be kept intact. [Erroneous] decisions in such constitutional cases are uniquely durable, because correction through legislative action, save for constitutional amendment, is impossible. . . .

The joint opinion discusses several stare decisis factors which, it asserts, point toward retaining a portion of Roe. Two of these factors are that the main "factual underpinning" of Roe has remained the same, and that its doctrinal foundation is no weaker now than it was in 1973. Of course, what might be called the basic facts which gave rise to Roe have remained the same — women become pregnant, there is a point somewhere, depending on medical technology, where a fetus becomes viable, and women give birth to children. But this is only to say that the same facts which gave rise to Roe will continue to give rise to similar cases. It is not a reason, in and of itself, why those cases must be decided in the same incorrect manner as was the first case to deal with the question. . . .

The joint opinion also points to the reliance interests involved in this context in its effort to explain why precedent must be followed for precedent's sake. Certainly it is true that where reliance is truly at issue, as in the case of judicial decisions that have formed the basis for private decisions, "considerations in favor of stare decisis are at their acme." But, as the joint opinion apparently agrees, ante, any traditional notion of reliance is not applicable here.

[In] the end, having failed to put forth any evidence to prove any true reliance, the joint opinion's argument is based solely on generalized assertions about the national psyche, on a belief that the people of this country have grown accustomed to the Roe decision over the last 19 years and have "ordered their thinking and living around" it. As an initial matter, one might inquire how the joint opinion can view the "central holding" of Roe as so deeply rooted in our constitutional culture, when it so casually uproots and disposes of that same decision's trimester framework. [However,] the simple fact that a generation or more had grown used to [Lochner and Plessy] did not prevent the Court from correcting its errors in those cases, nor should it prevent us from correctly interpreting the Constitution here.

Apparently realizing that conventional stare decisis principles do not support its position, the joint opinion advances a belief that retaining a portion of Roe is necessary to protect the "legitimacy" of this Court. Because the Court must take care to render decisions "grounded truly in principle," and not simply as political and social compromises, the joint opinion properly declares it to be this Court's duty to ignore the public criticism and protest that may arise as a result of a decision.

[But] the joint opinion goes on to state that when the Court "resolves the sort of intensely divisive controversy reflected in Roe and those rare, comparable cases," its decision is exempt from reconsideration under established principles of stare decisis in constitutional cases. [The] first difficulty with this principle lies in its assumption that cases which are "intensely divisive" can be readily distinguished from those that are not. The question of whether a particular issue is "intensely divisive" enough to qualify for special protection is entirely subjective and dependent on the individual assumptions of the members of this Court.

[The] joint opinion picks out and discusses two prior Court rulings that it believes are of the "intensely divisive" variety, and concludes that they are of comparable dimension to Roe. It appears to us very odd indeed that the joint opinion chooses as benchmarks two cases in which the Court chose not to adhere to erroneous constitutional precedent, but instead enhanced its stature by acknowledging and correcting its error, apparently in violation of the joint opinion's "legitimacy" principle. . . .

The joint opinion agrees that the Court's stature would have been seriously damaged if in Brown and West Coast Hotel it had dug in its heels and refused to apply normal principles of stare decisis to the earlier decisions. But the opinion contends that the Court was entitled to overrule Plessy and Lochner in those cases, despite the existence of opposition to the original decisions, only because both the Nation and the Court had learned new lessons in the interim. This is at best a feebly supported, post hoc rationalization for those decisions.

For example, the opinion asserts that the Court could justifiably overrule its decision in Lochner only because the Depression had convinced "most people" that constitutional protection of contractual freedom contributed to an economy that failed to protect the welfare of all. Surely the joint opinion does not mean to suggest that people saw this Court's failure to uphold minimum wage statutes as the cause of the Great Depression! In any event, the Lochner Court did not base its rule upon the policy judgment that an unregulated market was fundamental to a stable economy; it simply believed, erroneously, that "liberty" under the Due Process Clause protected the "right to make a contract." Lochner v. New York, 198 U.S., at 53. Nor is it the case that the people of this Nation only discovered the dangers of extreme laissez faire economics because of the Depression.

When the Court finally recognized its error in West Coast Hotel, it did not engage in the post hoc rationalization that the joint opinion attributes to it today; it did not state that Lochner had been based on an economic view that had fallen into disfavor, and that it therefore should be overruled. Chief Justice Hughes in his opinion for the Court simply recognized what Justice Holmes had previously recognized in his Lochner dissent, that "the Constitution does not speak of freedom of contract."

[The] joint opinion also agrees that the Court acted properly in rejecting the doctrine of "separate but equal" in Brown. In fact, the opinion lauds Brown in comparing it to Roe. This is strange, in that under the opinion's "legitimacy" principle the Court would seemingly have been forced to adhere to its erroneous decision in Plessy because of its "intensely divisive" character. To us, adherence to Roe today under the guise of "legitimacy" would seem to resemble more closely adherence to Plessy on the same ground. Fortunately, the Court did not choose that option in Brown, and instead frankly repudiated Plessy. [The] Court in Brown simply recognized, as Justice Harlan had recognized beforehand, that the Fourteenth Amendment does not permit racial segregation. The rule of Brown is not tied to popular opinion about the evils of segregation; it is a judgment that the Equal Protection Clause does not permit racial segregation, no matter whether the public might come to believe that it is beneficial. On that ground it stands, and on that ground alone the Court was justified in properly concluding that the Plessy Court had erred.

[The] end result of the joint opinion's paeans of praise for legitimacy is the enunciation of a brand new standard for evaluating state regulation of a woman's right to abortion — the "undue burden" standard. [In] evaluating abortion regulations under that standard, judges will have to decide whether they place a "substantial obstacle" in the path of a woman seeking an abortion. In that this standard is based even more on a judge's subjective determinations than was the trimester framework, the standard will do nothing to prevent "judges from roaming at large in the constitutional field" guided only by their personal views.

[We] have stated above our belief that the Constitution does not subject state abortion regulations to heightened scrutiny. Accordingly, we think that the correct analysis is that set forth by the plurality opinion in Webster. A woman's interest in having an abortion is a form of liberty protected by the Due Process Clause, but States may regulate abortion procedures in ways rationally related to a legitimate state interest. With this rule in mind, we examine each of the challenged provisions. . . .

The question before us is therefore whether the spousal notification requirement rationally furthers any legitimate state interests. We conclude that it does. First, a husband's interests in procreation within marriage and in the potential life of his unborn child are certainly substantial ones. [By] providing that a husband will usually know of his spouse's intent to have an abortion, the provision makes it more likely that the husband will participate in deciding the fate of his unborn child, a possibility that might otherwise have been denied him. This participation might in some cases result in a decision to proceed with the pregnancy.

[The] State also has a legitimate interest in promoting "the integrity of the marital relationship." [In] our view, the spousal notice requirement is a rational attempt by the State to improve truthful communication between spouses and encourage collaborative decisionmaking, and thereby fosters marital integrity.

[We would] hold that each of the challenged provisions of the Pennsylvania statute is consistent with the Constitution. It bears emphasis that our conclusion in this regard does not carry with it any necessary approval of these regulations. Our task is, as always, to decide only whether the challenged provisions of a law comport with the United States Constitution. If, as we believe, these do, their wisdom as a matter of public policy is for the people of Pennsylvania to decide.

Justice SCALIA, with whom THE CHIEF JUSTICE, Justice WHITE, and Justice THOMAS join, concurring in the judgment in part and dissenting in part. . . .

[A] State's choice between two positions on which reasonable people can disagree is constitutional even when (as is often the case) it intrudes upon a "liberty" in the absolute sense. Laws against bigamy, for example — which entire societies of reasonable people disagree with — intrude upon men and women's liberty to marry and live with one another. But bigamy happens not to be a liberty specially "protected" by the Constitution.

That is, quite simply, the issue in this case: not whether the power of a woman to abort her unborn child is a "liberty" in the absolute sense; or even whether it is a liberty of great importance to many women. Of course it is both. The issue is whether it is a liberty protected by the Constitution of the United States. I am sure it is not. I reach that conclusion [for] the same reason I reach the conclusion that bigamy is not constitutionally protected — because of two simple facts: (1) the Constitution says absolutely nothing about it, and (2) the longstanding traditions of American society have permitted it to be legally proscribed.

The Court destroys the proposition, evidently meant to represent my position, that "liberty" includes "only those practices, defined at the most specific level, that were protected against government interference by other rules of law when the Fourteenth Amendment was ratified." That is not, however, what Michael H. says; it merely observes that, in defining "liberty," we may not disregard a specific, "relevant tradition protecting, or denying protection to, the asserted right." But the Court does not wish to be fettered by any such limitations on its preferences. The Court's statement that it is "tempting" to acknowledge the authoritativeness of tradition in order to "curb the discretion of federal judges," is of course rhetoric rather than reality; no government official is "tempted" to place restraints upon his own freedom of action, which is why Lord Acton did not say "Power tends to purify." The Court's temptation is in the quite opposite and more natural direction — towards systematically eliminating checks upon its own power; and it succumbs.

Beyond that brief summary of the essence of my position, I will not swell the United States Reports with repetition of what I have said before; and applying the rational basis test, I would uphold the Pennsylvania statute in its entirety. I must, however, respond to a few of the more outrageous arguments in today's opinion, which it is beyond human nature to leave unanswered.

The inescapable fact is that adjudication of substantive due process claims may call upon the Court in interpreting the Constitution to exercise that same capacity which by tradition courts always have exercised: reasoned judgment. . . .

The emptiness of the "reasoned judgment" that produced Roe is displayed in plain view by the fact that, after more than 19 years of effort by some of the brightest (and most determined) legal minds in the country, after more than 10 cases upholding abortion rights in this Court, and after dozens upon dozens of amicus briefs submitted in this and other cases, the best the Court can do to explain how it is that the word "liberty" must be thought to include the right to destroy human fetuses is to rattle off a collection of adjectives that simply decorate a value judgment and conceal a political choice. . . .

"Liberty finds no refuge in a jurisprudence of doubt."

One might have feared to encounter this august and sonorous phrase in an opinion defending the real Roe v. Wade, rather than the revised version fabricated today by the authors of the joint opinion. The shortcomings of Roe did not include lack of clarity: Virtually all regulation of abortion before the third trimester was invalid. But to come across this phrase in the joint opinion — which calls upon federal district judges to apply an "undue burden" standard as doubtful in application as it is unprincipled in origin — is really more than one should have to bear. . . .

While we appreciate the weight of the arguments . . . that Roe should be overruled, the reservations any of us may have in reaffirming the central holding of Roe are outweighed by the explication of individual liberty we have given combined with the force of stare decisis.

The Court's reliance upon stare decisis can best be described as contrived. It insists upon the necessity of adhering not to all of Roe, but only to what it calls the "central holding." It seems to me that stare decisis ought to be applied even to the doctrine of stare decisis, and I confess never to have heard of this new, keep-what-you-want-and-throw-away-the-rest version. [I] am certainly not in a good position to dispute that the Court has saved the "central holding" of Roe, since to do that effectively I would have to know what the Court has saved, which in turn would require me to understand (as I do not) what the "undue burden" test means. I must confess, however, that I have always thought, and I think a lot of other people have always thought, that the arbitrary trimester framework, which the Court today discards, was quite as central to Roe as the arbitrary viability test, which the Court today retains. . . .

Where, in the performance of its judicial duties, the Court decides a case in such a way as to resolve the sort of intensely divisive controversy reflected in Roe . . . , its decision has a dimension that the resolution of the normal case does not carry. It is the dimension present whenever the Court's interpretation of the Constitution calls the contending sides of a national controversy to end their national division by accepting a common mandate rooted in the Constitution.

The Court's description of the place of Roe in the social history of the United States is unrecognizable. Not only did Roe not, as the Court suggests, resolve the deeply divisive issue of abortion; it did more than anything else to nourish it, by elevating it to the national level where it is infinitely more difficult to resolve. National politics were not plagued by abortion protests, national abortion lobbying, or abortion marches on Congress, before Roe v. Wade was decided. Profound disagreement existed among our citizens over the issue — as it does over other issues, such as the death penalty — but that disagreement was being worked out at the state level. As with many other issues, the division of sentiment within each State was not as closely balanced as it was among the population of the Nation as a whole, meaning not only that more people would be satisfied with the results of state-by-state resolution, but also that those results would be more stable. Pre-Roe, moreover, political compromise was possible. Roe's mandate for abortion-on-demand destroyed the compromises of the past, rendered compromise impossible for the future, and required the entire issue to be resolved uniformly, at the national level. At the same time, Roe created a vast new class of abortion consumers and abortion proponents by eliminating the moral opprobrium that had attached to the act. ("If the Constitution guarantees abortion, how can it be bad?" — not an accurate line of thought, but a natural one.) Many favor all of those developments, and it is not for me to say that they are wrong. But to portray Roe as the statesmanlike "settlement" of a divisive issue, a jurisprudential Peace of Westphalia that is worth preserving, is nothing less than Orwellian. Roe fanned into life an issue that has inflamed our national politics in general, and has obscured with its smoke the selection of Justices to this Court in particular, ever since.

[What] makes all this relevant to the bothersome application of "political pressure" against the Court are the twin facts that the American people love democracy and the American people are not fools. As long as this Court thought (and the people thought) that we Justices were doing essentially lawyers' work up here — reading text and discerning our society's traditional understanding of that text — the public pretty much left us alone. Texts and traditions are facts to study, not convictions to demonstrate about.

[There] is a poignant aspect to the Court's opinion. Its length, and what might be called its epic tone, suggest that its authors believe they are bringing to an end a troublesome era in the history of our Nation and of our Court. "It is the dimension" of authority, they say, to "call the contending sides of national controversy to end their national division by accepting a common mandate rooted in the Constitution."

There comes vividly to mind a portrait by Emanuel Leutze that hangs in the Harvard Law School: Roger Brooke Taney, painted in 1859, the 82d year of his life, the 24th of his Chief Justiceship, the second after his opinion in Dred Scott. He is all in black, sitting in a shadowed red armchair, left hand resting upon a pad of paper in his lap, right hand hanging limply, almost lifelessly, beside the inner arm of the chair. He sits facing the viewer, and staring straight out. There seems to be on his face, and in his deep-set eyes, an expression of profound sadness and disillusionment. Perhaps he always looked that way, even when dwelling upon the happiest of thoughts. But those of us who know how the lustre of his great Chief Justiceship came to be eclipsed by Dred Scott cannot help believing that he had that case — its already apparent consequences for the Court, and its soon-to-be-played-out consequences for the Nation — burning on his mind. I expect that two years earlier he, too, had thought himself "calling the contending sides of national controversy to end their national division by accepting a common mandate rooted in the Constitution."

It is no more realistic for us in this case, than it was for him in that, to think that an issue of the sort they both involved — an issue involving life and death, freedom and subjugation — can be "speedily and finally settled" by the Supreme Court, as President James Buchanan in his inaugural address said the issue of slavery in the territories would be. Quite to the contrary, by foreclosing all democratic outlet for the deep passions this issue arouses, by banishing the issue from the political forum that gives all participants, even the losers, the satisfaction of a fair hearing and an honest fight, by continuing the imposition of a rigid national rule instead of allowing for regional differences, the Court merely prolongs and intensifies the anguish.

We should get out of this area, where we have no right to be, and where we do neither ourselves nor the country any good by remaining.

Note: Stare Decisis after *Planned Parenthood v. Casey* but before *Dobbs v. Jackson Women's Health Organization*

The Court in its October 2019 term decided that Louisiana's jury practice allowing convictions for serious crimes by non-unanimous jury verdicts violated the Sixth Amendment on the grounds that it was a departure from the oft held standard that federal convictions must be accompanied by unanimous juries and that the practice of 48 states, save Louisiana and Oregon, also require unanimity. The decision in *Ramos v. Louisiana*, 590 U.S. ___, (2020) was based in large part on the also oft held standard that federal rights incorporated to the states should be implemented in identical fashion. But to arrive at its conclusion, the majority, in an opinion written by Justice Gorsuch, had to overrule *Apodaca v. Oregon*, 206 US 404 (1972), a notorious decision allowing Oregon's non-unanimous jury rule for serious crimes to stand. Justice Gorsuch, in his opinion, made the case that the *Casey* standard (interestingly without mentioning *Planned Parenthood v. Casey*) for overruling precedent under the principle of *stare decisis* applied in this case:

> To balance these considerations, when it revisits a precedent this Court has traditionally considered "the quality of the decision's reasoning; its consistency with related decisions; legal developments since the decision; and reliance on the decision." In this case, each factor points in the same direction.
>
> Start with the quality of the reasoning. Whether we look to the plurality opinion or Justice Powell's separate concurrence, Apodaca was gravely mistaken; again, no Member of the Court today defends either as rightly decided. Without repeating what we've already explained in detail, it's just an implacable fact that the plurality spent almost no time grappling with the historical meaning of the Sixth Amendment's jury trial right, this Court's long-repeated statements that it demands unanimity, or the racist origins of Louisiana's and Oregon's laws. Instead, the plurality subjected the Constitution's jury trial right to an incomplete functionalist analysis of its own creation for which it spared one paragraph. And, of course, five Justices expressly rejected the plurality's conclusion that the Sixth Amendment does not require unanimity. Meanwhile, Justice Powell refused to follow this Court's incorporation precedents. Nine Justices (including Justice Powell) recognized this for what it was; eight called it an error.
>
> Looking to *Apodaca's* consistency with related decisions and recent legal developments compounds the reasons for concern. *Apodaca* sits uneasily with 120 years of preceding case law. Given how unmoored it was from the start, it might seem unlikely that later developments could have done more to undermine the decision. Yet they have. While Justice Powell's dual-track theory of incorporation was already foreclosed in 1972, some at that time still argued that it might have a role to play outside the realm of criminal procedure. Since then, the Court has held otherwise. Until recently, dual-track incorporation attracted at least a measure of support in dissent. But this Court has now roundly rejected it. Nor has the plurality's rejection of the Sixth Amendment's historical unanimity requirement aged more gracefully. As we've seen, in the years since Apodaca, this Court has spoken inconsistently about its meaning— but nonetheless referred to the traditional unanimity requirement on at least eight occasions.64 In light of all this, calling Apodaca an outlier would be perhaps too suggestive of the possibility of company.
>
> When it comes to reliance interests, it's notable that neither Louisiana nor Oregon claims anything like the prospective economic, regulatory, or social disruption litigants seeking to preserve precedent usually invoke. No one, it seems, has signed a contract, entered a marriage, purchased a home, or opened a business based on the expectation that, should a crime occur, at least the accused may be sent away by a 10-to-2 verdict. Nor does anyone suggest that non-unanimous verdicts have "become part of our national

culture." It would be quite surprising if they had, given that non-unanimous verdicts are insufficient to convict in 48 States and federal court.

Instead, the only reliance interests that might be asserted here fall into two categories. The first concerns the fact Louisiana and Oregon may need to retry defendants convicted of felonies by non-unanimous verdicts whose cases are still pending on direct appeal.

[Louisiana and Oregon] credibly claim that the number of non-unanimous felony convictions still on direct appeal are somewhere in the hundreds, and retrying or plea bargaining these cases will surely impose a cost. But new rules of criminal procedures usually do, often affecting significant numbers of pending cases across the whole country. For example, after *Booker v. United States* held that the Federal Sentencing Guidelines must be advisory rather than mandatory, this Court vacated and remanded nearly 800 decisions to the courts of appeals. Similar consequences likely followed when *Crawford v. Washington* overturned prior interpretations of the Confrontation Clause or *Arizona v. Gant* changed the law for searches incident to arrests.70 Our decision here promises to cause less, and certainly nothing before us supports the dissent's surmise that it will cause wildly more, disruption than these other decisions.

The second and related reliance interest the dissent seizes upon involves the interest Louisiana and Oregon have in the security of their final criminal judgments. In light of our   decision today, the dissent worries that defendants whose appeals are already complete might seek to challenge their non-unanimous convictions through collateral (i.e., habeas) review.

But again the worries outstrip the facts. Under *Teague v. Lane*, newly recognized rules of criminal procedure do not normally apply in collateral review. True, Teague left open the possibility of an exception for "watershed rules" "implicat[ing] the fundamental fairness [and accuracy] of the trial." But, as this language suggests, Teague's test is a demanding one, so much so that this Court has yet to announce a new rule of criminal procedure capable of meeting it. And the test is demanding by design, expressly calibrated to address the reliance interests States have in the finality of their criminal judgments.

After reading *Dobbs* below, compare Justice Alito's take on stare decisis to both Justice Gorsuch's opinion in *Ramos*, and the opinion of Justices O'Connor, Kennedy, and Souter in *Casey*.

A word about *Dobbs*. *Dobbs* is easily the most significant overturning of precedent since the decision in *Brown v. Board of Education of Topeka Kansas*, 347 U.S. 483 (1954), overturned *Plessy v. Ferguson*, 163 U.S. 537 (1896) (see chapter 6 Equal Protection below). Both cases dealt with societal changing issues rife with controversy and national division. One key difference, however, between the two is worth noting. The *Brown* opinion, issued by a carefully constructed unanimous vote, actually acknowledged rights that had not been acknowledged before—the right against governmental discrimination on the basis of race. The decision below erased a right held by women for 50 years on the basis of a bitterly divided Supreme Court. The decision will be analyzed by generations of law students and legal scholars for what it did and did not do in arriving at the conclusion that the Constitution does not support a right to an abortion. In reading the case, consider the earlier materials on abortion and stare decisis, and try to draw your own conclusion about the decision.

THOMAS E. DOBBS, STATE HEALTH OFFICER OF THE MISSISSIPPI DEPARTMENT OF HEALTH, ET AL., PETITIONERS v. JACKSON WOMEN'S HEALTH ORGANIZATION
597 U.S. ____ (2022)

On Writ of Certiorari to the United States Court of Appeals for the Fifth Circuit Justice ALITO delivered the opinion of the Court.

Abortion presents a profound moral issue on which Americans hold sharply conflicting views. Some believe fervently that a human person comes into being at conception and that abortion ends an innocent life. Others feel just as strongly that any regulation of abortion invades a woman's right to control her own body and prevents women from achieving full equality. Still others in a third group think that abortion should be allowed under some but not all circumstances, and those within this group hold a variety of views about the particular restrictions that should be imposed.

For the first 185 years after the adoption of the Constitution, each State was permitted to address this issue in accordance with the views of its citizens. Then, in 1973, this Court decided *Roe v. Wade*, 410 U. S. 113. Even though the Constitution makes no mention of abortion, the Court held that it confers a broad right to obtain one. It did not claim that American law or the common law had ever recognized such a right, and its survey of history ranged from the constitutionally irrelevant (*e.g.*, its discussion of abortion in antiquity) to the plainly incorrect (*e.g.*, its assertion that abortion was probably never a crime under the common law). After cataloging a wealth of other information having no bearing on the meaning of the Constitution, the opinion concluded with a numbered set of rules much like those that might be found in a statute enacted by a legislature.

[At] the time of *Roe*, 30 States still prohibited abortion at all stages. In the years prior to that decision, about a third of the States had liberalized their laws, but *Roe* abruptly ended that political process. It imposed the same highly restrictive regime on the entire Nation, and it effectively struck down the abortion laws of every single State. As Justice Byron White aptly put it in his dissent, the decision represented the "exercise of raw judicial power," 410 U. S., at 222, and it sparked a national controversy that has embittered our political culture for a half century.

Eventually, in *Planned Parenthood of Southeastern Pa. v. Casey*, 505 U. S. 833 (1992), the Court revisited *Roe*, but the Members of the Court split three ways. Two Justices expressed no desire to change *Roe* in any way. Four others wanted to overrule the decision in its entirety. And the three remaining Justices, who jointly signed the controlling opinion, took a third position. Their opinion did not endorse *Roe*'s reasoning, and it even hinted that one or more of its authors might have "reservations" about whether the Constitution protects a right to abortion. But the opinion concluded that *stare decisis*, which calls for prior decisions to be followed in most instances, required adherence to what it called *Roe*'s "central holding"—that a State may not constitutionally protect fetal life before "viability"—even if that holding was wrong. Anything less, the opinion claimed, would undermine respect for this Court and the rule of law.

[Before] us now is one such state law. The State of Mississippi asks us to uphold the constitutionality of a law that generally prohibits an abortion after the 15th week of pregnancy—several weeks before the point at which a fetus is now regarded as "viable" outside the womb. In defending this law, the State's primary argument is that we should reconsider and overrule *Roe* and *Casey* and once again allow each State to regulate abortion as its citizens wish. On the other side, respondents and the Solicitor General ask us to reaffirm *Roe* and *Casey*, and they contend that the Mississippi law cannot stand if we do so. Allowing Mississippi to prohibit abortions after 15 weeks of pregnancy, they argue, "would be no different than overruling *Casey* and *Roe* entirely." Brief for Respondents 43. They contend that "no half-measures" are available and that we must either reaffirm or overrule *Roe* and *Casey*. Brief for Respondents 50.

We hold that *Roe* and *Casey* must be overruled. The Constitution makes no reference to abortion, and no such right is implicitly protected by any constitutional provision, including the one on which the defenders of *Roe* and *Casey* now chiefly rely—the Due Process Clause of the Fourteenth Amendment. That provision has been held to guarantee some rights that are not mentioned in the Constitution, but any such right must be "deeply rooted in this Nation's history and tradition" and "implicit in the concept of ordered liberty." *Washington* v. *Glucksberg*, 521 U. S. 702, 721 (1997) (internal quotation marks omitted).

The right to abortion does not fall within this category. Until the latter part of the 20th century, such a right was entirely unknown in American law. [*Stare] decisis*, the doctrine on which *Casey*'s controlling opinion was based, does not compel unending adherence to *Roe*'s abuse of judicial authority. *Roe* was egregiously wrong from the start. Its reasoning was exceptionally weak, and the decision has had damaging consequences. And far from bringing about a national settlement of the abortion issue, *Roe* and *Casey* have enflamed debate and deepened division.

It is time to heed the Constitution and return the issue of abortion to the people's elected representatives. "The permissibility of abortion, and the limitations, upon it, are to be resolved like most important questions in our democracy: by citizens trying to persuade one another and then voting." *Casey*, 505 U. S., at 979 (Scalia, J., concurring in judgment in part and dissenting in part). That is what the Constitution and the rule of law demand.

[II]

We begin by considering the critical question whether the Constitution, properly understood, confers a right to obtain an abortion. Skipping over that question, the controlling opinion in *Casey* reaffirmed *Roe*'s "central holding" based solely on the doctrine of *stare decisis*, but as we will explain, proper application of *stare decisis* required an assessment of the strength of the grounds on which *Roe* was based. See *infra*, at 45–56.

We therefore turn to the question that the *Casey* plurality did not consider, and we address that question in three steps. First, we explain the standard that our cases have used in determining whether the Fourteenth Amendment's reference to "liberty" protects a particular right. Second, we examine whether the right at issue in this case is rooted in our Nation's history and tradition and whether it is an essential component of what we have described as "ordered liberty." Finally, we consider whether a right to obtain an abortion is part of a broader entrenched right that is supported by other precedents.

A

1

Constitutional analysis must begin with "the language of the instrument," *Gibbons* v. *Ogden*, 9 Wheat. 1, 186–189 (1824), which offers a "fixed standard" for ascertaining what our founding document means, 1 J. Story, Commentaries on the Constitution of the United States §399, p. 383 (1833). The Constitution makes no express reference to a right to obtain an abortion, and therefore those who claim that it protects such a right must show that the right is somehow implicit in the constitutional text.

Roe, however, was remarkably loose in its treatment of the constitutional text. It held that the abortion right, which is not mentioned in the Constitution, is part of a right to privacy, which is also not mentioned. See 410 U. S., at 152–153. And that privacy right, *Roe* observed, had been found to spring from no fewer than five different constitutional provisions—the First, Fourth, Fifth, Ninth, and Fourteenth Amendments. *Id.*, at 152.

The Court's discussion left open at least three ways in which some combination of these provisions could protect the abortion right. One possibility was that the right was "founded . . . in the Ninth Amendment's reservation of rights to the people." *Id.,* at 153. Another was that the right was rooted in the First, Fourth, or Fifth Amendment, or in some combination of those provisions, and that this right had been "incorporated" into the Due Process Clause of the Fourteenth Amendment just as many other Bill of Rights provisions had by then been incorporated. *Ibid*; see also *McDonald* v. *Chicago*, 561 U. S. 742, 763–766 (2010) (majority opinion) (discussing incorporation). And a third path was that the First, Fourth, and Fifth Amendments played no role and that the right was simply a component of the "liberty" protected by the Fourteenth Amendment's Due Process Clause. *Roe*, 410 U. S., at 153. *Roe* expressed the "feel[ing]" that the Fourteenth Amendment was the provision that did the work, but its message seemed to be that the abortion right could be found *somewhere* in the Constitution and that specifying its exact location was not of paramount importance.[16] The *Casey* Court did not defend this unfocused analysis and instead grounded its decision solely on the theory that the right to obtain an abortion is part of the "liberty" protected by the Fourteenth Amendment's Due Process Clause.

2

The underlying theory on which this argument rests—that the Fourteenth Amendment's Due Process Clause provides substantive, as well as procedural, protection for "liberty"—has long been controversial. But our decisions have held that the Due Process Clause protects two categories of substantive rights.

The first consists of rights guaranteed by the first eight Amendments. Those Amendments originally applied only to the Federal Government, *Barron ex rel. Tiernan* v. *Mayor of Baltimore*, 7 Pet. 243, 247–251 (1833) (opinion for the Court by Marshall, C. J.), but this Court has held that the Due Process Clause of the Fourteenth Amendment "incorporates" the great majority of those rights and thus makes them equally applicable to the States. See *McDonald*, 561 U. S., at 763–767, and nn. 12–13. The second category—which is the one in question here—comprises a select list of fundamental rights that are not mentioned anywhere in the Constitution.

In deciding whether a right falls into either of these categories, the Court has long asked whether the right is "deeply rooted in [our] history and tradition" and whether it is essential to our Nation's "scheme of ordered liberty." *Timbs* v. *Indiana*, 586 U. S. ___, ___ (2019) (slip op., at 3) (internal quotation marks omitted); *McDonald*, 561 U. S., at 764, 767 (internal quotation marks omitted); *Glucksberg*, 521 U. S., at 721 (internal quotation marks omitted).[19] And in conducting this inquiry, we have engaged in a careful analysis of the history of the right at issue.

Justice Ginsburg's opinion for the Court in *Timbs* is a recent example. In concluding that the Eighth Amendment's protection against excessive fines is "fundamental to our scheme of ordered liberty" and "deeply rooted in this Nation's history and tradition," 586 U. S., at ___ (slip op., at 7) (internal quotation marks omitted), her opinion traced the right back to Magna Carta, Blackstone's Commentaries, and 35 of the 37 state constitutions in effect at the ratification of the Fourteenth Amendment. 586 U. S., at ___–___ (slip op., at 3–7).

A similar inquiry was undertaken in *McDonald*, which held that the Fourteenth Amendment protects the right to keep and bear arms. The lead opinion surveyed the origins of the Second Amendment, the debates in Congress about the adoption of the Fourteenth Amendment, the state constitutions in effect when that Amendment was ratified (at least 22 of the 37 States protected the right to keep and bear arms), federal laws enacted during the same period, and other relevant historical evidence. 561 U. S., at 767–777. Only then did the opinion conclude that "the Framers and ratifiers of the Fourteenth Amendment counted the right to keep and bear arms among those fundamental rights necessary to our system of ordered liberty." *Id.*, at 778; see also *id.*, at 822–850 (THOMAS, J., concurring in part and concurring in judgment) (surveying history and reaching the same result under the Fourteenth Amendment's Privileges or Immunities Clause).

[On] occasion, when the Court has ignored the "[a]ppropriate limits" imposed by "'respect for the teachings of history,'" *Moore,* 431 U. S., at 503 (plurality opinion), it has fallen into the freewheeling judicial policymaking that characterized discredited decisions such as *Lochner* v. *New York*, 198 U. S. 45 (1905). The Court must not fall prey to such an unprincipled approach. Instead, guided by the history and tradition that map the essential components of our Nation's concept of ordered liberty, we must ask what the *Fourteenth Amendment* means by the term "liberty." When we engage in that inquiry in the present case, the clear answer is that the Fourteenth Amendment does not protect the right to an abortion.[22]

B

1

Until the latter part of the 20th century, there was no support in American law for a constitutional right to obtain an abortion. No state constitutional provision had recognized such a right. Until a few years before *Roe* was handed down, no federal or state court had recognized such a right. Nor had any scholarly treatise of which we are aware. And although law review articles are not reticent about advocating new rights, the earliest article proposing a constitutional right to abortion that has come to our attention was published only a few years before *Roe*.[23]

---

[22] That is true regardless of whether we look to the Amendment's Due Process Clause or its Privileges or Immunities Clause. Some scholars and Justices have maintained that

the Privileges or Immunities Clause is the provision of the Fourteenth Amendment that guarantees substantive rights. See, *e.g., McDonald* v. *Chicago*, 561 U. S. 742, 813–850 (2010) (THOMAS, J., concurring in part and concurring in judgment); *Duncan*, 391 U. S., at 165–166 (Black, J., concurring); A. Amar, Bill of Rights: Creation and Reconstruction 163–180 (1998) (Amar); J. Ely, Democracy and Distrust 22–30 (1980); 2 W. Crosskey, Politics and the Constitution in the History of the United States 1089–1095 (1953). But even on that view, such a right would need to be rooted in the Nation's history and tradition. See *Corfield* v. *Coryell*, 6 F. Cas. 546, 551–552 (No. 3,230) (CC ED Pa. 1823) (describing unenumerated rights under the Privileges and Immunities Clause, Art. IV, §2, as those "fundamental" rights "which have, at all times, been enjoyed by the citizens of the several states"); Amar 176 (relying on *Corfield* to interpret the Privileges or Immunities Clause); cf. *McDonald*, 561 U. S., at 819–820, 832, 854 (opinion of THOMAS, J.)

Not only was there no support for such a constitutional right until shortly before *Roe*, but abortion had long been a crime in every single State. At common law, abortion was criminal in at least some stages of pregnancy and was regarded as unlawful and could have very serious consequences at all stages. American law followed the common law until a wave of statutory restrictions in the 1800s expanded criminal liability for abortions. By the time of the adoption of the Fourteenth Amendment, three-quarters of the States had made abortion a crime at any stage of pregnancy, and the remaining States would soon follow.

Roe either ignored or misstated this history, and *Casey* declined to reconsider *Roe*'s faulty historical analysis. It is therefore important to set the record straight.

2

a

We begin with the common law, under which abortion was a crime at least after "quickening"—*i.e.*, the first felt movement of the fetus in the womb, which usually occurs between the 16th and 18th week of pregnancy.[24]

The "eminent common-law authorities (Blackstone, Coke, Hale, and the like)," *Kahler* v. *Kansas*, 589 U. S. ___, ___ (2020) (slip op., at 7), *all* describe abortion after quickening as criminal. [E]nglish cases dating all the way back to the 13th century corroborate the treatises' statements that abortion was a crime.

[T]hat the common law did not condone even prequickening abortions is confirmed by what one might call a proto-felony-murder rule. Hale and Blackstone explained a way in which a pre-quickening abortion could rise to the level of a homicide. Hale wrote that if a physician gave a woman "with child*"* a "potion" to cause an abortion, and the woman died, it was "murder" because the potion was given "*unlawfully* to destroy her child within her." 1 Hale 429–430 (emphasis added). As Blackstone explained, to be "murder" a killing had to be done with "malice aforethought, . . . either express or implied." 4 Blackstone 198 (emphasis deleted). In the case of an abortionist, Blackstone wrote, "the law will imply [malice]" for the same reason that it would imply malice if a person who intended to kill one person accidentally killed a different person:

"[If] one shoots at A and misses *him*, but kills B, this is murder; because of the previous felonious intent, which the law transfers from one to the other. The same is the case, where one lays poison for A; and B, against whom the prisoner had no malicious intent, takes it, and it kills him; this is likewise murder. *So also*, if one gives *a woman with child* a medicine to procure abortion, and it operates so violently as to kill the woman, *this is murder* in the person who gave it." *Id.*, at 200–201 (emphasis added; footnote omitted).

[In] sum, although common-law authorities differed on the severity of punishment for abortions committed at different points in pregnancy, none endorsed the practice. Moreover, we are aware of no common-law case or authority, and the parties have not pointed to any, that remotely suggests a positive *right* to procure an abortion at any stage of pregnancy.

b

The few cases available from the early colonial period corroborate that abortion was a crime. See generally Dellapenna 215–228 (collecting cases). In Maryland in 1652, for example, an indictment charged that a man "Murtherously endeavoured to destroy or Murther the Child by him begotten in the Womb." *Proprietary* v. *Mitchell*, 10 Md. Archives 80, 183 (1652) (W. Browne ed. 1891). And by the 19th century, courts frequently explained that the common law made abortion of a quick child a crime. See, *e.g.*, *Smith* v. *Gaffard*, 31 Ala. 45, 51 (1857); *Smith* v. *State*, 33 Me. 48, 55 (1851); *State* v. *Cooper*, 22 N. J. L. 52, 52–55 (1849); *Commonwealth* v. *Parker*, 50 Mass. 263, 264–268 (1845).

c

[The] Solicitor General offers a different explanation of the basis for the quickening rule, namely, that before quickening the common law did not regard a fetus "as having a 'separate and independent existence.'" Brief for United States 26 (quoting *Parker*, 50 Mass., at 266). But the case on which the Solicitor General relies for this proposition also suggested that the criminal law's quickening rule was out of step with the treatment of prenatal life in other areas of law, noting that "to many purposes, in reference to civil rights, an infant *in ventre sa mere* is regarded as a person in being." *Ibid.* (citing 1 Blackstone 129); see also *Evans,* 49 N. Y., at 89; *Mills* v. *Commonwealth*, 13 Pa. 631, 633 (1850); *Morrow* v. *Scott*, 7 Ga. 535, 537 (1849); *Hall* v. *Hancock*, 32 Mass. 255, 258 (1834); *Thellusson* v. *Woodford*, 4 Ves. 227, 321–322, 31 Eng. Rep. 117, 163 (1789).

[In] this country during the 19th century, the vast majority of the States enacted statutes criminalizing abortion at all stages of pregnancy. See Appendix A, *infra* (listing state statutory provisions in chronological order). By 1868, the year when the Fourteenth Amendment was ratified, three-quarters of the States, 28 out of 37, had enacted statutes making abortion a crime even if it was performed before quickening. See *ibid.* Of the nine States that had not yet

[This] overwhelming consensus endured until the day *Roe* was decided. At that time, also by the *Roe* Court's own count, a substantial majority—30 States—still prohibited abortion at all stages except to save the life of the mother. See *id.*, at 118, and n. 2 (listing States). And though *Roe* discerned a "trend toward liberalization" in about "one-third of the States," those States still criminalized some abortions and regulated them more stringently than *Roe* would allow. *Id.*, at 140, and n. 37; Tribe 2. In short, the "Court's opinion in *Roe* itself convincingly refutes the notion that the abortion liberty is deeply rooted in the history or tradition of our people." *Thornburgh* v. *American College of Obstetricians and Gynecologists*, 476 U. S. 747, 793 (1986) (White, J., dissenting).

d

The inescapable conclusion is that a right to abortion is not deeply rooted in the Nation's history and traditions. On the contrary, an unbroken tradition of prohibiting abortion on pain of criminal punishment persisted from the earliest days of the common law until 1973. The Court in *Roe* could have said of abortion exactly what *Glucksberg* said of assisted suicide: "Attitudes toward [abortion] have changed since Bracton, but our laws have consistently condemned, and continue to prohibit, [that practice]." 521 U. S., at 719.

3

Respondents and their *amici* have no persuasive answer to this historical evidence.

Neither respondents nor the Solicitor General disputes the fact that by 1868 the vast majority of States criminalized abortion at all stages of pregnancy. See Brief for Petitioners 12–13; see also Brief for American Historical Association et al. as *Amici Curiae* 27–28, and nn. 14–15 (conceding that 26 out of 37 States prohibited abortion before quickening); Tr. of Oral Arg. 74–75 (respondents' counsel conceding the same). Instead, respondents are forced to argue that it "does [not] matter that some States prohibited abortion at the time *Roe* was decided or when the Fourteenth Amendment was adopted." Brief for Respondents 21. But that argument flies in the face of the standard we have applied in determining whether an asserted right that is nowhere mentioned in the Constitution is nevertheless protected by the Fourteenth Amendment.

Not only are respondents and their *amici* unable to show that a constitutional right to abortion was established when the Fourteenth Amendment was adopted, but they have found no support for the existence of an abortion right that predates the latter part of the 20th century—no state constitutional provision, no statute, no judicial decision, no learned treatise. The earliest sources called to our attention are a few district court and state court decisions decided shortly before *Roe* and a small number of law review articles from the same time period.

[One] *amicus* brief relied upon by respondents tries to dismiss the significance of the state criminal statutes that were in effect when the Fourteenth Amendment was adopted by suggesting that they were enacted for illegitimate reasons. According to this account, which is based almost entirely on statements made by one prominent proponent of the statutes, important motives for the laws were the fear that Catholic immigrants were having more babies than Protestants and that the availability of abortion was leading White Protestant women to "shir[k their] maternal duties." Brief for American Historical Association et al. as *Amici Curiae* 20.

Resort to this argument is a testament to the lack of any real historical support for the right that *Roe* and *Casey* recognized. This Court has long disfavored arguments based on alleged legislative motives. See, *e.g.*, *Erie v. Pap's A. M.*, 529 U. S. 277, 292 (2000) (plurality opinion); *Turner Broadcasting System, Inc. v. FCC*, 512 U. S. 622, 652 (1994); *United States v. O'Brien*, 391 U. S. 367, 383 (1968); *Arizona v. California*, 283 U. S. 423, 455 (1931) (collecting cases). The Court has recognized that inquiries into legislative motives "are a hazardous matter." *O'Brien*, 391 U. S., at 383. Even when an argument about legislative motive is backed by statements made by legislators who voted for a law, we have been reluctant to attribute those motives to the legislative body as a whole. "What motivates one legislator to make a speech about a statute is not necessarily what motivates scores of others to enact it." *Id.,* at 384.

One may disagree with this belief (and our decision is not based on any view about when a State should regard prenatal life as having rights or legally cognizable interests), but even *Roe* and *Casey* did not question the good faith of abortion opponents. See, *e.g., Casey,* 505 U. S., at 850 ("Men and women of good conscience can disagree . . . about the profound moral and spiritual implications of terminating a pregnancy even in its earliest stage"). And we see no reason to discount the significance of the state laws in question based on these *amici*'s suggestions about legislative motive.

C

1

Instead of seriously pressing the argument that the abortion right itself has deep roots, supporters of *Roe* and *Casey* contend that the abortion right is an integral part of a broader entrenched right. *Roe* termed this a right to privacy, 410 U. S., at 154, and *Casey* described it as the freedom to make "intimate and personal choices" that are "central to personal dignity and autonomy," 505 U. S., at 851.*Casey* elaborated: "At the heart of liberty is the right to define one's own concept of existence, of meaning, of the universe, and of the mystery of human life." *Ibid.*

The Court did not claim that this broadly framed right is absolute, and no such claim would be plausible. While individuals are certainly free *to think* and *to say* what they wish about "existence," "meaning," the "universe," and "the mystery of human life," they are not always free *to act* in accordance with those thoughts. License to act on the basis of such beliefs may correspond to one of the many understandings of "liberty," but it is certainly not "ordered liberty."

Ordered liberty sets limits and defines the boundary between competing interests. *Roe* and *Casey* each struck a particular balance between the interests of a woman who wants an abortion and the interests of what they termed "potential life." *Roe,* 410 U. S., at 150 (emphasis deleted); Casey, 505 U. S., at 852. But the people of the various States may evaluate those interests differently. In some States, voters may believe that the abortion right should be even more extensive than the right that *Roe* and *Casey* recognized. Voters in other States may wish to impose tight restrictions based on their belief that abortion destroys an "unborn human being." Miss. Code Ann. §41–41–191(4)(b). Our Nation's historical understanding of ordered liberty does not prevent the people's elected representatives from deciding how abortion should be regulated.

Nor does the right to obtain an abortion have a sound basis in precedent. *Casey* relied on cases involving the right to marry a person of a different race, *Loving* v. *Virginia,* 388 U. S. 1 (1967); the right to marry while in prison, *Turner* v. *Safley,* 482 U. S. 78 (1987); the right to obtain contraceptives, *Griswold* v. *Connecticut,* 381 U. S. 479 (1965), *Eisenstadt* v. *Baird,* 405 U. S. 438 (1972), *Carey* v. *Population Services Int'l,* 431 U. S. 678 (1977); the right to reside with relatives, *Moore* v. *East Cleveland,* 431 U. S. 494 (1977); the right to make decisions about the education of one's children, *Pierce* v. *Society of Sisters,* 268 U. S. 510 (1925), *Meyer* v. *Nebraska,* 262 U. S. 390 (1923); the right not to be sterilized without consent, *Skinner* v. *Oklahoma ex rel. Williamson,* 316 U. S. 535 (1942); and the right in certain circumstances not to undergo involuntary surgery, forced administration of drugs, or other substantially similar procedures, *Winston* v. *Lee*, 470 U. S. 753 (1985), *Washington* v. *Harper*, 494 U. S. 210 (1990), *Rochin* v. *California*, 342 U. S. 165 (1952). Respondents and the Solicitor General also rely on post-*Casey* decisions like *Lawrence* v. *Texas*, 539 U. S. 558 (2003) (right to engage in private, consensual sexual acts), and *Obergefell* v. *Hodges*, 576 U. S. 644 (2015) (right to marry a person of the same sex). See Brief for Respondents 18; Brief for United States 23–24.

These attempts to justify abortion through appeals to a broader right to autonomy and to define one's "concept of existence" prove too much. *Casey*, 505 U. S., at 851. Those criteria, at a high level of generality, could license fundamental rights to illicit drug use, prostitution, and the like. See *Compassion in Dying* v. *Washington*, 85 F. 3d 1440, 1444 (CA9 1996) (O'Scannlain, J., dissenting from denial of rehearing en banc). None of these rights has any claim to being deeply rooted in history. *Id.*, at 1440, 1445.

What sharply distinguishes the abortion right from the rights recognized in the cases on which *Roe* and *Casey* rely is something that both those decisions acknowledged: Abortion destroys what those decisions call "potential life" and what the law at issue in this case regards as the life of an "unborn human being." See *Roe*, 410 U. S., at 159 (abortion is "inherently different"); *Casey*, 505 U. S., at 852 (abortion is "a unique act"). None of the other decisions cited by *Roe* and *Casey* involved the critical moral question posed by abortion. They are therefore inapposite. They do not support the right to obtain an abortion, and by the same token, our conclusion that the Constitution does not confer such a right does not undermine them in any way.

2

In drawing this critical distinction between the abortion right and other rights, it is not necessary to dispute *Casey*'s claim (which we accept for the sake of argument) that "the specific practices of States at the time of the adoption of the Fourteenth Amendment" do not "mar[k] the outer limits of the substantive sphere of liberty which the Fourteenth Amendment protects." 505 U. S., at 848. Abortion is nothing new. It has been addressed by lawmakers for centuries, and the fundamental moral question that it poses is ageless.

Defenders of *Roe* and *Casey* do not claim that any new scientific learning calls for a different answer to the underlying moral question, but they do contend that changes in society require the recognition of a constitutional right to obtain an abortion. Without the availability of abortion, they maintain, people will be inhibited from exercising their freedom to choose the types of relationships they desire, and women will be unable to compete with men in the workplace and in other endeavors.

Americans who believe that abortion should be restricted press countervailing arguments about modern developments. They note that attitudes about the pregnancy of unmarried women have changed drastically; that federal and state laws ban discrimination on the basis of pregnancy;[42] that leave for pregnancy and childbirth are now guaranteed by law in many cases;[43] that the costs of medical care associated with pregnancy are covered by insurance or government assistance;[44] that States have increasingly adopted "safe haven" laws, which generally allow women to drop off babies anonymously;[45] and that a woman who puts her newborn up for adoption today has little reason to fear that the baby will not find a suitable home.[46] They also claim that many people now have a new appreciation of fetal life and that when prospective parents who want to have a child view a sonogram, they typically have no doubt that what they see is their daughter or son.

Both sides make important policy arguments, but supporters of *Roe* and *Casey* must show that this Court has the authority to weigh those arguments and decide how abortion may be regulated in the States. They have failed to make that showing, and we thus return the power to weigh those arguments to the people and their elected representatives.

D

1

The dissent is very candid that it cannot show that a constitutional right to abortion has any foundation, let alone a "'deeply rooted'" one, "'in this Nation's history and tradition.'" *Glucksberg*, 521 U. S., at 721; see *post*, at 12–14 (joint opinion of BREYER, SOTOMAYOR, and KAGAN, JJ.). [The] dissent's failure to engage with this long tradition is devastating to its position. We have held that the "established method of substantive-due-process analysis" requires that an unenumerated right be "'deeply rooted in this Nation's history and tradition'" before it can be recognized as a component of the "liberty" protected in the Due Process Clause. *Glucksberg*, 521 U. S., at 721; cf. *Timbs*, 586 U. S., at ___ (slip op., at 7). But despite the dissent's professed fidelity to *stare decisis*, it fails to seriously engage with that important precedent—which it cannot possibly satisfy.

[2]

Because the dissent cannot argue that the abortion right is rooted in this Nation's history and tradition, it contends that the "constitutional tradition" is "not captured whole at a single moment," and that its "meaning gains content from the long sweep of our history and from successive judicial precedents." *Post*, at 18 (internal quotation marks omitted). This vague formulation imposes no clear restraints on what Justice White called the "exercise of raw judicial power," *Roe*, 410 U. S., at 222 (dissenting opinion), and while the dissent claims that its standard "does not mean anything goes," *post*, at 17, any real restraints are hard to discern.

The largely limitless reach of the dissenters' standard is illustrated by the way they apply it here. First, if the "long sweep of history" imposes any restraint on the recognition of unenumerated rights, then *Roe* was surely wrong, since abortion was never allowed (except to save the life of the mother) in a majority of States for over 100 years before that decision was handed down. Second, it is impossible to defend *Roe* based on prior precedent because all of the precedents *Roe* cited, including *Griswold* and *Eisenstadt*, were critically different for a reason that we have explained: None of those cases involved the destruction of what *Roe* called "potential life." See *supra*, at 32.

So without support in history or relevant precedent, *Roe*'s reasoning cannot be defended even under the dissent's proposed test, and the dissent is forced to rely solely on the fact that a constitutional right to abortion was recognized in *Roe* and later decisions that accepted *Roe*'s interpretation. Under the doctrine of *stare decisis*, those precedents are entitled to careful and respectful consideration, and we engage in that analysis below.

[III]

[In] this case, five factors weigh strongly in favor of overruling *Roe* and *Casey*: the nature of their error, the quality of their reasoning, the "workability" of the rules they imposed on the country, their disruptive effect on other areas of the law, and the absence of concrete reliance.

A

The nature of the Court's error. An erroneous interpretation of the Constitution is always important, but some are more damaging than others.

The infamous decision in *Plessy* v. *Ferguson,* was one such decision. It betrayed our commitment to "equality before the law." 163 U. S., at 562 (Harlan, J., dissenting). It was "egregiously wrong" on the day it was decided, see *Ramos,* 590 U. S., at ___ (opinion of KAVANAUGH, J.) (slip op., at 7), and as the Solicitor General agreed at oral argument, it should have been overruled at the earliest opportunity.

Roe was also egregiously wrong and deeply damaging. For reasons already explained, *Roe*'s constitutional analysis was far outside the bounds of any reasonable interpretation of the various constitutional provisions to which it vaguely pointed.

Roe was on a collision course with the Constitution from the day it was decided, *Casey* perpetuated its errors, and those errors do not concern some arcane corner of the law of little importance to the American people. Rather, wielding nothing but "raw judicial power," *Roe,* 410 U. S., at 222 (White, J., dissenting), the Court usurped the power to address a question of profound moral and social importance that the Constitution unequivocally leaves for the people. *Casey* described itself as calling both sides of the national controversy to resolve their debate, but in doing so, *Casey* necessarily declared a winning side. Those on the losing side—those who sought to advance the State's interest in fetal life—could no longer seek to persuade their elected representatives to adopt policies consistent with their views. The Court short-circuited the democratic process by closing it to the large number of Americans who dissented in any respect from *Roe.* "*Roe* fanned into life an issue that has inflamed our national politics in general, and has obscured with its smoke the selection of Justices to this Court in particular, ever since." *Casey,* 505 U. S., at 995–996 (opinion of Scalia, J.). Together, *Roe* and *Casey* represent an error that cannot be allowed to stand.

As the Court's landmark decision in *West Coast Hotel* illustrates, the Court has previously overruled decisions that wrongly removed an issue from the people and the democratic process. As Justice White later explained, "decisions that find in the Constitution principles or values that cannot fairly be read into that document usurp the people's authority, for such decisions represent choices that the people have never made and that they cannot disavow through corrective legislation. For this reason, it is essential that this Court maintain the power to restore authority to its proper possessors by correcting constitutional decisions that, on reconsideration, are found to be mistaken." *Thornburgh,* 476 U. S., at 787 (dissenting opinion).

B

The quality of the reasoning. Under our precedents, the quality of the reasoning in a prior case has an important bearing on whether it should be reconsidered. See *Janus,* 585 U. S., at ___ (slip op., at 38); *Ramos,* 590 U. S., at ___ – ___ (opinion of KAVANAUGH, J.) (slip op., at 7–8). In Part II, *supra,* we explained why *Roe* was incorrectly decided, but that decision was more than just wrong. It stood on exceptionally weak grounds.

Roe found that the Constitution implicitly conferred a right to obtain an abortion, but it failed to ground its decision in text, history, or precedent. It relied on an erroneous historical narrative; it devoted great attention to and presumably relied on matters that have no bearing on the meaning of the Constitution; it disregarded the fundamental difference between the precedents on which it relied and the question before the Court; it concocted an elaborate set of rules, with different restrictions for each trimester of pregnancy, but it did not explain how this veritable code could be teased out of anything in the Constitution, the history of abortion laws, prior precedent, or any other cited source; and its most important rule (that States cannot protect fetal life prior to "viability") was never raised by any party and has never been plausibly explained. *Roe*'s reasoning quickly drew scathing scholarly criticism, even from supporters of broad access to abortion.

The *Casey* plurality, while reaffirming *Roe*'s central holding, pointedly refrained from endorsing most of its reasoning. It revised the textual basis for the abortion right, silently abandoned *Roe*'s erroneous historical narrative, and jettisoned the trimester framework. But it replaced that scheme with an arbitrary "undue burden" test and relied on an exceptional version of *stare decisis* that, as explained below, this Court had never before applied and has never invoked since.

1

a

The weaknesses in *Roe*'s reasoning are well-known. Without any grounding in the constitutional text, history, or precedent, it imposed on the entire country a detailed set of rules much like those that one might expect to find in a statute or regulation. See 410 U. S., at 163–164. Dividing pregnancy into three trimesters, the Court imposed special rules for each.

b

Not only did this scheme resemble the work of a legislature, but the Court made little effort to explain how these rules could be deduced from any of the sources on which constitutional decisions are usually based. We have already discussed *Roe*'s treatment of constitutional text, and the opinion failed to show that history, precedent, or any other cited source supported its scheme.

[Finally], after all this, the Court turned to precedent. Citing a broad array of cases, the Court found support for a constitutional "right of personal privacy," *id.,* at 152, but it conflated two very different meanings of the term: the right to shield information from disclosure and the right to make and implement important personal decisions without governmental interference. See *Whalen* v. *Roe*, 429 U. S. 589, 599–600 (1977). Only the cases involving this second sense of the term could have any possible relevance to the abortion issue, and some of the cases in that category involved personal decisions that were obviously very, very far afield. See *Pierce*, 268 U. S. 510 (right to send children to religious school); *Meyer*, 262 U. S. 390 (right to have children receive German language instruction).

What remained was a handful of cases having something to do with marriage, *Loving*, 388 U. S. 1 (right to marry a person of a different race), or procreation, *Skinner*, 316 U. S. 535 (right not to be sterilized); *Griswold*, 381 U. S. 479 (right of married persons to obtain contraceptives); *Eisenstadt*, 405 U. S. 438 (same, for unmarried persons). But none of these decisions involved what is distinctive about abortion: its effect on what *Roe* termed "potential life."

[2]

When *Casey* revisited *Roe* almost 20 years later, very little of *Roe*'s reasoning was defended or preserved. The Court abandoned any reliance on a privacy right and instead grounded the abortion right entirely on the Fourteenth Amendment's Due Process Clause. 505 U. S., at 846. The Court did not reaffirm *Roe*'s erroneous account of abortion history. In fact, none of the Justices in the majority said anything about the history of the abortion right. And as for precedent, the Court relied on essentially the same body of cases that *Roe* had cited. Thus, with respect to the standard grounds for constitutional decisionmaking— text, history, and precedent—*Casey* did not attempt to bolster *Roe*'s reasoning.

The Court also made no real effort to remedy one of the greatest weaknesses in *Roe*'s analysis: its much-criticized discussion of viability. The Court retained what it called *Roe*'s "central holding"—that a State may not regulate previability abortions for the purpose of protecting fetal life— but it provided no principled defense of the viability line. 505 U. S., at 860, 870–871. Instead, it merely rephrased what *Roe* had said, stating that viability marked the point at which "the independent existence of a second life can in reason and fairness be the object of state protection that now overrides the rights of the woman." 505 U. S., at 870. Why "reason and fairness" demanded that the line be drawn at viability the Court did not explain. And the Justices who authored the controlling opinion conspicuously failed to say that they agreed with the viability rule; instead, they candidly acknowledged "the reservations [some] of us may have in reaffirming [that] holding of *Roe*." *Id.*, at 853.

The controlling opinion criticized and rejected *Roe*'s trimester scheme, 505 U. S., at 872, and substituted a new "undue burden" test, but the basis for this test was obscure. And as we will explain, the test is full of ambiguities and is difficult to apply.

Casey, in short, either refused to reaffirm or rejected important aspects of *Roe*'s analysis, failed to remedy glaring deficiencies in *Roe*'s reasoning, endorsed what it termed *Roe*'s central holding while suggesting that a majority might not have thought it was correct, provided no new support for the abortion right other than *Roe*'s status as precedent, and imposed a new and problematic test with no firm grounding in constitutional text, history, or precedent.

As discussed below, *Casey* also deployed a novel version of the doctrine of *stare decisis*. See *infra*, at 64–69. This new doctrine did not account for the profound wrongness of the decision in *Roe*, and placed great weight on an intangible form of reliance with little if any basis in prior case law. *Stare decisis* does not command the preservation of such a decision.

C

Workability. Our precedents counsel that another important consideration in deciding whether a precedent should be overruled is whether the rule it imposes is workable—that is, whether it can be understood and applied in a consistent and predictable manner. *Casey*'s "undue burden" test has scored poorly on the workability scale.

1

Problems begin with the very concept of an "undue burden." As Justice Scalia noted in his *Casey* partial dissent, determining whether a burden is "due" or "undue" is "inherently standardless." 505 U. S., at 992; see also *June Medical Services L. L. C.* v. *Russo*, 591 U. S. ___, ___ (2020) (GORSUCH, J., dissenting) (slip op., at 17) ("[W]hether a burden is deemed undue depends heavily on which factors the judge considers and how much weight he accords each of them" (internal quotation marks and alterations omitted)).

The *Casey* plurality tried to put meaning into the "undue burden" test by setting out three subsidiary rules, but these rules created their own problems. The first rule is that "a provision of law is invalid, if its purpose or effect is to place a *substantial obstacle* in the path of a woman seeking an abortion before the fetus attains viability." 505 U. S., at 878 (emphasis added); see also *id.*, at 877. But whether a particular obstacle qualifies as "substantial" is often open to reasonable debate. In the sense relevant here, "substantial" means "of ample or considerable amount, quantity, or size." Random House Webster's Unabridged Dictionary 1897 (2d ed. 2001). Huge burdens are plainly "substantial," and trivial ones are not, but in between these extremes, there is a wide gray area.

This ambiguity is a problem, and the second rule, which applies at all stages of a pregnancy, muddies things further. It states that measures designed "to ensure that the woman's choice is informed" are constitutional so long as they do not impose "an undue burden on the right." *Casey*, 505 U. S., at 878. To the extent that this rule applies to previability abortions, it overlaps with the first rule and appears to impose a different standard. Consider a law that imposes an insubstantial obstacle but serves little purpose. As applied to a pre-viability abortion, would such a regulation be constitutional on the ground that it does not impose a "*substantial* obstacle"? Or would it be unconstitutional on the ground that it creates an "*undue* burden" because the burden it imposes, though slight, outweighs its negligible benefits? *Casey* does not say, and this ambiguity would lead to confusion down the line. Compare *June Medical*, 591 U. S., at ___–___ (plurality opinion) (slip op., at 1–2), with *id.,* at ___–___ (ROBERTS, C. J., concurring) (slip op., at 5– 6).

The third rule complicates the picture even more. Under that rule, *"[u]nnecessary health* regulations that have the purpose or effect of presenting a *substantial obstacle* to a woman seeking an abortion impose an *undue burden* on the right." *Casey*, 505 U. S., at 878 (emphasis added). This rule contains no fewer than three vague terms. It includes the two already discussed—"undue burden" and "substantial obstacle"—even though they are inconsistent. And it adds a third ambiguous term when it refers to "*unnecessary* health regulations." The term "necessary" has a range of meanings—from "essential" to merely "useful." See Black's Law Dictionary 928 (5th ed. 1979); American Heritage Dictionary of the English Language 877 (1971). *Casey* did not explain the sense in which the term is used in this rule.

In addition to these problems, one more applies to all three rules. They all call on courts to examine a law's effect on women, but a regulation may have a very different impact on different women for a variety of reasons, including their places of residence, financial resources, family situations, work and personal obligations, knowledge about fetal development and abortion, psychological and emotional disposition and condition, and the firmness of their desire to obtain abortions. In order to determine whether a regulation presents a substantial obstacle to women, a court needs to know which set of women it should have in mind and how many of the women in this set must find that an obstacle is "substantial."

Casey provided no clear answer to these questions. It said that a regulation is unconstitutional if it imposes a substantial obstacle "in a large fraction of cases in which [it] is relevant," 505 U. S., at 895, but there is obviously no clear line between a fraction that is "large" and one that is not. Nor is it clear what the Court meant by "cases in which" a regulation is "relevant." These ambiguities have caused confusion and disagreement. Compare *Whole Woman's Health* v. *Hellerstedt*, 579 U. S. 582, 627–628 (2016), with *id.,* at 666–667, and n. 11 (ALITO, J., dissenting).

2

The difficulty of applying *Casey*'s new rules surfaced in that very case. The controlling opinion found that Pennsylvania's 24-hour waiting period requirement and its informed-consent provision did not impose "undue burden[s]," *Casey*, 505 U. S., at 881–887, but Justice Stevens, applying the same test, reached the opposite result, *id.,* at 920–922 (opinion concurring in part and dissenting in part). That did not bode well, and then-Chief Justice Rehnquist aptly observed that "the undue burden standard presents nothing more workable than the trimester framework." *Id.,* at 964–966 (dissenting opinion).

The ambiguity of the "undue burden" test also produced disagreement in later cases. In *Whole Woman's Health*, the Court adopted the cost-benefit interpretation of the test, stating that "[t]he rule announced in *Casey* . . . requires that courts consider the burdens a law imposes on abortion access *together with the benefits those laws confer*." 579 U. S., at 607 (emphasis added). But five years later, a majority of the Justices rejected that interpretation. See *June Medical*, 591 U. S. ___. Four Justices reaffirmed *Whole Woman's Health*'s instruction to "weigh" a law's "benefits" against "the burdens it imposes on abortion access." 591 U. S., at ___ (plurality opinion) (slip op., at 2) (internal quotation marks omitted). But THE CHIEF JUSTICE—who cast the deciding vote—argued that "[n]othing about *Casey* suggested that a weighing of costs and benefits of an abortion regulation was a job for the courts." *Id.,* at ___ (opinion concurring in judgment) (slip op., at 6). And the four Justices in dissent rejected the plurality's interpretation of *Casey*. See 591 U. S., at ___ (opinion of ALITO, J., joined in relevant part by THOMAS, GORSUCH, and KAVANAUGH, JJ.) (slip op., at 4); *id.,* at ___–___ (opinion of GORSUCH, J.) (slip op., at 15–18); *id.,* at ___–___ (opinion of KAVANAUGH, J.) (slip op., at 1–2) ("[F]ive Members of the Court reject the *Whole Woman's Health* cost-benefit standard").
This Court's experience applying *Casey* has confirmed Chief Justice Rehnquist's prescient diagnosis that the undue-burden standard was "not built to last." *Casey*, 505 U. S., at 965 (opinion concurring in judgment in part and dissenting in part).

[D]

Effect on other areas of law. *Roe* and *Casey* have led to the distortion of many important but unrelated legal doctrines, and that effect provides further support for overruling those decisions. See *Ramos*, 590 U. S., at ___ (opinion of KAVANAUGH, J.) (slip op., at 8); *Janus*, 585 U. S., at ___ (slip op., at 34).

Members of this Court have repeatedly lamented that "no legal rule or doctrine is safe from ad hoc nullification by this Court when an occasion for its application arises in a case involving state regulation of abortion." *Thornburgh*, 476 U. S., at 814 (O'Connor, J., dissenting); see *Madsen* v. *Women's Health Center, Inc.*, 512 U. S. 753, 785 (1994) (Scalia, J., concurring in judgment in part and dissenting in part); *Whole Woman's Health*, 579 U.

S., at 631–633 (THOMAS, J., dissenting); *id.,* at 645–666, 678–684 (ALITO, J., dissenting); *June Medical,* 591 U.S., at ___–___ (GORSUCH, J., dissenting) (slip op., at 1–15).

The Court's abortion cases have diluted the strict standard for facial constitutional challenges. They have ignored the Court's third-party standing doctrine. They have disregarded standard *res judicata* principles. They have flouted the ordinary rules on the severability of unconstitutional provisions, as well as the rule that statutes should be read where possible to avoid unconstitutionality. And they have distorted First Amendment doctrines.

When vindicating a doctrinal innovation requires courts to engineer exceptions to longstanding background rules, the doctrine "has failed to deliver the 'principled and intelligible' development of the law that *stare decisis* purports to secure." *Id.,* at ___ (THOMAS, J., dissenting) (slip op., at 19) (quoting *Vasquez* v. *Hillery,* 474 U. S. 254, 265 (1986)).

E

Reliance interests. We last consider whether overruling *Roe* and *Casey* will upend substantial reliance interests.

1

Traditional reliance interests arise "where advance planning of great precision is most obviously a necessity." *Casey,* 505 U. S., at 856 (joint opinion); see also *Payne,* 501 U. S., at 828. In *Casey,* the controlling opinion conceded that those traditional reliance interests were not implicated because getting an abortion is generally "unplanned activity," and "reproductive planning could take virtually immediate account of any sudden restoration of state authority to ban abortions." 505 U. S., at 856. For these reasons, we agree with the *Casey* plurality that conventional, concrete reliance interests are not present here.

2

Unable to find reliance in the conventional sense, the controlling opinion in *Casey* perceived a more intangible form of reliance. It wrote that "people [had] organized intimate relationships and made choices that define their views of themselves and their places in society . . . in reliance on the availability of abortion in the event that contraception should fail" and that "[t]he ability of women to participate equally in the economic and social life of the Nation has been facilitated by their ability to control their reproductive lives." *Ibid.* But this Court is ill-equipped to assess "generalized assertions about the national psyche." *Id.,* at 957 (opinion of Rehnquist, C. J.). *Casey's* notion of reliance thus finds little support in our cases, which instead emphasize very concrete reliance interests, like those that develop in "cases involving property and contract rights." *Payne,* 501 U. S., at 828.

When a concrete reliance interest is asserted, courts are equipped to evaluate the claim, but assessing the novel and intangible form of reliance endorsed by the *Casey* plurality is another matter. That form of reliance depends on an empirical question that is hard for anyone—and in particular, for a court—to assess, namely, the effect of the abortion right on society and in particular on the lives of women. The contending sides in this case make impassioned and conflicting arguments about the effects of the abortion right on the lives of women. Compare Brief for Petitioners 34– 36; Brief for Women Scholars et al. as *Amici Curiae* 13–20, 29–41, with Brief for Respondents 36–41; Brief for National

Women's Law Center et al. as *Amici Curiae* 15–32. The contending sides also make conflicting arguments about the status of the fetus. This Court has neither the authority nor the expertise to adjudicate those disputes, and the *Casey* plurality's speculations and weighing of the relative importance of the fetus and mother represent a departure from the "original constitutional proposition" that "courts do not substitute their social and economic beliefs for the judgment of legislative bodies." *Ferguson* v. *Skrupa*, 372 U. S. 726, 729–730 (1963).

Our decision returns the issue of abortion to those legislative bodies, and it allows women on both sides of the abortion issue to seek to affect the legislative process by influencing public opinion, lobbying legislators, voting, and running for office.

[3]

Unable to show concrete reliance on *Roe* and *Casey* themselves, the Solicitor General suggests that overruling those decisions would "threaten the Court's precedents holding that the Due Process Clause protects other rights." Brief for United States 26 (citing *Obergefell*, 576 U. S. 644; *Lawrence*, 539 U. S. 558; *Griswold*, 381 U. S. 479). That is not correct for reasons we have already discussed. As even the *Casey* plurality recognized, "[a]bortion is a unique act" because it terminates "life or potential life." 505 U. S., at 852; see also *Roe*, 410 U. S., at 159 (abortion is "inherently different from marital intimacy," "marriage," or "procreation"). And to ensure that our decision is not misunderstood or mischaracterized, we emphasize that our decision concerns the constitutional right to abortion and no other right. Nothing in this opinion should be understood to cast doubt on precedents that do not concern abortion.

[VI]

We must now decide what standard will govern if state abortion regulations undergo constitutional challenge and whether the law before us satisfies the appropriate standard.

A

Under our precedents, rational-basis review is the appropriate standard for such challenges. As we have explained, procuring an abortion is not a fundamental constitutional right because such a right has no basis in the Constitution's text or in our Nation's history. See *supra,* at 8–39.

It follows that the States may regulate abortion for legitimate reasons, and when such regulations are challenged under the Constitution, courts cannot "substitute their social and economic beliefs for the judgment of legislative bodies." *Ferguson*, 372 U. S., at 729–730; see also *Dandridge* v. *Williams*, 397 U. S. 471, 484–486 (1970); *United States* v. *Carolene Products Co.*, 304 U. S. 144, 152 (1938). That respect for a legislature's judgment applies even when the laws at issue concern matters of great social significance and moral substance. See, *e.g., Board of Trustees of Univ. of Ala.* v. *Garrett*, 531 U. S. 356, 365–368 (2001) ("treatment of the disabled"); *Glucksberg*, 521 U. S., at 728 ("assisted suicide"); *San Antonio Independent School Dist.* v. *Rodriguez*, 411 U. S. 1, 32–35, 55 (1973) ("financing public education").

A law regulating abortion, like other health and welfare laws, is entitled to a "strong presumption of validity." *Heller* v. *Doe*, 509 U. S. 312, 319 (1993). It must be sustained if there is a rational basis on which the legislature could have thought that it would serve legitimate state interests. These legitimate interests include respect for and preservation of prenatal life at all stages of development, *Gonzales*, 550 U. S., at 157–158; the protection of maternal health and safety; the elimination of particularly gruesome or barbaric medical procedures; the preservation of the integrity of the medical profession; the mitigation of fetal pain; and the prevention of discrimination on the basis of race, sex, or disability. See *id.*, at 156– 157; *Roe*, 410 U. S., at 150; cf. *Glucksberg*, 521 U. S., at 728– 731 (identifying similar interests).

B

These legitimate interests justify Mississippi's Gestational Age Act. Except "in a medical emergency or in the case of a severe fetal abnormality," the statute prohibits abortion "if the probable gestational age of the unborn human being has been determined to be greater than fifteen (15) weeks." Miss. Code Ann. §41–41–191(4)(b). The Mississippi Legislature's findings recount the stages of "human prenatal development" and assert the State's interest in "protecting the life of the unborn." §2(b)(i). The legislature also found that abortions performed after 15 weeks typically use the dilation and evacuation procedure, and the legislature found the use of this procedure "for nontherapeutic or elective reasons [to be] a barbaric practice, dangerous for the maternal patient, and demeaning to the medical profession." §2(b)(i)(8); see also *Gonzales*, 550 U. S., at 135–143 (describing such procedures). These legitimate interests provide a rational basis for the Gestational Age Act, and it follows that respondents' constitutional challenge must fail.

VII

We end this opinion where we began. Abortion presents a profound moral question. The Constitution does not prohibit the citizens of each State from regulating or prohibiting abortion. *Roe* and *Casey* arrogated that authority. We now overrule those decisions and return that authority to the people and their elected representatives.

The judgment of the Fifth Circuit is reversed, and the case is remanded for further proceedings consistent with this opinion.

It is so ordered.

Justice THOMAS concurring.

I join the opinion of the Court because it correctly holds that there is no constitutional right to abortion.

As I have previously explained, "substantive due process" is an oxymoron that "lack[s] any basis in the Constitution." *Johnson*, 576 U. S., at 607–608 (opinion of THOMAS, J.); see also, *e.g., Vaello Madero*, 596 U. S., at ___ (THOMAS, J., concurring) (slip op., at 3) ("[T]ext and history provide little support for modern substantive due process doctrine"). "The notion that a constitutional provision that guarantees only 'process' before a person is deprived of life, liberty, or property could define the substance of those rights strains credulity for even the most casual user of words." *McDonald* v. *Chicago*, 561 U. S. 742, 811 (2010) (THOMAS, J., concurring in part and concurring in judgment); see also *United States* v. *Carlton*, 512 U. S. 26, 40 (1994) (Scalia, J., concurring in judgment). The resolution of this case is thus straightforward. Because the Due Process Clause does not secure *any* substantive rights, it does not secure a right to abortion.

The Court today declines to disturb substantive due process jurisprudence generally or the doctrine's application in other, specific contexts. Cases like *Griswold* v. *Connecticut*,

381 U. S. 479 (1965) (right of married persons to obtain contraceptives)*; *Lawrence* v. *Texas*, 539 U. S. 558 (2003) (right to engage in private, consensual sexual acts); and *Obergefell* v. *Hodges*, 576 U. S. 644 (2015) (right to same-sex marriage), are not at issue. The Court's abortion cases are unique, see *ante,* at 31–32, 66, 71–72, and no party has asked us to decide "whether our entire Fourteenth Amendment jurisprudence must be preserved or revised," *McDonald,* 561 U. S., at 813 (opinion of THOMAS, J.). Thus, I agree that "[n]othing in [the Court's] opinion should be understood to cast doubt on precedents that do not concern abortion." *Ante,* at 66.

For that reason, in future cases, we should reconsider all of this Court's substantive due process precedents, including *Griswold, Lawrence,* and *Obergefell.* Because any substantive due process decision is "demonstrably erroneous," *Ramos* v. *Louisiana,* 590 U. S. ___, ___ (2020) (THOMAS, J., concurring in judgment) (slip op., at 7), we have a duty to "correct the error" established in those precedents, *Gamble* v. *United States,* 587 U. S. ___, ___ (2019) (THOMAS, J., concurring) (slip op., at 9). After overruling these demonstrably erroneous decisions, the question would remain whether other constitutional provisions guarantee the myriad rights that our substantive due process cases have generated. For example, we could consider whether any of the rights announced in this Court's substantive due process cases are "privileges or immunities of citizens of the United States" protected by the Fourteenth Amendment. Amdt.14, §1; see *McDonald,* 561 U. S., at 806 (opinion of THOMAS, J.). To answer that question, we would need to decide important antecedent questions, including whether the Privileges or Immunities Clause protects *any* rights that are not enumerated in the Constitution and, if so, how to identify those rights. See *id.,* at 854. That said, even if the Clause does protect unenumerated rights, the Court conclusively demonstrates that abortion is not one of them under any plausible interpretive approach. See *ante,* at 15, n. 22.

Chief Justice ROBERTS concurring.

We granted certiorari to decide one question: "Whether all pre-viability prohibitions on elective abortions are unconstitutional." Pet. for Cert. i. That question is directly implicated here: Mississippi's Gestational Age Act, Miss. Code Ann. §41–41–191 (2018), generally prohibits abortion after the fifteenth week of pregnancy—several weeks before a fetus is regarded as "viable" outside the womb. In urging our review, Mississippi stated that its case was "an ideal vehicle" to "reconsider the bright-line viability rule," and that a judgment in its favor would "not require the Court to overturn" *Roe* v. *Wade,* 410 U. S. 113 (1973), and *Planned Parenthood of Southeastern Pa.* v. *Casey,* 505 U. S. 833 (1992). Pet. for Cert. 5.

Today, the Court nonetheless rules for Mississippi by doing just that. I would take a more measured course. I agree with the Court that the viability line established by *Roe* and *Casey* should be discarded under a straightforward *stare decisis* analysis. That line never made any sense. Our abortion precedents describe the right at issue as a woman's right to choose to terminate her pregnancy. That right should therefore extend far enough to ensure a reasonable opportunity to choose, but need not extend any further—certainly not all the way to viability. Mississippi's law allows a woman three months to obtain an abortion, well beyond the point at which it is considered "late" to discover a pregnancy.

See A. Ayoola, Late Recognition of Unintended Pregnancies, 32 Pub. Health Nursing 462 (2015) (pregnancy is discoverable and ordinarily discovered by six weeks of gestation). I see no sound basis for questioning the adequacy of that opportunity.

But that is all I would say, out of adherence to a simple yet fundamental principle of judicial restraint: If it is not necessary to decide more to dispose of a case, then it is necessary *not* to decide more. Perhaps we are not always perfect in following that command, and certainly there are cases that warrant an exception. But this is not one of them. Surely we should adhere closely to principles of judicial restraint here, where the broader path the Court chooses entails repudiating a constitutional right we have not only previously recognized, but also expressly reaffirmed applying the doctrine of *stare decisis*. The Court's opinion is thoughtful and thorough, but those virtues cannot compensate for the fact that its dramatic and consequential ruling is unnecessary to decide the case before us.

I

[The] viability line is a relic of a time when we recognized only two state interests warranting regulation of abortion: maternal health and protection of "potential life." *Roe*, 410 U. S., at 162–163. That changed with *Gonzales* v. *Carhart*, 550 U. S. 124 (2007). There, we recognized a broader array of interests, such as drawing "a bright line that clearly distinguishes abortion and infanticide," maintaining societal ethics, and preserving the integrity of the medical profession. *Id.*, at 157–160. The viability line has nothing to do with advancing such permissible goals. Cf. *id.*, at 171 (Ginsburg, J., dissenting) (*Gonzales* "blur[red] the line, firmly drawn in *Casey*, between previability and postviability abortions"); see also R. Beck, *Gonzales, Casey*, and the Viability Rule, 103 Nw. U. L. Rev. 249, 276–279 (2009).

[In] short, the viability rule was created outside the ordinary course of litigation, is and always has been completely unreasoned, and fails to take account of state interests since recognized as legitimate. It is indeed "telling that other countries almost uniformly eschew" a viability line. *Ante,* at 53 (opinion of the Court). Only a handful of countries, among them China and North Korea, permit elective abortions after twenty weeks; the rest have coalesced around a 12–week line. See The World's Abortion Laws, Center for Reproductive Rights (Feb. 23, 2021) (online source archived) (Canada, China, Iceland, Guinea-Bissau, the Netherlands, North Korea, Singapore, and Vietnam permit elective abortions after twenty weeks). The Court rightly rejects the arbitrary viability rule today.

[II]

None of this, however, requires that we also take the dramatic step of altogether eliminating the abortion right first recognized in *Roe*. Mississippi itself previously argued as much to this Court in this litigation. [And] it went out of its way to make clear that it was *not* asking the Court to repudiate entirely the right to choose whether to terminate a pregnancy: "To be clear, the questions presented in this petition do not require the Court to overturn *Roe* or *Casey*." *Id.,* at 5. Mississippi tempered that statement with an oblique one-sentence footnote intimating that, if the Court could not reconcile *Roe* and *Casey* with current facts or other cases, it "should not retain erroneous precedent." Pet. for Cert. 5–6, n. 1. But the State never argued that we should grant review for that purpose.

After we granted certiorari, however, Mississippi changed course. In its principal brief, the State bluntly announced that the Court should overrule *Roe* and *Casey*. The Constitution does not protect a right to an abortion, it argued, and a State should be able to prohibit elective abortions if a rational basis supports doing so. See Brief for Petitioners 12–13.

The Court now rewards that gambit, noting three times that the parties presented "no half-measures" and argued that "we must either reaffirm or overrule *Roe* and *Casey.*" *Ante*, at 5, 8, 72. Given those two options, the majority picks the latter.

[Following] that "fundamental principle of judicial restraint," *Washington State Grange*, 552 U. S., at 450, we should begin with the narrowest basis for disposition, proceeding to consider a broader one only if necessary to resolve the case at hand. [Here], there is a clear path to deciding this case correctly without overruling *Roe* all the way down to the studs: recognize that the viability line must be discarded, as the majority rightly does, and leave for another day whether to reject any right to an abortion at all.

Of course, such an approach would not be available if the rationale of *Roe* and *Casey* was inextricably entangled with and dependent upon the viability standard. It is not. Our precedents in this area ground the abortion right in a woman's "right to choose." [The] question in *Roe* was whether there was any right to abortion in the Constitution. See Brief for Appellants and Brief for Appellees, in *Roe* v. *Wade*, O. T. 1971, No. 70–18. How far the right extended was a concern that was separate and subsidiary, and—not surprisingly—entirely unbriefed.

The Court in *Roe* just chose to address both issues in one opinion: It first recognized a right to "choose to terminate [a] pregnancy" under the Constitution, see 410 U. S., at 129–159, and then, having done so, explained that a line should be drawn at viability such that a State could not proscribe abortion before that period, see *id.*, at 163. The viability line is a separate rule fleshing out the metes and bounds of *Roe*'s core holding. Applying principles of *stare decisis*, I would excise that additional rule—and only that rule—from our jurisprudence.

Overruling the subsidiary rule is sufficient to resolve this case in Mississippi's favor. The law at issue allows abortions up through fifteen weeks, providing an adequate opportunity to exercise the right *Roe* protects. By the time a pregnant woman has reached that point, her pregnancy is well into the second trimester. Pregnancy tests are now inexpensive and accurate, and a woman ordinarily discovers she is pregnant by six weeks of gestation.

[III]

Whether a precedent should be overruled is a question "entirely within the discretion of the court." *Hertz* v. *Woodman*, 218 U. S. 205, 212 (1910); see also *Payne* v. *Tennessee*, 501 U. S. 808, 828 (1991) (*stare decisis* is a "principle of policy"). In my respectful view, the sound exercise of that discretion should have led the Court to resolve the case on the narrower grounds set forth above, rather than overruling *Roe* and *Casey* entirely. The Court says there is no "principled basis" for this approach, *ante*, at 73, but in fact it is firmly grounded in basic principles of *stare decisis* and judicial restraint.

The Court's decision to overrule *Roe* and *Casey* is a serious jolt to the legal system—regardless of how you view those cases. A narrower decision rejecting the misguided viability line would be markedly less unsettling, and nothing more is needed to decide this case.

Our cases say that the effect of overruling a precedent on reliance interests is a factor to consider in deciding whether to take such a step, and respondents argue that generations of women have relied on the right to an abortion in organizing their relationships and planning their futures. Brief for Respondents 36–41; see also *Casey*, 505 U. S., at 856 (making the same point). The Court questions whether these concerns are pertinent under our precedents, see *ante*, at 64–65, but the issue would not even arise with a decision rejecting only the viability line: It cannot reasonably be argued that women have shaped their lives in part on the assumption that they would be able to abort up to viability, as opposed to fifteen weeks.

[Both] the Court's opinion and the dissent display a relentless freedom from doubt on the legal issue that I cannot share. I am not sure, for example, that a ban on terminating a pregnancy from the moment of conception must be treated the same under the Constitution as a ban after fifteen weeks. A thoughtful Member of this Court once counseled that the difficulty of a question "admonishes us to observe the wise limitations on our function and to confine ourselves to deciding only what is necessary to the disposition of the immediate case." *Whitehouse* v. *Illinois Central R. Co.*, 349 U. S. 366, 372–373 (1955) (Frankfurter, J., for the Court). I would decide the question we granted review to answer—whether the previously recognized abortion right bars all abortion restrictions prior to viability, such that a ban on abortions after fifteen weeks of pregnancy is necessarily unlawful. The answer to that question is no, and there is no need to go further to decide this case.
I therefore concur only in the judgment.

Justice BREYER, Justice SOTOMAYOR, and Justice KAGAN, dissenting.

For half a century, *Roe* v. *Wade*, 410 U. S. 113 (1973), and *Planned Parenthood of Southeastern Pa.* v. *Casey*, 505 U. S. 833 (1992), have protected the liberty and equality of women. *Roe* held, and *Casey* reaffirmed, that the Constitution safeguards a woman's right to decide for herself whether to bear a child. *Roe* held, and *Casey* reaffirmed, that in the first stages of pregnancy, the government could not make that choice for women. The government could not control a woman's body or the course of a woman's life: It could not determine what the woman's future would be. See *Casey*, 505 U. S., at 853; *Gonzales* v. *Carhart*, 550 U. S. 124, 171–172 (2007) (Ginsburg, J., dissenting). Respecting a woman as an autonomous being, and granting her full equality, meant giving her substantial choice over this most personal and most consequential of all life decisions.

[Today], the Court discards that balance. It says that from the very moment of fertilization, a woman has no rights to speak of. A State can force her to bring a pregnancy to term, even at the steepest personal and familial costs. An abortion restriction, the majority holds, is permissible whenever rational, the lowest level of scrutiny known to the law. And because, as the Court has often stated, protecting fetal life is rational, States will feel free to enact all manner of restrictions. The Mississippi law at issue here bars abortions after the 15th week of pregnancy. Under the majority's ruling, though, another State's law could do so after ten weeks, or five or three or one—or, again, from the moment of fertilization. States have already passed such laws, in anticipation of today's ruling. More will follow. [So] too, after today's ruling, some States may compel women to carry to term a fetus with severe physical anomalies—for example, one afflicted with Tay-Sachs disease, sure to die within a few years of birth. States may even argue that a prohibition on abortion need make no provision for protecting a woman from risk of death or physical harm. Across a vast array of circumstances, a State will be able to impose its moral choice on a woman and coerce her to give birth to a child.

Enforcement of all these draconian restrictions will also be left largely to the States' devices. A State can of course impose criminal penalties on abortion providers, including lengthy prison sentences. But some States will not stop there. Perhaps, in the wake of today's decision, a state law will criminalize the woman's conduct too, incarcerating or fining her for daring to seek or obtain an abortion. And as Texas has recently shown, a State can turn neighbor against neighbor, enlisting fellow citizens in the effort to root out anyone who tries to get an abortion, or to assist another in doing so.

[After] this decision, some States may block women from traveling out of State to obtain abortions, or even from receiving abortion medications from out of State. Some may criminalize efforts, including the provision of information or funding, to help women gain access to other States' abortion services. Most threatening of all, no language in today's decision stops the Federal Government from prohibiting abortions nationwide, once again from the moment of conception and without exceptions for rape or incest. If that happens, "the views of [an individual State's] citizens" will not matter.*Ante*, at 1. The challenge for a woman will be to finance a trip not to "New York [or] California" but to Toronto. *Ante*, at 4 (KAVANAUGH, J., concurring).

[And] no one should be confident that this majority is done with its work. The right *Roe* and *Casey* recognized does not stand alone. To the contrary, the Court has linked it for decades to other settled freedoms involving bodily integrity, familial relationships, and procreation. Most obviously, the right to terminate a pregnancy arose straight out of the right to purchase and use contraception. See *Griswold* v.*Connecticut*, 381 U. S. 479 (1965); *Eisenstadt* v. *Baird*, 405 U. S. 438 (1972). In turn, those rights led, more recently, to rights of same-sex intimacy and marriage. See *Lawrence* v. *Texas*, 539 U. S. 558 (2003); *Obergefell* v. *Hodges*, 576 U. S. 644 (2015). They are all part of the same constitutional fabric, protecting autonomous decision-making over the most personal of life decisions. The majority (or to be more accurate, most of it) is eager to tell us today that nothing it does "cast[s] doubt on precedents that do not concern abortion." *Ante*, at 66; cf. *ante*, at 3 (THOMAS, J., concurring) (advocating the overruling of *Griswold*, *Lawrence*, and *Obergefell*). But how could that be? The lone rationale for what the majority does today is that the right to elect an abortion is not "deeply rooted in history": Not until *Roe*, the majority argues, did people think abortion fell within the Constitution's guarantee of liberty. *Ante*, at 32. The same could be said, though, of most of the rights the majority claims it is not tampering with. The majority could write just as long an opinion showing, for example, that until the mid-20th century, "there was no support in American law for a constitutional right to obtain [contraceptives]." *Ante*, at 15. So one of two things must be true. Either the majority does not really believe in its own reasoning. Or if it does, all rights that have no history stretching back to the mid19th century are insecure. Either the mass of the majority's opinion is hypocrisy, or additional constitutional rights are under threat. It is one or the other.

[Roe] and *Casey* have been the law of the land for decades, shaping women's expectations of their choices when an unplanned pregnancy occurs. Women have relied on the availability of abortion both in structuring their relationships and in planning their lives. The legal framework *Roe* and *Casey* developed to balance the competing interests in this sphere has proved workable in courts across the country. No recent developments, in either law or fact, have eroded or cast doubt on those precedents. Nothing, in short, has changed. Indeed, the Court in *Casey* already found all of that to be true. *Casey* is a precedent about precedent. It reviewed the same arguments made here in support of overruling *Roe*, and it found that doing so was not warranted. The Court reverses course today for one reason and one reason only: because the composition of this Court has changed. *Stare decisis*, this Court has often said, "contributes to the actual and perceived integrity of the judicial process" by ensuring that decisions are "founded in the law rather than in the proclivities of individuals." *Payne* v. *Tennessee*, 501 U. S. 808, 827 (1991); *Vasquez* v. *Hillery*, 474 U. S. 254, 265 (1986). Today, the proclivities of individuals rule. The Court departs from its obligation to faithfully and impartially apply the law. We dissent.

I

We start with *Roe* and *Casey*, and with their deep connections to a broad swath of this Court's precedents. To hear the majority tell the tale, *Roe* and *Casey* are aberrations: They came from nowhere, went nowhere—and so are easy to excise from this Nation's constitutional law. That is not true. After describing the decisions themselves, we explain how they are rooted in—and themselves led to—other rights giving individuals control over their bodies and their most personal and intimate associations. The majority does not wish to talk about these matters for obvious reasons; to do so would both ground *Roe* and *Casey* in this Court's precedents and reveal the broad implications of today's decision. But the facts will not so handily disappear.

[A]

Some half-century ago, *Roe* struck down a state law making it a crime to perform an abortion unless its purpose was to save a woman's life. The *Roe* Court knew it was treading on difficult and disputed ground. It understood that different people's "experiences," "values," and "religious training" and beliefs led to "opposing views" about abortion. 410 U. S., at 116. But by a 7-to-2 vote, the Court held that in the earlier stages of pregnancy, that contested and contestable choice must belong to a woman, in consultation with her family and doctor. The Court explained that a long line of precedents, "founded in the Fourteenth Amendment's concept of personal liberty," protected individual decisionmaking related to "marriage, procreation, contraception, family relationships, and child rearing and education." *Id.*, at 152–153 (citations omitted). For the same reasons, the Court held, the Constitution must protect "a woman's decision whether or not to terminate her pregnancy." *Id.*, at 153. The Court recognized the myriad ways bearing a child can alter the "life and future" of a woman and other members of her family. *Ibid.* A State could not, "by adopting one theory of life," override all "rights of the pregnant woman." *Id.*, at 162.

[At] the same time, though, the Court recognized "valid interest[s]" of the State "in regulating the abortion decision." *Id.*, at 153. The Court noted in particular "important interests" in "protecting potential life," "maintaining medical standards," and "safeguarding [the] health" of the woman. *Id.*, at 154. No "absolut[ist]" account of the woman's right could wipe away those significant state claims. *Ibid.*

[In] *Casey*, the Court considered the matter anew, and again upheld *Roe*'s core precepts. *Casey* is in significant measure a precedent about the doctrine of precedent—until today, one of the Court's most important.

Central to that conclusion was a full-throated restatement of a woman's right to choose. Like *Roe*, *Casey* grounded that right in the Fourteenth Amendment's guarantee of "liberty." That guarantee encompasses realms of conduct not specifically referenced in the Constitution: "Marriage is mentioned nowhere" in that document, yet the Court was "no doubt correct" to protect the freedom to marry "against state interference." 505 U. S., at 847–848. And the guarantee of liberty encompasses conduct today that was not protected at the time of the Fourteenth Amendment. See *id.*, at 848. "It is settled now," the Court said—though it was not always so—that "the Constitution places limits on a State's right to interfere with a person's most basic decisions about family and parenthood, as well as bodily integrity." *Id.*, at 849 (citations omitted); see *id.*, at 851 (similarly describing the constitutional protection given to "personal decisions relating to marriage, procreation, contraception, [and] family relationships"). Especially important in this web of precedents protecting an individual's most "personal choices" were those guaranteeing the right to contraception. *Ibid.*; see *id.*, at 852–853. In those cases, the Court had recognized "the right of the individual" to make the vastly consequential "decision whether to bear" a child. *Id.*, at 851 (emphasis deleted). So too, *Casey* reasoned, the liberty clause protects the decision of a woman confronting an unplanned pregnancy. Her decision about abortion was central, in the same way, to her capacity to chart her life's course. See *id.*, at 853.

[At] the same time, *Casey* decided, based on two decades of experience, that the *Roe* framework did not give States sufficient ability to regulate abortion prior to viability. In that period, *Casey* now made clear, the State could regulate not only to protect the woman's health but also to "promot[e] prenatal life." 505 U. S., at 873 (plurality opinion). In particular, the State could ensure informed choice and could try to promote childbirth. See *id.*, at 877–878. But the State still could not place an "undue burden"—or "substantial obstacle"—"in the path of a woman seeking an abortion." *Id.*, at 878. Prior to viability, the woman, consistent with the constitutional "meaning of liberty," must "retain the ultimate control over her destiny and her body." *Id.*, at 869.

We make one initial point about this analysis in light of the majority's insistence that *Roe* and *Casey*, and we in defending them, are dismissive of a "State's interest in protecting prenatal life." *Ante*, at 38. Nothing could get those decisions more wrong. As just described, *Roe* and *Casey* invoked powerful state interests in that protection, operative at every stage of the pregnancy and overriding the woman's liberty after viability. The strength of those state interests is exactly why the Court allowed greater restrictions on the abortion right than on other rights deriving from the Fourteenth Amendment.[1] But what *Roe* and *Casey* also recognized—which today's majority does not—is that a woman's freedom and equality are likewise involved. That fact—the presence of countervailing interests—is what made the abortion question hard, and what necessitated balancing. [Today's] Court, that is, does not think there is anything of constitutional significance attached to a woman's control of her body and the path of her life. *Roe* and *Casey* thought that one-sided view misguided. In some sense, that is the difference in a nutshell between our precedents and the majority opinion. The constitutional regime we have lived in for the last 50 years recognized competing interests, and sought a balance between them. The constitutional regime we enter today erases the woman's interest and recognizes only the State's (or the Federal Government's).

B

The majority makes this change based on a single question: Did the reproductive right recognized in *Roe* and *Casey* exist in "1868, the year when the Fourteenth Amendment was ratified"? *Ante*, at 23. The majority says (and with this much we agree) that the answer to this question is no: In 1868, there was no nationwide right to end a pregnancy, and no thought that the Fourteenth Amendment provided one.

The majority's core legal postulate, then, is that we in the 21st century must read the Fourteenth Amendment just as its ratifiers did. And that is indeed what the majority emphasizes over and over again. See *ante*, at 47 ("[T]he most important historical fact [is] how the States regulated abortion when the Fourteenth Amendment was adopted"); see also *ante*, at 5, 16, and n. 24, 23, 25, 28. If the ratifiers did not understand something as central to freedom, then neither can we. Or said more particularly: If those people did not understand reproductive rights as part of the guarantee of liberty conferred in the Fourteenth Amendment, then those rights do not exist.

As an initial matter, note a mistake in the just preceding sentence. We referred there to the "people" who ratified the Fourteenth Amendment: What rights did those "people" have in their heads at the time? But, of course, "people" did not ratify the Fourteenth Amendment. Men did. So it is perhaps not so surprising that the ratifiers were not perfectly attuned to the importance of reproductive rights for women's liberty, or for their capacity to participate as equal members of our Nation. Indeed, the ratifiers—both in 1868 and when the original Constitution was approved in 1788—did not understand women as full members of the community embraced by the phrase "We the People." In 1868, the first wave of American feminists were explicitly told—of course by men—that it was not their time to seek constitutional protections. (Women would not get even the vote for another half-century.) To be sure, most women in 1868 also had a foreshortened view of their rights: If most men could not then imagine giving women control over their bodies, most women could not imagine having that kind of autonomy. But that takes away nothing from the core point. Those responsible for the original Constitution, including the Fourteenth Amendment, did not perceive women as equals, and did not recognize women's rights. When the majority says that we must read our foundational charter as viewed at the time of ratification (except that we may also check it against the Dark Ages), it consigns women to second-class citizenship.

[So] how is it that as *Casey* said, our Constitution, read now, grants rights to women, though it did not in 1868? [The] answer is that this Court has rejected the majority's pinched view [in the past, *eds.*] of how to read our Constitution. [In] the words of the great Chief Justice John Marshall, our Constitution is "intended to endure for ages to come," and must adapt itself to a future "seen dimly," if at all. *McCulloch* v. *Maryland*, 4 Wheat. 316, 415 (1819). That is indeed why our Constitution is written as it is. The Framers (both in 1788 and 1868) understood that the world changes. So they did not define rights by reference to the specific practices existing at the time. Instead, the Framers defined rights in general terms, to permit future evolution in their scope and meaning. And over the course of our history, this Court has taken up the Framers' invitation. It has kept true to the Framers' principles by applying them in new ways, responsive to new societal understandings and conditions.

Nowhere has that approach been more prevalent than in construing the majestic but open-ended words of the Fourteenth Amendment—the guarantees of "liberty" and "equality" for all. And nowhere has that approach produced prouder moments, for this country and the Court. Consider an example *Obergefell* used a few years ago. The Court there confronted a claim, based on *Washington* v. *Glucksberg*, 521 U. S. 702 (1997), that the Fourteenth Amendment "must be defined in a most circumscribed manner, with central reference to specific historical practices"—exactly the view today's majority follows. *Obergefell*, 576 U. S., at 671. And the Court specifically rejected that view.[4] In doing so, the Court reflected on what the proposed, historically circumscribed approach would have meant for interracial marriage. See *ibid.* The Fourteenth Amendment's ratifiers did not think it gave black and white people a right to marry each other. To the contrary, contemporaneous practice deemed that act quite as unprotected as abortion. Yet the Court in *Loving* v. *Virginia*, 388 U. S. 1 (1967), read the Fourteenth Amendment to embrace the Lovings' union. If, *Obergefell* explained, "rights were defined by who exercised them in the past, then received practices could serve as their own continued justification"—even when they conflict with "liberty" and "equality" as later and more broadly understood. 576 U. S., at 671. The Constitution does not freeze for all time the original view of what those rights guarantee, or how they apply.

That does not mean anything goes. The majority wishes people to think there are but two alternatives: (1) accept the original applications of the Fourteenth Amendment and no others, or (2) surrender to judges' "own ardent views," ungrounded in law, about the "liberty that Americans should enjoy." *Ante*, at 14. At least, that idea is what the majority *sometimes* tries to convey. At other times, the majority (or, rather, most of it) tries to assure the public that it has no designs on rights (for example, to contraception) that arose only in the back half of the 20th century—in other words, that it is happy to pick and choose, in accord with individual preferences. See *ante*, at 32, 66, 71–72; *ante*, at 10 (KAVANAUGH, J., concurring); but see *ante*, at 3 (THOMAS, J., concurring). But that is a matter we discuss later. See *infra*, at 24–29. For now, our point is different: It is that applications of liberty and equality can evolve while remaining grounded in constitutional principles, constitutional history, and constitutional precedents. The second Justice Harlan discussed how to strike the right balance when he explained why he would have invalidated a State's ban on contraceptive use. Judges, he said, are not "free to roam where unguided speculation might take them." *Poe* v. *Ullman*, 367 U. S. 497, 542 (1961) (dissenting opinion). Yet they also must recognize that the constitutional "tradition" of this country is not captured whole at a single moment. Rather, its meaning gains content from the long sweep of our history and from successive judicial precedents—each looking to the last and each seeking to apply the Constitution's most fundamental commitments to new conditions. That is why Americans, to go back to *Obergefell*'s example, have a right to marry across racial lines.

And it is why, to go back to Justice Harlan's case, Americans have a right to use contraceptives so they can choose for themselves whether to have children.

All that is what *Casey* understood. *Casey* explicitly rejected the present majority's method. "[T]he specific practices of States at the time of the adoption of the Fourteenth Amendment," *Casey* stated, do not "mark[ ] the outer limits of the substantive sphere of liberty which the Fourteenth Amendment protects." 505 U. S., at 848.[5] To hold otherwise—as the majority does today—"would be inconsistent with our law." *Id.*, at 847. Why? Because the Court has "vindicated [the] principle" over and over that (no matter the sentiment in 1868) "there is a realm of personal liberty which the government may not enter"—especially relating to "bodily integrity" and "family life." *Id.*, at 847, 849, 851.*Casey* described in detail the Court's contraception cases. See *id.*, at 848–849, 851–853. It noted decisions protecting the right to marry, including to someone of another race. See *id.*, at 847–848 ("[I]nterracial marriage was illegal in most States in the 19th century, but the Court was no doubt correct in finding it to be an aspect of liberty protected against state interference"). In reviewing decades and decades of constitutional law, *Casey* could draw but one conclusion: Whatever was true in 1868, "[i]t is settled now, as it was when the Court heard arguments in *Roe* v. *Wade*, that the Constitution places limits on a State's right to interfere with a person's most basic decisions about family and parenthood." *Id.*, at 849.

And that conclusion still held good, until the Court's intervention here. It was settled at the time of *Roe*, settled at the time of *Casey*, and settled yesterday that the Constitution places limits on a State's power to assert control over an individual's body and most personal decisionmaking. A multitude of decisions supporting that principle led to *Roe*'s recognition and *Casey*'s reaffirmation of the right to choose; and *Roe* and *Casey* in turn supported additional protections for intimate and familial relations.

---

[5] In a perplexing paragraph in its opinion, the majority declares that itneed not say whether that statement from *Casey* is true. See *ante*, at 32– 33. But how could that be? Has not the majority insisted for the prior 30 or so pages that the "specific practice[]" respecting abortion at the time of the Fourteenth Amendment precludes its recognition as a constitutional right? *Ante*, at 33. It has. And indeed, it has given no other reason for overruling *Roe* and *Casey. Ante*, at 15–16. We are not mindreaders, but here is our best guess as to what the majority means. It says next that "[a]bortion is nothing new." *Ante*, at 33. So apparently, the Fourteenth Amendment might provide protection for things wholly unknown in the 19th century; maybe one day there could be constitutional protection for, oh, time travel. But as to anything that was known back then (such as abortion or contraception), no such luck.

Consider first, then, the line of this Court's cases protecting "bodily integrity." *Casey*, 505 U. S., at 849. "No right," in this Court's time-honored view, "is held more sacred, or is more carefully guarded," than "the right of every individual to the possession and control of his own person." *Union Pacific R. Co.* v. *Botsford*, 141 U. S. 250, 251 (1891); see *Cruzan* v. *Director, Mo. Dept. of Health*, 497 U. S. 261, 269 (1990) (Every adult "has a right to determine what shall be done with his own body"). Or to put it more simply: Everyone, including women, owns their own bodies. So the Court has restricted the power of government to interfere with a person's medical decisions or compel her to undergo medical procedures or treatments. See, *e.g.*, *Winston* v. *Lee*, 470 U. S. 753, 766–767 (1985) (forced surgery); *Rochin* v. *California*, 342 U. S. 165, 166, 173–174 (1952) (forced stomach pumping); *Washington* v. *Harper*, 494 U. S. 210, 229, 236 (1990) (forced administration of antipsychotic drugs).

Casey recognized the "doctrinal affinity" between those precedents and *Roe*. 505 U. S., at 857. And that doctrinal affinity is born of a factual likeness. There are few greater incursions on a body than forcing a woman to complete a pregnancy and give birth. For every woman, those experiences involve all manner of physical changes, medical treatments (including the possibility of a cesarean section), and medical risk. Just as one example, an American woman is 14 times more likely to die by carrying a pregnancy to term than by having an abortion. See *Whole Woman's Health* v. *Hellerstedt*, 579 U. S. 582, 618 (2016). That women happily undergo those burdens and hazards of their own accord does not lessen how far a State impinges on a woman's body when it compels her to bring a pregnancy to term. And for some women, as *Roe* recognized, abortions are medically necessary to prevent harm. See 410 U. S., at 153. The majority does not say—which is itself ominous—whether a State may prevent a woman from obtaining an abortion when she and her doctor have determined it is a needed medical treatment.

So too, *Roe* and *Casey* fit neatly into a long line of decisions protecting from government intrusion a wealth of private choices about family matters, child rearing, intimate relationships, and procreation. See *Casey*, 505 U. S., at 851, 857; *Roe*, 410 U. S., at 152–153; see also *ante*, at 31–32 (listing the myriad decisions of this kind that *Casey* relied on). Those cases safeguard particular choices about whom to marry; whom to have sex with; what family members to live with; how to raise children—and crucially, whether and when to have children. In varied cases, the Court explained that those choices—"the most intimate and personal" a person can make—reflect fundamental aspects of personal identity; they define the very "attributes of personhood." *Casey*, 505 U. S., at 851. And they inevitably shape the nature and future course of a person's life (and often the lives of those closest to her). So, the Court held, those choices belong to the individual, and not the government. That is the essence of what liberty requires.

And liberty may require it, this Court has repeatedly said, even when those living in 1868 would not have recognized the claim—because they would not have seen the person making it as a full-fledged member of the community. Throughout our history, the sphere of protected liberty has expanded, bringing in individuals formerly excluded. In that way, the constitutional values of liberty and equality go hand in hand; they do not inhabit the hermetically sealed containers the majority portrays.

[Faced] with all these connections between *Roe/Casey* and judicial decisions recognizing other constitutional rights, the majority tells everyone not to worry. It can (so it says) neatly extract the right to choose from the constitutional edifice without affecting any associated rights. (Think of someone telling you that the Jenga tower simply will not collapse.) Today's decision, the majority first says, "does not undermine" the decisions cited by *Roe* and *Casey*—the ones involving "marriage, procreation, contraception, [and] family relationships"— "in any way." *Ante*, at 32; *Casey*, 505 U. S., at 851. Note that this first assurance does not extend to rights recognized after *Roe* and *Casey*, and partly based on them—in particular, rights to same-sex intimacy and marriage. See *supra*, at 23.[6] On its later tries, though, the majority includes those too: "Nothing in this opinion should be understood to cast doubt on precedents that do not concern abortion." *Ante*, at 66; see *ante*, at 71–72. That right is unique, the majority asserts, "because [abortion] terminates life or potential life." *Ante*, at 66 (internal quotation marks omitted); see *ante*, at 32, 71–72. So the majority depicts today's decision as "a restricted railroad ticket, good for this day and train only." *Smith* v. *Allwright*, 321 U. S. 649, 669 (1944) (Roberts, J., dissenting). Should the audience for these too-much-repeated protestations be duly satisfied? We think not.

The first problem with the majority's account comes from JUSTICE THOMAS's concurrence—which makes clear he is not with the program. In saying that nothing in today's opinion casts doubt on non-abortion precedents, JUSTICETHOMAS explains, he means only that they are not at issue in this very case. See *ante*, at 7 ("[T]his case does not present the opportunity to reject" those precedents). But he lets us know what he wants to do when they are. "[I]n future cases," he says, "we should reconsider all of this Court's substantive due process precedents, including *Griswold*, *Lawrence*, and *Obergefell*." *Ante*, at 3; see also *supra*, at 25, and n. 6. And when we reconsider them? Then "we have a duty" to "overrul[e] these demonstrably erroneous decisions." *Ante*, at 3. So at least one Justice is planning to use the ticket of today's decision again and again and again.

Even placing the concurrence to the side, the assurance in today's opinion still does not work. Or at least that is so if the majority is serious about its sole reason for overturning *Roe* and *Casey*: the legal status of abortion in the 19th century. Except in the places quoted above, the state interest in protecting fetal life plays no part in the majority's analysis. To the contrary, the majority takes pride in not expressing a view "about the status of the fetus." *Ante*, at 65; see *ante*, at 32 (aligning itself with *Roe*'s and *Casey*'s stance of not deciding whether life or potential life is involved); *ante*, at 38–39 (similar). The majority's departure from *Roe* and *Casey* rests instead—and only—on whether a woman's decision to end a pregnancy involves any Fourteenth Amendment liberty interest (against which *Roe* and *Casey* balanced the state interest in preserving fetal life).[7]

---

[6] And note, too, that the author of the majority opinion recently joined a statement, written by another member of the majority, lamenting that*Obergefell* deprived States of the ability "to resolve th[e] question [of same-sex marriage] through legislation." *Davis* v. *Ermold*, 592 U. S. ___, ___ (2020) (statement of THOMAS, J.) (slip op., at 1). That might sound familiar. Cf. *ante*, at 44 (lamenting that *Roe* "short-circuited the democratic process"). And those two Justices hardly seemed content to let the matter rest: The Court, they said, had "created a problem that only it can fix." *Davis*, 592 U. S., at ___ (slip op., at 4).

[7] Indulge a few more words about this point. The majority had a choice of two different ways to overrule *Roe* and *Casey*. It could claim that those cases underrated the State's interest in fetal life. Or it could claim that they overrated a woman's constitutional liberty interest in choosing an abortion. (Or both.) The majority here rejects the first path, and we can see why. Taking that route would have prevented the majority from claiming that it means only to leave this issue to the democratic process—that it does not have a dog in the fight. See *ante*, at 38–39, 65. And indeed, doing so might have suggested a revolutionary

proposition: that the fetus is itself a constitutionally protected "person," such that an abortion ban is constitutionally *mandated*. The majority therefore chooses the second path, arguing that the Fourteenth Amendment does not conceive of the abortion decision as implicating liberty, because the law in the 19th century gave that chouce no protection. The trouble is that the chosen path [provides no way to distinguish between the abortion right and a range of other rights including contraception. Eds.]

According to the majority, no liberty interest is present— because (and only because) the law offered no protection to the woman's choice in the 19th century. But here is the rub. The law also did not then (and would not for ages) protect a wealth of other things. It did not protect the rights recognized in *Lawrence* and *Obergefell* to same-sex intimacy and marriage. It did not protect the right recognized in *Loving* to marry across racial lines. It did not protect the right recognized in *Griswold* to contraceptive use. For that matter, it did not protect the right recognized in *Skinner* v. *Oklahoma ex rel. Williamson*, 316 U. S. 535 (1942), not to be sterilized without consent. So if the majority is right in its legal analysis, all those decisions were wrong, and all those matters properly belong to the States too— whatever the particular state interests involved. And if that is true, it is impossible to understand (as a matter of logic and principle) how the majority can say that its opinion today does not threaten—does not even "undermine"—any number of other constitutional rights. *Ante*, at 32.[8]

Nor does it even help just to take the majority at its word. Assume the majority is sincere in saying, for whatever reason, that it will go so far and no further. Scout's honor. Still, the future significance of today's opinion will be decided in the future. And law often has a way of evolving without regard to original intentions—a way of actually following where logic leads, rather than tolerating hard-toexplain lines. Rights can expand in that way. Dissenting in *Lawrence*, Justice Scalia explained why he took no comfort in the Court's statement that a decision recognizing the right to same-sex intimacy did "not involve" same-sex marriage. 539 U. S., at 604. That could be true, he wrote, "only if one entertains the belief that principle and logic have nothing to do with the decisions of this Court." *Id.*, at 605. Score one for the dissent, as a matter of prophecy. And logic and principle are not one-way ratchets. Rights can contract in the same way and for the same reason—because whatever today's majority might say, one thing really does lead to another. We fervently hope that does not happen because of today's decision. We hope that we will not join Justice Scalia in the book of prophets. But we cannot understand how anyone can be confident that today's opinion will be the last of its kind.

[As] a matter of constitutional substance, the majority's opinion has all the flaws its method would suggest. Because laws in 1868 deprived women of any control over their bodies, the majority approves States doing so today. Because those laws prevented women from charting the course of their own lives, the majority says States can do the same again. Because in 1868, the government could tell a pregnant woman—even in the first days of her pregnancy—that she could do nothing but bear a child, it can once more impose that command. Today's decision strips women of agency over what even the majority agrees is a contested and contestable moral issue. It forces her to carry out the State's will, whatever the circumstances and whatever the harm it will wreak on her and her family. In the

Fourteenth Amendment's terms, it takes away her liberty. Even before we get to *stare decisis*, we dissent.

II

By overruling *Roe*, *Casey*, and more than 20 cases reaffirming or applying the constitutional right to abortion, the majority abandons *stare decisis*, a principle central to the rule of law. "*Stare decisis*" means "to stand by things decided." Black's Law Dictionary 1696 (11th ed. 2019). Blackstone called it the "established rule to abide by former precedents." 1 Blackstone 69. *Stare decisis* "promotes the evenhanded, predictable, and consistent development of legal principles." *Payne*, 501 U. S., at 827. It maintains a stability that allows people to order their lives under the law. See H. Hart & A. Sacks, The Legal Process: Basic Problems in the Making and Application of Law 568–569 (1994).

That means the Court may not overrule a decision, even a constitutional one, without a "special justification." *Gamble* v. *United States*, 587 U. S. ___, ___ (2019) (slip op., at 11). *Stare decisis* is, of course, not an "inexorable command"; it is sometimes appropriate to overrule an earlier decision. *Pearson* v. *Callahan*, 555 U. S. 223, 233 (2009). But the Court must have a good reason to do so over and above the belief "that the precedent was wrongly decided." *Halliburton Co.* v. *Erica P. John Fund, Inc.*, 573 U. S. 258, 266 (2014). "[I]t is not alone sufficient that we would decide a case differently now than we did then." *Kimble* v. *Marvel Entertainment, LLC*, 576 U. S. 446, 455 (2015).

[The] majority has overruled *Roe* and *Casey* for one and only one reason: because it has always despised them, and now it has the votes to discard them. The majority thereby substitutes a rule by judges for the rule of law.

A

Contrary to the majority's view, there is nothing unworkable about *Casey*'s "undue burden" standard. Its primary focus on whether a State has placed a "substantial obstacle" on a woman seeking an abortion is "the sort of inquiry familiar to judges across a variety of contexts." *June Medical Services L. L. C.* v. *Russo*, 591 U. S. ___, ___ (2020) (slip op., at 6) (ROBERTS, C. J., concurring in judgment). And it has given rise to no more conflict in application than many standards this Court and others unhesitatingly apply every day.

[Anyone] concerned about workability should consider the majority's substitute standard. The majority says a law regulating or banning abortion "must be sustained if there is a rational basis on which the legislature could have thought that it would serve legitimate state interests." *Ante*, at 77. And the majority lists interests like "respect for and preservation of prenatal life," "protection of maternal health," elimination of certain "medical procedures," "mitigation of fetal pain," and others. *Ante*, at 78. This Court will surely face critical questions about how that test applies. Must a state law allow abortions when necessary to protect a woman's life and health? And if so, exactly when? How much risk to a woman's life can a State force her to incur, before the Fourteenth Amendment's protection of life kicks in? Suppose a patient with pulmonary hypertension has a 30-to-50 percent risk of dying with ongoing pregnancy; is that enough? And short of death, how much illness or injury can the State require her to accept, consistent with the Amendment's protection of liberty and equality? Further, the Court may face questions about the application of abortion regulations to medical care most people view as quite different from abortion. What about the morning-after pill? IUDs? In vitro fertilization? And how about the use of dilation and evacuation or medication for miscarriage management? See generally L. Harris, Navigating Loss of Abortion Services—A Large Academic Medical Center Prepares for the Overturn of *Roe* v. *Wade*, 386 New England J. Med. 2061 (2022).[12]

B

When overruling constitutional precedent, the Court has almost always pointed to major legal or factual changes undermining a decision's original basis. [But] it is not so today. Although nodding to some arguments others have made about "modern developments," the majority does not really rely on them, no doubt seeing their slimness. *Ante*, at 33; see *ante*, at 34. The majority briefly invokes the current controversy over abortion. See *ante*, at 70–71. But it has to acknowledge that the same dispute has existed for decades: Conflict over abortion is not a change but a constant.

[1]

Subsequent legal developments have only reinforced *Roe* and *Casey*. The Court has continued to embrace all the decisions *Roe* and *Casey* cited, decisions which recognize a constitutional right for an individual to make her own choices about "intimate relationships, the family," and contraception. *Casey*, 505 U. S., at 857. *Roe* and *Casey* have themselves formed the legal foundation for subsequent decisions protecting these profoundly personal choices. As discussed earlier, the Court relied on *Casey* to hold that the Fourteenth Amendment protects same-sex intimate relationships. See *Lawrence*, 539 U. S., at 578; *supra*, at 23. The Court later invoked the same set of precedents to accord constitutional recognition to same-sex marriage. See *Obergefell*, 576 U. S., at 665–666; *supra*, at 23. In sum, *Roe* and *Casey* are inextricably interwoven with decades of precedent about the meaning of the Fourteenth Amendment. See *supra*, at 21–24. While the majority might wish it otherwise, *Roe* and *Casey* are the very opposite of " 'obsolete constitutional thinking.' " *Agostini* v. *Felton*, 521 U. S. 203, 236 (1997) (quoting *Casey*, 505 U. S., at 857).

Moreover, no subsequent factual developments have undermined *Roe* and *Casey*. Women continue to experience unplanned pregnancies and unexpected developments in pregnancies. Pregnancies continue to have enormous physical, social, and economic consequences. Even an uncomplicated pregnancy imposes significant strain on the body, unavoidably involving significant physiological change and excruciating pain. For some women, pregnancy and childbirth can mean life-altering physical ailments or even death. Today, as noted earlier, the risks of carrying a pregnancy to term dwarf those of having an abortion. See *supra*, at 22. Experts estimate that a ban on abortions increases maternal mortality by 21 percent, with white women facing a 13 percent increase in maternal mortality while black women face a 33 percent increase.[13] Pregnancy and childbirth may also impose large-scale financial costs.

[The] majority briefly notes the growing prevalence of haven laws and demand for adoption, see *ante*, at 34, and nn. 45–46, but, to the degree that these are changes at all, they too are irrelevant.[16] Neither reduces the health risks or financial costs of going through pregnancy and childbirth. Moreover, the choice to give up parental rights after giving birth is altogether different from the choice not to carry a pregnancy to term. The reality is that few women denied an abortion will choose adoption.[17] The vast majority will continue, just as in *Roe* and *Casey*'s time, to shoulder the costs of childrearing. Whether or not they choose to parent, they will experience the profound loss of autonomy and dignity that coerced pregnancy and birth always impose.[18]

[The] majority can point to neither legal nor factual developments in support of its decision. Nothing that has happened in this country or the world in recent decades undermines the core insight of *Roe* and *Casey*. It continues to be true that, within the constraints those decisions established, a woman, not the government, should choose whether she will bear the burdens of pregnancy, childbirth, and parenting.

2

In support of its holding, see *ante*, at 40, the majority invokes two watershed cases overruling prior constitutional precedents: *West Coast Hotel Co.* v. *Parrish* and *Brown* v. *Board of Education*. But those decisions, unlike today's, responded to changed law and to changed facts and attitudes that had taken hold throughout society. As *Casey* recognized, the two cases are relevant only to show—by stark contrast—how unjustified overturning the right to choose is. See 505 U. S., at 861–864.

[West] Coast Hotel overruled *Adkins* v. *Children's Hospital of D. C.*, 261 U. S. 525 (1923), and a whole line of cases beginning with *Lochner* v. *New York*, 198 U. S. 45 (1905). *Adkins* had found a state minimum-wage law unconstitutional because, in the Court's view, the law interfered with a constitutional right to contract. [In] *West Coast Hotel*, the Court caught up, recognizing through the lens of experience the flaws of existing legal doctrine. See also *ante*, at 11 (ROBERTS, C. J., concurring in judgment). The havoc the Depression had worked on ordinary Americans, the Court noted, was "common knowledge through the length and breadth of the land." 300 U. S., at 399. The *laissez-faire* approach had led to "the exploiting of workers at wages so low as to be insufficient to meet the bare cost of living."

Brown v. *Board of Education* overruled *Plessy* v. *Ferguson*, 163 U. S. 537 (1896), along with its doctrine of "separate but equal." By 1954, decades of Jim Crow had made clear what *Plessy*'s turn of phrase actually meant: "inherent[ ] [in]equal[ity]." *Brown*, 347 U. S., at 495. Segregation was not, and could not ever be, consistent with the Reconstruction Amendments, ratified to give the former slaves full citizenship. Whatever might have been thought in *Plessy*'s time, the *Brown* Court explained, both experience and "modern authority" showed the "detrimental effect[s]" of state-sanctioned segregation: It "affect[ed] [children's] hearts and minds in a way unlikely ever to be undone." 347 U. S., at 494. By that point, too, the law had begun to reflect that understanding. In a series of decisions, the Court had held unconstitutional public graduate schools' exclusion of black students. See, *e.g.*, *Sweatt* v. *Painter*, 339 U. S. 629 (1950); *Sipuel* v. *Board of Regents of Univ. of Okla.*, 332 U. S. 631 (1948) (*per curiam*); *Missouri ex rel. Gaines* v. *Canada*, 305 U. S. 337 (1938). The logic of those cases, *Brown* held, "appl[ied] with added force to children in grade and high schools." 347 U. S., at 494. Changed facts and changed law required *Plessy*'s end.

[In contrast] *Roe* and *Casey* continue to reflect, not diverge from, broad trends in American society. It is, of course, true that many Americans, including many women, opposed those decisions when issued and do so now as well. Yet the fact remains: *Roe* and *Casey* were the product of a profound and ongoing change in women's roles in the latter part of the 20th century. Only a dozen years before *Roe*, the Court described women as "the center of home and family life," with "special responsibilities" that precluded their full legal status under the Constitution. *Hoyt* v. *Florida*, 368 U. S. 57, 62 (1961). By 1973, when the Court decided *Roe*, fundamental social change was underway regarding the place of women—and the law had begun to follow. See *Reed* v. *Reed*, 404 U. S. 71, 76 (1971) (recognizing that the Equal Protection Clause prohibits sex-based discrimination). By 1992, when the Court decided *Casey*, the traditional view of a woman's role as only a wife and mother was "no longer consistent with our understanding of the family, the individual, or the Constitution." 505 U. S., at 897; see *supra*, at 15, 23–24. Under that charter, *Casey* understood, women must take their place as full and equal citizens. And for that to happen, women must have control over their reproductive decisions. Nothing since *Casey*—no changed law, no changed fact—has undermined that promise.

C

[The] reasons for retaining *Roe* and *Casey* gain further strength from the overwhelming reliance interests those decisions have created. The Court adheres to precedent not just for institutional reasons, but because it recognizes that stability in the law is "an essential thread in the mantle of protection that the law affords the individual." *Florida Dept. of Health and Rehabilitative Servs.* v. *Florida Nursing Home Assn.*, 450 U. S. 147, 154 (1981) (Stevens, J., concurring). So when overruling precedent "would dislodge [individuals'] settled rights and expectations," *stare decisis* has "added force." *Hilton* v. *South Carolina Public Railways Comm'n*, 502 U. S. 197, 202 (1991). *Casey* understood that to deny individuals' reliance on *Roe* was to "refuse to face the fact[s]." 505 U. S., at 856. Today the majority refuses to face the facts. "The most striking feature of the [majority] is the absence of any serious discussion" of how its ruling will affect women. *Ante*, at 37. By characterizing *Casey*'s reliance arguments as "generalized assertions about the national psyche," *ante*, at 64, it reveals how little it knows or cares about women's lives or about the suffering its decision will cause.

In *Casey*, the Court observed that for two decades individuals "have organized intimate relationships and made" significant life choices "in reliance on the availability of abortion in the event that contraception should fail." 505 U. S., at 856. Over another 30 years, that reliance has solidified. For half a century now, in *Casey*'s words, "[t]he ability of women to participate equally in the economic and social life of the Nation has been facilitated by their ability to control their reproductive lives." *Ibid.*; see *supra*, at 23– 24. Indeed, all women now of childbearing age have grown up expecting that they would be able to avail themselves of *Roe*'s and *Casey*'s protections.

The disruption of overturning *Roe* and *Casey* will therefore be profound. Abortion is a common medical procedure and a familiar experience in women's lives. About 18 percent of pregnancies in this country end in abortion, and about one quarter of American women will have an abortion before the age of 45.[22] Those numbers reflect the predictable and life-changing effects of carrying a pregnancy, giving birth, and becoming a parent. As *Casey* understood, people today rely on their ability to control and time pregnancies when making countless life decisions: where to live, whether and how to invest in education or careers, how to allocate financial resources, and how to approach intimate and family relationships. Women may count on abortion access for when contraception fails. They may count on abortion access for when contraception cannot be used, for example, if they were raped.

They may count on abortion for when something changes in the midst of a pregnancy, whether it involves family or financial circumstances, unanticipated medical complications, or heartbreaking fetal diagnoses. Taking away the right to abortion, as the majority does today, destroys all those individual plans and expectations. In so doing, it diminishes women's opportunities to participate fully and equally in the Nation's political, social, and economic life. See Brief for Economists as *Amici Curiae* 13 (showing that abortion availability has "large effects on women's education, labor force participation, occupations, and earnings" (footnotes omitted)).

[When] we "count[] the cost of [*Roe*'s] repudiation" on women who once relied on that decision, it is not hard to see where the greatest burden will fall. *Casey*, 505 U. S., at 855. In States that bar abortion, women of means will still be able to travel to obtain the services they need.[25] It is women who cannot afford to do so who will suffer most. These are the women most likely to seek abortion care in the first place. Women living below the federal poverty line experience unintended pregnancies at rates five times higher than higher income women do, and nearly half of women who seek abortion care live in households below the poverty line. See Brief for 547 Deans 7; Brief for Abortion Funds and Practical Support Organizations as *Amici Curiae* 8 (Brief for Abortion Funds).

Even with *Roe*'s protection, these women face immense obstacles to raising the money needed to obtain abortion care early in their pregnancy. See Brief for Abortion Funds 7– 12.[26] After today, in States where legal abortions are not available, they will lose any ability to obtain safe, legal abortion care. They will not have the money to make the trip necessary; or to obtain childcare for that time; or to take time off work. Many will endure the costs and risks of pregnancy and giving birth against their wishes. Others will turn in desperation to illegal and unsafe abortions. They may lose not just their freedom, but their lives.[27]

[The] Court's failure to perceive the whole swath of expectations *Roe* and *Casey* created reflects an impoverished view of reliance. According to the majority, a reliance interest must be "very concrete," like those involving "property" or "contract." *Ante*, at 64. While many of this Court's cases addressing reliance have been in the "commercial context," *Casey*, 505 U. S., at 855, none holds that interests must be analogous to commercial ones to warrant *stare decisis* protection.[28]

[The] majority claims that the reliance interests women have in *Roe* and *Casey* are too "intangible" for the Court to consider, even if it were inclined to do so. *Ante*, at 65. This is to ignore as judges what we know as men and women. The interests women have in *Roe* and *Casey* are perfectly, viscerally concrete. Countless women will now make different decisions about careers, education, relationships, and whether to try to become pregnant than they would have when *Roe* served as a backstop. Other women will carry pregnancies to term, with all the costs and risk of harm that involves, when they would previously have chosen to obtain an abortion. For millions of women, *Roe* and *Casey* have been critical in giving them control of their bodies and their lives. Closing our eyes to the suffering today's decision will impose will not make that suffering disappear. The majority cannot escape its obligation to "count[ ] the cost[s]" of its decision by invoking the "conflicting arguments" of "contending sides." *Casey*, 505 U. S., at 855; *ante*, at 65. *Stare decisis* requires that the

Court calculate the costs of a decision's repudiation on those who have relied on the decision, not on those who have disavowed it. See *Casey*, 505 U. S., at 855.

[After] today, young women will come of age with fewer rights than their mothers and grandmothers had. The majority accomplishes that result without so much as considering how women have relied on the right to choose or what it means to take that right away. The majority's refusal even to consider the life-altering consequences of reversing *Roe* and *Casey* is a stunning indictment of its decision.

III

Casey explained the importance of *stare decisis*; the inappositeness of *West Coast Hotel* and *Brown*; the absence of any "changed circumstances" (or other reason) justifying the reversal of precedent. 505 U. S., at 864; see *supra*, at 30–33, 37–47. "[T]he Court," *Casey* explained, "could not pretend" that overruling *Roe* had any "justification beyond a present doctrinal disposition to come out differently from the Court of 1973." 505 U. S., at 864. And to overrule for that reason? Quoting Justice Stewart, *Casey* explained that to do so—to reverse prior law "upon a ground no firmer than a change in [the Court's] membership"— would invite the view that "this institution is little different from the two political branches of the Government." *Ibid.* No view, *Casey* thought, could do "more lasting injury to this Court and to the system of law which it is our abiding mission to serve." *Ibid.* For overruling *Roe*, *Casey* concluded, the Court would pay a "terrible price." 505 U. S., at 864.

The Justices who wrote those words—O'Connor, Kennedy, and Souter—they were judges of wisdom. They would not have won any contests for the kind of ideological purity some court watchers want Justices to deliver. But if there were awards for Justices who left this Court better than they found it? And who for that reason left this country better? And the rule of law stronger? Sign those Justices up.

They knew that "the legitimacy of the Court [is] earned over time." *Id.*, at 868. They also would have recognized that it can be destroyed much more quickly. They worked hard to avert that outcome in *Casey*. The American public, they thought, should never conclude that its constitutional protections hung by a thread—that a new majority, adhering to a new "doctrinal school," could "by dint of numbers" alone expunge their rights. *Id.*, at 864. It is hard—no, it is impossible—to conclude that anything else has happened here. One of us once said that "[i]t is not often in the law that so few have so quickly changed so much." S. Breyer, Breaking the Promise of *Brown*: The Resegregation of America's Schools 30 (2022). For all of us, in our time on this Court, that has never been more true than today. In overruling *Roe* and *Casey*, this Court betrays its guiding principles.

With sorrow—for this Court, but more, for the many millions of American women who have today lost a fundamental constitutional protection—we dissent.

[A concurrence by Justice Kavanaugh is omitted]

Abortion and Gender Equality. *Casey*, for the first time, speaks of a relationship between *Roe* and gender equality. Is there an argument that restrictions on abortion implicate the equal protection clause and gender? Could such a claim be made? Strauss in "Abortion, Toleration, and Moral Uncertainty," 1993 Sup. Ct. Rev. 1, 27, comments, "The

Court in Casey addressed, essentially for the first time, the issues that ought to be central to the legal debate over abortion: not whether there are 'unenumerated rights' in the Constitution, but how to deal with fetal life, on the one hand, and the effect of abortion laws on the status of women, on the other." The "Court adopted [a] plausible and coherent justification for a regime of toleration in the area of abortion. That justification is premised on, first, fundamental moral uncertainty about the status of fetal life; and, second, the danger that the political process will subordinate women, a danger that is the basis of the well established constitutional principles governing gender discrimination."

Does *Dobbs* speak to the issue of gender equality? Does it undermine any theory that may have developed from Casey on the issue? Is the opinion indifferent or irrelevant to the issue of gender equality?

Democracy and *Dobbs*. To what degree have the Court's abortion decisions been affected by the democratic process and political pressure? Is this healthy? Was *Casey* a response to these social pressures, both in regard to maintaining the precedential value of *Roe* and yet changing applicable judicial standards? Was *Dobbs* a response to social pressure? Should the confirmation process, even presidential elections, turn on likely Supreme Court votes and nominees? Is this one of the Constitution's democratic "inputs" to a non-elected Court made up of members with life tenure?

Several members of the Court who voted to overturn Roe expressed their belief that *Roe v. Wade* was an important precedent in response to questioning by Senators during their confirmation hearings. Did those Justices break a commitment, actual or implied, in *Dobbs*?

4. EXTENDING PRIVACY RIGHTS: FAMILY, MARRIAGE, PROCREATION, CHILD REARING

The unarticulated fundamental right of privacy can extend well beyond the rights articulated in *Griswold* and *Roe*. Given that there are innumerable privacy interests, the question becomes which of these privacy interests will be deemed fundamental, entitled to constitutional protection, and a compelling purpose/strict scrutiny standard of review. The issue that ensues is how the Court will go about deciding that question. The revival of substantive due process as a source for the right, with the "lessons of *Lochner*" lurking in the background, make this inquiry both significant and controversial. This is particularly the case when the decisions will be made by a conservative Supreme Court espousing judicial restraint. The cases that follow shape the nature of the inquiry.

MOORE v. CITY OF EAST CLEVELAND
431 U.S. 494 (1977)

Appellant lives in her East Cleveland, Ohio, home with her son and two grandsons (who are first cousins). An East Cleveland housing ordinance limits occupancy of a dwelling unit to members of a single family, but defines "family" in such a way that appellant's household does not qualify. Appellant was convicted of a criminal violation of the ordinance. Her conviction was upheld on appeal over her claim that the ordinance is unconstitutional. Appellee city contends that the ordinance should be sustained under

Village of Belle Terre v. Boraas, 416 U.S. 1, 94 S.Ct. 1536, 39 L.Ed.2d 797 which upheld an ordinance imposing limits on the types of groups that could occupy a single dwelling unit.

Mr. Justice POWELL, joined by Mr. Justice BRENNAN, Mr. Justice MARSHALL, and Mr. Justice BLACKMUN, concluded that the ordinance deprived appellant of her liberty in violation of the Due Process Clause of the Fourteenth Amendment.

East Cleveland's housing ordinance, like many throughout the country, limits occupancy of a dwelling unit to members of a single family. § 1351.02. But the ordinance contains an unusual and complicated definitional section that recognizes as a "family" only a few categories of related individuals, § 1341.08. Because her family, living together in her home, fits none of those categories, appellant stands convicted of a criminal offense. The question in this case is whether the ordinance violates the Due Process Clause of the Fourteenth Amendment.

Appellant, Mrs. Inez Moore, lives in her East Cleveland home together with her son, Dale Moore Sr., and her two grandsons, Dale, Jr., and John Moore, Jr. The two boys are first cousins rather than brothers; we are told that John came to live with his grandmother and with the elder and younger Dale Moores after his mother's death.

In early 1973, Mrs. Moore received a notice of violation from the city, stating that John was an "illegal occupant" and directing her to comply with the ordinance. When she failed to remove him from her home, the city filed a criminal charge. Mrs. Moore moved to dismiss, claiming that the ordinance was constitutionally invalid on its face. Her motion was overruled, and upon conviction she was sentenced to five days in jail and a $25 fine. The Ohio Court of Appeals affirmed after giving full consideration to her constitutional claims and the Ohio Supreme Court denied review. We noted probable jurisdiction of her appeal, 425 U.S. 949, 96 S.Ct. 1723, 48 L.Ed.2d 193 (1976).

East Cleveland's housing ordinance, like many throughout the country, limits occupancy of a dwelling unit to members of a single family. § 1351.02.   But the ordinance contains an unusual and complicated definitional section that recognizes as a "family" only a few categories of related individuals, § 1341.08.   Because her family, living together in her home, fits none of those categories, appellant stands convicted of a criminal offense. The question in this case is whether the ordinance violates the Due Process Clause of the Fourteenth Amendment.

[The] city argues that our decision in Village of Belle Terre v. Boraas, 416 U.S. 1 (1974), requires us to sustain the ordinance attacked here. Belle Terre, like East Cleveland, imposed limits on the types of groups that could occupy a single dwelling unit. [We] sustained the Belle Terre ordinance on the ground that it bore a rational relationship to permissible state objectives. But one overriding factor sets this case apart from Belle Terre. The ordinance there affected only unrelated individuals. It expressly allowed all who were related by "blood, adoption, or marriage" to live [together]. East Cleveland, in contrast, has chosen to regulate the occupancy of its housing by slicing deeply into the family itself. [The ordinance] selects certain categories of relatives who may live together and declares that others may not. In particular, it makes a crime of a grandmother's choice to live with her grandson in circumstances like those presented here.

When a city undertakes such intrusive regulation of the family, [Belle Terre does not govern, and] the usual judicial deference to the legislature is inappropriate. "This Court has long recognized that freedom of personal choice in matters of marriage and family life is one of the liberties protected by the Due Process Clause of the Fourteenth Amendment."

[Citing, e.g., Meyer; Pierce; Roe; Griswold; Skinner.] [When] government intrudes on choices concerning family living arrangements, this Court must examine carefully the importance of the governmental interests advanced and the extent to which they are served by the challenged regulation. When thus examined, this ordinance cannot survive. The city seeks to justify it as a means of preventing overcrowding, minimizing traffic and parking congestion, and avoiding an undue financial burden on [the] school system. Although these are legitimate goals, the ordinance [serves] them marginally, at best. . . .

Substantive due process has at times been a treacherous field for this Court. There are risks when the judicial branch gives enhanced protection to certain substantive liberties without the guidance of the more specific provisions of the Bill of Rights. As the history of the Lochner era demonstrates, there is reason for concern lest the only limits to such judicial intervention become the predilections of those who happen at the time to be Members of this Court. That history counsels caution and restraint. But it does not counsel abandonment, nor does it require what the city urges here: cutting off any protection of family rights at the first convenient, if arbitrary boundary of the nuclear family. . . .

Appropriate limits on substantive due process comes not from drawing arbitrary lines but rather from careful "respect for the teachings of history [and] solid recognition of the basic values that underlie our society." [Griswold (Harlan, J., concurring).] Our decisions establish that the Constitution protects the sanctity of the family precisely because the institution of the family is deeply rooted in this Nation's history and tradition. It is through the family that we inculcate and pass down many of our most cherished values, moral and cultural. [And ours] is by no means a tradition limited to respect for [the] nuclear family. The tradition of uncles, aunts, cousins, and especially grandparents sharing a household along with parents has roots equally venerable and equally deserving of constitutional recognition. Over the years millions of our citizens have grown up in just such an environment, and most, surely, have profited from it. Even if conditions of modern society have brought about a decline in extended family households, they have not erased the accumulated wisdom of civilization, gained over the centuries and honored throughout our history, that supports a larger conception of the family. Out of choice, necessity, or a sense of family responsibility, it has been common for close relatives to draw together and participate in the duties and the satisfactions of a common home. Especially in times of adversity, such as the death of a spouse or economic need, the broader family has tended to come together for mutual sustenance and to maintain or rebuild a secure home life. This is apparently what happened here.

Whether or not such a household is established because of personal tragedy, the choice of relatives in this degree of kinship to live together may not lightly be denied by the State. [The] Constitution prevents East Cleveland from standardizing its children and its adults by forcing all to live in certain narrowly defined family patterns.

Justice STEVENS concurred in the result on the ground that the challenged ordinance "constitutes a taking of property without due process and without just compensation."

Justice STEWART, joined by Justice REHNQUIST, dissented.

To suggest [that] related persons [have] constitutional rights of association superior to those of unrelated persons is to misunderstand the nature of the associational freedoms that the Constitution has been understood to protect. Freedom of association has been constitutionally recognized because it is often indispensable to effectuation of explicit First Amendment guarantees. [Citing, e.g., NAACP v. Alabama, 357 U.S. 449 (1958).] [The] "association" in this case is not for any purpose relating to the promotion of speech, assembly, the press, or religion.

[Appellant] is considerably closer to the constitutional mark in asserting that [the] ordinance intrudes upon "the private realm of family life which the state cannot enter." [But] appellant's desire to share a single-dwelling unit [can] hardly be equated with any of the interests protected in [our prior decisions].

Justice WHITE dissented:

What the deeply rooted traditions of the country are is arguable; which of them deserve the protection of the Due Process Clause is even more debatable. The suggested view would broaden enormously the horizons of the Clause; and, if the interest involved here is any measure of what the States would be forbidden to regulate, the courts would be substantively weighing and very likely invalidating a wide range of measures that Congress and state legislatures think appropriate to respond to a changing economic and social order.

[Although] the Due Process Clause extends substantial protection to various phases of family life, [the challenged] ordinance [merely] denies appellant the opportunity to live with all her grandchildren in this particular [suburb].

ZABLOCKI v. REDHAIL
434 U.S. 374 (1978)

A Wisconsin statute providing that any resident "having minor issue not in his custody and which he is under an obligation to support by court order" may not marry without a prior judicial determination that the support obligation has been met, and that the children "are not then and are not likely thereafter to become public charges." . . .

Mr. Justice MARSHALL, delivered the opinion of the Court.

[The] decisions of this Court confirm that the right to marry is of fundamental importance for all individuals. [Citing, e.g., Loving v. Virginia, 388 U.S. 1 (1967) (invalidating state miscegenation laws); Griswold; Skinner; Meyer.] It is not surprising that the decision to marry has been placed on the same level of importance as decisions relating to procreation, childbirth, child rearing, and family relationships. [It] would make little sense to recognize a right of privacy with respect to other matters of family life and not with respect to the decision to enter the relationship that is the foundation of the family in our society. [If the] right to procreate means anything at all, it must imply some right to enter the only relationship in which the [State] allows sexual relations legally to take place. [We] do not mean to suggest that every state regulation which relates in any way to the incidents of or prerequisites for marriage must be subjected to rigorous scrutiny. To the contrary, reasonable regulations that do not significantly interfere with decisions to enter into the marital relationship may legitimately be imposed. [Citing, e.g., Califano v. Jobst.]

The statutory classification at issue here, however, [interferes] directly and substantially with the right to marry. Under the challenged statute, [some persons] will never be able to obtain the necessary court order, because they either lack the financial means to meet their support obligations or cannot prove that their children will not become public charges. These persons are absolutely prevented from getting married. Many others, able in theory to satisfy the statute's requirements, will be sufficiently burdened by having to do so that they will [forgo] their right to marry. And even those who can [meet] the statute's requirements suffer a serious intrusion into their freedom of choice in an area in which we have held such freedom to be fundamental.

When a statutory classification significantly interferes with the exercise of a fundamental right, it cannot be upheld unless it is supported by sufficiently important state interests and is closely tailored to effectuate only those interests. [The State argues that the statute protects the welfare of the out-of-custody children, but this] "collection device" rationale cannot justify the statute's broad infringement on the right to marry. First, with respect to individuals who are unable to [pay], the statute merely prevents the applicant from getting married, without delivering any money at all into the hands of [the] children. More importantly, [the] State already has numerous other means for exacting compliance with support obligations [that] do not impinge upon the right to marry.

Mr. Justice Stewart, concurring in the judgment. . . .

To hold [that] the Wisconsin statute violates the Equal Protection Clause [misconceives] the meaning of that constitutional guarantee. [The] problem in this case is not one of discriminatory classifications, but of unwarranted encroachment upon a constitutionally protected freedom. [The] statute is unconstitutional because it exceeds the bounds of permissible state regulation of marriage, and invades the sphere of liberty protected by the Due Process Clause of the Fourteenth Amendment. [On] several occasions this Court has held that a person's inability to pay [does] not justify the total deprivation of a constitutionally protected liberty. [Citing Boddie.] The principle of [Boddie] applies [here]. We [may] assume that [the law is permissible] as applied to those who can afford to [pay] but choose not to do [so]. [But] some people simply cannot afford to [pay]. To deny these people permission to marry penalizes them for failing to do that which they cannot do. Insofar as it applies to indigents, the [law] is [irrational].

Mr. Justice POWELL, concurring in the judgment. . . .

The Court apparently would subject all state regulation which "directly and substantially" interferes with the decision to marry in a traditional family setting [to] "compelling state interest" analysis. [We must recognize, however, that] domestic relations [is "an area that has long been regarded as a virtually exclusive province of the States." [The] State, representing the collective expression of moral aspirations, has an undeniable interest in ensuring that its rules of domestic relations reflect the widely held values of its people. [State] regulation has included bans on incest, bigamy, and homosexuality, as well as various preconditions to marriage, such as blood tests. Likewise, a showing of fault [traditionally] has been a prerequisite to [divorce]. A "compelling state purpose" inquiry would cast doubt on [such restrictions].

[Justice Powell then argued for a more flexible approach:] The Due Process Clause requires a showing of justification "when the government intrudes on choices concerning family living arrangements" in a manner which is contrary to deeply rooted traditions. [Quoting his plurality opinion in Moore.] Furthermore, under the Equal Protection Clause the means chosen by the State in this case must bear "a fair and substantial relation" to the object of the legislation. [Quoting Reed v. Reed, 404 U.S. 71 (1971).] The [challenged statute] does not pass muster under either due process or equal protection standards. [I] do not agree with the [Court] that a State may never condition the right to marry on satisfaction of existing support obligations [where] the [person is] able to make the required support payments but simply wish[es] to shirk [his] moral and legal [obligation]. The vice inheres, not in the collection concept, but in the failure to [exempt] those without the means to [pay]. [Citing Boddie.]

Mr. Justice STEVENS, concurring in the judgment.

The individual's interest in making the marriage decision independently is sufficiently important to merit special constitutional protection. It is not, however, an interest which is constitutionally immune from evenhanded regulation. Thus, laws prohibiting marriage to a child, a close relative, or a person afflicted with venereal disease, are unchallenged even though they "interfere directly and substantially with the right to marry." [The challenged] statute has a different character. Under this statute, a person's economic status may determine his eligibility to [marry]. This type of statutory discrimination [is] inconsistent with our tradition of administering justice equally to the rich and to the poor. [Neither] the fact that the appellee's interest is constitutionally protected, nor the fact that the classification is based on economic status is sufficient to justify a "level of scrutiny" so strict that a holding of unconstitutionality is virtually foreordained. [But] the presence of these factors precludes a holding that [rational explanation] is [sufficient]. [Here, the] discrimination between the rich and the poor is irrational in so many ways that it cannot withstand scrutiny under the Equal Protection Clause.

Mr. Justice REHNQUIST, dissenting.

I would view this [statute] in the light of the traditional presumption of validity. [The] statute so viewed is a permissible exercise of the State's power to regulate family life and to assure the support of minor children.

"Tradition"! Do *Moore* and *Zablacki* indicate the direction the Court is taking in deciding which privacy interests are fundamental? Are you surprised that the "grandparents" sitting on the Court would conclude that grandparents are a part of the traditional American family, "precisely because the institution of the family is deeply rooted in this Nation's history and tradition," and thus afforded fundamental right protection? Or that the right to marriage (*Zablocki*) would be included as well? The nature of tradition and protection of privacy rights permeates the Court's opinion in *Michael H.*

MICHAEL H. v. GERALD D.
491 U.S. 110 (1989)

Justice SCALIA announced the judgment of the Court and delivered an opinion, in which THE CHIEF JUSTICE joins, and in all but footnote 6 of which Justice O'CONNOR and Justice KENNEDY join.

I

[The] facts of this case are, we must hope, extraordinary. On May 9, 1976, in Las Vegas, Nevada, Carole D., an international model, and Gerald D., a top executive in a French oil company, were married. The couple established a home in Playa del Rey, California, in which they resided as husband and wife when one or the other was not out of the country on business. In the summer of 1978, Carole became involved in an adulterous affair with a neighbor, Michael H. In September 1980, she conceived a child,

Victoria D., who was born on May 11, 1981. Gerald was listed as father on the birth certificate and has always held Victoria out to the world as his daughter. Soon after delivery of the child, however, Carole informed Michael that she believed he might be the father.

In the first three years of her life, Victoria remained always with Carole, but found herself within a variety of quasi-family units. In October 1981, Gerald moved to New York City to pursue his business interests, but Carole chose to remain in California. At the end of that month, Carole and Michael had blood tests of themselves and Victoria, which showed a 98.07% probability that Michael was Victoria's father. In January 1982, Carole visited Michael in St. Thomas, where his primary business interests were based. There Michael held Victoria out as his child.

[In] November 1982, rebuffed in his attempts to visit Victoria, Michael filed a filiation action in California Superior Court to establish his paternity and right to visitation. In March 1983, the court appointed an attorney and guardian ad litem to represent Victoria's interests. Victoria then filed a cross-complaint asserting that if she had more than one psychological or *de facto* father, she was entitled to maintain her filial relationship, with all of the attendant rights, duties, and obligations, with both. In May 1983, Carole filed a motion for summary judgment. During this period, from March through July 1983, Carole was again living with Gerald in New York. In August, however, she returned to California, became involved once again with Michael . . .

For the ensuing eight months, when Michael was not in St. Thomas he lived with Carole and Victoria in Carole's apartment in Los Angeles and held Victoria out as his daughter. [In] June 1984, Carole reconciled with Gerald and joined him in New York, where they now live with Victoria and two other children since born into the marriage.

In May 1984, Michael and Victoria, through her guardian ad litem, sought visitation rights for Michael. . . . On October 19, 1984, Gerald, who had intervened in the action, moved for summary judgment on the ground that under Cal.Evid.Code § 621 there were no triable issues of fact as to Victoria's paternity. [The California] Superior Court granted Gerald's motion for summary judgment, and [the] California Court of Appeal affirmed the judgment of the Superior Court and upheld the constitutionality of the statute.

III

We address first the claims of Michael. At the outset, it is necessary to clarify what he sought and what he was denied. California law, like nature itself, makes no provision for dual fatherhood. Michael was seeking to be declared *the* father of Victoria. The immediate benefit he evidently sought to obtain from that status was visitation rights. See Cal.Civ.Code Ann. § 4601 (West 1983) (parent has statutory right to visitation "unless it is shown that such visitation would be detrimental to the best interests of the child"). But if Michael were successful in being declared the father, other rights would follow — most importantly, the right to be considered as the parent who should have custody, Cal.Civ.Code Ann. § 4600 (West 1983), a status which "embrace[s] the sum of parental rights with respect to the rearing of a child, including the child's care; the right to the child's services and earnings; the right to direct the child's activities; the right to make decisions regarding the control, education, and health of the child; and the right, as well as the duty, to prepare the child for additional obligations, which includes the teaching of moral standards, religious beliefs, and elements of good citizenship." 4 California Family Law § 60.02[1][b] (C. Markey ed. 1987) (footnotes omitted). All parental rights, including visitation, were automatically denied by denying Michael status as the father.

[Michael] contends as a matter of substantive due process that, because he has established a parental relationship with Victoria, protection of Gerald's and Carole's marital union is an insufficient state interest to support termination of that relationship. This argument is, of course, predicated on the assertion that Michael has a constitutionally protected liberty interest in his relationship with Victoria.

It is an established part of our constitutional jurisprudence that the term "liberty" in the Due Process Clause extends beyond freedom from physical restraint. Without that core textual meaning as a limitation, defining the scope of the Due Process Clause "has at times been a treacherous field for this Court," giving "reason for concern lest the only limits to . . . judicial intervention become the predilections of those who happen at the time to be Members of this Court." Moore v. East Cleveland, 431 U.S. 494, 502, 97 S.Ct. 1932, 1937, 52 L.Ed.2d 531 (1977).

[In] an attempt to limit and guide interpretation of the Clause, we have insisted not merely that the interest denominated as a "liberty" be "fundamental" (a concept that, in isolation, is hard to objectify), but also that it be an interest traditionally protected by our society. As we have put it, the Due Process Clause affords only those protections "so rooted in the traditions and conscience of our people as to be ranked as fundamental." Our cases reflect "continual insistence upon respect for the teachings of history [and] solid recognition of the basic values that underlie our society. . . ." Griswold v. Connecticut, 381 U.S. 479, 501, 85 S.Ct. 1678, 1690, 14 L.Ed.2d 510 (1965) (Harlan, J., concurring in judgment).

This insistence that the asserted liberty interest be rooted in history and tradition is evident, as elsewhere, in our cases according constitutional protection to certain parental rights. Michael reads the landmark case of Stanley v. Illinois, 405 U.S. 645, 92 S.Ct. 1208, 31 L.Ed.2d 551 (1972), and the subsequent cases of Quilloin v. Walcott, 434 U.S. 246, 98 S.Ct. 549, 54 L.Ed.2d 511 (1978), Caban v. Mohammed, 441 U.S. 380, 99 S.Ct. 1760, 60 L.Ed.2d 297 (1979), and Lehr v. Robertson, 463 U.S. 248, 103 S.Ct. 2985, 77 L.Ed.2d 614 (1983), as establishing that a liberty interest is created by biological fatherhood plus an established parental relationship — factors that exist in the present case as well. We think that distorts the rationale of those cases. As we view them, they rest not upon such isolated factors but upon the historic respect — indeed, sanctity would not be too strong a term — traditionally accorded to the relationships that develop within the unitary family. See Stanley, supra, 405 U.S., at 651, 92 S.Ct., at 1212; Quilloin, supra, 434 U.S., at 254-255, 98 S.Ct., at 554-555; Caban, supra, 441 U.S., at 389, 99 S.Ct., at 1766; Lehr, supra, 463 U.S., at 261, 103 S.Ct., at 2993. In *Stanley,* for example, we forbade the destruction of such a family when, upon the death of the mother, the State had sought to remove children from the custody of a father who had lived with and supported them and their mother for 18 years. As Justice Powell stated for the plurality in Moore v. East Cleveland, supra, 431 U.S., at 503, 97 S.Ct., at 1938: "Our decisions establish that the Constitution protects the sanctity of the family precisely because the institution of the family is deeply rooted in this Nation's history and tradition."

Thus, the legal issue in the present case reduces to whether the relationship between persons in the situation of Michael and Victoria has been treated as a protected family unit under the historic practices of our society, or whether on any other basis it has been accorded special protection. We think it impossible to find that it has. In fact, quite to the contrary, our traditions have protected the marital family (Gerald, Carole, and the child they acknowledge to be theirs) against the sort of claim Michael asserts.

The presumption of legitimacy was a fundamental principle of the common law. H. Nicholas, Adulturine Bastardy 1 (1836). Traditionally, that presumption could be rebutted only by proof that a husband was incapable of procreation or had had no access to his wife during the relevant period. *Id.,* at 9-10 (citing Bracton, De Legibus et Consuetudinibus Angliae, bk. i, ch. 9, p. 6; bk. ii, ch. 29, p. 63, ch. 32, p. 70 (1569)). As explained by Blackstone, nonaccess could only be proved "if the husband be out of the kingdom of England (or, as the law somewhat loosely phrases it, *extra quatuor maria* [beyond the four seas]) for above nine months. . . ." 1 Blackstone's Commentaries 456 (J. Chitty ed. 1826). And, under the common law both in England and here, "neither husband nor wife [could] be a witness to prove access or nonaccess." J. Schouler, Law of the Domestic Relations § 225, p. 306 (3d ed. 1882); R. Graveson & F. Crane, A Century of Family Law: 1857-1957, p. 158 (1957). The primary policy rationale underlying the common law's severe restrictions on rebuttal of the presumption appears to have been an aversion to declaring children illegitimate, see Schouler, *supra,* § 225, at 306-307; M. Grossberg, Governing the Hearth 201 (1985), thereby depriving them of rights of inheritance and succession, 2 J. Kent, Commentaries on American Law *175, and likely making them wards of the state. A secondary policy concern was the interest in promoting the "peace and tranquillity of States and families," Schouler, *supra,* § 225, at 304, quoting Boullenois, Traite des Status, bk. 1, p. 62, a goal that is obviously impaired by facilitating suits against husband and wife asserting that their children are illegitimate. Even though, as bastardy laws became less harsh, "[j]udges in both [England and the United States] gradually widened the acceptable range of evidence that could be offered by spouses, and placed restraints on the 'four seas rule' . . . [,] the law retained a strong bias against ruling the children of married women illegitimate." Grossberg, *supra,* at 202.

We have found nothing in the older sources, nor in the older cases, addressing specifically the power of the natural father to assert parental rights over a child born into a woman's existing marriage with another man. Since it is Michael's burden to establish that such a power (at least where the natural father has established a relationship with the child) is so deeply embedded within our traditions as to be a fundamental right, the lack of evidence alone might defeat his case. But the evidence shows that even in modern times — when, as we have noted, the rigid protection of the marital family has in other respects been relaxed — the ability of a person in Michael's position to claim paternity has not been generally acknowledged.

Moreover, even if it were clear that one in Michael's position generally possesses, and has generally always possessed, standing to challenge the marital child's legitimacy, that would still not establish Michael's case. As noted earlier, what is at issue here is not entitlement to a state pronouncement that Victoria was begotten by Michael. It is no conceivable denial of constitutional right for a State to decline to declare facts unless some legal consequence hinges upon the requested declaration. What Michael asserts here is a right to have himself declared the natural father *and thereby to obtain parental prerogatives.* What he must establish, therefore, is not that our society has traditionally allowed a natural father in his circumstances to establish paternity, but that it has traditionally accorded such a father parental rights, or at least has not traditionally denied them. Even if the law in all States had always been that the entire world could challenge the marital presumption and obtain a declaration as to who was the natural father, that would not advance Michael's claim. Thus, it is ultimately irrelevant, even for purposes of determining *current* social attitudes towards the alleged substantive right Michael asserts, that the present law in a number of States appears to allow the natural father —

including the natural father who has not established a relationship with the child — the theoretical power to rebut the marital presumption, see Note, Rebutting the Marital Presumption: A Developed Relationship Test, 88 Colum. L. Rev. 369, 373 (1988). What counts is whether the States in fact award substantive parental rights to the natural father of a child conceived within, and born into, an extant marital union that wishes to embrace the child. We are not aware of a single case, old or new, that has done so. This is not the stuff of which fundamental rights qualifying as liberty interests are made.

We do not accept Justice Brennan's criticism that this result "squashes" the liberty that consists of "the freedom not to conform." *Post,* at 2351. It seems to us that reflects the erroneous view that there is only one side to this controversy — that one disposition can expand a "liberty" of sorts without contracting an equivalent "liberty" on the other side. Such a happy choice is rarely available. Here, to *provide* protection to an adulterous natural father is to *deny* protection to a marital father, and vice versa. If Michael has a "freedom not to conform" (whatever that means), Gerald must equivalently have a "freedom to conform." One of them will pay a price for asserting that "freedom" — Michael by being unable to act as father of the child he has adulterously begotten, or Gerald by being unable to preserve the integrity of the traditional family unit he and Victoria have established. Our disposition does not choose between these two "freedoms," but leaves that to the people of California. Justice Brennan's approach chooses one of them as the constitutional imperative, on no apparent basis except that the unconventional is to be preferred.

IV

We have never had occasion to decide whether a child has a liberty interest, symmetrical with that of her parent, in maintaining her filial relationship. We need not do so here because, even assuming that such a right exists, Victoria's claim must fail. Victoria's due process challenge is, if anything, weaker than Michael's. Her basic claim is not that California has erred in preventing her from establishing that Michael, not Gerald, should stand as her legal father. Rather, she claims a due process right to maintain filial relationships with both Michael and Gerald. This assertion merits little discussion, for, whatever the merits of the guardian ad litem's belief that such an arrangement can be of great psychological benefit to a child, the claim that a State must recognize multiple fatherhood has no support in the history or traditions of this country.

[We] apply, therefore, the ordinary "rational relationship" test to Victoria's equal protection challenge. The primary rationale underlying § 621's limitation on those who may rebut the presumption of legitimacy is a concern that allowing persons other than the husband or wife to do so may undermine the integrity of the marital union. When the husband or wife contests the legitimacy of their child, the stability of the marriage has already been shaken. In contrast, allowing a claim of illegitimacy to be pressed by the child — or, more accurately, by a court-appointed guardian ad litem — may well disrupt an otherwise peaceful union. Since it pursues a legitimate end by rational means, California's decision to treat Victoria differently from her parents is not a denial of equal protection.

The judgment of the California Court of Appeal is affirmed.

Justice O'CONNOR, with whom Justice KENNEDY joins, concurring in part.

I concur in all but footnote 6 of Justice Scalia's opinion. This footnote sketches a mode of historical analysis to be used when identifying liberty interests protected by the Due Process Clause of the Fourteenth Amendment that may be somewhat inconsistent with our past decisions in this area. On occasion the Court has characterized relevant traditions protecting asserted rights at levels of generality that might not be "the most specific level" available. I would not foreclose the unanticipated by the prior imposition of a single mode of historical analysis.

Justice STEVENS, concurring in the judgment.

On the second issue I do not agree with Justice Scalia's analysis. He seems to reject the possibility that a natural father might ever have a constitutionally protected interest in his relationship with a child whose mother was married, to and cohabiting with, another man at the time of the child's conception and birth. I think cases like Stanley v. Illinois, 405 U.S. 645, 92 S.Ct. 1208, 31 L.Ed.2d 551 (1972), and Caban v. Mohammed, 441 U.S. 380, 99 S.Ct. 1760, 60 L.Ed.2d 297 (1979), demonstrate that enduring "family" relationships may develop in unconventional settings. I therefore would not foreclose the possibility that a constitutionally protected relationship between a natural father and his child might exist in a case like this. Indeed, I am willing to assume for the purpose of deciding this case that Michael's relationship with Victoria is strong enough to give him a constitutional right to try to convince a trial judge that Victoria's best interest would be served by granting him visitation rights.

[Under] the circumstances of the case before us, Michael was given a fair opportunity to show that he is Victoria's natural father, that he had developed a relationship with her, and that her interests would be served by granting him visitation rights. On the other hand, the record also shows that after its rather shaky start, the marriage between Carole and Gerald developed a stability that now provides Victoria with a loving and harmonious family home. In the circumstances of this case, I find nothing fundamentally unfair about the exercise of a judge's discretion that, in the end, allows the mother to decide whether her child's best interests would be served by allowing the natural father visitation privileges. Because I am convinced that the trial judge had the authority under state law both to hear Michael's plea for visitation rights and to grant him such rights if Victoria's best interests so warranted, I am satisfied that the California statutory scheme is consistent with the Due Process Clause of the Fourteenth Amendment. I therefore concur in the Court's judgment of affirmance.

Justice BRENNAN, with whom Justice MARSHALL and Justice BLACKMUN join, dissenting.

In a case that has yielded so many opinions as has this one, it is fruitful to begin by emphasizing the common ground shared by a majority of this Court. Five Members of the Court refuse to foreclose "the possibility that a natural father might ever have a constitutionally protected interest in his relationship with a child whose mother was married to, and cohabiting with, another man at the time of the child's conception and birth." [Four] Members of the Court agree that Michael H. has a liberty interest in his relationship with Victoria, and one assumes for purposes of this case that he does.

In contrast, only one other Member of the Court fully endorses Justice Scalia's view of the proper method of analyzing questions arising under the Due Process Clause. See *ante,* at 2336; *ante,* at 2346 (O'Connor, J., concurring in part). Nevertheless, because the plurality opinion's exclusively historical analysis portends a significant and unfortunate departure from our prior cases and from sound constitutional decisionmaking, I devote a substantial portion of my discussion to it.

I

Once we recognized that the "liberty" protected by the Due Process Clause of the Fourteenth Amendment encompasses more than freedom from bodily restraint, today's plurality opinion emphasizes, the concept was cut loose from one natural limitation on its meaning. This innovation paved the way, so the plurality hints, for judges to substitute their own preferences for those of elected officials. Dissatisfied with this supposedly unbridled and uncertain state of affairs, the plurality casts about for another limitation on the concept of liberty.

It finds this limitation in "tradition." Apparently oblivious to the fact that this concept can be as malleable and as elusive as "liberty" itself, the plurality pretends that tradition places a discernible border around the Constitution. The pretense is seductive; it would be comforting to believe that a search for "tradition" involves nothing more idiosyncratic or complicated than poring through dusty volumes on American history. Yet, as Justice White observed in his dissent in Moore v. East Cleveland, 431 U.S. 494, 549, 97 S.Ct. 1932, 1961, 52 L.Ed.2d 531 (1977): "What the deeply rooted traditions of the country are is arguable." Indeed, wherever I would begin to look for an interest "deeply rooted in the country's traditions," one thing is certain: I would not stop (as does the plurality) at Bracton, or Blackstone, or Kent, or even the American Law Reports in conducting my search. Because reasonable people can disagree about the content of particular traditions, and because they can disagree even about which traditions are relevant to the definition of "liberty," the plurality has not found the objective boundary that it seeks.

Even if we could agree, moreover, on the content and significance of particular traditions, we still would be forced to identify the point at which a tradition becomes firm enough to be relevant to our definition of liberty and the moment at which it becomes too obsolete to be relevant any longer. The plurality supplies no objective means by which we might make these determinations. Indeed, as soon as the plurality sees signs that the tradition upon which it bases its decision (the laws denying putative fathers like Michael standing to assert paternity) is crumbling, it shifts ground and says that the case has nothing to do with that tradition, after all. "[W]hat is at issue here," the plurality asserts after canvassing the law on paternity suits, "is not entitlement to a state pronouncement that Victoria was begotten by Michael." *Ante,* at 2343. But that is precisely what is at issue here, and the plurality's last-minute denial of this fact dramatically illustrates the subjectivity of its own analysis.

It is ironic that an approach so utterly dependent on tradition is so indifferent to our precedents. Citing barely a handful of this Court's numerous decisions defining the scope of the liberty protected by the Due Process Clause to support its reliance on tradition, the plurality acts as though English legal treatises and the American Law Reports always have provided the sole source for our constitutional principles. They have not. Just as common-law notions no longer define the "property" that the Constitution protects, see Goldberg v. Kelly, 397 U.S. 254, 90 S.Ct. 1011, 25 L.Ed.2d 287 (1970), neither do they circumscribe the "liberty" that it guarantees. On the contrary, "'[l]iberty' and 'property' are broad and majestic terms. They are among the '[g]reat [constitutional] concepts . . . purposely left to gather meaning from experience. . . . [T]hey relate to the whole domain of social and economic fact, and the statesmen who founded this Nation knew too well that only a stagnant society remains unchanged.'" Board of Regents of State Colleges v. Roth, 408 U.S. 564, 571, 92 S.Ct. 2701, 2706, 33 L.Ed.2d 548 (1972), quoting National Ins. Co. v. Tidewater Co., 337 U.S. 582, 646, 69 S.Ct. 1173, 1209, 93 L.Ed. 1556 (1949) (Frankfurter, J., dissenting).

It is not that tradition has been irrelevant to our prior decisions. Throughout our decisionmaking in this important area runs the theme that certain interests and practices — freedom from physical restraint, marriage, childbearing, childrearing, and others — form the core of our definition of "liberty." Our solicitude for these interests is partly the result of the fact that the Due Process Clause would seem an empty promise if it did not protect them, and partly the result of the historical and traditional importance of these interests in our society. In deciding cases arising under the Due Process Clause, therefore, we have considered whether the concrete limitation under consideration impermissibly impinges upon one of these more generalized interests.

Today's plurality, however, does not ask whether parenthood is an interest that historically has received our attention and protection; the answer to that question is too clear for dispute. Instead, the plurality asks whether the specific variety of parenthood under consideration — a natural father's relationship with a child whose mother is married to another man — has enjoyed such protection.

If we had looked to tradition with such specificity in past cases, many a decision would have reached a different result. Surely the use of contraceptives by unmarried couples, Eisenstadt v. Baird, 405 U.S. 438, 92 S.Ct. 1029, 31 L.Ed.2d 349 (1972), or even by married couples, Griswold v. Connecticut, 381 U.S. 479, 85 S.Ct. 1678, 14 L.Ed.2d 510 (1965); the freedom from corporal punishment in schools, Ingraham v. Wright, 430 U.S. 651, 97 S.Ct. 1401, 51 L.Ed.2d 711 (1977); the freedom from an arbitrary transfer from a prison to a psychiatric institution, Vitek v. Jones, 445 U.S. 480, 100 S.Ct. 1254, 63 L.Ed.2d 552 (1980); and even the right to raise one's natural but illegitimate children, Stanley v. Illinois, 405 U.S. 645, 92 S.Ct. 1208, 31 L.Ed.2d 551 (1972), were not "interest[s] traditionally protected by our society," *ante,* at 2341, at the time of their consideration by this Court. If we had asked, therefore, in Eisenstadt, Griswold, Ingraham, Vitek, or Stanley itself whether the specific interest under consideration had been traditionally protected, the answer would have been a resounding "no." That we did not ask this question in those cases highlights the novelty of the interpretive method that the plurality opinion employs today.

The plurality's interpretive method is more than novel; it is misguided. It ignores the good reasons for limiting the role of "tradition" in interpreting the Constitution's deliberately capacious language. In the plurality's constitutional universe, we may not take notice of the fact that the original reasons for the conclusive presumption of paternity are out of place in a world in which blood tests can prove virtually beyond a shadow of a doubt who sired a particular child and in which the fact of illegitimacy no longer plays the burdensome and stigmatizing role it once did. Nor, in the plurality's world, may we deny "tradition" its full scope by pointing out that the rationale for the conventional rule has changed over the years, as has the rationale for Cal.Evid.Code Ann. § 621 (West Supp.1989); instead, our task is simply to identify a rule denying the asserted interest and not to ask whether the basis for that rule — which is the true reflection of the values undergirding it — has changed too often or too recently to call the rule embodying that rationale a "tradition." Moreover, by describing the decisive question as whether Michael's and Victoria's interest is one that has been "traditionally *protected by* our society," *ante,* at 2341 (emphasis added), rather than one that society traditionally has thought important (with or without protecting it), and by suggesting that our sole function is to "*discern* the society's views," *ante,* at 2345, n. 6 (emphasis added), the plurality acts as if the only purpose of the Due Process Clause is to confirm the importance of interests already protected by a majority of the States. Transforming the protection afforded by the

Due Process Clause into a redundancy mocks those who, with care and purpose, wrote the Fourteenth Amendment.

In construing the Fourteenth Amendment to offer shelter only to those interests specifically protected by historical practice, moreover, the plurality ignores the kind of society in which our Constitution exists. We are not an assimilative, homogeneous society, but a facilitative, pluralistic one, in which we must be willing to abide someone else's unfamiliar or even repellent practice because the same tolerant impulse protects our own idiosyncracies. Even if we can agree, therefore, that "family" and "parenthood" are part of the good life, it is absurd to assume that we can agree on the content of those terms and destructive to pretend that we do. In a community such as ours, "liberty" must include the freedom not to conform. The plurality today squashes this freedom by requiring specific approval from history before protecting anything in the name of liberty.

The document that the plurality construes today is unfamiliar to me. It is not the living charter that I have taken to be our Constitution; it is instead a stagnant, archaic, hidebound document steeped in the prejudices and superstitions of a time long past. *This* Constitution does not recognize that times change, does not see that sometimes a practice or rule outlives its foundations. I cannot accept an interpretive method that does such violence to the charter that I am bound by oath to uphold.

II

The plurality's reworking of our interpretive approach is all the more troubling because it is unnecessary. This is not a case in which we face a "new" kind of interest, one that requires us to consider for the first time whether the Constitution protects it. On the contrary, we confront an interest — that of a parent and child in their relationship with each other — that was among the first that this Court acknowledged in its cases defining the "liberty" protected by the Constitution, and I think I am safe in saying that no one doubts the wisdom or validity of those decisions. Where the interest under consideration is a parent-child relationship, we need not ask, over and over again, whether that interest is one that society traditionally protects.

Thus, to describe the issue in this case as whether the relationship existing between Michael and Victoria "has been treated as a protected family unit under the historic practices of our society, or whether on any other basis it has been accorded special protection," *ante,* at 2342, is to reinvent the wheel. The better approach — indeed, the one commanded by our prior cases and by common sense — is to ask whether the specific parent-child relationship under consideration is close enough to the interests that we already have protected to be deemed an aspect of "liberty" as well. On the facts before us, therefore, the question is not what "level of generality" should be used to describe the relationship between Michael and Victoria, see *ante,* at 2344, n. 6, but whether the relationship under consideration is sufficiently substantial to qualify as a liberty interest under our prior cases.

The evidence is undisputed that Michael, Victoria, and Carole did live together as a family; that is, they shared the same household, Victoria called Michael "Daddy," Michael contributed to Victoria's support, and he is eager to continue his relationship with her. Yet they are not, in the plurality's view, a "unitary family," whereas Gerald, Carole, and Victoria do compose such a family. The only difference between these two sets of relationships, however, is the fact of marriage. The plurality, indeed, expressly recognizes that marriage is the critical fact in denying Michael a constitutionally protected stake in his relationship with Victoria: no fewer than six times, the plurality refers to Michael as the "*adulterous* natural father" (emphasis added) or the like. *Ante,* at 2340;

2344, n. 6; 2345, n. 7; 2345.   See also *ante,* at 2343 (referring to the "*marital* family" of Gerald, Carole, and Victoria) (emphasis added); *ante,* at 2345 (plurality's holding limited to those situations in which there is "an extant marital family"). However, the very premise of Stanley and the cases following it is that marriage is not decisive in answering the question whether the Constitution protects the parental relationship under consideration. These cases are, after all, important precisely because they involve the rights of *unwed* fathers.

[The] plurality's exclusive rather than inclusive definition of the "unitary family" is out of step with other decisions as well. This pinched conception of "the family," crucial as it is in rejecting Michael's and Victoria's claims of a liberty interest, is jarring in light of our many cases preventing the States from denying important interests or statuses to those whose situations do not fit the government's narrow view of the family. . . .

IV

The atmosphere surrounding today's decision is one of make-believe.   Beginning with the suggestion that the situation confronting us here does not repeat itself every day in every corner of the country, *ante,* at 2336, moving on to the claim that it is tradition alone that supplies the details of the liberty that the Constitution protects, and passing finally to the notion that the Court always has recognized a cramped vision of "the family," today's decision lets stand California's pronouncement that Michael — whom blood tests show to a 98 percent probability to be Victoria's father — is not Victoria's father.   When and if the Court awakes to reality, it will find a world very different from the one it expects.

Justice WHITE, with whom Justice BRENNAN joins, dissenting.

California law, as the plurality describes it, *ante,* at 2340, tells us that, except in limited circumstances, California declares it to be "*irrelevant* for paternity purposes whether a child conceived during, and born into, an existing marriage was begotten by someone other than the husband" (emphasis in original). This I do not accept, for the fact that Michael H. is the biological father of Victoria is to me highly relevant to whether he has rights, as a father or otherwise, with respect to the child. Because I believe that Michael H. has a liberty interest that cannot be denied without due process of the law, I must dissent.

I

Like Justices Brennan, Marshall, Blackmun, and Stevens, I do not agree with the plurality opinion's conclusion that a natural father can never "have a constitutionally protected interest in his relationship with a child whose mother was married to, and cohabiting with, another man at the time of the child's conception and birth." *Ante,* at 2347 (Stevens, J., concurring in judgment). Prior cases here have recognized the liberty interest of a father in his relationship with his child. In none of these cases did we indicate that the father's rights were dependent on the marital status of the mother or biological father. The basic principle enunciated in the Court's unwed father cases is that an unwed father who has demonstrated a sufficient commitment to his paternity by way of personal, financial, or custodial responsibilities has a protected liberty interest in a relationship with his child.

We have not before faced the question of a biological father's relationship with his child when the child was born while the mother was married to another man. On several occasions however, we have considered whether a biological father has a constitutionally cognizable interest in an opportunity to establish paternity. . . .

[In] the case now before us, Michael H. is not a father unwilling to assume his responsibilities as a parent. To the contrary, he is a father who has asserted his interests in raising and providing for his child since the very time of the child's birth.   [The] facts in this case satisfy the Lehr criteria, which focused on the relationship between father and child, not on the relationship between father and mother. Under Lehr a "mere biological relationship" is not enough, but in light of Carole's vicissitudes, what more could Michael have done? It is clear enough that Michael more than meets the mark in establishing the constitutionally protected liberty interest discussed in Lehr and recognized in Stanley v. Illinois, supra, and Caban v. Mohammed, supra. He therefore has a liberty interest entitled to protection under the Due Process Clause of the Fourteenth Amendment.

II

California plainly denies Michael this protection, by refusing him the opportunity to rebut the State's presumption that the mother's husband is the father of the child. California law not only deprives Michael of a legal parent-child relationship with his daughter Victoria but even denies him the opportunity to introduce blood-test evidence to rebut the demonstrable fiction that Gerald is Victoria's father. . . .

The interest in protecting a child from the social stigma of illegitimacy lacks any real connection to the facts of a case where a father is seeking to establish, rather than repudiate, paternity. The "stigma of illegitimacy" argument harks back to ancient common law when there were no blood tests to ascertain that the husband could not "by the laws of nature" be the child's father. [I] see no reason to debate the plurality's multilingual explorations into "spousal nonaccess" and ancient policy concerns behind bastardy laws. It may be true that a child conceived in an extramarital relationship would be considered a "bastard" in the literal sense of the word, but whatever stigma remains in today's society is far less compelling in the context of a child of a married mother, especially when there is a father asserting paternity and seeking a relationship with his child. It is hardly rare in this world of divorce and remarriage for a child to live with the "father" to whom her mother is married, and still have a relationship with her biological father.

The State's professed interest in the preservation of the existing marital unit is a more significant concern. To be sure, the intrusion of an outsider asserting that he is the father of a child whom the husband believes to be his own would be disruptive to say the least. On the facts of this case, however, Gerald was well aware of the liaison between Carole and Michael. The conclusive presumption of evidentiary rule § 621 virtually eliminates the putative father's chances of succeeding in his effort to establish paternity, but it by no means prevents him from asserting the claim. It may serve as a deterrent to such claims but does not eliminate the threat. Further, the argument that the conclusive presumption preserved the sanctity of the marital unit had more sway in a time when the husband was similarly prevented from challenging paternity.

As the Court has said: "The significance of the biological connection is that it offers the natural father an opportunity that no other male possesses to develop a relationship with his offspring. If he grasps that opportunity and accepts some measure of responsibility for the child's future, he may enjoy the blessings of the parent-child relationship and make uniquely valuable contributions to the child's development." Lehr, 463 U.S., at 262, 103 S.Ct., at 2993. It is as if this passage was addressed to Michael. Yet the plurality today recants. Michael eagerly grasped the opportunity to have a relationship with his daughter (he lived with her; he declared her to be his child; he provided financial support for her) and still, with today's opinion, his opportunity has vanished. He has been rendered a stranger to his child. Because Cal.Evid.Code Ann. § 621, as applied, should be held unconstitutional under the Due Process Clause of the Fourteenth Amendment, I respectfully dissent.

Comments on *Michael H*. and Tradition.   Exactly what are the traditions "deeply rooted in our culture"?   Tradition has been defined as the "passing down of elements of a culture from generation to generation." *American Heritage Dictionary of the English Language* (4th ed. 2003).   Is it surprising that a "conservative" Court would apply substantive due process to secure conservative cultural values?   Do the cases cited above, in particular *Michael H.*, constitutionalize this inquiry?

Determining what privacy interests are "deeply rooted in this Nation's history and tradition" may not necessarily be as limiting as Justice Scalia suggests in *Michael H.* Justice Stevens, for example, commented in Whalen v. Roe, 429 U.S. 589 (1977) (a privacy case concerning personal data and computers), that the "privacy cases involved at least two different kinds of interests.   One is the individual interest in avoiding disclosure of personal matter [e.g., *Griswold*], and another is the interest in independence in making certain kinds of important decisions [e.g., *Roe*]."   Both of these "kinds of interest," though broader than Justice Scalia's inquiry, would nonetheless seem to be "rooted" in an American view of "limited" government that is "deeply rooted in the traditions of the nation."   One's sexual orientation (reviewed in the next section) might also be protected under this view of the *Griswold* lineage of cases.   Justice Brennan inferred such when he commented in   *Roberts v. United States Jaycees*, 468 U.S. 609 (1984), "The Court has long recognized that, because the Bill of Rights is designed to secure individual liberty, it must afford the formation and preservation of certain kinds of highly personal relationships a substantial measure of sanctuary from unjustified interference by the State.   [Protecting] these relationships from unwarranted state interference therefore safeguards the ability independently to define one's identity that is central to any concept of liberty."

Aware that even a "conserving" view of our cultural traditions might defend Justice Stevens and Justice Brennan's standards, Justice Scalia offered a more "limiting" retort in footnote 6 of his *Michael H.* opinion:

> Justice Brennan['s dissent] criticizes our methodology in using historical traditions specifically relating to the rights of an adulterous natural father, rather than inquiring more generally "whether parenthood is an interest that historically has received our attention and protection."   [We] do not understand why, having rejected our focus upon the societal tradition regarding the natural father's rights vis-à-vis a child whose mother is married to another man, Justice Brennan would choose to focus instead upon "parenthood."   Why should the relevant category not be even more general — perhaps "family relationships"; or "personal relationships"; or even "emotional attachments in general"?   Though the dissent has no basis for the level of generality it would select, we do: We refer to the most specific level at which a relevant tradition protecting, or denying protection to, the asserted right can be identified.   If, for example, there were no societal tradition, either way, regarding the rights of the natural father of a child adulterously conceived, we would have to consult, and (if possible) reason from, the traditions regarding natural fathers in general. But there is such a more specific tradition, and it unqualifiedly denies protection to such a parent.   [Because] such general traditions provide such imprecise guidance, they permit judges to dictate rather than discern the society's views.   [Although] assuredly having the virtue (if it be that) of leaving judges free to decide as they think best when the unanticipated occurs, a rule of law that binds neither by text nor by any particular, identifiable tradition is no rule of law at all.

Is Justice Scalia's inquiry to "the most specific level" of any tradition a means of limiting judicial activism, or a means of enforcing his more conservative moral views?

Justice O'Connor, joined by Justice Kennedy, refused to join in only this aspect of Justice Scalia's opinion. In rejecting this limitation Justice O'Connor stated, "I concur in all but footnote 6 of Justice Scalia's opinion. This footnote sketches a mode of historical analysis to be used when identifying liberty interests protected by the Due Process Clause of the Fourteenth Amendment that may be somewhat inconsistent with our past decisions in this area. See Griswold v. Connecticut, 381 U.S. 479, 85 S.Ct. 1678, 14 L.Ed.2d 510 (1965); Eisenstadt v. Baird, 405 U.S. 438, 92 S.Ct. 1029, 31 L.Ed.2d 349 (1972). On occasion the Court has characterized relevant traditions protecting asserted rights at levels of generality that might not be "the most specific level" available. See Loving v. Virginia, 388 U.S. 1, 12, 87 S.Ct. 1817, 1823, 18 L.Ed.2d 1010 (1967). I would not foreclose the unanticipated by the prior imposition of a single mode of historical analysis. Poe v. Ullman, 367 U.S. 497, 542, 544, 81 S.Ct. 1752, 1776, 1777, 6 L.Ed.2d 989 (1961) (Harlan, J., dissenting)."

All of this certainly set forth a background for the Court dealing with an issue that might mandate protection if tradition was definable at a general as opposed to a more specific level — sexual orientation.

JAMES OBERGEFELL v. RICHARD HODGES, DIRECTOR, OHIO DEPARTMENT OF HEALTH
576 U.S. 644 (2015)

JUSTICE KENNEDY delivered the opinion of the Court.

The Constitution promises liberty to all within its reach, a liberty that includes certain specific rights that allow persons, within a lawful realm, to define and express their identity. The petitioners in these cases seek to find that liberty by marrying someone of the same sex and having their marriages deemed lawful on the same terms and conditions as marriages between persons of the opposite sex.

[II]

Before addressing the principles and precedents that govern these cases, it is appropriate to note the history of the subject now before the Court.

A

From their beginning to their most recent page, the annals of human history reveal the transcendent importance of marriage. The lifelong union of a man and a woman always has promised nobility and dignity to all persons, without regard to their station in life. Marriage is sacred to those who live by their religions and offers unique fulfillment to those who find meaning in the secular realm. Its dynamic allows two people to find a life that could not be found alone, for a marriage becomes greater than just the two persons. Rising from the most basic human needs, marriage is essential to our most profound hopes and aspirations.

[That] history is the beginning of these cases. The respondents say it should be the end as well. To them, it would demean a timeless institution if the concept and lawful status of marriage were extended to two persons of the same sex. Marriage, in their view, is by its nature a gender-differentiated union of man and woman. This view long has been held—and continues to be held—in good faith by reasonable and sincere people here and throughout the world.

The petitioners acknowledge this history but contend that these cases cannot end there. Were their intent to demean the revered idea and reality of marriage, the petitioners' claims would be of a different order. But that is neither their purpose nor their submission. To the contrary, it is the enduring importance of marriage that underlies the petitioners' contentions. This, they say, is their whole point. Far from seeking to devalue marriage, the petitioners seek it for themselves because of their respect—and need—for its privileges and responsibilities. And their immutable nature dictates that same-sex marriage is their only real path to this profound commitment.

Recounting the circumstances of three of these cases illustrates the urgency of the petitioners' cause from their perspective. Petitioner James Obergefell, a plaintiff in the Ohio case, met John Arthur over two decades ago. They fell in love and started a life together, establishing a lasting, committed relation. In 2011, however, Arthur was diagnosed with amyotrophic lateral sclerosis, or ALS. This debilitating disease is progressive, with no known cure. Two years ago, Obergefell and Arthur decided to commit to one another, resolving to marry before Arthur died. To fulfill their mutual promise, they traveled from Ohio to Maryland, where same-sex marriage was legal. It was difficult for Arthur to move, and so the couple were wed inside a medical transport plane as it remained on the tarmac in Baltimore. Three months later, Arthur died. Ohio law does not permit Obergefell to be listed as the surviving spouse on Arthur's death certificate. By statute, they must remain strangers even in death, a state imposed separation Obergefell deems "hurtful for the rest of time." App. in No. 14–556 etc., p. 38. He brought suit to be shown as the surviving spouse on Arthur's death certificate.

[B]

[The] ancient origins of marriage confirm its centrality, but it has not stood in isolation from developments in law and society. The history of marriage is one of both continuity and change. That institution—even as confined to opposite-sex relations—has evolved over time.

For example, marriage was once viewed as an arrangement by the couple's parents based on political, religious, and financial concerns; but by the time of the Nation's founding it was understood to be a voluntary contract between a man and a woman. [These] and other developments in the institution of marriage over the past centuries were not mere superficial changes.

[These] new insights have strengthened, not weakened, the institution of marriage. Indeed, changed understandings of marriage are characteristic of a Nation where new dimensions of freedom become apparent to new generations, often through perspectives that begin in pleas or protests and then are considered in the political sphere and the judicial process.

This dynamic can be seen in the Nation's experiences with the rights of gays and lesbians. Until the mid-20th century, same-sex intimacy long had been condemned as immoral by the state itself in most Western nations, a belief often embodied in the criminal law. For this reason, among others, many persons did not deem homosexuals to have dignity in their own distinct identity. A truthful declaration by same-sex couples of what was in their hearts had to remain unspoken. Even when a greater awareness of the humanity and integrity of homosexual persons came in the period after World War II, the argument that gays and lesbians had a just claim to dignity was in conflict with both law and widespread social conventions. Same-sex intimacy remained a crime in many States. Gays and lesbians were prohibited from most government employment, barred from military service, excluded under immigration laws, targeted by police, and burdened in their rights to associate.

[Against] this background, the legal question of same-sex marriage arose. In 1993, the Hawaii Supreme Court held Hawaii's law restricting marriage to opposite-sex couples constituted a classification on the basis of sex and was therefore subject to strict scrutiny under the Hawaii Constitution.

[In] 2003, the Supreme Judicial Court of Massachusetts held the State's Constitution guaranteed same-sex couples the right to marry. See Goodridge v. Department of Public Health, 440 Mass. 309, 798 N. E. 2d 941 (2003). After that ruling, some additional States granted marriage rights to same sex couples, either through judicial or legislative processes. These decisions and statutes are cited in Appendix B, infra. Two Terms ago, in United States v. Windsor, 570 U. S. ___ (2013), this Court invalidated DOMA to the extent it barred the Federal Government from treating same-sex marriages as valid even when they were lawful in the State where they were licensed. DOMA, the Court held, impermissibly disparaged those same-sex couples "who wanted to affirm their commitment to one another before their children, their family, their friends, and their community."

[After] years of litigation, legislation, referenda, and the discussions that attended these public acts, the States are now divided on the issue of same-sex marriage.

[III]

Under the Due Process Clause of the Fourteenth Amendment, no State shall "deprive any person of life, liberty, or property, without due process of law." The fundamental liberties protected by this Clause include most of the rights enumerated in the Bill of Rights. See Duncan v. Louisiana, 391 U. S. 145, 147–149 (1968). In addition these liberties extend to certain personal choices central to individual dignity and autonomy, including intimate choices that define personal identity and beliefs. See, e.g., Eisenstadt v. Baird, 405 U. S. 438, 453 (1972); Griswold v. Connecticut, 381 U. S. 479, 484–486 (1965). The identification and protection of fundamental rights is an enduring part of the judicial duty to interpret the Constitution. That responsibility, however, "has not been reduced to any formula." Poe v. Ullman, 367 U. S. 497, 542 (1961) (Harlan, J., dissenting). Rather, it requires courts to exercise reasoned judgment in identifying interests of the person so fundamental that the State must accord them its respect. See ibid. That process is guided by many of the same considerations relevant to analysis of other constitutional provisions that set forth broad principles rather than specific requirements. History and tradition guide and discipline this inquiry but do not set its outer boundaries. See Lawrence, supra, at 572. That method respects our history and learns from it without allowing the past alone to rule the present.

The nature of injustice is that we may not always see it in our own times. The generations that wrote and ratified the Bill of Rights and the Fourteenth Amendment did not presume to know the extent of freedom in all of its dimensions, and so they entrusted to future generations a charter protecting the right of all persons to enjoy liberty as we learn its meaning. When new insight reveals discord between the Constitution's central protections and a received legal stricture, a claim to liberty must be addressed.

Applying these established tenets, the Court has long held the right to marry is protected by the Constitution. In Loving v. Virginia, 388 U. S. 1, 12 (1967), which invalidated bans on interracial unions, a unanimous Court held marriage is "one of the vital personal rights essential to the orderly pursuit of happiness by free men." The Court reaffirmed that holding in Zablocki v. Redhail, 434 U. S. 374, 384 (1978), which held the right to marry was burdened by a law prohibiting fathers who were behind on child support from marrying. The Court again applied this principle in Turner v. Safley, 482 U. S. 78, 95 (1987), which held the right to marry was abridged by regulations limiting the privilege of prison inmates to marry. Over time and in other contexts, the Court has reiterated that the right to marry is fundamental under the Due Process Clause.

[It] cannot be denied that this Court's cases describing the right to marry presumed a relationship involving opposite-sex partners. The Court, like many institutions, has made assumptions defined by the world and time of which it is a part. This was evident in Baker v. Nelson, 409 U. S. 810, a one-line summary decision issued in 1972, holding the exclusion of same-sex couples from marriage did not present a substantial federal question.

Still, there are other, more instructive precedents. This Court's cases have expressed constitutional principles of broader reach. In defining the right to marry these cases have identified essential attributes of that right based in history, tradition, and other constitutional liberties inherent in this intimate bond. See, e.g., Lawrence, 539 U. S., at 574; Turner, supra, at 95; Zablocki, supra, at 384; Loving, supra, at 12; Griswold, supra, at 486. And in assessing whether the force and rationale of its cases apply to same-sex couples, the Court must respect the basic reasons why the right to marry has been long protected. See, e.g., Eisenstadt, supra, at 453–454; Poe, supra, at 542–553 (Harlan, J., dissenting).

This analysis compels the conclusion that same-sex couples may exercise the right to marry. The four principles and traditions to be discussed demonstrate that the reasons marriage is fundamental under the Constitution apply with equal force to same-sex couples.

A first premise of the Court's relevant precedents is that the right to personal choice regarding marriage is inherent in the concept of individual autonomy. This abiding connection between marriage and liberty is why Loving invalidated interracial marriage bans under the Due Process Clause. See 388 U. S., at 12; see also Zablocki, supra, at 384 (observing Loving held "the right to marry is of fundamental importance for all individuals"). Like choices concerning contraception, family relationships, procreation, and childrearing, all of which are protected by the Constitution, decisions concerning marriage are among the most intimate that an individual can make. See Lawrence, supra, at 574. Indeed, the Court has noted it would be contradictory "to recognize a right of privacy with respect to other matters of family life and not with respect to the decision to enter the relationship that is the foundation of the family in our society." Zablocki, supra, at 386.

[A] second principle in this Court's jurisprudence is that the right to marry is fundamental because it supports a two-person union unlike any other in its importance to the committed individuals. This point was central to Griswold v. Connecticut, which held the Constitution protects the right of married couples to use contraception. 381 U. S., at 485. Suggesting that marriage is a right "older than the Bill of Rights," Griswold described marriage this way:

> "Marriage is a coming together for better or for worse, hopefully enduring, and intimate to the degree of being sacred. It is an association that promotes a way of life, not causes; a harmony in living, not political faiths; a bilateral loyalty, not commercial or social projects. Yet it is an association for as noble a purpose as any involved in our prior decisions. " Id., at 486.

And in Turner, the Court again acknowledged the intimate association protected by this right, holding prisoners could not be denied the right to marry because their committed relationships satisfied the basic reasons why marriage is a fundamental right. See 482 U. S., at 95–96. The right to marry thus dignifies couples who "wish to define themselves by their commitment to each other." Windsor, supra, at ___ (slip op., at 14). Marriage responds to the universal fear that a lonely person might call out only to find no one there. It offers the hope of companionship and understanding and assurance that while both still live there will be someone to care for the other.

As this Court held in Lawrence, same-sex couples have the same right as opposite-sex couples to enjoy intimate association. Lawrence invalidated laws that made same sex intimacy a criminal act. And it acknowledged that "[w]hen sexuality finds overt expression in intimate conduct with another person, the conduct can be but one element in a personal bond that is more enduring." 539 U. S., at 567. But while Lawrence confirmed a dimension of freedom that allows individuals to engage in intimate association without criminal liability, it does not follow that freedom stops there. Outlaw to outcast may be a step forward, but it does not achieve the full promise of liberty.

A third basis for protecting the right to marry is that it safeguards children and families and thus draws meaning from related rights of childrearing, procreation, and education. See Pierce v. Society of Sisters, 268 U. S. 510 (1925); Meyer, 262 U. S., at 399. The Court has recognized these connections by describing the varied rights as a unified whole: "[T]he right to 'marry, establish a home and bring up children' is a central part of the liberty protected by the Due Process Clause." Zablocki, 434 U. S., at 384 Cite as: 576 U. S. ____ (2015) 15 Opinion of the Court (quoting Meyer, supra, at 399). Under the laws of the several States, some of marriage's protections for children and families are material. But marriage also confers more profound benefits. By giving recognition and legal structure to their parents' relationship, marriage allows children "to understand the integrity and closeness of their own family and its concord with other families in their community and in their daily lives." Windsor, supra, at ___ (slip op., at 23). Marriage also affords the permanency and stability important to children's best interests. See Brief for Scholars of the Constitutional Rights of Children as Amici Curiae 22–27.

As all parties agree, many same-sex couples provide loving and nurturing homes to their children, whether biological or adopted. And hundreds of thousands of children are presently being raised by such couples. See Brief for Gary J. Gates as Amicus Curiae 4. Most States have allowed gays and lesbians to adopt, either as individuals or as couples, and many adopted and foster children have same-sex parents, see id., at 5. This provides powerful confirmation from the law itself that gays and lesbians can create loving, supportive families.

Excluding same-sex couples from marriage thus conflicts with a central premise of the right to marry. Without the recognition, stability, and predictability marriage offers, their children suffer the stigma of knowing their families are somehow lesser. They also suffer the significant material costs of being raised by unmarried parents, relegated through no fault of their own to a more difficult and uncertain family life. The marriage laws at issue here thus harm and humiliate the children of same-sex couples. See Windsor, supra, at ___ (slip op., at 23).

That is not to say the right to marry is less meaningful for those who do not or cannot have children. An ability, desire, or promise to procreate is not and has not been a prerequisite for a valid marriage in any State. In light of precedent protecting the right of a married couple not to procreate, it cannot be said the Court or the States have conditioned the right to marry on the capacity or commitment to procreate. The constitutional marriage right has many aspects, of which childbearing is only one.

Fourth and finally, this Court's cases and the Nation's traditions make clear that marriage is a keystone of our social order. Alexis de Tocqueville recognized this truth on his travels through the United States almost two centuries ago:

> "There is certainly no country in the world where the tie of marriage is so much respected as in America . . . [W]hen the American retires from the turmoil of public life to the bosom of his family, he finds in it the image of order and of peace . . . . [H]e afterwards carries [that image] with him into public affairs." 1 Democracy in America 309 (H. Reeve transl., rev. ed. 1990).

In Maynard v. Hill, 125 U. S. 190, 211 (1888), the Court echoed de Tocqueville, explaining that marriage is "the foundation of the family and of society, without which there would be neither civilization nor progress." Marriage, the Maynard Court said, has long been "'a great public institution, giving character to our whole civil polity.'" Id., at 213. This idea has been reiterated even as the institution has evolved in substantial ways over time, superseding rules related to parental consent, gender, and race once thought by many to be essential. See generally N. Cott, Public Vows. Marriage remains a building block of our national community.

For that reason, just as a couple vows to support each other, so does society pledge to support the couple, offering symbolic recognition and material benefits to protect and nourish the union. Indeed, while the States are in general free to vary the benefits they confer on all married couples, they have throughout our history made marriage the basis for an expanding list of governmental rights, benefits, and responsibilities. These aspects of marital status include: taxation; inheritance and property rights; rules of intestate succession; spousal privilege in the law of evidence; hospital access; medical decision-making authority; adoption rights; the rights and benefits of survivors; birth and death certificates; professional ethics rules; campaign finance restrictions; workers' compensation benefits; health insurance; and child custody, support, and visitation rules. See Brief for United States as Amicus Curiae 6–9; Brief for American Bar Association as Amicus Curiae 8–29. Valid marriage under state law is also a significant status for over a thousand provisions of federal law. See Windsor, 570 U. S., at ___ – ___ (slip op., at 15–16). The States have contributed to the fundamental character of the marriage right by placing that institution at the center of so many facets of the legal and social order.

There is no difference between same- and opposite-sex couples with respect to this principle. Yet by virtue of their exclusion from that institution, same-sex couples are denied the constellation of benefits that the States have linked to marriage. This harm results in more than just material burdens. Same-sex couples are consigned to an instability many opposite-sex couples would deem intolerable in their own lives. As the State itself makes marriage all the more precious by the significance it attaches to it, exclusion from that status has the effect of teaching that gays and lesbians are unequal in important respects. It demeans gays and lesbians for the State to lock them out of a central institution of the Nation's society. Same-sex couples, too, may aspire to the transcendent purposes of marriage and seek fulfillment in its highest meaning.

The limitation of marriage to opposite-sex couples may long have seemed natural and just, but its inconsistency with the central meaning of the fundamental right to marry is now manifest. With that knowledge must come the recognition that laws excluding same-sex couples from the marriage right impose stigma and injury of the kind prohibited by our basic charter.

Objecting that this does not reflect an appropriate framing of the issue, the respondents refer to Washington v. Glucksberg, 521 U. S. 702, 721 (1997), which called for a "'careful description'" of fundamental rights. They assert the petitioners do not seek to exercise the right to marry but rather a new and nonexistent "right to same-sex marriage." Brief for Respondent in No. 14–556, p. 8. Glucksberg did insist that liberty under the Due Process Clause must be defined in a most circumscribed manner, with central reference to specific historical practices. Yet while that approach may have been appropriate for the asserted right there involved (physician-assisted suicide), it is inconsistent with the approach this Court has used in discussing other fundamental rights, including marriage and intimacy. Loving did not ask about a "right to interracial marriage"; Turner did not ask about a "right of inmates to marry"; and Zablocki did not ask about a "right of fathers with unpaid child support duties to marry." Rather, each case inquired about the right to marry in its comprehensive sense, asking if there was a sufficient justification for excluding the relevant class from the right. See also Glucksberg, 521 U. S., at 752–773 (Souter, J., concurring in judgment); id., at 789–792 (BREYER, J., concurring in judgments).

That principle applies here. If rights were defined by who exercised them in the past, then received practices could serve as their own continued justification and new groups could not invoke rights once denied. This Court has rejected that approach, both with respect to the right to marry and the rights of gays and lesbians. See Loving 388 U. S., at 12; Lawrence, 539 U. S., at 566–567.

The right of same-sex couples to marry that is part of the liberty promised by the Fourteenth Amendment is derived, too, from that Amendment's guarantee of the equal protection of the laws. The Due Process Clause and the Equal Protection Clause are connected in a profound way, though they set forth independent principles. Rights implicit in liberty and rights secured by equal protection may rest on different precepts and are not always coextensive, yet in some instances each may be instructive as to the meaning and reach of the other. In any particular case one Clause may be thought to capture the essence of the right in a more accurate and comprehensive way, even as the two Clauses may converge in the identification and definition of the right. See M. L. B., 519 U. S., at 120–121; id., at 128–129 (KENNEDY, J., concurring in judgment); Bearden v. Georgia, 461 U. S. 660, 665 (1983). This interrelation of the two principles furthers our understanding of what freedom is and must become.

The Court's cases touching upon the right to marry reflect this dynamic. In Loving the Court invalidated a prohibition on interracial marriage under both the Equal Protection Clause and the Due Process Clause. The Court first declared the prohibition invalid because of its unequal treatment of interracial couples. It stated: "There can be no doubt that restricting the freedom to marry solely because of racial classifications violates the central meaning of the Equal Protection Clause." 388 U. S., at 12. With this link to equal protection the Court proceeded to hold the prohibition offended central precepts of liberty: "To deny this fundamental freedom on so unsupportable a basis as the racial classifications embodied in these statutes, classifications so directly subversive of the principle of equality at the heart of the Fourteenth Amendment, is surely to deprive all the State's citizens of liberty without due process of law." Ibid. The reasons why marriage is a fundamental right became more clear and compelling from a full awareness and understanding of the hurt that resulted from laws barring interracial unions.

The synergy between the two protections is illustrated further in Zablocki. There the Court invoked the Equal Protection Clause as its basis for invalidating the challenged law, which, as already noted, barred fathers who were behind on child-support payments from marrying without judicial approval. The equal protection analysis depended in central part on the Court's holding that the law burdened a right "of fundamental importance." 434 U. S., at 383. It was the essential nature of the marriage right, discussed at length in Zablocki, see id., at 383–387, that made apparent the law's incompatibility with requirements of equality. Each concept—liberty and equal protection—leads to a stronger understanding of the other.

[IV]

There may be an initial inclination in these cases to proceed with caution—to await further legislation, litigation, and debate. The respondents warn there has been insufficient democratic discourse before deciding an issue so basic as the definition of marriage.

[Yet] there has been far more deliberation than this argument acknowledges. There have been referenda, legislative debates, and grassroots campaigns, as well as countless studies, papers, books, and other popular and scholarly writings. There has been extensive litigation in state and federal courts.

[Of] course, the Constitution contemplates that democracy is the appropriate process for change, so long as that process does not abridge fundamental rights. Last Term, a plurality of this Court reaffirmed the importance of the democratic principle in Schuette v. BAMN, 572 U. S. ___ (2014), noting the "right of citizens to debate so they can learn and decide and then, through the political process, act in concert to try to shape the course of their own times." Id., at ___ – ___ (slip op., at 15–16). Indeed, it is most often through democracy that liberty is preserved and protected in our lives. But as Schuette also said, "[t]he freedom secured by the Constitution consists, in one of its essential dimensions, of the right of the individual not to be injured by the unlawful exercise of governmental power." Id., at ___ (slip op., at 15). Thus, when the rights of persons are violated, "the Constitution requires redress by the courts," notwithstanding the more general value of democratic decision-making. Id., at ___ (slip op., at 17). This holds true even when protecting individual rights affects issues of the utmost importance and sensitivity.

The dynamic of our constitutional system is that individuals need not await legislative action before asserting a fundamental right. The Nation's courts are open to injured individuals who come to them to vindicate their own direct, personal stake in our basic charter. An individual can invoke a right to constitutional protection when he or she is harmed, even if the broader public disagrees and even if the legislature refuses to act. The idea of the Constitution "was to withdraw certain subjects from the vicissitudes of political controversy, to place them beyond the reach of majorities and officials and to establish them as legal principles to be applied by the courts." West Virginia Bd. of Ed. v. Barnette, 319 U. S. 624, 638 (1943). This is why "fundamental rights may not be submitted to a vote; they depend on the outcome of no elections." Ibid. It is of no moment whether advocates of same-sex marriage now enjoy or lack momentum in the democratic process. The issue before the Court here is the legal question whether the Constitution protects the right of same sex couples to marry.

[The] respondents also argue allowing same-sex couples to wed will harm marriage as an institution by leading to fewer opposite-sex marriages. This may occur, the respondents contend, because licensing same-sex marriage severs the connection between natural procreation and marriage. That argument, however, rests on a counterintuitive view of opposite-sex couple's decision-making processes regarding marriage and parenthood. Decisions about whether to marry and raise children are based on many personal, romantic, and practical considerations; and it is unrealistic to conclude that an opposite-sex couple would choose not to marry simply because same-sex couples may do so. See Kitchen v.

Herbert, 755 F. 3d 1193, 1223 (CA10 2014) ("[I]t is wholly illogical to believe that state recognition of the love and commitment between same-sex couples will alter the most intimate and personal decisions of opposite-sex couples"). The respondents have not shown a foundation for the conclusion that allowing same-sex marriage will cause the harmful outcomes they describe. Indeed, with respect to this asserted basis for excluding same-sex couples from the right to marry, it is appropriate to observe these cases involve only the rights of two consenting adults whose marriages would pose no risk of harm to themselves or third parties.

Finally, it must be emphasized that religions, and those who adhere to religious doctrines, may continue to advocate with utmost, sincere conviction that, by divine precepts, same-sex marriage should not be condoned. The First Amendment ensures that religious organizations and persons are given proper protection as they seek to teach the principles that are so fulfilling and so central to their lives and faiths, and to their own deep aspirations to continue the family structure they have long revered. The same is true of those who oppose same-sex marriage for other reasons. In turn, those who believe allowing same sex marriage is proper or indeed essential, whether as a matter of religious conviction or secular belief, may engage those who disagree with their view in an open and searching debate. The Constitution, however, does not permit the State to bar same-sex couples from marriage on the same terms as accorded to couples of the opposite sex.

V

These cases also present the question whether the Constitution requires States to recognize same-sex marriages validly performed out of State. As made clear by the case of Obergefell and Arthur, and by that of DeKoe and Kostura, the recognition bans inflict substantial and continuing harm on same-sex couples.

[As] counsel for the respondents acknowledged at argument, if States are required by the Constitution to issue marriage licenses to same-sex couples, the justifications for refusing to recognize those marriages performed elsewhere are undermined. See Tr. of Oral Arg. on Question 2, p. 44. The Court, in this decision, holds same-sex couples may exercise the fundamental right to marry in all States. It follows that the Court also must hold—and it now does hold—that there is no lawful basis for a State to refuse to recognize a lawful same-sex marriage performed in another State on the ground of its same-sex character.

* * *

No union is more profound than marriage, for it embodies the highest ideals of love, fidelity, devotion, sacrifice, and family. In forming a marital union, two people become something greater than once they were. As some of the petitioners in these cases demonstrate, marriage embodies a love that may endure even past death. It would misunderstand these men and women to say they disrespect the idea of marriage. Their plea is that they do respect it, respect it so deeply that they seek to find its fulfillment for themselves. Their hope is not to be condemned to live in loneliness, excluded from one of civilization's oldest institutions. They ask for equal dignity in the eyes of the law. The Constitution grants them that right.

The judgment of the Court of Appeals for the Sixth Circuit is reversed.

It is so ordered.

CHIEF JUSTICE ROBERTS, with whom JUSTICE SCALIA and JUSTICE THOMAS join, dissenting.

[This] Court is not a legislature. Whether same-sex marriage is a good idea should be of no concern to us. Under the Constitution, judges have power to say what the law is, not what it should be. The people who ratified the Constitution authorized courts to exercise "neither force nor will but merely judgment." The Federalist No. 78, p. 465 (C. Rossiter ed. 1961) (A. Hamilton) (capitalization altered).

Although the policy arguments for extending marriage to same-sex couples may be compelling, the legal arguments for requiring such an extension are not.

[Today], however, the Court takes the extraordinary step of ordering every State to license and recognize same-sex marriage. Many people will rejoice at this decision, and I begrudge none their celebration. But for those who believe in a government of laws, not of men, the majority's approach is deeply disheartening. Supporters of same-sex marriage have achieved considerable success persuading their fellow citizens—through the democratic process—to adopt their view. That ends today. Five lawyers have closed the debate and enacted their own vision of marriage as a matter of constitutional law.

[The] majority's decision is an act of will, not legal judgment. The right it announces has no basis in the Constitution or this Court's precedent. The majority expressly disclaims judicial "caution" and omits even a pretense of humility, openly relying on its desire to remake society according to its own "new insight" into the "nature of injustice." Ante, at 11, 23. As a result, the Court invalidates the marriage laws of more than half the States and orders the transformation of a social institution that has formed the basis of human society for millennia, for the Kalahari Bushmen and the Han Chinese, the Carthaginians and the Aztecs. Just who do we think we are?

[I]

[The] Constitution itself says nothing about marriage, and the Framers thereby entrusted the States with "[t]he whole subject of the domestic relations of husband and wife." Windsor, 570 U. S., at ___ (slip op., at 17) (quoting In re Burrus, 136 U. S. 586, 593–594 (1890)). There is no dispute that every State at the founding—and every State throughout our history until a dozen years ago—defined marriage in the traditional, biologically rooted way. The four States in these cases are typical. Their laws, before and after statehood, have treated marriage as the union of a man and a woman. See DeBoer v. Snyder, 772 F. 3d 388, 396–399 (CA6 2014). Even when state laws did not specify this definition expressly, no one doubted what they meant. See Jones v. Hallahan, 501 S. W. 2d 588, 589 (Ky. App. 1973). The meaning of "marriage" went without saying.

[As] the majority notes, some aspects of marriage have changed over time. Arranged marriages have largely given way to pairings based on romantic love. States have replaced coverture, the doctrine by which a married man and woman became a single legal entity, with laws that respect each participant's separate status. Racial restrictions on marriage, which "arose as an incident to slavery" to promote "White Supremacy," were repealed by many States and ultimately struck down by this Court.   Loving, 388 U. S., at 6–7.

The majority observes that these developments "were not mere superficial changes" in marriage, but rather "worked deep transformations in its structure." Ante, at 6–7. They did not, however, work any transformation in the core structure of marriage as the union between a man and a woman. If you had asked a person on the street how marriage was defined, no one would ever have said, "Marriage is the union of a man and a woman, where the woman is subject to coverture." The majority may be right that the "history of marriage is one of both continuity and change," but the core meaning of marriage has endured.

[II]

Petitioners first contend that the marriage laws of their States violate the Due Process Clause. The Solicitor General of the United States, appearing in support of petitioners, expressly disowned that position before this Court. See Tr. of Oral Arg. on Question 1, at

38–39. The majority nevertheless resolves these cases for petitioners based almost entirely on the Due Process Clause.

The majority purports to identify four "principles and traditions" in this Court's due process precedents that support a fundamental right for same-sex couples to marry. Ante, at 12. In reality, however, the majority's approach has no basis in principle or tradition, except for the unprincipled tradition of judicial policymaking that characterized discredited decisions such as Lochner v. New York, 198 U. S. 45. Stripped of its shiny rhetorical gloss, the majority's argument is that the Due Process Clause gives same-sex couples a fundamental right to marry because it will be good for them and for society. If I were a legislator, I would certainly consider that view as a matter of social policy. But as a judge, I find the majority's position indefensible as a matter of constitutional law.

A

Petitioners' "fundamental right" claim falls into the most sensitive category of constitutional adjudication. Petitioners do not contend that their States' marriage laws violate an enumerated constitutional right, such as the freedom of speech protected by the First Amendment. There is, after all, no "Companionship and Understanding" or "Nobility and Dignity" Clause in the Constitution. See ante, at 3, 14. They argue instead that the laws violate a right implied by the Fourteenth Amendment's requirement that "liberty" may not be deprived without "due process of law."

This Court has interpreted the Due Process Clause to include a "substantive" component that protects certain liberty interests against state deprivation "no matter what process is provided." Reno v. Flores, 507 U. S. 292, 302 (1993). The theory is that some liberties are "so rooted in the traditions and conscience of our people as to be ranked as fundamental," and therefore cannot be deprived without compelling justification. *Snyder v. Massachusetts*, 291 U. S. 97, 105 (1934).

Allowing unelected federal judges to select which unenumerated rights rank as "fundamental"—and to strike down state laws on the basis of that determination—raises obvious concerns about the judicial role. Our precedents have accordingly insisted that judges "exercise the utmost care" in identifying implied fundamental rights, "lest the liberty protected by the Due Process Clause be subtly transformed into the policy preferences of the Members of this Court." Washington v. Glucksberg, 521 U. S. 702, 720 (1997) (internal quotation marks omitted); see Kennedy, Unenumerated Rights and the Dictates of Judicial Restraint 13 (1986) (Address at Stanford) ("One can conclude that certain essential, or fundamental, rights should exist in any just society. It does not follow that each of those essential rights is one that we as judges can enforce under the written Constitution. The Due Process Clause is not a guarantee of every right that should inhere in an ideal system.").

[The] Court first applied substantive due process to strike down a statute in Dred Scott v. Sandford, 19 How. 393 (1857). There the Court invalidated the Missouri Compromise on the ground that legislation restricting the institution of slavery violated the implied rights of slaveholders. The Court relied on its own conception of liberty and property in doing so. It asserted that "an act of Congress which deprives a citizen of the United States of his liberty or property, merely because he came himself or brought his property into a particular Territory of the United States . . . could hardly be dignified with the name of due process of law."

[In] a series of early 20th-century cases, most prominently Lochner v. New York, this Court invalidated state statutes that presented "meddlesome interferences with the rights of the individual," and "undue interference with liberty of person and freedom of contract."

198 U. S., at 60, 61. In Lochner itself, the Court struck down a New York law setting maximum hours for bakery employees, because there was "in our judgment, no reasonable foundation for holding this to be necessary or appropriate as a health law." Id., at 58.

The dissenting Justices in Lochner explained that the New York law could be viewed as a reasonable response to legislative concern about the health of bakery employees, an issue on which there was at least "room for debate and for an honest difference of opinion." Id., at 72 (opinion of Harlan, J.). The majority's contrary conclusion required adopting as constitutional law "an economic theory which a large part of the country does not entertain." Id., at 75 (opinion of Holmes, J.). As Justice Holmes memorably put it, "The Fourteenth Amendment does not enact Mr. Herbert Spencer's Social Statics," a leading work on the philosophy of Social Darwinism.

[Eventually], the Court recognized its error and vowed not to repeat it. "The doctrine that . . . due process authorizes courts to hold laws unconstitutional when they believe the legislature has acted unwisely," we later explained, "has long since been discarded. We have returned to the original constitutional proposition that courts do not substitute their social and economic beliefs for the judgment of legislative bodies, who are elected to pass laws." Ferguson v. Skrupa, 372 U. S. 726, 730 (1963).

[Rejecting] Lochner does not require disavowing the doctrine of implied fundamental rights, and this Court has not done so. But to avoid repeating Lochner's error of converting personal preferences into constitutional mandates, our modern substantive due process cases have stressed the need for "judicial self-restraint." Our precedents have required that implied fundamental rights be "objectively, deeply rooted in this Nation's history and tradition," and "implicit in the concept of ordered liberty, such that neither liberty nor justice would exist if they were sacrificed." Glucksberg, 521 U. S., at 720–721.

[Proper] reliance on history and tradition of course requires looking beyond the individual law being challenged, so that every restriction on liberty does not supply its own constitutional justification. The Court is right about that. Ante, at 18. But given the few "guideposts for responsible decision-making in this unchartered area," Collins, 503 U. S., at 125, "an approach grounded in history imposes limits on the judiciary that are more meaningful than any based on [an] abstract formula."

[B]

[1]

[The] majority's driving themes are that marriage is desirable and petitioners desire it. The opinion describes the "transcendent importance" of marriage and repeatedly insists that petitioners do not seek to "demean," "devalue," "denigrate," or "disrespect" the institution. Ante, at 3, 4, 6, 28. Nobody disputes those points. Indeed, the compelling personal accounts of petitioners and others like them are likely a primary reason why many Americans have changed their minds about whether same-sex couples should be allowed to marry. As a matter of constitutional law, however, the sincerity of petitioners' wishes is not relevant.

When the majority turns to the law, it relies primarily on precedents discussing the fundamental "right to marry." Turner v. Safley, 482 U. S. 78, 95 (1987); Zablocki, 434 U. S., at 383; see Loving, 388 U. S., at 12. These cases do not hold, of course, that anyone who wants to get married has a constitutional right to do so. They instead require a State to justify barriers to marriage as that institution has always been understood. In Loving, the Court held that racial restrictions on the right to marry lacked a compelling justification. In Zablocki, restrictions based on child support debts did not suffice. In Turner, restrictions based on status as a prisoner were deemed impermissible.

None of the laws at issue in those cases purported to change the core definition of marriage as the union of a man and a woman. The laws challenged in Zablocki and Turner did not define marriage as "the union of a man and a woman, where neither party owes child support or is in prison." Nor did the interracial marriage ban at issue in Loving define marriage as "the union of a man and a woman of the same race." See Tragen, Comment, Statutory Prohibitions Against Interracial Marriage, 32 Cal. L. Rev. 269 (1944) ("at common law there was no ban on interracial marriage"); post, at 11–12, n. 5 (THOMAS, J., dissenting). Removing racial barriers to marriage therefore did not change what a marriage was any more than integrating schools changed what a school was. As the majority admits, the institution of "marriage" discussed in every one of these cases "presumed a relationship involving opposite-sex partners." Ante, at 11.

In short, the "right to marry" cases stand for the important but limited proposition that particular restrictions on access to marriage as traditionally defined violate due process. These precedents say nothing at all about a right to make a State change its definition of marriage, which is the right petitioners actually seek here.

[2]

[The] majority suggests that "there are other, more instructive precedents" informing the right to marry. Ante, at 12. Although not entirely clear, this reference seems to correspond to a line of cases discussing an implied fundamental "right of privacy."

[The] Court also invoked the right to privacy in Lawrence v. Texas, 539 U. S. 558 (2003), which struck down a Texas statute criminalizing homosexual sodomy. Lawrence relied on the position that criminal sodomy laws, like bans on contraceptives, invaded privacy by inviting "unwarranted government intrusions" that "touc[h] upon the most private human conduct, sexual behavior . . . in the most private of places, the home." Id., at 562, 567.

Neither Lawrence nor any other precedent in the privacy line of cases supports the right that petitioners assert here. Unlike criminal laws banning contraceptives and sodomy, the marriage laws at issue here involve no government intrusion. They create no crime and impose no punishment. Same-sex couples remain free to live together, to engage in intimate conduct, and to raise their families as they see fit. No one is "condemned to live in loneliness" by the laws challenged in these cases—no one. Ante, at 28. At the same time, the laws in no way interfere with the "right to be let alone."

[In] sum, the privacy cases provide no support for the majority's position, because petitioners do not seek privacy. Quite the opposite, they seek public recognition of their relationships, along with corresponding government benefits. Our cases have consistently refused to allow litigants to convert the shield provided by constitutional liberties into a sword to demand positive entitlements from the State.

[3]

[Ultimately,] only one precedent offers any support for the majority's methodology: Lochner v. New York, 198 U. S. 45. The majority opens its opinion by announcing petitioners' right to "define and express their identity." Ante, at 1–2. The majority later explains that "the right to personal choice regarding marriage is inherent in the concept of individual autonomy." Ante, at 12. This freewheeling notion of individual autonomy echoes nothing so much as "the general right of an individual to be free in his person and in his power to contract in relation to his own labor." Lochner, 198 U. S., at 58.

[III]

In addition to their due process argument, petitioners contend that the Equal Protection Clause requires their States to license and recognize same-sex marriages. The majority does not seriously engage with this claim. Its discussion is, quite frankly, difficult to follow.

[The] majority goes on to assert in conclusory fashion that the Equal Protection Clause provides an alternative basis for its holding. Ante, at 22. Yet the majority fails to provide even a single sentence explaining how the Equal Protection Clause supplies independent weight for its position, nor does it attempt to justify its gratuitous violation of the canon against unnecessarily resolving constitutional questions. See Northwest Austin Municipal Util. Dist. No. One v. Holder, 557 U. S. 193, 197 (2009). In any event, the marriage laws at issue here do not violate the Equal Protection Clause, because distinguishing between opposite-sex and same-sex couples is rationally related to the States' "legitimate state interest" in "preserving the traditional institution of marriage." Lawrence, 539 U. S., at 585 (O'Connor, J., concurring in judgment).

[IV]

[In] the face of all this, a much different view of the Court's role is possible. That view is more modest and restrained. It is more skeptical that the legal abilities of judges also reflect insight into moral and philosophical issues. It is more sensitive to the fact that judges are unelected and unaccountable, and that the legitimacy of their power depends on confining it to the exercise of legal judgment. It is more attuned to the lessons of history, and what it has meant for the country and Court when Justices have exceeded their proper bounds. And it is less pretentious than to suppose that while people around the world have viewed an institution in a particular way for thousands of years, the present generation and the present Court are the ones chosen to burst the bonds of that history and tradition.

* * *

If you are among the many Americans—of whatever sexual orientation—who favor expanding same-sex marriage, by all means celebrate today's decision. Celebrate the achievement of a desired goal. Celebrate the opportunity for a new expression of commitment to a partner. Celebrate the availability of new benefits. But do not celebrate the Constitution. It had nothing to do with it.

I respectfully dissent.

JUSTICE SCALIA, with whom JUSTICE THOMAS joins, dissenting.

I join THE CHIEF JUSTICE's opinion in full. I write separately to call attention to this Court's threat to American democracy.

The substance of today's decree is not of immense personal importance to me.   [It] is of overwhelming importance, however, who it is that rules me. Today's decree says that my Ruler, and the Ruler of 320 million Americans coast-to-coast, is a majority of the nine lawyers on the Supreme Court. The opinion in these cases is the furthest extension in fact—and the furthest extension one can even imagine—of the Court's claimed power to create "liberties" that the Constitution and its Amendments neglect to mention. This practice of constitutional revision by an unelected committee of nine, always accompanied (as it is today) by extravagant praise of liberty, robs the People of the most important liberty they asserted in the Declaration of Independence and won in the Revolution of 1776: the freedom to govern themselves.

[I]

[The] Constitution places some constraints on self-rule—constraints adopted by the People themselves when they ratified the Constitution and its Amendments. Forbidden are laws "impairing the Obligation of Contracts," 3 denying "Full Faith and Credit" to the "public Acts" of other States, 4 prohibiting the free exercise of religion, 5 abridging the freedom of speech, 6 infringing the right to keep and bear arms, 7 authorizing unreasonable searches and seizures, 8 and so forth. Aside from these limitations, those powers "reserved to the States respectively, or to the people" 9 can be exercised as the States or the People desire. These cases ask us to decide whether the Fourteenth Amendment contains a limitation that requires the States to license and recognize marriages between two people of the same sex. Does it remove that issue from the political process?

Of course not. It would be surprising to find a prescription regarding marriage in the Federal Constitution since, as the author of today's opinion reminded us only two years ago (in an opinion joined by the same Justices who join him today):

> "[R]egulation of domestic relations is an area that has long been regarded as a virtually exclusive province of the States."
> "[T]he Federal Government, through our history, has deferred to state-law policy decisions with respect to domestic relations."

[The] Court ends this debate, in an opinion lacking even a thin veneer of law. Buried beneath the mummeries and straining-to-be-memorable passages of the opinion is a candid and startling assertion: No matter what it was the People ratified, the Fourteenth Amendment protects those rights that the Judiciary, in its "reasoned judgment," thinks the Fourteenth Amendment ought to protect. That is so because "[t]he generations that wrote and ratified the Bill of Rights and the Fourteenth Amendment did not presume to know the extent of freedom in all of its dimensions . . . . " One would think that sentence would continue: ". . . and therefore they provided for a means by which the People could amend the Constitution," or perhaps ". . . and therefore they left the creation of additional liberties, such as the freedom to marry someone of the same sex, to the People, through the never-ending process of legislation." But no. What logically follows, in the majority's judge-empowering estimation, is: "and so they entrusted to future generations a charter protecting the right of all persons to enjoy liberty as we learn its meaning." The "we," needless to say, is the nine of us. "History and tradition guide and discipline [our] inquiry but do not set its outer boundaries." Thus, rather than focusing on the People's understanding of "liberty"—at the time of ratification or even today—the majority focuses on four "principles and traditions" that, in the majority's view, prohibit States from defining marriage as an institution consisting of one man and one woman.

[Not] surprisingly then, the Federal Judiciary is hardly a cross-section of America. Take, for example, this Court, which consists of only nine men and women, all of them successful lawyers who studied at Harvard or Yale Law School. Four of the nine are natives of New York City. Eight of them grew up in east- and west-coast States. Only one hails from the vast expanse in-between. Not a single Southwesterner or even, to tell the truth, a genuine Westerner (California does not count). Not a single evangelical Christian (a group that comprises about one quarter of Americans), or even a Protestant of any denomination. The strikingly unrepresentative character of the body voting on today's social upheaval would be irrelevant if they were functioning as judges, answering the legal question whether the American people had ever ratified a constitutional provision that was understood to proscribe the traditional definition of marriage. But of course the Justices in today's majority are not voting on that basis; they say they are not. And to allow the policy question of same-sex marriage to be considered and resolved by a select, patrician, highly unrepresentative panel of nine is to violate a principle even more fundamental than no taxation without representation: no social transformation without representation.

II

But what really astounds is the hubris reflected in today's judicial Putsch.

[It] is one thing for separate concurring or dissenting opinions to contain extravagances, even silly extravagances, of thought and expression; it is something else for the official opinion of the Court to do so.   Of course the opinion's showy profundities are often profoundly incoherent. "The nature of marriage is that, through its enduring bond, two persons together can find other freedoms, such as expression, intimacy, and spirituality." (Really? Who ever thought that intimacy and spirituality [whatever that means] were freedoms? And if intimacy is, one would think Freedom of Intimacy is abridged rather than expanded by marriage. Ask the nearest hippie. Expression, sure enough, is a freedom, but anyone in a long-lasting marriage will attest that that happy state constricts, rather than expands, what one can prudently say.) Rights, we are told, can "rise . . . from a better informed understanding of how constitutional imperatives define a liberty that remains urgent in our own era." (Huh? How can a better informed understanding of how constitutional imperatives [whatever that means] define [whatever that means] an urgent liberty [never mind], give birth to a right?) And we are told that, "[i]n any particular case," either the Equal Protection or Due Process Clause "may be thought to capture the essence of [a] right in a more accurate and comprehensive way," than the other, "even as the two Clauses may converge in the identification and definition of the right." (What say? What possible "essence" does substantive due process "capture" in an "accurate and comprehensive way"? It stands for nothing whatever, except those freedoms and entitlements that this Court really likes. And the Equal Protection Clause, as employed today, identifies nothing except a difference in treatment that this Court really dislikes.

[Hubris] is sometimes defined as o'erweening pride; and pride, we know, goeth before a fall. The Judiciary is the "least dangerous" of the federal branches because it has "neither Force nor Will, but merely judgment; and must ultimately depend upon the aid of the executive arm" and the States, "even for the efficacy of its judgments." With each decision of ours that takes from the People a question properly left to them—with each decision that is unabashedly based not on law, but on the "reasoned judgment" of a bare majority of this Court—we move one step closer to being reminded of our impotence.

JUSTICE THOMAS, with whom JUSTICE SCALIA joins, dissenting.

The Court's decision today is at odds not only with the Constitution, but with the principles upon which our Nation was built. Since well before 1787, liberty has been understood as freedom from government action, not entitlement to government benefits.

[II]

Even if the doctrine of substantive due process were somehow defensible—it is not—petitioners still would not have a claim. To invoke the protection of the Due Process Clause at all—whether under a theory of "substantive" or "procedural" due process—a party must first identify a deprivation of "life, liberty, or property." The majority claims these state laws deprive petitioners of "liberty," but the concept of "liberty" it conjures up bears no resemblance to any plausible meaning of that word as it is used in the Due Process Clauses.

[IV]

Perhaps recognizing that these cases do not actually involve liberty as it has been understood, the majority goes to great lengths to assert that its decision will advance the "dignity" of same-sex couples. The flaw in that reasoning, of course, is that the Constitution contains no "dignity" Clause, and even if it did, the government would be incapable of bestowing dignity.

Human dignity has long been understood in this country to be innate. When the Framers proclaimed in the Declaration of Independence that "all men are created equal" and "endowed by their Creator with certain unalienable Rights," they referred to a vision of mankind in which all humans are created in the image of God and therefore of inherent worth. That vision is the foundation upon which this Nation was built.

The corollary of that principle is that human dignity cannot be taken away by the government. Slaves did not lose their dignity (any more than they lost their humanity) because the government allowed them to be enslaved. Those held in internment camps did not lose their dignity because the government confined them. And those denied governmental benefits certainly do not lose their dignity because the government denies them those benefits. The government cannot bestow dignity, and it cannot take it away.

[* * *]

Our Constitution—like the Declaration of Independence before it—was predicated on a simple truth: One's liberty, not to mention one's dignity, was something to be shielded from—not provided by—the State. Today's decision casts that truth aside. In its haste to reach a desired result, the majority misapplies a clause focused on "due process" to afford substantive rights, disregards the most plausible understanding of the "liberty" protected by that clause, and distorts the principles on which this Nation was founded. Its decision will have inestimable consequences for our Constitution and our society.

I respectfully dissent.

a. HOW FAR DOES OBERGEFELL GO [PART 1]?

Obviously the marriage relationship, found to be within the due process rights of all persons protected by the Constitution including the LGBT community, carries with it associated rights and obligations. In *Pavan v. Smith* 582 U. S. ____ (2017), the Court, sitting as a nine-person tribunal following the appointment of Justice Neil Gorsuch, in a per curiam opinion confirmed that rights associated with parenthood are included in the right to marry. The case was an appeal from the Arkansas Supreme Court decision that the state's birth certificate law limiting the listing of natural parents of children born to marriages did not violate the rights of same sex married couples when only the biological mothers of those children, and husbands (assumed to be the biological father) were listed on the certificate. Specifically, the Arkansas law recognizes the mother as the woman giving birth to the child, and "[i]f the mother was married at the time of either conception or birth," the statute instructs that "the name of [her] husband shall be entered on the certificate as the father of the child." Arkansas argued that the law was designed to be a record of biological parentage and thus was not in conflict of the *Obergefell* decision. This position was undercut by several exceptions in the law. Most relevant to the current case was the exception applying to cases of artificial insemination which provided for the listing of a mother's husband at the time of birth as the father of the child. Another exception for adoption provided for a sealed birth certificate for the natural parents, and an amended birth certificate listing the adoptive parents.

The Court noted the inconsistencies in its opinion:

> The Arkansas Supreme Court's decision, we conclude, denied married same-sex couples access to the "constellation of benefits that the Stat[e] ha[s] linked to marriage." *Obergefell*, 576 U. S., at ___ (slip op., at 17). As already explained, when a married woman in Arkansas conceives a child by means of artificial insemination, the State

will—indeed, *must*—list the name of her male spouse on the child's birth certificate. See §20-18-401(f)(1); see also §9-10-201; *supra,* at 2. And yet state law, as interpreted by the court below, allows Arkansas officials in those very same circumstances to omit a married woman's female spouse from her child's birth certificate. See 505 S. W. 3d, at 177-178. As a result, same-sex parents in Arkansas lack the same right as opposite-sex parents to be listed on a child's birth certificate, a document often used for important transactions like making medical decisions for a child or enrolling a child in school. See Pet. for Cert. 5-7 (listing situations in which a parent might be required to present a child's birth certificate).

    Obergefell proscribes such disparate treatment. As we explained there, a State may not "exclude same-sex couples from civil marriage on the same terms and conditions as opposite-sex couples." 576 U. S., at ___ (slip op., at 23). Indeed, in listing those terms and conditions—the "rights, benefits, and responsibilities" to which same-sex couples, no less than opposite-sex couples, must have access—we expressly identified "birth and death certificates." *Id.,* at ___ (slip op., at 17). That was no accident: Several of the plaintiffs in *Obergefell* challenged a State's refusal to recognize their same-sex spouses on their children's birth certificates. In considering those challenges, we held the relevant state laws unconstitutional to the extent they treated same-sex couples differently from opposite-sex couples. See 576 U. S., at ___ (slip op., at 23). That holding applies with equal force to §20-18-401.

Accordingly the Court reversed the decision of the Arkansas Supreme Court and remanded the matter for resolution consistent with the opinion.

In a dissent by Justice Gorsuch, joined by Justices Thomas and Alito, it was pointed out that Arkansas conceded the inconsistency in application of the exceptions and acknowledged that same sex couples should be covered by them. Justice Gorsuch would allow Arkansas to maintain its biological parentage based scheme of birth certificates, which he saw as rational, and allow the state to fairly apply its exceptions to same sex couples.

Justice Gorsuch did not point out that similar biology-based statutes that did not include such exceptions could continue to exclude the listing of non-biological parents, albeit with attendant costs to opposite sex couples accessing artificial insemination or adoption in their family planning. As a practical matter, would such a regime be politically realistic? Does Justice Gorsuch have a point?

b. HOW FAR DOES OBERGEFELL GO [PART 2]?

Under the Constitution, the LGBT community remains vulnerable to other kinds of governmental discrimination because in neither of these decisions did the Court through the opinions by retiring Justice Kennedy embrace sexual orientation as classification deserving the highest protection of the Constitution. And when local and state governments seek to protect members of that community from *private* discrimination, using their police powers to so legislate, their authority to do so was questioned in one of the final decisions of this last term. In *Masterpiece Cakeshop v. Colorado Civil Rights Commission* 584 U. S. ____ (2018), Justice Kennedy's opinion held that the state cannot force a baker with religious objections to same sex marriage to prepare a wedding cake with expressions of congratulations to a same sex couple. The Court ruled and Kennedy's decision held that the baker was protected by the First Amendment's protections against compelled speech as well as the free exercise of religion clause. In his opinion, Justice Kennedy noted that the petitioning baker declined to prepare the cake with congratulatory language to the same sex married couple before the *Obergefell* decision and before Colorado recognized same sex marriages and was at the time within the mainstream of legal and social thought. Moreover, though the Colorado Civil Rights Commission reasoned in its decision that the petitioner's religious beliefs were not being violated because the message on the cake was not attributable to the baker, the Court noted that the Commission had previously upheld decisions by bake shop owners to decline to prepare bake goods with anti-gay or anti-gay marriage messages on them and did not use similar reasoning. There are indications in Kennedy's facts that a less hostile treatment of the baker's religious views would go a long way toward allowing the state to protect gay persons from discriminations by private actors in this case. A less hostile approach to the state's regulation of private discrimination against the LGBT community could indicate state neutrality toward religious views. So perhaps a window of opportunity was left open by Justice Kennedy.

McDonald and Non-articulated Rights. McDonald v. City of Chicago, 130 S. Ct. 3020 (2010), while a definitive "incorporation decision," (See Chapter 4) also provided the occasion for a notable duel between Justices Stevens and Scalia about constitutional methodology and substantive due process. Much as his assertion regarding his "specific" and narrow view of "tradition," Scalia's assertion that "original intent" was applicable to determining which rights are fundamental in the application of substantive due process was most interesting, as was a pointed rejoinder from Justice Stevens. Since Scalia himself opens the "barn door," the editors take note of Scalia's and Stevens' opinions in *McDonald* regarding these issues, as these discussions are quite significant in regard to the legitimacy of protecting rights beyond those enumerated explicitly in the constitution. These themes are also apparent in the *Dobbs* opinion by Justice Alito, and in the joint dissent by Justices Breyer, Sotomayor, and Kagan.

McDONALD v. CITY OF CHICAGO
130 S. Ct. 3020 (2010)

. . . Justice SCALIA, concurring.

I join the Court's opinion. Despite my misgivings about Substantive Due Process as an original matter, I have acquiesced in the Court's incorporation of certain guarantees in the Bill of Rights "because it is both long established and narrowly limited." This case does not require me to reconsider that view, since straightforward application of settled doctrine suffices to decide it.

I write separately only to respond to some aspects of Justice Stevens' dissent. Not that aspect which disagrees with the majority's application of our precedents to this case, which is fully covered by the Court's opinion. But much of what Justice Stevens writes is a broad condemnation of the theory of interpretation which underlies the Court's opinion, a theory that makes the traditions of our people paramount. He proposes a different theory, which he claims is more "cautiou[s]" and respectful of proper limits on the judicial role. It is that claim I wish to address.

Justice Stevens' response to this concurrence, makes the usual rejoinder of "living Constitution" advocates to the criticism that it empowers judges to eliminate or expand what the people have prescribed: The traditional, historically focused method, he says, reposes discretion in judges as well. Historical analysis can be difficult; it sometimes requires resolving threshold questions, and making nuanced judgments about which evidence to consult and how to interpret it.

I will stipulate to that. But the question to be decided is not whether the historically focused method is a *perfect means* of restraining aristocratic judicial Constitution-writing; but whether it is the *best means available* in an imperfect world. Or indeed, even more narrowly than that: whether it is demonstrably much better than what Justice Stevens proposes. I think it beyond all serious dispute that it is much less subjective, and intrudes much less upon the democratic process. It is less subjective because it depends upon a body of evidence susceptible of reasoned analysis rather than a variety of vague ethico-political First Principles whose combined conclusion can be found to point in any direction the judges favor. In the most controversial matters brought before this Court — for example, the constitutionality of prohibiting abortion, assisted suicide, or homosexual sodomy, or the constitutionality of the death penalty — *any* historical methodology, under *any* plausible standard of proof, would lead to the same conclusion. Moreover, the methodological differences that divide historians, and the varying interpretive assumptions they bring to their work, are nothing compared to the differences among the American people (though perhaps not among graduates of prestigious law schools) with regard to the moral judgments Justice Stevens would have courts pronounce. And whether or not special expertise is needed to answer historical questions, judges most certainly have no "comparative . . . advantage" in resolving moral disputes. What is more, his approach would not eliminate, but multiply, the hard questions courts must confront, since he would not *replace* history with moral philosophy, but would have courts consider *both*.

And the Court's approach intrudes less upon the democratic process because the rights it acknowledges are those established by a constitutional history formed by democratic decisions; and the rights it fails to acknowledge are left to be democratically adopted or rejected by the people, with the assurance that their decision is not subject to judicial revision. Justice Stevens' approach, on the other hand, deprives the people of that power, since whatever the Constitution and laws may say, the list of protected rights will be whatever courts wish it to be. After all, he notes, the people have been wrong before, and courts may conclude they are wrong in the future. Justice Stevens abhors a system in which "majorities or powerful interest groups always get their way," but replaces it with a system in which unelected and life-tenured judges always get their way. That such usurpation is effected unabashedly — with "the judge's cards . . . laid on the table" — makes it even worse. In a vibrant democracy, usurpation should have to be accomplished in the dark. It is Justice Stevens' approach, not the Court's, that puts democracy in peril.

Justice STEVENS, dissenting.

The first, and most basic, principle established by our cases is that the rights protected by the Due Process Clause are not merely procedural in nature. At first glance, this proposition might seem surprising, given that the Clause refers to "process." But substance and procedure are often deeply entwined. Upon closer inspection, the text can be read to "impos[e] nothing less than an obligation to give substantive content to the words 'liberty' and 'due process of law,' lest superficially fair procedures be permitted to 'destroy the enjoyment' of life, liberty, and property," *Poe* v. *Ullman*, 367 U.S. 497, 541 (1961) (Harlan, J., dissenting), and the Clause's prepositional modifier be permitted to swallow its primary command. Procedural guarantees are hollow unless linked to substantive interests; and no amount of process can legitimize some deprivations.

I have yet to see a persuasive argument that the Framers of the Fourteenth Amendment thought otherwise. To the contrary, the historical evidence suggests that, at least by the time of the Civil War if not much earlier, the phrase "due process of law" had acquired substantive content as a term of art within the legal community. This understanding is consonant with the venerable "notion that governmental authority has implied limits which preserve private autonomy," a notion which predates the founding and which finds reinforcement in the Constitution's Ninth Amendment. The Due Process Clause cannot claim to be the source of our basic freedoms — no legal document ever could — but it stands as one of their foundational guarantors in our law. . . .

The second principle woven through our cases is that substantive due process is fundamentally a matter of personal liberty. For it is the liberty clause of the Fourteenth Amendment that grounds our most important holdings in this field. It is the liberty clause that enacts the Constitution's "promise" that a measure of dignity and self-rule will be afforded to all persons. It is the liberty clause that reflects and renews "the origins of the American heritage of freedom [and] the abiding interest in individual liberty that makes certain state intrusions on the citizen's right to decide how he will live his own life intolerable." Our substantive due process cases have episodically invoked values such as privacy and equality as well, values that in certain contexts may intersect with or complement a subject's liberty interests in profound ways. But as I have observed on numerous occasions, "most of the significant [20th-century] cases raising Bill of Rights issues have, in the final analysis, actually interpreted the word 'liberty' in the Fourteenth Amendment."

It follows that the term "incorporation," like the term "unenumerated rights," is something of a misnomer. Whether an asserted substantive due process interest is explicitly named in one of the first eight Amendments to the Constitution or is not mentioned, the underlying inquiry is the same: We must ask whether the interest is "comprised within the term liberty." As the second Justice Harlan has shown, ever since the Court began considering the applicability of the Bill of Rights to the States, "the Court's usual approach has been to ground the prohibitions against state action squarely on due process, without intermediate reliance on any of the first eight Amendments." . . .

So far, I have explained that substantive due process analysis generally requires us to consider the term "liberty" in the Fourteenth Amendment, and that this inquiry may be informed by but does not depend upon the content of the Bill of Rights. How should a court go about the analysis, then? Our precedents have established, not an exact methodology, but rather a framework for decision-making. In this respect, too, the Court's narrative fails to capture the continuity and flexibility in our doctrine. . . .

[A] rigid historical methodology is unfaithful to the Constitution's command. For if it were really the case that the Fourteenth Amendment's guarantee of liberty embraces only those rights "so rooted in our history, tradition, and practice as to require special protection," then the guarantee would serve little function, save to ratify those rights that state actors have *already* been according the most extensive protection. Cf. *Duncan*, 391 U.S., at 183 (Harlan, J., dissenting) (critiquing "circular[ity]" of historicized test for incorporation). That approach is unfaithful to the expansive principle Americans laid down when they ratified the Fourteenth Amendment and to the level of generality they chose when they crafted its language; it promises an objectivity it cannot deliver and masks the value judgments that pervade any analysis of what customs, defined in what manner, are sufficiently "'rooted'"; it countenances the most revolting injustices in the name of continuity, for we must never forget that not only slavery but also the subjugation of women and other rank forms of discrimination are part of our history; and it effaces this Court's distinctive role in saying what the law is, leaving the development and safekeeping of liberty to majoritarian political processes. It is judicial abdication in the guise of judicial modesty.

No, the liberty safeguarded by the Fourteenth Amendment is not merely preservative in nature but rather is a "dynamic concept." Its dynamism provides a central means through which the Framers enabled the Constitution to "endure for ages to come," *McCulloch* v. *Maryland*, 4 Wheat. 316, 415 (1819), a central example of how they "wisely spoke in general language and left to succeeding generations the task of applying that language to the unceasingly changing environment in which they would live," Rehnquist, The Notion of a Living Constitution, 54 Tex. L. Rev. 693, 694 (1976). "The task of giving concrete meaning to the term 'liberty,'" I have elsewhere explained at some length, "was a part of the work assigned to future generations." The judge who would outsource the interpretation of "liberty to historical sentiment has turned his back on a task the Constitution assigned to him and drained the document of its intended vitality. . . .

Rather than seek a categorical understanding of the liberty clause, our precedents have thus elucidated a conceptual core. The clause safeguards, most basically, "the ability independently to define one's identity," "the individual's right to make certain unusually important decisions that will affect his own, or his family's, destiny," and the right to be respected as a human being. Self-determination, bodily integrity, freedom of conscience, intimate relationships, political equality, dignity and respect — these are the central values we have found implicit in the concept of ordered liberty. . . .

While I agree with the Court that our substantive due process cases offer a principled basis for holding that petitioners have a constitutional right to possess a usable firearm in the home, I am ultimately persuaded that a better reading of our case law supports the city of Chicago. I would not foreclose the possibility that a particular plaintiff — say, an elderly widow who lives in a dangerous neighborhood and does not have the strength to operate a long gun — may have a cognizable liberty interest in possessing a handgun. But I cannot accept petitioners' broader submission. A number of factors, taken together, lead me to this conclusion.

First, firearms have a fundamentally ambivalent relationship to liberty. Just as they can help homeowners defend their families and property from intruders, they can help thugs and insurrectionists murder innocent victims. The threat that firearms will be misused is far from hypothetical, for gun crime has devastated many of our communities. . . .

Hence, in evaluating an asserted right to be free from particular gun control regulations, liberty is on both sides of the equation. Guns may be useful for self-defense, as well as for hunting and sport, but they also have a unique potential to facilitate death and destruction and thereby to destabilize ordered liberty. *Your* interest in keeping and bearing a certain firearm may diminish *my* interest in being and feeling safe from armed violence. And while granting you the right to own a handgun might make you safer on any given day — assuming the handgun's marginal contribution to self-defense outweighs its marginal contribution to the risk of accident, suicide, and criminal mischief — it may make you and the community you live in less safe overall, owing to the increased number of handguns in circulation. It is at least reasonable for a democratically elected legislature to take such concerns into account in considering what sorts of regulations would best serve the public welfare. . . .

The Court is surely correct that Americans' conceptions of the Second Amendment right evolved over time in a more individualistic direction; that Members of the

Reconstruction Congress were urgently concerned about the safety of the newly freed slaves; and that some Members believed that, following ratification of the Fourteenth Amendment, the Second Amendment would apply to the States. But it is a giant leap from these data points to the conclusion that the Fourteenth Amendment "incorporated" the Second Amendment as a matter of original meaning or post enactment interpretation. Consider, for example, that the text of the Fourteenth Amendment says nothing about the Second Amendment or firearms; that there is substantial evidence to suggest that, when the Reconstruction Congress enacted measures to ensure newly freed slaves and Union sympathizers in the South enjoyed the right to possess firearms, it was motivated by antidiscrimination and equality concerns rather than arms-bearing concerns *per se;* that many contemporaneous courts and commentators did not understand the Fourteenth Amendment to have had an "incorporating" effect; and that the States heavily regulated the right to keep and bear arms both before and after the Amendment's passage. The Court's narrative largely elides these facts. The complications they raise show why even the most dogged historical inquiry into the "fundamentality" of the Second Amendment right (or any other) necessarily entails judicial judgment — and therefore judicial discretion — every step of the way. . . .

The preceding sections have already addressed many of the points made by Justice Scalia in his concurrence. But in light of that opinion's fixation on this one, it is appropriate to say a few words about Justice Scalia's broader claim: that his preferred method of substantive due process analysis, a method "that makes the traditions of our people paramount," is both more restrained and more facilitative of democracy than the method I have outlined. Colorful as it is, Justice Scalia's critique does not have nearly as much force as does his rhetoric. His theory of substantive due process, moreover, comes with its own profound difficulties.

Although Justice Scalia aspires to an "objective," "neutral" method of substantive due process analysis, his actual method is nothing of the sort. Under the "historically focused" approach he advocates, numerous threshold questions arise before one ever gets to the history. At what level of generality should one frame the liberty interest in question? What does it mean for a right to be "'deeply rooted in this Nation's history and tradition,'"? By what standard will that proposition be   tested? Which types of sources will count, and how will those sources be weighed and aggregated? There is no objective, neutral answer to these questions. There is not even a theory — at least, Justice Scalia provides none — of how to go about answering them.

Nor is there any escaping *Palko*, it seems. To qualify for substantive due process protection, Justice Scalia has stated, an asserted liberty right must be not only deeply rooted in American tradition, "but it must *also* be implicit in the concept of ordered liberty." Applying the latter, *Palko* derived half of that test requires precisely the sort of reasoned judgment — the same multifaceted evaluation of the right's contours and consequences — that Justice Scalia mocks in his concurrence today.

So does applying the first half. It is hardly a novel insight that history is not an objective science, and that its use can therefore "point in any direction the judges favor." Yet 21 years after the point was brought to his attention by Justice Brennan, Justice Scalia remains "oblivious to the fact that [the concept of 'tradition'] can be as malleable and elusive as 'liberty' itself." Even when historical analysis is focused on a discrete proposition, such as the original public meaning of the Second Amendment, the evidence often points in different directions. The historian must choose which pieces to credit and which to discount, and then must try to assemble them into a coherent whole. In *Heller*, Justice

Scalia preferred to rely on sources created much earlier and later in time than the Second Amendment itself; I focused more closely on sources contemporaneous with the Amendment's drafting and ratification. No mechanical yardstick can measure which of us was correct, either with respect to the materials we chose to privilege or the insights we gleaned from them.

The malleability and elusiveness of history increase exponentially when we move from a pure question of original meaning, as in *Heller*, to Justice Scalia's theory of substantive due process. At least with the former sort of question, the judge can focus on a single legal provision; the temporal scope of the inquiry is (or should be) relatively bounded; and there is substantial agreement on what sorts of authorities merit consideration. With Justice Scalia's approach to substantive due process, these guideposts all fall away. The judge must canvas the entire landscape of American law as it has evolved through time, and perhaps older laws as well, pursuant to a standard (deeply rootedness) that has never been defined. In conducting this rudderless, panoramic tour of American legal history, the judge has more than ample opportunity to "look over the heads of the crowd and pick out [his] friends."

My point is not to criticize judges' use of history in general or to suggest that it always generates indeterminate answers; I have already emphasized that historical study can discipline as well as enrich substantive due process analysis. My point is simply that Justice Scalia's defense of his method, which holds out objectivity and restraint as its cardinal — and, it seems, only — virtues, is unsatisfying on its own terms. For a limitless number of subjective judgments may be smuggled into his historical analysis. Worse, they may be *buried* in the analysis. At least with my approach, the judge's cards are laid on the table for all to see, and to critique. The judge must exercise judgment, to be sure. When answering a constitutional question to which the text provides no clear answer, there is always some amount of discretion; our constitutional system has always depended on judges' filling in the document's vast open space. But there is also transparency.

The concern runs still deeper. Not only can historical views be less than completely clear or informative, but they can also be wrong. Some notions that many Americans deeply believed to be true, at one time, turned out not to be true. Some practices that many Americans believed to be consistent with the Constitution's guarantees of liberty and equality, at one time, turned out to be inconsistent with them. The fact that we have a written Constitution does not consign this Nation to a static legal existence. Although we should always "pa[y] a decent regard to the opinions of former times," it "is not the glory of the people of America" to have "suffered a blind veneration for antiquity." The Federalist No. 14, p. 99, 104 (C. Rossiter ed. 1961) (J. Madison). It is not the role of federal judges to be amateur historians. And it is not fidelity to the Constitution to ignore its use of deliberately capacious language, in an effort to transform foundational legal commitments into narrow rules of decision. . . .

It is worth pondering, furthermore, the vision of democracy that underlies Justice Scalia's critique. Because very few of us would welcome a system in which majorities or powerful interest groups always get their way. Under our constitutional scheme, I would have thought that a judicial approach to liberty claims such as the one I have outlined — an approach that investigates both the intrinsic nature of the claimed interest and the practical significance of its judicial enforcement, that is transparent in its reasoning and sincere in its effort to incorporate constraints, that is guided by history but not beholden to it, and that is willing to protect some rights even if they have not already received uniform protection from the elected branches — has the capacity to improve, rather than "[im]peril", our democracy. It all depends on judges' exercising careful, reasoned judgment. As it always has, and as it always will.

Although the Court's decision in this case might be seen as a mere adjunct to its decision in *Heller*, the consequences could prove far more destructive — quite literally — to our Nation's communities and to our constitutional structure. Thankfully, the Second Amendment right identified in *Heller* and its newly minted Fourteenth Amendment analogue are limited, at least for now, to the home. But neither the "assurances" provided by the plurality, nor the many historical sources cited in its opinion should obscure the reality that today's ruling marks a dramatic change in our law — or that the Justices who have joined it have brought to bear an awesome amount of discretion in resolving the legal question presented by this case.

I would proceed more cautiously. For the reasons set out at length above, I cannot accept either the methodology the Court employs or the conclusions it draws. Although impressively argued, the majority's decision to overturn more than a century of Supreme Court precedent and to unsettle a much longer tradition of state practice is not, in my judgment, built "upon respect for the teachings of history, solid recognition of the basic values that underlie our society, and wise appreciation of the great roles that the doctrines of federalism and separation of powers have played in establishing and preserving American freedoms.

5. SEXUAL ORIENTATION

This question appeared to have been answered in Bowers v. Hardwick, 478 U.S. 186 (1986), in an opinion that seemed to exemplify Justice Scalia's inquiry limited to "the most specific level" of a relevant tradition. In upholding a challenge to a Georgia statute criminalizing sodomy by committing that act with another adult male in the bedroom of respondent's home, the Court held that "we think it evident that none of the rights announced [bears] any resemblance to the claimed constitutional right of homosexuals to engage in acts of sodomy that is asserted in this case. No connection between family, marriage, or procreation on the one hand and homosexual activity on the other has been demonstrated, either by the Court of Appeals or by respondent. Moreover, any claim that . . . any kind of private sexual conduct between consenting adults is constitutionally insulated from state proscription is unsupportable." Rejecting a more general view that might protect such sexual orientation because "[i]f the right of privacy means anything, it is the right of the *individual,* married or single, to be free from unwarranted governmental intrusion into matters so fundamentally affecting a person" (*Eisenstadt v. Baird*, 405 U.S. 438, 453 (1972)), the Court, viewing homosexual orientation at its "most specific level," asked whether homosexual sodomy was "deeply rooted in this Nation's traditions" or "implicit in the concept of ordered liberty."

Much to the surprise of "Court watchers," the Court in the 2003 term, in the opinion that follows, struck down a "Texas statute making it a crime for two persons of the same sex to engage in certain intimate sexual conduct." The Court, with a 5–4 majority, overruled *Bowers* on substantive due process grounds. Recall that Justice Kennedy, as well as Justice O'Conner (she concurred on equal protection grounds), had refused to concur in Scalia's footnote 6, cited above, in *Michael H.*

LAWRENCE v. TEXAS
539 U.S. 558 (2003)

Justice KENNEDY delivered the opinion of the Court [in which STEVENS, SOUTER, GINSBURG, and BREYER, JJ., joined.]

Liberty protects the person from unwarranted government intrusions into a dwelling or other private places. In our tradition the State is not omnipresent in the home. And there are other spheres of our lives and existence, outside the home, where the State should not be a dominant presence. Freedom extends beyond spatial bounds. Liberty presumes an autonomy of self that includes freedom of thought, belief, expression, and certain intimate conduct. The instant case involves liberty of the person both in its spatial and more transcendent dimensions.

I

The question before the Court is the validity of a Texas statute making it a crime for two persons of the same sex to engage in certain intimate sexual conduct.

In Houston, Texas, officers of the Harris County Police Department were dispatched to a private residence in response to a reported weapons disturbance. They entered an apartment where one of the petitioners, John Geddes Lawrence, resided. The right of the police to enter does not seem to have been questioned. The officers observed Lawrence and another man, Tyron Garner, engaging in a sexual act. The two petitioners were arrested, held in custody over night, and charged and convicted before a Justice of the Peace.

The complaints described their crime as "deviate sexual intercourse, namely anal sex, with a member of the same sex (man)." App. to Pet. for Cert. 127a, 139a. The applicable state law is Tex. Penal Code Ann. § 21.06(a) (2003). It provides: "A person commits an offense if he engages in deviate sexual intercourse with another individual of the same sex." The statute defines "[d]eviate sexual intercourse" as follows: "(A) any contact between any part of the genitals of one person and the mouth or anus of another person; or "(B) the penetration of the genitals or the anus of another person with an object." § 21.01(1).

The petitioners, having entered a plea of *nolo contendere*, were each fined $200 and assessed court costs of $141.25. App. to Pet. for Cert. 107a-110a. [T]he petitioners were adults at the time of the alleged offense. Their conduct was in private and consensual.

II

We conclude the case should be resolved by determining whether the petitioners were free as adults to engage in the private conduct in the exercise of their liberty under the Due Process Clause of the Fourteenth Amendment to the Constitution. For this inquiry we deem it necessary to reconsider the Court's holding in Bowers. [T]he most pertinent beginning point is our decision in Griswold v. Connecticut, 381 U.S. 479, 85 S.Ct. 1678, 14 L.Ed.2d 510 (1965).

In Griswold the Court invalidated a state law prohibiting the use of drugs or devices of contraception and counseling or aiding and abetting the use of contraceptives. The Court described the protected interest as a right to privacy and placed emphasis on the marriage relation and the protected space of the marital bedroom. Id., at 485, 85 S.Ct. 1678. After Griswold it was established that the right to make certain decisions regarding sexual conduct extends beyond the marital relationship. In Eisenstadt v. Baird, 405 U.S. 438, 92 S.Ct. 1029, 31 L.Ed.2d 349 (1972), the Court invalidated a law prohibiting the distribution of contraceptives to unmarried persons. The case was decided under the

Equal Protection Clause, id., at 454, 92 S.Ct. 1029; but with respect to unmarried persons, the Court went on to state the fundamental proposition that the law impaired the exercise of their personal rights, ibid. It quoted from the statement of the Court of Appeals finding the law to be in conflict with fundamental human rights, and it followed with this statement of its own:

> It is true that in Griswold the right of privacy in question inhered in the marital relationship.
> . . . If the right of privacy means anything, it is the right of the *individual,* married or single, to be free from unwarranted governmental intrusion into matters so fundamentally affecting a person as the decision whether to bear or beget a child."

Id., at 453, 92 S.Ct. 1029.

The opinions in Griswold and Eisenstadt were part of the background for the decision in Roe v. Wade, 410 U.S. 113, 93 S.Ct. 705, 35 L.Ed.2d 147 (1973). [B]oth Eisenstadt and Carey, as well as the holding and rationale in Roe, confirmed that the reasoning of Griswold could not be confined to the protection of rights of married adults. This was the state of the law with respect to some of the most relevant cases when the Court considered Bowers v. Hardwick.

The facts in Bowers had some similarities to the instant case. A police officer, whose right to enter seems not to have been in question, observed Hardwick, in his own bedroom, engaging in intimate sexual conduct with another adult male. The conduct was in violation of a Georgia statute making it a criminal offense to engage in sodomy. One difference between the two cases is that the Georgia statute prohibited the conduct whether or not the participants were of the same sex, while the Texas statute, as we have seen, applies only to participants of the same sex. Hardwick was not prosecuted, but he brought an action in federal court to declare the state statute invalid. [T]he Court, in an opinion by Justice White, sustained the Georgia law.

The Court began its substantive discussion in Bowers as follows: "The issue presented is whether the Federal Constitution confers a fundamental right upon homosexuals to engage in sodomy and hence invalidates the laws of the many States that still make such conduct illegal and have done so for a very long time." That statement, we now conclude, discloses the Court's own failure to appreciate the extent of the liberty at stake. To say that the issue in Bowers was simply the right to engage in certain sexual conduct demeans the claim the individual put forward, just as it would demean a married couple were it to be said marriage is simply about the right to have sexual intercourse. The laws involved in Bowers and here are, to be sure, statutes that purport to do no more than prohibit a particular sexual act. Their penalties and purposes, though, have more far-reaching consequences, touching upon the most private human conduct, sexual behavior, and in the most private of places, the home. The statutes do seek to control a personal relationship that, whether or not entitled to formal recognition in the law, is within the liberty of persons to choose without being punished as criminals.

This, as a general rule, should counsel against attempts by the State, or a court, to define the meaning of the relationship or to set its boundaries absent injury to a person or abuse of an institution the law protects. It suffices for us to acknowledge that adults may choose to enter upon this relationship in the confines of their homes and their own private lives and still retain their dignity as free persons. When sexuality finds overt expression in intimate conduct with another person, the conduct can be but one element in a personal bond that is more enduring.   The liberty protected by the Constitution allows homosexual persons the right to make this choice.

Having misapprehended the claim of liberty there presented to it, and thus stating the claim to be whether there is a fundamental right to engage in consensual sodomy, the Bowers Court said: "Proscriptions against that conduct have ancient roots." Id., at 192, 106 S.Ct. 2841.   In academic writings, and in many of the scholarly *amicus* briefs filed to assist the Court in this case, there are fundamental criticisms of the historical premises relied upon by the majority and concurring opinions in Bowers.   We need not enter this debate in the attempt to reach a definitive historical judgment, but the following considerations counsel against adopting the definitive conclusions upon which Bowers placed such reliance.

At the outset it should be noted that there is no longstanding history in this country of laws directed at homosexual conduct as a distinct matter. Beginning in colonial times there were prohibitions of sodomy derived from the English criminal laws passed in the first instance by the Reformation Parliament of 1533.   The English prohibition was understood to include relations between men and women as well as relations between men and men. Nineteenth-century commentators similarly read American sodomy, buggery, and crime-against-nature statutes as criminalizing certain relations between men and women and between men and men.   The absence of legal prohibitions focusing on homosexual conduct may be explained in part by noting that according to some scholars the concept of the homosexual as a distinct category of person did not emerge until the late 19th century. Thus early American sodomy laws were not directed at homosexuals as such but instead sought to prohibit nonprocreative sexual activity more generally.   This does not suggest approval of homosexual conduct.   It does tend to show that this particular form of conduct was not thought of as a separate category from like conduct between heterosexual persons.

Laws prohibiting sodomy do not seem to have been enforced against consenting adults acting in private.   A substantial number of sodomy prosecutions and convictions for which there are surviving records were for predatory acts against those who could not or did not consent, as in the case of a minor or the victim of an assault.   As to these, one purpose for the prohibitions was to ensure there would be no lack of coverage if a predator committed a sexual assault that did not constitute rape as defined by the criminal law. [T]he infrequency of these prosecutions.   In all events that infrequency makes it difficult to say that society approved of a rigorous and systematic punishment of the consensual acts committed in private and by adults.   The longstanding criminal prohibition of homosexual sodomy upon which the Bowers decision placed such reliance is as consistent with a general condemnation of nonprocreative sex as it is with an established tradition of prosecuting acts because of their homosexual character.

The policy of punishing consenting adults for private acts was not much discussed in the early legal literature.   We can infer that one reason for this was the very private nature of the conduct.   Despite the absence of prosecutions, there may have been periods in which there was public criticism of homosexuals as such and an insistence that the criminal laws be enforced to discourage their practices.   But far from possessing "ancient roots," Bowers, 478 U.S., at 192, 106 S.Ct. 2841, American laws targeting same-sex couples did not develop until the last third of the 20th century.

It was not until the 1970's that any State singled out same-sex relations for criminal prosecution, and only nine States have done so.   Post-Bowers even some of these States did not adhere to the policy of suppressing homosexual conduct.   Over the course of the last decades, States with same-sex prohibitions have moved toward abolishing them.

It must be acknowledged, of course, that the Court in Bowers was making the broader point that for centuries there have been powerful voices to condemn homosexual conduct as immoral. The condemnation has been shaped by religious beliefs, conceptions of right and acceptable behavior, and respect for the traditional family. For many persons these are not trivial concerns but profound and deep convictions accepted as ethical and moral principles to which they aspire and which thus determine the course of their lives. These considerations do not answer the question before us, however. The issue is whether the majority may use the power of the State to enforce these views on the whole society through operation of the criminal law. "Our obligation is to define the liberty of all, not to mandate our own moral code." Planned Parenthood of Southeastern Pa. v. Casey, 505 U.S. 833, 850, 112 S.Ct. 2791, 120 L.Ed.2d 674 (1992).

Chief Justice Burger joined the opinion for the Court in Bowers and further explained his views as follows: "Decisions of individuals relating to homosexual conduct have been subject to state intervention throughout the history of Western civilization. Condemnation of those practices is firmly rooted in Judeao-Christian moral and ethical standards." As with Justice White's assumptions about history, scholarship casts some doubt on the sweeping nature of the statement by Chief Justice Burger as it pertains to private homosexual conduct between consenting adults. In all events we think that our laws and traditions in the past half century are of most relevance here. These references show an emerging awareness that liberty gives substantial protection to adult persons in deciding how to conduct their private lives in matters pertaining to sex. "[H]istory and tradition are the starting point but not in all cases the ending point of the substantive due process inquiry." County of Sacramento v. Lewis, 523 U.S. 833, 857, 118 S.Ct. 1708, 140 L.Ed.2d 1043 (1998) (Kennedy, J., concurring).

This emerging recognition should have been apparent when Bowers was decided. In 1955 the American Law Institute promulgated the Model Penal Code and made clear that it did not recommend or provide for "criminal penalties for consensual sexual relations conducted in private." It justified its decision on three grounds: (1) The prohibitions undermined respect for the law by penalizing conduct many people engaged in; (2) the statutes regulated private conduct not harmful to others; and (3) the laws were arbitrarily enforced and thus invited the danger of blackmail. In 1961 Illinois changed its laws to conform to the Model Penal Code. Other States soon followed.

[T]he sweeping references by Chief Justice Burger to the history of Western civilization and to Judeo-Christian moral and ethical standards did not take account of other authorities pointing in an opposite direction. A committee advising the British Parliament recommended in 1957 repeal of laws punishing homosexual conduct. Parliament enacted the substance of those recommendations 10 years later. Of even more importance, almost five years before Bowers was decided the European Court of Human Rights considered a case with parallels to Bowers and to today's case. An adult male resident in Northern Ireland alleged he was a practicing homosexual who desired to engage in consensual homosexual conduct. The laws of Northern Ireland forbade him that right. He alleged that he had been questioned, his home had been searched, and he feared criminal prosecution. The court held that the laws proscribing the conduct were invalid under the European Convention on Human Rights. *Dudgeon v. United Kingdom,* 45 Eur. Ct. H.R. (1981) & ¶ 52. Authoritative in all countries that are members of the Council of Europe (21 nations then, 45 nations now), the decision is at odds with the premise in Bowers that the claim put forward was insubstantial in our Western civilization.

In our own constitutional system the deficiencies in Bowers became even more apparent in the years following its announcement. The 25 States with laws prohibiting the relevant conduct referenced in the Bowers decision are reduced now to 13, of which 4 enforce their laws only against homosexual conduct. In those States where sodomy is still proscribed, whether for same-sex or heterosexual conduct, there is a pattern of nonenforcement with respect to consenting adults acting in private. The State of Texas admitted in 1994 that as of that date it had not prosecuted anyone under those circumstances.

Two principal cases decided after Bowers cast its holding into even more doubt. In Planned Parenthood of Southeastern Pa. v. Casey, 505 U.S. 833, 112 S.Ct. 2791, 120 L.Ed.2d 674 (1992), the Court reaffirmed the substantive force of the liberty protected by the Due Process Clause. The Casey decision again confirmed that our laws and tradition afford constitutional protection to personal decisions relating to marriage, procreation, contraception, family relationships, child rearing, and education. In explaining the respect the Constitution demands for the autonomy of the person in making these choices, we stated as follows:

> These matters, involving the most intimate and personal choices a person may make in a lifetime, choices central to personal dignity and autonomy, are central to the liberty protected by the Fourteenth Amendment. At the heart of liberty is the right to define one's own concept of existence, of meaning, of the universe, and of the mystery of human life. Beliefs about these matters could not define the attributes of personhood were they formed under compulsion of the State.

Persons in a homosexual relationship may seek autonomy for these purposes, just as heterosexual persons do. The decision in Bowers would deny them this right.

The second post-Bowers case of principal relevance is Romer v. Evans, 517 U.S. 620, 116 S.Ct. 1620, 134 L.Ed.2d 855 (1996). There the Court struck down class-based legislation directed at homosexuals as a violation of the Equal Protection Clause. Romer invalidated an amendment to Colorado's constitution which named as a solitary class persons who were homosexuals, lesbians, or bisexual either by "orientation, conduct, practices or relationships." We concluded that the provision was "born of animosity toward the class of persons affected" and further that it had no rational relation to a legitimate governmental purpose.

As an alternative argument in this case, counsel for the petitioners and some *amici* contend that Romer provides the basis for declaring the Texas statute invalid under the Equal Protection Clause. That is a tenable argument, but we conclude the instant case requires us to address whether Bowers itself has continuing validity. Were we to hold the statute invalid under the Equal Protection Clause some might question whether a prohibition would be valid if drawn differently, say, to prohibit the conduct both between same-sex and different-sex participants.

Equality of treatment and the due process right to demand respect for conduct protected by the substantive guarantee of liberty are linked in important respects, and a decision on the latter point advances both interests. If protected conduct is made criminal and the law which does so remains unexamined for its substantive validity, its stigma might remain even if it were not enforceable as drawn for equal protection reasons. When homosexual conduct is made criminal by the law of the State, that declaration in and of itself is an invitation to subject homosexual persons to discrimination both in the public and in the private spheres. The central holding of Bowers has been brought in question by this case, and it should be addressed. Its continuance as precedent demeans the lives of homosexual persons.

[The] foundations of Bowers have sustained serious erosion from our recent decisions in Casey and Romer. When our precedent has been thus weakened, criticism from other sources is of greater significance. In the United States criticism of Bowers has been substantial and continuing, disapproving of its reasoning in all respects, not just as to its historical assumptions. See, *e.g.,* C. Fried, Order and Law: Arguing the Reagan Revolution — A Firsthand Account 81-84 (1991); R. Posner, Sex and Reason 341-350 (1992). The courts of five different States have declined to follow it in interpreting provisions in their own state constitutions parallel to the Due Process Clause of the Fourteenth Amendment.

To the extent Bowers relied on values we share with a wider civilization, it should be noted that the reasoning and holding in Bowers have been rejected elsewhere. The European Court of Human Rights has followed not Bowers but its own decision in *Dudgeon v. United Kingdom.* Other nations, too, have taken action consistent with an affirmation of the protected right of homosexual adults to engage in intimate, consensual conduct. The right the petitioners seek in this case has been accepted as an integral part of human freedom in many other countries. There has been no showing that in this country the governmental interest in circumscribing personal choice is somehow more legitimate or urgent.

The doctrine of *stare decisis* is essential to the respect accorded to the judgments of the Court and to the stability of the law. It is not, however, an inexorable command. In Casey we noted that when a Court is asked to overrule a precedent recognizing a constitutional liberty interest, individual or societal reliance on the existence of that liberty cautions with particular strength against reversing course. The holding in Bowers, however, has not induced detrimental reliance comparable to some instances where recognized individual rights are involved. Indeed, there has been no individual or societal reliance on Bowers of the sort that could counsel against overturning its holding once there are compelling reasons to do so. Bowers itself causes uncertainty, for the precedents before and after its issuance contradict its central holding.

The rationale of Bowers does not withstand careful analysis. In his dissenting opinion in Bowers Justice Stevens came to these conclusions:

> Our prior cases make two propositions abundantly clear. First, the fact that the governing majority in a State has traditionally viewed a particular practice as immoral is not a sufficient reason for upholding a law prohibiting the practice; neither history nor tradition could save a law prohibiting miscegenation from constitutional attack. Second, individual decisions by married persons, concerning the intimacies of their physical relationship, even when not intended to produce offspring, are a form of "liberty" protected by the Due Process Clause of the Fourteenth Amendment. Moreover, this protection extends to intimate choices by unmarried as well as married persons.

Justice Stevens' analysis, in our view, should have been controlling in Bowers and should control here. Bowers was not correct when it was decided, and it is not correct today. It ought not to remain binding precedent. Bowers v. Hardwick should be and now is overruled.

The present case does not involve minors. It does not involve persons who might be injured or coerced or who are situated in relationships where consent might not easily be refused. It does not involve public conduct or prostitution. It does not involve whether the government must give formal recognition to any relationship that homosexual persons seek to enter. The case does involve two adults who, with full and mutual consent from each other, engaged in sexual practices common to a homosexual lifestyle. The petitioners are entitled to respect for their private lives. The State cannot demean their existence or control their destiny by making their private sexual conduct a crime. Their right to liberty under the Due Process Clause gives them the full right to engage in their conduct without intervention of the government. "It is a promise of the Constitution that there is a realm of personal liberty which the government may not enter." Casey, supra, at 847, 112 S.Ct. 2791. The Texas statute furthers no legitimate state interest which can justify its intrusion into the personal and private life of the individual.

Had those who drew and ratified the Due Process Clauses of the Fifth Amendment or the Fourteenth Amendment known the components of liberty in its manifold possibilities, they might have been more specific. They did not presume to have this insight. They knew times can blind us to certain truths and later generations can see that laws once thought necessary and proper in fact serve only to oppress. As the Constitution endures, persons in every generation can invoke its principles in their own search for greater freedom. The judgment of the Court of Appeals for the Texas Fourteenth District is reversed, and the case is remanded for further proceedings not inconsistent with this opinion.

Justice O'CONNOR, concurring in the judgment.

The Court today overrules Bowers v. Hardwick, 478 U.S. 186, 106 S.Ct. 2841, 92 L.Ed.2d 140 (1986). I joined Bowers, and do not join the Court in overruling it. Nevertheless, I agree with the Court that Texas' statute banning same-sex sodomy is unconstitutional. Rather than relying on the substantive component of the Fourteenth Amendment's Due Process Clause, as the Court does, I base my conclusion on the Fourteenth Amendment's Equal Protection Clause.

[We] have consistently held, however, that some objectives, such as "a bare . . . desire to harm a politically unpopular group," are not legitimate state interests. Department of Agriculture v. Moreno, supra, at 534, 93 S.Ct. 2821. See also Cleburne v. Cleburne Living Center, supra, at 446-447, 105 S.Ct. 3249; Romer v. Evans, supra, at 632, 116 S.Ct. 1620. When a law exhibits such a desire to harm a politically unpopular group, we have applied a more searching form of rational basis review to strike down such laws under the Equal Protection Clause.

The statute at issue here makes sodomy a crime only if a person "engages in deviate sexual intercourse with another individual of the same sex." Sodomy between opposite-sex partners, however, is not a crime in Texas. [T]he Texas statute makes homosexuals unequal in the eyes of the law by making particular conduct — and only that conduct — subject to criminal sanction. It appears that prosecutions under Texas' sodomy law are rare. See State v. Morales, 869 S.W.2d 941, 943 (Tex.1994) (noting in 1994 that § 21.06 "has not been, and in all probability will not be, enforced against private consensual conduct between adults"). This case shows, however, that prosecutions under § 21.06 *do* occur. And while the penalty imposed on petitioners in this case was relatively minor, the consequences of conviction are not. As the Court notes, see *ante,* at 2482, petitioners' convictions, if upheld, would disqualify them from or restrict their ability to engage in a variety of professions, including medicine, athletic training, and interior design. See, *e.g.,* Tex. Occ.Code Ann. § 164.051(a)(2)(B) (2003 Pamphlet) (physician); § 451.251(a)(1) (athletic trainer); § 1053.252(2) (interior designer). Indeed, were petitioners to move to one of four States, their convictions would require them to register as sex offenders to local law enforcement. See, *e.g.,* Idaho Code § 18-8304 (Cum.Supp.2002); La. Stat. Ann. § 15:542 (West Cum.Supp.2003); Miss.Code Ann. § 45-33-25 (West 2003); S.C.Code Ann. § 23-3-430 (West Cum.Supp.2002); cf. *ante,* at 2482.

And the effect of Texas' sodomy law is not just limited to the threat of prosecution or consequence of conviction. Texas' sodomy law brands all homosexuals as criminals, thereby making it more difficult for homosexuals to be treated in the same manner as everyone else. Indeed, Texas itself has previously acknowledged the collateral effects of the law, stipulating in a prior challenge to this action that the law "legally sanctions discrimination against [homosexuals] in a variety of ways unrelated to the criminal law," including in the areas of "employment, family issues, and housing."

Texas attempts to justify its law, and the effects of the law, by arguing that the statute satisfies rational basis review because it furthers the legitimate governmental interest of the promotion of morality. [This] case raises a different issue than Bowers: whether, under the Equal Protection Clause, moral disapproval is a legitimate state interest to justify by itself a statute that bans homosexual sodomy, but not heterosexual sodomy. It is not. Moral disapproval of this group, like a bare desire to harm the group, is an interest that is insufficient to satisfy rational basis review under the Equal Protection Clause. Indeed, we have never held that moral disapproval, without any other asserted state interest, is a sufficient rationale under the Equal Protection Clause to justify a law that discriminates among groups of persons.

Whether a sodomy law that is neutral both in effect and application, see Yick Wo v. Hopkins, 118 U.S. 356, 6 S.Ct. 1064, 30 L.Ed. 220 (1886), would violate the substantive component of the Due Process Clause is an issue that need not be decided today. I am confident, however, that so long as the Equal Protection Clause requires a sodomy law to apply equally to the private consensual conduct of homosexuals and heterosexuals alike, such a law would not long stand in our democratic society. In the words of Justice Jackson:

> The framers of the Constitution knew, and we should not forget today, that there is no more effective practical guaranty against arbitrary and unreasonable government than to require that the principles of law which officials would impose upon a minority be imposed generally. Conversely, nothing opens the door to arbitrary action so effectively as to allow those officials to pick and choose only a few to whom they will apply legislation and thus to escape the political retribution that might be visited upon them if larger numbers were affected.

Railway Express Agency, Inc. v. New York, 336 U.S. 106, 112-113, 69 S.Ct. 463, 93 L.Ed. 533 (1949) (concurring opinion).

Justice SCALIA, with whom THE CHIEF JUSTICE and Justice THOMAS join, dissenting.

"Liberty finds no refuge in a jurisprudence of doubt." Planned Parenthood of Southeastern Pa. v. Casey, 505 U.S. 833, 844, 112 S.Ct. 2791, 120 L.Ed.2d 674 (1992). That was the Court's sententious response, barely more than a decade ago, to those seeking to overrule Roe v. Wade, 410 U.S. 113, 93 S.Ct. 705, 35 L.Ed.2d 147 (1973). The Court's response today, to those who have engaged in a 17-year crusade to overrule Bowers v. Hardwick, 478 U.S. 186, 106 S.Ct. 2841, 92 L.Ed.2d 140 (1986), is very different. The need for stability and certainty presents no barrier.

I do not myself believe in rigid adherence to *stare decisis* in constitutional cases; but I do believe that we should be consistent rather than manipulative in invoking the doctrine. [Today's] approach to *stare decisis* invites us to overrule an erroneously decided precedent (including an "intensely divisive" decision) *if:* (1) its foundations have been "eroded" by subsequent decisions, *ante,* at 2482; (2) it has been subject to "substantial and continuing" criticism, ibid.; and (3) it has not induced "individual or societal reliance" that counsels against overturning, *ante,* at 2483. The problem is that Roe itself — which today's majority surely has no disposition to overrule — satisfies these conditions to at least the same degree as Bowers.

I do not quarrel with the Court's claim that Romer v. Evans, 517 U.S. 620, 116 S.Ct. 1620, 134 L.Ed.2d 855 (1996), "eroded" the "foundations" of Bowers' rational-basis holding. See Romer, supra, at 640-643, 116 S.Ct. 1620 (Scalia, J., dissenting). But Roe and Casey have been equally "eroded" by Washington v. Glucksberg, 521 U.S. 702, 721, 117 S.Ct. 2258, 138 L.Ed.2d 772 (1997), which held that *only* fundamental rights which are "'deeply rooted in this Nation's history and tradition'" qualify for anything other than rational basis scrutiny under the doctrine of "substantive due process." Roe and Casey, of course, subjected the restriction of abortion to heightened scrutiny without even attempting to establish that the freedom to abort *was* rooted in this Nation's tradition.

Bowers, the Court says, has been subject to "substantial and continuing [criticism], disapproving of its reasoning in all respects, not just as to its historical assumptions." Of course, Roe too (and by extension Casey) had been (and still is) subject to unrelenting criticism, including criticism from the two commentators cited by the Court today. See Fried, *supra,* at 75 ("Roe was a prime example of twisted judging"); Posner, *supra,* at 337 ("[The Court's] opinion in Roe (3)27 fails to measure up to professional expectations regarding judicial opinions"); Posner, Judicial Opinion Writing, 62 U. Chi. L.Rev. 1421, 1434 (1995) (describing the opinion in Roe as an "embarrassing performanc[e]").

[It] seems to me that the "societal reliance" on the principles confirmed in Bowers and discarded today has been overwhelming. Countless judicial decisions and legislative enactments have relied on the ancient proposition that a governing majority's belief that certain sexual behavior is "immoral and unacceptable" constitutes a rational basis for regulation. [State] laws against bigamy, same-sex marriage, adult incest, prostitution, masturbation, adultery, fornication, bestiality, and obscenity are likewise sustainable only in light of Bowers' validation of laws based on moral choices. Every single one of these laws is called into question by today's decision; the Court makes no effort to cabin the scope of its decision to exclude them from its holding.

Texas Penal Code Ann. § 21.06(a) (2003) undoubtedly imposes constraints on liberty. So do laws prohibiting prostitution, recreational use of heroin, and, for that matter, working more than 60 hours per week in a bakery. But there is no right to "liberty" under the Due Process Clause, though today's opinion repeatedly makes that claim. The Fourteenth Amendment *expressly allows* States to deprive their citizens of "liberty," *so long as "due process of law" is provided.* [Our] opinions applying the doctrine known as "substantive due process" hold that the Due Process Clause prohibits States from infringing *fundamental* liberty interests, unless the infringement is narrowly tailored to serve a compelling state interest. We have held repeatedly, in cases the Court today does not overrule, that *only* fundamental rights qualify for this so-called "heightened scrutiny" protection — that is, rights which are "'deeply rooted in this Nation's history and tradition,'" All other liberty interests may be abridged or abrogated pursuant to a validly enacted state law if that law is rationally related to a legitimate state interest.

Bowers held, first, that criminal prohibitions of homosexual sodomy are not subject to heightened scrutiny because they do not implicate a "fundamental right" under the Due Process Clause.   [The] Court today does not overrule this holding.   Not once does it describe homosexual sodomy as a "fundamental right" or a "fundamental liberty interest," nor does it subject the Texas statute to strict scrutiny.   Instead, having failed to establish that the right to homosexual sodomy is "'deeply rooted in this Nation's history and tradition,'" the Court concludes that the application of Texas's statute to petitioners' conduct fails the rational-basis test, and overrules Bowers' holding to the contrary.

The Court's description of "the state of the law" at the time of Bowers only confirms that Bowers was right.   [Our] Nation has a longstanding history of laws prohibiting *sodomy in general* — regardless of whether it was performed by same-sex or opposite-sex couples:

> *Sodomy* was a criminal offense at common law and was forbidden by the laws of the original 13 States when they ratified the Bill of Rights.   In 1868, when the Fourteenth Amendment was ratified, all but 5 of the 37 States in the Union had *criminal sodomy laws.* In fact, until 1961, all 50 States outlawed *sodomy,* and today, 24 States and the District of Columbia continue to provide criminal penalties for *sodomy* performed in private and between consenting adults.   Against this background, to claim that a right to engage in such conduct is "deeply rooted in this Nation's history and tradition" or "implicit in the concept of ordered liberty" is, at best, facetious.

Whether homosexual sodomy was prohibited by a law targeted at same-sex sexual relations or by a more general law prohibiting both homosexual and heterosexual sodomy, the only relevant point is that it *was* criminalized — which suffices to establish that homosexual sodomy is not a right "deeply rooted in our Nation's history and tradition."

In any event, an "emerging awareness" is by definition not "deeply rooted in this Nation's history and tradition[s]," as we have said "fundamental right" status requires. Constitutional entitlements do not spring into existence because some States choose to lessen or eliminate criminal sanctions on certain behavior.   Much less do they spring into existence, as the Court seems to believe, because *foreign nations* decriminalize conduct. The Court's discussion of these foreign views (ignoring, of course, the many countries that have retained criminal prohibitions on sodomy) is therefore meaningless dicta. Dangerous dicta, however, since "this Court . . . should not impose foreign moods, fads, or fashions on Americans."

I turn now to the ground on which the Court squarely rests its holding: the contention that there is no rational basis for the law here under attack.   This proposition is so out of accord with our jurisprudence — indeed, with the jurisprudence of *any* society we know — that it requires little discussion.

The Texas statute undeniably seeks to further the belief of its citizens that certain forms of sexual behavior are "immoral and unacceptable," — the same interest furthered by criminal laws against fornication, bigamy, adultery, adult incest, bestiality, and obscenity.   Bowers held that this *was* a legitimate state interest.   The Court today reaches the opposite conclusion.   The Texas statute, it says, "furthers *no legitimate state interest* which can justify its intrusion into the personal and private life of the individual," *ante,* at 2484 (emphasis addded).   The Court embraces instead Justice Stevens' declaration in his Bowers dissent, that "the fact that the governing majority in a State has traditionally viewed a particular practice as immoral is not a sufficient reason for upholding a law prohibiting the practice," *ante,* at 2483.   This effectively decrees the end of all morals legislation.   If, as the Court asserts, the promotion of majoritarian sexual morality is not even a *legitimate* state interest, none of the above-mentioned laws can survive rational-basis review.

Today's opinion is the product of a Court, which is the product of a law-profession culture, that has largely signed on to the so-called homosexual agenda, by which I mean the agenda promoted by some homosexual activists directed at eliminating the moral opprobrium that has traditionally attached to homosexual conduct.   I noted in an earlier opinion the fact that the American Association of Law Schools (to which any reputable law school *must* seek to belong) excludes from membership any school that refuses to ban from its job-interview facilities a law firm (no matter how small) that does not wish to hire as a prospective partner a person who openly engages in homosexual conduct.

It is clear from this that the Court has taken sides in the culture war, departing from its role of assuring, as neutral observer, that the democratic rules of engagement are observed. Many Americans do not want persons who openly engage in homosexual conduct as partners in their business, as scoutmasters for their children, as teachers in their children's schools, or as boarders in their home.   They view this as protecting themselves and their families from a lifestyle that they believe to be immoral and destructive.

[Let] me be clear that I have nothing against homosexuals, or any other group, promoting their agenda through normal democratic means.   Social perceptions of sexual and other morality change over time, and every group has the right to persuade its fellow citizens that its view of such matters is the best.   That homosexuals have achieved some success in that enterprise is attested to by the fact that Texas is one of the few remaining States that criminalize private, consensual homosexual acts.   But persuading one's fellow citizens is one thing, and imposing one's views in absence of democratic majority will is something else.   I would no more *require* a State to criminalize homosexual acts — or, for that matter, display *any* moral disapprobation of them — than I would *forbid* it to do so.   What Texas has chosen to do is well within the range of traditional democratic action, and its hand should not be stayed through the invention of a brand-new "constitutional right" by a Court that is impatient of democratic change.   It is indeed true that "later generations can see that laws once thought necessary and proper in fact serve only to oppress," *ante,* at 2484; and when that happens, later generations can repeal those laws. But it is the premise of our system that those judgments are to be made by the people, and not imposed by a governing caste that knows best.

Justice THOMAS, dissenting.

I join Justice Scalia's dissenting opinion.   I write separately to note that the law before the Court today "is . . . uncommonly silly."   Griswold v. Connecticut, 381 U.S. 479, 527, 85 S.Ct. 1678, 14 L.Ed.2d 510 (1965) (Stewart, J., dissenting).   If I were a member of the Texas Legislature, I would vote to repeal it. Punishing someone for expressing his sexual preference through noncommercial consensual conduct with another adult does not appear to be a worthy way to expend valuable law enforcement resources.

Notwithstanding this, I recognize that as a member of this Court I am not empowered to help petitioners and others similarly situated.   My duty, rather, is to "decide cases 'agreeably to the Constitution and laws of the United States.'" And, just like Justice Stewart, I "can find [neither in the Bill of Rights nor any other part of the Constitution a] general right of privacy," or as the Court terms it today, the "liberty of the person both in its spatial and more transcendent dimensions."

––––––––––

Comments on *Lawrence*. Is it fair to say that Justice Scalia's limitation to "the most specific level" of a relevant tradition is now a minority view? Note Justice Kennedy's finding on behalf of the new majority in *Lawrence*: "It suffices for us to acknowledge that adults may choose to enter upon this relationship in the confines of their homes and their own private lives and still retain their dignity as free persons. When sexuality finds overt expression in intimate conduct with another person, the conduct can be but one element in a personal bond that is more enduring." Also, note the majority's reliance on a more "general level" of a relevant tradition by citing to both *Griswold* and *Eisenstadt*.

What does this foretell for the future? What of "gay marriage"? Stay on board, it should be interesting. Consider, in regard to such, the following comment by Justice Kennedy in *Lawrence*: "This [opinion], as a general rule, should counsel against attempts by the State, or a court, to define the meaning of the relationship or to set its boundaries *absent injury to a person or abuse of an institution the law protects*" (emphasis added).

6. RIGHT TO DIE

Is "death" deeply rooted in our nation's history and tradition? More to the point, does the due process clause protect one's right to refuse unwanted medical treatment, or to seek a physician's assistance in terminating life quickly and with less suffering, or perhaps even suicide? In a carefully balanced approach, the Court dealt with these issues in the cases that follow.

CRUZAN v. DIRECTOR, MISSOURI DEPARTMENT OF HEALTH
497 U.S. 261 (1990)

Chief Justice REHNQUIST delivered the opinion of the Court.

On the night of January 11, 1983, Nancy Cruzan lost control of her car as she traveled down Elm Road in Jasper County, Missouri. The vehicle overturned, and Cruzan was discovered lying face down in a ditch without detectable respiratory or cardiac function. [She] remained in a coma for approximately three weeks and then progressed to an unconscious state in which she was able to orally ingest some nutrition. In order to ease feeding and further the recovery, surgeons implanted a gastrostomy feeding and hydration tube in Cruzan with the consent of her then husband. Subsequent rehabilitative efforts proved unavailing. She now lies in a Missouri state hospital in what is commonly referred to as a persistent vegetative state: generally, a condition in which a person exhibits motor reflexes but evinces no indications of significant cognitive function. The State of Missouri is bearing the cost of her care.

After it had become apparent that Nancy Cruzan has virtually no chance of regaining her mental faculties her parents asked hospital employees to terminate the artificial nutrition and hydration procedures. All agree that such a removal would cause her death. The employees refused to honor the request without court approval.

[We] granted certiorari to consider the question of whether Cruzan has a right under the United States Constitution which would require the hospital to withdraw life-sustaining treatment from her under these circumstances.

At common law, even the touching of one person by another without consent and without legal justification was a battery. [The] logical corollary of the doctrine of informed consent is that the patient generally possesses the right not to consent, that is, to refuse treatment. Until about 15 years ago and the seminal decision in In re Quinlan, 70 N.J. 10, 355 A.2d 647, cert. denied sub nom., Garger v. New Jersey, 429 U.S. 922 (1976), the number of right-to-refuse-treatment decisions were relatively few. Most of the earlier cases involved patients who refused medical treatment forbidden by their religious beliefs, thus implicating First Amendment rights as well as common law rights of self-determination. More recently, however, with the advance of medical technology capable of sustaining life well past the point where natural forces would have brought certain death in earlier times, cases involving the right to refuse life-sustaining treatment have burgeoned. [The] common-law doctrine of informed consent is viewed as generally encompassing the right of a competent individual to refuse medical treatment.

[In] this Court, the question is simply and starkly whether the United States Constitution prohibits Missouri from choosing the rule of decision which it did. [The] principle that a competent person has a constitutionally protected liberty interest in refusing unwanted medical treatment may be inferred from our prior decisions. In Jacobson v. Massachusetts, 197 U.S. 11, 24-30 (1905), for instance the Court balanced an individual's liberty interest in declining an unwanted smallpox vaccine against the State's interest in preventing disease. [Just] this Term, in the course of holding that a State's procedures for administering antipsychotic medication to prisoners were sufficient to satisfy due process concerns, we recognized that prisoners possess "a significant liberty interest in avoiding the unwanted administration of antipsychotic drugs under the Due Process Clause of the Fourteenth Amendment." Washington v. Harper.

[Petitioners] insist that under the general holdings of our cases, the forced administration of life-sustaining medical treatment, and even of artificially-delivered food and water essential to life, would implicate a competent person's liberty interest. Although we think the logic of the cases discussed above would embrace such a liberty interest, the dramatic consequences involved in refusal of such treatment would inform the inquiry as to whether the deprivation of that interest is constitutionally permissible. But for purposes of this case, we assume that the United States Constitution would grant a competent person a constitutionally protected right to refuse lifesaving hydration and nutrition.

Petitioners go on to assert that an incompetent person should possess the same right in this respect as is possessed by a competent person. [The] difficulty with petitioners' claim is that in a sense it begs the question: an incompetent person is not able to make an informed and voluntary choice to exercise a hypothetical right to refuse treatment or any other right. Such a "right" must be exercised for her, if at all, by some sort of surrogate. Here, Missouri has in effect recognized that under certain circumstances a surrogate may act for the patient in electing to have hydration and nutrition withdrawn in such a way as to cause death, but it has established a procedural safeguard to assure that the action of the surrogate conforms as best it may to the wishes expressed by the patient while competent. Missouri requires that evidence of the incompetent's wishes as to the withdrawal of treatment be proved by clear and convincing evidence. The question, then, is whether the United States Constitution forbids the establishment of this procedural requirement by the State. We hold that it does not.

[Missouri] relies on its interest in the protection and preservation of human life, and there can be no gainsaying this interest. [The] majority of States in this country have laws imposing criminal penalties on one who assists another to commit suicide. We do not think a State is required to remain neutral in the face of an informed and voluntary decision by a physically-able adult to starve to death. But in the context presented here, a State has more particular interests at stake. The choice between life and death is a deeply personal decision of obvious and overwhelming finality. We believe Missouri may legitimately seek to safeguard the personal element of this choice through the imposition of heightened evidentiary requirements. It cannot be disputed that the Due Process Clause protects an interest in life as well as an interest in refusing life-sustaining medical treatment. Not all incompetent patients will have loved ones available to serve as surrogate decisionmakers. And even where family members are present, "[t]here will, of course, be some unfortunate situations in which family members will not act to protect a patient." In re Jobes, 108 N.J. 394, 419, 529 A.2d 434, 477 (1987). A State is entitled to guard against potential abuses in such situations. Similarly a State is entitled to consider that a judicial proceeding to make a determination regarding an incompetent's wishes may very well not be an adversarial one, with the added guarantee of accurate factfinding that the adversary process brings with it. Finally, we think a State may properly decline to make judgments about the "quality" of life that a particular individual may enjoy, and simply assert an unqualified interest in the preservation of human life to be weighed against the constitutionally protected interests of the individual.

In our view, Missouri has permissibly sought to advance these interests through the adoption of a "clear and convincing" standard of proof to govern such proceedings. [We] think it self-evident that the interests at stake in the instant proceedings are more substantial, both on an individual and societal level, than those in a run-of-the-mine civil dispute. But not only does the standard of proof reflect the importance of a particular adjudication, it also serves as "a societal judgment about how the risk of error should be distributed between the litigants." The more stringent the burden of proof a party must bear, the more that party bears the risk of an erroneous decision. We believe that Missouri may permissibly place an increased risk of an erroneous decision on those seeking to terminate an incompetent individual's life-sustaining treatment. An erroneous decision not to terminate results in a maintenance of the status quo; the possibility of subsequent developments such as advancements in medical science, the discovery of new evidence regarding the patient's intent, changes in the law, or simply the unexpected death of the patient despite the administration of life-sustaining treatment at least create the potential that a wrong decision will eventually be corrected or its impact mitigated. An erroneous decision to withdraw life-sustaining treatment, however, is not susceptible of correction.

[It] is also worth noting that most, if not all, States simply forbid oral testimony entirely in determining the wishes of parties in transactions which, while important, simply do not have the consequences that a decision to terminate a person's life does. [There] is no doubt that statutes requiring wills to be in writing, and statutes of frauds which require that a contract to make a will be in writing, on occasion frustrate the effectuation of the intent of a particular decedent, just as Missouri's requirement of proof in this case may have frustrated the effectuation of the not-fully-expressed desires of Nancy Cruzan. But the Constitution does not require general rules to work faultlessly; no general rule can. In sum, we conclude that a State may apply a clear and convincing evidence standard in proceedings where a guardian seeks to discontinue nutrition and hydration of a person diagnosed to be in a persistent vegetative state.

[The] Supreme Court of Missouri held that in this case the testimony adduced at trial did not amount to clear and convincing proof of the patient's desire to have hydration and nutrition withdrawn. In so doing, it reversed a decision of the Missouri trial court which had found that the evidence "suggest[ed]" Nancy Cruzan would not have desired to continue such measures, but which had not adopted the standard of "clear and convincing evidence" enunciated by the Supreme Court. The testimony adduced at trial consisted primarily of Nancy Cruzan's statement made to a housemate about a year before her accident that she would not want to live should she face life as a "vegetable," and other observations to the same effect. The observations did not deal in terms with withdrawal of medical treatment or hydration and nutrition. We cannot say that the Supreme Court of Missouri committed constitutional error in reaching the conclusion that it did.

No doubt is engendered by anything in this record but that Nancy Cruzan's mother and father are loving and caring parents. If the State were required by the United States Constitution to repose a right of "substituted judgment" with anyone, the Cruzans would surely qualify. But we do not think the Due Process Clause requires the State to repose judgment on these matters with anyone but the patient herself. Close family members may have a strong feeling — a feeling not at all ignoble or unworthy, but not entirely disinterested, either — that they do not wish to witness the continuation of the life of a loved one which they regard as hopeless, meaningless, and even degrading. But there is no automatic assurance that the view of close family members will necessarily be the same as the patient's would have been had she been confronted with the prospect of her situation while competent.   [The] judgment of the Supreme Court of Missouri is affirmed.

Justice O'CONNOR, concurring.

I agree that a protected liberty interest in refusing unwanted medical treatment may be inferred from our prior decisions, and that the refusal of artificially delivered food and water is encompassed within that liberty interest. I write separately to clarify why I believe this to be so.

[The] liberty interest in refusing medical treatment flows from decisions involving the State's invasions into the body. Because our notions of liberty are inextricably entwined with our idea of physical freedom and self-determination, the Court has often deemed state incursions into the body repugnant to the interests protected by the Due Process Clause. [The] State's imposition of medical treatment on an unwilling competent adult necessarily involves some form of restraint and intrusion.   [Artificial] feeding cannot readily be distinguished from other forms of medical treatment.

[I] also write separately to emphasize that the Court does not today decide the issue whether a State must also give effect to the decisions of a surrogate decisionmaker. In my view, such a duty may well be constitutionally required to protect the patient's liberty interest in refusing medical treatment. Few individuals provide explicit oral or written instructions regarding their intent to refuse medical treatment should they become incompetent.

Justice SCALIA, concurring.

[I] would have preferred that we announce, clearly and promptly, that the federal courts have no business in this field; that American law has always accorded the State the power to prevent, by force if necessary, suicide — including suicide by refusing to take appropriate measures necessary to preserve one's life; that the point at which life becomes "worthless," and the point at which the means necessary to preserve it become "extraordinary" or "inappropriate," are neither set forth in the Constitution nor known to the nine Justices of this Court any better than they are known to nine people picked at random from the Kansas City telephone directory; and hence, that even when it is demonstrated by clear and convincing evidence that a patient no longer wishes certain measures to be taken to preserve her life, it is up to the citizens of Missouri to decide, through their elected representatives, whether that wish will be honored.

[The] text of the Due Process Clause does not protect individuals against deprivations of liberty simpliciter. It protects them against deprivations of liberty "without due process of law." To determine that such a deprivation would not occur if Nancy Cruzan were forced to take nourishment against her will, it is unnecessary to reopen the historically recurrent debate over whether "due process" includes substantive restrictions.

[It] is at least true that no "substantive due process" claim can be maintained unless the claimant demonstrates that the State has deprived him of a right historically and traditionally protected against State interference. That cannot possibly be established here.

At common law in England, a suicide — defined as one who "deliberately puts an end to his own existence, or commits any unlawful malicious act, the consequence of which is his own death," 4 W. Blackstone, Commentaries — was criminally liable. [And] most States that did not explicitly prohibit assisted suicide in 1868 recognized, when the issue arose in the 50 years following the Fourteenth Amendment's ratification, that assisted and (in some cases) attempted suicide were unlawful.

[Petitioners] rely on three distinctions to separate Nancy Cruzan's case from ordinary suicide: (1) that she is permanently incapacited and in pain; (2) that she would bring on her death not by any affirmative act but by merely declining treatment that provides nourishment; and (3) that preventing her from effectuating her presumed wish to die requires violation of her bodily integrity. None of these suffices. . . .

[Are] there, then, no reasonable and humane limits that ought not to be exceeded in requiring an individual to preserve his own life? There obviously are, but they are not set forth in the Due Process Clause. What assures us that those limits will not be exceeded is the same constitutional guarantee that is the source of most of our protection — what protects us, for example, from being assessed a tax of 100% of our income above the subsistence level, from being forbidden to drive cars, or from being required to send our children to school for 10 hours a day, none of which horribles is categorically prohibited by the Constitution. Our salvation is the Equal Protection Clause, which requires the democratic majority to accept for themselves and their loved ones what they impose on you and me. This Court need not, and has no authority to, inject itself into every field of human activity where irrationality and oppression may theoretically occur, and if it tries to do so it will destroy itself.

Justice BRENNAN, with whom Justice MARSHALL and Justice BLACKMUN join, dissenting.

[The] Court concedes that our prior decisions "support the recognition of a general liberty interest in refusing medical treatment." The Court, however, avoids discussing either the measure of that liberty interest or its application by assuming, for purposes of this case only, that a competent person has a constitutionally protected liberty interest in being free of unwanted artificial nutrition and hydration.

[But] if a competent person has a liberty interest to be free of unwanted medical treatment, as both the majority and Justice O'Connor concede, it must be fundamental. [Whatever] other liberties protected by the Due Process Clause are fundamental, "those liberties that are 'deeply rooted in this Nation's history and tradition'" are among them. [The] right to be free from unwanted medical attention is a right to evaluate the potential benefit of treatment and its possible consequences according to one's own values and to make a personal decision whether to subject oneself to intrusion. For a patient like Nancy Cruzan, the sole benefit of medical treatment is being kept metabolically alive. Neither artificial nutrition nor any other form of medical treatment available today can cure or in any way ameliorate her condition. Irreversibly vegetative patients are devoid of thought, emotion and sensation; they are permanently and completely unconscious.

[Although] the right to be free of unwanted medical intervention, like other constitutionally protected interests, may not be absolute, no State interest could outweigh the rights of an individual in Nancy Cruzan's position. Whatever a State's possible interests in mandating life-support treatment under other circumstances, there is no good to be obtained here by Missouri's insistence that Nancy Cruzan remain on life-support systems if it is indeed her wish not to do so. Missouri does not claim, nor could it, that society as a whole will be benefited by Nancy's receiving medical treatment. No third party's situation will be improved and no harm to others will be averted.

The only state interest asserted here is a general interest in the preservation of life. But the State has no legitimate general interest in someone's life, completely abstracted from the interest of the person living that life, that could outweigh the person's choice to avoid medical treatment.

[This] is not to say that the State has no legitimate interests to assert here. As the majority recognizes Missouri has a parens patriae interest in providing Nancy Cruzan, now incompetent, with as accurate as possible a determination of how she would exercise her rights under these circumstances. Second, if and when it is determined that Nancy Cruzan would want to continue treatment, the State may legitimately assert an interest in providing that treatment. But until Nancy's wishes have been determined, the only state interest that may be asserted is an interest in safeguarding the accuracy of that determination.

Accuracy, therefore, must be our touchstone. Missouri may constitutionally impose only those procedural requirements that serve to enhance the accuracy of a determination of Nancy Cruzan's wishes or are at least consistent with an accurate determination. The Missouri "safeguard" that the Court upholds today does not meet that standard. [Missouri's] rule of decision imposes a markedly asymmetrical evidentiary burden. Only evidence of specific statements of treatment choice made by the patient when competent is admissible to support a finding that the patient, now in a persistent vegetative state, would wish to avoid further medical treatment. Moreover, this evidence must be clear and convincing. No proof is required to support a finding that the incompetent person would wish to continue treatment.

[Even] more than its heightened evidentiary standard, the Missouri court's categorical exclusion of relevant evidence dispenses with any semblance of accurate factfinding. The court adverted to no evidence supporting its decision, but held that no clear and convincing, inherently reliable evidence has been presented to show that Nancy would want to avoid further treatment. In doing so, the court failed to consider statements Nancy had made to family members and a close friend. The court also failed to consider testimony from Nancy's mother and sister that they were certain that Nancy would want to discontinue artificial nutrition and hydration, even after the court found that Nancy's family was loving and without malignant motive.

[Too] few people execute living wills or equivalently formal directives for such an evidentiary rule to ensure adequately that the wishes of incompetent persons will be honored. While it might be a wise social policy to encourage people to furnish such instructions, no general conclusion about a patient's choice can be drawn from the absence of formalities. The probability of becoming irreversibly vegetative is so low that many people may not feel an urgency to marshal formal evidence of their preferences. Some may not wish to dwell on their own physical deterioration and mortality. Even someone with a resolute determination to avoid life-support under circumstances such as Nancy's would still need to know that such things as living wills exist and how to execute one. Often legal help would be necessary, especially given the majority's apparent willingness to permit States to insist that a person's wishes are not truly known unless the particular medical treatment is specified.

[To] be constitutionally permissible, Missouri's intrusion upon these fundamental liberties must, at a minimum, bear a reasonable relationship to a legitimate state end. Missouri asserts that its policy is related to a state interest in the protection of life. In my view, however, it is an effort to define life, rather than to protect it, that is the heart of Missouri's policy. Missouri insists, without regard to Nancy Cruzan's own interests, upon equating her life with the biological persistence of her bodily functions. Nancy Cruzan, it must be remembered, is not now simply incompetent. She is in a persistent vegetative state, and has been so for seven years. The trial court found, and no party contested, that Nancy has no possibility of recovery and no consciousness.

It seems to me that the Court errs insofar as it characterizes this case as involving "judgments about the 'quality' of life that a particular individual may enjoy." Nancy Cruzan is obviously "alive" in a physiological sense. But for patients like Nancy Cruzan, who have no consciousness and no chance of recovery, there is a serious question as to whether the mere persistence of their bodies is "life" as that word is commonly understood, or as it is used in both the Constitution and the Declaration of Independence. The State's unflagging determination to perpetuate Nancy Cruzan's physical existence is comprehensible only after an effort to define life's meaning, not as an attempt to preserve its sanctity.

[In] short, there is no reasonable ground for believing that Nancy Beth Cruzan has any personal interest in the perpetuation of what the State has decided is her life. As I have already suggested, it would be possible to hypothesize such an interest on the basis of theological or philosophical conjecture. But even to posit such a basis for the State's action is to condemn it. It is not within the province of secular government to circumscribe the liberties of the people by regulations designed wholly for the purposes of establishing a sectarian definition of life.

[Only] because Missouri has arrogated to itself the power to define life, and only because the Court permits this usurpation, are Nancy Cruzan's life and liberty put into disquieting conflict. If Nancy Cruzan's life were defined by reference to her own interests, so that her life expired when her biological existence ceased serving any of her own interests, then her constitutionally protected interest in freedom from unwanted treatment would not come into conflict with her constitutionally protected interest in life. Conversely, if there were any evidence that Nancy Cruzan herself defined life to encompass every form of biological persistence by a human being, so that the continuation of treatment would serve Nancy's own liberty, then once again there would be no conflict between life and liberty. The opposition of life and liberty in this case are thus not the result of Nancy Cruzan's tragic accident, but are instead the artificial consequence of Missouri's effort, and this Court's willingness, to abstract Nancy Cruzan's life from Nancy Cruzan's person.

[The] Cruzan family's continuing concern provides a concrete reminder that Nancy Cruzan's interests did not disappear with her vitality or her consciousness. [Lives] do not exist in abstraction from persons, and to pretend otherwise is not to honor but to desecrate the State's responsibility for protecting life. A State that seeks to demonstrate its commitment to life may do so by aiding those who are actively struggling for life and health. In this endeavor, unfortunately, no State can lack for opportunities: there can be no need to make an example of tragic cases like that of Nancy Cruzan.

I respectfully dissent.

WASHINGTON v. GLUCKSBERG

521 U.S. 702 (1997)

Chief Justice REHNQUIST delivered the opinion of the Court.

The question presented in this case is whether Washington's prohibition against "caus[ing]" or "aid[ing]" a suicide offends the Fourteenth Amendment to the United States Constitution. We hold that it does not.

It has always been a crime to assist a suicide in the State of Washington. In 1854, Washington's first Territorial Legislature outlawed "assisting another in the commission of self-murder." Today, Washington law provides: "A person is guilty of promoting a suicide attempt when he knowingly causes or aids another person to attempt suicide." "Promoting a suicide attempt" is a felony, punishable by up to five years' imprisonment and up to a $10,000 fine. At the same time, Washington's Natural Death Act, enacted in 1979, states that the "withholding or withdrawal of life-sustaining treatment" at a patient's direction "shall not, for any purpose, constitute a suicide."

Petitioners in this case are the State of Washington and its Attorney General. Respondents Harold Glucksberg, M. D., Abigail Halperin, M. D., Thomas A. Preston, M. D., and Peter Shalit, M. D., are physicians who practice in Washington. These doctors occasionally treat terminally ill, suffering patients, and declare that they would assist these patients in ending their lives if not for Washington's assisted-suicide ban. In January 1994, respondents, along with three gravely ill, pseudonymous plaintiffs who have since died and Compassion in Dying, a nonprofit organization that counsels people considering physician-assisted suicide, sued in the United States District Court, seeking a declaration that Wash.Rev.Code § 9A.36.060(1) (1994) is, on its face, unconstitutional.

The plaintiffs asserted "the existence of a liberty interest protected by the Fourteenth Amendment which extends to a personal choice by a mentally competent, terminally ill adult to commit physician-assisted suicide." Ibid. Relying primarily on Planned Parenthood of Southeastern Pa. v. Casey, 505 U.S. 833, 112 S.Ct. 2791, 120 L.Ed.2d 674 (1992), and Cruzan v. Director, Mo. Dept. of Health, 497 U.S. 261, 110 S.Ct. 2841, 111 L.Ed.2d 224 (1990), the District Court agreed, 850 F.Supp., at 1459-1462, and concluded that Washington's assisted-suicide ban is unconstitutional because it "places an undue burden on the exercise of [that] constitutionally protected liberty interest."

A panel of the Court of Appeals for the Ninth Circuit reversed, emphasizing that "[i]n the two hundred and five years of our existence no constitutional right to aid in killing oneself has ever been asserted and upheld by a court of final jurisdiction." The Ninth Circuit reheard the case en banc, reversed the panel's decision, and affirmed the District Court. The court . . . discussed what it described as "historical" and "current societal attitudes" toward suicide and assisted suicide, and concluded that "the Constitution encompasses a due process liberty interest in controlling the time and manner of one's death — that there is, in short, a constitutionally-recognized 'right to die.'" After "[w]eighing and then balancing" this interest against Washington's various interests, the court held that the State's assisted-suicide ban was unconstitutional "as applied to terminally ill competent adults who wish to hasten their deaths with medication prescribed by their physicians."[6]

---

[6] Although, as Justice Stevens observes, 521 U.S., at 739, 117 S.Ct., at 2304 (opinion concurring in judgments), "[the court's] analysis and eventual holding that the statute was unconstitutional was not limited to a particular set of plaintiffs before it," the court did note that "[d]eclaring a statute unconstitutional as applied to members of a group is atypical but not uncommon." 79 F.3d, at 798, n. 9, and emphasized that it was "not

We begin, as we do in all due process cases, by examining our Nation's history, legal traditions, and practices. In almost every State — indeed, in almost every western democracy — it is a crime to assist a suicide. The States' assisted-suicide bans are not innovations. Rather, they are longstanding expressions of the States' commitment to the protection and preservation of all human life. Indeed, opposition to and condemnation of suicide — and, therefore, of assisting suicide — are consistent and enduring themes of our philosophical, legal, and cultural heritages. More specifically, for over 700 years, the Anglo-American common-law tradition has punished or otherwise disapproved of both suicide and assisting suicide. In the 13th century, Henry de Bracton, one of the first legal-treatise writers, observed that "[j]ust as a man may commit felony by slaying another so may he do so by slaying himself." The real and personal property of one who killed himself to avoid conviction and punishment for a crime were forfeit to the King; however, thought Bracton, "if a man slays himself in weariness of life or because he is unwilling to endure further bodily pain . . . [only] his movable goods [were] confiscated." Thus, "[t]he principle that suicide of a sane person, for whatever reason, was a punishable felony was . . . introduced into English common law." Centuries later, Sir William Blackstone, whose Commentaries on the Laws of England not only provided a definitive summary of the common law but was also a primary legal authority for 18th- and 19th-century American lawyers, referred to suicide as "self-murder" and "the pretended heroism, but real cowardice, of the Stoic philosophers, who destroyed themselves to avoid those ills which they had not the fortitude to endure. . . ." 4 W. Blackstone, Commentaries *189. Blackstone emphasized that "the law has . . . ranked [suicide] among the highest crimes."

For the most part, the early American Colonies adopted the common-law approach. [Over] time, however, the American Colonies abolished these harsh common-law penalties. [The] movement away from the common law's harsh sanctions did not represent an acceptance of suicide; rather, as Chief Justice Swift observed, this change reflected the growing consensus that it was unfair to punish the suicide's family for his wrongdoing. [Courts] continued to condemn it as a grave public wrong.

That suicide remained a grievous, though nonfelonious, wrong is confirmed by the fact that colonial and early state legislatures and courts did not retreat from prohibiting assisting suicide. [And] the prohibitions against assisting suicide never contained exceptions for those who were near death. The earliest American statute explicitly to outlaw assisting suicide was enacted in New York in 1828, and many of the new States and Territories followed New York's example. [By] the time the Fourteenth Amendment was ratified, it was a crime in most States to assist a suicide. In this century, the Model Penal Code also prohibited "aiding" suicide, prompting many States to enact or revise their assisted-suicide bans.

[Though] deeply rooted, the States' assisted-suicide bans have in recent years been reexamined and, generally, reaffirmed. Because of advances in medicine and technology, Americans today are increasingly likely to die in institutions, from chronic illnesses. President's Comm'n for the Study of Ethical Problems in Medicine and Biomedical and Behavioral Research, Deciding to Forego Life-Sustaining Treatment 16-18 (1983). Public concern and democratic action are therefore sharply focused on how best to protect dignity and independence at the end of life, with the result that there have been many

---

deciding the facial validity of [the Washington statute]," id., at 797-798, and nn. 8-9. It is therefore the court's holding that Washington's physician-assisted suicide statute is unconstitutional as applied to the "class of terminally ill, mentally competent patients," 521 U.S., at 750, 117 S.Ct., at 2309 (Stevens, J., concurring in judgments), that is before us today.

significant changes in state laws and in the attitudes these laws reflect. Many States, for example, now permit "living wills," surrogate health-care decisionmaking, and the withdrawal or refusal of life-sustaining medical treatment. At the same time, however, voters and legislators continue for the most part to reaffirm their States' prohibitions on assisting suicide.

[In] 1991, Washington voters rejected a ballot initiative which, had it passed, would have permitted a form of physician-assisted suicide. Washington then added a provision to the Natural Death Act expressly excluding physician-assisted suicide. [California] voters rejected an assisted-suicide initiative similar to Washington's in 1993. On the other hand, in 1994, voters in Oregon enacted, also through ballot initiative, that State's "Death With Dignity Act," which legalized physician-assisted suicide for competent, terminally ill adults. Since the Oregon vote, many proposals to legalize assisted-suicide have been and continue to be introduced in the States' legislatures, but none has been enacted. And just last year, Iowa and Rhode Island joined the overwhelming majority of States explicitly prohibiting assisted suicide. Also, on April 30, 1997, President Clinton signed the Federal Assisted Suicide Funding Restriction Act of 1997, which prohibits the use of federal funds in support of physician-assisted suicide. Attitudes toward suicide itself have changed since Bracton, but our laws have consistently condemned, and continue to prohibit, assisting suicide.

The Due Process Clause guarantees more than fair process, and the "liberty" it protects includes more than the absence of physical restraint. [We] have also assumed, and strongly suggested, that the Due Process Clause protects the traditional right to refuse unwanted lifesaving medical treatment. But we "ha[ve] always been reluctant to expand the concept of substantive due process because guideposts for responsible decisionmaking in this unchartered area are scarce and open-ended." By extending constitutional protection to an asserted right or liberty interest, we, to a great extent, place the matter outside the arena of public debate and legislative action. We must therefore "exercise the utmost care whenever we are asked to break new ground in this field," lest the liberty protected by the Due Process Clause be subtly transformed into the policy preferences of the Members of this Court.

Our established method of substantive-due-process analysis has two primary features: First, we have regularly observed that the Due Process Clause specially protects those fundamental rights and liberties which are, objectively, "deeply rooted in this Nation's history and tradition," *Moore* ("so rooted in the traditions and conscience of our people as to be ranked as fundamental"), and "implicit in the concept of ordered liberty," such that "neither liberty nor justice would exist if they were sacrificed," *Palko* Second, we have required in substantive-due-process cases a "careful description" of the asserted fundamental liberty interest. Our Nation's history, legal traditions, and practices thus provide the crucial "guideposts for responsible decisionmaking," that direct and restrain our exposition of the Due Process Clause.

[Justice] Souter, relying on Justice Harlan's dissenting opinion in Poe v. Ullman, would largely abandon this restrained methodology, and instead ask "whether [Washington's] statute sets up one of those 'arbitrary impositions' or 'purposeless restraints' at odds with the Due Process Clause of the Fourteenth Amendment," *post,* at 2275 (quoting Poe, 367 U.S. 497, 543, 81 S.Ct. 1752, 1776-1777, 6 L.Ed.2d 989 (1961) (Harlan, J., dissenting)). In our view, however, the development of this Court's substantive-due-process jurisprudence, described briefly *supra,* at 2267, has been a process whereby the outlines of the "liberty" specially protected by the Fourteenth Amendment —

never fully clarified, to be sure, and perhaps not capable of being fully clarified — have at least been carefully refined by concrete examples involving fundamental rights found to be deeply rooted in our legal tradition. This approach tends to rein in the subjective elements that are necessarily present in due-process judicial review.

[The] question before us is whether the "liberty" specially protected by the Due Process Clause includes a right to commit suicide which itself includes a right to assistance in doing so. We now inquire whether this asserted right has any place in our Nation's traditions. Here we are confronted with a consistent and almost universal tradition that has long rejected the asserted right, and continues explicitly to reject it today, even for terminally ill, mentally competent adults. To hold for respondents, we would have to reverse centuries of legal doctrine and practice, and strike down the considered policy choice of almost every State. Respondents contend, however, that the liberty interest they assert *is* consistent with this Court's substantive-due-process line of cases, if not with this Nation's history and practice.

[Respondents] contend that in Cruzan we "acknowledged that competent, dying persons have the right to direct the removal of life-sustaining medical treatment and thus hasten death," Brief for Respondents 23, and that "the constitutional principle behind recognizing the patient's liberty to direct the withdrawal of artificial life support applies at least as strongly to the choice to hasten impending death by consuming lethal medication." [The] right assumed in Cruzan, however, was not simply deduced from abstract concepts of personal autonomy. Given the common-law rule that forced medication was a battery, and the long legal tradition protecting the decision to refuse unwanted medical treatment, our assumption was entirely consistent with this Nation's history and constitutional traditions. The decision to commit suicide with the assistance of another may be just as personal and profound as the decision to refuse unwanted medical treatment, but it has never enjoyed similar legal protection.

[Respondents] also rely on Casey. [The] Court of Appeals, like the District Court, found Casey "'highly instructive'" and "'almost prescriptive'" for determining "'what liberty interest may inhere in a terminally ill person's choice to commit suicide'": "Like the decision of whether or not to have an abortion, the decision how and when to die is one of 'the most intimate and personal choices a person may make in a lifetime,' a choice 'central to personal dignity and autonomy.'" By choosing this language, the Court's opinion in Casey described, in a general way and in light of our prior cases, those personal activities and decisions that this Court has identified as so deeply rooted in our history and traditions, or so fundamental to our concept of constitutionally ordered liberty, that they are protected by the Fourteenth Amendment. The opinion moved from the recognition that liberty necessarily includes freedom of conscience and belief about ultimate considerations to the observation that "though the abortion decision may originate within the zone of conscience and belief, it is *more than a philosophic exercise.*" (emphasis added). That many of the rights and liberties protected by the Due Process Clause sound in personal autonomy does not warrant the sweeping conclusion that any and all important, intimate, and personal decisions are so protected, and Casey did not suggest otherwise.

The history of the law's treatment of assisted suicide in this country has been and continues to be one of the rejection of nearly all efforts to permit it. That being the case, our decisions lead us to conclude that the asserted "right" to assistance in committing suicide is not a fundamental liberty interest protected by the Due Process Clause. The Constitution also requires, however, that Washington's assisted-suicide ban be rationally related to legitimate government interests. This requirement is unquestionably met here.

As the court below recognized, Washington's assisted-suicide ban implicates a number of state interests.

First, Washington has an "unqualified interest in the preservation of human life." Cruzan, 497 U.S., at 282, 110 S.Ct., at 2853. The State's prohibition on assisted suicide, like all homicide laws, both reflects and advances its commitment to this interest. This interest is symbolic and aspirational as well as practical. The Court of Appeals also recognized Washington's interest in protecting life, but held that the "weight" of this interest depends on the "medical condition and the wishes of the person whose life is at stake." As we have previously affirmed, the States "may properly decline to make judgments about the 'quality' of life that a particular individual may enjoy." This remains true, as Cruzan makes clear, even for those who are near death.

Relatedly, all admit that suicide is a serious public-health problem, especially among persons in otherwise vulnerable groups. The State has an interest in preventing suicide, and in studying, identifying, and treating its causes. Those who attempt suicide — terminally ill or not — often suffer from depression or other mental disorders. [Research] indicates, however, that many people who request physician-assisted suicide withdraw that request if their depression and pain are treated. Thus, legal physician-assisted suicide could make it more difficult for the State to protect depressed or mentally ill persons, or those who are suffering from untreated pain, from suicidal impulses.

The State also has an interest in protecting the integrity and ethics of the medical profession. [The] American Medical Association, like many other medical and physicians' groups, has concluded that "[p]hysician-assisted suicide is fundamentally incompatible with the physician's role as healer." And physician-assisted suicide could, it is argued, undermine the trust that is essential to the doctor-patient relationship by blurring the time-honored line between healing and harming.

Next, the State has an interest in protecting vulnerable groups — including the poor, the elderly, and disabled persons — from abuse, neglect, and mistakes. [We] have recognized, however, the real risk of subtle coercion and undue influence in end-of-life situations. Cruzan, 497 U.S., at 281, 110 S.Ct., at 2852. Similarly, the New York Task Force warned that "[l]egalizing physician-assisted suicide would pose profound risks to many individuals who are ill and vulnerable. . . . The risk of harm is greatest for the many individuals in our society whose autonomy and well-being are already compromised by poverty, lack of access to good medical care, advanced age, or membership in a stigmatized social group." If physician-assisted suicide were permitted, many might resort to it to spare their families the substantial financial burden of end-of-life health-care costs. The State's interest here goes beyond protecting the vulnerable from coercion; it extends to protecting disabled and terminally ill people from prejudice, negative and inaccurate stereotypes, and "societal indifference."

Finally, the State may fear that permitting assisted suicide will start it down the path to voluntary and perhaps even involuntary euthanasia. Thus, it turns out that what is couched as a limited right to "physician-assisted suicide" is likely, in effect, a much broader license, which could prove extremely difficult to police and contain. This concern is further supported by evidence about the practice of euthanasia in the Netherlands. The Dutch government's own study revealed that in 1990, there were 2,300 cases of voluntary euthanasia (defined as "the deliberate termination of another's life at his request"), 400 cases of assisted suicide, and more than 1,000 cases of euthanasia without an explicit request. In addition to these latter 1,000 cases, the study found an additional 4,941 cases where physicians administered lethal morphine overdoses without the patients' explicit consent. Physician-Assisted Suicide and Euthanasia in the Netherlands: A Report of Chairman Charles T. Canady, *supra*, at 12-13 (citing Dutch study). This study suggests that, despite the existence of various reporting procedures, euthanasia in the Netherlands has not been limited to competent, terminally ill adults who are enduring physical suffering, and that regulation of the practice may not have prevented abuses in cases involving vulnerable persons, including severely disabled neonates and elderly persons suffering from dementia. Washington, like most other States, reasonably ensures against this risk by banning, rather than regulating, assisting suicide.

We need not weigh exactly the relative strengths of these various interests. They are unquestionably important and legitimate, and Washington's ban on assisted suicide is at least reasonably related to their promotion and protection. We therefore hold that Wash. Rev.Code § 9A.36.060(1) (1994) does not violate the Fourteenth Amendment, either on its face or "as applied to competent, terminally ill adults who wish to hasten their deaths by obtaining medication prescribed by their doctors."[24]

Throughout the Nation, Americans are engaged in an earnest and profound debate about the morality, legality, and practicality of physician-assisted suicide. Our holding permits this debate to continue, as it should in a democratic society. [Reversed]

Justice O'CONNOR, concurring. [Justice Ginsburg concurs in the Court's judgments substantially for the reasons stated in this opinion. Justice Breyer joins this opinion except insofar as it joins the opinions of the Court.]

[I] join the Court's opinions because I agree that there is no generalized right to "commit suicide." But respondents urge us to address the narrower question whether a mentally competent person who is experiencing great suffering has a constitutionally cognizable interest in controlling the circumstances of his or her imminent death. I see no need to reach that question in the context of the facial challenges to the New York and Washington laws at issue here. The parties and *amici* agree that in these States a patient who is suffering from a terminal illness and who is experiencing great pain has no legal barriers to obtaining medication, from qualified physicians, to alleviate that suffering, even to the point of causing unconsciousness and hastening death. In this light, even assuming that we would recognize such an interest, I agree that the State's interests in protecting those who are not truly competent or facing imminent death, or those whose decisions to hasten death would not truly be voluntary, are sufficiently weighty to justify a prohibition against physician-assisted suicide.

Justice STEVENS, concurring in the judgments.

Today, the Court decides that Washington's statute prohibiting assisted suicide is not invalid "on its face," that is to say, in all or most cases in which it might be applied. That

---

[24] Justice Stevens states that "the Court does conceive of respondents' claim as a facial challenge — addressing not the application of the statute to a particular set of plaintiffs before it, but the constitutionality of the statute's categorical prohibition. . . ." 521 U.S., at 740, 117 S.Ct., at 2305 (opinion concurring in judgments). We emphasize that we today reject the Court of Appeals' specific holding that the statute is unconstitutional "as applied" to a particular class. See n. 6, *supra*. Justice Stevens agrees with this holding, see 521 U.S., at 750, 117 S.Ct., at 2309, but would not "foreclose the possibility that an individual plaintiff seeking to hasten her death, or a doctor whose assistance was sought, could prevail in a more particularized challenge," ibid. Our opinion does not absolutely foreclose such a claim. However, given our holding that the Due Process Clause of the Fourteenth Amendment does not provide heightened protection to the asserted liberty interest in ending one's life with a physician's assistance, such a claim would have to be quite different from the ones advanced by respondents here.

holding, however, does not foreclose the possibility that some applications of the statute might well be invalid.

[History] and tradition provide ample support for refusing to recognize an open-ended constitutional right to commit suicide. [The] State has an interest in preserving and fostering the benefits that every human being may provide to the community — a community that thrives on the exchange of ideas, expressions of affection, shared memories, and humorous incidents, as well as on the material contributions that its members create and support. The value to others of a person's life is far too precious to allow the individual to claim a constitutional entitlement to complete autonomy in making a decision to end that life. Thus, I fully agree with the Court that the "liberty" protected by the Due Process Clause does not include a categorical "right to commit suicide which itself includes a right to assistance in doing so."

But just as our conclusion that capital punishment is not always unconstitutional did not preclude later decisions holding that it is sometimes impermissibly cruel, so is it equally clear that a decision upholding a general statutory prohibition of assisted suicide does not mean that every possible application of the statute would be valid.

In Cruzan v. Director, Mo. Dept. of Health, 497 U.S. 261, 110 S.Ct. 2841, 111 L.Ed.2d 224 (1990), the Court assumed that the interest in liberty protected by the Fourteenth Amendment encompassed the right of a terminally ill patient to direct the withdrawal of life-sustaining treatment. [Nancy] Cruzan's interest in refusing medical care was incidental to her more basic interest in controlling the manner and timing of her death. [The] source of Nancy Cruzan's right to refuse treatment was not just a common-law rule. Rather, this right is an aspect of a far broader and more basic concept of freedom that is even older than the common law. This freedom embraces not merely a person's right to refuse a particular kind of unwanted treatment, but also her interest in dignity, and in determining the character of the memories that will survive long after her death. [Avoiding] intolerable pain and the indignity of living one's final days incapacitated and in agony is certainly "[a]t the heart of [the] liberty . . . to define one's own concept of existence, of meaning, of the universe, and of the mystery of human life." While I agree with the Court that Cruzan does not decide the issue presented by these cases, Cruzan did give recognition, not just to vague, unbridled notions of autonomy, but to the more specific interest in making decisions about how to confront an imminent death. Although there is no absolute right to physician-assisted suicide, Cruzan makes it clear that some individuals who no longer have the option of deciding whether to live or to die because they are already on the threshold of death have a constitutionally protected interest that may outweigh the State's interest in preserving life at all costs. The liberty interest at stake in a case like this differs from, and is stronger than, both the common-law right to refuse medical treatment and the unbridled interest in deciding whether to live or die. It is an interest in deciding how, rather than whether, a critical threshold shall be crossed.

The state interests supporting a general rule banning the practice of physician-assisted suicide do not have the same force in all cases. First and foremost of these interests is the "'unqualified interest in the preservation of human life.'" Although as a general matter the State's interest in the contributions each person may make to society outweighs the person's interest in ending her life, this interest does not have the same force for a terminally ill patient faced not with the choice of whether to live, only of how to die. Allowing the individual, rather than the State, to make judgments "'about the "quality" of life that a particular individual may enjoy," (quoting Cruzan, 497 U.S., at 282, 110 S.Ct., at 2853), does not mean that the lives of terminally ill, disabled people have less value than the lives of those who are healthy. Rather, it gives proper recognition to the individual's interest in choosing a final chapter that accords with her life story, rather than one that demeans her values and poisons memories of her.

Similarly, the State's legitimate interests in preventing suicide, protecting the vulnerable from coercion and abuse, and preventing euthanasia are less significant in this context. I agree that the State has a compelling interest in preventing persons from committing suicide because of depression or coercion by third parties. But the State's legitimate interest in preventing abuse does not apply to an individual who is not victimized by abuse, who is not suffering from depression, and who makes a rational and voluntary decision to seek assistance in dying. Relatedly, the State and *amici* express the concern that patients whose physical pain is inadequately treated will be more likely to request assisted suicide. [For] such an individual, the State's interest in preventing potential abuse and mistake is only minimally implicated.

The final major interest asserted by the State is its interest in preserving the traditional integrity of the medical profession. The fear is that a rule permitting physicians to assist in suicide is inconsistent with the perception that they serve their patients solely as healers. But for some patients, it would be a physician's refusal to dispense medication to ease their suffering and make their death tolerable and dignified that would be inconsistent with the healing role. [Furthermore], because physicians are already involved in making decisions that hasten the death of terminally ill patients — through termination of life support, withholding of medical treatment, and terminal sedation — there is in fact significant tension between the traditional view of the physician's role and the actual practice in a growing number of cases.

Although, as the Court concludes today, these *potential* harms are sufficient to support the State's general public policy against assisted suicide, they will not always outweigh the individual liberty interest of a particular patient. Unlike the Court of Appeals, I would not say as a categorical matter that these state interests are invalid as to the entire class of terminally ill, mentally competent patients. I do not, however, foreclose the possibility that an individual plaintiff seeking to hasten her death, or a doctor whose assistance was sought, could prevail in a more particularized challenge. Future cases will determine whether such a challenge may succeed.

Justice SOUTER, concurring in the judgment.

The question is whether the statute sets up one of those "arbitrary impositions" or "purposeless restraints" at odds with the Due Process Clause of the Fourteenth Amendment. Poe v. Ullman, 367 U.S. 497, 543, 81 S.Ct. 1752, 1776-1777, 6 L.Ed.2d 989 (1961) (Harlan, J., dissenting). For two centuries American courts, and for much of that time this Court, have thought it necessary to provide some degree of review over the substantive content of legislation under constitutional standards of textual breadth. The obligation was understood before Dred Scott and has continued after the repudiation of Lochner's progeny. This enduring tradition of American constitutional practice is, in Justice Harlan's view, nothing more than what is required by the judicial authority and obligation to construe constitutional text and review legislation for conformity to that text. Like many judges who preceded him and many who followed, he found it impossible to construe the text of due process without recognizing substantive, and not merely procedural, limitations. [The] business of such review is not the identification of extra textual absolutes but scrutiny of a legislative resolution (perhaps unconscious) of clashing principles, each quite possibly worthy in and of itself, but each to be weighed within the history of our values as a people. It is a comparison of the relative strengths of opposing claims that informs the judicial task, not a deduction from some first premise. Thus informed, judicial review still has no warrant to substitute one reasonable resolution of the contending positions for another, but authority to supplant the balance already struck between the contenders only when it falls outside the realm of the reasonable.

[My] understanding of unenumerated rights in the wake of the Poe dissent and subsequent cases avoids the absolutist failing of many older cases without embracing the opposite pole of equating reasonableness with past practice described at a very specific level. That understanding begins with a concept of "ordered liberty, comprising a continuum of rights to be free from "arbitrary impositions and purposeless restraints." [The] claims of arbitrariness that mark almost all instances of unenumerated substantive rights are those resting on "certain interests requir[ing] particularly careful scrutiny of the state needs asserted to justify their abridgment[,] that is, interests in liberty sufficiently important to be judged "fundamental," In the face of an interest this powerful a State may not rest on threshold rationality or a presumption of constitutionality, but may prevail only on the ground of an interest sufficiently compelling to place within the realm of the reasonable a refusal to recognize the individual right asserted.

[This] approach calls for a court to assess the relative "weights" or dignities of the contending interests, and to this extent the judicial method is familiar to the common law. Common-law method is subject, however, to two important constraints in the hands of a court engaged in substantive due process review. First, such a court is bound to confine the values that it recognizes to those truly deserving constitutional stature, either to those expressed in constitutional text, or those exemplified by "the traditions from which [the Nation] developed," or revealed by contrast with "the traditions from which it broke." *Poe* (Harlan, J., dissenting) [Second, it] is only when the legislation's justifying principle, critically valued, is so far from being commensurate with the individual interest as to be arbitrarily or pointlessly applied that the statute must give way. [Common-law] method tends to pay respect instead to detail, seeking to understand old principles afresh by new examples and new counterexamples. The "tradition is a living thing," Poe (Harlan, J., dissenting), albeit one that moves by moderate steps carefully taken. "The decision of an apparently novel claim must depend on grounds which follow closely on well-accepted principles and criteria. The new decision must take its place in relation to what went before and further [cut] a channel for what is to come." (Harlan, J., dissenting) (internal quotation marks omitted). Exact analysis and characterization of any due process claim are critical to the method and to the result.

The argument supporting respondents' position thus progresses through three steps of increasing forcefulness. First, it emphasizes the decriminalization of suicide. Reliance on this fact is sanctioned under the standard that looks not only to the tradition retained, but to society's occasional choices to reject traditions of the legal past. See Poe v. Ullman, 367 U.S., at 542, 81 S.Ct., at 1776 (Harlan, J., dissenting). While the common law prohibited both suicide and aiding a suicide, with the prohibition on aiding largely justified by the primary prohibition on self-inflicted death itself, see, *e.g.,* American Law Institute, Model Penal Code § 210.5, Comment 1, at 92-93, and n. 7, the State's rejection of the traditional treatment of the one leaves the criminality of the other open to questioning that previously would not have been appropriate. The second step in the argument is to emphasize that the State's own act of decriminalization gives a freedom of choice much like the individual's option in recognized instances of bodily autonomy. One of these, abortion, is a legal right to choose in spite of the interest a State may legitimately invoke in discouraging the practice, just as suicide is now subject to choice, despite a state interest in discouraging it. The third step is to emphasize that respondents claim a right to assistance not on the basis of some broad principle that would be subject to exceptions if that continuing interest of the State's in discouraging suicide were to be recognized at all. Respondents base their claim on the traditional right to medical care and counsel, subject to the limiting conditions of informed, responsible choice when death is imminent, conditions that support a strong analogy to rights of care in other situations in which medical counsel and assistance have been available as a matter of course. There can be no stronger claim to a physician's assistance than at the time when death is imminent, a moral judgment implied by the State's own recognition of the legitimacy of medical procedures necessarily hastening the moment of impending death.

In my judgment, the importance of the individual interest here, as within that class of "certain interests" demanding careful scrutiny of the State's contrary claim, see Poe, supra, at 543, 81 S.Ct., at 1776-1777, cannot be gainsaid. Whether that interest might in some circumstances, or at some time, be seen as "fundamental" to the degree entitled to prevail is not, however, a conclusion that I need draw here, for I am satisfied that the State's interests described in the following section are sufficiently serious to defeat the present claim that its law is arbitrary or purposeless.

The State has put forward several interests to justify the Washington law as applied to physicians treating terminally ill patients, even those competent to make responsible choices: protecting life generally, Brief for Petitioners 33, discouraging suicide even if knowing and voluntary, and protecting terminally ill patients from involuntary suicide and euthanasia, both voluntary and nonvoluntary. The third is dispositive for me. That third justification is different from the first two, for it addresses specific features of respondents' claim, and it opposes that claim not with a moral judgment contrary to respondents', but with a recognized state interest in the protection of nonresponsible individuals and those who do not stand in relation either to death or to their physicians as do the patients whom respondents describe. The argument is that a progression would occur, obscuring the line between the ill and the dying, and between the responsible and the unduly influenced, until ultimately doctors and perhaps others would abuse a limited freedom to aid suicides by yielding to the impulse to end another's suffering under conditions going beyond the narrow limits the respondents propose.

The mere assertion that the terminally sick might be pressured into suicide decisions by close friends and family members would not alone be very telling. [The] State, however, goes further, to argue that dependence on the vigilance of physicians will not be enough. First, the lines proposed here (particularly the requirement of a knowing and voluntary decision by the patient) would be more difficult to draw than the lines that have limited other recently recognized due process rights. Limiting a State from prosecuting use of artificial contraceptives by married couples posed no practical threat to the State's capacity to regulate contraceptives in other ways that were assumed at the time of Poe to be legitimate; the trimester measurements of Roe and the viability determination of Casey were easy to make with a real degree of certainty. But the knowing and responsible mind is harder to assess. Second, this difficulty could become the greater by combining with another fact within the realm of plausibility, that physicians simply would not be assiduous to preserve the line. Whether acting from compassion or under some other influence, a physician who would provide a drug for a patient to administer might well go the further step of administering the drug himself; so, the barrier between assisted suicide and euthanasia could become porous, and the line between voluntary and involuntary euthanasia as well.   The case for the slippery slope is fairly made out here, not because recognizing one due process right would leave a court with no principled basis to avoid recognizing another, but because there is a plausible case that the right claimed would not be readily containable by reference to facts about the mind that are matters of difficult judgment, or by gatekeepers who are subject to temptation, noble or not.

Respondents propose an answer to all this, the answer of state regulation with teeth. Legislation proposed in several States, for example, would authorize physician-assisted suicide but require two qualified physicians to confirm the patient's diagnosis, prognosis, and competence; and would mandate that the patient make repeated requests witnessed by at least two others over a specified timespan; and would impose reporting requirements and criminal penalties for various acts of coercion.

But at least at this moment there are reasons for caution in predicting the effectiveness of the teeth proposed.   Respondents' proposals, as it turns out, sound much like the guidelines now in place in the Netherlands, the only place where experience with physician-assisted suicide and euthanasia has yielded empirical evidence about how such regulations might affect actual practice.   Dutch physicians must engage in consultation before proceeding, and must decide whether the patient's decision is voluntary, well considered, and stable, whether the request to die is enduring and made more than once, and whether the patient's future will involve unacceptable suffering.   See C. Gomez, Regulating Death 40-43 (1991).   There is, however, a substantial dispute today about what the Dutch experience shows.   Some commentators marshall evidence that the Dutch guidelines have in practice failed to protect patients from involuntary euthanasia and have been violated with impunity.   This evidence is contested.   The day may come when we can say with some assurance which side is right, but for now it is the substantiality of the factual disagreement, and the alternatives for resolving it, that matter.   They are, for me, dispositive of the due process claim at this time.   While I do not decide for all time that respondents' claim should not be recognized, I acknowledge the legislative institutional competence as the better one to deal with that claim at this time.

Justice BREYER, concurring in the judgments.

I believe that Justice O'Connor's views, which I share, have greater legal significance than the Court's opinion suggests.   I join her separate opinion, except insofar as it joins the majority.   I do not agree, however, with the Court's formulation of that claimed "liberty" interest.   The Court describes it as a "right to commit suicide with another's assistance."   But I would not reject the respondents' claim without considering a different formulation, for which our legal tradition may provide greater support.   That formulation would use words roughly like a "right to die with dignity."   But irrespective of the exact words used, at its core would lie personal control over the manner of death, professional medical assistance, and the avoidance of unnecessary and severe physical suffering — combined.

As Justice Souter points out, (opinion concurring in judgment), Justice Harlan's dissenting opinion in Poe v. Ullman, 367 U.S. 497, 81 S.Ct. 1752, 6 L.Ed.2d 989 (1961), offers some support for such a claim.   In that opinion, Justice Harlan referred to the "liberty" that the Fourteenth Amendment protects as including "a freedom from all substantial arbitrary impositions and purposeless restraints" and also as recognizing that "*certain interests* require particularly careful scrutiny of the state needs asserted to justify their abridgment."   Id., at 543, 81 S.Ct., at 1777.   The "certain interests" to which Justice

Harlan referred may well be similar (perhaps identical) to the rights, liberties, or interests that the Court today, as in the past, regards as "fundamental."

Justice Harlan concluded that marital privacy was such a "special interest." He found in the Constitution a right of "privacy of the home" — with the home, the bedroom, and "intimate details of the marital relation" at its heart — by examining the protection that the law had earlier provided for related, but not identical, interests described by such words as "privacy," "home," and "family." The respondents here essentially ask us to do the same. They argue that one can find a "right to die with dignity" by examining the protection the law has provided for related, but not identical, interests relating to personal dignity, medical treatment, and freedom from state-inflicted pain. Cruzan v. Director, Mo. Dept. of Health, 497 U.S. 261, 110 S.Ct. 2841, 111 L.Ed.2d 224 (1990); Casey, supra.

I do not believe, however, that this Court need or now should decide whether or a not such a right is "fundamental." That is because, in my view, the avoidance of severe physical pain (connected with death) would have to constitute an essential part of any successful claim and because, as Justice O'Connor points out, the laws before us do not *force* a dying person to undergo that kind of pain. Ante, at 2303 (concurring opinion). Rather, the laws of New York and of Washington do not prohibit doctors from providing patients with drugs sufficient to control pain despite the risk that those drugs themselves will kill.

Medical technology, we are repeatedly told, makes the administration of pain-relieving drugs sufficient, except for a very few individuals for whom the ineffectiveness of pain control medicines can mean not pain, but the need for sedation.

VACCO v. QUILL
521 U.S. 793 (1997)

Chief Justice REHNQUIST delivered the opinion of the Court.

In New York, as in most States, it is a crime to aid another to commit or attempt suicide, but patients may refuse even lifesaving medical treatment. The question presented by this case is whether New York's prohibition on assisting suicide therefore violates the Equal Protection Clause of the Fourteenth Amendment. We hold that it does not.

Petitioners are various New York public officials. Respondents Timothy E. Quill, Samuel C. Klagsbrun, and Howard A. Grossman are physicians who practice in New York. They assert that although it would be "consistent with the standards of [their] medical practice[s]" to prescribe lethal medication for "mentally competent, terminally ill patients" who are suffering great pain and desire a doctor's help in taking their own lives, they are deterred from doing so by New York's ban on assisting suicide. Respondents, and three gravely ill patients who have since died, sued the State's Attorney General in the United States District Court. They urged that because New York permits a competent person to refuse life-sustaining medical treatment, and because the refusal of such treatment is "essentially the same thing" as physician-assisted suicide, New York's assisted-suicide ban violates the Equal Protection Clause.

The District Court disagreed: "[I]t is hardly unreasonable or irrational for the State to recognize a difference between allowing nature to take its course, even in the most severe situations, and intentionally using an artificial death-producing device." The court noted New York's "obvious legitimate interests in preserving life, and in protecting vulnerable persons," and concluded that "[u]nder the United States Constitution and the federal system it establishes, the resolution of this issue is left to the normal democratic processes within the State."

The Court of Appeals for the Second Circuit reversed. The court determined that, despite the assisted-suicide ban's apparent general applicability, "New York law does not treat equally all competent persons who are in the final stages of fatal illness and wish to hasten their deaths," because "those in the final stages of terminal illness who are on life-support systems are allowed to hasten their deaths by directing the removal of such systems; but those who are similarly situated, except for the previous attachment of life-sustaining equipment, are not allowed to hasten death by self-administering prescribed drugs."

The Equal Protection Clause commands that no State shall "deny to any person within its jurisdiction the equal protection of the laws." This provision creates no substantive rights. San Antonio Independent School Dist. v. Rodriguez, 411 U.S. 1, 33, 93 S.Ct. 1278, 1296-1297, 36 L.Ed.2d 16 (1973); id., at 59, 93 S.Ct., at 1310 (Stewart, J., concurring). Instead, it embodies a general rule that States must treat like cases alike but may treat unlike cases accordingly. Plyler v. Doe, 457 U.S. 202, 216, 102 S.Ct. 2382, 2394, 72 L.Ed.2d 786 (1982) ("'[T]he Constitution does not require things which are different in fact or opinion to be treated in law as though they were the same'") (quoting Tigner v. Texas, 310 U.S. 141, 147, 60 S.Ct. 879, 882, 84 L.Ed. 1124 (1940)). If a legislative classification or distinction "neither burdens a fundamental right nor targets a suspect class, we will uphold [it] so long as it bears a rational relation to some legitimate end." Romer v. Evans, 517 U.S. 620, 631, 116 S.Ct. 1620, 1627, 134 L.Ed.2d 855 (1996).

New York's statutes outlawing assisting suicide affect and address matters of profound significance to all New Yorkers alike. They neither infringe fundamental rights nor involve suspect classifications. Washington v. Glucksberg, at 719-728, 117 S.Ct., at 2267-2271 These laws are therefore entitled to a "strong presumption of validity."

On their faces, neither New York's ban on assisting suicide nor its statutes permitting patients to refuse medical treatment treat anyone differently from anyone else or draw any distinctions between persons. *Everyone,* regardless of physical condition, is entitled, if competent, to refuse unwanted lifesaving medical treatment; *no one* is permitted to assist a suicide. Generally speaking, laws that apply evenhandedly to all "unquestionably comply" with the Equal Protection Clause. New York City Transit Authority v. Beazer, 440 U.S. 568, 587, 99 S.Ct. 1355, 1366-1367, 59 L.Ed.2d 587 (1979); see Personnel Administrator of Mass. v. Feeney, 442 U.S. 256, 271-273, 99 S.Ct. 2282, 2292-2293, 60 L.Ed.2d 870 (1979) ("[M]any [laws] affect certain groups unevenly, even though the law itself treats them no differently from all other members of the class described by the law").

The Court of Appeals, however, concluded that some terminally ill people — those who are on life-support systems — are treated differently from those who are not, in that the former may "hasten death" by ending treatment, but the latter may not "hasten death" through physician-assisted suicide. This conclusion depends on the submission that ending or refusing lifesaving medical treatment "is nothing more nor less than assisted suicide." Unlike the Court of Appeals, we think the distinction between assisting suicide and withdrawing life-sustaining treatment, a distinction widely recognized and endorsed in the medical profession[6] and in our legal traditions, is both important and logical; it is

---

[6] The American Medical Association emphasizes the "fundamental difference between refusing life-sustaining treatment and demanding a life-ending treatment." American Medical Association, Council on Ethical and Judicial Affairs, Physician-Assisted Suicide, 10 Issues in Law & Medicine 91, 93 (1994); see also American Medical Association, Council on Ethical and Judicial Affairs, Decisions Near the End of Life, 267

certainly rational. See Feeney, supra, at 272, 99 S.Ct., at 2292 ("When the basic classification is rationally based, uneven effects upon particular groups within a class are ordinarily of no constitutional concern").

The distinction comports with fundamental legal principles of causation and intent. First, when a patient refuses life-sustaining medical treatment, he dies from an underlying fatal disease or pathology; but if a patient ingests lethal medication prescribed by a physician, he is killed by that medication. See, *e.g.,* People v. Kevorkian, 447 Mich. 436, 470-472, 527 N.W.2d 714, 728 (1994), cert. denied, 514 U.S. 1083, 115 S.Ct. 1795, 131 L.Ed.2d 723 (1995); Matter of Conroy, 98 N.J. 321, 355, 486 A.2d 1209, 1226 (1985) (when feeding tube is removed, death "result[s] . . . from [the patient's] underlying medical condition"); In re Colyer, 99 Wash.2d 114, 123, 660 P.2d 738, 743 (1983) ("[D]eath which occurs after the removal of life sustaining systems is from natural causes"); American Medical Association, Council on Ethical and Judicial Affairs, Physician-Assisted Suicide, 10 Issues in Law & Medicine 91, 93 (1994) ("When a life-sustaining treatment is declined, the patient dies primarily because of an underlying disease").

Furthermore, a physician who withdraws, or honors a patient's refusal to begin, life-sustaining medical treatment purposefully intends, or may so intend, only to respect his patient's wishes and "to cease doing useless and futile or degrading things to the patient when [the patient] no longer stands to benefit from them." The same is true when a doctor provides aggressive palliative care; in some cases, painkilling drugs may hasten a patient's death, but the physician's purpose and intent is, or may be, only to ease his patient's pain. A doctor who assists a suicide, however, "must, necessarily and indubitably, intend primarily that the patient be made dead." *Id.,* at 367. Similarly, a patient who commits suicide with a doctor's aid necessarily has the specific intent to end his or her own life, while a patient who refuses or discontinues treatment might not.

The law has long used actors' intent or purpose to distinguish between two acts that may have the same result. Put differently, the law distinguishes actions taken "because of" a given end from actions taken "in spite of" their unintended but foreseen consequences.

[Given] these general principles, it is not surprising that many courts, including New York courts, have carefully distinguished refusing life-sustaining treatment from suicide. And recently, the Michigan Supreme Court also rejected the argument that the distinction "between acts that artificially sustain life and acts that artificially curtail life" is merely a "distinction without constitutional significance — a meaningless exercise in semantic gymnastics," insisting that "the Cruzan majority disagreed and so do we."

Similarly, the overwhelming majority of state legislatures have drawn a clear line between assisting suicide and withdrawing or permitting the refusal of unwanted lifesaving medical treatment by prohibiting the former and permitting the latter. And "nearly all states expressly disapprove of suicide and assisted suicide either in statutes dealing with

---

JAMA 2229, 2230-2231, 2233 (1992) ("The withdrawing or withholding of life-sustaining treatment is not inherently contrary to the principles of beneficence and nonmaleficence," but assisted suicide "is contrary to the prohibition against using the tools of medicine to cause a patient's death"); New York State Task Force on Life and the Law, When Death is Sought: Assisted Suicide and Euthanasia in the Medical Context 108 (1994) ("[Professional organizations] consistently distinguish assisted suicide and euthanasia from the withdrawing or withholding of treatment, and from the provision of palliative treatments or other medical care that risk fatal side effects"); Brief for American Medical Association et al. as *Amici Curiae* 18-25. Of course, as respondents' lawsuit demonstrates, there are differences of opinion within the medical profession on this question. See New York Task Force, *supra,* at 104-109.

durable powers of attorney in health-care situations, or in 'living will' statutes." Thus, even as the States move to protect and promote patients' dignity at the end of life, they remain opposed to physician-assisted suicide.

New York is a case in point. The State enacted its current assisted-suicide statutes in 1965. Since then, New York has acted several times to protect patients' common-law right to refuse treatment. In so doing, however, the State has neither endorsed a general right to "hasten death" nor approved physician-assisted suicide. Quite the opposite: The State has reaffirmed the line between "killing" and "letting die." More recently, the New York State Task Force on Life and the Law studied assisted suicide and euthanasia and, in 1994, unanimously recommended against legalization. When Death is Sought: Assisted Suicide and Euthanasia in the Medical Context vii (1994). In the Task Force's view, "allowing decisions to forgo life-sustaining treatment and allowing assisted suicide or euthanasia have radically different consequences and meanings for public policy."

This Court has also recognized, at least implicitly, the distinction between letting a patient die and making that patient die. In Cruzan v. Director, Mo. Dept. of Health, 497 U.S. 261, 278, 110 S.Ct. 2841, 2851, 111 L.Ed.2d 224 (1990), we concluded that "[t]he principle that a competent person has a constitutionally protected liberty interest in refusing unwanted medical treatment may be inferred from our prior decisions," and we assumed the existence of such a right for purposes of that case. But our assumption of a right to refuse treatment was grounded not, as the Court of Appeals supposed, on the proposition that patients have a general and abstract "right to hasten death," but on well-established, traditional rights to bodily integrity and freedom from unwanted touching. In fact, we observed that "the majority of States in this country have laws imposing criminal penalties on one who assists another to commit suicide." Cruzan therefore provides no support for the notion that refusing life-sustaining medical treatment is "nothing more nor less than suicide."

For all these reasons, we disagree with respondents' claim that the distinction between refusing lifesaving medical treatment and assisted suicide is "arbitrary" and "irrational." Granted, in some cases, the line between the two may not be clear, but certainty is not required, even were it possible. Logic and contemporary practice support New York's judgment that the two acts are different, and New York may therefore, consistent with the Constitution, treat them differently. By permitting everyone to refuse unwanted medical treatment while prohibiting anyone from assisting a suicide, New York law follows a longstanding and rational distinction.

New York's reasons for recognizing and acting on this distinction — including prohibiting intentional killing and preserving life; preventing suicide; maintaining physicians' role as their patients' healers; protecting vulnerable people from indifference, prejudice, and psychological and financial pressure to end their lives; and avoiding a possible slide towards euthanasia — are discussed in greater detail in our opinion in Glucksberg, ante. These valid and important public interests easily satisfy the constitutional requirement that a legislative classification bear a rational relation to some legitimate end. The judgment of the Court of Appeals is reversed.

Justice SOUTER, concurring in the judgment.

Even though I do not conclude that assisted suicide is a fundamental right entitled to recognition at this time, I accord the claims raised by the patients and physicians in this case and Washington v. Glucksberg a high degree of importance, requiring a commensurate justification. The reasons that lead me to conclude in Glucksberg that the prohibition on assisted suicide is not arbitrary under the due process standard also support the distinction between assistance to suicide, which is banned, and practices such as termination of artificial life support and death-hastening pain medication, which are permitted. I accordingly concur in the judgment of the Court.

II. PROCEDURAL DUE PROCESS

No person shall . . . be deprived of life, liberty, or property, without due process of law. . . . [U.S. Const. art. 5.]

[N]or shall any state deprive any person of life, liberty, or property, without due process of law. [U.S. Const. amend. XIV.]

Perhaps among the least well-explained concepts in constitutional law pedagogy is the connection between the two types of due process. Despite the fact that the term itself implies some sort of process or procedure, the materials have up to this point covered substantive due process and the controversies surrounding the incorporation doctrine and economic and non-economic unenumerated rights. In the first year, procedural due process is studied in civil procedure courses where the kind of process and the form of that process is examined. On the other hand, constitutional law courses address which interests trigger the procedural safeguards of due process in the first place. What is often missing is the connective tissue between the two concepts. This section will supply that connection.

Substantive due process cases usually involve legislative acts, of general applicability, that prohibit certain individual activities. An aggrieved party in such cases will attempt to establish that his liberty right to engage in such activities is among the body of *fundamental rights* that have been identified through the years by the Supreme Court. If successful, the government must establish that its prohibition was in pursuit of a compelling purpose under a strict scrutiny analysis. Procedural due process cases, by contrast, usually deal with specific acts by government (like firings, defamation, or denial of welfare benefits), interfering with an individual's liberty or property interest[2] — such interests in order to be protected by procedural safeguards do not have to be fundamental. What interests are protected procedurally depends upon a pre-established entitlement to a particular *property* or *liberty* interest (typically established by the common law or federal or state statutory law)[3] as well as the body of fundamental rights established by the Constitution (such as freedom of speech). Although the government may take away or interfere with such an entitlement, an individual does have the right to proper procedures reviewing the government's action — either before or after depending upon the nature of that government action.

The common law roots of due process are in the Magna Carta declaration of rights of English noblemen and limitations on the King. The guiding idea was that the landholding class of 13th century England should have the right to a sovereign whose power to take away land and the benefits of land ownership was limited by the "law of the land," a

---

[2] Deprivation of life and liberty within the criminal justice system and an individual's due process rights are addressed under criminal procedure.

[3] *Board of Regents v. Roth*, 408 U.S. 564 (1972).

concept that came to be known as due process.   A bit of background was supplied by the Supreme Court in *Davidson v. New Orleans*, 96 U.S. 102 (1878):

> It is easy to see that when the great barons of England wrung from King John, at the point of the sword, the concession that neither their lives nor their property should be disposed of by the crown, except as provided by the law of the land, they meant by the "law of the land" the ancient and customary laws of the English people, or laws enacted by the Parliament of which those barons were a controlling element.   It was not in their minds, therefore to protect themselves against the enactment of laws by the Parliament of England.

By the Court's description, due process began as a guarantee of procedural rights.   But by the fact that protection against the sovereign's unlimited power was the original purpose, a substantive dimension — one addressing the government's power over basic fundamental rights beyond mere procedures — can be envisioned.

A good summary of the difference between the two can be found in Taylor Patrick Brooks, *Alabama Supreme Court Contravenes United States Supreme Court Due Process Jurisprudence: Stallworth v. City of Evergreen*, 49 Ala. L. Rev. 1081 (1998):

> The Due Process Clause of the Fourteenth Amendment to the United States Constitution provides, "nor shall any State deprive any person of life, liberty, or property, without due process of law. . . ." The United States Supreme Court's interpretation of this clause is that the amendment provides two different types of constitutional protection: procedural due process and substantive due process. Procedural due process bars the government from procedural irregularities only when life, liberty, or property is being taken. Property interests are not created by the Constitution, rather "they are created and their dimensions are defined by existing rules or understandings that stem from an independent source such as state law. . . ." A government employee's contractual or statutory right to continued employment is a property interest falling within the scope of the Fourteenth Amendment's protection.
>
> The substantive component of the Due Process Clause protects those rights that are "implicit in the concept of ordered liberty." The United States Supreme Court has deemed that most, but not all, of the rights enumerated in the Bill of Rights] are fundamental. Certain unenumerated rights, such as the penumbral right of privacy, also merit protection. A finding that a right merits substantive due process protection means that the right is protected against government actions regardless of the procedures the government employs.
>
> Substantive due process rights also differ from procedural due process rights in the manner in which the violation of the right occurs. A violation of a substantive due process right is complete when it occurs. Hence, the availability of an adequate postdeprivation state remedy is irrelevant. Since "this right is 'fundamental,' no amount of process can justify its infringement." By contrast, there is no procedural due process violation unless and until the State fails to provide due process. Thus, the State may cure a procedural deprivation by providing a later procedural remedy. Only when the State refuses to provide a process sufficient to cure the deprivation does a constitutional violation arise.
>
> Another important difference between substantive and procedural due process is the type of remedy generally awarded to aggrieved parties. Plaintiffs in substantive due process claims generally seek compensation in the form of damages for the value of the deprived right. While procedural due process plaintiffs may seek compensatory damages, they are primarily interested in equitable relief. For example, an employee who challenges his or her termination "typically seeks reinstatement and a properly conducted pretermination hearing." This equitable remedy is unique to procedural due process remedies because substantive due process rights are such that they "may not be violated

regardless of the process. Since "the relief awarded to a person claiming a substantive due process violation primarily is monetary, not equitable, a substantive due process deprivation likely is of substantially greater monetary value than a procedural due process deprivation.

Employees with a property right in employment are "protected only by the procedural component of the Due Process Clause, not its substantive component." Employment rights are state created rather than "fundamental" rights. Therefore, employment rights do not enjoy substantive due process protection. Thus, since a procedural right has not been violated unless and until the State fails to remedy the inadequacy, a terminated employee must utilize appropriate, available state remedial measures before suing in federal court. Furthermore, an employee's remedy is not potential lifetime earnings, but rather procedural equitable remedies such as "reinstatement and a directive that proper procedures should be used in any future termination proceedings.

Additional useful language can be found in Hon. Harvey Brown and Sarah V. Kerrigan, *42 U.S.C. 1983: The Vehicle for Protecting Public Employees' Constitutional Rights*, 47 Baylor L. Rev. 619:

> No discussion of substantive due process would be proper without first distinguishing procedural and substantive due process. Procedural due process concerns whether the state has provided procedures that adequately protect individuals from arbitrary or erroneous deprivations of their rights. A procedural due process claim focuses on whether or not the employer engaged in a process sufficient to guarantee fair treatment of the employee. Hence, an employee may be able to state a procedural due process claim even if the government's action is wholly rational.
>
> Substantive due process, on the other hand, provides an individual with the right to be free from arbitrary and capricious governmental power. A substantive due process claim focuses on the constitutionality of the action itself. Hence, a violation may occur regardless of the process extended. To the extent an employer provides elaborate procedural safeguards, however, the argument that the government's action was arbitrary and capricious is substantially weakened.

Essentially, those cases in the post-*Lochner* era in which rational basis was used for non-fundamental rights would theoretically be subject to a procedural due process challenge if the procedures are claimed not to be consistent with the procedural due process guarantees. This is covered, however, in more depth in civil procedure courses. Understanding the differences is important in constitutional law.

A. PROCEDURAL DUE PROCESS IN CIVIL PROCEDURE

With the basic differences spelled out, a brief overview of the roadmap to your exposure to due process of the procedural variety in first-year civil procedure may clarify the two separate treatments within the phrase "due process of law."

Jurisdiction. Early in your civil procedure course, sometimes at the beginning, you studied cases like *Pennoyer v. Neff*, 95 U.S. 714 (1878); *International Shoe v. Washington*, 326 U.S. 310 (1945); *Harris v. Balk*, 198 U.S. 215 (1905); and *Shaffer v. Heitner*, 433 U.S. 186 (1977). In these and other cases that followed their holdings, someone was faced with the threat of losing property, real or personal, through court proceedings. Civil procedure addresses property interests for the most part and some aspects of liberty, leaving due process questions regarding government-sanctioned loss of most liberty or life to criminal procedure or substantive due process considerations in constitutional law. Each of these cases dealt with perhaps a classic situation in which a person being sued for property might not be able to avail his right to protect his property interests — for example, by being out of state and not able to adequately protect that interest due to distance and inconvenience. If procedural due process is about procedures, then it would be important to ensure that the proper tribunal is actually administering those procedures in a lawsuit. Under our federal system, much of what is understood to be fair in terms of identifying the proper forum for hearing has to do with state jurisdiction and the proper respect each state is to have for the procedures and authority of sister states. Part of this respect is for a state not to assert its authority in another state, or over persons or property residing in another state, unless that person has made minimum contacts with the forum state. You will recall that there were many ways of interpreting minimum contacts such as contract, stream of commerce, and the effects test. You will also recall how minimum contacts became, after some initial confusion, a basic requirement for cases filed against property, or the so-called *in rem* actions.

Notice. Just like with regard to jurisdiction, there is a certain intuitive expectation that a person ought to have notice of threats to her property before that property is actually taken. Accordingly, proper notice is understood to be crucial to any government-sanctioned deprivation, whether it would occur as a result of a court proceeding or an administrative proceeding. As the Supreme Court stated in *Mullane v. Central Hanover Bank & Trust*, 339 U.S. 306 (1950), in order to meet the due process requirements of proper notice,

> [t]he means of notice must be of such nature as one desirous of actually informing the absentee might reasonably adopt to accomplish it. There must be an effort to reasonably convey the required info and afford a reasonable time for the interested to make their appearance. But there must be due regard for the practicalities and peculiarities of the case — constitutional requirements can be met with such regard. [*Id.* at 315.]

You will recall studying various tests of this standard within the context of prisons[5] and apartment buildings,[6] to name a couple of the examples.

1. OPPORTUNITY TO BE HEARD

Perhaps outside of jurisdiction, among the more controversial procedural due process areas has to do with when and whether a party facing deprivation has a right to be heard, to plead one's case against the deprivation of a property right — again, an intuitive requirement of fairness under due process. The discussion in the case law developed into

---

[5] Dusenbery v. United States, 534 U.S. 161 (2002).
[6] 456 U.S. 444 (1982).

one divided into three main categories: What kind of rights deprivations were subject to the hearing requirement? What kind of hearing?[7] When should the hearing be held?[8]

What Interests Are Protected? Though the procedural dimension of the Due Process Clause has long been a subject of Supreme Court litigation, the 1970s saw the introduction of a more expansive interpretation of the clause. The Court declined to limit its search for rights, the taking of which requiring appropriate procedures, to the Constitution, and began to find property and liberty interests worthy of procedural protections within the

---

[7] A decision that closely tracks the issues in this course and in Civil Procedure, is *Cleveland Board of Education v. Loudermill* 470 U.S. 532 (1985). The Court decided two cases involving firings of school district employees without prior hearing. In both cases the firings were pursuant to Ohio state civil service rules that employees could only be fired for cause and procedures for hearings to review terminations are set out in the statute. Both parties received post-termination hearings, one denying reinstatement and the other allowing reinstatement but without back pay. Despite lower court holdings in the two cases following a plurality opinion in an earlier Supreme Court case tying the quality of hearing rights to the grant of the right by statute[7], Justice White, writing for the Court made clear the role that the Constitution has in determining the type of hearing that would be appropriate:

the Due Process Clause provides that certain substantive rights — life, liberty, and property — cannot be deprived except pursuant to constitutionally adequate procedures. The categories of substance and procedure are distinct. Were the rule otherwise, the Clause would be reduced to a mere tautology. "Property" cannot be defined by the procedures provided for its deprivation any more than can life or liberty. The right to due process

"is conferred, not by legislative grace, but by constitutional guarantee. While the legislature may elect not to confer a property interest in [public] employment, it may not constitutionally authorize the deprivation of such an interest, once conferred, without appropriate procedural safeguards."

Arnett v. Kennedy, supra, at (POWELL, J., concurring in part and concurring in result in part); *see id.* at 416 U. S. 185 (WHITE, J., concurring in part and dissenting in part).

In short, once it is determined that the Due Process Clause applies, "the question remains what process is due." *Morrissey v. Brewer,* 408 U. S. 471, 408 U. S. 481 (1972). The answer to that question is not to be found in the Ohio statute.

In this case quality of the hearing, including whether it should occur prior to termination of the property interest, is determined by the significance of the property interest. Here, the proper hearing would have to be a pre-deprivation hearing in order to satisfy constitutional muster because of the balancing of the government's interest in removing an unsatisfactory employee matched against the need for a determination of whether there are reasonable grounds to believe that the charges against the employee are true and support the proposed action. These constitutional considerations, according to the Court, and not the Ohio statute determine the quality of the hearing.

[8] After much effort and a series of relatively unsatisfying decisions purporting to describe a standard for determining when a hearing would be appropriate, the Court finally agreed upon a balancing standard. Recognizing that a "one size fits all" approach to the timing of a Due Process hearing was unworkable, the Court announced the new approach in *Mathews v. Eldridge,* 424 U.S. 319 (1976):

[Prior decisions on hearings] underscore the truism that "'[d]ue process,' unlike some legal rules, is not a technical conception with a fixed content unrelated to time, place and circumstances." Cafeteria Workers v. McElroy, 367 U.S. 886, 895 (1961). "[D]ue process is flexible, and calls for such procedural protections as the particular situation demands." Morrissey v. Brewer, 408 U.S. 471, 481 (1972). Accordingly, resolution of the issue whether the administrative procedures provided here are constitutionally sufficient requires analysis of the governmental and private interests that are affected. Arnett v. Kennedy, supra at 167-168 (POWELL, J., concurring in part); Goldberg v. Kelly, supra at 263-266; Cafeteria Workers v. McElroy, supra at 895. More precisely, our prior decisions indicate that identification of the specific dictates of due process generally requires consideration of three distinct factors: first, the private interest that will be affected by the official action; second, the risk of an erroneous deprivation of such interest through the procedures used, and the probable value, if any, of additional or substitute procedural safeguards; and, finally, the Government's interest, including the function involved and the fiscal and administrative burdens that the additional or substitute procedural requirement would entail. See, e.g., Goldberg v. Kelly, supra at 263-271.

Mathews v. Eldridge at 334-335.

expectations that individuals have based upon the common law or state statutory law.[9] One way of putting it, if the state, through the common law or statutory law creates an expectation, it cannot take it away without proper procedures. The discussion of the content of those "proper procedures" was covered in your civil procedure course. For purposes of this course in Constitutional law we will discuss the Supreme Court's expansion of the content of the rights protected by the procedural requirements.

Property. Perhaps the clearest signal that the Court was moving in the direction of expanding access to hearings was in *Goldberg v. Kelly*, 397 U.S. 254 (1970). There the Court held that New York City's practice of providing an opportunity for individuals losing welfare benefits to a post-deprivation instead of a pre-deprivation hearing was inadequate under the Constitution. Writing for the Court, Justice Brennan established that welfare was a protected interest and a matter of a statutory entitlement requiring some sort of hearing. What the Court did in this case was to establish also that it was an important interest, one amounting to a property interest. To reach this conclusion, the majority relied on reasoning from an influential article defining property to include statutory or contractual entitlements to benefits such as professional licenses, farm subsidies, government contracts for defense, space and education, and welfare benefits.[10] By placing welfare within the category of property, Justice Brennan's majority opinion established the full protection of the clause for welfare benefits, which in this case considering the importance of personal livelihood, required a pre-termination hearing.

It is important to note that unlike substantive rights that are subject to strict scrutiny, the protection in this and similar cases is whether to afford an individual a hearing and whether that hearing should be prior to termination of an entitlement interest. Another case involving a claimed property interest in an entitlement from the state dealt with an

---

[9] The Court generally has based its assessments on the right to due process on whether there is a property or liberty entitlement at issue, and not simply whether a specific "right" is in jeopardy from governmental action. This may reflect a hesitance to give entitlements the title "rights" while at the same time recognizing the individual's "right" to procedural protections nonetheless. See Goldberg v. Kelly, 397 U.S. 254, 262 (1970).
The Court in Board of Regents v. Roth explained the expansion of coverage this way:

"Liberty" and "property" are broad and majestic terms. They are among the "[g]reat [constitutional] concepts . . . purposely left to gather meaning from experience. . . . [T]hey relate to the whole domain of social and economic fact, and the statesmen who founded this Nation knew too well that only a stagnant society remains unchanged." *National Ins. Co.* v. *Tidewater Co.,* 337 U. S. 582, 646 (Frankfurter, J., dissenting). For that reason, the Court has fully and finally rejected the wooden distinction between "rights" and "privileges" that once seemed to govern the applicability of procedural due process rights. The Court has also made clear that the property interests protected by procedural due process extend well beyond actual ownership of real estate, chattels, or money. By the same token, the Court has required due process protection for deprivations of liberty beyond the sort of formal constraints imposed by the criminal process.

[10] Charles Reich, *Individual Rights and Social Welfare: The Emerging Legal Issues*, 74 Yale L.J. 1245, 1255 (1965); see also Charles Reich, *The New Property*, 73 Yale L.J. 733, 733 (1964):

The valuables dispensed by government take many forms, but they all share one characteristic. They are steadily taking the place of traditional forms of wealth — forms which are held as private property. Social insurance substitutes for savings; a government contract replaces a businessman's customers and goodwill. The wealth of more and more Americans depends upon a relationship to government. Increasingly, Americans live on government largess — allocated by government on its own terms, and held by recipients subject to conditions which express "the public interest."

untenured university professor and his state university's decision not to renew his one-year contract. In *Board of Regents v. Roth*, 408 U.S. 564 (1972), the Court, in an opinion written by Justice Stewart, ruled that the respondent professor could not establish an interest in either property or liberty protected by the Due Process Clause.

The opinion reasoned that the professor's liberty interests were not threatened by the university's decision not to rehire since he was free to seek other employment and that there was no suggestion that the professor suffered any stigma as a result of the failure to renew that would interfere with his personal honor, integrity, reputation, or good name, each of which the Court has found to have liberty interest implications.[11]

On the issue of the professor's property interest in being rehired, Justice Stewart described the procedural protection of property as a safeguard of the security of interests that a person has already acquired in specific benefits — an entitlement so to speak. The opinion pointed out:

> Property interests, of course, are not created by the Constitution. Rather, they are created and their dimensions are defined by existing rules or understandings that stem from an independent source such as state law — rules or understandings that secure certain benefits and that support claims of entitlement to those benefits. Thus, the welfare recipients in Goldberg v. Kelly, supra, had a claim of entitlement to welfare payments that was grounded in the statute defining eligibility for them. The recipients had not yet shown that they were, in fact, within the statutory terms of eligibility. But we held that they had a right to a hearing at which they might attempt to do so. [*Id.* at 577.]

To the majority, the professor was not able to establish any basis for an expectation that he would be hired — one that could be translated into a property interest. His contract was specific to the term of one year and did not provide for any terms of rehiring that could be interpreted as a statutory or contractual property interest.

Justice Douglas would have required the University to provide a hearing in that a First Amendment violation claim had been made. Despite the fact that the litigation of the issue had been stayed, the dissent saw no reason for not requiring a due process hearing to address those issues from the standpoint of the professor's liberty interest.

Yet, in a companion case, *Perry v. Sinderman*, 408 U.S. 593 (1972), the Court did find sufficient basis for establishing a property interest in continued employment for another academic who was not renewed for a successive one-year contract after several years with the institution. Like *Roth*, free speech issues were part of the case, but Justice Stewart noted that the mere allegation of retaliation for the exercise of the First Amendment right did not, without more, implicate a liberty interest. However, the Court found that the hiring and retention policies of the state school did implicate the property interest protectable under the Due Process Clause. The university had a peculiar provision in the college faculty guide essentially granting permanent de facto tenure as long as teaching services were satisfactory. To the court, this created a university "common law" or expected practice that the professor in this case was entitled to rely upon. The Court reasoned that this reliance was sufficient to establish a right to a prior hearing under the Due Process Clause.

---

[11] The Professor claimed that he was not rehired because of his criticism of University policy. Justice Stewart noted that proceedings on the First Amendment issues had been stayed by the district court and were not before the court in this case.

How Broad Is the Entitlement Principle? Recently, the Court dispelled any notion that every relationship between an individual and a government involves a formal entitlement and a protected interest. The respondent in *Town of Castle Rock v. Gonzales*, 545 U.S. 748 (2005), Jessica Gonzales, sued the town for the failure of its police department to enforce a restraining order against her estranged husband, a failure that resulted in the murder of the respondent's three daughters by the husband who was eventually killed in a confrontation with police. Gonzales claimed that she had a constitutionally protected property interest in the enforcement of the restraining order, pointing out the statutory basis for restraining orders in Colorado. Writing for the Court, Justice Scalia discussed the usual discretion involved in police work, pointing out that enforcement of the restraining order was not made more mandatory by its language or that of the statute governing restraining orders. Furthermore, Justice Scalia expressed doubts as to the appropriateness of criminal enforcement being characterized as a property interest, noting that since the *Roth* decision, the existence of some sort of monetary value in the new property was an implicit part of the definition of the interest. Finally the Court noted that the benefit was at best indirect, involving the state's obligation to act on a third party, a fact that Justice Scalia claimed further diluted Gonzales's claim of a property interest.

Justice Stevens, in a dissent joined by Justice Ginsburg, pointed out that the purpose of the Colorado statute governing restraining orders in domestic abuse situations was precisely to remove the discretion alluded to by the Court's opinion. Colorado joined a growing number of states passing domestic abuse legislation, the purpose of which was "to make police enforcement, not 'more mandatory' but simply mandatory. If as the Court says, the existence of a protected 'entitlement' turns on whether 'government officials may grant or deny it in their discretion,' the new mandatory statutes undeniably create an entitlement to police enforcement of restraining orders."

Overview of the Property Decisions. The Supreme Court's innovation in the area of procedural protection of property interests is in the liberal application of statutory and similar sources to entitlement to state employment, welfare payments, and other government benefits. However, the Court did seem on course to slowing down this expansion in *Town of Castle Rock* by suggesting that monetary value was a precondition to establishing a property right for due process purposes, effectively eliminating such traditional services as police protection from the expansion. During the same period, the Court established that the right to be heard about a deprivation of a benefit in which a property interest is established must be provided before a deprivation occurs (*Loudermill*).

The Liberty Interest. Meyer v. Nebraska, 262 U.S. 390, 399 (1923):

> While this Court has not attempted to define with exactness the liberty . . . guaranteed [by the Fourteenth Amendment], the term has received much consideration and some of the included things have been definitely stated. Without doubt, it denotes not merely freedom from bodily restraint but also the right of the individual to contract, to engage in any of the common occupations of life, to acquire useful knowledge, to marry, establish a home and bring up children, to worship God according to the dictates of his own conscience, and generally to enjoy those privileges long recognized . . . as essential to the orderly pursuit of happiness by free men.

By its own acknowledgment, the Court did not provide an exhaustive list of liberties subject to due process protections. In any list of liberties would be those that cannot be taken away but for a compelling reason under strict scrutiny analysis (fundamental liberties) and those whose sources are traced to statutory law, common law, or local custom. In the latter category, subject only to procedural protections, the Court has been less anxious to expand the definition of liberty, seeking instead to limit it to deprivation of liberties guaranteed by the state. For example, in *Paul v. Davis*, 424 U.S. 693 (1976), then Associate Justice Rehnquist declined, in a majority opinion, to extend procedural protections to reputation. The case involved a flyer distributed to retail businesses by a local Kentucky police department identifying Davis, among others, as a shoplifter, despite the fact that he had not been convicted of such a crime. Noting that state tort law would provide a remedy for damage to Davis's reputation, Justice Rehnquist noted that in previous cases addressing due process procedural protection of liberty "a right or status previously recognized by state law was distinctly altered or extinguished. It was this alteration, officially removing the interest from the recognition and protection previously afforded by the State, which we found sufficient to invoke the procedural guarantees contained in the Due Process Clause of the Fourteenth Amendment."

Davis was seeking a remedy for damage to his reputation. His interest in employment, freedom from restraint, or other attributes of the liberty interest had not been affected. Noting that "Kentucky law does not extend to respondent any legal guarantee of present enjoyment of reputation which has been altered as a result of petitioners' action" the Court declined to extend the definition of liberty beyond tangible guarantees of the government.

Chapter 6
Constitutionally Protected Rights
— Equal Protection

The Fourteenth Amendment's guarantee that no state shall "deny to any person within its jurisdiction the equal protection of the laws," is perhaps America's greatest anomaly. In a society where privilege, particularly in regard to wealth, abounds, a grant of "equal protection" seems to conflict with our core socio-economic cultural values. To enforce the equalitarian mandate of this language on our society via judicial review would likely have a revolutionary impact. Consequently, and perhaps much the same as the unequivocal language of the First Amendment, the history of the equal protection clause has been centered around how to limit its meaning and avoid a judicially led reordering of American society.

The first argument for such a limitation is to infer that the framers of the Amendment meant to limit its enforcement to the racial inequality that dominated the post-Civil War era. Though no one could deny its particular relevancy to the inequality that the freed persons in the South faced, the very language of the Amendment seems to limit such an interpretation. In fact, and as further support for an equal protection clause that reached beyond post war racial issues, the framers expanded the applicability of the clause to "any person," thus beyond the privilege and immunities clause limitation to "citizens." Though the Amendment's first sentence overrule of *Dred Scott* ("All persons born or naturalized in the United States, and subject to the jurisdiction thereof, are citizens of the United States and of the State wherein they reside.") made clear that persons previously held in the bondage of slavery were now citizens.

Perhaps a more tenable argument is to recognize that almost all laws discriminate. This is an argument that if meritorious would seem to prove that the framers could not have meant what they said. In this regard, for example, any criminal sanction discriminates against the convicted. Whatever one says about incarceration, the state most certainly discriminates against the prisoner! Here, of course, the argument is that the state has a valid purpose in discriminating against the convicted, serving to justify the discrimination. Viewed in this sense the clause would be interpreted as allowing a state to deny equal protection depending upon its purpose. An article published by Tussman & Broek, "The Equal Protection of the Laws," 37 Calf.L.Rev. 341 (1949), has been very influential in advancing this thesis, and is worthy of your review.

With this in mind and despite the unequivocal language of the equal protection clause, the Court has interpreted the clause as if it read, "A state *may* deny to any person within its jurisdiction the equal protection of the laws if it has a sufficient purpose." This type of analysis has limited an application of the clause that would challenge the very ethic of privilege that abounds in America. Any study of equal protection is then an analytical inquiry into whether a state has a sufficient purpose to defend its discriminatory classification.

I. An Overview — The "Old" and the "New"

The standard the Court applies, particularly how closely it scrutinizes a state's purpose in discriminating, becomes the central issue in the application of equal protection doctrine. As a means of gaining a general understanding we shall commence with an historical overview of how the Court has so analyzed. The decisional law that follows this overview will then be instructive as an application of these ends. We start with what scholars and the Court have described as the "old" and the "new" equal protection.

A. SOMETHING "OLD"

If legislation can meet the requirements of equal protection, the degree of judicial scrutiny that the Court applies in reviewing a state's legislative purpose is critical to the inquiry. We have learned thus far, for example, that the "lessons of the Lochner" have mandated minimal scrutiny of the state purpose in cases concerning "socio-economics." Here, and much the same, the Court has applied a "rational purpose" review of a state's purpose which bows to the "legislative process." This minimum scrutiny has been dubbed the "old" equal protection. The rational purpose inquiry of the "old" equal protection was so deferential that it was described as "fatal in theory but not in fact."

B. SOMETHING "NEW"

If this was the only standard applied in equal protection analysis we might well be successful in limiting the impact of the clause, but perhaps to a degree that its powerful verbiage would become meaningless in application. Recall, once again, Justice Stone's footnote in *Carolene Products*, that while supporting the "deferential review" of socio-economics in the post *Lochner* era, questioned the applicability of the same standard in regard to all discriminatory classification. Justice Stone suggested that discrimination in denial of fundamental rights (the Bill of Rights, vote, speech, religion, etc.) and discrimination against "racial minorities" ("prejudice against discrete and insular minorities") might "be subjected to more exacting judicial scrutiny."

It is that tact, "a dual standard, two tier approach," that the Court, particularly in the 1960s and the "Warren era," pursued as a "new" application of the equal protection clause. Thus, the level of judicial scrutiny applied to a state's legislative purpose now depended upon *who* (racial classifications) or *what* (fundamental rights) the legislation discriminated against. If the "old" equal protection was the deferential rational purpose test, this dual standard test became the "new" equal protection. To any analysis of state legislation the Court would apply a post-*Lochner* rational purpose test, deferential and easily defended by the State, unless the state discriminated against a racial classification or denied a fundamental right, which would require the state to prove a compelling purpose where strict scrutiny made a successful defense of the statute almost impossible. The second tier of the new equal protection was usually "strict in theory and *fatal* in fact."

C. THE NEWER THAN NEW BUT OLDER THAN OLD EQUAL PROTECTION

In 1973, in his dissenting opinion in *San Antonio Independent School dist. v. Rodriguez*, 411 U.S. 1, 65, Justice Thurgood Marshall commented:

The Court apparently seeks to establish today that equal protection cases fall into one of two neat categories which dictate the appropriate standard of review — strict scrutiny or mere rationality. But this Court's decisions in the field of equal protection defy such easy categorization. A principled reading of what this Court has done reveals that it has applied a spectrum of standards in reviewing discrimination allegedly violative of the Equal Protection Clause. This spectrum clearly comprehends variations in the degree of care with which *the* Court will scrutinize particular classifications, depending, I believe, on the constitutional and societal importance of the interest adversely affected and the recognized invidiousness of the basis upon which the particular classification is drawn. I find in fact that many of the Court's recent decisions embody the very sort of reasoned approach to equal protection analysis for which I previously argued — that is, an approach in which concentration (is) placed upon the character of the classification in question, the relative importance to individuals in the class discriminated against of the governmental benefits that they do not receive, and the asserted state interests in support of the classification.

In one paragraph Justice Marshall arguably laid the predicate for equal protection analysis in the modern era. The contemporary standards applied by the Court would find outcomes more fact based on case by case inquires, as opposed to the "automatics" of the "two-tiered" equal protection.

In the materials that follow we will see the Court apply a rational purpose test with more "teeth," and rather than the test predetermining the outcome, may find the Court striking down legislation. This rational purpose inquiry is arguably similar to the "old" rational purpose inquiry as opposed to the absolute deference of the "two tiered" approach. Thus, tongue in check, an "older than the old equal protection." Next, and just as Justice Marshall suggested that there are "variations in the degree of care with which the Court will scrutinize particular classifications," the Court will add a new "middle scrutiny" approach when gender and nonmarital children are so classified. This new standard, resting between the compelling and rational purpose tests, seemed to mirror Justice Marshall's prognostication. Finally, though the compelling purpose test of the "new equal projection" would remain, the "fatal in theory and in fact" application seemed to give way to an application of strict scrutiny that allowed room for the state to prove that they did have a compelling purpose. Much as the *Roe v. Wade* inquiry and particularly in regard to race based affirmative action, the modern compelling purpose test allowed the state to meet the previously steep evidential challenge successfully. Thus, and once again "tongue in cheek," a newer than new equal protection.

These inquires respond to Justice Marshall's description of "concentration. . . placed upon the character of the classification in question, [and] the relative importance to individuals in the class discriminated against," and in doing such stress the factual basis for outcomes in individual cases as opposed to the rather automatic result of the "neat categories" in the "two tiered" approach. The present equal protection analysis is "older, than old" in that state legislation may now be sustained under the rational purpose test, but is also "newer than new" because of the addition of a middle or heightened standard of review and a compelling purpose inquiry that might find the state successful.

The language of each inquiry scrutinizes the means the state applies to accomplishes its end. In a rational purpose inquiry the Court requires that the state maintain a legitimate purpose and that they have chosen a means to accomplish such that is rationally related to attaining their end. The "ante" steps up when middle or heightened scrutiny is applied because the state must now cite to an *"important"* governmental purpose that is *"substantially"* related to achieving their end. Where suspect classifications and fundamental rights are concerned, the state must prove a compelling purpose the means of which are closely tailored to the achievement of their ends, and that there is no "less restrictive" means of achieving their purpose. This is the "liturgy" of equal protection.

II. DISCRIMINATORY CLASSIFICATIONS

It is important to recognize that the right granted by Fourteenth Amendment's equal protection clause is a personal right not to be discriminated against. To allege a violation of equal protection one must first cite to a discriminatory classification. If this is a right not to be discriminated against in relation to others, then this right cannot be violated without alleging the nature of the discriminatory classification. In this section we will review discriminatory classifications: economic, race, gender, alienage, nonmarital children, and other additional classes. In order to determine the appropriate standard of review for any given classification, we must first allege a classification that the state is discriminating against.

A. ECONOMIC REGULATIONS: THE RATIONAL PURPOSE TEST

KOTCH v. BOARD OF RIVER PORT PILOTS
330 U.S. 552 (1947)

Mr. Justice BLACK delivered the opinion of the Court.

Louisiana statutes provide in general that all seagoing vessels moving between New Orleans and foreign ports must be navigated through the Mississippi River approaches to the port of New Orleans and within it, exclusively by pilots who are State Officers. New State pilots are appointed by the governor only upon certification of a State Board of River Pilot Commissioners, themselves pilots. Only those who have served a six month apprenticeship under incumbent pilots and who possess other specific qualifications may be certified to the governor by the board Appellants here have had at least fifteen years experience in the river, the port, and elsewhere, as pilots of vessels whose pilotage was not governed by the State law in question. Although they possess all the statutory qualifications except that they have not served the requisite six months apprenticeship under Louisiana officer pilots, they have been denied appointment as State pilots. Seeking relief in a Louisiana state court, they alleged that the incumbent pilots, having unfettered discretion under the law in the selection of apprentices, had selected with occasional exception, only the relatives and friends of incumbents; that the selections were made by electing prospective apprentices into the pilots' association, which the pilots have formed by authority of State law; that since "membership . . . is closed to all except those having the favor of the pilots" the result is that only their relatives and friends have and can become State pilots. The Supreme Court of Louisiana has held that the pilotage law so administered does not violate the equal protection clause of the Fourteenth Amendment, 209 La. 737, 25 So.2d 527. The case is here on appeal from that decision under 28 U.S.C. § 344(a), 28 U.S.C.A. § 344(a).

The constitutional command for a state to afford "equal protection of the laws" sets a goal not attainable by the invention and application of a precise formula. This Court has never attempted that impossible task. A law which affects the activities of some groups differently from the way in which it affects the activities of other groups is not necessarily banned by the Fourteenth Amendment. Otherwise, effective regulation in the public interest could not be provided, however essential that regulation might be. For it is axiomatic that the consequence of regulating by setting apart a classified group is that those in it will be subject to some restrictions or receive certain advantages that do not apply to other groups or to all the public. This selective application of a regulation is discrimination in the broad sense, but it may or may not deny equal protection of the laws. Clearly, it might offend that constitutional safeguard if it rested on grounds wholly irrelevant to achievement of the regulation's objectives. An example would be a law applied to deny a person a right to earn a living or hold any job because of hostility to his particular race, religion, beliefs, or because of any other reason having no rational relation to the regulated activities.

The case of Yick Wo v. Hopkins, 118 U.S. 356, relied on by appellants, is an illustration of a type of discrimination which is incompatible with any fair conception of equal protection of the laws. Yick Wo was denied the right to engage in an occupation supposedly open to all who could conduct their business in accordance with the law's requirements. He could meet these requirements, but was denied the right to do so solely because he was Chinese. And it made no difference that under the law as written Yick Wo would have enjoyed the same protection as all others. Its unequal application to Yick Wo was enough to condemn it. But Yick Wo's case, as other cases have demonstrated, was tested by the language of the law there considered and the administration there shown. So here, we must consider the relationship of the method of appointing pilots to the broad objectives of the entire Louisiana pilotage law. In so doing we must view the appointment system in the context of the historical evolution of the laws and institution of pilotage in Louisiana and elsewhere.

Studies of the long history of pilotage reveal that it is a unique institution and must be judged as such. In order to avoid invisible hazards, vessels approaching and leaving ports must be conducted from and to open waters by persons intimately familiar with the local waters. The pilot's job generally requires that he go outside the harbor's entrance in a small boat to meet incoming ships, board them and direct their course from open waters to the port. The same service is performed for vessels leaving the port. Pilots are thus indispensable cogs in the transportation system of every maritime economy. Their work prevents traffic congestion and accidents which would impair navigation in and to the ports. It affects the safety of lives and cargo, the cost and time expended in port calls, and in some measure, the competitive attractiveness of particular ports. Thus, for the same reasons that governments of most maritime communities have subsidized, regulated, or have themselves operated docks and other harbor facilities and sought to improve the approaches to their ports, they have closely regulated and often operated their ports' pilotage system.

The history and practice of pilotage demonstrate that, although inextricably geared to a complex commercial economy, it is also a highly personalized calling. A pilot does not require a formalized technical education so much as a detailed and extremely intimate, almost intuitive, knowledge of the weather, waterways and conformation of the harbor or river which he serves. This seems to be particularly true of the approaches to New Orleans through the treacherous and shifting channel of the Mississippi River. Moreover, harbor entrances where pilots can most conveniently make their homes and still be close to places where they board incoming and leave outgoing ships are usually some distance from the port cities they serve. These 'pilot towns' have begun, and generally exist today, as small communities of pilots perhaps near, but usually distinct from the port cities. In these communities young men have an opportunity to acquire special knowledge of the weather and water hazards of the locality and seem to grow up with ambitions to become pilots in the traditions of their fathers, relatives, and neighbors. We are asked, in effect, to say that Louisiana is without constitutional authority to conclude that apprenticeship under persons specially interested in a pilot's future is the best way to fit him for duty as a pilot officer in the service of the State.

The States have had full power to regulate pilotage of certain kinds of vessels since 1789 when the first Congress decided that then existing state pilot laws were satisfactory and made federal regulation unnecessary. Louisiana legislation has controlled the activities and appointment of pilots since 1805 — even before the Territory was admitted as a State. The State pilotage system, as it has evolved since 1805, is typical of that which grew up in most seaboard states and in foreign countries. Since 1805 Louisiana pilots have been State officers whose work has been controlled by the State. That Act forbade all but a limited number of pilots appointed by the governor to serve in that capacity. The pilots so appointed were authorized to select their own deputies. But pilots, and through them, their deputies, were literally under the command of the master and the wardens of the port of New Orleans, appointed by the governor. The master and wardens were authorized to make rules governing the practices of pilots, specifically empowered to order pilots to their stations, and to fine them for disobedience to orders or rules. And the pilots were required to make official bond for faithful performance of their duty. Pilots' fees were fixed; ships coming to the Mississippi were required to pay pilotage whether they took on pilots or not. The pilots were authorized to organize an association whose membership they controlled in order 'to enforce the legal regulations, and add to the efficiency of the service required thereby. Moreover, efficient and adequate service was sought to be insured by requiring the Board of Pilot Commissioners to report to the governor and authorizing him summarily to remove any pilot guilty of 'neglect of duty, habitual intemperance, carelessness, incompetency, or any act of conduct . . . showing' that he 'ought to be removed.' La.Act. No. 113, § 20 (1857). These provisions have been carried over with some revision into the present comprehensive Louisiana pilotage law. 6 La.Gen.Stat., cc. 6, 8 (1939). Thus in Louisiana, as elsewhere, it seems to have been accepted at an early date that in pilotage, unlike other occupations, competition for appointment, for the opportunity to serve particular ships and for fees, adversely affects the public interest in pilotage.

The practice of nepotism in appointing public servants has been a subject of controversy in this country throughout our history. Some states have adopted constitutional amendments or statutes, to prohibit it. These have reflected state policies to wipe out the practice. But Louisiana and most other states have adopted no such general policy. We can only assume that the Louisiana legislature weighed the obvious possibility of evil against whatever useful function a closely knit pilotage system may serve. Thus the advantages of early experience under friendly supervision in the locality of the pilot's training, the benefits to morale and esprit de corps which family and neighborly tradition might contribute, the close association in which pilots must work and live in their pilot communities and on the water, and the discipline and regulation which is imposed to assure the State competent pilot service after appointment, might have prompted the legislature to permit Louisiana pilot officers to select those which whom they would serve.

The number of people, as a practical matter, who can be pilots is very limited. No matter what system of selection is adopted, all but the few occasionally selected must of necessity be excluded. We are aware of no decision of this Court holding that the Constitution requires a state governor, or subordinates responsible to him and removable by him for cause, to select state public servants by competitive tests or by any other particular method of selection. The object of the entire pilotage law, as we have pointed out, is to secure for the State and others interested the safest and most efficiently operated pilotage system practicable. We cannot say that the method adopted in Louisiana for the selection of pilots is unrelated to this objective. We do not need to consider hypothetical questions concerning any similar system of selection which might conceivably be practiced in other professions or businesses regulated or operated by state governments. It is enough here that considering the entirely unique institution of pilotage in the light of its history in Louisiana, we cannot say that the practice appellants attack is the kind of discrimination which violates the equal protection clause of the Fourteenth Amendment. Affirmed.

Mr. Justice RUTLEDGE, dissenting.

The result of the decision therefore is to approve as constitutional state regulation which makes admission to the ranks of pilots turn finally on consanguinity. Blood is, in effect, made the crux of selection. That, in my opinion, is forbidden by the Fourteenth Amendment's guaranty against denial of the equal protection of the laws. The door is thereby closed to all not having blood relationship to presently licensed pilots. Whether the occupation is considered as having the status of "public officer" or of highly regulated private employment, it is beyond legislative power to make entrance to it turn upon such a criterion. The Amendment makes no exception from its prohibitions against state action on account of the fact that public rather than private employment is affected by the forbidden discriminations. That fact simply makes violation all the more clear where those discriminations are shown to exist.

It is not enough to avoid the Amendment's force that a familial system may have a tendency or, as the Court puts it, a direct relationship to the end of securing an efficient pilotage system. Classification based on the purpose to be accomplished may be said abstractly to be sound. But when the test adopted and applied in fact is race or consanguinity, it cannot be used constitutionally to bar all except a group chosen by such a relationship from public employment. That is not a test; it is a wholly arbitrary exercise of power.

[It] is precisely because the Amendment forbids enclosing those areas by legislative lines drawn on the basis of race, color, creed, and the like, that, in cases like this, the possibly most efficient method of securing the highest development of skills cannot be established by law. Absent any such bar, the presence of such a tendency or direct relationship would be effective for sustaining the legislation. It cannot be effective to overcome the bar itself. The discrimination here is not shown to be consciously racial in character. But I am unable to differentiate in effects one founded on blood relationship.

Mr. Justice Reed, Mr. Justice Douglas and Mr. Justice Murphy join in this dissent.

RAILWAY EXPRESS AGENCY v. NEW YORK
336 U.S. 106 (1949)

Mr. Justice DOUGLAS delivered the opinion of the Court.

Section 124 of the Traffic Regulations of the City of New York promulgated by the Police Commissioner provides: "No person shall operate, or cause to be operated, in or upon any street an advertising vehicle; provided that nothing herein contained shall prevent the putting of business notices upon business delivery vehicles, so long as such vehicles are engaged in the usual business or regular work of the owner and not used merely or mainly for advertising."

Appellant is engaged in a nation-wide express business. It operates about 1,900 trucks in New York City and sells the space on the exterior sides of these trucks for advertising. That advertising is for the most part unconnected with its own business. It was convicted in the magistrates court and fined.

The Court of Special Sessions concluded that advertising on vehicles using the streets of New York City constitutes a distraction to vehicle drivers and to pedestrians alike and therefore affects the safety of the public in the use of the streets. We do not sit to weigh evidence on the due process issue in order to determine whether the regulation is sound or appropriate; nor is it our function to pass judgment on its wisdom.

The question of equal protection of the laws is pressed more strenuously on us. It is pointed out that the regulation draws the line between advertisements of products sold by the owner of the truck and general advertisements. It is argued that unequal treatment on the basis of such a distinction is not justified by the aim and purpose of the regulation. It is said, for example, that one of appellant's trucks carrying the advertisement of a commercial house would not cause any greater distraction of pedestrians and vehicle drivers than if the commercial house carried the same advertisement on its own truck. Yet the regulation allows the latter to do what the former is forbidden from doing. It is therefore contended that the classification which the regulation makes has no relation to the traffic problem since a violation turns not on what kind of advertisements are carried on trucks but on whose trucks they are carried.

That, however, is a superficial way of analyzing the problem, even if we assume that it is premised on the correct construction of the regulation. The local authorities may well have concluded that those who advertised their own wares on their trucks do not present the same traffic problem in view of the nature or extent of the advertising which they use. It would take a degree of omniscience which we lack to say that such is not the case.

We cannot say that that judgment is not an allowable one. Yet if it is, the classification has relation to the purpose for which it is made and does not contain the kind of discrimination against which the Equal Protection Clause affords protection. It is by such practical considerations based on experience rather than by theoretical inconsistencies that the question of equal protection is to be answered. And the fact that New York City sees fit to eliminate from traffic this kind of distraction but does not touch what may be even greater ones in a different category, such as the vivid displays on Times Square, is immaterial. It is no requirement of equal protection that all evils of the same genus be eradicated or none at all. Affirmed.

Mr. Justice JACKSON, concurring.

My philosophy as to the relative readiness with which we should resort to these two clauses is almost diametrically opposed to the philosophy which prevails on this Court. While claims of denial of equal protection are frequently asserted, they are rarely sustained. But the Court frequently uses the due process clause to strike down measures taken by municipalities to deal with activities in their streets and public places which the local authorities consider to create hazards, annoyances or discomforts to their inhabitants.

[The] burden should rest heavily upon one who would persuade us to use the due process clause to strike down a substantive law or ordinance. Even its provident use against municipal regulations frequently disables all government — state, municipal and federal — from dealing with the conduct in question because the requirement of due process is also applicable to State and Federal Governments. Invalidation of a statute or an ordinance on due process grounds leaves ungoverned and ungovernable conduct which many people find objectionable.

Invocation of the equal protection clause, on the other hand, does not disable any governmental body from dealing with the subject at hand. It merely means that the prohibition or regulation must have a broader impact. I regard it as a salutary doctrine that cities, states and the Federal Government must exercise their powers so as not to discriminate between their inhabitants except upon some reasonable differentiation fairly related to the object of regulation. This equality is not merely abstract justice. The framers of the Constitution knew, and we should not forget today, that there is no more effective practical guaranty against arbitrary and unreasonable government than to require that the principles of law which officials would impose upon a minority must be imposed generally. Conversely, nothing opens the door to arbitrary action so effectively as to allow those officials to pick and choose only a few to whom they will apply legislation and thus to escape the political retribution that might be visited upon them if larger numbers were affected. Courts can take no better measure to assure that laws will be just than to require that laws be equal in operation.

This case affords an illustration. Even casual observations from the sidewalks of New York will show that an ordinance which would forbid all advertising on vehicles would run into conflict with many interests, including some, if not all, of the great metropolitan newspapers, which use that advertising extensively. Their blandishment of the latest sensations is not less a cause of diverted attention and traffic hazard than the commonplace cigarette advertisement which this truck-owner is forbidden to display. But any regulation applicable to all such advertising would require much clearer justification in local conditions to enable its enactment than does some regulation applicable to a few. I do not mention this to criticize the motives of those who enacted this ordinance, but it dramatizes the point that we are much more likely to find arbitrariness in the regulation of the few than of the many.

In this case, if the City of New York should assume that display of any advertising on vehicles tends and intends to distract the attention of persons using the highways and to increase the dangers of its traffic, I should think it fully within its constitutional powers to forbid it all. Instead of such general regulation of advertising, however, the City seeks to reduce the hazard only by saying that while some may, others may not exhibit such appeals. The same display, for example, advertising cigarettes, which this appellant is forbidden to carry on its trucks, may be carried on the trucks of a cigarette dealer.

The City urges that this applies equally to all persons of a permissible classification, because all that it does is (1) forbid all inhabitants of New York City from engaging in the business of selling advertising space on trucks which move as part of the city traffic; (2) forbid all truck owners from incidentally employing their vehicles for such purpose, with the exception that all truck owners can advertise their own business on their own trucks. It is argued that, while this does not eliminate vehicular advertising, it does eliminate such advertising for hire and to this extent cuts down the hazard sought to be controlled.

That the difference between carrying on any business for hire and engaging in the same activity on one's own is a sufficient one to sustain some types of regulations of the one that is not applied to the other, is almost elementary. But it is usual to find such regulations applied to the very incidents wherein the two classes present different problems, such as in charges, liability and quality of service.

The difference, however, is invoked here to sustain a discrimination in a problem in which the two classes present identical dangers. The courts of New York have declared that the sole nature and purpose of the regulation before us is to reduce traffic hazards. There is not even a pretense here that the traffic hazard created by the advertising which is forbidden is in any manner or degree more hazardous than that which is permitted.

[I] do not think differences of treatment under law should be approved on classification because of differences unrelated to the legislative purpose. The equal protection clause ceases to assure either equality or protection if it is avoided by any conceivable difference that can be pointed out between those bound and those left free. This Court has often announced the principle that the differentiation must have an appropriate relation to the object of the legislation or ordinance.

The question in my mind comes to this. Where individuals contribute to an evil or danger in the same way and to the same degree, may those who do so for hire be prohibited, while those who do so for their own commercial ends but not for hire be allowed to continue? I think the answer has to be that the hireling may be put in a class by himself and may be dealt with differently than those who act on their own. But this is not merely because such a discrimination will enable the lawmaker to diminish the evil. That might be done by many classifications, which I should think wholly unsustainable. It is rather because there is a real difference between doing in self-interest and doing for hire, so that it is one thing to tolerate action from those who act on their own and it is another thing to permit the same action to be promoted for a price.

[It] is not difficult to see that, in a day of extravagant advertising more or less subsidized by tax deduction, the rental of truck space could become an obnoxious enterprise. While I do not think highly of this type of regulation, that is not my business, and in view of the control I would concede to cities to protect citizens in quiet and orderly use for their proper purposes of the highways and public place. I think the judgment below must be affirmed.

DANDRIDGE v. WILLIAMS
397 U.S. 471 (1970)

[The Court sustained the Maryland Aid to Families with Dependent Children (AFDC) program that granted most eligible families their computed "standard of need," but imposed a maximum monthly grant of $250 per family regardless of family size or computed need. This standard of need was defined by the Statute as a minimum "subsistence need." Consequently, the State would not provide the basic necessities of life (food, shelter, etc.) when family size exceeded $250 per month. As Justice Marshall pointed out in his dissent, "the record in this case indicates that the State spends an average of almost $40 per recipient per month," assuming that this "subsistence need" would care for six children, a seventh child would not find any more funding available, either for the child, or the remainder of the family.]

Justice STEWART delivered the opinion of the Court:.

[Though Justice Stewart admitted that,] "Although the appellees argue that the younger and more recently arrived children in such families are totally deprived of aid, a more realistic view (Stewart's) is that the lot of the entire family is diminished because of the presence of additional children without any increase in payments," [he nonetheless concluded that]:

[Here] we deal with state regulation in the social and economic field, not affecting freedoms guaranteed by the Bill of Rights, and claimed to violate the Fourteenth Amendment only because the regulation results in some disparity in grants of welfare payments to the largest AFDC families. For this Court to approve the invalidation of state economic or social regulation [here] would be far too reminiscent of an era when the Court thought the Fourteenth Amendment gave it power to strike down state laws "because they may be unwise, improvident, or out of harmony with a particular school of thought," [Williamson v. Lee Optical Co.].

In the area of economics and social welfare, a State does not violate the Equal Protection Clause merely because the classifications made by its laws are imperfect. If the classification has some "reasonable basis," it does not offend the [Constitution]. To be sure, the cases [enunciating] this [standard] have in the main involved state regulation of business or industry. The administration of public welfare assistance, by contrast, involves the most basic economic needs of impoverished human beings. We recognize the dramatically real factual difference between the [business] cases and this one, but we can find no basis for applying a different constitutional standard. . . .

[The] maximum grant regulation is constitutionally valid. [By] keying the maximum family AFDC grants to the minimum wage a steadily employed head of a household receives, [the regulation encourages employment and avoids discrimination between welfare families and the families of the working poor]. [Although the regulation may be both over- and underinclusive,] the Equal Protection Clause does not require that a State must choose between attacking every aspect of a problem or not attacking the problem at all. [It] is enough that the State's action be rationally based and free from invidious discrimination. The regulation before us meets that test.

Justice MARSHALL, joined by Justice BRENNAN, dissented.

[The] maximum grant regulation [creates] two classes of eligible families: those small families [who] receive payments to cover their subsistence needs and those large families who do not. This classification [produces] a basic denial of equal treatment. [The] Court [focuses] upon the abstract dichotomy between two different approaches to equal protection [problems]. . . .

This case simply defies easy characterization in terms of one or the other of these "tests." The cases [that used] a "mere rationality" test [involved] the regulation of business interests. [But this] case, involving the literally vital interests of a powerless minority — poor families without breadwinners — is far removed from the area of business regulation. [On the other hand, in] my view, equal protection analysis of this case is not appreciably advanced by the a priori definition of a "right," fundamental or otherwise. Rather, concentration must be placed upon the character of the classification in question, the relative importance to individuals in the class discriminated against of the governmental benefits that they do not receive, and the asserted state interests in support of the classification. . . .

It is the individual interests here at stake [that] most clearly distinguish this case from the 'business regulation' equal protection cases. AFDC support to needy dependent children provides the stuff that sustains those children's lives: food, clothing, shelter. And this Court has already recognized [that] when a benefit [is] necessary to sustain life, stricter constitutional standards, both procedural and substantive, are applied to the deprivation of that benefit. [Citing, e.g., Shapiro v. Thompson, section E3 supra; Goldberg v. Kelly, section G infra.]

In the final analysis, Maryland has set up an AFDC program structured to calculate and pay the minimum standard of need to dependent children. Having set up that program, however, the State denies some of those needy children the minimum subsistence standard of living, and it does so on the wholly arbitrary basis that they happen to be members of large families. One need not speculate too far on the actual reason for the regulation, for in the early stages of this litigation the State virtually conceded that it set out to limit the total cost of the program along the path of least resistance. Now, however, we are told that other rationales can be manufactured to support the regulation and to sustain it against a fundamental constitutional challenge.

In any event, it cannot suffice merely to invoke the specter of the past and to recite from Lindsley v. Natural Carbonic Gas Co. and Williamson v. Lee Optical of Oklahoma, Inc. to decide the case. Appellees are not a gas company or an optical dispenser; they are needy dependent children and families who are discriminated against by the State. The basis of that discrimination — the classification of individuals into large and small families — is too arbitrary and too unconnected to the asserted rationale, the impact on those discriminated against — the denial of even a subsistence existence — too great, and the supposed interests served too contrived and attenuated to meet the requirements of the Constitution.

B. "PROVING UP DISCRIMINATION, DISCRIMINATORY PURPOSE"

The first thing we must do in an equal protection action is prove up a discriminatory classification. Of consequence, the nature of the classification will decide the level of scrutiny that the Court will apply and have a significant effect on the likely outcome. The significance of this determination is thus quite apparent. Off hand, however, it hardly seems that proving up discrimination should be a problem, for the legislation itself should set forth the discriminatory classification on its face. Unfortunately, however, life and discrimination are more subtle. Is it possible for a state to discriminate without alleging any such discrimination on the face of the statute? Can a statute be "neutral on its face," yet have a discriminatory purpose? *Yick Wo* has been cited as the classic example of a statute that although neutral on its face, was actionable because it was administered in a discriminatory fashion against one ethnic group. Effect alone seemed to prove a discriminatory purpose even though the statute was neutral on its face.

Post-apartheid America was also so circumstanced. By definition, apartheid, forced segregation of the races by law, engendered race-based discrimination on the face of the statute. Yet, do you think that the purging of apartheid from the American legal system would put an end to all state attempts to racially discriminate? The dominant issue in post-apartheid America focused on what appeared to be the racially discriminatory effect of statues that were neutral on their face. Thus, the state might discriminate against an economically deprived racial minority via legislation that classified and discriminated on the basis of wealth. If there was a desire to racially discriminate, this could thus be accomplished by application of the deferential rational purpose test applied to wealth-based discrimination. The question simply put was whether statistical proof of a racially discriminatory effect was sufficient to apply the strict scrutiny that would be mandated by race based discrimination. *Washington v. Davis* and *Arlington Heights* set forth the Supreme Court's answer to these most important questions in post apartheid America. *Feeny and Rodger v. Lodge* review similar issues in regard to gender and voting rights.

YICK WO v. HOPKINS
118 U.S. 356 (1886)

[A facially neutral (in regard to race) San Francisco ordinance required permission from the Board of Supervisors before a wooden laundry (a laundry in a wooden as opposed to a brick or stone building) could be operated in the City. The Board granted permits to operate "wooden" laundries to all but one non-Chinese applicant, but denied such permits to all, about 200, Chinese applicants. Yick Wo, a Chinese alien who had operated a wooden laundry for many years was refused such a permit and imprisoned for operating such a laundry.]

Mr. Justice MATTHEWS, opinion for the Court.

In the present cases, we are not obliged to reason from the probable to the actual, and pass upon the validity of the ordinances complained of, as tried merely by the opportunities which their terms afford, of unequal and unjust discrimination in their administration; for the cases present the ordinances in actual operation, and the facts shown establish an administration directed so exclusively against a particular class of persons as to warrant and require the conclusion that, whatever may have been the intent of the ordinances as adopted, they are applied by the public authorities charged with their administration, and thus representing the state itself, with a mind so unequal and oppressive as to amount to a practical denial by the state of that equal protection of the laws which is secured to the petitioners, as to all other persons, by the broad and benign provisions of the fourteenth amendment to the constitution of the United States. Though the law itself be fair on its face, and impartial in appearance, yet, if it is applied and administered by public authority with an evil eye and an unequal hand, so as practically to make unjust and illegal discriminations between persons in similar circumstances, material to their rights, the denial of equal justice is still within the prohibition of the constitution.

The present cases, as shown by the facts disclosed in the record, are within this class. It appears that both petitioners have complied with every requisite deemed by the law, or by the public officers charged with its administration, necessary for the protection of neighboring property from fire, or as a precaution against injury to the public health. No reason whatever, except the will of the supervisors, is assigned why they should not be permitted to carry on, in the accustomed manner, their harmless and useful occupation, on which they depend for a livelihood; and while this consent of the supervisors is withheld from them, and from 200 others who have also petitioned, all of whom happen to be Chinese subjects, 80 others, not Chinese subjects, are permitted to carry on the same business under similar conditions. The fact of this discrimination is admitted. No reason for it is shown, and the conclusion cannot be resisted that no reason for it exists except hostility to the race and nationality to which the petitioners belong, and which, in the eye of the law, is not justified. The discrimination is therefore illegal, and the public administration which enforces it is a denial of the equal protection of the laws, and a violation of the fourteenth amendment of the constitution. The imprisonment of the petitioners is therefore illegal, and they must be discharged.

WASHINGTON v. DAVIS
426 U.S. 229 (1976)

Mr. Justice WHITE delivered the opinion of the Court.

This case involves the validity of a qualifying test administered to applicants for positions as police officers in the District of Columbia Metropolitan Police Department. The test was sustained by the District Court but invalidated by the Court of Appeals. We are in agreement with the District Court and hence reverse the judgment of the Court of Appeals.

I

This action began on April 10, 1970, when two Negro police officers filed suit against the then Commissioner of the District of Columbia, the Chief of the District's Metropolitan Police Department, and the Commissioners of the United States Civil Service Commission. An amended complaint, filed December 10, alleged that the promotion policies of the Department were racially discriminatory and sought a declaratory judgment and an injunction. The respondents Harley and Sellers were permitted to intervene, their amended complaint asserting that their applications to become officers in the Department had been rejected, and that the Department's recruiting procedures discriminated on the basis of race against black applicants by a series of practices including, but not limited to, a written personnel test which excluded a disproportionately high number of Negro applicants. These practices were asserted to violate respondents' rights "under the due process clause of the Fifth Amendment to the United States Constitution, under 42 U.S.C. § 1981 and under D.C.Code § 1-320." Defendants answered, and discovery and various other proceedings followed. Respondents then filed a motion for partial summary judgment with respect to the recruiting phase of the case, seeking a declaration that the test administered to those applying to become police officers is "unlawfully discriminatory and thereby in violation of the due process clause of the Fifth Amendment. . . ." No issue under any statute or regulation was raised by the motion. The District of Columbia defendants, petitioners here, and the federal parties also filed motions for summary judgment with respect to the recruiting aspects of the case, asserting that respondents were entitled to relief on neither constitutional nor statutory grounds. The District Court granted petitioners' and denied respondents' motions. 348 F.Supp. 15 (DC1972).

According to the findings and conclusions of the District Court, to be accepted by the Department and to enter an intensive 17-week training program, the police recruit was required to satisfy certain physical and character standards, to be a high school graduate or its equivalent, and to receive a grade of at least 40 out of 80 on "Test 21," which is "an examination that is used generally throughout the federal service," which "was developed by the Civil Service Commission, not the Police Department," and which was "designed to test verbal ability, vocabulary, reading and comprehension." *Id.,* at 16.

The validity of Test 21 was the sole issue before the court on the motions for summary judgment. The District Court noted that there was no claim of "an intentional discrimination or purposeful discriminatory acts" but only a claim that Test 21 bore no relationship to job performance and "has a highly discriminatory impact in screening out black candidates." Ibid. Respondents' evidence, the District Court said, warranted three conclusions: "(a) The number of black police officers, while substantial, is not proportionate to the population mix of the city. (b) A higher percentage of blacks fail the Test than whites. (c) The Test has not been validated to establish its reliability for measuring subsequent job performance." Ibid. This showing was deemed sufficient to shift the burden of proof to the defendants in the action, petitioners here; but the court nevertheless concluded that on the undisputed facts respondents were not entitled to relief. The District Court relied on several factors. Since August 1969, 44% Of new police force recruits had been black; that figure also represented the proportion of blacks on the total force and was roughly equivalent to 20- to 29-year-old blacks in the 50-mile radius in which the recruiting efforts of the Police Department had been concentrated. It was undisputed that the Department had systematically and affirmatively sought to enroll black officers many of whom passed the test but failed to report for duty. The District Court rejected the assertion that Test 21 was culturally slanted to favor whites and was "satisfied that the indisputable facts prove the test to be reasonably and directly related to the requirements of the police recruit training program and that it is neither so designed nor operates [sic] to discriminate against otherwise qualified blacks' Id., at 17. It was thus not necessary to show that Test 21 was not only a useful indicator of training school performance but had also been validated in terms of job performance "The lack of job performance validation does not defeat the Test, given its direct relationship to recruiting and the valid part it plays in this process." Ibid. The District Court ultimately concluded that "[t]he proof is wholly lacking that a police officer qualifies on the color of his skin rather than ability" and that the Department "should not be required on this showing to lower standards or to abandon efforts to achieve excellence." Id., at 18.

Having lost on both constitutional and statutory issues in the District Court, respondents brought the case to the Court of Appeals claiming that their summary judgment motion, which rested on purely constitutional grounds, should have been granted. The tendered constitutional issue was whether the use of Test 21 invidiously discriminated against Negroes and hence denied them due process of law contrary to the commands of the Fifth Amendment. The Court of Appeals, addressing that issue, announced that it would be guided by Griggs v. Duke Power Co., 401 U.S. 424, 91 S.Ct. 849, 28 L.Ed.2d 158 (1971), a case involving the interpretation and application of Title VII of the Civil Rights Act of 1964, and held that the statutory standards elucidated in that case were to govern the due process question tendered in this one. 168 U.S.App.D.C. 42, 512 F.2d 956 (1975). The court went on to declare that lack of discriminatory intent in designing and administering Test 21 was irrelevant; the critical fact was rather that a far greater proportion of blacks four times as many failed the test than did whites. This disproportionate impact, standing alone and without regard to whether it indicated a discriminatory purpose, was held sufficient to establish a constitutional violation, absent proof by petitioners that the test was an adequate measure of job performance in addition to being an indicator of probable success in the training program, a burden which the court ruled petitioners had failed to discharge.

We have never held that the constitutional standard for adjudicating claims of invidious racial discrimination is identical to the standards applicable under Title VII, and we decline to do so today.

The central purpose of the Equal Protection Clause of the Fourteenth Amendment is the prevention of official conduct discriminating on the basis of race. It is also true that the Due Process Clause of the Fifth Amendment contains an equal protection component prohibiting the United States from invidiously discriminating between individuals or groups. Bolling v. Sharpe, 347 U.S. 497, 74 S.Ct. 693, 98 L.Ed. 884 (1954). But our cases have not embraced the proposition that a law or other official act, without regard to whether it reflects a racially discriminatory purpose, is unconstitutional solely because it has a racially disproportionate impact.

Almost 100 years ago, Strauder v. West Virginia, 100 U.S. 303, 25 L.Ed. 664 (1880), established that the exclusion of Negroes from grand and petit juries in criminal proceedings violated the Equal Protection Clause, but the fact that a particular jury or a series of juries does not statistically reflect the racial composition of the community does not in itself make out an invidious discrimination forbidden by the Clause. "A purpose to discriminate must be present which may be proven by systematic exclusion of eligible jurymen of the proscribed race or by unequal application of the law to such an extent as to show intentional discrimination." Akins v. Texas, 325 U.S. 398, 403-404, 65 S.Ct. 1276, 1279, 89 L.Ed. 1692, 1696 (1945). A defendant in a criminal case is entitled "to require that the State not deliberately and systematically deny to members of his race the right to participate as jurors in the administration of justice." Alexander v. Louisiana, 405 U.S. 625, 628-629, 92 S.Ct. 1221, 1224, 31 L.Ed.2d 536 (1972). See also Carter v. Jury Comm'n, 396 U.S. 320, 335-337, 339, 90 S.Ct. 5, 526-528, 529, 24 L.Ed.2d 549, 560-561, 562 (1970); Cassell v. Texas, 339 U.S. 282, 287-290, 70 S.Ct. 629, 631-633, 94 L.Ed. 839, 847-849 (1950); Patton v. Mississippi, 332 U.S. 463, 468-469, 68 S.Ct. 184, 187, 92 L.Ed. 76, 80 (1947).

The rule is the same in other contexts. Wright v. Rockefeller, 376 U.S. 52, 84 S.Ct. 603, 11 L.Ed.2d 512 (1964), upheld a New York congressional apportionment statute against claims that district lines had been racially gerrymandered. The challenged districts were made up predominantly of whites or of minority races, and their boundaries were irregularly drawn. The challengers did not prevail because they failed to prove that the New York Legislature "was either motivated by racial considerations or in fact drew the districts on racial lines"; the plaintiffs had not shown that the statute "was the product of a state contrivance to segregate on the basis of race or place of origin." Id., at 56, 58, 84 S.Ct., at 605, 11 L.Ed.2d, at 515. The dissenters were in agreement that the issue was whether the "boundaries . . . were purposefully drawn on racial lines." Id., at 67, 84 S.Ct., at 611, 11 L.Ed.2d, at 522.

The school desegregation cases have also adhered to the basic equal protection principle that the invidious quality of a law claimed to be racially discriminatory must ultimately be traced to a racially discriminatory purpose. That there are both predominantly black and predominantly white schools in a community is not alone violative of the Equal Protection Clause. The essential element of De jure segregation is "a current condition of segregation resulting from intentional state action. Keyes v. School Dist. No. 1, 413 U.S. 189, 205, 93 S.Ct. 2686, 2696, 37 L.Ed.2d 548 (1973). The differentiating factor between De jure segregation and so-called De facto segregation . . . is Purpose or Intent to segregate." Id., at 208, 93 S.Ct., at 2696, 37 L.Ed.2d, at 561. See also Id., at 199, 211, 213, 93 S.Ct. at 2692, 2698, 2699, 37 L.Ed.2d, at 558, 564, 566. The Court has also recently rejected allegations of racial discrimination based solely on the statistically disproportionate racial impact of various provisions of the Social Security Act because "(t)he acceptance of appellants' constitutional theory would render suspect each difference in treatment among the grant classes, however lacking in racial motivation and however otherwise rational the treatment might be." Jefferson v. Hackney, 406 U.S. 535, 548, 92 S.Ct. 1724, 1732, 32 L.Ed.2d 285, 297 (1972). And compare Hunter v. Erickson, 393 U.S. 385, 89 S.Ct. 557, 21 L.Ed.2d 616 (1969), with James v. Valtierra, 402 U.S. 137, 91 S.Ct. 1331, 28 L.Ed.2d 678 (1971).

This is not to say that the necessary discriminatory racial purpose must be express or appear on the face of the statute, or that a law's disproportionate impact is irrelevant in cases involving Constitution-based claims of racial discrimination. A statute, otherwise neutral on its face, must not be applied so as invidiously to discriminate on the basis of race. Yick Wo v. Hopkins, 118 U.S. 356, 6 S.Ct. 1064, 30 L.Ed. 220 (1886). It is also clear from the cases dealing with racial discrimination in the selection of juries that the systematic exclusion of Negroes is itself such an "unequal application of the law . . . as to show intentional discrimination." Akins v. Texas, supra, 325 U.S., at 404, 65 S.Ct., at 1279, 89 L.Ed., at 1696. Smith v. Texas, 311 U.S. 128, 61 S.Ct. 164, 85 L.Ed. 84 (1940); Pierre v. Louisiana, 306 U.S. 354, 59 S.Ct. 536, 83 L.Ed. 757 (1939); Neal v. Delaware, 103 U.S. 370, 26 L.Ed. 567 (1881). A prima facie case of discriminatory purpose may be proved as well by the absence of Negroes on a particular jury combined with the failure of the jury commissioners to be informed of eligible Negro jurors in a community, Hill v. Texas, 316 U.S. 400, 404, 62 S.Ct. 1159, 1161, 86 L.Ed. 1559, 1562 (1942), or with racially non-neutral selection procedures, Alexander v. Louisiana, supra; Avery v. Georgia, 345 U.S. 559, 73 S.Ct. 891, 97 L.Ed. 1244 (1953); Whitus v. Georgia, 385 U.S. 545, 87 S.Ct. 643, 17 L.Ed.2d 599 (1967). With a prima facie case made out, "the burden of proof shifts to the State to rebut the presumption of unconstitutional action by showing that permissible racially neutral selection criteria and procedures have produced the monochromatic result."

Necessarily, an invidious discriminatory purpose may often be inferred from the totality of the relevant facts, including the fact, if it is true, that the law bears more heavily on one race than another. It is also not infrequently true that the discriminatory impact in the jury cases for example, the total or seriously disproportionate exclusion of Negroes from jury venires may for all practical purposes demonstrate unconstitutionality because in various circumstances the discrimination is very difficult to explain on nonracial grounds. Nevertheless, we have not held that a law, neutral on its face and serving ends otherwise within the power of government to pursue, is invalid under the Equal Protection Clause simply because it may affect a greater proportion of one race than of another. Disproportionate impact is not irrelevant, but it is not the sole touchstone of an invidious racial discrimination forbidden by the Constitution. Standing alone, it does not trigger the rule, McLaughlin v. Florida, 379 U.S. 184, 85 S.Ct. 283, 13 L.Ed.2d 222 (1964), that racial classifications are to be subjected to the strictest scrutiny and are justifiable only by the weightiest of considerations.

There are some indications to the contrary in our cases. In Palmer v. Thompson, 403 U.S. 217, 91 S.Ct. 1940, 29 L.Ed.2d 438 (1971), the city of Jackson, Miss., following a court decree to this effect, desegregated all of its public facilities save five swimming pools which had been operated by the city and which, following the decree, were closed by ordinance pursuant to a determination by the city council that closure was necessary to preserve peace and order and that integrated pools could not be economically operated. Accepting the finding that the pools were closed to avoid violence and economic loss, this Court rejected the argument that the abandonment of this service was inconsistent with the outstanding desegregation decree and that the otherwise seemingly permissible ends served by the ordinance could be impeached by demonstrating that racially invidious motivations had prompted the city council's action. The holding was that the city was not overtly or covertly operating segregated pools and was extending identical treatment to both whites and Negroes. The opinion warned against grounding decision on legislative purpose or motivation, thereby lending support for the proposition that the operative effect of the law rather than its purpose is the paramount factor. But the holding of the case was that the legitimate purposes of the ordinance to preserve peace and avoid deficits were not open to impeachment by evidence that the councilmen were actually motivated by racial considerations. Whatever dicta the opinion may contain, the decision did not involve, much less invalidate, a statute or ordinary having neutral purposes but disproportionate racial consequences.

Wright v. Council of City of Emporia, 407 U.S. 451, 92 S.Ct. 2196, 33 L.Ed.2d 51 (1972), also indicates that in proper circumstances, the racial impact of a law, rather than its discriminatory purpose, is the critical factor. That case involved the division of a school district. The issue was whether the division was consistent with an outstanding order of a federal court to desegregate the dual school system found to have existed in the area. The constitutional predicate for the District Court's invalidation of the divided district was "the enforcement until 1969 of racial segregation in a public school system of which Emporia had always been a part." Id., at 459, 92 S.Ct., at 2202, 33 L.Ed.2d, at 60. There was thus no need to find "an independent constitutional violation." Ibid. Citing Palmer v. Thompson, we agreed with the District Court that the division of the district had the effect of interfering with the federal decree and should be set aside.

That neither Palmer Nor Wright was understood to have changed the prevailing rule is apparent from Keyes v. School Dist. No. 1, supra, where the principal issue in litigation was whether to what extent there had been purposeful discrimination resulting in a partially or wholly segregated school system. Nor did other later cases, Alexander v. Louisiana, supra, and Jefferson v. Hackney, supra, indicate that either Palmer or Wright had worked a fundamental change in equal protection law.

Both before and after Palmer v. Thompson, however, various Courts of Appeals have held in several contexts, including public employment, that the substantially disproportionate racial impact of a statute or official practice standing alone and without regard to discriminatory purpose, suffices to prove racial discrimination violating the Equal Protection Clause absent some justification going substantially beyond what would be necessary to validate most other legislative classifications. The cases impressively demonstrate that there is another side to the issue; but, with all due respect, to the extent that those cases rested on or expressed the view that proof of discriminatory racial purpose is unnecessary in making out an equal protection violation, we are in disagreement.

As an initial matter, we have difficulty understanding how a law establishing a racially neutral qualification for employment is nevertheless racially discriminatory and denies "any person . . . equal protection of the laws" simply because a greater proportion of Negroes fail to qualify than members of other racial or ethnic groups. Had respondents, along with all others who had failed Test 21, whether white or black, brought an action claiming that the test denied each of them equal protection of the laws as compared with those who had passed with high enough scores to qualify them as police recruits, it is most unlikely that their challenge would have been sustained. Test 21, which is administered generally to prospective Government employees, concededly seeks to ascertain whether those who take it have acquired a particular level of verbal skill; and it is untenable that the Constitution prevents the Government from seeking modestly to upgrade the communicative abilities of its employees rather than to be satisfied with some lower level of competence, particularly where the job requires special ability to communicate orally and in writing. Respondents, as Negroes, could no more successfully claim that the test denied them equal protection than could white applicants who also failed. The conclusion would not be different in the face of proof that more Negroes than whites had been disqualified by Test 21. That other Negroes also failed to score well would, alone, not demonstrate that respondents individually were being denied equal protection of the laws by the application of an otherwise valid qualifying test being administered to prospective police recruits.

Nor on the facts of the case before us would the disproportionate impact of Test 21 warrant the conclusion that it is a purposeful device to discriminate against Negroes and hence an infringement of the constitutional rights of respondents as well as other black applicants. As we have said, the test is neutral on its face and rationally may be said to serve a purpose the Government is constitutionally empowered to pursue. Even agreeing with the District Court that the differential racial effect of Test 21 called for further inquiry, we think the District Court correctly held that the affirmative efforts of the Metropolitan Police Department to recruit black officers, the changing racial composition of the recruit classes and of the force in general, and the relationship of the test to the training program negated any inference that the Department discriminated on the basis of race or that "a police officer qualifies on the color of his skin rather than ability." 348 F.Supp., at 18.

Under Title VII, Congress provided that when hiring and promotion practices disqualifying substantially disproportionate numbers of blacks are challenged, discriminatory purpose need not be proved, and that it is an insufficient response to demonstrate some rational basis for the challenged practices. It is necessary, in addition, that they be "validated" in terms of job performance in any one of several ways, perhaps by ascertaining the minimum skill, ability, or potential necessary for the position at issue and determining whether the qualifying tests are appropriate for the selection of qualified applicants for the job in question. However this process proceeds, it involves a more probing judicial review of, and less deference to, the seemingly reasonable acts of administrators and executives than is appropriate under the Constitution where special racial impact, without discriminatory purpose, is claimed. We are not disposed to adopt this more rigorous standard for the purposes of applying the Fifth and the Fourteenth Amendments in cases such as this.

A rule that a statute designed to serve neutral ends is nevertheless invalid, absent compelling justification, if in practice it benefits or burdens one race more than another would be far-reaching and would raise serious questions about, and perhaps invalidate, a whole range of tax, welfare, public service, regulatory, and licensing statutes that may be more burdensome to the poor and to the average black than to the more affluent white.

Given that rule, such consequences would perhaps be likely to follow. However, in our view, extension of the rule beyond those areas where it is already applicable by reason of statute, such as in the field of public employment, should await legislative prescription.

Mr. Justice STEVENS, concurring.

The requirement of purposeful discrimination is a common thread running through the cases summarized in Part II. These cases include criminal convictions which were set aside because blacks were excluded from the grand jury, a reapportionment case in which political boundaries were obviously influenced to some extent by racial considerations, a school desegregation case, and a case involving the unequal administration of an ordinance purporting to prohibit the operation of laundries in frame buildings. Although it may be proper to use the same language to describe the constitutional claim in each of these contexts, the burden of proving a prima facie case may well involve differing evidentiary considerations. The extent of deference that one pays to the trial court's determination of the factual issue, and indeed, the extent to which one characterizes the intent issue as a question of fact or a question of law, will vary in different contexts.

Frequently the most probative evidence of intent will be objective evidence of what actually happened rather than evidence describing the subjective state of mind of the actor. For normally the actor is presumed to have intended the natural consequences of his deeds. This is particularly true in the case of governmental action which is frequently the product of compromise, of collective decisionmaking, and of mixed motivation. It is unrealistic, on the one hand, to require the victim of alleged discrimination to uncover the actual subjective intent of the decisionmaker or, conversely, to invalidate otherwise legitimate action simply because an improper motive affected the deliberation of a participant in the decisional process. A law conscripting clerics should not be invalidated because an atheist voted for it.

My point in making this observation is to suggest that the line between discriminatory purpose and discriminatory impact is not nearly as bright, and perhaps not quite as critical, as the reader of the Court's opinion might assume. I agree, of course, that a constitutional issue does not arise every time some disproportionate impact is shown. On the other hand, when the disproportion is as dramatic as in Gomillion v. Lightfoot, 364 U.S. 339, 81 S.Ct. 125, 5 L.Ed.2d 110 or Yick Wo v. Hopkins, 118 U.S. 356, 6 S.Ct. 1064, 30 L.Ed. 220 (1886), it really does not matter whether the standard is phrased in terms of purpose or effect. Therefore, although I accept the statement of the general rule in the Court's opinion, I am not yet prepared to indicate how that standard should be applied in the many cases which have formulated the governing standard in different language.

My agreement with the conclusion reached in Part II of the Court's opinion rests on a ground narrower than the Court describes. I do not rely at all on the evidence of good-faith efforts to recruit black police officers. In my judgment, neither those efforts nor the subjective good faith of the District administration, would save Test 21 if it were otherwise invalid.

There are two reasons why I am convinced that the challenge to Test 21 is insufficient. First, the test serves the neutral and legitimate purpose of requiring all applicants to meet a uniform minimum standard of literacy. Reading ability is manifestly relevant to the police function, there is no evidence that the required passing grade was set at an arbitrarily high level, and there is sufficient disparity among high schools and high school graduates to justify the use of a separate uniform test. Second, the same test is used throughout the federal service. The applicants for employment in the District of Columbia Police Department represent such a small fraction of the total number of persons who have taken the test that their experience is of minimal probative value in assessing the neutrality of the test itself.

ARLINGTON HEIGHTS v. METROPOLITAN HOUSING DEVELOPMENT CORP.
429 U.S. 252 (1977)

Respondent Metropolitan Housing Development Corp. (MHDC), a nonprofit developer, contracted to purchase a tract within the boundaries of petitioner Village in order to build racially integrated low- and moderate-income housing. The contract was contingent upon securing rezoning as well as federal housing assistance. MHDC applied to the Village for the necessary rezoning from a single-family to a multiple-family (R-5) classification. At a series of Village Plan Commission public meetings, both supporters and opponents touched upon the fact that the project would probably be racially integrated. Opponents also stressed zoning factors that pointed toward denial of MHDC's application: The location had always been zoned single-family, and the Village's apartment policy called for limited use of R-5 zoning, primarily as a buffer between single-family development and commercial or manufacturing districts, none of which adjoined the project's proposed location. After the Village denied rezoning, MHDC and individual minority respondents filed this suit for injunctive and declaratory relief, alleging that the denial was racially discriminatory and violated, inter alia, the Equal Protection Clause of the Fourteenth Amendment and the Fair Housing Act. The District Court held that the Village's rezoning denial was motivated not by racial discrimination but by a desire to protect property values and maintain the Village's zoning plan. Though approving those conclusions, the Court of Appeals reversed, finding that the "ultimate effect" of the rezoning denial was racially discriminatory and observing that the denial would disproportionately affect blacks, particularly in view of the fact that the general suburban area, though economically expanding, continued to be marked by residential segregation.

Mr. Justice POWELL delivered the opinion of the Court.

In 1971 respondent Metropolitan Housing Development Corporation (MHDC) applied to petitioner, the Village of Arlington Heights, Ill., for the rezoning of a 15-acre parcel from single-family to multiple-family classification. Using federal financial assistance, MHDC planned to build 190 clustered townhouse units for low- and moderate-income tenants. The Village denied the rezoning request. MHDC, joined by other plaintiffs who are also respondents here, brought suit in the United States District Court for the Northern District of Illinois. They alleged that the denial was racially discriminatory and that it violated, inter alia, the Fourteenth Amendment and the Fair Housing Act of 1968, 82 Stat. 81, 42 U.S.C. § 3601 et seq. Following a bench trial, the District Court entered judgment for the Village, 373 F.Supp. 208 (1974), and respondents appealed. The Court of Appeals for the Seventh Circuit reversed, finding that the "ultimate effect" of the denial was racially discriminatory, and that the refusal to rezone therefore violated the Fourteenth Amendment. 517 F.2d 409 (1975). We granted the Village's petition for certiorari, 423 U.S. 1030, 96 S.Ct. 560, 46 L.Ed.2d 404 (1975), and now reverse.

Arlington Heights is a suburb of Chicago, located about 26 miles northwest of the downtown Loop area. Most of the land in Arlington Heights is zoned for detached single-family homes, and this is in fact the prevailing land use. The Village experienced substantial growth during the 1960's, but, like other communities in northwest Cook County, its population of racial minority groups remained quite low. According to the 1970 census, only 27 of the Village's 64,000 residents were black.

[Our] decision last Term in Washington v. Davis, 426 U.S. 229, 96 S.Ct. 2040, 48 L.Ed.2d 597 (1976), made it clear that official action will not be held unconstitutional solely because it results in a racially disproportionate impact. "Disproportionate impact is not irrelevant, but it is not the sole touchstone of an invidious racial discrimination." Id., at 242, 96 S.Ct., at 2049. Proof of racially discriminatory intent or purpose is required to show a violation of the Equal Protection Clause. Although some contrary indications may be drawn from some of our cases, the holding in Davis reaffirmed a principle well established in a variety of contexts.

Davis does not require a plaintiff to prove that the challenged action rested solely on racially discriminatory purposes. Rarely can it be said that a legislature or administrative body operating under a broad mandate made a decision motivated solely by a single concern, or even that a particular purpose was the "dominant" or "primary" one. In fact, it is because legislators and administrators are properly concerned with balancing numerous competing considerations that courts refrain from reviewing the merits of their decisions, absent a showing of arbitrariness or irrationality. But racial discrimination is not just another competing consideration. When there is a proof that a discriminatory purpose has been a motivating factor in the decision, this judicial deference is no longer justified.

[Determining] whether invidious discriminatory purpose was a motivating factor demands a sensitive inquiry into such circumstantial and direct evidence of intent as may be available. The impact of the official action whether it "bears more heavily on one race than another," Washington v. Davis, supra, 426 U.S., at 242, 96 S.Ct., at 2049 may provide an important starting point. Sometimes a clear pattern, unexplainable on grounds other than race, emerges from the effect of the state action even when the governing legislation appears neutral on its face. Yick Wo v. Hopkins, 118 U.S. 356, 6 S.Ct. 1064, 30 L.Ed. 220 (1886); Guinn v. United States, 238 U.S. 347, 35 S.Ct. 926, 59 L.Ed. 1340 (1915); Lane v. Wilson, 307 U.S. 268, 59 S.Ct. 872, 83 L.Ed. 1281 (1939); Gomillion v. Lightfoot, 364 U.S. 339, 81 S.Ct. 125, 5 L.Ed.2d 110 (1960). The evidentiary inquiry is then relatively easy. But such cases are rare. Absent a pattern as stark as that in Gomillion or Yick Wo, impact alone is not determinative, and the Court must look to other evidence.

The historical background of the decision is one evidentiary source, particularly if it reveals a series of official actions taken for invidious purposes. The specific sequence of events leading up the challenged decision also may shed some light on the decisionmaker's purposes. Reitman v. Mulkey, 387 U.S. 369, 373-376, 87 S.Ct. 1627, 1629-1631, 18 L.Ed.2d 830 (1967); Grosjean v. American Press Co., 297 U.S. 233, 250, 56 S.Ct. 444, 449, 80 L.Ed. 660 (1936). For example, if the property involved here always had been zoned R-5 but suddenly was changed to R-3 when the town learned of MHDC's plans to erect integrated housing, we would have a far different case. Departures from the normal procedural sequence also might afford evidence that improper purposes are playing a role. Substantive departures too may be relevant, particularly if the factors usually considered important by the decisionmaker strongly favor a decision contrary to the one reached.

The legislative or administrative history may be highly relevant, especially where there are contemporary statements by members of the decisionmaking body, minutes of its meetings, or reports. In some extraordinary instances the members might be called to the stand at trial to testify concerning the purpose of the official action, although even then such testimony frequently will be privileged.

This case was tried in the District Court and reviewed in the Court of Appeals before our decision in Washington v. Davis, supra. The respondents proceeded on the erroneous theory that the Village's refusal to rezone carried a racially discriminatory effect and was, without more, unconstitutional. But both courts below understood that at least part of their function was to examine the purpose underlying the decision. In making its findings on this issue, the District Court noted that some of the opponents of Lincoln Green who spoke at the various hearings might have been motivated by opposition to minority groups. The court held, however, that the evidence "does not warrant the conclusion that this motivated the defendants."

On appeal the Court of Appeals focused primarily on respondents' claim that the Village's buffer policy had not been consistently applied and was being invoked with a strictness here that could only demonstrate some other underlying motive. The court concluded that the buffer policy, though not always applied with perfect consistency, had on several occasions formed the basis for the Board's decision to deny other rezoning proposals. "The evidence does not necessitate a finding that Arlington Heights administered this policy in a discriminatory manner." 517 F.2d, at 412. The Court of Appeals therefore approved the District Court's findings concerning the Village's purposes in denying rezoning to MHDC.

[In] sum, the evidence does not warrant overturning the concurrent findings of both courts below. Respondents simply failed to carry their burden of proving that discriminatory purpose was a motivating factor in the Village's decision. This conclusion ends the constitutional inquiry. The court of Appeals' further finding that the Village's decision carried a discriminatory "ultimate effect" is without independent constitutional significance.

Respondents' complaint also alleged that the refusal to rezone violated the Fair Housing Act of 1968, 42 U.S.C. § 3601 et seq. They continue to urge here that a zoning decision made by a public body may, and that petitioners' action did, violate § 3604 or § 3617. The Court of Appeals, however, proceeding in a somewhat unorthodox fashion, did not decide the statutory question. We remand the case for further consideration of respondents' statutory claims. Reversed and remanded.

Comments on *Davis* and *Arlington Heights*. How important are these cases? How difficult is the affirmative burden placed on plaintiffs? Congress, in civil rights legislation under Title VII, has allowed discriminatory effect to prove a prima facia case, permitting a defendant to rebut this presumption. Why did Congress so act? How difficult is it to prove discriminatory purpose? How difficult is it to prove anyone's "intent," or "state of mind"? Is that why we have negligence and foreseeability in tort law? What would happen if we only had intentional torts?

What do you think of these decisions viewed in this context? Given that in the post apartheid era race based discrimination on the face of a statute was likely unconstitutional, the ability to accomplish the same via statutes race neutral on there face, despite a racially discriminatory effect, arguably became the only means of perpetuating state based racial discrimination. Was the Court's conclusion in these cases a tip of their moral hand, or do the facts of *Davis* prove that what seems to be may not be? Keep in mind that the issue is "burden of proof," if a defendant can prove a neutral explanation for a discriminatory effect, the cause would not be actionable.

After these cases can "effect" alone, outside of Title VII, ever prove up a prima facia case? Is *Yick Wo* still good law?

**TEXAS DEPARTMENT OF HOUSING
AND COMMUNITY AFFAIRS ET AL. v.
INCLUSIVE COMMUNITIES PROJECT, INC., ET AL.**
576 U.S. 519 (2015)

JUSTICE KENNEDY delivered the opinion of the Court.

The underlying dispute in this case concerns where housing for low-income persons should be constructed in Dallas, Texas—that is, whether the housing should be built in the inner city or in the suburbs. This dispute comes to the Court on a disparate-impact theory of liability. In contrast to a disparate-treatment case, where a "plaintiff must establish that the defendant had a discriminatory intent or motive," a plaintiff bringing a disparate impact claim challenges practices that have a "disproportionately adverse effect on minorities" and are otherwise unjustified by a legitimate rationale. Ricci v. DeStefano, 557 U. S. 557, 577 (2009) (internal quotation marks omitted). The question presented for the Court's determination is whether disparate-impact claims are cognizable under the Fair Housing Act (or FHA), 82 Stat. 81, as amended, 42 U. S. C. §3601 et seq.

I

A

Before turning to the question presented, it is necessary to discuss a different federal statute that gives rise to this dispute. The Federal Government provides low-income housing tax credits that are distributed to developers through designated state agencies. 26 U. S. C. §42. Congress has directed States to develop plans identifying selection criteria for distributing the credits. §42(m)(1). Those plans must include certain criteria, such as public housing waiting lists, §42(m)(1)(C), as well as certain preferences, including that low-income housing units "contribut[e] to a concerted community revitalization plan" and be built in census tracts populated predominantly by low-income residents. §§42(m)(1)(B)(ii)(III), 42(d)(5)(ii)(I). Federal law thus favors the distribution of these tax credits for the development of housing units in low-income areas.

In the State of Texas these federal credits are distributed by the Texas Department of Housing and Community Affairs (Department). Under Texas law, a developer's application for the tax credits is scored under a point system that gives priority to statutory criteria, such as the financial feasibility of the development project and the income level of tenants. Tex. Govt. Code Ann. §§2306.6710(a)–(b) (West 2008). The Texas Attorney General has interpreted state law to permit the consideration of additional criteria, such as whether the housing units will be built in a neighborhood with good schools. Those criteria cannot be awarded more points than statutorily mandated criteria. Tex. Op. Atty. Gen. No. GA– 0208, pp. 2–6 (2004), 2004 WL 1434796, *4–*6.

The Inclusive Communities Project, Inc. (ICP), is a Texas-based nonprofit corporation that assists low-income families in obtaining affordable housing. In 2008, the ICP brought this suit against the Department and its officers in the United States District Court for the Northern District of Texas. As relevant here, it brought a disparate impact claim under §§804(a) and 805(a) of the FHA. The ICP alleged the Department has caused continued segregated housing patterns by its disproportionate allocation of the tax credits, granting too many credits for housing in predominantly black inner-city areas and too few in predominantly white suburban neighborhoods. The ICP contended that the Department must modify its selection criteria in order to encourage the construction of low-income housing in suburban communities.

The District Court concluded that the ICP had established a prima facie case of disparate impact. It relied on two pieces of statistical evidence. First, it found "from 1999–2008, [the Department] approved tax credits for 49.7% of proposed non-elderly units in 0% to 9.9% Caucasian areas, but only approved 37.4% of proposed nonelderly units in 90% to 100% Caucasian areas." 749 F. Supp. 2d 486, 499 (ND Tex. 2010) (footnote omitted). Second, it found "92.29% of [low-income housing tax credit] units in the city of Dallas were located in census tracts with less than 50% Caucasian residents." Ibid.

The District Court then placed the burden on the Department to rebut the ICP's prima facie showing of disparate impact. 860 F. Supp. 2d 312, 322–323 (2012). After assuming the Department's proffered interests were legitimate, id., at 326, the District Court held that a defendant—here the Department—must prove "that there are no other less discriminatory alternatives to advancing their proffered interests," ibid. Because, in its view, the Department "failed to meet [its] burden of proving that there are no less discriminatory alternatives," the District Court ruled for the ICP. Id., at 331.

The District Court's remedial order required the addition of new selection criteria for the tax credits. For instance, it awarded points for units built in neighborhoods with good schools and disqualified sites that are located adjacent to or near hazardous conditions, such as high crime areas or landfills. See 2012 WL 3201401 (Aug. 7, 2012). The remedial order contained no explicit racial targets or quotas.

While the Department's appeal was pending, the Secretary of Housing and Urban Development (HUD) issued a regulation interpreting the FHA to encompass disparate impact liability. See Implementation of the Fair Housing Act's Discriminatory Effects Standard, 78 Fed. Reg. 11460 (2013). The regulation also established a burden-shifting framework for adjudicating disparate-impact claims. Under the regulation, a plaintiff first must make a prima facie showing of disparate impact. That is, the plaintiff "has the burden of proving that a challenged practice caused or predictably will cause a discriminatory effect." 24 CFR §100.500(c)(1) (2014). If a statistical discrepancy is caused by factors other than the defendant's policy, a plaintiff cannot establish a prima facie case, and there is no liability. After a plaintiff does establish a prima facie showing of disparate impact, the burden shifts to the defendant to "prov[e] that the challenged practice is necessary to achieve one or more substantial, legitimate, nondiscriminatory interests." §100.500(c)(2). HUD has clarified that this step of the analysis "is analogous to the Title VII requirement that an employer's interest in an employment practice with a disparate impact be job related." 78 Fed. Reg. 11470. Once a defendant has satisfied its burden at step two, a plaintiff may "prevail upon proving that the substantial, legitimate, nondiscriminatory interests supporting the challenged practice could be served by another practice that has a less discriminatory effect." §100.500(c)(3).

The Court of Appeals for the Fifth Circuit held, consistent with its precedent, that disparate-impact claims are cognizable under the FHA. 747 F. 3d 275, 280 (2014). On the merits, however, the Court of Appeals reversed and remanded. Relying on HUD's regulation, the Court of Appeals held that it was improper for the District Court to have placed the burden on the Department to prove there were no less discriminatory alternatives for allocating low-income housing tax credits. Id., at 282–283.

[B]

De jure residential segregation by race was declared unconstitutional almost a century ago, Buchanan v. Warley, 245 U. S. 60 (1917), but its vestiges remain today, intertwined with the country's economic and social life. Some segregated housing patterns can be traced to conditions that arose in the mid-20th century. Rapid urbanization, concomitant with the rise of suburban developments accessible by car, led many white families to leave the inner cities. This often left minority families concentrated in the center of the Nation's cities. During this time, various practices were followed, sometimes with governmental support, to encourage and maintain the separation of the races: Racially restrictive covenants prevented the conveyance of property to minorities, see Shelley v. Kraemer, 334 U. S. 1 (1948); steering by real-estate agents led potential buyers to consider homes in racially homogenous areas; and discriminatory lending practices, often referred to as redlining, precluded minority families from purchasing homes in affluent areas. See, e.g., M. Klarman, Unfinished Business: Racial Equality in American History 140– 141 (2007); Brief for Housing Scholars as Amici Curiae 22–23. By the 1960's, these policies, practices, and prejudices had created many predominantly black inner cities surrounded by mostly white suburbs. See K. Clark, Dark Ghetto: Dilemmas of Social Power 11, 21–26 (1965).

The mid-1960's was a period of considerable social unrest; and, in response, President Lyndon Johnson established the National Advisory Commission on Civil Disorders, commonly known as the Kerner Commission. Exec. Order No. 11365, 3 CFR 674 (1966– 1970 Comp.). After extensive fact finding the Commission identified residential segregation and unequal housing and economic conditions in the inner cities as significant, underlying causes of the social unrest. See Report of the National Advisory Commission on Civil Disorders 91 (1968) (Kerner Commission Report). The Commission found that "[n]early two-thirds of all nonwhite families living in the central cities today live in neighborhoods marked by substandard housing and general urban blight." Id., at 13. The Commission further found that both open and covert racial discrimination prevented black families from obtaining better housing and moving to integrated communities. Ibid. The Commission concluded that "[o]ur Nation is moving toward two societies, one black, one white—separate and unequal." Id., at 1. To reverse "[t]his deepening racial division," ibid., it recommended enactment of "a comprehensive and enforceable open-occupancy law making it an offense to discriminate in the sale or rental of any housing . . . on the basis of race, creed, color, or national origin." Id., at 263.

In April 1968, Dr. Martin Luther King, Jr., was assassinated in Memphis, Tennessee, and the Nation faced a new urgency to resolve the social unrest in the inner cities. Congress responded by adopting the Kerner Commission's recommendation and passing the Fair Housing Act. The statute addressed the denial of housing opportunities on the basis of "race, color, religion, or national origin." Civil Rights Act of 1968, §804, 82 Stat. 83. Then, in 1988, Congress amended the FHA. Among other provisions, it created certain exemptions from liability and added "familial status" as a protected characteristic. See Fair Housing Amendments Act of 1988, 102 Stat. 1619.

II

The issue here is whether, under a proper interpretation of the FHA, housing decisions with a disparate impact are prohibited. Before turning to the FHA, however, it is necessary to consider two other antidiscrimination statutes that preceded it.

The first relevant statute is §703(a) of Title VII of the Civil Rights Act of 1964, 78 Stat. 255. The Court addressed the concept of disparate impact under this statute in Griggs v. Duke Power Co., 401 U. S. 424 (1971). There, the employer had a policy requiring its manual laborers to possess a high school diploma and to obtain satisfactory scores on two intelligence tests. The Court of Appeals held the employer had not adopted these job requirements for a racially discriminatory purpose, and the plaintiffs did not challenge that holding in this Court. Instead, the plaintiffs argued §703(a)(2) covers the discriminatory effect of a practice as well as the motivation behind the practice. Section 703(a), as amended, provides as follows:

> "It shall be an unlawful employer practice for an employer—
> "(1) to fail or refuse to hire or to discharge any individual, or otherwise to discriminate against any individual with respect to his compensation, terms, conditions, or privileges of employment, because of such individual's race, color, religion, sex, or national origin; or
> "(2) to limit, segregate, or classify his employees or applicants for employment in any way which would deprive or tend to deprive any individual of employment opportunities or otherwise adversely affect his status as an employee, because of such individual's race, color, religion, sex, or national origin." 42 U. S. C. §2000e–2(a).

The Court did not quote or cite the full statute, but rather relied solely on §703(a)(2). Griggs, 401 U. S., at 426, n. 1.

In interpreting §703(a)(2), the Court reasoned that disparate-impact liability furthered the purpose and design of the statute. The Court explained that, in §703(a)(2), Congress "proscribe[d] not only overt discrimination but also practices that are fair in form, but discriminatory in operation."

[The] Court put important limits on its holding: namely, not all employment practices causing a disparate impact impose liability under §703(a)(2). In this respect, the Court held that "business necessity" constitutes a defense to disparate-impact claims. Id., at 431. This rule provides, for example, that in a disparate-impact case, §703(a)(2) does not prohibit hiring criteria with a "manifest relationship" to job performance. Id., at 432; see also Ricci, 557 U. S., at 587–589 (emphasizing the importance of the business necessity defense to disparate-impact liability). On the facts before it, the Court in Griggs found a violation of Title VII because the employer could not establish that high school diplomas and general intelligence tests were related to the job performance of its manual laborers. See 401 U. S., at 431–432.

[The Court discusses a similar interpretation encompassing disparate impact of the Age Discrimination in Employment Act in Smith v. City of Jackson, 544 U.S. 228 (2005).]

Together, Griggs holds and the plurality in Smith instructs that antidiscrimination laws must be construed to encompass disparate-impact claims when their text refers to the consequences of actions and not just to the mindset of actors, and where that interpretation is consistent with statutory purpose. These cases also teach that disparate impact liability must be limited so employers and other regulated entities are able to make the practical business choices and profit-related decisions that sustain a vibrant and dynamic free-enterprise system. And before rejecting a business justification—or, in the case of a governmental entity, an analogous public interest—a court must determine that a plaintiff has shown that there is "an available alternative . . . practice that has less disparate impact and serves the [entity's] legitimate needs." Ricci, supra, at 578. The cases interpreting Title VII and the ADEA provide essential background and instruction in the case now before the Court.

Turning to the FHA, the ICP relies on two provisions.

Section 804(a) provides that it shall be unlawful:

> "To refuse to sell or rent after the making of a bona fide offer, or to refuse to negotiate for the sale or rental of, or otherwise make unavailable or deny, a dwelling to any person

because of race, color, religion, sex, familial status, or national origin." 42 U. S. C. §3604(a).

Here, the phrase "otherwise make unavailable" is of central importance to the analysis that follows.

Section 805(a), in turn, provides:

> "It shall be unlawful for any person or other entity whose business includes engaging in real estate related transactions to discriminate against any person in making available such a transaction, or in the terms or conditions of such a transaction, because of race, color, religion, sex, handicap, familial status, or national origin." §3605(a).

Applied here, the logic of Griggs and Smith provides strong support for the conclusion that the FHA encompasses disparate-impact claims. Congress' use of the phrase "otherwise make unavailable" refers to the consequences of an action rather than the actor's intent. See United States v. Giles, 300 U. S. 41, 48 (1937) (explaining that the "word 'make' has many meanings, among them '[t]o cause to exist, appear or occur'" (quoting Webster's New International Dictionary 1485 (2d ed. 1934))). This results-oriented language counsels in favor of recognizing disparate-impact liability. See Smith, supra, at 236. The Court has construed statutory language similar to §805(a) to include disparate-impact liability. See, e.g., Board of Ed. of City School Dist. of New York v. Harris, 444 U. S. 130, 140–141 (1979) (holding the term "discriminat[e]" encompassed disparate-impact liability in the context of a statute's text, history, purpose, and structure).

A comparison to the antidiscrimination statutes examined in Griggs and Smith is useful. Title VII's and the ADEA's "otherwise adversely affect" language is equivalent in function and purpose to the FHA's "otherwise make unavailable" language. In these three statutes the operative text looks to results.

[It] is true that Congress did not reiterate Title VII's exact language in the FHA, but that is because to do so would have made the relevant sentence awkward and unclear. A provision making it unlawful to "refuse to sell[,] . . . or otherwise [adversely affect], a dwelling to any person" because of a protected trait would be grammatically obtuse, difficult to interpret, and far more expansive in scope than Congress likely intended. Congress thus chose words that serve the same purpose and bear the same basic meaning but are consistent with the structure and objectives of the FHA.

Emphasizing that the FHA uses the phrase "because of race," the Department argues this language forecloses disparate-impact liability since "[a]n action is not taken 'because of race' unless race is a reason for the action." Brief for Petitioners 26. Griggs and Smith, however, dispose of this argument. Both Title VII and the ADEA contain identical "because of " language, see 42 U. S. C. §2000e–2(a)(2); 29 U. S. C. §623(a)(2), and the Court nonetheless held those statutes impose disparate-impact liability.

In addition, it is of crucial importance that the existence of disparate-impact liability is supported by amendments to the FHA that Congress enacted in 1988. By that time, all nine Courts of Appeals to have addressed the question had concluded the Fair Housing Act encompassed disparate impact claims.

[When] it amended the FHA, Congress was aware of this unanimous precedent. And with that understanding, it made a considered judgment to retain the relevant statutory text. See H. R. Rep. No. 100–711, p. 21, n. 52 (1988) (H. R. Rep.) (discussing suits premised on disparate impact claims and related judicial precedent); 134 Cong. Rec. 23711

(1988) (statement of Sen. Kennedy) (noting unanimity of Federal Courts of Appeals concerning disparate impact); Fair Housing Amendments Act of 1987: Hearings on S. 558 before the Subcommittee on the Constitution of the Senate Committee on the Judiciary, 100th Cong., 1st Sess., 529 (1987) (testimony of Professor Robert Schwemm) (describing consensus judicial view that the FHA imposed disparate-impact liability). Indeed, Congress rejected a proposed amendment that would have eliminated disparate-impact liability for certain zoning decisions. See H. R. Rep., at 89–93.

Against this background understanding in the legal and regulatory system, Congress' decision in 1988 to amend the FHA while still adhering to the operative language in §§804(a) and 805(a) is convincing support for the conclusion that Congress accepted and ratified the unanimous holdings of the Courts of Appeals finding disparate-impact liability.

[Further] and convincing confirmation of Congress' understanding that disparate-impact liability exists under the FHA is revealed by the substance of the 1988 amendments. The amendments included three exemptions from liability that assume the existence of disparate-impact claims.

[The] relevant 1988 amendments were as follows. First, Congress added a clarifying provision: "Nothing in [the FHA] prohibits a person engaged in the business of furnishing appraisals of real property to take into consideration factors other than race, color, religion, national origin, sex, handicap, or familial status." 42 U. S. C. §3605(c). Second, Congress provided: "Nothing in [the FHA] prohibits conduct against a person because such person has been convicted by any court of competent jurisdiction of the illegal manufacture or distribution of a controlled substance." §3607(b)(4). And finally, Congress specified: "Nothing in [the FHA] limits the applicability of any reasonable . . . restrictions regarding the maximum number of occupants permitted to occupy a dwelling." §3607(b)(1).

The exemptions embodied in these amendments would be superfluous if Congress had assumed that disparate impact liability did not exist under the FHA.

[But] the amendments do constrain disparate-impact liability. For instance, certain criminal convictions are correlated with sex and race. See, e.g., Kimbrough v. United States, 552 U. S. 85, 98 (2007) (discussing the racial disparity in convictions for crack cocaine offenses). By adding an exemption from liability for exclusionary practices aimed at individuals with drug convictions, Congress ensured disparate-impact liability would not lie if a landlord excluded tenants with such convictions. The same is true of the provision allowing for reasonable restrictions on occupancy. And the exemption from liability for real-estate appraisers is in the same section as §805(a)'s prohibition of discriminatory practices in real-estate transactions, thus indicating Congress' recognition that disparate-impact liability arose under §805(a). In short, the 1988 amendments signal that Congress ratified disparate-impact liability.

[From] the standpoint of determining advantage or disadvantage to racial minorities, it seems difficult to say as a general matter that a decision to build low-income housing in a blighted inner-city neighborhood instead of a suburb is discriminatory, or vice versa. If those sorts of judgments are subject to challenge without adequate safeguards, then there is a danger that potential defendants may adopt racial quotas—a circumstance that itself raises serious constitutional concerns.

Courts must therefore examine with care whether a plaintiff has made out a prima facie case of disparate impact and prompt resolution of these cases is important. A plaintiff who fails to allege facts at the pleading stage or produce statistical evidence demonstrating a causal connection cannot make out a prima facie case of disparate impact. For instance, a plaintiff challenging the decision of a private developer to construct a new building in one location rather than another will not easily be able to show this is a policy causing a disparate impact because such a one-time decision may not be a policy at all. It may also be difficult to establish causation because of the multiple factors that go into investment decisions about where to construct or renovate housing units.

The FHA imposes a command with respect to disparate impact liability. Here, that command goes to a state entity. In other cases, the command will go to a private person or entity. Governmental or private policies are not contrary to the disparate-impact requirement unless they are "artificial, arbitrary, and unnecessary barriers." Griggs, 401 U. S., at 431. Difficult questions might arise if disparate-impact liability under the FHA caused race to be used and considered in a pervasive and explicit manner to justify governmental or private actions that, in fact, tend to perpetuate race-based considerations rather than move beyond them. Courts should avoid interpreting disparate impact liability to be so expansive as to inject racial considerations into every housing decision.

[The] judgment of the Court of Appeals for the Fifth Circuit is affirmed, and the case is remanded for further proceedings consistent with this opinion.
It is so ordered.

[The dissenting opinions of Justices Thomas and Alito have been omitted. Eds]

1. NOTE ON DISPARATE IMPACT

In *Texas Department of Housing and Community Affairs v. Inclusive Communities Project* the majority draw on language from Title VII of the Civil Rights Act of 1964, and the decision in *Griggs v. Duke Power* to establish by analogy the applicability of the disparate impact principle to housing cases filed under the Fair Housing Act of 1968. The majority's reasoning is that Congress intended its civil rights legislation to encompass both disparate treatment (which is understood by the Court to mean intentional discrimination) and disparate impact treatment (which describes policies which, absent a valid non-discriminatory interest in pursuing such policies, impacts persons of a protected category (race, religion, national origin, gender) less favorably than other persons and that the Fair Housing Act should be so interpreted.

In the same term, the Court ruled in *Equal Employment Opportunity Commission v. Abercrombie and Fitch Stores, Inc.*, 576 U.S. 768 (2015), that the refusal by the retail clothing chain to hire a Muslim woman (Samantha Elauf) who wore a head covering because of her faith, in compliance with the company's dress code, was a violation of Title VII's disparate treatment provision despite there being no actual evidence of knowledge that the head covering was a part of the plaintiff's religious practice. In a decision authored by one of the Court's more conservative members, Justice Scalia, the majority noted that the statute does not:

> "limit disparate-treatment claims to only those employer policies that treat religious practices less favorably than similar secular practices. Abercrombie's argument that a neutral policy cannot constitute "intentional discrimination" may make sense in other contexts. But Title VII does not demand mere neutrality with regard to religious practices—that they be treated no worse than other practices. Rather, it gives them favored treatment, affirmatively obligating employers not "to fail or refuse to hire or discharge any individual . . . because of such individual's" "religious observance and practice." An

employer is surely entitled to have, for example, a no headwear policy as an ordinary matter. But when an applicant requires an accommodation as an "aspect[t] of religious . . . practice," it is no response that the subsequent "fail[ure] . . . to hire" was due to an otherwise-neutral policy. Title VII requires otherwise-neutral policies to give way to the need for an accommodation.

Justice Thomas, in an opinion concurring in part and dissenting in part, took issue with this approach:

> Unlike the majority, I adhere to what I had thought before today was an undisputed proposition: Mere application of a neutral policy cannot constitute "intentional discrimination." Because the Equal Employment Opportunity Commission (EEOC) can prevail here only if Abercrombie engaged in intentional discrimination, and because Abercrombie's application of its neutral Look Policy [Abercrombie and Fitch's employee dress code, Eds] does not meet that description, I would affirm the judgment of the Tenth Circuit.

Justice Thomas went on to explain:

> Abercrombie refused to create an exception to its neutral Look Policy for Samantha Elauf's religious practice of wearing a headscarf. *Ante,* at 2. In doing so, it did not treat religious practices less favorably than similar secular practices, but instead remained neutral with regard to religious practices. To be sure, the *effects* of Abercrombie's neutral Look Policy, absent an accommodation, fall more harshly on those who wear headscarves as an aspect of their faith. *But that is a classic case of an alleged disparate impact.* [emphasis supplied, Eds.] It is not what we have previously understood to be a case of disparate treatment because Elauf received the *same* treatment from Abercrombie as any other applicant who appeared unable to comply with the company's Look Policy. Because I cannot classify Abercrombie's conduct as "intentional discrimination," I would affirm.

Is Justice Thomas correct? Does the policy of Abercrombie and Fitch have more in common with the challenged policy in *Texas Department of Housing* than not? In other words, is this really a disparate impact case? It should be noted that the EEOC did not allege disparate impact in its brief to the Supreme Court. Does this explain Justice Thomas' dissent and his reasoning that the circuit court's decision should be affirmed?

PERSONNEL ADMINISTRATOR OF MASSACHUSETTS v. FEENEY
442 U.S. 256 (1979)

Mr. Justice STEWART delivered the opinion of the Court.

This case presents a challenge to the constitutionality of the Massachusetts veterans' preference statute, Mass.Gen.Laws Ann., ch. 31, § 23, on the ground that it discriminates against women in violation of the Equal Protection Clause of the Fourteenth Amendment. Under ch. 31, § 23, all veterans who qualify for state civil service positions must be considered for appointment ahead of any qualifying nonveterans. The preference operates overwhelmingly to the advantage of males.

The Appellee Helen B. Feeney is not a veteran. She brought this action pursuant to 42 U.S.C. § 1983, alleging that the absolute preference formula established in ch. 31, §

23, inevitably operates to exclude women from consideration for the best Massachusetts civil service jobs and thus unconstitutionally denies them the equal protection of the laws. The three-judge District Court agreed, one judge dissenting. Anthony v. Massachusetts, 415 F.Supp. 485 (Mass.1976).

Upon an appeal taken by the Attorney General of Massachusetts, this Court vacated the judgment and remanded the case for further consideration in light of our intervening decision in Washington v. Davis, 426 U.S. 229, 96 S.Ct. 2040, 48 L.Ed.2d 597. Massachusetts v. Feeney, 434 U.S. 884, 98 S.Ct. 252, 54 L.Ed.2d 169. The *Davis* case held that a neutral law does not violate the Equal Protection Clause solely because it results in a racially disproportionate impact; instead the disproportionate impact must be traced to a purpose to discriminate on the basis of race. 426 U.S., at 238-244, 96 S.Ct., at 2046-2050.

Upon remand, the District Court, one judge concurring and one judge again dissenting, concluded that a veterans' hiring preference is inherently nonneutral because it favors a class from which women have traditionally been excluded, and that the consequences of the Massachusetts absolute-preference formula for the employment opportunities of women were too inevitable to have been "unintended." Accordingly, the court reaffirmed its original judgment. Feeney v. Massachusetts, 451 F.Supp. 143.

IA. The Federal Government and virtually all of the States grant some sort of hiring preference to veterans. The Massachusetts preference, which is loosely termed an "absolute lifetime" preference, is among the most generous. It applies to all positions in the State's classified civil service, which constitute approximately 60% of the public jobs in the State. It is available to "any person, male or female, including a nurse," who was honorably discharged from the United States Armed Forces after at least 90 days of active service, at least one day of which was during "wartime." Persons who are deemed veterans and who are otherwise qualified for a particular civil service job may exercise the preference at any time and as many times as they wish.

Civil service positions in Massachusetts fall into two general categories, labor and official. For jobs in the official service, with which the proofs in this action were concerned, the preference mechanics are uncomplicated. All applicants for employment must take competitive examinations. Grades are based on a formula that gives weight both to objective test results and to training and experience. Candidates who pass are then ranked in the order of their respective scores on an "eligible list." Chapter 31, § 23, requires, however, that disabled veterans, veterans, and surviving spouses and surviving parents of veterans be ranked — in the order of their respective scores — above all other candidates.

Rank on the eligible list and availability for employment are the sole factors that determine which candidates are considered for appointment to an official civil service position. When a public agency has a vacancy, it requisitions a list of "certified eligibles" from the state personnel division. Under formulas prescribed by civil service rules, a small number of candidates from the top of an appropriate list, three if there is only one vacancy, are certified. The appointing agency is then required to choose from among these candidates. Although the veterans' preference thus does not guarantee that a veteran will be appointed, it is obvious that the preference gives to veterans who achieve passing scores a well-nigh absolute advantage.

B. The appellee has lived in Dracut, Mass., most of her life. She entered the work force in 1948, and for the next 14 years worked at a variety of jobs in the private sector. She first entered the state civil service system in 1963, having competed successfully for a position as Senior Clerk Stenographer in the Massachusetts Civil Defense Agency. There she worked for four years. In 1967, she was promoted to the position of Federal Funds and Personnel Coordinator in the same agency. The agency, and with it her job, was eliminated in 1975.

During her 12-year tenure as a public employee, Ms. Feeney took and passed a number of open competitive civil service examinations. On several she did quite well, receiving in 1971 the second highest score on an examination for a job with the Board of Dental Examiners, and in 1973 the third highest on a test for an Administrative Assistant position with a mental health center. Her high scores, however, did not win her a place on the certified eligible list. Because of the veterans' preference, she was ranked sixth behind five male veterans on the Dental Examiner list. She was not certified, and a lower scoring veteran was eventually appointed. On the 1973 examination, she was placed in a position on the list behind 12 male veterans, 11 of whom had lower scores. Following the other examinations that she took, her name was similarly ranked below those of veterans who had achieved passing grades.

Ms. Feeney's interest in securing a better job in state government did not wane. Having been consistently eclipsed by veterans, however, she eventually concluded that further competition for civil service positions of interest to veterans would be futile. In 1975, shortly after her civil defense job was abolished, she commenced this litigation.

C. The veterans' hiring preference in Massachusetts, as in other jurisdictions, has traditionally been justified as a measure designed to reward veterans for the sacrifice of military service, to ease the transition from military to civilian life, to encourage patriotic service, and to attract loyal and well-disciplined people to civil service occupations. See, e. g., Hutcheson v. Director of Civil Service, 361 Mass. 480, 281 N.E.2d 53 (1972). The Massachusetts law dates back to 1884, when the State, as part of its first civil service legislation, gave a statutory preference to civil service applicants who were Civil War veterans if their qualifications were equal to those of nonveterans. 1884 Mass. Acts, ch. 320, § 14 (sixth). This tie-breaking provision blossomed into a truly absolute preference in 1895, when the State enacted its first general veterans' preference law and exempted veterans from all merit selection requirements. 1895 Mass. Acts, ch. 501, § 2. In response to a challenge brought by a male non-veteran, this statute was declared violative of state constitutional provisions guaranteeing that government should be for the "common good" and prohibiting hereditary titles. Brown v. Russell, 166 Mass. 14, 43 N.E. 1005 (1896).

The current veterans' preference law has its origins in an 1896 statute, enacted to meet the state constitutional standards enunciated in *Brown v. Russell*. That statute limited the absolute preference to veterans who were otherwise qualified. A closely divided Supreme Judicial Court, in an advisory opinion issued the same year, concluded that the preference embodied in such a statute would be valid. Opinion of the Justices, 166 Mass. 589, 44 N.E. 625 (1896). In 1919, when the preference was extended to cover the veterans of World War I, the formula was further limited to provide for a priority in eligibility, in contrast to an absolute preference in hiring. See Corliss v. Civil Service Comm'rs, 242 Mass. 61, 136 N.E. 356 (1922). In Mayor of Lynn v. Commissioner of Civil Service, 269 Mass. 410, 414, 169 N.E. 502, 503-504 (1929), the Supreme Judicial Court, adhering to the views expressed in its 1896 advisory opinion, sustained this statute against a state constitutional challenge.

Since 1919, the preference has been repeatedly amended to cover persons who served in subsequent wars, declared or undeclared. See 1943 Mass. Acts, ch. 194; 1949 Mass. Acts, ch. 642, § 2 (World War II); 1954 Mass. Acts, ch. 627 (Korea); 1968 Mass. Acts, ch. 531, § 1 (Vietnam). The current preference formula in ch. 31, § 23, is substantially the same as that settled upon in 1919. This absolute preference — even as modified in 1919 — has never been universally popular. Over the years it has been subjected to repeated legal challenges, see *Hutcheson v. Director of Civil Service, supra* (collecting cases), to criticism by civil service reform groups, see, *e. g.*, Report of the Massachusetts Committee on Public Service on Initiative Bill Relative to Veterans' Preference, S.No. 279 (1926); Report of Massachusetts Special Commission on Civil Service and Public Personnel Administration 37-43 (June 15, 1967), and, in 1926, to a referendum in which it was reaffirmed by a majority of 51.9%. See *id.*, at 38. The present case is apparently the first to challenge the Massachusetts veterans' preference on the simple ground that it discriminates on the basis of sex.

D. The first Massachusetts veterans' preference statute defined the term "veterans" in gender-neutral language. See 1896 Mass. Acts, ch. 517, § 1 ("a person" who served in the United States Army or Navy), and subsequent amendments have followed this pattern, see, *e. g.*, 1919 Mass. Acts, ch. 150, § 1 ("any person who has served . . ."); 1954 Mass. Acts, ch. 627, § 1 ("any person, male or female, including a nurse"). Women who have served in official United States military units during wartime, then, have always been entitled to the benefit of the preference. In addition, Massachusetts, through a 1943 amendment to the definition of "wartime service," extended the preference to women who served in unofficial auxiliary women's units. 1943 Mass. Acts, ch. 194.

When the first general veterans' preference statute was adopted in 1896, there were no women veterans. The statute, however, covered only Civil War veterans. Most of them were beyond middle age, and relatively few were actively competing for public employment. Thus, the impact of the preference upon the employment opportunities of nonveterans as a group and women in particular was slight.

Notwithstanding the apparent attempts by Massachusetts to include as many military women as possible within the scope of the preference, the statute today benefits an overwhelmingly male class. This is attributable in some measure to the variety of federal statutes, regulations, and policies that have restricted the number of women who could enlist in the United States Armed Forces, and largely to the simple fact that women have never been subjected to a military draft. See generally Binkin and Bach 4-21.

When this litigation was commenced, then, over 98% of the veterans in Massachusetts were male; only 1.8% were female. And over one-quarter of the Massachusetts population were veterans. During the decade between 1963 and 1973 when the appellee was actively participating in the State's merit selection system, 47,005 new permanent appointments were made in the classified official service. Forty-three percent of those hired were women, and 57% were men. Of the women appointed, 1.8% were veterans, while 54% of the men had veteran status. A large unspecified percentage of the female appointees were serving in lower paying positions for which males traditionally had not applied. On each of 50 sample eligible lists that are part of the record in this case, one or more women who would have been certified as eligible for appointment on the basis of test results were displaced by veterans whose test scores were lower.

At the outset of this litigation appellants conceded that for "many of the permanent positions for which males and females have competed" the veterans' preference has "resulted in a substantially greater proportion of female eligibles than male eligibles" not being certified for consideration. The impact of the veterans' preference law upon the public employment opportunities of women has thus been severe. This impact lies at the heart of the appellee's federal constitutional claim.

II. The sole question for decision on this appeal is whether Massachusetts, in granting an absolute lifetime preference to veterans, has discriminated against women in violation of the Equal Protection Clause of the Fourteenth Amendment.

B. The cases of *Washington v. Davis, supra,* and *Arlington Heights v. Metropolitan Housing Dev. Corp., supra,* recognize that when a neutral law has a disparate impact upon a group that has historically been the victim of discrimination, an unconstitutional purpose may still be at work. But those cases signaled no departure from the settled rule that the Fourteenth Amendment guarantees equal laws, not equal results. *Davis* upheld a job-related employment test that white people passed in proportionately greater numbers than Negroes, for there had been no showing that racial discrimination entered into the establishment or formulation of the test. *Arlington Heights* upheld a zoning board decision that tended to perpetuate racially segregated housing patterns, since, apart from its effect, the board's decision was shown to be nothing more than an application of a constitutionally neutral zoning policy. Those principles apply with equal force to a case involving alleged gender discrimination.

When a statute gender-neutral on its face is challenged on the ground that its effects upon women are disproportionably adverse, a twofold inquiry is thus appropriate. The first question is whether the statutory classification is indeed neutral in the sense that it is not gender-based. If the classification itself, covert of overt, is not based upon gender, the second question is whether the adverse effect reflects invidious gender-based discrimination. See *Arlington Heights v. Metropolitan Housing Dev. Corp., supra.* In this second inquiry, impact provides an "important starting point," 429 U.S., at 266, 97 S.Ct., at 564, but purposeful discrimination is "the condition that offends the Constitution." Swann v. Charlotte-Mecklenburg Board of Education, 402 U.S. 1, 16, 91 S.Ct. 1267, 1276, 28 L.Ed.2d 554.

It is against this background of precedent that we consider the merits of the case before us.

III. A. The question whether ch. 31, § 23, establishes a classification that is overtly or covertly based upon gender must first be considered. The appellee has conceded that ch. 31, § 23, is neutral on its face. She has also acknowledged that state hiring preferences for veterans are not *per se* invalid, for she has limited her challenge to the absolute lifetime preference that Massachusetts provides to veterans. The District Court made two central findings that are relevant here: first, that ch. 31, § 23, serves legitimate and worthy purposes; second, that the absolute preference was not established for the purpose of discriminating against women. The appellee has thus acknowledged and the District Court has thus found that the distinction between veterans and nonveterans drawn by ch. 31, § 23, is not a pretext for gender discrimination. The appellee's concession and the District Court's finding are clearly correct.

If the impact of this statute could not be plausibly explained on a neutral ground, impact itself would signal that the real classification made by the law was in fact not neutral. See Washington v. Davis, 426 U.S., at 242, 96 S.Ct., at 2049; Arlington Heights v. Metropolitan Housing Dev. Corp., supra, 429 U.S., at 266, 97 S.Ct., at 564. But there can be but one answer to the question whether this veteran preference excludes significant numbers of women from preferred state jobs because they are women or because they are nonveterans. Apart from the facts that the definition of "veterans" in the statute has always been neutral as to gender and that Massachusetts has consistently defined veteran status in a way that has been inclusive of women who have served in the military, this is not a law that can plausibly be explained only as a gender-based classification. Indeed, it is not a law that can rationally be explained on that ground. Veteran status is not uniquely male. Although few women benefit from the preference the nonveteran class is not substantially all female. To the contrary, significant numbers of nonveterans are men, and all nonveterans — male as well as female — are placed at a disadvantage. Too many men are affected by ch. 31, § 23, to permit the inference that the statute is but a pretext for preferring men over women.

Moreover, as the District Court implicitly found, the purposes of the statute provide the surest explanation for its impact. Just as there are cases in which impact alone can unmask an invidious classification, cf. Yick Wo v. Hopkins, 118 U.S. 356, 6 S.Ct. 1064, 30 L.Ed. 220, there are others, in which — notwithstanding impact — the legitimate noninvidious purposes of a law cannot be missed. This is one. The distinction made by ch. 31, § 23, is, as it seems to be, quite simply between veterans and nonveterans, not between men and women.

B. The dispositive question, then, is whether the appellee has shown that a gender-based discriminatory purpose has, at least in some measure, shaped the Massachusetts veterans' preference legislation. As did the District Court, she points to two basic factors which in her view distinguish ch. 31, § 23, from the neutral rules at issue in the *Washington v. Davis* and *Arlington Heights* cases. The first is the nature of the preference, which is said to be demonstrably gender-biased in the sense that it favors a status reserved under federal military policy primarily to men. The second concerns the impact of the absolute lifetime preference upon the employment opportunities of women, an impact claimed to be too inevitable to have been unintended. The appellee contends that these factors, coupled with the fact that the preference itself has little if any relevance to actual job performance, more than suffice to prove the discriminatory intent required to establish a constitutional violation.

1. The contention that this veterans' preference is "inherently nonneutral" or "gender-biased" presumes that the State, by favoring veterans, intentionally incorporated into its public employment policies the panoply of sex-based and assertedly discriminatory federal laws that have prevented all but a handful of women from becoming veterans. There are two serious difficulties with this argument. First, it is wholly at odds with the District Court's central finding that Massachusetts has not offered a preference to veterans for the purpose of discriminating against women. Second, it cannot be reconciled with the assumption made by both the appellee and the District Court that a more limiting hiring preference for veterans could be sustained. Taken together, these difficulties are fatal.

To the extent that the status of veteran is one that few women have been enabled to achieve, every hiring preference for veterans, however, modest or extreme, is inherently gender-biased. If Massachusetts by offering such a preference can be said intentionally to have incorporated into its state employment policies the historical gender-based federal military personnel practices, the degree of the preference would or should make no constitutional difference. Invidious discrimination does not become less so because the discrimination accomplished is of a lesser magnitude. Discriminatory intent is simply not amenable to calibration. It either is a factor that has influenced the legislative choice or it is not. The District Court's conclusion that the absolute veterans' preference was not originally enacted or subsequently reaffirmed for the purpose of giving an advantage to males as such necessarily compels the conclusion that the State is intended nothing more than to prefer "veterans." Given this finding, simple logic suggests that an intent to exclude women from significant public jobs was not at work in this law. To reason that it was, by describing the preference as "inherently nonneutral" or "gender-biased," is merely to restate the fact of impact, not to answer the question of intent.

To be sure, this case is unusual in that it involves a law that by design is not neutral. The law overtly prefers veterans as such. As opposed to the written test at issue in *Davis,* it does not purport to define a job-related characteristic. To the contrary, it confers upon a specifically described group — perceived to be particularly deserving — a competitive head start. But the District Court found, and the appellee has not disputed, that this legislative choice was legitimate. The basic distinction between veterans and nonveterans, having been found not gender-based, and the goals of the preference having been found worthy, ch. 31 must be analyzed as is any other neutral law that casts a greater burden upon women as a group than upon men as a group. The enlistment policies of the Armed Services may well have discrimination on the basis of sex. See Frontiero v. Richardson, 411 U.S. 677, 93 S.Ct. 1764, 36 L.Ed.2d 583; cf. Schlesinger v. Ballard, 419 U.S. 498, 95 S.Ct. 572, 42 L.Ed.2d 610. But the history of discrimination against women in the military is not on trial in this case.

2. The appellee's ultimate argument rests upon the presumption, common to the criminal and civil law, that a person intends the natural and foreseeable consequences of his voluntary actions. Her position was well stated in the concurring opinion in the District Court: "Conceding . . . that the goal here was to benefit the veteran, there is no reason to absolve the legislature from awareness that the means chosen to achieve this goal would freeze women out of all those state jobs actively sought by men. To be sure, the legislature did not wish to harm women. But the cutting-off of women's opportunities was an inevitable concomitant of the chosen scheme — as inevitable as the proposition that if tails is up, heads must be down. Where a law's consequences are *that* inevitable, can they meaningfully be described as unintended?" 451 F.Supp., at 151.

This rhetorical question implies that a negative answer is obvious, but it is not. The decision to grant a preference to veterans was of course "intentional." So, necessarily, did an adverse impact upon nonveterans follow from that decision. And it cannot seriously be argued that the Legislature of Massachusetts could have been unaware that most veterans are men. It would thus be disingenuous to say that the adverse consequences of this legislation for women were unintended, in the sense that they were not volitional or in the sense that they were not foreseeable.

"Discriminatory purpose," however, implies more than intent as volition or intent as awareness of consequences. See United Jewish Organizations v. Carey, 430 U.S. 144,

179, 97 S.Ct. 996, 1016, 51 L.Ed.2d 229 (concurring opinion). It implies that the decisionmaker, in this case a state legislature, selected or reaffirmed a particular course of action at least in part "because of," not merely "in spite of," its adverse effects upon an identifiable group. Yet, nothing in the record demonstrates that this preference for veterans was originally devised or subsequently re-enacted because it would accomplish the collateral goal of keeping women in a stereotypic and predefined place in the Massachusetts Civil Service.

To the contrary, the statutory history shows that the benefit of the preference was consistently offered to "any person" who was a veteran. That benefit has been extended to women under a very broad statutory definition of the term veteran. The preference formula itself, which is the focal point of this challenge, was first adopted — so it appears from this record — out of a perceived need to help a small group of older Civil War veterans. It has since been reaffirmed and extended only to cover new veterans. When the totality of legislative actions establishing and extending the Massachusetts veterans' preference are considered, see Washington v. Davis, 426 U.S., at 242, 96 S.Ct., at 2049, the law remains what it purports to be: a preference for veterans of either sex over nonveterans of either sex, not for men over women.

IV. The appellee, however, has simply failed to demonstrate that the law in any way reflects a purpose to discriminate on the basis of sex. The judgment is reversed, and the case is remanded for further proceedings consistent with this opinion.

Mr. Justice STEVENS, with whom Mr. Justice WHITE joins, concurring.

[While] I concur in the Court's opinion, I confess that I am not at all sure that there is any difference between the two questions posed *ante*, at 2293. If a classification is not overtly based on gender, I am inclined to believe the question whether it is covertly gender based is the same as the question whether its adverse effects reflect invidious gender-based discrimination. However the question is phrased, for me the answer is largely provided by the fact that the number of males disadvantaged by Massachusetts' veterans' preference (1,867,000) is sufficiently large — and sufficiently close to the number of disadvantaged females (2,954,000) — to refute the claim that the rule was intended to benefit males as a class over females as a class.

Mr. Justice MARSHALL, with whom Mr. Justice BRENNAN joins, dissenting.

[Although] neutral in form, the statute is anything but neutral in application. It inescapably reserves a major sector of public employment to "an already established class which, as a matter of historical fact, is 98% male." *Ibid.* Where the foreseeable impact of a facially neutral policy is so disproportionate, the burden should rest on the State to establish that sex-based considerations played no part in the choice of the particular legislative scheme.

[The] legislative history of the statute reflects the Commonwealth's patent appreciation of the impact the preference system would have on women, and an equally evident desire to mitigate that impact only with respect to certain traditionally female occupations. Until 1971, the statute and implementing civil service regulations exempted from operation of the preference any job requisitions "especially calling for women." 1954 Mass. Acts, ch. 627, § 5. See also 1896 Mass. Acts, ch. 517, § 6; 1919 Mass. Acts, ch. 150, § 2; 1945 Mass. Acts, ch. 725, § 2(e); 1965 Mass. Acts, ch. 53; *ante*, at 2289 nn. 13, 14. In practice, this exemption, coupled with the absolute preference for veterans, has created a gender-based civil service hierarchy, with women occupying low-grade clerical and secretarial jobs and men holding more responsible and remunerative positions. See 415 F.Supp., at 488; 451 F.Supp., at 148 n. 9.

[Thus], for over 70 years, the Commonwealth has maintained, as an integral part of its veterans' preference system, an exemption relegating female civil service applicants to occupations traditionally filled by women. Such a statutory scheme both reflects and perpetuates precisely the kind of archaic assumptions about women's roles which we have previously held invalid. Particularly when viewed against the range of less discriminatory alternatives available to assist veterans, Massachusetts' choice of a formula that so severely restricts public employment opportunities for women cannot reasonably be thought gender-neutral. Cf. Albemarle Paper Co. v. Moody, supra, 422 U.S., at 425, 95 S.Ct., at 2375. The Court's conclusion to the contrary — that "nothing in the record" evinces a "collateral goal of keeping women in a stereotypic and predefined place in the Massachusetts Civil Service," *ante*, at 2296 — displays a singularly myopic view of the facts established below.

I would affirm the judgment of the court below.

ROGERS v. LODGE
458 U.S. 613 (1982)

Justice WHITE delivered the opinion of the Court.

The issue in this case is whether the at-large system of elections in Burke County, Ga., violates the Fourteenth Amendment rights of Burke County's black citizens.

I. Burke County is a large, predominately rural county located in eastern Georgia. According to the 1980 census, Burke County had a total population of 19,349, of whom 10,385, or 53.6%, were black. The average age of blacks living there is lower than the average age of whites and therefore whites constitute a slight majority of the voting age population. As of 1978, 6,373 persons were registered to vote in Burke County, of whom 38% were black.

The Burke County Board of Commissioners governs the county. It was created in 1911, and consists of five members elected at large to concurrent 4-year terms by all qualified voters in the county. The county has never been divided into districts, either for the purpose of imposing a residency requirement on candidates or for the purpose of requiring candidates to be elected by voters residing in a district. In order to be nominated or elected, a candidate must receive a majority of the votes cast in the primary or general election, and a runoff must be held if no candidate receives a majority in the first primary or general election. Each candidate must run for a specific seat on the Board, and a voter may vote only once for any candidate. No Negro has ever been elected to the Burke County Board of Commissioners.

Appellees, eight black citizens of Burke County filed this suit in 1976 in the United States District Court for the Southern District of Georgia. The suit was brought on behalf of all black citizens in Burke County. The class was certified in 1977. The complaint alleged that the county's system of at-large elections violates appellees' First, Thirteenth, Fourteenth, and Fifteenth Amendment rights, as well as their rights under 42 U.S.C. § § 1971, 1973, and 1983, by diluting the voting power of black citizens. [The] court issued an order on September 29, 1978, stating that appellees were entitled to prevail and ordering that Burke County be divided into five districts for purposes of electing County Commissioners. App. to Juris. Statement 62a. The court later issued detailed findings of fact and conclusions of law in which it stated that while the present method of electing County Commissioners was "racially neutral when adopted, [it] is being *maintained* for invidious purposes" in violation of appellees' Fourteenth and Fifteenth Amendment rights. *Id.*, at 71a, 96a.

The Court of Appeals affirmed. It stated that while the proceedings in the District Court took place prior to the decision in Mobile v. Bolden, 446 U.S. 55, 100 S.Ct. 1490, 64 L.Ed.2d 47 (1980), the District Court correctly anticipated *Mobile* and required appellees to prove that the at-large voting system was maintained for a discriminatory purpose. The Court of Appeals also held that the District Court's findings were not clearly erroneous, and that its conclusion that the at-large system was maintained for invidious purposes was "virtually mandated by the overwhelming proof." [We] affirm.

II. At-large voting schemes and multimember districts tend to minimize the voting strength of minority groups by permitting the political majority to elect *all* representatives of the district. A distinct minority, whether it be a racial, ethnic, economic, or political group, may be unable to elect any representatives in an at-large election, yet may be able to elect several representatives if the political unit is divided into single-member districts. The minority's voting power in a multimember district is particularly diluted when bloc voting occurs and ballots are cast along strict majority-minority lines. While multimember districts have been challenged for "their winner-take-all aspects, their tendency to submerge minorities and to over represent the winning party," Whitcomb v. Chavis, 403 U.S. 124, 158-159, 91 S.Ct. 1858, 1877, 29 L.Ed.2d 363 (1971), this Court has repeatedly held that they are not unconstitutional per se. Mobile v. Bolden, supra, 446 U.S., at 66, 100 S.Ct., at 1499; White v. Regester, 412 U.S. 755, 765, 93 S.Ct. 2332, 2339, 37 L.Ed.2d 314 (1973); Whitcomb v. Chavis, supra, 403 U.S., at 142, 91 S.Ct., at 1868. The Court has recognized, however, that multimember districts violate the Fourteenth Amendment if "conceived or operated as purposeful devices to further racial discrimination" by minimizing, canceling out or diluting the voting strength of racial elements in the voting population. Whitcomb v. Chavis, supra, 403 U.S., at 149, 91 S.Ct., at 1872. See also White v. Regester, supra, 412 U.S., at 765, 93 S.Ct., at 2339. Cases charging that multimember districts unconstitutionally dilute the voting strength of racial minorities are thus subject to the standard of proof generally applicable to Equal Protection Clause cases. Washington v. Davis, 426 U.S. 229, 96 S.Ct. 2040, 48 L.Ed.2d 597 (1976), and Arlington Heights v. Metropolitan Housing Dev. Corp., 429 U.S. 252, 97 S.Ct. 555, 50 L.Ed.2d 450 (1977), made it clear that in order for the Equal Protection Clause to be violated, "the invidious quality of a law claimed to be racially discriminatory must ultimately be traced to a racially discriminatory purpose." Washington v. Davis, supra, 426 U.S., at 240, 96 S.Ct., at 2048. Neither case involved voting dilution, but in both cases the Court observed that the requirement that racially discriminatory purpose or intent be proved applies to voting cases by relying upon, among others, a districting case, to illustrate that a showing of discriminatory intent has long been required in *all* types of equal protection cases charging racial discrimination. Arlington Heights, supra, 429 U.S., at 265, 97 S.Ct., at 563; Washington v. Davis, supra, 426 U.S., at 240, 96 S.Ct., at 2048.

Arlington Heights and *Washington v. Davis* both rejected the notion that a law is invalid under the Equal Protection Clause simply because it may affect a greater proportion of one race than another. *Arlington Heights*; Washington v. Davis. However, both cases recognized that discriminatory intent need not be proved by direct evidence. "Necessarily, an invidious discriminatory purpose may often be inferred from the totality of the relevant facts, including the fact, if it is true, that the law bears more heavily on one race than another." *Ibid.* Thus determining the existence of a discriminatory purpose "demands a sensitive inquiry into such circumstantial and direct evidence of intent as may be available."

In *Mobile v. Bolden, supra,* the Court was called upon to apply these principles to the at-large election system in Mobile, Ala. Mobile is governed by three commissioners who exercise all legislative, executive, and administrative power in the municipality. Each candidate for the City Commission runs for one of three numbered posts in an at-large election and can only be elected by a majority vote. Plaintiffs brought a class action on behalf of all Negro citizens of Mobile alleging that the at-large scheme diluted their voting strength in violation of several statutory and constitutional provisions. The District Court concluded that the at-large system "violates the constitutional rights of the plaintiffs by improperly restricting their access to the political process," Bolden v. Mobile, 423 F.Supp. 384, 399 (SD Ala.1976), and ordered that the commission form of government be replaced by a mayor and a nine-member City Council elected from single-member districts. The Court of Appeals affirmed. This Court reversed.

Justice Stewart, writing for himself and three other Justices, noted that to prevail in their contention that the at-large voting system violates the Equal Protection Clause of the Fourteenth Amendment, plaintiffs had to prove the system was "'conceived or operated as [a] purposeful devic[e] to further racial . . . discrimination.'" quoting Whitcomb v. Chavis, supra, 403 U.S., at 149, 91 S.Ct., at 1872. Such a requirement "is simply one aspect of the basic principle that only if there is purposeful discrimination can there be a violation of the Equal Protection Clause of the Fourteenth Amendment," Another Justice agreed with the standard of proof recognized by the plurality. (White, J., dissenting).

The plurality went on to conclude that the District Court had failed to comply with this standard. The District Court had analyzed plaintiffs' claims in light of the standard which had been set forth in Zimmer v. McKeithen, 485 F.2d 1297 (CA5 1973), aff'd on other grounds. *Zimmer* set out a list of factors[8] gleaned from *Whitcomb v. Chavis, supra,* and *White v. Regester, supra,* that a court should consider in assessing the constitutionality of at-large and multimember district voting schemes.

The plurality in *Mobile* was of the view that *Zimmer* was "decided upon the misunderstanding that it is not necessary to show a discriminatory purpose in order to prove a violation of the Equal Protection Clause — that proof of a discriminatory effect is sufficient." 446 U.S., at 71, 100 S.Ct., at 1502. The plurality observed that while "the presence of the indicia relied on in *Zimmer* may afford some evidence of a discriminatory purpose," the mere existence of those criteria is not a substitute for a finding of discriminatory purpose. Id., at 73, 100 S.Ct., at 1503. The District Court's standard in *Mobile* was likewise flawed.

Because the District Court in the present case employed the evidentiary factors outlined in *Zimmer,* it is urged that its judgment is infirm for the same reasons that led to the

---

[8] The primary factors listed in *Zimmer* include a lack of minority access to the candidate selection process, unresponsiveness of elected officials to minority interests, a tenuous state policy underlying the preference for multimember or at-large districting, and the existence of past discrimination which precludes effective participation in the elector process. 485 F.2d, at 1305. Factors which enhance the proof of voting dilution are the existence of large districts, anti-single-shot voting provisions, and the absence of any provision for at-large candidates to run from geographic subdistricts. *Ibid.*

reversal in *Mobile.* We do not agree. First, and fundamentally, we are unconvinced that the District Court in this case applied the wrong legal standard. Not only was the District Court's decision rendered a considerable time after *Washington v. Davis* and *Arlington Heights,* but the trial judge also had the benefit of Nevett v. Sides, 571 F.2d 209 (1978), where the Court of Appeals for the Fifth Circuit assessed the impact of *Washington v. Davis* and *Arlington Heights* and held that "a showing of racially motivated discrimination is a necessary element in an equal protection voting dilution claim. . . ." The court stated that "[t]he ultimate issue in a case alleging unconstitutional dilution of the votes of a racial group is whether the districting plan under attack exists because it was intended to diminish or dilute the political efficacy of that group." The Court of Appeals also explained that although the evidentiary factors outlined in *Zimmer* were important considerations in arriving at the ultimate conclusion of discriminatory intent, the plaintiff is not limited to those factors.

The District Court referred to *Nevett v. Sides* and demonstrated its understanding of the controlling standard by observing that a determination of discriminatory intent is "a requisite to a finding of unconstitutional vote dilution" under the Fourteenth and Fifteenth Amendments. Furthermore, while recognizing that the evidentiary factors identified in *Zimmer* were to be considered, the District Court was aware that it was "not limited in its determination only to the *Zimmer* factors" but could consider other relevant factors as well. The District Court then proceeded to deal with what it considered to be the relevant proof and concluded that the at-large scheme of electing commissioners, "although racially neutral when adopted, is being *maintained* for invidious purposes." That system "while neutral in origin . . . has been subverted to invidious purposes." *Id.,* at 90a. For the most part, the District Court dealt with the evidence in terms of the factors set out in *Zimmer* and its progeny, but as the Court of Appeals stated: "Judge Alaimo employed the constitutionally required standard. . . . [and] did not treat the *Zimmer* criteria as absolute, but rather considered them only to the extent they were relevant to the question of discriminatory intent." Although a tenable argument can be made to the contrary, we are not inclined to disagree with the Court of Appeals' conclusion that the District Court applied the proper legal standard.

III.A. We are also unconvinced that we should disturb the District Court's finding that the at-large system in Burke County was being maintained for the invidious purpose of diluting the voting strength of the black population. In White v. Regester, 412 U.S., at 769-770, 93 S.Ct., at 2341, we stated that we were not inclined to overturn the District Court's factual findings, "representing as they do a blend of history and an intensely local appraisal of the design and impact of the Bexar County multimember district in the light of past and present reality, political and otherwise." See also Columbus Board of Education v. Penick, 443 U.S. 449, 468, 99 S.Ct. 2941, 2952, 61 L.Ed.2d 666 (1979) (BURGER, C.J., concurring in judgment). Our recent decision in Pullman-Standard v. Swint, 456 U.S. 273, 102 S.Ct. 1781, 72 L.Ed.2d 66 (1982), emphasizes the deference Federal Rule of Civil Procedure 52 requires reviewing courts to give a trial court's findings of fact. "Rule 52a broadly requires that findings of fact not be set aside unless clearly erroneous. It does not make exceptions or purport to exclude certain categories of factual findings. . . ." The Court held that the issue of whether the differential impact of a seniority system resulted from an intent to discriminate on racial grounds "is a pure question of fact, subject to Rule 52a's clearly-erroneous standard." The *Swint* Court also noted that issues of intent are commonly treated as factual matters. We are of the view that the same clearly-erroneous standard applies to the trial court's finding in this case that the at-large system in Burke County is being maintained for discriminatory purposes, as well as to the court's subsidiary findings of fact. The Court of Appeals did not hold any of the District Court's findings of fact to be clearly erroneous, and this Court has frequently noted its reluctance to disturb findings of fact concurred in by two lower courts. We agree with the Court of Appeals that on the record before us, none of the factual findings are clearly erroneous.

B. The District Court found that blacks have always made up a substantial majority of the population in Burke County, but that they are a distinct minority of the registered voters. There was also overwhelming evidence of bloc voting along racial lines. Hence, although there had been black candidates, no black had ever been elected to the Burke County Commission. These facts bear heavily on the issue of purposeful discrimination. Voting along racial lines allows those elected to ignore black interests without fear of political consequences, and without bloc voting the minority candidates would not lose elections solely because of their race. Because it is sensible to expect that at least some blacks would have been elected in Burke County, the fact that none have ever been elected is important evidence of purposeful exclusion. Under our cases, however, such facts are insufficient in themselves to prove purposeful discrimination absent other evidence such as proof that blacks have less opportunity to participate in the political processes and to elect candidates of their choice. Both the District Court and the Court of Appeals thought the supporting proof in this case was sufficient to support an inference of intentional discrimination. These factors were primarily those suggested in Zimmer v. McKeithen, 485 F.2d 1297 (CA5 1973).

The District Court began by determining the impact of past discrimination on the ability of blacks to participate effectively in the political process. Past discrimination was found to contribute to low black voter registration, because prior to the Voting Rights Act of 1965, blacks had been denied access to the political process by means such as literacy tests, poll taxes, and white primaries. The result was that "Black suffrage in Burke County was virtually non-existent." Black voter registration in Burke County has increased following the Voting Rights Act to the point that some 38% of blacks eligible to vote are registered to do so. On that basis the District Court inferred that "past discrimination has had an adverse effect on black voter registration which lingers to this date." *Ibid.* Past discrimination against blacks in education also had the same effect. [The] District Court found further evidence of exclusion from the political process. Past discrimination had prevented blacks from effectively participating in Democratic Party affairs and in primary elections. There were also property ownership requirements that made it difficult for blacks to serve as chief registrar in the county. There had been discrimination in the selection of grand jurors, the hiring of county employees, and in the appointments to boards and committees which oversee the county government. The District Court thus concluded that historical discrimination had restricted the present opportunity of blacks effectively to participate in the political process. Evidence of historical discrimination is relevant to drawing an inference of purposeful discrimination, particularly in cases such as this one where the evidence shows that discriminatory practices were commonly utilized, that they were abandoned when enjoined by courts or made illegal by civil rights legislation, and that they were replaced by laws and practices which, though neutral on their face, serve to maintain the status quo.

Extensive evidence was cited by the District Court to support its finding that elected officials of Burke County have been unresponsive and insensitive to the needs of the black community, which increases the likelihood that the political process was not equally open to blacks. The District Court also considered the depressed socio-economic status of Burke County blacks. It found that proportionately more blacks than whites have incomes below the poverty level. Nearly 53% of all black families living in Burke County had incomes equal to or less than three-fourths of a poverty-level income. [Although finding that the state policy behind the at-large electoral system in Burke County was "neutral in origin," the District Court concluded that the policy "has been subverted to invidious purposes." As a practical matter, maintenance of the state statute providing for at-large elections in Burke County is determined by Burke County's state representatives, for the legislature defers to their wishes on matters of purely local application. The court found that Burke County's state representatives "have retained a system which has minimized the ability of Burke County Blacks to participate in the political system."

The trial court considered, in addition, several factors which this Court has indicated enhance the tendency of multimember districts to minimize the voting strength of racial minorities. See Whitcomb v. Chavis, 403 U.S., at 143-144, 91 S.Ct., at 1869. It found that the sheer geographic size of the county, which is nearly two-thirds the size of Rhode Island, "has made it more difficult for Blacks to get to polling places or to campaign for office." App. to Juris. Statement 91a. The court concluded, as a matter of law, that the size of the county tends to impair the access of blacks to the political process. Id., at 92a. The majority vote requirement, Ga.Code § 34-1513 (Supp.1980), was found "to submerge the will of the minority" and thus "deny the minority's access to the system." The court also found the requirement that candidates run for specific seats, enhances appellee's lack of access because it prevents a cohesive political group from concentrating on a single candidate. Because Burke County has no residency requirement, "[a]ll candidates could reside in Waynesboro, or in 'lilly-white' [sic] neighborhoods. To that extent, the denial of access becomes enhanced." None of the District Court's findings underlying its ultimate finding of intentional discrimination appears to us to be clearly erroneous; and as we have said, we decline to overturn the essential finding of the District Court, agreed to by the Court of Appeals, that the at-large system in Burke County has been maintained for the purpose of denying blacks equal access to the political processes in the county.

IV. We also find no reason to overturn the relief ordered by the District Court. Neither the District Court nor the Court of Appeals discerned any special circumstances that would militate against utilizing single-member districts. Where "a constitutional violation has been found, the remedy does not 'exceed' the violation if the remedy is tailored to cure the 'condition that offends the Constitution.'" Affirmed.

Justice POWELL, with whom Justice REHNQUIST joins, dissenting.

I. The District Court and Court of Appeals in this case based their findings of unconstitutional discrimination on the same factors held insufficient in *Mobile*. Yet the Court now finds their conclusion unexceptionable. The *Mobile* plurality also affirmed that the concept of "intent" was no mere fiction, and held that the District Court had erred in "its failure to identify the state officials whose intent it considered relevant." Although the courts below did not answer that question in this case, the Court today affirms their decision. Whatever the wisdom of *Mobile*, the Court's opinion cannot be reconciled persuasively with that case. There are some variances in the largely sociological evidence presented in the two cases. But *Mobile* held that this *kind* of evidence was not enough. Such evidence, we found in *Mobile*, did not merely fall short, but "fell *far* short[,] of showing that [an at-large electoral scheme was] 'conceived or operated [as a] purposeful devic[e] to further racial . . . discrimination.'" Id., at 70, 100 S.Ct., at 1501 (emphasis added), quoting Whitcomb v. Chavis, 403 U.S. 124, 149, 91 S.Ct., 1858, 1872, 29 L.Ed.2d 363 (1971). Because I believe that *Mobile* controls this case, I dissent.

II. The Court's decision today relies heavily on the capacity of the federal district courts — essentially free from any standards propounded by this Court — to determine whether at-large voting systems are "being maintained for the invidious purpose of diluting the voting strength of the black population." *Ante*, at 3278. Federal courts thus are invited to engage in deeply subjective inquiries into the motivations of local officials in structuring local governments. Inquiries of this kind not only can be "unseemly," see Karst, The Costs of Motive-Centered Inquiry, 15 San Diego L.Rev. 1163, 1164 (1978); they intrude the federal courts — with only the vaguest constitutional direction — into an area of intensely local and political concern. Emphasizing these considerations, Justice Stevens, *post*, at 3289-3293, argues forcefully that the Court's focus of inquiry is seriously mistaken. I agree with much of what he says. As I do not share his views entirely, however, I write separately.

A. As I understand it, Justice Stevens' critique of the Court's approach rests on three principles with which I am in fundamental agreement. First, it is appropriate to distinguish between "state action that inhibits an individual's right to vote and state action that affects the political strength of various groups." Mobile v. Bolden, supra, at 83, 100 S.Ct., at 1508 (Stevens, J., concurring in judgment); see *post*, at 3283, 3286, n. 16. Under this distinction, this case is fundamentally different from cases involving direct barriers to voting. There is no claim here that blacks may not register freely and vote for whom they choose. This case also differs from one-man, one-vote cases, in which districting practices make a person's vote less weighty in some districts than in others. Second, I agree with Justice Stevens that vote dilution cases of this kind are difficult if not impossible to distinguish — especially in their remedial aspect — from other actions to redress gerrymanders. Finally, Justice Stevens clearly is correct in arguing that the standard used to identify unlawful racial discrimination in this area should be defined in terms that are judicially manageable and reviewable. See *post*, at 3284, 3289-3293. In the absence of compelling reasons of both law and fact, the federal judiciary is unwarranted in undertaking to restructure state political systems. This is inherently a political area, where the identification of a seeming violation does not necessarily suggest an enforceable judicial remedy — or at least none short of a system of quotas or group representation. Any such system, of course, would be antithetical to the principles of our democracy.

B. Justice Stevens would accommodate these principles by holding that subjective intent is irrelevant to the establishment of a case of racial vote dilution under the Fourteenth Amendment. See *post*, at 3286. Despite sharing the concerns from which his position is developed, I would not accept this view. "The central purpose of the Equal Protection Clause of the Fourteenth Amendment is the prevention of official conduct discriminating on the basis of race." Washington v. Davis, 426 U.S. 229, 239, 96 S.Ct. 2040, 2047, 48 L.Ed.2d 597 (1976). Because I am unwilling to abandon this central principle in cases of this kind, I cannot join Justice Stevens' opinion. Nonetheless, I do agree with him that what he calls "objective" factors should be the focus of inquiry in vote-dilution cases. Unlike the considerations on which the lower courts relied in this case and in *Mobile*, the factors identified by Justice Stevens as "objective" in fact are direct, reliable, and unambiguous indices of discriminatory *intent*. If we held, as I think we should, that the district courts must place primary reliance on these factors to establish discriminatory intent, we would prevent federal — court inquiries into the *subjective* thought processes of local officials — at least until enough objective evidence had been presented to warrant discovery into subjective motivations in this complex, politically charged area. By prescribing such a rule we would hold federal courts to a standard that was judicially manageable. And we would remain faithful to the central protective purpose of the Equal Protection Clause.

In the absence of proof of discrimination by reliance on the kind of objective factors identified by Justice Stevens, I would hold that the factors cited by the Court of Appeals are too attenuated as a matter of law to support an inference of discriminatory intent. I would reverse its judgment on that basis.

C. RACE-BASED CLASSIFICATIONS

1. STRICT SCRUTINY

That the Supreme Court has closely scrutinized race-based discrimination should come as no surprise given the Civil War, adoption of the 14th Amendment, and the Equal Protection Clause. The Court's opinion in *Strauder v. West Virginia*, 100 U.S. 303 (1880) certainly exemplified such, "[What is equal protection] but declaring, [in] regard to the colored race, for whose protection the amendment was primarily designed, that no discrimination shall be made against them by law because of their color? [That] the West Virginia stature respecting juries [is] such a discrimination ought not to doubted."

Based upon this premise the Court has historically treated all disadvantaged racial classifications as inherently suspect, mandating close judicial scrutiny, and requiring the state to prove a compelling purpose. Recall our earlier discussion (Chapter 6) of *Korematsu v. United States*, where despite the Court's sustaining relocation of Japanese Americans to concentration camps during a "time of war," the Court nonetheless commented, "[All] legal restrictions which curtail the civil rights of a single racial groups are immediately suspect. That is not to say that all such restrictions are unconstitutional. It is to say that courts must subject them to the most rigid scrutiny." Thus, though the Equal Protection Clause has had particular relevancy to discrimination against African Americans, the Court has continually applied strict scrutiny to any race-based classification.

Traditionally, the closest scrutiny has been applied to what the Court has described as "discrete (easily identifiable) and insular (isolated) minorities who have a history of being discriminated against and being disadvantaged in the majoritarian process. The degree to which this approach would be applied to any racial group, as opposed to a "discrete and insular" racial minority, awaited the postmodern civil rights era and is discussed in the next section.

Why should race-based discrimination be viewed as "inherently suspect"? Can we say that given the nation's history and obsession with racial discrimination and oppression, from slavery to apartheid, that this history itself mandates that any such classifications have to be viewed as "inherently suspect? Much in the same vein, given this history, is "equal application equal protection"? The Supreme Court, at the height of the civil rights movement in the Warren era, faced this issue in the context of Virginia's miscegenation law.

LOVING v. VIRGINIA
388 U.S. 1 (1967)

Mr. Chief Justice WARREN delivered the opinion of the Court.

This case presents a constitutional question never addressed by this Court: whether a statutory scheme adopted by the State of Virginia to prevent marriages between persons solely on the basis of racial classifications violates the Equal Protection and Due Process Clauses of the Fourteenth Amendment. For reasons which seem to us to reflect the central meaning of those constitutional commands, we conclude that these statutes cannot stand consistently with the Fourteenth Amendment.

In June 1958, two residents of Virginia, Mildred Jeter, a Negro woman, and Richard Loving, a white man, were married in the District of Columbia pursuant to its laws. Shortly after their marriage, the Lovings returned to Virginia and established their marital abode in Caroline County. At the October Term, 1958, of the Circuit Court of Caroline County, a grand jury issued an indictment charging the Lovings with violating Virginia's ban on interracial marriages. On January 6, 1959, the Lovings pleaded guilty to the charge and were sentenced to one year in jail; however, the trial judge suspended the sentence for a period of 25 years on the condition that the Lovings leave the State and not return to Virginia together for 25 years. He stated in an opinion that: [The] two statutes under which appellants were convicted and sentenced are part of a comprehensive statutory scheme aimed at prohibiting and punishing interracial marriages.

[Virginia] is now one of 16 States which prohibit and punish marriages on the basis of racial classifications. Penalties for miscegenation arose as an incident to slavery and have been common in Virginia since the colonial period.

[The] State does not contend in its argument before this Court that its powers to regulate marriage are unlimited notwithstanding the commands of the Fourteenth Amendment. Nor could it do so in light of. Instead, the State argues that the meaning of the Equal Protection Clause, as illuminated by the statements of the Framers, is only that state penal laws containing an interracial element as part of the definition of the offense must apply equally to whites and Negroes in the sense that members of each race are punished to the same degree. Thus, the State contends that, because its miscegenation statutes punish equally both the white and the Negro participants in an interracial marriage, these statutes, despite their reliance on racial classifications do not constitute an invidious discrimination based upon race.

[Because] we reject the notion that the mere "equal application" of a statute containing racial classifications is enough to remove the classifications from the Fourteenth Amendment's proscription of all invidious racial discriminations, we do not accept the State's contention that these statutes should be upheld if there is any possible basis for concluding that they serve a rational purpose. [We] deal with statutes containing racial classifications, and the fact of equal application does not immunize the statute from the very heavy burden of justification which the Fourteenth Amendment has traditionally required of state statutes drawn according to race.

The State argues that statements in the Thirty-ninth Congress about the time of the passage of the Fourteenth Amendment indicate that the Framers did not intend the Amendment to make unconstitutional state miscegenation laws. [We] have said in connection with a related problem, that although these historical sources "cast some light" they are not sufficient to resolve the problem; "[a]t best, they are inconclusive. The most avid proponents of the post-War Amendments undoubtedly intended them to remove all legal distinctions among "all persons born or naturalized in the United States." Their opponents, just as certainly, were antagonistic to both the letter and the spirit of the Amendments and wished them to have the most limited purpose. Brown v. Board of Education of Topeka. We have rejected the proposition that the debates in the Thirty-ninth Congress or in the state legislatures which ratified the Fourteenth Amendment supported the theory advanced by the State, that the requirement of equal protection of the laws is satisfied by penal laws defining offenses based on racial classifications so long as white and Negro participants in the offense were similarly punished. McLaughlin v. State of Florida, 379 U.S. 184, 85 S.Ct. 283, 13 L.Ed.2d 222 (1964).

The State finds support for its "equal application" theory in the decision of the Court in Pace v. State of Alabama, 106 U.S. 583, 1 S.Ct. 637, 27 L.Ed. 207 (1883). In that case, the Court upheld a conviction under an Alabama statute forbidding adultery or fornication between a white person and a Negro which imposed a greater penalty than that of a statute proscribing similar conduct by members of the same race. The Court reasoned that the statute could not be said to discriminate against Negroes because the punishment for each participant in the offense was the same. However, as recently as the 1964 Term, in rejecting the reasoning of that case, we stated "Pace represents a limited view of the Equal Protection Clause which has not withstood analysis in the subsequent decisions of this Court." McLaughlin v. Florida, supra, 379 U.S. at 188, 85 S.Ct. at 286. As we there demonstrated, the Equal Protection Clause requires the consideration of whether the classifications drawn by any statute constitute an arbitrary and invidious discrimination. The clear and central purpose of the Fourteenth Amendment was to eliminate all official state sources of invidious racial discrimination in the States. Slaughter-House Cases, 16 Wall. 36, 71, 21 L.Ed. 394 (1873); Strauder v. State of West Virginia, 100 U.S. 303, 307-308, 25 L.Ed. 664 (1880).

There can be no question but that Virginia's miscegenation statutes rest solely upon distinctions drawn according to race. The statutes proscribe generally accepted conduct if engaged in by members of different races. Over the years, this Court has consistently repudiated "[d]istinctions between citizens solely because of their ancestry" as being "odious to a free people whose institutions are founded upon the doctrine of equality." Hirabayashi v. United States, 320 U.S. 81, 100, 63 S.Ct. 1375, 1385, 87 L.Ed. 1774 (1943). At the very least, the Equal Protection Clause demands that racial classifications, especially suspect in criminal statutes, be subjected to the "most rigid scrutiny," Korematsu v. United States, 323 U.S. 214, 216, 65 S.Ct. 193, 194, 89 L.Ed. 194 (1944), and, if they are ever to be upheld, they must be shown to be necessary to the accomplishment of some permissible state objective, independent of the racial discrimination which it was the object of the Fourteenth Amendment to eliminate.

[There] is patently no legitimate overriding purpose independent of invidious racial discrimination which justifies this classification. The fact that Virginia prohibits only interracial marriages involving white persons demonstrates that the racial classifications must stand on their own justification, as measures designed to maintain White Supremacy. We have consistently denied the constitutionality of measures which restrict the rights of citizens on account of race. There can be no doubt that restricting the freedom to marry solely because of racial classifications violates the central meaning of the Equal Protection Clause.

[Marriage] is one of the "basic civil rights of man," fundamental to our very existence and survival. Skinner v. State of Oklahoma, 316 U.S. 535, 541, 62 S.Ct. 1110, 1113, 86 L.Ed. 1655 (1942). See also Maynard v. Hill, 125 U.S. 190, 8 S.Ct. 723, 31 L.Ed. 654 (1888). To deny this fundamental freedom on so unsupportable a basis as the racial classifications embodied in these statutes, classifications so directly subversive of the principle of equality at the heart of the Fourteenth Amendment, is surely to deprive all the State's citizens of liberty without due process of law. The Fourteenth Amendment requires that the freedom of choice to marry not be restricted by invidious racial discriminations. Under our Constitution, the freedom to marry or not marry, a person of another race resides with the individual and cannot be infringed by the State.

These convictions must be reversed. It is so ordered. Reversed.

Comments on *Loving*. Is the law applied equally if whites cannot marry blacks, as well as limiting blacks from marrying whites? Are the parties not treated the "same"? Does the nation's abysmal record of racial discrimination against African Americans affect this conclusion? Was the real purpose of these laws to discriminate against African Americans, and so the Court's conclusion is supported by the same factors that make racial discrimination against this racial minority "inherently suspect"?

Racial Segregation — Still "Suspect": Johnson v. California, 503 U.S. 499 (2005). In *Johnson* the Court indicated once again that race-based segregation was "inherently suspect," mandating "strict judicial scrutiny." The California Department of Corrections' defended its unwritten policy of racially segregating prisoners in double cells for up to 60 days each time they enter a new correctional facility based on the asserted rationale that it prevented violence caused by racial gangs. The Ninth Circuit held that the applicable standard of review should be a deferential standard articulated in *Turner v. Safley*, 482 U.S. 78, not strict scrutiny, and that the policy survived *Turner* scrutiny.

The Supreme Court reversed and remanded in holding that "strict scrutiny is the proper standard of review for an equal protection challenge to the CDC's policy, [b]ecause the CDC's policy is "immediately suspect" as an express racial classification," and that, "the Ninth Circuit erred in failing to apply strict scrutiny and thereby to require the CDC to demonstrate that the policy is narrowly tailored to serve a compelling state interest. *[A]ll* racial classifications [imposed by government] . . . must be analyzed . . . under strict scrutiny," in order to "'smoke out' illegitimate uses of race by assuring that [government] is pursuing a goal important enough to warrant [such] a highly suspect tool." The CDC's claim that its policy should be exempt from this categorical rule because it is "neutral" — *i.e.*, because all prisoners are "equally" segregated — ignores this Court's repeated command that "racial classifications receive close scrutiny even when they may be said to burden or benefit the races equally," Indeed, the Court rejected the notion that separate can ever be equal — or "neutral" — 50 years ago in *Brown v. Board of Education*, 347 U.S. 483, and refuses to resurrect it today. Justice O'Connor delivered the opinion of the Court, in which Justices Kennedy, Souter, Ginsburg, and Breyer, joined. Justice Ginsburg filed a concurring opinion in which Justices Souter and Breyer joined. Justice Stevens filed a dissenting opinion. Justice Thomas filed a dissenting opinion in which Justice Scalia joined. The Chief Justice took no part in the decision.

2. Racial Segregation — Apartheid

Racial segregation by force of law is apartheid. Recall our discussion of *Plessy v. Ferguson*, where the Supreme Court found this practice constitutional and not violative of the Equal Protection Clause because "separate but equal was equal." Apartheid flourished in the South post-*Plessy*. The problem was, of course, that the social facts in the South were not reflective of the *Plessy* decision, — separate was *not* equal.

Based upon this disparity, the goal of attacking and finding segregation in the public schools unconstitutional commenced with a series of cases where the discrimination and disparity in equality between state-financed educational institutions was so great that it could be challenged based upon the separate but equal doctrine itself. In short, "make them eat *Plessy*."

The careful and successful planning aimed at attacking apartheid extended from the Howard University Law School, led by Professor Charles Houston, his pupil Thurgood Marshall, and the NAACP legal defense fund. Their use of the legal system as a tool for social progress is a singular triumph perhaps unmatched in our legal history. It is important to not only understand the success in result, but the skillful and incremental planning applied to achieve such. A fine work by Richard Kluger, *Simple Justice* (1976), presents a most thorough and outstanding review of these issues, and is a primary source for the material herein.

a. The Road to *Brown*

Gaines, *Sweatt*, and *McLaurin* are presented as representative "stepping stones to *Brown*" and reflect the strategy to challenge *Plessy*. If you wanted to prove that an educational entity was separate but not equal, what would be the best facts to support such? Would *Gaines*, so qualify? Why or why not? How are both *Sweat* and *McClaren* bridges from the finding in *Gaines* to the ultimate result in *Brown*?

STATE OF MISSOURI ex rel. GAINES v. CANADA
305 U.S. 337 (1938)

[Missouri, by force of its laws, mandated separate education for whites and blacks. The State's only Law School, at the University of Missouri, in accordance with such laws maintained racial segregation by denying admittance to black students. A Missouri statute, however, authorized the Board of Curators to arrange for attendance of black residents at institutions in neighboring states and to pay reasonable tuition rates for such attendance because no black in-state facility was available. Lloyd Gaines, a black denied admission at the University of Missouri law school, brought this action to compel the curators to admit him. The state court denied relief, holding that he should have applied for aid to attend an out-of-state institution.]

Mr. Chief Justice Hughes delivered the opinion of the court.

[The] basic consideration is not as to what sort of opportunities, other States provide, or whether they are as good as those in Missouri, but as to what opportunities Missouri itself furnishes to white students and denies to negroes solely upon the ground of color. The admissibility of laws separating the races in the enjoyment of privileges afforded by the State rests wholly upon the equality of the privileges which the laws give to the separated groups within the State. The question here is not of a duty of the State to supply legal training, or of the quality of the training which it does supply, but of its duty when it provides such training to furnish it to the residents of the State upon the basis of an equality of right. By the operation of the laws of Missouri a privilege has been created for white law students which is denied to negroes by reason of their race. The white resident is afforded legal education within the State; the negro resident having the same qualifications is refused it there and must go outside the State to obtain it. That is a denial of the equality of legal right to the enjoyment of the privilege which the State has set up, and the provision for the payment of tuition fees in another State does not remove the discrimination.

The equal protection of the laws is 'a pledge of the protection of equal laws'. Yick Wo v. Hopkins, 118 U.S. 356, 369, 6 S.Ct. 1064, 1070, 30 L.Ed. 220. Manifestly, the obligation of the State to give the protection of equal laws can be performed only where its laws operate, that is, within its own jurisdiction. It is there that the equality of legal right must be maintained. That obligation is imposed by the Constitution upon the States severally as governmental entities, — each responsible for its own laws establishing the rights and duties of persons within its borders. It is an obligation the burden of which cannot be cast by one State upon another, and no State can be excused from performance by what another State may do or fail to do. That separate responsibility of each State within its own sphere is of the essence of statehood maintained under our dual system. It seems to be implicit in respondents' argument that if other States did not provide courses for legal education, it would nevertheless be the constitutional duty of Missouri when it supplied such courses for white students to make equivalent provision for negroes. But that plain duty would exist because it rested upon the State independently of the action of other States. We find it impossible to conclude that what otherwise would be an unconstitutional discrimination, with respect to the legal right to the enjoyment of opportunities within the State, can be justified by requiring resort to opportunities elsewhere. That resort may mitigate the inconvenience of the discrimination but cannot serve to validate it.

Nor can we regard the fact that there is but a limited demand in Missouri for the legal education of negroes as excusing the discrimination in favor of whites. We had occasion to consider a cognate question in the case of McCabe v. Atchison, Topeka & Santa Fe Railway Co., supra. There the argument was advanced, in relation to the provision by a carrier of sleeping cars, dining and chair cars, that the limited demand by negroes justified the State in permitting the furnishing of such accommodations exclusively for white persons. We found that argument to be without merit. It made, we said, the constitutional right 'depend upon the number of persons who may be discriminated against, whereas the essence of the constitutional right is that it is a personal one. Whether or not particular facilities shall be provided may doubtless be conditioned upon there being a reasonable demand therefore; but, if facilities are provided, substantial equality of treatment of persons traveling under like conditions cannot be refused. It is the individual who is entitled to the equal protection of the laws, and if he is denied by a common carrier, acting in the matter under the authority of a state law, a facility or convenience in the course of his journey which, under substantially the same circumstances, is furnished to another traveler, he may properly complain that his constitutional privilege has been invaded'. Id., 235 U.S. pages 161, 162, 35 S.Ct. page 71.

Here, petitioner's right was a personal one. It was as an individual that he was entitled to the equal protection of the laws, and the State was bound to furnish him within its borders facilities for legal education substantially equal to those which the State there afforded for persons of the white race, whether or not other negroes sought the same opportunity.

It is urged, however, that the provision for tuition outside the State is a temporary one, — that it is intended to operate merely pending the establishment of a law department for negroes at Lincoln University. While in that sense the discrimination may be termed temporary, it may nevertheless continue for an indefinite period by reason of the discretion given to the curators of Lincoln University and the alternative of arranging for tuition in other States, as permitted by the state law as construed by the state court, so long as the curators find it unnecessary and impracticable to provide facilities for the legal instruction of negroes within the State. In that view, we cannot regard the discrimination as excused by what is called its temporary character.

Reversed and remanded.

SWEATT v. PAINTER
339 U.S. 629 (1950)

Mr. Chief Justice VINSON delivered the opinion of the Court.

This case and McLaurin v. Oklahoma State Regents, 339 U.S. 637, 70 S.Ct. 851, present different aspects of this general question: To what extent does the Equal Protection Clause of the Fourteenth Amendment limit the power of a state to distinguish between students of different races in professional and graduate education in a state university? Broader issues have been urged for our consideration, but we adhere to the principle of deciding constitutional questions only in the context of the particular case before the Court. We have frequently reiterated that this Court will decide constitutional questions only when necessary to the disposition of the case at hand, and that such decisions will be drawn as narrowly as possible. Rescue Army v. Municipal Court, 1947, 331 U.S. 549, 67 S.Ct. 1409, 91 L.Ed. 1666, and cases cited therein. Because of this traditional reluctance to extend constitutional interpretations to situations or facts which are not before the Court, much of the excellent research and detailed argument presented in these cases is unnecessary to their disposition.

In the instant case, petitioner filed an application for admission to the University of Texas Law School for the February, 1946 term. His application was rejected solely because he is a Negro.[1] Petitioner thereupon brought this suit for mandamus against the appropriate school officials, respondents here, to compel his admission. At that time, there was no law school in Texas which admitted Negroes.

The State trial court recognized that the action of the State in denying petitioner the opportunity to gain a legal education while granting it to others deprived him of the equal protection of the laws guaranteed by the Fourteenth Amendment. The court did not grant the relief requested, however, but continued the case for six months to allow the State to supply substantially equal facilities. At the expiration of the six months, in December, 1946, the court denied the writ on the showing that the authorized university officials had

---

[1] It appears that the University has been restricted to white students, in accordance with the State law. See Tex.Const. Art. VII, ss 7, 14; Tex.Rev.Civ.Stat. Arts. 2643b, 2719, 2900 (Vernon, 1925 and Supp.).

adopted an order calling for the opening of a law school for Negroes the following February. While petitioner's appeal was pending, such a school was made available, but petitioner refused to register therein. The Texas Court of Civil Appeals set aside the trial court's judgment and ordered the cause 'remanded generally to the trial court for further proceedings without prejudice to the rights of any party to this suit.'

On remand, a hearing was held on the issue of the equality of the educational facilities at the newly established school as compared with the University of Texas Law School. Finding that the new school offered petitioner "privileges, advantages, and opportunities for the study of law substantially equivalent to those offered by the State to white students at the University of Texas," the trial court denied mandamus. The Court of Civil Appeals affirmed. 1948, 210 S.W.2d 442. Petitioner's application for a writ of error was denied by the Texas Supreme Court. We granted certiorari, 1949, 338 U.S. 865, 70 S.Ct. 139, because of the manifest importance of the constitutional issues involved.

The University of Texas Law School, from which petitioner was excluded, was staffed by a faculty of sixteen full-time and three part-time professors, some of whom are nationally recognized authorities in their field. Its student body numbered 850. The library contained over 65,000 volumes. Among the other facilities available to the students were a law review, moot court facilities, scholarship funds, and Order of the Coif affiliation. The school's alumni occupy the most distinguished positions in the private practice of the law and in the public life of the State. It may properly be considered one of the nation's ranking law schools.

The law school for Negroes which was to have opened in February, 1947, would have had no independent faculty or library. The teaching was to be carried on by four members of the University of Texas Law School faculty, who were to maintain their offices at the University of Texas while teaching at both institutions. Few of the 10,000 volumes ordered for the library had arrived; nor was there any full-time librarian. The school lacked accreditation.

Since the trial of this case, respondents report the opening of a law school at the Texas State University for Negroes. It is apparently on the road to full accreditation. It has a faculty of five full-time professors; a student body of 23; a library of some 16,500 volumes serviced by a full-time staff; a practice court and legal aid association; and one alumnus who has become a member of the Texas Bar.

Whether the University of Texas Law School is compared with the original or the new law school for Negroes, we cannot find substantial equality in the educational opportunities offered white and Negro law students by the State. In terms of number of the faculty, variety of courses and opportunity for specialization, size of the student body, scope of the library, availability of law review and similar activities, the University of Texas Law School is superior. What is more important, the University of Texas Law School possesses to a far greater degree those qualities which are incapable of objective measurement but which make for greatness in a law school. Such qualities, to name but a few, include reputation of the faculty, experience of the administration, position and influence of the alumni, standing in the community, traditions and prestige. It is difficult to believe that one who had a free choice between these law schools would consider the question close.

Moreover, although the law is a highly learned profession, we are well aware that it is an intensely practical one. The law school, the proving ground for legal learning and practice, cannot be effective in isolation from the individuals and institutions with which the law interacts. Few students and no one who has practiced law would choose to study in an academic vacuum, removed from the interplay of ideas and the exchange of views with which the law is concerned. The law school to which Texas is willing to admit petitioner excludes from its student body members of the racial groups which number 85% of the population of the State and include most of the lawyers, witnesses, jurors, judges and other officials with whom petitioner will inevitably be dealing when he becomes a member of the Texas Bar. With such a substantial and significant segment of society excluded, we cannot conclude that the education offered petitioner is substantially equal to that which he would receive if admitted to the University of Texas Law School.

It may be argued that excluding petitioner from that school is no different from excluding white students from the new law school. This contention overlooks realities. It is unlikely that a member of a group so decisively in the majority, attending a school with rich traditions and prestige which only a history of consistently maintained excellence could command, would claim that the opportunities afforded him for legal education were unequal to those held open to petitioner. That such a claim, if made, would be dishonored by the State, is no answer. "Equal protection of the laws is not achieved through indiscriminate imposition of inequalities." Shelley v. Kraemer, 1948, 334 U.S. 1, 22, 68 S.Ct. 836, 846, 92 L.Ed. 1161, 3 A.L.R.2d 441.

It is fundamental that these cases concern rights which are personal and present. This Court has stated unanimously that "The State must provide (legal education) for (petitioner) in conformity with the equal protection clause of the Fourteenth Amendment and provide it as soon as it does for applicants of any other group." Sipuel v. Board of Regents, 1948, 332 U.S. 631, 633, 68 S.Ct. 299, 92 L.Ed. 247. That case "did not present the issue whether a state might not satisfy the equal protection clause of the Fourteenth Amendment by establishing a separate law school for Negroes." Fisher v. Hurst, 1948, 333 U.S. 147, 150, 68 S.Ct. 389, 390, 92 L.Ed. 604. In State of Missouri ex rel. Gaines v. Canada, 1938, 305 U.S. 337, 351, 59 S.Ct. 232, 237, 83 L.Ed. 208, the Court, speaking through Chief Justice Hughes, declared that "petitioner's right was a personal one. It was as an individual that he was entitled to the equal protection of the laws, and the State was bound to furnish him within its borders facilities for legal education substantially equal to those which the State there afforded for persons of the white race, whether or not other Negroes sought the same opportunity." These are the only cases in this Court which present the issue of the constitutional validity of race distinctions in state-supported graduate and professional education.

In accordance with these cases, petitioner may claim his full constitutional right: legal education equivalent to that offered by the State to students of other races. Such education is not available to him in a separate law school as offered by the State. We cannot, therefore, agree with respondents that the doctrine of Plessy v. Ferguson, 1896, 163 U.S. 537, 16 S.Ct. 1138, 41 L.Ed. 256, requires affirmance of the judgment below. Nor need we reach petitioner's contention that Plessy v. Ferguson should be reexamined in the light of contemporary knowledge respecting the purposes of the Fourteenth Amendment and the effects of racial segregation. See supra, 339 U.S. 631, 70 S.Ct. 849.

We hold that the Equal Protection Clause of the Fourteenth Amendment requires that petitioner be admitted to the University of Texas Law School. The judgment is reversed and the cause is remanded for proceedings not inconsistent with this opinion. Reversed.

McLAURIN v. OKLAHOMA STATE REGENTS FOR HIGHER EDUCATION
339 U.S. 637 (1950)

Mr. Chief Justice VINSON delivered the opinion of the Court.

In this case, we are faced with the question whether a state may, after admitting a student to graduate instruction in its state university, afford him different treatment from other students solely because of his race. We decide only this issue; see Sweatt v. Painter, 339 U.S. 629, 70 S.Ct. 848.

Appellant is a Negro citizen of Oklahoma. Possessing a Master's degree, he applied for admission to the University of Oklahoma in order to pursue studies and courses leading to a Doctorate in Education. At that time, his application was denied, solely because of his race. The school authorities were required to exclude him by the Oklahoma statutes, 70 Okl.Stat. (1941) §§ 455, 456, 457, which made it a misdemeanor to maintain or operate, teach or attend a school at which both whites and Negroes are enrolled or taught. Appellant filed a complaint requesting injunctive relief, alleging that the action of the school authorities and the statutes upon which their action was based were unconstitutional and deprived him of the equal protection of the laws. Citing our decisions in State of Missouri ex rel. Gaines v. Canada, 1938, 305 U.S. 337, 59 S.Ct. 232, 83 L.Ed. 208, and Sipuel v. Board of Regents, 1948, 332 U.S. 631, 68 S.Ct. 299, 92 L.Ed. 247, a statutory three-judge District Court held, 87 F.Supp. 526, that the State had a constitutional duty to provide him with the education he sought as soon as it provided that education for applicants of any other group. It further held that to the extent the Oklahoma statutes denied him admission they were unconstitutional and void. On the assumption, however, that the State would follow the constitutional mandate, the court refused to grant the injunction, retaining jurisdiction of the cause with full power to issue any necessary and proper orders to secure McLaurin the equal protection of the laws.

Following this decision, the Oklahoma legislature amended these statutes to permit the admission of Negroes to institutions of higher learning attended by white students, in cases where such institutions offered courses not available in the Negro schools. The amendment provided, however, that in such cases the program of instruction "shall be given at such colleges or institutions of higher education upon a segregated basis." Appellant was thereupon admitted to the University of Oklahoma Graduate School. In apparent conformity with the amendment, his admission was made subject to "such rules and regulations as to segregation as the President of the University shall consider to afford Mr. G. W. McLaurin substantially equal educational opportunities as are afforded to other persons seeking the same education in the Graduate College," a condition which does not appear to have been withdrawn. Thus he was required to sit apart at a designated desk in an anteroom adjoining the classroom; to sit at a designated desk on the mezzanine floor of the library, but not to use the desks in the regular reading room; and to sit at a designated table and to eat at a different time from the other students in the school cafeteria.

To remove these conditions, appellant filed a motion to modify the order and judgment of the District Court. That court held that such treatment did not violate the provisions of the Fourteenth Amendment and denied the motion. 87 F.Supp. 528. This appeal followed.

In the interval between the decision of the court below and the hearing in this Court, the treatment afforded appellant was altered. For some time, the section of the classroom in which appellant sat was surrounded by a rail on which there was a sign stating, "Reserved For Colored," but these have been removed. He is now assigned to a seat in the classroom in a row specified for colored students; he is assigned to a table in the library on the main floor; and he is permitted to eat at the same time in the cafeteria as other students, although here again he is assigned to a special table.

It is said that the separations imposed by the State in this case are in form merely nominal. McLaurin uses the same classroom, library and cafeteria as students of other races; there is no indication that the seats to which he is assigned in these rooms have any disadvantage of location. He may wait in line in the cafeteria and there stand and talk with his fellow students, but while he eats he must remain apart.

These restrictions were obviously imposed in order to comply, as nearly as could be, with the statutory requirements of Oklahoma. But they signify that the State, in administering the facilities it affords for professional and graduate study, sets McLaurin apart from the other students. The result is that appellant is handicapped in his pursuit of effective graduate instruction. Such restrictions impair and inhibit his ability to study, to engage in discussions and exchange views with other students, and, in general, to learn his profession.

Our society grows increasingly complex, and our need for trained leaders increases correspondingly. Appellant's case represents, perhaps, the epitome of that need, for he is attempting to obtain an advanced degree in education, to become, by definition, a leader and trainer of others. Those who will come under his guidance and influence must be directly affected by the education he receives. Their own education and development will necessarily suffer to the extent that his training is unequal to that of his classmates. State imposed restrictions which produce such inequalities cannot be sustained.

It may be argued that appellant will be in no better position when these restrictions are removed, for he may still be set apart by his fellow students. This we think irrelevant. There is a vast difference — a Constitutional difference — between restrictions imposed by the state which prohibit the intellectual commingling of students, and the refusal of individuals to commingle where the state presents no such bar. Shelley v. Kraemer, 1948, 334 U.S. 1, 13-14, 68 S.Ct. 836, 842, 92 L.Ed. 1161, 3 A.L.R.2d 441. The removal of the state restrictions will not necessarily abate individual and group predilections, prejudices and choices. But at the very least, the state will not be depriving appellant of the opportunity to secure acceptance by his fellow students on his own merits.

We conclude that the conditions under which this appellant is required to receive his education deprive him of his personal and present right to the equal protection of the laws. See Sweatt v. Painter, 339 U.S. 629, 70 S.Ct. 848. We hold that under these circumstances the Fourteenth Amendment precludes differences in treatment by the state based upon race. Appellant, having been admitted to a state-supported graduate school, must receive the same treatment at the hands of the state as students of other races. The judgment is reversed.

Hernandez v. Texas and discrimination based on custom. The several previous cases beginning with *Missouri ex rel Gaines v. Canada* (dubbed "The Road to Brown" in these pages), can be called the Brown jurisprudential canon, as they were part of a strategy to equalize opportunities for African Americans in this country. Too often overlooked is the case which was published right before Brown in the U.S. Reports. That case is *Hernandez v. Texas*. This case dealt with discrimination against Mexican Americans, the largest community within the larger Latinx community of the United States. In Texas, at the time of the decision, Mexican Americans, a multi-racial community, were categorized as white under state law though, as the opinion that follows demonstrates, seldom if ever were accorded the benefits traditionally available to Anglo whites in a manner no less serious and humiliating than the treatment received by African Americans during this same period. In the decision, the Court addresses this tradition by referencing the notion of *class* discrimination noting that the Fourteenth Amendment is not based on a two-class theory consisting of blacks and whites, and proceeded to deal with the discrimination in a manner consistent with the case law built from the earlier *racial* discrimination cases.

HERNANDEZ v. TEXAS
347 U.S. 475 (1954)

Mr. Chief Justice WARREN delivered the opinion of the Court.

The petitioner, Pete Hernandez, was indicted for the murder of one Joe Espinosa by a grand jury in Jackson County, Texas. He was convicted and sentenced to life imprisonment. The Texas Court of Criminal Appeals affirmed the judgment of the trial court. Prior to the trial, the petitioner, by his counsel, offered timely motions to quash the indictment and the jury panel. He alleged that persons of Mexican descent were systematically excluded from service as jury commissioners, grand jurors, and petit jurors, although there were such persons fully qualified to serve residing in Jackson County. The petitioner asserted that exclusion of this class deprived him, as a member of the class, of the equal protection of the laws guaranteed by the Fourteenth Amendment of the Constitution. After a hearing, the trial court denied the motions. At the trial, the motions were renewed, further evidence taken, and the motions again denied. An allegation that the trial court erred in denying the motions was the sole basis of petitioner's appeal. In affirming the judgment of the trial court, the Texas Court of Criminal Appeals considered and passed upon the substantial federal question raised by the petitioner. We granted a writ of certiorari to review that decision. 346 U.S. 811.

In numerous decisions, this Court has held that it is a denial of the equal protection of the laws to try a defendant of a particular race or color under an indictment issued by a grand jury, or before a petit jury, from which all persons of his race or color have, solely because of that race or color, been excluded by the State, whether acting through its legislature, its courts, or its executive or administrative officers. Although the Court has had little occasion to rule on the question directly, it has been recognized since *Strauder v. West Virginia,* that the exclusion of a class of persons from jury service on grounds other than race or color may also deprive a defendant who is a member of that class of the constitutional guarantee of equal protection of the laws. The State of Texas would have us hold that there are only two classes — white and Negro — within the contemplation of the Fourteenth Amendment. The decisions of this Court do not support that view. And, except where the question presented involves the exclusion of persons of Mexican descent from juries, Texas courts have taken a broader view of the scope of the equal protection clause.

Throughout our history, differences in race and color have defined easily identifiable groups which have at times required the aid of the courts in securing equal treatment under the laws. But community prejudices are not static, and, from time to time, other differences from the community norm may define other groups which need the same protection. Whether such a group exists within a community is a question of fact. When the existence of a distinct class is demonstrated, and it is further shown that the laws, as written or as applied, single out that class for different treatment not based on some reasonable classification, the guarantees of the Constitution have been violated. The Fourteenth Amendment is not directed solely against discrimination due to a "two-class theory" — that is, based upon differences between "white" and Negro.

As the petitioner acknowledges, the Texas system of selecting grand and petit jurors by the use of jury commissions is fair on its face and capable of being utilized without discrimination. But, as this Court has held, the system is susceptible to abuse, and can be employed in a discriminatory manner. The exclusion of otherwise eligible persons from jury service solely because of their ancestry or national origin is discrimination prohibited by the Fourteenth Amendment. The Texas statute makes no such discrimination, but the petitioner alleges that those administering the law do.

The petitioner's initial burden in substantiating his charge of group discrimination was to prove that persons of Mexican descent constitute a separate class in Jackson County, distinct from "whites." One method by which this may be demonstrated is by showing the attitude of the community. Here, the testimony of responsible officials and citizens contained the admission that residents of the community distinguished between "white" and "Mexican." The participation of persons of Mexican descent in business and community groups was shown to be slight. Until very recent times, children of Mexican descent were required to attend a segregated school for the first four grades. At least one restaurant in town prominently displayed a sign announcing "No Mexicans Served." On the courthouse grounds at the time of the hearing, there were two men's toilets, one unmarked, and the other marked "Colored Men" and "Hombres Aqui" ("Men Here"). No substantial evidence was offered to rebut the logical inference to be drawn from these facts, and it must be concluded that petitioner succeeded in his proof.

Having established the existence of a class, petitioner was then charged with the burden of proving discrimination. To do so, he relied on the pattern of proof established by *Norris v. Alabama*. In that case, proof that Negroes constituted a substantial segment of the population of the jurisdiction, that some Negroes were qualified to serve as jurors, and that none had been called for jury service over an extended period of time, was held to constitute *prima facie* proof of the systematic exclusion of Negroes from jury service. This holding, sometimes called the "rule of exclusion," has been applied in other cases, and it is available in supplying proof of discrimination against any delineated class.

The petitioner established that 14% of the population of Jackson County were persons with Mexican or Latin American surnames, and that 11% of the males over 21 bore such names. The County Tax Assessor testified that 6 or 7 percent of the freeholders on the tax rolls of the County were persons of Mexican descent. The State of Texas stipulated that," for the last twenty-five years, there is no record of any person with a Mexican or Latin American name having served on a jury commission, grand jury or petit jury in Jackson County."

The parties also stipulated that "there are some male persons of Mexican or Latin American descent in Jackson County who, by virtue of being citizens, freeholders, and having all other legal prerequisites to jury service, are eligible to serve as members of a jury commission, grand jury and/or petit jury."

The petitioner met the burden of proof imposed in *Norris v. Alabama, supra.* To rebut the strong *prima facie* case of the denial of the equal protection of the laws guaranteed by the Constitution thus established, the State offered the testimony of five jury commissioners that they had no discriminated against persons of Mexican or Latin American descent in selecting jurors. They stated that their only objective had been to select those whom they thought were best qualified. This testimony is not enough to overcome the petitioner's case. As the Court said in *Norris v. Alabama:*

> "That showing as to the long-continued exclusion of negroes from jury service, and as to the many negroes qualified for that service, could not be met by mere generalities. If, in the presence of such testimony as defendant adduced, the mere general assertions by officials of their performance of duty were to be accepted as an adequate justification for the complete exclusion of negroes from jury service, the constitutional provision . . . would be but a vain and illusory requirement."

The same reasoning is applicable to these facts.

Circumstances or chance may well dictate that no persons in a certain class will serve on a particular jury or during some particular period. But it taxes our credulity to say that mere chance resulted in their being no members of this class among the over six thousand jurors called in the past 25 years. The result bespeaks discrimination, whether or not it was a conscious decision on the part of any individual jury commissioner. The judgment of conviction must be reversed.

To say that this decision revives the rejected contention that the Fourteenth Amendment requires proportional representation of all the component ethnic groups of the community on every jury ignores the facts. The petitioner did not seek proportional representation, nor did he claim a right to have persons of Mexican descent sit on the particular juries which he faced.His only claim is the right to be indicted and tried by juries from which all members of his class are not systematically excluded — juries selected from among all qualified persons regardless of national origin or descent. To this much he is entitled by the Constitution.

Reversed.

BROWN v. BOARD OF EDUCATION (BROWN I)
347 U.S. 483 (1954)

Mr. Chief Justice WARREN delivered the opinion of the Court.

These cases come to us from the States of Kansas, South Carolina, Virginia, and Delaware. They are premised on different facts and different local conditions, but a common legal question justifies their consideration together in this consolidated opinion.

[In] each of the cases, minors of the Negro race, through their legal representatives, seek the aid of the courts in obtaining admission to the public schools of their community on a nonsegregated basis. In each instance, they have been denied admission to schools attended by white children under laws requiring or permitting segregation according to race. This segregation was alleged to deprive the plaintiffs of the equal protection of the laws under the Fourteenth Amendment. In each of the cases other than the Delaware case, a three-judge federal district court denied relief to the plaintiffs on the so-called "separate but equal" doctrine announced by this Court in Plessy v. Ferguson, 163 U.S. 537, 16 S.Ct. 1138, 41 L.Ed. 256.

[The] plaintiffs contend that segregated public schools are not 'equal' and cannot be made "equal," and that hence they are deprived of the equal protection of the laws. Because of the obvious importance of the question presented, the Court took jurisdiction.

Argument was heard in the 1952 Term, and reargument was heard this Term on certain questions propounded by the Court.

Reargument was largely devoted to the circumstances surrounding the adoption of the Fourteenth Amendment in 1868. It covered exhaustively consideration of the Amendment in Congress, ratification by the states, then existing practices in racial segregation, and the views of proponents and opponents of the Amendment. This discussion and our own investigation convince us that, although these sources cast some light, it is not enough to resolve the problem with which we are faced. At best, they are inconclusive. The most avid proponents of the post-War Amendments undoubtedly intended them to remove all legal distinctions among "all persons born or naturalized in the United States." Their opponents, just as certainly, were antagonistic to both the letter and the spirit of the Amendments and wished them to have the most limited effect. What others in Congress and the state legislatures had in mind cannot be determined with any degree of certainty.

An additional reason for the inconclusive nature of the Amendment's history, with respect to segregated schools, is the status of public education at that time. In the South, the movement toward free common schools, supported by general taxation, had not yet taken hold. Education of white children was largely in the hands of private groups. Education of Negroes was almost nonexistent, and practically all of the race were illiterate. In fact, any education of Negroes was forbidden by law in some states. Today, in contrast, many Negroes have achieved outstanding success in the arts and sciences as well as in the business and professional world. It is true that public school education at the time of the Amendment had advanced further in the North, but the effect of the Amendment on Northern States was generally ignored in the congressional debates. Even in the North, the conditions of public education did not approximate those existing today. The curriculum was usually rudimentary; ungraded schools were common in rural areas; the school term was but three months a year in many states; and compulsory school attendance was virtually unknown. As a consequence, it is not surprising that there should be so little in the history of the Fourteenth Amendment relating to its intended effect on public education.

[In] the first cases in this Court construing the Fourteenth Amendment, decided shortly after its adoption, the Court interpreted it as proscribing all state-imposed discriminations against the Negro race. The doctrine of "separate but equal" did not make its appearance in this court until 1896 in the case of Plessy v. Ferguson, supra, involving not education but transportation. American courts have since labored with the doctrine for over half a century. In this Court, there have been six cases involving the "separate but equal" doctrine in the field of public education. In Cumming v. Board of Education of Richmond County, 175 U.S. 528, 20 S.Ct. 197, 44 L.Ed. 262, and Gong Lum v. Rice, 275 U.S. 78, 48 S.Ct. 91, 72 L.Ed. 172, the validity of the doctrine itself was not challenged. In more recent cases, all on the graduate school level, inequality was found in that specific benefits enjoyed by white students were denied to Negro students of the same educational qualifications. State of Missouri ex rel. Gaines v. Canada, 305 U.S. 337, 59 S.Ct. 232, 83 L.Ed. 208; Sipuel v. Board of Regents of University of Oklahoma, 332 U.S. 631, 68 S.Ct. 299, 92 L.Ed. 247; Sweatt v. Painter, 339 U.S. 629, 70 S.Ct. 848, 94 L.Ed. 1114; McLaurin v. Oklahoma State Regents, 339 U.S. 637, 70 S.Ct. 851, 94 L.Ed. 1149. In none of these cases was it necessary to re-examine the doctrine to grant relief to the Negro plaintiff. And in Sweatt v. Painter, supra, the Court expressly reserved decision on the question whether Plessy v. Ferguson should be held inapplicable to public education.

[In] the instant cases, that question is directly presented. Here, unlike Sweatt v. Painter, there are findings below that the Negro and white schools involved have been equalized, or are being equalized, with respect to buildings, curricula, qualifications and salaries of teachers, and other "tangible" factors. Our decision, therefore, cannot turn on merely a comparison of these tangible factors in the Negro and white schools involved in each of the cases. We must look instead to the effect of segregation itself on public education.

[In] approaching this problem, we cannot turn the clock back to 1868 when the Amendment was adopted, or even to 1896 when Plessy v. Ferguson was written. We must consider public education in the light of its full development and its present place in American life throughout the Nation. Only in this way can it be determined if segregation in public schools deprives these plaintiffs of the equal protection of the laws.

Today, education is perhaps the most important function of state and local governments. Compulsory school attendance laws and the great expenditures for education both demonstrate our recognition of the importance of education to our democratic society. It is required in the performance of our most basic public responsibilities, even service in the armed forces. It is the very foundation of good citizenship. Today it is a principal instrument in awakening the child to cultural values, in preparing him for later professional training, and in helping him to adjust normally to his environment. In these days, it is doubtful that any child may reasonably be expected to succeed in life if he is denied the opportunity of an education. Such an opportunity, where the state has undertaken to provide it, is a right which must be made available to all on equal terms.

We come then to the question presented: Does segregation of children in public schools solely on the basis of race, even though the physical facilities and other 'tangible' factors may be equal, deprive the children of the minority group of equal educational opportunities? We believe that it does.

In Sweatt v. Painter, supra (339 U.S. 629, 70 S.Ct. 850), in finding that a segregated law school for Negroes could not provide them equal educational opportunities, this Court relied in large part on "those qualities which are incapable of objective measurement but which make for greatness in a law school." In McLaurin v. Oklahoma State Regents, supra (339 U.S. 637, 70 S.Ct. 853), the Court, in requiring that a Negro admitted to a white graduate school be treated like all other students, again resorted to intangible considerations: ". . . his ability to study, to engage in discussions and exchange views with other students, and, in general, to learn his profession." Such considerations apply with added force to children in grade and high schools. To separate them from others of similar age and qualifications solely because of their race generates a feeling of inferiority as to their status in the community that may affect their hearts and minds in a way unlikely ever to be undone. The effect of this separation on their educational opportunities was well stated by a finding in the Kansas case by a court which nevertheless felt compelled to rule against the Negro plaintiffs:

> Segregation of white and colored children in public schools has a detrimental effect upon the colored children. The impact is greater when it has the sanction of the law; for the policy of separating the races is usually interpreted as denoting the inferiority of the negro group. A sense of inferiority affects the motivation of a child to learn. Segregation with the sanction of law, therefore, has a tendency to (retard) the educational and mental development of Negro children and to deprive them of some of the benefits they would receive in a racial(ly) integrated school system.

[Whatever] may have been the extent of psychological knowledge at the time of Plessy v. Ferguson, this finding is amply supported by modern authority.[11] Any language in Plessy v. Ferguson contrary to this finding is rejected.

[We] conclude that in the field of public education the doctrine of "separate but equal" has no place. Separate educational facilities are inherently unequal. Therefore, we hold that the plaintiffs and others similarly situated for whom the actions have been brought are, by reason of the segregation complained of, deprived of the equal protection of the laws guaranteed by the Fourteenth Amendment. This disposition makes unnecessary any discussion whether such segregation also violates the Due Process Clause of the Fourteenth Amendment.

Because these are class actions, because of the wide applicability of this decision, and because of the great variety of local conditions, the formulation of decrees in these cases presents problems of considerable complexity. On reargument, the consideration of appropriate relief was necessarily subordinated to the primary question — the constitutionality of segregation in public education. We have now announced that such segregation is a denial of the equal protection of the laws. In order that we may have the full assistance of the parties in formulating decrees, the cases will be restored to the docket, and the parties are requested to present further argument on Questions 4 and 5 previously propounded by the Court for the reargument. It is so ordered

BROWN v. BOARD OF EDUCATION (BROWN II)
349 U.S. 294 (1955)

Mr. Chief Justice WARREN delivered the opinion of the Court.

These cases were decided on May 17, 1954. The opinions of that date, declaring the fundamental principle that racial discrimination in public education is unconstitutional, are incorporated herein by reference. All provisions of federal, state, or local law requiring or permitting such discrimination must yield to this principle. There remains for consideration the manner in which relief is to be accorded.

Because these cases arose under different local conditions and their disposition will involve a variety of local problems, we requested further argument on the question of relief.[2] In view of the nationwide importance of the decision, we invited the Attorney

---

[11] K. B. Clark, Effect of Prejudice and Discrimination on Personality Development (Midcentury White House Conference on Children and Youth, 1950); Witmer and Kotinsky, Personality in the Making (1952), c. VI; Deutscher and Chein, The Psychological Effects of Enforced Segregation: A Survey of Social Science Opinion, 26 J.Psychol. 259 (1948); Chein, What are the Psychological Effects of Segregation Under Conditions of Equal Facilities?, 3 Int. J. Opinion and Attitude Res. 229 (1949); Brameld, Educational Costs, in Discrimination and National Welfare (MacIver, ed., 1949), 44-48; Frazier, The Negro in the United States (1949), 674-681. And see generally Myrdal, An American Dilemma (1944).

[2] Further argument was requested on the following questions, previously propounded by the Court:

4. Assuming it is decided that segregation in public schools violates the Fourteenth Amendment

(a) would a decree necessarily follow providing that, within the limits set by normal geographic school districting, Negro children should forthwith be admitted to schools of their choice, or

(b) may this Court, in the exercise of its equity powers, permit an effective gradual ad-

General of the United States and the Attorneys General of all states requiring or permitting racial discrimination in public education to present their views on that question. The parties, the United States, and the States of Florida, North Carolina, Arkansas, Oklahoma, Maryland, and Texas filed briefs and participated in the oral argument.

These presentations were informative and helpful to the Court in its consideration of the complexities arising from the transition to a system of public education freed of racial discrimination. The presentations also demonstrated that substantial steps to eliminate racial discrimination in public schools have already been taken, not only in some of the communities in which these cases arose, but in some of the states appearing as amici curiae, and in other states as well. Substantial progress has been made in the District of Columbia and in the communities in Kansas and Delaware involved in this litigation. The defendants in the cases coming to us from South Carolina and Virginia are awaiting the decision of this Court concerning relief.

Full implementation of these constitutional principles may require solution of varied local school problems. School authorities have the primary responsibility for elucidating, assessing, and solving these problems; courts will have to consider whether the action of school authorities constitutes good faith implementation of the governing constitutional principles. Because of their proximity to local conditions and the possible need for further hearings, the courts which originally heard these cases can best perform this judicial appraisal. Accordingly, we believe it appropriate to remand the cases to those courts.

In fashioning and effectuating the decrees, the courts will be guided by equitable principles. Traditionally, equity has been characterized by a practical flexibility in shaping its remedies and by a facility for adjusting and reconciling public and private needs. These cases call for the exercise of these traditional attributes of equity power. At stake is the personal interest of the plaintiffs in admission to public schools as soon as practicable on a nondiscriminatory basis. To effectuate this interest may call for elimination of a variety of obstacles in making the transition to school systems operated in accordance with the constitutional principles set forth in our May 17, 1954, decision. Courts of equity may properly take into account the public interest in the elimination of such obstacles in a systematic and effective manner. But it should go without saying that the vitality of these constitutional principles cannot be allowed to yield simply because of disagreement with them.

While giving weight to these public and private considerations, the courts will require that the defendants make a prompt and reasonable start toward full compliance with our May 17, 1954, ruling. Once such a start has been made, the courts may find that additional time is necessary to carry out the ruling in an effective manner. The burden rests

---

justment to be brought about from existing segregated systems to a system not based on color distinctions?

5. On the assumption on which questions 4(a) and (b) are based, and assuming further that this Court will exercise its equity powers to the end described in question 4(b),

(a) should this Court formulate detailed decrees in these cases;

(b) if so, what specific issues should the decrees reach;

(c) should this Court appoint a special master to hear evidence with a view to recommending specific terms for such decrees;

(d) should this Court remand to the courts of first instance with directions to frame decrees in these cases, and if so what general directions should the decrees of this Court include and what procedures should the courts of first instance follow in arriving at the specific terms of more detailed decrees?

upon the defendants to establish that such time is necessary in the public interest and is consistent with good faith compliance at the earliest practicable date. To that end, the courts may consider problems related to administration, arising from the physical condition of the school plant, the school transportation system, personnel, revision of school districts and attendance areas into compact units to achieve a system of determining admission to the public schools on a nonracial basis, and revision of local laws and regulations which may be necessary in solving the foregoing problems. They will also consider the adequacy of any plans the defendants may propose to meet these problems and to effectuate a transition to a racially nondiscriminatory school system. During this period of transition, the courts will retain jurisdiction of these cases.

The judgments below, except that in the Delaware case, are accordingly reversed and the cases are remanded to the District Courts to take such proceedings and enter such orders and decrees consistent with this opinion as are necessary and proper to admit to public schools on a racially nondiscriminatory basis with all deliberate speed the parties to these cases. The judgment in the Delaware case — ordering the immediate admission of the plaintiffs to schools previously attended only by white children — is affirmed on the basis of the principles stated in our May 17, 1954, opinion, but the case is remanded to the Supreme Court of Delaware for such further proceedings as that Court may deem necessary in light of this opinion.

Comments on *Brown*. Is separate but equal "inherently" unequal? Is there a place for separate education? Did *Brown* deny such? Was *Brown* wrong in this regard? Do contemporary circumstances represent the failure rather than the success of *Brown*? A brief piece that the author has written commemorative of the fiftieth anniversary of the *Brown* decision, and addressing these issues, follows.

SEPARATE BUT EQUAL *IS* INHERENTLY UNEQUAL
Martin L. Levy

It is most appropriate, as we approach the fiftieth "anniversary" of *Brown v. Board of Education*, that its central, albeit oft criticized thesis, "SEPARATE BUT EQUAL *IS* INHERENTLY UNEQUAL," is re-evaluated against a modern landscape. I shall assert herein, that this premise of *Brown* is just as accurate now as it was then. That the criticisms attacking this thesis since the Court so held, are misplaced, and to a great degree a "smokescreen" making it difficult to grant this landmark decision its proper due. To me, these criticisms of *Brown* underscore the racism in American myth and culture. I will assert herein that the unrepentant meaning of *Brown* was the doom it spelled for American apartheid! It is time to speak out. It is time to celebrate this decision for its ultimate truth — a crushing blow to the most heinous practice, American apartheid, racial segregation imposed by the state through the force of its laws.

APARTHEID AND BROWN

There is, of course, a history of criticism regarding *Brown*. Some is illicit, and traceable to the racism of the South. Some is quite legitimate. Herbert Wechler's and Learned Hand's come easily to mind. But the issue I address is a singular criticism aimed at the jugular of the decision, that separate but equal is *not* inherently unequal, and can serve a greater good.

Thus, for example, it has been argued, "that separate schools are not inherently unequal; the inferiority described in *Brown* should be attributed to the notions of white superiority ingrained in the social structures that once demanded mandatory segregation," or,

[W]hen an African-American community responds to its own cultural alienation — Its loss of voice — by creating schools that affirm group bonds and empower the community, and everyone within the community who has experienced cultural victimization may choose to enroll in the schools, then separate is not inherently unequal. On the contrary, separate is an avenue to effective education.

While serving on the faculty of the nation's largest producer of African American lawyers for over thirty-years, and teaching *Brown* to thirty straight Constitutional Law classes, I have conducted my own empirical study, an informal study based upon observation. In each and every year, there is a large and dynamic resistance to the *Brown* metaphor, a clear bias and desire of the students to assert the benefit of "separate education," at the cost of *Brown's* tenet.

What is most concerning about this view of the decision is how the issue itself has been blurred. Students perceive and scholar's challenge *Brown's* core *meaning*. Thus, so it goes, if "separate is not inherently unequal" *Brown's* posterity and meaning must be negated. Can we take pride in a decision that is read as a rejection of any benefit of black separate action and unification?

My plea is pure and simple. This notion of *Brown* is inaccurate. This is the "Catch 22 of *Brown*," — we cannot benefit from "separate" action, even in education, and allow *Brown* to ring true. It is a syllogism where one must deny the other. This confusion is the shame of the American psyche. It portends that if the African-American community wants to act together, act separately, then it must reject the premise of *Brown*. This propaganda denies us all the reality of what *Brown* represents, something all of America can take pride in — the "smashing" of the ignoble American sin of this century, apartheid. Put simply, and despite the smokescreen to the contrary, the fact that "apartheid is inherently unequal," does not deny to us any benefit of racial separation.

As is often the case, at the bottom of what appears to be a most complex difficulty is a rather simple and straightforward answer. Such is the case in the matter at hand. When the Court in *Brown* held, "We conclude that in the field of public education the doctrine of "separate but equal" has no place. Separate educational facilities are inherently unequal," it could only speak to the facts before it, it could only conclude that such was the case when segregation was imposed by the force of state law. What the Court in fact held was that, "*apartheid* was inherently unequal." (emphasis added) Separate but equal is then "inherently unequal" when it is "sanctioned by law." Herein lies the rub. The criticism of *Brown* challenges this conclusion in regard to the benefits that racial separation may offer, when the opinion itself spoke only to apartheid, and never denied the conceivability of such benefits.

I think the Court's use of the term "inherently" also begs comment. This is a serious term. For something to be "inherent" it must be "intrinsic," or "in the nature of the thing." Inherent is "always," and always is forever. To describe anything forever is as absolute as language can be. In life there are very few absolutes. I am arguing that we have come upon one of them. Apartheid is an absolute. Apartheid is inherently unequal. Failing to understand such means one might conclude that by use of "inherently," the Court meant that "any separation was unequal." This is a misnomer.

What is important here is what the Court in *Brown* spoke to and what it did not. While the South was fashioning apartheid for South Africa to emulate, "choice" was not an issue. The facts were quite clear. Students could not choose or exercise volition regarding attending a racially segregated school. This was mandated by law. This is what the Court in *Brown* outlawed. To be sure, even if apartheid was purged from our legal system, we knew that discrimination would not be. Other more difficult questions laid ahead. What is choice? What is volition? Here are three scenarios that are apparent in regard to these questions and segregation in America:

1. Segregation "by law" — no choice.
2. Segregation by "apparent volition" — no choice. (The State imposes segregation by techniques that appear to be *ultra vires* the State, when they are not so in fact.)
3. Separation "by volition" — choice.

Distinguishing between 2 and 3 is as arduous as it gets. We have been attempting to define where we are in this regard for over forty years. The reality is that the Court in *Brown* did not speak to these issues. It did not even attempt to speak to these issues. The Court addressed 1, resolved it, and set forth a precedent which ultimately purged apartheid. We no longer maintain such practices — they are accepted as illegal and unconstitutional. Today we are mired in deciding whether we have apparent volition, but still no choice, or whether we do have volition — choice. Where we are may well depend upon your political persuasion. This much we know, we are more segregated today in housing and schools than we were thirty years ago! To be sure, not via apartheid, but arguably by legalizing the "surreptitiousness" detailed in 2 above.

Note that a decision based on 1, says nothing about 2 or 3. Why then should we reject *Brown's* premise of when the Court never addressed the issue or the degree to which the state could create and enforce segregation by surreptitious means (2)? Or, much the same, why should we reject the premise of *Brown* when the Court never addressed the meaning of separation by volition or choice (3)? Therefore, just as the opinion in *Brown* could not be held responsible for our present segregative circumstance, it could also not be criticized for denying any benefit of racial separation by choice. The Court held "apartheid" unequal, not all separation.

The fact that we have failed in achieving the ideal of an integrated community does not fall at the footsteps of *Brown*. It falls at the footsteps of the inherent racism in our society. But just the same, the Court in *Brown* never denied the possible benefits of racial separation for both educational and political purposes. It quite simply did not speak to these issues.

There is an issue of consequence, I have yet to address. My thesis is dependant upon it as well. If I have helped clarify what I have called the "Catch 22 of *Brown*," so that its vitality may remain with us today; then I must also address the veracity of the Court's conclusion that "apartheid *is* inherently unequal."

> [S]tate-sponsored segregation conveys a message of "inferiority" as to th[e] status [of Afro-American school children] in the community that may affect their hearts and minds in a way unlikely ever to be undone.

Much literature and debate has centered upon the Court's support for the above cited conclusion in *Brown*. Particular debate has focused on the Court's famous citation in footnote 11 to "psychological knowledge" in support of such. Scholars until today debate not only the degree to which the Court's decision rested upon "social science" empirical data, but the accuracy of it as well. Literature still abounds, for example, debating K.B. Clark's study on the, "Effect of Prejudice and Discrimination on Personality Development," cited in footnote 11.

But I have cast a "Photoshop mask" over this issue regarding *Brown*. Since the case dealt only with state enforced segregation, evaluating its actual impact on African-Americans, and in particular African-American children, must be so limited. As I have previously argued, confusion is the only by-product of an analysis not so limited. Once again, much of the "fog" in the air is cleared if we rid ourselves of the "baggage" that the Court in *Brown* spoke to all forms of separation. Thus viewed, I do not feel that the viability of the Court's finding that "apartheid is inherently unequal" lives or dies either on the degree to which the Court supported its decision based upon social science data, or even the veracity of that data.

I submit that the process of identifying one group of people in order to separate them from all other groups of people, by force of law, is inherently unequal. Any standard of living in the "ghetto" could not de-stigmatize the Jewish experience in Warsaw. To deny the stigma and inferiority of apartheid, particularly when it followed the enslavement of that very race, is both illogical and impious. The evident psychological impact of such separation of one race from all others, casts a pale of inferiority that no study need verify. The force of law alone conjures such result. How can you explain to a child why the law separates his race from all others? The mere fact that we placed a child in this circumstance is inhuman. The water at the "colored" fountain might be the same, but tell me how you explain to this child why the law mandates that as an African-American he or she must drink there, while *all* others may drink from another? You cannot so explain. To even suggest that it can be explained is offensive, for racism is the only defense, the only explanation. Kenneth Clark's "dolls" are not needed to understand state imposed racial inferiority. The stigma and inferiority that stems from apartheid stems from the crimes committed against this humanity. This is so and it should be said.

I submit that separating one racial group from all others by force of law is demeaning, dehumanizing, and imposes a state imposed inferiority on the race so effected. Apartheid can only be defended by that which brought it about — racism.

On this point the Court in *Brown* was clear. Whatever the extent of importance in the Court's citation in footnote 11, the Court rested its finding in the stigma of apartheid emphasized above:

> The Court based this conclusion on its recognition of the particular social harm that racially segregated schools inflict on Afro-American children. "To separate them from others of similar age and qualifications solely because of their race generates a feeling of inferiority as to their status in the community that may affect their hearts and minds in a way unlikely ever to be undone. The effect of this separation on their educational opportunities was well stated by a finding in the Kansas case by a court which nevertheless felt compelled to rule against the Negro plaintiffs: "'Segregation of white and colored children in public schools has a detrimental effect upon the colored children. The impact is greater when it has the sanction of law; for the policy of separating the races is usually interpreted as denoting the inferiority of the negro group. A sense of inferiority affects the motivation of a child to learn. Segregation with the sanction of law, therefore, has a tendency to [retard] the educational and mental development of negro children and to deprive them of some of the benefits they would receive in a racial[ly] integrated school

system.' (Justice Marshall's reference to *Brown*, while dissenting in, *Brd. of Educ. of Ok-lahoma City Pub. Sch. v. Dowell*).

Does segregation of children in public schools solely on the basis of race, even though the physical facilities and other 'tangible' factors may be equal, deprive the children of the minority group of equal educational opportunities? We believe that it does.

Just as slavery is inherently unequal, apartheid is inherently unequal. A defense of one is a defense of the other. They are of the same seed. There were both brought about by racism, and they can only be defended by racism. That is the truth.

THE FIFTIETH ANNIVERSARY OF BROWN V. BRD. OF EDUCATION:
THE DEATH KNELL OF AMERICAN APARTHEID

A line was drawn in American history in 1954. Historians view this date as a demarcation in America's social structure. 1954 was the "death knell" to American apartheid. This is the meaning and heritage of *Brown*. We can perhaps best understand this by exploring not only what *Brown* "was," but what it "was not":

The Court in *Brown* did not speak to a circumstance where state imposed segregation did not directly extend from the force of its laws. In a society where private discrimination is not a violation of Constitutional rights, and where many necessities that the public is dependent on are held in private hands, this is a dynamic question regarding segregation and racism. To assume that the reasoning in *Brown* is applicable to this question is an attempt to discredit the case that is undeserved. This, as a post-apartheid issue, was critical *after* the *Brown* decision, and our failure to deal with it is therefore not traceable to *Brown*.

The Court in *Brown* did not speak to either the value or constitutionality of racial separation by choice. The Court did not even address what choice meant. This is another significant post-apartheid issue. Where the line can or should be drawn in this regard is a question of consequence in our society today. But, and once again, the Court in *Brown* addressed separation imposed by the state and enforced by law, and did not even address "choice." As I have asserted herein, arguing the relevancy of *Brown* here is an illicit attempt to undermine its very meaning.

Finally, the Court in *Brown* did not speak to how either of the above referenced circumstances would effect desegregation or integration of the nation's public schools. Simply put, though we have not failed in putting an end to apartheid, we have failed in achieving noble goals in regard to the continued segregation in post-apartheid America. Once again, the problem here rests in the racial discrimination that is ingrained in and still pervades American culture, not in *Brown*.

Brown was the "death knell" to apartheid in America. As we approach its fiftieth anniversary, it is time that we recognize and acclaim it for such. The purpose of this piece has not only been to proclaim such, but to clear away the maze of confusion that has surrounded the opinion in this respect.

A unanimous Supreme Court stood proud in 1954. A Court, I might add, that had been a party in both the maintenance of slavery, as well as interpreting the great post war amendments so as to make Jim Crow and apartheid possible. We have debated our successes and failures in dealing with American racism ever since, but we must recognize the cause for what it is, a racist America, not the failure of *Brown*. To that end, avocation of the tenet that "separate but equal is inherently unequal" must no longer mandate any apologia, but rather instill in us the spirit of hope unto which it was intended, a recognition of the significant step in the progress of American history it represents. Sleep well Thurgood Marshall, *Brown v. Brd. of Educ.,* much thanks to you, mandated and foretold the end of American apartheid. SEPARATE BUT EQUAL *IS* INHERENTLY UNEQUAL — let us hail to *that* chief!

b. IMPLEMENTATION

The nation's response to the enforcement of *Brown* was deliberate only in the sense of noncompliance. Recall the challenge to *Brown* and the power of the Supreme Court as we introduced judicial review in *Cooper v. Aaron.* Though President Eisenhower called in federal troops to respond to the challenge of the very authority of the federal government, his Justice Department was no friend of the decision. In fact, Earl Warren comments in his *The Memoirs of Earl Warren* (1977), that "Eisenhower resented our decision in *Brown*," and even alludes to the fact that had Eisenhower publicly supported the decision "much of our racial strife could have been avoided." (*Id.* at 290-292.)

What did the "all deliberate speed" of *Brown II* mean in relation to southern non-compliance? History now tells us about ten years — ten years of non-involvement of the federal courts, ten years to allow the states to act on their own. But the reality was that if "all deliberate speed" meant ten years of non-interference, it meant ten years of inaction to southern school districts. Though the Court would always refer to compliance as if action should have commenced in 1954, these were nonetheless ten lost years. But by 1963 in *Goss v. Board of Educ*ation, 373 U.S. 683, and *Waston v. City of Memphis*, 373 U.S. 526, and certainly by 1968 in *Green v. County School Board*, 391 U.S. 430, the Court concluded that "delays [were] no longer tolerable." In *Alexander v. Holmes County School Board*, 396 U.S. 19, in 1969, the Court announced that the dual system must be "terminated" at once.

But by the end of the decade the mood of the government and the nation changed. First was the election of Richard Nixon as President in 1968, and the evolution of the Republican Party's "Southern strategy," aimed at seeking votes of disenchanted southern whites. In *Carter v. West Feliciana Parish*, 396 U.S. 290 (1970), in a narrow 5–4 decision, the Supreme Court found a "delay" tolerable for the first time, and the federal government (for the first time as well) argued in favor of such. Second, the determination that apartheid, or legally mandated segregation, was unconstitutional, did not mean the end of discrimination. The end of de jure (by law) school segregation did not mean the end of de facto (not by law, but in fact) segregation. Though most northern states did not mandate de jure segregation, segregation in fact (de facto) nonetheless existed. The focus on the north certainly changed the political face of desegregation and the fact that southern states that had maintained apartheid still maintained de facto segregation made the political climate even more difficult. We could purge the nation of apartheid but not discrimination and segregated schools. Somehow, the issue was different when it was Pontiac, Michigan and Boston, Massachusetts rather than Birmingham. Finally, the dismantling of segregated schools, and the efforts necessary to create desegregated schools, as against this political climate, made matters worse. Remedies such as busing children to desegregate, or spending money for necessary new schools, fueled the political fires.

In realty the nation had moved on to a more difficult issue, *Brown* had led the fight to strike apartheid, but segregation and discrimination still continued, and the degree to which a state should still be held responsible for de facto segregation was a new and more difficult question. Where should the line be drawn in making a state responsible for the racist views of its citizens? Was de facto segregation "voluntary" or simply a more covert form of state sponsored discrimination? Was the state still responsible and the segregation actionable? Viewed in this sense the right and wrong of fighting apartheid was easy, dealing with the remaining discrimination was not.

In 1971, with Earl Warren retired, and Richard Nixon's appointments shaping a Supreme Court that would break with the "new deal" and "Warren Court" legacy, the "Burger" Court responded to these issues in a series of school desegregation cases that began with *Swann v. Charlotte-Meckenburg Board of Education*. *Swann*, the "Burger" Court bible on intra-district enforcement and remedies, commenced a new era in school desegregation.

c. CONTEMPORARY STANDARDS

SWANN v. CHARLOTTE-MECKLENBURG BOARD OF EDUCATION
402 U.S. 1 (1971)

Mr. Chief Justice BURGER delivered the opinion of the Court.

We granted certiorari in this case to review important issues as to the duties of school authorities and the scope of powers of federal courts under this Court's mandates to eliminate racially separate public schools established and maintained by state action. Brown v. Board of Education, 347 U.S. 483, 74 S.Ct. 686, 98 L.Ed. 873 (1954) (Brown I).

The problems encountered by the district courts and courts of appeals make plain that we should now try to amplify guidelines, however incomplete and imperfect, for the assistance of school authorities and courts. The failure of local authorities to meet their constitutional obligations aggravated the massive problem of converting from the state-enforced discrimination of racially separate school systems. This process has been rendered more difficult by changes since 1954 in the structure and patterns of communities, the growth of student population, movement of families, and other changes, some of which had marked impact on school planning, sometimes neutralizing or negating remedial action before it was fully implemented. Rural areas accustomed for half a century to the consolidated school systems implemented by bus transportation could make adjustments more readily than metropolitan areas with dense and shifting population, numerous schools, congested and complex traffic patterns.

III. The objective today remains to eliminate from the public schools all vestiges of state-imposed segregation. Segregation was the evil struck down by Brown I as contrary to the equal protection guarantees of the Constitution. That was the violation sought to be corrected by the remedial measures of Brown II. That was the basis for the holding in Green that school authorities are "clearly charged with the affirmative duty to take whatever steps might be necessary to convert to a unitary system in which racial discrimination would be eliminated root and branch." 391 U.S., at 437-438, 88 S.Ct., at 1694.

If school authorities fail in their affirmative obligations under these holdings, judicial authority may be invoked. Once a right and a violation have been shown, the scope of a district court's equitable powers to remedy past wrongs is broad, for breadth and flexibility are inherent in equitable remedies.

The school authorities argue that the equity powers of federal district courts have been limited by Title IV of the Civil Rights Act of 1964, 42 U.S.C. § 2000c et seq. The language and the history of Title IV show that it was enacted not to limit but to define the role of the Federal Government in the implementation of the Brown I decision.

IV. In ascertaining the existence of legally imposed school segregation, the existence of a pattern of school construction and abandonment is thus a factor of great weight. In devising remedies where legally imposed segregation has been established, it is the responsibility of local authorities and district courts to see to it that future school construction and abandonment are not used and do not serve to perpetuate or re-establish the dual system. When necessary, district courts should retain jurisdiction to assure that these responsibilities are carried out. Cf. United States v. Board of Public Instruction, 395 F.2d 66 (CA5 1968); Brewer v. School Board, 397 F.2d 37 (CA4 1968).

V. The central issue in this case is that of student assignment, and there are essentially four problem areas:

- to what extent racial balance or racial quotas may be used as an implement in a remedial order to correct a previously segregated system;
- whether every all-Negro and all-white school must be eliminated as an indispensable part of a remedial process of desegregation;
- what the limits are, if any, on the rearrangement of school districts and attendance zones, as a remedial measure; and
- what the limits are, if any, on the use of transportation facilities to correct state-enforced racial school segregation.

(1) Racial Balances or Racial Quotas. [We] do not reach in this case the question whether a showing that school segregation is a consequence of other types of state action, without any discriminatory action by the school authorities, is a constitutional violation requiring remedial action by a school desegregation decree. In this case it is urged that the District Court has imposed a racial balance requirement of 71%–29% on individual schools. If we were to read the holding of the District Court to require, as a matter of substantive constitutional right, any particular degree of racial balance or mixing, that approach would be disapproved and we would be obliged to reverse. The constitutional command to desegregate schools does not mean that every school in every community must always reflect the racial composition of the school system as a whole. We see therefore that the use made of mathematical ratios was no more than a starting point in the process of shaping a remedy, rather than an inflexible requirement. As we said in Green, a school authority's remedial plan or a district court's remedial decree is to be judged by its effectiveness. Awareness of the racial composition of the whole school system is likely to be a useful starting point in shaping a remedy to correct past constitutional violations. In sum, the very limited use made of mathematical ratios was within the equitable remedial discretion of the District Court.

(2) One-race Schools. [The] existence of some small number of one-race, or virtually one-race, schools within a district is not in and of itself the mark of a system that still practices segregation by law. The court should scrutinize such schools, and the burden upon the school authorities will be to satisfy the court that their racial composition is not the result of present or past discriminatory action on their part.

An optional majority-to-minority transfer provision has long been recognized as a useful part of every desegregation plan. Provision for optional transfer of those in the majority racial group of a particular school to other schools where they will be in the minority is an indispensable remedy for those students willing to transfer to other schools in order to lessen the impact on them of the state-imposed stigma of segregation. In order to be effective, such a transfer arrangement must grant the transferring student free transportation and space must be made available in the school to which he desires to move.

(3) Remedial Altering of Attendance Zones. The maps submitted in these cases graphically demonstrate that one of the principal tools employed by school planners and by courts to break up the dual school system has been a frank — and sometimes drastic — gerrymandering of school districts and attendance zones. An additional step was pairing, "clustering," or "grouping" of schools with attendance assignments made deliberately to accomplish the transfer of Negro students out of formerly segregated Negro schools and transfer of white students to formerly all-Negro schools. More often than not, these zones are neither compact nor contiguous; indeed they may be on opposite ends of the city. As an interim corrective measure, this cannot be said to be beyond the broad remedial powers of a court.

Absent a constitutional violation there would be no basis for judicially ordering assignment of students on a racial basis. All things being equal, with no history of discrimination, it might well be desirable to assign pupils to schools nearest their homes. But all things are not equal in a system that has been deliberately constructed and maintained to enforce racial segregation. The remedy for such segregation may be administratively awkward, inconvenient, and even bizarre in some situations and may impose burdens on some; but all awkwardness and inconvenience cannot be avoided in the interim period when remedial adjustments are being made to eliminate the dual school systems.

No fixed or even substantially fixed guidelines can be established as to how far a court can go, but it must be recognized that there are limits. The objective is to dismantle the dual school system. "Racially neutral" assignment plans proposed by school authorities to a district court may be inadequate; such plans may fail to counteract the continuing effects of past school segregation resulting from discriminatory location of school sites or distortion of school size in order to achieve or maintain an artificial racial separation. When school authorities present a district court with a "loaded game board," affirmative action in the form of remedial altering of attendance zones is proper to achieve truly nondiscriminatory assignments.

We hold that the pairing and grouping of noncontiguous school zones is a permissible tool and such action is to be considered in light of the objectives sought. Judicial steps in shaping such zones going beyond combinations of contiguous areas should be examined in light of what is said in subdivisions (1), (2), and (3) of this opinion concerning the objectives to be sought.

Transportation of Students. The scope of permissible transportation of students as an implement of a remedial decree has never been defined by this Court and by the very nature of the problem it cannot be defined with precision. No rigid guidelines as to student transportation can be given for application to the infinite variety of problems presented in thousands of situations. Bus transportation has been an integral part of the public education system for years, and was perhaps the single most important factor in the transition from the one-room schoolhouse to the consolidated school. Eighteen million of the Nation's public school children, approximately 39% were transported to their schools by bus in 1969-1970 in all parts of the country. [We] find no basis for holding that the local school authorities may not be required to employ bus transportation as one tool of school desegregation. Desegregation plans cannot be limited to the walk-in school.

An objection to transportation of students may have validity when the time or distance of travel is so great as to either risk the health of the children or significantly impinge on the educational process. District courts must weigh the soundness of any transportation plan in light of what is said in subdivisions (1), (2), and (3) above. It hardly needs stating that the limits on time of travel will vary with many factors, but probably with none more than the age of the students. The reconciliation of competing values in a desegregation case is, of course, a difficult task with many sensitive facets but fundamentally no more so than remedial measures courts of equity have traditionally employed.

VI. At some point, these school authorities and others like them should have achieved full compliance with this Court's decision in Brown I. The systems would then be "unitary" in the sense required by our decisions in Green and Alexander. It does not follow that the communities served by such systems will remain demographically stable, for in a growing, mobile society, few will do so. Neither school authorities nor district courts are constitutionally required to make year-by-year adjustments of the racial composition of student bodies once the affirmative duty to desegregate has been accomplished and racial discrimination through official action is eliminated from the system. This does not mean that federal courts are without power to deal with future problems; but in the absence of a showing that either the school authorities or some other agency of the State has deliberately attempted to fix or alter demographic patterns to affect the racial composition of the schools, further intervention by a district court should not be necessary. It is so ordered.

d. "THE NORTH"

Prior to *Keyes* the Court had not faced a challenge to de facto segregation in a northern school district. This circumstance is much the same as the *Arlington Heights* and *Davis* cases, reviewed earlier — proving up discriminatory intent on behalf of the state when a statute is "race" neutral on its face. *Columbus Board* presents a more contemporary view of both "proof" and compliance by northern districts. Compare the burden of proof required in *Keyes* and *Columbus Board* to that required in *Davis* and *Arlington Heights*. Is there a difference in the plaintiff's burden of proof in the school desegregation cases, particularly in *Columbus Board*, which was decided after *Davis* and *Arlington Heights*?

Finally, when does a school board achieve compliance, or when is a dual district dismantled and unitary? If a district is held to have remedied its constitutional violation, but demographics indicate a return to a dual system, what is required to prove that the district is once again segregated? This was the circumstance in *Pasadena*, how to procede once a judge concludes that the original constitutional violation has been remedied.

KEYES v. SCHOOL DISTRICT NO. 1, DENVER
413 U.S. 189 (1973)

[Here, the Supreme Court, for the first time, considered the lawfulness of school segregation in a northern city that had never mandated segregated education by law. The district court found that the Denver School Board had for a period of ten years maintained deliberately segregated schools in the Park Hill section of the city through use of gerryman-dered attendance zones and similar devices. Although the district court ordered desegre-gation of the Park Hill schools, it held that the finding of purposeful segregation in this area did not require the board to remedy racial imbalance in other areas of the city. The court of appeals affirmed this portion of the district court's order, but the Supreme Court, in an opinion by Justice Brennan, reversed and held that system wide relief might be appropriate.

Since maintenance of a segregated system was not mandated by law it was assumed that the plaintiffs bore the burden of establishing that segregated schools had been brought about or maintained by intentional state action. The Court held, however, that once such a showing had been made with regard to a substantial portion of the system, plaintiffs need not bear the additional burden of showing deliberate segregation as to each school within the school system.]

Mr. Justice BRENNAN delivered the opinion of the Court.

[We] emphasize that the differentiating factor between de jure segregation and so-called de facto segregation to which we referred in Swann is purpose or intent to segre-gate. Where school authorities have been found to have practiced purposeful segregation in part of a school system, they may be expected to oppose system-wide desegregation, as did the respondents in this case, on the ground that their purposefully segregative actions were isolated and individual events, thus leaving plaintiffs with the burden of proving otherwise. But at that point where an intentionally segregative policy is practiced in a meaningful or significant segment of a school system, as in this case, the school authori-ties cannot be heard to argue that plaintiffs have proved only 'isolated and individual' unlawfully segregative actions. In that circumstance, it is both fair and reasonable to re-quire that the school authorities bear the burden of showing that their actions as to other segregated schools within the system were not also motivated by segregative intent.

[Where] plaintiffs prove that the school authorities have carried out a systematic program of segregation affecting a substantial portion of the students, schools, teachers, and facilities within the school system, it is only common sense to conclude that there exists a predicate for a finding of the existence of a dual school system.

[Common] sense dictates the conclusion that racially inspired school board actions have an impact beyond the particular schools that are subject to those actions. Although there might be "rare" cases where the effect of discriminatory conduct was isolated, in the more usual case, proof of unlawful segregation in a substantial portion of a district was sufficient to support a finding of the existence of a dual school system.

Moreover, even if the effect of discriminatory action in a part of the system was iso-lated, it might still serve as the evidentiary predicate for system-wide relief. This was so because "a finding of intentionally segregative school board actions in a meaningful por-tion of a school system, creates [a] prima facie case of unlawful segregative design on the part of school authorities, and shifts to those authorities the burden of proving that other segregated schools within the system are not also the result of intentionally segregative actions. This is true even if it is determined that different areas of the school district should be viewed independently of each other because, even in that situation, there is high probability that where school authorities have effectuated an intentionally segrega-tive policy in a meaningful portion of the school system, similar impermissible considera-tions have motivated their actions in other areas of the system. . . .

Justice POWELL concurred in part and dissented in part:

The situation in Denver is generally comparable to that in other large cities across the country in which there is a substantial minority population and where desegregation has not been ordered by the federal courts. There is segregation in the schools of many of these cities fully as pervasive as that in southern cities prior to the desegregation decrees of the past decade and a half. The focus of the school desegregation problem has now shifted from the South to the country as a whole.

Unwilling and footdragging as the process was in most places, substantial progress toward achieving integration has been made in Southern States. No comparable progress has been made in many non-southern cities with large minority populations primarily because of the de facto/de jure distinction nurtured by the courts and accepted complacently by many of the same voices which denounced the evils of segregated schools in the South. But if our national concern is for those who attend such schools, rather than for perpetuating a legalism rooted in history rather than present reality, we must recognize that the evil of operating separate schools is no less in Denver than in Atlanta. . . .

In my view we should abandon a distinction which long since has outlived its time, and formulate constitutional principles of national rather than merely regional application. . . .

Whereas Brown I rightly decreed the elimination of state-imposed segregation in that particular section of the country where it did exist, Swann imposed obligations on southern school districts to eliminate conditions which are not regionally unique but are similar both in origin and effect to conditions in the rest of the country. [I] would hold, quite simply, that where segregated public schools exist within a school district to a substantial degree, there is a prima facie case that the duly constituted public authorities [are] sufficiently responsible to warrant imposing upon them a nationally applicable burden to demonstrate they nevertheless are operating a genuinely integrated school system. [This] means that school authorities, consistent with the generally accepted educational goal of attaining quality education for all pupils, must make and implement their customary decisions with a view toward enhancing integrated school opportunities. . . .

An integrated school system does not mean — and indeed could not mean in view of the residential patterns of most of our major metropolitan areas — that every school must in fact be an integrated unit. A school which happens to be all or predominantly white or all or predominantly black is not a 'segregated' school in an unconstitutional sense if the system itself is a genuinely integrated one.

Public schools are creatures of the State, and whether the segregation is state-created or state-assisted or merely state-perpetuated should be irrelevant to constitutional principle. The school board exercises pervasive and continuing responsibility over the long-range planning as well as the daily operations of the public school system. [School] board decisions obviously are not the sole cause of segregated school conditions. But if, after such detailed and complete public supervision, substantial school segregation still persists, the presumption is strong that the school board, by its acts or omissions, is in some part responsible. . . .

Where school authorities have defaulted in their duty to operate an integrated school system, district courts must insure that affirmative desegregative steps ensue. Many of these can be taken effectively without damaging state and parental interests in having children attend schools within a reasonable vicinity of home. Where desegregative steps are possible within the framework of a system of "neighborhood education," school authorities must pursue them. . . .

A constitutional requirement of extensive student transportation solely to achieve integration presents a vastly more complex problem. It promises, on the one hand, a greater degree of actual desegregation, while it infringes on what may fairly be regarded as other important community aspirations and personal rights. Such a requirement is also likely to divert attention and resources from the foremost goal of any school system: the best quality education for all pupils. The Equal Protection Clause does, indeed, command that racial discrimination not be tolerated in the decisions of public school authorities. But it does not require that school authorities undertake widespread student transportation solely for the sake of maximizing integration.

"This obviously does not mean that bus transportation has no place in public school systems or is not a permissible means in the desegregative process. [The] crucial issue is when, under what circumstances, and to what extent such transportation may appropriately be ordered. The answer to this turns — as it does so often in the law — upon a sound exercise of discretion under the circumstances. . . .

"[This] would [require] that the legitimate community interests in neighborhood school systems be accorded far greater respect. [As] a minimum, this Court should not require school boards to engage in the unnecessary transportation away from their neighborhoods of elementary-age children. . . ."

Justice REHNQUIST dissented:

Underlying the Court's entire opinion is its apparent thesis that a district judge is at least permitted to find that if a single attendance zone between two individual schools in the large metropolitan district is found by him to have been "gerrymandered," the school district is guilty of operating a "dual" school system, and is apparently a candidate for what is in practice a federal receivership. [It] would therefore presumably be open to the District Court to require, inter alia, that pupils be transported great distances throughout the district to and from schools whose attendance zones have not been gerrymandered. Yet, unless the Equal Protection Clause of the Fourteenth Amendment now be held to embody a principle of "taint," found in some primitive legal systems but discarded centuries ago in ours, such a result can only be described as the product of judicial fiat. . . .

The Court has taken a long leap in this area of constitutional law in equating the district-wide consequences of gerrymandering individual attendance zones in a district where separation of the races was never required by law with statutes or ordinances in other jurisdictions which did so require. It then adds to this potpourri a confusing enunciation of evidentiary rules in order to make it more likely that the trial court will on remand reach the result which the Court apparently wants it to reach. Since I believe neither of these steps is justified by prior decisions of this Court. I dissent.

COLUMBUS BOARD OF EDUCATION v. PENICK
443 U.S. 449 (1979)

This class action was brought in 1973 by students in the Columbus, Ohio, school system, charging that the Columbus Board of Education (Board) and its officials had pursued and were pursuing a course of conduct having the purpose and effect of causing and perpetuating racial segregation in the public schools, contrary to the Fourteenth Amendment. The case was ultimately tried in April-June 1976, final arguments were heard in September 1976, and in March 1977 the District Court filed an opinion and order containing its findings of fact and conclusions of law. It found (1) that in 1954, when Brown v. Board of Education, 347 U.S. 483, 74 S.Ct. 686, 98 L.Ed. 873 (Brown I), was decided, the Board was not operating a racially neutral unitary school system, but was conducting "an enclave of separate, black schools on the near east side of Columbus" and that this was "the direct result of cognitive acts or omissions of those school board members and administrators who had originally intentionally caused and later perpetuated the racial isolation"; (2) that since the decision in Brown v. Board of Education, 349 U.S. 294, 75 S.Ct. 753, 99 L.Ed. 1083 *(Brown II)*, the Board had been under a continuous constitutional obligation to disestablish its dual system and that it has failed to discharge this duty; and (3) that in the intervening years since 1954 there had been a series of Board actions and practices that could not "reasonably be explained without reference to racial concerns" and that "intentionally aggravated, rather than alleviated," racial separation in the schools. Ultimately concluding that at the time of trial the racial segregation in the Columbus school system "directly resulted from [the Board's] intentional segregative acts and omissions," in violation of the Equal Protection Clause of the Fourteenth Amendment, the court, accordingly, enjoined the defendants from continuing to discriminate on the basis of race in operating the public schools and ordered the submission of a systemwide desegregation plan. Subsequently, following the decision in Dayton Board of Education v. Brinkman, 433 U.S. 406, 97 S.Ct. 2766, 53 L.Ed.2d 851 (Dayton I), the District Court rejected the Board's argument that that decision required or permitted modification of the court's finding or judgment. Based on its examination of the record, the Court of Appeals affirmed the judgments against the defendants.

Mr. Justice WHITE delivered the opinion of the Court.

We have discovered no reason, however, to disturb the judgment of the Court of Appeals, based on the findings and conclusions of the District Court, that the Board's conduct at the time of trial and before not only was animated by an unconstitutional, segregative purpose, but also had current, segregative impact that was sufficiently systemwide to warrant the remedy ordered by the District Court.

These ultimate conclusions were rooted in a series of constitutional violations that the District Court found the Board to have committed and that together dictated its judgment and decree. In each instance, the Court of Appeals found the District Court's conclusions to be factually and legally sound.

A. First, although at least since 1888 there had been no statutory requirement or authorization to operate segregated schools, the District Court found that in 1954, when Brown v. Board of Education, 347 U.S. 483, 74 S.Ct. 686, 98 L.Ed. 873 (*Brown I*), was decided, the Columbus Board was not operating a racially neutral, unitary school system, but was conducting "an enclave of separate, black schools on the near east side of Columbus," and that "[t]he then-existing racial separation was the direct result of cognitive acts or omissions of those school board members and administrators who had originally intentionally caused and later perpetuated the racial isolation . . . ." Such separateness could not "be said to have been the result of racially neutral official acts."

B. Second, both courts below declared that since the decision in Brown v. Board of Education, 349 U.S. 294, 75 S.Ct. 753, 99 L.Ed. 1083 (1955) (*Brown II*), the Columbus Board has been under a continuous constitutional obligation to disestablish its dual school system and that it has failed to discharge this duty.

Where a racially discriminatory school system has been found to exist, *Brown II* imposes the duty on local school boards to "effectuate a transition to a racially nondiscriminatory school system." 349 U.S., at 301, 75 S.Ct., at 756. "*Brown II* was a call for the dismantling of well-entrenched dual systems," and school boards operating such systems were "clearly charged with the affirmative duty to take whatever steps might be necessary to convert to a unitary system in which racial discrimination would be eliminated root and branch." Green v. County School Board, 391 U.S. 430, 437-438, 88 S.Ct. 1689, 1694, 20 L.Ed.2d 716 (1968). Each instance of a failure or refusal to fulfill this affirmative duty continues the violation of the Fourteenth Amendment. Dayton I, 433 U.S., at 413-414, 97 S.Ct., at 2771-2772; Wright v. Council of City of Emporia, 407 U.S. 451, 460, 92 S.Ct. 2196, 2202, 33 L.Ed.2d 51 (1972); United States v. Scotland Neck Board of Education, 407 U.S. 484, 92 S.Ct. 2214, 33 L.Ed.2d 75 (1972) (creation of a new school district in a city that had operated a dual school system but was not yet the subject of court-ordered desegregation).

The Board's continuing "affirmative duty to disestablish the dual school system" is therefore beyond question, McDaniel v. Barresi, 402 U.S. 39, 41, 91 S.Ct. 1287, 1288, 28 L.Ed.2d 582 (1971), and it has pointed to nothing in the record persuading us that at the time of trial the dual school system and its effects had been disestablished. The Board does not appear to challenge the finding of the District Court that at the time of trial most blacks were still going to black schools and most whites to white schools. Whatever the Board's current purpose with respect to racially separate education might be, it knowingly continued its failure to eliminate the consequences of its past intentionally segregative policies. The Board "never actively set out to dismantle this dual system." 429 F.Supp., at 260.

C. Third, the District Court not only found that the Board had breached its constitutional duty by failing effectively to eliminate the continuing consequences of its intentional systemwide segregation in 1954, but also found that in the intervening years there had been a series of Board actions and practices that could not "reasonably be explained without reference to racial concerns," and that "intentionally aggravated, rather than alleviated," racial separation in the schools. [The] court generally noted that "[s]ince the 1954 *Brown* decision, the Columbus defendants or their predecessors were adequately put on notice of the fact that action was required to correct and to prevent the increase in" segregation, yet failed to heed their duty to alleviate racial separation in the schools.

II. Against this background, we cannot fault the conclusion of the District Court and the Court of Appeals that at the time of trial there was systemwide segregation in the Columbus schools that was the result of recent and remote intentionally segregative actions of the Columbus Board. While appearing not to challenge most of the subsidiary findings of historical fact, Tr. of Oral Arg. 7, petitioners dispute many of the factual inferences drawn from these facts by the two courts below. On this record, however, there is no apparent reason to disturb the factual findings and conclusions entered by the District Court and strongly affirmed by the Court of Appeals after its own examination of the record.

Nor do we discern that the judgments entered below rested on any misapprehension of the controlling law. It is urged that the courts below failed to heed the requirements of Keyes, Washington v. Davis, 426 U.S. 229, 96 S.Ct. 2040, 48 L.Ed.2d 597 (1976), and Arlington Heights v. Metropolitan Housing Dev. Corp., 429 U.S. 252, 97 S.Ct. 555, 50 L.Ed.2d 450 (1977), that a plaintiff seeking to make out an equal protection violation on the basis of racial discrimination must show purpose. Both courts, it is argued, considered the requirement satisfied if it were shown that disparate impact would be the natural and foreseeable consequence of the practices and policies of the Board, which, it is said, is nothing more than equating impact with intent, contrary to the controlling precedent.

The District Court, however, was amply cognizant of the controlling cases. It is understood that to prevail the plaintiffs were required to "'prove not only that segregated schooling exists but also that it was brought about or maintained by intentional state action,'" 429 F.Supp., at 251, quoting Keyes, 413 U.S., at 198, 93 S.Ct., at 2692 — that is, that the school officials had "intended to segregate." 429 F.Supp., at 254. See also 583 F.2d, at 801. The District Court also recognized that under those cases disparate impact and foreseeable consequences, without more, do not establish a constitutional violation. See, e. g., 429 F.Supp., at 251. Nevertheless, the District Court correctly noted that actions having foreseeable and anticipated disparate impact are relevant evidence to prove the ultimate fact, forbidden purpose. Those cases do not forbid "the foreseeable effects standard from being utilized as one of the several kinds of proofs from which an inference of segregative intent may be properly drawn." Id., at 255. Adherence to a particular policy or practice, "with full knowledge of the predictable effects of such adherence upon racial imbalance in a school system is one factor among many others which may be considered by a court in determining whether an inference of segregative intent should be drawn." *Ibid.* The District Court thus stayed well within the requirements of *Washington v. Davis* and *Arlington Heights.* See Personnel Administrator of Massachusetts v. Feeney, 442 U.S. 256, 279 n. 25, 99 S.Ct. 2282, 2296, 60 L.Ed.2d 870 (1979).

It is also urged that the District Court and the Court of Appeals failed to observe the requirements of our recent decision in *Dayton I,* which reiterated the accepted rule that the remedy imposed by a court of equity should be commensurate with the violation ascertained, and held that the remedy for the violations that had then been established in that case should be aimed at rectifying the "incremental segregative effect" of the discriminatory acts identified. In *Dayton I,* only a few apparently isolated discriminatory practices had been found; yet a systemwide remedy had been imposed without proof of a systemwide impact. Here, however, the District Court repeatedly emphasized that it had found purposefully segregative practices with current, systemwide impact.

Nor do we perceive any misuse of *Keyes,* where we held that purposeful discrimination in a substantial part of a school system furnishes a sufficient basis for an inferential finding of a systemwide discriminatory intent unless otherwise rebutted, and that given the purpose to operate a dual school system one could infer a connection between such a purpose and racial separation in other parts of the school system. There was no undue reliance here on the inferences permitted by *Keyes,* or upon those recognized by *Swann.* Furthermore, the Board was given ample opportunity to counter the evidence of segregative purpose and current, systemwide impact, and the findings of the courts below were against it in both respects.

Because the District Court and the Court of Appeals committed no prejudicial errors of fact or law, the judgment appealed from must be affirmed. So ordered.

PASADENA CITY BOARD OF EDUCATION v. SPANGLER
427 U.S. 424 (1976)

In 1968, respondents, Pasadena, Cal., high school students and their parents, brought a purported class action against various school officials seeking injunctive relief from allegedly unconstitutional segregation of the public schools in Pasadena. The United States intervened as a party plaintiff pursuant to § 902 of the Civil Rights Act of 1964, which provides that upon intervention "the United States shall be entitled to the same relief as if it had instituted the action." Ultimately in 1970 the District Court, holding that the defendants' educational policies and procedures violated the Fourteenth Amendment, enjoined the defendants from failing to adopt a desegregation plan, ordered them to submit a plan for desegregating the Pasadena schools which would provide that beginning with the 1970-1971 school year there would be no school "with a majority of any minority students," and retained jurisdiction so as to see that such a plan was carried out. The defendants did not appeal from this decree, and subsequently submitted the "Pasadena Plan," which was approved by the District Court. In 1974, however, petitioner school officials, successors to the original defendants, filed a motion with the District Court seeking to modify the 1970 order by eliminating the "no majority" requirement, whose meaning was admittedly unclear to all the parties, dissolving the injunction, and terminating the court's retained jurisdiction, or, in the alternative, to obtain approval of the petitioners' proposed modifications of the "Pasadena Plan." The District Court denied the motion, largely on the grounds that petitioners had failed to comply with the 1970 order, that literal compliance with the "no majority" requirement had occurred only in the initial year of the "Pasadena Plan's" operation, that subsequently a number of schools had violated that requirement, and that such requirement was an inflexible one to be applied anew each school year even though subsequent changes in the racial mix in the schools were caused by factors for which petitioners might not be considered responsible. The Court of Appeals affirmed, but with reservations, which it felt the District Court would heed, as to that court's view that it had a lifetime commitment to the "no majority" requirement and as to the substance of such requirement.

Mr. Justice REHNQUIST delivered the opinion of the Court.

Because the case seemed to present issues of importance regarding the extent of a district court's authority in imposing a plan designed to achieve a unitary school system, we granted certiorari. 423 U.S. 945, 96 S.Ct. 355, 46 L.Ed.2d 276 (1975). We vacate the judgment of the Court of Appeals and remand the case to that court for further proceedings.

II. The District Court's conclusion that unconstitutional segregation existed in the PUSD; its decision to order a systemwide school reorganization plan based upon the guidelines which it submitted to the defendants; and the inclusion in those guidelines of the requirement that the plan contain provisions insuring that there be no majority of any minority in any Pasadena school, all became embodied in the 1970 decree. All that is now before us are the questions of whether the District Court was correct in denying relief when petitioners in 1974 sought to modify the "no majority" requirement as then interpreted by the District Court.

When the District Court's order in this case, as interpreted and applied by that court, is measured against what this Court said in its intervening decision in Swann v. Charlotte-Mecklenburg Board of Education, 402 U.S. 1, 91 S.Ct. 1267, 28 L.Ed.2d 554 (1971), regarding the scope of the judicially created relief which might be available to remedy violations of the Fourteenth Amendment, we think the inconsistency between the two is clear. The District Court's interpretation of the order appears to contemplate the "substantive constitutional right (to a) particular degree of racial balance or mixing" which the Court in Swann expressly disapproved. It became apparent, at least by the time of the 1974 hearing, that the District Court viewed this portion of its order not merely as a "starting point in the process of shaping a remedy," which Swann indicated would be appropriate; but instead as an "inflexible requirement," Ibid., to be applied anew each year to the school population within the attendance zone of each school.

The District Court apparently believed it had authority to impose this requirement even though subsequent changes in the racial mix in the Pasadena schools might be caused by factors for which the defendants could not be considered responsible. Whatever may have been the basis for such a belief in 1970, in Swann the Court cautioned that "it must be recognized that there are limits" beyond which a court may not go in seeking to dismantle a dual school system. These limits are in part tied to the necessity of establishing that school authorities have in some manner caused unconstitutional segregation, for "(a)bsent a constitutional violation there would be no basis for judicially ordering assignment of students on a racial basis." Ibid. While the District Court found such a violation in 1970, and while this unappealed finding afforded a basis for its initial requirement that the defendants prepare a plan to remedy such racial segregation, its adoption of the Pasadena Plan in 1970 established a racially neutral system of student assignment in the PUSD. Having done that, we think that in enforcing its order so as to require annual readjustment of attendance zones so that there would not be a majority of any minority in any Pasadena public school, the District Court exceeded its authority.

There was [no] showing in this case that those post-1971 changes in the racial mix of some Pasadena schools which were focused upon by the lower courts were in any manner caused by segregative actions chargeable to the defendants. The District Court rejected petitioners' assertion that the movement was caused by so-called "white flight" traceable to the decree itself. It stated that the "trends evidenced in Pasadena closely approximate the state-wide trends in California schools, both segregated and desegregated." 375 F.Supp., at 1306. The fact that black student enrollment at 5 out of 32 of the regular Pasadena schools came to exceed 50% During the 4-year period from 1970 to 1974 apparently resulted from people randomly moving into, out of, and around the PUSD area. This quite normal pattern of human migration resulted in some changes in the demographics of Pasadena's residential patterns, with resultant shifts in the racial makeup of some of the schools. But as these shifts were not attributed to any segregative actions on the part of the petitioners, we think this case comes squarely within the sort of situation foreseen in Swann: "It does not follow that the communities served by (unitary) systems will remain demographically stable, for in a growing, mobile society, few will do so. Neither school authorities nor district courts are constitutionally required to make year-by-year adjustments of the racial composition of student bodies once the affirmative duty to desegregate has been accomplished and racial discrimination through official action is eliminated from the system." 402 U.S., at 31-32, 91 S.Ct. at 1283-1284.

It may well be that petitioners have not yet totally achieved the unitary system contemplated by this quotation from Swann. There has been, for example, dispute as to the petitioners' compliance with those portions of the plan specifying procedures for hiring and promoting teachers and administrators. See 384 F.Supp. 846 (1974), vacated, 537

F.2d 1031 (1976). But that does not undercut the force of the principle underlying the quoted language from Swann. In this case the District Court approved a plan designed to obtain racial neutrality in the attendance of students at Pasadena's public schools. No one disputes that the initial implementation of this plan accomplished That objective. That being the case, the District Court was not entitled to require the PSUD to rearrange its attendance zones each year so as to ensure that the racial mix desired by the court was maintained in perpetuity. For having once implemented a racially neutral attendance pattern in order to remedy the perceived constitutional violations on the part of the defendants, the District Court had fully performed its function of providing the appropriate remedy for previous racially discriminatory attendance patterns.

At least one of the judges of the Court of Appeals expressed the view that while all of the petitioners' contentions which we have discussed might be sound, they were barred from asserting them by their predecessors' failure to appeal from the 1970 decree of the District Court. But this observation overlooks well-established rules governing modification of even a final decree entered by a court of equity. In the latter case this Court said: "There is also no dispute but that a sound judicial discretion may call for the modification of the terms of an injunctive decree if the circumstances, whether of law or fact, obtaining at the time of its issuance have changed, or new ones have since arisen. The source of the power to modify is of course the fact that an injunction often requires continuing supervision by the issuing court and always a continuing willingness to apply its powers and processes on behalf of the party who obtained that equitable relief."

Even had the District Court's decree been unambiguous and clearly understood by the parties to mean what that court declared it to mean in 1974, the "no majority of any minority" provision would, as we have indicated previously, be contrary to the intervening decision of this Court in *Swann, supra*. The ambiguity of the provision itself, and the fact that the parties to the decree interpreted it in a manner contrary to the interpretation ultimately placed upon it by the District Court, is an added factor in support of modification. The two factors taken together make a sufficiently compelling case so that such modification should have been ordered by the District Court. System Federation v. Wright, supra.

III. Because the case is to be returned to the Court of Appeals, that court will have an opportunity to reconsider its decision in light of our observations regarding the appropriate scope of equitable relief in this case. [The] record in this case reflects the situation in Pasadena as it was in 1974. At oral argent the Solicitor General discussed the Government's belief that if, as petitioners have represented, they have complied with the District Court's order during the intervening two years, they will probably be entitled to a lifting of the District Court's order in its entirety. Tr. of Oral Arg. 28-31. And while any determination of compliance or noncompliance must, of course, comport with our holding today, it must also depend on factual determinations which the Court of Appeals and the District Court are in a far better position than we are to make in the first instance. Accordingly the judgment of the Court of Appeals is vacated, and the case is remanded to that court for further proceedings not inconsistent with this opinion.

So ordered.

e. "INTER-DISTRICT RELIEF"

The cases that we have reviewed thus far concerned intra-district relief, or relief within a single district. In 1974 the Court, in *Milliken I*, decided when and what remedies would be available for "inter-district" relief, or remedial orders between two or more different school districts. The significance of this issue cannot be underestimated. To this day many scholars have argued that the "real future" of desegregation was decided in *Milliken*. Here, two meaningful social values came into conflict, the priority of the boundaries of local school districts versus the phenomenon of "white flight." Could integration be avoided if parents simply moved to an adjacent or likely suburban district? If such "white flight" left a district with no choice but to maintain "one race schools," what result? How significant were local school district boundaries as set against the ability to avoid the goals of *Brown*? Put briefly, for the first time since *Brown*, "could you run and hide?" With great impact on the future of desegregation, the "Burger Court" faced this issue in the opinion that follows.

MILLIKEN v. BRADLEY (MILLIKEN I)
418 U.S. 717 (1974)

[The Court held that federal courts lack the power to impose interdistrict remedies for school segregation absent an interdistrict violation or interdistrict effects. After a lengthy trial, the district court found that the Detroit schools had been deliberately segregated, and that any Detroit-only remedy "would make the Detroit school system more identifiably black [thereby] increasing the flight of whites from the city and the system." Consequently, the court ordered a desegregation plan encompassing fifty-three suburban school districts surrounding Detroit. The court of appeals affirmed after noting that "any less comprehensive [solution would] result in an all black school system immediately surrounded by practically all white suburban school systems, with an overwhelmingly white majority population in the local metropolitan area."]

Chief Justice BURGER delivered the opinion of the Court.

The notion that school district lines may be casually ignored or treated as a mere administrative convenience is contrary to the history of public education in our country. No single tradition in public education is more deeply rooted than local control over the operation of schools

The controlling principle consistently expounded in our holdings is that the scope of the remedy is determined by the nature and extent of the constitutional violation. Swann, 402 U.S., at 16, 91 S.Ct., at 1276. Before the boundaries of separate and autonomous school districts may be set aside by consolidating the separate units for remedial purposes or by imposing a cross-district remedy, it must first be shown that there has been a constitutional violation within one district that produces a significant segregative effect in another district. Specifically, it must be shown that racially discriminatory acts of the state or local school districts, or of a single school district have been a substantial cause of interdistrict segregation. Thus an interdistrict remedy might be in order where the racially discriminatory acts of one or more school districts caused racial segregation in an adjacent district, or where district lines have been deliberately drawn on the basis of race. In such circumstances an interdistrict remedy would be appropriate to eliminate the interdistrict segregation directly caused by the constitutional violation. Conversely, without an interdistrict violation and interdistrict effect, there is no constitutional wrong calling for an interdistrict remedy.

The constitutional right of the Negro respondents residing in Detroit is to attend a unitary school system in that district. Unless petitioners drew the district lines in a discriminatory fashion or arranged for white students residing in the Detroit district to attend schools in Oakland and Macomb Counties, they were under no constitutional duty to make provisions for Negro students to do so. The view of the dissenters, that the existence of a dual system in Detroit can be made the basis for a decree requiring cross-district transportation of pupils, cannot be supported on the grounds that it represents merely the devising of a suitably flexible remedy for the violation of rights already established by our prior decisions. It can be supported only by drastic expansion of the constitutional right itself, an expansion without any support in either constitutional principle or precedent.

We conclude that the relief ordered by the District Court and affirmed by the Court of Appeals was based upon an erroneous standard and was unsupported by record evidence that acts of the outlying districts effected the discrimination found to exist in the schools of Detroit. Accordingly, the judgment of the Court of Appeals is reversed and the case is remanded for further proceedings consistent with this opinion leading to prompt formulation of a decree directed to eliminating the segregation found to exist in Detroit city schools, a remedy which has been delayed since 1970.

Mr. Justice MARSHALL, with whom Mr. Justice DOUGLAS, Mr. Justice BRENNAN, and Mr. Justice WHITE join, dissenting.

In Brown v. Board of Education, 347 U.S. 483, 74 S.Ct. 686, 98 L.Ed. 873 (1954), this Court held that segregation of children in public schools on the basis of race deprives minority group children of equal educational opportunities and therefore denies them the equal protection of the laws under the Fourteenth Amendment. This Court recognized then that remedying decades of segregation in public education would not be an easy task. Subsequent events, unfortunately, have seen that prediction bear bitter fruit. But however imbedded old ways, however ingrained old prejudices, this Court has not been diverted from its appointed task of making "a living truth" of our constitutional ideal of equal justice under law. Cooper v. Aaron, 358 U.S. 1, 20, 78 S.Ct. 1401, 1410, 3 L.Ed.2d 5 (1958).

After 20 years of small, often difficult steps toward that great end, the Court today takes a giant step backwards. Notwithstanding a record showing widespread and pervasive racial segregation in the educational system provided by the State of Michigan for children in Detroit, this Court holds that the District Court was powerless to require the State to remedy its constitutional violation in any meaningful fashion. Ironically purporting to base its result on the principle that the scope of the remedy in a desegregation case should be determined by the nature and the extent of the constitutional violation, the Court's answer is to provide no remedy at all for the violation proved in this case, thereby guaranteeing that Negro children in Detroit will receive the same separate and inherently unequal education in the future as they have been unconstitutionally afforded in the past.

I cannot subscribe to this emasculation of our constitutional guarantee of equal protection of the laws and must respectfully dissent. Our precedents, in my view, firmly establish that where, as here, state-imposed segregation has been demonstrated, it becomes the duty of the State to eliminate root and branch all vestiges of racial discrimination and to achieve the greatest possible degree of actual desegregation. I agree with both the District Court and the Court of Appeals that, under the facts of this case, this duty cannot be fulfilled unless the State of Michigan involves outlying metropolitan area school districts in its desegregation remedy. Furthermore, I perceive no basis either in law or in the practicalities of the situation justifying the State's interposition of school district boundaries as absolute barriers to the implementation of an effective desegregation remedy. Under established and frequently used Michigan procedures, school district lines are both flexible and permeable for a wide variety of purposes, and there is no reason why they must now stand in the way of meaningful desegregation relief. [. . .]

These conclusions were unaffected by the fact that the state of Michigan had exercised substantial control over the activity of local school districts, and that state agencies had participated in the deliberate segregation of the Detroit schools. Despite this state activity, "[d]isparate treatment of white and Negro students occurred within the Detroit school system, and not elsewhere, and on this record the remedy must be limited to that system."

f. "RECENT ERA"

BOARD OF EDUCATION OF OKLAHOMA CITY v. DOWELL
498 U.S. 237 (1991)

In 1963, a district court found that Oklahoma City had intentionally segregated its schools and was currently operating a "dual school system." In 1972, after finding that previous desegregation efforts had failed, the court ordered adoption of a plan involving extensive busing of school children. In 1984, the school board adopted a new plan that relied on neighborhood assignments for students in lower grades. Plaintiffs challenged the plan on the ground that it amounted to a return to segregation, but the district court found that the school system was integrated, that unitariness had been achieved, and that court-ordered desegregation must therefore end. The court of appeals reversed, holding that a desegregation decree must remain in effect until a school district can show "grievous wrong evoked by new and unforseen conditions." The Court held that the court of appeals had applied the wrong standard.

Chief Justice REHNQUIST delivered the opinion of the Court.

From the very first, federal supervision of local school systems was intended as a temporary measure to remedy past discrimination. Brown considered the "complexities arising from the *transition* to a system of public education freed of racial discrimination" in holding that the implementation of desegregation was to proceed "with all deliberate speed." Green also spoke of the "*transition* to a unitary, nonracial system of public education."

[Injunctions] entered in school desegregation cases [not] intended to operate in perpetuity. Local control over the education of children allows citizens to participate in decisionmaking, and allows innovation so that school programs can fit local needs. The legal justification for displacement of local authority by an injunctive decree in a school desegregation case is a violation of the Constitution by the local authorities. Dissolving a desegregation decree after the local authorities have operated in compliance with it for a reasonable period of time properly recognizes that "necessary concern for the important values of local control of public school systems dictates that a federal court's regulatory control of such systems not extend beyond the time required to remedy the effects of past intentional discrimination.

A district court need not accept at face value the profession of a school board which has intentionally discriminated that it will cease to do so in the future. But in deciding whether to modify or dissolve a desegregation decree, a school board's compliance with previous court orders is obviously relevant. In this case the original finding of *de jure* segregation was entered in 1961, the injunctive decree from which the Board seeks relief was entered in 1972, and the Board complied with the decree in good faith until 1985. Not only do the personnel of school boards change over time, but the same passage of time enables the District Court to observe the good faith of the school board in complying with the decree. The test espoused by the Court of Appeals would condemn a school district, once governed by a board which intentionally discriminated, to judicial tutelage for the indefinite future. Neither the principles governing the entry and dissolution of injunctive decrees, nor the commands of the Equal Protection Clause of the Fourteenth Amendment, require any such Draconian result.

Petitioner urges that we reinstate the decision of the District Court terminating the injunction, but we think that the preferable course is to remand the case to that court so that it may decide, in accordance with this opinion, whether the Board made a sufficient showing of constitutional compliance as of 1985, when the SRP was adopted, to allow the injunction to be dissolved. The District Court should address itself to whether the Board had complied in good faith with the desegregation decree since it was entered, and whether the vestiges of past discrimination had been eliminated to the extent practicable.

In considering whether the vestiges of *de jure* segregation had been eliminated as far as practicable, the District Court should look not only at student assignments, but "to every facet of school operations — faculty, staff, transportation, extra-curricular activities and facilities." ("[E]xisting policy and practice with regard to faculty, staff, transportation, extra-curricular activities, and facilities" are "among the most important indicia of a segregated system").

After the District Court decides whether the Board was entitled to have the decree terminated, it should proceed to decide respondent's challenge to the SRP. A school district which has been released from an injunction imposing a desegregation plan no longer requires court authorization for the promulgation of policies and rules regulating matters such as assignment of students and the like, but it of course remains subject to the mandate of the Equal Protection Clause of the Fourteenth Amendment. If the Board was entitled to have the decree terminated as of 1985, the District Court should then evaluate the Board's decision to implement the SRP under appropriate equal protection principles. The judgment of the Court of Appeals is reversed, and the case is remanded to the District Court for further proceedings consistent with this opinion. It is so ordered.

Justice MARSHALL, with whom Justice BLACKMUN and Justice STEVENS join, dissenting.

Oklahoma gained statehood in 1907. For the next 65 years, the Oklahoma City School Board maintained segregated schools — initially relying on laws requiring dual school systems; thereafter, by exploiting residential segregation that had been created by legally enforced restrictive covenants. In 1972 — 18 years after this Court first found segregated schools unconstitutional — a federal court finally interrupted this cycle, enjoining the Oklahoma City School Board to implement a specific plan for achieving actual desegregation of its schools.

The practical question now before us is whether, 13 years after that injunction was imposed, the same School Board should have been allowed to return many of its elementary schools to their former one-race status. The majority today suggests that 13 years of desegregation was enough. The Court remands the case for further evaluation of whether the purposes of the injunctive decree were achieved sufficient to justify the decree's dissolution. However, the inquiry it commends to the District Court fails to recognize explicitly the threatened reemergence of one-race schools as a relevant "vestige" of *de jure* segregation.

In my view, the standard for dissolution of a school desegregation decree must reflect the central aim of our school desegregation precedents. In Brown v. Board of Education, 347 U.S. 483, 74 S.Ct. 686, 98 L.Ed. 873 (1954) (Brown I), a unanimous Court declared that racially "[s]eparate educational facilities are inherently unequal." Id., at 495, 74 S.Ct., at 692. This holding rested on the Court's recognition that state-sponsored segregation conveys a message of "inferiority as to th[e] status [of Afro-American school children] in the community that may affect their hearts and minds in a way unlikely ever to be undone." Remedying this evil and preventing its recurrence were the motivations animating our requirement that formerly *de jure* segregated school districts take all feasible steps to *eliminate* racially identifiable schools. [I] believe a desegregation decree cannot be lifted so long as conditions likely to inflict the stigmatic injury condemned in Brown I persist and there remain feasible methods of eliminating such conditions. Because the record here shows, and the Court of Appeals found, that feasible steps could be taken to avoid one-race schools, it is clear that the purposes of the decree have not yet been achieved and the Court of Appeals' reinstatement of the decree should be affirmed. I therefore dissent.

In order to assess the full consequence of lifting the decree at issue in this case, it is necessary to explore more fully than does the majority the history of racial segregation in the Oklahoma City schools. This history reveals nearly unflagging resistance by the Board to judicial efforts to dismantle the City's dual education system.

I agree with the majority that the proper standard for determining whether a school desegregation decree should be dissolved is whether the purposes of the desegregation litigation, as incorporated in the decree, have been fully achieved. I strongly disagree with the majority, however, on what must be shown to demonstrate that a decree's purposes have been fully realized. In my view, a standard for dissolution of a desegregation decree must take into account the unique harm associated with a system of racially identifiable schools and must expressly demand the elimination of such schools.

Our pointed focus in Brown I upon the stigmatic injury caused by segregated schools explains our unflagging insistence that formerly *de jure* segregated school districts extinguish all vestiges of school segregation. The concept of stigma also gives us guidance as to what conditions must be eliminated before a decree can be deemed to have served its purpose. In the decisions leading up to Brown I, the Court had attempted to curtail the ugly legacy of Plessy v. Ferguson, 163 U.S. 537, 16 S.Ct. 1138, 41 L.Ed. 256 (1896), by insisting on a searching inquiry into whether "separate" Afro-American schools were genuinely "equal" to white schools in terms of physical facilities, curricula, quality of the faculty and certain "intangible" considerations. In Brown I, the Court finally liberated the Equal Protection Clause from the doctrinal tethers of Plessy, declaring that "in the field of public education the doctrine of "separate but equal" has no place. Separate educational facilities are inherently unequal."

The Court based this conclusion on its recognition of the particular social harm that racially segregated schools inflict on Afro-American children. "To separate them from others of similar age and qualifications solely because of their race generates a feeling of inferiority as to their status in the community that may affect their hearts and minds in a way unlikely ever to be undone. The effect of this separation on their educational opportunities was well stated by a finding in the Kansas case by a court which nevertheless felt compelled to rule against the Negro plaintiffs: "'Segregation of white and colored children in public schools has a detrimental effect upon the colored children. The impact is greater when it has the sanction of law; for the policy of separating the races is usually interpreted as denoting the inferiority of the negro group. A sense of inferiority affects the motivation of a child to learn. Segregation with the sanction of law, therefore, has a tendency to [retard] the educational and mental development of negro children and to deprive them of some of the benefits they would receive in a racial[ly] integrated school system.'"

Remedying and avoiding the recurrence of this stigmatizing injury have been the guiding objectives of this Court's desegregation jurisprudence ever since. These concerns inform the standard by which the Court determines the effectiveness of a proposed desegregation remedy. By so construing the extent of a school board's obligations, the Court made clear that the Equal Protection Clause demands elimination of every indicium of a "[r]acial[ly] identifi[able]" school system that will inflict the stigmatizing injury that Brown I sought to cure.

The majority suggests a more vague and, I fear, milder standard. Ignoring the harm identified in Brown I, the majority asserts that the District Court should find that the purposes of the decree have been achieved so long as "the Oklahoma City School District [is now] being operated in compliance with the commands of the Equal Protection Clause" and "it [is] unlikely that the Board would return to its former ways." Insofar as the majority instructs the District Court, on remand, to "conside[r] whether the vestiges of *de jure* segregation ha[ve] been eliminated as far as practicable," the majority presumably views elimination of vestiges as part of "operat[ing] in compliance with the commands of the Equal Protection Clause." [In] sum, our school-desegregation jurisprudence establishes that the *effects* of past discrimination remain chargeable to the school district regardless of its lack of continued enforcement of segregation, and the remedial decree is required until those effects have been finally eliminated.

Applying the standard I have outlined, I would affirm the Court of Appeals' decision ordering the District Court to restore the desegregation decree. For it is clear on this record that removal of the decree will result in a significant number of racially identifiable schools that could be eliminated. Against the background of former state-sponsorship of one-race schools, the persistence of racially identifiable schools perpetuates the message of racial inferiority associated with segregation. Therefore, such schools must be eliminated whenever feasible.

Nonetheless, the majority hints that the District Court could ignore the effect of residential segregation in perpetuating racially identifiable schools if the court finds residential segregation to be "the result of private decisionmaking and economics." Finally, the majority warns against the application of a standard that would subject formerly segregated school districts to the "Draconian" fate of "judicial tutelage for the indefinite future."

I also reject the majority's suggestion that the length of federal judicial supervision is a valid factor in assessing a dissolution. The majority is correct that the Court has never contemplated perpetual judicial oversight of former *de jure* segregated school districts. Our jurisprudence requires, however, that the job of school desegregation be fully completed and maintained so that the stigmatic harm identified in Brown I will not recur upon lifting the decree. Any doubt on the issue whether the School Board has fulfilled its remedial obligations should be resolved in favor of the Afro-American children affected by this litigation. In its concern to spare local school boards the "Draconian" fate of "indefinite" "judicial tutelage," the majority risks subordination of the constitutional rights of Afro-American children to the interest of school board autonomy.

We should keep in mind that the court's active supervision of the desegregation process ceased in 1977. Consistent with the mandate of Brown I, our cases have imposed on school districts an unconditional duty to eliminate *any* condition that perpetuates the message of racial inferiority inherent in the policy of state-sponsored segregation. The racial identifiability of a district's schools is such a condition. Whether this "vestige" of state-sponsored segregation will persist cannot simply be ignored at the point where a district court is contemplating the dissolution of a desegregation decree. In a district with a history of state-sponsored school segregation, racial separation, in my view, *remains* inherently unequal.

MISSOURI v. JENKINS
515 U.S. 70 (1995)

Chief Justice REHNQUIST delivered the opinion of the Court.

As this school desegregation litigation enters its 18th year, we are called upon again to review the decisions of the lower courts. In this case, the State of Missouri has challenged the District Court's order of salary increases for virtually all instructional and non-instructional staff within the Kansas City, Missouri, School District (KCMSD) and the District Court's order requiring the State to continue to fund remedial "quality education" programs because student achievement levels were still "at or below national norms at many grade levels."

Instead of seeking to remove the racial identity of the various schools within the KCMSD, the District Court has set out on a program to create a school district that was equal to or superior to the surrounding SSD's. Its remedy has focused on "desegregative attractiveness," coupled with "suburban comparability." Examination of the District Court's reliance on "desegregative attractiveness" and "suburban comparability" is instructive for our ultimate resolution of the salary-order issue.

The purpose of desegregative attractiveness has been not only to remedy the systemwide reduction in student achievement, but also to attract nonminority students not presently enrolled in the KCMSD. This remedy has included an elaborate program of capital improvements, course enrichment, and extracurricular enhancement not simply in the formerly identifiable black schools, but in schools throughout the district. The District Court's remedial orders have converted every senior high school, every middle school, and one-half of the elementary schools in the KCMSD into "magnet" schools. The District Court's remedial order has all but made the KCMSD itself into a magnet district.

We previously have approved of intradistrict desegregation remedies involving magnet schools. See, *e.g.,* Milliken II, supra, 433 U.S., at 272, 97 S.Ct., at 2753. Magnet schools have the advantage of encouraging voluntary movement of students within a school district in a pattern that aids desegregation on a voluntary basis, without requiring extensive busing and redrawing of district boundary lines. Cf. Jenkins II, supra, 495 U.S., at 59-60, 110 S.Ct., at 1667-1668 (Kennedy, J., concurring in part and concurring in judgment) (citing Milliken II, supra, 433 U.S., at 272, 97 S.Ct., at 2753). As a component in an intradistrict remedy, magnet schools also are attractive because they promote desegregation while limiting the withdrawal of white student enrollment that may result from mandatory student reassignment.

The District Court's remedial plan in this case, however, is not designed solely to redistribute the students within the KCMSD in order to eliminate racially identifiable schools within the KCMSD. Instead, its purpose is to attract nonminority students from outside the KCMSD schools. But this *inter* district goal is beyond the scope of the *intra*district violation identified by the District Court. In effect, the District Court has devised a remedy to accomplish indirectly what it admittedly lacks the remedial authority to mandate directly: the interdistrict transfer of students.

[What] we meant in Milliken I by an interdistrict violation was a violation that caused segregation between adjoining districts. Nothing in Milliken I suggests that the District Court in that case could have circumvented the limits on its remedial authority by requiring the State of Michigan, a constitutional violator, to implement a magnet program designed to achieve the same interdistrict transfer of students that we held was beyond its remedial authority. Here, the District Court has done just that: created a magnet district of the KCMSD in order to serve the *inter*district goal of attracting nonminority students from the surrounding SSD's and redistributing them within the KCMSD. The District Court's pursuit of "desegregative attractiveness" is beyond the scope of its broad remedial authority.

The District Court's pursuit of the goal of "desegregative attractiveness" results in so many imponderables and is so far removed from the task of eliminating the racial identifiability of the schools within the KCMSD that we believe it is beyond the admittedly broad discretion of the District Court. In this posture, we conclude that the District Court's order of salary increases, which was "grounded in remedying the vestiges of segregation by improving the desegregative attractiveness of the KCMSD," App. to Pet. for Cert. A-90, is simply too far removed from an acceptable implementation of a permissible means to remedy previous legally mandated segregation.

Similar considerations lead us to conclude that the District Court's order requiring the State to continue to fund the quality education programs because student achievement levels were still "at or below national norms at many grade levels" cannot be sustained. The State does not seek from this Court a declaration of partial unitary status with respect to the quality education programs. Reply Brief for Petitioners 3. It challenges the requirement of indefinite funding of a quality education program until national norms are met, based on the assumption that while a mandate for significant educational improvement, both in teaching and in facilities, may have been justified originally, its indefinite extension is not.

Justice O'CONNOR, concurring.

What the District Court did in this case, however, and how it transgressed the constitutional bounds of its remedial powers, was to make desegregative attractiveness the underlying goal of its remedy for the specific purpose of reversing the trend of white flight. However troubling that trend may be, remedying it is within the District Court's authority only if it is "directly caused by the constitutional violation." The Court and the dissent attempt to reconcile the different statements by the lower courts as to whether white flight was caused by segregation or desegregation. See *ante,* at 2052-2053; *post,* at 2084-2086. One fact, however, is uncontroverted. When the District Court found that KCMSD was racially segregated, the constitutional violation from which all remedies flow in this case, it also found that there was neither an interdistrict violation nor significant interdistrict segregative effects. See Jenkins v. Missouri, 807 F.2d, at 672; *ante*, at 2053. Whether the white exodus that has resulted in a school district that is 68% black was caused by the District Court's remedial orders or by natural, if unfortunate, demographic forces, we have it directly from the District Court that the segregative effects of KCMSD's constitutional violation did not transcend its geographical boundaries. In light of that finding, the District Court cannot order remedies seeking to rectify regional demographic trends that go beyond the nature and scope of the constitutional violation.

Justice THOMAS, concurring.

It never ceases to amaze me that the courts are so willing to assume that anything that is predominantly black must be inferior. Instead of focusing on remedying the harm done to those black schoolchildren injured by segregation, the District Court here sought to convert the Kansas City, Missouri, School District (KCMSD) into a "magnet district" that would reverse the "white flight" caused by *de*segregation. In this respect, I join the Court's decision concerning the two remedial issues presented for review. I write separately, however, to add a few thoughts with respect to the overall course of this litigation.

The mere fact that a school is black does not mean that it is the product of a constitutional violation. A "racial imbalance does not itself establish a violation of the Constitution." Instead, in order to find unconstitutional segregation, we require that plaintiffs "prove all of the essential elements of *de jure* segregation — that is, stated simply, a current condition of segregation resulting from *intentional state action directed specifically* to the [allegedly segregated] schools."

[Without] a basis in any real finding of intentional government action, the District Court's imposition of liability upon the State of Missouri improperly rests upon a theory that racial imbalances are unconstitutional. That is, the court has "indulged the presumption, often irrebuttable in practice, that a presently observed [racial] imbalance has been proximately caused by intentional state action during the prior *de jure* era." In effect, the court found that racial imbalances constituted an ongoing constitutional violation that continued to inflict harm on black students. This position appears to rest upon the idea that any school that is black is inferior, and that blacks cannot succeed without the benefit of the company of whites. The District Court's willingness to adopt such stereotypes stemmed from a misreading of our earliest school desegregation case.

[Thus], the District Court seemed to believe that black students in the KCMSD would continue to receive an "inferior education" despite the end of *de jure* segregation, as long as *de facto* segregation persisted. As the District Court later concluded, compensatory educational programs were necessary "as a means of remedying many of the educational problems which go hand in hand with racially isolated minority student populations." Such assumptions and any social science research upon which they rely certainly cannot form the basis upon which we decide matters of constitutional principle.

Segregation was not unconstitutional because it might have caused psychological feelings of inferiority. Public school systems that separated blacks and provided them with superior educational resources — making blacks "feel" superior to whites sent to lesser schools — would violate the Fourteenth Amendment, whether or not the white students felt stigmatized, just as do school systems in which the positions of the races are reversed. Psychological injury or benefit is irrelevant to the question whether state actors have engaged in intentional discrimination — the critical inquiry for ascertaining violations of the Equal Protection Clause. The judiciary is fully competent to make independent determinations concerning the existence of state action without the unnecessary and misleading assistance of the social sciences.

Regardless of the relative quality of the schools, segregation violated the Constitution because the State classified students based on their race. Of course, segregation additionally harmed black students by relegating them to schools with substandard facilities and resources. But neutral policies, such as local school assignments, do not offend the Constitution when individual private choices concerning work or residence produce schools with high black populations. The Constitution does not prevent individuals from choosing to live together, to work together, or to send their children to school together, so long as the State does not interfere with their choices on the basis of race.

Given that desegregation has not produced the predicted leaps forward in black educational achievement, there is no reason to think that black students cannot learn as well when surrounded by members of their own race as when they are in an integrated environment. Indeed, it may very well be that what has been true for historically black colleges is true for black middle and high schools. Despite their origins in "the shameful history of state-enforced segregation," these institutions can be "'both a source of pride to blacks who have attended them and a source of hope to black families who want the benefits of . . . learning for their children.'"Because of their "distinctive histories and traditions," ibid., black schools can function as the center and symbol of black communities, and provide examples of independent black leadership, success, and achievement.

The District Court's unwarranted focus on the psychological harm to blacks and on racial imbalances has been only half of the tale. Not only did the court subscribe to a theory of injury that was predicated on black inferiority, it also married this concept of liability to our expansive approach to remedial powers. We have given the federal courts the freedom to use any measure necessary to reverse problems — such as racial isolation or low educational achievement — that have proven stubbornly resistant to government policies. We have not permitted constitutional principles such as federalism or the separation of powers to stand in the way of our drive to reform the schools. Thus, the District Court here ordered massive expenditures by local and state authorities, without congressional or executive authorization and without any indication that such measures would attract whites back to KCMSD or raise KCMSD test scores. The time has come for us to put the genie back in the bottle.

It is perhaps understandable that we permitted the lower courts to exercise such sweeping powers. Although we had authorized the federal courts to work toward "a system of determining admission to the public schools on a nonracial basis" in Brown v. Board of Education, 349 U.S. 294, 300-301, 75 S.Ct. 753, 756, 99 L.Ed. 1083 (1955) (Brown II), resistance to Brown I produced little desegregation by the time we decided Green v. School Bd. of New Kent Cty., supra. Our impatience with the pace of desegregation and with the lack of a good-faith effort on the part of school boards led us to approve such extraordinary remedial measures. But such powers should have been temporary and used only to overcome the widespread resistance to the dictates of the Constitution. The judicial overreaching we see before us today perhaps is the price we now pay for our approval of such extraordinary remedies in the past.

Justice SOUTER, with whom Justice STEVENS, Justice GINSBURG, and Justice BREYER join, dissenting.

On its face, the Court's opinion projects an appealing pragmatism in seeming to cut through the details of many facts by applying a rule of law that can claim both precedential support and intuitive sense, that there is error in imposing an interdistrict remedy to cure a merely intradistrict violation. Since the District Court has consistently described the violation here as solely intradistrict, and since the object of the magnet schools under its plan includes attracting students into the district from other districts, the Court's result seems to follow with the necessity of logic, against which arguments about detail or calls for fair warning may not carry great weight.

The attractiveness of the Court's analysis disappears, however, as soon as we recognize two things. First, the District Court did not mean by an "intradistrict violation" what the Court apparently means by it today. The District Court meant that the violation within the KCMSD had not led to segregation outside of it, and that no other school districts had played a part in the violation. It did not mean that the violation had not produced effects of any sort beyond the district. Indeed, the record that we have indicates that the District Court understood that the violation here did produce effects spanning district borders and leading to greater segregation within the KCMSD, the reversal of which the District Court sought to accomplish by establishing magnet schools. Insofar as the Court assumes that this was not so in fact, there is at least enough in the record to cast serious doubt on its assumption. Second, the Court violates existing case law even on its own apparent view of the facts, that the segregation violation within the KCMSD produced no proven effects, segregative or otherwise, outside it. Assuming this to be true, the Court's decision that the rule against interdistrict remedies for intradistrict violations applies to this case, solely because the remedy here is meant to produce effects outside the district in which the violation occurred, is flatly contrary to established precedent.

[The] Court, however, rejects the findings of the District Court, endorsed by the Court of Appeals, that segregation led to white flight from the KCMSD, and does so at the expense of another accepted norm of our appellate procedure. We have long adhered to the view that "[a] court of law, such as this Court is, rather than a court for correction of errors in factfinding, cannot undertake to review concurrent findings of fact by two courts below in the absence of a very obvious and exceptional showing of error." The Court fails to show any exceptional circumstance present here, however: it relies on a "contradiction" that is not an obvious contradiction at all, and on an arbitrary "supposition" that "'white flight' may result from desegregation, not *de jure* segregation," *ante,* at 2052, a supposition said to be bolstered by the District Court's statement that there was "an abundance of evidence that many residents of the KCMSD left the district and moved to the suburbs because of the district's efforts to integrate its schools."

Justice GINSBURG, dissenting.

I join Justice Souter's illuminating dissent and emphasize a consideration key to this controversy.

The Court stresses that the present remedial programs have been in place for seven years. But compared to more than two centuries of firmly entrenched official discrimination, the experience with the desegregation remedies ordered by the District Court has been evanescent.

In 1724, Louis XV of France issued the Code Noir, the first slave code for the Colony of Louisiana, an area that included Missouri. Violette, The Black Code in Missouri, in 6 Proceedings of the Mississippi Valley Historical Association 287, 288 (B. Shambaugh ed. 1913). When Missouri entered the Union in 1821, it entered as a slave State.

Before the Civil War, Missouri law prohibited the creation or maintenance of schools for educating blacks: "No person shall keep or teach any school for the instruction of negroes or mulattoes, in reading or writing, in this State."

Beginning in 1865, Missouri passed a series of laws requiring separate public schools for blacks. The Missouri Constitution first permitted, then required, separate schools.

After this Court announced its decision in Brown v. Board of Education, 347 U.S. 483, 74 S.Ct. 686, 98 L.Ed. 873 (1954), Missouri's Attorney General declared these provisions mandating segregated schools unenforceable. The statutes were repealed in 1957 and the constitutional provision was rescinded in 1976. Nonetheless, 30 years after Brown, the District Court found that "the inferior education indigenous of the state-compelled dual school system has lingering effects in the Kansas City, Missouri School District." The District Court concluded that "the State . . . cannot defend its failure to affirmatively act to eliminate the structure and effects of its past dual system on the basis of restrictive state law." Just ten years ago, in June 1985, the District Court issued its first remedial order.

Today, the Court declares illegitimate the goal of attracting non-minority students to the Kansas City, Missouri, School District, and thus stops the District Court's efforts to integrate a school district that was, in the 1984/1985 school year, sorely in need and 68.3% black. Given the deep, inglorious history of segregation in Missouri, to curtail desegregation at this time and in this manner is an action at once too swift and too soon.

g. USE OF THE POLITICAL PROCESS TO REPEAL REMEDIES

HUNTER v. ERICKSON
393 U.S. 385 (1969)

Mr. Justice WHITE delivered the opinion of the Court.

The question in this case is whether the City of Akron, Ohio, has denied a Negro citizen, Nellie Hunter, the equal protection of its laws by amending the city charter to prevent the city council from implementing any ordinance dealing with racial, religious, or ancestral discrimination in housing without the approval of the majority of the voters of Akron.

The proposal for the charter amendment had been placed on the ballot at a general election upon petition of more than 10% of Akron's voters, and the amendment had been duly passed by a majority.

[Only] laws to end housing discrimination based on "race, color, religion, national origin or ancestry" must run § 137's gantlet. It is true that the section draws no distinctions among racial and religious groups. Negroes and whites, Jews and Catholics are all subject to the same requirements if there is housing discrimination against them which they wish to end. But § 137 nevertheless disadvantages those who would benefit from laws barring racial, religious, or ancestral discriminations as against those who would bar other discriminations or who would otherwise regulate the real estate market in their favor. The automatic referendum system does not reach housing discrimination on sexual or political grounds, or against those with children or dogs, nor does it affect tenants seeking more heat or better maintenance from landlords, nor those seeking rent control, urban renewal, public housing, or new building codes.

Moreover, although the law on its face treats Negro and white, Jew and gentile in an identical manner, the reality is that the law's impact falls on the minority. The majority needs no protection against discrimination and if it did, a referendum might be bothersome but no more than that. Like the law requiring specification of candidates' race on the ballot, 137 places special burden on racial minorities within the governmental process. This is no more permissible than denying them the vote, on an equal basis with others. The preamble to the open housing ordinance which was suspended by § 137 recited that the population of Akron consists of "people of different race, color, religion, ancestry or national origin, many of whom live in circumscribed and segregated areas, under substandard unhealthful, unsafe, unsanitary and overcrowded conditions, because of discrimination in the sale, lease, rental and financing of housing." Such was the situation in Akron. It is against this background that the referendum required by § 137 must be assessed.

[We] are unimpressed with any of Akron's justifications for its discrimination. Characterizing it simply as a public decision to move slowly in the delicate area of race relations emphasizes the impact and burden of § 137, but does not justify it. The amendment was unnecessary either to implement a decision to go slowly, or to allow the people of Akron to participate in that decision. Likewise, insisting that a State may distribute legislative power as it desires and that the people may retain for themselves the power over certain subjects may generally be true, but these principles furnish no justification for a legislative structure which otherwise would violate the Fourteenth Amendment. Nor does the implementation of this change through popular referendum immunize it. The sovereignty of the people is itself subject to those constitutional limitations which have been duly adopted and remain unrepealed. Even though Akron might have proceeded by majority vote at town meeting on all its municipal legislation, it has instead chosen a more complex system. Having done so, the State may no more disadvantage any particular group by making it more difficult to enact legislation in its behalf than it may dilute any person's vote or give any group a smaller representation than another of comparable size.

We hold that § 137 discriminates against minorities, and constitutes a real, substantial, and invidious denial of the equal protection of the laws.

Reversed.

Mr. Justice HARLAN, whom Mr. Justice STEWART joins, concurring.

[In] the case before us, however, the city of Akron has not attempted to allocate governmental power on the basis of any general principle. Here, we have a provision that has the clear purpose of making it more difficult for certain racial and religious minorities to achieve legislation that is in their interest. Since the charter amendment is discriminatory on its face, Akron must "bear a far heavier burden of justification" than is required in the normal case. And Akron has failed to sustain this burden. The city's principal argument in support of the charter amendment relies on the undisputed fact that fair housing legislation may often be expected to raise the passions of the community to their highest pitch. It was not necessary, however, to pass this amendment in order to assure that particularly sensitive issues will ultimately be decided by the general electorate. Akron has already provided a procedure, which is grounded in neutral principle, that requires a general referendum on this issue if 10% of the voters insist. If the prospect of fair housing legislation really arouses passionate opposition, the voters will have the final say. Consequently, the charter amendment will have its real impact only when fair housing does not arouse extraordinary controversy. This being the case, I can perceive no legitimate state interest which in any degree vindicates the action taken by the City here.

As I read the Court's opinion to be entirely consistent with the basic principles which I believe control this case, I join in it.

WASHINGTON v. SEATTLE SCHOOL DISTRICT NO. 1
458 U.S. 457 (1982)

Justice BLACKMUN delivered the opinion of the Court.

We are presented here with an extraordinary question: whether an elected local school board may use the Fourteenth Amendment to defend its program of busing for integration from attack by the State. [In 1978, the Seattle School Board voluntarily adopted a plan to alleviate racial isolation in the schools. The plan made extensive use of busing and mandatory reassignment. Opponents of the plan responded by drafting a statewide initiative designed to terminate use of mandatory busing for purposes of racial integration. The proposal, known as Initiative 350, prohibited school boards from requiring students to attend schools not nearest or next nearest to their place of residence. The initiative included a series of exceptions, however, which permitted such assignments for a variety of nonracial reasons, such as overcrowding or special education needs. It also permitted racial reassignments when a court found that they were constitutionally required.

[The initiative was adopted by a substantial statewide majority, including a majority of Seattle voters. The Seattle School Board thereupon initiated this litigation challenging the constitutionality of the initiative under the equal protection clause of the fourteenth amendment. The district court held that the initiative was unconstitutional, and the court of appeals affirmed.]

II. The Equal Protection Clause of the Fourteenth Amendment guarantees racial minorities the right to full participation in the political life of the community. It is beyond dispute, of course, that given racial or ethnic groups may not be denied the franchise, or precluded from entering into the political process in a reliable and meaningful manner. But the Fourteenth Amendment also reaches "a political structure that treats all individuals as equals," Mobile v. Bolden, 446 U.S. 55, 84 (1980) (Stevens, J., concurring in the judgment), yet more subtly distorts governmental processes in such a way as to place special burdens on the ability of minority groups to achieve beneficial legislation.

This principle received its clearest expression in Hunter v. Erickson, [393 U.S. 385 (1969)], a case that involved attempts to overturn antidiscrimination legislation in Akron, Ohio. The Akron city council, pursuant to its ordinary legislative processes, had enacted a fair housing ordinance. In response, the local citizenry, using an established referendum procedure, amended the city charter to provide that ordinances regulating real estate transactions "'on the basis of race, color, religion, national origin or ancestry must first be approved by a majority of the electors voting on the question at a regular or general election before said ordinance shall be effective.'"This action "not only suspended the operation of the existing ordinance forbidding housing discrimination, but also required the approval of the electors before any future [fair housing] ordinance could take effect." In essence, the amendment changed the requirements for the adoption of one type of local legislation: to enact an ordinance barring housing discrimination on the basis of race or religion, proponents had to obtain the approval of the city council and of a majority of the voters citywide. To enact an ordinance preventing housing discrimination on other grounds, or to enact any other type of housing ordinance, proponents needed the support of only the city council.

In striking down the charter amendment, the Hunter Court recognized that, on its face, the provision "draws no distinctions among racial and religious groups." But it did differentiate "between those groups who sought the law's protection against racial . . . discriminations in the sale and rental of real estate and those who sought to regulate real property transactions in the pursuit of other ends," thus "disadvantag[ing] those who would benefit from laws barring racial . . . discriminations as against those who would bar other discriminations or who would otherwise regulate the real estate market in their favor." In "reality," the burden imposed by such an arrangement necessarily "falls on the minority. The majority needs no protection against discrimination and if it did, a referendum might be bothersome but no more than that." In effect, then, the charter amendment served as an "explicitly racial classification treating racial housing matters differently from other racial and housing matters." This made the amendment constitutionally suspect: "the State may no more disadvantage any particular group by making it more difficult to enact legislation in its behalf than it may dilute any person's vote or give any group a smaller representation than another of comparable size. . . .

[This case yields] a simple but central principle. [The] political majority may generally restructure the political process to place obstacles in the path of everyone seeking to secure the benefits of governmental action. But a different analysis is required when the State allocates governmental power non-neutrally, by explicitly using the racial nature of a decision to determine the decisionmaking process. State action of this kind, the Court said, "places special burdens on racial minorities within the governmental process. . . ."

III. In our view, Initiative 350 must fall because it does "not attemp[t] to allocate governmental power on the basis of any general principle." Hunter v. Erickson. Instead, it uses the racial nature of an issue to define the governmental decisionmaking structure, and thus imposes substantial and unique burdens on racial minorities.

A. Noting that Initiative 350 nowhere mentions "race" or "integration," appellants suggest that the legislation has no racial overtones; they maintain that Hunter is inapposite because the initiative simply permits busing for certain enumerated purposes while neutrally forbidding it for all other reasons. We find it difficult to believe that appellants' analysis is seriously advanced, however, for despite its facial neutrality there is little doubt that the initiative was effectively drawn for racial purposes. [It] is beyond reasonable dispute, then, that the initiative was enacted "'because of,' not merely 'in spite of,' its adverse effects upon" busing for integration. Personnel Administrator of Massachusetts v. Feeney. . . . [It] undoubtedly is true, as the United States suggests, that the proponents of mandatory integration cannot be classified by race: Negroes and whites may be counted among both the supporters and the opponents of Initiative 350. And it should be equally clear that white as well as Negro children benefit from exposure to "ethnic and racial diversity in the classroom." Columbus Board of Education v. Penick, 443 U.S. 449 (1979) (Powell, J., dissenting). But neither of these factors serves to distinguish Hunter, for we may fairly assume that members of the racial majority both favored and benefited from

Akron's fair housing ordinance. In any event, our cases suggest that desegregation of the public schools, like the Akron open housing ordinance, at bottom inures primarily to the benefit of the minority, and is designed for that purpose. . . .

B. We are also satisfied that the practical effect of Initiative 350 is to work a reallocation of power of the kind condemned in Hunter. The initiative removes the authority to address a racial problem — and only a racial problem — from the existing decisionmaking body, in such a way as to burden minority interests. . . . The state appellants and the United States, in response to this line of analysis, argue that Initiative 350 has not worked any reallocation of power. They note that the State necessarily retains plenary authority over Washington's system of education, and therefore they suggest that the initiative amounts to nothing more than an unexceptional example of a State's intervention in its own school system. . . . But "insisting that a State may distribute legislative power as it desires . . . furnish[es] no justification for a legislative structure which otherwise would violate the Fourteenth Amendment." [It] is irrelevant that the State might have vested all decisionmaking authority in itself, so long as the political structure it in fact erected imposes comparative burdens on minority interests; that much is settled by Hunter. And until the passage of Initiative 350, Washington law in fact had established the local school board, rather than the State, as the entity charged with making decisions of the type at issue here. . . .

[Before] adoption of the initiative, the power to determine what programs would most appropriately fill a school district's educational needs — including programs involving student assignment and desegregation — was firmly committed to the local board's discretion. The question whether to provide an integrated learning environment rather than a system of neighborhood schools surely involved a decision of that sort. After passage of Initiative 350, authority over all but one of those areas remained in the hands of the local board. By placing power over desegregative busing at the state level, then, Initiative 350 plainly "differentiates between the treatment of problems involving racial matters and that afforded other problems in the same area." . . .

C. To be sure, "the simple repeal or modification of desegregation or antidiscrimination laws, without more, never has been viewed as embodying a presumptively invalid racial classification." Initiative 350, however, works something more than the "mere repeal" of a desegregation law by the political entity that created it. It burdens all future attempts to integrate Washington schools in districts throughout the State, by lodging decisionmaking authority over the question at a new and remote level of government. Indeed, the initiative, like the charter amendment at issue in Hunter, has its most pernicious effect on integration programs that do "not arouse extraordinary controversy." In such situations the initiative makes the enactment of racially beneficial legislation difficult, though the particular program involved might not have inspired opposition had it been promulgated through the usual legislative processes used for comparable legislation. . . .

IV. In the end, appellants are reduced to suggesting that Hunter has been effectively overruled by more recent decisions of this Court. As they read it, Hunter applied a simple "disparate impact" analysis: it invalidated a facially neutral ordinance because of the law's adverse effects upon racial minorities. Appellants therefore contend that Hunter was swept away, along with the disparate impact approach to equal protection, in [Washington v. Davis]. . . .

There is one immediate and crucial difference between Hunter and the cases cited by appellants. While decisions such as [Washington v. Davis] considered classifications facially unrelated to race, the charter amendment at issue in Hunter dealt in explicitly racial terms with legislation designed to benefit minorities "as minorities," not legislation intended to benefit some larger group of underprivileged citizens among whom minorities were disproportionately represented. This does not mean, of course, that every attempt to address a racial issue gives rise to an impermissible racial classification. But when the political process or the decisionmaking mechanism used to address racially conscious legislation — and only such legislation — is singled out for peculiar and disadvantageous treatment, the governmental action plainly "rests on 'distinctions based on race.'"29 And when the State's allocation of power places unusual burdens on the ability of racial groups to enact legislation specifically designed to overcome the "special condition" of prejudice, the governmental action seriously "curtail[s] the operation of those political processes ordinarily to be relied upon to protect minorities." [Carolene Products] In a most direct sense, this implicates the judiciary's special role in safeguarding the interests of those groups that are "relegated to such a position of political powerlessness as to command extraordinary protection from the majoritarian political process." . . . Accordingly, the judgment of the Court of Appeals is affirmed.

Justice POWELL, with whom [Chief Justice BURGER], Justice REHNQUIST, and Justice O'CONNOR join, dissenting.

[In] the absence of a prior constitutional violation, the States are under no constitutional duty to adopt integration programs in their schools, and certainly they are under no duty to establish a regime of mandatory busing. Nor does the Federal Constitution require that particular decisions concerning the schools or any other matter be made on the local as opposed to the State level. . . .

Application of these settled principles demonstrates the serious error of today's decision — an error that cuts deeply into the heretofore unquestioned right of a State to structure the decisionmaking authority of its government. In this case, by Initiative 350, the State has adopted a policy of racial neutrality in student assignments. The policy in no way interferes with the power of State or Federal Courts to remedy constitutional violations. And if such a policy had been adopted by any of the school districts in this litigation there could have been no question that the policy was constitutional. The issue here arises only because the Seattle School District — in the absence of a then established State policy — chose to adopt race specific school assignments with extensive busing. It is not questioned that the District itself, at any time thereafter, could have changed its mind and cancelled its integration program without violating the Federal Constitution. Yet this Court holds that neither the legislature nor the people of the State of Washington could alter what the District had decided.

The Court argues that the people of Washington by Initiative 350 created a racial classification, and yet must agree that identical action by the Seattle School District itself would have created no such classification. This is not an easy argument to answer because it seems to make no sense. School boards are the creation of supreme State authority, whether in a State Constitution or by legislative enactment. Until today's decision no one would have questioned the authority of a State to abolish school boards altogether, or to require that they conform to any lawful State policy. And in the State of Washington, a neighborhood school policy would have been lawful.

Under today's decision this heretofore undoubted supreme authority of a State's electorate is to be curtailed whenever a school board — or indeed any other state board or local instrumentality — adopts a race specific program that arguably benefits racial minorities. Once such a program is adopted, only the local or subordinate entity that approved it will have authority to change it. The Court offers no authority or relevant explanation for this extraordinary subordination of the ultimate sovereign power of a State to act with respect to racial matters by subordinate bodies. It is a strange notion — alien to our system — that local governmental bodies can forever preempt the ability of a State — the sovereign power — to address a matter of compelling concern to the State. The Constitution of the United States does not require such a bizarre result. . . .

[Initiative] 350 places no "special burdens on racial minorities within the governmental process," [Hunter], such that interference with the State's distribution of authority is justified. Initiative 350 is simply a reflection of the State's political process at work. It does not alter that process in any respect. It does not require, for example, that all matters dealing with race — or with integration in the schools — must henceforth be submitted to a referendum of the people. Cf. Hunter v. Erickson, supra. The State has done no more than precisely what the Court has said that it should do: It has "resolved through the political process" the "desirability and efficacy of [mandatory] school desegregation" where there has been no unlawful segregation.

The political process in Washington, as in other States, permits persons who are dissatisfied at a local level to appeal to the State legislature or the people of the State for redress. It permits the people of a State to preempt local policies, and to formulate new programs and regulations. Such a process is inherent in the continued sovereignty of the States. This is our system. Any time a State chooses to address a major issue some persons or groups may be disadvantaged. In a democratic system there are winners and losers. But there is no inherent unfairness in this and certainly no Constitutional violation. . .

.

Nothing in Hunter supports the Court's extraordinary invasion into the State's distribution of authority. [In] this case, unlike in Hunter, the political system has not been redrawn or altered. The authority of the State over the public school system, acting through Initiative or the legislature, is plenary. Thus, the State's political system is not altered when it adopts for the first time a policy, concededly within the area of its authority, for the regulation of local school [districts.] Hunter, therefore, is simply irrelevant. It is the Court that by its decision today disrupts the normal course of State government. Under its unprecedented theory of a vested constitutional right to local decisionmaking, the State apparently is now forever barred from addressing the perplexing problems of how best to educate fairly all children in a multi-racial society where, as in this case, the local school board has acted first.

CRAWFORD v. LOS ANGELES BOARD OF EDUCATION
458 U.S. 527 (1982)

[In *Crawford*, decided on the same day as Seattle, petitioners challenged the constitutionality of an amendment to the California Constitution prohibiting state courts from ordering mandatory pupil assignment or transportation unless a federal court would do so to remedy a violation of the federal equal protection clause. The amendment followed a decision by the California Supreme Court interpreting the state constitution as prohibiting de facto segregation and ordering "reasonable steps" to alleviate it. Opponents of this decision succeeded in placing Proposition I, which embodied the amendment, on the ballot, and the proposition was approved in a statewide referendum.]

Justice POWELL delivered the opinion of the Court.

We agree with the California Court of Appeal in rejecting the contention that once a State chooses to do 'more' than the Fourteenth Amendment requires, it may never recede. We reject an interpretation of the Fourteenth Amendment so destructive of a State's democratic processes and of its ability to experiment. . . .

Proposition I does not inhibit enforcement of any federal law or constitutional requirement. Quite the contrary, by its plain language the Proposition seeks only to embrace the requirements of the Federal Constitution with respect to mandatory school assignments and transportation. It would be paradoxical to conclude that by adopting the Equal Protection Clause of the Fourteenth Amendment, the voters of the State thereby had violated it. . . .

We would agree that if Proposition I employed a racial classification it would be unconstitutional unless necessary to further a compelling state interest. [But] Proposition I does not embody a racial classification. It neither says nor implies that persons are to be treated differently on account of their race. It simply forbids state courts to order pupil school assignment or transportation in the absence of a Fourteenth Amendment violation. The benefit it seeks to confer — neighborhood schooling — is made available regardless of race in the discretion of school [boards].

Similarly, the Court has recognized that a distinction may exist between state action that discriminates on the basis of race and state action that addresses, in neutral fashion, race related matters. This distinction is implicit in the Court's repeated statement that the Equal Protection Clause is not violated by the mere repeal of race related legislation or policies that were not required by the Federal Constitution in the first place. . . .

Relying primarily on the decision in Hunter v. Erickson, [petitioners] contend that Proposition I does not simply repeal a state created right but fundamentally alters the judicial system so that "those seeking redress from racial isolation in violation of state law must be satisfied with less than full relief from a state court." We do not view Hunter as controlling here, nor are we persuaded by petitioners' characterization of Proposition I as something more than a mere repeal. . . .

[It cannot be said] that Proposition I distorts the political process for racial reasons or that it allocates governmental or judicial power on the basis of a discriminatory principle. . . .

[Having] gone beyond the requirements of the Federal Constitution, the State was free to return in part to the standard prevailing generally throughout the United States."

[Justice BLACKMUN, joined by Justice BRENNAN, concurred:] "While I join the opinion of the Court, I write separately to address what I believe are the critical distinctions between this case and Washington v. Seattle School District No. 1. . . .

State courts do not create the rights they enforce; those rights originate elsewhere — in the state legislature, in the State's political subdivisions, or in the state constitution itself. When one of those rights is repealed, and therefore is rendered unenforceable in the courts, that action hardly can be said to restructure the State's decisionmaking mechanism. While the California electorate may have made it more difficult to achieve desegregation when it enacted Proposition I, to my mind it did so not by working a structural change in the political process so much as by simply repealing the right to invoke a judicial busing remedy. Indeed, ruling for petitioners on a Hunter theory seemingly would mean that statutory affirmative action or antidiscrimination programs never could be repealed, for a repeal of the enactment would mean that enforcement authority previously lodged in the state courts was being removed by another political entity.

Justice MARSHALL, dissenting.

In my view [the principles announced in Seattle] lead to the conclusion that California's Proposition I works an unconstitutional reallocation of state power by depriving California courts of the ability to grant meaningful relief to those seeking to vindicate the State's guarantee against de facto segregation in the public schools. . . .

Prior to the enactment of Proposition I, those seeking to vindicate the rights enumerated by the California Supreme Court just as those interested in attaining any other educational objective, followed a two-stage procedure. First, California's minority community could attempt to convince the local school board voluntarily to comply with its constitutional obligation to take reasonably feasible steps to eliminate racial isolation in the public schools. If the board was either unwilling or unable to carry out its constitutional duty, those seeking redress could petition the California state courts to require school officials to live up to their obligations. Busing could be required as part of a judicial remedial order. . . .

Whereas Initiative 350 attempted to deny minority children the first step of this procedure, Proposition I eliminates by fiat the second stage: the ability of California courts to order meaningful compliance with the requirements of the State Constitution. After the adoption of Proposition I, the only method of enforcing against a recalcitrant school board the state constitutional duty to eliminate racial isolation is to petition either the state legislature or the electorate as a whole. Clearly, the rules of the game have been significantly changed for those attempting to vindicate this state constitutional right.

h. COLLEGES AND UNIVERSITIES

UNITED STATES v. FORDICE
505 U.S. 717 (1992)

Justice WHITE delivered the opinion of the Court.

Mississippi launched its public university system in 1848 by establishing the University of Mississippi, an institution dedicated to the higher education exclusively of white persons. In succeeding decades, the State erected additional postsecondary, single-race educational facilities. Alcorn State University opened its doors in 1871 as "an agricultural college for the education of Mississippi's black youth." Ayers v. Allain, 674 F.Supp. 1523, 1527 (ND Miss.1987). Creation of four more exclusively white institutions followed: Mississippi State University (1880), Mississippi University for Women (1885), University of Southern Mississippi (1912), and Delta State University (1925). The State added two more solely black institutions in 1940 and 1950: in the former year, Jackson State University, which was charged with training "black teachers for the black public schools," and in the latter year, Mississippi Valley State University, whose functions were to educate teachers primarily for rural and elementary schools and to provide vocational instruction to black students.

Despite this Court's decisions in Brown I and Brown II, Mississippi's policy of *de jure* segregation continued. The first black student was not admitted to the University of Mississippi until 1962, and then only by court order. For the next 12 years the segregated public university system in the State remained largely intact. [By] the mid-1980's, 30 years after *Brown,* more than 99 percent of Mississippi's white students were enrolled at University of Mississippi, Mississippi State, Southern Mississippi, Delta State, and Mississippi University for Women. The student bodies at these universities remained predominantly white, averaging between 80 and 91 percent white students. Seventy-one percent of the State's black students attended Jackson State, Alcorn State, and Mississippi Valley State, where the racial composition ranged from 92 to 99 percent black.

The Court of Appeals concluded that the State had fulfilled its affirmative obligation to disestablish its prior *de jure* segregated system by adopting and implementing race-neutral policies governing its college and university system. Because students seeking higher education had "real freedom" to choose the institution of their choice, the State need do no more. Even though neutral policies and free choice were not enough to dismantle a dual system of primary or secondary schools, Green v. School Bd. of New Kent County, 391 U.S. 430, 88 S.Ct. 1689, 20 L.Ed.2d 716 (1968), the Court of Appeals thought that universities "differ in character fundamentally" from lower levels of schools.

We do not agree with the Court of Appeals or the District Court, however, that the adoption and implementation of race-neutral policies alone suffice to demonstrate that the State has completely abandoned its prior dual system. That college attendance is by choice and not by assignment does not mean that a race-neutral admissions policy cures the constitutional violation of a dual system. In a system based on choice, student attendance is determined not simply by admissions policies, but also by many other factors. Although some of these factors clearly cannot be attributed to state policies, many can be. Thus, even after a State dismantles its segregative *admissions* policy, there may still be state action that is traceable to the State's prior *de jure* segregation and that continues to foster segregation. The Equal Protection Clause is offended by "sophisticated as well as simple-minded modes of discrimination." If policies traceable to the *de jure* system are still in force and have discriminatory effects, those policies too must be reformed to the extent practicable and consistent with sound educational practices.

[If] the State perpetuates policies and practices traceable to its prior system that continue to have segregative effects — whether by influencing student enrollment decisions or by fostering segregation in other facets of the university system — and such policies are without sound educational justification and can be practicably eliminated, the State has not satisfied its burden of proving that it has dismantled its prior system. Such policies run afoul of the Equal Protection Clause, even though the State has abolished the legal requirement that whites and blacks be educated separately and has established racially neutral policies not animated by a discriminatory purpose.

Had the Court of Appeals applied the correct legal standard, it would have been apparent from the undisturbed factual findings of the District Court that there are several surviving aspects of Mississippi's prior dual system which are constitutionally suspect; for even though such policies may be race neutral on their face, they substantially restrict a person's choice of which institution to enter, and they contribute to the racial identifiably of the eight public universities. Mississippi must justify these policies or eliminate them.

[We] deal first with the current admissions policies of Mississippi's public universities. As the District Court found, the three flagship historically white universities in the system University of Mississippi, Mississippi State University, and University of Southern Mississippi — enacted policies in 1963 requiring all entrants to achieve a minimum composite score of 15 on the test administered by the American College Testing Program (ACT). The court described the "discriminatory taint" of this policy, an obvious reference to the fact that, at the time, the average ACT score for white students was 18 and the average score for blacks was 7.

[The] present admissions standards are not only traceable to the *de jure* system and were originally adopted for a discriminatory purpose, but they also have present discriminatory effects. Every Mississippi resident under 21 seeking admission to the university system must take the ACT test. Any applicant who scores at least 15 qualifies for automatic admission to any of the five historically white institutions except Mississippi University for Women, which requires a score of 18 for automatic admission unless the student has a 3.0 high school grade average. Those scoring less than 15 but at least 13 automatically qualify to enter Jackson State University, Alcorn State University, and Mississippi Valley State University. Without doubt, these requirements restrict the range of choices of entering students as to which institution they may attend in a way that perpetuates segregation. Those scoring 13 or 14, must go to one of the historically black institutions or attend junior college with the hope of transferring to a historically white institution. Proportionately more blacks than whites face this choice: In 1985, 72 percent of Mississippi's white high school seniors achieved an ACT composite score of 15 or better, while less than 30 percent of black high school seniors earned that score. It is not surprising then that Mississippi's universities remain predominantly identifiable by race.

[A] second aspect of the present system that necessitates further inquiry is the widespread duplication of programs. [It] can hardly be denied that such duplication was part and parcel of the prior dual system of higher education — the whole notion of "separate but equal" required duplicative programs in two sets of schools — and that the present unnecessary duplication is a continuation of that practice. Brown and its progeny, however, established that the burden of proof falls on the *State,* and not the aggrieved plaintiffs, to establish that it has dismantled its prior *de jure* segregated system. Brown II, 349 U.S., at 300, 75 S.Ct., at 756. The court's holding that petitioners could not establish the constitutional defect of unnecessary duplication, therefore, improperly shifted the burden away from the State.

[The] institutional mission designations adopted in 1981 have as their antecedents the policies enacted to perpetuate racial separation during the *de jure* segregated regime. The Court of Appeals expressly disagreed with the District Court by recognizing that the "inequalities among the institutions largely follow the mission designations, and the mission designations to some degree follow the historical racial assignments." [We] do not suggest that absent discriminatory purpose the assignment of different missions to various institutions in a State's higher education system would raise an equal protection issue where one or more of the institutions become or remain predominantly black or white. But here the issue is whether the State has sufficiently dismantled its prior dual system; and when combined with the differential admission practices and unnecessary program duplication, it is likely that the mission designations interfere with student choice and tend to perpetuate the segregated system. On remand, the court should inquire whether it would be practicable and consistent with sound educational practices to eliminate any such discriminatory effects of the State's present policy of mission assignments.

Fourth, the State attempted to bring itself into compliance with the Constitution by continuing to maintain and operate all eight higher educational institutions. The existence of eight instead of some lesser number was undoubtedly occasioned by state laws forbidding the mingling of the races. And as the District Court recognized, continuing to maintain all eight universities in Mississippi is wasteful and irrational. The District Court pointed especially to the facts that Delta State and Mississippi Valley State are only 35 miles apart and that only 20 miles separate Mississippi State and Mississippi University for Women. It was evident to the District Court that "the defendants undertake to fund more institutions of higher learning than are justified by the amount of financial resources available to the state," but the court concluded that such fiscal irresponsibility was a policy choice of the legislature rather than a feature of a system subject to constitutional scrutiny.

Unquestionably, a larger rather than a smaller number of institutions from which to choose in itself makes for different choices, particularly when examined in the light of other factors present in the operation of the system, such as admissions, program duplication, and institutional mission designations. Though certainly closure of one or more institutions would decrease the discriminatory effects of the present system, based on the present record we are unable to say whether such action is constitutionally required. Elimination of program duplication and revision of admissions criteria may make institutional closure unnecessary. However, on remand this issue should be carefully explored by inquiring and determining whether retention of all eight institutions itself affects student choice and perpetuates the segregated higher education system, whether maintenance of each of the universities is educationally justifiable, and whether one or more of them can be practicably closed or merged with other existing institutions.

Because the former *de jure* segregated system of public universities in Mississippi impeded the free choice of prospective students, the State in dismantling that system must take the necessary steps to ensure that this choice now is truly free. The full range of policies and practices must be examined with this duty in mind. That an institution is predominantly white or black does not in itself make out a constitutional violation. But surely the State may not leave in place policies rooted in its prior officially segregated system that serve to maintain the racial identifiability of its universities if those policies can practicably be eliminated without eroding sound educational policies.

If we understand private petitioners to press us to order the upgrading of Jackson State, Alcorn State, and Mississippi Valley State *solely* so that they may be publicly financed, exclusively black enclaves by private choice, we reject that request. The State provides these facilities for *all* its citizens and it has not met its burden under Brown to take affirmative steps to dismantle its prior *de jure* system when it perpetuates a separate, but "more equal" one. Whether such an increase in funding is necessary to achieve a full dismantlement under the standards we have outlined, however, is a different question, and one that must be addressed on remand.

Justice THOMAS, concurring.

"We must rally to the defense of our schools. We must repudiate this unbearable assumption of the right to kill institutions unless they conform to one narrow standard." Du Bois, Schools, 13 The Crisis 111, 112 (1917).

I agree with the Court that a State does not satisfy its obligation to dismantle a dual system of higher education merely by adopting race-neutral policies for the future administration of that system. Today, we hold that "[i]f policies traceable to the *de jure* system are still in force and have discriminatory effects, those policies too must be reformed to the extent practicable and consistent with sound educational practices." I agree that this statement defines the appropriate standard to apply in the higher education context. I write separately to emphasize that this standard is far different from the one adopted to govern the grade-school context in Green v. School Bd. of New Kent County, 391 U.S. 430, 88 S.Ct. 1689, 20 L.Ed.2d 716 (1968), and its progeny. In particular, because it does not compel the elimination of all observed racial imbalance, it portends neither the destruction of historically black colleges nor the severing of those institutions from their distinctive histories and traditions.

[From] the beginning, we have recognized that desegregation remedies cannot be designed to ensure the elimination of any remnant at any price, but rather must display "a practical flexibility" and "a facility for adjusting and reconciling public and private needs." Quite obviously, one compelling need to be considered is the *educational* need of the present and future *students* in the Mississippi university system, for whose benefit the remedies will be crafted.

In particular, we do not foreclose the possibility that there exists "sound educational justification" for maintaining historically black colleges *as such*. Despite the shameful history of state-enforced segregation, these institutions have survived and flourished. Indeed, they have expanded as opportunities for blacks to enter historically white institutions have expanded. Between 1954 and 1980, for example, enrollment at historically black colleges increased from 70,000 to 200,000 students, while degrees awarded increased from 13,000 to 32,000.

I think it undisputable that these institutions have succeeded in part because of their distinctive histories and traditions; for many, historically black colleges have become "a symbol of the highest attainments of black culture." J. Preer, Lawyers v. Educators: Black Colleges and Desegregation in Public Higher Education 2 (1982). Obviously, a State cannot maintain such traditions by closing particular institutions, historically white or historically black, to particular racial groups. Nonetheless, it hardly follows that a State cannot operate a diverse assortment of institutions — including historically black institutions — open to all on a race-neutral basis, but with established traditions and programs that might disproportionately appeal to one race or another. No one, I imagine, would argue that such institutional *diversity* is without "sound educational justification," or that it is even remotely akin to program *duplication*, which is designed to separate the races for the sake of separating the races. The Court at least hints at the importance of this value when it distinguishes Green in part on the ground that colleges and universities "are not fungible." *Ante*, at 2736. Although I agree that a State is not constitutionally *required* to maintain its historically black institutions as such, see *ante*, at 2743, I do not understand our opinion to hold that a State is *forbidden* to do so. It would be ironic, to say the least, if the institutions that sustained blacks during segregation were themselves destroyed in an effort to combat its vestiges.

Justice SCALIA, concurring in the judgment in part and dissenting in part.

Before evaluating the Court's handiwork, it is no small task simply to comprehend it. The Court sets forth not one, but seemingly two different tests for ascertaining compliance with Brown I — though in the last analysis they come to the same. The Court initially announces the following test, in Part III of its opinion: All policies (i) "traceable to [the State's] prior [*de jure*] system" (ii) "that continue to have segregative effects — whether by influencing student enrollment decisions or by fostering segregation in other facets of the university system — "must be eliminated (iii) to the extent "practicabl[e]" and (iv) consistent with "sound educational" practices. *Ante,* at 2737. When the Court comes to applying its test, however, in Part IV of the opinion, "influencing student enrollment decisions" is not merely one example of a "segregative effec[t]," but is elevated to an independent and essential requirement of its own. The policies that must be eliminated are those that (i) are legacies of the dual system, (ii) "contribute to the racial identifiability" of the State's universities (the same as (i) and (ii) in Part III), and, in addition, (iii) do so in a way that "*substantially restrict[s] a person's choice of which institution to enter.*"

What the Court means by "substantially restrict[ing] a person's choice of which institution to enter" is not clear.

[Whether] one consults the Court's description of what it purports to be doing, in Part III, *ante,* at 2735-2737, or what the Court actually does, one must conclude that the Court is essentially applying to universities the amorphous standard adopted for primary and secondary schools in Green v. School Bd. of New Kent County, 391 U.S. 430, 88 S.Ct. 1689, 20 L.Ed.2d 716 (1968). Like that case, today's decision places upon the State the ordinarily unsustainable burden of proving the negative proposition that *it* is not responsible for extant racial disparity in enrollment. Green requires school boards to prove that racially identifiable schools are *not* the consequence of past or present discriminatory state action, today's opinion requires state university administrators to prove that racially identifiable schools are *not* the consequence of any practice or practices (in such impromptu "aggregation" as might strike the fancy of a district judge) held over from the prior *de jure* regime. This will imperil virtually any practice or program plaintiffs decide to challenge — just as Green has — so long as racial imbalance remains.

[The] constitutional evil of the "separate but equal" regime that we confronted in Brown I was that blacks were told to go to one set of schools, whites to another. See Plessy v. Ferguson, 163 U.S. 537, 16 S.Ct. 1138, 41 L.Ed. 256 (1896). What made this "even-handed" racial partitioning offensive to equal protection was its implicit stigmatization of minority students: "To separate [black students] from others of similar age and qualifications solely because of their race generates a feeling of inferiority as to their status in the community that may affect their hearts and minds in a way unlikely ever to be undone." Brown I, 347 U.S., at 494, 74 S.Ct., at 691. In the context of higher education, a context in which students decide whether to attend school and if so where, the only unconstitutional derivations of that bygone system are those that limit access on discriminatory bases; for only they have the potential to generate the harm Brown I condemned, and only they have the potential to deny students equal access to the best public education a State has to offer. Legacies of the dual system that permit (or even incidentally facilitate) free choice of racially identifiable schools — while still assuring each individual student the right to attend *whatever* school he wishes — do not have these consequences.

It is my view that the requirement of compelled integration (whether by student assignment, as in Green itself, or by elimination of nonintegrated options, as the Court today effectively decrees) does not apply to higher education. Only one aspect of a historically segregated university system need be eliminated: discriminatory admissions standards. The burden is upon the formerly *de jure* system to show that that has been achieved. Once that has been done, however, it is not just unprecedented, but illogical as well, to establish that former *de jure* States continue to deny equal protection of the law to students whose choices among public university offerings are unimpeded by discriminatory barriers.

[Moreover], equal funding, like program duplication, facilitates continued segregation — enabling students to attend schools where their own race predominates without paying a penalty in the quality of education. Nor could such an equal-funding policy be saved on the basis that it serves what the Court calls a "sound educational justification." The only conceivable *educational* value it furthers is that of fostering schools in which blacks receive their education in a "majority" setting; but to acknowledge that as a "value" would contradict the compulsory-integration philosophy that underlies Green. Just as vulnerable, of course, would be all other programs that have the effect of facilitating the continued existence of predominantly black institutions: elevating an HBI to comprehensive status (but see *ante,* at 2741-2742, where the Court inexplicably suggests that this action may be required); offering a so-called Afrocentric curriculum, as has been done recently on an experimental basis in some secondary and primary schools, see Jarvis, Brown and the Afrocentric Curriculum, 101 Yale L.J. 1285, 1287, and n. 12 (1992); preserving eight separate universities, see *ante,* at 2742-2743, which is perhaps Mississippi's single policy most segregative in effect; or providing funding for HBI's as HBI's, see 20 U.S.C. § § 1060-1063c, which does just that.

But this predictable impairment of HBI's should come as no surprise: for incidentally facilitating — indeed, even tolerating — the continued existence of HBI's is not what the Court's test is about, and has never been what Green is about. See Green, 391 U.S., at 442, 88 S.Ct., at 1696 ("The Board must be required to formulate a new plan and . . . fashion steps which promise realistically to convert promptly to a system without a 'white' school and a 'Negro' school") (footnote omitted). What the Court's test is designed to achieve is the elimination of predominantly black institutions. While that may be good social policy, the present petitioners, I suspect, would not agree; and there is much to be said for the Court of Appeals' perception in Ayers, 914 F.2d, at 687, that "if no [state] authority exists to deny [the student] the right to attend the institution of his choice, he is done a severe disservice by remedies which, in seeking to maximize integration, minimize diversity and vitiate his choices." But whether or not the Court's antagonism to unintegrated schooling is good policy, it is assuredly not good constitutional law. There is nothing unconstitutional about a "black" school in the sense, not of a school that blacks *must* attend and that whites *cannot,* but of a school that, as a consequence of private choice in residence or in school selection, contains, and has long contained, a large black majority. See McLaurin v. Oklahoma State Regents for Higher Ed., 339 U.S. 637, 641, 70 S.Ct. 851, 853, 94 L.Ed. 1149 (1950). (The Court says this, see *ante,* at 2743, but does not appear to mean it, see *ante,* at 2736, n. 4.) In a perverse way, in fact, the insistence, whether explicit or implicit, that such institutions not be permitted to endure perpetuates the very stigma of black inferiority that Brown I sought to destroy. . . .

I would not predict, however, that today's opinion will succeed in producing the same result as Green — viz., compelling the States to compel racial "balance" in their schools — because of several practical imperfections: because the Court deprives district judges of the most efficient (and perhaps the only effective) Green remedy, mandatory student assignment, see *ante,* at 2736, n. 4; because some contradictory elements of the opinion (its suggestion, for example, that Mississippi's mission designations foster, rather than deter, segregation) will prevent clarity of application; and because the virtually standardless discretion conferred upon district judges (see Part I, *supra*) will permit them to do pretty much what they please. What I do predict is a number of years of litigation-driven confusion and destabilization in the university systems of all the formerly *de jure* States, that will benefit neither blacks nor whites, neither predominantly black institutions nor predominantly white ones. Nothing good will come of this judicially ordained turmoil, except the public recognition that any court that would knowingly impose it must hate segregation. We must find some other way of making that point.

3. AFFIRMATIVE ACTION

Should discrimination against a racial majority be treated the same as discrimination against a disadvantaged racial minority? In post-apartheid America, when many states and the federal government attempted to offer "affirmative action" to remedy past discrimination against disadvantaged racial minorities, this became a significant social and constitutional question. The controversy extending from this debate may well have been the reason the Court "sidestepped" the merits of the University of Washington Law School's "preferential admissions program" in 1974. (See *DeFunis v. Odegarrd.*)

As reviewed in the previous section, the Court had traditionally applied strict scrutiny to racial classifications that were "inherently suspect" because they were "discrete and insular" minorities who had a past history of racial discrimination and had been denied participation in the majoritarian political process. This approach seemed to indicate that the "strictest" scrutiny would only be applied to discrimination against disadvantaged racial minorities. Offhand, it hardly seems odious for a racial majority to discriminate against itself. This is particularly the case when affirmative action plans are voluntary and not court ordered. Here the majoritarian political process would seem to offer protection against invidious purpose, since the majority could cease to discriminate against itself whenever it chose. Yet, given America's heinous history of racial discrimination it can certainly be argued that any racial discrimination should never be easily tolerated. Recall, in this regard, Justice Harlan's eloquent plea for a "color-blind" Constitution in his in his *Plessy* dissent. Justice Brennan, in his *Bakke* dissent, attempted to take all of these factors into account in arguing that a "heightened degree of scrutiny" should be applied to discrimination against a racial majority, but short of the strict scrutiny applied to disadvantaged racial minorities or traditional "inherently suspect classifications."

The Court formally began its foray into these issues in the *Bakke* opinion, which follows. As the Court's makeup and perhaps the concurrent attitudes of the nation changed toward a more conservative view of these issues, so did the Court's opinions. The *Croson* and *Adarand* decision are reflective of what appeared to be a more limited view of constitutionally permissible affirmative action programs post *Bakke*.

REGENTS OF THE UNIVERSITY OF CALIFORNIA v. BAKKE
438 U.S. 265 (1978)

Mr. Justice Brennan, Mr. Justice White, Mr. Justice Marshall and Mr. Justice Blackmun filed an opinion concurring in the judgment in part and dissenting.

Mr. Justice Marshall filed a separate opinion.

Mr. Justice Blackmun filed a separate opinion.

Mr. Justice Stevens concurred in the judgment in part and dissented in part and filed an opinion in which Mr. Chief Justice Burger, Mr. Justice Stewart and Mr. Justice Rehnquist joined.

Mr. Justice POWELL announced the judgment of the Court.

This case presents a challenge to the special admissions program of the petitioner, the Medical School of the University of California at Davis, which is designed to assure the admission of a specified number of students from certain minority groups. [The] Supreme Court of California affirmed those portions of the trial court's judgment declaring the special admissions program unlawful and enjoining petitioner from considering the race of any applicant. It modified that portion of the judgment denying respondent's requested injunction and directed the trial court to order his admission.

For the reasons stated in the following opinion, I believe that so much of the judgment of the California court as holds petitioner's special admissions program unlawful and directs that respondent be admitted to the Medical School must be affirmed. For the reasons expressed in a separate opinion, my Brothers The Chief Justice, Mr. Justice Stewart, Mr. Justice Rehnquist and Mr. Justice Stevens concur in this judgment.

I also conclude for the reasons stated in the following opinion that the portion of the court's judgment enjoining petitioner from according any consideration to race in its admissions process must be reversed. For reasons expressed in separate opinions, my Brothers Mr. Justice Brennan, Mr. Justice White, Mr. Justice Marshall, and Mr. Justice Blackmun concur in this judgment.

Affirmed in part and reversed in part.

The Medical School of the University of California at Davis opened in 1968 with an entering class of 50 students. In 1971, the size of the entering class was increased to 100 students, a level at which it remains. No admissions program for disadvantaged or minority students existed when the school opened, and the first class contained three Asians but no blacks, no Mexican-Americans, and no American Indians. Over the next two years, the faculty devised a special admissions program to increase the representation of "disadvantaged" students in each Medical School class. The special program consisted of a separate admissions system operating in coordination with the regular admissions process.

Under the regular admissions procedure, a candidate could submit his application to the Medical School beginning in July of the year preceding the academic year for which admission was sought. Record 149. Because of the large number of applications, the admissions committee screened each one to select candidates for further consideration. Candidates whose overall undergraduate grade point averages fell below 2.5 on a scale of 4.0 were summarily rejected. Id., at 63. About one out of six applicants was invited for a personal interview. *Ibid.* Following the interviews, each candidate was rated on a scale of 1 to 100 by his interviewers and four other members of the admissions committee. The rating embraced the interviewers' summaries, the candidate's overall grade point average, grade point average in science courses, scores on the Medical College Admissions Test (MCAT), letters of recommendation, extracurricular activities, and other biographical data. Id., at 62. The ratings were added together to arrive at each candidate's "benchmark" score. Since five committee members rated each candidate in 1973, a perfect score was 500; in 1974, six members rated each candidate, so that a perfect score was 600. The full committee then reviewed the file and scores of each applicant and made offers of admission on a "rolling" basis. The chairman was responsible for placing names on the waiting list. They were not placed in strict numerical order; instead, the chairman had discretion to include persons with "special skills." Id., at 63-64.

The special admissions program operated with a separate committee, a majority of whom were members of minority groups. On the 1973 application form, candidates were asked to indicate whether they wished to be considered as "economically and/or educationally disadvantaged" applicants; on the 1974 form the question was whether they wished to be considered as members of a "minority group," which the Medical School apparently viewed as "Blacks," "Chicanos," "Asians," and "American Indians." If these questions were answered affirmatively, the application was forwarded to the special admissions committee. No formal definition of "disadvantaged" was ever produced, but the chairman of the special committee screened each application to see whether it reflected economic or educational deprivation. Having passed this initial hurdle, the applications then were rated by the special committee in a fashion similar to that used by the general admissions committee, except that special candidates did not have to meet the 2.5 grade point average cutoff applied to regular applicants. About one-fifth of the total number of special applicants was invited for interviews in 1973 and 1974.

From the year of the increase in class size — 1971 through 1974, the special program resulted in the admission of 21 black students, 30 Mexican-Americans, and 12 Asians, for a total of 63 minority students. Over the same period, the regular admissions program produced 1 black, 6 Mexican-Americans, and 37 Asians, for a total of 44 minority students. Although disadvantaged whites applied to the special program in large numbers, see n. 5, *supra*, none received an offer of admission through that process. Indeed, in 1974, at least, the special committee explicitly considered only "disadvantaged" special applicants who were members of one of the designated minority groups. . . .

In both years, applicants were admitted under the special program with grade point averages, MCAT scores, and benchmark scores significantly lower than Bakke's.[**]

After the second rejection, Bakke filed the instant suit in the Superior Court of California. He sought mandatory, injunctive, and declaratory relief compelling his admission to the Medical School. He alleged that the Medical School's special admissions program operated to exclude him from the school on the basis of his race, in violation of his rights under the Equal Protection Clause of the Fourteenth Amendment, Art. I, § 21, of the California Constitution, and § 601 of Title VI of the Civil Rights Act of 1964, 78 Stat. 252, 42 U.S.C. § 2000d. The University cross-complained for a declaration that its special

---

[**] The following table compares Bakke's science grade point average, overall grade point average, and MCAT scores with the average scores of regular admittees and of special admittees in both 1973 and 1974.

Class Entering in 1973
MCAT (percentiles)

	SGPA	OGPA	Verbal	Quantitative	Science	Gen. Information.
Bakke	3.44	3.46	96	94	97	72
Average of regular admittees	3.51	3.49	81	76	83	69
Average of special admittees	2.62	2.88	46	24	35	33

Class Entering in 1974
MCAT (Percentiles)

	SGPA	OGPA	Verbal	Quantitative	Science	Gen. Information
Bakke	3.44	3.46	96	94	97	72
Average of regular admittees	3.36	3.29	69	67	82	72
Average of special admittees	2.42	2.62	34	30	37	18

Applicants admitted under the special program also had benchmark scores significantly lower than many students, including Bakke, rejected under the general admissions program, even though the special rating system apparently gave credit for overcoming "disadvantage." *Id.*, at 181, 388.

admissions program was lawful. The trial court found that the special program operated as a racial quota, because minority applicants in the special program were rated only against one another. Record 388 and 16 places in the class of 100 were reserved for them. Declaring that the University could not take race into account in making admissions decisions, the trial court held the challenged program violative of the Federal Constitution, the State Constitution, and Title VI. The court refused to order Bakke's admission, however, holding that he had failed to carry his burden of proving that he would have been admitted but for the existence of the special program.

Bakke appealed from the portion of the trial court judgment denying him admission, and the University appealed from the decision that its special admissions program was unlawful and the order enjoining it from considering race in the processing of applications. The Supreme Court of California transferred the case directly from the trial court, "because of the importance of the issues involved." The California court accepted the findings of the trial court with respect to the University's program. Because the special admissions program involved a racial classification, the Supreme Court held itself bound to apply strict scrutiny. It then turned to the goals the University presented as justifying the special program. Although the court agreed that the goals of integrating the medical profession and increasing the number of physicians willing to serve members of minority groups were compelling state interests, it concluded that the special admissions program was not the least intrusive means of achieving those goals. Without passing on the state constitutional or the federal statutory grounds cited in the trial court's judgment, the California court held that the Equal Protection Clause of the Fourteenth Amendment required that "no applicant may be rejected because of his race, in favor of another who is less qualified, as measured by standards applied without regard to race."

Turning to Bakke's appeal, the court ruled that since Bakke had established that the University had discriminated against him on the basis of his race, the burden of proof shifted to the University to demonstrate that he would not have been admitted even in the absence of the special admissions program. [On] this basis, the court initially ordered a remand for the purpose of determining whether, under the newly allocated burden of proof, Bakke would have been admitted to either the 1973 or the 1974 entering class in the absence of the special admissions program. In its petition for rehearing below, however, the University conceded its inability to carry that burden.[*] The California court

---

[*] Several *amici* suggest that Bakke lacks standing, arguing that he never showed that his injury — exclusion from the Medical School — will be redressed by a favorable decision, and that the petitioner "fabricated" jurisdiction by conceding its inability to meet its burden of proof. Petitioner does not object to Bakke's standing, but inasmuch as this charge concerns our jurisdiction under Art. III, it must be considered and rejected. First, there appears to be no reason to question the petitioner's concession. It was not an attempt to stipulate to a conclusion of law or to disguise actual facts of record. Cf. Swift & Co. v. Hocking Valley R. Co., 243 U.S. 281, 37 S.Ct. 287, 61 L.Ed. 722 (1917). Second, even if Bakke had been unable to prove that he would have been admitted in the absence of the special program, it would not follow that he lacked standing. The constitutional element of standing is plaintiff's demonstration of any injury to himself that is likely to be redressed by favorable decision of his claim. Warth v. Seldin, 422 U.S. 490, 498, 95 S.Ct. 2197, 2204, 45 L.Ed.2d 243 (1975). The trial court found such an injury, apart from failure to be admitted, in the University's decision not to permit Bakke to compete for all 100 places in the class, simply because of his race. Record 323. Hence the constitutional requirements of Art. III were met. The question of Bakke's admission *vel non* is merely one of relief. Nor is it fatal to Bakke's standing that he was not a "disadvantaged" applicant. Despite the program's purported emphasis on disadvantage, it was a minority enrollment program with a secondary disadvantage element. White disadvantaged students were never considered under the special program, and the University acknowledges that its goal in devising the program was to increase minority enrollment.

thereupon amended its opinion to direct that the trial court enter judgment ordering Bakke's admission to the Medical School. That order was stayed pending review in this Court. We granted certiorari to consider the important constitutional issue.

II. A. [We] assume, only for the purposes of this case, that respondent has a right of action under Title VI. [1964 Civil Rights Act]

B. The language of § 601, 78 Stat. 252, like that of the Equal Protection Clause, is majestic in its sweep: "No person in the United States shall, on the ground of race, color, or national origin, be excluded from participation in, be denied the benefits of, or be subjected to discrimination under any program or activity receiving Federal financial assistance."

[Examination] of the voluminous legislative history of Title VI reveals a congressional intent to halt federal funding of entities that violate a prohibition of racial discrimination similar to that of the Constitution. Although isolated statements of various legislators taken out of context, can be marshaled in support of the proposition that § 601 enacted a purely color-blind scheme, without regard to the reach of the Equal Protection Clause, these comments must be read against the background of both the problem that Congress was addressing and the broader view of the statute that emerges from a full examination of the legislative debates.

[In] view of the clear legislative intent, Title VI must be held to proscribe only those racial classifications that would violate the Equal Protection Clause or the Fifth Amendment.

III.A. The parties do disagree as to the level of judicial scrutiny to be applied to the special admissions program. Petitioner argues that the court below erred in applying strict scrutiny, as this inexact term has been applied in our cases. That level of review, petitioner asserts, should be reserved for classifications that disadvantage "discrete and insular minorities." SeeUnited States v. Carolene Products Co., 304 U.S. 144, 152 n. 4, 58 S.Ct. 778, 783, 82 L.Ed. 1234 (1938). Respondent, on the other hand, contends that the California court correctly rejected the notion that the degree of judicial scrutiny accorded a particular racial or ethnic classification hinges upon membership in a discrete and insular minority and duly recognized that the "rights established [by the Fourteenth Amendment] are personal rights." Shelley v. Kraemer, 334 U.S. 1, 22, 68 S.Ct. 836, 846, 92 L.Ed. 1161 (1948).

En route to this crucial battle over the scope of judicial review, the parties fight a sharp preliminary action over the proper characterization of the special admissions program. Petitioner prefers to view it as establishing a "goal" of minority representation in the Medical School. Respondent, echoing the courts below, labels it a racial quota.

This semantic distinction is beside the point: The special admissions program is undeniably a classification based on race and ethnic background. To the extent that there existed a pool of at least minimally qualified minority applicants to fill the 16 special admissions seats, white applicants could compete only for 84 seats in the entering class, rather than the 100 open to minority applicants. Whether this limitation is described as a quota or a goal, it is a line drawn on the basis of race and ethnic status.

The guarantees of the Fourteenth Amendment extend to all persons. Its language is explicit: "No State shall . . . deny to any person within its jurisdiction the equal protection of the laws." It is settled beyond question that the "rights created by the first section of the Fourteenth Amendment are, by its terms, guaranteed to the individual. The rights established are personal rights." Shelley v. Kraemer. The guarantee of equal protection cannot mean one thing when applied to one individual and something else when applied to a person of another color. If both are not accorded the same protection, then it is not equal.

Nevertheless, petitioner argues that the court below erred in applying strict scrutiny to the special admissions program because white males, such as respondent, are not a "discrete and insular minority" requiring extraordinary protection from the majoritarian political process. Carolene Products Co., supra, 304 U.S., at 152-153 n. 4, 58 S.Ct., at 783-784. This rationale, however, has never been invoked in our decisions as a prerequisite to subjecting racial or ethnic distinctions to strict scrutiny. [Racial] and ethnic distinctions of any sort are inherently suspect and thus call for the most exacting judicial examination.

B. This perception of racial and ethnic distinctions is rooted in our Nation's constitutional and demographic history. The Court's initial view of the Fourteenth Amendment was that its "one pervading purpose" was "the freedom of the slave race, the security and firm establishment of that freedom, and the protection of the newly-made freeman and citizen from the oppressions of those who had formerly exercised dominion over him." Slaughter-House Cases, 16 Wall. 36, 71, 21 L.Ed. 394 (1873). The Equal Protection Clause, however, was "[v]irtually strangled in infancy by post-civil-war judicial reactionism." It was relegated to decades of relative desuetude while the Due Process Clause of the Fourteenth Amendment, after a short germinal period, flourished as a cornerstone in the Court's defense of property and liberty of contract. It was only as the era of substantive due process came to a close, see, e. g., Nebbia v. New York, 291 U.S. 502, 54 S.Ct. 505, 78 L.Ed. 940 (1934); West Coast Hotel Co. v. Parrish, 300 U.S. 379, 57 S.Ct. 578, 81 L.Ed. 703 (1937), that the Equal Protection Clause began to attain a genuine measure of vitality.

By that time it was no longer possible to peg the guarantees of the Fourteenth Amendment to the struggle for equality of one racial minority. During the dormancy of the Equal Protection Clause, the United States had become a Nation of minorities. Each had to struggle — and to some extent struggles still — to overcome the prejudices not of a monolithic majority, but of a "majority" composed of various minority groups of whom it was said — perhaps unfairly in many cases — that a shared characteristic was a willingness to disadvantage other groups. As the Nation filled with the stock of many lands, the reach of the Clause was gradually extended to all ethnic groups seeking protection from official discrimination. See Strauder v. West Virginia, 100 U.S. 303, 308, 25 L.Ed. 664 (1880) (Celtic Irishmen) (dictum); Yick Wo v. Hopkins, 118 U.S. 356, 6 S.Ct. 1064, 30 L.Ed. 220 (1886) (Chinese); Truax v. Raich, 239 U.S. 33, 41, 36 S.Ct. 7, 10, 60 L.Ed. 131 (1915) (Austrian resident aliens); *Korematsu, supra* (Japanese); Hernandez v. Texas, 347 U.S. 475, 74 S.Ct. 667, 98 L.Ed. 866 (1954) (Mexican-Americans). The guarantees of equal protection, said the Court in *Yick Wo,* "are universal in their application, to all persons within the territorial jurisdiction, without regard to any differences of race, of color, or of nationality; and the equal protection of the laws is a pledge of the protection of equal laws." 118 U.S., at 369, 6 S.Ct., at 1070.

Although many of the Framers of the Fourteenth Amendment conceived of its primary function as bridging the vast distance between members of the Negro race and the white "majority," *Slaughter-House Cases, supra,* the Amendment itself was framed in universal terms, without reference to color, ethnic origin, or condition of prior servitude.

[Over] the past 30 years, this Court has embarked upon the crucial mission of interpreting the Equal Protection Clause with the view of assuring to all persons "the protection of equal laws," Yick Wo, supra, 118 U.S., at 369, 6 S.Ct., at 1070, in a Nation confronting a legacy of slavery and racial discrimination. See, e. g., Shelley v. Kraemer, 334 U.S. 1, 68 S.Ct. 836, 92 L.Ed. 1161 (1948); Brown v. Board of Education, 347 U.S. 483, 74 S.Ct. 686, 98 L.Ed. 873 (1954); Hills v. Gautreaux, 425 U.S. 284, 96 S.Ct. 1538, 47 L.Ed.2d 792 (1976). Because the landmark decisions in this area arose in response to the continued exclusion of Negroes from the mainstream of American society, they could be characterized as involving discrimination by the "majority" white race against the Negro minority. But they need not be read as depending upon that characterization for their results. It suffices to say that "[o]ver the years, this Court has consistently repudiated '[d]istinctions between citizens solely because of their ancestry' as being 'odious to a free people whose institutions are founded upon the doctrine of equality.'" Loving v. Virginia, 388 U.S. 1, 11, 87 S.Ct. 1817, 1823, 18 L.Ed.2d 1010 (1967), quoting Hirabayashi, 320 U.S., at 100, 63 S.Ct., at 1385.

Petitioner urges us to adopt for the first time a more restrictive view of the Equal Protection Clause and hold that discrimination against members of the white "majority" cannot be suspect if its purpose can be characterized as "benign." The clock of our liberties, however, cannot be turned back to 1868. Brown v. Board of Education, supra, 347 U.S., at 492, 74 S.Ct., at 690; accord, Loving v. Virginia, supra, 388 U.S., at 9, 87 S.Ct., at 1822. It is far too late to argue that the guarantee of equal protection to *all* persons permits the recognition of special wards entitled to a degree of protection greater than that accorded others. "The Fourteenth Amendment is not directed solely against discrimination due to a 'two-class theory' — that is, based upon differences between 'white' and Negro." Hernandez, 347 U.S., at 478, 74 S.Ct., at 670.

Once the artificial line of a "two-class theory" of the Fourteenth Amendment is put aside, the difficulties entailed in varying the level of judicial review according to a perceived "preferred" status of a particular racial or ethnic minority are intractable. The concepts of "majority" and "minority" necessarily reflect temporary arrangements and political judgments. As observed above, the white "majority" itself is composed of various minority groups, most of which can lay claim to a history of prior discrimination at the hands of the State and private individuals. Not all of these groups can receive preferential treatment and corresponding judicial tolerance of distinctions drawn in terms of race and nationality, for then the only "majority" left would be a new minority of white Anglo-Saxon Protestants. There is no principled basis for deciding which groups would merit "heightened judicial solicitude" and which would not.[36] Courts would be asked to evaluate the extent of the prejudice and consequent harm suffered by various minority groups. Those whose societal injury is thought to exceed some arbitrary level of tolerability then would be entitled to preferential classifications at the expense of individuals belonging to other groups. Those classifications would be free from exacting judicial scrutiny. As these preferences began to have their desired effect, and the consequences of past discrimination were undone, new judicial rankings would be necessary. The kind

---

[36] As I am in agreement with the view that race may be taken into account as a factor in an admissions program, I agree with my Brothers Brennan, White, Marshall, and Blackmun that the portion of the judgment that would proscribe all consideration of race must be reversed. See Part V, *infra.* But I disagree with much that is said in their opinion.

of variable sociological and political analysis necessary to produce such rankings simply does not lie within the judicial competence — even if they otherwise were politically feasible and socially desirable.

Moreover, there are serious problems of justice connected with the idea of preference itself. First, it may not always be clear that a so-called preference is in fact benign. Courts may be asked to validate burdens imposed upon individual members of a particular group in order to advance the group's general interest. See United Jewish Organizations v. Carey, 430 U.S., at 172-173, 97 S.Ct., at 1013. (Brennan, J., concurring in part). Nothing in the Constitution supports the notion that individuals may be asked to suffer otherwise impermissible burdens in order to enhance the societal standing of their ethnic groups. Second, preferential programs may only reinforce common stereotypes holding that certain groups are unable to achieve success without special protection based on a factor having no relationship to individual worth. See DeFunis v. Odegaard, 416 U.S. 312, 343, 94 S.Ct. 1704, 1719, 40 L.Ed.2d 164 (1974) (Douglas, J., dissenting). Third, there is a measure of inequity in forcing innocent persons in respondent's position to bear the burdens of redressing grievances not of their making.

By hitching the meaning of the Equal Protection Clause to these transitory considerations, we would be holding, as a constitutional principle, that judicial scrutiny of classifications touching on racial and ethnic background may vary with the ebb and flow of political forces. Disparate constitutional tolerance of such classifications well may serve to exacerbate racial and ethnic antagonisms rather than alleviate them. United Jewish Organizations, supra, 430 U.S., at 173-174, 97 S.Ct., at 1013-1014 (Brennan, J., concurring in part). Also, the mutability of a constitutional principle, based upon shifting political and social judgments, undermines the chances for consistent application of the Constitution from one generation to the next, a critical feature of its coherent interpretation. Pollock v. Farmers' Loan & Trust Co., 157 U.S. 429, 650-651, 15 S.Ct. 673, 716, 39 L.Ed. 759 (1895) (White, J., dissenting). In expounding the Constitution, the Court's role is to discern "principles sufficiently absolute to give them roots throughout the community and continuity over significant periods of time, and to lift them above the level of the pragmatic political judgments of a particular time and place." A. Cox, The Role of the Supreme Court in American Government 114 (1976).

If it is the individual who is entitled to judicial protection against classifications based upon his racial or ethnic background because such distinctions impinge upon personal rights, rather than the individual only because of his membership in a particular group, then constitutional standards may be applied consistently. Political judgments regarding the necessity for the particular classification may be weighed in the constitutional balance, Korematsu v. United States, 323 U.S. 214, 65 S.Ct. 193, 89 L.Ed. 194 (1944), but the standard of justification will remain constant. This is as it should be, since those political judgments are the product of rough compromise struck by contending groups within the democratic process. When they touch upon an individual's race or ethnic background, he is entitled to a judicial determination that the burden he is asked to bear on that basis is precisely tailored to serve a compelling governmental interest.

C. Petitioner contends that on several occasions this Court has approved preferential classifications without applying the most exacting scrutiny. Most of the cases upon which petitioner relies are drawn from three areas: school desegregation, employment discrimination, and sex discrimination. Each of the cases cited presented a situation materially different from the facts of this case.

The school desegregation cases are inapposite. Each involved remedies for clearly determined constitutional violations. E. g., Swann v. Charlotte-Mecklenburg Board of Education, 402 U.S. 1, 91 S.Ct. 1267, 28 L.Ed.2d 554 (1971); McDaniel v. Barresi, 402 U.S. 39, 91 S.Ct. 1287, 28 L.Ed.2d 582 (1971); Green v. County School Board, 391 U.S. 430, 88 S.Ct. 1689, 20 L.Ed.2d 716 (1968). Racial classifications thus were designed as remedies for the vindication of constitutional entitlement. Moreover, the scope of the remedies was not permitted to exceed the extent of the violations. E. g., Dayton Board of Education v. Brinkman, 433 U.S. 406, 97 S.Ct. 2766, 53 L.Ed.2d 851 (1977); Milliken v. Bradley, 418 U.S. 717, 94 S.Ct. 3112, 41 L.Ed.2d 1069 (1974); see Pasadena City Board of Education v. Spangler, 427 U.S. 424, 96 S.Ct. 2697, 49 L.Ed.2d 599 (1976). Here, there was no judicial determination of constitutional violation as a predicate for the formulation of a remedial classification.

The employment discrimination cases also do not advance petitioner's cause. For example, in Franks v. Bowman Transportation Co., 424 U.S. 747, 96 S.Ct. 1251, 47 L.Ed.2d 444 (1976), we approved a retroactive award of seniority to a class of Negro truck drivers who had been the victims of discrimination — not just by society at large, but by the respondent in that case. While this relief imposed some burdens on other employees, it was held necessary "'to make [the victims] whole for injuries suffered on account of unlawful employment discrimination.'." [But] we have never approved preferential classifications in the absence of proved constitutional or statutory violations.

Nor is petitioner's view as to the applicable standard supported by the fact that gender-based classifications are not subjected to this level of scrutiny. *E.G.,* Califano v. Webster, 430 U.S. 313, 316-317, 97 S.Ct. 1192, 1194-1195, 51 L.Ed.2d 360 (1977); Craig v. Boren, 429 U.S. 190, 211, 97 S.Ct. 451, 464, 50 L.Ed.2d 397 (1976) (Powell, J., concurring). Gender-based distinctions are less likely to create the analytical and practical problems present in preferential programs premised on racial or ethnic criteria. With respect to gender there are only two possible classifications. The incidence of the burdens imposed by preferential classifications is clear. There are no rival groups which can claim that they, too, are entitled to preferential treatment. Classwide questions as to the group suffering previous injury and groups which fairly can be burdened are relatively manageable for reviewing courts. See, e. g., Califano v. Goldfarb, 430 U.S. 199, 212-217, 97 S.Ct. 1021, 1029-1032, 51 L.Ed.2d 270 (1977); Weinberger v. Wiesenfeld, 420 U.S. 636, 645, 95 S.Ct. 1225, 1231, 43 L.Ed.2d 514 (1975). The resolution of these same questions in the context of racial and ethnic preferences presents far more complex and intractable problems than gender-based classifications. More importantly, the perception of racial classifications as inherently odious stems from a lengthy and tragic history that gender-based classifications do not share. In sum, the Court has never viewed such classification as inherently suspect or as comparable to racial or ethnic classifications for the purpose of equal protection analysis.

[P]etitioner contends that our recent decision in United Jewish Organizations v. Carey, 430 U.S. 144, 97 S.Ct. 996, 51 L.Ed.2d 229 (1977), indicates a willingness to approve racial classifications designed to benefit certain minorities, without denominating the classifications as "suspect." The State of New York had redrawn its reapportionment plan to meet objections of the Department of Justice under § 5 of the Voting Rights Act of 1965, 42 U.S.C. § 1973c (1970 ed., Supp. V). Specifically, voting districts were redrawn to enhance the electoral power of certain "nonwhite" voters found to have been the victims of unlawful "dilution" under the original reapportionment plan. *United Jewish Organizations,* like *Lau,* properly is viewed as a case in which the remedy for an administrative finding of discrimination encompassed measures to improve the previously disadvantaged group's ability to participate, without excluding individuals belonging to any other group from enjoyment of the relevant opportunity — meaningful participation in the electoral process.

In this case, unlike *Lau* and *United Jewish Organizations,* there has been no determination by the legislature or a responsible administrative agency that the University engaged in a discriminatory practice requiring remedial efforts. Moreover, the operation of petitioner's special admissions program is quite different from the remedial measures approved in those cases. It prefers the designated minority groups at the expense of other individuals who are totally foreclosed from competition for the 16 special admissions seats in every Medical School class. Because of that foreclosure, some individuals are excluded from enjoyment of a state-provided benefit — admission to the Medical School — they otherwise would receive. When a classification denies an individual opportunities or benefits enjoyed by others solely because of his race or ethnic background, it must be regarded as suspect. E. g., McLaurin v. Oklahoma State Regents, 339 U.S., at 641-642, 70 S.Ct., at 853-854.

IV. We have held that in "order to justify the use of a suspect classification, a State must show that its purpose or interest is both constitutionally permissible and substantial, and that its use of the classification is 'necessary . . . to the accomplishment' of its purpose or the safeguarding of its interest." In re Griffiths, 413 U.S. 717, 721-722, 93 S.Ct. 2851, 2855, 37 L.Ed.2d 910 (1973) (footnotes omitted); Loving v. Virginia, 388 U.S., at 11, 87 S.Ct., at 1823; McLaughlin v. Florida, 379 U.S. 184, 196, 85 S.Ct. 283, 290, 13 L.Ed.2d 222 (1964). The special admissions program purports to serve the purposes of: (i) "reducing the historic deficit of traditionally disfavored minorities in medical schools and in the medical profession," Brief for Petitioner 32; (ii) countering the effects of societal discrimination; (iii) increasing the number of physicians who will practice in communities currently underserved; and (iv) obtaining the educational benefits that flow from an ethnically diverse student body. It is necessary to decide which, if any, of these purposes is substantial enough to support the use of a suspect classification.

A. If petitioner's purpose is to assure within its student body some specified percentage of a particular group merely because of its race or ethnic origin, such a preferential purpose must be rejected not as insubstantial but as facially invalid. Preferring members of any one group for no reason other than race or ethnic origin is discrimination for its own sake. This the Constitution forbids. *E. g.,* Loving v. Virginia, supra, 388 U.S., at 11, 87 S.Ct., at 1823; McLaughlin v. Florida, supra, 379 U.S., at 196, 85 S.Ct., at 290; Brown v. Board of Education, 347 U.S. 483, 74 S.Ct. 686, 98 L.Ed. 873 (1954).

B. The State certainly has a legitimate and substantial interest in ameliorating, or eliminating where feasible, the disabling effects of identified discrimination. The line of school desegregation cases, commencing with *Brown,* attests to the importance of this state goal and the commitment of the judiciary to affirm all lawful means toward its attainment. In the school cases, the States were required by court order to redress the wrongs worked by specific instances of racial discrimination. That goal was far more focused than the remedying of the effects of "societal discrimination," an amorphous concept of injury that may be ageless in its reach into the past.

We have never approved a classification that aids persons perceived as members of relatively victimized groups at the expense of other innocent individuals in the absence of judicial, legislative, or administrative findings of constitutional or statutory violations. After such findings have been made, the governmental interest in preferring members of the injured groups at the expense of others is substantial, since the legal rights of the victims must be vindicated. In such a case, the extent of the injury and the consequent remedy will have been judicially, legislatively, or administratively defined. Also, the remedial action usually remains subject to continuing oversight to assure that it will work the least harm possible to other innocent persons competing for the benefit. Without such findings of constitutional or statutory violations, it cannot be said that the government has any greater interest in helping one individual than in refraining from harming another. Thus, the government has no compelling justification for inflicting such harm.

Petitioner does not purport to have made, and is in no position to make, such findings. Its broad mission is education, not the formulation of any legislative policy or the adjudication of particular claims of illegality. For reasons similar to those stated in Part III of this opinion, isolated segments of our vast governmental structures are not competent to make those decisions, at least in the absence of legislative mandates and legislatively determined criteria. Cf. Hampton v. Mow Sun Wong, 426 U.S. 88, 96 S.Ct. 1895, 48 L.Ed.2d 495 (1976) Before relying upon these sorts of findings in establishing a racial classification, a governmental body must have the authority and capability to establish, in the record, that the classification is responsive to identified discrimination. See, e. g., Califano v. Webster, 430 U.S., at 316-321, 97 S.Ct., at 1194-1197; Califano v. Goldfarb, 430 U.S., at 212-217, 97 S.Ct., at 1029-1032. Lacking this capability, petitioner has not carried its burden of justification on this issue.

Hence, the purpose of helping certain groups whom the faculty of the Davis Medical School perceived as victims of "societal discrimination" does not justify a classification that imposes disadvantages upon persons like respondent, who bear no responsibility for whatever harm the beneficiaries of the special admissions program are thought to have suffered. To hold otherwise would be to convert a remedy heretofore reserved for violations of legal rights into a privilege that all institutions throughout the Nation could grant at their pleasure to whatever groups are perceived as victims of societal discrimination. That is a step we have never approved. Cf. Pasadena City Board of Education v. Spangler, 427 U.S. 424, 96 S.Ct. 2697, 49 L.Ed.2d 599 (1976).

C. Petitioner identifies, as another purpose of its program, improving the delivery of health-care services to communities currently underserved. It may be assumed that in some situations a State's interest in facilitating the health care of its citizens is sufficiently compelling to support the use of a suspect classification. But there is virtually no evidence in the record indicating that petitioner's special admissions program is either needed or geared to promote that goal.

D. The fourth goal asserted by petitioner is the attainment of a diverse student body. This clearly is a constitutionally permissible goal for an institution of higher education. Academic freedom, though not a specifically enumerated constitutional right, long has been viewed as a special concern of the First Amendment. The freedom of a university to make its own judgments as to education includes the selection of its student body.

[The] atmosphere of "speculation, experiment and creation" — so essential to the quality of higher education — is widely believed to be promoted by a diverse student body. As the Court noted in *Keyishian*, it is not too much to say that the "nation's future depends upon leaders trained through wide exposure" to the ideas and mores of students as diverse as this Nation of many peoples.

Thus, in arguing that its universities must be accorded the right to select those students who will contribute the most to the "robust exchange of ideas," petitioner invokes a countervailing constitutional interest, that of the First Amendment. In this light, petitioner must be viewed as seeking to achieve a goal that is of paramount importance in the fulfillment of its mission.

It may be argued that there is greater force to these views at the undergraduate level than in a medical school where the training is centered primarily on professional competency. But even at the graduate level, our tradition and experience lend support to the view that the contribution of diversity is substantial. In Sweatt v. Painter, 339 U.S., at 634, 70 S.Ct., at 850, the Court made a similar point with specific reference to legal education:

> "The law school, the proving ground for legal learning and practice, cannot be effective in isolation from the individuals and institutions with which the law interacts. Few students and no one who has practiced law would choose to study in an academic vacuum, removed from the interplay of ideas and the exchange of views with which the law is concerned." Physicians serve a heterogeneous population. An otherwise qualified medical student with a particular background — whether it be ethnic, geographic, culturally advantaged or disadvantaged — may bring to a professional school of medicine experiences, outlooks, and ideas that enrich the training of its student body and better equip its graduates to render with understanding their vital service to humanity.

Ethnic diversity, however, is only one element in a range of factors a university properly may consider in attaining the goal of a heterogeneous student body. Although a university must have wide discretion in making the sensitive judgments as to who should be admitted, constitutional limitations protecting individual rights may not be disregarded. Respondent urges — and the courts below have held — that petitioner's dual admissions program is a racial classification that impermissibly infringes his rights under the Fourteenth Amendment. As the interest of diversity is compelling in the context of a university's admissions program, the question remains whether the program's racial classification is necessary to promote this interest.

V.A. It may be assumed that the reservation of a specified number of seats in each class for individuals from the preferred ethnic groups would contribute to the attainment of considerable ethnic diversity in the student body. But petitioner's argument that this is the only effective means of serving the interest of diversity is seriously flawed. In a most fundamental sense the argument misconceives the nature of the state interest that would justify consideration of race or ethnic background. It is not an interest in simple ethnic diversity, in which a specified percentage of the student body is in effect guaranteed to be members of selected ethnic groups, with the remaining percentage an undifferentiated aggregation of students. The diversity that furthers a compelling state interest encompasses a far broader array of qualifications and characteristics of which racial or ethnic origin is but a single though important element. Petitioner's special admissions program, focused *solely* on ethnic diversity, would hinder rather than further attainment of genuine diversity.

Nor would the state interest in genuine diversity be served by expanding petitioner's two-track system into a multitrack program with a prescribed number of seats set aside for each identifiable category of applicants. Indeed, it is inconceivable that a university would thus pursue the logic of petitioner's two-track program to the illogical end of insulating each category of applicants with certain desired qualifications from competition with all other applicants.

The experience of other university admissions programs, which take race into account in achieving the educational diversity valued by the First Amendment, demonstrates that the assignment of a fixed number of places to a minority group is not a necessary means toward that end. An illuminating example is found in the Harvard College program:

> "In recent years Harvard College has expanded the concept of diversity to include students from disadvantaged economic, racial and ethnic groups. Harvard College now recruits not only Californians or Louisianans but also blacks and Chicanos and other minority students. . . .
> "In practice, this new definition of diversity has meant that race has been a factor in some admission decisions. When the Committee on Admissions reviews the large middle group of applicants who are 'admissible' and deemed capable of doing good work in their courses, the race of an applicant may tip the balance in his favor just as geographic origin or a life spent on a farm may tip the balance in other candidates' cases. A farm boy from Idaho can bring something to Harvard College that a Bostonian cannot offer. Similarly, a black student can usually bring something that a white person cannot offer. [See Appendix hereto.] . . .
> "In Harvard College admissions the Committee has not set target-quotas for the number of blacks, or of musicians, football players, physicists or Californians to be admitted in a given year. . . . But that awareness [of the necessity of including more than a token number of black students] does not mean that the Committee sets a minimum number of blacks or of people from west of the Mississippi who are to be admitted. It means only that in choosing among thousands of applicants who are not only 'admissible' academically but have other strong qualities, the Committee, with a number of criteria in mind, pays some attention to distribution among many types and categories of students." App. to Brief for Columbia University, Harvard University, Stanford University, and the University of Pennsylvania, as *Amici Curiae* 2-3.

In such an admissions program, race or ethnic background may be deemed a "plus" in a particular applicant's file, yet it does not insulate the individual from comparison with all other candidates for the available seats. The file of a particular black applicant may be examined for his potential contribution to diversity without the factor of race being decisive when compared, for example, with that of an applicant identified as an Italian-American if the latter is thought to exhibit qualities more likely to promote beneficial educational pluralism. Such qualities could include exceptional personal talents, unique work or service experience, leadership potential, maturity, demonstrated compassion, a history of overcoming disadvantage, ability to communicate with the poor, or other qualifications deemed important. In short, an admissions program operated in this way is flexible enough to consider all pertinent elements of diversity in light of the particular qualifications of each applicant, and to place them on the same footing for consideration, although not necessarily according them the same weight. Indeed, the weight attributed to a particular quality may vary from year to year depending upon the "mix" both of the student body and the applicants for the incoming class.

This kind of program treats each applicant as an individual in the admissions process. The applicant who loses out on the last available seat to another candidate receiving a "plus" on the basis of ethnic background will not have been foreclosed from all consideration for that seat simply because he was not the right color or had the wrong surname. It would mean only that his combined qualifications, which may have included similar nonobjective factors, did not outweigh those of the other applicant. His qualifications would have been weighed fairly and competitively, and he would have no basis to complain of unequal treatment under the Fourteenth Amendment.

It has been suggested that an admissions program which considers race only as one factor is simply a subtle and more sophisticated — but no less effective — means of according racial preference than the Davis program. A facial intent to discriminate, however, is evident in petitioner's preference program and not denied in this case. No such facial infirmity exists in an admissions program where race or ethnic background is simply one element — to be weighedfairly against other elements — in the selection process. "A boundary line," as Mr. Justice Frankfurter remarked in another connection, "is none the worse for being narrow." McLeod v. Dilworth, 322 U.S. 327, 329, 64 S.Ct. 1023, 1025, 88 L.Ed. 1304 (1944). And a court would not assume that a university, professing to employ a facially nondiscriminatory admissions policy, would operate it as a cover for the functional equivalent of a quota system. In short, good faith would be presumed in the absence of a showing to the contrary in the manner permitted by our cases. See e. g., Arlington Heights v. Metropolitan Housing Dev. Corp., 429 U.S. 252, 97 S.Ct. 555, 50 L.Ed.2d 450 (1977); Washington v. Davis, 426 U.S. 229, 96 S.Ct. 2040, 48 L.Ed.2d 597 (1976); Swain v. Alabama, 380 U.S. 202, 85 S.Ct. 824, 13 L.Ed.2d 759 (1965).

B. In summary, it is evident that the Davis special admissions program involves the use of an explicit racial classification never before countenanced by this Court. It tells applicants who are not Negro, Asian, or Chicano that they are totally excluded from a specific percentage of the seats in an entering class. No matter how strong their qualifications, quantitative and extracurricular, including their own potential for contribution to educational diversity, they are never afforded the chance to compete with applicants from the preferred groups for the special admissions seats. At the same time, the preferred applicants have the opportunity to compete for every seat in the class.

The fatal flaw in petitioner's preferential program is its disregard of individual rights as guaranteed by the Fourteenth Amendment. Shelley v. Kraemer, 334 U.S., at 22, 68 S.Ct., at 846. Such rights are not absolute. But when a State's distribution of benefits or imposition of burdens hinges on ancestry or the color of a person's skin, that individual is entitled to a demonstration that the challenged classification is necessary to promote a substantial state interest. Petitioner has failed to carry this burden. For this reason, that portion of the California court's judgment holding petitioner's special admissions program invalid under the Fourteenth Amendment must be affirmed.

C. In enjoining petitioner from ever considering the race of any applicant, however, the courts below failed to recognize that the State has a substantial interest that legitimately may be served by a properly devised admissions program involving the competitive consideration of race and ethnic origin. For this reason, so much of the California court's judgment as enjoins petitioner from any consideration of the race of any applicant must be reversed.

VI. With respect to respondent's entitlement to an injunction directing his admission to the Medical School, petitioner has conceded that it could not carry its burden of proving that, but for the existence of its unlawful special admissions program, respondent still would not have been admitted. Hence, respondent is entitled to the injunction, and that portion of the judgment must be affirmed.

Opinion of Mr. Justice BRENNAN, Mr. Justice WHITE, Mr. Justice MARSHALL, and Mr. Justice BLACKMUN, concurring in the judgment in part and dissenting in part.

The Court today, in reversing in part the judgment of the Supreme Court of California, affirms the constitutional power of Federal and State Governments to act affirmatively to achieve equal opportunity for all. The [T]he difficulty of the issue presented — whether government may use race-conscious programs to redress the continuing effects of past discrimination — and the mature consideration which each of our Brethren has brought to it have resulted in many opinions, no single one speaking for the Court. But this should not and must not mask the central meaning of today's opinions: Government may take race into account when it acts not to demean or insult any racial group, but to remedy disadvantages cast on minorities by past racial prejudice, at least when appropriate findings have been made by judicial, legislative, or administrative bodies with competence to act in this area.

The Chief Justice and our Brothers Stewart, Rehnquist, and Stevens, have concluded that Title VI of the Civil Rights Act of 1964, 78 Stat. 252, as amended, 42 U.S.C. § 2000d *et seq.*, prohibits programs such as that at the Davis Medical School. On this statutory theory alone, they would hold that respondent Allan Bakke's rights have been violated and that he must, therefore, be admitted to the Medical School. Our Brother Powell, reaching the Constitution, concludes that, although race may be taken into account in university admissions, the particular special admissions program used by petitioner, which resulted in the exclusion of respondent Bakke, was not shown to be necessary to achieve petitioner's stated goals. Accordingly, these Members of the Court form a majority of five affirming the judgment of the Supreme Court of California insofar as it holds that respondent Bakke "is entitled to an order that he be admitted to the University.

We agree with Mr. Justice Powell that, as applied to the case before us, Title VI goes no further in prohibiting the use of race than the Equal Protection Clause of the Fourteenth Amendment itself. We also agree that the effect of the California Supreme Court's affirmance of the judgment of the Superior Court of California would be to prohibit the University from establishing in the future affirmative-action programs that take race into account. See *ante*, at 2738 n. **. Since we conclude that the affirmative admissions program at the Davis Medical School is constitutional, we would reverse the judgment below in all respects. Mr. Justice Powell agrees that some uses of race in university admissions are permissible and, therefore, he joins with us to make five votes reversing the judgment below insofar as it prohibits the University from establishing race-conscious programs in the future.[1]

---

[1] We also agree with Mr. Justice Powell that a plan like the "Harvard" plan, see *ante*, at 2762-2763, is constitutional under our approach, at least so long as the use of race to achieve an integrated student body is necessitated by the lingering effects of past discrimination.

I. Our Nation was founded on the principle that "all Men are created equal." Yet candor requires acknowledgment that the Framers of our Constitution, to forge the 13 Colonies into one Nation, openly compromised this principle of equality with its antithesis: slavery. The consequences of this compromise are well known and have aptly been called our "American Dilemma." Still, it is well to recount how recent the time has been, if it has yet come, when the promise of our principles has flowered into the actuality of equal opportunity for all regardless of race or color.

The Fourteenth Amendment, the embodiment in the Constitution of our abiding belief in human equality, has been the law of our land for only slightly more than half its 200 years. Worse than desuetude, the Clause was early turned against those whom it was intended to set free, condemning them to a "separate but equal" status before the law, a status always separate but seldom equal. Not until 1954 — only 24 years ago — was this odious doctrine interred by our decision in Brown v. Board of Education, 347 U.S. 483, 74 S.Ct. 686, 98 L.Ed. 873 (Brown I), and its progeny, which proclaimed that separate schools and public facilities of all sorts were inherently unequal and forbidden under our Constitution. Even then inequality was not eliminated with "all deliberate speed." Brown v. Board of Education, 349 U.S. 294, 301, 75 S.Ct. 753, 756, 99 L.Ed. 1083 (1955). In 1968 and again in 1971, for example, we were forced to remind school boards of their obligation to eliminate racial discrimination root and branch. And a glance at our docket and at dockets of lower courts will show that even today officially sanctioned discrimination is not a thing of the past.

Against this background, claims that law must be "color-blind" or that the datum of race is no longer relevant to public policy must be seen as aspiration rather than as description of reality. This is not to denigrate aspiration; for reality rebukes us that race has too often been used by those who would stigmatize and oppress minorities. Yet we cannot — and, as we shall demonstrate, need not under our Constitution or Title VI, which merely extends the constraints of the Fourteenth Amendment to private parties who receive federal funds — let color blindness become myopia which masks the reality that many "created equal" have been treated within our lifetimes as inferior both by the law and by their fellow citizens.

II. In our view, Title VI prohibits only those uses of racial criteria that would violate the Fourteenth Amendment if employed by a State or its agencies; it does not bar the preferential treatment of racial minorities as a means of remedying past societal discrimination to the extent that such action is consistent with the Fourteenth Amendment. The legislative history of Title VI, administrative regulations interpreting the statute, subsequent congressional and executive action, and the prior decisions of this Court compel this conclusion. None of these sources lends support to the proposition that Congress intended to bar all race-conscious efforts to extend the benefits of federally financed programs to minorities who have been historically excluded from the full benefits of American life.

We turn, therefore, to our analysis of the Equal Protection Clause of the Fourteenth Amendment.

III.A. The assertion of human equality is closely associated with the proposition that differences in color or creed, birth or status, are neither significant nor relevant to the way in which persons should be treated. Nonetheless, the position that such factors must be "constitutionally an irrelevance," Edwards v. California, 314 U.S. 160, 185, 62 S.Ct. 164,

172, 86 L.Ed. 119 (1941) (Jackson, J., concurring), summed up by the shorthand phrase "[o]ur Constitution is color-blind," Plessy v. Ferguson, 163 U.S. 537, 559, 16 S.Ct. 1138, 1146, 41 L.Ed. 256 (1896) (Harlan, J., dissenting), has never been adopted by this Court as the proper meaning of the Equal Protection Clause. In deed, we have expressly rejected this proposition on a number of occasions.

Our cases have always implied that an "overriding statutory purpose," McLaughlin v. Florida, 379 U.S. 184, 192, 85 S.Ct. 283, 288, 13 L.Ed.2d 222 (1964), could be found that would justify racial classifications. See, *e. g., ibid.;* Loving v. Virginia, 388 U.S. 1, 11, 87 S.Ct. 1817, 1823, 18 L.Ed.2d 1010 (1967); Korematsu v. United States, 323 U.S. 214, 216, 65 S.Ct. 193, 194, 89 L.Ed. 194 (1944); Hirabayashi v. United States, 320 U.S. 81, 100-101, 63 S.Ct. 1375, 1385-1386, 87 L.Ed. 1774 (1943). More recently, in McDaniel v. Barresi, 402 U.S. 39, 91 S.Ct. 1287, 28 L.Ed.2d 582 (1971), this Court unanimously reversed the Georgia Supreme Court which had held that a desegregation plan voluntarily adopted by a local school board, which assigned students on the basis of race, was *per se* invalid because it was not color-blind. And in *North Carolina Board of Education v. Swann* we held, again unanimously, that a statute mandating color-blind school-assignment plans could not stand "against the background of segregation," since such a limit on remedies would "render illusory the promise of *Brown [I]*." 402 U.S., at 45-46, 91 S.Ct., at 1286.

We conclude, therefore, that racial classifications are not *per se* invalid under the Fourteenth Amendment. Accordingly, we turn to the problem of articulating what our role should be in reviewing state action that expressly classifies by race.

B. Respondent argues that racial classifications are always suspect and, consequently, that this Court should weigh the importance of the objectives served by Davis' special admissions program to see if they are compelling. In addition, he asserts that this Court must inquire whether, in its judgment, there are alternatives to racial classifications which would suit Davis' purposes. Petitioner, on the other hand, states that our proper role is simply to accept petitioner's determination that the racial classifications used by its program are reasonably related to what it tells us are its benign purposes. We reject petitioner's view, but, because our prior cases are in many respects inapposite to that before us now, we find it necessary to define with precision the meaning of that inexact term, "strict scrutiny."

Unquestionably we have held that a government practice or statute which restricts "fundamental rights" or which contains "suspect classifications" is to be subjected to "strict scrutiny" and can be justified only if it furthers a compelling government purpose and, even then, only if no less restrictive alternative is available. See, e. g., San Antonio Independent School District v. Rodriguez, 411 U.S. 1, 16-17, 93 S.Ct. 1278, 1287-1288, 36 L.Ed.2d 16 (1973); Dunn v. Blumstein, 405 U.S. 330, 92 S.Ct. 995, 31 L.Ed.2d 274 (1972). But no fundamental right is involved here. See San Antonio, supra, 411 U.S., at 29-36, 93 S.Ct., at 1294-1298. Nor do whites as a class have any of the "traditional indicia of suspectness: the class is not saddled with such disabilities, or subjected to such a history of purposeful unequal treatment, or relegated to such a position of political powerlessness as to command extraordinary protection from the majoritarian political process." Id., at 28, 93 S.Ct., at 1294; see United States v. Carolene Products Co., 304 U.S. 144, 152 n. 4, 58 S.Ct. 778, 783, 82 L.Ed. 1234 (1938).[31]

Moreover, if the University's representations are credited, this is not a case where racial classifications are "irrelevant and therefore prohibited." Hirabayashi, supra, 320 U.S., at 100, 63 S.Ct., at 1385. Nor has anyone suggested that the University's purposes contravene the cardinal principle that racial classifications that stigmatize — because they are drawn on the presumption that one race is inferior to another or because they put the weight of government behind racial hatred and separatism — are invalid without more.

On the other hand, the fact that this case does not fit neatly into our prior analytic framework for race cases does not mean that it should be analyzed by applying the very loose rational-basis standard of review that is the very least that is always applied in equal protection cases. "'[T]he mere recitation of a benign, compensatory purpose is not an automatic shield which protects against any inquiry into the actual purposes underlying a statutory scheme.'" Califano v. Webster, 430 U.S. 313, 317, 97 S.Ct. 1192, 1194, 51 L.Ed.2d 360 (1977), quoting Weinberger v. Wiesenfeld, 420 U.S. 636, 648, 95 S.Ct. 1225, 1233, 43 L.Ed.2d 514 (1975). Instead, a number of considerations — developed in gender-discrimination cases but which carry even more force when applied to racial classifications — lead us to conclude that racial classifications designed to further remedial purposes "'must serve important governmental objectives and must be substantially related to achievement of those objectives.'" Califano v. Webster, supra, 430 U.S., at 317, 97 S.Ct., at 1194, quoting Craig v. Boren, 429 U.S. 190, 197, 97 S.Ct. 451, 457, 50 L.Ed.2d 397 (1976).[35]

> But, were we asked to decide whether any given rival group — German-Americans for example — must constitutionally be accorded preferential treatment, we do have a "principled basis," ante, at 2751, for deciding this question, one that is well established in our cases: The Davis program expressly sets out four classes which receive preferred status. Ante, at 2740. The program clearly distinguishes whites, but one cannot reason from this a conclusion that German-Americans, as a national group, are singled out for invidious treatment. And even if the Davis program had a differential impact on German-Americans, they would have no constitutional claim unless they could prove that Davis intended invidiously to discriminate against German-Americans. See Arlington Heights v. Metropolitan Housing Dev. Corp., 429 U.S. 252, 264-265, 97 S.Ct. 555, 562-563, 50 L.Ed.2d 450 (1977); Washington v. Davis, 426 U.S. 229, 238-241, 96 S.Ct. 2040, 2046, 2048, 48 L.Ed.2d 597 (1976). If this could not be shown, then "the principle that calls for the closest scrutiny of distinctions in laws *denying* fundamental rights . . . is inapplicable," Katzenbach v. Morgan, 384 U.S. 641, 657, 86 S.Ct. 1717, 1727, 16 L.Ed.2d 828 (1966), and the only question is whether it was rational for Davis to conclude that the groups it preferred had a greater claim to compensation than the groups it excluded. See

---

[31] Of course, the fact that whites constitute a political majority in our Nation does not necessarily mean that active judicial scrutiny of racial classifications that disadvantage whites is inappropriate. Cf. Castaneda v. Partida, 430 U.S. 482, 499-500, 97 S.Ct. 1272, 1282-1283, 51 L.Ed.2d 498 (1977); id., at 501, 97 S.Ct., at 1283 (Marshall, J., concurring).

[35] We disagree with our Brother POWELL's suggestion, ante, at 2755, that the presence of "rival groups which can claim that they, too, are entitled to preferential treatment" distinguishes the gender cases or is relevant to the question of scope of judicial review of race classifications. We are not asked to determine whether groups other than those favored by the Davis program should similarly be favored. All we are asked to do is to pronounce the constitutionality of what Davis has done.

ibid.; San Antonio Independent School District v. Rodriquez, 411 U.S. 1, 38-39, 93 S.Ct. 1278, 1299-1300, 36 L.Ed.2d 16 (1973) (applying *Katzenbach* test to state action intended to remove discrimination in educational opportunity). Thus, claims of rival groups, although they may create thorny political problems, create relatively simple problems for the courts.

First, race, like, "gender-based classifications too often [has] been inexcusably utilized to stereotype and stigmatize politically powerless segments of society." Kahn v. Shevin, 416 U.S. 351, 357, 94 S.Ct. 1734, 1738, 40 L.Ed.2d 189 (1974) (dissenting opinion). [Second], race, like gender and illegitimacy, see Weber v. Aetna Casualty & Surety Co., 406 U.S. 164, 92 S.Ct. 1400, 31 L.Ed.2d 768 (1972), is an immutable characteristic which its possessors are powerless to escape or set aside.

[In sum], because of the significant risk that racial classifications established for ostensibly benign purposes can be misused, causing effects not unlike those created by invidious classifications, it is inappropriate to inquire only whether there is any conceivable basis that might sustain such a classification. Instead, to justify such a classification an important and articulated purpose for its use must be shown. In addition, any statute must be stricken that stigmatizes any group or that singles out those least well represented in the political process to bear the brunt of a benign program. Thus, our review under the Fourteenth Amendment should be strict — not "'strict' in theory and fatal in fact," because it is stigma that causes fatality — but strict and searching nonetheless.

IV. Davis' articulated purpose of remedying the effects of past societal discrimination is, under our cases, sufficiently important to justify the use of race-conscious admissions programs where there is a sound basis for concluding that minority underrepresentation is substantial and chronic, and that the handicap of past discrimination is impeding access of minorities to the Medical School.

A. At least since Green v. County School Board, 391 U.S. 430, 88 S.Ct. 1689, 20 L.Ed.2d 716 (1968), it has been clear that a public body which has itself been adjudged to have engaged in racial discrimination cannot bring itself into compliance with the Equal Protection Clause simply by ending its unlawful acts and adopting a neutral stance. Three years later, Swann v. Charlotte-Mecklenburg Board of Education, 402 U.S. 1, 91 S.Ct. 1267, 28 L.Ed.2d 554 (1971), and its companion cases, Davis v. School Comm'rs of Mobile County, 402 U.S. 33, 91 S.Ct. 1289, 28 L.Ed.2d 577 (1971); McDaniel v. Barresi, 402 U.S. 39, 91 S.Ct. 1287, 28 L.Ed.2d 582 (1971), and North Carolina Board of Education v. Swann, 402 U.S. 43, 91 S.Ct. 1284, 28 L.Ed.2d 586 (1971), reiterated that racially neutral remedies for past discrimination were inadequate where consequences of past discriminatory acts influence or control present decisions. See, e. g., Charlotte-Mecklenburg, supra, 402 U.S., at 28, 91 S.Ct., at 1282. And the Court further held both that courts could enter desegregation orders which assigned students and faculty by reference to race, Charlotte-Mecklenburg, supra; Davis, supra; United States v. Montgomery County Board of Ed., 395 U.S. 225, 89 S.Ct. 1670, 23 L.Ed.2d 263 (1969), and that local school boards could *voluntarily* adopt desegregation plans which made express reference to race if this was necessary to remedy the effects of past discrimination. *McDaniel v. Barresi, supra.* Moreover, we stated that school boards, even in the absence of a judicial finding of past discrimination, could voluntarily adopt plans which assigned students with the end of creating racial pluralism by establishing fixed ratios of black and white students in each school. Charlotte-Mecklenburg, supra, 402 U.S., at 16, 91 S.Ct., at 1276.

In each instance, the creation of unitary school systems, in which the effects of past discrimination had been "eliminated root and branch," Green, supra, 391 U.S., at 438, 88 S.Ct., at 1694, was recognized as a compelling social goal justifying the overt use of race.

Finally, the conclusion that state educational institutions may constitutionally adopt admissions programs designed to avoid exclusion of historically disadvantaged minorities, even when such programs explicitly take race into account, finds direct support in our cases construing congressional legislation designed to overcome the present effects of past discrimination. Congress can and has outlawed actions which have a disproportionately adverse and unjustified impact upon members of racial minorities and has required or authorized race-conscious action to put individuals disadvantaged by such impact in the position they otherwise might have enjoyed. See Franks v. Bowman Transportation Co., 424 U.S. 747, 96 S.Ct. 1251, 47 L.Ed.2d 444 (1976); Teamsters v. United States, 431 U.S. 324, 97 S.Ct. 1843, 52 L.Ed.2d 396 (1977). Such relief does not require as a predicate proof that recipients of preferential advancement have been individually discriminated against; it is enough that each recipient is within a general class of persons likely to have been the victims of discrimination. See id., at 357-362, 97 S.Ct., at 1865-1868. Nor is it an objection to such relief that preference for minorities will upset the settled expectations of nonminorities. See Franks, supra. In addition, we have held that Congress, to remove barriers to equal opportunity, can and has required employers to use test criteria that fairly reflect the qualifications of minority applicants vis-à-vis nonminority applicants, even if this means interpreting the qualifications of an applicant in light of his race. See Albemarle Paper Co. v. Moody, 422 U.S. 405, 435, 95 S.Ct. 2362, 2380, 45 L.Ed.2d 280 (1975).

These cases cannot be distinguished simply by the presence of judicial findings of discrimination, for race-conscious remedies have been approved where such findings have not been made. McDaniel v. Barresi, supra; UJO; seeCalifano V. Webster, 430 U.S. 313, 97 S.Ct. 1192, 51 L.Ed.2d 360 (1977); Schlesinger v. Ballard, 419 U.S. 498, 95 S.Ct. 572, 42 L.Ed.2d 610 (1975); Kahn v. Shevin, 416 U.S. 351, 94 S.Ct. 1734, 40 L.Ed.2d 189 (1974). See also Katzenbach v. Morgan, 384 U.S. 641, 86 S.Ct. 1717, 16 L.Ed.2d 828 (1966). Indeed, the requirement of a judicial determination of a constitutional or statutory violation as a predicate for race-conscious remedial actions would be self-defeating. Such a requirement would severely undermine efforts to achieve voluntary compliance with the requirements of law. And our society and jurisprudence have always stressed the value of voluntary efforts to further the objectives of the law. Judicial intervention is a last resort to achieve cessation of illegal conduct or the remedying of its effects rather than a prerequisite to action.

Nor can our cases be distinguished on the ground that the entity using explicit racial classifications itself had violated § 1 of the Fourteenth Amendment or an antidiscrimination regulation, for again race-conscious remedies have been approved where this is not the case. See UJO, 430 U.S., at 157, 97 S.Ct., at 1005 (opinion of White, J., joined by Brennan, Blackmun, and Stevens, JJ.); id., at 167, 97 S.Ct., at 1010 (opinion of White, J., joined by Rehnquist and Stevens, JJ.); cf. Califano v. Webster, supra, 430 U.S., at 317, 97 S.Ct., at 1194; Kahn v. Shevin, supra. Moreover, the presence or absence of past discrimination by universities or employers is largely irrelevant to resolving respondent's constitutional claims. The claims of those burdened by the race-conscious actions of a university or employer who has never been adjudged in violation of an antidiscrimination law are not any more or less entitled to deference than the claims of the burdened nonminority workers in Franks v. Bowman Transportation Co., supra, in which the employer had violated Title VII, for in each case the employees are innocent of past discrimination. And, although it might be argued that, where an employer has violated an antidiscrimination law, the expectations of nonminority workers are themselves products of discrimination and hence "tainted," see Franks, supra, at 776, 96 S.Ct., at 1270, and therefore more easily upset, the same argument can be made with respect to respondent. If it was reasonable to conclude — as we hold that it was — that the failure of minorities to qualify for admission at Davis under regular procedures was due principally to the effects of past discrimination, then there is a reasonable likelihood that, but for pervasive racial discrimination, respondent would have failed to qualify for admission even in the absence of Davis' special admissions program.

Thus, our cases under Title VII of the Civil Rights Act have held that, in order to achieve minority participation in previously segregated areas of public life, Congress may require or authorize preferential treatment for those likely disadvantaged by societal racial discrimination. Such legislation has been sustained even without a requirement of findings of intentional racial discrimination by those required or authorized to accord preferential treatment, or a case-by-case determination that those to be benefited suffered from racial discrimination. These decisions compel the conclusion that States also may adopt race-conscious programs designed to overcome substantial, chronic minority underrepresentation where there is reason to believe that the evil addressed is a product of past racial discrimination.[42]

[Nothing] whatever in the legislative history of either the Fourteenth Amendment or the Civil Rights Acts even remotely suggests that the States are foreclosed from furthering the fundamental purpose of equal opportunity to which the Amendment and those

---

[42] We do not understand Mr. Justice Powell to disagree that providing a remedy for past racial prejudice can constitute a compelling purpose sufficient to meet strict scrutiny. See *ante,* at 2756. Yet, because petitioner is a corporation administering a university, he would not allow it to exercise such power in the absence of "judicial, legislative, or administrative findings of constitutional or statutory violations." *Ante,* at 2758. While we agree that reversal in this case would follow *a fortiori* had Davis been guilty of invidious racial discrimination or if a federal statute mandated that universities refrain from applying any admissions policy that had a disparate and unjustified racial impact, see, e. g., McDaniel v. Barresi, 402 U.S. 39, 91 S.Ct. 1287, 28 L.Ed.2d 582 (1971); Franks v. Bowman Transportation Co., 424 U.S. 747, 96 S.Ct. 1251, 47 L.Ed.2d 444 (1976), we do not think it of constitutional significance that Davis has not been so adjudged.

Generally, the manner in which a State chooses to delegate governmental functions is for it to decide. Cf. Sweezy v. New Hampshire, 354 U.S. 234, 256, 77 S.Ct. 1203, 1 L.Ed.2d 1311 (1957) (Frankfurter, J., concurring in result). California, by constitutional provision, has chosen to place authority over the operation of the University of California in the Board of Regents. See Cal.Const., Art. 9, § 9(a). Control over the University is to be found not in the legislature, but rather in the Regents who had been vested with full legislative (including policymaking), administrative, and adjudicative powers by the citizens of California. See ibid.; Ishimatsu v. Regents, 266 Cal.App.2d 854, 863-864, 72 Cal.Rptr. 756, 762-763 (1968); Goldberg v. Regents, 248 Cal.App.2d 867, 874, 57 Cal.Rptr. 463, 468 (1967); 30 Op.Cal.Atty.Gen. 162, 166 (1957) ("The Regents, not the legislature, have the general rule-making or policy-making power in regard to the University"). This is certainly a permissible choice, see *Sweezy, supra,* and we, unlike our Brother POWELL, find nothing in the Equal Protection Clause that requires us to depart from established principle by limiting the scope of power the Regents may exercise more narrowly than the powers that may constitutionally be wielded by the Assembly.

Because the Regents can exercise plenary legislative and administrative power, it elevates form over substance to insist that Davis could not use race-conscious remedial programs until it had been adjudged in violation of the Constitution or an antidiscrimination statute. For, if the Equal Protection Clause required such a violation as a predicate, the Regents could simply have promulgated a regulation prohibiting disparate treatment not justified by the need to admit only qualified students, and could have declared Davis to have been in violation of such a regulation on the basis of the exclusionary effect of the admissions policy applied during the first two years of its operation. See *infra,* at 2789-2790.

Acts are addressed. Indeed, voluntary initiatives by the States to achieve the national goal of equal opportunity have been recognized to be essential to its attainment. "To use the Fourteenth Amendment as a sword against such State power would stultify that Amendment." Railway Mail Assn. v. Corsi, 326 U.S. 88, 98, 65 S.Ct. 1483, 1489, 89 L.Ed. 2072 (1945) (Frankfurter, J., concurring). We therefore conclude that Davis' goal of admitting minority students disadvantaged by the effects of past discrimination is sufficiently important to justify use of race-conscious admissions criteria.

B. Properly construed, therefore, our prior cases unequivocally show that a state government may adopt race-conscious programs if the purpose of such programs is to remove the disparate racial impact its actions might otherwise have and if there is reason to believe that the disparate impact is itself the product of past discrimination, whether its own or that of society at large. There is no question that Davis' program is valid under this test.

Certainly, on the basis of the undisputed factual submissions before this Court, Davis had a sound basis for believing that the problem of underrepresentation of minorities was substantial and chronic and that the problem was attributable to handicaps imposed on minority applicants by past and present racial discrimination. Until at least 1973, the practice of medicine in this country was, in fact, if not in law, largely the prerogative of whites. In 1950, for example, while Negroes constituted 10% of the total population, Negro physicians constituted only 2.2% of the total number of physicians. The overwhelming majority of these, moreover, were educated in two predominantly Negro medical schools, Howard and Meharry. By 1970, the gap between the proportion of Negroes in medicine and their proportion in the population had widened: The number of Negroes employed in medicine remained frozen at 2.2% while the Negro population had increased to 11.1%. The number of Negro admittees to predominantly white medical schools, moreover, had declined in absolute numbers during the years 1955 to 1964. Odegaard 19.

Moreover, Davis had very good reason to believe that the national pattern of underrepresentation of minorities in medicine would be perpetuated if it retained a single admissions standard. For example, the entering classes in 1968 and 1969, the years in which such a standard was used, included only 1 Chicano and 2 Negroes out of the 50 admittees for each year. Nor is there any relief from this pattern of underrepresentation in the statistics for the regular admissions program in later years.

Davis clearly could conclude that the serious and persistent underrepresentation of minorities in medicine depicted by these statistics is the result of handicaps under which minority applicants labor as a consequence of a background of deliberate, purposeful discrimination against minorities in education and in society generally, as well as in the medical profession. From the inception of our national life, Negroes have been subjected to unique legal disabilities impairing access to equal educational opportunity.

[The] generation of minority students applying to Davis Medical School since it opened in 1968 — most of whom were born before or about the time *Brown I* was decided — clearly have been victims of this discrimination. Judicial decrees recognizing discrimination in public education in California testify to the fact of widespread discrimination suffered by California-born minority applicants; many minority group members living in California, moreover, were born and reared in school districts in Southern States segregated by law. Since separation of school-children by race "generates a feeling of inferiority as to their status in the community that may affect their hearts and minds in a way unlikely ever to be undone," Brown I, supra, 347 U.S., at 494, 74 S.Ct., at 691, the conclusion is inescapable that applicants to medical school must be few indeed who endured the effects of *de jure* segregation, the resistance to *Brown I,* or the equally debilitating pervasive private discrimination fostered by our long history of official discrimination, cf. Reitman v. Mulkey, 387 U.S. 369, 87 S.Ct. 1627, 18 L.Ed.2d 830 (1967), and yet come to the starting line with an education equal to whites.

C. The second prong of our test — whether the Davis program stigmatizes any discrete group or individual and whether race is reasonably used in light of the program's objectives — is clearly satisfied by the Davis program.

It is not even claimed that Davis' program in any way operates to stigmatize or single out any discrete and insular, or even any identifiable, nonminority group. Nor will harm comparable to that imposed upon racial minorities by exclusion or separation on grounds of race be the likely result of the program. It does not, for example, establish an exclusive preserve for minority students apart from and exclusive of whites. Rather, its purpose is to overcome the effects of segregation by bringing the races together. True, whites are excluded from participation in the special admissions program, but this fact only operates to reduce the number of whites to be admitted in the regular admissions program in order to permit admission of a reasonable percentage — less than their proportion of the California population — of otherwise underrepresented qualified minority applicants.

Nor was Bakke in any sense stamped as inferior by the Medical School's rejection of him. Indeed, it is conceded by all that he satisfied those criteria regarded by the school as generally relevant to academic performance better than most of the minority members who were admitted. Moreover, there is absolutely no basis for concluding that Bakke's rejection as a result of Davis' use of racial preference will affect him throughout his life in the same way as the segregation of the Negro schoolchildren in *Brown I* would have affected them. Unlike discrimination against racial minorities, the use of racial preferences for remedial purposes does not inflict a pervasive injury upon individual whites in the sense that wherever they go or whatever they do there is a significant likelihood that they will be treated as second-class citizens because of their color. This distinction does not mean that the exclusion of a white resulting from the preferential use of race is not sufficiently serious to require justification; but it does mean that the injury inflicted by such a policy is not distinguishable from disadvantages caused by a wide range of government actions, none of which has ever been thought impermissible for that reason alone.

E. The "Harvard" program, see *ante,* at 2762-2763, as those employing it readily concede, openly and successfully employs a racial criterion for the purpose of ensuring that some of the scarce places in institutions of higher education are allocated to disadvantaged minority students. That the Harvard approach does not also make public the extent of the preference and the precise workings of the system while the Davis program employs a specific, openly stated number, does not condemn the latter plan for purposes of Fourteenth Amendment adjudication. It may be that the Harvard plan is more acceptable to the public than is the Davis "quota." If it is, any State, including California, is free to adopt it in preference to a less acceptable alternative, just as it is generally free, as far as the Constitution is concerned, to abjure granting any racial preferences in its admissions program. But there is no basis for preferring a particular preference program simply because in achieving the same goals that the Davis Medical School is pursuing, it proceeds in a manner that is not immediately apparent to the public.

Mr. Justice MARSHALL.

I agree with the judgment of the Court only insofar as it permits a university to consider the race of an applicant in making admissions decisions. I do not agree that petitioner's admissions program violates the Constitution.

While I applaud the judgment of the Court that a university may consider race in its admissions process, it is more than a little ironic that, after several hundred years of class-based discrimination against Negroes, the Court is unwilling to hold that a class-based remedy for that discrimination is permissible. In declining to so hold, today's judgment ignores the fact that for several hundred years Negroes have been discriminated against, not as individuals, but rather solely because of the color of their skins. It is unnecessary in 20th-century America to have individual Negroes demonstrate that they have been victims of racial discrimination; the racism of our society has been so pervasive that none, regardless of wealth or position, has managed to escape its impact. The experience of Negroes in America has been different in kind, not just in degree, from that of other ethnic groups. It is not merely the history of slavery alone but also that a whole people were marked as inferior by the law. And that mark has endured. The dream of America as the great melting pot has not been realized for the Negro; because of his skin color he never even made it into the pot.

These differences in the experience of the Negro make it difficult for me to accept that Negroes cannot be afforded greater protection under the Fourteenth Amendment where it is necessary to remedy the effects of past discrimination.

I fear that we have come full circle. After the Civil War our Government started several "affirmative action" programs. This Court in the *Civil Rights Cases* and *Plessy v. Ferguson* destroyed the movement toward complete equality. For almost a century no action was taken, and this nonaction was with the tacit approval of the courts. Then we had *Brown v. Board of Education* and the Civil Rights Acts of Congress, followed by numerous affirmative-action programs. *Now*, we have this Court again stepping in, this time to stop affirmative-action programs of the type used by the University of California.

Mr. Justice BLACKMUN.

I participate fully, of course, in the opinion, *ante*, p. 2766, that bears the names of my Brothers Brennan, White, Marshall, and myself. I add only some general observations that hold particular significance for me, and then a few comments on equal protection.

I suspect that it would be impossible to arrange an affirmative-action program in a racially neutral way and have it successful. To ask that this be so is to demand the impossible. In order to get beyond racism, we must first take account of race. There is no other way. And in order to treat some persons equally, we must treat them differently. We cannot — we dare not — let the Equal Protection Clause perpetuate racial supremacy.

Mr. Justice STEVENS, with whom THE CHIEF JUSTICE, Mr. Justice STEWART, and Mr. Justice REHNQUIST join, concurring in the judgment in part and dissenting in part.

III. Section 601 of the Civil Rights Act of 1964, 78 Stat. 252, 42 U.S.C. § 2000d, provides: "No person in the United States shall, on the ground of race, color, or national origin, be excluded from participation in, be denied the benefits of, or be subjected to discrimination under any program or activity receiving Federal financial assistance."

The University, through its special admissions policy, excluded Bakke from participation in its program of medical education because of his race. The University also acknowledges that it was, and still is, receiving federal financial assistance. The plain language of the statute therefore requires affirmance of the judgment below. A different result cannot be justified unless that language misstates the actual intent of the Congress that enacted the statute or the statute is not enforceable in a private action. Neither conclusion is warranted.

Accordingly, I concur in the Court's judgment insofar as it affirms the judgment of the Supreme Court of California. To the extent that it purports to do anything else, I respectfully dissent.

CITY OF RICHMOND v. CROSON
488 U.S. 469 (1989)

Bidder brought suit challenging city's plan requiring prime contractors awarded city construction contracts to subcontract at least 30% of the dollar amount of each contract to one or more "Minority Business Enterprises." The United States District Court for the Eastern District of Virginia, Robert R. Merhige, Jr., J., ruled in favor of city. Bidder appealed. The Court of Appeals, Fourth Circuit, 779 F.2d 181, affirmed. Certiorari was granted. The Supreme Court, 106 S.Ct. 3327, remanded case for further consideration. On remand, the Court of Appeals, 822 F.2d 1355, struck down the set-aside program, and probable jurisdiction was noted.

Justice O'CONNOR announced the judgment of the Court and delivered the opinion of the Court with respect to Parts I, III-B, and IV, an opinion with respect to Part II, in which THE CHIEF JUSTICE and Justice WHITE join, and an opinion with respect to Parts III-A and V, in which THE CHIEF JUSTICE, Justice WHITE, and Justice KENNEDY join.

In this case, we confront once again the tension between the Fourteenth Amendment's guarantee of equal treatment to all citizens, and the use of race-based measures to ameliorate the effects of past discrimination on the opportunities enjoyed by members of minority groups in our society. Relying largely on our decision in Fullilove, some lower federal courts have applied a similar standard of review in assessing the constitutionality of state and local minority set-aside provisions under the Equal Protection Clause of the Fourteenth Amendment. Since our decision two Terms ago in Wygant v. Jackson Board of Education, 476 U.S. 267, 106 S.Ct. 1842, 90 L.Ed.2d 260 (1986), the lower federal courts have attempted to apply its standards in evaluating the constitutionality of state and local programs which allocate a portion of public contracting opportunities exclusively to minority-owned businesses. We noted probable jurisdiction in this case to consider the applicability of our decision in Wygant to a minority set-aside program adopted by the city of Richmond, Virginia.

I. The Plan was adopted by the Richmond City Council after a public hearing. Seven members of the public spoke to the merits of the ordinance: five were in opposition, two in favor. Proponents of the set-aside provision relied on a study which indicated that, while the general population of Richmond was 50% black, only 0.67% of the city's prime construction contracts had been awarded to minority businesses in the 5-year period from 1978 to 1983. It was also established that a variety of contractors' associations, whose representatives appeared in opposition to the ordinance, had virtually no minority businesses within their membership. The city's legal counsel indicated his view that the ordinance was constitutional under this Court's decision in Fullilove v. Klutznick, 448 U.S. 448, 100 S.Ct. 2758, 65 L.Ed.2d 902 (1980). App. 24. Councilperson Marsh, a proponent of the ordinance, made the following statement: "There is some information, however, that I want to make sure that we put in the record. I have been practicing law in this community since 1961, and I am familiar with the practices in the construction industry in this area, in the State, and around the nation. And I can say without equivocation, that the general conduct of the construction industry in this area, and the State, and around the nation, is one in which race discrimination and exclusion on the basis of race is widespread.

There was no direct evidence of race discrimination on the part of the city in letting contracts or any evidence that the city's prime contractors had discriminated against minority-owned subcontractors. See *Id.*, at 42 (statement of Councilperson Kemp) ("[The public witnesses] indicated that the minority contractors were just not available. There wasn't a one that gave any indication that a minority contractor would not have an opportunity, if he were available").

II. The parties and their supporting *amici* fight an initial battle over the scope of the city's power to adopt legislation designed to address the effects of past discrimination. Relying on our decision in Wygant, appellee argues that the city must limit any race-based remedial efforts to eradicating the effects of its own prior discrimination. This is essentially theposition taken by the Court of Appeals below. Appellant argues that our decision in Fullilove is controlling, and that as a result the city of Richmond enjoys sweeping legislative power to define and attack the effects of prior discrimination in its local construction industry. We find that neither of these two rather stark alternatives can withstand analysis.

Appellant and its supporting *amici* rely heavily on Fullilove for the proposition that a city council, like Congress, need not make specific findings of discrimination to engage in race-conscious relief. Thus, appellant argues "[I]t would be a perversion of federalism to hold that the federal government has a compelling interest in remedying the effects of racial discrimination in its own public works program, but a city government does not."

What appellant ignores is that Congress, unlike any State or political subdivision, has a specific constitutional mandate to enforce the dictates of the Fourteenth Amendment. The power to "enforce" may at times also include the power to define situations which *Congress* determines threaten principles of equality and to adopt prophylactic rules to deal with those situations.

That Congress may identify and redress the effects of society-wide discrimination does not mean that, *a fortiori,* the States and their political subdivisions are free to decide that such remedies are appropriate. Section 1 of the Fourteenth Amendment is an explicit *constraint* on state power, and the States must undertake any remedial efforts in accordance with that provision. To hold otherwise would be to cede control over the content of the Equal Protection Clause to the 50 state legislatures and their myriad political subdivisions. The mere recitation of a benign or compensatory purpose for the use of a racial classification would essentially entitle the States to exercise the full power of Congress under § 5 of the Fourteenth Amendment and insulate any racial classification from judicial scrutiny under § 1. We believe that such a result would be contrary to the intentions of the Framers of the Fourteenth Amendment, who desired to place clear limits on the States' use of race as a criterion for legislative action, and to have the federal courts enforce those limitations.

We do not, as Justice Marshall's dissent suggests, see *post,* at 755-757, find in § 5 of the Fourteenth Amendment some form of federal pre-emption in matters of race. We simply note what should be apparent to all — § 1 of the Fourteenth Amendment stemmed from a distrust of state legislative enactments based on race; § 5 is, as the dissent notes, "'a *positive* grant of legislative power'" to Congress. *Post,* at 755, quoting Katzenbach v. Morgan, supra, 384 U.S., at 651, 86 S.Ct., at 1723 (emphasis in dissent). Thus, our treatment of an exercise of congressional power in Fullilove cannot be dispositive here.

It would seem equally clear, however, that a state or local subdivision (if delegated the authority from the State) has the authority to eradicate the effects of private discrimination within its own legislative jurisdiction. This authority must, of course, be exercised within the constraints of § 1 of the Fourteenth Amendment. Our decision in Wygant is not to the contrary. As a matter of state law, the city of Richmond has legislative authority over its procurement policies, and can use its spending powers to remedy private discrimination, if it identifies that discrimination with the particularity required by the Fourteenth Amendment. To this extent, on the question of the city's competence, the Court of Appeals erred in following Wygant by rote in a case involving a state entity which has state-law authority to address discriminatory practices within local commerce under its jurisdiction.

Thus, if the city could show that it had essentially become a "passive participant" in a system of racial exclusion practiced by elements of the local construction industry, we think it clear that the city could take affirmative steps to dismantle such a system. It is beyond dispute that any public entity, state or federal, has a compelling interest in assuring that public dollars, drawn from the tax contributions of all citizens, do not serve to finance the evil of private prejudice.

III. A. The Richmond Plan denies certain citizens the opportunity to compete for a fixed percentage of public contracts based solely upon their race. To whatever racial group these citizens belong, their "personal rights" to be treated with equal dignity and respect are implicated by a rigid rule erecting race as the sole criterion in an aspect of public decisionmaking.

Absent searching judicial inquiry into the justification for such race-based measures, there is simply no way of determining what classifications are "benign" or "remedial" and what classifications are in fact motivated by illegitimate notions of racial inferiority or simple racial politics. Indeed, the purpose of strict scrutiny is to "smoke out" illegitimate uses of race by assuring that the legislative body is pursuing a goal important enough to warrant use of a highly suspect tool. The test also ensures that the means chosen "fit" this compelling goal so closely that there is little or no possibility that the motive for the classification was illegitimate racial prejudice or stereotype.

Classifications based on race carry a danger of stigmatic harm. Unless they are strictly reserved for remedial settings, they may in fact promote notions of racial inferiority and lead to a politics of racial hostility. We thus reaffirm the view expressed by the plurality in Wygant that the standard of review under the Equal Protection Clause is not dependent on the race of those burdened or benefited by a particular classification.

Our continued adherence to the standard of review employed in Wygant does not, as Justice Marshall's dissent suggests, see *post,* at 752, indicate that we view "racial discrimination as largely a phenomenon of the past" or that "government bodies need no longer preoccupy themselves with rectifying racial injustice." Rather, our interpretation of § 1 stems from our agreement with the view expressed by Justice Powell in Bakke that "[t]he guarantee of equal protection cannot mean one thing when applied to one individual and something else when applied to a person of another color." Bakke, supra, 438 U.S., at 289-290, 98 S.Ct., at 2748.

The dissent's watered-down version of equal protection review effectively assures that race will always be relevant in American life, and that the "ultimate goal" of "eliminat[ing] entirely from governmental decisionmaking such irrelevant factors as a human being's race," Wygant, supra, 476 U.S., at 320, 106 S.Ct., at 1871 (Stevens, J., dissenting) (footnote omitted), will never be achieved.

Even were we to accept a reading of the guarantee of equal protection under which the level of scrutiny varies according to the ability of different groups to defend their interests in the representative process, heightened scrutiny would still be appropriate in the circumstances of this case. One of the central arguments for applying a less exacting standard to "benign" racial classifications is that such measures essentially involve a choice made by dominant racial groups to disadvantage themselves. If one aspect of the judiciary's role under the Equal Protection Clause is to protect "discrete and insular minorities" from majoritarian prejudice or indifference, see United States v. Carolene Products Co., 304 U.S. 144, 153, n. 4, 58 S.Ct. 778, 784, n. 4, 82 L.Ed. 1234 (1938), some maintain that these concerns are not implicated when the "white majority" places burdens upon itself. See J. Ely, Democracy and Distrust 170 (1980).

In this case, blacks constitute approximately 50% of the population of the city of Richmond. Five of the nine seats on the city council are held by blacks. The concern that a political majority will more easily act to the disadvantage of a minority based on unwarranted assumptions or incomplete facts would seem to militate for, not against, the application of heightened judicial scrutiny in this case.

The District Court found the city council's "findings sufficient to ensure that, in adopting the Plan, it was remedying the present effects of past discrimination in the *construction industry.*" Like the "role model" theory employed in Wygant, a generalized assertion that there has been past discrimination in an entire industry provides no guidance for a legislative body to determine the precise scope of the injury it seeks to remedy. It "has no logical stopping point." Wygant, supra, at 275, 106 S.Ct., at 1847 (plurality opinion). "Relief" for such an ill-defined wrong could extend until the percentage of public contracts awarded to MBE's in Richmond mirrored the percentage of minorities in the population as a whole.

Appellant argues that it is attempting to remedy various forms of past discrimination that are alleged to be responsible for the small number of minority businesses in the local contracting industry. Among these the city cites the exclusion of blacks from skilled construction trade unions and training programs. This past discrimination has prevented them "from following the traditional path from laborer to entrepreneur." The city also lists a host of nonracial factors which would seem to face a member of any racial group attempting to establish a new business enterprise, such as deficiencies in working capital, inability to meet bonding requirements, unfamiliarity with bidding procedures, and disability caused by an inadequate track record.

While there is no doubt that the sorry history of both private and public discrimination in this country has contributed to a lack of opportunities for black entrepreneurs, this observation, standing alone, cannot justify a rigid racial quota in the awarding of public contracts in Richmond, Virginia. Like the claim that discrimination in primary and secondary schooling justifies a rigid racial preference in medical school admissions, an amorphous claim that there has been past discrimination in a particular industry cannot justify the use of an unyielding racial quota.

It is sheer speculation how many minority firms there would be in Richmond absent past societal discrimination, just as it was sheer speculation how many minority medical students would have been admitted to the medical school at Davis absent past discrimination in educational opportunities. Defining these sorts of injuries as "identified discrimination" would give local governments license to create a patchwork of racial preferences based on statistical generalizations about any particular field of endeavor.

These defects are readily apparent in this case. The 30% quota cannot in any realistic sense be tied to any injury suffered by anyone. The District Court relied upon five predicate "facts" in reaching its conclusion that there was an adequate basis for the 30% quota: (1) the ordinance declares itself to be remedial; (2) several proponents of the measure stated their views that there had been past discrimination in the construction industry; (3) minority businesses received 0.67% of prime contracts from the city while minorities constituted 50% of the city's population; (4) there were very few minority contractors in local and state contractors' associations; and (5) in 1977, Congress made a determination that the effects of past discrimination had stifled minority participation in the construction industry nationally.

None of these "findings," singly or together, provide the city of Richmond with a "strong basis in evidence for its conclusion that remedial action was necessary." There is nothing approaching a prima facie case of a constitutional or statutory violation by *anyone* in the Richmond construction industry.

The District Court accorded great weight to the fact that the city council designated the Plan as "remedial." But the mere recitation of a "benign" or legitimate purpose for a racial classification is entitled to little or no weight. See Weinberger v. Wiesenfeld, 420 U.S., at 648, n. 16, 95 S.Ct., at 1233, n. 16 ("This Court need not in equal protection cases accept at face value assertions of legislative purposes, when an examination of the legislative scheme and its history demonstrates that the asserted purpose could not have been a goal of the legislation"). Racial classifications are suspect, and that means that simple legislative assurances of good intention cannot suffice.

The District Court also relied on the highly conclusory statement of a proponent of the Plan that there was racial discrimination in the construction industry "in this area, and the State, and around the nation." App. 41 (statement of Councilperson Marsh). These statements are of little probative value in establishing identified discrimination in the Richmond construction industry. The fact finding process of legislative bodies is generally entitled to a presumption of regularity and deferential review by the judiciary. See Williamson v. Lee Optical of Oklahoma, Inc., 348 U.S. 483, 488-489, 75 S.Ct. 461, 464-465, 99 L.Ed. 563 (1955). But when a legislative body chooses to employ a suspect classification, it cannot rest upon a generalized assertion as to the classification's relevance to its goals. The history of racial classifications in this country suggests that blind judicial deference to legislative or executive pronouncements of necessity has no place in equal protection analysis. See Korematsu v. United States, 323 U.S. 214, 235-240, 65 S.Ct. 193, 202-205, 89 L.Ed. 194 (1944) (Murphy, J., dissenting).

Reliance on the disparity between the number of prime contracts awarded to minority firms and the minority population of the city of Richmond is similarly misplaced.

In this case, the city does not even know how many MBE's in the relevant market are qualified to undertake prime or subcontracting work in public construction projects. Nor does the city know what percentage of total city construction dollars minority firms now receive as subcontractors on prime contracts let by the city. Without any information on minority participation in subcontracting, it is quite simply impossible to evaluate overall minority representation in the city's construction expenditures.

The city and the District Court also relied on evidence that MBE membership in local contractors' associations was extremely low. Again, standing alone this evidence is not probative of any discrimination in the local construction industry. There are numerous explanations for this dearth of minority participation, including past societal discrimination in education and economic opportunities as well as both black and white career and entrepreneurial choices. For low minority membership in these associations to be relevant, the city would have to link it to the number of local MBE's eligible for membership. If the statistical disparity between eligible MBE's and MBE membership were great enough, an inference of discriminatory exclusion could arise.

Finally, the city and the District Court relied on Congress' finding in connection with the set-aside approved in Fullilove that there had been nationwide discrimination in the construction industry. The probative value of these findings for demonstrating the existence of discrimination in Richmond is extremely limited. By its inclusion of a waiver procedure in the national program addressed in Fullilove, Congress explicitly recognized that the scope of the problem would vary from market area to market area. See Fullilove, 448 U.S., at 487, 100 S.Ct., at 2779 (noting that the presumption that minority firms are disadvantaged by past discrimination may be rebutted by grantees in individual situations).

Moreover, as noted above, Congress was exercising its powers under § 5 of the Fourteenth Amendment in making a finding that past discrimination would cause federal funds to be distributed in a manner which reinforced prior patterns of discrimination. While the States and their subdivisions may take remedial action when they possess evidence that their own spending practices are exacerbating a pattern of prior discrimination, they must identify that discrimination, public or private, with some specificity before they may use race-conscious relief. Congress has made national findings that there has been societal discrimination in a host of fields. If all a state or local government need do is find a congressional report on the subject to enact a set-aside program, the constraints of the Equal Protection Clause will, in effect, have been rendered a nullity.

Justice Marshall apparently views the requirement that Richmond identify the discrimination it seeks to remedy in its own jurisdiction as a mere administrative headache, an "onerous documentary obligatio[n]." We cannot agree. The "evidence" relied upon by the dissent, the history of school desegregation in Richmond and numerous congressional reports, does little to define the scope of any injury to minority contractors in Richmond or the necessary remedy. The factors relied upon by the dissent could justify a preference of any size or duration.

Moreover, Justice Marshall's suggestion that findings of discrimination may be "shared" from jurisdiction to jurisdiction in the same manner as information concerning zoning and property values is unprecedented. We have never approved the extrapolation of discrimination in one jurisdiction from the experience of another. See Milliken v. Bradley, 418 U.S. 717, 746, 94 S.Ct. 3112, 3128, 41 L.Ed.2d 1069 (1974) ("Disparate treatment of white and Negro students occurred within the Detroit school system, and not elsewhere, and on this record the remedy must be limited to that system").

In sum, none of the evidence presented by the city points to any identified discrimination in the Richmond construction industry. We, therefore, hold that the city has failed to demonstrate a compelling interest in apportioning public contracting opportunities on the basis of race. To accept Richmond's claim that past societal discrimination alone can serve as the basis for rigid racial preferences would be to open the door to competing claims for "remedial relief" for every disadvantaged group. The dream of a Nation of equal citizens in a society where race is irrelevant to personal opportunity and achievement would be lost in a mosaic of shifting preferences based on inherently unmeasurable claims of past wrongs. "Courts would be asked to evaluate the extent of the prejudice and consequent harm suffered by various minority groups. Those whose societal injury is thought to exceed some arbitrary level of tolerability then would be entitled to preferential classifications. . . ." Bakke, 438 U.S., at 296-297, 98 S.Ct., at 2751 (Powell, J.). We think such a result would be contrary to both the letter and spirit of a constitutional provision whose central command is equality.

The foregoing analysis applies only to the inclusion of blacks within the Richmond set-aside program. There is *absolutely no evidence* of past discrimination against Spanish-speaking, Oriental, Indian, Eskimo, or Aleut persons in any aspect of the Richmond construction industry. The District Court took judicial notice of the fact that the vast majority of "minority" persons in Richmond were black. It may well be that Richmond has never had an Aleut or Eskimo citizen. The random inclusion of racial groups that, as a practical matter, may never have suffered from discrimination in the construction industry in Richmond suggests that perhaps the city's purpose was not in fact to remedy past discrimination.

If a 30% set-aside was "narrowly tailored" to compensate black contractors for past discrimination, one may legitimately ask why they are forced to share this "remedial relief" with an Aleut citizen who moves to Richmond tomorrow? The gross overinclusiveness of Richmond's racial preference strongly impugns the city's claim of remedial motivation.

IV. As noted by the court below, it is almost impossible to assess whether the Richmond Plan is narrowly tailored to remedy prior discrimination since it is not linked to identified discrimination in any way. We limit ourselves to two observations in this regard.

First, there does not appear to have been any consideration of the use of race-neutral means to increase minority business participation in city contracting. If MBE's disproportionately lack capital or cannot meet bonding requirements, a race-neutral program of city financing for small firms would, *a fortiori,* lead to greater minority participation. Second, the 30% quota cannot be said to be narrowly tailored to any goal, except perhaps outright racial balancing. It rests upon the "completely unrealistic" assumption that minorities will choose a particular trade in lockstep proportion to their representation in the local population.

Since the city must already consider bids and waivers on a case-by-case basis, it is difficult to see the need for a rigid numerical quota. As noted above, the congressional scheme upheld in Fullilove allowed for a waiver of the set-aside provision where an

MBE's higher price was not attributable to the effects of past discrimination. Based upon proper findings, such programs are less problematic from an equal protection standpoint because they treat all candidates individually, rather than making the color of an applicant's skin the sole relevant consideration. Unlike the program upheld in Fullilove, the Richmond Plan's waiver system focuses solely on the availability of MBE's; there is no inquiry into whether or not the particular MBE seeking a racial preference has suffered from the effects of past discrimination by the city or prime contractors.

Given the existence of an individualized procedure, the city's only interest in maintaining a quota system rather than investigating the need for remedial action in particular cases would seem to be simple administrative convenience. But the interest in avoiding the bureaucratic effort necessary to tailor remedial relief to those who truly have suffered the effects of prior discrimination cannot justify a rigid line drawn on the basis of a suspect classification. Under Richmond's scheme, a successful black, Hispanic, or Oriental entrepreneur from anywhere in the country enjoys an absolute preference over other citizens based solely on their race. We think it obvious that such a program is not narrowly tailored to remedy the effects of prior discrimination.

V. Nothing we say today precludes a state or local entity from taking action to rectify the effects of identified discrimination within its jurisdiction. If the city of Richmond had evidence before it that nonminority contractors were systematically excluding minority businesses from subcontracting opportunities it could take action to end the discriminatory exclusion. Where there is a significant statistical disparity between the number of qualified minority contractors willing and able to perform a particular service and the number of such contractors actually engaged by the locality or the locality's prime contractors, an inference of discriminatory exclusion could arise. See Bazemore v. Friday, 478 U.S., at 398, 106 S.Ct., at 3008; Teamsters v. United States, 431 U.S., at 337-339, 97 S.Ct., at 1856. Under such circumstances, the city could act to dismantle the closed business system by taking appropriate measures against those who discriminate on the basis of race or other illegitimate criteria. See, *e.g.,* New York State Club Assn. v. New York City, 487 U.S. 1, 10-11, 13-14, 108 S.Ct. 2225, 2232-2233, 2234-2235, 101 L.Ed.2d 1 (1988). In the extreme case, some form of narrowly tailored racial preference might be necessary to break down patterns of deliberate exclusion.

Nor is local government powerless to deal with individual instances of racially motivated refusals to employ minority contractors. Even in the absence of evidence of discrimination, the city has at its disposal a whole array of race-neutral devices to increase the accessibility of city contracting opportunities to small entrepreneurs of all races. Simplification of bidding procedures, relaxation of bonding requirements, and training and financial aid for disadvantaged entrepreneurs of all races would open the public contracting market to all those who have suffered the effects of past societal discrimination or neglect. The city may also act to prohibit discrimination in the provision of credit or bonding by local suppliers and banks. Business as usual should not mean business pursuant to the unthinking exclusion of certain members of our society from its rewards.

In the case at hand, the city has not ascertained how many minority enterprises are present in the local construction market nor the level of their participation in city construction projects. The city points to no evidence that qualified minority contractors have been passed over for city contracts or subcontracts, either as a group or in any individual case. Under such circumstances, it is simply impossible to say that the city has demonstrated "a strong basis in evidence for its conclusion that remedial action was necessary."

Proper findings in this regard are necessary to define both the scope of the injury and the extent of the remedy necessary to cure its effects. Such findings also serve to assure all citizens that the deviation from the norm of equal treatment of all racial and ethnic groups is a temporary matter, a measure taken in the service of the goal of equality itself. Absent such findings, there is a danger that a racial classification is merely the product of unthinking stereotypes or a form of racial politics. Because the city of Richmond has failed to identify the need for remedial action in the awarding of its public construction contracts, its treatment of its citizens on a racial basis violates the dictates of the Equal Protection Clause. Accordingly, the judgment of the Court of Appeals for the Fourth Circuit is affirmed.

Justice STEVENS, concurring in part and concurring in the judgment.

I do not agree with the premise that seems to underlie today's decision, as well as the decision in Wygant v. Jackson Board of Education, 476 U.S. 267, 106 S.Ct. 1842, 90 L.Ed.2d 260 (1986), that a governmental decision that rests on a racial classification is never permissible except as a remedy for a past wrong. See *ante,* at 721-722. I do, however, agree with the Court's explanation of why the Richmond ordinance cannot be justified as a remedy for past discrimination, and therefore join Parts I, III-B, and IV of its opinion. I write separately to emphasize three aspects of the case that are of special importance to me. First, the city makes no claim that the public interest in the efficient performance of its construction contracts will be served by granting a preference to minority-business enterprises. This case is therefore completely unlike Wygant, in which I thought it quite obvious that the school board had reasonably concluded that an integrated faculty could provide educational benefits to the entire student body that could not be provided by an all-white, or nearly all-white, faculty. Second, this litigation involves an attempt by a legislative body, rather than a court, to fashion a remedy for a past wrong. It is the judicial system, rather than the legislative process, that is best equipped to identify past wrongdoers and to fashion remedies that will create the conditions that presumably would have existed had no wrong been committed. Third, instead of engaging in a debate over the proper standard of review to apply in affirmative-action litigation, I believe it is more constructive to try to identify the characteristics of the advantaged and disadvantaged classes that may justify their disparate treatment. In this case that approach convinces me that, instead of carefully identifying the characteristics of the two classes of contractors that are respectively favored and disfavored by its ordinance, the Richmond City Council has merely engaged in the type of stereotypical analysis that is a hallmark of violations of the Equal Protection Clause. Whether we look at the class of persons benefited by the ordinance or at the disadvantaged class, the same conclusion emerges.

The justification for the ordinance is the fact that in the past white contractors — and presumably other white citizens in Richmond — have discriminated against black contractors. The class of persons benefited by the ordinance is not, however, limited to victims of such discrimination — it encompasses persons who have never been in business in Richmond as well as minority contractors who may have been guilty of discriminating against members of other minority groups. Indeed, for all the record shows, all of the minority-business enterprises that have benefited from the ordinance may be firms that have prospered notwithstanding the discriminatory conduct that may have harmed other minority firms years ago. Ironically, minority firms that have survived in the competitive struggle, rather than those that have perished, are most likely to benefit from an ordinance of this kind.

The ordinance is equally vulnerable because of its failure to identify the characteristics of the disadvantaged class of white contractors that justify the disparate treatment. The composition of the disadvantaged class of white contractors presumably includes some who have been guilty of unlawful discrimination, some who practiced discrimination before it was forbidden by law, and some who have never discriminated against anyone on the basis of race. Imposing a common burden on such a disparate class merely because each member of the class is of the same race stems from reliance on a stereotype rather than fact or reason. There is a special irony in the stereotypical thinking that prompts legislation of this kind. Although it stigmatizes the disadvantaged class with the unproven charge of past racial discrimination, it actually imposes a greater stigma on its supposed beneficiaries.

Justice KENNEDY, concurring in part and concurring in the judgment.

I join all but Part II of Justice O'Connor's opinion and give this further explanation.

The process by which a law that is an equal protection violation when enacted by a State becomes transformed to an equal protection guarantee when enacted by Congress poses a difficult proposition for me; but as it is not before us, any reconsideration of that issue must await some further case.

The moral imperative of racial neutrality is the driving force of the Equal Protection Clause. Justice Scalia's opinion underscores that proposition, quite properly in my view. The rule suggested in his opinion, which would strike down all preferences which are not necessary remedies to victims of unlawful discrimination, would serve important structural goals, as it would eliminate the necessity for courts to pass upon each racial preference that is enacted. Structural protections may be necessities if moral imperatives are to be obeyed. His opinion would make it crystal clear to the political branches, at least those of the States, that legislation must be based on criteria other than race.

Nevertheless, given that a rule of automatic invalidity for racial preferences in almost every case would be a significant break with our precedents that require a case-by-case test, I am not convinced we need adopt it at this point. On the assumption that it will vindicate the principle of race neutrality found in the Equal Protection Clause, I accept the less absolute rule contained in Justice O'Connor's opinion, a rule based on the proposition that any racial preference must face the most rigorous scrutiny by the courts. My reasons for doing so are as follows. First, I am confident that, in application, the strict scrutiny standard will operate in a manner generally consistent with the imperative of race neutrality, because it forbids the use even of narrowly drawn racial classifications except as a last resort. Second, the rule against race-conscious remedies is already less than an absolute one, for that relief may be the only adequate remedy after a judicial determination that a State or its instrumentality has violated the Equal Protection Clause. I note, in this connection, that evidence which would support a judicial finding of intentional discrimination may suffice also to justify remedial legislative action, for it diminishes the constitutional responsibilities of the political branches to say they must wait to act until ordered to do so by a court. Third, the strict scrutiny rule is consistent with our precedents, as Justice O'Connor's opinion demonstrates.

The ordinance before us falls far short of the standard we adopt. We are left with an ordinance and a legislative record open to the fair charge that it is not a remedy but is itself a preference which will cause the same corrosive animosities that the Constitution forbids.

Justice SCALIA, concurring in the judgment.

I agree with much of the Court's opinion, and, in particular, with Justice O'Connor's conclusion that strict scrutiny must be applied to all governmental classification by race, whether or not its asserted purpose is "remedial" or "benign." I do not agree, however, with Justice O'Connor's dictum suggesting that, despite the Fourteenth Amendment, state and local governments may in some circumstances discriminate on the basis of race in order (in a broad sense) "to ameliorate the effects of past discrimination." The benign purpose of compensating for social disadvantages, whether they have been acquired by reason of prior discrimination or otherwise, can no more be pursued by the illegitimate means of racial discrimination than can other assertedly benign purposes we have repeatedly rejected. The difficulty of overcoming the effects of past discrimination is as nothing compared with the difficulty of eradicating from our society the source of those effects, which is the tendency — fatal to a Nation such as ours — to classify and judge men and women on the basis of their country of origin or the color of their skin. A solution to the first problem that aggravates the second is no solution at all. At least where state or local action is at issue, only a social emergency rising to the level of imminent danger to life and limb — for example, a prison race riot, requiring temporary segregation of inmates, cf. Lee v. Washington, supra — can justify an exception to the principle embodied in the Fourteenth Amendment that "[o]ur Constitution is color-blind, and neither knows nor tolerates classes among citizens,"

We have in some contexts approved the use of racial classifications by the Federal Government to remedy the effects of past discrimination. I do not believe that we must or should extend those holdings to the States. A sound distinction between federal and state (or local) action based on race rests not only upon the substance of the Civil War Amendments, but upon social reality and governmental theory.

In my view there is only one circumstance in which the States may act *by race* to "undo the effects of past discrimination": where that is necessary to eliminate their own maintenance of a system of unlawful racial classification. If, for example, a state agency has a discriminatory pay scale compensating black employees in all positions at 20% less than their nonblack counterparts, it may assuredly promulgate an order raising the salaries of "all black employees" to eliminate the differential. Cf. Bazemore v. Friday, 478 U.S. 385, 395-396, 106 S.Ct. 3000, 3006, 92 L.Ed.2d 315 (1986). This distinction explains our school desegregation cases, in which we have made plain that States and localities sometimes have an obligation to adopt race-conscious remedies.

I agree with the Court's dictum that a fundamental distinction must be drawn between the effects of "societal" discrimination and the effects of "identified" discrimination, and that the situation would be different if Richmond's plan were "tailored" to identify those particular bidders who "suffered from the effects of past discrimination by the city or prime contractors." In my view, however, the reason that would make a difference is not, as the Court states, that it would justify race-conscious action — but rather that it would enable race-neutral remediation. Nothing prevents Richmond from according a contracting preference to identified victims of discrimination. While most of the beneficiaries might be black, neither the beneficiaries nor those disadvantaged by the preference would be identified *on the basis of their race.* In other words, far from justifying racial classification, identification of actual victims of discrimination makes it less supportable than ever, because more obviously unneeded.

When we depart from this American principle we play with fire, and much more than an occasional DeFunis, Johnson, or Croson burns. It is plainly true that in our society blacks have suffered discrimination immeasurably greater than any directed at other racial groups. But those who believe that racial preferences can help to "even the score" display, and reinforce, a manner of thinking by race that was the source of the injustice and that will, if it endures within our society, be the source of more injustice still. The relevant proposition is not that it was blacks, or Jews, or Irish who were discriminated against, but that it was individual men and women, "created equal," who were discriminated against. And the relevant resolve is that that should never happen again. Racial preferences appear to "even the score" (in some small degree) only if one embraces the proposition that our society is appropriately viewed as divided into races, making it right that an injustice rendered in the past to a black man should be compensated for by discriminating against a white. Nothing is worth that embrace. Since blacks have been disproportionately disadvantaged by racial discrimination, any race-neutral remedial program aimed at the disadvantaged *as such* will have a disproportionately beneficial impact on blacks. Only such a program, and not one that operates on the basis of race, is in accord with the letter and the spirit of our Constitution.

Justice MARSHALL, with whom Justice BRENNAN and Justice BLACKMUN join, dissenting.

It is a welcome symbol of racial progress when the former capital of the Confederacy acts forthrightly to confront the effects of racial discrimination in its midst. In my view, nothing in the Constitution can be construed to prevent Richmond, Virginia, from allocating a portion of its contracting dollars for businesses owned or controlled by members of minority groups. Indeed, Richmond's set-aside program is indistinguishable in all meaningful respects from — and in fact was patterned upon — the federal set-aside plan which this Court upheld in Fullilove v. Klutznick, 448 U.S. 448, 100 S.Ct. 2758, 65 L.Ed.2d 902 (1980).

A majority of this Court holds today, however, that the Equal Protection Clause of the Fourteenth Amendment blocks Richmond's initiative. Today's decision marks a deliberate and giant step backward in this Court's affirmative-action jurisprudence. Cynical of one municipality's attempt to redress the effects of past racial discrimination in a particular industry, the majority launches a grapeshot attack on race-conscious remedies in general. The majority's unnecessary pronouncements will inevitably discourage or prevent governmental entities, particularly States and localities, from acting to rectify the scourge of past discrimination. This is the harsh reality of the majority's decision, but it is not the Constitution's command.

I. As an initial matter, the majority takes an exceedingly myopic view of the factual predicate on which the Richmond City Council relied when it passed the Minority Business Utilization Plan. The majority's refusal to recognize that Richmond has proved itself no exception to the dismaying pattern of national exclusion which Congress so painstakingly identified infects its entire analysis of this case.

So long as one views Richmond's local evidence of discrimination against the backdrop of systematic nationwide racial discrimination which Congress had so painstakingly identified in this very industry, this case is readily resolved.

II. My view has long been that race-conscious classifications designed to further re-medial goals "must serve important governmental objectives and must be substantially related to achievement of those objectives" in order to withstand constitutional scrutiny. Analyzed in terms of this two-pronged standard, Richmond's set-aside, like the federal program on which it was modeled, is "plainly constitutional."

A.1. Turning first to the governmental interest inquiry, Richmond has two powerful interests in setting aside a portion of public contracting funds for minority-owned enter-prises. The first is the city's interest in eradicating the effects of past racial discrimina-tion. It is far too late in the day to doubt that remedying such discrimination is a compel-ling, let alone an important, interest. Richmond has a second compelling interest in set-ting aside, where possible, a portion of its contracting dollars. That interest is the pro-spective one of preventing the city's own spending decisions from reinforcing and per-petuating the exclusionary effects of past discrimination.

The majority pays only lip service to this additional governmental interest. But our decisions have often emphasized the danger of the government tacitly adopting, encour-aging, or furthering racial discrimination even by its own routine. When government channels all its contracting funds to a white-dominated community of established con-tractors whose racial homogeneity is the product of private discrimination, it does more than place its *imprimatur* on the practices which forged and which continue to define that community. It also provides a measurable boost to those economic entities that have thrived within it, while denying important economic benefits to those entities which, but for prior discrimination, might well be better qualified to receive valuable government contracts.

2. The remaining question with respect to the "governmental interest" prong of equal protection analysis is whether Richmond has proffered satisfactory proof of past racial discrimination to support its twin interests in remediation and in governmental nonperpetuation. The varied body of evidence on which Richmond relied provides a "strong," "firm," and "unquestionably legitimate" basis upon which the city council could determine that the effects of past racial discrimination warranted a remedial and prophylactic governmental response. The city's local evidence confirmed that Rich-mond's construction industry did not deviate from this pernicious national pattern. The fact that just 0.67% of public construction expenditures over the previous five years had gone to minority-owned prime contractors, despite the city's racially mixed population, strongly suggests that construction contracting in the area was rife with "present econom-ic inequities." To the extent this enormous disparity did not itself demonstrate that dis-crimination had occurred, the descriptive testimony of Richmond's elected and appointed leaders drew the necessary link between the pitifully small presence of minorities in con-struction contracting and past exclusionary practices. That *no one* who testified chal-lenged this depiction of widespread racial discrimination in area construction contracting lent significant weight to these accounts. The fact that area trade associations had virtual-ly no minority members dramatized the extent of present inequities and suggested the lasting power of past discriminatory systems. In sum, to suggest that the facts on which Richmond has relied do not provide a sound basis for its finding of past racial discrimina-tion simply blinks credibility.

Richmond's reliance on localized, industry-specific findings is a far cry from the reliance on generalized "societal discrimination" which the majority decries as a basis for remedial action. The majority also takes the disingenuous approach of disaggregating Richmond's local evidence, attacking it piecemeal, and thereby concluding that no *single* piece of evidence adduced by the city, "standing alone," see, *e.g., ante,* at 726, suffices to prove past discrimination. But items of evidence do not, of course, "stan[d] alone" or exist in alien juxtaposition; they necessarily work together, reinforcing or contradicting each other.

The majority's perfunctory dismissal of the testimony of Richmond's appointed and elected leaders is also deeply disturbing. No one, of course, advocates "blind judicial deference" to the findings of the city council or the testimony of city leaders. The majority's suggestion that wholesale deference is what Richmond seeks is a classic strawman argument.

Had the majority paused for a moment on the facts of the Richmond experience, it would have discovered that the city's leadership is deeply familiar with what racial discrimination is. When the legislatures and leaders of cities with histories of pervasive discrimination testify that past discrimination has infected one of their industries, armchair cynicism like that exercised by the majority has no place.

Finally, I vehemently disagree with the majority's dismissal of the congressional and Executive Branch findings noted in Fullilove as having "extremely limited" probative value in this case. No principle of federalism or of federal power, however, forbids a state or local government to draw upon a nationally relevant historical record prepared by the Federal Government. Of course, Richmond could have built an even more compendious record of past discrimination, one including additional stark statistics and additional individual accounts of past discrimination. But nothing in the Fourteenth Amendment imposes such onerous documentary obligations upon States and localities once the reality of past discrimination is apparent.

B. In my judgment, Richmond's set-aside plan also comports with the second prong of the equal protection inquiry, for it is substantially related to the interests it seeks to serve in remedying past discrimination and in ensuring that municipal contract procurement does not perpetuate that discrimination. The most striking aspect of the city's ordinance is the similarity it bears to the "appropriately limited" federal set-aside provision upheld in Fullilove. The majority takes issue, however, with two aspects of Richmond's tailoring: the city's refusal to explore the use of race-neutral measures to increase minority business participation in contracting, *ante,* at 729, and the selection of a 30% set-aside figure. *Ante,* at 729. The majority's first criticism is flawed in two respects. First, the majority overlooks the fact that since 1975, Richmond has barred both discrimination by the city in awarding public contracts and discrimination by public contractors. Second, the majority's suggestion that Richmond should have first undertaken such race-neutral measures as a program of city financing for small firms, *ante,* at 729, ignores the fact that such measures, while theoretically appealing, have been discredited by Congress as ineffectual in eradicating the effects of past discrimination in this very industry.

As for Richmond's 30% target, the majority states that this figure "cannot be said to be narrowly tailored to any goal, except perhaps outright racial balancing." *Ante,* at 729. The majority ignores two important facts. First, the set-aside measure affects only 3% of overall city contracting; thus, any imprecision in tailoring has far less impact than the majority suggests. But more important, the majority ignores the fact that Richmond's

30% figure was patterned directly on the Fullilove precedent. Congress' 10% figure fell "roughly halfway between the present percentage of minority contractors and the percentage of minority group members in the Nation." Fullilove, supra, 448 U.S., at 513-514, 100 S.Ct., at 2792-2793 (Powell, J., concurring). The Richmond City Council's 30% figure similarly falls roughly halfway between the present percentage of Richmond-based minority contractors (almost zero) and the percentage of minorities in Richmond (50%). In faulting Richmond for not presenting a different explanation for its choice of a set-aside figure, the majority honors Fullilove only in the breach.

III. I would ordinarily end my analysis at this point and conclude that Richmond's ordinance satisfies both the governmental interest and substantial relationship prongs of our Equal Protection Clause analysis. However, I am compelled to add more, for the majority has gone beyond the facts of this case to announce a set of principles which unnecessarily restricts the power of governmental entities to take race-conscious measures to redress the effects of prior discrimination.

A. Today, for the first time, a majority of this Court has adopted strict scrutiny as its standard of Equal Protection Clause review of race-conscious remedial measures. This is an unwelcome development. A profound difference separates governmental actions that themselves are racist, and governmental actions that seek to remedy the effects of prior racism or to prevent neutral governmental activity from perpetuating the effects of such racism.

Racial classifications "drawn on the presumption that one race is inferior to another or because they put the weight of government behind racial hatred and separatism" warrant the strictest judicial scrutiny because of the very irrelevance of these rationales. By contrast, racial classifications drawn for the purpose of remedying the effects of discrimination that itself was race based have a highly pertinent basis: the tragic and indelible fact that discrimination against blacks and other racial minorities in this Nation has pervaded our Nation's history and continues to scar our society.

In concluding that remedial classifications warrant no different standard of review under the Constitution than the most brutal and repugnant forms of state-sponsored racism, a majority of this Court signals that it regards racial discrimination as largely a phenomenon of the past, and that government bodies need no longer preoccupy themselves with rectifying racial injustice. I, however, do not believe this Nation is anywhere close to eradicating racial discrimination or its vestiges. In constitutionalizing its wishful thinking, the majority today does a grave disservice not only to those victims of past and present racial discrimination in this Nation whom government has sought to assist, but also to this Court's long tradition of approaching issues of race with the utmost sensitivity.

B. I am also troubled by the majority's assertion that, even if it did not believe generally in strict scrutiny of race-based remedial measures, "the circumstances of this case" require this Court to look upon the Richmond City Council's measure with the strictest scrutiny. The sole such circumstance which the majority cites, however, is the fact that blacks in Richmond are a "dominant racial grou[p]" in the city. In support of this characterization of dominance, the majority observes that "blacks constitute approximately 50% of the population of the city of Richmond" and that "[f]ive of the nine seats on the City Council are held by blacks."

While I agree that the numerical and political supremacy of a given racial group is a factor bearing upon the level of scrutiny to be applied, this Court has never held that numerical inferiority, standing alone, makes a racial group "suspect" and thus entitled to strict scrutiny review. Rather, we have identified *other* "traditional indicia of suspectness": whether a group has been "saddled with such disabilities, or subjected to such a history of purposeful unequal treatment, or relegated to such a position of political powerlessness as to command extraordinary protection from the majoritarian political process." San Antonio Independent School Dist. v. Rodriguez, 411 U.S. 1, 28, 93 S.Ct. 1278, 1294, 36 L.Ed.2d 16 (1973).

It cannot seriously be suggested that nonminorities in Richmond have any "history of purposeful unequal treatment." Nor is there any indication that they have any of the disabilities that have characteristically afflicted those groups this Court has deemed suspect. Indeed, the numerical and political dominance of nonminorities within the State of Virginia and the Nation as a whole provides an enormous political check against the "simple racial politics" at the municipal level which the majority fears.

In my view, the "circumstances of this case," underscore the importance of *not* subjecting to a strict scrutiny straitjacket the increasing number of cities which have recently come under minority leadership and are eager to rectify, or at least prevent the perpetuation of, past racial discrimination. In many cases, these cities will be the ones with the most in the way of prior discrimination to rectify. The majority's view that remedial measures undertaken by municipalities with black leadership must face a stiffer test of Equal Protection Clause scrutiny than remedial measures undertaken by municipalities with white leadership implies a lack of political maturity on the part of this Nation's elected minority officials that is totally unwarranted. Such insulting judgments have no place in constitutional jurisprudence.

C. Today's decision, finally, is particularly noteworthy for the daunting standard it imposes upon States and localities contemplating the use of race-conscious measures to eradicate the present effects of prior discrimination and prevent its perpetuation. The majority restricts the use of such measures to situations in which a State or locality can put forth "a prima facie case of a constitutional or statutory violation."

Nothing in the Constitution or in the prior decisions of this Court supports limiting state authority to confront the effects of past discrimination to those situations in which a prima facie case of a constitutional or statutory violation can be made out. To the degree that this parsimonious standard is grounded on a view that either § 1 or § 5 of the Fourteenth Amendment substantially disempowered States and localities from remedying past racial discrimination, the majority is seriously mistaken. With respect, first, to § 5, our precedents have never suggested that this provision — or, for that matter, its companion federal-empowerment provisions in the Thirteenth and Fifteenth Amendments — was meant to pre-empt or limit state police power to undertake race-conscious remedial measures.

As for § 1, it is too late in the day to assert seriously that the Equal Protection Clause prohibits States — or for that matter, the Federal Government, to whom the equal protection guarantee has largely been applied, see Bolling v. Sharpe, 347 U.S. 497, 74 S.Ct. 693, 98 L.Ed. 884 (1954) — from enacting race-conscious remedies. Our cases in the areas of school desegregation, voting rights, and affirmative action have demonstrated time and again that race is constitutionally germane, precisely because race remains dismayingly relevant in American life.

The fact is that Congress' concern in passing the Reconstruction Amendments, and particularly their congressional authorization provisions, was that States would *not* adequately respond to racial violence or discrimination against newly freed slaves. To interpret any aspect of these Amendments as proscribing state remedial responses to these very problems turns the Amendments on their heads.

IV. The majority today sounds a full-scale retreat from the Court's longstanding solicitude to race-conscious remedial efforts "directed toward deliverance of the century-old promise of equality of economic opportunity." Fullilove, 448 U.S., at 463, 100 S.Ct., at 2767. The new and restrictive tests it applies scuttle one city's effort to surmount its discriminatory past, and imperil those of dozens more localities. I, however, profoundly disagree with the cramped vision of the Equal Protection Clause which the majority offers today and with its application of that vision to Richmond, Virginia's, laudable set-aside plan. The battle against pernicious racial discrimination or its effects is nowhere near won. I must dissent.

Justice BLACKMUN, with whom Justice BRENNAN joins, dissenting.

I join Justice Marshall's perceptive and incisive opinion revealing great sensitivity toward those who have suffered the pains of economic discrimination in the construction trades for so long.

I never thought that I would live to see the day when the city of Richmond, Virginia, the cradle of the Old Confederacy, sought on its own, within a narrow confine, to lessen the stark impact of persistent discrimination. But Richmond, to its great credit, acted. Yet this Court, the supposed bastion of equality, strikes down Richmond's efforts as though discrimination had never existed or was not demonstrated in this particular litigation. Justice Marshall convincingly discloses the fallacy and the shallowness of that approach. History is irrefutable, even though one might sympathize with those who — though possibly innocent in themselves — benefit from the wrongs of past decades.

So the Court today regresses. I am confident, however, that, given time, it one day again will do its best to fulfill the great promises of the Constitution's Preamble and of the guarantees embodied in the Bill of Rights — a fulfillment that would make this Nation very special.

ADARAND CONSTRUCTORS, INC. v. PENA
515 U.S. 200 (1995)

Justice O'CONNOR announced the judgment of the Court and delivered an opinion with respect to Parts I, II, III-A, III-B, III-D, and IV, which is for the Court except insofar as it might be inconsistent with the views expressed in Justice SCALIA's concurrence, and an opinion with respect to Part III-C in which Justice KENNEDY joins.

Petitioner Adarand Constructors, Inc., claims that the Federal Government's practice of giving general contractors on Government projects a financial incentive to hire sub-contractors controlled by "socially and economically disadvantaged individuals," and in particular, the Government's use of race-based presumptions in identifying such individuals, violates the equal protection component of the Fifth Amendment's Due Process Clause. The Court of Appeals rejected Adarand's claim. We conclude, however, that courts should analyze cases of this kind under a different standard of review than the one the Court of Appeals applied. We therefore vacate the Court of Appeals' judgment and remand the case for further proceedings.

I. In 1989, the Central Federal Lands Highway Division (CFLHD), which is part of the United States Department of Transportation (DOT), awarded the prime contract for a highway construction project in Colorado to Mountain Gravel & Construction Company. Mountain Gravel then solicited bids from subcontractors for the guardrail portion of the contract. Adarand, a Colorado-based highway construction company specializing in guardrail work, submitted the low bid. Gonzales Construction Company also submitted a bid.

The prime contract's terms provide that Mountain Gravel would receive additional compensation if it hired subcontractors certified as small businesses controlled by "socially and economically disadvantaged individuals," App. 24. Gonzales is certified as such a business; Adarand is not. Mountain Gravel awarded the subcontract to Gonzales, despite Adarand's low bid, and Mountain Gravel's Chief Estimator has submitted an affidavit stating that Mountain Gravel would have accepted Adarand's bid, had it not been for the additional payment it received by hiring Gonzales instead. *Id.,* at 28-31. Federal law requires that a subcontracting clause similar to the one used here must appear in most federal agency contracts, and it also requires the clause to state that "[t]he contractor shall presume that socially and economically disadvantaged individuals include Black Americans, Hispanic Americans, Native Americans, Asian Pacific Americans, and other minorities, or any other individual found to be disadvantaged by the [Small Business] Administration pursuant to section 8(a) of the Small Business Act." 15 U.S.C. § § 637(d)(2), (3). Adarand claims that the presumption set forth in that statute discriminates on the basis of race in violation of the Federal Government's Fifth Amendment obligation not to deny anyone equal protection of the laws.

II. Adarand, in addition to its general prayer for "such other and further relief as to the Court seems just and equitable," specifically seeks declaratory and injunctive relief against any *future* use of subcontractor compensation clauses. App. 22-23 (complaint). Before reaching the merits of Adarand's challenge, we must consider whether Adarand has standing to seek forward-looking relief. Adarand's allegation that it has lost a contract in the past because of a subcontractor compensation clause of course entitles it to seek damages for the loss of that contract (we express no view, however, as to whether sovereign immunity would bar such relief on these facts). But as we explained in Los Angeles v. Lyons, 461 U.S. 95, 103 S.Ct. 1660, 75 L.Ed.2d 675 (1983), the fact of past injury, "while presumably affording [the plaintiff] standing to claim damages . . ., does nothing to establish a real and immediate threat that he would again" suffer similar injury in the future. Id., at 105, 103 S.Ct., at 1667.

III. Respondents urge that "[t]he Subcontracting Compensation Clause program is . . . a program based on *disadvantage,* not on race," and thus that it is subject only to "the most relaxed judicial scrutiny." Brief for Respondents 26. To the extent that the statutes and regulations involved in this case are race neutral, we agree. Respondents concede, however, that "the race-based rebuttable presumption used in some certification determinations under the Subcontracting Compensation Clause" is subject to some heightened level of scrutiny. *Id.,* at 27. The parties disagree as to what that level should be. (We note, incidentally, that this case concerns only classifications based explicitly on race, and presents none of the additional difficulties posed by laws that, although facially race neutral, result in racially disproportionate impact and are motivated by a racially discriminatory purpose. See generally Arlington Heights v. Metropolitan Housing Development Corp., 429 U.S. 252, 97 S.Ct. 555, 50 L.Ed.2d 450 (1977); Washington v. Davis, 426 U.S. 229, 96 S.Ct. 2040, 48 L.Ed.2d 597 (1976).)

Adarand's claim arises under the Fifth Amendment to the Constitution, which provides that "No person shall . . . be deprived of life, liberty, or property, without due process of law." Although this Court has always understood that Clause to provide some measure of protection against *arbitrary* treatment by the Federal Government, it is not as explicit a guarantee of *equal* treatment as the Fourteenth Amendment, which provides that "No *State* shall . . . deny to any person within its jurisdiction the equal protection of the laws" (emphasis added). Our cases have accorded varying degrees of significance to the difference in the language of those two Clauses. We think it necessary to revisit the issue here.

A. The Court reviewed cases involving laws disadvantaging minorities and found that these rulings "did not distinguish between the duties of the States and the Federal Government to avoid racial classifications." B. The Court then turned to cases involving the question whether "benign classifications should also be subject to rigid scrutiny." The Court's failure to produce a majority opinion in Bakke, Fullilove, and Wygant left unresolved the proper analysis for remedial race-based governmental action. With Croson, the court finally agreed that the Fourteenth Amendment requires strict scrutiny of all race-based action by state and local governments. But Croson of course had no occasion to declare what standard of review the Fifth Amendment requires for such action taken by the Federal Government. Croson observed simply that the Court's "treatment of an exercise of congressional power in Fullilove cannot be dispositive here," because the case did not implicate Congress' broad power under §5 of the Fourteenth Amendment. Thus, some uncertainty persisted with respect to the standard of review for federal racial classifications.

Despite lingering uncertainty in the details, however, the Court's cases through Croson had established three general propositions with respect to governmental racial classifications. First, skepticism: "'Any preference based on racial or ethnic criteria must necessarily receive a most searching examination,'" Wygant, 476 U.S., at 273, 106 S.Ct., at 1847 (plurality opinion of Powell, J.); Fullilove, 448 U.S., at 491, 100 S.Ct., at 2781 (opinion of Burger, C.J.); see also id., at 523, 100 S.Ct., at 2798 (Stewart, J., dissenting) ("[A]ny official action that treats a person differently on account of his race or ethnic origin is inherently suspect"); McLaughlin, 379 U.S., at 192, 85 S.Ct., at 288 ("[R]acial classifications [are] 'constitutionally suspect'"); Hirabayashi, 320 U.S., at 100, 63 S.Ct., at 1385 ("Distinctions between citizens solely because of their ancestry are by their very nature odious to a free people"). Second, consistency: "[T]he standard of review under the Equal Protection Clause is not dependent on the race of those burdened or benefited by a particular classification," Croson, 488 U.S., at 494, 109 S.Ct., at 722 (plurality opinion); id., at 520, 109 S.Ct., at 735 (SCALIA, J., concurring in judgment); see also Bakke, 438 U.S., at 289-290, 98 S.Ct., at 2747-2748 (opinion of Powell, J.), *i.e.,* all racial classifications reviewable under the Equal Protection Clause must be strictly scrutinized. And third, congruence: "Equal protection analysis in the Fifth Amendment area is the same as that under the Fourteenth Amendment," Buckley v. Valeo, 424 U.S., at 93, 96 S.Ct., at 670; see also Weinberger v. Wiesenfeld, 420 U.S., at 638, n. 2, 95 S.Ct., at 1228, n. 2;

Bolling v. Sharpe, 347 U.S., at 500, 74 S.Ct., at 694. Taken together, these three propositions lead to the conclusion that any person, of whatever race, has the right to demand that any governmental actor subject to the Constitution justify any racial classification subjecting that person to unequal treatment under the strictest judicial scrutiny.

A year later, however, the Court took a surprising turn. Metro Broadcasting, Inc. v. FCC, involved a Fifth Amendment challenge to two race-based policies of the Federal Communications Commission (FCC). In Metro Broadcasting, the Court repudiated the long-held notion that "it would be unthinkable that the same Constitution would impose a lesser duty on the Federal Government" than it does on a State to afford equal protection of the laws, Bolling, supra, at 500, 74 S.Ct., at 694. It did so by holding that "benign" federal racial classifications need only satisfy intermediate scrutiny, even though Croson had recently concluded that such classifications enacted by a State must satisfy strict scrutiny.

By adopting intermediate scrutiny as the standard of review for congressionally mandated "benign" racial classifications, Metro Broadcasting departed from prior cases in two significant respects. First, it turned its back on Croson's explanation of why strict scrutiny of all governmental racial classifications is essential: We adhere to that view today, despite the surface appeal of holding "benign" racial classifications to a lower standard, because "it may not always be clear that a so-called preference is in fact benign." Second, Metro Broadcasting squarely rejected one of the three propositions established by the Court's earlier equal protection cases, namely, congruence between the standards applicable to federal and state racial classifications, and in so doing also undermined the other two — skepticism of all racial classifications and consistency of treatment irrespective of the race of the burdened or benefited group. See supra, at 2110-2111. Under Metro Broadcasting, certain racial classifications ("benign" ones enacted by the Federal Government) should be treated less skeptically than others; and the race of the benefited group is critical to the determination of which standard of review to apply. Metro Broadcasting was thus a significant departure from much of what had come before it.

The three propositions undermined by Metro Broadcasting all derive from the basic principle that the Fifth and Fourteenth Amendments to the Constitution protect persons, not groups. It follows from that principle that all governmental action based on race — a group classification long recognized as "in most circumstances irrelevant and therefore prohibited," Hirabayashi, 320 U.S., at 100, 63 S.Ct., at 1385 — should be subjected to detailed judicial inquiry to ensure that the personal right to equal protection of the laws has not been infringed. These ideas have long been central to this Court's understanding of equal protection, and holding "benign" state and federal racial classifications to different standards does not square with them. "[A] free people whose institutions are founded upon the doctrine of equality," ibid., should tolerate no retreat from the principle that government may treat people differently because of their race only for the most compelling reasons. Accordingly, we hold today that all racial classifications, imposed by whatever federal, state, or local governmental actor, must be analyzed by a reviewing court under strict scrutiny. In other words, such classifications are constitutional only if they are narrowly tailored measures that further compelling governmental interests. To the extent that Metro Broadcasting is inconsistent with that holding, it is overruled.

Justice Stevens chides us for our "supposed inability to differentiate between 'invidious' and 'benign' discrimination," because it is in his view sufficient that "people understand the difference between good intentions and bad." Post, at 2121. But, as we have just explained, the point of strict scrutiny is to "differentiate between" permissible and impermissible governmental use of race. And Justice Stevens himself has already explained in his dissent in Fullilove why "good intentions" alone are not enough to sustain a supposedly "benign" racial classification:

Perhaps it is not the standard of strict scrutiny itself, but our use of the concepts of "consistency" and "congruence" in conjunction with it, that leads Justice Stevens to dissent. According to Justice Stevens, our view of consistency "equate[s] remedial preferences with invidious discrimination," and ignores the difference between "an engine of oppression" and an effort "to foster equality in society," or, more colorfully, "between a 'No Trespassing' sign and a welcome mat," *post.* It does nothing of the kind. The principle of consistency simply means that whenever the government treats any person unequally because of his or her race, that person has suffered an injury that falls squarely within the language and spirit of the Constitution's guarantee of equal protection. It says nothing about the ultimate validity of any particular law; that determination is the job of the court applying strict scrutiny. The principle of consistency explains the circumstances in which the injury requiring strict scrutiny occurs. The application of strict scrutiny, in turn, determines whether a compelling governmental interest justifies the infliction of that injury.

Requiring that Congress, like the States, enact racial classifications only when doing so is necessary to further a "compelling interest" does not contravene any principle of appropriate respect for a coequal branch of the Government. It is true that various Members of this Court have taken different views of the authority § 5 of the Fourteenth Amendment confers upon Congress to deal with the problem of racial discrimination, and the extent to which courts should defer to Congress' exercise of that authority. We need not, and do not, address these differences today. For now, it is enough to observe that Justice Stevens' suggestion that any Member of this Court has repudiated in this case his or her previously expressed views on the subject is incorrect.

D. Our action today makes explicit what Justice Powell thought implicit in the Fullilove lead opinion: Federal racial classifications, like those of a State, must serve a compelling governmental interest, and must be narrowly tailored to further that interest. It follows that to the extent (if any) that Fullilove held federal racial classifications to be subject to a less rigorous standard, it is no longer controlling. But we need not decide today whether the program upheld in Fullilove would survive strict scrutiny as our more recent cases have defined it.

Some have questioned the importance of debating the proper standard of review of race-based legislation. But we agree with Justice Stevens that, "[b]ecause racial characteristics so seldom provide a relevant basis for disparate treatment, and because classifications based on race are potentially so harmful to the entire body politic, it is especially important that the reasons for any such classification be clearly identified and unquestionably legitimate," and that "[r]acial classifications are simply too pernicious to permit any but the most exact connection between justification and classification." We think that requiring strict scrutiny is the best way to ensure that courts will consistently give racial classifications that kind of detailed examination, both as to ends and as to means. Korematsu demonstrates vividly that even "the most rigid scrutiny" can sometimes fail to detect an illegitimate racial classification. Any retreat from the most searching judicial inquiry can only increase the risk of another such error occurring in the future.

Finally, we wish to dispel the notion that strict scrutiny is "strict in theory, but fatal in fact." Fullilove, supra, at 519, 100 S.Ct., at 2795 (Marshall, J., concurring in judgment). The unhappy persistence of both the practice and the lingering effects of racial discrimination against minority groups in this country is an unfortunate reality, and government is not disqualified from acting in response to it. When race-based action is necessary to further a compelling interest, such action is within constitutional constraints if it satisfies the "narrow tailoring" test this Court has set out in previous cases.

IV. Because our decision today alters the playing field in some important respects, we think it best to remand the case to the lower courts for further consideration in light of the principles we have announced. The Court of Appeals, following Metro Broadcasting and Fullilove, analyzed the case in terms of intermediate scrutiny. It upheld the challenged statutes and regulations because it found them to be "narrowly tailored to achieve [their] *significant governmental purpose* of providing subcontracting opportunities for small disadvantaged business enterprises." 16 F.3d, at 1547 (emphasis added). The Court of Appeals did not decide the question whether the interests served by the use of subcontractor compensation clauses are properly described as "compelling." It also did not address the question of narrow tailoring in terms of our strict scrutiny cases, by asking, for example, whether there was "any consideration of the use of race-neutral means to increase minority business participation" in government contracting, Croson, supra, at 507, 109 S.Ct., at 729, or whether the program was appropriately limited such that it "will not last longer than the discriminatory effects it is designed to eliminate," Fullilove, supra, at 513, 100 S.Ct., at 2792-2793 (Powell, J., concurring).

The question whether any of the ways in which the Government uses subcontractor compensation clauses can survive strict scrutiny, and any relevance distinctions such as these may have to that question, should be addressed in the first instance by the lower courts.

Accordingly, the judgment of the Court of Appeals is vacated, and the case is remanded for further proceedings consistent with this opinion. It is so ordered.

Justice SCALIA, concurring in part and concurring in the judgment.

I join the opinion of the Court, except Part III-C, and except insofar as it may be inconsistent with the following: In my view, government can never have a "compelling interest" in discriminating on the basis of race in order to "make up" for past racial discrimination in the opposite direction. See Richmond v. J.A. Croson Co., 488 U.S. 469, 520, 109 S.Ct. 706, 735-736, 102 L.Ed.2d 854 (1989) (Scalia, J., concurring in judgment). Individuals who have been wronged by unlawful racial discrimination should be made whole; but under our Constitution there can be no such thing as either a creditor or a debtor race. That concept is alien to the Constitution's focus upon the individual. To pursue the concept of racial entitlement — even for the most admirable and benign of purposes — is to reinforce and preserve for future mischief the way of thinking that produced race slavery, race privilege and race hatred. In the eyes of government, we are just one race here. It is American.

It is unlikely, if not impossible, that the challenged program would survive under this understanding of strict scrutiny, but I am content to leave that to be decided on remand.

Justice THOMAS, concurring in part and concurring in the judgment.

I agree with the majority's conclusion that strict scrutiny applies to *all* government classifications based on race. I write separately, however, to express my disagreement with the premise underlying Justice Stevens' and Justice Ginsburg's dissents: that there is a racial paternalism exception to the principle of equal protection. I believe that there is a "moral [and] constitutional equivalence," *post,* at 2120 (Stevens, J., dissenting), between laws designed to subjugate a race and those that distribute benefits on the basis of race in order to foster some current notion of equality. Government cannot make us equal; it can only recognize, respect, and protect us as equal before the law.

That these programs may have been motivated, in part, by good intentions cannot provide refuge from the principle that under our Constitution, the government may not make distinctions on the basis of race. As far as the Constitution is concerned, it is irrelevant whether a government's racial classifications are drawn by those who wish to oppress a race or by those who have a sincere desire to help those thought to be disadvantaged. There can be no doubt that the paternalism that appears to lie at the heart of this program is at war with the principle of inherent equality that underlies and infuses our Constitution.

These programs not only raise grave constitutional questions, they also undermine the moral basis of the equal protection principle. Purchased at the price of immeasurable human suffering, the equal protection principle reflects our Nation's understanding that such classifications ultimately have a destructive impact on the individual and our society. Unquestionably, "[i]nvidious [racial discrimination is an engine of oppression," *post,* at 2120 (Stevens, J., dissenting). It is also true that "[r]emedial" racial preferences may reflect "a desire to foster equality in society," *ibid.* But there can be no doubt that racial paternalism and its unintended consequences can be as poisonous and pernicious as any other form of discrimination. So-called "benign" discrimination teaches many that because of chronic and apparently immutable handicaps, minorities cannot compete with them without their patronizing indulgence. Inevitably, such programs engender attitudes of superiority or, alternatively, provoke resentment among those who believe that they have been wronged by the government's use of race. These programs stamp minorities with a badge of inferiority and may cause them to develop dependencies or to adopt an attitude that they are "entitled" to preferences. Indeed, Justice Stevens once recognized the real harms stemming from seemingly"

In my mind, government-sponsored racial discrimination based on benign prejudice is just as noxious as discrimination inspired by malicious prejudice. In each instance, it is racial discrimination, plain and simple.

Justice STEVENS, with whom Justice GINSBURG joins, dissenting.

Instead of deciding this case in accordance with controlling precedent, the Court today delivers a disconcerting lecture about the evils of governmental racial classifications. For its text the Court has selected three propositions, represented by the bywords "skepticism," "consistency," and "congruence."

I. The Court's concept of skepticism is, at least in principle, a good statement of law and of common sense. Undoubtedly, a court should be wary of a governmental decision that relies upon a racial classification. "Because racial characteristics so seldom provide a relevant basis for disparate treatment, and because classifications based on race are potentially so harmful to the entire body politic," a reviewing court must satisfy itself that the reasons for any such But, as the opinions in Fullilove demonstrate, substantial agreement on the standard to be applied in deciding difficult cases does not necessarily lead to agreement on how those cases actually should or will be resolved. In my judgment, because uniform standards are often anything but uniform, we should evaluate the Court's comments on "consistency," "congruence," and *stare decisis* with the same type of skepticism that the Court advocates for the underlying issue.

II. The Court's concept of "consistency" assumes that there is no significant difference between a decision by the majority to impose a special burden on the members of a minority race and a decision by the majority to provide a benefit to certain members of that minority notwithstanding its incidental burden on some members of the majority. In my opinion that assumption is untenable. There is no moral or constitutional equivalence between a policy that is designed to perpetuate a caste system and one that seeks to eradicate racial subordination. Invidious discrimination is an engine of oppression, subjugating a disfavored group to enhance or maintain the power of the majority. Remedial race-based preferences reflect the opposite impulse: a desire to foster equality in society. No sensible conception of the Government's constitutional obligation to "govern impartially," Hampton v. Mow Sun Wong, 426 U.S. 88, 100, 96 S.Ct. 1895, 1903, 48 L.Ed.2d 495 (1976), should ignore this distinction.

The consistency that the Court espouses would disregard the difference between a "No Trespassing" sign and a welcome mat. It would treat a Dixiecrat Senator's decision to vote against Thurgood Marshall's confirmation in order to keep African-Americans off the Supreme Court as on a par with President Johnson's evaluation of his nominee's race as a positive factor. It would equate a law that made black citizens ineligible for military service with a program aimed at recruiting black soldiers. An attempt by the majority to exclude members of a minority race from a regulated market is fundamentally different from a subsidy that enables a relatively small group of newcomers to enter that market. An interest in "consistency" does not justify treating differences as though they were similarities.

The Court's explanation for treating dissimilar race-based decisions as though they were equally objectionable is a supposed inability to differentiate between "invidious" and "benign" discrimination. But the term "affirmative action" is common and well understood. Its presence in everyday parlance shows that people understand the difference between good intentions and bad. As with any legal concept, some cases may be difficult to classify, but our equal protection jurisprudence has identified a critical difference between state action that imposes burdens on a disfavored few and state action that benefits the few "in spite of" its adverse effects on the many.

Indeed, our jurisprudence has made the standard to be applied in cases of invidious discrimination turn on whether the discrimination is "intentional," or whether, by contrast, it merely has a discriminatory "effect." Washington v. Davis, 426 U.S. 229, 96 S.Ct. 2040, 48 L.Ed.2d 597 (1976). Surely this distinction is at least as subtle, and at least as difficult to apply, see id., at 253–254, 96 S.Ct., at 2054 (concurring opinion), as the usually obvious distinction between a measure intended to benefit members of a particular minority race and a measure intended to burden a minority race. A state actor inclined to subvert the Constitution might easily hide bad intentions in the guise of unintended "effects"; but I should think it far more difficult to enact a law intending to preserve the majority's hegemony while casting it plausibly in the guise of affirmative action for minorities.

Nothing is inherently wrong with applying a single standard to fundamentally different situations, as long as that standard takes relevant differences into account. For example, if the Court in all equal protection cases were to insist that differential treatment be justified by relevant characteristics of the members of the favored and disfavored classes that provide a legitimate basis for disparate treatment, such a standard would treat dissimilar cases differently while still recognizing that there is, after all, only one Equal Protection Clause. Under such a standard, subsidies for disadvantaged businesses may be constitutional though special taxes on such businesses would be invalid. But a single standard that purports to equate remedial preferences with invidious discrimination cannot be defended in the name of "equal protection."

Moreover, the Court may find that its new "consistency" approach to race-based classifications is difficult to square with its insistence upon rigidly separate categories for discrimination against different classes of individuals. For example, as the law currently stands, the Court will apply "intermediate scrutiny" to cases of invidious gender discrimination and "strict scrutiny" to cases of invidious race discrimination, while applying the same standard for benign classifications as for invidious ones. If this remains the law, then today's lecture about "consistency" will produce the anomalous result that the Government can more easily enact affirmative-action programs to remedy discrimination against women than it can enact affirmative-action programs to remedy discrimination against African-Americans — even though the primary purpose of the Equal Protection Clause was to end discrimination against the former slaves. When a court becomes preoccupied with abstract standards, it risks sacrificing common sense at the altar of formal consistency.

As a matter of constitutional and democratic principle, a decision by representatives of the majority to discriminate against the members of a minority race is fundamentally different from those same representatives' decision to impose incidental costs on the majority of their constituents in order to provide a benefit to a disadvantaged minority. Indeed, as I have previously argued, the former is virtually always repugnant to the principles of a free and democratic society, whereas the latter is, in some circumstances, entirely consistent with the ideal of equality. By insisting on a doctrinaire notion of "consistency" in the standard applicable to all race-based governmental actions, the Court obscures this essential dichotomy.

III. The Court's concept of "congruence" assumes that there is no significant difference between a decision by the Congress of the United States to adopt an affirmative-action program and such a decision by a State or a municipality.

The majority in Metro Broadcasting and the plurality in Fullilove were not alone in relying upon a critical distinction between federal and state programs. In his separate opinion in Richmond v. J.A. Croson Co., 488 U.S. 469, 520-524, 109 S.Ct. 706, 735-738, 102 L.Ed.2d 854 (1989), Justice Scalia discussed the basis for this distinction. He observed that "it is one thing to permit racially based conduct by the Federal Government — whose legislative powers concerning matters of race were explicitly enhanced by the Fourteenth Amendment, see U.S. Const., Amdt. 14, § 5 — and quite another to permit it by the precise entities against whose conduct in matters of race that Amendment was specifically directed, see Amdt. 14, § 1." Id., at 521-522, 109 S.Ct., at 736. Continuing, Justice Scalia explained why a "sound distinction between federal and state (or local) action based on race rests not only upon the substance of the Civil War Amendments, but upon social reality and governmental theory."

An additional reason for giving greater deference to the National Legislature than to a local lawmaking body is that federal affirmative-action programs represent the will of our entire Nation's elected representatives, whereas a state or local program may have an impact on nonresident entities who played no part in the decision to enact it. Thus, in the state or local context, individuals who were unable to vote for the local representatives who enacted a race-conscious program may nonetheless feel the effects of that program.

Presumably, the majority is now satisfied that its theory of "congruence" between the substantive rights provided by the Fifth and Fourteenth Amendments disposes of the objection based upon divided constitutional powers. But it is one thing to say (as no one seems to dispute) that the Fifth Amendment encompasses a general guarantee of equal protection as broad as that contained within the Fourteenth Amendment. It is another thing entirely to say that Congress' institutional competence and constitutional authority entitles it to no greater deference when it enacts a program designed to foster equality than the deference due a state legislature. The latter is an extraordinary proposition; and, as the foregoing discussion demonstrates, our precedents have rejected it explicitly and repeatedly.

In my judgment, the Court's novel doctrine of "congruence" is seriously misguided. Congressional deliberations about a matter as important as affirmative action should be accorded far greater deference than those of a State or municipality.

VI. My skeptical scrutiny of the Court's opinion leaves me in dissent. The majority's concept of "consistency" ignores a difference, fundamental to the idea of equal protection, between oppression and assistance. The majority's concept of "congruence" ignores a difference, fundamental to our constitutional system, between the Federal Government and the States. And the majority's concept of *stare decisis* ignores the force of binding precedent. I would affirm the judgment of the Court of Appeals.

Justice GINSBURG, with whom Justice BREYER joins, dissenting.

For the reasons stated by Justice Souter, and in view of the attention the political branches are currently giving the matter of affirmative action, I see no compelling cause for the intervention the Court has made in this case. I further agree with Justice Stevens that, in this area, large deference is owed by the Judiciary to "Congress' institutional competence and constitutional authority to overcome historic racial subjugation." I write separately to underscore not the differences the several opinions in this case display, but the considerable field of agreement — the common understandings and concerns — revealed in opinions that together speak for a majority of the Court.

I. The divisions in this difficult case should not obscure the Court's recognition of the persistence of racial inequality and a majority's acknowledgment of Congress' authority to act affirmatively, not only to end discrimination, but also to counteract discrimination's lingering effects. Those effects, reflective of a system of racial caste only recently ended, are evident in our workplaces, markets, and neighborhoods. Job applicants with identical resumes, qualifications, and interview styles still experience different receptions, depending on their race. White and African-American consumers still encounter different deals. People of color looking for housing still face discriminatory treatment by landlords, real estate agents, and mortgage lenders. Minority entrepreneurs sometimes fail to gain contracts though they are the low bidders, and they are sometimes refused work even after winning contracts. Bias both conscious and unconscious, reflecting traditional and unexamined habits of thought, keeps up barriers that must come down if equal opportunity and nondiscrimination are ever genuinely to become this country's law and practice.

Given this history and its practical consequences, Congress surely can conclude that a carefully designed affirmative action program may help to realize, finally, the "equal protection of the laws" the Fourteenth Amendment has promised since 1868.

II. The lead opinion uses one term, "strict scrutiny," to describe the standard of judicial review for all governmental classifications by race. *Ante,* at 2117-2118. But that opinion's elaboration strongly suggests that the strict standard announced is indeed "fatal" for classifications burdening groups that have suffered discrimination in our society. That seems to me, and, I believe, to the Court, the enduring lesson one should draw from Korematsu v. United States, 323 U.S. 214, 65 S.Ct. 193, 89 L.Ed. 194 (1944); for in that case, scrutiny the Court described as "most rigid," id., at 216, 65 S.Ct., at 194, nonetheless yielded a pass for an odious, gravely injurious racial classification. See *ante,* at 2106 (lead opinion). A Korematsu-type classification, as I read the opinions in this case, will never again survive scrutiny: Such a classification, history and precedent instruct, properly ranks as prohibited.

For a classification made to hasten the day when "we are just one race," *ante,* at 2119 (Scalia, J., concurring in part and concurring in judgment), however, the lead opinion has dispelled the notion that "strict scrutiny" is "'fatal in fact.'" Properly, a majority of the Court calls for review that is searching, in order to ferret out classifications in reality malign, but masquerading as benign. See *ante,* at 2113-2114 (lead opinion). The Court's once lax review of sex-based classifications demonstrates the need for such suspicion. Today's decision thus usefully reiterates that the purpose of strict scrutiny "is precisely to distinguish legitimate from illegitimate uses of race in governmental decisionmaking," *ante,* at 2113 (lead opinion), "to 'differentiate between' permissible and impermissible governmental use of race," *ibid.,* to distinguish "'between a "No Trespassing" sign and a welcome mat.

Close review also is in order for this further reason. As this very case shows, some members of the historically favored race can be hurt by catch-up mechanisms designed to cope with the lingering effects of entrenched racial subjugation. Court review can ensure that preferences are not so large as to trammel unduly upon the opportunities of others or interfere too harshly with legitimate expectations of persons in once-preferred groups.

While I would not disturb the programs challenged in this case, and would leave their improvement to the political branches, I see today's decision as one that allows our precedent to evolve, still to be informed by and responsive to changing conditions.

RICCI v. DeSTEFANO
557 U.S. 557 (2009)

Justice KENNEDY delivered the opinion of the Court.

In the fire department of New Haven, Connecticut — as in emergency service agencies throughout the Nation — firefighters prize their promotion to and within the officer ranks. . . . New Haven, like many cities, relies on objective examinations to identify the best qualified candidates.

In 2003, 118 New Haven firefighters took examinations to qualify for promotion to the rank of lieutenant or captain. . . . Many firefighters studied for months, at considerable personal and financial cost. When the examination results showed that white candidates had outperformed minority candidates, the mayor and other local politicians opened a public debate that turned rancorous. Some firefighters . . . threatened a discrimination lawsuit if the City made promotions based on the tests. Other firefighters said the exams were neutral and fair. And they, in turn, threatened a discrimination lawsuit if the City, relying on the statistical racial disparity, ignored the test results and denied promotions to the candidates who had performed well. In the end the City took the side of those who protested the test results. It threw out the examinations.

Certain white and Hispanic firefighters who likely would have been promoted based on their good test performance sued the City and some of its officials. Theirs is the suit now before us. The suit alleges that, by discarding the test results, the City and the named officials discriminated against the plaintiffs based on their race, in violation of both Title VII of the Civil Rights Act of 1964, and the Equal Protection Clause of the Fourteenth Amendment. The City and the officials defended their actions, arguing that if they had certified the results, they could have faced liability under Title VII for adopting a practice that had a disparate impact on the minority firefighters. The District Court granted summary judgment for the defendants, and the Court of Appeals affirmed.

We conclude that race-based action like the City's in this case is impermissible under Title VII unless the employer can demonstrate a strong basis in evidence that, had it not taken the action, it would have been liable under the disparate-impact statute. The respondents, we further determine, cannot meet that threshold standard. As a result, the City's action in discarding the tests was a violation of Title VII. In light of our ruling under the statutes, we need not reach the question whether respondents' actions may have violated the Equal Protection Clause.

This litigation comes to us after the parties' cross-motions for summary judgment, so we set out the facts in some detail. As the District Court noted, although "the parties strenuously dispute the relevance and legal import of, and inferences to be drawn from, many aspects of this case, the underlying facts are largely undisputed."

[T]he City hired Industrial/Organizational Solutions, Inc. (IOS) to develop and administer the [oral and written] examinations, at a cost to the City of $100,000. . . . At every stage of the job analyses, IOS, by deliberate choice, oversampled minority firefighters to ensure that the results — which IOS would use to develop the examinations — would not unintentionally favor white candidates. . . . Sixty-six percent of the panelists [judging the oral examination] were minorities, and each of the nine three-member assessment panels contained two minority members. . . .

Candidates took the examinations in November and December 2003. Seventy-seven candidates completed the lieutenant examination — 43 whites, 19 blacks, and 15 Hispanics. Of those, 34 candidates passed — 25 whites, 6 blacks, and 3 Hispanics. [T]he top 10 candidates were eligible for an immediate promotion to lieutenant. All 10 were white. Subsequent vacancies would have allowed at least 3 black candidates to be considered for promotion to lieutenant.

Forty-one candidates completed the captain examination — 25 whites, 8 blacks, and 8 Hispanics. Of those, 22 candidates passed — 16 whites, 3 blacks, and 3 Hispanics [and] 9 candidates were eligible for an immediate promotion to captain — 7 whites and 2 Hispanics. . . .

Although they did not know whether they had passed or failed, some firefighter-candidates spoke at the first CSB [the Civil Service Board of New Haven] meeting in favor of certifying the test results. . . . Frank Ricci stated that the test questions were based on the Department's own rules and procedures and on "nationally recognized" materials that represented the "accepted standard[s]" for firefighting. Ricci stated that he had "several learning disabilities," including dyslexia; that he had spent more than $1,000 to purchase the materials and pay his neighbor to read them on tape so he could "give it [his] best shot"; and that he had studied "8 to 13 hours a day to prepare" for the test. . . . "When your life's on the line, second best may not be good enough." Other firefighters spoke against certifying the test results. They described the test questions as outdated or not relevant to firefighting practices in New Haven. . . .

The CSB's decision not to certify the examination results led to this lawsuit. The plaintiffs — who are the petitioners here — are 17 white firefighters and 1 Hispanic firefighter who passed the examinations but were denied a chance at promotions when the CSB refused to certify the test results. . . .

The District Court granted summary judgment for respondents. [It] rejected petitioners' equal protection claim on the theory that respondents had not acted because of "discriminatory animus" toward petitioners. It concluded that respondents' actions were not "based on race" because "all applicants took the same test, and the result was the same for all because the test results were discarded and nobody was promoted."

[T]the Court of Appeals affirmed in a one-paragraph, unpublished summary order; it later withdrew that order, issuing in its place a nearly identical, one-paragraph *per curiam* opinion adopting the District Court's reasoning. Three days later, the Court of Appeals voted 7 to 6 to deny rehearing en banc, over written dissents by Chief Judge Jacobs and Judge Cabranes. . . .

Title VII of the Civil Rights Act of 1964 prohibits employment discrimination on the basis of race, color, religion, sex, or national origin. Title VII prohibits both intentional discrimination (known as "disparate treatment") as well as, in some cases, practices that are not intended to discriminate but in fact have a disproportionately adverse effect on minorities (known as "disparate impact").

[In] *Griggs* v. *Duke Power Co.*, 401 U. S. 424 (1971), the Court . . . stated that the "touchstone" for disparate-impact liability is the lack of "business necessity": "If an employment practice which operates to exclude [minorities] cannot be shown to be related to job performance, the practice is prohibited." [Congress later codified] the prohibition on disparate-impact discrimination. . . . Title VII is express in disclaiming any interpretation of its requirements as calling for outright racial balancing. § 2000e-2(j). The purpose of Title VII "is to promote hiring on the basis of job qualifications, rather than on the basis of race or color." *Griggs*.

[T]his Court has considered cases similar to this one, albeit in the context of the Equal Protection Clause of the Fourteenth Amendment. The Court has held that certain government actions to remedy past racial discrimination — actions that are themselves based on race — are constitutional only where there is a "'strong basis in evidence'" that the remedial actions were necessary. *Richmond* v. *J. A. Croson Co.* (1989) (quoting *Wygant* (1986) (plurality opinion)). This suit does not call on us to consider whether the statutory constraints under Title VII must be parallel in all respects to those under the Constitution. That does not mean the constitutional authorities are irrelevant, however. Our cases discussing constitutional principles can provide helpful guidance in this statutory context.

[The plurality in *Wygant*] required a strong basis in evidence because "[e]videntiary support for the conclusion that remedial action is warranted becomes crucial when the remedial program is challenged in court by nonminority employees." The Court applied the same standard in *Croson*, observing that "an amorphous claim that there has been past discrimination . . . cannot justify the use of an unyielding racial quota."

The same interests are at work in the interplay between the disparate-treatment and disparate-impact provisions of Title VII. Congress has imposed liability on employers for unintentional discrimination in order to rid the workplace of "practices that are fair in form, but discriminatory in operation." *Griggs*. But it has also prohibited employers from taking adverse employment actions "because of" race. § 2000e-2(a)(1). Applying the strong-basis-in-evidence standard to Title VII gives effect to both the disparate-treatment and disparate-impact provisions, allowing violations of one in the name of compliance with the other only in certain, narrow circumstances. The standard leaves ample room for employers' voluntary compliance efforts, which are essential to the statutory scheme and to Congress's efforts to eradicate workplace discrimination. And the standard appropriately constrains employers' discretion in making race-based decisions: It limits that discretion to cases in which there is a strong basis in evidence of disparate-impact liability, but it is not so restrictive that it allows employers to act only when there is a provable, actual violation.

. . . Employment tests can be an important part of a neutral selection system that safeguards against the very racial animosities Title VII was intended to prevent. Here, however, the firefighters saw their efforts invalidated by the City in sole reliance upon race-based statistics.

If an employer cannot rescore a test based on the candidates' race, § 2000e-2(*l*), then it follows *a fortiori* that it may not take the greater step of discarding the test altogether to achieve a more desirable racial distribution of promotion-eligible candidates — absent a strong basis in evidence that the test was deficient and that discarding the results is necessary to avoid violating the disparate-impact provision. Restricting an employer's ability to discard test results (and thereby discriminate against qualified candidates on the basis of their race) also is in keeping with Title VII's express protection of bona fide promotional examinations.

For the foregoing reasons, we adopt the strong-basis-in-evidence standard as a matter of statutory construction to resolve any conflict between the disparate-treatment and disparate-impact provisions of Title VII. Our statutory holding does not address the constitutionality of the measures taken here in purported compliance with Title VII. We also do not hold that meeting the strong-basis-in-evidence standard would satisfy the Equal Protection Clause in a future case. [B]ecause respondents have not met their burden under Title VII, we need not decide whether a legitimate fear of disparate impact is ever sufficient to justify discriminatory treatment under the Constitution.

[U]nder Title VII, before an employer can engage in intentional discrimination for the asserted purpose of avoiding or remedying an unintentional disparate impact, the employer must have a strong basis in evidence to believe it will be subject to disparate-impact liability if it fails to take the race-conscious, discriminatory action.

[T]he record makes clear there is no support for the conclusion that respondents had an objective, strong basis in evidence to find the tests inadequate, with some consequent disparate-impact liability in violation of Title VII. [A] prima facie case of disparate-impact liability — essentially, a threshold showing of a significant statistical disparity, and nothing more — is far from a strong basis in evidence that the City would have been liable under Title VII had it certified the results. [T]he City could be liable for disparate-impact discrimination only if the examinations were not job related and consistent with business necessity, or if there existed an equally valid, less-discriminatory alternative that served the City's needs but that the City refused to adopt. We conclude there is no strong basis in evidence to establish that the test was deficient in either of these respects. . . .

There is no genuine dispute that the examinations were job-related and consistent with business necessity. The City's assertions to the contrary are "blatantly contradicted by the record." The CSB heard statements from Chad Legel (the IOS vice president) as well as city officials outlining the detailed steps IOS took to develop and administer the examinations. IOS devised the written examinations, which were the focus of the CSB's inquiry, after painstaking analyses of the captain and lieutenant positions — analyses in which IOS made sure that minorities were overrepresented. And IOS drew the questions from source material approved by the Department. Of the outside witnesses who appeared before the CSB, only one, Vincent Lewis ["who is black," a "fire program specialist for the Department of Homeland Security and a retired fire captain from Michigan"], had reviewed the examinations in any detail, and he was the only one with any fire-fighting experience. Lewis stated that the "questions were relevant for both exams." The only other witness who had seen any part of the examinations, Christopher Hornick (a competitor of IOS's), criticized the fact that no one within the Department had reviewed the tests — a condition imposed by the City to protect the integrity of the exams in light of past alleged security breaches. But Hornick stated that the exams "appea[r] to be . . . reasonably good" and recommended that the CSB certify the results. . . .

The City, moreover, turned a blind eye to evidence that supported the exams' validity. . . . IOS stood ready to provide respondents with detailed information to establish the validity of the exams, but respondents did not accept that offer. . . .

On the record before us, there is no genuine dispute that the City lacked a strong basis in evidence to believe it would face disparate-impact liability if it certified the examination results. In other words, there is no evidence — let alone the required strong basis in evidence — that the tests were flawed because they were not job-related or because other, equally valid and less discriminatory tests were available to the City. Fear of litigation alone cannot justify an employer's reliance on race to the detriment of individuals who passed the examinations and qualified for promotions. The City's discarding the test results was impermissible under Title VII, and summary judgment is appropriate for petitioners on their disparate-treatment claim. . . .

[A]fter the tests were completed, the raw racial results became the predominant rationale for the City's refusal to certify the results. [I]ts hearings produced no strong evidence of a disparate-impact violation, and the City was not entitled to disregard the tests based solely on the racial disparity in the results.

Our holding today clarifies how Title VII applies to resolve competing expectations under the disparate-treatment and disparate-impact provisions. If, after it certifies the test results, the City faces a disparate-impact suit, then in light of our holding today it should be clear that the City would avoid disparate-impact liability based on the strong basis in evidence that, had it not certified the results, it would have been subject to disparate-treatment liability.

Petitioners are entitled to summary judgment on their Title VII claim, and we therefore need not decide the underlying constitutional question. The judgment of the Court of Appeals is reversed, and the cases are remanded for further proceedings consistent with this opinion.

It is so ordered.

Justice SCALIA, concurring.

I join the Court's opinion in full, but write separately to observe that its resolution of this dispute merely postpones the evil day on which the Court will have to confront the question: Whether, or to what extent, are the disparate-impact provisions of Title VII of the Civil Rights Act of 1964 consistent with the Constitution's guarantee of equal protection? The question is not an easy one.

The difficulty is this: Whether or not Title VII's disparate-treatment provisions forbid "remedial" race-based actions when a disparate-impact violation would *not* otherwise result — the question resolved by the Court today — it is clear that Title VII not only permits but affirmatively *requires* such actions when a disparate-impact violation *would* otherwise result. But if the Federal Government is prohibited from discriminating on the basis of race, then surely it is also prohibited from enacting laws mandating that third parties — *e.g.*, employers, whether private, State, or municipal — discriminate on the basis of race. As the facts of these cases illustrate, Title VII's disparate-impact provisions place a racial thumb on the scales, often requiring employers to evaluate the racial outcomes of their policies, and to make decisions based on (because of) those racial outcomes. That type of racial decisionmaking is, as the Court explains, discriminatory.

To be sure, the disparate-impact laws do not mandate imposition of quotas, but it is not clear why that should provide a safe harbor. Would a private employer not be guilty of unlawful discrimination if he refrained from establishing a racial hiring quota but intentionally designed his hiring practices to achieve the same end? [T]he war between disparate impact and equal protection will be waged sooner or later, and it behooves us to begin thinking about how — and on what terms — to make peace between them.

Justice ALITO, with whom Justice SCALIA and Justice THOMAS join, concurring.

I join the Court's opinion in full. I write separately only because the dissent, while claiming that "[t]he Court's recitation of the facts leaves out important parts of the story," provides an incomplete description of the events that led to New Haven's decision to reject the results of its exam. [E]ven the District Court admitted that "a jury could rationally infer that city officials worked behind the scenes to sabotage the promotional examinations because they knew that, were the exams certified, the Mayor would incur the wrath of [Rev. Boise] Kimber and other influential leaders of New Haven's African-American community."

This admission finds ample support in the record. Reverend Boise Kimber, to whom the District Court referred, is a politically powerful New Haven pastor and a self-professed "'kingmaker.'" . . . Reverend Kimber's personal ties with seven-term New Haven Mayor John DeStefano (Mayor) stretch back more than a decade. In 1996, for example, Mayor DeStefano testified for Rev. Kimber as a character witness when Rev. Kimber — then the manager of a funeral home — was prosecuted and convicted for stealing prepaid funeral expenses from an elderly woman and then lying about the matter under oath. . . . In 2002, the Mayor picked Rev. Kimber to serve as the Chairman of the New Haven Board of Fire Commissioners (BFC), "despite the fact that he had no experience in the profession, fire administration, [or] municipal management." In that capacity, Rev. Kimber told firefighters that certain new recruits would not be hired because "'they just have too many vowels in their name[s].'" After protests about this comment, Rev. Kimber stepped down as chairman of the BFC, but he remained on the BFC and retained "a direct line to the mayor." . . .

Four days after the CSB's first meeting, Mayor DeStefano's executive aide sent an e-mail [that] clearly indicated that the Mayor had made up his mind to oppose certification of the test results (but nevertheless wanted to conceal that fact from the public):

I wanted to make sure we are all on the same page for this meeting tomorrow. . . . *[L]et's remember, that these folks are not against certification yet. So we can't go in and tell them that is our position;* we have to deliberate and arrive there as the fairest and most cogent outcome. . . .

Petitioners are firefighters who seek only a fair chance to move up the ranks in their chosen profession. In order to qualify for promotion, they made personal sacrifices. Petitioner Frank Ricci, who is dyslexic, found it necessary to "hir[e] someone, at considerable expense, to read onto audiotape the content of the books and study materials." He "studied an average of eight to thirteen hours a day . . . , even listening to audio tapes while driving his car." Petitioner Benjamin Vargas, who is Hispanic, had to "give up a part-time job," and his wife had to "take leave from her own job in order to take care of their three young children while Vargas studied." "Vargas devoted countless hours to study . . . , missed two of his children's birthdays and over two weeks of vacation time," and "incurred significant financial expense" during the three-month study period.

Petitioners were denied promotions for which they qualified because of the race and ethnicity of the firefighters who achieved the highest scores on the City's exam. The District Court threw out their case on summary judgment, even though that court all but conceded that a jury could find that the City's asserted justification was pretextual. The Court of Appeals then summarily affirmed that decision.

The dissent grants that petitioners' situation is "unfortunate" and that they "understandably attract this Court's sympathy." But "sympathy" is not what petitioners have a right to demand. What they have a right to demand is evenhanded enforcement of the law-of Title VII's prohibition against discrimination based on race. And that is what, until today's decision, has been denied them.

Justice GINSBURG, with whom Justice STEVENS, Justice SOUTER, and Justice BREYER join, dissenting. . . .

By order of this Court, New Haven, a city in which African-Americans and Hispanics account for nearly 60 percent of the population, must today be served — as it was in the days of undisguised discrimination — by a fire department in which members of racial and ethnic minorities are rarely seen in command positions. . . .

Respondents were no doubt conscious of race during their decisionmaking process, the court acknowledged, but this did not mean they had engaged in racially disparate treatment. The conclusion they had reached and the action thereupon taken were race-neutral in this sense: "[A]ll the test results were discarded, no one was promoted, and firefighters of every race will have to participate in another selection process to be considered for promotion." . . .

Applying what I view as the proper standard to the record thus far made, I would hold that New Haven had ample cause to believe its selection process was flawed and not justified by business necessity. Judged by that standard, petitioners have not shown that New Haven's failure to certify the exam results violated Title VII's disparate-treatment provision. [T]he record solidly establishes that the City had good cause to fear disparate-impact liability.

It is indeed regrettable that the City's noncertification decision would have required all candidates to go through another selection process. But it would have been more regrettable to rely on flawed exams to shut out candidates who may well have the command presence and other qualities needed to excel as fire officers. Yet that is the choice the Court makes today. . . .

————————

Comment on *Ricci*. Though the majority interpreted the statute to avoid the constitutional issue, what does *Ricci* foretell if the Court decided on such a basis? If the Congress amends the voting rights act and adopts the dissent's test, in an effort to encourage voluntary compliance, so that an employer may discard the results of an examination if it has "ample cause to believe its selection process was flawed and not justified by business necessity," would such a statute be constitutional?

a. *BAKKE* REVISITED

Despite several decisions dealing with affirmative action the Court avoided reviewing the central issues of *Bakke* (1978) until 2003. The decisions in the intervening years seemed to question the contemporary vitality of the *Bakke* opinion. Foremost among such was a decision by the 5th Circuit Court Appeals reviewing the constitutionality of a preferential admission policy at the University of Texas Law School, *Hopwood v. Texas,* 78 F.3d 932 (1996). The 5th Circuit, in an opinion by Justice Smith, not only struck down the racial preference in the Texas program as violative of the Equal Protection Clause, but took a step out on its own, and held that *Bakke* was overruled, if not in their view, then in their view of what the Supreme Court's thoughts were. Justice Smith held that to the 5th Circuit, "[Justice] Powell's view in *Bakke* is not binding precedent on this issue." That, "any consideration of race or ethnicity by the law school for the purpose of achieving a diverse student body is not a compelling interest under the Fourteenth Amendment. [In] short, there has been no indication from the Supreme Court, other than Justice Powell's lonely opinion in *Bakke,* that the state's interest in diversity constitutes a compelling justification for governmental race-based discrimination. Subsequent Supreme Court case law strongly suggests, in fact, that it is not."

The *Hopwood* soup was thickened when the Supreme Court refused to grant certiorari. Notably, Justices Ginsburg and Souter concurred and commented in regard to the denial: "Whether it is constitutional for a public college or graduate school to use race or national origin as a factor in its admissions process is an issue of great national importance. The petition before us, however, does not challenge the lower courts' *judgments* that the particular admissions procedure used by the University of Texas Law School in 1992 was unconstitutional. Acknowledging that the 1992 admissions program "has long since been discontinued and will not be reinstated," the petitioners do not defend that program in this Court, ("We agree that the 1992 [admissions] policy was constitutionally flawed. . . ."). Instead, petitioners challenge the *rationale* relied on by the Court of Appeals. "[T]his Court," however, "reviews judgments, not opinions." Chevron U.S.A. Inc. v. Natural Resources Defense Council, Inc., 467 U.S. 837, 842, 104 S.Ct. 2778, 2781, 81 L.Ed.2d 694 (1984) (footnote omitted). Accordingly, we must await a final judgment on a program genuinely in controversy before addressing the important question raised in this petition. ("[A]ll concede this record is inadequate to assess definitively" the constitutionality of the law school's current consideration of race in its admissions process.)." *Hopwood v. Texas,* 518 U.S. 1033 (1996) cert. denied.

In two companion decisions in the 2003 term, however, the Court reviewed equal protection challenges to the use of race preferences in admissions at the University of

Michigan in both their undergraduate and law school programs. In these decisions, *Grutter* (Law School) and *Gratz* (Undergraduate), the Court reaffirmed and elaborated upon Justice Powell's opinion for the Court in *Bakke* finding diversity a compelling interest in the context of university admissions. In doing such the Court seemed to set aside any challenge to the relevancy of *Bakke*. Applying that standard, the Court issued split judgments, upholding the use of race preferences by the Law School on the ground that it was part of individualized review of files that was narrowly tailored to produce diversity, but invalidating the use of race preferences in undergraduate admissions on the ground that it involved too mechanical a procedure for taking race into account. These cases follow and undoubtedly set the modern standard in this area — at least for now!

GRUTTER v. BOLLINGER
539 U.S. 306 (2003)

Justice O'CONNOR delivered the opinion of the Court [in which Justices STEVENS, SOUTER, GINSBURG, and BREYER joined in full].

This case requires us to decide whether the use of race as a factor in student admissions by the University of Michigan Law School (Law School) is unlawful.

I. A. The Law School ranks among the Nation's top law schools. It receives more than 3,500 applications each year for a class of around 350 students. Seeking to "admit a group of students who individually and collectively are among the most capable," the Law School looks for individuals with "substantial promise for success in law school" and "a strong likelihood of succeeding in the practice of law and contributing in diverse ways to the well-being of others." [The Law School's admissions policy also] aspires to "achieve that diversity which has the potential to enrich everyone's education and thus make a law school class stronger than the sum of its parts." The policy does not restrict the types of diversity contributions eligible for "substantial weight" in the admissions process, but instead recognizes "many possible bases for diversity admissions." The policy does, however, reaffirm the Law School's longstanding commitment to "one particular type of diversity," that is, "racial and ethnic diversity with special reference to the inclusion of students from groups which have been historically discriminated against, like African-Americans, Hispanics and Native Americans, who without this commitment might not be represented in our student body in meaningful numbers." By enrolling a "'critical mass' of [underrepresented] minority students," the Law School seeks to "ensur[e] their ability to make unique contributions to the character of the Law School." The policy does not define diversity "solely in terms of racial and ethnic status."

B. Petitioner Barbara Grutter is a white Michigan resident who applied to the Law School in 1996 with a 3.8 grade point average and 161 LSAT score. The Law School initially placed petitioner on a waiting list, but subsequently rejected her application. In December 1997, petitioner filed suit [alleging] that respondents discriminated against her on the basis of race in violation of the Fourteenth Amendment. [After a 15-day bench trial,] the District Court concluded that the Law School's use of race as a factor in admissions decisions was unlawful. [Sitting] en bane, the Court of Appeals reversed.

II. A. We last addressed the use of race in public higher education over 25 years ago. In the landmark Bakke case [(1978); 14th ed. p. 752], we reviewed a racial set-aside program that reserved 16 out of 100 seats in a medical school class for members of certain minority groups. [Since] this Court's splintered decision in Bakke, Justice Powell's opinion announcing the judgment of the Court has served as the touchstone for constitutional analysis of race-conscious admissions policies. Public and private universities across the Nation have modeled their own admissions programs on Justice Powell's views on permissible race-conscious policies. [Today] we endorse Justice Powell's view that student body diversity is a compelling state interest that can justify the use of race in university admissions.

B. [We] have held that all racial classifications imposed by government "must be analyzed by a reviewing court under strict scrutiny." This means that such classifications are constitutional only if they are narrowly tailored to further compelling governmental interests. [Strict] scrutiny is not "strict in theory, but fatal in fact." Although all governmental uses of race are subject to strict scrutiny, not all are invalidated by it. [Context] matters when reviewing race-based governmental action under the Equal Protection Clause. [Not] every decision influenced by race is equally objectionable and strict scrutiny is designed to provide a framework for carefully examining the importance and the sincerity of the reasons advanced by the governmental decision maker for the use of race in that particular context.

III. A. With these principles in mind, we turn to the question whether the Law School's use of race is justified by a compelling state interest. Before this Court, as they have throughout this litigation, respondents assert only one justification for their use of race in the admissions process: obtaining "the educational benefits that flow from a diverse student body."

We first wish to dispel the notion that the Law School's argument has been foreclosed, either expressly or implicitly, by our affirmative-action cases decided since Bakke. It is true that some language in those opinions might be read to suggest that remedying past discrimination is the only permissible justification for race-based governmental action. See, e.g., Richmond v. J.A. Croson Co. (plurality opinion) [(1989); 14th ed., p. 770]. But we have never held that the only governmental use of race that can survive strict scrutiny is remedying past discrimination. Nor, since Bakke, have we directly addressed the use of race in the context of public higher education. Today, we hold that the Law School has a compelling interest in attaining a diverse student body.

The Law School's educational judgment that such diversity is essential to its educational mission is one to which we defer. [Our] scrutiny of the interest asserted by the Law School is no less strict for taking into account complex educational judgments in an area that lies primarily within the expertise of the university. Our holding today is in keeping with our tradition of giving a degree of deference to a university's academic decisions. [We] have long recognized that, given the important purpose of public education and the expansive freedoms of speech and thought associated with the university environment, universities occupy a special niche in our constitutional tradition. [Our] conclusion that the Law School has a compelling interest in a diverse student body is informed by our view that attaining a diverse student body is at the heart of the Law School's proper institutional mission.

[The] Law School seeks to "enroll a 'critical mass' of minority students." The Law School's interest is not simply "to assure within its student body some specified percentage of a particular group merely because of its race or ethnic origin." That would amount to outright racial balancing, which is patently unconstitutional. Rather, the Law School's concept of critical mass is defined by reference to the educational benefits that diversity is designed to produce. These benefits are substantial. [The] Law School's admissions policy promotes "cross-racial understanding," helps to break down racial stereotypes, and "enables [students] to better understand persons of different races." These benefits are "important and laudable," because "classroom discussion is livelier, more spirited, and simply more enlightening and interesting" when the students have "the greatest possible variety of backgrounds." [Student] body diversity promotes learning outcomes, and "better prepares students for an increasingly diverse workforce and society, and better prepares them as professionals." These benefits are not theoretical but real, as major American businesses have made clear [in their amicus briefs in support of the University] that the skills needed in today's increasingly global marketplace can only be developed through exposure to widely diverse people, cultures, ideas, and viewpoints. What is more, high-ranking retired officers and civilian leaders of the United States military assert [in their amicus brief] that, "[biased on [their] decades of experience," a "highly qualified, racially diverse officer corps . . . is essential to the military's ability to fulfill its principle mission to provide national security." [At] present, "the military cannot achieve an officer corps that is both highly qualified and racially diverse unless the service academies and the ROTC used limited race-conscious recruiting and admissions policies." [We] agree that "[it requires only a small step from this analysis to conclude that our country's other most selective institutions must remain both diverse and selective."

[Moreover,] universities, and in particular, law schools, represent the training ground for a large number of our Nation's leaders. Individuals with law degrees occupy roughly half the state governorships, more than half the seats in the United States Senate, and more than a third of the seats in the United States House of Representatives. The pattern is even more striking when it comes to highly selective law schools. A handful of these schools accounts for 25 of the 100 United States Senators, 74 United States Courts of Appeals judges, and nearly 200 of the more than 600 United States District Court judges. In order to cultivate a set of leaders with legitimacy in the eyes of the citizenry, it is necessary that the path to leadership be visibly open to talented and qualified individuals of every race and ethnicity.

B. [Even] in the limited circumstance when drawing racial distinctions is permissible to further a compelling state interest, [the means] must be specifically and narrowly framed. [We] find that the Law School's admissions program bears the hallmarks of a narrowly tailored plan. As Justice Powell made clear in Bakke, truly individualized consideration demands that race be used in a flexible, nonmechanical way. It follows from this mandate that universities cannot establish quotas for members of certain racial groups or put members of those groups on separate admissions tracks. Nor can universities insulate applicants who belong to certain racial or ethnic groups from the competition for admission. Universities can, however, consider race or ethnicity more flexibly as a "plus" factor in the context of individualized consideration of each and every applicant. We are satisfied that the Law School's admissions pro-gram, like the Harvard plan described by Justice Powell, does not operate as a quota. [The] Law School's goal of attaining a critical mass of underrepresented minority students does not transform its program into a quota.

[That] a race-conscious admissions program does not operate as a quota does not, by itself, satisfy the requirement of individualized consideration. When using race as a "plus" factor in university admissions, a university's admissions program must remain flexible enough to ensure that each applicant is evaluated as an individual and not in a way that makes an applicant's race or ethnicity the defining feature of his or her application. The importance of this individualized consideration in the context of a race-conscious admissions program is paramount.

Here, the Law School engages in a highly individualized, holistic review of each applicant's file, giving serious consideration to all the ways an applicant might contribute to a diverse educational environment. The Law School affords this individualized consideration to applicants of all races. [We] also find that [the] Law School's race-conscious admissions program adequately ensures that all factors that may contribute to student body diversity are meaningfully considered alongside race in admissions decisions. The Law School does not [limit] in any way the broad range of qualities and experiences that may be considered valuable contributions to student body diversity. To the contrary, the [admissions] policy makes clear "[t]here are many possible bases for diversity admissions," and provides examples of admittees who have lived or traveled widely abroad, are fluent in several languages, have overcome personal adversity and family hardship, have exceptional records of extensive community service, and have had successful careers in other fields. The Law School seriously considers each "applicant's promise of making a notable contribution to the class by way of a particular strength, attainment, or characteristic — e.g., an unusual intellectual achievement, employment experience, nonacademic performance, or personal background." All applicants have the opportunity to highlight their own potential diversity contributions through the submission of a personal statement, letters of recommendation, and an essay describing the ways in which the applicant will contribute to the life and diversity of the Law School.

[Petitioner] and the United States argue that the Law School's plan is not narrowly tailored because race-neutral means exist to obtain the educational benefits of student body diversity that the Law School seeks. We disagree. Narrow tailoring does not require exhaustion of every conceivable race-neutral alternative. Nor does it require a university to choose between maintaining a reputation for excellence or fulfilling a commitment to provide educational opportunities to members of all racial groups. Narrow tailoring does, however, require serious, good faith consideration of workable race-neutral alternatives that will achieve the diversity the university seeks.

We agree with the Court of Appeals that the Law School sufficiently considered workable race-neutral alternatives. The District Court took the Law School to task for failing to consider race-neutral alternatives such as "using a lottery system" or "decreasing the emphasis for all applicants on undergraduate GPA and LSAT scores." But these alternatives would require a dramatic sacrifice of diversity, the academic quality of all admitted students, or both. [The] United States advocates "percentage plans," recently adopted by public undergraduate institutions in Texas, Florida, and California to guarantee admission to all students above a certain class-rank threshold in every high school in the State. The United States does not, however, explain how such plans could work for graduate and professional schools. Moreover, even assuming such plans are race-neutral, they may preclude the university from conducting the individualized assessments necessary to assemble a student body that is not just racially diverse, but diverse along all the qualities valued by the university. We are satisfied that the Law School adequately considered race-neutral alternatives currently capable of producing a critical mass without forcing the Law School to abandon the academic selectivity that is the corner-stone of its educational mission.

[To] be narrowly tailored, a race-conscious admissions program must not "unduly burden individuals who are not members of the favored racial and ethnic groups." We are satisfied that the Law School's admissions program does not. Because the Law School considers "all pertinent elements of diversity," it can (and does) select nonminority applicants who have greater potential to enhance student body diversity over underrepresented minority applicants.

[We] are mindful, however, that "[a] core purpose of the Fourteenth Amendment was to do away with all governmentally imposed discrimination based on race." Accordingly, race-conscious admissions policies must be limited in time. [We] see no reason to exempt race-conscious admissions programs from the requirement that all governmental use of race must have a logical end point. [We] take the Law School at its word that it would "like nothing better than to find a race-neutral admissions formula" and will terminate its race-conscious admissions program as soon as practicable. It has been 25 years since Justice Powell first approved the use of race to further an interest in student body diversity in the context of public higher education. Since that time, the number of minority applicants with high grades and test scores has indeed increased. We expect that 25 years from now, the use of racial preferences will no longer be necessary to further the interest approved today.

IV. In summary, the Equal Protection Clause does not prohibit the Law School's narrowly tailored use of race in admissions decisions to further a compelling interest in obtaining the educational benefits that flow from a diverse student body. [Affirmed.]

Justice GINSBURG, with whom Justice BREYER joins, concurring.

[It] is well documented that conscious and unconscious race bias, even rank discrimination based on race, remains alive in our land, impeding realization of our highest values and ideals. As to public education, data for the years 2000-2001 show that 71.6% of African-American children and 76.3% of Hispanic children attended a school in which minorities made up a majority of the student body. And schools in predominantly minority communities lag far behind others measured by the educational resources available to them. However strong the public's desire for improved education systems may be, it remains the current reality that many minority students encounter markedly inadequate and unequal educational opportunities. [As] lower school education in minority communities improves, an increase in the number of such students may be anticipated. From today's vantage point, one may hope, but not firmly forecast, that over the next generation's span, progress toward nondiscrimination and genuinely equal opportunity will make it safe to sunset affirmative action.

Justice SCALIA, with whom Justice THOMAS joins, concurring in part and dissenting in part.

[Unlike] a clear constitutional holding that racial preferences in state educational institutions are impermissible, or even a clear anticonstitutional holding that racial preferences in state educational institutions are OK, today's Grutter-Gratz split double header [see Gratz v. Bollinger, the undergraduate admissions decision, below] seems perversely designed to prolong the controversy and the litigation. Some future lawsuits will presumably focus on whether the discriminatory scheme in question contains enough evaluation of the applicant "as an individual," and sufficiently avoids "separate admissions tracks" to fall under Grutter rather than Gratz. Some will focus on whether a university has gone beyond the bounds of a "'good faith effort'" and has so zealously pursued its "critical mass" as to make it an unconstitutional de facto quota system, rather than merely "'a permissible goal.'" Other lawsuits may focus on whether, in the particular setting at issue, any educational benefits flow from racial diversity. Still other suits may challenge the bona fides of the institution's expressed commitment to the educational benefits of diversity that immunize the discriminatory scheme in Grutter. (Tempting targets, one would suppose, will be those universities that talk the talk of multiculturalism and racial diversity in the courts but walk the walk of tribalism and racial segregation on their campuses — through minority-only student organizations, separate minority housing opportunities, separate minority student centers, even separate minority-only graduation ceremonies.) And still other suits may claim that the institution's racial preferences have gone below or above the mystical Grutter-approved "critical mass." Finally, litigation can be expected on behalf of minority groups intentionally short changed in the institution's composition of its generic minority "critical mass." I do not look forward to any of these cases. The Constitution proscribes government discrimination on the basis of race, and state-provided education is no exception.

Justice THOMAS, with whom Justice SCALIA joins as to Parts I-VII, concurring in part and dissenting in part.

Frederick Douglass, speaking to a group of abolitionists almost 140 years ago, delivered a message lost on today's majority:

[I]n regard to the colored people, there is always more that is benevolent, I perceive, than just, manifested towards us. What I ask for the negro is not benevolence, not pity, not sympathy, but simply justice. The American people have always been anxious to know what they shall do with us. . . . I have had but one answer from the beginning. Do nothing with us! Your doing with us has already played the mischief with us. Do nothing with us! If the apples will not remain on the tree of their own strength, if they are worm-eaten at the core, if they are early ripe and disposed to fall, let them fall! . . . And if the negro cannot stand on his own legs, let him fall also. All I ask is, give him a chance to stand on his own legs! Let him alone! . . . [Y]our interference is doing him positive injury.

Like Douglass, I believe blacks can achieve in every avenue of American life without the meddling of university administrators. Because I wish to see all students succeed whatever their color, I share, in some respect, the sympathies of those who sponsor the type of discrimination advanced by the University of Michigan Law School (Law School). The Constitution does not, however, tolerate institutional devotion to the status quo in admissions policies when such devotion ripens into racial discrimination. Nor does the Constitution countenance the unprecedented deference the Court gives to the Law School, an approach inconsistent with the very concept of "strict scrutiny."

I.

[The] Constitution abhors classifications based on race, not only because those classifications can harm favored races or are based on illegitimate motives, but also because every time the government places citizens on racial registers and makes race relevant to the provision of burdens or benefits, it demeans us all.

II.

[Unlike] the majority, I seek to define with precision the interest being asserted by the Law School before determining whether that interest is so compelling as to justify racial discrimination. The Law School maintains that it wishes to obtain "educational benefits that flow from student body diversity." [But attaining] "diversity," whatever it means,* is the mechanism by which the Law School obtains educational benefits, not an end of itself. [It] is the educational benefits that are the end, or allegedly compelling state interest, not "diversity." [But the] Law School [refuses] to entertain changes to its current admissions system that might produce the same educational benefits. The Law School adamantly disclaims any race-neutral alternative that would reduce "academic selectivity." [Instead] the Court upholds the use of racial discrimination as a tool to advance the Law School's interest in offering a marginally superior education while maintaining an elite institution.

III.

[Under] the proper standard, there is no pressing public necessity in maintaining a public law school at all and, it follows, certainly not an elite law school. [While] legal education at a public university may be good policy or otherwise laudable, it is obviously not a pressing public necessity.

IV.

[The] Court never explicitly holds that the Law School's desire to retain the status quo in "academic selectivity" is itself a compelling state interest. [Therefore], the Law School should be forced to choose between its classroom aesthetic and its exclusionary admissions system — it cannot have it both ways. With the adoption of different admissions methods, such as accepting all students who meet minimum qualifications, the Law School could achieve its vision of the racially aesthetic student body without the use of racial discrimination. [The] Court ignores the fact that other top law schools have succeeded in meeting their aesthetic demands without racial discrimination. [The] sky has not fallen at Boalt Hall at the University of California, Berkeley, for example. Prior to Proposition 209's adoption of Cal. Const., Art. 1, § 31(a), which bars the State from "grant[ing] preferential treatment . . . on the basis of race . . . in the operation of . . . public education," Boalt Hall enrolled 20 blacks and 28 Hispanics in its first-year class for 1996. In 2002, without deploying express racial discrimination in admissions, Boalt's entering class enrolled 14 blacks and 36 Hispanics. Total underrepresented minority student enrollment at Boalt Hall now exceeds 1996 levels. [The] Court will not even deign to make the Law School try other methods, however, preferring instead to grant a 25-year license to violate the Constitution.

V.

[The] rallying cry that in the absence of racial discrimination in admissions there would be a true meritocracy ignores the fact that the entire process is poisoned by numerous exceptions to "merit." For example, in the national debate on racial discrimination in

---

* "[D]iversity," for all of its devotees, is more a fashionable catchphrase than it is a useful term, especially when something as serious as racial discrimination is at issue. Because the Equal Protection Clause renders the color of one's skin constitutionally irrelevant to the Law School's mission, I refer to the Law School's interest as an "aesthetic." That is, the Law School wants to have a certain appearance, from the shape of the desks and tables in its classrooms to the color of the students sitting at them. [It] must be remembered that the Law School's racial discrimination does nothing for those too poor or uneducated to participate in elite higher education and therefore presents only an illusory solution to the challenges facing our Nation. [Footnote by Justice Thomas.]

higher education admissions, much has been made of the fact that elite institutions utilize a so-called "legacy" preference to give the children of alumni an advantage in admissions. This, and other, exceptions to a "true" meritocracy give the lie to protestations that merit admissions are in fact the order of the day at the Nation's universities. The Equal Protection Clause does not, however, prohibit the use of unseemly legacy preferences or many other kinds of arbitrary admissions procedures. What the Equal Protection Clause does prohibit are classifications made on the basis of race. So while legacy preferences can stand under the Constitution, racial discrimination cannot.[*]

VI.

[I must also] contest the notion that the Law School's discrimination benefits those admitted as a result of it. [The] Law School tantalizes unprepared students with the promise of a University of Michigan degree and all of the opportunities that it offers. These overmatched students take the bait, only to find that they cannot succeed in the cauldron of competition. [To] cover the tracks of the aestheticists, this cruel farce of racial discrimination must continue — in selection for the Michigan Law Review, and in hiring at law firms and for judicial clerkships — until the "beneficiaries" are no longer tolerated. While these students may graduate with law degrees, there is no evidence that they have received a qualitatively better legal education (or become better lawyers) than if they had gone to a less "elite" law school for which they were better prepared.

[Beyond] the harm the Law School's racial discrimination visits upon its test subjects, no social science has disproved the notion that this discrimination "engender[s] attitudes of superiority or, alternatively, provoke [s] resentment among those who believe that they have been wronged by the government's use of race." "These programs stamp minorities with a badge of inferiority and may cause them to develop dependencies or to adopt an attitude that they are 'entitled' to preferences." It is uncontested that each year, the Law School admits a handful of blacks who would be admitted in the absence of racial discrimination. Who can differentiate between those who belong and those who do not? The majority of blacks are admitted to the Law School because of discrimination, and because of this policy all are tarred as undeserving. This problem of stigma does not depend on determinacy as to whether those stigmatized are actually the "beneficiaries" of racial discrimination. When blacks take positions in the highest places of government, industry, or academia, it is an open question today whether their skin color played a part in their advancement. The question itself is the stigma — because either racial discrimination did play a role, in which case the person may be deemed "otherwise unqualified," or it did not, in which case asking the question itself unfairly marks those blacks who would succeed without discrimination.

VII.

As the foregoing makes clear, I believe the Court's opinion to be, in most respects, erroneous. I do, however, find two points on which I agree. First, I note that the issue of unconstitutional racial discrimination among the groups the Law School prefers is not presented in this case. [I] join the Court's opinion insofar as it confirms that this type of racial discrimination remains unlawful. Under today's decision, it is still the case that racial discrimination that does not help a university to enroll an unspecified number, or "critical mass," of underrepresented minority students is unconstitutional. Thus, the Law

---

[*] Were this Court to have the courage to forbid the use of racial discrimination in admissions, legacy preferences (and similar practices) might quickly become less popular — a possibility not lost, I am certain, on the elites (both individual and institutional) supporting the Law School in this case. [Footnote by Justice Thomas.]

School may not discriminate in admissions between similarly situated blacks and Hispanics, or between whites and Asians. [The] Court also holds that racial discrimination in admissions should be given another 25 years before it is deemed no longer narrowly tailored to the Law School's fabricated compelling state interest. While I agree that in 25 years the practices of the Law School will be illegal, they are, for the reasons I have given, illegal now.

[For] the immediate future, however, the majority has placed its imprimatur on a practice that can only weaken the principle of equality embodied in the Declaration of Independence and the Equal Protection Clause. "Our Constitution is color-blind, and neither knows nor tolerates classes among citizens." Plessy v. Ferguson, [(1896) (Harlan, J., dissenting)]. It has been nearly 140 years since Frederick Douglass asked the intellectual ancestors of the Law School to "[d]o nothing with us!" and the Nation adopted the Fourteenth Amendment. Now we must wait another 25 years to see this principle of equality vindicated. I therefore respectfully dissent from the remainder of the Court's opinion and the judgment.

Chief Justice REHNQUIST, with whom Justice SCALIA, Justice KENNEDY, and Justice THOMAS join, dissenting.

I agree with the Court that, "in the limited circumstance when drawing racial distinctions is permissible," the government must ensure that its means are narrowly tailored to achieve a compelling state interest. I do not believe, however, that the University of Michigan Law School's (Law School) means are narrowly tailored to the interest it asserts. The Law School claims it must take the steps it does to achieve a "'critical mass'" of underrepresented minority students. But its actual program bears no relation to this asserted goal.

[From] 1995 through 2000, the Law School admitted between 1,130 and 1,310 students. Of those, between 13 and 19 were Native American, between 91 and 108 were African-Americans, and between 47 and 56 were Hispanic. If the Law School is admitting between 91 and 108 African-Americans in order to achieve "critical mass," thereby preventing African-American students from feeling "isolated or like spokespersons for their race," one would think that a number of the same order of magnitude would be necessary to accomplish the same purpose for Hispanics and Native Americans. [In] order for this pattern of admission to be consistent with the Law School's explanation of "critical mass," one would have to believe that the objectives of "critical mass" offered by respondents are achieved with only half the number of Hispanics and one-sixth the number of Native Americans as compared to African-Americans. But respondents *offer* no race-specific reasons for such disparities. Instead, they simply 'emphasize the importance of achieving "critical mass," without any explanation of why that concept is applied differently among the three under-represented minority groups.

[Only] when the "critical mass" label is discarded does a likely explanation for these numbers emerge. The Court states that the Law School's goal of attaining a "critical mass" of underrepresented minority students is not an interest in merely" assur[ing] within its student body some specified percent-age of a particular group merely because of its race or ethnic origin.'" The Court recognizes that such an interest "would amount to outright racial balancing, which is patently unconstitutional." The Court concludes, however, that the Law School's use of race in admissions, consistent with Justice Powell's opinion in Bakke, only pays" [s]ome attention to numbers.'" But the correlation between the percentage of the Law School's pool of applicants who are members of the three minority groups and the percentage of the admitted applicants who are members of these same groups is far too precise to be dismissed as merely the result of the school paying "some attention to [the] numbers." [From] 1995 through 2000 the percentage of admitted applicants who were members of these minority groups closely tracked the percentage of individuals in the school's applicant pool who were from the same groups. [For] example, in 1995, when 9.7% of the applicant pool was African-American, 9.4% of the admitted class was African-American. By 2000, only 7.5% of the applicant pool was African-American, and 7.3% of the admitted class was African-American. This correlation is striking. [The] tight correlation between the percentage of applicants and admittees of a given race [must] result from careful race based planning by the Law School.

[I] do not believe that the Constitution gives the Law School such free rein in the use of race. The Law School has offered no explanation for its actual admissions practices and, unexplained, we are bound to conclude that the Law School has managed its admissions program, not to achieve a "critical mass," but to extend offers of admission to members of selected minority groups in proportion to their statistical representation in the applicant pool. But this is precisely the type of racial balancing that the Court itself calls "patently unconstitutional."

GRATZ v. BOLLINGER
539 U.S. 244 (2003)

Chief Justice REHNQUIST delivered the opinion of the Court [in which Justices O'CONNOR, SCALIA, KENNEDY, and THOMAS, joined].

[This case, like Grutter, involved a challenge by white students to an admissions policy of the University of Michigan, this time by the undergraduate College of Literature, Science, and the Arts (LSA). Although the college considered the challengers "qualified," they were ultimately denied admission. The college considered a number of factors in making admissions decisions, including high school grades, standardized test scores, high school quality, curriculum strength, geography, alumni relationships, leadership, and race. The college used a selection method under which every applicant from an underrepresented racial or ethnic minority group — namely, African-Americans, Hispanics, and Native Americans — was automatically awarded 20 points of the 100 needed to guarantee admission. It was undisputed that the University admitted virtually every qualified applicant from these groups. The majority opinion began by dismissing the dissenters' objections that the challengers lacked standing. The Chief Justice proceeded:]

Petitioners argue [that] the University's use of race in undergraduate admissions violates the Fourteenth Amendment [because] this Court has only sanctioned the use of racial classifications to remedy identified discrimination, a justification on which respondents have never relied, [and that] "diversity as a basis for employing racial preferences is simply too open-ended, ill-defined, and indefinite to constitute a compelling interest capable of supporting narrowly-tailored means." [For] the reasons set forth today in Grutter v. Bollinger [above] the Court has rejected these arguments. [But we] find that the University's policy, which automatically distributes 20 points, or one-fifth of the points needed to guarantee admission, to every single "underrepresented minority" applicant solely because of race, is not narrowly tailored to achieve the interest in educational diversity that respondents claim justifies their program.

[Justice] Powell's opinion in Bakke emphasized the importance of considering each particular applicant as an individual, assessing all of the qualities that individual possesses, and in turn, evaluating that individual's ability to contribute to the unique setting of higher education. The admissions program Justice Powell described, however, did not contemplate that any single characteristic automatically ensured a specific and identifiable contribution to a university's diversity. [The] current LSA policy does not provide such individualized consideration. The LSA's policy automatically distributes 20 points to every single applicant from an "underrepresented minority" group, as defined by the University. The only consideration that accompanies this distribution of points is a factual review of an application to determine whether an individual is a member of one of these minority groups. [Even if a student's] "extraordinary artistic talent" rivaled that of Monet or Picasso, the applicant would receive, at most, five points under the LSA's system. At the same time, every single underrepresented minority applicant [would] automatically receive 20 points for submitting an application. Clearly, the LSA's system does not offer applicants the individualized selection process.

[Respondents] contend that "[t]he volume of applications and the presentation of applicant information make it impractical for [LSA] to use the . . . admissions system" upheld by the Court today in Grutter. But the fact that the implementation of a program capable of providing individualized consideration might present administrative challenges does not render constitutional an otherwise problematic system. Nothing in Justice Powell's opinion in Bakke signaled that a university may employ whatever means it desires to achieve the stated goal of diversity without regard to the limits imposed by our strict scrutiny analysis. We conclude, therefore, that because the University's use of race in its current freshman admissions policy is not narrowly tailored to achieve respondents' asserted compelling interest in diversity, the admissions policy violates the Equal Protection Clause of the Fourteenth Amendment.

Justice O'CONNOR, concurring.

Unlike the law school admissions policy the Court upholds today in Grutter, the procedures employed by the University of Michigan's Office of Undergraduate Admissions do not provide for a meaningful individualized review of applicants. The law school considers the various diversity qualifications of each applicant, including race, on a case-by-case basis. By contrast, the Office of Undergraduate Admissions relies on the selection index to assign every underrepresented minority applicant the same, automatic 20-point bonus without consideration of the particular background, experiences, or qualities of each individual applicant. [Although] the Office of Undergraduate Admissions does assign 20 points to some "soft" variables other than race, the points available for other diversity contributions, such as leadership and service, personal achievement, and geographic diversity, are capped at much lower levels. Even the most outstanding national high school leader could never receive more than five points for his or her accomplishments — a mere quarter of the points automatically assigned to an underrepresented minority solely based on the fact of his or her race. [The] selection index, by setting up automatic, predetermined point allocations for the soft variables, ensures that the diversity contributions of applicants cannot be individually assessed. This policy stands in sharp contrast to the law school's admissions plan, which enables admissions officers to make nuanced judgments with respect to the contributions each applicant is likely to make to the diversity of the incoming class.

Justice THOMAS, concurring.

I join the Court's opinion because I believe it correctly applies our precedents, including today's decision in Grutter v. Bollinger. For similar reasons to those given in my separate opinion in that case, however, I would hold that a State's use of racial discrimination in higher education admissions is categorically prohibited by the Equal Protection Clause.

Justice SOUTER, dissenting.

[Even] if the merits were reachable, I would dissent from the Court's judgment. [The] cases now contain two pointers toward the line between the valid and the unconstitutional in race-conscious admissions schemes. Grutter reaffirms the permissibility of individualized consideration of race to achieve a diversity of students, at least where race is not assigned a preordained value in all cases. On the other hand, Justice Powell's opinion in [Bakke] rules out a racial quota or set-aside, in which race is the sole fact of eligibility for certain places in a class. Although the freshman admissions system here is subject to argument on the merits, I think it is closer to what Grutter approves than to what Bakke condemns, and should not be held unconstitutional on the current record.

The record does not describe a system with a quota like the one struck down in Bakke, which "insulate[d]" all nonminority candidates from competition from certain seats. [The] plan here, in contrast, lets all applicants compete for all places and values an applicant's offering for any place not only on grounds of race, but on grades, test scores, strength of high school, quality of course of study, residence, alumni relationships, leadership, personal character, socioeconomic disadvantage, athletic ability, and quality of a personal essay. [The] one qualification to this description of the admissions process is that membership in an underrepresented minority is given a weight of 20 points on the 150-point scale. On the face of things, however, this assignment of specific points does not set race apart from all other weighted considerations. Nonminority students may receive 20 points for athletic ability, socioeconomic disadvantage, attendance at a socioeconomically disadvantaged or predominantly minority high school, or at the Provost's discretion; they may also receive 10 points for being residents of Michigan, 6 for residence in an underrepresented Michigan county, 5 for leadership and service, and so on. [Since] college admission is not left entirely to inarticulate intuition, it is hard to see what is inappropriate in assigning some stated value to a relevant characteristic, whether it be reasoning ability, writing style, running speed, or minority race. [Nor] is it possible to say that the 20 points convert race into a decisive factor comparable to reserving minority places as in Bakke.

[It] seems especially unfair to treat the candor of the admissions plan as an Achilles' heel. In contrast to the college's forthrightness in saying just what plus factor it gives for membership in an underrepresented minority, it is worth considering the character of one alternative thrown up as preferable, because supposedly not based on race. Drawing on admissions systems used at public universities in California, Florida, and Texas, the United States contends that Michigan could get student diversity in satisfaction of its compelling interest by guaranteeing admission to a fixed percentage of the top students from each high school in Michigan. While there is nothing unconstitutional about such a practice, it nonetheless suffers from a serious disadvantage. It is the disadvantage of deliberate obfuscation. The "percentage plans" are just as race conscious as the point scheme (and fairly so), but they get their racially diverse results without saying directly what they are doing or why they are doing it. In contrast, Michigan states its purpose directly and, if this were a doubtful case for me, I would be tempted to give Michigan an extra point of its own for its frankness. Equal protection cannot become an exercise in which the winners are the ones who hide the ball.

Justice GINSBURG, with whom Justice SOUTER joins, dissenting.

[The] Court once again maintains that the same standard of review controls judicial inspection of all official race classifications. This insistence on "consistency" would be fitting were our Nation free of the vestiges of rank discrimination long reinforced by law. But we are not far distant from an overtly discriminatory past, and the effects of centuries of law-sanctioned inequality remain painfully evident in our communities and schools. [Unemployment], poverty, and access to health care vary disproportionately by race. Neighborhoods and schools remain racially divided. African-American and Hispanic children are all too often educated in poverty-stricken and underperforming institutions. Adult African-Americans and Hispanics generally earn less than whites with equivalent levels of education. Equally credentialed job applicants receive different receptions depending on their race. Irrational prejudice is still encountered in real estate markets and consumer transactions.

[The] Constitution instructs all who act for the government that they may not "deny to any person . . . the equal protection of the laws." Amdt. 14, § 1. In implementing this equality instruction, as I see it, government decision makers may properly distinguish between policies of exclusion and inclusion. Actions designed to burden groups long denied full citizenship stature are not sensibly ranked with measures taken to hasten the day when entrenched discrimination and its after effects have been extirpated. [Where] race is considered "for the purpose of achieving equality," no automatic proscription is in order.

[Examining] in this light the admissions policy employed by [LSA], I see no constitutional infirmity. Like other top-ranking institutions, the College has many more applicants for admission than it can accommodate in an entering class. Every applicant admitted under the current plan [is] qualified to attend the College. The racial and ethnic groups to which the College accords special consideration (African-Americans, Hispanics, and Native-Americans) historically have been relegated to inferior status by law and social practice; their members continue to experience class-based discrimination to this day. There is no suggestion that the College adopted its current policy in order to limit or decrease enrollment by any particular racial or ethnic group, and no seats are reserved on the basis of race. Nor has there been any demonstration that the College's program unduly constricts admissions opportunities for students who do not receive special consideration based on race.

The stain of generations of racial oppression is still visible in our society, and the determination to hasten its removal remains vital. One can reasonably anticipate, therefore, that colleges and universities will seek to maintain their minority enrollment — and the networks and opportunities thereby opened to minority graduates — whether or not they can do so in full candor through adoption of affirmative action plans of the kind here at issue. Without recourse to such plans, institutions of higher education may resort to camouflage. For example, schools may encourage applicants to write of their cultural traditions in the essays they submit, or to indicate whether English is their second language. Seeking to improve their chances for admission, applicants may highlight the minority group associations to which they belong, or the Hispanic surnames of their mothers or grandparents. [If] honesty is the best policy, surely Michigan's accurately described, fully disclosed College affirmative action program is preferable to achieving similar numbers through winks, nods, and disguises.

Comment on *Grutter* and *Gratz*. Is *Bakke* still good law? What are the differences between Justice Powell's opinion in *Bakke* and the majority's findings in *Grutter* and *Gratz*? How would you design an affirmative action program for your law school based upon these cases? What do you think of the "soul searching" in Justice Thomas's opinion? Does it have merit?

FISHER v. THE UNIVERSITY OF TEXAS AT AUSTIN
579 U.S. 365 (2016)

JUSTICE KENNEDY delivered the opinion of the Court.

The Court is asked once again to consider whether the race-conscious admissions program at the University of Texas is lawful under the Equal Protection Clause.

I

The University of Texas at Austin (or University) relies upon a complex system of admissions that has undergone significant evolution over the past two decades. Until 1996, the University made its admissions decisions primarily based on a measure called "Academic Index" (or AI), which it calculated by combining an applicant's SAT score and academic performance in high school. In assessing applicants, preference was given to racial minorities.

In 1996, the Court of Appeals for the Fifth Circuit invalidated this admissions system, holding that any consideration of race in college admissions violates the Equal Protection Clause. See Hopwood v. Texas, 78 F. 3d 932, 934–935, 948.

One year later the University adopted a new admissions policy. Instead of considering race, the University began making admissions decisions based on an applicant's AI and his or her "Personal Achievement Index" (PAI). The PAI was a numerical score based on a holistic review of an application. Included in the number were the applicant's essays, leadership and work experience, extracurricular activities, community service, and other "special characteristics" that might give the admissions committee insight into a student's background. Consistent with Hopwood, race was not a consideration in calculating an applicant's AI or PAI.

The Texas Legislature responded to Hopwood as well. It enacted H. B. 588, commonly known as the Top Ten Percent Law. Tex. Educ. Code Ann. §51.803 (West Cum. Supp. 2015). As its name suggests, the Top Ten Percent Law guarantees college admission to students who graduate from a Texas high school in the top 10 percent of their class. Those students may choose to attend any of the public universities in the State.

The University implemented the Top Ten Percent Law in 1998. After first admitting any student who qualified for admission under that law, the University filled the remainder of its incoming freshman class using a combination of an applicant's AI and PAI scores—again, without considering race.

The University used this admissions system until 2003, when this Court decided the companion cases of Grutter v. Bollinger, 539 U. S. 306, and Gratz v. Bollinger, 539 U. S. 244. In Gratz, this Court struck down the University of Michigan's undergraduate system of admissions, which at the time allocated predetermined points to racial minority candidates. See 539 U. S., at 255, 275–276. In Grutter, however, the Court upheld the University of Michigan Law School's system of holistic review—a system that did not mechanically assign points but rather treated race as a relevant feature within the broader context of a candidate's application. See 539 U. S., at 337, 343–344. In upholding this nuanced use of race, Grutter implicitly overruled Hopwood's categorical prohibition.

In the wake of Grutter, the … University concluded that its admissions policy was not providing these benefits. To change its system, the University submitted a proposal to the Board of Regents that requested permission to begin taking race into consideration as one of "the many ways in which [an] academically qualified individual might contribute to, and benefit from, the rich, diverse, and challenging educational environment of the University." Id., at 23a. After the board approved the proposal, the University adopted a new admissions policy to implement it. The University has continued to use that admissions policy to this day.

Although the University's new admissions policy was a direct result of Grutter, it is not identical to the policy this Court approved in that case. Instead, consistent with the State's legislative directive, the University continues to fill a significant majority of its class through the Top Ten Percent Plan (or Plan). Today, up to 75 percent of the places in the freshman class are filled through the Plan. As a practical matter, this 75 percent cap, which has now been fixed by statute, means that, while the Plan continues to be referenced as a "Top Ten Percent Plan," a student actually needs to finish in the top seven or eight percent of his or her class in order to be admitted under this category.

The University did adopt an approach similar to the one in Grutter for the remaining 25 percent or so of the incoming class. This portion of the class continues to be admitted based on a combination of their AI and PAI scores. Now, however, race is given weight as a subfactor within the PAI. The PAI is a number from 1 to 6 (6 is the best) that is based on two primary components. The first component is the average score a reader gives the applicant on two required essays. The second component is a full-file review that results in another 1-to-6 score, the "Personal Achievement Score" or PAS. The PAS is determined by a separate reader, who (1) rereads the applicant's required essays, (2) reviews any supplemental information the applicant submits (letters of recommendation, resumes, an additional optional essay, writing samples, artwork, etc.), and (3) evaluates the applicant's potential contributions to the University's student body based on the applicant's leadership experience, extracurricular activities, awards/honors, community service, and other "special circumstances."

"Special circumstances" include the socioeconomic status of the applicant's family, the socioeconomic status of the applicant's school, the applicant's family responsibilities, whether the applicant lives in a single-parent home, the applicant's SAT score in relation to the average SAT score at the applicant's school, the language spoken at the applicant's home, and, finally, the applicant's race. See App. 218a–220a, 430a.

[Once] the essay and full-file readers have calculated each applicant's AI and PAI scores, admissions officers from each school within the University set a cutoff PAI/AI score combination for admission, and then admit all of the applicants who are above that cutoff point. In setting the cutoff, those admissions officers only know how many applicants received a given PAI/AI score combination. They do not know what factors went into calculating those applicants' scores. The admissions officers who make the final decision as to whether a particular applicant will be admitted make that decision without knowing the applicant's race. Race enters the admissions process, then, at one stage and one stage only—the calculation of the PAS.

Therefore, although admissions officers can consider race as a positive feature of a minority student's application, there is no dispute that race is but a "factor of a factor of a factor" in the holistic-review calculus. 645 F. Supp. 2d 587, 608 (WD Tex. 2009). Furthermore, consideration of race is contextual and does not operate as a mechanical plus factor for underrepresented minorities. Id., at 606 ("Plaintiffs cite no evidence to show racial groups other than African-Americans and Hispanics are excluded from benefitting from UT's consideration of race in admissions. As the Defendants point out, the consideration of race, within the full context of the entire application, may be beneficial to any UT Austin applicant— including whites and Asian-Americans"); see also Brief for Asian American Legal Defense and Education Fund et al. as Amici Curiae 12 (the contention that the University discriminates against Asian-Americans is "entirely unsupported by evidence in the record or empirical data"). There is also no dispute, however, that race, when considered in conjunction with other aspects of an applicant's background, can alter an applicant's PAS score. Thus, race, in this indirect fashion, considered with all of the other factors that make up an applicant's AI and PAI scores, can make a difference to whether an application is accepted or rejected.

Petitioner Abigail Fisher applied for admission to the University's 2008 freshman class. She was not in the top 10 percent of her high school class, so she was evaluated for admission through holistic, full-file review. Petitioner's application was rejected.

Petitioner then filed suit alleging that the University's consideration of race as part of its holistic-review process disadvantaged her and other Caucasian applicants, in violation of the Equal Protection Clause. See U. S. Const., Amdt. 14, §1 (no State shall "deny to any person within its jurisdiction the equal protection of the laws"). The District Court entered summary judgment in the University's favor, and the Court of Appeals affirmed.

This Court granted certiorari and vacated the judgment of the Court of Appeals, Fisher v. University of Tex. at Austin, 570 U. S. ___ (2013) (Fisher I), because it had applied an overly deferential "good-faith" standard in assessing the constitutionality of the University's program. The Court remanded the case for the Court of Appeals to assess the parties' claims under the correct legal standard. Without further remanding to the District Court, the Court of Appeals again affirmed the entry of summary judgment in the University's favor. 758 F. 3d 633 (CA5 2014). This Court granted certiorari for a second time, 576 U. S. ___ (2015), and now affirms.

II

Fisher I set forth three controlling principles relevant to assessing the constitutionality of a public university's affirmative-action program. First, "because racial characteristics so seldom provide a relevant basis for disparate treatment," Richmond v. J. A. Croson Co., 488 U. S. 469, 505 (1989), "[r]ace may not be considered [by a university] unless the admissions process can withstand strict scrutiny," Fisher I, 570 U. S., at ___ (slip op., at 7). Strict scrutiny requires the university to demonstrate with clarity that its "'purpose or interest is both constitutionally permissible and substantial, and that its use of the classification is necessary . . . to the accomplishment of its purpose.'" Ibid.

Second, Fisher I confirmed that "the decision to pursue 'the educational benefits that flow from student body diversity' . . . is, in substantial measure, an academic judgment to which some, but not complete, judicial deference is proper." Id., at ___ (slip op, at 9). A university cannot impose a fixed quota or otherwise "define diversity as 'some specified percentage of a particular group merely because of its race or ethnic origin.'" Ibid. Once, however, a university gives "a reasoned, principled explanation" for its decision, deference must be given "to the University's conclusion, based on its experience and expertise, that a diverse student body would serve its educational goals." Ibid. (internal quotation marks and citation omitted).

Third, Fisher I clarified that no deference is owed when determining whether the use of race is narrowly tailored to achieve the university's permissible goals. Id., at ___ (slip op., at 10). A university, Fisher I explained, bears the burden of proving a "nonracial approach" would not promote its interest in the educational benefits of diversity "about as well and at tolerable administrative expense." Id., at ___ (slip op., at 11) (internal quotation marks omitted). Though "[n]arrow tailoring does not require exhaustion of every conceivable race-neutral alternative" or "require a university to choose between maintaining a reputation for excellence [and] fulfilling a commitment to provide educational opportunities to members of all racial groups," Grutter, 539 U. S., at 339, it does impose "on the university the ultimate burden of demonstrating" that "race-neutral alternatives" that are both "available" and "workable" "do not suffice." Fisher I, 570 U. S., at ___ (slip op., at 11).

Fisher I set forth these controlling principles, while taking no position on the constitutionality of the admissions program at issue in this case. The Court held only that the District Court and the Court of Appeals had "confined the strict scrutiny inquiry in too narrow a way by deferring to the University's good faith in its use of racial classifications." Id., at ___ (slip op., at 12) The Court remanded the case, with instructions to evaluate the record under the correct standard and to determine whether the University had made "a showing that its plan is narrowly tailored to achieve" the educational benefits that flow from diversity. Id., at ___ (slip op., at 13). On remand, the Court of Appeals determined that the program conformed with the strict scrutiny mandated by Fisher I. See 758 F. 3d, at 659–660. Judge Garza dissented.

III

The University's program is sui generis. Unlike other approaches to college admissions considered by this Court, it combines holistic review with a percentage plan. This approach gave rise to an unusual consequence in this case: The component of the University's admissions policy that had the largest impact on petitioner's chances of admission was not the school's consideration of race under its holistic-review process but rather the Top Ten Percent Plan. Because petitioner did not graduate in the top 10 percent of her high school class, she was categorically ineligible for more than three-fourths of the slots in the incoming freshman class. It seems quite plausible, then, to think that petitioner would have had a better chance of being admitted to the University if the school used race conscious holistic review to select its entire incoming class, as was the case in Grutter.

Despite the Top Ten Percent Plan's outsized effect on petitioner's chances of admission, she has not challenged it. For that reason, throughout this litigation, the Top Ten Percent Plan has been taken, somewhat artificially, as a given premise.

Petitioner's acceptance of the Top Ten Percent Plan complicates this Court's review. In particular, it has led to a record that is almost devoid of information about the students who secured admission to the University through the Plan. The Court thus cannot know how students admitted solely based on their class rank differ in their contribution to diversity from students admitted through holistic review.

In an ordinary case, this evidentiary gap perhaps could be filled by a remand to the district court for further fact-finding. When petitioner's application was rejected, however, the University's combined percentage-plan/holistic review approach to admission had been in effect for just three years. While studies undertaken over the eight years since then may be of significant value in determining the constitutionality of the University's current admissions policy, that evidence has little bearing on whether petitioner received equal treatment when her application was rejected in 2008. If the Court were to remand, therefore, further fact-finding would be limited to a narrow 3 year sample, review of which might yield little insight.

Under the circumstances of this case, then, a remand would do nothing more than prolong a suit that has already persisted for eight years and cost the parties on both sides significant resources. Petitioner long since has graduated from another college, and the University's policy—and the data on which it first was based—may have evolved or changed in material ways.

The fact that this case has been litigated on a somewhat artificial basis, furthermore, may limit its value for prospective guidance. The Texas Legislature, in enacting the Top Ten Percent Plan, cannot much be criticized, for it was responding to Hopwood, which at the time was binding law in the State of Texas. That legislative response, in turn, circumscribed the University's discretion in crafting its admissions policy. These circumstances refute any criticism that the University did not make good-faith efforts to comply with the law.

[IV]

In seeking to reverse the judgment of the Court of Appeals, petitioner makes four arguments. First, she argues that the University has not articulated its compelling interest with sufficient clarity. According to petitioner, the University must set forth more precisely the level of minority enrollment that would constitute a "critical mass." Without a clearer sense of what the University's ultimate goal is, petitioner argues, a reviewing court cannot assess whether the University's admissions program is narrowly tailored to that goal. As this Court's cases have made clear, however, the compelling interest that justifies consideration of race in college admissions is not an interest in enrolling a certain number of minority students. Rather, a university may institute a race-conscious admissions program as a means of obtaining "the educational benefits that flow from student body diversity." Fisher I, (internal quotation marks omitted); see also Grutter, 539 U. S., at 328. As this Court has said, enrolling a diverse student body "promotes cross-racial understanding, helps to break down racial stereotypes, and enables students to better understand persons of different races." Id., at 330 (internal quotation marks and alteration omitted). Equally important, "student body diversity promotes learning outcomes, and better prepares students for an increasingly diverse workforce and society." Ibid. (internal quotation marks omitted).

Increasing minority enrollment may be instrumental to these educational benefits, but it is not, as petitioner seems to suggest, a goal that can or should be reduced to pure numbers. Indeed, since the University is prohibited from seeking a particular number or quota of minority students, it cannot be faulted for failing to specify the particular level of minority enrollment at which it believes the educational benefits of diversity will be obtained.

On the other hand, asserting an interest in the educational benefits of diversity writ large is insufficient. A university's goals cannot be elusory or amorphous—they must be sufficiently measurable to permit judicial scrutiny of the policies adopted to reach them.

The record reveals that in first setting forth its current admissions policy, the University articulated concrete and precise goals. On the first page of its 2004 "Proposal to Consider Race and Ethnicity in Admissions," the University identifies the educational values it seeks to realize through its admissions process: the destruction of stereotypes, the "'promot[ion of] cross-racial understanding,'" the preparation of a student body "'for an increasingly diverse workforce and society,'" and the "'cultivat[ion of] a set of leaders with legitimacy in the eyes of the citizenry.'" Later in the proposal, the University explains that it strives to provide an "academic environment" that offers a "robust exchange of ideas, exposure to differing cultures, preparation for the challenges of an increasingly diverse workforce, and acquisition of competencies required of future leaders." Supp. App. 23a. All of these objectives, as a general matter, mirror the "compelling interest" this Court has approved in its prior cases.

The University has provided in addition a "reasoned, principled explanation" for its decision to pursue these goals. Fisher I, supra, at ___ (slip op., at 9). The University's 39-page proposal was written following a year-long study, which concluded that "[t]he use of race-neutral policies and programs ha[d] not been successful" in "provid[ing] an educational setting that fosters cross-racial understanding, provid[ing] enlightened discussion and learning, [or] prepar[ing] students to function in an increasingly diverse workforce and society." Supp. App. 25a; see also App. 481a–482a (Walker Aff. ¶¶8–12) (describing the "thoughtful review" the University undertook when it faced the "important decision . . . whether or not to use race in its admissions process"). Further support for the University's conclusion can be found in the depositions and affidavits from various admissions officers, all of whom articulate the same, consistent "reasoned, principled explanation." Petitioner's contention that the University's goal was insufficiently concrete is rebutted by the record.

Second, petitioner argues that the University has no need to consider race because it had already "achieved critical mass" by 2003 using the Top Ten Percent Plan and race-neutral holistic review. Brief for Petitioner 46. Petitioner is correct that a university bears a heavy burden in showing that it had not obtained the educational benefits of diversity before it turned to a race-conscious plan. The record reveals, however, that, at the time of petitioner's application, the University could not be faulted on this score. Before changing its policy the University conducted "months of study and deliberation, including retreats, interviews, [and] review of data," App. 446a, and concluded that "[t]he use of race-neutral policies and programs ha[d] not been successful in achieving" sufficient racial diversity at the University, Supp. App. 25a. At no stage in this litigation has petitioner challenged the University's good faith in conducting its studies, and the Court properly declines to consider the extra record materials the dissent relies upon, many of which are tangential to this case at best and none of which the University has had a full opportunity to respond to. See, e.g., post, at 45– 46 (opinion of ALITO, J.) (describing a 2015 report regarding the admission of applicants who are related to ''politically connected individuals'').

The record itself contains significant evidence, both statistical and anecdotal, in support of the University's position. To start, the demographic data the University has submitted show consistent stagnation in terms of the percentage of minority students enrolling at the University from 1996 to 2002. In 1996, for example, 266 African American freshmen enrolled, a total that constituted 4.1 percent of the incoming class. In 2003, the year Grutter was decided, 267 African-American students enrolled— again, 4.1 percent of the incoming class. The numbers for Hispanic and Asian-American students tell a similar story. See Supp. App. 43a. Although demographics alone are by no means dispositive, they do have some value as a gauge of the University's ability to enroll students who can offer underrepresented perspectives.

In addition to this broad demographic data, the University put forward evidence that minority students admitted under the Hopwood regime experienced feelings of loneliness and isolation.

This anecdotal evidence is, in turn, bolstered by further, more nuanced quantitative data. In 2002, 52 percent of undergraduate classes with at least five students had no African-American students enrolled in them, and 27 percent had only one African-American student. Supp. App. 140a. In other words, only 21 percent of undergraduate classes with five or more students in them had more than one African-American student enrolled. Twelve percent of these classes had no Hispanic students, as compared to 10 percent in 1996. Id., at 74a, 140a. Though a college must continually reassess its need for race-conscious review, here that assessment appears to have been done with care, and a reasonable determination was made that the University had not yet attained its goals.

Third, petitioner argues that considering race was not necessary because such consideration has had only a "'minimal impact' in advancing the [University's] compelling interest." Brief for Petitioner 46; see also Tr. of Oral Arg. 23:10–12; 24:13–25:2, 25:24–26:3. Again, the record does not support this assertion. In 2003, 11 percent of the Texas residents enrolled through holistic review were Hispanic and 3.5 percent were African-American. Supp. App. 157a. In 2007, by contrast, 16.9 percent of the Texas holistic-review freshmen were Hispanic and 6.8 percent were African-American. Ibid. Those increases—of 54 percent and 94 percent, respectively—show that consideration of race has had a meaningful, if still limited, effect on the diversity of the University's freshman class.

In any event, it is not a failure of narrow tailoring for the impact of racial consideration to be minor. The fact that race consciousness played a role in only a small portion of admissions decisions should be a hallmark of narrow tailoring, not evidence of unconstitutionality. Petitioner's final argument is that "there are numerous other available race-neutral means of achieving" the University's compelling interest. Brief for Petitioner 47. A review of the record reveals, however, that, at the time of petitioner's application, none of her proposed alternatives was a workable means for the University to attain the benefits of diversity it sought. For example, petitioner suggests that the University could intensify its outreach efforts to African-American and Hispanic applicants. But the University submitted extensive evidence of the many ways in which it already had intensified its outreach efforts to those students. The University has created three new scholarship programs, opened new regional admissions centers, increased its recruitment budget by half-a-million dollars, and organized over 1,000 recruitment events. Supp. App. 29a–32a; App. 450a–452a (citing affidavit of Michael Orr ¶¶4–20). Perhaps more significantly, in the wake of Hopwood, the University spent seven years attempting to achieve its compelling interest using race-neutral holistic review. None of these efforts succeeded, and petitioner fails to offer any meaningful way in which the University could have improved upon them at the time of her application.

Petitioner also suggests altering the weight given to academic and socioeconomic factors in the University's admissions calculus. This proposal ignores the fact that the University tried, and failed, to increase diversity through enhanced consideration of socioeconomic and other factors. And it further ignores this Court's precedent making clear that the Equal Protection Clause does not force universities to choose between a diverse student body and a reputation for academic excellence. Grutter, 539 U. S., at 339.

Petitioner's final suggestion is to uncap the Top Ten Percent Plan, and admit more—if not all—the University's students through a percentage plan. As an initial matter, petitioner overlooks the fact that the Top Ten Percent Plan, though facially neutral, cannot be understood apart from its basic purpose, which is to boost minority enrollment. Percentage plans are "adopted with racially segregated neighborhoods and schools front and center stage." Fisher I, 570 U. S., at ___ (GINSBURG, J., dissenting) (slip op., at 2). "It is race consciousness, not blindness to race, that drives such plans." Ibid. Consequently, petitioner cannot assert simply that increasing the University's reliance on a percentage plan would make its admissions policy more race neutral.

Even if, as a matter of raw numbers, minority enrollment would increase under such a regime, petitioner would be hard-pressed to find convincing support for the proposition that college admissions would be improved if they were a function of class rank alone. That approach would sacrifice all other aspects of diversity in pursuit of enrolling a higher number of minority students. A system that selected every student through class rank alone would exclude the star athlete or musician whose grades suffered because of daily practices and training. It would exclude a talented young biologist who struggled to maintain above-average grades in humanities classes. And it would exclude a student whose freshman-year grades were poor because of a family crisis but who got herself back on track in her last three years of school, only to find herself just outside of the top decile of her class.

These are but examples of the general problem. Class rank is a single metric, and like any single metric, it will capture certain types of people and miss others. This does not imply that students admitted through holistic review are necessarily more capable or more desirable than those admitted through the Top Ten Percent Plan. It merely reflects the fact that privileging one characteristic above all others does not lead to a diverse student body. Indeed, to compel universities to admit students based on class rank alone is in deep tension with the goal of educational diversity as this Court's cases have defined it. See Grutter, supra, at 340 (explaining that percentage plans "may preclude the university from conducting the individualized assessments necessary to assemble a student body that is not just racially diverse, but diverse along all the qualities valued by the university"); 758 F. 3d, at 653 (pointing out that the Top Ten Percent Law leaves out students "who fell outside their high school's top ten percent but excelled in unique ways that would enrich the diversity of [the University's] educational experience" and "leaves a gap in an admissions process seeking to create the multidimensional diversity that [Regents of Univ. of Cal. v. Bakke, 438 U. S. 265 (1978),] envisions"). At its center, the Top Ten Percent Plan is a blunt instrument that may well compromise the University's own definition of the diversity it seeks.

In addition to these fundamental problems, an admissions policy that relies exclusively on class rank creates perverse incentives for applicants. Percentage plans "encourage parents to keep their children in low performing segregated schools, and discourage students from taking challenging classes that might lower their grade point averages." Gratz, 539 U. S., at 304, n. 10 (GINSBURG, J., dissenting).

For all these reasons, although it may be true that the Top Ten Percent Plan in some instances may provide a path out of poverty for those who excel at schools lacking in resources, the Plan cannot serve as the admissions solution that petitioner suggests. Wherever the balance between percentage plans and holistic review should rest, an effective admissions policy cannot prescribe, realistically, the exclusive use of a percentage plan. In short, none of petitioner's suggested alternatives— nor other proposals considered or discussed in the course of this litigation—have been shown to be "available" and "workable" means through which the University could have met its educational goals, as it understood and defined them in 2008. Fisher I, supra, at ___ (slip op., at 11). The University has thus met its burden of showing that the admissions policy it used at the time it rejected petitioner's application was narrowly tailored.

[A] university is in large part defined by those intangible "qualities which are incapable of objective measurement but which make for greatness." Sweatt v. Painter, 339 U. S. 629, 634 (1950). Considerable deference is owed to a university in defining those intangible characteristics, like student body diversity, that are central to its identity and educational mission. But still, it remains an enduring challenge to our Nation's education system to reconcile the pursuit of diversity with the constitutional promise of equal treatment and dignity.

In striking this sensitive balance, public universities, like the States themselves, can serve as "laboratories for experimentation." United States v. Lopez, 514 U. S. 549, 581 (1995) (KENNEDY, J., concurring); see also New State Ice Co. v. Liebmann, 285 U. S. 262, 311 (1932) (Brandeis, J., dissenting). The University of Texas at Austin has a special opportunity to learn and to teach. The University now has at its disposal valuable data about the manner in which different approaches to admissions may foster diversity or instead dilute it. The University must continue to use this data to scrutinize the fairness of its admissions program; to assess whether changing demographics have undermined the need for a race-conscious policy; and to identify the effects, both positive and negative, of the affirmative-action measures it deems necessary.

The Court's affirmance of the University's admissions policy today does not necessarily mean the University may rely on that same policy without refinement. It is the University's ongoing obligation to engage in constant deliberation and continued reflection regarding its admissions policies. The judgment of the Court of Appeals is affirmed.

It is so ordered.

JUSTICE KAGAN took no part in the consideration or decision of this case.

JUSTICE ALITO, with whom THE CHIEF JUSTICE and JUSTICE THOMAS join, dissenting.

Something strange has happened since our prior decision in this case. See Fisher v. University of Tex. at Austin, 570 U. S. ___ (2013) (Fisher I). In that decision, we held that strict scrutiny requires the University of Texas at Austin (UT or University) to show that its use of race and ethnicity in making admissions decisions serves compelling interests and that its plan is narrowly tailored to achieve those ends. Rejecting the argument that we should defer to UT's judgment on those matters, we made it clear that UT was obligated (1) to identify the interests justifying its plan with enough specificity to permit a reviewing court to determine whether the requirements of strict scrutiny were met, and (2) to show that those requirements were in fact satisfied. On remand, UT failed to do what our prior decision demanded. The University has still not identified with any degree of specificity the interests that its use of race and ethnicity is supposed to serve. Its primary argument is that merely invoking "the educational benefits of diversity" is sufficient and that it need not identify any metric that would allow a court to determine whether its plan is needed to serve, or is actually serving, those interests. This is nothing less than the plea for deference that we emphatically rejected in our prior decision. Today, however, the Court inexplicably grants that request.

To the extent that UT has ever moved beyond a plea for deference and identified the relevant interests in more specific terms, its efforts have been shifting, unpersuasive, and, at times, less than candid. When it adopted its race based plan, UT said that the plan was needed to promote classroom diversity. See Supp. App. 1a, 24a–25a, 39a; App. 316a. It pointed to a study showing that African American, Hispanic, and Asian-American students were underrepresented in many classes. See Supp. App. 26a. But UT has never shown that its race-conscious plan actually ameliorates this situation. The University presents no evidence that its admissions officers, in administering the "holistic" component of its plan, make any effort to determine whether an African-American, Hispanic, or Asian-American student is likely to enroll in classes in which minority students are underrepresented. And although UT's records should permit it to determine without much difficulty whether holistic admittees are any more likely than students admitted through the Top Ten Percent Law, Tex. Educ. Code Ann. §51.803 (West Cum. Supp. 2015), to enroll in the classes lacking racial or ethnic diversity, UT either has not crunched those numbers or has not revealed what they show. Nor has UT explained why the underrepresentation of Asian-American students in many classes justifies its plan, which discriminates against those students.

[It] should not have been necessary for us to grant review a second time in this case, and I have no greater desire than the majority to see the case drag on. But that need not happen. When UT decided to adopt its race-conscious plan, it had every reason to know that its plan would have to satisfy strict scrutiny and that this meant that it would be its burden to show that the plan was narrowly tailored to serve compelling interests. UT has failed to make that showing. By all rights, judgment should be entered in favor of petitioner. But if the majority is determined to give UT yet another chance, we should reverse and send this case back to the District Court. What the majority has now done— awarding a victory to UT in an opinion that fails to address the important issues in the case—is simply wrong.

[II]

UT's race-conscious admissions program cannot satisfy strict scrutiny. UT says that the program furthers its interest in the educational benefits of diversity, but it has failed to define that interest with any clarity or to demonstrate that its program is narrowly tailored to achieve that or any other particular interest. By accepting UT's rationales as sufficient to meet its burden, the majority licenses UT's perverse assumptions about different groups of minority students—the precise assumptions strict scrutiny is supposed to stamp out. A "The moral imperative of racial neutrality is the driving force of the Equal Protection Clause." Richmond v. J. A. Croson Co., 488 U. S. 469, 518 (1989) (KENNEDY, J., concurring in part and concurring in judgment). "At the heart of the Constitution's guarantee of equal protection lies the simple command that the Government must treat citizens as individuals, not as simply components of a racial, religious, sexual or national class." Miller v. Johnson, 515 U. S. 900, 911 (1995) (internal quotation marks omitted). "Race-based assignments embody stereotypes that treat individuals as the product of their race, evaluating their thoughts and efforts—their very worth as citizens— according to a criterion barred to the Government by history and the Constitution." Id., at 912 (internal quotation marks omitted). Given our constitutional commitment to "the doctrine of equality," "'[d]istinctions between citizens solely because of their ancestry are by their very nature odious to a free people.'" Rice v. Cayetano, 528 U. S. 495, 517 (2000) (quoting Hirabayashi v. United States, 320 U. S. 81, 100 (1943)).

[B]

Here, UT has failed to define its interest in using racial preferences with clarity. As a result, the narrow tailoring inquiry is impossible, and UT cannot satisfy strict scrutiny.

When UT adopted its challenged policy, it characterized its compelling interest as obtaining a "'critical mass'" of underrepresented minorities. Id., at ___ (slip op., at 1). The 2004 Proposal claimed that "[t]he use of race-neutral policies and programs has not been successful in achieving a critical mass of racial diversity." Supp. App. 25a; see Fisher v. University of Tex. at Austin, 631 F. 3d 213, 226 (CA5 2011) ("[T]he 2004 Proposal explained that UT had not yet achieved the critical mass of underrepresented minority students needed to obtain the full educational benefits of diversity"). But to this day, UT has not explained in anything other than the vaguest terms what it means by "critical mass." In fact, UT argues that it need not identify any interest more specific than "securing the educational benefits of diversity." Brief for Respondents 15. UT has insisted that critical mass is not an absolute number. See Tr. of Oral Arg. 39 (Oct. 10, 2012) (declaring that UT is not working toward any particular number of African-American or Hispanic students); App. 315a (confirming that UT has not defined critical mass as a number and has not projected when it will attain critical mass). Instead, UT prefers a deliberately malleable "we'll know it when we see it" notion of critical mass. It defines "critical mass" as "an adequate representation of minority students so that the . . . educational benefits that can be derived from diversity can actually happen," and it declares that it "will . . . know [that] it has reached critical mass" when it "see[s] the educational benefits happening." Id., at 314a–315a. In other words: Trust us.

The majority acknowledges that "asserting an interest in the educational benefits of diversity writ large is insufficient," and that "[a] university's goals cannot be elusory or amorphous—they must be sufficiently measurable to permit judicial scrutiny of the policies adopted to reach them." Ante, at 12. According to the majority, however, UT has articulated the following "concrete and precise goals": "the destruction of stereotypes, the promot[ion of] cross-racial understanding, the preparation of a student body for an increasingly diverse workforce and society, and the cultivat[ion of] a set of leaders with legitimacy in the eyes of the citizenry." Ibid. (internal quotation marks omitted).

These are laudable goals, but they are not concrete or precise, and they offer no limiting principle for the use of racial preferences. For instance, how will a court ever be able to determine whether stereotypes have been adequately destroyed? Or whether cross-racial understanding has been adequately achieved? If a university can justify racial discrimination simply by having a few employees opine that racial preferences are necessary to accomplish these nebulous goals, see ante, at 12–13 (citing only self-serving statements from UT officials), then the narrow tailoring inquiry is meaningless. Courts will be required to defer to the judgment of university administrators, and affirmative-action policies will be completely insulated from judicial review.

By accepting these amorphous goals as sufficient for UT to carry its burden, the majority violates decades of precedent rejecting blind deference to government officials defending "'inherently suspect'" classifications. Miller, 515 U. S., at 904 (citing Regents of Univ. of Cal. v. Bakke, 438 U. S. 265, 291 (1978) (opinion of Powell, J.)); see also, e.g., Miller, supra, at 922 ("Our presumptive skepticism of all racial classifications . . . prohibits us . . . from accepting on its face the Justice Department's conclusion" (citation omitted)); Croson, 488 U. S., at 500 ("[T]he mere recitation of a 'benign' or legitimate purpose for a racial classification is entitled to little or no weight"); id., at 501 ("The history of racial classifications in this country suggests that blind judicial deference to legislative or executive pronouncements of necessity has no place in equal protection analysis"). Most troublingly, the majority's uncritical deference to UT's self-serving claims blatantly contradicts our decision in the prior iteration of this very case, in which we faulted the Fifth Circuit for improperly "deferring to the University's good faith in its use of racial classifications." Fisher I, 570 U. S., at ___ (slip op., at 12). As we emphasized just three years ago, our precedent "ma[kes] clear that it is for the courts, not for university administrators, to ensure that" an admissions process is narrowly tailored. Id., at ___ (slip op., at 10).

A court cannot ensure that an admissions process is narrowly tailored if it cannot pin down the goals that the process is designed to achieve. UT's vague policy goals are "so broad and imprecise that they cannot withstand strict scrutiny." Parents Involved, supra, at 785 (KENNEDY, J., concurring in part and concurring in judgment).

C

[2]

The other major explanation UT offered in the Proposal was its desire to promote classroom diversity. The Proposal stressed that UT "has not reached a critical mass at the classroom level." Supp. App. 24a (emphasis added). In support of this proposition, UT relied on a study of select classes containing five or more students. As noted above, the study indicated that 52% of these classes had no African Americans, 16% had no Asian-Americans, and 12% had no Hispanics. Supp. App. 26a. The study further suggested that only 21% of these classes had two or more African Americans, 67% had two or more Asian-Americans, and 70% had two or more Hispanics. See ibid. Based on this study, UT concluded that it had a "compelling educational interest" in employing racial preferences to ensure that it did not "have large numbers of classes in which there are no students—or only a single student—of a given underrepresented race or ethnicity." Id., at 25a. UT now equivocates, disclaiming any discrete interest in classroom diversity. See Brief for Respondents 26–27. Instead, UT has taken the position that the lack of classroom diversity was merely a "red flag that UT had not yet fully realized" "the constitutionally permissible educational benefits of diversity." Brief for Respondents in No. 11– 345, at 43. But UT has failed to identify the level of classroom diversity it deems sufficient, again making it impossible to apply strict scrutiny. A reviewing court cannot determine whether UT's race-conscious program was necessary to remove the so-called "red flag" without understanding the precise nature of that goal or knowing when the "red flag" will be considered to have disappeared.

Moreover, if UT is truly seeking to expose its students to a diversity of ideas and perspectives, its policy is poorly tailored to serve that end. UT's own study—which the majority touts as the best "nuanced quantitative data" supporting UT's position, ante, at 15—demonstrated that classroom diversity was more lacking for students classified as Asian-American than for those classified as Hispanic. Supp. App. 26a. But the UT plan discriminates against Asian-American students. UT is apparently unconcerned that Asian-Americans "may be made to feel isolated or may be seen as . . . 'spokesperson[s]' of their race or ethnicity." Id., at 69a; see id., at 25a. And unless the University is engaged in unconstitutional racial balancing based on Texas demographics (where Hispanics outnumber Asian-Americans), see Part II–C–1, supra, it seemingly views the classroom contributions of Asian American students as less valuable than those of Hispanic students. In UT's view, apparently, "Asian Americans are not worth as much as Hispanics in promoting 'cross-racial understanding,' breaking down 'racial stereotypes,' and enabling students to 'better understand persons of different races.'" Brief for Asian American Legal Foundation et al. as Amici Curiae 11 (representing 117 Asian American organizations). The majority opinion effectively endorses this view, crediting UT's reliance on the classroom study as proof that the University assessed its need for racial discrimination (including racial discrimination that undeniably harms Asian-Americans) "with care." Ante, at 15.

Perhaps the majority finds discrimination against Asian-American students benign, since Asian-Americans are "overrepresented" at UT. 645 F. Supp. 2d, at 606. But "[h]istory should teach greater humility." Metro Broadcasting, 497 U. S., at 609 (O'Connor, J., dissenting). "'[B]enign' carries with it no independent meaning, but reflects only acceptance of the current generation's conclusion that a politically acceptable burden, imposed on particular citizens on the basis of race, is reasonable." Id., at 610. Where, as here, the government has provided little explanation for why it needs to discriminate based on race, "'there is simply no way of determining what classifications are "benign" . . . and what classifications are in fact motivated by illegitimate notions of racial inferiority or simple racial politics.'" Parents Involved, 551 U. S., at 783 (opinion of KENNEDY, J.) (quoting Croson, 488 U. S., at 493 (plurality opinion of O'Connor, J.)). By accepting the classroom study as proof that UT satisfied strict scrutiny, the majority "move[s] us from 'separate but equal' to 'unequal but benign.'" Metro Broadcasting, supra, at 638 (KENNEDY, J., dissenting).

In addition to demonstrating that UT discriminates against Asian-American students, the classroom study also exhibits UT's use of a few crude, overly simplistic racial and ethnic categories. Under the UT plan, both the favored and the disfavored groups are broad and consist of students from enormously diverse backgrounds. See Supp. App. 30a; see also Fisher I, 570 U. S., at ___ (slip op., at 4) ("five predefined racial categories"). Because "[c]rude measures of this sort threaten to reduce [students] to racial chits," Parents Involved, 551 U. S., at 798 (opinion of KENNEDY, J.), UT's reliance on such measures further undermines any claim based on classroom diversity statistics, see id., at 723 (majority opinion) (criticizing school policies that viewed race in rough "white/nonwhite" or "black/'other'" terms); id., at 786 (opinion of KENNEDY, J.) (faulting government for relying on "crude racial categories"); Metro Broadcasting, supra, at 633, n. 1 (KENNEDY, J., dissenting) (concluding that "'the very attempt to define with precision a beneficiary's qualifying racial characteristics is repugnant to our constitutional ideals,'" and noting that if the government "'is to make a serious effort to define racial classes by criteria that can be administered objectively, it must study precedents such as the First Regulation to the Reichs Citizenship Law of November 14, 1935'").

For example, students labeled "Asian American," Supp. App. 26a, seemingly include "individuals of Chinese, Japanese, Korean, Vietnamese, Cambodian, Hmong, Indian and other backgrounds comprising roughly 60% of the world's population," Brief for Asian American Legal Foundation et al. as Amici Curiae, O. T. 2012, No. 11–345, p. 28. It would be ludicrous to suggest that all of these students have similar backgrounds and similar ideas and experiences to share. So why has UT lumped them together and concluded that it is appropriate to discriminate against Asian-American students because they are "overrepresented" in the UT student body? UT has no good answer. And UT makes no effort to ensure that it has a critical mass of, say, "Filipino Americans" or "Cambodian Americans." Tr. of Oral Arg. 52 (Oct. 10, 2012). As long as there are a sufficient number of "Asian Americans," UT is apparently satisfied.

UT's failure to provide any definition of the various racial and ethnic groups is also revealing. UT does not specify what it means to be "African-American," "Hispanic," "Asian American," "Native American," or "White." Supp. App. 30a. And UT evidently labels each student as falling into only a single racial or ethnic group, see, e.g., id., at

10a–13a, 30a, 43a–44a, 71a, 156a–157a, 169a–170a, without explaining how individuals with ancestors from different groups are to be characterized. As racial and ethnic prejudice recedes, more and more students will have parents (or grandparents) who fall into more than one of UT's five groups. According to census figures, individuals describing themselves as members of multiple races grew by 32% from 2000 to 2010.7 A recent survey reported that 26% of Hispanics and 28% of Asian Americans marry a spouse of a different race or ethnicity.

UT's crude classification system is ill suited for the more integrated country that we are rapidly becoming. UT assumes that if an applicant describes himself or herself as a member of a particular race or ethnicity, that applicant will have a perspective that differs from that of applicants who describe themselves as members of different groups. But is this necessarily so? If an applicant has one grandparent, great-grandparent, or great-great-grandparent who was a member of a favored group, is that enough to permit UT to infer that this student's classroom contribution will reflect a distinctive perspective or set of experiences associated with that group? UT does not say. It instead relies on applicants to "classify themselves." Fisher I, 570 U. S., at ___ (slip op., at 4). This is an invitation for applicants to game the system.

[3]

UT's purported interest in interracial diversity, or "diversity within diversity," Brief for Respondents 34, also falls short. At bottom, this argument relies on the unsupported assumption that there is something deficient or at least radically different about the African-American and Hispanic students admitted through the Top Ten Percent Plan.

Throughout this litigation, UT has repeatedly shifted its position on the need for interracial diversity. Initially, in the 2004 Proposal, UT did not rely on this alleged need at all. Rather, the Proposal "examined two metrics— classroom diversity and demographic disparities—that it concluded were relevant to its ability to provide [the] benefits of diversity." Brief for United States as Amicus Curiae 27–28. Those metrics looked only to the numbers of African-Americans and Hispanics, not to diversity within each group.

On appeal to the Fifth Circuit and in Fisher I, however, UT began to emphasize its interracial diversity argument. UT complained that the Top Ten Percent Law hinders its efforts to assemble a broadly diverse class because the minorities admitted under that law are drawn largely from certain areas of Texas where there are majority minority schools. These students, UT argued, tend to come from poor, disadvantaged families, and the University would prefer a system that gives it substantial leeway to seek broad diversity within groups of underrepresented minorities. In particular, UT asserted a need for more African-American and Hispanic students from privileged backgrounds. See, e.g., Brief for Respondents in No. 11– 345, at 34 (explaining that UT needs race-conscious admissions in order to admit "[t]he African-American or Hispanic child of successful professionals in Dallas"); ibid. (claiming that privileged minorities "have great potential for serving as a 'bridge' in promoting cross-racial understanding, as well as in breaking down racial stereotypes"); ibid. (intimating that the underprivileged minority students admitted under the Top Ten Percent Plan "reinforc[e]" "stereotypical assumptions"); Tr. of Oral Arg. 43– 45 (Oct. 10, 2012) ("[A]lthough the percentage plan certainly helps with minority admissions, by and large, the— the minorities who are admitted tend to come from segregated, racially-identifiable schools," and "we want minorities from different backgrounds"). Thus, the Top Ten Percent Law is faulted for admitting the wrong kind of African-American and Hispanic students.

The Fifth Circuit embraced this argument on remand, endorsing UT's claimed need to enroll minorities from "high-performing," "majority-white" high schools. 758 F. 3d, at 653. According to the Fifth Circuit, these more privileged minorities "bring a perspective not captured by" students admitted under the Top Ten Percent Law, who often come "from highly segregated, underfunded, and underperforming schools." Ibid. For instance, the court determined, privileged minorities "can enrich the diversity of the student body in distinct ways" because such students have "higher levels of preparation and better prospects for admission to UT Austin's more demanding colleges" than underprivileged minorities. Id., at 654; see also Fisher, 631 F. 3d, at 240, n. 149 (concluding that the Top Ten Percent Plan "widens the 'credentials gap' between minority and non-minority students at the University, which risks driving away matriculating minority students from difficult majors like business or the sciences").

Remarkably, UT now contends that petitioner has "fabricat[ed]" the argument that it is seeking affluent minorities. Brief for Respondents 2. That claim is impossible to square with UT's prior statements to this Court in the briefing and oral argument in Fisher I.9 Moreover, although UT reframes its argument, it continues to assert that it needs affirmative action to admit privileged minorities. For instance, UT's brief highlights its interest in admitting "[t]he black student with high grades from Andover." Brief for Respondents 33. Similarly, at oral argument, UT claimed that its "interests in the educational benefits of diversity would not be met if all of [the] minority students were . . . coming from depressed socioeconomic backgrounds."

Ultimately, UT's interracial diversity rationale relies on the baseless assumption that there is something wrong with African-American and Hispanic students admitted through the Top Ten Percent Plan, because they are "from the lower-performing, racially identifiable schools." Id., at 43; see id., at 42–43 (explaining that "the basis" for UT's conclusion that it was "not getting a variety of perspectives among African-Americans or Hispanics" was the fact that the Top Ten Percent Plan admits underprivileged minorities from highly segregated schools). In effect, UT asks the Court "to assume"—without any evidence—"that minorities admitted under the Top Ten Percent Law . . . are somehow more homogenous, less dynamic, and more undesirably stereotypical than those admitted under holistic review." 758 F. 3d, at 669–670 (Garza, J., dissenting). And UT's assumptions appear to be based on the pernicious stereotype that the African-Americans and Hispanics admitted through the Top Ten Percent Plan only got in because they did not have to compete against very many whites and Asian-Americans. See Tr. of Oral Arg. 42–43 (Dec. 9, 2015). These are "the very stereotypical assumptions [that] the Equal Protection Clause forbids." Miller, 515 U. S., at 914. UT cannot satisfy its burden by attempting to "substitute racial stereotype for evidence, and racial prejudice for reason." Calhoun v. United States, 568 U. S. ___, ___ (2013) (slip op., at 4) (SOTOMAYOR, J., respecting denial of certiorari).

In addition to relying on stereotypes, UT's argument that it needs racial preferences to admit privileged minorities turns the concept of affirmative action on its head. When affirmative action programs were first adopted, it was for the purpose of helping the disadvantaged. See, e.g., Bakke, 438 U. S., at 272–275 (opinion of Powell, J.) (explaining that the school's affirmative action program was designed "to increase the representation" of "'economically and/or educationally disadvantaged' applicants"). Now we are told that a program that tends to admit poor and disadvantaged minority students is inadequate because it does not work to the advantage of those who are more fortunate. This is affirmative action gone wild.

It is also far from clear that UT's assumptions about the socioeconomic status of minorities admitted through the Top Ten Percent Plan are even remotely accurate. Take, for example, parental education. In 2008, when petitioner applied to UT, approximately 79% of Texans aged 25 years or older had a high school diploma, 17% had a bachelor's degree, and 8% had a graduate or professional degree. Dept. of Educ., Nat. Center for Educ. Statistics, T. Snyder & S. Dillow, Digest of Education Statistics 2010, p. 29 (2011). In contrast, 96% of African-Americans admitted through the Top Ten Percent Plan had a parent with a high school diploma, 59% had a parent with a bachelor's degree, and 26% had a parent with a graduate or professional degree. See UT, Office of Admissions, Student Profile, Admitted Freshman Class of 2008, p. 8 (rev. Aug. 1, 2012) (2008 Student Profile)...Similarly, 83% of Hispanics admitted through the Top Ten Percent Plan had a parent with a high school diploma, 42% had a parent with a bachelor's degree, and 21% had a parent with a graduate or professional degree. Ibid. As these statistics make plain, the minorities that UT characterizes as "coming from depressed socioeconomic backgrounds," Tr. of Oral Arg. 53 (Dec. 9, 2015), generally come from households with education levels exceeding the norm in Texas.

[In] addition to using socioeconomic status to falsely denigrate the minority students admitted through the Top Ten Percent Plan, UT also argues that such students are academically inferior. See, e.g., Brief for Respondents in No. 11–345, at 33 ("[T]he top 10% law systematically hinders UT's efforts to assemble a class that is . . . academically excellent").

[This] argument fails for a number of reasons. First, it is simply not true that Top Ten Percent minority admittees are academically inferior to holistic admittees. In fact, as UT's president explained in 2000, "top 10 percent high school students make much higher grades in college than non-top 10 percent students," and "[s]trong academic performance in high school is an even better predictor of success in college than standardized test scores." App. 393a–394a; see also Lavergne Deposition 41–42 (agreeing that "it's generally true that students admitted pursuant to HB 588 [the Top Ten Percent Law] have a higher level of academic performance at the University than students admitted outside of HB 588"). Indeed, the statistics in the record reveal that, for each year between 2003 and 2007, African-American in-state freshmen who were admitted under the Top Ten Percent Law earned a higher mean grade point average than those admitted outside of the Top Ten Percent Law. Supp. App. 164a. The same is true for Hispanic students. Id., at 165a. These conclusions correspond to the results of nationwide studies showing that high school grades are a better predictor of success in college than SAT scores.

[UT] certainly has a compelling interest in admitting students who will achieve academic success, but it does not follow that it has a compelling interest in maximizing admittees' SAT scores. Approximately 850 4-year-degree institutions do not require the SAT or ACT as part of the admissions process. See J. Soares, SAT Wars: The Case for Test-Optional College Admissions 2 (2012). This includes many excellent schools.

[III]

The majority purports to agree with much of the above analysis. The Court acknowledges that "'because racial characteristics so seldom provide a relevant basis for disparate treatment,'" "'[r]ace may not be considered [by a university] unless the admissions process can withstand strict scrutiny.'" Ante, at 6–7. The Court admits that the burden of proof is on UT, ante, at 7, and that "a university bears a heavy burden in showing that it had not obtained the educational benefits of diversity before it turned to a race-conscious plan," ante, at 13–14. And the Court recognizes that the record here is "almost devoid of information about the students who secured admission to the University through the Plan," and that "[t]he Court thus cannot know how students admitted solely based on their class rank differ in their contribution to diversity from students admitted through holistic review." Ante, at 9. This should be the end of the case: Without identifying what was missing from the African-American and Hispanic students it was already admitting through its race-neutral process, and without showing how the use of race-based admissions could rectify the deficiency, UT cannot demonstrate that its procedure is narrowly tailored.

Yet, somehow, the majority concludes that petitioner must lose as a result of UT's failure to provide evidence justifying its decision to employ racial discrimination. Tellingly, the Court frames its analysis as if petitioner bears the burden of proof here. See ante, at 11–19. But it is not the petitioner's burden to show that the consideration of race is unconstitutional. To the extent the record is inadequate, the responsibility lies with UT. For "[w]hen a court subjects governmental action to strict scrutiny, it cannot construe ambiguities in favor of the State," Parents Involved, supra, at 786 (opinion of KENNEDY, J.), particularly where, as here, the summary judgment posture obligates the Court to view the facts in the light most favorable to petitioner, see Matsushita Elec. Industrial Co. v. Zenith Radio Corp., 475 U. S. 574, 587 (1986).

Given that the University bears the burden of proof, it is not surprising that UT never made the argument that it should win based on the lack of evidence. UT instead asserts that "if the Court believes there are any deficiencies in [the] record that cast doubt on the constitutionality of UT's policy, the answer is to order a trial, not to grant summary judgment." Brief for Respondents 51; see also id., at 52–53 ("[I]f this Court has any doubts about how the Top 10% Law works, or how UT's holistic plan offsets the tradeoffs of the Top 10% Law, the answer is to remand for a trial"). Nevertheless, the majority cites three reasons for breaking from the normal strict scrutiny standard. None of these is convincing.

[IV]

It is important to understand what is and what is not at stake in this case. What is not at stake is whether UT or any other university may adopt an admissions plan that results in a student body with a broad representation of students from all racial and ethnic groups. UT previously had a race-neutral plan that it claimed had "effectively compensated for the loss of affirmative action," and UT could have taken other steps that would have increased the diversity of its admitted students without taking race or ethnic background into account. What is at stake is whether university administrators may justify systematic racial discrimination simply by asserting that such discrimination is necessary to achieve "the educational benefits of diversity," without explaining—much less proving—why the discrimination is needed or how the discriminatory plan is well crafted to serve its objectives. Even though UT has never provided any coherent explanation for its asserted need to discriminate on the basis of race, and even though UT's position relies on a series of unsupported and noxious racial assumptions, the majority concludes that UT has met its heavy burden. This conclusion is remarkable—and remarkably wrong. Because UT has failed to satisfy strict scrutiny, I respectfully dissent.

[A dissent by Justice Thomas has been omitted]

SCHUETTE v. COALITION TO DEFEND AFFIRMATIVE ACTION, INTE-GRATION & IMMIGRANT RIGHTS & FIGHT FOR EQUALITY BY ANY MEANS NECESSARY (BAMN)
572 U.S. 291 (2014)

JUSTICE KENNEDY announced the judgment of the Court and delivered an opinion, in which [CHIEF JUSTICE ROBERTS] and JUSTICE ALITO join.

[Given the Court's decisions in *Gratz* and *Grutter,* in 2006 voters of Michigan adopted Proposal 2, which amended Michigan's constitution. The amendment provided as follows:]

"(1) The University of Michigan, Michigan State University, Wayne State University, and any other public college or university, community college, or school district shall not discriminate against, or grant preferential treatment to, any individual or group on the basis of race, sex, color, ethnicity, or national origin in the operation of public employment, public education, or public contracting.

"(2) The state shall not discriminate against, or grant preferential treatment to, any individual or group on the basis of race, sex, color, ethnicity, or national origin in the operation of public employment, public education, or public contracting.

"(3) For the purposes of this section "state" includes, but is not necessarily limited to, the state itself, any city, county, any public college, university, or community college, school district, or other political subdivision or governmental instrumentality of or within the State of Michigan not included in sub-section 1."

[The District Court rejected an equal protection challenge to the amendment, but the Court of Appeals reversed.]

Before the Court addresses the question presented, it is important to note what this case is not about. It is not about the constitutionality, or the merits, of race conscious admissions policies in higher education. [The] question here concerns not the permissibility of race-conscious admissions policies under the Constitution but whether, and in what manner, voters in the States may choose to prohibit the consideration of racial preferences in governmental decisions, in particular with respect to school admissions.

This Court has noted that some States have decided to prohibit race-conscious admissions policies. In *Grutter,* the Court noted: "Universities in California, Florida, and Washington State, where racial preferences in admissions are prohibited by state law, are currently engaged in experimenting with a wide variety of alternative approaches. Universities in other States can and should draw on the most promising aspects of these race-neutral alternatives as they develop." In this way, *Grutter* acknowledged the significance of a dialogue regarding this contested and complex policy question among and within States.

. . . [This] Court's decision in Reitman v. Mulkey, 387 U.S. 369 (1967), is a proper beginning point for discussing the controlling decisions. [*Mulkey* is discussed at page 1570 of the main volume.] In *Mulkey,* voters amended the California Constitution to prohibit any state legislative interference with an owner's prerogative to decline to sell or rent residential property on any basis. [The] Court agreed with the California Supreme Court that the amendment operated to insinuate the State into the decision to discriminate by encouraging that practice. The Court noted the "immediate design and intent" of the amendment was to "establis[h] a purported constitutional right to privately discriminate."

The Court agreed that the amendment "expressly authorized and constitutionalized the private right to discriminate." The effect of the state constitutional amendment was to "significantly encourage and involve the State in private racial discriminations." . . .

The next precedent of relevance, Hunter v. Erickson, 393 U.S. 385 (1969), is central to the arguments the respondents make in the instant case. [Hunter is discussed at page 537 of the main volume.] In Hunter, the Court for the first time elaborated what the Court of Appeals here styled the "political process" doctrine. There, the Akron City Council found that the citizens of Akron consisted of " 'people of different race[s], . . . many of whom live in circumscribed and segregated areas, under sub-standard unhealthful, unsafe, unsanitary and overcrowded conditions, because of discrimination in the sale, lease, rental and financing of housing.' " To address the problem, Akron enacted a fair housing ordinance to prohibit that sort of discrimination. In response, voters amended the city charter to overturn the ordinance and to require that any additional antidiscrimination housing ordinance be approved by referendum. But most other ordinances "regulating the real property market" were not subject to those threshold requirements. . . . Central to the Court's reasoning in Hunter was that the charter amendment was enacted in circumstances where widespread racial discrimination in the sale and rental of housing led to segregated housing, forcing many to live in " 'unhealthful, unsafe, unsanitary and overcrowded conditions.' " [The] Court found that the city charter amendment, by singling out antidiscrimination ordinances, "places special burden on racial minorities within the governmental process," thus becoming as impermissible as any other government action taken with the invidious intent to injure a racial minority. [Hunter] rests on the unremarkable principle that the State may not alter the procedures of government to target racial minorities. The facts in Hunter established that invidious discrimination would be the necessary result of the procedural restructuring. Thus, in Mulkey and Hunter, there was a demonstrated injury on the basis of race that, by reasons of state encouragement or participation, became more aggravated.

[Washington v. Seattle School District No. 1, 458 U.S. 457 (1982),] is the third case of principal relevance here. There, the school board adopted a mandatory busing program to alleviate racial isolation of minority students in local schools. Voters who opposed the school board's busing plan passed a state initiative that barred busing to desegregate. The Court first determined that, although "white as well as Negro children benefit from" diversity, the school board's plan "inures primarily to the benefit of the minority." The Court next found that "the practical effect" of the state initiative was to "remov[e] the authority to address a racial problem — and only a racial problem — from the existing decision-making body, in such a way as to burden minority interests" because advocates of busing "now must seek relief from the state legislature, or from the statewide electorate." The Court therefore found that the initiative had "explicitly us[ed] the racial nature of a decision to determine the decision-making process." . . .

Seattle is best understood as a case in which the state action in question (the bar on busing enacted by the State's voters) had the serious risk, if not purpose, of causing specific injuries on account of race, just as had been the case in Mulkey and Hunter. Although there had been no judicial finding of de jure segregation with respect to Seattle's school district, it appears as though school segregation in the district in the 1940's and 1950's may have been the partial result of school board policies that "permitted white students to transfer out of black schools while restricting the transfer of black students into white schools." Parents Involved in Community Schools v. Seattle School Dist. No. 1 (Breyer, J., dissenting). . . .

As this Court held in *Parents Involved,* the school board's purported remedial action would not be permissible today absent a showing of *de jure* segregation. That holding prompted Justice Breyer to observe in dissent, as noted above, that one permissible reading of the record was that the school board had maintained policies to perpetuate racial segregation in the schools. In all events we must understand *Seattle* as *Seattle* understood itself, as a case in which neither the State nor the United States "challenge[d] the propriety of race-conscious student assignments for the purpose of achieving integration, even absent a finding of prior *de jure* segregation." In other words the legitimacy and constitutionality of the remedy in question (busing for desegregation) was assumed, and *Seattle* must be understood on that basis. *Seattle* involved a state initiative that "was carefully tailored to interfere only with desegregative busing." The *Seattle* Court, accepting the validity of the school board's busing remedy as a predicate to its analysis of the constitutional question, found that the State's disapproval of the school board's busing remedy was an aggravation of the very racial injury in which the State itself was complicit.

The broad language used in *Seattle,* however, went well beyond the analysis needed to resolve the case. [*Seattle*] stated that where a government policy "inures primarily to the benefit of the minority" and "minorities . . . consider" the policy to be " 'in their interest,' " then any state action that "place[s] effective decision-making authority over" that policy "at a different level of government" must be reviewed under strict scrutiny. [In] essence, according to the broad reading of *Seattle,* any state action with a "racial focus" that makes it "more difficult for certain racial minorities than for other groups" to "achieve legislation that is in their interest" is subject to strict scrutiny. It is this reading of *Seattle* that the Court of Appeals found to be controlling here. And that reading must be rejected.

[To] the extent *Seattle* is read to require the Court to determine and declare which political policies serve the "interest" of a group defined in racial terms, that rationale was unnecessary to the decision in *Seattle*; it has no support in precedent; and it raises serious constitutional concerns. That expansive language does not provide a proper guide for decisions and should not be deemed authoritative or controlling. . . .

[It] cannot be entertained as a serious proposition that all individuals of the same race think alike. Yet that proposition would be a necessary beginning point were the *Seattle* formulation to control, as the Court of Appeals held it did in this case. And if it were deemed necessary to probe how some races define their own interest in political matters, still another beginning point would be to define individuals according to race. But in a society in which those lines are becoming more blurred, the attempt to define race-based categories also raises serious questions of its own. Government action that classifies individuals on the basis of race is inherently suspect and carries the danger of perpetuating the very racial divisions the polity seeks to transcend. [Were] courts to embark upon this venture not only would it be undertaken with no clear legal standards or accepted sources to guide judicial decision but also it would result in, or at least impose a high risk of, inquiries and categories dependent upon demeaning stereotypes, classifications of questionable constitutionality on their own terms.

Even assuming these initial steps could be taken in a manner consistent with a sound analytic and judicial framework, the court would next be required to determine the policy realms in which certain groups — groups defined by race — have a political interest. That undertaking, again without guidance from any accepted legal standards, would risk, in turn, the creation of incentives for those who support or oppose certain policies to cast the debate in terms of racial advantage or disadvantage. Thus could racial antagonisms and conflict tend to arise in the context of judicial decisions as courts undertook to announce what particular issues of public policy should be classified as advantageous to some group defined by race. . . .

[In] a nation in which governmental policies are wide ranging, those who seek to limit voter participation might be tempted, were this Court to adopt the *Seattle* formulation, to urge that a group they choose to define by race or racial stereotypes are advantaged or disadvantaged by any number of laws or decisions. Tax policy, housing subsidies, wage regulations, and even the naming of public schools, highways, and monuments are just a few examples of what could become a list of subjects that some organizations could insist should be beyond the power of voters to decide, or beyond the power of a legislature to decide when enacting limits on the power of local authorities or other governmental entities to address certain subjects. Racial division would be validated, not discouraged, were the *Seattle* formulation, and the reasoning of the Court of Appeals in this case, to remain in force.

[The] holding in the instant case is simply that the courts may not disempower the voters from choosing which path to follow. In the realm of policy discussions the regular give-and-take of debate ought to be a context in which rancor or discord based on race are avoided, not invited. And if these factors are to be interjected, surely it ought not to be at the invitation or insistence of the courts.

One response to these concerns may be that objections to the larger consequences of the *Seattle* formulation need not be confronted in this case, for here race was an undoubted subject of the ballot issue. But a number of problems raised by *Seattle,* such as racial definitions, still apply. And this principal flaw in the ruling of the Court of Appeals does remain: Here there was no infliction of a specific injury of the kind at issue in *Mulkey* and *Hunter* and in the history of the Seattle schools. Here there is no precedent for extending these cases to restrict the right of Michigan voters to determine that race-based preferences granted by Michigan governmental entities should be ended.

[By] approving Proposal 2 and thereby adding § 26 to their State Constitution, the Michigan voters exercised their privilege to enact laws as a basic exercise of their democratic power. [Michigan] voters used the initiative system to bypass public officials who were deemed not responsive to the concerns of a majority of the voters with respect to a policy of granting race-based preferences that raises difficult and delicate issues.

The freedom secured by the Constitution consists, in one of its essential dimensions, of the right of the individual not to be injured by the unlawful exercise of governmental power. [Yet] freedom does not stop with individual rights. Our constitutional system embraces, too, the right of citizens to debate so they can learn and decide and then, through the political process, act in concert to try to shape the course of their own times and the course of a nation that must strive always to make freedom ever greater and more secure. Here Michigan voters acted in concert and statewide to seek consensus and adopt a policy on a difficult subject against a historical background of race in America that has been a source of tragedy and persisting injustice. That history demands that we continue to learn, to listen, and to remain open to new approaches if we are to aspire always to a constitutional order in which all persons are treated with fairness and equal dignity. Were the Court to rule that the question addressed by Michigan voters is too sensitive or complex to be within the grasp of the electorate; or that the policies at issue remain too delicate to be resolved save by university officials or faculties, acting at some remove from immediate public scrutiny and control; or that these matters are so arcane that the electorate's power must be limited because the people cannot prudently exercise that power even after a full debate, that holding would be an unprecedented restriction on the exercise of a fundamental right held not just by one person but by all in common. It is the right to speak and debate and learn and then, as a matter of political will, to act through a lawful electoral process.

[It] is demeaning to the democratic process to presume that the voters are not capable of deciding an issue of this sensitivity on decent and rational grounds. The process of public discourse and political debate should not be foreclosed even if there is a risk that during a public campaign there will be those, on both sides, who seek to use racial division and discord to their own political advantage. An informed public can, and must, rise above this. The idea of democracy is that it can, and must, mature. Freedom embraces the right, indeed the duty, to engage in a rational, civic discourse in order to determine how best to form a consensus to shape the destiny of the Nation and its people. These First Amendment dynamics would be disserved if this Court were to say that the question here at issue is beyond the capacity of the voters to debate and then to determine.

These precepts are not inconsistent with the well-established principle that when hurt or injury is inflicted on racial minorities by the encouragement or command of laws or other state action, the Constitution requires redress by the courts. As already noted, those were the circumstances that the Court found present in *Mulkey, Hunter,* and *Seattle.* But those circumstances are not present here.

[What] is at stake here is not whether injury will be inflicted but whether government can be instructed not to follow a course that entails, first, the definition of racial categories and, second, the grant of favored status to persons in some racial categories and not others. The electorate's instruction to governmental entities not to embark upon the course of race-defined and race-based preferences was adopted, we must assume, because the voters deemed a preference system to be unwise, on account of what voters may deem its latent potential to become itself a source of the very resentments and hostilities based on race that this Nation seeks to put behind it. Whether those adverse results would follow is, and should be, the subject of debate. Voters might likewise consider, after debate and reflection, that programs designed to increase diversity — consistent with the Constitution — are a necessary part of progress to transcend the stigma of past racism.

This case is not about how the debate about racial preferences should be resolved. It is about who may resolve it. There is no authority in the Constitution of the United States or in this Court's precedents for the Judiciary to set aside Michigan laws that commit this policy determination to the voters. Deliberative debate on sensitive issues such as racial preferences all too often may shade into rancor. But that does not justify removing certain court-determined issues from the voters' reach. Democracy does not presume that some subjects are either too divisive or too profound for public debate. . . .

JUSTICE KAGAN took no part in the consideration or decision of this case.

CHIEF JUSTICE ROBERTS, concurring.

The dissent devotes 11 pages to expounding its own policy preferences in favor of taking race into account in college admissions, while nonetheless concluding that it "do[es] not mean to suggest that the virtues of adopting race-sensitive admissions policies should inform the legal question before the Court." The dissent concedes that the governing boards of the State's various universities could have implemented a policy making it illegal to "discriminate against, or grant preferential treatment to," any individual on the basis of race. On the dissent's view, if the governing boards conclude that drawing racial distinctions in university admissions is undesirable or counterproductive, they are permissibly exercising their policymaking authority. But others who might reach the same conclusion are failing to take race seriously.

The dissent states that "[t]he way to stop discrimination on the basis of race is to speak openly and candidly on the subject of race." And it urges that "[r]ace matters because of the slights, the snickers, the silent judgments that reinforce that most crippling of thoughts: 'I do not belong here.' " But it is not "out of touch with reality" to conclude that racial preferences may themselves have the debilitating effect of reinforcing precisely that doubt, and — if so — that the preferences do more harm than good. To disagree with the dissent's views on the costs and benefits of racial preferences is not to "wish away, rather than confront" racial inequality. People can disagree in good faith on this issue, but it similarly does more harm than good to question the openness and candor of those on either side of the debate.

JUSTICE SCALIA, with whom JUSTICE THOMAS joins, concurring in the judgment.

It has come to this. Called upon to explore the jurisprudential twilight zone between two errant lines of precedent, we confront a frighteningly bizarre question: Does the Equal Protection Clause of the Fourteenth Amendment *forbid* what its text plainly *requires*? Needless to say (except that this case obliges us to say it), the question answers itself. "The Constitution proscribes government discrimination on the basis of race, and state-provided education is no exception." [*Grutter* (Scalia, J., concurring in part and dissenting in part)]. It is precisely this understanding the correct understanding — of the federal Equal Protection Clause that the people of the State of Michigan have adopted for their own fundamental law. By adopting it, they did not simultaneously *offend* it.

Even taking this Court's sorry line of race-based-admissions cases as a given, I find the question presented only slightly less strange: Does the Equal Protection Clause forbid a State from banning a practice that the Clause barely — and only provisionally — permits? Reacting to those race-based-admissions decisions, some States — whether deterred by the prospect of costly litigation; aware that *Grutter*'s bell may soon toll; or simply opposed in principle to the notion of "benign" racial discrimination — have gotten out of the racial-preferences business altogether. And with our express encouragement: "Universities in California, Florida, and Washington State, where racial preferences in admissions are prohibited by state law, are currently engaging in experimenting with a wide variety of alternative approaches. Universities in other States can *and should* draw on the most promising aspects of these race-neutral alternatives as they develop." (emphasis added). Respondents seem to think this admonition was merely in jest.

The experiment, they maintain, is not only over; it never rightly began. Neither the people of the States nor their legislatures ever had the option of directing subordinate public-university officials to cease considering the race of applicants, since that would deny members of those minority groups the option of enacting a policy designed to further their interest, thus denying them the equal protection of the laws. Never mind that it is hotly disputed whether the practice of race-based admissions is *ever* in a racial minority's interest. And never mind that, were a public university to stake its defense of a race-based-admissions policy on the ground that it was *designed* to benefit primarily minorities (as opposed to all students, regardless of color, by enhancing diversity), *we would hold the policy unconstitutional.* . . .

But the battleground for this case is not the constitutionality of race-based admissions — at least, not quite. Rather, it is the so-called political-process doctrine, derived from this Court's opinions in *Washington v. Seattle School Dist. No. 1*, and *Hunter v. Erickson*. I agree with those parts of the plurality opinion that repudiate this doctrine. But I do not agree with its reinterpretation of *Seattle* and *Hunter*, which makes them stand in part for the cloudy and doctrinally anomalous proposition that whenever state action poses "the serious risk . . . of causing specific injuries on account of race," it denies equal protection. I would instead reaffirm that the "ordinary principles of our law [and] of our democratic heritage" require "plaintiffs alleging equal protection violations" stemming from facially neutral acts to "prove intent and causation and not merely the existence of racial disparity." Freeman v. Pitts, 503 U.S. 467, 506 (Scalia, J., concurring) (citing Washington v. Davis, 426 U.S. 229 (1976)). I would further hold that a law directing state actors to provide equal protection is (to say the least) facially neutral, and cannot violate the Constitution. Section 26 of the Michigan Constitution (formerly Proposal 2) rightly stands. . . .

[*Hunter, Seattle,* and, I think, the plurality] endorse[ ] a version of the proposition that a facially neutral law may deny equal protection solely because it has a disparate racial impact. Few equal-protection theories have been so squarely and soundly rejected. . . .

Notwithstanding our dozens of cases confirming the exception less nature of the *Washington v. Davis* rule, the plurality opinion leaves ajar an effects-test escape hatch modeled after *Hunter* and *Seattle*, suggesting that state action denies equal protection when it "ha[s] the *serious risk,* if not purpose, of causing specific injuries on account of race," or is either "designed to be used, or . . . *likely to be used,* to encourage infliction of injury by reason of race." (emphasis added). Since these formulations enable a determination of an equal-protection violation where there is no discriminatory intent, they are inconsistent with the long *Washington v. Davis* line of cases. [Thus,] the question in this case, as in every case in which neutral state action is said to deny equal protection on account of race, is whether the action reflects a racially discriminatory purpose. *Seattle* stresses that "singling out the political processes affecting racial issues for uniquely disadvantageous treatment inevitably raises dangers of impermissible motivation." True enough, but that motivation must be proved. And respondents do not have a prayer of proving it here. The District Court noted that, under "conventional equal protection" doctrine, the suit was "doom[ed]." Though the Court of Appeals did not opine on this question, I would not leave it for them on remand. In my view, any law expressly requiring state actors to afford all persons equal protection of the laws (such as Initiative 350 in *Seattle*, though not the charter amendment in *Hunter*) does not — *cannot* — deny "to any person . . . equal protection of the laws," U.S. Const., Amdt. 14, § 1, regardless of whatever evidence of seemingly foul purposes plaintiffs may cook up in the trial court.

* * *

As Justice Harlan observed over a century ago, "[o]ur Constitution is colorblind, and neither knows nor tolerates classes among citizens." (dissenting opinion). The people of Michigan wish the same for their governing charter. It would be shameful for us to stand in their way.

JUSTICE BREYER, concurring in the judgment. . . .

[I] agree with the plurality that the amendment is consistent with the Federal Equal Protection Clause. But I believe this for different reasons.

[We] do not address the amendment insofar as it forbids the use of race-conscious admissions programs designed to remedy past exclusionary racial discrimination or the direct effects of that discrimination. Application of the amendment in that context would present different questions which may demand different answers. . . .

I continue to believe that the Constitution permits, though it does not require, the use of the kind of race-conscious programs that are now barred by the Michigan Constitution.
. . .

The Constitution allows local, state, and national communities to adopt narrowly tailored race-conscious programs designed to bring about greater inclusion and diversity. But the Constitution foresees the ballot box, not the courts, as the normal instrument for resolving differences and debates about the merits of these programs. . . .

[Cases] such as *Hunter v. Erickson* and *Washington v. Seattle School Dist. No. 1* reflect an important principle, namely, that an individual's ability to participate meaningfully in the political process should be independent of his race. Although racial minorities, like other political minorities, will not always succeed at the polls, they must have the same opportunity as others to secure through the ballot box policies that reflect their preferences. In my view, however, neither *Hunter* nor *Seattle* applies here. And the parties do not here suggest that the amendment violates the Equal Protection Clause if not under the *Hunter-Seattle* doctrine.

[*Hunter* and *Seattle*] involved a restructuring of the political process that changed the political level at which policies were enacted. In *Hunter*, decision-making was moved from the elected city council to the local electorate at large. And in *Seattle*, decision-making by an elected school board was replaced with decision-making by the state legislature and electorate at large.

This case, in contrast, does not involve a reordering of the *political* process; it does not in fact involve the movement of decision-making from one political level to another. Rather, here, Michigan law delegated broad policymaking authority to elected university boards, but those boards delegated admissions-related decision-making authority to unelected university faculty members and administrators. Although the boards unquestionably retained the *power* to set policy regarding race-conscious admissions, in *fact* faculty members and administrators set the race-conscious admissions policies in question. [Thus], unelected faculty members and administrators, not voters or their elected representatives, adopted the race-conscious admissions programs affected by Michigan's constitutional amendment. The amendment took decision-making authority away from these unelected actors and placed it in the hands of the voters.

[The] doctrine set forth in *Hunter* and *Seattle* does not easily fit this case. In those cases minorities had participated in the political process and they had won. The majority's subsequent reordering of the political process repealed the minority's successes and made it more difficult for the minority to succeed in the future. [But] one cannot as easily characterize the movement of the decision-making mechanism at issue here — from an administrative process to an electoral process — as diminishing the minority's ability to participate meaningfully in the *political* process. There is no prior electoral process in which the minority participated.

For another thing, to extend the holding of *Hunter* and *Seattle* to reach situations in which decisionmaking authority is moved from an administrative body to a political one would pose significant difficulties. The administrative process encompasses vast numbers of decision makers answering numerous policy questions in hosts of different fields. Administrative bodies modify programs in detail, and decisionmaking authority within the administrative process frequently moves around — due to amendments to statutes, new administrative rules, and evolving agency practice. It is thus particularly difficult in this context for judges to determine when a change in the locus of decisionmaking authority places a comparative structural burden on a racial minority. And to apply *Hunter* and *Seattle* to the administrative process would, by tending to hinder change, risk discouraging experimentation, interfering with efforts to see when and how race-conscious policies work.

Finally, the principle that underlies *Hunter* and *Seattle* runs up against a competing principle, discussed above. This competing principle favors decision-making [through] the democratic process. Just as this principle strongly supports the right of the people, or their elected representatives, to adopt race-conscious policies for reasons of inclusion, so must it give them the right to vote not to do so. . . .

JUSTICE SOTOMAYOR, with whom JUSTICE GINSBURG joins, dissenting.

We are fortunate to live in a democratic society. But without checks, democratically approved legislation can oppress minority groups. For that reason, our Constitution places limits on what a majority of the people may do. This case implicates one such limit: the guarantee of equal protection of the laws. Although that guarantee is traditionally understood to prohibit intentional discrimination under existing laws, equal protection does not end there. Another fundamental strand of our equal protection jurisprudence focuses on process, securing to all citizens the right to participate meaningfully and equally in self-government. That right is the bedrock of our democracy, for it preserves all other rights.

Yet to know the history of our Nation is to understand its long and lamentable record of stymieing the right of racial minorities to participate in the political process. At first, the majority acted with an open, invidious purpose. Notwithstanding the command of the Fifteenth Amendment, certain States shut racial minorities out of the political process altogether by withholding the right to vote. This Court intervened to preserve that right. The majority tried again, replacing outright bans on voting with literacy tests, good character requirements, poll taxes, and gerrymandering. The Court was not fooled; it invalidated those measures, too. The majority persisted. This time, although it allowed the minority access to the political process, the majority changed the ground rules of the process so as to make it more difficult for the minority, and the minority alone, to obtain policies designed to foster racial integration. Although these political restructurings may not have been discriminatory in purpose, the Court reaffirmed the right of minority members of our society to participate meaningfully and equally in the political process.

This case involves this last chapter of discrimination: A majority of the Michigan electorate changed the basic rules of the political process in that State in a manner that uniquely disadvantaged racial minorities. [FN1] Prior to the enactment of the constitutional initiative at issue here, all of the admissions policies of Michigan's public colleges and universities — including race-sensitive admissions policies — were in the hands of each institution's governing board. The members of those boards are nominated by political parties and elected by the citizenry in statewide elections. After over a century of being shut out of Michigan's institutions of higher education, racial minorities in Michigan had succeeded in persuading the elected board representatives to adopt admissions policies that took into account the benefits of racial diversity. And this Court twice blessed such *efforts — first in Regents of Univ. of Cal. v. Bakke, and again in Grutter v. Bollinger,* a case that itself concerned a Michigan admissions policy.

[FN1] I of course do not mean to suggest that Michigan's voters acted with anything like the invidious intent, of those who historically stymied the rights of racial minorities. Contra, n. 11 (Scalia, J., concurring in judgment). But like earlier chapters of political restructuring, the Michigan amendment at issue in this case changed the rules of the political process to the disadvantage of minority members of our society.

In the wake o f *Grutter,* some voters in Michigan set out to eliminate the use of race-sensitive admissions policies. Those voters were of course free to pursue this end in any number of ways. For example, they could have persuaded existing board members to change their minds through individual or grassroots lobbying efforts, or through general public awareness campaigns. Or they could have mobilized efforts to vote uncooperative board members out of office, replacing them with members who would share their desire to abolish race-sensitive admissions policies. When this Court holds that the Constitution permits a particular policy, nothing prevents a majority of a State's voters from choosing not to adopt that policy. Our system of government encourages — and indeed, depends on — that type of democratic action.

But instead, the majority of Michigan voters changed the rules in the middle of the game, reconfiguring the existing political process in Michigan in a manner that burdened racial minorities. They did so in the 2006 election by amending the Michigan [Constitution]. As a result of § 26, there are now two very different processes through which a Michigan citizen is permitted to influence the admissions policies of the State's universities: one for persons interested in race-sensitive admissions policies and one for everyone else. A citizen who is a University of Michigan alumnus, for instance, can advocate for an admissions policy that considers an applicant's legacy status by meeting individually with members of the Board of Regents to convince them of her views, by joining with other legacy parents to lobby the Board, or by voting for and supporting Board candidates who share her position. The same options are available to a citizen who wants the Board to adopt admissions policies that consider athleticism, geography, area of study, and so on. The one and only policy a Michigan citizen may not seek through this long-established process is a race-sensitive admissions policy that considers race in an individualized manner when it is clear that race-neutral alternatives are not adequate to achieve diversity. For that policy alone, the citizens of Michigan must undertake the daunting task of amending the State Constitution.

Our precedents do not permit political restructurings that create one process for racial minorities and a separate, less burdensome process for everyone else. . . .

Today, disregarding *stare decisis,* a majority of the Court effectively discards those precedents. The plurality does so, it tells us, because the freedom actually secured by the Constitution is the freedom of self-government — because the majority of Michigan citizens "exercised their privilege to enact laws as a basic exercise of their democratic power." It would be "demeaning to the democratic process," the plurality concludes, to disturb that decision in any way. This logic embraces majority rule without an important constitutional limit.

The plurality's decision fundamentally misunderstands the nature of the injustice worked by § 26. This case is not, as the plurality imagines, about "who may resolve" the debate over the use of race in higher education admissions. I agree wholeheartedly that nothing vests the resolution of that debate exclusively in the courts or requires that we remove it from the reach of the electorate. Rather, this case is about *how* the debate over the use of race-sensitive admissions policies may be resolved — that is, it must be resolved in constitutionally permissible ways. While our Constitution does not guarantee minority groups victory in the political process, it does guarantee them meaningful and equal access to that process. It guarantees that the majority may not win by stacking the political process against minority groups permanently, forcing the minority alone to surmount unique obstacles in pursuit of its goals — here, educational diversity that cannot reasonably be accomplished through race-neutral measures. Today, by permitting a majority of the voters in Michigan to do what our Constitution forbids, the Court ends the debate over race-sensitive admissions policies in Michigan in a manner that contravenes constitutional protections long recognized in our precedents.

Like the plurality, I have faith that our citizenry will continue to learn from this Nation's regrettable history; that it will strive to move beyond those injustices towards a future of equality. And I, too, believe in the importance of public discourse on matters of public policy. But I part ways with the plurality when it suggests that judicial intervention in this case "impede[s]" rather than "advance[s]" the democratic process and the ultimate hope of equality. I firmly believe that our role as judges includes policing the process of self-government and stepping in when necessary to secure the constitutional guarantee of equal protection. Because I would do so here, I respectfully dissent. . . .

[Section] 26 has a "racial focus." *Seattle.* That is clear from its text, which prohibits Michigan's public colleges and universities from "grant[ing] preferential treatment to any individual or group on the basis of race." Like desegregation of public schools, race-sensitive admissions policies "inur[e] primarily to the benefit of the minority," [*Seattle,*] as they are designed to increase minorities' access to institutions of higher education.

Petitioner argues that race-sensitive admissions policies cannot "inur[e] primarily to the benefit of the minority," as the Court has upheld such policies only insofar as they further "the educational benefits that flow from a diverse student body," [*Grutter.*] But there is no conflict between this Court's pronouncement in *Grutter* and the common-sense reality that race-sensitive admissions policies benefit minorities. Rather, race-sensitive admissions policies further a compelling state interest in achieving a diverse student body precisely because they increase minority enrollment, which necessarily benefits minority groups. In other words, constitutionally permissible race-sensitive admissions policies can both serve the compelling interest of obtaining the educational benefits that flow from a diverse student body, and inure to the benefit of racial minorities. . . . Section 26 restructures the political process in Michigan in a manner that places unique burdens on racial minorities. It establishes a distinct and more burdensome political process for the enactment of admissions plans that consider racial diversity. . . .

[The] plurality sees it differently. [According] to the plurality, the *Hunter* and *Seattle* Courts were not concerned with efforts to reconfigure the political process to the detriment of racial minorities; rather, those cases invalidated governmental actions merely because they reflected an invidious purpose to discriminate. This is not a tenable reading of those cases.

The plurality identifies "invidious discrimination" as the "necessary result" of the restructuring in *Hunter*. It is impossible to assess whether the housing amendment in *Hunter* was motivated by discriminatory purpose, for the opinion does not discuss the question of intent. What is obvious, however, is that the possibility of invidious discrimination played no role in the Court's reasoning. We ordinarily understand our precedents to mean what they actually say, not what we later think they could or should have said. The *Hunter* Court was clear about why it invalidated the Akron charter amendment: It was impermissible as a restructuring of the political process, not as an action motivated by discriminatory intent.

Similarly, the plurality disregards what *Seattle* actually says and instead opines that "the political restriction in question was designed to be used, or was likely to be used, to encourage infliction of injury by reason of race." Here, the plurality derives its conclusion not from *Seattle* itself, but from evidence unearthed more than a quarter-century later in Parents Involved in Community Schools v. Seattle *School Dist. No. 1.* . . .

[Not] once did the [*Seattle*] Court suggest the presence of *de jure* segregation in Seattle. Quite the opposite: The opinion explicitly suggested the desegregation plan was adopted to remedy *de facto* rather than *de jure* segregation. The Court, moreover, assumed that no "constitutional violation" through *de jure* segregation had occurred. And it unmistakably rested its decision on *Hunter*, holding Seattle's initiative invalid because it "use[d] the racial nature of an issue to define the governmental decision-making structure, and thus impose[d] substantial and unique burdens on racial minorities." . . .

[Justice] Scalia disagrees with "the proposition that a facially neutral law may deny equal protection solely because it has a disparate racial impact." (opinion concurring in judgment). He would acknowledge, however, that an act that draws racial distinctions or makes racial classifications triggers strict scrutiny regardless of whether discriminatory intent is shown. That should settle the matter: Section 26 draws a racial distinction. As the *Seattle* Court explained, "when the political process or the decision-making mechanism used to *address* racially conscious legislation — and only such legislation — is singled out for peculiar and disadvantageous treatment, the governmental action plainly rests on 'distinctions based on race.' " . . .

[My] colleagues are of the view that we should leave race out of the picture entirely and let the voters sort it out. We have seen this reasoning before. See *Parents Involved* ("The way to stop discrimination on the basis of race is to stop discriminating on the basis of race"). It is a sentiment out of touch with reality, one not required by our Constitution, and one that has properly been rejected as "not sufficient" to resolve cases of this nature. Id. (Kennedy, J., concurring in part and concurring in judgment). While "[t]he enduring hope is that race should not matter[,] the reality is that too often it does." Id. "[R]acial discrimination . . . [is] not ancient history." Bartlett v. Strickland, 556 U.S. 1, 25 (2009) (plurality opinion).

Race matters. Race matters in part because of the long history of racial minorities' being denied access to the political process. And although we have made great strides, "voting discrimination still exists; no one doubts that." [Shelby Cnty. v. Holder, 133 S. Ct. 2612, 2619 (2012)].

Race also matters because of persistent racial inequality in society — inequality that cannot be ignored and that has produced stark socioeconomic disparities. . . .

And race matters for reasons that really are only skin deep, that cannot be discussed any other way, and that cannot be wished away. Race matters to a young man's view of society when he spends his teenage years watching others tense up as he passes, no matter the neighborhood where he grew up. Race matters to a young woman's sense of self when she states her hometown, and then is pressed, "No, where are you *really* from?", regardless of how many generations her family has been in the country. Race matters to a young person addressed by a stranger in a foreign language, which he does not understand because only English was spoken at home. Race matters because of the slights, the snickers, the silent judgments that reinforce that most crippling of thoughts: "I do not belong here."

In my colleagues' view, examining the racial impact of legislation only perpetuates racial discrimination. This refusal to accept the stark reality that race matters is regrettable. The way to stop discrimination on the basis of race is to speak openly and candidly on the subject of race, and to apply the Constitution with eyes open to the unfortunate effects of centuries of racial discrimination. As members of the judiciary tasked with intervening to carry out the guarantee of equal protection, we ought not sit back and wish away, rather than confront, the racial inequality that exists in our society. It is this view that works harm, by perpetuating the facile notion that what makes race matter is acknowledging the simple truth that race *does* matter. . . .

V

Although the only constitutional rights at stake in this case are process-based rights, the substantive policy at issue is undeniably of some relevance to my colleagues. I will therefore speak in response. . . .

[Justice Sotomayor outlines the history of segregation in Michigan's colleges and universities, the growing diversity of the student population during the period when the state used "race-sensitive" admissions policies, and the decline in diversity in Michigan and elsewhere after abandonment of "race-sensitive" policies.] These statistics may not influence the views of some of my colleagues, as they question the wisdom of adopting race-sensitive admissions policies and would prefer if our Nation's colleges and universities were to discard those policies altogether. See (Roberts, C.J., concurring) (suggesting that race-sensitive admissions policies might "do more harm than good"); (Scalia, J., concurring in judgment); *Grutter* (Thomas, J., concurring in part and dissenting in part); id. (Scalia, J., concurring in part and dissenting in part). That view is at odds with our recognition in *Grutter,* and more recently in *Fisher v. University of Texas at Austin,* that race-sensitive admissions policies are necessary to achieve a diverse student body when race-neutral alternatives have failed. More fundamentally, it ignores the importance of diversity in institutions of higher education and reveals how little my colleagues understand about the reality of race in America.

[To] be clear, I do not mean to suggest that the virtues of adopting race-sensitive admissions policies should inform the legal question before the Court today regarding the constitutionality of § 26. But I cannot ignore the unfortunate outcome of today's decision: Short of amending the State Constitution, a Herculean task, racial minorities in Michigan are deprived of even an opportunity to convince Michigan's public colleges and universities to consider race in their admissions plans when other attempts to achieve racial diversity have proved unworkable, and those institutions are unnecessarily hobbled in their pursuit of a diverse student body.

[Today's] decision eviscerates an important strand of our equal protection jurisprudence. For members of historically marginalized groups, which rely on the federal courts to protect their constitutional rights, the decision can hardly bolster hope for a vision of democracy that preserves for all the right to participate meaningfully and equally in self-government.

I respectfully dissent.

(i.) RACIAL DIVERSITY IN K-12 PUBLIC EDUCATION

Do the principles of *Grutter* and *Gratz* control when a public school district uses racial identity as one basis on which to assign students to schools within a district? Does diversity constitute a compelling interest in this context? Even if it does, are there more race-neutral means for achieving it? Does the K-12 context differ from the university context because all students are included and school assignments are a zero-sum game, as opposed to a selective process? These and related questions were raised in a pair of cases decided as the first major pronouncement by the new Roberts Court on issues of race and equal protection, with Chief Justice Roberts having succeeded Chief Justice Rehnquist and Justice Alito having succeeded Justice O'Connor, whose vote had pivotally determined the outcomes in *Grutter* and *Gratz*. The Court held equal protection violated by both Seattle's and Louisville's efforts at racial mixing of their K-12 school populations:

PARENTS INVOLVED IN COMMUNITY SCHOOLS v. SEATTLE SCHOOL DISTRICT
551 U.S. 701 (2007)

Chief Justice ROBERTS announced the judgment of the Court, and delivered the opinion of the Court with respect to Parts I, II, III-A, and III-C, and an opinion with respect to Parts III-B and IV, in which Justices SCALIA, THOMAS, and ALITO join.

The school districts in these cases voluntarily adopted student assignment plans that rely upon race to determine which public schools certain children may attend. The Seattle school district classifies children as white or nonwhite; the Jefferson County school district as black or "other." In Seattle, this racial classification is used to allocate slots in oversubscribed high schools. In Jefferson County, it is used to make certain elementary school assignments and to rule on transfer requests. In each case, the school district relies upon an individual student's race in assigning that student to a particular school, so that the racial balance at the school falls within a predetermined range based on the racial composition of the school district as a whole. Parents of students denied assignment to particular schools under these plans solely because of their race brought suit, contending that allocating children to different public schools on the basis of race violated the Fourteenth Amendment guarantee of equal protection. The Courts of Appeals below upheld the plans. We [reverse].

I. Both cases present the same underlying legal question — whether a public school that had not operated legally segregated schools or has been found to be unitary may choose to classify students by race and rely upon that classification in making school assignments. Although we examine the plans under the same legal framework, the specifics of the two plans, and the circumstances surrounding their adoption, are in some respects quite different.

Seattle School District operates 10 regular public high schools. In 1998, it adopted the plan at issue in this case for assigning students to these schools. The plan allows incoming ninth graders to choose from among any of the district's high schools, ranking however many schools they wish in order of preference. Some schools are more popular than others. If too many students list the same school as their first choice, the district employs a series of tiebreakers" to determine who will fill the open slots at the oversubscribed "tiebreaker selects for admission students who have a sibling school. The first tiebreaker depends upon the currently enrolled in the chosen school. The next racial composition of the particular school and the race of the individual student. In the district's public schools approximately 41 percent of enrolled students are white; the remaining 59 percent, comprising all other racial groups, are classified by Seattle for assignment purposes as nonwhite. If an oversubscribed school is not within 10 percentage points of the district's overall white/nonwhite racial balance, it is what the district calls "integration positive," and the district employs a tiebreaker that selects for assignment students whose race "will serve to bring the school into balance." [Seattle] has never operated segregated schools — legally separate schools for students of different races — nor has it ever been subject to court-ordered desegregation. It nonetheless employs the racial tiebreaker in an attempt to address the effects of racially identifiable housing patterns on school assignments.

Jefferson County Public Schools operates the public school system in metropolitan Louisville, Kentucky. In 1973 a federal court found that Jefferson County had maintained a segregated school system, and in 1975 the District Court entered a desegregation decree. Jefferson County operated under this decree until 2000, when the District Court dissolved the decree after finding that the district had achieved unitary status by eliminating "to the greatest extent practicable" the vestiges of its prior policy of segregation. In 2001, after the decree had been dissolved, Jefferson County adopted the voluntary student assignment plan at issue in this case. Approximately 34 percent of the district's 97,000 students are black; most of the remaining 66 percent are white. The plan requires all non-magnet schools to maintain a minimum black enrollment of 15 percent, and a maximum black enrollment of 50 percent.

III. A. It is well established that when the government distributes burdens or benefits on the basis of individual racial classifications, that action is reviewed under strict scrutiny. [In] order to satisfy this searching standard of review, the school districts must demonstrate that the use of individual racial classifications in the assignment plans here under review is "narrowly tailored" to achieve a "compelling" government interest. [Our] prior cases, in evaluating the use of racial classifications in the school context, have recognized two interests that qualify as compelling. The first is the compelling interest of remedying the effects of past intentional discrimination. Yet the Seattle public schools have not shown that they were ever segregated by law, and were not subject to court-ordered desegregation decrees. The Jefferson County public schools were previously segregated by law and were subject to a desegregation decree [but it has since] achieved "unitary" status.

[The] second government interest we have recognized as compelling for purposes of strict scrutiny is the interest in diversity in higher education upheld in Grutter. The entire gist of the analysis in Grutter was that the admissions program at issue there focused on each applicant as an individual, and not simply as a member of a particular racial group. [The] point of the narrow tailoring analysis in which the Grutter Court engaged was to ensure that the use of racial classifications was indeed part of a broader assessment of diversity, and not simply an effort to achieve racial balance, which the Court explained would be "patently unconstitutional." In the present cases, by contrast, race is not considered as part of a broader effort to achieve "exposure to widely diverse people, cultures, ideas, and viewpoints"; race, for some students, is determinative standing alone. The districts argue that other factors, such as student preferences, affect assignment decisions under their plans, but under each plan when race comes into play, it is decisive by itself. It is not simply one factor weighed with others in reaching a decision, as in Grutter; it is *the* factor. Like the University of Michigan undergraduate plan struck down in Gratz, the plans here "do not provide for a meaningful individualized review of applicants" but instead rely on racial classifications in a "nonindividualized, mechanical" way. [In] upholding the admissions plan in Grutter, [this] Court relied upon considerations unique to institutions of higher education. The present cases are not governed by Grutter.

B. Perhaps recognizing that reliance on Grutter cannot sustain their plans, both school districts assert additional interests, distinct from the interest upheld in Grutter, to justify their race-based assignments. [Seattle] contends that its use of race helps to reduce racial concentration in schools and to ensure that racially concentrated housing patterns do not prevent nonwhite students from having access to the most desirable schools. Jefferson County has articulated a similar goal, phrasing its interest in terms of educating its students "in a racially integrated environment." Each school district argues that educational and broader socialization benefits flow from a racially diverse learning environment, and each contends that because the diversity they seek is racial diversity — not the broader diversity at issue in Grutter — it makes sense to promote that interest directly by relying on race alone.

The parties and their amici dispute whether racial diversity in schools in fact has a marked impact on test scores and other objective yardsticks or achieves intangible socialization benefits. The debate is not one we need to resolve, however, because it is clear that the racial classifications employed by the districts are not narrowly tailored to the goal of achieving the educational and social benefits asserted to flow from racial diversity. In design and operation, the plans are directed only to racial balance, pure and simple, an objective this Court has repeatedly condemned as illegitimate.

The plans are tied to each district's specific racial demographics, rather than to any pedagogic concept of the level of diversity needed to obtain the asserted educational benefits. In Seattle, the district seeks white enrollment of between 31 and 51 percent (within 10 percent of "the district white average" of 41 percent), and nonwhite enrollment of between 49 and 69 percent (within 10 percent of "the district minority average" of 59 percent). In Jefferson County, by contrast, the district seeks black enrollment of no less than 15 or more than 50 percent, a range designed to be "equally above and below Black student enrollment systemwide" [of] 34 percent. [The] districts offer no evidence that the level of racial diversity necessary to achieve the asserted educational benefits happens to coincide with the racial demographics of the respective school districts. [Seattle did not] demonstrate in any way how the educational and social benefits of racial diversity or avoidance of racial isolation are more likely to be achieved at a school that is 50 percent white and 50 percent Asian-American, which would qualify as diverse under Seattle's plan, than at a school that is 30 percent Asian-American, 25 percent African-American, 25 percent Latino, and 20 percent white, which under Seattle's definition would be racially concentrated.

[This] working backward to achieve a particular type of racial balance, rather than working forward from some demonstration of the level of diversity that provides the purported benefits, is a fatal flaw under our existing precedent. We have many times over reaffirmed that "racial balance is not to be achieved for its own sake." [Accepting] racial balancing as a compelling state interest would justify the imposition of racial proportionality throughout American society. [The] principle that racial balancing is not permitted is one of substance, not semantics. Racial balancing is not transformed from "patently unconstitutional" to a compelling state interest simply by relabeling it "racial diversity." While the school districts use various verbal formulations to describe the interest they seek to promote — racial diversity, avoidance of racial isolation, racial integration — they offer no definition of the interest that suggests it differs from racial balance.

C. The districts assert, as they must, that the way in which they have employed individual racial classifications is necessary to achieve their stated ends. The minimal effect these classifications have on student assignments, however, suggests that other means would be effective. Seattle's racial tiebreaker results, in the end, only in shifting a small number of students between schools. [Similarly,] Jefferson County's use of racial classifications has only a minimal effect on the assignment of students. [While] we do not suggest that *greater* use of race would be preferable, the minimal impact of the districts' racial classifications on school enrollment casts doubt on the necessity of using racial classifications. [The] districts have also failed to show that they considered methods other than explicit racial classifications to achieve their stated goals. Narrow tailoring requires "serious, good faith consideration of workable race-neutral alternatives."

IV. [Justice Breyer's dissent] asserts that these cases are controlled by Grutter, claiming that the existence of a compelling interest in these cases "follows a fortiori" from Grutter, and accusing us of tacitly overruling that case. The dissent overreads Grutter, however. [The] Court was exceedingly careful in describing the interest furthered in Grutter as "not an interest in simple ethnic diversity" but rather a "far broader array of qualifications and characteristics" in which race was but a single element. We take the Grutter Court at its word.

[Justice Breyer] also suggests that other means for achieving greater racial diversity in schools are necessarily unconstitutional if the racial classifications at issue in these cases cannot survive strict scrutiny. These other means — e.g., where to construct new schools, how to allocate resources among schools, and which academic offerings to provide to attract students to certain schools — implicate different considerations than the explicit racial classifications at issue in these cases, and we express no opinion on their validity. [Rather,] we employ the familiar and well-established analytic approach of strict scrutiny to evaluate the plans at issue today, an approach that in no way warrants the dissent's cataclysmic concerns. Under that approach, the school districts have not carried their burden of showing that the ends they seek justify the particular extreme means they have chosen — classifying individual students on the basis of their race and discriminating among them on that basis.

[The] parties and their amici debate which side is more faithful to the heritage of Brown, but the position of the plaintiffs in Brown was spelled out in their brief and could not have been clearer: "The Fourteenth Amendment prevents states from according differential treatment to American children on the basis of their color or race." What do the racial classifications at issue here do, if not accord differential treatment on the basis of race? [Before] Brown, schoolchildren were told where they could and could not go to school based on the color of their skin. The school districts in these cases have not carried the heavy burden of demonstrating that we should allow this once again — even for very different reasons. For schools that never segregated on the basis of race, such as Seattle, or that have removed the vestiges of past segregation, such as Jefferson County, the way "to achieve a system of determining admission to the public schools on a nonracial basis," is to stop assigning students on a racial basis. The way to stop discrimination on the basis of race is to stop discriminating on the basis of race.

Justice THOMAS, concurring.

[The dissent] claims that the school districts are threatened with resegregation and that they will succumb to that threat if these plans are declared unconstitutional. It also argues that these plans can be justified as part of the school boards' attempts to "eradicate earlier school segregation." Contrary to the dissent's rhetoric, neither of these school dis-

1210 | Part II. Individual Rights and Liberties

tricts is threatened with resegregation, and neither is constitutionally compelled or permitted to undertake race-based remediation. Racial imbalance is not segregation. [In] the context of public schooling, segregation is the deliberate operation of a school system to "carry out a governmental policy to separate pupils in schools solely on the basis of race." Racial imbalance is the failure of a school district's individual schools to match or approximate the demographic makeup of the student population at large. [Although] presently observed racial imbalance might result from past *de jure* segregation, racial imbalance can also result from any number of innocent private decisions, including voluntary housing choices. Because racial imbalance is not inevitably linked to unconstitutional segregation, it is not unconstitutional in and of itself. [Although] there is arguably a danger of racial imbalance in schools in Seattle and Louisville, there is no danger of resegregation. No one contends that Seattle has established or that Louisville has reestablished a dual school system that separates students on the basis of race.

[It] is far from apparent that coerced racial mixing has any educational benefits, much less that integration is necessary to black achievement. [Even] after *Brown*, some schools with predominantly black enrollments have achieved outstanding educational results. There is also evidence that black students attending historically black colleges achieve better academic results than those attending predominantly white colleges. [Given] this tenuous relationship between forced racial mixing and improved educational results for black children, the dissent cannot plausibly maintain that an educational element supports the integration interest, let alone makes it compelling.

[Most] of the dissent's criticisms of today's result can be traced to its rejection of the color-blind Constitution. [But] I am quite comfortable in the company I keep. My view of the Constitution is Justice Harlan's view in Plessy: "Our Constitution is color-blind, and neither knows nor tolerates classes among citizens." And my view was the rallying cry for the lawyers who litigated Brown ("That the Constitution is color blind is our dedicated belief"). [What] was wrong in 1954 cannot be right today.

Justice KENNEDY, concurring in part and concurring in the judgment.

[Parts] of the opinion by the Chief Justice imply an all-too-unyielding insistence that race cannot be a factor in instances when, in my view, it may be taken into account. The plurality opinion is too dismissive of the legitimate interest government has in ensuring all people have equal opportunity regardless of their race. The plurality's postulate that "the way to stop discrimination on the basis of race is to stop discriminating on the basis of race," is not sufficient to decide these cases. Fifty years of experience since Brown should teach us that the problem before us defies so easy a solution. School districts can seek to reach Brown's objective of equal educational opportunity. The plurality opinion is at least open to the interpretation that the Constitution requires school districts to ignore the problem of *de facto* resegregation in schooling. I cannot endorse that conclusion. To the extent the plurality opinion suggests the Constitution mandates that state and local school authorities must accept the status quo of racial isolation in schools, it is, in my view, profoundly mistaken.

[In] the administration of public schools by the state and local authorities it is permissible to consider the racial makeup of schools and to adopt general policies to encourage a diverse student body, one aspect of which is its racial composition. If school authorities are concerned that the student-body compositions of certain schools interfere with the objective of offering an equal educational opportunity to all of their students, they are free to devise race conscious measures to address the problem in a general way and without treating each student in different fashion solely on the basis of a systematic, individual typing by race.

School boards may pursue the goal of bringing together students of diverse backgrounds and races through other means, including strategic site selection of new schools; drawing attendance zones with general recognition of the demographics of neighborhoods; allocating resources for special programs; recruiting students and faculty in a targeted fashion; and tracking enrollments, performance, and other statistics by race. These mechanisms are race conscious but do not lead to different treatment based on a classification that tells each student he or she is to be defined by race, so it is unlikely any of them would demand strict scrutiny to be found permissible. Executive and legislative branches, which for generations now have considered these types of policies and procedures, should be permitted to employ them with candor and with confidence that a constitutional violation does not occur whenever a decisionmaker considers the impact a given approach might have on students of different races. Assigning to each student a personal designation according to a crude system of individual racial classifications is quite a different matter; and the legal analysis changes accordingly.

[In] the cases before us it is noteworthy that the number of students whose assignment depends on express racial classifications is limited. I join Part III-C of the Court's opinion because I agree that in the context of these plans, the small number of assignments affected suggests that the schools could have achieved their stated ends through different means. These include the facially race-neutral means set forth above or, if necessary, a more nuanced, individual evaluation of school needs and student characteristics that might include race as a component. The latter approach would be informed by Grutter, though of course the criteria relevant to student placement would differ based on the age of the students, the needs of the parents, and the role of the schools.

[If] it is legitimate for school authorities to work to avoid racial isolation in their schools, must they do so only by indirection and general policies? Does the Constitution mandate this inefficient result? Why may the authorities not recognize the problem in candid fashion and solve it altogether through resort to direct assignments based on student racial classifications? So, the argument proceeds, if race is the problem, then perhaps race is the solution.

The argument ignores the dangers presented by individual classifications, dangers that are not as pressing when the same ends are achieved by more indirect means. When the government classifies an individual by race, it must first define what it means to be of a race. Who exactly is white and who is nonwhite? To be forced to live under a state-mandated racial label is inconsistent with the dignity of individuals in our society. And it is a label that an individual is powerless to change. Governmental classifications that command people to march in different directions based on racial typologies can cause a new divisiveness. The practice can lead to corrosive discourse, where race serves not as an element of our diverse heritage but instead as a bargaining chip in the political process. On the other hand race-conscious measures that do not rely on differential treatment based on individual classifications present these problems to a lesser degree.

[This] Nation has a moral and ethical obligation to fulfill its historic commitment to creating an integrated society that ensures equal opportunity for all of its children. A compelling interest exists in avoiding racial isolation, an interest that a school district, in its discretion and expertise, may choose to pursue. Likewise, a district may consider it a compelling interest to achieve a diverse student population. Race may be one component of that diversity, but other demographic factors, plus special talents and needs, should also be considered. What the government is not permitted to do, absent a showing of necessity not made here, is to classify every student on the basis of race and to assign each of them to schools based on that classification. Crude measures of this sort threaten to reduce children to racial chits valued and traded according to one school's supply and another's demand.

[The] decision today should not prevent school districts from continuing the important work of bringing together students of different racial, ethnic, and economic backgrounds. Due to a variety of factors — some influenced by government, some not — neighborhoods in our communities do not reflect the diversity of our Nation as a whole. Those entrusted with directing our public schools can bring to bear the creativity of experts, parents, administrators, and other concerned citizens to find a way to achieve the compelling interests they face without resorting to widespread governmental allocation of benefits and burdens on the basis of racial classifications.

Justice STEVENS, dissenting.

There is a cruel irony in the Chief Justice's reliance on our decision in Brown. [He] states: "Before Brown, schoolchildren were told where they could and could not go to school based on the color of their skin." This sentence reminds me of Anatole France's observation: "The majestic equality of the law, forbids rich and poor alike to sleep under bridges, to beg in the streets, and to steal their bread." The Chief Justice fails to note that it was only black schoolchildren who were so ordered; indeed, the history books do not tell stories of white children struggling to attend black schools. In this and other ways, the Chief Justice rewrites the history of one of this Court's most important decisions.

The Court has changed significantly since . . . 1968. It was then more faithful to Brown and more respectful of our precedent than it is today. It is my firm conviction that no member of the Court that I joined in 1975 would have agreed with today's decision.

Justice BREYER, with whom Justices STEVENS, SOUTER, and GINSBURG join, dissenting.

These cases consider the longstanding efforts of two local school boards to integrate their public schools. The school board plans before us resemble many others adopted in the last 50 years by primary and secondary schools throughout the Nation. All of those plans represent local efforts to bring about the kind of racially integrated education that Brown long ago promised — efforts that this Court has repeatedly required, permitted, and encouraged local authorities to undertake. This Court has recognized that the public interests at stake in such cases are "compelling." We have approved of "narrowly tailored" plans that are no less race-conscious than the plans before us. And we have understood that the Constitution *permits* local communities to adopt desegregation plans even where it does not *require* them to do so.

The plurality pays inadequate attention to this law, to past opinions' rationales, their language, and the contexts in which they arise. As a result, it reverses course and reaches the wrong conclusion. In doing so, it distorts precedent, it misapplies the relevant constitutional principles, it announces legal rules that will obstruct efforts by state and local governments to deal effectively with the growing resegregation of public schools, it threatens to substitute for present calm a disruptive round of race-related litigation, and it undermines *Brown*'s promise of integrated primary and secondary education that local communities have sought to make a reality. This cannot be justified in the name of the Equal Protection Clause.

A longstanding and unbroken line of legal authority tells us that the Equal Protection Clause permits local school boards to use race-conscious criteria to achieve positive race-related goals. Swann. [The principle] that the government may voluntarily adopt race-conscious measures to improve conditions of race even when it is not under a constitutional obligation to do so [has] been accepted by every branch of government and is rooted in the history of the Equal Protection Clause itself. [The] basic objective of those who wrote the Equal Protection Clause [was] forbidding practices that lead to racial exclusion. The Amendment sought to bring into American society as full members those whom the Nation had previously held in slavery. There is reason to believe that those who drafted an Amendment with this basic purpose in mind would have understood the legal and practical difference between the use of race-conscious criteria in defiance of that purpose, namely to keep the races apart, and the use of race-conscious criteria to further that purpose, namely to bring the races together.

[No] case — not Adarand, Gratz, Grutter, or any other — has ever held that the test of "strict scrutiny" means that all racial classifications — no matter whether they seek to include or exclude — must in practice be treated the same. [Rather,] they apply the strict scrutiny test in a manner that is "fatal in fact" only to racial classifications that harmfully *exclude;* they apply the test in a manner that is *not* fatal in fact to racial classifications that seek to *include.* [Today's] opinion reveals that the plurality would rewrite this Court's prior jurisprudence, at least in practical application, transforming the "strict scrutiny" test into a rule that is fatal in fact across the board. In doing so, the plurality parts company from this Court's prior cases, and it takes from local government the longstanding legal right to use race-conscious criteria for inclusive purposes in limited ways.

[Here,] the context is one in which school districts seek to advance or to maintain racial integration in primary and secondary schools. [This] context is *not* a context that involves the use of race to decide who will receive goods or services that are normally distributed on the basis of merit and which are in short supply. It is not one in which race-conscious limits stigmatize or exclude; the limits at issue do not pit the races against each other or otherwise significantly exacerbate racial tensions. They do not impose burdens unfairly upon members of one race alone but instead seek benefits for members of all races alike. The context here is one of racial limits that seek, not to keep the races apart, but to bring them together. In my view, this contextual approach to scrutiny is altogether fitting. I believe that the law requires application here of a standard of review that is not "strict" in the traditional sense of that word. [Apparently] Justice Kennedy also agrees that strict scrutiny would not apply in respect to certain "race-conscious" school board policies.

[The] interest at stake possesses three essential elements. First, there is a historical and remedial element: an interest in setting right the consequences of prior conditions of segregation. [Second,] there is an educational element: an interest in overcoming the adverse educational effects produced by and associated with highly segregated schools. Third, there is a democratic element: an interest in producing an educational environment that reflects the "pluralistic society" in which our children will live. It is an interest in helping our children learn to work and play together with children of different racial backgrounds. It is an interest in teaching children to engage in the kind of cooperation among Americans of all races that is necessary to make a land of three hundred million people one Nation. [In] light of this Court's conclusions in Grutter, the "compelling" nature of these interests in the context of primary and secondary public education follows here *a fortiori.*

[Several] factors, taken together, nonetheless lead me to conclude that the boards' use of race-conscious criteria in these plans passes even the strictest "tailoring" test. First, the race-conscious criteria at issue only help set the outer bounds of *broad* ranges. They constitute but one part of plans that depend primarily upon other, nonracial elements. To use race in this way is not to set a forbidden "quota." In fact, the defining feature of both plans is greater emphasis upon student choice. [Second,] broad-range limits on voluntary school choice plans are less burdensome, and [hence] *more narrowly tailored* than the race-conscious admission plans that this Court approved in Grutter. Here, race becomes a factor only in a fraction of students' non-merit-based assignments — not in large numbers of students' merit-based applications. Moreover, the effect of applying race-conscious criteria here affects potentially disadvantaged students *less severely,* not more severely, than the criteria at issue in Grutter. Disappointed students are not rejected from a State's flagship graduate program; they simply attend a different one of the district's many public schools. Third, [the] school boards' widespread consultation, their experimentation with numerous other plans, [make] clear that plans that are less explicitly race based are unlikely to achieve the board's "compelling" objectives. [Giving] some degree of weight to a local school board's knowledge, expertise, and concerns in these particular matters is not inconsistent with rigorous judicial scrutiny. It simply recognizes that judges are not well suited to act as school administrators. [In] sum, the districts' race-conscious plans satisfy "strict scrutiny" and are therefore lawful.

[*De facto*] resegregation is on the rise. Given the conditions in which school boards work to set policy, they may need all of the means presently at their disposal to combat those problems. Yet the plurality would deprive them of at least one tool that some districts now consider vital — the limited use of broad race-conscious student population ranges. [I] fear the consequences of doing so for the law, for the schools, for the democratic process, and for America's efforts to create, out of its diversity, one Nation.

(ii.) "DISPARATE IMPACT," TITLE VII, AND EMPLOYMENT PRACTICES

With Judge Sotomayor's appointment pending for confirmation before the Senate, a case in which she had participated as a member of a three-judge Second Circuit Panel, summarily affirming (without opinion) a district court dismissal of a reverse based discrimination claim by New Haven, Connecticut, firemen, was decided by the Court. In *Ricci,* (see above, this chapter) more interesting for what the Court did not say (it avoided the constitutional question posed), as well as its ideological taint (the majority (5–4) supported its decision by interpreting (amending?) the statute to require a "strong basis in evidence), the Court continued the contemporary controversy of affirmative action, diversity, and discrimination against whites. Once again, it was Justice Kennedy's vote that determined where the line was to be drawn in these circumstances, and although the decision would appear to have implications in Title VII employment practices, it was perhaps most significant as it foretold that these issues remain fertile ground for future controversy and litigation.

D. GENDER-BASED CLASSIFICATIONS

1. HEIGHTENED REVIEW

Perhaps no issue considered by the Supreme Court has better exemplified the concept of a "living constitution" than its treatment of gender-based discrimination. From the paternalistic protection of woman by the Michigan State Legislature in *Goesaert* (below) in 1948, to the evolvement of the "middle scrutiny" standard of review in *Craig v. Boren,* by 1976, to the requirement of an "exceedingly persuasive justification" and application of "skeptical scrutiny" in *United States v. Virginia* in 1996, the Court has undeniably reflected the changing and contemporary status of females in our society into constitutional law. As if to reinforce these contemporary values the Court has admonished states against attempts to reinforce "archaic and stereotypic concepts based on fixed notions concerning the roles of males and females." Even Justice Rehnquist, no traditional advocate of a living constitution has seen his own standards evolve as reflective of these changing social values. (See Justice Rehnquist's concurring opinion in *United States v. Virginia.*)

All of this has occurred despite the failure to adopt an "Equal Rights Amendment" ("Equality of rights under the law shall not be denied or abridged by the United States or any State on account of Sex") leaving the language of the Constitution unchanged. The only possible explanation for these evolving standards in Supreme Court decisional law is the changing roles of men and women in our society. The major controversy today surrounds to what degree "skeptical scrutiny" in fact differs from the "strict scrutiny" traditionally applied to suspect classifications. The cases below reflect this evolution and current debate.

GOESAERT v. CLEARY
335 U.S. 464 (1948)

Mr. Justice FRANKFURTER delivered the opinion of the Court.

As part of the Michigan system for controlling the sale of liquor, bartenders are required to be licensed in all cities having a population of 50,000, or more, but no female may be so licensed unless she be "the wife or daughter of the male owner" of a licensed liquor establishment. Section 19a of Act 133 of the Public Acts of Michigan 1945, Mich.Stat.Ann. § 18,990(1), Cum.Supp.1947. The case is here on direct appeal from an order of the District Court of three judges, convened under § 266 of the old Judicial Code, now 28 U.S.C. § 2284, 28 U.S.C.A. § 2284, denying an injunction to restrain the enforcement of the Michigan law. The claim, denied below, one judge dissenting, 74 F.Supp. 735, and renewed here, is that Michigan cannot forbid females generally from being barmaids and at the same time make an exception in favor of the wives and daughters of the owners of liquor establishments. Beguiling as the subject is, it need not detain us long. To ask whether or not the Equal Protection of the Laws Clause of the Fourteenth Amendment barred Michigan from making the classification the State has made between wives and daughters of owners of liquor places and wives and daughters of non-owners, is one of those rare instances where to state the question is in effect to answer it.

We are, to be sure, dealing with a historic calling. We meet the alewife, sprightly and ribald, in Shakespeare, but centuries before him she played a role in the social life of

England. See, e.g., Jusserand, English Wayfaring Life, 133, 134, 136-37 (1889). The Fourteenth Amendment did not tear history up by the roots, and the regulation of the liquor traffic is one of the oldest and most untrammeled of legislative powers. Michigan could, beyond question, forbid all women from working behind a bar. This is so despite the vast changes in the social and legal position of women. The fact that women may now have achieved the virtues that men have long claimed as their prerogatives and now indulge in vices that men have long practiced, does not preclude the States from drawing a sharp line between the sexes, certainly, in such matters as the regulation of the liquor traffic. See the Twenty-First Amendment and Carter v. Virginia, 321 U.S. 131, 64 S.Ct. 464, 88 L.Ed. 605. The Constitution does not require legislatures to reflect sociological insight, or shifting social standards, any more than it requires them to keep abreast of the latest scientific standards.

While Michigan may deny to all women opportunities for bartending, Michigan cannot play favorites among women without rhyme or reasons. The Constitution in enjoining the equal protection of the laws upon States precludes irrational discrimination as between persons or groups of persons in the incidence of a law. But the Constitution does not require situations "which are different in fact or opinion to be treated in law as though they were the same." Tigner v. State of Texas, 310 U.S. 141, 147, 60 S.Ct. 879, 882, 84 L.Ed. 1124, 130 A.L.R. 1321. Since bartending by women may, in the allowable legislative judgment, give rise to moral and social problems against which it may devise preventive measures, the legislature need not go to the full length of prohibition if it believes that as to a defined group of females other factors are operating which either eliminate or reduce the moral and social problems otherwise calling for prohibition. Michigan evidently believes that the oversight assured through ownership of a bar by a barmaid's husband or father minimizes hazards that may confront a barmaid without such protecting oversight. This Court is certainly not in a position to gainsay such belief by the Michigan legislature. If it is entertainable, as we think it is, Michigan has not violated its duty to afford equal protection of its laws. We cannot cross-examine either actually or argumentatively the mind of Michigan legislators nor question their motives. Since the line they have drawn is not without a basis in reason, we cannot give ear to the suggestion that the real impulse behind this legislation was an unchivalrous desire of male bartenders to try to monopolize the calling.

It would be an idle parade of familiar learning to review the multitudinous cases in which the constitutional assurance of the equal protection of the laws has been applied. The generalties on this subject are not in dispute; their application turns peculiarly on the particular circumstances of a case. Thus, it would be a sterile inquiry to consider whether this case is nearer to the nepotic pilotage law of Louisiana, sustained in Kotch v. River Port Pilot Commissioners, 330 U.S 552, 67 S.Ct. 910, 91 L.Ed. 1093, than it is to the Oklahoma sterilization law, which fell in Skinner v. State of Oklahoma ex rel. Williamson, 316 U.S. 535, 62 S.Ct. 1110, 86 L.Ed. 1655. Suffice it to say that "A statute is not invalid under the Constitution because it might have gone farther than it did, or because it may not succeed in bringing about the result that it tends to produce." Roschen v. Ward, 279 U.S. 337, 339, 49 S.Ct. 336, 73 L.Ed. 722.

Nor is it unconstitutional for Michigan to withdraw from women the occupation of bartending because it allows women to serve as waitresses where liquor is dispensed. The District Court has sufficiently indicated the reasons that may have influenced the legislature in allowing women to be waitresses in a liquor establishment over which a man's ownership provides control. Nothing need be added to what was said below as to the other grounds on which the Michigan law was assailed. Judgment affirmed.

Mr. Justice RUTLEDGE, with whom Mr. Justice DOUGLAS and Mr. Justice MURPHY join, dissenting.

While the equal protection clause does not require a legislature to achieve "abstract symmetry" or to classify with "mathematical nicety," that clause does require lawmakers to refrain from invidious distinctions of the sort drawn by the statute challenged in this case.

The statute arbitrarily discriminates between male and female owners of liquor establishments. A male owner, although he himself is always absent from his bar, may employ his wife and daughter as barmaids. A female owner may neither work as a barmaid herself nor employ her daughter in that position, even if a man is always present in the establishment to keep order. This inevitable result of the classification belies the assumption that the statute was motivated by a legislative solicitude for the moral and physical well-being of women who, but for the law, would be employed as barmaids. Since there could be no other conceivable justification for such discrimination against women owners of liquor establishments, the statute should be held invalid as a denial of equal protection.

CRAIG v. BOREN
429 U.S. 190 (1976)

Mr. Justice BRENNAN delivered the opinion of the Court.

The interaction of two sections of an Oklahoma statute, Okla.Stat., Tit. 37, §§ 241 and 245 (1958 and Supp.1976), prohibits the sale of "nonintoxicating" 3.2% beer to males under the age of 21 and to females under the age of 18. The question to be decided is whether such a gender-based differential constitutes a denial to males 18-20 years of age of the equal protection of the laws in violation of the Fourteenth Amendment.

[To] withstand constitutional challenge, previous cases establish that classifications by gender must serve important governmental objectives and must be substantially related to achievement of those objectives. Thus, in Reed, the objectives of "reducing the workload on probate courts," id., at 76, 92 S.Ct., at 254, and "avoiding intrafamily controversy," were deemed of insufficient importance to sustain use of an overt gender criterion in the appointment of administrators of intestate decedents' estates. Decisions following Reed similarly have rejected administrative ease and convenience as sufficiently important objectives to justify gender-based classifications. See, e. g., Stanley v. Illinois, 405 U.S. 645, 656, 92 S.Ct. 1208, 1215, 31 L.Ed.2d 551 (1972); Frontiero v. Richardson, 411 U.S. 677, 690, 93 S.Ct. 1764, 1772, 36 L.Ed.2d 583 (1973); cf. Schlesinger v. Ballard, 419 U.S. 498, 506-507, 95 S.Ct. 572, 576-577, 42 L.Ed.2d 610 (1975). And only two Terms ago, Stanton v. Stanton, 421 U.S. 7, 95 S.Ct. 1373, 43 L.Ed.2d 688 (1975), expressly stating that Reed v. Reed was "controlling," 421 U.S., at 13, 95 S.Ct., at 1377, held that Reed required invalidation of a Utah differential age-of-majority statute, notwithstanding the statute's coincidence with and furtherance of the State's purpose of fostering "old notions" of role typing and preparing boys for their expected performance in the economic and political worlds. 421 U.S., at 14-15, 95 S.Ct., at 1378.

Reed v. Reed has also provided the underpinning for decisions that have invalidated statutes employing gender as an inaccurate proxy for other, more germane bases of classification. Hence, "archaic and overbroad" generalizations, Schlesinger v. Ballard, supra, 419 U.S., at 508, 95 S.Ct., at 577, concerning the financial position of servicewomen, Frontiero v. Richardson, supra, 411 U.S., at 689 n. 23, 93 S.Ct., at 1772, and working women, Weinberger v. Wiesenfeld, 420 U.S. 636, 643, 95 S.Ct. 1225, 1230, 43 L.Ed.2d 514 (1975), could not justify use of a gender line in determining eligibility for certain governmental entitlements. Similarly, increasingly outdated misconceptions concerning the role of females in the home rather than in the "marketplace and world of ideas" were rejected as loose-fitting characterizations incapable of supporting state statutory schemes that were premised upon their accuracy. In light of the weak congruence between gender and the characteristic or trait that gender purported to represent, it was necessary that the legislatures choose either to realign their substantive laws in a gender-neutral fashion, or to adopt procedures for identifying those instances where the sex-centered generalization actually comported with fact.

In this case, too, "Reed, we feel is controlling . . . ," Stanton v. Stanton, supra, 421 U.S., at 13, 95 S.Ct., at 1377. We turn then to the question whether, under Reed, the difference between males and females with respect to the purchase of 3.2% beer warrants the differential in age drawn by the Oklahoma statute. We conclude that it does not.

We accept for purposes of discussion the District Court's identification of the objective underlying §§ 241 and 245 as the enhancement of traffic safety. However, appellees' statistics in our view cannot support the conclusion that the gender-based distinction closely serves to achieve that objective and therefore the distinction cannot under Reed withstand equal protection challenge. [Even] were this statistical evidence accepted as accurate, it nevertheless offers only a weak answer to the equal protection question presented here. The most focused and relevant of the statistical surveys, arrests of 18-20-year-olds for alcohol-related driving offenses, exemplifies the ultimate unpersuasiveness of this evidentiary record. Viewed in terms of the correlation between sex and the actual activity that Oklahoma seeks to regulate driving while under the influence of alcohol the statistics broadly establish that .18% of females and 2% of males in that age group were arrested for that offense. While such a disparity is not trivial in a statistical sense, it hardly can form the basis for employment of a gender line as a classifying device. Certainly if maleness is to serve as a proxy for drinking and driving, a correlation of 2% must be considered an unduly tenuous "fit." Indeed, prior cases have consistently rejected the use of sex as a decisionmaking factor even though the statutes in question certainly rested on far more predictive empirical relationships than this.

Moreover, the statistics exhibit a variety of other shortcomings that seriously impugn their value to equal protection analysis. Setting aside the obvious methodological problems, the surveys do not adequately justify the salient features of Oklahoma's gender-based traffic-safety law. None purports to measure the use and dangerousness of 3.2% beer as opposed to alcohol generally, a detail that is of particular importance since, in light of its low alcohol level, Oklahoma apparently considers the 3.2% beverage to be "nonintoxicating." [There] is no reason to belabor this line of analysis. It is unrealistic to expect either members of the judiciary or state officials to be well versed in the rigors of experimental or statistical technique. But this merely illustrates that proving broad sociological propositions by statistics is a dubious business, and one that inevitably is in tension with the normative philosophy that underlies the Equal Protection Clause. Suffice to say that the showing offered by the appellees does not satisfy us that sex represents a legitimate, accurate proxy for the regulation of drinking and driving. In fact, when it is further recognized that Oklahoma's statute prohibits only the selling of 3.2% beer to young males and not their drinking the beverage once acquired (even after purchase by their 18-20-year-old female companions), the relationship between gender and traffic safety becomes far too tenuous to satisfy Reed's requirement that the gender-based difference be substantially related to achievement of the statutory objective.

[In sum], the principles embodied in the Equal Protection Clause are not to be rendered inapplicable by statistically measured but loose-fitting generalities concerning the drinking tendencies of aggregate groups. We thus hold that the operation of the Twenty-first Amendment does not alter the application of equal protection standards that otherwise govern this case. We conclude that the gender-based differential contained in Okla.Stat., Tit. 37, § 245 (1976 Supp.) constitutes a denial of the equal protection of the laws to males aged 18-20 and reverse the judgment of the District Court. It is so ordered.

Mr. Justice POWELL, concurring.

I join the opinion of the Court as I am in general agreement with it. I do have reservations as to some of the discussion concerning the appropriate standard for equal protection analysis and the relevance of the statistical evidence. Accordingly, I add this concurring statement.

With respect to the equal protection standard, I agree that Reed v. Reed, 404 U.S. 71, 92 S.Ct. 251, 30 L.Ed.2d 225 (1971), is the most relevant precedent. But I find it unnecessary, in deciding this case, to read that decision as broadly as some of the Court's language may imply. Reed and subsequent cases involving gender-based classifications make clear that the Court subjects such classifications to a more critical examination than is normally applied when "fundamental" constitutional rights and "suspect classes" are not present.

I view this as a relatively easy case. The decision of the case turns on whether the state legislature, by the classification it has chosen, had adopted a means that bears a "'fair and substantial relation'" to this objective.

It seems to me that the statistics offered by appellees and relied upon by the District Court do tend generally to support the view that young men drive more, possibly are inclined to drink more, and for various reasons are involved in more accidents than young women. Even so, I am not persuaded that these facts and the inferences fairly drawn from them justify this classification based on a three-year age differential between the sexes, and especially one that it so easily circumvented as to be virtually meaningless. Putting it differently, this gender-based classification does not bear a fair and substantial relation to the object of the legislation.

Mr. Justice STEVENS, concurring.

There is only one Equal Protection Clause. I am inclined to believe that what has become known as the two-tiered analysis of equal protection claims does not describe a completely logical method of deciding cases, but rather is a method the Court has employed to explain decisions that actually apply a single standard in a reasonably consistent fashion. I also suspect that a careful explanation of the reasons motivating particular decisions may contribute more to an identification of that standard than an attempt to articulate it in all-encompassing terms. It may therefore be appropriate for me to state the principal reasons which persuaded me to join the Court's opinion.

In this case, the classification is not as obnoxious as some the Court has condemned, nor as inoffensive as some the Court has accepted. It is objectionable because it is based on an accident of birth, because it is a mere remnant of the now almost universally rejected tradition of discriminating against males in this age bracket, and because, to the extent it reflects any physical difference between males and females, it is actually perverse. The question then is whether the traffic safety justification put forward by the State is sufficient to make an otherwise offensive classification acceptable.

The classification is not totally irrational. For the evidence does indicate that there are more males than females in this age bracket who drive and also more who drink. Nevertheless, there are several reasons why I regard the justification as unacceptable. It is difficult to believe that the statute was actually intended to cope with the problem of traffic safety, since it has only a minimal effect on access to a not very intoxicating beverage and does not prohibit its consumption. Moreover, the empirical data submitted by the State accentuate the unfairness of treating all 18-21-year-old males as inferior to their female counterparts. The legislation imposes a restraint on 100% of the males in the class allegedly because about 2% of them have probably violated one or more laws relating to the consumption of alcoholic beverages. It is unlikely that this law will have a significant deterrent effect either on that 2% or on the law-abiding 98%. But even assuming some such slight benefit, it does not seem to me that an insult to all of the young men of the State can be justified by visiting the sins of the 2% on the 98%.

Mr. Justice REHNQUIST, dissenting.

The Court's disposition of this case is objectionable on two grounds. First is its conclusion that men challenging a gender-based statute which treats them less favorably than women may invoke a more stringent standard of judicial review than pertains to most other types of classifications. Second is the Court's enunciation of this standard, without citation to any source, as being that "classifications by gender must serve important governmental objectives and must be substantially related to achievement of those objectives." Ante at 457 (emphasis added). The only redeeming feature of the Court's opinion, to my mind, is that it apparently signals a retreat by those who joined the plurality opinion in Frontiero v. Richardson, 411 U.S. 677, 93 S.Ct. 1764, 36 L.Ed.2d 583 (1973), from their view that sex is a "suspect" classification for purposes of equal protection analysis. I think the Oklahoma statute challenged here need pass only the "rational basis" equal protection analysis expounded in cases such as McGowan v. Maryland, 366 U.S. 420, 81 S.Ct. 1101, 6 L.Ed.2d 393 (1961), and Williamson v. Lee Optical Co., 348 U.S. 483, 75 S.Ct. 461, 99 L.Ed. 563 (1955), and I believe that it is constitutional under that analysis.

There is no suggestion in the Court's opinion that males in this age group are in any way peculiarly disadvantaged, subject to systematic discriminatory treatment, or otherwise in need of special solicitude from the courts. It is true that a number of our opinions contain broadly phrased dicta implying that the same test should be applied to all classifications based on sex, whether affecting females or males. E.g., Frontiero v. Richardson, supra, 411 U.S., at 688, 93 S.Ct., at 1771; Reed v. Reed, 404 U.S. 71, 76, 92 S.Ct. 251, 254, 30 L.Ed.2d 225 (1971). However, before today, no decision of this Court has applied an elevated level of scrutiny to invalidate a statutory discrimination harmful to males. [There] being no such interest here, and there being no plausible argument that this is a discrimination against females, the Court's reliance on our previous sex-discrimination cases is ill-founded.

The Court's conclusion that a law which treats males less favorably than females "must serve important governmental objectives and must be substantially related to achievement of those objectives" apparently comes out of thin air. How is this Court to divine what objectives are important? How is it to determine whether a particular law is "substantially" related to the achievement of such objective, rather than related in some other way to its achievement? Both of the phrases used are so diaphanous and elastic as to invite subjective judicial preferences or prejudices relating to particular types of legislation, masquerading as judgments whether such legislation is directed at "important" objectives or, whether the relationship to those objectives is "substantial" enough.

The applicable rational-basis test is one which "permits the States a wide scope of discretion in enacting laws which affect some groups of citizens differently than others. The constitutional safeguard is offended only if the classification rests on grounds wholly irrelevant to the achievement of the State's objective. State legislatures are presumed to have acted within their constitutional power despite the fact that, in practice, their laws result in some inequality. A statutory discrimination will not be set aside if any state of facts reasonably may be conceived to justify it." McGowan v. Maryland, supra, 366 U.S., at 425-426, 81 S.Ct., at 1105 (citations omitted).

I believe that a more traditional type of scrutiny is appropriate in this case, and I think that the Court would have done well here to heed its own warning that "(i)t is unrealistic to expect . . . members of the judiciary . . . to be well versed in the rigors of experimental or statistical technique." [The] Court's criticism of the statistics relied on by the District Court conveys the impression that a legislature in enacting a new law is to be subjected to the judicial equivalent of a doctoral examination in statistics. Legislatures are not held to any rules of evidence such as those which may govern courts or other administrative bodies, and are entitled to draw factual conclusions on the basis of the determination of probable cause which an arrest by a police officer normally represents. In this situation, they could reasonably infer that the incidence of drunk driving is a good deal higher than the incidence of arrest. And while, as the Court observes, relying on a report to a Presidential Commission which it cites in a footnote, such statistics may be distorted as a result of stereotyping, the legislature is not required to prove before a court that its statistics are perfect. In any event, if stereotypes are as pervasive as the Court suggests, they may in turn influence the conduct of the men and women in question, and cause the young men to conform to the wild and reckless image which is their stereotype. [O]ur only appropriate course is to defer to the reasonable inference supporting the statute that taken in sufficient quantity this beer has the same effect as any alcoholic beverage. Notwithstanding the Court's critique of the statistical evidence, that evidence suggests clear differences between the drinking and driving habits of young men and women. Those differences are grounds enough for the State reasonably to conclude that young males pose by far the greater drunk-driving hazard, both in terms of sheer numbers and in terms of hazard on a per-driver basis. The gender-based difference in treatment in this case is therefore not irrational.

MISSISSIPPI UNIVERSITY FOR WOMEN v. HOGAN
458 U.S. 718 (1982)

Justice O'CONNOR delivered the opinion of the Court.

This case presents the narrow issue of whether a state statute that excludes males from enrolling in a state-supported professional nursing school violates the Equal Protection Clause of the Fourteenth Amendment.

I. The facts are not in dispute. In 1884, the Mississippi Legislature created the Mississippi Industrial Institute and College for the Education of White Girls of the State of Mississippi, now the oldest state-supported all-female college in the United States. The school, known today as Mississippi University for Women (MUW), has from its inception limited its enrollment to women. In 1971, MUW established a School of Nursing, initially offering a 2-year associate degree. Three years later, the school instituted a 4-year baccalaureate program in nursing and today also offers a graduate program. The School of Nursing has its own faculty and administrative officers and establishes its own criteria for admission.

Respondent, Joe Hogan, is a registered nurse but does not hold a baccalaureate degree in nursing. In 1979, Hogan applied for admission to the MUW School of Nursing's baccalaureate program. Although he was otherwise qualified, he was denied admission to the School of Nursing solely because of his sex. Hogan filed an action in the United States District Court for the Northern District of Mississippi, claiming the single-sex admissions policy of MUW's School of Nursing violated the Equal Protection Clause of the Fourteenth Amendment.

Following a hearing, the District Court denied preliminary injunctive relief. The court concluded that maintenance of MUW as a single-sex school bears a rational relationship to the State's legitimate interest "in providing the greatest practical range of educational opportunities for its female student population." The District Court entered summary judgment in favor of the State.

The Court of Appeals for the Fifth Circuit reversed, holding that, because the admissions policy discriminates on the basis of gender, the District Court improperly used a "rational relationship" test to judge the constitutionality of the policy. Instead, the Court of Appeals stated, the proper test is whether the State has carried the heavier burden of showing that the gender-based classification is substantially related to an important governmental objective. Recognizing that the State has a significant interest in providing educational opportunities for all its citizens, the court then found that the State had failed to show that providing a unique educational opportunity for females, but not for males, bears a substantial relationship to that interest. Holding that the policy excluding Hogan because of his sex denies him equal protection of the laws, the court vacated the summary judgment and remanded for entry of a declaratory judgment in conformity with its opinion and for further appropriate proceedings. We granted certiorari, and now affirm the judgment of the Court of Appeals.

II. We begin our analysis aided by several firmly established principles. That this statutory policy discriminates against males rather than against females does not exempt it from scrutiny or reduce the standard of review. Our decisions also establish that the party seeking to uphold a statute that classifies individuals on the basis of their gender must carry the burden of showing an "exceedingly persuasive justification" for the classification. The burden is met only by showing at least that the classification serves "important governmental objectives and that the discriminatory means employed" are "substantially related to the achievement of those objectives."

Although the test for determining the validity of a gender-based classification is straightforward, it must be applied free of fixed notions concerning the roles and abilities of males and females. Care must be taken in ascertaining whether the statutory objective itself reflects archaic and stereotypic notions. Thus, if the statutory objective is to exclude or "protect" members of one gender because they are presumed to suffer from an inherent handicap or to be innately inferior, the objective itself is illegitimate. If the State's objective is legitimate and important, we next determine whether the requisite direct, substantial relationship between objective and means is present. The purpose of requiring that close relationship is to assure that the validity of a classification is determined through reasoned analysis rather than through the mechanical application of traditional, often inaccurate, assumptions about the proper roles of men and women. The need for the requirement is amply revealed by reference to the broad range of statutes already invalidated by this Court, statutes that relied upon the simplistic, outdated assumption that gender could be used as a "proxy for other, more germane bases of classification."

III.A. The State's primary justification for maintaining the single-sex admissions policy of MUW's School of Nursing is that it compensates for discrimination against women and, therefore, constitutes educational affirmative action. In limited circumstances, a gender-based classification favoring one sex can be justified if it intentionally and directly assists members of the sex that is disproportionately burdened. However, we consistently have emphasized that "the mere recitation of a benign, compensatory purpose is not an automatic shield which protects against any inquiry into the actual purposes underlying a statutory scheme." The same searching analysis must be made, regardless of whether the State's objective is to eliminate family controversy, to achieve administrative efficiency, or to balance the burdens borne by males and females.

It is readily apparent that a State can evoke a compensatory purpose to justify an otherwise discriminatory classification only if members of the gender benefited by the classification actually suffer a disadvantage related to the classification. We considered such a situation in Califano v. Webster, 430 U.S. 313, 97 S.Ct. 1192, 51 L.Ed.2d 360 (1977), which involved a challenge to a statutory classification that allowed women to eliminate more low-earning years than men for purposes of computing Social Security retirement benefits. Although the effect of the classification was to allow women higher monthly benefits than were available to men with the same earning history, we upheld the statutory scheme, noting that it took into account that women "as such have been unfairly hindered from earning as much as men" and "work[ed] directly to remedy" the resulting economic disparity. Id., at 318, 97 S.Ct., at 1195.

A similar pattern of discrimination against women influenced our decision in *Schlesinger v. Ballard, supra*. There, we considered a federal statute that granted female Naval officers a 13-year tenure of commissioned service before mandatory discharge, but accorded male officers only a 9-year tenure. We recognized that, because women were barred from combat duty, they had had fewer opportunities for promotion than had their male counterparts. By allowing women an additional four years to reach a particular rank before subjecting them to mandatory discharge, the statute directly compensated for other statutory barriers to advancement.

In sharp contrast, Mississippi has made no showing that women lacked opportunities to obtain training in the field of nursing or to attain positions of leadership in that field when the MUW School of Nursing opened its door or that women currently are deprived of such opportunities. In fact, in 1970, the year before the School of Nursing's first class enrolled, women earned 94 percent of the nursing baccalaureate degrees conferred in Mississippi and 98.6 percent of the degrees earned nationwide. That year was not an aberration; one decade earlier, women had earned all the nursing degrees conferred in Mississippi and 98.9 percent of the degrees conferred nationwide. As one would expect, the labor force reflects the same predominance of women in nursing. When MUW's School of Nursing began operation, nearly 98 percent of all employed registered nurses were female.

Rather than compensate for discriminatory barriers faced by women, MUW's policy of excluding males from admission to the School of Nursing tends to perpetuate the stereotyped view of nursing as an exclusively woman's job. By assuring that Mississippi allots more openings in its state-supported nursing schools to women than it does to men, MUW's admissions policy lends credibility to the old view that women, not men, should become nurses, and makes the assumption that nursing is a field for women a self-fulfilling prophecy. Thus, we conclude that, although the State recited a "benign, compensatory purpose," it failed to establish that the alleged objective is the actual purpose underlying the discriminatory classification.

The policy is invalid also because it fails the second part of the equal protection test, for the State has made no showing that the gender-based classification is substantially and directly related to its proposed compensatory objective. To the contrary, MUW's policy of permitting men to attend classes as auditors fatally undermines its claim that women, at least those in the School of Nursing, are adversely affected by the presence of men.

The uncontroverted record reveals that admitting men to nursing classes does not affect teaching style. In sum, the record in this case is flatly inconsistent with the claim that excluding men from the School of Nursing is necessary to reach any of MUW's educational goals.

Thus, considering both the asserted interest and the relationship between the interest and the methods used by the State, we conclude that the State has fallen far short of establishing the "exceedingly persuasive justification" needed to sustain the gender-based classification. Accordingly, we hold that MUW's policy of denying males the right to enroll for credit in its School of Nursing violates the Equal Protection Clause of the Fourteenth Amendment.

Justice POWELL, with whom Justice REHNQUIST joins, dissenting.

The Court in effect holds today that no State now may provide even a single institution of higher learning open only to women students. At best this is anomalous. And ultimately the anomaly reveals legal error — that of applying a heightened equal protection standard, developed in cases of genuine sexual stereotyping, to a narrowly utilized state classification that provides an *additional* choice for women. Moreover, I believe that Mississippi's educational system should be upheld in this case even if this inappropriate method of analysis is applied.

In my view, the Court errs seriously by assuming — without argument or discussion — that the equal protection standard generally applicable to sex discrimination is appropriate here. That standard was designed to free women from "archaic and overbroad generalizations. . . ." In no previous case have we applied it to invalidate state efforts to *expand* women's choices. Nor are there prior sex discrimination decisions by this Court in which a male plaintiff, as in this case, had the choice of an equal benefit.

The cases cited by the Court therefore do not control the issue now before us. In most of them women were given no opportunity for the same benefit as men. Cases involving male plaintiffs are equally inapplicable. In Craig v. Boren, 429 U.S. 190, 97 S.Ct. 451, 50 L.Ed.2d 397 (1976), a male under 21 was not permitted to buy beer anywhere in the State, and women were afforded no choice as to whether they would accept the "statistically measured but loose-fitting generalities concerning the drinking tendencies of aggregate groups." A similar situation prevailed in Orr v. Orr, 440 U.S. 268, 279, 99 S.Ct. 1102, 1111, 59 L.Ed.2d 306 (1979), where men had no opportunity to seek alimony from their divorced wives, and women had no escape from the statute's stereotypical announcement of "the State's preference for an allocation of family responsibilities under which the wife plays a dependent role. . . ."

By applying heightened equal protection analysis to this case, the Court frustrates the liberating spirit of the Equal Protection Clause.

III. The Court views this case as presenting a serious equal protection claim of sex discrimination. I do not, and I would sustain Mississippi's right to continue MUW on a rational-basis analysis. But I need not apply this "lowest tier" of scrutiny. I can accept for present purposes the standard applied by the Court: that there is a gender-based distinction that must serve an important governmental objective by means that are substantially related to its achievement. And the State's purpose in preserving that choice is legitimate and substantial. Generations of our finest minds, both among educators and students, have believed that single-sex, college-level institutions afford distinctive benefits. But simply because there are these differences is no reason — certainly none of constitutional dimension — to conclude that no substantial state interest is served when such a choice is made available.

In sum, the practice of voluntarily chosen single-sex education is an honored tradition in our country, even if it now rarely exists in state colleges and universities. Mississippi's accommodation of such student choices is legitimate because it is completely consensual and is important because it permits students to decide for themselves the type of college education they think will benefit them most. Finally, Mississippi's policy is substantially related to its long-respected objective.

J.E.B. v. ALABAMA ex rel T.B.
511 U.S. 127 (1994)

The case concerned the constitutionality of the state's use of gender-based peremptory challenges in a trial to determine whether the defendant was the father of a child and the extent of his child support obligations. After the court excused three jurors for cause, only ten of the remaining thirty-three jurors were male. The state then used nine of its ten peremptory strikes to remove male jurors. The defendant used all but one of his strikes to remove female jurors. As a result, all the selected jurors were female. The Court held that gender-based peremptory challenges were unconstitutional:

Justice BLACKMUN delivered the opinion of the Court.

Under our equal protection jurisprudence, gender-based classifications require "an exceedingly persuasive justification" in order to survive constitutional scrutiny. Far from proffering an exceptionally persuasive justification for its gender-based peremptory challenges, respondent maintains that its decision to strike virtually all the males from the jury in this case "may reasonably have been based upon the perception, supported by history, that men otherwise totally qualified to serve upon a jury might be more sympathetic and receptive to the arguments of a man alleged in a paternity action to be the father of an out-of-wedlock child, while women equally qualified to serve upon a jury might be more sympathetic and receptive to the arguments of the complaining witness who bore the child."

We shall not accept as a defense to gender-based peremptory challenges "the very stereotype the law condemns." [Respondent] offers virtually no support for the conclusion that gender alone is an accurate predictor of juror's attitudes; yet it urges this Court to condone the same stereotypes that justified the wholesale exclusion of women from juries and the ballot box. Respondent seems to assume that gross generalizations that would be deemed impermissible if made on the basis of race are somehow permissible when made on the basis of gender.

Justice O'CONNOR concurring.

We know that like race, gender matters. A plethora of studies make clear that in rape cases, for example, female jurors are somewhat more likely to vote to convict than male jurors. Moreover, though there have been no similarly definitive studies regarding, for example, sexual harassment, child custody, or spousal or child abuse, one need not be a sexist to share the intuition that in certain cases a person's gender and resulting life experience will be relevant to his or her view of the case.

Today's decision severely limits a litigant's ability to act on this intuition. [But] to say that gender makes no difference as a matter of law is not to say that gender makes no difference as a matter of fact. [Today's] decision is a statement that, in an effort to eliminate the potential discriminatory use of the peremptory, gender is now governed by the special rule of relevance formerly reserved for race. Though we gain much from this statement, we cannot ignore what we lose.

Comments on *Hogan* and *J.E.B.* Does the "exceedingly persuasive justification" requirement change traditional middle scrutiny review? Is the Court applying a more stringent standard in regard to gender-based discrimination? If so, is this another application of Justice Marshall's approach to equal protection in his *Rodriquez* dissent? What will be the impact of this approach?

UNITED STATES v. VIRGINIA
518 U.S. 515 (1996)

Justice GINSBURG delivered the opinion of the Court.

I. Founded in 1839, VMI is today the sole single-sex school among Virginia's 15 public institutions of higher learning. VMI's distinctive mission is to produce "citizen-soldiers," men prepared for leadership in civilian life and in military service. VMI pursues this mission through pervasive training of a kind not available anywhere else in Virginia. Assigning prime place to character development, VMI uses an "adversative method" modeled on English public schools and once characteristic of military instruction. VMI constantly endeavors to instill physical and mental discipline in its cadets and impart to them a strong moral code. The school's graduates leave VMI with heightened comprehension of their capacity to deal with duress and stress, and a large sense of accomplishment for completing the hazardous course.

VMI has notably succeeded in its mission to produce leaders; among its alumni are military generals, Members of Congress, and business executives. The school's alumni overwhelmingly perceive that their VMI training helped them to realize their personal goals.

Neither the goal of producing citizen-soldiers nor VMI's implementing methodology is inherently unsuitable to women. And the school's impressive record in producing leaders has made admission desirable to some women. Nevertheless, Virginia has elected to preserve exclusively for men the advantages and opportunities a VMI education affords.

II. A. From its establishment in 1839 as one of the Nation's first state military colleges, VMI has remained financially supported by Virginia and "subject to the control of the [Virginia] General Assembly," VMI today enrolls about 1,300 men as cadets. Its academic offerings in the liberal arts, sciences, and engineering are also available at other public colleges and universities in Virginia. But VMI's mission is special. It is the mission of the school "'to produce educated and honorable men, prepared for the varied work of civil life, imbued with love of learning, confident in the functions and attitudes of leadership, possessing a high sense of public service, advocates of the American democracy and free enterprise system, and ready as citizen-soldiers to defend their country in time of national peril.'" VMI's program "is directed at preparation for both military and civilian life"; "[o]nly about 15% of VMI cadets enter career military service."

VMI produces its "citizen-soldiers" through "an adversative, or doubting, model of education" which features "[p]hysical rigor, mental stress, absolute equality of treatment, absence of privacy, minute regulation of behavior, and indoctrination in desirable values." VMI cadets live in spartan barracks where surveillance is constant and privacy nonexistent; they wear uniforms, eat together in the mess hall, and regularly participate in drills.

VMI's "adversative model" is further characterized by a hierarchical "class system" of privileges and responsibilities, a "dyke system" for assigning a senior class mentor to each entering class "rat," and a stringently enforced "honor code," which prescribes that a cadet "'does not lie, cheat, steal nor tolerate those who do.'" "[W]omen have no opportunity anywhere to gain the benefits of [the system of education at VMI]."

B. In 1990, prompted by a complaint filed with the Attorney General by a female high-school student seeking admission to VMI, the United States sued the Commonwealth of Virginia and VMI, alleging that VMI's exclusively male admission policy violated the Equal Protection Clause of the Fourteenth Amendment.

In the two years preceding the lawsuit, the District Court noted, VMI had received inquiries from 347 women, but had responded to none of them. "[S]ome women, at least," the court said, "would want to attend the school if they had the opportunity." The court further recognized that, with recruitment, VMI could "achieve at least 10% female enrollment" — "a sufficient 'critical mass' to provide the female cadets with a positive educational experience." And it was also established that "some women are capable of all of the individual activities required of VMI cadets." In addition, experts agreed that if VMI admitted women, "the VMI ROTC experience would become a better training program from the perspective of the armed forces, because it would provide training in dealing with a mixed-gender army."

C. Virginia proposed a parallel program for women: Virginia Women's Institute for Leadership (VWIL). The 4-year, state-sponsored undergraduate program would be located at Mary Baldwin College, a private liberal arts school for women, and would be open, initially, to about 25 to 30 students. Although VWIL would share VMI's mission — to produce "citizen-soldiers" — the VWIL program would differ, as does Mary Baldwin College, from VMI in academic offerings, methods of education, and financial resources.

The average combined SAT score of entrants at Mary Baldwin is about 100 points lower than the score for VMI freshmen. Mary Baldwin's faculty holds "significantly fewer Ph.D.'s than the faculty at VMI," and receives significantly lower salaries. While VMI offers degrees in liberal arts, the sciences, and engineering, Mary Baldwin, at the time of trial, offered only bachelor of arts degrees. A VWIL student seeking to earn an engineering degree could gain one, without public support, by attending Washington University in St. Louis, Missouri, for two years, paying the required private tuition.

Experts in educating women at the college level composed the Task Force charged with designing the VWIL program; Task Force members were drawn from Mary Baldwin's own faculty and staff. Training its attention on methods of instruction appropriate for "most women," the Task Force determined that a military model would be "wholly inappropriate" for VWIL. VWIL students would participate in ROTC programs and a newly established, "largely ceremonial" Virginia Corps of Cadets, but the VWIL House would not have a military format, and VWIL would not require its students to eat meals together or to wear uniforms during the school day. In lieu of VMI's adversative method, the VWIL Task Force favored "a cooperative method which reinforces self-esteem." In addition to the standard Bachelor of Arts program offered at Mary Baldwin, VWIL students would take courses in leadership, complete an off-campus leadership externship, participate in community service projects, and assist in arranging a speaker series.

Virginia represented that it will provide equal financial support for in-state VWIL students and VMI cadets, and the VMI Foundation agreed to supply a $5.4625 million endowment for the VWIL program. Mary Baldwin's own endowment is about $19 million; VMI's is $131 million. Mary Baldwin will add $35 million to its endowment based on future commitments; VMI will add $220 million.

D. [The] District Court Court [and the Court of Appeals] decided the plan met the requirements of the Equal Protection Clause. . . .

III. The cross-petitions in this suit present two ultimate issues. First, does Virginia's exclusion of women from the educational opportunities provided by VMI — extraordinary opportunities for military training and civilian leadership development — deny to women "capable of all of the individual activities required of VMI cadets," the equal protection of the laws guaranteed by the Fourteenth Amendment? Second, if VMI's "unique" situation, — as Virginia's sole single-sex public institution of higher education — offends the Constitution's equal protection principle, what is the remedial requirement? . . .

IV. We note, once again, the core instruction of this Court's pathmaking decisions in J.E.B. v. Alabama ex rel. T. B., 511 U.S. 127, 136-137, and n. 6, 114 S.Ct. 1419, 1425-1426, and n. 6, 128 L.Ed.2d 89 (1994), and Mississippi Univ. for Women, 458 U.S., at 724, 102 S.Ct., at 3336 (internal quotation marks omitted): Parties who seek to defend gender-based government action must demonstrate an "exceedingly persuasive justification" for that action.

Today's skeptical scrutiny of official action denying rights or opportunities based on sex responds to volumes of history. As a plurality of this Court acknowledged a generation ago, "our Nation has had a long and unfortunate history of sex discrimination." Frontiero v. Richardson, 411 U.S. 677, 684, 93 S.Ct. 1764, 1769, 36 L.Ed.2d 583 (1973). Through a century plus three decades and more of that history, women did not count among voters composing "We the People"; not until 1920 did women gain a constitutional right to the franchise. And for a half century thereafter, it remained the prevailing doctrine that government, both federal and state, could withhold from women opportunities accorded men so long as any "basis in reason" could be conceived for the discrimination.

Since *Reed,* the Court has repeatedly recognized that neither federal nor state government acts compatibly with the equal protection principle when a law or official policy denies to women, simply because they are women, full citizenship stature — equal opportunity to aspire, achieve, participate in and contribute to society based on their individual talents and capacities. Without equating gender classifications, for all purposes, to classifications based on race or national origin, the Court, in post-*Reed* decisions, has carefully inspected official action that closes a door or denies opportunity to women (or to men). To summarize the Court's current directions for cases of official classification based on gender: Focusing on the differential treatment or denial of opportunity for which relief is sought, the reviewing court must determine whether the proffered justification is "exceedingly persuasive." The burden of justification is demanding and it rests entirely on the State. The State must show "at least that the [challenged] classification serves 'important governmental objectives and that the discriminatory means employed' are 'substantially related to the achievement of those objectives.'" The justification must be genuine, not hypothesized or invented *post hoc* in response to litigation. And it must not rely on overbroad generalizations about the different talents, capacities, or preferences of males and females.

The heightened review standard our precedent establishes does not make sex a proscribed classification. Supposed "inherent differences" are no longer accepted as a ground for race or national origin classifications. Physical differences between men and women, however, are enduring: "[T]he two sexes are not fungible; a community made up exclusively of one [sex] is different from a community composed of both."

"Inherent differences" between men and women, we have come to appreciate, remain cause for celebration, but not for denigration of the members of either sex or for artificial constraints on an individual's opportunity. Sex classifications may be used to compensate women "for particular economic disabilities [they have] suffered," to "promot[e] equal employment opportunity," to advance full development of the talent and capacities of our Nation's people. But such classifications may not be used, as they once were, see *Goesaert,* to create or perpetuate the legal, social, and economic inferiority of women.

Measuring the record in this case against the review standard just described, we conclude that Virginia has shown no "exceedingly persuasive justification" for excluding all women from the citizen-soldier training afforded by VMI. We therefore affirm the Fourth Circuit's initial judgment, which held that Virginia had violated the Fourteenth Amendment's Equal Protection Clause. Because the remedy proffered by Virginia — the Mary Baldwin VWIL program — does not cure the constitutional violation, *i.e.,* it does not provide equal opportunity, we reverse the Fourth Circuit's final judgment in this case.

V. Virginia challenges that "liability" ruling and asserts two justifications in defense of VMI's exclusion of women. First, the Commonwealth contends, "single-sex education provides important educational benefits," and the option of single-sex education contributes to "diversity in educational approaches." Second, the Commonwealth argues, "the unique VMI method of character development and leadership training," the school's adversative approach, would have to be modified were VMI to admit women. We consider these two justifications in turn.

A. Single-sex education affords pedagogical benefits to at least some students, Virginia emphasizes, and that reality is uncontested in this litigation. Similarly, it is not disputed that diversity among public educational institutions can serve the public good. But Virginia has not shown that VMI was established, or has been maintained, with a view to diversifying, by its categorical exclusion of women, educational opportunities within the Commonwealth. In cases of this genre, our precedent instructs that "benign" justifications proffered in defense of categorical exclusions will not be accepted automatically; a tenable justification must describe actual state purposes, not rationalizations for actions in fact differently grounded.

Mississippi Univ. for Women is immediately in point. There the State asserted, in justification of its exclusion of men from a nursing school, that it was engaging in "educational affirmative action" by "compensat[ing] for discrimination against woman." Undertaking a "searching analysis,"the Court found no close resemblance between "the alleged objective" and "the actual purpose underlying the discriminatory classification." Pursuing a similar inquiry here, we reach the same conclusion.

Neither recent nor distant history bears out Virginia's alleged pursuit of diversity through single-sex educational options. In 1839, when the Commonwealth established VMI, a range of educational opportunities for men and women was scarcely contemplated. Higher education at the time was considered dangerous for women; reflecting widely held views about women's proper place, the Nation's first universities and colleges — for example, Harvard in Massachusetts, William and Mary in Virginia — admitted only men. VMI was not at all novel in this respect: In admitting no women, VMI followed the lead of the Commonwealth's flagship school, the University of Virginia, founded in 1819. "[N]o struggle for the admission of women to a state university," a historian has recounted, "was longer drawn out, or developed more bitterness, than that at the University of Virginia." In 1879, the State Senate resolved to look into the possibility of higher education for women, recognizing that Virginia "'has never, at any period of her history,'" provided for the higher education of her daughters, though she "'has liberally provided for the higher education of her sons.'" Despite this recognition, no new opportunities were instantly open to women.

Virginia eventually provided for several women's seminaries and colleges. Farmville Female Seminary became a public institution in 1884. Two women's schools, Mary Washington College and James Madison University, were founded in 1908; another, Radford University, was founded in 1910. By the mid-1970's, all four schools had become coeducational.

Virginia describes the current absence of public single-sex higher education for women as "an historical anomaly." But the historical record indicates action more deliberate than anomalous: First, protection of women against higher education; next, schools for women far from equal in resources and stature to schools for men; finally, conversion of the separate schools to coeducation. The state legislature, prior to the advent of this controversy, had repealed "[a]ll Virginia statutes requiring individual institutions to admit only men or women." And in 1990, an official commission, "legislatively established to chart the future goals of higher education in Virginia," reaffirmed the policy "'of affording broad access'" while maintaining "'autonomy and diversity.'" Significantly, the commission reported: "'Because colleges and universities provide opportunities for students to develop values and learn from role models, it is extremely important that they deal with faculty, staff, and students without regard to sex, race, or ethnic origin.'"

In sum, we find no persuasive evidence in this record that VMI's male-only admission policy "is in furtherance of a state policy of 'diversity.'" A purpose genuinely to advance an array of educational options, as the Court of Appeals recognized, is not served by VMI's historic and constant plan — a plan to "affor[d] a unique educational benefit only to males." However "liberally" this plan serves the Commonwealth's sons, it makes no provision whatever for her daughters. That is not *equal* protection.

B. Virginia next argues that VMI's adversative method of training provides educational benefits that cannot be made available, unmodified, to women. Alterations to accommodate women would necessarily be "radical," so "drastic," Virginia asserts, as to transform, indeed "destroy," VMI's program. See Brief for Cross-Petitioners 34-36. Neither sex would be favored by the transformation, Virginia maintains: Men would be deprived of the unique opportunity currently available to them; women would not gain that opportunity because their participation would "eliminat[e] the very aspects of [the] program that distinguish [VMI] from . . . other institutions of higher education in Virginia." *Id.*, at 34.

The District Court forecast from expert witness testimony, and the Court of Appeals accepted, that coeducation would materially affect "at least these three aspects of VMI's program — physical training, the absence of privacy, and the adversative approach." And it is uncontested that women's admission would require accommodations, primarily in arranging housing assignments and physical training programs for female cadets. It is also undisputed, however, that "the VMI methodology could be used to educate women." The District Court even allowed that some women may prefer it to the methodology a women's college might pursue. "[S]ome women, at least, would want to attend [VMI] if they had the opportunity," the District Court recognized, and "some women," the expert testimony established, "are capable of all of the individual activities required of VMI cadets." The parties, furthermore, agree that "*some* women can meet the physical standards [VMI] now impose[s] on men."

In support of its initial judgment for Virginia, a judgment rejecting all equal protection objections presented by the United States, the District Court made "findings" on "gender-based developmental differences." These "findings" restate the opinions of Virginia's expert witnesses, opinions about typically male or typically female "tendencies." For example, "[m]ales tend to need an atmosphere of adversativeness," while "[f]emales tend to thrive in a cooperative atmosphere." [The] United States emphasizes that time and again since this Court's turning point decision in Reed v. Reed, 404 U.S. 71, 92 S.Ct. 251, 30 L.Ed.2d 225 (1971), we have cautioned reviewing courts to take a "hard look" at generalizations or "tendencies" of the kind pressed by Virginia, and relied upon by the District Court. State actors controlling gates to opportunity, we have instructed, may not exclude qualified individuals based on "fixed notions concerning the roles and abilities of males and females."

It may be assumed, for purposes of this decision, that most women would not choose VMI's adversative method. As Fourth Circuit Judge Motz observed, however, in her dissent from the Court of Appeals' denial of rehearing en banc, it is also probable that "many men would not want to be educated in such an environment." (On that point, even our dissenting colleague might agree.) Education, to be sure, is not a "one size fits all" business. The issue, however, is not whether "women — or men — should be forced to attend VMI"; rather, the question is whether the Commonwealth can constitutionally deny to women who have the will and capacity, the training and attendant opportunities that VMI uniquely affords.

The notion that admission of women would downgrade VMI's stature, destroy the adversative system and, with it, even the school, is a judgment hardly proved, a prediction hardly different from other "self-fulfilling prophec[ies]," see Mississippi Univ. for Women, 458 U.S., at 730, 102 S.Ct., at 3339, once routinely used to deny rights or opportunities. When women first sought admission to the bar and access to legal education, concerns of the same order were expressed.

Medical faculties similarly resisted men and women as partners in the study of medicine. [Surely] that goal is great enough to accommodate women, who today count as citizens in our American democracy equal in stature to men. Just as surely, the Commonwealth's great goal is not substantially advanced by women's categorical exclusion, in total disregard of their individual merit, from the Commonwealth's premier "citizen-soldier" corps. Virginia, in sum, "has fallen far short of establishing the 'exceedingly persuasive justification,'" that must be the solid base for any gender-defined classification.

VI. In the second phase of the litigation, Virginia presented its remedial plan — maintain VMI as a male-only college and create VWIL as a separate program for women.

A remedial decree, this Court has said, must closely fit the constitutional violation; it must be shaped to place persons unconstitutionally denied an opportunity or advantage in "the position they would have occupied in the absence of [discrimination]." The constitutional violation in this suit is the categorical exclusion of women from an extraordinary educational opportunity afforded men. A proper remedy for an unconstitutional exclusion, we have explained, aims to "eliminate [so far as possible] the discriminatory effects of the past" and to "bar like discrimination in the future."

Virginia chose not to eliminate, but to leave untouched, VMI's exclusionary policy. For women only, however, Virginia proposed a separate program, different in kind from VMI and unequal in tangible and intangible facilities. Having violated the Constitution's equal protection requirement, Virginia was obliged to show that its remedial proposal "directly address[ed] and relate[d] to" the violation, i.e., the equal protection denied to women ready, willing, and able to benefit from educational opportunities of the kind VMI offers. Virginia described VWIL as a "parallel program," and asserted that VWIL shares VMI's mission of producing "citizen-soldiers" and VMI's goals of providing "education, military training, mental and physical discipline, character . . . and leadership development." Brief for Respondents 24 (internal quotation marks omitted). If the VWIL program could not "eliminate the discriminatory effects of the past," could it at least "bar like discrimination in the future"? A comparison of the programs said to be "parallel" informs our answer.

VWIL affords women no opportunity to experience the rigorous military training for which VMI is famed. Instead, the VWIL program "deemphasize[s]," and uses a "cooperative method" of education "which reinforces self-esteem. VWIL students participate in ROTC and a "largely ceremonial" Virginia Corps of Cadets, but Virginia deliberately did not make VWIL a military institute. VWIL students receive their "leadership training" in seminars, externships, and speaker series, see   episodes and encounters lacking the "[p]hysical rigor, mental stress, . . . minute regulation of behavior, and indoctrination in desirable values" made hallmarks of VMI's citizen-soldier training. Kept away from the pressures, hazards, and psychological bonding characteristic of VMI's adversative training, VWIL students will not know the "feeling of tremendous accomplishment" commonly experienced by VMI's successful cadets.

Virginia maintains that these methodological differences are "justified pedagogically," based on "important differences between men and women in learning and developmental needs," "psychological and sociological differences" Virginia describes as "real" and "not stereotypes." The Task Force charged with developing the leadership program for women, drawn from the staff and faculty at Mary Baldwin College, "determined that a military model and, especially VMI's adversative method, would be wholly inappropriate for educating and training *most women.*"

As earlier stated, see *supra,* at 2280, generalizations about "the way women are," estimates of what is appropriate for *most women,* no longer justify denying opportunity to women whose talent and capacity place them outside the average description. Notably, Virginia never asserted that VMI's method of education suits *most men.* It is also revealing that Virginia accounted for its failure to make the VWIL experience "the entirely militaristic experience of VMI" on the ground that VWIL "is planned for women who do not necessarily expect to pursue military careers." By that reasoning, VMI's "entirely militaristic" program would be inappropriate for men in general or *as a group,* for "[o]nly about 15% of VMI cadets enter career military service."

In contrast to the generalizations about women on which Virginia rests, we note again these dispositive realities: VMI's "implementing methodology" is not "inherently unsuitable to women;" "some women . . . do well under [the] adversative model;" "some women, at least, would want to attend [VMI] if they had the opportunity;" "some women are capable of all of the individual activities required of VMI cadets," and "can meet the physical standards [VMI] now impose[s] on men," It is on behalf of these women that the United States has instituted this suit, and it is for them that a remedy must be crafted.

B. In myriad respects other than military training, VWIL does not qualify as VMI's equal. VWIL's student body, faculty, course offerings, and facilities hardly match VMI's. Nor can the VWIL graduate anticipate the benefits associated with VMI's 157-year history, the school's prestige, and its influential alumni network.

[Virginia], in sum, while maintaining VMI for men only, has failed to provide any "comparable single-gender women's institution." Instead, the Commonwealth has created a VWIL program fairly appraised as a "pale shadow" of VMI in terms of the range of curricular choices and faculty stature, funding, prestige, alumni support and influence.

Virginia's VWIL solution is reminiscent of the remedy Texas proposed 50 years ago, in response to a state trial court's 1946 ruling that, given the equal protection guarantee, African-Americans could not be denied a legal education at a state facility. See Sweatt v. Painter, 339 U.S. 629, 70 S.Ct. 848, 94 L.Ed. 1114 (1950). Reluctant to admit African-Americans to its flagship University of Texas Law School, the State set up a separate school for Heman Sweatt and other black law students. As originally opened, the new school had no independent faculty or library, and it lacked accreditation. Nevertheless, the state trial and appellate courts were satisfied that the new school offered Sweatt opportunities for the study of law "substantially equivalent to those offered by the State to white students at the University of Texas." Before this Court considered the case, the new school had gained "a faculty of five full-time professors; a student body of 23; a library of some 16,500 volumes serviced by a full-time staff; a practice court and legal aid association; and one alumnus who ha[d] become a member of the Texas Bar." This Court contrasted resources at the new school with those at the school from which Sweatt had been excluded.

More important than the tangible features, the Court emphasized, are "those qualities which are incapable of objective measurement but which make for greatness" in a school, including "reputation of the faculty, experience of the administration, position and influence of the alumni, standing in the community, traditions and prestige." Facing the marked differences reported in the *Sweatt* opinion, the Court unanimously ruled that Texas had not shown "substantial equality in the [separate] educational opportunities" the State offered. Accordingly, the Court held, the Equal Protection Clause required Texas to admit African-Americans to the University of Texas Law School. In line with *Sweatt,* we rule here that Virginia has not shown substantial equality in the separate educational opportunities the Commonwealth supports at VWIL and VMI.

C. [The] Fourth Circuit plainly erred in exposing Virginia's VWIL plan to a deferential analysis, for "all gender-based classifications today" warrant "heightened scrutiny." Valuable as VWIL may prove for students who seek the program offered, Virginia's remedy affords no cure at all for the opportunities and advantages withheld from women who want a VMI education and can make the grade. In sum, Virginia's remedy does not match the constitutional violation; the Commonwealth has shown no "exceedingly persuasive justification" for withholding from women qualified for the experience premier training of the kind VMI affords.

For the reasons stated, the initial judgment of the Court of Appeals, is affirmed, the final judgment of the Court of Appeals, is reversed, and the case is remanded for further proceedings consistent with this opinion.

It is so ordered.

Justice Thomas took no part in the consideration or decision of these cases.

Chief Justice REHNQUIST, concurring in the judgment.

The Court holds first that Virginia violates the Equal Protection Clause by maintaining the Virginia Military Institute's (VMI's) all-male admissions policy, and second that establishing the Virginia Women's Institute for Leadership (VWIL) program does not remedy that violation. While I agree with these conclusions, I disagree with the Court's analysis and so I write separately.

I. Two decades ago in Craig v. Boren, 429 U.S. 190, 197, 97 S.Ct. 451, 456-457, 50 L.Ed.2d 397 (1976), we announced that "[t]o withstand constitutional challenge, . . . classifications by gender must serve important governmental objectives and must be substantially related to achievement of those objectives." We have adhered to that standard of scrutiny ever since. While the majority adheres to this test today, *ante,* at 2271, 2275, it also says that the Commonwealth must demonstrate an "'exceedingly persuasive justification'" to support a gender-based classification. See *ante,* at 2271, 2273, 2274, 2275,

2276, 2281, 2282, 2287. It is unfortunate that the Court thereby introduces an element of uncertainty respecting the appropriate test.

Before this Court, Virginia has sought to justify VMI's single-sex admissions policy primarily on the basis that diversity in education is desirable, and that while most of the public institutions of higher learning in the Commonwealth are coeducational, there should also be room for single-sex institutions. I agree with the Court that there is scant evidence in the record that this was the real reason that Virginia decided to maintain VMI as men only. But, unlike the majority, I would consider only evidence that postdates our decision in *Hogan,* and would draw no negative inferences from the Commonwealth's actions before that time. [Had] Virginia made a genuine effort to devote comparable public resources to a facility for women, and followed through on such a plan, it might well have avoided an equal protection violation. I do not believe the Commonwealth was faced with the stark choice of either admitting women to VMI, on the one hand, or abandoning VMI and starting from scratch for both men and women, on the other. . . .

Virginia offers a second justification for the single-sex admissions policy: maintenance of the adversative method. I agree with the Court that this justification does not serve an important governmental objective. A State does not have substantial interest in the adversative methodology unless it is pedagogically beneficial. While considerable evidence shows that a single-sex education is pedagogically beneficial for some students, and hence a State may have a valid interest in promoting that methodology, there is no similar evidence in the record that an adversative method is pedagogically beneficial or is any more likely to produce character traits than other methodologies.

II. The Court defines the constitutional violation in these cases as "the categorical exclusion of women from an extraordinary educational opportunity afforded to men." By defining the violation in this way, and by emphasizing that a remedy for a constitutional violation must place the victims of discrimination in "'the position they would have occupied in the absence of [discrimination],'" the Court necessarily implies that the only adequate remedy would be the admission of women to the all-male institution. As the foregoing discussion suggests, I would not define the violation in this way; it is not the "exclusion of women" that violates the Equal Protection Clause, but the maintenance of an all-men school without providing any — much less a comparable — institution for women.

Accordingly, the remedy should not necessarily require either the admission of women to VMI or the creation of a VMI clone for women. An adequate remedy in my opinion might be a demonstration by Virginia that its interest in educating men in a single-sex environment is matched by its interest in educating women in a single-sex institution. To demonstrate such, the Commonwealth does not need to create two institutions with the same number of faculty Ph.D.'s, similar SAT scores, or comparable athletic fields. Nor would it necessarily require that the women's institution offer the same curriculum as the men's; one could be strong in computer science, the other could be strong in liberal arts. It would be a sufficient remedy, I think, if the two institutions offered the same quality of education and were of the same overall caliber.

If a State decides to create single-sex programs, the State would, I expect, consider the public's interest and demand in designing curricula. And rightfully so. But the State should avoid assuming demand based on stereotypes; it must not assume *a priori,* without evidence, that there would be no interest in a women's school of civil engineering, or in a men's school of nursing.

In the end, the women's institution Virginia proposes, VWIL, fails as a remedy, because it is distinctly inferior to the existing men's institution and will continue to be for the foreseeable future. VWIL simply is not, in any sense, the institution that VMI is. In particular, VWIL is a program appended to a private college, not a self-standing institution; and VWIL is substantially underfunded as compared to VMI. I therefore ultimately agree with the Court that Virginia has not provided an adequate remedy.

Justice SCALIA, dissenting.

Today the Court shuts down an institution that has served the people of the Commonwealth of Virginia with pride and distinction for over a century and a half. To achieve that desired result, it rejects (contrary to our established practice) the factual findings of two courts below, sweeps aside the precedents of this Court, and ignores the history of our people. As to facts: It explicitly rejects the finding that there exist "gender-based developmental differences" supporting Virginia's restriction of the "adversative" method to only a men's institution, and the finding that the all-male composition of the Virginia Military Institute (VMI) is essential to that institution's character. As to precedent: It drastically revises our established standards for reviewing sex-based classifications. And as to history: It counts for nothing the long tradition, enduring down to the present, of men's military colleges supported by both States and the Federal Government.

The virtue of a democratic system with a First Amendment is that it readily enables the people, over time, to be persuaded that what they took for granted is not so, and to change their laws accordingly. That system is destroyed if the smug assurances of each age are removed from the democratic process and written into the Constitution. So to counterbalance the Court's criticism of our ancestors, let me say a word in their praise: They left us free to change. The same cannot be said of this most illiberal Court, which has embarked on a course of inscribing one after another of the current preferences of the society (and in some cases only the counter-majoritarian preferences of the society's law-trained elite) into our Basic Law. Today it enshrines the notion that no substantial educational value is to be served by an all-men's military academy — so that the decision by the people of Virginia to maintain such an institution denies equal protection to women who cannot attend that institution but can attend others.

[I] have no problem with a system of abstract tests such as rational basis, intermediate, and strict scrutiny (though I think we can do better than applying strict scrutiny and intermediate scrutiny whenever we feel like it). Such formulas are essential to evaluating whether the new restrictions that a changing society constantly imposes upon private conduct comport with that "equal protection" our society has always accorded in the past. But in my view the function of this Court is to *preserve* our society's values regarding (among other things) equal protection, not to *revise* them; to prevent backsliding from the degree of restriction the Constitution imposed upon democratic government, not to prescribe, on our own authority, progressively higher degrees. For that reason it is my view that, whatever abstract tests we may choose to devise, they cannot supersede — and indeed ought to be crafted *so as to reflect* — those constant and unbroken national traditions that embody the people's understanding of ambiguous constitutional texts. More specifically, it is my view that "when a practice not expressly prohibited by the text of the Bill of Rights bears the endorsement of a long tradition of open, widespread, and unchallenged use that dates back to the beginning of the Republic, we have no proper basis for striking it down." The same applies, *mutatis mutandis,* to a practice asserted to be in violation of the post-Civil War Fourteenth Amendment.

The all-male constitution of VMI comes squarely within such a governing tradition. Founded by the Commonwealth of Virginia in 1839 and continuously maintained by it since, VMI has always admitted only men. And in that regard it has not been unusual. For almost all of VMI's more than a century and a half of existence, its single-sex status reflected the uniform practice for government-supported military colleges. In other words, the tradition of having government-funded military schools for men is as well rooted in the traditions of this country as the tradition of sending only men into military combat. The people may decide to change the one tradition, like the other, through democratic processes; but the assertion that either tradition has been unconstitutional through the centuries is not law, but politics-smuggled-into-law. These traditions may of course be changed by the democratic decisions of the people, as they largely have been.

Today, however, change is forced upon Virginia, and reversion to single-sex education is prohibited nationwide, not by democratic processes but by order of this Court. Even while bemoaning the sorry, bygone days of "fixed notions" concerning women's education, see *ante*, at 2277-2278, and n. 10, 2277-2278, 2280-2282, the Court favors current notions so fixedly that it is willing to write them into the Constitution of the United States by application of custom-built "tests." This is not the interpretation of a Constitution, but the creation of one. . . .

II. To reject the Court's disposition today, however, it is not necessary to accept my view that the Court's made-up tests cannot displace longstanding national traditions as the primary determinant of what the Constitution means. It is only necessary to apply honestly the test the Court has been applying to sex-based classifications for the past two decades. It is well settled, as Justice O'Connor stated some time ago for a unanimous Court, that we evaluate a statutory classification based on sex under a standard that lies "[b]etween th[e] extremes of rational basis review and strict scrutiny." We have denominated this standard "intermediate scrutiny" and under it have inquired whether the statutory classification is "substantially related to an important governmental objective."

[Intermediate] scrutiny has never required a least-restrictive-means analysis, but only a "substantial relation" between the classification and the state interests that it serves. The reasoning in our other intermediate-scrutiny cases has similarly required only a substantial relation between end and means, not a perfect fit. There is simply no support in our cases for the notion that a sex-based classification is invalid unless it relates to characteristics that hold true in every instance.

Not content to execute a *de facto* abandonment of the intermediate scrutiny that has been our standard for sex-based classifications for some two decades, the Court purports to reserve the question whether, even in principle, a higher standard (*i.e.*, strict scrutiny) should apply, and it describes our earlier cases as having done no more than decline to "equat[e] gender classifications, *for all purposes*, to classifications based on race or national origin." The statements are irresponsible, insofar as they are calculated to destabilize current law.

The Court's intimations are particularly out of place because it is perfectly clear that, if the question of the applicable standard of review for sex-based classifications were to be regarded as an appropriate subject for reconsideration, the stronger argument would be not for elevating the standard to strict scrutiny, but for reducing it to rational-basis review. The latter certainly has a firmer foundation in our past jurisprudence: Whereas no majority of the Court has ever applied strict scrutiny in a case involving sex-based classifications, we routinely applied rational-basis review until the 1970's.

III. It is beyond question that Virginia has an important state interest in providing effective college education for its citizens. That single-sex instruction is an approach substantially related to that interest should be evident enough from the long and continuing history in this country of men's and women's colleges. But beyond that, as the Court of Appeals here stated: "That single-gender education at the college level is beneficial to both sexes is a *fact established in this case.*"

But besides its single-sex constitution, VMI is different from other colleges in another way. It employs a "distinctive educational method," sometimes referred to as the "adversative, or doubting, model of education." "Physical rigor, mental stress, absolute equality of treatment, absence of privacy, minute regulation of behavior, and indoctrination in desirable values are the salient attributes of the VMI educational experience." No one contends that this method is appropriate for all individuals; education is not a "one size fits all" business. Just as a State may wish to support junior colleges, vocational institutes, or a law school that emphasizes case practice instead of classroom study, so too a State's decision to maintain within its system one school that provides the adversative method is "substantially related" to its goal of good education. Moreover, it was uncontested that "if the state were to establish a women's VMI-type [*i.e.,* adversative] program, the program would attract an insufficient number of participants to make the program work," and it was found by the District Court that if Virginia were to include women in VMI, the school "would eventually find it necessary to drop the adversative system altogether." Thus, Virginia's options were an adversative method that excludes women or no adversative method at all.

In these circumstances, Virginia's election to fund one public all-male institution and one on the adversative model — and to concentrate its resources in a single entity that serves both these interests in diversity — is substantially related to the Commonwealth's important educational interests.

All-male character is "substantially related" to an important state goal. But VWIL now exists, and the Court's treatment of it shows how far reaching today's decision is.

Comments on *V.M.I.* Does Justice Ginsburg's description of the "exceedingly persuasive justification" standard as "[t]oday's skeptical scrutiny" reinforce the argument that the Court has upped the ante beyond "middle scrutiny" in gender-based discrimination? Justice Scalia, in his *V.M.I.* dissent, included a critique of Justice Ginsburg's opinion, arguing that she was applying a "strict" as opposed to "intermediate" scrutiny standard that "drastically revises our established standards for reviewing sex-based classifications." Do you agree?

a. ARE ALL DIFFERENCES BETWEEN MEN AND WOMAN ARCHAIC GENERALIZATIONS?

A significant question that remains, particularly given the "skeptical scrutiny" applied by the Court today, is when "archaic generalizations" stop and the state can distinguish between the sexes because they are not "similarly situated." Though there is no easy answer to this question as the roles of men and women are arguably ever changing, Justice Rehnquist speaks to these issues in *Michael M.*, which follows, and argues that equal protection does not require "things which are different in fact be treated in law as though they were the same."

MICHAEL M. v. SONOMA COUNTY SUPERIOR COURT
450 U.S. 464 (1981)

Justice REHNQUIST announced the judgment of the Court and delivered an opinion, in which [Chief Justice BURGER], Justice STEWART, and Justice POWELL joined.

[Petitioner, a seventeen-and-one-half-year-old male, was convicted of "statutory rape" for having intercourse with a sixteen-and-one-half-year-old female. California law defined this offense as "an act of sexual intercourse accomplished with a female not the wife of the perpetrator, where the female is under the age of 18 years." The statute thus made men alone criminally liable for the act of sexual intercourse. Petitioner claimed that the statute violated the equal protection clause by unlawfully discriminating on the basis of gender.]

[A] legislature may not "make overbroad generalizations based on sex which are entirely unrelated to any differences between men and women or which demean the ability or social status of the affected class." Parham v. Hughes, 441 U.S. 347, 354 (1979) (plurality opinion of Stewart, J.). But because the Equal Protection Clause does not "demand that a statute necessarily apply equally to all persons" or require "'things which are different in fact . . . to be treated in law as though they were the same,'" Rinaldi v. Yeager, 384 U.S. 305, 309 (1966), quoting Tigner v. Texas, 310 U.S. 141, 147 (1940), this Court has consistently upheld statutes where the gender classification is not invidious, but rather realistically reflects the fact that the sexes are not similarly situated in certain circumstances. . . .

Applying those principles to this case, the fact that the California Legislature criminalized the act of illicit sexual intercourse with a minor female is a sure indication of its intent or purpose to discourage that conduct. Precisely why the legislature desired that result is of course somewhat less clear. . . .

The justification for the statute offered by the State, and accepted by the Supreme Court of California, is that the legislature sought to prevent illegitimate teenage pregnancies. . . .

We are satisfied not only that the prevention of illegitimate pregnancy is at least one of the "purposes" of the statute, but also that the State has a strong interest in preventing such pregnancy. . . .

We need not be medical doctors to discern that young men and young women are not similarly situated with respect to the problems and the risks of sexual intercourse. Only women may become pregnant, and they suffer disproportionately the profound physical, emotional, and psychological consequences of sexual activity. The statute at issue here protects women from sexual intercourse at an age when those consequences are particularly severe.

The question thus boils down to whether a State may attack the problem of sexual intercourse and teenage pregnancy directly by prohibiting a male from having sexual intercourse with a minor female. We hold that such a statute is sufficiently related to the State's objectives to pass constitutional muster. Because virtually all of the significant harmful and inescapably identifiable consequences of teenage pregnancy fall on the young female, a legislature acts well within its authority when it elects to punish only the participant who, by nature, suffers few of the consequences of his conduct. It is hardly unreasonable for a legislature acting to protect minor females to exclude them from punishment. Moreover, the risk of pregnancy itself constitutes a substantial deterrence to young females. No similar natural sanctions deter males. A criminal sanction imposed solely on males thus serves to roughly "equalize" the deterrents on the sexes. . . .

[We] cannot say that a gender-neutral statute would be as effective as the statute California has chosen to enact. The State persuasively contends that a gender-neutral statute would frustrate its interest in effective enforcement. Its view is that a female is surely less likely to report violations of the statute if she herself would be subject to criminal prosecution. . . .

We similarly reject petitioner's argument that [the statute] is impermissibly overbroad because it makes unlawful sexual intercourse with prepubescent females, who are, by definition, incapable of becoming pregnant. Quite apart from the fact that the statute could well be justified on the grounds that very young females are particularly susceptible to physical injury from sexual intercourse, it is ludicrous to suggest that the Constitution requires the California Legislature to limit the scope of its rape statute to older teenagers and exclude young girls.

There remains only petitioner's contention that the statute is unconstitutional as it is applied to him because he, like [his partner], was under 18 at the time of sexual intercourse. Petitioner argues that the statute is flawed because it presumes that as between two persons under 18, the male is the culpable aggressor. We find petitioner's contentions unpersuasive. Contrary to his assertions, the statute does not rest on the assumption that males are generally the aggressors. It is instead an attempt by a legislature to prevent illegitimate teenage pregnancy by providing an additional deterrent for men. The age of the man is irrelevant since young men are as capable as older men of inflicting the harm sought to be prevented. . . .

Accordingly, the judgment of the California Supreme Court is affirmed.

[An opinion by Justice Stewart concurring in the judgment is omitted].

Justice BLACKMUN, concurring in the judgment.

It is gratifying that the plurality recognizes that "[a]t the risk of stating the obvious, teenage pregnancies . . . have increased dramatically over the last two decades" and "have significant social, medical, and economic consequences for both the mother and her child, and the State." There have been times when I have wondered whether the Court was capable of this perception, particularly when it has struggled with the different but not unrelated problems that attend abortion issues. . . .

I think too, that it is only fair, with respect to this particular petitioner, to point out that his partner, Sharon, appears not to have been an unwilling participant in at least the initial stages of the intimacies that took place the night of June 3, 1968. Petitioner's and Sharon's nonacquaintance with each other before the incident; their drinking; their withdrawal from the others of the group; their foreplay, in which she willingly participated and seems to have encouraged; and the closeness of their ages (a difference of only one year and 18 days) are factors that should make this case an unattractive one to prosecute at all, and especially to prosecute as a felony. [But] the State has chosen to prosecute in that manner, and the facts, I reluctantly conclude, may fit the crime.

Justice BRENNAN, with whom Justices WHITE and Justice MARSHALL join, dissenting. . .

.

The State of California vigorously asserts that the "important governmental objective" to be served by [the statute] is the prevention of teenage pregnancy. It claims that its statute furthers this goal by deterring sexual activity by males — the class of persons it considers more responsible for causing those pregnancies. But even assuming that prevention of teenage pregnancy is an important governmental objective and that it is in fact an objective of [the statute], California still has the burden of proving that there are fewer teenage pregnancies under its gender-based statutory rape law than there would be if the law were gender neutral. To meet this burden, the State must show that because its statutory rape law punishes only males, and not females, it more effectively deters minor females from having sexual intercourse.

The plurality assumes that a gender-neutral statute would be less effective than [this statute] in deterring sexual activity because a gender-neutral statute would create significant enforcement problems. [However,] a State's bare assertion that its gender-based statutory classification substantially furthers an important governmental interest is not enough to meet its burden of proof under Craig v. Boren. Rather, the State must produce evidence that will persuade the Court that its assertion is true. [Even] assuming that a gender-neutral statute would be more difficult to enforce, the State has still not shown that those enforcement problems would make such a statute less effective than a gender-based statute in deterring minor females from engaging in sexual intercourse. Common sense, however, suggests that a gender-neutral statutory rape law is potentially a greater deterrent of sexual activity than a gender-based law, for the simple reason that a gender-neutral law subjects both men and women to criminal sanctions and thus arguably has a deterrent effect on twice as many potential violators. Even if fewer persons were prosecuted under the gender-neutral law, as the State suggests, it would still be true that twice as many persons would be subject to arrest. . . .

Until very recently, no California court or commentator had suggested that the purpose of California's statutory rape law was to protect young women from the risk of pregnancy. Indeed, the historical development of [the statute] demonstrates that the law was initially enacted on the premise that young women, in contrast to young men, were to be deemed legally incapable of consenting to an act of sexual intercourse. Because their chastity was considered particularly precious, those young women were felt to be uniquely in need of the State's protection. In contrast, young men were assumed to be capable of making such decisions for themselves; the law therefore did not offer them any special protection. . . .

I would hold that [the statute] violates the Equal Protection Clause of the Fourteenth Amendment, and I would reverse the judgment of the California Supreme Court.

Justices STEVENS, dissenting. . . .

[I] think the plurality is quite correct in making the assumption that the joint act that this law seeks to prohibit creates a greater risk of harm for the female than for the male. But the plurality surely cannot believe that the risk of pregnancy confronted by the female — any more than the risk of venereal disease confronted by males as well as females — has provided an effective deterrent to voluntary female participation in the risk-creating conduct. Yet the plurality's decision seems to rest on the assumption that the California Legislature acted on the basis of that rather fanciful notion. In my judgment, the fact that a class of persons is especially vulnerable to a risk that a statute is designed to avoid is a reason for making the statute applicable to that class. The argument that a special need for protection provides a rational explanation for an exemption is one I simply do not comprehend. . . .

[If] we view the government's interest as that of a parens patriae seeking to protect its subjects from harming themselves, the discrimination is actually perverse. Would a rational parent making rules for the conduct of twin children of opposite sex simultaneously forbid the son and authorize the daughter to engage in conduct that is especially harmful to the daughter? That is the effect of this statutory classification.

In my opinion, the only acceptable justification for a general rule requiring disparate treatment of the two participants in a joint act must be a legislative judgment that one is more guilty than the other. [The] fact that the California Legislature has decided to apply its prohibition only to the male may reflect a legislative judgment that in the typical case the male is actually the more guilty party. Any such judgment must, in turn, assume that the decision to engage in the risk-creating conduct is always — or at least typically — a male decision. If that assumption is valid, the statutory classification should also be valid. But what is the support for the assumption? [The] possibility that such a habitual attitude may reflect nothing more than an irrational prejudice makes it an insufficient justification for discriminatory treatment that is otherwise blatantly unfair. . . .

Nor do I find at all persuasive the suggestion that this discrimination is adequately justified by the desire to encourage females to inform against their male partners. Even if the concept of a wholesale informant's exemption were an acceptable enforcement device, what is the justification for defining the exempt class entirely by reference to sex rather than by reference to a more neutral criterion such as relative innocence? Indeed, if the exempt class is to be composed entirely of members of one sex, what is there to support the view that the statutory purpose will be better served by granting the informing license to females rather than to males? If a discarded male partner informs on a promiscuous female, a timely threat of prosecution might well prevent the precise harm the statute is intended to minimize.

Finally, even if my logic is faulty and there actually is some speculative basis for treating equally guilty males and females differently, I still believe that any such speculative justification would be outweighed by the paramount interest in evenhanded enforcement of the law. A rule that authorizes punishment of only one of two equally guilty wrongdoers violates the essence of the constitutional requirement that the sovereign must govern impartially. I respectfully dissent.

2. AFFIRMATIVE ACTION

Can a gender-based classification be applied to remedy past discrimination against women without being an archaic generalization? Here, much as in race, there are two potentially conflicting constitutional theses. Initially it appeared that the Court would apply the more lenient rational purpose test to programs compensating women for past discrimination. See, for example, *Kahn v. Shevin*, 416 U.S. 351 (1974), property tax exemptions for widows as opposed to widowers, and *Orr v. Orr*, 440 U.S. 268 (1979), alimony for wives not husbands. In the modern era, however, the Court has been quite clear that the same scrutiny applies (heightened review) whether the alleged classification benefits women (affirmative action, benign discrimination) or discriminates against women (invidious discrimination). The cases that follow are reflective of such.

ROSTKER v. GOLDBERG
453 U.S. 57 (1981)

A three-judge panel of the United States District Court for the Eastern District of Pennsylvania, 509 F.Supp. 586, held that the Military Selective Service Act violated the due process clause of the Fifth Amendment and permanently enjoined the government from requiring registration under the Act and the government, which obtained a stay against enforcement of the injunction, appealed. The Supreme Court, Justice Rehnquist, held that: (1) women, who were excluded from combat service by statute or military policy, and men were not similarly situated for purposes of a draft or registration for a draft; thus Congress' decision to authorize registration of only men did not violate due process clause, and (2) Congress acted within its constitutional authority when it authorized registration of men, and not women, under Military Selective Service Act.

Justice REHNQUIST delivered the opinion of the Court.

[The] case arises in the context of Congress' authority over national defense and military affairs, and perhaps in no other area has the Court accorded Congress greater deference.

None of this is to say that Congress is free to disregard the Constitution when it acts in the area of military affairs, but the tests and limitations to be applied may differ because of the military context. We of course do not abdicate our ultimate responsibility to decide the constitutional question, but simply recognize that the Constitution itself requires such deference to congressional choice. In deciding the question before us we must be particularly careful not to substitute our judgment of what is desirable for that of Congress, or our own evaluation of evidence for a reasonable evaluation by the Legislative Branch.

No one could deny that under the test of *Craig v. Boren, supra,* the Government's interest in raising and supporting armies is an "important governmental interest." Congress and its Committees carefully considered and debated two alternative means of furthering that interest: the first was to register only males for potential conscription, and the other was to register both sexes.

In light of the floor debate and the Report of the Senate Armed Services Committee hereinafter discussed, it is apparent that Congress was fully aware not merely of the many facts and figures presented to it by witnesses who testified before its Committees, but of the current thinking as to the place of women in the Armed Services. In such a case, we cannot ignore Congress' broad authority conferred by the Constitution to raise and support armies.

This case is quite different from several of the gender-based discrimination cases we have considered in that, despite appellees' assertions, Congress did not act "unthinkingly" or "reflexively and not for any considered reason." Brief for Appellees 35. The question of registering women for the draft not only received considerable national attention and was the subject of wide-ranging public debate, but also was extensively considered by Congress.

[The] foregoing clearly establishes that the decision to exempt women from registration was not the "'accidental by-product of a traditional way of thinking about females. [Congress] determined that any future draft, which would be facilitated by the registration scheme, would be characterized by a need for combat troops. [Since] women are excluded from combat, Congress concluded that they would not be needed in the event of a draft, and therefore decided not to register them.

[This] is not a case of Congress arbitrarily choosing to burden one of two similarly situated groups, such as would be the case with an all-black or all-white, or an all-Catholic or all-Lutheran, or an all-Republican or all-Democratic registration. Men and women, because of the combat restrictions on women, are simply not similarly situated for purposes of a draft or registration for a draft.

[The] exemption of women from registration is not only sufficiently but also closely related to Congress' purpose in authorizing registration. As was the case in *Schlesinger v. Ballard, supra*, "the gender classification is not invidious, but rather realistically reflects the fact that the sexes are not similarly situated" in this case. Michael M., supra, at 469, 101 S.Ct., at 1204 (plurality opinion). The Constitution requires that Congress treat similarly situated persons similarly, not that it engage in gestures of superficial equality.

In holding the MSSA constitutionally invalid the District Court relied heavily on the President's decision to seek authority to register women and the testimony of members of the Executive Branch and the military in support of that decision. As stated by the administration's witnesses before Congress, however, the President's "decision to ask for authority to register women is based on equity." Congress was certainly entitled, in the exercise of its constitutional powers to raise and regulate armies and navies, to focus on the question of military need rather than "equity."

Although the military experts who testified in favor of registering women uniformly opposed the actual drafting of women, see, *e. g.*, Hearing on S. 109 and S. 226, at 11 (Gen. Rogers), there was testimony that in the event of a draft of 650,000 the military could absorb some 80,000 female inductees. The 80,000 would be used to fill noncombat positions, freeing men to go to the front. In relying on this testimony in striking down the MSSA, the District Court, palpably exceeded its authority when it ignored Congress' considered response to this line of reasoning.

In the first place, assuming that a small number of women could be drafted for noncombat roles, Congress simply did not consider it worth the added burdens of including women in draft and registration plans. Congress also concluded that whatever the need for women for noncombat roles during mobilization, whether 80,000 or less, it could be met by volunteers. Most significantly, Congress determined that staffing noncombat positions with women during a mobilization would be positively detrimental to the important goal of military flexibility.

The District Court was quite wrong in undertaking an independent evaluation of this evidence, rather than adopting an appropriately deferential examination of *Congress'* evaluation of that evidence. In light of the foregoing, we conclude that Congress acted well within its constitutional authority when it authorized the registration of men, and not women, under the Military Selective Service Act. The decision of the District Court holding otherwise is accordingly reversed.

Justice MARSHALL, with whom Justice BRENNAN joins, dissenting.

The Court today places its imprimatur on one of the most potent remaining public expressions of "ancient canards about the proper role of women."

[Although] the purpose of registration is to assist preparations for drafting civilians into the military, *we are not asked to rule on the constitutionality of a statute governing conscription.* Consequently, we are not called upon to decide whether either men or women can be drafted at all, whether they must be drafted in equal numbers, in what order they should be drafted, or, once inducted, how they are to be trained for their respective functions. In addition, this case does not involve a challenge to the statutes or policies that prohibit female members of the Armed Forces from serving in combat. It is with this understanding that I turn to the task at hand.

[In] my judgment, there simply is no basis for concluding in this case that excluding women from registration is substantially related to the achievement of a concededly important governmental interest in maintaining an effective defense.

[This] analysis, however, focuses on the wrong question. The relevant inquiry under the *Craig v. Boren* test is not whether a *gender-neutral* classification would substantially advance important governmental interests. Rather, the question is whether the gender-based classification is itself substantially related to the achievement of the asserted governmental interest. Thus, the Government's task in this case is to demonstrate that excluding women from registration substantially furthers the goal of preparing for a draft of combat troops. Or to put it another way, the Government must show that registering women would substantially impede its efforts to prepare for such a draft. Under our precedents, the Government cannot meet this burden without showing that a gender-neutral statute would be a less effective means of attaining this end.

[In] this case, the Government makes no claim that preparing for a draft of combat troops cannot be accomplished just as effectively by *registering* both men and women but *drafting* only men if only men turn out to be needed. Nor can the Government argue that this alternative entails the additional cost and administrative inconvenience of registering women. This Court has repeatedly stated that the administrative convenience of employing a gender classification is not an adequate constitutional justification under the *Craig v. Boren* test.

[Both] Congress and the Court have lost sight of the important distinction between *registration* and *conscription.* The fact that registration is a first step in the conscription process does not mean that a registration law expressly discriminating between men and women may be justified by a valid conscription program which would, in retrospect, make the current discrimination appear functionally related to the program that emerged.

But even addressing the Court's reasoning on its own terms, its analysis is flawed because the entire argument rests on a premise that is demonstrably false. As noted, the majority simply assumes that registration prepares for a draft in which *every* draftee must be available for assignment to combat. But the majority's draft scenario finds no support in either the testimony before Congress, or more importantly, in the findings of the Senate Report.

[Testimony] about personnel requirements in the event of a draft established that women could fill at least 80,000 of the 650,000 positions for which conscripts would be inducted. Thus, with respect to these 80,000 or more positions, the statutes and policies barring women from combat do not provide a reason for distinguishing between male and female potential conscripts; the two groups are, in the majority's parlance, "similarly situated." As such, the combat restrictions cannot by themselves supply the constitutionally required justification for the MSSA's gender-based classification.

[This] discussion confirms the Report's conclusion that drafting *"very large numbers* of women" would hinder military flexibility. The discussion does not, however, address the different question whether drafting only a *limited* number of women would similarly impede military flexibility.

[The] Senate Report establishes that induction of a large number of men but only a limited number of women, as determined by the military's personnel requirements, would be substantially related to important governmental interests. But the discussion and findings in the Senate Report do not enable the Government to carry its burden of demonstrating that *completely* excluding women from the draft by excluding them from registration substantially furthers important governmental objectives.

CALIFANO v. WEBSTER
430 U.S. 313 (1977)

Male recipient of old-age insurance benefits under the Social Security Act filed suit challenging the constitutionality of Act provision under which a female wage earner, in respect to the formula utilized in computing benefits, could exclude from the computation of her 'average monthly wage' three more lower earning years than a similarly situated male wage earner. The United States District Court for the Eastern District of New York, 413 F.Supp. 127, entered judgment in favor of claimant, and an appeal was taken by the Secretary of Health, Education, and Welfare. The Supreme Court held that the Social Security Act provision allowing women, who as such have been unfairly hindered from earning as much as men, to eliminate additional low-earning years from the calculation of their retirement benefit works directly to remedy some part of the effect of past discrimination and is not unconstitutional; furthermore, the fact that Congress changed its mind in 1972 and equalized the treatment of men and women did not constitute an admission by Congress that its previous policy was invidiously discriminatory, nor did the failure to make the 1972 amendment retroactive constitute discrimination on the basis of date of birth.

[To] withstand scrutiny under the equal protection component of the Fifth Amendment's Due Process Clause, classifications by gender must serve important governmental objectives and must be substantially related to achievement of those objectives. Reduction of the disparity in economic condition between men and women caused by the long history of discrimination against women has been recognized as such an important governmental objective. But 'the mere recitation of a benign, compensatory purpose is not an automatic shield which protects against any inquiry into the actual purposes underlying a statutory scheme. Accordingly, we have rejected attempts to justify gender classifications as compensation for past discrimination against women when the classifications in fact penalized women wage earners, or when the statutory structure and its legislative history revealed that the classification was not enacted as compensation for past discrimination.

The statutory scheme involved here is more analogous to those upheld in Kahn and Ballard than to those struck down in Wiesenfeld and Goldfarb. The more favorable treatment of the female wage earner enacted here was not a result of "archaic and overbroad generalizations" about women, Schlesinger v. Ballard, supra, at 508, 95 S.Ct., at 577, or of 'the role-typing society has long imposed' upon women, Stanton v. Stanton, 421 U.S. 7, 15, 95 S.Ct. 1373, 1378, 43 L.Ed.2d 688 (1975), such as casual assumptions that women are "the weaker sex" or are more likely to be child-rearers or dependents. Cf. Califano v. Goldfarb, supra; Weinberger v. Wiesenfeld, supra. Rather, "the only discernible purpose of (§ 215's more favorable treatment is) the permissible one of redressing our society's longstanding disparate treatment of women." Califano v. Goldfarb, supra, at 209 n. 8, 97 S.Ct., at 1028.

The challenged statute operated directly to compensate women for past economic discrimination. Allowing women, who as such have been unfairly hindered from earning as much as men, to eliminate additional low-earning years from the calculation of their retirement benefits works directly to remedy some part of the effect of past discrimination.

The legislative history of § 215(b)(3) also reveals that Congress directly addressed the justification for differing treatment of men and women in the former version of that section and purposely enacted the more favorable treatment for female wage earners to compensate for past employment discrimination against women.

E. ALIENAGE

Should alienage be a suspect classification? Does the fact that the Court has traditionally applied strict scrutiny to discrimination based upon "race, religion, and national origin" provide an answer? Is "national origin" distinguishable from "alienage"? How does the fact that citizenship may be required to exercise the right to vote affect your answer? Yet, are not aliens, precisely because of such, "politically powerless" and identifiable by national origin?

In *Graham v. Richardson*, 403 U.S. 365 (1971), the Court applied strict scrutiny to alienage in holding that the states could not deny welfare benefits to aliens. The Court reasoned that "alienage, like those based on nationality or race, are inherently suspect and subject to close judicial scrutiny. Aliens as a class are a prime example of a 'discrete and insular minority.'" This pattern continued in *Application of Griffiths*, 413 U.S. 717 (1973), when the Court, once again applying strict scrutiny, struck down Connecticut's exclusion of all resident aliens from the practice of law. But in 1978 in *Foley*, which follows, questions as to the appropriate standard of review for alienage were raised based upon a "government function" exception drawn from *Sugarman v. Dougall*, 413 U.S. 634 (1973).

FOLEY v. CONNELIE
435 U.S. 291 (1978)

Alien brought class action for declaration that New York statute limiting appointment of members of state police force to United States citizens was unconstitutional. A Three-Judge District Court, granted summary judgment to defendants, and plaintiff appealed. The Supreme Court, Mr. Chief Justice Burger, held that New York statute limiting appointment of members of state police force to citizens of United States does not violate equal protection clause.

Mr. Chief Justice BURGER delivered the opinion of the Court.
[It] would be inappropriate, however, to require every statutory exclusion of aliens to clear the high hurdle of "strict scrutiny," because to do so would "obliterate all the distinctions between citizens and aliens, and thus depreciate the historic values of citizenship."

The practical consequence of this theory is that "our scrutiny will not be so demanding where we deal with matters firmly within a State's constitutional prerogatives." Dougall, supra, at 648, 93 S.Ct. at 2850. The State need only justify its classification by a showing of some rational relationship between the interest sought to be protected and the limiting classification.

[Police] officers in the ranks do not formulate policy, *per se*, but they are clothed with authority to exercise an almost infinite variety of discretionary powers. The execution of the broad powers vested in them affects members of the public significantly and often in the most sensitive areas of daily life. Our Constitution, of course, provides safeguards to persons, homes and possessions, as well as guidance to police officers. And few countries, if any, provide more protection to individuals by limitations on the power and discretion of the police. Nonetheless, police may, in the exercise of their discretion, invade the privacy of an individual in public places.

[Clearly] the exercise of police authority calls for a very high degree of judgment and discretion, the abuse or misuse of which can have serious impact on individuals.

[In] the enforcement and execution of the laws the police function is one where citizenship bears a rational relationship to the special demands of the particular position. A State may, therefore, consonant with the Constitution, confine the performance of this important public responsibility to citizens of the United States.

Comments on *Foley*. The deferential review of *Foley* continued to be applied in other similar circumstances. See *Amback v. Norwich*, 441 U.S. 68 (1979), where the Court held that a state may refuse to employ aliens who refused to seek naturalization when eligible, as elementary and secondary school teachers. These cases continued to raise questions concerning the standard of review and level of scrutiny to be applied to aliens until the decision in *Bernal v. Fainter*.

BERNAL v. FAINTER
467 U.S. 216 (1984)

Resident alien who unsuccessfully applied to Texas Secretary of State to become a notary public brought action claiming that statute requiring that a notary public be United States citizen violates equal protection. The United States District Court for the Southern District of Texas, found the requirement constitutionally infirm. A divided panel of the Court of Appeals for the Fifth Circuit reversed, 710 F.2d 190. Certiorari was granted. The Supreme Court, Justice Marshall, held that: (1) the "public function" exception to strict judicial scrutiny was not applicable, notwithstanding that notaries authenticate witnesses, administer oaths and take out-of-court depositions; (2) possibility that some resident aliens were unsuitable would not justify wholesale ban against all resident aliens; and (3) the requirement violates equal protection.

Justice MARSHALL delivered the opinion of the Court.

As a general matter, a state law that discriminates on the basis of alienage can be sustained only if it can withstand strict judicial scrutiny. In order to withstand strict scrutiny, the law must advance a compelling state interest by the least restrictive means available. Applying this principle, we have invalidated an array of state statutes that denied aliens the right to pursue various occupations. In Sugarman v. Dougall, 413 U.S. 634, 93 S.Ct. 2842, 37 L.Ed.2d 853 (1973), we struck down a state statute barring aliens from employment in permanent positions in the competitive class of the state civil service. In In re Griffiths, 413 U.S. 717, 93 S.Ct. 2851, 37 L.Ed.2d 910 (1973), we nullified a state law excluding aliens from eligibility for membership in the State Bar. And in Examining

Board v. Flores de Otero, 426 U.S. 572, 96 S.Ct. 2264, 49 L.Ed.2d 65 (1976), we voided a state law that excluded aliens from the practice of civil engineering.

We have, however, developed a narrow exception to the rule that discrimination based on alienage triggers strict scrutiny. This exception has been labeled the "political function" exception and applies to laws that exclude aliens from positions intimately related to the process of democratic self-government. The contours of the "political function" exception are outlined by our prior decisions. In Foley v. Connelie, 435 U.S. 291, 98 S.Ct. 1067, 55 L.Ed.2d 287 (1978), we held that a State may require police to be citizens because, in performing a fundamental obligation of government, police "are clothed with authority to exercise an almost infinite variety of discretionary powers" often involving the most sensitive areas of daily life. Id., at 297, 98 S.Ct., at 1071. In Ambach v. Norwick, 441 U.S. 68, 99 S.Ct. 1589, 60 L.Ed.2d 49 (1979), we held that a State may bar aliens who have not declared their intent to become citizens from teaching in the public schools because teachers, like police, possess a high degree of responsibility and discretion in the fulfillment of a basic governmental obligation. They have direct, day-to-day contact with students, exercise unsupervised discretion over them, act as role models, and influence their students about the government and the political process. Id., at 78-79, 99 S.Ct., at 1595-1596. Finally, in Cabell v. Chavez-Salido, 454 U.S. 432, 102 S.Ct. 735, 70 L.Ed.2d 677 (1982), we held that a State may bar aliens from positions as probation officers because they, like police and teachers, routinely exercise discretionary power, involving a basic governmental function, that places them in a position of direct authority over other individuals.

The rationale behind the political-function exception is that within broad boundaries a State may establish its own form of government and limit the right to govern to those who are full-fledged members of the political community. Some public positions are so closely bound up with the formulation and implementation of self-government that the State is permitted to exclude from those positions persons outside the political community, hence persons who have not become part of the process of democratic self-determination.

> The exclusion of aliens from basic governmental processes is not a deficiency in the democratic system but a necessary consequence of the community's process of political self-definition. Self-government, whether direct or through representatives, begins by defining the scope of the community of the governed and thus of the governors as well: Aliens are by definition those outside of this community.

Id., at 439-440, 102 S.Ct., at 740.

We have therefore lowered our standard of review when evaluating the validity of exclusions that entrust only to citizens important elective and nonelective positions whose operations "go to the heart of representative government." Sugarman v. Dougall, supra, 413 U.S., at 647, 93 S.Ct., at 2850. "While not retreating from the position that restrictions on lawfully resident aliens that primarily affect economic interests are subject to heightened judicial scrutiny . . . we have concluded that strict scrutiny is out of place when the restriction primarily serves a political function. . . ." Cabell v. Chavez-Salido, supra, 454 U.S., at 439, 102 S.Ct., at 739 (citation omitted).

To determine whether a restriction based on alienage fits within the narrow political-function exception, we devised in Cabell a two-part test. "First, the specificity of the classification will be examined: a classification that is substantially overinclusive or underinclusive tends to undercut the governmental claim that the classification serves legitimate political ends. . . . Second, even if the classification is sufficiently tailored, it may be applied in the particular case only to 'persons holding state elective or important nonelective executive, legislative, and judicial positions,' those officers who 'participate directly in the formulation, execution, or review of broad public policy' and hence 'perform functions that go to the heart of representative government.'" 454 U.S., at 440, 102 S.Ct., at 740 (quoting Sugarman v. Dougall, supra, 413 U.S., at 647, 93 S.Ct., at 2850).

[The] focus of our inquiry has been whether a position was such that the officeholder would necessarily exercise broad discretionary power over the formulation or execution of public policies importantly affecting the citizen population — power of the sort that a self-governing community could properly entrust only to full-fledged members of that community.

[We] recognize the critical need for a notary's duties to be carried out correctly and with integrity. But a notary's duties, important as they are, hardly implicate responsibilities that go to the heart of representative government. Rather, these duties are essentially clerical and ministerial.

[We] conclude that Article 5949(2) violates the Fourteenth Amendment of the United States Constitution. Accordingly the judgment of the Court of Appeals is reversed, and the case is remanded for further proceedings consistent with this opinion.

Comments on *Bernal*. Is strict scrutiny now applied to alienage? Can a "lower" standard be applied? Where and when?

1. "FEDERAL GOVERNMENT"

Should the Court apply a different standard of review in regard to federal restrictions on alienage as opposed to state-based classifications? Why and on what basis should they be viewed differently? Both *Hampton* and *Diaz* make this difference most significant.

HAMPTON v. WONG
426 U.S. 88 (1976)

[In *Hampton*, the Court invalidated a Civil Service Commission policy excluding aliens from most civil service jobs.]

Justices STEVENS delivered the opinion of the Court.

[He acknowledged that] there may be overriding national interests which justify selective federal legislation that would be unacceptable for an individual State. [The] paramount federal power over immigration and naturalization [forecloses] a simple extension of the holding in Sugarman." [Nonetheless, the Court held that imposition of a citizenship requirement by the Civil Service Commission violated due process.]

When the Federal Government asserts an overriding national interest as justification for a discriminatory rule which would violate the Equal Protection Clause if adopted by a State, due process requires that there be a legitimate basis for presuming that the rule was actually intended to serve that interest. If the agency which promulgates the rule has direct responsibility for fostering or protecting that interest, it may reasonably be presumed that the asserted interest was the actual predicate for the rule. That presumption would, of course, be fortified by an appropriate statement of reasons identifying the relevant interest. Alternatively, if the rule were expressly mandated by the Congress or the President, we might presume that any interest which might rationally be served by the rule did in fact give rise to its adoption.

We may assume [that] if the Congress or the President had expressly imposed the citizenship requirement, it would be justified by the national interest in providing an incentive for aliens to become naturalized, or possibly even as providing the President with an expendable token for treaty negotiating purposes; but we are not willing to presume that the Chairman of the Civil Service Commission [was] deliberately fostering an interest so far removed from his normal responsibilities. [By] broadly denying this class substantial opportunities for employment, the Civil Service Commission rule deprives its members of an aspect of liberty. Since these residents were admitted as a result of decisions made by the Congress and the President, [due process] requires that the decision to impose that deprivation of an important liberty be made either at a comparable level of government or, if it is to be permitted to be made by the Civil Service Commission, that it be justified by reasons which are properly the concern of that agency.

Justice Rehnquist filed a dissenting opinion that was joined by Chief Justice Burger and Justices White and Blackmun.

MATHEWS v. DIAZ
426 U.S. 67 (1976)

[A unanimous Court upheld a federal statute limiting participation in a federal medical insurance program to citizens and aliens who had continuously resided in the United States for five years and had been admitted for permanent residence.]

Justice STEVENS delivered the opinion of the Court:
In the exercise of its broad power over naturalization and immigration, Congress regularly makes rules that would be unacceptable if applied to citizens. [In] particular, the fact that Congress has provided some welfare benefits for citizens does not require it to provide like benefits for all aliens. Neither the overnight visitor, the unfriendly agent of a hostile foreign power, the resident diplomat, nor the illegal entrant, can advance even a colorable constitutional claim to a share in the bounty that a conscientious sovereign makes available to its own citizens and some of its guests. The decision to share that bounty with our guests may take into account the character of the relationship between the alien and this country: Congress may decide that as the alien's tie grows stronger, so does the strength of his claim to an equal share of that munificence.

Graham v. Richardson, in the Court's view, was fully consistent with this analysis. Indeed, the federalism prong of the Graham holding "actually supports our holding today that it is the business of the political branches of the Federal Government, rather than that of either the States or the Federal Judiciary, to regulate the conditions of entry and residence of aliens." Moreover, the equal protection analysis in Graham involved "significantly different considerations." Whereas the states had little, if any, basis for treating persons who are citizens of another State differently from persons who are citizens of another country, [a] comparable classification by the Federal Government is a routine and normally legitimate part of its business. Furthermore, whereas the Constitution inhibits every State's power to restrict travel across its own borders, Congress is explicitly empowered to exercise that type of control over travel across the borders of the United States.

F. NONMARITAL CHILDREN

Though family law has traditionally been the province of the states, the equal protection clause is nonetheless applicable to discriminatory classifications therein. State governments have historically discriminated against nonmarital (illegitimate) children in regard to a variety of family and inheritance rights. The Court, in *Levy v. Louisiana*, 391 U.S. 68 (1968), at the height of the "Warren era," hinted at a "heightened" review standard in finding a state statute unconstitutional in denying nonmarital children the right to recover for the wrongful death of their mother.

A series of cases commencing in the early 1970s seemed to indicate the Court's withdrawal from the heightened scrutiny of *Levy*. Though these cases sometimes indicated a minimum rationality review, at other times they also appeared to apply a rationality review with a "bite" that found the Court determining state legislation unconstitutional. (*Labine v. Vincent*, 401 U.S. 532 (1971); *Weber v. Aetna*, 406 U.S. 164 (1972); *Mathews v. Lucas*, 427 U.S. (1976); *Trimble v. Gordon*, 430 U.S. 762 (1977); *Lilli v. Lalli*, 439 U.S. 259 (1978); *Mills v. Habluetzel*, 456 U.S. 91 (1982).) Finally, in 1988, in *Clark v. Jetter*, a unanimous Court seemed to clarify the hard-to-ascertain review applied in the above-cited cases, and agreed on the level of scrutiny to be applied in classifications dealing with nonmarital children.

CLARK v. JETER
486 U.S. 456 (1988)

Ten years after her illegitimate daughter's birth, petitioner filed a support complaint on the daughter's behalf in a Pennsylvania state court, naming respondent as the father. Although a blood test showed a 99.3% probability that respondent was the father, the court entered judgment for respondent on the basis of a state statute providing that actions to establish the paternity of an illegitimate child ordinarily must be commenced within six years of the child's birth. The court rejected petitioner's contentions that the statute violates the Equal Protection and Due Process Clauses of the Fourteenth Amendment to the Federal Constitution. While petitioner's appeal to the Superior Court of Pennsylvania was pending, the State adopted an 18-year statute of limitations for paternity actions, in order to comply with a requirement of the federal Child Support Enforcement Amendments of 1984 (federal Act). The Superior Court concluded, however, that the new 18-year statute of limitations did not apply retroactively, and that the 6-year period would continue to apply in cases like petitioner's. The court affirmed the trial court's conclusion that the 6-year statute of limitations was constitutional.

Justice O'CONNOR delivered the opinion of the Court.

In considering whether state legislation violates the Equal Protection Clause of the Fourteenth Amendment, U.S. Const., Amdt. 14, § 1, we apply different levels of scrutiny to different types of classifications. Between these extremes of rational basis review and strict scrutiny lies a level of intermediate scrutiny, which generally has been applied to discriminatory classifications based on sex or illegitimacy.

To withstand intermediate scrutiny, a statutory classification must be substantially related to an important governmental objective. Consequently we have invalidated classifications that burden illegitimate children for the sake of punishing the illicit relations of their parents, because "visiting this condemnation on the head of an infant is illogical and unjust."

This Court has developed a particular framework for evaluating equal protection challenges to statutes of limitations that apply to suits to establish paternity, and thereby limit the ability of illegitimate children to obtain support. "First, the period for obtaining support . . . must be sufficiently long in duration to present a reasonable opportunity for those with an interest in such children to assert claims on their behalf. Second, any time limitation placed on that opportunity must be substantially related to the State's interest in avoiding the litigation of stale or fraudulent claims." Mills v. Habluetzel, 456 U.S., at 99-100, 102 S.Ct., at 1554.

In *Mills,* we held that Texas' 1-year statute of limitations failed both steps of the analysis. We explained that paternity suits typically will be brought by the child's mother, who might not act swiftly amidst the emotional and financial complications of the child's first year. And, it is unlikely that the lapse of a mere 12 months will result in the loss of evidence or appreciably increase the likelihood of fraudulent claims. Id., at 100-101, 102 S.Ct., at 1555-56. [In] Pickett v. Brown, 462 U.S. 1, 103 S.Ct. 2199, 76 L.Ed.2d 372 (1983), the Court unanimously struck down Tennessee's 2-year statute of limitations for paternity and child support actions brought on behalf of certain illegitimate children. Adhering to the analysis developed in *Mills,* the Court first considered whether two years afforded a reasonable opportunity to bring such suits. The Tennessee statute was relatively more generous than the Texas statute considered in *Mills* because it did not limit actions against a father who had acknowledged his paternity in writing or by furnishing support; nor did it apply if the child was likely to become a public charge. Nevertheless, the Court concluded that the 2-year period was too short in light of the persisting financial and emotional problems that are likely to afflict the child's mother. Proceeding to the second step of the analysis, the Court decided that the 2-year statute of limitations was not substantially related to Tennessee's asserted interest in preventing stale and fraudulent claims. The period during which suit could be brought was only a year longer than the period considered in *Mills,* and this incremental difference would not create substantially greater proof and fraud problems. Furthermore, Tennessee tolled most other actions during a child's minority, and even permitted a support action to be brought on behalf of a child up to 18 years of age if the child was or was likely to become a public charge. Finally, scientific advances in blood testing had alleviated some problems of proof in paternity actions. For these reasons, the Tennessee statute failed to survive heightened scrutiny under the Equal Protection Clause.

In light of this authority, we conclude that Pennsylvania's 6-year statute of limitations violates the Equal Protection Clause. Even six years does not necessarily provide a reasonable opportunity to assert a claim on behalf of an illegitimate child. "The unwillingness of the mother to file a paternity action on behalf of her child, which could stem from her relationship with the natural father or . . . from the emotional strain of having an illegitimate child, or even from the desire to avoid community and family disapproval, may continue years after the child is born. The problem may be exacerbated if, as often happens, the mother herself is a minor." Mills, supra, at 105, n. 4, 102 S.Ct., at 1558, n.

4. (O'CONNOR, J., concurring). Not all of these difficulties are likely to abate in six years.

We do not rest our decision on this ground, however, for it is not entirely evident that six years would necessarily be an unreasonable limitations period for child support actions involving illegitimate children. We are, however, confident that the 6-year statute of limitations is not substantially related to Pennsylvania's interest in avoiding the litigation of stale or fraudulent claims. In a number of circumstances, Pennsylvania permits the issue of paternity to be litigated more than six years after the birth of an illegitimate child. The statute itself permits a suit to be brought more than six years after the child's birth if it is brought within two years of a support payment made by the father. And in other types of suits, Pennsylvania places no limits on when the issue of paternity may be litigated. For example, the intestacy statute, 20 Pa. Cons. Stat. § 2107(3) (1982), permits a child born out of wedlock to establish paternity as long as "there is clear and convincing evidence that the man was the father of the child." Likewise, no statute of limitations applies to a father's action to establish paternity. In *Pickett* and *Mills,* similar tolling statutes cast doubt on the State's purported interest in avoiding the litigation of stale or fraudulent claims. 462 U.S., at 15-16, 103 S.Ct., at 2207-08; 456 U.S., at 104-105, 102 S.Ct., at 1557-58 (O'CONNOR, J., concurring); id., at 106, 102 S.Ct., at 1558 (Powell, J., concurring in judgment). Pennsylvania's tolling statute has the same implications here.

We conclude that the Pennsylvania statute does not withstand heightened scrutiny under the Equal Protection Clause. We therefore find it unnecessary to reach Clark's due process claim. The judgment of the Superior Court is reversed, and the case is remanded for further proceedings not inconsistent with this opinion.

G. "ADDITIONAL CLASSES"?

What other classifications have received some form of "heightened" scrutiny review? In the cases that follow, dealing with disabilities, age, and sexual orientation — for what the Court takes they may also give! Though the Court seems hesitant about applying a stricter degree of scrutiny to additional classifications, the cases below nonetheless suggest that the Court may apply a rational purpose test with enough "bite" to strike down legislation.

1. DISABILITIES

CITY OF CLEBURNE v. CLEBURNE LIVING CENTER
473 U.S. 432 (1985)

Justice WHITE delivered the opinion of the Court.

A Texas city denied a special use permit for the operation of a group home for the mentally retarded, acting pursuant to a municipal zoning ordinance requiring permits for such homes. The Court of Appeals [held that] the ordinance violated the Equal Protection Clause. [We affirm.]

Respondent purchased a building with the intention of converting it into a group home for thirteen mentally retarded men and women who would reside there under the constant supervision of staff members. A city zoning ordinance permitted a wide variety of structures on the proposed site, including "[h]ospitals, sanitariums, nursing homes or homes for convalescents or aged." However, the ordinance specifically excepted "homes for [the] insane or feeble-minded or alcoholics or drug addicts.

The general rule is that legislation is presumed to be valid and will be sustained if the classification drawn by the statute is rationally related to a legitimate state interest. Schweiker v. Wilson, 450 U.S. 221, 230, 101 S.Ct. 1074, 1080, 67 L.Ed.2d 186 (1981); United States Railroad Retirement Board v. Fritz, 449 U.S. 166, 174-175, 101 S.Ct. 453, 459-460, 66 L.Ed.2d 368 (1980); Vance v. Bradley, 440 U.S. 93, 97, 99 S.Ct. 939, 942, 59 L.Ed.2d 171 (1979); New Orleans v. Dukes, 427 U.S. 297, 303, 96 S.Ct. 2513, 2516, 49 L.Ed.2d 511 (1976). When social or economic legislation is at issue, the Equal Protection Clause allows the States wide latitude, United States Railroad Retirement Board v. Fritz, supra, 449 U.S., at 174, 101 S.Ct., at 459; New Orleans v. Dukes, supra, 427 U.S., at 303, 96 S.Ct., at 2516, and the Constitution presumes that even improvident decisions will eventually be rectified by the democratic processes.

The general rule gives way, however, when a statute classifies by race, alienage, or national origin. These factors are so seldom relevant to the achievement of any legitimate state interest that laws grounded in such considerations are deemed to reflect prejudice and antipathy — a view that those in the burdened class are not as worthy or deserving as others. For these reasons and because such discrimination is unlikely to be soon rectified by legislative means, these laws are subjected to strict scrutiny and will be sustained only if they are suitably tailored to serve a compelling state interest. McLaughlin v. Florida, 379 U.S. 184, 192, 85 S.Ct. 283, 288, 13 L.Ed.2d 222 (1964); Graham v. Richardson, 403 U.S. 365, 91 S.Ct. 1848, 29 L.Ed.2d 534 (1971). Similar oversight by the courts is due when state laws impinge on personal rights protected by the Constitution. Kramer v. Union Free School District No. 15, 395 U.S. 621, 89 S.Ct. 1886, 23 L.Ed.2d 583 (1969); Shapiro v. Thompson, 394 U.S. 618, 89 S.Ct. 1322, 22 L.Ed.2d 600 (1969); Skinner v. Oklahoma ex rel. Williamson, 316 U.S. 535, 62 S.Ct. 1110, 86 L.Ed. 1655 (1942).

Legislative classifications based on gender also call for a heightened standard of review. That factor generally provides no sensible ground for differential treatment. "[W]hat differentiates sex from such nonsuspect statuses as intelligence or physical disability . . . is that the sex characteristic frequently bears no relation to ability to perform or contribute to society." Frontiero v. Richardson, 411 U.S. 677, 686, 93 S.Ct. 1764, 1770, 36 L.Ed.2d 583 (1973) (plurality opinion). Rather than resting on meaningful considerations, statutes distributing benefits and burdens between the sexes in different ways very likely reflect outmoded notions of the relative capabilities of men and women. A gender classification fails unless it is substantially related to a sufficiently important governmental interest. Mississippi University for Women v. Hogan, 458 U.S. 718, 102 S.Ct. 3331, 73 L.Ed.2d 1090 (1982); Craig v. Boren, 429 U.S. 190, 97 S.Ct. 451, 50 L.Ed.2d 397 (1976). Because illegitimacy is beyond the individual's control and bears "no relation to the individual's ability to participate in and contribute to society," Mathews v. Lucas, 427 U.S. 495, 505, 96 S.Ct. 2755, 2762, 49 L.Ed.2d 651 (1976), official discriminations resting on that characteristic are also subject to somewhat heightened review. Those restrictions "will survive equal protection scrutiny to the extent they are substantially related to a legitimate state interest." Mills v. Habluetzel, 456 U.S. 91, 99, 102 S.Ct. 1549, 1554, 71 L.Ed.2d 770 (1982).

We have declined, however, to extend heightened review to differential treatment based on age:

> While the treatment of the aged in this Nation has not been wholly free of discrimination, such persons, unlike, say, those who have been discriminated against on the basis of race or national origin, have not experienced a 'history of purposeful unequal treatment' or been subjected to unique disabilities on the basis of stereotyped characteristics not truly indicative of their abilities.

Massachusetts Board of Retirement v. Murgia, 427 U.S. 307, 313, 96 S.Ct. 2562, 2567, 49 L.Ed.2d 520 (1976).

The lesson of *Murgia* is that where individuals in the group affected by a law have distinguishing characteristics relevant to interests the State has the authority to implement, the courts have been very reluctant, as they should be in our federal system and with our respect for the separation of powers, to closely scrutinize legislative choices as to whether, how, and to what extent those interests should be pursued. In such cases, the Equal Protection Clause requires only a rational means to serve a legitimate end.

First, it is undeniable [that] those who are mentally retarded have a reduced ability to cope with and function in the everyday world. [They] are thus different, immutably so, in relevant respects, and the states' interest in dealing with and providing for them is plainly a legitimate one. How this large and diversified group is to be treated under the law is a difficult and often technical matter, very much a task for legislators guided by qualified professionals and not by the perhaps ill-informed opinions of the judiciary.

Second, the distinctive legislative response, both national and state, to the plight of those who are mentally retarded demonstrates not only that they have unique problems, but also that the lawmakers have been addressing their difficulties in a manner that belies a continuing antipathy or prejudice and a corresponding need for more intrusive oversight by the judiciary. Thus, the federal government has not only outlawed discrimination against the mentally retarded in federally funded programs, but it has also provided the retarded with the right to receive "appropriate treatment services and habilitation" in a setting that is "least restrictive of [their] personal liberty." . . .

Such legislation thus singling out the retarded for special treatment reflects the real and undeniable differences between the retarded and others. That a civilized and decent society expects and approves such legislation indicates that governmental consideration of those differences in the vast majority of situations is not only legitimate but desirable. [Even] assuming that many of these laws could be shown to be substantially related to an important governmental purpose, merely requiring the legislature to justify its efforts in these terms may lead it to refrain from acting at all. [Especially] given the wide variation in the abilities and needs of the retarded themselves, governmental bodies must have a certain amount of flexibility and freedom from judicial oversight in shaping and limiting their remedial efforts.

Third, the legislative response, which could hardly have occurred and survived without public support, negates any claim that the mentally retarded are politically powerless in the sense that they have no ability to attract the attention of lawmakers. . . .

Fourth, if the large and amorphous class of the mentally retarded were deemed quasi-suspect [it] would be difficult to find a principled way to distinguish a variety of other groups who have perhaps immutable disabilities setting them off from others, who cannot themselves mandate the desired legislative responses, and who can claim some degree of prejudice from at least part of the public at large. One need mention in this respect only the aging, the disabled, the mentally ill, and the infirm. We are reluctant to set out on that course, and we decline to do so.

Doubtless, there have been and there will continue to be instances of discrimination against the retarded that are in fact [invidious]. But the appropriate method of reaching such instances is not to create a new quasi-suspect classification and subject all governmental action based on that classification to more searching evaluation.

Our refusal to recognize the retarded as a quasi-suspect class does not leave them entirely unprotected from invidious discrimination. To withstand equal protection review, legislation that distinguishes between the mentally retarded and others must be rationally related to a legitimate governmental purpose. . . .

[The] mentally retarded as a group are indeed different from others not sharing their misfortune, and in this respect they may be different from those who would occupy other facilities that would be [permitted.] But this difference is largely irrelevant unless the [home] and those who would occupy it would threaten legitimate interests of the city in a way that other permitted uses such as boarding houses and hospitals would not. . . .

The District Court found that the City Council's insistence on the permit rested on several factors. [The] Council was concerned with the negative attitude of the majority of property owners located within 200 feet of the [facility], as well as with the fears of elderly residents of the neighborhood. But mere negative attitudes, or fear, unsubstantiated by factors which are properly cognizable in a zoning proceeding, are not permissible bases for treating a home for the mentally retarded differently from apartment houses, multiple dwellings, and the like. It is plain that the electorate as a whole [could] not order city action violative of the Equal Protection Clause, and the City may not avoid the strictures of that Clause by deferring to the wishes or objections of some fraction of the body politic. . . .

[The] Council had two objections to the location of the facility. It was concerned that the facility was across the street from a junior high school, and it feared that the students might harass the occupants of the [home]. But the school itself is attended by about 30 mentally retarded students, and denying a permit based on such vague, undifferentiated fears is again permitting some portion of the community to validate what would otherwise be an equal protection violation. The other objection to the home's location was that it was located on "a five hundred year flood plain." This concern with the possibility of a flood, however, can hardly be based on a distinction between the [home] and, for example, nursing homes, homes for convalescents or the aged, or sanitariums or hospitals, any of which could be located on the [site] without obtaining a special use permit. The same may be said of another concern of the Council — doubts about the legal responsibility for actions which the mentally retarded might take. If there is no concern about legal responsibility with respect to other uses that would be permitted in the area, such as boarding and fraternity houses, it is difficult to believe that the groups of mildly or moderately mentally retarded individuals who would live at [the home] would present any different or special hazard.

[The] Council was concerned with the size of the home and the number of people that would occupy it. [But], there would be no restrictions on the number of people who could occupy this home as a boarding house, nursing home, family dwelling, fraternity house, or dormitory. . . .

The short of it is that requiring the permit in this case appears to us to rest on an irrational prejudice against the mentally retarded, including those who would occupy the [facility] and who would live under the closely supervised and highly regulated conditions expressly provided for by state and federal law. . . .

Justices STEVENS, with whom [Chief Justice BURGER] joins, concurring.

[Our] cases reflect a continuum of judgmental responses to differing classifications which have been explained in opinions by terms ranging from "strict scrutiny" at one extreme to "rational basis" at the other. I have never been persuaded that these so called "standards" adequately explain the decisional process. [In] my own approach to these cases, I have always asked myself whether I could find a "rational basis" for the classification at issue. The term "rational," of course, includes a requirement that an impartial lawmaker could logically believe that the classification would serve a legitimate public purpose that transcends the harm to the members of the disadvantaged class. Thus, the word "rational" — for me at least — includes elements of legitimacy and neutrality that must always characterize the performance of the sovereign's duty to govern impartially. . . .

[The] Court of Appeals correctly observed that through ignorance and prejudice the mentally retarded "have been subjected to a history of unfair and often grotesque mistreatment." The discrimination against the mentally retarded that is at issue in this case is the city's decision to require an annual special use permit before property in an apartment house district may be used as a group home for persons who are mildly retarded. The record convinces me that this permit was required because of the irrational fears of neighboring property owners, rather than for the protection of the mentally retarded persons who would reside in [the] home.

Justice MARSHALL, with whom Justice BRENNAN and Justice BLACKMUN join, concurring in the judgment in part and dissenting in part. . . .

[The] mentally retarded have been subject to a 'lengthy and tragic history' of segregation and discrimination that can only be called grotesque. [By] the latter part of the [nineteenth] century and during the first decades of the new one, [social] views of the retarded underwent a radical transformation. Fueled by the rising tide of Social Darwinism, the 'science' of eugenics, and the extreme xenophobia of those years, leading medical authorities and others began to portray the 'feebleminded' as a 'menace to society and civilization [responsible] in a large degree for many, if not all, our social problems.' A regime of state-mandated segregation and degradation soon emerged that in its virulence and bigotry rivaled, and indeed paralleled, the worst excesses of Jim Crow. . . .

Prejudice, once let loose, is not easily cabined. As of 1979, most states still categorically disqualified 'idiots' from voting, without regard to individual capacity and with discretion to exclude left in the hands of low-level officials. Not until Congress enacted the Education of the Handicapped Act were 'the door[s] of public education' opened wide to handicapped children. But most important, lengthy and continuing isolation of the retarded has perpetuated the ignorance, irrational fears, and stereotyping that long have plagued them.

In light of the importance of the interest at stake and the history of discrimination the retarded have suffered, the Equal Protection Clause requires us to do more than review the distinctions drawn by Cleburne's zoning ordinance as if they appeared in a taxing statute or in economic or commercial legislation. The searching scrutiny I would give to restrictions on the ability of the retarded to establish community group homes leads me to conclude that Cleburne's vague generalizations for classifying the 'feeble minded' with drug addicts, alcoholics, and the insane, and excluding them where the elderly, the ill, the boarder, and the transient are allowed, are not substantial or important enough to overcome the suspicion that the ordinance rests on impermissible assumptions or outmoded and perhaps invidious stereotypes.

[The] Court holds the ordinance invalid on rational basis grounds and disclaims that anything special, in the form of heightened scrutiny, is taking place. Yet Cleburne's ordinance surely would be valid under the traditional rational basis test applicable to economic and commercial regulation. . . .

The Court, for example, concludes that legitimate concerns for fire hazards or the serenity of the neighborhood do not justify singling out respondents to bear the burdens of these concerns, for analogous permitted uses appear to pose similar threats. Yet under the traditional and most minimal version of the rational basis test, "reform may take one step at a time, addressing itself to the phase of the problem which seems most acute to the legislative mind." [Williamson.] The "record" is said not to support the ordinance's classifications, but under the traditional standard we do not sift through the record to determine whether policy decisions are squarely supported by a firm factual foundation. Finally, the Court further finds it "difficult to believe" that the retarded present different or special hazards than other groups. In normal circumstances, the burden is not on the legislature to convince the Court that the lines it has drawn are sensible; legislation is presumptively constitutional, and a State "is not required to resort to close distinctions or to maintain a precise, scientific uniformity with reference" to its goals. Allied Stores of Ohio, Inc. v. Bowers, 358 U.S. 522, 527 (1959).

I share the Court's criticisms of the overly broad lines that Cleburne's zoning ordinance has drawn. But if the ordinance is to be invalidated for its imprecise classifications, it must be pursuant to more powerful scrutiny than the minimal rational-basis test used to review classifications affecting only economic and commercial matters. The same imprecision in a similar ordinance that required opticians but not optometrists to be licensed to practice, see [Williamson], [would] hardly be fatal to the statutory scheme.

2. AGE

MASSACHUSETTS BOARD OF RETIREMENT v. MURGIA
427 U.S. 307 (1976)

PER CURIAM.

This case presents the question whether the provision of Mass.Gen.Laws Ann. c. 32, § 26(3)(a) (1969), that a uniformed state police officer "shall be retired . . . upon his attaining age fifty," denies appellee police officer equal protection of the laws in violation of the Fourteenth Amendment.

Appellee Robert Murgia was an officer in the Uniformed Branch of the Massachusetts State Police. The Massachusetts Board of Retirement retired him upon his 50th birthday. Appellee brought this civil action in the United States District Court for the District of Massachusetts, alleging that the operation of § 26(3)(a) denied him equal protection of the laws.

The primary function of the Uniformed Branch of the Massachusetts State Police is to protect persons and property and maintain law and order. Specifically, uniformed officers participate in controlling prison and civil disorders, respond to emergencies and natural disasters, patrol highways in marked cruisers, investigate crime, apprehend criminal suspects, and provide backup support for local law enforcement personnel. As the

District Court observed, "service in this branch is, or can be, arduous." 376 F.Supp., at 754. "[H]igh versatility is required, with few, if any, backwaters available for the partially superannuated." Ibid. Thus, "even (appellee's) experts concede that there is a general relationship between advancing age and decreasing physical ability to respond to the demands of the job." Id., at 755.

These considerations prompt the requirement that uniformed state officers pass a comprehensive physical examination biennially until age 40. After that, until mandatory retirement at age 50, uniformed officers must pass annually a more rigorous examination, including an electrocardiogram and tests for gastro-intestinal bleeding. Appellee Murgia had passed such an examination four months before he was retired, and there is no dispute that, when he retired, his excellent physical and mental health still rendered him capable of performing the duties of a uniformed officer.

The record includes the testimony of three physicians. [The] testimony clearly established that the risk of physical failure, particularly in the cardiovascular system, increases with age, and that the number of individuals in a given age group incapable of performing stress functions increases with the age of the group. The testimony also recognized that particular individuals over 50 could be capable of safely performing the functions of uniformed officers.

We agree that rationality is the proper standard by which to test whether compulsory retirement at age 50 violates equal protection. We disagree, however, with the District Court's determination that the age 50 classification is not rationally related to furthering a legitimate state interest.

[The] class of uniformed state police officers over 50 [does not] constitute a suspect class for purposes of equal protection analysis. Rodriguez, supra, 411 U.S. at 28, 93 S.Ct. at 1294, observed that a suspect class is one "saddled with such disabilities, or subjected to such a history of purposeful unequal treatment, or relegated to such a position of political powerlessness as to command extraordinary protection from the majoritarian political process." While the treatment of the aged in this Nation has not been wholly free of discrimination, such persons, unlike, say, those who have been discriminated against on the basis of race or national origin, have not experienced a "history of purposeful unequal treatment" or been subjected to unique disabilities on the basis of stereotyped characteristics not truly indicative of their abilities. The class subject to the compulsory retirement feature of the Massachusetts statute consists of uniformed state police officers over the age of 50. It cannot be said to discriminate only against the elderly. Rather, it draws the line at a certain age in middle life. But even old age does not define a "discrete and insular" group, United States v. Carolene Products Co., 304 U.S. 144, 152-153, n. 4, 58 S.Ct. 778, 783, 82 L.Ed. 1234 (1938), in need of "extraordinary protection from the majoritarian political process." Instead, it marks a stage that each of us will reach if we live out our normal span.

We turn then to examine this state classification under the rational-basis standard. This inquiry employs a relatively relaxed standard reflecting the Court's awareness that the drawing of lines that create distinctions is peculiarly a legislative task and an unavoidable one. Perfection in making the necessary classifications is neither possible nor necessary. Dandridge v. Williams, supra, 397 U.S., at 485, 90 S.Ct., at 1162. Such action by a legislature is presumed to be valid.

In this case, the Massachusetts statute clearly meets the requirements of the Equal Protection Clause, for the State's classification rationally furthers the purpose identified by the State: Through mandatory retirement at age 50, the legislature seeks to protect the public by assuring physical preparedness of its uniformed police. Since physical ability generally declines with age, mandatory retirement at 50 serves to remove from police service those whose fitness for uniformed work presumptively has diminished with age. This clearly is rationally related to the State's objective. There is no indication that s26(3)(a) has the effect of excluding from service so few officers who are in fact unqualified as to render age 50 a criterion wholly unrelated to the objective of the statute.

That the State chooses not to determine fitness more precisely through individualized testing after age 50 is not to say that the objective of assuring physical fitness is not rationally furthered by a maximum-age limitation. It is only to say that with regard to the interest of all concerned, the State perhaps has not chosen the best means to accomplish this purpose. But where rationality is the test, a State "does not violate the Equal Protection Clause merely because the classifications made by its laws are imperfect." Dandridge v. Williams, 397 U.S., at 485, 90 S.Ct., at 1161. The judgment is reversed.

Mr. Justice MARSHALL dissenting.

Of course, the Court is quite right in suggesting that distinctions exist between the elderly and traditional suspect classes such as Negroes, and between the elderly and "quasi-suspect" classes such as women or illegitimates. [The] elderly are not isolated in society, and discrimination against them is not pervasive but is centered primarily in employment. The advantage of a flexible equal protection standard, however, is that it can readily accommodate such variables. The elderly are undoubtedly discriminated against, and when legislation denies them an important benefit employment I conclude that to sustain the legislation appellants must show a reasonably substantial interest and a scheme reasonably closely tailored to achieving that interest. Cf. San Antonio School District v. Rodriguez, 411 U.S. at 124-126, 93 S.Ct. at 1343 (Marshall, J., dissenting). This inquiry, ultimately, is not markedly different from that undertaken by the Court in Reed v. Reed, 404 U.S. 71, 92 S.Ct. 251, 30 L.Ed.2d 225 (1971).

3. SEXUAL ORIENTATION

ROMER v. EVANS
517 U.S. 620 (1996)

After various Colorado municipalities passed ordinances banning discrimination based on sexual orientation in housing, employment, education, public accommodations, health and welfare services, and other transactions and activities, Colorado voters adopted by statewide referendum "Amendment 2" to the State Constitution, which precludes all legislative, executive, or judicial action at any level of state or local government designed to protect the status of persons based on their "homosexual, lesbian or bisexual orientation, conduct, practices or relationships." Respondents, who include aggrieved homosexuals and municipalities, commenced this litigation in state court against petitioner state parties to declare Amendment 2 invalid and enjoin its enforcement. The trial court's grant of a preliminary injunction was sustained by the Colorado Supreme Court, which held that Amendment 2 was subject to strict scrutiny under the Equal Protection Clause of the Fourteenth Amendment because it infringed the fundamental right of gays and lesbians to participate in the political process. On remand, the trial court found that the amendment failed to satisfy strict scrutiny. It enjoined Amendment 2's enforcement, and the State Supreme Court affirmed.

Justice KENNEDY delivered the opinion of the Court.

One century ago, the first Justice Harlan admonished this Court that the Constitution "neither knows nor tolerates classes among citizens." Plessy v. Ferguson, 163 U.S. 537, 559, 16 S.Ct. 1138, 1146, 41 L.Ed. 256 (1896) (dissenting opinion). Unheeded then, those words now are understood to state a commitment to the law's neutrality where the rights of persons are at stake. The Equal Protection Clause enforces this principle and today requires us to hold invalid a provision of Colorado's Constitution.

I. The enactment challenged in this case is an amendment to the Constitution of the State of Colorado, adopted in a 1992 statewide referendum. The parties and the state courts refer to it as "Amendment 2," its designation when submitted to the voters. The impetus for the amendment and the contentious campaign that preceded its adoption came in large part from ordinances that had been passed in various Colorado municipalities. For example, the cities of Aspen and Boulder and the city and County of Denver each had enacted ordinances which banned discrimination in many transactions and activities, including housing, employment, education, public accommodations, and health and welfare services. What gave rise to the statewide controversy was the protection the ordinances afforded to persons discriminated against by reason of their sexual orientation. [Yet] Amendment 2, in explicit terms, does more than repeal or rescind these provisions. It prohibits all legislative, executive or judicial action at any level of state or local government designed to protect the named class, a class we shall refer to as homosexual persons or gays and lesbians. The amendment reads: "No Protected Status Based on Homosexual, Lesbian or Bisexual Orientation. Neither the State of Colorado, through any of its branches or departments, nor any of its agencies, political subdivisions, municipalities or school districts, shall enact, adopt or enforce any statute, regulation, ordinance or policy whereby homosexual, lesbian or bisexual orientation, conduct, practices or relationships shall constitute or otherwise be the basis of or entitle any person or class of persons to have or claim any minority status, quota preferences, protected status or claim of discrimination. This Section of the Constitution shall be in all respects self-executing." [The] State Supreme Court held that Amendment 2 was subject to strict scrutiny under the Fourteenth Amendment because it infringed the fundamental right of gays and lesbians to participate in the political process. Hunter v. Erickson, 393 U.S. 385, 89 S.Ct. 557, 21 L.Ed.2d 616 (1969); Reitman v. Mulkey, 387 U.S. 369, 87 S.Ct. 1627, 18 L.Ed.2d 830 (1967); Washington v. Seattle School Dist. No. 1, 458 U.S. 457, 102 S.Ct. 3187, 73 L.Ed.2d 896 (1982) On remand, the State advanced various arguments in an effort to show that Amendment 2 was narrowly tailored to serve compelling interests, but the trial court found none sufficient. It enjoined enforcement of Amendment 2, and the Supreme Court of Colorado, in a second opinion, affirmed the ruling. We granted certiorari, and now affirm the judgment, but on a rationale different from that adopted by the State Supreme Court.

II. The State's principal argument in defense of Amendment 2 is that it puts gays and lesbians in the same position as all other persons. So, the State says, the measure does no more than deny homosexuals special rights. This reading of the amendment's language is implausible. We rely not upon our own interpretation of the amendment but upon the authoritative construction of Colorado's Supreme Court: ["The] immediate objective of Amendment 2 is, at a minimum, to repeal existing statutes, regulations, ordinances, and policies of state and local entities that barred discrimination based on sexual orientation; [and] various provisions prohibiting discrimination based on sexual orientation at state colleges. The 'ultimate effect' of Amendment 2 is to prohibit any governmental entity from adopting similar, or more protective statutes, regulations, ordinances, or policies in the future unless the state constitution is first amended to permit such measures." Sweeping and comprehensive is the change in legal status affected by this law. So much is evident from the ordinances the Colorado Supreme Court declared would be void by operation of Amendment 2. Homosexuals, by state decree, are put in a solitary class with respect to transactions and relations in both the private and governmental spheres. The amendment withdraws from homosexuals, but no others, specific legal protection from the injuries caused by discrimination, and it forbids reinstatement of these laws and policies.

The change Amendment 2 works in the legal status of gays and lesbians in the private sphere is far reaching, both on its own terms and when considered in light of the structure and operation of modern anti-discrimination laws. [Most] States have chosen to counter discrimination by enacting detailed statutory schemes. Colorado's state and municipal laws typify this emerging tradition of statutory protection and follow a consistent pattern. The laws first enumerate the persons or entities subject to a duty not to discriminate. The list goes well beyond the entities covered by the common law. The Boulder ordinance, for example, has a comprehensive definition of entities deemed places of "public accommodation." They include "any place of business engaged in any sales to the general public and any place that offers services, facilities, privileges, or advantages to the general public or that receives financial support through solicitation of the general public or through governmental subsidy of any kind." The Denver ordinance is of similar breadth, applying, for example, to hotels, restaurants, hospitals, dental clinics, theaters, banks, common carriers, travel and insurance agencies, and "shops and stores dealing with goods or services of any kind."

[These] statutes and ordinances also depart from the common law by enumerating the groups or persons within their ambit of protection. Enumeration is the essential device used to make the duty not to discriminate concrete and to provide guidance for those who must comply. In following this approach, Colorado's state and local governments have not limited antidiscrimination laws to groups that have so far been given the protection of heightened equal protection scrutiny under our cases. Rather, they set forth an extensive catalog of traits which cannot be the basis for discrimination, including age, military status, marital status, pregnancy, parenthood, custody of a minor child, political affiliation, physical or mental disability of an individual or of his or her associates — - and, in recent times, sexual orientation. Amendment 2 bars homosexuals from securing protection against the injuries that these public-accommodations laws address. That in itself is a severe consequence, but there is more. Amendment 2, in addition, nullifies specific legal protections for this targeted class in all transactions in housing, sale of real estate, insurance, health and welfare services, private education, and employment.

Not confined to the private sphere, Amendment 2 also operates to repeal and forbid all laws or policies providing specific protection for gays or lesbians from discrimination by every level of Colorado government. The State Supreme Court cited two examples of protections in the governmental sphere that are now rescinded and may not be reintroduced. The first is Colorado Executive Order D0035 (1990), which forbids employment discrimination against "'all state employees, classified and exempt' on the basis of sexual orientation." Also repealed, and now forbidden, are "various provisions prohibiting discrimination based on sexual orientation at state colleges." The repeal of these measures and the prohibition against their future reenactment demonstrate that Amendment 2 has the same force and effect in Colorado's governmental sector as it does elsewhere and that it applies to policies as well as ordinary legislation.

Amendment 2's reach may not be limited to specific laws passed for the benefit of gays and lesbians. It is a fair, if not necessary, inference from the broad language of the amendment that it deprives gays and lesbians even of the protection of general laws and policies that prohibit arbitrary discrimination in governmental and private settings. See, *e.g.,* Colo.Rev.Stat. § 24-4-106(7) (1988) (agency action subject to judicial review under arbitrary and capricious standard); § 18-8-405 (making it a criminal offense for a public servant knowingly, arbitrarily, or capriciously to refrain from performing a duty imposed on him by law); § 10-3-1104(1)(f) (prohibiting "unfair discrimination" in insurance); 4 Colo. Code of Regulations 801-1, Policy 11-1 (1983) (prohibiting discrimination in state employment on grounds of specified traits or "other non-merit factor"). At some point in the systematic administration of these laws, an official must determine whether homosexuality is an arbitrary and, thus, forbidden basis for decision. Yet a decision to that effect would itself amount to a policy prohibiting discrimination on the basis of homosexuality, and so would appear to be no more valid under Amendment 2 than the specific prohibitions against discrimination the state court held invalid.

If this consequence follows from Amendment 2, as its broad language suggests, it would compound the constitutional difficulties the law creates. The state court did not decide whether the amendment has this effect, however, and neither need we. In the course of rejecting the argument that Amendment 2 is intended to conserve resources to fight discrimination against suspect classes, the Colorado Supreme Court made the limited observation that the amendment is not intended to affect many anti-discrimination laws protecting nonsuspect classes. In our view that does not resolve the issue. In any event, even if, as we doubt, homosexuals could find some safe harbor in laws of general application, we cannot accept the view that Amendment 2's prohibition on specific legal protections does no more than deprive homosexuals of special rights. To the contrary, the amendment imposes a special disability upon those persons alone. Homosexuals are forbidden the safeguards that others enjoy or may seek without constraint. They can obtain specific protection against discrimination only by enlisting the citizenry of Colorado to amend the State Constitution or perhaps, on the State's view, by trying to pass helpful laws of general applicability. This is so no matter how local or discrete the harm, no matter how public and widespread the injury. We find nothing special in the protections Amendment 2 withholds. These are protections taken for granted by most people either because they already have them or do not need them; these are protections against exclusion from an almost limitless number of transactions and endeavors that constitute ordinary civic life in a free society.

III. The Fourteenth Amendment's promise that no person shall be denied the equal protection of the laws must coexist with the practical necessity that most legislation classifies for one purpose or another, with resulting disadvantage to various groups or persons. We have attempted to reconcile the principle with the reality by stating that, if a law neither burdens a fundamental right nor targets a suspect class, we will uphold the legislative classification so long as it bears a rational relation to some legitimate end.

Amendment 2 fails, indeed defies, even this conventional inquiry. First, the amendment has the peculiar property of imposing a broad and undifferentiated disability on a single named group, an exceptional and, as we shall explain, invalid form of legislation. Second, its sheer breadth is so discontinuous with the reasons offered for it that the amendment seems inexplicable by anything but animus toward the class it affects; it lacks a rational relationship to legitimate state interests.

Taking the first point, even in the ordinary equal protection case calling for the most deferential of standards, we insist on knowing the relation between the classification adopted and the object to be attained. The search for the link between classification and objective gives substance to the Equal Protection Clause; it provides guidance and discipline for the legislature, which is entitled to know what sorts of laws it can pass; and it marks the limits of our own authority. In the ordinary case, a law will be sustained if it can be said to advance a legitimate government interest, even if the law seems unwise or works to the disadvantage of a particular group, or if the rationale for it seems tenuous. See New Orleans v. Dukes, 427 U.S. 297, 96 S.Ct. 2513, 49 L.Ed.2d 511 (1976) (tourism benefits justified classification favoring pushcart vendors of certain longevity); Williamson v. Lee Optical of Okla., Inc., 348 U.S. 483, 75 S.Ct. 461, 99 L.Ed. 563 (1955) (assumed health concerns justified law favoring optometrists over opticians); Railway Express Agency, Inc. v. New York, 336 U.S. 106, 69 S.Ct. 463, 93 L.Ed. 533 (1949) (potential traffic hazards justified exemption of vehicles advertising the owner's products from general advertising ban); Kotch v. Board of River Port Pilot Comm'rs for Port of New Orleans, 330 U.S. 552, 67 S.Ct. 910, 91 L.Ed. 1093 (1947) (licensing scheme that disfavored persons unrelated to current river boat pilots justified by possible efficiency and safety benefits of a closely knit pilotage system). The laws challenged in the cases just cited were narrow enough in scope and grounded in a sufficient factual context for us to ascertain some relation between the classification and the purpose it served. By requiring that the classification bear a rational relationship to an independent and legitimate legislative end, we ensure that classifications are not drawn for the purpose of disadvantaging the group burdened by the law.

Amendment 2 confounds this normal process of judicial review. It is at once too narrow and too broad. It identifies persons by a single trait and then denies them protection across the board. The resulting disqualification of a class of persons from the right to seek specific protection from the law is unprecedented in our jurisprudence. The absence of precedent for Amendment 2 is itself instructive; "[d]iscriminations of an unusual character especially suggest careful consideration to determine whether they are obnoxious to the constitutional provision." It is not within our constitutional tradition to enact laws of this sort. Central both to the idea of the rule of law and to our own Constitution's guarantee of equal protection is the principle that government and each of its parts remain open on impartial terms to all who seek its assistance. [Respect] for this principle explains why laws singling out a certain class of citizens for disfavored legal status or general hardships are rare. A law declaring that in general it shall be more difficult for one group of citizens than for all others to seek aid from the government is itself a denial of equal protection of the laws in the most literal sense. [Davis v. Beason, 133 U.S. 333, 10 S.Ct. 299, 33 L.Ed. 637 (1890)], not cited by the parties but relied upon by the dissent, is not evidence that Amendment 2 is within our constitutional tradition, and any reliance upon it as authority for sustaining the amendment is misplaced. In Davis, the Court approved an Idaho territorial statute denying Mormons, polygamists, and advocates of polygamy the right to vote and to hold office because, as the Court construed the statute, it "simply excludes from the privilege of voting, or of holding any office of honor, trust or profit, those who have been convicted of certain offences, and those who advocate a practical resistance to the laws of the Territory and justify and approve the commission of crimes forbidden by it." To the extent Davis held that persons advocating a certain practice may be denied the right to vote, it is no longer good law. To the extent it held that the groups designated in the statute may be deprived of the right to vote because of their status, its ruling could not stand without surviving strict scrutiny, a most doubtful outcome. To the extent Davis held that a convicted felon may be denied the right to vote, its holding is not implicated by our decision and is unexceptionable.

A second and related point is that laws of the kind now before us raise the inevitable inference that the disadvantage imposed is born of animosity toward the class of persons affected. "[I]f the constitutional conception of 'equal protection of the laws' means anything, it must at the very least mean that a bare . . . desire to harm a politically unpopular group cannot constitute a *legitimate* governmental interest." Department of Agriculture v. Moreno, 413 U.S. 528, 534, 93 S.Ct. 2821, 2826, 37 L.Ed.2d 782 (1973). Even laws enacted for broad and ambitious purposes often can be explained by reference to legitimate public policies which justify the incidental disadvantages they impose on certain persons. Amendment 2, however, in making a general announcement that gays and lesbians shall not have any particular protections from the law, inflicts on them immediate, continuing, and real injuries that outrun and belie any legitimate justifications that may be claimed for it. We conclude that, in addition to the far-reaching deficiencies of Amendment 2 that we have noted, the principles it offends, in another sense, are conventional and venerable; a law must bear a rational relationship to a legitimate governmental purpose, and Amendment 2 does not.

The primary rationale the State offers for Amendment 2 is respect for other citizens' freedom of association, and in particular the liberties of landlords or employers who have personal or religious objections to homosexuality. Colorado also cites its interest in conserving resources to fight discrimination against other groups. The breadth of the amendment is so far removed from these particular justifications that we find it impossible to credit them. We cannot say that Amendment 2 is directed to any identifiable legitimate purpose or discrete objective. It is a status-based enactment divorced from any factual context from which we could discern a relationship to legitimate state interests; it is a classification of persons undertaken for its own sake, something the Equal Protection Clause does not permit. [We] must conclude that Amendment 2 classifies homosexuals not to further a proper legislative end but to make them unequal to everyone else. This Colorado cannot do. A State cannot so deem a class of persons a stranger to its laws. Amendment 2 violates the Equal Protection Clause, and the judgment of the Supreme Court of Colorado is affirmed. It is so ordered.

Justice SCALIA, with whom THE CHIEF JUSTICE and Justice THOMAS join, dissenting.

The Court has mistaken a Kulturkampf for a fit of spite. The constitutional amendment before us here is not the manifestation of a "'bare . . . desire to harm'" homosexuals, *ante,* at 1628, but is rather a modest attempt by seemingly tolerant Coloradans to preserve traditional sexual mores against the efforts of a politically powerful minority to revise those mores through use of the laws. That objective, and the means chosen to achieve it, are not only unimpeachable under any constitutional doctrine hitherto pronounced (hence the opinion's heavy reliance upon principles of righteousness rather than judicial holdings); they have been specifically approved by the Congress of the United States and by this Court.

In holding that homosexuality cannot be singled out for disfavorable treatment, the Court contradicts a decision, unchallenged here, pronounced only 10 years ago, see Bowers v. Hardwick, 478 U.S. 186, 106 S.Ct. 2841, 92 L.Ed.2d 140 (1986), and places the prestige of this institution behind the proposition that opposition to homosexuality is as reprehensible as racial or religious bias. Whether it is or not is *precisely* the cultural debate that gave rise to the Colorado constitutional amendment (and to the preferential laws against which the amendment was directed). Since the Constitution of the United States says nothing about this subject, it is left to be resolved by normal democratic means, including the democratic adoption of provisions in state constitutions. This Court has no business imposing upon all Americans the resolution favored by the elite class from which the Members of this institution are selected, pronouncing that "animosity" toward homosexuality, *ante,* at 1628, is evil. I vigorously dissent.

I. Let me first discuss Part II of the Court's opinion, its longest section, which is devoted to rejecting the State's arguments that Amendment 2 "puts gays and lesbians in the same position as all other persons," and "does no more than deny homosexuals special rights." The Court concludes that this reading of Amendment 2's language is "implausible" under the "authoritative construction" given Amendment 2 by the Supreme Court of Colorado.

In reaching this conclusion, the Court considers it unnecessary to decide the validity of the State's argument that Amendment 2 does not deprive homosexuals of the "protection [afforded by] general laws and policies that prohibit arbitrary discrimination in governmental and private settings." *Ante,* at 1626. I agree that we need not resolve that dispute, because the Supreme Court of Colorado has resolved it for us. In the case below, 882 P.2d 1335 (1994), the Colorado court stated: "[I]t is significant to note that Colorado law currently proscribes discrimination against persons who are not suspect classes, including discrimination based on age, § 24-34-402(1)(a), 10A C.R.S. (1994 Supp.); marital or family status, § 24-34-502(1)(a), 10A C.R.S. (1994 Supp.); veterans' status, § 28-3-506, 11B C.R.S. (1989); and for any legal, off-duty conduct such as smoking tobacco, § 24-34-402.5, 10A C. R.S. (1994 Supp.). *Of course Amendment 2 is not intended to have any effect on this legislation, but seeks only to prevent the adoption of antidiscrimination laws intended to protect gays, lesbians, and bisexuals.*" Id., at 1346, n. 9 (emphasis added).

The Court utterly fails to distinguish this portion of the Colorado court's opinion. The clear import of the Colorado court's conclusion that it is not affected is that "general laws and policies that prohibit arbitrary discrimination" would continue to prohibit discrimination on the basis of homosexual conduct as well. This analysis, which is fully in accord with (indeed, follows inescapably from) the text of the constitutional provision, lays to rest such horribles, raised in the course of oral argument, as the prospect that assaults upon homosexuals could not be prosecuted. The amendment prohibits *special treatment* of homosexuals, and nothing more. It would not affect, for example, a requirement of state law that pensions be paid to all retiring state employees with a certain length of service; homosexual employees, as well as others, would be entitled to that benefit. But it would prevent the State or any municipality from making death-benefit payments to the "life partner" of a homosexual when it does not make such payments to the long-time roommate of a nonhomosexual employee. Or again, it does not affect the requirement of the State's general insurance laws that customers be afforded coverage without discrimination unrelated to anticipated risk. Thus, homosexuals could not be denied coverage, or charged a greater premium, with respect to auto collision insurance; but neither the State nor any municipality could require that distinctive health insurance risks associated with homosexuality (if there are any) be ignored.

Despite all of its hand wringing about the potential effect of Amendment 2 on general antidiscrimination laws, the Court's opinion ultimately does not dispute all this, but assumes it to be true. See *ante,* at 1626. The only denial of equal treatment it contends homosexuals have suffered is this: They may not obtain *preferential* treatment without amending the State Constitution. That is to say, the principle underlying the Court's opinion is that one who is accorded equal treatment under the laws, but cannot as readily as others obtain *preferential* treatment under the laws, has been denied equal protection of the laws. If merely stating this alleged "equal protection" violation does not suffice to refute it, our constitutional jurisprudence has achieved terminal silliness.

The central thesis of the Court's reasoning is that any group is denied equal protection when, to obtain advantage (or, presumably, to avoid disadvantage), it must have recourse to a more general and hence more difficult level of political decisionmaking than others. The world has never heard of such a principle, which is why the Court's opinion is so long on emotive utterance and so short on relevant legal citation. And it seems to me most unlikely that any multilevel democracy can function under such a principle. For *whenever* a disadvantage is imposed, or conferral of a benefit is prohibited, at one of the higher levels of democratic decisionmaking (*i.e.,* by the state legislature rather than local government, or by the people at large in the state constitution rather than the legislature), the affected group has (under this theory) been denied equal protection. To take the simplest of examples, consider a state law prohibiting the award of municipal contracts to relatives of mayors or city councilmen. Once such a law is passed, the group composed of such relatives must, in order to get the benefit of city contracts, persuade the state legislature — unlike all other citizens, who need only persuade the municipality. It is ridiculous to consider this a denial of equal protection, which is why the Court's theory is unheard of.

The Court might reply that the example I have given is *not* a denial of equal protection only because the same "rational basis" (avoidance of corruption) which renders constitutional the *substantive discrimination* against relatives (*i.e.,* the fact that they alone cannot obtain city contracts) also automatically suffices to sustain what might be called the *electoral-procedural discrimination* against them (*i.e.,*the fact that they must go to the state level to get this changed). This is of course a perfectly reasonable response, and would explain why "electoral-procedural discrimination" has not hitherto been heard of: A law that is valid in its substance is automatically valid in its level of enactment. But the Court cannot afford to make this argument, for as I shall discuss next, there is no doubt of a rational basis for the substance of the prohibition at issue here. The Court's entire novel theory rests upon the proposition that there is something *special* — something that cannot be justified by normal "rational basis" analysis — in making a disadvantaged group (or a nonpreferred group) resort to a higher decisionmaking level. That proposition finds no support in law or logic.

II. I turn next to whether there was a legitimate rational basis for the substance of the constitutional amendment — for the prohibition of special protection for homosexuals. It is unsurprising that the Court avoids discussion of this question, since the answer is so obviously yes. The case most relevant to the issue before us today is not even mentioned in the Court's opinion: In Bowers v. Hardwick, 478 U.S. 186, 106 S.Ct. 2841, 92 L.Ed.2d 140 (1986), we held that the Constitution does not prohibit what virtually all States had done from the founding of the Republic until very recent years — making homosexual conduct a crime. That holding is unassailable, except by those who think that the Constitution changes to suit current fashions. But in any event it is a given in the present case: Respondents' briefs did not urge overruling Bowers, and at oral argument respondents' counsel expressly disavowed any intent to seek such overruling. If it is constitutionally permissible for a State to make homosexual conduct criminal, surely it is constitutionally permissible for a State to enact other laws merely *disfavoring* homosexual conduct. [And] *a fortiori* it is constitutionally permissible for a State to adopt a provision *not even* disfavoring homosexual conduct, but merely prohibiting all levels of state government from bestowing *special protections* upon homosexual conduct. Respondents (who, unlike the Court, cannot afford the luxury of ignoring inconvenient precedent) counter Bowers with the argument that a greater-includes-the-lesser rationale cannot justify Amendment 2's application to individuals who do not engage in homosexual acts, but are merely of homosexual "orientation."

But assuming that, in Amendment 2, a person of homosexual "orientation" is someone who does not engage in homosexual conduct but merely has a tendency or desire to do so, Bowers still suffices to establish a rational basis for the provision. If it is rational to criminalize the conduct, surely it is rational to deny special favor and protection to those with a self-avowed tendency or desire to engage in the conduct. Indeed, where criminal sanctions are not involved, homosexual "orientation" is an acceptable stand-in for homosexual conduct. A State "does not violate the Equal Protection Clause merely because the classifications made by its laws are imperfect," Dandridge v. Williams, 397 U.S. 471, 485, 90 S.Ct. 1153, 1161, 25 L.Ed.2d 491 (1970). Just as a policy barring the hiring of methadone users as transit employees does not violate equal protection simply because *some* methadone users pose no threat to passenger safety, see New York City Transit Authority v. Beazer, 440 U.S. 568, 99 S.Ct. 1355, 59 L.Ed.2d 587 (1979), and just as a mandatory retirement age of 50 for police officers does not violate equal protection even though it prematurely ends the careers of many policemen over 50 who still have the capacity to do the job, see Massachusetts Bd. of Retirement v. Murgia, 427 U.S. 307, 96 S.Ct. 2562, 49 L.Ed.2d 520 (1976) *(per curiam),* Amendment 2 is not constitutionally invalid simply because it could have been drawn more precisely so as to withdraw special antidiscrimination protections only from those of homosexual "orientation" who actually engage in homosexual conduct.

Moreover, even if the provision regarding homosexual "orientation" *were* invalid, respondents' challenge to Amendment 2 — which is a facial challenge — must fail. "A facial challenge to a legislative Act is, of course, the most difficult challenge to mount successfully, since the challenger must establish that no set of circumstances exists under which the Act would be valid." It would not be enough for respondents to establish (if they could) that Amendment 2 is unconstitutional as applied to those of homosexual "orientation"; since, under Bowers, Amendment 2 is unquestionably constitutional as applied to those who engage in homosexual conduct, the facial challenge cannot succeed.

III. The foregoing suffices to establish what the Court's failure to cite any case remotely in point would lead one to suspect: No principle set forth in the Constitution, nor even any imagined by this Court in the past 200 years, prohibits what Colorado has done here. But the case for Colorado is much stronger than that. What it has done is not only unprohibited, but eminently reasonable, with close, congressionally approved precedent in earlier constitutional practice.

First, as to its eminent reasonableness. The Court's opinion contains grim, disapproving hints that Coloradans have been guilty of "animus" or "animosity" toward homosexuality, as though that has been established as un-American. Of course it is our moral heritage that one should not hate any human being or class of human beings. But I had thought that one could consider certain conduct reprehensible — murder, for example, or polygamy, or cruelty to animals — and could exhibit even "animus" toward such conduct. Surely that is the only sort of "animus" at issue here: moral disapproval of homosexual conduct, the same sort of moral disapproval that produced the centuries-old criminal laws that we held constitutional in Bowers.

But though Coloradans are, as I say, *entitled* to be hostile toward homosexual conduct, the fact is that the degree of hostility reflected by Amendment 2 is the smallest conceivable. The Court's portrayal of Coloradans as a society fallen victim to pointless, hate-filled "gay-bashing" is so false as to be comical. Colorado not only is one of the 25 States that have repealed their antisodomy laws, but was among the first to do so. See 1971 Colo. Sess. Laws, ch. 121, § 1. But the society that eliminates criminal punishment for homosexual acts does not necessarily abandon the view that homosexuality is morally wrong and socially harmful; often, abolition simply reflects the view that enforcement of such criminal laws involves unseemly intrusion into the intimate lives of citizens.

There is a problem, however, which arises when criminal sanction of homosexuality is eliminated but moral and social disapprobation of homosexuality is meant to be retained. The Court cannot be unaware of that problem; it is evident in many cities of the country, and occasionally bubbles to the surface of the news, in heated political disputes over such matters as the introduction into local schools of books teaching that homosexuality is an optional and fully acceptable "alternative life style." The problem (a problem, that is, for those who wish to retain social disapprobation of homosexuality) is that, because those who engage in homosexual conduct tend to reside in disproportionate numbers in certain communities, see Record, Exh. MMM, have high disposable income, see *ibid.;* App. 254 (affidavit of Prof. James Hunter), and, of course, care about homosexual-rights issues much more ardently than the public at large, they possess political power much greater than their numbers, both locally and statewide. Quite understandably, they devote this political power to achieving not merely a grudging social toleration, but full social acceptance, of homosexuality. By the time Coloradans were asked to vote on Amendment 2, their exposure to homosexuals' quest for social endorsement was not limited to newspaper accounts of happenings in places such as New York, Los Angeles, San Francisco, and Key West. Three Colorado cities — Aspen, Boulder, and Denver — had enacted ordinances that listed "sexual orientation" as an impermissible ground for discrimination, equating the moral disapproval of homosexual conduct with racial and religious bigotry. The phenomenon had even appeared statewide: The Governor of Colorado had signed an executive order pronouncing that "in the State of Colorado we recognize the diversity in our pluralistic society and strive to bring an end to discrimination in any form," and directing state agency-heads to "ensure non-discrimination" in hiring and promotion based on, among other things, "sexual orientation." I do not mean to be critical of these legislative successes; homosexuals are as entitled to use the legal system for reinforcement of their moral sentiments as is the rest of society. But they are subject to being countered by lawful, democratic countermeasures as well.

That is where Amendment 2 came in. It sought to counter both the geographic concentration and the disproportionate political power of homosexuals by (1) resolving the controversy at the statewide level, and (2) making the election a single-issue contest for both sides. It put directly, to all the citizens of the State, the question: Should homosexuality be given special protection? They answered no. The Court today asserts that this most democratic of procedures is unconstitutional. Lacking any cases to establish that facially absurd proposition, it simply asserts that it *must* be unconstitutional, because it has never happened before. What the Court says is even demonstrably false at the constitutional level. The Eighteenth Amendment to the Federal Constitution, for example, deprived those who drank alcohol not only of the power to alter the policy of prohibition *locally* or through *state legislation,* but even of the power to alter it through *state constitutional amendment* or *federal legislation.* The Establishment Clause of the First Amendment prevents theocrats from having their way by converting their fellow citizens at the local, state, or federal statutory level; as does the Republican Form of Government Clause prevent monarchists.

But there is a much closer analogy, one that involves precisely the effort by the majority of citizens to preserve its view of sexual morality statewide, against the efforts of a geographically concentrated and politically powerful minority to undermine it. The Constitutions of the States of Arizona, Idaho, New Mexico, Oklahoma, and Utah *to this day* contain provisions stating that polygamy is "forever prohibited." The United States Congress, by the way, *required* the inclusion of these antipolygamy provisions in the Constitutions of Arizona, New Mexico, Oklahoma, and Utah, as a condition of their admission to statehood. Thus, this "singling out" of the sexual practices of a single group for statewide, democratic vote — so utterly alien to our constitutional system, the Court would have us believe — has not only happened, but has received the explicit approval of the United States Congress.

I cannot say that this Court has explicitly approved any of these state constitutional provisions; but it has approved a territorial statutory provision that went even further, depriving polygamists of the ability even to achieve a constitutional amendment, by depriving them of the power to vote. But the proposition that polygamy can be criminalized, and those engaging in that crime deprived of the vote, remains good law. See Richardson v. Ramirez, 418 U.S. 24, 53, 94 S.Ct. 2655, 2670, 41 L.Ed.2d 551 (1974). Beason rejected the argument that "such discrimination is a denial of the equal protection of the laws." Brief for Appellant in *Davis v. Beason,* O.T. 1889, No. 1261, p. 41. Among the Justices joining in that rejection were the two whose views in other cases the Court today treats as equal protection lodestars — Justice Harlan, who was to proclaim in Plessy v. Ferguson, 163 U.S. 537, 559, 16 S.Ct. 1138, 1146, 41 L.Ed. 256 (1896) (dissenting opinion), that the Constitution "neither knows nor tolerates classes among citizens," quoted *ante,* at 1623, and Justice Bradley, who had earlier declared that "class legislation . . . [is] obnoxious to the prohibitions of the Fourteenth Amendment," Civil Rights Cases, 109 U.S. 3, 24, 3 S.Ct. 18, 30, 27 L.Ed. 835 (1883), quoted *ante,* at 1629.

This Court cited Beason with approval as recently as 1993, in an opinion authored by the same Justice who writes for the Court today. That opinion said: "[A]dverse impact will not always lead to a finding of impermissible targeting. For example, a social harm may have been a legitimate concern of government for reasons quite apart from discrimination. . . . See, *e.g.,* . . . Davis v. Beason, 133 U.S. 333 [10 S.Ct. 299, 33 L.Ed. 637] (1890)." Church of Lukumi Babalu Aye, Inc. v. Hialeah, 508 U.S. 520, 535, 113 S.Ct. 2217, 2228, 124 L.Ed.2d 472 (1993). It remains to be explained how § 501 of the Idaho

Revised Statutes was not an "impermissible targeting" of polygamists, but (the much more mild) Amendment 2 is an "impermissible targeting" of homosexuals. Has the Court concluded that the perceived social harm of polygamy is a "legitimate concern of government," and the perceived social harm of homosexuality is not?

IV. I strongly suspect that the answer to the last question is yes, which leads me to the last point I wish to make: The Court today, announcing that Amendment 2 "defies . . . conventional [constitutional] inquiry," *ante,* at 1627, and "confounds [the] normal process of judicial review," *ante,* at 1628, employs a constitutional theory heretofore unknown to frustrate Colorado's reasonable effort to preserve traditional American moral values. [To] suggest, for example, that this constitutional amendment springs from nothing more than "'a bare . . . desire to harm a politically unpopular group,'" *ante,* at 1628, quoting Department of Agriculture v. Moreno, 413 U.S. 528, 534, 93 S.Ct. 2821, 2826, 37 L.Ed.2d 782 (1973), is nothing short of insulting. (It is also nothing short of preposterous to call "politically unpopular" a group which enjoys enormous influence in American media and politics, and which, as the trial court here noted, though composing no more than 4% of the population had the support of 46% of the voters on Amendment 2, see App. to Pet. for Cert. C-18.)

When the Court takes sides in the culture wars, it tends to be with the knights rather than the villans — and more specifically with the Templars, reflecting the views and values of the lawyer class from which the Court's Members are drawn. How that class feels about homosexuality will be evident to anyone who wishes to interview job applicants at virtually any of the Nation's law schools. The interviewer may refuse to offer a job because the applicant is a Republican; because he is an adulterer; because he went to the wrong prep school or belongs to the wrong country club; because he eats snails; because he is a womanizer; because she wears real-animal fur; or even because he hates the Chicago Cubs. But if the interviewer should wish not to be an associate or partner of an applicant because he disapproves of the applicant's homosexuality, *then* he will have violated the pledge which the Association of American Law Schools requires all its member schools to exact from job interviewers: "assurance of the employer's willingness" to hire homosexuals. Bylaws of the Association of American Law Schools, Inc. § 6-4(b); Executive Committee Regulations of the Association of American Law Schools § 6.19, in 1995 Handbook, Association of American Law Schools. This law-school view of what "prejudices" must be stamped out may be contrasted with the more plebeian attitudes that apparently still prevail in the United States Congress, which has been unresponsive to repeated attempts to extend to homosexuals the protections of federal civil rights laws. . .

Today's opinion has no foundation in American constitutional law, and barely pretends to. The people of Colorado have adopted an entirely reasonable provision which does not even disfavor homosexuals in any substantive sense, but merely denies them preferential treatment. Amendment 2 is designed to prevent piecemeal deterioration of the sexual morality favored by a majority of Coloradans, and is not only an appropriate means to that legitimate end, but a means that Americans have employed before. Striking it down is an act, not of judicial judgment, but of political will. I dissent.

———

a. COMMENTS CONCERNING *ROMER* AND SEXUAL ORIENTATION

How does the Court's opinion in *Lawrence v. Texas* affect the test applied in *Romer*? Recall that Justice O'Conner's concurrence in *Lawrence* was based upon the equal protection clause. Her vote was a sixth vote; a majority of five Justices appeared to support their decision based upon a substantive due process denial of a fundament right, thus apparently applying strict scrutiny in striking the Texas statute. Justice O'Conner's concurrence applied the "bite" of the *Romer* rational purpose test: "[We] have consistently held [that] some objectives, such as 'a bare . . . desire to harm a politically unpopular group,' are not legitimate state interests. When a law exhibits such a desire to harm a politically unpopular group, we have applied a more searching from of rational basis review to strike down such laws under the Equal Protection Clause."

Does this mean that homosexuals can receive close scrutiny review only when denied "a realm of personal liberty which the government may not enter," yet receive rational purpose review as an equal protection classification? Or, will *Lawrence* support the inclusion of homosexuals as a class for "heightened" equal protection review as well? Would it be inconsistent for the Court to not so hold? Note that Justice Scalia makes this argument in comparing *Romer* to the now overruled *Bowers v. Hardwick*: "In holding that homosexuality cannot be singled out for disfavorable treatment, the Court contradicts a decision, unchallenged here, pronounced only 10 years ago, see Bowers v. Hardwick, 478 U.S. 186, 106 S.Ct. 2841, 92 L.Ed.2d 140 (1986), and places the prestige of this institution behind the proposition that opposition to homosexuality is as reprehensible as racial or religious bias." Can this argument now be turned around on Justice Scalia?

UNITED STATES v. WINDSOR
570 U. S. ____ (2013)

JUSTICE KENNEDY delivered the opinion of the Court.

Two women then resident in New York were married in a lawful ceremony in Ontario, Canada, in 2007. Edith Windsor and Thea Spyer returned to their home in New York City. When Spyer died in 2009, she left her entire state to Windsor. Windsor sought to claim the estate tax exemption for surviving spouses. She was barred from doing so, however, by a federal law, the Defense of Marriage Act, which excludes a same-sex partner from the definition of "spouse" as that term is used in federal statutes. Windsor paid the taxes but filed suit to challenge the constitutionality of this provision. The United States District Court and the Court of Appeals ruled that this portion of the statute is unconstitutional and ordered the United States to pay Windsor a refund. This Court granted certiorari and now affirms the judgment in Windsor's favor.

I

In 1996, as some States were beginning to consider the concept of same-sex marriage, see, *e.g.*, *Baehr* v. *Lewin*, 74 Haw. 530, 852 P. 2d 44 (1993), and before any State had acted to permit it, Congress enacted the Defense of Marriage Act (DOMA), 110 Stat. 2419. DOMA contains two operative sections: Section 2, which has not been challenged here, allows States to refuse to recognize same-sex marriages performed under the laws of other States. See 28 U. S. C. §1738C.

Section 3 is at issue here. It amends the Dictionary Act in Title 1, §7, of the United States Code to provide a federal definition of "marriage" and "spouse." Section 3 of DOMA provides as follows:

> "In determining the meaning of any Act of Congress, or of any ruling, regulation, or interpretation of the various administrative bureaus and agencies of the United States, the word 'marriage' means only a legal union between one man and one woman as husband and wife, and the word 'spouse' refers only to a person of the opposite sex who is a husband or a wife." 1 U. S. C. §7.

The definitional provision does not by its terms forbid States from enacting laws permitting same-sex marriages or civil unions or providing state benefits to residents in that status. The enactment's comprehensive definition of marriage for purposes of all federal statutes and other regulations or directives covered by its terms, however, does control over 1,000 federal laws in which marital or spousal status is addressed as a matter of federal law. See GAO, D. Shah, Defense of Marriage Act: Update to Prior Report 1 (GAO–04–353R, 2004).

Edith Windsor and Thea Spyer met in New York City in 1963 and began a long-term relationship. Windsor and Spyer registered as domestic partners when New York City gave that right to same-sex couples in 1993. Concerned about Spyer's health, the couple made the 2007 trip to Canada for their marriage, but they continued to reside in New York City. The State of New York deems their Ontario marriage to be a valid one. See 699 F. 3d 169, 177–178 (CA2 2012).

Spyer died in February 2009, and left her entire estate to Windsor. Because DOMA denies federal recognition to same-sex spouses, Windsor did not qualify for the marital exemption from the federal estate tax, which excludes from taxation "any interest in property which passes or has passed from the decedent to his surviving spouse." 26 U. S. C. §2056(a). Windsor paid $363,053 in estate taxes and sought a refund. The Internal Revenue Service denied the refund, concluding that, under DOMA, Windsor was not a "surviving spouse." Windsor commenced this refund suit in the United States District Court for the Southern District of New York. She contended that DOMA violates the guarantee of equal protection, as applied to the Federal Government through the Fifth Amendment.

While the tax refund suit was pending, the Attorney General of the United States notified the Speaker of the House of Representatives, pursuant to 28 U. S. C. §530D, that the Department of Justice would no longer defend the constitutionality of DOMA's §3. Noting that "the Department has previously defended DOMA against . . . challenges involving legally married same-sex couples," App. 184, the Attorney General informed Congress that "the President has concluded that given a number of factors, including a documented history of discrimination, classifications based on sexual orientation should be subject to a heightened standard of scrutiny." *Id.*, at 191. The Department of Justice has submitted many §530D letters over the years refusing to defend laws it deems unconstitutional, when, for instance, a federal court has rejected the Government's defense of a statute and has issued a judgment against it. This case is unusual, however, because the §530D letter was not preceded by an adverse judgment. The letter instead reflected the Executive's own conclusion, relying on a definition still being debated and considered in the courts, that heightened equal protection scrutiny should apply to laws that classify on the basis of sexual orientation.

Although "the President . . . instructed the Department not to defend the statute in *Windsor*," he also decided "that Section 3 will continue to be enforced by the Executive Branch" and that the United States had an "interest in providing Congress a full and fair opportunity to participate in the litigation of those cases." *Id.,* at 191–193. The stated rationale for this dual-track procedure (determination of unconstitutionality coupled with ongoing enforcement) was to "recogniz[e] the judiciary as the final arbiter of the constitutional claims raised." *Id.,* at 192.

In response to the notice from the Attorney General, the Bipartisan Legal Advisory Group (BLAG) of the House of Representatives voted to intervene in the litigation to defend the constitutionality of §3 of DOMA. The Department of Justice did not oppose limited intervention by BLAG. The District Court denied BLAG's motion to enter the suit as of right, on the rationale that the United States already was represented by the Department of Justice. The District Court, however, did grant intervention by BLAG as an interested party. See Fed. Rule Civ. Proc. 24(a)(2).

On the merits of the tax refund suit, the District Court ruled against the United States. It held that §3 of DOMA is unconstitutional and ordered the Treasury to refund the tax with interest. Both the Justice Department and BLAG filed notices of appeal, and the Solicitor General filed a petition for certiorari before judgment. Before this Court acted on the petition, the Court of Appeals for the Second Circuit affirmed the District Court's judgment. It applied heightened scrutiny to classifications based on sexual orientation, as both the Department and Windsor had urged. The United States has not complied with the judgment. Windsor has not received her refund, and the Executive Branch continues to enforce §3 of DOMA.

In granting certiorari on the question of the constitutionality of §3 of DOMA, the Court requested argument on two additional questions: whether the United States' agreement with Windsor's legal position precludes further review and whether BLAG has standing to appeal the case. All parties agree that the Court has jurisdiction to decide this case; and, with the case in that framework, the Court appointed Professor Vicki Jackson as *amicus curiae* to argue the position that the Court lacks jurisdiction to hear the dispute. 568 U. S. ___ (2012). She has ably discharged her duties.

[III]

When at first Windsor and Spyer longed to marry, neither New York nor any other State granted them that right. After waiting some years, in 2007 they traveled to Ontario to be married there. It seems fair to conclude that, until recent years, many citizens had not even considered the possibility that two persons of the same sex might aspire to occupy the same status and dignity as that of a man and woman in lawful marriage. For marriage between a man and a woman no doubt had been thought of by most people as essential to the very definition of that term and to its role and function throughout the history of civilization. That belief, for many who long have held it, became even more urgent, more cherished when challenged. For others, however, came the beginnings of a new perspective, a new insight. Accordingly some States concluded that same-sex marriage ought to be given recognition and validity in the law for those same-sex couples who wish to define themselves by their commitment to each other. The limitation of lawful marriage to heterosexual couples, which for centuries had been deemed both necessary and fundamental, came to be seen in New York and certain other States as an unjust exclusion.

Slowly at first and then in rapid course, the laws of New York came to acknowledge the urgency of this issue for same-sex couples who wanted to affirm their commitment to one another before their children, their family, their friends, and their community. And so New York recognized same-sex marriages performed elsewhere; and then it later amended its own marriage laws to permit same sex marriage. New York, in common with, as of this writing, 11 other States and the District of Columbia, decided that same-sex couples should have the right to marry and so live with pride in themselves and their union and in a status of equality with all other married persons. After a statewide deliberative process that enabled its citizens to discuss and weigh arguments for and against same-sex marriage, New York acted to enlarge the definition of marriage to correct what its citizens and elected representatives perceived to be an injustice that they had not earlier known or understood. See Marriage Equality Act, 2011 N. Y. Laws 749 (codified at N. Y. Dom. Rel. Law Ann. §§10–a, 10–b, 13 (West 2013)).

Against this background of lawful same-sex marriage in some States, the design, purpose, and effect of DOMA should be considered as the beginning point in deciding whether it is valid under the Constitution. By history and tradition the definition and regulation of marriage, as will be discussed in more detail, has been treated as being within the authority and realm of the separate States. Yet it is further established that Congress, in enacting discrete statutes, can make determinations that bear on marital rights and privileges.

[Though] these discrete examples establish the constitutionality of limited federal laws that regulate the meaning of marriage in order to further federal policy, DOMA has a far greater reach; for it enacts a directive applicable to over 1,000 federal statutes and the whole realm of federal regulations. And its operation is directed to a class of persons that the laws of New York, and of 11 other States, have sought to protect.

[In] order to assess the validity of that intervention it is necessary to discuss the extent of the state power and authority over marriage as a matter of history and tradition. State laws defining and regulating marriage, of course, must respect the constitutional rights of persons, see, *e.g., Loving* v. *Virginia*, 388 U. S. 1 (1967); but, subject to those guarantees, "regulation of domestic relations" is "an area that has long been regarded as a virtually exclusive province of the States." *Sosna* v. *Iowa*, 419 U. S. 393, 404 (1975).

The recognition of civil marriages is central to state domestic relations law applicable to its residents and citizens.

[Against] this background DOMA rejects the long established precept that the incidents, benefits, and obligations of marriage are uniform for all married couples within each State, though they may vary, subject to constitutional guarantees, from one State to the next. Despite these considerations, it is unnecessary to decide whether this federal intrusion on state power is a violation of the Constitution because it disrupts the federal balance. The State's power in defining the marital relation is of central relevance in this case quite apart from principles of federalism. Here the State's decision to give this class of persons the right to marry conferred upon them a dignity and status of immense import. When the State used its historic and essential authority to define the marital relation in this way, its role and its power in making the decision enhanced the recognition, dignity, and protection of the class in their own community. DOMA, because of its reach and extent, departs from this history and tradition of reliance on state law to define marriage. "'[D]iscriminations of an unusual character especially suggest careful consideration to determine whether they are obnoxious to the constitutional provision.'" *Romer* v. *Evans*, 517 U. S. 620, 633 (1996) (quoting *Louisville Gas & Elec. Co.* v. *Coleman*, 277 U. S. 32, 37–38 (1928)).

The Federal Government uses this state-defined class for the opposite purpose—to impose restrictions and disabilities. That result requires this Court now to address whether the resulting injury and indignity is a deprivation of an essential part of the liberty protected by the Fifth Amendment. What the State of New York treats as alike the federal law deems unlike by a law designed to injure the same class the State seeks to protect.

In acting first to recognize and then to allow same-sex marriages, New York was responding "to the initiative of those who [sought] a voice in shaping the destiny of their own times." *Bond* v. *United States*, 564 U. S. ___, ___ (2011) (slip op., at 9). These actions were without doubt a proper exercise of its sovereign authority within our federal system, all in the way that the Framers of the Constitution intended. The dynamics of state government in the federal system are to allow the formation of consensus respecting the way the members of a discrete community treat each other in their daily contact and constant interaction with each other.

The States' interest in defining and regulating the marital relation, subject to constitutional guarantees, stems from the understanding that marriage is more than a routine classification for purposes of certain statutory benefits. Private, consensual sexual intimacy between two adult persons of the same sex may not be punished by the State, and it can form "but one element in a personal bond that is more enduring." *Lawrence* v. *Texas*, 539 U. S. 558, 567 (2003). By its recognition of the validity of same-sex marriages performed in other jurisdictions and then by authorizing same-sex unions and same-sex marriages, New York sought to give further protection and dignity to that bond. For same-sex couples who wished to be married, the State acted to give their lawful conduct a lawful status. This status is a far-reaching legal acknowledgment of the intimate relationship between two people, a relationship deemed by the State worthy of dignity in the community equal with all other marriages. It reflects both the community's considered perspective on the historical roots of the institution of marriage and its evolving understanding of the meaning of equality.

IV

DOMA seeks to injure the very class New York seeks to protect. By doing so it violates basic due process and equal protection principles applicable to the Federal Government. See U. S. Const., Amdt. 5; *Bolling* v. *Sharpe*, 347 U. S. 497 (1954). The Constitution's guarantee of equality "must at the very least mean that a bare congressional desire to harm a politically unpopular group cannot" justify disparate treatment of that group. *Department of Agriculture* v. *Moreno*, 413 U. S. 528, 534–535 (1973). In determining whether a law is motive by an improper animus or purpose,"'[d]iscriminations of an unusual character'" especially require careful consideration. *Supra,* at 19 (quoting *Romer, supra,* at 633). DOMA cannot survive under these principles. The responsibility of the States for the regulation of domestic relations is an important indicator of the substantial societal impact the State's classifications have in the daily lives and customs of its people. DOMA's unusual deviation from the usual tradition of recognizing and accepting state definitions of marriage here operates to deprive same-sex couples of the benefits and responsibilities that come with the federal recognition of their marriages. This is strong evidence of a law having the purpose and effect of disapproval of that class. The avowed purpose and practical effect of the law here in question are to impose a disadvantage, a separate status, and so a stigma upon all who enter into same-sex marriages made lawful by the unquestioned authority of the States.

The history of DOMA's enactment and its own text demonstrate that interference with the equal dignity of same-sex marriages, a dignity conferred by the States in the exercise of their sovereign power, was more than an incidental effect of the federal statute. It was its essence. The House Report announced its conclusion that "it is both appropriate and necessary for Congress to do what it can to defend the institution of traditional heterosexual marriage. . . . H. R. 3396 is appropriately entitled the 'Defense of Marriage Act.' The effort to redefine 'marriage' to extend to homosexual couples is a truly radical proposal that would fundamentally alter the institution of marriage." H. R. Rep. No. 104–664, pp. 12–13 (1996). The House concluded that DOMA expresses "both moral disapproval of homosexuality, and a moral conviction that heterosexuality better comports with traditional (especially Judeo-Christian) morality." *Id.,* at 16 (footnote deleted). The stated purpose of the law was to promote an "interest in protecting the traditional moral teachings reflected in heterosexual-only marriage laws." *Ibid.* Were there any doubt of this far-reaching purpose, the title of the Act confirms it: The Defense of Marriage.

The arguments put forward by BLAG are just as candid about the congressional purpose to influence or interfere with state sovereign choices about who may be married. As the title and dynamics of the bill indicate, its purpose is to discourage enactment of state same-sex marriage laws and to restrict the freedom and choice of couples married under those laws if they are enacted. The congressional goal was "to put a thumb on the scales and influence a state's decision as to how to shape its own marriage laws." *Massachusetts,* 682 F. 3d, at 12–13. The Act's demonstrated purpose is to ensure that if any State decides to recognize same-sex marriages, those unions will be treated as second-class marriages for purposes of federal law. This raises a most serious question under the Constitution's Fifth Amendment.

DOMA's operation in practice confirms this purpose. When New York adopted a law to permit same-sex marriage, it sought to eliminate inequality; but DOMA frustrates that objective through a system-wide enactment with no identified connection to any particular area of federal law. DOMA writes inequality into the entire United States Code. The particular case at hand concerns the estate tax, but DOMA is more than a simple determination of what should or should not be allowed as an estate tax refund. Among the over 1,000 statutes and numerous federal regulations that DOMA controls are laws pertaining to Social Security, housing, taxes, criminal sanctions, copyright, and veterans' benefits.

DOMA's principal effect is to identify a subset of state sanctioned marriages and make them unequal. The principal purpose is to impose inequality, not for other reasons like governmental efficiency. Responsibilities, as well as rights, enhance the dignity and integrity of the person. And DOMA contrives to deprive some couples married under the laws of their State, but not other couples, of both rights and responsibilities. By creating two contradictory marriage regimes within the same State, DOMA forces same-sex couples to live as married for the purpose of state law but unmarried for the purpose of federal law, thus diminishing the stability and predictability of basic personal relations the State has found it proper to acknowledge and protect. By this dynamic DOMA undermines both the public and private significance of state sanctioned same-sex marriages; for it tells those couples, and all the world, that their otherwise valid marriages are unworthy of federal recognition. This places same-sex couples in an unstable position of being in a second-tier marriage. The differentiation demeans the couple, whose moral and sexual choices the Constitution protects, see *Lawrence,* 539 U. S. 558, and whose relationship the State has sought to dignify. And it humiliates tens of thousands of children now being raised by same-sex couples. The law in question makes it even more difficult for the children to understand the integrity and closeness of their own family and its concord with other families in their community and in their daily lives.

Under DOMA, same-sex married couples have their lives burdened, by reason of government decree, in visible and public ways. By its great reach, DOMA touches many aspects of married and family life, from the mundane to the profound. It prevents same-sex married couples from obtaining government healthcare benefits they would otherwise receive. See 5 U. S. C. §§8901(5), 8905. It deprives them of the Bankruptcy Code's special protections for domestic-support obligations. See 11 U. S. C. §§101(14A), 507(a)(1)(A), 523(a)(5), 523(a)(15). It forces them to follow a complicated procedure to file their state and federal taxes jointly. Technical Bulletin TB–55, 2010 Vt. Tax LEXIS 6 (Oct. 7, 2010); Brief for Federalism Scholars as *Amici Curiae* 34. It prohibits them from being buried together in veterans' cemeteries. National Cemetery Administration Directive 3210/1, p. 37 (June 4, 2008).

For certain married couples, DOMA's unequal effects are even more serious. The federal penal code makes it a crime to "assaul[t], kidna[p], or murde[r] . . . a member of the immediate family" of "a United States official, a United States judge, [or] a Federal law enforcement officer," 18 U. S. C. §115(a)(1)(A), with the intent to influence or retaliate against that official, §115(a)(1). Although a "spouse" qualifies as a member of the officer's "immediate family," §115(c)(2), DOMA makes this protection inapplicable to same-sex spouses.

DOMA also brings financial harm to children of same sex couples. It raises the cost of health care for families by taxing health benefits provided by employers to their workers' same-sex spouses. See 26 U. S. C. §106; Treas.Reg. §1.106–1, 26 CFR §1.106–1 (2012); IRS Private Letter Ruling 9850011 (Sept. 10, 1998). And it denies or reduces benefits allowed to families upon the loss of a spouse and parent, benefits that are an integral part of family security.

[DOMA] divests married same-sex couples of the duties and responsibilities that are an essential part of married life and that they in most cases would be honored to accept were DOMA not in force. For instance, because it is expected that spouses will support each other as they pursue educational opportunities, federal law takes into consideration a spouse's income in calculating a student's federal financial aid eligibility. See 20 U. S. C. §1087nn(b). Same-sex married couples are exempt from this requirement.

[***]

The power the Constitution grants it also restrains. And though Congress has great authority to design laws tofit its own conception of sound national policy, it cannot deny the liberty protected by the Due Process Clause of the Fifth Amendment.

What has been explained to this point should more than suffice to establish that the principal purpose and the necessary effect of this law are to demean those persons who are in a lawful same-sex marriage. This requires the Court to hold, as it now does, that DOMA is unconstitutional as a deprivation of the liberty of the person protected by the Fifth Amendment of the Constitution.

The liberty protected by the Fifth Amendment's Due Process Clause contains within it the prohibition against denying to any person the equal protection of the laws. See *Bolling*, 347 U. S., at 499–500; *Adarand Constructors, Inc.* v. *Peña*, 515 U. S. 200, 217–218 (1995). While the Fifth Amendment itself withdraws from Government the power to degrade or demean in the way this law does, the equal protection guarantee of the Fourteenth Amendment makes that Fifth Amendment right all the more specific and all the better understood and preserved.

The class to which DOMA directs its restrictions and restraints are those persons who are joined in same-sex marriages made lawful by the State. DOMA singles out a class of persons deemed by a State entitled to recognition and protection to enhance their own liberty. It imposes a disability on the class by refusing to acknowledge a status the State finds to be dignified and proper. DOMA instructs all federal officials, and indeed all persons with whom same-sex couples interact, including their own children, that their marriage is less worthy than the marriages of others. The federal statute is invalid, for no legitimate purpose overcomes the purpose and effect to disparage and to injure those whom the State, by its marriage laws, sought to protect in personhood and dignity. By seeking to displace this protection and treating those persons as living in marriages less respected than others, the federal statute is in violation of the Fifth Amendment. This opinion and its holding are confined to those lawful marriages.

The judgment of the Court of Appeals for the Second Circuit is affirmed.

It is so ordered.

CHIEF JUSTICE ROBERTS, dissenting.

I agree with JUSTICE SCALIA [that] Congress acted constitutionally in passing the Defense of Marriage Act (DOMA). Interests in uniformity and stability am- ply justified Congress's decision to retain the definition of marriage that, at that point, had been adopted by every State in our Nation, and every nation in the world. *Post*, at 19–20 (dissenting opinion).

The majority sees a more sinister motive, pointing out that the Federal Government has generally (though not uniformly) deferred to state definitions of marriage in the past. That is true, of course, but none of those prior state-by-state variations had involved differences over something—as the majority puts it—"thought of by most people as essential to the very definition of [marriage] and to its role and function throughout the history of civilization." *Ante*, at 13. That the Federal Government treated this fundamental question differently than it treated variations over consanguinity or minimum age is hardly surprising—and hardly enough to support a conclusion that the "principal purpose," *ante*, at 22, of the 342 Representatives and 85 Senators who voted for it, and the President who signed it, was a bare desire to harm. Nor do the snip- pets of legislative history and the banal title of the Act to which the majority points suffice to make such a showing. At least without some more convincing evidence that the Act's principal purpose was to codify malice, and that it furthered *no* legitimate government interests, I would not tar the political branches with the brush of bigotry.

But while I disagree with the result to which the majority's analysis leads it in this case, I think it more important to point out that its analysis leads no further. The Court does not have before it, and the logic of its opinion does not decide, the distinct question whether the States, in the exercise of their "historic and essential authority to define the marital relation," *ante*, at 18, may continue to utilize the traditional definition of marriage.

The majority goes out of its way to make this explicit in the penultimate sentence of its opinion. It states that "[t]his opinion and its holding are confined to those lawful marriages," *ante*, at 26—referring to same-sex marriages that a State has already recognized as a result of the local "community's considered perspective on the historical roots of the institution of marriage and its evolving understanding of the meaning of equality." *Ante*, at 20. JUSTICE SCALIA believes this is a "'bald, unreasoned disclaime[r].'" *Post*, at 22. In my view, though, the disclaimer is a logical and necessary consequence of the argument the majority has chosen to adopt. The dominant theme of the majority opinion is that the Federal Government's intrusion into an area "central to state domestic relations law applicable to its residents and citizens" is sufficiently "unusual" to set off alarm bells. *Ante*, at 17, 20. I think the majority goes off course, as I have said, but it is undeniable that its judgment is based on federalism.

The majority extensively chronicles DOMA's departure from the normal allocation of responsibility between State and Federal Governments, emphasizing that DOMA "rejects the long-established precept that the incidents, benefits, and obligations of marriage are uniform for all married couples within each State." *Ante,* at 18. But there is no such departure when one State adopts or keeps a definition of marriage that differs from that of its neighbor, for it is entirely expected that state definitions would "vary, subject to constitutional guarantees, from one State to the next." *Ibid.* Thus, while "[t]he State's power in defining the marital relation is of central relevance" to the majority's decision to strike down DOMA here, *ibid.*, that power will come into play on the other side of the board in future cases about the constitutionality of state marriage definitions. So too will the concerns for state diversity and sovereignty that weigh against DOMA's constitutionality in this case. See *ante,* at 19.

It is not just this central feature of the majority's analysis that is unique to DOMA, but many considerations on the periphery as well. For example, the majority focuses on the legislative history and title of this particular Act, *ante*, at 21; those statute-specific considerations will, of course, be irrelevant in future cases about different statutes. The majority emphasizes that DOMA was a "system- wide enactment with no identified connection to any particular area of federal law," but a State's definition of marriage "is the foundation of the State's broader authority to regulate the subject of domestic relations with respect to the '[p]rotection of offspring, property interests, and the enforcement of marital responsibilities.'" *Ante*, at 22, 17. And the federal decision undermined (in the majority's view) the "dignity [already] conferred by the States in the exercise of their sovereign power," *ante*, at 21, whereas a State's decision whether to expand the definition of marriage from its traditional contours involves no similar concern.

We may in the future have to resolve challenges to state marriage definitions affecting same-sex couples. That issue, however, is not before us in this case, and we hold today that we lack jurisdiction to consider it in the particular context of *Hollingsworth* v. *Perry, ante*, p. ___. I write only to highlight the limits of the majority's holding and reasoning today, lest its opinion be taken to resolve not only a question that I believe is not properly before us—DOMA's constitutionality—but also a question that all agree, and the Court explicitly acknowledges, is not at issue.

JUSTICE SCALIA, with whom JUSTICE THOMAS joins, and with whom THE CHIEF JUSTICE joins as to Part I, dissenting.

[II]

[A]

There are many remarkable things about the majority's merits holding. The first is how rootless and shifting its justifications are. For example, the opinion starts with seven full pages about the traditional power of States to define domestic relations—initially fooling many readers, I am sure, into thinking that this is a federalism opinion. But we are eventually told that "it is unnecessary to decide whether this federal intrusion on state power is a violation of the Constitution," and that "[t]he State's power in defining the marital relation is of central relevance in this case quite apart from principles of federalism" because "the State's decision to give this class of persons the right to marry conferred upon them a dignity and status of immense import." *Ante*, at 18. But no one questions the power of the States to define marriage (with the concomitant conferral of dignity and status), so what is the point of devoting seven pages to describing how long and well established that power is? Even after the opinion has formally disclaimed reliance upon principles of federalism, mentions of "the usual tradition of recognizing and accepting state definitions of marriage" continue. See, *e.g., ante,* at 20. What to make of this? The opinion never explains. My guess is that the majority, while reluctant to suggest that defining the meaning of "marriage" in federal statutes is unsupported by any of the Federal Government's enumerated powers, nonetheless needs some rhetorical basis to support its pretense that today's prohibition of laws excluding same-sex marriage is confined to the Federal Government (leaving the second, state-law shoe to be dropped later, maybe next Term). But I am only guessing.

Equally perplexing are the opinion's references to "the Constitution's guarantee of equality." *Ibid.* Near the end of the opinion, we are told that although the "equal protection guarantee of the Fourteenth Amendment makes [the] Fifth Amendment [due process] right all the more specific and all the better understood and preserved"—what can *that* mean?—"the Fifth Amendment itself withdraws from Government the power to degrade or demean in the way this law does." *Ante,* at 25. The only possible interpretation of this statement is that the Equal Protection Clause, even the Equal Protection Clause as incorporated in the Due Process Clause, is not the basis for today's holding. But the portion of the majority opinion that explains why DOMA is unconstitutional (Part IV) begins by citing *Bolling* v. *Sharpe,* 347 U. S. 497 (1954), *Department of Agriculture* v. *Moreno,* 413 U. S. 528 (1973), and *Romer* v. *Evans,* 517 U. S. 620 (1996)—*all* of which are equal protection cases. And those three cases are the *only* authorities that the Court cites in Part IV about the Constitution's meaning, except for its citation of *Lawrence* v. *Texas,* 539 U. S. 558 (2003) (not an equal-protection case) to support its passing assertion that the Constitution protects the "moral and sexual choices" of same-sex couples, *ante,* at 23.

Moreover, if this is meant to be an equal-protection opinion, it is a confusing one. The opinion does not resolve and indeed does not even mention what had been the central question in this litigation: whether, under the Equal Protection Clause, laws restricting marriage to a man and a woman are reviewed for more than mere rationality. That is the issue that divided the parties and the court below…In accord with my previously expressed skepticism about the Court's "tiers of scrutiny" approach, I would review this classification only for its rationality. See *United States* v. *Virginia,* 518 U. S. 515, 567–570 (1996) (SCALIA, J., dissenting). As nearly as I can tell, the Court agrees with that; its opinion does not apply strict scrutiny, and its central propositions are taken from rational-basis cases like *Moreno.* But the Court certainly does not *apply* anything that resembles that deferential framework. See *Heller* v. *Doe,* 509 U. S. 312, 320 (1993) (a classification "'must be upheld . . . if there is any reason- ably conceivable state of facts'" that could justify it).

The majority opinion need not get into the strict vs. rational-basis scrutiny question, and need not justify its holding under either, because it says that DOMA is unconstitutional as "a deprivation of the liberty of the person protected by the Fifth Amendment of the Constitution," *ante,* at 25; that it violates "basic due process" principles, *ante,* at 20; and that it inflicts an "injury and indignity" of a kind that denies "an essential part of the liberty protected by the Fifth Amendment," *ante,* at 19. The majority never utters the dread words "substantive due process" perhaps sensing the disrepute into which that doctrine has fallen, but that is what those statements mean. Yet the opinion does not argue that same-sex marriage is "deeply rooted in this Nation's history and tradition," *Washington* v. *Glucksberg*, 521 U. S. 702, 720–721 (1997), a claim that would of course be quite absurd. So would the further suggestion (also necessary, under our substantive-due-process precedents) that a world in which DOMA exists is one bereft of "'ordered liberty.'" *Id.,* at 721 (quoting *Palko* v. *Connecticut,* 302 U. S. 319, 325 (1937)).

Some might conclude that this loaf could have used awhile longer in the oven. But that would be wrong; it is already overcooked. The most expert care in preparation cannot redeem a bad recipe. The sum of all the Court's nonspecific hand-waving is that this law is invalid (maybe on equal-protection grounds, maybe on substantive-due process grounds, and perhaps with some amorphous federalism component playing a role) because it is motivated by a "'bare . . . desire to harm'" couples in same-sex marriages. *Ante,* at 20. It is this proposition with which I will therefore engage.

B

As I have observed before, the Constitution does not forbid the government to enforce traditional moral and sexual norms. See *Lawrence* v. *Texas,* 539 U. S. 558, 599 (2003) (SCALIA, J., dissenting). I will not swell the U. S. Reports with restatements of that point. It is enough to say that the Constitution neither requires nor forbids our society to approve of same-sex marriage, much as it neither requires nor forbids us to approve of no-fault divorce, polygamy, or the consumption of alcohol.

However, even setting aside traditional moral disapproval of same-sex marriage (or indeed same-sex sex),there are many perfectly valid—indeed, downright boring—justifying rationales for this legislation. Their existence ought to be the end of this case. For they give the lie to the Court's conclusion that only those with hateful hearts could have voted "aye" on this Act. And more importantly, they serve to make the contents of the legislators' hearts quite irrelevant: "It is a familiar principle of constitutional law that this Court will not strike down an otherwise constitutional statute on the basis of an alleged illicit legislative motive." *United States* v. *O'Brien,* 391 U. S. 367, 383 (1968). Or at least it *was* a familiar principle. By holding to the contrary, the majority has declared open season on any law that (in the opinion of the law's opponents and any panel of like-minded federal judges) can be characterized as mean-spirited.

The majority concludes that the only motive for this Act was the "bare . . . desire to harm a politically unpopular group." *Ante,* at 20. Bear in mind that the object of this condemnation is not the legislature of some once-Confederate Southern state (familiar objects of the Court's scorn, see, *e.g., Edwards* v. *Aguillard,* 482 U. S. 578 (1987)), but our respected coordinate branches, the Congress and Presidency of the United States. Laying such a charge against them should require the most extraordinary evidence, and I would have thought that every attempt would be made to indulge a more anodyne explanation for the statute. The majority does the opposite—affirmatively concealing from the reader the arguments that exist in justification. It makes only a passing mention of the "arguments put forward" by the Act's defenders, and does not even trouble to paraphrase or describe them. See *ante,* at 21. I imagine that this is because it is harder to maintain the illusion of the Act's supporters as unhinged members of a wild-eyed lynch mob when one first describes their views as *they* see them.

[DOMA] preserves the intended effects of prior legislation against then-unforeseen changes in circumstance. When Congress provided (for example) that a special estate-tax exemption would exist for spouses, this exemption reached only *opposite-sex* spouses—those being the only sort that were recognized in *any* State at the time of DOMA's passage. When it became clear that changes instate law might one day alter that balance, DOMA's definitional section was enacted to ensure that state-level experimentation did not automatically alter the basic operation of federal law, unless and until Congress made the further judgment to do so on its own. That is not animus—just stabilizing prudence. Congress has hardly demonstrated itself unwilling to make such further, revising judgments upon due deliberation. See, *e.g.,* Don't Ask, Don't Tell Repeal Act of 2010, 124 Stat. 3515.

The Court mentions none of this. Instead, it accuses the Congress that enacted this law and the President who signed it of something much worse than, for example, having acted in excess of enumerated federal powers—or even having drawn distinctions that prove to be irrational. Those legal errors may be made in good faith, errors though they are. But the majority says that the supporters of this Act acted with *malice*—with *the "purpose"* (*ante,* at 25) "to disparage and to injure" same-sex couples. It says that the motivation for DOMA was to "demean," *ibid.*; to "impose inequality," *ante,* at 22; to "impose . . . a stigma," *ante,* at 21; to deny people "equal dignity," *ibid.*; to brand gay people as "unworthy," *ante,* at 23; and to "*humiliat[e]*" their children, *ibid.* (emphasis added).

I am sure these accusations are quite untrue. To be sure (as the majority points out), the legislation is called the Defense of Marriage Act. But to defend traditional marriage is not to condemn, demean, or humiliate those who would prefer other arrangements, any more than to defend the Constitution of the United States is to condemn, demean, or humiliate other constitutions. To hurl such accusations so casually demeans *this institution.* In the majority's judgment, any resistance to its holding is beyond the pale of reasoned disagreement. To question its high-handed invalidation of a presumptively valid statute is to act (the majority is sure) with *the purpose* to "disparage," "injure," "degrade," "demean," and "humiliate" our fellow human beings, our fellow citizens, who are homosexual. All that, simply for supporting an Act that did no more than codify an aspect of marriage that had been unquestioned in our society for most of its existence—indeed, had been unquestioned in virtually all societies for virtually all of human history. It is one thing for a society to elect change; it is another for a court of law to impose change by adjudging those who oppose it *hostes humani generis,* enemies of the human race.

* * *

The penultimate sentence of the majority's opinion is a naked declaration that "[t]his opinion and its holding are confined" to those couples "joined in same-sex marriages made lawful by the State." *Ante,* at 26, 25. I have heard such "bald, unreasoned disclaimer[s]" before. *Lawrence,* 539 U. S., at 604. When the Court declared a constitutional right to homosexual sodomy, we were assured that the case had nothing, nothing at all to do with "whether the government must give formal recognition to any relationship that homosexual persons seek to enter." *Id.,* at 578. Now we are told that DOMA is invalid because it "demeans the couple, whose moral and sexual choices the Constitution protects," *ante,* at 23—with an accompanying citation of *Lawrence.* It takes real cheek for today's majority to assure us, as it is going out the door, that a constitutional requirement to give formal recognition to same-sex marriage is not at issue here—when what has preceded that assurance is a lecture on how superior the majority's moral judgment in favor of same-sex marriage is to the Congress's hateful moral judgment against it. I promise you this: The only thing that will "confine" the Court's holding is its sense of what it can get away with.

I do not mean to suggest disagreement with THE CHIEF JUSTICE's view, *ante,* p. 2–4 (dissenting opinion), that lower federal courts and state courts can distinguish today's case when the issue before them is state denial of marital status to same-sex couples—or even that this Court could *theoretically* do so. Lord, an opinion with such scatter-shot rationales as this one (federalism noises among them) can be distinguished in many ways. And deserves to be. State and lower federal courts should take the Court at its word and distinguish away.

In my opinion, however, the view that *this* Court will take of state prohibition of same-sex marriage is indicated beyond mistaking by today's opinion. As I have said, the real rationale of today's opinion, whatever disappearing trail of its legalistic argle-bargle one chooses to follow, is that DOMA is motivated by "'bare . . . desire to harm'" couples in same-sex marriages. *Supra,* at 18. How easy it is, indeed how inevitable, to reach the same conclusion with regard to state laws denying same-sex couples marital status. Consider how easy (inevitable) it is to make the following substitutions in a passage from today's opinion *ante,* at 22:

> "~~DOMA's~~-*This state law's* principal effect is to identify a subset of ~~state-sanctioned~~ ~~marriages~~-*constitutionally protected sexual relationships,* see *Lawrence,* and make them unequal. The principal purpose is to impose inequality, not for other reasons like governmental efficiency. Responsibilities, as well as rights, enhance the dignity and integrity of the person. And ~~DOMA~~-*this state law* contrives to deprive some couples ~~married~~ ~~under the laws of their State~~-*enjoying constitutionally protected sexual relationships,* but not other couples, of both rights and responsibilities."

Or try this passage, from *ante,* at 22–23:

> "~~[DOMA]~~-*This state law* tells those couples, and all the world, that their otherwise valid ~~marriages~~-*relationships* are unworthy of ~~federal~~-*state* recognition. This places same-sex couples in an unstable position of being in a second-tier ~~marriage~~-*relationship*. The differentiation demeans the couple, whose moral and sexual choices the Constitution protects, see *Lawrence,* . . . ."

Or this, from *ante,* at 23—which does not even require alteration, except as to the invented number:

> "And it humiliates tens of thousands of children now being raised by same-sex couples. The law in question makes it even more difficult for the children to understand the integrity and closeness of their own family and its concord with other families in their community and in their daily lives."

Similarly transposable passages—deliberately transposable, I think—abound. In sum, that Court which finds it so horrific that Congress irrationally and hatefully robbed same-sex couples of the "personhood and dignity" which state legislatures conferred upon them, will of a certitude be similarly appalled by state legislatures' irrational and hateful failure to acknowledge that "personhood and dignity" in the first place. *Ante,* at 26. As far as this Court is concerned, no one should be fooled; it is just a matter of listening and waiting for the other shoe.

By formally declaring anyone opposed to same-sex marriage an enemy of human decency, the majority arms well every challenger to a state law restricting marriage to its traditional definition. Henceforth those challengers will lead with this Court's declaration that there is "no legitimate purpose" served by such a law, and will claim that the traditional definition has "the purpose and effect to disparage and to injure" the "personhood and dignity" of same-sex couples, see *ante,* at 25, 26. The majority's limiting assurance will be meaningless in the face of language like that, as the majority well knows. That is why the language is there. The result will be a judicial distortion of our society's debate over marriage—a debate that can seem in need of our clumsy "help" only to a member of this institution.

As to that debate: Few public controversies touch an institution so central to the lives of so many, and few inspire such attendant passion by good people on all sides. Few public controversies will ever demonstrate so vividly the beauty of what our Framers gave us, a gift the Court pawns today to buy its stolen moment in the spotlight: a system of government that permits us to rule *ourselves.* Since DOMA's passage, citizens on all sides of the question have seen victories and they have seen defeats. There have been plebiscites, legislation, persuasion, and loud voices—in other words, democracy. Victories in one place for some, *[citations to state laws omitted]* are offset by victories in other places for others, *[citations to state laws omitted].*

In the majority's telling, this story is black-and-white: Hate your neighbor or come along with us. The truth is more complicated. It is hard to admit that one's political opponents are not monsters, especially in a struggle like this one, and the challenge in the end proves more than today's Court can handle. Too bad. A reminder that disagreement over something so fundamental as marriage can still be politically legitimate would have been a fit task for what in earlier times was called the judicial temperament. We might have covered ourselves with honor today, by promising all sides of this debate that it was theirs to settle and that we would respect their resolution. We might have let the People decide.

But that the majority will not do. Some will rejoice in today's decision, and some will despair at it; that is the nature of a controversy that matters so much to so many. But the Court has cheated both sides, robbing the winners of an honest victory, and the losers of the peace that comes from a fair defeat. We owed both of them better.

I dissent.

[The dissent by Justice Alito is omitted. – Eds.]

III. DISCRIMINATION IN DENIAL OF FUNDAMENTAL RIGHTS: STRICT SCRUTINY

There are two conduits to strict scrutiny under equal protection analysis: suspect classifications and denial of a fundamental federal right. While the level of scrutiny applied to a classification depends on "who" (race, gender, wealth, etc.) alleges discrimination, when a fundamental federal right is denied, strict scrutiny is applied no matter what the discriminatory classification. Thus, for example, though deference is applied to wealth-based classifications, strict scrutiny will be applied if a fundamental federal right is denied to the poor as against the wealthy. Here, the inquiry is not "who" but "what."

This makes a determination of what rights are deemed fundamental of consequence. Since "explicit" constitutional rights are the rights most likely to be deemed "fundamental," the more particularized issue is once again what unarticulated rights will be deemed fundamental. A determination by the Court that these "implicit rights" are fundamental requires that the state prove a compelling purpose under a strict scrutiny analysis. Despite the inherent controversy of this process, the fact that a right to vote is not expressly articulated in the Constitution makes it almost impossible not to conclude that there are "implicit, unarticulated" fundamental rights. Much as in our discussion concerning the "implicit" fundamental right of privacy, we now make a similar inquiry as to other such rights.

This section first reviews the definitive Supreme Court opinion dealing with "implicit" fundamental rights, *San Antonio Independent School District v. Rodriquez*, and then turns to other implicit rights the Court has deemed fundamental: voting, access to courts, and interstate travel. While it seemed during the "Warren era" that a more active Court was willing to extend unarticulated fundamental rights, the *Rodriguez* opinion, perhaps because of a change in the makeup of the "Burger" Court, presents a more limited view of such rights.

SAN ANTONIO INDEPENDENT SCHOOL DISTRICT v. RODRIGUEZ
411 U.S. 1 (1973)

[Public school education has long been financed largely by means of property taxes imposed by local school districts. This suit challenged the constitutionality of Texas's use of this financing system on the ground that it produced substantial inter-district disparities in per-pupil expenditures. For example, the Edgewood Independent School District, the least affluent of the seven school districts in metropolitan San Antonio, had an assessed property value of $5,960 per student. By imposing a property tax of $1.05 per $100 of assessed property value — the highest rate in the metropolitan area — the district raised $26 per student in local funds. In contrast, the Alamo Heights Independent School District, the most affluent in the area, had an assessed property value per student of more than $49,000 and with a tax rate of only $.85 per $100 was able to raise $333 per student. Contributions from a state-funded "foundation program," whose purpose it was to reduce inter-district disparities, in fact contributed more funds to Alamo Heights than Edgewood leaving a final disparity of $248 per pupil in Edgewood as compared to $558 in Alamo Heights. A federal district court, applying strict scrutiny, held that the Texas scheme violated the equal protection clause. The Supreme Court reversed.]

Mr. Justice POWELL delivered the opinion of the Court.

I. [We] must decide, first, whether the Texas system of financing public education operates to the disadvantage of some suspect class or impinges upon a fundamental right explicitly or implicitly protected by the Constitution, thereby requiring strict judicial scrutiny. If so, the judgment of the District Court should be affirmed. If not, the Texas scheme must still be examined to determine whether it rationally furthers some legitimate, articulated state purpose and therefore does not constitute an invidious discrimination in violation of the Equal Protection Clause of the Fourteenth Amendment.

II. [We] find neither the suspect-classification nor the fundamental-interest analysis persuasive.

A. The wealth discrimination discovered by the District Court in this case, and by several other courts that have recently struck down school-financing laws in other States, is quite unlike any of the forms of wealth discrimination heretofore reviewed by this Court. [The] individuals, or groups of individuals, who constituted the class discriminated against in our prior cases shared two distinguishing characteristics: because of their impecunity they were completely unable to pay for some desired benefit, and as a consequence, they sustained an absolute deprivation of a meaningful opportunity to enjoy that benefit. [Even] a cursory examination, however, demonstrates that neither of the two distinguishing characteristics of wealth classifications can be found here. First, in support of their charge that the system discriminates against the "poor," appellees have made no effort to demonstrate that it operates to the peculiar disadvantage of any class fairly definable as indigent, or as composed of persons whose incomes are beneath any designated poverty level. Indeed, there is reason to believe that the poorest families are not necessarily clustered in the poorest property districts. A recent and exhaustive study of school districts in Connecticut concluded that "[i]t is clearly incorrect . . . to contend that the 'poor' live in 'poor' districts. . . . Thus, the major factual assumption of Serrano — that the educational financing system discriminates against the 'poor' — is simply false in Connecticut." Defining "poor" families as those below the Bureau of the Census "poverty level," the Connecticut study found, not surprisingly, that the poor were clustered around commercial and industrial areas — those same areas that provide the most attractive sources of property tax income for school districts. Whether a similar pattern would be discovered in Texas is not known, but there is no basis on the record in this case for assuming that the poorest people — defined by reference to any level of absolute impecunity — are concentrated in the poorest districts.

Second, neither appellees nor the District Court addressed the fact that, unlike each of the foregoing cases, lack of personal resources has not occasioned an absolute deprivation of the desired benefit. The argument here is not that the children in districts having relatively low assessable property values are receiving no public education; rather, it is that they are receiving a poorer quality education than that available to children in districts having more assessable wealth. Apart from the unsettled and disputed question whether the quality of education may be determined by the amount of money expended for it, a sufficient answer to appellees' argument is that, at least where wealth is involved, the Equal Protection Clause does not require absolute equality or precisely equal advantages. Nor indeed, in view of the infinite variables affecting the educational process, can any system assure equal quality of education except in the most relative sense.

For these two reasons — the absence of any evidence that the financing system discriminates against any definable category of "poor" people or that it results in the absolute deprivation of education — the disadvantaged class is not susceptible of identification in traditional terms.[60]

This brings us, then, to the third way in which the classification scheme might be defined — district wealth discrimination. Since the only correlation indicated by the evidence is between district property wealth and expenditures, it may be argued that discrimination might be found without regard to the individual income characteristics of district

---

[60] An educational financing system might be hypothesized, however, in which the analogy to the wealth discrimination cases would be considerably closer. If elementary and secondary education were made available by the State only to those able to pay a tuition assessed against each pupil, there would be a clearly defined class of 'poor' people — definable in terms of their inability to pay the prescribed sum — who would be absolutely precluded from receiving an education. That case would present a far more compelling set of circumstances for judicial assistance than the case before us today. After all, Texas has undertaken to do a good deal more than provide an education to those who can afford it. It has provided what it considers to be an adequate base education for all children and has attempted, though imperfectly, to ameliorate by state funding and by the local assessment program the disparities in local tax resources.

residents. However described, it is clear that appellees' suit asks this Court to extend its most exacting scrutiny to review a system that allegedly discriminates against a large, diverse, and amorphous class, unified only by the common factor of residence in districts that happen to have less taxable wealth than other districts. The system of alleged discrimination and the class it defines have none of the traditional indicia of suspectness: the class is not saddled with such disabilities, or subjected to such a history of purposeful unequal treatment, or relegated to such a position of political powerlessness as to command extraordinary protection from the majoritarian political process.

We thus conclude that the Texas system does not operate to the peculiar disadvantage of any suspect class. But in recognition of the fact that this Court has never heretofore held that wealth discrimination alone provides an adequate basis for invoking strict scrutiny, appellees have not relied solely on this contention. They also assert that the State's system impermissibly interferes with the exercise of a 'fundamental' right and that accordingly the prior decisions of this Court require the application of the strict standard of judicial review.

B. In Brown v. Board of Education, 347 U.S. 483, 74 S.Ct. 686, 98 L.Ed. 873 (1954), a unanimous Court recognized that "education is perhaps the most important function of state and local governments." [Nothing] this Court holds today in any way detracts from our historic dedication to public education. But the importance of a service performed by the State does not determine whether it must be regarded as fundamental for purposes of examination under the Equal Protection Clause.

The lesson of these cases [Shapiro; Lindsey; Dandridge] in addressing the question now before the Court is plain. It is not the province of this Court to create substantive constitutional rights in the name of guaranteeing equal protection of the laws. Thus, the key to discovering whether education is 'fundamental' is not to be found in comparisons of the relative societal significance of education as opposed to subsistence or housing. Nor is it to be found by weighing whether education is as important as the right to travel. Rather, the answer lies in assessing whether there is a right to education explicitly or implicitly guaranteed by the Constitution. [Education], of course, is not among the rights afforded explicit protection under our Federal Constitution. Nor do we find any basis for saying it is implicitly so protected. As we have said, the undisputed importance of education will not alone cause this Court to depart from the usual standard for reviewing a State's social and economic legislation. It is appellees' contention, however, that education is distinguishable from other services and benefits provided by the State because it bears a peculiarly close relationship to other rights and liberties accorded protection under the Constitution. Specifically, they insist that education is itself a fundamental personal right because it is essential to the effective exercise of First Amendment freedoms and to intelligent utilization of the right to vote. In asserting a nexus between speech and education, appellees urge that the right to speak is meaningless unless the speaker is capable of articulating his thoughts intelligently and persuasively. The 'marketplace of ideas' is an empty forum for those lacking basic communicative tools.

A similar line of reasoning is pursued with respect to the right to vote. Exercise of the franchise, it is contended, cannot be divorced from the educational foundation of the voter.

We need not dispute any of these propositions. The Court has long afforded zealous protection against unjustifiable governmental interference with the individual's rights to speak and to vote. Yet we have never presumed to possess either the ability or the authority to guarantee to the citizenry the most effective speech or the most informed electoral choice. That these may be desirable goals of a system of freedom of expression and of a representative form of government is not to be doubted. These are indeed goals to be pursued by a people whose thoughts and beliefs are freed from governmental interference. But they are not values to be implemented by judicial instruction into otherwise legitimate state activities.

[Whatever] merit appellees' argument might have if a State's financing system occasioned an absolute denial of educational opportunities to any of its children, that argument provides no basis for finding an interference with fundamental rights where only relative differences in spending levels are involved and where — as is true in the present case — no charge fairly could be made that the system fails to provide each child with an opportunity to acquire the basic minimal skills necessary for the enjoyment of the rights of speech and of full participation in the political process.

Furthermore, the logical limitations on appellees' nexus theory are difficult to perceive. How, for instance, is education to be distinguished from the significant personal interests in the basics of decent food and shelter? Empirical examination might well buttress an assumption that the ill-fed, ill-clothed, and ill-housed are among the most ineffective participants in the political process, and that they derive the least enjoyment from the benefits of the First Amendment. If so, appellees' thesis would cast serious doubt on the authority of Dandridge v. Williams, supra and Lindsey v. Normet. [The] present case, in another basic sense, is significantly different from any of the cases in which the Court has applied strict scrutiny to state or federal legislation touching upon constitutionally protected rights. Each of our prior cases involved legislation which "deprived," "infringed," or "interfered" with the free exercise of some such fundamental personal right or liberty. A critical distinction between those cases and the one now before us lies in what Texas is endeavoring to do with respect to education.

Every step leading to the establishment of the system Texas utilizes today — including the decisions permitting localities to tax and expend locally, and creating and continuously expanding the state aid — was implemented in an effort to extend public education and to improve its quality. Of course, every reform that benefits some more than others may be criticized for what it fails to accomplish. But we think it plain that, in substance, the thrust of the Texas system is affirmative and reformatory and, therefore, should be scrutinized under judicial principles sensitive to the nature of the State's efforts and to the rights reserved to the States under the Constitution.

C. We need not rest our decision, however, solely on the inappropriateness of the strict-scrutiny test. A century of Supreme Court adjudication under the Equal Protection Clause affirmatively supports the application of the traditional standard of review, which requires only that the State's system be shown to bear some rational relationship to legitimate state purposes. This case represents far more than a challenge to the manner in which Texas provides for the education of its children. We have here nothing less than a direct attack on the way in which Texas has chosen to raise and disburse state and local tax revenues. We are asked to condemn the State's judgment in conferring on political subdivisions the power to tax local property to supply revenues for local interests. In so doing, appellees would have the Court intrude in an area in which it has traditionally deferred to state legislatures. This Court has often admonished against such interferences with the State's fiscal policies under the Equal Protection Clause.

[Thus], we stand on familiar grounds when we continue to acknowledge that the Justices of this Court lack both the expertise and the familiarity with local problems so necessary to the making of wise decisions with respect to the raising and disposition of public revenues. Yet, we are urged to direct the States either to alter drastically the present system or to throw out the property tax altogether in favor of some other form of taxation. No scheme of taxation, whether the tax is imposed on property, income, or purchases of goods and services, has yet been devised which is free of all discriminatory impact.

In addition to matters of fiscal policy, this case also involves the most persistent and difficult questions of educational policy, another area in which this Court's lack of specialized knowledge and experience counsels against premature interference with the informed judgments made at the state and local levels. Education, perhaps even more than welfare assistance, presents a myriad of "intractable economic, social, and even philosophical problems." Dandridge v. Williams, 397 U.S., at 487, 90 S.Ct. at 1163. [In] such circumstances, the judiciary is well advised to refrain from imposing on the States inflexible constitutional restraints that could circumscribe or handicap the continued research and experimentation so vital to finding even partial solutions to educational problems and to keeping abreast of ever-changing conditions.

III. [The] Texas system of school finance is responsive to these two forces. While assuring a basis education for every child in the State, it permits and encourages a large measure of participation in and control of each district's schools at the local level. [Appellees] suggest that local control could be preserved and promoted under other financing systems that resulted in more equality in education expenditures. While it is no doubt true that reliance on local property taxation for school revenues provides less freedom of choice with respect to expenditures for some districts than for others, the existence of "some inequality" in the manner in which the State's rationale is achieved is not alone a sufficient basis for striking down the entire system. [Nor] must the financing system fail because, as appellees suggest, other methods of satisfying the State's interest, which occasion "less drastic" disparities in expenditures, might be conceived. Only where state action impinges on the exercise of fundamental constitutional rights or liberties must it be found to have chosen the least restrictive alternative. It is also well to remember that even those districts that have reduced ability to make free decisions with respect to how much they spend on education still retain under the present system a large measure of authority as to how available funds will be allocated. They further enjoy the power to make numerous other decisions with respect to the operation of the schools. The people of Texas may be justified in believing that other systems of school financing, which place more of the financial responsibility in the hands of the State, will result in a comparable lessening of desired local autonomy. That is, they may believe that along with increased control of the purse strings at the state level will go increased control over local policies. [Appellees] further urge that the Texas system is unconstitutionally arbitrary because it allows the availability of local taxable resources to turn on "happenstance." [But] any scheme of local taxation — indeed the very existence of identifiable local governmental units — requires the establishment of jurisdictional boundaries that are inevitably arbitrary. It is equally inevitable that some localities are going to be blessed with more taxable assets than others. Nor is local wealth a static quantity.

In sum, to the extent that the Texas system of school financing results in unequal expenditures between children who happen to reside in different districts, we cannot say that such disparities are the product of a system that is so irrational as to be invidiously discriminatory. The constitutional standard under the Equal Protection Clause is whether the challenged state action rationally furthers a legitimate state purpose or interest. We hold that the Texas plan abundantly satisfies this standard.

IV. [A] cautionary postscript seems appropriate. The complexity of these problems is demonstrated by the lack of consensus with respect to whether it may be said with any assurance that the poor, the racial minorities, or the children in over-burdened core-city school districts would be benefited by abrogation of traditional modes of financing education. We hardly need add that this Court's action today is not to be viewed as placing its judicial imprimatur on the status quo. The need is apparent for reform in tax systems which may well have relied too long and too heavily on the local property tax. And certainly innovative thinking as to public education, its methods, and its funding is necessary to assure both a higher level of quality and greater uniformity of opportunity. These matters merit the continued attention of the scholars who already have contributed much by their challenges. But the ultimate solutions must come from the lawmakers and from the democratic pressures of those who elect them.

Reversed.

Mr. Justice STEWART, concurring.

I join the opinion and judgment of the Court because I am convinced that any other course would mark an extraordinary departure from principled adjudication under the Equal Protection Clause of the Fourteenth Amendment. The unchartered directions of such a departure are suggested, I think, by the imaginative dissenting opinion my Brother Marshall has filed today.

Unlike other provisions of the Constitution, the Equal Protection Clause confers no substantive rights and creates no substantive liberties. The function of the Equal Protection Clause, rather, is simply to measure the validity of classifications created by state laws.

Moreover, quite apart from the Equal Protection Clause, a state law that impinges upon a substantive right or liberty created or conferred by the Constitution is, of course, presumptively invalid, whether or not the law's purpose or effect is to create any classifications. Numerous cases in this Court illustrate this principle. In refusing to invalidate the Texas system of financing its public schools, the Court today applies with thoughtfulness and understanding the basic principles of [equal protection].

Mr. Justice WHITE, with whom Mr. Justice DOUGLAS and Mr. Justice BRENNAN join, dissenting.

[This] case would be quite different if it were true that the Texas system, while insuring minimum educational expenditures in every district through state funding, extended a meaningful option to all local districts to increase their per-pupil expenditures and so to improve their children's education to the extent that increased funding would achieve that goal. The system would then arguably provide a rational and sensible method of achieving the stated aim of preserving an area for local initiative and decision.

The difficulty with the Texas system, however, is that it provides a meaningful option to Alamo Heights and like school districts but almost none to Edgewood and those other districts with a low per-pupil real estate tax base. In these latter districts, no matter how desirous parents are of supporting their schools with greater revenues, it is impossible to do so through the use of the real estate property tax. In these districts, the Texas system utterly fails to extend a realistic choice to parents because the property tax, which is the only revenue-raising mechanism extended to school districts, is practically and legally unavailable.

Requiring the State to establish only that unequal treatment is in furtherance of a permissible goal, without also requiring the State to show that the means chosen to effectuate that goal are rationally related to its achievement, makes equal protection analysis no more than an empty gesture.

Mr. Justice MARSHALL, with whom Mr. Justice DOUGLAS concurs, dissenting.

To begin, I must once more voice my disagreement with the Court's rigidified approach to equal protection analysis. See Dandridge v. Williams, 397 U.S. 471, 519-521, 90 S.Ct. 1153, 1178-1180, 25 L.Ed.2d 491 (1970) (dissenting opinion); Richardson v. Belcher, 404 U.S. 78, 90, 92 S.Ct. 254, 261, 30 L.Ed.2d 231 (1971) (dissenting opinion). The Court apparently seeks to establish today that equal protection cases fall into one of two neat categories which dictate the appropriate standard of review — strict scrutiny or mere rationality. But this Court's decisions in the field of equal protection defy such easy categorization. A principled reading of what this Court has done reveals that it has applied a spectrum of standards in reviewing discrimination allegedly violative of the Equal Protection Clause. This spectrum clearly comprehends variations in the degree of care with which the Court will scrutinize particular classifications, depending, I believe, on the constitutional and societal importance of the interest adversely affected and the recognized invidiousness of the basis upon which the particular classification is drawn. I find in fact that many of the Court's recent decisions embody the very sort of reasoned approach to equal protection analysis for which I previously argued — that is, an approach in which "concentration [is] placed upon the character of the classification in question, the relative importance to individuals in the class discriminated against of the governmental benefits that they do not receive, and the asserted state interests in support of the classification." Dandridge v. Williams, supra, 397 U.S., at 520-521, 90 S.Ct., at 1180 (dissenting opinion).

I therefore cannot accept the majority's labored efforts to demonstrate that fundamental interests, which call for strict scrutiny of the challenged classification, encompass only established rights which we are somehow bound to recognize from the text of the Constitution itself. But it will not do to suggest that the "answer" to whether an interest is fundamental for purposes of equal protection analysis is always determined by whether that interest "is a right . . . explicitly or implicitly guaranteed by the Constitution."

I would like to know where the Constitution guarantees the right to procreate, Skinner v. Oklahoma ex rel. Williamson, 316 U.S. 535, 541, 62 S.Ct. 1110, 1113, 86 L.Ed. 1655 (1942), or the right to vote in state elections, e.g., Reynolds v. Sims, 377 U.S. 533, 84 S.Ct. 1362, 12 L.Ed.2d 506 (1964), or the right to an appeal from a criminal conviction, e.g., Griffin v. Illinois, 351 U.S. 12, 76 S.Ct. 585, 100 L.Ed. 891 (1956). These are instances in which, due to the importance of the interests at stake, the Court has displayed a strong concern with the existence of discriminatory state treatment. But the Court has never said or indicated that these are interests which independently enjoy full blown constitutional protection.

The majority is, of course, correct when it suggests that the process of determining which interests are fundamental is a difficult one. But I do not think the problem is insurmountable. And I certainly do not accept the view that the process need necessarily degenerate into an unprincipled, subjective "picking-and-choosing" between various interests or that it must involve this Court in creating "substantive constitutional rights in the name of guaranteeing equal protection of the laws," ante, at 1297. Although not all fundamental interests are constitutionally guaranteed, the determination of which interests are fundamental should be firmly rooted in the text of the Constitution. The task in every case should be to determine the extent to which constitutionally guaranteed rights are dependent on interests not mentioned in the Constitution. As the nexus between the specific constitutional guarantee and the nonconstitutional interest draws closer, the nonconstitutional interest becomes more fundamental and the degree of judicial scrutiny applied when the interest is infringed on a discriminatory basis must be adjusted accordingly. Thus, it cannot be denied that interests such as procreation, the exercise of the state franchise, and access to criminal appellate processes are not fully guaranteed to the citizen by our Constitution. But these interests have nonetheless been afforded special judicial consideration in the face of discrimination because they are, to some extent, interrelated with constitutional guarantees. Procreation is now understood to be important because of its interaction with the established constitutional right of privacy. The exercise of the state franchise is closely tied to basic civil and political rights inherent in the First Amendment. And access to criminal appellate processes enhances the integrity of the range of rights implicit in the Fourteenth Amendment guarantee of due process of law. Only if we closely protect the related interests from state discrimination do we ultimately ensure the integrity of the constitutional guarantee itself. This is the real lesson that must be taken from our previous decisions involving interests deemed to be fundamental.

In summary, it seems to me inescapably clear that this Court has consistently adjusted the care with which it will review state discrimination in light of the constitutional significance of the interests affected and the invidiousness of the particular classification. [The] majority suggests, however, that a variable standard of review would give this Court the appearance of a "super-legislature." I cannot agree. Such an approach seems to me a part of the guarantees of our Constitution and of the historic experiences with oppression of and discrimination against discrete, powerless minorities which underlie that document. In truth, the Court itself will be open to the criticism raised by the majority so long as it continues on its present course of effectively selecting in private which cases will be afforded special consideration without acknowledging the true basis of its action. It is true that this Court has never deemed the provision of free public education to be required by the Constitution. [But] education directly affects the ability of a child to exercise his First Amendment rights, both as a source and as a receiver of information and ideas, whatever interests he may pursue in life. [Of] particular importance is the relationship between education and the political process and the demonstrated effect of education on the exercise of the franchise by the electorate. [It] is this very sort of intimate relationship between a particular personal interest and specific constitutional guarantees that has heretofore caused the Court to attach special significance, for purposes of equal protection analysis, to individual interests such as procreation and the exercise of the state franchise. The factors just considered, including the relationship between education and the social and political interests enshrined within the Constitution, compel us to recognize the fundamentality of education and to scrutinize with appropriate care the bases for state discrimination affecting equality of educational opportunity in Texas' school districts — a conclusion which is only strengthened when we consider the character of the classification in this case.

We are told that in every prior case involving a wealth classification, the members of the disadvantaged class have "shared two distinguishing characteristics: because of their impecunity they were completely unable to pay for some desired benefit, and as a consequence, they sustained an absolute deprivation of a meaningful opportunity to enjoy that benefit." I cannot agree. [Harper,] Griffin and Douglas refute the majority's contention that we have in the past required an absolute deprivation before subjecting wealth classifications to strict scrutiny. This is not to say that the form of wealth classification in this case does not differ significantly from those recognized in the previous decisions of this Court. Our prior cases have dealt essentially with discrimination on the basis of personal wealth. Here, by contrast, the children of the disadvantaged Texas school districts are being discriminated against not necessarily because of their personal wealth or the wealth of their families, but because of the taxable property wealth of the residents of the district in which they happen to live. The appropriate question, then, is whether the same degree of judicial solicitude and scrutiny that has previously been afforded wealth classifications is warranted here.

That wealth classifications alone have not necessarily been considered to bear the same high degree of suspectness as have classifications based on, for instance, race or alienage may be explainable on a number of grounds. The "poor" may not be seen as politically powerless as certain discrete and insular minority groups. Personal poverty may entail much the same social stigma as historically attached to certain racial or ethnic groups. But personal poverty is not a permanent disability; its shackles may be escaped. Perhaps most importantly, though, personal wealth may not necessarily share the general irrelevance as a basis for legislative action that race or nationality is recognized to have. While the "poor" have frequently been a legally disadvantaged group, it cannot be ignored that social legislation must frequently take cognizance of the economic status of our citizens. Thus, we have generally gauged the invidiousness of wealth classifications with an awareness of the importance of the interests being affected and the relevance of personal wealth to those interests.

When evaluated with these considerations in mind, it seems to me that discrimination on the basis of group wealth in this case likewise calls for careful judicial scrutiny. First, it must be recognized that while local district wealth may serve other interests, it bears no relationship whatsoever to the interest of Texas schoolchildren in the educational opportunity afforded them by the State of Texas. Given the importance of that interest, we must be particularly sensitive to the invidious characteristics of any form of discrimination that is not clearly intended to serve it, as opposed to some other distinct state interest. Discrimination on the basis of group wealth may not, to be sure, reflect the social stigma frequently attached to personal poverty. Nevertheless, insofar as group wealth discrimination involves wealth over which the disadvantaged individual has no significant control, it represents in fact a more serious basis of discrimination than does personal wealth. For such discrimination is no reflection of the individual's characteristics or his abilities. And thus — particularly in the context of a disadvantaged class composed of children — we have previously treated discrimination on a basis which the individual cannot control as constitutionally disfavored. Cf. Weber v. Aetna Casualty & Surety Co., 406 U.S. 164, 92 S.Ct. 1400, 31 L.Ed.2d 768 (1972); Levy v. Louisiana, 391 U.S. 68, 88 S.Ct. 1509, 20 L.Ed.2d 436 (1968).

Here, both the nature of the interest and the classification dictate close judicial scrutiny of the purposes which Texas seeks to serve with its present educational financing scheme and of the means it has selected to serve that purpose. But I need not now decide how I might ultimately strike the balance were we confronted with a situation where the State's sincere concern for local control inevitably produced educational inequality. For, on this record, it is apparent that the State's purported concern with local control is offered primarily as an excuse rather than as a justification for interdistrict inequality. [Local] school districts cannot choose to have the best education in the State by imposing the highest tax rate. Instead, the quality of the educational opportunity offered by any particular district is largely determined by the amount of taxable property located in the district — a factor over which local voters can exercise no control.

In my judgment, any substantial degree of scrutiny of the operation of the Texas financing scheme reveals that the State has selected means wholly inappropriate to secure its purported interest in assuring its school districts local fiscal control. At the same time, appellees have pointed out a variety of alternative financing schemes which may serve the State's purported interest in local control as well as, if not better than, the present scheme without the current impairment of the educational opportunity of vast numbers of Texas schoolchildren. I see no need, however, to explore the practical or constitutional merits of those suggested alternatives at this time for, whatever their positive or negative features, experience with the present financing scheme impugns any suggestion that it constitutes a serious effort to provide local fiscal control. If for the sake of local education control, this Court is to sustain interdistrict discrimination in the educational opportunity afforded Texas school children, it should require that the State present something more than the mere sham now before us.

III. In this case we have been presented with an instance of such discrimination, in a particularly invidious form, against an individual interest of large constitutional and practical importance. To support the demonstrated discrimination in the provision of educational opportunity the State has offered a justification which, on analysis, takes on at best an ephemeral character. Thus, I believe that the wide disparities in taxable district property wealth inherent in the local property tax element of the Texas financing scheme render that scheme violative of the Equal Protection Clause.

———————

Comments on *Rodriguez*. To what degree does Justice Powell's opinion limit extension of those rights deemed fundamental? Note his comments in *Rodriguez*: "Thus, the key to discovering whether education is 'fundamental' is not to be found in comparisons of the relative societal significance of education as opposed to subsistence or housing. Nor is it to be found by weighing whether education is as important as the right to travel. Rather, the answer lies in assessing whether there is a right to education explicitly or implicitly guaranteed by the Constitution." Given that the Court admits that there are "implicit" rights guaranteed by the Constitution, is it the Court's reasoning or the applied standard that is more limiting?

What if a state denied any public education? Note how Justice Powell avoids this "bottom line" issue by stating, "[Whatever] merit appellees' argument might have if a State's financing system occasioned an absolute denial of educational opportunities to any of its children, that argument provides no basis for finding an interference with fundamental rights where only relative differences in spending levels are involved and where — as is true in the present case — no charge fairly could be made that the system fails to provide each child with an opportunity to acquire the basic minimal skills necessary for the enjoyment of the rights of speech and of full participation in the political process." What if a state provides "an absolute denial of educational opportunities to any of its children" that "fails to provide each child with an opportunity to acquire the basic minimal skills necessary for the enjoyment of the rights of speech and of full participation in the political process"?

In the case that follows, Texas did just that by denying any "free public education to children who had not been 'legally admitted' into the United States."

PLYLER v. DOE
457 U.S. 202 (1982)

Justice BRENNAN delivered the opinion of the Court. . . .

[The Court held unconstitutional a Texas statute that authorized local school districts to deny free public education to children who had not been "legally admitted" into the United States. Pursuant to this statute, the Tyler Independent School District required "undocumented" children to pay a "tuition fee" in order to enroll.]

[In] applying the Equal Protection Clause to most forms of state action, we [seek] only the assurance that the classification at issue bears some fair relationship to a legitimate public purpose. But we would not be faithful to our obligations under the Fourteenth Amendment if we applied so deferential a standard to every classification. [With] respect to [some] classifications, it is appropriate to enforce the mandate of equal protection by requiring the State to demonstrate that its classification has been precisely tailored to serve a compelling governmental interest. In addition, we have recognized that certain forms of legislative classification, while not facially invidious, nonetheless give rise to recurring constitutional difficulties; in these limited circumstances we have sought the assurance that the classification reflects a reasoned judgment consistent with the ideal of equal protection by inquiring whether it may fairly be viewed as furthering a substantial interest of the State. We turn to a consideration of the standard appropriate for the evaluation of [the challenged law].

Sheer incapability or lax enforcement of the laws barring entry into this country, [has] resulted in the creation of a substantial "shadow population" of illegal migrants — numbering in the millions — within our borders. This situation raises the specter of a permanent caste of undocumented resident aliens, encouraged by some to remain here as a source of cheap labor, but nevertheless denied the benefits that our society makes available to citizens and lawful residents. [The Court rejected the claim that "illegal aliens" are a suspect class on the ground that illegal status is at least partly voluntary and that that status is not irrelevant to legitimate government purposes.]

The children who are plaintiffs in these cases are special members of this underclass. [Adults] who elect to enter our territory by stealth and in violation of our law should be prepared to bear the consequences, including, but not limited to, deportation. But the children [of] illegal entrants are not comparably situated. [They] "can affect neither their parents' conduct nor their own status." [Trimble v. Gordon.]

[Of] course, undocumented status is not irrelevant to any proper legislative goal. Nor is undocumented status an absolutely immutable characteristic since it is the product of conscious, indeed unlawful, action. But [the challenged law] is directed against children, and imposes its discriminatory burden on the basis of a legal characteristic over which children can have little control. It is thus difficult to conceive of a rational justification for penalizing these children for their presence within the United States. Yet that appears to be precisely the effect of [the law].

Public education is not a "right" granted to individuals by the Constitution. [Rodriguez.] But neither is it merely some governmental "benefit" indistinguishable from other forms of social welfare legislation. Both the importance of education in maintaining our basic institutions, and the lasting impact of its deprivation on the life of the child, mark the distinction. ["Some] degree of education is necessary to prepare citizens to participate effectively and intelligently in our open political system if we are to preserve freedom and independence." [In] addition, education provides the basic tools by which individuals might lead economically productive lives to the benefit of us all. In sum, education has a fundamental role in maintaining the fabric of our society. We cannot ignore the significant social costs borne by our Nation when select groups are denied the means to absorb the values and skills upon which our social order rests.

In addition to the pivotal role of education in sustaining our political and cultural heritage, denial of education to some isolated group of children poses an affront to one of the goals of the Equal Protection Clause: the abolition of governmental barriers presenting unreasonable obstacles to advancement on the basis of individual merit. [Illiteracy] is an enduring disability. The inability to read and write will handicap the individual deprived of a basic education each and every day of his life. The inestimable toll of that deprivation on the social, economic, intellectual, and psychological well-being of the individual, and the obstacle it poses to individual achievement, make it most difficult to reconcile [a] status-based denial of basic education with the framework of equality embodied in the Equal Protection Clause.

These well-settled principles allow us to determine the proper level of deference to be afforded [the Texas statute]. Undocumented aliens [are not] a suspect class [and] education [is not] a fundamental [right]. But more is involved in [this case] than the abstract question whether [the Texas statute] discriminates against a suspect class, or whether education is a fundamental right. [The statute] imposes a lifetime hardship on a discrete class of children not accountable for their disabling status. [In] determining the rationality of [the challenged statute], we may appropriately take into account its costs to the Nation and to the innocent children who are its victims. In light of these countervailing costs, the discrimination contained in [the statute] can hardly be considered rational unless it furthers some substantial goal of the State.

It is the State's principal argument [that] the undocumented status of these children establishes a sufficient rational basis for denying them benefits that a State might choose to afford other residents. The State notes that while other aliens are admitted "on an equality of legal privileges with all citizens under non-discriminatory laws," the asserted right of these children to an education can claim no implicit congressional imprimatur. Indeed, in the State's view, Congress' apparent disapproval of the presence of these children within the United States [provides] authority for its decision to impose upon them special disabilities. Faced with an equal protection challenge respecting the treatment of aliens, we agree that the courts must be attentive to congressional policy; [but] we are unable to find in the congressional immigration scheme any statement of policy that might weigh significantly in arriving at an equal protection balance concerning the State's authority to deprive these children of an education.

Congress has developed a complex scheme governing admission to our Nation and status within our borders. The obvious need for delicate policy judgments has counseled the Judicial Branch to avoid intrusion into this field. But this traditional caution does not persuade us that unusual deference must be shown the [challenged classification]. The States enjoy no power with respect to the classification of aliens. This power is "committed to the political branches of the Federal Government." [And although] the States do have some authority to act with respect to illegal aliens, at least where such action mirrors federal objectives and furthers a legitimate state [goal], there is no indication that the disability imposed by [the challenged law] corresponds to any identifiable congressional policy. . . .

To be sure, like all persons who have entered the United States unlawfully, these children are subject to deportation. But there is no assurance that a child subject to deportation will ever be deported. [We] are reluctant to impute to Congress the intention to withhold from these children, for so long as they are present in this country through no fault of their own, access to a basic education. In other contexts, undocumented status, coupled with some articulable federal policy, might enhance state authority with respect to the treatment of undocumented aliens. But in the area of special constitutional sensitivity presented by these cases, and in the absence of any contrary indication fairly discernible in the present legislative record, we perceive no national policy that supports the State in denying these children an elementary education. . . .

[The State argues further] that the classification at issue furthers an interest in the "preservation of the state's limited resources for the education of its lawful residents." [But the] State must do more than justify its classification with a concise expression of an intention to discriminate. [We] discern three colorable state interests that might support [the classification].

First, [the State suggests that it may] protect itself from an influx of illegal immigrants. [But there] is no evidence in the record suggesting that illegal entrants impose any significant burden on the State's economy. To the contrary, the available evidence suggests that illegal aliens underutilize public services, while contributing their labor to the local economy and tax money to the state.

[Second,] the State suggests that undocumented children are appropriately singled out for exclusion because of the special burdens they impose on the State's ability to provide high-quality public education. But the record in no way supports the claim that exclusion of undocumented children is likely to improve the overall quality of education in the State. [Moreover], even if improvement in the quality of education were a likely result of barring some number of children from the schools of the State, the State must support its selection of this group as the appropriate target for exclusion. In terms of educational cost and need, however, undocumented children are "basically indistinguishable" from legally resident alien children.

Finally, [the State suggests] that undocumented children are appropriately singled out because their unlawful presence within the United States renders them less likely than other children to remain within the [State], and to put their education to productive social or political use within the State. Even assuming that such an interest is legitimate, it is an interest that is most difficult to quantify. The State has no assurance that any child, citizen or not, will employ the education provided by the State within the confines of the State's borders. In any event, the record is clear that many of the undocumented children disabled by this classification will remain in this country indefinitely, and that some will become lawful residents or citizens of the United States. It is difficult to understand precisely what the State hopes to achieve by promoting the creation and perpetuation of a subclass of illiterates within our boundaries, surely adding to the problems and costs of unemployment, welfare, and crime. It is thus clear that whatever savings might be achieved by denying these children an education, they are wholly insubstantial in light of the costs involved to these children, the State, and the Nation.

If the State is to deny a discrete group of innocent children the free public education that it offers to other children residing within its borders, that denial must be justified by a showing that it furthers some substantial state interest. No such showing was made here. . . .

Affirmed.

Justice MARSHALL, concurring.

While I join the Court opinion, I do so without in any way retreating from my opinion in [Rodriguez]. [Furthermore], I believe that the facts of [this case] demonstrate the wisdom of rejecting a rigidified approach to equal protection analysis, and of employing an approach that allows for varying levels of scrutiny depending upon "the constitutional and societal importance of the interest adversely affected and the recognized invidiousness of the [classification]."

Justice BLACKMUN, concurring.

[Here the state] immediately and inevitably creates class distinctions of a type fundamentally inconsistent with [the purposes] of the Equal Protection Clause. Children denied an education are placed at a permanent and insurmountable competitive disadvantage, for an uneducated child is denied even the opportunity to achieve. And when those children are members of an identifiable group, that group — through the State's action — will have been converted into a discrete underclass. Other benefits provided by the State, such as housing and public assistance, are of course important; to an individual in immediate need, they may be more desirable than the right to be educated. But classifications involving the complete denial of education are in a sense unique, for they strike at the heart of equal protection values by involving the State in the creation of permanent class distinctions. In a sense, then, denial of an education is the analogue of denial of the right to vote: the former relegates the individual to second-class social status; the latter places him at a permanent political disadvantage.

This conclusion is fully consistent with Rodriguez, [for the] Court there reserved judgment on the constitutionality of a state system that "occasioned an absolute denial of educational opportunities to any of its children." . . .

Justice POWELL, concurring.

I join the opinion of the Court, and write separately to emphasize the unique character of the [case] before us. . . .

Although the analogy is not perfect, our holding today does find support in decisions of this Court with respect to the status of illegitimates. [In this case], Texas effectively denies to the school-age children of illegal aliens the opportunity to attend the free public schools that the State makes available to all residents. They are excluded only because of a status resulting from the violation by parents or guardians of our immigration laws and the fact that they remain in our country unlawfully. The appellee children are innocent in this respect.

[A] legislative classification that threatens the creation of an underclass of future citizens and residents cannot be reconciled with one of the fundamental purposes of the Fourteenth Amendment. In these unique circumstances, the Court properly may require that the State's interests be substantial and that the means bear a "fair and substantial relation" to these interests. . . .

Chief Justice BURGER, with whom Justice WHITE, Justice REHNQUIST, and Justice O'CONNOR join, dissenting.

[The] Court expressly — and correctly — rejects any suggestion that illegal aliens are a suspect class, or that education is a fundamental right. Yet by patching together bits and pieces of what might be termed quasi-suspect-class and quasi-fundamental-rights analysis, the Court spins out a theory custom-tailored to the facts of [this case]. If ever a court was guilty of an unabashedly result-oriented approach, this case is a prime example.

The Court first suggests that these illegal alien children, although not a suspect class, are entitled to special solicitude under the Equal Protection Clause because they lack "control" over or "responsibility" for their unlawful entry into this country. Similarly, the Court appears to take the position that [the law] is presumptively "irrational" because it has the effect of imposing "penalties" on "innocent" children. However, the Equal Protection Clause does not preclude legislators from classifying among persons on the basis of factors and characteristics over which individuals may be said to lack "control." [A] state legislature is not barred from considering, for example, relevant differences between the mentally healthy and the mentally ill, or between the residents of different counties, simply because these may be factors unrelated to individual choice or to any "wrongdoing."

[The] Court's analogy to cases involving discrimination against illegitimate children is grossly misleading. The State has not thrust any disabilities upon appellees due to their "status of birth." Rather, appellees' status is predicated upon the circumstances of their concededly illegal presence in this country. . . .

The second strand of the Court's analysis rests on the premise that, although public education is not a constitutionally guaranteed right, "neither is it merely some governmental 'benefit' indistinguishable from other forms of social welfare legislation." [This] opaque observation [has] no bearing on the issues at hand. [The] importance of education is beyond dispute. Yet we have held repeatedly that the importance of a governmental service does not elevate it to the status of a "fundamental right" for purposes of equal protection analysis. Moreover, the Court points to no meaningful way to distinguish between education and other governmental benefits in this context. Is the Court suggesting that education is more "fundamental" than food, shelter, or medical care? [The] Equal Protection Clause [does] not mandate a constitutional hierarchy of governmental services. . .

Once it is conceded [that] illegal aliens are not a suspect class, and that education is not a fundamental right, our inquiry should focus on and be limited to whether the legislative classification at issue bears a rational relationship to a legitimate state purpose. [Dandridge.] [It] simply is not "irrational" for a state to conclude that it does not have the same responsibility to provide benefits for persons whose very presence in the state and this country is illegal as it does to provide for persons lawfully present. [The] Federal Government has seen fit to exclude illegal aliens from numerous social welfare programs, such as the food stamp program, the old-age assistance, aid to families with dependent children, aid to the blind, aid to the permanently and totally disabled, and supplemental security income [programs]. [These] exclusions [support] the rationality of [the challenged statute]. . . .

Comments on *Plyler*. Is an absolute denial of education a fundamental right post-*Plyler*? If not, upon what basis does the Court strike the Texas statute? What is the meaning of *Plyler* as precedent?

A. VOTE

HARPER v. VIRGINIA STATE BOARD OF ELECTIONS
383 U.S. 663 (1966)

Mr. Justice DOUGLAS delivered the opinion of the Court.

[The] right to vote in state elections is nowhere expressly mentioned [in the Constitution]. It is argued that the right to vote in state elections is implicit, particularly by reason of the First Amendment. [We] do not stop to canvass the relation between voting and political expression. For it is enough to say that once the franchise is granted to the electorate, lines may not be drawn which are inconsistent with the Equal Protection Clause of the Fourteenth Amendment. . . .

[The] Lassiter case does not govern the result here, because, unlike a poll tax, the "ability to read and write . . . has some relation to standards designed to promote intelligent use of the ballot." [Voter] qualifications have no relation to wealth nor to paying or not paying this or any other tax. . . .

It is argued that a State may exact fees from citizens for many different kinds of licenses; that if it can demand from all an equal fee for a driver's license, it can demand from all an equal poll tax for voting. But we must remember that the interest of the State, when it comes to voting, is limited to the power to fix qualifications. Wealth, like race, creed, or color, is not germane to one's ability to participate intelligently in the electoral process. Lines drawn on the basis of wealth or property, like those of race [are] traditionally disfavored. See [Griffin v. Illinois and Douglas v. California, section E2 infra]. To introduce wealth or payment of a fee as a measure of a voter's qualifications is to introduce a capricious or irrelevant factor. . . .

We agree, of course, with Mr. Justice Holmes that the Due Process Clause of the Fourteenth Amendment "does not enact Mr. Herbert Spencer's Social Statics." [Lochner.] Likewise, the Equal Protection Clause is not shackled to the political theory of a particular era. In determining what lines are unconstitutionally discriminatory, we have never been confined to historic notions of [equality]. Notions of what constitutes equal treatment for purposes of the Equal Protection Clause do change. [Comparing Plessy v. Ferguson with Brown v. Board of Education.]

[We] have long been mindful that where fundamental rights and liberties are asserted under the Equal Protection Clause, classifications which might invade or restrain them must be closely scrutinized and carefully confined. See, e.g., [Skinner].

Those principles apply here. For to repeat, wealth or fee paying has, in our view, no relation to voting qualifications; the right to vote is too precious, too fundamental to be so burdened or conditioned. Reversed.

Mr. Justice BLACK, dissenting. . . .

[Under] a proper interpretation of the Equal Protection Clause States are to have the broadest kind of leeway in areas where they have a general constitutional competence to act. [State] poll tax legislation can "reasonably," "rationally" and without an "invidious" or evil purpose to injure anyone be found to rest on a number of state policies including (1) the State's desire to collect its revenue, and (2) its belief that voters who pay a poll tax will be interested in furthering the State's welfare when they vote. [And] history is on the side of "rationality" of the State's poll tax policy. Property qualifications existed in the Colonies and were continued by many States after the Constitution was adopted. . . .

Another reason for my dissent [is that the Court] seems to be using the old "natural-law-due-process formula" to justify striking down state laws as violations of the Equal Protection Clause. . . .

Mr. Justice HARLAN, whom Mr. Justice STEWART joins, dissenting. . . .

[The Court uses] captivating phrases, but they are wholly inadequate to satisfy the standard governing adjudication of the equal protection issue: Is there a rational basis for Virginia's poll tax as a voting qualification? I think the answer to that question is undoubtedly "yes." Property qualifications and poll taxes have been a traditional part of our political structure. In the Colonies the franchise was generally a restricted one. [It] is certainly a rational argument that payment of some minimal poll tax promotes civic responsibility, weeding out those who do not care enough about public affairs to pay $1.50 or thereabouts a year for the exercise of the franchise. It is also arguable, indeed it was probably accepted as sound political theory by a large percentage of Americans through most of our history, that people with some property have a deeper stake in community affairs, and are consequently more responsible, more educated, more knowledgeable, more worthy of confidence, than those without means, and that the community and Nation would be better managed if the franchise were restricted to such citizens. . . .

[It] was not too long ago that Mr. Justice Holmes felt impelled to remind the Court that the Due Process Clause of the Fourteenth Amendment does not enact the laissez-faire theory of society, [Lochner]. The times have changed, and perhaps it is appropriate to observe that neither does the Equal Protection Clause of that Amendment rigidly impose upon America an ideology of unrestrained egalitarianism. . . .

1. "REAPPORTIONMENT"

REYNOLDS v. SIMS
377 U.S. 533 (1964)

[Though the Court's decision in *Baker v. Carr* may have "opened the door," it wasn't until *Reynolds* (and five companion cases) that the Court held that the system of apportionment of one or both houses of the legislature was unconstitutional. The Court held: "Legislative apportionment in Alabama is signally illustrative and symptomatic of the seriousness of this problem in a number of States. [There has] been no reapportionment of seats in the Alabama Legislature for over 60 years. [This has resulted] in the perpetuated scheme becoming little more than an irrational anachronism [enabling] a minority stranglehold on the State Legislature."]

Mr. Chief Justice WARREN delivered the opinion of the Court. . . .

A predominant consideration in determining whether a State's legislative apportionment scheme constitutes an invidious discrimination violative of rights asserted under the Equal Protection Clause is that the rights allegedly impaired are individual and personal in nature. [Since] the right of suffrage is a fundamental matter in a free and democratic society [and] is preservative of other basic civil and political rights, any alleged infringement of the right of citizens to vote must be carefully and meticulously scrutinized. . . .

Legislators represent people, not trees or acres. Legislators are elected by voters, not farms or cities or economic interests. As long as ours is a representative form of government, [the] right to elect legislators in a free and unimpaired fashion is a bedrock of our political system. It could hardly be gainsaid that a constitutional claim had been asserted by an allegation that certain otherwise qualified voters had been entirely prohibited from voting for members of their state legislature. And, if a State should provide that the votes of citizens in one part of the State should be given two times, or five times, or 10 times the weight of votes of citizens in another part of the State, it could hardly be contended that the right to vote of those residing in the disfavored areas had not been effectively diluted. [Of] course, the effect of state legislative districting schemes which give the same number of representatives to unequal numbers of constituents is identical. . . .

Logically, in a society ostensibly grounded on representative government, it would seem reasonable that a majority of the people of a State could elect a majority of that State's legislators. [To] sanction minority control of state legislative bodies, would appear to deny majority rights in a way that far surpasses any possible denial of minority rights that might otherwise be thought to result. [The] concept of equal protection has been traditionally viewed as requiring the uniform treatment of persons standing in the same relation to the governmental action questioned or challenged. With respect to the allocation of legislative representation, all voters, as citizens of a State, stand in the same relation regardless of where they live. Any suggested criteria for the differentiation of citizens are insufficient to justify any discrimination, as to the weight of their votes, unless relevant to the permissible purposes of legislative apportionment. Since the achieving of fair and effective representation for all citizens is concededly the basic aim of legislative apportionment, we conclude that the Equal Protection Clause guarantees the opportunity for equal participation by all voters in the election of state legislators. Diluting the weight of votes because of place of residence impairs basic constitutional rights under the Fourteenth Amendment. [Our] constitutional system amply provides for the protection of minorities by means other than giving them majority control of state legislatures. . . .

We are told that the matter of apportioning representation in a state legislature is a complex and many-faceted one. We are advised that States can rationally consider factors other than population in apportioning legislative representation. We are admonished not to restrict the power of the States to impose differing views as to political philosophy on their citizens. We are cautioned about the dangers of entering into political thickets and mathematical quagmires. Our answer is this: a denial of constitutionally protected rights demands judicial protection; our oath and our office require no less of us. [To] the extent that a citizen's right to vote is debased, he is that much less a citizen. [The] weight of a citizen's vote cannot be made to depend on where he lives.

Population is, of necessity, the starting point for consideration and the controlling criterion for judgment in legislative apportionment controversies. A citizen, a qualified voter, is no more nor no less so because he lives in the city or on the farm. This is the clear and strong command of our Constitution's Equal Protection Clause. . . .

We hold that, as a basic constitutional standard, the Equal Protection Clause requires that the seats in both houses of a bicameral state legislature must be apportioned on a population basis. Simply stated, an individual's right to vote for state legislators is unconstitutionally impaired when its weight is in a substantial fashion diluted when compared with votes of citizens living in other parts of the State. . . . [We] find the federal analogy inapposite and irrelevant to state legislative districting schemes. . . . The system of representation in the two Houses of the Federal Congress is one ingrained in our Constitution [and] is based on the consideration that in establishing our type of federalism a group of formerly independent States bound themselves together under one national government. [A] compromise between the larger and smaller States on this matter averted a deadlock in the Constitutional Convention which had threatened to abort the birth of our Nation. . .

Political subdivisions of States — counties, cities, or whatever — never were and never have been considered as sovereign entities. . . . By holding that as a federal constitutional requisite both houses of a state legislature must be apportioned on a population basis, we mean that the Equal Protection Clause requires that a State make an honest and good faith effort to construct districts, in both houses of its legislature, as nearly of equal population as is practicable. We realize that it is a practical impossibility to arrange legislative districts so that each one has an identical number of residents, or citizens, or voters. [So] long as the divergences from a strict population standard are based on legitimate considerations incident to the effectuation of a rational state policy, some deviations from the equal-population principle are constitutionally permissible [but] neither history alone, nor economic or other sorts of group interests, are permissible factors in attempting to justify disparities from population-based representation. Citizens, not history or economic interests, cast votes. Considerations of area alone provide an insufficient justification for deviations from the equal-population principle. Again, people, not land or trees or pastures, vote. . . . A consideration that appears to be of more substance in justifying some deviations from population-based representation in state legislatures is that of insuring some voice to political subdivisions, as political subdivisions. [In] many States much of the legislature's activity involves the enactment of so-called local legislation, directed only to the concerns of particular political subdivisions. [But] if, even as a result of a clearly rational state policy of according some legislative representation to political subdivisions, population is submerged as the controlling consideration in the apportionment of seats in the particular legislative body, then the right of all of the State's citizens to cast an effective and adequately weighted vote would be unconstitutionally impaired. . . . [Affirmed and remanded.]

Mr. Justice HARLAN, dissenting
[The] history of the adoption of the Fourteenth Amendment provides conclusive evidence that neither those who proposed nor those who ratified the Amendment believed that the Equal Protection Clause limited the power of the States to apportion their legislatures as they saw fit. Moreover, the history demonstrates that the intention to leave this power undisturbed was deliberate and was widely believed to be essential to the adoption of the Amendment. It is difficult to imagine a more intolerable and inappropriate interference by the judiciary with the independent legislatures of the States. . . . Although the Court — necessarily, as I believe — provides only generalities in elaboration of its main thesis, its opinion nevertheless fully demonstrates how far removed these problems are from fields of judicial competence. [In] one or another of today's opinions, the Court declares it unconstitutional for a State to give effective consideration to any of the following in establishing legislative districts: (1) history; (2) "economic or other sorts of group interests"; (3) area; (4) geographical considerations; (5) a desire "to insure effective repre-

sentation for sparsely settled areas"; (6) "availability of access of citizens to their representatives"; (7) theories of bicameralism (except those approved by the Court); (8) occupation; (9) "an attempt to balance urban and rural power"; (10) the preference of a majority of voters in the State.

So far as presently appears, the only factor which a State may consider, apart from numbers, is political subdivisions. But even "a clearly rational state policy" recognizing this factor is unconstitutional if "population is submerged as the controlling consideration. . . ." I know of no principle of logic or practical or theoretical politics, still less any constitutional principle, which establishes all or any of these exclusions. [The] Court says [only] that "legislators represent people, not trees or acres." [This] may be conceded. But it is surely equally obvious, and, in the context of elections, more meaningful to note that people are not ciphers and that legislators can represent their electors only by speaking for their interests — economic, social, political — many of which do reflect the place where the electors live. . . .

Mr. Justice STEWART, whom Mr. Justice CLARK joins, dissenting [in the Colorado and New York cases].

[My] own understanding of the various theories of representative government is that no one theory has ever commanded unanimous assent. [But] even if it were thought that the rule announced today by the Court is, as a matter of political theory, the most desirable general rule which can be devised, [I] could not join in the fabrication of a constitutional mandate which imports and forever freezes one theory of political thought into our Constitution. . . . Representative government is a process of accommodating group interests through democratic institutional arrangements. [Appropriate] legislative apportionment, therefore, should ideally be designed to insure effective representation in the State's legislature, in cooperation with other organs of political power, of the various groups and interests making up the electorate. [Population] factors must often to some degree be subordinated in devising a legislative apportionment plan which is to achieve the important goal of ensuring a fair, effective, and balanced representation of the regional, social, and economic interests within a State. [What] constitutes a rational plan reasonably designed to achieve this objective will vary from State to State, since each State is unique, in terms of topography, geography, demography, history, heterogeneity and concentration of population, variety of social and economic interests, and in the operation and interrelation of its political institutions. But so long as a State's apportionment plan reasonably achieves, in the light of the State's own characteristics, effective and balanced representation of all substantial interests, without sacrificing the principle of effective majority rule, that plan cannot be considered irrational. [The] Equal Protection Clause demands but two basic attributes of any plan of state legislative apportionment. First, it demands that, in the light of the State's own characteristics and needs, the plan must be a rational one. Secondly, it demands that the plan must be such as not to permit the systematic frustration of the will of a majority of the electorate of the State. [But,] beyond this, I think there is nothing in the Federal Constitution to prevent a State from choosing any electoral legislative structure it thinks best suited to the interests, temper, and customs of its people. [Applying these standards, Justice Stewart voted to uphold the Colorado and New York plans of legislative apportionment. The Colorado House was apportioned on a population basis, but rural areas were significantly "overrepresented" in the Senate. Stewart maintained that this departure from a population-based apportionment was permissible because it had been adopted in a statewide referendum and because it accommodated the distinct interests and characteristics of the state's various regions. Stewart thought that smaller population districts were reasonable in sparsely populated areas, for example, to enable senators "to maintain close contact with [constituents]," and he thought they were reasonable in certain agricultural areas to prevent the grouping of this portion of the electorate "in districts with larger numbers of voters with wholly different interests." Moreover, Stewart noted, because of the strength of the urban areas, "no possible combination of Colorado senators from rural districts [could] control the Senate." Stewart thus concluded that the Colorado scheme represented a reasonable "choice to protect the minority's interests." The New York plan assured smaller counties greater representation in the Assembly than would be warranted under a population-based apportionment and limited representation of the largest counties. Justice Stewart argued that this was justified as a counterweight to New York City's "concentration of population, homogeneity of interest, and political cohesiveness."

Post-*Reynolds* "One Person One Vote" Reapportionment, and the Equal Protection Clause Fundamental Rights. The discussion in this section flows from the dual landmark changes ushered in by the *Baker v. Carr* and *Reynolds v. Sims* decisions. *Baker* established that the federal courts did indeed have a jurisdiction to hear cases involving state reapportionment and that such cases were justiciable and not rendered, because of the political question doctrine, out of the reach of the federal judiciary. *Reynolds v. Sims* established basic equal protection principles that federal courts would need to follow in examining state apportionment schemes. Yet while *Reynolds* tied the constitutionality of such schemes to equal weighting of individual votes within a state, the Court made allowances to two distinct considerations. First the Court reaffirmed that federal congressional districting is governed by the "by the people" clause of the federal Constitution, implying a more precise measure than required for state legislative districting. With that in mind, the Court allowed that mathematical exactness in state legislative apportionment, which the Court acknowledged was impossible, could give way to good faith efforts on the part of the state legislatures: "So long as the divergences from a strict population standard are based on legitimate considerations incident to the effectuation of a rational state policy, some deviations from the equal-population principle are constitutionally permissible with respect to the apportionment of seats in either or both of the two houses of a bicameral state legislature."

The following cases put these propositions by the Court to the test.

a. CONGRESSIONAL DISTRICTS

Article I section 2 of the Constitution's "by the people" clause describing the method of election of members of the House of Representatives was the basis for Court rulings on Congressional districts which are drawn by state legislatures. Despite the state's role in administering those districts and the voting process within them, the Court ruled in *Karcher v. Daggett* that voting ratios within the districts of a state would be allowed minimal variances from each other in order to be constitutional. Stating that there was no de minimis level of constitutional acceptability and that states would have to establish constitutional justifications for variances as low as, in the case of the New Jersey apportionment under consideration, .6984 where an even smaller variance was rejected by the state legislature.

b. STATE ELECTIVE DISTRICTING

In contrast to the tight rein required by the "by the people" clause, state districting, which is subject to Fourteenth Amendment Equal Protection scrutiny, was held in several cases to be subject to a looser standard of equality by the Court. The looser standard was based on language in Reynolds that acknowledged that certain legitimate policies of state legislatures could justify wider variances. Among these policies was the need to have districts for state offices to conform as closely as possible to political subdivisions within a state.

The imprecision of this formula subjected the process to the political philosophies of the majority of the Court at various times. An 11.9% variances was found acceptable in an opinion by Justice Marshall in Abate v. Mundt, 403 U.S. 182 (1971), to account for traditional cooperation between city and county governments in Rockland County, New York. A greater variance was allowed in *Mahan v. Howell*, 410 U.S. 315 (1973). The case involved a direct test to the political subdivision test laid out in *Reynolds*, and in Justice Rehnquist's opinion, 16.4% was held to be constitutional for the purpose of maintaining political subdivision lines. Soon the Court began crunching numbers to establish what amounted to a de minimis "no justification needed" standard in Gaffney v. Cummings, 412 U.S. 735 (1973) (8% maximum and 2% average statewide), White v. Regester 412 U.S. 755 (1973) (9.9% maximum, 2 % average). Though a precise de minimis figure was not offered in either opinion, Justice White's opinion in both cases stated that relatively minor deviations would fail to meet "a threshold requirement of invidious discrimination."

Nonetheless, larger variances still required justification as the Court established in Connor v. Finch, 431 U.S. 407 (1977). The Court rejected 16.5% and 19.3% variations in the Mississippi House and Senate respectively where an alternative plan less disruptive to political subdivision lines that would have produced a lower variance was rejected by the legislature.

c. GERRYMANDERING

In addition to population equality in voting, state legislatures have also been involved in gerrymandering for political and racial purposes. Gerrymandering, named for an early nineteenth century Massachusetts politician, Elbridge Gerry who spearheaded efforts by the Democratic-Republican party (a predecessor to the modern Democratic Party) to oust Federalists from office by drawing contorted voting district lines, is used to produce political advantage for a particular group. Professors Cox and Holden have described the process:

> Redistricting allocates voters to electoral districts. In the United States, where members of both state legislative assemblies and Congress are elected predominantly from single-member districts, the allocation of voters to districts plays a significant role in determining which candidates emerge and who ultimately wins each seat. Redistricting thus presents whoever controls the process with a tremendous opportunity to shape political outcomes. This fact is not lost on the state legislative assemblies that, throughout most of the United States, have initial authority to draw both state legislative and

congressional districts. As far back as 1812, Elbridge Gerry's Democratic-Republican-controlled government in Massachusetts drew contorted districts in an (ultimately unsuccessful) effort to fend off the Federalists. Today, the Democratic and Republican parties fight for the partisan gain that comes with control over the decennial redistricting required by the release of each new census.

Political gerrymandering, as in Gerry's case, focuses on giving an advantage to the political party in power in the state legislature, and racial gerrymandering is used to provide political power to a particular racial group. The term is usually viewed as a derogatory description of the redistricting process when it results in such power advantages, though in the case of political gerrymandering, political parties have often acknowledge their purpose as simply being the spoils of electoral victory. Though racial gerrymandering was originally characterized as giving white voters power over black voters, efforts to equalize minority group electoral power, usually stemming from statutory requirements under the Voting Rights Act have been characterized as gerrymandering and have received exacting scrutiny from the Court.

(i.) POLITICAL GERRYMANDERING

After Baker v. Carr and the population equality cases, it would seem that a case involving political gerrymandering through redistricting would be clearly justiciable. However, Baker was about population inequality as a result of the Tennessee Legislature's failure to stay current with population trends by reapportionment. By declaring that case justiciable, it opened the door to the population equality cases. However, the next two cases gave the Court the opportunity to apply Baker to political redistricting. As you will see, the playing field for this issue remains clouded.

DAVIS v. BANDEMER
478 U.S. 109 (1986)

Justice WHITE announced the judgment of the Court and delivered the opinion of the Court as to Part II and an opinion as to Parts I, III, and IV, in which Justice BRENNAN, Justice MARSHALL, and Justice BLACKMUN join.

In early 1981, the General Assembly initiated the process of reapportioning the State's legislative districts pursuant to the 1980 census. At this time, there were Republican majorities in both the House and the Senate, and the Governor was Republican. Bills were introduced in both Houses, and a reapportionment plan was duly passed and approved by the Governor. This plan provided 50 single-member districts for the Senate; for the House, it provided 7 triple-member, 9 double-member, and 61 single-member districts. In the Senate plan, the population deviation between districts was 1.15%; in the House plan, the deviation was 1.05%. The multimember districts generally included the more metropolitan areas of the State, although not every metropolitan area was in a multimember district. Marion County, which includes Indianapolis, was combined with portions of its neighboring counties to form five triple-member districts. Fort Wayne was divided into two parts, and each part was combined with portions of the surrounding county or counties to make two triple-member districts. On the other hand, South Bend was divided and put partly into a double-member district and partly into a single-member district (each part combined with part of the surrounding county or counties). Although county and city lines were not consistently followed, township lines generally were. The two plans, the Senate and the House, were not nested; that is, each Senate district was not divided exactly into two House districts. There appears to have been little relation between the lines drawn in the two plans.

In early 1982, this suit was filed by several Indiana Democrats (here the appellees) against various state officials (here the appellants), alleging that the 1981 reapportionment plans constituted a political gerrymander intended to disadvantage Democrats. Specifically, they contended that the particular district lines that were drawn and the mix of single-member and multimember districts were intended to and did violate their right, as Democrats, to equal protection under the Fourteenth Amendment. A three-judge District Court was convened to hear these claims.

[In] November 1982, before the case went to trial, elections were held under the new districting plan. All of the House seats and half of the Senate seats were up for election. Over all the House races statewide, Democratic candidates received 51.9% of the vote. Only 43 Democrats, however, were elected to the House. Over all the Senate races statewide, Democratic candidates received 53.1% of the vote. Thirteen (of twenty-five) Democrats were elected. In Marion and Allen Counties, both divided into multimember House districts, Democratic candidates drew 46.6% of the vote, but only 3 of the 21 House seats were filled by Democrats.

On December 13, 1984, a divided District Court issued a decision declaring the reapportionment to be unconstitutional, enjoining the appellants from holding elections pursuant to the 1981 redistricting, ordering the General Assembly to prepare a new plan, and retaining jurisdiction over the case. See 603 F. Supp. 1479.

II

We address first the question whether this case presents a justiciable controversy or a nonjusticiable political question. Although the District Court never explicitly stated that the case was justiciable, its holding clearly rests on such a finding. The appellees urge that this Court has in the past acknowledged and acted upon the justiciability of purely political gerrymandering claims. The appellants contend that we have affirmed on the merits decisions of lower courts finding such claims to be nonjusticiable.

A

Since *Baker* v. *Carr,* 369 U. S. 186 (1962), we have consistently adjudicated equal protection claims in the legislative districting context regarding inequalities in population between districts. In the course of these cases, we have developed and enforced the "one person, one vote" principle. See, *e. g., Reynolds* v. *Sims,* 377 U. S. 533 (1964).

Our past decisions also make clear that even where there is no population deviation among the districts, racial gerrymandering presents a justiciable equal protection claim. In the multimember district context, we have reviewed, and on occasion rejected, districting plans that unconstitutionally diminished the effectiveness of the votes of racial minorities. See *Rogers* v. *Lodge,* 458 U. S. 613 (1982); *Mobile* v. *Bolden,* 446 U. S. 55 (1980); *White* v. *Regester,* 412 U. S. 755 (1973); *Whitcomb* v. *Chavis,* 403 U. S. 124 (1971); *Burns* v. *Richardson,* 384 U. S. 73 (1966); *Fortson* v. *Dorsey,* 379 U. S. 433 (1965). We have also adjudicated claims that the configuration of single-member districts violated equal protection with respect to racial and ethnic minorities, although we have never struck down an apportionment plan because of such a claim. See *United Jewish Organi-*

zations of Williamsburgh, Inc. v. *Carey,* 430 U. S. 144 (1977); *Wright* v. *Rockefeller,* 376 U. S. 52 (1964).

In the multimember district cases, we have also repeatedly stated that districting that would "operate to minimize or cancel out the voting strength of racial *or political* elements of the voting population" would raise a constitutional question. *Fortson, supra,* at 439 (emphasis added). See also *Gaffney* v. *Cummings,* 412 U. S. 735, 751 (1973); *Whitcomb* v. *Chavis, supra,* at 143; *Burns* v. *Richardson, supra,* at 88. Finally, in *Gaffney* v. *Cummings, supra,* we upheld against an equal protection political gerrymandering challenge a state legislative single-member redistricting scheme that was formulated in a bipartisan effort to try to provide political representation on a level approximately proportional to the strength of political parties in the State. In that case, we adjudicated the type of purely political equal protection claim that is brought here, although we did not, as a threshold matter, expressly hold such a claim to be justiciable. Regardless of this lack of a specific holding, our consideration of the merits of the claim in *Gaffney* in the face of a discussion of justiciability in appellant's brief, combined with our repeated reference in other opinions to the constitutional deficiencies of plans that dilute the vote of political groups, at the least supports an inference that these cases are justiciable.

In the years since *Baker* v. *Carr,* both before and after *Gaffney,* however, we have also affirmed a number of decisions in which the lower courts rejected the justiciability of purely political gerrymandering claims. In *WMCA, Inc.* v. *Lomenzo,* 382 U. S. 4 (1965), summarily aff'g 238 F. Supp. 916 (SDNY), the most frequently cited of these cases, we affirmed the decision of a three-judge District Court upholding a temporary apportionment plan for the State of New York. The District Court had determined that political gerrymandering equal protection challenges to this plan were nonjusticiable. See *id.,* at 925-926. Justice Harlan, in his opinion concurring in the Court's summary affirmance, expressed his understanding that the affirmance was based on the Court's approval of the lower court's finding of nonjusticiability. See 382 U. S., at 6. See also *Jimenez* v. *Hidalgo County Water Improvement District No. 2,* 424 U. S. 950 (1976), summarily aff'g 68 F. R. D. 668 (SD Tex. 1975); *Ferrell* v. *Hall,* 406 U. S. 939 (1972), summarily aff'g 339 F. Supp. 73 (WD Okla.); *Wells* v. *Rockefeller,* 398 U. S. 901 (1970), summarily aff'g 311 F. Supp. 48 (SDNY). Although these summary affirmances arguably support an inference that these claims are not justiciable, there are other cases in which federal or state courts adjudicated political gerrymandering claims and we summarily affirmed or dismissed for want of a substantial federal question. See, *e. g., Wiser* v. *Hughes,* 459 U. S. 962 (1982), dismissing for want of a substantial federal question an appeal from *In re Legislative Districting,* 299 Md. 658, 475 A. 2d 428; *Kelly* v. *Bumpers,* 413 U. S. 901 (1973), summarily aff'g 340 F. Supp. 568 (ED Ark. 1972); *Archer* v. *Smith,* 409 U. S. 808 (1972), summarily aff'g *Graves* v. *Barnes,* 343 F. Supp. 704, 734 (WD Tex.).

These sets of cases may look in different directions, but to the extent that our summary affirmances indicate the nonjusticiability of political gerrymander cases, we are not bound by those decisions. As we have observed before, "[i]t is not at all unusual for the Court to find it appropriate to give full consideration to a question that has been the subject of previous summary action." *Washington* v. *Yakima Indian Nation,* 439 U. S. 463, 477, n. 20 (1979). See also *Edelman* v. *Jordan,* 415 U. S. 651, 670-671 (1974). The issue that the appellants would have us find to be precluded by these summary dispositions is an important one, and it deserves further consideration.

B

[D]isposition of this question does not involve us in a matter more properly decided by a coequal branch of our Government. There is no risk of foreign or domestic disturbance, and in light of our cases since *Baker* we are not persuaded that there are no judicially discernible and manageable standards by which political gerrymander cases are to be decided.

It is true that the type of claim that was presented in *Baker* v. *Carr* was subsequently resolved in this Court by the formulation of the "one person, one vote" rule. See, *e. g.,* *Reynolds* v. *Sims,* 377 U. S., at 557-561. The mere fact, however, that we may not now similarly perceive a likely arithmetic presumption in the instant context does not compel a conclusion that the claims presented here are nonjusticiable. The one person, one vote principle had not yet been developed when *Baker* was decided. At that time, the Court did not rely on the potential for such a rule in finding justiciability. Instead, as the language quoted above clearly indicates, the Court contemplated simply that legislative line drawing in the districting context would be susceptible of adjudication under the applicable constitutional criteria.

Furthermore, in formulating the one person, one vote formula, the Court characterized the question posed by election districts of disparate size as an issue of fair representation. In such cases, it is not that anyone is deprived of a vote or that any person's vote is not counted. Rather, it is that one electoral district elects a single representative and another district of the same size elects two or more — the elector's vote in the former district having less weight in the sense that he may vote for and his district be represented by only one legislator, while his neighbor in the adjoining district votes for and is represented by two or more. *Reynolds* accordingly observed:

> Since the achieving of fair and effective representation for all citizens is concededly the basic aim of legislative apportionment, we conclude that the Equal Protection Clause guarantees the opportunity for equal participation by all voters in the election of State legislators. Diluting the weight of votes because of place of residence impairs basic constitutional rights under the Fourteenth Amendment just as much as invidious discriminations based upon factors such as race. . . .

377 U. S., at 565-566.

Reynolds surely indicates the justiciability of claims going to the adequacy of representation in state legislatures.

The issue here is of course different from that adjudicated in *Reynolds*. It does not concern districts of unequal size. Not only does everyone have the right to vote and to have his vote counted, but each elector may vote for and be represented by the same number of lawmakers. Rather, the claim is that each political group in a State should have the same chance to elect representatives of its choice as any other political group. Nevertheless, the issue is one of representation, and we decline to hold that such claims are never justiciable.

Our racial gerrymander cases such as *White* v. *Regester* and *Whitcomb* v. *Chavis* indicate as much. In those cases, there was no population variation among the districts, and no one was precluded from voting. The claim instead was that an identifiable racial or ethnic group had an insufficient chance to elect a representative of its choice and that district lines should be redrawn to remedy this alleged defect. In both cases, we adjudicated the merits of such claims, rejecting the claim in *Whitcomb* and sustaining it in *Regester.* Just as clearly, in *Gaffney* v. *Cummings,* where the districts also passed muster under the *Reynolds* formula, the claim was that the legislature had manipulated district lines to afford political groups in various districts an enhanced opportunity to elect legislators of their choice. Although advising caution, we said that "we *must* . . . respond to [the] claims . . . that even if acceptable populationwise, the . . . plan was invidiously discriminatory because a 'political fairness principle' was followed. . . ." 412 U. S., at 751-752 (emphasis added). We went on to hold that the statute at issue did not violate the Equal Protection Clause.

These decisions support a conclusion that this case is justiciable. As *Gaffney* demonstrates, that the claim is submitted by a political group, rather than a racial group, does not distinguish it in terms of justiciability. That the characteristics of the complaining group are not immutable or that the group has not been subject to the same historical stigma may be relevant to the manner in which the case is adjudicated, but these differences do not justify a refusal to entertain such a case.

In fact, Justice O'Connor's attempt to distinguish this political gerrymandering claim from the racial gerrymandering claims that we have consistently adjudicated demonstrates the futility of such an effort. Her conclusion that the claim in this case is not justiciable seems to rest on a dual concern that no judicially manageable standards exist and that adjudication of such claims requires an initial policy decision that the judiciary should not make. Yet she does not point out how the standards that we set forth here for adjudicating this political gerrymandering claim are less manageable than the standards that have been developed for racial gerrymandering claims. Nor does she demonstrate what initial policy decision — regarding, for example, the desirability of fair group representation — we have made here that we have not made in the race cases. She merely asserts that because race has historically been a suspect classification individual minority voters' rights are more immediately related to a racial minority group's voting strength. This, in combination with "the greater warrant the Equal Protection Clause gives the federal courts to intervene for protection against racial discrimination, suffice to render racial gerrymandering claims justiciable." *Post,* at 151 (O'Connor, J., concurring in judgment).

Reliance on these assertions to determine justiciability would transform the narrow categories of "political questions" that *Baker* v. *Carr* carefully defined into an ad hoc litmus test of this Court's reactions to the desirability of and need for judicial application of constitutional or statutory standards to a given type of claim. Justice O'Connor's own discussion seems to reflect such an approach: She concludes that because political gerrymandering may be a "self-limiting enterprise" there is no need for judicial intervention. *Post,* at 152. She also expresses concern that our decision today will lead to "political instability and judicial malaise," *post,* at 147, because nothing will prevent members of other identifiable groups from bringing similar claims. To begin with, Justice O'Connor's factual assumptions are by no means obviously correct: It is not clear that political gerrymandering *is* a self-limiting enterprise or that other groups will have any great incentive to bring gerrymandering claims, given the requirement of a showing of discriminatory intent. At a more fundamental level, however, Justice O'Connor's analysis is flawed because it focuses on the perceived need for judicial review and on the potential practical problems with allowing such review. Validation of the consideration of such amorphous and wide-ranging factors in assessing justiciability would alter substantially the analysis the Court enunciated in *Baker* v. *Carr,* and we decline Justice O'Connor's implicit invitation to rethink that approach.

III

Having determined that the political gerrymandering claim in this case is justiciable, we turn to the question whether the District Court erred in holding that the appellees had alleged and proved a violation of the Equal Protection Clause.

A

Preliminarily, we agree with the District Court that the claim made by the appellees in this case is a claim that the 1981 apportionment discriminates against Democrats on a statewide basis. Both the appellees and the District Court have cited instances of individual districting within the State which they believe exemplify this discrimination, but the appellees' claim, as we understand it, is that Democratic voters over the State as a whole, not Democratic voters in particular districts, have been subjected to unconstitutional discrimination. See, *e. g.,* Complaint of Bandemer Plaintiffs 3-7. Although the statewide discrimination asserted here was allegedly accomplished through the manipulation of individual district lines, the focus of the equal protection inquiry is necessarily somewhat different from that involved in the review of individual districts.

We also agree with the District Court that in order to succeed the Bandemer plaintiffs were required to prove both intentional discrimination against an identifiable political group and an actual discriminatory effect on that group. See, *e. g., Mobile* v. *Bolden,* 446 U. S., at 67-68. Further, we are confident that if the law challenged here had discriminatory effects on Democrats, this record would support a finding that the discrimination was intentional. Thus, we decline to overturn the District Court's finding of discriminatory intent as clearly erroneous.

Indeed, quite aside from the anecdotal evidence, the shape of the House and Senate Districts, and the alleged disregard for political boundaries, we think it most likely that whenever a legislature redistricts, those responsible for the legislation will know the likely political composition of the new districts and will have a prediction as to whether a particular district is a safe one for a Democratic or Republican candidate or is a competitive district that either candidate might win.

[B]

We do not accept, however, the District Court's legal and factual bases for concluding that the 1981 Act visited a sufficiently adverse effect on the appellees' constitutionally protected rights to make out a violation of the Equal Protection Clause. The District Court held that because any apportionment scheme that purposely prevents proportional representation is unconstitutional, Democratic voters need only show that their proportionate voting influence has been adversely affected. 603 F. Supp., at 1492. Our cases, however, clearly foreclose any claim that the Constitution requires proportional representation or that legislatures in reapportioning must draw district lines to come as near as possible to allocating seats to the contending parties in proportion to what their anticipated statewide vote will be. *Whitcomb* v. *Chavis,* 403 U. S., at 153, 156, 160; *White* v. *Regester,* 412 U. S., at 765-766.

The typical election for legislative seats in the United States is conducted in described geographical districts, with the candidate receiving the most votes in each district winning the seat allocated to that district. If all or most of the districts are competitive — defined by the District Court in this case as districts in which the anticipated split in the party vote is within the range of 45% to 55% — even a narrow statewide preference for either party would produce an overwhelming majority for the winning party in the state legislature. This consequence, however, is inherent in winner-take-all, district-based elections, and we cannot hold that such a reapportionment law would violate the Equal Protection Clause because the voters in the losing party do not have representation in the legislature in proportion to the statewide vote received by their party candidates. As we have said: "[W]e are unprepared to hold that district-based elections decided by plurality vote are unconstitutional in either single-or multi-member districts simply because the supporters of losing candidates have no legislative seats assigned to them." *Whitcomb* v. *Chavis, supra,* at 160. This is true of a racial as well as a political group. *White* v. *Regester, supra,* at 765-766. It is also true of a statewide claim as well as an individual district claim.

To draw district lines to maximize the representation of each major party would require creating as many safe seats for each party as the demographic and predicted political characteristics of the State would permit. This in turn would leave the minority in each safe district without a representative of its choice. We upheld this "political fairness" approach in *Gaffney* v. *Cummings,* despite its tendency to deny safe district minorities any realistic chance to elect their own representatives. But *Gaffney* in no way suggested that the Constitution requires the approach that Connecticut had adopted in that case.

In cases involving individual multimember districts, we have required a substantially greater showing of adverse effects than a mere lack of proportional representation to support a finding of unconstitutional vote dilution. Only where there is evidence that excluded groups have "less opportunity to participate in the political processes and to elect candidates of their choice" have we refused to approve the use of multimember districts. *Rogers* v. *Lodge,* 458 U. S., at 624. See also *United Jewish Organizations of Williamsburgh, Inc.* v. *Carey,* 430 U. S., at 167; *White* v. *Regester, supra,* at 765-766; *Whitcomb* v. *Chavis, supra,* at 150. In these cases, we have also noted the lack of responsiveness by those elected to the concerns of the relevant groups. See *Rogers* v. *Lodge, supra,* at 625-627; *White* v. *Regester, supra,* at 766-767.

These holdings rest on a conviction that the mere fact that a particular apportionment scheme makes it more difficult for a particular group in a particular district to elect the representatives of its choice does not render that scheme constitutionally infirm. This conviction, in turn, stems from a perception that the power to influence the political process is not limited to winning elections. An individual or a group of individuals who votes for a losing candidate is usually deemed to be adequately represented by the winning candidate and to have as much opportunity to influence that candidate as other voters in the district. We cannot presume in such a situation, without actual proof to the contrary, that the candidate elected will entirely ignore the interests of those voters. This is true even in a safe district where the losing group loses election after election. Thus, a group's electoral power is not unconstitutionally diminished by the simple fact of an apportionment scheme that makes winning elections more difficult, and a failure of proportional representation alone does not constitute impermissible discrimination under the Equal Protection Clause. See *Mobile* v. *Bolden,* 446 U. S., at 111, n. 7 (Marshall, J., dissenting).

As with individual districts, where unconstitutional vote dilution is alleged in the form of statewide political gerrymandering, the mere lack of proportional representation will not be sufficient to prove unconstitutional discrimination. Again, without specific supporting evidence, a court cannot presume in such a case that those who are elected will disregard the disproportionately underrepresented group. Rather, unconstitutional discrimination occurs only when the electoral system is arranged in a manner that will consistently degrade a voter's or a group of voters' influence on the political process as a whole.

Although this is a somewhat different formulation than we have previously used in describing unconstitutional vote dilution in an individual district, the focus of both of these inquiries is essentially the same. In both contexts, the question is whether a particular group has been unconstitutionally denied its chance to effectively influence the political process. In a challenge to an individual district, this inquiry focuses on the opportunity of members of the group to participate in party deliberations in the slating and nomination of candidates, their opportunity to register and vote, and hence their chance to directly influence the election returns and to secure the attention of the winning candidate. Statewide, however, the inquiry centers on the voters' direct or indirect influence on the elections of the state legislature as a whole. And, as in individual district cases, an equal protection violation may be found only where the electoral system substantially disadvantages certain voters in their opportunity to influence the political process effectively. In this context, such a finding of unconstitutionality must be supported by evidence of continued frustration of the will of a majority of the voters or effective denial to a minority of voters of a fair chance to influence the political process.

Based on these views, we would reject the District Court's apparent holding that *any* interference with an opportunity to elect a representative of one's choice would be sufficient to allege or make out an equal protection violation, unless justified by some acceptable state interest that the State would be required to demonstrate. In addition to being contrary to the above-described conception of an unconstitutional political gerrymander, such a low threshold for legal action would invite attack on all or almost all reapportionment statutes. District-based elections hardly ever produce a perfect fit between votes and representation. The one person, one vote imperative often mandates departure from this result as does the no-retrogression rule required by § 5 of the Voting Rights Act. Inviting attack on minor departures from some supposed norm would too much embroil the judiciary in second-guessing what has consistently been referred to as a political task for the legislature, a task that should not be monitored too closely unless the express or tacit goal is to effect its removal from legislative halls. We decline to take a major step toward that end, which would be so much at odds with our history and experience.

The view that a prima facie case of illegal discrimination in reapportionment requires a showing of more than a *de minimis* effect is not unprecedented. Reapportionment cases involving the one person, one vote principle such as *Gaffney* v. *Cummings* and *White* v. *Regester* provide support for such a requirement. In the present, considerably more complex context, it is also appropriate to require allegations and proof that the challenged legislative plan has had or will have effects that are sufficiently serious to require intervention by the federal courts in state reapportionment decisions.

[I]n determining the constitutionality of multimember districts challenged as racial gerrymanders, we have rejected the view that "any group with distinctive interests must be represented in legislative halls if it is numerous enough to command at least one seat and represents a minority living in an area sufficiently compact to constitute a single-member district." *Whitcomb,* 403 U. S., at 156. Rather, we have required that there be proof that the complaining minority "had less opportunity . . . to participate in the political processes and to elect legislators of their choice." *Id.,* at 149. In *Whitcomb,* we went on to observe that there was no proof that blacks were not allowed to register or vote, to choose the political party they desired to support, to participate in its affairs or to be equally represented on those occasions when candidates were chosen, or to be included among the candidates slated by the Democratic Party. Against this background, we concluded that the failure of the minority "to have legislative seats in proportion to its population emerges more as a function of losing elections than of built-in bias against poor Negroes. The voting power of ghetto residents may have been 'cancelled out' as the District Court held, but this seems a mere euphemism for political defeat at the polls." *Id.,* at 153. *Whitcomb* accordingly rejected a challenge to multimember districts in Marion County, Indiana. A similar challenge was sustained in *White* v. *Regester,* but only by employing the same criterion, namely, that the plaintiffs must produce evidence to support a finding "that the political processes leading to nomination and election were not equally open to participation by the group in question — that its members had less opportunity than did other residents in the district to participate in the political processes and to elect legislators of their choice." 412 U. S., at 766.

This participatory approach to the legality of individual multimember districts is not helpful where the claim is that such districts discriminate against Democrats, for it could hardly be said that Democrats, any more than Republicans, are excluded from participating in the affairs of their own party or from the processes by which candidates are nominated and elected. For constitutional purposes, the Democratic claim in this case, insofar as it challenges *vel non* the legality of the multimember districts in certain counties, is like that of the Negroes in *Whitcomb* who failed to prove a racial gerrymander, for it boils down to a complaint that they failed to attract a majority of the voters in the challenged multimember districts.

In sum, we hold that political gerrymandering cases are properly justiciable under the Equal Protection Clause. We also conclude, however, that a threshold showing of discriminatory vote dilution is required for a prima facie case of an equal protection violation. In this case, the findings made by the District Court of an adverse effect on the appellees do not surmount the threshold requirement. Consequently, the judgment of the District Court is reversed.

Justice O'CONNOR, with whom THE CHIEF JUSTICE and Justice REHNQUIST join, concurring in the judgment.

Today the Court holds that claims of political gerrymandering lodged by members of one of the political parties that make up our two-party system are justiciable under the Equal Protection Clause of the Fourteenth Amendment. Nothing in our precedents compels us to take this step, and there is every reason not to do so. I would hold that the partisan gerrymandering claims of major political parties raise a nonjusticiable political question that the judiciary should leave to the legislative branch as the Framers of the Constitution unquestionably intended. Accordingly, I would reverse the District Court's judgment on the grounds that appellees' claim is nonjusticiable.

[To] turn these matters over to the federal judiciary is to inject the courts into the most heated partisan issues. It is predictable that the courts will respond by moving away from the nebulous standard a plurality of the Court fashions today and toward some form of rough proportional representation for all political groups. The consequences of this shift will be as immense as they are unfortunate. I do not believe, and the Court offers not a shred of evidence to suggest, that the Framers of the Constitution intended the judicial power to encompass the making of such fundamental choices about how this Nation is to be governed. Nor do I believe that the proportional representation towards which the Court's expansion of equal protection doctrine will lead is consistent with our history, our traditions, or our political institutions.

The step taken today is a momentous one, which if followed in the future can only lead to political instability and judicial malaise. If members of the major political parties are protected by the Equal Protection Clause from dilution of their voting strength, then members of every identifiable group that possesses distinctive interests and tends to vote on the basis of those interests should be able to bring similar claims. Federal courts will have no alternative but to attempt to recreate the complex process of legislative apportionment in the context of adversary litigation in order to reconcile the competing claims of political, religious, ethnic, racial, occupational, and socioeconomic groups. Even if there were some way of limiting such claims to organized political parties, the fact remains that the losing party or the losing group of legislators in every reapportionment will now be invited to fight the battle anew in federal court. Apportionment is so important to legislators and political parties that the burden of proof the plurality places on political gerrymandering plaintiffs is unlikely to deter the routine lodging of such complaints. Notwithstanding the plurality's threshold requirement of discriminatory effects, the Court's holding that political gerrymandering claims are justiciable has opened the door to pervasive and unwarranted judicial superintendence of the legislative task of apportionment. There is simply no clear stopping point to prevent the gradual evolution of a requirement of roughly proportional representation for every cohesive political group.

In my view, this enterprise is flawed from its inception. The Equal Protection Clause does not supply judicially manageable standards for resolving purely political gerrymandering claims, and no group right to an equal share of political power was ever intended by the Framers of the Fourteenth Amendment. The Court rests its case on precedent, but the cases on which the Court relies do not require that we take this next and most far-reaching step into the "political thicket." *Colegrove* v. *Green*, 328 U. S. 549, 556 (1946) (opinion of Frankfurter, J.).

Baker v. *Carr* reaffirmed that a lawsuit will be held to involve a political question where there is "a lack of judicially discoverable and manageable standards for resolving it," or where "the impossibility of deciding without an initial policy determination of a kind clearly for nonjudicial discretion" is apparent. 369 U. S., at 217. The Court first found a workable constitutional standard for applying the Equal Protection Clause to state legislative districting in *Reynolds* v. *Sims, supra.* But until today the Court has not extended the principles of *Baker* v. *Carr* and *Reynolds* v. *Sims* to test a legislative districting plan on grounds of partisan political gerrymandering. Indeed, one year after *Reynolds* v. *Sims,* the Court was unanimous in summarily affirming a judgment determining that a political gerrymandering challenge was nonjusticiable; as Justice Harlan pointed out, the Court's action constituted a rejection of "contentions that . . . partisan 'gerrymandering' may be subject to federal constitutional attack under the Fourteenth Amendment." *WMCA, Inc.* v. *Lomenzo,* 382 U. S. 4, 6 (1965) (concurring opinion).

[In Baker v. Carr] the Court in effect ruled that an arbitrary and capricious discrimination against individual voters with respect to the weight of their votes would state a cognizable claim under the Equal Protection Clause. See *id.,* at 226; *id.,* at 338-339 (Harlan, J., dissenting). That threshold determination about the reach and meaning of the

Equal Protection Clause was the basis for the Court's holding that the complaint of the Tennessee voters was justiciable. Even this "arbitrary and capricious" standard threatened to prove unmanageable, but the difficulty was pretermitted when a relatively simple and judicially manageable requirement of population equality among districts was adopted the following Term in *Reynolds* v. *Sims.* See Bickel, The Supreme Court and Reapportionment, in Reapportionment in the 1970's pp. 57, 64 (N. Polsby ed. 1971).

Baker v. *Carr* does not require that we hold that the right asserted in this case is similarly within the intendment of the Equal Protection Clause and determinable under the standards developed to enforce that Clause. The right asserted in *Baker* v. *Carr* was an individual right to a vote whose weight was not arbitrarily subjected to "debasement," 369 U. S., at 194. The rights asserted in this case are *group* rights to an equal share of political power and representation, and the "arbitrary and capricious" standard discussed in *Baker* v. *Carr* cannot serve as the basis for recognizing such rights. Indeed, the Court today does not rely on such a standard.

Instead, the Court justifies the extension of vote dilution claims to mainstream political groups with the pronouncement that "*Reynolds* surely indicates the justiciability of claims going to the adequacy of representation in state legislatures." *Ante,* at 124. But *Reynolds* makes plain that the one person, one vote principle safeguards the individual's right to vote, not the interests of political groups: "To the extent that a citizen's right to vote is debased, he is that much less a citizen. The fact that an individual lives here or there is not a legitimate reason for overweighting or diluting the efficacy of his vote." 377 U. S., at 567. For that reason, "an individual's right to vote for state legislators is unconstitutionally impaired when its weight is in a substantial fashion diluted when compared with votes of citizens living in other parts of the State." *Id.,* at 568. Thus, the right guaranteed by the Equal Protection Clause as interpreted in *Reynolds* is "the right of *each voter* to 'have his vote weighted equally with those of all other citizens.'" *Mobile* v. *Bolden,* 446 U. S. 55, 78 (1980) (plurality opinion).

In the case of mainstream political groups, the Court has not accepted the argument that an "asserted entitlement to group representation," *Bolden,* 446 U. S., at 77, can be traced to the one person, one vote principle.

In my view, where a racial minority group is characterized by "the traditional indicia of suspectness" and is vulnerable to exclusion from the political process, *San Antonio Independent School District* v. *Rodriguez,* 411 U. S. 1, 28 (1973); see also *Johnson* v. *Robison,* 415 U. S. 361, 375, n. 14 (1974), individual voters who belong to that group enjoy some measure of protection against intentional dilution of their group voting strength by means of racial gerrymandering. As a matter of past history and present reality, there is a direct and immediate relationship between the racial minority's group voting strength in a particular community and the individual rights of its members to vote and to participate in the political process. In these circumstances, the stronger nexus between individual rights and group interests, and the greater warrant the Equal Protection Clause gives the federal courts to intervene for protection against racial discrimination, suffice to render racial gerrymandering claims justiciable. Even so, the individual's right is infringed only if the racial minority group can prove that it has "essentially been shut out of the political process." *Ante,* at 139.

Clearly, members of the Democratic and Republican Parties cannot claim that they are a discrete and insular group vulnerable to exclusion from the political process by some dominant group: these political parties *are* the dominant groups, and the Court has offered no reason to believe that they are incapable of fending for themselves through the political process. Indeed, there is good reason to think that political gerrymandering is a self-limiting enterprise. See B. Cain, The Reapportionment Puzzle 151-159 (1984). In order to gerrymander, the legislative majority must weaken some of its safe seats, thus exposing its own incumbents to greater risks of defeat — risks they may refuse to accept past a certain point. *Id.,* at 154-155. Similarly, an overambitious gerrymander can lead to disaster for the legislative majority: because it has created more seats in which it hopes to win relatively narrow victories, the same swing in overall voting strength will tend to cost the legislative majority more and more seats as the gerrymander becomes more ambitious. *Id.,* at 152. More generally, each major party presumably has ample weapons at its disposal to conduct the partisan struggle that often leads to a partisan apportionment, but also often leads to a bipartisan one. There is no proof before us that political gerrymandering is an evil that cannot be checked or cured by the people or by the parties themselves. Absent such proof, I see no basis for concluding that there is a need, let alone a constitutional basis, for judicial intervention.

[I] would avoid the difficulties generated by the plurality's efforts to confine the effects of a generalized group right to equal representation by not recognizing such a right in the first instance. To allow district courts to strike down apportionment plans on the basis of their prognostications as to the outcome of future elections or future apportionments invites "findings" on matters as to which neither judges nor anyone else can have any confidence. Once it is conceded that "a group's electoral power is not unconstitutionally diminished by the simple fact of an apportionment scheme that makes winning elections more difficult," *ante,* at 132, the virtual impossibility of reliably predicting how difficult it will be to win an election in 2, or 4, or 10 years should, in my view, weigh in favor of holding such challenges nonjusticiable. Racial gerrymandering should remain justiciable, for the harms it engenders run counter to the central thrust of the Fourteenth Amendment. But no such justification can be given for judicial intervention on behalf of mainstream political parties, and the risks such intervention poses to our political institutions are unacceptable. "Political affiliation is the keystone of the political trade. Race, ideally, is not." *United Jewish Organizations of Williamsburgh, Inc.* v. *Carey,* 430 U. S., at 171, n. 1 (Brennan, J., concurring).

[A dissent by Justice Powell, joined by Justice Stevens is omitted as is a concurrence by Chief Justice Burger].

Eighteen years after Davis, the Supreme Court revisited the question of the justiciability of political gerrymander cases in the decision below.

VIETH v. JUBILIRER
541 U.S. 267 (2004)

Justice SCALIA announced the judgment of the Court and delivered an opinion, in which THE CHIEF JUSTICE, Justice O'CONNOR, and Justice THOMAS join.

[O]ver the dissent of three Justices, the Court held in *Davis* v. *Bandemer* that, since it was "not persuaded that there are no judicially discernible and manageable standards by which political gerrymander cases are to be decided," 478 U. S., at 123, such cases *were* justiciable. The clumsy shifting of the burden of proof for the premise (the Court was "not persuaded" that standards do not exist, rather than "persuaded" that they do) was necessitated by the uncomfortable fact that the six-Justice majority could not discern what the judicially discernable standards might be. There was no majority on that point. Four of the Justices finding justiciability believed that the standard was one thing, see *id.*, at 127 (plurality opinion of White, J., joined by Brennan, Marshall, and Blackmun, JJ.); two believed it was something else, see *id.*, at 161 (Powell, J., joined by Stevens, J., concurring in part and dissenting in part). The lower courts have lived with that assurance of a standard (or more precisely, lack of assurance that there is no standard), coupled with that inability to specify a standard, for the past 18 years. In that time, they have considered numerous political gerrymandering claims; this Court has never revisited the unanswered question of what standard governs.

Nor can it be said that the lower courts have, over 18 years, succeeded in shaping the standard that this Court was initially unable to enunciate. They have simply applied the standard set forth in *Bandemer*'s four-Justice plurality opinion. This might be thought to prove that the four-Justice plurality standard has met the test of time — but for the fact that its application has almost invariably produced the same result (except for the incurring of attorney's fees) as would have obtained if the question were nonjusticiable: Judicial intervention has been refused. As one commentary has put it, "[t]hroughout its subsequent history, *Bandemer* has served almost exclusively as an invitation to litigation without much prospect of redress." S. Issacharoff, P. Karlan, & R. Pildes, The Law of Democracy 886 (rev. 2d ed. 2002). The one case in which relief was provided (and merely preliminary relief, at that) did *not* involve the drawing of district lines; in *all* of the cases we are aware of involving that most common form of political gerrymandering, relief was denied. Moreover, although the case in which relief was provided seemingly involved the *ne plus ultra* of partisan manipulation, see n. 5, *supra*, we would be at a loss to explain why the *Bandemer* line should have been drawn just there, and should not have embraced several districting plans that were upheld despite allegations of extreme partisan discrimination, bizarrely shaped districts, and disproportionate results. See, *e. g., Session* v. *Perry*, 298 F. Supp. 2d 451 (ED Tex. 2004) (*per curiam*); *O'Lear* v. *Miller*, 222 F. Supp. 2d 850 (ED Mich.), summarily aff'd, 537 U. S. 997 (2002); *Badham* v. *Eu*, 694 F. Supp. 664, 670 (ND Cal. 1988), summarily aff'd, 488 U. S. 1024 (1989). To think that this lower court jurisprudence has brought forth "judicially discernible and manageable standards" would be fantasy.

While we do not lightly overturn one of our own holdings, "when governing decisions are unworkable or are badly reasoned, 'this Court has never felt constrained to follow precedent.'" 501 U. S., at 827 (quoting *Smith* v. *Allwright*, 321 U. S. 649, 665 (1944)). Eighteen years of essentially pointless litigation have persuaded us that *Bandemer* is incapable of principled application. We would therefore overrule that case, and decline to adjudicate these political gerrymandering claims.

The judgment of the District Court is affirmed.

It is so ordered.

Justice KENNEDY, concurring in the judgment.

A decision ordering the correction of all election district lines drawn for partisan reasons would commit federal and state courts to unprecedented intervention in the American political process. The Court is correct to refrain from directing this substantial intrusion into the Nation's political life. While agreeing with the plurality that the complaint the appellants filed in the District Court must be dismissed, and while understanding that great caution is necessary when approaching this subject, I would not foreclose all possibility of judicial relief if some limited and precise rationale were found to correct an established violation of the Constitution in some redistricting cases.

That courts can grant relief in districting cases where race is involved does not answer our need for fairness principles here. Those controversies implicate a different inquiry. They involve sorting permissible classifications in the redistricting context from impermissible ones. Race is an impermissible classification. See *Shaw* v. *Reno,* 509 U. S. 630 (1993). Politics is quite a different matter. See *Gaffney* v. *Cummings,* 412 U. S. 735, 752 (1973) ("It would be idle, we think, to contend that any political consideration taken into account in fashioning a reapportionment plan is sufficient to invalidate it").

A determination that a gerrymander violates the law must rest on something more than the conclusion that political classifications were applied. It must rest instead on a conclusion that the classifications, though generally permissible, were applied in an invidious manner or in a way unrelated to any legitimate legislative objective.

[T]he plurality says that 18 years, in effect, prove the negative. *Ante,* at 306 ("Eighteen years of essentially pointless litigation have persuaded us"). As Justice Souter is correct to point out, however, during these past 18 years the lower courts could do no more than follow *Davis* v. *Bandemer,* which formulated a single, apparently insuperable standard. See *post,* at 344-345 (dissenting opinion). Moreover, by the timeline of the law 18 years is rather a short period. In addition, the rapid evolution of technologies in the apportionment field suggests yet unexplored possibilities. Computer assisted districting has become so routine and sophisticated that legislatures, experts, and courts can use databases to map electoral districts in a matter of hours, not months. See, *e. g., Larios* v. *Cox,* 305 F. Supp. 2d 1335 (ND Ga. 2004) (*per curiam*). Technology is both a threat and a promise. On the one hand, if courts refuse to entertain any claims of partisan gerrymandering, the temptation to use partisan favoritism in districting in an unconstitutional manner will grow. On the other hand, these new technologies may produce new methods of analysis that make more evident the precise nature of the burdens gerrymanders impose on the representational rights of voters and parties. That would facilitate court efforts to identify and remedy the burdens, with judicial intervention limited by the derived standards.

If suitable standards with which to measure the burden a gerrymander imposes on representational rights did emerge, hindsight would show that the Court prematurely abandoned the field. That is a risk the Court should not take. Instead, we should adjudicate only what is in the papers before us. See *Baker,* 369 U. S., at 331 (Harlan, J., dissenting) (concluding that the malapportionment claim "should have been dismissed for 'failure to state a claim upon which relief can be granted'" because "[u]ntil it is first decided to what extent [the] right [to apportion] is limited by the Federal Constitution, and whether what [a State] has done or failed to do . . . runs afoul of any such limitation, we need not reach the issues of 'justiciability' or 'political question'").

[T]hough in the briefs and at argument the appellants relied on the Equal Protection Clause as the source of their substantive right and as the basis for relief, I note that the complaint in this case also alleged a violation of First Amendment rights. See Amended Complaint ¶ 48; Juris. Statement 145a. The First Amendment may be the more relevant constitutional provision in future cases that allege unconstitutional partisan gerrymandering. After all, these allegations involve the First Amendment interest of not burdening or penalizing citizens because of their participation in the electoral process, their voting history, their association with a political party, or their expression of political views. See *Elrod* v. *Burns*, 427 U. S. 347 (1976) (plurality opinion). Under general First Amendment principles those burdens in other contexts are unconstitutional absent a compelling government interest. See *id.*, at 362. "Representative democracy in any populous unit of governance is unimaginable without the ability of citizens to band together in promoting among the electorate candidates who espouse their political views." *California Democratic Party* v. *Jones*, 530 U. S. 567, 574 (2000). As these precedents show, First Amendment concerns arise where a State enacts a law that has the purpose and effect of subjecting a group of voters or their party to disfavored treatment by reason of their views. In the context of partisan gerrymandering, that means that First Amendment concerns arise where an apportionment has the purpose and effect of burdening a group of voters' representational rights. The ordered working of our Republic, and of the democratic process, depends on a sense of decorum and restraint in all branches of government, and in the citizenry itself. Here, one has the sense that legislative restraint was abandoned. That should not be thought to serve the interests of our political order. Nor should it be thought to serve our interest in demonstrating to the world how democracy works. Whether spoken with concern or pride, it is unfortunate that our legislators have reached the point of declaring that, when it comes to apportionment: "'We are in the business of rigging elections.'" Hoeffel, Six Incumbents Are a Week Away from Easy Election, Winston-Salem Journal, Jan. 27, 1998, p. B1 (quoting a North Carolina state senator). Still, the Court's own responsibilities require that we refrain from intervention in this instance. The failings of the many proposed standards for measuring the burden a gerrymander imposes on representational rights make our intervention improper. If workable standards do emerge to measure these burdens, however, courts should be prepared to order relief. With these observations, I join the judgment of the Court.

[Dissenting opinions by Justices Stevens, Souter (joined by Ginsburg) and Breyer are omitted.]

Comments on *Vieth v. Jubilirer* The lower court in this case left the challenged redistricting intact because the judges there were unable to agree on a workable solution to the problem. Justice Scalia and three others on the Court would have overruled *Davis* but did not garner the necessary five votes for that outcome. Justice Kennedy was of the opinion that though manageable standards may not be available in the present case, the possibility of using later developed methods of judging fairness in political gerrymanders should not be foreclosed by overruling *Davis*. In addition to his fifth vote for leaving the lower court ruling intact (and thus the challenged plan as well), Justice Kennedy's refusal to join the plurality in overruling *Davis* technically means that the earlier decision remains the law (the four dissenters, in addition to believing that standards were available would not have overruled *Davis*, making the score five votes to maintain *Davis* as precedent).

Two Terms after *Vieth*, in a case that fragmented the Court into multiple opinions, a majority once again failed to coalesce for either the proposition that political gerrymandering claims are nonjusticiable or that the constitutional limits of permissible political influence on districting had been reached. In a consolidated set of cases captioned *League of United Latin American Citizens v. Perry*, 548 U.S. 399 (2006), the Court considered the constitutionality of the Republican-dominated Texas legislature's 2003 redistricting plan, which took place in between regular decennial censuses and increased the Republican cohort in the state congressional delegation by six seats. Republicans defended the plan as helping to correct earlier gerrymandering that Democrats had engineered when they controlled the legislature but were losing their relative share of the voting population. Announcing the judgment of the Court and writing the controlling opinion, Justice Kennedy rejected the challengers' argument for a rule or presumption of constitutional invalidity "when a mid-decade redistricting plan is adopted solely for partisan motivations": "[W]e disagree with appellants' view that a legislature's decision to override a valid, court-drawn plan mid-decade is sufficiently suspect to give shape to a reliable standard for identifying unconstitutional political gerrymanders. We conclude that appellants have established no legally impermissible use of political classifications."

Dissenting from the portion of the decision upholding the constitutionality of the statewide plan, Justice Stevens, joined by Justice Breyer, would have found it "perfectly clear that judicially manageable standards enable us to decide the merits of a statewide challenge to a political gerrymander" and that the legislature's redrawing of an otherwise valid plan "for purely partisan purposes violated the State's constitutional duty to govern impartially." Justice Stevens noted that "although the Constitution places no *per se* ban on midcycle redistricting, a legislature's decision to redistrict in the middle of the census cycle, when the legislature is under no legal obligation to do so, makes the judicial task of identifying the legislature's motive simpler than it would otherwise be. [The] equal protection component of the Fourteenth Amendment requires actions taken by the sovereign to be supported by some legitimate interest, and [a] bare desire to harm a politically disfavored group is not a legitimate interest."

Justice Souter, joined by Justice Ginsburg, likewise filed a partial dissent reaffirming commitment to "the principle that partisan gerrymandering can be recognized as a violation of equal protection," but declining to state how he would apply the substantive test for such a violation that he suggested in *Vieth* because no standard could command a majority of the Court. Justice Breyer also wrote separately, emphasizing that "because the plan entrenches the Republican Party, the State cannot successfully defend it as an effort simply to *neutralize* the Democratic Party's previous political gerrymander," and concluding that "a plan that overwhelmingly relies upon the unjustified use of purely partisan line-drawing considerations [in] its entirety violates the Equal Protection Clause."

Chief Justice Roberts, joined by Justice Alito, filed a partial concurrence, stating, "I agree with the determination that appellants have not provided 'a reliable standard for identifying unconstitutional political gerrymanders. The question whether any such standard exists — that is, whether a challenge to a political gerrymander presents a justiciable case or controversy — has not been argued in these cases. I therefore take no position on that question, which has divided the Court." Justice Scalia, joined by Justice Thomas, concurred in part in the judgment but reiterated his view that "claims of unconstitutional partisan gerrymandering do not present a justiciable case or controversy."

In portions of the decision addressing purely statutory challenges under § 2 of the Voting Rights Act, Justice Kennedy spoke for one majority of the Court in invalidating a redrawn majority-Latino district, and for another majority of the Court in rejecting other Voting Rights Act challenges.

Race and Redistricting: Strict Scrutiny and the Voting Rights Act. The period immediately prior to the enactment of the Voting Rights Act of 1965 saw litigation over the right hamstrung by procedurally difficult statutes, in particular the Civil Rights Act of

1957. The act, based upon the enforcement provisions of both the Fourteenth and Fifteenth Amendments policed the enforcement of the anti-discriminatory amendments through injunction suits filed by the Justice Department and for private suits for money damages. The practical reality of the period was that as certain practices by states or subdivisions were eliminated, they were replaced by new discriminatory practices. As for private suits, civil rights activism at the time was dangerous business and the suits simply were not a reliable means of enforcement of the franchise. The results of this first experiment in voting rights enforcement resulted in little progress.

Following the Civil Rights Act of 1964, Congress passed the Voting Rights Act of 1965. Cognizant of the ineffectiveness of the previous effort in the direction of voting rights enforcement against discrimination, Congress did three things of significance. First it specifically prohibited any "practice, procedure . . . which results in a denial or abridgement of the right of any citizen of the United States to vote on account of race or color." The provision addressed generally practices that would result in either denial or abridgement of the franchise, giving Congress a broad authority over any discriminatory procedure. It also provided for federal observers in affected states and subdivisions, as well as the retention of court jurisdiction as needed.

Additionally, the law provided for preclearance of any "voting qualification or prerequisite to voting, or standard, practice or procedure with respect to voting different from that in force or effect on November 1, 1964 [and subsequent years identified in later renewals of the bill] by either the United States District Court for the District of Columbia, or the Attorney General." In effect, the law, in addition to broader congressional authority provided in the earlier sections, hedged against states and subdivisions practice of using new devices after former practices were ruled as discriminatory violations.

The effectiveness of the preclearance provision in the new law can be credited with the earlier decision of the Supreme Court in *Baker v. Carr* that state reapportionment plans could be reviewed by the federal courts and were not subject to the political question limitation on judicial review, opening that area of state control over political elections to federal scrutiny as "a voting qualification practice. . . or procedure with respect to voting different from that in force or effect on November 1, 1964."

Several key cases arose in the interim years following the initial passage and several subsequent renewals of the act. The cases can be categorized as cases involving state challenges to DOJ preclearance decisions and individual challenges to pre-cleared plans. Typically these cases had to do with re-apportionment or redistricting, but, as is the case in *Texas v. Holder*, other voting procedures were the subject of the litigation. The lynchpin in this litigation was the use of race in the process of developing a plan consistent with the VRA.

SHAW v. RENO
509 U.S. 630 (1993)

[F]orty of North Carolina's one hundred counties are covered by § 5 of the Voting Rights Act of 1965, 42 U.S.C. § 1973c which prohibits a jurisdiction subject to its provisions from implementing changes in a "standard, practice, or procedure with respect to voting" without federal authorization. *Ibid.* The jurisdiction must obtain either a judgment from the United States District Court for the District of Columbia declaring that the proposed change "does not have the purpose and will not have the effect of denying or abridging the right to vote on account of race or color" or administrative preclearance from the Attorney General. *Ibid.* Because the General Assembly's reapportionment plan affected the covered counties, the parties agree that § 5 applied. Tr. of Oral Arg. 14, 27-29. The State chose to submit its plan to the Attorney General for preclearance.

The Attorney General, acting through the Assistant Attorney General for the Civil Rights Division, interposed a formal objection to the General Assembly's plan. The Attorney General specifically objected to the configuration of boundary lines drawn in the south central to southeastern region of the State. In the AttorneyGeneral's view, the General Assembly could have created a second majority minority district "to give effect to black and Native American voting strength in this area" by using boundary lines "no more irregular than [those] found elsewhere in the proposed plan," but failed to do so for "pretextual reasons." See App. to Brief for Federal Appellees 10a-11a.

Under § 5, the State remained free to seek a declaratory judgment from the District Court for the District of Columbia notwithstanding the Attorney General's objection. It did not do so. Instead, the General Assembly enacted a revised redistricting plan, 1991 N. C. Extra Sess. Laws, ch. 7, that included a second majority black district. The General Assembly located the second district not in the south central to southeastern part of the State, but in the north central region along Interstate 85. See Appendix.

The first of the two majority black districts contained in the revised plan, District 1, is somewhat hook shaped. Centered in the northeast portion of the State, it moves southward until it tapers to a narrow band; then, with finger like extensions, it reaches far into the southern most part of the State near the South Carolina border. District 1 has been compared to a "Rorschach ink blot test," *Shaw* v. *Barr*, 808 F. Supp. 461, 476 (EDNC 1992) (Voorhees, C. J., concurring in part and dissenting in part), and a "bug splattered on a windshield," Wall Street Journal, Feb. 4, 1992, p. A14.

The second majority black district, District 12, is even more unusually shaped. It is approximately 160 miles long and, for much of its length, no wider than the I-85 corridor. It winds in snake like fashion through tobacco country, financial centers, and manufacturing areas "until it gobbles in enough enclaves of black neighborhoods." *Shaw* v. *Barr*, *supra*, at 476-477 (Voorhees, C. J., concurring in part and dissenting in part). Northbound and southbound drivers on I-85 sometimes findthemselves in separate districts in one county, only to "trade" districts when they enter the next county. Of the 10 counties through which District 12 passes, five are cut into three different districts; even towns are divided. At one point the district remains contiguous only because it intersects at a single point with two other districts before crossing over them.

[A]ppellants instituted the present action in the United States District Court for the Eastern District of North Carolina. Appellants alleged not that the revised plan constituted a political gerrymander, nor that it violated the "one person, one vote" principle, see *Reynolds* v. *Sims*, 377 U.S. 533, 558 (1964), but that the State had created an unconstitutional *racial* gerrymander. Appellants are five residents of Durham County, North Carolina, all registered to vote in that county. Under the General Assembly's plan, two will vote for congressional representatives in District 12 and three will vote in neighboring District 2. Appellants sued the Governor of North Carolina, the Lieutenant Governor, the Secretary of State, the Speaker of the North Carolina House of Representatives, and members of the North Carolina State Board of Elections (state appellees), together with two federal officials, the Attorney General and the Assistant Attorney General for the Civil Rights Division (federal appellees).

Appellants contended that the General Assembly's revised reapportionment plan violated several provisions of the United States Constitution, including the Fourteenth Amendment. They alleged that the General Assembly deliberately "create[d] two Congressional Districts in which a majority of black voters was concentrated arbitrarily — without regard to any other considerations, such as compactness, contiguousness, geographical boundaries, or political subdivisions" with the purpose "to create Congressional Districts along racial lines" and to assure the election of two black representatives to Congress. App. to Juris. Statement 102a. Appellants sought declaratory and injunctive relief against the state appellees. They sought similar relief against the federal appellees, arguing, alternatively, that the federal appellees had misconstrued the Voting Rights Act or that the Act itself was unconstitutional.

[T]he three judge District Court granted the [a]ppellees' motion to dismiss. [T]he majority found no support for appellants' contentions that race based districting is prohibited by Article I, § 4, or Article I, § 2, of the Constitution, or by the Privileges and Immunities Clause of the Fourteenth Amendment. It deemed appellants' claim under the Fifteenth Amendment essentially subsumed within their related claim under the Equal Protection Clause. 808 F. Supp., at 468-469. That claim, the majority concluded, was barred by *United Jewish Organizations of Williamsburgh, Inc.* v. *Carey*, 430 U.S. 144 (1977) *(UJO)*.

The majority read *UJO* to stand for the proposition that a redistricting scheme violates white voters' rights only if it is "adopted with the purpose and effect of discriminating against white voters . . . on account of their race." 808 F. Supp., at 472. The purposes of favoring minority voters and complying with the Voting Rights Act are not discriminatory in the constitutional sense, the court reasoned, and majority minority districts have an impermissibly discriminatory effect only when they unfairly dilute or cancel out white voting strength. Because the State's purpose here was to comply with the Voting Rights Act, and because the General Assembly's plan did not lead to proportional underrepresentation of white voters statewide, the majority concluded that appellants had failed to state an equal protection claim. *Id.*, at 472-473.

Chief Judge Voorhees agreed that race conscious redistricting is not *per se* unconstitutional but dissented from the rest of the majority's equal protection analysis. He read Justice White's opinion in *UJO* to authorize race based reapportionment only when the State employs traditional districting principles such as compactness and contiguity. 808 F. Supp., at 475-477 (Voorhees, C. J., concurring in part and dissenting in part). North Carolina's failure to respect these principles, in Judge Voorhees' view, "augur[ed] a constitutionally suspect, and potentially unlawful, intent" sufficient to defeat the state appellees' motion to dismiss. *Id.*, at 477.

We noted probable jurisdiction.

Our focus is on appellants' claim that the State engaged in unconstitutional racial gerrymandering. That argument strikes a powerful historical chord: It is unsettling how closely the North Carolina plan resembles the most egregious racial gerrymanders of the past.

An understanding of the nature of appellants' claim is critical to our resolution of the case. In their complaint, appellants did not claim that the General Assembly's reapportionment plan unconstitutionally "diluted" white voting strength. They did not even claim to be white. Rather, appellants' complaint alleged that the deliberatesegregation of voters into separate districts on the basis of race violated their constitutional right to participate in a "color blind" electoral process.

[N]o inquiry into legislative purpose is necessary when the racial classification appears on the face of the statute. See *Personnel Administrator of Massachusetts* v. *Feeney*, 442 U.S. 256, 272 (1979). Accord, *Washington* v. *SeattleSchool District No. 1*, 458 U.S. 457, 485 (1982). Express racial classifications are immediately suspect because, "[a]bsent searching judicial inquiry . . . , there is simply no way of determining what classifications are 'benign' or 'remedial' and what classifications are in fact motivated by illegitimate notions of racial inferiority or simple racial politics."

[The Court went on to establish that in its view, once racial motive is established in a redistricting case, the state's action should be subject to the same scrutiny that other state actions impacting race would receive — strict scrutiny.]

Put differently, we believe that reapportionment is one area in which appearances do matter. A reapportionment plan that includes in one district individuals who belongto the same race, but who are otherwise widely separated by geographical and political boundaries, and who may have little in common with one another but the color of their skin, bears an uncomfortable resemblance to political apartheid. It reinforces the perception that members of the same racial group — regardless of their age, education, economic status, or the community in which the live — think alike, share the same political interests, and will prefer the same candidates at the polls.

[T]he state appellees suggest that a covered jurisdiction may have a compelling interest in creating majority-minority districts in order to comply with the Voting Rights Act. The States certainly have a very strong interest in complying with federal antidiscrimination laws that are constitutionally valid as interpreted and as applied. But in the context of a Fourteenth Amendment challenge, courts must bear in mind the difference between what the law permits and what it requires.

A reapportionment plan would not be narrowly tailored to the goal of avoiding retrogression if the State went beyond what was reasonably necessary to avoid retrogression. Our conclusion is supported by the plurality opinion in *UJO,* in which four Justices determined that New York's creation of additional majority-minority districts was constitutional because the plaintiffs had failed to demonstrate that the State "did more than the Attorney General was authorized to *require* it to do under the nonretrogression principle.

. .

Before us, the state appellees contend that the General Assembly's revised plan was necessary not to prevent retrogression, but to avoid dilution of black voting strength in violation of § 2, as construed in *Thornburg* v. *Gingles*, 478 U.S. 30 (1986). In *Gingles* the Court considered a multimember redistricting plan for the North Carolina State Legislature. The Court held that members of a racial minority group claiming § 2 vote dilution through the use of multimember districts must prove three threshold conditions: that the minority group "is sufficiently large and geographically compact to constitute a majority in a single member district," that the minority group is "politically cohesive," and that "the white majority votes sufficiently as a bloc to enable it . . . usually to defeat the minority's preferred candidate." *Id.,* at 50-51. We have indicated that similar preconditions apply in §2 challenges to single member districts. See *Voinovich* v. *Quilter*, 507 U. S., at ___; *Growe* v. *Emison, supra,* at ___ (slip op., at 14-15).

Appellants maintain that the General Assembly's revised plan could not have been required by § 2. They contend that the State's black population is too dispersed to support two geographically compact majority black districts, as the bizarre shape of District 12 demonstrates, and that there is no evidence of black political cohesion. They also contend that recent black electoral successes demonstrate the willingness of white voters in North Carolina to vote for black candidates. Appellants point out that blacks currently hold the positions of State Auditor, Speaker of the North Carolina House of Representatives, and chair of the North Carolina State Board of Elections. They also point out that in 1990 a black candidate defeated a white opponent in the Democratic Party run off for a United States Senate seat before being defeated narrowly by the Republican incumbent in the general election. Appellants further argue that if § 2 did require adoption of North Carolina'srevised plan, § 2 is to that extent unconstitutional. These arguments were not developed below, and the issues remain open for consideration on remand.

The state appellees alternatively argue that the General Assembly's plan advanced a compelling interest entirely distinct from the Voting Rights Act. We previously have recognized a significant state interest in eradicating the effects of past racial discrimination. See, e. g., *Croson*, 488 U. S., at 491-493 (opinion of O'Connor, J., joined by Rehnquist, C. J., and White, J.); *id.*, at 518 (Kennedy, J., concurring in part and concurring in judgment); *Wygant*, 476 U. S., at 280-282 (plurality opinion); *id.*, at 286 (O'Connor, J., concurring in part and concurring in judgment). But the State must have a "'strong basis in evidence for [concluding] that remedial action [is] necessary.'" *Croson, supra,* at 500 (quoting *Wygant, supra,* at 277 (plurality opinion)).

The state appellees submit that two pieces of evidence gave the General Assembly a strong basis for believing that remedial action was warranted here: the Attorney General's imposition of the § 5 preclearance requirement on 40 North Carolina counties, and the *Gingles* District Court's findings of a long history of official racial discrimination in North Carolina's political system and of pervasive racial bloc voting. The state appellees assert that the deliberate creation of majority minority districts is the most precise way — indeed the only effective way — to overcome the effects of racially polarized voting. This question also need not be decided at this stage of the litigation. We note, however, that only three Justices in *UJO* were prepared to say that States have a significant interest in minimizing the consequences of racial bloc voting apart from the requirements of the Voting Rights Act. And those three Justices specifically concluded that race based districting, as a response to racially polarized voting, is constitutionally permissible only when the State "employ[s] sound districting principles," and only when the affected racial group's "residential patterns afford the opportunity of creating districts in which they will be in the majority." 430 U. S., at 167-168 (opinion of White, J., joined by Stevens and Rehnquist, JJ.).

[R]acial classifications of any sort pose the risk of lasting harm to our society. They reinforce the belief, held by too many for too much of our history, that individuals should be judged by the color of their skin. Racial classifications with respect to voting carry particular dangers. Racial gerrymandering, even for remedial purposes, may balkanize us into competing racial factions; it threatens to carry us further from the goal of a political system in which race no longer matters — a goal that the Fourteenth and Fifteenth Amendments embody, and to which the Nation continues to aspire. It is for these reasons that race based districting by our state legislatures demands close judicial scrutiny.

In this case, the Attorney General suggested that North Carolina could have created a reasonably compact second majority minority district in the south central to southeastern part of the State. We express no view as to whether appellants successfully could have challenged such a district under the Fourteenth Amendment. We also do not decide whether appellants' complaint stated a claim under constitutional provisions other than the Fourteenth Amendment. Today we hold only that appellants have stated a claim under the Equal Protection Clause by alleging that the North Carolina General Assembly adopted a reapportionment scheme so irrational on its face that it can be understood only as an effort to segregate voters into separate voting districts because of their race, and that the separation lacks sufficient justification. If the allegation of racial gerrymandering remains uncontradicted, the District Court further must determine whether the North Carolina plan is narrowly tailored tofurther a compelling governmental interest. Accordingly, we reverse the judgment of the District Court and remand the case for further proceedings consistent with this opinion.

Justice WHITE, with whom Justice BLACKMUN and Justices STEVENS join, dissenting.

The most compelling evidence of the Court's position prior to this day, for it is most directly on point, is *UJO*, 430 U.S. 144 (1977). The Court characterizes the decision as "highly fractured," *ante*, at 19, but that should not detract attention from the rejection by a majority in *UJO* of the claim that the State's intentional creation of majority minority districts transgressed constitutional norms. As stated above, five Justices were of the view that, absent any contention that the proposed plan was adopted with the intent, or had the effect, of unduly minimizing the white majority's voting strength, the Fourteenth Amendment was not implicated. Writing for three members of the Court, I justified this conclusion as follows:

> It is true that New York deliberately increased the nonwhite majorities in certain districts in order to enhance the opportunity for election of nonwhite representatives from those districts. Nevertheless, there was no fencing out of the white population from participation in the political processes of the county, and the plan did not minimize or unfairly cancel out white voting strength.

430 U. S., at 165 (opinion of White, J.).

In a similar vein, Justice Stewart was joined by Justice Powell in stating that:

> The petitioners have made no showing that a racial criterion was used as a basis for denying them their right to vote, in contravention of the Fifteenth Amendment. See *Gomillion* v. *Lightfoot*, 364 U.S. 339. They have made no showing that the redistricting scheme was employed as part of a 'contrivance to segregate'; to minimize or cancel out the voting strength of a minority class or interest; or otherwise to impair or burden the opportunity of affected persons to participate in the political process.

Id., at 179 (Stewart, J., concurring in judgment) (citations omitted).

Under either formulation, it is irrefutable that appellants in this proceeding likewise have failed to state a claim. As was the case in New York, a number of North Carolina's political subdivisions have interfered with black citizens' meaningful exercise of the franchise, and are therefore subject to §§ 4 and 5 of the Voting Rights Act. Compare

UJO, supra, at 148. In other words, North Carolina was found by Congress to have "'resorted to the extraordinary stratagem of contriving new rules of various kinds for the sole purpose of perpetuating voting discrimination in the face of adverse federal court decrees'" and therefore "would be likely to engage in 'similar maneuvers in the future in order to evade the remedies for voting discrimination contained in the Act itself.'" *McCain* v. *Lybrand,* 465 U.S. 236, 245 (1984) (quoting *South Carolina* v. *Katzenbach,* 383 U.S. 301, 334, 335 (1966)). Like New York, North Carolina failed to prove to the Attorney General's satisfaction that its proposed redistricting had neither the purpose nor the effect of abridging the right to vote on account of race or color. Compare *UJO, supra,* at 150. The Attorney General's interposition of a § 5 objection "properly is viewed" as "an administrative finding of discrimination" against a racial minority. *Regents of Univ. of California* v. *Bakke, supra,* at 305 (opinion of Powell, J.). Finally, like New York, North Carolina reacted by modifying its plan and creating additional majority minority districts. Compare *UJO,* 430 U. S., at 151-152.

In light of this background, it strains credulity to suggest that North Carolina's purpose in creating a second majority minority district was to discriminate against members of the majority group by "impair[ing] or burden[ing their] opportunity . . . to participate in the political process." *Id.,* at 179 (Stewart, J., concurring in judgment). The State has made no mystery of its intent, which was to respond to the Attorney General's objections, see Brief for State Appellees 13-14, by improving the minority group's prospects of electing a candidate of its choice. I doubt that this constitutes a discriminatory purpose as defined in the Court's equal protection cases — *i.e.,* an intent to aggravate "the unequal distribution of electoral power." *Post,* at 3 (Stevens, J., dissenting). But even assuming that it does, there is no question that appellants have not alleged the requisite discriminatory effects. Whites constitute roughly 76 percent of the total population and 79 percent of the voting age population in North Carolina. Yet, under the State's plan, they still constitute a voting majority in 10 (or 83 percent) of the 12 congressional districts. Though they might be dissatisfied at the prospect of casting a vote for a losing candidate — a lot shared by many, including a disproportionate number of minority voters — surely they cannot complain of discriminatory treatment.

[In previous cases,] we have put the plaintiff challenging the district lines to the burden of demonstrating that the plan was meant to, and did in fact, exclude an identifiable racial group from participation in the political process.

Not so, apparently, when the districting "segregates" by drawing odd shaped lines. In that case, we are told, such proof no longer is needed. Instead, it is the *State* that must rebut the allegation that race was taken into account, a fact that, together with the legislators' consideration of ethnic, religious, and other group characteristics, I had thought we practically took for granted, see *supra,* at 3. Part of the explanation for the majority's approach has to do, perhaps, with the emotions stirred by words such as "segregation" and "political apartheid." But their loose and imprecise use by today's majority has, I fear, led it astray. See n. 7, *supra.* The consideration of race in "segregation" cases is no different than in other race conscious districting; from the standpoint of the affected groups, moreover, the line drawings all act in similar fashion. A plan that "segregates" being functionally indistinguishable from any of the other varieties of gerrymandering, we should be consistent in what we require from a claimant: Proof of discriminatory purpose and effect.

[T]he other part of the majority's explanation of its holding is related to its simultaneous discomfort and fascination with irregularly shaped districts. Lack of compactness or contiguity, like uncouth district lines, certainly is a helpful indicator that some form of gerrymandering (racial or other) might have taken place and that "something may be amiss."

[B]ut while district irregularities may provide strong indicia of a potential gerrymander, they do no more than that. In particular, they have no bearing on whether the plan ultimately is found to violate the Constitution. Given two districts drawn on similar, race based grounds, the one does not become more injurious than the other simply by virtue of being snake like, at least so far as the Constitution is concerned and absent any evidence of differential racial impact. The majority's contrary view is perplexing in light of its concession that "compactness or attractiveness has never been held to constitute an independent federal constitutional requirement for state legislative districts." *Gaffney*, 412 U. S., at 752, n. 18; see *ante*, at __. It is shortsighted as well, for a regularly shaped district can just as effectively effectuate racially discriminatory gerrymandering as an odd shaped one. By focusing on looks rather than impact, the majority "immediately casts attention in the wrong direction — toward superficialities of shape and size, rather than toward the political realities of district composition." R. Dixon, Democratic Representation: Reapportionment in Law and Politics 459 (1968).

[S]ince I do not agree that petitioners alleged an Equal Protection violation and because the Court of Appeals faithfully followed the Court's prior cases, I dissent and would affirm the judgment below.

Basis for Claim. Justice O'Connor points out that the challengers do allege that a right to a color-blind electoral process is at issue, implicating fundamental interest analysis, and O'Connor does suggest that the challengers do not claim to be white. So is this really a *Bakke*-like challenge to a benign classification scheme? What is missing? Does Justice White's dissent give a clue to what's missing in Justice O'Connor's analysis? Do white voters in North Carolina stand to endure the same injury that Allen Bakke claimed in the *Bakke* case?

Standard for Determining Impermissible Use of Race. Here, according to the majority, we have a bizarrely shaped district created at the behest of the Bush (I) Justice Department to allow the election of black congressperson under the preclearance requirements of the Voting Rights Act. O'Connor applies strict scrutiny here. She notes that race-conscious state decision making on apportionment has never been disapproved by the Court. But here, the districting is so bizarre that it is unexplainable on grounds other than race. This puts the matter into the *Gomillion v. Lightfoot* category (see note 48).

Justice O'Connor went on to point out that "[w]hen members of a racial group live together in one community, a reapportionment plan that concentrates members of the group in one district and excludes them from others may reflect wholly legitimate purposes." Compactness, contiguity of territory, or maintenance of political subdivisions may explain such circumstances. These factors, though not required, may show that race was not a predominant reason for apportionment.

Voting Rights Act Compliance as a Compelling Purpose? Though Justice O'Connor does not rule on whether compliance with the Voting Rights Act is a compelling interest, she distinguishes between what the Act requires and what the Act permits. It may permit this kind of gerrymandering (an obvious slap at DOJ preclearance), but it may not be required. Whether it is required is not addressed in this opinion. Whether meeting Voting Rights Act requirements is a compelling interest is also not addressed here. The merits were not necessarily decided here. The case was whether the plaintiffs had stated a claim.

In *Miller v. Johnson*, 515 U.S. 900 (1995), the Court applied *Shaw* and moved forward with a ruling offering a continuing narrative on determining when a redistricting decision uses race to a constitutionally unacceptable degree, and on the relevance of the Voting Rights Act to determining a compelling purpose for state action.

Generally, whether race was a predominant factor in the drawing of the district can be determined by cosmetic and logistical factors. A third black district in Georgia, required for Justice Department preclearance, stretched from urban Atlanta to the Georgia coast, a distance of about 260 miles. The district was described as a monstrosity by one of the commentators selected by Justice Kennedy to use in his opinion.

The opinion stated:

> The distinction between being aware of racial considerations and being motivated by them may be difficult to make. This evidentiary difficulty, together with the sensitive nature of redistricting and the presumption of good faith that must be accorded legislative enactments, requires courts to exercise extraordinary caution in adjudicating claims that a State has drawn district lines on the basis of race. The plaintiff's burden is to show, either through circumstantial evidence of a district's shape and demographics or more direct evidence going to legislative purpose, that race was the predominant factor motivating the legislature's decision to place a significant number of voters within or without a particular district. To make this showing, a plaintiff must prove that the legislature subordinated traditional race-neutral districting principles, including but not limited to compactness, contiguity, and respect for political subdivisions or communities defined by actual shared interests, to racial considerations.

Justice Kennedy's opinion went on to at least partially answer the question left unanswered in *Shaw*:

> We do not accept the contention that the State has a compelling interest in complying with whatever preclearance mandates the Justice Department issues. When a state governmental entity seeks to justify race-based remedies to cure the effects of past discrimination, we do not accept the government's mere assertion that the remedial action is required. Rather, we insist on a strong basis in evidence of the harm being remedied. See, e.g., *Shaw, supra,* at 656; *Croson, supra,* at 500-501; *Wygant, supra,* at 276-277 (plurality opinion). "The history of racial classifications in this country suggests that blind judicial deference to legislative or executive pronouncements of necessity has no place in equal protection analysis." *Croson, supra,* at 501. Our presumptive skepticism of all racial classifications, see *Adarand, ante,* at 223-224, prohibits us as well from accepting on its face the Justice Department's conclusion that racial districting is necessary under the Act. Where a State relies on the Department's determination that race-based districting is necessary to comply with the Act, the judiciary retains an independent obligation in adjudicating consequent equal protection challenges to ensure that the State's actions are narrowly tailored to achieve a compelling interest. See *Shaw, supra,* at 654. Were we to ac-

cept the Justice Department's objection itself as a compelling interest adequate to insulate racial districting from constitutional review, we would be surrendering to the Executive Branch our role in enforcing the constitutional limits on race-based official action. We may not do so. See, *e. g., United States* v. *Nixon,* 418 U. S. 683, 704 (1974) (judicial power cannot be shared with Executive Branch); *Marbury* v. *Madison,* 1 Cranch 137, 177 (1803) ("It is emphatically the province and duty of the judicial department to say what the law is"); cf.*Baker* v. *Carr,* 369 U. S. 186, 211 (1962) (Supreme Court is "ultimate interpreter of the Constitution"); *Cooper* v. *Aaron,* 358 U. S. 1, 18 (1958) ("permanent and indispensable feature of our constitutional system" is that "the federal judiciary is supreme in the exposition of the law of the Constitution").

For the same reasons, we think it inappropriate for a court engaged in constitutional scrutiny to accord deference to the Justice Department's interpretation of the Act. Although we have deferred to the Department's interpretation in certain statutory cases, see, *e. g., Presley* v. *Etowah County Comm'n,* 502 U. S. 491, 508-509 (1992), and cases cited therein, we have rejected agency interpretations to which we would otherwise defer where they raise serious constitutional questions.

[I]nstead of grounding its objections on evidence of a discriminatory purpose, it would appear the Government was driven by its policy of maximizing majority-black districts. Although the Government now disavows having had that policy, and seems to concede its impropriety the District Court's well-documented factual finding was that the Department did adopt a maximization policy and followed it in objecting to Georgia's first two plans.

Does the Voting Rights Act anticipate Supreme Court review of pre-clearance requirements? Does it preclude review? The Court makes clear that it will be the final arbiter of constitutional standards, a conclusion that necessarily precludes the argument by states that a challenged redistricting plan should withstand strict scrutiny because compliance with the Voting Rights Act is a compelling purpose. Has the Court put itself up as a "shadow Justice Department" in matters involving pre-clearance? Does the fact that race is involved present particular problems with pre-clearance as a compelling purpose? Is this result required by *Marbury v. Madison? Baker v. Carr*? Has the Court answered the question as to whether compliance with the VRA is a compelling purpose under strict scrutiny? Or has it simply answered the quite obvious question that an unconstitutional redistricting plan could never be a compelling purpose for VRA compliance?

Shaw v. Hunt, 517 U.S. 899 (1996), is *Shaw v. Reno* (Shaw II) back up on appeal after remand and a subsequent plan was put in place. In rejecting yet another attempt by Georgia to gain VRA compliance, the Court, in an opinion by Chief Justice Rehnquist, examined three different possible compelling purposes raised by the state to survive strict scrutiny:

Appellees point to three separate compelling interests to sustain District 12: to eradicate the effects of past and present discrimination; to comply with §5 of the Voting Rights Act; and to comply with §2 of that Act. We address each in turn.

A State's interest in remedying the effects of past or present racial discrimination may in the proper case justify a government's use of racial distinctions. *Croson,* 488 U. S., at 498-506. For that interest to rise to the level of a compelling state interest, it must satisfy two conditions. First, the discrimination must be "'identified discrimination.'" *Id.,* at 499, 500, 505, 507, 509. "While the States and their subdivisions may take remedial action when they possess evidence" of past or present discrimination, "they must identify that discrimination, public or private, with some specificity before they may use race conscious relief." *Id.*, at 504. A generalized assertion of past discrimination in a particular industry or region is not adequate because it "provides no guidance for a legislative body to determine the precise scope of the injury it seeks to remedy." *Id.*, at 498 (opinion of O'Connor, J.). Accordingly, an effort to alleviate the effects of societal discrimination is not a compelling interest. *Wygant*, *supra*, at 274-275, 276, 288. Second, the institution that makes the racial distinction must have had a "strong basis in evidence" to conclude that remedial action was necessary, "*before* it embarks on an affirmative action program," 476 U. S., at 277 (plurality opinion) (emphasis added). In this case, the District Court found that an interest in ameliorating past discrimination did not actually precipitate the use of race in the redistricting plan. While some legislators invoked the State's history of discrimination as an argument for creating a second majority black district, the court found that these members did not have enough voting power to have caused the creation of the second district on that basis alone.

Chief Justice Rehnquist went on to explain that evidence utilized before the district court, because it was not evidence used by the legislature when it redistricted, cannot be the basis for proving that racial discrimination in voting ever existed North Carolina, commenting that:

> there is little to suggest that the legislature considered the historical events and social science data that the reports recount, beyond what individual members may have recalled from personal experience. We certainly cannot say on the basis of these reports that the District Court's findings on this point were clearly erroneous.

With regard to section 2 of the VRA, which addresses liability for constitutional violations, the Chief Justice noted "we find that creating an additional majority black district was not required under a correct reading of §5 and that District 12, as drawn, is not a remedy narrowly tailored to the State's professed interest in avoiding §2 liability."

Finally with respect to section 5 preclearance, the majority opinion stated:

> [W]ith respect to §5 of the Voting Rights Act, we believe our decision in *Miller* forecloses the argument, adopted by the District Court, that failure to engage in the race based districting would have violated that section.
>
> [N]orth Carolina's first plan, Chapter 601, indisputably was ameliorative, having created the first majority black district in recent history. Thus, that plan, "'even if [it] fall[s] short of what might be accomplished in terms of increasing minority representation,'" "'cannot violate §5 unless the new apportionment itself so discriminates on the basis of race or color as to violate the Constitution.'" *Miller*. . .
>
> [T]he United States relies on the purpose prong of §5 to explain the Department's preclearance objections, alleging that North Carolina, for pretextual reasons, did not create a second majority minority district . . . The General Assembly, in its submission filed with Chapter 601, explained . . . among its goals were "to keep precincts whole, to avoid dividing counties into more than two districts, and to give black voters a fair amount of influence by creating at least one district that was majority black in voter registration and by creating a substantial number of other districts in which black voters would exercise a significant influence over the choice of congressmen." . . . We have recognized that a "State's policy of adhering to other districting principles instead of creating as many majority minority districts as possible does not support an inference that the plan 'so discriminates on the basis of race or color as to violate the Constitution,' and thus cannot

provide any basis under §5 for the Justice Department's objection." *Miller, supra*, at ___ (slip op., at 23) (citations omitted).

It appears that the Justice Department was pursuing in North Carolina the same policy of maximizing the number of majority black districts that it pursued in Georgia. See *Miller, supra*, at ___, and n. (slip op., at 23-24, and n.).

DOJ argued to the Supreme Court that the liability requirements of section 2 and the preclearance requirement of section 5 include an obligation to gain majority minority districts; Chief Justice Rehnquist's conclusion was simply that this was not so. Not reached, however, is the issue of whether meeting what is required by the act (and by the Constitution) would be a compelling interest of the state.

Bush v. Vera, 517 U.S. 952 (1996) was a case affecting the 18th, 29th (Houston), and 30th congressional districts of Texas. As a result of the 1990 Census, Texas was slated to receive three additional congressional seats: The 29th and 30th were created and were both majority minority, and the 18th was reconfigured to achieve a minority district. Justice O'Connor, in a plurality, made the point that "strict scrutiny does not apply merely because redistricting is performed with consciousness of race. Nor does it apply to all cases of intentional creation of majority-minority districts. For strict scrutiny to apply, the plaintiffs must prove that other legitimate districting principles were 'subordinated' to race."

The plurality opinion found that Texas had substantially neglected traditional districting criteria such as compactness, while at the same time leaving room for the constitutional use of race as long as it was not the predominant factor in a redistricting plan.

How does all of this square when it comes to compliance with the Voting Rights Act (meaning achieving preclearance)? That this is and remains a dilemma for jurisdictions is underscored in the plurality:

> In 1982, Congress amended the VRA by changing the language of §2(a) and adding §2(b), which provides a "results" test for violation of §2(a). A violation exists if, "based on the totality of circumstances, it is shown that the political processes leading to nomination or election in the State or political subdivision are not equally open to participation by members of a class of citizens protected by subsection (a) of this section in that its members have less opportunity than other members of the electorate to participate in the political process and to elect representatives of their choice." 42 U.S.C. § 1973(b).
>
> Appellants contend that creation of each of the three majority minority districts at issue was justified by Texas' compelling state interest in complying with this results test.
>
> As we have done in each of our previous cases in which this argument has been raised as a defense to charges of racial gerrymandering, we assume without deciding that compliance with the results test, as interpreted by our precedents, see, *e.g., Growe* v. *Emison,* 507 U.S. 25, 37-42 (1993), can be a compelling state interest. See *Shaw II, ante,* at 13; *Miller,* 515 U. S., at ___ (slip op., at 19-20). We also reaffirm that the "narrow tailoring" requirement of strict scrutiny allows the States a limited degree of leeway in furthering such interests. If the State has a "strong basis in evidence," *Shaw I,* 509 U. S., at 656 (internal quotation marks omitted), for concluding that creation of a majority minority district is reasonably necessary to comply with §2, and the districting that is based on race "substantially addresses the §2 violation," *Shaw II, ante,* at 18, it satisfies strict scrutiny.
>
> [T]he final contention offered by the State and private appellants is that creation of District 18 (only) was justified by a compelling state interest in complying with VRA §5.

We have made clear that §5 has a limited substantive goal: "'to insure that no voting procedure changes would be made that would lead to a retrogression in the position of racial minorities with respect to their effective exercise of the electoral franchise.'" *Miller*. . .

[N]onretrogression is not a license for the State to do whatever it deems necessary to insure continued electoral *success;* it merely mandates that the minority's *opportunity* to elect representatives of its choice not be diminished, directly or indirectly, by the State's actions. We anticipated this problem in *Shaw I,* 509 U. S., at 655: "A reapportionment plan would not be narrowly tailored to the goal of avoiding retrogression if the State went beyond what was reasonably necessary to avoid retrogression." Applying that principle, it is clear that District 18 is not narrowly tailored to the avoidance of §5 liability.

Following the plurality written by Justice O'Connor, she also wrote a rare concurrence to her own opinion. Writing for herself alone, Justice O'Connor acknowledged that the Court has assumed without deciding that the results test of section 2 of the VRA is violated if, quoting from section 2,

based on the totality of circumstances, it is shown that the political processes leading to nomination or election in the State or political subdivision are not equally open to participation by members of [*e.g.,* a racial minority group] in that its members have less opportunity than other members of the electorate to participate in the political process and to elect representatives of their choice." 42 U.S.C. § 1973(b).

Additionally, the concurrence acknowledged the states obligation to follow legislation enacted. . . .

In my view, therefore, the States have a compelling interest in complying with the results test as this Court has interpreted it.

Although I agree with the dissenters about §2's role as part of our national commitment to racial equality, I differ from them in my belief that that commitment can and must be reconciled with the complementary commitment of our Fourteenth Amendment jurisprudence to eliminate the unjustified use of racial stereotypes. At the same time that we combat the symptoms of racial polarization in politics, we must strive to eliminate unnecessary race based state action that appears to endorse the disease.

Today's decisions, in conjunction with the recognition of the compelling state interest in compliance with the reasonably perceived requirements of §2, present a workable framework for the achievement of these twin goals. I would summarize that framework, and the rules governing the States' consideration of race in the districting process, as follows.

First, so long as they do not subordinate traditional districting criteria to the use of race for its own sake or as a proxy, States may intentionally create majority minority districts, and may otherwise take race into consideration, without coming under strict scrutiny. See *ante,* at 3-4 (plurality opinion); *post,* at 7-9 & n. 8, 26 (Stevens, J., dissenting); *post,* at 14, 23, 31 (Souter, J., dissenting). Only if traditional districting criteria are neglected *and* that neglect is predominantly due to the misuse of race does strict scrutiny apply. *Ante,* at 7, 9-10, 24 (plurality opinion).

Second, where voting is racially polarized, §2 prohibits States from adopting districting schemes that would have the effect that minority voters "have less opportunity than other members of the electorate to . . . elect representatives of their choice." §2(b). That principle may require a State to create a majority minority district where the three *Gingles* factors are present — viz., (i) the minority group "is sufficiently large and geographically compact to constitute a majority in a single member district," (ii) "it is politically cohesive," and (iii) "the white majority votes sufficiently as a bloc to enable it . . . usually to defeat the minority's preferred candidate," *Thornburg* v. *Gingles*, 478 U. S., at 50-51.

Third, the state interest in avoiding liability under VRA §2 is compelling. See *supra*, at 1-4; *post*, at 34 (Stevens, J., dissenting); *post*, at 23 (Souter, J., dissenting). If a State has a strong basis in evidence for concluding that the *Gingles* factors are present, it may create a majority minority district without awaiting judicial findings. Its "strong basis in evidence" need not take any particular form, although it cannot simply rely on generalized assumptions about the prevalence of racial bloc voting.

Fourth, if a State pursues that compelling interest by creating a district that "substantially addresses" the potential liability, *Shaw II, ante,* at ___ [draft op. at 18], and does not deviate substantially from a hypothetical court drawn §2 district for predominantly racial reasons, cf. *ante,* at 25 (plurality opinion) (explaining how District 30 fails to satisfy these criteria), its districting plan will be deemed narrowly tailored. Cf. *ante,* at 27 (plurality opinion) (acknowledging this possibility); *post,* at 26 (Souter, J., dissenting) (same); *post,* at 34-36 (Stevens, J., dissenting) (contending that it is applicable here).

Finally, however, districts that are bizarrely shaped and non compact, and that otherwise neglect traditional districting principles and deviate substantially from the hypothetical court drawn district, *for predominantly racial reasons,* are unconstitutional. See *ante,* at 25 (plurality opinion).

District 30 illustrates the application of these principles. Dallas County has a history of racially polarized voting. See, *e.g.,* *White* v. *Regester*, 412 U.S. 755, 765-767 (1973); *Lipscomb* v. *Wise*, 399 F. Supp. 782, 785-786 (ND Tex. 1975), rev'd, 551 F. 2d 1043 (CA5 1977), rev'd, 437 U.S. 535 (1978). One year before the redistricting at issue here, a district court invalidated under §2 the Dallas City Council election scheme, finding racial polarization and that candidates preferred by African American voters were consistently defeated.

Is Justice O'Connor trying to help the group that wants to see majority minority districts? Is she saying, in effect, "send up something that I can support, that is not predominantly about race even if it provides a majority minority district"? How are her concurrence and her plurality similar and different? Why did she write two opinions?

HUNT v. CROMARTIE
532 U.S. 234 (2001)

Justice BREYER delivered the opinion of the Court.

In this appeal, we review a three-judge District Court's determination that North Carolina's legislature used race as the "predominant factor" in drawing its 12th Congressional District's 1997 boundaries. The court's findings, in our view, are clearly erroneous. We therefore reverse its conclusion that the State violated the Equal Protection Clause. U.S. Const., Amdt. 14, §1.

I

This "racial districting" litigation is before us for the fourth time. Our first two holdings addressed North Carolina's former Congressional District 12, one of two North Carolina congressional districts drawn in 1992 that contained a majority of African-American voters. See Shaw v. Reno, 509 U.S. 630 (1993) (Shaw I); Shaw v. Hunt, 517 U.S. 899 (1996) (Shaw II).

A

In Shaw I, the Court considered whether plaintiffs' factual allegation — that the legislature had drawn the former district's boundaries for race-based reasons — if true, could underlie a legal holding that the legislature had violated the Equal Protection Clause. The Court held that it could. It wrote that a violation may exist where the legislature's boundary drawing, though "race neutral on its face," nonetheless can be understood only as an effort to "separate voters into different districts on the basis of race," and where the "separation lacks sufficient justification." 509 U.S., at 649.

In Shaw II, the Court reversed a subsequent three-judge District Court's holding that the boundary-drawing law in question did not violate the Constitution. This Court found that the district's "unconventional," snakelike shape, the way in which its boundaries split towns and counties, its predominately African-American racial make-up, and its history, together demonstrated a deliberate effort to create a "majority-black" district in which race "could not be compromised," not simply a district designed to "protec[t] Democratic incumbents." 517 U.S., at 902-903, 905-907. And the Court concluded that the legislature's use of racial criteria was not justified. Id., at 909-918.

B

Our third holding focused on a new District 12, the boundaries of which the legislature had redrawn in 1997. Hunt v. Cromartie, 526 U.S. 541 (1999). A three-judge District Court, with one judge dissenting, had granted summary judgment in favor of those challenging the district's boundaries. The court found that the legislature again had "used criteria . . . that are facially race driven," in violation of the Equal Protection Clause. App. to Juris. Statement 262a. It based this conclusion upon "uncontroverted material facts" showing that the boundaries created an unusually shaped district, split counties and cities,and in particular placed almost all heavily Democratic-registered, predominantly African-American voting precincts, inside the district while locating some heavily Democratic-registered, predominantly white precincts, outside the district. This latter circumstance, said the court, showed that the legislature was trying to maximize new District 12's African-American voting strength, not the district's Democratic voting strength. Ibid.

This Court reversed. We agreed with the District Court that the new district's shape, the way in which it split towns and counties, and its heavily African-American voting population all helped the plaintiffs' case. 526 U.S., at 547-549. But neither that evidence by itself, nor when coupled with the evidence of Democratic registration, was sufficient to show, on summary judgment, the unconstitutional race-based objective that plaintiffs claimed. That is because there was a genuine issue of material fact as to whether the evidence also was consistent with a constitutional political objective, namely, the creation of a safe Democratic seat. Id., at 549-551.

We pointed to the affidavit of an expert witness for defendants, Dr. David W. Peterson. Dr. Peterson offered to show that, because North Carolina's African-American voters are overwhelmingly Democratic voters, one cannot easily distinguish a legislative effort to create a majority-African-American district from a legislative effort to create a safely Democratic district. Id., at 550. And he also provided data showing that registration did not indicate how voters would actually vote. Id., at 550-551. We agreed that data showing how voters actually behave, not data showing only how those voters are registered, could affect the outcome of this litigation. Ibid. We concluded that the case was "not suited for summary disposition" and we reversed the District Court. Id., at 554.

C

On remand, the parties undertook additional discovery. The three-judge District Court held a 3-day trial. And the court again held (over a dissent) that the legislature had unconstitutionally drawn District 12's new 1997 boundaries. It found that the legislature had tried "(1) [to] cur[e] the [previous district's] constitutional defects" while also "(2) drawing the plan to maintain the existing partisan balance in the State's congressional delegation." App. to Juris. Statement 11a. It added that to "achieve the second goal," the legislature "drew the new plan (1) to avoid placing two incumbents in the same district and (2) to preserve the partisan core of the existing districts." Ibid. The court concluded that the "plan as enacted largely reflects these directives." Ibid. But the court also found "as a matter of fact that the General Assembly . . . used criteria . . . that are facially race driven" without any compelling justification for doing so. Id., at 28a.

The court based its latter, constitutionally critical, conclusion in part upon the district's snakelike shape, the way in which it split cities and towns, and its heavily African-American (47%) voting population, id., at 11a-17a — all matters that this Court had considered when it found summary judgment inappropriate, Cromartie, supra, at 544. The court also based this conclusion upon a specific finding — absent when we previously considered this litigation — that the legislature had drawn the boundaries in order "to collect precincts with high racial identification rather than political identification." App. to Juris. Statement 28a-29a (emphasis added).

This last-mentioned finding rested in turn upon five subsidiary determinations:

(1) that "the legislators excluded many heavily-Democratic precincts from District 12, even when those precincts immediately border the Twelfth and would have established a far more compact district," id., at 25a; see also id., at 29a ("more heavily Democratic precincts . . . were bypassed . . . in favor of precincts with a higher African-American population");

(2) that "[a]dditionally, Plaintiffs' expert, Dr. Weber, showed time and again how race trumped party affiliation in the construction of the 12th District and how political explanations utterly failed to explain the composition of the district," id., at 26a;

(3) that Dr. Peterson's testimony was "'unreliable' and not relevant," id., at 27a (citing testimony of Dr. Weber);

(4) that a legislative redistricting leader, Senator Roy Cooper, had alluded at the time of redistricting "to a need for 'racial and partisan' balance," ibid.; and

(5) that the Senate's redistricting coordinator, Gerry Cohen, had sent Senator Cooper an e-mail reporting that Cooper had "moved Greensboro Black community into the 12th, and now need[ed] to take [about] 60,000 out of the 12th," App. 369; App. to Juris. Statement 27a-28a.

The State and intervenors filed a notice of appeal. 28 U.S.C. § 1253. We noted probable jurisdiction. 530 U.S. 1260 (2000). And we now reverse.

II

The issue in this case is evidentiary. We must determine whether there is adequate support for the District Court's key findings, particularly the ultimate finding that the legislature's motive was predominantly racial, not political. In making this determination, we are aware that, under Shaw I and later cases, the burden of proof on the plaintiffs (who attack the district) is a "demanding one." Miller v. Johnson, 515 U.S. 900, 928 (1995) (O'Connor, J., concurring). The Court has specified that those who claim that a legislature has improperly used race as a criterion, in order, for example, to create a majority-minority district, must show at a minimum that the "legislature subordinated traditional race-neutral districting principles . . . to racial considerations." Id., at 916 (majority opinion). Race must not simply have been "a motivation for the drawing of a majority minority district," Bush v. Vera, 517 U.S. 952, 959 (1996) (O'Connor, J., principal opinion) (emphasis in original), but "the 'predominant factor' motivating the legislature's districting decision," Cromartie, 526 U.S., at 547 (quoting Miller, supra, at 916) (emphasis added). Plaintiffs must show that a facially neutral law "'is "unexplainable on grounds other than race."'" Cromartie, supra, at 546 (quoting Shaw I, 509 U.S., at 644, in turn quoting Arlington Heights v. Metropolitan Housing Development Corp., 429 U.S. 252, 266 (1977)).

The Court also has made clear that the underlying districting decision is one that ordinarily falls within a legislature's sphere of competence. Miller, 515 U.S., at 915. Hence, the legislature "must have discretion to exercise the political judgment necessary to balance competing interests," ibid., and courts must "exercise extraordinary caution in adjudicating claims that a State has drawn district lines on the basis of race," id., at 916 (emphasis added). Caution is especially appropriate in this case, where the State has articulated a legitimate political explanation for its districting decision, and the voting population is one in which race and political affiliation are highly correlated.

[W]e also are aware that we review the District Court's findings only for "clear error." In applying this standard, we, like any reviewing court, will not reverse a lower court's finding of fact simply because we "would have decided the case differently." Anderson v. Bessemer City, 470 U.S. 564, 573 (1985). Rather, a reviewing court must ask whether "on the entire evidence," it is "left with the definite and firm conviction that a mistake has been committed." United States v. United States Gypsum Co., 333 U.S. 364, 395 (1948).

Where an intermediate court reviews, and affirms, a trial court's factual findings, this Court will not "lightly overturn" the concurrent findings of the two lower courts. E.g., Neil v. Biggers, 409 U.S. 188, 193, n. 3 (1972). But in this instance there is no intermediate court, and we are the only court of review. Moreover, the trial here at issue was not lengthy and the key evidence consisted primarily of documents and expert testimony. Credibility evaluations played a minor role. Accordingly, we find that an extensive review of the District Court's findings, for clear error, is warranted. See Bose Corp. v. Consumers Union of United States, Inc., 466 U.S. 485, 500-501 (1984). That review leaves us "with the definite and firm conviction," United States Gypsum Co., supra, at 395, that the District Court's key findings are mistaken.

III

The critical District Court determination — the matter for which we remanded this litigation — consists of the finding that race *rather than* politics *predominantly* explains District 12's 1997 boundaries. That determination rests upon three findings (the district's shape, its splitting of towns and counties, and its high African-American voting population) that we previously found insufficient to support summary judgment. *Cromartie, supra*, at 547-549. Given the undisputed evidence that racial identification is highly correlated with political affiliation in North Carolina, these facts in and of themselves cannot, as a matter of law, support the District Court's judgment. See *Vera*, 517 U.S., at 968 (O'Connor, J., principal opinion) ("If district lines merely correlate with race because they are drawn on the basis of political affiliation, which correlates with race, there is no racial classification to justify"). The District Court rested, however, upon five new subsidiary findings to conclude that District 12's lines are the product of no "mer[e] correlat[ion]," *ibid.*, but are instead a result of the predominance of race in the legislature's line-drawing process. See *supra*, at 5.

First, the primary evidence upon which the District Court relied for its "race, not politics," conclusion is evidence of voting registration, not voting behavior; and that is precisely the kind of evidence that we said was inadequate the last time this case was before us. See *infra*, at 9-10. Second, the additional evidence to which appellees' expert, Dr. Weber, pointed, and the statements made by Senator Cooper and Gerry Cohen, simply do not provide significant additional support for the District Court's conclusion. See *infra*, at 10-15, 17-19. Third, the District Court, while not accepting the contrary conclusion of appellants' expert, Dr. Peterson, did not (and as far as the record reveals, could not) reject much of the significant supporting factual information he provided. See *infra*, at 15-17. Fourth, in any event, appellees themselves have provided us with charts summarizing evidence of voting behavior and those charts tend to refute the court's "race not politics" conclusion. See *infra*, at 19-21; Appendixes, *infra*.

A

The District Court primarily based its "race, not politics," conclusion upon its finding that "the legislators excluded many heavily-Democratic precincts from District 12, even when those precincts immediately border the Twelfth and would have established a far more compact district." . . . This finding, however — insofar as it differs from the remaining four — rests solely upon evidence that the legislature excluded heavily white precincts with high Democratic Party *registration*, while including heavily African-American precincts with equivalent, or lower, Democratic Party registration. See *id.*, at 13a-14a, 17a. Indeed, the District Court cites at length figures showing that the legislature included "several precincts with racial compositions of 40 to 100 percent African-American," while excluding certain adjacent precincts "with less than 35 percent African-American population" but which contain between 54% and 76% *registered* Democrats. *Id.*, at 13a-14a.

As we said before, the problem with this evidence is that it focuses upon party registration, not upon voting behavior. And we previously found the same evidence, compare *ibid.* (District Court's opinion after trial) with *id.*, at 249a — 250a (District Court's summary judgment opinion), inadequate because registration figures do not accurately predict preference at the polls. See *id.*, at 174a; see also *Cromartie*, 526 U.S., at 550-551 (describing Dr. Peterson's analysis as "more thorough" because in North Carolina, "party registration and party preference do not always correspond"). In part this is because white voters registered as Democrats "cross-over" to vote for a Republican candidate more often than do African-Americans, who register and vote Democratic between 95% and 97% of the time. See Record, Deposition of Gerry Cohen 37-42 (discussing data); App. 304 (stating that white voters cast about 60% to 70% of their votes for Republican candidates); *id.*, at 139 (Dr. Weber's testimony that 95% to 97% of African-Americans register and vote as Democrats); see also *id.*, at 118 (testimony by Dr. Weber that registration data were the least reliable information upon which to predict voter behavior). A legislature trying to secure a safe Democratic seat is interested in Democratic voting behavior. Hence, a legislature may, by placing reliable Democratic precincts within a district without regard to race, end up with a district containing more heavily African-American precincts, but the reasons would be political rather than racial.

Insofar as the District Court relied upon voting registration data, particularly data that were previously before us, it tells us nothing new; and the data do not help answer the question posed when we previously remanded this litigation. *Cromartie, supra*, at 551.

B

The District Court wrote that "[a]dditionally, [p]laintiffs' expert, Dr. Weber, showed time and again how race trumped party affiliation in the construction of the 12th District and how political explanations utterly failed to explain the composition of the district." App. to Juris. Statement 26a. In support of this conclusion, the court relied upon six different citations to Dr. Weber's trial testimony. We have examined each reference.

1

At the first cited pages of the trial transcript, Dr. Weber says that a reliably Democratic voting population of 60% is sufficient to create a safe Democratic seat. App. 91. Yet, he adds, the legislature created a more-than-60% reliable Democratic voting population in District 12. Hence (we read Dr. Weber to infer), the legislature likely was driven by race, not politics. Tr. 163; App. 314-315.

The record indicates, however, that, although Dr. Weber is right that District 12 is more than 60% reliably Democratic, it exceeds that figure by very little. Nor did Dr. Weber ask whether other districts, unchallenged by appellees, were significantly less "safe" than was District 12. *Id.,* at 148. In fact the figures the legislature used showed that District 12 would be 63% reliably Democratic. App. to Juris. Statement 80a (Democratic vote over three representative elections averaged 63%). By the same measures, at least two Republican districts (Districts 6 and 10) are 61% reliably Republican. *Ibid*. And, as Dr. Weber conceded, incumbents might have urged legislators (trying to maintain a six/six Democrat/Republican delegation split) to make their seats, not 60% safe, but as safe as possible. App. 149. In a field such as voting behavior, where figures are inherently uncertain, Dr. Weber's tiny calculated percentage differences are simply too small to carry significant evidentiary weight.

2

The District Court cited two parts of the transcript where Dr. Weber testified about a table he had prepared listing all precincts in the six counties, portions of which make up District 12. Tr. 204-205, 262. Dr. Weber said that District 12 contains between 39% and 56% of the precincts (depending on the county) that are more-than-40% reliably Democratic, but it contains almost every precinct with more-than-40% African-American voters. *Id.,* at 204-205. Why, he essentially asks, if the legislature had had politics primarily in mind, would its effort to place reliably Democratic precincts within District 12 not have produced a greater racial mixture?

Dr. Weber's own testimony provides an answer to this question. As Dr. Weber agreed, the precincts listed in the table were at least *40%* reliably Democratic, but virtually all the African-American precincts included in District 12 were *more* than 40% reliably Democratic. Moreover, *none* of the excluded white precincts were *as* reliably Democratic as the African-American precincts that were included in the district. App. 140. Yet the legislature sought precincts that were reliably Democratic, not precincts that were *40%*-reliably Democratic, for obvious political reasons.

Neither does the table specify whether the excluded white-reliably-Democratic precincts were located near enough to District 12's boundaries or each other for the legislature as a practical matter to have drawn District 12's boundaries to have included them, without sacrificing other important political goals. The contrary is suggested by the fact that Dr. Weber's own proposed alternative plan, see *id.,* at 106-107, would have pitted two incumbents against each other (Sue Myrick, a Republican from former District 9 and Mel Watt, a Democrat from former District 12). Dr. Weber testified that such a result — "a very competitive race with one of them losing their seat" — was desirable. *Id.,* at 153. But the legislature, for political, not racial, reasons, believed the opposite. And it drew its plan to protect incumbents — a legitimate political goal recognized by the District Court. App. to Juris. Statement 11a.

For these reasons, Dr. Weber's table offers little insight into the legislature's true motive.

3

The next part of the transcript the District Court cited contains Dr. Weber's testimony about a Mecklenburg County precinct (precinct 77) which the legislature split between Districts 9 and 12. Tr. 221. Dr. Weber apparently thought that the legislature did not have to split this precinct, placing the more heavily African-American segment within District 12 — unless, of course, its motive was racial rather than political. But Dr. Weber simultaneously conceded that he had not considered whether District 9's incumbent Republican would have wanted the whole of precinct 77 left in her own district where it would have burdened her with a significant additional number of reliably Democratic voters. App. 156-157. Nor had Dr. Weber "test[ed]" his conclusion that this split helped to show a racial (rather than political) motive, say, by adjusting other boundary lines and determining the political, or other nonracial, consequences of such adjustments. *Id.,* at 132.

The maps in evidence indicate that to have placed all of precinct 77 within District 12 would have created a District 12 peninsula that invaded District 9, neatly dividing that latter district in two, see *id.,* at 496 — a conclusive nonracial reason for the legislature's decision not to do so.

4

The District Court cited Dr. Weber's conclusion that "race is the predominant factor." Tr. 251. But this statement of the conclusion is no stronger than the evidence that underlies it.

5

The District Court's final citation is to Dr. Weber's assertion that there are other ways in which the legislature could have created a safely Democratic district without placing so many primarily African-American districts within District 12. *Id.,* at 288. And we recognize that *some* such other ways may exist. But, unless the evidence also shows that these hypothetical alternative districts would have better satisfied the legislature's other nonracial political goals as well as traditional nonracial districting principles, this fact alone cannot show an improper legislative motive. After all, the Constitution does not place an *affirmative* obligation upon the legislature to avoid creating districts that turn out to be heavily, even majority, minority. It simply imposes an obligation not to create such districts for predominantly racial, as opposed to political or traditional, districting motivations. And Dr. Weber's testimony does not, at the pages cited, provide evidence of a politically practical alternative plan that the legislature failed to adopt predominantly for racial reasons.

6

In addition, we have read the whole of Dr. Weber's testimony, including portions not cited by the District Court. Some of those portions further undercut Dr. Weber's conclusions. Dr. Weber said, for example, that he had developed those conclusions while under the erroneous impression that the legislature's computer-based districting program provided information about racial, but not political, balance. App. 137-138; see also *id.,* at 302 (reflecting Dr. Weber's erroneous impression in the declaration he submitted to the District Court). He also said he was not aware of "anything about political dynamics going on in the [l]egislature involving" District 12, *id.,* at 135, sometimes expressing disdain for a process that we have cautioned courts to respect, *id.,* at 150-151; *Miller,* 515 U.S., at 915-916.

Other portions support Dr. Weber's conclusions. Dr. Weber testified, for example, about a different alternative plan that, in his view, would have provided both greater racial balance and political security, namely, a plan that the legislature did enact in 1998, and which has been in effect during the time the courts have been reviewing the constitutionality of the 1997 plan. App. 156-157. The existence of this alternative plan, however, cannot help appellees significantly. Although it created a somewhat more compact district, it still divides many communities along racial lines, while providing fewer reliably Democratic District 12 voters and transferring a group of highly Democratic precincts into two safely Republican districts, namely, the 5th and 6th Districts, which political result the 1997 plan sought to avoid. See Tr. 352, 355. Furthermore, the 1997 plan before this Court, unlike the 1998 plan, joined three major cities in a manner legislators regarded as reflecting "a real commonality of urban interests, with inner city schools, urban health care . . . problems, public housing problems." App. 430 (statement of Sen. Winner); see also *id.,* at 421 (statement of Sen. Martin). Consequently, we cannot tell whether the existence of the 1998 plan shows that the 1997 plan was drawn with racial considerations predominant. And, in any event, the District Court did not rely upon the existence of the 1998 plan to support its ultimate conclusion. See *Kelley* v. *Everglades Drainage Dist.,* 319 U.S. 415, 420-422 (1943) *(per curiam).*

We do not see how Dr. Weber's testimony, taken as a whole, could have provided more than minimal support for the District Court's conclusion that race predominantly underlay the legislature's districting decision.

C

The District Court found that the testimony of the State's primary expert, Dr. Peterson, was "'unreliable' and not relevant. Dr. Peterson's testimony was designed to show that African-American Democratic voters were more reliably Democratic and that District 12's boundaries were drawn to include reliable Democrats. Specifically, Dr. Peterson compared precincts immediately within District 12 and those immediately without to determine whether the boundaries of the district corresponded better with race than with politics. The principle underlying Dr. Peterson's analysis is that if the district were drawn with race predominantly in mind, one would expect the boundaries of the district to correlate with race more than with politics.

The pages cited in support of the District Court's rejection of Dr. Peterson's conclusions contain testimony by Dr. Weber, who says that Dr. Peterson's analysis is unreliable because (1) it "ignor[es] the core" of the district, *id.,* at 223, and (2) it fails to take account of the fact that different precincts have different populations, *id.,* at 223-224. The first matter — ignoring the "core" — apparently reflects Dr. Weber's view that in context the fact that District 12's heart or "core" is heavily African-American by itself shows that the legislature's motive was predominantly racial, not political. The District Court did not argue that the racial makeup of a district's "core" is critical. Nor do we see why "core" makeup alone could help the court discern the relevant legislative motive. Nothing here suggests that only "core" makeup could answer the "political/racial" question that this Court previously found critical. *Cromartie*, 526 U.S., at 551-552.

[D]

The District Court also relied on two pieces of "direct" evidence of discriminatory intent.

1

The court found that a legislative redistricting leader, Senator Roy Cooper, when testifying before a legislative committee in 1997, had said that the 1997 plan satisfies a "need for 'racial and partisan' balance." App. to Juris. Statement 27a. The court concluded that the words "racial balance" referred to a 10-to-2 Caucasian/African-American balance in the State's 12-member congressional delegation. *Ibid*. Hence, Senator Cooper had admitted that the legislature had drawn the plan with race in mind.

Senator Cooper's full statement reads as follows:

> Those of you who dealt with Redistricting before realize that you cannot solve each problem that you encounter and everyone can find a problem with this Plan. However, I think that overall it provides for a fair, geographic, racial and partisan balance throughout the State of North Carolina. I think in order to come to an agreement all sides had to give a little bit, but I think we've reached an agreement that we can live with.

App. 460.

We agree that one can read the statement about "racial . . . balance" as the District Court read it — to refer to the current congressional delegation's racial balance. But even as so read, the phrase shows that the legislature considered race, along with other partisan and geographic considerations; and as so read it says little or nothing about whether race played a *predominant* role comparatively speaking. See *Vera*, 517 U.S., at 958 (O'Connor, J., principal opinion) ("Strict scrutiny does not apply merely because redistricting is performed with consciousness of race"); see also *Miller*, 515 U.S., at 916 (legislatures "will . . . almost always be aware of racial demographics"); *Shaw I*, 509 U.S., at 646 (same).

2

The second piece of "direct" evidence relied upon by the District Court is a February 10, 1997, e-mail sent from Gerry Cohen, a legislative staff member responsible for drafting districting plans, to Senator Cooper and Senator Leslie Winner. Cohen wrote: "I have moved Greensboro Black community into the 12th, and now need to take [about] 60,000 out of the 12th. I await your direction on this." App. 369.

The reference to race — *i.e.*, "Black community" — is obvious. But the e-mail does not discuss the point of the reference. It does not discuss why Greensboro's African-American voters were placed in the 12th District; it does not discuss the political consequences of failing to do so; it is addressed only to two members of the legislature; and it suggests that the legislature paid less attention to race in respect to the 12th District than in respect to the 1st District, where the e-mail provides a far more extensive, detailed discussion of racial percentages. It is less persuasive than the kinds of direct evidence we have found significant in other redistricting cases. See *Vera, supra*, at 959 (O'Connor, J., principal opinion) (State conceded that one of its goals was to create a majority-minority district); *Miller, supra*, at 907 (State set out to create majority-minority district); *Shaw II*,

517 U.S., at 906 (recounting testimony by Cohen that creating a majority-minority district was the "principal reason" for the 1992 version of District 12). Nonetheless, the e-mail offers some support for the District Court's conclusion.

E

As we have said, we assume that the maps appended to appellees' brief reflect the record insofar as that record describes the relation between District 12's boundaries and reliably Democratic voting behavior. Consequently we shall consider appellees' related claims, made on appeal, that the maps provide significant support for the District Court, in that they show how the legislature might have "swapped" several more heavily African-American District 12 precincts for other less heavily African-American adjacent precincts — without harming its basic "safely Democratic" political objective. Cf. *supra*, at 10-11.

First, appellees suggest, without identifying any specific swap, that the legislature could have brought within District 12 several reliably Democratic, primarily white, precincts in Forsyth County. See Brief for Appellees 30. None of these precincts, however, is more reliably Democratic than the precincts immediately adjacent and within District 12. See Appendix A, *infra* (showing Democratic strength reflected by Republican victories in each precinct); App. 484 (showing Democratic strength re-flected by Democratic registration). One of them, the Brown/Douglas Recreation Precinct, is heavily African-American. See *ibid.* And the remainder form a buffer between the home precinct of Fifth District Representative Richard Burr and the District 12 border, such that their removal from District 5 would deprive Representative Burr of a large portion of his own hometown, making him more vulnerable to a challenge from elsewhere within his district. App. to Juris. Statement 209a; App. 623. Consequently the Forsyth County precincts do not significantly help appellees'"race not politics" thesis.

[E]ven if our judgments in respect to a few of these precincts are wrong, a showing that the legislature might have "swapped" a handful of precincts out of a total of 154 precincts, involving a population of a few hundred out of a total population of about half a million, cannot significantly strengthen appellees' case.

IV

We concede the record contains a modicum of evidence offering support for the District Court's conclusion. That evidence includes the Cohen e-mail, Senator Cooper's reference to "racial balance," and to a minor degree, some aspects of Dr. Weber's testimony. The evidence taken together, however, does not show that racial considerations predominated in the drawing of District 12's boundaries. That is because race in this case correlates closely with political behavior. The basic question is whether the legislature drew District 12's boundaries because of race *rather than* because of political behavior (coupled with traditional, nonracial districting considerations). It is not, as the dissent contends, see *post*, at 9, whether a legislature may defend its districting decisions based on a "stereotype" about African-American voting behavior. And given the fact that the party attacking the legislature's decision bears the burden of proving that racial considerations are "dominant and controlling," *Miller*, 515 U.S., at 913, given the "demanding" nature of that burden of proof, *id.*, at 929 (O'Connor, J., concurring), and given the sensitivity, the "extraordinary caution," that district courts must show to avoid treading upon legislative prerogatives, *id.*, at 916 (majority opinion), the attacking party has not successfully shown that race, rather than politics, predominantly accounts for the result. The record leaves us with the "definite and firm conviction," *United States Gypsum Co.*, 333 U.S., at

395, that the District Court erred in finding to the contrary. And we do not believe that providing appellees a further opportunity to make their "precinct swapping" arguments in the District Court could change this result.

We can put the matter more generally as follows: In a case such as this one where majority-minority districts (or the approximate equivalent) are at issue and where racial identification correlates highly with political affiliation, the party attacking the legislatively drawn boundaries must show at the least that the legislature could have achieved its legitimate political objectives in alternative ways that are comparably consistent with traditional districting principles. That party must also show that those districting alternatives would have brought about significantly greater racial balance. Appellees failed to make any such showing here. We conclude that the District Court's contrary findings are clearly erroneous. Because of this disposition, we need not address appellants' alternative grounds for reversal.

The judgment of the District Court is reversed.

Comments on *Hunt v. Cromartie*: Justice Breyer's opinion for the majority basically conforms to the broad jurisprudential principles of the previous race and voting cases. However, this case is essentially a legislative case and certain facts when viewed from the standpoint of a Court liberal — giving credence to the state's expert to explain voting patterns over the plaintiff's expert — are interpreted differently than what one would expect from a Court conservative. Compare Justice Breyer's opinion here to Chief Justice Rehnquist conclusion in *Shaw v. Hunt* rejecting evidence that voting discrimination had occurred in North Carolina — many jurists would have assumed and taken judicial notice of this fact — on extraordinarily flimsy reasoning. Does this suggest that the Justices are engaged in a philosophical game among themselves as opposed to a legitimate search for legal truth? Or is this characterization a false critique on our part?

Justice Breyer's opinion says in so many words: Just because it looks like race was a predominant factor, does not mean that it was. Political gerrymandering may have been the reason. Democrats have the right to gerrymander in favor of strong and loyal Democratic voters. In North Carolina, that means more black districts.

As a result of strict scrutiny not used in this case.

A slightly different issue has been raised in recent VRA cases that has to do with the constitutionality of the total enterprise of preclearance. There are definitely federalism concerns as states have chafed over the need to report what may in some instances be merely administrative changes to the Justice Department or the District Court for the District of Columbia for VRA preclearance. This is particularly the case given the fact that Congress reauthorized the Voting Rights Act in 1970, 1982, and 2006. In 2006, even given the progress achieved under the Act, Congress extended the preclearance provisions of § 5 of the Voting Right Act for another 25 years. While the previous cases addressing race and voting dealt with how far a state could go in attempting to comply with Justice Department preclearance, these later cases addresses whether DOJ even has the authority under the enforcement provisions of the Fourteenth and Fifteenth Amendments to the Constitution. While these cases are best left for discussion in the section devoted to Enforcing the Civil War Amendments, a brief note here is in order.

In Northwest Utility District v. Holder, 557 U.S. 193 (2009), a political subdivision sought to bailout of coverage under the VRA and, in the alternative, sought to demonstrate that the preclearance requirement of section 5 of the Act was unconstitutional. However, the Court in an opinion by Chief Justice Roberts, declined to give the alternative relief under the principle of constitutional avoidance, and ruled that Northwest Austin and other similarly situated political subdivisions had the right to bailout from under the VRA. However, in a parting blow, the Chief Justice stated that the constitutionality of section 5 could depend upon whether it was needed for current times considering the changes in the previously covered jurisdictions:

> These improvements are no doubt due in significant part to the Voting Rights Act itself, and stand as a monument to its success. Past success alone, however, is not adequate justification to retain the preclearance requirements. It may be that these improvements are insufficient and that conditions continue to warrant preclearance under the Act. But the Act imposes current burdens and must be justified by current needs.
>
> The Act also differentiates between the States, despite our historic tradition that all the States enjoy "equal sovereignty." *United States v. Louisiana,* 363 U.S. 1, 16, 80 S.Ct. 961, 4 L.Ed.2d 1025 (1960). Distinctions can be justified in some cases. "The doctrine of the equality of States . . . does not bar . . . remedies for *local* evils which have subsequently appeared." *Katzenbach* (emphasis added). But a departure from the fundamental principle of equal sovereignty requires a showing that a statute's disparate geographic coverage is sufficiently related to the problem that it targets. . . .

ALABAMA LEGISLATIVE BLACK CAUCUS ET AL. v. ALABAMA ET AL.
575 U.S. 254 (2015)

JUSTICE BREYER delivered the opinion of the Court.

[The Court's opinion regarding the standing of the Alabama Democratic Caucus, one of the plaintiff in the case, can be found at pages ____.]

The Alabama Constitution requires the legislature to reapportion its State House and Senate electoral districts following each decennial census. Ala. Const., Art. IX, §§199–200. In 2012 Alabama redrew the boundaries of the State's 105 House districts and 35 Senate districts. 2012 Ala. Acts no. 602 (House plan); *id.,* at no. 603 (Senate plan) (Acts). In doing so, Alabama sought to achieve numerous traditional districting objectives, such as compactness, not splitting counties or precincts, minimizing change, and protecting incumbents. But it placed yet greater importance on achieving two other goals.

[First], it sought to minimize the extent to which a district might deviate from the theoretical ideal of precisely equal population.

[Second,] it sought to ensure compliance with federal law, and, in particular, the Voting Rights Act of 1965. 79 Stat. 439, as amended, 52 U. S. C. §10301 *et seq.* At the time of the redistricting Alabama was a covered jurisdiction under that Act. Accordingly §5 of the Act required Alabama to demonstrate that an electoral change, such as redistricting, would not bring about retrogression in respect to racial minorities' "ability . . . to elect their preferred candidates of choice." 52 U. S. C. §10304(b). Specifically, Alabama believed that, to avoid retrogression under §5, it was required to maintain roughly the same black population percentage in existing majority-minority districts.

Compliance with these two goals posed particular difficulties with respect to many of the State's 35 majority-minority districts (8 in the Senate, 27 in the House). That is because many of these districts were (compared with the average district) under populated. In order for Senate District 26, for example, to meet the State's no-more-than 1% population-deviation objective, the State would have to add about 16,000 individuals to the district. And, prior to redistricting, 72.75% of District 26's population was black. Accordingly, Alabama's plan added 15,785 new individuals, and only 36 of those newly added individuals were white.

This suit, as it appears before us, focuses in large part upon Alabama's efforts to achieve these two goals. The Caucus and the Conference basically claim that the State, in adding so many new minority voters to majority-minority districts (and to others), went too far. They allege the State created a constitutionally forbidden "racial gerrymander"—a gerrymander that (*e.g.*, when the State adds more minority voters than needed for a minority group to elect a candidate of its choice) might, among other things, harm the very minority voters that Acts such as the Voting Rights Act sought to help.

After a bench trial, the Federal District Court held in favor of the State, *i.e.*, against the Caucus and the Conference, with respect to their racial gerrymandering claims as well as with respect to several other legal claims that the Caucus and the Conference had made. With respect to racial gerrymandering, the District Court recognized that electoral districting violates the Equal Protection Clause when (1) race is the "dominant and controlling" or "predominant" consideration in deciding "to place a significant number of voters within or without a particular district," *Miller* v. *Johnson*, 515 U. S. 900, 913, 916 (1995), and (2) the use of race is not "narrowly tailored to serve a compelling state interest," *Shaw II*, 517 U. S., at 902; see also *Shaw* v. *Reno*, 509 U. S. 630, 649 (1993) (*Shaw I*) (Constitution forbids "separat[ion of] voters into different district son the basis of race" when the separation "lacks sufficient justification"); *Bush* v. *Vera*, 517 U. S. 952, 958–959, 976 (1996) (principal opinion of O'Connor, J.) (same). But, after trial the District Court held (2 to 1) that the Caucus and the Conference had failed to prove their racial gerrymandering claims. The Caucus along with the Conference(and several other plaintiffs) appealed. We noted probable jurisdiction with respect to the racial gerrymandering claims. 572 U. S. ___ (2014).

[II]

We begin by considering the geographical nature of the racial gerrymandering claims. The District Court repeatedly referred to the racial gerrymandering claims as claims that race improperly motivated the drawing of boundary lines of the State *considered as a whole*. See, *e.g.*, 989 F. Supp. 2d, at 1293 ("Race was not the predominant motivating factor for the Acts as a whole"); *id.*, at 1287 (construing plaintiffs' challenge as arguing that the "Acts as a whole constitute racial gerrymanders"); *id.*, at 1292 (describing the plaintiffs' challenge as a "claim of racial gerrymandering to the Acts as a whole"); cf. *supra*, at 4–5 (noting four exceptions).

A racial gerrymandering claim, however, applies to the boundaries of individual districts. It applies district-by-district. It does not apply to a State considered as an undifferentiated "whole." We have consistently described a claim of racial gerrymandering as a claim that race was improperly used in the drawing of the boundaries of one or more *specific electoral districts*. See, *e.g.*, *Shaw I*, 509 U. S., at 649 (violation consists of "separat[ing] voters *into different districts* on the basis of race" (emphasis added)); *Vera*, 517 U. S., at 965 (principal opinion) ("[Courts] must scrutinize *each challenged district . . .*" (emphasis added)). We have described the plaintiff's evidentiary burden similarly. See

Miller, supra, at 916 (plaintiff must show that "race was the predominant factor motivating the legislature's decision to place a significant number of voters within or without *a particular district*" (emphasis added)).

[IV]

The District Court held in the alternative that the claims of racial gerrymandering must fail because "[r]ace was not the predominant motivating factor" in the creation of any of the challenged districts. 989 F. Supp. 2d, at 1293. In our view, however, the District Court did not properly calculate "predominance." In particular, it judged race to lack "predominance" in part because it placed in the balance, among other nonracial factors, legislative efforts to create districts of approximately equal population. See, *e.g., id.,* at 1305 (the "need to bring the neighboring districts into compliance with the requirement of one person, one vote *served as the primary motivating factor* for the changes to [Senate] District 22" (emphasis added)); *id.,* at 1297 (the "constitutional requirement of one person, one vote trumped every other districting principle"); *id.,* at 1296 (the "record establishes that the drafters of the new districts, above all, had to correct [for] severe malapportionment . . ."); *id.,* at 1306 (the "inclusion of additional precincts [in Senate District 26] is a reasonable response to the under population of the District").

In our view, however, an equal population goal is not one factor among others to be weighed against the use of race to determine whether race "predominates." Rather, it is part of the redistricting background, taken as a given, when determining whether race, or other factors, predominate in a legislator's determination as to *how* equal population objectives will be met.

To understand this conclusion, recall what "predominance" is about: A plaintiff pursuing a racial gerrymandering claim must show that "race was the predominant factor motivating the legislature's decision to place a significant number of voters within or without a particular district." *Miller,* 515 U. S., at 916. To do so, the "plaintiff must prove that the legislature subordinated *traditional race-neutral districting principles* . . . to racial considerations." *Ibid.* (emphasis added).

Now consider the nature of those offsetting "traditional race-neutral districting principles." We have listed several, including "compactness, contiguity, respect for political subdivisions or communities defined by actual shared interests," *ibid.,* incumbency protection, and political affiliation, *Vera,* 517 U. S., at 964, 968 (principal opinion).

But we have not listed equal population objectives. And there is a reason for that omission. The reason that equal population objectives do not appear on this list of "traditional" criteria is that equal population objectives play a different role in a State's redistricting process. That role is not a minor one. Indeed, in light of the Constitution's demands, that role may often prove "predominant" in the ordinary sense of that word. But, as the United States points out, "predominance" in the context of a racial gerrymandering claim is special. It is not about whether a legislature believes that the need for equal population takes ultimate priority. Rather, it is, as we said, whether the legislature "placed" race "above traditional districting considerations in determining *which* persons were placed *in appropriately apportioned districts.*" Brief for United States as *Amicus Curiae* 19 (some emphasis added). In other words, if the legislature must place 1,000 or so additional voters in a particular in order to achieve an equal population goal, the "predominance" question concerns *which* voters the legislature decides to choose, and specifically whether the legislature predominately uses race as opposed to other, "traditional" factors when doing so.

Consequently, we agree with the United States that the requirement that districts have approximately equal populations is a background rule against which redistricting takes place. *Id.*, at 12. It is not a factor to be treated like other nonracial factors when a court determines whether race predominated over other, "traditional" factors in the drawing of district boundaries.

Had the District Court not taken a contrary view of the law, its "predominance" conclusions, including those concerning the four districts that the Conference specifically challenged, might well have been different. For example, once the legislature's "equal population" objectives are put to the side—*i.e.*, seen as a background principle—then there is strong, perhaps overwhelming, evidence that race did predominate as a factor when the legislature drew the boundaries of Senate District 26, the one district that the parties have discussed here in depth.

The legislators in charge of creating the redistricting plan believed, and told their technical adviser, that a primary redistricting goal was to maintain existing racial percentages in each majority-minority district, insofar as feasible. See *supra*, at 9–10 (compiling extensive record testimony in support of this point). There is considerable evidence that this goal had a direct and significant impact on the drawing of at least some of District 26's boundaries. [Transgressing] their own redistricting guidelines, Committee Guidelines 3–4, the drafters split seven precincts between the majority-black District 26 and the majority-white District 25, with the population in those precincts clearly divided on racial lines. [And] the District Court conceded that race "was a factor in the drawing of District 26," and that the legislature "preserved" "the percentage of the population that was black." 989 F. Supp. 2d, at 1306.

[All] this is to say that, with respect to District 26 and likely others as well, had the District Court treated equal population goals as background factors, it might have concluded that race was the predominant boundary-drawing consideration. Thus, on remand, the District Court should reconsider its "no predominance" conclusions with respect to Senate District 26 and others to which our analysis is applicable.

Finally, we note that our discussion in this section is limited to correcting the District Court's misapplication of the "predominance" test for strict scrutiny discussed in *Miller*, 515 U. S., at 916. It does not express a view on the question of whether the intentional use of race in redistricting, even in the absence of proof that traditional districting principles were subordinated to race, triggers strict scrutiny. See *Vera*, 517 U. S., at 996 (KENNEDY, J., concurring).

V

The District Court, in a yet further alternative holding, found that "[e]ven if the [State] subordinated traditional districting principles to racial considerations," the racial gerrymandering claims failed because, in any event, "the Districts would satisfy strict scrutiny." 989 F. Supp. 2d, at 1306. In the District Court's view, the "Acts are narrowly tailored to comply with Section 5" of the Voting Rights Act. *Id.*, at 1311. That provision "required the Legislature to maintain, where feasible, the existing number of majority-black districts and *not substantially reduce the relative percentages of black voters in those districts." Ibid.* (emphasis added). And, insofar as the State's redistricting embodied racial considerations, it did so in order to meet this §5 requirement.

In our view, however, this alternative holding rests upon a misperception of the law. Section 5, which covered particular States and certain other jurisdictions, does not require a covered jurisdiction to maintain a particular numerical minority percentage. It requires the jurisdiction to maintain a minority's ability to elect a preferred candidate of choice.

That is precisely what the language of the statute says. It prohibits a covered jurisdiction from adopting any change that "has the purpose of or will have the effect of diminishing the ability of [the minority group] to elect their preferred candidates of choice." 52 U. S. C.§10304(b); see also §10304(d) (the "purpose of subsection (b) . . . is to protect the ability of such citizens to elect their preferred candidates of choice").

That is also just what Department of Justice Guidelines say. The Guidelines state specifically that the Department's preclearance determinations are not based

> "on any predetermined or fixed demographic percentages. . . . Rather, in the Department's view, this determination requires a functional analysis of the electoral behavior within the particular jurisdiction or election district. . . . [C]ensus data alone may not provide sufficient indicia of electoral behavior to make the requisite determination." Guidance Concerning Redistricting Under Section 5 of the Voting Rights Act, 76 Fed. Reg. 7471 (2011).

Consistent with this view, the United States tells us that "Section 5" does not "requir[e] the State to maintain the same percentage of black voters in each of the majority-black districts as had existed in the prior districting plans." Brief for United States as *Amicus Curiae* 22. Rather, it "prohibits only those diminutions of a minority group's proportionate strength that strip the group within a district of its existing ability to elect its candidates of choice." *Id.*, at 22–23. We agree. Section 5 does not require maintaining the same population percentages in majority-minority districts as in the prior plan. Rather, §5 is satisfied if minority voters retain the ability to elect their preferred candidates.

The history of §5 further supports this view. In adopting the statutory language to which we referred above, Congress rejected this Court's decision in *Georgia* v. *Ashcroft*, 539 U. S. 461, 480 (2003) (holding that it is not necessarily retrogressive for a State to replace safe majority-minority districts with crossover or influence districts), and it adopted the views of the dissent. H. R. Rep. No. 109–478, pp. 68–69, and n. 183 (2006). While the thrust of Justice Souter's dissent was that, in a §5 retrogression case, courts should ask whether a new voting provision would likely deprive minority voters of their ability to elect a candidate of their choice—language that Congress adopted in revising §5—his dissent also made clear that courts should not mechanically rely upon numerical percentages but should take account of all significant circumstances. *Georgia* v. *Ashcroft*, *supra*, at 493, 498, 505, 509. And while the revised language of §5 may raise some interpretive questions—*e.g.*, its application to coalition, crossover, and influence districts—it is clear that Congress did not mandate that a 1% reduction in a 70% black population district would be necessarily retrogressive. See Persily, The Promises and Pitfalls of the New Voting Rights Act, 117 Yale L. J. 174, 218 (2007). Indeed, Alabama's mechanical interpretation of §5 can raise serious constitutional concerns. See *Miller*, *supra*, at 926.

The record makes clear that both the District Court and the legislature relied heavily upon a mechanically numerical view as to what counts as forbidden retrogression. See Appendix B, *infra*. And the difference between that view and the more purpose-oriented view reflected in the statute's language can matter. Imagine a majority-minority district with a 70% black population. Assume also that voting in that district, like that in the State itself, is racially polarized. And assume that the district has long elected to office black voters' preferred candidate. Other things being equal, it would seem highly unlikely that a redistricting plan that, while increasing the numerical size of the district, reduced the percentage of the black population from, say, 70% to 65% would have a significant impact on the black voters' ability to elect their preferred candidate. And, for that reason, it would be difficult to explain just why a plan that uses racial criteria predominately to maintain the black population at 70% is "narrowly tailored" to achieve a "compelling state interest," namely the interest in preventing §5 retrogression. The circumstances of this hypothetical example, we add, are close to those characterizing Senate District 26, as set forth in the District Court's opinion and throughout the record.

In saying this, we do not insist that a legislature guess precisely what percentage reduction a court or the Justice Department might eventually find to be retrogressive. The law cannot insist that a state legislature, when redistricting, determine *precisely* what percent minority population §5 demands. The standards of §5 are complex; they often require evaluation of controverted claims about voting behavior; the evidence may be unclear; and, with respect to any particular district, judges may disagree about the proper outcome. The law cannot lay a trap for an unwary legislature, condemning its redistricting plan as either (1) unconstitutional racial gerrymandering should the legislature place a few too many minority voters in a district or (2) retrogressive under §5 should the legislature place a few too few. See *Vera*, 517 U. S., at 977 (principal opinion). Thus, we agree with the United States that a court's analysis of the narrow tailoring requirement insists only that the legislature have a "strong basis in evidence" in support of the (race-based) choice that it has made. Brief for United States as *Amicus Curiae* 29 (citing *Ricci* v. *DeStefano*, 557 U. S. 557, 585 (2009)). This standard, as the United States points out, "does not demand that a State's actions actually be necessary to achieve a compelling state interest in order to be constitutionally valid." Brief for United States as *Amicus Curiae* 29. And legislators "may have a strong basis in evidence to use racial classifications in order to comply with a statute when they have *good reasons* to believe such use is required, even if a court does not find that the actions were necessary for statutory compliance." *Ibid.* (emphasis added).

Here the District Court enunciated a narrow tailoring standard close to the one we have just mentioned. It said that a plan is "narrowly tailored . . . when the race-based action taken was *reasonably necessary*" to achieve a compelling interest. 989 F. Supp. 2d, at 1307 (emphasis added). And it held that preventing retrogression is a compelling interest. *Id.*, at 1306–1307. While we do not here decide whether, given *Shelby County* v. *Holder*, 570 U. S. ___ (2013), continued compliance with §5 remains a compelling interest, we conclude that the District Court and the legislature asked the wrong question with respect to narrow tailoring. They asked: "How can we maintain present minority percentages in majority-minority districts?" But given §5's language, its purpose, the Justice Department Guidelines, and the relevant precedent, they should have asked: "To what extent must we preserve existing minority percentages in order to maintain the minority's present ability to elect the candidate of its choice?" Asking the wrong question may well have led to the wrong answer. Hence, we cannot accept the District Court's "compelling interest/narrow tailoring" conclusion.

* * *

For these reasons, the judgment of the District Court is vacated. We note that appellants have also raised additional questions in their jurisdictional statements, relating to their one-person, one-vote claims (Caucus) and vote dilution claims (Conference), which were also rejected by the District Court. We do not pass upon these claims. The District Court remains free to reconsider the claims should it find reconsideration appropriate. And the parties are free to raise them, including as modified by the District Court, on any further appeal.

The cases are remanded for further proceedings consistent with this opinion. *It is so ordered.*

JUSTICE THOMAS, dissenting.

[I] join JUSTICE SCALIA's dissent. I write only to point out that, as this case painfully illustrates, our jurisprudence in this area continues to be infected with error.

I

The Alabama Legislature faced a difficult situation in its 2010 redistricting efforts. It began with racially segregated district maps that were inherited from previous decades. The maps produced by the 2001 redistricting contained 27 majority-black House districts and 8 majority-black Senate districts—both at the time they were drawn, App. to Juris. Statement 47–48, and at the time of the 2010 Census, App. 103–108. Many of these majority-black districts were over 70% black when they were drawn in 2001, and even more were over 60% black. App. to Juris. Statement 47–48. Even after the 2010 Census, the population remained above 60% black in the majority of districts. App. 103–108.

Under the 2006 amendments to §5 of the Voting Rights Act of 1965, Alabama was also under a federal command to avoid drawing new districts that would "have the effect of diminishing the ability" of black voters "to elect their preferred candidates of choice." 52 U. S. C. §10304(b). To comply with §5, the legislature adopted a policy of maintaining the same percentage of black voters within each of those districts as existed in the 2001 plans. See *ante*, at 16. This, the districting committee thought, would preserve the ability of black voters to elect the same number of preferred candidates. App. to Juris. Statement 174– 175. The Department of Justice (DOJ) apparently agreed. Acting under its authority to administer §5 of the Voting Rights Act, the DOJ pre cleared Alabama's plans.[1] *Id.,* at 9.

Appellants—including the Alabama Legislative Black Caucus and the Alabama Democratic Conference—saw matters differently. They sued Alabama, and on appeal they argue that the State's redistricting plans are racially gerrymandered because many districts are highly packed with black voters. According to appellants, black voters would have more voting power if they were spread over more districts rather than concentrated in the same number of districts as in previous decades. The DOJ has entered the fray in support of appellants, arguing that the State's redistricting maps fail strict scrutiny because the State focused too heavily on a single racial characteristic—the number of black voters in majority-minority districts—which potentially resulted in impermissible packing of black voters.

Like the DOJ, today's majority sides with appellants, faulting Alabama for choosing the wrong percentage of blacks in the State's majority-black districts, or at least for arriving at that percentage using the wrong reasoning. In doing so, the Court—along with appellants and the DOJ—exacerbates a problem many years in the making. It seems fitting, then, to trace that history here. The practice of creating highly packed—"safe"— majority-minority districts is the product of our erroneous jurisprudence, which created a system that forces States to segregate voters into districts based on the color of their skin. Alabama's current legislative districts have their genesis in the "max-black" policy that the DOJ itself applied to §5 throughout the 1990's and early 2000's. The 2006 amendments to §5 then effectively locked in place Alabama's max-black districts that were established during the 1990's and 2000's. These three problems—a jurisprudence requiring segregated districts, the distortion created by the DOJ's max-black policy, and the ossifying effects of the 2006 amendments—are the primary culprits in this case, not Alabama's redistricting policy. Nor does this Court have clean hands.

II

This Court created the current system of race-based redistricting by adopting expansive readings of §2 and §5 of the Voting Rights Act. Both §2 and §5 prohibit States from implementing voting laws that "den[y] or abridg[e]the right to vote on account of race or color." §§10304(a), 10301(a). But both provisions extend to only certain types of voting laws: any "voting qualification or prerequisite to voting, or standard, practice, or procedure." *Ibid.* As I have previously explained, the terms "'standard, practice, or procedure' . . . refer only to practices that affect minority citizens' access to the ballot," such as literacy tests. *Holder*, 512 U. S. at 914 (opinion concurring in judgment). They do not apply to "[d]istricting systems and electoral mechanisms that may affect the 'weight' given to a ballot duly cast and counted." *Ibid.* Yet this Court has adopted far-reaching interpretations of both provisions, holding that they encompass legislative redistricting and other actions that might "dilute" the strength of minority votes.

[The] consequences have been as predictable and as they are unfortunate. In pursuing "undiluted" or maximized minority voting power, "we have devised a remedial mechanism that encourages federal courts to segregate voters into racially designated districts to ensure minority electoral success." *Holder, supra,* at 892 (THOMAS, J., concurring in judgment). Section 5, the provision at issue here, has been applied to require States that redistrict to maintain the number of pre-existing majority-minority districts, in which minority voters make up a large enough portion of the population to be able to elect their candidate of choice. See, *e.g., Miller, supra,* at 923–927 (rejecting the DOJ's policy of requiring States to increase the number of majority-black districts because maintaining the same number of majority-black districts would not violate §5).

[IV]

Alabama's quandary as it attempted to redraw its legislative districts after 2010 was exacerbated by the 2006 amendments to §5. Those amendments created an inflexible definition of "retrogression" that Alabama understandably took as requiring it to maintain the same percentages of minority voters in majority-minority districts. The amendments thus provide the last piece of the puzzle that explains why the State sought to maintain the same percentages of blacks in each majority-black district.

Congress passed the 2006 amendments in response to our attempt to define "retrogression" in *Georgia* v. *Ashcroft*, 539 U. S. 461. Prior to that decision, practically any reapportionment change could "be deemed 'retrogressive' under our vote dilution jurisprudence by a court inclined to find it so." *Bossier I*, 520 U. S., at 490–491 (THOMAS, J., concurring). "[A] court could strike down *any* reapportionment plan, either because it did not include enough majority-minority districts or because it did (and thereby diluted the minority vote in the remaining districts)." *Id.,* at 491. Our §5 jurisprudence thus "inevitably force[d] the courts to make political judgments regarding which type of apportionment best serves supposed minority interests—judgments courts are ill equipped to make." *Id.,* at 492.

We tried to pull the courts and the DOJ away from making these sorts of judgments in *Georgia* v. *Ashcroft, supra.* Insofar as §5 applies to the drawing of voting districts, we held that a District Court had wrongly rejected Georgia's reapportionment plan, and we adopted a retrogression standard that gave States flexibility in determining the percentage of black voters in each district. *Id.,* at 479–481. As we explained, "a State may choose to create a certain number of 'safe' districts, in which it is highly likely that minority voters will be able to elect the candidate of their choice." *Id.,* at 480. Alternatively, "a State may choose to create a greater number of districts in which it is likely—although perhaps not quite as likely as under the benchmark plan—that minority voters will be able to elect candidates of their choice." *Ibid.* We noted that "spreading out minority voters over a greater number of districts creates more districts in which minority voters may have the opportunity to elect a candidate of their choice," even if success is not guaranteed, and even if it diminished the chance of electing a representative in some districts. *Id.,* at 481. Thus, States would be permitted to make judgments about how best to prevent retrogression in a minority group's voting power, including assessing the range of appropriate minority population percentages within each district. *Id.,* at 480–481.

In response, Congress amended §5 and effectively overruled *Georgia* v. *Ashcroft.* See 120 Stat. 577. The 2006 amendments added subsection (b), which provides:

> "Any voting qualification or prerequisite to voting, or standard, practice or procedure with respect to voting that has the purpose or will have the effect of diminishing the ability of any citizens of the United States on account of race or color . . . to elect their preferred candidates of choice denies or abridges the right to vote within the meaning of . . . this section." 52 U. S. C. §10304(b). See §5, 120 Stat. 577.

Thus, any change that has the effect of "diminishing the ability" of a minority group to "elect their preferred candidate of choice" is retrogressive.

[[T]he] majority's solution to the appellants' gerrymandering claims requires States to analyze race even *more* exhaustively, not less, by accounting for black voter registration and turnout statistics. *Ante,* at 18–19. The majority's command to analyze black voting patterns in route to adopting the "correct" racial quota does nothing to ease the conflict between our color-blind Constitution and the "consciously segregated districting system" the Court has required in the name of equality. *Holder,* 512 U. S., at 907. Although I dissent today on procedural grounds, I also continue to disagree with the Court's misguided and damaging jurisprudence.

[A dissent by Justice Scalia is omitted.]

ARIZONA STATE LEGISLATURE v. ARIZONA INDEPENDENT REDISTRICTING COMMISSION ET AL.
576 U.S. __ (2015)

JUSTICE GINSBURG delivered the opinion of the Court. [See pages ___ for the Court's opinion on the standing issue.]

This case concerns an endeavor by Arizona voters to address the problem of partisan gerrymandering—the drawing of legislative district lines to subordinate adherents of one political party and entrench a rival party in power. "[P]artisan gerrymanders," this Court has recognized, "[are incompatible] with democratic principles." *Vieth* v. *Jubelirer,* 541 U. S. 267, 292 (2004) (plurality opinion); *id.,* at 316 (KENNEDY, J., concurring in judgment). Even so, the Court in *Vieth* did not grant relief on the plaintiffs' partisan gerrymander claim. The plurality held the matter nonjusticiable. *Id.,* at 281. JUSTICE KENNEDY found no standard workable in that case, but left open the possibility that a suitable standard might be identified in later litigation. *Id.,* at 317.

In 2000, Arizona voters adopted an initiative, Proposition 106, aimed at "ending the practice of gerrymandering and improving voter and candidate participation in elections." App. 50. Proposition 106 amended Arizona's Constitution to remove redistricting authority from the Arizona Legislature and vest that authority in an independent commission, the Arizona Independent Redistricting Commission (AIRC or Commission). After the 2010 census, as after the 2000 census, the AIRC adopted redistricting maps for congressional as well as state legislative districts.

The Arizona Legislature challenged the map the Commission adopted in January 2012 for congressional districts. Recognizing that the voters could control redistricting for state legislators, Brief for Appellant 42, 47; Tr. of Oral Arg. 3–4, the Arizona Legislature sued the AIRC in federal court seeking a declaration that the Commission and its map for congressional districts violated the "Elections Clause" of the U. S. Constitution. That Clause, critical to the resolution of this case, provides:

> "The Times, Places and Manner of holding Elections for Senators and Representatives, shall be prescribed in each State by the Legislature thereof; but the Congress may at any time by Law make or alter such Regulations . . . ." Art. I, §4, cl. 1.

The Arizona Legislature's complaint alleged that "[t]heword 'Legislature' in the Elections Clause means [specifically and only] the representative body which makes the laws of the people," App. 21, ¶37; so read, the Legislature urges, the Clause precludes resort to an independent commission, created by initiative, to accomplish redistricting. The AIRC responded that, for Elections Clause purposes, "the Legislature" is not confined to the elected representatives; rather, the term encompasses all legislative authority conferred by the State Constitution, including initiatives adopted by the people themselves.

A three-judge District Court held, unanimously, that the Arizona Legislature had standing to sue; dividing two to one, the Court rejected the Legislature's complaint on the merits. We postponed jurisdiction and instructed the parties to address two questions: (1) Does the Arizona Legislature have standing to bring this suit? (2) Do the Elections Clause of the United States Constitution and 2 U. S. C. §2a(c) permit Arizona's use of a commission to adopt congressional districts? 573 U. S. ___ (2014).

We now affirm the District Court's judgment. We hold, first, that the Arizona Legislature, having lost authority to draw congressional districts, has standing to contest the constitutionality of Proposition 106. Next, we hold that lawmaking power in Arizona includes the initiative process, and that both §2a(c) and the Elections Clause permit use of the AIRC in congressional districting in the same way the Commission is used in districting for Arizona's own Legislature.

I

[C]

Proposition 106, vesting redistricting authority in the AIRC, was adopted by citizen initiative in 2000 against a "background of recurring redistricting turmoil" in Arizona. Cain, Redistricting Commissions: A Better Political Buffer? 121 Yale L. J. 1808, 1831 (2012). Redistricting plans adopted by the Arizona Legislature sparked controversy in every redistricting cycle since the 1970's, and several of those plans were rejected by a federal court or refused preclearance by the Department of Justice under the Voting Rights Act of 1965. See *id.,* at 1830–1832.

Aimed at "ending the practice of gerrymandering and improving voter and candidate participation in elections," App. 50, Proposition 106 amended the Arizona Constitution to remove congressional redistricting authority from the state legislature, lodging that authority, instead, in a new entity, the AIRC. Ariz. Const., Art. IV, pt. 2, §1, ¶¶3– 23. The AIRC convenes after each census, establishes final district boundaries, and certifies the new districts to the Arizona Secretary of State. ¶¶16–17. The legislature may submit non-binding recommendations to the AIRC,¶16, and is required to make necessary appropriations for its operation, ¶18.

[D]

On January 17, 2012, the AIRC approved final congressional and state legislative maps based on the 2010 census. See Arizona Independent Redistricting, Final Maps, Less than four months later, on June 6, 2012, the Arizona Legislature filed suit in the United States District Court for the District of Arizona, naming as defendants the AIRC, its five members, and the Arizona Secretary of State. The Legislature sought both a declaration that Proposition 106 and congressional maps adopted by the AIRC are unconstitutional, and, as affirmative relief, an injunction against use of AIRC maps for any congressional election after the 2012 general election.

A three-judge District Court, convened pursuant to 28 U. S. C. §2284(a), unanimously denied a motion by the AIRC to dismiss the suit for lack of standing. The Arizona Legislature, the court determined, had "demonstrated that its loss of redistricting power constitute[d] a [sufficiently] concrete injury." 997 F. Supp. 2d 1047, 1050 (2014). On the merits, dividing two to one, the District Court granted the AIRC's motion to dismiss the complaint for failure to state a claim. Decisions of this Court, the majority concluded, "demonstrate that the word 'Legislature' in the Elections Clause refers to the legislative process used in [a] state, determined by that state's own constitution and laws." Id., at 1054. As the "lawmaking power" in Arizona" plainly includes the power to enact laws through initiative," the District Court held, the "Elections Clause permits [Arizona's] establishment and use" of the Commission. Id., at 1056. Judge Rosenblatt dissented in part. Proposition 106, in his view, unconstitutionally denied "the Legislature" of Arizona the "ability to have any outcome-defining effect on the congressional redistricting process." Id., at 1058.

We postponed jurisdiction, and now affirm.

[The Court's discussion of the standing issue can be found in Chapter 1, page 147.]

[III]

[The] Elections Clause is set out at the start of this opinion, *supra*, at 2. Section 2a(c) provides:

> "Until a State is redistricted in the manner provided by the law thereof after any apportionment, the Representatives to which such State is entitled under such apportionment shall be elected in the following manner: [setting out five federally prescribed redistricting procedures]."

Before focusing directly on the statute and constitutional prescriptions in point, we summarize this Court's precedent relating to appropriate state decision makers for redistricting purposes. Three decisions compose the relevant case law: *Ohio ex rel. Davis* v. *Hildebrant*, 241 U. S. 565 (1916); *Hawke* v. *Smith (No. 1)*, 253 U. S. 221 (1920); and *Smiley* v. *Holm*, 285 U. S. 355 (1932).

A

Davis v. *Hildebrant* involved an amendment to the Constitution of Ohio vesting in the people the right, exercisable by referendum, to approve or disapprove by popular vote any law enacted by the State's legislature. A 1915 Act redistricting the State for the purpose of congressional elections had been submitted to a popular vote, resulting in disapproval of the legislature's measure. State election officials asked the State's Supreme Court to declare the referendum void. That court rejected the request, holding that the referendum authorized by Ohio's Constitution, "was a part of the legislative power of the State," and "nothing in [federal statutory law] or in [the Elections Clause] operated to the contrary." 241 U. S., at 567. This Court affirmed the Ohio Supreme Court's judgment. In upholding the state court's decision, we recognized that the referendum was "part of the legislative power" in Ohio, *ibid.*, legitimately exercised by the people to disapprove the legislation creating congressional districts. For redistricting purposes, *Hildebrant* thus established, "the Legislature" did not mean the representative body alone. Rather, the word encompassed a veto power lodged in the people.

Hawke v. *Smith* involved the Eighteenth Amendment to the Federal Constitution. Ohio's Legislature had ratified the Amendment, and a referendum on that ratification was at issue. Reversing the Ohio Supreme Court's decision upholding the referendum, we held that "ratification by a State of a constitutional amendment is not an act of legislation within the proper sense of the word." 253 U. S., at 229. Instead, Article V governing ratification had lodged in "the legislatures of three-fourths of the several States" sole authority to assent to a proposed amendment. *Id.,* at 226. The Court contrasted the ratifying function, exercisable exclusively by a State's legislature, with "the ordinary business of legislation." *Id.,* at 229. *Davis* v. *Hildebrant*, the Court explained, involved the enactment of legislation, *i.e.*, a redistricting plan, and properly held that "the referendum [was] part of the legislative authority of the State for [that] purpose." 253 U. S., at 230.

[THE] CHIEF JUSTICE, in dissent, features, indeed trumpets repeatedly, the pre-Seventeenth Amendment regime in which Senators were "chosen [in each State] by the Legislature thereof." Art. I, §3; see *post,* at 1, 8–9, 19. If we are right, he asks, why did popular election proponents resort to the amending process instead of simply interpreting "the Legislature" to mean "the people"? *Post,* at 1. *Smiley*, as just indicated, answers that question. Article I, §3, gave state legislatures "a function different from that of lawgiver," 285 U. S., at 365; it made each of them "an electoral body" charged to perform that function to the exclusion of other participants, *ibid.* So too, of the ratifying function. As we explained in *Hawke*, "the power to legislate in the enactment of the laws of a State is derived from the people of the State." 253 U. S., at 230. Ratification, however, "has its source in the Federal Constitution" and is not "an act of legislation within the proper sense of the word." *Id.,* at 229–230.

Constantly resisted by THE CHIEF JUSTICE, but well understood in opinions that speak for the Court: "[T]he meaning of the word 'legislature,' used several times in the Federal Constitution, differs according to the connection in which it is employed, depend[ent] upon the character of the function which that body in each instance is called upon to exercise." *Atlantic Cleaners & Dyers, Inc.* v. *United States*, 286 U. S. 427, 434 (1932) (citing *Smiley*, 285 U. S. 355). Thus "the Legislature" comprises the referendum and the Governor's veto in the context of regulating congressional elections. *Hildebrant*, see *supra*, at 15–16; *Smiley*, see *supra*, at 17–18. In the context of ratifying constitutional amendments, in contrast, "the Legislature" has a different identity, one that excludes the referendum and the Governor's veto. *Hawke*, see *supra*, at 16.

In sum, our precedent teaches that redistricting is a legislative function, to be performed in accordance with the State's prescriptions for lawmaking, which may include the referendum and the Governor's veto. The exercise of the initiative, we acknowledge, was not at issue in our prior decisions. But as developed below, we see no constitutional barrier to a State's empowerment of its people by embracing that form of lawmaking.

[C]

[To] restate the key question in this case, the issue centrally debated by the parties: Absent congressional authorization, does the Elections Clause preclude the people of Arizona from creating a commission operating independently of the state legislature to establish congressional districts? The history and purpose of the Clause weigh heavily against such preclusion, as does the animating principle of our Constitution that the people themselves are the originating source of all the powers of government.

[1]

The dominant purpose of the Elections Clause, the historical record bears out, was to empower Congress to override state election rules, not to restrict the way States enact legislation.

[The] Clause was also intended to act as a safeguard against manipulation of electoral rules by politicians and factions in the States to entrench themselves or place their interests over those of the electorate.

[2]

The Arizona Legislature maintains that, by specifying" the Legislature thereof," the Elections Clause renders the State's representative body the sole "component of state government authorized to prescribe . . . regulations . . . for congressional redistricting." Brief for Appellant 30. THE CHIEF JUSTICE, in dissent, agrees. But it is characteristic of our federal system that States retain autonomy to establish their own governmental processes. See *Alden* v. *Maine*, 527 U. S. 706, 752 (1999) ("A State is entitled to order the processes of its own governance."); The Federalist No. 43, at 272 (J. Madison) ("Whenever the States may choose to substitute other republican forms, they have a right to do so.").

[We] resist reading the Elections Clause to single out federal elections as the one area in which States may not use citizen initiatives as an alternative legislative process. Nothing in that Clause instructs, nor has this Court ever held, that a state legislature may prescribe regulations on the time, place, and manner of holding federal elections in defiance of provisions of the State's constitution. See *Shiel*, H. R. Misc. Doc. No. 57, at 349–352 (concluding that Oregon's Constitution prevailed over any conflicting legislative measure setting the date for a congressional election).

THE CHIEF JUSTICE, in dissent, maintains that, under the Elections Clause, the state legislature can trump any initiative-introduced constitutional provision regulating federal elections. He extracts support for this position from *Baldwin* v. *Trowbridge*, 2 Bartlett Contested Election Cases, H. R. Misc. Doc. No. 152, 41st Cong., 2d Sess., 46–47 (1866). See *post*, at 15–16. There, Michigan voters had amended the State Constitution to require votes to be cast within a resident's township or ward. The Michigan Legislature, however, passed a law permitting soldiers to vote in other locations. One candidate would win if the State Constitution's requirement controlled; his opponent would prevail under the Michigan Legislature's prescription. The House Elections Committee, in a divided vote, ruled that, under the Elections Clause, the Michigan Legislature had the paramount power.

As the minority report in *Baldwin* pointed out, however, the Supreme Court of Michigan had reached the opposite conclusion, holding, as courts generally do, that state legislation in direct conflict with the State's constitution is void. *Baldwin*, H. R. Misc. Doc. No. 152, at 50. The *Baldwin* majority's ruling, furthermore, appears in tension with the Election Committee's unanimous decision in *Shiel* just five years earlier. [In] short, *Baldwin* is not a disposition that should attract this Court's reliance.

[***]

Invoking the Elections Clause, the Arizona Legislature instituted this lawsuit to disempower the State's voters from serving as the legislative power for redistricting purposes. But the Clause surely was not adopted to diminish a State's authority to determine its own lawmaking processes. Article I, §4, stems from a different view. Both parts of the Elections Clause are in line with the fundamental premise that all political power flows from the people. *McCulloch* v. *Maryland*, 4 Wheat. 316, 404–405 (1819). So comprehended, the Clause doubly empowers the people. They may control the State's lawmaking processes in the first instance, as Arizona voters have done, and they may seek Congress' correction of regulations prescribed by state legislatures.

The people of Arizona turned to the initiative to curb the practice of gerrymandering and, thereby, to ensure that Members of Congress would have "an habitual recollection of their dependence on the people." The Federalist No. 57, at 350 (J. Madison). In so acting, Arizona voters sought to restore "the core principle of republican government, "namely, "that the voters should choose their representatives, not the other way around." Berman, Managing Gerrymandering, 83 Texas L. Rev. 781 (2005). The Elections Clause does not hinder that endeavor.

For the reasons stated, the judgment of the United States District Court for the District of Arizona is *Affirmed*.

[Dissents by Chief Justice Roberts, Justice Scalia, and Justice Thomas have been omitted. Eds]

In the following case, the Court was asked to reconsider the concept of "one person, one vote" as that term applies to state legislative districts. The question raised is whether state legislative districts should be apportioned according to population or voting eligible population under the Equal Protection Clause. The decision was announced a little over a month following the death of Justice Antonin Scalia and was the product of an eight-person court. By this point in the course, you may be familiar with the jurisprudence of Justice Scalia. Do you think the absence of Justice Scalia affected the outcome of this decision?

EVENWEL ET AL. v. ABBOTT, GOVERNOR OF TEXAS
578 U. S. 54 (2016)

JUSTICE GINSBURG delivered the opinion of the Court.

Texas, like all other States, draws its legislative districts on the basis of total population. Plaintiffs appellants are Texas voters; they challenge this uniform method of districting on the ground that it produces unequal districts when measured by voter-eligible population. Voter-eligible population, not total population, they urge, must be used to ensure that their votes will not be devalued in relation to citizens' votes in other districts.

We hold, based on constitutional history, this Court's decisions, and longstanding practice, that a State may draw its legislative districts based on total population.

I

A

This Court long resisted any role in overseeing the process by which States draw legislative districts. "The remedy for unfairness in districting," the Court once held, "is to secure State legislatures that will apportion properly, or to invoke the ample powers of Congress." Colegrove v. Green, 328 U. S. 549, 556 (1946). "Courts ought not to enter this political thicket," as Justice Frankfurter put it.

Judicial abstention left pervasive malapportionment unchecked. In the opening half of the 20th century, there was a massive population shift away from rural areas and toward suburban and urban communities. Nevertheless, many States ran elections into the early 1960's based on maps drawn to equalize each district's population as it was composed around 1900. Other States used maps allocating a certain number of legislators to each county regardless of its population. These schemes left many rural districts significantly underpopulated in comparison with urban and suburban districts. But rural legislators who benefited from malapportionment had scant incentive to adopt new maps that might put them out of office.

The Court confronted this ingrained structural inequality in Baker v. Carr, 369 U. S. 186, 191–192 (1962). That case presented an equal protection challenge to a Tennessee state-legislative map that had not been redrawn since 1901. See also id., at 192 (observing that, in the meantime, there had been "substantial growth and redistribution" of the State's population). Rather than steering clear of the political thicket yet again, the Court held for the first time that malapportionment claims are justiciable. Id., at 237 ("We conclude that the complaint's allegations of a denial of equal protection present a justiciable constitutional cause of action upon which appellants are entitled to a trial and a decision.").

Although the Court in Baker did not reach the merits of the equal protection claim, Baker's justiciability ruling set the stage for what came to be known as the one-person, one-vote principle. Just two years after Baker, in Wesberry v. Sanders, 376 U. S. 1, 7–8 (1964), the Court invalidated Georgia's malapportioned congressional map, under which the population of one congressional district was "two to three times" larger than the population of the others. Relying on Article I, §2, of the Constitution, the Court required that congressional districts be drawn with equal populations. Id., at 7, 18. Later that same Term, in Reynolds v. Sims, 377 U. S. 533, 568 (1964), the Court upheld an equal protection challenge to Alabama's malapportioned state-legislative maps. "[T]he Equal Protection Clause," the Court concluded, "requires that the seats in both houses of a bicameral state legislature must be apportioned on a population basis." Ibid. Wesberry and Reynolds together instructed that jurisdictions must design both congressional and state-legislative districts with equal populations, and must regularly reapportion districts to prevent malapportionment.

Over the ensuing decades, the Court has several times elaborated on the scope of the one-person, one-vote rule. States must draw congressional districts with populations as close to perfect equality as possible. See Kirkpatrick v. Preisler, 394 U. S. 526, 530–531 (1969). But, when drawing state and local legislative districts, jurisdictions are permitted to deviate somewhat from perfect population equality to accommodate traditional districting objectives, among them, preserving the integrity of political subdivisions, maintaining communities of interest, and creating geographic compactness. See Brown v. Thomson, 462 U. S. 835, 842–843 (1983). Where the maximum population deviation between the largest and smallest district is less than 10%, the Court has held, a state or local legislative map presumptively complies with the one-person, onevote rule. Ibid. Maximum deviations above 10% are presumptively impermissible.

[I]n contrast to repeated disputes over the permissibility of deviating from perfect population equality, little controversy has centered on the population base jurisdictions must equalize. On rare occasions, jurisdictions have relied on the registered-voter or voter-eligible populations of districts. See Burns v. Richardson, 384 U. S. 73, 93–94 (1966) (holding Hawaii could use a registered-voter population base because of "Hawaii's special population problems"—in particular, its substantial temporary military population). But, in the overwhelming majority of cases, jurisdictions have equalized total population, as measured by the decennial census. Today, all States use total population numbers from the census when designing congressional and state-legislative districts, and only seven States adjust those census numbers in any meaningful way.

B

Appellants challenge that consensus. After the 2010 census, Texas redrew its State Senate districts using a total-population baseline. At the time, Texas was subject to the preclearance requirements of §5 of the Voting Rights Act of 1965. 52 U. S. C. §10304 (requiring jurisdictions to receive approval from the U. S. Department of Justice or the U. S. District Court for the District of Columbia before implementing certain voting changes). Once it became clear that the new Senate map, S148, would not receive preclearance in advance of the 2012 elections, the U. S. District Court for the Western District of Texas drew an interim Senate map, S164, which also equalized the total population of each district. See Davis v. Perry, No. SA–11–CV–788 (Nov. 23, 2011). On direct appeal, this Court observed that the District Court had failed to "take guidance from the State's recently enacted plan in drafting an interim plan," and therefore vacated the District Court's map. Perry v. Perez, 565 U. S. ___, ___, ___–___ (2012) (per curiam) (slip op., at 4, 8–10).

The District Court, on remand, again used census data to draw districts so that each included roughly the same size total population. Texas used this new interim map, S172, in the 2012 elections, and, in 2013, the Texas Legislature adopted S172 as the permanent Senate map. See App. to Brief for Texas Senate Hispanic Caucus et al. as Amici Curiae 5 (reproducing the current Senate map). The permanent map's maximum total-population deviation is 8.04%, safely within the presumptively permissible 10% range. But measured by a voter-population baseline—eligible voters or registered voters—the map's maximum population deviation exceeds 40%.

Appellants Sue Evenwel and Edward Pfenninger live in Texas Senate districts (one and four, respectively) with particularly large eligible- and registered-voter populations. Contending that basing apportionment on total population dilutes their votes in relation to voters in other Senate districts, in violation of the one-person, one-vote principle of the Equal Protection Clause, appellants filed suit in the U. S. District Court for the Western District of Texas. They named as defendants the Governor and Secretary of State of Texas, and sought a permanent injunction barring use of the existing Senate map in favor of a map that would equalize the voter population in each district.

The case was referred to a three-judge District Court for hearing and decision. See 28 U. S. C. §2284(a); Shapiro v. McManus, 577 U. S. ___, ___–___ (2015) (slip op., at 5–7). That court dismissed the complaint for failure to state a claim on which relief could be granted. Appellants, the District Court explained, "rel[y] upon a theory never before accepted by the Supreme Court or any circuit court: that the metric of apportionment employed by Texas (total population) results in an unconstitutional apportionment because it does not achieve equality as measured by Plaintiffs' chosen metric—voter population." Decisions of this Court, the District Court concluded, permit jurisdictions to use any neutral, nondiscriminatory population baseline, including total population, when drawing state and local legislative districts. Id., at 13a–14a.6

We noted probable jurisdiction, 575 U. S. ___ (2015), and now affirm.

II

The parties and the United States advance different positions in this case. As they did before the District Court, appellants insist that the Equal Protection Clause requires jurisdictions to draw state and local legislative districts with equal voter-eligible populations, thus protecting "voter equality," i.e., "the right of eligible voters to an equal vote." Brief for Appellants 14. To comply with their proposed rule, appellants suggest, jurisdictions should design districts based on citizen-voting-age-population (CVAP) data from the Census Bureau's American Community Survey (ACS), an annual statistical sample of the U. S. population. Texas responds that jurisdictions may, consistent with the Equal Protection Clause, design districts using any population baseline—including total population and voter-eligible population—so long as the choice is rational and not invidiously discriminatory. Although its use of total-population data from the census was permissible, Texas therefore argues, it could have used ACS CVAP data instead. Sharing Texas' position that the Equal Protection Clause does not mandate use of voter-eligible population, the United States urges us not to address Texas' separate assertion that the Constitution allows States to use alternative population baselines, including voter-eligible population. Equalizing total population, the United States maintains, vindicates the principle of representational equality by "ensur[ing] that the voters in each district have the power to elect a representative who represents the same number of constituents as all other representatives." Brief for United States as Amicus Curiae 5.

In agreement with Texas and the United States, we reject appellants' attempt to locate a voter-equality mandate in the Equal Protection Clause. As history, precedent, and practice demonstrate, it is plainly permissible for jurisdictions to measure equalization by the total population of state and local legislative districts.

A

We begin with constitutional history. At the time of the founding, the Framers confronted a question analogous to the one at issue here: On what basis should congressional districts be allocated to States? The Framers' solution, now known as the Great Compromise, was to provide each State the same number of seats in the Senate, and to allocate House seats based on States' total populations. "Representatives and direct Taxes," they wrote, "shall be apportioned among the several States which may be included within this Union, according to their respective Numbers." U. S. Const., Art. I, §2, cl. 3 (emphasis added). "It is a fundamental principle of the proposed constitution," James Madison explained in the Federalist Papers, "that as the aggregate number of representatives allotted to the several states, is to be . . . founded on the aggregate number of inhabitants; so, the right of choosing this allotted number in each state, is to be exercised by such part of the inhabitants, as the state itself may designate." The Federalist No. 54, p. 284 (G. Carey & J. McClellan eds. 2001). In other words, the basis of representation in the House was to include all inhabitants—although slaves were counted as only three-fifths of a person—even though States remained free to deny many of those inhabitants the right to participate in the selection of their representatives.

[Following a discussion of the debates leading to the drafting of the post Civil War Fourteenth Amendment, Justice Ginsburg continued:]

The product of these debates was §2 of the Fourteenth Amendment, which retained total population as the congressional apportionment base. See U. S. Const., Amdt. 14, §2 ("Representatives shall be apportioned among the several States according to their respective numbers, counting the whole number of persons in each State, excluding Indians not taxed."). Introducing the final version of the Amendment on the Senate floor, Senator Jacob Howard explained:

> "[The] basis of representation is numbers . . . ; that is, the whole population except untaxed Indians and persons excluded by the State laws for rebellion or other crime. . . . The committee adopted numbers as the most just and satisfactory basis, and this is the principle upon which the Constitution itself was originally framed, that the basis of representation should depend upon numbers; and such, I think, after all, is the safest and most secure principle upon which the Government can rest. Numbers, not voters; numbers, not property; this is the theory of the Constitution." Cong. Globe, 39th Cong., 1st Sess., 2766–2767 (1866).

Appellants ask us to find in the Fourteenth Amendment's Equal Protection Clause a rule inconsistent with this "theory of the Constitution." But, as the Court recognized in Wesberry, this theory underlies not just the method of allocating House seats to States; it applies as well to the method of apportioning legislative seats within States. "The debates at the [Constitutional] Convention," the Court explained, "make at least one fact abundantly clear: that when the delegates agreed that the House should represent 'people,' they intended that in allocating Congressmen the number assigned to each state should be determined solely by the number of inhabitants." 376 U. S., at 13. "While it may not be possible to draw congressional districts with mathematical precision," the Court acknowledged, "that is no excuse for ignoring our Constitution's plain objective of making equal representation for equal numbers of people the fundamental goal for the House of Representatives." Id., at 18 (emphasis added). It cannot be that the Fourteenth Amendment calls for the apportionment of congressional districts based on total population, but simultaneously prohibits States from apportioning their own legislative districts on the same basis.

Cordoning off the constitutional history of congressional districting, appellants stress two points. First, they draw a distinction between allocating seats to States, and apportioning seats within States. The Framers selected total population for the former, appellants and their amici argue, because of federalism concerns inapposite to intrastate districting. These concerns included the perceived risk that a voter-population base might encourage States to expand the franchise unwisely, and the hope that a total-population base might counter States' incentive to undercount their populations, thereby reducing their share of direct taxes. Wesberry, however, rejected the distinction appellants now press. See supra, at 12. Even without the weight of Wesberry, we would find appellants' distinction unconvincing. One can accept that federalism—or, as JUSTICE ALITO emphasizes, partisan and regional political advantage, see post, at 6–13—figured in the Framers' selection of total population as the basis for allocating congressional seats. Even so, it remains beyond doubt that the principle of representational equality figured prominently in the decision to count people, whether or not they qualify as voters.

Second, appellants and JUSTICE ALITO urge, see post, at 5–6, the Court has typically refused to analogize to features of the federal electoral system—here, the constitutional scheme governing congressional apportionment— when considering challenges to state and local election laws. True, in Reynolds, the Court rejected Alabama's argument that it had permissibly modeled its State Senate apportionment scheme—one Senator for each county—on the United States Senate. "[T]he federal analogy," the Court explained, "[is] inapposite and irrelevant to state legislative districting schemes" because "[t]he system of representation in the two Houses of the Federal Congress" arose "from unique historical circumstances." 377 U. S., at 573–574. Likewise, in Gray v. Sanders, 372 U. S. 368, 371–372, 378 (1963), Georgia unsuccessfully attempted to defend, by analogy to the electoral college, its scheme of assigning a certain number of "units" to the winner of each county in statewide elections.

Reynolds and Gray, however, involved features of the federal electoral system that contravene the principles of both voter and representational equality to favor interests that have no relevance outside the federal context. Senate seats were allocated to States on an equal basis to respect state sovereignty and increase the odds that the smaller States would ratify the Constitution. See Wesberry, 376 U. S., at 9–13 (describing the history of the Great Compromise). See also Reynolds, 377 U. S., at 575 ("Political subdivisions of States—counties, cities, or whatever— never were and never have been considered as sovereign entities. . . . The relationship of the States to the Federal Government could hardly be less analogous.").

[B]

Consistent with constitutional history, this Court's past decisions reinforce the conclusion that States and localities may comply with the one-person, one-vote principle by designing districts with equal total populations. Quoting language from those decisions that, in appellants' view, supports the principle of equal voting power—and emphasizing the phrase "one-person, one-vote"—appellants contend that the Court had in mind, and constantly meant, that States should equalize the voter-eligible population of districts. See Reynolds, 377 U. S., at 568 ("[A]n individual's right to vote for State legislators is unconstitutionally impaired when its weight is in a substantial fashion diluted when compared with votes of citizens living on other parts of the State."); Gray, 372 U. S., at 379–380 ("The concept of 'we the people' under the Constitution visualizes no preferred class of voters but equality among those who meet the basic qualifications.").

[F]or every sentence appellants quote from the Court's opinions, one could respond with a line casting the oneperson, one-vote guarantee in terms of equality of representation, not voter equality. In Reynolds, for instance, the Court described "the fundamental principle of representative government in this country" as "one of equal representation for equal numbers of people." 377 U. S., at 560–561. See also Davis v. Bandemer, 478 U. S. 109, 123 (1986) ("[I]n formulating the one person, one vote formula, the Court characterized the question posed by election districts of disparate size as an issue of fair representation."); Reynolds, 377 U. S., at 563 (rejecting state districting schemes that "give the same number of representatives to unequal numbers of constituents"). And the Court has suggested, repeatedly, that districting based on total population serves both the State's interest in preventing vote dilution and its interest in ensuring equality of representation. See Board of Estimate of City of New York v. Morris, 489 U. S. 688, 693–694 (1989).

[M]oreover, from Reynolds on, the Court has consistently looked to total-population figures when evaluating whether districting maps violate the Equal Protection Clause by deviating impermissibly from perfect population equality. See Brief for Appellees 29–31 (collecting cases brought under the Equal Protection Clause). See also id., at 31, n. 9 (collecting congressional-districting cases). Appellants point to no instance in which the

Court has determined the permissibility of deviation based on eligible- or registered-voter data. It would hardly make sense for the Court to have mandated voter equality sub silentio and then used a total-population baseline to evaluate compliance with that rule. More likely, we think, the Court has always assumed the permissibility of drawing districts to equalize total population.

[C]

What constitutional history and our prior decisions strongly suggest, settled practice confirms. Adopting voter-eligible apportionment as constitutional command would upset a well-functioning approach to districting that all 50 States and countless local jurisdictions have followed for decades, even centuries. Appellants have shown no reason for the Court to disturb this longstanding use of total population. See Walz v. Tax Comm'n of City of New York, 397 U. S. 664, 678 (1970) ("unbroken practice" followed "openly and by affirmative state action, not covertly or by state inaction, is not something to be lightly cast aside"). See also Burson v. Freeman, 504 U. S. 191, 203–206 (1992) (plurality opinion) (upholding a law limiting campaigning in areas around polling places in part because all 50 States maintain such laws, so there is a "widespread and time-tested consensus" that legislation of this order serves important state interests). As the Framers of the Constitution and the Fourteenth Amendment comprehended, representatives serve all residents, not just those eligible or registered to vote. See supra, at 8–12. Nonvoters have an important stake in many policy debates—children, their parents, even their grandparents, for example, have a stake in a strong public-education Cite as: 578 U. S. ____ (2016) 19 Opinion of the Court system—and in receiving constituent services, such as help navigating public-benefits bureaucracies. By ensuring that each representative is subject to requests and suggestions from the same number of constituents, totalpopulation apportionment promotes equitable and effective representation. See McCormick v. United States, 500 U. S. 257, 272 (1991) ("Serving constituents and supporting legislation that will benefit the district and individuals and groups therein is the everyday business of a legislator.").

In sum, the rule appellants urge has no mooring in the Equal Protection Clause. The Texas Senate map, we therefore conclude, complies with the requirements of the one-person, one-vote principle.15 Because history, precedent, and practice suffice to reveal the infirmity of appellants' claims, we need not and do not resolve whether, as Texas now argues, States may draw districts to equalize voter-eligible population rather than total population.

* * *

For the reasons stated, the judgment of the United States District Court for the Western District of Texas is *Affirmed.*

[The concurring opinion by Justice Thomas, and the dissenting opinion by Justice Alito have been omitted. *Eds.*]

ABBOTT v. PEREZ
585 U. S. ____ (2018)

JUSTICE ALITO delivered the opinion of the Court.

Before us for review are orders of a three-judge court in the Western District of Texas effectively directing the State not to conduct this year's elections using districting plans that the court itself adopted some years earlier. The court developed those plans for use in the 2012 elections pursuant to our directions in Perry v. Perez, 565 U. S. 388 (2012) (per curiam). We instructed the three-judge court to start with the plans adopted by the Texas Legislature in 2011 but to make adjustments as required by the Constitution and the Voting Rights Act. Id., at 392–396. After those plans were used in 2012, the Texas Legislature enacted them (with only minor modifications) in 2013, and the plans were used again in both 2014 and 2016.

Last year, however, the three-judge court reversed its prior analysis and held that some of the districts in those plans are unlawful. After reviewing the repealed 2011 plans, which had never been used, the court found that they were tainted by discriminatory intent and that the 2013 Legislature had not "cured" that "taint." We now hold that the three-judge court committed a fundamental legal error. It was the challengers' burden to show that the 2013 Legislature acted with discriminatory intent when it enacted plans that the court itself had produced. The 2013 Legislature was not obligated to show that it had "cured" the unlawful intent that the court attributed to the 2011 Legislature. Thus, the essential pillar of the three-judge court's reasoning was critically flawed. When the congressional and state legislative districts are reviewed under the proper legal standards, all but one of them, we conclude, are lawful.

[III]

[The] primary question is whether the Texas court erred when it required the State to show that the 2013 Legislature somehow purged the "taint" that the court attributed to the defunct and never-used plans enacted by a prior legislature in 2011.

[A]

Whenever a challenger claims that a state law was enacted with discriminatory intent, the burden of proof lies with the challenger, not the State. Reno v. Bossier Parish School Bd., 520 U. S. 471, 481 (1997). This rule takes on special significance in districting cases. Redistricting "is primarily the duty and responsibility of the State," and "[f]ederal-court review of districting legislation represents a serious intrusion on the most vital of local functions." Miller v. Johnson, 515 U. S. 900, 915 (1995) (internal quotation marks omitted). "[I]n assessing the sufficiency of a challenge to a districting plan," a court "must be sensitive to the complex interplay of forces that enter a legislature's redistricting calculus." Id., at 915– 916. And the "good faith of [the] state legislature must be presumed." Id., at 915. The allocation of the burden of proof and the presumption of legislative good faith are not changed by a finding of past discrimination. "[P]ast discrimination cannot, in the manner of original sin, condemn governmental action that is not itself unlawful." Mobile, 446 U. S., at 74 (plurality opinion). The "ultimate question remains whether a discriminatory intent has been proved in a given case." Ibid. The "historical background" of a legislative enactment is "one evidentiary source" relevant to the question of intent. Arlington Heights v. Metropolitan Housing Development Corp., 429 U. S. 252, 267 (1977). But we have never suggested that past discrimination flips the evidentiary burden on its head.

Neither the District Court nor appellees have pointed to any authority that would justify shifting the burden. The appellees rely primarily on Hunter v. Underwood, 471 U. S. 222 (1985), but that case addressed a very different situation. Hunter involved an equal protection challenge to an article of the Alabama Constitution adopted in 1901 at a constitutional convention avowedly dedicated to the establishment of white supremacy. Id., at 228–230. The article disenfranchised anyone convicted of any crime on a long list that included many minor offenses. Id., at 226– 227. The court below found that the article had been adopted with discriminatory intent, and this Court accepted that conclusion. Id., at 229. The article was never repealed, but over the years, the list of disqualifying offenses had been pruned, and the State argued that what remained was facially constitutional. Id., at 232–233. This Court rejected that argument because the amendments did not alter the intent with which the article, including the parts that remained, had been adopted. Id., at 233. But the Court specifically declined to address the question whether the then-existing version would have been valid if "[re]enacted today." Ibid.

In these cases, we do not confront a situation like the one in Hunter. Nor is this a case in which a law originally enacted with discriminatory intent is later reenacted by a different legislature. The 2013 Texas Legislature did not Neither the District Court nor appellees have pointed to any authority that would justify shifting the burden. The appellees rely primarily on Hunter v. Underwood, 471 U. S. 222 (1985), but that case addressed a very different situation. Hunter involved an equal protection challenge to an article of the Alabama Constitution adopted in 1901 at a constitutional convention avowedly dedicated to the establishment of white supremacy. Id., at 228–230. The article disenfranchised anyone convicted of any crime on a long list that included many minor offenses. Id., at 226– 227. The court below found that the article had been adopted with discriminatory intent, and this Court accepted that conclusion. Id., at 229. The article was never repealed, but over the years, the list of disqualifying offenses had been pruned, and the State argued that what remained was facially constitutional. Id., at 232–233. This Court rejected that argument because the amendments did not alter the intent with which the article, including the parts that remained, had been adopted. Id., at 233. But the Court specifically declined to address the question whether the then-existing version would have been valid if "[re]enacted today." Ibid. In these cases, we do not confront a situation like the one in Hunter. Nor is this a case in which a law originally enacted with discriminatory intent is later reenacted by a different legislature. The 2013 Texas Legislature did not reenact the plan previously passed by its 2011 predecessor. Nor did it use criteria that arguably carried forward the effects of any discriminatory intent on the part of the 2011 Legislature. Instead, it enacted, with only very small changes, plans that had been developed by the Texas court pursuant to instructions from this Court "not to incorporate . . . any legal defects." Perry, 565 U. S., at 394.

Under these circumstances, there can be no doubt about what matters: It is the intent of the 2013 Legislature. And it was the plaintiffs' burden to overcome the presumption of legislative good faith and show that the 2013 Legislature acted with invidious intent.

The Texas court contravened these basic principles. Instead of holding the plaintiffs to their burden of overcoming the presumption of good faith and proving discriminatory intent, it reversed the burden of proof. It imposed on the State the obligation of proving that the 2013 Legislature had experienced a true "change of heart" and had "engage[d] in a deliberative process to ensure that the 2013 plans cured any taint from the 2011 plans." 274 F. Supp. 3d, at 649.

The Texas court's references to the need to "cure" the earlier Legislature's "taint" cannot be dismissed as stray comments. On the contrary, they were central to the court's analysis. The court referred repeatedly to the 2013 Legislature's duty to expiate its predecessor's bad intent, and when the court summarized its analysis, it drove the point home. It stated: "The discriminatory taint [from the 2011 plans] was not removed by the Legislature's enactment of the Court's interim plans, because the Legislature engaged in no deliberative process to remove any such taint, and in fact intended any such taint to be maintained but be safe from remedy." Id., at 686.

[B]

In holding that the District Court disregarded the presumption of legislative good faith and improperly reversed the burden of proof, we do not suggest either that the intent of the 2011 Legislature is irrelevant or that the plans enacted in 2013 are unassailable because they were previously adopted on an interim basis by the Texas court. Rather, both the intent of the 2011 Legislature and the court's adoption of the interim plans are relevant to the extent that they naturally give rise to—or tend to refute—inferences regarding the intent of the 2013 Legislature. They must be weighed together with any other direct and circumstantial evidence of that Legislature's intent. But when all the relevant evidence in the record is taken into account, it is plainly insufficient to prove that the 2013 Legislature acted in bad faith and engaged in intentional discrimination.19 See, e.g., Ricci v. DeStefano, 557 U. S. 557, 585 (2009); McCleskey v. Zant, 499 U. S. 467, 497 (1991). There is thus no need for any further prolongation of this already protracted litigation.

The only direct evidence brought to our attention suggests that the 2013 Legislature's intent was legitimate. It wanted to bring the litigation about the State's districting plans to an end as expeditiously as possible. The attorney general advised the Legislature that the best way to do this was to adopt the interim, court-issued plans. The sponsor of the 2013 plans voiced the same objective, and the Legislature then adopted the court-approved plans.

On its face, this explanation of the Legislature's intent is entirely reasonable and certainly legitimate. The Legislature had reason to know that any new plans it devised were likely to be attacked by one group of plaintiffs or another. (The plaintiffs' conflicting positions with regard to some of the districts in the plans now before us bear this out.) Litigating districting cases is expensive and time consuming, and until the districts to be used in the next election are firmly established, a degree of uncertainty clouds the electoral process. Wishing to minimize these effects is understandable and proper.

[Not] only does the direct evidence suggest that the 2013 Legislature lacked discriminatory intent, but the circumstantial evidence points overwhelmingly to the same conclusion. Consider the situation when the Legislature adopted the court-approved interim plans. First, the Texas court had adopted those plans, and no one would claim that the court acted with invidious intent when it did so. Second, the Texas court approved those plans only after reviewing them and modifying them as required to comply with our instructions. Not one of the judges on that court expressed the view that the plans were unlawful. Third, we had directed the Texas court to make changes in response to any claims under the Equal Protection Clause and §2 of the Voting Rights Act if those claims were merely likely to prevail. Perry, 565 U. S., at 394. And the Texas court was told to accommodate any claim under §5 of the VRA unless it was "insubstantial." Id., at 395. Fourth, the Texas court had made a careful analysis of all the claims, had provided a detailed examination of individual districts, and had modified many districts. Its work was anything but slapdash. All these facts gave the Legislature good reason to believe that the court-approved interim plans were legally sound.

Is there any evidence from which a contrary inference can reasonably be drawn? Appellees stress the preliminary nature of the Texas court's approval of the interim plans, and as we have said, that fact is relevant. But in light of our instructions to the Texas court and the care with which the interim plans were developed, the court's approval still gave the Legislature a sound basis for thinking that the interim plans satisfied all legal requirements.

The court below and the dissent infer bad faith because the Legislature "pushed the redistricting bills through quickly in a special session." 274 F. Supp. 3d, at 649. But we do not see how the brevity of the legislative process can give rise to an inference of bad faith—and certainly not an inference that is strong enough to overcome the presumption of legislative good faith (a concept to which the dissent pays only the briefest lip service, post, at 21). The "special session" was necessary because the regular session had ended. As explained, the Legislature had good reason to believe that the interim plans were sound, and the adoption of those already-completed plans did not require a prolonged process. After all, part of the reason for adopting those plans was to avoid the time and expense of starting from scratch and leaving the electoral process in limbo while that occurred.

[IV]

Once the Texas court's intent finding is reversed, there remain only four districts that were invalidated on alternative grounds. For three of these districts, the District Court relied on the "effects" test of §2. We reverse as to each of these, but we affirm the District Court's final holding that HD90 is a racial gerrymander.

[A]

To make out a §2 "effects" claim, a plaintiff must establish the three so-called "Gingles factors." These are (1) a geographically compact minority population sufficient to constitute a majority in a single-member district, (2) political cohesion among the members of the minority group, and (3) bloc voting by the majority to defeat the minority's preferred candidate. Gingles, 478 U. S., at 48–51; LULAC, 548 U. S., at 425. If a plaintiff makes that showing, it must then go on to prove that, under the totality of the circumstances, the district lines dilute the votes of the members of the minority group. Id., at 425–426.

1

The Texas court held that CD27 violates §2 of the VRA because it has the effect of diluting the votes of Latino voters in Nueces County. C. J. S. 191a. CD27 is anchored in Nueces County (home to Corpus Christi) and follows the Gulf of Mexico to the northeast before taking a turn inland to the northwest in the direction of Austin. Nueces County contains a Latino population of roughly 200,000 (a little less than one-third the size of an ideal Texas congressional district), and the court held that the Nueces County Latinos should have been included in a Latino opportunity district, rather than CD27, which is not such a district. The court found that an area centered on Nueces County satisfies the Gingles factors and that, under the totality of the circumstances, the placement of the Nueces County Latinos in CD27 deprives them of the equal opportunity to elect candidates of their choice. C. J. S. 181a–195a.

The problem with this holding is that plaintiffs could not establish a violation of §2 of the VRA without showing that there is a "'possibility of creating more than the existing number of reasonably compact'" opportunity districts. LULAC, supra, at 430. And as the Texas court itself found, the geography and demographics of south and west Texas do not permit the creation of any more than the seven Latino opportunity districts that exist under the current plan. 274 F. Supp. 3d, at 684, and n. 85.

Attempting to get around this problem, the Texas court relied on our decision in LULAC, but it misapplied our holding. In LULAC, we held that the State should have created six proper Latino opportunity districts but instead drew only five. 548 U. S., at 435. Although the State claimed that the plan actually included a sixth opportunity district, that district failed to satisfy the Gingles factors. 548 U. S., at 430. We held that a

"State's creation of an opportunity district for those without a §2 right offers no excuse for its failure to provide an opportunity district for those with a §2 right." Ibid.

Here, the Texas court concluded that Texas committed the same violation as in LU-LAC: It created "an opportunity district for those without a §2 right" (the Latinos in CD35), while failing to create such a district "for those with a §2 right" (the Latinos of Nueces County). Ibid. This holding is based on a flawed analysis of CD35.

CD35 lies to the north of CD27 and runs along I–35 from San Antonio up to Austin, the center of Travis County. In the District Court's view, the Latinos of CD35 do not have a §2 right because one of the Gingles factors, majority bloc voting, is not present. The Court reached this conclusion because the non-Latino voters of Travis County tend to favor the same candidates as the great majority of Latinos. There are two serious problems with the District Court's analysis. First, the Court took the wrong approach in evaluating the presence of majority bloc voting in CD35. The Court looked at only one, small part of the district, the portion that falls within Travis County. 274 F. Supp. 3d, at 683; C. J. S. 175a–176a. But Travis County makes up only 21% of the district. We have made clear that redistricting analysis must take place at the district level. Bethune-Hill, 580 U. S., at ___ (slip op., at 12). In failing to perform that district-level analysis, the District Court went astray. Second, here, unlike in LULAC, the 2013 Legislature had "good reasons" to believe that the district at issue (here CD35) was a viable Latino opportunity district that satisfied the Gingles factors. CD35 was based on a concept proposed by MAL-DEF, C. J. S. Findings 315a–316a, and the Latino Redistricting Task Force (a plaintiff group) argued that the district is mandated by §2. C. J. S. 174a. The only Gingles factor disputed by the court was majority bloc voting, and there is ample evidence that this factor is met. Indeed, the court found that majority bloc voting exists throughout the State. C. J. S. Findings 467a. In addition, the District Court extensively analyzed CD35 in 2012 and determined that it was likely not a racial gerrymander and that even if it was, it likely satisfied strict scrutiny. C. J. S. 415a. In other words, the 2013 Legislature justifiably thought that it had placed a viable opportunity district along the I–35 corridor.

[The Court then proceeded to review a congressional district in Tarrant County Texas in which the District Court for the Western District of Texas (the Texas Court) found to be a racial gerrymander, basically a district drawn for in pursuit of no compelling state interest and for no reason than to favor a particular racial group. The Court upheld the District Court's decision. Eds.]

Except with respect to one Texas House district, we hold that the court below erred in effectively enjoining the use of the districting maps adopted by the Legislature in 2013. We therefore reverse with respect to No. 17–586; reverse in part and affirm in part with respect to No. 17–626; and remand for proceedings consistent with this opinion. It is so ordered.

GILL v. WHITFORD
585 U. S. ____ (2018)

CHIEF JUSTICE ROBERTS delivered the opinion of the Court.

The State of Wisconsin, like most other States, entrusts to its legislature the periodic task of redrawing the boundaries of the State's legislative districts. A group of Wisconsin Democratic voters filed a complaint in the District Court, alleging that the legislature carried out this task with an eye to diminishing the ability of Wisconsin Democrats to convert Democratic votes into Democratic seats in the legislature. The plaintiffs asserted that, in so doing, the legislature had infringed their rights under the First and Fourteenth Amendments.

But a plaintiff seeking relief in federal court must first demonstrate that he has standing to do so, including that he has "a personal stake in the outcome," Baker v. Carr, 369 U. S. 186, 204 (1962), distinct from a "generally available grievance about government," Lance v. Coffman, 549 U. S. 437, 439 (2007) (per curiam). That threshold requirement "ensures that we act as judges, and do not engage in policymaking properly left to elected representatives." Hollingsworth v. Perry, 570 U. S. 693, 700 (2013) Certain of the plaintiffs before us alleged that they had such a personal stake in this case, but never followed up with the requisite proof. The District Court and this Court therefore lack the power to resolve their claims. We vacate the judgment and remand the case for further proceedings, in the course of which those plaintiffs may attempt to demonstrate standing in accord with the analysis in this opinion.

I

[In] July 2015, twelve Wisconsin voters filed a complaint in the Western District of Wisconsin challenging Act 43. The plaintiffs identified themselves as "supporters of the public policies espoused by the Democratic Party and of Democratic Party candidates." 1 App. 32, Complaint ¶15. They alleged that Act 43 is a partisan gerrymander that "unfairly favor[s] Republican voters and candidates," and that it does so by "cracking" and "packing" Democratic voters around Wisconsin.

[The plaintiffs] alleged that, regardless of "whether they themselves reside in a district that has been packed or cracked," they have been "harmed by the manipulation of district boundaries" because Democrats statewide "do not have the same opportunity provided to Republicans to elect representatives of their choice to the Assembly." Id., at 33, ¶16. The plaintiffs argued that, on a statewide level, the degree to which packing and cracking has favored one party over another can be measured by a single calculation: an "efficiency gap" that compares each party's respective "wasted" votes across all legislative districts. "Wasted" votes are those cast for a losing candidate or for a winning candidate in excess of what that candidate needs to win. Id., at 28–29, ¶5. The plaintiffs alleged that Act 43 resulted in an unusually large efficiency gap that favored Republicans. Id., at 30, ¶7. They also submitted a "Demonstration Plan" that, they asserted, met all of the legal criteria for apportionment, but was at the same time "almost perfectly balanced in its partisan consequences." Id., at 31, ¶10. They argued that because Act 43 generated a large and unnecessary efficiency gap in favor of Republicans, it violated the First Amendment right of association of Wisconsin Democratic voters and their Fourteenth Amendment right to equal protection. The plaintiffs named several members of the state election commission as defendants in the action. Id., at 36,

The election officials moved to dismiss the complaint. They argued, among other things, that the plaintiffs lacked standing to challenge the constitutionality of Act 43 as a whole because, as individual voters, their legally protected interests extend only to the makeup of the legislative districts in which they vote. A three-judge panel of the District Court, see 28 U. S. C. §2284(a), denied the defendants' motion. In the District Court's view, the plaintiffs "identif[ied] their injury as not simply their inability to elect a representative in their own districts, but also their reduced opportunity to be represented by Democratic legislators across the state." Whitford v. Nichol, 151 F. Supp. 3d 918, 924 (WD Wis. 2015). It therefore followed, in the District Court's opinion, that "[b]ecause plaintiffs' alleged injury in this case relates to their statewide representation, . . . they should be permitted to bring a statewide claim." Id., at 926.

[On the issue of whether the districting plans constituted a political gerrymander, the District Court ruled for the plaintiffs. Eds.]

Regarding standing, the court held that the plaintiffs had a "cognizable equal protection right against state imposed barriers on [their] ability to vote effectively for the party of [their] choice." Id., at 928. It concluded that Act 43 "prevent[ed] Wisconsin Democrats from being able to translate their votes into seats as effectively as Wisconsin Republicans," and that "Wisconsin Democrats, therefore, have suffered a personal injury to their Equal Protection rights." Ibid. The court turned away the defendants' argument that the plaintiffs' injury was not sufficiently particularized by finding that "[t]he harm that the plaintiffs have experienced . . . is one shared by Democratic voters in the State of Wisconsin. The dilution of their votes is both personal and acute." Id., at 930.

[After discussing the state of the Court's decisions regarding political gerrymandering, the Court went on to discuss standing in districting cases. Eds]

To ensure that the Federal Judiciary respects "the proper—and properly limited—role of the courts in a democratic society," Allen v. Wright, 468 U. S. 737, 750 (1984), a plaintiff may not invoke federal-court jurisdiction unless he can show "a personal stake in the outcome of the controversy." Baker, 369 U. S., at 204. A federal court is not "a forum for generalized grievances," and the requirement of such a personal stake "ensures that courts exercise power that is judicial in nature." Lance, 549 U. S., at 439, 441. We enforce that requirement by insisting that a plaintiff satisfy the familiar three-part test for Article III standing: that he "(1) suffered an injury in fact, (2) that is fairly traceable to the challenged conduct of the defendant, and (3) that is likely to be redressed by a favorable judicial decision." Spokeo, Inc. v. Robins, 578 U. S. ___, ___ (2016) (slip op., at 6). Foremost among these requirements is injury in fact—a plaintiff 's pleading and proof that he has suffered the "invasion of a legally protected interest" that is "concrete and particularized," i.e., which "affect[s] the plaintiff in a personal and individual way." Lujan v. Defenders of Wildlife, 504 U. S. 555, 560, and n. 1 (1992).

We have long recognized that a person's right to vote is "individual and personal in nature." Reynolds v. Sims, 377 U. S. 533, 561 (1964). Thus, "voters who allege facts showing disadvantage to themselves as individuals have standing to sue" to remedy that disadvantage. Baker, 369 U. S., at 206. The plaintiffs in this case alleged that they suffered such injury from partisan gerrymandering, which works through "packing" and "cracking" voters of one party to disadvantage those voters. 1 App. 28–29, 32–33, Complaint ¶¶5, 15. That is, the plaintiffs claim a constitutional right not to be placed in legislative districts deliberately designed to "waste" their votes in elections where their chosen candidates will win in landslides (packing) or are destined to lose by closer margins (cracking). Id., at 32–33, ¶15.

To the extent the plaintiffs' alleged harm is the dilution of their votes, that injury is district specific. An individual voter in Wisconsin is placed in a single district. He votes for a single representative. The boundaries of the district, and the composition of its voters, determine whether and to what extent a particular voter is packed or cracked. This "disadvantage to [the voter] as [an] individual[]," Baker, 369 U. S., at 206, therefore results from the boundaries of the particular district in which he resides. And a plaintiff 's remedy must be "limited to the inadequacy that produced [his] injury in fact." Lewis v. Casey, 518 U. S. 343, 357 (1996). In this case the remedy that is proper and sufficient lies in the revision of the boundaries of the individual's own district. For similar reasons, we have held that a plaintiff who alleges that he is the object of a racial gerrymander—a drawing of district lines on the basis of race—has standing to assert only that his own district has been so gerrymandered. See United States v. Hays, 515 U. S. 737, 744–745 (1995). A plaintiff who complains of gerrymandering, but who does not live in a gerrymandered district, "assert[s] only a generalized grievance against governmental conduct of which he or she does not approve." Id., at 745. Plaintiffs who complain of racial gerrymandering in their State cannot sue to invalidate the whole State's legislative districting map; such complaints must proceed "district by-district." Alabama Legislative Black Caucus v. Alabama, 575 U. S. ___, ___ (2015) (slip op., at 6).

The plaintiffs argue that their claim of statewide injury is analogous to the claims presented in Baker and Reynolds, which they assert were "statewide in nature" because they rested on allegations that "districts throughout a state [had] been malapportioned." Brief for Appellees 29. But, as we have already noted, the holdings in Baker and Reynolds were expressly premised on the understanding that the injuries giving rise to those claims were "individual and personal in nature," Reynolds, 377 U. S., at 561, because the claims were brought by voters who alleged "facts showing disadvantage to themselves as individuals," Baker, 369 U. S., at 206.

The plaintiffs' mistaken insistence that the claims in Baker and Reynolds were "statewide in nature" rests on a failure to distinguish injury from remedy. In those malapportionment cases, the only way to vindicate an individual plaintiff's right to an equally weighted vote was through a wholesale "restructuring of the geographical distribution of seats in a state legislature." Reynolds, 377 U. S., at 561; see, e.g., Moss v. Burkhart, 220 F. Supp. 149, 156–160 (WD Okla. 1963) (directing the county-by-county reapportionment of the Oklahoma Legislature), aff'd sub nom. Williams v. Moss, 378 U. S. 558 (1964) (per curiam).

Here, the plaintiffs' partisan gerrymandering claims turn on allegations that their votes have been diluted. That harm arises from the particular composition of the voter's own district, which causes his vote—having been packed or cracked—to carry less weight than it would carry in another, hypothetical district. Remedying the individual voter's harm, therefore, does not necessarily require restructuring all of the State's legislative districts. It requires revising only such districts as are necessary to reshape the voter's district—so that the voter may be unpacked or untracked, as the case may be. Cf. Alabama Legislative Black Caucus, 575 U. S., at ___ (slip op., at 7). This fits the rule that a "remedy must of course be limited to the inadequacy that produced the injury in fact that the plaintiff has established." Lewis, 518 U. S., at 357.

The plaintiffs argue that their legal injury is not limited to the injury that they have suffered as individual voters, but extends also to the statewide harm to their interest "in their collective representation in the legislature," and in influencing the legislature's overall "composition and policymaking." Brief for Appellees 31. But our cases to date have not found that this presents an individual and personal injury of the kind required for Article III standing. On the facts of this case, the plaintiffs may not rely on "the kind of undifferentiated, generalized grievance about the conduct of government that we have refused to countenance in the past." Lance, 549 U. S., at 442. A citizen's interest in the overall composition of the legislature is embodied in his right to vote for his representative. And the citizen's abstract interest in policies adopted by the legislature on the facts here is a nonjusticiable "general interest common to all members of the public." Ex parte Lévitt, 302 U. S. 633, 634 (1937) (per curiam).

[The] sum of the standing principles articulated here, as applied to this case, is that the harm asserted by the plaintiffs is best understood as arising from a burden on those plaintiffs' own votes. In this gerrymandering context that burden arises through a voter's placement in a "cracked" or "packed" district.

[The Court went on to discuss plaintiffs who alleged that they lived in cracked or packed districts, but did not prove that the districts fit that description. Eds.]

[III]

In cases where a plaintiff fails to demonstrate Article III standing, we usually direct the dismissal of the plaintiff's claims. See, e.g., DaimlerChrysler Corp. v. Cuno, 547 U. S. 332, 354 (2006). This is not the usual case. It concerns an unsettled kind of claim this Court has not agreed upon, the contours and justiciability of which are unresolved. Under the circumstances, and in light of the plaintiffs' allegations that Donohue, Johnson, Mitchell, and Wallace live in districts where Democrats like them have been packed or cracked, we decline to direct dismissal. We therefore remand the case to the District Court so that the plaintiffs may have an opportunity to prove concrete and particularized injuries using evidence—unlike the bulk of the evidence presented thus far—that would tend to demonstrate a burden on their individual votes. Cf. Alabama Legislative Black Caucus, 575 U. S., at ____ (slip op., at 8) (remanding for further consideration of the plaintiffs' gerrymandering claims on a district-by-district basis). We express no view on the merits of the plaintiffs' case. We caution, however, that "standing is not dispensed in gross": A plaintiff's remedy must be tailored to redress the plaintiff's particular injury. Cuno, 547 U. S., at 353.

The judgment of the District Court is vacated, and the case is remanded for further proceedings consistent with this opinion.

It is so ordered.

COMMON CAUSE v. RUCHO
587 U.S. ___(2019)

Chief Justice ROBERTS delivered the opinion of the Court.

Voters and other plaintiffs in North Carolina and Maryland challenged their States' congressional districting maps as unconstitutional partisan gerrymanders. The North Carolina plaintiffs complained that the State's districting plan discriminated against Democrats; the Maryland plaintiffs complained that their State's plan discriminated against Republicans. The plaintiffs alleged that the gerrymandering violated the First Amendment, the Equal Protection Clause of the Fourteenth Amendment, the Elections Clause, and Article I, §2, of the Constitution.

[T]hese cases require us to consider once again whether claims of excessive partisanship in districting are "justiciable" that is, properly suited for resolution by the federal courts. This Court has not previously struck down a districting plan as an unconstitutional partisan gerrymander, and has struggled without success over the past several decades to discern judicially manageable standards for deciding such claims.

I

A

The first case involves a challenge to the congressional redistricting plan enacted by the Republican-controlled North Carolina General Assembly in 2016. Rucho v. Common Cause, No. 18–422. The Republican legislators leading the redistricting effort instructed their mapmaker to use political data to draw a map that would produce a congressional delegation of ten Republicans and three Democrats. 318 F. Supp. 3d 777, 807–808 (MDNC 2018). As one of the two Republicans chairing the redistricting committee stated, "I think electing Republicans is better than electing Democrats. So I drew this map to help foster what I think is better for the country." Id., at 809. He further explained that the map was drawn with the aim of electing ten Republicans and three Democrats because he did "not believe it [would be] possible to draw a map with 11 Republicans and 2 Democrats." Id., at 808. One Democratic state senator objected that entrenching the 10–3 advantage for Republicans was not "fair, reasonable, [or] balanced" because, as recently as 2012, "Democratic congressional candidates had received more votes on a statewide basis than Republican candidates." Ibid. The General Assembly was not swayed by that objection and approved the 2016 Plan by a party-line vote. Id., at 809.

In November 2016, North Carolina conducted congressional elections using the 2016 Plan, and Republican candidates won 10 of the 13 congressional districts. Id., at 810. [Eds. Note, the plan was struck down by the district court hearing a challenge to the gerrymander and along with a similar case from Maryland, favoring Democrats, both cases are before the Court for decision.]

II

B

Partisan gerrymandering is nothing new. Nor is frustration with it. The practice was known in the Colonies prior to Independence, and the Framers were familiar with it at the time of the drafting and ratification of the Constitution. See Vieth, 541 U. S., at 274 (plurality opinion). During the very first congressional elections, George Washington and his Federalist allies accused Patrick Henry of trying to gerrymander Virginia's districts against their candidates—in particular James Madison, who ultimately prevailed over fellow future President James Monroe. Hunter, The First Gerrymander? 9 Early Am. Studies 792–794, 811 (2011). See 5 Writings of Thomas Jefferson 71 (P. Ford ed. 1895) (Letter to W. Short (Feb. 9, 1789)) ("Henry has so modeled the districts for representatives as to tack Orange [county] to counties where he himself has great influence that Madison may not be elected into the lower federal house").

In 1812, Governor of Massachusetts and future Vice President Elbridge Gerry notoriously approved congressional districts that the legislature had drawn to aid the Democratic-Republican Party. The moniker "gerrymander" was born when an outraged Federalist newspaper observed that one of the misshapen districts resembled a salamander. See Vieth, 541 U. S., at 274 (plurality opinion); E. Griffith, The Rise and Development of the Gerrymander 17–19 (1907). "By 1840, the gerrymander was a recognized force in party politics and was generally at- tempted in all legislation enacted for the formation of election districts. It was generally conceded that each party would attempt to gain power which was not proportionate to its numerical strength." Id., at 123.

The Framers addressed the election of Representatives to Congress in the Elections Clause. Art. I, §4, cl. 1. That provision assigns to state legislatures the power to prescribe the "Times, Places and Manner of holding Elections" for Members of Congress, while giving Congress the power to "make or alter" any such regulations. Whether to give that supervisory authority to the National Government was debated at the Constitutional Convention. When those opposed to such congressional oversight moved to strike the relevant language, Madison came to its defense: "[T]he State Legislatures will sometimes fail or refuse to consult the common interest at the expense of their local coveniency or prejudices. . . . Whenever the State Legislatures had a favorite measure to carry, they would take care so to mould their regulations as to favor the candidates they wished to succeed." 2 Records of the Federal Convention of 1787, at 240– 241.

During the subsequent fight for ratification, the provision remained a subject of debate. Antifederalists predicted that Congress's power under the Elections Clause would allow Congress to make itself "omnipotent," setting the "time" of elections as never or the "place" in difficult to reach corners of the State. Federalists responded that, among other justifications, the revisionary power was necessary to counter state legislatures set on undermining fair representation, including through malapportionment. M. Klarman, The Framers' Coup: The Making of the United States Constitution 340–342 (2016). The Federalists were, for example, concerned that newly developing population centers would be deprived of their proper electoral weight, as some cities had been in Great Britain. See 6 The Documentary History of the Ratification of the Constitution: Massachusetts 1278– 1279 (J. Kaminski & G. Saladino eds. 2000).

Congress has regularly exercised its Elections Clause power, including to address partisan gerrymandering. The Apportionment Act of 1842, which required single-member districts for the first time, specified that those districts be "composed of contiguous territory," Act of June 25, 1842, ch. 47, 5 Stat. 491, in "an attempt to forbid the practice of the gerrymander," Griffith, supra, at 12. Later statutes added requirements of compactness and equality of population. Act of Jan. 16, 1901, ch. 93, §3, 31 Stat. 733; Act of Feb. 2, 1872, ch. 11, §2, 17 Stat. 28. (Only the single member district requirement remains in place today. 2 U. S. C. §2c.) See Vieth, 541 U. S., at 276 (plurality opinion). Congress also used its Elections Clause power in 1870, enacting the first comprehensive federal statute dealing with elections as a way to enforce the Fifteenth Amendment. Force Act of 1870, ch. 114, 16 Stat. 140. Starting in the 1950s, Congress enacted a series of laws to protect the right to vote through measures such as the suspension of literacy tests and the prohibition of English- only elections. See, e.g., 52 U. S. C. §10101 et seq.

Appellants suggest that, through the Elections Clause, the Framers set aside electoral issues such as the one before us as questions that only Congress can resolve. See Baker, 369 U. S., at 217. We do not agree. In two areas—one-person, one-vote and racial gerrymandering—our cases have held that there is a role for the courts with respect to at least some issues that could arise from a State's drawing of congressional districts. See Wesberry v. Sanders, 376 U. S. 1 (1964); Shaw v. Reno, 509 U. S. 630 (1993) (Shaw I).

[C]

[In] the leading case of Baker v. Carr, voters in Tennessee complained that the State's districting plan for state representatives "debase[d]" their votes, because the plan was predicated on a 60-year-old census that no longer reflected the distribution of population in the State. The plaintiffs argued that votes of people in overpopulated districts held less value than those of people in less-populated districts, and that this inequality violated the Equal Protection Clause of the Fourteenth Amendment. The District Court dismissed the action on the ground that the claim was not justiciable, relying on this Court's prec- edents, including Colegrove. Baker v. Carr, 179 F. Supp. 824, 825, 826 (MD Tenn. 1959). This Court reversed. It identified various considerations relevant to determining whether a claim is a nonjusticiable political question, including whether there is "a lack of judicially discoverable and manageable standards for resolving it." 369 U. S., at 217. The Court concluded that the claim of population inequality among districts did not fall into that category, because such a claim could be decided under basic equal protection principles. Id., at 226. In Wesberry v. Sanders, the Court extended its ruling to malapportionment of congressional districts, holding that Article I, §2, required that "one man's vote in a congressional election is to be worth as much as another's." 376 U. S., at 8.

Another line of challenges to districting plans has focused on race. Laws that explicitly discriminate on the basis of race, as well as those that are race neutral on their face but are unexplainable on grounds other than race, are of course presumptively invalid. The Court applied those principles to electoral boundaries in Gomillion v. Lightfoot, concluding that a challenge to an "un- couth twenty-eight sided" municipal boundary line that excluded black voters from city elections stated a constitutional claim. 364 U. S. 339, 340 (1960). In Wright v. Rockefeller, 376 U. S. 52 (1964), the Court extended the reasoning of Gomillion to congressional districting. See Shaw I, 509 U. S., at 645.

Partisan gerrymandering claims have proved far more difficult to adjudicate. The basic reason is that, while it is illegal for a jurisdiction to depart from the one-person, one-vote rule, or to engage in racial discrimination in districting, "a jurisdiction may engage in constitutional political gerrymandering." Hunt v. Cromartie, 526 U. S. 541, 551 (1999) (citing Bush v. Vera, 517 U. S. 952, 968 (1996); Shaw v. Hunt, 517 U. S. 899, 905 (1996) (Shaw II); Miller v. Johnson, 515 U. S. 900, 916 (1995); Shaw I, 509 U. S., at 646). See also Gaffney v. Cummings, 412 U. S. 735, 753 (1973) (recognizing that "[p]olitics and political considerations are inseparable from districting and apportionment").

To hold that legislators cannot take partisan interests into account when drawing district lines would essentially countermand the Framers' decision to entrust districting to political entities. The "central problem" is not deter- mining whether a jurisdiction has engaged in partisan gerrymandering. It is "determining when political gerrymandering has gone too far." Vieth, 541 U. S., at 296 (plurality opinion). See League of United Latin American Citizens v. Perry, 548 U. S. 399, 420 (2006) (LULAC) (opinion of Kennedy, J.) (difficulty is "providing a standard for deciding how much partisan dominance is too much").

We first considered a partisan gerrymandering claim in Gaffney v. Cummings in 1973. There we rejected an equal protection challenge to Connecticut's redistricting plan, which "aimed at a rough scheme of proportional representation of the two major political parties" by "wiggl[ing] and joggl[ing] boundary lines" to create the appropriate num- ber of safe seats for each party. 412 U. S., at 738, 752, n. 18 (internal quotation marks omitted). In upholding the State's plan, we reasoned that districting "inevitably has and is intended to have substantial political consequences." Id., at 753.

Thirteen years later, in Davis v. Bandemer, we addressed a claim that Indiana Republicans had cracked and packed Democrats in violation of the Equal Protection Clause. 478 U. S. 109, 116–117 (1986) (plurality opinion). A majority of the Court agreed that the case was justiciable, but the Court splintered over the proper standard to apply. Four Justices would have required proof of "intentional discrimination against an identifiable political group and an actual discriminatory effect on that group." Id., at 127. Two Justices would have focused on "whether the boundaries of the voting districts have been distorted deliberately and arbitrarily to achieve illegitimate ends." Id., at 165 (Powell, J., concurring in part and dissenting in part). Three Justices, meanwhile, would have held that the Equal Protection Clause simply "does not supply judicially manageable standards for resolving purely political gerrymandering claims." Id., at 147 (O'Connor, J., concurring in judgment). At the end of the day, there was "no 'Court' for a standard that properly should be applied in determining whether a challenged redistricting plan is an unconstitutional partisan political gerrymander." Id., at 185, n. 25 (opinion of Powell, J.). In any event, the Court held that the plaintiffs had failed to show that the plan violated the Constitution.

Eighteen years later, in Vieth, the plaintiffs complained that Pennsylvania's legislature "ignored all traditional redistricting criteria, including the preservation of local government boundaries," in order to benefit Republican congressional candidates. 541 U. S., at 272–273 (plurality opinion) (brackets omitted). Justice Scalia wrote for a four-Justice plurality. He would have held that the plain- tiffs' claims were nonjusticiable because there was no "judicially discernible and manageable standard" for deciding them. Id., at 306. Justice Kennedy, concurring in the judgment, noted "the lack of comprehensive and neutral principles for drawing electoral boundaries [and] the absence of rules to limit and confine judicial intervention." Id., at 306–307. He nonetheless left open the possibility that "in another case a standard might emerge." Id., at 312. Four Justices dissented.

In LULAC, the plaintiffs challenged a mid-decade redistricting map approved by the Texas Legislature. Once again a majority of the Court could not find a justiciable standard for resolving the plaintiffs' partisan gerrymandering claims. See 548 U. S., at 414 (noting that the "disagreement over what substantive standard to apply" that was evident in Bandemer "persists").

As we summed up last Term in Gill, our "considerable efforts in Gaffney, Bandemer, Vieth, and LULAC leave unresolved whether . . . claims [of legal right] may be brought in cases involving allegations of partisan gerrymandering." 585 U. S., at ___ (slip op., at 13). Two "threshold questions" remained: standing, which we ad- dressed in Gill, and "whether [such] claims are justiciable." Ibid.

III
A

[T]he question is one of degree: How to "provid[e] a standard for deciding how much partisan dominance is too much." LULAC, 548 U. S., at 420 (opinion of Kennedy, J.). And it is vital in such circumstances that the Court act only in accord with especially clear standards: "With uncertain limits, intervening courts— even when proceeding with best intentions—would risk assuming political, not legal, responsibility for a process that often produces ill will and distrust." Vieth, 541 U. S., at 307 (opinion of Kennedy, J.). If federal courts are to "inject [themselves] into the most heated partisan issues" by adjudicating partisan gerrymandering claims, Bandemer, 478 U. S., at 145 (opinion of O'Connor, J.), they must be armed with a standard that can reliably differentiate unconstitutional from "constitutional political gerrymandering." Cromartie, 526 U. S., at 551.

B

Partisan gerrymandering claims rest on an instinct that groups with a certain level of political support should enjoy a commensurate level of political power and influence. Explicitly or implicitly, a districting map is alleged to be unconstitutional because it makes it too difficult for one party to translate statewide support into seats in the legislature. But such a claim is based on a "norm that does not exist" in our electoral system— "statewide elections for representatives along party lines." Bandemer, 478 U. S., at 159 (opinion of O'Connor, J.).

Partisan gerrymandering claims invariably sound in a desire for proportional representation. As Justice O'Connor put it, such claims are based on "a conviction that the greater the departure from proportionality, the more suspect an apportionment plan becomes." Ibid. "Our cases, however, clearly foreclose any claim that the Constitution requires proportional representation or that legislatures in reapportioning must draw district lines to come as near as possible to allocating seats to the contend- ing parties in proportion to what their anticipated statewide vote will be." Id., at 130 (plurality opinion). See Mobile v. Bolden, 446 U. S. 55, 75–76 (1980) (plurality opinion) ("The Equal Protection Clause of the Fourteenth Amendment does not require proportional representation as an imperative of political organization.").

The Founders certainly did not think proportional representation was required. For more than 50 years after ratification of the Constitution, many States elected their congressional representatives through at-large or "general ticket" elections. Such States typically sent single-party delegations to Congress. See E. Engstrom, Partisan Gerrymandering and the Construction of American Democracy 43–51 (2013). That meant that a party could garner nearly half of the vote statewide and wind up without any seats in the congressional delegation. The Whigs in Alabama suffered that fate in 1840: "their party garnered 43 per- cent of the statewide vote, yet did not receive a single seat." Id., at 48. When Congress required single-member districts in the Apportionment Act of 1842, it was not out of a general sense of fairness, but instead a (mis)calculation by the Whigs that such a change would improve their electoral prospects. Id., at 43–44.

Unable to claim that the Constitution requires proportional representation outright, plaintiffs inevitably ask the courts to make their own political judgment about how much representation particular political parties deserve— based on the votes of their supporters—and to rearrange the challenged districts to achieve that end. But federal courts are not equipped to apportion political power as a matter of fairness, nor is there any basis for concluding that they were authorized to do so. As Justice Scalia put it for the plurality in Vieth: "'Fairness' does not seem to us a judicially manage- able standard. . . . Some criterion more solid and more demonstrably met than that seems to us necessary to enable the state legislatures to discern the limits of their districting discretion, to meaningfully constrain the discretion of the courts, and to win public acceptance for the courts' intrusion into a process that is the very foundation of democratic decision-making." 541 U. S., at 291.

The initial difficulty in settling on a "clear, manageable and politically neutral" test for fairness is that it is not even clear what fairness looks like in this context. There is a large measure of "unfairness" in any winner-take-all system. Fairness may mean a greater number of competitive districts. Such a claim seeks to undo packing and cracking so that supporters of the disadvantaged party have a better shot at electing their preferred candidates. But making as many districts as possible more competitive could be a recipe for disaster for the disadvantaged party. As Justice White has pointed out, "[i]f all or most of the districts are competitive . . . even a narrow statewide preference for either party would produce an overwhelm- ing majority for the winning party in the state legislature." Bandemer, 478 U. S., at 130 (plurality opinion).

On the other hand, perhaps the ultimate objective of a "fairer" share of seats in the congressional delegation is most readily achieved by yielding to the gravitational pull of proportionality and engaging in cracking and packing, to ensure each party its "appropriate" share of "safe" seats. See id., at 130–131 ("To draw district lines to maximize the representation of each major party would require creating as many safe seats for each party as the demo- graphic and predicted political characteristics of the State would permit."); Gaffney, 412 U. S., at 735–738. Such an approach, however, comes at the expense of competitive districts and of individuals in districts allocated to the opposing party.

Or perhaps fairness should be measured by adherence to "traditional" districting criteria, such as maintaining political subdivisions, keeping communities of interest together, and protecting incumbents. See Brief for Bipartisan Group of Current and Former

Members of the House of Representatives as Amici Curiae; Brief for Professor Wesley Pegden et al. as Amici Curiae in No. 18–422. But protecting incumbents, for example, enshrines a particular partisan distribution. And the "natural political geography" of a State—such as the fact that urban electoral districts are often dominated by one political party—can itself lead to inherently packed districts. As Justice Kennedy has explained, traditional criteria such as compactness and contiguity "cannot promise political neutrality when used as the basis for relief. Instead, it seems, a decision under these standards would unavoidably have significant political effect, whether intended or not." Vieth, 541 U. S., at 308–309 (opinion concurring in judgment). See id., at 298 (plurality opinion) ("[P]acking and cracking, whether intentional or no, are quite consistent with adherence to compactness and respect for political subdivision lines").

[And]it is only after determining how to define fairness that you can even begin to answer the determinative question: "How much is too much?" At what point does permissible partisanship become unconstitutional? If compliance with traditional districting criteria is the fairness touchstone, for example, how much deviation from those criteria is constitutionally acceptable and how should map drawers prioritize competing criteria? Should a court "reverse gerrymander" other parts of a State to counteract "natural" gerrymandering caused, for example, by the urban concentration of one party? If a districting plan protected half of the incumbents but redistricted the rest into head to head races, would that be constitutional? A court would have to rank the relative importance of those traditional criteria and weigh how much deviation from each to allow.

If a court instead focused on the respective number of seats in the legislature, it would have to decide the ideal number of seats for each party and determine at what point deviation from that balance went too far. If a 5–3 allocation corresponds most closely to statewide vote totals, is a 6–2 allocation permissible, given that legislatures have the authority to engage in a certain degree of partisan gerrymandering? Which seats should be packed and which cracked? Or if the goal is as many competitive districts as possible, how close does the split need to be for the district to be considered competitive? Presumably not all districts could qualify, so how to choose? Even assuming the court knew which version of fairness to be looking for, there are no discernible and manageable standards for deciding whether there has been a violation. The questions are "unguided and ill suited to the development of judicial standards," Vieth, 541 U. S., at 296 (plurality opinion), and "results from one gerrymandering case to the next would likely be disparate and inconsistent," id., at 308 (opinion of Kennedy, J.).

Appellees contend that if we can adjudicate one-person, one-vote claims, we can also assess partisan gerrymander- ing claims. But the one-person, one-vote rule is relatively easy to administer as a matter of math. The same cannot be said of partisan gerrymandering claims, because the Constitution supplies no objective measure for assessing whether a districting map treats a political party fairly. It hardly follows from the principle that each person must have an equal say in the election of representatives that a person is entitled to have his political party achieve representation in some way commensurate to its share of statewide support.

More fundamentally, "vote dilution" in the one-person, one-vote cases refers to the idea that each vote must carry equal weight. In other words, each representative must be accountable to (approximately) the same number of constituents. That requirement does not extend to political parties. It does not mean that each party must be influential in proportion to its number of supporters. As we stated unanimously in Gill, "this Court is not responsible for vindicating generalized partisan preferences. The Court's constitutionally prescribed role is to vindicate the individual rights of the people appearing before it." 585 U. S., at ___ (slip op., at 21). See also Bandemer, 478 U. S., at 150 (opinion of O'Connor, J.) ("[T]he Court has not accepted the argument that an 'asserted entitlement to group representation' . . . can be traced to the one per- son, one vote principle." (quoting Bolden, 446 U. S., at 77)).*

*The dissent's observation that the Framers viewed political parties "with deep suspicion, as fomenters of factionalism and symptoms of disease in the body politic" post, at 9, n. 1 (opinion of KAGAN, J.) (internal quotation marks and alteration omitted), is exactly right. Its inference from that fact is exactly wrong. The Framers would have been amazed at a constitutional theory that guarantees a certain degree of representation to political parties.

Nor do our racial gerrymandering cases provide an appropriate standard for assessing partisan gerrymander- ing. "[N]othing in our case law compels the conclusion that racial and political gerrymanders are subject to precisely the same constitutional scrutiny. In fact, our country's long and persistent history of racial discrimination in voting—as well as our Fourteenth Amendment jurisprudence, which always has reserved the strictest scrutiny for discrimination on the basis of race—would seem to compel the opposite conclusion." Shaw I, 509 U. S., at 650 (citation omitted). Unlike partisan gerrymandering claims, a racial gerrymandering claim does not ask for a fair share of political power and influence with all the justiciability conundrums that entails. It asks instead for the elimination of a racial classification. A partisan gerrymandering claim cannot ask for the elimination of partisanship.

IV

[D]

The North Carolina District Court further concluded that the 2016 Plan violated the Elections Clause and Article I, §2. We are unconvinced by that novel approach.

Article I, §2, provides that "[t]he House of Representatives shall be composed of Members chosen every second Year by the People of the several States." The Elections Clause provides that "[t]he Times, Places and Manner of holding Elections for Senators and Representatives, shall be prescribed in each State by the Legislature thereof; but the Congress may at any time by Law make or alter such Regulations, except as to the Places of choosing Senators." Art. I, §4, cl. 1.

The District Court concluded that the 2016 Plan exceeded the North Carolina General Assembly's Elections Clause authority because, among other reasons, "the Elections Clause did not empower State legislatures to disfavor the interests of supporters of a particular candidate or party in drawing congressional districts." 318 F. Supp. 3d, at 937. The court further held that partisan gerrymandering infringes the right of "the People" to select their representatives. Id., at 938–940. Before the District Court's decision, no court had reached a similar conclusion. In fact, the plurality in Vieth concluded—without objection from any other Justice—that neither §2 nor §4 of Article I "provides a judicially enforceable limit on the political considerations that the States and Congress may take into account when districting." 541 U. S., at 305.

The District Court nevertheless asserted that partisan gerrymanders violate "the core principle of [our] republican government" preserved in Art. I, §2, "namely, that the voters should choose their representatives, not the other way around." 318 F. Supp. 3d, at 940 (quoting Arizona State Legislature, 576 U. S., at ___ (slip op., at 35); internal quotation marks omitted; alteration in original). That seems like an objection more properly grounded in the Guarantee Clause of Article IV, §4, which "guarantee[s] to every State in

[the] Union a Republican Form of Govern-sent." This Court has several times concluded, however, that the Guarantee Clause does not provide the basis for a justiciable claim. See, e.g., Pacific States Telephone & Telegraph Co. v. Oregon, 223 U. S. 118 (1912).

V

Excessive partisanship in districting leads to results that reasonably seem unjust. But the fact that such gerrymandering is "incompatible with democratic principles," Arizona State Legislature, 576 U. S., at ___ (slip op., at 1), does not mean that the solution lies with the federal judiciary. We conclude that partisan gerrymandering claims present political questions beyond the reach of the federal courts. Federal judges have no license to reallocate political power between the two major political parties, with no plausible grant of authority in the Constitution, and no legal standards to limit and direct their decisions. "[J]udicial action must be governed by standard, by rule," and must be "principled, rational, and based upon reasoned distinctions" found in the Constitution or laws. Vieth, 541 U. S., at 278, 279 (plurality opinion). Judicial review of partisan gerrymandering does not meet those basic requirements.

[No] one can accuse this Court of having a crabbed view of the reach of its competence. But we have no commission to allocate political power and influence in the absence of a constitutional directive or legal standards to guide us in the exercise of such authority. "It is emphatically the province and duty of the judicial department to say what the law is." Marbury v. Madison, 1 Cranch, at 177. In this rare circumstance, that means our duty is to say "this is not law."

The judgments of the United States District Court for the Middle District of North Carolina and the United States District Court for the District of Maryland are vacated, and the cases are remanded with instructions to dismiss for lack of jurisdiction.

It is so ordered.

JUSTICE KAGAN, with whom JUSTICE GINSBURG, JUSTICE BREYER, and JUSTICE SOTOMAYOR join, dissenting.

For the first time ever, this Court refuses to remedy a constitutional violation because it thinks the task beyond judicial capabilities.

And not just any constitutional violation. The partisan gerrymanders in these cases deprived citizens of the most fundamental of their constitutional rights: the rights to participate equally in the political process, to join with others to advance political beliefs, and to choose their political representatives. In so doing, the partisan gerrymanders here debased and dishonored our democracy, turning upside-down the core American idea that all governmental power derives from the people.

[In] other words, [political gerrymanders eds.] allow courts to undo partisan gerrymanders of the kind we face today from North Carolina and Maryland. In giving such gerrymanders a pass from judicial review, the majority goes tragically wrong.

I

A

B

Now back to the question I asked before: Is that how American democracy is supposed to work? I have yet to meet the person who thinks so.

"Governments," the Declaration of Independence states, "deriv[e] their just Powers from the Consent of the Governed." The Constitution begins: "We the People of the United States." The Gettysburg Address (almost) ends: "[G]overnment of the people, by the people, for the people." If there is a single idea that made our Nation (and that our

Nation commended to the world), it is this one: The people are sovereign. The "power," James Madison wrote, "is in the people over the Government, and not in the Government over the people." 4 Annals of Cong. 934 (1794).

Free and fair and periodic elections are the key to that vision. The people get to choose their representatives. And then they get to decide, at regular intervals, whether to keep them. Madison again: "[R]epublican liberty" demands "not only, that all power should be derived from the people; but that those entrusted with it should be kept in dependence on the people." 2 The Federalist No. 37, p. 4 (J. & A. McLean eds. 1788). Members of the House of Representatives, in particular, are supposed to "recollect[ ] [that] dependence" every day. Id., No. 57, at 155. To retain an "intimate sympathy with the people," they must be "compelled to anticipate the moment" when their "exercise of [power] is to be reviewed." Id., Nos. 52, 57, at 124, 155. Election day—next year, and two years later, and two years after that—is what links the people to their representatives, and gives the people their sovereign power. That day is the foundation of democratic governance.

And partisan gerrymandering can make it meaningless. At its most extreme—as in North Carolina and Mary- land—the practice amounts to "rigging elections." Vieth v. Jubelirer, 541 U. S. 267, 317 (2004) (Kennedy, J., concur- ring in judgment) (internal quotation marks omitted). By drawing districts to maximize the power of some voters and minimize the power of others, a party in office at the right time can entrench itself there for a decade or more, no matter what the voters would prefer. Just ask the people of North Carolina and Maryland. The "core principle of republican government," this Court has recognized, is "that the voters should choose their representatives, not the other way around." Arizona State Legislature v. Arizona Independent Redistricting Comm'n, 576 U. S. ___, ___ (2015) (slip op., at 35) (internal quotation marks omitted). Partisan gerry- mandering turns it the other way around. By that mechanism, politicians can cherry-pick voters to ensure their reelection. And the power becomes, as Madison put it, "in the Gov- ernment over the people." 4 Annals of Cong. 934.

The majority disputes none of this. I think it important to underscore that fact: The majority disputes none of what I have said (or will say) about how gerrymanders under- mine democracy. Indeed, the majority concedes (really, how could it not?) that gerry- mandering is "incompatible with democratic principles." Ante, at 30 (quoting Arizona State Legislature, 576 U. S., at ___ (slip op., at 1)). And therefore what? That recognition would seem to demand a response. The majority offers two ideas that might qualify as such. One is that the political process can deal with the problem—a proposition so dubi- ous on its face that I feel secure in delaying my answer for some time. See ante, at 31–33; infra, at 29–31. The other is that political gerrymanders have always been with us. See ante, at 8, 24. To its credit, the majority does not frame that point as an originalist consti- tutional argument.

After all (as the majority rightly notes), racial and residential gerrymanders were also once with us, but the Court has done something about that fact. See ante, at 10.1 The ma- jority's idea instead seems to be that if we have lived with partisan gerrymanders so long, we will survive.

[C]

[Though] different Justices have described the constitutional harm in diverse ways, nearly all have agreed on this much: Extreme partisan gerrymandering (as happened in North Carolina and Maryland) violates the Constitution. See, e.g., Vieth, 541 U. S., at 293 (plurality opinion) ("[A]n excessive injection of politics [in districting] is unlawful" (emphasis deleted)); id., at 316 (opinion of Kennedy, J.) ("[P]artisan gerrymandering that disfavors one party is [im]permissible"); id., at 362 (BREYER, J., dissenting) (Gerrymandering causing political "entrenchment" is a "violat[ion of] the Constitution's Equal Protection Clause"); Davis v. Bandemer, 478 U. S. 109, 132 (1986) (plurality opinion) ("[U]nconstitutional discrimination" occurs "when the electoral system is arranged in a manner that will consistently degrade [a voter's] influence on the political process"); id., at 165 (Powell, J., concurring) ("Unconstitutional gerrymandering" occurs when "the boundaries of the voting districts have been distorted deliberately" to deprive voters of "an equal opportunity to participate in the State's legislative processes"). Once again, the majority never disagrees; it appears to accept the "principle that each person must have an equal say in the election of representatives." Ante, at 20. And indeed, without this settled and shared understanding that cases like these inflict constitutional injury, the question of whether there are judicially manageable standards for resolving them would never come up.

II

So the only way to understand the majority's opinion is as follows: In the face of grievous harm to democratic governance and flagrant infringements on individuals' rights—in the face of escalating partisan manipulation whose compatibility with this Nation's values and law no one defends—the majority declines to provide any remedy. For the first time in this Nation's history, the majority declares that it can do nothing about an acknowledged constitutional violation because it has searched high and low and cannot find a workable legal standard to apply.

The majority gives two reasons for thinking that the adjudication of partisan gerrymandering claims is beyond judicial capabilities. First and foremost, the majority says, it cannot find a neutral baseline—one not based on contestable notions of political fairness—from which to measure injury. See ante, at 15–19. According to the majority, "[p]artisan gerrymandering claims invariably sound in a desire for proportional representation." Ante, at 16. But the Constitution does not mandate proportional representation. So, the majority contends, resolving those claims "inevitably" would require courts to decide what is "fair" in the context of districting. Ante, at 17. They would have "to make their own political judgment about how much representation particular political parties deserve" and "to rearrange the challenged districts to achieve that end." Ibid. (emphasis in original). And second, the majority argues that even after establishing a baseline, a court would have no way to answer "the determinative question: 'How much is too much?'" Ante, at 19. No "discernible and manageable" standard is available, the majority claims—and so courts could willy-nilly be- come embroiled in fixing every districting plan. Ante, at 20; see ante, at 15–16.

I'll give the majority this one—and important—thing: It identifies some dangers everyone should want to avoid. Judges should not be apportioning political power based on their own vision of electoral fairness, whether proportional representation or any other. And judges should not be striking down maps left, right, and center, on the view that every smidgen of politics is a smidgen too much. Respect for state legislative processes—and restraint in the exercise of judicial authority—counsels intervention in only egregious cases.

But in throwing up its hands, the majority misses some- thing under its nose: What it says can't be done has been done. Over the past several years, federal courts across the country—including, but not exclusively, in the decisions below—have largely converged on a standard for adjudicating partisan gerrymandering claims (striking down both Democratic and Republican districting plans in the process). See also Ohio A. Philip Randolph Inst., 373 F. Supp. 3d 978; League of Women Voters of Michigan v. Benson, 373 F. Supp. 3d 867 (ED Mich. 2019). And that standard does what the majority says is impossible. The standard does not use any judge-made conception of electoral fairness—either proportional representation or any other; instead, it takes as its baseline a State's own criteria of fairness, apart from partisan gain. And by requiring plaintiffs to make difficult showings relating to both purpose and effects, the standard invalidates the most extreme, but only the most extreme, partisan gerrymanders.

[A]

Start with the standard the lower courts used. The majority disaggregates the opinions below, distinguishing the one from the other and then chopping up each into "a number of 'tests.'" Ante, at 22; see ante, at 22–30. But in doing so, it fails to convey the decisions' most significant— and common—features. Both courts focused on the harm of vote dilution, see supra, at 11, though the North Carolina court mostly grounded its analysis in the Fourteenth Amendment and the Maryland court in the First. And both courts (like others around the country) used basically the same three-part test to decide whether the plaintiffs had made out a vote dilution claim. As many legal standards do, that test has three parts: (1) intent; (2) effects; and (3) causation. First, the plaintiffs challenging a districting plan must prove that state officials' "predominant purpose" in drawing a district's lines was to "entrench [their party] in power" by diluting the votes of citizens favoring its rival. Rucho, 318 F. Supp. 3d, at 864 (quoting Arizona State Legislature, 576 U. S., at ___ (slip op., at 1)). Second, the plaintiffs must establish that the lines drawn in fact have the intended effect by "substantially" diluting their votes. Lamone, 348 F. Supp. 3d, at 498. And third, if the plaintiffs make those showings, the State must come up with a legitimate, non-partisan justification to save its map. See Rucho, 318 F. Supp. 3d, at 867.2 If you are a lawyer, you know that this test looks utterly ordinary. It is the sort of thing courts work with every day.

[The] majority's response to the District Courts' purpose analysis is discomfiting. The majority does not contest the lower courts' findings; how could it? Instead, the majority says that state officials' intent to entrench their party in power is perfectly "permissible," even when it is the pre- dominant factor in drawing district lines. Ante, at 23. But that is wrong. True enough, that the intent to inject "political considerations" into districting may not raise any constitutional concerns. In Gaffney v. Cummings, 412 U.S. 735 (1973), for example, we thought it non- problematic when state officials used political data to ensure rough proportional representation between the two parties. And true enough that even the naked purpose to gain partisan advantage may not rise to the level of constitutional notice when it is not the driving force in mapmaking or when the intended gain is slight. See Vieth, 541 U. S., at 286 (plurality opinion). But when political actors have a specific and predominant intent to entrench them- selves in power by manipulating district lines, that goes too far. Consider again Justice Kennedy's hypothetical of mapmakers who set out to maximally burden (i.e., make count for as little as possible) the votes going to a rival party. See supra, at 12. Does the majority really think that goal is permissible? But why even bother with hypotheticals? Just consider the purposes here. It cannot be permissible and thus irrelevant, as the majority claims, that state officials have as their purpose the kind of grotesquely gerrymandered map that, according to all this Court has ever said, violates the Constitution. See supra, at 13.

[Because] the Maryland gerrymander involved just one district, the evidence in that case was far simpler—but no less powerful for that. You've heard some of the numbers before. See supra, at 6. The 2010 census required only a minimal change in the Sixth District's population—the subtraction of about 10,000 residents from more than 700,000. But instead of making a correspondingly minimal adjustment, Democratic officials reconfigured the entire district. They moved 360,000 residents out and another 350,000 in, while splitting some counties for the first time in almost two centuries. The upshot was a district with 66,000 fewer Republican voters and 24,000 more Democratic ones.

4 The District Court also relied on actual election results (under both the new plan and the similar one preceding it) and on mathematical measurements of the new plan's "partisan asymmetry." See Rucho, 318 F. Supp. 3d, at 884–895. Those calculations assess whether supporters of the two parties can translate their votes into representation with equal ease. See Stephanopoulos & McGhee, The Measure of a Metric, 70 Stan. L. Rev. 1503, 1505–1507 (2018). The court found that the new North Carolina plan led to extreme asymmetry, compared both to plans used in the rest of the country and to plans previously used in the State. See Rucho, 318 F. Supp. 3d, at 886–887, 892–893.

In the old Sixth, 47% of registered voters were Republicans and only 36% Democrats. But in the new Sixth, 44% of registered voters were Democrats and only 33% Republicans. That reversal of the district's partisan composition translated into four consecutive Democratic victories, including in a wave election year for Republicans (2014). In what was once a party stronghold, Republicans now have little or no chance to elect their preferred candidate. The District Court thus found that the gerrymandered Maryland map substantially dilutes Republicans' votes. See Lamone, 348 F. Supp. 3d, at 519– 520.

[B]

[Contrary] to the majority's suggestion, the District Courts did not have to—and in fact did not—choose among competing visions of electoral fairness. That is because they did not try to compare the State's actual map to an "ideally fair" one (whether based on proportional representation or some other criterion). Instead, they looked at the difference between what the State did and what the State would have done if politicians hadn't been intent on partisan gain. Or put differently, the comparator (or baseline or touchstone) is the result not of a judge's philosophizing but of the State's own characteristics and judgments. The effects evidence in these cases accepted as a given the State's physical geography (e.g., where does the Chesapeake run?) and political geography (e.g., where do the Democrats live on top of each other?). So the courts did not, in the majority's words, try to "counteract 'natural' gerrymandering caused, for example, by the urban concentration of one party." Ante, at 19. Still more, the courts' analyses used the State's own criteria for electoral fairness—except for naked partisan gain. Under their approach, in other words, the State selected its own fairness baseline in the form of its other districting criteria. All the courts did was determine how far the State had gone off that track because of its politicians' effort to entrench themselves in office.

[The] majority's sole response misses the point. According to the majority, "it does not make sense to use" a State's own (non-partisan) districting criteria as the base- line from which to measure partisan gerrymandering because those criteria "will vary from State to State and year to year." Ante, at 27. But that is a virtue, not a vice—a feature, not a bug. Using the criteria the State itself has chosen at the relevant time prevents any judicial predilections from affecting the analysis—exactly what the majority claims it wants. At the same time, using those criteria enables a court to measure just what it should: the extent to which the pursuit of partisan advantage—by these legislators at this moment— has distorted the State's districting decisions. Sure, different non-partisan criteria could result, as the majority notes, in different partisan distributions to serve as the baseline.

Ante, at 28. But that in itself raises no issue: Everyone agrees that state officials using non-partisan criteria (e.g., must counties be kept together? should districts be compact?) have wide latitude in districting. The problem arises only when legislators or mapmakers substantially deviate from the baseline distribution by manipulating district lines for partisan gain. So once again, the majority's analysis falters because it equates the demand to eliminate partisan gerrymandering with a demand for a single partisan distribution—the one reflecting proportional representation. See ante, at 16–17. But those two demands are different, and only the former is at issue here.

[The] majority, in the end, fails to understand both the plaintiffs' claims and the decisions below. Everything in today's opinion assumes that these cases grew out of a "desire for proportional representation" or, more generally phrased, a "fair share of political power." Ante, at 16, 21. And everything in it assumes that the courts below had to (and did) decide what that fair share would be. But that is

not so. The plaintiffs objected to one specific practice—the extreme manipulation of district lines for partisan gain. Elimination of that practice could have led to proportional representation. Or it could have led to nothing close. What was left after the practice's removal could have been fair, or could have been unfair, by any number of measures. That was not the crux of this suit. The plaintiffs asked only that the courts bar politicians from entrenching themselves in power by diluting the votes of their rivals' supporters. And the courts, using neutral and manageable—and eminently legal—standards, provided that (and only that) relief. This Court should have cheered, not overturned, that restoration of the people's power to vote.

III

[Of] all times to abandon the Court's duty to declare the law, this was not the one. The practices challenged in these cases imperil our system of government. Part of the Court's role in that system is to defend its foundations. None is more important than free and fair elections. With respect but deep sadness, I dissent.

Notes and questions

The Court distinguishes Baker v. Carr and Reynolds v. Sims as "malapportionment cases," as opposed to the gerrymandering claims of the plaintiffs here. How is this relevant to the standing issue in this excerpt?

B. Access to Courts

M.L.B. v. S.L.J.
519 U.S. 102 (1996)

Justice GINSBURG delivered the opinion of the Court.

By order of a Mississippi Chancery Court, petitioner M. L. B.'s parental rights to her two minor children were forever terminated. M. L. B. sought to appeal from the termination decree, but Mississippi required that she pay in advance record preparation fees estimated at $2,352.36. Because M. L. B. lacked funds to pay the fees, her appeal was dismissed.

M. L. B. tenders this question, which we agreed to hear and decide: May a State, consistent with the Due Process and Equal Protection Clauses of the Fourteenth Amendment, condition appeals from trial court decrees terminating parental rights on the affected parent's ability to pay record preparation fees? We hold that, just as a State may not block an indigent petty offender's access to an appeal afforded others, so Mississippi may not deny M. L. B., because of her poverty, appellate review of the sufficiency of the evidence on which the trial court found her unfit to remain a parent.

[Courts] have confronted, in diverse settings, the "age-old problem" of "[p]roviding equal justice for poor and rich, weak and powerful alike." Griffin v. Illinois, 351 U.S. 12, 16, 76 S.Ct. 585, 589, 100 L.Ed. 891 (1956). Concerning access to appeal in general, and transcripts needed to pursue appeals in particular, Griffin is the foundation case.

Griffin involved an Illinois rule that effectively conditioned thoroughgoing appeals from criminal convictions on the defendant's procurement of a transcript of trial proceedings. Indigent defendants, other than those sentenced to death, were not excepted from the rule, so in most cases, defendants without means to pay for a transcript had no access to appellate review at all. Although the Federal Constitution guarantees no right to appellate review, once a State affords that right, Griffin held, the State may not "bolt the door to equal justice."

In contrast to the "flat prohibition" of "bolted doors" that the Griffin line of cases securely established, the right to counsel at state expense, as delineated in our decisions, is less encompassing. A State must provide trial counsel for an indigent defendant charged with a felony, Gideon v. Wainwright, 372 U.S. 335, 339, 83 S.Ct. 792, 793-794, 9 L.Ed.2d 799 (1963), but that right does not extend to nonfelony trials if no term of imprisonment is actually imposed, Scott v. Illinois, 440 U.S. 367, 373-374, 99 S.Ct. 1158, 1161-1162, 59 L.Ed.2d 383 (1979). A State's obligation to provide appellate counsel to poor defendants faced with incarceration applies to appeals of right. Douglas v. California, 372 U.S. 353, 357, 83 S.Ct. 814, 816-817, 9 L.Ed.2d 811 (1963). In Ross v. Moffitt, however, we held that neither the Due Process Clause nor the Equal Protection Clause requires a State to provide counsel at state expense to an indigent prisoner pursuing a discretionary appeal in the state system or petitioning for review in this Court.

We have also recognized a narrow category of civil cases in which the State must provide access to its judicial processes without regard to a party's ability to pay court fees. In Boddie v. Connecticut, 401 U.S. 371, 91 S.Ct. 780, 28 L.Ed.2d 113 (1971), we held that the State could not deny a divorce to a married couple based on their inability to pay approximately $60 in court costs. Crucial to our decision in Boddie was the fundamental interest at stake. "[G]iven the basic position of the marriage relationship in this society's hierarchy of values and the concomitant state monopolization of the means for legally dissolving this relationship," we said, due process "prohibit [s] a State from denying, solely because of inability to pay, access to its courts to individuals who seek judicial dissolution of their marriages." [In] United States v. Kras, 409 U.S. 434, 93 S.Ct. 631, 34 L.Ed.2d 626 (1973), the Court clarified that a constitutional requirement to waive court fees in civil cases is the exception, not the general rule. Kras concerned fees, totaling $50, required to secure a discharge in bankruptcy. The Court recalled in Kras that "[o]n many occasions we have recognized the fundamental importance . . . under our Constitution" of "the associational interests that surround the establishment and dissolution of th[e] [marital] relationship." But bankruptcy discharge entails no "fundamental interest," we said. Although "obtaining [a] desired new start in life [is] important," that interest, the Court explained, "does not rise to the same constitutional level" as the interest in establishing or dissolving a marriage. Nor is resort to court the sole path to securing debt forgiveness, we stressed; in contrast, termination of a marriage, we reiterated, requires access to the State's judicial machinery.

In sum, as Ortwein underscored, this Court has not extended Griffin to the broad array of civil cases. But tellingly, the Court has consistently set apart from the mine run of cases those involving state controls or intrusions on family relationships. In that domain, to guard against undue official intrusion, the Court has examined closely and contextually the importance of the governmental interest advanced in defense of the intrusion.

Does the Fourteenth Amendment require Mississippi to accord M. L. B. access to an appeal — available but for her inability to advance required costs — before she is forever branded unfit for affiliation with her children? Respondents urge us to classify M. L. B.'s case with the generality of civil cases, in which indigent persons have no constitutional right to proceed *in forma pauperis*. M. L. B., on the other hand, maintains that the accusatory state action she is trying to fend off is barely distinguishable from criminal condemnation in view of the magnitude and permanence of the loss she faces. [We agree with M.L.B.]

We observe first that the Court's decisions concerning access to judicial processes, commencing with Griffin and running through Mayer, reflect both equal protection and due process concerns. The equal protection concern relates to the legitimacy of fencing out would-be appellants based solely on their inability to pay core costs. The due process concern homes in on the essential fairness of the state-ordered proceedings anterior to adverse state action. Nevertheless, "[m]ost decisions in this area," we have recognized, "res[t] on an equal protection framework," as M. L. B.'s plea heavily does, for, as we earlier observed, see *supra,* at 560, due process does not independently require that the State provide a right to appeal.

We now focus on Mayer and the considerations linking that decision to M. L. B.'s case. Mayer, applied Griffin to a petty offender, fined a total of $500, who sought to appeal from the trial court's judgment. An "impecunious medical student," the defendant in Mayer could not pay for a transcript. We held that the State must afford him a record complete enough to allow fair appellate consideration of his claims. The defendant in Mayer faced no term of confinement, but the conviction, we observed, could affect his professional prospects and, possibly, even bar him from the practice of medicine. The State's pocketbook interest in advance payment for a transcript, we concluded, was unimpressive when measured against the stakes for the defendant.

Similarly here, the stakes for petitioner M. L. B. — forced dissolution of her parental rights — are large, "'more substantial than mere loss of money.'" In contrast to loss of custody, which does not sever the parent-child bond, parental status termination is "irretrievabl[y] destructi[ve]" of the most fundamental family relationship. And the risk of error, Mississippi's experience shows, is considerable. The countervailing government interest, as in Mayer, is financial. Mississippi urges, as the justification for its appeal cost prepayment requirement, the State's legitimate interest in offsetting the costs of its court system. But in the tightly circumscribed category of parental status termination cases, appeals are few, and not likely to impose an undue burden on the State.

In aligning M. L. B.'s case and Mayer — parental status termination decrees and criminal convictions that carry no jail time — for appeal access purposes, we do not question the general rule, stated in Ortwein, that fee requirements ordinarily are examined only for rationality. The State's need for revenue to offset costs, in the mine run of cases, satisfies the rationality requirement. States are not forced by the Constitution to adjust all tolls to account for "disparity in material circumstances." But our cases solidly establish two exceptions to that general rule. The basic right to participate in political processes as voters and candidates cannot be limited to those who can pay for a license. Nor may access to judicial processes in cases criminal or "quasi criminal in nature," turn on ability to pay. [We] place decrees forever terminating parental rights in the category of cases in which the State may not "bolt the door to equal justice,"

In numerous cases, respondents point out, the Court has held that government "need not provide funds so that people can exercise even fundamental rights." A decision for M. L. B., respondents contend, would dishonor our cases recognizing that the Constitution "generally confer[s] no affirmative right to governmental aid, even where such aid may be necessary to secure life, liberty, or property interests of which the government itself may not deprive the individual." DeShaney v. Winnebago County Dept. of Social Servs., 489 U.S. 189, 196, 109 S.Ct. 998, 1003, 103 L.Ed.2d 249 (1989). Complainants in the cases on which respondents rely sought state aid to subsidize their privately initiated action or to alleviate the consequences of differences in economic circumstances that existed apart from state action. M. L. B.'s complaint is of a different order. She is endeavoring to defend against the State's destruction of her family bonds, and to resist the brand associated with a parental unfitness adjudication. Like a defendant resisting criminal conviction, she seeks to be spared from the State's devastatingly adverse action.

[Respondents] and the dissenters urge that we will open floodgates if we do not rigidly restrict Griffin to cases typed "criminal." But we have repeatedly noticed what sets parental status termination decrees apart from mine run civil actions, even from other domestic relations matters such as divorce, paternity, and child custody. To recapitulate, termination decrees "wor[k] a unique kind of deprivation." In contrast to matters modifiable at the parties' will or based on changed circumstances, termination adjudications involve the awesome authority of the State "to destroy permanently all legal recognition of the parental relationship." We are therefore satisfied that the label "civil" should not entice us to leave undisturbed the Mississippi courts' disposition of this case. For the reasons stated, we hold that Mississippi may not withhold from M. L. B. "a 'record of sufficient completeness' to permit proper [appellate] consideration of [her] claims." Accordingly, we reverse the judgment of the Supreme Court of Mississippi and remand the case for further proceedings not inconsistent with this opinion.

Justice KENNEDY, concurring in the judgment.

In my view the cases most on point, and the ones which persuade me we must reverse the judgment now reviewed, are the decisions addressing procedures involving the rights and privileges inherent in family and personal relations. These are Boddie v. Connecticut, 401 U.S. 371, 91 S.Ct. 780, 28 L.Ed.2d 113 (1971); Lassiter v. Department of Social Servs. of Durham Cty., 452 U.S. 18, 101 S.Ct. 2153, 68 L.Ed.2d 640 (1981); and Santosky v. Kramer, 455 U.S. 745, 102 S.Ct. 1388, 71 L.Ed.2d 599 (1982), all cases resting exclusively upon the Due Process Clause. Here, due process is quite a sufficient basis for our holding.

Justice THOMAS, with whom Justice SCALIA joins, and with whom THE CHIEF JUSTICE joins except as to Part II, dissenting.

Today the majority holds that the Fourteenth Amendment requires Mississippi to afford petitioner a free transcript because her civil case involves a "fundamental" right. The majority seeks to limit the reach of its holding to the type of case we confront here, one involving the termination of parental rights. I do not think, however, that the newfound constitutional right to free transcripts in civil appeals can be effectively restricted to this case. The inevitable consequence will be greater demands on the States to provide free assistance to would-be appellants in all manner of civil cases involving interests that cannot, based on the test established by the majority, be distinguished from the admittedly important interest at issue here. The cases on which the majority relies, primarily cases requiring appellate assistance for indigent criminal defendants, were questionable when decided, and have, in my view, been undermined since. Even accepting those cases, however, I am of the view that the majority takes them too far. I therefore dissent.

I. Petitioner requests relief under both the Due Process and Equal Protection Clauses, though she does not specify how either Clause affords it. The majority accedes to petitioner's request. But, carrying forward the ambiguity in the cases on which it relies, the majority does not specify the source of the relief it grants.

Assuming that petitioner's interest may not be impinged without due process of law, I do not think that the Due Process Clause requires the result the majority reaches. Petitioner's largest obstacle to a due process appeal *gratis* is our oft-affirmed view that due process does not oblige States to provide for any appeal, even from a criminal conviction. [The] majority reaffirms that due process does not require an appeal. Indeed, as I noted above, it is not clear that the majority relies on the Due Process Clause at all. The majority does discuss, however, one case in which the Court stated its holding in terms of due process: Boddie v. Connecticut, 401 U.S. 371, 91 S.Ct. 780, 28 L.Ed.2d 113 (1971). In Boddie, the Court held violative of due process a Connecticut statute that exacted fees averaging $60 from persons seeking marital dissolution. Citing the importance of the interest in ending a marriage, and the State's monopoly over the mechanisms to accomplish it, we explained that, "at a minimum" and "absent a countervailing state interest of overriding significance, persons forced to settle their claims of right and duty through the judicial process must be given a meaningful opportunity to be heard." Boddie has little to do with this case. It, "of course, was not concerned with post-hearing review." Rather, the concern in Boddie was that indigent persons were deprived of "fundamental rights" with no hearing whatsoever. Petitioner, in contrast, received not merely a hearing, but in fact enjoyed procedural protections above and beyond what our parental termination cases have required. She received both notice and a hearing before a neutral, legally trained decisionmaker. She was represented by counsel — even though due process does not in every case require the appointment of counsel. Through her attorney, petitioner was able to confront the evidence and witnesses against her. And, in accordance with Santosky v. Kramer, 455 U.S. 745, 769, 102 S.Ct. 1388, 1403, 71 L.Ed.2d 599 (1982), the Chancery Court was required to find that petitioner's parental unfitness was proved by clear and convincing evidence. There seems, then, no place in the Due Process Clause — certainly as an original matter, and even as construed by this Court — for the constitutional "right" crafted by the majority today.

[I] do not think that the equal protection theory underlying the Griffin line of cases remains viable. In Griffin, the State of Illinois required all criminal appellants whose claims on appeal required review of a trial transcript to obtain it themselves. The plurality thought that this "discriminate[d] against some convicted defendants on account of their poverty." Justice Harlan, in dissent, perceived a troubling shift in this Court's equal protection jurisprudence. The Court, he noted, did not "dispute either the necessity for a bill of exceptions or the reasonableness of the general requirement that the trial transcript, if used in its preparation, be paid for by the appealing party." But, because requiring each would-be appellant to bear the costs of appeal hit the poor harder, the majority divined "an invidious classification between the 'rich' and the 'poor.'" Disputing this early manifestation of the "disparate impact" theory of equal protection, Justice Harlan argued: "[N]o economic burden attendant upon the exercise of a privilege bears equally upon all, and in other circumstances the resulting differentiation is not treated as an invidious classification by the State, even though discrimination against 'indigents' by name would be unconstitutional." Justice Harlan offered the example of a state university that conditions an education on the payment of tuition. If charging tuition did not create a discriminatory classification, then, Justice Harlan wondered, how did any other reasonable exaction by a State for a service it provides?

Justice Harlan's views were accepted by the Court in Washington v. Davis, 426 U.S. 229, 96 S.Ct. 2040, 48 L.Ed.2d 597 (1976), in which "[w]e rejected a disparate impact theory of the Equal Protection Clause altogether." We spurned the claim that "a law, neutral on its face and serving ends otherwise within the power of government to pursue, is invalid under the Equal Protection Clause simply because it may affect a greater proportion of one race than of another." Absent proof of discriminatory purpose, official action did not violate the Fourteenth Amendment "*solely* because it has a racially disparate impact." The lesson of Davis is that the Equal Protection Clause shields only against purposeful discrimination: A disparate impact, even upon members of a racial minority, the classification of which we have been most suspect, does not violate equal protection. The Clause is not a panacea for perceived social or economic inequity; it seeks to "guarante[e] equal laws, not equal results." I see no principled difference between a facially neutral rule that serves in some cases to prevent persons from availing themselves of state employment, or a state-funded education, or a state-funded abortion — each of which the State may, but is not required to, provide — and a facially neutral rule that prevents a person from taking an appeal that is available only because the State chooses to provide it.

The Griffin line of cases ascribed to — one might say announced — an equalizing notion of the Equal Protection Clause that would, I think, have startled the Fourteenth Amendment's Framers. In those cases, the Court did not find, nor did it seek, any purposeful discrimination on the part of the state defendants. That their statutes had disproportionate effect on poor persons was sufficient for us to find a constitutional violation. In Davis, among other cases, we began to recognize the potential mischief of a disparate impact theory writ large, and endeavored to contain it. In this case, I would continue that enterprise. Mississippi's requirement of prepaid transcripts in civil appeals seeking to contest the sufficiency of the evidence adduced at trial is facially neutral; it creates no classification. The transcript rule reasonably obliges would-be appellants to bear the costs of availing themselves of a service that the State chooses, but is not constitutionally required, to provide. Any adverse impact that the transcript requirement has on any person seeking to appeal arises not out of the State's action, but out of factors entirely unrelated to it.

If this case squarely presented the question, I would be inclined to vote to overrule Griffin and its progeny. Even were I convinced that the cases on which the majority today relies ought to be retained, I could not agree with the majority's extension of them. The interest at stake in this case differs in several important respects from that at issue in cases such as Griffin. Petitioner's interest in maintaining a relationship with her children is the subject of a civil, not criminal, action.

[Taking] the Griffin line as a given, however, and in the absence of any obvious limiting principle, I would restrict it to the criminal appeals to which its authors, see Boddie v. Connecticut, 401 U.S., at 389, 91 S.Ct., at 792 (Black, J., dissenting), sought to limit it.

TENNESSEE v. LANE
541 U.S. 509 (2004)

[See *Tennessee v. Lane*, infra, where the Court held that the fundamental right of access to the courts supported a challenge under the Americans with Disabilities Act of 1990 and was a valid exercise of Congress's authority under Sec. 5 of the Fourteenth Amendment to enforce that amendment's substantive guarantees.]

C. INTERSTATE TRAVEL

SHAPIRO v. THOMPSON
394 U.S. 618 (1969)

Mr. Justice BRENNAN delivered the opinion of the Court.

[Each] of these three appeals is] from a decision [holding] unconstitutional a State or District of Columbia statutory provision which denies welfare assistance to residents [who] have not resided within their jurisdictions for at least one year immediately preceding their applications for such assistance. We affirm. . . .

There is no dispute that the effect of the waiting-period requirement [is] to create two classes of needy resident families indistinguishable from each other except that one is composed of residents who have resided a year or more, and the second of residents who have resided less than a year, in the jurisdiction. [The] second class is denied welfare aid upon which may depend the ability of the families to obtain the very means to subsist — food, shelter, and other necessities of life. [This scheme] constitutes an invidious discrimination [denying] equal protection of the laws. [The] interests which appellants assert are promoted by the classification either may not constitutionally be promoted by government or are not compelling governmental interests.

Primarily, appellants justify the waiting-period requirement as a protective device to preserve the fiscal integrity of state public assistance programs. It is asserted that people who require welfare assistance during their first year of residence in a State are likely to become continuing burdens on state welfare programs. Therefore, the argument runs, if such people can be deterred from entering the jurisdiction by denying them welfare benefits during the first year, state programs to assist long-time residents will not be impaired by a substantial influx of indigent newcomers. . . .

We do not doubt that the one-year waiting-period device is well suited to discourage the influx of poor families in need of assistance. An indigent who desires to migrate, resettle, find a new job, and start a new life will doubtless hesitate if he knows that he must risk making the move without the possibility of falling back on state welfare assistance during his first year of residence, when his need may be most acute. But the purpose of inhibiting migration by needy persons into the State is constitutionally impermissible.

This Court long ago recognized that the nature of our Federal Union and our constitutional concepts of personal liberty unite to require that all citizens be free to travel throughout the length and breadth of our land uninhibited by statutes, rules, or regulations which unreasonably burden or restrict this movement. . . .

We have no occasion to ascribe the source of this right to travel interstate to a particular constitutional provision. It suffices that, as Mr. Justice Stewart said for the Court in United States v. Guest, 383 U.S. 745, 757-758 (1966): "The constitutional right to travel from one State to another . . . occupies a position fundamental to the concept of our Federal Union. It is a right that has been firmly established and repeatedly recognized. . . ."

Thus, the purpose of deterring the in-migration of indigents cannot serve as justification for the classification created by the one-year waiting period, since that purpose is constitutionally impermissible. If a law has "no other purpose . . . than to chill the assertion of constitutional rights by penalizing those who choose to exercise them, then it [is] patently unconstitutional."

Alternatively, appellants argue that even if it is impermissible for a State to attempt to deter the entry of all indigents, the challenged classification may be justified as a permissible state attempt to discourage those indigents who would enter the State solely to obtain larger benefits. [But] a State may no more try to fence out those indigents who seek higher welfare benefits than it may try to fence out indigents generally. [We] do not perceive why a mother who is seeking to make a new life for herself and her children should be regarded as less deserving because she considers, among other factors, the level of a State's public assistance. Surely such a mother is no less deserving than a mother who moves into a particular State in order to take advantage of its better educational facilities.

Appellants argue further that the challenged classification may be sustained as an attempt to distinguish between new and old residents on the basis of the contribution they have made to the community through the payment of taxes. [But this] would logically permit the State to bar new residents from schools, parks, and libraries or deprive them of police and fire protection. Indeed it would permit the State to apportion all benefits and services according to the past tax contributions of its citizens. The Equal Protection Clause prohibits such an apportionment of state services. We recognize that a State [may] legitimately attempt to limit its expenditures, whether for public assistance, public education, or any other program. But a State may not accomplish such a purpose by invidious distinctions between classes of its citizens. It could not, for example, reduce expenditures for education by barring indigent children from its schools. Similarly, [appellants] must do more than show that denying welfare benefits to new residents saves money. The saving of welfare costs cannot justify an otherwise invidious classification. . . .

Appellants next advance as justification certain administrative and related governmental objectives allegedly served by the waiting-period requirement. They argue that the requirement (1) facilitates the planning of the welfare budget; (2) provides an objective test of residency; (3) minimizes the opportunity for recipients fraudulently to receive payments from more than one jurisdiction; and (4) encourages early entry of new residents into the labor force.

At the outset, we reject appellants' argument that a mere showing of a rational relationship between the waiting period and these four admittedly permissible state objectives will suffice to justify the classification, [for] in moving from State to State or to the District of Columbia appellees were exercising a constitutional right, and any classification which serves to penalize the exercise of that right, unless shown to be necessary to promote a compelling governmental interest, is unconstitutional. Cf. [Skinner].

The argument that the waiting-period requirement facilitates budget predictability is wholly unfounded. The records [are] utterly devoid of evidence that either State or the District of Columbia in fact uses the one-year requirement as a means to predict the number of people who will require assistance in the budget year. . . .

The argument that the waiting period serves as an administratively efficient rule of thumb for determining residency similarly will not withstand scrutiny. [Before] granting an application, the welfare authorities investigate the applicant [and] in the course of the inquiry necessarily learn the facts upon which to determine whether the applicant is a resident.

Similarly, there is no need for a State to use the one-year waiting period as a safeguard against fraudulent receipt of benefits; for less drastic means are available, and are employed, to minimize that hazard. . . .

[Finally, a] state purpose to encourage employment provides no rational basis for imposing a one-year waiting-period restriction on new residents only, [for there is no reason not to require a similar waiting period for this reason for long-term residents].

We conclude therefore that appellants [have] no need to use the one-year requirement for the governmental purposes suggested. Thus, even under traditional equal protection tests a classification of welfare applicants according to whether they have lived in the State for one year would seem irrational and unconstitutional. But, of course, the traditional criteria do not apply in these cases. Since the classification here touches on the fundamental right of interstate movement, its constitutionality must be judged by the stricter standard of whether it promotes a compelling state interest. Under this standard, the waiting-period requirement clearly violates the Equal Protection Clause.

[The Court also rejected the states' argument that Congress had expressly authorized the one-year waiting period and added that, "even if . . . Congress did approve the imposition of a . . . waiting period," such an approval "would be unconstitutional," for "Congress may not authorize the States to violate the Equal Protection Clause."]

Mr. Justice STEWART, concurring.

The Court today does not "pick out particular human activities, characterize them as 'fundamental,' and give them added protection. . . ." To the contrary, the Court simply recognizes, as it must, an established constitutional right, and gives to that right no less protection than the Constitution itself demands. [As] Mr. Justice Harlan wrote for the Court more than a decade ago, "[T]o justify the deterrent effect . . . on the free exercise . . . of their constitutionally protected right . . . a '. . . subordinating interest of the State must be compelling.'" [NAACP v. Alabama.] . . .

Mr. Chief Justice WARREN, with whom Mr. Justice BLACK joins, dissenting. . . .

Congress has imposed a residence requirement in the District of Columbia and authorized the States to impose similar requirements. The issue before us must therefore be framed in terms of whether Congress may create minimal residence requirements, not whether the States, acting alone, may do so. . . .

Congress, pursuant to its commerce power, has enacted a variety of restrictions upon interstate travel. It has taxed air and rail fares and the gasoline needed to power cars and trucks which move interstate. Many of the federal safety regulations of common carriers which cross state lines burden the right to travel. And Congress has prohibited by criminal statute interstate travel for certain purposes. Although these restrictions operate as a limitation upon free interstate movement of persons, their constitutionality appears well settled. . . .

The Court's right-to-travel cases lend little support to the view that congressional action is invalid merely because it burdens the right to travel. Most of our cases fall into two categories: those in which state-imposed restrictions were involved, see, e.g., Edwards v. California, 314 U.S. 160 (1941); Crandall v. Nevada, 6 Wall. 35 (1868), and those concerning congressional decisions to remove impediments to interstate movement, see, e.g., United States v. Guest, 383 U.S. 745 (1966). [Here,] travel itself is not prohibited. Any burden inheres solely in the fact that a potential welfare recipient might take into consideration the loss of welfare benefits for a limited period of time if he changes his residence. . . .

[Our] cases require only that Congress have a rational basis for finding that a chosen regulatory scheme is necessary to the furtherance of interstate commerce. Certainly, a congressional finding that residence requirements allowed each State to concentrate its resources upon new and increased programs of rehabilitation ultimately resulting in an enhanced flow of commerce as the economic condition of welfare recipients progressively improved is rational and would justify imposition of residence requirements under the Commerce Clause.

Mr. Justice HARLAN, dissenting.

In upholding the equal protection argument, the Court has applied an equal protection doctrine of relatively recent vintage: the rule that statutory classifications which [affect] "fundamental rights" will be held to deny equal protection unless justified by a "compelling" governmental interest. [I] think this [doctrine] particularly unfortunate [because] it creates an exception which threatens to swallow the standard equal protection rule. Virtually every state statute affects important rights. [The] doctrine is also unnecessary. When the right affected is one assured by the Federal Constitution, any infringement can be dealt with under the Due Process Clause. But when a statute affects only matters not mentioned in the Federal Constitution and is not arbitrary or irrational, I must reiterate that I know of nothing which entitles this Court to pick out particular human activities, characterize them as "fundamental," and give them added protection under an unusually stringent equal protection test. . . .

[If] the issue is regarded purely as one of equal protection, [this] classification should be judged by ordinary equal protection standards. [And in] light of [the] undeniable relation of residence requirements to valid legislative aims, [I] can find no objection to these residence requirements under the Equal Protection Clause. . . .

The next issue [is] whether a one-year welfare residence requirement amounts to an undue burden upon the right of interstate travel [which I conclude] is a "fundamental" right [which] should be regarded as having its source in the Due Process Clause of the Fifth Amendment. . . .

[The decisive question is] whether the governmental interests served by residence requirements outweigh the burden imposed upon the right to travel. [Taking] all of [the] competing considerations into account, I believe that the balance definitely favors constitutionality. In reaching that conclusion, I do not minimize the importance of the right to travel interstate. However, the impact of residence conditions upon that right is indirect and apparently quite insubstantial. On the other hand, the governmental purposes served by the requirements are legitimate and real, and the residence requirements are clearly suited to their accomplishment. To abolish residence requirements might well discourage highly worthwhile experimentation in the welfare field. The statutes come to us clothed with the authority of Congress and attended by a correspondingly heavy presumption of constitutionality. Moreover, although [it is argued] that the same objectives could have been achieved by less restrictive means, this is an area in which the judiciary should be especially slow to fetter [legislative] judgment. . . . Residence requirements have advantages, such as administrative simplicity and relative certainty, which are not shared by the alternative solutions. . . . In these circumstances, I cannot find that the burden imposed by residence requirements upon ability to travel outweighs the governmental interests in their continued employment. . . .

SAENZ v. ROE
526 U.S. 489 (1999)

Justices STEVENS delivered the opinion of the Court.

In 1992, California enacted a statute limiting the maximum welfare benefits available to newly arrived residents. The scheme limits the amount payable to a family that has resided in the State for less than 12 months to the amount payable by the State of the family's prior residence. The questions presented by this case are whether the 1992 statute was constitutional when it was enacted and, if not, whether an amendment to the Social Security Act enacted by Congress in 1996 affects that determination.

[The plaintiffs who were] former residents of Louisiana and Oklahoma would receive $190 and $341 respectively for a family of three even though the full California grant was $641; the former resident of Colorado, who had just one child, was limited to $280 a month as opposed to the full California grant of $504 for a family of two. Relying primarily on our decisions in Shapiro v. Thompson, 394 U.S. 618, 89 S.Ct. 1322, 22 L.Ed.2d 600 (1969), and Zobel v. Williams, 457 U.S. 55, 102 S.Ct. 2309, 72 L.Ed.2d 672 (1982), he concluded that the statute placed "a penalty on the decision of new residents to migrate to the State and be treated on an equal basis with existing residents." [In 1996] Congress enacted the Personal Responsibility and Work Opportunity Reconciliation Act of 1996 (PRWORA), [which] expressly authorizes any State that receives a block grant under TANF to "apply to a family the rules (including benefit amounts) of the [TANF] program . . . of another State if the family has moved to the State from the other State and has resided in the State for less than 12 months." [The district court] concluded that the existence of the federal statute did not affect the legal analysis in his prior opinion. [The] Court of Appeals affirmed his issuance of a preliminary injunction. We now affirm.

The word "travel" is not found in the text of the Constitution. Yet the "constitutional right to travel from one State to another" is firmly embedded in our jurisprudence. Indeed, as Justice Stewart reminded us in Shapiro v. Thompson, 394 U.S. 618, 89 S.Ct. 1322, 22 L.Ed.2d 600 (1969), the right is so important that it is "assertable against private interference as well as governmental action . . . a virtually unconditional personal right, guaranteed by the Constitution to us all."

The "right to travel" discussed in our cases embraces at least three different components. It protects the right of a citizen of one State to enter and to leave another State, the right to be treated as a welcome visitor rather than an unfriendly alien when temporarily present in the second State, and, for those travelers who elect to become permanent residents, the right to be treated like other citizens of that State.

It was the right to go from one place to another, including the right to cross state borders while en route, that was vindicated in Edwards v. California, 314 U.S. 160, 62 S.Ct. 164, 86 L.Ed. 119 (1941), which invalidated a state law that impeded the free interstate passage of the indigent. We reaffirmed that right in United States v. Guest, 383 U.S. 745, 86 S.Ct. 1170, 16 L.Ed.2d 239 (1966), which afforded protection to the "'right to travel freely to and from the State of Georgia and to use highway facilities and other instrumentalities of interstate commerce within the State of Georgia.'" [The] second component of the right to travel is, however, expressly protected by the text of the Constitution. The first sentence of Article IV, § 2, provides: "The Citizens of each State shall be entitled to all Privileges and Immunities of Citizens in the several States."

Thus, by virtue of a person's state citizenship, a citizen of one State who travels in other States, intending to return home at the end of his journey, is entitled to enjoy the "Privileges and Immunities of Citizens in the several States" that he visits. This provision removes "from the citizens of each State the disabilities of alienage in the other States." Paul v. Virginia, 8 Wall. 168, 180, 19 L.Ed. 357 (1868).

What is at issue in this case, then, is this third aspect of the right to travel — the right of the newly arrived citizen to the same privileges and immunities enjoyed by other citizens of the same State. That right is protected not only by the new arrival's status as a state citizen, but also by her status as a citizen of the United States. That additional source of protection is plainly identified in the opening words of the Fourteenth Amendment: "All persons born or naturalized in the United States, and subject to the jurisdiction thereof, are citizens of the United States and of the State wherein they reside. No State shall make or enforce any law which shall abridge the privileges or immunities of citizens of the United States. . . ."

Despite fundamentally differing views concerning the coverage of the Privileges or Immunities Clause of the Fourteenth Amendment, most notably expressed in the majority and dissenting opinions in the Slaughter-House Cases, 16 Wall. 36, 21 L.Ed. 394 (1872), it has always been common ground that this Clause protects the third component of the right to travel. Writing for the majority in the Slaughter-House Cases, Justice Miller explained that one of the privileges conferred by this Clause "is that a citizen of the United States can, of his own volition, become a citizen of any State of the Union by a *bonâ fide* residence therein, with the same rights as other citizens of that State." Justice Bradley, in dissent, used even stronger language to make the same point: "The states have not now, if they ever had, any power to restrict their citizenship to any classes or persons. A citizen of the United States has a perfect constitutional right to go to and reside in any State he chooses, and to claim citizenship therein, and an equality of rights with every other citizen; and the whole power of the nation is pledged to sustain him in that right. He is not bound to cringe to any superior, or to pray for any act of grace, as a means of enjoying all the rights and privileges enjoyed by other citizens."

[Neither] mere rationality nor some intermediate standard of review should be used to judge the constitutionality of a state rule that discriminates against some of its citizens because they have been domiciled in the State for less than a year. The appropriate standard may be more categorical than that articulated in Shapiro, but it is surely no less strict. Because this case involves discrimination against citizens who have completed their interstate travel, the State's argument that its welfare scheme affects the right to travel only "incidentally" is beside the point. Were we concerned solely with actual deterrence to migration, we might be persuaded that a partial withholding of benefits constitutes a lesser incursion on the right to travel than an outright denial of all benefits. But since the right to travel embraces the citizen's right to be treated equally in her new State of residence, the discriminatory classification is itself a penalty.

It is undisputed that respondents and the members of the class that they represent are citizens of California and that their need for welfare benefits is unrelated to the length of time that they have resided in California. We thus have no occasion to consider what weight might be given to a citizen's length of residence if the bona fides of her claim to state citizenship were questioned. Moreover, because whatever benefits they receive will be consumed while they remain in California, there is no danger that recognition of their claim will encourage citizens of other States to establish residency for just long enough to acquire some readily portable benefit, such as a divorce or a college education, that will be enjoyed after they return to their original domicile. See, *e.g.,* Sosna v. Iowa, 419 U.S. 393, 95 S.Ct. 553, 42 L.Ed.2d 532 (1975); Vlandis v. Kline, 412 U.S. 441, 93 S.Ct. 2230, 37 L.Ed.2d 63 (1973).

The classifications challenged in this case [may] not be justified by a purpose to deter welfare applicants from migrating to California. [As] we squarely held in Shapiro v. Thompson, 394 U.S. 618, 89 S.Ct. 1322, 22 L.Ed.2d 600 (1969), such a purpose would be unequivocally impermissible. Disavowing any desire to fence out the indigent, California has instead advanced an entirely fiscal justification for its multitiered scheme. The enforcement of § 11450.03 will save the State approximately $10.9 million a year. The question is not whether such saving is a legitimate purpose but whether the State may accomplish that end by the discriminatory means it has chosen. An evenhanded, across-the-board reduction of about 72 cents per month for every beneficiary would produce the same result. But our negative answer to the question does not rest on the weakness of the State's purported fiscal justification. It rests on the fact that the Citizenship Clause of the Fourteenth Amendment expressly equates citizenship with residence: "That Clause does not provide for, and does not allow for, degrees of citizenship based on length of residence." Neither the duration of respondents' California residence, nor the identity of their prior States of residence, has any relevance to their need for benefits. [In] short, the State's legitimate interest in saving money provides no justification for its decision to discriminate among equally eligible citizens.

The question that remains is whether congressional approval of durational residency requirements in the 1996 amendment to the Social Security Act somehow resuscitates the constitutionality of § 11450.03. That question is readily answered, for we have consistently held that Congress may not authorize the States to violate the Fourteenth Amendment. Moreover, the protection afforded to the citizen by the Citizenship Clause of that Amendment is a limitation on the powers of the National Government as well as the States.

Citizens of the United States, whether rich or poor, have the right to choose to be citizens "of the State wherein they reside." U.S. Const., Amdt. 14, § 1. The States, however, do not have any right to select their citizens. The Fourteenth Amendment, like the Constitution itself, was, as Justice Cardozo put it, "framed upon the theory that the peoples of the several states must sink or swim together, and that in the long run prosperity and salvation are in union and not division." Baldwin v. G.A.F. Seelig, Inc., 294 U.S. 511, 523, 55 S.Ct. 497, 79 L.Ed. 1032 (1935).

The judgment of the Court of Appeals is affirmed. It is so ordered.

Chief Justice REHNQUIST, with whom Justice THOMAS joins, dissenting.

The right to travel clearly embraces the right to go from one place to another, and prohibits States from impeding the free interstate passage of citizens. [Nonresident] visitors of other States should not be subject to discrimination solely because they live out of State. [But] I cannot see how the right to become a citizen of another State is a necessary "component" of the right to travel, or why the Court tries to marry these separate and distinct rights. A person is no longer "traveling" in any sense of the word when he finishes his journey to a State which he plans to make his home. No doubt the Court has, in the past 30 years, essentially conflated the right to travel with the right to equal state citizenship in striking down durational residence requirements similar to the one challenged here. See, *e.g.,* Shapiro v. Thompson, 394 U.S. 618, 89 S.Ct. 1322, 22 L.Ed.2d 600 (1969) (striking down 1-year residence before receiving any welfare benefit); Dunn v. Blumstein, 405 U.S. 330, 92 S.Ct. 995, 31 L.Ed.2d 274 (1972) (striking down 1-year residence before receiving the right to vote in state elections); Maricopa County, 415 U.S., at 280-283, 94 S.Ct. 1076 (striking down 1-year county residence before receiving entitlement to nonemergency hospitalization or emergency care) [The] Court today tries to clear much of the underbrush created by these prior right-to-travel cases, abandoning its effort to define what residence requirements deprive individuals of "important rights and benefits" or "penalize" the right to travel. Under its new analytical framework, a State, outside certain ill-defined circumstances, cannot classify its citizens by the length of their residence in the State without offending the Privileges or Immunities Clause of the Fourteenth Amendment.

In unearthing from its tomb the right to become a state citizen and to be treated equally in the new State of residence, however, the Court ignores a State's need to assure that only persons who establish a bona fide residence receive the benefits provided to current residents of the State. [Thus], the Court has consistently recognized that while new citizens must have the same opportunity to enjoy the privileges of being a citizen of a State, the States retain the ability to use bona fide residence requirements to ferret out those who intend to take the privileges and run. [Recognizing] the practical appeal of such criteria, this Court has repeatedly sanctioned the State's use of durational residence requirements before new residents receive in-state tuition rates at state universities. The Court has done the same in upholding a 1-year residence requirement for eligibility to obtain a divorce in state courts, see Sosna v. Iowa, 419 U.S. 393, 406-409, 95 S.Ct. 553, 42 L.Ed.2d 532 (1975).

If States can require individuals to reside in-state for a year before exercising the right to educational benefits, the right to terminate a marriage, or the right to vote in primary elections that all other state citizens enjoy, then States may surely do the same for welfare benefits. The welfare payment here and in-state tuition rates are cash subsidies provided to a limited class of people, and California's standard of living and higher education system make both subsidies quite attractive. [The] Court tries to distinguish education and divorce benefits by contending that the welfare payment here will be consumed in California, while a college education or a divorce produces benefits that are "portable" and can be enjoyed after individuals return to their original domicile. But this "you can't take it with you" distinction is more apparent than real. [A] welfare subsidy is thus as much an investment in human capital as is a tuition subsidy, and their attendant benefits are just as "portable." I therefore believe that the durational residence requirement challenged here is a permissible exercise of the State's power to "assur[e] that services provided for its residents are enjoyed only by residents."

Finally, Congress' express approval in 42 U.S.C. § 604(c) of durational residence requirements for welfare recipients like the one established by California only goes to show the reasonableness of a law like § 11450.03. The National Legislature, where people from Mississippi as well as California are represented, has recognized the need to protect state resources in a time of experimentation and welfare reform. As States like California revamp their total welfare packages, see Brief for Petitioners 5-6, they should have the authority and flexibility to ensure that their new programs are not exploited. Congress has decided that it makes good welfare policy to give the States this power. California has reasonably exercised it through an objective, narrowly tailored residence requirement. I see nothing in the Constitution that should prevent the enforcement of that requirement.

Justice THOMAS, with whom THE CHIEF JUSTICE joins, dissenting.

I join The Chief Justice's dissent. I write separately to address the majority's conclusion that California has violated "the right of the newly arrived citizen to the same privileges and immunities enjoyed by other citizens of the same State." In my view, the majority attributes a meaning to the Privileges or Immunities Clause that likely was unintended when the Fourteenth Amendment was enacted and ratified.

[At] the time the Fourteenth Amendment was adopted, people understood that "privileges or immunities of citizens" were fundamental rights, rather than every public benefit established by positive law. Accordingly, the majority's conclusion — that a State violates the Privileges or Immunities Clause when it "discriminates" against citizens who have been domiciled in the State for less than a year in the distribution of welfare benefits — appears contrary to the original understanding and is dubious at best.

[Although] the majority appears to breathe new life into the Clause today, it fails to address its historical underpinnings or its place in our constitutional jurisprudence. Because I believe that the demise of the Privileges or Immunities Clause has contributed in no small part to the current disarray of our Fourteenth Amendment jurisprudence, I would be open to reevaluating its meaning in an appropriate case. Before invoking the Clause, however, we should endeavor to understand what the Framers of the Fourteenth Amendment thought that it meant.

IV. ENFORCEMENT LEGISLATION

A. POST-RECONSTRUCTION CIVIL RIGHTS LAWS

1. ENFORCING THE CIVIL WAR AMENDMENTS

Congress shall have power to enforce this article by appropriate legislation. [U.S. Const. amend. XIII, §2.]

The Congress shall have power to enforce, by appropriate legislation, the provisions of this article. [U.S. Const. amend. XIV, §2.]

The Congress shall have power to enforce this article by appropriate legislation. [U.S. Const. amend. XV, §2.]

a. Criminal Provisions

18 U.S.C. § 241. Conspiracy against rights [*derived from § 6 of the 1870 Act*]
If two or more persons conspire to injure, oppress, threaten, or intimidate any inhabitant of any State, Territory or District in the free exercise or enjoyment of any right or privilege secured to him by the Constitution or laws of the United States, or because of his having so exercised the same; or

If two or more persons go in disguise on the highway, or on the premises of another, with intent to prevent or hinder his free exercise or enjoyment of any right or privilege so secured

They shall be fined not more than $10,000 or imprisoned not more than ten years, or both; and if death results, they shall be subject to imprisonment for any term of years or for life.

18 U.S.C. § 242. Deprivation of rights under color of law. [*derived from § 2 of the 1866 Act*]
Whoever, under color of any law, statute, ordinance, regulation, or custom, willfully subjects any inhabitant of any State, Territory, or District to the deprivation of any rights, privileges, or immunities secured or protected by the [Constitution or laws], or to different punishments, pains, or penalties, on account of such inhabitant being an alien, or by reason of his color, or race, than are prescribed for the punishment of citizens, shall be fined not more than $1,000 or imprisoned not more than one year, or both; and if bodily injury results shall [be] imprisoned not more than ten [years]; and if death results shall be subject to imprisonment for any term of years or for life.

b. Civil Provisions

42 U.S.C. § 1981. Equal rights under the law. [*derived from the 1866 and 1870 Acts*]
All persons within the jurisdiction of the United States shall have the same right in every State and Territory to make and enforce contracts, to sue, be parties, give evidence, and to the full and equal benefit of all laws and proceedings for the security of persons and property as is enjoyed by white citizens, and shall be subject to like punishment, pains, penalties, taxes, licenses, and exactions of every kind, and to no other.

42 U.S.C. § 1982. Property rights of citizens. [*derived from the 1866 Act*]
All citizens of the United States shall have the same right, in every State and Territory, as is enjoyed by white citizens thereof to inherit, purchase, lease, sell, hold, and convey real and personal property.

42 U.S.C. § 1983. Civil action for deprivation of rights. [*derived from § 1 of the Civil Rights Act of 1871*]
Every person who, under color of any statute, ordinance, regulation, custom, or usage, of any State or Territory or the District of Columbia, subjects, or causes to be subjected, any citizen of the United States or other person within the jurisdiction thereof to the deprivation of any rights, privileges or immunities secured by the Constitution and laws, shall be liable to the party injured in an action at law, suit in equity, or other proper proceedings for redress.

42 U.S.C. § 1985(3). Conspiracy to interfere with civil rights. [*derived from Civil Rights Act of 1871*]

[If] two or more persons in any State or Territory conspire or go in disguise on the highway or on the premises of another, for the purpose of depriving, either directly or indirectly, any person or class of persons of the equal protection of the laws, or of equal privileges and immunities under the laws; Either party so injured or deprived may have an action for the recovery of damages occasioned by such injury or deprivation, against any one or more of the conspirators.

B. REACH OF THE ENFORCEMENT POWER

Each of the Civil War Amendments has a section granting Congress the power to enforce the provisions of the amendment. This simply means that Congress, under these enforcement sections, can pass legislation spelling out the procedures for enforcing the meaning of the amendments. Of course, neither amendment *requires* legislation to be enforced; the amendments stand on their own, as in case of *Brown v. Board of Education*, which found school segregation to be unconstitutional without prior congressional legislation.

These enforcement provisions are analogous to the enumerations of congressional authority under Article 1, section 8. One way to understand the scheme set up by the enforcement provisions is to distinguish between the Civil War Amendments' main provisions and the enumerations of congressional power. The amendments are declaratory of rights while the Article I authority is descriptive of Congress's power. For example, the Commerce Power ("[t]he Congress shall have power . . . To regulate commerce with foreign nations, and among the several states, and with the Indian tribes") is more like the enforcement provisions of the amendments than the main provisions, which are declarations of rights. Because the amendments are in two parts (the substantive portions and the enforcement portions), there has sometime been confusion as to whether the main provision stands alone without congressional implementation via the enforcement provision, and whether Congress can *interpret* the amendments by legislation without waiting on Court cases for guidance, or whether Congress's lawmaking function is limited to prescribing *remedial* (enforcement) measures for violations as determined by the Supreme Court. The Court has attempted to clear up this issue in the following cases. What lingers on as an unclear area is the extent to which Congress can interpret totally independent Supreme Court interpretation.

1. THE RIGHT TO VOTE AND THE FOURTEENTH AND FIFTEENTH AMENDMENTS

Several cases have addressed the issue of voting rights since the 1950s, a period coinciding with the American Civil Rights Movement. During this period, Congress passed the Voting Rights Act of 1965, which was a general law that prohibited practices that were racially discriminatory and provided for enforcement upon proof of violation by qualifying victims of discrimination to vote in the locale where the discrimination took place. What constituted discrimination was left open and for the federal courts to determine.

The practice in many southern states was to restrict the exercise of the voting franchise among African Americans through several devices, despite the fact that the Fifteenth Amendment prohibited discrimination "by the United States or by any state on account of race, color, or previous condition of servitude." A common device to get around this prohibition was to condition voting rights by requiring potential voters to pass a literacy test. In its first appearance before the Supreme Court, in *Lassiter v. Northhampton County Election Board*, 360 U.S. 45 (1959), it was approved as a reasonable exercise of the states' "broad powers to determine the conditions under which the right of suffrage may be exercised, absent of course the discrimination which the Constitution condemns." Justice Douglas reasoned that it was beyond the Court's role to sit in judgment of the policy, especially at a time when much of the debate on the issues addressed by elections required literacy. The Court was able to issue the ruling because the only prohibition on the use of literacy tests was that they not be used discriminatorily.

South Carolina v. Katzenbach, 383 U.S. 301 (1966). This case addressed the Voting Rights Act of 1965, legislation that interpreted the Fifteenth Amendment in a way to address a number of voting irregularities on account of race that were not sufficiently addressed by earlier voting and civil rights acts. Exercising its authority under section 2 of the Fifteenth Amendment, Congress based the law on its investigation of the conditions of voting in various states.

The Court sustained several provisions of the act, which were the subject of a challenge on the part of South Carolina, which requested an injunction against the implementation of the act on the basis of a bill of complaint. Among the provisions of the Act complained of were

> a complex scheme of stringent remedies aimed at areas where voting discrimination has been most flagrant. Section 4(a)-(d) lays down a formula defining the States and political subdivisions to which these new remedies apply. The first of the remedies, contained in § 4(a), is the suspension of literacy tests and similar voting qualifications for a period of five years from the last occurrence of substantial voting discrimination. Section 5 prescribes a second [p316] remedy, the suspension of all new voting regulations pending review by federal authorities to determine whether their use would perpetuate voting discrimination. The third remedy, covered in §§ 6(b), 7, 9, and 13(a), is the assignment of federal examiners on certification by the Attorney General to list qualified applicants who are thereafter entitled to vote in all elections.

Id. at 315.

In an opinion written by Chief Justice Earl Warren, the Court held that Congress may "use any rational means to effectuate the constitutional prohibition of racial discrimination in voting," speaking specifically of the enforcement power under section 2 of the Fifteenth Amendment. Noting that section 1 of the Fifteenth Amendment was fully self-executing, Congress had the chief responsibility under section 2 for implementing the prohibition of the amendment and that the Court would review whether Congress's interpretation was appropriate and rational. The Court did so and upheld the Act under the Fifteenth Amendment.

The Court extended that holding to the Fourteenth Amendment in another voting rights case, *Katzenbach v. Morgan* 384 U.S. 641 (1966). New York State's voting law required the ability to read and write English as a condition to voting in that state. It also allowed the franchise for individuals who had completed the sixth grade at an accredited school in Puerto Rico where the predominant language of instruction was English. However, section 4(e) of the Voting Rights Act of 1965, which by the language of that section was designed to enforce the Fourteenth Amendment (instead of the Fifteenth Amendment), states:

> Congress hereby declares that to secure the rights under the fourteenth amendment of persons educated in American-flag schools in which the predominant classroom language was other than English, it is necessary to prohibit the States from conditioning the right to vote of such persons on ability to read, write, understand, or interpret any matter in the English language. (2) No person who demonstrates that he has successfully completed the sixth primary grade in a public school in, or a private school accredited by, any State or territory, the District of Columbia, or the Commonwealth of Puerto Rico in which the predominant classroom language was other than English, shall be denied the right to vote in any Federal, State, or local election because of his inability to read, write, understand, or interpret any matter in the English language. . . .

Justice Brennan, writing for the Court, described the role of the Court as determining whether Congress had a rational basis for prohibiting the state practice, and not whether it would consider the state practice constitutional. He relied on *Ex parte Virginia*, 100 U.S. 339 (1879), for the proposition that the same standard of implementation of congressional powers under the Necessary and Proper Clause of Article 1 applied to the enforcement clauses, the 14th in particular, of the Civil War Amendments:

> Whatever legislation is appropriate, that is, adapted to carry out the objects the amendments have in view, whatever tends to enforce submission to the prohibitions they contain, and to secure to all persons the enjoyment of perfect equality of civil rights and the equal protection of the laws against State denial or invasion, if not prohibited, is brought within the domain of congressional power.

Id. at 345-346.

Consistent with *South Carolina v. Katzenbach*, the Court limited its inquiry into whether Congress acted rationally in prohibiting practice in furtherance of the goals of the Fourteenth Amendment, noting that Congress could rationally believe that such a prohibition was necessary for the purpose of securing non-discriminatory distribution of government services through the accumulation of political power, or that Congress could have believed the prohibition necessary to end discriminatory voting place treatment for the state's Puerto Rican community. Accordingly, that portion of the act was upheld.

Justice Harlan, joined by Justice Stewart, dissented on the basis that the Act's prohibition did amount to judicial interpretation on the part of the legislative branch, a point made stronger by Justice Harlan's review of the New York State practice as rational and not a violation of the Fourteenth Amendment's equal protection clause. To Harlan, for the Act to prohibit the English literacy requirement would amount to an interpretation of the Amendment by Congress and would not be like the remedial measures approved by the Court from other parts of Act in *South Carolina v. Katzenbach*. To Harlan, the remedial measures such as suspension of literacy tests and pre-approval of changes to state voting laws (and the prohibition of such laws if not approved), supported by a voluminous congressional record tending to confirm the discriminatory nature of the practices, amounted merely to remediating established violations of the Fifteenth Amendment, and not interpretation, a judicial function. In *Morgan*, Harlan believed that declaring language literacy requirements as violations of the Equal Protection clause, with little record establishing the discriminatory nature of the practice and no case law disapproving of the practice, crossed the line between remediation and interpretation. The dissenters would have found 4(e) to be an unconstitutional usurpation of the judicial function.

Notes

1. Are the dissenters correct? Are the holdings of the majorities in the *South Carolina* and *Morgan* cases different? The majority in the former does continually refer to the provisions in question as remedial and not interpretive. Are the measures at issue in the two cases really as different as Justice Harlan suggests?

2. Is there anything left for the Court to decide on the issue of whether Congress can rationally interpret the Civil War Amendments through legislation?

3. The Court had held on numerous occasions that discrimination in the distribution of government services was unconstitutional. In light of this, is the prohibition of English literacy as a condition of exercising the right to vote simply remedial legislation considering that providing the opportunity to vote is a government service? How does the *Lassiter* opinion, discussed earlier in this section, affect your answer?

4. Justice Harlan also claimed that Congress violated federalism principles under the Tenth Amendment. Do you agree?

Do these decisions establish the absolute authority of Congress to interpret the Civil War Amendments by way of enforcement? Can Congress simply declare a longstanding practice of a state practice violative of the Constitution through legislation? If this is what Congress did in *South Carolina* and *Morgan* involving arguably clear examples of discrimination, are there limits to the kind of situations in which Congress can "impose its will" on the states? One such limit was suggested in an opinion by Justice Hugo Black in *Oregon v. Mitchell*, 400 U.S. 112 (1970). The case addressed 1970 amendments to the Voting Rights Act, which lowered the voting age to 18 and suspended literacy tests throughout the country for five years, and not just in those areas with histories of voter discrimination. Though several separate opinions were written, the entire Court concurred in the judgment that Congress had the power to temporarily suspend literacy tests nationwide under the enforcement provisions. However, the Court was split on lowering the voting age. Justice Black's separate opinion reasoned that the federal act lowering the voting age in national elections was constitutional, but declined to find that any of the Civil War amendments granted power to Congress to adjust the voting age with respect to state and local elections. In Justice Black's view, despite the Fourteenth Amendment proscription against the denial of equal protection, the Clause was not intended to prohibit all discrimination absolutely under all conditions, and that Congress would have more authority to police and eliminate racial discrimination, the original focus of the Amendment, than any claim of age discrimination involved in the Act lowering the voting age in all elections.

CITY OF ROME v. UNITED STATES
446 U.S. 156 (1980)

Mr. Justice MARSHALL delivered the opinion of the Court.

At issue in this case is the constitutionality of the Voting Rights Act of 1965 and its applicability to electoral changes and annexations made by the city of Rome, Ga.

I

This is a declaratory judgment action brought by appellant city of Rome, a municipality in northwestern Georgia, under the Voting Rights Act of 1965, 79 Stat. 437, as amended, 42 U. S. C. § 1973 *et seq.* In 1970 the city had a population of 30,759, the racial composition of which was 76.6% white and 23.4% Negro. The voting-age population in 1970 was 79.4% white and 20.6% Negro.

The governmental structure of the city is established by a charter enacted in 1918 by the General Assembly of Georgia. Before the amendments at issue in this case, Rome's city charter provided for a nine-member City Commission and a five-member Board of Education to be elected concurrently on an at-large basis by a plurality of the vote. The city was divided into nine wards, with one city commissioner from each ward to be chosen in the citywide election. There was no residency requirement for Board of Education candidates.

In 1966, the General Assembly of Georgia passed several laws of local application that extensively amended the electoral provisions of the city's charter. These enactments altered the Rome electoral scheme in the following ways:

(1) the number of wards was reduced from nine to three;

(2) each of the nine commissioners would henceforth be elected at-large to one of three numbered posts established within each ward;

(3) each commissioner would be elected by majority rather than plurality vote, and if no candidate for a particular position received a majority, a runoff election would be held between the two candidates who had received the largest number of votes;

(4) the terms of the three commissioners from each ward would be staggered;

(5) the Board of Education was expanded from five to six members;

(6) each Board member would be elected at large, by majority vote, for one of two numbered posts created in each of the three wards, with runoff procedures identical to those applicable to City Commission elections;

(7) Board members would be required to reside in the wards from which they were elected;

(8) the terms of the two members from each ward would be staggered.

Section 5 of the Voting Rights Act of 1965 requires preclearance by the Attorney General or the United States District Court for the District of Columbia of any change in a "standard, practice, or procedure with respect to voting," 42 U. S. C. § 1973c, made after November 1, 1964, by jurisdictions that fall within the coverage formula set forth in § 4 (b) of the Act, 42 U. S. C. § 1973b (b). In 1965, the Attorney General designated Georgia a covered jurisdiction under the Act, 30 Fed. Reg. 9897, and the municipalities of that State must therefore comply with the preclearance procedure, *United States* v. *Board of Commissioners of Sheffield, Ala.,* 435 U. S. 110 (1978).

It is not disputed that the 1966 changes in Rome's electoral system were within the purview of the Act. *E. g., Allen* v. *State Board of Elections,* 393 U. S. 544 (1969). Nonetheless, the city failed to seek preclearance for them. In addition, the city did not seek preclearance for 60 annexations made between November 1, 1964, and February 10, 1975, even though required to do so because an annexation constitutes a change in a "standard, practice, or procedure with respect to voting" under the Act, *Perkins* v. *Matthews,* 400 U. S. 379 (1971).

In June 1974, the city did submit one annexation to the Attorney General for preclearance. The Attorney General discovered that other annexations had occurred, and, in response to his inquiries, the city submitted all the annexations and the 1966 electoral changes for preclearance. The Attorney General declined to preclear the provisions for majority vote, numbered posts, and staggered terms for City Commission and Board of Education elections, as well as the residency requirement for Board elections. He concluded that in a city such as Rome, in which the population is predominately white and racial bloc voting has been common, these electoral changes would deprive Negro voters of the opportunity to elect a candidate of their choice. The Attorney General also refused to preclear 13 of the 60 annexations in question. He found that the disapproved annexations either contained predominately white populations of significant size or were near predominately white areas and were zoned for residential subdivision development. Considering these factors in light of Rome's at-large electoral scheme and history of racial bloc voting, he determined that the city had not carried its burden of proving that the annexations would not dilute the Negro vote.

In response to the city's motion for reconsideration, the Attorney General agreed to clear the 13 annexations for School Board elections. He reasoned that his disapproval of the 1966 voting changes had resurrected the pre-existing electoral scheme and that the revivified scheme passed muster under the Act. At the same time, he refused to clear the annexations for City Commission elections because, in his view, the residency requirement for City Commission contained in the pre-existing electoral procedures could have a discriminatory effect.

The city and two of its officials then filed this action, seeking relief from the Act based on a variety of claims. A three-judge court, convened pursuant to 42 U. S. C. §§ 1973b (a) and 1973c, rejected the city's arguments and granted summary judgment for the defendants. 472 F. Supp. 221 (DC 1979). We noted probable jurisdiction, 443 U. S. 914 (1979), and now affirm.

III

The appellants raise five issues of law in support of their contention that the Act may not properly be applied to the electoral changes and annexations disapproved by the Attorney General.

A

The District Court found that the disapproved electoral changes and annexations had not been made for any discriminatory purpose, but did have a discriminatory effect. The appellants argue that § 5 of the Act may not be read as prohibiting voting practices that have only a discriminatory effect. The appellants do not dispute that the plain language of § 5 commands that the Attorney General may clear a practice only if it "does not have the purpose *and* will not have the effect of denying or abridging the right to vote on account of race or color." 42 U. S. C. § 1973c (emphasis added). By describing the elements of discriminatory purpose and effect in the conjunctive, Congress plainly intended that a voting practice not be precleared unless *both* discriminatory purpose and effect are absent. Our decisions have consistently interpreted § 5 in this fashion. *Beer* v. *United States,* 425 U. S. 130, 141 (1976); *City of Richmond* v. *United States,* 422 U. S. 358, 372 (1975); *Georgia* v. *United States, supra,* at 538; *Perkins* v. *Matthews,* 400 U. S. 379, 387, 388 (1971). Furthermore, Congress recognized that the Act prohibited both discriminatory purpose and effect when, in 1975, it extended the Act for another seven years. S. Rep.

No. 94-295, pp. 15-16 (1975) (hereinafter S. Rep.); H. R. Rep. No. 94-196, pp. 8-9 (1975) (hereinafter H. R. Rep.).

The appellants urge that we abandon this settled interpretation because in their view § 5, to the extent that it prohibits voting changes that have only a discriminatory effect, is unconstitutional. Because the statutory meaning and congressional intent are plain, however, we are required to reject the appellants' suggestion that we engage in a saving construction and avoid the constitutional issues they raise. See, *e. g., NLRB* v. *Catholic Bishop of Chicago,* 440 U. S. 490, 499-501 (1979); *id.,* at 508-511 (Brennan, J., dissenting). Instead, we now turn to their constitutional contentions.

B

Congress passed the Act under the authority accorded it by the Fifteenth Amendment. The appellants contend that the Act is unconstitutional because it exceeds Congress' power to enforce that Amendment. They claim that § 1 of the Amendment prohibits only purposeful racial discrimination in voting, and that in enforcing that provision pursuant to § 2, Congress may not prohibit voting practices lacking discriminatory intent even if they are discriminatory in effect. We hold that, even if § 1 of the Amendment prohibits only purposeful discrimination, the prior decisions of this Court foreclose any argument that Congress may not, pursuant to § 2, outlaw voting practices that are discriminatory in effect.

The appellants are asking us to do nothing less than overrule our decision in *South Carolina* v. *Katzenbach,* 383 U. S. 301 (1966), in which we upheld the constitutionality of the Act. The Court in that case observed that, after making an extensive investigation, Congress had determined that its earlier attempts to remedy the "insidious and pervasive evil" of racial discrimination in voting had failed because of "unremitting and ingenious defiance of the Constitution" in some parts of this country. *Id.,* at 309. Case-by-case adjudication had proved too ponderous a method to remedy voting discrimination, and, when it had produced favorable results, affected jurisdictions often "merely switched to discriminatory devices not covered by the federal decrees." *Id.,* at 314. In response to its determination that "sterner and more elaborate measures" were necessary, *id.,* at 309, Congress adopted the Act, a "complex scheme of stringent remedies aimed at areas where voting discrimination has been most flagrant," *id.,* at 315.

The Court then turned to the question whether the Fifteenth Amendment empowered Congress to impose the rigors of the Act upon the covered jurisdictions. The Court examined the interplay between the judicial remedy created by § 1 of the Amendment and the legislative authority conferred by § 2:

"By adding this authorization [in § 2], the Framers indicated that Congress was to be chiefly responsible for implementing the rights created in § 1. 'It is the power of Congress which has been enlarged. Congress is authorized to *enforce* the prohibitions by appropriate legislation. Some legislation is contemplated to make the [Civil War] amendments fully effective.' *Ex parte Virginia,* 100 U. S. 339, 345. Accordingly, in addition to the courts, Congress has full remedial powers to effectuate the constitutional prohibition against racial discrimination in voting." 383 U. S., at 325-326 (emphasis in original).

Congress' authority under § 2 of the Fifteenth Amendment, we held, was no less broad than its authority under the Necessary and Proper Clause, see *McCulloch* v. *Maryland,* 4 Wheat. 316, 421 (1819). This authority, as applied by longstanding precedent to congressional enforcement of the Civil War Amendments, is defined in these terms:

"'Whatever legislation is appropriate, that is, adapted to carry out the objects the [Civil War] amendments have in view, whatever tends to enforce submission to the prohibitions they contain, and to secure to all persons the enjoyment of perfect equality of civil rights and the equal protection of the laws against State denial or invasion, if not prohibited, is brought within the domain of congressional power.' *Ex parte Virginia,* 100 U. S. [339,] 345-346." *South Carolina* v. *Katzenbach, supra,* at 327.

Applying this standard, the Court held that the coverage formula of § 4 (b), the ban on the use of literacy tests and related devices, the requirement that new voting rules must be precleared and must lack both discriminatory purpose and effect, and the use of federal examiners were all appropriate methods for Congress to use to enforce the Fifteenth Amendment. 383 U. S., at 329-337.

The Court's treatment in *South Carolina* v. *Katzenbach* of the Act's ban on literacy tests demonstrates that, under the Fifteenth Amendment, Congress may prohibit voting practices that have only a discriminatory effect. The Court had earlier held in *Lassiter* v. *Northampton County Board of Elections,* 360 U. S. 45 (1959), that the use of a literacy test that was fair on its face and was not employed in a discriminatory fashion did not violate § 1 of the Fifteenth Amendment. In upholding the Act's *per se* ban on such tests in *South Carolina* v. *Katzenbach,* the Court found no reason to overrule *Lassiter.* Instead, the Court recognized that the prohibition was an appropriate method of enforcing the Fifteenth Amendment because for many years most of the covered jurisdictions had imposed such tests to effect voting discrimination and the continued use of even nondiscriminatory, fairly administered literacy tests would "freeze the effect" of past discrimination by allowing white illiterates to remain on the voting rolls while excluding illiterate Negroes. *South Carolina* v. *Katzenbach, supra,* at 334. This holding makes clear that Congress may, under the authority of § 2 of the Fifteenth Amendment, prohibit state action that, though in itself not violative of § 1, perpetuates the effects of past discrimination.

Other decisions of this Court also recognize Congress' broad power to enforce the Civil War Amendments. In *Katzenbach* v. *Morgan,* 384 U. S. 641 (1966), the Court held that legislation enacted under authority of § 5 of the Fourteenth Amendment would be upheld so long as the Court could find that the enactment "'is plainly adapted to [the] end'" of enforcing the Equal Protection Clause and "is not prohibited by but is consistent with 'the letter and spirit of the constitution,'" regardless of whether the practices outlawed by Congress in themselves violated the Equal Protection Clause. 384 U. S., at 651 (quoting *McCulloch* v. *Maryland, supra,* at 421). The Court stated that, "[c]orrectly viewed, § 5 is a positive grant of legislative power authorizing Congress to exercise its discretion in determining whether and what legislation is needed to secure the guarantees of the Fourteenth Amendment." 384 U. S., at 651. Four years later, in *Oregon* v. *Mitchell,* 400 U. S. 112 (1970), the Court unanimously upheld a provision of the Voting Rights Act Amendments of 1970, Pub. L. 91-285, 84 Stat. 314, imposing a 5-year nationwide ban on literacy tests and similar requirements for registering to vote in state and federal elections. The Court concluded that Congress could rationally have determined that these provisions were appropriate methods of attacking the perpetuation of earlier, purposeful racial discrimination, regardless of whether the practices they prohibited were discriminatory only in effect. See 400 U. S., at 132-133 (opinion of Black, J.); *id.,* at 144-147 (opinion of Douglas, J.); *id.,* at 216-217 (opinion of Harlan, J.); *id.,* at 231-236 (opinion of Brennan, White, and Marshall, JJ.); *id.,* at 282-284 (opinion of Stewart, J., joined by Burger, C. J., and Blackmun, J.).

It is clear, then, that under § 2 of the Fifteenth Amendment Congress may prohibit practices that in and of themselves do not violate § 1 of the Amendment, so long as the prohibitions attacking racial discrimination in voting are "appropriate," as that term is defined in *McCulloch* v. *Maryland* and *Ex parte Virginia,* 100 U. S. 339 (1880). In the present case, we hold that the Act's ban on electoral changes that are discriminatory in effect is an appropriate method of promoting the purposes of the Fifteenth Amendment, even if it is assumed that § 1 of the Amendment prohibits only intentional discrimination in voting. Congress could rationally have concluded that, because electoral changes by jurisdictions with a demonstrable history of intentional racial discrimination in voting create the risk of purposeful discrimination, it was proper to prohibit changes that have a discriminatory impact. See *South Carolina* v. *Katzenbach,* 383 U. S., at 335; *Oregon* v. *Mitchell, supra,* at 216 (opinion of Harlan, J.). We find no reason, then, to disturb Congress' considered judgment that banning electoral changes that have a discriminatory impact is an effective method of preventing States from "'undo[ing] or defeat[ing] the rights recently won' by Negroes." *Beer* v. *United States,* 425 U. S., at 140 (quoting H. R. Rep. No. 91-397, p. 8 (1969)).

CITY OF BOERNE v. FLORES, ARCHBISHOP OF SAN ANTONIO
521 U.S. 507 (1997)

KENNEDY, J., delivered the opinion of the Court, in which REHNQUIST, C.J., and STEVENS, THOMAS, and GINSBURG, JJ., joined, and in which SCALIA, J., joined as to all but Part III-A-1. STEVENS, J., filed a concurring opinion, *post,* p. 536. SCALIA, J., filed an opinion concurring in part, in which STEVENS, J., joined, *post,* p. 537. O'CONNOR, J., filed a dissenting opinion, in which BREYER, J., joined except as to the first paragraph of Part I, *post,* p. 544. SOUTER, J., *post,* p. 565, and BREYER, J., *post,* p. 566, filed dissenting opinions.

A decision by local zoning authorities to deny a church a building permit was challenged under the Religious Freedom Restoration Act of 1993 (RFRA or Act), 107 Stat. 1488, 42 U. S. C. § 2000bb *et seq.* The case calls into question the authority of Congress to enact RFRA. We conclude the statute exceeds Congress' power.

II

Congress enacted RFRA in direct response to the Court's decision in *Employment Div., Dept. of Human Resources of Ore.* v. *Smith,* 494 U. S. 872 (1990). There we considered a Free Exercise Clause claim brought by members of the Native American Church who were denied unemployment benefits when they lost their jobs because they had used peyote. Their practice was to ingest peyote for sacramental purposes, and they challenged an Oregon statute of general applicability which made use of the drug criminal. In evaluating the claim, we declined to apply the balancing test set forth in *Sherbert* v. *Verner,* 374 U. S. 398 (1963), under which we would have asked whether Oregon's prohibition substantially burdened a religious practice and, if it did, whether the burden was justified by a compelling government interest. We stated:

"[G]overnment's ability to enforce generally applicable prohibitions of socially harmful conduct . . . cannot depend on measuring the effects of a governmental action on a religious objector's spiritual development. To make an individual's obligation to obey such a law contingent upon the law's coincidence with his religious beliefs, except where the State's interest is 'compelling'. . . contradicts both constitutional tradition and common sense." 494 U. S., at 885 (internal quotation marks and citations omitted).

The application of the *Sherbert* test, the *Smith* decision explained, would have produced an anomaly in the law, a constitutional right to ignore neutral laws of general applicability. The anomaly would have been accentuated, the Court reasoned, by the difficulty of determining whether a particular practice was central to an individual's religion. We explained, moreover, that it "is not within the judicial ken to question the centrality of particular beliefs or practices to a faith, or the validity of particular litigants' interpretations of those creeds." 494 U. S., at 887 (internal quotation marks and citation omitted).

The only instances where a neutral, generally applicable law had failed to pass constitutional muster, the *Smith* Court noted, were cases in which other constitutional protections were at stake. *Id.*, at 881-882. In *Wisconsin* v. *Yoder*, 406 U. S. 205 (1972), for example, we invalidated Wisconsin's mandatory school-attendance law as applied to Amish parents who refused on religious grounds to send their children to school. That case implicated not only the right to the free exercise of religion but also the right of parents to control their children's education.

The *Smith* decision acknowledged the Court had employed the *Sherbert* test in considering free exercise challenges to state unemployment compensation rules on three occasions where the balance had tipped in favor of the individual. See *Sherbert, supra; Thomas* v. *Review Bd. of Indiana Employment Security Div.*, 450 U. S. 707 (1981); *Hobbie* v. *Unemployment Appeals Comm'n of Fla.*, 480 U. S. 136 (1987). Those cases, the Court explained, stand for "the proposition that where the State has in place a system of individual exemptions, it may not refuse to extend that system to cases of religious hardship without compelling reason." 494 U. S., at 884 (internal quotation marks omitted). By contrast, where a general prohibition, such as Oregon's, is at issue, "the sounder approach, and the approach in accord with the vast majority of our precedents, is to hold the test inapplicable to [free exercise] challenges." *Id.*, at 885. *Smith* held that neutral, generally applicable laws may be applied to religious practices even when not supported by a compelling governmental interest.

Four Members of the Court disagreed. They argued the law placed a substantial burden on the Native American Church members so that it could be upheld only if the law served a compelling state interest and was narrowly tailored to achieve that end. *Id.*, at 894. Justice O'Connor concluded Oregon had satisfied the test, while Justice Blackmun, joined by Justice Brennan and Justice Marshall, could see no compelling interest justifying the law's application to the members.

These points of constitutional interpretation were debated by Members of Congress in hearings and floor debates. Many criticized the Court's reasoning, and this disagreement resulted in the passage of RFRA. Congress announced:

"(1) [T]he framers of the Constitution, recognizing free exercise of religion as an unalienable right, secured its protection in the First Amendment to the Constitution;

"(2) laws 'neutral' toward religion may burden religious exercise as surely as laws intended to interfere with religious exercise;

"(3) governments should not substantially burden religious exercise without compelling justification;

"(4) in Employment Division v. Smith, 494 U. S. 872 (1990), the Supreme Court virtually eliminated the requirement that the government justify burdens on religious exercise imposed by laws neutral toward religion; and

"(5) the compelling interest test as set forth in prior Federal court rulings is a workable test for striking sensible balances between religious liberty and competing prior governmental interests." 42 U. S. C. § 2000bb(a).

The Act's stated purposes are:

"(1) to restore the compelling interest test as set forth in Sherbert v. Verner, 374 U. S. 398 (1963) and Wisconsin v. Yoder, 406 U. S. 205 (1972) and to guarantee its application in all cases where free exercise of religion is substantially burdened; and

"(2) to provide a claim or defense to persons whose religious exercise is substantially burdened by government." § 2000bb(b).

RFRA prohibits "[g]overnment" from "substantially burden[ing]" a person's exercise of religion even if the burden results from a rule of general applicability unless the government can demonstrate the burden "(1) is in furtherance of a compelling governmental interest; and (2) is the least restrictive means of furthering that compelling governmental interest." § 2000bb-1. The Act's mandate applies to any "branch, department, agency, instrumentality, and official (or other person acting under color of law) of the United States," as well as to any "State, or . . . subdivision of a State." § 2000bb-2(1). The Act's universal coverage is confirmed in § 2000bb-3(a), under which RFRA "applies to all Federal and State law, and the implementation of that law, whether statutory or otherwise, and whether adopted before or after [RFRA's enactment]." In accordance with RFRA's usage of the term, we shall use "state law" to include local and municipal ordinances.

III

A

Congress relied on its Fourteenth Amendment enforcement power in enacting the most far-reaching and substantial of RFRA's provisions, those which impose its requirements on the States. See Religious Freedom Restoration Act of 1993. The Fourteenth Amendment provides, in relevant part:

"Section 1. . . . No State shall make or enforce any law which shall abridge the privileges or immunities of citizens of the United States; nor shall any State deprive any person of life, liberty, or property, without due process of law; nor deny to any person within its jurisdiction the equal protection of the laws. . . .

"Section 5. The Congress shall have power to enforce, by appropriate legislation, the provisions of this article."

The parties disagree over whether RFRA is a proper exercise of Congress' § 5 power "to enforce" by "appropriate legislation" the constitutional guarantee that no State shall deprive any person of "life, liberty, or property, without due process of law," nor deny any person "equal protection of the laws."

In defense of the Act, respondent the Archbishop contends, with support from the United States, that RFRA is permissible enforcement legislation. Congress, it is said, is only protecting by legislation one of the liberties guaranteed by the Fourteenth Amendment's Due Process Clause, the free exercise of religion, beyond what is necessary under *Smith*. It is said the congressional decision to dispense with proof of deliberate or overt discrimination and instead concentrate on a law's effects accords with the settled understanding that § 5 includes the power to enact legislation designed to prevent, as well as remedy, constitutional violations. It is further contended that Congress' § 5 power is not limited to remedial or preventive legislation.

CHAPTER 6. CONSTITUTIONALLY PROTECTED RIGHTS – EQUAL PROTECTION | 1417

In *Ex parte Virginia,* 100 U. S. 339, 345-346 (1880), we explained the scope of Congress' § 5 power in the following broad terms:

"Whatever legislation is appropriate, that is, adapted to carry out the objects the amendments have in view, whatever tends to enforce submission to the prohibitions they contain, and to secure to all persons the enjoyment of perfect equality of civil rights and the equal protection of the laws against State denial or invasion, if not prohibited, is brought within the domain of congressional power."

Legislation which deters or remedies constitutional violations can fall within the sweep of Congress' enforcement power even if in the process it prohibits conduct which is not itself unconstitutional and intrudes into "legislative spheres of autonomy previously reserved to the States." *Fitzpatrick* v. *Bitzer,* 427 U. S. 445, 455 (1976). For example, the Court upheld a suspension of literacy tests and similar voting requirements under Congress' parallel power to enforce the provisions of the Fifteenth Amendment, see U. S. Const., Amdt. 15, § 2, as a measure to combat racial discrimination in voting, *South Carolina* v. *Katzenbach,* 383 U. S. 301, 308 (1966), despite the facial constitutionality of the tests under *Lassiter* v. *Northampton County Bd. of Elections,* 360 U. S. 45 (1959).

It is also true, however, that "[a]s broad as the congressional enforcement power is, it is not unlimited." *Oregon* v. *Mitchell, supra,* at 128 (opinion of Black, J.). In assessing the breadth of § 5's enforcement power, we begin with its text. Congress has been given the power "to enforce" the "provisions of this article."

Congress' power under § 5, however, extends only to "enforc[ing]" the provisions of the Fourteenth Amendment. The Court has described this power as "remedial," *South Carolina* v. *Katzenbach, supra,* at 326. The design of the Amendment and the text of § 5 are inconsistent with the suggestion that Congress has the power to decree the substance of the Fourteenth Amendment's restrictions on the States. Legislation which alters the meaning of the Free Exercise Clause cannot be said to be enforcing the Clause. Congress does not enforce a constitutional right by changing what the right is. It has been given the power "to enforce," not the power to determine what constitutes a constitutional violation. Were it not so, what Congress would be enforcing would no longer be, in any meaningful sense, the "provisions of [the Fourteenth Amendment]."

While the line between measures that remedy or prevent unconstitutional actions and measures that make a substantive change in the governing law is not easy to discern, and Congress must have wide latitude in determining where it lies, the distinction exists and must be observed. There must be a congruence and proportionality between the injury to be prevented or remedied and the means adopted to that end. Lacking such a connection, legislation may become substantive in operation and effect. History and our case law support drawing the distinction, one apparent from the text of the Amendment.

2

The remedial and preventive nature of Congress' enforcement power, and the limitation inherent in the power, were confirmed in our earliest cases on the Fourteenth Amendment. In the *Civil Rights Cases,* 109 U. S. 3 (1883), the Court invalidated sections of the Civil Rights Act of 1875 which prescribed criminal penalties for denying to any person "the full enjoyment of" public accommodations and conveyances, on the grounds that it exceeded Congress' power by seeking to regulate private conduct. The Enforcement Clause, the Court said, did not authorize Congress to pass "general legislation upon the rights of the citizen, but corrective legislation, that is, such as may be necessary and proper for counteracting such laws as the States may adopt or enforce, and which, by the amendment, they are prohibited from making or enforcing. . . ." *Id.,* at 13-14. The power to "legislate generally upon" life, liberty, and property, as opposed to the "power to provide modes of redress" against offensive state action, was "repugnant" to the Constitution. *Id.,* at 15.

Recent cases have continued to revolve around the question whether § 5 legislation can be considered remedial. In *South Carolina* v. *Katzenbach, supra,* we emphasized that "[t]he constitutional propriety of [legislation adopted under the Enforcement Clause] must be judged with reference to the historical experience . . . it reflects." 383 U. S., at 308. There we upheld various provisions of the Voting Rights Act of 1965, finding them to be "remedies aimed at areas where voting discrimination has been most flagrant," *id.,* at 315, and necessary to "banish the blight of racial discrimination in voting, which has infected the electoral process in parts of our country for nearly a century," *id.,* at 308. We noted evidence in the record reflecting the subsisting and pervasive discriminatory — and therefore unconstitutional — use of literacy tests. *Id.,* at 333-334. The Act's new remedies, which used the administrative resources of the Federal Government, included the suspension of both literacy tests and, pending federal review, all new voting regulations in covered jurisdictions, as well as the assignment of federal examiners to list qualified applicants enabling those listed to vote. The new, unprecedented remedies were deemed necessary given the ineffectiveness of the existing voting rights laws, see *id.,* at 313-315, and the slow, costly character of case-by-case litigation, *id.,* at 328.

3

Any suggestion that Congress has a substantive, nonremedial power under the Fourteenth Amendment is not supported by our case law. In *Oregon* v. *Mitchell,* a majority of the Court concluded Congress had exceeded its enforcement powers by enacting legislation lowering the minimum age of voters from 21 to 18 in state and local elections. The five Members of the Court who reached this conclusion explained that the legislation intruded into an area reserved by the Constitution to the States. See 400 U. S., at 125 (concluding that the legislation was unconstitutional because the Constitution "reserves to the States the power to set voter qualifications in state and local elections") (opinion of Black, J.); *id.,* at 154 (explaining that the "Fourteenth Amendment was never intended to restrict the authority of the States to allocate their political power as they see fit") (opinion of Harlan, J.); *id.,* at 294 (concluding that States, not Congress, have the power "to establish a qualification for voting based on age") (opinion of Stewart, J., joined by Burger, C. J., and Blackmun, J.). Four of these five were explicit in rejecting the position that § 5 endowed Congress with the power to establish the meaning of constitutional provisions. See *id.,* at 209 (opinion of Harlan, J.); *id.,* at 296 (opinion of Stewart, J.). Justice Black's rejection of this position might be inferred from his disagreement with Congress' interpretation of the Equal Protection Clause. See *id.,* at 125.

There is language in our opinion in *Katzenbach* v. *Morgan,* 384 U. S. 641 (1966), which could be interpreted as acknowledging a power in Congress to enact legislation that expands the rights contained in § 1 of the Fourteenth Amendment. This is not a necessary interpretation, however, or even the best one. In *Morgan,* the Court considered the constitutionality of § 4(e) of the Voting Rights Act of 1965, which provided that no person who had successfully completed the sixth primary grade in a public school in, or a private school accredited by, the Commonwealth of Puerto Rico in which the language of instruction was other than English could be denied the right to vote because of an inability to read or write English. New York's Constitution, on the other hand, required voters to be able to read and write English. The Court provided two related rationales for its conclusion that § 4(e) could "be viewed as a measure to secure for the Puerto Rican community residing in New York nondiscriminatory treatment by government." *Id.*, at 652. Under the first rationale, Congress could prohibit New York from denying the right to vote to large segments of its Puerto Rican community, in order to give Puerto Ricans "enhanced political power" that would be "helpful in gaining nondiscriminatory treatment in public services for the entire Puerto Rican community." *Ibid.* Section 4(e) thus could be justified as a remedial measure to deal with "discrimination in governmental services." *Id.*, at 653. The second rationale, an alternative holding, did not address discrimination in the provision of public services but "discrimination in establishing voter qualifications." *Id.*, at 654. The Court perceived a factual basis on which Congress could have concluded that New York's literacy requirement "constituted an invidious discrimination in violation of the Equal Protection Clause." *Id.*, at 656. Both rationales for upholding § 4(e) rested on unconstitutional discrimination by New York and Congress' reasonable attempt to combat it. As Justice Stewart explained in *Oregon* v. *Mitchell, supra,* at 296, interpreting *Morgan* to give Congress the power to interpret the Constitution "would require an enormous extension of that decision's rationale."

If Congress could define its own powers by altering the Fourteenth Amendment's meaning, no longer would the Constitution be "superior paramount law, unchangeable by ordinary means." It would be "on a level with ordinary legislative acts, and, like other acts, . . .alterable when the legislature shall please to alter it." *Marbury* v. *Madison,* 1 Cranch, at 177. Under this approach, it is difficult to conceive of a principle that would limit congressional power. Shifting legislative majorities could change the Constitution and effectively circumvent the difficult and detailed amendment process contained in Article V.

We now turn to consider whether RFRA can be considered enforcement legislation under § 5 of the Fourteenth Amendment.

B

Respondent contends that RFRA is a proper exercise of Congress' remedial or preventive power. The Act, it is said, is a reasonable means of protecting the free exercise of religion as defined by *Smith*. It prevents and remedies laws which are enacted with the unconstitutional object of targeting religious beliefs and practices. See *Church of Lukumi Babalu Aye, Inc.* v. *Hialeah,* 508 U. S. 520, 533 (1993) ("[A] law targeting religious beliefs as such is never permissible"). To avoid the difficulty of proving such violations, it is said, Congress can simply invalidate any law which imposes a substantial burden on a religious practice unless it is justified by a compelling interest and is the least restrictive means of accomplishing that interest. If Congress can prohibit laws with discriminatory effects in order to prevent racial discrimination in violation of the Equal Protection Clause, see *Fullilove* v. *Klutznick,* 448 U. S. 448, 477 (1980) (plurality opinion); *City of Rome* , 446 U. S., at 177, then it can do the same, respondent argues, to promote religious liberty.

While preventive rules are sometimes appropriate remedial measures, there must be a congruence between the means used and the ends to be achieved. The appropriateness of remedial measures must be considered in light of the evil presented. See *South Carolina* v. *Katzenbach,* 383 U. S., at 308. Strong measures appropriate to address one harm may be an unwarranted response to another, lesser one. *Id.,* at 334.

A comparison between RFRA and the Voting Rights Act is instructive. In contrast to the record which confronted Congress and the Judiciary in the voting rights cases, RFRA's legislative record lacks examples of modern instances of generally applicable laws passed because of religious bigotry. The history of persecution in this country detailed in the hearings mentions no episodes occurring in the past 40 years.

Regardless of the state of the legislative record, RFRA cannot be considered remedial, preventive legislation, if those terms are to have any meaning. RFRA is so out of proportion to a supposed remedial or preventive object that it cannot be understood as responsive to, or designed to prevent, unconstitutional behavior. It appears, instead, to attempt a substantive change in constitutional protections. Preventive measures prohibiting certain types of laws may be appropriate when there is reason to believe that many of the laws affected by the congressional enactment have a significant likelihood of being unconstitutional. See *City of Rome,* 446 U. S., at 177 (since "jurisdictions with a demonstrable history of intentional racial discrimination . . . create the risk of purposeful discrimination," Congress could "prohibit changes that have a discriminatory impact" in those jurisdictions). Remedial legislation under § 5 "should be adapted to the mischief and wrong which the [Fourteenth] [A]mendment was intended to provide against." *Civil Rights Cases,* 109 U. S., at 13.

RFRA is not so confined. Sweeping coverage ensures its intrusion at every level of government, displacing laws and prohibiting official actions of almost every description and regardless of subject matter. RFRA's restrictions apply to every agency and official of the Federal, State, and local Governments. 42 U. S. C. § 2000bb-2(1). RFRA applies to all federal and state law, statutory or otherwise, whether adopted before or after its enactment. § 2000bb-3(a). RFRA has no termination date or termination mechanism. Any law is subject to challenge at any time by any individual who alleges a substantial burden on his or her free exercise of religion.

The reach and scope of RFRA distinguish it from other measures passed under Congress' enforcement power, even in the area of voting rights. In *South Carolina* v. *Katzenbach,* the challenged provisions were confined to those regions of the country where voting discrimination had been most flagrant, see 383 U. S., at 315, and affected a discrete class of state laws, *i. e.,* state voting laws. Furthermore, to ensure that the reach of the Voting Rights Act was limited to those cases in which constitutional violations were most likely (in order to reduce the possibility of overbreadth), the coverage under the Act would terminate "at the behest of States and political subdivisions in which the danger of substantial voting discrimination has not materialized during the preceding five years." *Id.,* at 331. The provisions restricting and banning literacy tests, upheld in *Katzenbach* v. *Morgan,* 384 U. S. 641 (1966), and *Oregon* v. *Mitchell, supra,* attacked a particular type of voting qualification, one with a long history as a "notorious means to deny and abridge voting rights on racial grounds." *South Carolina* v. *Katzenbach,* 383 U. S., at 355 (Black, J., concurring and dissenting). In *City of Rome, supra,* the Court rejected a challenge to the constitutionality of a Voting Rights Act provision which required certain jurisdictions to submit changes in electoral practices to the Department of Justice for preimplementation review. The requirement was placed only on jurisdictions with a history of intentional racial discrimination in voting. *Id.,* at 177. Like the provisions at issue in *South Carolina* v. *Katzenbach,* this provision permitted a covered jurisdiction to avoid preclearance requirements under certain conditions and, moreover, lapsed in seven years. This is not to say, of course, that § 5 legislation requires termination dates, geographic restrictions, or egregious predicates. Where, however, a congressional enactment pervasively prohibits constitutional state action in an effort to remedy or to prevent unconstitutional state action, limitations of this kind tend to ensure Congress' means are proportionate to ends legitimate under § 5.

The stringent test RFRA demands of state laws reflects a lack of proportionality or congruence between the means adopted and the legitimate end to be achieved. If an objector can show a substantial burden on his free exercise, the State must demonstrate a compelling governmental interest and show that the law is the least restrictive means of furthering its interest. Claims that a law substantially burdens someone's exercise of religion will often be difficult to contest. See *Smith* , 494 U. S., at 887 ("What principle of law or logic can be brought to bear to contradict a believer's assertion that a particular act is 'central' to his personal faith?"); *id.,* at 907 ("The distinction between questions of centrality and questions of sincerity and burden is admittedly fine . . .") (O'Connor, J., concurring in judgment). Requiring a State to demonstrate a compelling interest and show that it has adopted the least restrictive means of achieving that interest is the most demanding test known to constitutional law. If "'compelling interest' really means what it says . . . , many laws will not meet the test. . . . [The test] would open the prospect of constitutionally required religious exemptions from civic obligations of almost every conceivable kind." *Id.,* at 888. Laws valid under *Smith* would fall under RFRA without regard to whether they had the object of stifling or punishing free exercise. We make these observations not to reargue the position of the majority in *Smith* but to illustrate the substantive alteration of its holding attempted by RFRA. Even assuming RFRA would be interpreted in effect to mandate some lesser test, say, one equivalent to intermediate scrutiny, the statute nevertheless would require searching judicial scrutiny of state law with the attendant likelihood of invalidation. This is a considerable congressional intrusion into the States' traditional prerogatives and general authority to regulate for the health and welfare of their citizens.

The substantial costs RFRA exacts, both in practical terms of imposing a heavy litigation burden on the States and in terms of curtailing their traditional general regulatory power, far exceed any pattern or practice of unconstitutional conduct under the Free Exercise Clause as interpreted in *Smith.* Simply put, RFRA is not designed to identify and counteract state laws likely to be unconstitutional because of their treatment of religion. In most cases, the state laws to which RFRA applies are not ones which will have been motivated by religious bigotry. . . .When the exercise of religion has been burdened in an incidental way by a law of general application, it does not follow that the persons affected have been burdened any more than other citizens, let alone burdened because of their religious beliefs. In addition, the Act imposes in every case a least restrictive means requirement — a requirement that was not used in the pre-*Smith* jurisprudence RFRA purported to codify — which also indicates that the legislation is broader than is appropriate if the goal is to prevent and remedy constitutional violations.

When Congress acts within its sphere of power and responsibilities, it has not just the right but the duty to make its own informed judgment on the meaning and force of the Constitution. This has been clear from the early days of the Republic. In 1789, when a Member of the House of Representatives objected to a debate on the constitutionality of legislation based on the theory that "it would be officious" to consider the constitutionality of a measure that did not affect the House, James Madison explained that "it is incontrovertibly of as much importance to this branch of the Government as to any other, that the constitution should be preserved entire. It is our duty." 1 Annals of Congress 500 (1789). Were it otherwise, we would not afford Congress the presumption of validity its enactments now enjoy.

Our national experience teaches that the Constitution is preserved best when each part of the Government respects both the Constitution and the proper actions and determinations of the other branches. When the Court has interpreted the Constitution, it has acted within the province of the Judicial Branch, which embraces the duty to say what the law is. *Marbury* v. *Madison,* 1 Cranch, at 177. When the political branches of the Government act against the background of a judicial interpretation of the Constitution already issued, it must be understood that in later cases and controversies the Court will treat its precedents with the respect due them under settled principles, including *stare decisis,* and contrary expectations must be disappointed. RFRA was designed to control cases and controversies, such as the one before us; but as the provisions of the federal statute here invoked are beyond congressional authority, it is this Court's precedent, not RFRA, which must control. . . .

It is for Congress in the first instance to "determin[e] whether and what legislation is needed to secure the guarantees of the Fourteenth Amendment," and its conclusions are entitled to much deference. *Katzenbach* v. *Morgan,* 384 U. S., at 651. Congress' discretion is not unlimited, however, and the courts retain the power, as they have since *Marbury* v. *Madison,* to determine if Congress has exceeded its authority under the Constitution. Broad as the power of Congress is under the Enforcement Clause of the Fourteenth Amendment, RFRA contradicts vital principles necessary to maintain separation of powers and the federal balance. The judgment of the Court of Appeals sustaining the Act's constitutionality is reversed.

It is so ordered.

Comments on Boerne. Does Justice Kennedy lay out a clear "limiting principle" for how far Congress can go under the enforcement provisions of the Civil Rights amendments? Consider the reasons given by Congress for RFRA: "laws neutral toward religion may burden religious exercise as surely as laws intended to interfere with religious exercise." Considering that the Free Exercise Clause says "Congress shall make no law . . . prohibiting the free exercise thereof [of religion]" (applicable to the states via the incorporation doctrine), has Congress interpreted the constitutional provision or expanded it? Or has it simply interpreted it under the Religious Freedom Restoration Act?

Consider that Congress admits that it is barring any practices that cannot be justified under the strict scrutiny test — including those of general applicability. Its stated reason is that a case by case examination of possibly offensive laws would be fraught with difficulty, so it is within Congress's power to bar all burdensome laws whether specifically targeting religion or not.

Congress has essentially subjected government actions that affect (with or without intent) religion to strict scrutiny. How is this different from Congress barring for a period of years all literacy tests without determination of racist intent, apparently in contrast to the holding in *Lassiter?*

UNITED STATES v. MORRISON
529 U.S. 598 (2000)

[Earlier in the semester we discussed this case as it relates to the Commerce Clause and how the Court decided that Congress's attempt under the Violence Against Women Act to provide the victim here of a remedy in federal court under Congress's Commerce Power was unconstitutional. This portion of the opinion addresses an alternative argument that Congress's power comes from the enforcement provision of the Fourteenth Amendment as Congress is enforcing the equal protection clause by providing a civil remedy to women subjected to gender motivated violence.]

Because we conclude that the Commerce Clause does not provide Congress with authority to enact §13981, we address petitioners' alternative argument that the section's civil remedy should be upheld as an exercise of Congress' remedial power under §5 of the Fourteenth Amendment. As noted above, Congress expressly invoked the Fourteenth Amendment as a source of authority to enact §13981.

The principles governing an analysis of congressional legislation under §5 are well settled. Section 5 states that Congress may "'enforce,' by 'appropriate legislation' the constitutional guarantee that no State shall deprive any person of 'life, liberty or property, without due process of law,' nor deny any person 'equal protection of the laws.'" *City of Boerne* v. *Flores*, 521 U.S. 507, 517 (1997). Section 5 is "a positive grant of legislative power," *Katzenbach* v. *Morgan*, 384 U.S. 641, 651 (1966), that includes authority to "prohibit conduct which is not itself unconstitutional and [to] intrud[e] into 'legislative spheres of autonomy previously reserved to the States.'"

Petitioners' §5 argument is founded on an assertion that there is pervasive bias in various state justice systems against victims of gender-motivated violence. This assertion is supported by a voluminous congressional record. Specifically, Congress received evidence that many participants in state justice systems are perpetuating an array of erroneous stereotypes and assumptions. Congress concluded that these discriminatory stereotypes often result in insufficient investigation and prosecution of gender-motivated crime, inappropriate focus on the behavior and credibility of the victims of that crime, and unacceptably lenient punishments for those who are actually convicted of gender-motivated violence. Petitioners contend that this bias denies victims of gender-motivated violence the equal protection of the laws and that Congress therefore acted appropriately in enacting a private civil remedy against the perpetrators of gender-motivated violence to both remedy the States' bias and deter future instances of discrimination in the state courts.

As our cases have established, state-sponsored gender discrimination violates equal protection unless it "'serves "important governmental objectives and . . . the discriminatory means employed" are "substantially related to the achievement of those objectives." However, the language and purpose of the Fourteenth Amendment place certain limitations on the manner in which Congress may attack discriminatory conduct. These limitations are necessary to prevent the Fourteenth Amendment from obliterating the Framers' carefully crafted balance of power between the States and the National Government. Foremost among these limitations is the time-honored principle that the Fourteenth Amendment, by its very terms, prohibits only state action. "[T]he principle has become firmly embedded in our constitutional law that the action inhibited by the first section of the Fourteenth Amendment is only such action as may fairly be said to be that of the

States. That Amendment erects no shield against merely private conduct, however discriminatory or wrongful." *Shelley* v. *Kraemer*, 334 U.S. 1, 13, and n. 12 (1948).

Shortly after the Fourteenth Amendment was adopted, we decided two cases interpreting the Amendment's provisions, *United States* v. *Harris*, 106 U.S. 629 (1883), and the *Civil Rights Cases*, 109 U.S. 3 (1883). In *Harris*, the Court considered a challenge to §2 of the Civil Rights Act of 1871. That section sought to punish "private persons" for "conspiring to deprive any one of the equal protection of the laws enacted by the State." 106 U.S., at 639. We concluded that this law exceeded Congress' §5 power because the law was "directed exclusively against the action of private persons, without reference to the laws of the State, or their administration by her officers." *Id.*, at 640. In so doing, we reemphasized our statement from *Virginia* v. *Rives*, 100 U.S. 313, 318 (1880), that "'these provisions of the fourteenth amendment have reference to State action exclusively, and not to any action of private individuals.'" *Harris*, *supra*, at 639 (misquotation in *Harris*).

We reached a similar conclusion in the *Civil Rights Cases*. In those consolidated cases, we held that the public accommodation provisions of the Civil Rights Act of 1875, which applied to purely private conduct, were beyond the scope of the §5 enforcement power. 109 U.S., at 11 ("Individual invasion of individual rights is not the subject-matter of the [Fourteenth] [A]mendment").

The force of the doctrine of *stare decisis* behind these decisions stems not only from the length of time they have been on the books, but also from the insight attributable to the Members of the Court at that time. Every Member had been appointed by President Lincoln, Grant, Hayes, Garfield, or Arthur — and each of their judicial appointees obviously had intimate knowledge and familiarity with the events surrounding the adoption of the Fourteenth Amendment.

Petitioners contend that two more recent decisions have in effect overruled this longstanding limitation on Congress' §5 authority. They rely on *United States* v. *Guest*, 383 U.S. 745 (1966), for the proposition that the rule laid down in the *Civil Rights Cases* is no longer good law. In *Guest*, the Court reversed the construction of an indictment under 18 U.S.C. § 241 saying in the course of its opinion that "we deal here with issues of statutory construction, not with issues of constitutional power." 383 U.S., at 749. Three Members of the Court, in a separate opinion by Justice Brennan, expressed the view that the *Civil Rights Cases* were wrongly decided, and that Congress could under §5 prohibit actions by private individuals. 383 U.S., at 774 (opinion concurring in part and dissenting in part). Three other Members of the Court, who joined the opinion of the Court, joined a separate opinion by Justice Clark which in two or three sentences stated the conclusion that Congress could "punis[h] all conspiracies — with or without state action — that interfere with Fourteenth Amendment rights." *Id.*, at 762 (concurring opinion). Justice Harlan, in another separate opinion, commented with respect to the statement by these Justices:

"The action of three of the Justices who joined the Court's opinion in nonetheless cursorily pronouncing themselves on the far-reaching constitutional questions deliberately not reached in Part II seems to me, to say the very least, extraordinary." *Id.*, at 762, n. 1 (opinion concurring in part and dissenting in part).

Though these three Justices saw fit to opine on matters not before the Court in *Guest*, the Court had no occasion to revisit the *Civil Rights Cases* and *Harris*, having determined "the indictment [charging private individuals with conspiring to deprive blacks of equal access to state facilities] in fact contain[ed] an express allegation of state involvement." 383 U.S., at 756. The Court concluded that the implicit allegation of "active connivance by agents of the State" eliminated any need to decide "the threshold level that state action must attain in order to create rights under the Equal Protection Clause." *Ibid.* All of this Justice Clark explicitly acknowledged. See *id.,* at 762 (concurring opinion) ("The Court's interpretation of the indictment clearly avoids the question whether Congress, by appropriate legislation, has the power to punish private conspiracies that interfere with Fourteenth Amendment rights, such as the right to utilize public facilities").

To accept petitioners' argument, moreover, one must add to the three Justices joining Justice Brennan's reasoned explanation for his belief that the *Civil Rights Cases* were wrongly decided, the three Justices joining Justice Clark's opinion who gave no explanation whatever for their similar view. This is simply not the way that reasoned constitutional adjudication proceeds. We accordingly have no hesitation in saying that it would take more than the naked dicta contained in Justice Clark's opinion, when added to Justice Brennan's opinion, to cast any doubt upon the enduring vitality of the *Civil Rights Cases* and *Harris.*

Petitioners alternatively argue that, unlike the situation in the *Civil Rights Cases,* here there has been gender-based disparate treatment by state authorities, whereas in those cases there was no indication of such state action. There is abundant evidence, however, to show that the Congresses that enacted the Civil Rights Acts of 1871 and 1875 had a purpose similar to that of Congress in enacting §13981: There were state laws on the books bespeaking equality of treatment, but in the administration of these laws there was discrimination against newly freed slaves.

But even if that distinction were valid, we do not believe it would save §13981's civil remedy. For the remedy is simply not "corrective in its character, adapted to counteract and redress the operation of such prohibited [s]tate laws or proceedings of [s]tate officers." *Civil Rights Cases,* 109 U.S., at 18. Or, as we have phrased it in more recent cases, prophylactic legislation under §5 must have a "'congruence and proportionality' between the injury to be prevented or remedied and the means adopted to that end." *Florida Prepaid Postsecondary Ed. Expense Bd.* v. *College Savings Bank,* 527 U.S. 627, 639 (1999); *Flores,* 521 U.S., at 526. Section 13981 is not aimed at proscribing discrimination by officials which the Fourteenth Amendment might not itself proscribe; it is directed not at any State or state actor, but at individuals who have committed criminal acts motivated by gender bias.

In the present cases, for example, §13981 visits no consequence whatever on any Virginia public official involved in investigating or prosecuting Brzonkala's assault. The section is, therefore, unlike any of the §5 remedies that we have previously upheld. For example, in *Katzenbach* v. *Morgan,* 384 U.S. 641 (1966), Congress prohibited New York from imposing literacy tests as a prerequisite for voting because it found that such a requirement disenfranchised thousands of Puerto Rican immigrants who had been educated in the Spanish language of their home territory. That law, which we upheld, was directed at New York officials who administered the State's election law and prohibited them from using a provision of that law. In *South Carolina* v. *Katzenbach,* 383 U.S. 301 (1966), Congress imposed voting rights requirements on States that, Congress found, had a history of discriminating against blacks in voting. The remedy was also directed at state officials in those States. Similarly, in *Ex parte Virginia,* 100 U.S. 339 (1880), Congress criminally punished state officials who intentionally discriminated in jury selection; again, the remedy was directed to the culpable state official.

Section 13981 is also different from these previously upheld remedies in that it applies uniformly throughout the Nation. Congress' findings indicate that the problem of discrimination against the victims of gender-motivated crimes does not exist in all States, or even most States. By contrast, the §5 remedy upheld in *Katzenbach* v. *Morgan, supra*, was directed only to the State where the evil found by Congress existed, and in *South Carolina* v. *Katzenbach, supra*, the remedy was directed only to those States in which Congress found that there had been discrimination.

For these reasons, we conclude that Congress' power under §5 does not extend to the enactment of §13981.

IV

Petitioner Brzonkala's complaint alleges that she was the victim of a brutal assault. But Congress' effort in §13981 to provide a federal civil remedy can be sustained neither under the Commerce Clause nor under §5 of the Fourteenth Amendment. If the allegations here are true, no civilized system of justice could fail to provide her a remedy for the conduct of respondent Morrison. But under our federal system that remedy must be provided by the Commonwealth of Virginia, and not by the United States. The judgment of the Court of Appeals is affirmed.

Justice BREYER, with whom Justice STEVENS joins, and with whom Justice SOUTER and Justice GINSBURG join as to Part I-A, dissenting.

Given my conclusion on the Commerce Clause question, I need not consider Congress' authority under §5 of the Fourteenth Amendment. Nonetheless, I doubt the Court's reasoning rejecting that source of authority. The Court points out that in *United States* v. *Harris,* 106 U.S. 629 (1883), and the *Civil Rights Cases,* 109 U.S. 3 (1883), the Court held that §5 does not authorize Congress to use the Fourteenth Amendment as a source of power to remedy the conduct of *private persons. Ante,* at 21-23. That is certainly so. The Federal Government's argument, however, is that Congress used §5 to remedy the actions of *state actors,* namely, those States which, through discriminatory design or the discriminatory conduct of their officials, failed to provide adequate (or any) state remedies for women injured by gender-motivated violence — a failure that the States, and Congress, documented in depth. See *ante,* at 3-4, n. 7, 27-28 (Souter, J., dissenting) (collecting sources).

Neither *Harris* nor the *Civil Rights Cases* considered this kind of claim. The Court in *Harris* specifically said that it treated the federal laws in question as "directed *exclusively* against the action of private persons, without reference to the laws of the State, or their administration by her officers." 106 U.S., at 640 (emphasis added); see also *Civil Rights Cases*, 109 U.S., at 14 (observing that the statute did "not profess to be corrective of any constitutional wrong committed by the States" and that it established "rules for the conduct of individuals in society towards each other, . . . without referring in any manner to any supposed action of the State or its authorities").

The Court responds directly to the relevant "state actor" claim by finding that the present law lacks "'congruence and proportionality'" to the state discrimination that it purports to remedy. *Ante,* at 26; see *City of Boerne* v. *Flores,* 521 U.S. 507, 526 (1997). That is because the law, unlike federal laws prohibiting literacy tests for voting, imposing voting rights requirements, or punishing state officials who intentionally discriminated in jury selection, *Katzenbach* v. *Morgan,* 384 U.S. 641 (1966); *South Carolina* v. *Katzenbach,* 383 U.S. 301 (1966); *Ex parte Virginia,* 100 U.S. 339 (1880), is not "directed . . . at any State or state actor." *Ante,* at 26.

But why can Congress not provide a remedy against private actors? Those private actors, of course, did not themselves violate the Constitution. But this Court has held that Congress at least sometimes can enact remedial "[l]egislation . . . [that] prohibits conduct which is not itself unconstitutional." *Flores,* 521 U.S., at 518; see also *Katzenbach* v. *Morgan, supra,* at 651; *South Carolina* v. *Katzenbach, supra,* at 308. The statutory remedy does not in any sense purport to "determine what constitutes a constitutional violation." *Flores, supra,* at 519. It intrudes little upon either States or private parties. It may lead state actors to improve their own remedial systems, primarily through example. It restricts private actors only by imposing liability for private conduct that is, in the main, already forbidden by state law. Why is the remedy "disproportionate"? And given the relation between remedy and violation — the creation of a federal remedy to substitute for constitutionally inadequate state remedies — where is the lack of "congruence"?

The majority adds that Congress found that the problem of inadequacy of state remedies "does not exist in all States, or even most States." *Ante,* at 27. But Congress had before it the task force reports of at least 21 States documenting constitutional violations. And it made its own findings about pervasive gender-based stereotypes hampering many state legal systems, sometimes unconstitutionally so. See, *e.g.,* S. Rep. No. 103-138, pp. 38, 41-42, 44-47 (1993); S. Rep. No. 102-197, pp. 39, 44-49 (1991); H. R. Conf. Rep. No. 103-711, p. 385 (1994). The record nowhere reveals a congressional finding that the problem "does not exist" elsewhere. Why can Congress not take the evidence before it as evidence of a national problem? This Court has not previously held that Congress must document the existence of a problem in every State prior to proposing a national solution. And the deference this Court gives to Congress' chosen remedy under §5, *Flores, supra,* at 536, suggests that any such requirement would be inappropriate.

Despite my doubts about the majority's §5 reasoning, I need not, and do not, answer the §5 question, which I would leave for more thorough analysis if necessary on another occasion. Rather, in my view, the Commerce Clause provides an adequate basis for the statute before us. And I would uphold its constitutionality as the "necessary and proper" exercise of legislative power granted to Congress by that Clause.

TENNESSEE v. LANE
541 U.S. 509 (2004)

STEVENS, J., delivered the opinion of the Court.

Title II of the Americans with Disabilities Act of 1990 (ADA or Act), 104 Stat. 337, 42 U. S. C. §§ 12131-12165, provides that "no qualified individual with a disability shall, by reason of such disability, be excluded from participation in or be denied the benefits of the services, programs or activities of a public entity, or be subjected to discrimination by any such entity." § 12132. The question presented in this case is whether Title II exceeds Congress' power under § 5 of the Fourteenth Amendment.

I

In August 1998, respondents George Lane and Beverly Jones filed this action against the State of Tennessee and a number of Tennessee counties, alleging past and ongoing violations of Title II. Respondents, both of whom are paraplegics who use wheelchairs for mobility, claimed that they were denied access to, and the services of, the state court system by reason of their disabilities. Lane alleged that he was compelled to appear to answer a set of criminal charges on the second floor of a county courthouse that had no elevator. At his first appearance, Lane crawled up two flights of stairs to get to the courtroom. When Lane returned to the courthouse for a hearing, he refused to crawl again or to be carried by officers to the courtroom; he consequently was arrested and jailed for failure to appear. Jones, a certified court reporter, alleged that she has not been able to gain access to a number of county courthouses, and, as a result, has lost both work and an opportunity to participate in the judicial process. Respondents sought damages and equitable relief.

The State moved to dismiss the suit on the ground that it was barred by the Eleventh Amendment. The District Court denied the motion without opinion, and the State appealed. The United States intervened to defend Title II's abrogation of the States' Eleventh Amendment immunity. On April 28, 2000, after the appeal had been briefed and argued, the Court of Appeals for the Sixth Circuit entered an order holding the case in abeyance pending our decision in Board of Trustees of Univ. of Ala. v. Garrett, 531 U. S. 356 (2001).

In Garrett, we concluded that the Eleventh Amendment bars private suits seeking money damages for state violations of Title I of the ADA. We left open, however, the question whether the Eleventh Amendment permits suits for money damages under Title II. Id., at 360, n. 1. Following the Garrett decision, the Court of Appeals, sitting en banc, heard argument in a Title II suit brought by a hearing-impaired litigant who sought money damages for the State's failure to accommodate his disability in a child custody proceeding. Popovich v. Cuyahoga County Court, 276 F. 3d 808 (CA6 2002). A divided court permitted the suit to proceed despite the State's assertion of Eleventh Amendment immunity. The majority interpreted Garrett to bar private ADA suits against States based on equal protection principles, but not those that rely on due process principles. 276 F. 3d, at 811-816. The minority concluded that Congress had not validly abrogated the States' Eleventh Amendment immunity for any Title II claims, id., at 821, while the concurring opinion concluded that Title II validly abrogated state sovereign immunity with respect to both equal protection and due process claims.

Following the en banc decision in Popovich, a panel of the Court of Appeals entered an order affirming the District Court's denial of the State's motion to dismiss in [the present case]. The order explained that respondents' claims were not barred because they were based on due process principles. In response to a petition for rehearing arguing that Popovich was not controlling because the complaint did not allege due process violations, the panel filed an amended opinion. It explained that the Due Process Clause protects the right of access to the courts, and that the evidence before Congress when it enacted Title II "established that physical barriers in government buildings, including courthouses and in the courtrooms themselves, have had the effect of denying disabled people the opportunity to access vital services and to exercise fundamental rights guaranteed by the Due Process Clause." 315 F. 3d 680, 682 (2003). Moreover, that "record demonstrated that public entities' failure to accommodate the needs of qualified persons with disabilities may result directly from unconstitutional animus and impermissible stereotypes." Id., at 683. The panel did not, however, categorically reject the State's submission. It instead noted that the case presented difficult questions that "cannot be clarified absent a factual record," and remanded for further proceedings. Ibid. We granted certiorari, 539 U. S. 941 (2003), and now affirm.

II

The ADA was passed by large majorities in both Houses of Congress after decades of deliberation and investigation into the need for comprehensive legislation to address discrimination against persons with disabilities. In the years immediately preceding the ADA's enactment, Congress held 13 hearings and created a special task force that gathered evidence from every State in the Union. The conclusions Congress drew from this evidence are set forth in the task force and Committee Reports, described in lengthy legislative hearings, and summarized in the preamble to the statute. Central among these conclusions was Congress' finding that "individuals with disabilities are a discrete and insular minority who have been faced with restrictions and limitations, subjected to a history of purposeful unequal treatment, and relegated to a position of political powerlessness in our society, based on characteristics that are beyond the control of such individuals and resulting from stereotypic assumptions not truly indicative of the individual ability of such individuals to participate in, and contribute to, society." 42 U. S. C. § 12101(a)(7).

Invoking "the sweep of congressional authority, including the power to enforce the fourteenth amendment and to regulate commerce," the ADA is designed "to provide a clear and comprehensive national mandate for the elimination of discrimination against individuals with disabilities." §§ 12101(b)(1), (b)(4). It forbids discrimination against persons with disabilities in three major areas of public life: employment, which is covered by Title I of the statute; public services, programs, and activities, which are the subject of Title II; and public accommodations, which are covered by Title III.

Title II, §§ 12131-12134, prohibits any public entity from discriminating against "qualified" persons with disabilities in the provision or operation of public services, programs, or activities. The Act defines the term "public entity" to include state and local governments, as well as their agencies and instrumentalities. § 12131(1). Persons with disabilities are "qualified" if they, "with or without reasonable modifications to rules, policies, or practices, the removal of architectural, communication, or transportation barriers, or the provision of auxiliary aids and services, mee[t] the essential eligibility requirements for the receipt of services or the participation in programs or activities provided by a public entity." § 12131(2). Title II's enforcement provision incorporates by reference § 505 of the Rehabilitation Act of 1973, 92 Stat. 2982, as added, 29 U. S. C. § 794a, which authorizes private citizens to bring suits for money damages. 42 U. S. C. § 12133.

III

The Eleventh Amendment renders the States immune from "any suit in law or equity, commenced or prosecuted . . . by Citizens of another State, or by Citizens or Subjects of any Foreign State." Even though the Amendment "by its terms . . . applies only to suits against a State by citizens of another State," our cases have repeatedly held that this immunity also applies to unconsented suits brought by a State's own citizens. Garrett, 531 U. S., at 363; Kimel v. Florida Bd. of Regents, 528 U. S. 62, 72-73 (2000). Our cases have also held that Congress may abrogate the State's Eleventh Amendment immunity. To determine whether it has done so in any given case, we "must resolve two predicate questions: first, whether Congress unequivocally expressed its intent to abrogate that immunity; and second, if it did, whether Congress acted pursuant to a valid grant of constitutional authority." Id., at 73.

The first question is easily answered in this case. The Act specifically provides: "A State shall not be immune under the eleventh amendment to the Constitution of the United States from an action in Federal or State court of competent jurisdiction for a violation of this chapter." 42 U. S. C. § 12202. As in Garrett, see 531 U. S., at 363-364, no party disputes the adequacy of that expression of Congress' intent to abrogate the States' Eleventh Amendment immunity. The question, then, is whether Congress had the power to give effect to its intent.

In Fitzpatrick v. Bitzer, 427 U. S. 445 (1976), we held that Congress can abrogate a State's sovereign immunity when it does so pursuant to a valid exercise of its power under § 5 of the Fourteenth Amendment to enforce the substantive guarantees of that Amendment. Id., at 456. This enforcement power, as we have often acknowledged, is a "broad power indeed." Mississippi Univ. for Women v. Hogan, 458 U. S. 718, 732 (1982), citing Ex parte Virginia, 100 U. S. 339, 346 (1880). It includes "the authority both to remedy and to deter violation of rights guaranteed [by the Fourteenth Amendment] by prohibiting a somewhat broader swath of conduct, including that which is not itself forbidden by the Amendment's text." Kimel, 528 U. S., at 81. We have thus repeatedly affirmed that "Congress may enact so-called prophylactic legislation that proscribes facially constitutional conduct, in order to prevent and deter unconstitutional conduct." Nevada Dept. of Human Resources v. Hibbs, 538 U. S. 721, 727-728 (2003). See also City of Boerne v. Flores, 521 U. S. 507, 518 (1997). The most recent affirmation of the breadth of Congress' § 5 power came in Hibbs, in which we considered whether a male state employee could recover money damages against the State for its failure to comply with the family-care leave provision of the Family and Medical Leave Act of 1993 (FMLA), 107 Stat. 6, 29 U. S. C. § 2601 et seq. We upheld the FMLA as a valid exercise of Congress' § 5 power to combat unconstitutional sex discrimination, even though there was no suggestion that the State's leave policy was adopted or applied with a discriminatory purpose that would render it unconstitutional under the rule of Personnel Administrator of Mass. v. Feeney, 442 U. S. 256 520 (1979). When Congress seeks to remedy or prevent unconstitutional discrimination, § 5 authorizes it to enact prophylactic legislation proscribing practices that are discriminatory in effect, if not in intent, to carry out the basic objectives of the Equal Protection Clause.

Congress' § 5 power is not, however, unlimited. While Congress must have a wide berth in devising appropriate remedial and preventative measures for unconstitutional actions, those measures may not work a "substantive change in the governing law." Boerne, 521 U. S., at 519. In Boerne, we recognized that the line between remedial legislation and substantive redefinition is "not easy to discern," and that "Congress must have wide latitude in determining where it lies." Id., at 519-520. But we also confirmed that "the distinction exists and must be observed," and set forth a test for so observing it: Section 5 legislation is valid if it exhibits "a congruence and proportionality between the injury to be prevented or remedied and the means adopted to that end." Id., at 520.

In Boerne, we held that Congress had exceeded its § 5 authority when it enacted the Religious Freedom Restoration Act of 1993 (RFRA), 107 Stat. 1488, 42 U. S. C. § 2000bb et seq. We began by noting that Congress enacted RFRA "in direct response" to our decision in Employment Div., Dept. of Human Resources of Ore. v. Smith, 494 U. S. 872 (1990), for the stated purpose of "restor[ing]" a constitutional rule that Smith had rejected. 521 U. S., at 512, 515 (internal quotation marks omitted). Though the respondent attempted to defend the statute as a reasonable means of enforcing the Free Exercise Clause as interpreted in Smith, we concluded that RFRA was "so out of proportion" to that objective that it could be understood only as an attempt to work a "substantive change in constitutional protections." 521 U. S., at 529, 532. Indeed, that was the very purpose of the law.

Applying the Boerne test in Garrett, we concluded that Title I of the ADA was not a valid exercise of Congress' § 5 power to enforce the Fourteenth Amendment's prohibition on unconstitutional disability discrimination in public employment. As in Florida Prepaid, we concluded Congress' exercise of its prophylactic § 5 power was unsupported by a relevant history and pattern of constitutional violations. 531 U. S., at 368, 374. Although the dissent pointed out that Congress had before it a great deal of evidence of discrimination by the States against persons with disabilities, id., at 379 (opinion of BREYER, J.), the Court's opinion noted that the "overwhelming majority" of that evidence related to "the provision of public services and public accommodations, which areas are addressed in Titles II and III," rather than Title I, id., at 371, n. 7. We also noted that neither the ADA's legislative findings nor its legislative history reflected a concern that the States had been engaging in a pattern of unconstitutional employment discrimination. We emphasized that the House and Senate Committee Reports on the ADA focused on "'[d]iscrimination [in] . . . employment in the private sector,'" and made no mention of discrimination in public employment. Id., at 371-372 (quoting S. Rep. No. 101-116, p. 6 (1989), and H. R. Rep. No. 101-485, pt. 2, p. 28 (1990)) (emphasis in Garrett). Finally, we concluded that Title I's broad remedial scheme was insufficiently targeted to remedy or prevent unconstitutional discrimination in public employment. Taken together, the historical record and the broad sweep of the statute suggested that Title I's true aim was not so much to enforce the Fourteenth Amendment's prohibitions against disability discrimination in public employment as it was to "rewrite" this Court's Fourteenth Amendment jurisprudence. 531 U. S., at 372-374.

In view of the significant differences between Titles I and II, however, Garrett left open the question whether Title II is a valid exercise of Congress' § 5 enforcement power. It is to that question that we now turn.

IV

The first step of the Boerne inquiry requires us to identify the constitutional right or rights that Congress sought to enforce when it enacted Title II. Garrett, 531 U. S., at 365. In Garrett we identified Title I's purpose as enforcement of the Fourteenth Amendment's command that "all persons similarly situated should be treated alike." Cleburne v. Cleburne Living Center, Inc., 473 U. S. 432, 439 (1985). As we observed, classifications based on disability violate that constitutional command if they lack a rational relationship to a legitimate governmental purpose. Garrett, 531 U. S., at 366 (citing Cleburne, 473 U. S., at 446).

Title II, like Title I, seeks to enforce this prohibition on irrational disability discrimination. But it also seeks to enforce a variety of other basic constitutional guarantees, infringements of which are subject to more searching judicial review. See, e. g., Dunn v. Blumstein, 405 U. S. 330, 336-337 (1972); Shapiro v. Thompson, 394 U. S. 618, 634 (1969); Skinner v. Oklahoma ex rel. Williamson, 316 U. S. 535, 541 (1942). These rights include some, like the right of access to the courts at issue in this case, that are protected by the Due Process Clause of the Fourteenth Amendment. The Due Process Clause and the Confrontation Clause of the Sixth Amendment, as applied to the States via the Fourteenth Amendment, both guarantee to a criminal defendant such as respondent Lane the "right to be present at all stages of the trial where his absence might frustrate the fairness of the proceedings." Faretta v. California, 422 U. S. 806, 819, n. 15 (1975). The Due Process Clause also requires the States to afford certain civil litigants a "meaningful opportunity to be heard" by removing obstacles to their full participation in judicial proceedings. Boddie v. Connecticut, 401 U. S. 371, 379 (1971); M. L. B. v. S. L. J., 519 U. S. 102 (1996). We have held that the Sixth Amendment guarantees to criminal defendants the right to trial by a jury composed of a fair cross section of the community, noting that the exclusion of "identifiable segments playing major roles in the community cannot be squared with the constitutional concept of jury trial." Taylor v. Louisiana, 419 U. S. 522, 530 (1975). And, finally, we have recognized that members of the public have a right of access to criminal proceedings secured by the First Amendment. Press-Enterprise Co. v. Superior Court of Cal., County of Riverside, 478 U. S. 1, 8-15 (1986).

Whether Title II validly enforces these constitutional rights is a question that "must be judged with reference to the historical experience which it reflects." South Carolina v. Katzenbach, 383 U. S. 301, 308 (1966). See also Florida Prepaid, 527 U. S., at 639-640; Boerne, 521 U. S., at 530. While § 5 authorizes Congress to enact reasonably prophylactic remedial legislation, the appropriateness of the remedy depends on the gravity of the harm it seeks to prevent. "Difficult and intractable problems often require powerful remedies," Kimel, 528 U. S., at 88, but it is also true that "[s]trong measures appropriate to address one harm may be an unwarranted response to another, lesser one," Boerne, 521 U. S., at 530.

It is not difficult to perceive the harm that Title II is designed to address. Congress enacted Title II against a backdrop of pervasive unequal treatment in the administration of state services and programs, including systematic deprivations of fundamental rights. For example, "[a]s of 1979, most States . . . categorically disqualified 'idiots' from voting, without regard to individual capacity." The majority of these laws remain on the books, and have been the subject of legal challenge as recently as 2001. Similarly, a number of States have prohibited and continue to prohibit persons with disabilities from engaging in activities such as marrying and serving as jurors. The historical experience that Title II reflects is also documented in this Court's cases, which have identified unconstitutional treatment of disabled persons by state agencies in a variety of settings, including unjustified commitment, e. g., Jackson v. Indiana, 406 U. S. 715 (1972); the abuse and neglect of persons committed to state mental health hospitals, Youngberg v. Romeo, 457 U. S. 307 (1982); and irrational discrimination in zoning decisions, Cleburne v. Cleburne Living Center, Inc., 473 U. S. 432 (1985). The decisions of other courts, too, document a pattern of unequal treatment in the administration of a wide range of public services, programs, and activities, including the penal system, public education, and voting. Notably, these decisions also demonstrate a pattern of unconstitutional treatment in the administration of justice.

This pattern of disability discrimination persisted despite several federal and state legislative efforts to address it. In the deliberations that led up to the enactment of the ADA, Congress identified important shortcomings in existing laws that rendered them "inadequate to address the pervasive problems of discrimination that people with disabilities are facing." S. Rep. No. 101-116, at 18. See also H. R. Rep. No. 101-485, pt. 2, at 47. It also uncovered further evidence of those shortcomings, in the form of hundreds of examples of unequal treatment of persons with disabilities by States and their political sub-divisions. See Garrett, 531 U. S., at 379 (Breyer, J., dissenting). See also id., at 391 (App. C to opinion of Breyer, J., dissenting). As the Court's opinion in Garrett observed, the "overwhelming majority" of these examples concerned discrimination in the administration of public programs and services. Id., at 371, n. 7; Government's Lodging in Garrett.

With respect to the particular services at issue in this case, Congress learned that many individuals, in many States across the country, were being excluded from court-houses and court proceedings by reason of their disabilities. A report before Congress showed that some 76% of public services and programs housed in state-owned buildings were inaccessible to and unusable by persons with disabilities, even taking into account the possibility that the services and programs might be restructured or relocated to other parts of the buildings. U. S. Commission on Civil Rights, Accommodating the Spectrum of Individual Abilities 39 (1983). Congress itself heard testimony from persons with disabilities who described the physical inaccessibility of local courthouses. Oversight Hearing on H. R. 4498 before the House Subcommittee on Select Education of the Committee on Education and Labor, 100th Cong., 2d Sess., 40-41, 48 (1988). And its appointed task force heard numerous examples of the exclusion of persons with disabilities from state judicial services and programs, including exclusion of persons with visual impairments and hearing impairments from jury service, failure of state and local governments to provide interpretive services for the hearing impaired, failure to permit the testimony of adults with developmental disabilities in abuse cases, and failure to make courtrooms accessible to witnesses with physical disabilities. Government's Lodging in Garrett, O. T. 2000, No. 99-1240. See also Task Force on the Rights and Empowerment of Americans with Disabilities, From ADA to Empowerment (Oct. 12, 1990).

Given the sheer volume of evidence demonstrating the nature and extent of unconstitutional discrimination against persons with disabilities in the provision of public services, the dissent's contention that the record is insufficient to justify Congress' exercise of its prophylactic power is puzzling, to say the least. Just last Term in Hibbs, we approved the family-care leave provision of the FMLA as valid § 5 legislation based primarily on evidence of disparate provision of parenting leave, little of which concerned unconstitutional state conduct. 538 U. S., at 728-733. We explained that because the FMLA was targeted at sex-based classifications, which are subject to a heightened standard of judicial scrutiny, "it was easier for Congress to show a pattern of state constitutional violations" than in Garrett or Kimel, both of which concerned legislation that targeted classifications subject to rational-basis review. 538 U. S., at 735-737. Title II is aimed at the enforcement of a variety of basic rights, including the right of access to the courts at issue in this case, that call for a standard of judicial review at least as searching, and in some cases more searching, than the standard that applies to sex-based classifications. And in any event, the record of constitutional violations in this case — including judicial findings of unconstitutional state action, and statistical, legislative, and anecdotal evidence of the widespread exclusion of persons with disabilities from the enjoyment of public services — far exceeds the record in Hibbs.

The conclusion that Congress drew from this body of evidence is set forth in the text of the ADA itself: "[D]iscrimination against individuals with disabilities persists in such critical areas as . . . education, transportation, communication, recreation, institutionalization, health services, voting, and access to public services." 42 U. S. C. § 12101(a)(3). This finding, together with the extensive record of disability discrimination that underlies it, makes clear beyond peradventure that inadequate provision of public services and access to public facilities was an appropriate subject for prophylactic legislation.

V

The only question that remains is whether Title II is an appropriate response to this history and pattern of unequal treatment. At the outset, we must determine the scope of that inquiry. Title II — unlike RFRA, the Patent Remedy Act, and the other statutes we have reviewed for validity under § 5 — reaches a wide array of official conduct in an effort to enforce an equally wide array of constitutional guarantees. Petitioner urges us both to examine the broad range of Title II's applications all at once, and to treat that breadth as a mark of the law's invalidity. According to petitioner, the fact that Title II applies not only to public education and voting-booth access but also to seating at state-owned hockey rinks indicates that Title II is not appropriately tailored to serve its objectives. But nothing in our case law requires us to consider Title II, with its wide variety of applications, as an undifferentiated whole. Whatever might be said about Title II's other applications, the question presented in this case is not whether Congress can validly subject the States to private suits for money damages for failing to provide reasonable access to hockey rinks, or even to voting booths, but whether Congress had the power under § 5 to enforce the constitutional right of access to the courts. Because we find that Title II unquestionably is valid § 5 legislation as it applies to the class of cases implicating the accessibility of judicial services, we need go no further. See United States v. Raines, 362 U. S. 17, 26 (1960).

Congress' chosen remedy for the pattern of exclusion and discrimination described above, Title II's requirement of program accessibility, is congruent and proportional to its object of enforcing the right of access to the courts. The unequal treatment of disabled persons in the administration of judicial services has a long history, and has persisted despite several legislative efforts to remedy the problem of disability discrimination. Faced with considerable evidence of the shortcomings of previous legislative responses, Congress was justified in concluding that this "difficult and intractable proble[m]" warranted "added prophylactic measures in response." Hibbs, 538 U. S., at 737 (internal quotation marks omitted).

The remedy Congress chose is nevertheless a limited one. Recognizing that failure to accommodate persons with disabilities will often have the same practical effect as outright exclusion, Congress required the States to take reasonable measures to remove architectural and other barriers to accessibility. 42 U. S. C. § 12131(2). But Title II does not require States to employ any and all means to make judicial services accessible to persons with disabilities, and it does not require States to compromise their essential eligibility criteria for public programs. It requires only "reasonable modifications" that would not fundamentally alter the nature of the service provided, and only when the individual seeking modification is otherwise eligible for the service. Ibid. As Title II's implementing regulations make clear, the reasonable modification requirement can be satisfied in a number of ways. In the case of facilities built or altered after 1992, the regulations require compliance with specific architectural accessibility standards. 28 CFR § 35.151 (2003). But in the case of older facilities, for which structural change is likely to be more difficult, a public entity may comply with Title II by adopting a variety of less costly measures, including relocating services to alternative, accessible sites and assigning aides to assist persons with disabilities in accessing services. § 35.150(b)(1). Only if these measures are ineffective in achieving accessibility is the public entity required to make reasonable structural changes. Ibid. And in no event is the entity required to undertake measures that would impose an undue financial or administrative burden, threaten historic preservation interests, or effect a fundamental alteration in the nature of the service. §§ 35.150(a)(2), (a)(3).

This duty to accommodate is perfectly consistent with the well-established due process principle that, "within the limits of practicability, a State must afford to all individuals a meaningful opportunity to be heard" in its courts. Boddie, 401 U. S., at 379 (internal quotation marks and citation omitted). Our cases have recognized a number of affirmative obligations that flow from this principle: the duty to waive filing fees in certain family-law and criminal cases, the duty to provide transcripts to criminal defendants seeking review of their convictions, and the duty to provide counsel to certain criminal defendants. Each of these cases makes clear that ordinary considerations of cost and convenience alone cannot justify a State's failure to provide individuals with a meaningful right of access to the courts. Judged against this backdrop, Title II's affirmative obligation to accommodate persons with disabilities in the administration of justice cannot be said to be "so out of proportion to a supposed remedial or preventive object that it cannot be understood as responsive to, or designed to prevent, unconstitutional behavior." Boerne, 521 U. S., at 532; Kimel, 528 U. S., at 86. It is, rather, a reasonable prophylactic measure, reasonably targeted to a legitimate end.

For these reasons, we conclude that Title II, as it applies to the class of cases implicating the fundamental right of access to the courts, constitutes a valid exercise of Congress' § 5 authority to enforce the guarantees of the Fourteenth Amendment. The judgment of the Court of Appeals is therefore affirmed.

2. CONGRESSIONAL PROTECTION OF VOTING RIGHTS — THE COURT IN THE 21ST CENTURY: "WINDS OF CHANGE A-SHIFT"?

Congruence, Proportionality, and the Voting Rights Act. Although in *Boerne*, Justice Kennedy took pains not to question congressional authority to enact, as civil rights remedies, the provisions of the Voting Rights Act of 1965 (VRA), the Court's scrutiny of legislation abrogating the 11th Amendment via Congress's enforcement power under the 14th amendment (congruence and proportionality) made this an issue "worth watching." This is particularly the case given the fact that Congress reauthorized the Voting Rights Act in 1970, 1982, and 2006. In 2006, even given the progress achieved under the Act, Congress extended the preclearance provisions of § 5 of the Voting Right Act for another 25 years. This extension continued to require covered (mostly southern) jurisdictions to obtain federal approval for changes in election procedures in order to ensure that those procedures did not discriminate on the basis of race. In *Northwest Austin Municipal Utility District Number One v. Holder* a Texas utility district sought to avail itself of the "bailout" provision of the Voting Rights Act. The district also argued in the alternative that the 2006 extension of the VRA preclearance provisions unconstitutionally exceeded Congress's civil rights enforcement authority under *Boerne*. When the Court granted certiorari in this matter in the case that follows, it appeared that the clash between the Court's deference to the enforcement power under *South Carolina* would finally conflict with the scrutiny of congressional choices by the Court in the *Boerne* line of cases. The Court avoided the controversial constitutional question since the majority chose not to "[rush] to decide it." After reading the opinion below, consider whether the extension of the bailout position to this "utility district" as a "political subdivision," reflects the intent of the legislation itself. Also consider comments concerning the future of the voting rights act by Chief Justice Roberts, and Justice Thomas. What do their comments suggests about the future of section 5 preclearance?

NORTHWEST AUSTIN MUNICIPAL UTILITY DISTRICT NUMBER ONE v. HOLDER
557 U.S. 193 (2009)

Chief Justice ROBERTS delivered the opinion of the Court.

The plaintiff in this case is a small utility district raising a big question — the constitutionality of § 5 of the Voting Rights Act. The district has an elected board, and is required by § 5 to seek preclearance from federal authorities in Washington, D. C., before it can change anything about those elections. This is required even though there has never been any evidence of racial discrimination in voting in the district.

The district filed suit seeking relief from these preclearance obligations under the "bailout" provision of the Voting Rights Act. That provision allows the release of a "political subdivision" from the preclearance requirements if certain rigorous conditions are met. The court below denied relief, concluding that bailout was unavailable to a political subdivision like the utility district that did not register its own voters. The district appealed, arguing that the Act imposes no such limitation on bailout, and that if it does, the preclearance requirements are unconstitutional.

That constitutional question has attracted ardent briefs from dozens of interested parties, but the importance of the question does not justify our rushing to decide it. Quite the contrary: Our usual practice is to avoid the unnecessary resolution of constitutional questions. We agree that the district is eligible under the Act to seek bailout. We therefore reverse, and do not reach the constitutionality of § 5.

The Fifteenth Amendment promises that the "right of citizens of the United States to vote shall not be denied or abridged . . . on account of race, color, or previous condition of servitude." U.S. Const., Amdt. 15, § 1. In addition to that self-executing right, the Amendment also gives Congress the "power to enforce this article by appropriate legislation." § 2. The first century of congressional enforcement of the Amendment, however, can only be regarded as a failure. . . .

Congress responded with the Voting Rights Act. Section 2 of the Act operates nationwide; as it exists today, that provision forbids any "standard, practice, or procedure" that "results in a denial or abridgment of the right of any citizen of the United States to vote on account of race or color." 42 U.S.C.A. § 1973(a). Section 2 is not at issue in this case.

The remainder of the Act constitutes a "scheme of stringent remedies aimed at areas where voting discrimination has been most flagrant." *Katzenbach*. Rather than continuing to depend on case-by-case litigation, the Act directly pre-empted the most powerful tools of black disenfranchisement in the covered areas. All literacy tests and similar voting qualifications were abolished by § 4 of the Act. Although such tests may have been facially neutral, they were easily manipulated to keep blacks from voting. The Act also empowered federal examiners to override state determinations about who was eligible to vote.

These two remedies were bolstered by § 5, which suspended all changes in state election procedure until they were submitted to and approved by a three-judge Federal District Court in Washington, D. C., or the Attorney General. Such preclearance is granted only if the change neither "has the purpose nor will have the effect of denying or abridging the right to vote on account of race or color." We have interpreted the requirements of § 5 to apply not only to the ballot-access rights guaranteed by § 4, but to drawing district lines as well.

To confine these remedies to areas of flagrant disenfranchisement, the Act applied them only to States that had used a forbidden test or device in November 1964, and had less than 50% voter registration or turnout in the 1964 Presidential election. Congress recognized that the coverage formula it had adopted "might bring within its sweep governmental units not guilty of any unlawful discriminatory voting practices." It therefore "afforded such jurisdictions immediately available protection in the form of . . . [a] 'bailout' suit." . . .

As enacted, §§ 4 and 5 of the Voting Rights Act were temporary provisions. They were expected to be in effect for only five years. We upheld the temporary Voting Rights Act of 1965 as an appropriate exercise of congressional power in *Katzenbach,* explaining that "[t]he constitutional propriety of the Voting Rights Act of 1965 must be judged with reference to the historical experience which it reflects." We concluded that the problems Congress faced when it passed the Act were so dire that "exceptional conditions [could] justify legislative measures not otherwise appropriate." Id.

Congress reauthorized the Act in 1970 (for 5 years), 1975 (for 7 years), and 1982 (for 25 years). The coverage formula remained the same, based on the use of voting-eligibility tests and the rate of registration and turnout among all voters, but the pertinent dates for assessing these criteria moved from 1964 to include 1968 and eventually 1972. We upheld each of these reauthorizations against constitutional challenges, finding that circumstances continued to justify the provisions. Most recently, in 2006, Congress extended § 5 for yet another 25 years. Fannie Lou Hamer, Rosa Parks, and Coretta Scott King Voting Rights Act Reauthorization and Amendments Act of 2006. The 2006 Act retained 1972 as the last baseline year for triggering coverage under § 5. It is that latest extension that is now before us.

Northwest Austin Municipal Utility District Number One was created in 1987 to deliver city services to residents of a portion of Travis County, Texas. It is governed by a board of five members, elected to staggered terms of four years. The district does not register voters but is responsible for its own elections; for administrative reasons, those elections are run by Travis County. Because the district is located in Texas, it is subject to the obligations of § 5, although there is no evidence that it has ever discriminated on the basis of race.

The district filed suit in the District Court for the District of Columbia, seeking relief under the statute's bailout provisions and arguing in the alternative that, if interpreted to render the district ineligible for bailout, § 5 was unconstitutional. The three-judge District Court rejected both claims. Under the statute, only a "State or political subdivision" is permitted to seek bailout, and the court concluded that the district was not a political subdivision because that term includes only "counties, parishes, and voter-registering subunits." Turning to the district's constitutional challenge, the court concluded that the 25-year extension of § 5 was constitutional both because "Congress . . . rationally concluded that extending [§]5 was necessary to protect minorities from continued racial discrimination in voting" and because "the 2006 Amendment qualifies as a congruent and proportional response to the continuing problem of racial discrimination in voting." We noted probable jurisdiction, and now reverse.

The historic accomplishments of the Voting Rights Act are undeniable. When it was first passed, unconstitutional discrimination was rampant and the "registration of voting-age whites ran roughly 50 percentage points or more ahead" of black registration in many covered States. *Katzenbach.* Today, the registration gap between white and black voters is in single digits in the covered States; in some of those States, blacks now register and vote at higher rates than whites. Similar dramatic improvements have occurred for other racial minorities. . . .

At the same time, § 5, "which authorizes federal intrusion into sensitive areas of state and local policymaking, imposes substantial 'federalism costs.' " These federalism costs have caused Members of this Court to express serious misgivings about the constitutionality of § 5. *Katzenbach* (Black, J., concurring and dissenting); *Allen v. State Board of Elections*, 393 U.S. 544, 89 S.Ct. 817, 22 L.Ed.2d 1 (1969) (Harlan, J., concurring in part and dissenting in part); *City of Rome v. United States*, 446 U.S. 156, 100 S.Ct. 1548, 64 L.Ed.2d 119 (1980) (Rehnquist, J., dissenting); (Powell, J., dissenting); *Lopez v. Monterey County*, 525 U.S. 266, 119 S.Ct. 693, 142 L.Ed.2d 728 (1999) (Thomas, J., dissenting); (Kennedy, J., concurring in judgment).

Section 5 goes beyond the prohibition of the Fifteenth Amendment by suspending *all* changes to state election law — however innocuous — until they have been precleared by federal authorities in Washington, D.C. The preclearance requirement applies broadly, and in particular to every political subdivision in a covered State, no matter how small.

Some of the conditions that we relied upon in upholding this statutory scheme in *Katzenbach* and *City of Rome* have unquestionably improved. Things have changed in the South. Voter turnout and registration rates now approach parity. Blatantly discriminatory evasions of federal decrees are rare. And minority candidates hold office at unprecedented levels.

These improvements are no doubt due in significant part to the Voting Rights Act itself, and stand as a monument to its success. Past success alone, however, is not adequate justification to retain the preclearance requirements. It may be that these improvements are insufficient and that conditions continue to warrant preclearance under the Act. But the Act imposes current burdens and must be justified by current needs.

The Act also differentiates between the States, despite our historic tradition that all the States enjoy "equal sovereignty." *United States v. Louisiana*, 363 U.S. 1, 16, 80 S.Ct. 961, 4 L.Ed.2d 1025 (1960). Distinctions can be justified in some cases. "The doctrine of the equality of States . . . does not bar . . . remedies for *local* evils which have subsequently appeared." *Katzenbach* (emphasis added). But a departure from the fundamental principle of equal sovereignty requires a showing that a statute's disparate geographic coverage is sufficiently related to the problem that it targets. . . .

The evil that § 5 is meant to address may no longer be concentrated in the jurisdictions singled out for preclearance. The statute's coverage formula is based on data that is now more than 35 years old, and there is considerable evidence that it fails to account for current political conditions. For example, the racial gap in voter registration and turnout is lower in the States originally covered by § 5 than it is nationwide. . . .

The parties do not agree on the standard to apply in deciding whether, in light of the foregoing concerns, Congress exceeded its Fifteenth Amendment enforcement power in extending the preclearance requirements. The district argues that "'[t]here must be a congruence and proportionality between the injury to be prevented or remedied and the means adopted to that end,'" Brief for Appellant, quoting *City of Boerne v. Flores,* 521 U.S. 507, 520, 117 S.Ct. 2157, 138 L.Ed.2d 624 (1997); the Federal Government asserts that it is enough that the legislation be a "'rational means to effectuate the constitutional prohibition,'" Brief for Federal Appellee, quoting *Katzenbach.* That question has been extensively briefed in this case, but we need not resolve it. The Act's preclearance requirements and its coverage formula raise serious constitutional questions under either test.

In assessing those questions, we are keenly mindful of our institutional role. [It] "is a well-established principle governing the prudent exercise of this Court's jurisdiction that normally the Court will not decide a constitutional question if there is some other ground upon which to dispose of the case." Here, the district also raises a statutory claim that it is eligible to bail out under §§ 4 and 5. Justice Thomas argues that the principle of constitutional avoidance has no pertinence here. He contends that even if we resolve the district's statutory argument in its favor, we would still have to reach the constitutional question, because the district's statutory argument would not afford it all the relief it seeks. *Post* (opinion concurring in judgment in part and dissenting in part).

We disagree. The district expressly describes its constitutional challenge to § 5 as being "in the alternative" to its statutory argument. . . . [The Court turned to the statute and concluded] that all political subdivisions — not only those described in § 14(c)(2) — are eligible to file a bailout suit. . . .

More than 40 years ago, this Court concluded that "exceptional conditions" prevailing in certain parts of the country justified extraordinary legislation otherwise unfamiliar to our federal system. *Katzenbach.* In part due to the success of that legislation, we are now a very different Nation. Whether conditions continue to justify such legislation is a difficult constitutional question we do not answer today. We conclude instead that the Voting Rights Act permits all political subdivisions, including the district in this case, to seek relief from its preclearance requirements.

The judgment of the District Court is reversed, and the case is remanded for further proceedings consistent with this opinion.

It is so ordered.

Justice THOMAS concurring in the judgment in part and dissenting in part.

This appeal presents two questions: first, whether appellant is entitled to bail out from coverage under the Voting Rights Act of 1965(VRA); and second, whether the preclearance requirement of § 5 of the VRA is unconstitutional. Because the Court's statutory decision does not provide appellant with full relief, I conclude that it is inappropriate to apply the constitutional avoidance doctrine in this case. I would therefore decide the constitutional issue presented and hold that § 5 exceeds Congress' power to enforce the Fifteenth Amendment. . . .

The extensive pattern of discrimination that led the Court to previously uphold § 5 as enforcing the Fifteenth Amendment no longer exists. There is thus currently no concerted effort in these jurisdictions to engage in the "unremitting and ingenious defiance of the Constitution," that served as the constitutional basis for upholding the "uncommon exercise of congressional power" embodied in § 5, id . . .

I conclude that the lack of current evidence of intentional discrimination with respect to voting renders § 5 unconstitutional. [The] burden remains with Congress to prove that the extreme circumstances warranting § 5's enactment persist today. A record of scattered infringement of the right to vote is not a constitutionally acceptable substitute."

SHELBY COUNTY, ALABAMA v. HOLDER

570 U. S. 529 (2013)

CHIEF JUSTICE ROBERTS delivered the opinion of the Court.

The Voting Rights Act of 1965 employed extraordinary measures to address an extraordinary problem. Section 5 of the Act required States to obtain federal permission before enacting any law related to voting—a drastic departure from basic principles of federalism. And §4 of the Act applied that requirement only to some States—an equally dramatic departure from the principle that all States enjoy equal sovereignty. This was strong medicine, but Congress determined it was needed to address entrenched racial discrimination in voting, "an insidious and pervasive evil which had been perpetuated in certain parts four country through unremitting and ingenious defiance of the Constitution." *South Carolina* v. *Katzenbach*, 383 U. S. 301, 309 (1966). As we explained in upholding the law, "exceptional conditions can justify legislative measures not otherwise appropriate." *Id.,* at 334. Reflecting the unprecedented nature of these measures, they were scheduled to expire after five years. See Voting Rights Act of 1965, §4(a), 79 Stat. 438.

Nearly 50 years later, they are still in effect; indeed, they have been made more stringent, and are now scheduled to last until 2031. There is no denying, however, that the conditions that originally justified these measures no longer characterize voting in the covered jurisdictions. By 2009, "the racial gap in voter registration and turnout[was] lower in the States originally covered by §5 than it [was] nationwide." *Northwest Austin Municipal Util. Dist. No. One* v. *Holder,* 557 U. S. 193, 203–204 (2009). Since that time, Census Bureau data indicate that African-American voter turnout has come to exceed white voter turnout in five of the six States originally covered by §5, with a gap in the sixth State of less than one half of one percent.

[At] the same time, voting discrimination still exists; no one doubts that. The question is whether the Act's extraordinary measures, including its disparate treatment of the States, continue to satisfy constitutional requirements. As we put it a short time ago, "the Act imposes current burdens and must be justified by current needs." *Northwest Austin,* 557 U. S., at 203.

I

A

The Fifteenth Amendment was ratified in 1870, in the wake of the Civil War. It provides that "[t]he right of citizens of the United States to vote shall not be denied or abridged by the United States or by any State on account of race, color, or previous condition of servitude," and it gives Congress the "power to enforce this article by appropriate legislation."

"The first century of congressional enforcement of the Amendment, however, can only be regarded as a failure." *Id.,* at 197. In the 1890s, Alabama, Georgia, Louisiana, Mississippi, North Carolina, South Carolina, and Virginia began to enact literacy tests for voter registration and to employ other methods designed to prevent African-Americans from voting. *Katzenbach,* 383 U. S., at 310. Congress passed statutes outlawing some of these practices and facilitating litigation against them, but litigation remained slow and expensive, and the States came up with new ways to discriminate as soon as existing ones were struck down. Voter registration of African-Americans barely improved. *Id.,* at 313–314.

Inspired to action by the civil rights movement, Congress responded in 1965 with the Voting Rights Act. Section 2 was enacted to forbid, in all 50 States, any "standard, practice, or procedure . . . imposed or applied . . . to deny or abridge the right of any citizen of the United States to vote on account of race or color." 79 Stat. 437. The current version forbids any "standard, practice, or procedure" that "results in a denial or abridgement of the right of any citizen of the United States to vote on account of race or color." 42 U. S. C. §1973(a). Both the Federal Government and individuals have sued to enforce §2, see, *e.g., Johnson* v. *De Grandy,* 512 U. S. 997 (1994), and injunctive relief is available in appropriate cases to block voting laws from going into effect, see 42 U. S. C. §1973j(d). Section 2 is permanent, applies nationwide, and is not at issue in this case.

Other sections targeted only some parts of the country. At the time of the Act's passage, these "covered" jurisdictions were those States or political subdivisions that had maintained a test or device as a prerequisite to voting as of November 1, 1964, and had less than 50 percent voter registration or turnout in the 1964 Presidential election. §4(b), 79 Stat. 438. Such tests or devices included literacy and knowledge tests, good moral character requirements, the need for vouchers from registered voters, and the like. §4(c), *id.,* at 438–439. A covered jurisdiction could "bail out" of coverage if it had not used a test or device in the preceding five years "for the purpose or with the effect of denying or abridging the right to vote on account of race or color." §4(a), *id.,* at 438. In 1965, the covered States included Alabama, Georgia, Louisiana, Mississippi, South Carolina, and Virginia. The additional covered subdivisions included 39 counties in North Carolina and one in Arizona. See 28 CFR pt. 51, App. (2012).

In those jurisdictions, §4 of the Act banned all such tests or devices. §4(a), 79 Stat. 438. Section 5 provided that no change in voting procedures could take effect until it was approved by federal authorities in Washington, D. C.—either the Attorney General or a court of three judges. *Id.,* at 439. A jurisdiction could obtain such "preclearance" only by proving that the change had neither "the purpose [nor] the effect of denying or abridging the right to vote on account of race or color." *Ibid.*

Sections 4 and 5 were intended to be temporary; they were set to expire after five years. See §4(a), *id.,* at 438; *Northwest Austin, supra,* at 199. In *South Carolina* v. *Katzenbach,* we upheld the 1965 Act against constitutional challenge, explaining that it was justified to address "voting discrimination where it persists on a pervasive scale." 383 U. S., at 308.

In 1970, Congress reauthorized the Act for another five years, and extended the coverage formula in §4(b) to jurisdictions that had a voting test and less than 50 percent voter registration or turnout as of 1968. Voting Rights Act Amendments of 1970, §§3–4, 84 Stat. 315. That swept in several counties in California, New Hampshire, and New York. See 28 CFR pt. 51, App. Congress also extended the ban in §4(a) on tests and devices nationwide. §6, 84 Stat. 315.

In 1975, Congress reauthorized the Act for seven more years, and extended its coverage to jurisdictions that had a voting test and less than 50 percent voter registration or turnout as of 1972. Voting Rights Act Amendments of 1975. Congress also amended the definition of "test or device" to include the practice of providing English-only voting materials in places where over five percent of voting-age citizens spoke a single language other than English. §203, *id.*, at 401–402. As a result of these amendments, the States of Alaska, Arizona, and Texas, as well as several counties in California, Florida, Michigan, New York, North Carolina, and South Dakota, became covered jurisdictions. Finally, Congress made the nationwide ban on tests and devices permanent. §102, *id.*, at 400.

In 1982, Congress reauthorized the Act for 25 years, but did not alter its coverage formula. See Voting Rights Act Amendments, 96 Stat. 131. Congress did, however, amend the bailout provisions, allowing political subdivisions of covered jurisdictions to bail out. Among other prerequisites for bailout, jurisdictions and their subdivisions must not have used a forbidden test or device, failed to receive preclearance, or lost a §2 suit, in the ten years prior to seeking bailout. §2, *id.,* at 131–133.

We upheld each of these reauthorizations against constitutional challenge.

[In] 2006, Congress again reauthorized the Voting Rights Act for 25 years, again without change to its coverage formula. Fannie Lou Hamer, Rosa Parks, and Coretta Scott King Voting Rights Act Reauthorization and Amendments Act, 120 Stat. 577. Congress also amended §5 to prohibit more conduct than before. [Section] 5 now forbids voting changes with "any discriminatory purpose" as well as voting changes that diminish the ability of citizens, on account of race, color, or language minority status, "to elect their preferred candidates of choice." 42 U. S. C. §§1973c(b)–(d).

Shortly after this reauthorization, a Texas utility district brought suit, seeking to bail out from the Act's cover- age and, in the alternative, challenging the Act's constitutionality. See *Northwest Austin*, 557 U. S., at 200–201. A three-judge District Court explained that only a State or political subdivision was eligible to seek bailout under the statute, and concluded that the utility district was not apolitical subdivision, a term that encompassed only "counties, parishes, and voter-registering subunits." *Northwest Austin Municipal Util. Dist. No. One* v. *Mukasey*, 573 F. Supp. 2d 221, 232 (DC 2008). The District Court also rejected the constitutional challenge. *Id.,* at 283.

We reversed. We explained that "'normally the Court will not decide a constitutional question if there is some other ground upon which to dispose of the case.'" *Northwest Austin, supra,* at 205 (quoting *Escambia County* v. *McMillan*, 466 U. S. 48, 51 (1984) (*per curiam*)). Concluding that "underlying constitutional concerns," among other things, "compel[led] a broader reading of the bailout provision," we construed the statute to allow the utility district to seek bailout. *Northwest Austin*, 557 U. S., at 207. In doing so we expressed serious doubts about the Act's continued constitutionality.

We explained that §5 "imposes substantial federalism costs" and "differentiates between the States, despite our historic tradition that all the States enjoy equal sovereignty." *Id.,* at 202, 203 (internal quotation marks omitted). We also noted that "[t]hings have changed in the South. Voter turnout and registration rates now approach parity. Blatantly discriminatory evasions of federal decrees are rare. And minority candidates hold office at unprecedented levels." *Id.,* at 202. Finally, we questioned whether the problems that §5 meant to address were still "concentrated in the jurisdictions singled out for preclearance." *Id.,* at 203.

Eight Members of the Court subscribed to these views, and the remaining Member would have held the Act unconstitutional. Ultimately, however, the Court's construction of the bailout provision left the constitutional issues for another day.

B

Shelby County is located in Alabama, a covered jurisdiction. It has not sought bailout, as the Attorney General has recently objected to voting changes proposed from within the county. See App. 87a–92a. Instead, in 2010, the county sued the Attorney General in Federal District Court in Washington, D. C., seeking a declaratory judgment that sections 4(b) and 5 of the Voting Rights Act are facially unconstitutional, as well as a permanent injunction against their enforcement. The District Court ruled against the county and upheld the Act. 811 F. Supp. 2d 424, 508 (2011). The court found that the evidence before Congress in 2006 was sufficient to justify reauthorizing §5 and continuing the §4(b) coverage formula.

The Court of Appeals for the D. C. Circuit affirmed. In assessing §5, the D. C. Circuit considered six primary categories of evidence: Attorney General objections to voting changes, Attorney General requests for more information regarding voting changes, successful §2 suits in covered jurisdictions, the dispatching of federal observers to monitor elections in covered jurisdictions, §5 preclearance suits involving covered jurisdictions, and the deterrent effect of §5. See 679 F. 3d 848, 862–863 (2012). After extensive analysis of the record, the court accepted Congress's conclusion that §2 litigation remained inadequate in the covered jurisdictions to protect the rights of minority voters, and that §5 was therefore still necessary. *Id.*, at 873.

Turning to §4, the D. C. Circuit noted that the evidence for singling out the covered jurisdictions was "less robust" and that the issue presented "a close question." *Id.*, at 879. But the court looked to data comparing the number of successful §2 suits in the different parts of the country. Coupling that evidence with the deterrent effect of §5, the court concluded that the statute continued "to single out the jurisdictions in which discrimination is concentrated," and thus held that the coverage formula passed constitutional muster. *Id.*, at 883.

[II]

In *Northwest Austin*, we stated that "the Act imposes current burdens and must be justified by current needs." 557 U. S., at 203. And we concluded that "a departure from the fundamental principle of equal sovereignty requires a showing that a statute's disparate geographic coverage is sufficiently related to the problem that it targets." *Ibid.* These basic principles guide our review of the question before us.

A

The Constitution and laws of the United States are "the supreme Law of the Land." U. S. Const., Art. VI, cl. 2. State legislation may not contravene federal law. The Federal Government does not, however, have a general right to review and veto state enactments before they go into effect. A proposal to grant such authority to "negative" state laws was considered at the Constitutional Convention, but rejected in favor of allowing state laws to take effect, subject to later challenge under the Supremacy Clause. See 1 Records of the Federal Convention of 1787, pp. 21, 164–168 (M. Farrand ed. 1911); 2 *id.*, at 27–29, 390–392.

[[T]he] federal balance "is not just an end in itself: Rather, federalism secures to citizens the liberties that derive from the diffusion of sovereign power." *Ibid.* (internal quotation marks omitted).

[II]

[A]

[More] specifically, "'the Framers of the Constitution intended the States to keep for themselves, as provided in the Tenth Amendment, the power to regulate elections.'" *Gregory* v. *Ashcroft*, 501 U. S. 452, 461–462 (1991) (quoting *Sugarman* v. *Dougall*, 413 U. S. 634, 647 (1973); some internal quotation marks omitted).

[Not] only do States retain sovereignty under the Constitution, there is also a "fundamental principle of *equal* sovereignty" among the States. [Over] a hundred years ago, this Court explained that our Nation "was and is a union of States, equal in power, dignity and authority." *Coyle* v. *Smith*, 221 U. S. 559, 567 (1911). Indeed, "the constitutional equality of the States is essential to the harmonious operation of the scheme upon which the Republic was organized." *Id.,* at 580. *Coyle* concerned the admission of new States, and *Katzenbach* rejected the notion that the principle operated as a *bar* on differential treatment outside that context. 383 U. S., at 328–329. At the same time, as we made clear in *Northwest Austin*, the fundamental principle of equal sovereignty remains highly pertinent in assessing subsequent disparate treatment of States. 557 U. S., at 203.

The Voting Rights Act sharply departs from these basic principles. It suspends "*all* changes to state election law—however innocuous—until they have been pre cleared by federal authorities in Washington, D. C." *Id.,* at 202. States must beseech the Federal Government for permission to implement laws that they would otherwise have the right to enact and execute on their own, subject of course to any injunction in a §2 action. The Attorney General has 60 days to object to a preclearance request, longer if he requests more information. See 28 CFR §§51.9, 51.37. If a State seeks preclearance from a three judge court, the process can take years.

And despite the tradition of equal sovereignty, the Act applies to only nine States (and several additional counties). While one State waits months or years and expends funds to implement a validly enacted law, its neighbor can typically put the same law into effect immediately, through the normal legislative process. Even if a noncovered jurisdiction is sued, there are important differences between those proceedings and preclearance proceedings; the preclearance proceeding "not only switches the burden of proof to the supplicant jurisdiction, but also applies substantive standards quite different from those governing the rest of the nation." 679 F. 3d, at 884 (Williams, J., dissenting) (case below).

All this explains why, when we first upheld the Act in 1966, we described it as "stringent" and "potent." *Katzenbach,* 383 U. S., at 308, 315, 337. We recognized that it "may have been an uncommon exercise of congressional power," but concluded that "legislative measures not otherwise appropriate" could be justified by "exceptional conditions." *Id.,* at 334. We have since noted that the Act "authorizes federal intrusion into sensitive areas of state and local policymaking," *Lopez*, 525 U. S., at 282, and represents an "extraordinary departure from the traditional course of relations between the States and the Federal Government," *Presley* v. *Etowah County Comm'n*, 502 U. S. 491, 500–501 (1992). As we reiterated in *Northwest Austin*, the Act constitutes "extraordinary legislation otherwise unfamiliar to our federal system." 557 U. S., at 211.

[C]

[Shelby] County contends that the preclearance requirement, even without regard to its disparate coverage, is now unconstitutional. Its arguments have a good deal of force. In the covered jurisdictions, "[v]oter turnout and registration rates now approach parity. Blatantly discriminatory evasions of federal decrees are rare. And minority candidates hold office at unprecedented levels." *Northwest Austin*, 557 U. S., at 202. The tests and devices that blocked access to the ballot have been forbidden nationwide for over 40 years.

[Yet] Those conclusions are not ours alone. Congress said the same when it reauthorized the Act in 2006, writing that"[s]ignificant progress has been made in eliminating first generation barriers experienced by minority voters, including increased numbers of registered minority voters, minority voter turnout, and minority representation in Congress, State legislatures, and local elected offices." §2(b)(1), 120 Stat. 577. The House Report elaborated that "the number of African-Americans who are registered and who turn out to cast ballots has increased significantly over the last 40 years, particularly since 1982," and noted that "[i]n some circumstances, minorities register to vote and cast ballots at levels that surpass those of white voters." H. R. Rep. No. 109–478, p. 12 (2006). That Report also explained that there have been "significant increases in the number of African-Americans serving in elected offices"; more specifically, there has been approximately a 1,000 percent increase since 1965 in the number of African-American elected officials in the six States originally covered by the Voting Rights Act. *Id.,* at 18.

[Yet] the Act has not eased the restrictions in §5 or narrowed the scope of the coverage formula in §4(b) along the way. Those extraordinary and unprecedented features were reauthorized—as if nothing had changed. In fact, the Act's unusual remedies have grown even stronger. When Congress reauthorized the Act in 2006, it did so for another 25 years on top of the previous 40—a far cry from the initial five-year period. See 42 U. S. C. §1973b(a)(8). Congress also expanded the prohibitions in §5. We had previously interpreted §5 to prohibit only those redistricting plans that would have the purpose or effect of worsening the position of minority groups. See *Bossier II*, 528 U. S., at 324, 335–336. In 2006, Congress amended §5 to prohibit laws that could have favored such groups but did not do so because of a discriminatory purpose, see 42 U. S. C. §1973c(c), even though we had stated that such broadening of §5 coverage would "exacerbate the substantial federalism costs that the preclearance procedure already exacts, perhaps to the extent of raising concerns about §5's constitutionality," *Bossier II, supra,* at 336 (citation and internal quotation marks omitted). In addition, Congress expanded §5 to prohibit any voting law "that has the purpose of or will have the effect of diminishing the ability of any citizens of the United States," on account of race, color, or language minority status, "to elect their preferred candidates of choice." §1973c(b). In light of those two amendments, the bar that covered jurisdictions must clear has been raised even as the conditions justifying that requirement have dramatically improved.

We have also previously highlighted the concern that "the preclearance requirements in one State [might] be unconstitutional in another." *Northwest Austin*, 557 U. S., at 203; see *Georgia* v. *Ashcroft*, 539 U. S., at 491 (KENNEDY, J., concurring) ("considerations of race that would doom a redistricting plan under the Fourteenth Amendment or §2 [of the Voting Rights Act] seem to be what save it under §5"). Nothing has happened since to alleviate this troubling concern about the current application of §5.

Respondents do not deny that there have been improvements on the ground, but argue that much of this can be attributed to the deterrent effect of §5, which dissuades covered jurisdictions from engaging in discrimination that they would resume should §5 be struck down. Under this theory, however, §5 would be effectively immune from scrutiny; no matter how "clean" the record of covered jurisdictions, the argument could always be made that it was deterrence that accounted for the good behavior.

The provisions of §5 apply only to those jurisdictions singled out by §4. We now consider whether that coverage formula is constitutional in light of current conditions.

III

A

When upholding the constitutionality of the coverage formula in 1966, we concluded that it was "rational in both practice and theory." *Katzenbach*, 383 U. S., at 330. The formula looked to cause (discriminatory tests) and effect (low voter registration and turnout), and tailored the remedy (preclearance) to those jurisdictions exhibiting both.

By 2009, however, we concluded that the "coverage formula raise[d] serious constitutional questions." *Northwest Austin*, 557 U. S., at 204. As we explained, a statute's "current burdens" must be justified by "current needs," and any "disparate geographic coverage" must be "sufficiently related to the problem that it targets." *Id.*, at 203. The coverage formula met that test in 1965, but no longer does so.

Coverage today is based on decades-old data and eradicated practices. The formula captures States by reference to literacy tests and low voter registration and turnout in the 1960s and early 1970s. But such tests have been banned nationwide for over 40 years. §6, 84 Stat. 315; §102, 89 Stat. 400. And voter registration and turnout numbers in the covered States have risen dramatically in the years since. H. R. Rep. No. 109–478, at 12. Racial disparity in those numbers was compelling evidence justifying the preclearance remedy and the coverage formula. See, *e.g., Katzenbach, supra*, at 313, 329–330. There is no longer such a disparity.

In 1965, the States could be divided into two groups: those with a recent history of voting tests and low voter registration and turnout, and those without those characteristics. Congress based its coverage formula on that distinction. Today the Nation is no longer divided along those lines, yet the Voting Rights Act continues to treat it as if it were.

[B]

[But] history did not end in 1965. By the time the Act was reauthorized in 2006, there had been 40 more years of it. In assessing the "current need[]" for a preclearance system that treats States differently from one another today, that history cannot be ignored. During that time, largely because of the Voting Rights Act, voting tests were abolished, disparities in voter registration and turnout due to race were erased, and African-Americans attained political office in record numbers. And yet the coverage formula that Congress reauthorized in 2006 ignores these developments, keeping the focus on decades-old data relevant to decades-old problems, rather than current data reflecting current needs.

[C]

In defending the coverage formula, the Government, the intervenors, and the dissent also rely heavily on data from the record that they claim justify disparate coverage. Congress compiled thousands of pages of evidence before reauthorizing the Voting Rights Act. The court below and the parties have debated what that record shows—they have gone back and forth about whether to compare covered to noncovered jurisdictions as blocks, how to disaggregate the data State by State, how to weigh §2 cases as evidence of ongoing discrimination, and whether to consider evidence not before Congress, among other issues. Compare, *e.g.,* 679 F. 3d, at 873–883 (case below), with *id.,* at 889–902 (Williams, J., dissenting). Regardless of how to look at the record, however, no one can fairly say that it shows anything approaching the "pervasive," "flagrant," "widespread," and "rampant" discrimination that faced Congress in 1965, and that clearly distinguished the covered jurisdictions from the rest of the Nation at that time. *Katzenbach, supra,* at 308, 315, 331; *Northwest Austin,* 557 U. S., at 201.

But a more fundamental problem remains: Congress did not use the record it compiled to shape a coverage formula grounded in current conditions. It instead reenacted a formula based on 40-year-old facts having no logical relation to the present day. The dissent relies on "second generation barriers," which are not impediments to the casting of ballots, but rather electoral arrangements that affect the weight of minority votes. That does not cure the problem. Viewing the preclearance requirements as targeting such efforts simply highlights the irrationality of continued reliance on the §4 coverage formula, which is based on voting tests and access to the ballot, not vote dilution. We cannot pretend that we are reviewing an updated statute, or try our hand at updating the statute ourselves, based on the new record compiled by Congress. Contrary to the dissent's contention, see *post,* at 23, we are not ignoring the record; we are simply recognizing that it played no role in shaping the statutory formula before us today.

[D]

[The] dissent treats the Act as if it were just like any other piece of legislation, but this Court has made clear from the beginning that the Voting Rights Act is far from ordinary. At the risk of repetition, *Katzenbach* indicated that the Act was "uncommon" and "not otherwise appropriate," but was justified by "exceptional" and "unique" conditions. 383 U. S., at 334, 335. Multiple decisions since have reaffirmed the Act's "extraordinary" nature. See, *e.g., Northwest Austin, supra,* at 211. Yet the dissent goes so far as to suggest instead that the preclearance requirement and disparate treatment of the States should be upheld into the future "unless there [is] no or almost no evidence of unconstitutional action by States." *Post,* at 33.

In other ways as well, the dissent analyzes the question presented as if our decision in *Northwest Austin* never happened. For example, the dissent refuses to consider the principle of equal sovereignty, despite *Northwest Austin*'s emphasis on its significance. *Northwest Austin* also emphasized the "dramatic" progress since 1965, 557 U. S., at 201, but the dissent describes current levels of discrimination as "flagrant," "widespread," and "pervasive," *post,* at 7, 17 (internal quotation marks omitted).Despite the fact that *Northwest Austin* requires an Act's "disparate geographic coverage" to be "sufficiently related" to its targeted problems, 557 U. S., at 203, the dissent maintains that an Act's limited coverage actually eases Congress's burdens, and suggests that a fortuitous relationship should suffice. Although *Northwest Austin* stated definitively that "current burdens" must be justified by "current needs," *ibid.,* the dissent argues that the coverage formula can be justified by history, and that the required showing can be weaker on reenactment than when the law was first passed.

There is no valid reason to insulate the coverage formula from review merely because it was previously enacted 40 years ago. If Congress had started from scratch in 2006, it plainly could not have enacted the present coverage formula. It would have been irrational for Congress to distinguish between States in such a fundamental way based on 40-year-old data, when today's statistics tell an entirely different story. And it would have been irrational to base coverage on the use of voting tests 40 years ago, when such tests have been illegal since that time. But that is exactly what Congress has done.

* * *

Striking down an Act of Congress "is the gravest and most delicate duty that this Court is called on to perform." *Blodgett* v. *Holden,* 275 U. S. 142, 148 (1927) (Holmes, J., concurring). We do not do so lightly. That is why, in 2009, we took care to avoid ruling on the constitutionality of the Voting Rights Act when asked to do so, and instead resolved the case then before us on statutory grounds. But in issuing that decision, we expressed our broader concerns about the constitutionality of the Act. Congress could have updated the coverage formula at that time, but did not do so. Its failure to act leaves us today with no choice but to declare §4(b) unconstitutional. The formula in that section can no longer be used as a basis for subjecting jurisdictions to preclearance.

Our decision in no way affects the permanent, nationwide ban on racial discrimination in voting found in §2. We issue no holding on §5 itself, only on the coverage formula. Congress may draft another formula based on current conditions. Such a formula is an initial prerequisite to a determination that exceptional conditions still exist justifying such an "extraordinary departure from the traditional course of relations between the States and the Federal Government." *Presley*, 502 U. S., at 500–501. Our country has changed, and while any racial discrimination in voting is too much, Congress must ensure that the legislation it passes to remedy that problem speaks to current conditions.

The judgment of the Court of Appeals is reversed.

It is so ordered.

JUSTICE GINSBURG, with whom JUSTICE BREYER, JUSTICE SOTOMAYOR, and JUSTICE KAGAN join, dissenting.

In the Court's view, the very success of §5 of the Voting Rights Act demands its dormancy. Congress was of another mind. Recognizing that large progress has been made, Congress determined, based on a voluminous record, that the scourge of discrimination was not yet extirpated. The question this case presents is who decides whether, as currently operative, §5 remains justifiable, [FN1] this Court, or a Congress charged with the obligation to enforce the post-Civil War Amendments "by appropriate legislation." With overwhelming support in both Houses, Congress concluded that, for two prime reasons, §5 should continue in force, unabated. First, continuance would facilitate completion of the impressive gains thus far made; and second, continuance would guard against backsliding. Those assessments were well within Congress' province to make and should elicit this Court's unstinting approbation.

> [FN1] The Court purports to declare unconstitutional only the coverage formula set out in §4(b). See *ante*, at 24. But without that formula, §5 is immobilized. *Ante*, at 2. But the Court today terminates the remedy that proved to be best suited to block that discrimination. The Voting Rights Act of 1965 (VRA) has worked to combat voting discrimination where other remedies had been tried and failed. Particularly effective is the VRA's requirement of federal preclearance for all changes to voting laws in the regions of the country with the most aggravated records of rank discrimination against minority voting rights.

I

"[V]oting discrimination still exists; no one doubts that." *Ante*, at 2. But the Court today terminates the remedy that proved to be best suited to block that discrimination. The Voting Rights Act of 1965 (VRA) has worked to combat voting discrimination where other remedies had been tried and failed. Particularly effective is the VRA's requirement of federal preclearance for all changes to voting laws in the regions of the country with the most aggravated records of rank discrimination against minority voting rights.

A century after the Fourteenth and Fifteenth Amendments guaranteed citizens the right to vote free of discrimination on the basis of race, the "blight of racial discrimination in voting" continued to "infec[t] the electoral process in parts of our country." *South Carolina* v. *Katzenbach*, 383 U. S. 301, 308 (1966). Early attempts to cope with this vile infection resembled battling the Hydra. Whenever one form of voting discrimination was identified and prohibited, others sprang up in its place. This Court repeatedly encountered the remarkable "variety and persistence" of laws disenfranchising minority citizens. *Id.,* at 311. To take just one example, the Court, in 1927, held unconstitutional a Texas law barring black voters from participating in primary elections, *Nixon* v. *Herndon*, 273 U. S. 536, 541; in 1944, the Court struck down a "reenacted" and slightly altered version of the same law, *Smith* v. *Allwright*, 321 U. S. 649, 658; and in 1953, the Court once again confronted an attempt by Texas to "circumven[t]" the Fifteenth Amendment by adopting yet another variant of the all-white primary, *Terry* v. *Adams*, 345 U. S. 461, 469.

During this era, the Court recognized that discrimination against minority voters was a quintessentially political problem requiring a political solution. As Justice Holmes explained: If "the great mass of the white population intends to keep the blacks from voting," "relief from [that] great political wrong, if done, as alleged, by the people of a State and the State itself, must be given by them or by the legislative and political department of the government of the United States." *Giles* v. *Harris*, 189 U. S. 475, 488 (1903).

Congress learned from experience that laws targeting particular electoral practices or enabling case-by-case litigation were inadequate to the task. In the Civil Rights Acts of 1957, 1960, and 1964, Congress authorized and then expanded the power of "the Attorney General to seek injunctions against public and private interference with the right to vote on racial grounds." *Katzenbach*, 383 U. S., at 313. But circumstances reduced the ameliorative potential of these legislative Acts:

> "Voting suits are unusually onerous to prepare, sometimes requiring as many as 6,000 man-hours spent combing through registration records in preparation for trial. Litigation has been exceedingly slow, in part because of the ample opportunities for delay afforded voting officials and others involved in the proceedings. Even when favorable decisions have finally been obtained, some of the States affected have merely switched to discriminatory devices not covered by the federal decrees or have enacted difficult new tests designed to prolong the existing disparity between white and Negro registration. Alternatively, certain local officials have defied and evaded court orders or have simply closed their registration offices to freeze the voting rolls." *Id.,* at 314 (footnote omitted).

Patently, a new approach was needed.

Answering that need, the Voting Rights Act became one of the most consequential, efficacious, and amply justified exercises of federal legislative power in our Nation's history. Requiring federal preclearance of changes in voting laws in the covered jurisdictions—those States and localities where opposition to the Constitution's commands were most virulent—the VRA provided a fit solution for minority voters as well as for States. Under the preclearance regime established by §5 of the VRA, covered jurisdictions must submit proposed changes in voting laws or procedures to the Department of Justice (DOJ), which has 60 days to respond to the changes. 79 Stat. 439, codified at 42 U. S. C. §1973c(a). A change will be approved unless DOJ finds it has "the purpose [or] . . . the effect of denying or abridging the right to vote on account of race or color." *Ibid.* In the alternative, the covered jurisdiction may seek approval by a three-judge District Court in the District of Columbia.

After a century's failure to fulfill the promise of the Fourteenth and Fifteenth Amendments, passage of the VRA finally led to signal improvement on this front. "The

Justice Department estimated that in the five years after[the VRA's] passage, almost as many blacks registered [to vote] in Alabama, Mississippi, Georgia, Louisiana, North Carolina, and South Carolina as in the entire century before 1965." Davidson, The Voting Rights Act: A Brief History, in Controversies in Minority Voting 7, 21 (B. Grofman & C. Davidson eds. 1992). And in assessing the overall effects of the VRA in 2006, Congress found that"[s]ignificant progress has been made in eliminating first generation barriers experienced by minority voters, including increased numbers of registered minority voters, minority voter turnout, and minority representation in Congress, State legislatures, and local elected offices. This progress is the direct result of the Voting Rights Act of 1965." Fannie Lou Hamer, Rosa Parks, and Coretta Scott King Voting Rights Act Reauthorization and Amendments Act of 2006 (hereinafter 2006 Reauthorization), §2(b)(1), 120 Stat. 577. On that matter of cause and effects there can be no genuine doubt.

Although the VRA wrought dramatic changes in the realization of minority voting rights, the Act, to date, surely has not eliminated all vestiges of discrimination against the exercise of the franchise by minority citizens. Jurisdictions covered by the preclearance requirement continued to submit, in large numbers, proposed changes to voting laws that the Attorney General declined to approve, auguring that barriers to minority voting would quickly resurface were the preclearance remedy eliminated. *City of Rome* v. *United States*, 446 U. S. 156, 181 (1980). Congress also found that as "registration and voting of minority citizens increas[ed], other measures may be resorted to which would dilute increasing minority voting strength." *Ibid.* (quoting H. R. Rep. No. 94–196, p. 10 (1975)). See also *Shaw* v. *Reno*, 509 U. S. 630, 640 (1993) ("[I]t soon became apparent that guaranteeing equal access to the polls would not suffice to root out other racially discriminatory voting practices" such as voting dilution). Efforts to reduce the impact of minority votes, in contrast to direct attempts to block access to the ballot, are aptly described as "second-generation barriers" to minority voting.

Second-generation barriers come in various forms. One of the blockages is racial gerrymandering, the redrawing of legislative districts in an "effort to segregate the races for purposes of voting." *Id.,* at 642. Another is adoption of a system of at-large voting in lieu of district-by-district voting in a city with a sizable black minority. By switching to at-large voting, the overall majority could control the election of each city council member, effectively eliminating the potency of the minority's votes. Grofman & Davidson, The Effect of Municipal Election Structure on Black Representation in Eight Southern States, in Quiet Revolution in the South 301, 319 (C. Davidson& B. Grofman eds. 1994) (hereinafter Quiet Revolution). A similar effect could be achieved if the city engaged in discriminatory annexation by incorporating majority white areas into city limits, thereby decreasing the effect of VRA-occasioned increases in black voting. Whatever the device employed, this Court has long recognized that vote dilution, when adopted with a discriminatory purpose, cuts down the right to vote as certainly as denial of access to the ballot. *Shaw*, 509 U. S., at 640–641; *Allen* v. *State Bd. of Elections*, 393 U. S. 544, 569 (1969); *Reynolds* v. *Sims*, 377 U. S. 533, 555 (1964). See also H. R. Rep. No. 109–478, p. 6 (2006) (although "[d]iscrimination today is more subtle than the visible methods used in 1965," "the effect and results are the same, namely a diminishing of the minority community's ability to fully participate in the electoral process and to elect their preferred candidates").

In response to evidence of these substituted barriers, Congress reauthorized the VRA for five years in 1970, for seven years in 1975, and for 25 years in 1982. *Ante,* at 4– 5. Each time, this Court upheld the reauthorization as a valid exercise of congressional power. *Ante*, at 5. As the 1982 reauthorization approached its 2007 expiration date, Congress again considered whether the VRA's preclearance mechanism remained an appropriate response to the problem of voting discrimination in covered jurisdictions.

[In] the long course of the legislative process, Congress "amassed a sizable record." *Northwest Austin Municipal Util. Dist. No. One* v. *Holder*, 557 U. S. 193, 205 (2009). [The] compilation presents countless "examples of flagrant racial discrimination" since the last reauthorization; Congress also brought to light systematic evidence that "intentional racial discrimination in voting remains so serious and widespread in covered jurisdictions that section 5 preclearance is still needed." 679 F. 3d, at 866.

After considering the full legislative record, Congress made the following findings: The VRA has directly caused significant progress in eliminating first-generation barriers to ballot access, leading to a marked increase in minority voter registration and turnout and the number of minority elected officials. 2006 Reauthorization §2(b)(1).But despite this progress, "second generation barriers constructed to prevent minority voters from fully participating in the electoral process" continued to exist, as well as racially polarized voting in the covered jurisdictions, which increased the political vulnerability of racial and language minorities in those jurisdictions. §§2(b)(2)–(3),120 Stat. 577. Extensive "[e]vidence of continued discrimination," Congress concluded, "clearly show[ed] the continued need for Federal oversight" in covered jurisdictions. §§2(b)(4)–(5), *id.,* at 577–578. The overall record demonstrated to the federal lawmakers that, "without the continuation of the Voting Rights Act of 1965 protections, racial and language minority citizens will be deprived of the opportunity to exercise their right to vote, or will have their votes diluted, undermining the significant gains made by minorities in the last 40 years." §2(b)(9), *id.,* at 578.

Based on these findings, Congress reauthorized preclearance for another 25 years, while also undertaking to reconsider the extension after 15 years to ensure that the provision was still necessary and effective. 42 U. S. C. §1973b(a)(7), (8) (2006 ed., Supp. V). The question before the Court is whether Congress had the authority under the Constitution to act as it did.

II

In answering this question, the Court does not write on a clean slate. It is well established that Congress' judgment regarding exercise of its power to enforce the Fourteenth and Fifteenth Amendments warrants substantial deference. The VRA addresses the combination of race discrimination and the right to vote, which is "preservative of all rights." *Yick Wo* v. *Hopkins*, 118 U. S. 356, 370 (1886). When confronting the most constitutionally invidious form of discrimination, and the most fundamental right in our democratic system, Congress' power to act is at its height.

The basis for this deference is firmly rooted in both constitutional text and precedent. The Fifteenth Amendment, which targets precisely and only racial discrimination in voting rights, states that, in this domain, "Congress shall have power to enforce this article by appropriate legislation." In choosing this language, the Amendment's framers invoked Chief Justice Marshall's formulation of the scope of Congress' powers under the Necessary and Proper Clause:

> "Let the end be legitimate, let it be within the scope of the constitution, and *all means which are appropriate, which are plainly adapted to that end*, which are not prohibited, but consist with the letter and spirit of the constitution, are constitutional." *McCulloch* v. *Maryland*, 4 Wheat. 316, 421 (1819) (emphasis added).

[The] stated purpose of the Civil War Amendments was to arm Congress with the power and authority to protect all persons within the Nation from violations of their rights by the States. In exercising that power, then, Congress may use "all means which are appropriate, which are plainly adapted" to the constitutional ends declared by these Amendments. *McCulloch*, 4 Wheat., at 421. So when Congress acts to enforce the right to vote free from racial discrimination, we ask not whether Congress has chosen the means most wise, but whether Congress has rationally selected means appropriate to a legitimate end. "It is not for us to review the congressional resolution of [the need for its chosen remedy]. It is enough that we be able to perceive a basis upon which the Congress might resolve the conflict as it did." *Katzenbach* v. *Morgan*, 384 U. S. 641, 653 (1966).

Until today, in considering the constitutionality of the VRA, the Court has accorded Congress the full measure of respect its judgments in this domain should garner. *South Carolina* v. *Katzenbach* supplies the standard of review: "As against the reserved powers of the States, Congress may use any rational means to effectuate the constitutional prohibition of racial discrimination in voting." 383 U. S., at 324. Faced with subsequent reauthorizations of the VRA, the Court has reaffirmed this standard. *E.g., City of Rome*, 446 U. S., at 178. Today's Court does not purport to alter settled precedent establishing that the dispositive question is whether Congress has employed "rational means."

[This] is not to suggest that congressional power in this area is limitless. It is this Court's responsibility to ensure that Congress has used appropriate means. The question meet for judicial review is whether the chosen means are "adapted to carry out the objects the amendments have in view." *Ex parte Virginia*, 100 U. S. 339, 346 (1880). The Court's role, then, is not to substitute its judgment for that of Congress, but to determine whether the legislative record sufficed to show that "Congress could rationally have determined that [its chosen] provisions were appropriate methods." *City of Rome*, 446 U. S., at 176–177.

In summary, the Constitution vests broad power in Congress to protect the right to vote, and in particular to combat racial discrimination in voting. This Court has repeatedly reaffirmed Congress' prerogative to use any rational means in exercise of its power in this area. And both precedent and logic dictate that the rational-means test should be easier to satisfy, and the burden on the statute's challenger should be higher, when what is at issue is the reauthorization of a remedy that the Court has previously affirmed, and that Congress found, from contemporary evidence, to be working to advance the legislature's legitimate objective.

III

The 2006 reauthorization of the Voting Rights Act fully satisfies the standard stated in *McCulloch*, 4 Wheat., at 421: Congress may choose any means "appropriate" and "plainly adapted to" a legitimate constitutional end. As we shall see, it is implausible to suggest otherwise.

A

I begin with the evidence on which Congress based its decision to continue the preclearance remedy. The surest way to evaluate whether that remedy remains in order is to see if preclearance is still effectively preventing discriminatory changes to voting laws. See *City of Rome*, 446 U. S., at 181. [On] that score, the record before Congress was huge. In fact, Congress found there were *more* DOJ objections between 1982 and 2004 (626) than there were between 1965 and the 1982 reauthorization (490). 1 Voting Rights Act: Evidence of Continued Need, Hearing before the Subcommittee on the Constitution of the House Committee on the Judiciary, 109th Cong., 2d Sess., p. 172 (2006) (hereinafter Evidence of Continued Need).

All told, between 1982 and 2006, DOJ objections blocked over 700 voting changes based on a determination that the changes were discriminatory. H. R. Rep. No. 109–478, at 21. Congress found that the majority of DOJ objections included findings of discriminatory intent, see 679 F. 3d, at 867, and that the changes blocked by preclearance were "calculated decisions to keep minority voters from fully participating in the political process." H. R. Rep. 109–478, at 21. On top of that, over the same time period the DOJ and private plaintiffs succeeded in more than 100 actions to enforce the §5 preclearance requirements. 1 Evidence of Continued Need 186, 250.

In addition to blocking proposed voting changes through preclearance, DOJ may request more information from a jurisdiction proposing a change. In turn, the jurisdiction may modify or withdraw the proposed change. The number of such modifications or withdrawals provides an indication of how many discriminatory proposals are deterred without need for formal objection. Congress received evidence that more than 800 proposed changes were altered or withdrawn since the last reauthorization in 1982. H. R. Rep. No. 109–478, at 40–41. Congress also received empirical studies finding that DOJ's requests for more information had a significant effect on the degree to which covered jurisdictions "compl[ied] with their obligatio[n]" to protect minority voting rights. 2 Evidence of Continued Need 2555.

Congress also received evidence that litigation under §2 of the VRA was an inadequate substitute for preclearance in the covered jurisdictions. Litigation occurs only after the fact, when the illegal voting scheme has already been put in place and individuals have been elected pursuant to it, thereby gaining the advantages of incumbency. 1 Evidence of Continued Need 97. An illegal scheme might be in place for several election cycles before a §2 plaintiff can gather sufficient evidence to challenge it. [And] litigation places a heavy financial burden on minority voters. See id., at 84. Congress also received evidence that preclearance lessened the litigation burden on covered jurisdictions themselves, because the preclearance process is far less costly than defending against a §2 claim, and clearance by DOJ substantially reduces the likelihood that a §2 claim will be mounted. Reauthorizing the Voting Rights Act's Temporary Provisions: Policy Perspectives and Views From the Field: Hearing before the Subcommittee on the Constitution, Civil Rights and Property Rights of the Senate Committee on the Judiciary, 109th Cong., 2d Sess., pp. 13, 120–121 (2006). See also Brief for States of New York, California, Mississippi, and North Carolina as *Amici Curiae* 8–9 (Section 5 "reduc[es] the likelihood that a jurisdiction will face costly and protracted Section 2 litigation").

The number of discriminatory changes blocked or deterred by the preclearance requirement suggests that the state of voting rights in the covered jurisdictions would have been significantly different absent this remedy. Surveying the type of changes stopped by the preclearance procedure conveys a sense of the extent to which §5 continues to protect minority voting rights. Set out below are characteristic examples of changes blocked in the years leading up to the 2006 reauthorization:

- In 1995, Mississippi sought to reenact a dual voter registration system, "which was initially enacted in 1892 to disenfranchise Black voters," and for that reason, was struck down by a federal court in 1987. H. R. Rep. No. 109–478, at 39.
- Following the 2000 census, the City of Albany, Georgia, proposed a redistricting plan that DOJ found to be "designed with the purpose to limit and retrogress the

increased black voting strength . . . in the city as a whole." *Id.*, at 37 (internal quotation marks omitted).

- [In 2006,] this Court found that Texas' attempt to redraw a congressional district to reduce the strength of Latino voters bore "the mark of intentional discrimination that could give rise to an equal protection violation," and ordered the district redrawn in compliance with the VRA. *League of United Latin American Citizens v. Perry*, 548 U. S. 399, 440 (2006). In response, Texas sought to undermine this Court's order by curtailing early voting in the district, but was blocked by an action to enforce the §5 preclearance requirement. See Order in *League of United Latin American Citizens v. Texas*, No. 06–cv–1046 (WD Tex.), Doc. 8.
- In 2003, after African-Americans won a majority of the seats on the school board for the first time in history, Charleston County, South Carolina, proposed an at-large voting mechanism for the board. The proposal, made without consulting any of the African-American members of the school board, was found to be an "'exact replica'" of an earlier voting scheme that, a federal court had determined, violated the VRA. 811 F. Supp. 2d 424, 483 (DDC 2011). See also S. Rep. No. 109–295, at 309. DOJ invoked §5 to block the proposal.
- In 1993, the City of Millen, Georgia, proposed to delay the election in a majority-black district by two years, leaving that district without representation on the city council while the neighboring majority white district would have three representatives. 1 Section 5 Hearing 744. DOJ blocked the proposal. The county then sought to move a polling place from a predominantly black neighborhood in the city to an inaccessible location in a predominantly white neighborhood outside city limits. *Id.*, at 816.
- In 2004, Waller County, Texas, threatened to prosecute two black students after they announced their intention to run for office. The county then attempted to reduce the availability of early voting in that election at polling places near a historically black university. 679 F. 3d, at 865–866.
- In 1990, Dallas County, Alabama, whose county seat is the City of Selma, sought to purge its voter rolls of many black voters. DOJ rejected the purge as discriminatory, noting that it would have disqualified many citizens from voting "simply because they failed to pick up or return a voter update form, when there was no valid requirement that they do so." 1 Section 5 Hearing 356.

These examples, and scores more like them, fill the pages of the legislative record. The evidence was indeed sufficient to support Congress' conclusion that "racial discrimination in voting in covered jurisdictions [remained] serious and pervasive." 679 F. 3d, at 865.[FN5]

[FN5] For an illustration postdating the 2006 reauthorization, see *South Carolina* v. *United States*, 898 F. Supp. 2d 30 (DC 2012), which involved a South Carolina voter-identification law enacted in 2011. Concerned that the law would burden minority voters, DOJ brought a§5 enforcement action to block the law's implementation. In the course of the litigation, South Carolina officials agreed to binding interpretations that made it "far easier than some might have expected or feared" for South Carolina citizens to vote. *Id.*, at 37. A three-judge panel precleared the law after adopting both interpretations as an express "condition of preclearance." *Id.*, at 37–38. Two of the judges commented that the case demonstrated "the continuing utility of Section 5 of the Voting Rights Act in deterring problematic, and hence encouraging non-discriminatory, changes in state and local voting laws." *Id.,* at 54 (opinion of Bates, J.).

[True,] conditions in the South have impressively improved since passage of the Voting Rights Act. Congress noted this improvement and found that the VRA was the driving force behind it. 2006 Reauthorization §2(b)(1). But Congress also found that voting discrimination had evolved into subtler second-generation barriers, and that eliminating preclearance would risk loss of the gains that had been made. §§2(b)(2), (9). Concerns of this order, the Court previously found, gave Congress adequate cause to reauthorize the VRA. *City of Rome,* 446 U. S., at 180–182 (congressional reauthorization of the preclearance requirement was justified based on "the number and nature of objections interposed by the Attorney General" since the prior reauthorization; extension was "necessary to preserve the limited and fragile achievements of the Act and to promote further amelioration of voting discrimination")(internal quotation marks omitted). Facing such evidence then, the Court expressly rejected the argument that disparities in voter turnout and number of elected officials were the only metrics capable of justifying reauthorization of the VRA. *Ibid.*

B

I turn next to the evidence on which Congress based its decision to reauthorize the coverage formula in §4(b).Because Congress did not alter the coverage formula, the same jurisdictions previously subject to preclearance continue to be covered by this remedy. The evidence just described, of preclearance's continuing efficacy in blocking constitutional violations in the covered jurisdictions, itself grounded Congress' conclusion that the remedy should be retained for those jurisdictions. There is no question, moreover, that the covered jurisdictions have a unique history of problems with racial discrimination in voting. *Ante,* at 12–13. Consideration of this long history, still in living memory, was altogether appropriate. The Court criticizes Congress for failing to recognize that "history did not end in 1965." *Ante,* at 20. But the Court ignores that "what's past is prologue." W. Shakespeare, The Tempest, act 2, sc. 1. And "[t]hose who cannot remember the past are condemned to repeat it."

[Of] particular importance, even after 40 years and thousands of discriminatory changes blocked by preclearance, conditions in the covered jurisdictions demonstrated that the formula was still justified by "current needs." *Northwest Austin,* 557 U. S., at 203.

Congress learned of these conditions through a report, known as the Katz study, that looked at §2 suits between 1982 and 2004. [Because] the private right of action authorized by §2 of the VRA applies nationwide, a comparison of §2 lawsuits in covered and noncovered jurisdictions provides an appropriate yardstick for measuring differences between covered and noncovered jurisdictions. If differences in the risk of voting discrimination between covered and noncovered jurisdictions had disappeared, one would expect that the rate of successful §2 lawsuits would be roughly the same in both areas. The study's findings, however, indicated that racial discrimination in voting remains "concentrated in the jurisdictions singled out for preclearance." *Northwest Austin,* 557 U. S., at 203.

Although covered jurisdictions account for less than 25 percent of the country's population, the Katz study revealed that they accounted for 56 percent of successful §2 litigation since 1982. Impact and Effectiveness 974. Controlling for population, there were nearly *four* times as many successful §2 cases in covered jurisdictions as there were in noncovered jurisdictions. 679 F. 3d, at 874. The Katz study further found that §2 law-suits are more likely to succeed when they are filed in covered jurisdictions than in non-covered jurisdictions. Impact and Effectiveness 974. From these findings—ignored by the Court—Congress reasonably concluded that the coverage formula continues to identify the jurisdictions of greatest concern.

The evidence before Congress, furthermore, indicated that voting in the covered ju-risdictions was more racially polarized than elsewhere in the country. H. R. Rep. No. 109–478, at 34–35. While racially polarized voting alone does not signal a constitutional violation, it is a factor that increases the vulnerability of racial minorities to discriminato-ry changes in voting law. [When] voting is racially polarized, efforts by the ruling party to pursue that incentive "will inevitably discriminate against a racial group." *Ibid.* Just as buildings in California have a greater need to be earth quakeproofed, places where there is greater racial polarization in voting have a greater need for prophylactic measures to prevent purposeful race discrimination. This point was understood by Congress and is well recognized in the academic literature. See 2006 Reauthorization §2(b)(3), 120 Stat. 577 ("The continued evidence of racially polarized voting in each of the jurisdictions covered by the [preclearance requirement] demonstrates that racial and language minori-ties remain politically vulnerable").

[Congress] was satisfied that the VRA's bailout mechanism provided an effective means of adjusting the VRA's coverage over time. H. R. Rep. No. 109–478, at 25 (the success of bailout "illustrates that: (1) covered status is neither permanent nor over-broad; and (2) covered status has been and continues to be within the control of the jurisdiction such that those jurisdictions that have a genuinely clean record and want to terminate coverage have the ability to do so"). Nearly 200 jurisdictions have successfully bailed out of the preclearance requirement, and DOJ has consented to every bailout application filed by an eligible jurisdiction since the current bailout procedure became effective in 1984. Brief for Federal Respondent 54. The bail-in mechanism has also worked. Several juris-dictions have been subject to federal preclearance by court orders, including the States of New Mexico and Arkansas. App. to Brief for Federal Respondent 1a–3a.

This experience exposes the inaccuracy of the Court's portrayal of the Act as static, unchanged since 1965. Congress designed the VRA to be a dynamic statute, capable of adjusting to changing conditions. True, many covered jurisdictions have not been able to bail out due to recent acts of noncompliance with the VRA, but that truth reinforces the congressional judgment that these jurisdictions were rightfully subject to preclearance, and ought to remain under that regime.

IV

Congress approached the 2006 reauthorization of the VRA with great care and seri-ousness. The same cannot be said of the Court's opinion today. The Court makes no gen-uine attempt to engage with the massive legislative record that Congress assembled. In-stead, it relies on increases in voter registration and turnout as if that were the whole sto-ry. See *supra,* at 18–19. Without even identifying a standard of review, the Court dis-missively brushes off arguments based on "data from the record," and declines to enter the "debat[e about] what [the] record shows." *Ante,* at 20–21. One would expect more from an opinion striking at the heart of the Nation's signal piece of civil-rights legisla-tion.

I note the most disturbing lapses. [Second], the Court veers away from controlling precedent regarding the "equal sovereignty" doctrine without even acknowledging that it is doing so. Third, hardly showing the respect ordinarily paid when Congress acts to implement the Civil War Amendments, and as just stressed, the Court does not even deign to grapple with the legislative record.

[B]

The Court stops any application of §5 by holding that §4(b)'s coverage formula is unconstitutional. It pins this result, in large measure, to "the fundamental principle of equal sovereignty." *Ante*, at 10–11, 23. In *Katzenbach*, however, the Court held, in no uncertain terms, that the principle "*applies only to the terms upon which States are admitted to the Union*, and not to the remedies for local evils which have subsequently appeared." 383 U. S., at 328–329 (emphasis added).

Katzenbach, the Court acknowledges, "rejected the notion that the [equal sovereignty] principle operate[s] as a bar on differential treatment outside [the] context [of the admission of new States]." *Ante*, at 11 (citing 383 U. S., at 328–329) (emphasis omitted). But the Court clouds that once clear understanding by citing dictum from *Northwest Austin* to convey that the principle of equal sovereignty "remains highly pertinent in assessing subsequent disparate treatment of States." *Ante*, at 11 (citing 557 U. S., at 203). See also *ante*, at 23 (relying on *Northwest Austin*'s "emphasis on [the] significance" of the equal-sovereignty principle). If the Court is suggesting that dictum in *Northwest Austin* silently overruled *Katzenbach*'s limitation of the equal sovereignty doctrine to "the admission of new States," the suggestion is untenable. *Northwest Austin* cited *Katzenbach*'s holding in the course of *declining to decide* whether the VRA was constitutional or even what standard of review applied to the question. 557 U. S., at 203–204. In today's decision, the Court ratchets up what was pure dictum in *Northwest Austin*, attributing breadth to the equal sovereignty principle in flat contradiction of *Katzenbach*. The Court does so with nary an explanation of why it finds *Katzenbach* wrong, let alone any discussion of whether *stare decisis* nonetheless counsels adherence to *Katzenbach*'s ruling on the limited "significance" of the equal sovereignty principle.

Today's unprecedented extension of the equal sovereignty principle outside its proper domain—the admission of new States—is capable of much mischief. Federal statutes that treat States disparately are hardly novelties. [Do] such provisions remain safe given the Court's expansion of equal sovereignty's sway?

Of gravest concern, Congress relied on our path marking *Katzenbach* decision in each reauthorization of the VRA. It had every reason to believe that the Act's limited geographical scope would weigh in favor of, not against, the Act's constitutionality. See, *e.g., United States* v. *Morrison*, 529 U. S. 598, 626–627 (2000) (confining preclearance regime to States with a record of discrimination bolstered the VRA's constitutionality). Congress could hardly have foreseen that the VRA's limited geographic reach would render the Act constitutionally suspect. See Persily 195("[S]upporters of the Act sought to develop an evidentiary record for the principal purpose of explaining why the covered jurisdictions should remain covered, rather than justifying the coverage of certain jurisdictions but not others.").

In the Court's conception, it appears, defenders of the VRA could not prevail upon showing what the record overwhelmingly bears out, *i.e.*, that there is a need for continuing the preclearance regime in covered States. In addition, the defenders would have to disprove the existence of a comparable need elsewhere. See Tr. of Oral Arg. 61–62 (suggesting that proof of egregious episodes of racial discrimination in covered jurisdictions would not suffice to carry the day for the VRA, unless such episodes are shown to be absent elsewhere). I am aware of no precedent for imposing such a double burden on defenders of legislation.

C

The Court has time and again declined to upset legislation of this genre unless there was no or almost no evidence of unconstitutional action by States. See, *e.g., City of Boerne* v. *Flores*, 521 U. S. 507, 530 (1997) (legislative record "mention[ed] no episodes [of the kind the legislation aimed to check] occurring in the past 40 years"). No such claim can be made about the congressional record for the 2006 VRA reauthorization. Given a record replete with examples of denial or abridgment of a paramount federal right, the Court should have left the matter where it belongs: in Congress' bailiwick.

Instead, the Court strikes §4(b)'s coverage provision because, in its view, the provision is not based on "current conditions." *Ante*, at 17. It discounts, however, that one such condition was the preclearance remedy in place in the covered jurisdictions, a remedy Congress designed both to catch discrimination before it causes harm, and to guard against return to old ways. 2006 Reauthorization §2(b)(3), (9). Volumes of evidence supported Congress' determination that the prospect of retrogression was real. Throwing out preclearance when it has worked and is continuing to work to stop discriminatory changes is like throwing away your umbrella in a rainstorm because you are not getting wet.

[For] the reasons stated, I would affirm the judgment of the Court of Appeals.

BRNOVICH v. DEMOCRATIC NATIONAL COMMITTEE
592 U.S.____(2021)

JUSTICE ALITO delivered the opinion of the Court.

In these cases, we are called upon for the first time to apply §2 of the Voting Rights Act of 1965 to regulations that govern how ballots are collected and counted. Arizona law generally makes it very easy to vote. All voters may vote by mail or in person for nearly a month before election day, but Arizona imposes two restrictions that are claimed to be unlawful. First, in some counties, voters who choose to cast a ballot in person on election day must vote in their own pre- cincts or else their ballots will not be counted. Second, mail- in ballots cannot be collected by anyone other than an election official, a mail carrier, or a voter's family member, household member, or caregiver.

[I]

A

Congress enacted the landmark Voting Rights Act of 1965, 79 Stat. 437, as amended, 52 U. S. C. §10301 et seq., in an effort to achieve at long last what the Fifteenth Amendment had sought to bring about 95 years earlier: an end to the denial of the right to vote based on race. Ratified in 1870, the Fifteenth Amendment provides in §1 that "[t]he right of citizens of the United States to vote shall not be denied or abridged by the United States or by any State on account of race, color, or previous condition of servitude." Section 2 of the Amendment then grants Congress the "power to enforce [the Amendment] by appropriate legislation."

Despite the ratification of the Fifteenth Amendment, the right of African-Americans to vote was heavily suppressed for nearly a century. States employed a variety of notorious methods, including poll taxes, literacy tests, property qualifications, " 'white primar[ies],' " and " 'grandfather clause[s].'"1 Challenges to some blatant efforts reached this Court and were held to violate the Fifteenth Amendment.

[Invoking] the power conferred by §2 of the Fifteenth Amendment, City of Rome v. United States, 446 U. S. 156, 173 (1980), Congress enacted the Voting Rights Act (VRA) to address this entrenched problem. The Act and its amendments in the 1970s specifically forbade some of the practices that had been used to suppress black voting. See 52 U. S. C. §§10303(a), (c), 10501 (prohibiting the denial of the right to vote in any election for failure to pass a test demonstrating literacy, educational achievement or knowledge of any particular subject, or good moral character); see also 52 U. S. C. §10306 (declaring poll taxes unlawful); 52 U. S. C. §10307 (prohibiting intimidation and the refusal to allow or count votes). Sections 4 and 5 of the VRA imposed special requirements for States and subdivisions where violations of the right to vote had been severe. And §2 addressed the denial or abridgment of the right to vote in any part of the country.

As originally enacted, §2 closely tracked the language of the Amendment it was adopted to enforce. Section 2 stated simply that "[n]o voting qualification or prerequisite to voting, or standard, practice, or procedure shall be imposed or applied by any State or political subdivision to deny or abridge the right of any citizen of the United States to vote on account of race or color." 79 Stat. 437.

[The Court describes the history of the development of the present day section 2]. Congress amended §2 of the VRA. The oft-cited Report of the Senate Judiciary Committee accompanying the 1982 Amendment stated that the amendment's purpose was to [replace] the phrase "to deny or abridge the right . . . to vote on account of race or color," the amendment substituted "in a manner which results in a denial or abridgement of the right . . . to vote on account of race or color." H. R. Rep. No. 97–227, p. 48 (1981) (emphasis added); H. R. 3112, 97th Cong., 1st Sess., §2, p. 8 (introduced Oct. 7, 1981).

The House bill "originally passed . . . under a loose understanding that §2 would prohibit all discriminatory 'effects' of voting practices, and that intent would be 'irrelevant,'" but "[t]his version met stiff resistance in the Senate." Mississippi Republican Executive Committee v. Brooks, 469 U. S. 1002, 1010 (1984) (Rehnquist, J., dissenting) (quoting H. R. Rep. No. 97–227, at 29). The House and Senate com- promised, and the final product included language proposed by Senator Dole.

What is now §2(b) was added, and that provision sets out what must be shown to prove a §2 violation. It requires consideration of "the totality of circumstances" in each case and demands proof that "the political processes leading to nomination or election in the State or political subdivision are not equally open to participation" by members of a protected class "in that its members have less opportunity than other members of the electorate to participate in the political process and to elect representatives of their choice." 52 U. S. C. §10301(b) (emphasis added).

This Court first construed the amended §2 in Thornburg v. Gingles, 478 U. S. 30 (1986)—another vote-dilution case. Justice Brennan's opinion for the Court set out three threshold requirements for proving a §2 vote-dilution claim, and, taking its cue from the Senate Report, provided a non- exhaustive list of factors to be considered in determining whether §2 had been violated. Id., at 44–45, 48–51, 80. "The essence of a §2 claim," the Court said, "is that a certain electoral law, practice, or structure interacts with social and historical conditions to cause an inequality in the opportunities" of minority and non-minority voters to elect their preferred representatives. Id., at 47.

In the years since Gingles, we have heard a steady stream of §2 vote-dilution cases, but until today, we have not considered how §2 applies to generally applicable time, place, or manner voting rules. In recent years, however, such claims have proliferated in the lower courts.

B

The present dispute concerns two features of Arizona voting law, which generally makes it quite easy for residents to vote. All Arizonans may vote by mail for 27 days before an election using an "early ballot." No special excuse is needed. In addition, during the 27 days before an election, Arizonans may vote in person at an early voting location in each county. And they may also vote in person on election day.

The regulations at issue in this suit govern precinct-based election-day voting and early mail-in voting. Voters who choose to vote in person on election day in a county that uses the precinct system must vote in their assigned precincts. If a voter goes to the wrong polling place, poll workers are trained to direct the voter to the right location. If a voter finds that his or her name does not appear on the register at what the voter believes is the right precinct, the voter ordinarily may cast a provisional ballot. That ballot is later counted if the voter's address is determined to be within the precinct. But if it turns out that the voter cast a ballot at the wrong precinct, that vote is not counted.

For those who choose to vote early by mail, Arizona has long required that "[o]nly the elector may be in possession of that elector's unvoted early ballot." In 2016, the state legislature enacted House Bill 2023 (HB 2023), which makes it a crime for any person other than a postal worker, an elections official, or a voter's caregiver, family member, or household member to knowingly collect an early ballot—either before or after it has been completed.

In 2016, the Democratic National Committee and certain affiliates brought this suit and named as defendants (among others) the Arizona attorney general and secretary of state in their official capacities. Among other things, the plaintiffs claimed that both the State's refusal to count ballots cast in the wrong precinct and its ballot-collection restriction "adversely and disparately affect Arizona's American Indian, Hispanic, and African American citizens," in violation of §2 of the VRA. Democratic Nat. Comm. v. Hobbs, 948 F. 3d 989, 998 (CA9 2020) (en banc). In addition, they alleged that the ballot-collection restriction was "enacted with discriminatory intent" and thus violated both §2 of the VRA and the Fifteenth Amendment.

[The District Court rejected plaintiff's claims regarding disparate impact with regard to the law regarding out of precinct voting and the ballot collection prohibition. In addition the District Court rejected the plaintiff's claim on discriminatory intent regarding the ballot collection law. On appeal to the Ninth Circuit Court of Appeals, that court, sitting en banc, held for the plaintiffs, reversing the District Court with regard to the out of precinct voting and ballot collection finding on the disparate impact. The panel also reversed on the issue of discriminatory intent on the issue of ballot collection. Editors.]

[III]

A

We start with the text of VRA §2. It now provides:

> "(a) No voting qualification or prerequisite to voting or standard, practice, or procedure shall be imposed or applied by any State or political subdivision in a manner which results in a denial or abridgement of the right of any citizen of the United States to vote on account of race or color, or in contravention of the guarantees set forth in section 10303(f)(2) of this title, as provided in subsection (b).
>
> "(b) A violation of subsection (a) is established if, based on the totality of circumstances, it is shown that the political processes leading to nomination or election in the State or political subdivision are not equally open to participation by members of a class of citizens protected by subsection (a) in that its members have less opportunity

than other members of the electorate to participate in the political process and to elect representatives of their choice. The extent to which members of a protected class have been elected to office in the State or political subdivision is one circumstance which may be considered: Provided, That nothing in this section establishes a right to have members of a protected class elected in numbers equal to their proportion in the population."

52 U. S. C. §10301.

In *Gingles* [*Thornburg v. Gingles*, 478 U. S. 30 (1986)] our seminal §2 vote-dilution case, the Court quoted the text of amended §2 and then jumped right to the Senate Judiciary Committee Report, which focused on the issue of vote dilution. 478 U. S., at 36–37, 43, and n. 7. Our many subsequent vote-dilution cases have largely followed the path that Gingles charted. But because this is our first §2 time, place, or manner case, a fresh look at the statutory text is appropriate. Today, our statutory interpretation cases almost always start with a careful consideration of the text, and there is no reason to do otherwise here.

B

Section 2(a), as noted, omits the phrase [from the pre-1982 version of the law] "to deny or abridge the right . . . to vote on account of race or color," which [decisions prior to the 1982 amendments] interpreted to require proof of discriminatory intent. In place of that language, §2(a) substitutes the phrase "in a manner which results in a denial or abridgement of the right . . . to vote on account of race or color." (Emphasis added.) We need not decide what this text would mean if it stood alone because §2(b), which was added to win Senate approval, explains what must be shown to establish a §2 violation. Section 2(b) states that §2 is violated only where "the political processes leading to nomination or election" are not "equally open to participation" by members of the relevant protected group "in that its members have less opportunity than other members of the electorate to participate in the political process and to elect representatives of their choice." (Emphasis added.)

[What] §2(b) means by voting that is not "equally open" is further explained by this language: "in that its members have less opportunity than other members of the electorate to participate in the political process and to elect representatives of their choice." The phrase "in that" is "used to specify the respect in which a statement is true." Thus, equal openness and equal opportunity are not separate requirements. Instead, equal opportunity helps to explain the meaning of equal openness. And the term "opportunity" means, among other things, "a combination of circum- stances, time, and place suitable or favorable for a particular activity or action." Id., at 1583; see also Random House Dictionary of the English Language, at 1010 ("an appropriate or favorable time or occasion," "a situation or condition favorable for attainment of a goal").

Putting these terms together, it appears that the core of §2(b) is the requirement that voting be "equally open." The statute's reference to equal "opportunity" may stretch that concept to some degree to include consideration of a person's ability to use the means that are equally open. But equal openness remains the touchstone.

C

One other important feature of §2(b) stands out. The provision requires consideration of "the totality of circumstances." Thus, any circumstance that has a logical bearing on whether voting is "equally open" and affords equal "opportunity" may be considered. We will not attempt to com- pile an exhaustive list, but several important circumstances should be mentioned.

1

1. First, the size of the burden imposed by a challenged voting rule is highly relevant. The concepts of "open[ness]" and "opportunity" connote the absence of obstacles and burdens that block or seriously hinder voting, and therefore the size of the burden imposed by a voting rule is important. After all, every voting rule imposes a burden of some sort.

Voting takes time and, for almost everyone, some travel, even if only to a nearby mailbox. Casting a vote, whether by following the directions for using a voting machine or completing a paper ballot, requires compliance with certain rules. But because voting necessarily requires some effort and compliance with some rules, the concept of a voting system that is "equally open" and that furnishes an equal "opportunity" to cast a ballot must tolerate the "usual burdens of voting." Crawford v. Marion County Election Bd., 553 U. S. 181, 198 (2008) (opinion of Stevens, J.). Mere inconvenience cannot be enough to demonstrate a violation of §2.

2. For similar reasons, the degree to which a voting rule departs from what was standard practice when §2 was amended in 1982 is a relevant consideration. Because every voting rule imposes a burden of some sort, it is useful to have benchmarks with which the burdens imposed by a challenged rule can be compared. The burdens associated with the rules in widespread use when §2 was adopted are therefore useful in gauging whether the burdens imposed by a challenged rule are sufficient to prevent voting from being equally "open" or furnishing an equal "opportunity" to vote in the sense meant by §2. Therefore, it is relevant that in 1982 States typically required nearly all voters to cast their ballots in person on election day and allowed only narrow and tightly defined categories of voters to cast absentee ballots. [We] doubt that Congress intended to uproot facially neutral time, place, and manner regulations that have a long pedigree or are in widespread use in the United States. We have no need to decide whether adherence to, or a return to, a 1982 framework is necessarily lawful under §2, but the degree to which a challenged rule has a long pedigree or is in widespread use in the United States is a circumstance that must be taken into account.15

3. The size of any disparities in a rule's impact on members of different racial or ethnic groups is also an important factor to consider. Small disparities are less likely than large ones to indicate that a system is not equally open. To the extent that minority and non-minority groups differ with respect to employment, wealth, and education, even neutral regulations, no matter how crafted, may well result in some predictable disparities in rates of voting and non- compliance with voting rules. But the mere fact there is some disparity in impact does not necessarily mean that a system is not equally open or that it does not give everyone an equal opportunity to vote. The size of any disparity matters.

[4]. Next, courts must consider the opportunities provided by a State's entire system of voting when assessing the burden imposed by a challenged provision. This follows from §2(b)'s reference to the collective concept of a State's "political processes" and its "political process" as a whole. Thus, where a State provides multiple ways to vote, any burden imposed on voters who choose one of the available options cannot be evaluated without also taking into account the other available means.

5. Finally, the strength of the state interests served by a challenged voting rule is also an important factor that must be taken into account. As noted, every voting rule imposes a burden of some sort, and therefore, in determining "based on the totality of circumstances" whether a rule goes too far, it is important to consider the reason for the rule. Rules that are supported by strong state interests are less likely to violate §2.

One strong and entirely legitimate state interest is the prevention of fraud. Fraud can affect the outcome of a close election, and fraudulent votes dilute the right of citizens to cast ballots that carry appropriate weight. Fraud can also undermine public confidence in the fairness of elections and the perceived legitimacy of the announced outcome.

Ensuring that every vote is cast freely, without intimidation or undue influence, is also a valid and important state interest. This interest helped to spur the adoption of what soon became standard practice in this country and in other democratic nations the world round: the use of private voting booths. See Burson v. Freeman, 504 U. S. 191, 202–205 (1992) (plurality opinion).

2.

[The Court noted that the caselaw regarding section 2 has centered on vote dilution cases and that some of the standards used in those cases would not be appropriate or would need to be modified for time place and manner cases such as the present. It also noted that with regard to disparate impact, federal laws on fair housing and employment which employ that standard would not be an appropriate model for voting cases. The Court explains its reasoning below. Editors.]

[For] example, we think it inappropriate to read §2 to impose a strict "necessity requirement" that would force States to demonstrate that their legitimate interests can be accomplished only by means of the voting regulations in question. Stephanopoulos, Disparate Impact, Unified Law, 128 Yale L. J. 1566, 1617–1619 (2019) (advocating such a requirement). Demanding such a tight fit would have the effect of invalidating a great many neutral voting regulations with long pedigrees that are reasonable means of pursuing legitimate interests. It would also transfer much of the authority to regulate election procedures from the States to the federal courts. For those reasons, the Title VII and Fair Housing Act models are unhelpful in §2 cases.

D

[The majority provided a lengthy critique of points made by the dissent summarizing its disagreement with the dissenting opinion as follows. Editors.] Section 2 of the Voting Rights Act provides vital protection against discriminatory voting rules, and no one suggests that discrimination in voting has been extirpated or that the threat has been eliminated. But §2 does not deprive the States of their authority to establish nondiscriminatory voting rules, and that is precisely what the dissent's radical interpretation would mean in practice. The dissent is correct that the Voting Rights Act exemplifies our country's commitment to democracy, but there is nothing democratic about the dissent's attempt to bring about a wholesale transfer of the authority to set voting rules from the States to the federal courts.

IV

A

In light of the principles set out above, neither Arizona's out-of-precinct rule nor its ballot-collection law violates §2 of the VRA. Arizona's out-of-precinct rule enforces the requirement that voters who choose to vote in person on election day must do so in their assigned precincts. Having to identify one's own polling place and then travel there to vote does not exceed the "usual burdens of voting." Crawford, 553 U. S., at 198 (opinion of Stevens, J.) (noting the same about making a trip to the department of motor vehicles). On the contrary, these tasks are quintessential examples of the usual burdens of voting.

Not only are these unremarkable burdens, but the District Court's uncontested findings show that the State made extensive efforts to reduce their impact on the number of valid votes ultimately cast. The State makes accurate precinct information available to all voters. When precincts or polling places are altered between elections, each registered voter is sent a notice showing the voter's new polling place. 329 F. Supp. 3d, at 859. Arizona law also mandates that election officials send a sample ballot to each household that includes a registered voter who has not opted to be placed on the permanent early voter list, and this mailing also identifies the voter's proper polling location. In addition, the Arizona secretary of state's office sends voters pamphlets that include information (in both English and Spanish) about how to identify their assigned precinct.

[The] burdens of identifying and traveling to one's assigned precinct are also modest when considering Arizona's "political processes" as a whole. The Court of Appeals noted that Arizona leads other States in the rate of votes rejected on the ground that they were cast in the wrong precinct, and the court attributed this to frequent changes in polling locations, confusing placement of polling places, and high levels of residential mobility. 948 F. 3d, at 1000–1004. But even if it is marginally harder for Arizona voters to find their assigned polling places, the State offers other easy ways to vote. Any voter can request an early ballot without excuse. Any voter can ask to be placed on the permanent early voter list so that an early ballot will be mailed automatically. Voters may drop off their early ballots at any polling place, even one to which they are not assigned. And for nearly a month before election day, any voter can vote in person at an early voting location in his or her county. The availability of those options likely explains why out-of-precinct votes on election day make up such a small and apparently diminishing portion of overall ballots cast— 0.47% of all ballots in the 2012 general election and just 0.15% in 2016. 329 F. Supp. 3d, at 872.

Next, the racial disparity in burdens allegedly caused by the out-of-precinct policy is small in absolute terms. The District Court accepted the plaintiffs' evidence that, of the Arizona counties that reported out-of-precinct ballots in the 2016 general election, a little over 1% of Hispanic voters, 1% of African-American voters, and 1% of Native American voters who voted on election day cast an out-of-precinct ballot. For non-minority voters, the rate was around 0.5%. A policy that appears to work for 98% or more of voters to whom it applies—minority and non-minority alike—is unlikely to render a system unequally open.

[The] Court of Appeals' decision also failed to give appropriate weight to the state interests that the out-of-precinct rule serves. Not counting out-of-precinct votes induces compliance with the requirement that Arizonans who choose to vote in-person on election day do so at their assigned polling places. And as the District Court recognized, precinct-based voting furthers important state interests. It helps to distribute voters more evenly among polling places and thus reduces wait times. It can put polling places closer to voter residences than would a more centralized voting-center model. In addition, precinct-based voting helps to ensure that each voter receives a ballot that lists only the candidates and public questions on which he or she can vote, and this orderly administration tends to decrease voter confusion and increase voter confidence in elections. It is also significant that precinct-based voting has a long pedigree in the United States. And the policy of not counting out-of-precinct ballots is widespread.

The Court of Appeals discounted the State's interests because, in its view, there was no evidence that a less restrictive alternative would threaten the integrity of precinct-based voting. The court thought the State had no good reason for not counting an out-of-precinct voter's choices with respect to the candidates and issues also on the ballot in the voter's proper precinct. We disagree with this reasoning.

Section 2 does not require a State to show that its chosen policy is absolutely necessary or that a less restrictive means would not adequately serve the State's objectives. And the Court of Appeals' preferred alternative would have obvious disadvantages. Partially counting out-of-precinct ballots would complicate the process of tabulation and could lead to disputes and delay. In addition, as one of the en banc dissenters noted, it would tend to encourage voters who are primarily interested in only national or statewide elections to vote in whichever place is most convenient even if they know that it is not their assigned polling place. In light of the modest burdens allegedly imposed by Arizona's out-of-precinct policy, the small size of its disparate impact, and the State's justifications, we conclude the rule does not violate §2 of the VRA. 18

[The ballot collection restrictions] likewise passes muster under the results test of §2. Arizonans who receive early ballots can submit them by going to a mailbox, a post office, an early ballot drop box, or an authorized election official's office within the 27-day early voting period. They can also drop off their ballots at any polling place or voting center on election day, and in order to do so, they can skip the line of voters waiting to vote in person. Making any of these trips—much like traveling to an assigned polling place—falls squarely within the heartland of the "usual burdens of voting." Crawford, 553 U. S., at 198 (opinion of Stevens, J.). And voters can also ask a statutorily authorized proxy—a family member, a household member, or a caregiver—to mail a ballot or drop it off at any time within 27 days of an election.

The plaintiffs were unable to provide statistical evidence showing that [HB2023—the ballot collection restrictions] had a disparate impact on minority voters. Instead, they called witnesses who testified that third-party ballot collection tends to be used most heavily in disadvantaged communities and that minorities in Arizona—especially Native Americans—are disproportionately disadvantaged. But from that evidence the District Court could conclude only The plaintiffs were unable to provide statistical evidence showing that [HB2023—the ballot collection restrictions] had a disparate impact on minority voters. Instead, they called witnesses who testified that third-party ballot collection tends to be used most heavily in disadvantaged communities and that minorities in Arizona—especially Native Americans—are disproportionately disadvantaged. But from that evidence the District Court could conclude only that prior to HB 2023's enactment, "minorities generically were more likely than non-minorities to return their early ballots with the assistance of third parties." Id., at 870. How much more, the court could not say from the record. Neither can we. And without more concrete evidence, we cannot conclude that HB 2023 results in less opportunity to participate in the political process.

Even if the plaintiffs had shown a disparate burden caused by HB 2023, the State's justifications would suffice to avoid §2 liability. [Limiting] the classes of persons who may handle early ballots to those less likely to have ulterior motives deters potential fraud and improves voter confidence. That was the view of the bipartisan Commission on Federal Election Reform chaired by former President Jimmy Carter and former Secretary of State James Baker. The Carter-Baker Commission noted that "[a]bsentee balloting is vulnerable to abuse in several ways: . . . Citizens who vote at home, at nursing homes, at the workplace, or in church are more susceptible to pressure, overt and subtle, or to intimidation." Report of the Comm'n on Fed. Election Reform, Building Confidence in U. S. Elections 46 (Sept. 2005).

[As] with the out-of-precinct policy, the modest evidence of racially disparate burdens caused by HB 2023, in light of the State's justifications, leads us to the conclusion that the law does not violate §2 of the VRA.

V

We also granted certiorari to review whether the Court of Appeals erred in concluding that HB 2023 was enacted with a discriminatory purpose. The District Court found that it The plaintiffs were unable to provide statistical evidence showing that [HB2023—the ballot collection restrictions] had a disparate impact on minority voters. Instead, they called witnesses who testified that third-party ballot collection tends to be used most heavily in disadvantaged communities and that minorities in Arizona—especially Native Americans—are disproportionately disadvantaged. But from that evidence the District Court could conclude only that prior to HB 2023's enactment, "minorities generically were more likely than non-minorities to return their early ballots with the assistance of third parties." Id., at 870. How much more, the court could not say from the record. Neither can we. And without more concrete evidence, we cannot conclude that HB 2023 results in less opportunity to participate in the political process. [note 19]

――――

[Note 19] Not one to let the absence of a key finding get in the way, the dissent concludes from its own review of the evidence that HB 2023 "prevents many Native Americans from making effective use of one of the principal means of voting in Arizona," and that "[w]hat is an inconsequential burden for others is for these citizens a severe hardship." Post, at 38. What is missing from those statements is any evidence about the actual size of the disparity. (For that matter, by the time the dissent gets around to assessing HB 2023, it appears to have lost its zeal for statistical significance, which is nowhere to be seen. See post, at 35–40, and n. 13.)

――――

[The majority opinion described the District Court's conclusion that the ballot collection restriction law was not based on discriminatory intent on the part of the Arizona Legislature. The law was passed on the heels of what both the District Court and the majority acknowledged to be a racially tinged effort by a state senator to eliminate the ballot collection practice. However the District Court concluded that during the deliberations on the measure, it could not find evidence of a racial discriminatory intent on the part of the entire legislature. Editors]

[Arizona's] out-of-precinct policy and HB 2023 do not violate §2 of the VRA, and HB 2023 was not enacted with a racially discriminatory purpose. The judgment of the Court of Appeals is reversed, and the cases are remanded for further proceedings consistent with this opinion.

It is so ordered.

[A concurrence by Justice Gorsuch, joined by Justice Thomas is omitted]
JUSTICE KAGAN, with whom JUSTICE BREYER and JUSTICE SOTOMAYOR join, dissenting.

If a single statute represents the best of America, it is the Voting Rights Act. It marries two great ideals: democracy and racial equality. And it dedicates our country to carrying them out. Section 2, the provision at issue here, guarantees that members of every racial group will have equal voting opportunities. Citizens of every race will have the same shot to participate in the political process and to elect representatives of their choice. They will all own our democracy together—no one more and no one less than any other.

If a single statute reminds us of the worst of America, it is the Voting Rights Act. Because it was—and remains—so necessary. Because a century after the Civil War was fought, at the time of the Act's passage, the promise of political equality remained a distant dream for African American citizens. Because States and localities continually "contriv[ed] new rules," mostly neutral on their face but discriminatory in operation, to keep minority voters from the polls. South Carolina v. Katzenbach, 383 U. S. 301, 335 (1966). Because "Congress had reason to suppose" that States would "try similar maneuvers in the future"— "pour[ing] old poison into new bottles" to suppress minority votes. Because Congress has been proved right.

I

The Voting Rights Act of 1965 is an extraordinary law. Rarely has a statute required so much sacrifice to ensure its passage. Never has a statute done more to advance the Nation's highest ideals. And few laws are more vital in the current moment. Yet in the last decade, this Court has treated no statute worse. To take the measure of today's harm, a look to the Act's past must come first. The idea is not to recount, as the majority hurriedly does, some bygone era of voting discrimination. See ante, at 2–3. It is instead to describe the electoral practices that the Act targets—and to show the high stakes of the present controversy.

A

Democratic ideals in America got off to a glorious start; democratic practice not so much. The Declaration of Independence made an awe-inspiring promise: to institute a government "deriving [its] just powers from the consent of the governed." But for most of the Nation's first century, that pledge ran to white men only. The earliest state election laws excluded from the franchise African Americans, Native Americans, women, and those without property.

In 1855, on the precipice of the Civil War, only five States permitted African Americans to vote. And at the federal level, our Court's most deplorable holding made sure that no black people could enter the voting booth. See Dred Scott v. Sandford, 19 How. 393 (1857).

But the "American ideal of political equality . . . could not forever tolerate the limitation of the right to vote" to whites only. Mobile v. Bolden, 446 U. S. 55, 103–104 (1980) (Marshall, J., dissenting). And a civil war, dedicated to ensuring "government of the people, by the people, for the people," brought constitutional change. In 1870, after a hard-fought battle over ratification, the Fifteenth Amendment carried the Nation closer to its founding aspirations. "The right of citizens of the United States to vote shall not be denied or abridged by the United States or by any State on account of race, color, or previous condition of servitude." Those words promised to enfranchise millions of black citizens who only a decade earlier had been slaves. Frederick Douglass held that the Amendment "means that we are placed upon an equal footing with all other men"—that with the vote, "liberty is to be the right of all." President Grant had seen much blood spilled in the Civil War; now he spoke of the fruits of that sacrifice. In a self- described "unusual" message to Congress, he heralded the Fifteenth Amendment as "a measure of grander importance than any other one act of the kind from the foundation of our free Government"—as "the most important event that has occurred since the nation came into life."

Momentous as the Fifteenth Amendment was, celebration of its achievements soon proved premature. The Amendment's guarantees "quickly became dead letters in much of the country." African Americans daring to go to the polls often "met with coordinated intimidation and violence." Northwest Austin Municipal Util. Dist. No. One v. Holder, 557 U. S. 193, 218–219 (2009) (THOMAS, J., concurring in judgment in part and dissenting in part). And almost immediately, legislators discovered that bloodless actions could also suffice to limit the electorate to white citizens. Many States, especially in the South, suppressed the black vote through a dizzying array of methods: literacy tests, poll taxes, registration requirements, and property qualifications. See Katzenbach, 383 U. S., at 310–312. Most of those laws, though facially neutral, gave enough discretion to election officials to prevent significant effects on poor or uneducated whites. The idea, as one Virginia representative put it, was "to disfranchise every negro that [he] could disfranchise," and "as few white people as possible." Decade after decade after decade, election rules blocked African Americans—and in some States, Hispanics and Native Americans too—from making use of the ballot. See Oregon v. Mitchell, 400 U. S. 112,

132 (1970) (opinion of Black, J.) (discussing treatment of non-black groups). By 1965, only 27% of black Georgians, 19% of black Alabamians, and 7%—yes, 7%—of black Mississippians were registered to vote. See C. Bullock, R. Gaddie, & J. Wert, The Rise and Fall of the Voting Rights Act 23 (2016).

The civil rights movement, and the events of a single Bloody Sunday, created pressure for change. Selma was the heart of an Alabama county whose 15,000 black citizens included, in 1961, only 156 on the voting rolls. See D. Garrow, Protest at Selma 31 (1978). In the first days of 1965, the city became the epicenter of demonstrations meant to force Southern election officials to register African American voters. As weeks went by without results, organizers announced a march from Selma to Birmingham. On March 7, some 600 protesters, led by future Congressman John Lewis, sought to cross the Edmund Pettus Bridge. State troopers in riot gear responded brutally: "Turning their nightsticks horizontally, they rushed into the crowd, knocking people over like bowling pins." G. May, Bending Toward Justice 87 (2013). Then came men on horseback, "swinging their clubs and ropes like cowboys driving cattle to market." Ibid. The protestors were beaten, knocked unconscious, and bloodied. Lewis's skull was fractured. "I thought I was going to die on this bridge," he later recalled.

A galvanized country responded. Ten days after the Selma march, President Johnson wrote to Congress proposing legislation to "help rid the Nation of racial discrimination in every aspect of the electoral process and thereby in- sure the right of all to vote." H. R. Doc. No. 120, at 1. (To his attorney general, Johnson was still more emphatic: "I want you to write the goddamnedest toughest voting rights act that you can devise." H. Raines, My Soul Is Rested 337 (1983).) And in August 1965, after the bill's supporters overcame a Senate filibuster, Johnson signed the Voting Rights Act into law. Echoing Grant's description of the Fifteenth Amendment, Johnson called the statute "one of the most monumental laws in the entire history of American freedom." "After a century's failure to fulfill the promise" of the Fifteenth Amendment, "passage of the VRA finally led to signal improvement." Shelby County, 570 U. S., at 562 (Ginsburg, J., dissenting). In the five years after the statute's passage, almost as many African Americans registered to vote in six Southern States as in the entire century before 1965. See Davidson, The Voting Rights Act: A Brief History, in Controversies in Minority Voting 21 (B. Grofman & C. Davidson eds. 1992). The crudest attempts to block voting access, like literacy tests and poll taxes, disappeared. Legislatures often replaced those vote denial schemes with new measures—mostly to do with districting—designed to dilute the impact of minority votes. But the Voting Rights Act, operating for decades at full strength, stopped many of those measures too. As a famed dissent assessed the situation about a half-century after the statute's enactment: The Voting Rights Act had become "one of the most consequential, efficacious, and amply justified exercises of federal legislative power in our Nation's history." Shelby County, 570 U. S., at 562 (Ginsburg, J., dissenting).

B

Much of the Voting Rights Act's success lay in its capacity to meet ever-new forms of discrimination. Experience showed that "[w]henever one form of voting discrimination was identified and prohibited, others sprang up in its place." Shelby County, 570 U. S., at 560 (Ginsburg, J., dissenting). Combating those efforts was like "battling the Hydra"—or to use a less cultured reference, like playing a game of whack-a-mole. So Congress, in Section 5 of the Act, gave the Department of Justice authority to review all new rules devised by jurisdictions with a history of voter suppression—and to block any that would have discriminatory effects. See 52 U. S. C. §§10304(a)–(b). In that way, the Act would prevent the use of new, more nuanced methods to restrict the voting opportunities of non-white citizens.

And for decades, Section 5 operated as intended. Between 1965 and 2006, the Department stopped almost 1200 voting laws in covered areas from taking effect. See Shelby County, 570 U. S., at 571 (Ginsburg, J., dissenting). Some of those laws used districting to dilute minority voting strength—making sure that the votes of minority citizens would carry less weight than the votes of whites in electing candidates. Other laws, even if facially neutral, disproportionately curbed the ability of non-white citizens to cast a ballot at all. So, for example, a jurisdiction might require forms of identification that those voters were less likely to have; or it might limit voting places and times convenient for those voters; or it might purge its voter rolls through mechanisms especially likely to ensnare them. See id., at 574–575. In reviewing mountains of such evidence in 2006, Congress saw a continuing need for Section 5. Although "discrimination today is more subtle than the visible methods used in 1965," Congress found, it still produces "the same [effects], namely a diminishing of the minority com- munity's ability to fully participate in the electoral process." H. R. Rep. No. 109–478, p. 6 (2006). Congress thus reauthorized the preclearance scheme for 25 years.

But this Court took a different view. Finding that "[o]ur country has changed," the Court saw only limited instances of voting discrimination—and so no further need for preclearance. Shelby County, 570 U. S., at 547–549, 557. Displacing Congress's contrary judgment, the Court struck down the coverage formula essential to the statute's operation. The legal analysis offered was perplexing: The Court based its decision on a "principle of equal [state] sovereignty" that a prior decision of ours had rejected—and that has not made an appearance since. Id., at 544 (majority opinion); see id., at 587–588 (Ginsburg, J., dissenting). Worse yet was the Court's blithe confidence in assessing what was needed and what was not. "[T]hings have changed dramatically," the Court reiterated, id., at 547: The statute that was once a necessity had become an imposition. But how did the majority know there was nothing more for Section 5 to do—that the (undoubted) changes in the country went so far as to make the provision unnecessary? It didn't, as Justice Ginsburg explained in dissent. The majority's faith that discrimination was almost gone derived, at least in part, from the success of Section 5—from its record of blocking discriminatory voting schemes. Discarding Section 5 because those schemes had diminished was "like throwing away your umbrella in a rainstorm because you are not getting wet." Id., at 590.

The rashness of the act soon became evident. Once Section 5's strictures came off, States and localities put in place new restrictive voting laws, with foreseeably adverse effects on minority voters. On the very day Shelby County issued, Texas announced that it would implement a strict voter-identification requirement that had failed to clear Section 5.

[And] that was just the first wave of post-Shelby County laws. In recent months, State after State has taken up or enacted legislation erecting new barriers to voting. See Brennan Center for Justice, Voting Laws Roundup: May 2021 (online source archived at www.supremecourt.gov) (compiling legislation). Those laws shorten the time polls are open, both on Election Day and before. They impose new prerequisites to voting by mail, and shorten the win- dows to apply for and return mail ballots. They make it harder to register to vote, and easier to purge voters from the rolls. Two laws even ban handing out food or water to voters standing in line. Some of those restrictions may be lawful under the Voting Rights Act. But chances are that some have the kind of impact the Act was designed to prevent—that they make the political process less open to minority voters than to others.

[II]

[A]

Section 2, as relevant here, has two interlocking parts. Subsection (a) states the law's basic prohibition: "No voting qualification or prerequisite to voting or standard, practice, or procedure shall be imposed or applied by any State or political subdivision in a manner which results in a denial or abridgement of the right of any citizen of the United States to vote on account of race or color." 52 U. S. C. §10301(a). Subsection (b) then tells courts how to apply that bar—or otherwise said, when to find that an infringement of the voting right has occurred: "A violation of subsection (a) is established if, based on the totality of circumstances, it is shown that the political processes leading to nomination or election in the State or political subdivision are not equally open to participation by members of [a given race] in that [those] members have less opportunity than other members of the electorate to participate in the political process and to elect representatives of their choice." §10301(b).

[The] first thing to note about Section 2 is how far its prohibitory language sweeps. The provision bars any "voting qualification," any "prerequisite to voting," or any "standard, practice, or procedure" that "results in a denial or abridgement of the right" to "vote on account of race." The overlapping list of covered state actions makes clear that Section 2 extends to every kind of voting or election rule. Congress carved out nothing pertaining to "voter qualifications or the manner in which elections are conducted." Holder v. Hall, 512 U. S. 874, 922 (1994) (THOMAS, J., concurring in judgment). So, for example, the provision "covers all manner of registration requirements, the practices surrounding registration," the "locations of polling places, the times polls are open, the use of paper ballots as opposed to voting machines, and other similar aspects of the voting process that might be manipulated to deny any citizen the right to cast a ballot and have it properly counted." All those rules and more come within the statute—so long as they result in a race-based "denial or abridgement" of the voting right. And the "denial or abridgement" phrase speaks broadly too. "[A]bridgment necessarily means something more subtle and less drastic than the complete denial of the right to cast a ballot, denial being separately forbidden." Bossier, 528 U. S., at 359 (Souter, J., concurring in part and dissenting in part). It means to "curtail," rather than take away, the voting right. American Heritage Dictionary 4 (1969).

The "results in" language, connecting the covered voting rules to the prohibited voting abridgement, tells courts that they are to focus on the law's effects. [But] when to conclude—looking to effects, not purposes—that a denial or abridgment has occurred? Again, answering that question is subsection (b)'s function. It teaches that a violation is established when, "based on the totality of circumstances," a State's electoral system is "not equally open" to members of a racial group. And then the subsection tells us what that means. A system is not equally open if members of one race have "less opportunity" than others to cast votes, to participate in politics, or to elect representatives. The key demand, then, is for equal political opportunity across races.

That equal "opportunity" is absent when a law or practice makes it harder for members of one racial group, than for others, to cast ballots. When Congress amended Section 2, the word "opportunity" meant what it also does today: "a favorable or advantageous combination of circumstances" for some action. See American Heritage Dictionary, at 922. In using that word, Congress made clear that the Voting Rights Act does not demand equal outcomes. If members of different races have the same opportunity to vote, but go to the ballot box at different rates, then so be it—that is their preference, and Section 2 has nothing to say. But if a law produces different voting opportunities across races—if it establishes rules and conditions of political participation that are less favorable (or advantageous) for one racial group than for others—then Section 2 kicks in. It applies, in short, whenever the law makes it harder for citizens of one race than of others to cast a vote.

[Suppose], as Justice Scalia once did, that a county has a law limiting "voter registration [to] only three hours one day a week." And suppose that policy makes it "more difficult for blacks to register than whites"—say, because the jobs African Americans disproportionately hold make it harder to take time off in that window. Ibid. Those citizens, Justice Scalia concluded, would then "have less opportunity 'to participate in the political process' than whites, and §2 would therefore be violated." Ibid. (emphasis deleted). In enacting Section 2, Congress documented many similar (if less extreme) facially neutral rules—"registration requirements," "voting and registration hours," voter "purging" policies, and so forth—that create disparities in voting opportunities. Those laws, Congress thought, would violate Section 2, though they were not facially discriminatory, because they gave voters of different races unequal access to the political process.

Congress also made plain, in calling for a totality-of- circumstances inquiry, that equal voting opportunity is a function of both law and background conditions—in other words, that a voting rule's validity depends on how the rule operates in conjunction with facts on the ground. "[T]otality review," this Court has explained, stems from Congress's recognition of "the demonstrated ingenuity of state and local governments in hobbling minority voting power." Johnson v. De Grandy, 512 U. S. 997, 1018 (1994). Sometimes, of course, state actions overtly target a single race: For example, Congress was acutely aware, in amending Section 2, of the elimination of polling places in African American neighborhoods. But sometimes government officials enact facially neutral laws that leverage—and become discriminatory by dint of pre-existing social and economic conditions. The classic historical cases are literacy tests and poll taxes. A more modern example is the one Justice Scalia gave, of limited registration hours. Congress knew how those laws worked: It saw that "inferior education, poor employment opportunities, and low incomes"—all conditions often correlated with race—could turn even an ordinary- seeming election rule into an effective barrier to minority voting in certain circumstances. Thornburg v. Gingles, 478 U. S. 30, 69 (1986) (plurality opinion). So Congress demanded, as this Court has recognized, "an intensely local appraisal" of a rule's impact—"a searching practical evaluation of the 'past and present reality.'"

At the same time, the totality inquiry enables courts to take into account strong state interests supporting an election rule. [But] in making that assessment of state interests, a court must keep in mind—just as Congress did—the ease of "offer[ing] a non-racial rationalization" for even blatantly discriminatory laws. State interests do not get accepted on faith. And even a genuine and strong interest will not suffice if a plaintiff can prove that it can be accomplished in a less discriminatory way. As we have put the point before: When a less racially biased law would not "significantly impair[] the State's interest," the discriminatory election rule must fall. Houston Lawyers' Assn., 501 U. S., at 428. [note 5].

So the text of Section 2, as applied in our precedents, tells us the following, every part of which speaks to the ambition of Congress's action. Section 2 applies to any voting rule, of any kind. The provision prohibits not just the denial but also the abridgment of a citizen's voting rights on account of race. The inquiry is focused on effects: It asks not about why state officials enacted a rule, but about whether that rule results in racial discrimination. The discrimination that is of concern is inequality of voting opportunity. That kind of discrimination can arise from facially neutral (not just targeted) rules. There is a Section 2 problem when an election rule, operating against a backdrop of historical the backdrop of historical, social, and economic conditions, makes it harder for minority citizens than for others to cast ballots. And strong state interests may save an otherwise discriminatory rule, but only if that rule is needed to achieve them—that is, only if a less discriminatory rule will not attain the State's goal.

---

5 The majority pretends that Houston Lawyers' Assn. did not ask about the availability of a less discriminatory means of serving the State's end, see ante, at 23, n. 16—but the inquiry is right there on page 428 (examining "if [the] impairment of a minority group's voting strength could be remedied without significantly impairing the State's interest in electing judges on a district-wide basis"). In posing that question, the Court did what Congress wanted, because absent a necessity test, States could too easily get away with offering "non-racial" but pretextual "rationalization[s]." S. Rep., at 37; see supra, at 14. And the Court did what it always does in applying laws barring discriminatory effects—ask whether a challenged policy is necessary to achieve the asserted goal.

Contrary to the majority's view, that kind of inquiry would not result in "invalidat[ing] just about any voting rule a State adopts." A plaintiff bears the burden of showing that a less discriminatory law would be "at least as effective in achieving the [State's] legitimate purpose." Reno v. American Civil Liberties Union, 521 U. S. 844, 874 (1997). [Given] those features of the alternative-means inquiry, a State that tries both to serve its electoral interests and to give its minority citizens equal electoral access will rarely have anything to fear from a Section 2 suit.

[B]

The majority's opinion mostly inhabits a law-free zone. It congratulates itself in advance for giving Section 2's text "careful consideration." And then it leaves that language almost wholly behind. (Every once in a while, when its lawmaking threatens to leap off the page, it thinks to sprinkle in a few random statutory words.) So too the majority barely mentions this Court's precedents construing Section 2's text. [The] majority instead founds its decision on a list of mostly made-up factors, at odds with Section 2 itself. To excuse this unusual free-form exercise, the majority notes that Section 2 authorizes courts to conduct a "totality of circumstances" analysis. But as described above, Congress mainly added that language so that Section 2 could protect against "the demonstrated ingenuity of state and local governments in hobbling minority voting power." De Grandy, 512 U. S., at 1018; see supra, at 16–17. The totality inquiry requires courts to explore how ordinary-seeming laws can interact with local conditions—economic, social, historical—to produce race-based voting inequalities. That inquiry hardly gives a court the license to devise whatever limitations on Section 2's reach it would have liked Congress to enact.

[Start] with the majority's first idea: a "[m]ere inconvenience[ ]" exception to Section 2. Voting, the majority says, imposes a set of "usual burdens": Some time, some travel, some rule compliance. And all of that is beneath the notice of Section 2—even if those burdens fall highly unequally on members of different races. But that categorical exclusion, for seemingly small (or "[un]usual" or "[un]serious") burdens, is nowhere in the provision's text. To the contrary (and as this Court has recognized before), Section 2 allows no "safe harbor[s]" for election rules resulting in disparate voting opportunities.

[And] what is a "mere inconvenience" or "usual burden" anyway? The drafters of the Voting Rights Act understood that "social and historical conditions," including disparities in education, wealth, and employment, often affect opportunities to vote. Gingles, 478 U. S., at 47; see supra, at 16– 17. What does not prevent one citizen from casting a vote might prevent another. How is a judge supposed to draw an "inconvenience" line in some reasonable place, taking those differences into account? Consider a law banning the handing out of water to voters. No more than—or not even—an inconvenience when lines are short; but what of when they are, as in some neighborhoods, hours-long? The point here is that judges lack an objective way to decide which voting obstacles are "mere" and which are not, for all voters at all times. And so Section 2 does not ask the question.

The majority's "multiple ways to vote" factor is similarly flawed. True enough, a State with three ways to vote (say, on Election Day; early in person; or by mail) may be more "open" than a State with only one (on Election Day). And some other statute might care about that. But Section 2 does not. What it cares about is that a State's "political processes" are "equally open" to voters of all races. And a State's electoral process is not equally open if, for example, the State "only" makes Election Day voting by members of one race peculiarly difficult.

[The] majority's history-and-commonality factor also pushes the inquiry away from what the statute demands. The oddest part of the majority's analysis is the idea that "what was standard practice when §2 was amended in 1982 is a relevant consideration." The 1982 state of the world is no part of the Section 2 test. An election rule prevalent at that time may make voting harder for minority than for white citizens; Section 2 then covers such a rule, as it covers any other. And contrary to the majority's unsupported speculation, Congress "intended" exactly that. See H. R. Rep., at 14 (explaining that the Act aimed to eradicate the "numerous practices and procedures which act as continued barriers to registration and voting"). Section 2 was meant to disrupt the status quo, not to preserve it—to eradicate then-current discriminatory practices, not to set them in amber.

[That] leaves only the majority's discussion of state interests, which is again skewed so as to limit Section 2 liability. No doubt that under our precedent, a state interest in an election rule "is a legitimate factor to be considered." Houston Lawyers' Assn., 501 U. S., at 426. But the majority wrongly dismisses the need for the closest possible fit between means and end—that is, between the terms of the rule and the State's asserted interest. In the past, this Court has stated that a discriminatory election rule must fall, no matter how weighty the interest claimed, if a less biased law would not "significantly impair[that] interest." Houston Lawyers' Assn., 501 U. S., at 428; see supra, at 17–18, and n. 5.

[The] Voting Rights Act was meant to replace state and local election rules that needlessly make voting harder for members of one race than for others. The text of the Act perfectly reflects that objective. The "democratic" principle it upholds is not one of States' rights as against federal courts. The democratic principle it upholds is the right of every American, of every race, to have equal access to the ballot box. The majority today undermines that principle as it refuses to apply the terms of the statute. By declaring some racially discriminatory burdens inconsequential, and by refusing to subject asserted state interests to serious means-end scrutiny, the majority enables voting discrimination.

III

Just look at Arizona. Two of that State's policies disproportionately affect minority citizens' opportunity to vote. The first—the out-of-precinct policy—results in Hispanic and African American voters' ballots being thrown out at a statistically higher rate than those of whites. And whatever the majority might say about the ordinariness of such a rule, Arizona applies it in extra-ordinary fashion: Arizona is the national outlier in dealing with out-of-precinct votes, with the next-worst offender nowhere in sight. The second rule—the ballot-collection ban—makes voting meaningfully more difficult for Native American citizens than for others. And nothing about how that ban is applied is "usual" either—this time because of how many of the State's Native American citizens need to travel long distances to use the mail. Both policies violate Section 2, on a straightforward application of its text. Considering the "totality of circumstances," both "result in" members of some races having "less opportunity than other members of the electorate to participate in the political process and to elect a representative of their choice." §10301(b). The majority reaches the opposite conclusion because it closes its eyes to the facts on the ground.10

A

Arizona's policy [of discarding out-of-precinct ballots] creates a statistically significant disparity between minority and white voters: Because of the policy, members of different racial groups do not in fact have an equal likelihood of having their ballots counted. Suppose a State decided to throw out 1% of the Hispanic vote each election. Presumably, the majority would not approve the action just because 99% of the Hispanic vote is unaffected. Nor would the majority say that Hispanics in that system have an equal shot of casting an effective ballot. Here, the policy is not so overt; but under Section 2, that difference does not matter. Because the policy "results in" statistically significant inequality, it implicates Section 2. And the kind of inequality that the policy produces is not the kind only a statistician could see. A rule that throws out, each and every election, thousands of votes cast by minority citizens is a rule that can affect election outcomes. If you were a minority vote suppressor in Arizona or elsewhere, you would want that rule in your bag of tricks. You would not think it remotely irrelevant.

[And], critically, Maricopa's relocations hit minority voters harder than others. In 2012, the county moved polling stations in African American and Hispanic neighborhoods 30% more often than in white ones. See App. 110–111. The odds of those changes leading to mistakes increased yet further because the affected areas are home to citizens with relatively low education and income levels. See id., at 170–171. And even putting relocations aside, the sitting of polling stations in minority areas caused significant out-of-precinct voting. Hispanic and Native American voters had to travel further than white voters did to their assigned polling places. See id., at 109. And all minority voters were disproportionately likely to be assigned to polling places other than the ones closest to where they lived. See id., at 109, and n. 30, 175–176. Small wonder, given such sitting decisions, that minority voters found it harder to identify and get to their correct precincts. But the majority does not address these matters.11

---

[10] Because I would affirm the Court of Appeals' holding that the effects of these policies violate Section 2, I need not pass on that court's alternative holding [regarding] discriminatory intent.

[11] The majority's excuse for failing to consider the plaintiffs' evidence on Arizona's sitting of polling places is that the plaintiffs did not bring a separate claim against those practices. See ante, at 30, n. 18. If that sounds odd, it is. The majority does not contest that the evidence on polling-place sitting is relevant to the plaintiffs' challenge to the out-of- precinct policy. Nor could the majority do so. The sitting practices are one of the background conditions against which the out-of-precinct policy operates—exactly the kind of thing that a totality-of-circumstances analysis demands a court take into account. To refuse to think about those practices because the plaintiffs might have brought a free-standing claim against them is to impose an out-of-thin-air pleading requirement that operates to exclude exactly the evidence that most strongly signals a Section 2 violation.

Facts also undermine the State's asserted interests, which the majority hangs its hat on. A government interest, as even the majority recognizes, is "merely one factor to be considered" in Section 2's totality analysis. Houston Lawyers' Assn., 501 U. S., at 427; see ante, at 19. Here, the State contends that it needs the out-of-precinct policy to support a precinct-based voting system. But 20 other States combine precinct-based systems with mechanisms for partially counting out-of-precinct ballots (that is, counting the votes for offices like President or Governor). And the District Court found that it would be "administratively feasible" for Arizona to join that group. 329 F. Supp. 3d, at 860. Arizona—echoed by the majority—objects that adopt- ing a partial-counting approach would decrease compliance with the vote-in-your-precinct rule (by reducing the penalty for a voter's going elsewhere). But there is more than a little paradox in that response. We know from the extraordinary number of ballots Arizona discards that its current system fails utterly to "induce[] compliance." Ante, at 28–29; see supra, at 30–31. Presumably, that is because the system—most notably, its placement and shifting of polling places—sows an unparalleled level of voter confusion. A State that makes compliance with an election rule so unusually hard is in no position to claim that its interest in "induc[ing] compliance" outweighs the need to remedy the race-based discrimination that rule has caused.

B

Arizona's law mostly banning third-party ballot collection also results in a significant race-based disparity in voting opportunities. The problem with that law again lies in facts nearly unique to Arizona—here, the presence of rural Native American communities that lack ready access to mail service. [Most] Arizonans vote by mail. But many rural Native American voters lack access to mail service, to a degree hard for most of us to fathom. Only 18% of Native voters in rural counties receive home mail delivery, compared to 86% of white voters living in those counties. See 329 F. Supp. 3d, at 836. And for many or most, there is no nearby post office. Native Americans in rural Arizona "often must travel 45 minutes to 2 hours just to get to a mailbox." [As] the District Court found: "[F]or many Native Americans living in rural locations," voting "is an activity that requires the active assistance of friends and neighbors." Ibid. So in some Native communities, third-party collection of ballots—mostly by fellow clan members—became "standard practice." Ibid. And stopping it, as one tribal election official testified, "would be a huge devastation." Ibid.; see Brief for Navajo Nation as Amicus Curiae 19–20 (explaining that ballot collection is how Navajo voters "have historically handled their mail-in ballots").

Arizona has always regulated these activities to prevent fraud. State law makes it a felony offense for a ballot collector to fail to deliver a ballot. See Ariz. Rev. Stat. Ann. §16–1005 (Cum. Supp. 2020). It is also a felony for a ballot collector to tamper with a ballot in any manner. See ibid. And as the District Court found, "tamper evident envelopes and a rigorous voter signature verification procedure" protect against any such attempts. 329 F. Supp. 3d, at 854. For those reasons and others, no fraud involving ballot collection has ever come to light in the State. Id., at 852.

Still, Arizona enacted—with full knowledge of the likely discriminatory consequences—the near-blanket ballot-collection ban challenged here.

[Put] all of that together, and Arizona's ballot-collection ban violates Section 2. The ban interacts with conditions on the ground—most crucially, disparate access to mail service—to create unequal voting opportunities for Native Americans.

[In] the majority's alternate world collection ban is just a "usual burden[ ] of voting" for every- one. Ante, at 30. And in that world, "[f]raud is a real risk" of ballot collection—as to every community, in every circumstance—just because the State in litigation asserts that it is. Ante, at 33. The State need not even show that the discriminatory rule it enacted is necessary to prevent the fraud it purports to fear. So the State has no duty to substitute a non-discriminatory rule that would adequately serve its professed goal. Like the rest of today's opinion, the majority's treatment of the collection ban thus flouts what Section 2 commands: the eradication of election rules resulting in unequal opportunities for minority voters.

IV

Congress enacted the Voting Rights Act to address a deep fault of our democracy—the historical and continuing attempt to withhold from a race of citizens their fair share of influence on the political process. For a century, African Americans had struggled and sacrificed to wrest their voting rights from a resistant Nation. The statute they and their allies at long last attained made a promise to all Americans. From then on, Congress demanded, the political process would be equally open to every citizen, regardless of race.

One does not hear much in the majority opinion about that promise. One does not hear much about what brought Congress to enact the Voting Rights Act, what Congress hoped for it to achieve, and what obstacles to that vision remain today. One would never guess that the Act is, as the President who signed it wrote, "monumental." Johnson Papers 841.

[This] Court has no right to remake Section 2. Maybe some think that vote suppression is a relic of history—and so the need for a potent Section 2 has come and gone. Cf. Shelby County, 570 U. S., at 547 ("[T]hings have changed dramatically"). But Congress gets to make that call. Because it has not done so, this Court's duty is to apply the law as it is written. The law that confronted one of this country's most enduring wrongs; pledged to give every American, of every race, an equal chance to participate in our democracy; and now stands as the crucial tool to achieve that goal. That law, of all laws, deserves the sweep and power Congress gave it. That law, of all laws, should not be diminished by this Court.

Notes

1. Justice Kagan does not end her dissent with the customary "I respectfully dissent." Could this be an indicator of some tension on the Court? Do you think Kagan was unduly harsh to Justice Alito? Which had the better argument? Why? Think about that and discuss.

2. It is likely that this Kagan dissent will be remembered for its tone, breadth, and critique of the majority opinion. It is also likely that it will be compared to the late Justice Ginsburg's dissent in *Shelby County v. Holder* ("Throwing out pre-clearance when it has worked and is continuing to work to stop discriminatory changes is like throwing away your umbrella in a rainstorm because you are not getting wet."). Can you think of other historic dissents to compare it to? Does it rank with Justice John Marshall Harlan's (the first) dissent in *Plessy v. Ferguson*? Justice Scalia's dissent in *Lawrence v. Texas*?

3. How does Justice Alito understand the term "totality of the circumstances"? How does Justice Kagan understand this term? Are their understandings crucial to their conclusions about Section 2?

4. Two approaches to Section 2 flow from the two opinions. The first Justice Alito focuses on alternative voting options under the totality of circumstances rule. Justice Kagan focuses on whether a particular rule on a voting method has a disparate impact on minorities with regard to that method. Whose position do you prefer?

Here are some notable quotations from the full opinion selected by the editors:

[**Justice Alito**] "The Court of Appeals viewed the State's justifications for HB 2023 as tenuous largely because there was no evidence of early ballot fraud in Arizona. But prevention of fraud is not the only legitimate interest served by restrictions on ballot collection. Third-party ballot collection can lead to pressure and intimidation. Further, a State may take action to prevent election fraud without waiting for it to occur within its own borders." Pp. 30–34.

[**Justice Kagan**] "But in making that assessment of state interests, a court must keep in mind—just as Congress did—the ease of 'offer[ing] a non-racial rationalization' for even blatantly discriminatory laws. S. Rep., at 37; see supra, at 14. State interests do not get accepted on faith. And even a genuine and strong interest will not suffice if a plaintiff can prove that it can be accomplished in a less discriminatory way. As we have put the point before: When a less racially biased law would not 'significantly impair[] the State's interest,' the discriminatory election rule must fall." Houston Lawyers' Assn., 501 U. S., at 428.5

So much for balls and strikes: "And what is a 'mere inconvenience' or 'usual burden' anyway? The drafters of the Voting Rights Act understood that "social and historical conditions," including disparities in education, wealth, and employment, often affect opportunities to vote. *Gingles*, 478 U. S., at 47; see supra, at 16–17. What does not prevent one citizen from casting a vote might prevent another. How is a judge supposed to draw an 'inconvenience' line in some reasonable place, taking those differences into account? Consider a law banning the handing out of water to voters. No more than—or not even—an inconvenience when lines are short; but what of when they are, as in some neighborhoods, hours-long? The point here is that judges lack an objective way to decide which voting obstacles are 'mere' and which are not for all voters at all times. And so Section 2 does not ask the question."

The dissent seeks to rehabilitate this statement by focusing on the last part of this sentence, in which the District Court stated that the Legislature "intended [the] taint to be maintained but safe from remedy." Post, at 33–34. In making this argument, the dissent, like the District Court, refuses to heed the presumption of legislative good faith and the allocation of the burden of proving intentional discrimination. We do not dispute that the District Court purportedly found that the 2013 Legislature acted with discriminatory intent. The problem is that, in making that finding, it relied overwhelmingly on what it perceived to be the 2013 Legislature's duty to show that it had purged the bad intent of its predecessor.

The Constitution
of the United States

WE THE PEOPLE of the United States, in Order to form a more perfect Union, establish Justice, insure domestic Tranquility, provide for the common defense, promote the general Welfare, and secure the Blessings of Liberty to ourselves and our Posterity, do ordain and establish this Constitution for the United States of America.

ARTICLE I

Section 1. All legislative Powers herein granted shall be vested in a Congress of the United States which shall consist of a Senate and House of Representatives.

Section 2. [1] The House of Representatives shall be composed of Members chosen every second Year by the People of the several States, and the Electors in each State shall have the Qualifications requisite for Electors of the most numerous Branch of the State Legislature. [2] No Person shall be a Representative who shall not have attained to the Age of twenty five Years, and been seven Years a Citizen of the United States, and who shall not, when elected, be an Inhabitant of that State in which he shall be chosen. [3] Representatives and direct Taxes shall be apportioned among the several States which may be included within this Union, according to their respective Numbers, which shall be determined by adding to the whole Number of free Persons, including those bound to Service for a Term of Years, and excluding Indians not taxed, three fifths of all other Persons. The actual Enumeration shall be made within three Years after the first Meeting of the Congress of the United States, and within every subsequent Term of ten Years, in such Manner as they shall by Law direct. The Number of Representatives shall not exceed one for every thirty Thousand, but each State shall have at Least One Representative; and until such enumeration shall be made, the State of New Hampshire shall be entitled to chuse three, Massachusetts eight, Rhode Island and Providence Plantations one, Connecticut five, New York six, New Jersey four, Pennsylvania eight, Delaware one, Maryland six, Virginia ten, North Carolina five, South Carolina five, and Georgia three. [4] When vacancies happen in the Representation from any State, the Executive Authority thereof shall issue Writs of Election to fill such Vacancies. [5] The House of Representatives shall chuse their Speaker and other Officers; and shall have the sole Power of Impeachment.

Section 3. [1] The Senate of the United States shall be composed of two Senators from each State, chosen by the Legislature thereof, for six Years; and each Senator shall have one Vote. [2] Immediately after they shall be assembled in Consequence of the first Election, they shall be divided as equally as may be into three Classes. The Seats of the Senators of the first Class shall be vacated at the Expiration of the second Year, of the second Class at the Expiration of the fourth Year, and of the third Class at the Expiration of the sixth Year, so that one third may be chosen every second Year; and if Vacancies happen by Resignation, or otherwise, during the Recess of the Legislature of any State, the Executive thereof may make temporary Appointments until the next Meeting of the Legislature, which shall then fill such Vacancies. [3] No Person shall be a Senator who shall not have attained to the Age of thirty Years, and been nine Years a Citizen of the United States, and who shall not, when elected, be an Inhabitant of that State for which he shall be chosen. [4] The Vice President of the United States shall be President of the Senate, but shall have no Vote, unless they be equally divided. [5] The Senate shall chuse their other Officers, and also a President pro tempore, in the absence of the Vice President, or when he shall exercise the Office of President of the United States. [6] The Senate shall have the sole Power to try all Impeachments. When sitting for that Purpose, they shall be on Oath or Affirmation. When the President of the United States is tried, the Chief Justice shall preside: And no Person shall be convicted without the Concurrence of two thirds of the Members present. [7] Judgment in Cases of Impeachment shall not extend further than to removal from Office, and disqualification to hold and enjoy any Office of honor, Trust or Profit under the United States: but the Party convicted shall nevertheless be liable and subject to Indictment, Trial, Judgment and Punishment, according to Law.

Section 4. [1] The Times, Places and Manner of holding Elections for Senators and Representatives, shall be prescribed in each State by the Legislature thereof; but the Congress may at any time by Law make or alter such Regulations, except as to the Places of chusing Senators. [2] The Congress shall assemble at least once in every Year, and such Meeting shall be on the first Monday in December, unless they shall by Law appoint a different Day.

Section 5. [1] Each House shall be the Judge of the Elections, Returns and Qualifications of its own Members, and a Majority of each shall constitute a Quorum to do Business; but a smaller Number may adjourn from day to day, and may be authorized to compel the Attendance of absent Members, in such Manner, and under such Penalties as each House may provide. [2] Each House may determine the Rules of its Proceedings, punish its Members for disorderly Behavior, and, with the Concurrence of two thirds, expel a Member. [3] Each House shall keep a Journal of its Proceedings, and from time to time publish the same, excepting such Parts as may in their Judgment require Secrecy; and the Yeas and Nays of the Members of either House on any question shall, at the Desire of one fifth of those Present, be entered on the Journal. [4] Neither House, during the Session of Congress, shall, without the Consent of the other, adjourn for more than three days, nor to any other Place than that in which the two Houses shall be sitting.

Section 6. [1] The Senators and Representatives shall receive a Compensation for their Services, to be ascertained by Law, and paid out of the Treasury of the United States. They shall in all Cases, except Treason, Felony and Breach of the Peace, be privileged from Arrest during their Attendance at the Session of their respective Houses, and in going to and returning from the same; and for any Speech or Debate in either House, they shall not be questioned in any other Place. [2] No Senator or Representative shall, during the Time for which he was elected, be appointed to any civil Office under the Authority of the United States, which shall have been created, or the Emoluments whereof shall have been encreased during such time; and no Person holding any Office under the United States, shall be a Member of either House during his Continuance in Office.

Section 7. [1] All Bills for raising Revenue shall originate in the House of Representatives; but the Senate may propose or concur with Amendments as on other Bills. [2] Every Bill which shall have passed the House of Representatives and the Senate, shall, before it becomes a Law, be presented to the President of the United States; If he approve he shall sign it, but if not he shall return it, with his Objections to the House in which it shall have originated, who shall enter the Objections at large on their Journal, and proceed to reconsider it. If after such Reconsideration two thirds of that House shall agree to pass the Bill, it shall be sent, together with the Objections, to the other House, by which it shall likewise be reconsidered, and if approved by two thirds of that House, it shall become a Law. But in all such Cases the Votes of both Houses shall be determined by yeas and Nays, and the Names of the Persons voting for and against the Bill shall be entered on the Journal of each House respectively. If any Bill shall not be returned by the President within ten Days (Sundays excepted) after it shall have been presented to him, the Same shall be a Law, in like Manner as if he had signed it, unless the Congress by their Adjournment prevents its Return, in which Case it shall not be a Law. [3] Every Order, Resolution, or Vote to Which the Concurrence of the Senate and House of Representatives may be necessary (except on a question of Adjournment) shall be presented to the President of the United States; and before the Same shall take Effect, shall be approved by him, or being disapproved by him, shall be repassed by two thirds of the Senate and House of Representatives, according to the Rules and Limitations prescribed in the Case of a Bill.

Section 8. [1] The Congress shall have Power To lay and collect Taxes, Duties, Imposts and Excises, to pay the Debts and provide for the common Defence and general Welfare of the United States; but all Duties, Imposts and Excises shall be uniform throughout the United States; [2] To borrow money on the credit of the United States; [3] To regulate Commerce with foreign Nations, and among the several States, and with the Indian Tribes; [4] To establish an uniform Rule of Naturalization, and uniform Laws on the subject of Bankruptcies throughout the United States; [5] To coin Money, regulate the value thereof, and of foreign Coin, and fix the Standard of Weights and Measures; [6] To provide the Punishment of counterfeiting the Securities and current Coin of the United States; [7] To establish Post Offices and post Roads; [8] To promote the Progress of Science and useful Arts, by securing for limited Times to Authors and Inventors the exclusive Right to their respective Writings and Discoveries; [9] To constitute Tribunals inferior to the supreme Court; [10] To define and punish Piracies and Felonies committed on the high Seas, and Offenses against the Law of Nations; [11] To declare War, grant Letters of Marque and Reprisal, and make Rules concerning Captures on Land and Water; [12] To raise and support Armies, but no Appropriation of Money to that Use shall be for a longer Term than two Years; [13] To provide and maintain a Navy; [14] To make Rules for the Government and Regulation of the land and naval Forces; [15] To provide for calling forth the Militia to execute the Laws of the Union, suppress Insurrections and repel Invasions; [16] To provide for organizing, arming, and disciplining, the Militia, and for governing such Part of them as may be employed in the Service of the United States, reserving to the States respectively, the Appointment of the Officers, and the Authority of training the Militia according to the discipline prescribed by Congress; [17] To exercise exclusive Legislation in all Cases whatsoever, over such

District (not exceeding ten Miles square) as may, by Cession of particular States, and the Acceptance of Congress, become the Seat of the Government of the United States, and to exercise like Authority over all Places purchased by the Consent of the Legislature of the State in which the Same shall be, for the Erection of Forts, Magazines, Arsenals, dock-Yards, and other needful Buildings;--And [18] To make all Laws which shall be necessary and proper for carrying into Execution the foregoing Powers, and all other Powers vested by this Constitution in the Government of the United States, or in any Department or Officer thereof.

Section 9. [1] The Migration or Importation of such Persons as any of the States now existing shall think proper to admit, shall not be prohibited by the Congress prior to the Year one thousand eight hundred and eight, but a Tax or duty may be imposed on such Importation, not exceeding ten dollars for each Person. [2] The privilege of the Writ of Habeas Corpus shall not be suspended, unless when in Cases of Rebellion or Invasion the public Safety may require it. [3] No Bill of Attainder or ex post facto Law shall be passed. [4] No Capitation, or other direct, Tax shall be laid, unless in Proportion to the Census or Enumeration herein before directed to be taken. [5] No Tax or Duty shall be laid on Articles exported from any State. [6] No Preference shall be given by any Regulation of Commerce or Revenue to the Ports of one State over those of another: nor shall Vessels bound to, or from, one State, be obliged to enter, clear, or pay Duties in another. [7] No Money shall be drawn from the Treasury, but in Consequence of Appropriations made by Law; and a regular Statement and Account of the Receipts and Expenditures of all public Money shall be published from time to time. [8] No Title of Nobility shall be granted by the United States: And no Person holding any Office of Profit or Trust under them, shall, without the Consent of the Congress, accept of any present, Emolument, Office, or Title, of any kind whatever, from any King, Prince, or foreign State.

Section 10. [1] No State shall enter into any Treaty, Alliance, or Confederation; grant Letters of Marque and Reprisal; coin Money; emit Bills of Credit; make any Thing but gold and silver Coin a Tender in Payment of Debts; pass any Bill of Attainder, ex post facto Law, or Law impairing the Obligation of Contracts, or grant any Title of Nobility. [2] No State shall, without the Consent of the Congress, lay any Imposts or Duties on Imports or Exports, except what may be absolutely necessary for executing its inspection Laws: and the net Produce of all Duties and Imposts, laid by any State on Imports or Exports, shall be for the Use of the Treasury of the United States; and all such Laws shall be subject to the Revision and Controul of the Congress. [3] No State shall, without the Consent of Congress, lay any Duty of Tonnage, keep Troops, or Ships of War in time of Peace, enter into any Agreement or Compact with another State, or with a foreign Power, or engage in War, unless actually invaded, or in such imminent Danger as will not admit of delay.

ARTICLE II

Section 1. [1] The executive Power shall be vested in a President of the United States of America. He shall hold his Office during the Term of four Years, and, together with the Vice President, chosen for the same Term, be elected, as follows: [2] Each State shall appoint, in such Manner as the Legislature thereof may direct, a Number of Electors, equal to the whole Number of Senators and Representatives to which the State may be entitled in the Congress: but no Senator or Representative, or Person holding an Office of

Trust or Profit under the United States, shall be appointed an Elector. [3] The Electors shall meet in their respective States, and vote by Ballot for two Persons, of whom one at least shall not be an Inhabitant of the same State with themselves. And they shall make a List of all the Persons voted for, and of the Number of Votes for each; which List they shall sign and certify, and transmit sealed to the Seat of the Government of the United States, directed to the President of the Senate. The President of the Senate shall, in the Presence of the Senate and House of Representatives, open all the Certificates, and the Votes shall then be counted. The Person having the greatest Number of Votes shall be the President, if such Number be a Majority of the whole Number of Electors appointed; and if there be more than one who have such Majority, and have an equal Number of Votes, then the House of Representatives shall immediately chuse by Ballot one of them for President; and if no Person have a Majority, then from the five highest on the List the said House shall in like Manner chuse the President. But in chusing the President, the Votes shall be taken by States, the Representation from each State having one Vote; a quorum for this Purpose shall consist of a Member or Members from two thirds of the States, and a Majority of all the States shall be necessary to a Choice. In every Case, after the Choice of the President, the Person having the greatest Number of Votes of the Electors shall be the Vice President. But if there should remain two or more who have equal Votes, the Senate shall chuse from them by Ballot the Vice President. [4] The Congress may determine the Time of chusing the Electors, and the Day on which they shall give their Votes; which Day shall be the same throughout the United States. [5] No person except a natural born Citizen, or a Citizen of the United States, at the time of the Adoption of this Constitution, shall be eligible to the Office of President; neither shall any Person be eligible to that Office who shall not have attained to the Age of thirty five Years, and been fourteen Years a Resident within the United States. [6] In case of the removal of the President from Office, or of his Death, Resignation or Inability to discharge the Powers and Duties of the said Office, the Same shall devolve on the Vice President, and the Congress may by Law provide for the Case of Removal, Death, Resignation or Inability, both of the President and Vice President, declaring what Officer shall then act as President, and such Officer shall act accordingly, until the Disability be removed, or a President shall be elected. [7] The President shall, at stated Times, receive for his Services, a Compensation, which shall neither be increased nor diminished during the Period for which he shall have been elected, and he shall not receive within that Period any other Emolument from the United States, or any of them. [8] Before he enter on the Execution of his Office, he shall take the following Oath or Affirmation: "I do solemnly swear (or affirm) that I will faithfully execute the Office of President of the United States, and will to the best of my Ability, preserve, protect and defend the Constitution of the United States."

Section 2. [1] The President shall be Commander in Chief of the Army and Navy of the United States, and of the Militia of the several States, when called into the actual Service of the United States; he may require the Opinion, in writing, of the principal Officer in each of the executive Departments, upon any subject relating to the Duties of their respective Offices, and he shall have Power to grant Reprieves and Pardons for Offenses against the United States, except in Cases of Impeachment. [2] He shall have Power, by and with the Advice and Consent of the Senate, to make Treaties, provided two thirds of the Senators present concur; and he shall nominate, and by and with the Advice and Consent of the Senate, shall appoint Ambassadors, other public Ministers and Consuls,

Judges of the supreme Court, and all other Officers of the United States, whose Appointments are not herein otherwise provided for, and which shall be established by Law: but the Congress may by Law vest the Appointment of such inferior Officers, as they think proper, in the President alone, to the Courts of Law, or in the Heads of Departments. [3] The President shall have Power to fill up all Vacancies that may happen during the Recess of the Senate, by granting Commissions which shall expire at the End of their next Session.

Section 3. He shall from time to time give to the Congress Information of the State of the Union, and recommend to their Consideration such Measures as he shall judge necessary and expedient; he may, on extraordinary occasions, convene both Houses, or either of them, and in Case of Disagreement between them, with Respect to the time of Adjournment, he may adjourn them to such Time as he shall think proper; he shall receive Ambassadors and other public Ministers; he shall take Care that the Laws be faithfully executed, and shall Commission all the Officers of the United States.

Section 4. The President, Vice President and all civil Officers of the United States, shall be removed from Office on Impeachment for, and Conviction of, Treason, Bribery, or other high Crimes and Misdemeanors.

ARTICLE III

Section 1. The judicial Power of the United States, shall be vested in one supreme Court, and in such inferior Courts as the Congress may from time to time ordain and establish. The Judges, both of the supreme and inferior Courts, shall hold their Offices during good Behaviour, and shall, at stated Times, receive for their Services, a Compensation, which shall not be diminished during their Continuance in Office.

Section 2. [1] The Judicial Power shall extend to all Cases, in Law and Equity, arising under this Constitution, the Laws of the United States, and Treaties made, or which shall be made, under their Authority;--to all Cases affecting Ambassadors, other public Ministers and Consuls;--to all Cases of admiralty and maritime Jurisdiction;--to Controversies to which the United States shall be a Party;--to Controversies between two or more States;--between a State and Citizens of another State;--between Citizens of different States;--between Citizens of the same State claiming Lands under Grants of different States, and between a State, or the Citizens thereof, and foreign States, Citizens or Subjects. [2] In all Cases affecting Ambassadors, other public Ministers and Consuls, and those in which a State shall be a Party, the supreme Court shall have original Jurisdiction. In all the other Cases before mentioned, the supreme Court shall have appellate Jurisdiction, both as to Law and Fact, with such Exceptions, and under such Regulations as the Congress shall make. [3] The trial of all Crimes, except in Cases of Impeachment, shall be by Jury; and such Trial shall be held in the State where the said Crimes shall have been committed; but when not committed within any State, the Trial shall be at such Place or Places as the Congress may by Law have directed.

Section 3. [1] Treason against the United States, shall consist only in levying War against them, or in adhering to their Enemies, giving them Aid and Comfort. No person shall be convicted of Treason unless on the Testimony of two Witnesses to the same overt Act, or on Confession in open Court. [2] The Congress shall have Power to declare the Punishment of Treason, but no Attainder of Treason shall work Corruption of Blood, or Forfeiture except during the Life of the Person attainted.

ARTICLE IV

Section 1. Full Faith and Credit shall be given in each State to the public Acts, Records, and judicial Proceedings of every other State. And the Congress may by general Laws prescribe the Manner in which such Acts, Records and Proceedings shall be proved, and the Effect thereof.

Section 2. [1] The Citizens of each State shall be entitled to all Privileges and Immunities of Citizens in the several States. [2] A Person charged in any State with Treason, Felony, or other Crime, who shall flee from Justice, and be found in another State, shall on demand of the executive Authority of the State from which he fled, be delivered up, to be removed to the State having Jurisdiction of the Crime. [3] No Person held to Service or Labour in one State, under the Laws thereof, escaping into another, shall, in Consequence of any Law or Regulation therein, be discharged from such Service or Labour, but shall be delivered up on Claim of the Party to whom such Service or Labour may be due.

Section 3. [1] New States may be admitted by the Congress into this Union; but no new State shall be formed or erected within the Jurisdiction of any other State; nor any State be formed by the Junction of two or more States, or Parts of States, without the Consent of the Legislatures of the States concerned as well as of the Congress. [2] The Congress shall have Power to dispose of and make all needful Rules and Regulations respecting the Territory or other Property belonging to the United States; and nothing in this Constitution shall be so construed as to Prejudice any Claims of the United States, or of any particular State.

Section 4. The United States shall guarantee to every State in this Union a Republican Form of Government, and shall protect each of them against Invasion; and on Application of the Legislature, or of the Executive (when the Legislature cannot be convened) against domestic Violence.

ARTICLE V

The Congress, whenever two thirds of both Houses shall deem it necessary, shall propose Amendments to this Constitution, or, on the Application of the Legislatures of two thirds of the several States, shall call a Convention for proposing Amendments, which, in either Case, shall be valid to all Intents and Purposes, as part of this Constitution, when ratified by the Legislatures of three fourths of the several States, or by Conventions in three fourths thereof, as the one or the other Mode of Ratification may be proposed by the Congress; Provided that no Amendment which may be made prior to the Year One thousand eight hundred and eight shall in any Manner affect the first and fourth Clauses in the Ninth Section of the first Article; and that no State, without its Consent, shall be deprived of its equal Suffrage in the Senate.

ARTICLE VI

[1] All Debts contracted and Engagements entered into, before the Adoption of this Constitution, shall be as valid against the United States under this Constitution, as under the Confederation. [2] This Constitution, and the Laws of the United States which shall be made in Pursuance thereof; and all Treaties made, or which shall be made, under the Authority of the United States, shall be the supreme Law of the Land; and the Judges in every State shall be bound thereby, any Thing in the Constitution or Laws of any State to the Contrary notwithstanding. [3] The Senators and Representatives before mentioned,

and the Members of the several State Legislatures, and all executive and judicial Officers, both of the United States and of the several States, shall be bound by Oath or Affirmation, to support this Constitution; but no religious Test shall ever be required as a Qualification to any Office or public Trust under the United States.

ARTICLE VII

The Ratification of the Conventions of nine States shall be sufficient for the Establishment of this Constitution between the States so ratifying the Same

ARTICLES IN ADDITION TO, AND AMENDMENT OF, THE CONSTITUTION OF THE UNITED STATES OF AMERICA, PROPOSED BY CONGRESS, AND RATIFIED BY THE LEGISLATURES OF THE SEVERAL STATES, PURSUANT TO THE FIFTH ARTICLE OF THE ORIGINAL CONSTITUTION

AMENDMENT I [1791]

Congress shall make no law respecting an establishment of religion, or prohibiting the free exercise thereof; or abridging the freedom of speech, or of the press; or the right of the people peaceably to assemble, and to petition the Government for a redress of grievances.

AMENDMENT II [1791]

A well regulated Militia, being necessary to the security of a free State, the right of the people to keep and bear Arms, shall not be infringed.

AMENDMENT III [1791]

No Soldier shall, in time of peace be quartered in any house, without the consent of the Owner, nor in time of war, but in a manner to be prescribed by law.

AMENDMENT IV [1791]

The right of the people to be secure in their persons, houses, papers, and effects, against unreasonable searches and seizures, shall not be violated, and no Warrants shall issue, but upon probable cause, supported by Oath or affirmation, and particularly describing the place to be searched, and the persons or things to be seized.

AMENDMENT V [1791]

No person shall be held to answer for a capital, or otherwise infamous crime, unless on a presentment or indictment of a Grand Jury, except in cases arising in the land or naval forces, or in the Militia, when in actual service in time of War or public danger; nor shall any person be subject for the same offence to be twice put in jeopardy of life or limb; nor shall be compelled in any criminal case to be a witness against himself, nor be deprived of life, liberty, or property, without due process of law; nor shall private property be taken for public use, without just compensation.

AMENDMENT VI [1791]

In all criminal prosecutions, the accused shall enjoy the right to a speedy and public trial, by an impartial jury of the State and district wherein the crime shall have been committed, which district shall have been previously ascertained by law, and to be informed of the nature and cause of the accusation; to be confronted with the witnesses against him; to have compulsory process for obtaining witnesses in his favor, and to have the Assistance of Counsel for his defence.

AMENDMENT VII [1791]

In Suits at common law, where the value in controversy shall exceed twenty dollars, the right of trial by jury shall be preserved, and no fact tried by a jury, shall be otherwise re-examined in any Court of the United States, than according to the rules of the common law.

AMENDMENT VIII [1791]

Excessive bail shall not be required, nor excessive fines imposed, nor cruel and unusual punishments inflicted.

AMENDMENT IX [1791]

The enumeration in the Constitution, of certain rights, shall not be construed to deny or disparage others retained by the people.

AMENDMENT X [1791]

The powers not delegated to the United States by the Constitution, nor prohibited by it to the States, are reserved to the States respectively, or to the people.

AMENDMENT XI [1798]

The Judicial power of the United States shall not be construed to extend to any suit in law or equity, commenced or prosecuted against one of the United States by Citizens of another State, or by Citizens or Subjects of any Foreign State.

AMENDMENT XII [1804]

The Electors shall meet in their respective states and vote by ballot for President and Vice-President, one of whom, at least, shall not be an inhabitant of the same state with themselves; they shall name in their ballots the person voted for as President, and in distinct ballots the person voted for as Vice-President, and they shall make distinct lists of all persons voted for as President, and of all persons voted for as Vice-President, and of the number of votes for each, which lists they shall sign and certify, and transmit sealed to the seat of the government of the United States, directed to the President of the Senate;--The President of the Senate shall, in the presence of the Senate and House of Representatives, open all the certificates and the votes shall then be counted;--The person having the greatest number of votes for President, shall be the President, if such number be a majority of the whole number of Electors appointed; and if no person have such majority, then from the persons having the highest numbers not exceeding three on the list of those voted for as President, the House of Representatives shall choose immediately, by ballot, the President. But in choosing the President, the votes shall be taken by states, the representation from each state having one vote; a quorum for this purpose shall consist of a member or members from two-thirds of the states, and a majority of all the states shall be necessary to a choice. And if the House of Representatives shall not choose a President whenever the right of choice shall devolve upon them, before the fourth day of March next following, then the Vice-President shall act as President, as in the case of the death or other constitutional disability of the President.--The person having the greatest number of votes as Vice-President, shall be the

Vice-President, if such number be a majority of the whole number of Electors appointed, and if no person have a majority, then from the two highest numbers on the list, the Senate shall choose the Vice-President; a quorum for the purpose shall consist of two-thirds of the whole number of Senators, and a majority of the whole number shall be necessary to a choice. But no person constitutionally ineligible to the office of President shall be eligible to that of Vice-President of the United States.

AMENDMENT XIII [1865]

Section 1. Neither slavery nor involuntary servitude, except as a punishment for crime whereof the party shall have been duly convicted, shall exist within the United States, or any place subject to their jurisdiction.

Section 2. Congress shall have power to enforce this article by appropriate legislation.

AMENDMENT XIV [1868]

Section 1. All persons born or naturalized in the United States, and subject to the jurisdiction thereof, are citizens of the United States and of the State wherein they reside. No State shall make or enforce any law which shall abridge the privileges or immunities of citizens of the United States; nor shall any State deprive any person of life, liberty, or property, without due process of law; nor deny to any person within its jurisdiction the equal protection of the laws.

Section 2. Representatives shall be apportioned among the several States according to their respective numbers, counting the whole number of persons in each State, excluding Indians not taxed. But when the right to vote at any election for the choice of electors for President and Vice President of the United States, Representatives in Congress, the Executive and Judicial officers of a State, or the members of the Legislature thereof, is denied to any of the male inhabitants of such State, being twenty-one years of age, and citizens of the United States, or in any way abridged, except for participation in rebellion, or other crime, the basis of representation therein shall be reduced in the proportion which the number of such male citizens shall bear to the whole number of male citizens twenty-one years of age in such State.

Section 3. No person shall be a Senator or Representative in Congress, or elector of President and Vice President, or hold any office, civil or military, under the United States, or under any State, who, having previously taken an oath, as a member of Congress, or as an officer of the United States, or as a member of any State legislature, or as an executive or judicial officer of any State, to support the Constitution of the United States, shall have engaged in insurrection or rebellion against the same, or given aid or comfort to the enemies thereof. But Congress may by a vote of two-thirds of each House, remove such disability.

Section 4. The validity of the public debt of the United States, authorized by law, including debts incurred for payment of pensions and bounties for services in suppressing insurrection or rebellion, shall not be questioned. But neither the United States nor any State shall assume or pay any debt or obligation incurred in aid of insurrection or rebellion against the United States, or any claim for the loss of emancipation of any slave; but all such debts, obligations and claims shall be held illegal and void.

Section 5. The Congress shall have power to enforce, by appropriate legislation, the provisions of this article.

AMENDMENT XV [1870]

Section 1. The right of citizens of the United States to vote shall not be denied or abridged by the United States or by any State on account of race, color, or previous condition of servitude.

Section 2. The Congress shall have power to enforce this article by appropriate legislation.

AMENDMENT XVI [1913]

The Congress shall have power to lay and collect taxes on incomes, from whatever source derived, without apportionment among the several States, and without regard to any census or enumeration.

AMENDMENT XVII [1913]

[1] The Senate of the United States shall be composed of two Senators from each State, elected by the people thereof, for six years, and each Senator shall have one vote. The electors in each State shall have the qualifications requisite for electors of the most numerous branch of the State legislatures.   [2] When vacancies happen in the representation of any State in the Senate, the executive authority of such State shall issue writs of election to fill such vacancies: Provided, That the legislature of any State may empower the executive thereof to make temporary appointments until the people fill the vacancies by election as the legislature may direct. [3] This amendment shall not be so construed as to affect the election or term of any Senator chosen before it becomes valid as part of the Constitution.

AMENDMENT XVIII [1919]

Section 1. After one year from the ratification of this article the manufacture, sale, or transportation of intoxicating liquors within, the importation thereof into, or the exportation thereof from the United States and all territory subject to the jurisdiction thereof for beverage purposes is hereby prohibited.

Section 2. The Congress and the several States shall have concurrent power to enforce this article by appropriate legislation.

Section 3. This article shall be inoperative unless it shall have been ratified as an amendment to the Constitution by the legislatures of the several States, as provided in the Constitution, within seven years from the date of the submission hereof to the States by the Congress.

AMENDMENT XIX [1920]

[1] The right of citizens of the United States to vote shall not be denied or abridged by the United States or by any State on account of sex. [2] Congress shall have power to enforce this article by appropriate legislation.

AMENDMENT XX [1933]

Section 1. The terms of the President and Vice President shall end at noon on the 20th day of January, and the terms of Senators and Representatives at noon on the 3d day of January, of the years in which such terms would have ended if this article had not been ratified; and the terms of their successors shall then begin.

Section 2. The Congress shall assemble at least once in every year, and such meeting shall begin at noon on the 3d day of January, unless they shall by law appoint a different day.

Section 3. If, at the time fixed for the beginning of the term of the President, the President elect shall have died, the Vice President elect shall become President. If a President shall not have been chosen before the time fixed for the beginning of his term, or if the President elect shall have failed to qualify, then the Vice President elect shall act as President until a President shall have qualified; and the Congress may by law provide for the case wherein neither a President elect nor a Vice President elect shall have qualified, declaring who shall then act as President, or the manner in which one who is to act shall be selected, and such person shall act accordingly until a President or Vice President shall have qualified.

Section 4. The Congress may by law provide for the case of the death of any of the persons from whom the House of Representatives may choose a President whenever the right of choice shall have devolved upon them, and for the case of the death of any of the persons from whom the Senate may choose a Vice President whenever the right of choice shall have devolved upon them.

Section 5. Sections 1 and 2 shall take effect on the 15th day of October following the ratification of this article.

Section 6. This article shall be inoperative unless it shall have been ratified as an amendment to the Constitution by the legislatures of three-fourths of the several States within seven years from the date of its submission.

AMENDMENT XXI [1933]

Section 1. The eighteenth article of amendment to the Constitution of the United States is hereby repealed.

Section 2. The transportation or importation into any State, Territory, or possession of the United States for delivery or use therein of intoxicating liquors, in violation of the laws thereof, is hereby prohibited.

Section 3. This article shall be inoperative unless it shall have been ratified as an amendment to the Constitution by conventions in the several States, as provided in the Constitution, within seven years from the date of the submission hereof to the States by the Congress.

AMENDMENT XXII [1951]

Section 1. No person shall be elected to the office of the President more than twice, and no person who has held the office of President, or acted as President, for more than two years of a term to which some other person was elected President shall be elected to the office of the President more than once. But this Article shall not apply to any person holding the office of President when this Article was proposed by the Congress, and shall not prevent any person who may be holding the office of President, or acting as President, during the term within which the Article becomes operative from holding the office of President or acting as President during the remainder of such term.

Section 2. This article shall be inoperative unless it shall have been ratified as an amendment to the Constitution by the legislatures of three-fourths of the several States within seven years from the date of its submission to the States by the Congress.

AMENDMENT XXIII [1961]

Section 1. The District constituting the seat of Government of the United States shall appoint in such manner as the Congress may direct: A number of electors of President and Vice President equal to the whole number of Senators and Representatives in Congress to which the District would be entitled if it were a State, but in no event more than the least populous State; they shall be in addition to those appointed by the States, but they shall be considered, for the purposes of the election of President and Vice President, to be electors appointed by a State; and they shall meet in the District and perform such duties as provided by the twelfth article of amendment.

Section 2. The Congress shall have power to enforce this article by appropriate legislation.

AMENDMENT XXIV [1964]

Section 1. The right of citizens of the United States to vote in any primary or other election for President or Vice President, for electors for President or Vice President, or for Senator or Representative in Congress, shall not be denied or abridged by the United States or any State by reason of failure to pay any poll tax or other tax.

Section 2. The Congress shall have power to enforce this article by appropriate legislation.

AMENDMENT XXV [1967]

Section 1. In case of the removal of the President from office or of his death or resignation, the Vice President shall become President.

Section 2. Whenever there is a vacancy in the office of the Vice President, the President shall nominate a Vice President who shall take office upon confirmation by a majority vote of both Houses of Congress.

Section 3. Whenever the President transmits to the President pro tempore of the Senate and the Speaker of the House of Representatives his written declaration that he is unable to discharge the powers and duties of his office, and until he transmits to them a written declaration to the contrary, such powers and duties shall be discharged by the Vice President as Acting President.

Section 4. Whenever the Vice President and a Majority of either the principal officers of the executive departments or of such other body as Congress may by law provide, transmit to the President pro tempore of the Senate and the Speaker of the House of Representatives their written declaration that the President is unable to discharge the powers and duties of his office, the Vice President shall immediately assume the powers and duties of the office as Acting President. Thereafter, when the President transmits to the President pro tempore of the Senate and the Speaker of the House of Representatives his written declaration that no inability exists, he shall resume the powers and duties of his office unless the Vice President and a majority of either the principal officers of the executive department or of such other body as Congress may by law provide, transmit within four days to the President pro tempore of the Senate and the Speaker of the House of Representatives their written declaration that the President is unable to discharge the powers and duties of his office. Thereupon Congress shall decide the issue, assembling within forty-eight hours for that purpose if not in session. If the Congress, within twenty-one days after receipt of the latter written declaration, or, if Congress is not in session, within twenty-one days after Congress is required to assemble, determines by two-thirds vote of both Houses that the President is unable to discharge the powers and duties of his office, the Vice President shall continue to discharge the same as Acting President; otherwise, the President shall resume the powers and duties of his office.

AMENDMENT XXVI [1971]

Section 1. The right of citizens of the United States, who are eighteen years of age or older, to vote shall not be denied or abridged by the United States or by any State on account of age.

Section 2. The Congress shall have power to enforce this article by appropriate legislation.

AMENDMENT XXVII [1992]

No law varying the Compensation for the services of the Senators and Representatives shall take effect, unless an election of Representatives shall have intervened.

Table of Cases

Index